Precious Oyebanjo B

Collins

Spanish

Dictionary

BESTSELLING BILINGUAL DICTIONARIES

Published by Collins
An imprint of HarperCollins Publishers
Westerhill Road
Bishopbriggs
Glasgow G64 2QT
www.harpercollins.co.uk

This Edition 2014

10 9 8 7 6 5 4 3

© HarperCollins Publishers 2011, 2014

ISBN 978-0-00-789782-7

www.collinsdictionary.com
www.collins.co.uk

Typeset by Davidson Publishing Solutions,
Glasgow

Printed in Great Britain by Clays Ltd,
St Ives plc

A catalogue record for this book is
available from the British Library.

If you would like to comment on any
aspect of this book, please contact us at
the above address or online.
E-mail: dictionaries@harpercollins.co.uk

Acknowledgements
We would like to thank those authors and
publishers who kindly gave permission for
copyright material to be used in the
Collins Corpus. We would also like to
thank Times Newspapers Ltd for providing
valuable data.

Índice de materias

Contents

William Collins' dream of knowledge for all began with the publication of his first book in 1819. A self-educated mill worker, he not only enriched millions of lives, but also founded a flourishing publishing house. Today, staying true to this spirit, Collins books are packed with inspiration, innovation, and practical expertise. They place you at the centre of a world of possibility and give you exactly what you need to explore it.

Language is the key to this exploration, and at the heart of Collins Dictionaries is language as it is really used. New words, phrases, and meanings spring up every day, and all of them are captured and analysed by the Collins Word Web. Constantly updated, and with over 2.5 billion entries, this living language resource is unique to our dictionaries.

Words are tools for life. And a Collins Dictionary makes them work for you.

Collins. Do more.

Introduction

You may be starting Spanish for the first time, or you may wish to extend your knowledge of the language. Perhaps you want to read and study Spanish books, newspapers and magazines, or perhaps simply have a conversation with Spanish speakers. Whatever the reason, whether you're a student, a tourist or want to use Spanish for business, this is the ideal book to help you understand and communicate. This modern, user-friendly dictionary gives priority to everyday vocabulary and the language of current affairs, business, computing and tourism, and, as in all Collins dictionaries, the emphasis is firmly placed on contemporary language and expressions.

How to use the dictionary

Below you will find an outline of how information is presented in your dictionary. Our aim is to give you the maximum amount of detail in the clearest and most helpful way.

Entries

A typical entry in your dictionary will be made up of the following elements:

Phonetic transcription

Phonetics appear in square brackets immediately after the headword. They are shown using the International Phonetic Alphabet (IPA), and a complete list of the symbols used in this system can be found on page x. The pronunciation given is for Castilian Spanish except where a word is solely used in Latin America, when we give the Latin American pronunciation. A further guide to the differences in types of Spanish pronunciation is given on page x.

Grammatical information

All words belong to one of the following parts of speech: noun, verb, adjective, adverb, pronoun, article, conjunction, preposition, abbreviation. Nouns can be singular or plural and, in Spanish, masculine or feminine. Verbs can be transitive, intransitive, reflexive or impersonal. Parts of speech appear in *italics* immediately after the phonetic spelling of the headword. The gender of the translation also appears in *italics* immediately following the key element of the translation, except where this is a regular masculine singular noun ending in "o", or a regular feminine singular noun ending in "a".

Often a word can have more than one part of speech. Just as the English word **chemical** can be an adjective or a noun, the Spanish word **conocido** can be an adjective ("(well-) known") or a noun ("acquaintance"). In the same way the verb **to walk** is sometimes transitive, ie it takes an object ("to walk the dog") and sometimes intransitive, ie it doesn't take an object ("to walk to school"). To help you find the meaning you are looking for quickly and for clarity of presentation, the different part of speech categories are separated by a shaded square ■.

Meaning divisions

Most words have more than one meaning. Take, for example, **punch** which can be, amongst other things, a blow with the fist or an object used for making holes. Other words are translated differently depending on the context in which they are used. The transitive verb **to put on**, for example, can be translated by "ponerse", "encender" etc depending on *what* it is you are putting on. To help you select the most appropriate translation in every context, entries are divided according to meaning. Each different meaning is introduced by an "indicator" in *italics* and in brackets. Thus, the examples given above will be shown as follows:

> **punch** [pʌntʃ] *n* (*blow*) golpe *m*, puñetazo; (*tool*) punzón *m*

Likewise, some words can have a different meaning when used to talk about a specific subject area or field. For example **bishop**, which in a religious context means a high-ranking clergyman, is also the name of a chess piece. To show English speakers which translation to use, we have added "subject field labels" in brackets, in this case (*Chess*):

> **bishop** ['bɪʃəp] *n* obispo; (*Chess*) alfil *m*

Field labels are often shortened to save space. You will find a complete list of abbreviations used in the dictionary on pages viii and ix.

Translations

Most English words have a direct translation in Spanish and vice versa, as shown in the examples given above. Sometimes, however, no exact equivalent exists in the target language. In such cases we have given an approximate equivalent, indicated by the sign ≈. An example is **Health Service**, the Spanish equivalent of which is "Insalud". There is no exact equivalent since the bodies in the two countries are quite different:

> **Health Service** *n* (*Brit*) servicio de salud pública, ≈ Insalud *m* (*SP*)

On occasion it is impossible to find even an approximate equivalent. This may be the case, for example, with the names of types of food:

> **fabada** [fa'βaða] *nf* *bean and sausage stew*

Here the translation (which doesn't exist) is replaced by an explanation. For increased clarity, the explanation, or "gloss", is shown in *italics*.

It is often the case that a word, or a particular meaning of a word, cannot be translated in isolation. The translation of **Dutch**, for example, is "holandés/esa". However, the phrase **to go Dutch** is rendered by "pagar cada uno lo suyo". Even an expression as simple as **washing powder** needs a separate translation since it translates as "detergente (en polvo)", not "polvo para lavar". This is where your dictionary will prove to be particularly informative and useful since it contains an abundance of compounds, phrases and idiomatic expressions.

Levels of formality and familiarity

In English you instinctively know when to say **I'm broke** or **I'm a bit short of cash** and when to say **I don't have any money**. When you are trying to understand someone who is speaking Spanish, however, or when you yourself try to speak Spanish, it is important to know what is polite and what is less so, and what you can say in a relaxed situation but not in a formal context. To help you with this, on the Spanish-English side we have added the label (*fam*) to show that a Spanish meaning or expression is colloquial, while those meanings or expressions which are vulgar are given an exclamation mark (*fam!*), warning you they can cause serious offence. Note also that on the English-Spanish side, translations which are vulgar are followed by an exclamation mark in brackets.

Keywords

Words labelled in the text as KEYWORDS, such as **have** and **do** or their Spanish equivalents **tener** and **hacer**, have been given special treatment because they form the basic elements of the language. This extra help will ensure that you know how to use these complex words with confidence.

Cultural information

Entries which are marked in the main text by a column of dots explain aspects of culture in Spanish and English-speaking countries. Subject areas covered include politics, education, media and national festivals.

Spanish alphabetical order

In 1994 the **Real Academia Española** and the Spanish American language academies jointly decided to stop treating CH and LL as separate letters in Spanish, thereby bringing it into line with European spelling norms. This means that **chapa** and **lluvia** will appear in letters C and L respectively. Of course, it should also be remembered that words like **cancha** and **callar**, with **ch** and **ll** in the middle of the words, will also have changed places alphabetically, now being found after **cáncer** and **cáliz** respectively. Spanish, however still has one more letter than English with Ñ treated separately, between N and O.

Abreviaturas | # Abbreviations

abreviatura	*ab(b)r*	abbreviation
adjetivo, locución adjetiva	*adj*	adjective, adjectival phrase
administración, lenguaje administrativo	*Admin*	administration
adverbio, locución adverbial	*adv*	adverb, adverbial phrase
agricultura	*Agr*	agriculture
alguien	*algn*	
América Latina	*Am*	Latin America
anatomía	*Anat*	anatomy
arquitectura	*Arq, Arch*	architecture
astrología, astronomía	*Astro*	astrology, astronomy
el automóvil	*Aut(o)*	the motor car and motoring
aviación, viajes en avión	*Aviat*	flying, air travel
biología	*Bio(l)*	biology
botánica, flores	*Bot*	botany
inglés británico	*Brit*	British English
química	*Chem*	chemistry
cine	*Cine*	cinema
lenguaje familiar (! vulgar)	*col (!)*	colloquial usage (! particularly offensive)
comercio, finanzas, banca	*Com(m)*	commerce, finance, banking
informática	*Comput*	computing
conjunción	*conj*	conjunction
construcción	*Constr*	building
compuesto	*cpd*	compound element
cocina	*Culin*	cookery
economía	*Econ*	economics
electricidad, electrónica	*Elec*	electricity, electronics
enseñanza, sistema escolar	*Escol*	schooling, schools
España	*Esp*	Spain
especialmente	*esp*	especially
exclamación, interjección	*excl*	exclamation, interjection
femenino	*f*	feminine
lenguaje familiar (! vulgar)	*fam (!)*	colloquial usage (! particularly offensive)
ferrocarril	*Ferro*	railways
uso figurado	*fig*	figurative use
fotografía	*Foto*	photography
(verbo inglés) del cual la partícula es inseparable	*fus*	(phrasal verb) where the particle is inseparable
generalmente	*gen*	generally
geografía, geología	*Geo*	geography, geology
geometría	*Geom*	geometry
informática	*Inform*	computing
invariable	*inv*	invariable
irregular	*irreg*	irregular
lo jurídico	*Jur*	law
América Latina	*LAm*	Latin America
gramática, lingüística	*Ling*	grammar, linguistics

literatura	*Lit*	literature
masculino	*m*	masculine
matemáticas	*Mat(h)*	mathematics
medicina	*Med*	medical term, medicine
masculino/femenino	*m/f*	masculine/feminine
lo militar, el ejército	*Mil*	military matters
música	*Mus*	music
sustantivo	*n*	noun
navegación, náutica	*Naut*	sailing, navigation
sustantivo no empleado en el plural	*no pl*	collective (uncountable) noun, not used in plural
sustantivo numérico	*num*	numeral noun
complemento	*obj*	(grammatical) object
	o.s.	oneself
peyorativo	*pey, pej*	derogatory, pejorative
fotografía	*Phot*	photography
fisiología	*Physiol*	physiology
plural	*pl*	plural
política	*Pol*	politics
participio de pasado	*pp*	past participle
prefijo	*pref*	prefix
preposición	*prep*	preposition
pronombre	*pron*	pronoun
psicología, psiquiatría	*Psico, Psych*	psychology, psychiatry
tiempo pasado	*pt*	past tense
ferrocarril	*Rail*	railways
religión, lo eclesiástico	*Rel*	religion, church service
	sb	somebody
enseñanza, sistema escolar	*Scol*	schooling, schools
singular	*sg*	singular
España	*SP*	Spain
	sth	something
subjuntivo	*subjun*	subjunctive
sujeto	*su(b)j*	(grammatical) subject
sufijo	*suff*	suffix
tauromaquia	*Taur*	bullfighting
también	*tb*	also
teatro	*Teat*	
técnica, tecnología	*Tec(h)*	technical term, technology
telecomunicaciones	*Telec, Tel*	telecommunications
	Theat	theatre
imprenta, tipografía	*Tip, Typ*	typography, printing
televisión	*TV*	television
sistema universitario	*Univ*	universities
inglés norteamericano	*US*	American English
verbo	*vb*	verb
verbo intransitivo	*vi*	intransitive verb
verbo pronominal	*vr*	reflexive verb
verbo transitivo	*vt*	transitive verb
zoología, animales	*Zool*	zoology
marca registrada	®	registered trademark
indica un equivalente cultural	≈	introduces a cultural equivalent

Spanish Pronunciation

Consonants

b	[b] [β]	See notes on *v* below	*bomba* *labor*
c	[k]	*c* before *a, o* or *u* is pronounced as in *cat*	*caja*
ce, ci	[θe,θi] [se,si']	*c* before *e* or *i* is pronounced as in *thin* and as *s* in *sin* in Latin America and parts of Spain	*cero, cielo* *vocero, noticiero*
ch	[tʃ]	*ch* is pronounced as *ch* in *chair*	*chiste*
d	[d] [ð]	at the beginning of a word or after *l* or *n*, *d* is pronounced as in English. In any other position it is like *th* in *the*	*danés* *ciudad*
g	[g] [ɣ]	*g* before *a, o* or *u* is pronounced as in *gap* if at the beginning of a word or after *n*. In other positions the sound is softened.	*gafas, guerra* *paga*
ge, gi	[xe, xi]	*g* before *e* or *i* is pronounced similar to *ch* in Scottish lo*ch*	*gente, girar*
h		*h* is always silent in Spanish	*haber*
j	[x]	*j* is pronounced like *ch* in Scottish lo*ch*	*jugar*
ll	[ʎ]	*ll* is pronounced like the *lli* in mi*lli*on	*talle*
ñ	[ɲ]	*ñ* is pronounced like the *ni* in o*ni*on	*niño*
q	[k]	*q* is pronounced as *k* in *king*	*que*
r, rr	[r] [rr]	*r* is always pronounced in Spanish, unlike the *r* in dancer. *rr* and *r* at the beginning of a word are trilled, like a Scottish *r*	*quitar* *garra*
s	[s] [z]	*s* is usually pronounced as in *pass*, but before *b, d, g, l, m* or *n* it is pronounced as in *rose*	*quizás* *isla*
v	[b] [β]	*v* is pronounced something like *b*. At the beginning of a word or after *m* or *n* it is pronounced as *b* in *boy*. In any other position it is pronounced with the lips in position to pronounce *b* of *boy*, but not meeting	*vía* *dividir*
w	[b] [w]	pronounced either like Spanish *b*, or like English *w*	*wáter* *whiskey*

z	[θ]	z is pronounced as th in thin and as s in sin in	tenaz
	[s']	Latin America and parts of Spain	izada
	[ks]	x is pronounced as in toxin except in informal	tóxico
	[s]	Spanish or at the beginning of a word	xenofobia

f, k, l, m, n, p and t are pronounced as in English
' Only shown in Latin American entries.

Vowels

a	[a]	Not as long as a in far. When followed by a consonant in the same syllable (ie in a closed syllable), as in amante, the a is short as in bat	pata
e	[e]	like e in they. In a closed syllable, as in gente, the e is short as in pet	me
i	[i]	as in mean or machine	pino
o	[o]	as in local. In a closed syllable, as in control, the o is short as in cot	lo
u	[u]	As in rule. It is silent after q, and in gue, gui, unless marked güe, güi eg antigüedad, when it is pronounced like w in wolf	lunes

Semi-vowels

| i, y | [j] | pronounced like y in yes | bien, hielo, yunta |
| u | [w] | unstressed u between consonant and vowel is pronounced like w in well. See also notes on u above | huevo, fuente, antigüedad |

Diphthongs

ai, ay	[ai]	as i in ride	baile
au	[au]	as ou in shout	auto
ei, ey	[ei]	as ey in grey	buey
eu	[eu]	both elements pronounced independently [e] + [u]	deuda
oi, oy	[oi]	as oy in toy	hoy

Stress

The rules of stress in Spanish are as follows:

(a)   when a word ends in a vowel or in *n* or *s*, the second last syllable is stressed: pa*tata*, pa*tatas*, *come*, *comen*

(b)   when a word ends in a consonant other than *n* or *s*, the stress falls on the last syllable: pa*red*, ha*blar*

(c)   when the rules set out in (a) and (b) are not applied, an acute accent appears over the stressed vowel: común, geografía, inglés

In the phonetic transcription, the symbol ['] precedes the syllable on which the stress falls.

In general, we give the pronunciation of each entry in square brackets after the word in question.

Spanish Verb Forms

1 Gerund **2** Imperative **3** Present **4** Preterite **5** Future **6** Present subjunctive **7** Imperfect subjunctive **8** Past participle **9** Imperfect

acertar 2 acierta **3** acierto, aciertas, acierta, aciertan **6** acierte, aciertes, acierte, acierten

acordar 2 acuerda **3** acuerdo, acuerdas, acuerda, acuerdan **6** acuerde, acuerdes, acuerde, acuerden

advertir 1 advirtiendo **2** advierte **3** advierto, adviertes, advierte, advierten **4** advirtió, advirtieron **6** advierta, adviertas, advierta, advirtamos, advirtáis, adviertan **7** advirtiera *etc*

agradecer 3 agradezco **6** agradezca *etc*

andar 4 anduve, anduviste, anduvo, anduvimos, anduvisteis, anduvieron **7** anduviera *or* anduviese *etc*

aparecer 3 aparezco **6** aparezca *etc*

aprobar 2 aprueba **3** apruebo, apruebas, aprueba, aprueban **6** apruebe, apruebes, apruebe, aprueben

atravesar 2 atraviesa **3** atravieso, atraviesas, atraviesa, atraviesan **6** atraviese, atravieses, atraviese, atraviesen

caber 3 quepo **4** cupe, cupiste, cupo, cupimos, cupisteis, cupieron **5** cabré *etc* **6** quepa *etc* **7** cupiera *etc*

caer 1 cayendo **3** caigo **4** cayó, cayeron **6** caiga *etc* **7** cayera *etc*

calentar 2 calienta **3** caliento, calientas, calienta, calientan **6** caliente, calientes, caliente, calienten

cerrar 2 cierra **3** cierro, cierras, cierra, cierran **6** cierre, cierres, cierre, cierren

COMER 1 comiendo **2** come, comed **3** como, comes, come, comemos, coméis, comen **4** comí, comiste, comió, comimos, comisteis, comieron **5** comeré, comerás, comerá, comeremos, comeréis, comerán **6** coma, comas, coma, comamos, comáis, coman **7** comiera, comieras, comiera, comiéramos, comierais, comieran **8** comido **9** comía, comías, comía, comíamos, comíais, comían

conocer 3 conozco **6** conozca *etc*

contar 2 cuenta **3** cuento, cuentas, cuenta, cuentan **6** cuente, cuentes, cuente, cuenten

costar 2 cuesta **3** cuesto, cuestas, cuesta, cuestan **6** cueste, cuestes, cueste, cuesten

dar 3 doy **4** di, diste, dio, dimos, disteis, dieron **7** diera *etc*

decir 2 di **3** digo **4** dije, dijiste, dijo, dijimos, dijisteis, dijeron **5** diré *etc* **6** diga *etc* **7** dijera *etc* **8** dicho

despertar 2 despierta **3** despierto, despiertas, despierta, despiertan **6** despierte, despiertes, despierte, despierten

divertir 1 divirtiendo **2** divierte **3** divierto, diviertes, divierte, divierten **4** divirtió, divirtieron **6** divierta, diviertas, divierta, divirtamos, divirtáis, diviertan **7** divirtiera *etc*

dormir 1 durmiendo **2** duerme **3** duermo, duermes, duerme, duermen **4** durmió, durmieron **6** duerma, duermas, duerma, durmamos, durmáis, duerman **7** durmiera *etc*

empezar 2 empieza **3** empiezo, empiezas, empieza, empiezan **4** empecé **6** empiece, empieces, empiece, empecemos, empecéis, empiecen

entender 2 entiende **3** entiendo, entiendes, entiende, entienden **6** entienda, entiendas, entienda, entiendan

ESTAR 2 está **3** estoy, estás, está, están **4** estuve, estuviste, estuvo, estuvimos, estuvisteis, estuvieron **6** esté, estés, esté, estén **7** estuviera *etc*

HABER 3 he, has, ha, hemos, habéis, han **4** hube, hubiste, hubo, hubimos, hubisteis, hubieron **5** habré *etc* **6** haya *etc* **7** hubiera *etc*

HABLAR 1 hablando **2** habla, hablad **3** hablo, hablas, habla, hablamos, habláis, hablan **4** hablé, hablaste, habló, hablamos, hablasteis, hablaron **5** hablaré, hablarás, hablará, hablaremos, hablaréis, hablarán **6** hable, hables, hable, hablemos, habléis, hablen **7** hablara *or* hablase, hablaras *or* hablases, habláramos *or* hablásemos, hablarais *or* hablaseis, hablaran *or* hablasen **8** hablado **9** hablaba, hablabas, hablaba, hablábamos, hablabais, hablaban

hacer 2 haz **3** hago **4** hice, hiciste, hizo, hicimos, hicisteis, hicieron **5** haré *etc* **6** haga *etc* **7** hiciera *etc* **8** hecho

instruir 1 instruyendo **2** instruye **3** instruyo, instruyes, instruye, instruyen **4** instruyó, instruyeron **6** instruya *etc* **7** instruyera *etc*

ir 1 yendo **2** ve **3** voy, vas, va, vamos, vais, van **4** fui, fuiste, fue, fuimos, fuisteis, fueron **6** vaya, vayas, vaya, vayamos, vayáis, vayan **7** fuera *etc* **9** iba, ibas, iba, íbamos, ibais, iban

jugar 2 juega 3 juego, juegas, juega, juegan 4 jugué 6 juegue *etc*

leer 1 leyendo 4 leyó, leyeron 7 leyera *etc*

morir 1 muriendo 2 muere 3 muero, mueres, muere, mueren 4 murió, murieron 6 muera, mueras, muera, muramos, muráis, mueran 7 muriera *etc* 8 muerto

mostrar 2 muestra 3 muestro, muestras, muestra, muestran 6 muestre, muestres, muestre, muestren

mover 2 mueve 3 muevo, mueves, mueve, mueven 6 mueva, muevas, mueva, muevan

negar 2 niega 3 niego, niegas, niega, niegan 4 negué 6 niegue, niegues, · niegue, neguemos, neguéis, nieguen

ofrecer 3 ofrezco 6 ofrezca *etc*

oír 1 oyendo 2 oye 3 oigo, oyes, oye, oyen 4 oyó, oyeron 6 oiga *etc* 7 oyera *etc*

oler 2 huele 3 huelo, hueles, huele, huelen 6 huela, huelas, huela, huelan

parecer 3 parezco 6 parezca *etc*

pedir 1 pidiendo 2 pide 3 pido, pides, pide, piden 4 pidió, pidieron 6 pida *etc* 7 pidiera *etc*

pensar 2 piensa 3 pienso, piensas, piensa, piensan 6 piense, pienses, piense, piensen

perder 2 pierde 3 pierdo, pierdes, pierde, pierden 6 pierda, pierdas, pierda, pierdan

poder 1 pudiendo 2 puede 3 puedo, puedes, puede, pueden 4 pude, pudiste, pudo, pudimos, pudisteis, pudieron 5 podré *etc* 6 pueda, puedas, pueda, puedan 7 pudiera *etc*

poner 2 pon 3 pongo 4 puse, pusiste, puso, pusimos, pusisteis, pusieron 5 pondré *etc* 6 ponga *etc* 7 pusiera *etc* 8 puesto

preferir 1 prefiriendo 2 prefiere 3 prefiero, prefieres, prefiere, prefieren 4 prefirió, prefirieron 6 prefiera, prefieras, prefiera, prefiramos, prefiráis, prefieran 7 prefiriera *etc*

querer 2 quiere 3 quiero, quieres, quiere, quieren 4 quise, quisiste, quiso, quisimos, quisisteis, quisieron 5 querré *etc* 6 quiera, quieras, quiera, quieran 7 quisiera *etc*

reir 2 ríe 3 río, ríes, ríe, ríen 4 rió, rieron 6 ría, rías, ría, riamos, riáis, rían 7 riera *etc*

repetir 1 repitiendo 2 repite 3 repito, repites, repite, repiten 4 repitió, repitieron 6 repita *etc* 7 repitiera *etc*

rogar 2 ruega 3 ruego, ruegas, ruega, ruegan 4 rogué 6 ruegue, ruegues, ruegue, roguemos, roguéis, rueguen

saber 3 sé 4 supe, supiste, supo, supimos, supisteis, supieron 5 sabré *etc* 6 sepa *etc* 7 supiera *etc*

salir 2 sal 3 salgo 5 saldré *etc* 6 salga *etc*

seguir 1 siguiendo 2 sigue 3 sigo, sigues, sigue, siguen 4 siguió, siguieron 6 siga *etc* 7 siguiera *etc*

sentar 2 sienta 3 siento, sientas, sienta, sientan 6 siente, sientes, siente, sienten

sentir 1 sintiendo 2 siente 3 siento, sientes, siente, sienten 4 sintió, sintieron 6 sienta, sientas, sienta, sintamos, sintáis, sientan 7 sintiera *etc*

SER 2 sé 3 soy, eres, es, somos, sois, son 4 fui, fuiste, fue, fuimos, fuisteis, fueron 6 sea *etc* 7 fuera *etc* 9 era, eras, era, éramos, erais, eran

servir 1 sirviendo 2 sirve 3 sirvo, sirves, sirve, sirven 4 sirvió, sirvieron 6 sirva *etc* 7 sirviera *etc*

soñar 2 sueña 3 sueño, sueñas, sueña, sueñan 6 sueñe, sueñes, sueñe, sueñen

tener 2 ten 3 tengo, tienes, tiene, tienen 4 tuve, tuviste, tuvo, tuvimos, tuvisteis, tuvieron 5 tendré *etc* 6 tenga *etc* 7 tuviera *etc*

traer 1 trayendo 3 traigo 4 traje, trajiste, trajo, trajimos, trajisteis, trajeron 6 traiga *etc* 7 trajera *etc*

valer 2 val 3 valgo 5 valdré *etc* 6 valga *etc*

venir 2 ven 3 vengo, vienes, viene, vienen 4 vine, viniste, vino, vinimos, vinisteis, vinieron 5 vendré *etc* 6 venga *etc* 7 viniera *etc*

ver 3 veo 6 vea *etc* 8 visto 9 veía *etc*

vestir 1 vistiendo 2 viste 3 visto, vistes, viste, visten 4 vistió, vistieron 6 vista *etc* 7 vistiera *etc*

VIVIR 1 viviendo 2 vive, vivid 3 vivo, vives, vive, vivimos, vivís, viven 4 viví, viviste, vivió, vivimos, vivisteis, vivieron 5 viviré, vivirás, vivirá, viviremos, viviréis, vivirán 6 viva, vivas, viva, vivamos, viváis, vivan 7 viviera *or* viviese, vivieras *or* vivieses, viviera *or* viviese, viviéramos *or* viviésemos, vivierais *or* vivieseis, vivieran *or* viviesen 8 vivido 9 vivía, vivías, vivía, vivíamos, vivías, vivían

volcar 2 vuelca 3 vuelco, vuelcas, vuelca, vuelcan 4 volqué 6 vuelque, vuelques, vuelque, volquemos, volquéis, vuelquen

volver 2 vuelve 3 vuelvo, vuelves, vuelve, vuelven 6 vuelva, vuelvas, vuelva, vuelvan 8 vuelto

For additional information on Spanish verb formation, see pp 6 – 161 of the Grammar section.

Números

Numbers

uno (un, una)*	1	one
dos	2	two
tres	3	three
cuatro	4	four
cinco	5	five
seis	6	six
siete	7	seven
ocho	8	eight
nueve	9	nine
diez	10	ten
once	11	eleven
doce	12	twelve
trece	13	thirteen
catorce	14	fourteen
quince	15	fifteen
dieciséis	16	sixteen
diecisiete	17	seventeen
dieciocho	18	eighteen
diecinueve	19	nineteen
veinte	20	twenty
veintiuno(-un, -una)*	21	twenty-one
veintidós	22	twenty-two
treinta	30	thirty
treinta y uno(un, una)*	31	thirty-one
treinta y dos	32	thirty-two
cuarenta	40	forty
cincuenta	50	fifty
sesenta	60	sixty
setenta	70	seventy
ochenta	80	eighty
noventa	90	ninety
cien(ciento)**	100	a hundred, one hundred
ciento uno(un, una)*	101	a hundred and one
ciento dos	102	a hundred and two
ciento cincuenta y seis	156	a hundred and fifty-six
doscientos(-as)	200	two hundred
trescientos(-as)	300	three hundred
quinientos(-as)	500	five hundred
mil	1,000	a thousand
mil tres	1,003	a thousand and three
dos mil	2,000	two thousand
un millón	1,000,000	a million

*'uno' (+'veintiuno' etc) agrees in gender (but not number) with its noun: **treinta y una personas**; the masculine form is shortened to 'un' unless it stands alone: **veintiún caballos, veintiuno.**

'ciento' is used in compound numbers, except when it multiplies: **ciento diez, but **cien mil**. 'Cien' is used before nouns: **cien hombres, cien casas.**

Números

Numbers

primero (primer, primera) 1º, 1er/1^a, 1^{era}	first, 1st
segundo(-a) 2º/2^a	second, 2nd
tercero (tercer, tercera) 3º, 3er/3^a, 3^{era}	third, 3rd
cuarto(-a) 4º/4^a	fourth, 4th
quinto(-a)	fifth, 5th
sexto(-a)	sixth, 6th
séptimo(-a)	seventh
octavo(-a)	eighth
noveno(-a); nono(-a)	ninth
décimo(-a)	tenth
undécimo(-a)	eleventh
duodécimo(-a)	twelfth
decimotercero(-a)	thirteenth
decimocuarto(-a)	fourteenth
decimoquinto(-a)	fifteenth
decimosexto(-a)	sixteenth
decimoséptimo(-a)	seventeenth
decimoctavo(-a)	eighteenth
decimonoveno(-a)	nineteenth
vigésimo(-a)	twentieth
vigésimo(-a) primero(-a)	twenty-first
vigésimo(-a) segundo(-a)	twenty-second
trigésimo(-a)	thirtieth
trigésimo(-a) primero(-a)	thirty-first
trigésimo(-a) segundo(-a)	thirty-second
cuadragésimo(-a)	fortieth
quincuagésimo(-a)	fiftieth
sexagésimo(-a)	sixtieth
septuagésimo(-a)	seventieth
octogésimo(-a)	eightieth
nonagésimo(-a)	ninetieth
centésimo(-a)	hundredth
centésimo(-a) primero(-a)	hundred-and-first
milésimo(-a)	thousandth

La hora

The time

¿qué hora es? — *what time is it?*

es la una	it's one o'clock
son las cuatro	it's four o'clock
medianoche, las doce de la noche	midnight
la una (de la madrugada)	one o'clock (in the morning), one (a.m.)
la una y cinco	five past one
la una y diez	ten past one
la una y cuarto *or* quince	a quarter past one, one fifteen
la una y veinticinco	twenty-five past one, one twenty-five
la una y media *or* treinta	half past one, one thirty
las dos menos veinticinco, la una treinta y cinco	twenty-five to two, one thirty-five
las dos menos veinte, la una cuarenta	twenty to two, one forty
las dos menos cuarto, la una cuarenta y cinco	a quarter to two, one forty-five
las dos menos diez, la una cincuenta	ten to two, one fifty
mediodía, las doce (de la mañana)	twelve o'clock, midday, noon
la dos (de la tarde)	
two o'clock (in the afternoon)	two (p.m.)
la siete (de la tarde), seven o'clock (in the evening)	seven (p.m.)

¿a qué hora? — *at what time?*

a medianoche	at midnight
a las siete	at seven o'clock
a la una	at one o'clock
en veinte minutos	in twenty minutes
hace diez minutos	ten minutes ago

La fecha

The date

hoy	today
mañana	tomorrow
pasado mañana	the day after tomorrow
ayer	yesterday
antes de ayer, anteayer	the day before yesterday
la víspera	the day before, the previous day
el día siguiente	the next *or* following day
la mañana	morning
la tarde	evening
esta mañana	this morning
esta tarde	this evening, this afternoon
ayer por la mañana	yesterday morning
ayer por la tarde	yesterday evening

mañana por la mañana	tomorrow morning
mañana por la tarde	tomorrow evening, tomorrow afternoon
en la noche del sábado al domingo	during Saturday night, during the night of Saturday to Sunday
vendrá el sábado	he's coming on Saturday
los sábados	on Saturdays
todos los sábados	every Saturday
el sábado pasado	last Saturday
el sábado que viene, el próximo sábado	next Saturday
ocho días a partir del sábado	a week on Saturday
quince días a partir del sábado	a fortnight *or* two weeks on Saturday
de lunes a sábado	from Monday to Saturday
todos las días	every day
una vez a la semana	once a week
una vez al mes	once a month
dos veces a la semana	twice a week
hace una semana *u* ocho días	a week ago
hace quince días	a fortnight *or* two weeks ago
el año pasado	last year
dentro de dos días	in two days
dentro de ocho días *o* una semana	in a week
dentro de quince días	in a fortnight *or* two weeks
el mes que viene, el próximo mes	next month
el año que viene, el próximo año	next year
¿a qué o a cuántos estamos?	*what day is it?*
el 1/22 octubre de 2008	the 1st/22nd of October 2008, October 1st/22nd 2008
en 2008	in 2008
mil novicientos noventa y cinco	nineteen ninety-five
44 a. de J.C.	44 BC
14 d. de J.C.	14 AD
en el (siglo) XIX	in the nineteenth century
en los años treinta	in the thirties
érase una vez ...	once upon a time ...

Aa

A, a [a] *nf* (*letra*) A, a; **A de Antonio** A for Andrew (*Brit*) *o* Able (*US*)
A. *abr* (*Escol*: = *aprobado*) pass

○ **PALABRA CLAVE**

a [a] *prep* (**a + el = al**) **1** (*dirección*) to; **fueron a Madrid/Grecia** they went to Madrid/Greece; **me voy a casa** I'm going home
2 (*distancia*): **está a 15 km de aquí** it's 15 kms from here
3 (*posición*): **estar a la mesa** to be at table; **al lado de** next to, beside; **a la derecha/izquierda** on the right/left; *ver tb* **puerta**
4 (*tiempo*): **a las 10/a medianoche** at 10/midnight; **¿a qué hora?** (at) what time?; **a la mañana siguiente** the following morning; **a los pocos días** after a few days; **estamos a 9 de julio** it's the 9th of July; **a los 24 años** at the age of 24; **ocho horas al día** eight hours a day; **al año/a la semana** (*Am*) a year/week later
5 (*manera*): **a la francesa** the French way; **a caballo** on horseback; **a oscuras** in the dark; **a rayas** striped; **le echaron a patadas** they kicked him out
6 (*medio, instrumento*): **a lápiz** in pencil; **a mano** by hand; **cocina a gas** gas stove
7 (*razón*): **a dos euros el kilo** at two euros a kilo; **a más de 50 kms por hora** at more than 50 kms per hour; **poco a poco** little by little
8 (*dativo*): **se lo di a él** I gave it to him; **se lo compré a él** I bought it from him
9 (*complemento directo*): **vi al policía** I saw the policeman
10 (*tras ciertos verbos*): **voy a verle** I'm going to see him; **empezó a trabajar** he started working *o* to work; **sabe a queso** it tastes of cheese
11 (+*infin*): **al verle, le reconocí inmediatamente** when I saw him I recognized him at once; **el camino a** recorrer the distance we (*etc*) have to travel; **¡a callar!** keep quiet!; **¡a comer!** let's eat!
12 (*a+que*): **¡a que llueve!** I bet it's going to rain!; **¿a qué viene eso?** what's the meaning of this?; **¿a que sí va a venir?** he IS coming, isn't he?; **¿a que no lo haces?** — **¡a que sí!** bet you don't do it! — yes, I WILL !

AA *nfpl abr* = **Aerolíneas Argentinas**
AA EE *abr* (= *Asuntos Exteriores*): **Min. de ~** ≈ FO (*Brit*)
ab. *abr* (= *abril*) Apr
abad, esa [a'βað, 'ðesa] *nm/f* abbot/abbess
abadía [aβa'ðia] *nf* abbey
abajo [a'βaxo] *adv* (*situación*) (down) below, underneath; (*en edificio*) downstairs; (*dirección*) down, downwards; **~ de** *prep* below, under; **el piso de ~** the downstairs flat; **la parte de ~** the lower part; **¡~ el gobierno!** down with the government!; **cuesta/río ~** downhill/downstream; **de arriba ~** from top to bottom; **el ~ firmante** the undersigned; **más ~** lower *o* further down
abalance *etc* [aβa'lanθe] *vb ver* **abalanzarse**
abalanzarse [aβalan'θarse] *vr*: **~ sobre** *o* **contra** to throw o.s. at
abalear [aβale'ar] *vt* (*Am fam*) to shoot
abalorios [aβa'lorjos] *nmpl* (*chucherías*) trinkets
abanderado [aβande'raðo] *nm* standard bearer
abandonado, -a [aβando'naðo, a] *adj* derelict; (*desatendido*) abandoned; (*desierto*) deserted; (*descuidado*) neglected
abandonar [aβando'nar] *vt* to leave; (*persona*) to abandon, desert; (*cosa*) to abandon, leave behind; (*descuidar*) to neglect; (*renunciar a*) to give up; (*Inform*) to quit; **abandonarse** *vr*: **abandonarse a** to abandon o.s. to; **abandonarse al alcohol** to take to drink
abandono [aβan'dono] *nm* (*acto*) desertion, abandonment; (*estado*) abandon, neglect;

(*renuncia*) withdrawal, retirement; **ganar por ~** to win by default

abanicar [aβani'kar] *vt* to fan

abanico [aβa'niko] *nm* fan; (*Naut*) derrick; **en ~** fan-shaped

abanique *etc* [aβa'nike] *vb ver* **abanicar**

abaratar [aβara'tar] *vt* to lower the price of ■ *vi*, **abaratarse** *vr* to go *o* come down in price

abarcar [aβar'kar] *vt* to include, embrace; (*contener*) to comprise; (*Am*) to monopolize; **quien mucho abarca poco aprieta** don't bite off more than you can chew

abarque *etc* [a'βarke] *vb ver* **abarcar**

abarrotado, -a [aβarro'taðo, a] *adj* packed; **~ de** packed *o* bursting with

abarrote [aβa'rrote] *nm* packing; **abarrotes** *nmpl* (*Am*) groceries, provisions

abarrotería [aβarrote'ria] *nf* (*Am*) grocery store

abarrotero, -a [aβarro'tero, a] *nm/f* (*Am*) grocer

abastecedor, a [aβasteθe'ðor, a] *adj* supplying ■ *nm/f* supplier

abastecer [aβaste'θer] *vt*: **~ (de)** to supply (with)

abastecimiento [aβasteθi'mjento] *nm* supply

abastezca *etc* [aβas'teθka] *vb ver* **abastecer**

abasto [a'βasto] *nm* supply; (*abundancia*) abundance; **no dar ~ a algo** not to be able to cope with sth

abatible [aβa'tiβle] *adj*: **asiento ~** tip-up seat

abatido, -a [aβa'tiðo, a] *adj* dejected, downcast; **estar muy ~** to be very depressed

abatimiento [aβati'mjento] *nm* (*depresión*) dejection, depression

abatir [aβa'tir] *vt* (*muro*) to demolish; (*pájaro*) to shoot *o* bring down; (*fig*) to depress; **abatirse** *vr* to get depressed; **abatirse sobre** to swoop *o* pounce on

abdicación [aβðika'θjon] *nf* abdication

abdicar [aβði'kar] *vi* to abdicate; **~ en algn** to abdicate in favour of sb

abdique *etc* [aβ'ðike] *vb ver* **abdicar**

abdomen [aβ'ðomen] *nm* abdomen

abdominal [aβðomi'nal] *adj* abdominal ■ *nm*: **abdominales** (*Deporte*) abdominals; (*Anat*) abdominals, stomach muscles

abecedario [aβeθe'ðarjo] *nm* alphabet

abedul [aβe'ðul] *nm* birch

abeja [a'βexa] *nf* bee; (*fig: hormiguita*) hard worker

abejorro [aβe'xorro] *nm* bumblebee

aberración [aβerra'θjon] *nf* aberration

aberrante [aβe'rrante] *adj* (*disparatado*) ridiculous

abertura [aβer'tura] *nf* = **apertura**

abertzale [aβer'tʃale] *adj*, *nm/f* Basque nationalist

abeto [a'βeto] *nm* fir

abierto, -a [a'βjerto, a] *pp de* **abrir** ■ *adj* open; (*fig: carácter*) frank

abigarrado, -a [aβiɣa'rraðo, a] *adj* multicoloured; (*fig*) motley

abismal [aβis'mal] *adj* (*fig*) vast, enormous

abismar [aβis'mar] *vt* to humble, cast down; **abismarse** *vr* to sink; (*Am*) to be amazed; **abismarse en** (*fig*) to be plunged into

abismo [a'βismo] *nm* abyss; **de sus ideas a las mías hay un ~** our views are worlds apart

abjurar [aβxu'rar] *vt* to abjure, forswear ■ *vi*: **~ de** to abjure, forswear

ablandar [aβlan'dar] *vt* to soften up; (*conmover*) to touch; (*Culin*) to tenderize ■ *vi*, **ablandarse** *vr* to get softer

abnegación [aβneɣa'θjon] *nf* self-denial

abnegado, -a [aβne'ɣaðo, a] *adj* self-sacrificing

abobado, -a [aβo'βaðo, a] *adj* silly

abobamiento [aβoβa'mjento] *nm* (*asombro*) bewilderment

abocado, -a [aβo'kaðo, a] *adj*: **verse ~ al desastre** to be heading for disaster

abochornar [aβotʃor'nar] *vt* to embarrass; **abochornarse** *vr* to get flustered; (*Bot*) to wilt; **abochornarse de** to get embarrassed about

abofetear [aβofete'ar] *vt* to slap (in the face)

abogacía [aβoɣa'θia] *nf* legal profession; (*ejercicio*) practice of the law

abogado, -a [aβo'ɣaðo, a] *nm/f* lawyer; (*notario*) solicitor; (*asesor*) counsel; (*en tribunal*) barrister, advocate, attorney (*US*); **~ defensor** defence lawyer *o* attorney (*US*); **~ del diablo** devil's advocate

abogar [aβo'ɣar] *vi*: **~ por** to plead for; (*fig*) to advocate

abogue *etc* [a'βoɣe] *vb ver* **abogar**

abolengo [aβo'lengo] *nm* ancestry, lineage

abolición [aβoli'θjon] *nf* abolition

abolir [aβo'lir] *vt* to abolish; (*cancelar*) to cancel

abolladura [aβoʎa'ðura] *nf* dent

abollar [aβo'ʎar] *vt* to dent

abominable [aβomi'naβle] *adj* abominable

abominación [aβomina'θjon] *nf* abomination

abonado, -a [aβo'naðo, a] *adj* (*deuda*) paid (-up) ■ *nm/f* subscriber

abonar [aβo'nar] *vt* to pay; (*deuda*) to settle; (*terreno*) to fertilize; (*idea*) to endorse; **abonarse** *vr* to subscribe; **~ dinero en una cuenta** to pay money into an account, credit money to an account

abono [a'βono] *nm* payment; fertilizer; subscription

abordable [aβor'ðaβle] *adj* (*persona*) approachable

abordar [aβor'ðar] *vt* (*barco*) to board; (*asunto*) to broach; (*individuo*) to approach

aborigen [aβo'rixen] *nm/f* aborigine

aborrecer [aβorre'θer] *vt* to hate, loathe

aborrezca *etc* [aβo'rreθka] *vb ver* **aborrecer**

abortar [aβor'tar] *vi* (*malparir*) to have a miscarriage; (*deliberadamente*) to have an abortion

aborto [a'βorto] *nm* miscarriage; abortion

abotagado, -a [aβota'ɣaðo, a] *adj* swollen

abotonar [aβoto'nar] *vt* to button (up), do up

abovedado, -a [aβoβe'ðaðo, a] *adj* vaulted, domed

abr. *abr* (= *abril*) Apr

abrace *etc* [a'βraθe] *vb ver* **abrazar**

abrasar [aβra'sar] *vt* to burn (up); (*Agr*) to dry up, parch

abrazadera [aβraθa'ðera] *nf* bracket

abrazar [aβra'θar] *vt* to embrace, hug; **abrazarse** *vr* to embrace, hug each other

abrazo [a'βraθo] *nm* embrace, hug; **un ~** (*en carta*) with best wishes

abrebotellas [aβreβo'teʎas] *nm inv* bottle opener

abrecartas [aβre'kartas] *nm inv* letter opener

abrelatas [aβre'latas] *nm inv* tin (*Brit*) *o* can (*US*) opener

abrevadero [aβreβa'ðero] *nm* watering place

abreviar [aβre'βjar] *vt* to abbreviate; (*texto*) to abridge; (*plazo*) to reduce ■ *vi*: **bueno, para ~** well, to cut a long story short

abreviatura [aβreβja'tura] *nf* abbreviation

abridor [aβri'ðor] *nm* (*de botellas*) bottle opener; (*de latas*) tin (*Brit*) *o* can (*US*) opener

abrigar [aβri'ɣar] *vt* (*proteger*) to shelter; (*suj: ropa*) to keep warm; (*fig*) to cherish; **abrigarse** *vr* (*con ropa*) to cover (o.s.) up; **abrigarse (de)** to take shelter (from), protect o.s. (from); **¡abrígate bien!** wrap up well!

abrigo [a'βriɣo] *nm* (*prenda*) coat, overcoat; (*lugar protegido*) shelter; **al ~ de** in the shelter of

abrigue *etc* [a'βriɣe] *vb ver* **abrigar**

abril [a'βril] *nm* April; *ver tb* **julio**

abrillantar [aβriʎan'tar] *vt* (*pulir*) to polish; (*fig*) to enhance

abrir [a'βrir] *vt* to open (up); (*camino etc*) to open up; (*apetito*) to whet; (*lista*) to head ■ *vi* to open; **abrirse** *vr* to open (up); (*extenderse*) to open out; (*cielo*) to clear; **~ un negocio** to start up a business; **en un ~ y cerrar de ojos** in the twinkling of an eye; **abrirse paso** to find *o* force a way through

abrochar [aβro'tʃar] *vt* (*con botones*) to button (up); (*zapato, con broche*) to do up; **abrocharse** *vr*: **abrocharse los zapatos** to tie one's shoelaces

abrogación [aβroɣa'θjon] *nf* repeal

abrogar [aβro'ɣar] *vt* to repeal

abrumador, a [aβruma'ðor, a] *adj* (*mayoría*) overwhelming

abrumar [aβru'mar] *vt* to overwhelm; (*sobrecargar*) to weigh down

abrupto, -a [a'βrupto, a] *adj* abrupt; (*empinado*) steep

absceso [aβs'θeso] *nm* abscess

absentismo [aβsen'tismo] *nm* (*de obreros*) absenteeism

absolución [aβsolu'θjon] *nf* (*Rel*) absolution; (*Jur*) acquittal

absoluto, -a [aβso'luto, a] *adj* absolute; (*total*) utter, complete; **en ~** *adv* not at all

absolver [aβsol'βer] *vt* to absolve; (*Jur*) to pardon; (*: acusado*) to acquit

absorbente [aβsor'βente] *adj* absorbent; (*interesante*) absorbing, interesting; (*exigente*) demanding

absorber [aβsor'βer] *vt* to absorb; (*embeber*) to soak up; **absorberse** *vr* to become absorbed

absorción [aβsor'θjon] *nf* absorption; (*Com*) takeover

absorto, -a [aβ'sorto, a] *pp de* **absorber** ■ *adj* absorbed, engrossed

abstemio, -a [aβs'temjo, a] *adj* teetotal

abstención [aβsten'θjon] *nf* abstention

abstendré *etc* [aβsten'dre] *vb ver* **abstenerse**

abstenerse [aβste'nerse] *vr*: **~ (de)** to abstain *o* refrain (from)

abstenga *etc* [aβs'tenga] *vb ver* **abstenerse**

abstinencia [aβsti'nenθja] *nf* abstinence; (*ayuno*) fasting

abstracción [aβstrak'θjon] *nf* abstraction

abstracto, -a [aβ'strakto, a] *adj* abstract; **en ~** in the abstract

abstraer [aβstra'er] *vt* to abstract; **abstraerse** *vr* to be *o* become absorbed

abstraído, -a [aβstra'iðo, a] *adj* absent-minded

abstraiga *etc* [aβs'traiɣa], **abstraje** *etc* [aβs'traxe], **abstrayendo** *etc* [aβstra'jendo] *vb ver* **abstraer**

abstuve *etc* [aβs'tuβe] *vb ver* **abstenerse**

absuelto [aβ'swelto] *pp de* **absolver**

absurdo, -a [aβ'surðo, a] *adj* absurd; **lo ~ es que ...** the ridiculous thing is that ... ■ *nm* absurdity

abuchear [aβutʃe'ar] *vt* to boo

abucheo [aβu'tʃeo] *nm* booing; **ganarse un ~** (*Teat*) to be booed

abuela [a'βwela] *nf* grandmother;

¡cuéntaselo a tu ~! (*fam!*) do you think I was born yesterday? (*fam*); **no tener/necesitar ~** (*fam*) to be full of o.s./blow one's own trumpet

abuelita [aβwe'lita] *nf* granny

abuelo [a'βwelo] *nm* grandfather; (*antepasado*) ancestor; **abuelos** *nmpl* grandparents

abulense [aβu'lense] *adj* of Ávila ■ *nm/f* native o inhabitant of Ávila

abulia [a'βulja] *nf* lethargy

abúlico, -a [a'βuliko, a] *adj* lethargic

abultado, -a [aβul'taðo, a] *adj* bulky

abultar [aβul'tar] *vt* to enlarge; (*aumentar*) to increase; (*fig*) to exaggerate ■ *vi* to be bulky

abundancia [aβun'danθja] *nf:* **una ~ de** plenty of; **en ~** in abundance

abundante [aβun'dante] *adj* abundant, plentiful

abundar [aβun'dar] *vi* to abound, be plentiful; **~ en una opinión** to share an opinion

aburguesarse [aβurɣe'sarse] *vr* to become middle-class

aburrido, -a [aβu'rriðo, a] *adj* (*hastiado*) bored; (*que aburre*) boring

aburrimiento [aβurri'mjento] *nm* boredom, tedium

aburrir [aβu'rrir] *vt* to bore; **aburrirse** *vr* to be bored, get bored; **aburrirse como una almeja** u **ostra** to be bored stiff

abusar [aβu'sar] *vi* to go too far; **~ de** to abuse

abusivo, -a [aβu'siβo, a] *adj* (*precio*) exorbitant

abuso [a'βuso] *nm* abuse; **~ de confianza** betrayal of trust

abyecto, -a [aβ'jekto, a] *adj* wretched, abject

a. C. *abr* (= *antes de Cristo*) B.C.

a/c *abr* (= *al cuidado de*) c/o; (= *a cuenta*) on account

acá [a'ka] *adv* (*lugar*) here; **pasearse de acá para allá** to walk up and down; **¡vente para acá!** come over here!; **¿de cuándo acá?** since when?

acabado, -a [aka'βaðo, a] *adj* finished, complete; (*perfecto*) perfect; (*agotado*) worn out; (*fig*) masterly ■ *nm* finish

acabar [aka'βar] *vt* (*llevar a su fin*) to finish, complete; (*consumir*) to use up; (*rematar*) to finish off ■ *vi* to finish, end; (*morir*) to die; **acabarse** *vr* to finish, stop; (*terminarse*) to be over; (*agotarse*) to run out; **~ con** to put an end to; **~ mal** to come to a sticky end; **esto ~á conmigo** this will be the end of me; **~ de llegar** to have just arrived; **acababa de hacerlo** I had just done it; **~ haciendo** o **por hacer algo** to end up (by) doing sth; **¡se**

acabó! (*¡basta!*) that's enough!; (*se terminó*) it's all over!; **se me acabó el tabaco** I ran out of cigarettes

acabóse [aka'βose] *nm:* **esto es el ~** this is the limit

acacia [a'kaθja] *nf* acacia

academia [aka'ðemja] *nf* academy; (*Escol*) private school; *ver tb* **colegio**

académico, -a [aka'ðemiko, a] *adj* academic

acaecer [akae'θer] *vi* to happen, occur

acaezca *etc* [aka'eθka] *vb ver* **acaecer**

acallar [aka'ʎar] *vt* (*silenciar*) to silence; (*calmar*) to pacify

acalorado, -a [akalo'raðo, a] *adj* (*discusión*) heated

acalorarse [akalo'rarse] *vr* (*fig*) to get heated

acampada [akam'paða] *nf:* **ir de ~** to go camping

acampanado, -a [akampa'naðo, a] *adj* flared

acampar [akam'par] *vi* to camp

acanalado, -a [akana'laðo, a] *adj* (*hierro*) corrugated

acanalar [akana'lar] *vt* to groove; (*ondular*) to corrugate

acantilado [akanti'laðo] *nm* cliff

acaparador, a [akapara'ðor, a] *nm/f* monopolizer

acaparar [akapa'rar] *vt* to monopolize; (*acumular*) to hoard

acápite [a'kapite] *nm* (*Am*) paragraph; **punto ~** full stop, new paragraph

acaramelado, -a [akarame'laðo, a] *adj* (*Culin*) toffee-coated; (*fig*) sugary

acariciar [akari'θjar] *vt* to caress; (*esperanza*) to cherish

acarrear [akarre'ar] *vt* to transport; (*fig*) to cause, result in; **le acarreó muchos disgustos** it brought him lots of problems

acaso [a'kaso] *adv* perhaps, maybe ■ *nm* chance; **¿~ es mi culpa?** (*Am fam*) what makes you think it's my fault?; **(por) si ~** (just) in case

acatamiento [akata'mjento] *nm* respect; (*de la ley*) observance

acatar [aka'tar] *vt* to respect; (*ley*) to obey, observe

acatarrarse [akata'rrarse] *vr* to catch a cold

acaudalado, -a [akauða'laðo, a] *adj* well-off

acaudillar [akauði'ʎar] *vt* to lead, command

acceder [akθe'ðer] *vi* to accede, agree; **~ a** (*Inform*) to access

accesible [akθe'siβle] *adj* accessible; **~ a** open to

accésit [ak'θesit] (*pl* **accésits** [ak'θesits]) *nm* consolation prize

acceso [ak'θeso] *nm* access, entry; (*camino*)

access road; (*Med*) attack, fit; (*de cólera*) fit; (*Pol*) accession; (*Inform*) access; ~ **aleatorio/ directo/secuencial** *o* **en serie** (*Inform*) random/direct/sequential *o* serial access; **de ~ múltiple** multi-access

accesorio, -a [akθe'sorjo, a] *adj* accessory ◼ *nm* accessory; **accesorios** *nmpl* (*Auto*) accessories, extras; (*Teat*) props

accidentado, -a [akθiðen'taðo, a] *adj* uneven; (*montañoso*) hilly; (*azaroso*) eventful ◼ *nm/f* accident victim

accidental [akθiðen'tal] *adj* accidental; (*empleo*) temporary

accidentarse [akθiðen'tarse] *vr* to have an accident

accidente [akθi'ðente] *nm* accident; **por ~** by chance; **accidentes** *nmpl* unevenness *sg*, roughness *sg*

acción [ak'θjon] *nf* action; (*acto*) action, act; (*Teat*) plot; (*Com*) share; (*Jur*) action, lawsuit; **capital en acciones** share capital; ~ **liberada/ordinaria/preferente** fully-paid/ordinary/preference share

accionamiento [akθjona'mjento] *nm* (*de máquina*) operation

accionar [akθjo'nar] *vt* to work, operate

accionista [akθjo'nista] *nm/f* shareholder

acebo [a'θeβo] *nm* holly; (*árbol*) holly tree

acechanza [aθe'tʃanθa] *nf* = **acecho**

acechar [aθe'tʃar] *vt* to spy on; (*aguardar*) to lie in wait for

acecho [a'θetʃo] *nm*: **estar al ~ (de)** to lie in wait (for)

acedera [aθe'ðera] *nf* sorrel

aceitar [aθei'tar] *vt* to oil, lubricate

aceite [a'θeite] *nm* oil; (*de oliva*) olive oil; ~ **de hígado de bacalao** cod-liver oil

aceitera [aθei'tera] *nf* oilcan

aceitoso, -a [aθei'toso, a] *adj* oily

aceituna [aθei'tuna] *nf* olive

aceitunado, -a [aθeitu'naðo, a] *adj* olive *cpd*; **de tez aceitunada** olive-skinned

acelerador [aθelera'ðor] *nm* accelerator

acelerar [aθele'rar] *vt* to accelerate; **acelerarse** *vr* to hurry

acelga [a'θelɣa] *nf* chard, beet

acendrado, -a [aθen'draðo, a] *adj*: **de ~ carácter español** typically Spanish

acendrar [aθen'drar] *vt* to purify

acento [a'θento] *nm* accent; (*acentuación*) stress; ~ **cerrado** strong *o* thick accent

acentuar [aθen'twar] *vt* to accent; to stress; (*fig*) to accentuate

acepción [aθep'θjon] *nf* meaning

aceptación [aθepta'θjon] *nf* acceptance; (*aprobación*) approval

aceptar [aθep'tar] *vt* to accept; to approve

acequia [a'θekja] *nf* irrigation ditch

acera [a'θera] *nf* pavement (*Brit*), sidewalk (*US*)

acerado, -a [aθe'raðo, a] *adj* steel; (*afilado*) sharp; (*fig: duro*) steely; (: *mordaz*) biting

acerbo, -a [a'θerβo, a] *adj* bitter; (*fig*) harsh

acerca [a'θerka]: ~ **de** *prep* about, concerning

acercar [aθer'kar] *vt* to bring *o* move nearer; **acercarse** *vr* to approach, come near

acerico [aθe'riko] *nm* pincushion

acero [a'θero] *nm* steel; ~ **inoxidable** stainless steel

acerque *etc* [a'θerke] *vb ver* **acercar**

acérrimo, -a [a'θerrimo, a] *adj* (*partidario*) staunch; (*enemigo*) bitter

acertado, -a [aθer'taðo, a] *adj* correct; (*apropiado*) apt; (*sensato*) sensible

acertar [aθer'tar] *vt* (*blanco*) to hit; (*solución*) to get right; (*adivinar*) to guess ◼ *vi* to get it right, be right; ~ **a** to manage to; ~ **con** to happen *o* hit on

acertijo [aθer'tixo] *nm* riddle, puzzle

acervo [a'θerβo] *nm* heap; ~ **común** undivided estate

achacar [atʃa'kar] *vt* to attribute

achacoso, -a [atʃa'koso, a] *adj* sickly

achantar [atʃan'tar] *vt* (*fam*) to scare, frighten; **achantarse** *vr* to back down

achaque *etc* [a'tʃake] *vb ver* **achacar** ◼ *nm* ailment

achatar [atʃa'tar] *vt* to flatten

achicar [atʃi'kar] *vt* to reduce; (*humillar*) to humiliate; (*Naut*) to bale out; **achicarse** *vr* (*ropa*) to shrink; (*fig*) to humble o.s.

achicharrar [atʃitʃa'rrar] *vt* to scorch, burn

achicoria [atʃi'korja] *nf* chicory

achinado, -a [atʃi'naðo, a] *adj* (*ojos*) slanting; (*Am*) half-caste

achique *etc* [a'tʃike] *vb ver* **achicar**

acholado, -a [atʃo'laðo, a] *adj* (*Am*) half-caste

achuchar [atʃu'tʃar] *vt* to crush

achuchón [atʃu'tʃon] *nm* shove; **tener un ~** (*Med*) to be poorly

achuras [a'tʃuras] *nf* (*Am, Culin*) offal

aciago, -a [a'θjaɣo, a] *adj* ill-fated, fateful

acicalar [aθika'lar] *vt* to polish; (*adornar*) to bedeck; **acicalarse** *vr* to get dressed up

acicate [aθi'kate] *nm* spur; (*fig*) incentive

acidez [aθi'ðeθ] *nf* acidity

ácido, -a ['aθiðo, a] *adj* sour, acid ◼ *nm* acid; (*fam: droga*) LSD

acierto *etc* [a'θjerto] *vb ver* **acertar** ◼ *nm* success; (*buen paso*) wise move; (*solución*) solution; (*habilidad*) skill, ability; (*al adivinar*) good guess; **fue un ~ suyo** it was a sensible choice on his part

aclamación [aklama'θjon] *nf* acclamation; (*aplausos*) applause

aclamar [akla'mar] *vt* to acclaim; to applaud

aclaración [aklara'θjon] *nf* clarification, explanation

aclarar [akla'rar] *vt* to clarify, explain; (*ropa*) to rinse ■ *vi* to clear up; **aclararse** *vr* (*suj: persona: explicarse*) to understand; (*fig: asunto*) to become clear; **aclararse la garganta** to clear one's throat

aclaratorio, -a [aklara'torjo, a] *adj* explanatory

aclimatación [aklimata'θjon] *nf* acclimatization

aclimatar [aklima'tar] *vt* to acclimatize; **aclimatarse** *vr* to become o get acclimatized; **aclimatarse a algo** to get used to sth

acné [ak'ne] *nm* acne

ACNUR *nm abr* (= *Alto Comisionado de las Naciones Unidas para los Refugiados*) UNHCR *f*

acobardar [akoβar'ðar] *vt* to daunt, intimidate; **acobardarse** *vr* (*atemorizarse*) to be intimidated; (*echarse atrás*): **acobardarse (ante)** to shrink back (from)

acodarse [ako'ðarse] *vr*: **~ en** to lean on

acogedor, a [akoxe'ðor, a] *adj* welcoming; (*hospitalario*) hospitable

acoger [ako'xer] *vt* to welcome; (*abrigar*) to shelter; **acogerse** *vr* to take refuge; **acogerse a** (*pretexto*) to take refuge in; (*ley*) to resort to

acogida [ako'xiða] *nf* reception; refuge

acoja *etc* [a'koxa] *vb ver* **acoger**

acojonante [akoxo'nante] *adj* (*Esp fam*) tremendous

acolchar [akol'tʃar] *vt* to pad; (*fig*) to cushion

acólito [a'kolito] *nm* (*Rel*) acolyte; (*fig*) minion

acometer [akome'ter] *vt* to attack; (*emprender*) to undertake

acometida [akome'tiða] *nf* attack, assault

acomodado, -a [akomo'ðaðo, a] *adj* (*persona*) well-to-do

acomodador, a [akomoða'ðor, a] *nm/f* usher(ette)

acomodar [akomo'ðar] *vt* to adjust; (*alojar*) to accommodate; **acomodarse** *vr* to conform; (*instalarse*) to install o.s.; (*adaptarse*) to adapt o.s.; **¡acomódese a su gusto!** make yourself comfortable!

acomodaticio, -a [akomoða'tiθjo, a] *adj* (*pey*) accommodating, obliging; (*manejable*) pliable

acompañamiento [akompaɲa'mjento] *nm* (*Mus*) accompaniment

acompañante, -a [akompa'ɲante, a] *nm/f* companion

acompañar [akompa'ɲar] *vt* to accompany, go with; (*documentos*) to enclose; **¿quieres que te acompañe?** do you want me to come with you?; **~ a algn a la puerta** to see sb to the door o out; **le acompaño en el sentimiento** please accept my condolences

acompasar [akompa'sar] *vt* (*Mus*) to mark the rhythm of

acomplejado, -a [akomple'xaðo, a] *adj* neurotic

acomplejar [akomple'xar] *vt* to give a complex to; **acomplejarse** *vr*: **acomplejarse (con)** to get a complex (about)

acondicionado, -a [akondiθjo'naðo, a] *adj* (*Tec*) in good condition

acondicionador [akondiθjona'ðor] *nm* conditioner

acondicionar [akondiθjo'nar] *vt* to get ready, prepare; (*pelo*) to condition

acongojar [akongo'xar] *vt* to distress, grieve

aconsejable [akonse'xaβle] *adj* advisable

aconsejar [akonse'xar] *vt* to advise, counsel; **aconsejarse** *vr*: **aconsejarse con** o **de** to consult

acontecer [akonte'θer] *vi* to happen, occur

acontecimiento [akonteθi'mjento] *nm* event

acontezca *etc* [akon'teθka] *vb ver* **acontecer**

acopiar [ako'pjar] *vt* (*recoger*) to gather; (*Com*) to buy up

acopio [a'kopjo] *nm* store, stock

acoplador [akopla'ðor] *nm*: **~ acústico** (*Inform*) acoustic coupler

acoplamiento [akopla'mjento] *nm* coupling, joint

acoplar [ako'plar] *vt* to fit; (*Elec*) to connect; (*vagones*) to couple

acoquinar [akoki'nar] *vt* to scare; **acoquinarse** *vr* to get scared

acorazado, -a [akora'θaðo, a] *adj* armour-plated, armoured ■ *nm* battleship

acordar [akor'ðar] *vt* (*resolver*) to agree, resolve; **acordarse** *vr* to agree; **acordarse (de algo)** to remember (sth)

acorde [a'korðe] *adj* (*Mus*) harmonious; **~ con** (*medidas etc*) in keeping with ■ *nm* chord

acordeón [akorðe'on] *nm* accordion

acordonado, -a [akorðo'naðo, a] *adj* (*calle*) cordoned-off

acorralar [akorra'lar] *vt* to round up, corral; (*fig*) to intimidate

acortar [akor'tar] *vt* to shorten; (*duración*) to cut short; (*cantidad*) to reduce; **acortarse** *vr* to become shorter

acosar [ako'sar] *vt* to pursue relentlessly; (*fig*) to hound, pester; **~ a algn a preguntas** to pester sb with questions

acoso [a'koso] *nm* relentless pursuit; (*fig*) hounding; **~ sexual** sexual harassment

acostar [akos'tar] *vt* (*en cama*) to put to bed; (*en suelo*) to lay down; (*barco*) to bring alongside; **acostarse** *vr* to go to bed; to lie down

acostumbrado, -a [akostum'braðo, a] *adj* (*habitual*) usual; **estar ~ a (hacer) algo** to be used to (doing) sth

acostumbrar [akostum'brar] *vt*: **~ a algn a algo** to get sb used to sth ■ *vi*: **~ (a hacer algo)** to be in the habit (of doing sth); **acostumbrarse** *vr*: **acostumbrarse a** to get used to

acotación [akota'θjon] *nf* (*apunte*) marginal note; (*Geo*) elevation mark; (*de límite*) boundary mark; (*Teat*) stage direction

acotar [ako'tar] *vt* (*terreno*) to mark out; (*fig*) to limit; (*caza*) to protect

acotejar [akote'xar] *vt* (*Am*) to put in order, arrange

ácrata ['akrata] *adj, nm/f* anarchist

acre ['akre] *adj* (*sabor*) sharp, bitter; (*olor*) acrid; (*fig*) biting ■ *nm* acre

acrecentar [akreθen'tar] *vt* to increase, augment

acreciente *etc* [akre'θjente] *vb ver* **acrecentar**

acreditado, -a [akreði'taðo, a] *adj* (*Pol*) accredited; (*Com*): **una casa acreditada** a reputable firm

acreditar [akreði'tar] *vt* (*garantizar*) to vouch for, guarantee; (*autorizar*) to authorize; (*dar prueba de*) to prove; (*Com: abonar*) to credit; (*embajador*) to accredit; **acreditarse** *vr* to become famous; (*demostrar valía*) to prove one's worth; **acreditarse de** to get a reputation for

acreedor, a [akree'ðor, a] *adj*: **~ a** worthy of ■ *nm/f* creditor; **~ común/diferido/con garantía** (*Com*) unsecured/deferred/secured creditor

acribillar [akriβi'ʎar] *vt*: **~ a balazos** to riddle with bullets

acrimonia [akri'monja], **acritud** [akri'tuð] *nf* acrimony

acrobacia [akro'βaθja] *nf* acrobatics; **~ aérea** aerobatics

acróbata [a'kroβata] *nm/f* acrobat

acta ['akta] *nf* certificate; (*de comisión*) minutes *pl*, record; **~ de nacimiento/de matrimonio** birth/marriage certificate; **~ notarial** affidavit; **levantar ~** (*Jur*) to make a formal statement *o* deposition

actitud [akti'tuð] *nf* attitude; (*postura*) posture; **adoptar una ~ firme** to take a firm stand

activar [akti'βar] *vt* to activate; (*acelerar*) to speed up

actividad [aktiβi'ðað] *nf* activity; **estar en plena ~** to be in full swing

activo, -a [ak'tiβo, a] *adj* active; (*vivo*) lively ■ *nm* (*Com*) assets *pl*; **~ y pasivo** assets and liabilities; **~ circulante/fijo/inmaterial/ invisible** (*Com*) current/fixed/intangible/ invisible assets; **~ realizable** liquid assets; **activos congelados** *o* **bloqueados** frozen assets; **~ tóxico** toxic asset; **estar en ~** (*Mil*) to be on active service

acto ['akto] *nm* act, action; (*ceremonia*) ceremony; (*Teat*) act; **en el ~** immediately; **hacer ~ de presencia** (*asistir*) to attend (formally)

actor [ak'tor] *nm* actor; (*Jur*) plaintiff

actora [ak'tora] *adj*: **parte ~** prosecution; (*demandante*) plaintiff

actriz [ak'triθ] *nf* actress

actuación [aktwa'θjon] *nf* action; (*comportamiento*) conduct, behaviour; (*Jur*) proceedings *pl*; (*desempeño*) performance

actual [ak'twal] *adj* present(-day), current; **el 6 del ~** the 6th of this month

actualice *etc* [aktwa'liθe] *vb ver* **actualizar**

actualidad [aktwali'ðað] *nf* present; **actualidades** *nfpl* news *sg*; **en la ~** nowadays, at present; **ser de gran ~** to be current

actualización [aktwaliθa'θjon] *nf* updating, modernization

actualizar [aktwali'θar] *vt* to update, modernize

actualmente [aktwal'mente] *adv* at present; (*hoy día*) nowadays

actuar [ak'twar] *vi* (*obrar*) to work, operate; (*actor*) to act, perform ■ *vt* to work, operate; **~ de** to act as

actuario, -a [ak'twarjo, a] *nm/f* clerk; (*Com*) actuary

acuarela [akwa'rela] *nf* watercolour

acuario [a'kwarjo] *nm* aquarium; **A~** (*Astro*) Aquarius

acuartelar [akwarte'lar] *vt* (*Mil: alojar*) to quarter

acuático, -a [a'kwatiko, a] *adj* aquatic

acuchillar [akutʃi'ʎar] *vt* (*Tec*) to plane (down), smooth

acuciar [aku'θjar] *vt* to urge on

acuclillarse [akukli'ʎarse] *vr* to crouch down

ACUDE [a'kuðe] *nf abr* = **Asociación de Consumidores y Usuarios de España**

acudir [aku'ðir] *vi* to attend, turn up; **~ a** to turn to; **~ en ayuda de** to go to the aid of; **~ a una cita** to keep an appointment; **~ a una llamada** to answer a call; **no tener a quién ~** to have nobody to turn to

acuerdo *etc* [a'kwerðo] *vb ver* **acordar** ■ *nm* agreement; (*Pol*) resolution; **~ de**

7

pago respectivo (*Com*) knock-for-knock agreement; **A~ general sobre aranceles aduaneros y comercio** (*Com*) General Agreement on Tariffs and Trade; **tomar un ~** to pass a resolution; **¡de ~!** agreed!; **de ~ con** (*persona*) in agreement with; (*acción, documento*) in accordance with; **de común ~** by common consent; **estar de ~** (*persona*) to agree; **llegar a un ~** to come to an understanding

acueste *etc* [aˈkweste] *vb ver* **acostar**

acullá [akuˈʎa] *adv* over there

acumular [akumuˈlar] *vt* to accumulate, collect

acunar [akuˈnar] *vt* to rock (to sleep)

acuñar [akuˈɲar] *vt* (*moneda*) to mint; (*frase*) to coin

acuoso, -a [aˈkwoso, a] *adj* watery

acupuntura [akupunˈtura] *nf* acupuncture

acurrucarse [akurruˈkarse] *vr* to crouch; (*ovillarse*) to curl up

acurruque *etc* [akuˈrruke] *vb ver* **acurrucarse**

acusación [akusaˈθjon] *nf* accusation

acusado, -a [akuˈsaðo, a] *adj* (*Jur*) accused; (*marcado*) marked; (*acento*) strong

acusar [akuˈsar] *vt* to accuse; (*revelar*) to reveal; (*denunciar*) to denounce; (*emoción*) to show; **~ recibo** to acknowledge receipt; **su rostro acusó extrañeza** his face registered surprise; **acusarse** *vr*: **acusarse (de)** to confess (to)

acuse [aˈkuse] *nm*: **~ de recibo** acknowledgement of receipt

acústico, -a [aˈkustiko, a] *adj* acoustic ■ *nf* (*de una sala etc*) acoustics *pl*; (*ciencia*) acoustics *sg*

ADA [ˈaða] *nf abr* (*Esp*: = *Ayuda del Automovilista*) ≈ AA, RAC (*Brit*), AAA (*US*)

adagio [aˈðaxjo] *nm* adage; (*Mus*) adagio

adalid [aðaˈlið] *nm* leader, champion

adaptación [aðaptaˈθjon] *nf* adaptation

adaptador [aðaptaˈðor] *nm* (*Elec*) adapter; **~ universal** universal adapter

adaptar [aðapˈtar] *vt* to adapt; (*acomodar*) to fit; (*convertir*): **~ (para)** to convert (to)

adecentar [aðeθenˈtar] *vt* to tidy up

adecuado, -a [aðeˈkwaðo, a] *adj* (*apto*) suitable; (*oportuno*) appropriate; **el hombre ~ para el puesto** the right man for the job

adecuar [aðeˈkwar] *vt* (*adaptar*) to adapt; (*hacer apto*) to make suitable

adefesio [aðeˈfesjo] *nm* (*fam*): **estaba hecha un ~** she looked a sight

a. de J.C. *abr* (= *antes de Jesucristo*) B.C.

adelantado, -a [aðelanˈtaðo, a] *adj* advanced; (*reloj*) fast; **pagar por ~** to pay in advance

adelantamiento [aðelantaˈmjento] *nm* advance, advancement; (*Auto*) overtaking

adelantar [aðelanˈtar] *vt* to move forward; (*avanzar*) to advance; (*acelerar*) to speed up; (*Auto*) to overtake ■ *vi* (*ir delante*) to go ahead; (*progresar*) to improve; **adelantarse** *vr* (*tomar la delantera*) to go forward, advance; **adelantarse a algn** to get ahead of sb; **adelantarse a los deseos de algn** to anticipate sb's wishes

adelante [aðeˈlante] *adv* forward(s), onward(s), ahead ■ *excl* come in!; **de hoy en ~** from now on; **más ~** later on; (*más allá*) further on

adelanto [aðeˈlanto] *nm* advance; (*mejora*) improvement; (*progreso*) progress; (*dinero*) advance; **los adelantos de la ciencia** the advances of science

adelgace *etc* [aðelˈɣaθe] *vb ver* **adelgazar**

adelgazar [aðelɣaˈθar] *vt* to thin (down); (*afilar*) to taper ■ *vi* to get thin; (*con régimen*) to slim down, lose weight

ademán [aðeˈman] *nm* gesture; **ademanes** *nmpl* manners; **en ~ de** as if to

además [aðeˈmas] *adv* besides; (*por otra parte*) moreover; (*también*) also; **~ de** besides, in addition to

ADENA [aˈðena] *nf abr* (*Esp*: = *Asociación para la Defensa de la Naturaleza*) organization for nature conservation

adentrarse [aðenˈtrarse] *vr*: **~ en** to go into, get inside; (*penetrar*) to penetrate (into)

adentro [aˈðentro] *adv* inside, in; **mar ~** out at sea; **tierra ~** inland ■ *nm*: **dijo para sus adentros** he said to himself

adepto, -a [aˈðepto, a] *nm/f* supporter

aderece *etc* [aðeˈreθe] *vb ver* **aderezar**

aderezar [aðereˈθar] *vt* (*ensalada*) to dress; (*comida*) to season

aderezo [aðeˈreθo] *nm* dressing; seasoning

adeudar [aðeuˈðar] *vt* to owe; **adeudarse** *vr* to run into debt; **~ una suma en una cuenta** to debit an account with a sum

adherirse [aðeˈrirse] *vr*: **~ a** to adhere to; (*fig*) to follow

adhesión [aðeˈsjon] *nf* adhesion; (*fig*) adherence

adhesivo, -a [aðeˈsiβo, a] *adj* adhesive ■ *nm* sticker

adhiera *etc* [aˈðjera], **adhiriendo** *etc* [aðiˈrjendo] *vb ver* **adherirse**

adicción [aðikˈθjon] *nf* addiction

adición [aðiˈθjon] *nf* addition

adicional [aðiθjoˈnal] *adj* additional; (*Inform*) add-on

adicionar [aðiθjoˈnar] *vt* to add

adicto, -a [aˈðikto, a] *adj*: **~ a** (*droga etc*) addicted to; (*dedicado*) devoted to ■ *nm/f* supporter, follower; (*toxicómano etc*) addict

adiestrar [aðjes'trar] *vt* to train, teach; (*conducir*) to guide, lead; **adiestrarse** *vr* to practise; (*aprender*) to train o.s.

adinerado, -a [aðine'raðo, a] *adj* wealthy

adiós [a'ðjos] *excl* (*para despedirse*) goodbye!, cheerio!; (*al pasar*) hello!

aditivo [aði'tiβo] *nm* additive

adivinanza [aðiβi'nanθa] *nf* riddle

adivinar [aðiβi'nar] *vt* (*profetizar*) to prophesy; (*conjeturar*) to guess

adivino, -a [aði'βino, a] *nm/f* fortune-teller

adj *abr* (= *adjunto*) encl; (= *adjetivo*) adj

adjetivo [aðxe'tiβo] *nm* adjective

adjudicación [aðxuðika'θjon] *nf* award; (Com) adjudication

adjudicar [aðxuði'kar] *vt* to award; **adjudicarse** *vr*: to appropriate

adjudique *etc* [aðxu'ðike] *vb ver* **adjudicar**

adjuntar [aðxun'tar] *vt* to attach, enclose

adjunto, -a [að'xunto, a] *adj* attached, enclosed ◼ *nm/f* assistant

adminículo [aðmi'nikulo] *nm* gadget

administración [aðministra'θjon] *nf* administration; (*dirección*) management; **~ pública** civil service; **A~ de Correos** General Post Office

administrador, a [aðministra'ðor, a] *nm/f* administrator; manager(ess)

administrar [aðminis'trar] *vt* to administer

administrativo, -a [aðministra'tiβo, a] *adj* administrative

admirable [aðmi'raβle] *adj* admirable

admiración [aðmira'θjon] *nf* admiration; (*asombro*) wonder; (Ling) exclamation mark

admirar [aðmi'rar] *vt* to admire; (*extrañar*) to surprise; **admirarse** *vr* to be surprised; **se admiró de saberlo** he was amazed to hear it; **no es de ~ que ...** it's not surprising that ...

admisible [aðmi'siβle] *adj* admissible

admisión [aðmi'sjon] *nf* admission; (*reconocimiento*) acceptance

admitir [aðmi'tir] *vt* to admit; (*aceptar*) to accept; (*dudas*) to leave room for; **esto no admite demora** this must be dealt with immediately

admón. *abr* (= *administración*) admin

admonición [aðmoni'θjon] *nf* warning

ADN *nm abr* (= *acido desoxirribonucleico*) DNA

adobar [aðo'βar] *vt* (*preparar*) to prepare; (*cocinar*) to season

adobe [a'ðoβe] *nm* adobe, sun-dried brick

adocenado, -a [aðoθe'naðo, a] *adj* (*fam*) mediocre

adoctrinar [aðoktri'nar] *vt* to indoctrinate

adolecer [aðole'θer] *vi*: **~ de** to suffer from

adolescente [aðoles'θente] *nm/f* adolescent, teenager ◼ *adj* adolescent, teenage

adolezca *etc* [aðo'leθka] *vb ver* **adolecer**

adonde [a'ðonde] *adv* (to) where

adónde [a'ðonde] *adv* = **dónde**

adondequiera [aðonde'kjera] *adv* wherever

adopción [aðop'θjon] *nf* adoption

adoptar [aðop'tar] *vt* to adopt

adoptivo, -a [aðop'tiβo, a] *adj* (*padres*) adoptive; (*hijo*) adopted

adoquín [aðo'kin] *nm* paving stone

adorar [aðo'rar] *vt* to adore

adormecer [aðorme'θer] *vt* to put to sleep; **adormecerse** *vr* to become sleepy; (*dormirse*) to fall asleep

adormezca *etc* [aðor'meθka] *vb ver* **adormecer**

adormilarse [aðormi'larse] *vr* to doze

adornar [aðor'nar] *vt* to adorn

adorno [a'ðorno] *nm* adornment; (*decoración*) decoration

adosado, -a [aðo'saðo, a] *adj* (*casa*) semidetached

adquiera *etc* [að'kjera] *vb ver* **adquirir**

adquirir [aðki'rir] *vt* to acquire, obtain

adquisición [aðkisi'θjon] *nf* acquisition; (*compra*) purchase

adrede [a'ðreðe] *adv* on purpose

Adriático [að'rjatiko] *nm*: **el (Mar) ~** the Adriatic (Sea)

adscribir [aðskri'βir] *vt* to appoint; **estuvo adscrito al servicio de ...** he was attached to ...

adscrito [að'skrito] *pp de* **adscribir**

ADSL *nm abr* ADSL

aduana [a'ðwana] *nf* customs *pl*; (*impuesto*) (customs) duty

aduanero, -a [aðwa'nero, a] *adj* customs *cpd* ◼ *nm/f* customs officer

aducir [aðu'θir] *vt* to adduce; (*dar como prueba*) to offer as proof

adueñarse [aðwe'ɲarse] *vr*: **~ de** to take possession of

adulación [aðula'θjon] *nf* flattery

adular [aðu'lar] *vt* to flatter

adulterar [aðulte'rar] *vt* to adulterate ◼ *vi* to commit adultery

adulterio [aðul'terjo] *nm* adultery

adúltero, -a [a'ðultero, a] *adj* adulterous ◼ *nm/f* adulterer/adulteress

adulto, -a [a'ðulto, a] *adj, nm/f* adult

adusto, -a [a'ðusto, a] *adj* stern; (*austero*) austere

aduzca *etc* [a'ðuθka] *vb ver* **aducir**

advenedizo, -a [aðβene'ðiθo, a] *nm/f* upstart

advenimiento [aðβeni'mjento] *nm* arrival; (*al trono*) accession

adverbio [að'βerβjo] *nm* adverb
adversario, -a [aðβer'sarjo, a] *nm/f*
adversary
adversidad [aðβersi'ðað] *nf* adversity;
(*contratiempo*) setback
adverso, -a [að'βerso, a] *adj* adverse; (*suerte*)
bad
advertencia [aðβer'tenθja] *nf* warning;
(*prefacio*) preface, foreword
advertir [aðβer'tir] *vt* (*observar*) to notice;
(*avisar*): ~ **a algn de** to warn sb about o of
Adviento [að'βjento] *nm* Advent
advierta *etc* [að'βjerta], **advirtiendo** *etc*
[aðβir'tjendo] *vb ver* **advertir**
adyacente [aðja'θente] *adj* adjacent
aéreo, -a [a'ereo, a] *adj* aerial; (*tráfico*) air *cpd*
aerobic [ae'roβik] *nm* aerobics *sg*
aerodeslizador [aeroðesliða'ðor] *nm*
hovercraft
aerodinámico, -a [aeroði'namiko, a] *adj*
aerodynamic
aeródromo [ae'roðromo] *nm* aerodrome
aerograma [aero'ɣrama] *nm* airmail letter
aeromodelismo [aeromoðe'lismo] *nm*
model aircraft making, aeromodelling
aeromozo, -a [aero'moso, a] *nm/f* (*Am*) flight
attendant, air steward(ess)
aeronáutico, -a [aero'nautiko, a] *adj*
aeronautical
aeronave [aero'naβe] *nm* spaceship
aeroplano [aero'plano] *nm* aeroplane
aeropuerto [aero'pwerto] *nm* airport
aerosol [aero'sol] *nm* aerosol, spray
a/f *abr* (= *a favor*) in favour
afabilidad [afaβili'ðað] *nf* affability,
pleasantness
afable [a'faβle] *adj* affable, pleasant
afamado, -a [afa'maðo, a] *adj* famous
afán [a'fan] *nm* hard work; (*deseo*) desire;
con ~ keenly
afanar [afa'nar] *vt* to harass; (*fam*) to pinch;
afanarse *vr*: **afanarse por** to strive to
afanoso, -a [afa'noso, a] *adj* (*trabajo*) hard;
(*trabajador*) industrious
AFE ['afe] *nf abr* (= *Asociación de Futbolistas*
Españoles) ≈ F.A
afear [afe'ar] *vt* to disfigure
afección [afek'θjon] *nf* affection; (*Med*)
disease
afectación [afekta'θjon] *nf* affectation
afectado, -a [afek'taðo, a] *adj* affected
afectar [afek'tar] *vt* to affect, have an effect
on; (*Am: dañar*) to hurt; **por lo que afecta a**
esto as far as this is concerned
afectísimo, -a [afek'tisimo, a] *adj*
affectionate; **suyo ~** yours truly
afectivo, -a [afek'tiβo, a] *adj* affective

afecto, -a [a'fekto, a] *adj*: ~ **a** fond of; (*Jur*)
subject to ■ *nm* affection; **tenerle ~ a algn**
to be fond of sb
afectuoso, -a [afek'twoso, a] *adj*
affectionate
afeitar [afei'tar] *vt* to shave; **afeitarse** *vr*
to shave
afeminado, -a [afemi'naðo, a] *adj*
effeminate
aferrar [afe'rrar] *vt* to moor; (*fig*) to grasp
■ *vi* to moor; **aferrarse** *vr* (*agarrarse*) to cling
on; **aferrarse a un principio** to stick to a
principle; **aferrarse a una esperanza** to
cling to a hope
Afganistán [afɣanis'tan] *nm* Afghanistan
afgano, -a [af'ɣano, a] *adj, nm/f* Afghan
afiance *etc* [a'fjanθe] *vb ver* **afianzar**
afianzamiento [afjanθa'mjento] *nm*
strengthening; security
afianzar [afjan'θar] *vt* to strengthen, secure;
afianzarse *vr* to steady o.s.; (*establecerse*) to
become established
afiche [a'fitʃe] *nm* (*Am*) poster
afición [afi'θjon] *nf*: ~ **a** fondness o liking
for; **la ~** the fans *pl*; **pinto por ~** I paint as a
hobby
aficionado, -a [afiθjo'naðo, a] *adj* keen,
enthusiastic; (*no profesional*) amateur ■ *nm/f*
enthusiast, fan; amateur
aficionar [afiθjo'nar] *vt*: ~ **a algn a algo**
to make sb like sth; **aficionarse** *vr*:
aficionarse a algo to grow fond of sth
afilado, -a [afi'laðo, a] *adj* sharp
afilador [afila'ðor] *nm* knife grinder
afilalápices [afila'lapiθes] *nm inv* pencil
sharpener
afilar [afi'lar] *vt* to sharpen; **afilarse** *vr* (*cara*)
to grow thin
afiliación [afilja'θjon] *nf* (*de sindicatos*)
membership
afiliado, -a [afi'ljaðo, a] *adj* subsidiary
■ *nm/f* affiliate
afiliarse [afi'ljarse] *vr* to affiliate
afín [a'fin] *adj* (*parecido*) similar; (*conexo*)
related
afinar [afi'nar] *vt* (*Tec*) to refine; (*Mus*) to tune
■ *vi* to play/sing in tune
afincarse [afin'karse] *vr* to settle
afinidad [afini'ðað] *nf* affinity; (*parentesco*)
relationship; **por ~** by marriage
afirmación [afirma'θjon] *nf* affirmation
afirmar [afir'mar] *vt* to affirm, state;
(*sostener*) to strengthen; **afirmarse** *vr*
(*recuperar el equilibrio*) to steady o.s.; **afirmarse**
en lo dicho to stand by what one has said
afirmativo, -a [afirma'tiβo, a] *adj*
affirmative

aflicción [aflik'θjon] *nf* affliction; (*dolor*) grief

afligir [afli'xir] *vt* to afflict; (*apenar*) to distress; **afligirse** *vr*: **afligirse (por** *o* **con** *o* **de)** to grieve (about *o* at); **no te aflijas tanto** you must not let it affect you like this

aflija *etc* [a'flixa] *vb ver* **afligir**

aflojar [aflo'xar] *vt* to slacken; (*desatar*) to loosen, undo; (*relajar*) to relax ■ *vi* (*amainar*) to drop; (*bajar*) to go down; **aflojarse** *vr* to relax

aflorar [aflo'rar] *vi* (*Geo, fig*) to come to the surface, emerge

afluencia [aflu'enθja] *nf* flow

afluente [aflu'ente] *adj* flowing ■ *nm* (*Geo*) tributary

afluir [aflu'ir] *vi* to flow

afluya *etc* [a'fluja], **afluyendo** *etc* [aflu'jendo] *vb ver* **afluir**

afmo., -a. *abr* (= *afectísimo, a suyo, a*) Yours

afónico, -a [a'foniko, a] *adj*: **estar ~** to have a sore throat; to have lost one's voice

aforar [afo'rar] *vt* (*Tec*) to gauge; (*fig*) to value

aforo [a'foro] *nm* (*Tec*) gauging; (*de teatro etc*) capacity; **el teatro tiene un ~ de 2,000** the theatre can seat 2,000

afortunado, -a [afortu'naðo, a] *adj* fortunate, lucky

afrancesado, -a [afranθe'saðo, a] *adj* francophile; (*pey*) Frenchified

afrenta [a'frenta] *nf* affront, insult; (*deshonra*) dishonour (*Brit*), dishonor (*US*), shame

afrentoso, -a [afren'toso, a] *adj* insulting; shameful

África ['afrika] *nf* Africa; **África del Sur** South Africa

africano, -a [afri'kano, a] *adj, nm/f* African

afrontar [afron'tar] *vt* to confront; (*poner cara a cara*) to bring face to face

after ['after] (*pl* **afters** *o* **~**) *nm*, **afterhours** ['afterauars] *nm inv* after-hours club

afuera [a'fwera] *adv* out, outside; **por ~** on the outside; **afueras** *nfpl* outskirts

ag. *abr* (= *agosto*) Aug

agachar [aɣa'tʃar] *vt* to bend, bow; **agacharse** *vr* to stoop, bend

agalla [a'ɣaʎa] *nf* (*Zool*) gill; **agallas** *nfpl* (*Med*) tonsillitis *sg*; (*Anat*) tonsils; **tener agallas** (*fam*) to have guts

agarradera [aɣarra'ðera] *nf* (*Am*), **agarradero** [aɣarra'ðero] *nm* handle; **agarraderas** *nfpl* pull *sg*, influence *sg*

agarrado, -a [aɣa'rraðo, a] *adj* mean, stingy

agarrar [aɣa'rrar] *vt* to grasp, grab; (*Am*) to take, catch ■ *vi* (*planta*) to take root; **agarrarse** *vr* to hold on (tightly); (*meterse*

uno con otro) to grapple (with each other); **agarrársela con algn** (*Am*) to pick on sb; **agarró y se fue** (*esp Am fam*) he upped and went

agarrotar [aɣarro'tar] *vt* (*lío*) to tie tightly; (*persona*) to squeeze tightly; (*reo*) to garrotte; **agarrotarse** *vr* (*motor*) to seize up; (*Med*) to stiffen

agasajar [aɣasa'xar] *vt* to treat well, fête

agave [a'ɣaβe] *nf* agave

agazapar [aɣaθa'par] *vt* (*coger*) to grab hold of; **agazaparse** *vr* (*agacharse*) to crouch down

agencia [a'xenθja] *nf* agency; **~ de créditos/ publicidad/viajes** credit/advertising/travel agency; **~ inmobiliaria** estate agent's (office) (*Brit*), real estate office (*US*); **~ matrimonial** marriage bureau

agenciar [axen'θjar] *vt* to bring about; **agenciarse** *vr* to look after o.s.; **agenciarse algo** to get hold of sth

agenda [a'xenda] *nf* diary; **~ electrónica** PDA; **~ telefónica** telephone directory

agente [a'xente] *nm* agent; (*de policía*) policeman; **~ femenino** policewoman; **~ de bolsa** stockbroker; **~ inmobiliario** estate agent (*Brit*), realtor (*US*); **~ de negocios** (*Com*) business agent; **~ de seguros** insurance broker; **~ de viajes** travel agent; **agentes sociales** social partners

ágil ['axil] *adj* agile, nimble

agilidad [axili'ðað] *nf* agility, nimbleness

agilizar [axili'θar] *vt* to speed up

agitación [axita'θjon] *nf* (*de mano etc*) shaking, waving; (*de líquido etc*) stirring; agitation

agitar [axi'tar] *vt* to wave, shake; (*líquido*) to stir; (*fig*) to stir up, excite; **agitarse** *vr* to get excited; (*inquietarse*) to get worried *o* upset

aglomeración [aɣlomera'θjon] *nf*: **~ de tráfico/gente** traffic jam/mass of people

aglomerar [aɣlome'rar] *vt*, **aglomerarse** *vr* to crowd together

agnóstico, -a [aɣ'nostiko, a] *adj, nm/f* agnostic

agobiante [aɣo'βjante] *adj* (*calor*) oppressive

agobiar [aɣo'βjar] *vt* to weigh down; (*oprimir*) to oppress; (*cargar*) to burden; **sentirse agobiado por** to be overwhelmed by

agobio [a'ɣoβjo] *nm* (*peso*) burden; (*fig*) oppressiveness

agolpamiento [aɣolpa'mjento] *nm* crush

agolparse [aɣol'parse] *vr* to crowd together

agonía [aɣo'nia] *nf* death throes *pl*; (*fig*) agony, anguish

agonice *etc* [aɣo'niθe] *vb ver* **agonizar**

agonizante [aɣoni'θante] *adj* dying

agonizar [aɣoni'θar] *vi* (*tb*: **estar**

11

agonizando) to be dying

agorero, -a [aɣo'rero, a] adj ominous ▪ nm/f soothsayer; **ave agorera** bird of ill omen

agostar [aɣo'star] vt (quemar) to parch; (fig) to wither

agosto [a'ɣosto] nm August; (fig) harvest; **hacer su ~** to make one's pile; ver tb **julio**

agotado, -a [aɣo'taðo, a] adj (persona) exhausted; (acabado) finished; (Com) sold out; (: libros) out of print; (pila) flat

agotador, a [aɣota'ðor, a] adj exhausting

agotamiento [aɣota'mjento] nm exhaustion

agotar [aɣo'tar] vt to exhaust; (consumir) to drain; (recursos) to use up, deplete; **agotarse** vr to be exhausted; (acabarse) to run out; (libro) to go out of print

agraciado, -a [aɣra'θjaðo, a] adj (atractivo) attractive; (en sorteo etc) lucky

agraciar [aɣra'θjar] vt (Jur) to pardon; (con premio) to reward; (hacer más atractivo) to make more attractive

agradable [aɣra'ðaβle] adj pleasant, nice

agradar [aɣra'ðar] vt, vi to please; **agradarse** vr to like each other

agradecer [aɣraðe'θer] vt to thank; (favor etc) to be grateful for; **le ~ía me enviara ...** I would be grateful if you would send me ...; **agradecerse** vr: **¡se agradece!** much obliged!

agradecido, -a [aɣraðe'θiðo, a] adj grateful; **¡muy ~!** thanks a lot!

agradecimiento [aɣraðeθi'mjento] nm thanks pl; gratitude

agradezca etc [aɣra'ðeθka] vb ver **agradecer**

agrado [a'ɣraðo] nm: **ser de tu** etc **~** to be to your etc liking

agrandar [aɣran'dar] vt to enlarge; (fig) to exaggerate; **agrandarse** vr to get bigger

agrario, -a [a'ɣrarjo, a] adj agrarian, land cpd; (política) agricultural, farming cpd

agravante [aɣra'βante] adj aggravating ▪ nf complication; **con la ~ de que ...** with the further difficulty that ...

agravar [aɣra'βar] vt (pesar sobre) to make heavier; (irritar) to aggravate; **agravarse** vr to worsen, get worse

agraviar [aɣra'βjar] vt to offend; (ser injusto con) to wrong; **agraviarse** vr to take offence

agravio [a'ɣraβjo] nm offence; wrong; (Jur) grievance

agraz [a'ɣraθ] nm (uva) sour grape; **en ~** (fig) immature

agredir [aɣre'ðir] vt to attack

agregado [aɣre'ɣaðo] nm aggregate; (persona) attaché; (profesor) assistant professor

agregar [aɣre'ɣar] vt to gather; (añadir) to add; (persona) to appoint

agregue etc [a'ɣreɣe] vb ver **agregar**

agresión [aɣre'sjon] nf aggression; (ataque) attack

agresivo, -a [aɣre'siβo, a] adj aggressive

agreste [a'ɣreste] adj (rural) rural; (fig) rough

agriar [a'ɣrjar] vt (fig) to (turn) sour; **agriarse** vr to turn sour

agrícola [a'ɣrikola] adj farming cpd, agricultural

agricultor, a [aɣrikul'tor, a] nm/f farmer

agricultura [aɣrikul'tura] nf agriculture, farming

agridulce [aɣri'ðulθe] adj bittersweet; (Culin) sweet and sour

agrietarse [aɣrje'tarse] vr to crack; (la piel) to chap

agrimensor, a [aɣrimen'sor, a] nm/f surveyor

agringado, -a [aɣrin'gaðo, a] adj gringolike

agrio, -a ['aɣrjo, a] adj bitter

agronomía [aɣrono'mia] nf agronomy, agriculture

agrónomo, -a [a'ɣronomo, a] nm/f agronomist, agricultural expert

agropecuario, -a [aɣrope'kwarjo, a] adj farming cpd, agricultural

agrupación [aɣrupa'θjon] nf group; (acto) grouping

agrupar [aɣru'par] vt to group; (Inform) to block; **agruparse** vr (Pol) to form a group; (juntarse) to gather

agua ['aɣwa] nf water; (Naut) wake; (Arq) slope of a roof; **aguas** nfpl (de joya) water sg, sparkle sg; (Med) water sg, urine sg; (Naut) waters; **aguas abajo/arriba** downstream/upstream; **~ bendita/destilada/potable** holy/distilled/drinking water; **~ caliente** hot water; **~ corriente** running water; **~ de colonia** eau de cologne; **~ mineral (con/sin gas)** (fizzy/non-fizzy) mineral water; **aguas jurisdiccionales** territorial waters; **aguas mayores** excrement sg; **~ pasada no mueve molino** it's no use crying over spilt milk; **estar con el ~ al cuello** to be up to one's neck; **venir como ~ de mayo** to be a godsend

aguacate [aɣwa'kate] nm avocado (pear)

aguacero [aɣwa'θero] nm (heavy) shower, downpour

aguachirle [aɣwa'tʃirle] nm (bebida) slops pl

aguado, -a [a'ɣwaðo, a] adj watery, watered down ▪ nf (Agr) watering place; (Naut) water supply; (Arte) watercolour

aguafiestas [aɣwa'fjestas] nm/f inv spoilsport

aguafuerte [aɣwa'fwerte] nf etching

aguaitar [aɣwai'tar] vt (Am) to watch

aguanieve [aɣwa'njeβe] nf sleet

aguantable [aɣwan'taβle] *adj* bearable, tolerable

aguantar [aɣwan'tar] *vt* to bear, put up with; (*sostener*) to hold up ■ *vi* to last; **aguantarse** *vr* to restrain o.s.; **no sé cómo aguanta** I don't know how he can take it

aguante [a'ɣwante] *nm* (*paciencia*) patience; (*resistencia*) endurance; (*Deporte*) stamina

aguar [a'ɣwar] *vt* to water down; (*fig*): ~ **la fiesta a algn** to spoil sb's fun

aguardar [aɣwar'ðar] *vt* to wait for

aguardentoso, -a [aɣwarðen'toso, a] *adj* (*pey: voz*) husky, gruff

aguardiente [aɣwar'ðjente] *nm* brandy, liquor

aguarrás [aɣwa'rras] *nm* turpentine

aguce *etc* [a'ɣuθe] *vb ver* **aguzar**

agudeza [aɣu'ðeθa] *nf* sharpness; (*ingenio*) wit

agudice *etc* [aɣu'ðiθe] *vb ver* **agudizar**

agudizar [aɣuði'θar] *vt* to sharpen; (*crisis*) to make worse; **agudizarse** *vr* to worsen, deteriorate

agudo, -a [a'ɣuðo, a] *adj* sharp; (*voz*) high-pitched, piercing; (*dolor, enfermedad*) acute

agüe *etc* ['aɣwe] *vb ver* **aguar**

agüero [a'ɣwero] *nm*: **buen/mal** ~ good/bad omen; **ser de buen** ~ to augur well; **pájaro de mal** ~ bird of ill omen

aguerrido, -a [aɣe'rriðo, a] *adj* hardened; (*fig*) experienced

aguijar [aɣi'xar] *vt* to goad; (*incitar*) to urge on ■ *vi* to hurry along

aguijón [aɣi'xon] *nm* sting; (*fig*) spur

aguijonear [aɣixone'ar] *vt* = **aguijar**

águila ['aɣila] *nf* eagle; (*fig*) genius

aguileño, -a [aɣi'leɲo, a] *adj* (*nariz*) aquiline; (*rostro*) sharp-featured

aguinaldo [aɣi'naldo] *nm* Christmas box

aguja [a'ɣuxa] *nf* needle; (*de reloj*) hand; (*Arq*) spire; (*Tec*) firing-pin; **agujas** *nfpl* (*Zool*) ribs; (*Ferro*) points

agujerear [aɣuxere'ar] *vt* to make holes in; (*penetrar*) to pierce

agujero [aɣu'xero] *nm* hole; (*Com*) deficit

agujetas [aɣu'xetas] *nfpl* stitch *sg*; (*rigidez*) stiffness *sg*

aguzar [aɣu'θar] *vt* to sharpen; (*fig*) to incite; ~ **el oído** to prick up one's ears

aherrumbrarse [aerrum'brarse] *vr* to get rusty

ahí [a'i] *adv* there; (*allá*) over there; **de ahí que** so that, with the result that; **ahí llega** here he comes; **por ahí** (*dirección*) that way; **¡hasta ahí hemos llegado!** so it has come to this!; **¡ahí va!** (*objeto*) here it comes!; (*individuo*) there he goes!; **ahí donde le ve** as sure as he's standing there

ahijado, -a [ai'xaðo, a] *nm/f* godson/daughter

ahijar [ai'xar] *vt*: ~ **algo a algn** (*fig*) to attribute sth to sb

ahínco [a'inko] *nm* earnestness; **con** ~ eagerly

ahíto, -a [a'ito, a] *adj*: **estoy** ~ I'm full up

ahogado, -a [ao'ɣaðo, a] *adj* (*en agua*) drowned; (*emoción*) pent-up; (*grito*) muffled

ahogar [ao'ɣar] *vt* (*en agua*) to drown; (*asfixiar*) to suffocate, smother; (*fuego*) to put out; **ahogarse** *vr* (*en agua*) to drown; (*por asfixia*) to suffocate

ahogo [a'oɣo] *nm* (*Med*) breathlessness; (*fig*) distress; (*problema económico*) financial difficulty

ahogue *etc* [a'oɣe] *vb ver* **ahogar**

ahondar [aon'dar] *vt* to deepen, make deeper; (*fig*) to go deeply into ■ *vi*: ~ **en** to go deeply into

ahora [a'ora] *adv* now; (*hace poco*) a moment ago, just now; (*dentro de poco*) in a moment; ~ **voy** I'm coming; ~ **mismo** right now; ~ **bien** now then; **por** ~ for the present

ahorcado, -a [aor'kaðo, a] *nm/f* hanged person

ahorcar [aor'kar] *vt* to hang; **ahorcarse** *vr* to hang o.s.

ahorita [ao'rita], **ahoritita** [aori'tita] *adv* (*esp Am: fam*) right now

ahorque *etc* [a'orke] *vb ver* **ahorcar**

ahorrar [ao'rrar] *vt* (*dinero*) to save; (*esfuerzos*) to save, avoid; **ahorrarse** *vr*: **ahorrarse molestias** to save o.s. trouble

ahorrativo, -a [aorra'tiβo, a] *adj* thrifty

ahorro [a'orro] *nm* (*acto*) saving; (*frugalidad*) thrift; **ahorros** *nmpl* savings

ahuecar [awe'kar] *vt* to hollow (out); (*voz*) to deepen ■ *vi*: **¡ahueca!** (*fam*) beat it! (*fam*); **ahuecarse** *vr* to give o.s. airs

ahueque *etc* [a'weke] *vb ver* **ahuecar**

ahumar [au'mar] *vt* to smoke, cure; (*llenar de humo*) to fill with smoke ■ *vi* to smoke; **ahumarse** *vr* to fill with smoke

ahuyentar [aujen'tar] *vt* to drive off, frighten off; (*fig*) to dispel

AI *nf abr* (= *Amnistía Internacional*) AI

aimara [ai'mara], **aimará** [aima'ra] *adj, nm/f* Aymara

aindiado, -a [aindi'aðo, a] *adj* (*Am*) Indian-like

airado, -a [ai'raðo, a] *adj* angry

airar [ai'rar] *vt* to anger; **airarse** *vr* to get angry

aire ['aire] *nm* air; (*viento*) wind; (*corriente*) draught; (*Mus*) tune; **aires** *nmpl*: **darse**

aires to give o.s. airs; **al ~ libre** in the open air; **~ aclimatizado** *o* **acondicionado** air conditioning; **tener ~ de** to look like; **estar de buen/mal ~** to be in a good/bad mood; **estar en el ~** (*Radio*) to be on the air; (*fig*) to be up in the air

airear [aire'ar] *vt* to ventilate; (*fig: asunto*) to air; **airearse** *vr* to take the air

airoso, -a [ai'roso, a] *adj* windy; draughty; (*fig*) graceful

aislado, -a [ais'laðo, a] *adj* (*remoto*) isolated; (*incomunicado*) cut off; (*Elec*) insulated

aislante [ais'lante] *nm* (*Elec*) insulator

aislar [ais'lar] *vt* to isolate; (*Elec*) to insulate; **aislarse** *vr* to cut o.s. off

ajar [a'xar] *vt* to spoil; (*fig*) to abuse; **ajarse** *vr* to get crumpled; (*fig: piel*) to get wrinkled

ajardinado, -a [axarði'naðo, a] *adj* landscaped

ajedrez [axe'ðreθ] *nm* chess

ajenjo [a'xenxo] *nm* (*bebida*) absinth(e)

ajeno, -a [a'xeno, a] *adj* (*que pertenece a otro*) somebody else's; **~ a** foreign to; **~ de** free from, devoid of; **por razones ajenas a nuestra voluntad** for reasons beyond our control

ajetreado, -a [axetre'aðo, a] *adj* busy

ajetrearse [axetre'arse] *vr* (*atarearse*) to bustle about; (*fatigarse*) to tire o.s. out

ajetreo [axe'treo] *nm* bustle

ají [a'xi] *nm* chil(l)i, red pepper; (*salsa*) chil(l)i sauce

ajiaco [axi'ako] *nm* (*Am*) potato and chil(l)i stew

ajilimoje [axili'moxe] *nm* sauce of garlic and pepper; **ajilimojes** *nmpl* (*fam*) odds and ends

ajo ['axo] *nm* garlic; **~ porro** *o* **puerro** leek; **(tieso) como un ~** (*fam*) snobbish; **estar en el ~** to be mixed up in it

ajorca [a'xorka] *nf* bracelet

ajuar [a'xwar] *nm* household furnishings *pl*; (*de novia*) trousseau; (*de niño*) layette

ajustado, -a [axus'taðo, a] *adj* (*tornillo*) tight; (*cálculo*) right; (*ropa*) tight(-fitting); (*Deporte: resultado*) close

ajustar [axus'tar] *vt* (*adaptar*) to adjust; (*encajar*) to fit; (*Tec*) to engage; (*Tip*) to make up; (*apretar*) to tighten; (*concertar*) to agree (on); (*reconciliar*) to reconcile; (*cuenta*) to settle ■ *vi* to fit

ajuste [a'xuste] *nm* adjustment; (*Costura*) fitting; (*acuerdo*) compromise; (*de cuenta*) settlement

al [al] = **a+el**; *ver* **a**

ala ['ala] *nf* wing; (*de sombrero*) brim; (*futbolista*) winger; **~ delta** hang-glider; **andar con el ~ caída** to be downcast; **cortar**

las alas a algn to clip sb's wings; **dar alas a algn** to encourage sb

alabanza [ala'βanθa] *nf* praise

alabar [ala'βar] *vt* to praise

alacena [ala'θena] *nf* cupboard (*Brit*), closet (*US*)

alacrán [ala'kran] *nm* scorpion

ALADI [a'laði] *nf abr* = **Asociación Latinoamericana de Integración**

alado, -a [a'laðo, a] *adj* winged

ALALC [a'lalk] *nf abr* (= *Asociación Latinoamericana de Libre Comercio*) LAFTA

alambicado, -a [alambi'kaðo, a] *adj* distilled; (*fig*) affected

alambicar [alambi'kar] *vt* to distil

alambique *etc* [alam'bike] *vb ver* **alambicar** ■ *nm* still

alambrada [alam'braða] *nf*, **alambrado** [alam'braðo] *nm* wire fence; (*red*) wire netting

alambre [a'lambre] *nm* wire; **~ de púas** barbed wire

alambrista [alam'brista] *nm/f* tightrope walker

alameda [ala'meða] *nf* (*plantío*) poplar grove; (*lugar de paseo*) avenue, boulevard

álamo ['alamo] *nm* poplar; **álamo temblón** aspen

alano [a'lano] *nm* mastiff

alarde [a'larðe] *nm* show, display; **hacer ~ de** to boast of

alardear [alarðe'ar] *vi* to boast

alargador [alarɣa'ðor] *nm* extension cable *o* lead

alargar [alar'ɣar] *vt* to lengthen, extend; (*paso*) to hasten; (*brazo*) to stretch out; (*cuerda*) to pay out; (*conversación*) to spin out; **alargarse** *vr* to get longer

alargue *etc* [a'larɣe] *vb ver* **alargar**

alarido [ala'riðo] *nm* shriek

alarma [a'larma] *nf* alarm; **voz de ~** warning note; **dar la ~** to raise the alarm

alarmante [alar'mante] *adj* alarming

alarmar [alar'mar] *vt* to alarm; **alarmarse** *vr* to get alarmed

alavés, -esa [ala'βes, esa] *adj* of Álava ■ *nm/f* native *o* inhabitant of Álava

alba ['alβa] *nf* dawn

albacea [alβa'θea] *nm/f* executor/executrix

albaceteño, -a [alβaθe'teɲo, a] *adj* of Albacete ■ *nm/f* native *o* inhabitant of Albacete

albahaca [al'βaka] *nf* (*Bot*) basil

Albania [al'βanja] *nf* Albania

albañal [alβa'ɲal] *nm* drain, sewer

albañil [alβa'ɲil] *nm* bricklayer; (*cantero*) mason

albarán [alβa'ran] *nm* (*Com*) invoice
albarda [al'βarða] *nf* packsaddle
albaricoque [alβari'koke] *nm* apricot
albedrío [alβe'ðrio] *nm*: **libre ~** free will
alberca [al'βerka] *nf* reservoir; (*Am*)
swimming pool
albergar [alβer'ɣar] *vt* to shelter; (*esperanza*)
to cherish; **albergarse** *vr* (*refugiarse*) to
shelter; (*alojarse*) to lodge
albergue *etc* [al'βerɣe] *vb ver* **albergar** ▪ *nm*
shelter, refuge; **~ de juventud** youth hostel
albis ['alβis] *adv*: **quedarse en ~** not to have
a clue
albóndiga [al'βondiɣa] *nf* meatball
albor [al'βor] *nm* whiteness; (*amanecer*) dawn
alborada [alβo'raða] *nf* dawn; (*diana*) reveille
alborear [alβore'ar] *vi* to dawn
albornoz [alβor'noθ] *nm* (*de los árabes*)
burnous; (*para el baño*) bathrobe
alboroce *etc* [alβo'roθe] *vb ver* **alborozar**
alborotar [alβoro'tar] *vi* to make a row
▪ *vt* to agitate, stir up; **alborotarse** *vr* to get
excited; (*mar*) to get rough
alboroto [alβo'roto] *nm* row, uproar
alborozar [alβoro'θar] *vt* to gladden;
alborozarse *vr* to rejoice, be overjoyed
alborozo [alβo'roθo] *nm* joy
albricias [al'βriθjas] *nfpl*: **¡~!** good news!
álbum ['alβum] (*pl* **álbums** *o* **álbumes**) *nm*
album
albumen [al'βumen] *nm* egg white, albumen
alcabala [alka'βala] *nf* (*Am*) roadblock
alcachofa [alka'tʃofa] *nf* (globe) artichoke;
(*Tip*) golf ball; (*de ducha*) shower head
alcahueta [alka'weta] *nf* procuress
alcahuete [alka'wete] *nm* pimp
alcalde, -esa [al'kalde, alkal'desa] *nm/f*
mayor(ess)
alcaldía [alkal'dia] *nf* mayoralty; (*lugar*)
mayor's office
álcali ['alkali] *nm* (*Química*) alkali
alcance *etc* [al'kanθe] *vb ver* **alcanzar** ▪ *nm*
(*Mil*: *Radio*) range; (*fig*) scope; (*Com*) adverse
balance, deficit; **estar al/fuera del ~ de**
algn to be within/beyond one's reach; (*fig*) to
be within one's powers/over one's head; **de**
gran ~ (*Mil*) long-range; (*fig*) far-reaching
alcancía [alkan'θia] *nf* money box
alcanfor [alkan'for] *nm* camphor
alcantarilla [alkanta'riʎa] *nf* (*de aguas*
cloacales) sewer; (*en la calle*) gutter
alcanzar [alkan'θar] *vt* (*algo: con la mano, el*
pie) to reach; (*alguien: en el camino etc*) to catch
up (with); (*autobús*) to catch; (*suj: bala*) to hit,
strike ▪ *vi* (*ser suficiente*) to be enough; **~ algo**
a algn to hand sth to sb; **alcánzame la sal,**
por favor pass the salt please; **~ a hacer** to

manage to do
alcaparra [alka'parra] *nf* (*Bot*) caper
alcatraz [alka'traθ] *nm* gannet
alcayata [alka'jata] *nf* hook
alcázar [al'kaθar] *nm* fortress; (*Naut*)
quarter-deck
alce *etc* ['alθe] *vb ver* **alzar**
alcista [al'θista] *adj* (*Com: Econ*): **mercado**
~ bull market; **la tendencia ~** the upward
trend ▪ *nm* speculator
alcoba [al'koβa] *nf* bedroom
alcohol [al'kol] *nm* alcohol; **no bebe ~** he
doesn't drink (alcohol)
alcoholemia [alkoo'lemia] *nf* blood alcohol
level; **prueba de la ~** breath test
alcoholice *etc* [alko'liθe] *vb ver* **alcoholizarse**
alcohólico, -a [al'koliko, a] *adj, nm/f*
alcoholic
alcoholímetro [alko'limetro] *nm*
Breathalyser®, drunkometer (*US*)
alcoholismo [alko'lismo] *nm* alcoholism
alcoholizarse [alkoli'θarse] *vr* to become an
alcoholic
alcornoque [alkor'noke] *nm* cork tree; (*fam*)
idiot
alcotana [alko'tana] *nf* pickaxe; (*Deporte*)
ice-axe
alcurnia [al'kurnja] *nf* lineage
alcuza [al'kusa] *nf* (*Am*) cruet
aldaba [al'daβa] *nf* (door) knocker
aldea [al'dea] *nf* village
aldeano, -a [alde'ano, a] *adj* village *cpd*
▪ *nm/f* villager
ale ['ale] *excl* come on!, let's go!
aleación [alea'θjon] *nf* alloy
aleatorio, -a [alea'torjo, a] *adj* random,
contingent; **acceso ~** (*Inform*) random access
aleccionador, a [alekθjona'ðor, a] *adj*
instructive
aleccionar [alekθjo'nar] *vt* to instruct;
(*adiestrar*) to train
aledaño, -a [ale'ðaɲo, a] *adj*: **~ a** bordering
on ▪ *nmpl*: **aledaños** outskirts
alegación [aleɣa'θjon] *nf* allegation
alegar [ale'ɣar] *vt* (*dificultad etc*) to plead; (*Jur*)
to allege ▪ *vi* (*Am*) to argue; **~ que ...** to give
as an excuse that ...
alegato [ale'ɣato] *nm* (*Jur*) allegation; (*escrito*)
indictment; (*declaración*) statement; (*Am*)
argument
alegoría [aleɣo'ria] *nf* allegory
alegrar [ale'ɣrar] *vt* (*causar alegría*) to cheer
(up); (*fuego*) to poke; (*fiesta*) to liven up;
alegrarse *vr* (*fam*) to get merry *o* tight;
alegrarse de to be glad about
alegre [a'leɣre] *adj* happy, cheerful; (*fam*)
merry, tight; (*licencioso*) risqué, blue

alegría | alienación

alegría [ale'ɣria] *nf* happiness; merriment;
~ **vital** joie de vivre
alegrón [ale'ɣron] *nm* (*fig*) sudden joy
alegue *etc* [a'leɣe] *vb ver* **alegar**
alejamiento [alexa'mjento] *nm* removal;
(*distancia*) remoteness
alejar [ale'xar] *vt* to move away, remove; (*fig*)
to estrange; **alejarse** *vr* to move away
alelado, -a [ale'laðo, a] *adj* (*bobo*) foolish
alelar [ale'lar] *vt* to bewilder
aleluya [ale'luja] *nm* (*canto*) hallelujah
alemán, -ana [ale'man, ana] *adj, nm/f*
German ∎ *nm* (*lengua*) German
Alemania [ale'manja] *nf* Germany; ~
Occidental/Oriental West/East Germany
alentador, a [alenta'ðor, a] *adj* encouraging
alentar [alen'tar] *vt* to encourage
alergia [a'lerxja] *nf* allergy
alero [a'lero] *nm* (*de tejado*) eaves *pl*; (*de foca,
Deporte*) flipper; (*Auto*) mudguard
alerta [a'lerta] *adj inv, nm* alert
aleta [a'leta] *nf* (*de pez*) fin; (*de ave*) wing;
(*de coche*) mudguard
aletargar [aletar'ɣar] *vt* to make drowsy;
(*entumecer*) to make numb; **aletargarse** *vr*
to grow drowsy; to become numb
aletargue *etc* [ale'tarɣe] *vb ver* **aletargar**
aletear [alete'ar] *vi* to flutter; (*ave*) to flap its
wings; (*individuo*) to wave one's arms
alevín [ale'βin] *nm* fry, young fish
alevosía [aleβo'sia] *nf* treachery
alfabetización [alfaβetiθa'θjon] *nf*:
campaña de ~ literacy campaign
alfabeto [alfa'βeto] *nm* alphabet
alfajor [alfa'xor] *nm* (*Esp: polvorón*) *cake eaten at
Christmas time*
alfalfa [al'falfa] *nf* alfalfa, lucerne
alfaque [al'fake] *nm* (*Naut*) bar, sandbank
alfar [al'far] *nm* (*taller*) potter's workshop;
(*arcilla*) clay
alfarería [alfare'ria] *nf* pottery; (*tienda*)
pottery shop
alfarero [alfa'rero] *nm* potter
alféizar [al'feiθar] *nm* window-sill
alférez [al'fereθ] *nm* (*Mil*) second lieutenant;
(*Naut*) ensign
alfil [al'fil] *nm* (*Ajedrez*) bishop
alfiler [alfi'ler] *nm* pin; (*broche*) clip; (*pinza*)
clothes peg (*Brit*) *o* pin (*US*); ~ **de gancho**
(*Am*) safety pin; **prendido con alfileres**
shaky
alfiletero [alfile'tero] *nm* needle case
alfombra [al'fombra] *nf* carpet; (*más pequeña*)
rug
alfombrar [alfom'brar] *vt* to carpet
alfombrilla [alfom'briʎa] *nf* rug, mat;
(*Inform*) mouse mat *o* pad

alforja [al'forxa] *nf* saddlebag
alforza [al'forθa] *nf* pleat
algarabía [alɣara'βia] *nf* (*fam*) gibberish;
(*griterío*) hullabaloo
algarada [alɣa'raða] *nf* outcry; **hacer** *o*
levantar una ~ to kick up a tremendous fuss
Algarbe [al'ɣarβe] *nm*: **el ~** the Algarve
algarroba [alɣa'rroβa] *nf* carob
algarrobo [alɣa'rroβo] *nm* carob tree
algas ['alɣas] *nfpl* seaweed *sg*
algazara [alɣa'θara] *nf* din, uproar
álgebra ['alxeβra] *nf* algebra
álgido, -a ['alxiðo, a] *adj* icy; (*momento etc*)
crucial, decisive
algo ['alɣo] *pron* something; (*en frases
interrogativas*) anything ∎ *adv* somewhat,
rather; **por ~ será** there must be some
reason for it; **es ~ difícil** it's a bit awkward
algodón [alɣo'ðon] *nm* cotton; (*planta*) cotton
plant; ~ **de azúcar** candy floss (*Brit*), cotton
candy (*US*); ~ **hidrófilo** cotton wool (*Brit*),
absorbent cotton (*US*)
algodonero, -a [alɣoðo'nero, a] *adj* cotton
cpd ∎ *nm/f* cotton grower ∎ *nm* cotton plant
algoritmo [alɣo'ritmo] *nm* algorithm
alguacil [alɣwa'θil] *nm* bailiff; (*Taur*)
mounted official
alguien ['alɣjen] *pron* someone, somebody;
(*en frases interrogativas*) anybody
alguno, -a [al'ɣuno, a] *adj* (*antes de nmsg*
algún) some; (*después de n*): **no tiene talento**
~ he has no talent, he hasn't any talent
∎ *pron* (*alguien*) someone, somebody; **algún
que otro libro** some book or other; **algún
día iré** I'll go one *o* some day; **sin interés ~**
without the slightest interest; ~ **que otro**
an occasional one; **algunos piensan** some
(people) think; ~ **de ellos** one of them
alhaja [a'laxa] *nf* jewel; (*tesoro*) precious
object, treasure
alhelí [ale'li] *nm* wallflower, stock
aliado, -a [a'ljaðo, a] *adj* allied
alianza [a'ljanθa] *nf* (*Pol etc*) alliance; (*anillo*)
wedding ring
aliar [a'ljar] *vt* to ally; **aliarse** *vr* to form an
alliance
alias ['aljas] *adv* alias
alicaído, -a [alika'iðo, a] *adj* (*Med*) weak; (*fig*)
depressed
alicantino, -a [alikan'tino, a] *adj* of Alicante
∎ *nm/f* native *o* inhabitant of Alicante
alicatar [alika'tar] *vt* to tile
alicate [ali'kate] *nm*, **alicates** [ali'kates]
nmpl pliers *pl*; ~**(s) de uñas** nail clippers
aliciente [ali'θjente] *nm* incentive; (*atracción*)
attraction
alienación [aljena'θjon] *nf* alienation

aliento etc [a'ljento] vb ver **alentar** ▪ nm
breath; (respiración) breathing; **sin** ~ breathless;
de un ~ in one breath; (fig) in one go

aligerar [alixe'rar] vt to lighten; (reducir) to
shorten; (aliviar) to alleviate; (mitigar) to ease

alijo [a'lixo] nm (Naut) unloading;
(contrabando) smuggled goods

alimaña [ali'maɲa] nf pest

alimentación [alimenta'θjon] nf (comida)
food; (acción) feeding; (tienda) grocer's (shop);
~ **continua** (en fotocopiadora etc) stream feed

alimentador [alimenta'ðor] nm: ~ **de papel**
sheet-feeder

alimentar [alimen'tar] vt to feed; (nutrir) to
nourish; **alimentarse** vr: **alimentarse (de)**
to feed (on)

alimenticio, -a [alimen'tiθjo, a] adj food cpd;
(nutritivo) nourishing, nutritious

alimento [ali'mento] nm food; (nutrición)
nourishment; **alimentos** nmpl (Jur)
alimony sg

alimón [ali'mon]: **al** ~ adv jointly, together

alineación [alinea'θjon] nf alignment;
(Deporte) line-up

alineado, -a [aline'aðo, a] adj (Tip): **(no)** ~
(un)justified; ~ **a la izquierda/derecha**
ranged left/right

alinear [aline'ar] vt to align; (Tip) to justify;
alinearse vr to line up; **alinearse en** to fall
in with

aliñar [ali'ɲar] vt (Culin) to dress

aliño [a'liɲo] nm (Culin) dressing

alisar [ali'sar] vt to smooth

aliso [a'liso] nm alder

alistamiento [alista'mjento] nm
recruitment

alistar [ali'star] vt to recruit; **alistarse** vr to
enlist; (inscribirse) to enrol; (Am: prepararse) to
get ready

aliviar [ali'βjar] vt (carga) to lighten; (persona)
to relieve; (dolor) to relieve, alleviate

alivio [a'liβjo] nm alleviation, relief; ~ **de
luto** half-mourning

aljibe [al'xiβe] nm cistern

allá [a'ʎa] adv (lugar) there; (por ahí) over there;
(tiempo) then; **allá abajo** down there; **más
allá** further on; **más allá de** beyond; **¡allá
tú!** that's your problem!

allanamiento [aʎana'mjento] nm (Am Policía)
raid, search; ~ **de morada** housebreaking

allanar [aʎa'nar] vt to flatten, level (out);
(igualar) to smooth (out); (fig) to subdue; (Jur)
to burgle, break into; (Am Policía) to raid,
search; **allanarse** vr to fall down; **allanarse
a** to submit to, accept

allegado, -a [aʎe'ɣaðo, a] adj near, close
▪ nm/f relation

allende [a'ʎende] adv on the other side
▪ prep: ~ **los mares** beyond the seas

allí [a'ʎi] adv there; **allí mismo** right there;
por allí over there; (por ese camino) that way

alma ['alma] nf soul; (persona) person; (Tec)
core; **se le cayó el** ~ **a los pies** he became
very disheartened; **entregar el** ~ to pass
away; **estar con el** ~ **en la boca** to be scared
to death; **lo siento en el** ~ I am truly sorry;
tener el ~ **en un hilo** to have one's heart
in one's mouth; **estar como** ~ **en pena** to
suffer; **ir como** ~ **que lleva el diablo** to go at
breakneck speed

almacén [alma'θen] nm (depósito) warehouse,
store; (Mil) magazine; (Am) grocer's shop,
food store, grocery store (US); **(grandes)
almacenes** nmpl department store sg;
~ **depositario** (Com) depository

almacenaje [almaθe'naxe] nm storage;
~ **secundario** backup storage

almacenamiento [almaθena'mjento] nm
(Inform) storage; ~ **temporal en disco** disk
spooling

almacenar [almaθe'nar] vt to store, put in
storage; (Inform) to store; (proveerse) to stock
up with

almacenero [almaθe'nero] nm
warehouseman; (Am) grocer, shopkeeper

almanaque [alma'nake] nm almanac

almeja [al'mexa] nf clam

almenas [al'menas] nfpl battlements

almendra [al'mendra] nf almond

almendro [al'mendro] nm almond tree

almeriense [alme'rjense] adj of Almería
▪ nm/f native o inhabitant of Almería

almiar [al'mjar] nm haystack

almíbar [al'miβar] nm syrup

almidón [almi'ðon] nm starch

almidonado, -a [almiðo'naðo, a] adj
starched

almidonar [almiðo'nar] vt to starch

almirantazgo [almiran'taθɣo] nm admiralty

almirante [almi'rante] nm admiral

almirez [almi'reθ] nm mortar

almizcle [al'miθkle] nm musk

almizclero [almiθ'klero] nm musk deer

almohada [almo'aða] nf pillow; (funda)
pillowcase

almohadilla [almoa'ðiʎa] nf cushion; (Tec)
pad; (Am) pincushion; (Inform) hash key

almohadillado, -a [almoaði'ʎaðo, a] adj
(acolchado) padded

almohadón [almoa'ðon] nm large pillow

almorcé [almor'θe], **almorcemos** etc
[almor'θemos] vb ver **almorzar**

almorranas [almo'rranas] nfpl piles,
haemorrhoids (Brit), hemorrhoids (US)

almorzar [almor'θar] vt: ~ **una tortilla** to have an omelette for lunch ■ vi to (have) lunch

almuerce etc [al'mwerθe] vb ver **almorzar**

almuerzo etc [al'mwerθo] vb ver **almorzar** ■ nm lunch

aló [a'lo] excl (esp Am Telec) hello!

alocado, -a [alo'kaðo, a] adj crazy

alojamiento [aloxa'mjento] nm lodging(s) (pl); (viviendas) housing

alojar [alo'xar] vt to lodge; **alojarse** vr: **alojarse en** to stay at; (bala) to lodge in

alondra [a'londra] nf lark, skylark

alpaca [al'paka] nf alpaca

alpargata [alpar'ɣata] nf espadrille

Alpes ['alpes] nmpl: **los ~** the Alps

alpinismo [alpi'nismo] nm mountaineering, climbing

alpinista [alpi'nista] nm/f mountaineer, climber

alpino, -a [al'pino, a] adj alpine

alpiste [al'piste] nm (semillas) birdseed; (Am fam: dinero) dough; (fam: alcohol) booze

alquería [alke'ria] nf farmhouse

alquilar [alki'lar] vt (suj: propietario: inmuebles) to let, rent (out); (: coche) to hire out; (: TV) to rent (out); (suj: alquilador: inmuebles, TV) to rent; (: coche) to hire; **"se alquila casa"** "house to let (Brit) o to rent (US)"

alquiler [alki'ler] nm renting, letting; hiring; (arriendo) rent; hire charge; **de ~** for hire; **~ de automóviles** car hire

alquimia [al'kimja] nf alchemy

alquitrán [alki'tran] nm tar

alrededor [alreðe'ðor] adv around, about; **alrededores** nmpl surroundings; **~ de** prep around, about; **mirar a su ~** to look (round) about one

Alsacia [al'saθja] nf Alsace

alta ['alta] nf (certificate of) discharge; **dar a algn de ~** to discharge sb; **darse de ~** (Mil) to join, enrol; (Deporte) to declare o.s. fit

altanería [altane'ria] nf haughtiness, arrogance

altanero, -a [alta'nero, a] adj haughty, arrogant

altar [al'tar] nm altar

altavoz [alta'βoθ] nm loudspeaker; (amplificador) amplifier

alteración [altera'θjon] nf alteration; (alboroto) disturbance; **~ del orden público** breach of the peace

alterar [alte'rar] vt to alter; to disturb; **alterarse** vr (persona) to get upset

altercado [alter'kaðo] nm argument

alternar [alter'nar] vt to alternate ■ vi, **alternarse** vr to alternate; (turnar) to take turns; **~ con** to mix with

alternativo, -a [alterna'tiβo, a] adj alternative; (alterno) alternating ■ nf alternative; (elección) choice; **alternativas** nfpl ups and downs; **tomar la alternativa** (Taur) to become a fully-qualified bullfighter

alterno, -a [al'terno, a] adj (Bot: Mat) alternate; (Elec) alternating

alteza [al'teθa] nf (tratamiento) highness

altibajos [alti'βaxos] nmpl ups and downs

altillo [al'tiʎo] nm (Geo) small hill; (Am) attic

altiplanicie [altipla'niθje] nf, **altiplano** [alti'plano] nm high plateau

altisonante [altiso'nante] adj high-flown, high-sounding

altitud [alti'tuð] nf altitude, height; **a una ~ de** at a height of

altivez [alti'βeθ] nf haughtiness, arrogance

altivo, -a [al'tiβo, a] adj haughty, arrogant

alto, -a ['alto, a] adj high; (persona) tall; (sonido) high, sharp; (noble) high, lofty; (Geo, clase) upper ■ nm halt; (Mus) alto; (Geo) hill; (Am) pile ■ adv (estar) high; (hablar) loud, loudly ■ excl halt!; **la pared tiene dos metros de ~** the wall is two metres high; **en alta mar** on the high seas; **en voz alta** in a loud voice; **las altas horas de la noche** the small (Brit) o wee (US) hours; **en lo ~ de** at the top of; **pasar por ~** to overlook; **altos y bajos** ups and downs; **poner la radio más ~** to turn the radio up; **¡más ~, por favor!** louder, please!

altoparlante [altopar'lante] nm (Am) loudspeaker

altramuz [altra'muθ] nm lupin

altruismo [al'truismo] nm altruism

altura [al'tura] nf height; (Naut) depth; (Geo) latitude; **la pared tiene 1.80 de ~** the wall is 1 metre 80 (cm) high; **a esta ~ del año** at this time of the year; **estar a la ~ de las circunstancias** to rise to the occasion; **ha sido un partido de gran ~** it has been a terrific match

alubia [a'luβja] nf French bean, kidney bean

alucinación [aluθina'θjon] nf hallucination

alucinante [aluθi'nante] adj (fam: estupendo) great, super

alucinar [aluθi'nar] vi to hallucinate ■ vt to deceive; (fascinar) to fascinate

alud [a'luð] nm avalanche; (fig) flood

aludir [alu'ðir] vi: **~ a** to allude to; **darse por aludido** to take the hint; **no te des por aludido** don't take it personally

alumbrado [alum'braðo] nm lighting

alumbramiento [alumbra'mjento] nm lighting; (Med) childbirth, delivery

alumbrar [alum'brar] vt to light (up) ■ vi (iluminar) to give light; (Med) to give birth

aluminio [alu'minjo] *nm* aluminium (*Brit*), aluminum (*US*)

alumnado [alum'naðo] *nm* (*Univ*) student body; (*Escol*) pupils *pl*

alumno, -a [a'lumno, a] *nm/f* pupil, student

alunice *etc* [alu'niθe] *vb ver* **alunizar**

alunizar [aluni'θar] *vi* to land on the moon

alusión [alu'sjon] *nf* allusion

alusivo, -a [alu'siβo, a] *adj* allusive

aluvión [alu'βjon] *nm* (*Geo*) alluvium; (*fig*) flood; ~ **de improperios** torrent of abuse

alvéolo [al'βeolo] *nm* (*Anat*) alveolus; (*fig*) network

alza ['alθa] *nf* rise; (*Mil*) sight; **alzas fijas/graduables** fixed/adjustable sights; **al** *o* **en** ~ (*precio*) rising; **jugar al** ~ to speculate on a rising *o* bull market; **cotizarse** *o* **estar en** ~ to be rising

alzado, -a [al'θaðo, a] *adj* (*gen*) raised; (*Com: precio*) fixed; (*: quiebra*) fraudulent; **por un tanto** ~ for a lump sum ■ *nf* (*de caballos*) height; (*Jur*) appeal

alzamiento [alθa'mjento] *nm* (*aumento*) rise, increase; (*acción*) lifting, raising; (*mejor postura*) higher bid; (*rebelión*) rising; (*Com*) fraudulent bankruptcy

alzar [al'θar] *vt* to lift (up); (*precio, muro*) to raise; (*cuello de abrigo*) to turn up; (*Agr*) to gather in; (*Tip*) to gather; **alzarse** *vr* to get up, rise; (*rebelarse*) to revolt; (*Com*) to go fraudulently bankrupt; (*Jur*) to appeal; **alzarse con el premio** to carry off the prize

a.m. *abr* (*Am*: = *ante meridiem*) a.m.

ama ['ama] *nf* lady of the house; (*dueña*) owner; (*institutriz*) governess; (*madre adoptiva*) foster mother; ~ **de casa** housewife; ~ **de cría** *o* **de leche** wet-nurse; ~ **de llaves** housekeeper

amabilidad [amaβili'ðað] *nf* kindness; (*simpatía*) niceness

amabilísimo, -a [amaβi'lisimo, a] *adj* superlativo *de* **amable**

amable [a'maβle] *adj* kind; nice

amaestrado, -a [amaes'traðo, a] *adj* (*animal*) trained; (*: en circo etc*) performing

amaestrar [amaes'trar] *vt* to train

amagar [ama'ɣar] *vt, vi* to threaten

amago [a'maɣo] *nm* threat; (*gesto*) threatening gesture; (*Med*) symptom

amague *etc* [a'maɣe] *vb ver* **amagar**

amainar [amai'nar] *vt* (*Naut*) to lower, take in; (*fig*) to calm ■ *vi*, **amainarse** *vr* to drop, die down; **el viento amaina** the wind is dropping

amalgama [amal'ɣama] *nf* amalgam

amalgamar [amalɣa'mar] *vt* to amalgamate; (*combinar*) to combine, mix

amamantar [amaman'tar] *vt* to suckle, nurse

amancebarse [amanθe'βarse] *vr* (*pareja*) to live together

amanecer [amane'θer] *vi* to dawn; (*fig*) to appear, begin to show ■ *nm* dawn; **el niño amaneció afiebrado** the child woke up with a fever

amanerado, -a [amane'raðo, a] *adj* affected

amanezca *etc* [ama'neθka] *vb ver* **amanecer**

amansar [aman'sar] *vt* to tame; (*persona*) to subdue; **amansarse** *vr* (*persona*) to calm down

amante [a'mante] *adj*: ~ **de** fond of ■ *nm/f* lover

amanuense [ama'nwense] *nm* (*escribiente*) scribe; (*copista*) copyist; (*Pol*) secretary

amañar [ama'ɲar] *vt* (*gen*) to do skilfully; (*pey: resultado*) to alter

amaño [a'maɲo] *nm* (*habilidad*) skill; **amaños** *nmpl* (*Tec*) tools; (*fig*) tricks

amapola [ama'pola] *nf* poppy

amar [a'mar] *vt* to love

amargado, -a [amar'ɣaðo, a] *adj* bitter; embittered

amargar [amar'ɣar] *vt* to make bitter; (*fig*) to embitter; **amargarse** *vr* to become embittered

amargo, -a [a'marɣo, a] *adj* bitter

amargor [amar'ɣor] *nm* (*sabor*) bitterness; (*fig*) grief

amargue *etc* [a'marɣe] *vb ver* **amargar**

amargura [amar'ɣura] *nf* = **amargor**

amarillento, -a [amari'ʎento, a] *adj* yellowish; (*tez*) sallow

amarillismo [amari'ʎismo] *nm* (*de prensa*) sensationalist journalism

amarillo, -a [ama'riʎo, a] *adj, nm* yellow

amarra [a'marra] *nf* (*Naut*) mooring line; **amarras** *nfpl* (*fig*) protection *sg*; **tener buenas amarras** to have good connections; **soltar amarras** to set off

amarrar [ama'rrar] *vt* to moor; (*sujetar*) to tie up

amartillar [amarti'ʎar] *vt* (*fusil*) to cock

amasar [ama'sar] *vt* to knead; (*mezclar*) to mix, prepare; (*confeccionar*) to concoct

amasijo [ama'sixo] *nm* kneading; mixing; (*fig*) hotchpotch

amateur ['amatur] *nm/f* amateur

amatista [ama'tista] *nf* amethyst

amazacotado, -a [amaθako'taðo, a] *adj* (*terreno, arroz etc*) lumpy

amazona [ama'θona] *nf* horsewoman

Amazonas [ama'θonas] *nm*: **el (Río)** ~ the Amazon

ambages [am'baxes] *nmpl*: **sin** ~ in plain language

ámbar ['ambar] *nm* amber
Amberes [am'beres] *nm* Antwerp
ambición [ambi'θjon] *nf* ambition
ambicionar [ambiθjo'nar] *vt* to aspire to
ambicioso, -a [ambi'θjoso, a] *adj* ambitious
ambidextro, -a [ambi'ðekstro, a] *adj* ambidextrous
ambientación [ambjenta'θjon] *nf* (*Cine: Lit etc*) setting; (*Radio etc*) sound effects *pl*
ambientador [ambjenta'ðor] *nm* air freshener
ambientar [ambjen'tar] *vt* (*gen*) to give an atmosphere to; (*Lit etc*) to set
ambiente [am'bjente] *nm* (*tb fig*) atmosphere; (*medio*) environment; (*Am*) room
ambigüedad [ambiɣwe'ðað] *nf* ambiguity
ambiguo, -a [am'biɣwo, a] *adj* ambiguous
ámbito ['ambito] *nm* (*campo*) field; (*fig*) scope
ambos, -as ['ambos, as] *adj pl, pron pl* both
ambulancia [ambu'lanθja] *nf* ambulance
ambulante [ambu'lante] *adj* travelling, itinerant; (*biblioteca*) mobile
ambulatorio [ambula'torio] *nm* state health-service clinic
ameba [a'meβa] *nf* amoeba
amedrentar [ameðren'tar] *vt* to scare
amén [a'men] *excl* amen; ~ **de** *prep* besides, in addition to; **en un decir** ~ in the twinkling of an eye; **decir** ~ **a todo** to have no mind of one's own
amenace *etc* [ame'naθe] *vb ver* **amenazar**
amenaza [ame'naθa] *nf* threat
amenazar [amena'θar] *vt* to threaten ■ *vi*: ~ **con hacer** to threaten to do
amenidad [ameni'ðað] *nf* pleasantness
ameno, -a [a'meno, a] *adj* pleasant
América [a'merika] *nf* (*continente*) America, the Americas; (*EEUU*) America; (*Hispanoamérica*) Latin *o* South America; ~ **del Norte/del Sur** North/South America; ~ **Central/Latina** Central/Latin America
americanismo [amerika'nismo] *nm* Americanism
americano, -a [ameri'kano, a] *adj, nm/f ver* **América** American; Latin *o* South American ■ *nf* coat, jacket
americe *etc* [ame'riθe] *vb ver* **amerizar**
amerindio, -a [ame'rindjo, a] *adj, nm/f* Amerindian, American Indian
amerizaje [ameri'θaxe] *nm* (*Aviat*) landing (on the sea)
amerizar [ameri'θar] *vi* (*Aviat*) to land (on the sea)
ametralladora [ametraʎa'ðora] *nf* machine gun
amianto [a'mjanto] *nm* asbestos
amigable [ami'ɣaβle] *adj* friendly

amígdala [a'miɣðala] *nf* tonsil
amigdalitis [amiɣða'litis] *nf* tonsillitis
amigo, -a [a'miɣo, a] *adj* friendly ■ *nm/f* friend; (*amante*) lover; ~ **de lo ajeno** thief; ~ **corresponsal** penfriend; **hacerse amigos** to become friends; **ser** ~ **de** to like, be fond of; **ser muy amigos** to be close friends
amigote [ami'ɣote] *nm* mate (*Brit*), buddy
amilanar [amila'nar] *vt* to scare; **amilanarse** *vr* to get scared
aminorar [amino'rar] *vt* to diminish; (*reducir*) to reduce; ~ **la marcha** to slow down
amistad [amis'tað] *nf* friendship; **amistades** *nfpl* friends
amistoso, -a [ami'stoso, a] *adj* friendly
amnesia [am'nesja] *nf* amnesia
amnistía [amnis'tia] *nf* amnesty
amnistiar [amnis'tjar] *vt* to amnesty, grant an amnesty to
amo ['amo] *nm* owner; (*jefe*) boss
amodorrarse [amoðo'rrarse] *vr* to get sleepy
amolar [amo'lar] *vt* to annoy
amoldar [amol'dar] *vt* to mould; (*adaptar*) to adapt
amonestación [amonesta'θjon] *nf* warning; **amonestaciones** *nfpl* marriage banns
amonestar [amone'star] *vt* to warn; to publish the banns of
amoniaco [amo'njako] *nm* ammonia
amontonar [amonto'nar] *vt* to collect, pile up; **amontonarse** *vr* (*gente*) to crowd together; (*acumularse*) to pile up; (*datos*) to accumulate; (*desastres*) to come one on top of another
amor [a'mor] *nm* love; (*amante*) lover; **hacer el** ~ to make love; ~ **interesado** cupboard love; ~ **propio** self-respect; **por (el)** ~ **de Dios** for God's sake; **estar al** ~ **de la lumbre** to be close to the fire
amoratado, -a [amora'taðo, a] *adj* purple, blue with cold; (*con cardenales*) bruised
amordace *etc* [amor'ðaθe] *vb ver* **amordazar**
amordazar [amorða'θar] *vt* to muzzle; (*fig*) to gag
amorfo, -a [a'morfo, a] *adj* amorphous, shapeless
amorío [amo'rio] *nm* (*fam*) love affair
amoroso, -a [amo'roso, a] *adj* affectionate, loving
amortajar [amorta'xar] *vt* (*fig*) to shroud
amortice *etc* [amor'tiθe] *vb ver* **amortizar**
amortiguador [amortiɣwa'ðor] *nm* shock absorber; (*parachoques*) bumper; (*silenciador*) silencer; **amortiguadores** *nmpl* (*Auto*) suspension *sg*
amortiguar [amorti'ɣwar] *vt* to deaden; (*ruido*) to muffle; (*color*) to soften

amortigüe *etc* [amor'tiɣwe] *vb ver*
amortiguar
amortización [amortiθa'θjon] *nf*
redemption; repayment; (*Com*) capital
allowance
amortizar [amorti'θar] *vt* (*Econ*: *bono*) to
redeem; (: *capital*) to write off; (: *préstamo*)
to pay off
amoscarse [amos'karse] *vr* to get cross
amosque *etc* [a'moske] *vb ver* **amoscarse**
amotinar [amoti'nar] *vt* to stir up, incite
(to riot); **amotinarse** *vr* to mutiny
amparar [ampa'rar] *vt* to protect;
ampararse *vr* to seek protection; (*de la lluvia*
etc) to shelter
amparo [am'paro] *nm* help, protection;
al ~ de under the protection of
amperímetro [ampe'rimetro] *nm* ammeter
amperio [am'perjo] *nm* ampère, amp
ampliable [am'pljaβle] *adj* (*Inform*)
expandable
ampliación [amplja'θjon] *nf* enlargement;
(*extensión*) extension
ampliar [am'pljar] *vt* to enlarge; to extend
amplificación [amplifika'θjon] *nf*
enlargement
amplificador [amplifika'ðor] *nm* amplifier
amplificar [amplifi'kar] *vt* to amplify
amplifique *etc* [ampli'fike] *vb ver* **amplificar**
amplio, -a ['ampljo, a] *adj* spacious; (*falda*
etc) full; (*extenso*) extensive; (*ancho*) wide
amplitud [ampli'tuð] *nf* spaciousness;
extent; (*fig*) amplitude; **~ de miras**
broadmindedness; **de gran ~** far-reaching
ampolla [am'poʎa] *nf* blister; (*Med*) ampoule
ampolleta [ampo'ʎeta] *nf* (*Am*) (light) bulb
ampuloso, -a [ampu'loso, a] *adj* bombastic,
pompous
amputar [ampu'tar] *vt* to cut off, amputate
amueblar [amwe'βlar] *vt* to furnish
amuleto [amu'leto] *nm* (lucky) charm
amurallar [amura'ʎar] *vt* to wall up *o* in
anacarado, -a [anaka'raðo, a] *adj* mother-
of-pearl *cpd*
anacardo [ana'karðo] *nm* cashew (nut)
anaconda [ana'konda] *nf* anaconda
anacronismo [anakro'nismo] *nm*
anachronism
ánade ['anaðe] *nm* duck
anagrama [ana'ɣrama] *nm* anagram
anales [a'nales] *nmpl* annals
analfabetismo [analfaβe'tismo] *nm*
illiteracy
analfabeto, -a [analfa'βeto, a] *adj*, *nm/f*
illiterate
analgésico [anal'xesiko] *nm* painkiller,
analgesic

analice *etc* [ana'liθe] *vb ver* **analizar**
análisis [a'nalisis] *nm inv* analysis; **~ de**
costos-beneficios cost-benefit analysis;
~ de mercados market research; **~ de**
sangre blood test
analista [ana'lista] *nm/f* (*gen*) analyst; (*Pol*:
Historia) chronicler; **~ de sistemas** (*Inform*)
systems analyst
analizar [anali'θar] *vt* to analyse
analogía [analo'xia] *nf* analogy; **por ~ con**
on the analogy of
analógico, -a [ana'loxico, a] *adj* analogue
análogo, -a [a'naloɣo, a] *adj* analogous,
similar
ananá [ana'na], **ananás** [ana'nas] *nm*
pineapple
anaquel [ana'kel] *nm* shelf
anaranjado, -a [anaran'xaðo, a] *adj* orange
(-coloured)
anarquía [anar'kia] *nf* anarchy
anarquismo [anar'kismo] *nm* anarchism
anarquista [anar'kista] *nm/f* anarchist
anatematizar [anatemati'θar] *vt* (*Rel*)
to anathematize; (*fig*) to curse
anatemice *etc* [anate'miθe] *vb ver*
anatemizar
anatomía [anato'mia] *nf* anatomy
anca ['anka] *nf* rump, haunch; **ancas** *nfpl*
(*fam*) behind *sg*; **llevar a algn en ancas**
to carry sb behind one
ancestral [anθes'tral] *adj* (*costumbre*) age-old
ancho, -a ['antʃo, a] *adj* wide; (*falda*) full; (*fig*)
liberal ■ *nm* width; (*Ferro*) gauge; **le viene**
muy ~ el cargo (*fig*) the job is too much for
him; **ponerse ~** to get conceited; **quedarse**
tan ~ to go on as if nothing had happened;
estar a sus anchas to be at one's ease
anchoa [an'tʃoa] *nf* anchovy
anchura [an'tʃura] *nf* width; (*amplitud*)
wideness
anchuroso, -a [antʃu'roso, a] *adj* wide
anciano, -a [an'θjano, a] *adj* old, aged
■ *nm/f* old man/woman ■ *nm* elder
ancla ['ankla] *nf* anchor; **levar anclas** to
weigh anchor
ancladero [ankla'ðero] *nm* anchorage
anclar [an'klar] *vi* to (drop) anchor
andadas [an'daðas] *nfpl* (*aventuras*)
adventures; **volver a las ~** to backslide
andaderas [anda'ðeras] *nfpl* baby-walker *sg*
andadura [anda'ðura] *nf* gait; (*de caballo*)
pace
Andalucía [andalu'θia] *nf* Andalusia
andaluz, a [anda'luθ, a] *adj*, *nm/f* Andalusian
andamio [an'damjo] *nm*, **andamiaje**
[anda'mjaxe] *nm* scaffold(ing)
andanada [anda'naða] *nf* (*fig*) reprimand;

soltarle a algn una ~ to give sb a rocket
andante [an'dante] *adj*: **caballero ~** knight errant
andar [an'dar] *vt* to go, cover, travel ■ *vi* to go, walk, travel; (*funcionar*) to go, work; (*estar*) to be ■ *nm* walk, gait, pace; **andarse** *vr* (*irse*) to go away *o* off; **~ a pie/a caballo/en bicicleta** to go on foot/on horseback/by bicycle; **¡anda!** (*sorpresa*) go on!; **anda en** *o* **por los 40** he's about 40; **¿en qué andas?** what are you up to?; **andamos mal de dinero/tiempo** we're badly off for money/we're short of time; **andarse por las ramas** to beat about the bush; **no andarse con rodeos** to call a spade a spade (*fam*); **todo se ~á** all in good time; **anda por aquí** it's round here somewhere; **~ haciendo algo** to be doing sth
andariego, -a [anda'rjeɣo, a] *adj* fond of travelling
andas ['andas] *nfpl* stretcher *sg*
andén [an'den] *nm* (*Ferro*) platform; (*Naut*) quayside; (*Am: acera*) pavement (*Brit*), sidewalk (*US*)
Andes ['andes] *nmpl*: **los ~** the Andes
andinismo [andin'ismo] *nm* (*Am*) mountaineering, climbing
andino, -a [an'dino, a] *adj* Andean, of the Andes
Andorra [an'dorra] *nf* Andorra
andrajo [an'draxo] *nm* rag
andrajoso, -a [andra'xoso, a] *adj* ragged
andurriales [andu'rrjales] *nmpl* out-of-the-way place *sg*, the sticks; **en esos ~** in that godforsaken spot
anduve [an'duβe], **anduviera** *etc* [andu'βjera] *vb ver* **andar**
anécdota [a'nekðota] *nf* anecdote, story
anegar [ane'ɣar] *vt* to flood; (*ahogar*) to drown; **anegarse** *vr* to drown; (*hundirse*) to sink
anegue *etc* [a'neɣe] *vb ver* **anegar**
anejo, -a [a'nexo, a] *adj* attached ■ *nm* (*Arq*) annexe
anemia [a'nemja] *nf* anaemia
anestesia [anes'tesja] *nf* anaesthetic; **~ general/local** general/local anaesthetic
anestesiar [aneste'sjar] *vt* to anaesthetize (*Brit*), anesthetize (*US*)
anestésico [anes'tesiko] *nm* anaesthetic
anexar [anek'sar] *vt* to annex; (*documento*) to attach; (*Inform*) to append
anexión [anek'sjon] *nf*, **anexionamiento** [aneksjona'mjento] *nm* annexation
anexionar [aneksjo'nar] *vt* to annex; **anexionarse** *vr*: **anexionarse un país** to annex a country

anexo, -a [a'nekso, a] *adj* attached ■ *nm* annexe
anfetamina [anfeta'mina] *nf* amphetamine
anfibio, -a [an'fiβjo, a] *adj* amphibious ■ *nm* amphibian
anfiteatro [anfite'atro] *nm* amphitheatre; (*Teat*) dress circle
anfitrión, -ona [anfi'trjon, ona] *nm/f* host(ess)
ángel ['anxel] *nm* angel; **ángel de la guarda** guardian angel; **tener ángel** to have charm
Ángeles ['anxeles] *nmpl*: **los Ángeles** Los Angeles
angélico, -a [an'xeliko, a], **angelical** [anxeli'kal] *adj* angelic(al)
angina [an'xina] *nf* (*Med*): **~ de pecho** angina; **tener anginas** to have a sore throat *o* throat infection
anglicano, -a [angli'kano, a] *adj, nm/f* Anglican
anglicismo [angli'θismo] *nm* anglicism
anglosajón, -ona [anglosa'xon, 'xona] *adj, nm/f* Anglo-Saxon
Angola [an'gola] *nf* Angola
angoleño, -a [ango'leɲo, a] *adj, nm/f* Angolan
angosto, -a [an'gosto, a] *adj* narrow
anguila [an'gila] *nf* eel; **anguilas** *nfpl* slipway *sg*
angula [an'gula] *nf* elver, baby eel
ángulo ['angulo] *nm* angle; (*esquina*) corner; (*curva*) bend
angustia [an'gustja] *nf* anguish
angustiar [angus'tjar] *vt* to distress, grieve; **angustiarse** *vr*: **angustiarse (por)** to be distressed (at, on account of)
anhelante [ane'lante] *adj* eager; (*deseoso*) longing
anhelar [ane'lar] *vt* to be eager for; to long for, desire ■ *vi* to pant, gasp
anhelo [a'nelo] *nm* eagerness; desire
anhídrido [a'niðriðo] *nm*: **~ carbónico** carbon dioxide
anidar [ani'ðar] *vt* (*acoger*) to take in, shelter ■ *vi* to nest; (*fig*) to make one's home
anilina [ani'lina] *nf* aniline
anilla [a'niʎa] *nf* ring; **(las) anillas** (*Deporte*) the rings
anillo [a'niʎo] *nm* ring; **~ de boda** wedding ring; **~ de compromiso** engagement ring; **venir como ~ al dedo** to suit to a tee
ánima ['anima] *nf* soul; **las ánimas** the Angelus (bell) *sg*
animación [anima'θjon] *nf* liveliness; (*vitalidad*) life; (*actividad*) bustle
animado, -a [ani'maðo, a] *adj* (*vivo*) lively; (*vivaz*) animated; (*concurrido*) bustling; (*alegre*) in high spirits; **dibujos animados** cartoon *sg*

a

animador, a [anima'ðor, a] *nm/f* (TV) host(ess) ▪ *nf* (*Deporte*) cheerleader

animadversión [animaðβer'sjon] *nf* ill-will, antagonism

animal [ani'mal] *adj* animal; (*fig*) stupid ▪ *nm* animal; (*fig*) fool; (*bestia*) brute

animalada [anima'laða] *nf* (*gen*) silly thing (to do *o* say); (*ultraje*) disgrace

animar [ani'mar] *vt* (*Bio*) to animate, give life to; (*fig*) to liven up, brighten up, cheer up; (*estimular*) to stimulate; **animarse** *vr* to cheer up, feel encouraged; (*decidirse*) to make up one's mind

ánimo ['animo] *nm* soul, mind; (*valentía*) courage ▪ *excl* cheer up!; **cobrar ánimo** to take heart; **dar ánimo(s) a** to encourage

animoso, -a [ani'moso, a] *adj* brave; (*vivo*) lively

aniñado, -a [ani'ɲaðo, a] *adj* (*facción*) childlike; (*carácter*) childish

aniquilar [aniki'lar] *vt* to annihilate, destroy

anís [a'nis] *nm* (*grano*) aniseed; (*licor*) anisette

aniversario [aniβer'sarjo] *nm* anniversary

Ankara [an'kara] *nf* Ankara

ano ['ano] *nm* anus

anoche [a'notʃe] *adv* last night; **antes de ~** the night before last

anochecer [anotʃe'θer] *vi* to get dark ▪ *nm* nightfall, dark; **al ~** at nightfall

anochezca *etc* [ano'tʃeθka] *vb ver* **anochecer**

anodino, -a [ano'ðino, a] *adj* dull, anodyne

anomalía [anoma'lia] *nf* anomaly

anonadado, -a [anona'ðaðo, a] *adj* stunned

anonimato [anoni'mato] *nm* anonymity

anónimo, -a [a'nonimo, a] *adj* anonymous; (*Com*) limited ▪ *nm* (*carta*) anonymous letter; (: *maliciosa*) poison-pen letter

anorak [ano'rak] (*pl* **anoraks**) *nm* anorak

anorexia [ano'reksja] *nf* anorexia

anormal [anor'mal] *adj* abnormal

anotación [anota'θjon] *nf* note; annotation

anotar [ano'tar] *vt* to note down; (*comentar*) to annotate

anquilosado, -a [ankilo'saðo, a] *adj* (*fig*) stale, out of date

anquilosamiento [ankilosa'mjento] *nm* (*fig*) paralysis, stagnation

ansia ['ansja] *nf* anxiety; (*añoranza*) yearning

ansiar [an'sjar] *vt* to long for

ansiedad [ansje'ðað] *nf* anxiety

ansioso, -a [an'sjoso, a] *adj* anxious; (*anhelante*) eager; **~ de** *o* **por algo** greedy for sth

antagónico, -a [anta'ɣoniko, a] *adj* antagonistic; (*opuesto*) contrasting

antagonista [antaɣo'nista] *nm/f* antagonist

antaño [an'taɲo] *adv* long ago

Antártico [an'tartiko] *nm*: **el (océano) ~** the Antarctic (Ocean)

Antártida [an'tartiða] *nf* Antarctica

ante ['ante] *prep* before, in the presence of; (*encarado con*) faced with ▪ *nm* suede; **~ todo** above all

anteanoche [antea'notʃe] *adv* the night before last

anteayer [antea'jer] *adv* the day before yesterday

antebrazo [ante'βraθo] *nm* forearm

antecámara [ante'kamara] *nf* (*Arq*) anteroom; (*antesala*) waiting room; (*Pol*) lobby

antecedente [anteθe'ðente] *adj* previous ▪ *nm*: **antecedentes** *nmpl* (*profesionales*) background *sg*; **antecedentes penales** criminal record; **no tener antecedentes** to have a clean record; **estar en antecedentes** to be well-informed; **poner a algn en antecedentes** to put sb in the picture

anteceder [anteθe'ðer] *vt* to precede, go before

antecesor, a [anteθe'sor, a] *nm/f* predecessor

antedicho, -a [ante'ðitʃo, a] *adj* aforementioned

antelación [antela'θjon] *nf*: **con ~** in advance

antemano [ante'mano]: **de ~** *adv* beforehand, in advance

antena [an'tena] *nf* antenna; (*de televisión etc*) aerial

anteojeras [anteo'xeras] *nfpl* blinkers (*Brit*), blinders (*US*)

anteojo [ante'oxo] *nm* eyeglass; **anteojos** *nmpl* (*esp Am*) glasses, spectacles

antepasados [antepa'saðos] *nmpl* ancestors

antepecho [ante'petʃo] *nm* guardrail, parapet; (*repisa*) ledge, sill

antepondré *etc* [antepon'dre] *vb ver* **anteponer**

anteponer [antepo'ner] *vt* to place in front; (*fig*) to prefer

anteponga *etc* [ante'ponɣa] *vb ver* **anteponer**

anteproyecto [antepro'jekto] *nm* preliminary sketch; (*fig*) blueprint; (*Pol*): **~ de ley** draft bill

antepuesto, -a [ante'pwesto, a] *pp de* **anteponer**

antepuse *etc* [ante'puse] *vb ver* **anteponer**

anterior [ante'rjor] *adj* preceding, previous

anterioridad [anterjori'ðað] *nf*: **con ~ a** prior to, before

anteriormente [anterjor'mente] *adv* previously, before

antes ['antes] *adv* sooner; (*primero*) first; (*con anterioridad*) before; (*hace tiempo*) previously, once; (*más bien*) rather ▪ *prep*: **~ de** before

■ *conj*: ~ **(de) que** before; ~ **bien** (but) rather;
dos días ~ two days before o previously;
mucho/poco ~ long/shortly before;
~ **muerto que esclavo** better dead than
enslaved; **tomo el avión ~ que el barco**
I take the plane rather than the boat;
cuanto ~, **lo ~ posible** as soon as possible;
cuanto ~ mejor the sooner the better
antesala [ante'sala] *nf* anteroom
antiadherente [antiaðe'rente] *adj* non-stick
antiaéreo, -a [antia'ereo, a] *adj* anti-aircraft
antialcohólico, -a [antial'koliko, a] *adj*:
centro ~ (*Med*) detoxification unit
antibalas [anti'βalas] *adj inv*: **chaleco ~**
bulletproof jacket
antibiótico [anti'βjotiko] *nm* antibiotic
anticiclón [antiθi'klon] *nm* (*Meteorología*)
anti-cyclone
anticipación [antiθipa'θjon] *nf* anticipation;
con 10 minutos de ~ 10 minutes early
anticipado, -a [antiθi'paðo, a] *adj* (in)
advance; **por ~** in advance
anticipar [antiθi'par] *vt* to anticipate;
(*adelantar*) to bring forward; (*Com*) to
advance; **anticiparse** *vr*: **anticiparse a su
época** to be ahead of one's time
anticipo [anti'θipo] *nm* (*Com*) advance
anticonceptivo, -a [antikonθep'tiβo, a] *adj*,
nm contraceptive; **métodos
anticonceptivos** methods of birth control
anticongelante [antikonxe'lante] *nm*
antifreeze
anticonstitucional [antikonstituθjo'nal] *adj*
unconstitutional
anticuado, -a [anti'kwaðo, a] *adj* out-of-
date, old-fashioned; (*desusado*) obsolete
anticuario [anti'kwarjo] *nm* antique dealer
anticuerpo [anti'kwerpo] *nm* (*Med*) antibody
antidemocrático, -a [antiðemo'kratiko, a]
adj undemocratic
antideportivo, -a [antiðepor'tiβo, a] *adj*
unsporting
antidepresivo [antiðepre'siβo] *nm*
antidepressant
antideslumbrante [antiðeslum'brante] *adj*
(*Inform*) anti-dazzle
antidoping [anti'ðopin] *adj inv* anti-drug
antídoto [an'tiðoto] *nm* antidote
antidroga [anti'ðroɣa] *adj inv* anti-drug;
brigada ~ drug squad
antiestético, -a [anties'tetiko, a] *adj*
unsightly
antifaz [anti'faθ] *nm* mask; (*velo*) veil
antigás [anti'gas] *adj inv*: **careta ~** gas mask
antiglobalización [antiglobaliθa'θjon] *n*
anti-globalization; **manifestantes ~** anti-
globalization protesters

antigualla [anti'ɣwaʎa] *nf* antique; (*reliquia*)
relic; **antiguallas** *nfpl* old things
antiguamente [antiɣwa'mente] *adv*
formerly; (*hace mucho tiempo*) long ago
antigüedad [antiɣwe'ðað] *nf* antiquity;
(*artículo*) antique; (*rango*) seniority
antiguo, -a [an'tiɣwo, a] *adj* old, ancient;
(*que fue*) former; **a la antigua** in the old-
fashioned way
antihigiénico, -a [anti'xjeniko, a] *adj*
unhygienic
antihistamínico, -a [antista'miniko, a] *adj*,
nm antihistamine
antiinflacionista [antinflaθjo'nista] *adj*
anti-inflationary, counter-inflationary
antillano, -a [anti'ʎano, a] *adj*, *nm/f* West
Indian
Antillas [an'tiʎas] *nfpl*: **las ~** the West Indies,
the Antilles; **el mar de las ~** the Caribbean Sea
antílope [an'tilope] *nm* antelope
antimonopolios [antimono'poljos] *adj inv*:
ley ~ anti-trust law
antinatural [antinatu'ral] *adj* unnatural
antiparras [anti'parras] *nfpl* (*fam*) specs
antipatía [antipa'tia] *nf* antipathy, dislike
antipático, -a [anti'patiko, a] *adj*
disagreeable, unpleasant
Antípodas [an'tipoðas] *nfpl*: **las ~** the
Antipodes
antiquísimo, -a [anti'kisimo, a] *adj* ancient
antirreglamentario, -a
[antirreɣlamen'tarjo, a] *adj* (*gen*) unlawful;
(*Pol etc*) unconstitutional
antirrobo [anti'rroβo] *nm* (*tb*: **dispositivo
antirrobo**: *para casas etc*) burglar alarm;
(*para coches*) car alarm
antisemita [antise'mita] *adj* anti-Semitic
■ *nm/f* anti-Semite
antiséptico, -a [anti'septiko, a] *adj*, *nm*
antiseptic
antiterrorista [antiterro'rista] *adj*
antiterrorist; **la lucha ~** the fight against
terrorism
antítesis [an'titesis] *nf inv* antithesis
antivírico, -a [anti'βiriko, a] *adj* (*Med*) antiviral
antojadizo, -a [antoxa'ðiθo, a] *adj*
capricious
antojarse [anto'xarse] *vr* (*desear*): **se me
antoja comprarlo** I have a mind to buy it;
(*pensar*): **se me antoja que** I have a feeling
that
antojo [an'toxo] *nm* caprice, whim; (*rosa*)
birthmark; (*lunar*) mole; **hacer a su ~** to do
as one pleases
antología [antolo'xia] *nf* anthology
antonomasia [antono'masja] *nf*: **por ~**
par excellence

antorcha [an'tortʃa] *nf* torch
antro ['antro] *nm* cavern; ~ **de corrupción** (*fig*) den of iniquity
antropófago, -a [antro'pofaɣo, a] *adj, nm/f* cannibal
antropología [antropolo'xia] *nf* anthropology
antropólogo, -a [antro'poloɣo, a] *nm/f* anthropologist
anual [a'nwal] *adj* annual
anualidad [anwali'ðað] *nf* annuity, annual payment; ~ **vitalicia** life annuity
anuario [a'nwarjo] *nm* yearbook
anublado, -a [anu'βlaðo, a] *adj* overcast
anudar [anu'ðar] *vt* to knot, tie; (*unir*) to join; **anudarse** *vr* to get tied up; **se me anudó la voz** I got a lump in my throat
anulación [anula'θjon] *nf* annulment; cancellation; repeal
anular [anu'lar] *vt* to annul, cancel; (*suscripción*) to cancel; (*ley*) to repeal ■ *nm* ring finger
anunciación [anunθja'θjon] *nf* announcement; **A~** (*Rel*) Annunciation
anunciante [anun'θjante] *nm/f* advertiser
anunciar [anun'θjar] *vt* to announce; (*proclamar*) to proclaim; (*Com*) to advertise
anuncio [a'nunθjo] *nm* announcement; (*señal*) sign; (*Com*) advertisement; (*cartel*) poster; (*Teat*) bill; **anuncios por palabras** classified ads
anverso [am'berso] *nm* obverse
anzuelo [an'θwelo] *nm* hook; (*para pescar*) fish hook; **tragar el ~** to swallow the bait
añadido [aɲa'ðiðo] *nm* addition
añadidura [aɲaði'ðura] *nf* addition, extra; **por ~** besides, in addition
añadir [aɲa'ðir] *vt* to add
añejo, -a [a'ɲexo, a] *adj* old; (*vino*) vintage; (*jamón*) well-cured
añicos [a'ɲikos] *nmpl*: **hacer ~** to smash, shatter; **hacerse ~** to smash, shatter
añil [a'ɲil] *nm* (*Bot, color*) indigo
año ['aɲo] *nm* year; **¡Feliz A~ Nuevo!** Happy New Year!; **tener 15 años** to be 15 (years old); **los años 80** the eighties; ~ **bisiesto/escolar** leap/school year; ~ **fiscal** fiscal *o* tax year; **estar de buen ~** to be in good shape; **en el ~ de la nana** in the year dot; **el ~ que viene** next year
añoranza [aɲo'ranθa] *nf* nostalgia; (*anhelo*) longing
añorar [aɲo'rar] *vt* to long for
añoso, -a [a'ɲoso, a] *adj* ancient, old
aovado, -a [ao'βaðo, a] *adj* oval
aovar [ao'βar] *vi* to lay eggs
apabullar [apaβu'ʎar] *vt* (*lit, fig*) to crush

apacentar [apaθen'tar] *vt* to pasture, graze
apacible [apa'θiβle] *adj* gentle, mild
apaciente *etc* [apa'θjente] *vb ver* **apacentar**
apaciguar [apaθi'ɣwar] *vt* to pacify, calm (down)
apacigüe *etc* [apa'θiɣwe] *vb ver* **apaciguar**
apadrinar [apaðri'nar] *vt* to sponsor, support; (*Rel*) to act as godfather to
apagado, -a [apa'ɣaðo, a] *adj* (*volcán*) extinct; (*color*) dull; (*voz*) quiet; (*sonido*) muted, muffled; (*persona: apático*) listless; **estar ~** (*fuego, luz*) to be out; (*radio, TV etc*) to be off
apagar [apa'ɣar] *vt* to put out; (*color*) to tone down; (*sonido*) to silence, muffle; (*sed*) to quench; (*Inform*) to toggle off; **apagarse** *vr* (*luz, fuego*) to go out; (*sonido*) to die away; (*pasión*) to wither; ~ **el sistema** (*Inform*) to close *o* shut down
apagón [apa'ɣon] *nm* blackout, power cut
apague *etc* [a'paɣe] *vb ver* **apagar**
apaisado, -a [apai'saðo, a] *adj* (*papel*) landscape *cpd*
apalabrar [apala'βrar] *vt* to agree to; (*obrero*) to engage
Apalaches [apa'latʃes] *nmpl*: (**Montes**) **~** Appalachians
apalear [apale'ar] *vt* to beat, thrash; (*Agr*) to winnow
apañado, -a [apa'ɲaðo, a] *adj* (*mañoso*) resourceful; (*arreglado*) tidy; (*útil*) handy
apañar [apa'ɲar] *vt* to pick up; (*asir*) to take hold of, grasp; (*reparar*) to mend, patch up; **apañarse** *vr* to manage, get along; **apañárselas por su cuenta** to look after number one (*fam*)
apaño [a'paɲo] *nm* (*Costura*) patch; (*maña*) skill; **esto no tiene ~** there's no answer to this one
aparador [apara'ðor] *nm* sideboard; (*escaparate*) shop window
aparato [apa'rato] *nm* apparatus; (*máquina*) machine; (*doméstico*) appliance; (*boato*) ostentation; (*Inform*) device; **al ~** (*Telec*) speaking; ~ **de facsímil** facsimile (machine), fax; ~ **respiratorio** respiratory system; **aparatos de mando** (*Aviat etc*) controls
aparatoso, -a [apara'toso, a] *adj* showy, ostentatious
aparcamiento [aparka'mjento] *nm* car park (*Brit*), parking lot (*US*)
aparcar [apar'kar] *vt, vi* to park
aparear [apare'ar] *vt* (*objetos*) to pair, match; (*animales*) to mate; **aparearse** *vr* to form a pair; to mate
aparecer [apare'θer] *vi*, **aparecerse** *vr* to appear; **apareció borracho** he turned up drunk

aparejado, -a [apare'xaðo, a] *adj* fit, suitable; **ir ~ con** to go hand in hand with; **llevar** *o* **traer ~** to involve

aparejador, a [aparexa'ðor, a] *nm/f (Arq)* quantity surveyor

aparejar [apare'xar] *vt* to prepare; *(caballo)* to saddle, harness; *(Naut)* to fit out, rig out

aparejo [apa'rexo] *nm* preparation; *(de caballo)* harness; *(Naut)* rigging; *(de poleas)* block and tackle

aparentar [aparen'tar] *vt (edad)* to look; *(fingir):* **~ tristeza** to pretend to be sad

aparente [apa'rente] *adj* apparent; *(adecuado)* suitable

aparezca *etc* [apa'reθka] *vb ver* **aparecer**

aparición [apari'θjon] *nf* appearance; *(de libro)* publication; *(de fantasma)* spectre

apariencia [apa'rjenθja] *nf* (outward) appearance; **en ~** outwardly, seemingly

aparque *etc* [a'parke] *vb ver* **aparcar**

apartado, -a [apar'taðo, a] *adj* separate; *(lejano)* remote ■ *nm (tipográfico)* paragraph; **~ (de correos)** post office box

apartamento [aparta'mento] *nm* apartment, flat *(Brit)*

apartamiento [aparta'mjento] *nm* separation; *(aislamiento)* remoteness; *(Am)* apartment, flat *(Brit)*

apartar [apar'tar] *vt* to separate; *(quitar)* to remove; *(Mineralogía)* to extract; **apartarse** *vr (separarse)* to separate, part; *(irse)* to move away; *(mantenerse aparte)* to keep away

aparte [a'parte] *adv (separadamente)* separately; *(además)* besides ■ *prep:* **~ de** apart from ■ *nm (Teat)* aside; *(tipográfico)* new paragraph; **"punto y ~"** "new paragraph"

apasionado, -a [apasjo'naðo, a] *adj* passionate; *(pey)* biassed, prejudiced ■ *nm/f* admirer

apasionante [apasjo'nante] *adj* exciting

apasionar [apasjo'nar] *vt* to arouse passion in; **apasionarse** *vr* to get excited; **le apasiona el fútbol** she's crazy about football

apatía [apa'tia] *nf* apathy

apático, -a [a'patiko, a] *adj* apathetic

apátrida [a'patriða] *adj* stateless

Apdo. *nm abr* (= *Apartado (de Correos)*) P.O. Box

apeadero [apea'ðero] *nm* halt, stopping place

apearse [ape'arse] *vr (jinete)* to dismount; *(bajarse)* to get down *o* out; *(de coche)* to get out, alight; **no ~ del burro** to refuse to climb down

apechugar [apetʃu'ɣar] *vi:* **~ con algo** to face up to sth

apechugue *etc* [ape'tʃuɣe] *vb ver* **apechugar**

apedrear [apeðre'ar] *vt* to stone

apegarse [ape'ɣarse] *vr:* **~ a** to become attached to

apego [a'peɣo] *nm* attachment, devotion

apegue *etc* [a'peɣe] *vb ver* **apegarse**

apelación [apela'θjon] *nf* appeal

apelar [ape'lar] *vi* to appeal; **~ a** *(fig)* to resort to

apelativo [apela'tiβo] *nm (Ling)* appellative; *(Am)* surname

apellidar [apeʎi'ðar] *vt* to call, name; **apellidarse** *vr:* **se apellida Pérez** her (sur)name's Pérez

apellido [ape'ʎiðo] *nm* surname; *see note*

● APELLIDO
●
● In the Spanish-speaking world most
● people use two *apellidos*, the first being
● their father's first surname, and the
● second their mother's first surname:
● eg the children of Juan García López,
● married to Carmen Pérez Rodríguez
● would have as their surname García
● Pérez. Married women retain their own
● surname(s) and sometimes add their
● husband's first surname on to theirs: eg
● Carmen Pérez de García. She could also
● be referred to as (la) Señora de García. In
● Latin America it is usual for the second
● surname to be shortened to an initial in
● correspondence eg: Juan García L.

apelmazado, -a [apelma'θaðo, a] *adj* compact, solid

apelotonar [apeloto'nar] *vt* to roll into a ball; **apelotonarse** *vr (gente)* to crowd together

apenar [ape'nar] *vt* to grieve, trouble; *(Am: avergonzar)* to embarrass; **apenarse** *vr* to grieve; *(Am)* to be embarrassed

apenas [a'penas] *adv* scarcely, hardly ■ *conj* as soon as, no sooner

apéndice [a'pendiθe] *nm* appendix

apendicitis [apendi'θitis] *nf* appendicitis

Apeninos [ape'ninos] *nmpl* Apennines

apercibimiento [aperθiβi'mjento] *nm (aviso)* warning

apercibir [aperθi'βir] *vt* to prepare; *(avisar)* to warn; *(Jur)* to summon; *(Am)* to notice, see; **apercibirse** *vr* to get ready; **apercibirse de** to notice

aperitivo [aperi'tiβo] *nm (bebida)* aperitif; *(comida)* appetizer

apero [a'pero] *nm (Agr)* implement; **aperos** *nmpl* farm equipment *sg*

apertura [aper'tura] *nf (gen)* opening;

(Pol) openness, liberalization; (Teat etc) beginning; ~ **de un juicio hipotecario** (Com) foreclosure

aperturismo [apertu'rismo] nm (Pol) (policy of) liberalization

apesadumbrar [apesaðum'brar] vt to grieve, sadden; **apesadumbrarse** vr to distress o.s.

apestar [apes'tar] vt to infect ■ vi: ~ **(a)** to stink (of)

apestoso, -a [apes'toso, a] adj (hediondo) stinking; (asqueroso) sickening

apetecer [apete'θer] vt: ¿**te apetece una tortilla?** do you fancy an omelette?

apetecible [apete'θiβle] adj desirable; (comida) tempting

apetezca etc [ape'teθka] vb ver **apetecer**

apetito [ape'tito] nm appetite

apetitoso, -a [apeti'toso, a] adj (gustoso) appetizing; (fig) tempting

apiadarse [apja'ðarse] vr: ~ **de** to take pity on

ápice ['apiθe] nm apex; (fig) whit, iota; **ni un ápice** not a whit; **no ceder un ápice** not to budge an inch

apicultor, a [apikul'tor, a] nm/f beekeeper, apiarist

apicultura [apikul'tura] nf beekeeping

apiladora [apila'ðora] nf (para máquina impresora) stacker

apilar [api'lar] vt to pile o heap up; **apilarse** vr to pile up

apiñado, -a [api'ɲaðo, a] adj (apretado) packed

apiñar [api'ɲar] vt to crowd; **apiñarse** vr to crowd o press together

apio ['apjo] nm celery

apisonadora [apisona'ðora] nf (máquina) steamroller

aplacar [apla'kar] vt to placate; **aplacarse** vr to calm down

aplace etc [a'plaθe] vb ver **aplazar**

aplanamiento [aplana'mjento] nm smoothing, levelling

aplanar [apla'nar] vt to smooth, level; (allanar) to roll flat, flatten; **aplanarse** vr (edificio) to collapse; (persona) to get discouraged

aplaque etc [a'plake] vb ver **aplacar**

aplastar [aplas'tar] vt to squash (flat); (fig) to crush

aplatanarse [aplata'narse] vr to get lethargic

aplaudir [aplau'ðir] vt to applaud

aplauso [a'plauso] nm applause; (fig) approval, acclaim

aplazamiento [aplaθa'mjento] nm postponement

aplazar [apla'θar] vt to postpone, defer

aplicación [aplika'θjon] nf application; (esfuerzo) effort; **aplicaciones de gestión** business applications

aplicado, -a [apli'kaðo, a] adj diligent, hard-working

aplicar [apli'kar] vt (gen) to apply; (poner en vigor) to put into effect; (esfuerzos) to devote; **aplicarse** vr to apply o.s.

aplique etc [a'plike] vb ver **aplicar** ■ nm wall light o lamp

aplomo [a'plomo] nm aplomb, self-assurance

apocado, -a [apo'kaðo, a] adj timid

apocamiento [apoka'mjento] nm timidity; (depresión) depression

apocarse [apo'karse] vr to feel small o humiliated

apocopar [apoko'par] vt (Ling) to shorten

apócope [a'pokope] nf apocopation; **gran es ~ de grande** "gran" is the shortened form of "grande"

apócrifo, -a [a'pokrifo, a] adj apocryphal

apodar [apo'ðar] vt to nickname

apoderado [apoðe'raðo] nm agent, representative

apoderar [apoðe'rar] vt to authorize, empower; (Jur) to grant (a) power of attorney to; **apoderarse** vr: **apoderarse de** to take possession of

apodo [a'poðo] nm nickname

apogeo [apo'xeo] nm peak, summit

apolillado, -a [apoli'ʎaðo, a] adj moth-eaten

apolillarse [apoli'ʎarse] vr to get moth-eaten

apología [apolo'xia] nf eulogy; (defensa) defence

apoltronarse [apoltro'narse] vr to get lazy

apoplejía [aople'xia] nf apoplexy, stroke

apoque etc [a'poke] vb ver **apocarse**

apoquinar [apoki'nar] vt (fam) to cough up, fork out

aporrear [aporre'ar] vt to beat (up)

aportación [aporta'θjon] nf contribution

aportar [apor'tar] vt to contribute ■ vi to reach port

aposentar [aposen'tar] vt to lodge, put up

aposento [apo'sento] nm lodging; (habitación) room

apósito [a'posito] nm (Med) dressing

aposta [a'posta] adv on purpose

apostar [apos'tar] vt to bet, stake; (tropas etc) to station, post ■ vi to bet

apostatar [aposta'tar] vi (Rel) to apostatize; (fig) to change sides

a posteriori [aposte'rjori] adv at a later date o stage; (Lógica) a posteriori

apostilla [apos'tiʎa] nf note, comment

apóstol [a'postol] nm apostle

apóstrofo [a'postrofo] nm apostrophe

apostura [apos'tura] *nf* neatness, elegance

apoteósico, -a [apote'osiko, a] *adj* tremendous

apoyar [apo'jar] *vt* to lean, rest; (*fig*) to support, back; **apoyarse** *vr*: **apoyarse en** to lean on

apoyo [a'pojo] *nm* support, backing

apreciable [apre'θjaβle] *adj* considerable; (*fig*) esteemed

apreciación [apreθja'θjon] *nf* appreciation; (*Com*) valuation

apreciar [apre'θjar] *vt* to evaluate, assess; (*Com*) to appreciate, value ∎ *vi* (*Econ*) to appreciate

aprecio [a'preθjo] *nm* valuation, estimate; (*fig*) appreciation

aprehender [apreen'der] *vt* to apprehend, detain; (*ver*) to see, observe

aprehensión [apreen'sjon] *nf* detention, capture

apremiante [apre'mjante] *adj* urgent, pressing

apremiar [apre'mjar] *vt* to compel, force ∎ *vi* to be urgent, press

apremio [a'premjo] *nm* urgency; **~ de pago** demand note

aprender [apren'der] *vt, vi* to learn; **~ a conducir** to learn to drive; **aprenderse** *vr*: **aprenderse algo** to learn sth (off) by heart

aprendiz, a [apren'diθ, a] *nm/f* apprentice; (*principiante*) learner, trainee; **~ de comercio** business trainee

aprendizaje [aprendi'θaxe] *nm* apprenticeship

aprensión [apren'sjon] *nm* apprehension, fear

aprensivo, -a [apren'siβo, a] *adj* apprehensive

apresar [apre'sar] *vt* to seize; (*capturar*) to capture

aprestar [apres'tar] *vt* to prepare, get ready; (*Tec*) to prime, size; **aprestarse** *vr* to get ready

apresto [a'presto] *nm* (*gen*) preparation; (*sustancia*) size

apresurado, -a [apresu'raðo, a] *adj* hurried, hasty

apresuramiento [apresura'mjento] *nm* hurry, haste

apresurar [apresu'rar] *vt* to hurry, accelerate; **apresurarse** *vr* to hurry, make haste; **me apresuré a sugerir que ...** I hastily suggested that ...

apretado, -a [apre'taðo, a] *adj* tight; (*escritura*) cramped

apretar [apre'tar] *vt* to squeeze, press; (*mano*) to clasp; (*dientes*) to grit; (*Tec*) to tighten; (*presionar*) to press together, pack ∎ *vi* to be too tight; **apretarse** *vr* to crowd together; **~ la mano a algn** to shake sb's hand; **~ el paso** to quicken one's step

apretón [apre'ton] *nm* squeeze; **~ de manos** handshake

aprieto *etc* [a'prjeto] *vb ver* **apretar** ∎ *nm* squeeze; (*dificultad*) difficulty, jam; **estar en un ~** to be in a jam; **ayudar a algn a salir de un ~** to help sb out of trouble

a priori [apri'ori] *adv* beforehand; (*Lógica*) a priori

aprisa [a'prisa] *adv* quickly, hurriedly

aprisionar [aprisjo'nar] *vt* to imprison

aprobación [aproβa'θjon] *nf* approval

aprobado [apro'βaðo] *nm* (*nota*) pass mark

aprobar [apro'βar] *vt* to approve (of); (*examen, materia*) to pass ∎ *vi* to pass

apropiación [apropja'θjon] *nf* appropriation

apropiado, -a [apro'pjaðo, a] *adj* appropriate

apropiarse [apro'pjarse] *vr*: **~ de** to appropriate

aprovechado, -a [aproβe'tʃaðo, a] *adj* industrious, hardworking; (*económico*) thrifty; (*pey*) unscrupulous

aprovechamiento [aproβetʃa'mjento] *nm* use, exploitation

aprovechar [aproβe'tʃar] *vt* to use; (*explotar*) to exploit; (*experiencia*) to profit from; (*oferta, oportunidad*) to take advantage of ∎ *vi* to progress, improve; **aprovecharse** *vr*: **aprovecharse de** to make use of; (*pey*) to take advantage of; **¡que aproveche!** enjoy your meal!

aprovisionar [aproβisjo'nar] *vt* to supply

aproximación [aproksima'θjon] *nf* approximation; (*de lotería*) consolation prize

aproximadamente [aproksimaða'mente] *adv* approximately

aproximado, -a [aproksi'maðo, a] *adj* approximate

aproximar [aproksi'mar] *vt* to bring nearer; **aproximarse** *vr* to come near, approach

apruebe *etc* [a'prweβe] *vb ver* **aprobar**

aptitud [apti'tuð] *nf* aptitude; (*capacidad*) ability; **~ para los negocios** business sense

apto, -a ['apto, a] *adj* (*hábil*) capable; (*apropiado*): **~ (para)** fit (for), suitable (for); **~/no ~ para menores** (*Cine*) suitable/unsuitable for children

apuesto, -a *etc* [a'pwesto, a] *vb ver* **apostar** ∎ *adj* neat, elegant ∎ *nf* bet, wager

apuntador [apunta'ðor] *nm* prompter

apuntalar [apunta'lar] *vt* to prop up

apuntar [apun'tar] *vt* (*con arma*) to aim at; (*con dedo*) to point at *o* to; (*anotar*) to note (down); (*datos*) to record; (*Teat*) to prompt;

apuntarse vr (Deporte: tanto, victoria) to score; (Escol) to enrol; **~ una cantidad en la cuenta de algn** to charge a sum to sb's account; **apuntarse en un curso** to enrol on a course; **¡yo me apunto!** count me in!

apunte [a'punte] nm note; (Teat: voz) prompt; (: texto) prompt book

apuñalar [apuɲa'lar] vt to stab

apurado, -a [apu'raðo, a] adj needy; (difícil) difficult; (peligroso) dangerous; (Am) hurried, rushed; **estar en una situación apurada** to be in a tight spot; **estar ~** to be in a hurry

apurar [apu'rar] vt (agotar) to drain; (recursos) to use up; (molestar) to annoy; **apurarse** vr (preocuparse) to worry; (esp Am: darse prisa) to hurry

apuro [a'puro] nm (aprieto) fix, jam; (escasez) want, hardship; (vergüenza) embarrassment; (Am) haste, urgency

aquejado, -a [ake'xaðo, a] adj: **~ de** (Med) afflicted by

aquejar [ake'xar] vt (afligir) to distress; **le aqueja una grave enfermedad** he suffers from a serious disease

aquel, aquella, aquellos, -as [a'kel, a'keʎa, a'keʎos, as] adj that, those pl

aquél, aquélla, aquéllos, -as [a'kel, a'keʎa, a'keʎos, as] pron that (one), those (ones) pl

aquello [a'keʎo] pron that, that business

aquí [a'ki] adv (lugar) here; (tiempo) now; **aquí arriba** up here; **aquí mismo** right here; **aquí yace** here lies; **de aquí a siete días** a week from now

aquietar [akje'tar] vt to quieten (down), calm (down)

Aquisgrán [akis'ɣran] nm Aachen, Aix-la-Chapelle

A.R. abr (= Alteza Real) R.H.

ara ['ara] nf (altar) altar; **en aras de** for the sake of

árabe ['araβe] adj Arab, Arabian, Arabic ■ nm/f Arab ■ nm (Ling) Arabic

Arabia [a'raβja] nf Arabia; **~ Saudí** o **Saudita** Saudi Arabia

arábigo, -a [a'raβiɣo, a] adj Arab, Arabian, Arabic

arácnido [a'rakniðo] nm arachnid

arado [a'raðo] nm plough

aragonés, -esa [araɣo'nes, esa] adj, nm/f Aragonese ■ nm (Ling) Aragonese

arancel [aran'θel] nm tariff, duty; **~ de aduanas** (customs) duty

arandela [aran'dela] nf (Tec) washer; (chorrera) frill

araña [a'raɲa] nf (Zool) spider; (lámpara) chandelier

arañar [ara'ɲar] vt to scratch

arañazo [ara'ɲaθo] nm scratch

arar [a'rar] vt to plough, till

araucano, -a [arau'kano, a] adj, nm/f Araucanian

arbitraje [arβi'traxe] nm arbitration

arbitrar [arβi'trar] vt to arbitrate in; (recursos) to bring together; (Deporte) to referee ■ vi to arbitrate

arbitrariedad [arβitrarje'ðað] nf arbitrariness; (acto) arbitrary act

arbitrario, -a [arβi'trarjo, a] adj arbitrary

arbitrio [ar'βitrjo] nm free will; (Jur) adjudication, decision; **dejar al ~ de algn** to leave to sb's discretion

árbitro ['arβitro] nm arbitrator; (Deporte) referee; (Tenis) umpire

árbol ['arβol] nm (Bot) tree; (Naut) mast; (Tec) axle, shaft

arbolado, -a [arβo'laðo, a] adj wooded; (camino) tree-lined ■ nm woodland

arboladura [arβola'ðura] nf rigging

arbolar [arβo'lar] vt to hoist, raise

arboleda [arβo'leða] nf grove, plantation

arbusto [ar'βusto] nm bush, shrub

arca ['arka] nf chest, box; **A~ de la Alianza** Ark of the Covenant; **A~ de Noé** Noah's Ark

arcada [ar'kaða] nf arcade; (de puente) arch, span; **arcadas** nfpl retching sg

arcaico, -a [ar'kaiko, a] adj archaic

arce ['arθe] nm maple tree

arcén [ar'θen] nm (de autopista) hard shoulder; (de carretera) verge

archiconocido, -a [artʃikono'θiðo, a] adj extremely well-known

archipiélago [artʃi'pjelaɣo] nm archipelago

archisabido, -a [artʃisa'βiðo, a] adj extremely well-known

archivador [artʃiβa'ðor] nm filing cabinet; **~ colgante** suspension file

archivar [artʃi'βar] vt to file (away); (Inform) to archive

archivo [ar'tʃiβo] nm archive(s) (pl); (Inform) file; **A~ Nacional** Public Record Office; **archivos policíacos** police files; **nombre de ~** (Inform) filename; **~ adjunto** (Inform) attachment; **~ de seguridad** (Inform) backup file

arcilla [ar'θiʎa] nf clay

arco ['arko] nm arch; (Mat) arc; (Mil: Mus) bow; (Am Deporte) goal; **~ iris** rainbow

arcón [ar'kon] nm large chest

arder [ar'ðer] vt to burn; **~ sin llama** to smoulder; **estar que arde** (persona) to fume

ardid [ar'ðið] nm ruse

ardiente [ar'ðjente] adj ardent

ardilla [ar'ðiʎa] nf squirrel

ardor [ar'ðor] nm (calor) heat, warmth; (fig)

ardour; **~ de estómago** heartburn

ardoroso, -a [arðo'roso, a] *adj* passionate

arduo, -a ['arðwo, a] *adj* arduous

área ['area] *nf* area; (*Deporte*) penalty area

arena [a'rena] *nf* sand; (*de una lucha*) arena

arenal [are'nal] *nm* (*arena movediza*) quicksand

arenga [a'renga] *nf* (*fam*) sermon

arengar [aren'gar] *vt* to harangue

arengue *etc* [a'renge] *vb ver* **arengar**

arenillas [are'niʎas] *nfpl* (*Med*) stones

arenisca [are'niska] *nf* sandstone; (*cascajo*) grit

arenoso, -a [are'noso, a] *adj* sandy

arenque [a'renke] *nm* herring

arepa [a'repa] *nf* (*Am*) corn pancake

arete [a'rete] *nm* earring

argamasa [arɣa'masa] *nf* mortar, plaster

Argel [ar'xel] *n* Algiers

Argelia [ar'xelja] *nf* Algeria

argelino, -a [arxe'lino, a] *adj, nm/f* Algerian

Argentina [arxen'tina] *nf*: **(la)** ~ the Argentine, Argentina

argentino, -a [arxen'tino, a] *adj* Argentinian; (*de plata*) silvery ■ *nm/f* Argentinian

argolla [ar'ɣoʎa] *nf* (large) ring; (*Am: de matrimonio*) wedding ring

argot [ar'ɣo] *nm* (*pl* **argots** [ar'ɣo, ar'ɣos]) slang

argucia [ar'ɣuθja] *nf* subtlety, sophistry

argüir [ar'ɣwir] *vt* to deduce; (*discutir*) to argue; (*indicar*) to indicate, imply; (*censurar*) to reproach ■ *vi* to argue

argumentación [arɣumenta'θjon] *nf* (line of) argument

argumentar [arɣumen'tar] *vt, vi* to argue

argumento [arɣu'mento] *nm* argument; (*razonamiento*) reasoning; (*de novela etc*) plot; (*Cine: TV*) storyline

arguyendo *etc* [arɣu'jendo] *vb ver* **argüir**

aria ['arja] *nf* aria

aridez [ari'ðeθ] *nf* aridity, dryness

árido, -a ['ariðo, a] *adj* arid, dry; **áridos** *nmpl* dry goods

Aries ['arjes] *nm* Aries

ariete [a'rjete] *nm* battering ram

ario, -a ['arjo, a] *adj* Aryan

arisco, -a [a'risko, a] *adj* surly; (*insociable*) unsociable

aristocracia [aristo'kraθja] *nf* aristocracy

aristócrata [aris'tokrata] *nm/f* aristocrat

aristocrático, -a [aristo'kratiko, a] *adj* aristocratic

aritmética [arit'metika] *nf* arithmetic

aritmético, -a [arit'metiko, a] *adj* arithmetic(al) ■ *nm/f* arithmetician

arma ['arma] *nf* arm; **armas** *nfpl* arms;

~ blanca blade, knife; (*espada*) sword; **~ de fuego** firearm; **armas cortas** small arms; **armas de destrucción masiva** weapons of mass destruction; **rendir las armas** to lay down one's arms; **ser de armas tomar** to be somebody to be reckoned with

armada [ar'maða] *nf* armada; (*flota*) fleet; *ver tb* **armado**

armadillo [arma'ðiʎo] *nm* armadillo

armado, -a [ar'maðo, a] *adj* armed; (*Tec*) reinforced

armador [arma'ðor] *nm* (*Naut*) shipowner

armadura [arma'ðura] *nf* (*Mil*) armour; (*Tec*) framework; (*Zool*) skeleton; (*Física*) armature

armamentista [armamen'tista], **armamentístico, a** [armamen'tistiko, a] *adj* arms *cpd*

armamento [arma'mento] *nm* armament; (*Naut*) fitting-out

armar [ar'mar] *vt* (*soldado*) to arm; (*máquina*) to assemble; (*navío*) to fit out; **armarla, ~ un lío** to start a row; **armarse** *vr*: **armarse de valor** to summon up one's courage

armario [ar'marjo] *nm* wardrobe; **salir del ~** to come out (of the closet)

armatoste [arma'toste] *nm* (*mueble*) monstrosity; (*máquina*) contraption

armazón [arma'θon] *nf o m* body, chassis; (*de mueble etc*) frame; (*Arq*) skeleton

Armenia [ar'menja] *nf* Armenia

armería [arme'ria] *nf* (*museo*) military museum; (*tienda*) gunsmith's

armiño [ar'miɲo] *nm* stoat; (*piel*) ermine

armisticio [armis'tiθjo] *nm* armistice

armonía [armo'nia] *nf* harmony

armónica [ar'monika] *nf* harmonica; *ver tb* **armónico**

armonice *etc* [armo'niθe] *vb ver* **armonizar**

armónico, -a [ar'moniko, a] *adj* harmonic

armonioso, -a [armo'njoso, a] *adj* harmonious

armonizar [armoni'θar] *vt* to harmonize; (*diferencias*) to reconcile ■ *vi* to harmonize; **~ con** (*fig*) to be in keeping with; (*colores*) to tone in with

arnés [ar'nes] *nm* armour; **arneses** *nmpl* harness *sg*

aro ['aro] *nm* ring; (*tejo*) quoit; (*Am: pendiente*) earring; **entrar por el ~** to give in

aroma [a'roma] *nm* aroma

aromaterapia [aromate'rapja] *nf* aromatherapy

aromático, -a [aro'matiko, a] *adj* aromatic

arpa ['arpa] *nf* harp

arpegio [ar'pexjo] *nm* (*Mus*) arpeggio

arpía [ar'pia] *nf* (*fig*) shrew

arpillera [arpi'ʎera] *nf* sacking, sackcloth

arpón [ar'pon] *nm* harpoon

arquear [arke'ar] *vt* to arch, bend;
arquearse *vr* to arch, bend

arqueo [ar'keo] *nm* (*gen*) arching; (*Naut*)
tonnage

arqueología [arkeolo'xia] *nf* archaeology

arqueológico, -a [arkeo'loxiko, a] *adj*
archaeological

arqueólogo, -a [arke'oloɣo, a] *nm/f*
archaeologist

arquero [ar'kero] *nm* archer, bowman;
(*Am Deporte*) goalkeeper

arquetipo [arke'tipo] *nm* archetype

arquitecto, -a [arki'tekto, a] *nm/f* architect;
~ **paisajista** *o* **de jardines** landscape
gardener

arquitectónico, -a [arkitek'toniko, a] *adj*
architectural

arquitectura [arkitek'tura] *nf* architecture

arrabal [arra'βal] *nm* suburb; **arrabales** *nmpl*
outskirts

arrabalero, -a [arraβa'lero, a] *adj* (*fig*)
common, coarse

arracimarse [arraθi'marse] *vr* to cluster
together

arraigado, -a [arrai'ɣaðo, a] *adj* deep-rooted;
(*fig*) established

arraigar [arrai'ɣar] *vt* to establish ■ *vi*,
arraigarse *vr* to take root; (*persona*) to settle

arraigo [a'rraiɣo] *nm* (*raíces*) roots *pl*; (*bienes*)
property; (*influencia*) hold; **hombre de** ~ man
of property

arraigue *etc* [a'rraiɣe] *vb ver* **arraigar**

arrancada [arran'kaða] *nf* (*arranque*) sudden
start

arrancar [arran'kar] *vt* (*sacar*) to extract, pull
out; (*arrebatar*) to snatch (away); (*pedazo*) to
tear off; (*página*) to rip out; (*suspiro*) to heave;
(*Auto*) to start; (*Inform*) to boot; (*fig*) to extract
■ *vi* (*Auto, máquina*) to start; (*ponerse en marcha*)
to get going; ~ **información a algn** to
extract information from sb; ~ **de** to stem
from

arranque *etc* [a'rranke] *vb ver* **arrancar** ■ *nm*
sudden start; (*Auto*) start; (*fig*) fit, outburst

arras ['arras] *nfpl* pledge *sg*, security *sg*

arrasar [arra'sar] *vt* (*aplanar*) to level, flatten;
(*destruir*) to demolish

arrastrado, -a [arras'traðo, a] *adj* poor,
wretched

arrastrador [arrastra'ðor] *nm* (*en máquina
impresora*) tractor

arrastrar [arras'trar] *vt* to drag (along); (*fig*)
to drag down, degrade; (*suj: agua, viento*) to
carry away ■ *vi* to drag, trail on the ground;
arrastrarse *vr* to crawl; (*fig*) to grovel; **llevar
algo arrastrado** to drag sth along

arrastre [a'rrastre] *nm* drag, dragging;
(*Deporte*) crawl; **estar para el** ~ (*fig*) to have
had it

array [a'rrai] *nm* (*Inform*) array; ~
empaquetado (*Inform*) packed array

arrayán [arra'jan] *nm* myrtle

arre ['arre] *excl* gee up!

arrear [arre'ar] *vt* to drive on, urge on
■ *vi* to hurry along

arrebañar [arreβa'ɲar] *vt* (*juntar*) to scrape
together

arrebatado, -a [arreβa'taðo, a] *adj* rash,
impetuous; (*repentino*) sudden, hasty

arrebatar [arreβa'tar] *vt* to snatch (away),
seize; (*fig*) to captivate; **arrebatarse** *vr* to get
carried away, get excited

arrebato [arre'βato] *nm* fit of rage, fury;
(*éxtasis*) rapture; **en un** ~ **de cólera** in an
outburst of anger

arrebolar [arreβo'lar] *vt* to redden;
arrebolarse *vr* (*enrojecer*) to blush

arrebujar [arreβu'xar] *vt* (*objetos*) to jumble
together; **arrebujarse** *vr* to wrap o.s. up

arrechar [arre'tʃar] (*Am*) *vt* to arouse, excite;
arrecharse *vr* to become aroused

arrechucho [arre'tʃutʃo] *nm* (*Med*) turn

arreciar [arre'θjar] *vi* to get worse; (*viento*) to
get stronger

arrecife [arre'θife] *nm* reef

arredrar [arre'ðrar] *vt* (*hacer retirarse*) to drive
back; **arredrarse** *vr* (*apartarse*) to draw back;
arredrarse ante algo to shrink away from sth

arreglado, -a [arre'ɣlaðo, a] *adj* (*ordenado*)
neat, orderly; (*moderado*) moderate,
reasonable

arreglar [arre'ɣlar] *vt* (*poner orden*) to tidy up;
(*algo roto*) to fix, repair; (*problema*) to solve;
arreglarse *vr* to reach an understanding;
arreglárselas (*fam*) to get by, manage

arreglo [a'rreɣlo] *nm* settlement; (*orden*)
order; (*acuerdo*) agreement; (*Mus*)
arrangement, setting; (*Inform*) array; **con** ~ **a**
in accordance with; **llegar a un** ~ to reach a
compromise

arrellanarse [arreʎa'narse] *vr* to sprawl;
~ **en el asiento** to lie back in one's chair

arremangar [arreman'gar] *vt* to roll up, turn
up; **arremangarse** *vr* to roll up one's sleeves

arremangue *etc* [arre'mange] *vb ver*
arremangar

arremeter [arreme'ter] *vt* to attack, assault;
~ **contra algn** to attack sb

arremetida [arreme'tiða] *nf* assault

arremolinarse [arremoli'narse] *vr* to crowd
around, mill around; (*corriente*) to swirl, eddy

arrendador, a [arrenda'ðor, a] *nm/f*
landlord/lady

arrendamiento [arrenda'mjento] *nm*
letting; (*el alquilar*) hiring; (*contrato*) lease;
(*alquiler*) rent

arrendar [arren'dar] *vt* to let; to hire; to lease;
to rent

arrendatario, -a [arrenda'tarjo, a] *nm/f*
tenant

arreos [a'rreos] *nmpl* harness *sg*, trappings

arrepentido, -a [arrepen'tiðo, a] *nm/f* (*Pol*)
reformed terrorist

arrepentimiento [arrepenti'mjento] *nm*
regret, repentance

arrepentirse [arrepen'tirse] *vr* to repent;
~ **de (haber hecho) algo** to regret (doing) sth

arrepienta *etc* [arre'pjenta], **arrepintiendo**
etc [arrepin'tjendo] *vb ver* **arrepentirse**

arrestar [arres'tar] *vt* to arrest; (*encarcelar*)
to imprison

arresto [a'rresto] *nm* arrest; (*Mil*) detention;
(*audacia*) boldness, daring; ~ **domiciliario**
house arrest

arriar [a'rrjar] *vt* (*velas*) to haul down;
(*bandera*) to lower, strike; (*un cable*) to pay out

arriate [a'rrjate] *nm* (*Bot*) bed; (*camino*) road

⬤ PALABRA CLAVE

arriba [a'rriβa] *adv* **1** (*posición*) above; **desde
arriba** from above; **arriba del todo** at the
very top, right on top; **Juan está arriba**
Juan is upstairs; **lo arriba mencionado** the
aforementioned; **aquí/allí arriba** up here/
there; **está hasta arriba de trabajo** (*fam*)
he's up to his eyes in work (*fam*)
2 (*dirección*) up, upwards; **más arriba** higher
o further up; **calle arriba** up the street
3: **de arriba abajo** from top to bottom;
mirar a algn de arriba abajo to look sb up
and down
4: **para arriba**: **de 50 euros para arriba**
from 50 euros up(wards); **de la cintura
(para) arriba** from the waist up
■ *adj*: **de arriba**: **el piso de arriba** the
upstairs flat (*Brit*) *o* apartment; **la parte de
arriba** the top *o* upper part
■ *prep*: **arriba de** (*Am*) above; **arriba de 200
dólares** more than 200 dollars
■ *excl*: ¡**arriba**! up!; ¡**manos arriba**! hands
up!; ¡**arriba España**! long live Spain!

arribar [arri'βar] *vi* to put into port; (*esp Am*:
llegar) to arrive

arribista [arri'βista] *nm/f* parvenu(e), upstart

arribo [a'rriβo] *nm* (*esp Am*) arrival

arriendo *etc* [a'rrjendo] *vb ver* **arrendar** ■ *nm*
= **arrendamiento**

arriero [a'rrjero] *nm* muleteer

arriesgado, -a [arrjes'ɣaðo, a] *adj* (*peligroso*)
risky; (*audaz*) bold, daring

arriesgar [arrjes'ɣar] *vt* to risk; (*poner en
peligro*) to endanger; **arriesgarse** *vr* to take
a risk

arriesgue *etc* [a'rrjesɣe] *vb ver* **arriesgar**

arrimar [arri'mar] *vt* (*acercar*) to bring close;
(*poner de lado*) to set aside; **arrimarse** *vr* to
come close *o* closer; **arrimarse a** to lean on;
(*fig*) to keep company with; (*buscar ayuda*)
to seek the protection of; **arrímate a mí**
cuddle up to me

arrinconado, -a [arrinko'naðo, a] *adj*
forgotten, neglected

arrinconar [arrinko'nar] *vt* to put in a
corner; (*fig*) to put on one side; (*abandonar*)
to push aside

arriscado, -a [arris'kaðo, a] *adj* (*Geo*) craggy;
(*fig*) bold, resolute

arroba [a'rroβa] *nf* (*peso*) 25 pounds; (*Inform: en
dirección electrónica*) at sign, @; **tiene talento
por arrobas** he has loads *o* bags of talent

arrobado, -a [arro'βaðo, a] *adj* entranced,
enchanted

arrobamiento [arroβa'mjento] *nm* ecstasy

arrobar [arro'βar] *vt* to enchant; **arrobarse**
vr to be enraptured; (*místico*) to go into a
trance

arrodillarse [arroði'ʎarse] *vr* to kneel (down)

arrogancia [arro'ɣanθja] *nf* arrogance

arrogante [arro'ɣante] *adj* arrogant

arrojar [arro'xar] *vt* to throw, hurl; (*humo*)
to emit, give out; (*Com*) to yield, produce;
arrojarse *vr* to throw *o* hurl o.s.

arrojo [a'rroxo] *nm* daring

arrollador, a [arroʎa'ðor, a] *adj* crushing,
overwhelming

arrollar [arro'ʎar] *vt* (*enrollar*) to roll up; (*suj:
inundación*) to wash away; (*Auto*) to run over;
(*Deporte*) to crush

arropar [arro'par] *vt* to cover (up), wrap up;
arroparse *vr* to wrap o.s. up

arrostrar [arros'trar] *vt* to face (up to);
arrostrarse *vr*: **arrostrarse con algn** to face
up to sb

arroyo [a'rrojo] *nm* stream; (*de la calle*) gutter;
poner a algn en el ~ to turn sb onto the
streets

arroz [a'rroθ] *nm* rice; ~ **con leche** rice
pudding

arrozal [arro'θal] *nm* paddy field

arruga [a'rruɣa] *nf* fold; (*de cara*) wrinkle;
(*de vestido*) crease

arrugar [arru'ɣar] *vt* to fold; to wrinkle; to
crease; **arrugarse** *vr* to get wrinkled; to get
creased

arrugue *etc* [a'rruɣe] *vb ver* **arrugar**

arruinar [arrwi'nar] *vt* to ruin, wreck; **arruinarse** *vr* to be ruined

arrullar [arru'ʎar] *vi* to coo ◼ *vt* to lull to sleep

arrumaco [arru'mako] *nm* (*caricia*) caress; (*halago*) piece of flattery

arrumbar [arrum'bar] *vt* (*objeto*) to discard; (*individuo*) to silence

arrurruz [arru'rruθ] *nm* arrowroot

arsenal [arse'nal] *nm* naval dockyard; (*Mil*) arsenal

arsénico [ar'seniko] *nm* arsenic

arte ['arte] *nm* (*gen m en sg, f en pl*) art; (*maña*) skill, guile; **por ~ de magia** (as if) by magic; **no tener ~ ni parte en algo** to have nothing whatsoever to do with sth; **artes** *nfpl* arts; **Bellas Artes** Fine Art *sg*; **artes y oficios** arts and crafts

artefacto [arte'fakto] *nm* appliance; (*Arqueología*) artefact

arteria [ar'terja] *nf* artery

arterial [arte'rjal] *adj* arterial; (*presión*) blood *cpd*

arterioesclerosis [arterjoeskle'rosis], **arteriosclerosis** [arterjoskle'rosis] *nf inv* hardening of the arteries, arteriosclerosis

artesa [ar'tesa] *nf* trough

artesanía [artesa'nia] *nf* craftsmanship; (*artículos*) handicrafts *pl*

artesano, -a [arte'sano, a] *nm/f* artisan, craftsman/woman

ártico, -a ['artiko, a] *adj* Arctic ◼ *nm*: **el (océano) Ártico** the Arctic (Ocean)

articulación [artikula'θjon] *nf* articulation; (*Med: Tec*) joint

articulado, -a [artiku'laðo, a] *adj* articulated; jointed

articular [artiku'lar] *vt* to articulate; to join together

articulista [artiku'lista] *nm/f* columnist, contributor (to a newspaper)

artículo [ar'tikulo] *nm* article; (*cosa*) thing, article; (*TV*) feature, report; **~ de fondo** leader, editorial; **artículos** *nmpl* goods; **artículos de marca** (*Com*) proprietary goods

artífice [ar'tifiθe] *nm* artist, craftsman; (*fig*) architect

artificial [artifi'θjal] *adj* artificial

artificio [arti'fiθjo] *nm* art, skill; (*artesanía*) craftsmanship; (*astucia*) cunning

artillería [artiʎe'ria] *nf* artillery

artillero [arti'ʎero] *nm* artilleryman, gunner

artilugio [arti'luxjo] *nm* gadget

artimaña [arti'maɲa] *nf* trap, snare; (*astucia*) cunning

artista [ar'tista] *nm/f* (*pintor*) artist, painter; (*Teat*) artist, artiste

artístico, -a [ar'tistiko, a] *adj* artistic

artritis [ar'tritis] *nf* arthritis

artrosis [ar'trosis] *nf* osteoarthritis

arveja [ar'βexa] *nf* (*Am*) pea

Arz. *abr* (= *Arzobispo*) Abp

arzobispo [arθo'βispo] *nm* archbishop

as [as] *nm* ace; **as del fútbol** star player

asa ['asa] *nf* handle; (*fig*) lever

asado [a'saðo] *nm* roast (meat); (*Am: barbacoa*) barbecue

asador [asa'ðor] *nm* (*varilla*) spit; (*aparato*) spit roaster

asadura [asa'ðura] *nf*, **asaduras** [asa'ðuras] *nfpl* entrails *pl*, offal *sg*; (*Culin*) chitterlings *pl*

asaetear [asaete'ar] *vt* (*fig*) to bother

asalariado, -a [asala'rjaðo, a] *adj* paid, wage-earning, salaried ◼ *nm/f* wage earner

asaltador, a [asalta'ðor, a], **asaltante** [asal'tante] *nm/f* assailant

asaltar [asal'tar] *vt* to attack, assault; (*fig*) to assail

asalto [a'salto] *nm* attack, assault; (*Deporte*) round

asamblea [asam'blea] *nf* assembly; (*reunión*) meeting

asar [a'sar] *vt* to roast; **~ al horno/a la parrilla** to bake/grill; **asarse** *vr* (*fig*): **me aso de calor** I'm roasting; **aquí se asa uno vivo** it's boiling hot here

asbesto [as'βesto] *nm* asbestos

ascendencia [asθen'denθja] *nf* ancestry; **de ~ francesa** of French origin

ascender [asθen'der] *vi* (*subir*) to ascend, rise; (*ser promovido*) to gain promotion ◼ *vt* to promote; **~ a** to amount to

ascendiente [asθen'djente] *nm* influence ◼ *nm/f* ancestor

ascensión [asθen'sjon] *nf* ascent; **la A~** the Ascension

ascenso [as'θenso] *nm* ascent; (*promoción*) promotion

ascensor [asθen'sor] *nm* lift (*Brit*), elevator (*US*)

ascético, -a [as'θetiko, a] *adj* ascetic

ascienda *etc* [as'θjenda] *vb ver* **ascender**

asco ['asko] *nm*: **el ajo me da ~** I hate o loathe garlic; **hacer ascos de algo** to turn up one's nose at sth; **estar hecho un ~** to be filthy; **poner a algn de ~** to call sb all sorts of names o every name under the sun; **¡qué ~!** how revolting o disgusting!

ascua ['askwa] *nf* ember; **arrimar el ~ a su sardina** to look after number one; **estar en ascuas** to be on tenterhooks

aseado, -a [ase'aðo, a] *adj* clean; (*arreglado*) tidy; (*pulcro*) smart

asear [ase'ar] *vt* (*lavar*) to wash; (*ordenar*) to tidy (up)

asechanza [ase't∫anθa] *nf* trap, snare

asediar [ase'ðjar] *vt* (*Mil*) to besiege, lay siege to; (*fig*) to chase, pester

asedio [a'seðjo] *nm* siege; (*Com*) run

asegurado, a [aseɣu'raðo, a] *adj* insured

asegurador, -a [aseɣura'ðor, a] *nm/f* insurer

asegurar [aseɣu'rar] *vt* (*consolidar*) to secure, fasten; (*dar garantía de*) to guarantee; (*preservar*) to safeguard; (*afirmar: dar por cierto*) to assure, affirm; (*tranquilizar*) to reassure; (*hacer un seguro*) to insure; **asegurarse** *vr* to assure o.s., make sure

asemejarse [aseme'xarse]˙ *vr* to be alike; ~ **a** to be like, resemble

asentado, -a [asen'taðo, a] *adj* established, settled

asentar [asen'tar] *vt* (*sentar*) to seat, sit down; (*poner*) to place, establish; (*alisar*) to level, smooth down *o* out; (*anotar*) to note down ■ *vi* to be suitable, suit

asentimiento [asenti'mjento] *nm* assent, agreement

asentir [asen'tir] *vi* to assent, agree

aseo [a'seo] *nm* cleanliness; **aseos** *nmpl* toilet *sg* (*Brit*), restroom *sg* (*US*), cloakroom *sg*

aséptico, -a [a'septiko, a] *adj* germ-free, free from infection

asequible [ase'kiβle] *adj* (*precio*) reasonable; (*meta*) attainable; (*persona*) approachable

aserradero [aserra'ðero] *nm* sawmill

aserrar [ase'rrar] *vt* to saw

asesinar [asesi'nar] *vt* to murder; (*Pol*) to assassinate

asesinato [asesi'nato] *nm* murder; assassination

asesino, -a [ase'sino, a] *nm/f* murderer, killer; (*Pol*) assassin

asesor, a [ase'sor, a] *nm/f* adviser, consultant; (*Com*) assessor, consultant; ~ **administrativo** management consultant

asesorar [aseso'rar] *vt* (*Jur*) to advise, give legal advice to; (*Com*) to act as consultant to; **asesorarse** *vr*: **asesorarse con** *o* **de** to take advice from, consult

asesoría [aseso'ria] *nf* (*cargo*) consultancy; (*oficina*) consultant's office

asestar [ases'tar] *vt* (*golpe*) to deal; (*arma*) to aim; (*tiro*) to fire

aseverar [aseβe'rar] *vt* to assert

asfaltado, -a [asfal'taðo, a] *adj* asphalted ■ *nm* (*pavimiento*) asphalt

asfalto [as'falto] *nm* asphalt

asfixia [as'fiksja] *nf* asphyxia, suffocation

asfixiar [asfik'sjar] *vt* to asphyxiate, suffocate

asga *etc* ['asɣa] *vb ver* **asir**

así [a'si] *adv* (*de esta manera*) in this way, like this, thus; (*aunque*) although; (*tan pronto como*) as soon as; **así que** so; **así como** as well as; **así y todo** even so; **¿no es así?** isn't it?, didn't you? *etc*; **así de grande** this big; **¡así sea!** so be it!; **así es la vida** such is life, that's life

Asia ['asja] *nf* Asia

asiático, -a [a'sjatiko, a] *adj, nm/f* Asian, Asiatic

asidero [asi'ðero] *nm* handle

asiduidad [asiðwi'ðað] *nf* assiduousness

asiduo, -a [a'siðwo, a] *adj* assiduous; (*frecuente*) frequent ■ *nm/f* regular (customer)

asiento *etc* [a'sjento] *vb ver* **asentar**; **asentir** ■ *nm* (*mueble*) seat, chair; (*de coche, en tribunal etc*) seat; (*localidad*) seat, place; (*fundamento*) site; ~ **delantero/trasero** front/back seat

asierre *etc* [a'sjerre] *vb ver* **aserrar**

asignación [asiɣna'θjon] *nf* (*atribución*) assignment; (*reparto*) allocation; (*Com*) allowance; ~ (**semanal**) pocket money; ~ **de presupuesto** budget appropriation

asignar [asiɣ'nar] *vt* to assign, allocate

asignatura [asiɣna'tura] *nf* subject; (*curso*) course; ~ **pendiente** (*fig*) matter pending

asilado, -a [asi'laðo, a] *nm/f* refugee

asilo [a'silo] *nm* (*refugio*) asylum, refuge; (*establecimiento*) home, institution; ~ **político** political asylum

asimilación [asimila'θjon] *nf* assimilation

asimilar [asimi'lar] *vt* to assimilate

asimismo [asi'mismo] *adv* in the same way, likewise

asintiendo *etc* [asin'tjendo] *vb ver* **asentir**

asir [a'sir] *vt* to seize, grasp; **asirse** *vr* to take hold; **asirse a** *o* **de** to seize

asistencia [asis'tenθja] *nf* presence; (*Teat*) audience; (*Med*) attendance; (*ayuda*) assistance; ~ **social** social *o* welfare work

asistente, -a [asis'tente, a] *nm/f* assistant ■ *nm* (*Mil*) orderly ■ *nf* daily help; **los asistentes** those present; ~ **social** social worker

asistido, -a [asis'tiðo, a] *adj* (*Auto: dirección*) power-assisted; ~ **por ordenador** computer-assisted

asistir [asis'tir] *vt* to assist, help ■ *vi*: ~ **a** to attend, be present at

asma ['asma] *nf* asthma

asno ['asno] *nm* donkey; (*fig*) ass

asociación [asoθja'θjon] *nf* association; (*Com*) partnership

asociado, -a [aso'θjaðo, a] *adj* associate ■ *nm/f* associate; (*Com*) partner

asociar [aso'θjar] *vt* to associate; **asociarse** *vr* to become partners

asolar [aso'lar] *vt* to destroy

asolear [asole'ar] *vt* to put in the sun;
asolearse *vr* to sunbathe

asomar [aso'mar] *vt* to show, stick out ■ *vi*
to appear; **asomarse** *vr* to appear, show up;
~ **la cabeza por la ventana** to put one's head
out of the window

asombrar [asom'brar] *vt* to amaze,
astonish; **asombrarse** *vr*: **asombrarse (de)**
(*sorprenderse*) to be amazed (at); (*asustarse*) to
be frightened (at)

asombro [a'sombro] *nm* amazement,
astonishment

asombroso, -a [asom'broso, a] *adj* amazing,
astonishing

asomo [a'somo] *nm* hint, sign; **ni por** ~ by
no means

asonancia [aso'nanθja] *nf* (*Lit*) assonance;
(*fig*) connection; **no tener** ~ **con** to bear no
relation to

asorocharse [asoro'tʃarse] *vr* (*Am*) to get
mountain sickness

aspa ['aspa] *nf* (*cruz*) cross; (*de molino*) sail;
en ~ X-shaped

aspaviento [aspa'βjento] *nm* exaggerated
display of feeling; (*fam*) fuss

aspecto [as'pekto] *nm* (*apariencia*) look,
appearance; (*fig*) aspect; **bajo ese** ~ from
that point of view

aspereza [aspe'reθa] *nf* roughness; (*de fruta*)
sharpness; (*de carácter*) surliness

áspero, -a ['aspero, a] *adj* rough; sharp;
harsh

aspersión [asper'sjon] *nf* sprinkling; (*Agr*)
spraying

aspersor [asper'sor] *nm* sprinkler

aspiración [aspira'θjon] *nf* breath,
inhalation; (*Mus*) short pause; **aspiraciones**
nfpl aspirations

aspiradora [aspira'ðora] *nf* vacuum cleaner,
Hoover®

aspirante [aspi'rante] *nm/f* (*candidato*)
candidate; (*Deporte*) contender

aspirar [aspi'rar] *vt* to breathe in ■ *vi*: ~ **a**
to aspire to

aspirina [aspi'rina] *nf* aspirin

asquear [aske'ar] *vt* to sicken ■ *vi* to be
sickening; **asquearse** *vr* to feel disgusted

asquerosidad [askerosi'ðað] *nf* (*suciedad*)
filth; (*dicho*) obscenity; (*faena*) dirty trick

asqueroso, -a [aske'roso, a] *adj* disgusting,
sickening

asta ['asta] *nf* lance; (*arpón*) spear; (*mango*)
shaft, handle; (*Zool*) horn; **a media** ~ at half
mast

astado, -a [as'taðo, a] *adj* horned ■ *nm* bull

asterisco [aste'risko] *nm* asterisk

asteroide [aste'roiðe] *nm* asteroid

astigmatismo [astiɣma'tismo] *nm*
astigmatism

astilla [as'tiʎa] *nf* splinter; (*pedacito*) chip;
astillas *nfpl* firewood *sg*

astillarse [asti'ʎarse] *vr* to splinter; (*fig*)
to shatter

astillero [asti'ʎero] *nm* shipyard

astringente [astrin'xente] *adj, nm* astringent

astro ['astro] *nm* star

astrología [astrolo'xia] *nf* astrology

astrólogo, -a [as'troloɣo, a] *nm/f* astrologer

astronauta [astro'nauta] *nm/f* astronaut

astronave [astro'naβe] *nm* spaceship

astronomía [astrono'mia] *nf* astronomy

astronómico, -a [astro'nomiko, a] *adj* (*tb fig*)
astronomical

astrónomo, -a [as'tronomo, a] *nm/f*
astronomer

astroso, -a [as'troso, a] *adj* (*desaliñado*)
untidy; (*vil*) contemptible

astucia [as'tuθja] *nf* astuteness; (*destreza*)
clever trick

asturiano, -a [astu'rjano, a] *adj, nm/f*
Asturian

Asturias [as'turjas] *nfpl* Asturias; **Príncipe
de** ~ crown prince

astuto, -a [as'tuto, a] *adj* astute; (*taimado*)
cunning

asueto [a'sweto] *nm* holiday; (*tiempo libre*)
time off; **día de** ~ day off; **tarde de** ~ (*trabajo*)
afternoon off; (*Escol*) half-holiday

asumir [asu'mir] *vt* to assume

asunción [asun'θjon] *nf* assumption

asunto [a'sunto] *nm* (*tema*) matter, subject;
(*negocio*) business; **¡eso es** ~ **mío!** that's my
business!; **asuntos exteriores** foreign
affairs; **asuntos a tratar** agenda *sg*

asustadizo, -a [asusta'ðiθo, a] *adj* easily
frightened

asustar [asus'tar] *vt* to frighten; **asustarse**
vr to be/become frightened

atacante [ata'kante] *nm/f* attacker

atacar [ata'kar] *vt* to attack

atadura [ata'ðura] *nf* bond, tie

atajar [ata'xar] *vt* (*gen*) to stop; (*ruta de fuga*)
to cut off; (*discurso*) to interrupt ■ *vi* to take
a short cut

atajo [a'taxo] *nm* short cut; (*Deporte*) tackle

atalaya [ata'laja] *nf* watchtower

atañer [ata'ɲer] *vi*: ~ **a** to concern; **en lo que
atañe a eso** with regard to that

ataque *etc* [a'take] *vb ver* **atacar** ■ *nm* attack;
~ **cardíaco** heart attack

atar [a'tar] *vt* to tie, tie up; ~ **la lengua a algn**
(*fig*) to silence sb

atardecer [atarðe'θer] *vi* to get dark ■ *nm*

evening; (*crepúsculo*) dusk

atardezca *etc* [atar'ðeθka] *vb ver* **atardecer**

atareado, -a [atare'aðo, a] *adj* busy

atascar [atas'kar] *vt* to clog up; (*obstruir*) to jam; (*fig*) to hinder; **atascarse** *vr* to stall; (*cañería*) to get blocked up; (*fig*) to get bogged down; (*en discurso*) to dry up

atasco [a'tasko] *nm* obstruction; (*Auto*) traffic jam

atasque *etc* [a'taske] *vb ver* **atascar**

ataúd [ata'uð] *nm* coffin

ataviar [ata'βjar] *vt* to deck, array; **ataviarse** *vr* to dress up

atavío [ata'βio] *nm* attire, dress; **atavíos** *nmpl* finery *sg*

ateísmo [ate'ismo] *nm* atheism

atemorice *etc* [atemo'riθe] *vb ver* **atemorizar**

atemorizar [atemori'θar] *vt* to frighten, scare; **atemorizarse** *vr* to get frightened *o* scared

Atenas [a'tenas] *nf* Athens

atención [aten'θjon] *nf* attention; (*bondad*) kindness ■ *excl* (be) careful!, look out!; **en ~ a esto** in view of this

atender [aten'der] *vt* to attend to, look after; (*Tec*) to service; (*enfermo*) to care for; (*ruego*) to comply with ■ *vi* to pay attention; **~ a** to attend to; (*detalles*) to take care of

atendré *etc* [aten'dre] *vb ver* **atenerse**

atenerse [ate'nerse] *vr*: **~ a** to abide by, adhere to

atenga *etc* [a'tenga] *vb ver* **atenerse**

ateniense [ate'njense] *adj, nm/f* Athenian

atentado [aten'taðo] *nm* crime, illegal act; (*asalto*) assault; (*terrorista*) attack; **~ contra la vida de algn** attempt on sb's life; **~ golpista** attempted coup; **~ suicida** suicide bombing, suicide attack

atentamente [atenta'mente] *adv*: **le saluda ~** Yours faithfully

atentar [aten'tar] *vi*: **~ a** *o* **contra** to commit an outrage against

atento, -a [a'tento, a] *adj* attentive, observant; (*cortés*) polite, thoughtful; **su atenta (carta)** (*Com*) your letter

atenuante [ate'nwante] *adj*: **circunstancias atenuantes** extenuating *o* mitigating circumstances ■ *nfpl*: **atenuantes** extenuating *o* mitigating circumstances

atenuar [ate'nwar] *vt* to attenuate; (*disminuir*) to lessen, minimize

ateo, -a [a'teo, a] *adj* atheistic ■ *nm/f* atheist

aterciopelado, -a [aterθjope'laðo, a] *adj* velvety

aterido, -a [ate'riðo, a] *adj*: **~ de frío** frozen stiff

aterrador, a [aterra'ðor, a] *adj* frightening

aterrar [ate'rrar] *vt* to frighten; (*aterrorizar*) to terrify; **aterrarse** *vr* to be frightened; to be terrified

aterrice *etc* [ate'rriθe] *vb ver* **aterrizar**

aterrizaje [aterri'θaxe] *nm* landing; **~ forzoso** forced landing

aterrizar [aterri'θar] *vi* to land

aterrorice *etc* [aterro'riθe] *vb ver* **aterrorizar**

aterrorizar [aterrori'θar] *vt* to terrify

atesorar [ateso'rar] *vt* to hoard, store up

atestado, -a [ates'taðo, a] *adj* packed ■ *nm* (*Jur*) affidavit

atestar [ates'tar] *vt* to pack, stuff; (*Jur*) to attest, testify to

atestiguar [atesti'ɣwar] *vt* to testify to, bear witness to

atestigüe *etc* [ates'tiɣwe] *vb ver* **atestiguar**

atiborrar [atiβo'rrar] *vt* to fill, stuff; **atiborrarse** *vr* to stuff o.s.

atice *etc* [a'tiθe] *vb ver* **atizar**

ático ['atiko] *nm* attic; **~ de lujo** penthouse flat

atienda *etc* [a'tjenda] *vb ver* **atender**

atildar [atil'dar] *vt* to criticize; (*Tip*) to put a tilde over; **atildarse** *vr* to spruce o.s. up

atinado, -a [ati'naðo, a] *adj* correct; (*sensato*) sensible

atinar [ati'nar] *vi* (*acertar*) to be right; **~ con** *o* **en** (*solución*) to hit upon; **~ a hacer** to manage to do

atípico, -a [a'tipiko, a] *adj* atypical

atiplado, -a [ati'plaðo, a] *adj* (*voz*) high-pitched

atisbar [atis'βar] *vt* to spy on; (*echar ojeada*) to peep at

atizar [ati'θar] *vt* to poke; (*horno etc*) to stoke; (*fig*) to stir up, rouse

atlántico, -a [at'lantiko, a] *adj* Atlantic ■ *nm*: **el (océano) A~** the Atlantic (Ocean)

atlas ['atlas] *nm inv* atlas

atleta [at'leta] *nm/f* athlete

atlético, -a [at'letiko, a] *adj* athletic

atletismo [atle'tismo] *nm* athletics *sg*

atmósfera [at'mosfera] *nf* atmosphere

atmosférico, -a [atmos'feriko, a] *adj* atmospheric

atol [a'tol], **atole** [a'tole] *nm* (*Am*) cornflour drink

atolladero [atoʎa'ðero] *nm*: **estar en un ~** to be in a jam

atollarse [ato'ʎarse] *vr* to get stuck; (*fig*) to get into a jam

atolondrado, -a [atolon'draðo, a] *adj* scatterbrained

atolondramiento [atolondra'mjento] *nm* bewilderment; (*insensatez*) silliness

atómico, -a [a'tomiko, a] *adj* atomic

atomizador [atomiθa'ðor] *nm* atomizer

átomo ['atomo] *nm* atom

atónito, -a [a'tonito, a] *adj* astonished, amazed

atontado, -a [aton'taðo, a] *adj* stunned; (*bobo*) silly, daft

atontar [aton'tar] *vt* to stun; **atontarse** *vr* to become confused

atorar [ato'rar] *vt* to obstruct; **atorarse** *vr* (*atragantarse*) to choke

atormentar [atormen'tar] *vt* to torture; (*molestar*) to torment; (*acosar*) to plague, harass

atornillar [atorni'ʎar] *vt* to screw on *o* down

atorón [ato'ron] *nm* (*Am*) traffic jam

atosigar [atosi'ɣar] *vt* to harass

atosigue *etc* [ato'siɣe] *vb ver* **atosigar**

atrabiliario, -a [atraβi'ljarjo, a] *adj* bad-tempered

atracadero [atraka'ðero] *nm* pier

atracador, a [atraka'ðor, a] *nm/f* robber

atracar [atra'kar] *vt* (*Naut*) to moor; (*robar*) to hold up, rob ▪ *vi* to moor; **atracarse** *vr* (*hartarse*) to stuff o.s.

atracción [atrak'θjon] *nf* attraction

atraco [a'trako] *nm* holdup, robbery

atracón [atra'kon] *nm*: **darse** *o* **pegarse un ~ (de)** (*fam*) to pig out (on)

atractivo, -a [atrak'tiβo, a] *adj* attractive ▪ *nm* attraction; (*belleza*) attractiveness

atraer [atra'er] *vt* to attract; **dejarse ~ por** to be tempted by

atragantarse [atraɣan'tarse] *vr*: **~ (con algo)** to choke (on sth); **se me ha atragantado el chico ese/el inglés** I don't take to that boy/English

atraiga *etc* [a'traiɣa], **atraje** *etc* [a'traxe] *vb ver* **atraer**

atrancar [atran'kar] *vt* (*con tranca, barra*) to bar, bolt

atranque *etc* [a'tranke] *vb ver* **atrancar**

atrapar [atra'par] *vt* to trap; (*resfriado etc*) to catch

atraque *etc* [a'trake] *vb ver* **atracar**

atrás [a'tras] *adv* (*movimiento*) back(wards); (*lugar*) behind; (*tiempo*) previously; **ir hacia ~** to go back(wards); to go to the rear; **estar ~** to be behind *o* at the back

atrasado, -a [atra'saðo, a] *adj* slow; (*pago*) overdue, late; (*país*) backward

atrasar [atra'sar] *vi* to be slow; **atrasarse** *vr* to remain behind; (*llegar tarde*) to arrive late

atraso [a'traso] *nm* slowness; lateness, delay; (*de país*) backwardness; **atrasos** *nmpl* arrears

atravesado, -a [atraβe'saðo, a] *adj*: **un tronco ~ en la carretera** a tree trunk lying across the road

atravesar [atraβe'sar] *vt* (*cruzar*) to cross (over); (*traspasar*) to pierce; (*período*) to go through; (*poner al través*) to lay *o* put across; **atravesarse** *vr* to come in between; (*intervenir*) to interfere

atraviese *etc* [atra'βjese] *vb ver* **atravesar**

atrayendo [atra'jendo] *vb ver* **atraer**

atrayente [atra'jente] *adj* attractive

atreverse [atre'βerse] *vr* to dare; (*insolentarse*) to be insolent

atrevido, -a [atre'βiðo, a] *adj* daring; insolent

atrevimiento [atreβi'mjento] *nm* daring; insolence

atribución [atriβu'θjon] *nf* (*Lit*) attribution; **atribuciones** *nfpl* (*Pol*) functions; (*Admin*) responsibilities

atribuir [atriβu'ir] *vt* to attribute; (*funciones*) to confer

atribular [atriβu'lar] *vt* to afflict, distress

atributo [atri'βuto] *nm* attribute

atribuya *etc* [atri'βuja], **atribuyendo** *etc* [atriβu'jendo] *vb ver* **atribuir**

atril [a'tril] *nm* lectern; (*Mus*) music stand

atrincherarse [atrintʃe'rarse] *vr* (*Mil*) to dig (o.s.) in; **~ en** (*fig*) to hide behind

atrio ['atrjo] *nm* (*Rel*) porch

atrocidad [atroθi'ðað] *nf* atrocity, outrage

atrofiado, -a [atro'fjaðo, a] *adj* (*extremidad*) withered

atrofiarse [atro'fjarse] *vr* (*tb fig*) to atrophy

atronador, a [atrona'ðor, a] *adj* deafening

atropellar [atrope'ʎar] *vt* (*derribar*) to knock over *o* down; (*empujar*) to push (aside); (*Auto*) to run over *o* down; (*agraviar*) to insult; **atropellarse** *vr* to act hastily

atropello [atro'peʎo] *nm* (*Auto*) accident; (*empujón*) push; (*agravio*) wrong; (*atrocidad*) outrage

atroz [a'troθ] *adj* atrocious, awful

A.T.S. *nm/f abr* (= *Ayudante Técnico Sanitario*) nurse

attrezzo [a'treθo] *nm* props *pl*

atuendo [a'twendo] *nm* attire

atufar [atu'far] *vt* (*suj: olor*) to overcome; (*molestar*) to irritate; **atufarse** *vr* (*fig*) to get cross

atún [a'tun] *nm* tuna, tunny

aturdir [atur'ðir] *vt* to stun; (*suj: ruido*) to deafen; (*fig*) to dumbfound, bewilder

aturrullar, aturullar [atur(r)u'ʎar] *vt* to bewilder

atusar [atu'sar] *vt* (*cortar*) to trim; (*alisar*) to smooth (down)

atuve *etc* [a'tuβe] *vb ver* **atenerse**

audacia [au'ðaθja] *nf* boldness, audacity

audaz [au'ðaθ] *adj* bold, audacious

audible [au'ðiβle] *adj* audible
audición [auði'θjon] *nf* hearing; (*Teat*) audition; ~ **radiofónica** radio concert
audiencia [au'ðjenθja] *nf* audience; (*Jur*) high court; (*Pol*): ~ **pública** public inquiry
audífono [au'ðifono] *nm* hearing aid
audiovisual [auðjoβi'swal] *adj* audio-visual
auditivo, -a [auði'tiβo, a] *adj* hearing *cpd*; (*conducto, nervio*) auditory
auditor [auði'tor] *nm* (*Jur*) judge-advocate; (*Com*) auditor
auditoría [auðito'ria] *nf* audit; (*profesión*) auditing
auditorio [auði'torjo] *nm* audience; (*sala*) auditorium
auge ['auxe] *nm* boom; (*clímax*) climax; (*Econ*) expansion; **estar en** ~ to thrive
augurar [auɣu'rar] *vt* to predict; (*presagiar*) to portend
augurio [au'ɣurjo] *nm* omen
aula ['aula] *nf* classroom
aullar [au'ʎar] *vi* to howl, yell
aullido [au'ʎiðo] *nm* howl, yell
aumentar [aumen'tar] *vt* to increase; (*precios*) to put up; (*producción*) to step up; (*con microscopio, anteojos*) to magnify ▪ *vi*, **aumentarse** *vr* to increase, be on the increase
aumento [au'mento] *nm* increase; rise
aún [a'un] *adv* still, yet
aun [a'un] *adv* even
aunque [a'unke] *conj* though, although, even though
aúpa [a'upa] *excl* up!, come on!; (*fam*): **una función de** ~ a slap-up do; **una paliza de** ~ a good hiding
aupar [au'par] *vt* (*levantar*) to help up; (*fig*) to praise
aura ['aura] *nf* (*atmósfera*) aura
aureola [aure'ola] *nf* halo
auricular [auriku'lar] *nm* earpiece, receiver; **auriculares** *nmpl* headphones
aurora [au'rora] *nf* dawn; ~ **boreal(is)** northern lights *pl*
auscultar [auskul'tar] *vt* (*Med*: *pecho*) to listen to, sound
ausencia [au'senθja] *nf* absence
ausentarse [ausen'tarse] *vr* to go away; (*por poco tiempo*) to go out
ausente [au'sente] *adj* absent ▪ *nm/f* (*Escol*) absentee; (*Jur*) missing person
auspiciar [auspi'sjar] *vt* (*Am*) to back, sponsor
auspicios [aus'piθjos] *nmpl* auspices; (*protección*) protection *sg*
austeridad [austeri'ðað] *nf* austerity
austero, -a [aus'tero, a] *adj* austere
austral [aus'tral] *adj* southern ▪ *nm* monetary

unit of Argentina (1985-1991)
Australia [aus'tralja] *nf* Australia
australiano, -a [austra'ljano, a] *adj, nm/f* Australian
Austria ['austrja] *nf* Austria
austriaco, -a [aus'trjako, a], **austríaco a** [aus'triako, a] *adj, nm/f* Austrian
autenticar [autenti'kar] *vt* to authenticate
auténtico, -a [au'tentiko, a] *adj* authentic
autentificar [autentifi'kar] *vt* to authenticate
autentique *etc* [auten'tike] *vb ver* **autenticar**
auto ['auto] *nm* (*coche*) car; (*Jur*) edict, decree; (: *orden*) writ; **autos** *nmpl* (*Jur*) proceedings; (: *acta*) court record *sg*; ~ **de comparecencia** summons, subpoena; ~ **de ejecución** writ of execution
autoadhesivo, -a [autoaðe'siβo, a] *adj* self-adhesive; (*sobre*) self-sealing
autoalimentación [autoalimenta'θjon] *nf* (*Inform*): ~ **de hojas** automatic paper feed
autobiografía [autoβjoɣra'fia] *nf* autobiography
autobronceador [autoβronθea'ðor] *adj* self-tanning
autobús [auto'βus] *nm* bus (*Brit*), (passenger) bus (*US*)
autocar [auto'kar] *nm* coach; ~ **de línea** intercity coach
autocomprobación [autokomproβa'θjon] *nf* (*Inform*) self-test
autóctono, -a [au'toktono, a] *adj* native, indigenous
autodefensa [autoðe'fensa] *nf* self-defence
autodeterminación [autoðetermina'θjon] *nf* self-determination
autodidacta [autoði'ðakta] *adj* self-taught ▪ *nm/f*: **ser un(a)** ~ to be self-taught
autoescuela [autoes'kwela] *nf* driving school
autofinanciado, -a [autofinan'θjaðo, a] *adj* self-financing
autogestión [autoxes'tjon] *nf* self-management
autógrafo [au'toɣrafo] *nm* autograph
automación [automa'θjon] *nf* = **automatización**
autómata [au'tomata] *nm* automaton
automáticamente [auto'matikamente] *adv* automatically
automatice *etc* [automa'tiθe] *vb ver* **automatizar**
automático, -a [auto'matiko, a] *adj* automatic ▪ *nm* press stud
automatización [automatiθa'θjon] *nf*: ~ **de fábricas** factory automation; ~ **de oficinas** office automation

automatizar [automati'θar] vt to automate

automontable [automon'taβle] adj self-assembly

automotor, -triz [automo'tor, 'triz] adj self-propelled ■ nm diesel train

automóvil [auto'moβil] nm (motor) car (Brit), automobile (US)

automovilismo [automoβi'lismo] nm (Deporte) (sports) car racing

automovilista [automoβi'lista] nm/f motorist, driver

automovilístico, -a [automoβi'listiko, a] adj (industria) car cpd

autonomía [autono'mia] nf autonomy; (Esp Pol) autonomy, self-government; (: comunidad) autonomous region

autonómico, -a [auto'nomiko, a] adj (Esp Pol) relating to autonomy, autonomous; **gobierno** ~ autonomous government

autónomo, -a [au'tonomo, a] adj autonomous; (Inform) stand-alone, offline

autopista [auto'pista] nf motorway (Brit), freeway (US)

autopsia [au'topsja] nf autopsy

autor, a [au'tor, a] nm/f author; **los autores del atentado** those responsible for the attack

autorice etc [auto'riθe] vb ver **autorizar**

autoridad [autori'ðað] nf authority; ~ **local** local authority

autoritario, -a [autori'tarjo, a] adj authoritarian

autorización [autoriθa'θjon] nf authorization

autorizado, -a [autori'θaðo, a] adj authorized; (aprobado) approved

autorizar [autori'θar] vt to authorize; to approve

autorretrato [autorre'trato] nm self-portrait

autoservicio [autoser'βiθjo] nm self-service shop o store; (restaurante) self-service restaurant

autostop [auto'stop] nm hitch-hiking; **hacer** ~ to hitch-hike

autostopista [autosto'pista] nm/f hitch-hiker

autosuficiencia [autosufi'θjenθja] nf self-sufficiency

autosuficiente [autosufi'θjente] adj self-sufficient; (pey) smug

autosugestión [autosuxes'tjon] nf autosuggestion

autovía [auto'βia] nf ≈ dual carriageway (Brit), ≈ separated highway (US)

auxiliar [auksi'ljar] vt to help ■ nm/f assistant

auxilio [auk'siljo] nm assistance, help; **primeros auxilios** first aid sg

Av abr (= Avenida) Av(e)

a/v abr (Com: = a vista) at sight

aval [a'βal] nm guarantee; (persona) guarantor

avalancha [aβa'lantʃa] nf avalanche

avalar [aβa'lar] vt (Com etc) to underwrite; (fig) to endorse

avalista [aβa'lista] nm (Com) endorser

avance etc [a'βanθe] vb ver **avanzar** ■ nm advance; (pago) advance payment; (Cine) trailer

avanzado, -a [aβan'θaðo, a] adj advanced; **de edad avanzada**, ~ **de edad** elderly

avanzar [aβan'θar] vt, vi to advance

avaricia [aβa'riθja] nf avarice, greed

avaricioso, -a [aβari'θjoso, a] adj avaricious, greedy

avaro, -a [a'βaro, a] adj miserly, mean ■ nm/f miser

avasallar [aβasa'ʎar] vt to subdue, subjugate

avatar [aβa'tar] nm change; **avatares** ups and downs

Avda abr (= Avenida) Av(e)

AVE ['aβe] nm abr (= Alta Velocidad Española) ≈ Bullet train

ave ['aβe] nf bird; ~ **de rapiña** bird of prey

avecinarse [aβeθi'narse] vr (tormenta, fig) to approach, be on the way

avejentar [aβexen'tar] vt, vi, **avejentarse** vr to age

avellana [aβe'ʎana] nf hazelnut

avellano [aβe'ʎano] nm hazel tree

avemaría [aβema'ria] nm Hail Mary, Ave Maria

avena [a'βena] nf oats pl

avendré etc [aβen'dre], **avenga** etc [a'βenga] vb ver **avenir**

avenida [aβe'niða] nf (calle) avenue

avenir [aβe'nir] vt to reconcile; **avenirse** vr to come to an agreement, reach a compromise

aventado, -a [aβen'taðo, a] adj (Am) daring

aventajado, -a [aβenta'xaðo, a] adj outstanding

aventajar [aβenta'xar] vt (sobrepasar) to surpass, outstrip

aventar [aβen'tar] vt to fan, blow; (grano) to winnow; (Am fam: echar) to chuck out

aventón [aβen'ton] nm (Am) push; **pedir** ~ to hitch a lift

aventura [aβen'tura] nf adventure; ~ **sentimental** love affair

aventurado, -a [aβentu'raðo, a] adj risky

aventurar [aβentu'rar] vt to risk; **aventurarse** vr to dare; **aventurarse a hacer algo** to venture to do sth

aventurero, -a [aβentu'rero, a] adj adventurous

a

avergoncé [aβerɣonˈθe], **avergoncemos** etc [aβerɣonˈθemos] vb ver **avergonzar**

avergonzar [aβerɣonˈθar] vt to shame; (desconcertar) to embarrass; **avergonzarse** vr to be ashamed; to be embarrassed

avergüence etc [aβerˈɣwenθe] vb ver **avergonzar**

avería [aβeˈria] nf (Tec) breakdown, fault

averiado, -a [aβeˈrjaðo, a] adj broken-down

averiar [aβeˈrjar] vt to break; **averiarse** vr to break down

averiguación [aβeriɣwaˈθjon] nf investigation

averiguar [aβeriˈɣwar] vt to investigate; (descubrir) to find out, ascertain

averigüe etc [aβeˈriɣwe] vb ver **averiguar**

aversión [aβerˈsjon] nf aversion, dislike; **cobrar ~ a** to take a strong dislike to

avestruz [aβesˈtruθ] nm ostrich

aviación [aβjaˈθjon] nf aviation; (fuerzas aéreas) air force

aviado, -a [aˈβjaðo, a] adj: **estar ~** to be in a mess

aviador, a [aβjaˈðor, a] nm/f aviator, airman/woman

aviar [aˈβjar] vt to prepare, get ready

avícola [aˈβikola] adj poultry cpd

avicultura [aβikulˈtura] nf poultry farming

avidez [aβiˈðeθ] nf avidity, eagerness

ávido, -a [ˈaβiðo, a] adj avid, eager

aviente etc [aˈβjente] vb ver **aventar**

avieso, -a [aˈβjeso, a] adj (torcido) distorted; (perverso) wicked

avinagrado, -a [aβinaˈɣraðo, a] adj sour, acid

avinagrarse [aβinaˈɣrarse] vr to go o turn sour

avine etc [aˈβine] vb ver **avenir**

Aviñón [aβiˈɲon] nm Avignon

avío [aˈβio] nm preparation; **avíos** nmpl gear sg, kit sg

avión [aˈβjon] nm aeroplane; (ave) martin; **~ de reacción** jet (plane); **por ~** (Correos) by air mail

avioneta [aβjoˈneta] nf light aircraft

avisar [aβiˈsar] vt (advertir) to warn, notify; (informar) to tell; (aconsejar) to advise, counsel

aviso [aˈβiso] nm warning; (noticia) notice; (Com) demand note; (Inform) prompt; **~ escrito** notice in writing; **sin previo ~** without warning; **estar sobre ~** to be on the look-out

avispa [aˈβispa] nf wasp

avispado, -a [aβisˈpaðo, a] adj sharp, clever

avispero [aβisˈpero] nm wasp's nest

avispón [aβisˈpon] nm hornet

avistar [aβisˈtar] vt to sight, spot

avitaminosis [aβitamiˈnosis] nf inv vitamin deficiency

avituallar [aβitwaˈʎar] vt to supply with food

avivar [aβiˈβar] vt to strengthen, intensify; **avivarse** vr to revive, acquire new life

avizor [aβiˈθor] adj: **estar ojo ~** to be on the alert

avizorar [aβiθoˈrar] vt to spy on

axila [akˈsila] nf armpit

axioma [akˈsjoma] nm axiom

ay [ai] excl (dolor) ow!, ouch!; (aflicción) oh!, oh dear!; **¡ay de mi!** poor me!

aya [ˈaja] nf governess; (niñera) nanny

ayer [aˈjer] adv, nm yesterday; **antes de ~** the day before yesterday; **~ por la tarde** yesterday afternoon/evening

aymara, aymará [aiˈmara] [aimaˈra] adj, nm/f Aymara

ayo [ˈajo] nm tutor

ayote [aˈjote] nm (Am) pumpkin

Ayto. abr = **Ayuntamiento**

ayuda [aˈjuða] nf help, assistance; (Med) enema ■ nm page; **~ humanitaria** humanitarian aid

ayudante, -a [ajuˈðante, a] nm/f assistant, helper; (Escol) assistant; (Mil) adjutant

ayudar [ajuˈðar] vt to help, assist

ayunar [ajuˈnar] vi to fast

ayunas [aˈjunas] nfpl: **estar en ~** (no haber comido) to be fasting; (ignorar) to be in the dark

ayuno [aˈjuno] nm fasting

ayuntamiento [ajuntaˈmjento] nm (consejo) town/city council; (edificio) town/city hall; (cópula) sexual intercourse

azabache [aθaˈβatʃe] nm jet

azada [aˈθaða] nf hoe

azafata [aθaˈfata] nf air hostess (Brit) o stewardess

azafate [asaˈfate] nm (Am) tray

azafrán [aθaˈfran] nm saffron

azahar [aθaˈar] nm orange/lemon blossom

azalea [aθaˈlea] nf azalea

azar [aˈθar] nm (casualidad) chance, fate; (desgracia) misfortune, accident; **por ~** by chance; **al ~** at random

azaroso, -a [aθaˈroso, a] adj (arriesgado) risky; (vida) eventful

Azerbaiyán [aθerbaˈjan] nm Azerbaijan

azerbaiyano, -a [aθerbaˈjano, a], **azerí** [aθeˈri] adj, nm/f Azerbaijani, Azeri

azogue [aˈθoɣe] nm mercury

azor [aˈθor] nm goshawk

azoramiento [aθoraˈmjento] nm alarm; (confusión) confusion

azorar [aθoˈrar] vt to alarm; **azorarse** vr to get alarmed

Azores [a'θores] *nfpl*: **las (Islas)** ~ the Azores
azotaina [aθo'taina] *nf* beating
azotar [aθo'tar] *vt* to whip, beat; (*pegar*) to spank
azote [a'θote] *nm* (*látigo*) whip; (*latigazo*) lash, stroke; (*en las nalgas*) spank; (*calamidad*) calamity
azotea [aθo'tea] *nf* (flat) roof
azteca [aθ'teka] *adj, nm/f* Aztec
azúcar [a'θukar] *nm* sugar
azucarado, -a [aθuka'raðo, a] *adj* sugary, sweet

azucarero, -a [aθuka'rero, a] *adj* sugar *cpd*
■ *nm* sugar bowl
azuce *etc* [a'θuθe] *vb ver* **azuzar**
azucena [aθu'θena] *nf* white lily
azufre [a'θufre] *nm* sulphur
azul [a'θul] *adj, nm* blue; ~ **celeste/marino** sky/navy blue
azulejo [aθu'lexo] *nm* tile
azulgrana [aθul'ɣrana] *adj inv* of Barcelona Football Club ■ *nm*: **los A** ~ the Barcelona F.C. players *o* team
azuzar [aθu'θar] *vt* to incite, egg on

a

41

Bb

B, b (*Esp*) [be] (*Am*) [be'larɣa] *nf* (*letra*) B, b;
B de Barcelona B for Benjamin (*Brit*) *o* Baker
(*US*)

baba ['baβa] *nf* spittle, saliva; **se le caía la ~**
(*fig*) he was thrilled to bits

babear [baβe'ar] *vi* (*echar saliva*) to slobber;
(*niño*) to dribble; (*fig*) to drool, slaver

babel [ba'βel] *nm o f* bedlam

babero [ba'βero] *nm* bib

Babia ['baβja] *nf*: **estar en ~** to be
daydreaming

bable ['baβle] *nm* Asturian (dialect)

babor [ba'βor] *nm* port (side); **a ~** to port

babosada [baβo'saða] *nf*: **decir babosadas**
(*Am fam*) to talk rubbish

baboso, -a [ba'βoso, a] *adj* slobbering; (*Zool*)
slimy; (*Am*) silly ■ *nm/f* (*Am*) fool

babucha [ba'βutʃa] *nf* slipper

baca ['baka] *nf* (*Auto*) luggage *o* roof rack

bacalao [baka'lao] *nm* cod(fish)

bacanal [baka'nal] *nf* orgy

bache ['batʃe] *nm* pothole, rut; (*fig*) bad patch

bachillerato [batʃiʎe'rato] *nm* two-year
secondary school course; *ver tb* **sistema educativo**

bacilo [ba'θilo] *nm* bacillus, germ

bacinica [baθi'nika] *nf*, **bacinilla** [baθi'niʎa]
nf chamber pot

bacteria [bak'terja] *nf* bacterium, germ

bacteriológico, -a [bakterjo'loxiko, a] *adj*
bacteriological; **guerra bacteriológica**
germ warfare

báculo ['bakulo] *nm* stick, staff; (*fig*) support

badajo [ba'ðaxo] *nm* clapper (*of a bell*)

bádminton ['baðminton] *nm* badminton

bafle ['bafle], **baffle** ['baffle] *nm* (*Elec*)
speaker

bagaje [ba'ɣaxe] *nm* baggage; (*fig*)
background

bagatela [baɣa'tela] *nf* trinket, trifle

Bahama [ba'ama]: **las (Islas) ~, las
Bahamas** *nfpl* the Bahamas

bahía [ba'ia] *nf* bay

bailar [bai'lar] *vt, vi* to dance

bailarín, -ina [baila'rin, ina] *nm/f* dancer;
(*de ballet*) ballet dancer

baile ['baile] *nm* dance; (*formal*) ball

baja ['baxa] *nf* drop, fall; (*Econ*) slump;
(*Mil*) casualty; (*paro*) redundancy; **dar de ~**
(*soldado*) to discharge; (*empleado*) to dismiss,
sack; **darse de ~** (*retirarse*) to drop out; (*Med*)
to go sick; (*dimitir*) to resign; **estar de ~**
(*enfermo*) to be off sick; (*Bolsa*) to be dropping
o falling; **jugar a la ~** (*Econ*) to speculate on a
fall in prices; *ver tb* **bajo**

bajada [ba'xaða] *nf* descent; (*camino*) slope;
(*de aguas*) ebb

bajamar [baxa'mar] *nf* low tide

bajar [ba'xar] *vi* to go *o* come down;
(*temperatura, precios*) to drop, fall ■ *vt* (*cabeza*)
to bow; (*escalera*) to go *o* come down; (*radio
etc*) to turn down; (*precio, voz*) to lower; (*llevar
abajo*) to take down; **bajarse** *vr* (*de vehículo*)
to get out; (*de autobús*) to get off; **~ de** (*coche*)
to get out of; (*autobús*) to get off; **bajarle los
humos a algn** (*fig*) to cut sb down to size;
bajarse algo de Internet to download sth
from the Internet

bajeza [ba'xeθa] *nf* baseness; (*una bajeza*) vile
deed

bajío [ba'xio] *nm* shoal, sandbank; (*Am*)
lowlands *pl*

bajista [ba'xista] *nm/f* (*Mus*) bassist ■ *adj*
(*Bolsa*) bear *cpd*

bajo, -a ['baxo, a] *adj* (*terreno*) low(-lying);
(*mueble, número, precio*) low; (*piso*) ground *cpd*;
(*de estatura*) small, short; (*color*) pale; (*sonido*)
faint, soft, low; (*voz, tono*) deep; (*metal*) base
■ *adv* (*hablar*) softly, quietly; (*volar*) low ■ *prep*
under, below, underneath ■ *nm* (*Mus*) bass;
hablar en voz baja to whisper; **~ la lluvia**
in the rain

bajón [ba'xon] *nm* fall, drop

bajura [ba'xura] *nf*: **pesca de ~** coastal
fishing

bakalao [baka'lao] *nm* (*Mus*) rave music

bala ['bala] *nf* bullet; **~ de goma** plastic bullet

balacera [bala'sera] *nf* (*Am*) shoot-out

balada [ba'laða] *nf* ballad

baladí [bala'ði] *adj* trivial

baladronada [balaðro'naða] *nf* (*dicho*) boast, brag; (*hecho*) piece of bravado

balance [ba'lanθe] *nm* (*Com*) balance; (: *libro*) balance sheet; (: *cuenta general*) stocktaking; ~ **de comprobación** trial balance; ~ **consolidado** consolidated balance sheet; **hacer** ~ to take stock

balancear [balanθe'ar] *vt* to balance ■ *vi*, **balancearse** *vr* to swing (to and fro); (*vacilar*) to hesitate

balanceo [balan'θeo] *nm* swinging

balandro [ba'landro] *nm* yacht

balanza [ba'lanθa] *nf* scales *pl*, balance; ~ **comercial** balance of trade; ~ **de pagos/ de poder(es)** balance of payments/of power; (*Astro*): **B~** Libra

balar [ba'lar] *vi* to bleat

balaustrada [balaus'traða] *nf* balustrade; (*pasamanos*) banister

balazo [ba'laθo] *nm* (*tiro*) shot; (*herida*) bullet wound

balboa [bal'βoa] *nf* Panamanian currency unit

balbucear [balβuθe'ar] *vi, vt* to stammer, stutter

balbuceo [balβu'θeo] *nm* stammering, stuttering

balbucir [balβu'θir] *vi, vt* to stammer, stutter

balbuzca *etc* [bal'βuθka] *vb ver* **balbucir**

Balcanes [bal'kanes] *nmpl*: **los (Montes)** ~ the Balkans, the Balkan Mountains; **la Península de los** ~ the Balkan Peninsula

balcánico, -a [bal'kaniko, a] *adj* Balkan

balcón [bal'kon] *nm* balcony

balda ['balda] *nf* (*estante*) shelf

baldar [bal'dar] *vt* to cripple; (*agotar*) to exhaust

balde ['balde] *nm* (*esp Am*) bucket, pail; **de** ~ *adv* (for) free, for nothing; **en** ~ *adv* in vain

baldío, -a [bal'dio, a] *adj* uncultivated; (*terreno*) waste; (*inútil*) vain ■ *nm* wasteland

baldosa [bal'dosa] *nf* (*azulejo*) floor tile; (*grande*) flagstone

baldosín [baldo'sin] *nm* wall tile

balear [bale'ar] *adj* Balearic, of the Balearic Islands ■ *nm/f* native *o* inhabitant of the Balearic Islands ■ *vt* (*Am*) to shoot (at)

Baleares [bale'ares] *nfpl*: **las (Islas)** ~ the Balearics, the Balearic Islands

balido [ba'liðo] *nm* bleat, bleating

balín [ba'lin] *nm* pellet; **balines** *nmpl* buckshot *sg*

balística [ba'listika] *nf* ballistics *pl*

baliza [ba'liθa] *nf* (*Aviat*) beacon; (*Naut*) buoy

ballena [ba'ʎena] *nf* whale

ballenero, -a [baʎe'nero, a] *adj*: **industria ballenera** whaling industry ■ *nm* (*pescador*) whaler; (*barco*) whaling ship

ballesta [ba'ʎesta] *nf* crossbow; (*Auto*) spring

ballet (*pl* **ballets**) [ba'le, ba'les] *nm* ballet

balneario, -a [balne'arjo, a] *adj*: **estación balnearia** (bathing) resort ■ *nm* spa, health resort

balompié [balom'pje] *nm* football

balón [ba'lon] *nm* ball

baloncesto [balon'θesto] *nm* basketball

balonmano [balon'mano] *nm* handball

balonred [balon'reð] *nm* netball

balonvolea [balombo'lea] *nm* volleyball

balsa ['balsa] *nf* raft; (*Bot*) balsa wood

bálsamo ['balsamo] *nm* balsam, balm

balsón [bal'son] *nm* (*Am*) swamp, bog

báltico, -a ['baltiko, a] *adj* Baltic; **el (Mar) B~** the Baltic (Sea)

baluarte [ba'lwarte] *nm* bastion, bulwark

bambolearse [bambole'arse] *vr* to swing, sway; (*silla*) to wobble

bamboleo [bambo'leo] *nm* swinging, swaying; wobbling

bambú [bam'bu] *nm* bamboo

banal [ba'nal] *adj* banal, trivial

banana [ba'nana] *nf* (*Am*) banana

bananal [bana'nal] *nm* (*Am*) banana plantation

banano [ba'nano] *nm* (*Am*) banana tree

banasta [ba'nasta] *nf* large basket, hamper

banca ['banka] *nf* bench; (*Com*) banking

bancario, -a [ban'karjo, a] *adj* banking *cpd*, bank *cpd*; **giro** ~ bank draft

bancarrota [banka'rrota] *nf* bankruptcy; **declararse en** *o* **hacer** ~ to go bankrupt

banco ['banko] *nm* bench; (*Escol*) desk; (*Com*) bank; (*Geo*) stratum; ~ **comercial** *o* **mercantil** commercial bank; ~ **por acciones** joint-stock bank; ~ **de crédito/de ahorros** credit/savings bank; ~ **de arena** sandbank; ~ **de datos** (*Inform*) data bank; ~ **de hielo** iceberg

banda ['banda] *nf* band; (*cinta*) ribbon; (*pandilla*) gang; (*Mus*) brass band; (*Naut*) side, edge; **la** ~ **ancha** broadband; **la B~ Oriental** Uruguay; ~ **sonora** soundtrack; ~ **transportadora** conveyor belt

bandada [ban'daða] *nf* (*de pájaros*) flock; (*de peces*) shoal

bandazo [ban'daθo] *nm*: **dar bandazos** (*coche*) to veer from side to side

bandeja [ban'dexa] *nf* tray; ~ **de entrada/ salida** in-tray/out-tray

bandera [ban'dera] *nf* (*de tela*) flag; (*estandarte*) banner; **izar la** ~ to hoist the flag

banderilla [bande'riʎa] *nf* banderilla; *(tapa)* savoury appetizer *(served on a cocktail stick)*
banderín [bande'rin] *nm* pennant, small flag
banderola [bande'rola] *nf* (Mil) pennant
bandido [ban'diðo] *nm* bandit
bando ['bando] *nm* (edicto) edict, proclamation; *(facción)* faction; **pasar al otro ~** to change sides; **los bandos** (Rel) the banns
bandolera [bando'lera] *nf*: **bolsa de ~** shoulder bag
bandolero [bando'lero] *nm* bandit, brigand
bandoneón [bandone'on] *nm* (Am) large accordion
banquero [ban'kero] *nm* banker
banqueta [ban'keta] *nf* stool; *(Am: acera)* pavement (Brit), sidewalk (US)
banquete [ban'kete] *nm* banquet; *(para convidados)* formal dinner; **~ de boda** wedding breakfast
banquillo [ban'kiʎo] *nm* (Jur) dock, prisoner's bench; *(banco)* bench; *(para los pies)* footstool
bañadera [baɲa'ðera] *nf* (Am) bath(tub)
bañado [ba'ɲaðo] *nm* (Am) swamp
bañador [baɲa'ðor] *nm* swimming costume (Brit), bathing suit (US)
bañar [ba'ɲar] *vt* (niño) to bath, bathe; *(objeto)* to dip; *(de barniz)* to coat; **bañarse** *vr* (en el mar) to bathe, swim; *(en la bañera)* to have a bath
bañero, -a [ba'ɲero, a] *nm/f* lifeguard ▪ *nf* bath(tub)
bañista [ba'ɲista] *nm/f* bather
baño ['baɲo] *nm* (en bañera) bath; *(en río, mar)* dip, swim; *(cuarto)* bathroom; *(bañera)* bath(tub); *(capa)* coating; **ir a tomar los baños** to take the waters
baptista [bap'tista] *nm/f* Baptist
baqueano, -a, baquiano, -a [bake'ano, a] [baki'ano, a] *nm/f* (Am) guide
baqueta [ba'keta] *nf* (Mus) drumstick
bar [bar] *nm* bar
barahúnda [bara'unda] *nf* uproar, hubbub
baraja [ba'raxa] *nf* pack (of cards); *see note*

● **BARAJA ESPAÑOLA**

The *baraja española* is the traditional Spanish deck of cards and differs from a standard poker deck. The four *palos* (suits) are *oros* (golden coins), *copas* (goblets), *espadas* (swords), and *bastos* ("clubs", but not like the clubs in a poker pack). Every suit has 9 numbered cards, although for certain games only 7 are used, and 3 face cards: *sota* (Jack), *caballo* (queen) and *rey* (king).

barajar [bara'xar] *vt* (naipes) to shuffle; *(fig)* to jumble up
baranda [ba'randa], **barandilla** [baran'diʎa] *nf* rail, railing
baratija [bara'tixa] *nf* trinket; *(fig)* trifle; **baratijas** *nfpl* (Com) cheap goods
baratillo [bara'tiʎo] *nm* (tienda) junk shop; *(subasta)* bargain sale; *(conjunto de cosas)* second-hand goods *pl*
barato, -a [ba'rato, a] *adj* cheap ▪ *adv* cheap, cheaply
baratura [bara'tura] *nf* cheapness
baraúnda [bara'unda] *nf* = **barahúnda**
barba ['barβa] *nf* (mentón) chin; *(pelo)* beard; **tener ~** to be unshaven; **hacer algo en las barbas de algn** to do sth under sb's very nose; **reírse en las barbas de algn** to laugh in sb's face
barbacoa [barβa'koa] *nf* (parrilla) barbecue; *(carne)* barbecued meat
barbaridad [barβari'ðað] *nf* barbarity; *(acto)* barbarism; *(atrocidad)* outrage; **una ~ de** *(fam)* loads of; **¡qué ~!** *(fam)* how awful!; **cuesta una ~** *(fam)* it costs a fortune
barbarie [bar'βarje] *nf*, **barbarismo** [barβa'rismo] *nm* barbarism; *(crueldad)* barbarity
bárbaro, -a ['barβaro, a] *adj* barbarous, cruel; *(grosero)* rough, uncouth ▪ *nm/f* barbarian ▪ *adv*: **lo pasamos ~** *(fam)* we had a great time; **¡qué ~!** *(fam)* how marvellous!; **un éxito ~** *(fam)* a terrific success; **es un tipo ~** *(fam)* he's a great bloke
barbecho [bar'βetʃo] *nm* fallow land
barbero [bar'βero] *nm* barber, hairdresser
barbilampiño [barβilam'piɲo] *adj* smooth-faced; *(fig)* inexperienced
barbilla [bar'βiʎa] *nf* chin, tip of the chin
barbitúrico [barβi'turiko] *nm* barbiturate
barbo ['barβo] *nm*: **~ de mar** red mullet
barbotar [barβo'tar], **barbotear** [barβote'ar] *vt, vi* to mutter, mumble
barbudo, -a [bar'βuðo, a] *adj* bearded
barbullar [barβu'ʎar] *vi* to jabber away
barca ['barka] *nf* (small) boat; **~ pesquera** fishing boat; **~ de pasaje** ferry
barcaza [bar'kaθa] *nf* barge; **~ de desembarco** landing craft
Barcelona [barθe'lona] *nf* Barcelona
barcelonés, -esa [barθelo'nes, esa] *adj* of o from Barcelona ▪ *nm/f* native o inhabitant of Barcelona
barco ['barko] *nm* boat; *(buque)* ship; *(Com etc)* vessel; **~ de carga** cargo boat; **~ de guerra** warship; **~ de vela** sailing ship; **ir en ~** to go by boat
baremo [ba'remo] *nm* scale; *(tabla de cuentas)*

ready reckoner

barítono [ba'ritono] *nm* baritone

barman ['barman] *nm* barman

Barna *abr* = **Barcelona**

barnice *etc* [bar'niθe] *vb ver* **barnizar**

barniz [bar'niθ] *nm* varnish; (*en la loza*) glaze; (*fig*) veneer

barnizar [barni'θar] *vt* to varnish; (*loza*) to glaze

barómetro [ba'rometro] *nm* barometer

barón [ba'ron] *nm* baron

baronesa [baro'nesa] *nf* baroness

barquero [bar'kero] *nm* boatman

barquilla [bar'kiʎa] *nf* (*Naut*) log

barquillo [bar'kiʎo] *nm* cone, cornet

barra ['barra] *nf* bar, rod; (*Jur*) rail; (:*banquillo*) dock; (*de un bar, café*) bar; (*de pan*) French loaf; (*palanca*) lever; **~ de carmín** *o* **de labios** lipstick; **~ de herramientas** (*Inform*) toolbar; **~ de espaciado** (*Inform*) space bar; **~ inversa** backslash; **~ libre** free bar; **no pararse en barras** to stick *o* stop at nothing

barrabasada [barraβa'saða] *nf* (piece of) mischief

barraca [ba'rraka] *nf* hut, cabin; (*en Valencia*) thatched farmhouse; (*en feria*) booth

barracón [barra'kon] *nm* (*caseta*) big hut

barragana [barra'ɣana] *nf* concubine

barranca [ba'rranka] *nf* ravine, gully

barranco [ba'rranko] *nm* ravine; (*fig*) difficulty

barrena [ba'rrena] *nf* drill

barrenar [barre'nar] *vt* to drill (through), bore

barrendero, -a [barren'dero, a] *nm/f* street-sweeper

barreno [ba'rreno] *nm* large drill

barreño [ba'rreɲo] *nm* washing-up bowl

barrer [ba'rrer] *vt* to sweep; (*quitar*) to sweep away; (*Mil: Naut*) to sweep, rake (with gunfire) ■ *vi* to sweep up

barrera [ba'rrera] *nf* barrier; (*Mil*) barricade; (*Ferro*) crossing gate; **poner barreras a** to hinder; **~ arancelaria** (*Com*) tariff barrier; **~ comercial** (*Com*) trade barrier

barriada [ba'rrjaða] *nf* quarter, district

barricada [barri'kaða] *nf* barricade

barrida [ba'rriða] *nf*, **barrido** [ba'rriðo] *nm* sweep, sweeping

barriga [ba'rriɣa] *nf* belly; (*panza*) paunch; (*vientre*) guts *pl*; **echar ~** to get middle-age spread

barrigón, -ona [barri'ɣon, ona], **barrigudo, -a** [barri'ɣuðo, a] *adj* potbellied

barril [ba'rril] *nm* barrel, cask; **cerveza de ~** draught beer

barrio ['barrjo] *nm* (*vecindad*) area,

neighborhood (US); (*en las afueras*) suburb; **barrios bajos** poor quarter *sg*; **~ chino** red-light district

barriobajero, -a [barrjobβa'xero, a] *adj* (*vulgar*) common

barro ['barro] *nm* (*lodo*) mud; (*objetos*) earthenware; (*Med*) pimple

barroco, -a [ba'rroko, a] *adj* Baroque; (*fig*) elaborate ■ *nm* Baroque

barrote [ba'rrote] *nm* (*de ventana etc*) bar

barruntar [barrun'tar] *vt* (*conjeturar*) to guess; (*presentir*) to suspect

barrunto [ba'rrunto] *nm* guess; suspicion

bartola [bar'tola]: **a la ~** *adv*: **tirarse a la ~** to take it easy, be lazy

bártulos ['bartulos] *nmpl* things, belongings

barullo [ba'ruʎo] *nm* row, uproar

basa ['basa] *nf* (*Arq*) base

basamento [basa'mento] *nm* base, plinth

basar [ba'sar] *vt* to base; **basarse** *vr*: **basarse en** to be based on

basca ['baska] *nf* nausea

báscula ['baskula] *nf* (platform) scales *pl*

base ['base] *nf* base; **a ~ de** on the basis of, based on; (*mediante*) by means of; **a ~ de bien** in abundance; **~ de conocimiento** knowledge base; **~ de datos** database

básico, -a ['basiko, a] *adj* basic

Basilea [basi'lea] *nf* Basle

basílica [ba'silika] *nf* basilica

basilisco [basi'lisko] *nm* (*Am*) iguana; **estar hecho un ~** to be hopping mad

basket, básquet ['basket] *nm* basketball

 PALABRA CLAVE

bastante [bas'tante] *adj* **1** (*suficiente*) enough; **bastante dinero** enough *o* sufficient money; **bastantes libros** enough books
2 (*valor intensivo*): **bastante gente** quite a lot of people; **tener bastante calor** to be rather hot; **hace bastante tiempo que ocurrió** it happened quite *o* rather a long time ago
■ *adv*: **bastante bueno/malo** quite good/ rather bad; **bastante rico** pretty rich; **(lo) bastante inteligente (como) para hacer algo** clever enough *o* sufficiently clever to do sth; **voy a tardar bastante** I'm going to be a while *o* quite some time

bastar [bas'tar] *vi* to be enough *o* sufficient; **bastarse** *vr* to be self-sufficient; **~ para** to be enough to; **¡basta!** (that's) enough!

bastardilla [bastar'ðiʎa] *nf* italics *pl*

bastardo, -a [bas'tarðo, a] *adj, nm/f* bastard

bastidor [basti'ðor] *nm* frame; (*de coche*) chassis; (*Arte*) stretcher; (*Teat*) wing; **entre**

bastidores behind the scenes

basto, -a ['basto, a] *adj* coarse, rough ■ *nmpl*: **bastos** (*Naipes*) one of the suits in the Spanish card deck; *ver tb* **baraja española**

bastón [bas'ton] *nm* stick, staff; (*para pasear*) walking stick; ~ **de mando** baton

bastonazo [basto'naθo] *nm* blow with a stick

bastoncillo [baston'θiʎo] *nm* (*tb*: **bastoncillo de algodón**) cotton bud

basura [ba'sura] *nf* rubbish, refuse (*Brit*), garbage (*US*) ■ *adj*: **comida/televisión ~** junk food/TV

basurero [basu'rero] *nm* (*hombre*) dustman (*Brit*), garbage collector *o* man (*US*); (*lugar*) rubbish dump; (*cubo*) (rubbish) bin (*Brit*), trash can (*US*)

bata ['bata] *nf* (*gen*) dressing gown; (*cubretodo*) smock, overall; (*Med: Tec etc*) lab(oratory) coat

batacazo [bata'kaθo] *nm* bump

batalla [ba'taʎa] *nf* battle; **de ~** for everyday use

batallar [bata'ʎar] *vi* to fight

batallón [bata'ʎon] *nm* battalion

batata [ba'tata] *nf* (*Am: Culin*) sweet potato

bate ['bate] *nm* (*Deporte*) bat

batea [ba'tea] *nf* (*Am*) washing trough

bateador [batea'ðor] *nm* (*Deporte*) batter, batsman

batería [bate'ria] *nf* battery; (*Mus*) drums *pl*; (*Teat*) footlights *pl*; ~ **de cocina** kitchen utensils *pl*

batiburrillo [batiβu'rriʎo] *nm* hotchpotch

batido, -a [ba'tiðo, a] *adj* (*camino*) beaten, well-trodden ■ *nm* (*Culin*) batter; ~ (**de leche**) milk shake ■ *nf* (*Am*) (police) raid

batidora [bati'ðora] *nf* beater, mixer; ~ **eléctrica** food mixer, blender

batir [ba'tir] *vt* to beat, strike; (*vencer*) to beat, defeat; (*revolver*) to beat, mix; (*pelo*) to backcomb; **batirse** *vr* to fight; ~ **palmas** to clap, applaud

baturro, -a [ba'turro, a] *nm/f* Aragonese peasant

batuta [ba'tuta] *nf* baton; **llevar la ~** (*fig*) to be the boss

baudio ['bauðjo] *nm* (*Inform*) baud

baúl [ba'ul] *nm* trunk; (*Am Auto*) boot (*Brit*), trunk (*US*)

bautice *etc* [bau'tiθe] *vb ver* **bautizar**

bautismo [bau'tismo] *nm* baptism, christening

bautista [bau'tista] *adj, nm/f* Baptist

bautizar [bauti'θar] *vt* to baptize, christen; (*fam: diluir*) to water down; (*dar apodo*) to dub

bautizo [bau'tiθo] *nm* baptism, christening

bávaro, -a ['baβaro, a] *adj, nm/f* Bavarian

Baviera [ba'βjera] *nf* Bavaria

baya ['baja] *nf* berry; *ver tb* **bayo**

bayeta [ba'jeta] *nf* (*trapo*) floor cloth; (*Am: pañal*) nappy (*Brit*), diaper (*US*)

bayo, -a ['bajo, a] *adj* bay

bayoneta [bajo'neta] *nf* bayonet

baza ['baθa] *nf* trick; **meter ~** to butt in

bazar [ba'θar] *nm* bazaar

bazo ['baθo] *nm* spleen

bazofia [ba'θofja] *nf* pigswill (*Brit*), hogwash (*US*); (*libro etc*) trash

BCE *nm abr* (= *Banco Central Europeo*) ECB

beatificar [beatifi'kar] *vt* to beatify

beato, -a [be'ato, a] *adj* blessed; (*piadoso*) pious

bebe (*Am*) (*pl* **bebes**) ['beβe, 'beβes], **bebé** (*pl* **bebés**) [be'βe, be'βes] *nm* baby; ~ **de diseño** designer baby

bebedero, -a [beβe'ðero, a] *nm* (*para animales*) drinking trough

bebedizo, -a [beβe'ðiθo, a] *adj* drinkable ■ *nm* potion

bebedor, a [beβe'ðor, a] *adj* hard-drinking

bebé-probeta [be'βe-pro'βeta] (*pl* **bebés-probeta**) *nm/f* test-tube baby

beber [be'βer] *vt, vi* to drink; ~ **a sorbos/tragos** to sip/gulp; **se lo bebió todo** he drank it all up

bebido, -a [be'βiðo, a] *adj* drunk ■ *nf* drink

beca ['beka] *nf* grant, scholarship

becado, -a [be'kaðo, a] *nm/f*, **becario, a** [be'karjo, a] *nm/f* scholarship holder

becerro [be'θerro] *nm* yearling calf

bechamel [betʃa'mel] *nf* = **besamel**

becuadro [be'kwaðro] *nm* (*Mus*) natural sign

bedel [be'ðel] *nm* porter, janitor

beduino, -a [be'ðwino, a] *adj, nm/f* Bedouin

befarse [be'farse] *vr*: ~ **de algo** to scoff at sth

beige ['beix], **beis** ['beis] *adj, nm* beige

béisbol ['beisβol] *nm* baseball

bejuco [be'xuko] *nm* (*Am*) reed, liana

beldad [bel'dað] *nf* beauty

Belén [be'len] *nm* Bethlehem; **belén** (*de Navidad*) nativity scene, crib

belga ['belɣa] *adj, nm/f* Belgian

Bélgica ['belxika] *nf* Belgium

Belgrado [bel'ɣraðo] *nm* Belgrade

Belice [be'liθe] *nm* Belize

bélico, -a ['beliko, a] *adj* (*actitud*) warlike

belicoso, -a [beli'koso, a] *adj* (*guerrero*) warlike; (*agresivo*) aggressive, bellicose

beligerante [belixe'rante] *adj* belligerent

bellaco, -a [be'ʎako, a] *adj* sly, cunning ■ *nm* villain, rogue

belladona [beʎa'ðona] *nf* deadly nightshade

bellaquería [beʎake'ria] *nf* (*acción*) dirty trick; (*calidad*) wickedness

belleza [be'ʎeθa] *nf* beauty

bello, -a ['beʎo, a] *adj* beautiful, lovely;
  Bellas Artes Fine Art *sg*
bellota [be'ʎota] *nf* acorn
bemol [be'mol] *nm* (*Mus*) flat; **esto tiene
  bemoles** (*fam*) this is a tough one
bencina [ben'sina] *nf* (*Am*) petrol (*Brit*), gas
  (*US*)
bendecir [bende'θir] *vt* to bless; ~ **la mesa**
  to say grace
bendición [bendi'θjon] *nf* blessing
bendiga *etc* [ben'diɣa], **bendije** *etc* [ben'dixe]
  vb ver **bendecir**
bendito, -a [ben'dito, a] *pp de* **bendecir** ■ *adj*
  (*santo*) blessed; (*agua*) holy; (*afortunado*) lucky;
  (*feliz*) happy; (*sencillo*) simple ■ *nm/f* simple
  soul; **¡~ sea Dios!** thank goodness!; **es un ~**
  he's sweet; **dormir como un ~** to sleep like
  a log
benedictino, -a [beneðik'tino, a] *adj, nm*
  Benedictine
benefactor, a [benefak'tor, a] *nm/f*
  benefactor/benefactress
beneficencia [benefi'θenθja] *nf* charity
beneficiar [benefi'θjar] *vt* to benefit, be of
  benefit to; **beneficiarse** *vr* to benefit, profit
beneficiario, -a [benefi'θjarjo, a] *nm/f*
  beneficiary; (*de cheque*) payee
beneficio [bene'fiθjo] *nm* (*bien*) benefit,
  advantage; (*Com*) profit, gain; **a ~ de** for
  the benefit of; **en ~ propio** to one's own
  advantage; **~ bruto/neto** gross/net profit;
  ~ por acción earnings *pl* per share
beneficioso, -a [benefi'θjoso, a] *adj*
  beneficial
benéfico, -a [be'nefiko, a] *adj* charitable;
  sociedad benéfica charity (organization)
benemérito, -a [bene'merito, a] *adj*
  meritorious ■ *nf*: **la Benemérita** (*Esp*) the
  Civil Guard; *ver tb* **Guardia Civil**
beneplácito [bene'plaθito] *nm* approval,
  consent
benevolencia [beneβo'lenθja] *nf*
  benevolence, kindness
benévolo, -a [be'neβolo, a] *adj* benevolent,
  kind
Bengala [ben'gala] *nf* Bengal; **el Golfo de ~**
  the Bay of Bengal
bengala [ben'gala] *nf* (*Mil*) flare; (*fuego*)
  Bengal light; (*materia*) rattan
bengalí [benga'li] *adj, nm/f* Bengali
benignidad [beniɣni'ðað] *nf* (*afabilidad*)
  kindness; (*suavidad*) mildness
benigno, -a [be'niɣno, a] *adj* kind; (*suave*)
  mild; (*Med: tumor*) benign, non-malignant
benjamín [benxa'min] *nm* youngest child
beodo, -a [be'oðo, a] *adj* drunk ■ *nm/f*
  drunkard

berberecho [berβe'retʃo] *nm* cockle
berenjena [beren'xena] *nf* aubergine (*Brit*),
  eggplant (*US*)
berenjenal [berenxe'nal] *nm* (*Agr*) aubergine
  bed; (*fig*) mess; **en buen ~ nos hemos
  metido** we've got ourselves into a fine mess
bergantín [berɣan'tin] *nm* brig(antine)
Berlín [ber'lin] *nm* Berlin
berlinés, -esa [berli'nes, esa] *adj* of o from
  Berlin ■ *nm/f* Berliner
bermejo, -a [ber'mexo, a] *adj* red
bermellón [berme'ʎon] *nm* vermilion
bermudas [ber'muðas] *nfpl* Bermuda shorts
berrear [berre'ar] *vi* to bellow, low
berrido [be'rriðo] *nm* bellow(ing)
berrinche [be'rrintʃe] *nm* (*fam*) temper,
  tantrum
berro ['berro] *nm* watercress
berza ['berθa] *nf* cabbage; **~ lombarda** red
  cabbage
besamel [besa'mel], **besamela** [besa'mela]
  nf (*Culin*) white sauce, bechamel sauce
besar [be'sar] *vt* to kiss; (*fig: tocar*) to graze;
  besarse *vr* to kiss (one another)
beso ['beso] *nm* kiss
bestia ['bestja] *nf* beast, animal; (*fig*) idiot;
  ~ de carga beast of burden; **¡~!** you idiot!; **¡no
  seas ~!** (*bruto*) don't be such a brute!; (*idiota*)
  don't be such an idiot!
bestial [bes'tjal] *adj* bestial; (*fam*) terrific
bestialidad [bestjali'ðað] *nf* bestiality; (*fam*)
  stupidity
besugo [be'suɣo] *nm* sea bream; (*fam*) idiot
besuguera [besu'ɣera] *nf* (*Culin*) fish pan
besuquear [besuke'ar] *vt* to cover with
  kisses; **besuquearse** *vr* to kiss and cuddle
bético, -a ['betiko, a] *adj* Andalusian
betún [be'tun] *nm* shoe polish; (*Química*)
  bitumen, asphalt
Bib. *abr* = **Biblioteca**
biberón [biβe'ron] *nm* feeding bottle
Biblia ['biβlja] *nf* Bible
bíblico, -a ['biβliko, a] *adj* biblical
bibliografía [biβljoɣra'fia] *nf* bibliography
biblioteca [biβljo'teka] *nf* library; (*estantes*)
  bookcase, bookshelves *pl*; **~ de consulta**
  reference library
bibliotecario, -a [biβljote'karjo, a] *nm/f*
  librarian
B.I.C. [bik] *nf abr* (= *Brigada de Investigación
  Criminal*) ≈ CID (*Brit*), FBI (*US*)
bicarbonato [bikarβo'nato] *nm* bicarbonate
bíceps ['biθeps] *nm inv* biceps
bicho ['bitʃo] *nm* (*animal*) small animal;
  (*sabandija*) bug, insect; (*Taur*) bull; **~ raro**
  (*fam*) queer fish
bici ['biθi] *nf* (*fam*) bike

b

47

bicicleta [biθi'kleta] *nf* bicycle, cycle;
~ **estática/de montaña** exercise/mountain
bike
bicoca [bi'koka] *nf* (*Esp fam*) cushy job
bidé [bi'ðe] *nm* bidet
bidireccional [biðirekθjo'nal] *adj*
bidirectional
bidón [bi'ðon] *nm* (*grande*) drum; (*pequeño*) can
Bielorrusia [bjelo'rrusja] *nf* Belarus,
Byelorussia
bielorruso, -a [bjelo'rruso, a] *adj, nm/f*
Belarussian, Belorussian ▪ *nm* (*Ling*)
Belarussian, Belorussian

 PALABRA CLAVE

bien [bjen] *nm* **1** (*bienestar*) good; **te lo digo
por tu bien** I'm telling you for your own
good; **el bien y el mal** good and evil
2 (*posesión*): **bienes** goods; **bienes de
consumo/equipo** consumer/capital
goods; **bienes inmuebles** *o* **raíces/bienes
muebles** real estate *sg*/personal property *sg*
▪ *adv* **1** (*de manera satisfactoria, correcta etc*) well;
trabaja/come bien she works/eats well;
contestó bien he answered correctly; **oler
bien** to smell nice *o* good; **me siento bien** I
feel fine; **no me siento bien** I don't feel very
well; **se está bien aquí** it's nice here
2 (*frases*): **hiciste bien en llamarme** you
were right to call me
3 (*valor intensivo*) very; **un cuarto bien
caliente** a nice warm room; **bien de veces**
lots of times; **bien se ve que ...** it's quite
clear that ...
4: **estar bien**: **estoy muy bien aquí** I feel
very happy here; **¿te encuentras bien?**
are you all right?; **te está bien la falda** (*ser
la talla*) the skirt fits you; (*sentar*) the skirt
suits you; **el libro está muy bien** the book
is really good; **está bien que vengan** it's all
right for them to come; **¡está bien! lo haré**
oh all right, I'll do it; **ya está bien de quejas**
that's quite enough complaining
5 (*de buena gana*): **yo bien que iría pero ...**
I'd gladly go but ...
▪ *excl*: **¡bien!** (*aprobación*) OK!; **¡muy bien!**
well done!; **¡qué bien!** great!; **bien, gracias,
¿y usted?** fine thanks, and you?
▪ *adj inv*: **niño bien** rich kid; **gente bien**
posh people
▪ *conj* **1**: **bien ... bien**: **bien en coche bien
en tren** either by car or by train
2: **no bien** (*esp Am*): **no bien llegue te
llamaré** as soon as I arrive I'll call you
3: **si bien** even though; *ver tb* **más**

bienal [bje'nal] *adj* biennial
bienaventurado, -a [bjenaβentu'raðo, a]
adj (*feliz*) happy; (*afortunado*) fortunate; (*Rel*)
blessed
bienestar [bjenes'tar] *nm* well-being;
estado de ~ welfare state
bienhechor, a [bjene'tʃor, a] *adj* beneficent
▪ *nm/f* benefactor/benefactress
bienio ['bjenjo] *nm* two-year period
bienvenido, -a [bjembe'niðo, a] *adj* welcome
▪ *excl* welcome! ▪ *nf* welcome; **dar la
bienvenida a algn** to welcome sb
bies ['bjes] *nm*: **falda al ~** bias-cut skirt;
cortar al ~ to cut on the bias
bifásico, -a [bi'fasiko, a] *adj* (*Elec*) two-phase
bife ['bife] *nm* (*Am*) steak
bifocal [bifo'kal] *adj* bifocal
bifurcación [bifurka'θjon] *nf* fork; (*Ferro*:
Inform) branch
bifurcarse [bifur'karse] *vr* to fork
bigamia [bi'ɣamja] *nf* bigamy
bígamo, -a ['biɣamo, a] *adj* bigamous ▪ *nm/f*
bigamist
bígaro ['biɣaro] *nm* winkle
bigote [bi'ɣote] *nm* (*tb*: **bigotes**) moustache
bigotudo, -a [biɣo'tuðo, a] *adj* with a big
moustache
bigudí [biɣu'ði] *nm* (hair-)curler
bikini [bi'kini] *nm* bikini; (*Culin*) toasted
cheese and ham sandwich
bilateral [bilate'ral] *adj* bilateral
bilbaíno, -a [bilβa'ino, a] *adj* of *o* from Bilbao
▪ *nm/f* native *o* inhabitant of Bilbao
bilingüe [bi'lingwe] *adj* bilingual
bilis ['bilis] *nf inv* bile
billar [bi'ʎar] *nm* billiards *sg*; (*lugar*) billiard
hall; (*galería de atracciones*) amusement
arcade; **~ americano** pool
billete [bi'ʎete] *nm* ticket; (*de banco*) banknote
(*Brit*), bill (*US*); (*carta*) note; **~ sencillo, ~ de
ida solamente/~ de ida y vuelta** single (*Brit*)
o one-way (*US*) ticket/return (*Brit*) *o* round-
trip (*US*) ticket; **sacar (un) ~** to get a ticket;
un ~ de cinco libras a five-pound note
billetera [biʎe'tera] *nf*, **billetero** [biʎe'tero]
nm wallet
billón [bi'ʎon] *nm* billion
bimensual [bimen'swal] *adj* twice monthly
bimestral [bimes'tral] *adj* bimonthly
bimestre [bi'mestre] *nm* two-month period
bimotor [bimo'tor] *adj* twin-engined ▪ *nm*
twin-engined plane
binario, -a [bi'narjo, a] *adj* (*Inform*) binary
bingo ['bingo] *nm* (*juego*) bingo; (*sala*) bingo
hall
binóculo [bi'nokulo] *nm* pince-nez
binomio [bi'nomjo] *nm* (*Mat*) binomial

biodegradable [bioðeɣra'ðaβle] *adj* biodegradable
biodiversidad [bioðiβersi'ðað] *nf* biodiversity
biografía [bjoɣra'fia] *nf* biography
biográfico, -a [bio'ɣrafiko, a] *adj* biographical
biógrafo, -a [bi'oɣrafo, a] *nm/f* biographer
biología [biolo'xia] *nf* biology
biológico, -a [bio'loxiko, a] *adj* biological; (*cultivo, producto*) organic; **guerra biológica** biological warfare
biólogo, -a [bi'oloɣo, a] *nm/f* biologist
biombo ['bjombo] *nm* (folding) screen
biopsia [bi'opsja] *nf* biopsy
bioquímico, -a [bio'kimiko, a] *adj* biochemical ■ *nm/f* biochemist ■ *nf* biochemistry
biosfera [bios'fera] *nf* biosphere
bioterrorismo [bioterro'rismo] *nm* bioterrorism
bióxido [bi'oksiðo] *nm* dioxide
bipartidismo [biparti'ðismo] *nm* (*Pol*) two-party system
biquini [bi'kini] *nm* = **bikini**
birlar [bir'lar] *vt* (*fam*) to pinch
birlibirloque [birliβir'loke] *nm*: **por arte de ~** (as if) by magic
Birmania [bir'manja] *nf* Burma
birmano, -a [bir'mano, a] *adj, nm/f* Burmese
birrete [bi'rrete] *nm* (*Jur*) judge's cap
birria ['birrja] *nf* (*fam*): **ser una ~** to be rubbish; **ir hecho una ~** to be o look a sight
bis [bis] *excl* encore! ■ *nm* encore ■ *adv* (*dos veces*) twice; **viven en el 27 ~** they live at 27a
bisabuelo, -a [bisa'βwelo, a] *nm/f* great-grandfather/mother; **bisabuelos** *nmpl* great-grandparents
bisagra [bi'saɣra] *nf* hinge
bisbisar [bisβi'sar], **bisbisear** [bisβise'ar] *vt* to mutter, mumble
bisbiseo [bisβi'seo] *nm* muttering
biselar [bise'lar] *vt* to bevel
bisexual [bisek'swal] *adj, nm/f* bisexual
bisiesto [bi'sjesto] *adj*: **año ~** leap year
bisnieto, -a [bis'njeto, a] *nm/f* great-grandson/daughter; **bisnietos** *nmpl* great-grandchildren
bisonte [bi'sonte] *nm* bison
bisoñé [biso'ɲe] *nm* toupée
bisoño, -a [bi'soɲo, a] *adj* green, inexperienced
bistec [bis'tek], **bisté** [bis'te] *nm* steak
bisturí [bistu'ri] *nm* scalpel
bisutería [bisute'ria] *nf* imitation o costume jewellery
bit [bit] *nm* (*Inform*) bit; **~ de parada** stop bit; **~ de paridad** parity bit

bizantino, -a [biθan'tino, a] *adj* Byzantine; (*fig*) pointless
bizarría [biθa'rria] *nf* (*valor*) bravery; (*generosidad*) generosity
bizarro, -a [bi'θarro, a] *adj* brave; generous
bizco, -a ['biθko, a] *adj* cross-eyed
bizcocho [biθ'kotʃo] *nm* (*Culin*) sponge cake
biznieto, -a [biθ'njeto, a] *nm/f* = **bisnieto**
bizquear [biθke'ar] *vi* to squint
blanco, -a ['blanko, a] *adj* white ■ *nm/f* white man/woman, white ■ *nm* (*color*) white; (*en texto*) blank; (*Mil, fig*) target ■ *nf* (*Mus*) minim; **en ~** blank; **cheque en ~** blank cheque; **votar en ~** to spoil one's vote; **quedarse en ~** to be disappointed; **noche en ~** sleepless night; **ser el ~ de las burlas** to be the butt of jokes; **sin blanca** broke
blancura [blan'kura] *nf* whiteness
blandengue [blan'denge] *adj* (*fam*) soft, weak
blandir [blan'dir] *vt* to brandish
blando, -a ['blando, a] *adj* soft; (*tierno*) tender, gentle; (*carácter*) mild; (*fam*) cowardly ■ *nm/f* (*Pol etc*) soft-liner
blandura [blan'dura] *nf* softness; tenderness; mildness
blanquear [blanke'ar] *vt* to whiten; (*fachada*) to whitewash; (*paño*) to bleach; (*dinero*) to launder ■ *vi* to turn white
blanquecino, -a [blanke'θino, a] *adj* whitish
blanqueo [blan'keo] *nm* (*de pared*) whitewashing; (*de dinero*) laundering
blasfemar [blasfe'mar] *vi* to blaspheme; (*fig*) to curse
blasfemia [blas'femja] *nf* blasphemy
blasfemo, -a [blas'femo, a] *adj* blasphemous ■ *nm/f* blasphemer
blasón [bla'son] *nm* coat of arms; (*fig*) honour
blasonar [blaso'nar] *vt* to emblazon ■ *vi* to boast, brag
bledo ['bleðo] *nm*: **(no) me importa un ~** I couldn't care less
blindado, -a [blin'daðo, a] *adj* (*Mil*) armour-plated; (*antibalas*) bulletproof; **coche** o (*Am*) **carro ~** armoured car; **puertas blindadas** security doors
blindaje [blin'daxe] *nm* armour, armour-plating
bloc (*pl* **blocs**) [blok, blos] *nm* writing pad; (*Escol*) jotter; **~ de dibujos** sketch pad
blog [bloɣ] (*pl* **blogs**) *nm* blog
blogging ['bloɣin] *nm* blogging
bloguear [bloɣe'ar] *vi* to blog
bloque ['bloke] *nm* (*tb Inform*) block; (*Pol*) bloc; **~ de cilindros** cylinder block
bloquear [bloke'ar] *vt* (*Naut etc*) to blockade; (*aislar*) to cut off; (*Com, Econ*) to freeze; **fondos bloqueados** frozen assets

bloqueo [blo'keo] *nm* blockade; (*Com*) freezing, blocking

bluejean [blu'jin] *nm* (*Am*) jeans *pl*, denims *pl*

blusa ['blusa] *nf* blouse

B.° *abr* (*Finanzas*: = *banco*) bank; (*Com*: = *beneficiario*) beneficiary

boa ['boa] *nf* boa

boato [bo'ato] *nm* show, ostentation

bobada [bo'βaða] *nf* foolish action (*o* statement); **decir bobadas** to talk nonsense

bobalicón, -ona [boβali'kon, ona] *adj* utterly stupid

bobería [boβe'ria] *nf* = **bobada**

bobina [bo'βina] *nf* (*Tec*) bobbin; (*Foto*) spool; (*Elec*) coil, winding

bobo, -a ['boβo, a] *adj* (*tonto*) daft, silly; (*cándido*) naïve ■ *nm/f* fool, idiot ■ *nm* (*Teat*) clown, funny man

boca ['boka] *nf* mouth; (*de crustáceo*) pincer; (*de cañón*) muzzle; (*entrada*) mouth, entrance; **bocas** *nfpl* (*de río*) mouth *sg*; **~ abajo/arriba** face down/up; **a ~ jarro** point-blank; **se me hace la ~ agua** my mouth is watering; **todo salió a pedir de ~** it all turned out perfectly; **en ~ de** (*esp Am*) according to; **la cosa anda de ~ en ~** the story is going the rounds; **¡cállate la ~!** (*fam*) shut up!; **quedarse con la ~ abierta** to be dumbfounded; **no abrir la ~** to keep quiet; **~ del estómago** pit of the stomach; **~ de metro** tube (*Brit*) *o* subway (*US*) entrance

bocacalle [boka'kaʎe] *nf* side street; **la primera ~** the first turning *o* street

bocadillo [boka'ðiʎo] *nm* sandwich

bocado [bo'kaðo] *nm* mouthful, bite; (*de caballo*) bridle; **~ de Adán** Adam's apple

bocajarro [boka'xarro]: **a ~** *adv* (*Mil*) at point-blank range; **decir algo a ~** to say sth bluntly

bocanada [boka'naða] *nf* (*de vino*) mouthful, swallow; (*de aire*) gust, puff

bocata [bo'kata] *nm* (*fam*) sandwich

bocazas [bo'kaθas] *nm/f inv* (*fam*) bigmouth

boceto [bo'θeto] *nm* sketch, outline

bocha ['botʃa] *nf* bowl; **bochas** *nfpl* bowls *sg*

bochinche [bo'tʃintʃe] *nm* (*fam*) uproar

bochorno [bo'tʃorno] *nm* (*vergüenza*) embarrassment; (*calor*): **hace ~** it's very muggy

bochornoso, -a [botʃor'noso, a] *adj* muggy; embarrassing

bocina [bo'θina] *nf* (*Mus*) trumpet; (*Auto*) horn; (*para hablar*) megaphone; **tocar la ~** (*Auto*) to sound *o* blow one's horn

bocinazo [boθi'naθo] *nm* (*Auto*) toot

bocio ['boθjo] *nm* (*Med*) goitre

boda ['boða] *nf* (*tb*: **bodas**) wedding, marriage; (*fiesta*) wedding reception; **bodas de plata/de oro** silver/golden wedding *sg*

bodega [bo'ðeɣa] *nf* (*de vino*) (wine) cellar; (*bar*) bar; (*restaurante*) restaurant; (*depósito*) storeroom; (*de barco*) hold

bodegón [boðe'ɣon] *nm* (*Arte*) still life

bodrio [bo'ðrio] *nm*: **el libro es un ~** the book is awful *o* rubbish

B.O.E. ['boe] *nm abr* = **Boletín Oficial del Estado**

bofe ['bofe] *nm* (*tb*: **bofes**: *de res*) lights *pl*; **echar los bofes** to slave (away)

bofetada [bofe'taða] *nf* slap (in the face); **dar de bofetadas a algn** to punch sb

bofetón [bofe'ton] *nm* = **bofetada**

boga ['boɣa] *nf*: **en ~** in vogue

bogar [bo'ɣar] *vi* (*remar*) to row; (*navegar*) to sail

bogavante [boɣa'βante] *nm* (*Naut*) stroke, first rower; (*Zool*) lobster

Bogotá [boɣo'ta] *n* Bogota

bogotano, -a [boɣo'tano, a] *adj* of *o* from Bogota ■ *nm/f* native *o* inhabitant of Bogota

bogue *etc* ['boɣe] *vb ver* **bogar**

bohemio, -a [bo'emjo, a] *adj, nm/f* Bohemian

boicot [boi'ko(t)] (*pl* **boicots**) *nm* boycott

boicotear [boikote'ar] *vt* to boycott

boicoteo [boiko'teo] *nm* boycott

boina ['boina] *nf* beret

bola ['bola] *nf* ball; (*canica*) marble; (*Naipes*) (grand) slam; (*betún*) shoe polish; (*mentira*) tale, story; **bolas** *nfpl* (*Am*) bolas; **~ de billar** billiard ball; **~ de nieve** snowball

bolchevique [boltʃe'βike] *adj, nm/f* Bolshevik

boleadoras [bolea'ðoras] *nfpl* (*Am*) bolas *sg*

bolera [bo'lera] *nf* skittle *o* bowling alley

bolero [bo'lero] *nm* bolero

boleta [bo'leta] *nf* (*Am*: *permiso*) pass, permit; (: *para votar*) ballot

boletería [bolete'ria] *nf* (*Am*) ticket office

boletero, -a [bole'tero, a] *nm/f* (*Am*) ticket seller

boletín [bole'tin] *nm* bulletin; (*periódico*) journal, review; **~ escolar** (*Esp*) school report; **~ de noticias** news bulletin; **~ de pedido** application form; **~ de precios** price list; **~ de prensa** press release; *see note*

BOLETÍN

The *Boletín Oficial del Estado*, abbreviated to *BOE*, is the official government record of all laws and resolutions passed by *las Cortes* (Spanish Parliament). It is widely consulted, mainly because it also publishes the announcements for the *oposiciones* (public competitive examinations).

boleto [bo'leto] *nm* (*esp Am*) ticket; **~ de apuestas** betting slip

boli ['boli] *nm* Biro®

boliche [bo'litʃe] *nm* (*bola*) jack; (*juego*) bowls *sg*; (*lugar*) bowling alley; (*Am: tienda*) small grocery store

bólido ['boliðo] *nm* meteorite; (*Auto*) racing car

bolígrafo [bo'liɣrafo] *nm* ball-point pen, Biro®

bolillo [bo'liʎo] *nm* (*Costura*) bobbin (for lacemaking)

bolívar [bo'liβar] *nm* monetary unit of Venezuela

Bolivia [bo'liβja] *nf* Bolivia

boliviano, -a [boli'βjano, a] *adj, nm/f* Bolivian

bollo ['boʎo] *nm* (*de pan*) roll; (*dulce*) scone; (*chichón*) bump, lump; (*abolladura*) dent; **bollos** *nmpl* (*Am*) troubles

bolo ['bolo] *nm* skittle; (*píldora*) (large) pill; **(juego de) bolos** skittles *sg*

Bolonia [bo'lonja] *nf* Bologna

bolsa ['bolsa] *nf* (*cartera*) purse; (*saco*) bag; (*Am*) pocket; (*Anat*) cavity, sac; (*Com*) stock exchange; (*Minería*) pocket; **~ de agua caliente** hot water bottle; **~ de aire** air pocket; **~ de (la) basura** bin-liner; **~ de dormir** (*Am*) sleeping bag; **~ de papel** paper bag; **~ de plástico** plastic (*o* carrier) bag; **"B~ de la propiedad"** "Property Mart"; **~ de trabajo** employment bureau; **jugar a la ~** to play the market

bolsillo [bol'siʎo] *nm* pocket; (*cartera*) purse; **de ~** pocket *cpd*; **meterse a algn en el ~** to get sb eating out of one's hand

bolsista [bol'sista] *nm/f* stockbroker

bolso ['bolso] *nm* (*bolsa*) bag; (*de mujer*) handbag

boludo, -a [bo'luðo, a] (*Am fam!*) *adj* stupid ■ *nm/f* prat (!)

bomba ['bomba] *nf* (*Mil*) bomb; (*Tec*) pump; (*Am: borrachera*) drunkenness ■ *adj* (*fam*): **noticia ~** bombshell ■ *adv* (*fam*): **pasarlo ~** to have a great time; **~ atómica/de humo/ de retardo** atomic/smoke/time bomb; **~ de gasolina** petrol pump; **~ de incendios** fire engine

bombacho, -a [bom'batʃo, a] *adj* baggy

bombardear [bombarðe'ar] *vt* to bombard; (*Mil*) to bomb

bombardeo [bombar'ðeo] *nm* bombardment; bombing

bombardero [bombar'ðero] *nm* bomber

bombear [bombe'ar] *vt* (*agua*) to pump (out *o* up); (*Mil*) to bomb; (*Fútbol*) to lob; **bombearse** *vr* to warp

bombero [bom'bero] *nm* fireman; **(cuerpo de) bomberos** fire brigade

bombilla [bom'biʎa] *nf* (*Esp*), **bombillo** [bom'biʎo] *nm* (*Am*) (light) bulb

bombín [bom'bin] *nm* bowler hat

bombo ['bombo] *nm* (*Mus*) bass drum; (*Tec*) drum; (*fam*) exaggerated praise; **hacer algo a ~ y platillo** to make a great song and dance about sth; **tengo la cabeza hecha un ~** I've got a splitting headache

bombón [bom'bon] *nm* chocolate; (*belleza*) gem

bombona [bom'bona] *nf*: **~ de butano** gas cylinder

bombonería [bombone'ria] *nf* sweetshop

bonachón, -ona [bona'tʃon, ona] *adj* good-natured

bonaerense [bonae'rense] *adj* of *o* from Buenos Aires ■ *nm/f* native *o* inhabitant of Buenos Aires

bonancible [bonan'θiβle] *adj* (*tiempo*) fair, calm

bonanza [bo'nanθa] *nf* (*Naut*) fair weather; (*fig*) bonanza; (*Minería*) rich pocket *o* vein

bondad [bon'dað] *nf* goodness, kindness; **tenga la ~ de** (please) be good enough to

bondadoso, -a [bonda'ðoso, a] *adj* good, kind

bongo ['bonɣo] *nm* large canoe

boniato [bo'njato] *nm* sweet potato, yam

bonificación [bonifika'θjon] *nf* (*Com*) allowance, discount; (*pago*) bonus; (*Deporte*) extra points *pl*

bonito, -a [bo'nito, a] *adj* (*lindo*) pretty; (*agradable*) nice ■ *adv* (*Am fam*) well ■ *nm* (*atún*) tuna (fish)

bono ['bono] *nm* voucher; (*Finanzas*) bond; **~ de billetes de metro** booklet of metro tickets; **~ del Tesoro** treasury bill

bonobús [bono'βus] *nm* (*Esp*) bus pass

Bono Loto, bonoloto [bono'loto] *nm o f* (*Esp*) state-run weekly lottery; *ver tb* **lotería**

boom (*pl* **booms**) [bum, bums] *nm* boom

boquear [boke'ar] *vi* to gasp

boquerón [boke'ron] *nm* (*pez*) (kind of) anchovy; (*agujero*) large hole

boquete [bo'kete] *nm* gap, hole

boquiabierto, -a [bokia'βjerto, a] *adj* open-mouthed (in astonishment); **quedar ~** to be left aghast

boquilla [bo'kiʎa] *nf* (*de riego*) nozzle; (*de cigarro*) cigarette holder; (*Mus*) mouthpiece

borbollar [borβo'ʎar], **borbollear** [borβoʎe'ar] *vi* to bubble

borbollón [borβo'ʎon] *nm* bubbling; **hablar a borbollones** to gabble; **salir a borbollones** (*agua*) to gush out

borbotar [borβo'tar] *vi* = **borbollar**

borbotón [borβo'ton] *nm*: **salir a borbotones** to gush out

borda ['borða] nf (Naut) gunwale; **echar** o **tirar algo por la ~** to throw sth overboard
bordado [bor'ðaðo] nm embroidery
bordar [bor'ðar] vt to embroider
borde ['borðe] nm edge, border; (de camino etc) side; (en la costura) hem; **al ~ de** (fig) on the verge o brink of; **ser ~** (Esp fam) to be a pain in the neck
bordear [borðe'ar] vt to border
bordillo [bor'ðiʎo] nm kerb (Brit), curb (US)
bordo ['borðo] nm (Naut) side; **a ~** on board
Borgoña [bor'ɣoɲa] nf Burgundy
borgoña [bor'ɣoɲa] nm burgundy
boricua [bo'rikwa], **borinqueño, -a** [borin'keɲo, a] adj, nm/f Puerto Rican
borla ['borla] nf (gen) tassel; (de gorro) pompon
borra ['borra] nf (pelusa) fluff; (sedimento) sediment
borrachera [borra'tʃera] nf (ebriedad) drunkenness; (orgía) spree, binge
borracho, -a [bo'rratʃo, a] adj drunk ■ nm/f (que bebe mucho) drunkard, drunk; (temporalmente) drunk, drunk man/woman ■ nm (Culin) cake soaked in liqueur or spirit
borrador [borra'ðor] nm (escritura) first draft, rough sketch; (cuaderno) scribbling pad; (goma) rubber (Brit), eraser; (Com) daybook; (para pizarra) duster; **hacer un nuevo ~ de** (Com) to redraft
borrar [bo'rrar] vt to erase, rub out; (tachar) to delete; (cinta) to wipe out; (Inform: archivo) to delete, erase; (Pol etc: eliminar) to deal with
borrasca [bo'rraska] nf (Meteorología) storm
borrascoso, -a [borras'koso, a] adj stormy
borrego, -a [bo'rreɣo, a] nm/f lamb; (oveja) sheep; (fig) simpleton
borricada [borri'kaða] nf foolish action/ statement
borrico, -a [bo'rriko, a] nm donkey; (fig) stupid man ■ nf she-donkey; (fig) stupid woman
borrón [bo'rron] nm (mancha) stain; **~ y cuenta nueva** let bygones be bygones
borroso, -a [bo'rroso, a] adj vague, unclear; (escritura) illegible; (escrito) smudgy; (Foto) blurred
Bósforo ['bosforo] nm: **el (Estrecho del) ~** the Bosp(h)orus
Bosnia ['bosnja] nf Bosnia
bosnio, -a ['bosnjo, a] adj, nm/f Bosnian
bosque ['boske] nm wood; (grande) forest
bosquejar [boske'xar] vt to sketch
bosquejo [bos'kexo] nm sketch
bosta ['bosta] nf dung, manure
bostece etc [bos'teθe] vb ver **bostezar**
bostezar [boste'θar] vi to yawn
bostezo [bos'teθo] nm yawn

bota ['bota] nf (calzado) boot; (de vino) leather wine bottle; **ponerse las botas** (fam) to strike it rich
botadura [bota'ðura] nf launching
botanas [bo'tanas] nfpl (Am) hors d'œuvres
botánico, -a [bo'taniko, a] adj botanical ■ nm/f botanist ■ nf botany
botar [bo'tar] vt to throw, hurl; (Naut) to launch; (esp Am fam) to throw out ■ vi to bounce
botarate [bota'rate] nm (imbécil) idiot
bote ['bote] nm (salto) bounce; (golpe) thrust; (vasija) tin, can; (embarcación) boat; **de ~ en ~** packed, jammed full; **~ salvavidas** lifeboat; **dar un ~** to jump; **dar botes** (Auto etc) to bump; **~ de la basura** (Am) dustbin (Brit), trash can (US)
botella [bo'teʎa] nf bottle; **~ de vino** (contenido) bottle of wine; (recipiente) wine bottle
botellero [bote'ʎero] nm wine rack
botellín [bote'ʎin] nm small bottle
botellón [bote'ʎon] nm (Esp: fam) outdoor drinking session (involving groups of young people)
botica [bo'tika] nf chemist's (shop) (Brit), pharmacy
boticario, -a [boti'karjo, a] nm/f chemist (Brit), pharmacist
botijo [bo'tixo] nm (earthenware) jug; (tren) excursion train
botín [bo'tin] nm (calzado) half boot; (polaina) spat; (Mil) booty; (de ladrón) loot
botiquín [boti'kin] nm (armario) medicine chest; (portátil) first-aid kit
botón [bo'ton] nm button; (Bot) bud; (de florete) tip; **~ de arranque** (Auto etc) starter; **~ de oro** buttercup; **pulsar el ~** to press the button
botones [bo'tones] nm inv bellboy, bellhop (US)
botulismo [botu'lismo] nm botulism, food poisoning
bóveda ['boβeða] nf (Arq) vault
bovino, -a [bo'βino, a] adj bovine; (Agr): **ganado ~** cattle
box [boks] nm (Am) boxing
boxeador [boksea'ðor] nm boxer
boxear [bokse'ar] vi to box
boxeo [bok'seo] nm boxing
boya ['boja] nf (Naut) buoy; (flotador) float
boyante [bo'jante] adj (Naut) buoyant; (feliz) buoyant; (próspero) prosperous
bozal [bo'θal] nm (de caballo) halter; (de perro) muzzle
bozo ['boθo] nm (pelusa) fuzz; (boca) mouth
bracear [braθe'ar] vi (agitar los brazos) to wave one's arms

bracero [bra'θero] *nm* labourer; (*en el campo*) farmhand

braga ['braɣa] *nf* (*cuerda*) sling, rope; (*de bebé*) nappy, diaper (*US*); **bragas** *nfpl* (*de mujer*) panties

braguero [bra'ɣero] *nm* (*Med*) truss

bragueta [bra'ɣeta] *nf* fly (*Brit*), flies *pl* (*Brit*), zipper (*US*)

braguetazo [braɣe'taθo] *nm* marriage of convenience

braille [breil] *nm* braille

bramante [bra'mante] *nm* twine, string

bramar [bra'mar] *vi* to bellow, roar

bramido [bra'miðo] *nm* bellow, roar

branquias ['brankjas] *nfpl* gills

brasa ['brasa] *nf* live o hot coal; **carne a la ~** grilled meat; **dar la ~** (*col: dar la lata, molestar*) to be a pain (*col*); **dar la ~ a algn** to go on at sb (*col*); **¡deja de darme la ~!** stop going on at me! (*col*)

brasero [bra'sero] *nm* brazier; (*Am: chimenea*) fireplace

Brasil [bra'sil] *nm:* (**el**) **~** Brazil

brasileño, -a [brasi'leɲo, a] *adj, nm/f* Brazilian

bravata [bra'βata] *nf* boast

braveza [bra'βeθa] *nf* (*valor*) bravery; (*ferocidad*) ferocity

bravío, -a [bra'βio, a] *adj* wild; (*feroz*) fierce

bravo, -a ['braβo, a] *adj* (*valiente*) brave; (*bueno*) fine, splendid; (*feroz*) ferocious; (*salvaje*) wild; (*mar etc*) rough, stormy; (*Culin*) hot, spicy ▪ *excl* bravo!

bravucón, -ona [braβu'kon, ona] *adj* swaggering ▪ *nm/f* braggart

bravura [bra'βura] *nf* bravery; ferocity; (*pey*) boast

braza ['braθa] *nf* fathom; **nadar a la ~** to swim (the) breast-stroke

brazada [bra'θaða] *nf* stroke

brazalete [braθa'lete] *nm* (*pulsera*) bracelet; (*banda*) armband

brazo ['braθo] *nm* arm; (*Zool*) foreleg; (*Bot*) limb, branch; **brazos** *nmpl* (*braceros*) hands, workers; **~ derecho** (*fig*) right-hand man; **a ~ partido** hand-to-hand; **cogidos etc del ~** arm in arm; **no dar su ~ a torcer** not to give way easily; **huelga de brazos caídos** sit-down strike

brea ['brea] *nf* pitch, tar

brebaje [bre'βaxe] *nm* potion

brecha ['bretʃa] *nf* breach; (*hoyo vacío*) gap, opening

brécol ['brekol] *nm* broccoli

brega ['breɣa] *nf* (*lucha*) struggle; (*trabajo*) hard work

bregar [bre'ɣar] *vi* (*luchar*) to struggle; (*trabajar mucho*) to slog away

bregue *etc* ['breɣe] *vb ver* **bregar**

breña ['breɲa] *nf* rough ground

Bretaña [bre'taɲa] *nf* Brittany

brete ['brete] *nm* (*cepo*) shackles *pl*; (*fig*) predicament; **estar en un ~** to be in a jam

breteles [bre'teles] *nmpl* (*Am*) straps

bretón, -ona [bre'ton, ona] *adj, nm/f* Breton

breva ['breβa] *nf* (*Bot*) early fig; (*puro*) flat cigar; **¡no caerá esa ~!** no such luck!

breve ['breβe] *adj* short, brief; **en ~** (*pronto*) shortly; (*en pocas palabras*) in short ▪ *nf* (*Mus*) breve

brevedad [breβe'ðað] *nf* brevity, shortness; **con o a la mayor ~** as soon as possible

breviario [bre'βjarjo] *nm* (*Rel*) breviary

brezal [bre'θal] *nm* moor(land), heath

brezo ['breθo] *nm* heather

bribón, -ona [bri'βon, ona] *adj* idle, lazy ▪ *nm/f* (*vagabundo*) vagabond; (*pícaro*) rascal, rogue

bricolaje [briko'laxe] *nm* do-it-yourself, DIY

brida ['briða] *nf* bridle, rein; (*Tec*) clamp; **a toda ~** at top speed

bridge [britʃ] *nm* (*Naipes*) bridge

brigada [bri'ɣaða] *nf* (*unidad*) brigade; (*trabajadores*) squad, gang ▪ *nm* warrant officer

brigadier [briɣa'ðjer] *nm* brigadier(-general)

brillante [bri'ʎante] *adj* brilliant; (*color*) bright; (*joya*) sparkling ▪ *nm* diamond

brillantez [briʎan'teθ] *nf* (*de color etc*) brightness; (*fig*) brilliance

brillar [bri'ʎar] *vi* (*tb fig*) to shine; (*joyas*) to sparkle; **~ por su ausencia** to be conspicuous by one's absence

brillo ['briʎo] *nm* shine; (*brillantez*) brilliance; (*fig*) splendour; **sacar ~ a** to polish

brilloso, -a [bri'ʎoso, a] *adj* (*Am*) = **brillante**

brincar [brin'kar] *vi* to skip about, hop about, jump about; **está que brinca** he's hopping mad

brinco ['brinko] *nm* jump, leap; **a brincos** by fits and starts; **de un ~** at one bound

brindar [brin'dar] *vi:* **~ a o por** to drink (a toast) to ▪ *vt* to offer, present; **le brinda la ocasión de** it offers o affords him the opportunity to; **brindarse** *vr:* **brindarse a hacer algo** to offer to do sth

brindis ['brindis] *nm inv* toast; (*Taur*) (ceremony of) dedication

brinque *etc* ['brinke] *vb ver* **brincar**

brío ['brio] *nm* spirit, dash

brioso, -a [bri'oso, a] *adj* spirited, dashing

brisa ['brisa] *nf* breeze

británico, -a [bri'taniko, a] *adj* British ▪ *nm/f* Briton, British person; **los británicos** the British

brizna ['briθna] *nf* (*hebra*) strand, thread; (*de hierba*) blade; (*trozo*) piece

broca ['broka] *nf* (*Costura*) bobbin; (*Tec*) drill bit; (*clavo*) tack

brocado [bro'kaðo] *nm* brocade

brocal [bro'kal] *nm* rim

brocha ['brotʃa] *nf* (large) paintbrush; **~ de afeitar** shaving brush; **pintor de ~ gorda** painter and decorator; (*fig*) poor painter

brochazo [bro'tʃaθo] *nm* brush-stroke; **a grandes brochazos** (*fig*) in general terms

broche ['brotʃe] *nm* brooch

broma ['broma] *nf* joke; (*inocentada*) practical joke; **en ~** in fun, as a joke; **gastar una ~ a algn** to play a joke on sb; **tomar algo a ~** to take sth as a joke

bromear [brome'ar] *vi* to joke

bromista [bro'mista] *adj* fond of joking ▪ *nm/f* joker, wag

bromuro [bro'muro] *nm* bromide

bronca ['bronka] *nf* row; (*regañada*) ticking-off; **armar una ~** to kick up a fuss; **echar una ~ a algn** to tell sb off

bronce ['bronθe] *nm* bronze; (*latón*) brass

bronceado, -a [bronθe'aðo, a] *adj* bronze *cpd*; (*por el sol*) tanned ▪ *nm* (sun)tan; (*Tec*) bronzing

bronceador [bronθea'ðor] *nm* suntan lotion

broncearse [bronθe'arse] *vr* to get a suntan

bronco, -a ['bronko, a] *adj* (*manera*) rude, surly; (*voz*) harsh

bronquios ['bronkjos] *nmpl* bronchial tubes

bronquitis [bron'kitis] *nf inv* bronchitis

brotar [bro'tar] *vt* (*tierra*) to produce ▪ *vi* (*Bot*) to sprout; (*aguas*) to gush (forth); (*lágrimas*) to well up; (*Med*) to break out

brote ['brote] *nm* (*Bot*) shoot; (*Med, fig*) outbreak

broza ['broθa] *nf* (*Bot*) dead leaves *pl*; (*fig*) rubbish

bruces ['bruθes]: **de ~** *adv*: **caer** *o* **dar de ~** to fall headlong, fall flat

bruja ['bruxa] *nf* witch

Brujas ['bruxas] *nf* Bruges

brujería [bruxe'ria] *nf* witchcraft

brujo ['bruxo] *nm* wizard, magician

brújula ['bruxula] *nf* compass

bruma ['bruma] *nf* mist

brumoso, -a [bru'moso, a] *adj* misty

bruñendo *etc* [bru'ɲendo] *vb ver* **bruñir**

bruñido [bru'ɲiðo] *nm* polish

bruñir [bru'ɲir] *vt* to polish

brusco, -a ['brusko, a] *adj* (*súbito*) sudden; (*áspero*) brusque

Bruselas [bru'selas] *nf* Brussels

brusquedad [bruske'ðað] *nf* suddenness; brusqueness

brutal [bru'tal] *adj* brutal

brutalidad [brutali'ðað] *nf* brutality

bruto, -a ['bruto, a] *adj* (*idiota*) stupid; (*bestial*) brutish; (*peso*) gross ▪ *nm* brute; **a la bruta, a lo ~** roughly; **en ~** raw, unworked

Bs. *abr* = **bolívares**

Bs.As. *abr* = **Buenos Aires**

bucal [bu'kal] *adj* oral; **por vía ~** orally

bucanero [buka'nero] *nm* buccaneer

bucear [buθe'ar] *vi* to dive ▪ *vt* to explore

buceo [bu'θeo] *nm* diving; (*fig*) investigation

buche ['butʃe] *nm* (*de ave*) crop; (*Zool*) maw; (*fam*) belly

bucle ['bukle] *nm* curl; (*Inform*) loop

budín [bu'ðin] *nm* pudding

budismo [bu'ðismo] *nm* Buddhism

budista [bu'ðista] *adj, nm/f* Buddhist

buen [bwen] *adj ver* **bueno**

buenamente [bwena'mente] *adv* (*fácilmente*) easily; (*voluntariamente*) willingly

buenaventura [bwenaβen'tura] *nf* (*suerte*) good luck; (*adivinación*) fortune; **decir** *o* **echar la ~ a algn** to tell sb's fortune

 PALABRA CLAVE

bueno, -a ['bweno, a] (*antes de nmsg* **buen**) *adj*
1 (*excelente etc*) good; (*Med*) well; **es un libro bueno, es un buen libro** it's a good book; **hace bueno, hace buen tiempo** the weather is fine, it is fine; **es buena persona** he's a good sort; **el bueno de Paco** good old Paco; **fue muy bueno conmigo** he was very nice *o* kind to me; **ya está bueno** he's fine now
2 (*apropiado*): **ser bueno para** to be good for; **creo que vamos por buen camino** I think we're on the right track
3 (*irónico*): **le di un buen rapapolvo** I gave him a good *o* real ticking off; **¡buen conductor estás hecho!** some driver *o* a fine driver you are!; **¡estaría bueno que ...!** a fine thing it would be if ...!
4 (*atractivo, sabroso*): **está bueno este bizcocho** this sponge is delicious; **Julio está muy bueno** (*fam*) Julio is a bit of alright
5 (*grande*) good, big; **un buen número de ...** a good number of ...; **un buen trozo de ...** a nice big piece of ...
6 (*saludos*): **¡buen día!** (*Am*), **¡buenos días!** (good) morning!; **¡buenas (tardes)!** good afternoon!; (*más tarde*) good evening!; **¡buenas noches!** good night!
7 (*otras locuciones*): **estar de buenas** to be in a good mood; **por las buenas o por las malas** by hook or by crook; **de buenas a primeras** all of a sudden

b

■ *excl*: ¡**bueno!** all right!; **bueno, ¿y qué?** well, so what?; **bueno, lo que pasa es que ...** well, the thing is ...; **pero ¡bueno!** well, I like that!; **bueno, pues ...** right, (then) ...

Buenos Aires [bweno'saires] *nm* Buenos Aires
buey [bwei] *nm* ox
búfalo ['bufalo] *nm* buffalo
bufanda [bu'fanda] *nf* scarf
bufar [bu'far] *vi* to snort
bufete [bu'fete] *nm* (*despacho de abogado*) lawyer's office; **establecer su ~** to set up in legal practice
buffer ['bufer] *nm* (*Inform*) buffer
bufón [bu'fon] *nm* clown
bufonada [bufo'naða] *nf* (*dicho*) jest; (*hecho*) piece of buffoonery; (*Teat*) farce
buhardilla [buar'ðiʎa] *nf* attic
búho ['buo] *nm* owl; (*fig*) hermit, recluse
buhonero [buo'nero] *nm* pedlar
buitre ['bwitre] *nm* vulture
bujía [bu'xia] *nf* (*vela*) candle; (*Elec*) candle (power); (*Auto*) spark plug
bula ['bula] *nf* (*papal*) bull
bulbo ['bulβo] *nm* (*Bot*) bulb
bulevar [bule'βar] *nm* boulevard
Bulgaria [bul'ɣarja] *nf* Bulgaria
búlgaro, -a ['bulɣaro, a] *adj, nm/f* Bulgarian
bulimia [bu'limja] *nf* bulimia
bulla ['buʎa] *nf* (*ruido*) uproar; (*de gente*) crowd; **armar** *o* **meter ~** to kick up a row
bullendo *etc* [bu'ʎendo] *vb ver* **bullir**
bullicio [bu'ʎiθjo] *nm* (*ruido*) uproar; (*movimiento*) bustle
bullicioso, -a [buʎi'θjoso, a] *adj* (*ruidoso*) noisy; (*calle*) busy; (*situación*) turbulent
bullir [bu'ʎir] *vi* (*hervir*) to boil; (*burbujear*) to bubble; (*moverse*) to move, stir; (*insectos*) to swarm; **~ de** (*fig*) to teem *o* seethe with
bulo ['bulo] *nm* false rumour
bulto ['bulto] *nm* (*paquete*) package; (*fardo*) bundle; (*tamaño*) size, bulkiness; (*Med*) swelling, lump; (*silueta*) vague shape; (*estatua*) bust, statue; **hacer ~** to take up space; **escurrir el ~** to make o.s. scarce; (*fig*) to dodge the issue
buñuelo [bu'ɲwelo] *nm* ≈ doughnut, ≈ donut (*US*)
buque ['buke] *nm* ship, vessel; **~ de guerra** warship; **~ mercante** merchant ship; **~ de vela** sailing ship
burbuja [bur'βuxa] *nf* bubble; **hacer burbujas** to bubble; (*gaseosa*) to fizz
burbujear [burβuxe'ar] *vi* to bubble
burdel [bur'ðel] *nm* brothel

Burdeos [bur'ðeos] *nm* Bordeaux
burdo, -a ['burðo, a] *adj* coarse, rough
burgalés, -esa [burɣa'les, esa] *adj* of *o* from Burgos ■ *nm/f* native *o* inhabitant of Burgos
burgués, -esa [bur'ɣes, esa] *adj* middle-class, bourgeois; **pequeño ~** lower middle-class; (*Pol, pey*) petty bourgeois
burguesía [burɣe'sia] *nf* middle class, bourgeoisie
burla ['burla] *nf* (*mofa*) gibe; (*broma*) joke; (*engaño*) trick; **hacer ~ de** to make fun of
burladero [burla'ðero] *nm* (bullfighter's) refuge
burlador, a [burla'ðor, a] *adj* mocking ■ *nm/f* mocker; (*bromista*) joker ■ *nm* (*libertino*) seducer
burlar [bur'lar] *vt* (*engañar*) to deceive; (*seducir*) to seduce ■ *vi*, **burlarse** *vr* to joke; **burlarse de** to make fun of
burlesco, -a [bur'lesko, a] *adj* burlesque
burlón, -ona [bur'lon, ona] *adj* mocking
buró [bu'ro] *nm* bureau
burocracia [buro'kraθja] *nf* bureaucracy
burócrata [bu'rokrata] *nm/f* bureaucrat
buromática [buro'matika] *nf* office automation
burrada [bu'rraða] *nf* stupid act; **decir burradas** to talk nonsense
burro, -a ['burro, a] *nm/f* (*Zool*) donkey; (*fig*) ass, idiot ■ *adj* stupid; **caerse del ~** to realise one's mistake; **no ver tres en un ~** to be as blind as a bat
bursátil [bur'satil] *adj* stock-exchange *cpd*
bus [bus] *nm* bus
busca ['buska] *nf* search, hunt ■ *nm* bleeper, pager; **en ~ de** in search of
buscador, a [buska'ðor, a] *nm/f* searcher ■ *nm* (*Internet*) search engine
buscapiés [buska'pjes] *nm inv* jumping jack (*Brit*), firecracker (*US*)
buscapleitos [buska'pleitos] *nm/f inv* troublemaker
buscar [bus'kar] *vt* to look for; (*objeto perdido*) to have a look for; (*beneficio*) to seek; (*enemigo*) to seek out; (*traer*) to bring, fetch; (*provocar*) to provoke; (*Inform*) to search ■ *vi* to look, search, seek; **ven a buscarme a la oficina** come and pick me up at the office; **buscarle 3 *o* 4 pies al gato** to split hairs; **"~ y reemplazar"** (*Inform*) "search and replace"; **se busca secretaria** secretary wanted; **se la buscó** he asked for it
buscavidas [buska'βiðas] *nm/f inv* snooper; (*persona ambiciosa*) go-getter
buscona [bus'kona] *nf* whore
busilis [bu'silis] *nm inv* (*fam*) snag
busque *etc* ['buske] *vb ver* **buscar**

búsqueda ['buskeða] *nf* = **busca**

busto ['busto] *nm* (*Anat:Arte*) bust

butaca [bu'taka] *nf* armchair; (*de cine, teatro*) stall, seat

butano [bu'tano] *nm* butane (gas); **bombona de ~** gas cylinder

butifarra [buti'farra] *nf* Catalan sausage

buzo ['buθo] *nm* diver; (*Am: chandal*) tracksuit

buzón [bu'θon] *nm* (*gen*) letter box; (*en la calle*) pillar box (*Brit*); (*Telec*) mailbox; **echar al ~** to post

buzonear [buθone'ar] *vt* to leaflet

byte [bait] *nm* (*Inform*) byte

Cc

C, c [θe] [se] (*esp Am*) *nf* (*letra*) C, c; **C de Carmen** C for Charlie

C. *abr* (= *centígrado*) C.; (= *compañía*) Co

c. *abr* (= *capítulo*) ch

C/ *abr* (= *calle*) St, Rd

c/ *abr* (*Com*: = *cuenta*) a/c

ca [ka] *excl* not a bit of it!

c.a. *abr* (= *corriente alterna*) A.C.

cabal [ka'βal] *adj* (*exacto*) exact; (*correcto*) right, proper; (*acabado*) finished, complete; **cabales** *nmpl*: **estar en sus cabales** to be in one's right mind

cábala ['kaβala] *nf* (*Rel*) cab(b)ala; (*fig*) cabal, intrigue; **cábalas** *nfpl* guess *sg*, supposition *sg*

cabalgadura [kaβalɣa'ðura] *nf* mount, horse

cabalgar [kaβal'ɣar] *vt, vi* to ride

cabalgata [kaβal'ɣata] *nf* procession; *ver tb* **Reyes Magos**

cabalgue *etc* [ka'βalɣe] *vb ver* **cabalgar**

cabalístico, -a [kaβa'listiko, a] *adj* (*fig*) mysterious

caballa [ka'βaʎa] *nf* mackerel

caballeresco, -a [kaβaʎe'resko, a] *adj* noble, chivalrous

caballería [kaβaʎe'ria] *nf* mount; (*Mil*) cavalry

caballeriza [kaβaʎe'riθa] *nf* stable

caballerizo [kaβaʎe'riθo] *nm* groom, stableman

caballero [kaβa'ʎero] *nm* gentleman; (*de la orden de caballería*) knight; (*trato directo*) sir; **"Caballeros"** "Gents"

caballerosidad [kaβaʎerosi'ðað] *nf* chivalry

caballete [kaβa'ʎete] *nm* (*Agr*) ridge; (*Arte*) easel

caballito [kaβa'ʎito] *nm* (*caballo pequeño*) small horse, pony; (*juguete*) rocking horse; **caballitos** *nmpl* merry-go-round *sg*; ~ **de mar** seahorse; ~ **del diablo** dragonfly

caballo [ka'βaʎo] *nm* horse; (*Ajedrez*) knight; (*Naipes*) ≈ queen; ~ **de vapor** *o* **de fuerza** horsepower; **es su** ~ **de batalla** it's his hobby-horse; ~ **blanco** (*Com*) backer; *ver tb* **Baraja Española**

cabaña [ka'βaɲa] *nf* (*casita*) hut, cabin

cabaré, cabaret (*pl* **cabarets**) [kaβa're, kaβa'res] *nm* cabaret

cabecear [kaβeθe'ar] *vi* to nod

cabecera [kaβe'θera] *nf* (*gen*) head; (*de distrito*) chief town; (*de cama*) headboard; (*Imprenta*) headline

cabecilla [kaβe'θiʎa] *nm* ringleader

cabellera [kaβe'ʎera] *nf* (head of) hair; (*de cometa*) tail

cabello [ka'βeʎo] *nm* (*tb*: **cabellos**) hair *sg*

cabelludo [kaβe'ʎuðo] *adj ver* **cuero**

caber [ka'βer] *vi* (*entrar*) to fit, go; **caben tres más** there's room for three more; **cabe preguntar si...** one might ask whether...; **cabe que venga más tarde** he may come later

cabestrillo [kaβes'triʎo] *nm* sling

cabestro [ka'βestro] *nm* halter

cabeza [ka'βeθa] *nf* head; (*Pol*) chief, leader ▪ *nm/f*: ~ **rapada** skinhead; **caer de** ~ to fall head first; **sentar la** ~ to settle down; ~ **de lectura/escritura** read/write head; ~ **impresora** *o* **de impresión** printhead

cabezada [kaβe'θaða] *nf* (*golpe*) butt; **dar una** ~ to nod off

cabezal [kaβe'θal] *nm*: ~ **impresor** print head

cabezazo [kaβe'θaθo] *nm* (*golpe*) headbutt; (*Fútbol*) header

cabezón, -ona [kaβe'θon, ona] *adj* with a big head; (*vino*) heady; (*obstinado*) obstinate, stubborn

cabezota [kaβe'θota] *adj inv* obstinate, stubborn

cabezudo, -a [kaβe'θuðo, a] *adj* with a big head; (*obstinado*) obstinate, stubborn

cabida [ka'βiða] *nf* space; **dar** ~ **a** to make room for; **tener** ~ **para** to have room for

cabildo [ka'βildo] *nm* (*de iglesia*) chapter; (*Pol*) town council

cabina [ka'βina] *nf* (*de camión*) cabin; ~ **telefónica** (tele)phone box (*Brit*) o booth

cabizbajo, -a [kaβiθ'βaxo, a] *adj* crestfallen

cable ['kaβle] *nm* cable; (*de aparato*) lead; ~ **aéreo** (*Elec*) overhead cable; **conectar con** ~ (*Inform*) to hardwire

cabo ['kaβo] *nm* (*de objeto*) end, extremity; (*Mil*) corporal; (*Naut*) rope, cable; (*Geo*) cape; (*Tec*) thread; **al** ~ **de tres días** after three days; **de** ~ **a rabo** o ~ from beginning to end; (*libro: leer*) from cover to cover; **llevar a** ~ to carry out; **atar cabos** to tie up the loose ends; **C~ de Buena Esperanza** Cape of Good Hope; **C~ de Hornos** Cape Horn; **las Islas de C~ Verde** the Cape Verde Islands

cabra ['kaβra] *nf* goat; **estar como una** ~ (*fam*) to be nuts

cabré *etc* [ka'βre] *vb ver* **caber**

cabrear [kaβre'ar] *vt* to annoy; **cabrearse** *vr* to fly off the handle

cabrío, -a [ka'βrio, a] *adj* goatish; **macho** ~ (he-)goat, billy goat

cabriola [ka'βrjola] *nf* caper

cabritilla [kaβri'tiʎa] *nf* kid, kidskin

cabrito [ka'βrito] *nm* kid

cabrón [ka'βron] *nm* (*fig: fam!*) bastard (!)

cabronada [kaβro'naða] *nf* (*fam!*): **hacer una** ~ **a algn** to be a bastard to sb

caca ['kaka] *nf* (*palabra de niños*) pooh ■ *excl*: **no toques, ¡~!** don't touch, it's dirty!

cacahuete [kaka'wete] *nm* (*Esp*) peanut

cacao [ka'kao] *nm* cocoa; (*Bot*) cacao

cacarear [kakare'ar] *vi* (*persona*) to boast; (*gallina*) to cackle

cacatúa [kaka'tua] *nf* cockatoo

cacereño, -a [kaθe'reɲo, a] *adj* of o from Cáceres ■ *nm/f* native o inhabitant of Cáceres

cacería [kaθe'ria] *nf* hunt

cacerola [kaθe'rola] *nf* pan, saucepan

cacha ['katʃa] *nf* (*mango*) handle; (*nalga*) buttock

cachalote [katʃa'lote] *nm* sperm whale

cacharro [ka'tʃarro] *nm* (*cazo*) pot; (*cerámica*) piece of pottery; (*fam*) useless object; **cacharros** *nmpl* pots and pans

cachear [katʃe'ar] *vt* to search, frisk

cachemir [katʃe'mir] *nm* cashmere

cacheo [ka'tʃeo] *nm* searching, frisking

cachete [ka'tʃete] *nm* (*Anat*) cheek; (*bofetada*) slap (in the face)

cachimba [ka'tʃimba] *nf*, **cachimbo** [ka'tʃimbo] *nm* (*Am*) pipe

cachiporra [katʃi'porra] *nf* truncheon

cachivache [katʃi'βatʃe] *nm* piece of junk; **cachivaches** *nmpl* trash *sg*, junk *sg*

cacho ['katʃo] *nm* (small) bit; (*Am: cuerno*)

horn

cachondearse [katʃonde'arse] *vr*: ~ **de algn** to tease sb

cachondeo [katʃon'deo] *nm* (*fam*) farce, joke; (*guasa*) laugh

cachondo, -a [ka'tʃondo, a] *adj* (*Zool*) on heat; (*caliente*) randy, sexy; (*gracioso*) funny

cachorro, -a [ka'tʃorro, a] *nm/f* (*de perro*) pup, puppy; (*de león*) cub

cachucha [ka'tʃutʃa] (*Méx fam*) *nf* cap

cacique [ka'θike] *nm* chief, local ruler; (*Pol*) local party boss; (*fig*) despot

caco ['kako] *nm* pickpocket

cacofonía [kakofo'nia] *nf* cacophony

cacto ['kakto] *nm*, **cactus** ['kaktus] *nm inv* cactus

cada ['kaða] *adj inv* each; (*antes de número*) every; ~ **día** each day, every day; ~ **dos días** every other day; ~ **uno/a** each one, every one; ~ **vez más/menos** more and more/less and less; **uno de** ~ **diez** one out of every ten; **¿~ cuánto?** how often?

cadalso [ka'ðalso] *nm* scaffold

cadáver [ka'ðaβer] *nm* (dead) body, corpse

cadavérico, -a [kaða'βeriko, a] *adj* cadaverous; (*pálido*) deathly pale

cadena [ka'ðena] *nf* chain; (*TV*) channel; **reacción en** ~ chain reaction; **trabajo en** ~ assembly line work; ~ **midi/mini** (*Mus*) midi/mini system; ~ **perpetua** (*Jur*) life imprisonment; ~ **de caracteres** (*Inform*) character string

cadencia [ka'ðenθja] *nf* cadence, rhythm

cadera [ka'ðera] *nf* hip

cadete [ka'ðete] *nm* cadet

Cádiz ['kaðiθ] *nm* Cadiz

caducar [kaðu'kar] *vi* to expire

caducidad [kaðuθi'ðað] *nf*: **fecha de** ~ expiry date; (*de comida*) sell-by date

caduco, -a [ka'ðuko, a] *adj* (*idea etc*) outdated, outmoded; **de hoja caduca** deciduous

caduque *etc* [ka'ðuke] *vb ver* **caducar**

caer [ka'er] *vi* to fall; (*premio*) to go; (*sitio*) to be, lie; (*pago*) to fall due; **caerse** *vr* to fall (down); **dejar** ~ to drop; **estar al** ~ to be due to happen; (*persona*) to be about to arrive; **me cae bien/mal** I like/don't like him; ~ **en la cuenta** to catch on; **su cumpleaños cae en viernes** her birthday falls on a Friday; **se me ha caído el guante** I've dropped my glove

café (*pl* ~**s**) [ka'fe, ka'fes] *nm* (*bebida, planta*) coffee; (*lugar*) café ■ *adj* (*color*) brown; **café con leche** white coffee; **café solo**, **café negro** (*Am*) (small) black coffee

cafeína [kafe'ina] *nf* caffein(e)

cafetal [kafe'tal] *nm* coffee plantation

cafetera [kafe'tera] *nf ver* **cafetero**

cafetería [kafete'ria] *nf* cafe

cafetero, -a [kafe'tero, a] *adj* coffee *cpd* ■ *nf* coffee pot; **ser muy ~** to be a coffee addict

cagalera [kaɣa'lera] *nf* (*fam!*): **tener ~** to have the runs

cagar [ka'ɣar] (*fam!*) *vt* to shit (*!*); (*fig*) to bungle, mess up ■ *vi* to have a shit (*!*); **cagarse** *vr*: ¡me cago en diez *etc*! Christ! (*!*)

cague *etc* ['kaɣe] *vb ver* **cagar**

caído, -a [ka'iðo, a] *adj* fallen; (*Inform*) down ■ *nf* fall; (*declive*) slope; (*disminución*) fall, drop; **~ del cielo** out of the blue; **a la caída del sol** at sunset; **sufrir una caída** to have a fall

caiga *etc* ['kaiɣa] *vb ver* **caer**

caimán [kai'man] *nm* alligator

Cairo ['kairo] *nm*: **el ~** Cairo

caja ['kaxa] *nf* box; (*ataúd*) coffin, casket (*US*); (*para reloj*) case; (*de ascensor*) shaft; (*Com*) cash box; (*Econ*) fund; (*donde se hacen los pagos*) cashdesk; (*en supermercado*) checkout, till; (*Tip*) case; (*de parking*) pay station; **~ de ahorros** savings bank; **~ de cambios** gearbox; **~ fuerte, ~ de caudales** safe, strongbox; **ingresar en ~** to be paid in

cajero, -a [ka'xero, a] *nm/f* cashier; (*en banco*) teller ■ *nm*: **~ automático** cash dispenser, automatic telling machine, ATM

cajetilla [kaxe'tiʎa] *nf* (*de cigarrillos*) packet

cajista [ka'xista] *nm/f* typesetter

cajón [ka'xon] *nm* big box; (*de mueble*) drawer

cajuela [kax'wela] (*Méx*) *nf* (*Auto*) boot (*Brit*), trunk (*US*)

cal [kal] *nf* lime; **cerrar algo a ~ y canto** to shut sth firmly

cal. *abr* (= *caloría(s)*) cal. (= *calorie(s)*)

cala ['kala] *nf* (*Geo*) cove, inlet; (*de barco*) hold

calabacín [kalaβa'θin] *nm* (*Bot*) baby marrow, courgette, zucchini (*US*)

calabaza [kala'βaθa] *nf* (*Bot*) pumpkin; **dar calabazas a** (*candidato*) to fail

calabozo [kala'βoθo] *nm* (*cárcel*) prison; (*celda*) cell

calado, -a [ka'laðo, a] *adj* (*prenda*) lace *cpd* ■ *nm* (*Tec*) fretwork; (*Naut*) draught ■ *nf* (*de cigarrillo*) puff; **estar ~ (hasta los huesos)** to be soaked (to the skin)

calamar [kala'mar] *nm* squid

calambre [ka'lambre] *nm* (*tb*: **calambres**) cramp

calamidad [kalami'ðað] *nf* calamity, disaster; (*persona*): **es una ~** he's a dead loss

calamina [kala'mina] *nf* calamine

cálamo ['kalamo] *nm* (*Bot*) stem; (*Mus*) reed

calaña [ka'laɲa] *nf* model, pattern; (*fig*) nature, stamp

calar [ka'lar] *vt* to soak, drench; (*penetrar*) to pierce, penetrate; (*comprender*) to see through; (*vela, red*) to lower; **calarse** *vr* (*Auto*) to stall; **calarse las gafas** to stick one's glasses on

calavera [kala'βera] *nf* skull

calcañal [kalka'ɲal], **calcañar** [kalka'ɲar] *nm* heel

calcar [kal'kar] *vt* (*reproducir*) to trace; (*imitar*) to copy

calce *etc* ['kalθe] *vb ver* **calzar**

cal. cen. *abr* = **calefacción central**

calceta [kal'θeta] *nf* (knee-length) stocking; **hacer ~** to knit

calcetín [kalθe'tin] *nm* sock

calcinar [kalθi'nar] *vt* to burn, blacken

calcio ['kalθjo] *nm* calcium

calco ['kalko] *nm* tracing

calcomanía [kalkoma'nia] *nf* transfer

calculador, a [kalkula'ðor, a] *adj* calculating ■ *nf* calculator

calcular [kalku'lar] *vt* (*Mat*) to calculate, compute; **~ que ...** to reckon that ...

cálculo ['kalkulo] *nm* calculation; (*Med*) (gall)stone; (*Mat*) calculus; **~ de costo** costing; **~ diferencial** differential calculus; **obrar con mucho ~** to act cautiously

caldear [kalde'ar] *vt* to warm (up), heat (up); (*metales*) to weld

caldera [kal'dera] *nf* boiler

calderero [kalde'rero] *nm* boilermaker

calderilla [kalde'riʎa] *nf* small change

caldero [kal'dero] *nm* small boiler

caldo ['kaldo] *nm* stock; (*consomé*) consommé; **~ de cultivo** (*Bio*) culture medium; **poner a ~ a** algn to tear sb off a strip; **los caldos jerezanos** sherries

caldoso, -a [kal'doso, a] *adj* (*guisado*) juicy; (*sopa*) thin

calé [ka'le] *adj* gipsy *cpd*

calefacción [kalefak'θjon] *nf* heating; **~ central** central heating

caleidoscopio [kaleiðos'kopjo] *nm* kaleidoscope

calendario [kalen'darjo] *nm* calendar

calentador [kalenta'ðor] *nm* heater

calentamiento [kalenta'mjento] *nm* (*Deporte*) warm-up

calentar [kalen'tar] *vt* to heat (up); (*fam: excitar*) to turn on; (*Am: enfurecer*) to anger; **calentarse** *vr* to heat up, warm up; (*fig: discusión etc*) to get heated

calentón, -ona [kalen'ton, ona] (*RPl fam*) *adj* (*sexualmente*) horny, randy (*Brit*)

calentura [kalen'tura] *nf* (*Med*) fever, (high) temperature; (*de boca*) mouth sore

calenturiento, -a [kalentu'rjento, a] *adj* (*mente*) overactive

calibrar [kali'βrar] vt to gauge, measure
calibre [ka'liβre] nm (de cañón) calibre, bore; (diámetro) diameter; (fig) calibre
calidad [kali'ðað] nf quality; **de ~** quality cpd; **~ de borrador** (Inform) draft quality; **~ de carta** o **de correspondencia** (Inform) letter quality; **~ texto** (Inform) text quality; **~ de vida** quality of life; **en ~ de** in the capacity of
cálido, -a ['kaliðo, a] adj hot; (fig) warm
caliente etc [ka'ljente] vb ver **calentar** ■ adj hot; (fig) fiery; (disputa) heated; (fam: cachondo) randy
califa [ka'lifa] nm caliph
calificación [kalifika'θjon] nf qualification; (de alumno) grade, mark; **~ de sobresaliente** first-class mark
calificar [kalifi'kar] vt to qualify; (alumno) to grade, mark; **~ de** to describe as
calificativo, -a [kalifika'tiβo, a] adj qualifying ■ nm qualifier, epithet
califique etc [kali'fike] vb ver **calificar**
californiano, -a [kalifor'njano, a] adj, nm/f Californian
caligrafía [kaliɣra'fia] nf calligraphy
calima [ka'lima] nf mist
calina [ka'lina] nf haze
cáliz ['kaliθ] nm (Bot) calyx; (Rel) chalice
caliza [ka'liθa] nf limestone
callado, -a [ka'ʎaðo, a] adj quiet, silent
callar [ka'ʎar] vt (asunto delicado) to keep quiet about, say nothing about; (omitir) to pass over in silence; (persona, oposición) to silence ■ vi, **callarse** vr to keep quiet, be silent; (dejar de hablar) to stop talking; **¡calla!** be quiet!; **¡cállate!, ¡cállese!** shut up!; **¡cállate la boca!** shut your mouth!
calle ['kaʎe] nf street; (Deporte) lane; **~ arriba/abajo** up/down the street; **~ de sentido único** one-way street; **poner a algn (de patitas) en la ~** to kick sb out
calleja [ka'ʎexa] nf alley, narrow street
callejear [kaʎexe'ar] vi to wander (about) the streets
callejero, -a [kaʎe'xero, a] adj street cpd ■ nm street map
callejón [kaʎe'xon] nm alley, passage; (Geo) narrow pass; **~ sin salida** cul-de-sac; (fig) blind alley
callejuela [kaʎe'xwela] nf side-street, alley
callista [ka'ʎista] nm/f chiropodist
callo ['kaʎo] nm callus; (en el pie) corn; **callos** nmpl (Culin) tripe sg
callosidad [kaʎosi'ðað] nf (de pie) corn; (de mano) callus
calloso, -a [ka'ʎoso, a] adj horny, rough
calma ['kalma] nf calm; (pachorra) slowness; (Com: Econ) calm, lull; **~ chicha** dead calm;

¡~!, ¡con ~! take it easy!
calmante [kal'mante] adj soothing ■ nm sedative, tranquillizer
calmar [kal'mar] vt to calm, calm down; (dolor) to relieve ■ vi, **calmarse** vr (tempestad) to abate; (mente etc) to become calm
calmoso, -a [kal'moso, a] adj calm, quiet
caló [ka'lo] nm (de gitanos) gipsy language, Romany; (argot) slang
calor [ka'lor] nm heat; (calor agradable) warmth; **entrar en ~** to get warm; **tener ~** to be o feel hot
caloría [kalo'ria] nf calorie
calorífero, -a [kalo'rifero, a] adj heat-producing, heat-giving ■ nm heating system
calque etc ['kalke] vb ver **calcar**
calumnia [ka'lumnja] nf slander; (por escrito) libel
calumniar [kalum'njar] vt to slander; to libel
calumnioso, -a [kalum'njoso, a] adj slanderous; libellous
caluroso, -a [kalu'roso, a] adj hot; (sin exceso) warm; (fig) enthusiastic
calva ['kalβa] nf bald patch; (en bosque) clearing
calvario [kal'βarjo] nm stations pl of the cross; (fig) cross, heavy burden
calvicie [kal'βiθje] nf baldness
calvo, -a ['kalβo, a] adj bald; (terreno) bare, barren; (tejido) threadbare ■ nm bald man
calza ['kalθa] nf wedge, chock
calzado, -a [kal'θaðo, a] adj shod ■ nm footwear ■ nf roadway, highway
calzador [kalθa'ðor] nm shoehorn
calzar [kal'θar] vt (zapatos etc) to wear; (un mueble) to put a wedge under; (Tec: rueda etc) to scotch; **calzarse** vr: **calzarse los zapatos** to put on one's shoes; **¿qué (número) calza?** what size do you take?
calzón [kal'θon] nm (tb: **calzones**) shorts pl; (Am: de hombre) pants pl; (: de mujer) panties pl
calzoncillos [kalθon'θiʎos] nmpl underpants
cama ['kama] nf bed; (Geo) stratum; **~ individual/de matrimonio** single/double bed; **guardar ~** to be ill in bed
camada [ka'maða] nf litter; (de personas) gang, band
camafeo [kama'feo] nm cameo
camaleón [kamale'on] nm chameleon
cámara ['kamara] nf (Pol etc) chamber; (habitación) room; (sala) hall; (Cine) cine camera; (fotográfica) camera; **~ de aire** inner tube; **~ alta/baja** upper/lower house; **~ de comercio** chamber of commerce; **~ digital** digital camera; **~ de gas** gas chamber; **~ de video** video camera; **a ~ lenta** in slow motion

camarada [kama'raða] *nm* comrade, companion

camaradería [kamaraðe'ria] *nf* comradeship

camarero, -a [kama'rero, a] *nm* waiter ■ *nf* (*en restaurante*) waitress; (*en casa, hotel*) maid

camarilla [kama'riʎa] *nf* (*clan*) clique; (*Pol*) lobby

camarín [kama'rin] *nm* (*Teat*) dressing room

camarón [kama'ron] *nm* shrimp

camarote [kama'rote] *nm* (*Naut*) cabin

cambiable [kam'bjaβle] *adj* (*variable*) changeable, variable; (*intercambiable*) interchangeable

cambiante [kam'bjante] *adj* variable

cambiar [kam'bjar] *vt* to change; (*trocar*) to exchange ■ *vi* to change; **cambiarse** *vr* (*mudarse*) to move; (*de ropa*) to change; ~**(se) de ...** to change one's ...; ~ **de idea/de ropa** to change one's mind/clothes

cambiazo [kam'bjaθo] *nm*: **dar el ~ a algn** to swindle sb

cambio ['kambjo] *nm* change; (*trueque*) exchange; (*Com*) rate of exchange; (*oficina*) bureau de change; (*dinero menudo*) small change; **en ~** on the other hand; (*en lugar de eso*) instead; ~ **de divisas** (*Com*) foreign exchange; ~ **de línea** (*Inform*) line feed; ~ **de página** (*Inform*) form feed; ~ **a término** (*Com*) forward exchange; ~ **de velocidades** gear lever; ~ **de vía** points *pl*

cambista [kam'bista] *nm* (*Com*) exchange broker

Camboya [kam'boja] *nf* Cambodia, Kampuchea

camboyano, -a [kambo'jano, a] *adj, nm/f* Cambodian, Kampuchean

camelar [kame'lar] *vt* (*con mujer*) to flirt with; (*persuadir*) to cajole

camelia [ka'melia] *nf* camellia

camello [ka'meʎo] *nm* camel; (*fam: traficante*) pusher

camelo [ka'melo] *nm*: **me huele a ~** it smells fishy

camerino [kame'rino] *nm* (*Teat*) dressing room

camilla [ka'miʎa] *nf* (*Med*) stretcher

caminante [kami'nante] *nm/f* traveller

caminar [kami'nar] *vi* (*marchar*) to walk, go; (*viajar*) to travel, journey ■ *vt* (*recorrer*) to cover, travel

caminata [kami'nata] *nf* long walk

camino [ka'mino] *nm* way, road; (*sendero*) track; **a medio ~** halfway (there); **en el ~** on the way, en route; ~ **de** on the way to; ~ **particular** private road; ~ **vecinal** country road; **Caminos, Canales y Puertos** (*Univ*) Civil Engineering; **ir por buen ~** (*fig*) to be on the right track; **C~ de Santiago** *see note*

● **CAMINO DE SANTIAGO**

The *Camino de Santiago* is a medieval pilgrim route stretching from the Pyrenees to Santiago de Compostela in north-west Spain, where tradition has it the body of the Apostle James is buried. Nowadays it is a popular tourist route as well as a religious one. The *concha* (cockleshell) is a symbol of the *Camino de Santiago*, because it is said that when St James' body was found it was covered in shells.

camión [ka'mjon] *nm* lorry, truck (*US*); (*Am: autobús*) bus; ~ **de bomberos** fire engine

camionero [kamjo'nero] *nm* lorry o truck (*US*) driver, trucker (*esp US*)

camioneta [kamjo'neta] *nf* van, transit®

camionista [kamjo'nista] *nmf* lorry o truck driver

camisa [ka'misa] *nf* shirt; (*Bot*) skin; ~ **de dormir** nightdress; ~ **de fuerza** straitjacket

camisería [kamise'ria] *nf* outfitter's (shop)

camiseta [kami'seta] *nf* tee-shirt; (*ropa interior*) vest; (*de deportista*) top

camisón [kami'son] *nm* nightdress, nightgown

camomila [kamo'mila] *nf* camomile

camorra [ka'morra] *nf*: **armar ~** to kick up a row; **buscar ~** to look for trouble

camorrista [kamo'rrista] *nm/f* thug

camote [ka'mote] *nm* (*Am*) sweet potato

campal [kam'pal] *adj*: **batalla ~** pitched battle

campamento [kampa'mento] *nm* camp

campana [kam'pana] *nf* bell

campanada [kampa'naða] *nf* peal

campanario [kampa'narjo] *nm* belfry

campanilla [kampa'niʎa] *nf* small bell

campante [kam'pante] *adj*: **siguió tan ~** he went on as if nothing had happened

campaña [kam'paɲa] *nf* (*Mil: Pol*) campaign; **hacer ~ (en pro de/contra)** to campaign (for/against); ~ **de venta** sales campaign

campechano, -a [kampe'tʃano, a] *adj* open

campeón, -ona [kampe'on, ona] *nm/f* champion

campeonato [kampeo'nato] *nm* championship

campesino, -a [kampe'sino, a] *adj* country *cpd*, rural; (*gente*) peasant *cpd* ■ *nm/f* countryman/woman; (*agricultor*) farmer

campestre [kam'pestre] *adj* country *cpd*, rural

camping ['kampin] *nm* camping; (*lugar*) campsite; **ir de** o **hacer ~** to go camping

campiña [kam'piɲa] *nf* countryside

campista [kam'pista] nm/f camper

campo ['kampo] nm (fuera de la ciudad) country, countryside; (Agr: Elec: Inform) field; (de fútbol) pitch; (de golf) course; (Mil) camp; ~ de batalla battlefield; ~ de minas minefield; ~ petrolífero oilfield; ~ visual field of vision; ~ de concentración/de internación/de trabajo concentration/internment/labour camp

camposanto [kampo'santo] nm cemetery

campus ['kampus] nm inv (Univ) campus

camuflaje [kamu'flaxe] nm camouflage

camuflar [kamu'flar] vt to camouflage

can [kan] nm dog, mutt (fam)

cana ['kana] nf ver cano

Canadá [kana'ða] nm Canada

canadiense [kana'ðjense] adj, nm/f Canadian ■ nf fur-lined jacket

canal [ka'nal] nm canal; (Geo) channel, strait; (de televisión) channel; (de tejado) gutter; **C~ de la Mancha** English Channel; **C~ de Panamá** Panama Canal

canalice etc [kana'liθe] vb ver canalizar

canalizar [kanali'θar] vt to channel

canalla [ka'naʎa] nf rabble, mob ■ nm swine

canallada [kana'ʎaða] nf (hecho) dirty trick

canalón [kana'lon] nm (conducto vertical) drainpipe; (del tejado) gutter; **canalones** nmpl (Culin) cannelloni

canapé (pl ~s) [kana'pe, kana'pes] nm sofa, settee; (Culin) canapé

Canarias [ka'narjas] nfpl: **las (Islas) ~** the Canaries, the Canary Isles

canario, -a [ka'narjo, a] adj of o from the Canary Isles ■ nm/f native o inhabitant of the Canary Isles ■ nm (Zool) canary

canasta [ka'nasta] nf (round) basket

canastilla [kanas'tiʎa] nf small basket; (de niño) layette

canasto [ka'nasto] nm large basket

cancela [kan'θela] nf (wrought-iron) gate

cancelación [kanθela'θjon] nf cancellation

cancelar [kanθe'lar] vt to cancel; (una deuda) to write off

cáncer ['kanθer] nm (Med) cancer; **C~** (Astro) Cancer

cancerígeno, -a [kanθe'rixeno, a] adj carcinogenic

cancha ['kantʃa] nf (de baloncesto, tenis etc) court; (Am: de fútbol etc) pitch

canciller [kanθi'ʎer] nm chancellor; **C~** (Am) Foreign Minister, ≈ Foreign Secretary (Brit)

Cancillería [kansiʎe'ria] nf (Am) Foreign Ministry, ≈ Foreign Office (Brit)

canción [kan'θjon] nf song; **~ de cuna** lullaby

cancionero [kanθjo'nero] nm song book

candado [kan'daðo] nm padlock

candela [kan'dela] nf candle

candelabro [kande'laβro] nm candelabra

candelero [kande'lero] nm (para vela) candlestick; (de aceite) oil lamp

candente [kan'dente] adj red-hot; (tema) burning

candidato, -a [kandi'ðato, a] nm/f candidate; (para puesto) applicant

candidatura [kandiða'tura] nf candidature

candidez [kandi'ðeθ] nf (sencillez) simplicity; (simpleza) naiveté

cándido, -a ['kandiðo, a] adj simple; naive

candil [kan'dil] nm oil lamp

candilejas [kandi'lexas] nfpl (Teat) footlights

candor [kan'dor] nm (sinceridad) frankness; (inocencia) innocence

canela [ka'nela] nf cinnamon

canelo [ka'nelo] nm: **hacer el ~** to act the fool

canelones [kane'lones] nmpl cannelloni

cangrejo [kan'grexo] nm crab

canguro [kan'guro] nm (Zool) kangaroo; (de niños) baby-sitter; **hacer de ~** to baby-sit

caníbal [ka'niβal] adj, nm/f cannibal

canica [ka'nika] nf marble

caniche [ka'nitʃe] nm poodle

canícula [ka'nikula] nf midsummer heat

canijo, -a [ka'nixo, a] adj frail, sickly

canilla [ka'niʎa] nf (Tec) bobbin

canino, -a [ka'nino, a] adj canine ■ nm canine (tooth)

canje [kan'xe] nm exchange; (trueque) swap

canjear [kanxe'ar] vt to exchange; (trocar) to swap

cano, -a ['kano, a] adj grey-haired, white-haired ■ nf (tb: canas) white o grey hair; **tener canas** to be going grey

canoa [ka'noa] nf canoe

canon ['kanon] nm canon; (pensión) rent; (Com) tax

canonice etc [kano'niθe] vb ver canonizar

canónico, -a [ka'noniko, a] adj: **derecho ~** canon law

canónigo [ka'noniyo] nm canon

canonizar [kanoni'θar] vt to canonize

canoro, -a [ka'noro, a] adj melodious

canoso, -a [ka'noso, a] adj (pelo) grey (Brit), gray (US); (persona) grey-haired

cansado, -a [kan'saðo, a] adj tired, weary; (tedioso) tedious, boring; **estoy ~ de hacerlo** I'm sick of doing it

cansancio [kan'sanθjo] nm tiredness, fatigue

cansar [kan'sar] vt (fatigar) to tire, tire out; (aburrir) to bore; (fastidiar) to bother; **cansarse** vr to tire, get tired; (aburrirse) to get bored

cantábrico, -a [kan'taβriko, a] *adj* Cantabrian; **Mar C~** Bay of Biscay; **(Montes) Cantábricos, Cordillera Cantábrica** Cantabrian Mountains

cántabro, -a ['kantaβro, a] *adj, nm/f* Cantabrian

cantante [kan'tante] *adj* singing ∎ *nm/f* singer

cantaor, a [kanta'or, a] *nm/f* Flamenco singer

cantar [kan'tar] *vt* to sing ∎ *vi* to sing; *(insecto)* to chirp; *(rechinar)* to squeak; *(fam: criminal)* to squeal ∎ *nm (acción)* singing; *(canción)* song; *(poema)* poem; **~ a algn las cuarenta** to tell sb a few home truths; **~ a dos voces** to sing a duet

cántara ['kantara] *nf* large pitcher

cántaro ['kantaro] *nm* pitcher, jug

cantautor, a [kantau'tor, a] *nm/f* singer-songwriter

cante ['kante] *nm*: **~ jondo** flamenco singing

cantera [kan'tera] *nf* quarry

cantidad [kanti'ðað] *nf* quantity, amount; *(Econ)* sum ∎ *adv (fam)* a lot; **~ alzada** lump sum; **~ de** lots of

cantilena [kanti'lena] *nf* = **cantinela**

cantimplora [kantim'plora] *nf* water bottle

cantina [kan'tina] *nf* canteen; *(de estación)* buffet; *(esp Am)* bar

cantinela [kanti'nela] *nf* ballad, song

canto ['kanto] *nm* singing; *(canción)* song; *(borde)* edge, rim; *(de un cuchillo)* back; **~ rodado** boulder

cantón [kan'ton] *nm* canton

cantor, a [kan'tor, a] *nm/f* singer

canturrear [kanturre'ar] *vi* to sing softly

canutas [ka'nutas] *nfpl*: **pasarlas ~** *(fam)* to have a rough time (of it)

canuto [ka'nuto] *nm (tubo)* small tube; *(fam: porro)* joint

caña ['kaɲa] *nf (Bot: tallo)* stem, stalk; *(carrizo)* reed; *(vaso)* tumbler; *(de cerveza)* glass of beer; *(Anat)* shinbone; *(Am: aguardiente)* cane liquor; **~ de azúcar** sugar cane; **~ de pescar** fishing rod

cañada [ka'ɲaða] *nf (entre dos montañas)* gully, ravine; *(camino)* cattle track

cáñamo ['kaɲamo] *nm (Bot)* hemp

cañaveral [kaɲaβe'ral] *nm (Bot)* reedbed; *(Agr)* sugar-cane field

cañería [kaɲe'ria] *nf* piping; *(tubo)* pipe

caño ['kaɲo] *nm (tubo)* tube, pipe; *(de aguas servidas)* sewer; *(Mus)* pipe; *(Naut)* navigation channel; *(de fuente)* jet

cañón [ka'ɲon] *nm (Mil)* cannon; *(de fusil)* barrel; *(Geo)* canyon, gorge

cañonazo [kaɲo'naθo] *nm (Mil)* gunshot

cañonera [kaɲo'nera] *nf (tb:* **lancha cañonera)** gunboat

caoba [ka'oβa] *nf* mahogany

caos ['kaos] *nm* chaos

caótico, -a [ka'otiko, a] *adj* chaotic

C.A.P. *nm abr* (= *Certificado de Aptitud Pedagógica*) teaching certificate

cap. *abr* (= *capítulo*) ch.

capa ['kapa] *nf* cloak, cape; *(Culin)* coating; *(Geo)* layer, stratum; *(de pintura)* coat; **de ~ y espada** cloak-and-dagger; **so ~ de** under the pretext of; **~ de ozono** ozone layer; **capas sociales** social groups

capacho [ka'patʃo] *nm* wicker basket

capacidad [kapaθi'ðað] *nf (medida)* capacity; *(aptitud)* capacity, ability; **una sala con ~ para 900** a hall seating 900; **~ adquisitiva** purchasing power

capacitación [kapaθita'θjon] *nf* training

capacitar [kapaθi'tar] *vt*: **~ a algn para algo** to qualify sb for sth; *(Tec)* to train sb for sth; **capacitarse** *vr*: **capacitarse para algo** to qualify for sth

capar [ka'par] *vt* to castrate, geld

caparazón [kapara'θon] *nm (Zool)* shell

capataz [kapa'taθ] *nm* foreman, charge hand

capaz [ka'paθ] *adj* able, capable; *(amplio)* capacious, roomy; **es ~ que venga mañana** *(Am)* he'll probably come tomorrow

capcioso, -a [kap'θjoso, a] *adj* wily, deceitful; **pregunta capciosa** trick question

capea [ka'pea] *nf (Taur)* bullfight with young bulls

capear [kape'ar] *vt (dificultades)* to dodge; **~ el temporal** to weather the storm

capellán [kape'ʎan] *nm* chaplain; *(sacerdote)* priest

caperuza [kape'ruθa] *nf* hood; *(de bolígrafo)* cap

capi ['kapi] *nf (esp Am fam)* capital (city)

capicúa [kapi'kua] *nf* reversible number, e.g. 1441

capilar [kapi'lar] *adj* hair *cpd*

capilla [ka'piʎa] *nf* chapel

capital [kapi'tal] *adj* capital ∎ *nm (Com)* capital ∎ *nf (de nación)* capital (city); *(tb:* **capital de provincia)** provincial capital, ≈ county town; **~ activo/en acciones** working/share o equity capital; **~ arriesgado** venture capital; **~ autorizado** o **social** authorised capital; **~ emitido** issued capital; **~ improductivo** idle money; **~ invertido** o **utilizado** capital employed; **~ pagado** paid-up capital; **~ de riesgo** risk capital; **~ social** equity o share capital; **inversión de capitales** capital investment; *ver tb* **provincia**

capitalice *etc* [kapita'liθe] *vb ver* **capitalizar**

capitalino, -a [kapita'lino, a] *adj* (*Am*) of o from the capital ■ *nm/f* native o inhabitant of the capital

capitalismo [kapita'lismo] *nm* capitalism

capitalista [kapita'lista] *adj, nm/f* capitalist

capitalizar [kapitali'θar] *vt* to capitalize

capitán [kapi'tan] *nm* captain; (*fig*) leader

capitana [kapi'tana] *nf* flagship

capitanear [kapitane'ar] *vt* to captain

capitanía [kapita'nia] *nf* captaincy

capitel [kapi'tel] *nm* (*Arq*) capital

capitolio [kapi'toljo] *nm* capitol

capitulación [kapitula'θjon] *nf* (*rendición*) capitulation, surrender; (*acuerdo*) agreement, pact; **capitulaciones matrimoniales** marriage contract *sg*

capitular [kapitu'lar] *vi* to come to terms, make an agreement; (*Mil*) to surrender

capítulo [ka'pitulo] *nm* chapter

capo [ka'po] *nm* drugs baron

capó [ka'po] *nm* (*Auto*) bonnet (*Brit*), hood (*US*)

capón [ka'pon] *nm* capon

caporal [kapo'ral] *nm* chief, leader

capota [ka'pota] *nf* (*de mujer*) bonnet; (*Auto*) hood (*Brit*), top (*US*)

capote [ka'pote] *nm* (*abrigo: de militar*) greatcoat; (*de torero*) cloak

capricho [ka'pritʃo] *nm* whim, caprice

caprichoso, -a [kapri'tʃoso, a] *adj* capricious

Capricornio [kapri'kornjo] *nm* Capricorn

cápsula ['kapsula] *nf* capsule; **~ espacial** space capsule

captar [kap'tar] *vt* (*comprender*) to understand; (*Radio*) to pick up; (*atención, apoyo*) to attract

captura [kap'tura] *nf* capture; (*Jur*) arrest

capturar [kaptu'rar] *vt* to capture; (*Jur*) to arrest; (*datos*) to input

capucha [ka'putʃa] *nf* hood, cowl

capullo [ka'puʎo] *nm* (*Zool*) cocoon; (*Bot*) bud; (*fam!*) berk (*Brit*), jerk (*US*)

caqui ['kaki] *nm* khaki

cara ['kara] *nf* (*Anat, de moneda*) face; (*aspecto*) appearance; (*de disco*) side; (*fig*) boldness; (*descaro*) cheek, nerve ■ *prep*: **~ a** facing; **de ~ a** opposite, facing; **dar la ~ a** to face the consequences; **echar algo en ~ a algn** to reproach sb for sth; **¿~ o cruz?** heads or tails?; **¡qué ~ más dura!** what a nerve!; **de una ~** (*disquete*) single-sided

carabina [kara'βina] *nf* carbine, rifle; (*persona*) chaperone

carabinero [karaβi'nero] *nm* (*de aduana*) customs officer; (*Am*) gendarme

Caracas [ka'rakas] *nm* Caracas

caracol [kara'kol] *nm* (*Zool*) snail; (*concha*) (sea)shell; **escalera de ~** spiral staircase

caracolear [karakole'ar] *vi* (*caballo*) to prance about

carácter (*pl* **caracteres**) [ka'rakter, karak'teres] *nm* character; **caracteres de imprenta** (*Tip*) type(face) *sg*; **~ libre** (*Inform*) wildcard character; **tener buen/mal ~** to be good-natured/bad tempered

caracterice *etc* [karakte'riθe] *vb ver* **caracterizar**

característico, -a [karakte'ristiko, a] *adj* characteristic ■ *nf* characteristic

caracterizar [karakteri'θar] *vt* (*distinguir*) to characterize, typify; (*honrar*) to confer a distinction on

caradura [kara'ðura] *nm/f* cheeky person; **es un ~** he's got a nerve

carajillo [kara'xiʎo] *nm* black coffee with brandy

carajo [ka'raxo] *nm* (*esp Am fam!*): **¡~!** shit! (*!*); **¡qué ~!** what the hell!; **me importa un ~** I don't give a damn

caramba [ka'ramba] *excl* well!, good gracious!

carámbano [ka'rambano] *nm* icicle

carambola [karam'bola] *nf*: **por ~** by a fluke

caramelo [kara'melo] *nm* (*dulce*) sweet; (*azúcar fundido*) caramel

carantoñas [karan'toɲas] *nfpl*: **hacer ~ a algn** to (try to) butter sb up

caraqueño, -a [kara'keɲo, a] *adj* of o from Caracas ■ *nm/f* native o inhabitant of Caracas

carátula [ka'ratula] *nf* (*máscara*) mask; (*Teat*): **la ~** the stage

caravana [kara'βana] *nf* caravan; (*fig*) group; (*de autos*) tailback

carbón [kar'βon] *nm* coal; **~ de leña** charcoal; **papel ~** carbon paper

carbonatado, -a [karβono'taðo, a] *adj* carbonated

carbonato [karβo'nato] *nm* carbonate; **~ sódico** sodium carbonate

carboncillo [karβon'θiʎo] *nm* (*Arte*) charcoal

carbonice *etc* [karβo'niθe] *vb ver* **carbonizar**

carbonilla [karβo'niʎa] *nf* coal dust

carbonizar [karβoni'θar] *vt* to carbonize; (*quemar*) to char; **quedar carbonizado** (*Elec*) to be electrocuted

carbono [kar'βono] *nm* carbon

carburador [karβura'ðor] *nm* carburettor

carburante [karβu'rante] *nm* fuel

carca ['karka] *adj, nm/f inv* reactionary

carcajada [karka'xaða] *nf* (loud) laugh, guffaw

carcajearse [karkaxe'arse] *vr* to roar with laughter

cárcel ['karθel] *nf* prison, jail; (*Tec*) clamp

carcelero, -a [karθe'lero, a] *adj* prison *cpd* ■ *nm/f* warder

carcoma [kar'koma] *nf* woodworm
carcomer [karko'mer] *vt* to bore into, eat into; *(fig)* to undermine; **carcomerse** *vr* to become worm-eaten; *(fig)* to decay
carcomido, -a [karko'miðo, a] *adj* worm-eaten; *(fig)* rotten
cardar [kar'ðar] *vt* (*Tec*) to card, comb
cardenal [karðe'nal] *nm* (*Rel*) cardinal; (*Med*) bruise
cárdeno, -a ['karðeno, a] *adj* purple; (*lívido*) livid
cardiaco, -a [kar'ðjako, a], **cardíaco, a** [kar'ðiako, a] *adj* cardiac; (*ataque*) heart *cpd*
cardinal [karði'nal] *adj* cardinal
cardiólogo, -a [karðj'oloɣo, a] *nm/f* cardiologist
cardo ['karðo] *nm* thistle
carear [kare'ar] *vt* to bring face to face; (*comparar*) to compare; **carearse** *vr* to come face to face, meet
carecer [kare'θer] *vi*: ~ **de** to lack, be in need of
carencia [ka'renθja] *nf* lack; (*escasez*) shortage; (*Med*) deficiency
carente [ka'rente] *adj*: ~ **de** lacking in, devoid of
carestía [kares'tia] *nf* (*escasez*) scarcity, shortage; (*Com*) high cost; **época de** ~ period of shortage
careta [ka'reta] *nf* mask
carey [ka'rei] *nm* (*tortuga*) turtle; (*concha*) tortoiseshell
carezca *etc* [ka'reθka] *vb ver* **carecer**
carga ['karɣa] *nf* (*peso, Elec*) load; (*de barco*) cargo, freight; (*Finanzas*) tax, duty; (*Mil*) charge; (*Inform*) loading; (*obligación, responsabilidad*) duty, obligation; ~ **aérea** (*Com*) air cargo; ~ **útil** (*Com*) payload; **la** ~ **fiscal** the tax burden
cargadero [karɣa'ðero] *nm* goods platform, loading bay
cargado, -a [kar'ɣaðo, a] *adj* loaded; (*Elec*) live; (*café, té*) strong; (*cielo*) overcast
cargador, a [karɣa'ðor, a] *nm/f* loader; (*Naut*) docker ■ *nm* (*Inform*): ~ **de discos** disk pack; (*Telec: del móvil*) charger
cargamento [karɣa'mento] *nm* (*acción*) loading; (*mercancías*) load, cargo
cargante [kar'ɣante] *adj* (*persona*) trying
cargar [kar'ɣar] *vt* (*barco, arma*) to load; (*Elec*) to charge; (*impuesto*) to impose; (*Com: algo en cuenta*) to charge, debit; (*Mil: enemigo*) to charge ■ *vi* (*Auto*) to load (up); (*inclinarse*) to lean; (*Inform*) to load, feed in; ~ **con** to pick up, carry away; **cargarse** *vr* (*fam: estropear*) to break; (: *matar*) to bump off; (*Elec*) to become charged
cargo ['karɣo] *nm* (*Com etc*) charge, debit;

(*puesto*) post, office; (*responsabilidad*) duty, obligation; (*fig*) weight, burden; (*Jur*) charge; **altos cargos** high-ranking officials; **una cantidad en ~ a algn** a sum chargeable to sb; **hacerse ~ de** to take charge of *o* responsibility for
cargue *etc* ['karɣe] *vb ver* **cargar**
carguero [kar'ɣero] *nm* freighter, cargo boat; (*avión*) freight plane
Caribe [ka'riβe] *nm*: **el** ~ the Caribbean
caribeño, -a [kari'βeɲo, a] *adj* Caribbean
caricatura [karika'tura] *nf* caricature
caricia [ka'riθja] *nf* caress; (*a animal*) pat, stroke
caridad [kari'ðað] *nf* charity
caries ['karjes] *nf inv* (*Med*) tooth decay
cariño [ka'riɲo] *nm* affection, love; (*caricia*) caress; (*en carta*) love ...
cariñoso, -a [kari'ɲoso, a] *adj* affectionate
carioca [ka'rjoka] *adj* (*Am*) of *o* from Rio de Janeiro ■ *nm/f* native *o* inhabitant of Rio de Janeiro
carisma [ka'risma] *nm* charisma
carismático, -a [karis'matiko, a] *adj* charismatic
caritativo, -a [karita'tiβo, a] *adj* charitable
cariz [ka'riθ] *nm*: **tener** *o* **tomar buen/mal ~** to look good/bad
carmesí [karme'si] *adj, nm* crimson
carmín [kar'min] *nm* (*color*) carmine; ~ **(de labios)** lipstick
carnal [kar'nal] *adj* carnal; **primo ~** first cousin
carnaval [karna'βal] *nm* carnival; *see note*

CARNAVAL

The 3 days before *miércoles de ceniza* (Ash Wednesday), when fasting traditionally starts, are the time for *carnaval*, an exuberant celebration which dates back to pre-Christian times. Although in decline during the Franco years, the *carnaval* has grown in popularity recently in Spain, Cádiz and Tenerife being particularly well-known for their celebrations. *El martes de carnaval* (Shrove Tuesday) is the biggest day, with colourful street parades, fancy dress, fireworks and a general party atmosphere.

carne ['karne] *nf* flesh; (*Culin*) meat; ~ **de cerdo/de cordero/de ternera/de vaca** pork/lamb/veal/beef; ~ **picada** mince; ~ **de gallina** (*fig*) gooseflesh
carné [kar'ne] *nm* = **carnet**

carnero [kar'nero] *nm* sheep, ram; (*carne*) mutton

carnet (*pl* **carnets**) [kar'ne, kar'nes] *nm*: **~ de conducir** driving licence; **~ de identidad** identity card; *ver tb* **Documento Nacional de Identidad**

carnicería [karniθe'ria] *nf* butcher's (shop); (*fig: matanza*) carnage, slaughter

carnicero, -a [karni'θero, a] *adj* carnivorous ■ *nm/f* (*tb fig*) butcher ■ *nm* carnivore

carnívoro, -a [kar'niβoro, a] *adj* carnivorous ■ *nm* carnivore

carnoso, -a [kar'noso, a] *adj* beefy, fat

caro, -a ['karo, a] *adj* dear; (*Com*) dear, expensive ■ *adv* dear, dearly; **vender ~** to sell at a high price

carpa ['karpa] *nf* (*pez*) carp; (*de circo*) big top; (*Am: de camping*) tent

carpeta [kar'peta] *nf* folder, file

carpintería [karpinte'ria] *nf* carpentry

carpintero [karpin'tero] *nm* carpenter; **pájaro ~** woodpecker

carraspear [karraspe'ar] *vi* (*aclararse la garganta*) to clear one's throat

carraspera [karras'pera] *nf* hoarseness

carrera [ka'rrera] *nf* (*acción*) run(ning); (*espacio recorrido*) run; (*certamen*) race; (*trayecto*) course; (*profesión*) career; (*Escol: Univ*) course; (*de taxi*) ride; (*en medias*) ladder; **a la ~** at (full) speed; **caballo de ~(s)** racehorse; **~ de armamentos** arms race

carrerilla [karre'riʎa] *nf*: **decir algo de ~** to reel sth off; **tomar ~** to get up speed

carreta [ka'rreta] *nf* wagon, cart

carrete [ka'rrete] *nm* reel, spool; (*Tec*) coil

carretera [karre'tera] *nf* (*main*) road, highway; **~ nacional** ≈ A road (*Brit*), ≈ state highway (*US*); **~ de circunvalación** ring road

carretilla [karre'tiʎa] *nf* trolley; (*Agr*) (wheel)barrow

carril [ka'rril] *nm* furrow; (*de autopista*) lane; (*Ferro*) rail

carril bici [karil'βiθi] (*pl* **carriles bici** [kariles'βiθi]) *nm* cycle lane, bikeway (*US*)

carrillo [ka'rriʎo] *nm* (*Anat*) cheek; (*Tec*) pulley

carro ['karro] *nm* cart, wagon; (*Mil*) tank; (*Am: coche*) car; (*Tip*) carriage; **~ blindado** armoured car

carrocería [karroθe'ria] *nf* body, bodywork *no pl* (*Brit*)

carroña [ka'rroɲa] *nf* carrion *no pl*

carroza [ka'rroθa] *nf* (*vehículo*) coach ■ *nm/f* (*fam*) old fogey

carruaje [ka'rrwaxe] *nm* carriage

carrusel [karru'sel] *nm* merry-go-round, roundabout (*Brit*)

carta ['karta] *nf* letter; (*Culin*) menu; (*naipe*) card; (*mapa*) map; (*Jur*) document; **~ de crédito** credit card; **~ de crédito documentaria** (*Com*) documentary letter of credit; **~ de crédito irrevocable** (*Com*) irrevocable letter of credit; **~ certificada/urgente** registered/special delivery letter; **~ marítima** chart; **~ de pedido** (*Com*) order; **~ verde** (*Auto*) green card; **~ de vinos** wine list; **echar una ~ al correo** to post a letter; **echar las cartas a algn** to tell sb's fortune

cartabón [karta'βon] *nm* set square

cartearse [karte'arse] *vr* to correspond

cartel [kar'tel] *nm* (*anuncio*) poster, placard; (*Escol*) wall chart; (*Com*) cartel

cartelera [karte'lera] *nf* hoarding, billboard; (*en periódico etc*) listings *pl*, entertainments guide; **"en ~"** "showing"

cartera [kar'tera] *nf* (*de bolsillo*) wallet; (*de colegial, cobrador*) satchel; (*Am: de señora*) handbag (*Brit*), purse (*US*); (*para documentos*) briefcase; **ministro sin ~** (*Pol*) minister without portfolio; **ocupa la ~ de Agricultura** he is Minister of Agriculture; **~ de pedidos** (*Com*) order book; **efectos en ~** (*Econ*) holdings

carterista [karte'rista] *nm/f* pickpocket

cartero [kar'tero] *nm* postman

cartílago [kar'tilaɣo] *nm* cartilage

cartilla [kar'tiʎa] *nf* (*Escol*) primer, first reading book; **~ de ahorros** bank book

cartografía [kartoɣra'fia] *nf* cartography

cartón [kar'ton] *nm* cardboard

cartucho [kar'tutʃo] *nm* (*Mil*) cartridge; (*bolsita*) paper cone; **~ de datos** (*Inform*) data cartridge; **~ de tinta** ink cartridge

cartulina [kartu'lina] *nf* fine cardboard, card

CASA ['kasa] *nf abr* (*Esp Aviat*) = **Construcciones Aeronáuticas S.A.**

casa ['kasa] *nf* house; (*hogar*) home; (*edificio*) building; (*Com*) firm, company; **~ consistorial** town hall; **~ de huéspedes** ≈ guest house; **~ de socorro** first aid post; **~ de citas** (*fam*) brothel; **~ independiente** detached house; **~ rural** (*de alquiler*) holiday cottage; (*pensión*) rural B&B; **ir a ~** to go home; **salir de ~** to go out; (*para siempre*) to leave home; **echar la ~ por la ventana** (*gastar*) to spare no expense; *ver tb* **hotel**

casadero, -a [kasa'ðero, a] *adj* marriageable

casado, -a [ka'saðo, a] *adj* married ■ *nm/f* married man/woman

casamiento [kasa'mjento] *nm* marriage, wedding

casar [ka'sar] *vt* to marry; (*Jur*) to quash, annul; **casarse** *vr* to marry, get married;

casarse por lo civil to have a civil wedding, get married in a registry office (*Brit*)

cascabel [kaska'βel] *nm* (small) bell; (*Zool*) rattlesnake

cascada [kas'kaða] *nf* waterfall

cascajo [kas'kaxo] *nm* gravel, stone chippings *pl*

cascanueces [kaska'nweθes] *nm inv*: **un ~** a pair of nutcrackers

cascar [kas'kar] *vt* to split; (*nuez*) to crack ■ *vi* to chatter; **cascarse** *vr* to crack, split, break (open)

cáscara ['kaskara] *nf* (*de huevo, fruta seca*) shell; (*de fruta*) skin; (*de limón*) peel

cascarón [kaska'ron] *nm* (broken) eggshell

cascarrabias [kaska'rraβjas] *nm/f inv* (*fam*) hothead

casco ['kasko] *nm* (*de bombero, soldado*) helmet; (*cráneo*) skull; (*Naut: de barco*) hull; (*Zool: de caballo*) hoof; (*botella*) empty bottle; (*de ciudad*): **el ~ antiguo** the old part; **el ~ urbano** the town centre; **los cascos azules** the UN peace-keeping force, the blue helmets

cascote [kas'kote] *nm* piece of rubble; **cascotes** *nmpl* rubble *sg*

caserío [kase'rio] *nm* hamlet, group of houses; (*casa*) country house

casero, -a [ka'sero, a] *adj*: **ser muy ~** (*persona*) to be homeloving; **"comida casera"** "home cooking" ■ *nm/f* (*propietario*) landlord/lady; (*Com*) house agent

caserón [kase'ron] *nm* large (ramshackle) house

caseta [ka'seta] *nf* hut; (*para bañista*) cubicle; (*de feria*) stall

casete [ka'sete] *nm o f* cassette; **~ digital** digital audio tape, DAT

casi ['kasi] *adv* almost; **~ nunca** hardly ever, almost never; **~ nada** next to nothing; **~ te caes** you almost o nearly fell

casilla [ka'siʎa] *nf* (*casita*) hut, cabin; (*Teat*) box office; (*para cartas*) pigeonhole; (*Ajedrez*) square; **C~ postal** o **de Correo(s)** (*Am*) P.O. Box; **sacar a algn de sus casillas** to drive sb round the bend (*fam*), make sb lose his temper

casillero [kasi'ʎero] *nm* pigeonholes

casino [ka'sino] *nm* club; (*de juego*) casino

caso ['kaso] *nm* case; (*suceso*) event; **en ~ de ...** in case of ...; **el ~ es que** the fact is that; **en el mejor de los casos** at best; **en ese ~** in that case; **en todo ~** in any case; **en último ~** as a last resort; **hacer ~ a** to pay attention to; **hacer ~ omiso de** to fail to mention, pass over; **hacer** o **venir al ~** to be relevant

caspa ['kaspa] *nf* dandruff

Caspio ['kaspjo] *adj*: **Mar ~** Caspian Sea

casque *etc* ['kaske] *vb ver* **cascar**

casquillo [kas'kiʎo] *nm* (*de bombilla*) fitting; (*de bala*) cartridge case

cassette [ka'set] *nf o m* = **casete**

casta ['kasta] *nf* caste; (*raza*) breed

castaña [kas'taɲa] *nf ver* **castaño**

castañetear [kastaɲete'ar] *vi* (*dientes*) to chatter

castaño, -a [kas'taɲo, a] *adj* chestnut (-coloured), brown ■ *nm* chestnut tree ■ *nf* chestnut; (*fam: golpe*) punch; **~ de Indias** horse chestnut tree

castañuelas [kasta'ɲwelas] *nfpl* castanets

castellano, -a [kaste'ʎano, a] *adj* Castilian; (*fam*) Spanish ■ *nm/f* Castilian; (*fam*) Spaniard ■ *nm* (*Ling*) Castilian, Spanish; *see note*

CASTELLANO

The term *castellano* is now the most widely used term in Spain and Spanish America to refer to the Spanish language, since *español* is too closely associated with Spain as a nation. Of course some people maintain that *castellano* should only refer to the type of Spanish spoken in Castilla.

castellonense [kasteʎo'nense] *adj* of o from Castellón de la Plana ■ *nm/f* native o inhabitant of Castellón de la Plana

castidad [kasti'ðað] *nf* chastity, purity

castigar [kasti'ɣar] *vt* to punish; (*Deporte*) to penalize; (*afligir*) to afflict

castigo [kas'tiɣo] *nm* punishment; (*Deporte*) penalty

castigue *etc* [kas'tiɣe] *vb ver* **castigar**

Castilla [kas'tiʎa] *nf* Castile

castillo [kas'tiʎo] *nm* castle

castizo, -a [kas'tiθo, a] *adj* (*Ling*) pure; (*de buena casta*) purebred, pedigree; (*auténtico*) genuine

casto, -a ['kasto, a] *adj* chaste, pure

castor [kas'tor] *nm* beaver

castrar [kas'trar] *vt* to castrate; (*gato*) to doctor; (*Bot*) to prune

castrense [kas'trense] *adj* army *cpd*, military

casual [ka'swal] *adj* chance, accidental

casualidad [kaswali'ðað] *nf* chance, accident; (*combinación de circunstancias*) coincidence; **¡qué ~!** what a coincidence!

casualmente [kaswal'mente] *adv* by chance

cataclismo [kata'klismo] *nm* cataclysm

catador [kata'ðor] *nm* taster

catadura [kata'ðura] *nf* (*aspecto*) looks *pl*

catalán, -ana [kata'lan, ana] *adj, nm/f*

Catalan ■ *nm* (*Ling*) Catalan; *ver tb* **lenguas cooficiales**

catalejo [kata'lexo] *nm* telescope

catalizador [kataliθa'ðor] *nm* catalyst; (*Auto*) catalytic converter

catalogar [katalo'ɣar] *vt* to catalogue; ~ **(de)** (*fig*) to classify as

catálogo [ka'taloɣo] *nm* catalogue

catalogue *etc* [kata'loɣe] *vb ver* **catalogar**

Cataluña [kata'luɲa] *nf* Catalonia

cataplasma [kata'plasma] *nf* (*Med*) poultice

catapulta [kata'pulta] *nf* catapult

catar [ka'tar] *vt* to taste, sample

catarata [kata'rata] *nf* (*Geo*) (water)fall; (*Med*) cataract

catarro [ka'tarro] *nm* catarrh; (*constipado*) cold

catarsis [ka'tarsis] *nf* catharsis

catastro [ka'tastro] *nm* property register

catástrofe [ka'tastrofe] *nf* catastrophe

catear [kate'ar] *vt* (*fam*) to flunk

catecismo [kate'θismo] *nm* catechism

cátedra ['kateðra] *nf* (*Univ*) chair, professorship; (*Escol*) principal teacher's post; **sentar ~ sobre un argumento** to take one's stand on an argument

catedral [kate'ðral] *nf* cathedral

catedrático, -a [kate'ðratiko, a] *nm/f* professor; (*Escol*) principal teacher

categoría [kateɣo'ria] *nf* category; (*rango*) rank, standing; (*calidad*) quality; **de ~** (*hotel*) top-class; **de baja ~** (*oficial*) low-ranking; **de segunda ~** second-rate; **no tiene ~** he has no standing

categórico, -a [kate'ɣoriko, a] *adj* categorical

catequesis [kate'kesis] *nf* catechism lessons

caterva [ka'terβa] *nf* throng, crowd

cateto, -a [ka'teto, a] *nm/f* yokel

cátodo ['katoðo] *nm* cathode

catolicismo [katoli'θismo] *nm* Catholicism

católico, -a [ka'toliko, a] *adj, nm/f* Catholic

catorce [ka'torθe] *num* fourteen

catre ['katre] *nm* camp bed (*Brit*), cot (*US*); (*fam*) pit

Cáucaso ['kaukaso] *nm* Caucasus

cauce ['kauθe] *nm* (*de río*) riverbed; (*fig*) channel

caucho ['kautʃo] *nm* rubber; (*Am: llanta*) tyre

caución [kau'θjon] *nf* bail

caucionar [kauθjo'nar] *vt* (*Jur*) to bail (out), go bail for

caudal [kau'ðal] *nm* (*de río*) volume, flow; (*fortuna*) wealth; (*abundancia*) abundance

caudaloso, -a [kauða'loso, a] *adj* (*río*) large; (*persona*) wealthy, rich

caudillaje [kauði'ʎaxe] *nm* leadership

caudillo [kau'ðiʎo] *nm* leader, chief

causa ['kausa] *nf* cause; (*razón*) reason; (*Jur*) lawsuit, case; **a** *o* **por ~ de** because of, on account of

causar [kau'sar] *vt* to cause

cáustico, -a ['kaustiko, a] *adj* caustic

cautela [kau'tela] *nf* caution, cautiousness

cauteloso, -a [kaute'loso, a] *adj* cautious, wary

cautivar [kauti'βar] *vt* to capture; (*fig*) to captivate

cautiverio [kauti'βerjo] *nm*, **cautividad** [kautiβi'ðað] *nf* captivity

cautivo, -a [kau'tiβo, a] *adj, nm/f* captive

cauto, -a ['kauto, a] *adj* cautious, careful

cava ['kaβa] *nf* (*bodega*) (wine) cellar ■ *nm* (*vino*) champagne-type wine

cavar [ka'βar] *vt* to dig; (*Agr*) to dig over

caverna [ka'βerna] *nf* cave, cavern

cavernoso, -a [kaβer'noso, a] *adj* cavernous; (*voz*) resounding

caviar [ka'βjar] *nm* caviar(e)

cavidad [kaβi'ðað] *nf* cavity

cavilación [kaβila'θjon] *nf* deep thought

cavilar [kaβi'lar] *vt* to ponder

cayado [ka'jaðo] *nm* (*de pastor*) crook; (*de obispo*) crozier

cayendo *etc* [ka'jendo] *vb ver* **caer**

caza ['kaθa] *nf* (*acción: gen*) hunting; (: *con fusil*) shooting; (*una caza*) hunt, chase; (*animales*) game; **coto de ~** hunting estate ■ *nm* (*Aviat*) fighter

cazabe [ka'saβe] *nm* (*Am*) cassava bread *o* flour

cazador, a [kaθa'ðor, a] *nm/f* hunter/huntress ■ *nf* jacket

cazaejecutivos [kaθaexeku'tiβos] *nm inv* (*Com*) headhunter

cazar [ka'θar] *vt* to hunt; (*perseguir*) to chase; (*prender*) to catch; **cazarlas al vuelo** to be pretty sharp

cazasubmarinos [kaθasuβma'rinos] *nm inv* (*Naut*) destroyer; (*Aviat*) anti-submarine craft

cazo ['kaθo] *nm* saucepan

cazuela [ka'θwela] *nf* (*vasija*) pan; (*guisado*) casserole

cazurro, -a [ka'θurro, a] *adj* surly

CC *nm abr* (*Pol*: = *Comité Central*) Central Committee

c/c. *abr* (*Com*: = *cuenta corriente*) current account

CCAA *abr* (*Esp*) = **Comunidades Autónomas**

CCI *nf abr* (*Com*: = *Cámara de Comercio Internacional*) ICC

CC.OO. *nfpl abr* = **Comisiones Obreras**

c/d *abr* (= *en casa de*) c/o, care of

CD *nm abr* (= *compact disc*) CD ■ *abr* (*Pol*: = *Cuerpo Diplomático*) CD (= *Diplomatic Corps*)

CDN *nm abr* (= *Centro Dramático Nacional*) ≈ RADA (*Brit*)

CD-Rom *nm abr* CD-Rom

CE *nm abr* (= *Consejo de Europa*) Council of Europe ∎ *nf abr* (= *Comunidad Europea*) EC

cebada [θe'βaða] *nf* barley

cebar [θe'βar] *vt* (*animal*) to fatten (up); (*anzuelo*) to bait; (*Mil: Tec*) to prime; **cebarse** *vr*: **cebarse en** to vent one's fury on, take it out on

cebo ['θeβo] *nm* (*gen: para animales*) feed, food; (*para peces, fig*) bait; (*de arma*) charge

cebolla [θe'βoʎa] *nf* onion

cebolleta [θeβo'ʎeta] *nf* spring onion

cebollino [θeβo'ʎino] *nm* spring onion

cebón, -ona [θe'βon, ona] *adj* fat, fattened

cebra ['θeβra] *nf* zebra; **paso de ~** zebra crossing

CECA ['θeka] *nf abr* (= *Comunidad Europea del Carbón y del Acero*) ECSC

ceca ['θeka] *nf*: **andar** *o* **ir de la ~ a la Meca** to chase about all over the place

cecear [θeθe'ar] *vi* to lisp

ceceo [θe'θeo] *nm* lisp

cecina [θe'θina] *nf* cured *o* smoked meat

cedazo [θe'ðaθo] *nm* sieve

ceder [θe'ðer] *vt* (*entregar*) to hand over; (*renunciar a*) to give up, part with ∎ *vi* (*renunciar*) to give in, yield; (*disminuir*) to diminish, decline; (*romperse*) to give way; (*viento*) to drop; (*fiebre etc*) to abate; **"ceda el paso"** (*Auto*) "give way"

cederom [θeðe'rom] *nm* CD-ROM

cedro ['θeðro] *nm* cedar

cédula ['θeðula] *nf* certificate, document; **~ de identidad** (*Am*) identity card; **~ en blanco** blank cheque; *ver tb* **Documento Nacional de Identidad**

CEE *nf abr* (= *Comunidad Económica Europea*) EEC

cegar [θe'ɣar] *vt* to blind; (*tubería etc*) to block up, stop up ∎ *vi* to go blind; **cegarse** *vr*: **cegarse (de)** to be blinded (by)

cegué *etc* [θe'ɣe] *vb ver* **cegar**

ceguera [θe'ɣera] *nf* blindness

CEI *nf abr* (= *Comunidad de Estados Independientes*) CIS

Ceilán [θei'lan] *nm* Ceylon, Sri Lanka

ceja ['θexa] *nf* eyebrow; **cejas pobladas** bushy eyebrows; **arquear las cejas** to raise one's eyebrows; **fruncir las cejas** to frown

cejar [θe'xar] *vi* (*fig*) to back down; **no ~** to keep it up, stick at it

cejijunto, -a [θexi'xunto, a] *adj* with bushy eyebrows; (*fig*) scowling

celada [θe'laða] *nf* ambush, trap

celador, a [θela'ðor, a] *nm/f* (*de edificio*) watchman; (*de museo etc*) attendant; (*de cárcel*) warder

celda ['θelda] *nf* cell

celebérrimo, -a [θele'βerrimo, a] *adj* superlativo de **célebre**

celebración [θeleβra'θjon] *nf* celebration

celebrar [θele'βrar] *vt* to celebrate; (*alabar*) to praise ∎ *vi* to be glad; **celebrarse** *vr* to occur, take place

célebre ['θeleβre] *adj* celebrated, renowned

celebridad [θeleβri'ðað] *nf* fame; (*persona*) celebrity

celeridad [θeleri'ðað] *nf*: **con ~** promptly

celeste [θe'leste] *adj* sky-blue; (*cuerpo etc*) heavenly ∎ *nm* sky blue

celestial [θeles'tjal] *adj* celestial, heavenly

celibato [θeli'βato] *nm* celibacy

célibe ['θeliβe] *adj, nm/f* celibate

celo ['θelo] *nm* zeal; (*Rel*) fervour; (*pey*) envy; **celos** *nmpl* jealousy *sg*; **dar celos a algn** to make sb jealous; **tener celos de algn** to be jealous of sb; **en ~** (*animales*) on heat

celofán [θelo'fan] *nm* Cellophane®

celosía [θelo'sia] *nf* lattice (window)

celoso, -a [θe'loso, a] *adj* (*envidioso*) jealous; (*trabajador*) zealous; (*desconfiado*) suspicious

celta ['θelta] *adj* Celtic ∎ *nm/f* Celt

célula ['θelula] *nf* cell

celular [θelu'lar] *adj*: **tejido ~** cell tissue

celulitis [θelu'litis] *nf* (*enfermedad*) cellulitis; (*grasa*) cellulite

celuloide [θelu'loiðe] *nm* celluloid

celulosa [θelu'losa] *nf* cellulose

cementerio [θemen'terjo] *nm* cemetery, graveyard; **~ de coches** scrap yard

cemento [θe'mento] *nm* cement; (*hormigón*) concrete; (*Am: cola*) glue

CEN *nm abr* (*Esp*) = **Consejo de Economía Nacional**

cena ['θena] *nf* evening meal, dinner

cenagal [θena'ɣal] *nm* bog, quagmire

cenar [θe'nar] *vt* to have for dinner, dine on ∎ *vi* to have dinner, dine

cencerro [θen'θerro] *nm* cowbell; **estar como un ~** (*fam*) to be round the bend

cenicero [θeni'θero] *nm* ashtray

ceniciento, -a [θeni'θjento, a] *adj* ash-coloured, ashen

cenit [θe'nit] *nm* zenith

ceniza [θe'niθa] *nf* ash, ashes *pl*

censar [θen'sar] *vt* to take a census of

censo ['θenso] *nm* census; **~ electoral** electoral roll

censor [θen'sor] *nm* censor; **~ de cuentas** (*Com*) auditor; **~ jurado de cuentas** chartered (*Brit*) *o* certified public (*US*) accountant

censura [θen'sura] *nf* (*Pol*) censorship; (*moral*) censure, criticism

censurable [θensu'raβle] *adj* reprehensible

censurar [θensu'rar] *vt* (*idea*) to censure; (*cortar: película*) to censor

centavo [θen'taβo] *nm* hundredth (part); (*Am*) cent

centella [θen'teʎa] *nf* spark

centellear [θenteʎe'ar] *vi* (*metal*) to gleam; (*estrella*) to twinkle; (*fig*) to sparkle

centelleo [θente'ʎeo] *nm* gleam(ing); twinkling; sparkling

centena [θen'tena] *nf* hundred

centenar [θente'nar] *nm* hundred

centenario, -a [θente'narjo, a] *adj* one hundred years old ∎ *nm* centenary

centeno [θen'teno] *nm* rye

centésimo, -a [θen'tesimo, a] *adj, nm* hundredth

centígrado [θen'tiɣraðo] *adj* centigrade

centigramo [θenti'ɣramo] *nm* centigramme

centilitro [θenti'litro] *nm* centilitre (*Brit*), centiliter (*US*)

centímetro [θen'timetro] *nm* centimetre (*Brit*), centimeter (*US*)

céntimo, -a ['θentimo, a] *adj* hundredth ∎ *nm* cent

centinela [θenti'nela] *nm* sentry, guard

centollo, -a [θen'toʎo, a] *nm/f* large (*o* spider) crab

central [θen'tral] *adj* central ∎ *nf* head office; (*Tec*) plant; (*Telec*) exchange; ~ **nuclear** nuclear power station

centralice *etc* [θentra'liθe] *vb ver* **centralizar**

centralita [θentra'lita] *nf* switchboard

centralización [θentraliθa'θjon] *nf* centralization

centralizar [θentrali'θar] *vt* to centralize

centrar [θen'trar] *vt* to centre

céntrico, -a ['θentriko, a] *adj* central

centrifugar [θentrifu'ɣar] *vt* (*ropa*) to spin-dry

centrífugo, -a [θent'rifuɣo, a] *adj* centrifugal

centrifugue *etc* [θentri'fuɣe] *vb ver* **centrifugar**

centrista [θen'trista] *adj* centre *cpd*

centro ['θentro] *nm* centre; **ser de ~** (*Pol*) to be a moderate; ~ **de acogida (para niños)** children's home; ~ **de beneficios** (*Com*) profit centre; ~ **cívico** community centre; ~ **comercial** shopping centre; ~ **de informática** computer centre; ~ **(de determinación) de costos** (*Com*) cost centre; ~ **delantero** (*Deporte*) centre forward; ~ **docente** teaching institution; ~ **juvenil** youth club; ~ **de llamadas** call centre; ~ **social** community centre

centroafricano, -a [θentroafri'kano, a] *adj*: **la República Centroafricana** the Central African Republic

centroamericano, -a [θentroameri'kano, a] *adj, nm/f* Central American

centrocampista [θentrokam'pista] *nm/f* (*Deporte*) midfielder

ceñido, -a [θe'ɲiðo, a] *adj* tight

ceñir [θe'ɲir] *vt* (*rodear*) to encircle, surround; (*ajustar*) to fit (tightly); (*apretar*) to tighten; **ceñirse** *vr*: **ceñirse algo** to put sth on; **ceñirse al asunto** to stick to the matter in hand

ceño ['θeɲo] *nm* frown, scowl; **fruncir el ~** to frown, knit one's brow

CEOE *nf abr* (= *Confederación Española de Organizaciones Empresariales*) ≈ CBI (*Brit*)

cepa ['θepa] *nf* (*de vid, fig*) stock; (*Bio*) strain

CEPAL [θe'pal] *nf abr* (= *Comisión Económica de las Naciones Unidas para la América Latina*) ECLA

cepillar [θepi'ʎar] *vt* to brush; (*madera*) to plane (down)

cepillo [θe'piʎo] *nm* brush; (*para madera*) plane; (*Rel*) poor box, alms box; ~ **de dientes** toothbrush

cepo ['θepo] *nm* (*de caza*) trap

CEPSA ['θepsa] *nf abr* (*Com*) = **Compañía Española de Petróleos, S.A.**

CEPYME *nf abr* = **Confederación Española de la Pequeña y Mediana Empresa**

cera ['θera] *nf* wax; ~ **de abejas** beeswax

cerámica [θe'ramika] *nf* pottery; (*arte*) ceramics *sg*

ceramista [θera'mista] *nm/f* potter

cerbatana [θerβa'tana] *nf* blowpipe

cerca ['θerka] *nf* fence ∎ *adv* near, nearby, close; **por aquí ~** nearby ∎ *prep*: ~ **de** (*cantidad*) nearly, about; (*distancia*) near, close to ∎ *nmpl*: **cercas** foreground *sg*

cercado [θer'kaðo] *nm* enclosure

cercanía [θerka'nia] *nf* nearness, closeness; **cercanías** *nfpl* outskirts, suburbs; **tren de cercanías** commuter *o* local train

cercano, -a [θer'kano, a] *adj* close, near; (*pueblo etc*) nearby; **C~ Oriente** Near East

cercar [θer'kar] *vt* to fence in; (*rodear*) to surround

cerciorar [θerθjo'rar] *vt* (*asegurar*) to assure; **cerciorarse** *vr*: **cerciorarse (de)** (*descubrir*) to find out (about); (*asegurarse*) to make sure (of)

cerco ['θerko] *nm* (*Agr*) enclosure; (*Am*) fence; (*Mil*) siege

cerda ['θerða] *nf* (*de cepillo*) bristle; (*Zool*) sow

cerdada [θer'ðaða] *nf* (*fam*): **hacer una ~ a algn** to play a dirty trick on sb

Cerdeña [θer'ðeɲa] *nf* Sardinia

cerdo ['θerðo] *nm* pig; **carne de ~** pork

cereal [θere'al] *nm* cereal; **cereales** *nmpl* cereals, grain *sg*

cerebral [θere'βral] *adj* (*tb fig*) cerebral;
(*tumor*) brain *cpd*
cerebro [θe'reβro] *nm* brain; (*fig*) brains *pl*;
ser un ~ (*fig*) to be brilliant
ceremonia [θere'monja] *nf* ceremony;
reunión de ~ formal meeting; **hablar sin ~**
to speak plainly
ceremonial [θeremo'njal] *adj, nm* ceremonial
ceremonioso, -a [θeremo'njoso, a] *adj*
ceremonious; (*cumplido*) formal
cereza [θe'reθa] *nf* cherry
cerezo [θe'reθo] *nm* cherry tree
cerilla [θe'riʎa] *nf*, **cerillo** [se'riʎo] *nm* (*Am*)
match
cerner [θer'ner] *vt* to sift, sieve; **cernerse** *vr*
to hover
cero ['θero] *nm* nothing, zero; (*Deporte*) nil; **8
grados bajo ~** 8 degrees below zero; **a partir
de ~** from scratch
cerque *etc* ['θerke] *vb ver* **cercar**
cerrado, -a [θe'rraðo, a] *adj* closed, shut;
(*con llave*) locked; (*tiempo*) cloudy, overcast;
(*curva*) sharp; (*acento*) thick, broad; **a puerta
cerrada** (*Jur*) in camera
cerradura [θerra'ðura] *nf* (*acción*) closing;
(*mecanismo*) lock
cerrajería [θerraxe'ria] *nf* locksmith's craft;
(*tienda*) locksmith's (shop)
cerrajero, -a [θerra'xero, a] *nm/f* locksmith
cerrar [θe'rrar] *vt* to close, shut; (*paso,
carretera*) to close; (*grifo*) to turn off; (*trato,
cuenta, negocio*) to close ∎ *vi* to close, shut;
(*la noche*) to come down; **~ con llave** to lock;
~ el sistema (*Inform*) to close o shut down
the system; **~ un trato** to strike a bargain;
cerrarse *vr* to close, shut; (*herida*) to heal
cerro ['θerro] *nm* hill; **andar por las cerros
de Úbeda** to wander from the point, digress
cerrojo [θe'rroxo] *nm* (*herramienta*) bolt; (*de
puerta*) latch
certamen [θer'tamen] *nm* competition,
contest
certero, -a [θer'tero, a] *adj* accurate
certeza [θer'teθa], **certidumbre**
[θerti'ðumbre] *nf* certainty
certificación [θertifika'θjon] *nf*
certification; (*Jur*) affidavit
certificado, -a [θertifi'kaðo, a] *adj* certified;
(*Correos*) registered ∎ *nm* certificate
certificar [θertifi'kar] *vt* (*asegurar, atestar*) to
certify
certifique *etc* [θerti'fike] *vb ver* **certificar**
cervatillo [θerβa'tiʎo] *nm* fawn
cervecería [θerβeθe'ria] *nf* (*fábrica*) brewery;
(*taberna*) public house
cerveza [θer'βeθa] *nf* beer; **~ de barril**
draught beer

cervical [θerβi'kal] *adj* cervical
cerviz [θer'βiθ] *nf* nape of the neck
cesación [θesa'θjon] *nf* cessation,
suspension
cesante [θe'sante] *adj* redundant;
(*Am*) unemployed; (*ministro*) outgoing;
(*diplomático*) recalled ∎ *nm/f* redundant
worker
cesantía [θesan'tia] *nf* (*Am*) unemployment
cesar [θe'sar] *vi* to cease, stop; (*de un trabajo*) to
leave ∎ *vt* (*en el trabajo*) to dismiss; (*alto cargo*)
to remove from office
cesárea [θe'sarea] *nf* Caesarean (section)
cese ['θese] *nm* (*de trabajo*) dismissal; (*de pago*)
suspension
CESID [θe'sið] *nm abr* (*Esp:* = *Centro Superior
de Investigación de la Defensa Nacional*) *military
intelligence service*
cesión [θe'sjon] *nf:* **~ de bienes** surrender of
property
césped ['θespeð] *nm* grass, lawn
cesta ['θesta] *nf* basket
cesto ['θesto] *nm* (large) basket, hamper
cetrería [θetre'ria] *nf* falconry
cetrino, -a [θe'trino, a] *adj* (*tez*) sallow
cetro ['θetro] *nm* sceptre
Ceuta [θe'uta] *nf* Ceuta
ceutí [θeu'ti] *adj* of o from Ceuta ∎ *nm/f*
native o inhabitant of Ceuta
C.F. *nm abr* (= *Club de Fútbol*) F.C.
CFC *nm abr* (= *clorofluorocarbono*) CFC
cfr *abr* (= *confróntese, compárese*) cf
cg *abr* (= *centígramo*) cg
CGPJ *nm abr* (= *Consejo General del Poder Judicial*)
governing body of Spanish legal system
CGS *nf abr* (*Guatemala: El Salvador*)
= **Confederación General de Sindicatos**
CGT *nf abr* (*Colombia: México: Nicaragua: Esp:*
= **Confederación General de Trabajadores**)
(*Argentina:* = **Confederación General del
Trabajo**)
Ch, ch [tʃe] *nf former letter in the Spanish alphabet*
chabacano, -a [tʃaβa'kano, a] *adj* vulgar,
coarse
chabola [tʃa'βola] *nf* shack; **chabolas** *nfpl*
shanty town *sg*
chabolismo [tʃaβo'lismo] *nm:* **el problema
del ~** the problem of substandard housing,
the shanty town problem
chacal [tʃa'kal] *nm* jackal
chacarero [tʃaka'rero] *nm* (*Am*) small farmer
chacha ['tʃatʃa] *nf* (*fam*) maid
cháchara ['tʃatʃara] *nf* chatter; **estar de ~**
to chatter away
chacra ['tʃakra] *nf* (*Am*) smallholding
chafar [tʃa'far] *vt* (*aplastar*) to crush, flatten;
(*arruinar*) to ruin

chaflán [tʃaˈflan] *nm* (*Tec*) bevel
chal [tʃal] *nm* shawl
chalado, -a [tʃaˈlaðo, a] *adj* (*fam*) crazy
chalé (*pl* ~**s**) [tʃaˈle, tʃaˈles] *nm* = **chalet**
chaleco [tʃaˈleko] *nm* waistcoat, vest (*US*); ~
  antibala bulletproof vest; ~ **salvavidas** life
  jacket; ~ **reflectante** (*Aut*) high-visibility
  vest
chalet (*pl* **chalets**) [tʃaˈle, tʃaˈles] *nm* villa,
  ≈ detached house; ~ **adosado** semi-detached
  house
chalupa [tʃaˈlupa] *nf* launch, boat
chamaco, -a [tʃaˈmako, a] *nm/f* (*Am*) boy/girl
chamarra [tʃaˈmarra] *nf* sheepskin jacket;
  (*Am: poncho*) blanket
champán [tʃamˈpan] *nm*, **champaña**
  [tʃamˈpaɲa] *nm* champagne
champiñón [tʃampiˈɲon] *nm* mushroom
champú [tʃamˈpu] (*pl* ~**es** o ~**s**) *nm* shampoo
chamuscar [tʃamusˈkar] *vt* to scorch, singe
chamusque *etc* [tʃaˈmuske] *vb ver* **chamuscar**
chamusquina [tʃamusˈkina] *nf* singeing
chance [ˈtʃanθe] *nm* (*a veces nf*) (*Am*) chance,
  opportunity
chanchada [tʃanˈtʃaða] *nf* (*Am fam*) dirty trick
chancho, -a [ˈtʃantʃo, a] *nm/f* (*Am*) pig
chanchullo [tʃanˈtʃuʎo] *nm* (*fam*) fiddle,
  wangle
chancla [ˈtʃankla] *nf*, **chancleta** [tʃanˈkleta]
  nf flip-flop; (*zapato viejo*) old shoe
chandal [tʃanˈdal] *nm* tracksuit; ~ (**de tactel**)
  shellsuit
chantaje [tʃanˈtaxe] *nm* blackmail; **hacer ~ a**
  uno to blackmail sb
chanza [ˈtʃanθa] *nf* joke
chao [tʃao] *excl* (*fam*) cheerio
chapa [ˈtʃapa] *nf* (*de metal*) plate, sheet; (*de
  madera*) board, panel; (*de botella*) bottle top;
  (*insignia*) (lapel) badge; (*Am: Auto: tb*: **chapa de
  matrícula**) number (*Brit*) o license (*US*) plate;
  (*Am: cerradura*) lock; **de 3 chapas** (*madera*)
  3-ply
chapado, -a [tʃaˈpaðo, a] *adj* (*metal*) plated;
  (*muebles etc*) finished
chaparro, -a [tʃaˈparro, a] *adj* squat; (*Am:
  bajito*) short
chaparrón [tʃapaˈrron] *nm* downpour,
  cloudburst
chapotear [tʃapoteˈar] *vt* to sponge down
  ■ *vi* (*fam*) to splash about
chapucero, -a [tʃapuˈθero, a] *adj* rough,
  crude ■ *nm/f* bungler
chapurrar [tʃapurˈrar], **chapurrear**
  [tʃapurreˈar] *vt* (*idioma*) to speak badly
chapuza [tʃaˈpuθa] *nf* botched job
chapuzón [tʃapuˈθon] *nm*: **darse un ~** to go
  for a dip

chaqué [tʃaˈke] *nm* morning coat
chaqueta [tʃaˈketa] *nf* jacket; **cambiar la ~**
  (*fig*) to change sides
chaquetón [tʃakeˈton] *nm* three-quarter-
  length coat
charca [ˈtʃarka] *nf* pond, pool
charco [ˈtʃarko] *nm* pool, puddle
charcutería [tʃarkuteˈria] *nf* (*tienda*) shop
  selling chiefly pork meat products; (*productos*)
  cooked pork meats *pl*
charla [ˈtʃarla] *nf* talk, chat; (*conferencia*)
  lecture
charlar [tʃarˈlar] *vi* to talk, chat
charlatán, -ana [tʃarlaˈtan, ana] *nm/f*
  chatterbox; (*estafador*) trickster
charol¹ [tʃaˈrol] *nm* varnish; (*cuero*) patent
  leather
charol² [tʃaˈrol] *nm* (*Am*), **charola** [tʃaˈrola]
  nf (*Am*) tray
charqui [ˈtʃarki] *nm* (*Am*) dried beef, jerky (*US*)
charro, -a [ˈtʃarro, a] *adj* Salamancan; (*Am*)
  Mexican; (*ropa*) loud, gaudy; (*Am: costumbres*)
  traditional ■ *nm/f* Salamancan; Mexican
chárter [ˈtʃarter] *adj inv*: **vuelo ~** charter
  flight
chascarrillo [tʃaskaˈrriʎo] *nm* (*fam*) funny
  story
chasco [ˈtʃasko] *nm* (*broma*) trick, joke;
  (*desengaño*) disappointment
chasis [ˈtʃasis] *nm inv* (*Auto*) chassis; (*Foto*)
  plate holder
chasquear [tʃaskeˈar] *vt* (*látigo*) to crack;
  (*lengua*) to click
chasquido [tʃasˈkiðo] *nm* (*de lengua*) click;
  (*de látigo*) crack
chat [tʃat] *nm* (*Internet*) chat room
chatarra [tʃaˈtarra] *nf* scrap (metal)
chatero, -a [tʃaˈtero, a] *adj* chat *cpd* ■ *nm/f*
  chat-room user
chato, -a [ˈtʃato, a] *adj* flat; (*nariz*) snub ■ *nm*
  wine tumbler; **beber unos chatos** to have a
  few drinks
chau [tʃau], **chaucito** [tʃauˈsito] *excl* (*fam*)
  cheerio
chauvinismo [tʃoβiˈnismo] *nm* chauvinism
chauvinista [tʃoβiˈnista] *adj, nm/f* chauvinist
chaval, a [tʃaˈβal, a] *nm/f* kid (*fam*), lad/lass
chavo [ˈtʃaβo] *nm* (*Am: fam*) bloke (*Brit*), guy
checo, -a [ˈtʃeko, a] *adj, nm/f* Czech ■ *nm*
  (*Ling*) Czech
checoeslovaco, -a [tʃekoesloˈβako, a],
  checoslovaco, -a [tʃekosloˈβako, a] *adj, nm/f*
  Czech, Czechoslovak
Checoeslovaquia [tʃekoesloˈβakja],
  Checoslovaquia [tʃekosloˈβakja] *nf*
  Czechoslovakia
chepa [ˈtʃepa] *nf* hump

cheque ['tʃeke] *nm* cheque (*Brit*), check (*US*);
~ **abierto/en blanco/cruzado** open/blank/crossed cheque; ~ **al portador** cheque payable to bearer; ~ **de viajero** traveller's cheque

chequeo [tʃe'keo] *nm* (*Med*) check-up; (*Auto*) service

chequera [tʃe'kera] *nf* (*Am*) chequebook (*Brit*), checkbook (*US*)

chévere ['tʃeβere] *adj* (*Am*) great, fabulous (*fam*)

chicano, -a [tʃi'kano, a] *adj, nm/f* chicano, Mexican-American

chicha ['tʃitʃa] *nf* (*Am*) maize liquor

chícharo ['tʃitʃaro] *nm* (*Am*) pea

chicharra [tʃi'tʃarra] *nf* harvest bug, cicada

chicharrón [tʃitʃa'rron] *nm* (pork) crackling

chichón [tʃi'tʃon] *nm* bump, lump

chicle ['tʃikle] *nm* chewing gum

chico, -a ['tʃiko, a] *adj* small, little ■ *nm/f* child; (*muchacho*) boy; (*muchacha*) girl

chicote [tʃi'kote] *nm* (*Am*) whip

chiflado, -a [tʃi'flaðo, a] *adj* (*fam*) crazy, round the bend ■ *nm/f* nutcase

chiflar [tʃi'flar] *vt* to hiss, boo ■ *vi* (*esp Am*) to whistle

Chile ['tʃile] *nm* Chile

chile ['tʃile] *nm* chilli, pepper

chileno, -a [tʃi'leno, a] *adj, nm/f* Chilean

chillar [tʃi'ʎar] *vi* (*persona*) to yell, scream; (*animal salvaje*) to howl; (*cerdo*) to squeal; (*puerta*) to creak

chillido [tʃi'ʎiðo] *nm* (*de persona*) yell, scream; (*de animal*) howl; (*de frenos*) screech(ing)

chillón, -ona [tʃi'ʎon, ona] *adj* (*niño*) noisy; (*color*) loud, gaudy

chimenea [tʃime'nea] *nf* chimney; (*hogar*) fireplace

chimpancé (*pl* ~**s**) [tʃimpan'θe, tʃimpan'θes] *nm* chimpanzee

China ['tʃina] *nf*: (**la**) ~ China

china ['tʃina] *nf* pebble

chinchar [tʃin'tʃar] (*fam*) *vt* to pester, annoy; **chincharse** *vr* to get cross; **¡chínchate!** tough!

chinche ['tʃintʃe] *nf* bug; (*Tec*) drawing pin (*Brit*), thumbtack (*US*) ■ *nm/f* nuisance, pest

chincheta [tʃin'tʃeta] *nf* drawing pin (*Brit*), thumbtack (*US*)

chinchorro [tʃin'tʃorro] *nm* (*Am*) hammock

chingado, -a [tʃin'gaðo, a] *adj* (*esp Am fam!*) lousy, bloody (!); **hijo de la chingada** bastard (!), son of a bitch (*US!*)

chingar [tʃin'gar] *vt* (*Am: fam!*) to fuck (up) (!), screw (up) (!); **chingarse** *vr* (*Am: emborracharse*) to get pissed (*Brit*), get plastered (: *fracasar*) to fail

chingue *etc* ['tʃinge] *vb ver* **chingar**

chino, -a ['tʃino, a] *adj, nm/f* Chinese ■ *nm* (*Ling*) Chinese; (*Culin*) chinois, conical strainer

chip [tʃip] *nm* (*Inform*) chip

chipirón [tʃipi'ron] *nm* squid

Chipre ['tʃipre] *nf* Cyprus

chipriota [tʃi'prjota], **chipriote** [tʃi'prjote] *adj* Cypriot, Cyprian ■ *nm/f* Cypriot

chiquillada [tʃiki'ʎaða] *nf* childish prank; (*Am: chiquillos*) kids *pl*

chiquillo, -a [tʃi'kiʎo, a] *nm/f* kid (*fam*), youngster, child

chiquito, -a [tʃi'kito, a] *adj* very small, tiny ■ *nm/f* kid (*fam*)

chirigota [tʃiri'ɣota] *nf* joke

chirimbolo [tʃirim'bolo] *nm* thingummyjig (*fam*)

chirimoya [tʃiri'moja] *nf* custard apple

chiringuito [tʃirin'gito] *nm* refreshment stall o stand

chiripa [tʃi'ripa] *nf* fluke; **por** ~ by chance

chirona [tʃi'rona], **chirola** (*Am*) [tʃi'rola] *nf* (*fam*) clink, jail

chirriar [tʃi'rrjar] *vi* (*goznes*) to creak, squeak; (*pájaros*) to chirp, sing

chirrido [tʃi'rriðo] *nm* creak(ing), squeak(ing); (*de pájaro*) chirp(ing)

chis [tʃis] *excl* sh!

chisme ['tʃisme] *nm* (*habladurías*) piece of gossip; (*fam: objeto*) thingummyjig

chismoso, -a [tʃis'moso, a] *adj* gossiping ■ *nm/f* gossip

chispa ['tʃispa] *nf* spark; (*fig*) sparkle; (*ingenio*) wit; (*fam*) drunkenness

chispeante [tʃispe'ante] *adj* (*tb fig*) sparkling

chispear [tʃispe'ar] *vi* to spark; (*lloviznar*) to drizzle

chisporrotear [tʃisporrote'ar] *vi* (*fuego*) to throw out sparks; (*leña*) to crackle; (*aceite*) to hiss, splutter

chistar [tʃistar] *vi*: **no** ~ not to say a word

chiste ['tʃiste] *nm* joke, funny story; ~ **verde** blue joke

chistera [tʃis'tera] *nf* top hat

chistoso, -a [tʃis'toso, a] *adj* (*gracioso*) funny, amusing; (*bromista*) witty

chistu ['tʃistu] *nm* = **txistu**

chivarse [tʃi'βarse] *vr* (*fam*) to grass

chivatazo [tʃiβa'taθo] *nm* (*fam*) tip-off; **dar** ~ to inform

chivo, -a ['tʃiβo, a] *nm/f* (billy/nanny-)goat; ~ **expiatorio** scapegoat

chocante [tʃo'kante] *adj* startling; (*extraño*) odd; (*ofensivo*) shocking

chocar [tʃo'kar] *vi* (*coches etc*) to collide, crash; (*Mil, fig*) to clash ■ *vt* to shock; (*sorprender*) to startle; **~ con** to collide with; (*fig*) to run into, run up against; **¡chócala!** (*fam*) put it there!

chochear [tʃotʃe'ar] *vi* to dodder, be senile

chocho, -a ['tʃotʃo, a] *adj* doddering, senile; (*fig*) soft, doting

chocolate [tʃoko'late] *adj* chocolate ▪ *nm* chocolate; (*fam*) dope, marijuana

chocolatería [tʃokolate'ria] *nf* chocolate factory (*o* shop)

chófer ['tʃofer], **chofer** [tʃo'fer] (*esp Am*) *nm* driver

chollo ['tʃoʎo] *nm* (*fam*) bargain, snip

chomba ['tʃomba], **chompa** ['tʃompa] *nf* (*Am*) jumper, sweater

chopo ['tʃopo] *nm* black poplar

choque *etc* ['tʃoke] *vb ver* **chocar** ▪ *nm* (*impacto*) impact; (*golpe*) jolt; (*Auto*) crash; (*fig*) conflict

chorizo [tʃo'riθo] *nm* hard pork sausage (type of salami); (*ladrón*) crook

chorra ['tʃorra] *nf* luck

chorrada [tʃo'rraða] *nf* (*fam*): **¡es una ~!** that's crap! (!); **decir chorradas** to talk crap (!)

chorrear [tʃorre'ar] *vt* to pour ▪ *vi* to gush (out), spout (out); (*gotear*) to drip, trickle

chorreras [tʃo'rreras] *nfpl* (*adorno*) frill *sg*

chorro ['tʃorro] *nm* jet; (*caudalito*) dribble, trickle; (*fig*) stream; **salir a chorros** to gush forth; **con propulsión a ~** jet-propelled

chotearse [tʃote'arse] *vr* to joke

choto ['tʃoto] *nm* (*cabrito*) kid

chovinismo [tʃoβi'nismo] *nm* = **chauvinismo**

chovinista [tʃoβi'nista] *adj*, *nm/f* = **chauvinista**

choza ['tʃoθa] *nf* hut, shack

chubasco [tʃu'βasko] *nm* squall

chubasquero [tʃuβas'kero] *nm* oilskins *pl*

chuchería [tʃutʃe'ria] *nf* trinket

chucho ['tʃutʃo] *nm* (*Zool*) mongrel

chufa ['tʃufa] *nf* chufa, earth almond, tiger nut; **horchata de chufas** drink made from chufas

chuleta [tʃu'leta] *nf* chop, cutlet; (*Escol etc: fam*) crib

chulo, -a ['tʃulo, a] *adj* (*encantador*) charming; (*aire*) proud; (*pey*) fresh; (*fam: estupendo*) great, fantastic ▪ *nm* (*pícaro*) rascal; (*madrileño*) working-class Madrilenian; (*rufián: tb:* **chulo de putas**) pimp

chumbera [tʃum'bera] *nf* prickly pear

chungo, -a ['tʃungo, a] (*fam*) *adj* lousy ▪ *nf*: **estar de chunga** to be in a merry mood

chupa ['tʃupa] *nf* (*fam*) jacket

chupado, -a [tʃu'paðo, a] *adj* (*delgado*) skinny, gaunt; **está ~** (*fam*) it's simple, it's dead easy

chupar [tʃu'par] *vt* to suck; (*absorber*) to

absorb; **chuparse** *vr* to grow thin; **para chuparse los dedos** mouthwatering

chupatintas [tʃupa'tintas] *nm inv* penpusher

chupe ['tʃupe] *nm* (*Am*) stew

chupete [tʃu'pete] *nm* dummy (*Brit*), pacifier (*US*)

chupetón [tʃupe'ton] *nm* suck

churrasco [tʃu'rrasko] *nm* (*Am*) barbecue, barbecued meat

churrería [tʃurre'ria] *nf* stall or shop which sells "churros"

churrete [tʃu'rrete] *nm* grease spot

churretón [tʃurre'ton] *nm* stain

churrigueresco, -a [tʃurrige'resko, a] *adj* (*Arq*) baroque; (*fig*) excessively ornate

churro, -a ['tʃurro, a] *adj* coarse ▪ *nm* (*Culin*) (type of) fritter; *see note*; (*chapuza*) botch, mess

CHURRO

Churros, long fritters made with flour and water, are very popular in much of Spain and are often eaten with thick hot chocolate, either for breakfast or as a snack. In Madrid, they eat a thicker variety of *churro* called *porra*.

churruscar [tʃurrus'kar] *vt* to fry crisp

churrusque *etc* [tʃu'rruske] *vb ver* **churruscar**

churumbel [tʃurum'bel] *nm* (*fam*) kid

chus [tʃus] *excl*: **no decir ni ~ ni mus** not to say a word

chusco, -a ['tʃusko, a] *adj* funny

chusma ['tʃusma] *nf* rabble, mob

chutar [tʃu'tar] *vi* (*Deporte*) to shoot (at goal); **esto va que chuta** it's going fine

chuzo ['tʃuθo] *nm*: **llueve a chuzos, llueven chuzos de punta** it's raining cats and dogs

C.I. *nm abr* = **coeficiente intelectual** *o* de **inteligencia**

Cía *abr* (= compañía) Co.

cianuro [θja'nuro] *nm* cyanide

ciática ['θjatika] *nf* sciatica

cibercafé [θiβerka'fe] *nm* cybercafé

ciberespacio [θiβeres'paθjo] *nm* cyberspace

cibernauta [θiβer'nauta] *nmf* cybernaut

cibernética [θiβer'netika] *nf* cybernetics *sg*

cicatrice *etc* [θika'triθe] *vb ver* **cicatrizar**

cicatriz [θika'triθ] *nf* scar

cicatrizar [θikatri'θar] *vt* to heal; **cicatrizarse** *vr* to heal (up), form a scar

cíclico, -a ['θikliko, a] *adj* cyclical

ciclismo [θi'klismo] *nm* cycling

ciclista [θi'klista] *nm/f* cyclist

ciclo ['θiklo] *nm* cycle

ciclomotor [θiklomo'tor] *nm* moped

ciclón [θi'klon] *nm* cyclone

cicloturismo [θiklotu'rismo] *nm* touring by bicycle

cicuta [θi'kuta] *nf* hemlock

ciego, -a *etc* ['θjeɣo, a] *vb ver* **cegar** ■ *adj* blind ■ *nm/f* blind man/woman; **a ciegas** blindly; **me puse ciega mariscos** (*fam*) I stuffed myself with seafood

ciegue *etc* ['θjeɣe] *vb ver* **cegar**

cielo ['θjelo] *nm* sky; (*Rel*) heaven; (*Arq: tb:* **cielo raso**) ceiling; **¡cielos!** good heavens!; **ver el ~ abierto** to see one's chance

ciempiés [θjem'pjes] *nm inv* centipede

cien [θjen] *num ver* **ciento**

ciénaga ['θjenaɣa] *nf* marsh, swamp

ciencia ['θjenθja] *nf* science; **ciencias** *nfpl* science *sg*; **saber algo a ~ cierta** to know sth for certain

ciencia-ficción ['θjenθjafik'θjon] *nf* science fiction

cieno ['θjeno] *nm* mud, mire

científico, -a [θjen'tifiko, a] *adj* scientific ■ *nm/f* scientist

ciento ['θjento], **cien** *num* hundred; **pagar al 10 por ~** to pay at 10 per cent

cierne *etc* ['θjerne] *vb ver* **cerner** ■ *nm*: **en ~** in blossom; **en ~(s)** (*fig*) in its infancy

cierre *etc* ['θjerre] *vb ver* **cerrar** ■ *nm* closing, shutting; (*con llave*) locking; (*Radio: TV*) close-down; **~ de cremallera** zip (fastener); **precios de ~** (*Bolsa*) closing prices; **~ del sistema** (*Inform*) system shutdown

cierto, -a ['θjerto, a] *adj* sure, certain; (*un tal*) a certain; (*correcto*) right, correct; **~ hombre** a certain man; **ciertas personas** certain *o* some people; **sí, es ~** yes, that's correct; **por ~** by the way; **lo ~ es que ...** the fact is that ...; **estar en lo ~** to be right

ciervo ['θjerβo] *nm* (*Zool*) deer; (*: macho*) stag

cierzo ['θjerθo] *nm* north wind

CIES *nm abr* = **Consejo Interamericano Económico y Social**

cifra ['θifra] *nf* number, figure; (*cantidad*) number, quantity; (*secreta*) code; **~ global** lump sum; **~ de negocios** (*Com*) turnover; **en cifras redondas** in round figures; **~ de referencia** (*Com*) bench mark; **~ de ventas** (*Com*) sales figures

cifrado, -a [θi'fraðo, a] *adj* in code

cifrar [θi'frar] *vt* to code, write in code; (*resumir*) to abridge; (*calcular*) to reckon

cigala [θi'ɣala] *nf* Norway lobster

cigarra [θi'ɣarra] *nf* cicada

cigarrera [θiɣa'rrera] *nf* cigar case

cigarrillo [θiɣa'rriʎo] *nm* cigarette

cigarro [θi'ɣarro] *nm* cigarette; (*puro*) cigar

cigüeña [θi'ɣweɲa] *nf* stork

cilíndrico, -a [θi'lindriko, a] *adj* cylindrical

cilindro [θi'lindro] *nm* cylinder

cima ['θima] *nf* (*de montaña*) top, peak; (*de árbol*) top; (*fig*) height

címbalo ['θimbalo] *nm* cymbal

cimbrear [θimbre'ar] *vt* to brandish; **cimbrearse** *vr* to sway

cimentar [θimen'tar] *vt* to lay the foundations of; (*fig: reforzar*) to strengthen; (*: fundar*) to found

cimiento *etc* [θi'mjento] *vb ver* **cimentar** ■ *nm* foundation

cinc [θink] *nm* zinc

cincel [θin'θel] *nm* chisel

cincelar [θinθe'lar] *vt* to chisel

cincha ['θintʃa] *nf* girth, saddle strap

cincho ['θintʃo] *nm* sash, belt

cinco ['θinko] *num* five; (*fecha*) fifth; **las ~** five o'clock; **no estar en sus ~** (*fam*) to be off one's rocker

cincuenta [θin'kwenta] *num* fifty

cincuentón, -ona [θinkwen'ton, ona] *adj*, *nm/f* fifty-year-old

cine ['θine] *nm* cinema; **el ~ mudo** silent films *pl*; **hacer ~** to make films

cineasta [θine'asta] *nm/f* (*director de cine*) film-maker *o* director

cine-club ['θine'klub] *nm* film club

cinéfilo, -a [θi'nefilo, a] *nm/f* film buff

cinematográfico, -a [θinemato'ɣrafiko, a] *adj* cine-, film *cpd*

cínico, -a ['θiniko, a] *adj* cynical; (*descarado*) shameless ■ *nm/f* cynic

cinismo [θi'nismo] *nm* cynicism

cinta ['θinta] *nf* band, strip; (*de tela*) ribbon; (*película*) reel; (*de máquina de escribir*) ribbon; (*métrica*) tape measure; (*magnetofónica*) tape; **~ adhesiva** sticky tape; **~ aislante** insulating tape; **~ de carbón** carbon ribbon; **~ magnética** (*Inform*) magnetic tape; **~ métrica** tape measure; **~ de múltiples impactos** (*en impresora*) multistrike ribbon; **~ de tela** (*para máquina de escribir*) fabric ribbon; **~ transportadora** conveyor belt

cinto ['θinto] *nm* belt, girdle

cintura [θin'tura] *nf* waist; (*medida*) waistline

cinturón [θintu'ron] *nm* belt; (*fig*) belt, zone; **~ salvavidas** lifebelt; **~ de seguridad** safety belt

ciña *etc* ['θiɲa], **ciñendo** *etc* [θi'ɲendo] *vb ver* **ceñir**

ciprés [θi'pres] *nm* cypress (tree)

circo ['θirko] *nm* circus

circuito [θir'kwito] *nm* circuit; (*Deporte*) lap; **TV por ~ cerrado** closed-circuit TV; **~ experimental** (*Inform*) breadboard; **~ impreso** printed circuit; **~ lógico** (*Inform*) logical circuit

circulación [θirkula'θjon] *nf* circulation; (*Auto*) traffic; **"cerrado a la ~ rodada"** "closed to vehicles"

circular [θirku'lar] *adj, nf* circular ■ *vt* to circulate ■ *vi* to circulate; (*dinero*) to be in circulation; (*Auto*) to drive; (*autobús*) to run

círculo ['θirkulo] *nm* circle; (*centro*) clubhouse; (*Pol*) political group

circuncidar [θirkunθi'dar] *vt* to circumcise

circunciso, -a [θirkun'θiso, a] *pp de* **circuncidar**

circundante [θirkun'dante] *adj* surrounding

circundar [θirkun'dar] *vt* to surround

circunferencia [θirkunfe'renθja] *nf* circumference

circunloquio [θirkun'lokjo] *nm* circumlocution

circunscribir [θirkunskri'βir] *vt* to circumscribe; **circunscribirse** *vr* to be limited

circunscripción [θirkunskrip'θjon] *nf* division; (*Pol*) constituency

circunscrito [θirkuns'krito] *pp de* **circunscribir**

circunspección [θirkunspek'θjon] *nf* circumspection, caution

circunspecto, -a [θirkuns'pekto, a] *adj* circumspect, cautious

circunstancia [θirkuns'tanθja] *nf* circumstance; **circunstancias agravantes/ extenuantes** aggravating/extenuating circumstances; **estar a la altura de las circunstancias** to rise to the occasion

circunvalación [θirkumbala'θjon] *nf*: **carretera de ~** ring road

cirio ['θirjo] *nm* (wax) candle

cirrosis [θi'rrosis] *nf* cirrhosis (of the liver)

ciruela [θi'rwela] *nf* plum; **~ pasa** prune

ciruelo [θi'rwelo] *nm* plum tree

cirugía [θiru'xia] *nf* surgery; **~ estética** *o* **plástica** plastic surgery

cirujano [θiru'xano] *nm* surgeon

cisco ['θisko] *nm*: **armar un ~** to kick up a row; **estar hecho ~** to be a wreck

cisma ['θisma] *nm* schism; (*Pol etc*) split

cisne ['θisne] *nm* swan; **canto de ~** swan song

cisterna [θis'terna] *nf* cistern, tank

cistitis [θis'titis] *nf* cystitis

cita ['θita] *nf* appointment, meeting; (*de novios*) date; (*referencia*) quotation; **acudir/ faltar a una ~** to turn up for/miss an appointment

citación [θita'θjon] *nf* (*Jur*) summons *sg*

citadino, -a [sita'ðino, a] (*Am*) *adj* urban ■ *nm/f* urban *o* city dweller

citar [θi'tar] *vt* to make an appointment with, arrange to meet; (*Jur*) to summons; (*un autor, texto*) to quote; **citarse** *vr*: **citarse con algn** to arrange to meet sb; **se citaron en el cine** they arranged to meet at the cinema

cítara ['θitara] *nf* zither

citología [θitolo'xia] *nf* smear test

cítrico, -a ['θitriko, a] *adj* citric ■ *nm*: **cítricos** citrus fruits

CiU *nm abr* (*Pol*) = **Convergència i Unió**

ciudad [θju'ðað] *nf* town; (*capital de país etc*) city; **~ universitaria** university campus; **C~ del Cabo** Cape Town; **la C~ Condal** Barcelona

ciudadanía [θjuðaða'nia] *nf* citizenship

ciudadano, -a [θjuða'ðano, a] *adj* civic ■ *nm/f* citizen

ciudadrealeño, -a [θjuðaðrea'leɲo, a] *adj* of *o* from Ciudad Real ■ *nm/f* native *o* inhabitant of Ciudad Real

cívico, -a ['θiβiko, a] *adj* civic; (*fig*) public-spirited

civil [θi'βil] *adj* civil ■ *nm* (*guardia*) policeman

civilice *etc* [θiβi'liθe] *vb ver* **civilizar**

civilización [θiβiliθa'θjon] *nf* civilization

civilizar [θiβili'θar] *vt* to civilize

civismo [θi'βismo] *nm* public spirit

cizaña [θi'θaɲa] *nf* (*fig*) discord; **sembrar ~** to sow discord

cl *abr* (= *centilitro*) cl.

clamar [kla'mar] *vt* to clamour for, cry out for ■ *vi* to cry out, clamour

clamor [kla'mor] *nm* (*grito*) cry, shout; (*fig*) clamour, protest

clamoroso, -a [klamo'roso, a] *adj* (*éxito etc*) resounding

clan [klan] *nm* clan; (*de gángsters*) gang

· **clandestinidad** [klandestini'ðað] *nf* secrecy

clandestino, -a [klandes'tino, a] *adj* clandestine; (*Pol*) underground

clara ['klara] *nf* (*de huevo*) egg white

claraboya [klara'βoja] *nf* skylight

clarear [klare'ar] *vi* (*el día*) to dawn; (*el cielo*) to clear up, brighten up; **clarearse** *vr* to be transparent

clarete [kla'rete] *nm* rosé (wine)

claridad [klari'ðað] *nf* (*del día*) brightness; (*de estilo*) clarity

clarificar [klarifi'kar] *vt* to clarify

clarifique *etc* [klari'fike] *vb ver* **clarificar**

clarín [kla'rin] *nm* bugle

clarinete [klari'nete] *nm* clarinet

clarividencia [klariβi'ðenθja] *nf* clairvoyance; (*fig*) far-sightedness

claro, -a ['klaro, a] *adj* clear; (*luminoso*) bright; (*color*) light; (*evidente*) clear, evident; (*poco espeso*) thin ■ *nm* (*en bosque*) clearing

■ *adv* clearly ■ *excl* of course!; **hablar ~** (*fig*) to speak plainly; **a las claras** openly; **no sacamos nada en ~** we couldn't get anything definite

clase ['klase] *nf* class; (*tipo*) kind, sort; (*Escol etc*) class; (: *aula*) classroom; **~ alta/media/obrera** upper/middle/working class; **dar clases** to teach

clásico, -a ['klasiko, a] *adj* classical; (*fig*) classic

clasificable [klasifi'kaβle] *adj* classifiable

clasificación [klasifika'θjon] *nf* classification; (*Deporte*) league (table); (*Com*) ratings *pl*

clasificador [klasifika'ðor] *nm* filing cabinet

clasificar [klasifi'kar] *vt* to classify; (*Inform*) to sort; **clasificarse** *vr* (*Deporte: en torneo*) to qualify

clasifique *etc* [klasi'fike] *vb ver* **clasificar**

clasista [kla'sista] *adj* (*fam: actitud*) snobbish

claudicar [klauði'kar] *vi* (*fig*) to back down

claudique *etc* [klau'ðike] *vb ver* **claudicar**

claustro ['klaustro] *nm* cloister; (*Univ*) staff; (*junta*) senate

claustrofobia [klaustro'foβja] *nf* claustrophobia

cláusula ['klausula] *nf* clause; **~ de exclusión** (*Com*) exclusion clause

clausura [klau'sura] *nf* closing, closure

clausurar [klausu'rar] *vt* (*congreso etc*) to close, bring to a close; (*Pol etc*) to adjourn; (*cerrar*) to close (down)

clavado, -a [kla'βaðo, a] *adj* nailed ■ *excl* exactly!, precisely!

clavar [kla'βar] *vt* (*tablas etc*) to nail (together); (*con alfiler*) to pin; (*clavo*) to hammer in; (*cuchillo*) to stick, thrust; (*mirada*) to fix; (*fam: estafar*) to cheat

clave ['klaβe] *nf* key; (*Mus*) clef ■ *adj inv* key *cpd*; **~ de acceso** password

clavel [kla'βel] *nm* carnation

clavicémbalo [klaβi'θembalo] *nm* harpsichord

clavicordio [klaβikor'ðjo] *nm* clavicord

clavícula [kla'βikula] *nf* collar bone

clavija [kla'βixa] *nf* peg, pin; (*Mus*) peg; (*Elec*) plug

clavo ['klaβo] *nm* (*de metal*) nail; (*Bot*) clove; **dar en el ~** (*fig*) to hit the nail on the head

claxon ['klakson] (*pl* **claxons**) *nm* horn; **tocar el ~** to sound one's horn

clemencia [kle'menθja] *nf* mercy, clemency

clemente [kle'mente] *adj* merciful, clement

cleptómano, -a [klep'tomano, a] *nm/f* kleptomaniac

clerical [kleri'kal] *adj* clerical

clérigo ['kleriɣo] *nm* priest, clergyman

clero ['klero] *nm* clergy

clic [klik] *nm* click; **hacer ~/doble ~ en algo** to click/double-click on sth

clicar [kli'kar] *vi* (*Inform*) to click; **clica en el icono** click on the icon

cliché [kli'tʃe] *nm* cliché; (*Tip*) stencil; (*Foto*) negative

cliente, -a ['kljente, a] *nm/f* client, customer

clientela [kljen'tela] *nf* clientele, customers *pl*; (*Com*) goodwill; (*Med*) patients *pl*

clima ['klima] *nm* climate

climatizado, -a [klimati'θaðo, a] *adj* air-conditioned

clímax ['klimaks] *nm inv* climax

clínico, -a ['kliniko, a] *adj* clinical ■ *nf* clinic; (*particular*) private hospital

clip (*pl* **clips**) [klip, klis] *nm* paper clip

cliquear [klike'ar] *vi* (*Inform*) to click; **cliquea en el icono** click on the icon

clítoris ['klitoris] *nm inv* clitoris

cloaca [klo'aka] *nf* sewer, drain

clonación [klona'θjon] *nf* cloning

clorhídrico, -a [klo'ridriko, a] *adj* hydrochloric

cloro ['kloro] *nm* chlorine

clorofila [kloro'fila] *nf* chlorophyl(l)

cloroformo [kloro'formo] *nm* chloroform

cloruro [klo'ruro] *nm* chloride; **~ sódico** sodium chloride

club (*pl* **clubs** *o* **clubes**) [klub, klus, 'kluβes] *nm* club; **~ de jóvenes** youth club

cm *abr* (= *centímetro*) cm

C.N.T. *nf abr* (*Esp*: = *Confederación Nacional de Trabajo*) Anarchist Union Confederation; (*Am*) = **Confederación Nacional de Trabajadores**

coacción [koak'θjon] *nf* coercion, compulsion

coaccionar [koakθjo'nar] *vt* to coerce, compel

coagular [koaɣu'lar] *vt*, **coagularse** *vr* (*sangre*) to clot; (*leche*) to curdle

coágulo [ko'aɣulo] *nm* clot

coalición [koali'θjon] *nf* coalition

coartada [koar'taða] *nf* alibi

coartar [koar'tar] *vt* to limit, restrict

coba ['koβa] *nf*: **dar ~ a algn** to soft-soap sb

cobarde [ko'βarðe] *adj* cowardly ■ *nm/f* coward

cobardía [koβar'ðia] *nf* cowardice

cobaya [ko'βaja] *nf* guinea pig

cobertizo [koβer'tiθo] *nm* shelter

cobertor [koβer'tor] *nm* bedspread

cobertura [koβer'tura] *nf* cover; (*Com*) coverage; **~ de dividendo** (*Com*) dividend cover; **estar fuera de ~** (*Telec*) to be out of range; **no tengo ~** (*Telec*) I'm out of range

cobija [ko'βixa] *nf* (*Am*) blanket

cobijar [koβi'xar] vt (cubrir) to cover; (abrigar) to shelter; **cobijarse** vr to take shelter
cobijo [ko'βixo] nm shelter
cobra ['koβra] nf cobra
cobrador, a [koβra'ðor, a] nm/f (de autobús) conductor/conductress; (de impuestos, gas) collector
cobrar [ko'βrar] vt (cheque) to cash; (sueldo) to collect, draw; (objeto) to recover; (precio) to charge; (deuda) to collect ■ vi to draw one's pay; **cobrarse** vr to recover, get on well; **cóbrese al entregar** cash on delivery (COD) (Brit), collect on delivery (COD) (US); **a ~** (Com) receivable; **cantidades por ~** sums due
cobre ['koβre] nm copper; (Am fam) cent
cobrizo, -a [ko'βriθo, a] adj coppery
cobro ['koβro] nm (de cheque) cashing; (pago) payment; **presentar al ~** to cash; ver tb **llamada**
coca ['koka] nf coca; (droga) coke
cocaína [koka'ina] nf cocaine
cocainómano, -a [kokai'nomano, a] nm/f cocaine addict
cocción [kok'θjon] nf (Culin) cooking; (el hervir) boiling
cocear [koθe'ar] vi to kick
cocer [ko'θer] vt, vi to cook; (en agua) to boil; (en horno) to bake
coche ['kotʃe] nm (Auto) car, automobile (US); (de tren, de caballos) coach, carriage; (para niños) pram (Brit), baby carriage (US); **~ de bomberos** fire engine; **~ celular** Black Maria, prison van; **~ (comedor)** (Ferro) (dining) car; **~ fúnebre** hearse
coche-bomba ['kotʃe'βomba] (pl **coches-bomba**) nm car bomb
coche-cama ['kotʃe'kama] (pl **coches-cama**) nm (Ferro) sleeping car, sleeper
coche-escuela ['kotʃees'kwela] nm inv learner car
cochera [ko'tʃera] nf garage; (de autobuses, trenes) depot
coche-restaurante ['kotʃerestau'rante] (pl **coches-restaurante**) nm (Ferro) dining-car
cochinada [kotʃi'naða] nf dirty trick
cochinillo [kotʃi'niʎo] nm piglet, suckling pig
cochino, -a [ko'tʃino, a] adj filthy, dirty ■ nm/f pig
cocido, -a [ko'θiðo, a] adj boiled; (fam) plastered ■ nm stew
cociente [ko'θjente] nm quotient
cocina [ko'θina] nf kitchen; (aparato) cooker, stove; (actividad) cookery; **~ casera** home cooking; **~ eléctrica** electric cooker; **~ francesa** French cuisine; **~ de gas** gas cooker
cocinar [koθi'nar] vt, vi to cook
cocinero, -a [koθi'nero, a] nm/f cook

coco ['koko] nm coconut; (fantasma) bogeyman; (fam: cabeza) nut; **comer el ~ a algn** (fam) to brainwash sb
cocodrilo [koko'ðrilo] nm crocodile
cocotero [koko'tero] nm coconut palm
cóctel ['koktel] nm (bebida) cocktail; (reunión) cocktail party; **~ Molotov** Molotov cocktail, petrol bomb
coctelera [kokte'lera] nf cocktail shaker
cod. abr (= código) code
codazo [ko'ðaθo] nm: **dar un ~ a algn** to nudge sb
codear [koðe'ar] vi to elbow, jostle; **codearse** vr: **codearse con** to rub shoulders with
códice ['koðiθe] nm manuscript, codex
codicia [ko'ðiθja] nf greed; (fig) lust
codiciar [koði'θjar] vt to covet
codicioso, -a [koði'θjoso, a] adj covetous
codificador [koðifika'ðor] nm (Inform) encoder; **~ digital** digitizer
codificar [koðifi'kar] vt (mensaje) to (en)code; (leyes) to codify
código ['koðiɣo] nm code; **~ de barras** (Com) bar code; **~ binario** binary code; **~ de caracteres** (Inform) character code; **~ de (la) circulación** highway code; **~ civil** common law; **~ de control** (Inform) control code; **~ máquina** (Inform) machine code; **~ militar** military law; **~ de operación** (Inform) operational o machine code; **~ penal** penal code; **~ de práctica** code of practice
codillo [ko'ðiʎo] nm (Zool) knee; (Tec) elbow
codo ['koðo] nm (Anat, de tubo) elbow; (Zool) knee; **hablar por los codos** to talk nineteen to the dozen
codorniz [koðor'niθ] nf quail
coeficiente [koefi'θjente] nm (Mat) coefficient; (Econ etc) rate; **~ intelectual o de inteligencia** I.Q.
coerción [koer'θjon] nf coercion
coercitivo, -a [koerθi'tiβo, a] adj coercive
coetáneo, -a [koe'taneo, a] nm/f: **coetáneos** contemporaries
coexistencia [koeksis'tenθja] nf coexistence
coexistir [koeksis'tir] vi to coexist
cofia ['kofja] nf (de enfermera) (white) cap
cofradía [kofra'ðia] nf brotherhood, fraternity; ver tb **Semana Santa**
cofre ['kofre] nm (baúl) trunk; (de joyas) box; (Am Auto) bonnet (Brit), hood (US)
cogedor [koxe'ðor] nm dustpan
coger [ko'xer] vt (Esp) to take (hold of); (objeto caído) to pick up; (frutas) to pick, harvest; (resfriado, ladrón, pelota) to catch; (Am fam!) to lay (!) ■ vi: **~ por el buen camino** to take the right road; **cogerse** vr (el dedo) to catch;

~ **a algn desprevenido** to take sb unawares; **cogerse a algo** to get hold of sth

cogida [ko'xiða] *nf* gathering, harvesting; *(de peces)* catch; *(Taur)* goring

cogollo [ko'ɣoʎo] *nm (de lechuga)* heart; *(fig)* core, nucleus

cogorza [ko'ɣorθa] *nf (fam)*: **agarrar una** ~ to get smashed

cogote [ko'ɣote] *nm* back o nape of the neck

cohabitar [koaβi'tar] *vi* to live together, cohabit

cohecho [ko'etʃo] *nm (acción)* bribery; *(soborno)* bribe

coherencia [koe'renθja] *nf* coherence

coherente [koe'rente] *adj* coherent

cohesión [koe'sjon] *nm* cohesion

cohete [ko'ete] *nm* rocket

cohibido, -a [koi'βiðo, a] *adj (Psico)* inhibited; *(tímido)* shy; **sentirse** ~ to feel embarrassed

cohibir [koi'βir] *vt* to restrain, restrict; **cohibirse** *vr* to feel inhibited

COI *nm abr* (= *Comité Olímpico Internacional*) IOC

coima ['koima] *nf (Am fam)* bribe

coincidencia [koinθi'ðenθja] *nf* coincidence

coincidir [koinθi'ðir] *vi (en idea)* to coincide, agree; *(en lugar)* to coincide

coito ['koito] *nm* intercourse, coitus

cojear [koxe'ar] *vi (persona)* to limp, hobble; *(mueble)* to wobble, rock

cojera [ko'xera] *nf* lameness; *(andar cojo)* limp

cojín [ko'xin] *nm* cushion

cojinete [koxi'nete] *nm* small cushion, pad; *(Tec)* (ball) bearing

cojo, -a *etc* ['koxo, a] *vb ver* **coger** ■ *adj (que no puede andar)* lame, crippled; *(mueble)* wobbly ■ *nm/f* lame person, cripple

cojón [ko'xon] *nm (fam!)* ball (!), testicle; **¡cojones!** shit! (!)

cojonudo, -a [koxo'nuðo, a] *adj (Esp fam)* great, fantastic

col [kol] *nf* cabbage; **coles de Bruselas** Brussels sprouts

cola ['kola] *nf* tail; *(de gente)* queue; *(lugar)* end, last place; *(para pegar)* glue, gum; *(de vestido)* train; **hacer** ~ to queue (up)

colaboración [kolaβora'θjon] *nf (gen)* collaboration; *(en periódico)* contribution

colaborador, a [kolaβora'ðor, a] *nm/f* collaborator; contributor

colaborar [kolaβo'rar] *vi* to collaborate

colación [kola'θjon] *nf*: **sacar a** ~ to bring up

colado, -a [ko'laðo, a] *adj (metal)* cast ■ *nf*: **hacer la colada** to do the washing

colador [kola'ðor] *nm (de té)* strainer; *(para verduras etc)* colander

colapsar [kolap'sar] *vt (tráfico etc)* to bring to a standstill

colapso [ko'lapso] *nm* collapse; ~ **nervioso** nervous breakdown

colar [ko'lar] *vt (líquido)* to strain off; *(metal)* to cast ■ *vi* to ooze, seep (through); **colarse** *vr* to jump the queue; *(en mitin)* to sneak in; *(equivocarse)* to slip up; **colarse en** to get into without paying; *(en una fiesta)* to gatecrash

colateral [kolate'ral] *nm* collateral

colcha ['koltʃa] *nf* bedspread

colchón [kol'tʃon] *nm* mattress; ~ **inflable** inflatable mattress

colchoneta [koltʃo'neta] *nf (en gimnasio)* mattress; ~ **hinchable** airbed

colear [kole'ar] *vi (perro)* to wag its tail

colección [kolek'θjon] *nf* collection

coleccionar [kolekθjo'nar] *vt* to collect

coleccionista [kolekθjo'nista] *nm/f* collector

colecta [ko'lekta] *nf* collection

colectivo, -a [kolek'tiβo, a] *adj* collective, joint ■ *nm (Am: autobús)* (small) bus; *(taxi)* collective taxi

colector [kolek'tor] *nm* collector; *(sumidero)* sewer

colega [ko'leɣa] *nm/f* colleague

colegiado, -a [kole'xjaðo, a] *adj (profesional)* registered ■ *nm/f* referee

colegial, a [kole'xjal, a] *adj (Escol etc)* school *cpd*, college *cpd* ■ *nm/f* schoolboy/girl

colegio [ko'lexjo] *nm* college; *(escuela)* school; *(de abogados etc)* association; ~ **de internos** boarding school; **ir al** ~ to go to school; *see note*

● COLEGIO

A *colegio* is normally a private primary or secondary school. In the state system it means a primary school although these are also called *escuela*. State secondary schools are called *institutos*. Extracurricular subjects, such as computing or foreign languages, are offered in private schools called *academias*.

---

colegir [kole'xir] *vt (juntar)* to collect, gather; *(deducir)* to infer, conclude

cólera ['kolera] *nf (ira)* anger; **montar en** ~ to get angry ■ *nm (Med)* cholera

colérico, -a [ko'leriko, a] *adj* angry, furious

colesterol [koleste'rol] *nm* cholesterol

coleta [ko'leta] *nf* pigtail

coletazo [kole'taθo] *nm*: **dar un** ~ *(animal)* to flap its tail; **los últimos coletazos** death throes

coletilla [kole'tiʎa] *nf (en carta)* postscript; *(en conversación)* filler phrase

colgado, -a [kol'ɣaðo, a] *pp de* **colgar** ■ *adj*

hanging; (*ahorcado*) hanged; **dejar ~ a algn** to let sb down

colgajo [kol'ɣaxo] *nm* tatter

colgante [kol'ɣante] *adj* hanging; *ver* **puente** ■ *nm* (*joya*) pendant

colgar [kol'ɣar] *vt* to hang (up); (*tender: ropa*) to hang out ■ *vi* to hang; (*teléfono*) to hang up; **no cuelgue** please hold

colgué [kol'ɣe], **colguemos** *etc* [kol'ɣemos] *vb ver* **colgar**

colibrí [koli'βri] *nm* hummingbird

cólico ['koliko] *nm* colic

coliflor [koli'flor] *nf* cauliflower

coligiendo *etc* [koli'xjenðo] *vb ver* **colegir**

colija *etc* [ko'lixa] *vb ver* **colegir**

colilla [ko'liʎa] *nf* cigarette end, butt

colina [ko'lina] *nf* hill

colindante [kolin'dante] *adj* adjacent, neighbouring

colindar [kolin'dar] *vi* to adjoin, be adjacent

colisión [koli'sjon] *nf* collision; **~ de frente** head-on crash

colitis [ko'litis] *nf inv*: **tener ~** to have diarrhoea

collar [ko'ʎar] *nm* necklace; (*de perro*) collar

colmado, -a [kol'maðo, a] *adj* full ■ *nm* grocer's (shop) (*Brit*), grocery store (*US*)

colmar [kol'mar] *vt* to fill to the brim; (*fig*) to fulfil, realize

colmena [kol'mena] *nf* beehive

colmillo [kol'miʎo] *nm* (*diente*) eye tooth; (*de elefante*) tusk; (*de perro*) fang

colmo ['kolmo] *nm* height, summit; **para ~ de desgracias** to cap it all; **¡eso es ya el ~!** that's beyond a joke!

colocación [koloka'θjon] *nf* (*acto*) placing; (*empleo*) job, position; (*situación*) place, position; (*Com*) placement

colocar [kolo'kar] *vt* to place, put, position; (*poner en empleo*) to find a job for; **~ dinero** to invest money; **colocarse** *vr* to place o.s.; (*conseguir trabajo*) to find a job

colofón [kolo'fon] *nm*: **como ~ de las conversaciones** as a sequel to o following the talks

Colombia [ko'lombja] *nf* Colombia

colombiano, -a [kolom'bjano, a] *adj, nm/f* Colombian

colon ['kolon] *nm* colon

colón [ko'lon] *nm* (*Am*) *monetary unit of Costa Rica and El Salvador*

Colonia [ko'lonja] *nf* Cologne

colonia [ko'lonja] *nf* colony; (*de casas*) housing estate; (*agua de colonia*) cologne; **~ escolar** summer camp (for schoolchildren)

colonice *etc* [kolo'niθe] *vb ver* **colonizar**

colonización [koloniθa'θjon] *nf* colonization

colonizador, a [koloniθa'ðor, a] *adj* colonizing ■ *nm/f* colonist, settler

colonizar [koloni'θar] *vt* to colonize

colono [ko'lono] *nm* (*Pol*) colonist, settler; (*Agr*) tenant farmer

coloque *etc* [ko'loke] *vb ver* **colocar**

coloquial [kolo'kjal] *adj* colloquial

coloquio [ko'lokjo] *nm* conversation; (*congreso*) conference

color [ko'lor] *nm* colour; **a todo ~** in full colour; **verlo todo ~ de rosa** to see everything through rose-coloured spectacles; **le salieron los colores** she blushed

colorado, -a [kolo'raðo, a] *adj* (*rojo*) red; (*Am: chiste*) rude, blue; **ponerse ~** to blush

colorante [kolo'rante] *nm* colouring (matter)

colorar [kolo'rar] *vt* to colour; (*teñir*) to dye

colorear [kolore'ar] *vt* to colour

colorete [kolo'rete] *nm* blusher

colorido [kolo'riðo] *nm* colour(ing)

coloso [ko'loso] *nm* colossus

columbrar [kolum'brar] *vt* to glimpse, spy

columna [ko'lumna] *nf* column; (*pilar*) pillar; (*apoyo*) support; **~ blindada** (*Mil*) armoured column; **~ vertebral** spine, spinal column

columpiar [kolum'pjar] *vt*, **columpiarse** *vr* to swing

columpio [ko'lumpjo] *nm* swing

colza ['kolθa] *nf* rape; **aceite de ~** rapeseed oil

coma ['koma] *nf* comma ■ *nm* (*Med*) coma

comadre [ko'maðre] *nf* (*madrina*) godmother; (*vecina*) neighbour; (*chismosa*) gossip

comadrear [komaðre'ar] *vi* (*esp Am*) to gossip

comadreja [koma'ðrexa] *nf* weasel

comadrona [koma'ðrona] *nf* midwife

comandancia [koman'danθja] *nf* command

comandante [koman'dante] *nm* commandant; (*grado*) major

comandar [koman'dar] *vt* to command

comando [ko'mando] *nm* (*Mil: mando*) command; (: *grupo*) commando unit; (*Inform*) command; **~ de búsqueda** search command

comarca [ko'marka] *nf* region; *ver tb* **provincia**

comarcal [komar'kal] *adj* local

comba ['komba] *nf* (*curva*) curve; (*en viga*) warp; (*cuerda*) skipping rope; **saltar a la ~** to skip

combar [kom'bar] *vt* to bend, curve

combate [kom'bate] *nm* fight; (*fig*) battle; **fuera de ~** out of action

combatiente [komba'tjente] *nm* combatant

combatir [komba'tir] *vt* to fight, combat

combatividad [kombatiβi'ðað] *nf* (*actitud*) fighting spirit; (*agresividad*) aggressiveness

combativo, -a [komba'tiβo, a] *adj* full of fight
combi ['kombi] *nm* fridge-freezer
combinación [kombina'θjon] *nf*
combination; (*Química*) compound; (*bebida*)
cocktail; (*plan*) scheme, setup; (*prenda*) slip
combinado, -a [kombi'naðo, a] *adj*: **plato ~**
main course served with vegetables
combinar [kombi'nar] *vt* to combine; (*colores*)
to match
combustible [kombus'tiβle] *nm* fuel
combustión [kombus'tjon] *nf* combustion
comedia [ko'meðja] *nf* comedy; (*Teat*) play,
drama; (*fig*) farce
comediante [kome'ðjante] *nm/f* (comic)
actor/actress
comedido, -a [kome'ðiðo, a] *adj* moderate
comedirse [kome'ðirse] *vr* to behave
moderately; (*ser cortés*) to be courteous
comedor, a [kome'ðor, a] *nm/f* (*persona*)
glutton ■ *nm* (*habitación*) dining room;
(*restaurante*) restaurant; (*cantina*) canteen
comencé [komen'θe], **comencemos** *etc*
[komen'θemos] *vb ver* **comenzar**
comensal [komen'sal] *nm/f* fellow guest/
diner
comentar [komen'tar] *vt* to comment on;
(*fam*) to discuss; **comentó que...** he made
the comment that...
comentario [komen'tarjo] *nm* comment,
remark; (*Lit*) commentary; **comentarios**
nmpl gossip *sg*; **dar lugar a comentarios**
to cause gossip
comentarista [komenta'rista] *nm/f*
commentator
comenzar [komen'θar] *vt, vi* to begin, start,
commence; **~ a hacer algo** to begin *o* start
doing *o* to do sth
comer [ko'mer] *vt* to eat; (*Damas: Ajédrez*) to
take, capture ■ *vi* to eat; (*almorzar*) to have
lunch; **comerse** *vr* to eat up; (*párrafo etc*) to
skip; **~ el coco a** (*fam*) to brainwash; **¡a ~!**
food's ready!
comercial [komer'θjal] *adj* commercial;
(*relativo al negocio*) business *cpd*
comerciante [komer'θjante] *nm/f* trader,
merchant; (*tendero*) shopkeeper; **~ exclusivo**
(*Com*) sole trader
comerciar [komer'θjar] *vi* to trade, do
business
comercio [ko'merθjo] *nm* commerce, trade;
(*negocio*) business; (*grandes empresas*) big
business; (*fig*) dealings *pl*; **~ autorizado**
(*Com*) licensed trade; **~ electrónico**
e-commerce; **~ exterior** foreign trade
comestible [komes'tiβle] *adj* eatable, edible
■ *nm*: **comestibles** food *sg*, foodstuffs; (*Com*)
groceries

cometa [ko'meta] *nm* comet ■ *nf* kite
cometer [kome'ter] *vt* to commit
cometido [kome'tiðo] *nm* (*misión*) task,
assignment; (*deber*) commitment
comezón [kome'θon] *nf* itch, itching
cómic (*pl* **cómics**) ['komik, 'komiks] *nm*
comic
comicios [ko'miθjos] *nmpl* elections; (*voto*)
voting *sg*
cómico, -a ['komiko, a] *adj* comic(al) ■ *nm/f*
comedian; (*de teatro*) (comic) actor/actress
comida *etc* [ko'miða] *vb ver* **comedirse** ■ *nf*
(*alimento*) food; (*almuerzo, cena*) meal; (*de
mediodía*) lunch; (*Am*) dinner
comidilla [komi'ðiʎa] *nf*: **ser la ~ de la
ciudad** to be the talk of the town
comience *etc* [ko'mjenθe] *vb ver* **comenzar**
comienzo *etc* [ko'mjenθo] *vb ver* **comenzar**
■ *nm* beginning, start; **dar ~ a un acto** to
begin a ceremony; **~ del archivo** (*Inform*)
top-of-file
comillas [ko'miʎas] *nfpl* quotation marks
comilón, -ona [komi'lon, ona] *adj* greedy
■ *nf* (*fam*) blow-out
comino [ko'mino] *nm* cumin (seed); **no me
importa un ~** I don't give a damn!
comisaría [komisa'ria] *nf* police station,
precinct (*US*); (*Mil*) commissariat
comisario [komi'sarjo] *nm* (*Mil etc*)
commissary; (*Pol*) commissar
comisión [komi'sjon] *nf* (*Com: pago*)
commission, rake-off (*fam*); (: *junta*) board;
(*encargo*) assignment; **~ mixta/permanente**
joint/standing committee; **Comisiones
Obreras** (*Esp*) *formerly Communist Union
Confederation*
comisura [komi'sura] *nf*: **~ de los labios**
corner of the mouth
comité (*pl* **~s**) *nm* [komi'te, komi'tes]
committee; **comité de empresa** works
council
comitiva [komi'tiβa] *nf* suite, retinue
como ['komo] *adv* as; (*tal como*) like;
(*aproximadamente*) about, approximately
■ *conj* (*ya que, puesto que*) as, since; (*en seguida
que*) as soon as; (*si: +subjun*) if; **¡~ no!** of
course!; **~ no lo haga hoy** unless he does it
today; **~ si** as if; **es tan alto ~ ancho** it is as
high as it is wide
cómo ['komo] *adv* how?, why? ■ *excl* what?,
I beg your pardon? ■ *nm*: **el ~ y el porqué**
the whys and wherefores; **¿~ está Ud?** how
are you?; **¿~ no?** why not?; **¡~ no!** (*esp Am*) of
course!; **¿~ son?** what are they like?
cómoda ['komoða] *nf* chest of drawers
comodidad [komoði'ðað] *nf* comfort; **venga
a su ~** come at your convenience

comodín [komoˈðin] *nm* joker; (*Inform*) wild card; **símbolo** ~ wild-card character

cómodo, -a [ˈkomoðo, a] *adj* comfortable; (*práctico, de fácil uso*) convenient

comodón, -ona [komoˈðon, ona] *adj* comfort-loving ■ *nm/f*: **ser un(a) ~/ona** to like one's home comforts

comoquiera [comoˈkjera] *conj*: ~ **que** (+*subjun*) in whatever way; ~ **que sea eso** however that may be

comp. *abr* (= *compárese*) cp

compacto, -a [komˈpakto, a] *adj* compact

compadecer [kompaðeˈθer] *vt* to pity, be sorry for; **compadecerse** *vr*: **compadecerse de** to pity, be sorry for

compadezca *etc* [kompaˈðeθka] *vb ver* **compadecer**

compadre [komˈpaðre] *nm* (*padrino*) godfather; (*esp Am: amigo*) friend, pal

compaginar [kompaxiˈnar] *vt*: ~ **A con B** to bring A into line with B; **compaginarse** *vr*: **compaginarse con** to tally with, square with

compañerismo [kompaɲeˈrismo] *nm* comradeship

compañero, -a [kompaˈɲero, a] *nm/f* companion; (*novio*) boyfriend/girlfriend; ~ **de clase** classmate

compañía [kompaˈɲia] *nf* company; ~ **afiliada** associated company; ~ **concesionaria** franchiser; ~ **(no) cotizable** (un)listed company; ~ **inversionista** investment trust; **hacer ~ a algn** to keep sb company

comparación [komparaˈθjon] *nf* comparison; **en ~ con** in comparison with

comparar [kompaˈrar] *vt* to compare

comparativo, -a [komparaˈtiβo, a] *adj* comparative

comparecencia [kompareˈθenθja] *nf* (*Jur*) appearance (in court); **orden de ~** summons *sg*

comparecer [kompareˈθer] *vi* to appear (in court)

comparezca *etc* [kompaˈreθka] *vb ver* **comparecer**

comparsa [komˈparsa] *nm/f* extra

compartimento [kompartiˈmento], **compartimiento** [kompartiˈmjento] *nm* (*Ferro*) compartment; (*de mueble, cajón*) section; ~ **estanco** (*fig*) watertight compartment

compartir [komparˈtir] *vt* to divide (up), share (out)

compás [komˈpas] *nm* (*Mus*) beat, rhythm; (*Mat*) compasses *pl*; (*Naut etc*) compass; **al ~** in time

compasión [kompaˈsjon] *nf* compassion, pity

compasivo, -a [kompaˈsiβo, a] *adj* compassionate

compatibilidad [kompatiβiliˈðað] *nf* (*tb Inform*) compatibility

compatible [kompaˈtiβle] *adj* compatible

compatriota [kompaˈtrjota] *nm/f* compatriot, fellow countryman/woman

compendiar [kompenˈdjar] *vt* to summarize; (*libro*) to abridge

compendio [komˈpendjo] *nm* summary; abridgement

compenetración [kompenetraˈθjon] *nf* (*fig*) mutual understanding

compenetrarse [kompeneˈtrarse] *vr* (*fig*): ~ **(muy) bien** to get on (very) well together

compensación [kompensaˈθjon] *nf* compensation; (*Jur*) damages *pl*; (*Com*) clearing

compensar [kompenˈsar] *vt* to compensate; (*pérdida*) to make up for

competencia [kompeˈtenθja] *nf* (*incumbencia*) domain, field; (*Com*) receipt; (*Jur, habilidad*) competence; (*rivalidad*) competition

competente [kompeˈtente] *adj* (*Jur, persona*) competent; (*conveniente*) suitable

competer [kompeˈter] *vi*: ~ **a** to be the responsibility of, fall to

competición [kompetiˈθjon] *nf* competition

competidor, a [kompetiˈðor, a] *nm/f* competitor

competir [kompeˈtir] *vi* to compete

competitivo, -a [kompetiˈtiβo, a] *adj* competitive

compilación [kompilaˈθjon] *nf* compilation; **tiempo de ~** (*Inform*) compile time

compilador [kompilaˈðor] *nm* compiler

compilar [kompiˈlar] *vt* to compile

compinche [komˈpintʃe] *nm/f* (*fam*) crony

compita *etc* [komˈpita] *vb ver* **competir**

complacencia [komplaˈθenθja] *nf* (*placer*) pleasure; (*satisfacción*) satisfaction; (*buena voluntad*) willingness

complacer [komplaˈθer] *vt* to please; **complacerse** *vr* to be pleased

complaciente [komplaˈθjente] *adj* kind, obliging, helpful

complazca *etc* [komˈplaθka] *vb ver* **complacer**

complejo, -a [komˈplexo, a] *adj, nm* complex

complementario, -a [komplemenˈtarjo, a] *adj* complementary

complemento [kompleˈmento] *nm* (*de moda, diseño*) accessory; (*Ling*) complement

completar [kompleˈtar] *vt* to complete

completo, -a [komˈpleto, a] *adj* complete; (*perfecto*) perfect; (*lleno*) full ■ *nm* full complement

complexión [komple'ksjon] nf constitution
complicación [komplika'θjon] nf complication
complicado, -a [kompli'kaðo, a] adj complicated; **estar ~ en** to be involved in
complicar [kompli'kar] vt to complicate
cómplice ['kompliθe] nm/f accomplice
complique etc [kom'plike] vb ver **complicar**
complot (pl **complots**) [kom'plo(t), kom'plos] nm plot; (conspiración) conspiracy
compondré etc [kompon'dre] vb ver **componer**
componenda [kompo'nenda] nf compromise; (pey) shady deal
componente [kompo'nente] adj, nm component
componer [kompo'ner] vt to make up, put together; (Mus: Lit: Imprenta) to compose; (algo roto) to mend, repair; (adornar) to adorn; (arreglar) to arrange; (reconciliar) to reconcile; **componerse** vr: **componerse de** to consist of; **componérselas para hacer algo** to manage to do sth
componga etc [kom'ponga] vb ver **componer**
comportamiento [komporta'mjento] nm behaviour, conduct
comportarse [kompor'tarse] vr to behave
composición [komposi'θjon] nf composition
compositor, a [komposi'tor, a] nm/f composer
compostelano, -a [komposte'lano, a] adj of o from Santiago de Compostela ■ nm/f native o inhabitant of Santiago de Compostela
compostura [kompos'tura] nf (reparación) mending, repair; (composición) composition; (acuerdo) agreement; (actitud) composure
compota [kom'pota] nf compote, preserve
compra ['kompra] nf purchase; **compras** nfpl purchases, shopping sg; **hacer la ~/ir de compras** to do the/go shopping; **~ a granel** (Com) bulk buying; **~ proteccionista** (Com) support buying
comprador, a [kompra'ðor, a] nm/f buyer, purchaser
comprar [kom'prar] vt to buy, purchase; **~ deudas** (Com) to factor
compraventa [kompra'βenta] nf (Jur) contract of sale
comprender [kompren'der] vt to understand; (incluir) to comprise, include
comprensible [kompren'siβle] adj understandable
comprensión [kompren'sjon] nf understanding; (totalidad) comprehensiveness
comprensivo, -a [kompren'siβo, a] adj comprehensive; (actitud) understanding

compresa [kom'presa] nf compress; **~ higiénica** sanitary towel (Brit) o napkin (US)
compresión [kompre'sjon] nf compression
comprimido, -a [kompri'miðo] adj compressed ■ nm (Med) pill, tablet; **en caracteres comprimidos** (Tip) condensed
comprimir [kompri'mir] vt to compress; (fig) to control; (Inform) to pack
comprobación [komproβa'θjon] nf: **~ general de cuentas** (Com) general audit
comprobante [kompro'βante] nm proof; (Com) voucher; **~ (de pago)** receipt
comprobar [kompro'βar] vt to check; (probar) to prove; (Tec) to check, test
comprometedor, a [kompromete'ðor, a] adj compromising
comprometer [komprome'ter] vt to compromise; (exponer) to endanger; **comprometerse** vr to compromise o.s.; (involucrarse) to get involved
comprometido, -a [komprome'tiðo, a] adj (situación) awkward; (escritor etc) committed
compromiso [kompro'miso] nm (obligación) obligation; (cita) engagement, date; (cometido) commitment; (convenio) agreement; (dificultad) awkward situation; **libre de ~** (Com) without obligation
comprueba etc [kom'prweβa] vb ver **comprobar**
compuerta [kom'pwerta] nf (en canal) sluice, floodgate; (Inform) gate
compuesto, -a [kom'pwesto, a] pp de **componer** ■ adj: **~ de** composed of, made up of ■ nm compound; (Med) preparation
compulsar [kompul'sar] vt (cotejar) to collate, compare; (Jur) to make an attested copy of
compulsivo, -a [kompul'siβo, a] adj compulsive
compungido, -a [kompun'xiðo, a] adj remorseful
compuse etc [com'puse] vb ver **componer**
computador [komputa'ðor] nm, **computadora** [komputa'ðora] nf computer; **~ central** mainframe computer; **~ especializado** dedicated computer; **~ personal** personal computer
computar [kompu'tar] vt to calculate, compute
cómputo ['komputo] nm calculation
comulgar [komul'ɣar] vi to receive communion
comulgue etc [ko'mulɣe] vb ver **comulgar**
común [ko'mun] adj (gen) common; (corriente) ordinary; **por lo ~** generally ■ nm: **el ~** the community
comuna [ko'muna] nf commune; (Am) district

comunicación [komunika'θjon] *nf* communication; (*informe*) report

comunicado [komuni'kaðo] *nm* announcement; ~ **de prensa** press release

comunicar [komuni'kar] *vt* to communicate; (*Arq*) to connect ∎ *vi* to communicate; to send a report; **comunicarse** *vr* to communicate; **está comunicando** (*Telec*) the line's engaged (*Brit*) o busy (*US*)

comunicativo, -a [komunika'tiβo, a] *adj* communicative

comunidad [komuni'ðað] *nf* community; ~ **autónoma** autonomous region; ~ **de vecinos** residents' association; **C~ Económica Europea (CEE)** European Economic Community (EEC); *see note*

COMUNIDAD

The 1978 Constitution provides for a degree of self-government for the 19 regions, called *comunidades autónomas* or *autonomías*. Some, such as Catalonia and the Basque Country, with their own language, history and culture, have long felt separate from the rest of Spain. This explains why some of the autonomías have more devolved powers than others, in all matters except foreign affairs and national defence. The regions are: Andalucía, Aragón, Asturias, Islas Baleares, Canarias, Cantabria, Castilla y León, Castilla-La Mancha, Cataluña, Extremadura, Galicia, Madrid, Murcia, Navarra, País Vasco, La Rioja, Comunidad Valenciana, Ceuta, Melilla.

comunión [komu'njon] *nf* communion

comunique *etc* [komu'nike] *vb ver* **comunicar**

comunismo [komu'nismo] *nm* communism

comunista [komu'nista] *adj, nm/f* communist

comunitario, -a [komuni'tarjo, a] *adj* (*de la* CE) Community *cpd*, EC *cpd*

PALABRA CLAVE

con [kon] *prep* **1** (*medio, compañía, modo*) with; **comer con cuchara** to eat with a spoon; **café con leche** white coffee; **estoy con un catarro** I've got a cold; **pasear con algn** to go for a walk with sb; **con habilidad** skilfully

2 (*a pesar de*): **con todo, merece nuestros respetos** all the same o even so, he deserves our respect

3 (*para con*): **es muy bueno para con los niños** he's very good with (the) children

4 (*+infin*): **con llegar tan tarde se quedó sin comer** by arriving o because he arrived so late he missed out on eating; **con estudiar un poco apruebas** with a bit of studying you should pass

5 (*queja*): **¡con las ganas que tenía de ir!** and I really wanted to go (too)!

∎ *conj*: **con que: será suficiente con que le escribas** it will be enough if you write to her

conato [ko'nato] *nm* attempt; ~ **de robo** attempted robbery

cóncavo, -a ['konkaβo, a] *adj* concave

concebir [konθe'βir] *vt* to conceive; (*imaginar*) to imagine ∎ *vi* to conceive

conceder [konθe'ðer] *vt* to concede

concejal, a [konθe'xal, a] *nm/f* town councillor

concejo [kon'θexo] *nm* council

concentración [konθentra'θjon] *nf* concentration

concentrar [konθen'trar] *vt*, **concentrarse** *vr* to concentrate

concéntrico, -a [kon'θentriko, a] *adj* concentric

concepción [konθep'θjon] *nf* conception

concepto [kon'θepto] *nm* concept; **por ~ de** as, by way of; **tener buen ~ de algn** to think highly of sb; **bajo ningún ~** under no circumstances

conceptuar [konθep'twar] *vt* to judge

concernir [konθer'nir] *vi*: **en lo que concierne a** concerning

concertar [konθer'tar] *vt* (*Mus*) to harmonize; (*acordar: precio*) to agree; (: *tratado*) to conclude; (*trato*) to arrange, fix up; (*combinar: esfuerzos*) to coordinate; (*reconciliar: personas*) to reconcile ∎ *vi* to harmonize, be in tune

concesión [konθe'sjon] *nf* concession; (*Com: fabricación*) licence

concesionario, -a [konθesjo'narjo, a] *nm/f* (*Com*) (licensed) dealer, agent, concessionaire; (: *de venta*) franchisee; (: *de transportes etc*) contractor

concha ['kontʃa] *nf* shell; (*Am fam!*) cunt (!)

conchabarse [kontʃa'βarse] *vr*: ~ **contra** to gang up on

conciencia [kon'θjenθja] *nf* (*moral*) conscience; (*conocimiento*) awareness; **libertad de ~** freedom of worship; **tener/tomar ~ de** to be/become aware of; **tener la ~ limpia** o **tranquila** to have a clear conscience; **tener plena ~ de** to be fully aware of

concienciar [konθjen'θjar] *vt* to make aware; **concienciarse** *vr* to become aware

concienzudo, -a [konθjen'θuðo, a] *adj* conscientious

concierne *etc* [kon'θjerne] *vb ver* **concernir**

concierto *etc* [kon'θjerto] *vb ver* **concertar** ■ *nm* concert; (*obra*) concerto

conciliación [konθilja'θjon] *nf* conciliation

conciliar [konθi'ljar] *vt* to reconcile ■ *adj* (*Rel*) of a council; ~ **el sueño** to get to sleep

concilio [kon'θiljo] *nm* council

concisión [konθi'sjon] *nf* conciseness

conciso, -a [kon'θiso, a] *adj* concise

conciudadano, -a [konθjuða'ðano, a] *nm/f* fellow citizen

concluir [konklu'ir] *vt* (*acabar*) to conclude; (*inferir*) to infer, deduce ■ *vi*, **concluirse** *vr* to conclude; **todo ha concluido** it's all over

conclusión [konklu'sjon] *nf* conclusion; **llegar a la ~ de que ...** to come to the conclusion that ...

concluya *etc* [kon'kluja] *vb ver* **concluir**

concluyente [konklu'jente] *adj* (*prueba, información*) conclusive

concordancia [konkor'ðanθja] *nf* agreement

concordar [konkor'ðar] *vt* to reconcile ■ *vi* to agree, tally

concordia [kon'korðja] *nf* harmony

concretamente [konkreta'mente] *adv* specifically, to be exact

concretar [konkre'tar] *vt* to make concrete, make more specific; (*problema*) to pinpoint; **concretarse** *vr* to become more definite

concreto, -a [kon'kreto, a] *adj, nm* (*Am*) concrete; **en ~** (*en resumen*) to sum up; (*específicamente*) specifically; **no hay nada en ~** there's nothing definite

concubina [konku'βina] *nf* concubine

concuerde *etc* [kon'kwerðe] *vb ver* **concordar**

concupiscencia [konkupis'θenθja] *nf* (*avaricia*) greed; (*lujuria*) lustfulness

concurrencia [konku'rrenθja] *nf* turnout

concurrido, -a [konku'rriðo, a] *adj* (*calle*) busy; (*local: reunión*) crowded

concurrir [konku'rrir] *vi* (*juntarse: ríos*) to meet, come together; (: *personas*) to gather, meet

concursante [konkur'sante] *nm* competitor

concursar [konkur'sar] *vi* to compete

concurso [kon'kurso] *nm* (*de público*) crowd; (*Escol: Deporte, competición*) competition; (*Com*) invitation to tender; (*examen*) open competition; (*TV etc*) quiz; (*ayuda*) help, cooperation

condado [kon'daðo] *nm* county

condal [kon'dal] *adj*: **la ciudad ~** Barcelona

conde ['konde] *nm* count

condecoración [kondekora'θjon] *nf* (*Mil*) medal, decoration

condecorar [kondeko'rar] *vt* to decorate

condena [kon'dena] *nf* sentence; **cumplir una ~** to serve a sentence

condenación [kondena'θjon] *nf* condemnation; (*Rel*) damnation

condenado, -a [konde'naðo, a] *adj* (*Jur*) condemned; (*fam: maldito*) damned ■ *nm/f* (*Jur*) convicted person

condenar [konde'nar] *vt* to condemn; (*Jur*) to convict; **condenarse** *vr* (*Jur*) to confess (one's guilt); (*Rel*) to be damned

condensar [konden'sar] *vt* to condense

condesa [kon'desa] *nf* countess

condescendencia [kondesθen'denθja] *nf* condescension; **aceptar algo por ~** to accept sth so as not to hurt feelings

condescender [kondesθen'der] *vi* to acquiesce, comply

condescienda *etc* [kondes'θjenda] *vb ver* **condescender**

condición [kondi'θjon] *nf* (*gen*) condition; (*rango*) social class; **condiciones** *nfpl* (*cualidades*) qualities; (*estado*) condition; **a ~ de que ...** on condition that ...; **las condiciones del contrato** the terms of the contract; **condiciones de trabajo** working conditions; **condiciones de venta** conditions of sale

condicional [kondiθjo'nal] *adj* conditional

condicionamiento [kondiθjona'mjento] *nm* conditioning

condicionar [kondiθjo'nar] *vt* (*acondicionar*) to condition; ~ **algo a algo** to make sth conditional *o* dependent on sth

condimento [kondi'mento] *nm* seasoning

condiscípulo, -a [kondis'θipulo, a] *nm/f* fellow student

condolerse [kondo'lerse] *vr* to sympathize

condominio [kondo'minjo] *nm* (*Com*) joint ownership; (*Am*) condominium, apartment

condón [kon'don] *nm* condom

condonar [kondo'nar] *vt* (*Jur: reo*) to reprieve; (*Com: deuda*) to cancel

cóndor ['kondor] *nm* condor

conducente [kondu'θente] *adj*: ~ **a** conducive to, leading to

conducir [kondu'θir] *vt* to take, convey; (*Elec etc*) to carry; (*Auto*) to drive; (*negocio*) to manage ■ *vi* to drive; (*fig*) to lead; **conducirse** *vr* to behave

conducta [kon'dukta] *nf* conduct, behaviour

conducto [kon'dukto] *nm* pipe, tube; (*fig*) channel; (*Elec*) lead; **por ~ de** through

conductor, a [konduk'tor, a] *adj* leading, guiding ■ *nm* (*Física*) conductor; (*de vehículo*) driver

conduela *etc* [kon'dwela] *vb ver* **condolerse**

conduje *etc* [kon'duxe] *vb ver* **conducir**
conduzca *etc* [kon'duθka] *vb ver* **conducir**
conectado, -a [konek'taðo, a] *adj* (*Elec*) connected, plugged in; (*Inform*) on-line
conectar [konek'tar] *vt* to connect (up), plug in; (*Inform*) to toggle on; **conectarse** *vr* (*Inform*) to log in *or* on
conejillo [kone'xiʎo] *nm*: ~ **de Indias** guinea pig
conejo [ko'nexo] *nm* rabbit
conexión [konek'sjon] *nf* connection; (*Inform*) logging in *or* on
confabularse [konfaβu'larse] *vr*: ~ (**para hacer algo**) to plot *o* conspire (to do sth)
confección [konfek'θjon] *nf* (*preparación*) preparation, making-up; (*industria*) clothing industry; (*producto*) article; **de ~** (*ropa*) off-the-peg
confeccionar [konfe(k)θjo'nar] *vt* to make (up)
confederación [konfeðera'θjon] *nf* confederation
conferencia [konfe'renθja] *nf* conference; (*lección*) lecture; (*Telec*) call; ~ **de cobro revertido** (*Telec*) reversed-charge (*Brit*) *o* collect (*US*) call; ~ **cumbre** summit (conference)
conferenciante [konferen'θjante] *nm/f* lecturer
conferir [konfe'rir] *vt* to award
confesar [konfe'sar] *vt* (*admitir*) to confess, admit; (*error*) to acknowledge; (*crimen*) to own up to
confesión [konfe'sjon] *nf* confession
confesionario [konfesjo'narjo] *nm* confessional
confeso, -a [kon'feso, a] *adj* (*Jur etc*) self-confessed
confeti [kon'feti] *nm* confetti
confiado, -a [kon'fjaðo, a] *adj* (*crédulo*) trusting; (*seguro*) confident; (*presumido*) conceited, vain
confianza [kon'fjanθa] *nf* trust; (*aliento, confidencia*) confidence; (*familiaridad*) intimacy, familiarity; (*pey*) vanity, conceit; **margen de ~** credibility gap; **tener ~ con algn** to be on close terms with sb
confiar [kon'fjar] *vt* to entrust ■ *vi* (*fiarse*) to trust; (*contar con*) to rely; **confiarse** *vr* to put one's trust in
confidencia [konfi'ðenθja] *nf* confidence
confidencial [konfiðen'θjal] *adj* confidential
confidente [konfi'ðente] *nm/f* confidant/confidante; (*policial*) informer
confiera *etc* [kon'fjera] *vb ver* **conferir**
confiese *etc* [kon'fjese] *vb ver* **confesar**
configuración [konfiɣura'θjon] *nf* (*tb Inform*) configuration; **la ~ del terreno** the lie of the

land; ~ **de bits** (*Inform*) bit pattern
configurar [konfiɣu'rar] *vt* to shape, form
confín [kon'fin] *nm* limit; **confines** *nmpl* confines, limits
confinar [konfi'nar] *vi* to confine; (*desterrar*) to banish
confiriendo *etc* [konfi'rjendo] *vb ver* **conferir**
confirmación [konfirma'θjon] *nf* confirmation; (*Rel*) Confirmation
confirmar [konfir'mar] *vt* to confirm; (*Jur etc*) to corroborate; **la excepción confirma la regla** the exception proves the rule
confiscar [konfis'kar] *vt* to confiscate
confisque *etc* [kon'fiske] *vb ver* **confiscar**
confitado, -a [konfi'taðo, a] *adj*: **fruta confitada** crystallized fruit
confite [kon'fite] *nm* sweet (*Brit*), candy (*US*)
confitería [konfite'ria] *nf* confectionery; (*tienda*) confectioner's (shop)
confitura [konfi'tura] *nf* jam
conflagración [konflaɣra'θjon] *nf* conflagration
conflictivo, -a [konflik'tiβo, a] *adj* (*asunto, propuesta*) controversial; (*país, situación*) troubled
conflicto [kon'flikto] *nm* conflict; (*fig*) clash; (: *dificultad*): **estar en un** ~ to be in a jam; ~ **laboral** labour dispute
confluir [konflu'ir] *vi* (*ríos etc*) to meet; (*gente*) to gather
confluya *etc* [kon'fluja] *vb ver* **confluir**
conformar [konfor'mar] *vt* to shape, fashion ■ *vi* to agree; **conformarse** *vr* to conform; (*resignarse*) to resign o.s.
conforme [kon'forme] *adj* alike, similar; (*de acuerdo*) agreed, in agreement; (*satisfecho*) satisfied ■ *adv* as ■ *excl* agreed! ■ *nm* agreement ■ *prep*: ~ **a** in accordance with
conformidad [konformi'ðað] *nf* (*semejanza*) similarity; (*acuerdo*) agreement; (*resignación*) resignation; **de/en ~ con** in accordance with; **dar su ~** to consent
conformismo [konfor'mismo] *nm* conformism
conformista [konfor'mista] *nm/f* conformist
confort (*pl* **conforts**) [kon'for, kon'for(t)s] *nm* comfort
confortable [konfor'taβle] *adj* comfortable
confortar [konfor'tar] *vt* to comfort
confraternidad [konfraterni'ðað] *nf* brotherhood; **espíritu de** ~ feeling of unity
confraternizar [konfraterni'θar] *vi* to fraternize
confrontación [konfronta'θjon] *nf* confrontation
confrontar [konfron'tar] *vt* to confront; (*dos personas*) to bring face to face; (*cotejar*) to

compare ▪ vi to border

confundir [konfun'dir] vt (borrar) to blur; (equivocar) to mistake, confuse; (mezclar) to mix; (turbar) to confuse; **confundirse** vr (hacerse borroso) to become blurred; (turbarse) to get confused; (equivocarse) to make a mistake; (mezclarse) to mix

confusión [konfu'sjon] nf confusion

confusionismo [konfusjo'nismo] nm confusion, uncertainty

confuso, -a [kon'fuso, a] adj (gen) confused; (recuerdo) hazy; (estilo) obscure

congelación [konxela'θjon] nf freezing; ~ **de créditos** credit freeze

congelado, -a [konxe'laðo, a] adj frozen ▪ nmpl: **congelados** frozen food sg o foods

congelador [konxela'ðor] nm freezer, deep freeze

congelar [konxe'lar] vt to freeze; **congelarse** vr (sangre, grasa) to congeal

congénere [kon'xenere] nm/f: **sus congéneres** his peers

congeniar [konxe'njar] vi to get on (Brit) o along (US) (well)

congénito, -a [kon'xenito, a] adj congenital

congestión [konxes'tjon] nf congestion

congestionado, -a [konxestjo'naðo, a] adj congested

congestionar [konxestjo'nar] vt to congest; **congestionarse** vr to become congested; **se le congestionó la cara** his face became flushed

conglomerado [konglome'raðo] nm conglomerate

Congo ['kongo] nm: **el** ~ the Congo

congoja [kon'goxa] nf distress, grief

congraciarse [kongra'θjarse] vr to ingratiate o.s.

congratular [kongratu'lar] vt to congratulate

congregación [kongreɣa'θjon] nf congregation

congregar [kongre'ɣar] vt, **congregarse** vr to gather together

congregue etc [kon'greɣe] vb ver **congregar**

congresista [kongre'sista] nm/f delegate, congressman/woman

congreso [kon'greso] nm congress; **C~ de los Diputados** (Esp Pol) ≈ House of Commons (Brit), House of Representatives (US); ver tb **Las Cortes (españolas)**

congrio ['kongrjo] nm conger (eel)

congruente [kon'grwente] adj congruent, congruous

conífera [ko'nifera] nf conifer

conjetura [konxe'tura] nf guess; (Com) guesstimate

conjeturar [konxetu'rar] vt to guess

conjugación [konxuɣa'θjon] nf conjugation

conjugar [konxu'ɣar] vt to combine, fit together; (Ling) to conjugate

conjugue etc [kon'xuɣe] vb ver **conjugar**

conjunción [konxun'θjon] nf conjunction

conjunctivitis [konxunti'βitis] nf conjunctivitis

conjunto, -a [kon'xunto, a] adj joint, united ▪ nm whole; (Mus) band; (de ropa) ensemble; (Inform) set; **en** ~ as a whole; ~ **integrado de programas** (Inform) integrated software suite

conjura [kon'xura] nf plot, conspiracy

conjurar [konxu'rar] vt (Rel) to exorcise; (peligro) to ward off ▪ vi to plot

conjuro [kon'xuro] nm spell

conllevar [konʎe'βar] vt to bear; (implicar) to imply, involve

conmemoración [konmemora'θjon] nf commemoration

conmemorar [konmemo'rar] vt to commemorate

conmigo [kon'miɣo] pron with me

conminar [konmi'nar] vt to threaten

conmiseración [konmisera'θjon] nf pity, commiseration

conmoción [konmo'θjon] nf shock; (Pol) disturbance; (fig) upheaval; ~ **cerebral** (Med) concussion

conmovedor, a [konmoβe'ðor, a] adj touching, moving; (emocionante) exciting

conmover [konmo'βer] vt to shake, disturb; (fig) to move; **conmoverse** vr (fig) to be moved

conmueva etc [kon'mweβa] vb ver **conmover**

conmutación [konmuta'θjon] nf (Inform) switching; ~ **de mensajes** message switching; ~ **por paquetes** packet switching

conmutador [konmuta'ðor] nm switch; (Am Telec) switchboard

conmutar [konmu'tar] vt (Jur) to commute

connivencia [konni'βenθja] nf: **estar en** ~ **con** to be in collusion with

connotación [konnota'θjon] nf connotation

cono ['kono] nm cone; **C~ Sur** Southern Cone

conocedor, a [konoθe'ðor, a] adj expert, knowledgeable ▪ nm/f expert, connoisseur

conocer [kono'θer] vt to know; (por primera vez) to meet, get to know; (entender) to know about; (reconocer) to recognize; **conocerse** vr (una persona) to know o.s.; (dos personas) to (get to) know each other; **darse a** ~ (presentarse) to make o.s. known; **se conoce que ...** (parece) apparently ...

conocido, -a [kono'θiðo, a] adj (well-)known ▪ nm/f acquaintance

conocimiento [konoθi'mjento] *nm*
knowledge; (*Med*) consciousness; (*Naut*:
tb: **conocimiento de embarque**) bill of
lading; **conocimientos** *nmpl* (*personas*)
acquaintances; (*saber*) knowledge *sg*;
hablar con ~ de causa to speak from
experience; **~ (de embarque) aéreo** (*Com*)
air waybill
conozca *etc* [ko'noθka] *vb ver* **conocer**
conque ['konke] *conj* and so, so then
conquense [kon'kense] *adj* of *o* from Cuenca
■ *nm/f* native *o* inhabitant of Cuenca
conquista [kon'kista] *nf* conquest
conquistador, a [konkista'ðor, a] *adj*
conquering ■ *nm* conqueror
conquistar [konkis'tar] *vt* (*Mil*) to conquer;
(*puesto, simpatía*) to win; (*enamorar*) to win the
heart of
consabido, -a [konsa'βiðo, a] *adj* (*frase etc*)
old; (*pey*): **las consabidas excusas** the same
old excuses
consagrado, -a [konsa'ɣraðo, a] *adj* (*Rel*)
consecrated; (*actor*) established
consagrar [konsa'ɣrar] *vt* (*Rel*) to consecrate;
(*fig*) to devote
consciente [kons'θjente] *adj* conscious; **ser** *o*
estar ~ de to be aware of
consecución [konseku'θjon] *nf* acquisition;
(*de fin*) attainment
consecuencia [konse'kwenθja] *nf*
consequence, outcome; (*firmeza*) consistency;
de ~ of importance
consecuente [konse'kwente] *adj* consistent
consecutivo, -a [konseku'tiβo, a] *adj*
consecutive
conseguir [konse'ɣir] *vt* to get, obtain;
(*sus fines*) to attain
consejería [konsexe'ria] *nf* (*Pol*) ministry
(*in a regional government*)
consejero, -a [konse'xero, a] *nm/f* adviser,
consultant; (*Pol*) minister (*in a regional
government*); (*Com*) director; (*en comisión*)
member
consejo [kon'sexo] *nm* advice; (*Pol*) council;
(*Com*) board; **un ~** a piece of advice; **~ de
administración** board of directors; **~
de guerra** court-martial; **C~ de Europa**
Council of Europe
consenso [kon'senso] *nm* consensus
consentido, -a [konsen'tiðo, a] *adj* (*mimado*)
spoiled
consentimiento [konsenti'mjento] *nm*
consent
consentir [konsen'tir] *vt* (*permitir, tolerar*)
to consent to; (*mimar*) to pamper, spoil
■ *vi* to agree, consent; **~ que algn haga algo**
to allow sb to do sth

conserje [kon'serxe] *nm* caretaker; (*portero*)
porter
conserva [kon'serβa] *nf*: **en ~** (*alimentos*)
tinned (*Brit*), canned; **conservas** tinned *o*
canned foods
conservación [konserβa'θjon] *nf*
conservation; (*de alimentos, vida*) preservation
conservador, a [konserβa'ðor, a] *adj* (*Pol*)
conservative ■ *nm/f* conservative
conservadurismo [konserβaðu'rismo] *nm*
(*Pol etc*) conservatism
conservante [konser'βante] *nm* preservative
conservar [konser'βar] *vt* (*gen*) to preserve;
(*recursos*) to conserve, keep; (*alimentos, vida*) to
preserve; **conservarse** *vr* to survive
conservas [kon'serβas] *nfpl*: **~ (alimenticias)**
tinned (*Brit*) *o* canned goods
conservatorio [konserβa'torjo] *nm* (*Mus*)
conservatoire; (*Am*) greenhouse
considerable [konsiðe'raβle] *adj*
considerable
consideración [konsiðera'θjon] *nf*
consideration; (*estimación*) respect; **de ~**
important; **De mi** *o* **nuestra (mayor) ~** (*Am*)
Dear Sir(s) *o* Madam; **tomar en ~** to take into
account
considerado, -a [konsiðe'raðo, a] *adj* (*atento*)
considerate; (*respetado*) respected
considerar [konsiðe'rar] *vt* (*gen*) to consider;
(*meditar*) to think about; (*tener en cuenta*) to
take into account
consienta *etc* [kon'sjenta] *vb ver* **consentir**
consigna [kon'siɣna] *nf* (*orden*) order,
instruction; (*para equipajes*) left-luggage
office (*Brit*), checkroom (*US*)
consignación [konsiɣna'θjon] *nf*
consignment; **~ de créditos** allocation of
credits
consignador [konsiɣna'ðor] *nm* (*Com*)
consignor
consignar [konsiɣ'nar] *vt* (*Com*) to send;
(*créditos*) to allocate
consignatario, -a [konsiɣna'tarjo, a] *nm/f*
(*Com*) consignee
consigo *etc* [kon'siɣo] *vb ver* **conseguir** ■ *pron*
(*m*) with him; (*f*) with her; (*usted*) with you;
(*reflexivo*) with o.s.
consiguiendo *etc* [konsi'ɣjendo] *vb ver*
conseguir
consiguiente [konsi'ɣjente] *adj* consequent;
por ~ and so, therefore, consequently
consintiendo *etc* [konsin'tjendo] *vb ver*
consentir
consistente [konsis'tente] *adj* consistent;
(*sólido*) solid, firm; (*válido*) sound; **~ en**
consisting of
consistir [konsis'tir] *vi*: **~ en** (*componerse de*)

to consist of; (*ser resultado de*) to be due to

consola [kon'sola] *nf* console, control panel; (*mueble*) console table; **~ de juegos** games console; **~ de mandos** (*Inform*) control console; **~ de visualización** visual display console

consolación [konsola'θjon] *nf* consolation

consolar [konso'lar] *vt* to console

consolidar [konsoli'ðar] *vt* to consolidate

consomé (*pl ~s*) [konso'me, konso'mes] *nm* consommé, clear soup

consonancia [konso'nanθja] *nf* harmony; **en ~ con** in accordance with

consonante [konso'nante] *adj* consonant, harmonious ■ *nf* consonant

consorcio [kon'sorθjo] *nm* (*Com*) consortium, syndicate

consorte [kon'sorte] *nm/f* consort

conspicuo, -a [kons'pikwo, a] *adj* conspicuous

conspiración [konspira'θjon] *nf* conspiracy

conspirador, a [konspira'ðor, a] *nm/f* conspirator

conspirar [konspi'rar] *vi* to conspire

constancia [kons'tanθja] *nf* (*gen*) constancy; (*certeza*) certainly; **dejar ~ de algo** to put sth on record

constante [kons'tante] *adj, nf* constant

constar [kons'tar] *vi* (*evidenciarse*) to be clear o evident; **~ (en)** to appear (in); **~ de** to consist of; **hacer ~** to put on record; **me consta que ...** I have evidence that ...; **que conste que lo hice por ti** believe me, I did it for your own good

constatar [konsta'tar] *vt* (*controlar*) to check; (*observar*) to note

constelación [konstela'θjon] *nf* constellation

consternación [konsterna'θjon] *nf* consternation

constipado, -a [konsti'paðo, a] *adj*: **estar ~** to have a cold ■ *nm* cold

constiparse [konsti'parse] *vr* to catch a cold

constitución [konstitu'θjon] *nf* constitution; **Día de la C~** (*Esp*) Constitution Day (*6th December*)

constitucional [konstituθjo'nal] *adj* constitutional

constituir [konstitu'ir] *vt* (*formar, componer*) to constitute, make up; (*fundar, erigir, ordenar*) to constitute, establish; (*ser*) to be; **constituirse** *vr* (*Pol etc: cuerpo*) to be composed; (*: fundarse*) to be established

constitutivo, -a [konstitu'tiβo, a] *adj* constitutive, constituent

constituya *etc* [konsti'tuja] *vb ver* **constituir**

constituyente [konstitu'jente] *adj* constituent

constreñir [konstre'ɲir] *vt* (*obligar*) to compel, oblige; (*restringir*) to restrict

constriño *etc* [kons'triɲo], **constriñendo** *etc* [konstri'ɲendo] *vb ver* **constreñir**

construcción [konstruk'θjon] *nf* construction, building

constructivo, -a [konstruk'tiβo, a] *adj* constructive

constructor, a [konstruk'tor, a] *nm/f* builder

construir [konstru'ir] *vt* to build, construct

construyendo *etc* [konstru'jendo] *vb ver* **construir**

consuelo *etc* [kon'swelo] *vb ver* **consolar** ■ *nm* consolation, solace

consuetudinario, -a [konswetuði'narjo, a] *adj* customary; **derecho ~** common law

cónsul ['konsul] *nm* consul

consulado [konsu'laðo] *nm* (*sede*) consulate; (*cargo*) consulship

consulta [kon'sulta] *nf* consultation; (*Med: consultorio*) consulting room; (*Inform*) enquiry; **horas de ~** surgery hours; **obra de ~** reference book

consultar [konsul'tar] *vt* to consult; **~ un archivo** (*Inform*) to interrogate a file

consultor, a [konsul'tor, a] *nm*: **~ en dirección de empresas** management consultant

consultorio [konsul'torjo] *nm* (*Med*) surgery

consumado, -a [konsu'maðo, a] *adj* perfect; (*bribón*) out-and-out

consumar [konsu'mar] *vt* to complete, carry out; (*crimen*) to commit; (*sentencia*) to carry out

consumición [konsumi'θjon] *nf* consumption; (*bebida*) drink; (*comida*) food; **~ mínima** cover charge

consumido, -a [konsu'miðo, a] *adj* (*flaco*) skinny

consumidor, a [konsumi'ðor, a] *nm/f* consumer

consumir [konsu'mir] *vt* to consume; **consumirse** *vr* to be consumed; (*persona*) to waste away

consumismo [konsu'mismo] *nm* (*Com*) consumerism

consumo [kon'sumo] *nm* consumption; **bienes de ~** consumer goods

contabilice *etc* [konta'βiliθe] *vb ver* **contabilizar**

contabilidad [kontaβili'ðað] *nf* accounting, book-keeping; (*profesión*) accountancy; (*Com*): **~ analítica** variable costing; **~ de costos** cost accounting; **~ de doble partida** double-entry book-keeping; **~ de gestión** management accounting; **~ por partida simple** single-entry book-keeping

contabilizar [kontaβi'liθar] *vt* to enter in the accounts

contable [kon'taβle] *nm/f* bookkeeper; (*licenciado*) accountant; **~ de costos** (*Com*) cost accountant

contactar [kontak'tar] *vi*: **~ con algn** to contact sb

contacto [kon'takto] *nm* contact; **lentes de ~** contact lenses; **estar en ~ con** to be in touch with

contado, -a [kon'taðo, a] *adj*: **contados** (*escasos*) numbered, scarce, few ■ *nm*: **al ~** for cash; **pagar al ~** to pay (in) cash; **precio al ~** cash price

contador [konta'ðor] *nm* (*aparato*) meter; (*Am*: *contable*) accountant

contaduría [kontaðu'ria] *nf* accountant's office

contagiar [konta'xjar] *vt* (*enfermedad*) to pass on, transmit; (*persona*) to infect; **contagiarse** *vr* to become infected

contagio [kon'taxjo] *nm* infection

contagioso, -a [konta'xjoso, a] *adj* infectious; (*fig*) catching

contaminación [kontamina'θjon] *nf* (*gen*) contamination; (*del ambiente etc*) pollution

contaminar [kontami'nar] *vt* (*gen*) to contaminate; (*aire, agua*) to pollute; (*fig*) to taint

contante [kon'tante] *adj*: **dinero ~ (y sonante)** hard cash

contar [kon'tar] *vt* (*páginas, dinero*) to count; (*anécdota etc*) to tell ■ *vi* to count; **contarse** *vr* to be counted, figure; **~ con** to rely on, count on; **sin ~** not to mention; **le cuento entre mis amigos** I reckon him among my friends

contemplación [kontempla'θjon] *nf* contemplation; **no andarse con contemplaciones** not to stand on ceremony

contemplar [kontem'plar] *vt* to contemplate; (*mirar*) to look at

contemporáneo, -a [kontempo'raneo, a] *adj, nm/f* contemporary

contemporizar [kontempori'θar] *vi*: **~ con** to keep in with

contención [konten'θjon] *nf* (*Jur*) suit; **muro de ~** retaining wall

contencioso, -a [konten'θjoso, a] *adj* (*Jur etc*) contentious ■ *nm* (*Pol*) conflict, dispute

contender [konten'der] *vi* to contend; (*en un concurso*) to compete

contendiente [konten'djente] *nm/f* contestant

contendrá *etc* [konten'dra] *vb ver* **contener**

contenedor [kontene'ðor] *nm* container; (*de escombros*) skip; **~ de (la) basura** wheelie-bin

(*Brit*); **~ de vidrio** bottle bank

contener [konte'ner] *vt* to contain, hold; (*risa etc*) to hold back, contain; **contenerse** *vr* to control o restrain o.s.

contenga *etc* [kon'tenga] *vb ver* **contener**

contenido, -a [konte'niðo, a] *adj* (*moderado*) restrained; (*risa etc*) suppressed ■ *nm* contents *pl*, content

contentar [konten'tar] *vt* (*satisfacer*) to satisfy; (*complacer*) to please; (*Com*) to endorse; **contentarse** *vr* to be satisfied

contento, -a [kon'tento, a] *adj* contented, content; (*alegre*) pleased; (*feliz*) happy

contestación [kontesta'θjon] *nf* answer, reply; **~ a la demanda** (*Jur*) defence plea

contestador [kontesta'ðor] *nm*: **~ automático** answering machine

contestar [kontes'tar] *vt* to answer (back), reply; (*Jur*) to corroborate, confirm

contestatario, -a [kontesta'tarjo, a] *adj* anti-establishment, nonconformist

contexto [kon'teksto] *nm* context

contienda [kon'tjenda] *nf* contest, struggle

contiene *etc* [kon'tjene] *vb ver* **contener**

contigo [kon'tiɣo] *pron* with you

contiguo, -a [kon'tiɣwo, a] *adj* (*de al lado*) next; (*vecino*) adjacent, adjoining

continental [kontinen'tal] *adj* continental

continente [konti'nente] *adj, nm* continent

contingencia [kontin'xenθja] *nf* contingency; (*riesgo*) risk; (*posibilidad*) eventuality

contingente [kontin'xente] *adj* contingent ■ *nm* contingent; (*Com*) quota

continuación [kontinwa'θjon] *nf* continuation; **a ~** then, next

continuamente [kon'tinwamente] *adv* (*sin interrupción*) continuously; (*a todas horas*) constantly

continuar [konti'nwar] *vt* to continue, go on with; (*reanudar*) to resume ■ *vi* to continue, go on; **~ hablando** to continue talking o to talk

continuidad [kontinwi'ðað] *nf* continuity

continuo, -a [kon'tinwo, a] *adj* (*sin interrupción*) continuous; (*acción perseverante*) continual

contonearse [kontone'arse] *vr* (*hombre*) to swagger; (*mujer*) to swing one's hips

contorno [kon'torno] *nm* outline; (*Geo*) contour; **contornos** *nmpl* neighbourhood *sg*, surrounding area *sg*

contorsión [kontor'sjon] *nf* contortion

contra ['kontra] *prep* against; (*Com: giro*) on ■ *adv* against ■ *adj, nm/f* (*Pol fam*) counter-revolutionary ■ *nm* con ■ *nf*: **la C~ (nicaragüense)** the Contras *pl*

contraalmirante [kontraalmi'rante] *nm* rear admiral

contraanálisis [kontraa'nalisis] *nm* follow-up test, countertest

contraataque [kontraa'take] *nm* counterattack

contrabajo [kontra'βaxo] *nm* double bass

contrabandista [kontraβan'dista] *nm/f* smuggler

contrabando [kontra'βando] *nm* (*acción*) smuggling; (*mercancías*) contraband; **~ de armas** gun-running

contracción [kontrak'θjon] *nf* contraction

contrachapado [kontratʃa'paðo] *nm* plywood

contracorriente [kontrako'rrjente] *nf* cross-current

contradecir [kontraðe'θir] *vt* to contradict

contradicción [kontraðik'θjon] *nf* contradiction; **espíritu de ~** contrariness

contradicho [kontra'ðitʃo] *pp de* **contradecir**

contradiciendo *etc* [kontraði'θjendo] *vb ver* **contradecir**

contradictorio, -a [kontraðik'torjo, a] *adj* contradictory

contradiga *etc* [kontra'ðiɣa], **contradije** [kontra'ðixe], **contradirá** *etc* [kontraði'ra] *vb ver* **contradecir**

contraer [kontra'er] *vt* to contract; (*hábito*) to acquire; (*limitar*) to restrict; **contraerse** *vr* to contract; (*limitarse*) to limit o.s.

contraespionage [kontraespjo'naxe] *nm* counter-espionage

contrafuerte [kontra'fwerte] *nm* (*Arq*) buttress

contragolpe [kontra'ɣolpe] *nm* backlash

contrahacer [kontraa'θer] *vb* (*copiar*) to copy, imitate; (*moneda*) to conterfeit; (*documento*) to forge, fake; (*libro*) to pirate

contrahaga *etc* [kontra'aɣa], **contraharé** *etc* [kontraa're] *vb ver* **contrahacer**

contrahecho, -a [kontra'etʃo, a] *pp de* **contrahacer** ■ *adj* fake; (*Anat*) hunchbacked

contrahice *etc* [kontra'iθe] *vb ver* **contrahacer**

contraiga *etc* [kon'traiɣa] *vb ver* **contraer**

contraindicaciones [kontraindika'θjones] *nfpl* (*Med*) contraindications

contraje *etc* [kon'traxe] *vb ver* **contraer**

contralor [kontra'lor] *nm* (*Am*) government accounting inspector

contraluz [kontra'luθ] *nf* (*Foto etc*) back lighting; **a ~** against the light

contramaestre [kontrama'estre] *nm* foreman

contraofensiva [kontraofen'siβa] *nf* counteroffensive

contraorden [kontra'orðen] *nf* counter-order, countermand

contrapartida [kontrapar'tiða] *nf* (*Com*) balancing entry; **como ~ (de)** in return (for), as o in compensation (for)

contrapelo [kontra'pelo]: **a ~** *adv* the wrong way

contrapesar [kontrape'sar] *vt* to counterbalance; (*fig*) to offset

contrapeso [kontra'peso] *nm* counterweight; (*fig*) counterbalance; (*Com*) makeweight

contrapondré *etc* [kontrapon'dre] *vb ver* **contraponer**

contraponer [kontrapo'ner] *vt* (*cotejar*) to compare; (*oponer*) to oppose

contraponga *etc* [kontra'ponga] *vb ver* **contraponer**

contraportada [kontrapor'taða] *nf* (*de revista*) back page

contraproducente [kontraproðu'θente] *adj* counterproductive

contrapuesto [kontra'pwesto] *pp de* **contraponer**

contrapunto [kontra'punto] *nm* counterpoint

contrapuse *etc* [kontra'puse] *vb ver* **contraponer**

contrariar [kontra'rjar] *vt* (*oponerse*) to oppose; (*poner obstáculo*) to impede; (*enfadar*) to vex

contrariedad [kontrarje'ðað] *nf* (*oposición*) opposition; (*obstáculo*) obstacle, setback; (*disgusto*) vexation, annoyance

contrario, -a [kon'trarjo, a] *adj* contrary; (*persona*) opposed; (*sentido, lado*) opposite ■ *nm/f* enemy, adversary; (*Deporte*) opponent; **al ~**, **por el ~** on the contrary; **de lo ~** otherwise

Contrarreforma [kontrarre'forma] *nf* Counter-Reformation

contrarreloj [kontrarre'lo(x)] *nf* (*tb*: **prueba contrarreloj**) time trial

contrarrestar [kontrarres'tar] *vt* to counteract

contrarrevolución [kontrarreβolu'θjon] *nf* counter-revolution

contrasentido [kontrasen'tiðo] *nm* contradiction; **es un ~ que él ...** it doesn't make sense for him to ...

contraseña [kontra'seɲa] *nf* countersign; (*frase*) password

contrastar [kontras'tar] *vt* to resist ■ *vi* to contrast

contraste [kon'traste] *nm* contrast

contrata [kon'trata] *nf* (*Jur*) written contract; (*empleo*) hiring

contratar [kontra'tar] *vt* (*firmar un acuerdo para*) to contract for; (*empleados, obreros*) to hire, engage; (*Deporte*) to sign up; **contratarse** *vr* to sign on

contratiempo [kontra'tjempo] *nm* (*revés*) setback; (*accidente*) mishap; **a ~** (*Mus*) offbeat

contratista [kontra'tista] *nm/f* contractor

contrato [kon'trato] *nm* contract; **~ de compraventa** contract of sale; **~ a precio fijo** fixed-price contract; **~ a término** forward contract; **~ de trabajo** contract of employment *o* service

contravalor [kontraβa'lor] *nm* exchange value

contravención [kontraβen'θjon] *nf* contravention, violation

contravendré *etc* [kontraβen'dre], **contravenga** *etc* [kontra'βenga] *vb ver* **contravenir**

contravenir [kontraβe'nir] *vi*: **~ a** to contravene, violate

contraventana [kontraβen'tana] *nf* shutter

contraviene *etc* [kontra'βjene], **contraviniendo** *etc* [kontraβi'njendo] *vb ver* **contravenir**

contrayendo [kontra'jendo] *vb ver* **contraer**

contribución [kontriβu'θjon] *nf* (*municipal etc*) tax; (*ayuda*) contribution; **exento de contribuciones** tax-free

contribuir [kontriβu'ir] *vt, vi* to contribute; (*Com*) to pay (in taxes)

contribuyendo *etc* [kontriβu'jendo] *vb ver* **contribuir**

contribuyente [kontriβu'jente] *nm/f* (*Com*) taxpayer; (*que ayuda*) contributor

contrincante [kontrin'kante] *nm* opponent, rival

control [kon'trol] *nm* control; (*inspección*) inspection, check; (*Com*): **~ de calidad** quality control; **~ de cambios** exchange control; **~ de costos** cost control; **~ de créditos** credit control; **~ de existencias** stock control; **~ de precios** price control

controlador, a [kontrola'ðor, a] *nm/f* controller; **~ aéreo** air-traffic controller

controlar [kontro'lar] *vt* to control; to inspect, check; (*Com*) to audit

controversia [kontro'βersja] *nf* controversy

contubernio [kontu'βernjo] *nm* ring, conspiracy

contumaz [kontu'maθ] *adj* obstinate, stubbornly disobedient

contundente [kontun'dente] *adj* (*prueba*) conclusive; (*fig: argumento*) convincing; **instrumento ~** blunt instrument

contusión [kontu'sjon] *nf* bruise

contuve *etc* [kon'tuβe] *vb ver* **contener**

convalecencia [kombale'θenθja] *nf* convalescence

convalecer [kombale'θer] *vi* to convalesce, get better

convaleciente [kombale'θjente] *adj, nm/f* convalescent

convalezca *etc* [komba'leθka] *vb ver* **convalecer**

convalidar [kombali'ðar] *vt* (*título*) to recognize

convencer [komben'θer] *vt* to convince; (*persuadir*) to persuade

convencimiento [kombenθi'mjento] *nm* (*acción*) convincing; (*persuasión*) persuasion; (*certidumbre*) conviction; **tener el ~ de que ...** to be convinced that ...

convención [komben'θjon] *nf* convention

convencional [kombenθjo'nal] *adj* conventional

convendré *etc* [komben'dre], **convenga** *etc* [kom'benga] *vb ver* **convenir**

conveniencia [kombe'njenθja] *nf* suitability; (*conformidad*) agreement; (*utilidad, provecho*) usefulness; **conveniencias** *nfpl* conventions; (*Com*) property *sg*; **ser de la ~ de algn** to suit sb

conveniente [kombe'njente] *adj* suitable; (*útil*) useful; (*correcto*) fit, proper; (*aconsejable*) advisable

convenio [kom'benjo] *nm* agreement, treaty; **~ de nivel crítico** threshold agreement

convenir [kombe'nir] *vi* (*estar de acuerdo*) to agree; (*ser conveniente*) to suit, be suitable; **"sueldo a ~"** "salary to be agreed"; **conviene recordar que ...** it should be remembered that ...

convento [kom'bento] *nm* monastery; (*de monjas*) convent

convenza *etc* [kom'benθa] *vb ver* **convencer**

convergencia [komber'xenθja] *nf* convergence

converger [komber'xer], **convergir** [komber'xir] *vi* to converge; **sus esfuerzos convergen a un fin común** their efforts are directed towards the same objective

converja *etc* [kom'berxa] *vb ver* **converger**; **convergir**

conversación [kombersa'θjon] *nf* conversation

conversar [komber'sar] *vi* to talk, converse

conversión [komber'sjon] *nf* conversion

converso, -a [kom'berso, a] *nm/f* convert

convertir [komber'tir] *vt* to convert; (*transformar*) to transform, turn; (*Com*) to (ex)change; **convertirse** *vr* (*Rel*) to convert

convexo, -a [kom'bekso, a] *adj* convex

convicción [kombik'θjon] *nf* conviction

convicto, -a [kom'bikto, a] *adj* convicted; (*condenado*) condemned

convidado, -a [kombi'ðaðo, a] *nm/f* guest

convidar [kombi'ðar] *vt* to invite

conviene *etc* [kom'bjene] *vb ver* **convenir**

convierta *etc* [kom'bjerta] *vb ver* **convertir**

convincente [kombin'θente] *adj* convincing

conviniendo *etc* [kombi'njendo] *vb ver* **convenir**

convirtiendo *etc* [kombir'tjendo] *vb ver* **convertir**

convite [kom'bite] *nm* invitation; (*banquete*) banquet

convivencia [kombi'βenθja] *nf* coexistence, living together

convivir [kombi'βir] *vi* to live together; (*Pol*) to coexist

convocar [kombo'kar] *vt* to summon, call (together)

convocatoria [komboka'torja] *nf* summons *sg*; (*anuncio*) notice of meeting; (*Escol*) examination session

convoque *etc* [kom'boke] *vb ver* **convocar**

convoy [kom'boj] *nm* (*Ferro*) train

convulsión [kombul'sjon] *nf* convulsion; (*Pol etc*) upheaval

conyugal [konju'ɣal] *adj* conjugal; **vida ~** married life

cónyuge ['konyuxe] *nm/f* spouse, partner

coña ['koɲa] *nf*: **tomar algo a ~** (*fam!*) to take sth as a joke

coñac (*pl* **coñacs**) ['koɲa(k), 'koɲas] *nm* cognac, brandy

coñazo [ko'ɲaθo] *nm* (*fam*) pain; **dar el ~** to be a real pain

coño ['koɲo] (*fam!*) *nm* cunt (!); (*Am pey*) Spaniard ■ *excl* (*enfado*) shit (!); (*sorpresa*) bloody hell (!); **¡qué ~!** what a pain in the arse! (!)

cookie ['kuki] *nm* (*Inform*) cookie

cooperación [koopera'θjon] *nf* cooperation

cooperar [koope'rar] *vi* to cooperate

cooperativo, -a [koopera'tiβo, a] *adj* cooperative ■ *nf* cooperative

coordenada [koorðe'naða] *nf* (*Mat*) coordinate; (*fig*): **coordenadas** *nfpl* guidelines, framework *sg*

coordinación [koorðina'θjon] *nf* coordination

coordinador, a [koorðina'ðor, a] *nm/f* coordinator ■ *nf* coordinating committee

coordinar [koorði'nar] *vt* to coordinate

copa ['kopa] *nf* (*tb Deporte*) cup; (*vaso*) glass; (*de árbol*) top; (*de sombrero*) crown; **copas** *nfpl* (*Naipes*) one of the suits in the Spanish card deck; (**tomar una**) **~** (to have a) drink; **ir de copas**

to go out for a drink; *ver tb* **Baraja Española**

copar [ko'par] *vt* (*puestos*) to monopolize

coparticipación [kopartiθipa'θjon] *nf* (*Com*) co-ownership

COPE *nf abr* (= *Cadena de Ondas Populares Españolas*) *Spanish radio network*

Copenhague [kope'naɣe] *n* Copenhagen

copete [ko'pete] *nm* tuft (of hair); **de alto ~** aristocratic, upper-crust (*fam*)

copia ['kopja] *nf* copy; (*Arte*) replica; (*Com etc*) duplicate; (*Inform*): **~ impresa** hard copy; **~ de respaldo** *o* **de seguridad** backup copy; **hacer ~ de seguridad** to back up; **~ de trabajo** working copy

copiadora [kopja'ðora] *nf* photocopier

copiar [ko'pjar] *vt* to copy; **~ al pie de la letra** to copy word for word

copiloto [kopi'loto] *nm* (*Aviat*) co-pilot; (*Auto*) co-driver

copioso, -a [ko'pjoso, a] *adj* copious, plentiful

copita [ko'pita] *nf* (small) glass; (*Golf*) tee

copla ['kopla] *nf* verse; (*canción*) (popular) song

copo ['kopo] *nm*: **copos de maíz** cornflakes; **~ de nieve** snowflake

coprocesador [koproθesa'ðor] *nm* (*Inform*) co-processor

coproducción [koproðuk'θjon] *nf* (*Cine etc*) joint production

copropietarios [kopropje'tarjos] *nmpl* (*Com*) joint owners

cópula ['kopula] *nf* copulation

copular [kopu'lar] *vi* to copulate

coqueta [ko'keta] *adj* flirtatious, coquettish ■ *nf* (*mujer*) flirt

coquetear [kokete'ar] *vi* to flirt

coraje [ko'raxe] *nm* courage; (*ánimo*) spirit; (*ira*) anger

coral [ko'ral] *adj* choral ■ *nf* choir ■ *nm* (*Zool*) coral

Corán [ko'ran] *nm*: **el ~** the Koran

coraza [ko'raθa] *nf* (*armadura*) armour; (*blindaje*) armour-plating

corazón [kora'θon] *nm* heart; (*Bot*) core; **corazones** *nmpl* (*Naipes*) hearts; **de buen ~** kind-hearted; **de todo ~** wholeheartedly; **estar mal del ~** to have heart trouble

corazonada [koraθo'naða] *nf* impulse; (*presentimiento*) presentiment, hunch

corbata [kor'βata] *nf* tie

corbeta [kor'βeta] *nf* corvette

Córcega ['korθeɣa] *nf* Corsica

corcel [kor'θel] *nm* steed

corchea [kor'tʃea] *nf* quaver

corchete [kor'tʃete] *nm* catch, clasp; **corchetes** *nmpl* (*Tip*) square brackets

corcho ['kortʃo] nm cork; (Pesca) float
corcovado, -a [korko'βaðo, a] adj
hunchbacked ■ nm/f hunchback
cordel [kor'ðel] nm cord, line
cordero [kor'ðero] nm lamb; (piel) lambskin
cordial [kor'ðjal] adj cordial ■ nm cordial,
tonic
cordialidad [korðjali'ðað] nf warmth,
cordiality
cordillera [korði'ʎera] nf range (of
mountains)
Córdoba ['korðoβa] nf Cordova
cordobés, -esa [korðo'βes, esa] adj, nm/f
Cordovan
cordón [kor'ðon] nm (cuerda) cord, string;
(de zapatos) lace; (Elec) flex, wire (US); (Mil etc)
cordon
cordura [kor'ðura] nf (Med) sanity; (fig) good
sense
Corea [ko'rea] nf Korea; ~ del Norte/Sur
North/South Korea
coreano, -a [kore'ano, a] adj, nm/f Korean
corear [kore'ar] vt to chorus
coreografía [koreoɣra'fia] nf choreography
corista [ko'rista] nf (Teat etc) chorus girl
cornada [kor'naða] nf (Taur etc) butt, goring
córner (pl **córners**) ['korner, 'korners] nm
corner (kick)
corneta [kor'neta] nf bugle
cornisa [kor'nisa] nf cornice
Cornualles [kor'nwaʎes] nm Cornwall
cornudo, -a [kor'nuðo, a] adj (Zool) horned;
(marido) cuckolded
coro ['koro] nm chorus; (conjunto de cantores)
choir
corolario [koro'larjo] nm corollary
corona [ko'rona] nf crown; (de flores) garland
coronación [korona'θjon] nf coronation
coronar [koro'nar] vt to crown
coronel [koro'nel] nm colonel
coronilla [koro'niʎa] nf (Anat) crown (of the
head); **estar hasta la ~ (de)** to be utterly fed
up (with)
corpiño [kor'piɲo] nm bodice; (Am: sostén) bra
corporación [korpora'θjon] nf corporation
corporal [korpo'ral] adj corporal, bodily
corporativo, -a [korpora'tiβo, a] adj
corporate
corpulento, -a [korpu'lento, a] adj (persona)
well-built
corral [ko'rral] nm (patio) farmyard; (Agr: de
aves) poultry yard; (redil) pen
correa [ko'rrea] nf strap; (cinturón) belt;
(de perro) lead, leash; ~ **transportadora**
conveyor belt
correaje [korre'axe] nm (Agr) harness
corrección [korrek'θjon] nf correction;

(reprensión) rebuke; (cortesía) good manners;
(Inform): ~ **por líneas** line editing; ~ **en
pantalla** screen editing; ~ **(de pruebas)**
(Tip) proofreading
correccional [korrekθjo'nal] nm reformatory
correcto, -a [ko'rrekto, a] adj correct;
(persona) well-mannered
corrector, a [korrek'tor, a] nm/f: ~ **de
pruebas** proofreader
corredera [korre'ðera] nf: **puerta de ~**
sliding door
corredizo, -a [korre'ðiθo, a] adj (puerta etc)
sliding; (nudo) running
corredor, a [korre'ðor, a] adj running;
(rápido) fast ■ nm/f (Deporte) runner ■ nm
(pasillo) corridor; (balcón corrido) gallery; (Com)
agent, broker; ~ **de bienes raíces** real-
estate broker; ~ **de bolsa** stockbroker; ~ **de
seguros** insurance broker
corregir [korre'xir] vt (error) to correct;
(amonestar, reprender) to rebuke, reprimand;
corregirse vr to reform
correo [ko'rreo] nm post, mail; (persona)
courier; **Correos** nmpl Post Office sg; ~ **aéreo**
airmail; ~ **basura** (por carta) junk mail; (por
Internet) spam; ~ **certificado** registered
mail; ~ **electrónico** email, electronic mail;
~ **urgente** special delivery; **a vuelta de ~** by
return (of post)
correr [ko'rrer] vt to run; (viajar) to cover,
travel; (riesgo) to run; (aventura) to have;
(cortinas) to draw; (cerrojo) to shoot ■ vi to
run; (líquido) to run, flow; (rumor) to go round;
correrse vr to slide, move; (colores) to run;
(fam: tener orgasmo) to come; **echar a ~** to
break into a run; ~ **con los gastos** to pay the
expenses; **eso corre de mi cuenta** I'll take
care of that
correspondencia [korrespon'denθja]
nf correspondence; (Ferro) connection;
(reciprocidad) return; ~ **directa** (Com) direct
mail
corresponder [korrespon'der] vi to
correspond; (convenir) to be suitable;
(pertenecer) to belong; (tocar) to concern;
(favor) to repay; **corresponderse** vr (por
escrito) to correspond; (amarse) to love one
another; **"a quien corresponda"** "to whom
it may concern"
correspondiente [korrespon'djente] adj
corresponding; (respectivo) respective
corresponsal [korrespon'sal] nm/f
(newspaper) correspondent; (Com) agent
corretaje [korre'taxe] nm (Com) brokerage
corretear [korrete'ar] vi to loiter
corrido, -a [ko'rriðo, a] adj (avergonzado)
abashed; (fluido) fluent ■ nf run, dash;

(*de toros*) bullfight; **de ~** fluently; **tres noches corridas** three nights running; **un kilo ~** a good kilo

corriente [ko'rrjente] *adj* (*agua*) running; (*fig*) flowing; (*cuenta etc*) current; (*común*) ordinary, normal ■ *nf* current; (*fig: tendencia*) course ■ *nm* current month; **~ de aire** draught; **~ eléctrica** electric current; **las corrientes modernas del arte** modern trends in art; **estar al ~ de** to be informed about

corrigiendo *etc* [korri'xjendo] *vb ver* **corregir**

corrija *etc* [ko'rrixa] *vb ver* **corregir**

corrillo [ko'rriʎo] *nm* ring, circle (of people); (*fig*) clique

corro ['korro] *nm* ring, circle (of people); (*baile*) ring-a-ring-a-roses; **la gente hizo ~** the people formed a ring

corroborar [korroβo'rar] *vt* to corroborate

corroer [korro'er] *vt* (*tb fig*) to corrode, eat away; (*Geo*) to erode

corromper [korrom'per] *vt* (*madera*) to rot; (*fig*) to corrupt

corrompido, -a [korrom'piðo, a] *adj* corrupt

corrosivo, -a [korro'siβo, a] *adj* corrosive

corroyendo *etc* [korro'jendo] *vb ver* **corroer**

corrupción [korrup'θjon] *nf* rot, decay; (*fig*) corruption

corrupto, -a [ko'rrupto, a] *adj* corrupt

corsario [kor'sarjo] *nm* privateer, corsair

corsé [kor'se] *nm* corset

corso, -a ['korso, a] *adj, nm/f* Corsican

cortacésped [korta'θespeð] *nm* lawn mower

cortado, -a [kor'taðo, a] *adj* (*con cuchillo*) cut; (*leche*) sour; (*confuso*) confused; (*desconcertado*) embarrassed; (*tímido*) shy ■ *nm* white coffee (with a little milk)

cortadora [korta'ðora] *nf* cutter, slicer

cortadura [korta'ðura] *nf* cut

cortalápices [korta'lapiθes], **cortalápiz** [korta'lapiθ] *nm inv* (*pencil*) sharpener

cortante [kor'tante] *adj* (*viento*) biting; (*frío*) bitter

cortapisa [korta'pisa] *nf* (*restricción*) restriction; (*traba*) snag

cortar [kor'tar] *vt* to cut; (*suministro*) to cut off; (*un pasaje*) to cut out; (*comunicación, teléfono*) to cut off ■ *vi* to cut; (*Am Telec*) to hang up; **cortarse** *vr* (*turbarse*) to become embarrassed; (*leche*) to turn, curdle; **~ por lo sano** to settle things once and for all; **cortarse el pelo** to have one's hair cut; **se cortó la línea** *o* **el teléfono** I got cut off

cortauñas [korta'uɲas] *nm inv* nail clippers *pl*

corte ['korte] *nm* cut, cutting; (*filo*) edge; (*de tela*) piece, length; (*Costura*) tailoring ■ *nf* (*real*) (royal) court; **~ y confección** dressmaking; **~ de corriente** *o* **luz** power

cut; **~ de pelo** haircut; **me da ~ pedírselo** I'm embarrassed to ask him for it; **¡qué ~ le di!** I left him with no comeback!; **C~ Internacional de Justicia** International Court of Justice; **las Cortes** the Spanish Parliament *sg*; **hacer la ~ a** to woo, court; *see note*

cortejar [korte'xar] *vt* to court

cortejo [kor'texo] *nm* entourage; **~ fúnebre** funeral procession, cortège

cortés [kor'tes] *adj* courteous, polite

cortesano, -a [korte'sano, a] *adj* courtly

cortesía [korte'sia] *nf* courtesy

corteza [kor'teθa] *nf* (*de árbol*) bark; (*de pan*) crust; (*de fruta*) peel, skin; (*de queso*) rind

cortijo [kor'tixo] *nm* farmhouse

cortina [kor'tina] *nf* curtain; **~ de humo** smoke screen

corto, -a ['korto, a] *adj* short; (*tímido*) bashful; **~ de luces** not very bright; **~ de oído** hard of hearing; **~ de vista** short-sighted; **estar ~ de fondos** to be short of funds

cortocircuito [kortoθir'kwito] *nm* short-circuit

cortometraje [kortome'traxe] *nm* (*Cine*) short

Coruña [ko'ruɲa] *nf*: **La ~** Corunna

coruñés, -esa [koru'ɲes, esa] *adj* of *o* from Corunna ■ *nm/f* native *o* inhabitant of Corunna

corvo, -a ['korβo, a] *adj* curved; (*nariz*) hooked ■ *nf* back of knee

cosa ['kosa] *nf* thing; (*asunto*) affair; **~ de** about; **eso es ~ mía** that's my business; **es poca ~** it's not important; **¡qué ~ más rara!** how strange!

cosaco, -a [ko'sako, a] *adj, nm/f* Cossack

coscorrón [kosko'rron] *nm* bump on the head

cosecha [ko'setʃa] *nf* (*Agr*) harvest; (*acto*) harvesting; (*de vino*) vintage; (*producción*) yield

cosechadora [kosetʃa'ðora] *nf* combine harvester

cosechar [kose'tʃar] *vt* to harvest, gather (in)

coser [ko'ser] *vt* to sew; (*Med*) to stitch (up)

cosido [ko'siðo] *nm* sewing

cosmético, -a [kos'metiko, a] *adj, nm* cosmetic ∎ *nf* cosmetics *pl*

cosmopolita [kosmopo'lita] *adj* cosmopolitan

cosmos ['kosmos] *nm* cosmos

coso ['koso] *nm* bullring

cosquillas [kos'kiʎas] *nfpl*: **hacer** ~ to tickle; **tener** ~ to be ticklish

cosquilleo [koski'ʎeo] *nm* tickling (sensation)

costa ['kosta] *nf* (*Geo*) coast; **C~ Brava** Costa Brava; **C~ Cantábrica** Cantabrian Coast; **C~ de Marfil** Ivory Coast; **C~ del Sol** Costa del Sol; **a** ~ (*Com*) at cost; **a ~ de** at the expense of; **a toda** ~ at any price

costado [kos'taðo] *nm* side; **de** ~ (*dormir*) on one's side; **español por los 4 costados** Spanish through and through

costal [kos'tal] *nm* sack

costalada [kosta'laða] *nf* bad fall

costanera [kosta'nera] *nf* (*Am*) (seaside) promenade

costar [kos'tar] *vt* (*valer*) to cost; **me cuesta hablarle** I find it hard to talk to him; **¿cuánto cuesta?** how much does it cost?

Costa Rica [kosta'rika] *nf* Costa Rica

costarricense [kostarri'θense], **costarriqueño, -a** [kostarri'keɲo, a] *adj, nm/f* Costa Rican

coste ['koste] *nm* (*Com*): ~ **promedio** average cost; **costes fijos** fixed costs; *ver tb* **costo**

costear [koste'ar] *vt* to pay for; (*Com etc*) to finance; (*Naut*) to sail along the coast of; **costearse** *vr* (*negocio*) to pay for itself, cover its costs

costeño, -a [kos'teɲo, a] *adj* coastal

costero [kos'tero, a] *adj* coastal, coast *cpd*

costilla [kos'tiʎa] *nf* rib; (*Culin*) cutlet

costo ['kosto] *nm* cost, price; ~ **directo** direct cost; ~ **de expedición** shipping charges; ~ **de sustitución** replacement cost; ~ **unitario** unit cost; ~ **de la vida** cost of living

costoso, -a [kos'toso, a] *adj* costly, expensive

costra ['kostra] *nf* (*corteza*) crust; (*Med*) scab

costumbre [kos'tumbre] *nf* custom, habit; **como de** ~ as usual

costura [kos'tura] *nf* sewing, needlework; (*confección*) dressmaking; (*zurcido*) seam

costurera [kostu'rera] *nf* dressmaker

costurero [kostu'rero] *nm* sewing box *o* case

cota ['kota] *nf* (*Geo*) height above sea level; (*fig*) height

cotarro [ko'tarro] *nm*: **dirigir el** ~ (*fam*) to rule the roost

cotejar [kote'xar] *vt* to compare

cotejo [ko'texo] *nm* comparison

cotice *etc* [ko'tiθe] *vb ver* **cotizar**

cotidiano, -a [koti'ðjano, a] *adj* daily, day to day

cotilla [ko'tiʎa] *nf* busybody, gossip

cotillear [kotiʎe'ar] *vi* to gossip

cotilleo [koti'ʎeo] *nm* gossip(ing)

cotización [kotiθa'θjon] *nf* (*Com*) quotation, price; (*de club*) dues *pl*

cotizado, -a [koti'θaðo, a] *adj* (*fig*) highly-prized

cotizar [koti'θar] *vt* (*Com*) to quote, price; **cotizarse** *vr* (*fig*) to be highly prized; **cotizarse a** to sell at, fetch; (*Bolsa*) to stand at, be quoted at

coto ['koto] *nm* (*terreno cercado*) enclosure; (*de caza*) reserve; (*Com*) price-fixing agreement; **poner** ~ **a** to put a stop to

cotorra [ko'torra] *nf* (*Zool: loro*) parrot; (*fam: persona*) windbag

coyote [ko'jote] *nm* coyote, prairie wolf

coyuntura [kojun'tura] *nf* (*Anat*) joint; (*fig*) juncture, occasion; **esperar una** ~ **favorable** to await a favourable moment

coz [koθ] *nf* kick

CP *nm abr* (= *computador personal*) PC

C.P. *abr* (*Esp*) = **Caja Postal**

C.P.A. *nf abr* (= *Caja Postal de Ahorros*) Post Office Savings Bank

CP/M *nm abr* (= *Programa de control para microprocesadores*) CP/M

CPN *nm abr* (*Esp*) = **Cuerpo de la Policía Nacional**

cps *abr* (= *caracteres por segundo*) c.p.s.

crac [krak] *nm* (*Econ*) crash

cráneo ['kraneo] *nm* skull, cranium

crápula ['krapula] *nf* drunkenness

cráter ['krater] *nm* crater

creación [krea'θjon] *nf* creation

creador, a [krea'ðor, a] *adj* creative ∎ *nm/f* creator

crear [kre'ar] *vt* to create, make; (*originar*) to originate; (*Inform: archivo*) to create; **crearse** *vr* (*comité etc*) to be set up

creativo, -a [krea'tiβo, a] *adj* creative

crecer [kre'θer] *vi* to grow; (*precio*) to rise; **crecerse** *vr* (*engreírse*) to get cocky

creces ['kreθes]: **con** ~ *adv* amply, fully

crecido, -a [kre'θiðo, a] *adj* (*persona, planta*) full-grown; (*cantidad*) large ∎ *nf* (*de río*) spate, flood

creciente [kre'θjente] *adj* growing; (*cantidad*) increasing; (*luna*) crescent ∎ *nm* crescent

crecimiento [kreθi'mjento] *nm* growth;

(*aumento*) increase; (*Com*) rise

credenciales [kreðen'θjales] *nfpl* credentials

crédito ['kreðito] *nm* credit; **a** ~ on credit; **dar** ~ **a** to believe (in); ~ **al consumidor** consumer credit; ~ **rotativo** *o* **renovable** revolving credit

credo ['kreðo] *nm* creed

crédulo, -a ['kreðulo, a] *adj* credulous

creencia [kre'enθja] *nf* belief

creer [kre'er] *vt, vi* to think, believe; (*considerar*) to think, consider; **creerse** *vr* to believe o.s. (to be); ~ **en** to believe in; **¡ya lo creo!** I should think so!

creíble [kre'iβle] *adj* credible, believable

creído, -a [kre'iðo, a] *adj* (*engreído*) conceited

crema ['krema] *adj inv* cream (coloured) ∎ *nf* cream; (*natillas*) custard; **la ~ de la sociedad** the cream of society

cremallera [krema'ʎera] *nf* zip (fastener) (*Brit*), zipper (*US*)

crematorio [krema'torjo] *nm* crematorium (*Brit*), crematory (*US*)

cremoso, -a [kre'moso, a] *adj* creamy

crepitar [krepi'tar] *vi* (*fuego*) to crackle

crepúsculo [kre'puskulo] *nm* twilight, dusk

crespo, -a ['krespo, a] *adj* (*pelo*) curly

crespón [kres'pon] *nm* crêpe

cresta ['kresta] *nf* (*Geo: Zool*) crest

Creta ['kreta] *nf* Crete

cretino, -a [kre'tino, a] *adj* cretinous ∎ *nm/f* cretin

creyendo *etc* [kre'jendo] *vb ver* **creer**

creyente [kre'jente] *nm/f* believer

crezca *etc* ['kreθka] *vb ver* **crecer**

cría *etc* ['kria] *vb ver* **criar** ∎ *nf ver* **crío, a**

criada [kri'aða] *nf ver* **criado, a**

criadero [kria'ðero] *nm* nursery; (*Zool*) breeding place

criadillas [kria'ðiʎas] *nfpl* (*Culin*) bull's (*o* sheep's) testicles

criado, -a [kri'aðo, a] *nm* servant ∎ *nf* servant, maid

criador [kria'ðor] *nm* breeder

crianza [kri'anθa] *nf* rearing, breeding; (*fig*) breeding; (*Med*) lactation

criar [kri'ar] *vt* (*amamantar*) to suckle, feed; (*educar*) to bring up; (*producir*) to grow, produce; (*animales*) to breed; **criarse** *vr* to grow (up); ~ **cuervos** to nourish a viper in one's bosom; **Dios los cría y ellos se juntan** birds of a feather flock together

criatura [kria'tura] *nf* creature; (*niño*) baby, (small) child

criba ['kriβa] *nf* sieve

cribar [kri'βar] *vt* to sieve

crimen ['krimen] *nm* crime; ~ **pasional** crime of passion

criminal [krimi'nal] *adj, nm/f* criminal

crin [krin] *nf* (*tb:* **crines**) mane

crío, -a ['krio, a] *nm/f* (*fam: chico*) kid ∎ *nf* (*de animales*) rearing, breeding; (*animal*) young

criollo, -a [kri'oʎo, a] *adj* (*gen*) Creole; (*Am*) native (to America), national ∎ *nm/f* (*gen*) Creole; (*Am*) native American

cripta ['kripta] *nf* crypt

crisis ['krisis] *nf inv* crisis; ~ **nerviosa** nervous breakdown

crisma ['krisma] *nf:* **romperle la ~ a algn** (*fam*) to knock sb's block off

crisol [kri'sol] *nm* (*Tec*) crucible; (*fig*) melting pot

crispación [krispa'θjon] *nf* tension

crispar [kris'par] *vt* (*músculo*) to cause to contract; (*nervios*) to set on edge

cristal [kris'tal] *nm* crystal; (*de ventana*) glass, pane; (*lente*) lens; **de ~** glass *cpd*; ~ **ahumado/ tallado** smoked/cut glass

cristalería [kristale'ria] *nf* (*tienda*) glassware shop; (*objetos*) glassware

cristalice *etc* [krista'liθe] *vb ver* **cristalizar**

cristalino, -a [krista'lino, a] *adj* crystalline; (*fig*) clear ∎ *nm* lens of the eye

cristalizar [kristali'θar] *vt, vi* to crystallize

cristiandad [kristjan'dað] *nf*, **cristianismo** [kristja'nismo] *nm* Christianity

cristiano, -a [kris'tjano, a] *adj, nm/f* Christian; **hablar en ~** to speak proper Spanish; (*fig*) to speak clearly

Cristo ['kristo] *nm* (*dios*) Christ; (*crucifijo*) crucifix

Cristóbal [kris'toβal] *nm:* ~ **Colón** Christopher Columbus

criterio [kri'terjo] *nm* criterion; (*juicio*) judgement; (*enfoque*) attitude, approach; (*punto de vista*) view, opinion; ~ **de clasificación** (*Inform*) sort criterion

criticar [kriti'kar] *vt* to criticize

crítico, -a ['kritiko, a] *adj* critical ∎ *nm* critic ∎ *nf* criticism; (*Teat etc*) review, notice; **la crítica** the critics *pl*

critique *etc* [kri'tike] *vb ver* **criticar**

Croacia [kro'aθja] *nf* Croatia

croar [kro'ar] *vi* to croak

croata [kro'ata] *adj, nm/f* Croat(ian) ∎ *nm* (*Ling*) Croat(ian)

croissan, croissant [krwa'san] *nm* croissant

crol ['krol] *nm* crawl

cromado [kro'maðo] *nm* chromium plating, chrome

cromo ['kromo] *nm* chrome; (*Tip*) coloured print

cromosoma [kromo'soma] *nm* chromosome

crónico, -a ['kroniko, a] *adj* chronic ∎ *nf* chronicle, account; (*de periódico*) feature, article

cronología [kronolo'xia] *nf* chronology
cronológico, -a [krono'loxiko, a] *adj* chronological
cronometraje [kronome'traxe] *nm* timing
cronometrar [kronome'trar] *vt* to time
cronómetro [kro'nometro] *nm* (*Deporte*) stopwatch; (*Tec etc*) chronometer
croqueta [kro'keta] *nf* croquette, rissole
croquis ['krokis] *nm inv* sketch
cruce *etc* ['kruθe] *vb ver* **cruzar** ■ *nm* crossing; (*de carreteras*) crossroads; (*Auto etc*) junction, intersection; (*Bio: proceso*) crossbreeding; **luces de ~** dipped headlights
crucero [kru'θero] *nm* (*Naut: barco*) cruise ship; (*: viaje*) cruise
crucial [kru'θjal] *adj* crucial
crucificar [kruθifi'kar] *vt* to crucify; (*fig*) to torment
crucifijo [kruθi'fixo] *nm* crucifix
crucifique *etc* [kruθi'fike] *vb ver* **crucificar**
crucigrama [kruθi'ɣrama] *nm* crossword (puzzle)
crudeza [kru'ðeθa] *nf* (*rigor*) harshness; (*aspereza*) crudeness
crudo, -a ['kruðo, a] *adj* raw; (*no maduro*) unripe; (*petróleo*) crude; (*rudo, cruel*) cruel; (*agua*) hard; (*clima etc*) harsh ■ *nm* crude (oil)
cruel [krwel] *adj* cruel
crueldad [krwel'ðað] *nf* cruelty
cruento, -a ['krwento, a] *adj* bloody
crujido [kru'xiðo] *nm* (*de madera etc*) creak
crujiente [kru'xjente] *adj* (*galleta etc*) crunchy
crujir [kru'xir] *vi* (*madera etc*) to creak; (*dedos*) to crack; (*dientes*) to grind; (*nieve, arena*) to crunch
cruz [kruθ] *nf* cross; (*de moneda*) tails *sg*; (*fig*) burden; **~ gamada** swastika; **C~ Roja** Red Cross
cruzado, -a [kru'θaðo, a] *adj* crossed ■ *nm* crusader ■ *nf* crusade
cruzar [kru'θar] *vt* to cross; (*palabras*) to exchange; **cruzarse** *vr* (*líneas etc*) to cross, intersect; (*personas*) to pass each other; **cruzarse de brazos** to fold one's arms; (*fig*) not to lift a finger to help; **cruzarse con algn en la calle** to pass sb in the street
CSIC [θe'sik] *nm abr* (*Esp Escol*) = **Consejo Superior de Investigaciones Científicas**
cta, c.[ta] *nf abr* (= *cuenta*) a/c
cta. cto. *abr* (= *carta de crédito*) L.C.
cte. *abr* (= *corriente, de los corrientes*) inst.
CTNE *nf abr* (*Telec*) = **Compañía Telefónica Nacional de España**
c/u *abr* (= *cada uno*) ea
cuaco ['kwako] *nm* (*Am*) nag
cuaderno [kwa'ðerno] *nm* notebook; (*de escuela*) exercise book; (*Naut*) logbook

cuadra ['kwaðra] *nf* (*caballeriza*) stable; (*Am*) (city) block
cuadrado, -a [kwa'ðraðo, a] *adj* square ■ *nm* (*Mat*) square
cuadragésimo, -a [kwaðra'xesimo, a] *num* fortieth
cuadrángulo [kwa'ðrangulo] *nm* quadrangle
cuadrante [kwa'ðrante] *nm* quadrant
cuadrar [kwa'ðrar] *vt* to square; (*Tip*) to justify ■ *vi*: **~ con** (*cuenta*) to square with, tally with; **cuadrarse** *vr* (*soldado*) to stand to attention; **~ por la derecha/izquierda** to right-/left-justify
cuadrícula [kwa'ðrikula] *nf* (*Tip etc*) grid, ruled squares
cuadriculado, -a [kwaðriku'laðo, a] *adj*: **papel ~** squared *o* graph paper
cuadrilátero [kwaðri'latero] *nm* (*Deporte*) boxing ring; (*Geom*) quadrilateral
cuadrilla [kwa'ðriʎa] *nf* (*de amigos*) party, group; (*de delincuentes*) gang; (*de obreros*) team
cuadro ['kwaðro] *nm* square; (*Pintura*) painting; (*Teat*) scene; (*diagrama: tb:* **cuadro sinóptico**) chart, table, diagram; (*Deporte: Med*) team; (*Pol*) executive; **~ de mandos** control panel; **a cuadros** check *cpd*
cuadruplicarse [kwaðrupli'karse] *vr* to quadruple
cuádruplo, -a ['kwaðruplo, a], **cuádruple** ['kwaðruple] *adj* quadruple
cuajado, -a [kwa'xaðo, a] *adj*: **~ de** (*fig*) full of ■ *nf* (*de leche*) curd
cuajar [kwa'xar] *vt* to thicken; (*leche*) to curdle; (*sangre*) to congeal; (*adornar*) to adorn; (*Culin*) to set ■ *vi* (*nieve*) to lie; (*fig*) to become set, become established; (*idea*) to be received, be acceptable; **cuajarse** *vr* to curdle; to congeal; (*llenarse*) to fill up
cuajo ['kwaxo] *nm*: **arrancar algo de ~** to tear sth out by its roots
cual [kwal] *adv* like, as ■ *pron*: **el ~** *etc* which; (*persona: sujeto*) who; (*: objeto*) whom; **lo ~** (*relativo*) which; **allá cada ~** every man to his own taste; **son a ~ más gandul** each is as idle as the other; **cada ~** each one ■ *adj* such as; **tal ~** just as it is
cuál [kwal] *pron interrogativo* which (one), what
cualesquier [kwales'kjer], **cualesquiera** [kwales'kjera] *adj pl, pron pl de* **cualquier; cualquiera**
cualidad [kwali'ðað] *nf* quality
cualificado, -a [kwalifi'kaðo, a] *adj* (*obrero*) skilled, qualified
cualquiera [kwal'kjera], **cualquier** [kwal'kjer] (*pl* **cualesquier(a)**) *adj* any ■ *pron* anybody, anyone; (*quienquiera*) whoever;

en cualquier momento any time; **en cualquier parte** anywhere; **~ que sea** whichever it is; (*persona*) whoever it is

cuán [kwan] *adv* how

cuando ['kwando] *adv* when; (*aún si*) if, even if ■ *conj* (*puesto que*) since ■ *prep*: **yo, ~ niño ...** when I was a child *o* as a child I ...; **~ no sea así** even if it is not so; **~ más** at (the) most; **~ menos** at least; **~ no** if not, otherwise; **de ~ en ~** from time to time; **ven ~ quieras** come when(ever) you like

cuándo ['kwando] *adv* when; **¿desde ~?, ¿de ~ acá?** since when?

cuantía [kwan'tia] *nf* (*alcance*) extent; (*importancia*) importance

cuantioso, -a [kwan'tjoso, a] *adj* substantial

○ **PALABRA CLAVE**

cuanto, -a ['kwanto, a] *adj* 1 (*todo*): **tiene todo cuanto desea** he's got everything he wants; **le daremos cuantos ejemplares necesite** we'll give him as many copies as *o* all the copies he needs; **cuantos hombres la ven** all the men who see her
2: **unos cuantos**: **había unos cuantos periodistas** there were (quite) a few journalists
3 (+*más*): **cuanto más vino bebas peor te sentirás** the more wine you drink the worse you'll feel; **cuantos más, mejor** the more the merrier
■ *pron*: **tiene cuanto desea** he has everything he wants; **tome cuanto/ cuantos quiera** take as much/many as you want
■ *adv*: **en cuanto**: **en cuanto profesor** as a teacher; **en cuanto a mí** as for me; *ver tb* **antes**
■ *conj* 1: **cuanto más gana menos gasta** the more he earns the less he spends; **cuanto más joven se es más se es confiado** the younger you are the more trusting you are
2: **en cuanto**: **en cuanto llegue/llegué** as soon as I arrive/arrived

cuánto, -a ['kwanto, a] *adj* (*exclamación*) what a lot of; (*interrogativo*: *sg*) how much?; (: *pl*) how many? ■ *pron, adv* how; (*interrogativo*: *sg*) how much?; (: *pl*) how many? ■ *excl*: **¡~ me alegro!** I'm so glad!; **¡~ gente!** what a lot of people!; **¿~ tiempo?** how long?; **¿~ cuesta?** how much does it cost?; **¿a ~s estamos?** what's the date?; **¿~ hay de aquí a Bilbao?** how far is it from here to Bilbao?; **Señor no sé ~s** Mr. So-and-So

cuarenta [kwa'renta] *num* forty

cuarentena [kwaren'tena] *nf* (*Med etc*) quarantine; (*conjunto*) forty(-odd)

cuarentón, -ona [kwaren'ton, ona] *adj* forty-year-old, fortyish ■ *nm/f* person of about forty

cuaresma [kwa'resma] *nf* Lent

cuarta ['kwarta] *nf ver* **cuarto**

cuartear [kwarte'ar] *vt* to quarter; (*dividir*) to divide up; **cuartearse** *vr* to crack, split

cuartel [kwar'tel] *nm* (*de ciudad*) quarter, district; (*Mil*) barracks *pl*; **~ general** headquarters *pl*

cuartelazo [kwarte'laθo] *nm* coup, military uprising

cuarteto [kwar'teto] *nm* quartet

cuartilla [kwar'tiʎa] *nf* (*hoja*) sheet (of paper); **cuartillas** *nfpl* (*Tip*) copy *sg*

cuarto, -a ['kwarto, a] *adj* fourth ■ *nm* (*Mat*) quarter, fourth; (*habitación*) room ■ *nf* (*Mat*) quarter, fourth; (*palmo*) span; **~ de baño** bathroom; **~ de estar** living room; **~ de hora** quarter (of an) hour; **~ de kilo** quarter kilo; **no tener un ~** to be broke (*fam*)

cuarzo ['kwarθo] *nm* quartz

cuatrero [kwa'trero] *nm* (*Am*) rustler, stock thief

cuatrimestre [kwatri'mestre] *nm* four-month period

cuatro ['kwatro] *num* four; **las ~** four o'clock; **el ~ de octubre** (on) the fourth of October; *ver tb* **seis**

cuatrocientos, -as [kwatro'θjentos, as] *num* four hundred; *ver tb* **seiscientos**

Cuba ['kuβa] *nf* Cuba

cuba ['kuβa] *nf* cask, barrel; **estar como una ~** (*fam*) to be sloshed

cubalibre [kuβa'liβre] *nm* (white) rum and coke®

cubano, -a [ku'βano, a] *adj, nm/f* Cuban

cubata [ku'βata] *nm* = **cubalibre**

cubertería [kuβerte'ria] *nf* cutlery

cúbico, -a ['kuβiko, a] *adj* cubic

cubierto, -a [ku'βjerto, a] *pp de* **cubrir** ■ *adj* covered; (*cielo*) overcast ■ *nm* cover; (*en la mesa*) place ■ *nf* cover, covering; (*neumático*) tyre; (*Naut*) deck; **cubiertos** *nmpl* cutlery *sg*; **a ~ de** covered with *o* in; **precio del ~** cover charge

cubil [ku'βil] *nm* den

cubilete [kuβi'lete] *nm* (*en juegos*) cup

cubito [ku'βito] *nm*: **~ de hielo** ice cube

cubo ['kuβo] *nm* cube; (*balde*) bucket, tub; (*Tec*) drum; **~ de (la) basura** dustbin

cubrecama [kuβre'kama] *nm* bedspread

cubrir [ku'βrir] *vt* to cover; (*vacante*) to fill; (*Bio*) to mate with; (*gastos*) to meet; **cubrirse** *vr* (*cielo*) to become overcast; (*Com*: *gastos*) to

be met o paid; (: *deuda*) to be covered;
~ las formas to keep up appearances; **lo
cubrieron las aguas** the waters closed over
it; **el agua casi me cubría** I was almost out
of my depth

cucaracha [kuka'ratʃa] *nf* cockroach

cuchara [ku'tʃara] *nf* spoon; (*Tec*) scoop

cucharada [kutʃa'raða] *nf* spoonful; **~
colmada** heaped spoonful

cucharadita [kutʃara'ðita] *nf* teaspoonful

cucharilla [kutʃa'riʎa] *nf* teaspoon

cucharita [kutʃa'rita] *nf* teaspoon

cucharón [kutʃa'ron] *nm* ladle

cuchichear [kutʃitʃe'ar] *vi* to whisper

cuchicheo [kutʃi'tʃeo] *nm* whispering

cuchilla [ku'tʃiʎa] *nf* (large) knife; (*de arma
blanca*) blade; **~ de afeitar** razor blade; **pasar
a ~** to put to the sword

cuchillada [kutʃi'ʎaða] *nf* (*golpe*) stab; (*herida*)
knife o stab wound

cuchillo [ku'tʃiʎo] *nm* knife

cuchitril [kutʃi'tril] *nm* hovel; (*habitación etc*)
pigsty

cuclillas [ku'kliʎas] *nfpl*: **en ~** squatting

cuco, -a ['kuko, a] *adj* pretty; (*astuto*) sharp
■ *nm* cuckoo

cucurucho [kuku'rutʃo] *nm* paper cone,
cornet

cuece *etc* ['kweθe] *vb ver* **cocer**

cuele *etc* ['kwele] *vb ver* **colar**

cuelgue *etc* ['kwelɣe] *vb ver* **colgar**

cuello ['kweʎo] *nm* (*Anat*) neck; (*de vestido,
camisa*) collar

cuenca ['kwenka] *nf* (*Anat*) eye socket; (*Geo:
valle*) bowl, deep valley; (: *fluvial*) basin

cuenco ['kwenko] *nm* (earthenware) bowl

cuenta *etc* ['kwenta] *vb ver* **contar** ■ *nf*
(*cálculo*) count, counting; (*en café, restaurante*)
bill; (*Com*) account; (*de collar*) bead; (*fig*)
account; **a fin de ~s** in the end; **en
resumidas ~s** in short; **caer en la ~** to catch
on; **dar ~ a algn de sus actos** to account to
sb for one's actions; **darse ~ de** to realize;
tener en ~ to bear in mind; **echar ~s** to take
stock; **~ atrás** countdown; **~ corriente/de
ahorros/a plazo (fijo)** current/savings/
deposit account; **~ de caja** cash account;
~ de capital capital account; **~ por cobrar**
account receivable; **~ de correo** (*Internet*)
email account; **~ de crédito** credit o loan
account; **~ de gastos e ingresos** income and
expenditure account; **~ por pagar** account
payable; **abonar una cantidad en ~ a algn**
to credit a sum to sb's account; **ajustar o
liquidar una ~** to settle an account; **pasar la
~** to send the bill

cuentagotas [kwenta'ɣotas] *nm inv* (*Med*)

dropper; **a o con ~** (*fam, fig*) drop by drop, bit
by bit

cuentakilómetros [kwentaki'lometros]
nm inv (*de distancias*) ≈ milometer, clock;
(*velocímetro*) speedometer

cuentista [kwen'tista] *nm/f* gossip; (*Lit*)
short-story writer

cuento *etc* ['kwento] *vb ver* **contar** ■ *nm*
story; (*Lit*) short story; **~ de hadas** fairy
story; **es el ~ de nunca acabar** it's an
endless business; **eso no viene a ~** that's
irrelevant

cuerda ['kwerða] *nf* rope; (*hilo*) string; (*de
reloj*) spring; (*Mus: de violín etc*) string; (*Mat*)
chord; (*Anat*) cord; **~ floja** tightrope;
cuerdas vocales vocal cords; **dar ~ a un
reloj** to wind up a clock

cuerdo, -a ['kwerðo, a] *adj* sane; (*prudente*)
wise, sensible

cuerear [kwere'ar] *vt* (*Am*) to skin

cuerno ['kwerno] *nm* (*Zool: gen*) horn; (: *de
ciervo*) antler; **poner los cuernos a** (*fam*) to
cuckold; **saber a ~ quemado** to leave a nasty
taste

cuero ['kwero] *nm* (*Zool*) skin, hide; (*Tec*)
leather; **en cueros** stark naked; **~ cabelludo**
scalp

cuerpo ['kwerpo] *nm* body; (*cadáver*) corpse;
(*fig*) main part; **~ de bomberos** fire brigade;
~ diplomático diplomatic corps; **luchar ~ a
~** to fight hand-to-hand; **tomar ~** (*plan etc*)
to take shape

cuervo ['kwerβo] *nm* (*Zool*) raven, crow; *ver*
criar

cuesta *etc* ['kwesta] *vb ver* **costar** ■ *nf* slope;
(*en camino etc*) hill; **~ arriba/abajo** uphill/
downhill; **a ~s** on one's back

cuestión [kwes'tjon] *nf* matter, question,
issue; (*riña*) quarrel, dispute; **eso es otra ~**
that's another matter

cuestionar [kwestjo'nar] *vt* to question

cuestionario [kwestjo'narjo] *nm*
questionnaire

cueva ['kweβa] *nf* cave

cueza *etc* ['kweθa] *vb ver* **cocer**

cuidado [kwi'ðaðo] *nm* care, carefulness;
(*preocupación*) care, worry ■ *excl* careful!, look
out!; **eso me tiene sin ~** I'm not worried
about that

cuidadoso, -a [kwiða'ðoso, a] *adj* careful;
(*preocupado*) anxious

cuidar [kwi'ðar] *vt* (*Med*) to care for; (*ocuparse
de*) to take care of, look after; (*detalles*) to
pay attention to ■ *vi*: **~ de** to take care of,
look after; **cuidarse** *vr* to look after o.s.;
cuidarse de hacer algo to take care to do
something

cuita ['kwita] *nf* (*preocupación*) worry, trouble; (*pena*) grief

culata [ku'lata] *nf* (*de fusil*) butt

culatazo [kula'taθo] *nm* kick, recoil

culebra [ku'leβra] *nf* snake; ~ **de cascabel** rattlesnake

culebrear [kuleβre'ar] *vi* to wriggle along; (*río*) to meander

culebrón [kule'βron] *nm* (*fam*) soap (opera)

culinario, -a [kuli'narjo, a] *adj* culinary, cooking *cpd*

culminación [kulmina'θjon] *nf* culmination

culminante [kulmi'nante] *adj*: **momento ~** climax, highlight, highspot

culminar [kulmi'nar] *vi* to culminate

culo ['kulo] *nm* (*fam: asentaderas*) bottom, backside, bum (*Brit*); (: *ano*) arse(hole) (*Brit!*), ass(hole) (*US!*); (*de vaso*) bottom

culpa ['kulpa] *nf* fault; (*Jur*) guilt; **culpas** *nfpl* sins; **por ~ de** through, because of; **tener la ~ (de)** to be to blame (for)

culpabilidad [kulpaβili'ðað] *nf* guilt

*culpable [kul'paβle] *adj* guilty ■ *nm/f* culprit; **confesarse ~** to plead guilty; **declarar ~ a algn** to find sb guilty

culpar [kul'par] *vt* to blame; (*acusar*) to accuse

cultivadora [kultiβa'ðora] *nf* cultivator

cultivar [kulti'βar] *vt* to cultivate; (*cosecha*) to raise; (*talento*) to develop

cultivo [kul'tiβo] *nm* (*acto*) cultivation; (*plantas*) crop; (*Bio*) culture

culto, -a ['kulto, a] *adj* (*cultivado*) cultivated; (*que tiene cultura*) cultured, educated ■ *nm* (*homenaje*) worship; (*religión*) cult; (*Pol etc*) cult

cultura [kul'tura] *nf* culture

cultural [kultu'ral] *adj* cultural

culturismo [kultu'rismo] *nm* body-building

cumbre ['kumbre] *nf* summit, top; (*fig*) top, height; **conferencia (en la) ~** summit (conference)

cumpleaños [kumple'aɲos] *nm inv* birthday

cumplido, -a [kum'pliðo, a] *adj* complete, perfect; (*abundante*) plentiful; (*cortés*) courteous ■ *nm* compliment; **visita de ~** courtesy call

cumplidor, a [kumpli'ðor, a] *adj* reliable

cumplimentar [kumplimen'tar] *vt* to congratulate; (*órdenes*) to carry out

cumplimiento [kumpli'mjento] *nm* (*de un deber*) fulfilment, execution, performance; (*acabamiento*) completion; (*Com*) expiry, end

cumplir [kum'plir] *vt* (*orden*) to carry out, obey; (*promesa*) to carry out, fulfil; (*condena*) to serve; (*años*) to reach, attain ■ *vi* (*pago*) to fall due; (*plazo*) to expire; **cumplirse** *vr* (*plazo*) to expire; (*plan etc*) to be fulfilled; (*vaticinio*) to come true; **hoy cumple**

dieciocho años he is eighteen today; ~ **con** (*deber*) to carry out, fulfil

cúmulo ['kumulo] *nm* (*montón*) heap; (*nube*) cumulus

cuna ['kuna] *nf* cradle, cot; **canción de ~** lullaby

cundir [kun'dir] *vi* (*noticia, rumor, pánico*) to spread; (*rendir*) to go a long way

cuneta [ku'neta] *nf* ditch

cuña ['kuɲa] *nf* (*Tec*) wedge; (*Com*) advertising spot; (*Med*) bedpan; **tener cuñas** to have influence

cuñado, -a [ku'ɲaðo, a] *nm/f* brother/sister-in-law

cuño ['kuɲo] *nm* (*Tec*) die-stamp; (*fig*) stamp

cuota ['kwota] *nf* (*parte proporcional*) share; (*cotización*) fee, dues *pl*; ~ **inicial** (*Com*) down payment

cupo *etc* ['kupo] *vb ver* **caber** ■ *nm* quota, share; (*Com*): ~ **de importación** import quota; ~ **de ventas** sales quota

cupón [ku'pon] *nm* coupon; ~ **de la ONCE** *o* **de los ciegos** ONCE lottery ticket; *ver tb* **lotería**

cúpula ['kupula] *nf* (*Arq*) dome

cura ['kura] *nf* (*curación*) cure; (*método curativo*) treatment ■ *nm* priest; ~ **de emergencia** emergency treatment

curación [kura'θjon] *nf* cure; (*acción*) curing

curado, -a [ku'raðo, a] *adj* (*Culin*) cured; (*pieles*) tanned

curandero, -a [kuran'dero, a] *nm/f* healer

curar [ku'rar] *vt* (*Med: herida*) to treat, dress; (: *enfermo*) to cure; (*Culin*) to cure, salt; (*cuero*) to tan ■ *vi*, **curarse** *vr* to get well, recover

curda ['kurða] (*fam*) *nm* drunk ■ *nf*: **agarrar una/estar ~** to get/be sloshed

curiosear [kurjose'ar] *vt* to glance at, look over ■ *vi* to look round, wander round; (*explorar*) to poke about

curiosidad [kurjosi'ðað] *nf* curiosity

curioso, -a [ku'rjoso, a] *adj* curious; (*aseado*) neat ■ *nm/f* bystander, onlooker; **¡qué ~!** how odd!

curita [ku'rita] *nf* (*Am*) sticking plaster

currante [ku'rrante] *nm/f* (*fam*) worker

currar [ku'rrar] *vi* (*fam*), **currelar** [kurre'lar] *vi* (*fam*) to work

currículo [ku'rrikulo] *nm*, **currículum** [ku'rrikulum] *nm* curriculum vitae

curro ['kurro] *nm* (*fam*) work, job

cursar [kur'sar] *vt* (*Escol*) to study

cursi ['kursi] *adj* (*fam*) pretentious; (: *amanerado*) affected

cursilada [kursi'laða] *nf*: **¡qué ~!** how tacky!

cursilería [kursile'ria] *nf* (*vulgaridad*) bad taste; (*amaneramiento*) affectation

cursillo [kur'siʎo] *nm* short course

cursiva [kur'siβa] *nf* italics *pl*

curso ['kurso] *nm* (*dirección*) course; (*fig*) progress; (*Escol*) school year; (*Univ*) academic year; **en ~** (*año*) current; (*proceso*) going on, under way; **moneda de ~ legal** legal tender

cursor [kur'sor] *nm* (*Inform*) cursor; (*Tec*) slide

curtido, -a [kur'tiðo, a] *adj* (*cara etc*) weather-beaten; (*fig: persona*) experienced

curtir [kur'tir] *vt* (*piel*) to tan; (*fig*) to harden

curvo, -a ['kurβo, a] *adj* (*gen*) curved; (*torcido*) bent ▪ *nf* (*gen*) curve, bend; **curva de rentabilidad** (*Com*) break-even chart

cúspide ['kuspiðe] *nf* (*Geo*) summit, peak; (*fig*) top, pinnacle

custodia [kus'toðja] *nf* (*cuidado*) safekeeping; (*Jur*) custody

custodiar [kusto'ðjar] *vt* (*conservar*) to keep, take care of; (*vigilar*) to guard

custodio [kus'toðjo] *nm* guardian, keeper

cutáneo, -a [ku'taneo, a] *adj* skin *cpd*

cutícula [ku'tikula] *nf* cuticle

cutis ['kutis] *nm inv* skin, complexion

cutre ['kutre] *adj* (*fam: lugar*) grotty; (: *persona*) naff

cuyo, -a ['kujo, a] *pron* (*de quien*) whose; (*de que*) whose, of which; **la señora en cuya casa me hospedé** the lady in whose house I stayed; **el asunto cuyos detalles conoces** the affair the details of which you know; **por ~ motivo** for which reason

C.V. *abr* (= *Curriculum Vitae*) CV; (= *caballos de vapor*) H.P.

Dd

D, d [de] *nf* (*letra*) D, d; **D de Dolores** D for David (*Brit*), D for Dog (*US*)

D. *abr* = **Don**

D.ª *abr* = **Doña**

dactilar [dakti'lar] *adj*: **huellas dactilares** fingerprints

dactilógrafo, -a [dakti'loɣrafo, a] *nm/f* typist

dádiva ['daðiβa] *nf* donation; (*regalo*) gift

dadivoso, -a [daði'βoso, a] *adj* generous

dado, -a ['daðo, a] *pp de* **dar** ■ *nm* die; **dados** *nmpl* dice ■ *adj*: **en un momento ~** at a certain point; **ser ~ a (hacer algo)** to be very fond of (doing sth); **~ que** *conj* given that

daga ['daɣa] *nf* dagger

daltónico, -a [dal'toniko, a] *adj* colour-blind

daltonismo [dalto'nismo] *nm* colour blindness

dama ['dama] *nf* (*gen*) lady; (*Ajedrez*) queen; **damas** *nfpl* draughts; **primera ~** (*Teat*) leading lady; (*Pol*) president's wife, first lady (*US*); **~ de honor** (*de reina*) lady-in-waiting; (*de novia*) bridesmaid

damasco [da'masko] *nm* (*tela*) damask; (*Am*: *árbol*) apricot tree; (: *fruta*) apricot

damnificado, -a [damnifi'kaðo, a] *nm/f*: **los damnificados** the victims

damnificar [damnifi'kar] *vt* to harm; (*persona*) to injure

damnifique *etc* [damni'fike] *vb ver* **damnificar**

dance *etc* ['danθe] *vb ver* **danzar**

danés, -esa [da'nes, esa] *adj* Danish ■ *nm/f* Dane ■ *nm* (*Ling*) Danish

Danubio [da'nuβjo] *nm* Danube

danza ['danθa] *nf* (*gen*) dancing; (*una danza*) dance

danzar [dan'θar] *vt, vi* to dance

danzarín, -ina [danθa'rin, ina] *nm/f* dancer

dañar [da'ɲar] *vt* (*objeto*) to damage; (*persona*) to hurt; (*estropear*) to spoil; **dañarse** *vr* (*objeto*) to get damaged

dañino, -a [da'ɲino, a] *adj* harmful

daño ['daɲo] *nm* (*a un objeto*) damage; (*a una persona*) harm, injury; **daños y perjuicios** (*Jur*) damages; **hacer ~ a** to damage; (*persona*) to hurt, injure; **hacerse ~** to hurt o.s.

dañoso, -a [da'ɲoso, a] *adj* harmful

DAO *abr* (= *Diseño Asistido por Ordenador*) CAD

 PALABRA CLAVE

dar [dar] *vt* **1** (*gen*) to give; (*obra de teatro*) to put on; (*film*) to show; (*fiesta*) to have; **dar algo a algn** to give sb sth o sth to sb; **dar una patada a algn/algo** to kick sb/sth, give sb/sth a kick; **dar un susto a algn** to give sb a fright; **dar de beber a algn** to give sb a drink; **dar de comer** to feed

2 (*intereses*) to yield; (*fruta*) to produce

3 (*locuciones +n*): **da gusto escucharle** it's a pleasure to listen to him; **me da pena/asco** it frightens/sickens me; *ver tb* **paseo** *y otros sustantivos*

4 (*considerar*): **dar algo por descontado/entendido** to take sth for granted/as read; **dar algo por concluido** to consider sth finished; **le dieron por desaparecido** they gave him up as lost

5 (*hora*): **el reloj dio las seis** the clock struck six (o'clock)

6: **me da lo mismo** it's all the same to me; *ver tb* **igual**; **más**

7: **¡y dale!** (*¡otra vez!*) not again!; **estar/seguir dale que dale** o **dale que te pego** o (*Am*) **dale y dale** to go/keep on and on

■ *vi* **1**: **dar a** (*habitación*) to overlook, look on to; (*accionar: botón etc*) to press, hit

2: **dar con**: **dimos con él dos horas más tarde** we came across him two hours later; **al final di con la solución** I eventually came up with the answer

3: **dar en** (*blanco, suelo*) to hit; **el sol me da en la cara** the sun is shining (right) in my face

4: **dar de sí** (*zapatos etc*) to stretch, give

5: **dar para** to be enough for; **nuestro**

presupuesto no da para más our budget's really tight

6: **dar por**: **le ha dado por estudiar música** now he's into studying music

7: **dar que hablar** to set people talking; **una película que da que pensar** a thought-provoking film

darse *vr* **1**: **darse un baño** to have a bath; **darse un golpe** to hit o.s.

2: **darse por vencido** to give up; **con eso me doy por satisfecho** I'd settle for that

3 (*ocurrir*): **se han dado muchos casos** there have been a lot of cases

4: **darse a**: **se ha dado a la bebida** he's taken to drinking

5: **se me dan bien/mal las ciencias** I'm good/bad at science

6: **dárselas de**: **se las da de experto** he fancies himself *o* poses as an expert

dardo ['darðo] *nm* dart
dársena ['darsena] *nf* (*Naut*) dock
datar [da'tar] *vi*: ~ **de** to date from
dátil ['datil] *nm* date
dativo [da'tiβo] *nm* (*Ling*) dative
dato ['dato] *nm* fact, piece of information; (*Mat*) datum; **datos** *nmpl* (*Inform*) data; **datos de entrada/salida** input/output data; **datos personales** personal particulars
dcha. *abr* (= *derecha*) r (= *right*)
d. de J. C. *abr* (= *después de Jesucristo*) A.D. (= *Anno Domini*)

 PALABRA CLAVE

de [de] *prep* (*de+el* = *del*) **1** (*posesión, pertenencia*) of; **la casa de Isabel/mis padres** Isabel's/my parents' house; **es de ellos/ella** it's theirs/hers; **un libro de Unamuno** a book by Unamuno

2 (*origen, distancia, con números*) from; **soy de Gijón** I'm from Gijón; **de 8 a 20** from 8 to 20; **5 metros de largo** 5 metres long; **salir del cine** to go out of *o* leave the cinema; **de ... en ... ** from ... to ...; **de 2 en 2** 2 by 2, 2 at a time; **9 de cada 10** 9 out of every 10

3 (*valor descriptivo*): **una copa de vino** a glass of wine; **una silla de madera** a wooden chair; **la mesa de la cocina** the kitchen table; **un viaje de dos días** a two-day journey; **un billete de 50 euros** a 50-euro note; **un niño de tres años** a three-year-old (child); **una máquina de coser** a sewing machine; **la ciudad de Madrid** the city of Madrid; **el tonto de Juan** that idiot Juan; **ir vestido de gris** to be dressed in grey; **la niña del vestido azul** the girl in the blue

dress; **la chica del pelo largo** the girl with long hair; **trabaja de profesora** she works as a teacher; **de lado** sideways; **de atrás/delante** rear/front

4 (*hora, tiempo*): **a las 8 de la mañana** at 8 o'clock in the morning; **de día/noche** by day/night; **de hoy en ocho días** a week from now; **de niño era gordo** as a child he was fat

5 (*comparaciones*): **más/menos de cien personas** more/less than a hundred people; **el más caro de la tienda** the most expensive in the shop; **menos/más de lo pensado** less/more than expected

6 (*causa*): **del calor** from the heat; **de puro tonto** out of sheer stupidity

7 (*tema*) about; **clases de inglés** English classes; **¿sabes algo de él?** do you know anything about him?; **un libro de física** a physics book

8 (*adj+de+infin*): **fácil de entender** easy to understand

9 (*oraciones pasivas*): **fue respetado de todos** he was loved by all

10 (*condicional+infin*): if; **de ser posible** if possible; **de no terminarlo hoy** if I *etc* don't finish it today

dé [de] *vb ver* **dar**
deambular [deambu'lar] *vi* to stroll, wander
debajo [de'βaxo] *adv* underneath; ~ **de** below, under; **por** ~ **de** beneath
debate [de'βate] *nm* debate
debatir [deβa'tir] *vt* to debate; **debatirse** *vr* to struggle
debe ['deβe] *nm* (*en cuenta*) debit side; ~ **y haber** debit and credit
deber [de'βer] *nm* duty ■ *vt* to owe ■ *vi*: **debe (de)** it must, it should; **deberse** *vr*: **deberse a** to be owing *o* due to; **deberes** *nmpl* (*Escol*) homework *sg*; **debo hacerlo** I must do it; **debe de ir** he should go; **¿qué** *o* **cuánto le debo?** how much is it?
debidamente [deβiða'mente] *adv* properly; (*rellenar*) duly
debido, -a [de'βiðo, a] *adj* proper, due; ~ **a** due to, because of; **en debida forma** duly
débil ['deβil] *adj* weak; (*persona: físicamente*) feeble; (*salud*) poor; (*voz, ruido*) faint; (*luz*) dim
debilidad [deβili'ðað] *nf* weakness; feebleness; dimness; **tener** ~ **por algn** to have a soft spot for sb
debilitar [deβili'tar] *vt* to weaken; **debilitarse** *vr* to grow weak
débito ['deβito] *nm* debit; (*deuda*) debt
debutante [deβu'tante] *nm/f* beginner
debutar [deβu'tar] *vi* to make one's debut

década ['dekaða] nf decade
decadencia [deka'ðenθja] nf (estado)
decadence; (proceso) decline, decay
decadente [deca'ðente] adj decadent
decaer [deka'er] vi (declinar) to decline;
(debilitarse) to weaken; (salud) to fail; (negocio)
to fall off
decaído, -a [deka'iðo, a] adj: **estar ~** (persona)
to be down
decaiga etc [de'kaiɣa] vb ver **decaer**
decaimiento [dekai'mjento] nm (declinación)
decline; (desaliento) discouragement; (Med:
depresión) depression
decanato [deka'nato] nm (cargo) deanship;
(despacho) dean's office
decano, -a [de'kano, a] nm/f (Univ etc) dean;
(de grupo) senior member
decantar [dekan'tar] vt (vino) to decant
decapitar [dekapi'tar] vt to behead
decayendo etc [deka'jendo] vb ver **decaer**
decena [de'θena] nf: **una ~** ten (or so)
decencia [de'θenθja] nf (modestia) modesty;
(honestidad) respectability
decenio [de'θenjo] nm decade
decente [de'θente] adj (correcto) proper;
(honesto) respectable
decepción [deθep'θjon] nf disappointment
decepcionante [deθepθjo'nante] adj
disappointing
decepcionar [deθepθjo'nar] vt to disappoint
decibelio [deθi'βeljo] nm decibel
decidido, -a [deθi'ðiðo, a] adj decided;
(resuelto) resolute
decidir [deθi'ðir] vt (persuadir) to convince,
persuade; (resolver) to decide ■ vi to decide;
decidirse vr: **decidirse a** to make up one's
mind to; **decidirse por** to decide o settle on,
choose
decimal [deθi'mal] adj, nm decimal
décimo, -a ['deθimo, a] num tenth ■ nf (Mat)
tenth; **tiene unas décimas de fiebre** he has
a slight temperature
decimoctavo, -a [deθimok'taβo, a] num
eighteenth; ver tb **sexto**
decimocuarto, -a [deθimo'kwarto, a] num
fourteenth; ver tb **sexto**
decimonoveno, -a [deθimono'βeno, a] num
nineteenth; ver tb **sexto**
decimoquinto, -a [deθimo'kinto, a] num
fifteenth; ver tb **sexto**
decimoséptimo, -a [deθimo'septimo, a] num
seventeenth; ver tb **sexto**
decimosexto, -a [deθimo'seksto, a] num
sixteenth; ver tb **sexto**
decimotercero, -a [deθimoter'θero, a] num
thirteenth; ver tb **sexto**
decir [de'θir] vt (expresar) to say; (contar) to
tell; (hablar) to speak; (indicar) to show;
(revelar) to reveal; (fam: nombrar) to call ■ nm
saying; **decirse** vr: **se dice** it is said, they
say; (se cuenta) the story goes; **¿cómo se dice
en inglés "cursi"?** what's the English for
"cursi"?; **~ para o entre sí** to say to o.s.; **~
por ~** to talk for talking's sake; **dar que ~
(a la gente)** to make people talk; **querer ~**
to mean; **es ~** that is to say, namely; **ni que
~ tiene que ...** it goes without saying that
...; **como quien dice** so to speak; **¡quién lo
diría!** would you believe it!; **el qué dirán**
gossip; **¡diga!, ¡dígame!** (en tienda etc) can I
help you?; (Telec) hello?; **le dije que fuera
más tarde** I told her to go later; **es un ~** it's
just a phrase
decisión [deθi'sjon] nf decision; (firmeza)
decisiveness; (voluntad) determination
decisivo, -a [deθi'siβo, a] adj decisive
declamar [dekla'mar] vt, vi to declaim;
(versos etc) to recite
declaración [deklara'θjon] nf (manifestación)
statement; (explicación) explanation; (Jur:
testimonio) evidence; **~ de derechos** (Pol)
bill of rights; **~ de impuestos** (Com) tax
return; **~ de ingresos o de la renta** income
tax return; **~ jurada** affidavit; **falsa ~** (Jur)
misrepresentation
declarar [dekla'rar] vt to declare ■ vi to
declare; (Jur) to testify; **declararse** vr (a una
chica) to propose; (guerra, incendio) to break
out; **~ culpable/inocente a algn** to find sb
guilty/not guilty; **declararse culpable/
inocente** to plead guilty/not guilty
declinación [deklina'θjon] nf (decaimiento)
decline; (Ling) declension
declinar [dekli'nar] vt (gen, Ling) to decline;
(Jur) to reject ■ vi (el día) to draw to a close
declive [de'kliβe] nm (cuesta) slope;
(inclinación) incline; (fig) decline; (Com: tb:
declive económico) slump
decodificador [dekoðifika'ðor] nm (Inform)
decoder
decolorarse [dekolo'rarse] vr to become
discoloured
decomisar [dekomi'sar] vt to seize,
confiscate
decomiso [deko'miso] nm seizure
decoración [dekora'θjon] nf decoration;
(Teat) scenery, set; **~ de escaparates** window
dressing
decorado [deko'raðo] nm (Cine, Teat) scenery,
set
decorador, a [dekora'ðor, a] nm/f (de
interiores) (interior) decorator; (Teat) stage o
set designer
decorar [deko'rar] vt to decorate

decorativo, -a [dekora'tiβo, a] *adj* ornamental, decorative

decoro [de'koro] *nm* (*respeto*) respect; (*dignidad*) decency; (*recato*) propriety

decoroso, -a [deko'roso, a] *adj* (*decente*) decent; (*modesto*) modest; (*digno*) proper

decrecer [dekre'θer] *vi* to decrease, diminish; (*nivel de agua*) to go down; (*días*) to draw in

decrépito, -a [de'krepito, a] *adj* decrepit

decretar [dekre'tar] *vt* to decree

decreto [de'kreto] *nm* decree; (*Pol*) act

decreto-ley [dekreto'lei] (*pl* **decretos-leyes**) *nm* decree

decrezca *etc* [de'kreθka] *vb ver* **decrecer**

decúbito [de'kuβito] *nm* (*Med*): ~ **prono/ supino** prone/supine position

dedal [de'ðal] *nm* thimble

dedalera [deða'lera] *nf* foxglove

dédalo ['deðalo] *nm* (*laberinto*) labyrinth; (*fig*) tangle, mess

dedicación [deðika'θjon] *nf* dedication; **con ~ exclusiva** o **plena** full-time

dedicar [deði'kar] *vt* (*libro*) to dedicate; (*tiempo, dinero*) to devote; **dedicarse** *vr*: **dedicarse a (hacer algo)** to devote o.s. to (doing sth); (*carrera, estudio*) to go in for (doing sth), take up (doing sth); **¿a qué se dedica usted?** what do you do (for a living)?

dedicatoria [deðika'torja] *nf* (*de libro*) dedication

dedillo [de'ðiʎo] *nm*: **saber algo al ~** to have sth at one's fingertips

dedique *etc* [de'ðike] *vb ver* **dedicar**

dedo ['deðo] *nm* finger; (*de vino etc*) drop; ~ **(del pie)** toe; ~ **pulgar** thumb; ~ **índice** index finger; ~ **mayor** o **cordial** middle finger; ~ **anular** ring finger; ~ **meñique** little finger; **contar con los dedos** to count on one's fingers; **comerse los dedos** to get very impatient; **entrar a ~** to get a job by pulling strings; **hacer ~** (*fam*) to hitch (a lift); **poner el ~ en la llaga** to put one's finger on it; **no tiene dos dedos de frente** he's pretty dim

deducción [deðuk'θjon] *nf* deduction

deducir [deðu'θir] *vt* (*concluir*) to deduce, infer; (*Com*) to deduct

deduje *etc* [de'ðuxe], **dedujera** *etc* [deðu'xera], **deduzca** *etc* [de'ðuθka] *vb ver* **deducir**

defección [defek'θjon] *nf* defection, desertion

defecto [de'fekto] *nm* defect, flaw; (*de cara*) imperfection; ~ **de pronunciación** speech defect; **por ~** (*Inform*) default; ~ **latente** (*Com*) latent defect

defectuoso, -a [defek'twoso, a] *adj* defective, faulty

defender [defen'der] *vt* to defend; (*ideas*) to uphold; (*causa*) to champion; (*amigos*) to stand up for; **defenderse** *vr* to defend o.s.; **defenderse bien** to give a good account of o.s.; **me defiendo en inglés** (*fig*) I can get by in English

defendible [defen'diβle] *adj* defensible

defensa [de'fensa] *nf* defence; (*Naut*) fender ■ *nm* (*Deporte*) back; **en ~ propia** in self-defence

defensivo, -a [defen'siβo, a] *adj* defensive ■ *nf*: **a la defensiva** on the defensive

defensor, -a [defen'sor, a] *adj* defending ■ *nm/f* (*abogado defensor*) defending counsel; (*protector*) protector; ~ **del pueblo** (*Esp*) ≈ ombudsman

deferente [defe'rente] *adj* deferential

deferir [defe'rir] *vt* (*Jur*) to refer, delegate ■ *vi*: ~ **a** to defer to

deficiencia [defi'θjenθja] *nf* deficiency

deficiente [defi'θjente] *adj* (*defectuoso*) defective; ~ **en** lacking o deficient in ■ *nm/f*: **ser un ~ mental** to be mentally handicapped

déficit (*pl* **déficits**) ['defiθit] *nm* (*Com*) deficit; (*fig*) lack, shortage; ~ **presupuestario** budget deficit

deficitario, -a [defiθi'tarjo, a] *adj* (*Com*) in deficit; (: *empresa*) loss-making

defienda *etc* [de'fjenda] *vb ver* **defender**

defiera *etc* [de'fjera] *vb ver* **deferir**

definición [defini'θjon] *nf* definition; (*Inform: de pantalla*) resolution

definido, -a [defi'niðo, a] *adj* (*tb Ling*) definite; **bien ~** well o clearly defined; ~ **por el usuario** (*Inform*) user-defined

definir [defi'nir] *vt* (*determinar*) to determine, establish; (*decidir, Inform*) to define; (*aclarar*) to clarify

definitivo, -a [defini'tiβo, a] *adj* (*edición, texto*) definitive; (*fecha*) definite; **en definitiva** definitively; (*en conclusión*) finally; (*en resumen*) in short

defiriendo *etc* [defi'rjendo] *vb ver* **deferir**

deflacionario, -a [deflaθjo'narjo, a], **deflacionista** [deflaθjo'nista] *adj* deflationary

deflector [deflek'tor] *nm* (*Tec*) baffle

deforestación [deforesta'θjon] *nf* deforestation

deformación [deforma'θjon] *nf* (*alteración*) deformation; (*Radio etc*) distortion

deformar [defor'mar] *vt* (*gen*) to deform; **deformarse** *vr* to become deformed

deforme [de'forme] *adj* (*informe*) deformed; (*feo*) ugly; (*mal hecho*) misshapen

deformidad [deformi'ðað] *nf* (*forma anormal*) deformity; (*fig: defecto*) (moral) shortcoming

defraudar [defrau'ðar] *vt* (*decepcionar*) to disappoint; (*estafar*) to cheat; to defraud; ~ **impuestos** to evade tax

defunción [defun'θjon] *nf* decease, demise

degeneración [dexenera'θjon] *nf* (*de las células*) degeneration; (*moral*) degeneracy

degenerar [dexene'rar] *vi* to degenerate; (*empeorar*) to get worse

deglutir [deɣlu'tir] *vt, vi* to swallow

degolladero [deɣoʎa'ðero] *nm* (*Anat*) throat; (*cadalso*) scaffold; (*matadero*) slaughterhouse

degollar [deɣo'ʎar] *vt* to slaughter

degradar [deɣra'ðar] *vt* to debase, degrade; (*Inform: datos*) to corrupt; **degradarse** *vr* to demean o.s.

degüelle *etc* [de'ɣweʎe] *vb ver* **degollar**

degustación [deɣusta'θjon] *nf* sampling, tasting

deificar [deifi'kar] *vt* (*persona*) to deify

deifique *etc* [dei'fike] *vb ver* **deificar**

dejadez [dexa'ðeθ] *nf* (*negligencia*) neglect; (*descuido*) untidiness, carelessness

dejado, -a [de'xaðo, a] *adj* (*desaliñado*) slovenly; (*negligente*) careless; (*indolente*) lazy

dejar [de'xar] *vt* (*gen*) to leave; (*permitir*) to allow, let; (*abandonar*) to abandon, forsake; (*actividad, empleo*) to give up; (*beneficios*) to produce, yield ■ *vi*: ~ **de** (*parar*) to stop; **dejarse** *vr* (*abandonarse*) to let o.s. go; **no puedo ~ de fumar** I can't give up smoking; **no dejes de visitarles** don't fail to visit them; **no dejes de comprar un billete** make sure you buy a ticket; ~ **a un lado** to leave *o* set aside; ~ **caer** to drop; ~ **entrar/salir** to let in/out; ~ **pasar** to let through; **¡déjalo!** (*no te preocupes*) don't worry about it; **te dejo en tu casa** I'll drop you off at your place; **deja mucho que desear** it leaves a lot to be desired; **dejarse persuadir** to allow o.s. to *o* let o.s. be persuaded; **¡déjate de tonterías!** stop messing about!

deje ['dexe] *nm* (trace of) accent

dejo ['dexo] *nm* (*Ling*) accent

del [del] = **de** + **el**; *ver* **de**

del. *abr* (*Admin*: = *Delegación*) district office

delantal [delan'tal] *nm* apron

delante [de'lante] *adv* in front; (*enfrente*) opposite; (*adelante*) ahead ■ *prep*: ~ **de** in front of, before; **la parte de** ~ the front part; **estando otros** ~ with others present

delantero, -a [delan'tero, a] *adj* front; (*patas de animal*) fore ■ *nm* (*Deporte*) forward ■ *nf* (*de vestido, casa etc*) front part; (*Teat*) front row; (*Deporte*) forward line; **llevar la delantera (a algn)** to be ahead (of sb)

delatar [dela'tar] *vt* to inform on *o* against, betray; **los delató a la policía** he reported them to the police

delator, -a [dela'tor, a] *nm/f* informer

delegación [deleɣa'θjon] *nf* (*acción: delegados*) delegation; (*Com: oficina*) district office, branch; ~ **de poderes** (*Pol*) devolution; ~ **de policía** police station

delegado, -a [dele'ɣaðo, a] *nm/f* delegate; (*Com*) agent

delegar [dele'ɣar] *vt* to delegate

delegue *etc* [de'leɣe] *vb ver* **delegar**

deleitar [delei'tar] *vt* to delight; **deleitarse** *vr*: **deleitarse con** *o* **en** to delight in, take pleasure in

deleite [de'leite] *nm* delight, pleasure

deletrear [deletre'ar] *vt* (*tb fig*) to spell (out)

deletreo [dele'treo] *nm* spelling; (*fig*) interpretation, decipherment

deleznable [deleθ'naβle] *adj* (*frágil*) fragile; (*fig: malo*) poor; (: *excusa*) feeble

delfín [del'fin] *nm* dolphin

delgadez [delɣa'ðeθ] *nf* thinness, slimness

delgado, -a [del'ɣaðo, a] *adj* thin; (*persona*) slim, thin; (*tierra*) poor; (*tela etc*) light, delicate ■ *adv*: **hilar (muy)** ~ (*fig*) to split hairs

deliberación [deliβera'θjon] *nf* deliberation

deliberar [deliβe'rar] *vt* to debate, discuss ■ *vi* to deliberate

delicadeza [delika'ðeθa] *nf* delicacy; (*refinamiento, sutileza*) refinement

delicado, -a [deli'kaðo, a] *adj* delicate; (*sensible*) sensitive; (*rasgos*) dainty; (*gusto*) refined; (*situación: difícil*) tricky; (: *violento*) embarrassing; (*punto, tema*) sore; (*persona: difícil de contentar*) hard to please; (: *sensible*) touchy, hypersensitive; (: *atento*) considerate

delicia [de'liθja] *nf* delight

delicioso, -a [deli'θjoso, a] *adj* (*gracioso*) delightful; (*exquisito*) delicious

delictivo, -a [delik'tiβo, a] *adj* criminal *cpd*

delimitar [delimi'tar] *vt* to delimit

delincuencia [delin'kwenθja] *nf*: ~ **juvenil** juvenile delinquency; **cifras de la** ~ crime rate

delincuente [delin'kwente] *nm/f* delinquent; (*criminal*) criminal; ~ **sin antecedentes** first offender; ~ **habitual** hardened criminal

delineante [deline'ante] *nm/f* draughtsman

delinear [deline'ar] *vt* to delineate; (*dibujo*) to draw; (*contornos, fig*) to outline; ~ **un proyecto** to outline a project

delinquir [delin'kir] *vi* to commit an offence

delirante [deli'rante] *adj* delirious

delirar [deli'rar] *vi* to be delirious, rave; (*fig: desatinar*) to talk nonsense

d

delirio [de'lirjo] *nm* (*Med*) delirium; (*palabras insensatas*) ravings *pl*; **~ de grandeza** megalomania; **~ de persecución** persecution mania; **con ~** (*fam*) madly; **¡fue el ~!** (*fam*) it was great!

delito [de'lito] *nm* (*gen*) crime; (*infracción*) offence

delta ['delta] *nm* delta

demacrado, -a [dema'kraðo, a] *adj* emaciated

demagogia [dema'ɣoxja] *nf* demagogy, demagoguery

demagogo [dema'ɣoɣo] *nm* demagogue

demanda [de'manda] *nf* (*pedido, Com*) demand; (*petición*) request; (*pregunta*) inquiry; (*reivindicación*) claim; (*Jur*) action, lawsuit; (*Teat*) call; (*Elec*) load; **~ de pago** demand for payment; **escribir en ~ de ayuda** to write asking for help; **entablar ~** (*Jur*) to sue; **presentar ~ de divorcio** to sue for divorce; **~ final** final demand; **~ indirecta** derived demand; **~ de mercado** market demand

demandado, -a [deman'daðo, a] *nm/f* defendant; (*en divorcio*) respondent

demandante [deman'dante] *nm/f* claimant; (*Jur*) plaintiff

demandar [deman'dar] *vt* (*gen*) to demand; (*Jur*) to sue, file a lawsuit against, start proceedings against; **~ a algn por calumnia/daños y perjuicios** to sue sb for libel/damages

demarcación [demarka'θjon] *nf* (*de terreno*) demarcation

demás [de'mas] *adj*: **los ~ niños** the other children, the remaining children ■ *pron*: **los/las ~** the others, the rest (of them); **lo ~** the rest (of it); **por ~** moreover; (*en vano*) in vain; **y ~** etcetera

demasía [dema'sia] *nf* (*exceso*) excess, surplus; **comer en ~** to eat to excess

demasiado, -a [dema'sjaðo, a] *adj*: **~ vino** too much wine ■ *adv* (*antes de adj, adv*) too; **demasiados libros** too many books; **¡es ~!** it's too much!; **es ~ pesado para levantar** it is too heavy to lift; **~ lo sé** I know it only too well; **hace ~ calor** it's too hot

demencia [de'menθja] *nf* (*locura*) madness

demencial [demen'θjal] *adj* crazy

demente [de'mente] *adj* mad, insane ■ *nm/f* lunatic

democracia [demo'kraθja] *nf* democracy

demócrata [de'mokrata] *nm/f* democrat

democratacristiano, -a [demokratakris'tjano, a], **democristiano, -a** [demokris'tjano, a] *adj, nm/f* Christian Democrat

democrático, -a [demo'kratiko, a] *adj* democratic

demográfico, -a [demo'ɣrafiko, a] *adj* demographic, population *cpd*; **la explosión demográfica** the population explosion

demoledor, a [demole'ðor, a] *adj* (*fig: argumento*) overwhelming; (: *ataque*) shattering

demoler [demo'ler] *vt* to demolish; (*edificio*) to pull down

demolición [demoli'θjon] *nf* demolition

demonio [de'monjo] *nm* devil, demon; **¡demonios!** hell!; **¿cómo demonios?** how the hell?; **¿qué demonios será?** what the devil can it be?; **¿dónde ~ lo habré dejado?** where the devil can I have left it?; **tener el ~ en el cuerpo** (*no parar*) to be always on the go

demora [de'mora] *nf* delay

demorar [demo'rar] *vt* (*retardar*) to delay, hold back; (*dilatar*) to hold up ■ *vi* to linger, stay on; **demorarse** *vr* to linger, stay on; (*retrasarse*) to take a long time; **demorarse en hacer algo** (*esp Am*) to take time doing sth

demos ['demos] *vb ver* **dar**

demostración [demostra'θjon] *nf* (*gen, Mat*) demonstration; (*de cariño, fuerza*) show; (*de teorema*) proof; (*de amistad*) gesture; (*de cólera, gimnasia*) display; **~ comercial** commercial exhibition

demostrar [demos'trar] *vt* (*probar*) to prove; (*mostrar*) to show; (*manifestar*) to demonstrate

demostrativo, -a [demostra'tiβo, a] *adj* demonstrative

demudado, -a [demu'ðaðo, a] *adj* (*rostro*) pale; (*fig*) upset; **tener el rostro ~** to look pale

demudar [demu'ðar] *vt* to change, alter; **demudarse** *vr* (*expresión*) to alter; (*perder color*) to change colour

demuela *etc* [de'mwela] *vb ver* **demoler**

demuestre *etc* [de'mwestre] *vb ver* **demostrar**

den [den] *vb ver* **dar**

denegación [deneɣa'θjon] *nf* refusal

denegar [dene'ɣar] *vt* (*rechazar*) to refuse; (*negar*) to deny; (*Jur*) to reject

denegué [dene'ɣe], **deneguemos** *etc* [dene'ɣemos], **deniego** *etc* [de'njeɣo], **deniegue** *etc* [de'njeɣe] *vb ver* **denegar**

dengue ['denɣe] *nm* dengue *o* breakbone fever

denigrante [deni'ɣrante] *adj* (*injurioso*) insulting; (*deshonroso*) degrading

denigrar [deni'ɣrar] *vt* (*desacreditar*) to denigrate; (*injuriar*) to insult

denodado, -a [deno'ðaðo, a] *adj* bold, brave

denominación [denomina'θjon] *nf* (*acto*) naming; (*clase*) denomination; *see note*

DENOMINACIÓN

The *denominación de origen*, often abbreviated to D.O., is a prestigious product classification given to designated regions by the awarding body, the *Consejo Regulador de la Denominación de Origen*, when their produce meets the required quality and production standards. It is often associated with *manchego* cheeses and many of the wines from the Rioja and Ribera de Duero regions.

denominador [denomina'ðor] *nm*: **~ común** common denominator

denostar [denos'tar] *vt* to insult

denotar [deno'tar] *vt* (*indicar*) to indicate, denote

densidad [densi'ðað] *nf* (*Física*) density; (*fig*) thickness

denso, -a ['denso, a] *adj* (*apretado*) solid; (*espeso, pastoso*) thick; (*fig*) heavy

dentado, -a [den'taðo, a] *adj* (*rueda*) cogged; (*filo*) jagged; (*sello*) perforated; (*Bot*) dentate

dentadura [denta'ðura] *nf* (set of) teeth *pl*; **~ postiza** false teeth *pl*

dental [den'tal] *adj* dental

dentellada [dente'ʎaða] *nf* (*mordisco*) bite, nip; (*señal*) tooth mark; **partir algo a dentelladas** to sever sth with one's teeth

dentera [den'tera] *nf* (*sensación desgradable*) the shivers *pl*

dentición [denti'θjon] *nf* (*acto*) teething; (*Anat*) dentition; **estar con la ~** to be teething

dentífrico, -a [den'tifriko, a] *adj* dental, tooth *cpd* ■ *nm* toothpaste; **pasta dentífrica** toothpaste

dentista [den'tista] *nm/f* dentist

dentro ['dentro] *adv* inside ■ *prep*: **~ de** in, inside, within; **allí ~** in there; **mirar por ~** to look inside; **~ de lo posible** as far as possible; **~ de todo** all in all; **~ de tres meses** within three months

denuedo [de'nweðo] *nm* boldness, daring

denuesto [de'nwesto] *nm* insult

denuncia [de'nunθja] *nf* (*delación*) denunciation; (*acusación*) accusation; (*de accidente*) report; **hacer *o* poner una ~** to report an incident to the police

denunciable [denun'θjaβle] *adj* indictable, punishable

denunciante [denun'θjante] *nm/f* accuser; (*delator*) informer

denunciar [denun'θjar] *vt* to report; (*delatar*) to inform on *o* against

Dep. *abr* (= *Departamento*) Dept.; (= *Depósito*) dep.

deparar [depa'rar] *vt* (*brindar*) to provide *o* furnish with; (*futuro, destino*) to have in store for; **los placeres que el viaje nos deparó** the pleasures which the trip afforded us

departamento [departa'mento] *nm* (*sección*) department, section; (*Am: piso*) flat (*Brit*), apartment (*US*); (*distrito*) department, province; **~ de envíos** (*Com*) dispatch department; **~ de máquinas** (*Naut*) engine room

departir [depar'tir] *vi* to talk, converse

dependencia [depen'denθja] *nf* dependence; (*Pol*) dependency; (*Com*) office, section; (*sucursal*) branch office; (*Arq: cuarto*) room; **dependencias** *nfpl* outbuildings

depender [depen'der] *vi*: **~ de** to depend on; (*contar con*) to rely on; (*autoridad*) to be under, be answerable to; **depende** it (all) depends; **no depende de mí** it's not up to me

dependienta [depen'djenta] *nf* saleswoman, shop assistant

dependiente [depen'djente] *adj* dependent ■ *nm* salesman, shop assistant

depilación [depila'θjon] *nf* hair removal

depilar [depi'lar] *vt* (*con cera: piernas*) to wax; (*cejas*) to pluck

depilatorio, -a [depila'torjo, a] *adj* depilatory ■ *nm* hair remover

deplorable [deplo'raβle] *adj* deplorable

deplorar [deplo'rar] *vt* to deplore

depondré *etc* [depon'dre] *vb ver* **deponer**

deponer [depo'ner] *vt* (*armas*) to lay down; (*rey*) to depose; (*gobernante*) to oust; (*ministro*) to remove from office ■ *vi* (*Jur*) to give evidence; (*declarar*) to make a statement

deponga *etc* [de'ponga] *vb ver* **deponer**

deportación [deporta'θjon] *nf* deportation

deportar [depor'tar] *vt* to deport

deporte [de'porte] *nm* sport

deportista [depor'tista] *adj* sports *cpd* ■ *nm/f* sportsman(-woman)

deportivo, -a [depor'tiβo, a] *adj* (*club, periódico*) sports *cpd* ■ *nm* sports car

deposición [deposi'θjon] *nf* (*de funcionario etc*) removal from office; (*Jur: testimonio*) evidence

depositante [deposi'tante] *nm/f* depositor

depositar [deposi'tar] *vt* (*dinero*) to deposit; (*mercaderías*) to put away, store; **depositarse** *vr* to settle; **~ la confianza en algn** to place one's trust in sb

depositario, -a [deposi'tarjo, a] *nm/f* trustee; **~ judicial** official receiver

depósito [de'posito] *nm* (*gen*) deposit; (*de mercaderías*) warehouse, store; (*de animales, coches*) pound; (*de agua, gasolina etc*) tank; (*en retrete*) cistern; **~ afianzado** bonded warehouse; **~ bancario** bank deposit; **~ de**

cadáveres mortuary; ~ **de maderas** timber yard; ~ **de suministro** feeder bin

depravar [depra'βar] vt to deprave, corrupt; **depravarse** vr to become depraved

depreciación [depreθja'θjon] nf depreciation

depreciar [depre'θjar] vt to depreciate, reduce the value of; **depreciarse** vr to depreciate, lose value

depredador, a [depreða'ðor, a] (Zool) adj predatory ■ nm predator

depredar [depre'ðar] vt to pillage

depresión [depre'sjon] nf (gen, Med) depression; (hueco) hollow; (en horizonte, camino) dip; (merma) drop; (Econ) slump, recession; ~ **nerviosa** nervous breakdown

deprimente [depri'mente] adj depressing

deprimido, -a [depri'miðo, a] adj depressed

deprimir [depri'mir] vt to depress; **deprimirse** vr (persona) to become depressed

deprisa [de'prisa] adv ver **prisa**

depuesto [de'pwesto] pp de **deponer**

depuración [depura'θjon] nf purification; (Pol) purge

depurador [depura'ðor] nm purifier

depuradora [depura'ðora] nf (de agua) water-treatment plant; (tb: **depuradora de aguas residuales**) sewage farm

depurar [depu'rar] vt to purify; (purgar) to purge

depuse etc [de'puse] vb ver **deponer**

der., der.° abr (= derecho) r

der.ª abr (= derecha) r

derecha [de'retʃa] nf ver **derecho, a**

derechazo [dere'tʃaθo] nm (Boxeo) right; (Tenis) forehand drive; (Taur) a pass with the cape

derechista [dere'tʃista] (Pol) adj right-wing ■ nm/f right-winger

derecho, -a [de'retʃo, a] adj right, right-hand ■ nm (privilegio) right; (título) claim, title; (lado) right(-hand) side; (leyes) law ■ nf right(-hand) side ■ adv straight, directly; **derechos** nmpl dues; (profesionales) fees; (impuestos) taxes; (de autor) royalties; **la(s) derecha(s)** (Pol) the Right; **derechos civiles** civil rights; **derechos de patente** patent rights; **derechos portuarios** (Com) harbour dues; ~ **de propiedad literaria** copyright; ~ **de timbre** (Com) stamp duty; ~ **de votar** right to vote; ~ **a voto** voting right; **Facultad de D~** Faculty of Law; **a derechas** rightly, correctly; **de derechas** (Pol) right-wing; **"reservados todos los derechos"** "all rights reserved"; **¡no hay ~!** it's not fair!; **tener ~ a** to have a right to; **a la derecha** on the right; (dirección) to the right; **siga todo ~** carry o (Brit) go straight on

deriva [de'riβa] nf: **ir** o **estar a la ~** to drift, be adrift

derivación [deriβa'θjon] nf derivation

derivado, -a [deri'βaðo, a] adj derived ■ nm (Ling) derivative; (Industria, Química) by-product

derivar [deri'βar] vt to derive; (desviar) to direct ■ vi, **derivarse** vr to derive, be derived; ~**(se) de** (consecuencia) to spring from

dermatólogo, -a [derma'toloɣo, a] nm/f dermatologist

dérmico, -a ['dermiko, a] adj skin cpd

dermoprotector, a [dermoprotek'tor, a] adj protective

derogación [deroɣa'θjon] nf repeal

derogar [dero'ɣar] vt (ley) to repeal; (contrato) to revoke

derogue etc [de'roɣe] vb ver **derogar**

derramamiento [derrama'mjento] nm (dispersión) spilling; (fig) squandering; ~ **de sangre** bloodshed

derramar [derra'mar] vt to spill; (verter) to pour out; (esparcir) to scatter; **derramarse** vr to pour out; ~ **lágrimas** to weep

derrame [de'rrame] nm (de líquido) spilling; (de sangre) shedding; (de tubo etc) overflow; (pédida) leakage; (Med) discharge; (declive) slope; ~ **cerebral** brain haemorrhage; ~ **sinovial** water on the knee

derrapar [derra'par] vi to skid

derredor [derre'ðor] adv: **al** o **en ~ de** around, about

derrengado, -a [derren'gaðo, a] adj (torcido) bent; (cojo) crippled; **estar ~** (fig) to ache all over; **dejar ~ a algn** (fig) to wear sb out

derretido, -a [derre'tiðo, a] adj melted; (metal) molten; **estar ~ por algn** (fig) to be crazy about sb

derretir [derre'tir] vt (gen) to melt; (nieve) to thaw; (fig) to squander; **derretirse** vr to melt

derribar [derri'βar] vt to knock down; (construcción) to demolish; (persona, gobierno, político) to bring down

derribo [de'rriβo] nm (de edificio) demolition; (Lucha) throw; (Aviat) shooting down; (Pol) overthrow; **derribos** nmpl rubble sg, debris sg

derrita etc [de'rrita] vb ver **derretir**

derrocar [derro'kar] vt (gobierno) to bring down, overthrow; (ministro) to oust

derrochador, a [derrotʃa'ðor, a] adj, nm/f spendthrift

derrochar [derro'tʃar] vt (dinero, recursos) to squander; (energía, salud) to be bursting with o full of

derroche [de'rrotʃe] nm (despilfarro) waste, squandering; (exceso) extravagance; **con un**

~ de buen gusto with a fine display of good taste

derroque *etc* [de'rroke] *vb ver* **derrocar**

derrota [de'rrota] *nf* (*Naut*) course; (*Mil*) defeat, rout; **sufrir una grave ~** (*fig*) to suffer a grave setback

derrotar [derro'tar] *vt* (*gen*) to defeat

derrotero [derro'tero] *nm* (*rumbo*) course; **tomar otro ~** (*fig*) to adopt a different course

derrotista [derro'tista] *adj, nm/f* defeatist

derruir [derru'ir] *vt* to demolish, tear down

derrumbamiento [derrumba'mjento] *nm* (*caída*) plunge; (*demolición*) demolition; (*desplome*) collapse; **~ de tierra** landslide

derrumbar [derrum'bar] *vt* to throw down; (*despeñar*) to fling o hurl down; (*volcar*) to upset; **derrumbarse** *vr* (*hundirse*) to collapse; (: *techo*) to fall in, cave in; (*fig: esperanzas*) to collapse

derrumbe [de'rrumbe] *nm* = **derrumbamiento**

derruyendo *etc* [derru'jendo] *vb ver* **derruir**

des [des] *vb ver* **dar**

desabastecido, -a [desaβaste'θiðo, a] *adj*: **estar ~ de algo** to be short of o out of sth

desabotonar [desaβoto'nar] *vt* to unbutton, undo ■ *vi* (*flores*) to blossom; **desabotonarse** *vr* to come undone

desabrido, -a [desa'βriðo, a] *adj* (*comida*) insipid, tasteless; (*persona: soso*) dull; (: *antipático*) rude, surly; (*respuesta*) sharp; (*tiempo*) unpleasant

desabrigado, -a [desaβri'ɣaðo, a] *adj* (*sin abrigo*) not sufficiently protected; (*fig*) exposed

desabrigar [desaβri'ɣar] *vt* (*quitar ropa a*) to remove the clothing of; (*descubrir*) to uncover; (*fig*) to deprive of protection; **desabrigarse** *vr*: **me desabrigué en la cama** the bedclothes came off

desabrigue *etc* [desa'βriɣe] *vb ver* **desabrigar**

desabrochar [desaβro'tʃar] *vt* (*botones, broches*) to undo, unfasten; **desabrocharse** *vr* (*ropa etc*) to come undone

desacatar [desaka'tar] *vt* (*ley*) to disobey

desacato [desa'kato] *nm* (*falta de respeto*) disrespect; (*Jur*) contempt

desacertado, -a [desaθer'taðo, a] *adj* (*equivocado*) mistaken; (*inoportuno*) unwise

desacierto [desa'θjerto] *nm* (*error*) mistake, error; (*dicho*) unfortunate remark

desaconsejable [desakonse'xaβle] *adj* inadvisable

desaconsejado, -a [desakonse'xaðo, a] *adj* ill-advised

desaconsejar [desakonse'xar] *vt*: **~ algo a algn** to advise sb against sth

desacoplar [desako'plar] *vt* (*Elec*) to disconnect; (*Tec*) to take apart

desacorde [desa'korðe] *adj* (*Mus*) discordant; (*fig: opiniones*) conflicting; **estar ~ con algo** to disagree with sth

desacreditar [desakreði'tar] *vt* (*desprestigiar*) to discredit, bring into disrepute; (*denigrar*) to run down

desactivar [desakti'βar] *vt* to deactivate; (*bomba*) to defuse

desacuerdo [desa'kwerðo] *nm* (*conflicto*) disagreement, discord; (*error*) error, blunder; **en ~** out of keeping

desafiante [desa'fjante] *adj* (*insolente*) defiant; (*retador*) challenging ■ *nm/f* challenger

desafiar [desa'fjar] *vt* (*retar*) to challenge; (*enfrentarse a*) to defy

desafilado, -a [desafi'laðo, a] *adj* blunt

desafinado, -a [desafi'naðo, a] *adj*: **estar ~** to be out of tune

desafinar [desafi'nar] *vi* to be out of tune; **desafinarse** *vr* to go out of tune

desafío [desa'fio] *nm* (*reto*) challenge; (*combate*) duel; (*resistencia*) defiance

desaforadamente [desafuraða'mente] *adv*: **gritar ~** to shout one's head off

desaforado, -a [desafo'raðo, a] *adj* (*grito*) ear-splitting; (*comportamiento*) outrageous

desafortunadamente [desafortunaða'mente] *adv* unfortunately

desafortunado, -a [desafortu'naðo, a] *adj* (*desgraciado*) unfortunate, unlucky

desagradable [desaɣra'ðaβle] *adj* (*fastidioso, enojoso*) unpleasant; (*irritante*) disagreeable; **ser ~ con algn** to be rude to sb

desagradar [desaɣra'ðar] *vi* (*disgustar*) to displease; (*molestar*) to bother

desagradecido, -a [desaɣraðe'θiðo, a] *adj* ungrateful

desagrado [desa'ɣraðo] *nm* (*disgusto*) displeasure; (*contrariedad*) dissatisfaction; **con ~** unwillingly

desagraviar [desaɣra'βjar] *vt* to make amends to

desagravio [desa'ɣraβjo] *nm* (*satisfacción*) amends; (*compensación*) compensation

desaguadero [desaɣwa'ðero] *nm* drain

desagüe [de'saɣwe] *nm* (*de un líquido*) drainage; (*cañería: tb*: **tubo de desagüe**) drainpipe; (*salida*) outlet, drain

desaguisado, -a [desaɣi'saðo, a] *adj* illegal ■ *nm* outrage

desahogado, -a [desao'ɣaðo, a] *adj* (*holgado*) comfortable; (*espacioso*) roomy

desahogar [desao'ɣar] *vt* (*aliviar*) to ease, relieve; (*ira*) to vent; **desahogarse** *vr* (*distenderse*) to relax; (*desfogarse*) to let off steam (*fam*); (*confesarse*) to confess, get sth off one's chest (*fam*)

d

desahogo [desa'oɣo] *nm* (*alivio*) relief; (*comodidad*) comfort, ease; **vivir con ~** to be comfortably off

desahogue *etc* [desa'oɣe] *vb ver* **desahogar**

desahuciado, -a [desau'θjaðo, a] *adj* hopeless

desahuciar [desau'θjar] *vt* (*enfermo*) to give up hope for; (*inquilino*) to evict

desahucio [de'sauθjo] *nm* eviction

desairado, -a [desai'raðo, a] *adj* (*menospreciado*) disregarded; (*desgarbado*) shabby; (*sin éxito*) unsuccessful; **quedar ~** to come off badly

desairar [desai'rar] *vt* (*menospreciar*) to slight, snub; (*cosa*) to disregard; (*Com*) to default on

desaire [des'aire] *nm* (*menosprecio*) slight; (*falta de garbo*) unattractiveness; **dar** *o* **hacer un ~ a algn** to offend sb; **¿me va usted a hacer ese ~?** I won't take no for an answer!

desajustar [desaxus'tar] *vt* (*desarreglar*) to disarrange; (*desconcertar*) to throw off balance; (*fig: planes*) to upset; **desajustarse** *vr* to get out of order; (*aflojarse*) to loosen

desajuste [desa'xuste] *nm* (*de máquina*) disorder; (*avería*) breakdown; (*situación*) imbalance; (*desacuerdo*) disagreement

desalentador, -a [desalenta'ðor, a] *adj* discouraging

desalentar [desalen'tar] *vt* (*desanimar*) to discourage; **desalentarse** *vr* to get discouraged

desaliento *etc* [desa'ljento] *vb ver* **desalentar** ■ *nm* discouragement; (*abatimiento*) depression

desaliñado, -a [desali'ɲaðo, a] *adj* (*descuidado*) slovenly; (*raído*) shabby; (*desordenado*) untidy; (*negligente*) careless

desaliño [desa'liɲo] *nm* (*descuido*) slovenliness; (*negligencia*) carelessness

desalmado, -a [desal'maðo, a] *adj* (*cruel*) cruel, heartless

desalojar [desalo'xar] *vt* (*gen*) to remove, expel; (*expulsar, echar*) to eject; (*abandonar*) to move out of ■ *vi* to move out; **la policía desalojó el local** the police cleared people out of the place

desalquilar [desalki'lar] *vt* to vacate, move out; **desalquilarse** *vr* to become vacant

desamarrar [desama'rrar] *vt* to untie; (*Naut*) to cast off

desamor [desa'mor] *nm* (*frialdad*) indifference; (*odio*) dislike

desamparado, -a [desampa'raðo, a] *adj* (*persona*) helpless; (*lugar: expuesto*) exposed; (*: desierto*) deserted

desamparar [desampa'rar] *vt* (*abandonar*) to desert, abandon; (*Jur*) to leave defenceless; (*barco*) to abandon

desamparo [desam'paro] *nm* (*acto*) desertion; (*estado*) helplessness

desamueblado, -a [desamwe'βlaðo, a] *adj* unfurnished

desandar [desan'dar] *vt*: **~ lo andado** *o* **el camino** to retrace one's steps

desanduve *etc* [desan'duβe], **desanduviera** *etc* [desandu'βjera] *vb ver* **desandar**

desangelado, -a [desanxe'laðo, a] *adj* (*habitación, edificio*) lifeless

desangrar [desan'grar] *vt* to bleed; (*fig: persona*) to bleed dry; (*lago*) to drain; **desangrarse** *vr* to lose a lot of blood; (*morir*) to bleed to death

desanimado, -a [desani'maðo, a] *adj* (*persona*) downhearted; (*espectáculo, fiesta*) dull

desanimar [desani'mar] *vt* (*desalentar*) to discourage; (*deprimir*) to depress; **desanimarse** *vr* to lose heart

desánimo [de'sanimo] *nm* despondency; (*abatimiento*) dejection; (*falta de animación*) dullness

desanudar [desanu'ðar] *vt* to untie; (*fig*) to clear up

desapacible [desapa'θiβle] *adj* unpleasant

desaparecer [desapare'θer] *vi* to disappear; (*el sol, la luz*) to vanish; (*desaparecer de vista*) to drop out of sight; (*efectos, señales*) to wear off ■ *vt* (*esp Am Pol*) to cause to disappear; (*: eufemismo*) to murder

desaparecido, -a [desapare'θiðo, a] *adj* missing; (*especie*) extinct ■ *nm/f* (*Am Pol*) kidnapped *o* missing person

desaparezca *etc* [desapa'reθka] *vb ver* **desaparecer**

desaparición [desapari'θjon] *nf* disappearance; (*de especie etc*) extinction

desapasionado, -a [desapasjo'naðo, a] *adj* dispassionate, impartial

desapego [desa'peɣo] *nm* (*frialdad*) coolness; (*distancia*) detachment

desapercibido, -a [desaperθi'βiðo, a] *adj* unnoticed; (*desprevenido*) unprepared; **pasar ~** to go unnoticed

desaplicado, -a [desapli'kaðo, a] *adj* slack, lazy

desaprensivo, -a [desapren'siβo, a] *adj* unscrupulous

desaprobar [desapro'βar] *vt* (*reprobar*) to disapprove of; (*condenar*) to condemn; (*no consentir*) to reject

desaprovechado, -a [desaproβe'tʃaðo, a] *adj* (*oportunidad, tiempo*) wasted; (*estudiante*) slack

desaprovechar [desaproβe'tʃar] *vt* to waste; (*talento*) not to use to the full ■ *vi* (*perder terreno*) to lose ground

desapruebe *etc* [desa'prweβe] *vb ver*
  desaprobar
desarmar [desar'mar] *vt* (*Mil, fig*) to disarm;
  (*Tec*) to take apart, dismantle
desarme [de'sarme] *nm* disarmament
desarraigado, -a [desarrai'ɣaðo, a] *adj*
  (*persona*) without roots, rootless
desarraigar [desarrai'ɣar] *vt* to uproot; (*fig:*
  costumbre) to root out; (: *persona*) to banish
desarraigo [desa'rraiɣo] *nm* uprooting
desarraigue *etc* [desa'rraiɣe] *vb ver*
  desarraigar
desarrapado, -a [desarra'paðo, a] *adj*
  ragged; **(de aspecto)** ~ shabby
desarreglado, -a [desarre'ɣlaðo, a] *adj*
  (*desordenado*) disorderly, untidy; (*hábitos*)
  irregular
desarreglar [desarre'ɣlar] *vt* to mess up;
  (*desordenar*) to disarrange; (*trastocar*) to upset,
  disturb
desarreglo [desa'rreɣlo] *nm* (*de casa, persona*)
  untidiness; (*desorden*) disorder; (*Tec*) trouble;
  (*Med*) upset; **viven en el mayor** ~ they live in
  complete chaos
desarrollado, -a [desarro'ʎaðo, a] *adj*
  developed
desarrollar [desarro'ʎar] *vt* (*gen*) to develop;
  (*extender*) to unfold; (*teoría*) to explain;
  desarrollarse *vr* to develop; (*extenderse*) to
  open (out); (*film*) to develop; (*fig*) to grow;
  (*tener lugar*) to take place; **aquí desarrollan
  un trabajo muy importante** they carry on
  o out very important work here; **la acción se
  desarrolla en Roma** (*Cine etc*) the scene is
  set in Rome
desarrollo [desa'rroʎo] *nm* development;
  (*de acontecimientos*) unfolding; (*de industria,
  mercado*) expansion, growth; **país en vías de**
  ~ developing country; **la industria está en
  pleno** ~ industry is expanding steadily; ~
  sostenible sustainable development
desarrugar [desarru'ɣar] *vt* (*alisar*) to smooth
  (out); (*ropa*) to remove the creases from
desarrugue *etc* [desa'rruɣe] *vb ver* **desarrugar**
desarticulado, -a [desartiku'laðo, a] *adj*
  disjointed
desarticular [desartiku'lar] *vt* (*huesos*) to
  dislocate, put out of joint; (*objeto*) to take
  apart; (*grupo terrorista etc*) to break up
desaseado, -a [desase'aðo, a] *adj* (*sucio*) dirty;
  (*desaliñado*) untidy
desaseo [desa'seo] *nm* (*suciedad*) dirtiness;
  (*desarreglo*) untidiness
desasga *etc* [de'sasɣa] *vb ver* **desasir**
desasir [desa'sir] *vt* to loosen; **desasirse** *vr*
  to extricate o.s.; **desasirse de** to let go, give up
desasosegar [desasose'ɣar] *vt* (*inquietar*) to

disturb, make uneasy; **desasosegarse** *vr*
  to become uneasy
desasosegué [desasose'ɣe], **desasoseguemos**
  etc [desasose'ɣemos] *vb ver* **desasosegar**
desasosiego *etc* [desaso'sjeɣo] *vb ver*
  desasosegar ■ *nm* (*intranquilidad*)
  uneasiness, restlessness; (*ansiedad*) anxiety;
  (*Pol etc*) unrest
desasosiegue *etc* [desaso'sjeɣe] *vb ver*
  desasosegar
desastrado, -a [desas'traðo, a] *adj*
  (*desaliñado*) shabby; (*sucio*) dirty
desastre [de'sastre] *nm* disaster; **¡un ~!** how
  awful!; **la función fue un** ~ the show was a
  shambles
desastroso, -a [desas'troso, a] *adj* disastrous
desatado, -a [desa'taðo, a] *adj* (*desligado*)
  untied; (*violento*) violent, wild
desatar [desa'tar] *vt* (*nudo*) to untie; (*paquete*)
  to undo; (*perro, odio*) to unleash; (*misterio*)
  to solve; (*separar*) to detach; **desatarse** *vr*
  (*zapatos*) to come untied; (*tormenta*) to break;
  (*perder control de sí mismo*) to lose self-control;
  desatarse en injurias to pour out a stream
  of insults
desatascar [desatas'kar] *vt* (*cañería*) to
  unblock, clear
desatasque *etc* [desa'taske] *vb ver* **desatascar**
desatención [desaten'θjon] *nf* (*descuido*)
  inattention; (*distracción*) absent-mindedness
desatender [desaten'der] *vt* (*no prestar atención
  a*) to disregard; (*abandonar*) to neglect
desatento, -a [desa'tento, a] *adj* (*distraído*)
  inattentive; (*descortés*) discourteous
desatienda *etc* [desa'tjenda] *vb ver*
  desatender
desatinado, -a [desati'naðo, a] *adj* foolish,
  silly
desatino [desa'tino] *nm* (*idiotez*) foolishness,
  folly; (*error*) blunder; **desatinos** *nmpl*
  nonsense *sg*; **¡qué ~!** how silly!, what
  rubbish!
desatornillar [desatorni'ʎar] *vt* to unscrew
desatrancar [desatran'kar] *vt* (*puerta*) to
  unbolt; (*cañería*) to unblock
desatranque *etc* [desa'tranke] *vb ver*
  desatrancar
desautorice *etc* [desauto'riθe] *vb ver*
  desautorizar
desautorizado, -a [desautori'θaðo, a] *adj*
  unauthorized
desautorizar [desautori'θar] *vt* (*oficial*) to
  deprive of authority; (*informe*) to deny
desavendré *etc* [desaβen'dre] *vb ver*
  desavenir
desavenencia [desaβe'nenθja] *nf* (*desacuerdo*)
  disagreement; (*discrepancia*) quarrel

desavenga etc [desa'βenga] vb ver **desavenir**

desavenido, -a [desaβe'niðo, a] adj (opuesto) contrary; (reñido) in disagreement; **ellos están desavenidos** they are at odds

desavenir [desaβe'nir] vt (enemistar) to make trouble between; **desavenirse** vr to fall out

desaventajado, -a [desaβenta'xaðo, a] adj (inferior) inferior; (poco ventajoso) disadvantageous

desaviene etc [desa'βjene], **desaviniendo** etc [desaβi'njendo] vb ver **desavenir**

desayunar [desaju'nar] vi, **desayunarse** vr to have breakfast ∎ vt to have for breakfast; **~ con café** to have coffee for breakfast; **~ con algo** (fig) to get the first news of sth

desayuno [desa'juno] nm breakfast

desazón [desa'θon] nf (angustia) anxiety; (Med) discomfort; (fig) annoyance

desazonar [desaθo'nar] vt (fig) to annoy, upset; **desazonarse** vr (enojarse) to be annoyed; (preocuparse) to worry, be anxious

desbancar [desβan'kar] vt (quitar el puesto a) to oust; (suplantar) to supplant (in sb's affections)

desbandada [desβan'daða] nf rush; **~ general** mass exodus; **a la ~** in disorder

desbandarse [desβan'darse] vr (Mil) to disband; (fig) to flee in disorder

desbanque etc [des'βanke] vb ver **desbancar**

desbarajuste [desβara'xuste] nm confusion, disorder; **¡qué ~!** what a mess!

desbaratar [desβara'tar] vt (gen) to mess up; (plan) to spoil; (deshacer, destruir) to ruin ∎ vi to talk nonsense; **desbaratarse** vr (máquina) to break down; (persona: irritarse) to fly off the handle (fam)

desbarrar [desβa'rrar] vi to talk nonsense

desbloquear [desβloke'ar] vt (negociaciones, tráfico) to get going again; (Com: cuenta) to unfreeze

desbocado, -a [desβo'kaðo, a] adj (caballo) runaway; (herramienta) worn

desbocar [desβo'kar] vt (vasija) to break the rim of; **desbocarse** vr (caballo) to bolt; (persona: soltar injurias) to let out a stream of insults

desboque etc [des'βoke] vb ver **desbocar**

desbordamiento [desβorða'mjento] nm (de río) overflowing; (Inform) overflow; (de cólera) outburst; (de entusiasmo) upsurge

desbordar [desβor'ðar] vt (sobrepasar) to go beyond; (exceder) to exceed ∎ vi, **desbordarse** vr (líquido, río) to overflow; (entusiasmo) to erupt; (persona: exaltarse) to get carried away

desbravar [desβra'βar] vt (caballo) to break in; (animal) to tame

descabalgar [deskaβal'ɣar] vi to dismount

descabalgue etc [deska'βalɣe] vb ver **descabalgar**

descabellado, -a [deskaβe'ʎaðo, a] adj (disparatado) wild, crazy; (insensato) preposterous

descabellar [deskaβe'ʎar] vt to ruffle; (Taur: toro) to give the coup de grace to

descabezado, -a [deskaβe'θaðo, a] adj (sin cabeza) headless; (insensato) wild

descafeinado, -a [deskafei'naðo, a] adj decaffeinated ∎ nm decaffeinated coffee, de-caff

descalabrar [deskala'βrar] vt to smash; (persona) to hit; (: en la cabeza) to hit on the head; (Naut) to cripple; (dañar) to harm, damage; **descalabrarse** vr to hurt one's head

descalabro [deska'laβro] nm blow; (desgracia) misfortune

descalce etc [des'kalθe] vb ver **descalzar**

descalificación [deskalifika'θjon] nf disqualification; **descalificaciones** nfpl discrediting sg

descalificar [deskalifi'kar] vt to disqualify; (desacreditar) to discredit

descalifique etc [deskali'fike] vb ver **descalificar**

descalzar [deskal'θar] vt (persona) to take the shoes off

descalzo, -a [des'kalθo, a] adj barefoot(ed); (fig) destitute; **estar (con los pies) ~(s)** to be barefooted

descambiar [deskam'bjar] vt to exchange

descaminado, -a [deskami'naðo, a] adj (equivocado) on the wrong road; (fig) misguided; **en eso no anda usted muy ~** you're not far wrong there

descamisado, -a [deskami'saðo, a] adj bare-chested

descampado [deskam'paðo] nm open space, piece of empty ground; **comer al ~** to eat in the open air

descansado, -a [deskan'saðo, a] adj (gen) rested; (que tranquiliza) restful

descansar [deskan'sar] vt (gen) to rest; (apoyar): **~ (sobre)** to lean (on) ∎ vi to rest, have a rest; (echarse) to lie down; (cadáver, restos) to lie; **¡que usted descanse!** sleep well!; **~ en** (argumento) to be based on

descansillo [deskan'siʎo] nm (de escalera) landing

descanso [des'kanso] nm (reposo) rest; (alivio) relief; (pausa) break; (Deporte) interval, half time; **día de ~** day off; **~ de enfermedad/ maternidad** sick/maternity leave; **tomarse unos días de ~** to take a few days' leave o rest

descapitalizado, -a [deskapitali'θaðo, a] adj undercapitalized

descapotable [deskapo'taβle] *nm* (*tb*: **coche descapotable**) convertible

descarado, -a [deska'raðo, a] *adj* (*sin vergüenza*) shameless; (*insolente*) cheeky

descarga [des'karɣa] *nf* (*Arq, Elec, Mil*) discharge; (*Naut*) unloading; (*Inform*) download

descargable [deskar'ɣaβle] *adj* downloadable

descargador [deskarɣa'ðor] *nm* docker

descargar [deskar'ɣar] *vt* to unload; (*golpe*) to let fly; (*arma*) to fire; (*Elec*) to discharge; (*pila*) to run down; (*conciencia*) to relieve; (*Com*) to take up; (*persona: de una obligación*) to release; (: *de una deuda*) to free; (*Jur*) to clear ◼ *vi* (*río*): **~ (en)** to flow (into); **descargarse** *vr* to unburden o.s.; **descargarse de algo** to get rid of sth; **descargarse algo de Internet** to download sth from the Internet

descargo [des'karɣo] *nm* (*de obligación*) release; (*Com: recibo*) receipt; (: *de deuda*) discharge; (*Jur*) evidence; **~ de una acusación** acquittal on a charge

descargue *etc* [des'karɣe] *vb ver* **descargar**

descarnado, -a [deskar'naðo, a] *adj* scrawny; (*fig*) bare; (*estilo*) straightforward

descaro [des'karo] *nm* nerve

descarriar [deska'rrjar] *vt* (*descaminar*) to misdirect; (*fig*) to lead astray; **descarriarse** *vr* (*perderse*) to lose one's way; (*separarse*) to stray; (*pervertirse*) to err, go astray

descarrilamiento [deskarrila'mjento] *nm* (*de tren*) derailment

descarrilar [deskarri'lar] *vi* to be derailed

descartable [deskar'taβle] *adj* (*Inform*) temporary

descartar [deskar'tar] *vt* (*rechazar*) to reject; (*eliminar*) to rule out; **descartarse** *vr* (*Naipes*) to discard; **descartarse de** to shirk

descascarar [deskaska'rar] *vt* (*naranja, limón*) to peel; (*nueces, huevo duro*) to shell; **descascararse** *vr* to peel (off)

descascarillado, -a [deskaskari'ʎaðo, a] *adj* (*paredes*) peeling

descendencia [desθen'denθja] *nf* (*origen*) origin, descent; (*hijos*) offspring; **morir sin dejar ~** to die without issue

descendente [desθen'dente] *adj* (*cantidad*) diminishing; (*Inform*) top-down

descender [desθen'der] *vt* (*bajar: escalera*) to go down ◼ *vi* to descend; (*temperatura, nivel*) to fall, drop; (*líquido*) to run; (*cortina etc*) to hang; (*fuerzas, persona*) to fail, get weak; **~ de** to be descended from

descendiente [desθen'djente] *nm/f* descendant

descenso [des'θenso] *nm* descent; (*de temperatura*) drop; (*de producción*) downturn;

(*de calidad*) decline; (*Minería*) collapse; (*bajada*) slope; (*fig: decadencia*) decline; (*de empleado etc*) demotion

descentrado, -a [desθen'traðo, a] *adj* (*pieza de una máquina*) off-centre; (*rueda*) out of true; (*persona*) bewildered; (*desequilibrado*) unbalanced; (*problema*) out of focus; **todavía está algo ~** he is still somewhat out of touch

descentralice *etc* [desθentra'liθe] *vb ver* **descentralizar**

descentralizar [desθentrali'θar] *vt* to decentralize

descerrajar [desθerra'xar] *vt* (*puerta*) to break open

descienda *etc* [des'θjenda] *vb ver* **descender**

descifrable [desθi'fraβle] *adj* (*gen*) decipherable; (*letra*) legible

descifrar [desθi'frar] *vt* (*escritura*) to decipher; (*mensaje*) to decode; (*problema*) to puzzle out; (*misterio*) to solve

descocado, -a [desko'kaðo, a] *adj* (*descarado*) cheeky; (*desvergonzado*) brazen

descoco [des'koko] *nm* (*descaro*) cheek; (*atrevimiento*) brazenness

descodificador [deskoðifika'ðor] *nm* decoder

descodificar [deskoðifi'kar] *vt* to decode

descolgar [deskol'ɣar] *vt* (*bajar*) to take down; (*desde una posición alta*) to lower; (*de una pared etc*) to unhook; (*teléfono*) to pick up; **descolgarse** *vr* to let o.s. down; **descolgarse por** (*bajar escurriéndose*) to slip down; (*pared*) to climb down; **dejó el teléfono descolgado** he left the phone off the hook

descolgué [deskol'ɣe] *etc vb ver* **descolgar**

descollar [desko'ʎar] *vi* (*sobresalir*) to stand out; (*montaña etc*) to rise; **la obra que más descuella de las suyas** his most outstanding work

descolocado, -a [deskolo'kaðo, a] *adj*: **estar ~** (*cosa*) to be out of place; (*criada*) to be unemployed

descolorido, -a [deskolo'riðo, a] *adj* (*color, tela*) faded; (*pálido*) pale; (*fig: estilo*) colourless

descompaginar [deskompaxi'nar] *vt* (*desordenar*) to disarrange, mess up

descompasado, -a [deskompa'saðo, a] *adj* (*sin proporción*) out of all proportion; (*excesivo*) excessive; (*hora*) unearthly

descompensar [deskompen'sar] *vt* to unbalance

descompondré *etc* [deskompon'dre] *vb ver* **descomponer**

descomponer [deskompo'ner] *vt* (*gen, Ling, Mat*) to break down; (*desordenar*) to disarrange, disturb; (*materia orgánica*) to rot, decompose; (*Tec*) to put out of order; (*facciones*) to distort; (*estómago etc*) to upset;

(: *planes*) to mess up; (*persona*: *molestar*) to upset; (*irritar*) to annoy; **descomponerse** *vr* (*corromperse*) to rot, decompose; (*estómago*) to get upset; (*el tiempo*) to change (for the worse); (*Tec*) to break down

descomponga *etc* [deskom'ponga] *vb ver* **descomponer**

descomposición [deskomposi'θjon] *nf* (*gen*) breakdown; (*de fruta etc*) decomposition; (*putrefacción*) rotting; (*de cara*) distortion; ~ **de vientre** (*Med*) stomach upset, diarrhoea

descompostura [deskompos'tura] *nf* (*Tec*) breakdown; (*desorganización*) disorganization; (*desorden*) untidiness

descompuesto, -a [deskom'pwesto, a] *pp de* **descomponer** ■ *adj* (*corrompido*) decomposed; (*roto*) broken (down)

descompuse *etc* [deskom'puse] *vb ver* **descomponer**

descomunal [deskomu'nal] *adj* (*enorme*) huge; (*fam*: *excelente*) fantastic

desconcertado, -a [deskonθer'taðo, a] *adj* disconcerted, bewildered

desconcertar [deskonθer'tar] *vt* (*confundir*) to baffle; (*incomodar*) to upset, put out; (*orden*) to disturb; **desconcertarse** *vr* (*turbarse*) to be upset; (*confundirse*) to be bewildered

desconchado, -a [deskon'tʃaðo, a] *adj* (*pintura*) peeling

desconchar [deskon'tʃar] *vt* (*pared*) to strip off; (*loza*) to chip off

desconcierto *etc* [deskon'θjerto] *vb ver* **desconcertar** ■ *nm* (*gen*) disorder; (*desorientación*) uncertainty; (*inquietud*) uneasiness; (*confusión*) bewilderment

desconectado, -a [deskonek'taðo, a] *adj* (*Elec*) disconnected, switched off; (*Inform*) offline; **estar ~ de** (*fig*) to have no contact with

desconectar [deskonek'tar] *vt* to disconnect; (*desenchufar*) to unplug; (*radio, televisión*) to switch off; (*Inform*) to toggle off

desconfiado, -a [deskon'fjaðo, a] *adj* suspicious

desconfianza [deskon'fjanθa] *nf* distrust

desconfiar [deskon'fjar] *vi* to be distrustful; ~ **de** (*sospechar*) to mistrust, suspect; (*no tener confianza en*) to have no faith o confidence in; **desconfío de ello** I doubt it; **desconfíe de las imitaciones** (*Com*) beware of imitations

desconforme [deskon'forme] *adj* = **disconforme**

descongelar [deskonxe'lar] *vt* (*nevera*) to defrost; (*comida*) to thaw; (*Auto*) to de-ice; (*Com, Pol*) to unfreeze

descongestionar [desconxestjo'nar] *vt* (*cabeza, tráfico*) to clear; (*calle, ciudad*) to relieve congestion in; (*fig: despejar*) to clear

desconocer [deskono'θer] *vt* (*ignorar*) not to know, be ignorant of; (*no aceptar*) to deny; (*repudiar*) to disown

desconocido, -a [deskono'θiðo, a] *adj* unknown; (*que no se conoce*) unfamiliar; (*no reconocido*) unrecognized ■ *nm/f* stranger; (*recién llegado*) newcomer; **está ~** he is hardly recognizable

desconocimiento [deskonoθi'mjento] *nm* (*falta de conocimientos*) ignorance; (*repudio*) disregard

desconozca *etc* [desko'noθka] *vb ver* **desconocer**

desconsiderado, -a [deskonsiðe'raðo, a] *adj* inconsiderate; (*insensible*) thoughtless

desconsolado, -a [deskonso'laðo, a] *adj* (*afligido*) disconsolate; (*cara*) sad; (*desanimado*) dejected

desconsolar [deskonso'lar] *vt* to distress; **desconsolarse** *vr* to despair

desconsuelo *etc* [deskon'swelo] *vb ver* **desconsolar** ■ *nm* (*tristeza*) distress; (*desesperación*) despair

descontado, -a [deskon'taðo, a] *adj*: **por ~** of course; **dar por ~ (que)** to take it for granted (that)

descontar [deskon'tar] *vt* (*deducir*) to take away, deduct; (*rebajar*) to discount

descontento, -a [deskon'tento, a] *adj* dissatisfied ■ *nm* dissatisfaction, discontent

descontrol [deskon'trol] *nm* (*fam*) lack of control

descontrolado, -a [deskontro'laðo, a] *adj* uncontrolled

descontrolarse [deskontro'larse] *vr* (*persona*) to lose control

desconvenir [deskombe'nir] *vi* (*personas*) to disagree; (*no corresponder*) not to fit; (*no convenir*) to be inconvenient

desconvocar [deskombo'kar] *vt* to call off

descorazonar [deskoraθo'nar] *vt* to discourage, dishearten; **descorazonarse** *vr* to get discouraged, lose heart

descorchador [deskortʃa'ðor] *nm* corkscrew

descorchar [deskor'tʃar] *vt* to uncork, open

descorrer [desko'rrer] *vt* (*cortina, cerrojo*) to draw back; (*velo*) to remove

descortés [deskor'tes] *adj* (*mal educado*) discourteous; (*grosero*) rude

descortesía [deskorte'sia] *nf* discourtesy; (*grosería*) rudeness

descoser [desko'ser] *vt* to unstitch; **descoserse** *vr* to come apart (at the seams); (*fam: descubrir un secreto*) to blurt out a secret; **descoserse de risa** to split one's sides laughing

descosido, -a [desko'siðo, a] *adj (costura)* unstitched; *(desordenado)* disjointed ■ *nm*: **como un ~** *(obrar)* wildly; *(beber, comer)* to excess; *(estudiar)* like mad

descoyuntar [deskojun'tar] *vt (Anat)* to dislocate; *(hechos)* to twist; **descoyuntarse** *vr*: **descoyuntarse un hueso** *(Anat)* to put a bone out of joint; **descoyuntarse de risa** *(fam)* to split one's sides laughing; **estar descoyuntado** *(persona)* to be double-jointed

descrédito [des'kreðito] *nm* discredit; **caer en ~** to fall into disrepute; **ir en ~ de** to be to the discredit of

descreído, -a [deskre'iðo, a] *adj (incrédulo)* incredulous; *(falto de fe)* unbelieving

descremado, -a [deskre'maðo, a] *adj* skimmed

descremar [deskre'mar] *vt (leche)* to skim

describir [deskri'βir] *vt* to describe

descripción [deskrip'θjon] *nf* description

descrito [des'krito] *pp de* **describir**

descuajar [deskwa'xar] *vt (disolver)* to melt; *(planta)* to pull out by the roots; *(extirpar)* to eradicate, wipe out; *(desanimar)* to dishearten

descuajaringarse [deskwaxarin'garse] *vr* to fall to bits

descuajaringue *etc* [deskwaxa'ringe] *vb ver* **descuajaringarse**

descuartice *etc* [deskwar'tiθe] *vb ver* **descuartizar**

descuartizar [deskwarti'θar] *vt (animal)* to carve up, cut up; *(fig: hacer pedazos)* to tear apart

descubierto, -a [desku'βjerto, a] *pp de* **descubrir** ■ *adj* uncovered, bare; *(persona)* bare-headed; *(cielo)* clear; *(coche)* open; *(campo)* treeless ■ *nm (lugar)* open space; *(Com: en el presupuesto)* shortage; *(: bancario)* overdraft; **al ~** in the open; **poner al ~** to lay bare; **quedar al ~** to be exposed; **estar en ~** to be overdrawn

descubridor, a [desku'βri'ðor, a] *nm/f* discoverer

descubrimiento [deskuβri'mjento] *nm* *(hallazgo)* discovery; *(de criminal, fraude)* detection; *(revelación)* revelation; *(de secreto etc)* disclosure; *(de estatua etc)* unveiling

descubrir [desku'βrir] *vt* to discover, find; *(petróleo)* to strike; *(inaugurar)* to unveil; *(vislumbrar)* to detect; *(sacar a luz: crimen)* to bring to light; *(revelar)* to reveal, show; *(poner al descubierto)* to expose to view; *(naipes)* to lay down; *(quitar la tapa de)* to uncover; *(cacerola)* to take the lid off; *(enterarse de: causa, solución)* to find out; *(divisar)* to see, make out; *(delatar)* to give away, betray; **descubrirse** *vr* to reveal o.s.; *(quitarse sombrero)* to take off one's

hat; *(confesar)* to confess; *(fig: salir a luz)* to come out o to light

descuelga *etc* [des'kwelɣa], **descuelgue** *etc* [des'kwelɣe] *vb ver* **descolgar**

descuelle *etc* [des'kweʎe] *vb ver* **descollar**

descuento *etc* [des'kwento] *vb ver* **descontar** ■ *nm* discount; **~ del 3%** 3% off; **con ~** at a discount; **~ por pago al contado** *(Com)* cash discount; **~ por volumen de compras** *(Com)* volume discount

descuidado, -a [deskwi'ðaðo, a] *adj (sin cuidado)* careless; *(desordenado)* untidy; *(olvidadizo)* forgetful; *(dejado)* neglected; *(desprevenido)* unprepared

descuidar [deskwi'ðar] *vt (dejar)* to neglect; *(olvidar)* to overlook ■ *vi*, **descuidarse** *vr* *(distraerse)* to be careless; *(estar desaliñado)* to let o.s. go; *(desprevenirse)* to drop one's guard; **¡descuida!** don't worry!

descuido [des'kwiðo] *nm (dejadez)* carelessness; *(olvido)* negligence; *(un descuido)* oversight; **al ~** casually; *(sin cuidado)* carelessly; **al menor ~** if my *etc* attention wanders for a minute; **con ~** thoughtlessly; **por ~** by an oversight

 PALABRA CLAVE

desde ['desðe] *prep* **1** *(lugar)* from; **desde Burgos hasta mi casa hay 30 km** it's 30 kms from Burgos to my house; **desde lejos** from a distance

2 *(posición)*: **hablaba desde el balcón** she was speaking from the balcony

3 *(tiempo: +adv, n)*: **desde ahora** from now on; **desde entonces/la boda** since then/the wedding; **desde niño** since I *etc* was a child; **desde tres años atrás** since three years ago

4 *(tiempo: +vb)* since; for; **nos conocemos desde 1978/desde hace 20 años** we've known each other since 1978/for 20 years; **no le veo desde 1983/desde hace 5 años** I haven't seen him since 1983/for 5 years; **¿desde cuándo vives aquí?** how long have you lived here?

5 *(gama)*: **desde los más lujosos hasta los más económicos** from the most luxurious to the most reasonably priced

6: **desde luego (que no)** of course (not) ■ *conj*: **desde que**: **desde que recuerdo** for as long as I can remember; **desde que llegó no ha salido** he hasn't been out since he arrived

desdecir [desðe'θir] *vi*: **~ de** *(no merecer)* to be unworthy of; *(no corresponder)* to clash with; **desdecirse** *vr*: **desdecirse de** to go back on

desdén [des'ðen] nm scorn
desdentado, -a [desðen'taðo, a] adj toothless
desdeñable [desðe'ɲaβle] adj contemptible; **nada ~** far from negligible, considerable
desdeñar [desðe'ɲar] vt (despreciar) to scorn
desdeñoso, -a [desðe'ɲoso, a] adj scornful
desdibujar [desðiβu'xar] vt to blur (the outlines of); **desdibujarse** vr to get blurred, fade (away); **el recuerdo se ha desdibujado** the memory has become blurred
desdichado, -a [desði'tʃaðo, a] adj (sin suerte) unlucky; (infeliz) unhappy; (día) ill-fated ■ nm/f (pobre desgraciado) poor devil
desdicho, -a [des'ðitʃo, a] pp de **desdecir** ■ nf (desgracia) misfortune; (infelicidad) unhappiness
desdiciendo etc [desði'θjendo] vb ver **desdecir**
desdiga etc [des'ðiɣa], **desdije** etc [des'dixe] vb ver **desdecir**
desdoblado, -a [desðo'βlaðo, a] adj (personalidad) split
desdoblar [desðo'βlar] vt (extender) to spread out; (desplegar) to unfold
deseable [dese'aβle] adj desirable
desear [dese'ar] vt to want, desire, wish for; **¿qué desea la señora?** (tienda etc) what can I do for you, madam?; **estoy deseando que esto termine** I'm longing for this to finish
desecar [dese'kar] vt, **desecarse** vr to dry up
desechable [dese'tʃaβle] adj (envase etc) disposable
desechar [dese'tʃar] vt (basura) to throw out o away; (ideas) to reject, discard; (miedo) to cast aside; (plan) to drop
desecho [de'setʃo] nm (desprecio) contempt; (lo peor) dregs pl; **desechos** nmpl rubbish sg, waste sg; **de ~** (hierro) scrap; (producto) waste; (ropa) cast-off
desembalar [desemba'lar] vt to unpack
desembarace etc [desemba'raθe] vb ver **desembarazar**
desembarazado, -a [desembara'θaðo, a] adj (libre) clear, free; (desenvuelto) free and easy
desembarazar [desembara'θar] vt (desocupar) to clear; (desenredar) to free; **desembarazarse** vr: **desembarazarse de** to free o.s. of, get rid of
desembarazo [desemba'raθo] nm (acto) clearing; (Am: parto) birth; (desenfado) ease
desembarcadero [desembarka'ðero] nm quay
desembarcar [desembar'kar] vt (personas) to land; (mercancías etc) to unload ■ vi, **desembarcarse** vr (de barco, avión) to disembark
desembarco [desem'barko] nm landing

desembargar [desembar'ɣar] vt (gen) to free; (Jur) to remove the embargo on
desembargue etc [desem'βarɣe] vb ver **desembargar**
desembarque etc [desem'barke] vb ver **desembarcar** ■ nm disembarkation; (de pasajeros) landing; (de mercancías) unloading
desembocadura [desemboka'ðura] nf (de río) mouth; (de calle) opening
desembocar [desembo'kar] vi: **~ en** to flow into; (fig) to result in
desemboce etc [desem'boθe] vb ver **desembozar**
desembolsar [desembol'sar] vt (pagar) to pay out; (gastar) to lay out
desembolso [desem'bolso] nm payment
desemboque etc [desem'boke] vb ver **desembocar**
desembozar [desembo'θar] vt to unmask
desembragar [desembra'ɣar] vt (Tec) to disengage, release ■ vi (Auto) to declutch
desembrague etc [desem'βraɣe] vb ver **desembragar**
desembrollar [desembro'ʎar] vt (madeja) to unravel; (asunto, malentendido) to sort out
desembuchar [desembu'tʃar] vt to disgorge; (fig) to come out with ■ vi (confesar) to spill the beans (fam); **¡desembucha!** out with it!
desemejante [deseme'xante] adj dissimilar; **~ de** different from, unlike
desemejanza [deseme'xanθa] nf dissimilarity
desempacar [desempa'kar] vt (esp Am) to unpack
desempañar [desempa'ɲar] vt (cristal) to clean, demist
desempaque etc [desem'pake] vb ver **desempacar**
desempaquetar [desempake'tar] vt to unpack, unwrap
desempatar [desempa'tar] vi to break a tie; **volvieron a jugar para ~** they held a play-off
desempate [desem'pate] nm (Fútbol) play-off; (Tenis) tie-break(er)
desempeñar [desempe'ɲar] vt (cargo) to hold; (papel) to play; (deber, función) to perform, carry out; (lo empeñado) to redeem; **desempeñarse** vr to get out of debt; **~ un papel** (fig) to play (a role)
desempeño [desem'peɲo] nm occupation; (de lo empeñado) redeeming; **de mucho ~** very capable
desempleado, -a [desemple'aðo, a] adj unemployed, out of work ■ nm/f unemployed person
desempleo [desem'pleo] nm unemployment
desempolvar [desempol'βar] vt (muebles etc)

to dust; (*lo olvidado*) to revive

desencadenar [desenkaðe'nar] *vt* to unchain; (*ira*) to unleash; (*provocar*) to cause, set off; **desencadenarse** *vr* to break loose; (*tormenta*) to burst; (*guerra*) to break out; **se desencadenó una lucha violenta** a violent struggle ensued

desencajar [desenka'xar] *vt* (*hueso*) to put out of joint; (*mandíbula*) to dislocate; (*mecanismo, pieza*) to disconnect, disengage

desencantar [desenkan'tar] *vt* to disillusion, disenchant

desencanto [desen'kanto] *nm* disillusionment, disenchantment

desenchufar [desentʃu'far] *vt* to unplug, disconnect

desenfadado, -a [desenfa'ðaðo, a] *adj* (*desenvuelto*) uninhibited; (*descarado*) forward; (*en el vestir*) casual

desenfado [desen'faðo] *nm* (*libertad*) freedom; (*comportamiento*) free and easy manner; (*descaro*) forwardness; (*desenvoltura*) self-confidence

desenfocado, -a [desenfo'kaðo, a] *adj* (Foto) out of focus

desenfrenado, -a [desenfre'naðo, a] *adj* (*descontrolado*) uncontrolled; (*inmoderado*) unbridled

desenfrenarse [desenfre'narse] *vr* (*persona: desmandarse*) to lose all self-control; (*multitud*) to run riot; (*tempestad*) to burst; (*viento*) to rage

desenfreno [desen'freno] *nm* (*vicio*) wildness; (*falta de control*) lack of self-control; (*de pasiones*) unleashing

desenganchar [desengan'tʃar] *vt* (*gen*) to unhook; (*Ferro*) to uncouple; (*Tec*) to disengage

desengañar [desenga'ɲar] *vt* to disillusion; (*abrir los ojos a*) to open the eyes of; **desengañarse** *vr* to become disillusioned; **¡desengáñate!** don't you believe it!

desengaño [desen'gaɲo] *nm* disillusionment; (*decepción*) disappointment; **sufrir un ~ amoroso** to be disappointed in love

desengrasar [desengra'sar] *vt* to degrease

desenlace *etc* [desen'laθe] *vb ver* **desenlazar** ▪ *nm* outcome; (Lit) ending

desenlazar [desenla'θar] *vt* (*desatar*) to untie; (*problema*) to solve; (*aclarar: asunto*) to unravel; **desenlazarse** *vr* (*desatarse*) to come undone; (Lit) to end

desenmarañar [desenmara'ɲar] *vt* (*fig*) to unravel

desenmascarar [desenmaska'rar] *vt* to unmask, expose

desenredar [desenre'ðar] *vt* to resolve

desenrollar [desenro'ʎar] *vt* to unroll, unwind

desenroscar [desenros'kar] *vt* (*tornillo etc*) to unscrew

desenrosque *etc* [desen'roske] *vb ver* **desenroscar**

desentenderse [desenten'derse] *vr*: ~ **de** to pretend not to know about; (*apartarse*) to have nothing to do with

desentendido, -a [desenten'diðo, a] *adj*: **hacerse el ~** to pretend not to notice; **se hizo el ~** he didn't take the hint

desenterrar [desente'rrar] *vt* to exhume; (*tesoro, fig*) to unearth, dig up

desentierre *etc* [desen'tjerre] *vb ver* **desenterrar**

desentonar [desento'nar] *vi* (Mus) to sing (o play) out of tune; (*no encajar*) to be out of place; (*color*) to clash

desentorpecer [desentorpe'θer] *vt* (*miembro*) to stretch; (*fam: persona*) to polish up

desentorpezca *etc* [desentor'peθka] *vb ver* **desentorpecer**

desentrañar [desentra'ɲar] *vt* (*misterio*) to unravel

desentrenado, -a [desentre'naðo, a] *adj* out of training

desentumecer [desentume'θer] *vt* (*pierna etc*) to stretch; (Deporte) to loosen up

desentumezca *etc* [desentu'meθka] *vb ver* **desentumecer**

desenvainar [desembai'nar] *vt* (*espada*) to draw, unsheathe

desenvoltura [desembol'tura] *nf* (*libertad, gracia*) ease; (*descaro*) free and easy manner; (*al hablar*) fluency

desenvolver [desembol'βer] *vt* (*paquete*) to unwrap; (*fig*) to develop; **desenvolverse** *vr* (*desarrollarse*) to unfold, develop; (*suceder*) to go off; (*prosperar*) to prosper; (*arreglárselas*) to cope

desenvolvimiento [desembolβi'mjento] *nm* (*desarrollo*) development; (*de idea*) exposition

desenvuelto, -a [desem'bwelto, a] *pp de* **desenvolver** ▪ *adj* (*suelto*) easy; (*desenfadado*) confident; (*al hablar*) fluent; (*pey*) forward

desenvuelva *etc* [desem'buelβa] *vb ver* **desenvolver**

deseo [de'seo] *nm* desire, wish; ~ **de saber** thirst for knowledge; **buen ~** good intentions *pl*; **arder en deseos de algo** to yearn for sth

deseoso, -a [dese'oso, a] *adj*: **estar ~ de hacer** to be anxious to do

deseque *etc* [de'seke] *vb ver* **desecar**

desequilibrado, -a [desekili'βraðo, a] *adj* unbalanced ▪ *nm/f* unbalanced person; ~ **mental** mentally disturbed person

d

119

desequilibrar [desekili'βrar] *vt* (*mente*) to unbalance; (*objeto*) to throw out of balance; (*persona*) to throw off balance

desequilibrio [deseki'liβrio] *nm* (*mental*) unbalance; (*entre cantidades*) imbalance; (*Med*) unbalanced mental condition

desertar [deser'tar] *vt* (*Jur: derecho de apelación*) to forfeit ■ *vi* to desert; ~ **de sus deberes** to neglect one's duties

desértico, -a [de'sertiko, a] *adj* desert *cpd*; (*vacío*) deserted

desertor, a [deser'tor, a] *nm/f* deserter

desesperación [desespera'θjon] *nf* desperation, despair; (*irritación*) fury; **es una ~** it's maddening; **es una ~ tener que ...** it's infuriating to have to ...

desesperado, -a [desespe'raðo, a] *adj* (*persona: sin esperanza*) desperate; (*caso, situación*) hopeless; (*esfuerzo*) furious ■ *nm*: **como un ~** like mad ■ *nf*: **hacer algo a la desesperada** to do sth as a last resort *o* in desperation

desesperance *etc* [desespe'ranθe] *vb ver* **desesperanzar**

desesperante [desespe'rante] *adj* (*exasperante*) infuriating; (*persona*) hopeless

desesperanzar [desesperan'θar] *vt* to drive to despair; **desesperanzarse** *vr* to lose hope, despair

desesperar [desespe'rar] *vt* to drive to despair; (*exasperar*) to drive to distraction ■ *vi*: ~ **de** to despair of; **desesperarse** *vr* to despair, lose hope

desespero [deses'pero] *nm* (*Am*) despair

desestabilice *etc* [desestaβi'liθe] *vb ver* **desestabilizar**

desestabilizar [desestaβili'θar] *vt* to destabilize

desestimar [desesti'mar] *vt* (*menospreciar*) to have a low opinion of; (*rechazar*) to reject

desfachatez [desfatʃa'teθ] *nf* (*insolencia*) impudence; (*descaro*) rudeness

desfalco [des'falko] *nm* embezzlement

desfallecer [desfaʎe'θer] *vi* (*perder las fuerzas*) to become weak; (*desvanecerse*) to faint

desfallecido, -a [desfaʎe'θiðo, a] *adj* (*débil*) weak

desfallezca *etc* [desfa'ʎeθka] *vb ver* **desfallecer**

desfasado, -a [desfa'saðo, a] *adj* (*anticuado*) old-fashioned; (*Tec*) out of phase

desfasar [desfa'sar] *vt* to phase out

desfase [des'fase] *nm* (*diferencia*) gap

desfavorable [desfaβo'raβle] *adj* unfavourable

desfavorecer [desfaβore'θer] *vt* (*sentar mal*) not to suit

desfavorezca *etc* [desfaβo'reθka] *vb ver* **desfavorecer**

desfiguración [desfiɣura'θjon] *nf*, **desfiguramiento** [desfiɣura'mjento] *nm* (*de persona*) disfigurement; (*de monumento*) defacement; (*Foto*) blurring

desfigurar [desfiɣu'rar] *vt* (*cara*) to disfigure; (*cuerpo*) to deform; (*cuadro, monumento*) to deface; (*Foto*) to blur; (*sentido*) to twist; (*suceso*) to misrepresent

desfiladero [desfila'ðero] *nm* gorge, defile

desfilar [desfi'lar] *vi* to parade; **desfilaron ante el general** they marched past the general

desfile [des'file] *nm* procession; (*Mil*) parade; ~ **de modelos** fashion show

desflorar [desflo'rar] *vt* (*mujer*) to deflower; (*arruinar*) to tarnish; (*asunto*) to touch on

desfogar [desfo'ɣar] *vt* (*fig*) to vent ■ *vi* (*Naut: tormenta*) to burst; **desfogarse** *vr* (*fig*) to let off steam

desfogue *etc* [des'foɣe] *vb ver* **desfogar**

desgajar [desɣa'xar] *vt* (*arrancar*) to tear off; (*romper*) to break off; (*naranja*) to split into segments; **desgajarse** *vr* to come off

desgana [des'ɣana] *nf* (*falta de apetito*) loss of appetite; (*renuencia*) unwillingness; **hacer algo a ~** to do sth unwillingly

desganado, -a [desɣa'naðo, a] *adj*: **estar ~** (*sin apetito*) to have no appetite; (*sin entusiasmo*) to have lost interest

desgañitarse [desɣaɲi'tarse] *vr* to shout o.s. hoarse

desgarbado, -a [desɣar'βaðo, a] *adj* (*sin gracia*) clumsy, ungainly

desgarrador, a [desɣarra'ðor, a] *adj* heartrending

desgarrar [desɣa'rrar] *vt* to tear (up); (*fig*) to shatter

desgarro [des'ɣarro] *nm* (*en tela*) tear; (*aflicción*) grief; (*descaro*) impudence

desgastar [desɣas'tar] *vt* (*deteriorar*) to wear away *o* down; (*estropear*) to spoil; **desgastarse** *vr* to get worn out

desgaste [des'ɣaste] *nm* wear (and tear); (*de roca*) erosion; (*de cuerda*) fraying; (*de metal*) corrosion; ~ **económico** drain on one's resources

desglosar [desɣlo'sar] *vt* to detach

desgobernar [desɣoβer'nar] *vb* (*Pol*) to misgovern, misrule; (*asunto*) to handle badly; (*Anat*) to dislocate

desgobierno *etc* [desɣo'βjerno] *vb ver* **desgobernar** ■ *nm* (*Pol*) misgovernment, misrule

desgracia [des'ɣraθja] *nf* misfortune; (*accidente*) accident; (*vergüenza*) disgrace;

(*contratiempo*) setback; **por ~** unfortunately; **en el accidente no hay que lamentar desgracias personales** there were no casualties in the accident; **caer en ~** to fall from grace; **tener la ~ de** to be unlucky enough to

desgraciadamente [desɣraθjaða'mente] *adv* unfortunately

desgraciado, -a [desɣra'θjaðo, a] *adj* (*sin suerte*) unlucky, unfortunate; (*miserable*) wretched; (*infeliz*) miserable ▪ *nm/f* (*malvado*) swine; (*infeliz*) poor creature; **¡esa radio desgraciada!** (*esp Am*) that lousy radio!

desgraciar [desɣra'θjar] *vt* (*estropear*) to spoil; (*ofender*) to displease

desgranar [desɣra'nar] *vt* (*trigo*) to thresh; (*guisantes*) to shell; **~ un racimo** to pick the grapes from a bunch; **~ mentiras** to come out with a string of lies

desgravación [desɣraβa'θjon] *nf* (*Com*): **~ de impuestos** tax relief; **~ personal** personal allowance

desgravar [desɣra'βar] *vt* (*producto*) to reduce the tax o duty on

desgreñado, -a [desɣre'ɲaðo, a] *adj* dishevelled

desguace [des'ɣwaθe] *nm* (*de coches*) scrapping; (*lugar*) scrapyard

desguazar [desɣwa'θar] *vt* (*coche*) to scrap

deshabitado, -a [desaβi'taðo, a] *adj* uninhabited

deshabitar [desaβi'tar] *vt* (*casa*) to leave empty; (*despoblar*) to depopulate

deshacer [desa'θer] *vt* (*lo hecho*) to undo, unmake; (*proyectos: arruinar*) to spoil; (*casa*) to break up; (*Tec*) to take apart; (*enemigo*) to defeat; (*diluir*) to melt; (*contrato*) to break; (*intriga*) to solve; (*cama*) to strip; (*maleta*) to unpack; (*paquete*) to unwrap; (*nudo*) to untie; (*costura*) to unpick; **deshacerse** *vr* (*desatarse*) to come undone; (*estropearse*) to be spoiled; (*descomponerse*) to fall to pieces; (*disolverse*) to melt; (*despedazarse*) to come apart o undone; **deshacerse de** to get rid of; (*Com*) to dump, unload; **deshacerse en** (*cumplidos, elogios*) to be lavish with; **deshacerse en lágrimas** to burst into tears; **deshacerse por algo** to be crazy about sth

deshaga *etc* [de'saɣa], **desharé** *etc* [desa're] *vb ver* **deshacer**

desharrapado, -a [desarra'paðo, a] *adj* = **desarrapado**

deshecho, -a [de'setʃo, a] *pp de* **deshacer** ▪ *adj* (*lazo, nudo*) undone; (*roto*) smashed; (*despedazado*) in pieces; (*cama*) unmade; (*Med: persona*) weak, emaciated; (: *salud*) broken; **estoy ~** I'm shattered

deshelar [dese'lar] *vt* (*cañería*) to thaw; (*heladera*) to defrost

desheredar [desere'ðar] *vt* to disinherit

deshice *etc* [de'siθe] *vb ver* **deshacer**

deshidratación [desiðrata'θjon] *nf* dehydration

deshidratar [desiðra'tar] *vt* to dehydrate

deshielo *etc* [des'jelo] *vb ver* **deshelar** ▪ *nm* thaw

deshilachar [desila'tʃar] *vt*, **deshilacharse** *vr* to fray

deshilar [desi'lar] *vt* (*tela*) to unravel

deshilvanado, -a [desilβa'naðo, a] *adj* (*fig*) disjointed, incoherent

deshinchar [desin'tʃar] *vt* (*neumático*) to let down; (*herida etc*) to reduce (the swelling of); **deshincharse** *vr* (*neumático*) to go flat; (*hinchazón*) to go down

deshojar [deso'xar] *vt* (*árbol*) to strip the leaves off; (*flor*) to pull the petals off; **deshojarse** *vr* to lose its leaves *etc*

deshollinar [desoʎi'nar] *vt* (*chimenea*) to sweep

deshonesto, -a [deso'nesto, a] *adj* (*no honrado*) dishonest; (*indecente*) indecent

deshonor [deso'nor] *nm* dishonour, disgrace; (*un deshonor*) insult, affront

deshonra [de'sonra] *nf* (*deshonor*) dishonour; (*vergüenza*) shame

deshonrar [deson'rar] *vt* to dishonour

deshonroso, -a [deson'roso, a] *adj* dishonourable, disgraceful

deshora [de'sora]: **a ~** *adv* at the wrong time; (*llegar*) unexpectedly; (*acostarse*) at some unearthly hour

deshuesar [deswe'sar] *vt* (*carne*) to bone; (*fruta*) to stone

desidia [de'siðja] *nf* (*pereza*) idleness

desierto, -a [de'sjerto, a] *adj* (*casa, calle, negocio*) deserted; (*paisaje*) bleak ▪ *nm* desert

designación [desiɣna'θjon] *nf* (*para un cargo*) appointment; (*nombre*) designation

designar [desiɣ'nar] *vt* (*nombrar*) to designate; (*indicar*) to fix

designio [de'siɣnjo] *nm* plan; **con el ~ de** with the intention of

desigual [desi'ɣwal] *adj* (*lucha*) unequal; (*diferente*) different; (*terreno*) uneven; (*tratamiento*) unfair; (*cambiadizo: tiempo*) changeable; (: *carácter*) unpredictable

desigualdad [desiɣwal'ðað] *nf* (*Econ, Pol*) inequality; (*de carácter, tiempo*) unpredictability; (*de escritura*) unevenness; (*de terreno*) roughness

desilusión [desilu'sjon] *nf* disillusionment; (*decepción*) disappointment

desilusionar [desilusjo'nar] *vt* to disillusion;

(*decepcionar*) to disappoint; **desilusionarse** *vr* to become disillusioned

desinencia [desi'nenθja] *nf* (*Ling*) ending

desinfectar [desinfek'tar] *vt* to disinfect

desinfestar [desinfes'tar] *vt* to decontaminate

desinflación [desinfla'θjon] *nf* (*Com*) disinflation

desinflar [desin'flar] *vt* to deflate; **desinflarse** *vr* (*neumático*) to go down *o* flat

desintegración [desinteɣra'θjon] *nf* disintegration; **~ nuclear** nuclear fission

desintegrar [desinte'ɣrar] *vt* (*gen*) to disintegrate; (*átomo*) to split; (*grupo*) to break up; **desintegrarse** *vr* to disintegrate; to split; to break up

desinterés [desinte'res] *nm* (*objetividad*) disinterestedness; (*altruismo*) unselfishness

desinteresado, -a [desinte're'saðo, a] *adj* (*imparcial*) disinterested; (*altruista*) unselfish

desintoxicar [desintoksi'kar] *vt* to detoxify; **desintoxicarse** *vr* (*drogadicto*) to undergo treatment for drug addiction; **desintoxicarse de** (*rutina, trabajo*) to get away from

desintoxique *etc* [desintok'sike] *vb ver* **desintoxicar**

desistir [desis'tir] *vi* (*renunciar*) to stop, desist; **~ de** (*empresa*) to give up; (*derecho*) to waive

deslavazado, -a [deslaβa'θaðo, a] *adj* (*lacio*) limp; (*desteñido*) faded; (*insípido*) colourless; (*incoherente*) disjointed

desleal [desle'al] *adj* (*infiel*) disloyal; (*Com: competencia*) unfair

deslealtad [desleal'tað] *nf* disloyalty

desleído, -a [desle'iðo, a] *adj* weak, woolly

desleír [desle'ir] *vt* (*líquido*) to dilute; (*sólido*) to dissolve

deslenguado, -a [deslen'gwaðo, a] *adj* (*grosero*) foul-mouthed

deslía *etc* [des'lia] *vb ver* **desleír**

desliar [des'ljar] *vt* (*desatar*) to untie; (*paquete*) to open; **desliarse** *vr* to come undone

deslice *etc* [des'liθe] *vb ver* **deslizar**

desliendo *etc* [desli'endo] *vb ver* **desleír**

desligar [desli'ɣar] *vt* (*desatar*) to untie, undo; (*separar*) to separate; **desligarse** *vr* (*de un compromiso*) to extricate o.s.

desligue *etc* [des'liɣe] *vb ver* **desligar**

deslindar [deslin'dar] *vt* (*señalar las lindes de*) to mark out, fix the boundaries of; (*fig*) to define

desliz [des'liθ] *nm* (*fig*) lapse; **~ de lengua** slip of the tongue; **cometer un ~** to slip up

deslizar [desli'θar] *vt* to slip, slide; **deslizarse** *vr* (*escurrirse: persona*) to slip, slide; (*: coche*) to skid; (*aguas mansas*) to flow gently;

(*error*) to creep in; (*tiempo*) to pass; (*persona: irse*) to slip away; **deslizarse en un cuarto** to slip into a room

deslomar [deslo'mar] *vt* (*romper el lomo de*) to break the back of; (*fig*) to wear out; **deslomarse** *vr* (*fig, fam*) to work one's guts out

deslucido, -a [deslu'θiðo, a] *adj* dull; (*torpe*) awkward, graceless; (*deslustrado*) tarnished; (*fracasado*) unsuccessful; **quedar ~** to make a poor impression

deslucir [deslu'θir] *vt* (*deslustrar*) to tarnish; (*estropear*) to spoil, ruin; (*persona*) to discredit; **la lluvia deslució el acto** the rain ruined the ceremony

deslumbrar [deslum'brar] *vt* (*con la luz*) to dazzle; (*cegar*) to blind; (*impresionar*) to dazzle; (*dejar perplejo a*) to puzzle, confuse

deslustrar [deslus'trar] *vt* (*vidrio*) to frost; (*quitar lustre a*) to dull; (*reputación*) to sully

desluzca *etc* [des'luθka] *vb ver* **deslucir**

desmadrarse [desma'ðrarse] *vr* (*fam*) to run wild

desmadre [des'maðre] *nm* (*fam: desorganización*) chaos; (*: jaleo*) commotion

desmán [des'man] *nm* (*exceso*) outrage; (*abuso de poder*) abuse

desmandarse [desman'darse] *vr* (*portarse mal*) to behave badly; (*excederse*) to get out of hand; (*caballo*) to bolt

desmano [des'mano]: **a ~** *adv*: **me coge** *o* **pilla a desmano** it's out of my way

desmantelar [desmante'lar] *vt* (*deshacer*) to dismantle; (*casa*) to strip; (*organización*) to disband; (*Mil*) to raze; (*andamio*) to take down; (*Naut*) to unrig

desmaquillador [desmakiʎa'ðor] *nm* make-up remover

desmaquillarse [desmaki'ʎarse] *vr* to take off one's make-up

desmarcarse [desmar'karse] *vr*: **~ de** (*Deporte*) to get clear of; (*fig*) to distance o.s. from

desmayado, -a [desma'jaðo, a] *adj* (*sin sentido*) unconscious; (*carácter*) dull; (*débil*) faint, weak; (*color*) pale

desmayar [desma'jar] *vi* to lose heart; **desmayarse** *vr* (*Med*) to faint

desmayo [des'majo] *nm* (*Med: acto*) faint; (*estado*) unconsciousness; (*depresión*) dejection; (*de voz*) faltering; **sufrir un ~** to have a fainting fit

desmedido, -a [desme'ðiðo, a] *adj* excessive; (*ambición*) boundless

desmejorado, -a [desmexo'raðo, a] *adj*: **está muy desmejorada** (*Med*) she's not looking too well

desmejorar [desmexo'rar] *vt* (*dañar*) to impair, spoil; (*Med*) to weaken

desmembración [desmembra'θjon] *nf* dismemberment; (*fig*) break-up

desmembrar [desmem'brar] *vt* (*Med*) to dismember; (*fig*) to separate

desmemoriado, -a [desmemo'rjaðo, a] *adj* forgetful, absent-minded

desmentir [desmen'tir] *vt* (*contradecir*) to contradict; (*refutar*) to deny; (*rumor*) to scotch ■ *vi:* ~ **de** to refute; **desmentirse** *vr* to contradict o.s.

desmenuce *etc* [desme'nuθe] *vb ver* **desmenuzar**

desmenuzar [desmenu'θar] *vt* (*deshacer*) to crumble; (*carne*) to chop; (*examinar*) to examine closely

desmerecer [desmere'θer] *vt* to be unworthy of ■ *vi* (*deteriorarse*) to deteriorate

desmerezca *etc* [desme'reθka] *vb ver* **desmerecer**

desmesurado, -a [desmesu'raðo, a] *adj* (*desmedido*) disproportionate; (*enorme*) enormous; (*ambición*) boundless; (*descarado*) insolent

desmiembre *etc* [des'mjembre] *vb ver* **desmembrar**

desmienta *etc* [des'mjenta] *vb ver* **desmentir**

desmigajar [desmiɣa'xar], **desmigar** [desmi'ɣar] *vt* to crumble

desmigue *etc* [des'miɣe] *vb ver* **desmigar**

desmilitarice *etc* [desmilita'riθe] *vb ver* **desmilitarizar**

desmilitarizar [desmilitari'θar] *vt* to demilitarize

desmintiendo *etc* [desmin'tjendo] *vb ver* **desmentir**

desmochar [desmo'tʃar] *vt* (*árbol*) to lop; (*texto*) to cut, hack about

desmontable [desmon'taβle] *adj* (*que se quita*) detachable; (*en compartimientos*) sectional; (*que se puede plegar etc*) collapsible

desmontar [desmon'tar] *vt* (*deshacer*) to dismantle; (*motor*) to strip down; (*máquina*) to take apart; (*escopeta*) to uncock; (*tienda de campaña*) to take down; (*tierra*) to level; (*quitar los árboles a*) to clear; (*jinete*) to throw ■ *vi* to dismount

desmonte [des'monte] *nm* (*de tierra*) levelling; (*de árboles*) clearing; (*terreno*) levelled ground; (*Ferro*) cutting

desmoralice *etc* [desmora'liθe] *vb ver* **desmoralizar**

desmoralizador, a [desmoraliθa'ðor, a] *adj* demoralizing

desmoralizar [desmorali'θar] *vt* to demoralize

desmoronado, -a [desmoro'naðo, a] *adj* (*casa, edificio*) dilapidated

desmoronamiento [desmorona'mjento] *nm* (*tb fig*) crumbling

desmoronar [desmoro'nar] *vt* to wear away, erode; **desmoronarse** *vr* (*edificio, dique*) to fall into disrepair; (*economía*) to decline

desmovilice *etc* [desmoβi'liθe] *vb ver* **desmovilizar**

desmovilizar [desmoβili'θar] *vt* to demobilize

desnacionalización [desnaθjonaliθa'θjon] *nf* denationalization

desnacionalizado, -a [desnaθjonali'θaðo, a] *adj* (*industria*) denationalized; (*persona*) stateless

desnatado, -a [desna'taðo, a] *adj* skimmed; (*yogur*) low-fat

desnatar [desna'tar] *vt* (*leche*) to skim; **leche sin ~** whole milk

desnaturalice *etc* [desnatura'liθe] *vb ver* **desnaturalizar**

desnaturalizado, -a [desnaturali'θaðo, a] *adj* (*persona*) unnatural; **alcohol ~** methylated spirits

desnaturalizar [desnaturali'θar] *vt* (*Química*) to denature; (*corromper*) to pervert; (*sentido de algo*) to distort; **desnaturalizarse** *vr* (*perder la nacionalidad*) to give up one's nationality

desnivel [desni'βel] *nm* (*de terreno*) unevenness; (*Pol*) inequality; (*diferencia*) difference

desnivelar [desniβe'lar] *vt* (*terreno*) to make uneven; (*fig: desequilibrar*) to unbalance; (*balanza*) to tip

desnuclearizado, -a [desnukleari'θaðo, a] *adj:* **región desnuclearizada** nuclear-free zone

desnudar [desnu'ðar] *vt* (*desvestir*) to undress; (*despojar*) to strip; **desnudarse** *vr* (*desvestirse*) to get undressed

desnudez [desnu'ðeθ] *nf* (*de persona*) nudity; (*fig*) bareness

desnudo, -a [des'nuðo, a] *adj* (*cuerpo*) naked; (*árbol, brazo*) bare; (*paisaje*) flat; (*estilo*) unadorned; (*verdad*) plain ■ *nm/f* nude; **~ de** devoid o bereft of; **la retrató al ~** he painted her in the nude; **poner al ~** to lay bare

desnutrición [desnutri'θjon] *nf* malnutrition

desnutrido, -a [desnu'triðo, a] *adj* undernourished

desobedecer [desoβeðe'θer] *vt, vi* to disobey

desobedezca *etc* [desoβe'ðeθka] *vb ver* **desobedecer**

desobediencia [desoβe'ðjenθja] *nf* disobedience

desocupación [desokupa'θjon] *nf* (*Am*) unemployment

desocupado, -a [desoku'paðo, a] *adj* at leisure; (*desempleado*) unemployed; (*deshabitado*) empty, vacant

desocupar [desoku'par] *vt* to vacate; **desocuparse** *vr* (*quedar libre*) to be free; **se ha desocupado aquella mesa** that table's free now

desodorante [desoðo'rante] *nm* deodorant

desoiga *etc* [de'soiɣa] *vb ver* **desoír**

desoír [deso'ir] *vt* to ignore, disregard

desolación [desola'θjon] *nf* (*de lugar*) desolation; (*fig*) grief

desolar [deso'lar] *vt* to ruin, lay waste

desollar [deso'ʎar] *vt* (*quitar la piel a*) to skin; (*criticar*): ~ **vivo a** to criticize unmercifully

desorbitado, -a [desorβi'taðo, a] *adj* (*excesivo*) excessive; (*precio*) exorbitant; **con los ojos desorbitados** pop-eyed

desorbitar [desorβi'tar] *vt* (*exagerar*) to exaggerate; (*interpretar mal*) to misinterpret; **desorbitarse** *vr* (*persona*) to lose one's sense of proportion; (*asunto*) to get out of hand

desorden [de'sorðen] *nm* confusion; (*de casa, cuarto*) mess; (*político*) disorder; **desórdenes** *nmpl* (*alborotos*) disturbances; (*excesos*) excesses; **en ~** (*gente*) in confusion

desordenado, -a [desorðe'naðo, a] *adj* (*habitación, persona*) untidy; (*objetos revueltos*) in a mess, jumbled; (*conducta*) disorderly

desordenar [desorðe'nar] *vt* (*gen*) to disarrange; (*pelo*) to mess up; (*cuarto*) to make a mess in; (*causar confusión a*) to throw into confusion

desorganice *etc* [desorɣa'niθe] *vb ver* **desorganizar**

desorganizar [desorɣani'θar] *vt* to disorganize

desorientar [desorjen'tar] *vt* (*extraviar*) to mislead; (*confundir, desconcertar*) to confuse; **desorientarse** *vr* (*perderse*) to lose one's way

desovar [deso'βar] *vi* (*peces*) to spawn; (*insectos*) to lay eggs

desoyendo *etc* [deso'jendo] *vb ver* **desoír**

despabilado, -a [despaβi'laðo, a] *adj* (*despierto*) wide-awake; (*fig*) alert, sharp

despabilar [despaβi'lar] *vt* (*despertar*) to wake up; (*fig: persona*) to liven up; (*trabajo*) to get through quickly ▪ *vi*, **despabilarse** *vr* to wake up; (*fig*) to get a move on

despachar [despa'tʃar] *vt* (*negocio*) to do, complete; (*resolver: problema*) to settle; (*correspondencia*) to deal with; (*fam: comida*) to polish off; (: *bebida*) to knock back; (*enviar*) to send, dispatch; (*vender*) to sell, deal in; (*Com: cliente*) to attend to; (*billete*) to issue; (*mandar ir*) to send away ▪ *vi* (*decidirse*) to get things settled; (*apresurarse*) to hurry up; **despacharse** *vr* to finish off; (*apresurarse*) to hurry up; **despacharse de algo** to get rid of sth; **despacharse a su gusto con algn** to give sb a piece of one's mind; **¿quién despacha?** is anybody serving?

despacho [des'patʃo] *nm* (*oficina*) office; (: *en una casa*) study; (*de paquetes*) dispatch; (*Com: venta*) sale (of goods); (*comunicación*) message; **~ de billetes** *o* **boletos** (*Am*) booking office; **~ de localidades** box office; **géneros sin ~** unsaleable goods; **tener buen ~** to find a ready sale

despachurrar [despatʃu'rrar] *vt* (*aplastar*) to crush; (*persona*) to flatten

despacio [des'paθjo] *adv* (*lentamente*) slowly; (*esp Am: en voz baja*) softly; **¡~!** take it easy!

despacito [despa'θito] *adv* (*fam*) slowly; (*suavemente*) softly

despampanante [despampa'nante] *adj* (*fam: chica*) stunning

desparejado, -a [despare'xaðo, a] *adj* odd

desparpajo [despar'paxo] *nm* (*desenvoltura*) self-confidence; (*pey*) nerve

desparramar [desparra'mar] *vt* (*esparcir*) to scatter; (*líquido*) to spill

despatarrarse [despata'rrarse] *vr* (*abrir las piernas*) to open one's legs wide; (*caerse*) to tumble; (*fig*) to be flabbergasted

despavorido, -a [despaβo'riðo, a] *adj* terrified

despecho [des'petʃo] *nm* spite; **a ~ de** in spite of; **por ~** out of (sheer) spite

despectivo, -a [despek'tiβo, a] *adj* (*despreciativo*) derogatory; (*Ling*) pejorative

despedace *etc* [despe'ðaθe] *vb ver* **despedazar**

despedazar [despeða'θar] *vt* to tear to pieces

despedida [despe'ðiða] *nf* (*adiós*) goodbye, farewell; (*antes de viaje*) send-off; (*en carta*) closing formula; (*de obrero*) sacking; (*Inform*) logout; **cena/función de ~** farewell dinner/performance; **regalo de ~** parting gift; **~ de soltero/soltera** stag/hen party

despedir [despe'ðir] *vt* (*visita*) to see off, show out; (*empleado*) to dismiss; (*inquilino*) to evict; (*objeto*) to hurl; (*olor etc*) to give out *o* off; **despedirse** *vr* (*dejar un empleo*) to give up one's job; (*Inform*) to log out *o* off; **despedirse de** to say goodbye to; **se despidieron** they said goodbye to each other

despegado, -a [despe'ɣaðo, a] *adj* (*separado*) detached; (*persona: poco afectuoso*) cold, indifferent ▪ *nm/f*: **es un ~** he has cut himself off from his family

despegar [despe'ɣar] *vt* to unstick; (*sobre*) to open ▪ *vi* (*avión*) to take off; (*cohete*) to blast off; **despegarse** vr to come loose, come unstuck; **sin ~ los labios** without uttering a word

despego [des'peɣo] nm detachment

despegue etc [des'peɣe] vb ver **despegar** ■ nm takeoff; (de cohete) blast-off

despeinado, -a [despei'naðo, a] adj dishevelled, unkempt

despeinar [despei'nar] vt (pelo) to ruffle; **¡me has despeinado todo!** you've completely ruined my hairdo!

despejado, -a [despe'xaðo, a] adj (lugar) clear, free; (cielo) clear; (persona) wide-awake, bright

despejar [despe'xar] vt (gen) to clear; (misterio) to clarify, clear up; (Mat: incógnita) to find ■ vi (el tiempo) to clear; **despejarse** vr (tiempo, cielo) to clear (up); (misterio) to become clearer; (cabeza) to clear; **¡despejen!** (moverse) move along!; (salirse) everybody out!

despeje [des'pexe] nm (Deporte) clearance

despellejar [despeʎe'xar] vt (animal) to skin; (criticar) to criticize unmercifully; (fam: arruinar) to fleece

despelotarse [despelo'tarse] vr (fam) to strip off; (fig) to let one's hair down

despelote [despe'lote] nm (Am: fam: lío) mess; **¡qué** o **vaya ~!** what a riot o laugh!

despenalizar [despenali'θar] vt to decriminalize

despensa [des'pensa] nf (armario) larder; (Naut) storeroom; (provisión de comestibles) stock of food

despeñadero [despeɲa'ðero] nm (Geo) cliff, precipice

despeñar [despe'ɲar] vt (arrojar) to fling down; **despeñarse** vr to fling o.s. down; (caer) to fall headlong

desperdiciar [desperði'θjar] vt (comida, tiempo) to waste; (oportunidad) to throw away

desperdicio [desper'ðiθjo] nm (despilfarro) squandering; (residuo) waste; **desperdicios** nmpl (basura) rubbish sg, refuse sg, garbage sg (US); (residuos) waste sg; **desperdicios de cocina** kitchen scraps; **el libro no tiene ~** the book is excellent from beginning to end

desperdigar [desperði'ɣar] vt (esparcir) to scatter; (energía) to dissipate; **desperdigarse** vr to scatter

desperdigue etc [desper'ðiɣe] vb ver **desperdigar**

desperece etc [despe'reθe] vb ver **desperezarse**

desperezarse [despere'θarse] vr to stretch

desperfecto [desper'fekto] nm (deterioro) slight damage; (defecto) flaw, imperfection

despertador [desperta'ðor] nm alarm clock; **~ de viaje** travelling clock

despertar [desper'tar] vt (persona) to wake up; (recuerdos) to revive; (esperanzas) to raise; (sentimiento) to arouse ■ vi, **despertarse** vr to awaken, wake up ■ nm awakening; **despertarse a la realidad** to wake up to reality

despiadado a [despja'ðaðo, a] adj (ataque) merciless; (persona) heartless

despido etc [des'piðo] vb ver **despedir** ■ nm dismissal, sacking; **~ improcedente** o **injustificado** wrongful dismissal; **~ injusto** unfair dismissal; **~ libre** right to hire and fire; **~ voluntario** voluntary redundancy

despierto, -a [des'pjerto, a] pp de **despertar** ■ adj awake; (fig) sharp, alert

despilfarrar [despilfa'rrar] vt (gen) to waste; (dinero) to squander

despilfarro [despil'farro] nm (derroche) squandering; (lujo desmedido) extravagance

despintar [despin'tar] vt (quitar pintura a) to take the paint off; (hechos) to distort ■ vi: **A no despinta a B** A is in no way inferior to B; **despintarse** vr (desteñir) to fade

despiojar [despjo'xar] vt to delouse

despistado, -a [despis'taðo, a] adj (distraído) vague, absent-minded; (poco práctico) unpractical; (confuso) confused; (desorientado) off the track ■ nm/f (persona distraída) scatterbrain, absent-minded person

despistar [despis'tar] vt to throw off the track o scent; (fig) to mislead, confuse; **despistarse** vr to take the wrong road; (fig) to become confused

despiste [des'piste] nm (Auto etc) swerve; (error) slip; (distracción) absent-mindedness; **tiene un terrible ~** he's terribly absent-minded

desplace etc [des'plaθe] vb ver **desplazar**

desplante [des'plante] nm: **hacer un ~ a algn** to be rude to sb

desplazado, -a [despla'θaðo, a] adj (pieza) wrongly placed ■ nm/f (inadaptado) misfit; **sentirse un poco ~** to feel rather out of place

desplazamiento [desplaθa'mjento] nm displacement; (viaje) journey; (de opinión, votos) shift, swing; (Inform) scrolling; **~ hacia arriba/abajo** (Inform) scroll up/down

desplazar [despla'θar] vt (gen) to move; (Física, Naut, Tec) to displace; (tropas) to transfer; (suplantar) to take the place of; (Inform) to scroll; **desplazarse** vr (persona, vehículo) to travel, go; (objeto) to move, shift; (votos, opinión) to shift, swing

desplegar [desple'ɣar] vt (tela, papel) to unfold, open out; (bandera) to unfurl; (alas) to spread; (Mil) to deploy; (manifestar) to display

desplegué [desple'ɣe], **despleguemos** etc [desple'ɣemos] vb ver **desplegar**

despliegue etc [des'pljeɣe] vb ver **desplegar** ▪ nm unfolding, opening; deployment, display

desplomarse [desplo'marse] vr (edificio, gobierno, persona) to collapse; (derrumbarse) to topple over; (precios) to slump; **se ha desplomado el techo** the ceiling has fallen in

desplumar [desplu'mar] vt (ave) to pluck; (fam: estafar) to fleece

despoblado, -a [despo'βlaðo, a] adj (sin habitantes) uninhabited; (con pocos habitantes) depopulated; (con insuficientes habitantes) underpopulated ▪ nm deserted spot

despojar [despo'xar] vt (a alguien: de sus bienes) to divest of, deprive of; (casa) to strip, leave bare; (de su cargo) to strip of; **despojarse** vr (desnudarse) to undress; **despojarse de** (ropa, hojas) to shed; (poderes) to relinquish

despojo [des'poxo] nm (acto) plundering; (objetos) plunder, loot; **despojos** nmpl (de ave, res) offal sg

desposado, -a [despo'saðo, a] adj, nm/f newly-wed

desposar [despo'sar] vt (sacerdote: pareja) to marry; **desposarse** vr (casarse) to marry, get married

desposeer [despose'er] vt (despojar) to dispossess; ~ **a algn de su autoridad** to strip sb of his authority

desposeído, -a [despose'iðo, a] nm/f: **los desposeídos** the have-nots

desposeyendo etc [despose'jendo] vb ver **desposeer**

desposorios [despo'sorjos] nmpl (esponsales) betrothal sg; (boda) marriage ceremony sg

déspota ['despota] nm/f despot

despotismo [despo'tismo] nm despotism

despotricar [despotri'kar] vi: ~ **contra** to moan o complain about

despotrique etc [despo'trike] vb ver **despotricar**

despreciable [despre'θjaβle] adj (moralmente) despicable; (objeto) worthless; (cantidad) negligible

despreciar [despre'θjar] vt (desdeñar) to despise, scorn; (afrentar) to slight

despreciativo, -a [despreθja'tiβo, a] adj (observación, tono) scornful, contemptuous; (comentario) derogatory

desprecio [des'preθjo] nm scorn, contempt; slight

desprender [despren'der] vt (soltar) to loosen; (separar) to separate; (desatar) to unfasten; (olor) to give off; **desprenderse** vr (botón: caerse) to fall off; (: abrirse) to unfasten; (olor, perfume) to be given off; **desprenderse de** to follow from; **desprenderse de algo** (ceder) to give sth up; (desembarazarse) to get rid of sth; **se desprende que ...** it transpires that ...

desprendido, -a [despren'dido, a] adj (pieza) loose; (sin abrochar) unfastened; (desinteresado) disinterested; (generoso) generous

desprendimiento [desprendi'mjento] nm (gen) loosening; (generosidad) disinterestedness; (indiferencia) detachment; (de gas) leak; (de tierra, rocas) landslide

despreocupado, -a [despreoku'paðo, a] adj (sin preocupación) unworried, unconcerned; (tranquilo) nonchalant; (en el vestir) casual; (negligente) careless

despreocuparse [despreoku'parse] vr to be carefree; (dejar de inquietarse) to stop worrying; (ser indiferente) to be unconcerned; ~ **de** to have no interest in

desprestigiar [despresti'xjar] vt (criticar) to run down, disparage; (desacreditar) to discredit

desprestigio [despres'tixjo] nm (denigración) disparagement; (impopularidad) unpopularity

desprevenido, -a [despreβe'niðo, a] adj (no preparado) unprepared, unready; **coger** (Esp) o **agarrar** (Am) **a algn** ~ to catch sb unawares

desproporción [despropor'θjon] nf disproportion, lack of proportion

desproporcionado, -a [desproporθjo'naðo, a] adj disproportionate, out of proportion

despropósito [despro'posito] nm (salida de tono) irrelevant remark; (disparate) piece of nonsense

desprovisto, -a [despro'βisto, a] adj: ~ **de** devoid of; **estar ~ de** to lack

después [des'pwes] adv afterwards, later; (desde entonces) since (then); (próximo paso) next; **poco** ~ soon after; **un año** ~ a year later; ~ **se debatió el tema** next the matter was discussed ▪ prep: ~ **de** (tiempo) after, since; (orden) next (to); ~ **de comer** after lunch; ~ **de corregido el texto** after the text had been corrected; ~ **de esa fecha** (pasado) since that date; (futuro) from o after that date; ~ **de todo** after all; ~ **de verlo** after seeing it, after I etc saw it; **mi nombre está ~ del tuyo** my name comes next to yours ▪ conj: ~ **(de) que** after; ~ **(de) que lo escribí** after o since I wrote it, after writing it

despuntar [despun'tar] vt (lápiz) to blunt ▪ vi (Bot: plantas) to sprout; (: flores) to bud; (alba) to break; (día) to dawn; (persona: descollar) to stand out

desquiciar [deski'θjar] vt (puerta) to take off its hinges; (descomponer) to upset; (persona: turbar) to disturb; (: volver loco a) to unhinge

desquitarse [deski'tarse] *vr* to obtain satisfaction; (*Com*) to recover a debt; (*fig: vengarse de*) to get one's own back; **~ de una pérdida** to make up for a loss

desquite [des'kite] *nm* (*satisfacción*) satisfaction; (*venganza*) revenge

Dest. *abr* = **destinatario**

destacado, -a [desta'kaðo, a] *adj* outstanding

destacamento [destaka'mento] *nm* (*Mil*) detachment

destacar [desta'kar] *vt* (*Arte: hacer resaltar*) to make stand out; (*subrayar*) to emphasize, point up; (*Mil*) to detach, detail; (*Inform*) to highlight ▪ *vi*, **destacarse** *vr* (*resaltarse*) to stand out; (*persona*) to be outstanding *o* exceptional; **quiero ~ que...** I wish to emphasize that...; **~(se) contra** *o* **en** *o* **sobre** to stand out *o* be outlined against

destajo [des'taxo] *nm*: **a ~** (*por pieza*) by the job; (*con afán*) eagerly; **trabajar a ~** to do piecework; (*fig*) to work one's fingers to the bone

destapar [desta'par] *vt* (*botella*) to open; (*cacerola*) to take the lid off; (*descubrir*) to uncover; **destaparse** *vr* (*descubrirse*) to get uncovered; (*revelarse*) to reveal one's true character

destape [des'tape] *nm* nudity; (*fig*) permissiveness; **el ~ español** the process of liberalization in Spain after Franco's death

destaque *etc* [des'take] *vb ver* **destacar**

destartalado, -a [destarta'laðo, a] *adj* (*desordenado*) untidy; (*casa etc: grande*) rambling; (: *ruinoso*) tumbledown

destellar [deste'ʎar] *vi* (*diamante*) to sparkle; (*metal*) to glint; (*estrella*) to twinkle

destello [des'teʎo] *nm* (*de diamante*) sparkle; (*de metal*) glint; (*de estrella*) twinkle; (*de faro*) signal light; **no tiene un ~ de verdad** there's not a grain of truth in it

destemplado, -a [destem'plaðo, a] *adj* (*Mus*) out of tune; (*voz*) harsh; (*Med*) out of sorts; (*Meteorología*) unpleasant, nasty

destemplar [destem'plar] *vt* (*Mus*) to put out of tune; (*alterar*) to upset; **destemplarse** *vr* (*Mus*) to lose its pitch; (*descomponerse*) to get out of order; (*persona: irritarse*) to get upset; (*Med*) to get out of sorts

desteñir [deste'ɲir] *vt* to fade ▪ *vi*, **desteñirse** *vr* to fade; **esta tela no destiñe** this fabric will not run

desternillarse [desterni'ʎarse] *vr*: **~ de risa** to split one's sides laughing

desterrado, -a [deste'rraðo, a] *nm/f* (*exiliado*) exile

desterrar [deste'rrar] *vt* (*exilar*) to exile; (*fig*) to banish, dismiss

destetar [deste'tar] *vt* to wean

destiempo [des'tjempo]: **a ~** *adv* at the wrong time

destierro *etc* [des'tjerro] *vb ver* **desterrar** ▪ *nm* exile; **vivir en el ~** to live in exile

destilar [desti'lar] *vt* to distil; (*pus, sangre*) to ooze; (*fig: rebosar*) to exude; (: *revelar*) to reveal ▪ *vi* (*gotear*) to drip

destilería [destile'ria] *nf* distillery; **~ de petróleo** oil refinery

destinar [desti'nar] *vt* (*funcionario*) to appoint, assign; (*fondos*) to set aside; **es un libro destinado a los niños** it is a book (intended *o* meant) for children; **una carta que viene destinada a usted** a letter for you, a letter addressed to you

destinatario, -a [destina'tarjo, a] *nm/f* addressee; (*Com*) payee

destino [des'tino] *nm* (*suerte*) destiny; (*de viajero*) destination; (*función*) use; (*puesto*) post, placement; **~ público** public appointment; **salir con ~ a** to leave for; **con ~ a Londres** (*avión, barco*) (bound) for London; (*carta*) to London

destiña *etc* [des'tiɲa], **destiñendo** *etc* [desti'ɲendo] *vb ver* **desteñir**

destitución [destitu'θjon] *nf* dismissal, removal

destituir [destitu'ir] *vt* (*despedir*) to dismiss; (: *ministro, funcionario*) to remove from office

destituyendo *etc* [destitu'jendo] *vb ver* **destituir**

destornillador [destorniʎa'ðor] *nm* screwdriver

destornillar [destorni'ʎar] *vt*, **destornillarse** *vr* (*tornillo*) to unscrew

destreza [des'treθa] *nf* (*habilidad*) skill; (*maña*) dexterity

destripar [destri'par] *vt* (*animal*) to gut; (*reventar*) to mangle

destroce *etc* [des'troθe] *vb ver* **destrozar**

destronar [destro'nar] *vt* (*rey*) to dethrone; (*fig*) to overthrow

destroncar [destron'kar] *vt* (*árbol*) to chop off, lop; (*proyectos*) to ruin; (*discurso*) to interrupt

destronque *etc* [des'tronke] *vb ver* **destroncar**

destrozar [destro'θar] *vt* (*romper*) to smash, break (up); (*estropear*) to ruin; (*nervios*) to shatter; **~ a algn en una discusión** to crush sb in an argument

destrozo [des'troθo] *nm* (*acción*) destruction; (*desastre*) smashing; **destrozos** *nmpl* (*pedazos*) pieces; (*daños*) havoc *sg*

destrucción [destruk'θjon] *nf* destruction

destructor, a [destruk'tor, a] *adj* destructive ▪ *nm* (*Naut*) destroyer

d

destruir [destru'ir] vt to destroy; (casa) to demolish; (equilibrio) to upset; (proyecto) to spoil; (esperanzas) to dash; (argumento) to demolish

destruyendo etc [destru'jendo] vb ver **destruir**

desuelle etc [de'sweʎe] vb ver **desollar**

desueve etc [de'sweβe] vb ver **desovar**

desunión [desu'njon] nf (separación) separation; (discordia) disunity

desunir [desu'nir] vt to separate; (Tec) to disconnect; (fig) to cause a quarrel o rift between

desuso [de'suso] nm disuse; **caer en ~** to fall into disuse, become obsolete; **una expresión caída en ~** an obsolete expression

desvaído, -a [desβa'iðo, a] adj (color) pale; (contorno) blurred

desvalido, -a [desβa'liðo, a] adj (desprotegido) destitute; (sin fuerzas) helpless; **niños desvalidos** waifs and strays

desvalijar [desβali'xar] vt (persona) to rob; (casa, tienda) to burgle; (coche) to break into

desvalorice etc [desβalo'riθe] vb ver **desvalorizar**

desvalorizar [desβalori'θar] vt to devalue

desván [des'βan] nm attic

desvanecer [desβane'θer] vt (disipar) to dispel; (recuerdo, temor) to banish; (borrar) to blur; **desvanecerse** vr (humo etc) to vanish, disappear; (duda) to be dispelled; (color) to fade; (recuerdo, sonido) to fade away; (Med) to pass out

desvanecido, -a [desβane'θiðo, a] adj (Med) faint; **caer ~** to fall in a faint

desvanecimiento [desβaneθi'mjento] nm (desaparición) disappearance; (de dudas) dispelling; (de colores) fading; (evaporación) evaporation; (Med) fainting fit

desvanezca etc [desβa'neθka] vb ver **desvanecer**

desvariar [desβa'rjar] vi (enfermo) to be delirious; (delirar) to talk nonsense

desvarío [desβa'rio] nm delirium; (desatino) absurdity; **desvaríos** nmpl ravings

desvelar [desβe'lar] vt to keep awake; **desvelarse** vr (no poder dormir) to stay awake; (vigilar) to be vigilant o watchful; **desvelarse por algo** (inquietarse) to be anxious about sth; (poner gran cuidado) to take great care over sth

desvelo [des'βelo] nm lack of sleep; (insomnio) sleeplessness; (fig) vigilance; **desvelos** nmpl (preocupación) anxiety sg, effort sg

desvencijado, -a [desβenθi'xaðo, a] adj (silla) rickety; (máquina) broken-down

desvencijar [desβenθi'xar] vt (romper) to break; (soltar) to loosen; (persona: agotar) to exhaust; **desvencijarse** vr to come apart

desventaja [desβen'taxa] nf disadvantage; (inconveniente) drawback

desventajoso, -a [desβenta'xoso, a] adj disadvantageous, unfavourable

desventura [desβen'tura] nf misfortune

desventurado, -a [desβentu'raðo, a] adj (desgraciado) unfortunate; (de poca suerte) ill-fated

desvergonzado, -a [desβerɣon'θaðo, a] adj (sin vergüenza) shameless; (descarado) insolent ▪ nm/f shameless person

desvergüenza [desβer'ɣwenθa] nf (descaro) shamelessness; (insolencia) impudence; (mala conducta) effrontery; **esto es una ~** this is disgraceful; **¡qué ~!** what a nerve!

desvestir [desβes'tir] vt, **desvestirse** vr to undress

desviación [desβja'θjon] nf deviation; (Auto: rodeo) diversion, detour; (: carretera de circunvalación) ring road (Brit), circular route (US); **~ de la circulación** traffic diversion; **es una ~ de sus principios** it is a departure from his usual principles

desviar [des'βjar] vt to turn aside; (balón, flecha, golpe) to deflect; (pregunta) to parry; (ojos) to avert, turn away; (río) to alter the course of; (navío) to divert, re-route; (conversación) to sidetrack; **desviarse** vr (apartarse del camino) to turn aside; (: barco) to go off course; (Auto: dar un rodeo) to make a detour; **desviarse de un tema** to get away from the point

desvincular [desβinku'lar] vt to free, release; **desvincularse** vr (aislarse) to be cut off; (alejarse) to cut o.s. off

desvío etc [des'βio] vb ver **desviar** ▪ nm (desviación) detour, diversion; (fig) indifference

desvirgar [desβir'ɣar] vt to deflower

desvirtuar [desβir'twar] vt (estropear) to spoil; (argumento, razonamiento) to detract from; (efecto) to counteract; (sentido) to distort; **desvirtuarse** vr to spoil

desvistiendo etc [desβis'tjendo] vb ver **desvestir**

desvitalizar [desβitali'θar] vt (nervio) to numb

desvivirse [desβi'βirse] vr: **~ por** to long for, crave for; **~ por los amigos** to do anything for one's friends

detalladamente [detaʎaða'mente] adv (en detalle) in detail; (extensamente) at great length

detallar [deta'ʎar] vt to detail; (asunto por asunto) to itemize

detalle [de'taʎe] nm detail; (fig) gesture,

token; **al ~** in detail; (*Com*) retail *cpd*;
comercio al ~ retail trade; **vender al ~** to sell
retail; **no pierde ~** he doesn't miss a trick;
me observaba sin perder ~ he watched my
every move; **tiene muchos detalles** she is
very considerate

detallista [detaˈʎista] *nm/f* retailer ■ *adj*
(*meticuloso*) meticulous; **comercio ~** retail
trade

detectar [detekˈtar] *vt* to detect

detective [detekˈtiβe] *nm/f* detective; **~
privado** private detective

detector [detekˈtor] *nm* (*Naut, Tec etc*)
detector; **~ de mentiras/de minas** lie/mine
detector

detención [detenˈθjon] *nf* (*acción*) stopping;
(*estancamiento*) stoppage; (*retraso*) holdup,
delay; (*Jur: arresto*) arrest; (*cuidado*) care; **~ de
juego** (*Deporte*) stoppage of play; **~ ilegal**
unlawful detention

detendré *etc* [detenˈdre] *vb ver* **detener**

detener [deteˈner] *vt* (*gen*) to stop; (*Jur:
arrestar*) to arrest; (*: encarcelar*) to detain;
(*objeto*) to keep; (*retrasar*) to hold up, delay;
(*aliento*) to hold; **detenerse** *vr* to stop;
detenerse en (*demorarse*) to delay over, linger
over

detenga *etc* [deˈtenga] *vb ver* **detener**

detenidamente [deteniðaˈmente] *adv*
(*minuciosamente*) carefully; (*extensamente*) at
great length

detenido, -a [deteˈniðo, a] *adj* (*arrestado*)
under arrest; (*minucioso*) detailed; (*examen*)
thorough; (*tímido*) timid ■ *nm/f* person
under arrest, prisoner

detenimiento [deteniˈmjento] *nm* care; **con
~** thoroughly

detentar [detenˈtar] *vt* to hold; (*sin derecho:
título*) to hold unlawfully; (*: puesto*) to occupy
unlawfully

detergente [deterˈxente] *adj, nm* detergent

deteriorado, -a [deterjoˈraðo, a] *adj*
(*estropeado*) damaged; (*desgastado*) worn

deteriorar [deterjoˈrar] *vt* to spoil, damage;
deteriorarse *vr* to deteriorate

deterioro [deteˈrjoro] *nm* deterioration

determinación [determinaˈθjon] *nf* (*empeño*)
determination; (*decisión*) decision; (*de fecha,
precio*) settling, fixing

determinado, -a [determiˈnaðo, a] *adj*
(*preciso*) fixed, set; (*Ling: artículo*) definite;
(*persona: resuelto*) determined; **un día ~** on a
certain day; **no hay ningún tema ~** there is
no particular theme

determinar [determiˈnar] *vt* (*plazo*) to
fix; (*precio*) to settle; (*daños, impuestos*) to
assess; (*pleito*) to decide; (*causar*) to cause;

determinarse *vr* to decide; **el reglamento
determina que ...** the rules lay it down *or*
state that ...; **aquello determinó la caída
del gobierno** that brought about the fall of
the government; **esto le determinó** this
decided him

detestable [detesˈtaβle] *adj* (*persona*) hateful;
(*acto*) detestable

detestar [detesˈtar] *vt* to detest

detonación [detonaˈθjon] *nf* detonation;
(*sonido*) explosion

detonante [detoˈnante] *nm* (*fig*) trigger

detonar [detoˈnar] *vi* to detonate

detractor, a [detrakˈtor, a] *adj* disparaging
■ *nm/f* detractor

detrás [deˈtras] *adv* behind; (*atrás*) at the
back ■ *prep*: **~ de** behind; **por ~ de algn** (*fig*)
behind sb's back; **salir de ~** to come out
from behind; **por ~** behind

detrasito [detraˈsito] *adv* (*Am fam*) behind

detrimento [detriˈmento] *nm*: **en ~ de** to the
detriment of

detuve *etc* [deˈtuβe] *vb ver* **detener**

deuda [deˈuða] *nf* (*condición*) indebtedness,
debt; (*cantidad*) debt; **~ a largo plazo** long-
term debt; **~ exterior/pública** foreign/
national debt; **~ incobrable** *o* **morosa**
bad debt; **deudas activas/pasivas** assets/
liabilities; **contraer deudas** to get into debt

deudor, a [deuˈðor, a] *nm/f* debtor; **~
hipotecario** mortgager; **~ moroso** slow payer

devaluación [deβalwaˈθjon] *nf* devaluation

devaluar [deβaluˈar] *vt* to devalue

devanar [deβaˈnar] *vt* (*hilo*) to wind;
devanarse *vr*: **devanarse los sesos** to rack
one's brains

devaneo [deβaˈneo] *nm* (*Med*) delirium;
(*desatino*) nonsense; (*fruslería*) idle pursuit;
(*amorío*) flirtation

devastar [deβasˈtar] *vt* (*destruir*) to devastate

devendré *etc* [deβenˈdre], **devenga** *etc*
[deˈβenga] *vb ver* **devenir**

devengar [deβenˈgar] *vt* (*salario: ganar*) to
earn; (*: tener que cobrar*) to be due; (*intereses*) to
bring in, accrue, earn

devengue *etc* [deˈβenge] *vb ver* **devengar**

devenir [deβeˈnir] *vi*: **~ en** to become,
turn into ■ *nm* (*movimiento progresivo*)
process of development; (*transformación*)
transformation

deviene *etc* [deˈβjene], **deviniendo** *etc*
[deβiˈnjendo] *vb ver* **devenir**

devoción [deβoˈθjon] *nf* devotion; (*afición*)
strong attachment

devolución [deβoluˈθjon] *nf* (*reenvío*) return,
sending back; (*reembolso*) repayment; (*Jur*)
devolution

129

devolver [deβol'βer] *vt* (*lo extraviado, prestado*) to give back; (*a su sitio*) to put back; (*carta al correo*) to send back; (*Com*) to repay, refund; (*visita, la palabra*) to return; (*salud, vista*) to restore; (*fam: vomitar*) to throw up ■ *vi* (*fam*) to be sick; **devolverse** *vr* (*Am*) to return; **~ mal por bien** to return ill for good; **~ la pelota a algn** to give sb tit for tat

devorar [deβo'rar] *vt* to devour; (*comer ávidamente*) to gobble up; (*fig: fortuna*) to run through; **todo lo devoró el fuego** the fire consumed everything; **le devoran los celos** he is consumed with jealousy

devoto, -a [de'βoto, a] *adj* (*Rel: persona*) devout; (: *obra*) devotional; (*amigo*): **~ (de algn)** devoted (to sb) ■ *nm/f* admirer; **los devotos** *nmpl* (*Rel*) the faithful; **su muy ~** your devoted servant

devuelto [de'βwelto], **devuelva** *etc* [de'βwelβa] *vb ver* **devolver**

D.F. *abr* (*México*) = **Distrito Federal**

dg *abr* (= *decigramo*) dg

D.G. *abr* (= *Dirección General, Director General*) DG

DGT *nf abr* (= *Dirección General de Tráfico*) = **Dirección General de Turismo**

di [di] *vb ver* **dar**; **decir**

día ['dia] *nm* day; **~ de asueto** day off; **~ feriado** (*Am*) *o* **festivo** (public) holiday; **~ hábil/inhábil** working/non-working day; **~ lunes** (*Am*) Monday; **~ lectivo** teaching day; **~ libre** day off; **D~ de Reyes** Epiphany (6 January); **¿qué ~ es?** what's the date?; **estar/poner al ~** to be/keep up to date; **el ~ de hoy/de mañana** today/tomorrow; **el ~ menos pensado** when you least expect it; **al ~ siguiente** on the following day; **todos los días** every day; **un ~ sí y otro no** every other day; **vivir al ~** to live from hand to mouth; **de ~** during the day, by day; **es de ~** it's daylight; **del ~** (*estilos*) fashionable; (*menú*) today's; **de un ~ para otro** any day now; **en pleno ~** in full daylight; **en su ~** in due time; **¡hasta otro ~!** so long!

diabetes [dja'betes] *nf* diabetes *sg*

diabético, -a [dja'betiko, a] *adj, nm/f* diabetic

diablo ['djaβlo] *nm* (*tb fig*) devil; **pobre ~** poor devil; **hace un frío de todos los diablos** it's hellishly cold

diablura [dja'βlura] *nf* prank; (*travesura*) mischief

diabólico, -a [dja'βoliko, a] *adj* diabolical

diadema [dja'ðema] *nf* (*para el pelo*) Alice band, headband; (*joya*) tiara

diáfano, -a ['djafano, a] *adj* (*tela*) diaphanous; (*agua*) crystal-clear

diafragma [dja'frayma] *nm* diaphragm

diagnosis [djay'nosis] *nf inv*, **diagnóstico** [djay'nostiko] *nm* diagnosis

diagnosticar [djaynosti'kar] *vt* to diagnose

diagonal [djayo'nal] *adj* diagonal ■ *nf* (*Geom*) diagonal; **en ~** diagonally

diagrama [dja'yrama] *nm* diagram; **~ de barras** (*Com*) bar chart; **~ de dispersión** (*Com*) scatter diagram; **~ de flujo** (*Inform*) flowchart

dial [di'al] *nm* dial

dialecto [dja'lekto] *nm* dialect

dialogar [djalo'yar] *vt* to write in dialogue form ■ *vi* (*conversar*) to have a conversation; **~ con** (*Pol*) to hold talks with

diálogo ['djaloyo] *nm* dialogue

dialogue *etc* [dja'loye] *vb ver* **dialogar**

diamante [dja'mante] *nm* diamond

diametralmente [djametral'mente] *adv* diametrically; **~ opuesto a** diametrically opposed to

diámetro [di'ametro] *nm* diameter; **~ de giro** (*Auto*) turning circle; **faros de gran ~** wide-angle headlights

diana ['djana] *nf* (*Mil*) reveille; (*de blanco*) centre, bull's-eye

diantre ['djantre] *nm*: **¡~!** (*fam*) oh hell!

diapasón [djapa'son] *nm* (*instrumento*) tuning fork; (*de violín etc*) fingerboard; (*de voz*) tone

diapositiva [djaposi'tiβa] *nf* (*Foto*) slide, transparency

diario, -a ['djarjo, a] *adj* daily ■ *nm* newspaper; (*libro diario*) diary; (: *Com*) daybook; (*Com: gastos*) daily expenses; **~ de navegación** (*Naut*) logbook; **~ hablado** (*Radio*) news (bulletin); **~ de sesiones** parliamentary report; **a ~** daily; **de** *o* **para ~** everyday

diarrea [dja'rrea] *nf* diarrhoea

diatriba [dja'triβa] *nf* diatribe, tirade

dibujante [diβu'xante] *nm/f* (*de bosquejos*) sketcher; (*de dibujos animados*) cartoonist; (*de moda*) designer; **~ de publicidad** commercial artist

dibujar [diβu'xar] *vt* to draw, sketch; **dibujarse** *vr* (*emoción*) to show; **dibujarse contra** to be outlined against

dibujo [di'βuxo] *nm* drawing; (*Tec*) design; (*en papel, tela*) pattern; (*en periódico*) cartoon; (*fig*) description; **dibujos animados** cartoons; **~ del natural** drawing from life

dic., dic.ᵉ *abr* (= *diciembre*) Dec.

diccionario [dikθjo'narjo] *nm* dictionary

dicharachero, -a [ditʃara'tʃero, a] *adj* talkative ■ *nm/f* (*con ingenio*) wit; (*parlanchín*) chatterbox

dicho, -a ['ditʃo, a] *pp de* **decir** ■ *adj* (*susodicho*) aforementioned ■ *nm* saying; (*proverbio*) proverb; (*ocurrencia*) bright remark

■ *nf* (*buena suerte*) good luck; **mejor** ~ rather; ~ **y hecho** no sooner said than done

dichoso, -a [di'tʃoso, a] *adj* (*feliz*) happy; (*afortunado*) lucky; ¡aquel ~ **coche!** (*fam*) that blessed car!

diciembre [di'θjembre] *nm* December; *ver tb* **julio**

diciendo *etc* [di'θjendo] *vb ver* **decir**

dictado [dik'taðo] *nm* dictation; **escribir al** ~ to take dictation; **los dictados de la conciencia** (*fig*) the dictates of conscience

dictador [dikta'ðor] *nm* dictator

dictadura [dikta'ðura] *nf* dictatorship

dictáfono® [dik'tafono] *nm* Dictaphone®

dictamen [dik'tamen] *nm* (*opinión*) opinion; (*informe*) report; ~ **contable** auditor's report; ~ **facultativo** (*Med*) medical report

dictar [dik'tar] *vt* (*carta*) to dictate; (*Jur: sentencia*) to pass; (*decreto*) to issue; (*Am: clase*) to give; (: *conferencia*) to deliver

didáctico, -a [di'ðaktiko, a] *adj* didactic; (*material*) teaching *cpd*; (*juguete*) educational

diecinueve [djeθinu'eβe] *num* nineteen; (*fecha*) nineteenth; *ver tb* **seis**

dieciochesco, -a [djeθio'tʃesko, a] *adj* eighteenth-century

dieciocho [djeθi'otʃo] *num* eighteen; (*fecha*) eighteenth; *ver tb* **seis**

dieciséis [djeθi'seis] *num* sixteen; (*fecha*) sixteenth; *ver tb* **seis**

diecisiete [djeθi'sjete] *num* seventeen; (*fecha*) seventeenth; *ver tb* **seis**

diente ['djente] *nm* (*Anat, Tec*) tooth; (*Zool*) fang; (: *de elefante*) tusk; (*de ajo*) clove; ~ **de león** dandelion; **dientes postizos** false teeth; **enseñar los dientes** (*fig*) to show one's claws; **hablar entre dientes** to mutter, mumble; **hincar el** ~ **en** (*comida*) to bite into

diera *etc* ['djera] *vb ver* **dar**

diéresis [di'eresis] *nf* diaeresis

dieron ['djeron] *vb ver* **dar**

diesel ['disel] *adj*: **motor** ~ diesel engine

diestro, -a ['djestro, a] *adj* (*derecho*) right; (*hábil*) skilful; (: *con las manos*) handy ■ *nm* (*Taur*) matador ■ *nf* right hand; **a** ~ **y siniestro** (*sin método*) wildly

dieta ['djeta] *nf* diet; **dietas** *nfpl* expenses; **estar a** ~ to be on a diet

dietético, -a [dje'tetiko, a] *adj* dietetic ■ *nm/f* dietician ■ *nf* dietetics *sg*

dietista [dje'tista] *nm/f* dietician

diez [djeθ] *num* ten; (*fecha*) tenth; **hacer las** ~ **de últimas** (*Naipes*) to sweep the board; *ver tb* **seis**

diezmar [djeθ'mar] *vt* to decimate

difamación [difama'θjon] *nf* slander; libel

difamar [difa'mar] *vt* (*Jur: hablando*) to slander; (: *por escrito*) to libel

difamatorio, -a [difama'torjo, a] *adj* slanderous; libellous

diferencia [dife'renθja] *nf* difference; **a** ~ **de** unlike; **hacer** ~ **entre** to make a distinction between; ~ **salarial** (*Com*) wage differential

diferencial [diferen'θjal] *nm* (*Auto*) differential

diferenciar [diferen'θjar] *vt* to differentiate between ■ *vi* to differ; **diferenciarse** *vr* to differ, be different; (*distinguirse*) to distinguish o.s.

diferente [dife'rente] *adj* different

diferido [dife'riðo] *nm*: **en** ~ (*TV etc*) recorded

diferir [dife'rir] *vt* to defer

difícil [di'fiθil] *adj* difficult; (*tiempos, vida*) hard; (*situación*) delicate; **es un hombre** ~ he's a difficult man to get on with

difícilmente [di'fiθilmente] *adv* (*con dificultad*) with difficulty; (*apenas*) hardly

dificultad [difikul'taθ] *nf* difficulty; (*problema*) trouble; (*objeción*) objection

dificultar [difikul'tar] *vt* (*complicar*) to complicate, make difficult; (*estorbar*) to obstruct; **las restricciones dificultan el comercio** the restrictions hinder trade

dificultoso, -a [difikul'toso, a] *adj* (*difícil*) difficult, hard; (*fam: cara*) odd, ugly; (*persona: exigente*) fussy

difiera *etc* [di'fjera], **difiriendo** *etc* [difi'rjendo] *vb ver* **diferir**

difuminar [difumi'nar] *vt* to blur

difundir [difun'dir] *vt* (*calor, luz*) to diffuse; (*Radio*) to broadcast; **difundirse** *vr* to spread (out); ~ **una noticia** to spread a piece of news

difunto, a [di'funto, a] *adj* dead, deceased ■ *nm/f*: **el** ~ the deceased

difusión [difu'sjon] *nf* (*de calor, luz*) diffusion; (*de noticia, teoría*) dissemination; (*de programa*) broadcasting; (*programa*) broadcast

difuso, -a [di'fuso, a] *adj* (*luz*) diffused; (*conocimientos*) widespread; (*estilo, explicación*) wordy

diga *etc* ['diɣa] *vb ver* **decir**

digerir [dixe'rir] *vt* to digest; (*fig*) to absorb; (*reflexionar sobre*) to think over

digestión [dixes'tjon] *nf* digestion; **corte de** ~ indigestion

digestivo, -a [dixes'tiβo, a] *adj* digestive ■ *nm* (*bebida*) liqueur, digestif

digiera *etc* [di'xjera], **digiriendo** *etc* [dixi'rjendo] *vb ver* **digerir**

digital [dixi'tal] *adj* (*Inform*) digital; (*dactilar*) finger *cpd* ■ *nf* (*Bot*) foxglove; (*droga*) digitalis

digitalizador [dixitaliθa'ðor] *nm* (*Inform*) digitizer
dignarse [diɣ'narse] *vr* to deign to
dignidad [diɣni'ðað] *nf* dignity; (*honra*) honour; (*rango*) rank; (*persona*) dignitary; **herir la ~ de algn** to hurt sb's pride
dignificar [diɣnifi'kar] *vt* to dignify
dignifique *etc* [diɣni'fike] *vb ver* **dignificar**
digno, -a ['diɣno, a] *adj* worthy; (*persona: honesto*) honourable; **~ de elogio** praiseworthy; **~ de mención** worth mentioning; **es ~ de verse** it is worth seeing; **poco ~** unworthy
digresión [diɣre'sjon] *nf* digression
dije *etc* ['dixe], **dijera** *etc* [di'xera] *vb ver* **decir**
dilación [dila'θjon] *nf* delay; **sin ~** without delay, immediately
dilapidar [dilapi'ðar] *vt* to squander, waste
dilatación [dilata'θjon] *nf* (*expansión*) dilation
dilatado, -a [dila'taðo, a] *adj* dilated; (*período*) long drawn-out; (*extenso*) extensive
dilatar [dila'tar] *vt* (*gen*) to dilate; (*prolongar*) to prolong; (*aplazar*) to delay; **dilatarse** *vr* (*pupila etc*) to dilate; (*agua*) to expand
dilema [di'lema] *nm* dilemma
diligencia [dili'xenθja] *nf* diligence; (*rapidez*) speed; (*ocupación*) errand, job; (*carruaje*) stagecoach; **diligencias** *nfpl* (*Jur*) formalities; **diligencias judiciales** judicial proceedings; **diligencias previas** inquest *sg*
diligente [dili'xente] *adj* diligent; **poco ~** slack
dilucidar [diluθi'ðar] *vt* (*aclarar*) to elucidate, clarify; (*misterio*) to clear up
diluir [dilu'ir] *vt* to dilute; (*aguar, fig*) to water down
diluviar [dilu'βjar] *vi* to pour with rain
diluvio [di'luβjo] *nm* deluge, flood; **un ~ de cartas** (*fig*) a flood of letters
diluyendo *etc* [dilu'jendo] *vb ver* **diluir**
dimanar [dima'nar] *vi*: **~ de** to arise o spring from
dimensión [dimen'sjon] *nf* dimension; **dimensiones** *nfpl* size *sg*; **tomar las dimensiones de** to take the measurements of
dimes ['dimes] *nmpl*: **andar en ~ y diretes con algn** to bicker o squabble with sb
diminutivo [diminu'tiβo] *nm* diminutive
diminuto, -a [dimi'nuto, a] *adj* tiny, diminutive
dimisión [dimi'sjon] *nf* resignation
dimitir [dimi'tir] *vt* (*cargo*) to give up; (*despedir*) to sack ◾ *vi* to resign
dimos ['dimos] *vb ver* **dar**
Dinamarca [dina'marka] *nf* Denmark
dinamarqués, -esa [dinamar'kes, esa] *adj* Danish ◾ *nm/f* Dane ◾ *nm* (*Ling*) Danish

dinámico, -a [di'namiko, a] *adj* dynamic ◾ *nf* dynamics *sg*
dinamita [dina'mita] *nf* dynamite
dinamitar [dinami'tar] *vt* to dynamite
dinamo [di'namo], **dínamo** ['dinamo] *nf, nm en AM* dynamo
dinastía [dinas'tia] *nf* dynasty
dineral [dine'ral] *nm* fortune
dinero [di'nero] *nm* money; (*dinero en circulación*) currency; **~ caro** (*Com*) dear money; **~ contante (y sonante)** hard cash; **~ de curso legal** legal tender; **~ efectivo** cash, ready cash; **es hombre de ~** he is a man of means; **andar mal de ~** to be short of money; **ganar ~ a espuertas** to make money hand over fist
dinosaurio [dino'saurjo] *nm* dinosaur
dintel [din'tel] *nm* lintel; (*umbral*) threshold
diñar [di'ɲar] *vt* (*fam*) to give; **diñarla** to kick the bucket
dio [djo] *vb ver* **dar**
diócesis ['djoθesis] *nf inv* diocese
Dios [djos] *nm* God; **~ mediante** God willing; **a ~ gracias** thank heaven; **a la buena de ~** any old how; **una de ~ es Cristo** an almighty row; **~ los cría y ellos se juntan** birds of a feather flock together; **como ~ manda** as is proper; **¡~ mío!** (oh) my God!; **¡por ~!** for God's sake!; **¡válgame ~!** bless my soul!
dios [djos] *nm* god
diosa ['djosa] *nf* goddess
Dip. *abr* (= *Diputación*) ≈ CC
diploma [di'ploma] *nm* diploma
diplomacia [diplo'maθja] *nf* diplomacy; (*fig*) tact
diplomado, -a [diplo'maðo, a] *adj* qualified ◾ *nm/f* holder of a diploma; (*Univ*) graduate; *ver tb* **licenciado**
diplomático, -a [diplo'matiko, a] *adj* (*cuerpo*) diplomatic; (*que tiene tacto*) tactful ◾ *nm/f* diplomat
diptongo [dip'tongo] *nm* diphthong
diputación [diputa'θjon] *nf* deputation; **~ permanente** (*Pol*) standing committee; **~ provincial** ≈ county council
diputado, -a [dipu'taðo, a] *nm/f* delegate; (*Pol*) ≈ member of parliament (*Brit*), ≈ representative (*US*); *ver tb* **Corte**
dique ['dike] *nm* dyke; (*rompeolas*) breakwater; **~ de contención** dam
Dir. *abr* = **dirección**; (= *director*) Mgr
diré *etc* [di're] *vb ver* **decir**
dirección [direk'θjon] *nf* direction; (*fig: tendencia*) trend; (*señas, tb Inform*) address; (*Auto*) steering; (*gerencia*) management; (*de periódico*) editorship; (*en escuela*)

headship; (*Pol*) leadership; (*junta*) board of directors; (*despacho*) director's/manager's/headmaster's/editor's office; **~ administrativa** office management; **~ asistida** power-assisted steering; **D~ General de Seguridad/Turismo** State Security/Tourist Office; **~ única** *o* **prohibida** one-way; **tomar la ~ de una empresa** to take over the running of a company

direccionamiento [direkθjonaˈmjento] *nm* (*Inform*) addressing

directivo, -a [direkˈtiβo, a] *adj* (*junta*) managing; (*función*) administrative ■ *nm/f* (*Com*) manager ■ *nf* (*norma*) directive; (*tb:* **junta directiva**) board of directors

directo, -a [diˈrekto, a] *adj* direct; (*línea*) straight; (*inmediato*) immediate; (*tren*) through; (*TV*) live; **programa en ~** live programme; **transmitir en ~** to broadcast live

director, a [direkˈtor, a] *adj* leading ■ *nm/f* director; (*Escol*) head (teacher) (*Brit*), principal (*US*); (*gerente*) manager/manageress; (*de compañía*) president; (*jefe*) head; (*Prensa*) editor; (*de prisión*) governor; (*Mus*) conductor; **~ adjunto** assistant manager; **~ de cine** film director; **~ comercial** marketing manager; **~ ejecutivo** executive director; **~ de empresa** company director; **~ general** general manager; **~ gerente** managing director; **~ de sucursal** branch manager

directorio [direkˈtorjo] *nm* (*Inform*) directory

directrices [direkˈtriθes] *nfpl* guidelines

dirigente [diriˈxente] *adj* leading ■ *nm/f* (*Pol*) leader; **los dirigentes del partido** the party leaders

dirigible [diriˈxiβle] *adj* (*Aviat, Naut*) steerable ■ *nm* airship

dirigir [diriˈxir] *vt* to direct; (*acusación*) to level; (*carta*) to address; (*obra de teatro, film*) to direct; (*Mus*) to conduct; (*comercio*) to manage; (*expedición*) to lead; (*sublevación*) to head; (*periódico*) to edit; (*guiar*) to guide; **dirigirse** *vr*: **dirigirse a** to go towards, make one's way towards; (*hablar con*) to speak to; **dirigirse a algn solicitando algo** to apply to sb for sth; **"diríjase a ..."** "apply to ..."

dirigismo [diriˈxismo] *nm* management, control; **~ estatal** state control

dirija *etc* [diˈrixa] *vb ver* **dirigir**

dirimir [diriˈmir] *vt* (*contrato, matrimonio*) to dissolve

discado [disˈkaðo] *nm*: **~ automático** autodial

discernir [disθerˈnir] *vt* to discern ■ *vi* to distinguish

discierna *etc* [disˈθjerna] *vb ver* **discernir**

disciplina [disθiˈplina] *nf* discipline

disciplinar [disθipliˈnar] *vt* to discipline; (*enseñar*) to school; (*Mil*) to drill; (*azotar*) to whip

discípulo, -a [disˈθipulo, a] *nm/f* disciple; (*seguidor*) follower; (*Escol*) pupil

Discman® [ˈdiskman] *nm* Discman®, personal CD player

disco [ˈdisko] *nm* disc (*Brit*), disk (*US*); (*Deporte*) discus; (*Telec*) dial; (*Auto: semáforo*) light; (*Mus*) record; (*Inform*) disk; **~ de arranque** boot disk; **~ compacto** compact disc; **~ de densidad sencilla/doble** single/double density disk; **~ de larga duración** long-playing record (LP); **~ flexible** *o* **floppy** floppy disk; **~ de freno** brake disc; **~ maestro** master disk; **~ de reserva** backup disk; **~ rígido** hard disk; **~ de una cara/dos caras** single-/double-sided disk; **~ virtual** RAMdisk

discóbolo [disˈkoβolo] *nm* discus thrower

discográfico, -a [diskoˈɣrafiko, a] *adj* record *cpd*; **casa discográfica** record company; **sello ~** label

díscolo, -a [ˈdiskolo, a] *adj* (*rebelde*) unruly

disconforme [diskonˈforme] *adj* differing; **estar ~ (con)** to be in disagreement (with)

discontinuo, -a [diskonˈtinwo, a] *adj* discontinuous; (*Auto: línea*) broken

discordar [diskorˈðar] *vi* (*Mus*) to be out of tune; (*estar en desacuerdo*) to disagree; (*colores, opiniones*) to clash

discorde [disˈkorðe] *adj* (*sonido*) discordant; (*opiniones*) clashing

discordia [disˈkorðja] *nf* discord

discoteca [diskoˈteka] *nf* disco(theque)

discreción [diskreˈθjon] *nf* discretion; (*reserva*) prudence; **¡a ~!** (*Mil*) stand easy!; **añadir azúcar a ~** (*Culin*) add sugar to taste; **comer a ~** to eat as much as one wishes

discrecional [diskreθjoˈnal] *adj* (*facultativo*) discretionary; **parada ~** request stop

discrepancia [diskreˈpanθja] *nf* (*diferencia*) discrepancy; (*desacuerdo*) disagreement

discrepante [diskreˈpante] *adj* divergent; **hubo varias voces discrepantes** there were some dissenting voices

discrepar [diskreˈpar] *vi* to disagree

discreto, -a [disˈkreto, a] *adj* (*diplomático*) discreet; (*sensato*) sensible; (*reservado*) quiet; (*sobrio*) sober; (*mediano*) fair, fairly good; **le daremos un plazo ~** we'll allow him a reasonable time

discriminación [diskriminaˈθjon] *nf* discrimination

discriminar [diskrimiˈnar] *vt* to discriminate

against; (*diferenciar*) to discriminate between

discuerde *etc* [dis'kwerðe] *vb ver* **discordar**

disculpa [dis'kulpa] *nf* excuse; (*pedir perdón*) apology; **pedir disculpas a/por** to apologize to/for

disculpar [diskul'par] *vt* to excuse, pardon; **disculparse** *vr* to excuse o.s.; to apologize

discurrir [disku'rrir] *vt* to contrive, think up ■ *vi* (*pensar, reflexionar*) to think, meditate; (*recorrer*) to roam, wander; (*río*) to flow; (*el tiempo*) to pass, flow by

discurso [dis'kurso] *nm* speech; ~ **de clausura** closing speech; **pronunciar un ~** to make a speech; **en el ~ del tiempo** with the passage of time

discusión [disku'sjon] *nf* (*diálogo*) discussion; (*riña*) argument; **tener una ~** to have an argument

discutible [disku'tiβle] *adj* debatable; **de mérito ~** of dubious worth

discutido, -a [disku'tiðo, a] *adj* controversial

discutir [disku'tir] *vt* (*debatir*) to discuss; (*pelear*) to argue about; (*contradecir*) to argue against ■ *vi* to discuss; (*disputar*) to argue; **~ de política** to argue about politics; **¡no discutas!** don't argue!

disecar [dise'kar] *vt* (*para conservar: animal*) to stuff; (: *planta*) to dry

diseminar [disemi'nar] *vt* to disseminate, spread

disentir [disen'tir] *vi* to dissent, disagree

diseñador, a [diseɲa'dor, a] *nm/f* designer

diseñar [dise'ɲar] *vt* to design

diseño [di'seɲo] *nm* (*Tec*) design; (*Arte*) drawing; (*Costura*) pattern; **de ~ italiano** Italian-designed; **~ asistido por ordenador** computer-assisted design, CAD

diseque *etc* [di'seke] *vb ver* **disecar**

disertar [diser'tar] *vi* to speak

disfrace *etc* [dis'fraθe] *vb ver* **disfrazar**

disfraz [dis'fraθ] *nm* (*máscara*) disguise; (*traje*) fancy dress; (*excusa*) pretext; **bajo el ~ de** under the cloak of

disfrazado, -a [disfra'θaðo, a] *adj* disguised; **ir ~ de** to masquerade as

disfrazar [disfra'θar] *vt* to disguise; **disfrazarse** *vr* to dress (o.s.) up; **disfrazarse de** to disguise o.s. as

disfrutar [disfru'tar] *vt* to enjoy ■ *vi* to enjoy o.s.; **¡que disfrutes!** have a good time!; **~ de** to enjoy, possess; **~ de buena salud** to enjoy good health

disfrute [dis'frute] *nm* (*goce*) enjoyment; (*aprovechamiento*) use

disgregar [disɣre'ɣar] *vt* (*desintegrar*) to disintegrate; (*manifestantes*) to disperse; **disgregarse** *vr* to disintegrate, break up

disgregue *etc* [dis'ɣreɣe] *vb ver* **disgregar**

disgustar [disɣus'tar] *vt* (*no gustar*) to displease; (*contrariar, enojar*) to annoy; to upset; **disgustarse** *vr* to be annoyed; (*dos personas*) to fall out; **estaba muy disgustado con el asunto** he was very upset about the affair

disgusto [dis'ɣusto] *nm* (*repugnancia*) disgust; (*contrariedad*) annoyance; (*desagrado*) displeasure; (*tristeza*) grief; (*riña*) quarrel; (*desgracia*) misfortune; **hacer algo a ~** to do sth unwillingly; **matar a algn a disgustos** to drive sb to distraction

disidente [disi'ðente] *nm* dissident

disienta *etc* [di'sjenta] *vb ver* **disentir**

disimulado, -a [disimu'laðo, a] *adj* (*solapado*) furtive, underhand; (*oculto*) covert; **hacerse el ~** to pretend not to notice

disimular [disimu'lar] *vt* (*ocultar*) to hide, conceal ■ *vi* to dissemble

disimulo [disi'mulo] *nm* (*fingimiento*) dissimulation; **con ~** cunningly

disipar [disi'par] *vt* (*duda, temor*) to dispel; (*esperanza*) to destroy; (*fortuna*) to squander; **disiparse** *vr* (*nubes*) to vanish; (*dudas*) to be dispelled; (*indisciplinarse*) to dissipate

diskette [dis'ket] *nm* (*Inform*) diskette, floppy disk

dislate [dis'late] *nm* (*absurdo*) absurdity; **dislates** *nmpl* nonsense *sg*

dislexia [dis'leksja] *nf* dyslexia

dislocar [dislo'kar] *vt* (*gen*) to dislocate; (*tobillo*) to sprain

disloque *etc* [dis'loke] *vb ver* **dislocar** ■ *nm*: **es el ~** (*fam*) it's the last straw

disminución [disminu'θjon] *nf* diminution

disminuido, -a [disminu'iðo, a] *nm/f*: **~ mental/físico** mentally/physically-handicapped person

disminuir [disminu'ir] *vt* to decrease, diminish; (*estrechar*) to lessen; (*temperatura*) to lower; (*gastos, raciones*) to cut down; (*dolor*) to relieve; (*autoridad, prestigio*) to weaken; (*entusiasmo*) to damp ■ *vi* (*días*) to grow shorter; (*precios, temperatura*) to drop, fall; (*velocidad*) to slacken; (*población*) to decrease; (*beneficios, número*) to fall off; (*memoria, vista*) to fail

disminuyendo *etc* [disminu'jendo] *vb ver* **disminuir**

disociar [diso'θjar] *vt* to disassociate; **disociarse** *vr* to disassociate o.s.

disoluble [diso'luβle] *adj* soluble

disolución [disolu'θjon] *nf* (*acto*) dissolution; (*Química*) solution; (*Com*) liquidation; (*moral*) dissoluteness

disoluto, -a [diso'luto, a] *adj* dissolute

disolvente [disol'βente] *nm* solvent, thinner
disolver [disol'βer] *vt* (*gen*) to dissolve; (*manifestación*) to break up; **disolverse** *vr* to dissolve; (*Com*) to go into liquidation
disonar [diso'nar] *vb* (*Mus*) to be out of tune; (*no armonizar*) to lack harmony; ~ **con** to be out of keeping with, clash with
dispar [dis'par] *adj* (*distinto*) different; (*irregular*) uneven
disparado, -a [dispa'raðo, a] *adj*: **entrar** ~ to shoot in; **salir** ~ to shoot out; **ir** ~ to go like mad
disparador [dispara'ðor] *nm* (*de arma*) trigger; (*Foto, Tec*) release; ~ **atómico** aerosol; ~ **de bombas** bomb release
disparar [dispa'rar] *vt, vi* to shoot, fire; **dispararse** *vr* (*arma de fuego*) to go off; (*persona: marcharse*) to rush off; (: *enojarse*) to lose control; (*caballo*) to bolt
disparatado, -a [dispara'taðo, a] *adj* crazy
disparate [dispa'rate] *nm* (*tontería*) foolish remark; (*error*) blunder; **decir disparates** to talk nonsense; **¡qué ~!** how absurd!; **costar un ~** to cost a hell of a lot
disparo [dis'paro] *nm* shot; (*acto*) firing; **disparos** *nmpl* shooting *sg*, exchange *sg* of shots, shots; ~ **inicial** (*de cohete*) blast-off
dispendio [dis'pendjo] *nm* waste
dispensar [dispen'sar] *vt* to dispense; (*ayuda*) to give; (*honores*) to grant; (*disculpar*) to excuse; **¡usted dispense!** I beg your pardon!; ~ **a algn de hacer algo** to excuse sb from doing sth
dispensario [dispen'sarjo] *nm* (*clínica*) community clinic; (*de hospital*) outpatients' department
dispersar [disper'sar] *vt* to disperse; (*manifestación*) to break up; **dispersarse** *vr* to scatter
disperso, -a [dis'perso, a] *adj* scattered
displicencia [displi'θenθja] *nf* (*mal humor*) peevishness; (*desgana*) lack of enthusiasm
displicente [displi'θente] *adj* (*malhumorado*) peevish; (*poco entusiasta*) unenthusiastic
dispondré *etc* [dispon'dre] *vb ver* **disponer**
disponer [dispo'ner] *vt* (*arreglar*) to arrange; (*ordenar*) to put in order; (*preparar*) to prepare, get ready ■ *vi*: ~ **de** to have, own; **disponerse** *vr*: **disponerse para** to prepare to, prepare for; **la ley dispone que ...** the law provides that ...; **no puede ~ de esos bienes** she cannot dispose of those properties
disponga *etc* [dis'ponga] *vb ver* **disponer**
disponibilidad [disponiβili'ðað] *nf* availability; **disponibilidades** *nfpl* (*Com*) resources, financial assets
disponible [dispo'niβle] *adj* available;

(*tiempo*) spare; (*dinero*) on hand
disposición [disposi'θjon] *nf* arrangement, disposition; (*de casa, Inform*) layout; (*ley*) order; (*cláusula*) provision; (*aptitud*) aptitude; ~ **de ánimo** attitude of mind; **última** ~ last will and testament; **a la ~ de** at the disposal of; **a su** ~ at your service
dispositivo [disposi'tiβo] *nm* device, mechanism; ~ **de alimentación** hopper; ~ **de almacenaje** storage device; ~ **periférico** peripheral (device); ~ **de seguridad** safety catch; (*fig*) security measure
dispuesto, -a [dis'pwesto, a] *pp de* **disponer** ■ *adj* (*arreglado*) arranged; (*preparado*) disposed; (*persona: dinámico*) bright; **estar ~/poco ~ a hacer algo** to be inclined/reluctant to do sth
dispuse *etc* [dis'puse] *vb ver* **disponer**
disputa [dis'puta] *nf* (*discusión*) dispute, argument; (*controversia*) controversy
disputar [dispu'tar] *vt* (*discutir*) to dispute, question; (*contender*) to contend for ■ *vi* to argue
disquete [dis'kete] *nm* (*Inform*) diskette, floppy disk
disquetera [diske'tera] *nf* disk drive
Dist. *abr* (= *Distrito*) dist.
distancia [dis'tanθja] *nf* distance; (*de tiempo*) interval; ~ **de parada** braking distance; ~ **del suelo** (*Auto etc*) height off the ground; **a gran** *o* **a larga** ~ long-distance; **mantenerse a** ~ to keep one's distance; (*fig*) to remain aloof; **guardar las distancias** to keep one's distance
distanciado, -a [distan'θjaðo, a] *adj* (*remoto*) remote; (*fig: alejado*) far apart; **estamos distanciados en ideas** our ideas are poles apart
distanciamiento [distanθja'mjento] *nm* (*acto*) spacing out; (*estado*) remoteness; (*fig*) distance
distanciar [distan'θjar] *vt* to space out; **distanciarse** *vr* to become estranged
distante [dis'tante] *adj* distant
distar [dis'tar] *vi*: **dista 5 kms de aquí** it is 5 kms from here; **¿dista mucho?** is it far?; **dista mucho de la verdad** it's very far from the truth
diste ['diste], **disteis** ['disteis] *vb ver* **dar**
distensión [disten'sjon] *nf* distension; (*Pol*) détente; ~ **muscular** (*Med*) muscular strain
distinción [distin'θjon] *nf* distinction; (*elegancia*) elegance; (*honor*) honour; **a ~ de** unlike; **sin ~** indiscriminately; **sin ~ de edades** irrespective of age
distinga *etc* [dis'tinga] *vb ver* **distinguir**
distinguido, -a [distin'giðo, a] *adj*

distinguished; (*famoso*) prominent, well-known; (*elegante*) elegant

distinguir [distin'gir] *vt* to distinguish; (*divisar*) to make out; (*escoger*) to single out; (*caracterizar*) to mark out; **distinguirse** *vr* to be distinguished; (*destacarse*) to distinguish o.s.; **a lo lejos no se distingue** it's not visible from a distance

distintivo, -a [distin'tiβo, a] *adj* distinctive; (*signo*) distinguishing ■ *nm* (*de policía etc*) badge; (*fig*) characteristic

distinto, -a [dis'tinto, a] *adj* different; (*claro*) clear; **distintos** several, various

distorsión [distor'sjon] *nf* (*Anat*) twisting; (*Radio etc*) distortion

distorsionar [distorsjo'nar] *vt, vi* to distort

distracción [distrak'θjon] *nf* distraction; (*pasatiempo*) hobby, pastime; (*olvido*) absent-mindedness, distraction

distraer [distra'er] *vt* (*atención*) to distract; (*divertir*) to amuse; (*fondos*) to embezzle ■ *vi* to be relaxing; **distraerse** *vr* (*entretenerse*) to amuse o.s.; (*perder la concentración*) to allow one's attention to wander; ~ **a algn de su pensamiento** to divert sb from his train of thought; **el pescar distrae** fishing is a relaxation

distraído, -a [distra'iðo, a] *adj* (*gen*) absent-minded; (*desatento*) inattentive; (*entretenido*) amusing ■ *nm*: **hacerse el** ~ to pretend not to notice; **con aire** ~ idly; **me miró distraída** she gave me a casual glance

distraiga *etc* [dis'traiɣa], **distraje** *etc* [dis'traxe], **distrajera** *etc* [distra'xera], **distrayendo** [distra'jendo] *vb ver* **distraer**

distribución [distriβu'θjon] *nf* distribution; (*entrega*) delivery; (*en estadística*) distribution, incidence; (*Arq*) layout; ~ **de premios** prize giving; **la ~ de los impuestos** the incidence of taxes

distribuidor, a [distriβui'ðor, a] *nm/f* (*persona: gen*) distributor; (: *Correos*) sorter; (: *Com*) dealer; **su ~ habitual** your regular dealer

distribuir [distriβu'ir] *vt* to distribute; (*prospectos*) to hand out; (*cartas*) to deliver; (*trabajo*) to allocate; (*premios*) to award; (*dividendos*) to pay; (*peso*) to distribute; (*Arq*) to plan

distribuyendo *etc* [distriβu'jendo] *vb ver* **distribuir**

distrito [dis'trito] *nm* (*sector, territorio*) region; (*barrio*) district; ~ **electoral** constituency; ~ **postal** postal district

disturbio [dis'turβjo] *nm* disturbance; (*desorden*) riot; **los disturbios** *nmpl* the troubles

disuadir [diswa'ðir] *vt* to dissuade

disuasión [diswa'sjon] *nf* dissuasion; (*Mil*) deterrent; ~ **nuclear** nuclear deterrent

disuasivo, -a [diswa'siβo, a] *adj* dissuasive; **arma disuasiva** deterrent

disuasorio, -a [diswa'sorjo, a] *adj* = **disuasivo**

disuelto [di'swelto] *pp de* **disolver**

disuelva *etc* [di'swelβa] *vb ver* **disolver**

disuene *etc* [di'swene] *vb ver* **disonar**

disyuntiva [disjun'tiβa] *nf* (*dilema*) dilemma

DIU ['diu] *nm abr* (= *dispositivo intrauterino*) IUD

diurno, -a ['djurno, a] *adj* day *cpd*, diurnal

diva ['diβa] *nf* prima donna

divagar [diβa'ɣar] *vi* (*desviarse*) to digress

divague *etc* [di'βaɣe] *vb ver* **divagar**

diván [di'βan] *nm* divan

divergencia [diβer'xenθja] *nf* divergence

divergir [diβer'xir] *vi* (*líneas*) to diverge; (*opiniones*) to differ; (*personas*) to disagree

diverja *etc* [di'βerxa] *vb ver* **divergir**

diversidad [diβersi'ðað] *nf* diversity, variety

diversificación [diβersifika'θjon] *nf* (*Com*) diversification

diversificar [diβersifi'kar] *vt* to diversify

diversifique *etc* [diβersi'fike] *vb ver* **diversificar**

diversión [diβer'sjon] *nf* (*gen*) entertainment; (*actividad*) hobby, pastime

diverso, -a [di'βerso, a] *adj* diverse; (*diferente*) different ■ *nm*: **diversos** (*Com*) sundries; **diversos libros** several books

divertido, -a [diβer'tiðo, a] *adj* (*chiste*) amusing, funny; (*fiesta etc*) enjoyable; (*película, libro*) entertaining; **está** ~ (*irónico*) this is going to be fun

divertir [diβer'tir] *vt* (*entretener, recrear*) to amuse, entertain; **divertirse** *vr* (*pasarlo bien*) to have a good time; (*distraerse*) to amuse o.s.

dividendo [diβi'ðendo] *nm* (*Com*): **dividendos** *nmpl* dividends; **dividendos por acción** earnings per share; ~ **definitivo** final dividend

dividir [diβi'ðir] *vt* (*gen*) to divide; (*separar*) to separate; (*distribuir*) to distribute, share out

divierta *etc* [di'βjerta] *vb ver* **divertir**

divinidad [diβini'ðað] *nf* (*esencia divina*) divinity; **la D~** God

divino, -a [di'βino, a] *adj* divine; (*fig*) lovely

divirtiendo *etc* [diβir'tjendo] *vb ver* **divertir**

divisa [di'βisa] *nf* (*emblema*) emblem, badge; **divisas** *nfpl* currency *sg*; (*Com*) foreign exchange *sg*; **control de divisas** exchange control; ~ **de reserva** reserve currency

divisar [diβi'sar] *vt* to make out

división [diβi'sjon] *nf* division; (*de partido*) split; (*de país*) partition

divisorio, -a [diβi'sorjo, a] *adj* (*línea*) dividing; **línea divisoria de las aguas** watershed

divorciado, -a [diβor'θjaðo, a] *adj* divorced; (*opinión*) split ∎ *nm/f* divorcé(e)

divorciar [diβor'θjar] *vt* to divorce; **divorciarse** *vr* to get divorced

divorcio [di'βorθjo] *nm* divorce; (*fig*) split

divulgación [diβulɣa'θjon] *nf* (*difusión*) spreading; (*popularización*) popularization

divulgar [diβul'ɣar] *vt* (*desparramar*) to spread; (*popularizar*) to popularize; (*hacer circular*) to divulge, circulate; **divulgarse** *vr* (*secreto*) to leak out; (*rumor*) to get about

divulgue *etc* [di'βulɣe] *vb ver* **divulgar**

dizque ['diske] *adv* (*Am fam*) apparently

Dls., dls *abr* (*Am*) = **dólares**

dm *abr* (= *decímetro*) dm

DNI *nm abr* (*Esp*) = **Documento Nacional de Identidad**

Dña. *abr* (= *Doña*) Mrs

do [do] *nm* (*Mus*) C

D.O. *abr* = **Denominación de Origen**; *ver* **denominación**

dobladillo [doβla'ðiʎo] *nm* (*de vestido*) hem; (*de pantalón: vuelta*) turn-up (*Brit*), cuff (*US*)

doblaje [do'βlaxe] *nm* (*Cine*) dubbing

doblar [do'βlar] *vt* to double; (*papel*) to fold; (*caño*) to bend; (*la esquina*) to turn, go round; (*film*) to dub ∎ *vi* to turn; (*campana*) to toll; **doblarse** *vr* (*plegarse*) to fold (up), crease; (*encorvarse*) to bend

doble ['doβle] *adj* (*gen*) double; (*de dos aspectos*) dual; (*cuerda*) thick; (*fig*) two-faced ∎ *nm* double ∎ *nm/f* (*Teat*) double, stand-in; **dobles** *nmpl* (*Deporte*) doubles *sg*; **~ o nada** double or quits; **~ página** double-page spread; **con ~ sentido** with a double meaning; **el ~** twice the quantity *o* as much; **su sueldo es el ~ del mío** his salary is twice (as much as) mine; (*Inform*): **~ cara** double-sided; **~ densidad** double density; **~ espacio** double spacing

doblegar [doβle'ɣar] *vt* to fold, crease; **doblegarse** *vr* to yield

doblegue *etc* [do'βleɣe] *vb ver* **doblegar**

doblez [do'βleθ] *nm* (*pliegue*) fold, hem ∎ *nf* (*falsedad*) duplicity

doc. *abr* (= *docena*) doz.; (= *documento*) doc.

doce ['doθe] *num* twelve; (*fecha*) twelfth; **las ~** twelve o'clock; *ver tb* **seis**

docena [do'θena] *nf* dozen; **por docenas** by the dozen

docente [do'θente] *adj*: **centro/personal ~** teaching institution/staff

dócil ['doθil] *adj* (*pasivo*) docile; (*manso*) gentle; (*obediente*) obedient

docto, -a ['dokto, a] *adj* learned, erudite ∎ *nm/f* scholar

doctor, a [dok'tor, a] *nm/f* doctor; **~ en filosofía** Doctor of Philosophy

doctorado [dokto'raðo] *nm* doctorate

doctorarse [dokto'rarse] *vr* to get a doctorate

doctrina [dok'trina] *nf* doctrine, teaching

documentación [dokumenta'θjon] *nf* documentation; (*de identidad etc*) papers *pl*

documental [dokumen'tal] *adj, nm* documentary

documentar [dokumen'tar] *vt* to document; **documentarse** *vr* to gather information

documento [doku'mento] *nm* (*certificado*) document; (*Jur*) exhibit; **documentos** *nmpl* papers; **~ adjunto** (*Inform*) attachment; **~ justificativo** voucher; **D~ Nacional de Identidad** national identity card; *see note*

DOCUMENTO

A laminated plastic ID card with the holder's personal details and photograph, the *Documento Nacional de Identidad* is renewed every 10 years. People are required to carry it at all times and to produce it on request for the police. In Spain it is commonly known as the DNI or *carnet de identidad*. In Spanish America a similar card is called the *cédula (de identidad)*.

dogma ['doɣma] *nm* dogma

dogmático, -a [doɣ'matiko, a] *adj* dogmatic

dogo ['doɣo] *nm* bulldog

dólar ['dolar] *nm* dollar

dolencia [do'lenθja] *nf* (*achaque*) ailment; (*dolor*) ache

doler [do'ler] *vt, vi* to hurt; (*fig*) to grieve; **dolerse** *vr* (*de su situación*) to grieve, feel sorry; (*de las desgracias ajenas*) to sympathize; (*quejarse*) to complain; **me duele el brazo** my arm hurts; **no me duele el dinero** I don't mind about the money; **¡ahí le duele!** you've put your finger on it!

doliente [do'ljente] *adj* (*enfermo*) sick; (*dolorido*) aching; (*triste*) sorrowful; **la familia ~** the bereaved family

dolor [do'lor] *nm* pain; (*fig*) grief, sorrow; **~ de cabeza** headache; **~ de estómago** stomach ache; **~ de oídos** earache; **~ sordo** dull ache

dolorido, -a [dolo'riðo, a] *adj* (*Med*) sore; **la parte dolorida** the part which hurts

doloroso, -a [dolo'roso, a] *adj* (*Med*) painful; (*fig*) distressing

dom. *abr* (= *domingo*) Sun.

domar [do'mar] *vt* to tame

domesticado, -a [domesti'kaðo, a] *adj*
(*amansado*) tame

domesticar [domesti'kar] *vt* to tame

doméstico, -a [do'mestiko, a] *adj* domestic
■ *nm/f* servant; **economía doméstica** home
economy; **gastos domésticos** household
expenses

domestique *etc* [domes'tike] *vb ver*
domesticar

domiciliación [domiθilja'θjon] *nf*: ~ **de**
pagos (*Com*) direct debit

domiciliar [domiθi'ljar] *vt* to domicile;
domiciliarse *vr* to take up (one's) residence

domiciliario, -a [domiθi'ljarjo, a] *adj*:
arresto ~ house arrest

domicilio [domi'θiljo] *nm* home; ~
particular private residence; ~ **social** (*Com*)
head office, registered office; **servicio a** ~
delivery service; **sin** ~ **fijo** of no fixed abode

dominante [domi'nante] *adj* dominant;
(*person*) domineering

dominar [domi'nar] *vt* (*gen*) to dominate;
(*países*) to rule over; (*adversario*) to overpower;
(*caballo, nervios, emoción*) to control; (*incendio,
epidemia*) to bring under control; (*idiomas*)
to be fluent in ■ *vi* to dominate, prevail;
dominarse *vr* to control o.s.

domingo [do'mingo] *nm* Sunday; **D~ de**
Ramos Palm Sunday; **D~ de Resurrección**
Easter Sunday; *ver tb* **sábado**; **Semana Santa**

dominguero, -a [domin'gero, a] *adj* Sunday
cpd

dominical [domini'kal] *adj* Sunday *cpd*;
periódico ~ Sunday newspaper

dominicano, -a [domini'kano, a] *adj, nm/f*
Dominican

dominio [do'minjo] *nm* (*tierras*) domain; (*Pol*)
dominion; (*autoridad*) power, authority;
(*supremacía*) supremacy; (*de las pasiones*)
grip, hold; (*de idioma*) command; **ser del** ~
público to be widely known

dominó [domi'no] *nm* (*pieza*) domino; (*juego*)
dominoes

don [don] *nm* (*talento*) gift; **D~ Juan Gómez**
Mr Juan Gómez, Juan Gómez Esq. (*Brit*);
tener ~ **de gentes** to know how to handle
people; ~ **de lenguas** gift for languages;
~ **de mando** (qualities of) leadership;
~ **de palabra** gift of the gab; *see note*

● **DON**
●
● Don or *doña* is a term used before
● someone's first name – eg Don Diego,
● Doña Inés – when showing respect or
● being polite to someone of a superior
● social standing or to an older person.

● It is becoming somewhat rare, but it does
● however continue to be used with names
● and surnames in official documents
● and in correspondence: eg Sr. D. Pedro
● Rodríguez Hernández, Sra. Dña Inés
● Rodríguez Hernández.

donación [dona'θjon] *nf* donation

donaire [do'naire] *nm* charm

donante [do'nante] *nm/f* donor; ~ **de sangre**
blood donor

donar [do'nar] *vt* to donate

donativo [dona'tiβo] *nm* donation

doncella [don'θeʎa] *nf* (*criada*) maid

donde ['donde] *adv* where ■ *prep*: **el coche**
está allí ~ **el farol** the car is over there by
the lamppost o where the lamppost is; **por** ~
through which; **a** ~ to where, to which; **en**
~ where, in which; **es a** ~ **vamos nosotros**
that's where we're going

dónde ['donde] *adv interrogativo* where?; **¿a** ~
vas? where are you going (to)?; **¿de** ~ **vienes?**
where have you come from?; **¿en** ~**?** where?;
¿por ~**?** where?, whereabouts?; **¿por** ~ **se va**
al estadio? how do you get to the stadium?

dondequiera [donde'kjera] *adv* anywhere
■ *conj*: ~ **que** wherever; **por** ~ everywhere, all
over the place

donostiarra [donos'tjarra] *adj* of o from San
Sebastián ■ *nm/f* native o inhabitant of San
Sebastián

doña ['doɲa] *nf*: **D~ Carmen Gómez** Mrs
Carmen Gómez; *ver tb* **don**

dopar [do'par] *vt* to dope, drug

doping ['dopin] *nm* doping, drugging

doquier [do'kjer] *adv*: **por** ~ all over,
everywhere

dorado, -a [do'raðo, a] *adj* (*color*) golden;
(*Tec*) gilt

dorar [do'rar] *vt* (*Tec*) to gild; (*Culin*) to brown,
cook lightly; ~ **la píldora** to sweeten the pill

dormilón, -ona [dormi'lon, ona] *adj* fond of
sleeping ■ *nm/f* sleepyhead

dormir [dor'mir] *vt*: ~ **la siesta por la tarde**
to have an afternoon nap ■ *vi* to sleep;
dormirse *vr* (*persona, brazo, pierna*) to fall
asleep; **dormirla** (*fam*) to sleep it off;
~ **la mona** (*fam*) to sleep off a hangover;
~ **como un lirón** o **tronco** to sleep like a log;
~ **a pierna suelta** to sleep soundly

dormitar [dormi'tar] *vi* to doze

dormitorio [dormi'torjo] *nm* bedroom;
~ **común** dormitory

dorsal [dor'sal] *adj* dorsal ■ *nm* (*Deporte*)
number

dorso ['dorso] *nm* back; **escribir algo al** ~
to write sth on the back; **"vease al** ~**"** "see

other side", "please turn over"

DOS *nm abr* (= *sistema operativo de disco*) DOS

dos [dos] *num* two; (*fecha*) second; **los ~** the two of them, both of them; **cada ~ por tres** every five minutes; **de ~ en ~** in twos; **estamos a ~** (*Tenis*) the score is deuce; *ver tb* **seis**

doscientos, -as [dos'θjentos, as] *num* two hundred

dosel [do'sel] *nm* canopy

dosificar [dosifi'kar] *vt* (*Culin, Med, Química*) to measure out; (*no derrochar*) to be sparing with

dosifique *etc* [dosi'fike] *vb ver* **dosificar**

dosis ['dosis] *nf inv* dose, dosage

dossier [do'sjer] *nm* dossier, file

dotación [dota'θjon] *nf* (*acto, dinero*) endowment; (*plantilla*) staff; (*Naut*) crew; **la ~ es insuficiente** we are understaffed

dotado, -a [do'taðo, a] *adj* gifted; **~ de** (*persona*) endowed with; (*máquina*) equipped with

dotar [do'tar] *vt* to endow; (*Tec*) to fit; (*barco*) to man; (*oficina*) to staff

dote ['dote] *nf* (*de novia*) dowry; **dotes** *nfpl* (*talentos*) gifts

doy [doj] *vb ver* **dar**

Dpto. *abr* (= *Departamento*) dept.

Dr., Dra. *abr* (= *Doctor, Doctora*) Dr

draga ['draɣa] *nf* dredge

dragado [dra'ɣaðo] *nm* dredging

dragar [dra'ɣar] *vt* to dredge; (*minas*) to sweep

dragón [dra'ɣon] *nm* dragon

drague *etc* ['draɣe] *vb ver* **dragar**

drama ['drama] *nm* drama; (*obra*) play

dramático, -a [dra'matiko, a] *adj* dramatic ■ *nm/f* dramatist; (*actor*) actor; **obra dramática** play

dramaturgo, -a [drama'turɣo, a] *nm/f* dramatist, playwright

dramón [dra'mon] *nm* (*Teat*) melodrama; **¡qué ~!** what a scene!

drástico, -a ['drastiko, a] *adj* drastic

drenaje [dre'naxe] *nm* drainage

drenar [dre'nar] *vt* to drain

droga ['droɣa] *nf* drug; (*Deporte*) dope; **el problema de la ~** the drug problem

drogadicto, -a [droɣa'ðikto, a] *nm/f* drug addict

drogar [dro'ɣar] *vt* to drug; (*Deporte*) to dope; **drogarse** *vr* to take drugs

drogodependencia [droɣoðepen'denθja] *nf* drug addiction

drogue *etc* ['droɣe] *vb ver* **drogar**

droguería [droɣe'ria] *nf* ≈ hardware shop (*Brit*) o store (*US*)

dromedario [drome'ðarjo] *nm* dromedary

Dto. *abr* = descuento

Dtor., Dtora. *abr* (= *Director, Directora*) Dir.

ducado [du'kaðo] *nm* duchy, dukedom

ducha ['dutʃa] *nf* (*baño*) shower; (*Med*) douche

ducharse [du'tʃarse] *vr* to take a shower

ducho, -a ['dutʃo, a] *adj*: **~ en** (*experimentado*) experienced in; (*hábil*) skilled at

dúctil ['duktil] *adj* (*metal*) ductile; (*persona*) easily influenced

duda ['duða] *nf* doubt; **sin ~** no doubt, doubtless; **¡sin ~!** of course!; **no cabe ~** there is no doubt about it; **no le quepa ~** make no mistake about it; **no quiero poner en ~ su conducta** I don't want to call his behaviour into question; **sacar a algn de la ~** to settle sb's doubts; **tengo una ~** I have a query

dudar [du'ðar] *vt* to doubt ■ *vi* to doubt, have doubts; **~ acerca de algo** to be uncertain about sth; **dudó en comprarlo** he hesitated to buy it; **dudan que sea verdad** they doubt whether o if it's true

dudoso, -a [du'ðoso, a] *adj* (*incierto*) hesitant; (*sospechoso*) doubtful; (*conducta*) dubious

duelo *etc* ['dwelo] *vb ver* **doler** ■ *nm* (*combate*) duel; (*luto*) mourning; **batirse en** *etc* to fight a duel

duende ['dwende] *nm* imp, goblin; **tiene ~** he's got real soul

dueño, -a ['dweɲo, a] *nm/f* (*propietario*) owner; (*de pensión, taberna*) landlord(-lady); (*de casa, perro*) master/mistress; (*empresario*) employer; **ser ~ de sí mismo** to have self-control; (*libre*) to be one's own boss; **eres ~ de hacer como te parezca** you're free to do as you think fit; **hacerse ~ de una situación** to take command of a situation

duerma *etc* ['dwerma] *vb ver* **dormir**

duermevela [dwerme'βela] *nf* (*fam*) nap, snooze

Duero ['dwero] *nm* Douro

dulce ['dulθe] *adj* sweet; (*carácter, clima*) gentle, mild ■ *adv* gently, softly ■ *nm* sweet

dulcificar [dulθifi'kar] *vt* (*fig*) to soften

dulcifique *etc* [dulθi'fike] *vb ver* **dulcificar**

dulzón, -ona [dul'θon, ona] *adj* (*alimento*) sickly-sweet, too sweet; (*canción etc*) gooey

dulzura [dul'θura] *nf* sweetness; (*ternura*) gentleness

duna ['duna] *nf* dune

Dunquerque [dun'kerke] *nm* Dunkirk

dúo ['duo] *nm* duet, duo

duodécimo, -a [duo'deθimo, a] *adj* twelfth; *ver tb* **sexto, a**

dup., dup.do *abr* (= *duplicado*) duplicated

dúplex ['dupleks] *nm inv* (*piso*) duplex (apartment); (*Telec*) link-up; (*Inform*): **~ integral** full duplex

duplicar [dupli'kar] *vt* (*hacer el doble de*) to duplicate; (*cantidad*) to double; **duplicarse** *vr* to double

duplique etc [du'plike] vb ver **duplicar**

duque ['duke] nm duke

duquesa [du'kesa] nf duchess

durable [du'raβle] adj durable

duración [dura'θjon] nf duration, length; (de máquina) life; ~ **media de la vida** average life expectancy; **de larga** ~ (enfermedad) lengthy; (pila) long-life; (disco) long-playing; **de poca** ~ short

duradero, -a [dura'ðero, a] adj (tela) hard-wearing; (fe, paz) lasting

durante [du'rante] adv during; ~ **toda la noche** all night long; **habló** ~ **una hora** he spoke for an hour

durar [du'rar] vi (permanecer) to last; (recuerdo) to remain; (ropa) to wear (well)

durazno [du'rasno] nm (Am: fruta) peach;

(: árbol) peach tree

durex ['dureks] nm (Am: tira adhesiva) Sellotape® (Brit), Scotch tape® (US)

dureza [du'reθa] nf (cualidad) hardness; (de carácter) toughness

durmiendo etc [dur'mjendo] vb ver **dormir**

durmiente [dur'mjente] adj sleeping ■ nm/f sleeper

duro, -a ['duro, a] adj hard; (carácter) tough; (pan) stale; (cuello, puerta) stiff; (clima, luz) harsh ■ adv hard ■ nm (moneda) five peseta coin; **el sector** ~ **del partido** the hardliners pl in the party; **ser** ~ **con algn** to be tough with o hard on sb; ~ **de mollera** (torpe) dense; ~ **de oído** hard of hearing; **trabajar** ~ to work hard; **estar sin un** ~ to be broke

DVD nm abr (= disco de vídeo digital) DVD

Ee

E, e [e] *nf* (*letra*) E, e; **E de Enrique** E for
Edward (*Brit*) *o* Easy (*US*)

E *abr* (= *este*) E

e [e] *conj* (*delante de* **i-** *e* **hi-** *pero no* **hie-**) and;
ver tb **y**

e/ *abr* (*Com*: = *envío*) shpt.

EA *abr* = **Ejército del Aire**

EAU *nmpl abr* (= *Emiratos Árabes Unidos*) UAE

ebanista [eβa'nista] *nm/f* cabinetmaker

ébano ['eβano] *nm* ebony

ebrio, -a ['eβrjo, a] *adj* drunk

Ebro ['eβro] *nm* Ebro

ebullición [eβuʎi'θjon] *nf* boiling; **punto
de ~** boiling point

eccema [ek'θema] *nm* (*Med*) eczema

echar [e'tʃar] *vt* to throw; (*agua, vino*) to pour
(out); (*Culin*) to put in, add; (*dientes*) to cut;
(*discurso*) to give; (*empleado: despedir*) to fire,
sack; (*hojas*) to sprout; (*cartas*) to post; (*humo*)
to emit, give out; (*reprimenda*) to deal out;
(*cuenta*) to make up; (*freno*) to put on ◼ *vi*:
~ a correr/llorar to break into a run/burst
into tears; **~ a reír** to burst out laughing;
echarse *vr* to lie down; **~ abajo** (*gobierno*) to
overthrow; (*edificio*) to demolish; **~ la
buenaventura a algn** to tell sb's fortune;
~ la culpa a to lay the blame on; **~ de menos**
to miss; **~ una mirada** to give a look; **~ sangre**
to bleed; **echarse atrás** to throw o.s.
back(wards); (*fig*) to go back on what one has
said; **echarse una novia** to get o.s. a girlfriend;
echarse una siestecita to have a nap

echarpe [e'tʃarpe] *nm* (woman's) stole

eclesiástico, -a [ekle'sjastiko, a] *adj*
ecclesiastical; (*autoridades etc*) church *cpd*
◼ *nm* clergyman

eclipsar [eklip'sar] *vt* to eclipse; (*fig*) to
outshine, overshadow

eclipse [e'klipse] *nm* eclipse

eco ['eko] *nm* echo; **encontrar un ~ en**
to produce a response from; **hacerse ~ de
una opinión** to echo an opinion; **tener ~**
to catch on

ecografía [ekoɣra'fia] *nf* ultrasound

ecología [ekolo'xia] *nf* ecology

ecológico, -a [eko'loxiko, a] *adj* ecological;
(*producto, método*) environmentally-friendly;
(*agricultura*) organic

ecologista [ekolo'xista] *adj* environmental,
conservation *cpd* ◼ *nm/f* environmentalist

economato [ekono'mato] *nm* cooperative
store

economía [ekono'mia] *nf* (*sistema*) economy;
(*cualidad*) thrift; **~ dirigida** planned
economy; **~ doméstica** housekeeping;
~ de mercado market economy; **~ mixta**
mixed economy; **~ sumergida** black
economy; **hacer economías** to economize;
economías de escala economies of scale

economice *etc* [ekono'miθe] *vb ver*
economizar

económico, -a [eko'nomiko, a] *adj* (*barato*)
cheap, economical; (*persona*) thrifty; (*Com*:
año etc) financial; (: *situación*) economic

economista [ekono'mista] *nm/f* economist

economizar [ekonomi'θar] *vt* to economize
on ◼ *vi* (*ahorrar*) to save up; (*pey*) to be miserly

ecosistema [ekosis'tema] *nm* ecosystem

ecu ['eku] *nm* ecu

ecuación [ekwa'θjon] *nf* equation

ecuador [ekwa'ðor] *nm* equator; **(el) E~**
Ecuador

ecuánime [e'kwanime] *adj* (*carácter*) level-
headed; (*estado*) calm

ecuatorial [ekwato'rjal] *adj* equatorial

ecuatoriano, -a [ekwato'rjano, a] *adj, nm/f*
Ecuador(i)an

ecuestre [e'kwestre] *adj* equestrian

eczema [ek'θema] *nm* = **eccema**

ed. *abr* (= *edición*) ed.

edad [e'ðað] *nf* age; **¿qué ~ tienes?** how
old are you?; **tiene ocho años de ~** he is
eight (years old); **de ~ corta** young; **ser de
~ mediana/avanzada** to be middle-aged/
getting on; **ser mayor de ~** to be of age;
llegar a mayor ~ to come of age; **ser menor**

de ~ to be under age; **la E~ Media** the Middle Ages; **la E~ de Oro** the Golden Age

Edén [e'ðen] *nm* Eden

edición [eði'θjon] *nf* (*acto*) publication; (*ejemplar*) edition; **"al cerrar la ~"** (*Tip*) "stop press"

edicto [e'ðikto] *nm* edict, proclamation

edificante [eðifi'kante] *adj* edifying

edificar [eðifi'kar] *vt* (*Arq*) to build

edificio [eði'fiθjo] *nm* building; (*fig*) edifice, structure

edifique *etc* [eði'fike] *vb ver* **edificar**

Edimburgo [eðim'burɣo] *nm* Edinburgh

editar [eði'tar] *vt* (*publicar*) to publish; (*preparar textos, tb Inform*) to edit

editor, a [eði'tor, a] *nm/f* (*que publica*) publisher; (*redactor*) editor ■ *adj:* **casa editora** publishing company

editorial [eðito'rjal] *adj* editorial ■ *nm* leading article, editorial ■ *nf* (*tb:* **casa editorial**) publisher

editorialista [eðitorja'lista] *nm/f* leader-writer

edredón [eðre'ðon] *nm* eiderdown, quilt; **~ nórdico** continental quilt, duvet

educación [eðuka'θjon] *nf* education; (*crianza*) upbringing; (*modales*) (good) manners *pl*; (*formación*) training; **sin ~** ill-mannered; **¡qué falta de ~!** how rude!

educado, -a [eðu'kaðo, a] *adj* well-mannered; **mal ~** ill-mannered

educar [eðu'kar] *vt* to educate; (*criar*) to bring up; (*voz*) to train

educativo, -a [eðuka'tiβo, a] *adj* educational; (*política*) education *cpd*

eduque *etc* [e'ðuke] *vb ver* **educar**

EE UU *nmpl abr* (= *Estados Unidos*) USA

efectista [efek'tista] *adj* sensationalist

efectivamente [efektiβa'mente] *adv* (*como respuesta*) exactly, precisely; (*verdaderamente*) really; (*de hecho*) in fact

efectivo, -a [efek'tiβo, a] *adj* effective; (*real*) actual, real ■ *nm:* **pagar en ~** to pay (in) cash; **hacer ~ un cheque** to cash a cheque

efecto [e'fekto] *nm* effect, result; (*objetivo*) purpose, end; **efectos** *nmpl* (*personales*) effects; (*bienes*) goods; (*Com*) assets; (*Econ*) bills, securities; **~ 2000** millennium bug; **~ invernadero** greenhouse effect; **efectos de consumo** consumer goods; **efectos a cobrar** bills receivable; **efectos especiales** special effects; **efectos personales** personal effects; **efectos secundarios** (*Com*) spin-off effects; **efectos sonoros** sound effects; **hacer o surtir ~** to have the desired effect; **hacer ~** (*impresionar*) to make an impression; **llevar algo a ~** to carry sth out; **en ~** in fact; (*respuesta*) exactly, indeed

efectuar [efek'twar] *vt* to carry out; (*viaje*) to make

efervescente [eferβes'θente] *adj* (*bebida*) fizzy, bubbly

eficacia [efi'kaθja] *nf* (*de persona*) efficiency; (*de medicamento etc*) effectiveness

eficaz [efi'kaθ] *adj* (*persona*) efficient; (*acción*) effective

eficiencia [efi'θjenθja] *nf* efficiency

eficiente [efi'θjente] *adj* efficient

efigie [e'fixje] *nf* effigy

efímero, -a [e'fimero, a] *adj* ephemeral

EFTA *sigla f* = **Asociación Europea de Libre Comercio**

efusión [efu'sjon] *nf* outpouring; (*en el trato*) warmth; **con ~** effusively

efusivo, -a [efu'siβo, a] *adj* effusive; **mis más efusivas gracias** my warmest thanks

EGB *nf abr* (*Esp Escol*: = *Educación General Básica*) primary education for six- to fourteen-year olds; *ver tb* **sistema educativo**

Egeo [e'xeo] *nm:* **(Mar) ~** Aegean (Sea)

egipcio, -a [e'xipθjo, a] *adj, nm/f* Egyptian

Egipto [e'xipto] *nm* Egypt

egocéntrico, -a [eɣo'θentriko, a] *adj* self-centred

egoísmo [eɣo'ismo] *nm* egoism

egoísta [eɣo'ista] *adj* egoistical, selfish ■ *nm/f* egoist

ególatra [e'ɣolatra] *adj* big-headed

egregio, -a [e'ɣrexjo, a] *adj* eminent, distinguished

egresado, -a [eɣre'saðo, a] *nm/f* (*Am*) graduate

egresar [eɣre'sar] *vi* (*Am*) to graduate

eh [e] *excl* hey!, hi!

Eire ['eire] *nm* Eire

ej. *abr* (= *ejemplo*) ex.

eje ['exe] *nm* (*Geo, Mat*) axis; (*Pol, fig*) axis, main line; (*de rueda*) axle; (*de máquina*) shaft, spindle

ejecución [exeku'θjon] *nf* execution; (*cumplimiento*) fulfilment; (*actuación*) performance; (*Jur: embargo de deudor*) attachment

ejecutar [exeku'tar] *vt* to execute, carry out; (*matar*) to execute; (*cumplir*) to fulfil; (*Mus*) to perform; (*Jur: embargar*) to attach, distrain; (*deseos*) to fulfil; (*Inform*) to run

ejecutivo, -a [exeku'tiβo, a] *adj, nm/f* executive; **el (poder) ~** the Executive (Power)

ejecutor [exeku'tor] *nm* (*tb:* **ejecutor testamentario**) executor

ejecutoria [exeku'torja] *nf* (*Jur*) final judgment

ejemplar [exem'plar] *adj* exemplary ■ *nm* example; (*Zool*) specimen; (*de libro*) copy;

(*de periódico*) number, issue; ~ **de regalo**
complimentary copy; **sin** ~ unprecedented
ejemplificar [exemplifi'kar] *vt* to exemplify,
illustrate
ejemplifique *etc* [exempli'fike] *vb ver*
ejemplificar
ejemplo [e'xemplo] *nm* example; (*caso*)
instance; **por** ~ for example; **dar** ~ to set an
example
ejercer [exer'θer] *vt* to exercise; (*funciones*) to
perform; (*negocio*) to manage; (*influencia*) to
exert; (*un oficio*) to practise; (*poder*) to wield
■ *vi*: ~ **de** to practise as
ejercicio [exer'θiθjo] *nm* exercise; (*Mil*) drill;
(*Com*) fiscal *o* financial year; (*período*) tenure;
~ **acrobático** (*Aviat*) stunt; ~ **comercial**
business year; **ejercicios espirituales** (*Rel*)
retreat *sg*; **hacer** ~ to take exercise
ejercitar [exerθi'tar] *vt* to exercise; (*Mil*) to
drill
ejército [e'xerθito] *nm* army; **E~ del Aire/de
Tierra** Air Force/Army; ~ **de ocupación**
army of occupation; ~ **permanente**
standing army; **entrar en el** ~ to join the
army, join up
ejerza *etc* [e'xerθa] *vb ver* **ejercer**
ejote [e'xote] *nm* (*Am*) green bean

⬤ **PALABRA CLAVE**

el, la, lo [el, la] (*pl* **los, las**) *artículo definido*
1 the; **el libro/la mesa/los estudiantes/las
flores** the book/table/students/flowers; **me
gusta el fútbol** I like football; **está en la
cama** she's in bed
2 (*con n abstracto o propio: no se traduce*): **el amor/
la juventud** love/youth; **el Conde Drácula**
Count Dracula
3 (*posesión: se traduce a menudo por adj posesivo*):
romperse el brazo to break one's arm;
levantó la mano he put his hand up;
se puso el sombrero she put her hat on
4 (*valor descriptivo*): **tener la boca grande/los
ojos azules** to have a big mouth/blue eyes
5 (*con días*) on; **me iré el viernes** I'll leave on
Friday; **los domingos suelo ir a nadar** on
Sundays I generally go swimming
6 (*lo + adj*): **lo difícil/caro** what is difficult/
expensive; (*cuán*): **no se da cuenta de lo
pesado que es** he doesn't realize how boring
he is
■ *pron demostrativo* **1**: **mi libro y el de
usted** my book and yours; **las de Pepe
son mejores** Pepe's are better; **no la(s)
blanca(s) sino la(s) gris(es)** not the white
one(s) but the grey one(s)
2: **lo de**: **lo de ayer** what happened

yesterday; **lo de las facturas** that business
about the invoices
■ *pron relativo*: **el que** *etc* **1** (*indef*): **el (los) que
quiera(n) que se vaya(n)** anyone who wants
to can leave; **llévese el/la que más le guste**
take the one you like best
2 (*def*): **el que compré ayer** the one I bought
yesterday; **los que se van** those who leave
3: **lo que**: **lo que pienso yo/más me gusta**
what I think/like most
■ *conj*: **el que**: **el que lo diga** the fact that he
says so; **el que sea tan vago me molesta** his
being so lazy bothers me
■ *excl*: **¡el susto que me diste!** what a fright
you gave me!
■ *pron personal* **1** (*persona: m*) him; (: *f*) her; (: *pl*)
them; **lo/las veo** I can see him/them
2 (*animal, cosa: sg*) it; (: *pl*) them; **lo** (*o* **la**) **veo** I
can see it; **los** (*o* **las**) **veo** I can see them
3: **lo** (*como sustituto de frase*): **no lo sabía** I
didn't know; **ya lo entiendo** I understand
now

él [el] *pron* (*persona*) he; (*cosa*) it; (*después de prep*:
persona) him; (: *cosa*) it; **mis libros y los de él**
my books and his
elaboración [elaβora'θjon] *nf* (*producción*)
manufacture; ~ **de presupuestos** (*Com*)
budgeting
elaborar [elaβo'rar] *vt* (*producto*) to make,
manufacture; (*preparar*) to prepare; (*madera,
metal etc*) to work; (*proyecto etc*) to work on *o* out
elasticidad [elastiθi'ðað] *nf* elasticity
elástico, -a [e'lastiko, a] *adj* elastic; (*flexible*)
flexible ■ *nm* elastic; (*gomita*) elastic band
elección [elek'θjon] *nf* election; (*selección*)
choice, selection; **elecciones parciales** by-
election *sg*; **elecciones generales** general
election *sg*
electo, -a [e'lekto, a] *adj* elect; **el presidente**
~ the president-elect
electorado [elekto'raðo] *nm* electorate,
voters *pl*
electoral [elekto'ral] *adj* electoral
electrice *etc* [elek'triθe] *vb ver* **electrizar**
electricidad [elektriθi'ðað] *nf* electricity
electricista [elektri'θista] *nm/f* electrician
eléctrico, -a [e'lektriko, a] *adj* electric
electrificar [elektrifi'kar] *vt* to electrify
electrizar [elektri'θar] *vt* (*Ferro, fig*) to electrify
electro... [elektro] *pref* electro...
electrocardiograma [elektrokarðjo'ɣrama]
nm electrocardiogram
electrocución [elektroku'θjon] *nf*
electrocution
electrocutar [elektroku'tar] *vt* to electrocute
electrodo [elek'troðo] *nm* electrode

e

electrodomésticos [elektroðo'mestikos] *nmpl* (electrical) household appliances; (Com) white goods

electroimán [electroi'man] *nm* electromagnet

electromagnético, -a [elektromaɣ'netiko, a] *adj* electromagnetic

electrón [elek'tron] *nm* electron

electrónico, -a [elek'troniko, a] *adj* electronic ■ *nf* electronics *sg*

electrotecnia [elektro'teknja] *nf* electrical engineering

electrotécnico, -a [elektro'tekniko, a] *nm/f* electrical engineer

electrotren [elektro'tren] *nm* express electric train

elefante [ele'fante] *nm* elephant

elegancia [ele'ɣanθja] *nf* elegance, grace; (*estilo*) stylishness

elegante [ele'ɣante] *adj* elegant, graceful; (*traje etc*) smart; (*decoración*) tasteful

elegía [ele'xia] *nf* elegy

elegir [ele'xir] *vt* (*escoger*) to choose, select; (*optar*) to opt for; (*presidente*) to elect

elemental [elemen'tal] *adj* (*claro, obvio*) elementary; (*fundamental*) elemental, fundamental

elemento [ele'mento] *nm* element; (*fig*) ingredient; (*Am*) person, individual; (*tipo raro*) odd person; (*de pila*) cell; **elementos** *nmpl* elements, rudiments; **estar en su ~** to be in one's element; **vino a verle un ~** someone came to see you

elenco [e'lenko] *nm* catalogue, list; (*Teat*) cast; (*Am: equipo*) team

elevación [eleβa'θjon] *nf* elevation; (*acto*) raising, lifting; (*de precios*) rise; (*Geo etc*) height, altitude

elevado, -a [ele'βaðo, a] *pp de* **elevar** ■ *adj* high

elevador [eleβa'ðor] *nm* (*Am*) lift (Brit), elevator (US)

elevar [ele'βar] *vt* to raise, lift (up); (*precio*) to put up; (*producción*) to step up; (*informe etc*) to present; **elevarse** *vr* (*edificio*) to rise; (*precios*) to go up; (*transportarse, enajenarse*) to get carried away; **la cantidad se eleva a ...** the total amounts to ...

eligiendo *etc* [eli'xjenðo], **elija** *etc* [e'lixa] *vb ver* **elegir**

eliminar [elimi'nar] *vt* to eliminate, remove; (*olor, persona*) to get rid of; (*Deporte*) to eliminate, knock out

eliminatoria [elimina'torja] *nf* heat, preliminary (round)

elite [e'lite], **élite** ['elite] *nf* elite, élite

elitista [eli'tista] *adj* elitist

elixir [elik'sir] *nm* elixir; (*tb*: **elixir bucal**) mouthwash

ella ['eʎa] *pron* (*persona*) she; (*cosa*) it; (*después de prep: persona*) her; (*cosa*) it; **de ~** hers

ellas ['eʎas] *pron ver* **ellos**

ello ['eʎo] *pron neutro* it; **es por ~ que ...** that's why ...

ellos, -as ['eʎos, as] *pron personal pl* they; (*después de prep*) them; **de ~** theirs

elocuencia [elo'kwenθja] *nf* eloquence

elocuente [elo'kwente] *adj* eloquent; (*fig*) significant; **un dato ~** a fact which speaks for itself

elogiar [elo'xjar] *vt* to praise, eulogize

elogio [e'loxjo] *nm* praise; **queda por encima de todo ~** it's beyond praise; **hacer ~ de** to sing the praises of

elote [e'lote] *nm* (*Am*) corn on the cob

El Salvador *nm* El Salvador

eludir [elu'ðir] *vt* (*evitar*) to avoid, evade; (*escapar*) to escape, elude

Em.ª *abr* (= *Eminencia*) Mgr

email ['imeil] *nm* (*gen*) email *m*; (*dirección*) email address; **mandar un ~ a algn** to email sb, send sb an email

emanar [ema'nar] *vi*: **~ de** to emanate from, come from; (*derivar de*) to originate in

emancipar [emanθi'par] *vt* to emancipate; **emanciparse** *vr* to become emancipated, free o.s.

embadurnar [embaður'nar] *vt* to smear

embajada [emba'xaða] *nf* embassy

embajador, a [embaxa'ðor, a] *nm/f* ambassador/ambassadress

embaladura [embala'ðura] *nf* (*Am*), **embalaje** [emba'laxe] *nm* packing

embalar [emba'lar] *vt* (*envolver*) to parcel, wrap (up); (*envasar*) to package ■ *vi* to sprint

embalsamar [embalsa'mar] *vt* to embalm

embalsar [embal'sar] *vt* (*río*) to dam (up); (*agua*) to retain

embalse [em'balse] *nm* (*presa*) dam; (*lago*) reservoir

embarace *etc* [emba'raθe] *vb ver* **embarazar**

embarazada [embara'θaða] *adj f* pregnant ■ *nf* pregnant woman

embarazar [embara'θar] *vt* to obstruct, hamper; **embarazarse** *vr* to become embarrassed; (*confundirse*) to get into a mess

embarazo [emba'raθo] *nm* (*de mujer*) pregnancy; (*impedimento*) obstacle, obstruction; (*timidez*) embarrassment

embarazoso, -a [embara'θoso, a] *adj* (*molesto*) awkward; (*violento*) embarrassing

embarcación [embarka'θjon] *nf* (*barco*) boat, craft; (*acto*) embarkation; **~ de arrastre** trawler; **~ de cabotaje** coasting vessel

embarcadero [embarka'ðero] *nm* pier, landing stage

embarcar [embar'kar] *vt* (*cargamento*) to ship, stow; (*persona*) to embark, put on board; (*fig*): ~ **a algn en una empresa** to involve sb in an undertaking; **embarcarse** *vr* to embark, go on board; (*marinero*) to sign on; (*Am: en tren etc*) to get on, get in

embargar [embar'ɣar] *vt* (*frenar*) to restrain; (*sentidos*) to overpower; (*Jur*) to seize, impound

embargo [em'barɣo] *nm* (*Jur*) seizure; (*Com etc*) embargo; **sin** ~ still, however, nonetheless

embargue *etc* [em'barɣe] *vb ver* **embargar**

embarque *etc* [em'barke] *vb ver* **embarcar** ■ *nm* shipment, loading

embarrancar [embarran'kar] *vt, vi* (*Naut*) to run aground; (*Auto etc*) to run into a ditch

embarranque *etc* [emba'rranke] *vb ver* **embarrancar**

embarullar [embaru'ʎar] *vt* to make a mess of

embate [em'bate] *nm* (*de mar, viento*) beating, violence

embaucador, a [embauka'ðor, a] *nm/f* (*estafador*) trickster; (*impostor*) impostor

embaucar [embau'kar] *vt* to trick, fool

embauque *etc* [em'bauke] *vb ver* **embaucar**

embeber [embe'βer] *vt* (*absorber*) to absorb, soak up; (*empapar*) to saturate ■ *vi* to shrink; **embeberse** *vr*: **embeberse en un libro** to be engrossed *o* absorbed in a book

embelesado, -a [embele'saðo, a] *adj* spellbound

embelesar [embele'sar] *vt* to enchant; **embelesarse** *vr*: **embelesarse (con)** to be enchanted (by)

embellecer [embeʎe'θer] *vt* to embellish, beautify

embellezca *etc* [embe'ʎeθka] *vb ver* **embellecer**

embestida [embes'tiða] *nf* attack, onslaught; (*carga*) charge

embestir [embes'tir] *vt* to attack, assault; to charge, attack ■ *vi* to attack

embistiendo *etc* [embis'tjendo] *vb ver* **embestir**

emblanquecer [emblanke'θer] *vt* to whiten, bleach; **emblanquecerse** *vr* to turn white

emblanquezca *etc* [emblan'keθka] *vb ver* **emblanquecer**

emblema [em'blema] *nm* emblem

embobado, -a [embo'βaðo, a] *adj* (*atontado*) stunned, bewildered

embobar [embo'βar] *vt* (*asombrar*) to amaze; (*fascinar*) to fascinate; **embobarse** *vr*:

embobarse con *o* **de** *o* **en** to be amazed at; to be fascinated by

embocadura [emboka'ðura] *nf* narrow entrance; (*de río*) mouth; (*Mus*) mouthpiece

embolado [embo'laðo] *nm* (*Teat*) bit part, minor role; (*fam*) trick

embolia [em'bolja] *nf* (*Med*) embolism; ~ **cerebral** clot on the brain

émbolo ['embolo] *nm* (*Auto*) piston

embolsar [embol'sar] *vt* to pocket

emboquillado, -a [emboki'ʎaðo, a] *adj* (*cigarrillo*) tipped, filter *cpd*

emborrachar [emborra'tʃar] *vt* to make drunk; **emborracharse** *vr* to get drunk

emboscada [embos'kaða] *nf* (*celada*) ambush

embotar [embo'tar] *vt* to blunt, dull; **embotarse** *vr* (*adormecerse*) to go numb

embotellamiento [emboteʎa'mjento] *nm* (*Auto*) traffic jam

embotellar [embote'ʎar] *vt* to bottle; **embotellarse** *vr* (*circulación*) to get into a jam

embozo [em'boθo] *nm* muffler, mask; (*de sábana*) turnover

embragar [embra'ɣar] *vt* (*Auto, Tec*) to engage; (*partes*) to connect ■ *vi* to let in the clutch

embrague *etc* [em'braɣe] *vb ver* **embragar** ■ *nm* (*tb*: **pedal de embrague**) clutch

embravecer [embraβe'θer] *vt* to enrage, infuriate; **embravecerse** *vr* to become furious; (*mar*) to get rough; (*tormenta*) to rage

embravecido, -a [embraβe'θiðo, a] *adj* (*mar*) rough; (*persona*) furious

embriagador, a [embrjaɣa'ðor, a] *adj* intoxicating

embriagar [embrja'ɣar] *vt* (*emborrachar*) to make drunk; (*alegrar*) to delight; **embriagarse** *vr* (*emborracharse*) to get drunk

embriague *etc* [em'brjaɣe] *vb ver* **embriagar**

embriaguez [embrja'ɣeθ] *nf* (*borrachera*) drunkenness

embrión [em'brjon] *nm* embryo

embrionario, -a [embrjo'narjo, a] *adj* embryonic

embrollar [embro'ʎar] *vt* (*asunto*) to confuse, complicate; (*persona*) to involve, embroil; **embrollarse** *vr* (*confundirse*) to get into a muddle *o* mess

embrollo [em'broʎo] *nm* (*enredo*) muddle, confusion; (*aprieto*) fix, jam

embromado, -a [embro'maðo, a] *adj* (*Am fam*) tricky, difficult

embromar [embro'mar] *vt* (*burlarse de*) to tease, make fun of; (*Am fam: molestar*) to annoy

embrujado, -a [embru'xaðo, a] *adj* (*persona*) bewitched; **casa embrujada** haunted house

embrujo [em'bruxo] *nm* (*de mirada etc*) charm, magic

embrutecer [embrute'θer] *vt* (*atontar*) to stupefy; **embrutecerse** *vr* to be stupefied

embrutezca *etc* [embru'teθka] *vb ver* **embrutecer**

embudo [em'buðo] *nm* funnel

embuste [em'buste] *nm* trick; (*mentira*) lie; (*humorístico*) fib

embustero, -a [embus'tero, a] *adj* lying, deceitful ■ *nm/f* (*tramposo*) cheat; (*mentiroso*) liar; (*humorístico*) fibber

embutido [embu'tiðo] *nm* (*Culin*) sausage

embutir [embu'tir] *vt* to insert; (*Tec*) to inlay; (*llenar*) to pack tight, cram

emergencia [emer'xenθja] *nf* emergency; (*surgimiento*) emergence

emergente [emer'xente] *adj* resultant, consequent; (*nación*) emergent; (*Inform*) pop-up *cpd*; **menú/ventana ~** pop-up menu/window

emerger [emer'xer] *vi* to emerge, appear

emeritense [emeri'tense] *adj* of o from Mérida ■ *nm/f* native o inhabitant of Mérida

emerja *etc* [e'merxa] *vb ver* **emerger**

emigración [emiɣra'θjon] *nf* emigration; (*de pájaros*) migration

emigrado, -a [emi'ɣraðo, a] *nm/f* emigrant; (*Pol etc*) émigré(e)

emigrante [emi'ɣrante] *adj, nm/f* emigrant

emigrar [emi'ɣrar] *vi* (*personas*) to emigrate; (*pájaros*) to migrate

eminencia [emi'nenθja] *nf* eminence; (*en títulos*): **Su E~** His Eminence; **Vuestra E~** Your Eminence

eminente [emi'nente] *adj* eminent, distinguished; (*elevado*) high

emisario [emi'sarjo] *nm* emissary

emisión [emi'sjon] *nf* (*acto*) emission; (*Com etc*) issue; (*Radio, TV: acto*) broadcasting; (: *programa*) broadcast, programme, program (*US*); **~ de acciones** (*Com*) share issue; **~ gratuita de acciones** (*Com*) rights issue; **~ de valores** (*Com*) flotation

emisor, a [emi'sor, a] *nm* transmitter ■ *nf* radio o broadcasting station

emitir [emi'tir] *vt* (*olor etc*) to emit, give off; (*moneda etc*) to issue; (*opinión*) to express; (*voto*) to cast; (*señal*) to send out; (*Radio*) to broadcast; **~ una señal sonora** to beep

emoción [emo'θjon] *nf* emotion; (*excitación*) excitement; (*sentimiento*) feeling; **¡qué ~!** how exciting!; (*irónico*) what a thrill!

emocionado, -a [emoθjo'naðo, a] *adj* deeply moved, stirred

emocionante [emoθjo'nante] *adj* (*excitante*) exciting, thrilling

emocionar [emoθjo'nar] *vt* (*excitar*) to excite, thrill; (*conmover*) to move, touch; (*impresionar*) to impress; **emocionarse** *vr* to get excited

emoticón [emoti'kon] *nm* smiley, emoticon

emotivo, -a [emo'tiβo, a] *adj* emotional

empacar [empa'kar] *vt* (*gen*) to pack; (*en caja*) to bale, crate

empacharse [empa'tʃarse] *vr* (*Med*) to get indigestion

empacho [em'patʃo] *nm* (*Med*) indigestion; (*fig*) embarrassment

empadronamiento [empaðrona'mjento] *nm* census; (*de electores*) electoral register

empadronarse [empaðro'narse] *vr* (*Pol: como elector*) to register

empalagar [empala'ɣar] *vt* (*comida*) to cloy; (*hartar*) to pall on ■ *vi* to pall

empalagoso, -a [empala'ɣoso, a] *adj* cloying; (*fig*) tiresome

empalague *etc* [empa'laɣe] *vb ver* **empalagar**

empalizada [empali'θaða] *nf* fence; (*Mil*) palisade

empalmar [empal'mar] *vt* to join, connect ■ *vi* (*dos caminos*) to meet, join

empalme [em'palme] *nm* joint, connection; (*de vías*) junction; (*de trenes*) connection

empanada [empa'naða] *nf* pie, pasty

empanar [empa'nar] *vt* (*Culin*) to cook o roll in breadcrumbs o pastry

empantanarse [empanta'narse] *vr* to get swamped; (*fig*) to get bogged down

empañarse [empa'ɲarse] *vr* (*nublarse*) to get misty, steam up

empapar [empa'par] *vt* (*mojar*) to soak, saturate; (*absorber*) to soak up, absorb; **empaparse** *vr*: **empaparse de** to soak up

empapelar [empape'lar] *vt* (*paredes*) to paper

empaque *etc* [em'pake] *vb ver* **empacar**

empaquetar [empake'tar] *vt* to pack, parcel up; (*Com*) to package

emparedado [empare'ðaðo] *nm* sandwich

emparejar [empare'xar] *vt* to pair ■ *vi* to catch up

emparentar [emparen'tar] *vi*: **~ con** to marry into

empariente *etc* [empa'rjente] *vb ver* **emparentar**

empastar [empas'tar] *vt* (*embadurnar*) to paste; (*diente*) to fill

empaste [em'paste] *nm* (*de diente*) filling

empatar [empa'tar] *vi* to draw, tie

empate [em'pate] *nm* draw, tie; **un ~ a cero** a no-score draw

empecé [empe'θe], **empecemos** *etc* [empe'θemos] *vb ver* **empezar**

empecinado, -a [empeθi'naðo, a] *adj* stubborn

empedernido, -a [empeðer'niðo, a] *adj* hard, heartless; *(fijado)* hardened, inveterate; **un fumador ~** a heavy smoker

empedrado, -a [empe'ðraðo, a] *adj* paved ■ *nm* paving

empedrar [empe'ðrar] *vt* to pave

empeine [em'peine] *nm (de pie, zapato)* instep

empellón [empe'ʎon] *nm* push, shove; **abrirse paso a empellones** to push *o* shove one's way past *o* through

empeñado, -a [empe'ɲaðo, a] *adj (persona)* determined; *(objeto)* pawned

empeñar [empe'ɲar] *vt (objeto)* to pawn, pledge; *(persona)* to compel; **empeñarse** *vr (obligarse)* to bind o.s., pledge o.s.; *(endeudarse)* to get into debt; **empeñarse en hacer** to be set on doing, be determined to do

empeño [em'peɲo] *nm (determinación)* determination; *(cosa prendada)* pledge; **casa de empeños** pawnshop; **con ~** insistently; *(con celo)* eagerly; **tener ~ en hacer algo** to be bent on doing sth

empeoramiento [empeora'mjento] *nm* worsening

empeorar [empeo'rar] *vt* to make worse, worsen ■ *vi* to get worse, deteriorate

empequeñecer [empekeɲe'θer] *vt* to dwarf; *(fig)* to belittle

empequeñezca *etc* [empeke'ɲeθka] *vb ver* **empequeñecer**

emperador [empera'ðor] *nm* emperor

emperatriz [empera'triθ] *nf* empress

emperrarse [empe'rrarse] *vr* to get stubborn; **~ en algo** to persist in sth

empezar [empe'θar] *vt, vi* to begin, start; **empezó a llover** it started to rain; **bueno, para ~** well, to start with

empiece *etc* [em'pjeθe] *vb ver* **empezar**

empiedre *etc* [em'pjeðre] *vb ver* **empedrar**

empiezo *etc* [em'pjeθo] *vb ver* **empezar**

empinado, -a [empi'naðo, a] *adj* steep

empinar [empi'nar] *vt* to raise; *(botella)* to tip up; **empinarse** *vr (persona)* to stand on tiptoe; *(animal)* to rear up; *(camino)* to climb steeply; **~ el codo** to booze *(fam)*

empingorotado, -a [empingoro'taðo, a] *adj (fam)* stuck-up

empírico, -a [em'piriko, a] *adj* empirical

emplace *etc* [em'plaθe] *vb ver* **emplazar**

emplaste [em'plaste], **emplasto** [em'plasto] *nm (Med)* plaster

emplazamiento [emplaθa'mjento] *nm* site, location; *(Jur)* summons *sg*

emplazar [empla'θar] *vt (ubicar)* to site, place, locate; *(Jur)* to summons; *(convocar)* to summon

empleado, -a [emple'aðo, a] *nm/f (gen)* employee; *(de banco etc)* clerk; **~ público** civil servant

emplear [emple'ar] *vt (usar)* to use, employ; *(dar trabajo a)* to employ; **emplearse** *vr (conseguir trabajo)* to be employed; *(ocuparse)* to occupy o.s.; **~ mal el tiempo** to waste time; **¡te está bien empleado!** it serves you right!

empleo [em'pleo] *nm (puesto)* job; *(puestos: colectivamente)* employment; *(uso)* use, employment; **"modo de ~"** "instructions for use"

emplumar [emplu'mar] *vt (estafar)* to swindle

empobrecer [empoβre'θer] *vt* to impoverish; **empobrecerse** *vr* to become poor *o* impoverished

empobrecimiento [empoβreθi'mjento] *nm* impoverishment

empobrezca *etc* [empo'βreθka] *vb ver* **empobrecer**

empollar [empo'ʎar] *vt* to incubate; *(Escol fam)* to swot (up) ■ *vi (gallina)* to brood; *(Escol fam)* to swot

empollón, -ona [empo'ʎon, ona] *nm/f (Escol fam)* swot

empolvar [empol'βar] *vt (cara)* to powder; **empolvarse** *vr* to powder one's face; *(superficie)* to get dusty

emponzoñar [emponθo'ɲar] *vt (esp fig)* to poison

emporio [em'porjo] *nm* emporium, trading centre; *(Am: gran almacén)* department store

empotrado, -a [empo'traðo, a] *adj (armario etc)* built-in

empotrar [empo'trar] *vt* to embed; *(armario etc)* to build in

emprendedor, a [emprende'ðor, a] *adj* enterprising

emprender [empren'der] *vt* to undertake; *(empezar)* to begin, embark on; *(acometer)* to tackle, take on; **~ marcha a** to set out for

empresa [em'presa] *nf* enterprise; *(Com: sociedad)* firm, company; *(: negocio)* business; *(esp Teat)* management; **~ filial** *(Com)* affiliated company; **~ matriz** *(Com)* parent company

empresarial [empresa'rjal] *adj (función, clase)* managerial; **sector ~** business sector

empresariales [empresa'rjales] *nfpl* business studies

empresario, -a [empre'sarjo, a] *nm/f (Com)* businessman(-woman), entrepreneur; *(Tec)* manager; *(Mus: de ópera etc)* impresario; **~ de pompas fúnebres** undertaker (Brit), mortician (US)

empréstito [em'prestito] *nm (public)* loan; *(Com)* loan capital

empujar | encanezca

empujar [empu'xar] *vt* to push, shove

empuje [em'puxe] *nm* thrust; (*presión*) pressure; (*fig*) vigour, drive

empujón [empu'xon] *nm* push, shove; **abrirse paso a empujones** to shove one's way through

empuñadura [empuɲa'ðura] *nf* (*de espada*) hilt; (*de herramienta etc*) handle

empuñar [empu'ɲar] *vt* (*asir*) to grasp, take (firm) hold of; **~ las armas** (*fig*) to take up arms

emulación [emula'θjon] *nf* emulation

emular [emu'lar] *vt* to emulate; (*rivalizar*) to rival

émulo, -a ['emulo, a] *nm/f* rival, competitor

emulsión [emul'sjon] *nf* emulsion

○ **PALABRA CLAVE**

en [en] *prep* **1** (*posición*) in; (: *sobre*) on; **está en el cajón** it's in the drawer; **en Argentina/La Paz** in Argentina/La Paz; **en el colegio/la oficina** at school/the office; **en casa** at home; **está en el suelo/quinto piso** it's on the floor/the fifth floor; **en el periódico** in the paper

2 (*dirección*) into; **entró en el aula** she went into the classroom; **meter algo en el bolso** to put sth into one's bag; **ir de puerta en puerta** to go from door to door

3 (*tiempo*) in; on; **en 1605/3 semanas/invierno** in 1605/3 weeks/winter; **en (el mes de) enero** in (the month of) January; **en aquella ocasión/época** on that occasion/at that time

4 (*precio*) for; **lo vendió en 20 dólares** he sold it for 20 dollars

5 (*diferencia*) by; **reducir/aumentar en una tercera parte/un 20 por ciento** to reduce/increase by a third/20 per cent

6 (*manera, forma*): **en avión/autobús** by plane/bus; **escrito en inglés** written in English; **en serio** seriously; **en espiral/círculo** in a spiral/circle

7 (*después de vb que indica gastar etc*) on; **han cobrado demasiado en dietas** they've charged too much to expenses; **se le va la mitad del sueldo en comida** half his salary goes on food

8 (*tema, ocupación*): **experto en la materia** expert on the subject; **trabaja en la construcción** he works in the building industry

9 (*adj + en + infin*): **lento en reaccionar** slow to react

enagua [ena'ɣwa] *nf*, **enaguas** [ena'ɣwas] *nfpl* (*esp Am*) petticoat

enajenación [enaxena'θjon] *nf*, **enajenamiento** [enaxena'mjento] ■ *nm* alienation; (*fig: distracción*) absent-mindedness; (: *embelesamiento*) rapture, trance; **~ mental** mental derangement

enajenar [enaxe'nar] *vt* to alienate; (*fig*) to carry away

enamorado, -a [enamo'raðo, a] *adj* in love ■ *nm/f* lover; **estar ~ (de)** to be in love (with)

enamorar [enamo'rar] *vt* to win the love of; **enamorarse** *vr*: **enamorarse (de)** to fall in love (with)

enano, -a [e'nano, a] *adj* tiny, dwarf ■ *nm/f* dwarf; (*pey*) runt

enarbolar [enarβo'lar] *vt* (*bandera etc*) to hoist; (*espada etc*) to brandish

enardecer [enarðe'θer] *vt* (*pasiones*) to fire, inflame; (*persona*) to fill with enthusiasm; **enardecerse** *vr* to get excited; **enardecerse por** to get enthusiastic about

enardezca *etc* [enar'deθka] *vb ver* **enardecer**

encabece *etc* [enka'βeθe] *vb ver* **encabezar**

encabezado [enkaβe'θaðo] *nm* (*Com*) header

encabezamiento [enkaβeθa'mjento] *nm* (*de carta*) heading; (*Com*) billhead, letterhead; (*de periódico*) headline; (*preámbulo*) foreword, preface; **~ normal** (*Tip etc*) running head

encabezar [enkaβe'θar] *vt* (*movimiento, revolución*) to lead, head; (*lista*) to head; (*carta*) to put a heading to; (*libro*) to entitle

encadenar [enkaðe'nar] *vt* to chain (together); (*poner grilletes a*) to shackle

encajar [enka'xar] *vt* (*ajustar*): **~ en** to fit (into); (*meter a la fuerza*) to push in; (*máquina etc*) to house; (*partes*) to join; (*fam: golpe*) to give, deal; (*entremeter*) to insert ■ *vi* to fit (well); (*fig: corresponder a*) to match; **encajarse** *vr*: **encajarse en un sillón** to squeeze into a chair

encaje [en'kaxe] *nm* (*labor*) lace

encajonar [enkaxo'nar] *vt* to box (up), put in a box

encalar [enka'lar] *vt* (*pared*) to whitewash

encallar [enka'ʎar] *vi* (*Naut*) to run aground

encaminado, -a [enkami'naðo, a] *adj*: **medidas encaminadas a ...** measures designed to o aimed at ...

encaminar [enkami'nar] *vt* to direct, send; **encaminarse** *vr*: **encaminarse a** to set out for; **~ por** (*expedición etc*) to route via

encandilar [enkandi'lar] *vt* to dazzle; (*persona*) to daze, bewilder

encanecer [enkane'θer] *vi*, **encanecerse** *vr* (*pelo*) to go grey

encanezca *etc* [enka'neθka] *vb ver* **encanecer**

encantado, -a [enkan'taðo, a] *adj* delighted; ¡~! how do you do!, pleased to meet you

encantador, a [enkanta'ðor, a] *adj* charming, lovely ∎ *nm/f* magician, enchanter/enchantress

encantar [enkan'tar] *vt* to charm, delight; (*cautivar*) to fascinate; (*hechizar*) to bewitch, cast a spell on

encanto [en'kanto] *nm* (*magia*) spell, charm; (*fig*) charm, delight; (*expresión de ternura*) sweetheart; **como por ~** as if by magic

encapotado, -a [enkapo'taðo, a] *adj* (*cielo*) overcast

encapricharse [enkapri'tʃarse] *vr*: **se ha encaprichado con ir** he's taken it into his head to go; **se ha encaprichado** he's digging his heels in

encaramar [enkara'mar] *vt* (*subir*) to raise, lift up; **encaramarse** *vr* (*subir*) to perch; **encaramarse a** (*árbol etc*) to climb

encararse [enka'rarse] *vr*: **~ a** o **con** to confront, come face to face with

encarcelar [enkarθe'lar] *vt* to imprison, jail

encarecer [enkare'θer] *vt* to put up the price of ∎ *vi*, **encarecerse** *vr* to get dearer

encarecidamente [enkareθiða'mente] *adv* earnestly

encarecimiento [enkareθi'mjento] *nm* price increase

encarezca *etc* [enka're θka] *vb ver* **encarecer**

encargado, -a [enkar'ɣaðo, a] *adj* in charge ∎ *nm/f* agent, representative; (*responsable*) person in charge

encargar [enkar'ɣar] *vt* to entrust; (*Com*) to order; (*recomendar*) to urge, recommend; **encargarse** *vr*: **encargarse de** to look after, take charge of; **~ algo a algn** to put sb in charge of sth

encargo [en'karɣo] *nm* (*pedido*) assignment, job; (*responsabilidad*) responsibility; (*recomendación*) recommendation; (*Com*) order

encargue *etc* [en'karɣe] *vb ver* **encargar**

encariñarse [enkari'ɲarse] *vr*: **~ con** to grow fond of, get attached to

encarnación [enkarna'θjon] *nf* incarnation, embodiment

encarnado, -a [enkar'naðo, a] *adj* (*color*) red; **ponerse ~** to blush

encarnar [enkar'nar] *vt* to personify; (*Teat: papel*) to play ∎ *vi* (*Rel etc*) to become incarnate

encarnizado, -a [enkarni'θaðo, a] *adj* (*lucha*) bloody, fierce

encarrilar [enkarri'lar] *vt* (*tren*) to put back on the rails; (*fig*) to correct, put on the right track

encasillar [enkasi'ʎar] *vt* (*Teat*) to typecast; (*clasificar: pey*) to pigeonhole

encasquetar [enkaske'tar] *vt* (*sombrero*) to pull down o on; **encasquetarse** *vr*: **encasquetarse el sombrero** to pull one's hat down o on; **~ algo a algn** to offload sth onto sb

encauce *etc* [en'kauθe] *vb ver* **encauzar**

encausar [enkau'sar] *vt* to prosecute, sue

encauzar [enkau'θar] *vt* to channel; (*fig*) to direct

encendedor [enθende'ðor] *nm* lighter

encender [enθen'der] *vt* (*con fuego*) to light; (*incendiar*) to set fire to; (*luz, radio*) to put on, switch on; (*Inform*) to toggle on, switch on; (*avivar: pasiones etc*) to inflame; (*despertar: entusiasmo*) to arouse; (*odio*) to awaken; **encenderse** *vr* to catch fire; (*excitarse*) to get excited; (*de cólera*) to flare up; (*el rostro*) to blush

encendidamente [enθendiða'mente] *adv* passionately

encendido, -a [enθen'diðo, a] *adj* alight; (*aparato*) (switched) on; (*mejillas*) glowing; (*cara: por el vino etc*) flushed; (*mirada*) passionate ∎ *nm* (*Auto*) ignition; (*de faroles*) lighting

encerado, -a [enθe'raðo, a] *adj* (*suelo*) waxed, polished ∎ *nm* (*Escol*) blackboard; (*hule*) oilcloth

encerar [enθe'rar] *vt* (*suelo*) to wax, polish

encerrar [enθe'rrar] *vt* (*confinar*) to shut in o up; (*con llave*) to lock in o up; (*comprender, incluir*) to include, contain; **encerrarse** *vr* to shut o lock o.s. up o in

encerrona [enθe'rrona] *nf* trap

encestar [enθes'tar] *vi* to score a basket

encharcar [entʃar'kar] *vt* to swamp, flood; **encharcarse** *vr* to become flooded

encharque *etc* [en'tʃarke] *vb ver* **encharcar**

enchufar [entʃu'far] *vt* (*Elec*) to plug in; (*Tec*) to connect, fit together; (*Com*) to merge

enchufe [en'tʃufe] *nm* (*Elec: clavija*) plug; (*: toma*) socket; (*de dos tubos*) joint, connection; (*fam: influencia*) contact, connection; (*puesto*) cushy job; **~ de clavija** jack plug; **tiene un ~ en el ministerio** he can pull strings at the ministry

encía [en'θia] *nf* (*Anat*) gum

enciclopedia [enθiklo'peðja] *nf* encyclopaedia

encienda *etc* [en'θjenda] *vb ver* **encender**

encierro *etc* [en'θjerro] *vb ver* **encerrar** ∎ *nm* shutting in o up; (*calabozo*) prison; (*Agr*) pen; (*Taur*) penning

encima [en'θima] *adv* (*sobre*) above, over; (*además*) besides; **~ de** (*en*) on, on top of; (*sobre*) above, over; (*además de*) besides, on top of; **por ~ de** over; **¿llevas dinero ~?** have you (got) any money on you?; **se me vino ~** it took me by surprise

encina [en'θina] *nf* (holm) oak

encinta [en'θinta] *adj f* pregnant

enclave [en'klaβe] *nm* enclave

enclenque [en'klenke] *adj* weak, sickly

encoger [enko'xer] *vt* (*gen*) to shrink, contract; (*fig: asustar*) to scare; (*: desanimar*) to discourage; **encogerse** *vr* to shrink, contract; (*fig*) to cringe; **encogerse de hombros** to shrug one's shoulders

encoja *etc* [en'koxa] *vb ver* **encoger**

encolar [enko'lar] *vt* (*engomar*) to glue, paste; (*pegar*) to stick down

encolerice *etc* [enkole'riθe] *vb ver* **encolerizar**

encolerizar [enkoleri'θar] *vt* to anger, provoke; **encolerizarse** *vr* to get angry

encomendar [enkomen'dar] *vt* to entrust, commend; **encomendarse** *vr*: **encomendarse a** to put one's trust in

encomiar [enko'mjar] *vt* to praise, pay tribute to

encomienda *etc* [enko'mjenda] *vb ver* **encomendar** ■ *nf* (*encargo*) charge, commission; (*elogio*) tribute; (*Am*) parcel, package; **~ postal** (*Am*) parcel post

encomio [en'komjo] *nm* praise, tribute

encono [en'kono] *nm* (*rencor*) rancour, spite

encontrado, -a [enkon'traðo, a] *adj* (*contrario*) contrary, conflicting; (*hostil*) hostile

encontrar [enkon'trar] *vt* (*hallar*) to find; (*inesperadamente*) to meet, run into; **encontrarse** *vr* to meet (each other); (*situarse*) to be (situated); (*persona*) to find o.s., be; (*entrar en conflicto*) to crash, collide; **encontrarse con** to meet; **encontrarse bien (de salud)** to feel well; **no se encuentra aquí en este momento** he's not in at the moment

encontronazo [enkontro'naθo] *nm* collision, crash

encorvar [enkor'βar] *vt* to curve; (*inclinar*) to bend (down); **encorvarse** *vr* to bend down, bend over

encrespado, -a [enkres'paðo, a] *adj* (*pelo*) curly; (*mar*) rough

encrespar [enkres'par] *vt* (*cabellos*) to curl; (*fig*) to anger, irritate; **encresparse** *vr* (*el mar*) to get rough; (*fig*) to get cross o irritated

encrucijada [enkruθi'xaða] *nf* crossroads *sg*; (*empalme*) junction

encuadernación [enkwaðerna'θjon] *nf* binding; (*taller*) binder's

encuadernador, a [enkwaðerna'ðor, a] *nm/f* bookbinder

encuadrar [enkwa'ðrar] *vt* (*retrato*) to frame; (*ajustar*) to fit, insert; (*encerrar*) to contain

encubierto [enku'βjerto] *pp de* **encubrir**

encubrir [enku'βrir] *vt* (*ocultar*) to hide, conceal; (*criminal*) to harbour, shelter; (*ayudar*) to be an accomplice in

encuentro *etc* [en'kwentro] *vb ver* **encontrar** ■ *nm* (*de personas*) meeting; (*Auto etc*) collision, crash; (*Deporte*) match, game; (*Mil*) encounter

encuesta [en'kwesta] *nf* inquiry, investigation; (*sondeo*) public opinion poll; **~ judicial** post-mortem

encumbrado, -a [enkum'braðo, a] *adj* eminent, distinguished

encumbrar [enkum'brar] *vt* (*persona*) to exalt; **encumbrarse** *vr* (*fig*) to become conceited

endeble [en'deβle] *adj* (*argumento, excusa, persona*) weak

endémico, -a [en'demiko, a] *adj* endemic

endemoniado, -a [endemo'njaðo, a] *adj* possessed (of the devil); (*travieso*) devilish

enderece *etc* [ende'reθe] *vb ver* **enderezar**

enderezar [endere'θar] *vt* (*poner derecho*) to straighten (out); (*: verticalmente*) to set upright; (*fig*) to straighten o sort out; (*dirigir*) to direct; **enderezarse** *vr* (*persona sentada*) to sit up straight

endeudarse [endeu'ðarse] *vr* to get into debt

endiablado, -a [endja'βlaðo, a] *adj* devilish, diabolical; (*humorístico*) mischievous

endibia [en'diβja] *nf* endive

endilgar [endil'yar] *vt* (*fam*): **~ algo a algn** to lumber sb with sth; **~ un sermón a algn** to give sb a lecture

endilgue *etc* [en'dilɣe] *vb ver* **endilgar**

endiñar [endi'ɲar] *vt*: **~ algo a algn** to land sth on sb

endomingarse [endomin'garse] *vr* to dress up, put on one's best clothes

endomingue *etc* [endo'minge] *vb ver* **endomingarse**

endosar [endo'sar] *vt* (*cheque etc*) to endorse

endulce *etc* [en'dulθe] *vb ver* **endulzar**

endulzar [endul'θar] *vt* to sweeten; (*suavizar*) to soften

endurecer [endure'θer] *vt* to harden; **endurecerse** *vr* to harden, grow hard

endurecido, -a [endure'θiðo, a] *adj* (*duro*) hard; (*fig*) hardy, tough; **estar ~ a algo** to be hardened o used to sth

endurezca *etc* [endu're θka] *vb ver* **endurecer**

ene. *abr* (= *enero*) Jan.

enemigo, -a [ene'miɣo, a] *adj* enemy, hostile ■ *nm/f* enemy ■ *nf* enmity, hostility; **ser ~ de** (*persona*) to dislike; (*tendencia*) to be inimical to

enemistad [enemis'tað] *nf* enmity

enemistar [enemis'tar] *vt* to make enemies of, cause a rift between; **enemistarse** *vr* to become enemies; (*amigos*) to fall out

energético, -a [ener'xetiko, a] *adj*: **política energética** energy policy

energía [ener'xia] *nf* (*vigor*) energy, drive; (*Tec, Elec*) energy, power; **~ atómica/eléctrica/ eólica** atomic/electric/wind power; **energías renovables** renewable energy sources

enérgico, -a [e'nerxiko, a] *adj* (*gen*) energetic; (*ataque*) vigorous; (*ejercicio*) strenuous; (*medida*) bold; (*voz, modales*) forceful

energúmeno, -a [ener'ɣumeno, a] *nm/f* madman(-woman); **ponerse como un ~ con algn** to get furious with sb

enero [e'nero] *nm* January; *ver tb* **julio**

enervar [ener'βar] *vt* (*poner nervioso a*) to get on sb's nerves

enésimo, -a [e'nesimo, a] *adj* (*Mat*) nth; **por enésima vez** (*fig*) for the umpteenth time

enfadado, -a [enfa'ðaðo, a] *adj* angry, annoyed

enfadar [enfa'ðar] *vt* to anger, annoy; **enfadarse** *vr* to get angry o annoyed

enfado [en'faðo] *nm* (*enojo*) anger, annoyance; (*disgusto*) trouble, bother

énfasis ['enfasis] *nm* emphasis, stress; **poner énfasis en** to stress

enfático, -a [en'fatiko, a] *adj* emphatic

enfatizado, -a [enfati'θaðo, a] *adj*: **en caracteres enfatizados** (*Inform*) emphasized

enfermar [enfer'mar] *vt* to make ill ▪ *vi* to fall ill, be taken ill; **su actitud me enferma** his attitude makes me sick; **~ del corazón** to develop heart trouble

enfermedad [enferme'ðað] *nf* illness; **~ venérea** venereal disease

enfermera [enfer'mera] *nf ver* **enfermero**

enfermería [enferme'ria] *nf* infirmary; (*de colegio etc*) sick bay

enfermero, -a [enfer'mero, a] *nm* (male) nurse ▪ *nf* nurse; **enfermera jefa** matron

enfermizo, -a [enfer'miθo, a] *adj* (*persona*) sickly, unhealthy; (*fig*) unhealthy

enfermo, -a [en'fermo, a] *adj* ill, sick ▪ *nm/f* invalid, sick person; (*en hospital*) patient

enfilar [enfi'lar] *vt* (*aguja*) to thread; (*calle*) to go down

enflaquecer [enflake'θer] *vt* (*adelgazar*) to make thin; (*debilitar*) to weaken

enflaquezca *etc* [enfla'keθka] *vb ver* **enflaquecer**

enfocar [enfo'kar] *vt* (*foto etc*) to focus; (*problema etc*) to consider, look at

enfoque *etc* [en'foke] *vb ver* **enfocar** ▪ *nm* focus; (*acto*) focusing; (*óptica*) approach

enfrascado, -a [enfras'kaðo, a] *adj*: **estar ~ en algo** (*fig*) to be wrapped up in sth

enfrascarse [enfras'karse] *vr*: **~ en un libro** to bury o.s. in a book

enfrasque *etc* [en'fraske] *vb ver* **enfrascarse**

enfrentamiento [enfrenta'mjento] *nm* confrontation

enfrentar [enfren'tar] *vt* (*peligro*) to face (up to), confront; (*oponer*) to bring face to face; **enfrentarse** *vr* (*dos personas*) to face o confront each other; (*Deporte: dos equipos*) to meet; **enfrentarse a** o **con** to face up to, confront

enfrente [en'frente] *adv* opposite; **~ de** *prep* opposite, facing; **la casa de ~** the house opposite, the house across the street

enfriamiento [enfria'mjento] *nm* chilling, refrigeration; (*Med*) cold, chill

enfriar [enfri'ar] *vt* (*alimentos*) to cool, chill; (*algo caliente*) to cool down; (*habitación*) to air, freshen; (*entusiasmo*) to dampen; **enfriarse** *vr* to cool down; (*Med*) to catch a chill; (*amistad*) to cool

enfurecer [enfure'θer] *vt* to enrage, madden; **enfurecerse** *vr* to become furious, fly into a rage; (*mar*) to get rough

enfurezca *etc* [enfu're θka] *vb ver* **enfurecer**

engalanar [engala'nar] *vt* (*adornar*) to adorn; (*ciudad*) to decorate; **engalanarse** *vr* to get dressed up

enganchar [engan'tʃar] *vt* to hook; (*ropa*) to hang up; (*dos vagones*) to hitch up; (*Tec*) to couple, connect; (*Mil*) to recruit; (*fam: atraer: persona*) to rope into; **engancharse** *vr* (*Mil*) to enlist, join up; **engancharse (a)** (*drogas*) to get hooked (on)

enganche [en'gantʃe] *nm* hook; (*Tec*) coupling, connection; (*acto*) hooking (up); (*Mil*) recruitment, enlistment; (*Am: depósito*) deposit

engañar [enga'ɲar] *vt* to deceive; (*estafar*) to cheat, swindle ▪ *vi*: **las apariencias engañan** appearances are deceptive; **engañarse** *vr* (*equivocarse*) to be wrong; (*asimismo*) to deceive o kid o.s.; **engaña a su mujer** he's unfaithful to o cheats on his wife

engaño [en'gaɲo] *nm* deceit; (*estafa*) trick, swindle; (*error*) mistake, misunderstanding; (*ilusión*) delusion

engañoso, -a [enga'ɲoso, a] *adj* (*tramposo*) crooked; (*mentiroso*) dishonest, deceitful; (*aspecto*) deceptive; (*consejo*) misleading

engarce *etc* [en'garθe] *vb ver* **engarzar**

engarzar [engar'θar] *vt* (*joya*) to set, mount; (*fig*) to link, connect

engatusar [engatu'sar] *vt* (*fam*) to coax

engendrar [enxen'drar] *vt* to breed; (*procrear*) to beget; (*fig*) to cause, produce

engendro [en'xendro] *nm* (*Bio*) foetus; (*fig*) monstrosity; (: *idea*) brainchild

englobar [englo'βar] *vt* (*comprender*) to include, comprise; (*incluir*) to lump together

engomar [engo'mar] *vt* to glue, stick

engordar [engor'ðar] *vt* to fatten ■ *vi* to get fat, put on weight

engorro [en'gorro] *nm* bother, nuisance

engorroso, -a [engo'rroso, a] *adj* bothersome, trying

engranaje [engra'naxe] *nm* (*Auto*) gear; (*juego*) gears *pl*

engrandecer [engrande'θer] *vt* to enlarge, magnify; (*alabar*) to praise, speak highly of; (*exagerar*) to exaggerate

engrandezca *etc* [engran'deθka] *vb ver* **engrandecer**

engrasar [engra'sar] *vt* (*Tec*: *poner grasa*) to grease; (: *lubricar*) to lubricate, oil; (*manchar*) to make greasy

engrase [en'grase] *nm* greasing, lubrication

engreído, -a [engre'iðo, a] *adj* vain, conceited

engrosar [engro'sar] *vt* (*ensanchar*) to enlarge; (*aumentar*) to increase; (*hinchar*) to swell

engrudo [en'gruðo] *nm* paste

engruese *etc* [en'grwese] *vb ver* **engrosar**

engullir [engu'ʎir] *vt* to gobble, gulp (down)

enhebrar [ene'βrar] *vt* to thread

enhiesto, -a [e'njesto, a] *adj* (*derecho*) erect; (*bandera*) raised; (*edificio*) lofty

enhorabuena [enora'βwena] *excl* congratulations

enigma [e'niɣma] *nm* enigma; (*problema*) puzzle; (*misterio*) mystery

enigmático, -a [eniɣ'matiko, a] *adj* enigmatic

enjabonar [enxaβo'nar] *vt* to soap; (*barba*) to lather; (*fam*: *adular*) to soft-soap; (: *regañar*) to tick off

enjalbegar [enxalβe'ɣar] *vt* (*pared*) to whitewash

enjalbegue *etc* [enxal'βeɣe] *vb ver* **enjalbegar**

enjambre [en'xamβre] *nm* swarm

enjaular [enxau'lar] *vt* to (put in a) cage; (*fam*) to jail, lock up

enjuagar [enxwa'ɣar] *vt* (*ropa*) to rinse (out)

enjuague *etc* [en'xwaɣe] *vb ver* **enjuagar** ■ *nm* (*Med*) mouthwash; (*de ropa*) rinse, rinsing

enjugar [enxu'ɣar] *vt* to wipe (off); (*lágrimas*) to dry; (*déficit*) to wipe out

enjugue *etc* [en'xuɣe] *vb ver* **enjugar**

enjuiciar [enxwi'θjar] *vt* (*Jur*: *procesar*) to prosecute, try; (*fig*) to judge

enjuto, -a [en'xuto, a] *adj* dry, dried up; (*fig*) lean, skinny

enlace *etc* [en'laθe] *vb ver* **enlazar** ■ *nm* link, connection; (*relación*) relationship; (*tb*: ~ **matrimonial**) marriage; (*de trenes*) connection; ~ **de datos** data link; ~ **sindical** shop steward; ~ **telefónico** telephone link-up

enlazar [enla'θar] *vt* (*unir con lazos*) to bind together; (*atar*) to tie; (*conectar*) to link, connect; (*Am*) to lasso

enlodar [enlo'ðar] *vt* to cover in mud; (*fig*: *manchar*) to stain; (: *rebajar*) to debase

enloquecer [enloke'θer] *vt* to drive mad ■ *vi*, **enloquecerse** *vr* to go mad

enloquezca *etc* [enlo'keθka] *vb ver* **enloquecer**

enlutado, -a [enlu'taðo, a] *adj* (*persona*) in mourning

enlutar [enlu'tar] *vt* to dress in mourning; **enlutarse** *vr* to go into mourning

enmarañar [enmara'ɲar] *vt* (*enredar*) to tangle up, entangle; (*complicar*) to complicate; (*confundir*) to confuse; **enmarañarse** *vr* (*enredarse*) to become entangled; (*confundirse*) to get confused

enmarcar [enmar'kar] *vt* (*cuadro*) to frame; (*fig*) to provide a setting for

enmarque *etc* [en'marke] *vb ver* **enmarcar**

enmascarar [enmaska'rar] *vt* to mask; (*intenciones*) to disguise; **enmascararse** *vr* to put on a mask

enmendar [enmen'dar] *vt* to emend, correct; (*constitución etc*) to amend; (*comportamiento*) to reform; **enmendarse** *vr* to reform, mend one's ways

enmienda *etc* [en'mjenda] *vb ver* **enmendar** ■ *nf* correction; amendment; reform

enmohecerse [enmoe'θerse] *vr* (*metal*) to rust, go rusty; (*muro, plantas*) to go mouldy

enmohezca *etc* [enmo'eθka] *vb ver* **enmohecerse**

enmudecer [enmuðe'θer] *vt* to silence ■ *vi*, **enmudecerse** *vr* (*perder el habla*) to fall silent; (*guardar silencio*) to remain silent; (*por miedo*) to be struck dumb

enmudezca *etc* [enmu'ðeθka] *vb ver* **enmudecer**

ennegrecer [enneɣre'θer] *vt* (*poner negro*) to blacken; (*oscurecer*) to darken; **ennegrecerse** *vr* to turn black; (*oscurecerse*) to get dark, darken

ennegrezca *etc* [enne'ɣreθka] *vb ver* **ennegrecer**

ennoblecer [ennoβle'θer] *vt* to ennoble

ennoblezca *etc* [enno'βleθka] *vb ver* **ennoblecer**

en.° abr (= enero) Jan.

enojadizo, -a [enoxa'ðiθo, a] adj irritable, short-tempered

enojar [eno'xar] (esp Am) vt (encolerizar) to anger; (disgustar) to annoy, upset; **enojarse** vr to get angry; to get annoyed

enojo [e'noxo] nm (esp Am: cólera) anger; (irritación) annoyance; **enojos** nmpl trials, problems

enojoso, -a [eno'xoso, a] adj annoying

enorgullecerse [enorɣuʎe'θerse] vr to be proud; ~ **de** to pride o.s. on, be proud of

enorgullezca etc [enorɣu'ʎeθka] vb ver **enorgullecerse**

enorme [e'norme] adj enormous, huge; (fig) monstrous

enormidad [enormi'ðað] nf hugeness, immensity

enraice etc [en'raiθe] vb ver **enraizar**

enraizar [enrai'θar] vi to take root

enrarecido, -a [enrare'θiðo, a] adj rarefied

enredadera [enreða'ðera] nf (Bot) creeper, climbing plant

enredar [enre'ðar] vt (cables, hilos etc) to tangle (up), entangle; (situación) to complicate, confuse; (meter cizaña) to sow discord among o between; (implicar) to embroil, implicate; **enredarse** vr to get entangled, get tangled (up); (situación) to get complicated; (persona) to get embroiled

enredo [en'reðo] nm (maraña) tangle; (confusión) mix-up, confusion; (intriga) intrigue; (apuro) jam; (amorío) love affair

enrejado [enre'xaðo] nm grating; (de ventana) lattice; (en jardín) trellis

enrevesado, -a [enreβe'saðo, a] adj (asunto) complicated, involved

enriquecer [enrike'θer] vt to make rich; (fig) to enrich; **enriquecerse** vr to get rich

enriquezca etc [enri'keθka] vb ver **enriquecer**

enrojecer [enroxe'θer] vt to redden ∎ vi, **enrojecerse** vr (persona) to blush

enrojezca etc [enro'xeθka] vb ver **enrojecer**

enrolar [enro'lar] vt (Mil) to enlist; (reclutar) to recruit; **enrolarse** vr (Mil) to join up; (afiliarse) to enrol, sign on

enrollar [enro'ʎar] vt to roll (up), wind (up); **enrollarse** vr: **enrollarse con algn** to get involved with sb

enroque [en'roke] nm (Ajedrez) castling

enroscar [enros'kar] vt (torcer, doblar) to twist; (arrollar) to coil (round), wind; (tornillo, rosca) to screw in; **enroscarse** vr to coil, wind

enrosque etc [en'roske] vb ver **enroscar**

ensalada [ensa'laða] nf salad; (lío) mix-up

ensaladilla [ensala'ðiʎa] nf (tb: **ensaladilla rusa**) ≈ Russian salad

ensalce etc [en'salθe] vb ver **ensalzar**

ensalzar [ensal'θar] vt (alabar) to praise, extol; (exaltar) to exalt

ensamblador [ensambla'ðor] nm (Inform) assembler

ensambladura [ensambla'ðura] nf, **ensamblaje** [ensam'blaxe] nm assembly; (Tec) joint

ensamblar [ensam'blar] vt (montar) to assemble; (madera etc) to join

ensanchar [ensan'tʃar] vt (hacer más ancho) to widen; (agrandar) to enlarge, expand; (Costura) to let out; **ensancharse** vr to get wider, expand; (pey) to give o.s. airs

ensanche [en'santʃe] nm (de calle) widening; (de negocio) expansion

ensangrentado, -a [ensangren'taðo, a] adj bloodstained, covered with blood

ensangrentar [ensangren'tar] vt to stain with blood

ensangriente etc [ensan'grjente] vb ver **ensangrentar**

ensañarse [ensa'ɲarse] vr: ~ **con** to treat brutally

ensartar [ensar'tar] vt (gen) to string (together); (carne) to spit, skewer

ensayar [ensa'jar] vt to test, try (out); (Teat) to rehearse

ensayista [ensa'jista] nm/f essayist

ensayo [en'sajo] nm test, trial; (Química) experiment; (Teat) rehearsal; (Deporte) try; (Escol, Lit) essay; **pedido de ~** (Com) trial order; ~ **general** (Teat) dress rehearsal; (Mus) full rehearsal

enseguida [ense'ɣuiða] adv at once, right away; ~ **termino** I've nearly finished, I shan't be long now

ensenada [ense'naða] nf inlet, cove

enseña [en'seɲa] nf ensign, standard

enseñante [ense'ɲante] nm/f teacher

enseñanza [ense'ɲanθa] nf (educación) education; (acción) teaching; (doctrina) teaching, doctrine; ~ **primaria/secundaria/ superior** primary/secondary/higher education

enseñar [ense'ɲar] vt (educar) to teach; (instruir) to teach, instruct; (mostrar, señalar) to show

enseres [en'seres] nmpl belongings

ensillar [ensi'ʎar] vt to saddle (up)

ensimismarse [ensimis'marse] vr (abstraerse) to become lost in thought; (estar absorto) to be lost in thought; (Am) to become conceited

ensopar [enso'par] vt (Am) to soak

ensordecer [ensorðe'θer] vt to deafen ∎ vi to go deaf

ensordezca etc [ensor'ðeθka] vb ver **ensordecer**

ensortijado, -a [ensorti'xaðo, a] *adj* (*pelo*) curly

ensuciar [ensu'θjar] *vt* (*manchar*) to dirty, soil; (*fig*) to defile; **ensuciarse** *vr* (*mancharse*) to get dirty; (*niño*) to dirty (*o* wet) o.s.

ensueño [en'sweɲo] *nm* (*sueño*) dream, fantasy; (*ilusión*) illusion; (*soñando despierto*) daydream; **de** ~ dream-like

entablado [enta'βlaðo] *nm* (*piso*) floorboards *pl*; (*armazón*) boarding

entablar [enta'βlar] *vt* (*recubrir*) to board (up); (*Ajedrez, Damas*) to set up; (*conversación*) to strike up; (*Jur*) to file ■ *vi* to draw

entablillar [entaβli'ʎar] *vt* (*Med*) to (put in a) splint

entallado, -a [enta'ʎaðo, a] *adj* waisted

entallar [enta'ʎar] *vt* (*traje*) to tailor ■ *vi*: **el traje entalla bien** the suit fits well

ente ['ente] *nm* (*organización*) body, organization; (*compañía*) company; (*fam: persona*) odd character; (*ser*) being; ~ **público** (*Esp*) state(-owned) body

entender [enten'der] *vt* (*comprender*) to understand; (*darse cuenta*) to realize; (*querer decir*) to mean ■ *vi* to understand; (*creer*) to think, believe ■ *nm*: **a mi** ~ in my opinion; ~ **de** to know all about; ~ **algo de** to know a little about; ~ **en** to deal with, have to do with; **entenderse** *vr* (*comprenderse*) to be understood; (*2 personas*) to get on together; (*ponerse de acuerdo*) to agree, reach an agreement; **dar a** ~ **que ...** to lead to believe that ...; **entenderse mal** to get on badly; **¿entiendes?** (do you) understand?

entendido, -a [enten'diðo, a] *adj* (*comprendido*) understood; (*hábil*) skilled; (*inteligente*) knowledgeable ■ *nm/f* (*experto*) expert ■ *excl* agreed!

entendimiento [entendi'mjento] *nm* (*comprensión*) understanding; (*inteligencia*) mind, intellect; (*juicio*) judgement

enterado, -a [ente'raðo, a] *adj* well-informed; **estar** ~ **de** to know about, be aware of; **no darse por** ~ to pretend not to understand

enteramente [entera'mente] *adv* entirely, completely

enterarse [ente'rarse] *vr*: ~ **(de)** to find out (about); **para que te enteres ...** (*fam*) for your information ...

entereza [ente'reθa] *nf* (*totalidad*) entirety; (*fig: de carácter*) strength of mind; (*honradez*) integrity

enternecedor, a [enterneθe'ðor, a] *adj* touching

enternecer [enterne'θer] *vt* (*ablandar*) to soften; (*apiadar*) to touch, move;

enternecerse *vr* to be touched, be moved

enternezca *etc* [enter'neθka] *vb ver* **enternecer**

entero, -a [en'tero, a] *adj* (*total*) whole, entire; (*fig: recto*) honest; (: *firme*) firm, resolute ■ *nm* (*Mat*) integer; (*Com: punto*) point; (*Am: pago*) payment; **las acciones han subido dos enteros** the shares have gone up two points

enterrador [enterra'ðor] *nm* gravedigger

enterrar [ente'rrar] *vt* to bury; (*fig*) to forget

entibiar [enti'βjar] *vt* (*enfriar*) to cool; (*calentar*) to warm; **entibiarse** *vr* (*fig*) to cool

entidad [enti'ðað] *nf* (*empresa*) firm, company; (*organismo*) body; (*sociedad*) society; (*Filosofía*) entity

entienda *etc* [en'tjenda] *vb ver* **entender**

entierro *etc* [en'tjerro] *vb ver* **enterrar** ■ *nm* (*acción*) burial; (*funeral*) funeral

entomología [entomolo'xia] *nf* entomology

entomólogo, -a [ento'moloɣo, a] *nm/f* entomologist

entonación [entona'θjon] *nf* (*Ling*) intonation; (*fig*) conceit

entonar [ento'nar] *vt* (*canción*) to intone; (*colores*) to tone; (*Med*) to tone up ■ *vi* to be in tune; **entonarse** *vr* (*engreírse*) to give o.s. airs

entonces [en'tonθes] *adv* then, at that time; **desde** ~ since then; **en aquel** ~ at that time; **(pues)** ~ and so; **el** ~ **embajador de España** the then Spanish ambassador

entornar [entor'nar] *vt* (*puerta, ventana*) to half close, leave ajar; (*los ojos*) to screw up

entorno [en'torno] *nm* setting, environment; ~ **de redes** (*Inform*) network environment

entorpecer [entorpe'θer] *vt* (*entendimiento*) to dull; (*impedir*) to obstruct, hinder; (: *tránsito*) to slow down, delay

entorpezca *etc* [entor'peθka] *vb ver* **entorpecer**

entrado, -a [en'traðo, a] *adj*: ~ **en años** elderly; **(una vez)** ~ **el verano** in the summer(time), when summer comes ■ *nf* (*acción*) entry, access; (*sitio*) entrance, way in; (*principio*) beginning; (*Com*) receipts *pl*, takings *pl*; (*Culin*) entrée; (*Deporte*) innings *sg*; (*Teat*) house, audience; (*para el cine etc*) ticket; (*Inform*) input; (*Econ*): **entradas** *nfpl* income *sg*; **entradas brutas** gross receipts; **entradas y salidas** (*Com*) income and expenditure; **entrada de aire** (*Tec*) air intake *o* inlet; **de entrada** right away; **"entrada gratis"** "admission free"; **tiene entradas** he's losing his hair

entrante [en'trante] *adj* next, coming; (*Pol*) incoming ■ *nm* inlet; (*Culin*) starter; **mes/año** ~ next month/year

entraña [en'traɲa] *nf* (*fig: centro*) heart, core; (*raíz*) root; **entrañas** *nfpl* (*Anat*) entrails; (*fig*) heart *sg*

entrañable [entra'ɲaβle] *adj* (*persona, lugar*) dear; (*relación*) close; (*acto*) intimate

entrañar [entra'ɲar] *vt* to entail

entrar [en'trar] *vt* (*introducir*) to bring in; (*persona*) to show in; (*Inform*) to input ▪ *vi* (*meterse*) to go *o* come in, enter; (*comenzar*): **~ diciendo** to begin by saying; **entré en** *o* **a** (*Am*) **la casa** I went into the house; **le entraron ganas de reír** he felt a sudden urge to laugh; **no me entra** I can't get the hang of it

entre ['entre] *prep* (*dos*) between; (*en medio de*) among(st); (*por*): **se abrieron paso ~ la multitud** they forced their way through the crowd; **~ una cosa y otra** what with one thing and another; **~ más estudia más aprende** (*Am*) the more he studies the more he learns

entreabierto [entrea'βjerto] *pp de* **entreabrir**

entreabrir [entrea'βrir] *vt* to half-open, open halfway

entreacto [entre'akto] *nm* interval

entrecano, -a [entre'kano, a] *adj* greying; **ser ~** (*persona*) to be going grey

entrecejo [entre'θexo] *nm*: **fruncir el ~** to frown

entrechocar [entretʃo'kar] *vi* (*dientes*) to chatter

entrechoque *etc* [entre'tʃoke] *vb ver* **entrechocar**

entrecomillado, -a [entrekomi'ʎaðo, a] *adj* in inverted commas

entrecortado, -a [entrekor'taðo, a] *adj* (*respiración*) laboured, difficult; (*habla*) faltering

entrecot [entre'ko(t)] *nm* (*Culin*) sirloin steak

entrecruce *etc* [entre'kruθe] *vb ver* **entrecruzarse**

entrecruzarse [entrekru'θarse] *vr* (*Bio*) to interbreed

entredicho [entre'ðitʃo] *nm* (*Jur*) injunction; **poner en ~** to cast doubt on; **estar en ~** to be in doubt

entrega [en'treɣa] *nf* (*de mercancías*) delivery; (*de premios*) presentation; (*de novela etc*) instalment; **"~ a domicilio"** "door-to-door delivery service"

entregar [entre'ɣar] *vt* (*dar*) to hand (over), deliver; (*ejercicios*) to hand in; **entregarse** *vr* (*rendirse*) to surrender, give in, submit; **entregarse a** (*dedicarse*) to devote o.s. to; **a ~** (*Com*) to be supplied

entregue *etc* [en'treɣe] *vb ver* **entregar**

entrelace *etc* [entre'laθe] *vb ver* **entrelazar**

entrelazar [entrela'θar] *vt* to entwine

entremedias [entre'meðjas] *adv* (*en medio*) in between, halfway

entremeses [entre'meses] *nmpl* hors d'œuvres

entremeter [entreme'ter] *vt* to insert, put in; **entremeterse** *vr* to meddle, interfere

entremetido, -a [entreme'tiðo, a] *adj* meddling, interfering

entremezclar [entremeθ'klar] *vt*, **entremezclarse** *vr* to intermingle

entrenador, a [entrena'ðor, a] *nm/f* trainer, coach

entrenamiento [entrena'mjento] *nm* training

entrenar [entre'nar] *vt* (*Deporte*) to train; (*caballo*) to exercise ▪ *vi*, **entrenarse** *vr* to train

entrepierna [entre'pjerna] *nf* (*tb*: **entrepiernas**) crotch, crutch

entresacar [entresa'kar] *vt* to pick out, select

entresaque *etc* [entre'sake] *vb ver* **entresacar**

entresuelo [entre'swelo] *nm* mezzanine, entresol; (*Teat*) dress *o* first circle

entretanto [entre'tanto] *adv* meanwhile, meantime

entretejer [entrete'xer] *vt* to interweave

entretela [entre'tela] *nf* (*de ropa*) interlining; **entretelas** *nfpl* heartstrings

entretención [entreten'sjon] *nf* (*Am*) entertainment

entretendré *etc* [entreten'dre] *vb ver* **entretener**

entretener [entrete'ner] *vt* (*divertir*) to entertain, amuse; (*detener*) to hold up, delay; (*mantener*) to maintain; **entretenerse** *vr* (*divertirse*) to amuse o.s.; (*retrasarse*) to delay, linger; **no le entretengo más** I won't keep you any longer

entretenga *etc* [entre'tenga] *vb ver* **entretener**

entretenido, -a [entrete'niðo, a] *adj* entertaining, amusing

entretenimiento [entreteni'mjento] *nm* entertainment, amusement; (*mantenimiento*) upkeep, maintenance

entretiempo [entre'tjempo] *nm*: **ropa de ~** *clothes for spring and autumn*

entretiene *etc* [entre'tjene], **entretuve** *etc* [entre'tuβe] *vb ver* **entretener**

entreveía *etc* [entreβe'ia] *vb ver* **entrever**

entrever [entre'βer] *vt* to glimpse, catch a glimpse of

entrevista [entre'βista] *nf* interview

entrevistar [entreβis'tar] *vt* to interview; **entrevistarse** *vr*: **entrevistarse con** to have an interview with, see; **el ministro**

se entrevistó con el Rey ayer the minister had an audience with the King yesterday

entrevisto [entre'βisto] *pp de* **entrever**

entristecer [entriste'θer] *vt* to sadden, grieve; **entristecerse** *vr* to grow sad

entristezca *etc* [entris'teθka] *vb ver* **entristecer**

entrometerse [entrome'terse] *vr:* ~ **(en)** to interfere (in *o* with)

entrometido, -a [entrome'tiðo, a] *adj* interfering, meddlesome

entroncar [entron'kar] *vi* to be connected *o* related

entronque *etc* [en'tronke] *vb ver* **entroncar**

entuerto [en'twerto] *nm* wrong, injustice; **entuertos** *nmpl* (*Med*) afterpains

entumecer [entume'θer] *vt* to numb, benumb; **entumecerse** *vr* (*por el frío*) to go *o* become numb

entumecido, -a [entume'θiðo, a] *adj* numb, stiff

entumezca *etc* [entu'meθka] *vb ver* **entumecer**

enturbiar [entur'βjar] *vt* (*el agua*) to make cloudy; (*fig*) to confuse; **enturbiarse** *vr* (*oscurecerse*) to become cloudy; (*fig*) to get confused, become obscure

entusiasmar [entusjas'mar] *vt* to excite, fill with enthusiasm; (*gustar mucho*) to delight; **entusiasmarse** *vr:* **entusiasmarse con** *o* **por** to get enthusiastic *o* excited about

entusiasmo [entu'sjasmo] *nm* enthusiasm; (*excitación*) excitement

entusiasta [entu'sjasta] *adj* enthusiastic ■ *nm/f* enthusiast

enumerar [enume'rar] *vt* to enumerate

enunciación [enunθja'θjon] *nf*, **enunciado** [enun'θjaðo] *nm* enunciation; (*declaración*) declaration, statement

enunciar [enun'θjar] *vt* to enunciate; to declare, state

envainar [embai'nar] *vt* to sheathe

envalentonar [embalento'nar] *vt* to give courage to; **envalentonarse** *vr* (*pey: jactarse*) to boast, brag

envanecer [embane'θer] *vt* to make conceited; **envanecerse** *vr* to grow conceited

envanezca *etc* [emba'neθka] *vb ver* **envanecer**

envasar [emba'sar] *vt* (*empaquetar*) to pack, wrap; (*enfrascar*) to bottle; (*enlatar*) to can; (*embolsar*) to pocket

envase [em'base] *nm* packing, wrapping; bottling; canning; pocketing; (*recipiente*) container; (*paquete*) package; (*botella*) bottle; (*lata*) tin (*Brit*), can

envejecer [embexe'θer] *vt* to make old, age ■ *vi*, **envejecerse** *vr* (*volverse viejo*) to grow old; (*parecer viejo*) to age

envejecido, -a [embexe'θiðo, a] *adj* old, aged; (*de aspecto*) old-looking

envejezca *etc* [embe'xeθka] *vb ver* **envejecer**

envenenar [embene'nar] *vt* to poison; (*fig*) to embitter

envergadura [emberɣa'ðura] *nf* (*expansión*) expanse; (*Naut*) breadth; (*fig*) scope; **un programa de gran** ~ a wide-ranging programme

envés [em'bes] *nm* (*de tela*) back, wrong side

enviado, -a [em'bjaðo, a] *nm/f* (*Pol*) envoy; ~ **especial** (*de periódico, TV*) special correspondent

enviar [em'bjar] *vt* to send; ~ **un mensaje a algn** (*por móvil*) to text sb, send sb a text message

enviciar [embi'θjar] *vt* to corrupt ■ *vi* (*trabajo etc*) to be addictive; **enviciarse** *vr:* **enviciarse (con** *o* **en)** to get addicted (to)

envidia [em'biðja] *nf* envy; **tener** ~ **a** to envy, be jealous of

envidiar [embi'ðjar] *vt* (*desear*) to envy; (*tener celos de*) to be jealous of

envidioso, -a [embi'ðjoso, a] *adj* envious, jealous

envío [em'bio] *nm* (*acción*) sending; (*de mercancías*) consignment; (*de dinero*) remittance; (*en barco*) shipment; **gastos de** ~ postage and packing; ~ **contra reembolso** COD shipment

enviudar [embju'ðar] *vi* to be widowed

envoltura [embol'tura] *nf* (*cobertura*) cover; (*embalaje*) wrapper, wrapping

envolver [embol'βer] *vt* to wrap (up); (*cubrir*) to cover; (*enemigo*) to surround; (*implicar*) to involve, implicate

envuelto [em'bwelto], **envuelva** *etc* [em'bwelβa] *vb ver* **envolver**

enyesar [enje'sar] *vt* (*pared*) to plaster; (*Med*) to put in plaster

enzarzarse [enθar'θarse] *vr:* ~ **en algo** to get mixed up in sth

epa ['epa], **épale** ['epale] (*Am*) *excl* hey!, wow!

E.P.D. *abr* (= *en paz descanse*) RIP

epicentro [epi'θentro] *nm* epicentre

épico, -a ['epiko, a] *adj* epic ■ *nf* epic (poetry)

epidemia [epi'ðemja] *nf* epidemic

epidémico, -a [epi'ðemiko, a] *adj* epidemic

epidermis [epi'ðermis] *nf* epidermis

epifanía [epifa'nia] *nf* Epiphany

epilepsia [epi'lepsja] *nf* epilepsy

epiléptico, -a [epi'leptiko, a] *adj, nm/f* epileptic

epílogo [e'piloɣo] *nm* epilogue

episcopado [episko'paðo] *nm* (*cargo*) bishopric; (*obispos*) bishops *pl* (*collectively*)
episodio [epi'soðjo] *nm* episode; (*suceso*) incident
epístola [e'pistola] *nf* epistle
epitafio [epi'tafjo] *nm* epitaph
epíteto [e'piteto] *nm* epithet
época ['epoka] *nf* period, time; (*temporada*) season; (*Historia*) age, epoch; **hacer ~** to be epoch-making
equidad [eki'ðað] *nf* equity, fairness
equilibrar [ekili'βrar] *vt* to balance
equilibrio [eki'liβrjo] *nm* balance, equilibrium; **~ político** balance of power
equilibrista [ekili'βrista] *nm/f* (*funámbulo*) tightrope walker; (*acróbata*) acrobat
equinoccio [eki'nokθjo] *nm* equinox
equipaje [eki'paxe] *nm* luggage (*Brit*), baggage (*US*); (*avíos*) equipment, kit; **~ de mano** hand luggage; **hacer el ~** to pack
equipar [eki'par] *vt* (*proveer*) to equip
equiparar [ekipa'rar] *vt* (*igualar*) to put on the same level; (*comparar*): **~ con** to compare with; **equipararse** *vr*: **equipararse con** to be on a level with
equipo [e'kipo] *nm* (*conjunto de cosas*) equipment; (*Deporte, grupo*) team; (*de obreros*) shift; (*de máquinas*) plant; (*turbinas etc*) set; **~ de caza** hunting gear; **~ físico** (*Inform*) hardware; **~ médico** medical team; **~ de música** music centre
equis ['ekis] *nf* (the letter) X
equitación [ekita'θjon] *nf* (*acto*) riding; (*arte*) horsemanship
equitativo, -a [ekita'tiβo, a] *adj* equitable, fair
equivaldré *etc* [ekiβal'dre] *vb ver* **equivaler**
equivalencia [ekiβa'lenθja] *nf* equivalence
equivalente [ekiβa'lente] *adj, nm* equivalent
equivaler [ekiβa'ler] *vi*: **~ a** to be equivalent *o* equal to; (*en rango*) to rank as
equivalga *etc* [eki'βalɣa] *vb ver* **equivaler**
equivocación [ekiβoka'θjon] *nf* mistake, error; (*malentendido*) misunderstanding
equivocado, -a [ekiβo'kaðo, a] *adj* wrong, mistaken
equivocarse [ekiβo'karse] *vr* to be wrong, make a mistake; **~ de camino** to take the wrong road
equívoco, -a [e'kiβoko, a] *adj* (*dudoso*) suspect; (*ambiguo*) ambiguous ■ *nm* ambiguity; (*malentendido*) misunderstanding
equivoque *etc* [eki'βoke] *vb ver* **equivocarse**
era ['era] *vb ver* **ser** ■ *nf* era, age; (*Agr*) threshing floor
erais ['erais], **éramos** ['eramos], **eran** ['eran] *vb ver* **ser**

erario [e'rarjo] *nm* exchequer, treasury
eras ['eras], **eres** ['eres] *vb ver* **ser**
erección [erek'θjon] *nf* erection
ergonomía [erɣono'mia] *nf* ergonomics *sg*, human engineering
erguir [er'ɣir] *vt* to raise, lift; (*poner derecho*) to straighten; **erguirse** *vr* to straighten up
erice *etc* [e'riθe] *vb ver* **erizarse**
erigir [eri'xir] *vt* to erect, build; **erigirse** *vr*: **erigirse en** to set o.s. up as
erija *etc* [e'rixa] *vb ver* **erigir**
erizado, -a [eri'θaðo, a] *adj* bristly
erizarse [eri'θarse] *vr* (*pelo: de perro*) to bristle; (*: de persona*) to stand on end
erizo [e'riθo] *nm* hedgehog; **~ de mar** sea urchin
ermita [er'mita] *nf* hermitage
ermitaño, -a [ermi'taɲo, a] *nm/f* hermit
erosión [ero'sjon] *nf* erosion
erosionar [erosjo'nar] *vt* to erode
erótico, -a [e'rotiko, a] *adj* erotic
erotismo [ero'tismo] *nm* eroticism
erradicar [erraði'kar] *vt* to eradicate
erradique *etc* [erra'ðike] *vb ver* **erradicar**
errado, -a [e'rraðo, a] *adj* mistaken, wrong
errante [e'rrante] *adj* wandering, errant
errar [e'rrar] *vi* (*vagar*) to wander, roam; (*equivocarse*) to be mistaken ■ *vt*: **~ el camino** to take the wrong road; **~ el tiro** to miss
errata [e'rrata] *nf* misprint
erre ['erre] *nf* (the letter) R; **~ que ~** stubbornly
erróneo, -a [e'rroneo, a] *adj* (*equivocado*) wrong, mistaken; (*falso*) false, untrue
error [e'rror] *nm* error, mistake; (*Inform*) bug; **~ de imprenta** misprint; **~ de lectura/escritura** (*Inform*) read/write error; **~ sintáctico** syntax error; **~ judicial** miscarriage of justice
Ertzaintza [er'tʃantʃa] *nf* Basque police; *ver tb* **policía**
eructar [eruk'tar] *vt* to belch, burp
eructo [e'rukto] *nm* belch
erudición [eruði'θjon] *nf* erudition, learning
erudito, -a [eru'ðito, a] *adj* erudite, learned ■ *nm/f* scholar; **los eruditos en esta materia** the experts in this field
erupción [erup'θjon] *nf* eruption; (*Med*) rash; (*de violencia*) outbreak; (*de ira*) outburst
es [es] *vb ver* **ser**
E/S *abr* (*Inform*: = *entrada/salida*) I/O
esa ['esa], **esas** ['esas] *adj demostrativo ver* **ese**
ésa ['esa], **ésas** ['esas] *pron ver* **ése**
esbelto, -a [es'βelto, a] *adj* slim, slender
esbirro [es'βirro] *nm* henchman
esbozar [esβo'θar] *vt* to sketch, outline
esbozo [es'βoθo] *nm* sketch, outline**

escabeche [eska'βetʃe] nm brine; (de aceitunas etc) pickle; **en ~** pickled

escabechina [eskaβe'tʃina] nf (batalla) massacre; **hacer una ~** (Escol) to fail a lot of students

escabroso, -a [eska'βroso, a] adj (accidentado) rough, uneven; (fig) tough, difficult; (: atrevido) risqué

escabullirse [eskaβu'ʎirse] vr to slip away; (largarse) to clear out

escacharrar [eskatʃa'rrar] vt (fam) to break; **escacharrarse** vr to get broken

escafandra [eska'fandra] nf (buzo) diving suit; (escafandra espacial) spacesuit

escala [es'kala] nf (proporción, Mus) scale; (de mano) ladder; (Aviat) stopover; (de colores etc) range; **~ de tiempo** time scale; **~ de sueldos** salary scale; **una investigación a ~ nacional** a nationwide inquiry; **reproducir a ~** to reproduce to scale; **hacer ~ en** to stop off o over at

escalada [eska'laða] nf (de montaña) climb; (de pared) scaling

escalafón [eskala'fon] nm salary o wage scale

escalar [eska'lar] vt to climb, scale ■ vi (Mil, Pol) to escalate

escaldar [eskal'dar] vt (quemar) to scald; (escarmentar) to teach a lesson

escalera [eska'lera] nf stairs pl, staircase; (escala) ladder; (Naipes) run; (de camión) tailboard; **~ mecánica** escalator; **~ de caracol** spiral staircase; **~ de incendios** fire escape

escalerilla [eskale'riʎa] nf (de avión) steps pl

escalfar [eskal'far] vt (huevos) to poach

escalinata [eskali'nata] nf staircase

escalofriante [eskalo'frjante] adj chilling

escalofrío [eskalo'frio] nm (Med) chill; **escalofríos** nmpl (fig) shivers

escalón [eska'lon] nm step, stair; (de escalera) rung; (fig: paso) step; (al éxito) ladder

escalonar [eskalo'nar] vt to spread out; (tierra) to terrace; (horas de trabajo) to stagger

escalope [eska'lope] nm (Culin) escalope

escama [es'kama] nf (de pez, serpiente) scale; (de jabón) flake; (fig) resentment

escamar [eska'mar] vt (pez) to scale; (producir recelo) to make wary

escamotear [eskamote'ar] vt (fam: robar) to lift, swipe; (hacer desaparecer) to make disappear

escampar [eskam'par] vb impersonal to stop raining

escanciar [eskan'θjar] vt (vino) to pour (out)

escandalice etc [eskanda'liθe] vb ver **escandalizar**

escandalizar [eskandali'θar] vt to scandalize, shock; **escandalizarse** vr to be shocked; (ofenderse) to be offended

escándalo [es'kandalo] nm scandal; (alboroto, tumulto) row, uproar; **armar un ~** to make a scene; **¡es un ~!** it's outrageous!

escandaloso, -a [eskanda'loso, a] adj scandalous, shocking; (risa) hearty; (niño) noisy

Escandinavia [eskandi'naβja] nf Scandinavia

escandinavo, -a [eskandi'naβo, a] adj, nm/f Scandinavian

escaneo [es'kaneo] nm scanning

escáner [es'kaner] nm scanner

escaño [es'kaɲo] nm bench; (Pol) seat

escapada [eska'paða] nf (huida) escape, flight; (Deporte) breakaway; (viaje) quick trip

escapar [eska'par] vi (gen) to escape, run away; (Deporte) to break away; **escaparse** vr to escape, get away; (agua, gas, noticias) to leak (out); **se me escapa su nombre** his name escapes me

escaparate [eskapa'rate] nm shop window; (Com) showcase; **ir de escaparates** to go window shopping

escapatoria [eskapa'torja] nf: **no tener ~** (fig) to have no way out

escape [es'kape] nm (huida) escape; (de agua, gas) leak; (de motor) exhaust; **salir a ~** to rush out

escapismo [eska'pismo] nm escapism

escaquearse [eskake'arse] vr (fam) to duck out

escarabajo [eskara'βaxo] nm beetle

escaramuza [eskara'muθa] nf skirmish; (fig) brush

escarbar [eskar'βar] vt (gallina) to scratch; (fig) to inquire into, investigate

escarceos [eskar'θeos] nmpl: **en sus ~ con la política** in his occasional forays into politics; **~ amorosos** flirtations

escarcha [es'kartʃa] nf frost

escarlata [eskar'lata] adj inv scarlet

escarlatina [eskarla'tina] nf scarlet fever

escarmentar [eskarmen'tar] vt to punish severely ■ vi to learn one's lesson; **¡para que escarmientes!** that'll teach you!

escarmiento etc [eskar'mjento] vb ver **escarmentar** ■ nm (ejemplo) lesson; (castigo) punishment

escarnio [es'karnjo] nm mockery; (injuria) insult

escarola [eska'rola] nf (Bot) endive

escarpado, -a [eskar'paðo, a] adj (pendiente) sheer, steep; (rocas) craggy

escasamente [eskasa'mente] adv (insuficientemente) scantily; (apenas) scarcely

escasear [eskase'ar] *vi* to be scarce

escasez [eska'seθ] *nf* (*falta*) shortage, scarcity; (*pobreza*) poverty; **vivir con ~** to live on the breadline

escaso, -a [es'kaso, a] *adj* (*poco*) scarce; (*raro*) rare; (*ralo*) thin, sparse; (*limitado*) limited; (*recursos*) scanty; (*público*) sparse; (*posibilidad*) slim; (*visibilidad*) poor

escatimar [eskati'mar] *vt* (*limitar*) to skimp (on), be sparing with; **no ~ esfuerzos (para)** to spare no effort (to)

escayola [eska'jola] *nf* plaster

escayolar [eskajo'lar] *vt* to put in plaster

escena [es'θena] *nf* scene; (*decorado*) scenery; (*escenario*) stage; **poner en ~** to put on

escenario [esθe'narjo] *nm* (Teat) stage; (Cine) set; (*fig*) scene; **el ~ del crimen** the scene of the crime; **el ~ político** the political scene

escenografía [esθenoɣra'fia] *nf* set o stage design

escepticismo [esθepti'θismo] *nm* scepticism

escéptico, -a [es'θeptiko, a] *adj* sceptical ▪ *nm/f* sceptic

escindir [esθin'dir] *vt* to split; **escindirse** *vr* (*facción*) to split off; **escindirse en** to split into

escisión [esθi'sjon] *nf* (Med) excision; (*fig*, Pol) split; **~ nuclear** nuclear fission

esclarecer [esklare'θer] *vt* (*iluminar*) to light up, illuminate; (*misterio, problema*) to shed light on

esclarezca *etc* [eskla'reθka] *vb ver* **esclarecer**

esclavice *etc* [eskla'βiθe] *vb ver* **esclavizar**

esclavitud [esklaβi'tuð] *nf* slavery

esclavizar [esklaβi'θar] *vt* to enslave

esclavo, -a [es'klaβo, a] *nm/f* slave

esclusa [es'klusa] *nf* (*de canal*) lock; (*compuerta*) floodgate

escoba [es'koβa] *nf* broom; **pasar la ~** to sweep up

escobazo [esko'βaθo] *nm* (*golpe*) blow with a broom; **echar a algn a escobazos** to kick sb out

escobilla [esko'βiʎa] *nf* brush

escocer [esko'θer] *vi* to burn, sting; **escocerse** *vr* to chafe, get chafed

escocés, -esa [esko'θes, esa] *adj* Scottish; (*whisky*) Scotch ▪ *nm/f* Scotsman(-woman), Scot ▪ *nm* (Ling) Scots *sg*; **tela escocesa** tartan

Escocia [es'koθja] *nf* Scotland

escoger [esko'xer] *vt* to choose, pick, select

escogido, -a [esko'xiðo, a] *adj* chosen, selected; (*calidad*) choice, select; (*persona*): **ser muy ~** to be very fussy

escoja *etc* [es'koxa] *vb ver* **escoger**

escolar [esko'lar] *adj* school *cpd* ▪ *nm/f* schoolboy(-girl), pupil

escolaridad [eskolari'ðað] *nf* schooling; **libro de ~** school record

escolarización [eskolariθa'θjon] *nf*: **~ obligatoria** compulsory education

escolarizado, -a [eskolari'θaðo, a] *adj, nm/f*: **los escolarizados** those in o attending school

escollo [es'koʎo] *nm* (*arrecife*) reef, rock; (*fig*) pitfall

escolta [es'kolta] *nf* escort

escoltar [eskol'tar] *vt* to escort; (*proteger*) to guard

escombros [es'kombros] *nmpl* (*basura*) rubbish *sg*; (*restos*) debris *sg*

esconder [eskon'der] *vt* to hide, conceal; **esconderse** *vr* to hide

escondidas [eskon'diðas] *nfpl* (Am) hide-and-seek *sg*; **a ~** secretly; **hacer algo a ~ de algn** to do sth behind sb's back

escondite [eskon'dite] *nm* hiding place; (*juego*) hide-and-seek

escondrijo [eskon'drixo] *nm* hiding place, hideout

escopeta [esko'peta] *nf* shotgun; **~ de aire comprimido** air gun

escoria [es'korja] *nf* (*desecho mineral*) slag; (*fig*) scum, dregs *pl*

Escorpio [es'korpjo] *nm* (Astro) Scorpio

escorpión [eskor'pjon] *nm* scorpion

escotado, -a [esko'taðo, a] *adj* low-cut

escotar [esko'tar] *vt* (*vestido: ajustar*) to cut to fit; (*cuello*) to cut low

escote [es'kote] *nm* (*de vestido*) low neck; **pagar a ~** to share the expenses

escotilla [esko'tiʎa] *nf* (Naut) hatchway

escotillón [eskoti'ʎon] *nm* trapdoor

escozor [esko'θor] *nm* (*dolor*) sting(ing)

escribano, -a [eskri'βano, a], **escribiente** [eskri'βjente] *nm/f* clerk; (*secretario judicial*) court o lawyer's clerk

escribir [eskri'βir] *vt, vi* to write; **~ a máquina** to type; **¿cómo se escribe?** how do you spell it?

escrito, -a [es'krito, a] *pp de* **escribir** ▪ *adj* written, in writing; (*examen*) written ▪ *nm* (*documento*) document; (*manuscrito*) text, manuscript; **por ~** in writing

escritor, a [eskri'tor, a] *nm/f* writer

escritorio [eskri'torjo] *nm* desk; (*oficina*) office

escritura [eskri'tura] *nf* (*acción*) writing; (*caligrafía*) (hand)writing; (Jur: *documento*) deed; (Com) indenture; **~ de propiedad** title deed; **Sagrada E~** (Holy) Scripture; **~ social** articles *pl* of association

escroto [es'kroto] *nm* scrotum

escrúpulo [es'krupulo] *nm* scruple; (*minuciosidad*) scrupulousness

escrupuloso, -a [eskrupu'loso, a] *adj* scrupulous

escrutar [eskru'tar] *vt* to scrutinize, examine; (*votos*) to count

escrutinio [eskru'tinjo] *nm* (*examen atento*) scrutiny; (*Pol: recuento de votos*) count(ing)

escuadra [es'kwaðra] *nf* (*Tec*) square; (*Mil etc*) squad; (*Naut*) squadron; (*de coches etc*) fleet

escuadrilla [eskwa'ðriʎa] *nf* (*de aviones*) squadron

escuadrón [eskwa'ðron] *nm* squadron

escuálido, -a [es'kwaliðo, a] *adj* skinny, scraggy; (*sucio*) squalid

escucha [es'kutʃa] *nf* (*acción*) listening ■ *nm* (*Telec: sistema*) monitor; (*oyente*) listener; **estar a la ~** to listen in; **estar de ~** to spy; **escuchas telefónicas** (phone)tapping *sg*

escuchar [esku'tʃar] *vt* to listen to; (*consejo*) to heed; (*esp Am: oír*) to hear ■ *vi* to listen; **escucharse** *vr*: **se escucha muy mal** (*Telec*) it's a very bad line

escudarse [esku'ðarse] *vr*: **~ en** (*fig*) to hide behind

escudería [eskuðe'ria] *nf*: **la ~ Ferrari** the Ferrari team

escudero [esku'ðero] *nm* squire

escudilla [esku'ðiʎa] *nf* bowl, basin

escudo [es'kuðo] *nm* shield; **~ de armas** coat of arms

escudriñar [eskuðri'ɲar] *vt* (*examinar*) to investigate, scrutinize; (*mirar de lejos*) to scan

escuece *etc* [es'kweθe] *vb ver* **escocer**

escuela [es'kwela] *nf* (*tb fig*) school; **~ normal** teacher training college; **~ técnica superior** *university offering five-year courses in engineering and technical subjects*; **~ universitaria** *university offering three-year diploma courses*; **~ de párvulos** kindergarten; *ver tb* **colegio**

escueto, -a [es'kweto, a] *adj* plain; (*estilo*) simple; (*explicación*) concise

escueza *etc* [es'kweθa] *vb ver* **escocer**

escuincle [es'kwinkle] *nm* (*Am fam*) kid

esculpir [eskul'pir] *vt* to sculpt; (*grabar*) to engrave; (*tallar*) to carve

escultor, a [eskul'tor, a] *nm/f* sculptor

escultura [eskul'tura] *nf* sculpture

escupidera [eskupi'ðera] *nf* spittoon

escupir [esku'pir] *vt* to spit (out) ■ *vi* to spit

escupitajo [eskupi'taxo] *nm* (*fam*) gob of spit

escurreplatos [eskurre'platos] *nm inv* plate rack

escurridizo, -a [eskurri'ðiθo, a] *adj* slippery

escurrir [esku'rrir] *vt* (*ropa*) to wring out; (*verduras, platos*) to drain ■ *vi* (*los líquidos*) to drip; **escurrirse** *vr* (*secarse*) to drain; (*resbalarse*) to slip, slide; (*escaparse*) to slip away

ese¹ ['ese] *nf* (the letter) S; **hacer eses** (*carretera*) to zigzag; (*borracho*) to reel about

ese² ['ese], **esa** ['esa], **esos** ['esos], **esas** ['esas] *adj demostrativo* that *sg*, those *pl*

ése ['ese], **ésa** ['esa], **ésos** ['esos], **ésas** ['esas] *pron* that (one) *sg*, those (ones) *pl*; **ése ... éste ...** the former ... the latter ...; **¡no me vengas con ésas!** don't give me any more of that nonsense!

esencia [e'senθja] *nf* essence

esencial [esen'θjal] *adj* essential; (*principal*) chief; **lo ~** the main thing

esfera [es'fera] *nf* sphere; (*de reloj*) face; **~ de acción** scope; **~ terrestre** globe

esférico, -a [es'feriko, a] *adj* spherical

esfinge [es'finxe] *nf* sphinx

esforcé [esfor'θe], **esforcemos** *etc* [esfor'θemos] *vb ver* **esforzarse**

esforzado, -a [esfor'θaðo, a] *adj* (*enérgico*) energetic, vigorous

esforzarse [esfor'θarse] *vr* to exert o.s., make an effort

esfuerce *etc* [es'fwerθe] *vb ver* **esforzarse**

esfuerzo *etc* [es'fwerθo] *vb ver* **esforzarse** ■ *nm* effort; **sin ~** effortlessly

esfumarse [esfu'marse] *vr* (*apoyo, esperanzas*) to fade away; (*persona*) to vanish

esgrima [es'ɣrima] *nf* fencing

esgrimidor [esɣrimi'ðor] *nm* fencer

esgrimir [esɣri'mir] *vt* (*arma*) to brandish; (*argumento*) to use ■ *vi* to fence

esguince [es'ɣinθe] *nm* (*Med*) sprain

eslabón [esla'βon] *nm* link; **~ perdido** (*Bio, fig*) missing link

eslabonar [eslaβo'nar] *vt* to link, connect

eslálom [es'lalom] *nm* slalom

eslavo, -a [es'laβo, a] *adj* Slav, Slavonic ■ *nm/f* Slav ■ *nm* (*Ling*) Slavonic

eslogan [es'loɣan] *nm* (*pl* **eslogans**) slogan

eslora [es'lora] *nf* (*Naut*) length

eslovaco, -a [eslo'βako, a] *adj*, *nm/f* Slovak, Slovakian ■ *nm* (*Ling*) Slovak, Slovakian

Eslovaquia [eslo'βakja] *nf* Slovakia

Eslovenia [eslo'βenja] *nf* Slovenia

esloveno, -a [eslo'βeno, a] *adj*, *nm/f* Slovene, Slovenian ■ *nm* (*Ling*) Slovene, Slovenian

esmaltar [esmal'tar] *vt* to enamel

esmalte [es'malte] *nm* enamel; **~ de uñas** nail varnish *o* polish

esmerado, -a [esme'raðo, a] *adj* careful, neat

esmeralda [esme'ralda] *nf* emerald

esmerarse [esme'rarse] *vr* (*aplicarse*) to take great pains, exercise great care; (*afanarse*) to work hard; (*hacer lo mejor*) to do one's best

esmero [es'mero] *nm* (great) care

esmirriado, -a [esmi'rrjaðo, a] *adj* puny

esmoquin [es'mokin] *nm* dinner jacket (*Brit*), tuxedo (*US*)

esnob [es'nob] *adj inv (persona)* snobbish; *(coche etc)* posh ■ *nm/f* snob
esnobismo [esno'βismo] *nm* snobbery
eso ['eso] *pron* that, that thing *o* matter; ~ **de su coche** that business about his car; ~ **de ir al cine** all that about going to the cinema; **a ~ de las cinco** at about five o'clock; **en ~** thereupon, at that point; **por ~** therefore; ~ **es** that's it; **nada de ~** far from it; ¡~ **sí que es vida!** now this is really living!; **por ~ te lo dije** that's why I told you; **y ~ que llovía** in spite of the fact it was raining
esófago [e'sofaɣo] *nm (Anat)* oesophagus
esos ['esos] *adj demostrativo ver* **ese**
ésos ['esos] *pron ver* **ése**
esotérico, -a [eso'teriko, a] *adj* esoteric
esp. *abr (= español)* Sp., Span.; = **especialmente**
espabilado, -a [espaβi'laðo, a] *adj* quick-witted
espabilar [espaβi'lar] *vt,* **espabilarse** *vr* = **despabilar(se)**
espachurrar [espatʃu'rrar] *vt* to squash; **espachurrarse** *vr* to get squashed
espaciado [espa'θjaðo] *nm (Inform)* spacing
espacial [espa'θjal] *adj (del espacio)* space *cpd*
espaciar [espa'θjar] *vt* to space (out)
espacio [es'paθjo] *nm* space; *(Mus)* interval; *(Radio, TV)* programme, program *(US)*; **el ~** space; **ocupar mucho ~** to take up a lot of room; **a dos espacios, a doble ~** *(Tip)* double-spaced; **por ~ de** during, for
espacioso, -a [espa'θjoso, a] *adj* spacious, roomy
espada [es'paða] *nf* sword ■ *nm* swordsman; *(Taur)* matador; **espadas** *nfpl (Naipes) one of the suits in the Spanish card deck;* **estar entre la ~ y la pared** to be between the devil and the deep blue sea; *ver tb* **baraja española**
espadachín [espaða'tʃin] *nm (esgrimidor)* skilled swordsman
espaguetis [espa'ɣetis] *nmpl* spaghetti *sg*
espalda [es'palda] *nf (gen)* back; *(Natación)* backstroke; **espaldas** *nfpl (hombros)* shoulders; **a espaldas de algn** behind sb's back; **estar de espaldas** to have one's back turned; **tenderse de espaldas** to lie (down) on one's back; **volver la ~ a algn** to cold-shoulder sb
espaldarazo [espalda'raθo] *nm (tb fig)* slap on the back
espaldilla [espal'ðiʎa] *nf* shoulder blade
espantadizo, -a [espanta'ðiθo, a] *adj* timid, easily frightened
espantajo [espan'taxo] *nm,* **espantapájaros** [espanta'paxaros] *nm inv* scarecrow
espantar [espan'tar] *vt (asustar)* to frighten, scare; *(ahuyentar)* to frighten off; *(asombrar)*

to horrify, appal; **espantarse** *vr* to get frightened *o* scared; to be appalled
espanto [es'panto] *nm (susto)* fright; *(terror)* terror; *(asombro)* astonishment; ¡**qué ~!** how awful!
espantoso, -a [espan'toso, a] *adj* frightening, terrifying; *(ruido)* dreadful
España [es'paɲa] *nf* Spain; **la ~ de pandereta** touristy Spain
español, a [espa'ɲol, a] *adj* Spanish ■ *nm/f* Spaniard ■ *nm (Ling)* Spanish; *ver tb* **castellano**
españolice *etc* [espaɲo'liθe] *vb ver* **españolizar**
españolizar [espaɲoli'θar] *vt* to make Spanish, Hispanicize; **españolizarse** *vr* to adopt Spanish ways
esparadrapo [espara'ðrapo] *nm* (sticking) plaster, Band-Aid® *(US)*
esparcido, -a [espar'θiðo, a] *adj* scattered
esparcimiento [esparθi'mjento] *nm (dispersión)* spreading; *(derramamiento)* scattering; *(fig)* cheerfulness
esparcir [espar'θir] *vt* to spread; *(derramar)* to scatter; **esparcirse** *vr* to spread (out); to scatter; *(divertirse)* to enjoy o.s.
espárrago [es'parraɣo] *nm (tb:* **espárragos)** asparagus; **estar hecho un ~** to be as thin as a rake; ¡**vete a freír espárragos!** *(fam)* go to hell!
esparto [es'parto] *nm* esparto (grass)
esparza *etc* [es'parθa] *vb ver* **esparcir**
espasmo [es'pasmo] *nm* spasm
espátula [es'patula] *nf (Med)* spatula; *(Arte)* palette knife; *(Culin)* fish slice
especia [es'peθja] *nf* spice
especial [espe'θjal] *adj* special
especialidad [espeθjali'ðað] *nf* speciality, specialty *(US)*; *(Escol: ramo)* specialism
especialista [espeθja'lista] *nm/f* specialist; *(Cine)* stuntman(-woman)
especializado, -a [espeθjali'θaðo, a] *adj* specialized; *(obrero)* skilled
especialmente [espeθjal'mente] *adv* particularly, especially
especie [es'peθje] *nf (Bio)* species; *(clase)* kind, sort; **pagar en ~** to pay in kind
especificar [espeθifi'kar] *vt* to specify
específico, -a [espe'θifiko, a] *adj* specific
especifique *etc* [espeθi'fike] *vb ver* **especificar**
espécimen [es'peθimen] *(pl* **especímenes)** *nm* specimen
espectáculo [espek'takulo] *nm (gen)* spectacle; *(Teat etc)* show; *(función)* performance; **dar un ~** to make a scene
espectador, a [espekta'ðor, a] *nm/f* spectator; *(de incidente)* onlooker; **los**

e

espectadores *nmpl* (*Teat*) the audience *sg*
espectro [es'pektro] *nm* ghost; (*fig*) spectre
especulación [espekula'θjon] *nf*
speculation; ~ **bursátil** speculation on the
Stock Market
especular [espeku'lar] *vt, vi* to speculate
especulativo, -a [espekula'tiβo, a] *adj*
speculative
espejismo [espe'xismo] *nm* mirage
espejo [es'pexo] *nm* mirror; (*fig*) model;
~ **retrovisor** rear-view mirror; **mirarse al ~**
to look (at o.s.) in the mirror
espeleología [espeleolo'xia] *nf* potholing
espeluznante [espeluθ'nante] *adj*
horrifying, hair-raising
espera [es'pera] *nf* (*pausa, intervalo*) wait;
(*Jur: plazo*) respite; **en ~ de** waiting for;
(*con expectativa*) expecting; **en ~ de su
contestación** awaiting your reply
esperance *etc* [espe'ranθe] *vb ver* **esperanzar**
esperanza [espe'ranθa] *nf* (*confianza*)
hope; (*expectativa*) expectation; **hay pocas
esperanzas de que venga** there is little
prospect of his coming
esperanzador, a [esperanθa'ðor, a] *adj*
hopeful, encouraging
esperanzar [esperan'θar] *vt* to give hope to
esperar [espe'rar] *vt* (*aguardar*) to wait for;
(*tener expectativa de*) to expect; (*desear*) to
hope for ∎ *vi* to wait; to expect; to hope;
esperarse *vr*: **como podía esperarse** as
was to be expected; **hacer ~ a uno** to keep sb
waiting; **ir a ~ a uno** to go and meet sb; ~ **un
bebé** to be expecting (a baby)
esperma [es'perma] *nf* sperm
espermatozoide [espermato'θoiðe] *nm*
spermatozoid
esperpento [esper'pento] *nm* (*persona*) sight
(*fam*); (*disparate*) (piece of) nonsense
espesar [espe'sar] *vt* to thicken; **espesarse**
vr to thicken, get thicker
espeso, -a [es'peso, a] *adj* thick; (*bosque*)
dense; (*nieve*) deep; (*sucio*) dirty
espesor [espe'sor] *nm* thickness; (*de nieve*)
depth
espesura [espe'sura] *nf* (*de bosque*) thicket
espetar [espe'tar] *vt* (*reto, sermón*) to give
espía [es'pia] *nm/f* spy
espiar [espi'ar] *vt* (*observar*) to spy on
∎ *vi*: ~ **para** to spy for
espiga [es'piɣa] *nf* (*Bot: de trigo etc*) ear;
(: *de flores*) spike
espigado, -a [espi'ɣaðo, a] *adj* (*Bot*) ripe; (*fig*)
tall, slender
espigón [espi'ɣon] *nm* (*Bot*) ear; (*Naut*)
breakwater
espina [es'pina] *nf* thorn; (*de pez*) bone;

~ **dorsal** (*Anat*) spine; **me da mala ~** I don't
like the look of it
espinaca [espi'naka] *nf* (*tb*: **espinacas**)
spinach
espinar [espi'nar] *nm* (*matorral*) thicket
espinazo [espi'naθo] *nm* spine, backbone
espinilla [espi'niʎa] *nf* (*Anat: tibia*)
shin(bone); (: *en la piel*) blackhead
espino [es'pino] *nm* hawthorn
espinoso, -a [espi'noso, a] *adj* (*planta*) thorny,
prickly; (*fig*) bony; (*problema*) knotty
espionaje [espjo'naxe] *nm* spying,
espionage
espiral [espi'ral] *adj, nf* spiral; **la ~
inflacionista** the inflationary spiral
espirar [espi'rar] *vt, vi* to breathe out, exhale
espiritista [espiri'tista] *adj, nm/f* spiritualist
espíritu [es'piritu] *nm* spirit; (*mente*) mind;
(*inteligencia*) intelligence; (*Rel*) spirit, soul;
E~ Santo Holy Ghost; **con ~ amplio** with an
open mind
espiritual [espiri'twal] *adj* spiritual
espita [es'pita] *nf* tap (*Brit*), faucet (*US*)
esplendidez [esplendi'ðeθ] *nf* (*abundancia*)
lavishness; (*magnificencia*) splendour
espléndido, -a [es'plendiðo, a] *adj* (*magnífico*)
magnificent, splendid; (*generoso*) generous,
lavish
esplendor [esplen'dor] *nm* splendour
espliego [es'pljeɣo] *nm* lavender
espolear [espole'ar] *vt* to spur on
espoleta [espo'leta] *nf* (*de bomba*) fuse
espolvorear [espolβore'ar] *vt* to dust,
sprinkle
esponja [es'ponxa] *nf* sponge; (*fig*) sponger
esponjoso, -a [espon'xoso, a] *adj* spongy
esponsales [espon'sales] *nmpl* betrothal *sg*
espontaneidad [espontanei'ðað] *nf*
spontaneity
espontáneo, -a [espon'taneo, a] *adj*
spontaneous; (*improvisado*) impromptu;
(*persona*) natural
espora [es'pora] *nf* spore
esporádico, -a [espo'raðiko, a] *adj* sporadic
esposa [es'posa] *nf ver* **esposo**
esposar [espo'sar] *vt* to handcuff
esposo, -a [es'poso, a] *nm* husband ∎ *nf*
wife; **esposas** *nfpl* handcuffs
espuela [es'pwela] *nf* spur; (*fam: trago*) one
for the road
espuerta [es'pwerta] *nf* basket, pannier
espuma [es'puma] *nf* foam; (*de cerveza*) froth,
head; (*de jabón*) lather; (*de olas*) surf
espumadera [espuma'ðera] *nf* skimmer
espumarajo [espuma'raxo] *nm* froth, foam;
echar espumarajos (de rabia) to splutter
with rage

espumoso, -a [espu'moso, a] adj frothy, foamy; (vino) sparkling

esputo [es'puto] nm (de saliva) spit; (Med) sputum

esqueje [es'kexe] nm (Bot) cutting

esquela [es'kela] nf: ~ **mortuoria** announcement of death

esquelético, -a [eske'letiko, a] adj (fam) skinny

esqueleto [eske'leto] nm skeleton; (lo esencial) bare bones (of a matter); **en** ~ unfinished

esquema [es'kema] nm (diagrama) diagram; (dibujo) plan; (plan) scheme; (Filosofía) schema

esquemático, -a [eske'matiko, a] adj schematic; **un resumen** ~ a brief outline

esquí [es'ki] (pl ~s) nm (objeto) ski; (deporte) skiing; ~ **acuático** water-skiing; **hacer** ~ to go skiing

esquiador, a [eskja'ðor, a] nm/f skier

esquiar [es'kjar] vi to ski

esquila [es'kila] nf (campanilla) small bell; (encerro) cowbell

esquilar [eski'lar] vt to shear

esquimal [eski'mal] adj, nm/f Eskimo

esquina [es'kina] nf corner; **doblar la** ~ to turn the corner

esquinazo [eski'naθo] nm: **dar** ~ **a algn** to give sb the slip

esquirla [es'kirla] nf splinter

esquirol [eski'rol] nm blackleg

esquivar [eski'βar] vt to avoid; (evadir) to dodge, elude

esquivo, -a [es'kiβo, a] adj (altanero) aloof; (desdeñoso) scornful, disdainful

esquizofrenia [eskiθo'frenja] nf schizophrenia

esta ['esta] adj demostrativo ver **este**

ésta ['esta] pron ver **éste**

está [es'ta] vb ver **estar**

estabilice etc [estaβi'liθe] vb ver **estabilizar**

estabilidad [estaβili'ðað] nf stability

estabilización [estaβiliθa'θjon] nf (Com) stabilization

estabilizar [estaβili'θar] vt to stabilize; (fijar) to make steady; (precios) to peg; **estabilizarse** vr to become stable

estable [es'taβle] adj stable

establecer [estaβle'θer] vt to establish; (fundar) to set up; (colonos) to settle; (récord) to set (up); **establecerse** vr to establish o.s.; (echar raíces) to settle (down); (Com) to start up

establecimiento [estaβleθi'mjento] nm establishment; (fundación) institution; (de negocio) start-up; (de colonias) settlement; (local) establishment; ~ **comercial** business house

establezca etc [esta'βleθka] vb ver **establecer**

establo [es'taβlo] nm (Agr) stall; (: esp Am) barn

estaca [es'taka] nf stake, post; (de tienda de campaña) peg

estacada [esta'kaða] nf (cerca) fence, fencing; (palenque) stockade; **dejar a algn en la** ~ to leave sb in the lurch

estación [esta'θjon] nf station; (del año) season; ~ **de autobuses/ferrocarril** bus/railway station; ~ **balnearia (de turistas)** seaside resort; ~ **de servicio** service station; ~ **terminal** terminus; ~ **de trabajo** (Com) work station; ~ **transmisora** transmitter; ~ **de visualización** display unit

estacionamiento [estaθjona'mjento] nm (Auto) parking; (Mil) stationing

estacionar [estaθjo'nar] vt (Auto) to park; (Mil) to station

estacionario, -a [estaθjo'narjo, a] adj stationary; (Com: mercado) slack

estada [es'taða], **estadía** [esta'ðia] nf (Am) stay

estadio [es'taðjo] nm (fase) stage, phase; (Deporte) stadium

estadista [esta'ðista] nm (Pol) statesman; (Estadística) statistician

estadística [esta'ðistika] nf (una estadística) figure, statistic; (ciencia) statistics sg

estado [es'taðo] nm (Pol: condición) state; ~ **civil** marital status; ~ **de cuenta(s)** bank statement, statement of accounts; ~ **de excepción** (Pol) state of emergency; ~ **financiero** (Com) financial statement; ~ **mayor** (Mil) staff; ~ **de pérdidas y ganancias** (Com) profit and loss statement, operating statement; **Estados Unidos (EE. UU.)** United States (of America) (USA); **estar en** ~ **(de buena esperanza)** to be pregnant

estadounidense [estaðouni'ðense] adj United States cpd, American ◼ nm/f United States citizen, American

estafa [es'tafa] nf swindle, trick; (Com etc) racket

estafar [esta'far] vt to swindle, defraud

estafeta [esta'feta] nf (oficina de correos) post office; ~ **diplomática** diplomatic bag

estalactita [estalak'tita] nf stalactite

estalagmita [estalaɣ'mita] nf stalagmite

estallar [esta'ʎar] vi to burst; (bomba) to explode, go off; (volcán) to erupt; (vidrio) to shatter; (látigo) to crack; (epidemia, guerra, rebelión) to break out; ~ **en llanto** to burst into tears

estallido [esta'ʎiðo] nm explosion; (de látigo, trueno) crack; (fig) outbreak

estambre [es'tambre] nm (tela) worsted; (Bot) stamen

Estambul [estam'bul] nm Istanbul

estamento [esta'mento] nm (social) class

estampa [es'tampa] nf (impresión, imprenta) print, engraving; (imagen, figura: de persona) appearance

estampado, -a [estam'paðo, a] adj printed ■ nm (impresión: acción) printing; (: efecto) print; (marca) stamping

estampar [estam'par] vt (imprimir) to print; (marcar) to stamp; (metal) to engrave; (poner sello en) to stamp; (fig) to stamp, imprint

estampida [estam'piða] nf stampede

estampido [estam'piðo] nm bang, report

estampilla [estam'piʎa] nf (sello de goma) (rubber) stamp; (Am) (postage) stamp

están [es'tan] vb ver **estar**

estancado, -a [estan'kaðo, a] adj (agua) stagnant

estancamiento [estanka'mjento] nm stagnation

estancar [estan'kar] vt (aguas) to hold up, hold back; (Com) to monopolize; (fig) to block, hold up; **estancarse** vr to stagnate

estancia [es'tanθja] nf (permanencia) stay; (sala) room; (Am) farm, ranch

estanciero [estan'sjero] nm (Am) farmer, rancher

estanco, -a [es'tanko, a] adj watertight ■ nm tobacconist's (shop); see note

estándar [es'tandar] adj, nm standard

estandarice etc [estanda'riθe] vb ver **estandarizar**

estandarizar [estandari'θar] vt to standardize

estandarte [estan'darte] nm banner, standard

estanque etc [es'tanke] vb ver **estancar** ■ nm (lago) pool, pond; (Agr) reservoir

estanquero, -a [estan'kero, a] nm/f tobacconist

estante [es'tante] nm (armario) rack, stand; (biblioteca) bookcase; (anaquel) shelf; (Am) prop

estantería [estante'ria] nf shelving, shelves pl

estaño [es'taɲo] nm tin

PALABRA CLAVE

estar [es'tar] vi 1 (posición) to be; **está en la plaza** it's in the square; **¿está Juan?** is Juan in?; **estamos a 30 km de Junín** we're 30 kms from Junín

2 (+ adj o adv: estado) to be; **estar enfermo** to be ill; **está muy elegante** he's looking very smart; **estar lejos** to be far (away); **¿cómo estás?** how are you keeping?

3 (+ gerundio) to be; **estoy leyendo** I'm reading

4 (uso pasivo): **está condenado a muerte** he's been condemned to death; **está envasado en ...** it's packed in ...

5: **estar a**: **¿a cuántos estamos?** what's the date today?; **estamos a 9 de mayo** it's the 9th of May; **las manzanas están a 1,50 euros** apples are (selling at) 1.5 euros; **estamos a 25 grados** it's 25 degrees today

6 (locuciones): **¿estamos?** (¿de acuerdo?) okay?; (¿listo?) ready?; **¡ya está bien!** that's enough!; **¿está la comida?** is dinner ready?; **¡ya está!, ¡ya estuvo!** (Am) that's it!

7: **estar con**: **está con gripe** he's got (the) flu

8: **estar de**: **estar de vacaciones/viaje** to be on holiday/away o on a trip; **está de camarero** he's working as a waiter

9: **estar para**: **está para salir** he's about to leave; **no estoy para bromas** I'm not in the mood for jokes

10: **estar por** (propuesta etc) to be in favour of; (persona etc) to support, side with; **está por limpiar** it still has to be cleaned; **¡estoy por dejarlo!** I think I'm going to leave this!

11 (+ que): **está que rabia** (fam) he's hopping mad (fam); **estoy que me caigo de sueño** I'm terribly sleepy, I can't keep my eyes open

12: **estar sin**: **estar sin dinero** to have no money; **está sin terminar** it isn't finished yet

estarse vr: **se estuvo en la cama toda la tarde** he stayed in bed all afternoon; **¡estáte quieto!** stop fidgeting!

estárter [es'tarter] nm (Auto) choke

estas ['estas] adj demostrativo ver **este**

éstas ['estas] pron ver **éste**

estás [es'tas] vb ver **estar**

estatal [esta'tal] adj state cpd

estático, -a [es'tatiko, a] adj static

estatua [es'tatwa] nf statue

estatura [esta'tura] nf stature, height

estatus [es'tatus] nm inv status

estatutario, -a [estatu'tarjo, a] adj statutory

estatuto [esta'tuto] nm (Jur) statute; (de

ciudad) bye-law; (*de comité*) rule; **estatutos sociales** (*Com*) articles of association

este¹ ['este] *adj* (*lado*) east; (*dirección*) easterly ◼ *nm* east; **en la parte del ~** in the eastern part

este² ['este], **esta** ['esta], **estos** ['estos], **estas** ['estas] *adj demostrativo* this *sg*, these *pl*; (*Am: como muletilla*) er, um

éste ['este], **ésta** ['esta], **éstos** ['estos], **éstas** ['estas] *pron* this (one) *sg*, these (ones) *pl*; **ése ... éste ...** the former ... the latter ...

esté [es'te] *vb ver* **estar**

estela [es'tela] *nf* wake, wash; (*fig*) trail

estelar [este'lar] *adj* (*Astro*) stellar; (*Teat*) star *cpd*

estén [es'ten] *vb ver* **estar**

estenografía [estenoɣra'fia] *nf* shorthand

estentóreo, -a [esten'toreo, a] *adj* (*sonido*) strident; (*voz*) booming

estepa [es'tepa] *nf* (*Geo*) steppe

estera [es'tera] *nf* (*alfombra*) mat; (*tejido*) matting

estercolero [esterko'lero] *nm* manure heap, dunghill

estéreo [es'tereo] *adj inv*, *nm* stereo

estereofónico, -a [estereo'foniko, a] *adj* stereophonic

estereotipar [estereoti'par] *vt* to stereotype

estereotipo [estereo'tipo] *nm* stereotype

estéril [es'teril] *adj* sterile, barren; (*fig*) vain, futile

esterilice *etc* [esteri'liθe] *vb ver* **esterilizar**

esterilizar [esterili'θar] *vt* to sterilize

esterilla [este'riʎa] *nf* (*alfombrilla*) small mat

esterlina [ester'lina] *adj*: **libra ~** pound sterling

esternón [ester'non] *nm* breastbone

estero [es'tero] *nm* (*Am*) swamp

estertor [ester'tor] *nm* death rattle

estés [es'tes] *vb ver* **estar**

esteta [es'teta] *nm/f* aesthete

esteticienne [esteti'θjen] *nf* beautician

estético, -a [es'tetiko, a] *adj* aesthetic ◼ *nf* aesthetics *sg*

estetoscopio [estetos'kopjo] *nm* stethoscope

estibador [estiβa'ðor] *nm* stevedore

estibar [esti'βar] *vt* (*Naut*) to stow

estiércol [es'tjerkol] *nm* dung, manure

estigma [es'tiɣma] *nm* stigma

estigmatice *etc* [estiɣma'tiθe] *vb ver* **estigmatizar**

estigmatizar [estiɣmati'θar] *vt* to stigmatize

estilarse [esti'larse] *vr* (*estar de moda*) to be in fashion; (*usarse*) to be used

estilice *etc* [esti'liθe] *vb ver* **estilizar**

estilizar [estili'θar] *vt* to stylize; (*Tec*) to design

estilo [es'tilo] *nm* style; (*Tec*) stylus; (*Natación*) stroke; **~ de vida** lifestyle; **al ~ de** in the style of; **algo por el ~** something along those lines

estilográfica [estilo'ɣrafika] *nf* fountain pen

estima [es'tima] *nf* esteem, respect

estimación [estima'θjon] *nf* (*evaluación*) estimation; (*aprecio, afecto*) esteem, regard

estimado, -a [esti'maðo, a] *adj* esteemed; **"E~ Señor"** "Dear Sir"

estimar [esti'mar] *vt* (*evaluar*) to estimate; (*valorar*) to value; (*apreciar*) to esteem, respect; (*pensar, considerar*) to think, reckon

estimulante [estimu'lante] *adj* stimulating ◼ *nm* stimulant

estimular [estimu'lar] *vt* to stimulate; (*excitar*) to excite; (*animar*) to encourage

estímulo [es'timulo] *nm* stimulus; (*ánimo*) encouragement

estío [es'tio] *nm* summer

estipendio [esti'pendjo] *nm* salary; (*Com*) stipend

estipulación [estipula'θjon] *nf* stipulation, condition

estipular [estipu'lar] *vt* to stipulate

estirado, -a [esti'raðo, a] *adj* (*tenso*) (stretched *o* drawn) tight; (*fig: persona*) stiff, pompous; (*engreído*) stuck-up

estirar [esti'rar] *vt* to stretch; (*dinero, suma etc*) to stretch out; (*cuello*) to crane; (*discurso*) to spin out; **~ la pata** (*fam*) to kick the bucket; **estirarse** *vr* to stretch

estirón [esti'ron] *nm* pull, tug; (*crecimiento*) spurt, sudden growth; **dar un ~** (*niño*) to shoot up

estirpe [es'tirpe] *nf* stock, lineage

estival [esti'βal] *adj* summer *cpd*

esto ['esto] *pron* this, this thing *o* matter; (*como muletilla*) er, um; **~ de la boda** this business about the wedding; **en ~** at this *o* that point; **por ~** for this reason

estocada [esto'kaða] *nf* (*acción*) stab; (*Taur*) death blow

Estocolmo [esto'kolmo] *nm* Stockholm

estofa [es'tofa] *nf*: **de baja ~** poor-quality

estofado [esto'faðo] *nm* stew

estofar [esto'far] *vt* (*bordar*) to quilt; (*Culin*) to stew

estoico, -a [es'toiko, a] *adj* (*Filosofía*) stoic(al); (*fig*) cold, indifferent

estomacal [estoma'kal] *adj* stomach *cpd*; **trastorno ~** stomach upset

estómago [es'tomaɣo] *nm* stomach; **tener ~** to be thick-skinned

Estonia [es'tonja] *nf* Estonia

estonio, -a [es'tonjo, a] *adj, nm/f* Estonian ◼ *nm* (*Ling*) Estonian

estoque [es'toke] nm rapier, sword
estorbar [estor'βar] vt to hinder, obstruct; (fig) to bother, disturb ▪ vi to be in the way
estorbo [es'torβo] nm (molestia) bother, nuisance; (obstáculo) hindrance, obstacle
estornino [estor'nino] nm starling
estornudar [estornu'ðar] vi to sneeze
estornudo [estor'nuðo] nm sneeze
estos ['estos] adj demostrativo ver **este**
éstos ['estos] pron ver **éste**
estoy [es'toi] vb ver **estar**
estrabismo [estra'βismo] nm squint
estrado [es'traðo] nm (tarima) platform; (Mus) bandstand; **estrados** nmpl law courts
estrafalario, -a [estrafa'larjo, a] adj odd, eccentric; (desarreglado) slovenly, sloppy
estrago [es'trayo] nm ruin, destruction; **hacer estragos en** to wreak havoc among
estragón [estra'yon] nm (Culin) tarragon
estrambótico, -a [estram'botiko, a] adj odd, eccentric
estrangulación [estrangula'θjon] nf strangulation
estrangulador, -a [estrangula'ðor, a] nm/f strangler ▪ nm (Tec) throttle; (Auto) choke
estrangulamiento [estrangula'mjento] nm (Auto) bottleneck
estrangular [estrangu'lar] vt (persona) to strangle; (Med) to strangulate
estraperlista [estraper'lista] nm/f black marketeer
estraperlo [estra'perlo] nm black market
estratagema [estrata'xema] nf (Mil) stratagem; (astucia) cunning
estratega [estra'teγa] nm/f strategist
estrategia [estra'texja] nf strategy
estratégico, -a [estra'texiko, a] adj strategic
estratificar [estratifi'kar] vt to stratify
estratifique etc [estrati'fike] vb ver **estratificar**
estrato [es'trato] nm stratum, layer
estratosfera [estratos'fera] nf stratosphere
estrechar [estre'tʃar] vt (reducir) to narrow; (vestido) to take in; (persona) to hug, embrace; **estrecharse** vr (reducirse) to narrow, grow narrow; (2 personas) to embrace; **~ la mano** to shake hands
estrechez [estre'tʃeθ] nf narrowness; (de ropa) tightness; (intimidad) intimacy; (Com) want o shortage of money; **estrecheces** nfpl financial difficulties
estrecho, -a [es'tretʃo, a] adj narrow; (apretado) tight; (íntimo) close, intimate; (miserable) mean ▪ nm strait; **~ de miras** narrow-minded; **E~ de Gibraltar** Straits of Gibraltar
estrella [es'treʎa] nf star; **~ fugaz** shooting

star; **~ de mar** starfish; **tener (buena)/ mala ~** to be lucky/unlucky
estrellado, -a [estre'ʎaðo, a] adj (forma) star-shaped; (cielo) starry; (huevos) fried
estrellar [estre'ʎar] vt (hacer añicos) to smash (to pieces); (huevos) to fry; **estrellarse** vr to smash; (chocarse) to crash; (fracasar) to fail
estrellato [estre'ʎato] nm stardom
estremecer [estreme'θer] vt to shake; **estremecerse** vr to shake, tremble; **~ de** (horror) to shudder with; (frío) to shiver with
estremecimiento [estremeθi'mjento] nm (temblor) trembling, shaking
estremezca etc [estre'meθka] vb ver **estremecer**
estrenar [estre'nar] vt (vestido) to wear for the first time; (casa) to move into; (película, obra de teatro) to present for the first time; **estrenarse** vr (persona) to make one's début; (película) to have its première; (Teat) to open
estreno [es'treno] nm (primer uso) first use; (Cine etc) première
estreñido, -a [estre'ɲiðo, a] adj constipated
estreñimiento [estreɲi'mjento] nm constipation
estreñir [estre'ɲir] vt to constipate
estrépito [es'trepito] nm noise, racket; (fig) fuss
estrepitoso, -a [estrepi'toso, a] adj noisy; (fiesta) rowdy
estrés [es'tres] nm stress
estresante [estre'sante] adj stressful
estría [es'tria] nf groove; **estrías (en el cutis)** stretchmarks
estribación [estriβa'θjon] nf (Geo) spur; **estribaciones** nfpl foothills
estribar [estri'βar] vi: **~ en** to rest on, be supported by; **la dificultad estriba en el texto** the difficulty lies in the text
estribillo [estri'βiʎo] nm (Lit) refrain; (Mus) chorus
estribo [es'triβo] nm (de jinete) stirrup; (de coche, tren) step; (de puente) support; (Geo) spur; **perder los estribos** to fly off the handle
estribor [estri'βor] nm (Naut) starboard
estricnina [estrik'nina] nf strychnine
estricto, -a [es'trikto, a] adj (riguroso) strict; (severo) severe
estridente [estri'ðente] adj (color) loud; (voz) raucous
estro ['estro] nm inspiration
estrofa [es'trofa] nf verse
estropajo [estro'paxo] nm scourer
estropeado, -a [estrope'aðo, a] adj: **está ~** it's not working
estropear [estrope'ar] vt (arruinar) to spoil;

(*dañar*) to damage; (: *máquina*) to break;
estropearse *vr* (*objeto*) to get damaged;
(*coche*) to break down; (*la piel etc*) to be ruined
estropicio [estro'piθjo] *nm* (*rotura*) breakage;
(*efectos*) harmful effects *pl*
estructura [estruk'tura] *nf* structure
estruendo [es'trwendo] *nm* (*ruido*) racket,
din; (*fig: alboroto*) uproar, turmoil
estrujar [estru'xar] *vt* (*apretar*) to squeeze;
(*aplastar*) to crush; (*fig*) to drain, bleed
estuario [es'twarjo] *nm* estuary
estuche [es'tutʃe] *nm* box, case
estudiante [estu'ðjante] *nm/f* student
estudiantil [estuðjan'til] *adj inv* student *cpd*
estudiantina [estuðjan'tina] *nf* student
music group
estudiar [estu'ðjar] *vt* to study; (*propuesta*) to
think about *o* over; ~ **para abogado** to study
to become a lawyer
estudio [es'tuðjo] *nm* study; (*encuesta*)
research; (*proyecto*) plan; (*piso*) studio
flat; (*Cine, Arte, Radio*) studio; **estudios**
nmpl studies; (*erudición*) learning *sg*;
cursar *o* **hacer estudios** to study; ~
de casos prácticos case study; ~ **de**
desplazamientos y tiempos (*Com*) time
and motion study; **estudios de motivación**
motivational research *sg*; ~ **del trabajo**
(*Com*) work study; ~ **de viabilidad** (*Com*)
feasibility study
estudioso, -a [estu'ðjoso, a] *adj* studious
estufa [es'tufa] *nf* heater, fire
estulticia [estul'tiθja] *nf* foolishness
estupefaciente [estupefa'θjente] *adj, nm*
narcotic
estupefacto, -a [estupe'fakto, a] *adj*
speechless, thunderstruck
estupendamente [estupenda'mente] *adv*
(*fam*): **estoy** ~ I feel great; **le salió** ~ he did it
very well
estupendo, -a [estu'pendo, a] *adj*
wonderful, terrific; (*fam*) great; ¡~! that's
great!, fantastic!
estupidez [estupi'ðeθ] *nf* (*torpeza*) stupidity;
(*acto*) stupid thing (to do); **fue una ~ mía**
that was a silly thing for me to do *o* say
estúpido, -a [es'tupiðo, a] *adj* stupid, silly
estupor [estu'por] *nm* stupor; (*fig*)
astonishment, amazement
estupro [es'tupro] *nm* rape
estuve *etc* [es'tuβe], **estuviera** *etc*
[estu'βjera] *vb ver* **estar**
esvástica [es'βastika] *nf* swastika
ET *abr* = **Ejército de Tierra**
ETA ['eta] *nf abr* (Pol: = *Euskadi Ta Askatasuna*)
ETA
etapa [e'tapa] *nf* (*de viaje*) stage; (*Deporte*) leg;

(*parada*) stopping place; (*fig*) stage, phase;
por etapas gradually, in stages
etarra [e'tarra] *adj* ETA *cpd* ■ *nm/f* member
of ETA
etc. *abr* (= *etcétera*) etc
etcétera [et'θetera] *adv* etcetera
etéreo, -a [e'tereo, a] *adj* ethereal
eternice *etc* [eter'niθe] *vb ver* **eternizarse**
eternidad [eterni'ðað] *nf* eternity
eternizarse [eterni'θarse] *vr*: ~ **en hacer algo**
to take ages to do sth
eterno, -a [e'terno, a] *adj* eternal,
everlasting; (*despectivo*) never-ending
ético, -a ['etiko, a] *adj* ethical ■ *nf* ethics
etimología [etimolo'xia] *nf* etymology
etiqueta [eti'keta] *nf* (*modales*) etiquette;
(*rótulo*) label, tag; **de** ~ formal
etnia ['etnja] *nf* ethnic group
étnico, -a ['etniko, a] *adj* ethnic
ETS *sigla f* (= *Enfermedad de Transmisión Sexual*)
STD
EU(A) *nmpl abr* (*esp Am*: = *Estados Unidos (de*
América)) US(A)
eucalipto [euka'lipto] *nm* eucalyptus
Eucaristía [eukaris'tia] *nf* Eucharist
eufemismo [eufe'mismo] *nm* euphemism
euforia [eu'forja] *nf* euphoria
eufórico, -a [eu'foriko, a] *adj* euphoric
eunuco [eu'nuko] *nm* eunuch
euro ['euro] *nm* (*moneda*) euro
eurodiputado, -a [euroðipu'taðo, a] *nm/f*
Euro MP, MEP
Eurolandia [euro'landja] *nf* Euroland
Europa [eu'ropa] *nf* Europe
europeice *etc* [euro'peiθe] *vb ver* **europeizar**
europeizar [europei'θar] *vt* to Europeanize;
europeizarse *vr* to become Europeanized
europeo, -a [euro'peo, a] *adj, nm/f* European
Eurotúnel [euro'tunel] *nm* (*estructura*)
Channel Tunnel
eurozona [euro'θona] *nf* Eurozone
Euskadi [eus'kaði] *nm* the Basque Provinces *pl*
euskera, eusquera [eus'kera] *nm* (*Ling*)
Basque; *ver tb* **Lengua**
eutanasia [euta'nasja] *nf* euthanasia
evacuación [eβakwa'θjon] *nf* evacuation
evacuar [eβa'kwar] *vt* to evacuate
evadir [eβa'ðir] *vt* to evade, avoid; **evadirse**
vr to escape
evaluación [eβalwa'θjon] *nf* evaluation,
assessment
evaluar [eβa'lwar] *vt* to evaluate, assess
evangélico, -a [eβan'xeliko, a] *adj*
evangelical
evangelio [eβan'xeljo] *nm* gospel
evaporación [eβapora'θjon] *nf* evaporation
evaporar [eβapo'rar] *vt* to evaporate;

evaporarse *vr* to vanish

evasión [eβa'sjon] *nf* escape, flight; (*fig*) evasion; ~ **fiscal** *o* **tributaria** tax evasion

evasivo, -a [eβa'siβo, a] *adj* evasive, non-committal ■ *nf* (*pretexto*) excuse; **contestar con evasivas** to avoid giving a straight answer

evento [e'βento] *nm* event; (*eventualidad*) eventuality

eventual [eβen'twal] *adj* possible, conditional (upon circumstances); (*trabajador*) casual, temporary

Everest [eβe'rest] *nm*: **el (Monte) ~** (Mount) Everest

evidencia [eβi'ðenθja] *nf* evidence, proof; **poner en ~** to make clear; **ponerse en ~** (*persona*) to show o.s. up

evidenciar [eβiðen'θjar] *vt* (*hacer patente*) to make evident; (*probar*) to prove, show; **evidenciarse** *vr* to be evident

evidente [eβi'ðente] *adj* obvious, clear, evident

evitar [eβi'tar] *vt* (*evadir*) to avoid; (*impedir*) to prevent; (*peligro*) to escape; (*molestia*) to save; (*tentación*) to shun; **si puedo evitarlo** if I can help it

evocador, a [eβoka'ðor, a] *adj* (*sugestivo*) evocative

evocar [eβo'kar] *vt* to evoke, call forth

evolución [eβolu'θjon] *nf* (*desarrollo*) evolution, development; (*cambio*) change; (*Mil*) manoeuvre

evolucionar [eβoluθjo'nar] *vi* to evolve; (*Mil, Aviat*) to manoeuvre

evoque *etc* [e'βoke] *vb ver* **evocar**

ex [eks] *adj* ex-; **el ex ministro** the former minister, the ex-minister

exabrupto [eksa'βrupto] *nm* interjection

exacción [eksak'θjon] *nf* (*acto*) exaction; (*de impuestos*) demand

exacerbar [eksaθer'βar] *vt* to irritate, annoy

exactamente [eksakta'mente] *adv* exactly

exactitud [eksakti'tuð] *nf* exactness; (*precisión*) accuracy; (*puntualidad*) punctuality

exacto, -a [ek'sakto, a] *adj* exact; accurate; punctual; **¡~!** exactly!; **eso no es del todo ~** that's not quite right; **para ser ~** to be precise

exageración [eksaxera'θjon] *nf* exaggeration

exagerado, -a [eksaxe'raðo, a] *adj* (*relato*) exaggerated; (*precio*) excessive; (*persona*) over-demonstrative; (*gesto*) theatrical

exagerar [eksaxe'rar] *vt* to exaggerate; (*exceder*) to overdo

exaltado, -a [eksal'taðo, a] *adj* (*apasionado*) over-excited, worked up; (*exagerado*) extreme;

(*fanático*) hot-headed; (*discurso*) impassioned ■ *nm/f* (*fanático*) hothead; (*Pol*) extremist

exaltar [eksal'tar] *vt* to exalt, glorify; **exaltarse** *vr* (*excitarse*) to get excited *o* worked up

examen [ek'samen] *nm* examination; (*de problema*) consideration; ~ **de** (*encuesta*) inquiry into; ~ **de ingreso** entrance examination; ~ **de conducir** driving test; ~ **eliminatorio** qualifying examination

examinar [eksami'nar] *vt* to examine; (*poner a prueba*) to test; (*inspeccionar*) to inspect; **examinarse** *vr* to be examined, take an examination

exánime [ek'sanime] *adj* lifeless; (*fig*) exhausted

exasperar [eksaspe'rar] *vt* to exasperate; **exasperarse** *vr* to get exasperated, lose patience

Exc.ª *abr* = **Excelencia**

excarcelar [ekskarθe'lar] *vt* to release (from prison)

excavador, a [ekskaβa'ðor, a] *nm/f* (*persona*) excavator ■ *nf* (*Tec*) digger

excavar [ekska'βar] *vt* to excavate, dig (out)

excedencia [eksθe'ðenθja] *nf* (*Mil*) leave; (*Escol*) sabbatical

excedente [eksθe'ðente] *adj, nm* excess, surplus

exceder [eksθe'ðer] *vt* to exceed, surpass; **excederse** *vr* (*extralimitarse*) to go too far; (*sobrepasarse*) to excel o.s.

excelencia [eksθe'lenθja] *nf* excellence; **E~ Excellency**; **por ~** par excellence

excelente [eksθe'lente] *adj* excellent

excelso, -a [eks'θelso, a] *adj* lofty, sublime

excentricidad [eksθentriθi'ðað] *nf* eccentricity

excéntrico, -a [eks'θentriko, a] *adj, nm/f* eccentric

excepción [eksθep'θjon] *nf* exception; **la ~ confirma la regla** the exception proves the rule

excepcional [eksθepθjo'nal] *adj* exceptional

excepto [eks'θepto] *adv* excepting, except (for)

exceptuar [eksθep'twar] *vt* to except, exclude

excesivo, -a [eksθe'siβo, a] *adj* excessive

exceso [eks'θeso] *nm* excess; (*Com*) surplus; ~ **de equipaje/peso** excess luggage/weight; ~ **de velocidad** speeding; **en** *o* **por ~** excessively

excitación [eksθita'θjon] *nf* (*sensación*) excitement; (*acción*) excitation

excitado, -a [eksθi'taðo, a] *adj* excited; (*emociones*) aroused

excitante [eksθi'tante] *adj* exciting; (*Med*) stimulating ∎ *nm* stimulant

excitar [eksθi'tar] *vt* to excite; (*incitar*) to urge; (*emoción*) to stir up; (*esperanzas*) to raise; (*pasión*) to arouse; **excitarse** *vr* to get excited

exclamación [eksklama'θjon] *nf* exclamation

exclamar [ekskla'mar] *vi* to exclaim; **exclamarse** *vr*: **exclamarse (contra)** to complain (about)

excluir [eksklu'ir] *vt* to exclude; (*dejar fuera*) to shut out; (*solución*) to reject; (*posibilidad*) to rule out

exclusión [eksklu'sjon] *nf* exclusion

exclusiva [eksklu'siβa] *nf ver* **exclusivo**

exclusive [eksklu'siβe] *prep* exclusive of, not counting

exclusivo, -a [eksklu'siβo, a] *adj* exclusive ∎ *nf* (*Prensa*) exclusive, scoop; (*Com*) sole right *o* agency; **derecho ~** sole *o* exclusive right

excluyendo *etc* [eksklu'jendo] *vb ver* **excluir**

Excma., Excmo. *abr* (= *Excelentísima, Excelentísimo*) *courtesy title*

excombatiente [ekskomba'tjente] *nm* ex-serviceman, war veteran (*US*)

excomulgar [ekskomul'ɣar] *vt* (*Rel*) to excommunicate

excomulgue *etc* [eksko'mulɣe] *vb ver* **excomulgar**

excomunión [ekskomu'njon] *nf* excommunication

excoriar [eksko'rjar] *vt* to flay, skin

excremento [ekskre'mento] *nm* excrement

exculpar [ekskul'par] *vt* to exonerate; (*Jur*) to acquit; **exculparse** *vr* to exonerate o.s.

excursión [ekskur'sjon] *nf* excursion, outing; **ir de ~** to go (off) on a trip

excursionista [ekskursjo'nista] *nm/f* (*turista*) sightseer

excusa [eks'kusa] *nf* excuse; (*disculpa*) apology; **presentar sus excusas** to excuse o.s.

excusado, -a [eksku'saðo, a] *adj* unnecessary; (*disculpado*) excused, forgiven

excusar [eksku'sar] *vt* to excuse; (*evitar*) to avoid, prevent; **excusarse** *vr* (*disculparse*) to apologize

execrable [ekse'kraβle] *adj* appalling

exención [eksen'θjon] *nf* exemption

exento, -a [ek'sento, a] *pp de* **eximir** ∎ *adj* exempt

exequias [ek'sekjas] *nfpl* funeral rites

exfoliar [eksfo'ljar] *vt* to exfoliate

exhalación [eksala'θjon] *nf* (*del aire*) exhalation; (*de vapor*) fumes *pl*, vapour; (*rayo*) shooting star; **salir como una ~** to shoot out

exhalar [eksa'lar] *vt* to exhale, breathe out; (*olor etc*) to give off; (*suspiro*) to breathe, heave

exhaustivo, -a [eksaus'tiβo, a] *adj* exhaustive

exhausto, -a [ek'sausto, a] *adj* exhausted, worn-out

exhibición [eksiβi'θjon] *nf* exhibition; (*demostración*) display, show; (*de película*) showing; (*de equipo*) performance

exhibicionista [eksiβiθjo'nista] *adj, nm/f* exhibitionist

exhibir [eksi'βir] *vt* to exhibit; to display, show; (*cuadros*) to exhibit; (*artículos*) to display; (*pasaporte*) to show; (*película*) to screen; (*mostrar con orgullo*) to show off; **exhibirse** *vr* (*mostrarse en público*) to show o.s. off; (*fam: indecentemente*) to expose o.s.

exhortación [eksorta'θjon] *nf* exhortation

exhortar [eksor'tar] *vt*: **~ a** to exhort to

exhumar [eksu'mar] *vt* to exhume

exigencia [eksi'xenθja] *nf* demand, requirement

exigente [eksi'xente] *adj* demanding; (*profesor*) strict; **ser ~ con algn** to be hard on sb

exigir [eksi'xir] *vt* (*gen*) to demand, require; (*impuestos*) to exact, levy; **~ el pago** to demand payment

exiguo, -a [ek'siɣwo, a] *adj* (*cantidad*) meagre; (*objeto*) tiny

exija *etc* [e'ksixa] *vb ver* **exigir**

exiliado, -a [eksi'ljaðo, a] *adj* exiled, in exile ∎ *nm/f* exile

exiliar [eksi'ljar] *vt* to exile; **exiliarse** *vr* to go into exile

exilio [ek'siljo] *nm* exile

eximio, -a [ek'simjo, a] *adj* (*eminente*) distinguished, eminent

eximir [eksi'mir] *vt* to exempt

existencia [eksis'tenθja] *nf* existence; **existencias** *nfpl* stock *sg*; **~ de mercancías** (*Com*) stock-in-trade; **tener en ~** to have in stock; **amargar la ~ a algn** to make sb's life a misery

existir [eksis'tir] *vi* to exist, be

éxito ['eksito] *nm* (*resultado*) result, outcome; (*triunfo*) success; (*Mus, Teat*) hit; **éxito editorial** bestseller; **éxito rotundo** smash hit; **tener éxito** to be successful

exitoso, -a [eksi'toso, a] *adj* (*esp Am*) successful

éxodo ['eksoðo] *nm* exodus; **el éxodo rural** the drift from the land

ex oficio [ekso'fiθjo] *adj, adv* ex officio

exonerar [eksone'rar] *vt* to exonerate; **~ de una obligación** to free from an obligation

exorcice *etc* [eksor'θiθe] *vb ver* **exorcizar**

exorcismo [eksor'θismo] *nm* exorcism

exorcizar [eksorθi'θar] *vt* to exorcize

exótico, -a [ek'sotiko, a] *adj* exotic

expandido, -a [ekspan'diðo, a] *adj*: **en caracteres expandidos** (*Inform*) double width

expandir [ekspan'dir] *vt* to expand; (*Com*) to expand, enlarge; **expandirse** *vr* to expand, spread

expansión [ekspan'sjon] *nf* expansion; (*recreo*) relaxation; **la ~ económica** economic growth; **economía en ~** expanding economy

expansionarse [ekspansjo'narse] *vr* (*dilatarse*) to expand; (*recrearse*) to relax

expansivo, -a [ekspan'siβo, a] *adj* expansive; (*efusivo*) communicative

expatriado, -a [ekspa'trjaðo, a] *nm/f* (*emigrado*) expatriate; (*exiliado*) exile

expatriarse [ekspa'trjarse] *vr* to emigrate; (*Pol*) to go into exile

expectación [ekspekta'θjon] *nf* (*esperanza*) expectation; (*ilusión*) excitement

expectativa [ekspekta'tiβa] *nf* (*espera*) expectation; (*perspectiva*) prospect; **~ de vida** life expectancy; **estar a la ~** to wait and see (what will happen)

expedición [ekspeði'θjon] *nf* (*excursión*) expedition; **gastos de ~** shipping charges

expedientar [ekspeðjen'tar] *vt* to open a file on; (*funcionario*) to discipline, start disciplinary proceedings against

expediente [ekspe'ðjente] *nm* expedient; (*Jur: procedimiento*) action, proceedings *pl*; (: *papeles*) dossier, file, record; **~ judicial** court proceedings *pl*; **~ académico** (student's) record

expedir [ekspe'ðir] *vt* (*despachar*) to send, forward; (*pasaporte*) to issue; (*cheque*) to make out

expedito, -a [ekspe'ðito, a] *adj* (*libre*) clear, free

expeler [ekspe'ler] *vt* to expel, eject

expendedor, a [ekspende'ðor, a] *nm/f* (*vendedor*) dealer; (*Teat*) ticket agent ▪ *nm* (*aparato*) (vending) machine; **~ de cigarrillos** cigarette machine

expendeduría [ekspendedu'ria] *nf* (*estanco*) tobacconist's (shop) (*Brit*), cigar store (*US*)

expendio [eks'pendjo] *nm* (*Am*) small shop (*Brit*) *o* store (*US*)

expensas [eks'pensas] *nfpl* (*Jur*) costs; **a ~ de** at the expense of

experiencia [ekspe'rjenθja] *nf* experience

experimentado, -a [eksperimen'taðo, a] *adj* experienced

experimentar [eksperimen'tar] *vt* (*en laboratorio*) to experiment with; (*probar*) to test, try out; (*notar, observar*) to experience;

(*deterioro, pérdida*) to suffer; (*aumento*) to show; (*sensación*) to feel

experimento [eksperi'mento] *nm* experiment

experto, -a [eks'perto, a] *adj* expert ▪ *nm/f* expert

expiar [ekspi'ar] *vt* to atone for

expida *etc* [eks'piða] *vb ver* **expedir**

expirar [ekspi'rar] *vi* to expire

explanada [ekspla'naða] *nf* (*paseo*) esplanade; (*a orillas del mar*) promenade

explayarse [ekspla'jarse] *vr* (*en discurso*) to speak at length; **~ con algn** to confide in sb

explicación [eksplika'θjon] *nf* explanation

explicar [ekspli'kar] *vt* to explain; (*teoría*) to expound; (*Univ*) to lecture in; **explicarse** *vr* to explain (o.s.); **no me lo explico** I can't understand it

explícito, -a [eks'pliθito, a] *adj* explicit

explique *etc* [eks'plike] *vb ver* **explicar**

exploración [eksplora'θjon] *nf* exploration; (*Mil*) reconnaissance

explorador, a [eksplora'ðor, a] *nm/f* (*pionero*) explorer; (*Mil*) scout ▪ *nm* (*Med*) probe; (*radar*) (radar) scanner

explorar [eksplo'rar] *vt* to explore; (*Med*) to probe; (*radar*) to scan

explosión [eksplo'sjon] *nf* explosion

explosivo, -a [eksplo'siβo, a] *adj* explosive

explotación [eksplota'θjon] *nf* exploitation; (*de planta etc*) running; (*de mina*) working; (*de recurso*) development; **~ minera** mine; **gastos de ~** operating costs

explotar [eksplo'tar] *vt* to exploit; (*planta*) to run, operate; (*mina*) to work ▪ *vi* (*bomba etc*) to explode, go off

expondré *etc* [ekspon'dre] *vb ver* **exponer**

exponer [ekspo'ner] *vt* to expose; (*cuadro*) to display; (*vida*) to risk; (*idea*) to explain; (*teoría*) to expound; (*hechos*) to set out; **exponerse** *vr*: **exponerse a (hacer) algo** to run the risk of (doing) sth

exponga *etc* [eks'ponga] *vb ver* **exponer**

exportación [eksporta'θjon] *nf* (*acción*) export; (*mercancías*) exports *pl*

exportador, a [eksporta'ðor, a] *adj* (*país*) exporting ▪ *nm/f* exporter

exportar [ekspor'tar] *vt* to export

exposición [eksposi'θjon] *nf* (*gen*) exposure; (*de arte*) show, exhibition; (*Com*) display; (*feria*) show, fair; (*explicación*) explanation; (*de teoría*) exposition; (*narración*) account, statement

exprés [eks'pres] *adj inv* (*café*) espresso ▪ *nm* (*Ferro*) express (train)

expresamente [ekspresa'mente] *adv* (*concretamente*) expressly; (*a propósito*) on purpose

expresar [ekspre'sar] *vt* to express; (*redactar*) to phrase, put; (*emoción*) to show; **expresarse** *vr* to express o.s.; (*dato*) to be stated; **como abajo se expresa** as stated below

expresión [expre'sjon] *nf* expression; ~ **familiar** colloquialism

expresivo, -a [ekspre'siβo, a] *adj* expressive; (*cariñoso*) affectionate

expreso, -a [eks'preso, a] *adj* (*explícito*) express; (*claro*) specific, clear; (*tren*) fast ■ *nm* (*Ferro*) fast train ■ *adv*: **mandar** ~ to send by express (delivery)

exprimidor [eksprimi'ðor] *nm* (lemon) squeezer

exprimir [ekspri'mir] *vt* (*fruta*) to squeeze; (*zumo*) to squeeze out

ex profeso [ekspro'feso] *adv* expressly

expropiar [ekspro'pjar] *vt* to expropriate

expuesto, -a [eks'pwesto, a] *pp de* **exponer** ■ *adj* exposed; (*cuadro etc*) on show, on display; **según lo ~ arriba** according to what has been stated above

expulsar [ekspul'sar] *vt* (*echar*) to eject, throw out; (*alumno*) to expel; (*despedir*) to sack, fire; (*Deporte*) to send off

expulsión [ekspul'sjon] *nf* expulsion; sending-off

expurgar [ekspur'ɣar] *vt* to expurgate

expuse *etc* [eks'puse] *vb ver* **exponer**

exquisito, -a [ekski'sito, a] *adj* exquisite; (*comida*) delicious; (*afectado*) affected

Ext. *abr* (= *Exterior*) ext.; (= *Extensión*) ext.

éxtasis ['ekstasis] *nm* (*tb droga*) ecstasy

extemporáneo, -a [ekstempo'raneo, a] *adj* unseasonal

extender [eksten'der] *vt* to extend; (*los brazos*) to stretch out, hold out; (*mapa, tela*) to spread (out), open (out); (*mantequilla*) to spread; (*certificado*) to issue; (*cheque, recibo*) to make out; (*documento*) to draw up; **extenderse** *vr* to extend; (*terreno*) to stretch o spread (out); (*persona: en el suelo*) to stretch out; (*en el tiempo*) to extend, last; (*costumbre, epidemia*) to spread; (*guerra*) to escalate; **extenderse sobre un tema** to enlarge on a subject

extendido, -a [eksten'diðo, a] *adj* (*abierto*) spread out, open; (*brazos*) outstretched; (*costumbre etc*) widespread

extensible [eksten'siβle] *adj* extending

extensión [eksten'sjon] *nf* (*de terreno, mar*) expanse, stretch; (*Mus*) range; (*de conocimientos*) extent; (*de programa*) scope; (*de tiempo*) length, duration; (*Telec*) extension; ~ **de plazo** (*Com*) extension; **en toda la ~ de la palabra** in every sense of the word; **de** ~ (*Inform*) add-on

extenso, -a [eks'tenso, a] *adj* extensive

extenuar [ekste'nwar] *vt* (*debilitar*) to weaken

exterior [ekste'rjor] *adj* (*de fuera*) external; (*afuera*) outside, exterior; (*apariencia*) outward; (*deuda, relaciones*) foreign ■ *nm* exterior, outside; (*aspecto*) outward appearance; (*Deporte*) wing(er); (*países extranjeros*) abroad; **asuntos exteriores** foreign affairs; **al** ~ outwardly, on the outside; **en el** ~ abroad; **noticias del** ~ foreign o overseas news

exteriorice *etc* [eksterjo'riθe] *vb ver* **exteriorizar**

exteriorizar [eksterjori'θar] *vt* (*emociones*) to show, reveal

exteriormente [eksterjor'mente] *adv* outwardly

exterminar [ekstermi'nar] *vt* to exterminate

exterminio [ekster'minjo] *nm* extermination

externo, -a [eks'terno, a] *adj* (*exterior*) external, outside; (*superficial*) outward ■ *nm/f* day pupil

extienda *etc* [eks'tjenda] *vb ver* **extender**

extinción [ekstin'θjon] *nf* extinction

extinga *etc* [eks'tinga] *vb ver* **extinguir**

extinguido, -a [ekstin'giðo, a] *adj* (*animal, volcán*) extinct; (*fuego*) out, extinguished

extinguir [ekstin'gir] *vt* (*fuego*) to extinguish, put out; (*raza, población*) to wipe out; **extinguirse** *vr* (*fuego*) to go out; (*Bio*) to die out, become extinct

extinto, -a [eks'tinto, a] *adj* extinct

extintor [ekstin'tor] *nm* (fire) extinguisher

extirpar [ekstir'par] *vt* (*vicios*) to eradicate, stamp out; (*Med*) to remove (surgically)

extorsión [ekstor'sjon] *nf* blackmail

extra ['ekstra] *adj inv* (*tiempo*) extra; (*vino*) vintage; (*chocolate*) good-quality; (*gasolina*) high-octane ■ *nm/f* extra ■ *nm* (*bono*) bonus; (*periódico*) special edition

extracción [ekstrak'θjon] *nf* extraction; (*en lotería*) draw; (*de carbón*) mining

extracto [eks'trakto] *nm* extract

extractor [ekstrak'tor] *nm* (*tb*: **extractor de humos**) extractor fan

extradición [ekstraði'θjon] *nf* extradition

extraditar [ekstraði'tar] *vt* to extradite

extraer [ekstra'er] *vt* to extract, take out

extrafino, -a [ekstra'fino, a] *adj* extra-fine; **azúcar** ~ caster sugar

extraiga *etc* [eks'traiɣa], **extraje** *etc* [eks'traxe], **extrajera** *etc* [ekstra'xera] *vb ver* **extraer**

extralimitarse [ekstralimi'tarse] *vr* to go too far

extranjerismo [ekstranxe'rismo] *nm* foreign word o phrase *etc*

extranjero, -a [ekstran'xero, a] *adj* foreign
■ *nm/f* foreigner ■ *nm* foreign lands *pl*; **en el ~** abroad

extrañamiento [ekstraɲa'mjento] *nm* estrangement

extrañar [ekstra'ɲar] *vt* (*sorprender*) to find strange *o* odd; (*echar de menos*) to miss;
extrañarse *vr* (*sorprenderse*) to be amazed, be surprised; (*distanciarse*) to become estranged, grow apart; **me extraña** I'm surprised

extrañeza [ekstra'ɲeθa] *nf* (*rareza*) strangeness, oddness; (*asombro*) amazement, surprise

extraño, -a [eks'traɲo, a] *adj* (*extranjero*) foreign; (*raro, sorprendente*) strange, odd

extraoficial [ekstraofi'θjal] *adj* unofficial, informal

extraordinario, -a [ekstraorði'narjo, a] *adj* extraordinary; (*edición, número*) special ■ *nm* (*de periódico*) special edition; **horas extraordinarias** overtime *sg*

extrarradio [ekstra'rraðjo] *nm* suburbs *pl*

extrasensorial [ekstrasenso'rjal] *adj*: **percepción ~** extrasensory perception

extraterrestre [ekstrate'rrestre] *adj* of *o* from outer space ■ *nm/f* creature from outer space

extravagancia [ekstraβa'ɣanθja] *nf* oddness; outlandishness; (*rareza*) peculiarity; **extravagancias** *nfpl* (*tonterías*) nonsense *sg*

extravagante [ekstraβa'ɣante] *adj* (*excéntrico*) eccentric; (*estrafalario*) outlandish

extraviado, -a [ekstra'βjaðo, a] *adj* lost, missing

extraviar [ekstra'βjar] *vt* to mislead, misdirect; (*perder*) to lose, misplace;
extraviarse *vr* to lose one's way, get lost; (*objeto*) to go missing, be mislaid

extravío [ekstra'βio] *nm* loss; (*fig*) misconduct

extrayendo [ekstra'jendo] *vb ver* **extraer**

extremado, -a [ekstre'maðo, a] *adj* extreme, excessive

Extremadura [ekstrema'ðura] *nf* Estremadura

extremar [ekstre'mar] *vt* to carry to extremes; **extremarse** *vr* to do one's utmost, make every effort

extremaunción [ekstremaun'θjon] *nf* extreme unction, last rites *pl*

extremidad [ekstremi'ðað] *nf* (*punta*) extremity; (*fila*) edge; **extremidades** *nfpl* (*Anat*) extremities

extremista [ekstre'mista] *adj, nm/f* extremist

extremo, -a [eks'tremo, a] *adj* extreme; (*más alejado*) furthest; (*último*) last ■ *nm* end; (*situación*) extreme; **E~ Oriente** Far East; **en último ~** as a last resort; **pasar de un ~ a otro** (*fig*) to go from one extreme to the other; **con ~** in the extreme; **la extrema derecha** (*Pol*) the far right; **~ derecho/izquierdo** (*Deporte*) outside right/left

extrínseco, -a [eks'trinseko, a] *adj* extrinsic

extrovertido, -a [ekstroβer'tiðo, a] *adj* extrovert, outgoing ■ *nm/f* extrovert

exuberancia [eksuβe'ranθja] *nf* exuberance

exuberante [eksuβe'rante] *adj* exuberant; (*fig*) luxuriant, lush

exudar [eksu'ðar] *vt, vi* to exude

exultar [eksul'tar] *vi*: **~ (en)** to exult (in); (*pey*) to gloat (over)

exvoto [eks'βoto] *nm* votive offering

eyaculación [ejakula'θjon] *nf* ejaculation

eyacular [ejaku'lar] *vt, vi* to ejaculate

Ff

F, f ['efe] *nf* (*letra*) F, f; **F de Francia** F for Frederick (*Brit*), F for Fox (*US*)

fa [fa] *nm* (*Mus*) F

f.ª *abr* (*Com*: = *factura*) Inv.

fabada [fa'βaða] *nf* bean and sausage stew

fábrica ['faβrika] *nf* factory; **~ de moneda** mint; **marca de ~** trademark; **precio de ~** factory price

fabricación [faβrika'θjon] *nf* (*manufactura*) manufacture; (*producción*) production; **de ~ casera** home-made; **de ~ nacional** home produced; **~ en serie** mass production

fabricante [faβri'kante] *nm/f* manufacturer

fabricar [faβri'kar] *vt* (*manufacturar*) to manufacture, make; (*construir*) to build; (*cuento*) to fabricate, devise; **~ en serie** to mass-produce

fabril [fa'βril] *adj*: **industria ~** manufacturing industry

fabrique etc [fa'βrike] *vb ver* **fabricar**

fábula ['faβula] *nf* (*cuento*) fable; (*chisme*) rumour; (*mentira*) fib

fabuloso, -a [faβu'loso, a] *adj* fabulous, fantastic

facción [fak'θjon] *nf* (*Pol*) faction; **facciones** *nfpl* (*del rostro*) features

faceta [fa'θeta] *nf* facet

facha ['fatʃa] (*fam*) *nm/f* fascist, right-wing extremist ■ *nf* (*aspecto*) look; (*cara*) face; **¡qué ~ tienes!** you look a sight!

fachada [fa'tʃaða] *nf* (*Arq*) façade, front; (*Tip*) title page; (*fig*) façade, outward show

facial [fa'θjal] *adj* facial

fácil ['faθil] *adj* (*simple*) easy; (*sencillo*) simple, straightforward; (*probable*) likely; (*respuesta*) facile; **~ de usar** (*Inform*) user-friendly

facilidad [faθili'ðað] *nf* (*capacidad*) ease; (*sencillez*) simplicity; (*de palabra*) fluency; **facilidades** *nfpl* facilities; **"facilidades de pago"** (*Com*) "credit facilities", "payment terms"

facilitar [faθili'tar] *vt* (*hacer fácil*) to make easy; (*proporcionar*) to provide; (*documento*) to issue; **le agradecería me facilitara …** I would be grateful if you could let me have …

fácilmente ['faθilmente] *adv* easily

facsímil [fak'simil] *nm* (*documento*) facsimile; **enviar por ~** to fax

factible [fak'tiβle] *adj* feasible

factor [fak'tor] *nm* factor; (*Com*) agent; (*Ferro*) freight clerk

factoría [fakto'ria] *nf* (*Com: fábrica*) factory

factura [fak'tura] *nf* (*cuenta*) bill; (*nota de pago*) invoice; (*hechura*) manufacture; **presentar ~ a** to invoice

facturación [faktura'θjon] *nf* (*Com*) invoicing; (: *ventas*) turnover; **~ de equipajes** luggage check-in; **~ online** online check-in

facturar [faktu'rar] *vt* (*Com*) to invoice, charge for; (*Aviat*) to check in; (*equipaje*) to register, check (*US*)

facultad [fakul'tað] *nf* (*aptitud, Escol etc*) faculty; (*poder*) power

facultativo, -a [fakulta'tiβo, a] *adj* optional; (*de un oficio*) professional; **prescripción facultativa** medical prescription

FAD *nm abr* (*Esp*) = **Fondo de Ayuda y Desarrollo**

faena [fa'ena] *nf* (*trabajo*) work; (*quehacer*) task, job; **faenas domésticas** housework *sg*

faenar [fae'nar] *vi* to fish

fagot [fa'ɣot] *nm* (*Mus*) bassoon

faisán [fai'san] *nm* pheasant

faja ['faxa] *nf* (*para la cintura*) sash; (*de mujer*) corset; (*de tierra*) strip

fajo ['faxo] *nm* (*de papeles*) bundle; (*de billetes*) role, wad

falange [fa'lanxe] *nf*: **la F~** (*Pol*) the Falange

falda ['falda] *nf* (*prenda de vestir*) skirt; (*Geo*) foothill; **~ escocesa** kilt

fálico, -a ['faliko, a] *adj* phallic

falla ['faʎa] *nf* (*defecto*) fault, flaw

fallar [fa'ʎar] *vt* (*Jur*) to pronounce sentence on; (*Naipes*) to trump ■ *vi* (*memoria*) to fail; (*plan*) to go wrong; (*motor*) to miss; **~ a algn** to let sb down

Fallas ['faʎas] *nfpl see note*

● **FALLAS**
●
● In the week of the 19th of March (the
● feast of St Joseph, San José), Valencia
● honours its patron saint with a
● spectacular *fiesta* called *las Fallas*. The
● *Fallas* are huge sculptures, made of wood,
● cardboard, paper and cloth, depicting
● famous politicians and other targets for
● ridicule, which are set alight and burned
● by the *falleros*, members of the competing
● local groups who have just spent months
● preparing them.

fallecer [faʎe'θer] *vi* to pass away, die
fallecido, -a [faʎe'θiðo, a] *adj* late ■ *nm/f*
deceased
fallecimiento [faʎeθi'mjento] *nm* decease,
demise
fallero, -a [fa'ʎero, a] *nm/f* maker of "Fallas"
fallezca *etc* [fa'ʎeθka] *vb ver* **fallecer**
fallido, -a [fa'ʎiðo, a] *adj* vain; (*intento*)
frustrated, unsuccessful
fallo ['faʎo] *nm* (*Jur*) verdict, ruling; (*decisión*)
decision; (*de jurado*) findings; (*fracaso*) failure;
(*Deporte*) miss; (*Inform*) bug
falo ['falo] *nm* phallus
falsear [false'ar] *vt* to falsify; (*firma etc*) to
forge ■ *vi* (*Mus*) to be out of tune
falsedad [false'ðað] *nf* falseness; (*hipocresía*)
hypocrisy; (*mentira*) falsehood
falsificación [falsifika'θjon] *nf* (*acto*)
falsification; (*objeto*) forgery
falsificar [falsifi'kar] *vt* (*firma etc*) to forge;
(*voto etc*) to rig; (*moneda*) to counterfeit
falsifique *etc* [falsi'fike] *vb ver* **falsificar**
falso, -a ['falso, a] *adj* false; (*erróneo*) wrong,
mistaken; (*firma, documento*) forged; (*moneda*
etc) fake; **en ~** falsely; **dar un paso en ~** to
trip; (*fig*) to take a false step
falta ['falta] *nf* (*defecto*) fault, flaw; (*privación*)
lack, want; (*ausencia*) absence; (*carencia*)
shortage; (*equivocación*) mistake; (*Jur*) default;
(*Deporte*) foul; (*Tenis*) fault; **~ de ortografía**
spelling mistake; **~ de respeto** disrespect;
echar en ~ to miss; **hacer ~ hacer algo** to be
necessary to do sth; **me hace ~ una pluma**
I need a pen; **sin ~** without fail; **por ~ de**
through o for lack of
faltar [fal'tar] *vi* (*escasear*) to be lacking,
be wanting; (*ausentarse*) to be absent, be
missing; **¿falta algo?** is anything missing?;
falta mucho todavía there's plenty of time
yet; **¿falta mucho?** is there long to go?;
faltan dos horas para llegar there are two
hours to go till arrival; **~ (al respeto) a algn**
to be disrespectful to sb; **~ a una cita** to miss

an appointment; **~ a la verdad** to lie;
¡no faltaba más! that's the last straw!
falto, -a ['falto, a] *adj* (*desposeído*) deficient,
lacking; (*necesitado*) poor, wretched; **estar ~**
de to be short of
fama ['fama] *nf* (*renombre*) fame; (*reputación*)
reputation
famélico, -a [fa'meliko, a] *adj* starving
familia [fa'milja] *nf* family; **~ política**
in-laws *pl*
familiar [fami'ljar] *adj* (*relativo a la familia*)
family *cpd*; (*conocido, informal*) familiar; (*estilo*)
informal; (*Ling*) colloquial ■ *nm/f* relative,
relation
familiarice *etc* [familja'riθe] *vb ver*
familiarizarse
familiaridad [familjari'ðað] *nf* familiarity;
(*informalidad*) homeliness
familiarizarse [familjari'θarse] *vr:* **~ con**
to familiarize o.s. with
famoso, -a [fa'moso, a] *adj* (*renombrado*)
famous
fan (*pl* **fans**) [fan, fans] *nm* fan
fanático, -a [fa'natiko, a] *adj* fanatical
■ *nm/f* fanatic; (*Cine, Deporte etc*) fan
fanatismo [fana'tismo] *nm* fanaticism
fanfarrón, -ona [fanfa'rron, ona] *adj*
boastful; (*pey*) showy
fanfarronear [fanfarrone'ar] *vi* to boast
fango ['fango] *nm* mud
fangoso, -a [fan'goso, a] *adj* muddy
fantasear [fantase'ar] *vi* to fantasize; **~ con**
una idea to toy with an idea
fantasía [fanta'sia] *nf* fantasy, imagination;
(*Mus*) fantasia; (*capricho*) whim; **joyas de ~**
imitation jewellery *sg*
fantasma [fan'tasma] *nm* (*espectro*) ghost,
apparition; (*presumido*) show-off
fantástico, -a [fan'tastiko, a] *adj* (*irreal, fam*)
fantastic
fanzine [fan'θine] *nm* fanzine
FAO ['fao] *nf abr* (= *Organización de las Naciones*
Unidas para la Agricultura y la Alimentación) FAO
faquir [fa'kir] *nm* fakir
faraón [fara'on] *nm* Pharaoh
faraónico, -a [fara'oniko, a] *adj* Pharaonic;
(*fig*) grandiose
fardar [far'ðar] *vi* to show off; **~ de** to boast
about
fardo ['farðo] *nm* bundle; (*fig*) burden
faringe [fa'rinxe] *nf* pharynx
faringitis [farin'xitis] *nf* pharyngitis
farmacéutico, -a [farma'θeutiko, a] *adj*
pharmaceutical ■ *nm/f* chemist (*Brit*),
pharmacist
farmacia [far'maθja] *nf* (*ciencia*) pharmacy;
(*tienda*) chemist's (shop) (*Brit*), pharmacy,

drugstore (US); **~ de turno** duty chemist

fármaco ['farmako] *nm* medicine, drug

faro ['faro] *nm* (*Naut: torre*) lighthouse; (*señal*) beacon; (*Auto*) headlamp; **faros antiniebla** fog lamps; **faros delanteros/traseros** headlights/rear lights

farol [fa'rol] *nm* (*luz*) lantern, lamp; (*Ferro*) headlamp; (*poste*) lamppost; **echarse un ~** (*fam*) to show off

farola [fa'rola] *nf* street lamp (*Brit*) *o* light (US), lamppost

farruco, -a [fa'rruko, a] *adj* (*fam*): **estar** *o* **ponerse ~** to get aggressive

farsa ['farsa] *nf* farce

farsante [far'sante] *nm/f* fraud, fake

FASA ['fasa] *nf abr* (*Esp Auto*) = **Fábrica de Automóviles, S.A.**

fascículo [fas'θikulo] *nm* part, instalment (*Brit*), installment (US)

fascinante [fasθi'nante] *adj* fascinating

fascinar [fasθi'nar] *vt* to fascinate; (*encantar*) to captivate

fascismo [fas'θismo] *nm* fascism

fascista [fas'θista] *adj, nm/f* fascist

fase ['fase] *nf* phase

fastidiar [fasti'ðjar] *vt* (*disgustar*) to annoy, bother; (*estropear*) to spoil; **fastidiarse** *vr* (*disgustarse*) to get annoyed *o* cross; **¡no fastidies!** you're joking!; **¡que se fastidie!** (*fam*) he'll just have to put up with it!

fastidio [fas'tiðjo] *nm* (*disgusto*) annoyance

fastidioso, -a [fasti'ðjoso, a] *adj* (*molesto*) annoying

fastuoso, -a [fas'twoso, a] *adj* (*espléndido*) magnificent; (*banquete etc*) lavish

fatal [fa'tal] *adj* (*gen*) fatal; (*desgraciado*) ill-fated; (*fam: malo, pésimo*) awful ■ *adv* terribly; **lo pasó ~** he had a terrible time (of it)

fatalidad [fatali'ðað] *nf* (*destino*) fate; (*mala suerte*) misfortune

fatídico, -a [fa'tiðiko, a] *adj* fateful

fatiga [fa'tiɣa] *nf* (*cansancio*) fatigue, weariness; **fatigas** *nfpl* hardships

fatigar [fati'ɣar] *vt* to tire, weary; **fatigarse** *vr* to get tired

fatigoso, -a [fati'ɣoso, a] *adj* (*que cansa*) tiring

fatigue *etc* [fa'tiɣe] *vb ver* **fatigar**

fatuo, -a ['fatwo, a] *adj* (*vano*) fatuous; (*presuntuoso*) conceited

fauces ['fauθes] *nfpl* (*Anat*) gullet *sg*; (*fam*) jaws

fauna ['fauna] *nf* fauna

favor [fa'βor] *nm* favour (*Brit*), favor (US); **haga el ~ de ...** would you be so good as to ..., kindly ...; **por ~** please; **a ~** in favo(u)r; **a ~ de** in favo(u)r of; (*Com*) to the order of

favorable [faβo'raβle] *adj* favourable (*Brit*),

favorable (US); (*condiciones etc*) advantageous

favorecer [faβore'θer] *vt* to favour (*Brit*), favor (US); (*amparar*) to help; (*vestido etc*) to become, flatter; **este peinado le favorece** this hairstyle suits him

favorezca *etc* [faβo'reθka] *vb ver* **favorecer**

favorito, -a [faβo'rito, a] *adj, nm/f* favourite (*Brit*), favorite (US)

fax [faks] *nm inv* fax; **mandar por ~** to fax

faz [faθ] *nf* face; **la ~ de la tierra** the face of the earth

FBI *nm abr* FBI

F.C., f.c. *abr* = **ferrocarril**; (= *Fútbol Club*) FC

FE *nf abr* = **Falange Española**

fe [fe] *nf* (*Rel*) faith; (*confianza*) belief; (*documento*) certificate; **de buena fe** (*Jur*) bona fide; **prestar fe a** to believe, credit; **actuar con buena/mala fe** to act in good/bad faith; **dar fe de** to bear witness to; **fe de erratas** errata

fealdad [feal'dað] *nf* ugliness

feb., feb.º *abr* (= *febrero*) Feb.

febrero [fe'βrero] *nm* February; *ver tb* **julio**

febril [fe'βril] *adj* feverish; (*movido*) hectic

fecha ['fetʃa] *nf* date; **~ límite** *o* **tope** closing *o* last date; **~ límite de venta** (*de alimentos*) sell-by date; **~ de caducidad** (*de alimentos*) sell-by date; (*de contrato*) expiry date; **en ~ próxima** soon; **hasta la ~** to date, so far; **~ de vencimiento** (*Com*) due date; **~ de vigencia** (*Com*) effective date

fechar [fe'tʃar] *vt* to date

fechoría [fetʃo'ria] *nf* misdeed

fécula ['fekula] *nf* starch

fecundación [fekunda'θjon] *nf* fertilization; **~ in vitro** in vitro fertilization, I.V.F.

fecundar [fekun'dar] *vt* (*generar*) to fertilize, make fertile

fecundidad [fekundi'ðað] *nf* fertility; (*fig*) productiveness

fecundo, -a [fe'kundo, a] *adj* (*fértil*) fertile; (*fig*) prolific; (*productivo*) productive

FED *nm abr* (= *Fondo Europeo de Desarrollo*) EDF

FEDER *nm abr* (= *Fondo Europeo de Desarrollo Regional*) ERDF

federación [feðera'θjon] *nf* federation

federal [feðe'ral] *adj* federal

federalismo [feðera'lismo] *nm* federalism

FEF [fef] *nf abr* = **Federación Española de Fútbol**

felicidad [feliθi'ðað] *nf* (*satisfacción, contento*) happiness; **felicidades** *nfpl* best wishes, congratulations

felicitación [feliθita'θjon] *nf* (*tarjeta*) greetings card; **felicitaciones** *nfpl* (*enhorabuena*) congratulations; **~ navideña** *o* **de Navidad** Christmas Greetings

felicitar [feliθi'tar] *vt* to congratulate

feligrés, -esa [feli'ɣres, esa] *nm/f* parishioner

felino, -a [fe'lino, a] *adj* cat-like; (*Zool*) feline ■ *nm* feline

feliz [fe'liθ] *adj* (*contento*) happy; (*afortunado*) lucky

felonía [felo'nia] *nf* felony, crime

felpa ['felpa] *nf* (*terciopelo*) plush; (*toalla*) towelling

felpudo [fel'puðo] *nm* doormat

femenino, -a [feme'nino, a] *adj* feminine; (*Zool etc*) female ■ *nm* (*Ling*) feminine

feminismo [femi'nismo] *nm* feminism

feminista [femi'nista] *adj, nm/f* feminist

fenomenal [fenome'nal] *adj* phenomenal; (*fam*) great, terrific

fenómeno [fe'nomeno] *nm* phenomenon; (*fig*) freak, accident ■ *adv*: **lo pasamos ~** we had a great time ■ *excl* great!, marvellous!

feo, -a ['feo, a] *adj* (*gen*) ugly; (*desagradable*) bad, nasty ■ *nm* insult; **hacer un ~ a algn** to offend sb; **más ~ que Picio** as ugly as sin

féretro ['feretro] *nm* (*ataúd*) coffin; (*sarcófago*) bier

feria ['ferja] *nf* (*gen*) fair; (*Am: mercado*) market; (*descanso*) holiday, rest day; (*Am: cambio*) small change; **~ comercial** trade fair; **~ de muestras** trade show

feriado, -a [fe'rjaðo, a] (*Am*) *adj*: **día ~** (public) holiday ■ *nm* (public) holiday

fermentar [fermen'tar] *vi* to ferment

fermento [fer'mento] *nm* leaven, leavening

ferocidad [feroθi'ðað] *nf* fierceness, ferocity

ferocísimo, -a [fero'θisimo, a] *adj superlativo de* **feroz**

feroz [fe'roθ] *adj* (*cruel*) cruel; (*salvaje*) fierce

férreo, -a ['ferreo, a] *adj* iron *cpd*; (*Tec*) ferrous; (*fig*) (of) iron

ferretería [ferrete'ria] *nf* (*tienda*) ironmonger's (shop) (*Brit*), hardware store

ferretero [ferre'tero] *nm* ironmonger

ferrocarril [ferroka'rril] *nm* railway, railroad (*US*); **~ de vía estrecha/única** narrow-gauge/single-track railway *o* line

ferroviario, -a [ferrovja'rjo, a] *adj* rail *cpd*, railway *cpd* (*Brit*), railroad *cpd* (*US*) ■ *nm*: **ferroviarios** railway (*Brit*) *o* railroad (*US*) workers

fértil ['fertil] *adj* (*productivo*) fertile; (*rico*) rich

fertilice *etc* [ferti'liθe] *vb ver* **fertilizar**

fertilidad [fertili'ðað] *nf* (*gen*) fertility; (*productividad*) fruitfulness

fertilizante [fertili'θante] *nm* fertilizer

fertilizar [fertili'θar] *vt* to fertilize

ferviente [fer'βjente] *adj* fervent

fervor [fer'βor] *nm* fervour (*Brit*), fervor (*US*)

fervoroso, -a [ferβo'roso, a] *adj* fervent

festejar [feste'xar] *vt* (*agasajar*) to wine and dine; (*galantear*) to court; (*celebrar*) to celebrate

festejo [fes'texo] *nm* (*diversión*) entertainment; (*galanteo*) courtship; (*fiesta*) celebration

festín [fes'tin] *nm* feast, banquet

festival [festi'βal] *nm* festival

festividad [festiβi'ðað] *nf* festivity

festivo, -a [fes'tiβo, a] *adj* (*de fiesta*) festive; (*fig*) witty; (*Cine, Lit*) humorous; **día ~** holiday

fetiche [fe'titʃe] *nm* fetish

fetichista [feti'tʃista] *adj* fetishistic ■ *nm/f* fetishist

fétido, -a ['fetiðo, a] *adj* (*hediondo*) foul-smelling

feto ['feto] *nm* foetus; (*fam*) monster

F.E.V.E. *nf abr* (= *Ferrocarriles Españoles de Vía Estrecha*) Spanish narrow-gauge railways

FF.AA. *nfpl abr* (*Mil*) = **Fuerzas Armadas**

FF.CC. *nmpl abr* (= *Ferrocarriles*) *ver* **ferrocarril**

fiable [fi'aβle] *adj* (*persona*) trustworthy; (*máquina*) reliable

fiado [fi'aðo] *nm*: **comprar al ~** to buy on credit; **en ~** on bail

fiador, a [fia'ðor, a] *nm/f* (*Jur*) surety, guarantor; (*Com*) backer; **salir ~ por algn** to stand bail for sb

fiambre ['fjambre] *adj* (*Culin*) served cold ■ *nm* (*Culin*) cold meat (*Brit*), cold cut (*US*); (*fam*) corpse, stiff

fiambrera [fjam'brera] *nf* ≈ lunch box, ≈ dinner pail (*US*)

fianza ['fjanθa] *nf* surety; (*Jur*): **libertad bajo ~** release on bail

fiar [fi'ar] *vt* (*salir garante de*) to guarantee; (*Jur*) to stand bail *o* bond (*US*) for; (*vender a crédito*) to sell on credit; (*secreto*) to confide ■ *vi*: **~ (de)** to trust (in); **ser de ~** to be trustworthy; **fiarse** *vr*: **fiarse de** to trust (in), rely on

fiasco ['fjasko] *nm* fiasco

fibra ['fiβra] *nf* fibre (*Brit*), fiber (*US*); (*fig*) vigour (*Brit*), vigor (*US*); **~ óptica** (*Inform*) optical fibre (*Brit*) *o* fiber (*US*)

ficción [fik'θjon] *nf* fiction

ficha ['fitʃa] *nf* (*Telec*) token; (*en juegos*) counter, marker; (*en casino*) chip; (*Com, Econ*) tally, check (*US*); (*Inform*) file; (*tarjeta*) (index) card; (*Elec*) plug; (*en hotel*) registration form; **~ policíaca** police dossier

fichaje [fi'tʃaxe] *nm* signing(-up)

fichar [fi'tʃar] *vt* (*archivar*) to file, index; (*Deporte*) to sign (up) ■ *vi* (*deportista*) to sign (up); (*obrero*) to clock in *o* on; **estar fichado** to have a record

fichero [fi'tʃero] *nm* card index; (*archivo*) filing cabinet; (*Com*) box file; (*Inform*) file, archive; (*de policía*) criminal records; **~ activo**

(*Inform*) active file; ~ **archivado** (*Inform*) archived file; ~ **indexado** (*Inform*) index file; ~ **de reserva** (*Inform*) backup file; ~ **de tarjetas** card index; **nombre de** ~ filename

ficticio, -a [fik'tiθjo, a] *adj* (*imaginario*) fictitious; (*falso*) fabricated

ficus ['fikus] *nm inv* (*Bot*) rubber plant

fidedigno, -a [fiðe'ðiɣno, a] *adj* reliable

fideicomiso [fiðeiko'miso] *nm* (*Com*) trust

fidelidad [fiðeli'ðað] *nf* (*lealtad*) fidelity, loyalty; (*exactitud: de dato etc*) accuracy; **alta** ~ high fidelity, hi-fi

fidelísimo, -a [fiðe'lisimo, a] *adj superlativo de* **fiel**

fideos [fi'ðeos] *nmpl* noodles

fiduciario, -a [fiðu'θjarjo, a] *nm/f* fiduciary

fiebre ['fjeβre] *nf* (*Med*) fever; (*fig*) fever, excitement; ~ **amarilla/del heno** yellow/hay fever; ~ **palúdica** malaria; **tener** ~ to have a temperature

fiel [fjel] *adj* (*leal*) faithful, loyal; (*fiable*) reliable; (*exacto*) accurate ■ *nm* (*aguja*) needle, pointer; **los fieles** *nmpl* the faithful

fieltro ['fjeltro] *nm* felt

fiera ['fjera] *nf ver* **fiero**

fiereza [fje'reθa] *nf* (*Zool*) wildness; (*bravura*) fierceness

fiero, -a ['fjero, a] *adj* (*cruel*) cruel; (*feroz*) fierce; (*duro*) harsh ■ *nm/f* (*fig*) fiend ■ *nf* (*animal feroz*) wild animal o beast; (*fig*) dragon

fierro ['fjerro] *nm* (*Am*) iron

fiesta ['fjesta] *nf* party; (*de pueblo*) festival; **la** ~ **nacional** bullfighting; (**día de**) ~ (public) holiday; **mañana es** ~ it's a holiday tomorrow; ~ **de guardar** (*Rel*) day of obligation; *see note*

● **FIESTA**
●
● *Fiestas* can be official public holidays
● (such as the *Día de la Constitución*), or special
● holidays for each *comunidad autónoma*,
● many of which are religious feast days.
● All over Spain there are also special local
● *fiestas* for a patron saint or the Virgin
● Mary. These often last several days
● and can include religious processions,
● carnival parades, bullfights, dancing and
● feasts of typical local produce.

FIFA *nf abr* (= *Federación Internacional de Fútbol Asociación*) FIFA

figura [fi'ɣura] *nf* (*gen*) figure; (*forma, imagen*) shape, form; (*Naipes*) face card

figurado, -a [fiɣu'raðo, a] *adj* figurative

figurante [fiɣu'rante] *nm/f* (*Teat*) walk-on part; (*Cine*) extra

figurar [fiɣu'rar] *vt* (*representar*) to represent; (*fingir*) to feign ■ *vi* to figure; **figurarse** *vr* (*imaginarse*) to imagine; (*suponer*) to suppose; **ya me lo figuraba** I thought as much

fijador [fixa'ðor] *nm* (*Foto etc*) fixative; (*de pelo*) gel

fijar [fi'xar] *vt* (*gen*) to fix; (*cartel*) to post, put up; (*estampilla*) to affix, stick (on); (*pelo*) to set; (*fig*) to settle (on), decide; **fijarse** *vr*: **fijarse en** to notice; **¡fíjate!** just imagine!; **¿te fijas?** see what I mean?

fijo, -a ['fixo, a] *adj* (*gen*) fixed; (*firme*) firm; (*permanente*) permanent; (*trabajo*) steady; (*colorfast*) fast ■ *adv*: **mirar** ~ to stare

fila ['fila] *nf* row; (*Mil*) rank; (*cadena*) line; (*en marcha*) file; ~ **india** single file; **ponerse en** ~ to line up, get into line; **primera** ~ front row

filántropo, -a [fi'lantropo, a] *nm/f* philanthropist

filarmónico, a [filar'moniko, a] *adj, nf* philharmonic

filatelia [fila'telja] *nf* philately, stamp collecting

filatelista [filate'lista] *nm/f* philatelist, stamp collector

filete [fi'lete] *nm* (*de carne*) fillet steak; (*de cerdo*) tenderloin; (*pescado*) fillet; (*Mecánica: rosca*) thread

filiación [filja'θjon] *nf* (*Pol etc*) affiliation; (*señas*) particulars *pl*; (*Mil, Policía*) records *pl*

filial [fi'ljal] *adj* filial ■ *nf* subsidiary; (*sucursal*) branch

Filipinas [fili'pinas] *nfpl*: **las (Islas)** ~ the Philippines

filipino, -a [fili'pino, a] *adj, nm/f* Philippine

film [film] (*pl* **films**) *nm* = **filme**

filmación [filma'θjon] *nf* filming, shooting

filmar [fil'mar] *vt* to film, shoot

filme ['filme] *nm* film, movie (*US*)

filmoteca [filmo'teka] *nf* film library

filo ['filo] *nm* (*gen*) edge; **sacar** ~ **a** to sharpen; **al** ~ **del medio día** at about midday; **de doble** ~ double-edged

filología [filolo'xia] *nf* philology

filólogo, -a [fi'loloɣo, a] *nm/f* philologist

filón [fi'lon] *nm* (*Minería*) vein, lode; (*fig*) gold mine

filoso, -a [fi'loso, a] *adj* (*Am*) sharp

filosofía [filoso'fia] *nf* philosophy

filosófico, -a [filo'sofiko, a] *adj* philosophic(al)

filósofo, -a [fi'losofo, a] *nm/f* philosopher

filtración [filtra'θjon] *nf* (*Tec*) filtration; (*Inform*) sorting; (*fig: de fondos*) misappropriation; (*de datos*) leak

filtrar [fil'trar] *vt, vi* to filter, strain; (*información*) to leak; **filtrarse** *vr* to filter;

(*fig*: *dinero*) to dwindle

filtro ['filtro] *nm* (*Tec*, *utensilio*) filter

filudo, -a [fi'luðo, a] *adj* (*Am*) sharp

fin [fin] *nm* end; (*objetivo*) aim, purpose; **a ~ de cuentas** at the end of the day; **al ~ y al cabo** when all's said and done; **a ~ de** in order to; **por ~** finally; **en ~** (*resumiendo*) in short; **¡en ~!** (*resignación*) oh, well!; **~ de archivo** (*Inform*) end-of-file; **~ de semana** weekend; **sin ~** endless(ly)

final [fi'nal] *adj* final ■ *nm* end, conclusion ■ *nf* (*Deporte*) final

finalice *etc* [fina'liθe] *vb ver* **finalizar**

finalidad [finali'ðað] *nf* finality; (*propósito*) purpose, aim

finalista [fina'lista] *nm/f* finalist

finalizar [finali'θar] *vt* to end, finish ■ *vi* to end, come to an end; **~ la sesión** (*Inform*) to log out *o* off

financiación [finanθja'θjon] *nf* financing

financiar [finan'θjar] *vt* to finance

financiero, -a [finan'θjero, a] *adj* financial ■ *nm/f* financier

financista [finan'sista] *nm/f* (*Am*) financier

finanzas [fi'nanθas] *nfpl* finances

finca ['finka] *nf* country estate

finde ['finde] *nm abbr* (*fam*: = *fin de semana*) weekend

fineza [fi'neθa] *nf* (*cualidad*) fineness; (*de modales*) refinement

fingir [fin'xir] *vt* (*simular*) to simulate, feign; (*pretextar*) to sham, fake ■ *vi* (*aparentar*) to pretend; **fingirse** *vr*: **fingirse dormido** to pretend to be asleep

finiquitar [finiki'tar] *vt* (*Econ*: *cuenta*) to settle and close

Finisterre [finis'terre] *nm*: **el cabo de ~** Cape Finisterre

finja *etc* ['finxa] *vb ver* **fingir**

finlandés, -esa [finlan'des, esa] *adj* Finnish ■ *nm/f* Finn ■ *nm* (*Ling*) Finnish

Finlandia [fin'landja] *nf* Finland

fino, -a ['fino, a] *adj* fine; (*delgado*) slender; (*de buenas maneras*) polite, refined; (*inteligente*) shrewd; (*punta*) sharp; (*gusto*) discriminating; (*oído*) sharp; (*jerez*) fino, dry ■ *nm* (*jerez*) dry sherry

finura [fi'nura] *nf* (*calidad*) fineness; (*cortesía*) politeness; (*elegancia*) elegance; (*agudeza*) shrewdness

FIP [fip] *nf abr* (*Esp*) = **Formación Intensiva Profesional**

firma ['firma] *nf* signature; (*Com*) firm, company

firmamento [firma'mento] *nm* firmament

firmante [fir'mante] *adj, nm/f* signatory; **los abajo firmantes** the undersigned

firmar [fir'mar] *vt* to sign; **~ un contrato** (*Com*: *colocarse*) to sign on; **firmado y sellado** signed and sealed

firme ['firme] *adj* firm; (*estable*) stable; (*sólido*) solid; (*constante*) steady; (*decidido*) resolute; (*duro*) hard; **¡firmes!** (*Mil*) attention!; **oferta en ~** (*Com*) firm offer ■ *nm* road (surface)

firmemente [firme'mente] *adv* firmly

firmeza [fir'meθa] *nf* firmness; (*constancia*) steadiness; (*solidez*) solidity

fiscal [fis'kal] *adj* fiscal ■ *nm* (*Jur*) ≈ Crown Prosecutor, ≈ Procurator Fiscal (*Escocia*), ≈ district attorney (*US*)

fiscalice *etc* [fiska'liθe] *vb ver* **fiscalizar**

fiscalizar [fiskali'θar] *vt* (*controlar*) to control; (*registrar*) to inspect (officially); (*fig*) to criticize

fisco ['fisko] *nm* (*hacienda*) treasury, exchequer; **declarar algo al ~** to declare sth for tax purposes

fisgar [fis'ɣar] *vt* to pry into

fisgón, -ona [fis'ɣon, ona] *adj* nosey

fisgue *etc* ['fisɣe] *vb ver* **fisgar**

físico, -a ['fisiko, a] *adj* physical ■ *nm* physique; (*aspecto*) appearance, looks *pl* ■ *nm/f* physicist ■ *nf* physics *sg*

fisioterapeuta [fisjotera'peuta] *nm/f* physiotherapist

fisioterapia [fisjote'rapja] *nf* physiotherapy

fisioterapista [fisjotera'pista] *nm/f* (*Am*) physiotherapist

fisonomía [fisono'mia] *nf* physiognomy, features *pl*

fisonomista [fisono'mista] *nm/f*: **ser buen ~** to have a good memory for faces

flaccidez [flakθi'ðeθ], **flacidez** [flaθi'ðeθ] *nf* softness, flabbiness

fláccido, -a ['flakθiðo, a], **flácido, -a** ['flaθiðo, a] *adj* flabby

flaco, -a ['flako, a] *adj* (*muy delgado*) skinny, thin; (*débil*) weak, feeble

flagrante [fla'ɣrante] *adj* flagrant

flamante [fla'mante] *adj* (*fam*) brilliant; (: *nuevo*) brand-new

flamear [flame'ar] *vt* (*Culin*) to flambé

flamenco, -a [fla'menko, a] *adj* (*de Flandes*) Flemish; (*baile, música*) gipsy ■ *nm/f* Fleming; **los flamencos** the Flemish ■ *nm* (*Ling*) Flemish; (*baile, música*) flamenco; (*Zool*) flamingo

flan [flan] *nm* creme caramel

flanco ['flanko] *nm* side; (*Mil*) flank

Flandes ['flandes] *nm* Flanders

flanquear [flanke'ar] *vt* to flank; (*Mil*) to outflank

flaquear [flake'ar] *vi* (*debilitarse*) to weaken; (*persona*) to slack

flaqueza [flaˈkeθa] *nf* (*delgadez*) thinness, leanness; (*fig*) weakness

flaquísimo, -a [flaˈkisimo, a] *adj superlativo de* **flaco**

flash [flas] (*pl* **flashes**) [flas] *nm* (*Foto*) flash

flato [ˈflato] *nm*: **el** (*o* **un**) ~ the (*o* a) stitch

flauta [ˈflauta] (*Mus*) *nf* flute ◼ *nm/f* flautist, flute player; **¡la gran ~!** (*Am*) my God!; **hijo de la gran ~** (*Am fam!*) bastard (!), son of a bitch (US!)

flecha [ˈfletʃa] *nf* arrow

flechazo [fleˈtʃaθo] *nm* (*acción*) bowshot; (*fam*): **fue un ~** it was love at first sight

fleco [ˈfleko] *nm* fringe

flema [ˈflema] *nm* phlegm

flemático, -a [fleˈmatiko, a] *adj* phlegmatic; (*tono etc*) matter-of-fact

flemón [fleˈmon] *nm* (*Med*) gumboil

flequillo [fleˈkiʎo] *nm* (*de pelo*) fringe, bangs (US)

fletar [fleˈtar] *vt* (*Com*) to charter; (*embarcar*) to load; (*Auto*) to lease(-purchase)

flete [ˈflete] *nm* (*carga*) freight; (*alquiler*) charter; (*precio*) freightage; ~ **debido** (*Com*) freight forward; ~ **sobre compras** (*Com*) freight inward

flexible [flekˈsiβle] *adj* flexible; (*individuo*) compliant

flexión [flekˈsjon] *nf* (*Deporte*) bend; (: *en el suelo*) press-up

flexo [ˈflekso] *nm* adjustable table lamp

flipper [ˈfliper] *nm* pinball machine

flirtear [flirteˈar] *vi* to flirt

FLN *nm abr* (*Pol*: *Esp, Perú, Venezuela*: = *Frente de Liberación Nacional*) political party

flojear [floxeˈar] *vi* (*piernas: al andar*) to give way; (*alumno*) to do badly; (*cosecha, mercado*) to be poor

flojera [floˈxera] *nf* (*Am*) laziness; **me da ~** I can't be bothered

flojo, -a [ˈfloxo, a] *adj* (*gen*) loose; (*sin fuerzas*) limp; (*débil*) weak; (*viento*) light; (*bebida*) weak; (*trabajo*) poor; (*actitud*) slack; (*precio*) low; (*Com: mercado*) dull, slack; (*Am*) lazy

flor [flor] *nf* flower; (*piropo*) compliment; **la ~ y nata de la sociedad** (*fig*) the cream of society; **en la ~ de la vida** in the prime of life; **a ~ de** on the surface of

flora [ˈflora] *nf* flora

florecer [floreˈθer] *vi* (*Bot*) to flower, bloom; (*fig*) to flourish

floreciente [floreˈθjente] *adj* (*Bot*) in flower, flowering; (*fig*) thriving

Florencia [floˈrenθja] *nf* Florence

florero [floˈrero] *nm* vase

florezca *etc* [floˈreθka] *vb ver* **florecer**

florista [floˈrista] *nm/f* florist

floristería [floristeˈria] *nf* florist's (shop)

flota [ˈflota] *nf* fleet

flotación [flotaˈθjon] *nf* (*Com*) flotation

flotador [flotaˈðor] *nm* (*gen*) float; (*para nadar*) rubber ring; (*de cisterna*) ballcock

flotante [floˈtante] *adj* floating; (*Inform*): **de coma ~** floating-point

flotar [floˈtar] *vi* to float

flote [ˈflote] *nm*: **a ~** afloat; **ponerse a ~** (*fig*) to get back on one's feet

FLS *nm abr* (*Pol*: *Nicaragua*) = **Frente de Liberación Sandinista**

fluctuación [fluktwaˈθjon] *nf* fluctuation

fluctuante [flukˈtwante] *adj* fluctuating

fluctuar [flukˈtwar] *vi* (*oscilar*) to fluctuate

fluidez [fluiˈðeθ] *nf* fluidity; (*fig*) fluency

fluido, -a [ˈflwiðo, a] *adj* fluid; (*lenguaje*) fluent; (*estilo*) smooth ◼ *nm* (*líquido*) fluid

fluir [fluˈir] *vi* to flow

flujo [ˈfluxo] *nm* flow; (*Pol*) swing; (*Naut*) rising tide; ~ **y reflujo** ebb and flow; ~ **de sangre** (*Med*) haemorrhage (*Brit*), hemorrhage (US); ~ **positivo/negativo de efectivo** (*Com*) positive/negative cash flow

flúor [ˈfluor] *nm* fluorine; (*en dentífrico*) fluoride

fluorescente [flworesˈθente] *adj* fluorescent ◼ *nm* (*tb*: **tubo fluorescente**) fluorescent tube

fluoruro [flwoˈruro] *nm* fluoride

fluvial [fluβiˈal] *adj* fluvial, river *cpd*

fluyendo *etc* [fluˈjendo] *vb ver* **fluir**

FM *nf abr* (= *Frecuencia Modulada*) FM

FMI *nm abr* (= *Fondo Monetario Internacional*) IMF

F.N. *nf abr* (*Esp Pol*) = **Fuerza Nueva** ◼ *nm abr* = **Frente Nacional**

f.° *abr* (= *folio*) fo., fol.

foca [ˈfoka] *nf* seal

foco [ˈfoko] *nm* focus; (*centro*) focal point; (*fuente*) source; (*de incendio*) seat; (*Elec*) floodlight; (*Teat*) spotlight; (*Am*) (light) bulb, light

fofo, -a [ˈfofo, a] *adj* (*esponjoso*) soft, spongy; (*músculo*) flabby

fogata [foˈɣata] *nf* (*hoguera*) bonfire

fogón [foˈɣon] *nm* (*de cocina*) ring, burner

fogoso, -a [foˈɣoso, a] *adj* spirited

foja [ˈfoxa] *nf* (*Am*) sheet (of paper); ~ **de servicios** record (file)

fol. *abr* (= *folio*) fo., fol.

folder, fólder [ˈfolder] *nm* (*Am*) folder

folio [ˈfoljo] *nm* folio; (*hoja*) leaf

folklore [folˈklore] *nm* folklore

folklórico, -a [folˈkloriko, a] *adj* traditional

follaje [foˈʎaxe] *nm* foliage

follar [foˈʎar] *vt, vi* (*fam!*) to fuck (!)

folletinesco, -a [foʎetinˈesko, a] *adj* melodramatic

folleto [fo'ʎeto] *nm* pamphlet; (*Com*) brochure; (*prospecto*) leaflet; (*Escol etc*) handout

follón [fo'ʎon] *nm* (*fam: lío*) mess; (: *conmoción*) fuss, rumpus, shindy; **armar un ~** to kick up a fuss; **se armó un ~** there was a hell of a row

fomentar [fomen'tar] *vt* (*Med*) to foment; (*fig: promover*) to promote, foster; (*odio etc*) to stir up

fomento [fo'mento] *nm* (*fig: ayuda*) fostering; (*promoción*) promotion

fonda ['fonda] *nf* ≈ guest house; *ver tb* **hotel**

fondear [fonde'ar] *vt* (*Naut: sondear*) to sound; (*barco*) to search

fondo ['fondo] *nm* (*de caja etc*) bottom; (*medida*) depth; (*de coche, sala*) back; (*Arte etc*) background; (*reserva*) fund; (*fig: carácter*) nature; **fondos** *nmpl* (*Com*) funds, resources; **~ de escritorio** (*Inform*) wallpaper; **F~ Monetario Internacional** International Monetary Fund; **~ del mar** sea bed *o* floor; **una investigación a ~** a thorough investigation; **en el ~** at bottom, deep down; **tener buen ~** to be good-natured

fonética [fo'netika] *nf* phonetics *sg*

fono ['fono] *nm* (*Am*) telephone (number)

fonobuzón [fonoβu'θon] *nm* voice mail

fonógrafo [fo'noɣrafo] *nm* (*esp Am*) gramophone, phonograph (US)

fonología [fonolo'xia] *nf* phonology

fontanería [fontane'ria] *nf* plumbing

fontanero [fonta'nero] *nm* plumber

footing ['futin] *nm* jogging; **hacer ~** to jog

F.O.P. [fop] *nfpl abr* (*Esp*) = **Fuerza del Orden Público**

forajido [fora'xiðo] *nm* outlaw

foráneo, -a [fo'raneo, a] *adj* foreign ■ *nm/f* outsider

forastero, -a [foras'tero, a] *nm/f* stranger

forcé [for'θe] *vb ver* **forzar**

forcejear [forθexe'ar] *vi* (*luchar*) to struggle

forcemos *etc* [for'θemos] *vb ver* **forzar**

fórceps ['forθeps] *nm inv* forceps *pl*

forense [fo'rense] *adj* forensic ■ *nm/f* pathologist

forestal [fores'tal] *adj* forest *cpd*

forjar [for'xar] *vt* to forge; (*formar*) to form

forma ['forma] *nf* (*figura*) form, shape; (*molde*) mould, pattern; (*Med*) fitness; (*método*) way, means; **estar en ~** to be fit; **~ de pago** (*Com*) method of payment; **las formas** the conventions; **de ~ que …** so that …; **de todas formas** in any case

formación [forma'θjon] *nf* (*gen*) formation; (*enseñanza*) training; **~ profesional** vocational training; **~ fuera del trabajo** off-the-job training; **~ en el trabajo** *o* **sobre la práctica** on-the-job training

formal [for'mal] *adj* (*gen*) formal; (*fig: persona*) serious; (: *de fiar*) reliable; (*conducta*) steady

formalice *etc* [forma'liθe] *vb ver* **formalizar**

formalidad [formali'ðað] *nf* formality; seriousness; reliability; steadiness

formalizar [formali'θar] *vt* (*Jur*) to formalize; (*plan*) to draw up; (*situación*) to put in order, regularize; **formalizarse** *vr* (*situación*) to be put in order, be regularized

formar [for'mar] *vt* (*componer*) to form, shape; (*constituir*) to make up, constitute; (*Escol*) to train, educate ■ *vi* (*Mil*) to fall in; (*Deporte*) to line up; **formarse** *vr* (*Escol*) to be trained (*o* educated); (*cobrar forma*) to form, take form; (*desarrollarse*) to develop

formatear [formate'ar] *vt* (*Inform*) to format

formateo [forma'teo] *nm* (*Inform*) formatting

formato [for'mato] *nm* (*Inform*): **sin ~** (*disco, texto*) unformatted; **~ de registro** record format

formidable [formi'ðaβle] *adj* (*temible*) formidable; (*asombroso*) tremendous

fórmula ['formula] *nf* formula

formular [formu'lar] *vt* (*queja*) to lodge; (*petición*) to draw up; (*pregunta*) to pose, formulate; (*idea*) to formulate

formulario [formu'larjo] *nm* form; **~ de solicitud/de pedido** (*Com*) application/order form; **llenar un ~** to fill in a form; **~ continuo desplegable** (*Inform*) fanfold paper

fornicar [forni'kar] *vi* to fornicate

fornido, -a [for'niðo, a] *adj* well-built

fornique *etc* [for'nike] *vb ver* **fornicar**

foro ['foro] *nm* (*gen*) forum; (*Jur*) court; **~ de discusión** (*Internet*) discussion forum

forofo, -a [fo'rofo, a] *nm/f* fan

FORPPA ['forpa] *nm abr* (*Esp*) = **Fondo de Ordenación y Regulación de Productos y Precios Agrarios**

FORPRONU [for'pronu] *nf abr* (= *Fuerza de Protección de las Naciones Unidas*) UNPROFOR

forrado, -a [fo'rraðo, a] *adj* (*ropa*) lined; (*fam*) well-heeled

forrar [fo'rrar] *vt* (*abrigo*) to line; (*libro*) to cover; (*coche*) to upholster; **forrarse** *vr* (*fam*) to line one's pockets

forro ['forro] *nm* (*de cuaderno*) cover; (*costura*) lining; (*de sillón*) upholstery; **~ polar** fleece

fortalecer [fortale'θer] *vt* to strengthen; **fortalecerse** *vr* to fortify o.s.; (*opinión etc*) to become stronger

fortaleza [forta'leθa] *nf* (*Mil*) fortress, stronghold; (*fuerza*) strength; (*determinación*) resolution

fortalezca etc [forta'leθka] vb ver **fortalecer**

fortificar [fortifi'kar] vt to fortify; (fig) to strengthen

fortifique etc [forti'fike] vb ver **fortificar**

fortísimo, -a [for'tisimo, a] adj superlativo de **fuerte**

fortuito, -a [for'twito, a] adj accidental, chance cpd

fortuna [for'tuna] nf (suerte) fortune, (good) luck; (riqueza) fortune, wealth

forzar [for'θar] vt (puerta) to force (open); (compeler) to compel; (violar) to rape; (ojos etc) to strain

forzoso, -a [for'θoso, a] adj necessary; (inevitable) inescapable; (obligatorio) compulsory

forzudo, -a [for'θuðo, a] adj burly

fosa ['fosa] nf (sepultura) grave; (en tierra) pit; (Med) cavity; **fosas nasales** nostrils

fosfato [fos'fato] nm phosphate

fosforescente [fosfores'θente] adj phosphorescent

fósforo ['fosforo] nm (Química) phosphorus; (esp Am: cerilla) match

fósil ['fosil] adj fossil, fossilized ▪ nm fossil

foso ['foso] nm ditch; (Teat) pit; (Auto): ~ **de reconocimiento** inspection pit

foto ['foto] nf photo, snap(shot); **sacar una ~** to take a photo o picture

fotocopia [foto'kopja] nf photocopy

fotocopiadora [fotokopja'ðora] nf photocopier

fotocopiar [fotoko'pjar] vt to photocopy

fotogénico, -a [foto'xeniko, a] adj photogenic

fotografía [fotoɣra'fia] nf (arte) photography; (una fotografía) photograph

fotografiar [fotoɣra'fjar] vt to photograph

fotógrafo, -a [fo'toɣrafo, a] nm/f photographer

fotomatón [fotoma'ton] nm (cabina) photo booth

fotómetro [fo'tometro] nm (Foto) light meter

fotonovela [fotono'βela] nf photo-story

foulard [fu'lar] nm (head)scarf

FP nf abr (Esp: Escol, Com) = **Formación Profesional** ▪ nm abr (Pol) = **Frente Popular**

FPLP nm abr (Pol: = Frente Popular para la Liberación de Palestina) PFLP

Fr. abr (= Fray) Fr.

fra. abr = **factura**

frac (pl fracs o fraques) [frak, 'frakes] nm dress coat, tails

fracasar [fraka'sar] vi (gen) to fail; (plan etc) to fall through

fracaso [fra'kaso] nm (desgracia, revés) failure; (de negociaciones etc) collapse, breakdown

fracción [frak'θjon] nf fraction; (Pol) faction, splinter group

fraccionamiento [fraksjona'mjento] nm (Am) housing estate

fractura [frak'tura] nf fracture, break

fragancia [fra'ɣanθja] nf (olor) fragrance, perfume

fragante [fra'ɣante] adj fragrant, scented

fraganti [fra'ɣanti]: **in ~** adv: **coger a algn in fraganti** to catch sb red-handed

fragata [fra'ɣata] nf frigate

frágil ['fraxil] adj (débil) fragile; (Com) breakable; (fig) frail, delicate

fragilidad [fraxili'ðað] nf fragility; (de persona) frailty

fragmento [fraɣ'mento] nm fragment; (pedazo) piece; (de discurso) excerpt; (de canción) snatch

fragor [fra'ɣor] nm (ruido intenso) din

fragua ['fraɣwa] nf forge

fraguar [fra'ɣwar] vt to forge; (fig) to concoct ▪ vi to harden

fragüe etc ['fraɣwe] vb ver **fraguar**

fraile ['fraile] nm (Rel) friar; (: monje) monk

frambuesa [fram'bwesa] nf raspberry

francés, -esa [fran'θes, esa] adj French ▪ nm/f Frenchman(-woman) ▪ nm (Ling) French

Francia ['franθja] nf France

franco, -a ['franko, a] adj (cándido) frank, open; (Com: exento) free ▪ nm (moneda) franc; ~ **de derechos** duty-free; ~ **al costado del buque** (Com) free alongside ship; ~ **puesto sobre vagón** (Com) free on rail; ~ **a bordo** free on board

francotirador, a [frankotira'ðor, a] nm/f sniper

franela [fra'nela] nf flannel

franja ['franxa] nf fringe; (de uniforme) stripe; (de tierra etc) strip

franquear [franke'ar] vt (camino) to clear; (carta, paquete) to frank, stamp; (obstáculo) to overcome; (Com etc) to free, exempt

franqueo [fran'keo] nm postage

franqueza [fran'keθa] nf frankness

franquicia [fran'kiθja] nf exemption; ~ **aduanera** exemption from customs duties

franquismo [fran'kismo] nm: **el ~** (sistema) the Franco system; (período) the Franco years; see note

● **FRANQUISMO**
●
● The political reign and style of
● government of Francisco Franco (from
● the end of the Spanish Civil War in 1939
● until his death in 1975) are commonly

called *franquismo*. He was a powerful, authoritarian, right-wing dictator, who promoted a traditional, Catholic and self-sufficient country. From the 1960s Spain gradually opened its doors to the international community, coinciding with a rise in economic growth and internal political opposition. On his death Spain became a democratic constitutional monarchy.

franquista [franˈkista] *adj* pro-Franco ■ *nm/f* supporter of Franco

frasco [ˈfrasko] *nm* bottle, flask; ~ **al vacio** (vacuum) flask

frase [ˈfrase] *nf* sentence; *(locución)* phrase, expression; ~ **hecha** set phrase

fraternal [fraterˈnal] *adj* brotherly, fraternal

fraude [ˈfrauðe] *nm (cualidad)* dishonesty; *(acto)* fraud, swindle

fraudulento, -a [frauðuˈlento, a] *adj* fraudulent

frazada [fraˈsaða] *nf (Am)* blanket

frecuencia [freˈkwenθja] *nf* frequency; **con** ~ frequently, often; ~ **de red** *(Inform)* mains frequency; ~ **del reloj** *(Inform)* clock speed; ~ **telefónica** voice frequency

frecuentar [frekwenˈtar] *vt (lugar)* to frequent; *(persona)* to see frequently *o* often; ~ **la buena sociedad** to mix in high society

frecuente [freˈkwente] *adj* frequent; *(costumbre)* common; *(vicio)* rife

fregadero [freɣaˈðero] *nm* (kitchen) sink

fregado, -a [freˈɣaðo, a] *adj (Am fam!)* damn, bloody (!)

fregar [freˈɣar] *vt (frotar)* to scrub; *(platos)* to wash (up); *(Am)* to annoy

fregón, -ona [freˈɣon, ona] *adj* = **fregado** ■ *nf (utensilio)* mop; *(pey: sirvienta)* skivvy

fregué *etc* [freˈɣe] *vb ver* **fregar**

freidora [freiˈðora] *nf* deep-fat fryer

freír [freˈir] *vt* to fry

fréjol [ˈfrexol] *nm* = **fríjol**

frenar [freˈnar] *vt* to brake; *(fig)* to check

frenazo [freˈnaθo] *nm*: **dar un** ~ to brake sharply

frenesí [freneˈsi] *nm* frenzy

frenético, -a [freˈnetiko, a] *adj* frantic; **ponerse** ~ to lose one's head

freno [ˈfreno] *nm (Tec, Auto)* brake; *(de cabalgadura)* bit; *(fig)* check

frente [ˈfrente] *nm (Arq, Mil, Pol)* front; *(de objeto)* front part ■ *nf* forehead, brow; ~ **de batalla** battle front; **hacer** ~ **común con algn** to make common cause with sb; ~ **a** in front of; *(en situación opuesta a)* opposite; **chocar de** ~ to crash head-on; **hacer** ~ **a**

to face up to

fresa [ˈfresa] *nf (Esp: fruta)* strawberry; *(de dentista)* drill

fresco, -a [ˈfresko, a] *adj (nuevo)* fresh; *(huevo)* newly-laid; *(frío)* cool; *(descarado)* cheeky, bad-mannered ■ *nm (aire)* fresh air; *(Arte)* fresco; *(Am: bebida)* fruit juice *o* drink ■ *nm/f (fam)* shameless person; *(persona insolente)* impudent person; **tomar el** ~ to get some fresh air; **¡qué** ~! what a cheek!

frescor [fresˈkor] *nm* freshness

frescura [fresˈkura] *nf* freshness; *(descaro)* cheek, nerve; *(calma)* calmness

fresno [ˈfresno] *nm* ash (tree)

fresón [freˈson] *nm* strawberry

frialdad [frjalˈdað] *nf (gen)* coldness; *(indiferencia)* indifference

fricción [frikˈθjon] *nf (gen)* friction; *(acto)* rub(bing); *(Med)* massage; *(Pol, fig etc)* friction, trouble

friega *etc* [ˈfrjeɣa], **friegue** *etc* [ˈfrjeɣe] *vb ver* **fregar**

friendo *etc* [friˈendo] *vb ver* **freír**

frigidez [frixiˈðeθ] *nf* frigidity

frígido, -a [ˈfrixiðo, a] *adj* frigid

frigo [ˈfriɣo] *nm* fridge

frigorífico, -a [friɣoˈrifiko, a] *adj* refrigerating ■ *nm* refrigerator; *(camión)* freezer lorry *o* truck (US); **instalación frigorífica** cold-storage plant

frijol [friˈxol], **fríjol** [ˈfrixol] *nm* kidney bean

friki *(col)* *adj* weird *(col)*; **me pasó una cosa muy** ~ something really weird *(col)* happened to me; **¡qué tío más** ~! What a weirdo! *(col)* ■ *nmf* weirdo *(col)*

frió [friˈo] *vb ver* **freír**

frío, -a *etc* [ˈfrio, a] *vb ver* **freír** ■ *adj* cold; *(fig: indiferente)* unmoved, indifferent; *(poco entusiasta)* chilly ■ *nm* cold(ness); indifference; **¡qué** ~! how cold it is!

friolento, -a [frjoˈlento, a], *(Am)* **friolero, -a** [frjoˈlero, a] *adj* sensitive to cold

frito, -a [ˈfrito, a] *pp de* **freír** ■ *adj* fried ■ *nm* fry; **me trae** ~ **ese hombre** I'm sick and tired of that man; **fritos variados** mixed grill

frívolo, -a [ˈfriβolo, a] *adj* frivolous

frondoso, -a [fronˈdoso, a] *adj* leafy

frontal [fronˈtal] *nm*: **choque** ~ head-on collision

frontera [fronˈtera] *nf* frontier; *(línea divisoria)* border; *(zona)* frontier area

fronterizo, -a [fronteˈriθo, a] *adj* frontier *cpd*; *(contiguo)* bordering

frontón [fronˈton] *nm (Deporte: cancha)* pelota court; *(: juego)* pelota

frotar [froˈtar] *vt* to rub; *(fósforo)* to strike;

frotarse vr: **frotarse las manos** to rub one's hands

fructífero, -a [fruk'tifero, a] adj productive, fruitful

frugal [fru'ɣal] adj frugal

fruncir [frun'θir] vt (Costura) to gather; (ceño) to frown; (labios) to purse

frunza etc ['frunθa] vb ver **fruncir**

frustración [frustra'θjon] nf frustration

frustrar [frus'trar] vt to frustrate; **frustrarse** vr to be frustrated; (plan etc) to fail

fruta ['fruta] nf fruit

frutal [fru'tal] adj fruit-bearing, fruit cpd ▪ nm: (**árbol**) ~ fruit tree

frutería [frute'ria] nf fruit shop

frutero, -a [fru'tero, a] adj fruit cpd ▪ nm/f fruiterer ▪ nm fruit dish o bowl

frutilla [fru'tiʎa] nf (Am) strawberry

fruto ['fruto] nm (Bot) fruit; (fig: resultado) result, outcome; **frutos secos** ≈ nuts and raisins

FSLN nm abr (Pol: Nicaragua) = **Frente Sandinista de Liberación Nacional**

fue [fwe] vb ver **ser**; **ir**

fuego ['fweɣo] nm (gen) fire; (Culin: gas) burner, ring; (Mil) fire; (fig: pasión) fire, passion; ~ **amigo** friendly fire; **fuegos artificiales** o **de artificio** fireworks; **prender** ~ **a** to set fire to; **a** ~ **lento** on a low flame o gas; ¡**alto el** ~! cease fire!; **estar entre dos fuegos** to be in the crossfire; ¿**tienes** ~? have you (got) a light?

fuelle ['fweʎe] nm bellows pl

fuel-oil [fuel'oil] nm paraffin (Brit), kerosene (US)

fuente ['fwente] nf fountain; (manantial, fig) spring; (origen) source; (plato) large dish; ~ **de alimentación** (Inform) power supply; **de** ~ **desconocida/fidedigna** from an unknown/reliable source

fuera etc ['fwera] vb ver **ser**; **ir** ▪ adv out(side); (en otra parte) away; (excepto, salvo) except, save ▪ prep: ~ **de** outside; (fig) besides; ~ **de alcance** out of reach; ~ **de combate** out of action; (boxeo) knocked out; ~ **de sí** beside o. s.; **por** ~ (on the) outside; **los de** ~ strangers, newcomers; **estar** ~ (en el extranjero) to be abroad

fuera-borda [fwera'βorða] nm inv outboard engine o motor

fuerce etc ['fwerθe] vb ver **forzar**

fuereño, -a [fwe'reɲo, a] nm/f (Am) outsider

fuero ['fwero] nm (carta municipal) municipal charter; (leyes locales) local o regional law code; (privilegio) privilege; (autoridad) jurisdiction; (fig): **en mi** etc ~ **interno ...** in my etc heart of hearts ..., deep down ...

fuerte ['fwerte] adj strong; (golpe) hard; (ruido) loud; (comida) rich; (lluvia) heavy; (dolor) intense ▪ adv strongly; hard; loud(ly) ▪ nm (Mil) fort, strongpoint; (fig): **ser** ~ **en** to be good at; **el canto no es mi** ~ singing is not my strong point

fuerza etc ['fwerθa] vb ver **forzar** ▪ nf (fortaleza) strength; (Tec, Elec) power; (coacción) force; (violencia) violence; (Mil: tb: **fuerzas**) forces pl; ~ **de arrastre** (Tec) pulling power; ~ **de brazos** manpower; ~ **mayor** force majeure; ~ **bruta** brute force; **F**~ **Armadas (FF.AA.)** armed forces; **F**~ **del Orden Público (F.O.P.)** police (forces); ~ **vital** vitality; **a** ~ **de** by (dint of); **cobrar** ~**s** to recover one's strength; **tener** ~**s para** to have the strength to; **hacer algo a la** ~ to be forced to do sth; **con** ~ **legal** (Com) legally binding; **a la** ~, **por** ~ of necessity; ~ **de voluntad** willpower

fuete ['fwete] nm (Am) whip

fuga ['fuɣa] nf (huida) flight, escape; (de enamorados) elopement; (de gas etc) leak; ~ **de cerebros** (fig) brain drain

fugarse [fu'ɣarse] vr to flee, escape

fugaz [fu'ɣaθ] adj fleeting

fugitivo, -a [fuxi'tiβo, a] adj fugitive, fleeing ▪ nm/f fugitive

fugue etc ['fuɣe] vb ver **fugarse**

fui etc [fwi] vb ver **ser**; **ir**

fulano, -a [fu'lano, a] nm/f so-and-so, what's-his-name/what's-her-name

fulgor [ful'ɣor] nm brilliance

fulminante [fulmi'nante] adj (pólvora) fulminating; (fig: mirada) withering; (Med) fulminant; (fam) terrific, tremendous

fulminar [fulmi'nar] vt: **caer fulminado por un rayo** to be struck down by lightning; ~ **a algn con la mirada** to look daggers at sb

fumador, a [fuma'ðor, a] nm/f smoker; **no** ~ non-smoker

fumar [fu'mar] vt, vi to smoke; **fumarse** vr (disipar) to squander; ~ **en pipa** to smoke a pipe

fumigar [fumi'ɣar] vt to fumigate

funámbulo, -a [fu'nambulo, a], **funambulista** [funambu'lista] nm/f tightrope walker

función [fun'θjon] nf function; (de puesto) duties pl; (Teat etc) show; **entrar en funciones** to take up one's duties; ~ **de tarde/de noche** matinée/evening performance

funcional [funθjo'nal] adj functional

funcionamiento [funθjona'mjento] nm functioning; (Tec) working; **en** ~ (Com) on stream; **entrar en** ~ to come into operation

funcionar [funθjo'nar] *vi* (*gen*) to function; (*máquina*) to work; **"no funciona"** "out of order"

funcionario, -a [funθjo'narjo, a] *nm/f* official; (*público*) civil servant

funda ['funda] *nf* (*gen*) cover; (*de almohada*) pillowcase; ~ **protectora del disco** (*Inform*) disk-jacket

fundación [funda'θjon] *nf* foundation

fundado, -a [fun'daðo, a] *adj* (*justificado*) well-founded

fundamental [fundamen'tal] *adj* fundamental, basic

fundamentalismo [fundamenta'lismo] *nm* fundamentalism

fundamentalista [fundamenta'lista] *adj, nm/f* fundamentalist

fundamentar [fundamen'tar] *vt* (*poner base*) to lay the foundations of; (*establecer*) to found; (*fig*) to base

fundamento [funda'mento] *nm* (*base*) foundation; (*razón*) grounds *pl*; **eso carece de** ~ that is groundless

fundar [fun'dar] *vt* to found; (*crear*) to set up; (*fig: basar*): ~ **(en)** to base *o* found (on); **fundarse** *vr*: **fundarse en** to be founded on

fundición [fundi'θjon] *nf* (*acción*) smelting; (*fábrica*) foundry; (*Tip*) fount (*Brit*), font

fundir [fun'dir] *vt* (*gen*) to fuse; (*metal*) to smelt, melt down; (*Com*) to merge; (*estatua*) to cast; **fundirse** *vr* (*colores etc*) to merge, blend; (*unirse*) to fuse together; (*Elec: fusible, lámpara etc*) to blow; (*nieve etc*) to melt

fúnebre ['funeβre] *adj* funeral *cpd*, funereal

funeral [fune'ral] *nm* funeral

funeraria [fune'rarja] *nf* undertaker's (*Brit*), mortician's (*US*)

funesto, -a [fu'nesto, a] *adj* ill-fated; (*desastroso*) fatal

fungir [fun'xir] *vi*: ~ **de** (*Am*) to act as

furgón [fur'ɣon] *nm* wagon

furgoneta [furɣo'neta] *nf* (*Auto, Com*) (transit) van (*Brit*), pickup (truck) (*US*)

furia ['furja] *nf* (*ira*) fury; (*violencia*) violence

furibundo, -a [furi'βundo, a] *adj* furious

furioso, -a [fu'rjoso, a] *adj* (*iracundo*) furious; (*violento*) violent

furor [fu'ror] *nm* (*cólera*) rage; (*pasión*) frenzy, passion; **hacer** ~ to be a sensation

furtivo, -a [fur'tiβo, a] *adj* furtive ◾ *nm* poacher

furúnculo [fu'runkulo] *nm* (*Med*) boil

fuselaje [fuse'laxe] *nm* fuselage

fusible [fu'siβle] *nm* fuse

fusil [fu'sil] *nm* rifle

fusilamiento [fusila'mjento] *nm* (*Jur*) execution by firing squad

fusilar [fusi'lar] *vt* to shoot

fusión [fu'sjon] *nf* (*gen*) melting; (*unión*) fusion; (*Com*) merger, amalgamation

fusionar [fusjo'nar] *vt* to fuse (together); (*Com*) to merge; **fusionarse** *vr* (*Com*) to merge, amalgamate

fusta ['fusta] *nf* (*látigo*) riding crop

fútbol ['futβol] *nm* football

futbolín [futβo'lin] *nm* table football

futbolista [futβo'lista] *nm/f* footballer

fútil ['futil] *adj* trifling

futilidad [futili'ðað], **futileza** [futi'leθa] *nf* triviality

futón [fu'ton] *nm* futon

futuro, -a [fu'turo, a] *adj* future ◾ *nm* future; (*Ling*) future tense; **futuros** *nmpl* (*Com*) futures

Gg

G, g [xe] *nf* (*letra*) G, g; **G de Gerona** G for George

gabacho, -a [ga'βatʃo, a] *adj* Pyrenean; (*fam*) Frenchified ■ *nm/f* Pyrenean villager; (*fam*) Frenchy

gabán [ga'βan] *nm* overcoat

gabardina [gaβar'ðina] *nf* (*tela*) gabardine; (*prenda*) raincoat

gabinete [gaβi'nete] *nm* (*Pol*) cabinet; (*estudio*) study; (*de abogados etc*) office; **~ de consulta/ de lectura** consulting/reading room

gacela [ga'θela] *nf* gazelle

gaceta [ga'θeta] *nf* gazette

gacetilla [gaθe'tiʎa] *nf* (*en periódico*) news in brief; (*de personalidades*) gossip column

gachas ['gatʃas] *nfpl* porridge *sg*

gacho, -a ['gatʃo, a] *adj* (*encorvado*) bent down; (*orejas*) drooping

gaditano, -a [gaði'tano, a] *adj* of o from Cadiz ■ *nm/f* native o inhabitant of Cadiz

gaélico, -a [ga'eliko, a] *adj* Gaelic ■ *nm/f* Gael ■ *nm* (*Ling*) Gaelic

gafar [ga'far] *vt* (*fam: traer mala suerte*) to put a jinx on

gafas ['gafas] *nfpl* glasses; **~ oscuras** dark glasses; **~ de sol** sunglasses

gafe ['gafe] *adj*: **ser ~** to be jinxed ■ *nm* (*fam*) jinx

gaita ['gaita] *nf* flute; (*tb*: **gaita gallega**) bagpipes *pl*; (*dificultad*) bother; (*cosa engorrosa*) tough job

gajes ['gaxes] *nmpl* (*salario*) pay *sg*; **los ~ del oficio** occupational hazards; **~ y emolumentos** perquisites

gajo ['gaxo] *nm* (*gen*) bunch; (*de árbol*) bough; (*de naranja*) segment

gala ['gala] *nf* full dress; (*fig: lo mejor*) cream, flower; **galas** *nfpl* finery *sg*; **estar de ~** to be in one's best clothes; **hacer ~ de** to display, show off; **tener algo a ~** to be proud of sth

galaico, -a [ga'laiko, a] *adj* Galician

galán [ga'lan] *nm* lover, gallant; (*hombre atractivo*) ladies' man; (*Teat*): **primer ~** leading man

galante [ga'lante] *adj* gallant; (*atento*) charming; (*cortés*) polite

galantear [galante'ar] *vt* (*hacer la corte a*) to court, woo

galanteo [galan'teo] *nm* (*coqueteo*) flirting; (*de pretendiente*) wooing

galantería [galante'ria] *nf* (*caballerosidad*) gallantry; (*cumplido*) politeness; (*piropo*) compliment

galápago [ga'lapaɣo] *nm* (*Zool*) freshwater tortoise

galardón [galar'ðon] *nm* award, prize

galardonar [galarðo'nar] *vt* (*premiar*) to reward; (*una obra*) to award a prize for

galaxia [ga'laksja] *nf* galaxy

galbana [gal'βana] *nf* (*pereza*) sloth, laziness

galeote [gale'ote] *nm* galley slave

galera [ga'lera] *nf* (*nave*) galley; (*carro*) wagon; (*Med*) hospital ward; (*Tip*) galley

galería [gale'ria] *nf* (*gen*) gallery; (*balcón*) veranda(h); (*de casa*) corridor; (*fam: público*) audience; **~ secreta** secret passage

Gales ['gales] *nm*: (**el País de**) **~** Wales

galés, -esa [ga'les, esa] *adj* Welsh ■ *nm/f* Welshman(-woman) ■ *nm* (*Ling*) Welsh

galgo, -a ['galɣo, a] *nm/f* greyhound

Galia ['galja] *nf* Gaul

Galicia [ga'liθja] *nf* Galicia

galicismo [gali'θismo] *nm* gallicism

Galilea [gali'lea] *nf* Galilee

galimatías [galima'tias] *nm inv* (*asunto*) rigmarole; (*lenguaje*) gibberish, nonsense

gallardía [gaʎar'ðia] *nf* (*galantería*) dash; (*gracia*) gracefulness; (*valor*) bravery; (*elegancia*) elegance; (*nobleza*) nobleness

gallego, -a [ga'ʎeɣo, a] *adj* Galician; (*Am pey*) Spanish ■ *nm/f* Galician; (*Am pey*) Spaniard ■ *nm* (*Ling*) Galician; *ver tb* **Lengua**

galleta [ga'ʎeta] *nf* biscuit; (*fam: bofetada*) whack, slap

gallina [ga'ʎina] *nf* hen ■ *nm* (*fam*) coward; **~ ciega** blind man's buff; **~ llueca** broody hen

gallinazo [gaʎiˈnaso] *nm* (*Am*) turkey buzzard
gallinero [gaʎiˈnero] *nm* (*criadero*) henhouse; (*Teat*) gods *sg*, top gallery; (*voces*) hubbub
gallo [ˈgaʎo] *nm* cock, rooster; (*Mus*) false o wrong note; (*cambio de voz*) break in the voice; **en menos que canta un ~** in an instant
galo, -a [ˈgalo, a] *adj* Gallic; (= *francés*) French ◼ *nm/f* Gaul
galón [gaˈlon] *nm* (*Costura*) braid; (*Mil*) stripe; (*medida*) gallon
galopante [galoˈpante] *adj* galloping
galopar [galoˈpar] *vi* to gallop
galope [gaˈlope] *nm* gallop; **al ~** (*fig*) in great haste; **a ~ tendido** at full gallop
galvanice *etc* [galβaˈniθe] *vb ver* **galvanizar**
galvanizar [galβaniˈθar] *vt* to galvanize
gama [ˈgama] *nf* (*Mus*) scale; (*fig*) range; (*Zool*) doe
gamba [ˈgamba] *nf* prawn
gamberrada [gambeˈrraða] *nf* act of hooliganism
gamberro, -a [gamˈberro, a] *nm/f* hooligan, lout
gamo [ˈgamo] *nm* (*Zool*) buck
gamuza [gaˈmuθa] *nf* chamois; (*bayeta*) duster; (*Am: piel*) suede
gana [ˈgana] *nf* (*deseo*) desire, wish; (*apetito*) appetite; (*voluntad*) will; (*añoranza*) longing; **de buena ~** willingly; **de mala ~** reluctantly; **me dan ganas de** I feel like, I want to; **tener ganas de** to feel like; **no me da la (real) ~** I don't (damned well) want to; **son ganas de molestar** they're just trying to be awkward
ganadería [ganaðeˈria] *nf* (*ganado*) livestock; (*ganado vacuno*) cattle *pl*; (*cría, comercio*) cattle raising
ganadero, -a [ganaˈðero, a] *adj* stock *cpd* ◼ *nm* stockman
ganado [gaˈnaðo] *nm* livestock; **~ caballar/cabrío** horses *pl*/goats *pl*; **~ lanar** u **ovejuno** sheep *pl*; **~ porcino/vacuno** pigs *pl*/cattle *pl*
ganador, -a [ganaˈðor, a] *adj* winning ◼ *nm/f* winner; (*Econ*) earner
ganancia [gaˈnanθja] *nf* (*lo ganado*) gain; (*aumento*) increase; (*beneficio*) profit; **ganancias** *nfpl* (*ingresos*) earnings; (*beneficios*) profit *sg*, winnings; **ganancias y pérdidas** profit and loss; **~ bruta/líquida** gross/net profit; **ganancias de capital** capital gains; **sacar ~ de** to draw profit from
ganapán [ganaˈpan] *nm* (*obrero casual*) odd-job man; (*individuo tosco*) lout
ganar [gaˈnar] *vt* (*obtener*) to get, obtain; (*sacar ventaja*) to gain; (*Com*) to earn; (*Deporte, premio*) to win; (*derrotar*) to beat; (*alcanzar*) to reach; (*Mil: objetivo*) to take; (*apoyo*) to gain, win ◼ *vi* (*Deporte*) to win; **ganarse** *vr*: **ganarse la**

vida to earn one's living; **se lo ha ganado** he deserves it; **~ tiempo** to gain time
ganchillo [ganˈtʃiʎo] *nm* (*para croché*) crochet hook; (*arte*) crochet work
gancho [ˈgantʃo] *nm* (*gen*) hook; (*colgador*) hanger; (*pey: revendedor*) tout; (*fam: atractivo*) sex appeal; (*Boxeo: golpe*) hook
gandul, -a [ganˈdul, a] *adj, nm/f* good-for-nothing
ganga [ˈganga] *nf* (*cosa*) bargain; (*chollo*) cushy job
Ganges [ˈganxes] *nm*: **el (Río) ~** the Ganges
ganglio [ˈgangljo] *nm* (*Anat*) ganglion; (*Med*) swelling
gangrena [ganˈgrena] *nf* gangrene
gansada [ganˈsaða] *nf* (*fam*) stupid thing (to do)
ganso, -a [ˈganso, a] *nm/f* (*Zool*) gander/goose; (*fam*) idiot
ganzúa [ganˈθua] *nf* skeleton key ◼ *nm/f* burglar
gañán [gaˈɲan] *nm* farmhand, farm labourer
garabatear [garaβateˈar] *vt* to scribble, scrawl
garabato [garaˈβato] *nm* (*gancho*) hook; (*garfio*) grappling iron; (*escritura*) scrawl, scribble; (*fam*) sex appeal
garaje [gaˈraxe] *nm* garage
garajista [garaˈxista] *nmf* mechanic
garante [gaˈrante] *adj* responsible ◼ *nm/f* guarantor
garantía [garanˈtia] *nf* guarantee; (*seguridad*) pledge; (*compromiso*) undertaking; (*Jur: caución*) warranty; **de máxima ~** absolutely guaranteed; **~ de trabajo** job security
garantice *etc* [garanˈtiθe] *vb ver* **garantizar**
garantizar [garantiˈθar] *vt* (*hacerse responsable de*) to vouch for; (*asegurar*) to guarantee
garbanzo [garˈβanθo] *nm* chickpea
garbeo [garˈβeo] *nm*: **darse un ~** to go for a walk
garbo [ˈgarβo] *nm* grace, elegance; (*desenvoltura*) jauntiness; (*de mujer*) glamour; **andar con ~** to walk gracefully
garboso, -a [garˈβoso, a] *adj* graceful, elegant
garete [gaˈrete] *nm*: **irse al ~** to go to the dogs
garfio [ˈgarfjo] *nm* grappling iron; (*gancho*) hook; (*Alpinismo*) climbing iron
gargajo [garˈɣaxo] *nm* phlegm, sputum
garganta [garˈɣanta] *nf* (*interna*) throat; (*externa, de botella*) neck; (*Geo: barranco*) ravine; (*desfiladero*) narrow pass
gargantilla [garɣanˈtiʎa] *nf* necklace
gárgara [ˈgarɣara] *nf* gargle, gargling; **hacer gárgaras** to gargle; **¡vete a hacer gárgaras!** (*fam*) go to blazes!

gárgola ['garɣola] nf gargoyle
garita [ga'rita] nf cabin, hut; (Mil) sentry box; (puesto de vigilancia) lookout post
garito [ga'rito] nm (lugar) gaming house o den
garra ['garra] nf (de gato, Tec) claw; (de ave) talon; (fam) hand, paw; (fig: de canción etc) bite; **caer en las garras de algn** to fall into sb's clutches
garrafa [ga'rrafa] nf carafe, decanter
garrafal [garra'fal] adj enormous, terrific; (error) terrible
garrapata [garra'pata] nf (Zool) tick
garrotazo [garro'taθo] nm blow with a stick o club
garrote [ga'rrote] nm (palo) stick; (porra) club, cudgel; (suplicio) garrotte
garza ['garθa] nf heron
gas [gas] nm gas; (vapores) fumes pl; **gases de escape** exhaust (fumes)
gasa ['gasa] nf gauze; (de pañal) nappy liner
gaseoso, -a [gase'oso, a] adj gassy, fizzy ▪ nf lemonade, pop (fam)
gasoducto [gaso'ðukto] nm gas pipeline
gasoil [ga'soil], **gasóleo** [ga'soleo] nm diesel (oil)
gasolina [gaso'lina] nf petrol, gas(oline) (US); ~ **sin plomo** unleaded petrol
gasolinera [gasoli'nera] nf petrol (Brit) o gas (US) station
gastado, -a [gas'taðo, a] adj (ropa) worn out; (usado: frase etc) trite
gastar [gas'tar] vt (dinero, tiempo) to spend; (consumir) to use (up), consume; (desperdiciar) to waste; (llevar) to wear; **gastarse** vr to wear out; (terminarse) to run out; (estropearse) to waste; ~ **bromas** to crack jokes; **¿qué número gastas?** what size (shoe) do you take?
gasto ['gasto] nm (desembolso) expenditure, spending; (cantidad gastada) outlay, expense; (consumo, uso) use; (desgaste) waste; **gastos** nmpl (desembolsos) expenses; (cargos) charges, costs; ~ **corriente** (Com) revenue expenditure; ~ **fijo** (Com) fixed charge; **gastos bancarios** bank charges; **gastos corrientes** running expenses; **gastos de distribución** (Com) distribution costs; **gastos generales** overheads; **gastos de mantenimiento** maintenance expenses; **gastos operacionales** operating costs; **gastos de tramitación** (Com) handling charge sg; **gastos vencidos** (Com) accrued charges; **cubrir gastos** to cover expenses; **meterse en gastos** to incur expense
gastronomía [gastrono'mia] nf gastronomy
gata ['gata] nf (Zool) she-cat; **andar a gatas** to go on all fours

gatear [gate'ar] vi to go on all fours
gatillo [ga'tiʎo] nm (de arma de fuego) trigger; (de dentista) forceps
gato ['gato] nm (Zool) cat; (Tec) jack; ~ **de Angora** Angora cat; ~ **montés** wildcat; **dar a algn ~ por liebre** to take sb in; **aquí hay ~ encerrado** there's something fishy here
GATT [gat] sigla m (= Acuerdo General sobre Aranceles Aduaneros y Comercio) GATT
gatuno, -a [ga'tuno, a] adj feline
gaucho, -a ['gautʃo, a] adj, nm/f gaucho
gaveta [ga'βeta] nf drawer
gavilán [gaβi'lan] nm sparrowhawk
gavilla [ga'βiʎa] nf sheaf
gaviota [ga'βjota] nf seagull
gay [ge] adj, nm gay, homosexual
gazapo [ga'θapo] nm young rabbit
gaznate [gaθ'nate] nm (pescuezo) gullet; (garganta) windpipe
gazpacho [gaθ'patʃo] nm gazpacho
gel [xel] nm gel
gelatina [xela'tina] nf jelly; (polvos etc) gelatine
gema ['xema] nf gem
gemelo, -a [xe'melo, a] adj, nm/f twin; **gemelos** nmpl (de camisa) cufflinks; **gemelos de campo** field glasses, binoculars; **gemelos de teatro** opera glasses
gemido [xe'miðo] nm (quejido) moan, groan; (lamento) wail, howl
Géminis ['xeminis] nm (Astro) Gemini
gemir [xe'mir] vi (quejarse) to moan, groan; (animal) to whine; (viento) to howl
gen [xen] nm gene
gen. abr (Ling) = **género**; **genitivo**
gendarme [xen'darme] nm (Am) policeman
genealogía [xenealo'xia] nf genealogy
generación [xenera'θjon] nf generation; **primera/segunda/tercera/cuarta ~** (Inform) first/second/third/fourth generation
generado, -a [xene'raðo, a] adj (Inform): ~ **por ordenador** computer generated
generador [xenera'ðor] nm generator; ~ **de programas** (Inform) program generator
general [xene'ral] adj general; (común) common; (pey: corriente) rife; (frecuente) usual ▪ nm general; ~ **de brigada/de división** brigadier-/major-general; **por lo** o **en ~** in general
generalice etc [xenera'liθe] vb ver **generalizar**
generalidad [xenerali'ðað] nf generality
Generalitat [jenerali'tat] nf regional government of Catalonia; ~ **Valenciana** regional government of Valencia
generalización [xeneraliθa'θjon] nf generalization
generalizar [xenerali'θar] vt to generalize;

generalizarse vr to become generalized, spread; (difundirse) to become widely known
generalmente [xeneral'mente] adv generally
generar [xene'rar] vt to generate
genérico, -a [xe'neriko, a] adj generic
género ['xenero] nm (clase) kind, sort; (tipo) type; (Bio) genus; (Ling) gender; (Com) material; **géneros** nmpl (productos) goods; **~ humano** human race; **~ chico** (zarzuela) Spanish operetta; **géneros de punto** knitwear sg
generosidad [xenerosi'ðað] nf generosity
generoso, -a [xene'roso, a] adj generous
genético, -a [xe'netiko, a] adj genetic ▪ nf genetics sg
genial [xe'njal] adj inspired; (idea) brilliant; (afable) genial
genialidad [xenjali'ðað] nf (singularidad) genius; (acto genial) stroke of genius; **es una ~ suya** it's one of his brilliant ideas
genio ['xenjo] nm (carácter) nature, disposition; (humor) temper; (facultad creadora) genius; **mal ~** bad temper; **~ vivo** quick o hot temper; **de mal ~** bad-tempered
genital [xeni'tal] adj genital ▪ nm: **genitales** genitals, genital organs
genitivo [xeni'tiβo] nm (Ling) genitive
genocidio [xeno'θiðjo] nm genocide
Génova ['xenoβa] nf Genoa
genovés, -esa [xeno'βes, esa] adj, nm/f Genoese
gente ['xente] nf (personas) people pl; (raza) race; (nación) nation; (parientes) relatives pl; **~ bien/baja** posh/lower-class people pl; **~ menuda** (niños) children pl; **es buena ~** (fam: esp Am) he's a good sort; **una ~ como Vd** (Am) a person like you
gentil [xen'til] adj (elegante) graceful; (encantador) charming; (Rel) gentile
gentileza [xenti'leθa] nf grace; charm; (cortesía) courtesy; **por ~ de** by courtesy of
gentilicio, -a [xenti'liθjo, a] adj (familiar) family cpd
gentío [xen'tio] nm crowd, throng
gentuza [xen'tuθa] nf (pey: plebe) rabble; (: chusma) riffraff
genuflexión [xenuflek'sjon] nf genuflexion
genuino, -a [xe'nwino, a] adj genuine
GEO ['xeo] nmpl abr (Esp: = Grupos Especiales de Operaciones) Special Police Units used in anti-terrorist operations etc
geografía [xeoɣra'fia] nf geography
geográfico, -a [xeo'ɣrafiko, a] adj geographic(al)
geología [xeolo'xia] nf geology
geólogo, -a [xe'oloɣo, a] nm/f geologist

geometría [xeome'tria] nf geometry
geométrico, -a [xeo'metriko, a] adj geometric(al)
Georgia [xe'orxja] nf Georgia
georgiano, -a [xeor'xjano, a] adj, nm/f Georgian ▪ nm (Ling) Georgian
geranio [xe'ranjo] nm (Bot) geranium
gerencia [xe'renθja] nf management; (cargo) post of manager; (oficina) manager's office
gerente [xe'rente] nm/f (supervisor) manager; (jefe) director
geriatría [xerja'tria] nf (Med) geriatrics sg
geriátrico, -a [xer'jatriko, a] adj geriatric
germano, -a [xer'mano, a] adj German, Germanic ▪ nm/f German
germen ['xermen] nm germ
germinar [xermi'nar] vi to germinate; (brotar) to sprout
gerundense [xerun'dense] adj of o from Gerona ▪ nm/f native o inhabitant of Gerona
gerundio [xe'rundjo] nm (Ling) gerund
gestación [xesta'θjon] nf gestation
gesticulación [xestikula'θjon] nf (ademán) gesticulation; (mueca) grimace
gesticular [xestiku'lar] vi (con ademanes) to gesture; (con muecas) to make faces
gestión [xes'tjon] nf management; (diligencia, acción) negotiation; **hacer las gestiones preliminares** to do the groundwork; **~ de cartera** (Com) portfolio management; **~ financiera** (Com) financial management; **~ interna** (Inform) housekeeping; **~ de personal** personnel management; **~ de riesgos** (Com) risk management
gestionar [xestjo'nar] vt (tratar de arreglar) to try to arrange; (llevar) to manage
gesto ['xesto] nm (mueca) grimace; (ademán) gesture; **hacer gestos** to make faces
gestor, a [xes'tor, a] adj managing ▪ nm/f manager; (promotor) promoter; (agente) business agent
gestoría [xesto'ria] nf agency undertaking business with government departments, insurance companies etc
Gibraltar [xiβral'tar] nm Gibraltar
gibraltareño, -a [xiβralta'reɲo, a] adj of o from Gibraltar ▪ nm/f native o inhabitant of Gibraltar
gigante [xi'ɣante] adj, nm/f giant
gijonés, -esa [xixo'nes, esa] adj of o from Gijón ▪ nm/f native o inhabitant of Gijón
gilipollas [xili'poʎas] (fam) adj inv daft ▪ nm/f berk
gilipollez [xilipo'ʎez] nf (fam): **es una ~** that's a load of crap (!); **decir gilipolleces** to talk crap (!)
gima etc ['xima] vb ver **gemir**

gimnasia [xim'nasja] *nf* gymnastics *pl*; **confundir la ~ con la magnesia** to get things mixed up

gimnasio [xim'nasjo] *nm* gym(nasium)

gimnasta [xim'nasta] *nm/f* gymnast

gimnástica [xim'nastika] *nf* gymnastics *sg*

gimotear [ximote'ar] *vi* to whine, whimper; (*lloriquear*) to snivel

Ginebra [xi'neβra] *n* Geneva

ginebra [xi'neβra] *nf* gin

ginecología [xinekolo'xia] *nf* gyn(a)ecology

ginecológico, -a [xineko'loxiko, a] *adj* gyn(a)ecological

ginecólogo, -a [xine'koloɣo, a] *nm/f* gyn(a)ecologist

gira ['xira] *nf* tour, trip

girar [xi'rar] *vt* (*dar la vuelta*) to turn (around); (: *rápidamente*) to spin; (*Com*: *giro postal*) to draw; (*comerciar*: *letra de cambio*) to issue ■ *vi* to turn (round); (*dar vueltas*) to rotate; (*rápido*) to spin; **la conversación giraba en torno a las elecciones** the conversation centred on the election; **~ en descubierto** to overdraw

giratorio, -a [xira'torjo, a] *adj* (*gen*) revolving; (*puente*) swing *cpd*; (*silla*) swivel *cpd*

giro ['xiro] *nm* (*movimiento*) turn, revolution; (*Ling*) expression; (*Com*) draft; (*de sucesos*) trend, course; **~ bancario** money order, bank giro; **~ de existencias** (*Com*) stock turnover; **~ postal** postal order

gis [xis] *nm* (*Am*) chalk

gitano, -a [xi'tano, a] *adj, nm/f* gypsy

glacial [gla'θjal] *adj* icy, freezing

glaciar [gla'θjar] *nm* glacier

glándula ['glandula] *nf* (*Anat, Bot*) gland

glicerina [gliθe'rina] *nf* (*Tec*) glycerin(e)

global [glo'βal] *adj* (*en conjunto*) global; (*completo*) total; (*investigación*) full; (*suma*) lump *cpd*

globalización [gloβaliθa'θjon] *nf* globalization

globo ['gloβo] *nm* (*esfera*) globe, sphere; (*aeróstato, juguete*) balloon

glóbulo ['gloβulo] *nm* globule; (*Anat*) corpuscle; **~ blanco/rojo** white/red corpuscle

gloria ['glorja] *nf* glory; (*fig*) delight; (*delicia*) bliss

glorieta [glo'rjeta] *nf* (*de jardín*) bower, arbour, arbor (*US*); (*Auto*) roundabout (*Brit*), traffic circle (*US*); (*plaza redonda*) circus; (*cruce*) junction

glorificar [glorifi'kar] *vt* (*enaltecer*) to glorify, praise

glorifique *etc* [glori'fike] *vb ver* **glorificar**

glorioso, -a [glo'rjoso, a] *adj* glorious

glosa ['glosa] *nf* comment; (*explicación*) gloss

glosar [glo'sar] *vt* (*comentar*) to comment on

glosario [glo'sarjo] *nm* glossary

glotón, -ona [glo'ton, ona] *adj* gluttonous, greedy ■ *nm/f* glutton

glotonería [glotone'ria] *nf* gluttony, greed

glúteo ['gluteo] *nm* (*fam*: *nalga*) buttock

G.N. *abr* (*Nicaragua, Panamá*: = *Guardia Nacional*) police

gnomo ['nomo] *nm* gnome

gobernación [goβerna'θjon] *nf* government, governing; (*Pol*) Provincial Governor's office; **Ministro de la G~** Minister of the Interior, Home Secretary (*Brit*)

gobernador, -a [goβerna'ðor, a] *adj* governing ■ *nm/f* governor

gobernanta [goβer'nanta] *nf* (*esp Am*: *niñera*) governess

gobernante [goβer'nante] *adj* governing ■ *nm* ruler ■ *nf* (*en hotel etc*) housekeeper

gobernar [goβer'nar] *vt* (*dirigir*) to guide, direct; (*Pol*) to rule, govern ■ *vi* to govern; (*Naut*) to steer; **~ mal** to misgovern

gobierno *etc* [go'βjerno] *vb ver* **gobernar** ■ *nm* (*Pol*) government; (*gestión*) management; (*dirección*) guidance, direction; (*Naut*) steering; (*puesto*) governorship

goce *etc* ['goθe] *vb ver* **gozar** ■ *nm* enjoyment

godo, -a ['goðo, a] *nm/f* Goth; (*Am pey*) Spaniard

gol [gol] *nm* goal

golear [gole'ar] *vt* (*marcar*) to score a goal against

golf [golf] *nm* golf

golfo, -a ['golfo, a] *nm/f* (*pilluelo*) street urchin; (*vagabundo*) tramp; (*gorrón*) loafer; (*gamberro*) lout ■ *nm* (*Geo*) gulf ■ *nf* (*fam*: *prostituta*) slut, whore, hooker (*US*)

golondrina [golon'drina] *nf* swallow

golosina [golo'sina] *nf* titbit; (*dulce*) sweet

goloso, -a [go'loso, a] *adj* sweet-toothed; (*fam*: *glotón*) greedy

golpe ['golpe] *nm* blow; (*de puño*) punch; (*de mano*) smack; (*de remo*) stroke; (*Fútbol*) kick; (*Tenis etc*) hit, shot; (*mala suerte*) misfortune; (*fam*: *atraco*) job, heist (*US*); (*fig*: *choque*) clash; **no dar ~** to be bone idle; **de un ~** with one blow; **de ~** suddenly; **~ (de estado)** coup (d'état); **~ de gracia** coup de grâce (*tb fig*); **~ de fortuna/maestro** stroke of luck/genius; **cerrar una puerta de ~** to slam a door

golpear [golpe'ar] *vt, vi* to strike, knock; (*asestar*) to beat; (*de puño*) to punch; (*golpetear*) to tap; (*mesa*) to bang

golpista [gol'pista] *adj*: **intentona ~** coup attempt ■ *nm/f* participant in a coup (d'état)

golpiza [gol'pisa] *nf*: **dar una ~ a algn** (*Am*) to beat sb up

goma ['goma] nf (caucho) rubber; (elástico) elastic; (tira) rubber o elastic (Brit) band; (fam: preservativo) condom; (droga) hashish; (explosivo) plastic explosive; ~ **(de borrar)** eraser, rubber (Brit); ~ **de mascar** chewing gum; ~ **de pegar** gum, glue

goma-espuma [gomaes'puma] nf foam rubber

gomina [go'mina] nf hair gel

gomita [go'mita] nf rubber o elastic (Brit) band

góndola ['gondola] nf (barco) gondola; (de tren) goods wagon

gordo, -a ['gorðo, a] adj (gen) fat; (persona) plump; (agua) hard; (fam) enormous ■ nm/f fat man o woman; **el (premio)** ~ (en lotería) first prize; ¡~! (fam) fatty!

gordura [gor'ðura] nf fat; (corpulencia) fatness, stoutness

gorgojo [gor'ɣoxo] nm (insecto) grub

gorgorito [gorɣo'rito] nm (gorjeo) trill, warble

gorila [go'rila] nm gorilla; (fam) tough, thug; (guardaespaldas) bodyguard

gorjear [gorxe'ar] vi to twitter, chirp

gorjeo [gor'xeo] nm twittering, chirping

gorra ['gorra] nf (gen) cap; (de niño) bonnet; (militar) bearskin; ~ **de montar/de paño/de punto/de visera** riding/cloth/knitted/peaked cap; **andar** o **ir** o **vivir de** ~ to sponge, scrounge; **entrar de** ~ (fam) to gatecrash

gorrión [go'rrjon] nm sparrow

gorro ['gorro] nm cap; (de niño, mujer) bonnet; **estoy hasta el** ~ I am fed up

gorrón, -ona [go'rron, ona] nm pebble; (Tec) pivot ■ nm/f scrounger

gorronear [gorrone'ar] vi (fam) to sponge, scrounge

gota ['gota] nf (gen) drop; (de pintura) blob; (de sudor) bead; (Med) gout; ~ **a** ~ drop by drop; **caer a gotas** to drip

gotear [gote'ar] vi to drip; (escurrir) to trickle; (salirse) to leak; (cirio) to gutter; (lloviznar) to drizzle

gotera [go'tera] nf leak

gótico, -a ['gotiko, a] adj Gothic

gozar [go'θar] vi to enjoy o.s.; ~ **de** (disfrutar) to enjoy; (poseer) to possess; ~ **de buena salud** to enjoy good health

gozne ['goθne] nm hinge

gozo ['goθo] nm (alegría) joy; (placer) pleasure; ¡**mi** ~ **en el pozo!** that's torn it!, just my luck!

g.p. nm abr (= giro postal) m.o.

gr abr (= gramo(s)) g

grabación [graβa'θjon] nf recording

grabado, -a [gra'βaðo, a] adj (Mus) recorded; (en cinta) taped, on tape ■ nm print, engraving; ~ **al agua fuerte** etching; ~ **al**

aguatinta aquatint; ~ **en cobre** copperplate; ~ **en madera** woodcut; ~ **rupestre** rock carving

grabador, -a [graβa'ðor, a] nm/f engraver ■ nf tape-recorder; **grabadora de cassettes** cassette recorder

grabar [gra'βar] vt to engrave; (discos, cintas) to record; (impresionar) to impress

gracejo [gra'θexo] nm (ingenio) wit, humour; (elegancia) grace

gracia ['graθja] nf (encanto) grace, gracefulness; (Rel) grace; (chiste) joke; (humor) humour, wit; ¡**muchas gracias!** thanks very much!; **gracias a** thanks to; **tener** ~ (chiste etc) to be funny; ¡**qué** ~! how funny!; (irónico) what a nerve!; **no me hace** ~ (broma) it's not funny; (plan) I am not too keen; **con gracias anticipadas/repetidas** thanking you in advance/again; **dar las gracias a algn por algo** to thank sb for sth

grácil ['graθil] adj (sutil) graceful; (delgado) slender; (delicado) delicate

gracioso, -a [gra'θjoso, a] adj (garboso) graceful; (chistoso) funny; (cómico) comical; (agudo) witty; (título) gracious ■ nm/f (Teat) comic character, fool; **su graciosa Majestad** His/Her Gracious Majesty

grada ['graða] nf (de escalera) step; (de anfiteatro) tier, row; **gradas** nfpl (de estadio) terraces

gradación [graða'θjon] nf gradation; (serie) graded series

gradería [graðe'ria] nf (gradas) (flight of) steps pl; (de anfiteatro) tiers pl, rows pl; ~ **cubierta** covered stand

grado ['graðo] nm degree; (etapa) stage, step; (nivel) rate; (de parentesco) order of lineage; (de aceite, vino) grade; (grada) step; (Escol) class, year, grade (US); (Univ) degree; (Ling) degree of comparison; (Mil) rank; **de buen** ~ willingly; **en sumo** ~, **en** ~ **superlativo** in the highest degree

graduación [graðwa'θjon] nf (acto) gradation; (clasificación) rating; (del alcohol) proof, strength; (Escol) graduation; (Mil) rank; **de alta** ~ high-ranking

gradual [gra'ðwal] adj gradual

graduar [gra'ðwar] vt (gen) to graduate; (medir) to gauge; (Tec) to calibrate; (Univ) to confer a degree on; (Mil) to commission; **graduarse** vr to graduate; **graduarse la vista** to have one's eyes tested

grafía [gra'fia] nf (escritura) writing; (ortografía) spelling

gráfico, -a ['grafiko, a] adj graphic; (fig: vívido) vivid, lively ■ nm diagram ■ nf graph; ~ **de barras** (Com) bar chart;

~ de sectores *o* **de tarta** (*Com*) pie chart; **gráficos** *nmpl* (*tb Inform*) graphics; **gráficos empresariales** (*Com*) business graphics

grafito [gra'fito] *nm* (*Tec*) graphite, black lead

grafología [grafolo'xia] *nf* graphology

gragea [gra'xea] *nf* (*Med*) pill; (*caramelo*) dragée

grajo ['graxo] *nm* rook

Gral. *abr* (*Mil*: = *General*) Gen.

gramático, -a [gra'matiko, a] *nm/f* (*persona*) grammarian ■ *nf* grammar

gramo ['gramo] *nm* gramme (*Brit*), gram (*US*)

gran [gran] *adj ver* **grande**

grana ['grana] *nf* (*Bot*) seedling; (*color*) scarlet; **ponerse como la ~** to go as red as a beetroot

granada [gra'naða] *nf* pomegranate; (*Mil*) grenade; **~ de mano** hand grenade; **~ de metralla** shrapnel shell

granadilla [grana'ðiʎa] *nf* (*Am*) passion fruit

granadino, -a [grana'ðino, a] *adj* of *o* from Granada ■ *nm/f* native *o* inhabitant of Granada ■ *nf* grenadine

granar [gra'nar] *vi* to seed

granate [gra'nate] *adj inv* maroon ■ *nm* garnet; (*color*) maroon

Gran Bretaña [grambre'taɲa] *nf* Great Britain

Gran Canaria [granka'narja] *nf* Grand Canary

grancanario, -a [granka'narjo, a] *adj* of *o* from Grand Canary ■ *nm/f* native *o* inhabitant of Grand Canary

grande ['grande], **gran** *adj* (*de tamaño*) big, large; (*alto*) tall; (*distinguido*) great; (*impresionante*) grand ■ *nm* grandee; **¿cómo es de ~?** how big is it?, what size is it?; **pasarlo en ~** to have a tremendous time

grandeza [gran'deθa] *nf* greatness; (*tamaño*) bigness; (*esplendor*) grandness; (*nobleza*) nobility

grandioso, -a [gran'djoso, a] *adj* magnificent, grand

grandullón, -ona [granðu'ʎon, ona] *adj* oversized

granel [gra'nel] *nm* (*montón*) heap; **a ~** (*Com*) in bulk

granero [gra'nero] *nm* granary, barn

granice *etc* [gra'niθe] *vb ver* **granizar**

granito [gra'nito] *nm* (*Agr*) small grain; (*roca*) granite

granizada [grani'θaða] *nf* hailstorm; (*fig*) hail; **una ~ de balas** a hail of bullets

granizado [grani'θaðo] *nm* iced drink; **~ de café** iced coffee

granizar [grani'θar] *vi* to hail

granizo [gra'niθo] *nm* hail

granja ['granxa] *nf* (*gen*) farm; **~ avícola** chicken *o* poultry farm

granjear [granxe'ar] *vt* (*cobrar*) to earn; (*ganar*) to win; (*avanzar*) to gain; **granjearse** *vr* (*amistad etc*) to gain for o.s.

granjero, -a [gran'xero, a] *nm/f* farmer

grano ['grano] *nm* grain; (*semilla*) seed; (*baya*) berry; (*Med*) pimple, spot; (*partícula*) particle; (*punto*) speck; **granos** *nmpl* cereals; **~ de café** coffee bean; **ir al ~** to get to the point

granuja [gra'nuxa] *nm* rogue; (*golfillo*) urchin

grapa ['grapa] *nf* staple; (*Tec*) clamp; (*sujetador*) clip, fastener; (*Arq*) cramp

grapadora [grapa'ðora] *nf* stapler

GRAPO ['grapo] *nm abr* (*Esp Pol*) = **Grupo de Resistencia Antifascista Primero de Octubre**

grasa ['grasa] *nf ver* **graso**

grasiento, -a [gra'sjento, a] *adj* greasy; (*de aceite*) oily; (*mugriento*) filthy

graso, -a ['graso, a] *adj* fatty; (*aceitoso*) greasy, oily ■ *nf* (*gen*) grease; (*de cocina*) fat, lard; (*sebo*) suet; (*mugre*) filth; (*Auto*) oil; (*lubricante*) grease; **grasa de ballena** blubber; **grasa de pescado** fish oil

grasoso, -a [gra'soso, a] *adj* (*Am*) greasy, sticky

gratificación [gratifika'θjon] *nf* (*propina*) tip; (*aguinaldo*) gratuity; (*bono*) bonus; (*recompensa*) reward

gratificar [gratifi'kar] *vt* (*dar propina*) to tip; (*premiar*) to reward; **"se ~á"** "a reward is offered"

gratifique *etc* [grati'fike] *vb ver* **gratificar**

gratinar [grati'nar] *vt* to cook au gratin

gratis ['gratis] *adv* free, for nothing

gratitud [grati'tuð] *nf* gratitude

grato, -a ['grato, a] *adj* (*agradable*) pleasant, agreeable; (*bienvenido*) welcome; **nos es ~ informarle que ...** we are pleased to inform you that ...

gratuito, -a [gra'twito, a] *adj* (*gratis*) free; (*sin razón*) gratuitous; (*acusación*) unfounded

grava ['graβa] *nf* (*guijos*) gravel; (*piedra molida*) crushed stone; (*en carreteras*) road metal

gravamen [gra'βamen] *nm* (*carga*) burden; (*impuesto*) tax; **libre de ~** (*Econ*) free from encumbrances

gravar [gra'βar] *vt* to burden; (*Com*) to tax; (*Econ*) to assess for tax; **~ con impuestos** to burden with taxes

grave ['graβe] *adj* heavy; (*fig, Med*) grave, serious; (*importante*) important; (*herida*) severe; (*Mus*) low, deep; (*Ling: acento*) grave; **estar ~** to be seriously ill

gravedad [graβe'ðað] *nf* gravity; (*fig*) seriousness; (*grandeza*) importance; (*dignidad*) dignity; (*Mus*) depth

grávido, -a ['graβiðo, a] *adj* (*preñada*) pregnant
gravilla [gra'βiʎa] *nf* gravel
gravitación [graβita'θjon] *nf* gravitation
gravitar [graβi'tar] *vi* to gravitate; **~ sobre** to rest on
gravoso, -a [gra'βoso, a] *adj* (*pesado*) burdensome; (*costoso*) costly
graznar [graθ'nar] *vi* (*cuervo*) to squawk; (*pato*) to quack; (*hablar ronco*) to croak
graznido [graθ'niðo] *nm* squawk; croak
Grecia ['greθja] *nf* Greece
gregario, -a [gre'ɣarjo, a] *adj* gregarious; **instinto ~** herd instinct
gremio ['gremjo] *nm* (*asociación*) professional association, guild
greña ['greɲa] *nf* (*cabellos*) shock of hair; (*maraña*) tangle; **andar a la ~** to bicker, squabble
greñudo, -a [gre'ɲuðo, a] *adj* (*persona*) dishevelled; (*pelo*) tangled
gresca ['greska] *nf* uproar; (*trifulca*) row
griego, -a ['grjeɣo, a] *adj* Greek, Grecian ■ *nm/f* Greek ■ *nm* (*Ling*) Greek
grieta ['grjeta] *nf* crack; (*hendidura*) chink; (*quiebra*) crevice; (*Med*) chap; (*Pol*) rift
grifa ['grifa] *nf* (*fam: droga*) marijuana
grifo ['grifo] *nm* tap (*Brit*), faucet (*US*); (*Am*) petrol (*Brit*) *o* gas (*US*) station
grilletes [gri'ʎetes] *nmpl* fetters, shackles
grillo ['griʎo] *nm* (*Zool*) cricket; (*Bot*) shoot; **grillos** *nmpl* shackles, irons
grima ['grima] *nf* (*horror*) loathing; (*desagrado*) reluctance; (*desazón*) uneasiness; **me da ~** it makes me sick
gringo, -a ['gringo, a] (*Am*) *adj* (*pey: extranjero*) foreign; (*: norteamericano*) Yankee; (*idioma*) foreign ■ *nm/f* foreigner; Yank
gripa ['gripa] *nf* (*Am*) flu, influenza
gripe ['gripe] *nf* flu, influenza; **~ porcina** swine flu
gris [gris] *adj* grey
grisáceo, -a [gri'saθeo, a] *adj* greyish
grisoso, -a [gri'soso, a] *adj* (*Am*) greyish
gritar [gri'tar] *vt, vi* to shout, yell; **¡no grites!** stop shouting!
grito ['grito] *nm* shout, yell; (*de horror*) scream; **a ~ pelado** at the top of one's voice; **poner el ~ en el cielo** to scream blue murder; **es el último ~** (*de moda*) it's all the rage
groenlandés, -esa [groenlan'des, esa] *adj* Greenland *cpd* ■ *nm/f* Greenlander
Groenlandia [groen'landja] *nf* Greenland
grosella [gro'seʎa] *nf* (red)currant; **~ negra** blackcurrant
grosería [grose'ria] *nf* (*actitud*) rudeness; (*comentario*) vulgar comment; (*palabrota*) swearword

grosero, -a [gro'sero, a] *adj* (*poco cortés*) rude, bad-mannered; (*ordinario*) vulgar, crude
grosor [gro'sor] *nm* thickness
grotesco, -a [gro'tesko, a] *adj* grotesque; (*absurdo*) bizarre
grúa ['grua] *nf* (*Tec*) crane; (*de petróleo*) derrick; **~ corrediza** *o* **móvil/de pescante/puente/de torre** travelling/jib/overhead/tower crane
grueso, -a ['grweso, a] *adj* thick; (*persona*) stout; (*calidad*) coarse ■ *nm* bulk; (*espesor*) thickness; (*densidad*) density; (*de gente*) main body, mass; **el ~ de** the bulk of
grulla ['gruʎa] *nf* (*Zool*) crane
grumete [gru'mete] *nm* (*Naut*) cabin *o* ship's boy
grumo ['grumo] *nm* (*coágulo*) clot, lump; (*masa*) dollop
gruñido [gru'ɲiðo] *nm* grunt, growl; (*fig*) grumble
gruñir [gru'ɲir] *vi* (*animal*) to grunt, growl; (*fam*) to grumble
gruñón, -ona [gru'ɲon, ona] *adj* grumpy ■ *nm/f* grumbler
grupa ['grupa] *nf* (*Zool*) rump
grupo ['grupo] *nm* group; (*Tec*) unit, set; (*de árboles*) cluster; **~ sanguíneo** blood group
gruta ['gruta] *nf* grotto
Gta. *abr* (*Auto*) = **Glorieta**
guaca ['gwaka] *nf* Indian tomb
guacamole [gwaka'mole] *nm* (*Am*) avocado salad
guachimán [gwatʃi'man] *nm* (*Am*) night watchman
guadalajareño, -a [gwaðalaxa'reɲo, a] *adj* of *o* from Guadalajara ■ *nm/f* native *o* inhabitant of Guadalajara
Guadalquivir [gwaðalki'βir] *nm*: **el (Río) ~** the Guadalquivir
guadaña [gwa'ðaɲa] *nf* scythe
guadañar [gwaða'ɲar] *vt* to scythe, mow
Guadiana [gwa'ðjana] *nm*: **el (Río) ~** the Guadiana
guagua ['gwaɣwa] *nf* (*Am, Canarias*) bus; (*Am: criatura*) baby
guajolote [gwaxo'lote] *nm* (*Am*) turkey
guano ['gwano] *nm* guano
guantada [gwan'taða] *nf*, **guantazo** [gwan'taθo] *nm* slap
guante ['gwante] *nm* glove; **se ajusta como un ~** it fits like a glove; **echar el ~ a algn** to catch hold of sb; (*fig: policía*) to catch sb
guapo, -a ['gwapo, a] *adj* good-looking; (*mujer*) pretty, attractive; (*hombre*) handsome; (*elegante*) smart ■ *nm* lover, gallant; (*Am fam*) tough guy, bully
guaraní [gwara'ni] *adj, nm/f* Guarani ■ *nm* (*moneda*) monetary unit of Paraguay

guarapo [gwa'rapo] *nm* (*Am*) fermented cane juice

guarda ['gwarða] *nm/f* (*persona*) warden, keeper ■ *nf* (*acto*) guarding; (*custodia*) custody; (*Tip*) flyleaf, endpaper; ~ **forestal** game warden

guardaagujas [gwarda'ɣuxas] *nm inv* (*Ferro*) switchman

guardabarros [gwarða'βarros] *nm inv* mudguard (*Brit*), fender (*US*)

guardabosques [gwarda'βoskes] *nm inv* gamekeeper

guardacoches [gwarða'kotʃes] *nm/f inv* (*celador*) parking attendant

guardacostas [gwarda'kostas] *nm inv* coastguard vessel

guardador, a [gwarða'ðor, a] *adj* protective; (*tacaño*) mean, stingy ■ *nm/f* guardian, protector

guardagujas [gwarda'ɣuxas] *nm inv* = **guardaagujas**

guardaespaldas [gwardaes'paldas] *nm/f inv* bodyguard

guardameta [gwarða'meta] *nm* goalkeeper

guardapolvo [gwarda'polβo] *nm* dust cover; (*prenda de vestir*) overalls *pl*

guardar [gwar'ðar] *vt* (*gen*) to keep; (*vigilar*) to guard, watch over; (*conservar*) to put away; (*dinero: ahorrar*) to save; (*promesa etc*) to keep; (*ley*) to observe; (*rencor*) to bear, harbour; (*Inform: archivo*) to save; **guardarse** *vr* (*preservarse*) to protect o.s.; **guardarse de algo** (*evitar*) to avoid sth; (*abstenerse*) to refrain from sth; **guardarse de hacer algo** to be careful not to do sth; **guardársela a algn** to have it in for sb

guardarropa [gwarða'rropa] *nm* (*armario*) wardrobe; (*en establecimiento público*) cloakroom

guardería [gwarðe'ria] *nf* nursery

guardia ['gwarðja] *nf* (*Mil*) guard; (*cuidado*) care, custody ■ *nm/f* guard; (*policía*) policeman(-woman); **estar de ~** to be on guard; **montar ~** to mount guard; **la G~ Civil** the Civil Guard; **~ municipal** *o* **urbana** municipal police; **un ~ civil** a Civil Guard(sman); **un(a) ~ nacional** a policeman(-woman); **~ urbano** traffic policeman; *see note*

guardián, -ana [gwar'ðjan, ana] *nm/f* (*gen*) guardian, keeper

guarecer [gware'θer] *vt* (*proteger*) to protect; (*abrigar*) to shelter; **guarecerse** *vr* to take refuge

guarezca *etc* [gwa're θka] *vb ver* **guarecer**

guarida [gwa'riða] *nf* (*de animal*) den, lair; (*de persona*) haunt, hideout; (*refugio*) refuge

guarnecer [gwarne'θer] *vt* (*equipar*) to provide; (*adornar*) to adorn; (*Tec*) to reinforce

guarnezca *etc* [gwar'neθka] *vb ver* **guarnecer**

guarnición [gwarni'θjon] *nf* (*de vestimenta*) trimming; (*de piedra*) mount; (*Culin*) garnish; (*arneses*) harness; (*Mil*) garrison

guarrada [gwa'rraða] (*fam*) *nf* (*cosa sucia*) dirty mess; (*acto o dicho obsceno*) obscenity; **hacer una ~ a algn** to do the dirty on sb

guarrería [gwarre'ria] *nf* = **guarrada**

guarro, -a ['gwarro, a] *nm/f* (*fam*) pig; (*fig*) dirty *o* slovenly person

guasa ['gwasa] *nf* joke; **con** *o* **de ~** jokingly, in fun

guasón, -ona [gwa'son, ona] *adj* witty; (*bromista*) joking ■ *nm/f* wit; joker

Guatemala [gwate'mala] *nf* Guatemala

guatemalteco, -a [gwatemal'teko, a] *adj, nm/f* Guatemalan

guateque [gwa'teke] *nm* (*fiesta*) party

guay [gwai] *adj* (*fam*) super, great

guayaba [gwa'jaβa] *nf* (*Bot*) guava

Guayana [gwa'jana] *nf* Guyana, Guiana

gubernamental [guβernamen'tal], **gubernativo, -a** [guβerna'tiβo, a] *adj* governmental

guedeja [ge'ðexa] *nf* long hair

guerra ['gerra] *nf* war; (*arte*) warfare; (*pelea*) struggle; **~ atómica/bacteriológica/nuclear/de guerrillas** atomic/germ/nuclear/guerrilla warfare; **Primera/Segunda G~ Mundial** First/Second World War; **~ de precios** (*Com*) price war; **~ civil/fría** civil/cold war; **~ a muerte** fight to the death; **de ~** military, war *cpd*; **estar en ~** to be at war; **dar ~** to be annoying

guerrear [gerre'ar] *vi* to wage war

guerrero, -a [ge'rrero, a] *adj* fighting; (*carácter*) warlike ■ *nm/f* warrior

guerrilla [ge'rriʎa] *nf* guerrilla warfare; (*tropas*) guerrilla band *o* group

guerrillero, -a [gerri'ʎero, a] *nm/f* guerrilla (fighter); (*contra invasor*) partisan

gueto ['geto] *nm* ghetto

guía *etc* ['gia] *vb ver* **guiar** ■ *nm/f* (*persona*) guide ■ *nf* (*libro*) guidebook; (*manual*) handbook; **~ de ferrocarriles** railway timetable; **~ telefónica** telephone directory; **~ del turista/del viajero** tourist/traveller's guide

g

guiar [gi'ar] *vt* to guide, direct; (*dirigir*) to lead; (*orientar*) to advise; (*Auto*) to steer; **guiarse** *vr*: **guiarse por** to be guided by

guijarro [gi'xarro] *nm* pebble

guillotina [giʎo'tina] *nf* guillotine

guinda ['ginda] *nf* morello cherry; (*licor*) cherry liqueur

guindar [gin'dar] *vt* to hoist; (*fam: robar*) to nick

guindilla [gin'diʎa] *nf* chil(l)i pepper

Guinea [gi'nea] *nf* Guinea

guineo, -a [gi'neo, a] *adj* Guinea *cpd*, Guinean ▪ *nm/f* Guinean

guiñapo [gi'ɲapo] *nm* (*harapo*) rag; (*persona*) rogue

guiñar [gi'ɲar] *vi* to wink

guiño ['giɲo] *nm* (*parpadeo*) wink; (*muecas*) grimace; **hacer guiños a** (*enamorados*) to make eyes at

guiñol [gi'ɲol] *nm* (*Teat*) puppet theatre

guión [gi'on] *nm* (*Ling*) hyphen, dash; (*esquema*) summary, outline; (*Cine*) script

guionista [gjo'nista] *nm/f* scriptwriter

guipuzcoano, -a [gipuθko'ano, a] *adj* of o from Guipúzcoa ▪ *nm/f* native o inhabitant of Guipúzcoa

guiri ['giri] *nm/f* (*fam, pey*) foreigner

guirigay [giri'gai] *nm* (*griterío*) uproar; (*confusión*) chaos

guirnalda [gir'nalda] *nf* garland

guisa ['gisa] *nf*: **a ~ de** as, like

guisado [gi'saðo] *nm* stew

guisante [gi'sante] *nm* pea

guisar [gi'sar] *vt, vi* to cook; (*fig*) to arrange

guiso ['giso] *nm* cooked dish

guita ['gita] *nf* twine; (*fam: dinero*) dough

guitarra [gi'tarra] *nf* guitar

guitarrista [gita'rrista] *nm/f* guitarist

gula ['gula] *nf* gluttony, greed

gusano [gu'sano] *nm* maggot, worm; (*de mariposa, polilla*) caterpillar; (*fig*) worm; (*ser despreciable*) creep; **~ de seda** silk-worm

gustar [gus'tar] *vt* to taste, sample ▪ *vi* to please, be pleasing; **~ de algo** to like o enjoy sth; **me gustan las uvas** I like grapes; **le gusta nadar** she likes o enjoys swimming; **¿gusta Ud?** would you like some?; **como Ud guste** as you wish

gusto ['gusto] *nm* (*sentido, sabor*) taste; (*agrado*) liking; (*placer*) pleasure; **tiene un ~ amargo** it has a bitter taste; **tener buen ~** to have good taste; **sobre gustos no hay nada escrito** there's no accounting for tastes; **de buen/mal ~** in good/bad taste; **sentirse a ~** to feel at ease; **¡mucho o tanto ~ (en conocerle)!** how do you do?, pleased to meet you; **el ~ es mío** the pleasure is mine; **tomar ~ a** to take a liking to; **con ~** willingly, gladly

gustoso, -a [gus'toso, a] *adj* (*sabroso*) tasty; (*agradable*) pleasant; (*con voluntad*) willing, glad; **lo hizo ~** he did it gladly

gutural [gutu'ral] *adj* guttural

guyanés, -esa [gwaja'nes, esa] *adj, nm/f* Guyanese

Hh

H, h ['atʃe] *nf* (*letra*) H, h; **H de Historia** H for Harry (*Brit*) *o* How (*US*)

H. *abr* (*Química*: = *Hidrógeno*) H; (= *Hectárea(s)*) ha.

h. *abr* (= *hora(s)*) h., hr(s). ■ *nmpl abr* (= *habitantes*) pop.

ha¹ [a] *vb ver* **haber**

ha² *abr* (= *Hectárea(s)*) ha.

haba ['aβa] *nf* bean; **son habas contadas** it goes without saying; **en todas partes cuecen habas** it's the same (story) the whole world over

Habana [a'βana] *nf*: **la ~** Havana

habanero, -a [aβa'nero, a] *adj* of *o* from Havana ■ *nm/f* native *o* inhabitant of Havana ■ *nf* (*Mus*) habanera

habano [a'βano] *nm* Havana cigar

habeas corpus [a'βeas'korpus] *nm* (*Law*) habeas corpus

⬤ **PALABRA CLAVE**

haber [a'βer] *vb auxiliar* **1** (*tiempos compuestos*) to have; **había comido** I have/had eaten; **antes/después de haberlo visto** before seeing/after seeing *o* having seen it; **si lo hubiera sabido habría ido** if I had known I would have gone

2: **¡haberlo dicho antes!** you should have said so before!; **¿habráse visto (cosa igual)?** have you ever seen anything like it?

3: **haber de**: **he de hacerlo** I must do it; **ha de llegar mañana** it should arrive tomorrow

■ *vb impersonal* **1** (*existencia*: *sg*) there is; (: *pl*) there are; **hay un hermano/dos hermanos** there is one brother/there are two brothers; **¿cuánto hay de aquí a Sucre?** how far is it from here to Sucre?; **habrá unos 4 grados** it must be about 4 degrees; **no hay quien te entienda** there's no understanding you

2 (*obligación*): **hay que hacer algo** something must be done; **hay que apuntarlo para acordarse** you have to write it down to remember

3: **¡hay que ver!** well I never!

4: **¡no hay de** *o* **por** (*Am*) **qué!** don't mention it!, not at all!

5: **¿qué hay?** (*¿qué pasa?*) what's up?, what's the matter?; (*¿qué tal?*) how's it going?

■ *vt*: **he aquí unas sugerencias** here are some suggestions; **todos los inventos habidos y por haber** all inventions present and future; **en el encuentro habido ayer** in yesterday's game

haberse *vr*: **habérselas con algn** to have it out with sb

■ *nm* (*en cuenta*) credit side

haberes *nmpl* assets; **¿cuánto tengo en el haber?** how much do I have in my account?; **tiene varias novelas en su haber** he has several novels to his credit

habichuela [aβi'tʃwela] *nf* kidney bean

hábil ['aβil] *adj* (*listo*) clever, smart; (*capaz*) fit, capable; (*experto*) expert; **día ~** working day

habilidad [aβili'ðað] *nf* (*gen*) skill, ability; (*inteligencia*) cleverness; (*destreza*) expertness, expertise; (*Jur*) competence; **~ (para)** fitness (for); **tener ~ manual** to be clever with one's hands

habilitación [aβilita'θjon] *nf* qualification; (*colocación de muebles*) fitting out; (*financiamiento*) financing; (*oficina*) paymaster's office

habilitado [aβili'taðo] *nm* paymaster

habilitar [aβili'tar] *vt* to qualify; (*autorizar*) to authorize; (*capacitar*) to enable; (*dar instrumentos*) to equip; (*financiar*) to finance

hábilmente [aβil'mente] *adv* skilfully, expertly

habitable [aβi'taβle] *adj* inhabitable

habitación [aβita'θjon] *nf* (*cuarto*) room; (*casa*) dwelling, abode; (*Bio*: *morada*) habitat; **~ sencilla** *o* **individual** single room; **~ doble** *o* **de matrimonio** double room

habitante [aβi'tante] *nm/f* inhabitant

habitar [aβi'tar] *vt* (*residir en*) to inhabit; (*ocupar*) to occupy ■ *vi* to live

hábitat (*pl* **hábitats**) ['aβitat, 'aβitats] *nm* habitat

hábito ['aβito] *nm* habit; **tener el ~ de hacer algo** to be in the habit of doing sth

habitual [aβi'twal] *adj* habitual

habituar [aβi'twar] *vt* to accustom; **habituarse** *vr*: **habituarse a** to get used to

habla ['aβla] *nf* (*capacidad de hablar*) speech; (*idioma*) language; (*dialecto*) dialect; **perder el ~** to become speechless; **de ~ francesa** French-speaking; **estar al ~** to be in contact; (*Telec*) to be on the line; **¡González al ~!** (*Telec*) Gonzalez speaking!

hablador, a [aβla'ðor, a] *adj* talkative ■ *nm/f* chatterbox

habladuría [aβlaðu'ria] *nf* rumour; **habladurías** *nfpl* gossip *sg*

hablante [a'βlante] *adj* speaking ■ *nm/f* speaker

hablar [a'βlar] *vt* to speak, talk ■ *vi* to speak; **hablarse** *vr* to speak to each other; **~ con** to speak to; **¡hable!, ¡puede ~!** (*Telec*) you're through!; **de eso ni ~** no way, that's not on; **~ alto/bajo/claro** to speak loudly/quietly/plainly *o* bluntly; **~ de** to speak of *o* about; **"se habla inglés"** "English spoken here"; **no se hablan** they are not on speaking terms

habré *etc* [a'βre] *vb ver* **haber**

hacedor, a [aθe'ðor, a] *nm/f* maker

hacendado, -a [aθen'daðo, a] *adj* property-owning ■ *nm* (*terrateniente*) large landowner

hacendoso, -a [aθen'doso, a] *adj* industrious, hard-working

 PALABRA CLAVE

hacer [a'θer] *vt* **1** (*fabricar, producir, conseguir*) to make; (*construir*) to build; **hacer una película/un ruido** to make a film/noise; **el guisado lo hice yo** I made *o* cooked the stew; **hacer amigos** to make friends

2 (*ejecutar: trabajo etc*) to do; **hacer la colada** to do the washing; **hacer la comida** to do the cooking; **¿qué haces?** what are you doing?; **¡eso está hecho!** you've got it!; **hacer el tonto/indio** to act the fool/clown; **hacer el malo** *o* **el papel del malo** (*Teat*) to play the villain

3 (*estudios, algunos deportes*) to do; **hacer español/económicas** to do *o* study Spanish/economics; **hacer yoga/gimnasia** to do yoga/go to the gym

4 (*transformar, incidir en*): **esto lo hará más difícil** this will make it more difficult; **salir te hará sentir mejor** going out will make you feel better; **te hace más joven** it makes you look younger

5 (*cálculo*): **2 y 2 hacen 4** 2 and 2 make 4; **éste hace 100** this one makes 100

6 (+*sub*): **esto hará que ganemos** this will make us win; **harás que no quiera venir** you'll stop him wanting to come

7 (*como sustituto de vb*) to do; **él bebió y yo hice lo mismo** he drank and I did likewise

8: **no hace más que criticar** all he does is criticize

■ *vb semi-auxiliar* (+*infin*) **1** (*directo*): **les hice venir** I made *o* had them come; **hacer trabajar a los demás** to get others to work

2 (*por intermedio de otros*): **hacer reparar algo** to get sth repaired

■ *vi* **1**: **haz como que no lo sabes** act as if you don't know; **hiciste bien en decírmelo** you were right to tell me

2 (*ser apropiado*): **si os hace** if it's alright with you

3: **hacer de**: **hacer de madre para uno** to be like a mother to sb; (*Teat*): **hacer de Otelo** to play Othello; **la tabla hace de mesa** the board does as a table

■ *vb impersonal* **1**: **hace calor/frío** it's hot/cold; *ver tb* **bueno**; **sol**; **tiempo**

2 (*tiempo*): **hace tres años** three years ago; **hace un mes que voy/no voy** I've been going/I haven't been for a month; **no le veo desde hace mucho** I haven't seen him for a long time

3: **¿cómo has hecho para llegar tan rápido?** how did you manage to get here so quickly?

hacerse *vr* **1** (*volverse*) to become; **se hicieron amigos** they became friends; **hacerse viejo** to get *o* grow old; **se hace tarde** it's getting late

2: **hacerse algo**: **me hice un traje** I got a suit made

3 (*acostumbrarse*): **hacerse a** to get used to; **hacerse a la idea** to get used to the idea

4: **se hace con huevos y leche** it's made out of eggs and milk; **eso no se hace** that's not done

5 (*obtener*): **hacerse de** *o* **con algo** to get hold of sth

6 (*fingirse*): **hacerse el sordo/sueco** to turn a deaf ear/pretend not to notice

hacha ['atʃa] *nf* axe; (*antorcha*) torch

hachazo [a'tʃaθo] *nm* axe blow

hache ['atʃe] *nf* (the letter) H; **llámele usted ~** call it what you will

hachís [a'tʃis] *nm* hashish

hacia ['aθja] *prep (en dirección de, actitud)* towards; *(cerca de)* near; **~ arriba/abajo** up(wards)/down(wards); **~ mediodía** about noon

hacienda [a'θjenda] *nf (propiedad)* property; *(finca)* farm; *(Am)* ranch; **~ pública** public finance; **(Ministerio de) H~** Exchequer *(Brit)*, Treasury Department *(US)*

hacinar [aθi'nar] *vt* to pile (up); *(Agr)* to stack; *(fig)* to overcrowd

hada ['aða] *nf* fairy; **~ madrina** fairy godmother

hado ['aðo] *nm* fate, destiny

haga *etc* ['aɣa] *vb ver* **hacer**

Haití [ai'ti] *nm* Haiti

haitiano, -a [ai'tjano, a] *adj, nm/f* Haitian

hala ['ala] *excl (vamos)* come on!; *(anda)* get on with it!

halagar [ala'ɣar] *vt (lisonjear)* to flatter

halago [a'laɣo] *nm (adulación)* flattery

halague *etc* [a'laɣe] *vb ver* **halagar**

halagüeño, -a [ala'ɣweɲo, a] *adj* flattering

halcón [al'kon] *nm* falcon, hawk

hálito ['alito] *nm* breath

halitosis [ali'tosis] *nf* halitosis, bad breath

hallar [a'ʎar] *vt (gen)* to find; *(descubrir)* to discover; *(toparse con)* to run into; **hallarse** *vr* to be (situated); *(encontrarse)* to find o.s.; **se halla fuera** he is away; **no se halla** he feels out of place

hallazgo [a'ʎaθɣo] *nm* discovery; *(cosa)* find

halo ['alo] *nm* halo

halógeno, a [a'loxeno, a] *adj:* **faro ~** halogen lamp

halterofilia [altero'filja] *nf* weightlifting

hamaca [a'maka] *nf* hammock

hambre ['ambre] *nf* hunger; *(carencia)* famine; *(inanición)* starvation; *(fig)* longing; **tener ~** to be hungry

hambriento, -a [am'brjento, a] *adj* hungry, starving ■ *nm/f* starving person; **los hambrientos** the hungry; **~ de** hungry *o* longing for

hambruna [am'bruna] *nf* famine

Hamburgo [am'burɣo] *nm* Hamburg

hamburguesa [ambur'ɣesa] *nf* hamburger, burger

hampa ['ampa] *nf* underworld

hampón [am'pon] *nm* thug

hámster ['xamster] *nm* hamster

han [an] *vb ver* **haber**

haragán, -ana [ara'ɣan, ana] *adj, nm/f* good-for-nothing

haraganear [araɣane'ar] *vi* to idle, loaf about

harapiento, -a [ara'pjento, a] *adj* tattered, in rags

harapo [a'rapo] *nm* rag

hardware ['xardwer] *nm (Inform)* hardware

haré *etc* [a're] *vb ver* **hacer**

harén [a'ren] *nm* harem

harina [a'rina] *nf* flour; **eso es ~ de otro costal** that's another kettle of fish

harinero, -a [ari'nero, a] *nm/f* flour merchant

harinoso, -a [ari'noso, a] *adj* floury

hartar [ar'tar] *vt* to satiate, glut; *(fig)* to tire, sicken; **hartarse** *vr (de comida)* to gorge o.s.; *(cansarse):* **hartarse de** to get fed up with

hartazgo [ar'taθɣo] *nm* surfeit, glut

harto, -a ['arto, a] *adj (lleno)* full; *(cansado)* fed up ■ *adv (bastante)* enough; *(muy)* very; **estar ~ de** to be fed up with; **¡estoy ~ de decírtelo!** I'm sick and tired of telling you (so)!

hartura [ar'tura] *nf (exceso)* surfeit; *(abundancia)* abundance; *(satisfacción)* satisfaction

has¹ [as] *vb ver* **haber**

has² *abr* (= **Hectáreas**) ha.

hasta ['asta] *adv* even ■ *prep (alcanzando a)* as far as, up/down to; *(de tiempo: a tal hora)* till, until; *(: antes de)* before ■ *conj:* **~ que** until; **~ luego** *o* **ahora/el sábado** *(fam)* see you soon/on Saturday; **~ la fecha** (up) to date; **~ nueva orden** until further notice; **~ en Valencia hiela a veces** even in Valencia it freezes sometimes

hastiar [as'tjar] *vt (gen)* to weary; *(aburrir)* to bore; **hastiarse** *vr:* **hastiarse de** to get fed up with

hastío [as'tio] *nm* weariness; boredom

hatajo [a'taxo] *nm:* **un ~ de gamberros** a bunch of hooligans

hatillo [a'tiʎo] *nm* belongings *pl*, kit; *(montón)* bundle, heap

Hawai [a'wai] *nm (tb:* **las Islas Hawai**) Hawaii

hawaianas [awa'janas] *nfpl (esp Am)* flip-flops *(Brit)*, thongs

hawaiano, -a [awa'jano, a] *adj, nm/f* Hawaiian

hay [ai] *vb ver* **haber**

Haya ['aja] *nf:* **la ~** The Hague

haya *etc* ['aja] *vb ver* **haber** ■ *nf* beech tree

hayal [a'jal] *nm* beech grove

haz [aθ] *vb ver* **hacer** ■ *nm* bundle, bunch; *(rayo: de luz)* beam ■ *nf:* **~ de la tierra** face of the earth

hazaña [a'θaɲa] *nf* feat, exploit; **sería una ~** it would be a great achievement

hazmerreír [aθmerre'ir] *nm inv* laughing stock

he [e] *vb ver* **haber** ■ *adv:* **he aquí** here is, here are; **he aquí por qué ...** that is why ...

hebilla [e'βiʎa] *nf* buckle, clasp

hebra ['eβra] *nf* thread; *(Bot: fibra)* fibre, grain

hebreo, -a [e'βreo, a] *adj, nm/f* Hebrew ■ *nm* (*Ling*) Hebrew

Hébridas ['eβriðas] *nfpl*: **las ~** the Hebrides

hechice *etc* [e'tʃiθe] *vb ver* **hechizar**

hechicero, -a [etʃi'θero, a] *nm/f* sorcerer/ sorceress

hechizar [etʃi'θar] *vt* to cast a spell on, bewitch

hechizo [e'tʃiθo] *nm* witchcraft, magic; (*acto de magia*) spell, charm

hecho, -a ['etʃo, a] *pp de* **hacer** ■ *adj* complete; (*maduro*) mature; (*Costura*) ready-to-wear ■ *nm* deed, act; (*dato*) fact; (*cuestión*) matter; (*suceso*) event ■ *excl* agreed!, done!; **¡bien ~!** well done!; **de ~** in fact, as a matter of fact; (*Pol etc*: *adj, adv*) de facto; **de ~ y de derecho** de facto and de jure; **~ a la medida** made-to-measure; **a lo ~, pecho** it's no use crying over spilt milk

hechura [e'tʃura] *nf* making, creation; (*producto*) product; (*forma*) form, shape; (*de persona*) build; (*Tec*) craftsmanship

hectárea [ek'tarea] *nf* hectare

heder [e'ðer] *vi* to stink, smell; (*fig*) to be unbearable

hediondez [eðjon'deθ] *nf* stench, stink; (*cosa*) stinking thing

hediondo, -a [e'ðjondo, a] *adj* stinking

hedor [e'ðor] *nm* stench

hegemonía [exemo'nia] *nf* hegemony

helada [e'laða] *nf* frost

heladera [ela'ðera] *nf* (*Am*: *refrigerador*) refrigerator

heladería [elaðe'ria] *nf* ice-cream stall (*o* parlour)

helado, -a [e'laðo, a] *adj* frozen; (*glacial*) icy; (*fig*) chilly, cold ■ *nm* ice-cream; **dejar ~ a algn** to dumbfound sb

helador, a [ela'ðor, a] *adj* (*viento etc*) icy

helar [e'lar] *vt* to freeze, ice (up); (*dejar atónito*) to amaze; (*desalentar*) to discourage ■ *vi*, **helarse** *vr* to freeze; (*Aviat, Ferro etc*) to ice (up), freeze up; (*líquido*) to set

helecho [e'letʃo] *nm* bracken, fern

hélice ['eliθe] *nf* spiral; (*Tec*) propeller; (*Mat*) helix

helicóptero [eli'koptero] *nm* helicopter

helio ['eljo] *nm* helium

helmántico, -a [el'mantiko, a] *adj* of *o* from Salamanca

helvético, -a [el'βetiko, a] *adj, nm/f* Swiss

hematoma [ema'toma] *nm* bruise

hembra ['embra] *nf* (*Bot, Zool*) female; (*mujer*) woman; (*Tec*) nut; **un elefante ~** a she-elephant

hemeroteca [emero'teka] *nf* newspaper library

hemiciclo [emi'θiklo] *nm*: **el ~** (*Pol*) the floor

hemisferio [emis'ferjo] *nm* hemisphere

hemofilia [emo'filja] *nf* haemophilia (*Brit*), hemophilia (*US*)

hemorragia [emo'rraxja] *nf* haemorrhage (*Brit*), hemorrhage (*US*)

hemorroides [emo'rroiðes] *nfpl* haemorrhoids (*Brit*), hemorrhoids (*US*)

hemos ['emos] *vb ver* **haber**

henar [e'nar] *nm* meadow, hayfield

henchir [en'tʃir] *vt* to fill, stuff; **henchirse** *vr* (*llenarse de comida*) to stuff o.s. (with food); (*inflarse*) to swell (up)

Hendaya [en'daja] *nf* Hendaye

hender [en'der] *vt* to cleave, split

hendidura [endi'ðura] *nf* crack, split; (*Geo*) fissure

henequén [ene'ken] *nm* (*Am*) henequen

heno ['eno] *nm* hay

hepatitis [epa'titis] *nf inv* hepatitis

herbario, -a [er'βarjo, a] *adj* herbal ■ *nm* (*colección*) herbarium; (*especialista*) herbalist; (*botánico*) botanist

herbicida [erβi'θiða] *nm* weedkiller

herbívoro, -a [er'βiβoro, a] *adj* herbivorous

herboristería [erβoriste'ria] *nf* herbalist's shop

heredad [ere'ðað] *nf* landed property; (*granja*) farm

heredar [ere'ðar] *vt* to inherit

heredero, -a [ere'ðero, a] *nm/f* heir(ess); **~ del trono** heir to the throne

hereditario, -a [ereði'tarjo, a] *adj* hereditary

hereje [e'rexe] *nm/f* heretic

herejía [ere'xia] *nf* heresy

herencia [e'renθja] *nf* inheritance; (*fig*) heritage; (*Bio*) heredity

herético, -a [e'retiko, a] *adj* heretical

herido, -a [e'riðo, a] *adj* injured, wounded; (*fig*) offended ■ *nm/f* casualty ■ *nf* injury

herir [e'rir] *vt* to wound, injure; (*fig*) to offend; (*conmover*) to touch, move

hermana [er'mana] *nf ver* **hermano**

hermanación [ermana'θjon] *nf* (*de ciudades*) twinning

hermanado, -a [erma'naðo, a] *adj* (*ciudad*) twinned

hermanar [erma'nar] *vt* to match; (*unir*) to join; (*ciudades*) to twin

hermanastro, -a [erma'nastro, a] *nm/f* stepbrother(-sister)

hermandad [erman'dað] *nf* brotherhood; (*de mujeres*) sisterhood; (*sindicato etc*) association

hermano, -a [er'mano, a] *adj* similar ■ *nm* brother ■ *nf* sister; **~ gemelo** twin brother; **~ político** brother-in-law; **~ primo** first cousin; **mis hermanos** my brothers, my brothers and sisters; **hermana política** sister-in-law

hermético, -a [er'metiko, a] *adj* hermetic;
(*fig*) watertight

hermoso, -a [er'moso, a] *adj* beautiful,
lovely; (*estupendo*) splendid; (*guapo*)
handsome

hermosura [ermo'sura] *nf* beauty; (*de hombre*)
handsomeness

hernia ['ernja] *nf* hernia, rupture; ~ **discal**
slipped disc

herniarse [er'njarse] *vr* to rupture o.s.; (*fig*)
to break one's back

héroe ['eroe] *nm* hero

heroicidad [eroiθi'ðað] *nf* heroism; (*una
heroicidad*) heroic deed

heroico, -a [e'roiko, a] *adj* heroic

heroína [ero'ina] *nf* (*mujer*) heroine; (*droga*)
heroin

heroinómano, -a [eroi'nomano, a] *nm/f*
heroin addict

heroísmo [ero'ismo] *nm* heroism

herpes ['erpes] *nmpl o nfpl* (*Med: gen*) herpes *sg*;
(: *de la piel*) shingles *sg*

herradura [erra'ðura] *nf* horseshoe

herraje [e'rraxe] *nm* (*trabajos*) ironwork

herramienta [erra'mjenta] *nf* tool

herrería [erre'ria] *nf* smithy; (*Tec*) forge

herrero [e'rrero] *nm* blacksmith

herrumbre [e'rrumbre] *nf* rust

herrumbroso, -a [errum'broso, a] *adj* rusty

hervidero [erβi'ðero] *nm* (*fig*) swarm; (*Pol etc*)
hotbed

hervir [er'βir] *vi* to boil; (*burbujear*) to bubble;
(*fig*): ~ **de** to teem with; ~ **a fuego lento** to
simmer

hervor [er'βor] *nm* boiling; (*fig*) ardour, fervour

heterogéneo, -a [etero'xeneo, a] *adj*
heterogeneous

heterosexual [eterosek'swal] *adj, nm/f*
heterosexual

hez [eθ] *nf* (*tb*: **heces**) dregs

hibernar [iβer'nar] *vi* to hibernate

híbrido, -a ['iβriðo, a] *adj* hybrid

hice *etc* ['iθe] *vb ver* **hacer**

hidalgo, -a [i'ðalɣo, a] *adj* noble; (*honrado*)
honourable (*Brit*), honorable (*US*) ◾ *nm/f*
noble(man(-woman))

hidratante [iðra'tante] *adj*: **crema** ~
moisturizing cream, moisturizer

hidratar [iðra'tar] *vt* to moisturize

hidrato [i'ðrato] *nm* hydrate; ~ **de carbono**
carbohydrate

hidráulico, -a [i'ðrauliko, a] *adj* hydraulic
◾ *nf* hydraulics *sg*

hidro... [iðro] *pref* hydro..., water-...

hidroavión [iðroa'βjon] *nm* seaplane

hidrodeslizador [iðrodesliθa'ðor] *nm*
hovercraft

hidroeléctrico, -a [iðroe'lektriko, a] *adj*
hydroelectric

hidrófilo, -a [i'ðrofilo, a] *adj* absorbent;
algodón ~ cotton wool (*Brit*), absorbent
cotton (*US*)

hidrofobia [iðro'foβja] *nf* hydrophobia, rabies

hidrófugo, -a [i'ðrofuɣo, a] *adj* damp-proof

hidrógeno [i'ðroxeno] *nm* hydrogen

hieda *etc* ['jeða] *vb ver* **heder**

hiedra ['jeðra] *nf* ivy

hiel [jel] *nf* gall, bile; (*fig*) bitterness

hielo *etc* ['jelo] *vb ver* **helar** ◾ *nm* (*gen*) ice;
(*escarcha*) frost; (*fig*) coldness, reserve;
romper el ~ (*fig*) to break the ice

hiena ['jena] *nf* (*Zool*) hyena

hiera *etc* ['jera] *vb ver* **herir**

hierba ['jerβa] *nf* (*pasto*) grass; (*Culin, Med*:
planta) herb; **mala** ~ weed; (*fig*) evil influence

hierbabuena [jerβa'βwena] *nf* mint

hierro ['jerro] *nm* (*metal*) iron; (*objeto*) iron
object; ~ **acanalado** corrugated iron; ~
colado *o* **fundido** cast iron; **de** ~ iron *cpd*

hierva *etc* ['jerβa] *vb ver* **hervir**

hígado ['iɣaðo] *nm* liver; **hígados** *nmpl* (*fig*)
guts; **echar los hígados** to wear o.s. out

higiene [i'xjene] *nf* hygiene

higiénico, -a [i'xjeniko, a] *adj* hygienic

higo ['iɣo] *nm* fig; ~ **seco** dried fig; ~ **chumbo**
prickly pear; **de higos a brevas** once in a
blue moon

higuera [i'ɣera] *nf* fig tree

hijastro, -a [i'xastro, a] *nm/f*
stepson(-daughter)

hijo, -a ['ixo, a] *nm/f* son/daughter, child;
(*uso vocativo*) dear; **hijos** *nmpl* children, sons
and daughters; **sin hijos** childless; ~/**hija
político/a** son-/daughter-in-law; ~ **pródigo**
prodigal son; ~ **de papá/mamá** daddy's/
mummy's boy; ~ **de puta** (*fam!*) bastard (!),
son of a bitch (!); ~ **único** only child; **cada** ~
de vecino any Tom, Dick or Harry

hilacha [i'latʃa] *nf* ravelled thread

hilado, -a [i'laðo, a] *adj* spun

hilandero, -a [ilan'dero, a] *nm/f* spinner

hilar [i'lar] *vt* to spin; (*fig*) to reason, infer;
~ **delgado** to split hairs

hilera [i'lera] *nf* row, file

hilo ['ilo] *nm* thread; (*Bot*) fibre; (*tela*) linen;
(*de metal*) wire; (*de agua*) trickle, thin stream;
(*de luz*) beam, ray; (*de conversación*) thread,
theme; (*de pensamientos*) train; ~ **dental**
dental floss; **colgar de un** ~ (*fig*) to hang by a
thread; **traje de** ~ linen suit

hilvanar [ilβa'nar] *vt* (*Costura*) to tack (*Brit*),
baste (*US*); (*fig*) to do hurriedly

Himalaya [ima'laja] *nm*: **el** ~, **los Montes
Himalaya** the Himalayas

h

himno ['imno] *nm* hymn; ~ **nacional** national anthem

hincapié [inka'pje] *nm*: **hacer hincapié en** to emphasize, stress

hincar [in'kar] *vt* to drive (in), thrust (in); (*diente*) to sink; **hincarse** *vr*: **hincarse de rodillas** (*esp Am*) to kneel down

hincha ['intʃa] *nm/f* (*fam: Deporte*) fan

hinchado, -a [in'tʃaðo, a] *adj* (*gen*) swollen; (*persona*) pompous ▪ *nf* (group of) supporters o fans

hinchar [in'tʃar] *vt* (*gen*) to swell; (*inflar*) to blow up, inflate; (*fig*) to exaggerate; **hincharse** *vr* (*inflarse*) to swell up; (*fam: llenarse*) to stuff o.s.; (*fig*) to get conceited; **hincharse de reír** to have a good laugh

hinchazón [intʃa'θon] *nf* (*Med*) swelling; (*protuberancia*) bump, lump; (*altivez*) arrogance

hindú [in'du] *adj, nm/f* Hindu

hinojo [i'noxo] *nm* fennel

hinque *etc* ['inke] *vb ver* **hincar**

hipar [i'par] *vi* to hiccup

hiper... [iper] *pref* hyper...

hiperactivo, -a [iperak'tiβo, a] *adj* hyperactive

hipermercado [ipermer'kaðo] *nm* hypermarket, superstore

hipersensible [ipersen'siβle] *adj* hypersensitive

hipertensión [iperten'sjon] *nf* high blood pressure, hypertension

hípico, -a ['ipiko, a] *adj* horse *cpd*, equine; **club** ~ riding club

hipnosis [ip'nosis] *nf inv* hypnosis

hipnotice *etc* [ipno'tiθe] *vb ver* **hipnotizar**

hipnotismo [ipno'tismo] *nm* hypnotism

hipnotizar [ipnoti'θar] *vt* to hypnotize

hipo ['ipo] *nm* hiccups *pl*; **quitar el ~ a algn** to cure sb's hiccups

hipocondría [ipokon'dria] *nf* hypochondria

hipocondríaco, -a [ipokon'driako, a] *adj, nm/f* hypochondriac

hipocresía [ipokre'sia] *nf* hypocrisy

hipócrita [i'pokrita] *adj* hypocritical ▪ *nm/f* hypocrite

hipodérmico, -a [ipo'ðermiko, a] *adj*: **aguja hipodérmica** hypodermic needle

hipódromo [i'poðromo] *nm* racetrack

hipopótamo [ipo'potamo] *nm* hippopotamus

hipoteca [ipo'teka] *nf* mortgage; **redimir una** ~ to pay off a mortgage

hipotecar [ipote'kar] *vt* to mortgage; (*fig*) to jeopardize

hipotecario, -a [ipote'karjo, a] *adj* mortgage *cpd*

hipótesis [i'potesis] *nf inv* hypothesis; **es una** ~ **(nada más)** that's just a theory

hipotético, -a [ipo'tetiko, a] *adj* hypothetic(al)

hiriendo *etc* [i'rjendo] *vb ver* **herir**

hiriente [i'rjente] *adj* offensive, wounding

hirsuto, -a [ir'suto, a] *adj* hairy

hirviendo *etc* [ir'βjendo] *vb ver* **hervir**

hisopo [i'sopo] *nm* (*Rel*) sprinkler; (*Bot*) hyssop; (*de algodón*) swab

hispánico, -a [is'paniko, a] *adj* Hispanic, Spanish

hispanidad [ispani'ðað] *nf* (*cualidad*) Spanishness; (*Pol*) Spanish o Hispanic world

hispanista [ispa'nista] *nm/f* (*Univ etc*) Hispan(ic)ist

hispano, -a [is'pano, a] *adj* Hispanic, Spanish, Hispano- ▪ *nm/f* Spaniard

Hispanoamérica [ispanoa'merika] *nf* Spanish o Latin America

hispanoamericano, -a [ispanoameri'kano, a] *adj, nm/f* Spanish o Latin American

hispanohablante [ispanoa'βlante], **hispanoparlante** [ispanopar'lante] *adj* Spanish-speaking

histeria [is'terja] *nf* hysteria

histérico, -a [is'teriko, a] *adj* hysterical

histerismo [iste'rismo] *nm* (*Med*) hysteria; (*fig*) hysterics

histograma [isto'ɣrama] *nm* histogram

historia [is'torja] *nf* history; (*cuento*) story, tale; **historias** *nfpl* (*chismes*) gossip *sg*; **dejarse de historias** to come to the point; **pasar a la** ~ to go down in history

historiador, a [istorja'ðor, a] *nm/f* historian

historial [isto'rjal] *nm* record; (*profesional*) curriculum vitae, c.v., résumé (*US*); (*Med*) case history

histórico, -a [is'toriko, a] *adj* historical; (*fig*) historic

historieta [isto'rjeta] *nf* tale, anecdote; (*de dibujos*) comic strip

histrionismo [istrjo'nismo] *nm* (*Teat*) acting; (*fig*) histrionics *pl*

hito ['ito] *nm* (*fig*) landmark; (*objetivo*) goal, target; (*fig*) milestone

hizo ['iθo] *vb ver* **hacer**

Hna., Hnas. *abr* (= *Hermana(s)*) Sr(s).

Hno., Hnos. *abr* (= *Hermano(s)*) Bro(s).

hocico [o'θiko] *nm* snout; (*fig*) grimace

hockey ['xoki] *nm* hockey; ~ **sobre hielo** ice hockey

hogar [o'ɣar] *nm* fireplace, hearth; (*casa*) home; (*vida familiar*) home life

hogareño, -a [oɣa'reɲo, a] *adj* home *cpd*; (*persona*) home-loving

hogaza [o'ɣaθa] *nf* (*de pan*) large loaf

hoguera [o'ɣera] *nf* (*gen*) bonfire; (*para herejes*) stake

hoja ['oxa] nf (gen) leaf; (de flor) petal; (de hierba) blade; (de papel) sheet; (página) page; (formulario) form; (de puerta) leaf; ~ **de afeitar** razor blade; ~ **de cálculo electrónica** spreadsheet; ~ **de ruta** road map; ~ **de solicitud** application form; ~ **de trabajo** (Inform) worksheet; **de ~ ancha** broad-leaved; **de ~ caduca/perenne** deciduous/evergreen

hojalata [oxa'lata] nf tin(plate)

hojaldre [o'xaldre] nm (Culin) puff pastry

hojarasca [oxa'raska] nf (hojas) dead o fallen leaves pl; (fig) rubbish

hojear [oxe'ar] vt to leaf through, turn the pages of

hola ['ola] excl hello!

Holanda [o'landa] nf Holland

holandés, -esa [olan'des, esa] adj Dutch ■ nm/f Dutchman(-woman); **los holandeses** the Dutch ■ nm (Ling) Dutch

holgado, -a [ol'ɣaðo, a] adj loose, baggy; (rico) well-to-do

holgar [ol'ɣar] vi (descansar) to rest; (sobrar) to be superfluous; **huelga decir que** it goes without saying that

holgazán, -ana [olɣa'θan, ana] adj idle, lazy ■ nm/f loafer

holgazanear [olɣaθane'ar] vi to laze o loaf around

holgura [ol'ɣura] nf looseness, bagginess; (Tec) play, free movement; (vida) comfortable living, luxury

hollar [o'ʎar] vt to tread (on), trample

hollín [o'ʎin] nm soot

hombre ['ombre] nm man; (raza humana): **el ~** man(kind) ■ excl: **¡sí ~!** (claro) of course!; (para énfasis) man, old chap; ~ **de negocios** businessman; ~**-rana** frogman; ~ **de bien** o **pro** honest man; ~ **de confianza** right-hand man; ~ **de estado** statesman; **el ~ medio** the average man

hombrera [om'brera] nf shoulder strap

hombro ['ombro] nm shoulder; **arrimar el ~** to lend a hand; **encogerse de hombros** to shrug one's shoulders

hombruno, -a [om'bruno, a] adj mannish

homenaje [ome'naxe] nm (gen) homage; (tributo) tribute; **un partido ~** a benefit match

homeopatía [omeopa'tia] nf hom(o)eopathy

homeopático, -a [omeo'patiko, a] adj hom(o)eopathic

homicida [omi'θiða] adj homicidal ■ nm/f murderer

homicidio [omi'θiðjo] nm murder, homicide; (involuntario) manslaughter

homologación [omoloɣa'θjon] nf (de sueldo, condiciones) parity

homologar [omolo'ɣar] vt (Com) to standardize; (Escol) to officially approve; (Deporte) to officially recognize; (sueldos) to equalize

homólogo, -a [o'moloɣo, a] nm/f counterpart, opposite number

homónimo [o'monimo] nm (tocayo) namesake

homosexual [omosek'swal] adj, nm/f homosexual

hondo, -a ['ondo, a] adj deep; **lo ~** the depth(s) (pl), the bottom; **con ~ pesar** with deep regret

hondonada [ondo'naða] nf hollow, depression; (cañón) ravine; (Geo) lowland

hondura [on'dura] nf depth, profundity

Honduras [on'duras] nf Honduras

hondureño, -a [ondu'reno, a] adj, nm/f Honduran

honestidad [onesti'ðað] nf purity, chastity; (decencia) decency

honesto, -a [o'nesto, a] adj chaste; decent, honest; (justo) just

hongo ['ongo] nm (Bot: gen) fungus; (: comestible) mushroom; (: venenoso) toadstool; (sombrero) bowler (hat) (Brit), derby (US); **hongos del pie** foot rot sg, athlete's foot sg

honor [o'nor] nm (gen) honour (Brit), honor (US); (gloria) glory; ~ **profesional** professional etiquette; **en ~ a la verdad** to be fair

honorable [ono'raβle] adj honourable (Brit), honorable (US)

honorario, -a [ono'rarjo, a] adj honorary ■ nm: **honorarios** fees

honorífico, -a [ono'rifiko, a] adj honourable (Brit), honorable (US); **mención honorífica** hono(u)rable mention

honra ['onra] nf (gen) honour (Brit), honor (US); (renombre) good name; **honras fúnebres** funeral rites; **tener algo a mucha ~** to be proud of sth

honradez [onra'ðeθ] nf honesty; (de persona) integrity

honrado, -a [on'raðo, a] adj honest, upright

honrar [on'rar] vt to honour (Brit) o honor (US); **honrarse** vr: **honrarse con algo/de hacer algo** to be honoured by sth/to do sth

honroso, -a [on'roso, a] adj (honrado) honourable (Brit), honorable (US); (respetado) respectable

hora ['ora] nf hour; (tiempo) time; **¿qué ~ es?** what time is it?; **¿a qué ~?** at what time?; **media ~** half an hour; **a la ~ de comer/de recreo** at lunchtime/at playtime; **a primera ~** first thing (in the morning); **a última ~** at

the last moment; **"última ~"** "stop press";
noticias de última ~ last-minute news; **a
altas horas** in the small hours; **a la ~ en
punto** on the dot; **¡a buena ~!** about time,
too!; **en mala ~** unluckily; **dar la ~** to strike
the hour; **poner el reloj en ~** to set one's
watch; **horas de oficina/de trabajo** office/
working hours; **horas de visita** visiting
times; **horas extras** o **extraordinarias**
overtime *sg*; **horas punta** rush hours; **no
ver la ~ de** to look forward to; **¡ya era ~!** and
about time too!

horadar [ora'ðar] *vt* to drill, bore
horario, -a [o'rarjo, a] *adj* hourly, hour *cpd*
■ *nm* timetable; **~ comercial** business hours
horca ['orka] *nf* gallows *sg*; (*Agr*) pitchfork
horcajadas [orka'xaðas]: **a ~** *adv* astride
horchata [or'tʃata] *nf* cold drink made from tiger
nuts and water, tiger nut milk
horda ['orða] *nf* horde
horizontal [oriθon'tal] *adj* horizontal
horizonte [ori'θonte] *nm* horizon
horma ['orma] *nf* mould; **~ (de calzado)** last;
~ de sombrero hat block
hormiga [or'miɣa] *nf* ant; **hormigas** *nfpl*
(*Med*) pins and needles
hormigón [ormi'ɣon] *nm* concrete; **~
armado/pretensado** reinforced/prestressed
concrete
hormigueo [ormi'ɣeo] *nm* (*comezón*) itch; (*fig*)
uneasiness
hormiguero [ormi'ɣero] *nm* (*Zool*) ant's nest;
era un ~ it was swarming with people
hormona [or'mona] *nf* hormone
hornada [or'naða] *nf* batch of loaves (*etc*)
hornillo [or'niʎo] *nm* (*cocina*) portable stove
horno ['orno] *nm* (*Culin*) oven; (*Tec*)
furnace; (*para cerámica*) kiln; **~ microondas**
microwave (oven); **alto ~** blast furnace; **~
crematorio** crematorium
horóscopo [o'roskopo] *nm* horoscope
horquilla [or'kiʎa] *nf* hairpin; (*Agr*) pitchfork
horrendo, -a [o'rrendo, a] *adj* horrendous,
frightful
horrible [o'rriβle] *adj* horrible, dreadful
horripilante [orripi'lante] *adj* hair-raising,
horrifying
horripilar [orripi'lar] *vt*: **~ a algn** to horrify
sb; **horripilarse** *vr* to be horrified
horror [o'rror] *nm* horror, dread; (*atrocidad*)
atrocity; **¡qué ~!** (*fam*) how awful!; **estudia
horrores** he studies a hell of a lot
horrorice *etc* [orro'riθe] *vb ver* **horrorizar**
horrorizar [orrori'θar] *vt* to horrify, frighten;
horrorizarse *vr* to be horrified
horroroso, -a [orro'roso, a] *adj* horrifying,
ghastly

hortaliza [orta'liθa] *nf* vegetable
hortelano, -a [orte'lano, a] *nm/f* (market)
gardener
hortera [or'tera] *adj* (*fam*) vulgar, naff
horterada [orte'raða] *nf* (*fam*): **es una ~** it's
really naff
hortícola [or'tikola] *adj* horticultural
horticultura [ortikul'tura] *nf* horticulture
hortofrutícola [ortofru'tikola] *adj* fruit and
vegetable *cpd*
hosco, -a ['osko, a] *adj* dark; (*persona*) sullen,
gloomy
hospedaje [ospe'ðaxe] *nm* (cost of) board and
lodging
hospedar [ospe'ðar] *vt* to put up;
hospedarse *vr*: **hospedarse (con/en)** to stay
o lodge (with/at)
hospedería [ospeðe'ria] *nf* (*edificio*) inn;
(*habitación*) guest room
hospicio [os'piθjo] *nm* (*para niños*) orphanage
hospital [ospi'tal] *nm* hospital
hospitalario, -a [ospita'larjo, a] *adj* (*acogedor*)
hospitable
hospitalice *etc* [ospita'liθe] *vb ver*
hospitalizar
hospitalidad [ospitali'ðað] *nf* hospitality
hospitalizar [ospitali'θar] *vt* to send o take to
hospital, hospitalize
hosquedad [oske'ðað] *nf* sullenness
hostal [os'tal] *nm* small hotel; *ver tb* **hotel**
hostelería [ostele'ria] *nf* hotel business o
trade
hostia ['ostja] *nf* (*Rel*) host, consecrated
wafer; (*fam: golpe*) whack, punch ■ *excl*: **¡~(s)!**
(*fam!*) damn!
hostigar [osti'ɣar] *vt* to whip; (*fig*) to harass,
pester
hostigue *etc* [os'tiɣe] *vb ver* **hostigar**
hostil [os'til] *adj* hostile
hostilidad [ostili'ðað] *nf* hostility
hotel [o'tel] *nm* hotel; *see note*

HOTEL

In Spain you can choose from the
following categories of accommodation,
in descending order of quality and price:
hotel (from 5 stars to 1), *hostal, pensión,
casa de huéspedes, fonda*. Quality can vary
widely even within these categories.
The State also runs luxury hotels called
paradores, which are usually sited in places
of particular historical interest and are
often historic buildings themselves.

hotelero, -a [ote'lero, a] *adj* hotel *cpd* ■ *nm/f*
hotelier

hoy [oi] *adv* (*este día*) today; (*en la actualidad*) now(adays) ∎ *nm* present time; ~ **(en) día** now(adays); **el día de ~**, **~ día** (*Am*) this very day; **~ por ~** right now; **de ~ en ocho días** a week today; **de ~ en adelante** from now on

hoya ['oja] *nf* pit; (*sepulcro*) grave; (*Geo*) valley

hoyo ['ojo] *nm* hole, pit; (*tumba*) grave; (*Golf*) hole; (*Med*) pockmark

hoyuelo [oj'welo] *nm* dimple

hoz [oθ] *nf* sickle

hube *etc* ['uβe] *vb ver* **haber**

hucha ['utʃa] *nf* money box

hueco, -a ['weko, a] *adj* (*vacío*) hollow, empty; (*resonante*) booming; (*sonido*) resonant; (*persona*) conceited; (*estilo*) pompous ∎ *nm* hollow, cavity; (*agujero*) hole; (*de escalera*) well; (*de ascensor*) shaft; (*vacante*) vacancy; **~ de la mano** hollow of the hand

huela *etc* ['wela] *vb ver* **oler**

huelga *etc* ['welɣa] *vb ver* **holgar** ∎ *nf* strike; **declararse en ~** to go on strike, come out on strike; **~ general** general strike; **~ de hambre** hunger strike; **~ oficial** official strike

huelgue *etc* ['welɣe] *vb ver* **holgar**

huelguista [wel'ɣista] *nm/f* striker

huella ['weʎa] *nf* (*acto de pisar, pisada*) tread(ing); (*marca del paso*) footprint, footstep; (: *de animal, máquina*) track; **~ digital** fingerprint; **sin dejar ~** without leaving a trace

huérfano, -a ['werfano, a] *adj* orphan(ed); (*fig*) unprotected ∎ *nm/f* orphan

huerta ['werta] *nf* market garden (*Brit*), truck farm (*US*); (*de Murcia, Valencia*) irrigated region

huerto ['werto] *nm* kitchen garden; (*de árboles frutales*) orchard

hueso ['weso] *nm* (*Anat*) bone; (*de fruta*) stone, pit (*US*); **sin ~** (*carne*) boned; **estar en los huesos** to be nothing but skin and bone; **ser un ~** (*profesor*) to be terribly strict; **un ~ duro de roer** a hard nut to crack

huesoso, -a [we'soso, a] *adj* (*esp Am*) bony

huésped, a ['wespeð, a] *nm/f* (*invitado*) guest; (*habitante*) resident; (*anfitrión*) host(ess)

huesudo, -a [we'suðo, a] *adj* bony, big-boned

huevas ['weβas] *nfpl* eggs, roe *sg*; (*Am: fam!*) balls (!)

huevera [we'βera] *nf* eggcup

huevo ['weβo] *nm* egg; (*fam!*) ball (!), testicle; **~ duro/escalfado/estrellado** o **frito/pasado por agua** hard-boiled/poached/fried/soft-boiled egg; **huevos revueltos** scrambled eggs; **me costó un ~** (*fam!*) it was hard work; **tener huevos** (*fam!*) to have guts

huevón, -ona [we'βon, ona] *nm/f* (*Am fam!*)

stupid bastard (!), stupid idiot

huida [u'iða] *nf* escape, flight; **~ de capitales** (*Com*) flight of capital

huidizo, -a [ui'ðiθo, a] *adj* (*tímido*) shy; (*pasajero*) fleeting

huir [u'ir] *vt* (*escapar*) to flee, escape; (*evadir*) to avoid ∎ *vi* to flee, run away

hule ['ule] *nm* (*encerado*) oilskin; (*esp Am*) rubber

hulla ['uʎa] *nf* bituminous coal

humanice *etc* [uma'niθe] *vb ver* **humanizar**

humanidad [umani'ðað] *nf* (*género humano*) man(kind); (*cualidad*) humanity; (*fam: gordura*) corpulence

humanitario, -a [umani'tarjo, a] *adj* humanitarian; (*benévolo*) humane

humanizar [umani'θar] *vt* to humanize; **humanizarse** *vr* to become more human

humano, -a [u'mano, a] *adj* (*gen*) human; (*humanitario*) humane ∎ *nm* human; **ser ~** human being

humareda [uma'reða] *nf* cloud of smoke

humeante [ume'ante] *adj* smoking, smoky

humedad [ume'ðað] *nf* (*del clima*) humidity; (*de pared etc*) dampness; **a prueba de ~** damp-proof

humedecer [umeðe'θer] *vt* to moisten, wet; **humedecerse** *vr* to get wet

humedezca *etc* [ume'ðeθka] *vb ver* **humedecer**

húmedo, -a ['umeðo, a] *adj* (*mojado*) damp, wet; (*tiempo etc*) humid

humildad [umil'dað] *nf* humility, humbleness

humilde [u'milde] *adj* humble, modest; (*clase etc*) low, modest

humillación [umiʎa'θjon] *nf* humiliation

humillante [umi'ʎante] *adj* humiliating

humillar [umi'ʎar] *vt* to humiliate; **humillarse** *vr* to humble o.s., grovel

humo ['umo] *nm* (*de fuego*) smoke; (*gas nocivo*) fumes *pl*; (*vapor*) steam, vapour; **humos** *nmpl* (*fig*) conceit *sg*; **irse todo en ~** (*fig*) to vanish without trace; **bajar los humos a algn** to take sb down a peg or two

humor [u'mor] *nm* (*disposición*) mood, temper; (*lo que divierte*) humour; **de buen/mal ~** in a good/bad mood

humorismo [umo'rismo] *nm* humour

humorista [umo'rista] *nm/f* comic

humorístico, -a [umo'ristiko, a] *adj* funny, humorous

hundimiento [undi'mjento] *nm* (*gen*) sinking; (*colapso*) collapse

hundir [un'dir] *vt* to sink; (*edificio, plan*) to ruin, destroy; **hundirse** *vr* to sink, collapse; (*fig: arruinarse*) to be ruined; (*desaparecer*) to

h

disappear; **se hundió la economía** the economy collapsed; **se hundieron los precios** prices slumped

húngaro, -a ['ungaro, a] *adj, nm/f* Hungarian ■ *nm* (*Ling*) Hungarian, Magyar

Hungría [un'gria] *nf* Hungary

huracán [ura'kan] *nm* hurricane

huraño, -a [u'raɲo, a] *adj* shy; (*antisocial*) unsociable

hurgar [ur'ɣar] *vt* to poke, jab; (*remover*) to stir (up); **hurgarse** *vr*: **hurgarse (las narices)** to pick one's nose

hurgonear [urɣone'ar] *vt* to poke

hurgue *etc* ['urɣe] *vb ver* **hurgar**

hurón [u'ron] *nm* (*Zool*) ferret

hurra ['urra] *excl* hurray!, hurrah!

hurtadillas [urta'ðiʎas]: **a ~** *adv* stealthily, on the sly

hurtar [ur'tar] *vt* to steal; **hurtarse** *vr* to hide, keep out of the way

hurto ['urto] *nm* theft, stealing; (*lo robado*) (piece of) stolen property, loot

husmear [usme'ar] *vt* (*oler*) to sniff out, scent; (*fam*) to pry into ■ *vi* to smell bad

huso ['uso] *nm* (*Tec*) spindle; (*de torno*) drum

huy ['ui] *excl* (*dolor*) ow!, ouch!; (*sorpresa*) well!; (*alivio*) phew!; **¡~, perdona!** oops, sorry!

huyendo *etc* [u'jendo] *vb ver* **huir**

I i

I, i [i] *nf (letra)* I, i; **I de Inés** I for Isaac *(Brit)* o Item *(US)*
IA *abr* = **inteligencia artificial**
iba *etc* ['iβa] *vb ver* **ir**
Iberia [i'βerja] *nf* Iberia
ibérico, -a [i'βeriko, a] *adj* Iberian; **la Península ibérica** the Iberian Peninsula
ibero, -a [i'βero, a], **íbero, -a** ['iβero, a] *adj, nm/f* Iberian
iberoamericano, -a [iβeroameri'kano, a] *adj, nm/f* Latin American
íbice ['iβiθe] *nm* ibex
ibicenco, -a [iβi'θenko, a] *adj* o from Ibiza ■ *nm/f* native o inhabitant of Ibiza
Ibiza [i'βiθa] *nf* Ibiza
ice *etc* ['iθe] *vb ver* **izar**
iceberg [iθe'ber] *nm* iceberg
ICONA [i'kona] *nm abr (Esp)* = **Instituto Nacional para la Conservación de la Naturaleza**
icono [i'kono] *nm (tb Inform)* icon
iconoclasta [ikono'klasta] *adj* iconoclastic ■ *nm/f* iconoclast
ictericia [ikte'riθja] *nf* jaundice
íd. *abr* = **ídem**
I+D *nf abr (= Investigación y Desarrollo)* R&D
ida ['iða] *nf* going, departure; **~ y vuelta** round trip, return; **idas y venidas** comings and goings
IDE ['iðe] *nf abr (= Iniciativa de Defensa Estratégica)* SDI
idea [i'ðea] *nf* idea; *(impresión)* opinion; *(propósito)* intention; **~ genial** brilliant idea; **a mala ~** out of spite; **no tengo la menor ~** I haven't a clue
ideal [iðe'al] *adj, nm* ideal
idealice *etc* [iðea'liθe] *vb ver* **idealizar**
idealista [iðea'lista] *adj* idealistic ■ *nm/f* idealist
idealizar [iðeali'θar] *vt* to idealize
idear [iðe'ar] *vt* to think up; *(aparato)* to invent; *(viaje)* to plan
ídem ['iðem] *pron* ditto

idéntico, -a [i'ðentiko, a] *adj* identical
identidad [iðenti'ðað] *nf* identity; **~ corporativa** corporate identity o image
identificación [iðentifika'θjon] *nf* identification
identificador de llamadas [iðentifika'ðor-] *nm* caller ID
identificar [iðentifi'kar] *vt* to identify; **identificarse** *vr*: **identificarse con** to identify with
identifique *etc* [iðenti'fike] *vb ver* **identificar**
ideología [iðeolo'xia] *nf* ideology
ideológico, -a [iðeo'loxiko, a] *adj* ideological
idílico, -a [i'ðiliko, a] *adj* idyllic
idilio [i'ðiljo] *nm* love affair
idioma [i'ðjoma] *nm* language
idiomático, -a [iðjo'matiko, a] *adj* idiomatic
idiota [i'ðjota] *adj* idiotic ■ *nm/f* idiot
idiotez [iðjo'teθ] *nf* idiocy
idolatrar [iðola'trar] *vt (fig)* to idolize
ídolo ['iðolo] *nm (tb fig)* idol
idoneidad [iðonei'ðað] *nf* suitability; *(capacidad)* aptitude
idóneo, -a [i'ðoneo, a] *adj* suitable
I.E.S. *nm abr* = **Instituto de Enseñanza Secundaria**
iglesia [i'ɣlesja] *nf* church; **~ parroquial** parish church; **¡con la ~ hemos topado!** now we're really up against it!
iglú [i'ɣlu] *nm* igloo; *(contenedor)* bottle bank
IGME *nm abr* = **Instituto Geográfico y Minero**
ignición [iɣni'θjon] *nf* ignition
ignominia [iɣno'minja] *nf* ignominy
ignominioso, -a [iɣnomi'njoso, a] *adj* ignominious
ignorado, -a [iɣno'raðo, a] *adj* unknown; *(dato)* obscure
ignorancia [iɣno'ranθja] *nf* ignorance; **por ~** through ignorance
ignorante [iɣno'rante] *adj* ignorant, uninformed ■ *nm/f* ignoramus
ignorar [iɣno'rar] *vt* not to know, be ignorant of; *(no hacer caso a)* to ignore; **ignoramos su**

paradero we don't know his whereabouts
ignoto, -a [iɣ'noto, a] *adj* unknown
igual [i'ɣwal] *adj* equal; (*similar*) like, similar; (*mismo*) (the) same; (*constante*) constant; (*temperatura*) even ■ *nm/f* equal; **al ~ que** *prep, conj* like, just like; **~ que** the same as; **sin ~** peerless; **me da** *o* **es ~** I don't care, it makes no difference; **no tener ~** to be unrivalled; **son iguales** they're the same
iguala [i'ɣwala] *nf* equalization; (*Com*) agreement
igualada [iɣwa'laða] *nf* equalizer
igualar [iɣwa'lar] *vt* (*gen*) to equalize, make equal; (*terreno*) to make even; (*Com*) to agree upon; **igualarse** *vr* (*platos de balanza*) to balance out; **igualarse (a)** (*equivaler*) to be equal (to)
igualdad [iɣwal'dað] *nf* equality; (*similaridad*) sameness; (*uniformidad*) uniformity; **en ~ de condiciones** on an equal basis
igualmente [iɣwal'mente] *adv* equally; (*también*) also, likewise ■ *excl* the same to you!
iguana [i'ɣwana] *nf* iguana
ikurriña [iku'rriɲa] *nf* Basque flag
ilegal [ile'ɣal] *adj* illegal
ilegitimidad [ilexitimi'ðað] *nf* illegitimacy
ilegítimo, -a [ile'xitimo, a] *adj* illegitimate
ileso, -a [i'leso, a] *adj* unhurt, unharmed
ilícito, -a [i'liθito, a] *adj* illicit
ilimitado, -a [ilimi'taðo, a] *adj* unlimited
Ilma., Ilmo. *abr* (= *Ilustrísima, Ilustrísimo*) *courtesy title*
ilógico, -a [i'loxiko, a] *adj* illogical
iluminación [ilumina'θjon] *nf* illumination; (*alumbrado*) lighting; (*fig*) enlightenment
iluminar [ilumi'nar] *vt* to illuminate, light (up); (*fig*) to enlighten
ilusión [ilu'sjon] *nf* illusion; (*quimera*) delusion; (*esperanza*) hope; (*emoción*) excitement, thrill; **hacerse ilusiones** to build up one's hopes; **no te hagas ilusiones** don't build up your hopes *o* get too excited
ilusionado, -a [ilusjo'naðo, a] *adj* excited
ilusionar [ilusjo'nar] *vt*: **~ a algn** (*falsamente*) to build up sb's hopes; **ilusionarse** *vr* (*falsamente*) to build up one's hopes; (*entusiasmarse*) to get excited; **me ilusiona mucho el viaje** I'm really excited about the trip
ilusionista [ilusjo'nista] *nm/f* conjurer
iluso, -a [i'luso, a] *adj* gullible, easily deceived ■ *nm/f* dreamer, visionary
ilusorio, -a [ilu'sorjo, a] *adj* (*de ilusión*) illusory, deceptive; (*esperanza*) vain
ilustración [ilustra'θjon] *nf* illustration; (*saber*) learning, erudition; **la I~** the Enlightenment

ilustrado, -a [ilus'traðo, a] *adj* illustrated; learned
ilustrar [ilus'trar] *vt* to illustrate; (*instruir*) to instruct; (*explicar*) to explain, make clear; **ilustrarse** *vr* to acquire knowledge
ilustre [i'lustre] *adj* famous, illustrious
imagen [i'maxen] *nf* (*gen*) image; (*dibujo, TV*) picture; (*Rel*) statue; **ser la viva ~ de** to be the spitting *o* living image of; **a su ~** in one's own image
imaginación [imaxina'θjon] *nf* imagination; (*fig*) fancy; **ni por ~** on no account; **no se me pasó por la ~ que ...** it never even occurred to me that ...
imaginar [imaxi'nar] *vt* (*gen*) to imagine; (*idear*) to think up; (*suponer*) to suppose; **imaginarse** *vr* to imagine; **¡imagínate!** just imagine!, just fancy!; **imagínese que ...** suppose that ...; **me imagino que sí** I should think so
imaginario, -a [imaxi'narjo, a] *adj* imaginary
imaginativo, -a [imaxina'tiβo, a] *adj* imaginative ■ *nf* imagination
imán [i'man] *nm* magnet
imanar [ima'nar], **imantar** [ima'ntar] *vt* to magnetize
imbécil [im'beθil] *nm/f* imbecile, idiot
imbecilidad [imbeθili'ðað] *nf* imbecility, stupidity
imberbe [im'berβe] *adj* beardless
imborrable [imbo'rraβle] *adj* indelible; (*inolvidable*) unforgettable
imbuir [imbu'ir] *vi* to imbue
imbuyendo *etc* [imbu'jendo] *vb ver* **imbuir**
imitación [imita'θjon] *nf* imitation; (*parodia*) mimicry; **a ~ de** in imitation of; **desconfíe de las imitaciones** (*Com*) beware of copies *o* imitations
imitador, a [imita'ðor, a] *adj* imitative ■ *nm/f* imitator; (*Teat*) mimic
imitar [imi'tar] *vt* to imitate; (*parodiar, remedar*) to mimic, ape; (*copiar*) to follow
impaciencia [impa'θjenθja] *nf* impatience
impacientar [impaθjen'tar] *vt* to make impatient; (*enfadar*) to irritate; **impacientarse** *vr* to get impatient; (*inquietarse*) to fret
impaciente [impa'θjente] *adj* impatient; (*nervioso*) anxious
impacto [im'pakto] *nm* impact; (*esp Am: fig*) shock
impagado, -a [impa'ɣaðo, a] *adj* unpaid, still to be paid
impar [im'par] *adj* odd ■ *nm* odd number
imparable [impa'raβle] *adj* unstoppable
imparcial [impar'θjal] *adj* impartial, fair

imparcialidad [imparθjali'ðað] *nf*
impartiality, fairness

impartir [impar'tir] *vt* to impart, give

impasible [impa'siβle] *adj* impassive

impávido, -a [im'paβiðo, a] *adj* fearless,
intrepid

IMPE ['impe] *nm abr* (*Esp, Com*) = **Instituto de
la Mediana y Pequeña Empresa**

impecable [impe'kaβle] *adj* impeccable

impedido, -a [impe'ðiðo, a] *adj*: **estar** ~ to
be an invalid ■ *nm/f*: **ser un** ~ **físico** to be
an invalid

impedimento [impeði'mento] *nm*
impediment, obstacle

impedir [impe'ðir] *vt* (*obstruir*) to impede,
obstruct; (*estorbar*) to prevent; ~ **el tráfico** to
block the traffic

impeler [impe'ler] *vt* to drive, propel; (*fig*) to
impel

impenetrabilidad [impenetraβili'ðað] *nf*
impenetrability

impenetrable [impene'traβle] *adj*
impenetrable; (*fig*) incomprehensible

impensable [impen'saβle] *adj* unthinkable

impepinable [impepi'naβle] *adj* (*fam*)
certain, inevitable

imperante [impe'rante] *adj* prevailing

imperar [impe'rar] *vi* (*reinar*) to rule, reign;
(*fig*) to prevail, reign; (*precio*) to be current

imperativo, -a [impera'tiβo, a] *adj* (*persona*)
imperious; (*urgente, Ling*) imperative

imperceptible [imperθep'tiβle] *adj*
imperceptible

imperdible [imper'ðiβle] *nm* safety pin

imperdonable [imperðo'naβle] *adj*
unforgivable, inexcusable

imperecedero, -a [impereθe'ðero, a] *adj*
undying

imperfección [imperfek'θjon] *nf*
imperfection; (*falla*) flaw, fault

imperfecto, -a [imper'fekto, a] *adj* faulty,
imperfect ■ *nm* (*Ling*) imperfect tense

imperial [impe'rjal] *adj* imperial

imperialismo [imperja'lismo] *nm*
imperialism

imperialista [imperja'lista] *adj*
imperialist(ic) ■ *nm/f* imperialist

impericia [impe'riθja] *nf* (*torpeza*)
unskilfulness; (*inexperiencia*) inexperience

imperio [im'perjo] *nm* empire; (*autoridad*)
rule, authority; (*fig*) pride, haughtiness;
vale un ~ (*fig*) it's worth a fortune

imperioso, -a [impe'rjoso, a] *adj* imperious;
(*urgente*) urgent; (*imperativo*) imperative

impermeable [imperme'aβle] *adj* (*a prueba de
agua*) waterproof ■ *nm* raincoat, mac (*Brit*)

impersonal [imperso'nal] *adj* impersonal

impertérrito, -a [imper'territo, a] *adj*
undaunted

impertinencia [imperti'nenθja] *nf*
impertinence

impertinente [imperti'nente] *adj*
impertinent

imperturbable [impertur'βaβle] *adj*
imperturbable; (*sereno*) unruffled; (*impasible*)
impassive

ímpetu ['impetu] *nm* (*impulso*) impetus,
impulse; (*impetuosidad*) impetuosity;
(*violencia*) violence

impetuosidad [impetwosi'ðað] *nf*
impetuousness; (*violencia*) violence

impetuoso, -a [impe'twoso, a] *adj*
impetuous; (*río*) rushing; (*acto*) hasty

impida *etc* [im'piða] *vb ver* **impedir**

impío, -a [im'pio, a] *adj* impious, ungodly;
(*cruel*) cruel, pitiless

implacable [impla'kaβle] *adj* implacable,
relentless

implantación [implanta'θjon] *nf*
introduction; (*Bio*) implantation

implantar [implan'tar] *vt* (*costumbre*) to
introduce; (*Bio*) to implant; **implantarse** *vr*
to be introduced

implicar [impli'kar] *vt* to involve; (*entrañar*) to
imply; **esto no implica que ...** this does not
mean that ...

implícito, -a [im'pliθito, a] *adj* (*tácito*)
implicit; (*sobreentendido*) implied

implique *etc* [im'plike] *vb ver* **implicar**

implorar [implo'rar] *vt* to beg, implore

impondré *etc* [impon'dre] *vb ver* **imponer**

imponente [impo'nente] *adj* (*impresionante*)
impressive, imposing; (*solemne*) grand
■ *nm/f* (*Com*) depositor

imponer [impo'ner] *vt* (*gen*) to impose; (*tarea*)
to set; (*exigir*) to exact; (*miedo*) to inspire;
(*Com*) to deposit; **imponerse** *vr* to assert o.s.;
(*prevalecer*) to prevail; (*costumbre*) to grow up;
imponerse un deber to assume a duty

imponga *etc* [im'ponga] *vb ver* **imponer**

imponible [impo'niβle] *adj* (*Com*) taxable,
subject to tax; (*importación*) dutiable, subject
to duty; **no** ~ tax-free, tax-exempt (*US*)

impopular [impopu'lar] *adj* unpopular

importación [importa'θjon] *nf* (*acto*)
importing; (*mercancías*) imports *pl*

importancia [impor'tanθja] *nf* importance;
(*valor*) value, significance; (*extensión*)
size, magnitude; **no dar** ~ **a** to consider
unimportant; (*fig*) to make light of; **no
tiene** ~ it's nothing

importante [impor'tante] *adj* important;
valuable, significant

importar [impor'tar] *vt* (*del extranjero*) to

import; (*costar*) to amount to; (*implicar*) to involve ■ *vi* to be important, matter; **me importa un bledo** I don't give a damn; **¿le importa que fume?** do you mind if I smoke?; **¿te importa prestármelo?** would you mind lending it to me?; **¿qué importa?** what difference does it make?; **no importa** it doesn't matter; **no le importa** he doesn't care, it doesn't bother him; **"no importa precio"** "cost no object"

importe [im'porte] *nm* (*cantidad*) amount; (*valor*) value

importunar [importu'nar] *vt* to bother, pester

importuno, -a [impor'tuno, a] *adj* (*inoportuno, molesto*) inopportune; (*indiscreto*) troublesome

imposibilidad [imposiβili'ðað] *nf* impossibility; **mi ~ para hacerlo** my inability to do it

imposibilitado, -a [imposiβili'taðo, a] *adj*: **verse ~ para hacer algo** to be unable to do sth

imposibilitar [imposiβili'tar] *vt* to make impossible, prevent

imposible [impo'siβle] *adj* impossible; (*insoportable*) unbearable, intolerable; **es ~** it's out of the question; **es ~ de predecir** it's impossible to forecast *o* predict

imposición [imposi'θjon] *nf* imposition; (*Com*) tax; (*inversión*) deposit; **efectuar una ~** to make a deposit

impostor, a [impos'tor, a] *nm/f* impostor

impostura [impos'tura] *nf* fraud, imposture

impotencia [impo'tenθja] *nf* impotence

impotente [impo'tente] *adj* impotent

impracticable [imprakti'kaβle] *adj* (*irrealizable*) impracticable; (*intransitable*) impassable

imprecar [impre'kar] *vi* to curse

imprecisión [impreθi'sjon] *nf* lack of precision, vagueness

impreciso, -a [impre'θiso, a] *adj* imprecise, vague

impredecible [impreðe'θiβle], **impredictible** [impreðik'tiβle] *adj* unpredictable

impregnar [impreɣ'nar] *vt* to impregnate; (*fig*) to pervade; **impregnarse** *vr* to become impregnated

imprenta [im'prenta] *nf* (*acto*) printing; (*aparato*) press; (*casa*) printer's; (*letra*) print

impreque *etc* [im'preke] *vb ver* **imprecar**

imprescindible [impresθin'diβle] *adj* essential, vital

impresión [impre'sjon] *nf* impression; (*Imprenta*) printing; (*edición*) edition; (*Foto*) print; (*marca*) imprint; **~ digital** fingerprint

impresionable [impresjo'naβle] *adj* (*sensible*) impressionable

impresionado, -a [impresjo'naðo, a] *adj* impressed; (*Foto*) exposed

impresionante [impresjo'nante] *adj* impressive; (*tremendo*) tremendous; (*maravilloso*) great, marvellous

impresionar [impresjo'nar] *vt* (*conmover*) to move; (*afectar*) to impress, strike; (*película fotográfica*) to expose; **impresionarse** *vr* to be impressed; (*conmoverse*) to be moved

impresionista [impresjo'nista] *adj* impressionist(ic); (*Arte*) impressionist ■ *nm/f* impressionist

impreso, -a [im'preso, a] *pp de* **imprimir** ■ *adj* printed ■ *nm* printed paper/book *etc*; **impresos** *nmpl* printed matter *sg*; **~ de solicitud** application form

impresora [impre'sora] *nf* (*Inform*) printer; **~ de chorro de tinta** ink-jet printer; **~ (por) láser** laser printer; **~ de línea** line printer; **~ de matriz (de agujas)** dot-matrix printer; **~ de rueda** *o* **de margarita** daisy-wheel printer

imprevisible [impreβi'siβle] *adj* unforeseeable; (*individuo*) unpredictable

imprevisión [impreβi'sjon] *nf* short-sightedness; (*irreflexión*) thoughtlessness

imprevisto, -a [impre'βisto, a] *adj* unforeseen; (*inesperado*) unexpected ■ *nm*: **imprevistos** (*dinero*) incidentals, unforeseen expenses

imprimir [impri'mir] *vt* to stamp; (*textos*) to print; (*Inform*) to output, print out

improbabilidad [improβaβili'ðað] *nf* improbability, unlikelihood

improbable [impro'βaβle] *adj* improbable; (*inverosímil*) unlikely

improcedente [improθe'ðente] *adj* inappropriate; (*Jur*) inadmissible

improductivo, -a [improðuk'tiβo, a] *adj* unproductive

impronunciable [impronun'θjaβle] *adj* unpronounceable

improperio [impro'perjo] *nm* insult; **improperios** *nmpl* abuse *sg*

impropiedad [impropje'ðað] *nf* impropriety (of language)

impropio, -a [im'propjo, a] *adj* improper; (*inadecuado*) inappropriate

improvisación [improβisa'θjon] *nf* improvization

improvisado, -a [improβi'saðo, a] *adj* improvised, impromptu

improvisar [improβi'sar] *vt* to improvise; (*comida*) to rustle up ■ *vi* to improvise; (*Mus*) to extemporize; (*Teat etc*) to ad-lib

improviso [impro'βiso] *adv*: **de ~** unexpectedly, suddenly; (*Mus etc*) impromptu

imprudencia [impru'ðenθja] *nf* imprudence; (*indiscreción*) indiscretion; (*descuido*) carelessness

imprudente [impru'ðente] *adj* imprudent; indiscreet

Impte. *abr* (= *Importe*) amt.

impúdico, -a [im'puðiko, a] *adj* shameless; (*lujurioso*) lecherous

impudor [impu'ðor] *nm* shamelessness; (*lujuria*) lechery

impuesto, -a [im'pwesto, a] *pp de* **imponer** ■ *adj* imposed ■ *nm* tax; **anterior al ~** pre-tax; **sujeto a ~** taxable; **~ de lujo** luxury tax; **~ de plusvalía** capital gains tax; **~ sobre la propiedad** property tax; **~ sobre la renta** income tax; **~ sobre la renta de las personas físicas (IRPF)** personal income tax; **~ sobre la riqueza** wealth tax; **~ de transferencia de capital** capital transfer tax; **~ de venta** sales tax; **~ sobre el valor añadido (IVA)** value added tax (VAT)

impugnar [impuɣ'nar] *vt* to oppose, contest; (*refutar*) to refute, impugn

impulsar [impul'sar] *vt* to promote

impulsivo, -a [impul'siβo, a] *adj* impulsive

impulso [im'pulso] *nm* impulse; (*fuerza, empuje*) thrust, drive; (*fig: sentimiento*) urge, impulse; **a impulsos del miedo** driven on by fear

impune [im'pune] *adj* unpunished

impunemente [impune'mente] *adv* with impunity

impureza [impu're θa] *nf* impurity; (*fig*) lewdness

impuro, -a [im'puro, a] *adj* impure; lewd

impuse *etc* [im'puse] *vb ver* **imponer**

imputación [imputa'θjon] *nf* imputation

imputar [impu'tar] *vt*: **~ a** to attribute to, to impute to

inabordable [inaβor'ðaβle] *adj* unapproachable

inacabable [inaka'βaβle] *adj* (*infinito*) endless; (*interminable*) interminable

inaccesible [inakθe'siβle] *adj* inaccessible; (*fig: precio*) beyond one's reach, prohibitive; (*individuo*) aloof

inacción [inak'θjon] *nf* inactivity

inaceptable [inaθep'taβle] *adj* unacceptable

inactividad [inaktiβi'ðað] *nf* inactivity; (*Com*) dullness

inactivo, -a [inak'tiβo, a] *adj* inactive; (*Com*) dull; (*población*) non-working

inadaptación [inaðapta'θjon] *nf* maladjustment

inadaptado, -a [inaðap'taðo, a] *adj* maladjusted ■ *nm/f* misfit

inadecuado, -a [inaðe'kwaðo, a] *adj* (*insuficiente*) inadequate; (*inapto*) unsuitable

inadmisible [inaðmi'siβle] *adj* inadmissible

inadvertido, -a [inaðβer'tiðo, a] *adj* (*no visto*) unnoticed

inagotable [inaɣo'taβle] *adj* inexhaustible

inaguantable [inaɣwan'taβle] *adj* unbearable

inalámbrico, -a [ina'lambriko, a] *adj* cordless, wireless

inalcanzable [inalkan'θaβle] *adj* unattainable

inalterable [inalte'raβle] *adj* immutable, unchangeable

inamovible [inamo'βiβle] *adj* fixed, immovable; (*Tec*) undetachable

inanición [inani'θjon] *nf* starvation

inanimado, -a [inani'maðo, a] *adj* inanimate

inapelable [inape'laβle] *adj* (*Jur*) unappealable; (*fig*) irremediable

inapetencia [inape'tenθja] *nf* lack of appetite

inaplicable [inapli'kaβle] *adj* not applicable

inapreciable [inapre'θjaβle] *adj* invaluable

inarrugable [inarru'ɣaβle] *adj* crease-resistant

inasequible [inase'kiβle] *adj* unattainable

inaudito, -a [inau'ðito, a] *adj* unheard-of

inauguración [inauɣura'θjon] *nf* inauguration; (*de exposición*) opening

inaugurar [inauɣu'rar] *vt* to inaugurate; to open

I.N.B.A. *abr* (*Am*) = **Instituto Nacional de Bellas Artes**

inca ['inka] *nm/f* Inca

INCAE [in'kae] *nm abr* = **Instituto Centroamericano de Administración de Empresas**

incaico, -a [in'kaiko, a] *adj* Inca

incalculable [inkalku'laβle] *adj* incalculable

incandescente [inkandes'θente] *adj* incandescent

incansable [inkan'saβle] *adj* tireless, untiring

incapacidad [inkapaθi'ðað] *nf* incapacity; (*incompetencia*) incompetence; **~ física/mental** physical/mental disability

incapacitar [inkapaθi'tar] *vt* (*inhabilitar*) to incapacitate, handicap; (*descalificar*) to disqualify

incapaz [inka'paθ] *adj* incapable; **~ de hacer algo** unable to do sth

incautación [inkauta'θjon] *nf* seizure, confiscation

incautarse [inkau'tarse] vr: ~ **de** to seize, confiscate

incauto, -a [in'kauto, a] adj (imprudente) incautious, unwary

incendiar [inθen'djar] vt to set fire to; (fig) to inflame; **incendiarse** vr to catch fire

incendiario, -a [inθen'djarjo, a] adj incendiary ■ nm/f fire-raiser, arsonist

incendio [in'θendjo] nm fire; ~ **intencionado** arson

incentivo [inθen'tiβo] nm incentive

incertidumbre [inθerti'ðumbre] nf (inseguridad) uncertainty; (duda) doubt

incesante [inθe'sante] adj incessant

incesto [in'θesto] nm incest

incidencia [inθi'ðenθja] nf (Mat) incidence; (fig) effect

incidente [inθi'ðente] nm incident

incidir [inθi'ðir] vi: ~ **en** (influir) to influence; (afectar) to affect; ~ **en un error** to be mistaken

incienso [in'θjenso] nm incense

incierto, -a [in'θjerto, a] adj uncertain

incineración [inθinera'θjon] nf incineration; (de cadáveres) cremation

incinerar [inθine'rar] vt to burn; to cremate

incipiente [inθi'pjente] adj incipient

incisión [inθi'sjon] nf incision

incisivo, -a [inθi'siβo, a] adj sharp, cutting; (fig) incisive

inciso [in'θiso] nm (Ling) clause, sentence; (coma) comma; (Jur) subsection

incitante [inθi'tante] adj (estimulante) exciting; (provocativo) provocative

incitar [inθi'tar] vt to incite, rouse

incivil [inθi'βil] adj rude, uncivil

inclemencia [inkle'menθja] nf (severidad) harshness, severity; (del tiempo) inclemency

inclemente [inkle'mente] adj harsh, severe; inclement

inclinación [inklina'θjon] nf (gen) inclination; (de tierras) slope, incline; (de cabeza) nod, bow; (fig) leaning, bent

inclinado, -a [inkli'naðo, a] adj (objeto) leaning; (superficie) sloping

inclinar [inkli'nar] vt to incline; (cabeza) to nod, bow; **inclinarse** vr to lean, slope; (en reverencia) to bow; (encorvarse) to stoop; **inclinarse a** (parecerse) to take after, resemble; **inclinarse ante** to bow down to; **me inclino a pensar que ...** I'm inclined to think that ...

incluir [inklu'ir] vt to include; (incorporar) to incorporate; (meter) to enclose; **todo incluido** (Com) inclusive, all-in

inclusive [inklu'siβe] adv inclusive ■ prep including

incluso, -a [in'kluso, a] adj included ■ adv inclusively; (hasta) even

incluyendo etc [inklu'jendo] vb ver **incluir**

incobrable [inko'βraβle] adj irrecoverable; (deuda) bad

incógnita [in'koɣnita] nf (fig) mystery

incógnito [in'koɣnito]: **de ~** adv incognito

incoherencia [inkoe'renθja] nf incoherence; (falta de conexión) disconnectedness

incoherente [inkoe'rente] adj incoherent

incoloro, -a [inko'loro, a] adj colourless

incólume [in'kolume] adj safe; (indemne) unhurt, unharmed

incombustible [inkombus'tiβle] adj (gen) fire-resistant; (telas) fireproof

incomodar [inkomo'ðar] vt to inconvenience; (molestar) to bother, trouble; (fastidiar) to annoy; **incomodarse** vr to put o.s. out; (fastidiarse) to get annoyed; **no se incomode** don't bother

incomodidad [inkomoði'ðað] nf inconvenience; (fastidio, enojo) annoyance; (de vivienda) discomfort

incómodo, -a [in'komoðo, a] adj (inconfortable) uncomfortable; (molesto) annoying; (inconveniente) inconvenient; **sentirse ~** to feel ill at ease

incomparable [inkompa'raβle] adj incomparable

incomparecencia [inkompare'θenθja] nf (Jur etc) failure to appear

incompatible [inkompa'tiβle] adj incompatible

incompetencia [inkompe'tenθja] nf incompetence

incompetente [inkompe'tente] adj incompetent

incompleto, -a [inkom'pleto, a] adj incomplete, unfinished

incomprendido, -a [inkompren'diðo, a] adj misunderstood

incomprensible [inkompren'siβle] adj incomprehensible

incomunicado, -a [inkomuni'kaðo, a] adj (aislado) cut off, isolated; (confinado) in solitary confinement

incomunicar [inkomuni'kar] vt (gen) to cut off; (preso) to put into solitary confinement; **incomunicarse** vr (fam) to go into one's shell

incomunique etc [inkomu'nike] vb ver **incomunicar**

inconcebible [inkonθe'βiβle] adj inconceivable

inconcluso, -a [inkon'kluso, a] adj (inacabado) unfinished

incondicional [inkondiθjo'nal] adj unconditional; (apoyo) wholehearted; (partidario) staunch

inconexo, -a [inko'nekso, a] *adj* unconnected; (*desunido*) disconnected; (*incoherente*) incoherent

inconfeso, -a [inkon'feso, a] *adj* unconfessed; **un homosexual ~** a closet homosexual

inconformista [inkonfor'mista] *adj, nm/f* nonconformist

inconfundible [inkonfun'diβle] *adj* unmistakable

incongruente [inkon'grwente] *adj* incongruous

inconmensurable [inkonmensu'raβle] *adj* immeasurable, vast

inconsciencia [inkons'θjenθja] *nf* unconsciousness; (*fig*) thoughtlessness

inconsciente [inkons'θjente] *adj* unconscious; thoughtless; (*ignorante*) unaware; (*involuntario*) unwitting

inconsecuencia [inkonse'kwenθja] *nf* inconsistency

inconsecuente [inkonse'kwente] *adj* inconsistent

inconsiderado, -a [inkonsiðe'raðo, a] *adj* inconsiderate

inconsistente [inkonsis'tente] *adj* inconsistent; (*Culin*) lumpy; (*endeble*) weak; (*tela*) flimsy

inconstancia [inkons'tanθja] *nf* inconstancy; (*de tiempo*) changeability; (*capricho*) fickleness

inconstante [inkons'tante] *adj* inconstant; changeable; fickle

incontable [inkon'taβle] *adj* countless, innumerable

incontestable [inkontes'taβle] *adj* unanswerable; (*innegable*) undeniable

incontinencia [inkonti'nenθja] *nf* incontinence

incontrolado, -a [inkontro'laðo, a] *adj* uncontrolled

incontrovertible [inkontroβer'tiβle] *adj* undeniable, incontrovertible

inconveniencia [inkombe'njenθja] *nf* unsuitability, inappropriateness; (*falta de cortesía*) impoliteness

inconveniente [inkombe'njente] *adj* unsuitable; impolite ■ *nm* obstacle; (*desventaja*) disadvantage; **el ~ es que ...** the trouble is that ...; **no hay ~ en** o **para hacer eso** there is no objection to doing that; **no tengo ~** I don't mind

incordiar [inkor'ðjar] *vt* (*fam*) to hassle

incorporación [inkorpora'θjon] *nf* incorporation; (*fig*) inclusion

incorporado, -a [inkorpo'raðo, a] *adj* (*Tec*) built-in

incorporar [inkorpo'rar] *vt* to incorporate; (*abarcar*) to embody; (*Culin*) to mix; **incorporarse** *vr* to sit up; **incorporarse a** to join

incorrección [inkorrek'θjon] *nf* incorrectness, inaccuracy; (*descortesía*) bad-mannered behaviour

incorrecto, -a [inko'rrekto, a] *adj* incorrect, wrong; (*comportamiento*) bad-mannered

incorregible [inkorre'xiβle] *adj* incorrigible

incorruptible [inkorrup'tiβle] *adj* incorruptible

incorrupto, -a [inko'rrupto, a] *adj* uncorrupted; (*fig*) pure

incredulidad [inkreðuli'ðað] *nf* incredulity; (*escepticismo*) scepticism

incrédulo, -a [in'kreðulo, a] *adj* incredulous, unbelieving; sceptical

increíble [inkre'iβle] *adj* incredible

incrementar [inkremen'tar] *vt* (*aumentar*) to increase; (*alzar*) to raise; **incrementarse** *vr* to increase

incremento [inkre'mento] *nm* increment; (*aumento*) rise, increase; **~ de precio** rise in price

increpar [inkre'par] *vt* to reprimand

incriminar [inkrimi'nar] *vt* (*Jur*) to incriminate

incruento, -a [in'krwento, a] *adj* bloodless

incrustar [inkrus'tar] *vt* to incrust; (*piedras: en joya*) to inlay; (*fig*) to graft; (*Tec*) to set

incubar [inku'βar] *vt* to incubate; (*fig*) to hatch

incuestionable [inkwestjo'naβle] *adj* unchallengeable

inculcar [inkul'kar] *vt* to inculcate

inculpar [inkul'par] *vt*: **~ de** (*acusar*) to accuse of; (*achacar, atribuir*) to charge with, blame for

inculque *etc* [in'kulke] *vb ver* **inculcar**

inculto, -a [in'kulto, a] *adj* (*persona*) uneducated, uncultured; (*fig: grosero*) uncouth ■ *nm/f* ignoramus

incumbencia [inkum'benθja] *nf* obligation; **no es de mi ~** it is not my field

incumbir [inkum'bir] *vi*: **~ a** to be incumbent upon; **no me incumbe a mí** it is no concern of mine

incumplimiento [inkumpli'mjento] *nm* non-fulfilment; (*Com*) repudiation; **~ de contrato** breach of contract; **por ~** by default

incurable [inku'raβle] *adj* (*enfermedad*) incurable; (*paciente*) incurably ill

incurrir [inku'rrir] *vi*: **~ en** to incur; (*crimen*) to commit; **~ en un error** to make a mistake

indagación [indaɣa'θjon] *nf* investigation; (*búsqueda*) search; (*Jur*) inquest

indagar | indispensable

indagar [inda'ɣar] vt to investigate; to search; (averiguar) to ascertain
indague etc [in'daɣe] vb ver **indagar**
indebido, -a [inde'βiðo, a] adj undue; (dicho) improper
indecencia [inde'θenθja] nf indecency; (dicho) obscenity
indecente [inde'θente] adj indecent, improper; (lascivo) obscene
indecible [inde'θiβle] adj unspeakable; (indescriptible) indescribable
indeciso, -a [inde'θiso, a] adj (por decidir) undecided; (vacilante) hesitant
indefenso, -a [inde'fenso, a] adj defenceless
indefinido, -a [indefi'niðo, a] adj indefinite; (vago) vague, undefined
indeleble [inde'leβle] adj indelible
indemne [in'demne] adj (objeto) undamaged; (persona) unharmed, unhurt
indemnice etc [indem'niθe] vb ver **indemnizar**
indemnización [indemniθa'θjon] nf (acto) indemnification; (suma) indemnity; ~ de cese redundancy payment; ~ de despido severance pay; doble ~ double indemnity
indemnizar [indemni'θar] vt to indemnify; (compensar) to compensate
independencia [indepen'denθja] nf independence
independice etc [indepen'diθe] vb ver **independizar**
independiente [indepen'djente] adj (libre) independent; (autónomo) self-sufficient; (Inform) stand-alone
independizar [independi'θar] vt to make independent; **independizarse** vr to become independent
indescifrable [indesθi'fraβle] adj (Mil: código) indecipherable; (fig: misterio) impenetrable
indeseable [indese'aβle] adj, nm/f undesirable
indeterminado, -a [indetermi'naðo, a] adj (tb Ling) indefinite; (desconocido) indeterminate
India ['indja] nf: la ~ India
indiano, -a [in'djano, a] adj (Spanish-) American ■ nm Spaniard who has made good in America
indicación [indika'θjon] nf indication; (dato) piece of information; (señal) sign; (sugerencia) suggestion, hint; **indicaciones** nfpl (Com) instructions
indicado, -a [indi'kaðo, a] adj (apto) right, appropriate
indicador [indika'ðor] nm indicator; (Tec) gauge, meter; (aguja) hand, pointer; (de carretera) roadsign; ~ de encendido (Inform) power-on indicator

indicar [indi'kar] vt (mostrar) to indicate, show; (suj: termómetro etc) to read, register; (señalar) to point to
indicativo, -a [indika'tiβo, a] adj indicative ■ nm (Radio) call sign; ~ de nacionalidad (Auto) national identification plate
índice ['indiθe] nm index; (catálogo) catalogue; (Anat) index finger, forefinger; ~ del coste de (la) vida cost-of-living index; ~ de crédito credit rating; ~ de materias table of contents; ~ de natalidad birth rate; ~ de precios al por menor (IPM) (Com) retail price index (RPI)
indicio [in'diθjo] nm indication, sign; (en pesquisa etc) clue
indiferencia [indife'renθja] nf indifference; (apatía) apathy
indiferente [indife'rente] adj indifferent; me es ~ it makes no difference to me
indígena [in'dixena] adj indigenous, native ■ nm/f native
indigencia [indi'xenθja] nf poverty, need
indigenista [indixe'nista] (Am) adj pro-Indian ■ nm/f (estudiante) student of Indian cultures; (Pol etc) promoter of Indian cultures
indigestar [indixes'tar] vt to cause indigestion to; **indigestarse** vr to get indigestion
indigestión [indixes'tjon] nf indigestion
indigesto, -a [indi'xesto, a] adj undigested; (indigerible) indigestible; (fig) turgid
indignación [indiɣna'θjon] nf indignation
indignante [indiɣ'nante] adj outrageous, infuriating
indignar [indiɣ'nar] vt to anger, make indignant; **indignarse** vr: **indignarse por** to get indignant about
indigno, -a [in'diɣno, a] adj (despreciable) low, contemptible; (inmerecido) unworthy
indio, -a ['indjo, a] adj, nm/f Indian
indique etc [in'dike] vb ver **indicar**
indirecto, -a [indi'rekto, a] adj indirect ■ nf insinuation, innuendo; (sugerencia) hint
indisciplina [indisθi'plina] nf (gen) lack of discipline; (Mil) insubordination
indiscreción [indiskre'θjon] nf (imprudencia) indiscretion; (irreflexión) tactlessness; (acto) gaffe, faux pas; ..., si no es ~ ..., if I may say so
indiscreto, -a [indis'kreto, a] adj indiscreet
indiscriminado, -a [indiskrimi'naðo, a] adj indiscriminate
indiscutible [indisku'tiβle] adj indisputable, unquestionable
indispensable [indispen'saβle] adj indispensable

indispondré etc [indispon'dre] vb ver **indisponer**

indisponer [indispo'ner] vt to spoil, upset; (salud) to make ill; **indisponerse** vr to fall ill; **indisponerse con algn** to fall out with sb

indisponga etc [indis'ponga] vb ver **indisponer**

indisposición [indisposi'θjon] nf indisposition; (desgana) unwillingness

indispuesto, -a [indis'pwesto, a] pp de **indisponer** ■ adj indisposed; **sentirse ~** to feel unwell o indisposed

indispuse etc [indis'puse] vb ver **indisponer**

indistinto, -a [indis'tinto, a] adj indistinct; (vago) vague

individual [indiβi'ðwal] adj individual; (habitación) single ■ nm (Deporte) singles sg

individuo, -a [indi'βiðwo, a] adj individual ■ nm individual

Indochina [indo'tʃina] nf Indochina

indocumentado, -a [indokumen'taðo, a] adj without identity papers

indoeuropeo, -a [indoeuro'peo, a] adj, nm/f Indo-European

índole ['indole] nf (naturaleza) nature; (clase) sort, kind

indolencia [indo'lenθja] nf indolence, laziness

indoloro, -a [in'doloro, a] adj painless

indomable [indo'maβle] adj (animal) untameable; (espíritu) indomitable

indómito, -a [in'domito, a] adj indomitable

Indonesia [indo'nesja] nf Indonesia

indonesio, -a [indo'nesjo, a] adj, nm/f Indonesian

inducción [induk'θjon] nf (Filosofía, Elec) induction; **por ~** by induction

inducir [indu'θir] vt to induce; (inferir) to infer; (persuadir) to persuade; **~ a algn en el error** to mislead sb

indudable [indu'ðaβle] adj undoubted; (incuestionable) unquestionable; **es ~ que ...** there is no doubt that ...

indulgencia [indul'xenθja] nf indulgence; (Jur etc) leniency; **proceder sin ~ contra** to proceed ruthlessly against

indultar [indul'tar] vt (perdonar) to pardon, reprieve; (librar de pago) to exempt

indulto [in'dulto] nm pardon; exemption

indumentaria [indumen'tarja] nf (ropa) clothing, dress

industria [in'dustrja] nf industry; (habilidad) skill; **~ agropecuaria** farming and fishing; **~ pesada** heavy industry; **~ petrolífera** oil industry

industrial [indus'trjal] adj industrial ■ nm industrialist

industrializar [industrjali'θar] vt to industrialize; **industrializarse** vr to become industrialized

INE ['ine] nm abr (Esp) = **Instituto Nacional de Estadística**

inédito, -a [i'neðito, a] adj (libro) unpublished; (nuevo) unheard-of

inefable [ine'faβle] adj ineffable, indescribable

ineficacia [inefi'kaθja] nf (de medida) ineffectiveness; (de proceso) inefficiency

ineficaz [inefi'kaθ] adj (inútil) ineffective; (ineficiente) inefficient

ineludible [inelu'ðiβle] adj inescapable, unavoidable

INEM [i'nem] nm abr (Esp: = Instituto Nacional de Empleo) ≈ Department of Employment (Brit)

INEN ['inen] nm abr (México) = **Instituto Nacional de Energía Nuclear**

inenarrable [inena'rraβle] adj inexpressible

ineptitud [inepti'tuð] nf ineptitude, incompetence

inepto, -a [i'nepto, a] adj inept, incompetent

inequívoco, -a [ine'kiβoko, a] adj unequivocal; (inconfundible) unmistakable

inercia [i'nerθja] nf inertia; (pasividad) passivity

inerme [i'nerme] adj (sin armas) unarmed; (indefenso) defenceless

inerte [i'nerte] adj inert; (inmóvil) motionless

inescrutable [ineskru'taβle] adj inscrutable

inesperado, -a [inespe'raðo, a] adj unexpected, unforeseen

inestable [ines'taβle] adj unstable

inestimable [inesti'maβle] adj inestimable; **de valor ~** invaluable

inevitable [ineβi'taβle] adj inevitable

inexactitud [ineksakti'tuð] nf inaccuracy

inexacto, -a [inek'sakto, a] adj inaccurate; (falso) untrue

inexistente [ineksis'tente] adj non-existent

inexorable [inekso'raβle] adj inexorable

inexperiencia [inekspe'rjenθja] nf inexperience, lack of experience

inexperto, -a [ineks'perto, a] adj (novato) inexperienced

inexplicable [inekspli'kaβle] adj inexplicable

inexpresable [inekspre'saβle] adj inexpressible

inexpresivo, -a [inekspre'siβo, a] adj inexpressive; (ojos) dull; (cara) wooden

inexpugnable [inekspuɣ'naβle] adj (Mil) impregnable; (fig) firm

infalible [infa'liβle] adj infallible; (indefectible) certain, sure; (plan) foolproof

infame [in'fame] adj infamous

infamia [in'famja] nf infamy; (deshonra) disgrace

infancia [in'fanθja] nf infancy, childhood; **jardín de la ~** nursery school

infanta [in'fanta] nf (hija del rey) infanta, princess

infante [in'fante] nm (hijo del rey) infante, prince

infantería [infante'ria] nf infantry

infantil [infan'til] adj child's, children's; (pueril, aniñado) infantile; (cándido) childlike

infarto [in'farto] nm (tb: **infarto de miocardio**) heart attack

infatigable [infati'γaβle] adj tireless, untiring

infección [infek'θjon] nf infection

infeccioso, -a [infek'θjoso, a] adj infectious

infectar [infek'tar] vt to infect; **infectarse** vr: **infectarse (de)** (tb fig) to become infected (with)

infecundidad [infekundi'ðað] nf (de tierra) infertility, barrenness; (de mujer) sterility

infecundo, -a [infe'kundo, a] adj infertile, barren; sterile

infeliz [infe'liθ] adj (desgraciado) unhappy, wretched; (inocente) gullible ▪ nm/f (desgraciado) wretch; (inocentón) simpleton

inferior [infe'rjor] adj inferior; (situación, Mat) lower ▪ nm/f inferior, subordinate; **cualquier número ~ a nueve** any number less than 0 under 0 below nine; **una cantidad ~** a lesser quantity

inferioridad [inferjori'ðað] nf inferiority; **estar en ~ de condiciones** to be at a disadvantage

inferir [infe'rir] vt (deducir) to infer, deduce; (causar) to cause

infernal [infer'nal] adj infernal

infértil [in'fertil] adj infertile

infestar [infes'tar] vt to infest

infidelidad [infiðeli'ðað] nf infidelity, unfaithfulness

infiel [in'fjel] adj unfaithful, disloyal; (falso) inaccurate ▪ nm/f infidel, unbeliever

infiera etc [in'fjera] vb ver **inferir**

infierno [in'fjerno] nm hell; **¡vete al ~!** go to hell; **está en el quinto ~** it's at the back of beyond

infiltrar [infil'trar] vt to infiltrate; **infiltrarse** vr to infiltrate, filter; (líquidos) to percolate

ínfimo, -a ['infimo, a] adj (vil) vile, mean; (más bajo) lowest; (peor) worst; (miserable) wretched

infinidad [infini'ðað] nf infinity; (abundancia) great quantity; **~ de** vast numbers of; **~ de veces** countless times

infinitivo [infini'tiβo] nm infinitive

infinito, -a [infi'nito, a] adj infinite; (fig)

boundless ▪ adv infinitely ▪ nm infinite; (Mat) infinity; **hasta lo ~** ad infinitum

infiriendo etc [infi'rjendo] vb ver **inferir**

inflación [infla'θjon] nf (hinchazón) swelling; (monetaria) inflation; (fig) conceit

inflacionario, -a [inflaθjo'narjo, a] adj inflationary

inflacionismo [inflaθjo'nismo] nm (Econ) inflation

inflacionista [inflaθjo'nista] adj inflationary

inflamar [infla'mar] vt to set on fire; (Med, fig) to inflame; **inflamarse** vr to catch fire; to become inflamed

inflar [in'flar] vt (hinchar) to inflate, blow up; (fig) to exaggerate; **inflarse** vr to swell (up); (fig) to get conceited

inflexible [inflek'siβle] adj inflexible; (fig) unbending

infligir [infli'xir] vt to inflict

inflija etc [in'flixa] vb ver **infligir**

influencia [in'flwenθja] nf influence

influenciar [inflwen'θjar] vt to influence

influir [influ'ir] vt to influence ▪ vi to have influence, carry weight; **~ en** 0 **sobre** to influence, affect; (contribuir a) to have a hand in

influjo [in'fluxo] nm influence; **~ de capitales** (Econ etc) capital influx

influyendo etc [influ'jendo] vb ver **influir**

influyente [influ'jente] adj influential

información [informa'θjon] nf information; (noticias) news sg; (informe) report; (Inform: datos) data; (Jur) inquiry; **I~** (oficina) Information; (Telec) Directory Enquiries (Brit), Directory Assistance (US); (mostrador) Information Desk; **una ~** a piece of information; **abrir una ~** (Jur) to begin proceedings; **~ deportiva** (en periódico) sports section

informal [infor'mal] adj informal

informante [infor'mante] nm/f informant

informar [infor'mar] vt (gen) to inform; (revelar) to reveal, make known ▪ vi (Jur) to plead; (denunciar) to inform; (dar cuenta de) to report on; **informarse** vr to find out; **informarse de** to inquire into

informática [infor'matika] nf ver **informático**

informatice etc [informa'tiθe] vb ver **informatizar**

informático, -a [infor'matiko, a] adj computer cpd ▪ nf (Tec) information technology; computing; (Escol) computer science 0 studies; **~ de gestión** commercial computing

informativo, -a [informa'tiβo, a] adj (libro) informative; (folleto) information cpd;

(*Radio,TV*) news *cpd* ∎ *nm* (*Radio,TV*) news programme

informatización [informatiθa'θjon] *nf* computerization

informatizar [informati'θar] *vt* to computerize

informe [in'forme] *adj* shapeless ∎ *nm* report; (*dictamen*) statement; (*Mil*) briefing; (*Jur*) plea; **informes** *nmpl* information *sg*; (*datos*) data; ~ **anual** annual report; ~ **del juez** summing-up

infortunio [infor'tunjo] *nm* misfortune

infracción [infrak'θjon] *nf* infraction, infringement; (*Auto*) offence

infraestructura [infraestruk'tura] *nf* infrastructure

in fraganti [infra'ɣanti] *adv*: **pillar a algn** ~ to catch sb red-handed

infranqueable [infranke'aβle] *adj* impassable; (*fig*) insurmountable

infrarrojo, -a [infra'rroxo, a] *adj* infrared

infravalorar [infraβalo'rar] *vt* to undervalue; (*Finanzas*) to underestimate

infringir [infrin'xir] *vt* to infringe, contravene

infrinja *etc* [in'frinxa] *vb ver* **infringir**

infructuoso, -a [infruk'twoso, a] *adj* fruitless, unsuccessful

infundado, -a [infun'daðo, a] *adj* groundless, unfounded

infundir [infun'dir] *vt* to infuse, instil; ~ **ánimo a algn** to encourage sb; ~ **miedo a algn** to intimidate sb

infusión [infu'sjon] *nf* infusion; ~ **de manzanilla** camomile tea

Ing. *abr* (*Am*) = **Ingeniero**

ingeniar [inxe'njar] *vt* to think up, devise; **ingeniarse** *vr* to manage; **ingeniarse para** to manage to

ingeniería [inxenje'ria] *nf* engineering; ~ **genética** genetic engineering; ~ **de sistemas** (*Inform*) systems engineering

ingeniero, -a [inxe'njero, a] *nm/f* engineer; (*Am*) *courtesy title*; ~ **de sonido** sound engineer; ~ **de caminos** civil engineer

ingenio [in'xenjo] *nm* (*talento*) talent; (*agudeza*) wit; (*habilidad*) ingenuity, inventiveness; (*Tec*): ~ **azucarero** sugar refinery

ingenioso, -a [inxe'njoso, a] *adj* ingenious, clever; (*divertido*) witty

ingente [in'xente] *adj* huge, enormous

ingenuidad [inxenwi'ðað] *nf* ingenuousness; (*sencillez*) simplicity

ingenuo, -a [in'xenwo, a] *adj* ingenuous

ingerir [inxe'rir] *vt* to ingest; (*tragar*) to swallow; (*consumir*) to consume

ingiera *etc* [in'xjera], **ingiriendo** *etc* [inxi'rjenðo] *vb ver* **ingerir**

Inglaterra [ingla'terra] *nf* England

ingle ['ingle] *nf* groin

inglés, -esa [in'gles, esa] *adj* English ∎ *nm/f* Englishman(-woman) ∎ *nm* (*Ling*) English; **los ingleses** the English

ingratitud [ingrati'tuð] *nf* ingratitude

ingrato, -a [in'grato, a] *adj* ungrateful; (*tarea*) thankless

ingravidez [ingraβi'ðeθ] *nf* weightlessness

ingrediente [ingre'ðjente] *nm* ingredient; **ingredientes** *nmpl* (*Am: tapas*) titbits

ingresar [ingre'sar] *vt* (*dinero*) to deposit ∎ *vi* to come *o* go in; ~ **a** (*esp Am*) to enter; ~ **en** (*club*) to join; (*Mil, Escol*) to enrol in; ~ **en el hospital** to go into hospital

ingreso [in'greso] *nm* (*entrada*) entry; (: *en hospital etc*) admission; (*Mil, Escol*) enrolment; **ingresos** *nmpl* (*dinero*) income *sg*; (: *Com*) takings *pl*; ~ **gravable** taxable income *sg*; **ingresos accesorios** fringe benefits; **ingresos brutos** gross receipts; **ingresos devengados** earned income *sg*; **ingresos exentos de impuestos** non-taxable income *sg*; **ingresos personales disponibles** disposable personal income *sg*

íngrimo, -a ['ingrimo, a] *adj* (*Am: tb*: **íngrimo y solo**) all alone

inhábil [i'naβil] *adj* unskilful, clumsy

inhabilitar [inaβili'tar] *vt* (*Pol, Med*): ~ **a algn (para hacer algo)** to disqualify sb (from doing sth)

inhabitable [inaβi'taβle] *adj* uninhabitable

inhabituado, -a [inaβi'twaðo, a] *adj* unaccustomed

inhalador [inala'ðor] *nm* (*Med*) inhaler

inhalar [ina'lar] *vt* to inhale

inherente [ine'rente] *adj* inherent

inhibición [iniβi'θjon] *nf* inhibition

inhibir [ini'βir] *vt* to inhibit; (*Rel*) to restrain; **inhibirse** *vr* to keep out

inhospitalario, -a [inospita'larjo, a], **inhóspito, -a** [i'nospito, a] *adj* inhospitable

inhumación [inuma'θjon] *nf* burial, interment

inhumano, -a [inu'mano, a] *adj* inhuman

INI ['ini] *nm abr* = **Instituto Nacional de Industria**

inicial [ini'θjal] *adj, nf* initial

inicialice *etc* [iniθja'liθe] *vb ver* **inicializar**

inicializar [iniθjali'θar] *vt* (*Inform*) to initialize

iniciar [ini'θjar] *vt* (*persona*) to initiate; (*empezar*) to begin, commence; (*conversación*) to start up; ~ **a algn en un secreto** to let sb into a secret; ~ **la sesión** (*Inform*) to log in *o* on

215

iniciativa [iniθja'tiβa] *nf* initiative; (*liderazgo*) leadership; **la ~ privada** private enterprise

inicio [i'niθjo] *nm* start, beginning

inicuo, -a [i'nikwo, a] *adj* iniquitous

inigualado, -a [iniɣwa'laðo, a] *adj* unequalled

ininteligible [ininteli'xiβle] *adj* unintelligible

ininterrumpido, -a [ininterrum'piðo, a] *adj* uninterrupted; (*proceso*) continuous; (*progreso*) steady

injerencia [inxe'renθja] *nf* interference

injertar [inxer'tar] *vt* to graft

injerto [in'xerto] *nm* graft; **~ de piel** skin graft

injuria [in'xurja] *nf* (*agravio, ofensa*) offence; (*insulto*) insult; **injurias** *nfpl* abuse *sg*

injuriar [inxu'rjar] *vt* to insult

injurioso, -a [inxu'rjoso, a] *adj* offensive; insulting

injusticia [inxus'tiθja] *nf* injustice, unfairness; **con ~** unjustly

injusto, -a [in'xusto, a] *adj* unjust, unfair

inmaculado, -a [inmaku'laðo, a] *adj* immaculate, spotless

inmadurez [inmaðu'reθ] *nf* immaturity

inmaduro, -a [inma'ðuro, a] *adj* immature; (*fruta*) unripe

inmediaciones [inmeðja'θjones] *nfpl* neighbourhood *sg*, environs

inmediatez [inmeðja'teθ] *nf* immediacy

inmediato, -a [inme'ðjato, a] *adj* immediate; (*contiguo*) adjoining; (*rápido*) prompt; (*próximo*) neighbouring, next; **de ~** (*esp Am*) immediately

inmejorable [inmexo'raβle] *adj* unsurpassable; (*precio*) unbeatable

inmemorable [inmemo'raβle], **inmemorial** [inmemo'rjal] *adj* immemorial

inmenso, -a [in'menso, a] *adj* immense, huge

inmerecido, -a [inmere'θiðo, a] *adj* undeserved

inmersión [inmer'sjon] *nf* immersion; (*buzo*) dive

inmigración [inmiɣra'θjon] *nf* immigration

inmigrante [inmi'ɣrante] *adj, nm/f* immigrant

inminente [inmi'nente] *adj* imminent, impending

inmiscuirse [inmisku'irse] *vr* to interfere, meddle

inmiscuyendo *etc* [inmisku'jendo] *vb ver* **inmiscuirse**

inmobiliario, -a [inmoβi'ljarjo, a] *adj* real-estate *cpd*, property *cpd* ■ *nf* estate agency

inmolar [inmo'lar] *vt* to immolate, sacrifice

inmoral [inmo'ral] *adj* immoral

inmortal [inmor'tal] *adj* immortal

inmortalice *etc* [inmorta'liθe] *vb ver* **inmortalizar**

inmortalizar [inmortali'θar] *vt* to immortalize

inmotivado, -a [inmoti'βaðo, a] *adj* motiveless; (*sospecha*) groundless

inmóvil [in'moβil] *adj* immobile

inmovilizar [inmoβili'θar] *vt* to immobilize; (*paralizar*) to paralyse; **inmovilizarse** *vr*: **se le ha inmovilizado la pierna** her leg was paralysed

inmueble [in'mweβle] *adj*: **bienes inmuebles** real estate *sg*, landed property *sg* ■ *nm* property

inmundicia [inmun'diθja] *nf* filth

inmundo, -a [in'mundo, a] *adj* filthy

inmune [in'mune] *adj* (*Med*) immune

inmunidad [inmuni'ðað] *nf* immunity; (*fisco*) exemption; **~ diplomática/ parlamentaria** diplomatic/parliamentary immunity

inmunitario, -a [inmuni'tarjo, a] *adj*: **sistema ~** immune system

inmunización [inmuniθa'θjon] *nf* immunization

inmunizar [inmuni'θar] *vt* to immunize

inmutable [inmu'taβle] *adj* immutable; **permaneció ~** he didn't flinch

inmutarse [inmu'tarse] *vr*: **siguió sin ~** he carried on unperturbed

innato, -a [in'nato, a] *adj* innate

innecesario, -a [inneθe'sarjo, a] *adj* unnecessary

innegable [inne'ɣaβle] *adj* undeniable

innoble [in'noβle] *adj* ignoble

innovación [innoβa'θjon] *nf* innovation

innovador, a [innoβa'ðor, a] *adj* innovatory, innovative ■ *nm/f* innovator

innovar [inno'βar] *vt* to introduce

innumerable [innume'raβle] *adj* countless

inocencia [ino'θenθja] *nf* innocence

inocentada [inoθen'taða] *nf* practical joke

inocente [ino'θente] *adj* (*ingenuo*) naive, innocent; (*no culpable*) innocent; (*sin malicia*) harmless ■ *nm/f* simpleton; **día de los (Santos) Inocentes** ≈ April Fool's Day; *see note*

○ **INOCENTE**
○
○ The 28th December, *el día de los*
○ *(Santos) Inocentes*, is when the Church
○ commemorates the story of Herod's
○ slaughter of the innocent children of
○ Judea in the time of Christ. On this day

Spaniards play *inocentadas* (practical
jokes) on each other, much like our April
Fools' Day pranks, eg typically sticking
a *monigote* (cut-out paper figure) on
someone's back, or broadcasting unlikely
news stories.

inocuidad [inokwi'ðað] *nf* harmlessness
inocular [inoku'lar] *vt* to inoculate
inocuo, -a [i'nokwo, a] *adj (sustancia)*
harmless
inodoro, -a [ino'ðoro, a] *adj* odourless ■ *nm*
toilet (*Brit*), lavatory (*Brit*), washroom (*US*)
inofensivo, -a [inofen'siβo, a] *adj*
inoffensive
inolvidable [inolβi'ðaβle] *adj* unforgettable
inoperante [inope'rante] *adj* ineffective
inopinado, -a [inopi'naðo, a] *adj* unexpected
inoportuno, -a [inopor'tuno, a] *adj*
untimely; *(molesto)* inconvenient;
(inapropiado) inappropriate
inoxidable [inoksi'ðaβle] *adj* stainless;
acero ~ stainless steel
inquebrantable [inkeβran'taβle] *adj*
unbreakable; *(fig)* unshakeable
inquiera *etc* [in'kjera] *vb ver* **inquirir**
inquietante [inkje'tante] *adj* worrying
inquietar [inkje'tar] *vt* to worry, trouble;
inquietarse *vr* to worry, get upset
inquieto, -a [in'kjeto, a] *adj* anxious,
worried; **estar ~ por** to be worried about
inquietud [inkje'tuð] *nf* anxiety, worry
inquilino, -a [inki'lino, a] *nm/f* tenant; *(Com)*
lessee
inquiriendo *etc* [inki'rjendo] *vb ver* **inquirir**
inquirir [inki'rir] *vt* to enquire into,
investigate
insaciable [insa'θjaβle] *adj* insatiable
insalubre [insa'luβre] *adj* unhealthy;
(condiciones) insanitary
INSALUD [insa'luð] *nm abr (Esp)* = **Instituto
Nacional de la Salud**
insano, -a [in'sano, a] *adj (loco)* insane;
(malsano) unhealthy
insatisfacción [insatisfak'θjon] *nf*
dissatisfaction
insatisfecho, -a [insatis'fetʃo, a] *adj*
(condición) unsatisfied; *(estado de ánimo)*
dissatisfied
inscribir [inskri'βir] *vt* to inscribe; *(en lista)*
to put; *(en censo)* to register; **inscribirse** *vr* to
register; *(Escol etc)* to enrol
inscripción [inskrip'θjon] *nf* inscription;
(Escol etc) enrolment; *(en censo)* registration
inscrito [ins'krito] *pp de* **inscribir**
insecticida [insekti'θiða] *nm* insecticide
insecto [in'sekto] *nm* insect

inseguridad [inseɣuri'ðað] *nf* insecurity
inseguro, -a [inse'ɣuro, a] *adj* insecure;
(inconstante) unsteady; *(incierto)* uncertain
inseminación [insemina'θjon] *nf*: ~
artificial artificial insemination (A.I.)
inseminar [insemi'nar] *vt* to inseminate,
fertilize
insensato, -a [insen'sato, a] *adj* foolish,
stupid
insensibilice *etc* [insensiβi'liθe] *vb ver*
insensibilizar
insensibilidad [insensiβili'ðað] *nf (gen)*
insensitivity; *(dureza de corazón)* callousness
insensibilizar [insensiβili'θar] *vt* to
desensitize; *(Med)* to anaesthetize (*Brit*),
anesthetize (*US*); *(eufemismo)* to knock out *o*
unconscious
insensible [insen'siβle] *adj (gen)* insensitive;
(movimiento) imperceptible; *(sin sensación)*
numb
inseparable [insepa'raβle] *adj* inseparable
INSERSO [in'serso] *nm abr* (= *Instituto Nacional
de Servicios Sociales*) branch of social services
insertar [inser'tar] *vt* to insert
inservible [inser'βiβle] *adj* useless
insidioso, -a [insi'ðjoso, a] *adj* insidious
insigne [in'siɣne] *adj* distinguished; *(famoso)*
notable
insignia [in'siɣnja] *nf (señal distintiva)* badge;
(estandarte) flag
insignificante [insiɣnifi'kante] *adj*
insignificant
insinuar [insi'nwar] *vt* to insinuate, imply;
insinuarse *vr*: **insinuarse con algn** to
ingratiate o.s. with sb
insípido, -a [in'sipiðo, a] *adj* insipid
insistencia [insis'tenθja] *nf* insistence
insistir [insis'tir] *vi* to insist; **~ en algo** to
insist on sth; *(enfatizar)* to stress sth
in situ [in'situ] *adv* on the spot, in situ
insobornable [insoβor'naβle] *adj*
incorruptible
insociable [inso'θjaβle] *adj* unsociable
insolación [insola'θjon] *nf (Med)* sunstroke
insolencia [inso'lenθja] *nf* insolence
insolente [inso'lente] *adj* insolent
insólito, -a [in'solito, a] *adj* unusual
insoluble [inso'luβle] *adj* insoluble
insolvencia [insol'βenθja] *nf* insolvency
insomne [in'somne] *adj* sleepless ■ *nm/f*
insomniac
insomnio [in'somnjo] *nm* insomnia
insondable [inson'daβle] *adj* bottomless
insonorización [insonoriθa'θjon] *nf*
soundproofing
insonorizado, -a [insonori'θaðo, a] *adj*
(cuarto etc) soundproof

insoportable [insopor'taβle] *adj* unbearable
insoslayable [insosla'jaβle] *adj* unavoidable
insospechado, -a [insospe'tʃaðo, a] *adj*
(*inesperado*) unexpected
insostenible [insoste'niβle] *adj* untenable
inspección [inspek'θjon] *nf* inspection,
check; **I~** inspectorate; **~ técnica (de
vehículos)** ≈ MOT (test) (*Brit*)
inspeccionar [inspekθjo'nar] *vt* (*examinar*) to
inspect, examine; (*controlar*) to check
inspector, a [inspek'tor, a] *nm/f* inspector
inspectorado [inspekto'raðo] *nm*
inspectorate
inspiración [inspira'θjon] *nf* inspiration
inspirador, a [inspira'ðor, a] *adj* inspiring
inspirar [inspi'rar] *vt* to inspire; (*Med*) to
inhale; **inspirarse** *vr*: **inspirarse en** to be
inspired by
instalación [instala'θjon] *nf* (*equipo*) fittings
pl, equipment; **~ eléctrica** wiring
instalar [insta'lar] *vt* (*establecer*) to instal;
(*erguir*) to set up, erect; **instalarse** *vr* to
establish o.s.; (*en una vivienda*) to move into
instancia [ins'tanθja] *nf* (*solicitud*)
application; (*ruego*) request; (*Jur*) petition;
a ~ de at the request of; **en última ~** in the
last resort
instantáneo, -a [instan'taneo, a] *adj*
instantaneous ■ *nf* snap(shot); **café ~**
instant coffee
instante [ins'tante] *nm* instant, moment;
en un ~ in a flash
instar [ins'tar] *vt* to press, urge
instaurar [instau'rar] *vt* (*establecer*) to
establish, set up
instigador, a [instiɣa'ðor, a] *nm/f* instigator;
~ de un delito (*Jur*) accessory before the fact
instigar [insti'ɣar] *vt* to instigate
instintivo, -a [instin'tiβo, a] *adj* instinctive
instinto [ins'tinto] *nm* instinct; **por ~**
instinctively
institución [institu'θjon] *nf* institution,
establishment; **~ benéfica** charitable
foundation
instituir [institu'ir] *vt* to establish; (*fundar*)
to found
instituto [insti'tuto] *nm* (*gen*) institute;
I~ Nacional de Enseñanza (*Esp*)
≈ comprehensive (*Brit*) *o* high (*US*) school;
I~ Nacional de Industria (INI) (*Esp Com*)
≈ National Enterprise Board (*Brit*)
institutriz [institu'triθ] *nf* governess
instituyendo *etc* [institu'jendo] *vb ver*
instituir
instrucción [instruk'θjon] *nf* instruction;
(*enseñanza*) education, teaching; (*Jur*)
proceedings *pl*; (*Mil*) training; (*Deporte*)

coaching; (*conocimientos*) knowledge;
(*Inform*) statement; **instrucciones para el
uso** directions for use; **instrucciones de
funcionamiento** operating instructions
instructivo, -a [instruk'tiβo, a] *adj*
instructive
instructor [instruk'to] *nm* instructor
instruir [instru'ir] *vt* (*gen*) to instruct;
(*enseñar*) to teach, educate; (*Jur: proceso*) to
prepare, draw up; **instruirse** *vr* to learn,
teach o.s.
instrumento [instru'mento] *nm* (*gen, Mus*)
instrument; (*herramienta*) tool, implement;
(*Com*) indenture; (*Jur*) legal document; **~
de percusión/cuerda/viento** percussion/
string(ed)/wind instrument
instruyendo *etc* [instru'jendo] *vb ver* **instruir**
insubordinarse [insuβorði'narse] *vr* to rebel
insuficiencia [insufi'θjenθja] *nf* (*carencia*)
lack; (*inadecuación*) inadequacy; **~ cardíaca/
renal** heart/kidney failure
insuficiente [insufi'θjente] *adj* (*gen*)
insufficient; (*Escol: nota*) unsatisfactory
insufrible [insu'friβle] *adj* insufferable
insular [insu'lar] *adj* insular
insulina [insu'lina] *nf* insulin
insulso, -a [in'sulso, a] *adj* insipid; (*fig*) dull
insultar [insul'tar] *vt* to insult
insulto [in'sulto] *nm* insult
insumisión [insumi'sjon] *nf refusal to do
military service or community service*
insumiso, -a [insu'miso, a] *adj* (*rebelde*)
rebellious ■ *nm/f* (*Pol*) *person who refuses to do
military service or community service*; *ver tb* **mili**
insuperable [insupe'raβle] *adj*
(*excelente*) unsurpassable; (*problema etc*)
insurmountable
insurgente [insur'xente] *adj, nm/f* insurgent
insurrección [insurrek'θjon] *nf* insurrection,
rebellion
insustituible [insusti'twiβle] *adj*
irreplaceable
intachable [inta'tʃaβle] *adj* irreproachable
intacto, -a [in'takto, a] *adj* (*sin tocar*)
untouched; (*entero*) intact
integrado, -a [inte'ɣraðo, a] *adj* (*Inform*):
circuito ~ integrated circuit
integral [inte'ɣral] *adj* integral; (*completo*)
complete; (*Tec*) built-in; **pan ~** wholemeal
bread
integrante [inte'ɣrante] *adj* integral ■ *nm/f*
member
integrar [inte'ɣrar] *vt* to make up, compose;
(*Mat, fig*) to integrate
integridad [inteɣri'ðað] *nf* wholeness;
(*carácter, tb Inform*) integrity; **en su ~**
completely

integrismo [inte'ɣrismo] *nm*
fundamentalism
integrista [inte'ɣrista] *adj, nm/f*
fundamentalist
íntegro, -a ['inteɣro, a] *adj* whole, entire;
(*texto*) uncut, unabridged; (*honrado*) honest
intelectual [intelek'twal] *adj, nm/f*
intellectual
intelectualidad [intelektwali'ðað] *nf*
intelligentsia, intellectuals *pl*
inteligencia [inteli'xenθja] *nf* intelligence;
(*ingenio*) ability; **~ artificial** artificial
intelligence
inteligente [inteli'xente] *adj* intelligent
inteligible [inteli'xiβle] *adj* intelligible
intemperancia [intempe'ranθja] *nf* excess,
intemperance
intemperie [intem'perje] *nf*: **a la ~** outdoors,
in the open air
intempestivo, -a [intempes'tiβo, a] *adj*
untimely
intención [inten'θjon] *nf* intention, purpose;
con segundas intenciones maliciously;
con ~ deliberately
intencionado, -a [intenθjo'naðo, a] *adj*
deliberate; **bien ~** well-meaning; **mal ~** ill-
disposed, hostile
intendencia [inten'denθja] *nf* management,
administration; (*Mil: tb:* **cuerpo de
intendencia**) ≈ service corps
intensidad [intensi'ðað] *nf* (*gen*) intensity;
(*Elec, Tec*) strength; (*de recuerdo*) vividness;
llover con ~ to rain hard
intensificar [intensifi'kar] *vt,* **intensificarse**
vr to intensify
intensifique *etc* [intensi'fike] *vb ver*
intensificar
intensivo, -a [inten'siβo, a] *adj* intensive;
curso ~ crash course
intenso, -a [in'tenso, a] *adj* intense;
(*impresión*) vivid; (*sentimiento*) profound, deep
intentar [inten'tar] *vt* (*tratar*) to try, attempt
intento [in'tento] *nm* (*intención*) intention,
purpose; (*tentativa*) attempt
intentona [inten'tona] *nf* (*Pol*) attempted
coup
interaccionar [interakθjo'nar] *vi* (*Inform*) to
interact
interactivo, -a [interak'tiβo, a] *adj*
interactive; (*Inform*): **computación
interactiva** interactive computing
intercalación [interkala'θjon] *nf* (*Inform*)
merging
intercalar [interka'lar] *vt* to insert; (*Inform:
archivos, texto*) to merge
intercambiable [interkam'bjaβle] *adj*
interchangeable

intercambio [inter'kambjo] *nm* (*canje*)
exchange; (*trueque*) swap
interceder [interθe'ðer] *vi* to intercede
interceptar [interθep'tar] *vt* to intercept, cut
off; (*Auto*) to hold up
interceptor [interθep'tor] *nm* interceptor;
(*Tec*) trap
intercesión [interθe'sjon] *nf* intercession
interés [inte'res] *nm* (*gen, Com*) interest;
(*importancia*) concern; (*parte*) share, part;
(*pey*) self-interest; **~ compuesto** compound
interest; **~ simple** simple interest; **con un ~
de 9 por ciento** at an interest of 9%; **dar a ~**
to lend at interest; **tener ~ en** (*Com*) to hold
a share in; **intereses acumulados** accrued
interest *sg*; **intereses por cobrar** interest
receivable *sg*; **intereses creados** vested
interests; **intereses por pagar** interest
payable *sg*
interesado, -a [intere'saðo, a] *adj* interested;
(*prejuiciado*) prejudiced; (*pey*) mercenary, self-
seeking ■ *nm/f* person concerned; (*firmante*)
the undersigned
interesante [intere'sante] *adj* interesting
interesar [intere'sar] *vt* to interest, be of
interest to ■ *vi* to interest, be of interest;
(*importar*) to be important; **interesarse** *vr*:
interesarse en *o* **por** to take an interest in;
no me interesan los toros bullfighting
does not appeal to me
interestatal [interesta'tal] *adj* inter-state
interface [inter'faθe], **interfase** [inter'fase]
nm (*Inform*) interface; **~ hombre/máquina/
por menús** man/machine/menu interface
interfaz [inter'faθ] *nm* = **interface**
interferencia [interfe'renθja] *nf*
interference
interferir [interfe'rir] *vt* to interfere with;
(*Telec*) to jam ■ *vi* to interfere
interfiera *etc* [inter'fjera], **interfiriendo** *etc*
[interfi'rjendo] *vb ver* **interferir**
interfono [inter'fono] *nm* intercom
ínterin ['interin] *adv* meanwhile ■ *nm*
interim; **en el ínterin** in the meantime
interino, -a [inte'rino, a] *adj* temporary;
(*empleado etc*) provisional ■ *nm/f* temporary
holder of a post; (*Med*) locum; (*Escol*) supply
teacher; (*Teat*) stand-in
interior [inte'rjor] *adj* inner, inside; (*Com*)
domestic, internal ■ *nm* interior, inside;
(*fig*) soul, mind; (*Deporte*) inside forward;
Ministerio del I~ ≈ Home Office (*Brit*),
Ministry of the Interior; **dije para mi ~**
I said to myself
interjección [interxek'θjon] *nf* interjection
interlínea [inter'linea] *nf* (*Inform*) line feed
interlocutor, a [interloku'tor, a] *nm/f*

speaker; (al teléfono) person at the other end (of the line); **mi** ~ the person I was speaking to

intermediario, -a [interme'ðjarjo, a] adj (mediador) mediating ∎ nm/f intermediary, go-between; (mediador) mediator

intermedio, -a [inter'meðjo, a] adj intermediate; (tiempo) intervening ∎ nm interval; (Pol) recess

interminable [intermi'naβle] adj endless, interminable

intermitente [intermi'tente] adj intermittent ∎ nm (Auto) indicator

internacional [internaθjo'nal] adj international

internado [inter'naðo] nm boarding school

internamiento [interna'mjento] nm internment

internar [inter'nar] vt to intern; (en un manicomio) to commit; **internarse** vr (penetrar) to penetrate; **internarse en** to go into o right inside; **internarse en un estudio** to study a subject in depth

internauta [inter'nauta] nmf Internet user

Internet [inter'net] nm o nf Internet

interno, -a [in'terno, a] adj internal, interior; (Pol etc) domestic ∎ nm/f (alumno) boarder

interpelación [interpela'θjon] nf appeal, plea

interpelar [interpe'lar] vt (rogar) to implore; (hablar) to speak to; (Pol) to ask for explanations, question formally

interpondré etc [interpon'dre] vb ver interponer

interponer [interpo'ner] vt to interpose, put in; **interponerse** vr to intervene

interponga etc [inter'ponga] vb ver interponer

interposición [interposi'θjon] nf insertion

interpretación [interpreta'θjon] nf interpretation; (Mus, Teat) performance; **mala** ~ misinterpretation

interpretar [interpre'tar] vt to interpret

intérprete [in'terprete] nm/f (Ling) interpreter, translator; (Mus, Teat) performer, artist(e)

interpuesto [inter'pwesto], **interpuse** etc [inter'puse] vb ver interponer

interrogación [interroɣa'θjon] nf interrogation; (Ling: tb: **signo de interrogación**) question mark; (Telec) polling

interrogante [interro'ɣante] adj questioning ∎ nm question mark; (fig) question mark, query

interrogar [interro'ɣar] vt to interrogate, question

interrogatorio [interroɣa'torjo] nm interrogation; (Mil) debriefing; (Jur) examination

interrogue etc [inte'rroɣe] vb ver interrogar

interrumpir [interrum'pir] vt to interrupt; (vacaciones) to cut short; (servicio) to cut off; (tráfico) to block

interrupción [interrup'θjon] nf interruption

interruptor [interrup'tor] nm (Elec) switch

intersección [intersek'θjon] nf intersection; (Auto) junction

interurbano, -a [interur'βano, a] adj inter-city; (Telec) long-distance

intervalo [inter'βalo] nm interval; (descanso) break; **a intervalos** at intervals, every now and then

intervención [interβen'θjon] nf supervision; (Com) audit(ing); (Med) operation; (Telec) tapping; (participación) intervention; ~ **quirúrgica** surgical operation; **la política de no** ~ the policy of non-intervention

intervencionista [interβenθjo'nista] adj: **no** ~ (Com) laissez-faire

intervendré etc [interβen'dre], **intervenga** etc [inter'βenga] vb ver intervenir

intervenir [interβe'nir] vt (controlar) to control, supervise; (Com) to audit; (Med) to operate on; (Telec) to tap ∎ vi (participar) to take part, participate; (mediar) to intervene

interventor, a [interβen'tor, a] nm/f inspector; (Com) auditor

interviniendo etc [interβi'njendo] vb ver intervenir

interviú [inter'βju] nf interview

intestino [intes'tino] nm intestine

inti ['inti] nm monetary unit of Peru

intimar [inti'mar] vt to intimate, announce; (mandar) to order ∎ vi, **intimarse** vr to become friendly

intimidad [intimi'ðað] nf intimacy; (familiaridad) familiarity; (vida privada) private life; (Jur) privacy

intimidar [intimi'ðar] vt to intimidate, scare

íntimo, -a ['intimo, a] adj intimate; (pensamientos) innermost; (vida) personal, private; **una boda íntima** a quiet wedding

intolerable [intole'raβle] adj intolerable, unbearable

intolerancia [intole'ranθja] nf intolerance

intoxicación [intoksika'θjon] nf poisoning; ~ **alimenticia** food poisoning

intraducible [intraðu'θiβle] adj untranslatable

intranet [intra'net] nf intranet

intranquilice etc [intranki'liθe] vb ver intranquilizarse

intranquilizarse [intrankili'θarse] vr to get worried o anxious

intranquilo, -a [intran'kilo, a] adj worried

intranscendente [intransθen'dente] adj unimportant

intransferible [intransfe'riβle] *adj* not transferable

intransigente [intransi'xente] *adj* intransigent

intransitable [intransi'taβle] *adj* impassable

intransitivo, -a [intransi'tiβo, a] *adj* intransitive

intratable [intra'taβle] *adj* (*problema*) intractable; (*dificultad*) awkward; (*individuo*) unsociable

intrepidez [intrepi'ðeθ] *nf* courage, bravery

intrépido, -a [in'trepiðo, a] *adj* intrepid, fearless

intriga [in'triɣa] *nf* intrigue; (*plan*) plot

intrigar [intri'ɣar] *vt, vi* to intrigue

intrigue *etc* [in'triɣe] *vb ver* **intrigar**

intrincado, -a [intrin'kaðo, a] *adj* intricate

intrínseco, -a [in'trinseko, a] *adj* intrinsic

introducción [introðuk'θjon] *nf* introduction; (*de libro*) foreword; (*Inform*) input

introducir [introðu'θir] *vt* (*gen*) to introduce; (*moneda*) to insert; (*Inform*) to input, enter

introduje *etc* [intro'ðuxe], **introduzca** *etc* [intro'ðuθka] *vb ver* **introducir**

intromisión [intromi'sjon] *nf* interference, meddling

introvertido, -a [introβer'tiðo, a] *adj, nm/f* introvert

intruso, -a [in'truso, a] *adj* intrusive ▪ *nm/f* intruder

intuición [intwi'θjon] *nf* intuition

intuir [intu'ir] *vt* to know by intuition, intuit

intuyendo *etc* [intu'jendo] *vb ver* **intuir**

inundación [inunda'θjon] *nf* flood(ing)

inundar [inun'dar] *vt* to flood; (*fig*) to swamp, inundate

inusitado, -a [inusi'taðo, a] *adj* unusual

inútil [i'nutil] *adj* useless; (*esfuerzo*) vain, fruitless

inutilice *etc* [inuti'liθe] *vb ver* **inutilizar**

inutilidad [inutili'ðað] *nf* uselessness

inutilizar [inutili'θar] *vt* to make unusable, put out of action; (*incapacitar*) to disable; **inutilizarse** *vr* to become useless

invadir [imba'ðir] *vt* to invade

invalidar [imbali'ðar] *vt* to invalidate

invalidez [imbali'ðeθ] *nf* (*Med*) disablement; (*Jur*) invalidity

inválido, -a [im'baliðo, a] *adj* invalid; (*Jur*) null and void ▪ *nm/f* invalid

invariable [imba'rjable] *adj* invariable

invasión [imba'sjon] *nf* invasion

invasor, a [imba'sor, a] *adj* invading ▪ *nm/f* invader

invencible [imben'θiβle] *adj* invincible; (*timidez, miedo*) unsurmountable

invención [imben'θjon] *nf* invention

inventar [imben'tar] *vt* to invent

inventario [imben'tarjo] *nm* inventory; (*Com*) stocktaking

inventiva [imben'tiβa] *nf* inventiveness

invento [im'bento] *nm* invention; (*fig*) brainchild; (*pey*) silly idea

inventor, a [imben'tor, a] *nm/f* inventor

invernadero [imberna'ðero] *nm* greenhouse

invernal [imber'nal] *adj* wintry, winter *cpd*

invernar [imber'nar] *vi* (*Zool*) to hibernate

inverosímil [imbero'simil] *adj* implausible

inversión [imber'sjon] *nf* (*Com*) investment; **~ de capitales** capital investment; **inversiones extranjeras** foreign investment *sg*

inverso, a [im'berso, a] *adj* inverse, opposite; **en el orden ~** in reverse order; **a la inversa** inversely, the other way round

inversor, -a [imber'sor, a] *nm/f* (*Com*) investor

invertebrado, -a [imberte'βraðo, a] *adj, nm* invertebrate

invertido, -a [imber'tiðo, a] *adj* inverted; (*al revés*) reversed; (*homosexual*) homosexual ▪ *nm/f* homosexual

invertir [imber'tir] *vt* (*Com*) to invest; (*volcar*) to turn upside down; (*tiempo etc*) to spend

investigación [imbestiɣa'θjon] *nf* investigation; (*indagación*) inquiry; (*Univ*) research; **~ y desarrollo** (*Com*) research and development (R & D); **~ de los medios de publicidad** media research; **~ del mercado** market research

investigador, a [imbestiɣa'ðor, a] *nm/f* investigator; (*Univ*) research fellow

investigar [imbesti'ɣar] *vt* to investigate; (*estudiar*) to do research into

investigue *etc* [imbes'tiɣe] *vb ver* **investigar**

investir [imbes'tir] *vt*: **~ a algn con algo** to confer sth on sb; **fue investido Doctor Honoris Causa** he was awarded an honorary doctorate

invicto, -a [im'bikto, a] *adj* unconquered

invidente [imbi'ðente] *adj* sightless ▪ *nm/f* blind person; **los invidentes** the sightless

invierno [im'bjerno] *nm* winter

invierta *etc* [im'bjerta] *vb ver* **invertir**

inviolabilidad [imbjolaβili'ðað] *nf* inviolability; **~ parlamentaria** parliamentary immunity

invirtiendo *etc* [imbir'tjendo] *vb ver* **invertir**

invisible [imbi'siβle] *adj* invisible; **exportaciones/importaciones invisibles** invisible exports/imports

invitación [imbita'θjon] *nf* invitation

invitado, -a [imbi'taðo, a] *nm/f* guest

invitar [imbi'tar] vt to invite; (incitar) to entice; ~ **a algn a hacer algo** to invite sb to do sth; ~ **a algo** to pay for sth; **nos invitó a cenar fuera** she took us out for dinner; **invito yo** it's on me

in vitro [im'bitro] adv in vitro

invocar [imbo'kar] vt to invoke, call on

involucrar [imbolu'krar] vt: ~ **algo en un discurso** to bring something irrelevant into a discussion; ~ **a algn en algo** to involve sb in sth; **involucrarse** vr (interesarse) to get involved

involuntario, -a [imbolun'tarjo, a] adj involuntary; (ofensa etc) unintentional

invoque etc [im'boke] vb ver **invocar**

inyección [injek'θjon] nf injection

inyectar [injek'tar] vt to inject

ión [i'on] nm ion

IPC nm abr (Esp: = índice de precios al consumo) CPI

IPM nm abr (= índice de precios al por menor) RPI

 PALABRA CLAVE

ir [ir] vi **1** to go; (a pie) to walk; (viajar) to travel; **ir caminando** to walk; **fui en tren** I went o travelled by train; **voy a la calle** I'm going out; **ir en coche/en bicicleta** to drive/cycle; **ir a pie** to walk, go on foot; **ir de pesca** to go fishing; **¡(ahora) voy!** (I'm just) coming!

2: **ir (a) por**: **ir (a) por el médico** to fetch the doctor

3 (progresar: persona, cosa) to go; **el trabajo va muy bien** work is going very well; **¿cómo te va?** how are things going?; **me va muy bien** I'm getting on very well; **le fue fatal** it went awfully badly for him

4 (funcionar): **el coche no va muy bien** the car isn't running very well

5 (sentar): **me va estupendamente** (ropa, color) it suits me really well; (medicamento) it works really well for me; **ir bien con algo** to go well with sth

6 (aspecto): **iba muy bien vestido** he was very well dressed; **ir con zapatos negros** to wear black shoes

7 (locuciones): **¿vino? — ¡que va!** did he come? — of course not!; **vamos, no llores** come on, don't cry; **¡vaya coche!** (admiración) what a car!, that's some car!; (desprecio) that's a terrible car!; **¡vaya!** (regular) so so; (desagrado) come on!; **¡vamos!** come on!; **¡que le vaya bien!** (adiós) take care!

8: **no vaya a ser**: **tienes que correr, no vaya a ser que pierdas el tren** you'll have to run so as not to miss the train

9: **no me** etc **va ni me viene** I etc don't care

■ vb auxiliar **1**: **ir a**: **voy/iba a hacerlo hoy** I am/was going to do it today

2 (+gerundio): **iba anocheciendo** it was getting dark; **todo se me iba aclarando** everything was gradually becoming clearer to me

3 (+pp = pasivo) **van vendidos 300 ejemplares** 300 copies have been sold so far

irse vr **1**: **¿por dónde se va al zoológico?** which is the way to the zoo?

2 (marcharse) to leave; **ya se habrán ido** they must already have left o gone; **¡vámonos!**, **¡nos fuimos!** (Am) let's go!; **¡vete!** go away!; **¡vete a saber!** your guess is as good as mine!, who knows!

IRA ['ira] nm abr (= Irish Republican Army) IRA

ira ['ira] nf anger, rage

iracundo, -a [ira'kundo, a] adj irascible

Irak [i'rak] nm = **Iraq**

Irán [i'ran] nm Iran

iraní [ira'ni] adj, nm/f Iranian

Iraq [i'rak] nm Iraq

iraquí [ira'ki] adj, nm/f Iraqi

irascible [iras'θiβle] adj irascible

irguiendo etc [ir'ɣjendo] vb ver **erguir**

iris ['iris] nm inv (arco iris) rainbow; (Anat) iris

Irlanda [ir'landa] nf Ireland; ~ **del Norte** Northern Ireland, Ulster

irlandés, -esa [irlan'des, esa] adj Irish ■ nm/f Irishman(-woman) ■ nm (Ling) Gaelic, Irish; **los irlandeses** nmpl the Irish

ironía [iro'nia] nf irony

irónico, -a [i'roniko, a] adj ironic(al)

IRPF nm abr (Esp) = **impuesto sobre la renta de las personas físicas**

irracional [irraθjo'nal] adj irrational

irrazonable [irraθo'naβle] adj unreasonable

irreal [irre'al] adj unreal

irrealizable [irreali'θaβle] adj (gen) unrealizable; (meta) unrealistic

irrebatible [irreβa'tiβle] adj irrefutable

irreconocible [irrekono'θiβle] adj unrecognizable

irrecuperable [irrekupe'raβle] adj irrecoverable, irretrievable

irreembolsable [irreembol'saβle] adj (Com) non-returnable

irreflexión [irreflek'sjon] nf thoughtlessness; (ímpetu) rashness

irregular [irreɣu'lar] adj irregular; (situación) abnormal, anomalous; **margen izquierdo/derecho** ~ (texto) ragged left/right (margin)

irregularidad [irreɣulari'ðað] nf irregularity

irremediable [irreme'ðjaβle] adj irremediable; (vicio) incurable

irreprochable [irrepro'tʃaβle] adj

irreproachable

irresistible [irresis'tiβle] *adj* irresistible

irresoluto, -a [irreso'luto, a] *adj* irresolute, hesitant; (*sin resolver*) unresolved

irrespetuoso, -a [irrespe'twoso, a] *adj* disrespectful

irresponsable [irrespon'saβle] *adj* irresponsible

irreverente [irreβe'rente] *adj* disrespectful

irreversible [irreβer'siβle] *adj* irreversible

irrevocable [irreβo'kaβle] *adj* irrevocable

irrigar [irri'ɣar] *vt* to irrigate

irrigue *etc* [i'rriɣe] *vb ver* **irrigar**

irrisorio, -a [irri'sorjo, a] *adj* derisory, ridiculous; (*precio*) bargain *cpd*

irritación [irrita'θjon] *nf* irritation

irritar [irri'tar] *vt* to irritate, annoy; **irritarse** *vr* to get angry, lose one's temper

irrompible [irrom'piβle] *adj* unbreakable

irrumpir [irrum'pir] *vi*: ~ **en** to burst o rush into

irrupción [irrup'θjon] *nf* irruption; (*invasión*) invasion

IRTP *nm abr* (*Esp*: = *impuesto sobre el rendimiento del trabajo personal*) ≈ PAYE

ISBN *nm abr* (= *International Standard Book Number*) ISBN

isla ['isla] *nf* (*Geo*) island; **Islas Británicas** British Isles; **Islas Filipinas/Malvinas/Canarias** Philippines/Falklands/Canaries

Islam [is'lam] *nm* Islam

islámico, -a [is'lamiko, a] *adj* Islamic

islandés, -esa [islan'des, esa] *adj* Icelandic ■ *nm/f* Icelander ■ *nm* (*Ling*) Icelandic

Islandia [is'landja] *nf* Iceland

isleño, -a [is'leɲo, a] *adj* island *cpd* ■ *nm/f* islander

islote [is'lote] *nm* small island

isotónico, -a [iso'toniko, a] *adj* isotonic

isótopo [i'sotopo] *nm* isotope

Israel [isra'el] *nm* Israel

israelí [israe'li] *adj, nm/f* Israeli

istmo ['istmo] *nm* isthmus; **el I~ de Panamá** the Isthmus of Panama

Italia [i'talja] *nf* Italy

italiano, -a [ita'ljano, a] *adj, nm/f* Italian ■ *nm* (*Ling*) Italian

itinerante [itine'rante] *adj* travelling; (*embajador*) roving

itinerario [itine'rarjo] *nm* itinerary, route

ITV *nf abr* (= *Inspección Técnica de Vehículos*) ≈ MOT (test) (*Brit*)

IVA ['iβa] *nm abr* (*Esp Com*: = *Impuesto sobre el Valor Añadido*) VAT

IVP *nm abr* = **Instituto Venezolano de Petroquímica**

izada [i'saða] *nf* (*Am*) lifting, raising

izar [i'θar] *vt* to hoist

izda, izq.ª *abr* (= *izquierda*) L, l

izdo, izq.º *abr* (= *izquierdo*) L, l

izquierda [iθ'kjerða] *nf ver* **izquierdo**

izquierdista [iθkjer'ðista] *adj* leftist, left-wing ■ *nm/f* left-winger, leftist

izquierdo, -a [iθ'kjerðo, a] *adj* left ■ *nf* left; (*Pol*) left (wing); **a la izquierda** on the left; **es un cero a la izquierda** (*fam*) he is a nonentity; **conducción por la izquierda** left-hand drive

Jj

J, j ['xota] *nf* (*letra*) J, j; **J de José** J for Jack (*Brit*) *o* Jig (*US*)

J *abr* (= *julio(s)*) J

jabalí [xaβa'li] *nm* wild boar

jabalina [xaβa'lina] *nf* javelin

jabato, -a [xa'βato, a] *adj* brave, bold ■ *nm* young wild boar

jabón [xa'βon] *nm* soap; (*fam: adulación*) flattery; **~ de afeitar** shaving soap; **~ de tocador** toilet soap; **dar ~ a algn** to soft-soap sb

jabonar [xaβo'nar] *vt* to soap

jaca ['xaka] *nf* pony

jacinto [xa'θinto] *nm* hyacinth

jactancia [xak'tanθja] *nf* boasting, boastfulness

jactarse [xak'tarse] *vr*: **~ (de)** to boast *o* brag (about *o* of)

jadear [xaðe'ar] *vi* to pant, gasp for breath

jadeo [xa'ðeo] *nm* panting, gasping

jaguar [xa'ɣwar] *nm* jaguar

jalar [xa'lar] *vt* (*Am*) to pull

jalbegue [xal'βeɣe] *nm* whitewash

jalea [xa'lea] *nf* jelly

jaleo [xa'leo] *nm* racket, uproar; **armar un ~** to kick up a racket

jalón [xa'lon] *nm* (*Am*) tug

jalonar [xalo'nar] *vt* to stake out; (*fig*) to mark

Jamaica [xa'maika] *nf* Jamaica

jamaicano, -a [xamai'kano, a] *adj, nm/f* Jamaican

jamás [xa'mas] *adv* never, not ... ever; (*interrogativo*) ever; **¿~ se vio tal cosa?** did you ever see such a thing?

jamón [xa'mon] *nm* ham; **~ (de) York** boiled ham; **~ dulce/serrano** boiled/cured ham

Japón [xa'pon] *nm*: **el ~** Japan

japonés, -esa [xapo'nes, esa] *adj, nm/f* Japanese ■ *nm* (*Ling*) Japanese

jaque ['xake] *nm*: **~ mate** checkmate

jaqueca [xa'keka] *nf* (very bad) headache, migraine

jarabe [xa'raβe] *nm* syrup; **~ para la tos** cough syrup *o* mixture

jarana [xa'rana] *nf* (*juerga*) spree (*fam*); **andar/ir de ~** to be/go on a spree

jardín [xar'ðin] *nm* garden; **~ botánico** botanical garden; **~ de (la) infancia** (*Esp*) *o* **de niños** (*Am*) *o* **infantil** (*Am*) kindergarten, nursery school

jardinaje [xarði'nay] *nm* gardening

jardinería [xarðine'ria] *nf* gardening

jardinero, -a [xarði'nero, a] *nm/f* gardener

jarra ['xarra] *nf* jar; (*jarro*) jug; (*de leche*) churn; (*de cerveza*) mug; **de *o* en jarras** with arms akimbo

jarro ['xarro] *nm* jug

jarrón [xa'rron] *nm* vase; (*Arqueología*) urn

jaspeado, -a [xaspe'ado, a] *adj* mottled, speckled

jaula ['xaula] *nf* cage; (*embalaje*) crate

jauría [xau'ria] *nf* pack of hounds

jazmín [xaθ'min] *nm* jasmine

J. C. *abr* = **Jesucristo**

jeep® (*pl* **jeeps**) [jip, jips] *nm* jeep®

jefa ['xefa] *nf ver* **jefe**

jefatura [xefa'tura] *nf* (*liderazgo*) leadership; (*sede*) central office; **J~ de la aviación civil** ≈ Civil Aviation Authority; **~ de policía** police headquarters *sg*

jefazo [xe'faθo] *nm* bigwig

jefe, -a ['xefe, a] *nm/f* (*gen*) chief, head; (*patrón*) boss; (*Pol*) leader; (*Com*) manager(ess); **~ de camareros** head waiter; **~ de cocina** chef; **~ ejecutivo** (*Com*) chief executive; **~ de estación** stationmaster; **~ de estado** head of state; **~ de oficina** (*Com*) office manager; **~ de producción** (*Com*) production manager; **~ supremo** commander-in-chief; **ser el ~** (*fig*) to be the boss

JEN [xen] *nf abr* (*Esp*) = **Junta de Energía Nuclear**

jengibre [xen'xiβre] *nm* ginger

jeque ['xeke] *nm* sheik(h)

jerarquía [xerar'kia] *nf* (*orden*) hierarchy; (*rango*) rank

jerárquico, -a [xe'rarkiko, a] *adj* hierarchic(al)

jerez [xe'reθ] *nm* sherry; **J~ de la Frontera** Jerez

jerezano, -a [xere'θano, a] *adj* of o from Jerez ▪ *nm/f* native o inhabitant of Jerez

jerga ['xerɣa] *nf* (*tela*) coarse cloth; (*lenguaje*) jargon; **~ informática** computer jargon

jerigonza [xeri'ɣonθa] *nf* (*jerga*) jargon, slang; (*galimatías*) nonsense, gibberish

jeringa [xe'ringa] *nf* syringe; (*Am*) annoyance, bother; **~ de engrase** grease gun

jeringar [xerin'gar] *vt* to annoy, bother

jeringue *etc* [xe'ringe] *vb ver* **jeringar**

jeringuilla [xerin'guiʎa] *nf* hypodermic (syringe)

jeroglífico [xero'ɣlifiko] *nm* hieroglyphic

jersey [xer'sei] (*pl* **jerseys**) *nm* jersey, pullover, jumper

Jerusalén [xerusa'len] *n* Jerusalem

Jesucristo [xesu'kristo] *nm* Jesus Christ

jesuita [xe'swita] *adj, nm* Jesuit

Jesús [xe'sus] *nm* Jesus; ¡~! good heavens!; (*al estornudar*) bless you!

jet (*pl* **jets**) [jet, jet] *nm* jet (plane) ▪ *nf*: **la ~** the jet set

jeta ['xeta] *nf* (*Zool*) snout; (*fam: cara*) mug; **¡que ~ tienes!** (*fam: insolencia*) you've got a nerve!

jíbaro, -a ['xiβaro, a] *adj, nm/f* Jíbaro (Indian)

jícara ['xikara] *nf* small cup

jiennense [xjen'nense] *adj* of o from Jaén ▪ *nm/f* native o inhabitant of Jaén

jilguero [xil'ɣero] *nm* goldfinch

jinete, -a [xi'nete, a] *nm/f* horseman(-woman)

jipijapa [xipi'xapa] *nm* (*Am*) straw hat

jira ['xira] *nf* (*de tela*) strip; (*excursión*) picnic

jirafa [xi'rafa] *nf* giraffe

jirón [xi'ron] *nm* rag, shred

JJ.OO. *nmpl abr* = **Juegos Olímpicos**

jocosidad [xokosi'ðað] *nf* humour; (*chiste*) joke

jocoso, -a [xo'koso, a] *adj* humorous, jocular

joder [xo'ðer] (*fam!*) *vt* to fuck (!), screw (!); (*fig: fastidiar*) to piss off (!), bug; **joderse** *vr* (*fracasar*) to fail; **¡~!** damn it!; **se jodió todo** everything was ruined

jodido, -a [xo'ðiðo, a] *adj* (*fam!: difícil*) awkward; **estoy ~** I'm knackered

jofaina [xo'faina] *nf* washbasin

jojoba [xo'xoβa] *nf* jojoba

jolgorio [xol'ɣorjo] *nm* (*juerga*) fun, revelry

jonrón [xon'ron] *nm* home run

Jordania [xor'ðanja] *nf* Jordan

jornada [xor'naða] *nf* (*viaje de un día*) day's journey; (*camino o viaje entero*) journey; (*día de trabajo*) working day; **~ de 8 horas** 8-hour day; (**trabajar a**) **~ partida** (to work a) split shift

jornal [xor'nal] *nm* (day's) wage

jornalero, -a [xorna'lero, a] *nm/f* (day) labourer

joroba [xo'roβa] *nf* hump

jorobado, -a [xoro'βaðo, a] *adj* hunchbacked ▪ *nm/f* hunchback

jorobar [xoro'βar] *vt* to annoy, pester, bother; **jorobarse** *vr* to get cross; **¡hay que jorobarse!** to hell with it!; **esto me joroba!** ¡I'm fed up with this!

jota ['xota] *nf* letter J; (*danza*) Aragonese dance; (*fam*) jot, iota; **no saber ni ~** to have no idea

joven ['xoβen] *adj* young ▪ *nm* young man, youth ▪ *nf* young woman, girl

jovencito, -a [xoβen'θito, a] *nm/f* youngster

jovial [xo'βjal] *adj* cheerful, jolly

jovialidad [xoβjali'ðað] *nf* cheerfulness

joya ['xoja] *nf* jewel, gem; (*fig: persona*) gem; **joyas de fantasía** imitation jewellery *sg*

joyería [xoje'ria] *nf* (*joyas*) jewellery; (*tienda*) jeweller's (shop)

joyero [xo'jero] *nm* (*persona*) jeweller; (*caja*) jewel case

Juan [xwan] *nm*: **Noche de San ~** *see note*

● NOCHE DE SAN JUAN

The *Noche de San Juan* (evening of the Feast of Saint John) on the 24th June is a *fiesta* coinciding with the summer solstice, and which has taken the place of other ancient pagan festivals. Traditionally fire plays a major part in these festivities, which can last for days in certain areas. Celebrations and dancing take place around *hogueras* (bonfires) in towns and villages across the country.

juanete [xwa'nete] *nm* (*del pie*) bunion

jubilación [xuβila'θjon] *nf* (*retiro*) retirement

jubilado, -a [xuβi'laðo, a] *adj* retired ▪ *nm/f* retired person, pensioner (*Brit*), senior citizen

jubilar [xuβi'lar] *vt* to pension off, retire; (*fam*) to discard; **jubilarse** *vr* to retire

jubileo [xuβi'leo] *nm* jubilee

júbilo ['xuβilo] *nm* joy, rejoicing

jubiloso, -a [xuβi'loso, a] *adj* jubilant

judaísmo [xuða'ismo] *nm* Judaism

judía [xu'ðia] *nf ver* **judío**

judicatura [xuðika'tura] *nf* (*cargo de juez*) office of judge; (*cuerpo de jueces*) judiciary

judicial [xuði'θjal] *adj* judicial
judío, -a [xu'ðio, a] *adj* Jewish ■ *nm* Jew ■ *nf* Jewess, Jewish woman; (*Culin*) bean; **judía blanca** haricot bean; **judía verde** French *o* string bean
juego *etc* ['xweɣo] *vb ver* **jugar** ■ *nm* (*gen*) play; (*pasatiempo, partido*) game; (*en casino*) gambling; (*deporte*) sport; (*conjunto*) set; (*herramientas*) kit; **~ de azar** game of chance; **~ de café** coffee set; **~ de caracteres** (*Inform*) font; **~ limpio/sucio** fair/foul *o* dirty play; **~ de mesa** board game; **J~s Olímpicos** Olympic Games; **~ de programas** (*Inform*) suite of programs; **fuera de ~** (*Deporte: persona*) offside; (*: pelota*) out of play; **por ~** in fun, for fun
juegue *etc* ['xweɣe] *vb ver* **jugar**
juerga ['xwerɣa] *nf* binge; (*fiesta*) party; **ir de ~** to go out on a binge
juerguista [xwer'ɣista] *nm/f* reveller
jueves ['xweβes] *nm inv* Thursday; *ver tb* **sábado**
juez [xweθ] *nm/f* judge; (*Tenis*) umpire; **~ de línea** linesman; **~ de paz** justice of the peace; **~ de salida** starter
jueza [xweθa] *nf ver* **juez**
jugada [xu'ɣaða] *nf* play; **buena ~** good move (*o* shot *o* stroke) *etc*
jugador, a [xuɣa'ðor, a] *nm/f* player; (*en casino*) gambler
jugar [xu'ɣar] *vt* to play; (*en casino*) to gamble; (*apostar*) to bet ■ *vi* to play; to gamble; (*Com*) to speculate; **jugarse** *vr* to gamble (away); **jugarse el todo por el todo** to stake one's all, go for bust; **¿quién juega?** whose move is it?; **¡me la han jugado!** (*fam*) I've been had!
jugarreta [xuɣa'rreta] *nf* (*mala jugada*) bad move; (*trampa*) dirty trick; **hacer una ~ a algn** to play a dirty trick on sb
juglar [xu'ɣlar] *nm* minstrel
jugo ['xuɣo] *nm* (*Bot, de fruta*) juice; (*fig*) essence, substance; **~ de naranja** (*esp Am*) orange juice
jugoso, -a [xu'ɣoso, a] *adj* juicy; (*fig*) substantial, important
jugué [xu'ɣe], **juguemos** *etc* [xu'ɣemos] *vb ver* **jugar**
juguete [xu'ɣete] *nm* toy
juguetear [xuɣete'ar] *vi* to play
juguetería [xuɣete'ria] *nf* toyshop
juguetón, -ona [xuɣe'ton, ona] *adj* playful
juicio ['xwiθjo] *nm* judgement; (*sana razón*) sanity, reason; (*opinión*) opinion; (*Jur: proceso*) trial; **estar fuera de ~** to be out of one's mind; **a mi ~** in my opinion
juicioso, -a [xwi'θjoso, a] *adj* wise, sensible
JUJEM [xu'xem] *nf abr* (*Esp Mil*) = **Junta de Jefes del Estado Mayor**

jul. *abr* (= *julio*) Jul.
julio ['xuljo] *nm* July; **el uno** *o* **el primero de ~** the first of July; **en el mes de ~** during July; **en ~ del año que viene** in July of next year
jumento, -a [xu'mento, a] *nm/f* donkey
jun. *abr* (= *junio*) Jun.
junco ['xunko] *nm* rush, reed
jungla ['xungla] *nf* jungle
junio ['xunjo] *nm* June; *ver tb* **julio**
junta ['xunta] *nf ver* **junto**
juntar [xun'tar] *vt* to join, unite; (*maquinaria*) to assemble, put together; (*dinero*) to collect; **juntarse** *vr* to join, meet; (*reunirse: personas*) to meet, assemble; (*arrimarse*) to approach, draw closer; **juntarse con algn** to join sb
junto, -a ['xunto, a] *adj* joined; (*unido*) united; (*anexo*) near, close; (*contiguo, próximo*) next, adjacent ■ *nf* (*asamblea*) meeting, assembly; (*comité, consejo*) board, council, committee; (*Mil, Pol*) junta; (*articulación*) joint ■ *adv*: **todo ~** all at once ■ *prep*: **~ a** near (to), next to; **juntos** together; **junta constitutiva** (*Com*) statutory meeting; **junta directiva** (*Com*) board of management; **junta general extraordinaria** (*Com*) extraordinary general meeting
juntura [xun'tura] *nf* (*punto de unión*) join, junction; (*articulación*) joint
jura ['xura] *nf* oath, pledge; **~ de bandera** (ceremony of taking the) oath of allegiance
jurado [xu'raðo] *nm* (*Jur: individuo*) juror; (*: grupo*) jury; (*de concurso: grupo*) panel (of judges); (*: individuo*) member of a panel
juramentar [xuramen'tar] *vt* to swear in, administer the oath to; **juramentarse** *vr* to be sworn in, take the oath
juramento [xura'mento] *nm* oath; (*maldición*) oath, curse; **bajo ~** on oath; **prestar ~** to take the oath; **tomar ~ a** to swear in, administer the oath to
jurar [xu'rar] *vt, vi* to swear; **~ en falso** to commit perjury; **jurárselas a algn** to have it in for sb
jurídico, -a [xu'riðiko, a] *adj* legal, juridical
jurisdicción [xurisðik'θjon] *nf* (*poder, autoridad*) jurisdiction; (*territorio*) district
jurisprudencia [xurispru'ðenθja] *nf* jurisprudence
jurista [xu'rista] *nm/f* jurist
justamente [xusta'mente] *adv* justly, fairly; (*precisamente*) just, exactly
justicia [xus'tiθja] *nf* justice; (*equidad*) fairness, justice; **de ~** deservedly
justiciero, -a [xusti'θjero, a] *adj* just, righteous
justificable [xustifi'kaβle] *adj* justifiable

justificación [xustifika'θjon] *nf*
justification; ~ **automática** (*Inform*)
automatic justification

justificado, -a [xustifi'kaðo, a] *adj* (*Tip*): (**no**)
~ (un)justified

justificante [xustifi'kante] *nm* voucher;
~ **médico** sick note

justificar [xustifi'kar] *vt* (*tb Tip*) to justify;
(*probar*) to verify

justifique *etc* [xusti'fike] *vb ver* **justificar**

justo, -a ['xusto, a] *adj* (*equitativo*) just, fair,
right; (*preciso*) exact, correct; (*ajustado*) tight

■ *adv* (*precisamente*) exactly, precisely; (*apenas
a tiempo*) just in time; **¡~!** that's it!, correct!;
llegaste muy ~ you just made it; **vivir muy
~** to be hard up

juvenil [xuβe'nil] *adj* youthful

juventud [xuβen'tuð] *nf* (*adolescencia*) youth;
(*jóvenes*) young people *pl*

juzgado [xuθ'ɣaðo] *nm* tribunal; (*Jur*) court

juzgar [xuθ'ɣar] *vt* to judge; **a ~ por ...**
to judge by ..., judging by ...; **~ mal** to
misjudge; **júzguelo usted mismo** see for
yourself

j

Kk

K, k [ka] nf (letra) K, k; **K de Kilo** K for King
K abr (= 1.000) K; (Inform: = 1.024) K
Kampuchea [kampu'tʃea] nf Kampuchea
karaoke [kara'oke] nm karaoke
kárate ['karate], **karate** [ka'rate] nm karate
KAS nf abr (= Koordinadora Abertzale Sozialista)
  Basque nationalist umbrella group
Kazajstán [kaθaxs'tan] nm Kazakhstan
k/c. abr (= kilociclos) kc.
Kenia ['kenja] nf Kenya
keniata [ke'njata] adj, nm/f Kenyan
kepí, kepis [ke'pi, 'kepis] nm (esp Am) kepi,
  military hat
kerosene [kero'sene] nm kerosene
Kg, kg abr (= kilogramo(s)) K, kg
KGB sigla m KGB
kilate [ki'late] nm = **quilate**
kilo ['kilo] nm kilo
kilobyte ['kiloβait] nm (Inform) kilobyte
kilogramo [kilo'ɣramo] nm kilogramme
  (Brit), kilogram (US)
kilolitro [kilo'litro] nm kilolitre (Brit),
  kiloliter (US)
kilometraje [kilome'traxe] nm distance in
  kilometres, ≈ mileage

kilométrico, -a [kilo'metriko, a] adj
  kilometric; (fam) very long; **(billete)** ~ (Ferro)
  mileage ticket
kilómetro [ki'lometro] nm kilometre (Brit),
  kilometer (US)
kiloocteto [kilook'teto] nm (Inform)
  kilobyte
kilovatio [kilo'βatjo] nm kilowatt
kiosco ['kjosko] nm = **quiosco**
Kirguizistán [kirɣiθis'tan] nm Kirghizia
kiwi ['kiwi] nm kiwi (fruit)
km abr (= kilómetro(s)) km
km/h abr (= kilómetros por hora) km/h
knock-out ['nokau], **K.O.** ['kao] nm
  knockout; (golpe) knockout blow; **dejar** o
  poner a algn ~ to knock sb out
kosovar [koso'βar] adj Kosovan
Kosovo [koso'βo] nm Kosovo
k.p.h. abr (= kilómetros por hora) km/h
k.p.l. abr (= kilómetros por litro) ≈ mpg
kurdo, -a ['kurðo, a] adj Kurdish ■ nm/f
  Kurd ■ nm (Ling) Kurdish
kuwaití [kuβai'ti] adj, nm/f Kuwaiti
kv abr (= kilovatio) kw
kv/h abr (= kilovatios-hora) kw-h

Ll

L, l ['ele] *nf* (*letra*) L, l; **L de Lorenzo** L for Lucy (*Brit*) o Love (*US*)

l *abr* (= *litro(s)*) l; (= *libro*) bk

L/ *abr* (*Com*) = **letra**

la [la] *artículo definido fsg* the ■ *pron* her; (*en relación a usted*) you; (*en relación a una cosa*) it ■ *nm* (*Mus*) A; **está en la cárcel** he's in jail; **la del sombrero rojo** the woman/girl/one in the red hat

laberinto [laβe'rinto] *nm* labyrinth

labia ['laβja] *nf* fluency; (*pey*) glibness; **tener mucha ~** to have the gift of the gab

labial [la'βjal] *adj* labial

labio ['laβjo] *nm* lip; (*de vasija etc*) edge, rim; **~ inferior/superior** lower/upper lip

labor [la'βor] *nf* labour; (*Agr*) farm work; (*tarea*) job, task; (*Costura*) needlework, sewing; (*punto*) knitting; **~ de equipo** teamwork; **~ de ganchillo** crochet

laborable [laβo'raβle] *adj* (*Agr*) workable; **día ~** working day

laboral [laβo'ral] *adj* (*accidente, conflictividad*) industrial; (*jornada*) working; (*derecho, relaciones*) labour *cpd*

laboralista [laβora'lista] *adj*: **abogado ~** labour lawyer

laborar [laβo'rar] *vi* to work

laboratorio [laβora'torjo] *nm* laboratory

laborioso, -a [laβo'rjoso, a] *adj* (*persona*) hard-working; (*trabajo*) tough

laborista [laβo'rista] (*Pol*) *adj*: **Partido L~** Labour Party ■ *nm/f* Labour Party member o supporter

labrado, -a [la'βraðo, a] *adj* worked; (*madera*) carved; (*metal*) wrought ■ *nm* (*Agr*) cultivated field

Labrador [laβra'ðor] *nm* Labrador

labrador, a [laβra'ðor, a] *nm/f* farmer

labranza [la'βranθa] *nf* (*Agr*) cultivation

labrar [la'βrar] *vt* (*gen*) to work; (*madera etc*) to carve; (*fig*) to cause, bring about

labriego, -a [la'βrjeɣo, a] *nm/f* peasant

laca ['laka] *nf* lacquer; (*de pelo*) hairspray; **~ de uñas** nail varnish

lacayo [la'kajo] *nm* lackey

lacerar [laθe'rar] *vt* to lacerate

lacio, -a ['laθjo, a] *adj* (*pelo*) lank, straight

lacón [la'kon] *nm* shoulder of pork

lacónico, -a [la'koniko, a] *adj* laconic

lacra ['lakra] *nf* (*defecto*) blemish; **~ social** social disgrace

lacrar [la'krar] *vt* (*cerrar*) to seal (with sealing wax)

lacre ['lakre] *nm* sealing wax

lacrimógeno, -a [lakri'moxeno, a] *adj* (*fig*) sentimental; **gas ~** tear gas

lacrimoso, -a [lakri'moso, a] *adj* tearful

lactancia [lak'tanθja] *nf* breast-feeding

lactar [lak'tar] *vt, vi* to suckle, breast-feed

lácteo, -a ['lakteo, a] *adj*: **productos lácteos** dairy products

ladear [laðe'ar] *vt* to tip, tilt ■ *vi* to tilt; **ladearse** *vr* to lean; (*Deporte*) to swerve; (*Aviat*) to bank, turn

ladera [la'ðera] *nf* slope

ladino, -a [la'ðino, a] *adj* cunning

lado ['laðo] *nm* (*gen*) side; (*fig*) protection; (*Mil*) flank; **~ izquierdo** left(-hand) side; **~ a ~** side by side; **al ~ de** next to, beside; **hacerse a un ~** to stand aside; **poner de ~** to put on its side; **poner a un ~** to put aside; **me da de ~** I don't care; **por un ~ ..., por otro ~ ...** on the one hand ..., on the other (hand) ...; **por todos lados** on all sides, all round (*Brit*)

ladrar [la'ðrar] *vi* to bark

ladrido [la'ðriðo] *nm* bark, barking

ladrillo [la'ðriʎo] *nm* (*gen*) brick; (*azulejo*) tile

ladrón, -ona [la'ðron, ona] *nm/f* thief

lagar [la'ɣar] *nm* (wine/oil) press

lagartija [laɣar'tixa] *nf* (small) lizard, wall lizard

lagarto [la'ɣarto] *nm* (*Zool*) lizard; (*Am*) alligator

lago ['laɣo] *nm* lake

Lagos ['laɣos] *nm* Lagos

lágrima ['laɣrima] *nf* tear

lagrimal [laɣri'mal] *nm* (inner) corner of the eye

lagrimear [laɣrime'ar] *vi* to weep; (*ojos*) to water

laguna [la'ɣuna] *nf* (*lago*) lagoon; (*en escrito, conocimientos*) gap

laico, -a ['laiko, a] *adj* lay ■ *nm/f* layman(-woman)

laja ['laxa] *nf* rock

lamber [lam'ber] *vt* (*Am*) to lick

lambiscón, -ona [lambis'kon, ona] *adj* flattering ■ *nm/f* flatterer

lameculos [lame'kulos] *nm/f inv* (*fam*) arse licker (!), crawler

lamentable [lamen'taβle] *adj* lamentable, regrettable; (*miserable*) pitiful

lamentación [lamenta'θjon] *nf* lamentation; **ahora no sirven lamentaciones** it's no good crying over spilt milk

lamentar [lamen'tar] *vt* (*sentir*) to regret; (*deplorar*) to lament; **lamentarse** *vr* to lament; **lo lamento mucho** I'm very sorry

lamento [la'mento] *nm* lament

lamer [la'mer] *vt* to lick

lámina ['lamina] *nf* (*plancha delgada*) sheet; (*para estampar, estampa*) plate; (*grabado*) engraving

laminar [lami'nar] *vt* (*en libro*) to laminate; (*Tec*) to roll

lámpara ['lampara] *nf* lamp; **~ de alcohol/ gas** spirit/gas lamp; **~ de pie** standard lamp

lamparilla [lampa'riʎa] *nf* night-light

lamparón [lampa'ron] *nm* (*Med*) scrofula; (*mancha*) (large) grease spot

lampiño, -a [lam'piɲo, a] *adj* (*sin pelo*) hairless

lana ['lana] *nf* wool; (*tela*) woollen (*Brit*) o woolen (*US*) cloth; (*Am fam: dinero*) dough; **(hecho) de ~** wool *cpd*

lance *etc* ['lanθe] *vb ver* **lanzar** ■ *nm* (*golpe*) stroke; (*suceso*) event, incident

lanceta [lan'seta] *nf* (*Am*) sting

lancha ['lantʃa] *nf* launch; **~ motora** motorboat; **~ de pesca** fishing boat; **~ salvavidas/torpedera** lifeboat/torpedo boat; **~ neumática** rubber dinghy

lanero, -a [la'nero, a] *adj* wool *cpd*

langosta [lan'gosta] *nf* (*insecto*) locust; (*crustáceo*) lobster; (*: de río*) crayfish

langostino [langos'tino] *nm* prawn; (*de agua dulce*) crayfish

languidecer [langiðe'θer] *vi* to languish

languidez [langi'ðeθ] *nf* languor

languidezca *etc* [langi'ðeθka] *vb ver* **languidecer**

lánguido, -a ['langiðo, a] *adj* (*gen*) languid; (*sin energía*) listless

lanilla [la'niʎa] *nf* nap; (*tela*) thin flannel cloth

lanolina [lano'lina] *nf* lanolin(e)

lanudo, -a [la'nuðo, a] *adj* woolly, fleecy

lanza ['lanθa] *nf* (*arma*) lance, spear; **medir lanzas** to cross swords

lanzacohetes [lanθako'etes] *nm inv* rocket launcher

lanzadera [lanθa'ðera] *nf* shuttle

lanzado, -a [lan'θaðo, a] *adj* (*atrevido*) forward; (*decidido*) determined; **ir ~** (*rápido*) to fly along

lanzallamas [lanθa'ʎamas] *nm inv* flamethrower

lanzamiento [lanθa'mjento] *nm* (*gen*) throwing; (*Naut, Com*) launch, launching; **~ de pesos** putting the shot

lanzar [lan'θar] *vt* (*gen*) to throw; (*con violencia*) to fling; (*Deporte: pelota*) to bowl, to pitch (*US*) (*Naut, Com*) to launch; (*Jur*) to evict; (*grito*) to give, utter; **lanzarse** *vr* to throw o.s.; (*fig*) to take the plunge; **lanzarse a** (*fig*) to embark upon

Lanzarote [lanθa'rote] *nm* Lanzarote

lanzatorpedos [lanθator'peðos] *nm inv* torpedo tube

lapa ['lapa] *nf* limpet

La Paz *nf* La Paz

lapicero [lapi'θero] *nm* pencil; (*Am*) propelling (*Brit*) o mechanical (*US*) pencil; (*: bolígrafo*) Biro®

lápida ['lapiða] *nf* stone; **~ conmemorativa** memorial stone; **~ mortuoria** headstone

lapidar [lapi'ðar] *vt* to stone; (*Tec*) to polish, lap

lapidario, -a [lapi'ðarjo, a] *adj, nm* lapidary

lápiz ['lapiθ] *nm* pencil; **~ de color** coloured pencil; **~ de labios** lipstick; **~ óptico** o **luminoso** light pen

lapón, -ona [la'pon, ona] *adj* Lapp ■ *nm/f* Laplander, Lapp ■ *nm* (*Ling*) Lapp

Laponia [la'ponja] *nf* Lapland

lapso ['lapso] *nm* lapse; (*error*) error; **~ de tiempo** interval of time

lapsus ['lapsus] *nm inv* error, mistake

LAR [lar] *nf abr* (*Esp Jur*) = **Ley de Arrendamientos Rústicos**

largamente [larɣa'mente] *adv* for a long time; (*relatar*) at length

largar [lar'ɣar] *vt* (*soltar*) to release; (*aflojar*) to loosen; (*lanzar*) to launch; (*fam*) to let fly; (*velas*) to unfurl; (*Am*) to throw; **largarse** *vr* (*fam*) to beat it; **largarse a** (*Am*) to start to

largo, -a ['larɣo, a] *adj* (*longitud*) long; (*tiempo*) lengthy; (*persona: alta*) tall; (*: fig*) generous

■ *nm* length; (*Mus*) largo; **dos años largos** two long years; **a ~ plazo** in the long term; **tiene nueve metros de ~** it is nine metres long; **a lo ~** (*posición*) lengthways; **a lo ~ de** along; (*tiempo*) all through, throughout; **a la larga** in the long run; **me dio largas con una promesa** she put me off with a promise; **¡~ de aquí!** (*fam*) clear off!

largometraje [larɣome'traxe] *nm* full-length *o* feature film

largüe *etc* ['larɣe] *vb ver* **largar**

larguero [lar'ɣero] *nm* (*Arq*) main beam, chief support; (*de puerta*) jamb; (*Deporte*) crossbar; (*de cama*) bolster

largueza [lar'ɣeθa] *nf* generosity

larguirucho, -a [larɣi'rutʃo, a] *adj* lanky, gangling

larguísimo, -a [lar'ɣisimo, a] *adj superlativo de* **largo**

largura [lar'ɣura] *nf* length

laringe [la'rinxe] *nf* larynx

laringitis [larin'xitis] *nf* laryngitis

larva ['larβa] *nf* larva

las [las] *artículo definido fpl* the ■ *pron* them; **~ que cantan** the ones/women/girls who sing

lasaña [la'saɲa] *nf* lasagne, lasagna

lasca ['laska] *nf* chip of stone

lascivia [las'θiβja] *nf* lewdness; (*lujuria*) lust; (*fig*) playfulness

lascivo, -a [las'θiβo, a] *adj* lewd

láser ['laser] *nm* laser

Las Palmas *nf* Las Palmas

lástima ['lastima] *nf* (*pena*) pity; **dar ~** to be pitiful; **es una ~ que** it's a pity that; **¡qué ~!** what a pity!; **estar hecho una ~** to be a sorry sight

lastimar [lasti'mar] *vt* (*herir*) to wound; (*ofender*) to offend; **lastimarse** *vr* to hurt o.s.

lastimero, -a [lasti'mero, a] *adj* pitiful, pathetic

lastre ['lastre] *nm* (*Tec, Naut*) ballast; (*fig*) dead weight

lata ['lata] *nf* (*metal*) tin; (*envase*) tin, can; (*fam*) nuisance; **en ~** tinned; **dar (la) ~** to be a nuisance

latente [la'tente] *adj* latent

lateral [late'ral] *adj* side, lateral ■ *nm* (*Teat*) wings *pl*

latido [la'tiðo] *nm* (*del corazón*) beat; (*de herida*) throb(bing)

latifundio [lati'fundjo] *nm* large estate

latifundista [latifun'dista] *nm/f* owner of a large estate

latigazo [lati'ɣaθo] *nm* (*golpe*) lash; (*sonido*) crack; (*fig: regaño*) dressing-down

látigo ['latiɣo] *nm* whip

latiguillo [lati'ɣiʎo] *nm* (*Teat*) hamming

latín [la'tin] *nm* Latin; **saber (mucho) ~** (*fam*) to be pretty sharp

latinajo [lati'naxo] *nm* dog Latin; **echar latinajos** to come out with Latin words

latino, -a [la'tino, a] *adj* Latin

Latinoamérica [latinoa'merika] *nf* Latin America

latinoamericano, -a [latinoameri'kano, a] *adj, nm/f* Latin American

latir [la'tir] *vi* (*corazón, pulso*) to beat

latitud [lati'tuð] *nf* (*Geo*) latitude; (*fig*) breadth, extent

lato, -a ['lato, a] *adj* broad

latón [la'ton] *nm* brass

latoso, -a [la'toso, a] *adj* (*molesto*) annoying; (*aburrido*) boring

latrocinio [latro'θinjo] *nm* robbery

LAU *nf abr* (*Esp Jur*) = **Ley de Arrendamientos Urbanos**

laúd [la'uð] *nm* lute

laudatorio, -a [lauða'torjo, a] *adj* laudatory

laudo ['lauðo] *nm* (*Jur*) decision, finding

laurear [laure'ar] *vt* to honour, reward

laurel [lau'rel] *nm* (*Bot*) laurel; (*Culin*) bay

Lausana [lau'sana] *nf* Lausanne

lava ['laβa] *nf* lava

lavable [la'βaβle] *adj* washable

lavabo [la'βaβo] *nm* (*jofaina*) washbasin; (*retrete*) lavatory (*Brit*), toilet (*Brit*), washroom (*US*)

lavadero [laβa'ðero] *nm* laundry

lavado [la'βaðo] *nm* washing; (*de ropa*) wash, laundry; (*Arte*) wash; **~ de cerebro** brainwashing

lavadora [laβa'ðora] *nf* washing machine

lavanda [la'βanda] *nf* lavender

lavandería [laβande'ria] *nf* laundry; **~ automática** launderette

lavaparabrisas [laβapara'βrisas] *nm inv* windscreen washer

lavaplatos [laβa'platos] *nm inv* dishwasher

lavar [la'βar] *vt* to wash; (*borrar*) to wipe away; **lavarse** *vr* to wash o.s.; **lavarse las manos** to wash one's hands; (*fig*) to wash one's hands of it; **~ y marcar** (*pelo*) to shampoo and set; **~ en seco** to dry-clean

lavativa [laβa'tiβa] *nf* (*Med*) enema

lavavajillas [laβaβa'xiʎas] *nm inv* dishwasher

laxante [lak'sante] *nm* laxative

laxitud [laksi'tuð] *nf* laxity, slackness

lazada [la'θaða] *nf* bow

lazarillo [laθa'riʎo] *nm*: **perro de ~** guide dog

lazo ['laθo] *nm* knot; (*lazada*) bow; (*para animales*) lasso; (*trampa*) snare; (*vínculo*) tie; **~ corredizo** slipknot

lb *abr* = **libra**

LBE *nf abr* (*Esp Jur*) = **Ley Básica de Empleo**
lbs *abr* = **libras**
L/C *abr* (= *Letra de Crédito*) B/E
Lda., Ldo. *abr* = **Licenciado, a**
le [le] *pron* (*directo*) him (*o* her); (: *en relación a usted*) you; (*indirecto*) to him (*o* her *o* it); (: *a usted*) to you
leal [le'al] *adj* loyal
lealtad [leal'tað] *nf* loyalty
lebrel [le'βrel] *nm* greyhound
lección [lek'θjon] *nf* lesson; ~ **práctica** object lesson; **dar lecciones** to teach, give lessons; **dar una ~ a algn** (*fig*) to teach sb a lesson
leche ['letʃe] *nf* milk; (*fam!*) semen, spunk (!); **dar una ~ a algn** (*fam*) to belt sb; **estar de mala ~** (*fam*) to be in a foul mood; **tener mala ~** (*fam*) to be a nasty piece of work; **~ condensada/en polvo** condensed/powdered milk; **~ desnatada** skimmed milk; **~ de magnesia** milk of magnesia; **¡~!** hell!
lechera [le'tʃera] *nf ver* **lechero**
lechería [letʃe'ria] *nf* dairy
lechero, -a [le'tʃero, a] *adj* milk *cpd* ■ *nm* milkman ■ *nf* (*vendedora*) milkwoman; (*recipiente*) milk pan; (*para servir*) milk churn
lecho ['letʃo] *nm* (*cama, de río*) bed; (*Geo*) layer; **~ mortuorio** deathbed
lechón [le'tʃon] *nm* sucking (*Brit*) *o* suckling (*US*) pig
lechoso, -a [le'tʃoso, a] *adj* milky
lechuga [le'tʃuɣa] *nf* lettuce
lechuza [le'tʃuθa] *nf* (barn) owl
lectivo, -a [lek'tiβo, a] *adj* (*horas*) teaching *cpd*; **año** *o* **curso ~** (*Escol*) school year; (*Univ*) academic year
lector, a [lek'tor, a] *nm/f* reader; (*Escol, Univ*) (conversation) assistant ■ *nm*: **~ óptico de caracteres** (*Inform*) optical character reader ■ *nf*: **lectora de fichas** (*Inform*) card reader
lectura [lek'tura] *nf* reading; **~ de marcas sensibles** (*Inform*) mark sensing
leer [le'er] *vt* to read; **~ entre líneas** to read between the lines
legación [leɣa'θjon] *nf* legation
legado [le'ɣaðo] *nm* (*don*) bequest; (*herencia*) legacy; (*enviado*) legate
legajo [le'ɣaxo] *nm* file, bundle (of papers)
legal [le'ɣal] *adj* legal, lawful; (*persona*) trustworthy
legalice *etc* [leɣa'liθe] *vb ver* **legalizar**
legalidad [leɣali'ðað] *nf* legality
legalizar [leɣali'θar] *vt* to legalize; (*documento*) to authenticate
legaña [le'ɣaɲa] *nf* sleep (*in eyes*)
legar [le'ɣar] *vt* to bequeath, leave
legatario, -a [leɣa'tarjo, a] *nm/f* legatee
legendario, -a [lexen'darjo, a] *adj* legendary

legible [le'xiβle] *adj* legible; **~ por máquina** (*Inform*) machine-readable
legión [le'xjon] *nf* legion
legionario, -a [lexjo'narjo, a] *adj* legionary ■ *nm* legionnaire
legislación [lexisla'θjon] *nf* legislation; (*leyes*) laws *pl*; **~ antimonopolio** (*Com*) anti-trust legislation
legislar [lexis'lar] *vt* to legislate
legislativo, -a [lexisla'tiβo, a] *adj*: (**elecciones**) **legislativas** ≈ general election
legislatura [lexisla'tura] *nf* (*Pol*) period of office
legitimar [lexiti'mar] *vt* to legitimize
legítimo, -a [le'xitimo, a] *adj* (*genuino*) authentic; (*legal*) legitimate, rightful
lego, -a ['leɣo, a] *adj* (*Rel*) secular; (*ignorante*) ignorant ■ *nm* layman
legua ['leɣwa] *nf* league; **se ve** (*o* **nota**) **a la ~** you can tell (it) a mile off
legue *etc* ['leɣe] *vb ver* **legar**
leguleyo [leɣu'lejo] *nm* (*pey*) petty *o* shyster (*US*) lawyer
legumbres [le'ɣumbres] *nfpl* pulses
leído, -a [le'iðo, a] *adj* well-read
lejanía [lexa'nia] *nf* distance
lejano, -a [le'xano, a] *adj* far-off; (*en el tiempo*) distant; (*fig*) remote; **L~ Oriente** Far East
lejía [le'xia] *nf* bleach
lejísimos [le'xisimos] *adv* a long, long way
lejos ['lexos] *adv* far, far away; **a lo ~** in the distance; **de** *o* **desde ~** from a distance; **está muy ~** it's a long way (away); **¿está ~?** is it far?; **~ de** *prep* far from
lelo, -a ['lelo, a] *adj* silly ■ *nm/f* idiot
lema ['lema] *nm* motto; (*Pol*) slogan
lencería [lenθe'ria] *nf* (*telas*) linen, drapery; (*ropa interior*) lingerie
lendakari [lenda'kari] *nm* *head of the Basque Autonomous Government*
lengua ['lengwa] *nf* tongue; **~ materna** mother tongue; **~ de tierra** (*Geo*) spit *o* tongue of land; **dar a la ~** to chatter; **morderse la ~** to hold one's tongue; **sacar la ~ a algn** (*fig*) to cock a snook at sb; *see note*

● **LENGUA**

● Under the Spanish constitution *lenguas*
● *cooficiales* or *oficiales* enjoy the same status
● as *castellano* in those regions which have
● retained their own distinct language,
● ie in Galicia, *gallego*; in the Basque
● Country, *euskera*; in Catalonia and the
● Balearic Islands, *catalán*. The regional
● governments actively promote their own
● language through the media and the

education system. Of the three regions with their own language, Catalonia has the highest number of people who speak the *lengua cooficial*.

lenguado [len'gwaðo] *nm* sole

lenguaje [len'gwaxe] *nm* language; (*forma de hablar*) (mode of) speech; ~ **comercial** business language; ~ **ensamblador** *o* **de alto nivel** (*Inform*) high-level language; ~ **máquina** (*Inform*) machine language; ~ **original** source language; ~ **periodístico** journalese; ~ **de programación** (*Inform*) programming language; **en ~ llano** ≈ in plain English

lenguaraz [lengwa'raθ] *adj* talkative; (*pey*) foul-mouthed

lengüeta [len'gweta] *nf* (*Anat*) epiglottis; (*de zapatos, Mus*) tongue

lenidad [leni'ðað] *nf* lenience

Leningrado [lenin'graðo] *nm* Leningrad

lente ['lente] *nm o nf* lens; (*lupa*) magnifying glass; **lentes** *nmpl* glasses; **lentes de contacto** contact lenses; **lentes progresivas** varifocal lenses

lenteja [len'texa] *nf* lentil

lentejuela [lente'xwela] *nf* sequin

lentilla [len'tiʎa] *nf* contact lens

lentitud [lenti'tuð] *nf* slowness; **con ~** slowly

lento, -a ['lento, a] *adj* slow

leña ['leɲa] *nf* firewood; **dar ~ a** to thrash; **echar ~ al fuego** to add fuel to the flames

leñador, a [leɲa'ðor, a] *nm/f* woodcutter

leño ['leɲo] *nm* (*trozo de árbol*) log; (*madera*) timber; (*fig*) blockhead

Leo ['leo] *nm* (*Astro*) Leo

león [le'on] *nm* lion; ~ **marino** sea lion

leonera [leo'nera] *nf* (*jaula*) lion's cage; **parece una ~** it's shockingly dirty

leonés, -esa [leo'nes, esa] *adj, nm/f* Leonese ■ *nm* (*Ling*) Leonese

leonino, -a [leo'nino, a] *adj* leonine

leopardo [leo'parðo] *nm* leopard

leotardos [leo'tarðos] *nmpl* tights

lepra ['lepra] *nf* leprosy

leprosería [leprose'ria] *nf* leper colony

leproso, -a [le'proso, a] *nm/f* leper

lerdo, -a ['lerðo, a] *adj* (*lento*) slow; (*patoso*) clumsy

leridano, -a [leri'ðano, a] *adj* of *o* from Lérida ■ *nm/f* native *o* inhabitant of Lérida

les [les] *pron* (*directo*) them; (: *en relación a ustedes*) you; (*indirecto*) to them; (: *a ustedes*) to you

lesbiana [les'βjana] *nf* lesbian

lesión [le'sjon] *nf* wound, lesion; (*Deporte*) injury

lesionado, -a [lesjo'naðo, a] *adj* injured ■ *nm/f* injured person

lesionar [lesjo'nar] *vt* (*dañar*) to hurt; (*herir*) to wound; **lesionarse** *vr* to get hurt

letal [le'tal] *adj* lethal

letanía [leta'nia] *nf* litany; (*retahíla*) long list

letárgico, -a [le'tarxiko, a] *adj* lethargic

letargo [le'tarɣo] *nm* lethargy

letón, -ona [le'ton, ona] *adj, nm/f* Latvian ■ *nm* (*Ling*) Latvian

Letonia [le'tonja] *nf* Latvia

letra ['letra] *nf* letter; (*escritura*) handwriting; (*Com*) letter, bill, draft; (*Mus*) lyrics *pl*; **letras** *nfpl* (*Univ*) arts; ~ **bastardilla/negrilla** italics *pl*/bold type; ~ **de cambio** bill of exchange; ~ **de imprenta** print; ~ **inicial/mayúscula/minúscula** initial/capital/small letter; **lo tomó al pie de la ~** he took it literally; ~ **bancaria** (*Com*) bank draft; ~ **de patente** (*Com*) letters patent *pl*; **escribir cuatro letras a algn** to drop a line to sb

letrado, -a [le'traðo, a] *adj* learned; (*fam*) pedantic ■ *nm/f* lawyer

letrero [le'trero] *nm* (*cartel*) sign; (*etiqueta*) label

letrina [le'trina] *nf* latrine

leucemia [leu'θemja] *nf* leukaemia

leucocito [leuko'θito] *nm* white blood cell, leucocyte

leva ['leβa] *nf* (*Naut*) weighing anchor; (*Mil*) levy; (*Tec*) lever

levadizo, -a [leβa'ðiθo, a] *adj*: **puente ~** drawbridge

levadura [leβa'ðura] *nf* yeast, leaven; ~ **de cerveza** brewer's yeast

levantamiento [leβanta'mjento] *nm* raising, lifting; (*rebelión*) revolt, rising; (*Geo*) survey; ~ **de pesos** weightlifting

levantar [leβan'tar] *vt* (*gen*) to raise; (*del suelo*) to pick up; (*hacia arriba*) to lift (up); (*plan*) to make, draw up; (*mesa*) to clear; (*campamento*) to strike; (*fig*) to cheer up, hearten; **levantarse** *vr* to get up; (*enderezarse*) to straighten up; (*rebelarse*) to rebel; (*sesión*) to be adjourned; (*niebla*) to lift; (*viento*) to rise; **levantarse (de la cama)** to get up, get out of bed; ~ **el ánimo** to cheer up

levante [le'βante] *nm* east; (*viento*) east wind; **el L~** *region of Spain extending from Castellón to Murcia*

levantino, -a [leβan'tino, a] *adj* of *o* from the *Levante* ■ *nm/f*: **los levantinos** the people of the *Levante*

levar [le'βar] *vi* to weigh anchor

leve ['leβe] *adj* light; (*fig*) trivial; (*mínimo*) slight

levedad [leβe'ðað] *nf* lightness; (*fig*) levity

levita [le'βita] *nf* frock coat
léxico, -a ['leksiko, a] *adj* lexical ■ *nm*
(*vocabulario*) vocabulary; (*Ling*) lexicon
ley [lei] *nf* (*gen*) law; (*metal*) standard;
decreto-~ decree law; **de buena ~** (*fig*)
genuine; **según la ~** in accordance with the
law, by law, in law
leyenda [le'jenda] *nf* legend; (*Tip*)
inscription
leyendo *etc* [le'jendo] *vb ver* **leer**
liar [li'ar] *vt* to tie (up); (*unir*) to bind; (*envolver*)
to wrap (up); (*enredar*) to confuse; (*cigarrillo*)
to roll; **liarse** *vr* (*fam*) to get involved;
(*confundirse*) to get mixed up; **liarse a palos**
to get involved in a fight
lib. *abr* (= *libro*) bk.
libanés, -esa [liβa'nes, esa] *adj, nm/f*
Lebanese
Líbano ['liβano] *nm*: **el ~** the Lebanon
libar [li'βar] *vt* to suck
libelo [li'βelo] *nm* satire, lampoon; (*Jur*)
petition
libélula [li'βelula] *nf* dragonfly
liberación [liβera'θjon] *nf* liberation; (*de la
cárcel*) release
liberado, -a [liβe'raðo, a] *adj* liberated; (*Com*)
paid-up, paid-in (*US*)
liberal [liβe'ral] *adj, nm/f* liberal
liberar [liβe'rar] *vt* to liberate
libertad [liβer'tað] *nf* liberty, freedom;
**~ de asociación/de culto/de prensa/
de comercio/de palabra** freedom of
association/of worship/of the press/of trade/
of speech; **~ condicional** probation; **~ bajo
palabra** parole; **~ bajo fianza** bail; **estar en
~** to be free; **poner a algn en ~** to set sb free
libertador, a [liβerta'ðor, a] *adj* liberating
■ *nm/f* liberator; **El L~** (*Am*) The Liberator
libertar [liβer'tar] *vt* (*preso*) to set free; (*de una
obligación*) to release; (*eximir*) to exempt
libertinaje [liβerti'naxe] *nm* licentiousness
libertino, -a [liβer'tino, a] *adj* permissive
■ *nm/f* permissive person
Libia ['liβja] *nf* Libya
libidinoso, -a [liβiði'noso, a] *adj* lustful;
(*viejo*) lecherous
libido [li'βiðo] *nf* libido
libio, -a ['liβjo, a] *adj, nm/f* Libyan
libra ['liβra] *nf* pound; **L~** (*Astro*) Libra;
~ esterlina pound sterling
librador, a [liβra'ðor, a] *nm/f* drawer
libranza [li'βranθa] *nf* (*Com*) draft; (*letra de
cambio*) bill of exchange
librar [li'βrar] *vt* (*de peligro*) to save; (*batalla*) to
wage, fight; (*de impuestos*) to exempt; (*cheque*)
to make out; (*Jur*) to exempt; **librarse** *vr*:
librarse de to escape from, free o.s. from;

de buena nos hemos librado we're well
out of that
libre ['liβre] *adj* (*gen*) free; (*lugar*) unoccupied;
(*tiempo*) spare; (*asiento*) vacant; (*Com*): **~ a
bordo** free on board; **~ de franqueo** post-
free; **~ de impuestos** free of tax; **tiro ~**
free kick; **los 100 metros ~** the 100 metres
freestyle (race); **al aire ~** in the open air;
¿estás ~? are you free?
librecambio [liβre'kambjo] *nm* free trade
librecambista [liβrekam'bista] *adj* free-
trade *cpd* ■ *nm* free-trader
librería [liβre'ria] *nf* (*tienda*) bookshop;
(*estante*) bookcase; **~ de ocasión** secondhand
bookshop
librero, -a [li'βrero, a] *nm/f* bookseller
libreta [li'βreta] *nf* notebook; (*pan*) one-
pound loaf; **~ de ahorros** savings book
libro ['liβro] *nm* book; **~ de actas** minute
book; **~ de bolsillo** paperback; **~ de
cabecera** bedside book; **~ de caja** (*Com*)
cashbook; **~ de caja auxiliar** (*Com*) petty
cash book; **~ de cocina** cookery book (*Brit*),
cookbook (*US*); **~ de consulta** reference
book; **~ de cuentas** account book; **~ de
cuentos** storybook; **~ de cheques** cheque
(*Brit*) *o* check (*US*) book; **~ diario** journal;
~ de entradas y salidas (*Com*) daybook;
~ de honor visitors' book; **~ electrónico**
e-book; **~ mayor** (*Com*) general ledger; **~ de
reclamaciones** complaints book; **~ de texto**
textbook
Lic. *abr* = **Licenciado, a**
licencia [li'θenθja] *nf* (*gen*) licence; (*permiso*)
permission; **~ por enfermedad/con goce de
sueldo** sick/paid leave; **~ de armas/de caza**
gun/game licence; **~ de exportación** (*Com*)
export licence; **~ poética** poetic licence
licenciado, -a [liθen'θjaðo, a] *adj* licensed
■ *nm/f* graduate; **L~ en Filosofía y Letras**
≈ Bachelor of Arts; *see note*

● **LICENCIADO**
●
● When students finish University after
● an average of five years they receive the
● degree of *licenciado*. If the course is only
● three years such as Nursing, or if they
● choose not to do the optional two-year
● specialization, they are awarded the
● degree of *diplomado*. *Cursos de posgrado*,
● postgraduate courses, are becoming
● increasingly popular, especially one-year
● specialist courses called *masters*.

licenciar [liθen'θjar] *vt* (*empleado*) to dismiss;
(*permitir*) to permit, allow; (*soldado*) to

discharge; (*estudiante*) to confer a degree upon; **licenciarse** *vr*: **licenciarse en letras** to get an arts degree

licenciatura [liθenθja'tura] *nf* (*título*) degree; (*estudios*) degree course

licencioso, -a [liθen'θjoso, a] *adj* licentious

liceo [li'θeo] *nm* (*esp Am*) (high) school

licitación [liθita'θjon] *nf* bidding; (*oferta*) tender, offer

licitador [liθita'ðor] *nm* bidder

licitar [liθi'tar] *vt* to bid for ▪ *vi* to bid

lícito, -a ['liθito, a] *adj* (*legal*) lawful; (*justo*) fair, just; (*permisible*) permissible

licor [li'kor] *nm* spirits *pl* (*Brit*), liquor (*US*); (*con hierbas etc*) liqueur

licra® ['likra] *nf* Lycra®

licuadora [likwa'ðora] *nf* blender

licuar [li'kwar] *vt* to liquidize

lid [lið] *nf* combat; (*fig*) controversy

líder ['liðer] *nm/f* leader

liderato [liðe'rato] *nm* = **liderazgo**

liderazgo [liðe'raθɣo] *nm* leadership

lidia ['liðja] *nf* bullfighting; (*una lidia*) bullfight; **toros de** ~ fighting bulls

lidiar [li'ðjar] *vt*, *vi* to fight

liebre ['ljeβre] *nf* hare; **dar gato por** ~ to con

Lieja ['ljexa] *nf* Liège

lienzo ['ljenθo] *nm* linen; (*Arte*) canvas; (*Arq*) wall

lifting ['liftin] *nm* facelift

liga ['liɣa] *nf* (*de medias*) garter, suspender; (*confederación*) league; (*Am: gomita*) rubber band

ligadura [liɣa'ðura] *nf* bond, tie; (*Med, Mus*) ligature

ligamento [liɣa'mento] *nm* (*Anat*) ligament; (*atadura*) tie; (*unión*) bond

ligar [li'ɣar] *vt* (*atar*) to tie; (*unir*) to join; (*Med*) to bind up; (*Mus*) to slur; (*fam*) to get off with, pick up ▪ *vi* to mix, blend; (*fam*) to get off with sb; (2 *personas*) to get off with one another; **ligarse** *vr* (*fig*) to commit o.s.; ~ **con** (*fam*) to get off with, pick up; **ligarse a algn** to get off with o pick up sb

ligereza [lixe'reθa] *nf* lightness; (*rapidez*) swiftness; (*agilidad*) agility; (*superficialidad*) flippancy

ligero, -a [li'xero, a] *adj* (*de peso*) light; (*tela*) thin; (*rápido*) swift, quick; (*ágil*) agile, nimble; (*de importancia*) slight; (*de carácter*) flippant, superficial ▪ *adv* quickly, swiftly; **a la ligera** superficially; **juzgar a la ligera** to jump to conclusions

light ['lait] *adj inv* (*cigarrillo*) low-tar; (*comida*) diet *cpd*

ligón [li'ɣon] *nm* (*fam*) Romeo

ligue *etc* ['liɣe] *vb ver* **ligar** ▪ *nm/f* boyfriend/girlfriend ▪ *nm* (*persona*) pick-up

liguero [li'ɣero] *nm* suspender (*Brit*) o garter (*US*) belt

lija ['lixa] *nf* (*Zool*) dogfish; (**papel de**) ~ sandpaper

lijar [li'xar] *vt* to sand

lila ['lila] *adj inv*, *nf* lilac ▪ *nm* (*fam*) twit

lima ['lima] *nf* file; (*Bot*) lime; ~ **de uñas** nail file; **comer como una** ~ to eat like a horse

limar [li'mar] *vt* to file; (*alisar*) to smooth over; (*fig*) to polish up

limbo ['limbo] *nm* (*Rel*) limbo; **estar en el** ~ to be on another planet

limitación [limita'θjon] *nf* limitation, limit; ~ **de velocidad** speed limit

limitado, -a [limi'taðo, a] *adj* limited; **sociedad limitada** (*Com*) limited company

limitar [limi'tar] *vt* to limit; (*reducir*) to reduce, cut down ▪ *vi*: ~ **con** to border on; **limitarse** *vr*: **limitarse a** to limit o confine o.s. to

límite ['limite] *nm* (*gen*) limit; (*fin*) end; (*frontera*) border; **como** ~ at (the) most; (*fecha*) at the latest; **no tener límites** to know no bounds; ~ **de crédito** (*Com*) credit limit; ~ **de página** (*Inform*) page break; ~ **de velocidad** speed limit

limítrofe [li'mitrofe] *adj* bordering, neighbouring

limón [li'mon] *nm* lemon ▪ *adj*: **amarillo** ~ lemon-yellow

limonada [limo'naða] *nf* lemonade

limonero [limo'nero] *nm* lemon tree

limosna [li'mosna] *nf* alms *pl*; **pedir** ~ to beg; **vivir de** ~ to live on charity

limpiabotas [limpja'βotas] *nm/f inv* bootblack (*Brit*), shoeshine boy/girl

limpiacristales [limpjakris'tales] *nm inv* (*detergente*) window cleaner

limpiador, a [limpja'ðor, a] *adj* cleaning, cleansing ▪ *nm/f* cleaner

limpiaparabrisas [limpjapara'βrisas] *nm inv* windscreen (*Brit*) o windshield (*US*) wiper

limpiar [lim'pjar] *vt* to clean; (*con trapo*) to wipe; (*quitar*) to wipe away; (*zapatos*) to shine, polish; (*casa*) to tidy up; (*Inform*) to debug; (*fig*) to clean up; (: *purificar*) to cleanse, purify; (*Mil*) to mop up; ~ **en seco** to dry-clean

limpieza [lim'pjeθa] *nf* (*estado*) cleanliness; (*acto*) cleaning; (: *de las calles*) cleansing; (: *de zapatos*) polishing; (*habilidad*) skill; (*fig: Policía*) clean-up; (*pureza*) purity; (*Mil*): **operación de** ~ mopping-up operation; ~ **étnica** ethnic cleansing; ~ **en seco** dry cleaning

limpio, -a ['limpjo, a] *adj* clean; (*moralmente*) pure; (*ordenado*) tidy; (*despejado*) clear; (*Com*) clear, net; (*fam*) honest ▪ *adv*: **jugar** ~ to play fair; **pasar a** ~ to make a fair copy; **sacar**

algo en ~ to get benefit from sth; **~ de** free from

linaje [li'naxe] *nm* lineage, family

linaza [li'naθa] *nf* linseed; **aceite de ~** linseed oil

lince ['linθe] *nm* lynx; **ser un ~** (*fig: observador*) to be very observant; (*: astuto*) to be shrewd

linchar [lin'tʃar] *vt* to lynch

lindante [lin'dante] *adj* adjoining; **~ con** bordering on

lindar [lin'dar] *vi* to adjoin; **~ con** to border on; (*Arq*) to abut on

linde ['linde] *nm o nf* boundary

lindero, -a [lin'dero, a] *adj* adjoining ■ *nm* boundary

lindo, -a ['lindo, a] *adj* pretty, lovely ■ *adv* (*esp Am: fam*) nicely, very well; **canta muy ~** (*Am*) he sings beautifully; **se divertían de lo ~** they enjoyed themselves enormously

línea ['linea] *nf* (*gen, moral, Pol etc*) line; (*talle*) figure; (*Inform*): **en ~** on line; **fuera de ~** off line; **~ de estado** status line; **~ de formato** format line; **~ aérea** airline; **~ de alto el fuego** ceasefire line; **~ de fuego** firing line; **~ de meta** goal line; (*de carrera*) finishing line; **~ de montaje** assembly line; **~ dura** (*Pol*) hard line; **~ recta** straight line; **la ~ de 2008** (*moda*) the 2008 look

lineal [line'al] *adj* linear

lingote [lin'gote] *nm* ingot

lingüista [lin'gwista] *nm/f* linguist

lingüística [lin'gwistika] *nf* linguistics *sg*

linimento [lini'mento] *nm* liniment

lino ['lino] *nm* linen; (*Bot*) flax

linóleo [li'noleo] *nm* lino, linoleum

linterna [lin'terna] *nf* lantern, lamp; **~ eléctrica** o **a pilas** torch (*Brit*), flashlight (*US*)

lío ['lio] *nm* bundle; (*desorden*) muddle, mess; (*fam: follón*) fuss; (*: relación amorosa*) affair; **armar un ~** to make a fuss; **meterse en un ~** to get into a jam; **tener un ~ con algn** to be having an affair with sb

lipotimia [lipo'timja] *nf* blackout

liquen ['liken] *nm* lichen

liquidación [likiða'θjon] *nf* liquidation; (*de cuenta*) settlement; **venta de ~** clearance sale

liquidar [liki'ðar] *vt* (*Química*) to liquefy; (*Com*) to liquidate; (*deudas*) to pay off; (*empresa*) to wind up; **~ a algn** to bump sb off, rub sb out (*fam*)

liquidez [liki'ðeθ] *nf* liquidity

líquido, -a ['likiðo, a] *adj* liquid; (*ganancia*) net ■ *nm* liquid; (*Com: efectivo*) ready cash o money; (*: ganancia*) net amount o profit; **~ imponible** net taxable income

lira ['lira] *nf* (*Mus*) lyre; (*moneda*) lira

lírico, -a ['liriko, a] *adj* lyrical

lirio ['lirjo] *nm* (*Bot*) iris

lirismo [li'rismo] *nm* lyricism; (*sentimentalismo*) sentimentality

lirón [li'ron] *nm* (*Zool*) dormouse; (*fig*) sleepyhead

Lisboa [lis'βoa] *nf* Lisbon

lisboeta [lisβo'eta] *adj* of o from Lisbon ■ *nm/f* native o inhabitant of Lisbon

lisiado, -a [li'sjaðo, a] *adj* injured ■ *nm/f* cripple

lisiar [li'sjar] *vt* to maim; **lisiarse** *vr* to injure o.s.

liso, -a ['liso, a] *adj* (*terreno*) flat; (*cabello*) straight; (*superficie*) even; (*tela*) plain; **lisa y llanamente** in plain language, plainly

lisonja [li'sonxa] *nf* flattery

lisonjear [lisonxe'ar] *vt* to flatter; (*fig*) to please

lisonjero, -a [lison'xero, a] *adj* flattering; (*agradable*) gratifying, pleasing ■ *nm/f* flatterer

lista ['lista] *nf* list; (*de alumnos*) school register; (*de libros*) catalogue; (*de correos*) poste restante; (*de platos*) menu; (*de precios*) price list; **pasar ~** to call the roll; (*Escol*) to call the register; **~ de correos** poste restante; **~ de direcciones** mailing list; **~ electoral** electoral roll; **~ de espera** waiting list; **tela a listas** striped material

listado, -a [lis'taðo, a] *adj* striped ■ *nm* (*Com, Inform*) listing; **~ paginado** (*Inform*) paged listing

listar [lis'tar] *vt* (*Inform*) to list

listo, -a ['listo, a] *adj* (*perspicaz*) smart, clever; (*preparado*) ready; **~ para usar** ready-to-use; **¿estás ~?** are you ready?; **pasarse de ~** to be too clever by half

listón [lis'ton] *nm* (*de tela*) ribbon; (*de madera, metal*) strip

litera [li'tera] *nf* (*en barco, tren*) berth; (*en dormitorio*) bunk, bunk bed

literal [lite'ral] *adj* literal

literario, -a [lite'rarjo, a] *adj* literary

literato, -a [lite'rato, a] *nm/f* writer

literatura [litera'tura] *nf* literature

litigante [liti'ɣante] *nm/f* litigant, claimant

litigar [liti'ɣar] *vt* to fight ■ *vi* (*Jur*) to go to law; (*fig*) to dispute, argue

litigio [li'tixjo] *nm* (*Jur*) lawsuit; (*fig*): **en ~ con** in dispute with

litigue *etc* [li'tiɣe] *vb ver* **litigar**

litografía [litoɣra'fia] *nf* lithography; (*una litografía*) lithograph

litoral [lito'ral] *adj* coastal ■ *nm* coast, seaboard

litro ['litro] *nm* litre, liter (*US*)

Lituania [li'twanja] *nf* Lithuania

lituano, -a [li'twano, a] *adj, nm/f* Lithuanian ■ *nm* (*Ling*) Lithuanian

liturgia [li'turxja] *nf* liturgy

liviano, -a [li'βjano, a] *adj* (*persona*) fickle; (*cosa, objeto*) trivial; (*Am*) light

lívido, -a ['liβiðo, a] *adj* livid

living ['liβin] (*pl* **livings**) *nm* (*esp Am*) sitting room

Ll, ll ['eʎe] *nf former letter in the Spanish alphabet*

llaga ['ʎaɣa] *nf* wound

llagar [ʎa'ɣar] *vt* to make sore; (*herir*) to wound

llague *etc* ['ʎaɣe] *vb ver* **llagar**

llama ['ʎama] *nf* flame; (*fig*) passion; (*Zool*) llama; **en llamas** burning, ablaze

llamada [ʎa'maða] *nf* call; (*a la puerta*) knock; (: *al timbre*) ring; **~ a cobro revertido** reverse-charge call; **~ al orden** call to order; **~ a pie de página** reference note; **~ a procedimiento** (*Inform*) procedure call; **~ interurbana** trunk call

llamado [ʎa'maðo] *nm* (*Am*) (telephone) call; (*llamamiento*) appeal, call

llamamiento [ʎama'mjento] *nm* call; **hacer un ~ a algn para que haga algo** to appeal to sb to do sth

llamar [ʎa'mar] *vt* to call; (*convocar*) to summon; (*invocar*) to invoke; (*atraer con gesto*) to beckon; (*atención*) to attract; (*Telec: tb:* **llamar por teléfono**) to call, ring up, telephone; (*Mil*) to call up ■ *vi* (*por teléfono*) to phone; (*a la puerta*) to knock (*o* ring); (*por señas*) to beckon; **llamarse** *vr* to be called, be named; **¿cómo se llama usted?** what's your name?; **¿quién llama?** (*Telec*) who's calling?, who's that?; **no me llama la atención** (*fam*) I don't fancy it

llamarada [ʎama'raða] *nf* (*llamas*) blaze; (*rubor*) flush; (*fig*) flare-up

llamativo, -a [ʎama'tiβo, a] *adj* showy; (*color*) loud

llamear [ʎame'ar] *vi* to blaze

llanamente [ʎana'mente] *adv* (*lisamente*) smoothly; (*sin ostentaciones*) plainly; (*sinceramente*) frankly; *ver tb* **liso**

llaneza [ʎa'neθa] *nf* (*gen*) simplicity; (*honestidad*) straightforwardness, frankness

llano, -a ['ʎano, a] *adj* (*superficie*) flat; (*persona*) straightforward; (*estilo*) clear ■ *nm* plain, flat ground

llanta ['ʎanta] *nf* (wheel) rim; (*Am: neumático*) tyre; (: *cámara*) (inner) tube

llanto ['ʎanto] *nm* weeping; (*fig*) lamentation; (*canción*) dirge, lament

llanura [ʎa'nura] *nf* (*lisura*) flatness, smoothness; (*Geo*) plain

llave ['ʎaβe] *nf* key; (*de gas, agua*) tap (Brit), faucet (US); (*Mecánica*) spanner; (*de la luz*) switch; (*Mus*) key; **~ inglesa** monkey wrench; **~ maestra** master key; **~ de contacto** (*Auto*) ignition key; **~ de paso** stopcock; **echar ~ a** to lock up

llavero [ʎa'βero] *nm* keyring

llavín [ʎa'βin] *nm* latchkey

llegada [ʎe'ɣaða] *nf* arrival

llegar [ʎe'ɣar] *vt* to bring up, bring over ■ *vi* to arrive; (*bastar*) to be enough; **llegarse** *vr*: **llegarse a** to approach; **~ a** (*alcanzar*) to reach; to manage to, succeed in; **~ a saber** to find out; **~ a ser famoso/el jefe** to become famous/the boss; **~ a las manos** to come to blows; **~ a las manos de** to come into the hands of; **no llegues tarde** don't be late; **esta cuerda no llega** this rope isn't long enough

llegue *etc* ['ʎeɣe] *vb ver* **llegar**

llenar [ʎe'nar] *vt* to fill; (*superficie*) to cover; (*espacio, tiempo*) to fill, take up; (*formulario*) to fill in *o* out; (*fig*) to heap; **llenarse** *vr* to fill (up); **llenarse de** (*fam*) to stuff o.s. with

lleno, -a ['ʎeno, a] *adj* full, filled; (*repleto*) full up ■ *nm* (*abundancia*) abundance; (*Teat*) full house; **dar de ~ contra un muro** to hit a wall head-on

llevadero, -a [ʎeβa'ðero, a] *adj* bearable, tolerable

llevar [ʎe'βar] *vt* to take; (*ropa*) to wear; (*cargar*) to carry; (*quitar*) to take away; (*en coche*) to drive; (*transportar*) to transport; (*ruta*) to follow, keep to; (*traer: dinero*) to carry; (*suj: camino etc*): **~ a** to lead to; (*Mat*) to carry; (*aguantar*) to bear; (*negocio*) to conduct, direct; to manage; **llevarse** *vr* to carry off, take away; **llevamos dos días aquí** we have been here for two days; **él me lleva dos años** he's two years older than me; **~ adelante** (*fig*) to carry forward; **~ por delante a uno** (*en coche etc*) to run sb over; (*fig*) to ride roughshod over sb; **~ la ventaja** to be winning *o* in the lead; **~ los libros** (*Com*) to keep the books; **llevo las de perder** I'm likely to lose; **no las lleva todas consigo** he's not all there; **nos llevó a cenar fuera** she took us out for a meal; **llevarse a uno por delante** (*atropellar*) to run sb over; **llevarse bien** to get on well (together)

llorar [ʎo'rar] *vt* to cry, weep ■ *vi* to cry, weep; (*ojos*) to water; **~ a moco tendido** to sob one's heart out; **~ de risa** to cry with laughter

lloriquear [ʎorike'ar] *vi* to snivel, whimper

lloro ['ʎoro] *nm* crying, weeping

llorón, -ona [ʎo'ron, ona] *adj* tearful ■ *nm/f* cry-baby

lloroso, -a [ʎo'roso, a] *adj* (*gen*) weeping,

tearful; (triste) sad, sorrowful

llover [ʎo'βer] vi to rain; **~ a cántaros** o **a cubos** o **a mares** to rain cats and dogs, pour (down); **ser una cosa llovida del cielo** to be a godsend; **llueve sobre mojado** it never rains but it pours

llovizna [ʎo'βiθna] nf drizzle

llovizna [ʎoβiθ'nar] vi to drizzle

llueve etc ['ʎweβe] vb ver **llover**

lluvia ['ʎuβja] nf rain; (cantidad) rainfall; (fig: de balas etc) hail, shower; **~ radioactiva** radioactive fallout; **día de ~** rainy day; **una ~ de regalos** a shower of gifts

lluvioso, -a [ʎu'βjoso, a] adj rainy

lo [lo] artículo definido neutro: **lo bueno** the good ▪ pron (en relación a una persona) him; (en relación a una cosa) it; **lo mío** what is mine; **lo difícil es que ...** the difficult thing about it is that ...; **no saben lo aburrido que es** they don't know how boring it is; **viste a lo americano** he dresses in the American style; **lo de** that matter of; **lo que** what, that which; **toma lo que quieras** take what(ever) you want; **lo que sea** whatever; **¡toma lo que he dicho!** I stand by what I said!

loa ['loa] nf praise

loable [lo'aβle] adj praiseworthy

LOAPA [lo'apa] nf abr (Esp Jur) = **Ley Orgánica de Armonización del Proceso Autónomo**

loar [lo'ar] vt to praise

lobato [lo'βato] nm (Zool) wolf cub

lobo ['loβo] nm wolf; **~ de mar** (fig) sea dog; **~ marino** seal

lóbrego, -a ['loβreɣo, a] adj dark; (fig) gloomy

lóbulo ['loβulo] nm lobe

LOC nm abr (= lector óptico de caracteres) OCR

local [lo'kal] adj local ▪ nm place, site; (oficinas) premises pl

localice etc [loka'liθe] vb ver **localizar**

localidad [lokali'ðað] nf (barrio) locality; (lugar) location; (Teat) seat, ticket

localizador nm (de un vuelo) booking reference, reservation code

localizar [lokali'θar] vt (ubicar) to locate, find; (encontrar) to find, track down; (restringir) to localize; (situar) to place

loción [lo'θjon] nf lotion, wash

loco, -a ['loko, a] adj mad; (fig) wild, mad ▪ nm/f lunatic, madman(-woman); **~ de atar, ~ de remate, ~ rematado** raving mad; **a lo ~** without rhyme or reason; **ando ~ con el examen** the exam is driving me crazy; **estar ~ de alegría** to be overjoyed o over the moon

locomoción [lokomo'θjon] nf locomotion

locomotora [lokomo'tora] nf engine, locomotive

locuaz [lo'kwaθ] adj loquacious, talkative

locución [loku'θjon] nf expression

locura [lo'kura] nf madness; (acto) crazy act

locutor, a [loku'tor, a] nm/f (Radio) announcer; (comentarista) commentator; (TV) newscaster, newsreader

locutorio [loku'torjo] nm (Telec) telephone box o booth; (negocio) shop or internet café providing telephone services

lodo ['lodo] nm mud

logia ['loxja] nf (Mil, de masones) lodge; (Arq) loggia

lógico, -a ['loxiko, a] adj logical; (correcto) natural; (razonable) reasonable ▪ nm logician ▪ nf logic; **es ~ que ...** it stands to reason that ...; **ser de una lógica aplastante** to be as clear as day

logístico, -a [lo'xistiko, a] adj logistical ▪ nf logistics pl

logotipo [loɣo'tipo] nm logo

logrado, -a [lo'ɣraðo, a] adj accomplished

lograr [lo'ɣrar] vt (obtener) to get, obtain; (conseguir) to achieve, attain; **~ hacer** to manage to do; **~ que algn venga** to manage to get sb to come; **~ acceso a** (Inform) to access

logro ['loɣro] nm achievement, success; (Com) profit

logroñés, -esa [logro'ɲes, esa] adj of o from Logroño ▪ nm/f native o inhabitant of Logroño

Loira ['loira] nm Loire

loma ['loma] nf hillock, low ridge

Lombardía [lombar'ðia] nf Lombardy

lombriz [lom'briθ] nf (earth)worm

lomo ['lomo] nm (de animal) back; (Culin: de cerdo) pork loin; (: de vaca) rib steak; (de libro) spine

lona ['lona] nf canvas

loncha ['lontʃa] nf = **lonja**

lonche ['lontʃe] nm (Am) lunch

lonchería [lontʃe'ria] nf (Am) snack bar, diner (US)

londinense [londi'nense] adj London cpd, of o from London ▪ nm/f Londoner

Londres ['londres] nm London

longaniza [longa'niθa] nf pork sausage

longevidad [lonxeβi'ðað] nf longevity

longitud [lonxi'tuð] nf length; (Geo) longitude; **tener tres metros de ~** to be three metres long; **~ de onda** wavelength; **salto de ~** long jump

longitudinal [lonxituði'nal] adj longitudinal

lonja ['lonxa] nf slice; (de tocino) rasher; (Com) market, exchange; **~ de pescado** fish market

lontananza [lonta'nanθa] nf background; **en ~** far away, in the distance

Lorena [lo'rena] nf Lorraine

loro ['loro] *nm* parrot
los [los] *artículo definido mpl* the ■ *pron* them; (*en relación a ustedes*) you; **mis libros y ~ de usted** my books and yours
losa ['losa] *nf* stone; **~ sepulcral** gravestone
lote ['lote] *nm* portion, share; (*Com*) lot; (*Inform*) batch
lotería [lote'ria] *nf* lottery; (*juego*) lotto; **le tocó la ~** he won a big prize in the lottery; (*fig*) he struck lucky; **~ nacional** national lottery; **~ primitiva** (*Esp*) *type of state-run lottery; see note*

  ● **LOTERÍA**
  ●
  ● Millions of pounds are spent every year
  ● on *loterías*, lotteries. There is the weekly
  ● *Lotería Nacional* which is very popular
  ● especially at Christmas. Other weekly
  ● lotteries are the *Bono Loto* and the (*Lotería*)
  ● *Primitiva*. One of the most famous lotteries
  ● is run by the wealthy and influential
  ● society for the blind, *la ONCE*, and the
  ● form is called *el cupón de la ONCE* or *el cupón*
  ● *de los ciegos*.

lotero, -a [lo'tero, a] *nm/f* seller of lottery tickets
Lovaina [lo'βaina] *nf* Louvain
loza ['loθa] *nf* crockery; **~ fina** china
lozanía [loθa'nia] *nf* (*lujo*) luxuriance
lozano, -a [lo'θano, a] *adj* luxuriant; (*animado*) lively
LPA *sigla f* (= *Ley del Proceso Autonómico*) *law for the autonomy of the regions*
LRA *sigla f* = **Ley de Reforma Agraria**
LRU *sigla f* = **Ley de Reforma Universitaria**
LSD *sigla m* (= *Dietilamida del Acido Lisérgico*) LSD
lubina [lu'βina] *nf* (*Zool*) sea bass
lubricante [luβri'kante] *adj, nm* lubricant
lubricar [luβri'kar], **lubrificar** [luβrifi'kar] *vt* to lubricate
lubrique *etc* [lu'βrike] *vb ver* **lubricar**
lucense [lu'θense] *adj* of o from Lugo ■ *nm/f* native o inhabitant of Lugo
Lucerna [lu'θerna] *nf* Lucerne
lucero [lu'θero] *nm* (*Astro*) bright star; (*fig*) brilliance; **~ del alba/de la tarde** morning/evening star
luces ['luθes] *nfpl de* **luz**
lucha ['lutʃa] *nf* fight, struggle; **~ de clases** class struggle; **~ libre** wrestling
luchar [lu'tʃar] *vi* to fight
lucidez [luθi'ðeθ] *nf* lucidity
lucido, -a [lu'θiðo, a] *adj* (*espléndido*) splendid, brilliant; (*elegante*) elegant; (*exitoso*) successful

lúcido, -a ['luθiðo, a] *adj* lucid
luciérnaga [lu'θjernaɣa] *nf* glow-worm
lucimiento [luθi'mjento] *nm* (*brillo*) brilliance; (*éxito*) success
lucio ['luθjo] *nm* (*Zool*) pike
lucir [lu'θir] *vt* to illuminate, light (up); (*ostentar*) to show off ■ *vi* (*brillar*) to shine; (*Am: parecer*) to look, seem; **lucirse** *vr* (*irónico*) to make a fool of o.s.; (*presumir*) to show off; **la casa luce limpia** the house looks clean
lucrativo, -a [lukra'tiβo, a] *adj* lucrative, profitable; **institución no lucrativa** non profit-making institution
lucro ['lukro] *nm* profit, gain; **lucros y daños** (*Com*) profit and loss *sg*
luctuoso, -a [luk'twoso, a] *adj* mournful
lúdico, -a ['luðiko, a] *adj* playful; (*actividad*) recreational
ludopatía [luðopa'tia] *nf* addiction to gambling (o videogames)
luego ['lweɣo] *adv* (*después*) next; (*más tarde*) later, afterwards; (*Am fam: en seguida*) at once, immediately; **desde ~** of course; **¡hasta ~!** see you later!, so long!; **¿y ~?** what next?
lugar [lu'ɣar] *nm* place; (*sitio*) spot; (*pueblo*) village, town; **en ~ de** instead of; **en primer ~** in the first place, firstly; **dar ~ a** to give rise to; **hacer ~** to make room; **fuera de ~** out of place; **tener ~** to take place; **~ común** commonplace; **yo en su ~** if I were him; **no hay ~ para preocupaciones** there is no cause for concern
lugareño, -a [luɣa'reɲo, a] *adj* village *cpd* ■ *nm/f* villager
lugarteniente [luɣarte'njente] *nm* deputy
lúgubre ['luɣuβre] *adj* mournful
lujo ['luxo] *nm* luxury; (*fig*) profusion, abundance; **de ~** luxury *cpd*, de luxe
lujoso, -a [lu'xoso, a] *adj* luxurious
lujuria [lu'xurja] *nf* lust
lumbago [lum'baɣo] *nm* lumbago
lumbre ['lumbre] *nf* (*luz*) light; (*fuego*) fire; **cerca de la ~** near the fire, at the fireside; **¿tienes ~?** (*para cigarro*) have you got a light?
lumbrera [lum'brera] *nf* luminary; (*fig*) leading light
luminoso, -a [lumi'noso, a] *adj* luminous, shining; (*idea*) bright, brilliant
luna ['luna] *nf* moon; (*vidrio: escaparate*) plate glass; (: *de un espejo*) glass; (: *de gafas*) lens; (*fig*) crescent; **~ creciente/llena/menguante/nueva** crescent/full/waning/new moon; **~ de miel** honeymoon; **estar en la ~** to have one's head in the clouds
lunar [lu'nar] *adj* lunar ■ *nm* (*Anat*) mole; **tela a lunares** spotted material
lunes ['lunes] *nm inv* Monday; *ver tb* **sábado**

luneta [luˈneta] *nf* lens
lupa [ˈlupa] *nf* magnifying glass
lusitano, -a [lusiˈtano, a], **luso, -a** [ˈluso, a] *adj, nm/f* Portuguese
lustrador [lustraˈðor] *nm* (*Am*) bootblack
lustrar [lusˈtrar] *vt* (*esp Am: mueble*) to polish; (*zapatos*) to shine
lustre [ˈlustre] *nm* polish; (*fig*) lustre; **dar ~ a** to polish
lustro [ˈlustro] *nm* period of five years
lustroso, -a [lusˈtroso, a] *adj* shining
luterano, -a [luteˈrano, a] *adj* Lutheran
luto [ˈluto] *nm* mourning; (*congoja*) grief, sorrow; **llevar el** *o* **vestirse de ~** to be in mourning
luxación [luksaˈθjon] *nf* (*Med*) dislocation; **tener una ~ de tobillo** to have a dislocated ankle
Luxemburgo [luksemˈburɣo] *nm* Luxembourg

luz [luθ] (*pl* **luces**) *nf* (*tb fig*) light; (*fam*) electricity; **dar a ~ un niño** to give birth to a child; **sacar a la ~** to bring to light; **dar la ~** to switch on the light; **encender** (*Esp*) *o* **prender** (*Am*)/**apagar la ~** to switch the light on/off; **les cortaron la ~** their (electricity) supply was cut off; **a la ~ de** in the light of; **a todas luces** by any reckoning; **hacer la ~ sobre** to shed light on; **tener pocas luces** to be dim *o* stupid; **~ de la luna/del sol** *o* **solar** moonlight/sunlight; **~ eléctrica** electric light; **~ roja/verde** red/green light; **~ de cruce** (*Auto*) dipped headlight; **~ de freno** brake light; **~ intermitente/trasera** flashing/rear light; **luces de tráfico** traffic lights; **el Siglo de las Luces** the Age of Enlightenment; **traje de luces** bullfighter's costume

Mm

M, m ['eme] *nf* (*letra*) M, m; **M de Madrid** M
for Mike

M. *abr* (*Ferro*) = **Metro**; (= *mujer*) F

m *abr* (= *metro(s)*) m; (= *minuto(s)*) min., m;
(= *masculino*) m., masc

M.ª *abr* = **María**

macabro, -a [ma'kaβro, a] *adj* macabre

macaco [ma'kako] *nm* (*Zool*) rhesus monkey;
(*fam*) runt, squirt

macana [ma'kana] *nf* (*Am: porra*) club;
(: *mentira*) lie, fib; (: *tontería*) piece of nonsense

macanudo, -a [maka'nuðo, a] *adj* (*Am fam*)
great

macarra [ma'karra] *nm* (*fam*) thug

macarrones [maka'rrones] *nmpl* macaroni *sg*

Macedonia [maθe'ðonja] *nf* Macedonia

macedonia [maθe'ðonja] *nf*: ~ **de frutas**
fruit salad

macedonio [maθe'ðonjo] *adj, nm/f*
Macedonian ■ *nm* (*Ling*) Macedonian

macerar [maθe'rar] *vt* (*Culin*) to soak,
macerate; **macerarse** *vr* to soak, soften

maceta [ma'θeta] *nf* (*de flores*) pot of flowers;
(*para plantas*) flowerpot

macetero [maθe'tero] *nm* flowerpot stand
o holder

machacar [matʃa'kar] *vt* to crush, pound;
(*moler*) to grind (up); (*aplastar*) to mash
■ *vi* (*insistir*) to go on, keep on

machacón, -ona [matʃa'kon, ona] *adj*
(*pesado*) tiresome; (*insistente*) insistent;
(*monótono*) monotonous

machamartillo [matʃamar'tiʎo]: **a** ~ *adv*:
creer a machamartillo (*firmemente*) to
believe, firmly

machaque *etc* [ma'tʃake] *vb ver* **machacar**

machete [ma'tʃete] *nm* machete, (large)
knife

machismo [ma'tʃismo] *nm* sexism; male
chauvinism

machista [ma'tʃista] *adj, nm* sexist; male
chauvinist

macho ['matʃo] *adj* male; (*fig*) virile ■ *nm*

male; (*fig*) he-man, tough guy (*US*); (*Tec*:
perno) pin, peg; (*Elec*) pin, plug; (*Costura*) hook

macilento, -a [maθi'lento, a] *adj* (*pálido*)
pale; (*ojeroso*) haggard

macizo, -a [ma'θiθo, a] *adj* (*grande*) massive;
(*fuerte, sólido*) solid ■ *nm* mass, chunk; (*Geo*)
massif

macramé [makra'me] *nm* macramé

macrobiótico, -a [makro'βjotiko, a] *adj*
macrobiotic

macrocomando [makroko'mando] *nm*
(*Inform*) macro (command)

macroeconomía [makroekono'mia] *nf* (*Com*)
macroeconomics *sg*

mácula ['makula] *nf* stain, blemish

macuto [ma'kuto] *nm* (*Mil*) knapsack

Madagascar [madaɣas'kar] *nm* Madagascar

madeja [ma'ðexa] *nf* (*de lana*) skein, hank

madera [ma'ðera] *nf* wood; (*fig*) nature,
character; (: *aptitud*) aptitude; **una** ~ a piece
of wood; ~ **contrachapada** *o* **laminada**
plywood; **tiene buena** ~ he's made of solid
stuff; **tiene** ~ **de futbolista** he's got the
makings of a footballer

maderaje [maðe'raxe], **maderamen**
[maðe'ramen] *nm* timber; (*trabajo*)
woodwork, timbering

maderero [maðe'rero] *nm* timber merchant

madero [ma'ðero] *nm* beam; (*fig*) ship

madrastra [ma'ðrastra] *nf* stepmother

madre ['maðre] *adj* mother *cpd*; (*Am*)
tremendous ■ *nf* mother; (*de vino etc*) dregs
pl; ~ **adoptiva/política/soltera** foster
mother/mother-in-law/unmarried mother;
la M~ Patria the Mother Country; **sin** ~
motherless; **¡~ mía!** oh dear!; **¡tu ~!** (*fam!*)
fuck off! (!); **salirse de** ~ (*río*) to burst its
banks; (*persona*) to lose all self-control

madreperla [maðre'perla] *nf* mother-of-
pearl

madreselva [maðre'selβa] *nf* honeysuckle

Madrid [ma'ðrið] *n* Madrid

madriguera [maðri'ɣera] *nf* burrow

madrileño | mal

madrileño, -a [maðri'leɲo, a] *adj* of *o* from Madrid ■ *nm/f* native *o* inhabitant of Madrid

Madriles [ma'ðriles] *nmpl*: **Los ~** *(fam)* Madrid *sg*

madrina [ma'ðrina] *nf* godmother; *(Arq)* prop, shore; *(Tec)* brace; **~ de boda** bridesmaid

madroño [ma'ðroɲo] *nm (Bot)* strawberry tree, arbutus

madrugada [maðru'ɣaða] *nf* early morning, small hours; *(alba)* dawn, daybreak; **a las cuarto de la ~** at four o'clock in the morning

madrugador, a [maðruɣa'ðor, a] *adj* early-rising

madrugar [maðru'ɣar] *vi* to get up early; *(fig)* to get a head start

madrugue *etc* [ma'ðruɣe] *vb ver* **madrugar**

madurar [maðu'rar] *vt, vi (fruta)* to ripen; *(fig)* to mature

madurez [maðu're θ] *nf* ripeness; *(fig)* maturity

maduro, -a [ma'ðuro, a] *adj* ripe; *(fig)* mature; **poco ~** unripe

MAE *nm abr (Esp Pol)* = **Ministerio de Asuntos Exteriores**

maestra [ma'estra] *nf ver* **maestro**

maestría [maes'tria] *nf* mastery; *(habilidad)* skill, expertise; *(Am)* Master's Degree

maestro, -a [ma'estro, a] *adj* masterly; *(perito)* skilled, expert; *(principal)* main; *(educado)* trained ■ *nm/f* master/mistress; *(profesor)* teacher ■ *nm (autoridad)* authority; *(Mus)* maestro; *(obrero)* skilled workman; **~ albañil** master mason; **~ de obras** foreman

mafia ['mafja] *nf* mafia; **la M~** the Mafia

mafioso [ma'fjoso] *nm* gangster

Magallanes [maɣa'ʎanes] *nm*: **Estrecho de ~** Strait of Magellan

magia ['maxja] *nf* magic

mágico, -a ['maxiko, a] *adj* magic(al) ■ *nm/f* magician

magisterio [maxis'terjo] *nm (enseñanza)* teaching; *(profesión)* teaching profession; *(maestros)* teachers *pl*

magistrado [maxis'traðo] *nm* magistrate; **Primer M~** *(Am)* President, Prime Minister

magistral [maxis'tral] *adj* magisterial; *(fig)* masterly

magistratura [maxistra'tura] *nf* magistracy; **M~ del Trabajo** *(Esp)* ≈ Industrial Tribunal

magnánimo, -a [maɣ'nanimo, a] *adj* magnanimous

magnate [maɣ'nate] *nm* magnate, tycoon; **~ de la prensa** press baron

magnesio [maɣ'nesjo] *nm (Química)* magnesium

magnetice *etc* [maɣne'tiθe] *vb ver* **magnetizar**

magnético, -a [maɣ'netiko, a] *adj* magnetic

magnetismo [maɣne'tismo] *nm* magnetism

magnetizar [maɣneti'θar] *vt* to magnetize

magnetofón [maɣneto'fon], **magnetófono** [maɣne'tofono] *nm* tape recorder

magnetofónico, -a [maɣneto'foniko, a] *adj*: **cinta magnetofónica** recording tape

magnicidio [maɣni'θiðjo] *nm* assassination *(of an important person)*

magnífico, -a [maɣ'nifiko, a] *adj* splendid, magnificent

magnitud [maɣni'tuð] *nf* magnitude

mago, -a ['maɣo, a] *nm/f* magician, wizard; **los Reyes Magos** the Magi, the Three Wise Men; *ver tb* **Reyes Magos**

magrear [maɣre'ar] *vt (fam)* to touch up

magro, -a ['maɣro, a] *adj (persona)* thin, lean; *(carne)* lean

maguey [ma'ɣei] *nm (Bot)* agave

magulladura [maɣuʎa'ðura] *nf* bruise

magullar [maɣu'ʎar] *vt (amoratar)* to bruise; *(dañar)* to damage; *(fam: golpear)* to bash, beat

Maguncia [ma'ɣunθja] *nf* Mainz

mahometano, -a [maome'tano, a] *adj* Mohammedan

mahonesa [mao'nesa] *nf* = **mayonesa**

maicena [mai'θena] *nf* cornflour, corn starch *(US)*

mail [meil] *nm (fam)* email

maillot [ma'jot] *nm* swimming costume; *(Deporte)* vest

maître ['metre] *nm* head waiter

maíz [ma'iθ] *nm* maize *(Brit)*, corn *(US)*; sweet corn

maizal [mai'θal] *nm* maize field, cornfield

majadero, -a [maxa'ðero, a] *adj* silly, stupid

majar [ma'xar] *vt* to crush, grind

majareta [maxa'reta] *adj (fam)* cracked, potty

majestad [maxes'tað] *nf* majesty; **Su M~** His/Her Majesty; **(Vuestra) M~** Your Majesty

majestuoso, -a [maxes'twoso, a] *adj* majestic

majo, -a ['maxo, a] *adj* nice; *(guapo)* attractive, good-looking; *(elegante)* smart

mal [mal] *adv* badly; *(equivocadamente)* wrongly; *(con dificultad)* with difficulty ■ *adj* = **malo, a** ■ *nm* evil; *(desgracia)* misfortune; *(daño)* harm, damage; *(Med)* illness ■ *conj*: **~ que le pese** whether he likes it or not; **me entendió ~** he misunderstood me; **hablar ~ de algn** to speak ill of sb; **huele ~** it smells bad; **ir de ~ en peor** to go from bad to worse; **oigo/veo ~** I can't hear/see very well; **si ~ no recuerdo** if my memory serves me right;

¡menos ~! just as well!; **~ que bien** rightly or wrongly; **no hay ~ que por bien no venga** every cloud has a silver lining; **~ de ojo** evil eye

malabarismo [malaβa'rismo] *nm* juggling

malabarista [malaβa'rista] *nm/f* juggler

malaconsejado, -a [malakonse'xaðo, a] *adj* ill-advised

malacostumbrado, -a [malakostum'braðo, a] *adj* (*consentido*) spoiled

malacostumbrar [malakostum'brar] *vt*: **~ a algn** to get sb into bad habits

malagueño, -a [mala'ɣeɲo, a] *adj* of *o* from Málaga ■ *nm/f* native *o* inhabitant of Málaga

Malaisia [ma'laisja] *nf* Malaysia

malaria [ma'larja] *nf* malaria

Malasia [ma'lasja] *nf* Malaysia

malavenido, -a [malaβe'niðo, a] *adj* incompatible

malayo, -a [ma'lajo, a] *adj* Malay(an) ■ *nm/f* Malay ■ *nm* (*Ling*) Malay

Malaysia [ma'laisia] *nf* Malaysia

malcarado, -a [malka'raðo, a] *adj* ugly, grim-faced

malcriado, -a [mal'krjaðo, a] *adj* (*consentido*) spoiled

malcriar [mal'krjar] *vt* to spoil, pamper

maldad [mal'dað] *nf* evil, wickedness

maldecir [malde'θir] *vt* to curse ■ *vi*: **~ de** to speak ill of

maldiciendo *etc* [maldi'θjendo] *vb ver* **maldecir**

maldición [maldi'θjon] *nf* curse; **¡~!** curse it!, damn!

maldiga *etc* [mal'diɣa], **maldije** *etc* [mal'dixe] *vb ver* **maldecir**

maldito, -a [mal'dito, a] *adj* (*condenado*) damned; (*perverso*) wicked ■ *nm*: **el ~** the devil; **¡~ sea!** damn it!; **no le hace ~ (el) caso** he doesn't take a blind bit of notice

maleable [male'aβle] *adj* malleable

maleante [male'ante] *adj* wicked ■ *nm/f* criminal, crook

malecón [male'kon] *nm* pier, jetty

maledicencia [maleði'θenθja] *nf* slander, scandal

maleducado, -a [maleðu'kaðo, a] *adj* bad-mannered, rude

maleficio [male'fiθjo] *nm* curse, spell

malentendido [malenten'diðo] *nm* misunderstanding

malestar [males'tar] *nm* (*gen*) discomfort; (*enfermedad*) indisposition; (*fig: inquietud*) uneasiness; (*Pol*) unrest; **siento un ~ en el estómago** my stomach is upset

maleta [ma'leta] *nf* case, suitcase; (*Auto*) boot (*Brit*), trunk (*US*); **hacer la ~** to pack

maletera [male'tera] *nf* (*Am Auto*) boot (*Brit*), trunk (*US*)

maletero [male'tero] *nm* (*Auto*) boot (*Brit*), trunk (*US*); (*persona*) porter

maletín [male'tin] *nm* small case, bag; (*portafolio*) briefcase

malevolencia [maleβo'lenθja] *nf* malice, spite

malévolo, -a [ma'leβolo, a] *adj* malicious, spiteful

maleza [ma'leθa] *nf* (*malas hierbas*) weeds *pl*; (*arbustos*) thicket

malgache [mal'ɣatʃe] *adj* of *o* from Madagascar ■ *nm/f* native *o* inhabitant of Madagascar

malgastar [malɣas'tar] *vt* (*tiempo, dinero*) to waste; (*recursos*) to squander; (*salud*) to ruin

malhaya [ma'laja] *excl* (*esp Am: fam!*) damn (it)! (!); **¡~ sea/sean!** damn it/them! (!)

malhechor, a [male'tʃor, a] *nm/f* delinquent; (*criminal*) criminal

malherido, -a [male'riðo, a] *adj* badly injured

malhumorado, -a [malumo'raðo, a] *adj* bad-tempered

malicia [ma'liθja] *nf* (*maldad*) wickedness; (*astucia*) slyness, guile; (*mala intención*) malice, spite; (*carácter travieso*) mischievousness

malicioso, -a [mali'θjoso, a] *adj* wicked, evil; sly, crafty; malicious, spiteful; mischievous

malignidad [maliɣni'ðað] *nf* (*Med*) malignancy; (*malicia*) malice

maligno, -a [ma'liɣno, a] *adj* evil; (*dañino*) pernicious, harmful; (*malévolo*) malicious; (*Med*) malignant ■ *nm*: **el ~** the devil

malintencionado, -a [malintenθjo'naðo, a] *adj* (*comentario*) hostile; (*persona*) malicious

malla ['maʎa] *nf* (*de una red*) mesh; (*red*) network; (*Am: de baño*) swimsuit; (*de ballet, gimnasia*) leotard; **mallas** *nfpl* tights; **~ de alambre** wire mesh

Mallorca [ma'ʎorka] *nf* Majorca

mallorquín, -ina [maʎor'kin, ina] *adj, nm/f* Majorcan ■ *nm* (*Ling*) Majorcan

malnutrido, -a [malnu'triðo, a] *adj* undernourished

malo, -a ['malo, a] *adj* (**mal** *before nmsg*) bad; (*calidad*) poor; (*falso*) false; (*espantoso*) dreadful; (*niño*) naughty ■ *nm/f* villain ■ *nm* (*Cine fam*) bad guy ■ *nf* spell of bad luck; **estar ~** to be ill; **andar a malas con algn** to be on bad terms with sb; **estar de malas** (*mal humor*) to be in a bad mood; **lo ~ es que ...** the trouble is that ...

malograr [malo'ɣrar] *vt* to spoil; (*plan*) to upset; (*ocasión*) to waste; **malograrse** *vr*

m

(*plan etc*) to fail, come to grief; (*persona*) to die before one's time

maloliente [malo'ljente] *adj* stinking, smelly

malparado, -a [malpa'raðo, a] *adj*: **salir ~** to come off badly

malpensado, -a [malpen'saðo, a] *adj* evil-minded

malquerencia [malke'renθja] *nf* dislike

malquistar [malkis'tar] *vt*: **~ a dos personas** to cause a rift between two people; **malquistarse** *vr* to fall out

malsano, -a [mal'sano, a] *adj* unhealthy

malsonante [malso'nante] *adj* (*palabra*) nasty, rude

Malta ['malta] *nf* Malta

malta ['malta] *nf* malt

malteada [malte'aða] *nf* (*Am*) milk shake

maltés, -esa [mal'tes, esa] *adj, nm/f* Maltese

maltraer [maltra'er] *vt* (*abusar*) to insult, abuse; (*maltratar*) to ill-treat

maltratar [maltra'tar] *vt* to ill-treat, mistreat

maltrecho, -a [mal'tretʃo, a] *adj* battered, damaged

malva ['malβa] *nf* mallow; **~ loca** hollyhock; (**de color de**) **~** mauve

malvado, -a [mal'βaðo, a] *adj* evil, villainous

malvavisco [malβa'βisko] *nm* marshmallow

malvender [malβen'der] *vt* to sell off cheap *o* at a loss

malversación [malβersa'θjon] *nf* embezzlement, misappropriation

malversar [malβer'sar] *vt* to embezzle, misappropriate

Malvinas [mal'βinas] *nfpl*: **Islas ~** Falkland Islands

mama ['mama] (*pl* **mamás**) *nf* (*de animal*) teat; (*de mujer*) breast

mamá [ma'ma] *nf* (*fam*) mum, mummy

mamacita [mama'sita] *nf* (*Am fam*) mum, mummy

mamadera [mama'dera] *nf* (*Am*) baby's bottle

mamagrande [mama'grande] *nf* (*Am*) grandmother

mamar [ma'mar] *vt* (*pecho*) to suck; (*fig*) to absorb, assimilate ■ *vi* to suck; **dar de ~** to (breast-)feed; (*animal*) to suckle

mamarracho [mama'rratʃo] *nm* sight, mess

mambo ['mambo] *nf* (*Mus*) mambo

mamífero, -a [ma'mifero, a] *adj* mammalian, mammal *cpd* ■ *nm* mammal

mamón, -ona [ma'mon, ona] *adj* small, baby *cpd* ■ *nm/f* small baby; (*fam!*) wanker (!)

mamotreto [mamo'treto] *nm* hefty volume; (*fam*) whacking great thing

mampara [mam'para] *nf* (*entre habitaciones*) partition; (*biombo*) screen

mamporro [mam'porro] *nm* (*fam*): **dar un ~ a** to clout

mampostería [mamposte'ria] *nf* masonry

mamut [ma'mut] *nm* mammoth

maná [ma'na] *nm* manna

manada [ma'naða] *nf* (*Zool*) herd; (*: de leones*) pride; (*: de lobos*) pack; **llegaron en manadas** (*fam*) they came in droves

Managua [ma'naɣwa] *n* Managua

manantial [manan'tjal] *nm* spring; (*fuente*) fountain; (*fig*) source

manar [ma'nar] *vt* to run with, flow with ■ *vi* to run, flow; (*abundar*) to abound

manaza [ma'naθa] *nf* big hand ■ *adj, nm/f inv*: **manazas**: **ser un manazas** to be clumsy

mancebo [man'θeβo] *nm* (*joven*) young man

mancha ['mantʃa] *nf* stain, mark; (*de tinta*) blot; (*de vegetación*) patch; (*imperfección*) stain, blemish, blot; (*boceto*) sketch, outline; **la M~** La Mancha

manchado, -a [man'tʃaðo, a] *adj* (*sucio*) dirty; (*animal*) spotted; (*ave*) speckled; (*de tinta*) smudged

manchar [man'tʃar] *vt* to stain, mark; (*Zool*) to patch; (*ensuciar*) to soil, dirty; **mancharse** *vr* to get dirty; (*fig*) to dirty one's hands

manchego, -a [man'tʃeɣo, a] *adj* of *o* from La Mancha ■ *nm/f* native *o* inhabitant of La Mancha

mancilla [man'θiʎa] *nf* stain, blemish

mancillar [manθi'ʎar] *vt* to stain, sully

manco, -a ['manko, a] *adj* one-armed; one-handed; (*fig*) defective, faulty; **no ser ~** to be useful *o* active

mancomunar [mankomu'nar] *vt* to unite, bring together; (*recursos*) to pool; (*Jur*) to make jointly responsible

mancomunidad [mankomuni'ðað] *nf* union, association; (*comunidad*) community; (*Jur*) joint responsibility

mandado [man'daðo] *nm* (*orden*) order; (*recado*) commission, errand

mandamás [manda'mas] *adj, nm/f inv* boss; **ser un ~** to be very bossy

mandamiento [manda'mjento] *nm* (*orden*) order, command; (*Rel*) commandment; **~ judicial** warrant

mandar [man'dar] *vt* (*ordenar*) to order; (*dirigir*) to lead, command; (*país*) to rule over; (*enviar*) to send; (*pedir*) to order, ask for ■ *vi* to be in charge; (*pey*) to be bossy; **mandarse** *vr*: **mandarse mudar** (*Am fam*) to go away, clear off; **¿mande?** pardon?, excuse me? (*US*); **¿manda usted algo más?** is there anything else?; **~ a algn a paseo** *o* **a la porra** to tell sb to go to hell; **se lo mandaremos por correo** we'll post it to you; **~ hacer un traje** to have a suit made

mandarín [manda'rin] *nm* petty bureaucrat

mandarina [manda'rina] *nf* (*fruta*) tangerine, mandarin (orange)

mandatario, -a [manda'tarjo, a] *nm/f* (*representante*) agent; **primer ~** (*esp Am*) head of state

mandato [man'dato] *nm* (*orden*) order; (*Pol: período*) term of office; (*: territorio*) mandate; **~ judicial** (search) warrant

mandíbula [man'diβula] *nf* jaw

mandil [man'dil] *nm* (*delantal*) apron

Mandinga [man'dinɣa] *nm* (*Am*) Devil

mandioca [man'djoka] *nf* cassava

mando ['mando] *nm* (*Mil*) command; (*de país*) rule; (*el primer lugar*) lead; (*Pol*) term of office; (*Tec*) control; **~ a la izquierda** left-hand drive; **los altos mandos** the high command *sg*; **~ por botón** push-button control; **al ~ de** in charge of; **tomar el ~** to take the lead

mandolina [mando'lina] *nf* mandolin(e)

mandón, -ona [man'don, ona] *adj* bossy, domineering

manecilla [mane'θiʎa] *nf* (*Tec*) pointer; (*de reloj*) hand

manejable [mane'xaβle] *adj* manageable; (*fácil de usar*) handy

manejar [mane'xar] *vt* to manage; (*máquina*) to work, operate; (*caballo etc*) to handle; (*casa*) to run, manage; (*Am Auto*) to drive ■ *vi* (*Am Auto*) to drive; **manejarse** *vr* (*comportarse*) to act, behave; (*arreglárselas*) to manage; **"~ con cuidado"** "handle with care"

manejo [ma'nexo] *nm* management; handling; running; driving; (*facilidad de trato*) ease, confidence; (*de idioma*) command; **manejos** *nmpl* intrigues; **tengo ~ del francés** I have a good command of French

manera [ma'nera] *nf* way, manner, fashion; (*Arte, Lit etc: estilo*) manner, style; **maneras** *nfpl* (*modales*) manners; **su ~ de ser** the way he is; (*aire*) his manner; **de mala ~** (*fam*) badly, unwillingly; **de ninguna ~** no way, by no means; **de otra ~** otherwise; **de todas maneras** at any rate; **en gran ~** to a large extent; **sobre ~** exceedingly; **a mi ~ de ver** in my view; **no hay ~ de persuadirle** there's no way of convincing him

manga ['manga] *nf* (*de camisa*) sleeve; (*de riego*) hose; **de ~ corta/larga** short-/long-sleeved; **andar ~ por hombro** (*desorden*) to be topsy-turvy; **tener ~ ancha** to be easy-going

mangante [man'gante] *adj* (*descarado*) brazen ■ *nm* (*mendigo*) beggar

mangar [man'gar] *vt* (*unir*) to plug in; (*fam:*

birlar) to pinch, nick, swipe; (*mendigar*) to beg

mango ['mango] *nm* handle; (*Bot*) mango; **~ de escoba** broomstick

mangonear [mangone'ar] *vt* to boss about ■ *vi* to be bossy

mangue *etc* ['mange] *vb ver* **mangar**

manguera [man'gera] *nf* (*de riego*) hose; (*tubo*) pipe; **~ de incendios** fire hose

maní [ma'ni] *nm* (*pl ~es o manises*) (*Am: cacahuete*) peanut; (*: planta*) groundnut plant

manía [ma'nia] *nf* (*Med*) mania; (*fig: moda*) rage, craze; (*disgusto*) dislike; (*malicia*) spite; **tiene manías** she's a bit fussy; **tener ~ a algn** to dislike sb

maníaco, -a [ma'niako, a] *adj* maniac(al) ■ *nm/f* maniac

maniatar [manja'tar] *vt* to tie the hands of

maniático, -a [ma'njatiko, a] *adj* maniac(al); (*loco*) crazy; (*tiquismiquis*) fussy ■ *nm/f* maniac

manicomio [mani'komjo] *nm* mental hospital (*Brit*), insane asylum (*US*)

manicuro, -a [mani'kuro, a] *nm/f* manicurist ■ *nf* manicure

manido, -a [ma'niðo, a] *adj* (*tema etc*) trite, stale

manifestación [manifesta'θjon] *nf* (*declaración*) statement, declaration; (*demostración*) show, display; (*Pol*) demonstration

manifestante [manifes'tante] *nm/f* demonstrator

manifestar [manifes'tar] *vt* to show, manifest; (*declarar*) to state, declare; **manifestarse** *vr* to show, become apparent; (*Pol: desfilar*) to demonstrate; (*: reunirse*) to hold a mass meeting

manifiesto, -a *etc* [mani'fjesto, a] *vb ver* **manifestar** ■ *adj* clear, manifest ■ *nm* manifesto; (*Anat, Naut*) manifest; **poner algo de ~** (*aclarar*) to make sth clear; (*revelar*) to reveal sth; **quedar ~** to be plain o clear

manija [ma'nixa] *nf* handle

manilla [ma'niʎa] *nf* (*de reloj*) hand; (*Am*) handle, lever; **manillas (de hierro)** *nfpl* handcuffs

manillar [mani'ʎar] *nm* handlebars *pl*

maniobra [ma'njoβra] *nf* manœuvring; (*manejo*) handling; (*fig: movimiento*) manœuvre, move; (*: estratagema*) trick, stratagem; **maniobras** *nfpl* manœuvres

maniobrar [manio'βrar] *vt* to manœuvre; (*manejar*) to handle ■ *vi* to manœuvre

manipulación [manipula'θjon] *nf* manipulation; (*Com*) handling

manipular [manipu'lar] *vt* to manipulate; (*manejar*) to handle

maniquí [mani'ki] nm/f model ■ nm dummy

manirroto, -a [mani'rroto, a] adj lavish, extravagant ■ nm/f spendthrift

manita [ma'nita] nf little hand; **manitas de plata** artistic hands

manitas [ma'nitas] adj inv good with one's hands ■ nm/f inv: **ser un ~** to be very good with one's hands

manito [ma'nito] nm (Am: en conversación) mate (fam), chum

manivela [mani'βela] nf crank

manjar [man'xar] nm (tasty) dish

mano[1] ['mano] nf hand; (Zool) foot, paw; (de pintura) coat; (serie) lot, series; **a ~** by hand; **a ~ derecha/izquierda** on (o to) the right(-hand side)/left(-hand side); **hecho a ~** handmade; **a manos llenas** lavishly, generously; **de primera ~** (at) first hand; **de segunda ~** (at) second hand; **robo a ~ armada** armed robbery; **Pedro es mi ~ derecha** Pedro is my right-hand man; **~ de obra** labour, manpower; **~ de santo** sure remedy; **darse la(s) ~(s)** to shake hands; **echar una ~** to lend a hand; **echar una ~ a** to lay hands on; **echar ~ de** to make use of; **estrechar la ~ a algn** to shake sb's hand; **traer o llevar algo entre manos** to deal o be busy with sth; **está en tus manos** it's up to you; **se le fue la ~** his hand slipped; (fig) he went too far; **¡manos a la obra!** to work!

mano[2] ['mano] nm (Am fam) friend, mate

manojo [ma'noxo] nm handful, bunch; **~ de llaves** bunch of keys

manómetro [ma'nometro] nm (pressure) gauge

manopla [ma'nopla] nf (paño) flannel; **manoplas** nfpl mittens

manoseado, -a [manose'aðo, a] adj well-worn

manosear [manose'ar] vt (tocar) to handle, touch; (desordenar) to mess up, rumple; (insistir en) to overwork; (acariciar) to caress, fondle; (pey: persona) to feel o touch up

manotazo [mano'taθo] nm slap, smack

mansalva [man'salβa]: **a ~** adv indiscriminately

mansedumbre [manse'ðumbre] nf gentleness, meekness; (de animal) tameness

mansión [man'sjon] nf mansion

manso, -a ['manso, a] adj gentle, mild; (animal) tame

manta ['manta] nf blanket; (Am) poncho

manteca [man'teka] nf fat; (Am) butter; **~ de cacahuete/cacao** peanut/cocoa butter; **~ de cerdo** lard

mantecado [mante'kaðo] nm ice cream

mantecoso, -a [mante'koso, a] adj fat, greasy; **queso ~** soft cheese

mantel [man'tel] nm tablecloth

mantelería [mantele'ria] nf table linen

mantendré etc [manten'dre] vb ver **mantener**

mantener [mante'ner] vt to support, maintain; (alimentar) to sustain; (conservar) to keep; (Tec) to maintain, service; **mantenerse** vr (seguir de pie) to be still standing; (no ceder) to hold one's ground; (subsistir) to sustain o.s., keep going; **~ algo en equilibrio** to keep sth balanced; **mantenerse a distancia** to keep one's distance; **mantenerse firme** to hold one's ground

mantenga etc [man'tenga] vb ver **mantener**

mantenimiento [manteni'mjento] nm maintenance; sustenance; (sustento) support

mantequería [manteke'ria] nf (ultramarinos) grocer's (shop)

mantequilla [mante'kiʎa] nf butter

mantilla [man'tiʎa] nf mantilla; **mantillas** nfpl baby clothes; **estar en mantillas** (persona) to be terribly innocent; (proyecto) to be in its infancy

manto ['manto] nm (capa) cloak; (de ceremonia) robe, gown

mantón [man'ton] nm shawl

mantuve etc [man'tuβe] vb ver **mantener**

manual [ma'nwal] adj manual ■ nm manual, handbook; **habilidad ~** manual skill

manubrio [ma'nuβrio] nm (Am Auto) steering wheel

manufactura [manufak'tura] nf manufacture; (fábrica) factory

manufacturado, -a [manufaktu'raðo, a] adj manufactured

manuscrito, -a [manus'krito, a] adj handwritten ■ nm manuscript

manutención [manuten'θjon] nf maintenance; (sustento) support

manzana [man'θana] nf apple; (Arq) block; **~ de la discordia** (fig) bone of contention

manzanal [manθa'nal] nm apple orchard

manzanilla [manθa'niʎa] nf (planta) camomile; (infusión) camomile tea; (vino) manzanilla

manzano [man'θano] nm apple tree

maña ['maɲa] nf (gen) skill, dexterity; (pey) guile; (costumbre) habit; (una maña) trick, knack; **con ~** craftily

mañana [ma'ɲana] adv tomorrow ■ nm future ■ nf morning; **de o por la ~** in the morning; **¡hasta ~!** see you tomorrow!; **pasado ~** the day after tomorrow; **~ por la ~** tomorrow morning

mañanero, -a [maɲa'nero, a] adj early-rising

maño, -a ['maɲo, a] adj Aragonese ■ nm/f

native o inhabitant of Aragon

mañoso, -a [ma'ɲoso, a] adj (hábil) skilful; (astuto) smart, clever

mapa ['mapa] nm map

mapuche, -a [ma'putʃe, a] adj, nm/f Mapuche, Araucanian

maqueta [ma'keta] nf (scale) model

maquiavélico, -a [makja'βeliko, a] adj Machiavellian

maquillador, a [makiʎa'ðor, a] nm/f (Teat etc) make-up artist

maquillaje [maki'ʎaxe] nm make-up; (acto) making up

maquillar [maki'ʎar] vt to make up; **maquillarse** vr to put on (some) make-up

máquina ['makina] nf machine; (de tren) locomotive, engine; (Foto) camera; (Am: coche) car; (fig) machinery; (: proyecto) plan, project; **a toda ~** at full speed; **escrito a ~** typewritten; **~ de afeitar** electric razor; **~ de escribir** typewriter; **~ de coser/lavar** sewing/washing machine; **~ de facsímil** facsimile (machine), fax; **~ de franqueo** franking machine; **~ tragaperras** fruit machine; (Com) slot machine

maquinación [makina'θjon] nf machination, plot

maquinal [maki'nal] adj (fig) mechanical, automatic

maquinar [maki'nar] vt, vi to plot

maquinaria [maki'narja] nf (máquinas) machinery; (mecanismo) mechanism, works pl

maquinilla [maki'niʎa] nf small machine; (torno) winch; **~ de afeitar** razor; **~ eléctrica** electric razor

maquinista [maki'nista] nm (Ferro) engine driver (Brit), engineer (US); (Tec) operator; (Naut) engineer

mar [mar] nm sea; **~ de fondo** groundswell; **~ llena** high tide; **~ adentro** o **afuera** out at sea; **en alta ~** on the high seas; **por ~** by sea o boat; **hacerse a la ~** to put to sea; **a mares** in abundance; **un ~ de** lots of; **es la ~ de guapa** she is ever so pretty; **el M~ Negro/Báltico** the Black/Baltic Sea; **el M~ Muerto/Rojo** the Dead/Red Sea; **el M~ del Norte** the North Sea

mar. abr (= marzo) Mar.

maraca [ma'raka] nf maraca

maraña [ma'raɲa] nf (maleza) thicket; (confusión) tangle

maravilla [mara'βiʎa] nf marvel, wonder; (Bot) marigold; **hacer maravillas** to work wonders; **a (las mil) maravillas** wonderfully well

maravillar [maraβi'ʎar] vt to astonish, amaze; **maravillarse** vr to be astonished, be amazed

maravilloso, -a [maraβi'ʎoso, a] adj wonderful, marvellous

marbellí [marβe'ʎi] adj of o from Marbella ■ nm/f native o inhabitant of Marbella

marca ['marka] nf mark; (sello) stamp; (Com) make, brand; (de ganado) brand; (: acto) branding; (Deporte) record; **de ~** excellent; **~ de fábrica** trademark; **~ propia** own brand; **~ registrada** registered trademark

marcación [marka'θjon] nf (Telec): **~ automática** autodial

marcado, -a [mar'kaðo, a] adj marked, strong

marcador [marka'ðor] nm marker; (rotulador) marker (pen); (de libro) bookmark; (Deporte) scoreboard; (: persona) scorer

marcapasos [marka'pasos] nm inv pacemaker

marcar [mar'kar] vt to mark; (número de teléfono) to dial; (gol) to score; (números) to record, keep a tally of; (el pelo) to set; (ganado) to brand; (suj: termómetro) to read, register; (: reloj) to show; (tarea) to assign; (Com) to put a price on ■ vi (Deporte) to score; (Telec) to dial; **mi reloj marca las dos** it's two o'clock by my watch; **~ el compás** (Mus) to keep time; **~ el paso** (Mil) to mark time

marcha ['martʃa] nf march; (Deporte) walk; (Tec) running, working; (Auto) gear; (velocidad) speed; (fig) progress; (curso) course; **dar ~ atrás** to reverse, put into reverse; **estar en ~** to be under way, be in motion; **hacer algo sobre la ~** to do sth as you etc go along; **poner en ~** to put into gear; **ponerse en ~** to start, get going; **a marchas forzadas** (fig) with all speed; **¡en ~!** (Mil) forward march!; (fig) let's go!; **"~ moderada"** (Auto) "drive slowly"; **que tiene** o **de mucha ~** (fam) very lively

marchante, -a [mar'tʃante, a] nm/f dealer, merchant

marchar [mar'tʃar] vi (ir) to go; (funcionar) to work, go; (fig) to go, proceed; **marcharse** vr to go (away), leave; **todo marcha bien** everything is going well

marchitar [martʃi'tar] vt to wither, dry up; **marchitarse** vr (Bot) to wither; (fig) to fade away

marchito, -a [mar'tʃito, a] adj withered, faded; (fig) in decline

marchoso, -a [mar'tʃoso, a] adj (fam: animado) lively; (: moderno) modern

marcial [mar'θjal] adj martial, military

marciano, -a [mar'θjano, a] adj Martian, of o from Mars

marco ['marko] nm frame; (Deporte) goalposts

pl; (*moneda*) mark; (*fig*) setting; (*contexto*)
framework; **~ de chimenea** mantelpiece

marea [ma'rea] *nf* tide; (*llovizna*) drizzle; **~
alta/baja** high/low tide; **~ negra** oil slick

mareado, -a [mare'aðo, a] *adj*: **estar ~** (*con
náuseas*) to feel sick; (*aturdido*) to feel dizzy

marear [mare'ar] *vt* (*fig: irritar*) to annoy,
upset; (*Med*): **~ a algn** to make sb feel sick;
marearse *vr* (*tener náuseas*) to feel sick;
(*desvanecerse*) to feel faint; (*aturdirse*) to feel
dizzy; (*fam: emborracharse*) to get tipsy

marejada [mare'xaða] *nf* (*Naut*) swell, heavy
sea

maremágnum [mare'maɣnum] *nm* (*fig*)
ocean, abundance

maremoto [mare'moto] *nm* tidal wave

mareo [ma'reo] *nm* (*náusea*) sick feeling;
(*aturdimiento*) dizziness; (*fam: lata*) nuisance

marfil [mar'fil] *nm* ivory

margarina [marɣa'rina] *nf* margarine

margarita [marɣa'rita] *nf* (*Bot*) daisy;
(**rueda**) ~ (*en máquina impresora*) daisy wheel

margen ['marxen] *nm* (*borde*) edge, border;
(*fig*) margin, space ■ *nf* (*de río etc*) bank; **~
de beneficio** *o* **de ganancia** profit margin;
~ comercial mark-up; **~ de confianza**
credibility gap; **dar ~ para** to give an
opportunity for; **dejar a algn al ~** to leave sb
out (in the cold); **mantenerse al ~** to keep
out (of things); **al ~ de lo que digas** despite
what you say

marginado, -a [marxi'naðo, a] *nm/f* outcast

marginal [marxi'nal] *adj* (*tema, error*) minor;
(*grupo*) fringe *cpd*; (*anotación*) marginal

marginar [marxi'nar] *vt* to exclude

maría [ma'ria] *nf* (*fam: mujer*) housewife

mariachi [ma'rjatʃi] *nm* (*música*) mariachi
music; (*grupo*) mariachi band; (*persona*)
mariachi player

marica [ma'rika] *nm* (*fam*) sissy; (*homosexual*)
queer

Maricastaña [marikas'taɲa] *nf*: **en los días**
o **en tiempos de ~** way back, in the good old
days

maricón [mari'kon] *nm* (*fam*) queer

marido [ma'riðo] *nm* husband

marihuana [mari'wənə] *nf* marijuana,
cannabis

marimacho [mari'matʃo] *nf* (*fam*) mannish
woman

marimorena [marimo'rena] *nf* fuss, row;
armar una ~ to kick up a row

marina [ma'rina] *nf* navy; **~ mercante**
merchant navy

marinero, -a [mari'nero, a] *adj* sea *cpd*;
(*barco*) seaworthy ■ *nm* sailor, seaman

marino, -a [ma'rino, a] *adj* sea *cpd*, marine

■ *nm* sailor; **~ de agua dulce/de cubierta/
de primera** landlubber/deckhand/able
seaman

marioneta [marjo'neta] *nf* puppet

mariposa [mari'posa] *nf* butterfly

mariposear [maripose'ar] *vi* (*revolotear*) to
flutter about; (*ser inconstante*) to be fickle;
(*coquetear*) to flirt

mariquita [mari'kita] *nm* (*fam*) sissy;
(*homosexual*) queer ■ *nf* (*Zool*) ladybird (*Brit*),
ladybug (*US*)

marisco [ma'risko] *nm* (*tb*: **mariscos**)
shellfish, seafood

marisma [ma'risma] *nf* marsh, swamp

marisquería [mariske'ria] *nf* shellfish bar,
seafood restaurant

marítimo, -a [ma'ritimo, a] *adj* sea *cpd*,
maritime

marmita [mar'mita] *nf* pot

mármol ['marmol] *nm* marble

marmóreo, -a [mar'moreo, a] *adj* marble

marmota [mar'mota] *nf* (*Zool*) marmot; (*fig*)
sleepyhead

maroma [ma'roma] *nf* rope

marque *etc* ['marke] *vb ver* **marcar**

marqués, -esa [mar'kes, esa] *nm/f* marquis/
marchioness

marquesina [marke'sina] *nf* (*de parada*) bus-
shelter

marquetería [markete'ria] *nf* marquetry,
inlaid work

marranada [marra'naða] *nf* (*fam*): **es una ~**
that's disgusting; **hacer una ~ a algn** to do
the dirty on sb

marrano, -a [ma'rrano, a] *adj* filthy, dirty
■ *nm* (*Zool*) pig; (*malo*) swine; (*sucio*) dirty pig

marras ['marras]: **de ~** *adv*: **es el problema
de ~** it's the same old problem

marrón [ma'rron] *adj* brown

marroquí [marro'ki] *adj, nm/f* Moroccan
■ *nm* Morocco (leather)

Marruecos [ma'rrwekos] *nm* Morocco

marta ['marta] *nf* (*animal*) (pine) marten;
(*piel*) sable

Marte ['marte] *nm* Mars

martes ['martes] *nm inv* Tuesday; **~ de
carnaval** Shrove Tuesday; *ver tb* **Carnaval;
sábado**

martillar [marti'ʎar], **martillear**
[martiʎe'ar] *vt* to hammer

martilleo [marti'ʎeo] *nm* hammering

martillo [mar'tiʎo] *nm* hammer; (*de presidente
de asamblea, comité*) gavel; **~ neumático**
pneumatic drill (*Brit*), jackhammer (*US*)

Martinica [marti'nika] *nf* Martinique

mártir ['martir] *nm/f* martyr

martirice *etc* [marti'riθe] *vb ver* **martirizar**

martirio [mar'tirjo] *nm* martyrdom; *(fig)* torture, torment

martirizar [martiri'θar] *vt (Rel)* to martyr; *(fig)* to torture, torment

maruja [ma'ruxa] *nf (fam)* = **maría**

marxismo [mark'sismo] *nm* Marxism

marxista [mark'sista] *adj, nm/f* Marxist

marzo ['marθo] *nm* March; **11-M** (= 11 *de marzo*) *the Madrid train bombings of 11th March 2004; ver tb* **julio**

mas [mas] *conj* but

○ **PALABRA CLAVE**

más [mas] *adj, adv* **1**: ~ **(que, de)** *(compar)* more (than), …+ er (than); ~ **grande/inteligente** bigger/more intelligent; **trabaja ~ (que yo)** he works more (than me); ~ **de seis** more than six; **es ~ de medianoche** it's after midnight; **durar ~** to last longer; *ver tb* **cada**

2 *(superl)*: **el ~** the most, …+ est; **el ~ grande/inteligente (de)** the biggest/most intelligent (in)

3 *(negativo)*: **no tengo ~ dinero** I haven't got any more money; **no viene ~ por aquí** he doesn't come round here any more; **no sé ~** I don't know any more, that's all I know

4 *(adicional)*: **un kilómetro ~** one more kilometre; **no le veo ~ solución que …** I see no other solution than to …; **¿algo ~?** anything else?; *(en tienda)* will that be all?; **¿quién ~?** anybody else?

5 (+ *adj: valor intensivo*): **¡qué perro ~ sucio!** what a filthy dog!; **¡es ~ tonto!** he's so stupid!

6 *(locuciones)*: ~ **o menos** more or less; **los ~** most people; **es ~** in fact, furthermore; ~ **bien** rather; **¡qué ~ da!** what does it matter!; *ver tb* **no**

7: **por ~**: **por más que lo intento** no matter how much o hard I try; **por ~ que quisiera ayudar** much as I should like to help

8: **de ~**: **veo que aquí estoy de más** I can see I'm not needed here; **tenemos uno de ~** we've got one extra

9 *(Am)*: **no ~** only, just; **ayer no ~** just yesterday ■ *prep*: **2 ~ 2 son 4** 2 and 0 plus 2 are 4

■ *nm inv*: **este trabajo tiene sus ~ y sus menos** this job's got its good points and its bad points

masa ['masa] *nf (mezcla)* dough; *(volumen)* volume, mass; *(Física)* mass; **en ~** en masse; **las masas** *(Pol)* the masses

masacrar [masa'krar] *vt* to massacre

masacre [ma'sakre] *nf* massacre

masaje [ma'saxe] *nm* massage; **dar ~ a** to massage

masajista [masa'xista] *nm/f* masseur/masseuse

mascar [mas'kar] *vt, vi* to chew; *(fig)* to mumble, mutter

máscara ['maskara] *nf (tb Inform)* mask ■ *nm/f* masked person; ~ **antigás** gas mask

mascarada [maska'raða] *nf* masquerade

mascarilla [maska'riʎa] *nf* mask; *(vaciado)* deathmask; *(de maquillaje)* face pack

mascarón [maska'ron] *nm* large mask; ~ **de proa** figurehead

mascota [mas'kota] *nf* mascot

masculino, -a [masku'lino, a] *adj* masculine; *(Bio)* male ■ *nm (Ling)* masculine

mascullar [masku'ʎar] *vt* to mumble, mutter

masificación [masifika'θjon] *nf* overcrowding

masilla [ma'siʎa] *nf* putty

masivo, -a [ma'siβo, a] *adj (en masa)* mass

masón [ma'son] *nm* (free)mason

masonería [masone'ria] *nf* (free)masonry

masoquista [maso'kista] *adj* masochistic ■ *nm/f* masochist

masque *etc* ['maske] *vb ver* **mascar**

mastectomía [mastekto'mia] *nf* mastectomy

máster (*pl* **masters**) ['master, 'masters] *nm* postgraduate degree; *ver tb* **licenciado**

masticar [masti'kar] *vt* to chew; *(fig)* to ponder over

mástil ['mastil] *nm (de navío)* mast; *(de guitarra)* neck

mastín [mas'tin] *nm* mastiff

mastique *etc* [mas'tike] *vb ver* **masticar**

masturbación [masturβa'θjon] *nf* masturbation

masturbarse [mastur'βarse] *vr* to masturbate

Mat. *abr* = **Matemáticas**

mata ['mata] *nf (arbusto)* bush, shrub; *(de hierbas)* tuft; *(campo)* field; *(manojo)* tuft, blade; **matas** *nfpl* scrub *sg*; ~ **de pelo** mop of hair; **a salto de ~** *(día a día)* from day to day; *(al azar)* haphazardly

matadero [mata'ðero] *nm* slaughterhouse, abattoir

matador, a [mata'ðor, a] *adj* killing ■ *nm/f* killer ■ *nm (Taur)* matador, bullfighter

matamoscas [mata'moskas] *nm inv (palo)* fly swat

matanza [ma'tanθa] *nf* slaughter

matar [ma'tar] *vt* to kill; *(tiempo, pelota)* to kill ■ *vi* to kill; **matarse** *vr (suicidarse)* to kill o.s., commit suicide; *(morir)* to be o get killed;

(*gastarse*) to wear o.s. out; ~ **el hambre** to stave off hunger; ~ **a algn a disgustos** to make sb's life a misery; **matarlas callando** to go about things slyly; **matarse trabajando** to kill o.s. with work; **matarse por hacer algo** to struggle to do sth

matarife [mata'rife] *nm* slaughterman

matasanos [mata'sanos] *nm inv* quack

matasellos [mata'seʎos] *nm inv* postmark

mate ['mate] *adj* (*sin brillo: color*) dull, matt ■ *nm* (*en ajedrez*) (check)mate; (*Am: hierba*) maté; (: *vasija*) gourd

matemático, -a [mate'matiko, a] *adj* mathematical ■ *nm/f* mathematician; **matemáticas** *nfpl* mathematics *sg*

materia [ma'terja] *nf* (*gen*) matter; (*Tec*) material; (*Escol*) subject; **en ~ de** on the subject of; (*en cuanto a*) as regards; ~ **prima** raw material; **entrar en ~** to get down to business

material [mate'rjal] *adj* material; (*dolor*) physical; (*real*) real; (*literal*) literal ■ *nm* material; (*Tec*) equipment; ~ **de construcción** building material; **materiales de derribo** rubble *sg*

materialismo [materja'lismo] *nm* materialism

materialista [materja'lista] *adj* materialist(ic)

materialmente [materjal'mente] *adv* materially; (*fig*) absolutely

maternal [mater'nal] *adj* motherly, maternal

maternidad [materni'ðað] *nf* motherhood, maternity

materno, -a [ma'terno, a] *adj* maternal; (*lengua*) mother *cpd*

matice *etc* [ma'tiθe] *vb ver* **matizar**

matinal [mati'nal] *adj* morning *cpd*

matiz [ma'tiθ] *nm* shade; (*de sentido*) shade, nuance; (*de ironía etc*) touch

matizar [mati'θar] *vt* (*variar*) to vary; (*Arte*) to blend; ~ **de** to tinge with

matón [ma'ton] *nm* bully

matorral [mato'rral] *nm* thicket

matraca [ma'traka] *nf* rattle; (*fam*) nuisance

matraz [ma'traθ] *nm* (*Química*) flask

matriarcado [matrjar'kaðo] *nm* matriarchy

matrícula [ma'trikula] *nf* (*registro*) register; (*Escol: inscripción*) registration; (*Auto*) registration number; (: *placa*) number plate

matricular [matriku'lar] *vt* to register, enrol

matrimonial [matrimo'njal] *adj* matrimonial

matrimonio [matri'monjo] *nm* (*pareja*) (married) couple; (*acto*) marriage; ~ **civil/ clandestino** civil/secret marriage; **contraer ~ (con)** to marry

matriz [ma'triθ] *nf* (*Anat*) womb; (*Tec*) mould; (*Mat*) matrix; **casa ~** (*Com*) head office

matrona [ma'trona] *nf* (*mujer de edad*) matron

matutino, -a [matu'tino, a] *adj* morning *cpd*

maula ['maula] *adj* (*persona*) good-for-nothing ■ *nm/f* (*vago*) idler, slacker ■ *nf* (*persona*) dead loss (*fam*)

maullar [mau'ʎar] *vi* to mew, miaow

maullido [mau'ʎiðo] *nm* mew(ing), miaow(ing)

Mauricio [mau'riθjo] *nm* Mauritius

Mauritania [mauri'tanja] *nf* Mauritania

mausoleo [mauso'leo] *nm* mausoleum

max. *abr* (= *máximo*) max.

maxilar [maksi'lar] *nm* jaw(bone)

máxima ['maksima] *nf ver* **máximo**

máxime ['maksime] *adv* especially

máximo, -a ['maksimo, a] *adj* maximum; (*más alto*) highest; (*más grande*) greatest ■ *nm* maximum ■ *nf* maxim; ~ **jefe** *o* **líder** (*Am*) President, leader; **como ~** at most; **al ~** to the utmost

maxisingle [maksi'singel] *nm* twelve-inch (single)

maya ['maja] *adj* Mayan ■ *nm/f* Maya(n)

mayo ['majo] *nm* May; *ver tb* **julio**

mayonesa [majo'nesa] *nf* mayonnaise

mayor [ma'jor] *adj* main, chief; (*adulto*) grown-up, adult; (*Jur*) of age; (*de edad avanzada*) elderly; (*Mus*) major; (*comparativo: de tamaño*) bigger; (: *de edad*) older; (*superlativo: de tamaño*) biggest; (*tb fig*) greatest; (: *de edad*) oldest ■ *nm* chief, boss; (*adulto*) adult; **al por ~** wholesale; ~ **de edad** adult; *ver tb* **mayores**

mayoral [majo'ral] *nm* foreman

mayordomo [major'ðomo] *nm* butler

mayoreo [majo'reo] *nm* (*Am*) wholesale (trade)

mayores [ma'jores] *nmpl* grown-ups; **llegar a ~** to get out of hand

mayoría [majo'ria] *nf* majority, greater part; **en la ~ de los casos** in most cases; **en su ~** on the whole

mayorista [majo'rista] *nm/f* wholesaler

mayoritario, -a [majori'tarjo, a] *adj* majority *cpd*; **gobierno ~** majority government

mayúsculo, -a [ma'juskulo, a] *adj* (*fig*) big, tremendous ■ *nf* capital (letter); **mayúsculas** *nfpl* capitals; (*Tip*) upper case *sg*

maza ['maθa] *nf* (*arma*) mace; (*Deporte*) bat; (*Polo*) stick

mazacote [maθa'kote] *nm* hard mass; (*Culin*) dry doughy food; (*Arte, Lit etc*) mess, hotchpotch

mazapán [maθa'pan] *nm* marzipan

mazmorra [maθ'morra] *nf* dungeon

mazo ['maθo] *nm* (*martillo*) mallet; (*de mortero*) pestle; (*de flores*) bunch; (*Deporte*) bat

mazorca [ma'θorka] *nf* (*Bot*) spike; (*de maíz*) cob, ear

Mb *abr* (= *megabyte*) Mb

MCAC *nm abr* = **Mercado Común de la América Central**

m.c.d. *abr* (= *mínimo común denominador*) lcd

MCI *nm abr* = **Mercado Común Iberoamericano**

m.c.m. *abr* = **mínimo común múltiplo**

me [me] *pron* (*directo*) me; (*indirecto*) (to) me; (*reflexivo*) (to) myself; **¡dámelo!** give it to me!; **me lo compró** (*de mí*) he bought it from me; (*para mí*) he bought it for me

meandro [me'andro] *nm* meander

mear [me'ar] (*fam*) *vt* to piss on (!) ■ *vi* to pee, piss (!), have a piss (!); **mearse** *vr* to wet o.s.

Meca ['meka] *nf:* **La ~** Mecca

mecánica [me'kanika] *nf ver* **mecánico**

mecanice *etc* [meka'niθe] *vb ver* **mecanizar**

mecánico, -a [me'kaniko, a] *adj* mechanical; (*repetitivo*) repetitive ■ *nm/f* mechanic ■ *nf* (*estudio*) mechanics *sg*; (*mecanismo*) mechanism

mecanismo [meka'nismo] *nm* mechanism; (*engranaje*) gear

mecanizar [mekani'θar] *vt* to mechanize

mecanografía [mekanoɣra'fia] *nf* typewriting

mecanografiado, -a [mekanoɣra'fjaðo, a] *adj* typewritten ■ *nm* typescript

mecanógrafo, -a [meka'noɣrafo, a] *nm/f* (*copy*) typist

mecate [me'kate] *nm* (*Am*) rope

mecedor [mese'ðor] *nm* (*Am*), **mecedora** [meθe'ðora] *nf* rocking chair

mecenas [me'θenas] *nm inv* patron

mecenazgo [meθe'naθɣo] *nm* patronage

mecer [me'θer] *vt* (*cuna*) to rock; **mecerse** *vr* to rock; (*rama*) to sway

mecha ['metʃa] *nf* (*de vela*) wick; (*de bomba*) fuse; **a toda ~** at full speed; **ponerse mechas** to streak one's hair

mechero [me'tʃero] *nm* (cigarette) lighter

mechón [me'tʃon] *nm* (*gen*) tuft; (*manojo*) bundle; (*de pelo*) lock

medalla [me'ðaʎa] *nf* medal

media ['meðja] *nf ver* **medio**

mediación [meða'θjon] *nf* mediation; **por ~ de** through

mediado, -a [me'ðjaðo, a] *adj* half-full; (*trabajo*) half-completed; **a mediados de** in the middle of, halfway through

medianamente [meðjana'mente] *adv* (*moderadamente*) moderately, fairly; (*regularmente*) moderately well

mediano, -a [me'ðjano, a] *adj* (*regular*) medium, average; (*mediocre*) mediocre ■ *nf* (*Aut*) central reservation, median (*US*); (**de tamaño**) ~ medium-sized

medianoche [meðja'notʃe] *nf* midnight

mediante [me'ðjante] *adv* by (means of), through

mediar [me'ðjar] *vi* (*tiempo*) to elapse; (*interceder*) to mediate, intervene; (*existir*) to exist; **media el hecho de que ...** there is the fact that ...

medicación [meðika'θjon] *nf* medication, treatment

medicamento [meðika'mento] *nm* medicine, drug

medicina [meði'θina] *nf* medicine

medicinal [meðiθi'nal] *adj* medicinal

medición [meði'θjon] *nf* measurement

médico, -a ['meðiko, a] *adj* medical ■ *nm/f* doctor; **~ de cabecera** family doctor; **~ pediatra** paediatrician; **~ residente** house physician, intern (*US*)

medida [me'ðiða] *nf* measure; (*medición*) measurement; (*de camisa, zapato etc*) size, fitting; (*moderación*) moderation, prudence; **en cierta/gran ~** up to a point/to a great extent; **un traje a la ~** made-to-measure suit; **~ de cuello** collar size; **a ~ de** in proportion to; (*de acuerdo con*) in keeping with; **con ~** with restraint; **sin ~** immoderately; **a ~ que ...** (at the same time) as ...; **tomar medidas** to take steps

medieval [meðje'βal] *adj* medieval

medio, -a ['meðjo, a] *adj* half (a); (*punto*) mid, middle; (*promedio*) average ■ *adv* half-; (*esp Am: un tanto*) rather, quite ■ *nm* (*centro*) middle, centre; (*método*) means, way; (*ambiente*) environment ■ *nf* (*prenda de vestir*) stocking; (*Am*) sock; (*promedio*) average; **medias** *nfpl* tights; **media hora** half an hour; **~ litro** half a litre; **las tres y media** half past three; **M~ Oriente** Middle East; **a ~ camino** halfway (there); **~ dormido** half asleep; **~ enojado** (*esp Am*) rather annoyed; **lo dejó a medios** he left it half-done; **ir a medios** to go fifty-fifty; **a ~ terminar** half finished; **en ~** in the middle; (*entre*) in between; **por ~ de** by (means of), through; **en los medios financieros** in financial circles; **encontrarse en su ~** to be in one's element; **~ ambiente** environment; **~ circulante** (*Com*) money supply; *ver tb* **medios**

medioambiental [meðjoambjen'tal] *adj* environmental

mediocre [me'ðjokre] *adj* middling, average; (*pey*) mediocre

mediocridad [meðjokri'ðað] *nf* middling quality; (*pey*) mediocrity

mediodía [meðjo'ðia] *nm* midday, noon

mediopensionista [meðjopensjo'nista] *nm/f* day boy (girl)

medios ['meðjos] *nmpl* means, resources; **los ~ de comunicación** the media

medir [me'ðir] *vt* (*gen*) to measure ▪ *vi* to measure; **medirse** *vr* (*moderarse*) to be moderate, act with restraint; **¿cuánto mides? — mido 1.50 m** how tall are you? — I am 1.50 m tall

meditabundo, -a [meðita'βundo, a] *adj* pensive

meditar [meði'tar] *vt* to ponder, think over, meditate on; (*planear*) to think out ▪ *vi* to ponder, think, meditate

mediterráneo, -a [meðite'rraneo, a] *adj* Mediterranean ▪ *nm*: **el (mar) M~** the Mediterranean (Sea)

medrar [me'ðrar] *vi* to increase, grow; (*mejorar*) to improve; (*prosperar*) to prosper, thrive; (*animal, planta etc*) to grow

medroso, -a [me'ðroso, a] *adj* fearful, timid

médula ['meðula] *nf* (*Anat*) marrow; (*Bot*) pith; **~ espinal** spinal cord; **hasta la ~** (*fig*) to the core

medusa [me'ðusa] *nf* (*Esp*) jellyfish

megabyte ['meɣaβait] *nm* (*Inform*) megabyte

megafonía [meɣafo'nia] *nf* PA o public address system

megáfono [me'ɣafono] *nm* public address system

megalomanía [meɣaloma'nia] *nf* megalomania

megalómano, -a [meɣa'lomano, a] *nm/f* megalomaniac

megaocteto [meɣaok'teto] *nm* (*Inform*) megabyte

mejicano, -a [mexi'kano, a] *adj, nm/f* Mexican

Méjico ['mexiko] *nm* Mexico

mejilla [me'xiʎa] *nf* cheek

mejillón [mexi'ʎon] *nm* mussel

mejor [me'xor] *adj, adv* (*comparativo*) better; (*superlativo*) best; **lo ~** the best thing; **lo ~ de la vida** the prime of life; **a lo ~** probably; (*quizá*) maybe; **~ dicho** rather; **tanto ~** so much the better; **es el ~ de todos** he's the best of all

mejora [me'xora] *nf*, **mejoramiento** [mexora'mjento] *nm* improvement

mejorar [mexo'rar] *vt* to improve, make better ▪ *vi*, **mejorarse** *vr* to improve, get better; (*Com*) to do well, prosper; **~ a** to be better than; **los negocios mejoran** business is picking up

mejoría [mexo'ria] *nf* improvement; (*restablecimiento*) recovery

mejunje [me'xunxe] *nm* (*pey*) concoction

melancolía [melanko'lia] *nf* melancholy

melancólico, -a [melan'koliko, a] *adj* (*triste*) sad, melancholy; (*soñador*) dreamy

melena [me'lena] *nf* (*de persona*) long hair; (*Zool*) mane

melillense [meli'ʎense] *adj* of o from Melilla ▪ *nm/f* native o inhabitant of Melilla

mella ['meʎa] *nf* (*rotura*) notch, nick; **hacer ~** (*fig*) to make an impression

mellizo, -a [me'ʎiθo, a] *adj, nm/f* twin

melocotón [meloko'ton] *nm* (*Esp*) peach

melodía [melo'ðia] *nf* melody; (*tonada*) tune; (*de móvil*) ringtone

melodrama [melo'ðrama] *nm* melodrama

melodramático, -a [meloðra'matiko, a] *adj* melodramatic

melón [me'lon] *nm* melon

melopea [melo'pea] *nf* (*fam*): **tener una ~** to be sloshed

meloso, -a [me'loso, a] *adj* honeyed, sweet; (*empalagoso*) sickly, cloying; (*voz*) sweet; (*zalamero*) smooth

membrana [mem'brana] *nf* membrane

membrete [mem'brete] *nm* letterhead; **papel con ~** headed notepaper

membrillo [mem'briʎo] *nm* quince; **carne de ~** quince jelly

memo, -a ['memo, a] *adj* silly, stupid ▪ *nm/f* idiot

memorable [memo'raβle] *adj* memorable

memorándum [memo'randum] *nm* (*libro*) notebook; (*comunicación*) memorandum

memoria [me'morja] *nf* (*gen*) memory; (*artículo*) (learned) paper; **memorias** *nfpl* (*de autor*) memoirs; **~ anual** annual report; **aprender algo de ~** to learn sth by heart; **si tengo buena ~** if my memory serves me right; **venir a la ~** to come to mind; (*Inform*): **~ de acceso aleatorio** random access memory, RAM; **~ auxiliar** backing storage; **~ fija** read-only memory, ROM; **~ del teclado** keyboard memory

memorice *etc* [memo'riθe] *vb ver* **memorizar**

memorizar [memori'θar] *vt* to memorize

menaje [me'naxe] *nm* (*muebles*) furniture; (*utensilios domésticos*) household equipment; **~ de cocina** kitchenware

mención [men'θjon] *nf* mention; **digno de ~** noteworthy; **hacer ~ de** to mention

mencionar [menθjo'nar] *vt* to mention; (*nombrar*) to name; **sin ~ ...** let alone ...

mendicidad [mendiθi'ðað] *nf* begging

mendigar [mendi'ɣar] *vt* to beg (for)

mendigo, -a [men'diɣo, a] *nm/f* beggar

mendigue etc [men'diɣe] vb ver **mendigar**

mendrugo [men'druɣo] nm crust

menear [mene'ar] vt to move; (cola) to wag; (cadera) to swing; (fig) to handle; **menearse** vr to shake; (balancearse) to sway; (moverse) to move; (fig) to get a move on

menester [menes'ter] nm (necesidad) necessity; **menesteres** nmpl (deberes) duties; **es ~ hacer algo** it is necessary to do sth, sth must be done

menestra [me'nestra] nf: **~ de verduras** vegetable stew

mengano, -a [men'gano, a] nm/f Mr (o Mrs o Miss) So-and-so

mengua ['mengwa] nf (disminución) decrease; (falta) lack; (pobreza) poverty; (fig) discredit; **en ~ de** to the detriment of

menguante [men'gwante] adj decreasing, diminishing; (luna) waning; (marea) ebb cpd

menguar [men'gwar] vt to lessen, diminish; (fig) to discredit ■ vi to diminish, decrease; (fig) to decline

mengüe etc ['mengwe] vb ver **menguar**

menopausia [meno'pausja] nf menopause

menor [me'nor] adj (más pequeño: comparativo) smaller; (número) less, lesser; (: superlativo) smallest; (número) least; (más joven: comparativo) younger; (: superlativo) youngest; (Mus) minor ■ nm/f (joven) young person, juvenile; **Juanito es ~ que Pepe** Juanito is younger than Pepe; **ella es la ~ de todas** she is the youngest of all; **no tengo la ~ idea** I haven't the faintest idea; **al por ~** retail; **~ de edad** under age

Menorca [me'norka] nf Minorca

menorquín, -ina [menor'kin, ina] adj, nm/f Minorcan

 PALABRA CLAVE

menos [menos] adj **1**: **~ (que/de)** (compar: cantidad) less (than); (: número) fewer (than); **con ~ entusiasmo** with less enthusiasm; **~ gente** fewer people; ver tb **cada**
2 (superl): **es el que ~ culpa tiene** he is the least to blame; **donde ~ problemas hay** where there are fewest problems
■ adv **1** (compar): **~ (que/de)** less (than); **me gusta ~ que el otro** I like it less than the other one; **~ de cinco** less than five; **~ de lo que piensas** less than you think
2 (superl): **es el ~ listo (de su clase)** he's the least bright (in his class); **de todas ellas es la que ~ me agrada** out of all of them she's the one I like least; **(por) lo ~** at (the very) least; **es lo ~ que puedo hacer** it's the least I can do; **lo ~ posible** as little as possible

3 (locuciones): **no quiero verle y ~ visitarle** I don't want to see him let alone visit him; **tenemos siete (de) ~** we're seven short; **eso es lo de ~** that's the least of it; **¡todo ~ eso!** anything but that!; **al/por lo ~** at (the very) least; **si al ~** if only
■ prep except; (cifras) minus; **todos ~ él** everyone except (for) him; **5 ~ 2** 5 minus 2; **las 7 ~ 20** (hora) 20 to 7
■ conj: **a ~ que**: **a menos que venga mañana** unless he comes tomorrow

menoscabar [menoska'βar] vt (estropear) to damage, harm; (fig) to discredit

menospreciar [menospre'θjar] vt to underrate, undervalue; (despreciar) to scorn, despise

menosprecio [menos'preθjo] nm (subestimación) underrating, undervaluation; (desdén) scorn, contempt

mensaje [men'saxe] nm message; **~ de error** (Inform) error message; **~ de texto** text message; **~ electrónico** email

mensajero, -a [mensa'xero, a] nm/f messenger

menstruación [menstrwa'θjon] nf menstruation

menstruar [mens'trwar] vi to menstruate

mensual [men'swal] adj monthly; **10 euros mensuales** 10 euros a month

mensualidad [menswali'ðað] nf (salario) monthly salary; (Com) monthly payment o instalment

menta ['menta] nf mint

mentado, -a [men'taðo, a] adj (mencionado) aforementioned; (famoso) well-known ■ nf: **hacerle una mentada a algn** (Am fam) to (seriously) insult sb

mental [men'tal] adj mental

mentalidad [mentali'ðað] nf mentality

mentalizar [mentali'θar] vt (sensibilizar) to make aware; (convencer) to convince; (preparar mentalmente) to psych up; **mentalizarse** vr (concienciarse) to become aware; (prepararse mentalmente) to get psyched up; **mentalizarse de que …** (convencerse) to get it into one's head that …

mentar [men'tar] vt to mention, name; **~ la madre a algn** to swear at sb

mente ['mente] nf mind; (inteligencia) intelligence; **no tengo en ~ hacer eso** it is not my intention to do that

mentecato, -a [mente'kato, a] adj silly, stupid ■ nm/f fool, idiot

mentir [men'tir] vi to lie; **¡miento!** sorry, I'm wrong!

mentira [men'tira] nf (una mentira) lie; (acto)

m

lying; (*invención*) fiction; ~ **piadosa** white lie; **una ~ como una casa** a whopping great lie (*fam*); **parece ~ que ...** it seems incredible that ..., I can't believe that ...

mentiroso, -a [menti'roso, a] *adj* lying; (*falso*) deceptive ■ *nm/f* liar

mentís [men'tis] *nm inv* denial; (*tb*: **dar el mentís a**) to deny

mentón [men'ton] *nm* chin

menú [me'nu] *nm* (*tb Inform*) menu; (*tb*: **menú del día**) set meal; **guiado por menú** (*Inform*) menu-driven

menudear [menuðe'ar] *vt* (*repetir*) to repeat frequently ■ *vi* (*ser frecuente*) to be frequent; (*detallar*) to go into great detail

menudencia [menu'ðenθja] *nf* (*bagatela*) trifle; **menudencias** *nfpl* odds and ends

menudeo [menu'ðeo] *nm* retail sales *pl*

menudillos [menu'ðiʎos] *nmpl* giblets

menudo, -a [me'nuðo, a] *adj* (*pequeño*) small, tiny; (*sin importancia*) petty, insignificant; **¡~ negocio!** (*fam*) some deal!; **a ~** often, frequently

meñique [me'ɲike] *nm* little finger

meollo [me'oʎo] *nm* (*fig*) essence, core

mequetrefe [meke'trefe] *nm* good-for-nothing, whippersnapper

mercader [merka'ðer] *nm* merchant

mercadería [merkaðe'ria] *nf* commodity; **mercaderías** *nfpl* goods, merchandise *sg*

mercado [mer'kaðo] *nm* market; **~ en baja** falling market; **M~ Común** Common Market; **~ de demanda/de oferta** seller's/buyer's market; **~ laboral** labour market; **~ objetivo** target market; **~ de productos básicos** commodity market; **~ de valores** stock market; **~ exterior/interior** *o* **nacional/libre** overseas/home/free market

mercancía [merkan'θia] *nf* commodity; **mercancías** *nfpl* goods, merchandise *sg*; **mercancías en depósito** bonded goods; **mercancías perecederas** perishable goods

mercancías [merkan'θias] *nm inv* goods train, freight train (*US*)

mercantil [merkan'til] *adj* mercantile, commercial

mercenario, -a [merθe'narjo, a] *adj, nm* mercenary

mercería [merθe'ria] *nf* (*artículos*) haberdashery (*Brit*), notions *pl* (*US*); (*tienda*) haberdasher's shop (*Brit*), drapery (*Brit*), notions store (*US*)

Mercosur [merko'sur] *nm abr* (*Argentina, Brasil, Paraguay, Uruguay*) = **Mercado Común del Sur**

mercurio [mer'kurjo] *nm* mercury

merecedor, a [mereθe'ðor, a] *adj* deserving; **~ de confianza** trustworthy

merecer [mere'θer] *vt* to deserve, merit ■ *vi* to be deserving, be worthy; **merece la pena** it's worthwhile

merecido, -a [mere'θiðo, a] *adj* (well) deserved; **llevarse su ~** to get one's deserts

merendar [meren'dar] *vt* to have for tea ■ *vi* to have tea; (*en el campo*) to have a picnic

merendero [meren'dero] *nm* (*café*) tearoom; (*en el campo*) picnic spot

merengue [me'renge] *nm* meringue

merezca *etc* [me'reθka] *vb ver* **merecer**

meridiano [meri'ðjano] *nm* (*Astro, Geo*) meridian; **la explicación es de una claridad meridiana** the explanation is as clear as day

meridional [meriðjo'nal] *adj* Southern ■ *nm/f* Southerner

merienda *etc* [me'rjenda] *vb ver* **merendar** ■ *nf* (light) tea, afternoon snack; (*de campo*) picnic; **~ de negros** free-for-all

mérito ['merito] *nm* merit; (*valor*) worth, value; **hacer méritos** to make a good impression; **restar ~ a** to detract from

meritorio, -a [meri'torjo, a] *adj* deserving

merluza [mer'luθa] *nf* hake; **coger una ~** (*fam*) to get sozzled

merma ['merma] *nf* decrease; (*pérdida*) wastage

mermar [mer'mar] *vt* to reduce, lessen ■ *vi* to decrease, dwindle

mermelada [merme'laða] *nf* jam; **~ de naranja** marmalade

mero, -a ['mero, a] *adj* mere, simple; (*Am fam*) real ■ *adv* (*Am*) just, right ■ *nm* (*Zool*) grouper; **el ~ ~** (*Am fam*) the boss

merodear [meroðe'ar] *vi* (*Mil*) to maraud; (*de noche*) to prowl (about); (*curiosear*) to snoop around

mes [mes] *nm* month; (*salario*) month's pay; **el ~ corriente** this *o* the current month

mesa ['mesa] *nf* table; (*de trabajo*) desk; (*Com*) counter; (*en mitin*) platform; (*Geo*) plateau; (*Arq*) landing; **~ de noche/de tijera/de operaciones** *u* **operatoria** bedside/folding/operating table; **~ redonda** (*reunión*) round table; **~ digitalizadora** (*Inform*) graph pad; **~ directiva** board; **~ y cama** bed and board; **poner/quitar la ~** to lay/clear the table

mesarse [me'sarse] *vr*: **~ el pelo** *o* **los cabellos** to tear one's hair

mesera [me'sera] *nf* (*Am*) waitress

mesero [me'sero] *nm* (*Am*) waiter

meseta [me'seta] *nf* (*Geo*) tableland; (*Arq*) landing

mesilla [me'siʎa], **mesita** [me'sita] *nf*: **~ de noche** bedside table

mesón [me'son] *nm* inn

mestizo, -a [mes'tiθo, a] *adj* half-caste, of mixed race; (*Zool*) crossbred ∎ *nm/f* half-caste

mesura [me'sura] *nf* (*calma*) calm; (*moderación*) moderation, restraint; (*cortesía*) courtesy

mesurar [mesu'rar] *vt* (*contener*) to restrain; **mesurarse** *vr* to restrain o.s.

meta ['meta] *nf* goal; (*de carrera*) finish; (*fig*) goal, aim, objective

metabolismo [metaβo'lismo] *nm* metabolism

metafísico, -a [meta'fisiko, a] *adj* metaphysical ∎ *nf* metaphysics *sg*

metáfora [me'tafora] *nf* metaphor

metafórico, -a [meta'foriko, a] *adj* metaphorical

metal [me'tal] *nm* (*materia*) metal; (*Mus*) brass

metálico, -a [me'taliko, a] *adj* metallic; (*de metal*) metal ∎ *nm* (*dinero contante*) cash

metalurgia [meta'lurxja] *nf* metallurgy

metalúrgico, -a [meta'lurxiko, a] *adj* metallurgic(al); **industria metalúrgica** engineering industry

metamorfosear [metamorfose'ar] *vt*: ~ **(en)** to metamorphose o transform (into)

metamorfosis [metamor'fosis] *nf inv* metamorphosis, transformation

metedura [mete'ðura] *nf*: ~ **de pata** (*fam*) blunder

meteorito [meteo'rito] *nm* meteorite

meteoro [mete'oro] *nm* meteor

meteorología [meteorolo'xia] *nf* meteorology

meteorólogo, -a [meteo'roloɣo, a] *nm/f* meteorologist; (*Radio, TV*) weather reporter

meter [me'ter] *vt* (*colocar*) to put, place; (*introducir*) to put in, insert; (*involucrar*) to involve; **meterse** *vr*: **meterse en** to go into, enter; (*fig*) to interfere in, meddle in; **meterse a** to start; **meterse a escritor** to become a writer; **meterse con algn** to provoke sb, pick a quarrel with sb; ~ **prisa a algn** to hurry sb up

meticuloso, -a [metiku'loso, a] *adj* meticulous, thorough

metido, -a [me'tiðo, a] *adj*: **estar muy ~ en un asunto** to be deeply involved in a matter; ~ **en años** elderly; ~ **en carne** plump

metódico, -a [me'toðiko, a] *adj* methodical

metodismo [meto'ðismo] *nm* Methodism

método ['metoðo] *nm* method

metodología [metoðolo'xia] *nf* methodology

metomentodo [metomen'toðo] *nm inv* meddler, busybody

metraje [me'traxe] *nm* (*Cine*) length; **cinta de largo/corto** ~ full-length film/short

metralla [me'traʎa] *nf* shrapnel

metralleta [metra'ʎeta] *nf* sub-machine-gun

métrico, -a ['metriko, a] *adj* metric ∎ *nf* metrics *pl*; **cinta métrica** tape measure

metro ['metro] *nm* metre; (*tren: tb:* **metropolitano**) underground (*Brit*), subway (*US*); (*instrumento*) rule; ~ **cuadrado/cúbico** square/cubic metre

metrópoli [me'tropoli], **metrópolis** [me'tropolis] *nf* (*ciudad*) metropolis; (*colonial*) mother country

mexicano, -a [mexi'kano, a] *adj, nm/f* (*Am*) Mexican

México ['mexiko] *nm* (*Am*) Mexico; **Ciudad de ~** Mexico City

mezcla ['meθkla] *nf* mixture; (*fig*) blend

mezclar [meθ'klar] *vt* to mix (up); (*armonizar*) to blend; (*combinar*) to merge; **mezclarse** *vr* to mix, mingle; ~ **en** to get mixed up in, get involved in

mezcolanza [meθko'lanθa] *nf* hotchpotch, jumble

mezquindad [meθkin'dað] *nf* (*cicatería*) meanness; (*miras estrechas*) pettiness; (*acto*) mean action

mezquino, -a [meθ'kino, a] *adj* (*cicatero*) mean ∎ *nm/f* (*avaro*) mean person; (*miserable*) petty individual

mezquita [meθ'kita] *nf* mosque

mg *abr* (= *miligramo(s)*) mg

mi [mi] *adj posesivo* my ∎ *nm* (*Mus*) E

mí [mi] *pron* me, myself; **¿y a mí qué?** so what?

miaja ['mjaxa] *nf* crumb; **ni una ~** (*fig*) not the least little bit

miau [mjau] *nm* miaow

michelín [mitʃe'lin] *nm* (*fam*) spare tyre

mico ['miko] *nm* monkey

micro ['mikro] *nm* (*Radio*) mike, microphone; (*Am: pequeño*) minibus; (: *grande*) coach, bus

microbio [mi'kroβjo] *nm* microbe

microbús [mikro'βus] *nm* minibus

microchip [mikro'tʃip] *nm* microchip

microcomputador [mikrokomputa'ðor] *nm*, **microcomputadora** [mikrokomputa'ðora] *nf* micro(computer)

microeconomía [mikroekono'mia] *nf* microeconomics *sg*

microficha [mikro'fitʃa] *nf* microfiche

microfilm (*pl* **microfilms**) [mikro'film, mikro'films] *nm* microfilm

micrófono [mi'krofono] *nm* microphone

microinformática [mikroinfor'matika] *nf* microcomputing

micrómetro [mi'krometro] *nm* micrometer

microonda [mikro'onda] *nf* microwave;

255

(horno) microondas microwave (oven)
microordenador [mikroordena'ðor] *nm*
microcomputer
micropastilla [mikropas'tiʎa],
microplaqueta [mikropla'keta] *nf* (*Inform*)
chip, wafer
microplaquita [mikropla'kita] *nf*: **~ de
silicio** silicon chip
microprocesador [mikroprocesa'ðor] *nm*
microprocessor
microscópico, -a [mikros'kopiko, a] *adj*
microscopic
microscopio [mikros'kopjo] *nm* microscope
midiendo *etc* [mi'ðjendo] *vb ver* **medir**
miedo ['mjeðo] *nm* fear; (*nerviosismo*)
apprehension, nervousness; **meter ~ a** to
scare, frighten; **tener ~** to be afraid; **de ~**
wonderful, marvellous; **¡qué ~!** (*fam*) how
awful!; **me da ~** it scares me; **hace un frío
de ~** (*fam*) it's terribly cold
miedoso, -a [mje'ðoso, a] *adj* fearful, timid
miel [mjel] *nf* honey; **no hay ~ sin hiel**
there's no rose without a thorn
miembro ['mjembro] *nm* limb; (*socio*)
member; (*de institución*) fellow; **~ viril** penis
mientes *etc* ['mjentes] *vb ver* **mentar**; **mentir**
■ *nfpl*: **no parar ~ en** to pay no attention to;
traer a las ~ to recall
mientras ['mjentras] *conj* while; (*duración*) as
long as ■ *adv* meanwhile; **~ (que)** whereas;
~ tanto meanwhile; **~ más tiene, más
quiere** the more he has, the more he wants
miércoles ['mjerkoles] *nm inv* Wednesday; **~
de ceniza** Ash Wednesday; *ver tb* **Carnaval;
sábado**
mierda ['mjerða] *nf* (*fam!*) shit (!), crap (!); (*fig*)
filth, dirt; **¡vete a la ~!** go to hell!
mies [mjes] *nf* (ripe) corn, wheat, grain
miga ['miɣa] *nf* crumb; (*fig: meollo*) essence;
hacer buenas migas (*fam*) to get on well;
esto tiene su ~ there's more to this than
meets the eye
migaja [mi'ɣaxa] *nf*: **una ~ de** (*un poquito*) a
little; **migajas** *nfpl* crumbs; (*pey*) left-overs
migración [miɣra'θjon] *nf* migration
migratorio, -a [miɣra'torjo, a] *adj* migratory
mil [mil] *num* thousand; **dos ~ libras** two
thousand pounds
milagro [mi'laɣro] *nm* miracle; **hacer
milagros** (*fig*) to work wonders
milagroso, -a [mila'ɣroso, a] *adj* miraculous
Milán [mi'lan] *nm* Milan
milenario, -a [mile'narjo, a] *adj* millennial;
(*fig*) very ancient
milenio [mi'lenjo] *nm* millennium
milésimo, -a [mi'lesimo, a] *num* thousandth
mileurista *nmf person earning around a thousand*

euros or less; **un ~ no puede comprar ese piso**
no one on a salary of a thousand euros could
afford that flat ■ *adj* of (around) a thousand
euros; **un sueldo ~** a salary of (around) a
thousand euros
mili ['mili] *nf*: **hacer la ~** (*fam*) to do one's
military service; *see note*

● **MILI**
●
● *La mili*, military service, is compulsory in
● Spain although the number of months'
● service has been reduced and recruits are
● now posted close to their home town.
● There continues to be strong opposition
● from *objetores de conciencia*, conscientious
● objectors, who are obliged to do *Prestación
● Social Sustitutoria* in place of military
● service; this usually involves doing
● community service and lasts longer.
● Those who refuse to do either of these, *los
● insumisos*, can be sent to prison.

milicia [mi'liθja] *nf* (*Mil*) militia; (*servicio
militar*) military service
miligramo [mili'ɣramo] *nm* milligram
milímetro [mi'limetro] *nm* millimetre (*Brit*),
millimeter (*US*)
militante [mili'tante] *adj* militant
militar [mili'tar] *adj* military ■ *nm/f* soldier
■ *vi* to serve in the army; (*fig*) to militate, fight
militarismo [milita'rismo] *nm* militarism
milla ['miʎa] *nf* mile; **~ marina** nautical mile
millar [mi'ʎar] *num* thousand; **a millares** in
thousands
millón [mi'ʎon] *num* million
millonario, -a [miʎo'narjo, a] *nm/f*
millionaire
millonésimo, -a [miʎo'nesimo, a] *num*
millionth
mimado, -a [mi'maðo, a] *adj* spoiled
mimar [mi'mar] *vt* to spoil, pamper
mimbre ['mimbre] *nm* wicker; **de ~** wicker
cpd, wickerwork
mimetismo [mime'tismo] *nm* mimicry
mímica ['mimika] *nf* (*para comunicarse*) sign
language; (*imitación*) mimicry
mimo ['mimo] *nm* (*caricia*) caress; (*de niño*)
spoiling; (*Teat*) mime; (: *actor*) mime artist
mina ['mina] *nf* mine; (*pozo*) shaft; (*de lápiz*)
lead refill; **hullera o ~ de carbón** coalmine
minar [mi'nar] *vt* to mine; (*fig*) to undermine
mineral [mine'ral] *adj* mineral ■ *nm* (*Geo*)
mineral; (*mena*) ore
minería [mine'ria] *nf* mining
minero, -a [mi'nero, a] *adj* mining *cpd*
■ *nm/f* miner

miniatura [minja'tura] *adj inv, nf* miniature

minicadena [minika'ðena] *nf* (*Mus*) mini hi-fi

minicomputador [minikomputa'ðor] *nm* minicomputer

MiniDisc® [mini'disk] *nm* MiniDisc®

minidisco [mini'ðisko] *nm* diskette

minifalda [mini'falda] *nf* miniskirt

minifundio [mini'fundjo] *nm* smallholding, small farm

minimizar [minimi'θar] *vt* to minimize

mínimo, -a ['minimo, a] *adj* minimum; (*insignificante*) minimal ∎ *nm* minimum; **precio/salario** ~ minimum price/wage; **lo ~ que pueden hacer** the least they can do

minino, -a [mi'nino, a] *nm/f* (*fam*) puss, pussy

ministerio [minis'terjo] *nm* ministry (*Brit*), department (*US*); **M~ de Asuntos Exteriores** Foreign Office (*Brit*), State Department (*US*); **M~ del Comercio e Industria** Department of Trade and Industry; **M~ de (la) Gobernación** *o* **del Interior** ≈ Home Office (*Brit*), Ministry of the Interior; **M~ de Hacienda** Treasury (*Brit*), Treasury Department (*US*)

ministro, -a [mi'nistro, a] *nm/f* minister, secretary (*esp US*); **M~ de Hacienda** Chancellor of the Exchequer, Secretary of the Treasury (*US*); **M~ de (la) Gobernación** *o* **del Interior** ≈ Home Secretary (*Brit*), Secretary of the Interior (*US*)

minoría [mino'ria] *nf* minority

minorista [mino'rista] *nm* retailer

mintiendo *etc* [min'tjendo] *vb ver* **mentir**

minucia [mi'nuθja] *nf* (*detalle insignificante*) trifle; (*bagatela*) mere nothing

minuciosidad [minuθjosi'ðað] *nf* (*meticulosidad*) thoroughness, meticulousness

minucioso, -a [minu'θjoso, a] *adj* thorough, meticulous; (*prolijo*) very detailed

minúsculo, -a [mi'nuskulo, a] *adj* tiny, minute ∎ *nf* small letter; **minúsculas** *nfpl* (*Tip*) lower case *sg*

minusvalía [minusβa'lia] *nf* physical handicap; (*Com*) depreciation, capital loss

minusválido, -a [minus'βaliðo, a] *adj* (physically) handicapped *o* disabled ∎ *nm/f* disabled person

minuta [mi'nuta] *nf* (*de comida*) menu; (*de abogado etc*) fee

minutero [minu'tero] *nm* minute hand

minuto [mi'nuto] *nm* minute

Miño ['miɲo] *nm*: **el (río)** ~ the Miño

mío, -a ['mio, a] *adj, pron*: **el** ~ mine; **un amigo** ~ a friend of mine; **lo** ~ what is mine; **los míos** my people, my relations

miope ['mjope] *adj* short-sighted

miopía [mjo'pia] *nf* near- *o* short-sightedness

MIR [mir] *nm abr* (*Pol*) = **Movimiento de Izquierda Revolucionaria**; (*Esp Med*) = **Médico Interno y Residente**

mira ['mira] *nf* (*de arma*) sight(s) *pl*; (*fig*) aim, intention; **de amplias/estrechas miras** broad-/narrow-minded

mirada [mi'raða] *nf* look, glance; (*expresión*) look, expression; ~ **de soslayo** sidelong glance; ~ **fija** stare, gaze; ~ **perdida** distant look; **echar una** ~ **a** to glance at; **levantar/bajar la** ~ to look up/down; **resistir la** ~ **de algn** to stare sb out

mirado, -a [mi'raðo, a] *adj* (*sensato*) sensible; (*considerado*) considerate; **bien/mal** ~ well/not well thought of

mirador [mira'ðor] *nm* viewpoint, vantage point

miramiento [mira'mjento] *nm* (*consideración*) considerateness; **tratar sin miramientos a algn** to ride roughshod over sb

mirar [mi'rar] *vt* to look at; (*observar*) to watch; (*considerar*) to consider, think over; (*vigilar, cuidar*) to watch, look after ∎ *vi* to look; (*Arq*) to face; **mirarse** *vr* (*dos personas*) to look at each other; ~ **algo/a algn de reojo** *o* **de través** to look askance at sth/sb; ~ **algo/a algn por encima del hombro** to look down on sth/sb; ~ **bien/mal** to think highly of/have a poor opinion of; ~ **fijamente** to stare *o* gaze at; ~ **por** (*fig*) to look after; ~ **por la ventana** to look out of the window; **mirarse al espejo** to look at o.s. in the mirror; **mirarse a los ojos** to look into each other's eyes

mirilla [mi'riʎa] *nf* (*agujero*) spyhole, peephole

mirlo ['mirlo] *nm* blackbird

misa ['misa] *nf* mass; ~ **del gallo** midnight mass (*on Christmas Eve*); ~ **de difuntos** requiem mass; **como en** ~ in dead silence; **estos datos van a** ~ (*fig*) these facts are utterly trustworthy

misántropo [mi'santropo] *nm* misanthrope, misanthropist

miscelánea [misθe'lanea] *nf* miscellany

miserable [mise'raβle] *adj* (*avaro*) mean, stingy; (*nimio*) miserable, paltry; (*lugar*) squalid; (*fam*) vile, despicable ∎ *nm/f* (*malvado*) rogue

miseria [mi'serja] *nf* misery; (*pobreza*) poverty; (*tacañería*) meanness, stinginess; (*condiciones*) squalor; **una** ~ a pittance

misericordia [miseri'korðja] *nf* (*compasión*) compassion, pity; (*perdón*) forgiveness, mercy

misil [mi'sil] *nm* missile

misión [mi'sjon] *nf* mission; (*tarea*) job,

duty; (Pol) assignment; **misiones** nfpl (Rel) overseas missions

misionero, -a [misjo'nero, a] nm/f missionary

mismamente [misma'mente] adv (fam: sólo) only, just

mismísimo, -a [mis'misimo, a] adj superlativo selfsame, very (same)

mismo, -a ['mismo, a] adj (semejante) same; (después de pronombre) -self; (para énfasis) very ■ adv: **aquí/ayer/hoy ~** right here/only yesterday/this very day; **ahora ~** right now ■ conj: **lo ~ que** just like, just as; **por lo ~** for the same reason; **el ~ traje** the same suit; **en ese ~ momento** at that very moment; **vino el ~ Ministro** the Minister himself came; **yo ~ lo vi** I saw it myself; **lo hizo por sí ~** he did it by himself; **lo ~** the same (thing); **da lo ~** it's all the same; **quedamos en las mismas** we're no further forward

misógino [mi'soxino] nm misogynist

miss [mis] nf beauty queen

misterio [mis'terjo] nm mystery; (lo secreto) secrecy

misterioso, -a [miste'rjoso, a] adj mysterious; (inexplicable) puzzling

misticismo [misti'θismo] nm mysticism

místico, -a ['mistiko, a] adj mystic(al) ■ nm/f mystic ■ nf mysticism

mitad [mi'tað] nf (medio) half; (centro) middle; **~ (y) ~** half-and-half; (fig) yes and no; **a ~ de precio** (at) half-price; **en o a ~ del camino** halfway along the road; **cortar por la ~** to cut through the middle

mítico, -a ['mitiko, a] adj mythical

mitigar [miti'ɣar] vt to mitigate; (dolor) to relieve; (sed) to quench; (ira) to appease; (preocupación) to allay; (soledad) to alleviate

mitigue etc [mi'tiɣe] vb ver **mitigar**

mitin ['mitin] nm (esp Pol) meeting

mito ['mito] nm myth

mitología [mitolo'xia] nf mythology

mitológico, -a [mito'loxiko, a] adj mythological

mixto, -a ['miksto, a] adj mixed; (comité) joint

ml abr (= mililitro(s)) ml

mill. abr (= millón, millones) M

mm abr (= milímetro(s)) mm

MMS nm abr (= multimedia message service) MMS m

M.N. (Am), **m/n** abr (Econ) = **moneda nacional**

M.° abr (Pol: = Ministerio) Min

m/o abr (Com) = **mi orden**

mobiliario [moβi'ljarjo] nm furniture

mocasín [moka'sin] nm moccasin

mocedad [moθe'ðað] nf youth

mochila [mo'tʃila] nf rucksack (Brit), backpack

moción [mo'θjon] nf motion; **~ compuesta** (Pol) composite motion

moco ['moko] nm mucus; **limpiarse los mocos** to blow one's nose; **no es ~ de pavo** it's no trifle

mocoso, -a [mo'koso, a] adj snivelling; (fig) ill-bred ■ nm/f (fam) brat

moda ['moða] nf fashion; (estilo) style; **de o a la ~** in fashion, fashionable; **pasado de ~** out of fashion; **vestido a la última ~** trendily dressed

modal [mo'ðal] adj modal ■ nm: **modales** manners

modalidad [moðali'ðað] nf (clase) kind, variety; (manera) way; (Inform) mode; **~ de texto** (Inform) text mode

modelar [moðe'lar] vt to model

modelo [mo'ðelo] adj inv model ■ nm/f model ■ nm (patrón) pattern; (norma) standard

módem ['moðem] nm (Inform) modem

moderado, -a [moðe'raðo, a] adj moderate

moderar [moðe'rar] vt to moderate; (violencia) to restrain, control; (velocidad) to reduce; **moderarse** vr to restrain o.s., control o.s

modernice etc [moðer'niθe] vb ver **modernizar**

modernizar [moðerni'θar] vt to modernize; (Inform) to upgrade

moderno, -a [mo'ðerno, a] adj modern; (actual) present-day; (equipo etc) up-to-date

modestia [mo'ðestja] nf modesty

modesto, -a [mo'ðesto, a] adj modest

módico, -a ['moðiko, a] adj moderate, reasonable

modificar [moðifi'kar] vt to modify

modifique etc [moði'fike] vb ver **modificar**

modismo [mo'ðismo] nm idiom

modisto, -a [mo'ðisto, a] nm/f dressmaker

modo ['moðo] nm (manera, forma) way, manner; (Inform, Mus) mode; (Ling) mood; **modos** nmpl manners; **"~ de empleo"** "instructions for use"; **~ de gobierno** form of government; **a ~ de** like; **de este ~** in this way; **de ningún ~** in no way; **de todos modos** at any rate; **de un ~ u otro** (in) one way or another

modorra [mo'ðorra] nf drowsiness

modoso, -a [mo'ðoso, a] adj (educado) quiet, well-mannered

modulación [moðula'θjon] nf modulation; **~ de frecuencia** (Radio) frequency modulation, FM

módulo ['moðulo] *nm* module; (*de mueble*) unit

mofarse [mo'farse] *vr*: ~ **de** to mock, scoff at

moflete [mo'flete] *nm* fat cheek, chubby cheek

mogollón [moɣo'ʎon] (*fam*) *nm*: ~ **de discos** *etc* loads of records *etc* ■ *adv*: **un** ~ a hell of a lot

mohín [mo'in] *nm* (*mueca*) (wry) face; (*pucheros*) pout

mohíno, -a [mo'ino, a] *adj* (*triste*) gloomy, depressed; (*enojado*) sulky

moho ['moo] *nm* (*Bot*) mould, mildew; (*en metal*) rust

mohoso, -a [mo'oso, a] *adj* mouldy; rusty

mojado, -a [mo'xaðo, a] *adj* wet; (*húmedo*) damp; (*empapado*) drenched

mojar [mo'xar] *vt* to wet; (*humedecer*) to damp(en), moisten; (*calar*) to soak; **mojarse** *vr* to get wet; ~ **el pan en el café** to dip *o* dunk one's bread in one's coffee

mojigato, -a [moxi'ɣato, a] *adj* (*hipócrita*) hypocritical; (*santurrón*) sanctimonious; (*gazmoño*) prudish ■ *nm/f* hypocrite; sanctimonious person; prude

mojón [mo'xon] *nm* (*hito*) landmark; (*en un camino*) signpost; (*tb:* **mojón kilométrico**) milestone

mol. *abr* (= *molécula*) mol

molar [mo'lar] *nm* molar ■ *vt* (*fam*): **lo que más me mola es ...** what I'm really into is ...; **¿te mola un pitillo?** do you fancy a smoke?

Moldavia [mol'ðaβja], **Moldova** [mol'ðoβa] *nf* Moldavia, Moldova

moldavo, -a [mol'ðaβo, a] *adj, nm/f* Moldavian, Moldovan

molde ['molde] *nm* mould; (*vaciado*) cast; (*de costura*) pattern; (*fig*) model

moldear [molde'ar] *vt* to mould; (*en yeso etc*) to cast

mole ['mole] *nf* mass, bulk; (*edificio*) pile

molécula [mo'lekula] *nf* molecule

moler [mo'ler] *vt* to grind, crush; (*pulverizar*) to pound; (*trigo etc*) to mill; (*cansar*) to tire out, exhaust; ~ **a algn a palos** to give sb a beating

molestar [moles'tar] *vt* to bother; (*fastidiar*) to annoy; (*incomodar*) to inconvenience, put out; (*perturbar*) to trouble, upset ■ *vi* to be a nuisance; **molestarse** *vr* to bother; (*incomodarse*) to go to a lot of trouble; (*ofenderse*) to take offence; **¿le molesta el ruido?** do you mind the noise?; **siento molestarle** I'm sorry to trouble you

molestia [mo'lestja] *nf* bother, trouble; (*incomodidad*) inconvenience; (*Med*) discomfort; **no es ninguna** ~ it's no trouble at all

molesto, -a [mo'lesto, a] *adj* (*que fastidia*) annoying; (*incómodo*) inconvenient; (*inquieto*) uncomfortable, ill at ease; (*enfadado*) annoyed; **estar** ~ (*Med*) to be in some discomfort; **estar** ~ **con algn** (*fig*) to be cross with sb; **me sentí** ~ I felt embarrassed

molido, -a [mo'liðo, a] *adj* (*machacado*) ground; (*pulverizado*) powdered; **estar** ~ (*fig*) to be exhausted *o* dead beat

molinero [moli'nero] *nm* miller

molinillo [moli'niʎo] *nm* hand mill; ~ **de carne/café** mincer/coffee grinder

molino [mo'lino] *nm* (*edificio*) mill; (*máquina*) grinder

mollera [mo'ʎera] *nf* (*Anat*) crown of the head; (*fam: seso*) brains *pl*; **duro de** ~ (*estúpido*) thick

Molucas [mo'lukas] *nfpl*: **las (Islas)** ~ the Moluccas, the Molucca Islands

molusco [mo'lusko] *nm* mollusc

momentáneo, -a [momen'taneo, a] *adj* momentary

momento [mo'mento] *nm* (*gen*) moment; (*Tec*) momentum; **de** ~ at the moment, for the moment; **en ese** ~ at that moment, just then; **por el** ~ for the time being

momia ['momja] *nf* mummy

mona ['mona] *nf ver* **mono**

Mónaco ['monako] *nm* Monaco

monada [mo'naða] *nf* (*gracia*) charming habit; (*cosa primorosa*) lovely thing; (*chica*) pretty girl; **¡qué** ~! isn't it cute?

monaguillo [mona'ɣiʎo] *nm* altar boy

monarca [mo'narka] *nm/f* monarch, ruler

monarquía [monar'kia] *nf* monarchy

monárquico, -a [mo'narkiko, a] *nm/f* royalist, monarchist

monasterio [monas'terjo] *nm* monastery

Moncloa [mon'kloa] *nf*: **la** ~ *official residence of the Spanish Prime Minister*

monda ['monda] *nf* (*poda*) pruning; (: *de árbol*) lopping; (: *de fruta*) peeling; (*cáscara*) skin; **¡es la** ~! (*fam: fantástico*) it's great!; (: *el colmo*) it's the limit!; (: *persona: gracioso*) he's a knockout!

mondadientes [monda'ðjentes] *nm inv* toothpick

mondar [mon'dar] *vt* (*limpiar*) to clean; (*pelar*) to peel; **mondarse** *vr*: **mondarse de risa** (*fam*) to split one's sides laughing

moneda [mo'neða] *nf* (*tipo de dinero*) currency, money; (*pieza*) coin; **una** ~ **de 50 céntimos** a 50-cent coin; ~ **de curso** legal tender; ~ **extranjera** foreign exchange; ~ **única** single currency; **es** ~ **corriente** (*fig*) it's common knowledge

monedero [mone'ðero] *nm* purse

monegasco, -a [mone'ɣasko, a] *adj* of *o* from

Monaco, Monegasque ■ *nm/f* Monegasque

monetario, -a [mone'tarjo, a] *adj* monetary, financial

monetarista [moneta'rista] *adj, nm/f* monetarist

mongólico, -a [mon'goliko, a] *adj, nm/f* Mongol

monigote [moni'ɣote] *nm* (*dibujo*) doodle; (*de papel*) cut-out figure; (*pey*) wimp; *ver tb* **inocente**

monitor [moni'tor] *nm* (*Inform*) monitor; **~ en color** colour monitor

monja ['monxa] *nf* nun

monje ['monxe] *nm* monk

mono, -a ['mono, a] *adj* (*bonito*) lovely, pretty; (*gracioso*) nice, charming ■ *nm/f* monkey, ape ■ *nm* dungarees *pl*; (*traje de faena*) overalls *pl*; (*fam: de drogadicto*) cold turkey; **una chica muy mona** a very pretty girl; **dormir la ~** to sleep it off

monóculo [mo'nokulo] *nm* monocle

monografía [monoɣra'fia] *nf* monograph

monolingüe [mono'lingwe] *adj* monolingual

monólogo [mo'noloɣo] *nm* monologue

monomando [mono'mando] *nm* (*tb:* **grifo monomando**) mixer tap

monoparental [monoparen'tal] *adj:* **familia ~** single-parent family

monopatín [monopa'tin] *nm* skateboard

monopolice *etc* [monopo'liθe] *vb ver* **monopolizar**

monopolio [mono'poljo] *nm* monopoly; **~ total** absolute monopoly

monopolista [monopo'lista] *adj, nm/f* monopolist

monopolizar [monopoli'θar] *vt* to monopolize

monosílabo, -a [mono'silaβo, a] *adj* monosyllabic ■ *nm* monosyllable

monotonía [monoto'nia] *nf* (*sonido*) monotone; (*fig*) monotony

monótono, -a [mo'notono, a] *adj* monotonous

mono-usuario, -a [monou'swarjo, a] *adj* (*Inform*) single-user

monóxido [mo'noksiðo] *nm* monoxide; **~ de carbono** carbon monoxide

Mons. *abr* (*Rel*) = **Monseñor**

monseñor [monse'ɲor] *nm* monsignor

monserga [mon'serɣa] *nf* (*lenguaje confuso*) gibberish; (*tonterías*) drivel

monstruo ['monstrwo] *nm* monster ■ *adj inv* fantastic

monstruoso, -a [mons'trwoso, a] *adj* monstrous

monta ['monta] *nf* total, sum; **de poca ~** unimportant, of little account

montacargas [monta'karɣas] *nm inv* service lift (*Brit*), freight elevator (*US*)

montador [monta'ðor] *nm* (*para montar*) mounting block; (*profesión*) fitter; (*Cine*) film editor

montaje [mon'taxe] *nm* assembly; (*organización*) fitting up; (*Teat*) décor; (*Cine*) montage

montante [mon'tante] *nm* (*poste*) upright; (*soporte*) stanchion; (*Arq: de puerta*) transom; (*: de ventana*) mullion; (*suma*) amount, total

montaña [mon'taɲa] *nf* (*monte*) mountain; (*sierra*) mountains *pl*, mountainous area; (*Am: selva*) forest; **~ rusa** roller coaster

montañero, -a [monta'ɲero, a] *adj* mountain *cpd* ■ *nm/f* mountaineer, climber

montañés, -esa [monta'ɲes, esa] *adj* mountain *cpd*; (*de Santander*) of o from the Santander region ■ *nm/f* highlander; native o inhabitant of the Santander region

montañismo [monta'ɲismo] *nm* mountaineering, climbing

montañoso, -a [monta'ɲoso, a] *adj* mountainous

montar [mon'tar] *vt* (*subir a*) to mount, get on; (*caballo etc*) to ride; (*Tec*) to assemble, put together; (*negocio*) to set up; (*colocar*) to lift on to; (*Cine: película*) to edit; (*Teat: obra*) to stage, put on; (*Culin: batir*) to whip, beat ■ *vi* to mount, get on; (*sobresalir*) to overlap; **~ en cólera** to get angry; **~ un número** o **numerito** to make a scene; **tanto monta** it makes no odds

montaraz [monta'raθ] *adj* mountain *cpd*, highland *cpd*; (*pey*) uncivilized

monte ['monte] *nm* (*montaña*) mountain; (*bosque*) woodland; (*área sin cultivar*) wild area, wild country; **~ de piedad** pawnshop; **~ alto** forest; **~ bajo** scrub(land)

montera [mon'tera] *nf* (*sombrero*) cloth cap; (*de torero*) bullfighter's hat

monto ['monto] *nm* total, amount

montón [mon'ton] *nm* heap, pile; **un ~ de** (*fig*) heaps of, lots of; **a montones** by the score, galore

montura [mon'tura] *nf* (*cabalgadura*) mount; (*silla*) saddle; (*arreos*) harness; (*de joya*) mounting; (*de gafas*) frame

monumental [monumen'tal] *adj* (*tb fig*) monumental; **zona ~** area of historical interest

monumento [monu'mento] *nm* monument; (*de conmemoración*) memorial

monzón [mon'θon] *nm* monsoon

moña ['moɲa] *nf* hair ribbon

moño ['moɲo] *nm* (*de pelo*) bun; **estar hasta**

el ~ (fam) to be fed up to the back teeth

MOPTMA nm abr = **Ministerio de Obras Públicas, Transporte y Medio Ambiente**

moqueta [mo'keta] nf fitted carpet

moquillo [mo'kiʎo] nm (enfermedad) distemper

mora ['mora] nf (Bot) mulberry; (: zarzamora) blackberry; (Com): **en ~** in arrears

morado, -a [mo'raðo, a] adj purple, violet ■ nm bruise ■ nf (casa) dwelling, abode; **pasarlas moradas** to have a tough time of it

moral [mo'ral] adj moral ■ nf (ética) ethics pl; (moralidad) morals pl, morality; (ánimo) morale; **tener baja la ~** to be in low spirits

moraleja [mora'lexa] nf moral

moralice etc [mora'liθe] vb ver **moralizar**

moralidad [morali'ðað] nf morals pl, morality

moralizar [morali'θar] vt to moralize

morar [mo'rar] vi to live, dwell

moratón [mora'ton] nm bruise

moratoria [mora'torja] nf moratorium

morbo ['morβo] nm (fam) morbid pleasure

morbosidad [morβosi'ðað] nf morbidity

morboso, -a [mor'βoso, a] adj morbid

morcilla [mor'θiʎa] nf blood sausage, ≈ black pudding (Brit)

mordaz [mor'ðaθ] adj (crítica) biting, scathing

mordaza [mor'ðaθa] nf (para la boca) gag; (Tec) clamp

morder [mor'ðer] vt to bite; (mordisquear) to nibble; (fig: consumir) to eat away, eat into ■ vi, **morderse** vr to bite; **está que muerde** he's hopping mad; **morderse la lengua** to hold one's tongue

mordida [mor'ðiða] nf (Am fam) bribe

mordisco [mor'ðisko] nm bite

mordisquear [morðiske'ar] vt to nibble at

moreno, -a [mo'reno, a] adj (color) (dark) brown; (de tez) dark; (de pelo moreno) dark-haired; (negro) black ■ nm/f (de tez) dark-skinned man/woman; (de pelo) dark-haired man/woman

morfina [mor'fina] nf morphine

morfinómano, -a [morfi'nomano, a] adj addicted to hard drugs ■ nm/f drug addict

morgue ['morgue] nf (Am) mortuary (Brit), morgue (US)

moribundo, -a [mori'βundo, a] adj dying ■ nm/f dying person

morir [mo'rir] vi to die; (fuego) to die down; (luz) to go out; **morirse** vr to die; (fig) to be dying; (Ferro etc: vías) to end; (calle) to come out; **fue muerto a tiros/en un accidente** he was shot (dead)/was killed in an accident; **~ de frío/hambre** to die of cold/starve to death; **¡me muero de hambre!** (fig) I'm starving!; **morirse por algo** to be dying for sth; **morirse por algn** to be crazy about sb

mormón, -ona [mor'mon, ona] nm/f Mormon

moro, -a ['moro, a] adj Moorish ■ nm/f Moor; **¡hay moros en la costa!** watch out!

moroso, -a [mo'roso, a] adj (lento) slow ■ nm (Com) bad debtor, defaulter; **deudor ~** (Com) slow payer

morral [mo'rral] nm haversack

morriña [mo'rriɲa] nf homesickness; **tener ~** to be homesick

morro ['morro] nm (Zool) snout, nose; (Auto, Aviat) nose; (fam: labio) (thick) lip; **beber a ~** to drink from the bottle; **caer de ~** to nosedive; **estar de morros (con algn)** to be in a bad mood (with sb); **tener ~** to have a nerve

morrocotudo, -a [morroko'tuðo, a] adj (fam: fantástico) smashing; (riña, golpe) tremendous; (fuerte) strong; (pesado) heavy; (difícil) awkward

morsa ['morsa] nf walrus

morse ['morse] nm Morse (code)

mortadela [morta'ðela] nf mortadella, bologna sausage

mortaja [mor'taxa] nf shroud; (Tec) mortise; (Am) cigarette paper

mortal [mor'tal] adj mortal; (golpe) deadly

mortalidad [mortali'ðað], **mortandad** [mortan'dað] nf mortality

mortecino, -a [morte'θino, a] adj (débil) weak; (luz) dim; (color) dull

mortero [mor'tero] nm mortar

mortífero, -a [mor'tifero, a] adj deadly, lethal

mortificar [mortifi'kar] vt to mortify; (atormentar) to torment

mortifique etc [morti'fike] vb ver **mortificar**

mortuorio, -a [mor'tworjo, a] adj mortuary, death cpd

Mosa ['mosa] nm: **el (Río) ~** the Meuse

mosaico [mo'saiko] nm mosaic

mosca ['moska] nf fly; **por si las moscas** just in case; **estar ~** (desconfiar) to smell a rat; **tener la ~ en** o **detrás de la oreja** to be wary

moscovita [mosko'βita] adj Muscovite, Moscow cpd ■ nm/f Muscovite

Moscú [mos'ku] nm Moscow

mosquear [moske'ar] (fam) vt (hacer sospechar) to make suspicious; (fastidiar) to annoy; **mosquearse** vr (enfadarse) to get annoyed; (ofenderse) to take offence

mosquita [mos'kita] nf: **parece una ~ muerta** he looks as though butter wouldn't melt in his mouth

mosquitero [moski'tero] nm mosquito net

mosquito [mos'kito] *nm* mosquito
Mossos ['mosos] *nmpl*: ~ **d'Esquadra** Catalan police; *ver tb* **policía**
mostaza [mos'taθa] *nf* mustard
mosto ['mosto] *nm* unfermented grape juice
mostrador [mostra'ðor] *nm* (*de tienda*) counter; (*de café*) bar
mostrar [mos'trar] *vt* to show; (*exhibir*) to display, exhibit; (*explicar*) to explain; **mostrarse** *vr*: **mostrarse amable** to be kind; to prove to be kind; **no se muestra muy inteligente** he doesn't seem (to be) very intelligent; ~ **en pantalla** (*Inform*) to display
mota ['mota] *nf* speck; (*en diseño*) dot
mote ['mote] *nm* (*apodo*) nickname
motín [mo'tin] *nm* (*del pueblo*) revolt, rising; (*del ejército*) mutiny
motivación [motiβa'θjon] *nf* motivation
motivar [moti'βar] *vt* (*causar*) to cause, motivate; (*explicar*) to explain, justify
motivo [mo'tiβo] *nm* motive, reason; (*Arte, Mus*) motif; **con ~ de** (*debido a*) because of; (*en ocasión de*) on the occasion of; (*con el fin de*) in order to; **sin ~** for no reason at all
moto ['moto] *nf*, **motocicleta** [motoθi'kleta] *nf* motorbike (*Brit*), motorcycle
motociclista [motoθi'klista] *nmf* motorcyclist, biker
motoneta [moto'neta] *nf* (*Am*) Vespa®
motor, a [mo'tor, a] *adj* (*Tec*) motive; (*Anat*) motor ■ *nm* motor, engine; ~ **a chorro** o **de reacción/de explosión** jet engine/internal combustion engine; ~ **de búsqueda** (*Internet*) search engine ■ *nf* motorboat
motorismo [moto'rismo] *nm* motorcycling
motorista [moto'rista] *nm/f* (*esp Am: automovilista*) motorist; (: *motociclista*) motorcyclist
motorizado, -a [motori'θaðo, a] *adj* motorized
motosierra [moto'sjerra] *nf* mechanical saw
motriz [mo'triz] *adj*: **fuerza ~** motive power; (*fig*) driving force
movedizo, -a [moβe'ðiθo, a] *adj* (*inseguro*) unsteady; (*fig*) unsettled, changeable; (*persona*) fickle
mover [mo'βer] *vt* to move; (*cambiar de lugar*) to shift; (*cabeza: para negar*) to shake; (: *para asentir*) to nod; (*accionar*) to drive; (*fig*) to cause, provoke; **moverse** *vr* to move; (*mar*) to get rough; (*viento*) to rise; (*fig: apurarse*) to get a move on; (: *transformarse*) to be on the move
movible [mo'βiβle] *adj* (*no fijo*) movable; (*móvil*) mobile; (*cambiadizo*) changeable
movido, -a [mo'βiðo, a] *adj* (*Foto*) blurred;

(*persona: activo*) active; (*mar*) rough; (*día*) hectic ■ *nf* move; **la movida madrileña** the Madrid scene
móvil ['moβil] *adj* mobile; (*pieza de máquina*) moving; (*mueble*) movable ■ *nm* (*motivo*) motive; (*teléfono*) mobile, cellphone (*US*)
movilice *etc* [moβi'liθe] *vb ver* **movilizar**
movilidad [moβili'ðað] *nf* mobility
movilizar [moβili'θar] *vt* to mobilize
movimiento [moβi'mjento] *nm* movement; (*Tec*) motion; (*actividad*) activity; (*Mus*) tempo; **el M~** the Falangist Movement; ~ **de bloques** (*Inform*) block move; ~ **de mercancías** (*Com*) turnover, volume of business; ~ **obrero/sindical** workers'/trade union movement; ~ **sísmico** earth tremor
Mozambique [moθam'bike] *nm* Mozambique
mozambiqueño, -a [moθambi'keɲo, a] *adj*, *nm/f* Mozambican
mozo, -a ['moθo, a] *adj* (*joven*) young; (*soltero*) single, unmarried ■ *nm/f* (*joven*) youth, young man (girl); (*camarero*) waiter; (*camarera*) waitress; ~ **de estación** porter
MP3 *nm* MP3; **reproductor (de)** ~ MP3 player
MPAIAC [emepa'jak] *nm abr* (*Esp Pol*) = **Movimiento para la Autodeterminación y la Independencia del Archipiélago Canario**
mucama [mu'kama] *nf* (*Am*) maid
muchacho, -a [mu'tʃatʃo, a] *nm/f* (*niño*) boy/girl; (*criado*) servant/servant o maid
muchedumbre [mutʃe'ðumbre] *nf* crowd
muchísimo, -a [mu'tʃisimo, a] *adj superlativo de* **mucho** lots and lots of, ever so much ■ *adv* ever so much

 PALABRA CLAVE

mucho, -a ['mutʃo, a] *adj* **1** (*cantidad*) a lot of, much; (*número*) lots of, a lot of, many; ~ **dinero** a lot of money; **hace ~ calor** it's very hot; **muchas amigas** lots o a lot of o many friends
2 (*sg: fam*): **ésta es mucha casa para él** this house is much too big for him; **había ~ borracho** there were a lot o lots of drunks ■ *pron*: **tengo ~ que hacer** I've got a lot to do; **muchos dicen que ...** a lot of people say that ...; *ver tb* **tener**
■ *adv* **1**: **me gusta ~** I like it a lot o very much; **lo siento ~** I'm very sorry; **come ~** he eats a lot; **trabaja ~** he works hard; **¿te vas a quedar ~?** are you going to be staying long?; ~ **más/menos** much o a lot more/less
2 (*respuesta*) very; **¿estás cansado? — ¡~!** are you tired? — very!
3 (*locuciones*): **como ~** at (the) most; **el mejor**

con ~ by far the best; ¡ni ~ **menos!** far from it!; **no es rico ni ~ menos** he's far from being rich

4: **por ~ que**: **por mucho que le creas** however much o no matter how much you believe him

muda ['muða] nf (de ropa) change of clothing; (Zool) moult; (de serpiente) slough

mudanza [mu'ðanθa] nf (cambio) change; (de casa) move; **estar de ~** to be moving

mudar [mu'ðar] vt to change; (Zool) to shed ■ vi to change; **mudarse** vr (la ropa) to change; **mudarse de casa** to move house

mudo, -a ['muðo, a] adj dumb; (callado: película) silent; (Ling: letra) mute; (: consonante) voiceless; **quedarse ~ (de)** (fig) to be dumb with; **quedarse ~ de asombro** to be speechless

mueble ['mweβle] nm piece of furniture; **muebles** nmpl furniture sg

mueble-bar [mweβle'βar] nm cocktail cabinet

mueca ['mweka] nf face, grimace; **hacer muecas a** to make faces at

muela etc ['mwela] vb ver **moler** ■ nf (diente) tooth; (: de atrás) molar; (de molino) millstone; (de afilar) grindstone; **~ del juicio** wisdom tooth

muelle ['mweʎe] adj (blando) soft; (fig) soft, easy ■ nm spring; (Naut) wharf; (malecón) jetty

muera etc ['mwera] vb ver **morir**

muerda etc ['mwerða] vb ver **morder**

muermo ['mwermo] nm (fam) wimp

muerte ['mwerte] nf death; (homicidio) murder; **dar ~ a** to kill; **de mala ~** (fam) lousy, rotten; **es la ~** (fam) it's deadly boring

muerto, -a ['mwerto, a] pp de **morir** ■ adj dead; (color) dull ■ nm/f dead man(-woman); (difunto) deceased; (cadáver) corpse; **cargar con el ~** (fam) to carry the can; **echar el ~ a algn** to pass the buck; **hacer el ~** (nadando) to float; **estar ~ de cansancio** to be dead tired

muesca ['mweska] nf nick

muestra etc ['mwestra] vb ver **mostrar** ■ nf (señal) indication, sign; (demostración) demonstration; (prueba) proof; (estadística) sample; (modelo) model, pattern; (testimonio) token; **dar ~s de** to show signs of; **~ al azar** (Com) random sample

muestrario [mwes'trarjo] nm collection of samples; (exposición) showcase

muestreo [mwes'treo] nm sample, sampling

mueva etc ['mweβa] vb ver **mover**

mugir [mu'xir] vi (vaca) to moo

mugre ['muɣre] nf dirt, filth, muck

mugriento, -a [mu'ɣrjento, a] adj dirty, filthy, mucky

mugroso, -a [mu'ɣroso, a] adj (Am) filthy, grubby

muja etc ['muxa] vb ver **mugir**

mujer [mu'xer] nf woman; (esposa) wife

mujeriego [muxe'rjeɣo] nm womaniser

mula ['mula] nf mule

mulato, -a [mu'lato, a] adj, nm/f mulatto

muleta [mu'leta] nf (para andar) crutch; (Taur) stick with red cape attached

muletilla [mule'tiʎa] nf (palabra) pet word, tag; (de cómico) catch phrase

mullido, -a [mu'ʎiðo, a] adj (cama) soft; (hierba) soft, springy

multa ['multa] nf fine; **echar o poner una ~ a** to fine

multar [mul'tar] vt to fine; (Deporte) to penalize

multiacceso [multjak'θeso] adj (Inform) multi-access

multicine [multi'θine] nm multiscreen cinema

multicolor [multiko'lor] adj multicoloured

multimillonario, -a [multimiʎo'narjo, a] adj (contrato) multimillion pound o dollar cpd ■ nm/f multimillionaire/-millionairess

multinacional [multinaθjo'nal] adj, nf multinational

múltiple ['multiple] adj multiple, many pl, numerous; **de tarea ~** (Inform) multi-tasking; **de usuario ~** (Inform) multi-user

multiplicar [multipli'kar] vt (Mat) to multiply; (fig) to increase; **multiplicarse** vr (Bio) to multiply; (fig) to be everywhere at once

multiplique etc [multi'plike] vb ver **multiplicar**

múltiplo ['multiplo] adj, nm multiple

multitud [multi'tuð] nf (muchedumbre) crowd; **~ de** lots of

multitudinario, -a [multituði'narjo, a] adj (numeroso) multitudinous; (de masas) mass cpd

mundanal [munda'nal] adj worldly; **alejarse del ~ ruido** to get away from it all

mundano, -a [mun'dano, a] adj worldly; (de moda) fashionable

mundial [mun'djal] adj world-wide, universal; (guerra, récord) world cpd

mundialización [mundjaliθa'θjon] nf globalization

mundialmente [mundjal'mente] adv worldwide; **~ famoso** world-famous

mundo ['mundo] nm world; (ámbito) world, circle; **el otro ~** the next world; **el ~ del espectáculo** show business; **todo el ~** everybody; **tener ~** to be experienced, know one's way around; **el ~ es un pañuelo** it's a small world; **no es nada del otro ~** it's nothing special; **se le cayó el ~ (encima)** his world fell apart

Munich ['munitʃ] *nm* Munich

munición [muni'θjon] *nf* (*Mil: provisiones*) stores *pl*, supplies *pl*; (: *de armas*) ammunition

municipal [muniθi'pal] *adj* (*elección*) municipal; (*concejo*) town *cpd*, local; (*piscina etc*) public ▪ *nm* (*guardia*) policeman

municipio [muni'θipjo] *nm* (*ayuntamiento*) town council, corporation; (*territorio administrativo*) town, municipality

muñeca [mu'ɲeka] *nf* (*Anat*) wrist; (*juguete*) doll

muñeco [mu'ɲeko] *nm* (*figura*) figure; (*marioneta*) puppet; (*fig*) puppet, pawn; (*niño*) pretty little boy; **~ de nieve** snowman

muñequera [muɲe'kera] *nf* wristband

muñón [mu'ɲon] *nm* (*Anat*) stump

mural [mu'ral] *adj* mural, wall *cpd* ▪ *nm* mural

muralla [mu'raʎa] *nf* (*city*) wall(s) *pl*

murciano, -a [mur'θjano, a] *adj* of *o* from Murcia ▪ *nm/f* native *o* inhabitant of Murcia

murciélago [mur'θjelaɣo] *nm* bat

murga ['murɣa] *nf* (*banda*) band of street musicians; **dar la ~** to be a nuisance

murmullo [mur'muʎo] *nm* murmur(ing); (*cuchicheo*) whispering; (*de arroyo*) murmur, rippling; (*de hojas, viento*) rustle, rustling; (*ruido confuso*) hum(ming)

murmuración [murmura'θjon] *nf* gossip; (*críticas*) backbiting

murmurador, a [murmura'ðor, a] *adj* gossiping; (*criticón*) backbiting ▪ *nm/f* gossip; backbiter

murmurar [murmu'rar] *vi* to murmur, whisper; (*criticar*) to criticize; (*cotillear*) to gossip

muro ['muro] *nm* wall; **~ de contención** retaining wall

mus [mus] *nm* card game

musaraña [musa'raɲa] *nf* (*Zool*) shrew; (*insecto*) creepy-crawly; **pensar en las musarañas** to daydream

muscular [musku'lar] *adj* muscular

músculo ['muskulo] *nm* muscle

musculoso, -a [musku'loso, a] *adj* muscular

museo [mu'seo] *nm* museum; **~ de arte** *o* **de pintura** art gallery; **~ de cera** waxworks

musgo ['musɣo] *nm* moss

musical [musi'kal] *adj, nm* musical

músico, -a ['musiko, a] *adj* musical ▪ *nm/f* musician ▪ *nf* music; **irse con la música a otra parte** to clear off

musitar [musi'tar] *vt, vi* to mutter, mumble

muslo ['muslo] *nm* thigh; (*de pollo*) leg, drumstick

mustio, -a ['mustjo, a] *adj* (*persona*) depressed, gloomy; (*planta*) faded, withered

musulmán, -ana [musul'man, ana] *nm/f* Moslem, Muslim

mutación [muta'θjon] *nf* (*Bio*) mutation; (: *cambio*) (sudden) change

mutilar [muti'lar] *vt* to mutilate; (*a una persona*) to maim

mutis ['mutis] *nm inv* (*Teat*) exit; **hacer ~** (*Teat: retirarse*) to exit, go off; (*fig*) to say nothing

mutismo [mu'tismo] *nm* silence

mutualidad [mutwali'ðað] *nf* (*reciprocidad*) mutual character; (*asociación*) friendly *o* benefit (*US*) society

mutuamente [mutwa'mente] *adv* mutually

mutuo, -a ['mutwo, a] *adj* mutual

muy [mwi] *adv* very; (*demasiado*) too; **M~ Señor mío** Dear Sir; **~ bien** (*de acuerdo*) all right; **~ de noche** very late at night; **eso es ~ de él** that's just like him; **eso es ~ español** that's typically Spanish

Nn

N, n ['ene] *nf* (*letra*) N, n; **N de Navarra** N for Nellie (*Brit*) *o* Nan (*US*)

N *abr* (= *norte*) N

N. *abr* = **carretera nacional** (*Am*: = *moneda nacional*) local currency; **le entregaron sólo N.$2.000** they only gave him $2000 pesos

N.° *abr* (= *número*) No

n. *abr* (*Ling*: = *nombre*) n; = **nacido, a**

n/ *abr* = **nuestro, a**

nabo ['naβo] *nm* turnip

nácar ['nakar] *nm* mother-of-pearl

nacer [na'θer] *vi* to be born; (*huevo*) to hatch; (*vegetal*) to sprout; (*río*) to rise; (*fig*) to begin, originate, have its origins; **nació para poeta** he was born to be a poet; **nadie nace enseñado** we all have to learn; **nació una sospecha en su mente** a suspicion formed in her mind

nacido, -a [na'θiðo, a] *adj* born; **recién ~** newborn

naciente [na'θjente] *adj* new, emerging; (*sol*) rising

nacimiento [naθi'mjento] *nm* birth; (*fig*) birth, origin; (*de Navidad*) Nativity; (*linaje*) descent, family; (*de río*) source; **ciego de ~** blind from birth

nación [na'θjon] *nf* nation; (*pueblo*) people; **Naciones Unidas** United Nations

nacional [naθjo'nal] *adj* national; (*Com, Econ*) domestic, home *cpd*

nacionalice *etc* [naθjona'liθe] *vb ver* **nacionalizar**

nacionalidad [naθjonali'ðað] *nf* nationality; (*Esp, Pol*) autonomous region

nacionalismo [naθjona'lismo] *nm* nationalism

nacionalista [naθjona'lista] *adj, nm/f* nationalist

nacionalizar [naθjonali'θar] *vt* to nationalize; **nacionalizarse** *vr* (*persona*) to become naturalized

nada ['naða] *pron* nothing ■ *adv* not at all, in no way ■ *nf* nothingness; **no decir ~ (más)**

to say nothing (else), not to say anything (else); **¡~ más!** that's all; **de ~** don't mention it; **~ de eso** nothing of the kind; **antes de ~** right away; **como si ~** as if it didn't matter; **no ha sido ~** it's nothing; **la ~** the void

nadador, a [naða'ðor, a] *nm/f* swimmer

nadar [na'ðar] *vi* to swim; **~ en la abundancia** (*fig*) to be rolling in money

nadie ['naðje] *pron* nobody, no-one; **~ habló** nobody spoke; **no había ~** there was nobody there, there wasn't anybody there; **es un don ~** he's a nobody *o* nonentity

nadita [na'ðita] (*esp Am*: *fam*) = **nada**

nado ['naðo]: **a ~** *adv*: **pasar a ~** to swim across

nafta ['nafta] *nf* (*Am*) petrol (*Brit*), gas(oline) (*US*)

naftalina [nafta'lina] *nf*: **bolas de ~** mothballs

náhuatl ['nawatl] *adj, nm* Nahuatl

naipe ['naipe] *nm* (playing) card; **naipes** *nmpl* cards

nal. *abr* (= *nacional*) nat

nalgas ['nalɣas] *nfpl* buttocks

Namibia [na'miβja] *nf* Namibia

nana ['nana] *nf* lullaby

napias ['napjas] *nfpl* (*fam*) conk *sg*

Nápoles ['napoles] *nf* Naples

napolitano, -a [napoli'tano, a] *adj* of *o* from Naples, Neapolitan ■ *nm/f* Neapolitan

naranja [na'ranxa] *adj inv, nf* orange; **media ~** (*fam*) better half; **¡naranjas de la China!** nonsense!

naranjada [naran'xaða] *nf* orangeade

naranjo [na'ranxo] *nm* orange tree

Narbona [nar'βona] *nf* Narbonne

narcisista [narθi'sista] *adj* narcissistic

narciso [nar'θiso] *nm* narcissus

narcotice *etc* [narko'tiθe] *vb ver* **narcotizar**

narcótico, -a [nar'kotiko, a] *adj, nm* narcotic

narcotizar [narkoti'θar] *vt* to drug

narcotraficante [narkotrafi'kante] *nm/f* narcotics *o* drug trafficker

narcotráfico [narko'trafiko] *nm* narcotics *o* drug trafficking

nardo ['narðo] *nm* lily

narices [na'riθes] *nfpl ver* **nariz**

narigón, -ona [nari'ɣon, ona], **narigudo, a** [nari'ɣuðo, a] *adj* big-nosed

nariz [na'riθ] *nf* nose; **narices** *nfpl* nostrils; ¡**narices!** (*fam*) rubbish!; **delante de las narices de algn** under one's (very) nose; **estar hasta las narices** to be completely fed up; **meter las narices en algo** to poke one's nose into sth

narración [narra'θjon] *nf* narration

narrador, a [narra'ðor, a] *nm/f* narrator

narrar [na'rrar] *vt* to narrate, recount

narrativo, -a [narra'tiβo, a] *adj* narrative ■ *nf* narrative, story

nasal [na'sal] *adj* nasal

N.ª *abr* = **Nuestra Señora**

nata ['nata] *nf* cream (*tb fig*); (*en leche cocida etc*) skin; ~ **batida** whipped cream

natación [nata'θjon] *nf* swimming

natal [na'tal] *adj* natal; (*país*) native; **ciudad** ~ home town

natalicio [nata'liθjo] *nm* birthday

natalidad [natali'ðað] *nf* birth rate

natillas [na'tiʎas] *nfpl* (egg) custard *sg*

natividad [natiβi'ðað] *nf* nativity

nativo, -a [na'tiβo, a] *adj, nm/f* native

nato, -a ['nato, a] *adj* born; **un músico** ~ a born musician

natural [natu'ral] *adj* natural; (*fruta etc*) fresh ■ *nm/f* native ■ *nm* disposition, temperament; **buen** ~ good nature; **fruta al** ~ fruit in its own juice

naturaleza [natura'leθa] *nf* nature; (*género*) nature, kind; ~ **muerta** still life

naturalice *etc* [natura'liθe] *vb ver* **naturalizarse**

naturalidad [naturali'ðað] *nf* naturalness

naturalización [naturaliθa'θjon] *nf* naturalization

naturalizarse [naturali'θarse] *vr* to become naturalized; (*aclimatarse*) to become acclimatized

naturalmente [natural'mente] *adv* naturally; ¡~! of course!

naturista [natu'rista] *adj* (*Med*) naturopathic ■ *nm/f* naturopath

naufragar [naufra'ɣar] *vi* (*barco*) to sink; (*gente*) to be shipwrecked; (*fig*) to fail

naufragio [nau'fraxjo] *nm* shipwreck

náufrago, -a ['naufraɣo, a] *nm/f* castaway, shipwrecked person

naufrague *etc* [nau'fraɣe] *vb ver* **naufragar**

náusea ['nausea] *nf* nausea; **me da náuseas** it makes me feel sick

nauseabundo, -a [nausea'βundo, a] *adj* nauseating, sickening

náutico, -a ['nautiko, a] *adj* nautical; **club** ~ sailing *o* yacht club ■ *nf* navigation, seamanship

navaja [na'βaxa] *nf* (*cortaplumas*) clasp knife (*Brit*), penknife; ~ (**de afeitar**) razor

navajazo [naβa'xaθo] *nm* (*herida*) gash; (*acto*) slash

naval [na'βal] *adj* (*Mil*) naval; **construcción** ~ shipbuilding; **sector** ~ shipbuilding industry

Navarra [na'βarra] *nf* Navarre

navarro, -a [na'βarro, a] *adj* of *o* from Navarre, Navarrese ■ *nm/f* Navarrese ■ *nm* (*Ling*) Navarrese

nave ['naβe] *nf* (*barco*) ship, vessel; (*Arq*) nave; ~ **espacial** spaceship; **quemar las naves** to burn one's boats

navegación [naβeɣa'θjon] *nf* navigation; (*viaje*) sea journey; ~ **aérea** air traffic; ~ **costera** coastal shipping; ~ **fluvial** river navigation

navegador [naβeɣa'ðor] *nm* (*Inform*) browser; (*de coche*) sat nav

navegante [naβe'ɣante] *nm/f* navigator

navegar [naβe'ɣar] *vi* (*barco*) to sail; (*avión*) to fly ■ *vt* to sail; to fly; (*dirigir el rumbo de*) to navigate

navegue *etc* [na'βeɣe] *vb ver* **navegar**

navidad [naβi'ðað] *nf* Christmas; **navidades** *nfpl* Christmas time *sg*; **día de** ~ Christmas Day; **por navidades** at Christmas (time); ¡**felices navidades!** Merry Christmas

navideño, -a [naβi'ðeɲo, a] *adj* Christmas *cpd*

navío [na'βio] *nm* ship

nazi ['naθi] *adj, nm/f* Nazi

nazismo [na'θismo] *nm* Nazism

N. de la R. *abr* (= *nota de la redacción*) editor's note

N. de la T./del T. *abr* (= *nota de la traductora/del traductor*) translator's note

NE *abr* (= *nor(d)este*) NE

neblina [ne'βlina] *nf* mist

nebuloso, -a [neβu'loso, a] *adj* foggy; (*calinoso*) misty; (*indefinido*) nebulous, vague ■ *nf* nebula

necedad [neθe'ðað] *nf* foolishness; (*una necedad*) foolish act

necesario, -a [neθe'sarjo, a] *adj* necessary; **si fuera** *o* **fuese** ~ if need(s) be

neceser [neθe'ser] *nm* vanity case; (*bolsa grande*) holdall

necesidad [neθesi'ðað] *nf* need; (*lo inevitable*) necessity; (*miseria*) poverty, need; **en caso de** ~ in case of need *o* emergency; **hacer sus necesidades** to relieve o.s.

necesitado, -a [neθesi'taðo, a] *adj* needy, poor; ~ **de** in need of

necesitar [neθesi'tar] *vt* to need, require ∎ *vi*: ~ **de** to have need of; **necesitarse** *vr* to be needed; (*en anuncios*): **"necesítase coche"** "car wanted"

necio, -a ['neθjo, a] *adj* foolish ∎ *nm/f* fool

necrología [nekrolo'xia] *nf* obituary

necrópolis [ne'kropolis] *nf inv* cemetery

néctar ['nektar] *nm* nectar

nectarina [nekta'rina] *nf* nectarine

neerlandés, -esa [neerlan'des, esa] *adj* Dutch ∎ *nm/f* Dutchman(-woman) ∎ *nm* (*Ling*) Dutch; **los neerlandeses** the Dutch

nefando, -a [ne'fando, a] *adj* unspeakable

nefasto, -a [ne'fasto, a] *adj* ill-fated, unlucky

negación [neɣa'θjon] *nf* negation; (*Ling*) negative; (*rechazo*) refusal, denial

negado, -a [ne'ɣaðo, a] *adj*: ~ **para** inept at, unfitted for

negar [ne'ɣar] *vt* (*renegar, rechazar*) to refuse; (*prohibir*) to refuse, deny; (*desmentir*) to deny; **negarse** *vr*: **negarse a hacer algo** to refuse to do sth

negativo, -a [neɣa'tiβo, a] *adj* negative ∎ *nm* (*Foto*) negative; (*Mat*) minus ∎ *nf* (*gen*) negative; (*rechazo*) refusal, denial; **negativa rotunda** flat refusal

negligencia [neɣli'xenθja] *nf* negligence

negligente [neɣli'xente] *adj* negligent

negociable [neɣo'θjaβle] *adj* negotiable

negociación [neɣoθja'θjon] *nf* negotiation

negociado [neɣo'θjaðo] *nm* department, section

negociante [neɣo'θjante] *nm/f* businessman(-woman)

negociar [neɣo'θjar] *vt, vi* to negotiate; ~ **en** to deal in, trade in

negocio [ne'ɣoθjo] *nm* (*Com*) business; (*asunto*) affair, business; (*operación comercial*) deal, transaction; (*Am*) shop, store; (*lugar*) place of business; **los negocios** business *sg*; **hacer** ~ to do business; **el** ~ **del libro** the book trade; ~ **autorizado** licensed trade; **hombre de negocios** businessman; ~ **sucio** shady deal; **hacer un buen** ~ to pull off a profitable deal; **¡mal** ~! it looks bad!

negra ['neɣra] *nf ver* **negro** ∎ *nf* (*Mus*) crotchet

negrita [ne'ɣrita] *nf* (*Tip*) bold face; **en** ~ in bold (type)

negro, -a ['neɣro, a] *adj* black; (*suerte*) awful, atrocious; (*humor etc*) sad; (*lúgubre*) gloomy ∎ *nm* (*color*) black ∎ *nm/f* Black person ∎ *nf* (*Mus*) crotchet; ~ **como la boca del lobo** pitch-black; **estoy** ~ **con esto** I'm getting desperate about it; **ponerse** ~ (*fam*) to get cross

negrura [ne'ɣrura] *nf* blackness

negué [ne'ɣe], **neguemos** *etc* [ne'ɣemos] *vb ver* **negar**

nene, -a ['nene, a] *nm/f* baby, small child

nenúfar [ne'nufar] *nm* water lily

neologismo [neolo'xismo] *nm* neologism

neón [ne'on] *nm* neon

neoyorquino, -a [neojor'kino, a] *adj* New York *cpd* ∎ *nm/f* New Yorker

neozelandés, -esa [neoθelan'des, esa] *adj* New Zealand *cpd* ∎ *nm/f* New Zealander

nepotismo [nepo'tismo] *nm* nepotism

nervio ['nerβjo] *nm* (*Anat*) nerve; (: *tendón*) tendon; (*fig*) vigour; (*Tec*) rib; **crispar los nervios a algn, poner los nervios de punta a algn** to get on sb's nerves

nerviosismo [nerβjo'sismo] *nm* nervousness, nerves *pl*

nervioso, -a [ner'βjoso, a] *adj* nervous; (*sensible*) nervy, highly-strung; (*impaciente*) restless; **¡no te pongas ~!** take it easy!

nervudo, -a [ner'βuðo, a] *adj* tough; (*mano*) sinewy

netiqueta [neti'keta] *n* netiquette

neto, -a ['neto, a] *adj* clear; (*limpio*) clean; (*Com*) net

neumático, -a [neu'matiko, a] *adj* pneumatic ∎ *nm* (*Esp*) tyre (*Brit*), tire (*US*); ~ **de recambio** spare tyre

neumonía [neumo'nia] *nf* pneumonia; ~ **asiática** SARS

neura ['neura] (*fam*) *nm/f* (*persona*) neurotic ∎ *nf* (*obsesión*) obsession

neuralgia [neu'ralxja] *nf* neuralgia

neurálgico, -a [neu'ralxiko, a] *adj* neuralgic; (*fig: centro*) nerve *cpd*

neurastenia [neuras'tenja] *nf* neurasthenia; (*fig*) excitability

neurasténico, -a [neuras'teniko, a] *adj* neurasthenic; excitable

neurólogo, -a [neu'roloɣo, a] *nm/f* neurologist

neurona [neu'rona] *nf* neuron

neurosis [neu'rosis] *nf inv* neurosis

neurótico, -a [neu'rotiko, a] *adj, nm/f* neurotic

neutral [neu'tral] *adj* neutral

neutralice *etc* [neutra'liθe] *vb ver* **neutralizar**

neutralizar [neutrali'θar] *vt* to neutralize; (*contrarrestar*) to counteract

neutro, -a ['neutro, a] *adj* (*Bio, Ling*) neuter

neutrón [neu'tron] *nm* neutron

nevado, -a [ne'βaðo, a] *adj* snow-covered; (*montaña*) snow-capped; (*fig*) snowy, snow-white ∎ *nf* snowstorm; (*caída de nieve*) snowfall

nevar [ne'βar] *vi* to snow ∎ *vt* (*fig*) to whiten

nevera [ne'βera] *nf* (*Esp*) refrigerator (*Brit*), icebox (*US*)

n

nevisca [ne'βiska] *nf* flurry of snow

nexo ['nekso] *nm* link, connection

n/f *abr* (*Com*) = **nuestro favor**

ni [ni] *conj* nor, neither; (*tb*: **ni siquiera**) not even; **ni que** not even if; **ni blanco ni negro** neither white nor black; **ni el uno ni el otro** neither one nor the other

Nicaragua [nika'raγwa] *nf* Nicaragua

nicaragüense [nikara'ɣwense] *adj, nm/f* Nicaraguan

nicho ['nitʃo] *nm* niche

nick [nik] *nm* (*Internet*) nickname, user name, nick

nicotina [niko'tina] *nf* nicotine

nido ['niðo] *nm* nest; (*fig*) hiding place; **~ de ladrones** den of thieves

niebla ['njeβla] *nf* fog; (*neblina*) mist; **hay ~** it is foggy

niego *etc* ['njeγo], **niegue** *etc* ['njeγe] *vb ver* **negar**

nieto, -a ['njeto, a] *nm/f* grandson/ granddaughter; **nietos** *nmpl* grandchildren

nieve *etc* ['njeβe] *vb ver* **nevar** ■ *nf* snow; (*Am*) ice cream; **copo de ~** snowflake

N.I.F. *nm abr* (= *Número de Identificación Fiscal*) ID number used for tax purposes

Nigeria [ni'xerja] *nf* Nigeria

nigeriano, -a [nixe'rjano, a] *adj, nm/f* Nigerian

nigromancia [niɣro'manθja] *nf* necromancy, black magic

nihilista [nii'lista] *adj* nihilistic ■ *nm* nihilist

Nilo ['nilo] *nm*: **el (Río) ~** the Nile

nimbo ['nimbo] *nm* (*aureola*) halo; (*nube*) nimbus

nimiedad [nimje'ðað] *nf* small-mindedness; (*trivialidad*) triviality; (*una nimiedad*) trifle, tiny detail

nimio, -a ['nimjo, a] *adj* trivial, insignificant

ninfa ['ninfa] *nf* nymph

ninfómana [nin'fomana] *nf* nymphomaniac

ninguno, -a [nin'guno, a] *adj* (*antes de nmsg* **ningún**) no ■ *pron* (*nadie*) nobody; (*ni uno*) none, not one; (*ni uno ni otro*) neither; **de ninguna manera** by no means, not at all; **no voy a ninguna parte** I'm not going anywhere

niña ['niɲa] *nf ver* **niño**

niñera [ni'ɲera] *nf* nursemaid, nanny

niñería [niɲe'ria] *nf* childish act

niñez [ni'ɲeθ] *nf* childhood; (*infancia*) infancy

niño, -a ['niɲo, a] *adj* (*joven*) young; (*inmaduro*) immature ■ *nm* (*chico*) boy, child ■ *nf* girl, child; (*Anat*) pupil; **los niños** the children; **~ bien** rich kid; **~ expósito** foundling; **~ de pecho** babe-in-arms; **~ prodigio** child

prodigy; **de ~** as a child; **ser el ~ mimado de algn** to be sb's pet; **ser la niña de los ojos de algn** to be the apple of sb's eye

nipón, -ona [ni'pon, ona] *adj, nm/f* Japanese; **los nipones** the Japanese

níquel ['nikel] *nm* nickel

niquelar [nike'lar] *vt* (*Tec*) to nickel-plate

níspero ['nispero] *nm* medlar

nitidez [niti'ðeθ] *nf* (*claridad*) clarity; (: *de atmósfera*) brightness; (: *de imagen*) sharpness

nítido, -a ['nitiðo, a] *adj* bright; (*fig*) pure; (*imagen*) clear, sharp

nitrato [ni'trato] *nm* nitrate

nitrógeno [ni'troxeno] *nm* nitrogen

nitroglicerina [nitroɣliθe'rina] *nf* nitroglycerine

nivel [ni'βel] *nm* (*Geo*) level; (*norma*) level, standard; (*altura*) height; **~ de aceite** oil level; **~ de aire** spirit level; **~ de vida** standard of living; **al ~ de** on a level with, at the same height as; (*fig*) on a par with; **a 900m sobre el ~ del mar** at 900m above sea level

nivelado, -a [niβe'laðo, a] *adj* level, flat; (*Tec*) flush

nivelar [niβe'lar] *vt* to level out; (*fig*) to even up; (*Com*) to balance

Niza ['niθa] *nf* Nice

n/l. *abr* (*Com*) = **nuestra letra**

NNE *abr* (= *nornordeste*) NNE

NNO *abr* (= *nornoroeste*) NNW

NN. UU. *nfpl abr* (= *Naciones Unidas*) UN *sg*

NO *abr* (= *noroeste*) NW

no [no] *adv* no; (*con verbo*) not ■ *excl* no!; **no tengo nada** I don't have anything, I have nothing; **no es el mío** it's not mine; **ahora no** not now; **¿no lo sabes?** don't you know?; **no mucho** not much; **no bien termine, lo entregaré** as soon as I finish I'll hand it over; **¡a que no lo sabes!** I bet you don't know!; **¡cómo no!** of course!; **pacto de no agresión** non-aggression pact; **los países no alineados** the non-aligned countries; **el no va más** the ultimate; **la no intervención** non-intervention

n/o *abr* (*Com*) = **nuestra orden**

noble ['noβle] *adj, nm/f* noble; **los nobles** the nobility *sg*

nobleza [no'βleθa] *nf* nobility

noche ['notʃe] *nf* night, night-time; (*la tarde*) evening; (*fig*) darkness; **de ~, por la ~** at night; **ayer por la ~** last night; **esta ~** tonight; **(en) toda la ~** all night; **hacer ~ en un sitio** to spend the night in a place; **se hace de ~** it's getting dark

Nochebuena [notʃe'βwena] *nf* Christmas Eve; *see note*

● **NOCHEBUENA**

On *Nochebuena* in Spanish homes there
is normally a large supper when family
members come from all over to be
together. The more religiously inclined
attend *la misa del gallo* at midnight. The
tradition of receiving Christmas presents
from Santa Claus that night is becoming
more and more widespread and gradually
replacing the tradition of *los Reyes Magos*
(The Three Wise Men) on the 6th of
January.

Nochevieja [notʃe'βjexa] *nf* New Year's Eve;
ver tb **uvas**

noción [no'θjon] *nf* notion; **nociones** *nfpl*
elements, rudiments

nocivo, -a [no'θiβo, a] *adj* harmful

noctambulismo [noktambu'lismo] *nm*
sleepwalking

noctámbulo, -a [nok'tambulo, a] *nm/f*
sleepwalker

nocturno, -a [nok'turno, a] *adj* (*de la noche*)
nocturnal, night *cpd*; (*de la tarde*) evening *cpd*
■ *nm* nocturne

Noé [no'e] *nm* Noah

nogal [no'ɣal] *nm* walnut tree; (*madera*)
walnut

nómada ['nomaða] *adj* nomadic ■ *nm/f*
nomad

nomás [no'mas] *adv* (*Am: gen*) just; (*: tan sólo*)
only; **así ~** (*Am fam*) just like that; **ayer ~**
only yesterday ■ *conj* (*Am: en cuanto*): **~ se fue
se acordó** no sooner had she left than she
remembered

nombramiento [nombra'mjento] *nm*
naming; (*para un empleo*) appointment; (*Pol
etc*) nomination; (*Mil*) commission

nombrar [nom'brar] *vt* (*gen*) to name;
(*mencionar*) to mention; (*designar*) to appoint,
nominate; (*Mil*) to commission

nombre ['nombre] *nm* name; (*sustantivo*)
noun; (*fama*) renown; **~ y apellidos** name
in full; **~ común/propio** common/proper
noun; **~ de pila/de soltera** Christian/
maiden name; **~ de fichero** (*Inform*) file
name; **en ~ de** in the name of, on behalf of;
sin ~ nameless; **su conducta no tiene ~** his
behaviour is utterly despicable

nomenclatura [nomenkla'tura] *nf*
nomenclature

nomeolvides [nomeol'βiðes] *nm inv* forget-
me-not

nómina ['nomina] *nf* (*lista*) list; (*Com: tb:*
nóminas) payroll

nominal [nomi'nal] *adj* nominal; (*valor*) face

cpd; (*Ling*) noun *cpd*, substantival

nominar [nomi'nar] *vt* to nominate

nominativo, -a [nomina'tiβo, a] *adj* (*Ling*)
nominative; (*Com*): **un cheque ~ a X** a
cheque made out to X

non [non] *adj* odd, uneven ■ *nm* odd
number; **pares y nones** odds and evens

nonagésimo, -a [nona'xesimo, a] *num*
ninetieth

nono, -a ['nono, a] *num* ninth

nordeste [nor'ðeste] *adj* north-east, north-
eastern, north-easterly ■ *nm* north-east;
(*viento*) north-east wind, north-easterly

nórdico, -a ['norðiko, a] *adj* (*del norte*)
northern, northerly; (*escandinavo*) Nordic,
Norse ■ *nm/f* northerner; (*escandinavo*)
Norseman/-woman ■ *nm* (*Ling*) Norse

noreste [no'reste] *adj, nm* = **nordeste**

noria ['norja] *nf* (*Agr*) waterwheel; (*de
carnaval*) big (*Brit*) o Ferris (*US*) wheel

norma ['norma] *nf* standard, norm, rule;
(*patrón*) pattern; (*método*) method

normal [nor'mal] *adj* (*corriente*) normal;
(*habitual*) usual, natural; (*Tec*) standard;
Escuela N~ teacher training college;
(**gasolina**) **~** two-star petrol

normalice *etc* [norma'liθe] *vb ver* **normalizar**

normalidad [normali'ðað] *nf* normality

normalización [normaliθa'θjon] *nf* (*Com*)
standardization

normalizar [normali'θar] *vt* (*reglamentar*)
to normalize; (*Com, Tec*) to standardize;
normalizarse *vr* to return to normal

normalmente [normal'mente] *adv* (*con
normalidad*) normally; (*habitualmente*) usually

Normandía [norman'dia] *nf* Normandy

normando, -a [nor'mando, a] *adj, nm/f*
Norman

normativo, -a [norma'tiβo, a] *adj*: **es ~ en
todos los coches nuevos** it is standard in all
new cars ■ *nf* regulations *pl*

noroeste [noro'este] *adj* north-west, north-
western, north-westerly ■ *nm* north-west;
(*viento*) north-west wind, north-westerly

norte ['norte] *adj* north, northern, northerly
■ *nm* north; (*fig*) guide

Norteamérica [nortea'merika] *nf* North
America

norteamericano, -a [norteameri'kano, a]
adj, nm/f (North) American

norteño, -a [nor'teɲo, a] *adj* northern
■ *nm/f* northerner

Noruega [no'rweɣa] *nf* Norway

noruego, -a [no'rweɣo, a] *adj, nm/f*
Norwegian ■ *nm* (*Ling*) Norwegian

nos [nos] *pron* (*directo*) us; (*indirecto*) (to) us;
(*reflexivo*) (to) ourselves; (*recíproco*) (to) each

n

other; **~ levantamos a las siete** we get up at seven

nosocomio [noso'komjo] *nm (Am)* hospital

nosotros, -as [no'sotros, as] *pron (sujeto)* we; *(después de prep)* us; **~ (mismos)** ourselves

nostalgia [nos'talxja] *nf* nostalgia, homesickness

nostálgico, -a [nos'talxiko, a] *adj* nostalgic, homesick

nota ['nota] *nf* note; *(Escol)* mark; *(de fin de año)* report; *(Univ etc)* footnote; *(Com)* account; **~ de aviso** advice note; **~ de crédito/débito** credit/debit note; **~ de gastos** expenses claim; **~ de sociedad** gossip column; **tomar notas** to take notes

notable [no'taβle] *adj* noteworthy, notable; *(Escol etc)* outstanding ■ *nm/f* notable

notar [no'tar] *vt* to notice, note; *(percibir)* to feel; *(ver)* to see; **notarse** *vr* to be obvious; **se nota que ...** one observes that ...

notaría [nota'ria] *nf (profesión)* profession of notary; *(despacho)* notary's office

notarial [nota'rjal] *adj (estilo)* legal; **acta ~** affidavit

notario [no'tarjo] *nm* notary; *(abogado)* solicitor

noticia [no'tiθja] *nf (información)* piece of news; *(TV etc)* news item; **las noticias** the news *sg*; **según nuestras noticias** according to our information; **tener noticias de algn** to hear from sb

noticiario [noti'θjarjo] *nm (Cine)* newsreel; *(TV)* news bulletin

noticiero [noti'θjero] *nm* newspaper; *(Am: tb:* **noticiero telediario**) news bulletin

notificación [notifika'θjon] *nf* notification

notificar [notifi'kar] *vt* to notify, inform

notifique *etc* [noti'fike] *vb ver* **notificar**

notoriedad [notorje'ðað] *nf* fame, renown

notorio, -a [no'torjo, a] *adj (público)* well-known; *(evidente)* obvious

nov. *abr (= noviembre)* Nov.

novatada [noβa'taða] *nf (burla)* teasing, hazing (US); **pagar la ~** to learn the hard way

novato, -a [no'βato, a] *adj* inexperienced ■ *nm/f* beginner, novice

novecientos, -as [noβe'θjentos, as] *num* nine hundred

novedad [noβe'ðað] *nf (calidad de nuevo)* newness, novelty; *(noticia)* piece of news; *(cambio)* change, (new) development; *(sorpresa)* surprise; **novedades** *nfpl (noticia)* latest (news) *sg*

novedoso, -a [noβe'ðoso, a] *adj* novel

novel [no'βel] *adj* new; *(inexperto)* inexperienced ■ *nm/f* beginner

novela [no'βela] *nf* novel; **~ policíaca** detective story

novelero, -a [noβe'lero, a] *adj* highly imaginative

novelesco, -a [noβe'lesko, a] *adj* fictional; *(romántico)* romantic; *(fantástico)* fantastic

novelista [noβe'lista] *nm/f* novelist

novelística [noβe'listika] *nf:* **la ~** fiction, the novel

noveno, -a [no'βeno, a] *num* ninth

noventa [no'βenta] *num* ninety

novia ['noβja] *nf ver* **novio**

noviazgo [no'βjaθɣo] *nm* engagement

novicio, -a [no'βiθjo, a] *nm/f* novice

noviembre [no'βjembre] *nm* November; *ver tb* **julio**

novilla [no'βiʎa] *nf* heifer

novillada [noβi'ʎaða] *nf (Taur)* bullfight with young bulls

novillero [noβi'ʎero] *nm* novice bullfighter

novillo [no'βiʎo] *nm* young bull, bullock; **hacer novillos** *(fam)* to play truant (Brit) *o* hooky (US)

novio, -a ['noβjo, a] *nm/f* boyfriend/ girlfriend; *(prometido)* fiancé/fiancée; *(recién casado)* bridegroom/bride; **los novios** the newly-weds

novísimo, -a [no'βisimo, a] *adj superlativo de* **nuevo, a**

NPI *nm abr (Inform: = número personal de identificación)* PIN

N. S. *abr* = **Nuestro Señor**

ns/nc *abr* = **no sabe(n)/no contesta(n)**

ntra., ntro. *abr* = **nuestra, nuestro**

Ntro. Sr. *abr* = **Nuestro Señor**

NU *nfpl abr (= Naciones Unidas)* UN *sg*

nubarrón [nuβa'rron] *nm* storm cloud

nube ['nuβe] *nf* cloud; *(Med: ocular)* cloud, film; *(fig)* mass; **una ~ de críticas** a storm of criticism; **los precios están por las nubes** prices are sky-high; **estar en las nubes** to be away with the fairies

nublado, -a [nu'βlaðo, a] *adj* cloudy ■ *nm* storm cloud

nublar [nu'βlar] *vt (oscurecer)* to darken; *(confundir)* to cloud; **nublarse** *vr* to cloud over

nuboso, -a [nu'βoso, a] *adj* cloudy

nuca ['nuka] *nf* nape of the neck

nuclear [nukle'ar] *adj* nuclear

nuclearizado, -a [nukleari'θaðo, a] *adj:* **países nuclearizados** countries possessing nuclear weapons

núcleo ['nukleo] *nm (centro)* core; *(Física)* nucleus

nudillo [nu'ðiʎo] *nm* knuckle

nudista [nu'dista] *adj, nm/f* nudist

nudo ['nuðo] *nm* knot; *(unión)* bond; *(de problema)* crux; *(Ferro)* junction; *(fig)* lump;

~ **corredizo** slipknot; **con un ~ en la
garganta** with a lump in one's throat
nudoso, -a [nu'ðoso, a] *adj* knotty; (*tronco*)
gnarled; (*bastón*) knobbly
nueces ['nweθes] *nfpl de* **nuez**
nuera ['nwera] *nf* daughter-in-law
nuestro, -a ['nwestro, a] *adj posesivo* our
■ *pron* ours; ~ **padre** our father; **un amigo**
~ a friend of ours; **es el** ~ it's ours; **los
nuestros** our people; (*Deporte*) our *o* the local
team *o* side
nueva ['nweβa] *nf ver* **nuevo**
Nueva Escocia *nf* Nova Scotia
nuevamente [nweβa'mente] *adv* (*otra vez*)
again; (*de nuevo*) anew
Nueva York [-'jork] *nf* New York
Nueva Zelanda [-θe'landa], **Nueva
Zelandia** [-θe'landja] *nf* New Zealand
nueve ['nweβe] *num* nine
nuevo, -a ['nweβo, a] *adj* (*gen*) new ■ *nf*
piece of news; **¿qué hay de ~?** (*fam*) what's
new?; **de** ~ again
Nuevo Méjico *nm* New Mexico
nuez [nweθ] (*pl* **nueces**) *nf* nut; (*del nogal*)
walnut; ~ **de Adán** Adam's apple; ~
moscada nutmeg
nulidad [nuli'ðað] *nf* (*incapacidad*)
incompetence; (*abolición*) nullity; (*individuo*)
nonentity; **es una** ~ he's a dead loss
nulo, -a ['nulo, a] *adj* (*inepto, torpe*) useless;
(*inválido*) (null and) void; (*Deporte*) drawn, tied
núm. *abr* (= *número*) no.
numen ['numen] *nm* inspiration
numeración [numera'θjon] *nf* (*cifras*)
numbers *pl*; (*arábiga, romana etc*) numerals *pl*;
~ **de línea** (*Inform*) line numbering
numerador [numera'ðor] *nm* (*Mat*) numerator
numeral [nume'ral] *nm* numeral

numerar [nume'rar] *vt* to number;
numerarse *vr* (*Mil etc*) to number off
numerario, -a [nume'rarjo, a] *adj* numerary;
profesor ~ permanent *o* tenured member of
teaching staff ■ *nm* hard cash
numérico, -a [nu'meriko, a] *adj* numerical
número ['numero] *nm* (*gen*) number; (*tamaño:
de zapato*) size; (*ejemplar: de diario*) number,
issue; (*Teat etc*) turn, act, number; **sin**
~ numberless, unnumbered; ~ **binario**
(*Inform*) binary number; ~ **de matrícula/de
teléfono** registration/telephone number;
~ **personal de identificación** (*Inform etc*)
personal identification number; ~ **de
serie** (*Com*) serial number; ~ **atrasado** back
number
numeroso, -a [nume'roso, a] *adj* numerous;
familia numerosa large family
numerus ['numerus] *nm*: ~ **clausus** (*Univ*)
restricted *o* selective entry
nunca ['nunka] *adv* (*jamás*) never; (*con verbo
negativo*) ever; ~ **lo pensé** I never thought
it; **no viene** ~ he never comes; ~ **más** never
again
nuncio ['nunθjo] *nm* (*Rel*) nuncio
nupcial [nup'θjal] *adj* wedding *cpd*
nupcias ['nupθjas] *nfpl* wedding *sg*, nuptials
nutria ['nutrja] *nf* otter
nutrición [nutri'θjon] *nf* nutrition
nutrido, -a [nu'triðo, a] *adj* (*alimentado*)
nourished; (*fig: grande*) large; (*abundante*)
abundant; **mal** ~ undernourished; ~ **de**
full of
nutrir [nu'trir] *vt* to feed, nourish; (*fig*) to
feed, strengthen
nutritivo, -a [nutri'tiβo, a] *adj* nourishing,
nutritious
nylon [ni'lon] *nm* nylon

n

Ñ, ñ ['eɲe] *nf* (*letra*) Ñ ñ
ñato, -a ['ɲato, a] *adj* (*Am*) snub-nosed
ñoñería [ɲoɲe'ria], **ñoñez** [ɲo'ɲeθ] *nf*
  insipidness

ñoño, -a ['ɲoɲo, a] *adj* (*soso*) insipid;
  (*persona: débil*) spineless
ñoquis ['ɲokis] *nmpl* (*Culin*) gnocchi

Oo

O, o [o] *nf* (*letra*) O, o; **O de Oviedo** O for Oliver (*Brit*) o Oboe (*US*)

O *abr* (= *oeste*) W

o [o] *conj* or; **o ... o** either ... or; **o sea** that is

ó [o] *conj* (*en números para evitar confusión*) or; **cinco ó seis** five or six

o/ *nm* (*Com*: = *orden*) o

OACI *nf abr* (= *Organización de la Aviación Civil Internacional*) ICAO

oasis [o'asis] *nm inv* oasis

obcecado, -a [oβθe'kaðo, a] *adj* blind; (*terco*) stubborn

obcecarse [oβθe'karse] *vr* to be obstinate; **~ en hacer** to insist on doing

obceque *etc* [oβ'θeke] *vb ver* **obcecarse**

obedecer [oβeðe'θer] *vt* to obey; **~ a** (*Med etc*) to yield to; (*fig*): **~ a ...**, **~ al hecho de que ...** to be due to ..., arise from ...

obedezca *etc* [oβe'ðeθka] *vb ver* **obedecer**

obediencia [oβe'ðjenθja] *nf* obedience

obediente [oβe'ðjente] *adj* obedient

obertura [oβer'tura] *nf* overture

obesidad [oβesi'ðað] *nf* obesity

obeso, -a [o'βeso, a] *adj* obese

óbice ['oβiθe] *nm* obstacle, impediment

obispado [oβis'paðo] *nm* bishopric

obispo [o'βispo] *nm* bishop

óbito ['oβito] *nm* demise

objeción [oβxe'θjon] *nf* objection; **hacer una ~**, **poner objeciones** to raise objections, object

objetar [oβxe'tar] *vt, vi* to object

objetivo, -a [oβxe'tiβo, a] *adj* objective ■ *nm* objective; (*fig*) aim; (*Foto*) lens

objeto [oβ'xeto] *nm* (*cosa*) object; (*fin*) aim

objetor, a [oβxe'tor, a] *nm/f* objector; **~ de conciencia** conscientious objector; *ver tb* **mili**

oblea [o'βlea] *nf* (*Rel, fig*) wafer

oblicuo, -a [o'βlikwo, a] *adj* oblique; (*mirada*) sidelong

obligación [oβliɣa'θjon] *nf* obligation; (*Com*) bond, debenture

obligar [oβli'ɣar] *vt* to force; **obligarse** *vr*: **obligarse a** to commit o.s. to

obligatorio, -a [oβliɣa'torjo, a] *adj* compulsory, obligatory

obligue *etc* [o'βliɣe] *vb ver* **obligar**

oboe [o'βoe] *nm* oboe; (*músico*) oboist

Ob.° *abr* (= *Obispo*) Bp

obra ['oβra] *nf* work; (*producción*) piece of work; (*Arq*) construction, building; (*libro*) book; (*Mus*) opus; (*Teat*) play; **~ de arte** work of art; **~ maestra** masterpiece; **~ de consulta** reference book; **obras completas** complete works; **~ benéfica** charity; **"obras"** (*en carretera*) "men at work"; **obras públicas** public works; **por ~ de** thanks to (the efforts of); **obras son amores y no buenas razones** actions speak louder than words

obrar [o'βrar] *vt* to work; (*tener efecto*) to have an effect on ■ *vi* to act, behave; (*tener efecto*) to have an effect; **la carta obra en su poder** the letter is in his/her possession

Ob.ᵖᵒ *abr* = **obispo**

obr. cit. *abr* (= *obra citada*) op. cit.

obrero, -a [o'βrero, a] *adj* working; (*movimiento*) labour *cpd*; **clase obrera** working class ■ *nm/f* (*gen*) worker; (*sin oficio*) labourer

obscenidad [oβsθeni'ðað] *nf* obscenity

obsceno, -a [oβs'θeno, a] *adj* obscene

obscu... *pref* = **oscu...**

obsequiar [oβse'kjar] *vt* (*ofrecer*) to present; (*agasajar*) to make a fuss of, lavish attention on

obsequio [oβ'sekjo] *nm* (*regalo*) gift; (*cortesía*) courtesy, attention

obsequioso, -a [oβse'kjoso, a] *adj* attentive

observación [oβserβa'θjon] *nf* observation; (*reflexión*) remark; (*objeción*) objection

observador, a [oβserβa'ðor, a] *adj* observant ■ *nm/f* observer

observancia [oβser'βanθja] *nf* observance

observar [oβser'βar] *vt* to observe; (*notar*) to notice; (*leyes*) to observe, respect; (*reglas*) to abide by

O

observatorio [oβserβa'torjo] *nm*
observatory; **~ del tiempo** weather station
obsesión [oβse'sjon] *nf* obsession
obsesionar [oβsesjo'nar] *vt* to obsess
obseso, -a [oβ'seso, a] *nm/f* (*sexual*) sex
maniac
obsolescencia [oβsoles'θenθja] *nf*: ~
incorporada (*Com*) built-in obsolescence
obsoleto, -a [oβso'leto, a] *adj* obsolete
obstaculice *etc* [oβstaku'liθe] *vb ver*
obstaculizar
obstaculizar [oβstakuli'θar] *vt* (*dificultar*) to
hinder, hamper
obstáculo [oβs'takulo] *nm* (*gen*) obstacle;
(*impedimento*) hindrance, drawback
obstante [oβs'tante]: **no ~** *adv* nevertheless;
(*de todos modos*) all the same *prep* in spite of
obstetra [oβs'tetra] *nm/f* obstetrician
obstetricia [oβste'triθja] *nf* obstetrics *sg*
obstinado, -a [oβsti'naðo, a] *adj* (*gen*)
obstinate; (*terco*) stubborn
obstinarse [oβsti'narse] *vr* to dig one's heels
in; **~ en** to persist in
obstrucción [oβstruk'θjon] *nf* obstruction
obstruir [oβstru'ir] *vt* to obstruct; (*bloquear*)
to block; (*estorbar*) to hinder
obstruyendo *etc* [oβstru'jendo] *vb ver*
obstruir
obtención [oβten'θjon] *nf* (*Com*)
procurement
obtendré *etc* [oβten'dre] *vb ver* **obtener**
obtener [oβte'ner] *vt* (*conseguir*) to obtain;
(*ganar*) to gain
obtenga *etc* [oβ'tenga] *vb ver* **obtener**
obturación [oβtura'θjon] *nf* plugging,
stopping; (*Foto*): **velocidad de ~** shutter speed
obturador [oβtura'ðor] *nm* (*Foto*) shutter
obtuso, -a [oβ'tuso, a] *adj* (*filo*) blunt; (*Mat*,
fig) obtuse
obtuve *etc* [oβ'tuβe] *vb ver* **obtener**
obús [o'βus] *nm* (*Mil*) shell
obviar [oβ'βjar] *vt* to obviate, remove
obvio, -a ['oββjo, a] *adj* obvious
oca ['oka] *nf* goose; (*tb*: **juego de la oca**)
≈ snakes and ladders
ocasión [oka'sjon] *nf* (*oportunidad*)
opportunity, chance; (*momento*) occasion,
time; (*causa*) cause; **de ~** secondhand; **con ~
de** on the occasion of; **en algunas ocasiones**
sometimes; **aprovechar la ~** to seize one's
opportunity
ocasionar [okasjo'nar] *vt* to cause
ocaso [o'kaso] *nm* sunset; (*fig*) decline
occidental [okθiðen'tal] *adj* western ▪ *nm/f*
westerner ▪ *nm* west
occidente [okθi'ðente] *nm* west; **el O~** the
West

occiso, -a [ok'θiso, a] *nm/f*: **el ~** the deceased;
(*de asesinato*) the victim
O.C.D.E. *nf abr* (= *Organización de Cooperación y
Desarrollo Económicos*) OECD
océano [o'θeano] *nm* ocean; **el ~ Índico** the
Indian Ocean
ochenta [o'tʃenta] *num* eighty
ocho ['otʃo] *num* eight; (*fecha*) eighth; **~ días**
a week
ochocientos, -as [otʃo'θjentos, as] *num*
eight hundred
OCI ['oθi] *nf abr* (*Pol: Venezuela, Perú*) = **Oficina
Central de Información**
ocio ['oθjo] *nm* (*tiempo*) leisure; (*pey*) idleness;
"guía del ~" "what's on"
ociosidad [oθjosi'ðað] *nf* idleness
ocioso, -a [o'θjoso, a] *adj* (*inactivo*) idle; (*inútil*)
useless
oct. *abr* (= *octubre*) Oct.
octanaje [okta'naxe] *nm*: **de alto ~** high
octane
octano [ok'tano] *nm* octane
octavilla [okta'βiʎa] *nm* leaflet, pamphlet
octavo, -a [ok'taβo, a] *num* eighth
octeto [ok'teto] *nm* (*Inform*) byte
octogenario, -a [oktoxe'narjo, a] *adj*, *nm/f*
octogenarian
octubre [ok'tuβre] *nm* October; *ver tb* **julio**
OCU ['oku] *nf abr* (*Esp*: = *Organización de
Consumidores y Usuarios*) ≈ Consumers'
Association
ocular [oku'lar] *adj* ocular, eye *cpd*; **testigo ~**
eyewitness
oculista [oku'lista] *nm/f* oculist
ocultar [okul'tar] *vt* (*esconder*) to hide; (*callar*)
to conceal; (*disfrazar*) to screen; **ocultarse** *vr*
to hide (o.s.); **ocultarse a la vista** to keep
out of sight
oculto, -a [o'kulto, a] *adj* hidden; (*fig*) secret
ocupación [okupa'θjon] *nf* occupation;
(*tenencia*) occupancy
ocupado, -a [oku'paðo, a] *adj* (*persona*) busy;
(*plaza*) occupied, taken; (*teléfono*) engaged;
¿está ocupada la silla? is that seat taken?
ocupar [oku'par] *vt* (*gen*) to occupy; (*puesto*)
to hold, fill; (*individuo*) to engage; (*obreros*)
to employ; (*confiscar*) to seize; **ocuparse**
vr: **ocuparse de** *o* **en** to concern o.s. with;
(*cuidar*) to look after; **ocuparse de lo suyo** to
mind one's own business
ocurrencia [oku'rrenθja] *nf* (*ocasión*)
occurrence; (*agudeza*) witticism
ocurrir [oku'rrir] *vi* to happen; **ocurrirse**
vr: **se me ocurrió que ...** it occurred to me
that ...; **¿se te ocurre algo?** can you think
of *o* come up with anything?; **¿qué ocurre?**
what's going on?

oda ['oða] *nf* ode

ODECA [o'ðeka] *nf abr* = **Organización de Estados Centroamericanos**

odiar [o'ðjar] *vt* to hate

odio ['oðjo] *nm* (*gen*) hate, hatred; (*disgusto*) dislike

odioso, -a [o'ðjoso, a] *adj* (*gen*) hateful; (*malo*) nasty

odisea [oði'sea] *nf* odyssey

odontología [oðontolo'xia] *nf* dentistry, dental surgery

odontólogo, -a [oðon'toloɣo, a] *nm/f* dentist, dental surgeon

odre ['oðre] *nm* wineskin

O.E.A. *nf abr* (= *Organización de Estados Americanos*) O.A.S.

OECE *nf abr* (= *Organización Europea de Cooperación Económica*) OEEC

OELA [o'ela] *nf abr* = **Organización de Estados Latinoamericanos**

oeste [o'este] *nm* west; **una película del ~** a western

ofender [ofen'der] *vt* (*agraviar*) to offend; (*insultar*) to insult; **ofenderse** *vr* to take offence

ofensa [o'fensa] *nf* offence; (*insulto*) slight

ofensivo, -a [ofen'siβo, a] *adj* (*insultante*) insulting; (*Mil*) offensive ■ *nf* offensive

oferta [o'ferta] *nf* offer; (*propuesta*) proposal; (*para contrato*) bid, tender; **la ~ y la demanda** supply and demand; **artículos en ~** goods on offer; **~ excedentaria** (*Com*) excess supply; **~ monetaria** money supply; **~ pública de adquisición (OPA)** (*Com*) takeover bid; **ofertas de trabajo** (*en periódicos*) situations vacant column

offset ['ofset] *nm* offset

oficial [ofi'θjal] *adj* official ■ *nm* official; (*Mil*) officer

oficialista [ofisja'lista] *adj* (*Am*) (pro-) government; **el candidato ~** the governing party's candidate

oficiar [ofi'θjar] *vt* to inform officially ■ *vi* (*Rel*) to officiate

oficina [ofi'θina] *nf* office; **~ de empleo** employment agency; **~ de información** information bureau; **~ de objetos perdidos** lost property office (*Brit*), lost-and-found department (*US*); **~ de turismo** tourist office; **~ principal** (*Com*) head office, main branch

oficinista [ofiθi'nista] *nm/f* clerk; **los oficinistas** white-collar workers

oficio [o'fiθjo] *nm* (*profesión*) profession; (*puesto*) post; (*Rel*) service; (*función*) function; (*comunicado*) official letter; **ser del ~** to be an old hand; **tener mucho ~** to have a lot of experience; **~ de difuntos** funeral service; **de ~** officially

oficioso, -a [ofi'θjoso, a] *adj* (*pey*) officious; (*no oficial*) unofficial, informal

ofimática [ofi'matika] *nf* office automation

ofrecer [ofre'θer] *vt* (*dar*) to offer; (*proponer*) to propose; **ofrecerse** *vr* (*persona*) to offer o.s., volunteer; (*situación*) to present itself; **¿qué se le ofrece?, ¿se le ofrece algo?** what can I do for you?, can I get you anything?

ofrecimiento [ofreθi'mjento] *nm* offer, offering

ofrendar [ofren'dar] *vt* to offer, contribute

ofrezca *etc* [o'freθka] *vb ver* **ofrecer**

oftalmología [oftalmolo'xia] *nf* ophthalmology

oftalmólogo, -a [oftal'moloɣo, a] *nm/f* ophthalmologist

ofuscación [ofuska'θjon] *nf*, **ofuscamiento** [ofuska'mjento] *nm* (*fig*) bewilderment

ofuscar [ofus'kar] *vt* (*confundir*) to bewilder; (*enceguecer*) to dazzle, blind

ofusque *etc* [o'fuske] *vb ver* **ofuscar**

ogro ['oɣro] *nm* ogre

OIC *nf abr* (= *Organización Interamericana del Café*: *Com*) = **Organización Internacional del Comercio**

oída [o'iða] *nf*: **de oídas** by hearsay

oído [o'iðo] *nm* (*Anat, Mus*) ear; (*sentido*) hearing; **~ interno** inner ear; **de ~** by ear; **apenas pude dar crédito a mis oídos** I could scarcely believe my ears; **hacer oídos sordos a** to turn a deaf ear to

OIEA *nm abr* (= *Organismo Internacional de Energía Atómica*) IAEA

oiga *etc* ['oiɣa] *vb ver* **oír**

OIR [o'ir] *nf abr* (= *Organización Internacional para los Refugiados*) IRO; = **Organización Internacional de Radiodifusión**

oír [o'ir] *vt* (*gen*) to hear; (*esp Am*: *escuchar*) to listen to; **¡oye!** (*sorpresa*) I say!, say! (*US*); **¡oiga!** (*Telec*) hullo?; **~ misa** to attend mass; **como quien oye llover** without paying (the slightest) attention

O.I.T. *nf abr* (= *Organización Internacional del Trabajo*) ILO

ojal [o'xal] *nm* buttonhole

ojalá [oxa'la] *excl* if only (it were so)!, some hope! ■ *conj* if only...!, would that...!; **ojalá que venga hoy** I hope he comes today; **¡ojalá pudiera!** I wish I could!

ojeada [oxe'aða] *nf* glance; **echar una ~ a** to take a quick look at

ojera [o'xera] *nf*: **tener ojeras** to have bags under one's eyes

ojeriza [oxe'riθa] *nf* ill-will; **tener ~ a** to have a grudge against, have it in for

ojeroso, -a [oxe'roso, a] *adj* haggard
ojete [o'xete] *nm* eye(let)
ojo ['oxo] *nm* eye; (*de puente*) span; (*de cerradura*) keyhole ∎ *excl* careful!; **tener ~ para** to have an eye for; **ojos saltones** bulging *o* goggle eyes; **~ de buey** porthole; **~ por ~** an eye for an eye; **en un abrir y cerrar de ojos** in the twinkling of an eye; **a ojos vistas** openly; (*crecer etc*) before one's (very) eyes; **a ~ (de buen cubero)** roughly; **ojos que no ven, corazón que no siente** out of sight, out of mind; **ser el ~ derecho de algn** (*fig*) to be the apple of sb's eye
okupa [o'kupa] *nm/f* (*fam*) squatter
OL *abr* (= *onda larga*) LW, long wave
ola ['ola] *nf* wave; **~ de calor/frío** heatwave/cold spell; **la nueva ~** the latest fashion; (*Cine, Mus*) (the) new wave
OLADE [o'laðe] *nf abr* = **Organización Latinoamericana de Energía**
olé [o'le] *excl* bravo!, olé!
oleada [ole'aða] *nf* big wave, swell; (*fig*) wave
oleaje [ole'axe] *nm* swell
óleo ['oleo] *nm* oil
oleoducto [oleo'ðukto] *nm* (oil) pipeline
oler [o'ler] *vt* (*gen*) to smell; (*inquirir*) to pry into; (*fig: sospechar*) to sniff out ∎ *vi* to smell; **~ a** to smell of; **huele mal** it smells bad, it stinks
olfatear [olfate'ar] *vt* to smell; (*fig: sospechar*) to sniff out; (*inquirir*) to pry into
olfato [ol'fato] *nm* sense of smell
oligarquía [oliɣar'kia] *nf* oligarchy
olimpiada [olim'piaða] *nf*: **la ~ o las olimpiadas** the Olympics
olímpicamente [o'limpikamente] *adv*: **pasar ~ de algo** to totally ignore sth
olímpico, -a [o'limpiko, a] *adj* Olympian; (*deportes*) Olympic
oliva [o'liβa] *nf* (*aceituna*) olive; **aceite de ~** olive oil
olivar [oli'βar] *nm* olive grove *o* plantation
olivo [o'liβo] *nm* olive tree
olla ['oʎa] *nf* pan; (*para hervir agua*) kettle; (*comida*) stew; **~ a presión** pressure cooker
olmo ['olmo] *nm* elm (tree)
olor [o'lor] *nm* smell
oloroso, -a [olo'roso, a] *adj* scented
OLP *nf abr* (= *Organización para la Liberación de Palestina*) PLO
olvidadizo, -a [olβiða'ðiθo, a] *adj* (*desmemoriado*) forgetful; (*distraído*) absent-minded
olvidar [olβi'ðar] *vt* to forget; (*omitir*) to omit; (*abandonar*) to leave behind; **olvidarse** *vr* (*fig*) to forget o.s.; **se me olvidó** I forgot
olvido [ol'βiðo] *nm* oblivion; (*acto*) oversight;

(*descuido*) slip; **caer en el ~** to fall into oblivion
O.M. *abr* (= *onda media*) MW, medium wave; (= *Oriente Medio*) Middle East; (*Pol*) = **Orden Ministerial**
ombligo [om'bliɣo] *nm* navel
OMI *nf abr* (= *Organización Marítima Internacional*) IMO
ominoso, -a [omi'noso, a] *adj* ominous
omisión [omi'sjon] *nf* (*abstención*) omission; (*descuido*) neglect
omiso, -a [o'miso, a] *adj*: **hacer caso ~ de** to ignore, pass over
omitir [omi'tir] *vt* to leave *o* miss out, omit
ómnibus ['omniβus] *nm* (*Am*) bus
omnipotente [omnipo'tente] *adj* omnipotent
omnipresente [omnipre'sente] *adj* omnipresent
omnívoro, -a [om'niβoro, a] *adj* omnivorous
omoplato [omo'plato], **omóplato** [o'moplato] *nm* shoulder-blade
OMS *nf abr* (= *Organización Mundial de la Salud*) WHO
ONCE ['onθe] *nf abr* (= *Organización Nacional de Ciegos Españoles*) *charity for the blind*
once ['onθe] *num* eleven ∎ *nm* (*Am*); **onces** *nfpl* tea break *sg*
onda ['onda] *nf* wave; **~ corta/larga/media** short/long/medium wave; **ondas acústicas/hertzianas** acoustic/Hertzian waves; **~ sonora** sound wave
ondear [onde'ar] *vi* to wave; (*tener ondas*) to be wavy; (*agua*) to ripple; **ondearse** *vr* to swing, sway
ondulación [ondula'θjon] *nf* undulation
ondulado, -a [ondu'laðo, a] *adj* wavy ∎ *nm* wave
ondulante [ondu'lante] *adj* undulating
ondular [ondu'lar] *vt* (*el pelo*) to wave ∎ *vi*, **ondularse** *vr* to undulate
oneroso, -a [one'roso, a] *adj* onerous
ONG *nf abr* (= *organización no gubernamental*) NGO
onomástico, -a [ono'mastiko, a] *adj*: **fiesta onomástica** saint's day ∎ *nm* saint's day
ONU ['onu] *nf abr ver* **Organización de las Naciones Unidas**
onubense [onu'βense] *adj* of *o* from Huelva ∎ *nm/f* native *o* inhabitant of Huelva
ONUDI [o'nuði] *nf abr* (= *Organización de las Naciones Unidas para el Desarrollo Industrial*) UNIDO (= *United Nations Industrial Development Organization*)
onza ['onθa] *nf* ounce
O.P. *nfpl abr* = **Obras Públicas**; (*Com*) = **Oficina Principal**

OPA ['opa] *nf abr* (= *Oferta Pública de Adquisición*) takeover bid

opaco, -a [o'pako, a] *adj* opaque; (*fig*) dull

ópalo ['opalo] *nm* opal

opción [op'θjon] *nf* (*gen*) option; (*derecho*) right, option; **no hay ~** there is no alternative

opcional [opθjo'nal] *adj* optional

O.P.E.P. [o'pep] *nf abr* (= *Organización de Países Exportadores de Petróleo*) OPEC

ópera ['opera] *nf* opera; **ópera bufa** o **cómica** comic opera

operación [opera'θjon] *nf* (*gen*) operation; (*Com*) transaction, deal; **~ a plazo** (*Com*) forward transaction; **operaciones accesorias** (*Inform*) housekeeping; **operaciones a término** (*Com*) futures

operador, a [opera'ðor, a] *nm/f* operator; (*Cine: proyección*) projectionist; (: *rodaje*) cameraman

operar [ope'rar] *vt* (*producir*) to produce, bring about; (*Med*) to operate on ■ *vi* (*Com*) to operate, deal; **operarse** *vr* to occur; (*Med*) to have an operation; **se han operado grandes cambios** great changes have been made o have taken place

operario, -a [ope'rarjo, a] *nm/f* worker

opereta [ope'reta] *nf* operetta

opinar [opi'nar] *vt* (*estimar*) to think ■ *vi* (*enjuiciar*) to give one's opinion; **~ bien de** to think well of

opinión [opi'njon] *nf* (*creencia*) belief; (*criterio*) opinion; **la ~ pública** public opinion

opio ['opjo] *nm* opium

opíparo, -a [o'piparo, a] *adj* sumptuous

opondré *etc* [opon'dre] *vb ver* **oponer**

oponente [opo'nente] *nm/f* opponent

oponer [opo'ner] *vt* (*resistencia*) to put up, offer; (*negativa*) to raise; **oponerse** *vr* (*objetar*) to object; (*estar frente a frente*) to be opposed; (*dos personas*) to oppose each other; **~ A a B** to set A against B; **me opongo a pensar que ...** I refuse to believe o think that ...

oponga *etc* [o'ponga] *vb ver* **oponer**

Oporto [o'porto] *nm* Oporto

oporto [o'porto] *nm* port

oportunidad [oportuni'ðað] *nf* (*ocasión*) opportunity; (*posibilidad*) chance

oportunismo [oportu'nismo] *nm* opportunism

oportunista [oportu'nista] *nm/f* opportunist; (*infección*) opportunistic

oportuno, -a [opor'tuno, a] *adj* (*en su tiempo*) opportune, timely; (*respuesta*) suitable; **en el momento ~** at the right moment

oposición [oposi'θjon] *nf* opposition; **oposiciones** *nfpl* public examinations;

ganar un puesto por oposiciones to win a post by public competitive examination; **hacer oposiciones a**, **presentarse a unas oposiciones a** to sit a competitive examination for; *see note*

OPOSICIÓN

The *oposiciones* are exams held every year for posts nationally and locally in the public sector, State education, the Judiciary etc. These posts are permanent and the number of candidates is high so the exams are tough. The candidates, *opositores*, have to study a great number of subjects relating to their field and also the Constitution. People can spend years studying and resitting exams.

opositar [oposi'tar] *vi* to sit a public entrance examination

opositor, -a [oposi'tor, a] *nm/f* (*Admin*) candidate to a public examination; (*adversario*) opponent

opresión [opre'sjon] *nf* oppression

opresivo, -a [opre'siβo, a] *adj* oppressive

opresor, a [opre'sor, a] *nm/f* oppressor

oprimir [opri'mir] *vt* to squeeze; (*asir*) to grasp; (*pulsar*) to press; (*fig*) to oppress

optar [op'tar] *vi* (*elegir*) to choose; **~ a** o **por** to opt for

optativo, -a [opta'tiβo, a] *adj* optional

óptico, -a ['optiko, a] *adj* optic(al) ■ *nm/f* optician ■ *nf* optics *sg*; (*fig*) viewpoint

optimismo [opti'mismo] *nm* optimism

optimista [opti'mista] *nm/f* optimist

óptimo, -a ['optimo, a] *adj* (*el mejor*) very best

opuesto, -a [o'pwesto, a] *pp de* **oponer** ■ *adj* (*contrario*) opposite; (*antagónico*) opposing

opulencia [opu'lenθja] *nf* opulence

opulento, -a [opu'lento, a] *adj* opulent

opuse *etc* [o'puse] *vb ver* **oponer**

ora ['ora] *adv*: **~ tú ~ yo** now you, now me

oración [ora'θjon] *nf* (*Rel*) prayer; (*Ling*) sentence

oráculo [o'rakulo] *nm* oracle

orador, a [ora'ðor, a] *nm/f* orator; (*conferenciante*) speaker

oral [o'ral] *adj* oral; **por vía ~** (*Med*) orally

orangután [orangu'tan] *nm* orang-utan

orar [o'rar] *vi* (*Rel*) to pray

oratoria [ora'torja] *nf* oratory

orbe ['orβe] *nm* orb, sphere; (*fig*) world; **en todo el ~** all over the globe

órbita ['orβita] *nf* orbit; (*Anat: ocular*) (eye-)socket

orden ['orðen] *nm* (*gen*) order; (*Inform*)

command; ~ **público** public order, law and order; (*números*): **del ~ de** about; **de primer** ~ first-rate; **en ~ de prioridad** in order of priority ▪ *nf* (*gen*) order; ~ **bancaria** banker's order; ~ **de compra** (*Com*) purchase order; ~ **del día** agenda; **eso ahora está a la ~ del día** that is now the order of the day; **a la ~ de usted** at your service; **dar la ~ de hacer algo** to give the order to do sth

ordenación [orðena'θjon] *nf* (*estado*) order; (*acto*) ordering; (*Rel*) ordination

ordenado, -a [orðe'naðo, a] *adj* (*metódico*) methodical; (*arreglado*) orderly

ordenador [orðena'ðor] *nm* computer; ~ **central** mainframe computer; ~ **de gestión** business computer; ~ **portátil** laptop (computer); ~ **de sobremesa** desktop computer

ordenamiento [orðena'mjento] *nm* legislation

ordenanza [orðe'nanθa] *nf* ordinance; **ordenanzas municipales** by-laws ▪ *nm* (*Com etc*) messenger; (*Mil*) orderly; (*bedel*) porter

ordenar [orðe'nar] *vt* (*mandar*) to order; (*poner orden*) to put in order, arrange; **ordenarse** *vr* (*Rel*) to be ordained

ordeñadora [orðeɲa'ðora] *nf* milking machine

ordeñar [orðe'ɲar] *vt* to milk

ordinariez [orðina'rjeθ] *nf* (*cualidad*) coarseness, vulgarity; (*una ordinariez*) coarse remark *o* joke *etc*

ordinario, -a [orði'narjo, a] *adj* (*común*) ordinary, usual; (*vulgar*) vulgar, common

ordinograma [orðino'ɣrama] *nm* flowchart

orear [ore'ar] *vt* to air; **orearse** *vr* (*ropa*) to air

orégano [o'reɣano] *nm* oregano

oreja [o'rexa] *nf* ear; (*Mecánica*) lug, flange

orensano, -a [oren'sano, a] *adj* of *o* from Orense ▪ *nm/f* native *o* inhabitant of Orense

orfanato [orfa'nato] *nm*, **orfanatorio** [orfana'torjo] *nm* orphanage

orfandad [orfan'dað] *nf* orphanhood

orfebre [or'feβre] *nm* gold-/silversmith

orfebrería [orfeβre'ria] *nf* gold/silver work

orfelinato [orfeli'nato] *nm* orphanage

orfeón [orfe'on] *nm* (*Mus*) choral society

organice *etc* [orɣa'niθe] *vb ver* **organizar**

orgánico, -a [or'ɣaniko, a] *adj* organic

organigrama [orɣani'ɣrama] *nm* flow chart; (*de organización*) organization chart

organillo [orɣa'niʎo] *nm* barrel organ

organismo [orɣa'nismo] *nm* (*Bio*) organism; (*Pol*) organization; **O~ Internacional de Energía Atómica** International Atomic Energy Agency

organista [orɣa'nista] *nm/f* organist

organización [orɣaniθa'θjon] *nf* organization; **O~ de las Naciones Unidas (ONU)** United Nations Organization; **O~ del Tratado del Atlántico Norte (OTAN)** North Atlantic Treaty Organization (NATO)

organizador, a [orɣaniθa'ðor, a] *adj* organizing; **el comité** ~ the organizing committee ▪ *nm/f* organizer

organizar [orɣani'θar] *vt* to organize

órgano ['orɣano] *nm* organ

orgasmo [or'ɣasmo] *nm* orgasm

orgía [or'xia] *nf* orgy

orgullo [or'ɣuʎo] *nm* (*altanería*) pride; (*autorespeto*) self-respect

orgulloso, -a [orɣu'ʎoso, a] *adj* (*gen*) proud; (*altanero*) haughty

orientación [orjenta'θjon] *nf* (*posición*) position; (*dirección*) direction; ~ **profesional** occupational guidance

oriental [orjen'tal] *adj* oriental; (*región etc*) eastern ▪ *nm/f* oriental

orientar [orjen'tar] *vt* (*situar*) to orientate; (*señalar*) to point; (*dirigir*) to direct; (*guiar*) to guide; **orientarse** *vr* to get one's bearings; (*decidirse*) to decide on a course of action

oriente [o'rjente] *nm* east; **el O~** the East, the Orient; **Cercano/Medio/Lejano O~** Near/Middle/Far East

orificio [ori'fiθjo] *nm* orifice

origen [o'rixen] *nm* origin; (*nacimiento*) lineage, birth; **dar ~ a** to cause, give rise to

original [orixi'nal] *adj* (*nuevo*) original; (*extraño*) odd, strange ▪ *nm* original; (*Tip*) manuscript; (*Tec*) master (copy)

originalidad [orixinali'ðað] *nf* originality

originar [orixi'nar] *vt* to originate; **originarse** *vr* to originate

originario, -a [orixi'narjo, a] *adj* (*nativo*) native; (*primordial*) original; **ser ~ de** to originate from; **país** ~ country of origin

orilla [o'riʎa] *nf* (*borde*) border; (*de río*) bank; (*de bosque, tela*) edge; (*de mar*) shore; **a orillas de** on the banks of

orillar [ori'ʎar] *vt* (*bordear*) to skirt, go round; (*Costura*) to edge; (*resolver*) to wind up; (*tocar: asunto*) to touch briefly on; (*dificultad*) to avoid

orín [o'rin] *nm* rust

orina [o'rina] *nf* urine

orinal [ori'nal] *nm* (chamber) pot

orinar [ori'nar] *vi* to urinate; **orinarse** *vr* to wet o.s.

orines [o'rines] *nmpl* urine *sg*

oriundo, -a [o'rjundo, a] *adj*: ~ **de** native of

orla ['orla] *nf* edge, border; (*Escol*) graduation photograph

ornamentar [ornamen'tar] *vt* (*adornar,*

ataviar) to adorn; (*revestir*) to bedeck
ornar [or'nar] *vt* to adorn
ornitología [ornitolo'xia] *nf* ornithology, bird watching
ornitólogo, -a [orni'toloɣo, a] *nm/f* ornithologist
oro ['oro] *nm* gold; **~ en barras** gold ingots; **de ~** gold, golden; **no es ~ todo lo que reluce** all that glitters is not gold; **hacerse de ~** to make a fortune; *ver tb* **oros**
orondo, -a [o'rondo, a] *adj* (*vasija*) rounded; (*individuo*) smug, self-satisfied
oropel [oro'pel] *nm* tinsel
oros ['oros] *nmpl* (*Naipes*) one of the suits in the Spanish card deck; *ver tb* **Baraja Española**
orquesta [or'kesta] *nf* orchestra; **~ de cámara/sinfónica** chamber/symphony orchestra; **~ de jazz** jazz band
orquestar [orkes'tar] *vt* to orchestrate
orquídea [or'kiðea] *nf* orchid
ortiga [or'tiɣa] *nf* nettle
ortodoncia [orto'ðonθja] *nf* orthodontics *sg*
ortodoxo, -a [orto'ðokso, a] *adj* orthodox
ortografía [ortoɣra'fia] *nf* spelling
ortopedia [orto'peðja] *nf* orthop(a)edics *sg*
ortopédico, -a [orto'peðiko, a] *adj* orthop(a)edic
oruga [o'ruɣa] *nf* caterpillar
orujo [o'ruxo] *nm* type of strong grape liqueur made from grape pressings
orzuelo [or'θwelo] *nm* (*Med*) stye
os [os] *pron* (*gen*) you; (*a vosotros*) (to) you; (*reflexivo*) (to) yourselves; (*mutuo*) (to) each other; **vosotros os laváis** you wash yourselves; **¡callaros!** (*fam*) shut up!
osa ['osa] *nf* (she-)bear; **O~ Mayor/Menor** Great/Little Bear, Ursa Major/Minor
osadía [osa'ðia] *nf* daring; (*descaro*) impudence
osamenta [osa'menta] *nf* skeleton
osar [o'sar] *vi* to dare
oscense [os'θense] *adj* of *o* from Huesca ■ *nm/f* native *o* inhabitant of Huesca
oscilación [osθila'θjon] *nf* (*movimiento*) oscillation; (*fluctuación*) fluctuation; (*vacilación*) hesitation; (*de columpio*) swinging, movement to and fro
oscilar [osθi'lar] *vi* to oscillate; to fluctuate; to hesitate
ósculo ['oskulo] *nm* kiss
oscurecer [oskure'θer] *vt* to darken ■ *vi* to grow dark; **oscurecerse** *vr* to grow *o* get dark
oscurezca *etc* [osku'reθka] *vb ver* **oscurecer**
oscuridad [oskuri'ðað] *nf* obscurity; (*tinieblas*) darkness
oscuro, -a [os'kuro, a] *adj* dark; (*fig*) obscure;

(*indefinido*) confused; (*cielo*) overcast, cloudy; (*futuro etc*) uncertain; **a oscuras** in the dark
óseo, -a ['oseo, a] *adj* bony; (*Med etc*) bone *cpd*
oso ['oso] *nm* bear; **~ blanco/gris/pardo** polar/grizzly/brown bear; **~ de peluche** teddy bear; **~ hormiguero** anteater; **hacer el ~** to play the fool
Ostende [os'tende] *nm* Ostend
ostensible [osten'siβle] *adj* obvious
ostensiblemente [ostensiβle'mente] *adv* perceptibly, visibly
ostentación [ostenta'θjon] *nf* (*gen*) ostentation; (*acto*) display
ostentar [osten'tar] *vt* (*gen*) to show; (*pey*) to flaunt, show off; (*poseer*) to have, possess
ostentoso, -a [osten'toso, a] *adj* ostentatious, showy
osteópata [oste'opata] *nm/f* osteopath
ostra ['ostra] *nf* oyster ■ *excl:* **¡ostras!** (*fam*) sugar!
ostracismo [ostra'θismo] *nm* ostracism
OTAN ['otan] *nf abr ver* **Organización del Tratado del Atlántico Norte**
OTASE [o'tase] *nf abr* (= *Organización del Tratado del Sudeste Asiático*) SEATO
otear [ote'ar] *vt* to observe; (*fig*) to look into
otero [o'tero] *nm* low hill, hillock
otitis [o'titis] *nf* earache
otoñal [oto'ɲal] *adj* autumnal
otoño [o'toɲo] *nm* autumn, fall (*US*)
otorgamiento [otorɣa'mjento] *nm* conferring, granting; (*Jur*) execution
otorgar [otor'ɣar] *vt* (*conceder*) to concede; (*dar*) to grant; (*poderes*) to confer; (*premio*) to award
otorgue *etc* [o'torɣe] *vb ver* **otorgar**
otorrinolaringólogo, -a [otorrinolarin'go loɣo, a] *nm/f* (*Med: tb:* **otorrino**) ear, nose and throat specialist

 PALABRA CLAVE

otro, -a ['otro, a] *adj* **1** (*distinto: sg*) another; (*: pl*) other; **otra cosa/persona** something/someone else; **con otros amigos** with other *o* different friends; **a/en otra parte** elsewhere, somewhere else
2 (*adicional*): **tráigame ~ café (más), por favor** can I have another coffee please; **otros 10 días más** another 10 days
■ *pron* **1** (*sg*) another one; **el ~** the other one; **(los) otros** (the) others; **¡otra!** (*Mus*) more!; **de ~** somebody *o* someone else's; **que lo haga ~** let somebody *o* someone else do it; **ni uno ni ~** neither one nor the other
2 (*recíproco*): **se odian (la) una a (la) otra** they hate one another *o* each other

3: ~ **tanto**: **comer otro tanto** to eat the same *o* as much again; **recibió una decena de telegramas y otras tantas llamadas** he got about ten telegrams and as many calls

otrora [o'trora] *adv* formerly; **el ~ señor del país** the one-time ruler of the country
OUA *nf abr* (= *Organización de la Unidad Africana*) OAU
ovación [oβa'θjon] *nf* ovation
ovacionar [oβaθjo'nar] *vt* to cheer
oval [o'βal], **ovalado, a** [oβa'laðo, a] *adj* oval
óvalo ['oβalo] *nm* oval
ovario [o'βarjo] *nm* ovary
oveja [o'βexa] *nf* sheep; ~ **negra** (*fig*) black sheep (of the family)
overol [oβe'rol] *nm* (*Am*) overalls *pl*
ovetense [oβe'tense] *adj* of *o* from Oviedo
  ■ *nm/f* native *o* inhabitant of Oviedo

ovillo [o'βiʎo] *nm* (*de lana*) ball; (*fig*) tangle; **hacerse un ~** to curl up (into a ball)
OVNI ['oβni] *nm abr* (= *objeto volante* (*o volador*) *no identificado*) UFO
ovulación [oβula'θjon] *nf* ovulation
óvulo ['oβulo] *nm* ovum
oxidación [oksiða'θjon] *nf* rusting
oxidar [oksi'ðar] *vt* to rust; **oxidarse** *vr* to go rusty; (*Tec*) to oxidize
óxido ['oksiðo] *nm* oxide
oxigenado, -a [oksixe'naðo, a] *adj* (*Química*) oxygenated; (*pelo*) bleached
oxigenar [oksixe'nar] *vt* to oxygenate; **oxigenarse** *vr* to become oxygenated; (*fam*) to get some fresh air
oxígeno [ok'sixeno] *nm* oxygen
oyendo *etc* [o'jendo] *vb ver* **oír**
oyente [o'jente] *nm/f* listener, hearer; (*Escol*) unregistered *o* occasional student

Pp

P, p [pe] *nf* (*letra*) P, p; **P de París** P for Peter
P *abr* (*Rel*: = *padre*) Fr.; = **papa**; (= *pregunta*) Q
p. *abr* (= *página*) p; (*Costura*) = **punto**
p.a. *abr* = **por autorización; por ausencia**
pabellón [paβe'ʎon] *nm* bell tent; (*Arq*)
pavilion; (*de hospital etc*) block, section;
(*bandera*) flag; ~ **de conveniencia** (*Com*) flag
of convenience; ~ **de la oreja** outer ear
pábilo ['paβilo] *nm* wick
pábulo ['paβulo] *nm* food; **dar ~ a** to feed,
encourage
PAC *nf abr* (= *Política Agrícola Común*) CAP
pacense [pa'θense] *adj* of o from Badajoz
■ *nm/f* native o inhabitant of Badajoz
paceño, -a [pa'θeɲo, a] *adj* of o from La Paz
■ *nm/f* native o inhabitant of La Paz
pacer [pa'θer] *vi* to graze ■ *vt* to graze on
pachá [pa'tʃa] *nm*: **vivir como un pachá** to
live like a king
pachanguero, -a [patʃan'gero, a] *adj* (*pey*:
música) noisy and catchy
pachorra [pa'tʃorra] *nf* (*indolencia*) slowness;
(*tranquilidad*) calmness
pachucho, -a [pa'tʃutʃo, a] *adj* (*fruta*)
overripe; (*persona*) off-colour, poorly
paciencia [pa'θjenθja] *nf* patience; **¡~!** be
patient!; **¡~ y barajar!** don't give up!; **perder
la ~** to lose one's temper
paciente [pa'θjente] *adj, nm/f* patient
pacificación [paθifika'θjon] *nf* pacification
pacificar [paθifi'kar] *vt* to pacify; (*tranquilizar*)
to calm
pacífico, -a [pa'θifiko, a] *adj* peaceful;
(*persona*) peace-loving; (*existencia*) pacific;
el (Océano) P~ the Pacific (Ocean)
pacifique *etc* [paθi'fike] *vb ver* **pacificar**
pacifismo [paθi'fismo] *nm* pacifism
pacifista [paθi'fista] *nm/f* pacifist
pack [pak] *nm* (*de yogures, latas*) pack; (*de
vacaciones*) package
pacotilla [pako'tiʎa] *nf* trash; **de ~** shoddy
pactar [pak'tar] *vt* to agree to, agree on ■ *vi*
to come to an agreement

pacto ['pakto] *nm* (*tratado*) pact; (*acuerdo*)
agreement
padecer [paðe'θer] *vt* (*sufrir*) to suffer;
(*soportar*) to endure, put up with; (*ser víctima
de*) to be a victim of ■ *vi*: ~ **de** to suffer from
padecimiento [paðeθi'mjento] *nm* suffering
pádel ['paðel] *nm* paddle tennis
padezca *etc* [pa'ðeθka] *vb ver* **padecer**
padrastro [pa'ðrastro] *nm* stepfather
padre ['paðre] *nm* father ■ *adj* (*fam*): **un
éxito ~** a tremendous success; **padres** *nmpl*
parents; ~ **espiritual** confessor; **P~ Nuestro**
Lord's Prayer; ~ **político** father-in-law;
García ~ García senior; **¡tu ~!** (*fam!*) up
yours! (!)
padrino [pa'ðrino] *nm* godfather; (*fig*)
sponsor, patron; **padrinos** *nmpl* godparents;
~ **de boda** best man
padrón [pa'ðron] *nm* (*censo*) census, roll; (*de
socios*) register
paella [pa'eʎa] *nf* paella,, dish of rice with meat,
shellfish etc
paga ['paɣa] *nf* (*dinero pagado*) payment;
(*sueldo*) pay, wages *pl*
pagadero, -a [paɣa'ðero, a] *adj* payable; ~ **a
la entrega/a plazos** payable on delivery/in
instalments
pagano, -a [pa'ɣano, a] *adj, nm/f* pagan,
heathen
pagar [pa'ɣar] *vt* (*gen*) to pay; (*las compras,
crimen*) to pay for; (*deuda*) to pay (off); (*fig:
favor*) to repay ■ *vi* to pay; **pagarse** *vr*:
pagarse con algo to be content with sth;
¡me las ~ás! I'll get you for this!
pagaré [paɣa're] *nm* I.O.U
página ['paxina] *nf* page; ~ **de inicio** (*Inform*)
home page; ~ **personal** (*Internet*) personal
web page
páginas amarillas *nfpl* Yellow Pages®;
página web web page
paginación [paxina'θjon] *nf* (*Inform, Tip*)
pagination
paginar [paxi'nar] *vt* (*Inform, Tip*) to paginate

P

pago ['paɣo] *nm* (*dinero*) payment; (*fig*) return; ~ **anticipado/a cuenta/a la entrega/en especie/inicial** advance payment/payment on account/cash on delivery/payment in kind/down payment; ~ **a título gracioso** ex gratia payment; **en ~ de** in return for

pág(s). *abr* (= *página(s)*) p(p)

pague *etc* ['paɣe] *vb ver* **pagar**

paila ['paila] *nf* (*Am*) frying pan

país [pa'is] *nm* (*gen*) country; (*región*) land; **los Países Bajos** the Low Countries; **el P~ Vasco** the Basque Country

paisaje [pai'saxe] *nm* countryside, landscape; (*vista*) scenery

paisano, -a [pai'sano, a] *adj* of the same country ■ *nm/f* (*compatriota*) fellow countryman(-woman); **vestir de ~** (*soldado*) to be in civilian clothes; (*guardia*) to be in plain clothes

paja ['paxa] *nf* straw; (*fig*) trash, rubbish; (*en libro, ensayo*) padding, waffle; **riñeron por un quítame allá esas pajas** they quarrelled over a trifle

pajar [pa'xar] *nm* hay loft

pajarita [paxa'rita] *nf* bow tie

pájaro ['paxaro] *nm* bird; (*fam: astuto*) clever fellow; **tener la cabeza a pájaros** to be featherbrained

pajita [pa'xita] *nf* (drinking) straw

pajizo, -a [pa'xiθo, a] *adj* (*de paja*) straw *cpd*; (*techo*) thatched; (*color*) straw-coloured

pakistaní [pakista'ni] *adj, nm/f* Pakistani

pala ['pala] *nf* (*de mango largo*) spade; (*de mango corto*) shovel; (*raqueta etc*) bat; (: *de tenis*) racquet; (*Culin*) slice; ~ **matamoscas** fly swat

palabra [pa'laβra] *nf* (*gen, promesa*) word; (*facultad*) (power of) speech; (*derecho de hablar*) right to speak; **faltar a su ~** to go back on one's word; **quedarse con la ~ en la boca** to stop short; (*en reunión, comité etc*): **tomar la ~** to speak, take the floor; **pedir la ~** to ask to be allowed to speak; **tener la ~** to have the floor; **no encuentro palabras para expresarme** words fail me

palabrería [palaβre'ria] *nf* hot air

palabrota [pala'βrota] *nf* swearword

palacio [pa'laθjo] *nm* palace; (*mansión*) mansion, large house; ~ **de justicia** courthouse; ~ **municipal** town/city hall

palada [pa'laða] *nf* shovelful, spadeful; (*de remo*) stroke

paladar [pala'ðar] *nm* palate

paladear [palaðe'ar] *vt* to taste

palanca [pa'lanka] *nf* lever; (*fig*) pull, influence; ~ **de cambio** (*Auto*) gear lever, gearshift (*US*); ~ **de freno** (*Auto*) brake lever; ~ **de gobierno** *o* **de control** (*Inform*) joystick

palangana [palan'gana] *nf* washbasin

palco ['palko] *nm* box

palenque [pa'lenke] *nm* (*cerca*) stockade, fence; (*área*) arena, enclosure; (*de gallos*) pit

palentino, -a [palen'tino, a] *adj* of *o* from Palencia ■ *nm/f* native *o* inhabitant of Palencia

paleolítico, -a [paleo'litiko, a] *adj* paleolithic

paleontología [paleontolo'xia] *nf* paleontology

Palestina [pales'tina] *nf* Palestine

palestino, -a [pales'tino, a] *adj, nm/f* Palestinian

palestra [pa'lestra] *nf*: **salir** *o* **saltar a la ~** to come into the spotlight

paleto, -a [pa'leto, a] *nm/f* yokel, hick (*US*) ■ *nf* (*pala*) small shovel; (*Arte*) palette; (*Anat*) shoulder blade; (*Am*) ice lolly

paliar [pa'ljar] *vt* (*mitigar*) to mitigate; (*disfrazar*) to conceal

paliativo [palja'tiβo] *nm* palliative

palidecer [paliðe'θer] *vi* to turn pale

palidez [pali'ðeθ] *nf* paleness

palidezca *etc* [pali'ðeθka] *vb ver* **palidecer**

pálido, -a [pa'liðo, a] *adj* pale

palillo [pa'liʎo] *nm* small stick; (*para dientes*) toothpick; **palillos (chinos)** chopsticks; **estar hecho un ~** to be as thin as a rake

palio ['paljo] *nm* canopy

palique [pa'like] *nm*: **estar de ~** (*fam*) to have a chat

paliza [pa'liθa] *nf* beating, thrashing; **dar** *o* **propinar > una ~ a algn** (*fam*) to give sb a thrashing

palma ['palma] *nf* (*Anat*) palm; (*árbol*) palm tree; **batir** *o* **dar palmas** to clap, applaud; **llevarse la ~** to triumph, win

palmada [pal'maða] *nf* slap; **palmadas** *nfpl* clapping *sg*, applause *sg*

Palma de Mallorca *nf* Palma

palmar [pal'mar] *vi* (*tb*: **palmarla**) to die, kick the bucket

palmarés [palma'res] *nm* (*lista*) list of winners; (*historial*) track record

palmear [palme'ar] *vi* to clap

palmero, -a [pal'mero, a] *adj* of the island of Palma ■ *nm/f* native *o* inhabitant of the island of Palma ■ *nm* (*Am*) ■ *nf* palm tree

palmo ['palmo] *nm* (*medida*) span; (*fig*) small amount; ~ **a ~** inch by inch

palmotear [palmote'ar] *vi* to clap, applaud

palmoteo [palmo'teo] *nm* clapping, applause

palo ['palo] *nm* stick; (*poste*) post, pole; (*mango*) handle, shaft; (*golpe*) blow, hit; (*de golf*) club; (*de béisbol*) bat; (*Naut*) mast; (*Naipes*) suit; **vermut a ~ seco** straight vermouth; **de tal ~ tal astilla** like father like son

paloma [pa'loma] *nf* dove, pigeon; ~ **mensajera** carrier *o* homing pigeon

palomilla [palo'miʎa] *nf* moth; (*Tec: tuerca*) wing nut; (*soporte*) bracket

palomitas [palo'mitas] *nfpl* popcorn *sg*

palpable [pal'paβle] *adj* palpable; (*fig*) tangible

palpar [pal'par] *vt* to touch, feel

palpitación [palpita'θjon] *nf* palpitation

palpitante [palpi'tante] *adj* palpitating; (*fig*) burning

palpitar [palpi'tar] *vi* to palpitate; (*latir*) to beat

palta ['palta] *nf* (*Am*) avocado

palúdico, -a [pa'luðiko, a] *adj* marshy

paludismo [palu'ðismo] *nm* malaria

palurdo, -a [pa'lurðo, a] *adj* coarse, uncouth ■ *nm/f* yokel, hick (*US*)

pamela [pa'mela] *nf* sun hat

pampa ['pampa] *nf* (*Am*) pampa(s), prairie

pamplinas [pam'plinas] *nfpl* nonsense *sg*

pamplonés, -esa [pamplo'nes, esa], **pamplonica** [pamplo'nika] *adj* of *o* from Pamplona ■ *nm/f* native *o* inhabitant of Pamplona

pan [pan] *nm* bread; (*una barra*) loaf; ~ **de molde** sliced loaf; ~ **integral** wholemeal bread; ~ **rallado** breadcrumbs *pl*; **eso es ~ comido** it's a cinch; **llamar al ~ ~ y al vino vino** to call a spade a spade

pana ['pana] *nf* corduroy

panadería [panaðe'ria] *nf* baker's (shop)

panadero, -a [pana'ðero, a] *nm/f* baker

panal [pa'nal] *nm* honeycomb

Panamá [pana'ma] *nm* Panama

panameño, -a [pana'meɲo, a] *adj* Panamanian

pancarta [pan'karta] *nf* placard, banner

pancho, -a ['pantʃo, a] *adj*: **estar tan ~** to remain perfectly calm

pancito [pan'sito] *nm* (*Am*) (bread) roll

páncreas ['pankreas] *nm* pancreas

panda ['panda] *nm* panda ■ *nf* gang

pandemia [pan'demja] *nf* pandemic

pandereta [pande'reta] *nf* tambourine

pandilla [pan'diʎa] *nf* set, group; (*de criminales*) gang; (*pey*) clique

pando, -a ['pando, a] *adj* sagging

panecillo [pane'θiʎo] *nm* (bread) roll

panel [pa'nel] *nm* panel; ~ **acústico** acoustic screen

panera [pa'nera] *nf* bread basket

panfleto [pan'fleto] *nm* (*Pol etc*) pamphlet; lampoon

pánico ['paniko] *nm* panic

panificadora [panifika'ðora] *nf* bakery

panorama [pano'rama] *nm* panorama; (*vista*) view

panqué [pan'ke] *nm* (*Am*) pancake

pantaletas [panta'letas] *nfpl* (*Am*) panties

pantalla [pan'taʎa] *nf* (*de cine*) screen; (*cubreluz*) lampshade; (*Inform*) screen, display; **servir de ~ a** to be a blind for; ~ **de cristal líquido** liquid crystal display; ~ **táctil** touch screen; ~ **de ayuda** help screen

pantalón [panta'lon] *nm*, **pantalones** [panta'lones] *nmpl* trousers *pl*, pants *pl* (*US*); **pantalones cortos** shorts *pl*; **pantalones vaqueros** jeans *pl*

pantano [pan'tano] *nm* (*ciénaga*) marsh, swamp; (*depósito: de agua*) reservoir; (*fig*) jam, fix, difficulty

pantera [pan'tera] *nf* panther

pantis ['pantis] *nmpl* tights

pantomima [panto'mima] *nf* pantomime

pantorrilla [panto'rriʎa] *nf* calf (of the leg)

pantufla [pan'tufla] *nf* slipper

panty ['panti] *nm* = **pantis**

panza ['panθa] *nf* belly, paunch

panzón, -ona [pan'θon, ona], **panzudo, -a** [pan'θuðo, a] *adj* fat, potbellied

pañal [pa'ɲal] *nm* nappy, diaper (*US*); **estar todavía en pañales** to be still wet behind the ears

pañería [paɲe'ria] *nf* (*artículos*) drapery; (*tienda*) draper's (shop), dry-goods store (*US*)

paño ['paɲo] *nm* (*tela*) cloth; (*pedazo de tela*) (piece of) cloth; (*trapo*) duster, rag; ~ **de cocina** dishcloth; ~ **higiénico** sanitary towel; **paños menores** underclothes; **paños calientes** (*fig*) half-measures; **no andarse con paños calientes** to pull no punches

pañuelo [pa'ɲwelo] *nm* handkerchief, hanky (*fam*); (*para la cabeza*) (head)scarf

papa ['papa] *nf* (*Am*) potato ■ *nm*: **el P~** the Pope

papá [pa'pa] *nm* (*pl* ~**s**) (*fam*) dad, daddy, pop (*US*); **papás** *nmpl* parents; **hijo de papá** Hooray Henry (*fam*)

papada [pa'paða] *nf* double chin

papagayo [papa'yajo] *nm* parrot

papanatas [papa'natas] *nm inv* (*fam*) sucker, simpleton

paparrucha [papa'rrutʃa] *nf* (*tontería*) piece of nonsense

papaya [pa'paja] *nf* papaya

papear [pape'ar] *vt, vi* (*fam*) to eat

papel [pa'pel] *nm* (*gen*) paper; (*hoja de papel*) sheet of paper; (*Teat*) part, role; **papeles** *nmpl* identification papers; ~ **de calco/ carbón/de cartas** tracing paper/carbon paper/stationery; ~ **continuo** (*Inform*) continuous stationery; ~ **de envolver/de**

P

empapelar brown paper/wrapping paper/ wallpaper; **~ de aluminio/higiénico** tinfoil/ toilet paper; **~ del o de pagos al Estado** government bonds *pl*; **~ de lija** sandpaper; **~ moneda** paper money; **~ plegado (en abanico o en acordeón)** fanfold paper; **~ pintado** wallpaper; **~ secante** blotting paper; **~ térmico** thermal paper

papeleo [pape'leo] *nm* red tape

papelera [pape'lera] *nf (cesto)* wastepaper basket; *(escritorio)* desk; **~ de reciclaje** *(Inform)* wastebasket

papelería [papele'ria] *nf (tienda)* stationer's *(shop)*

papeleta [pape'leta] *nf (pedazo de papel)* slip o bit of paper; *(Pol)* ballot paper; *(Escol)* report; **¡vaya ~!** this is a tough one!

paperas [pa'peras] *nfpl* mumps *sg*

papilla [pa'piʎa] *nf (de bebé)* baby food; *(pey)* mush; **estar hecho ~** to be dog-tired

paquete [pa'kete] *nm (caja)* packet; *(bulto)* parcel; *(Am fam)* nuisance, bore; *(Inform)* package *(of software)*; *(de vacaciones)* package tour; **~ de aplicaciones** *(Inform)* applications package; **~ integrado** *(Inform)* integrated package; **~ de gestión integrado** combined management suite; **paquetes postales** parcel post *sg*

paquistaní [pakista'ni] = **pakistaní**

par [par] *adj (igual)* like, equal; *(Mat)* even ■ *nm* equal; *(de guantes)* pair; *(de veces)* couple; *(título)* peer; *(Golf, Com)* par ■ *nf* par; **pares o nones** odds or evens; **abrir de ~ en ~** to open wide; **a la ~** par; **sobre/bajo la ~** above/ below par

para ['para] *prep* for; **no es ~ comer** it's not for eating; **decir ~ sí** to say to o.s.; **¿~ qué lo quieres?** what do you want it for?; **se casaron ~ separarse otra vez** they married only to separate again; **~ entonces** by then o that time; **lo tendré ~ mañana** I'll have it for tomorrow; **ir ~ casa** to go home, head for home; **~ profesor es muy estúpido** he's very stupid for a teacher; **¿quién es usted ~ gritar así?** who are you to shout like that?; **tengo bastante ~ vivir** I have enough to live on

parabellum [paraβe'lum] *nm* (automatic) pistol

parabién [para'βjen] *nm* congratulations *pl*

parábola [pa'raβola] *nf* parable; *(Mat)* parabola

parabólica [para'βolika] *nf (tb: **antena parabólica**)* satellite dish

parabrisas [para'βrisas] *nm inv* windscreen, windshield *(US)*

paracaídas [paraka'iðas] *nm inv* parachute

paracaidista [parakai'ðista] *nm/f* parachutist; *(Mil)* paratrooper

parachoques [para'tʃokes] *nm inv* bumper, fender *(US)*; shock absorber

parada [pa'raða] *nf ver* **parado**

paradero [para'ðero] *nm* stopping-place; *(situación)* whereabouts

parado, -a [pa'raðo, a] *adj (persona)* motionless, standing still; *(fábrica)* closed, at a standstill; *(coche)* stopped; *(Am: de pie)* standing (up); *(sin empleo)* unemployed, idle; *(confuso)* confused ■ *nf (gen)* stop; *(acto)* stopping; *(de industria)* shutdown, stoppage; *(lugar)* stopping-place; **salir bien ~** to come off well; **parada de autobús** bus stop; **parada discrecional** request stop; **parada en seco** sudden stop; **parada de taxis** taxi rank

paradoja [para'ðoxa] *nf* paradox

paradójico, -a [para'ðoxiko, a] *adj* paradoxical

parador [para'ðor] *nm* (luxury) hotel

parafrasear [parafrase'ar] *vt* to paraphrase

paráfrasis [pa'rafrasis] *nf inv* paraphrase

paraguas [pa'raɣwas] *nm inv* umbrella

Paraguay [para'ɣwai] *nm*: **el ~** Paraguay

paraguayo, -a [para'ɣwajo, a] *adj, nm/f* Paraguayan

paraíso [para'iso] *nm* paradise, heaven; **~ fiscal** *(Com)* tax haven

paraje [pa'raxe] *nm* place, spot

paralelo, -a [para'lelo, a] *adj, nm* parallel; **en ~** *(Elec, Inform)* (in) parallel

paralice *etc* [para'liθe] *vb ver* **paralizar**

parálisis [pa'ralisis] *nf inv* paralysis; **~ cerebral** cerebral palsy; **~ progresiva** creeping paralysis

paralítico, -a [para'litiko, a] *adj, nm/f* paralytic

paralizar [parali'θar] *vt* to paralyse; **paralizarse** *vr* to become paralysed; *(fig)* to come to a standstill

parámetro [pa'rametro] *nm* parameter

paramilitar [paramili'tar] *adj* paramilitary

páramo ['paramo] *nm* bleak plateau

parangón [paran'gon] *nm*: **sin ~** incomparable

paraninfo [para'ninfo] *nm (Escol)* assembly hall

paranoia [para'noia] *nf* paranoia

paranoico, -a [para'noiko, a] *adj, nm/f* paranoid

paranormal [paranor'mal] *adj* paranormal

parapetarse [parape'tarse] *vr* to shelter

parapléjico, -a [para'plexiko, a] *adj, nm/f* paraplegic

parar [pa'rar] *vt* to stop; *(progreso etc)* to

check, halt; (*golpe*) to ward off ∎ *vi* to stop; (*hospedarse*) to stay, put up; **pararse** *vr* to stop; (*Am*) to stand up; **no ~ de hacer algo** to keep on doing sth; **ha parado de llover** it has stopped raining; **van a ~ en la comisaría** they're going to end up in the police station; **no sabemos en qué va a ~ todo esto** we don't know where all this is going to end; **pararse a hacer algo** to stop to do sth; **pararse en** to pay attention to

pararrayos [para'rrajos] *nm inv* lightning conductor

parásito, -a [pa'rasito, a] *nm/f* parasite

parasol [para'sol] *nm* parasol, sunshade

parcela [par'θela] *nf* plot, piece of ground, smallholding

parche ['partʃe] *nm* patch

parchís [par'tʃis] *nm* ludo

parcial [par'θjal] *adj* (*pago*) part-; (*eclipse*) partial; (*juez*) prejudiced, biased

parcialidad [parθjali'ðað] *nf* (*prejuicio*) prejudice, bias

parco, -a ['parko, a] *adj* (*frugal*) sparing; (*moderado*) moderate

pardillo, -a [par'ðiʎo, a] *adj* (*pey*) provincial ∎ *nm/f* (*pey*) country bumpkin ∎ *nm* (*Zool*) linnet

pardo, -a ['parðo, a] *adj* (*color*) brown; (*cielo*) overcast; (*voz*) flat, dull

parear [pare'ar] *vt* (*juntar, hacer par*) to match, put together; (*calcetines*) to put into pairs; (*Bio*) to mate, pair

parecer [pare'θer] *nm* (*opinión*) opinion, view; (*aspecto*) looks *pl* ∎ *vi* (*tener apariencia*) to seem, look; (*asemejarse*) to look like, seem like; (*aparecer, llegar*) to appear; **parecerse** *vr* to look alike, resemble each other; **parecerse a** to look like, resemble; **al ~** apparently; **me parece que** I think (that), it seems to me that

parecido, -a [pare'θiðo, a] *adj* similar ∎ *nm* similarity, likeness, resemblance; **~ a** like, similar to; **bien ~** good-looking, nice-looking

pared [pa'reð] *nf* wall; **~ divisoria/medianera** dividing/party wall; **subirse por las paredes** (*fam*) to go up the wall

paredón [pare'ðon] *nm*: **llevar a algn al ~** to put sb up against a wall, shoot sb

parejo, -a [pa'rexo, a] *adj* (*igual*) equal; (*liso*) smooth, even ∎ *nf* (*dos*) pair; (: *de personas*) couple; (*el otro: de un par*) other one (of a pair); (: *persona*) partner; (*de Guardias*) Civil Guard patrol

parentela [paren'tela] *nf* relations *pl*

parentesco [paren'tesko] *nm* relationship

paréntesis [pa'rentesis] *nm inv* parenthesis;

(*digresión*) digression; (*en escrito*) bracket

parezca *etc* [pa'reθka] *vb ver* **parecer**

parida [pa'riða] *nf*: **~ mental** (*fam*) dumb idea

paridad [pari'ðað] *nf* (*Econ*) parity

pariente, -a [pa'rjente, a] *nm/f* relative, relation

parihuela [pari'wela] *nf* stretcher

paripé [pari'pe] *nm*: **hacer el ~** to put on an act

parir [pa'rir] *vt* to give birth to ∎ *vi* (*mujer*) to give birth, have a baby; (*yegua*) to foal; (*vaca*) to calve

París [pa'ris] *nm* Paris

parisiense [pari'sjense] *adj, nm/f* Parisian

paritario, -a [pari'tarjo, a] *adj* equal

parking ['parkin] *nm* car park, parking lot (*US*)

parlamentar [parlamen'tar] *vi* (*negociar*) to parley

parlamentario, -a [parlamen'tarjo, a] *adj* parliamentary ∎ *nm/f* member of parliament

parlamento [parla'mento] *nm* (*Pol*) parliament; (*Jur*) speech

parlanchín, -ina [parlan'tʃin, ina] *adj* loose-tongued, indiscreet ∎ *nm/f* chatterbox

parlante [par'lante] *nm* (*Am*) loudspeaker

parlar [par'lar] *vi* to chatter (away)

parlotear [parlote'ar] *vi* to chatter, prattle

parloteo [parlo'teo] *nm* chatter, prattle

paro ['paro] *nm* (*huelga*) stoppage (of work), strike; (*desempleo*) unemployment; **~ cardiaco** cardiac arrest; **subsidio de ~** unemployment benefit; **hay ~ en la industria** work in the industry is at a standstill; **~ del sistema** (*Inform*) system shutdown

parodia [pa'roðja] *nf* parody

parodiar [paro'ðjar] *vt* to parody

parpadear [parpaðe'ar] *vi* (*los ojos*) to blink; (*luz*) to flicker

parpadeo [parpa'ðeo] *nm* (*de ojos*) blinking, winking; (*de luz*) flickering

párpado ['parpaðo] *nm* eyelid

parque ['parke] *nm* (*lugar verde*) park; **~ de atracciones/de bomberos/zoológico** fairground/fire station/zoo; **~ infantil** children's playground; **~ temático** theme park

parqué, parquet [par'ke] *nm* parquet

parqueadero [parkea'ðero] *nm* (*Am*) car park, parking lot (*US*)

parquímetro [par'kimetro] *nm* parking meter

parra ['parra] *nf* grapevine

párrafo ['parrafo] *nm* paragraph; **echar un ~** (*fam*) to have a chat

P

parranda [pa'rranda] *nf* (*fam*) spree, binge
parrilla [pa'rriʎa] *nf* (*Culin*) grill; (*Am Auto*)
roof-rack; ~ **(de salida)** (*Auto*) starting grid;
carne a la ~ grilled meat
parrillada [parri'ʎaða] *nf* barbecue
párroco ['parroko] *nm* parish priest
parroquia [pa'rrokja] *nf* parish; (*iglesia*)
parish church; (*Com*) clientele, customers *pl*
parroquiano, -a [parro'kjano, a] *nm/f*
parishioner; client, customer
parsimonia [parsi'monja] *nf* (*frugalidad*)
sparingness; (*calma*) deliberateness; **con** ~
calmly
parte ['parte] *nm* message; (*informe*) report; ~
meteorológico weather forecast ▪ *nf* part;
(*lado, cara*) side; (*de reparto*) share; (*Jur*) party;
en alguna ~ **de Europa** somewhere in
Europe; **en cualquier** ~ anywhere; **por ahí
no se va a ninguna** ~ that leads nowhere;
(*fig*) this is getting us nowhere; **en** *o* **por
todas partes** everywhere; **en gran** ~ to a
large extent; **la mayor** ~ **de los españoles**
most Spaniards; **de algún tiempo a esta**
~ for some time past; **de** ~ **de algn** on sb's
behalf; **¿de** ~ **de quién?** (*Telec*) who is
speaking?; **por** ~ **de** on the part of; **yo por
mi** ~ I for my part; **por una** ~ ... **por otra** ~ on
the one hand, ... on the other (hand); **dar** ~ **a
algn** to report to sb; **tomar** ~ to take part
partera [par'tera] *nf* midwife
parterre [par'terre] *nm* (flower)bed
partición [parti'θjon] *nf* division, sharing-
out; (*Pol*) partition
participación [partiθipa'θjon] *nf* (*acto*)
participation, taking part; (*parte*) share;
(*Com*) share, stock (*US*); (*de lotería*) shared
prize; (*aviso*) notice, notification; ~ **en los
beneficios** profit-sharing; ~ **minoritaria**
minority interest
participante [partiθi'pante] *nm/f*
participant
participar [partiθi'par] *vt* to notify, inform
▪ *vi* to take part, participate; ~ **en una
empresa** (*Com*) to invest in an enterprise;
le participo que ... I have to tell you that ...
partícipe [par'tiθipe] *nm/f* participant;
hacer ~ **a algn de algo** to inform sb of sth
participio [parti'θipjo] *nm* participle; ~ **de
pasado/presente** past/present participle
partícula [par'tikula] *nf* particle
particular [partiku'lar] *adj* (*especial*)
particular, special; (*individual, personal*)
private, personal ▪ *nm* (*punto, asunto*)
particular, point; (*individuo*) individual;
tiene coche ~ he has a car of his own; **no
dijo mucho sobre el** ~ he didn't say much
about the matter

particularice *etc* [partikula'riθe] *vb ver*
particularizar
particularidad [partikulari'ðað] *nf*
peculiarity; **tiene la** ~ **de que** ... one of its
special features is (that) ...
particularizar [partikulari'θar] *vt* to
distinguish; (*especificar*) to specify; (*detallar*)
to give details about
partida [par'tiða] *nf* (*salida*) departure; (*Com*)
entry, item; (*juego*) game; (*grupo, bando*) band,
group; **mala** ~ dirty trick; ~ **de nacimiento/
matrimonio/defunción** birth/marriage/
death certificate; **echar una** ~ to have a
game
partidario, -a [parti'ðarjo, a] *adj* partisan
▪ *nm/f* (*Deporte*) supporter; (*Pol*) partisan
partidismo [parti'ðismo] *nm* (*Jur*)
partisanship, bias; (*Pol*) party politics
partido [par'tiðo] *nm* (*Pol*) party; (*encuentro*)
game, match; (*apoyo*) support; (*equipo*) team;
~ **amistoso** (*Deporte*) friendly (game); ~ **de
fútbol** football match; **sacar** ~ **de** to profit
from, benefit from; **tomar** ~ to take sides
partir [par'tir] *vt* (*dividir*) to split, divide;
(*compartir, distribuir*) to share (out), distribute;
(*romper*) to break open, split open; (*rebanada*)
to cut (off); (*vi: ponerse en camino*) to set off, set
out; (*comenzar*) to start (off *o* out); **partirse**
vr to crack *o* split *o* break (in two *etc*); **a** ~ **de**
(starting) from; **partirse de risa** to split
one's sides (laughing)
partitura [parti'tura] *nf* score
parto ['parto] *nm* birth, delivery; (*fig*)
product, creation; **estar de** ~ to be in labour
parvulario [parβu'larjo] *nm* nursery school,
kindergarten
párvulo, -a ['parβulo, a] *nm/f* infant
pasa ['pasa] *nf ver* **paso**
pasable [pa'saβle] *adj* passable
pasada [pa'saða] *nf ver* **pasado**
pasadizo [pasa'ðiθo] *nm* (*pasillo*) passage,
corridor; (*callejuela*) alley
pasado, -a [pa'saðo, a] *adj* past; (*malo: comida,
fruta*) bad; (*muy cocido*) overdone; (*anticuado*)
out of date ▪ *nm* past; (*Ling*) past (tense)
▪ *nf* passing, passage; (*acción de pulir*) rub,
polish; ~ **mañana** the day after tomorrow;
el mes ~ last month; **pasados dos días** after
two days; **lo** ~, ~ let bygones be bygones; ~
de moda old-fashioned; ~ **por agua** (*huevo*)
boiled; **estar** ~ **de vueltas** *o* **de rosca** (*grifo,
tuerca*) to be worn; **de pasada** in passing,
incidentally; **una mala pasada** a dirty trick
pasador [pasa'ðor] *nm* (*gen*) bolt; (*de pelo*) pin,
grip, slide; **pasadores** *nmpl* (*Am: cordones*)
shoelaces
pasaje [pa'saxe] *nm* (*gen*) passage; (*pago de*

viaje) fare; (*los pasajeros*) passengers *pl*; (*pasillo*) passageway

pasajero, -a [pasa'xero, a] *adj* passing; (*ave*) migratory ■ *nm/f* passenger; (*viajero*) traveller

pasamanos [pasa'manos] *nm inv* rail, handrail; (*de escalera*) banister

pasamontañas [pasamon'taɲas] *nm inv* balaclava (helmet)

pasaporte [pasa'porte] *nm* passport

pasar [pa'sar] *vt* (*gen*) to pass; (*tiempo*) to spend; (*durezas*) to suffer, endure; (*noticia*) to give, pass on; (*película*) to show; (*persona*) to take, conduct; (*río*) to cross; (*barrera*) to pass through; (*falta*) to overlook, tolerate; (*contrincante*) to surpass, do better than; (*coche*) to overtake; (*contrabando*) to smuggle (in/out); (*enfermedad*) to give, infect with ■ *vi* (*gen*) to pass, go; (*terminarse*) to be over; (*ocurrir*) to happen; **pasarse** *vr* (*efectos*) to pass, be over; (*flores*) to fade; (*comida*) to go bad, go off; (*fig*) to overdo it, go too far *o* over the top; **~ la aspiradora** to do the vacuuming *o* hoovering, to hoover; **~ de** to go beyond, exceed; **¡pase!** come in!; **nos hicieron ~** they showed us in; **~ por** to fetch; **~ por alto** to skip; **~ por una crisis** to go through a crisis; **se hace ~ por médico** he passes himself off as a doctor; **pasarlo bien/bomba** *o* **de maravilla** to have a good/great time; **¡que lo pases bien!** have a good time!; **pasarse al enemigo** to go over to the enemy; **pasarse de la raya** to go too far; **¡no te pases!** don't try me!; **se me pasó** I forgot; **se me pasó el turno** I missed my turn; **no se le pasa nada** nothing escapes him, he misses nothing; **ya se te ~á** you'll get over it; **¿qué pasa?** what's happening?, what's going on?, what's up?; **¡cómo pasa el tiempo!** time just flies!; **pase lo que pase** come what may; **el autobús pasa por nuestra casa** the bus goes past our house

pasarela [pasa'rela] *nf* footbridge; (*en barco*) gangway

pasatiempo [pasa'tjempo] *nm* pastime, hobby; (*distracción*) amusement

Pascua, pascua ['paskwa] *nf*: **~ (de Resurrección)** Easter; **~ de Navidad** Christmas; **Pascuas** *nfpl* Christmas time *sg*; **¡felices Pascuas!** Merry Christmas!; **de Pascuas a Ramos** once in a blue moon; **hacer la ~ a** (*fam*) to annoy, bug

pase ['pase] *nm* pass; (*Cine*) performance, showing; (*Com*) permit; (*Jur*) licence

pasear [pase'ar] *vt* to take for a walk; (*exhibir*) to parade, show off ■ *vi*, **pasearse** *vr* to walk, go for a walk; **~ en coche** to go for a drive

paseo [pa'seo] *nm* avenue; (*distancia corta*) short walk; **~ marítimo** promenade; **dar un ~** to go for a walk; **~ en bicicleta** (bike) ride; **~ en barco** boat trip; **mandar a algn a ~** to tell sb to go to blazes; **¡vete a ~!** get lost!

pasillo [pa'siʎo] *nm* passage, corridor

pasión [pa'sjon] *nf* passion

pasional [pasjo'nal] *adj* passionate; **crimen ~** crime of passion

pasivo, -a [pa'siβo, a] *adj* passive; (*inactivo*) inactive ■ *nm* (*Com*) liabilities *pl*, debts *pl*; (*de cuenta*) debit side; **~ circulante** current liabilities

pasma ['pasma] *nm* (*fam*) cop

pasmado, -a [pas'maðo, a] *adj* (*asombrado*) astonished; (*atontado*) bewildered

pasmar [pas'mar] *vt* (*asombrar*) to amaze, astonish; **pasmarse** *vr* to be amazed *o* astonished

pasmo ['pasmo] *nm* amazement, astonishment; (*fig*) wonder, marvel

pasmoso, -a [pas'moso, a] *adj* amazing, astonishing

paso, -a ['paso, a] *adj* dried ■ *nm* (*gen, de baile*) step; (*modo de andar*) walk; (*huella*) footprint; (*rapidez*) speed, pace, rate; (*camino accesible*) way through, passage; (*cruce*) crossing; (*pasaje*) passing, passage; (*Rel*) *religious float or sculpture*; (*Geo*) pass; (*estrecho*) strait; (*fig*) step, measure; (*apuro*) difficulty ■ *nf* raisin; **pasa de Corinto/de Esmirna** currant/sultana; **~ a ~** step by step; **a ese ~** (*fig*) at that rate; **salir al ~ de** *o* **a** to waylay; **salir del ~** to get out of trouble; **dar un ~ en falso** to trip; (*fig*) to take a false step; **estar de ~** to be passing through; **~ atrás** step backwards; (*fig*) backward step; **~ elevado/subterráneo** flyover/subway, underpass (US); **prohibido el ~** no entry; **ceda el ~** give way; *ver tb* **Semana Santa**

pasota [pa'sota] *adj, nm/f* (*fam*) ≈ dropout; **ser un (tipo) ~** to be a bit of a dropout; (*ser indiferente*) not to care about anything

pasotismo [paso'tismo] *nm* underground *o* alternative culture

pasta ['pasta] *nf* (*gen*) paste; (*Culin: masa*) dough; (: *de bizcochos etc*) pastry; (*fam*) money, dough; (*encuadernación*) hardback; **pastas** *nfpl* (*bizcochos*) pastries, small cakes; (*espaguetis etc*) pasta *sg*; **~ de dientes** *o* **dentífrica** toothpaste; **~ de madera** wood pulp

pastar [pas'tar] *vt, vi* to graze

pastel [pas'tel] *nm* (*dulce*) cake; (*de carne*) pie; (*Arte*) pastel; (*fig*) plot; **pasteles** *nmpl* pastry *sg*, confectionery *sg*

pastelería [pastele'ria] *nf* cake shop, pastry shop

P

pasteurizado, -a [pasteuri'θaðo, a] *adj* pasteurized

pastilla [pas'tiʎa] *nf* (*de jabón, chocolate*) cake, bar; (*píldora*) tablet, pill

pastizal [pasti'θal] *nm* pasture

pasto ['pasto] *nm* (*hierba*) grass; (*lugar*) pasture, field; (*fig*) food, nourishment

pastor, a [pas'tor, a] *nm/f* shepherd(ess) ■ *nm* clergyman, pastor; (*Zool*) sheepdog; ~ **alemán** Alsatian

pastoso, -a [pas'toso, a] *adj* (*material*) doughy, pasty; (*lengua*) furry; (*voz*) mellow

pat. *abr* (= *patente*) pat

pata ['pata] *nf* (*pierna*) leg; (*pie*) foot; (*de muebles*) leg; **patas arriba** upside down; **a cuatro patas** on all fours; **meter la ~** to put one's foot in it; **~ de cabra** (*Tec*) crowbar; **patas de gallo** crow's feet; **tener buena/ mala ~** to be lucky/unlucky

patada [pa'taða] *nf* stamp; (*puntapié*) kick; **a patadas** in abundance; (*trato*) roughly; **echar a algn a patadas** to kick sb out

patagón, -ona [pata'ɣon, ona] *adj, nm/f* Patagonian

Patagonia [pata'ɣonja] *nf*: **la ~** Patagonia

patalear [patale'ar] *vi* to stamp one's feet

pataleo [pata'leo] *nm* stamping

patán [pa'tan] *nm* rustic, yokel

patata [pa'tata] *nf* potato; **patatas fritas** *o* **a la española** chips, French fries; **patatas a la inglesa** crisps; **ni ~** (*fam*) nothing at all; **no entendió ni ~** he didn't understand a single word

paté [pa'te] *nm* pâté

patear [pate'ar] *vt* (*pisar*) to stamp on, trample (on); (*pegar con el pie*) to kick ■ *vi* to stamp (with rage), stamp one's foot

patentar [paten'tar] *vt* to patent

patente [pa'tente] *adj* obvious, evident; (*Com*) patent ■ *nf* patent

patera [pa'tera] *nf* boat

paternal [pater'nal] *adj* fatherly, paternal

paternalista [paterna'lista] *adj* (*tono, actitud etc*) patronizing

paternidad [paterni'ðað] *nf* fatherhood, parenthood; (*Jur*) paternity

paterno, -a [pa'terno, a] *adj* paternal

patético, -a [pa'tetiko, a] *adj* pathetic, moving

patíbulo [pa'tiβulo] *nm* scaffold, gallows *sg*

patilla [pa'tiʎa] *nf* (*de gafas*) arm; (*de pelo*) sideburn

patín [pa'tin] *nm* skate; (*de tobogán*) runner; **~ de hielo** ice skate; **~ de ruedas** roller skate

patinaje [pati'naxe] *nm* skating

patinar [pati'nar] *vi* to skate; (*resbalarse*) to skid, slip; (*fam*) to slip up, blunder

patinazo [pati'naθo] *nm* (*Auto*) skid; **dar un ~** (*fam*) to blunder

patio ['patjo] *nm* (*de casa*) patio, courtyard; **~ de recreo** playground

pato ['pato] *nm* duck; **pagar el ~** (*fam*) to take the blame, carry the can

patológico, -a [pato'loxiko, a] *adj* pathological

patoso, -a [pa'toso, a] *adj* awkward, clumsy

patraña [pa'traɲa] *nf* story, fib

patria ['patrja] *nf* native land, mother country; **~ chica** home town

patrimonio [patri'monjo] *nm* inheritance; (*fig*) heritage; (*Com*) net worth

patriota [pa'trjota] *nm/f* patriot

patriotero, -a [patrjo'tero, a] *adj* chauvinistic

patriótico, -a [pa'trjotiko, a] *adj* patriotic

patriotismo [patrjo'tismo] *nm* patriotism

patrocinador, a [patroθina'ðor, a] *nm/f* sponsor

patrocinar [patroθi'nar] *vt* to sponsor; (*apoyar*) to back, support

patrocinio [patro'θinjo] *nm* sponsorship; backing, support

patrón, -ona [pa'tron, ona] *nm/f* (*jefe*) boss, chief, master/mistress; (*propietario*) landlord(-lady); (*Rel*) patron saint ■ *nm* (*Costura*) pattern; (*Tec*) standard; **~ oro** gold standard

patronal [patro'nal] *adj*: **la clase ~** management; **cierre ~** lockout

patronato [patro'nato] *nm* sponsorship; (*acto*) patronage; (*Com*) employers' association; (*fundación*) trust; **el ~ de turismo** the tourist board

patrulla [pa'truʎa] *nf* patrol

patrullar [patru'ʎar] *vi* to patrol

paulatino, -a [paula'tino, a] *adj* gradual, slow

paupérrimo, -a [pau'perrimo, a] *adj* very poor, poverty-stricken

pausa ['pausa] *nf* pause; (*intervalo*) break; (*interrupción*) interruption; (*Tec: en videograbadora*) hold; **con ~** slowly

pausado, -a [pau'saðo, a] *adj* slow, deliberate

pauta ['pauta] *nf* line, guide line

pavimento [paβi'mento] *nm* (*Arq*) flooring

pavo ['paβo] *nm* turkey; (*necio*) silly thing, idiot; **~ real** peacock; **¡no seas ~!** don't be silly!

pavonearse [paβone'arse] *vr* to swagger, show off

pavor [pa'βor] *nm* dread, terror

payasada [paja'saða] *nf* ridiculous thing (to do); **payasadas** *nfpl* clowning *sg*

payaso, -a [pa'jaso, a] *nm/f* clown

payo, -a ['pajo, a] *adj, nm/f* non-gipsy

paz [paθ] *nf* peace; (*tranquilidad*) peacefulness, tranquillity; **dejar a algn en ~** to leave sb alone *o* in peace; **hacer las paces** to make peace; (*fig*) to make up; **¡haya ~!** stop it!

pazca *etc* ['paθka] *vb ver* **pacer**

PC *nm abr* (*Pol*: = *Partido Comunista*) CP

P.C.E. *nm abr* = **Partido Comunista Español**

PCL *nf abr* (= *pantalla de cristal líquido*) LCD

P.D. *abr* (= *posdata*) P.S.

peaje [pe'axe] *nm* toll; **autopista de ~** toll motorway, turnpike (*US*)

peatón [pea'ton] *nm* pedestrian; **paso de peatones** pedestrian crossing, crosswalk (*US*)

peca ['peka] *nf* freckle

pecado [pe'kaðo] *nm* sin

pecador, a [peka'ðor, a] *adj* sinful ■ *nm/f* sinner

pecaminoso, -a [pekami'noso, a] *adj* sinful

pecar [pe'kar] *vi* (*Rel*) to sin; (*fig*): **~ de generoso** to be too generous

pecera [pe'θera] *nf* goldfish bowl

pecho ['petʃo] *nm* (*Anat*) chest; (*de mujer*) breast(*s pl*), bosom; (*corazón*) heart, breast; (*valor*) courage, spirit; **dar el ~ a** to breast-feed; **tomar algo a ~** to take sth to heart; **no le cabía en el ~** he was bursting with happiness

pechuga [pe'tʃuɣa] *nf* breast (of chicken *etc*)

pecoso, -a [pe'koso, a] *adj* freckled

peculiar [peku'ljar] *adj* special, peculiar; (*característico*) typical, characteristic

peculiaridad [pekuljari'ðað] *nf* peculiarity; special feature, characteristic

pedagogía [peðaɣo'ɣia] *nf* education

pedagogo [peða'ɣoɣo] *nm* pedagogue, teacher

pedal [pe'ðal] *nm* pedal; **~ de embrague** clutch (pedal); **~ de freno** footbrake

pedalear [peðale'ar] *vi* to pedal

pédalo ['peðalo] *nm* pedalo, pedal boat

pedante [pe'ðante] *adj* pedantic ■ *nm/f* pedant

pedantería [peðante'ria] *nf* pedantry

pedazo [pe'ðaθo] *nm* piece, bit; **hacerse pedazos** to fall to pieces; (*romperse*) to smash, shatter; **un ~ de pan** a scrap of bread; (*fig*) a terribly nice person

pedernal [peðer'nal] *nm* flint

pedestal [peðes'tal] *nm* base; **tener/poner a algn en un ~** to put sb on a pedestal

pedestre [pe'ðestre] *adj* pedestrian; **carrera ~** foot race

pediatra [pe'ðjatra] *nm/f* paediatrician (*Brit*), pediatrician (*US*)

pediatría [peðja'tria] *nf* paediatrics *sg* (*Brit*), pediatrics *sg* (*US*)

pedicuro, -a [peði'kuro, a] *nm/f* chiropodist (*Brit*), podiatrist (*US*)

pedido [pe'ðiðo] *nm* (*Com*: *mandado*) order; (*petición*) request; **pedidos en cartera** (*Com*) backlog *sg*

pedigrí [peði'ɣri] *nm* pedigree

pedir [pe'ðir] *vt* to ask for, request; (*comida, Com*: *mandar*) to order; (*exigir*: *precio*) to ask; (*necesitar*) to need, demand, require ■ *vi* to ask; **~ prestado** to borrow; **~ disculpas** to apologize; **me pidió que cerrara la puerta** he asked me to shut the door; **¿cuánto piden por el coche?** how much are they asking for the car?

pedo ['peðo] (*fam*) *adj inv*: **estar ~** to be pissed (!) ■ *nm* fart (!)

pedrada [pe'ðraða] *nf* throw of a stone; (*golpe*) blow from a stone; **herir a algn de una ~** to hit sb with a stone

pedrea [pe'ðrea] *nf* (*granizada*) hailstorm; (*de lotería*) minor prizes

pedrisco [pe'ðrisko] *nm* (*granizo*) hail; (*granizada*) hailstorm

Pedro ['peðro] *nm* Peter; **entrar como ~ por su casa** to come in as if one owned the place

pega ['peɣa] *nf* (*dificultad*) snag; **de ~** false, dud; **poner pegas** to raise objections

pegadizo, -a [peɣa'ðiθo, a] *adj* (*canción etc*) catchy

pegajoso, -a [peɣa'xoso, a] *adj* sticky, adhesive

pegamento [peɣa'mento] *nm* gum

pegar [pe'ɣar] *vt* (*papel, sellos*) to stick (on); (*con cola*) to glue; (*cartel*) to post, stick up; (*coser*) to sew (on); (*unir*: *partes*) to join, fix together; (*Inform*) to paste; (*Med*) to give, infect with; (*dar*: *golpe*) to give, deal ■ *vi* (*adherirse*) to stick, adhere; (*Inform*) to paste; (*ir juntos*: *colores*) to match, go together; (*golpear*) to hit; (*quemar*: *el sol*) to strike hot, burn; (*fig*); **pegarse** *vr* (*gen*) to stick; (*dos personas*) to hit each other, fight; **pegarle a algo** to be a great one for sth; **~ un grito** to let out a yell; **~ un salto** to jump (with fright); **~ fuego** to catch fire; **~ en** to touch; **pegarse un tiro** to shoot o.s.; **no pega** that doesn't seem right; **ese sombrero no pega con el abrigo** that hat doesn't go with the coat

pegatina [peɣa'tina] *nf* (*Pol etc*) sticker

pego ['peɣo] *nm*: **dar el ~** (*pasar por verdadero*) to look like the real thing

pegote [pe'ɣote] *nm* (*fig*) patch, ugly mend; **tirarse pegotes** (*fam*) to come on strong

pegue *etc* ['peɣe] *vb ver* **pegar**

peinado [pei'naðo] *nm* (*en peluquería*) hairdo; (*estilo*) hair style

p

peinar [pei'nar] *vt* to comb sb's hair; *(con un cierto estilo)* to style; **peinarse** *vr* to comb one's hair

peine ['peine] *nm* comb

peineta [pei'neta] *nf* ornamental comb

p.ej. *abr* (= *por ejemplo*) e.g.

Pekín [pe'kin] *n* Peking

pela ['pela] *nf* (*Esp fam*) peseta; *ver tb* **pelas**

pelado, -a [pe'laðo, a] *adj* (*cabeza*) shorn; (*fruta*) peeled; (*campo, fig*) bare; (*fam: sin dinero*) broke

pelaje [pe'laxe] *nm* (*Zool*) fur, coat; (*fig*) appearance

pelambre [pe'lambre] *nm* long hair, mop

pelar [pe'lar] *vt* (*fruta, patatas*) to peel; (*cortar el pelo a*) to cut the hair of; (*quitar la piel: animal*) to skin; (*ave*) to pluck; (*habas etc*) to shell; **pelarse** *vr* (*la piel*) to peel off; **corre que se las pela** (*fam*) he runs like nobody's business

pelas ['pelas] *nfpl* (*Esp fam*) dough

peldaño [pel'daɲo] *nm* step; (*de escalera portátil*) rung

pelea [pe'lea] *nf* (*lucha*) fight; (*discusión*) quarrel, row

peleado, -a [pele'aðo, a] *adj*: **estar ~ (con algn)** to have fallen out (with sb)

pelear [pele'ar] *vi* to fight; **pelearse** *vr* to fight; (*reñir*) to fall out, quarrel

pelele [pe'lele] *nm* (*figura*) guy, dummy; (*fig*) puppet

peletería [pelete'ria] *nf* furrier's, fur shop

peliagudo, -a [pelja'ɣuðo, a] *adj* tricky

pelícano [pe'likano] *nm* pelican

película [pe'likula] *nf* (*Cine*) film, movie (*US*); (*cobertura ligera*) film, thin covering; (*Foto: rollo*) roll o reel of film; **~ de dibujos (animados)** cartoon film; **~ muda** silent film; **de ~** (*fam*) astonishing, out of this world

peligrar [peli'ɣrar] *vi* to be in danger

peligro [pe'liɣro] *nm* danger; (*riesgo*) risk; **"~ de muerte"** "danger"; **correr ~ de** to be in danger of; **con ~ de la vida** at the risk of one's life

peligrosidad [peliɣrosi'ðað] *nf* danger, riskiness

peligroso, -a [peli'ɣroso, a] *adj* dangerous; risky

pelirrojo, -a [peli'rroxo, a] *adj* red-haired, red-headed

pellejo [pe'ʎexo] *nm* (*de animal*) skin, hide; **salvar el ~** to save one's skin

pellizcar [peʎiθ'kar] *vt* to pinch, nip

pellizco [pe'ʎiθko] *nm* pinch

pellizque *etc* [pe'ʎiθke] *vb ver* **pellizcar**

pelma ['pelma] *nm/f*, **pelmazo** [pel'maθo] *nm* (*fam*) pest

pelo ['pelo] *nm* (*cabellos*) hair; (*de barba, bigote*) whisker; (*de animal: piel*) fur, coat; (*de perro etc*) hair, coat; (*de ave*) down; (*de tejido*) nap; (*Tec*) fibre; **a ~** bareheaded; (*desnudo*) naked; **al ~** just right; **venir al ~** to be exactly what one needs; **por los pelos** by the skin of one's teeth; **escaparse por un ~** to have a close shave; **se me pusieron los pelos de punta** my hair stood on end; **no tener pelos en la lengua** to be outspoken, not mince words; **tomar el ~ a algn** to pull sb's leg

pelón, -ona [pe'lon, ona] *adj* hairless, bald

pelota [pe'lota] *nf* ball; (*fam: cabeza*) nut (*fam*); **en ~(s)** stark naked; **~ vasca** pelota; **devolver la ~ a algn** (*fig*) to turn the tables on sb; **hacer la ~ (a algn)** to creep (to sb)

pelotera [pelo'tera] *nf* (*fam*) barney

pelotón [pelo'ton] *nm* (*Mil*) squad, detachment

peluca [pe'luka] *nf* wig

peluche [pe'lutʃe] *nm*: **muñeco de ~** soft toy

peludo, -a [pe'luðo, a] *adj* hairy, shaggy

peluquería [peluke'ria] *nf* hairdresser's; (*para hombres*) barber's (shop)

peluquero, -a [pelu'kero, a] *nm/f* hairdresser; barber

peluquín [pelu'kin] *nm* toupée

pelusa [pe'lusa] *nf* (*Bot*) down; (*Costura*) fluff

pelvis ['pelβis] *nf* pelvis

PEMEX [pe'meks] *nm abr* = **Petróleos Mejicanos**

PEN [pen] *nm abr* (*Esp*: = *Plan Energético Nacional*: *Arg*) = **Poder Ejecutivo Nacional**

pena ['pena] *nf* (*congoja*) grief, sadness; (*remordimiento*) regret; (*dificultad*) trouble; (*dolor*) pain; (*Am: vergüenza*) shame; (*Jur*) sentence; (*Deporte*) penalty; **~ capital** capital punishment; **~ de muerte** death penalty; **~ pecuniaria** fine; **merecer** o **valer la ~** to be worthwhile; **a duras penas** with great difficulty; **so ~ de** on pain of; **me dan ~** I feel sorry for them; **¿no te da ~ hacerlo?** (*Am*) aren't you embarrassed doing that?; **¡qué ~!** what a shame o pity!

penal [pe'nal] *adj* penal ■ *nm* (*cárcel*) prison

penalidad [penali'ðað] *nf* (*problema, dificultad*) trouble, hardship; (*Jur*) penalty, punishment

penalizar [penali'θar] *vt* to penalize

penalti, penalty [pe'nalti] *nm* (*Deporte*) penalty

penar [pe'nar] *vt* to penalize; (*castigar*) to punish ■ *vi* to suffer

pendejo, -a [pen'dexo, a] *nm/f* (*Am fam!*) wanker (*Brit*) (!), jerk (*US*) (!)

pender [pen'der] *vi* (*colgar*) to hang; (*Jur*) to be pending

pendiente [pen'djente] *adj* pending,

unsettled ■ *nm* earring ■ *nf* hill, slope; **tener una asignatura ~** to have to resit a subject

pendón [pen'don] *nm* banner, standard

péndulo ['pendulo] *nm* pendulum

pene ['pene] *nm* penis

penene [pe'nene] *nm/f* = **PNN**

penetración [penetra'θjon] *nf* (*acto*) penetration; (*agudeza*) sharpness, insight

penetrante [pene'trante] *adj* (*herida*) deep; (*persona, arma*) sharp; (*sonido*) penetrating, piercing; (*mirada*) searching; (*viento, ironía*) biting

penetrar [pene'trar] *vt* to penetrate, pierce; (*entender*) to grasp ■ *vi* to penetrate, go in; (*líquido*) to soak in; (*emoción*) to pierce

penicilina [peniθi'lina] *nf* penicillin

península [pe'ninsula] *nf* peninsula; **P~ Ibérica** Iberian Peninsula

peninsular [peninsu'lar] *adj* peninsular

penique [pe'nike] *nm* penny; **peniques** *nmpl* pence

penitencia [peni'tenθja] *nf* (*remordimiento*) penitence; (*castigo*) penance; **en ~** as a penance

penitencial [peniten'θjal] *adj* penitential

penitenciaría [penitenθja'ria] *nf* prison, penitentiary

penitenciario, -a [peniten'θjarjo, a] *adj* prison *cpd*

penoso, -a [pe'noso, a] *adj* laborious, difficult

pensado, -a [pen'saðo, a] *adj*: **bien/mal ~** well intentioned/cynical; **en el momento menos ~** when least expected

pensador, a [pensa'ðor, a] *nm/f* thinker

pensamiento [pensa'mjento] *nm* (*gen*) thought; (*mente*) mind; (*idea*) idea; (*Bot*) pansy; **no se le pasó por el ~** it never occurred to him

pensar [pen'sar] *vt* to think; (*considerar*) to think over, think out; (*proponerse*) to intend, plan, propose; (*imaginarse*) to think up, invent ■ *vi* to think; **~ en** to think of o about; (*anhelar*) to aim at, aspire to; **dar que ~ a algn** to give sb food for thought

pensativo, -a [pensa'tiβo, a] *adj* thoughtful, pensive

pensión [pen'sjon] *nf* (*casa*) ≈ guest house; (*dinero*) pension; (*cama y comida*) board and lodging; **~ de jubilación** retirement pension; **~ escalada** graduated pension; **~ completa** full board; **media ~** half board

pensionista [pensjo'nista] *nm/f* (*jubilado*) (old-age) pensioner; (*el que vive en una pensión*) lodger; (*Escol*) boarder

pentágono [pen'taɣono] *nm* pentagon; **el P~** the Pentagon

pentagrama [penta'ɣrama] *nm* (*Mus*) stave, staff

penúltimo, -a [pe'nultimo, a] *adj* penultimate, second last

penumbra [pe'numbra] *nf* half-light, semi-darkness

penuria [pe'nurja] *nf* shortage, want

peña ['peɲa] *nf* (*roca*) rock; (*acantilado*) cliff, crag; (*grupo*) group, circle; (*Deporte*) supporters' club

peñasco [pe'ɲasko] *nm* large rock, boulder

peñón [pe'ɲon] *nm* crag; **el P~** the Rock (of Gibraltar)

peón [pe'on] *nm* labourer; (*Am*) farm labourer, farmhand; (*Tec*) spindle, shaft; (*Ajedrez*) pawn

peonza [pe'onθa] *nf* spinning top

peor [pe'or] *adj* (*comparativo*) worse; (*superlativo*) worst ■ *adv* worse; worst; **de mal en ~** from bad to worse; **tanto ~** so much the worse; **A es ~ que B** A is worse than B; **Z es el ~ de todos** Z is the worst of all

pepenar [pepe'nar] *vi* (*Am*) to sift through rubbish o garbage

pepinillo [pepi'niʎo] *nm* gherkin

pepino [pe'pino] *nm* cucumber; **(no) me importa un ~** I don't care two hoots

pepita [pe'pita] *nf* (*Bot*) pip; (*Minería*) nugget

pepito [pe'pito] *nm* meat sandwich

peque *etc* ['peke] *vb ver* **pecar**

pequeñez [peke'ɲeθ] *nf* smallness, littleness; (*trivialidad*) trifle, triviality

pequeño, -a [pe'keɲo, a] *adj* small, little; (*cifra*) small, low; (*bajo*) short; **~ burgués** lower middle-class

pequinés, -esa [peki'nes, esa] *adj, nm/f* Pekinese

pera ['pera] *adj inv* classy; **niño ~** spoiled upper-class brat ■ *nf* pear; **eso es pedir peras al olmo** that's asking the impossible

peral [pe'ral] *nm* pear tree

percance [per'kanθe] *nm* setback, misfortune

per cápita [per'kapita] *adj*: **renta ~** per capita income

percatarse [perka'tarse] *vr*: **~ de** to notice, take note of

percebe [per'θeβe] *nm* (*Zool*) barnacle; (*fam*) idiot

percepción [perθep'θjon] *nf* (*vista*) perception; (*idea*) notion, idea; (*Com*) collection

perceptible [perθep'tiβle] *adj* perceptible, noticeable; (*Com*) payable, receivable

percha ['pertʃa] *nf* (*poste*) pole, support; (*gancho*) peg; (*de abrigos*) coat stand; (*colgador*) coat hanger; (*de ave*) perch

P

perchero [per'tʃero] nm clothes rack

percibir [perθi'βir] vt to perceive, notice; (ver) to see; (peligro etc) to sense; (Com) to earn, receive, get

percusión [perku'sjon] nf percussion

percusor [perku'sor], **percutor** [perku'tor] nm (Tec) hammer; (de arma) firing pin

perdedor, a [perðe'ðor, a] adj losing ■ nm/f loser

perder [per'ðer] vt to lose; (tiempo, palabras) to waste; (oportunidad) to lose, miss; (tren) to miss ■ vi to lose; **perderse** vr (extraviarse) to get lost; (desaparecer) to disappear, be lost to view; (arruinarse) to be ruined; **echar a ~** (comida) to spoil, ruin; (oportunidad) to waste; **tener buen ~** to be a good loser; **¡no te lo pierdas!** don't miss it!; **he perdido la costumbre** I have got out of the habit

perdición [perði'θjon] nf perdition; (fig) ruin

pérdida ['perðiða] nf loss; (de tiempo) waste; (Com) net loss; **pérdidas** nfpl (Com) losses; **¡no tiene ~!** you can't go wrong!; **~ contable** (Com) book loss

perdido, -a [per'ðiðo, a] adj lost; **estar ~ por** to be crazy about; **es un caso ~** he is a hopeless case

perdigón [perði'ɣon] nm pellet

perdiz [per'ðiθ] nf partridge

perdón [per'ðon] nm (disculpa) pardon, forgiveness; (clemencia) mercy; **¡~!** sorry!, I beg your pardon!; **con ~** if I may, if you don't mind

perdonar [perðo'nar] vt to pardon, forgive; (la vida) to spare; (excusar) to exempt, excuse ■ vi to pardon, forgive; **¡perdone (usted)!** sorry!, I beg your pardon!; **perdone, pero me parece que ...** excuse me, but I think ...

perdurable [perðu'raβle] adj lasting; (eterno) everlasting

perdurar [perðu'rar] vi (resistir) to last, endure; (seguir existiendo) to stand, still exist

perecedero, -a [pereθe'ðero, a] adj perishable

perecer [pere'θer] vi to perish, die

peregrinación [pereɣrina'θjon] nf (Rel) pilgrimage

peregrino, -a [pere'ɣrino] adj (extraño) strange; (singular) rare ■ nm/f pilgrim

perejil [pere'xil] nm parsley

perenne [pe'renne] adj perennial

perentorio, -a [peren'torjo, a] adj (urgente) urgent; (terminante) peremptory; (fijo) set, fixed

pereza [pe'reθa] nf (flojera) laziness; (lentitud) sloth, slowness

perezca etc [pe'reθka] vb ver **perecer**

perezoso, -a [pere'θoso, a] adj lazy; slow, sluggish

perfección [perfek'θjon] nf perfection; **a la ~** to perfection

perfeccionar [perfekθjo'nar] vt to perfect; (acabar) to complete, finish

perfecto, -a [per'fekto, a] adj perfect ■ nm (Ling) perfect (tense)

perfidia [per'fiðja] nf perfidy, treachery

pérfido, -a ['perfiðo, a] adj perfidious, treacherous

perfil [per'fil] nm (parte lateral) profile; (silueta) silhouette, outline; (Tec) (cross) section; **perfiles** nmpl features; (fig) social graces; **~ del cliente** (Com) customer profile; **en ~** from the side, in profile

perfilado, -a [perfi'laðo, a] adj (bien formado) well-shaped; (largo: cara) long

perfilar [perfi'lar] vt (trazar) to outline; (dar carácter a) to shape, give character to; **perfilarse** vr to be silhouetted (en against); **el proyecto se va perfilando** the project is taking shape

perforación [perfora'θjon] nf perforation; (con taladro) drilling

perforadora [perfora'ðora] nf drill; **~ de fichas** card-punch

perforar [perfo'rar] vt to perforate; (agujero) to drill, bore; (papel) to punch a hole in ■ vi to drill, bore

perfumar [perfu'mar] vt to scent, perfume

perfume [per'fume] nm perfume, scent

perfumería [perfume'ria] nf perfume shop

pergamino [perɣa'mino] nm parchment

pericia [pe'riθja] nf skill, expertise

periferia [peri'ferja] nf periphery; (de ciudad) outskirts pl

periférico, -a [peri'feriko, a] adj peripheral ■ nm (Inform) peripheral; (Am: Auto) ring road; **barrio ~** outlying district

perilla [pe'riʎa] nf goatee

perímetro [pe'rimetro] nm perimeter

periódico, -a [pe'rjoðiko, a] adj periodic(al) ■ nm (news)paper; **~ dominical** Sunday (news)paper

periodismo [perjo'ðismo] nm journalism

periodista [perjo'ðista] nm/f journalist

periodístico, -a [perjo'ðistiko, a] adj journalistic

periodo [pe'rjoðo], **período** [pe'rioðo] nm period; **~ contable** (Com) accounting period

peripecias [peri'peθjas] nfpl adventures

peripuesto, -a [peri'pwesto, a] adj dressed up; **tan ~** all dressed up (to the nines)

periquito [peri'kito] nm budgerigar, budgie (fam)

perito, -a [pe'rito, a] adj (experto) expert; (diestro) skilled, skilful ■ nm/f expert; skilled worker; (técnico) technician

perjudicar [perxuði'kar] vt (gen) to damage, harm; (fig) to prejudice

perjudicial [perxuði'θjal] adj damaging, harmful; (en detrimento) detrimental

perjudique etc [perxu'ðike] vb ver **perjudicar**

perjuicio [per'xwiθjo] nm damage, harm; **en/sin ~ de** to the detriment of/without prejudice to

perjurar [perxu'rar] vi to commit perjury

perla ['perla] nf pearl; **me viene de perlas** it suits me fine

permanecer [permane'θer] vi (quedarse) to stay, remain; (seguir) to continue to be

permanencia [perma'nenθja] nf (duración) permanence; (estancia) stay

permanente [perma'nente] adj (que queda) permanent; (constante) constant; (comisión etc) standing ■ nf perm; **hacerse una ~** to have one's hair permed

permanezca etc [perma'neθka] vb ver **permanecer**

permisible [permi'siβle] adj permissible, allowable

permiso [per'miso] nm permission; (licencia) permit, licence (Brit), license (US); **con ~** excuse me; **estar de ~** (Mil) to be on leave; **~ de conducir** o **conductor** driving licence (Brit), driver's license (US); **~ de exportación/importación** export/import licence; **~ por asuntos familiares** compassionate leave

permitir [permi'tir] vt to permit, allow; **permitirse** vr: **permitirse algo** to allow o.s. sth; **no me puedo ~ ese lujo** I can't afford that; **¿me permite?** may I?; **si lo permite el tiempo** weather permitting

permuta [per'muta] nf exchange

permutar [permu'tar] vt to switch, exchange; **~ destinos con algn** to swap o exchange jobs with sb

pernicioso, -a [perni'θjoso, a] adj (maligno, Med) pernicious; (persona) wicked

perno ['perno] nm bolt

pernoctar [pernok'tar] vi to stay for the night

pero ['pero] conj but; (aún) yet ■ nm (defecto) flaw, defect; (reparo) objection; **¡no hay ~ que valga!** there are no buts about it

perogrullada [peroɣru'ʎaða] nf platitude, truism

perol [pe'rol] nm, **perola** [pe'rola] nf pan

peronista [pero'nista] adj, nm/f Peronist

perorata [pero'rata] nf long-winded speech

perpendicular [perpendiku'lar] adj perpendicular; **el camino es ~ al río** the road is at right angles to the river

perpetrar [perpe'trar] vt to perpetrate

perpetuamente [perpetwa'mente] adv perpetually

perpetuar [perpe'twar] vt to perpetuate

perpetuo, -a [per'petwo, a] adj perpetual; (Jur etc: condena) life cpd

Perpiñán [perpi'ɲan] nm Perpignan

perplejo, -a [per'plexo, a] adj perplexed, bewildered

perra ['perra] nf bitch; (fam: dinero) money; (: manía) mania, crazy idea; (: rabieta) tantrum; **estar sin una ~** to be flat broke

perrera [pe'rrera] nf kennel

perro ['perro] nm dog; **~ caliente** hot dog; **"~ peligroso"** "beware of the dog"; **ser ~ viejo** to be an old hand; **tiempo de perros** filthy weather; **~ que ladra no muerde** his bark is worse than his bite

persa ['persa] adj, nm/f Persian ■ nm (Ling) Persian

persecución [perseku'θjon] nf pursuit, hunt, chase; (Rel, Pol) persecution

perseguir [perse'ɣir] vt to pursue, hunt; (cortejar) to chase after; (molestar) to pester, annoy; (Rel, Pol) to persecute; (Jur) to prosecute

perseverante [perseβe'rante] adj persevering, persistent

perseverar [perseve'rar] vi to persevere, persist; **~ en** to persevere in, persist with

persiana [per'sjana] nf (Venetian) blind

persiga etc [per'siɣa] vb ver **perseguir**

persignarse [persiɣ'narse] vr to cross o.s.

persiguiendo etc [persi'ɣjenðo] vb ver **perseguir**

persistente [persis'tente] adj persistent

persistir [persis'tir] vi to persist

persona [per'sona] nf person; **10 personas** 10 people; **tercera ~** third party; (Ling) third person; **en ~** in person o the flesh; **por ~** a head; **es buena ~** he's a good sort

personaje [perso'naxe] nm important person, celebrity; (Teat) character

personal [perso'nal] adj (particular) personal; (para una persona) single, for one person ■ nm (plantilla) personnel, staff; (Naut) crew; (fam: gente) people

personalidad [personali'ðað] nf personality; (Jur) status

personalizar [personali'θar] vt to personalize ■ vi (al hablar) to name names

personarse [perso'narse] vr to appear in person; **~ en** to present o.s. at, report to

personero, -a [perso'nero, a] nm/f (Am) (government) official

personificar [personifi'kar] vt to personify

personifique etc [personi'fike] vb ver **personificar**

p

perspectiva [perspek'tiβa] *nf* perspective; (*vista, panorama*) view, panorama; (*posibilidad futura*) outlook, prospect; **tener algo en ~** to have sth in view

perspicacia [perspi'kaθja] *nf* discernment, perspicacity

perspicaz [perspi'kaθ] *adj* shrewd

persuadir [perswa'ðir] *vt* (*gen*) to persuade; (*convencer*) to convince; **persuadirse** *vr* to become convinced

persuasión [perswa'sjon] *nf* (*acto*) persuasion; (*convicción*) conviction

persuasivo, -a [perwa'siβo, a] *adj* persuasive; convincing

pertenecer [pertene'θer] *vi*: **~ a** to belong to; (*fig*) to concern

perteneciente [pertene'θjente] *adj*: **~ a** belonging to

pertenencia [perte'nenθja] *nf* ownership; **pertenencias** *nfpl* possessions, property *sg*

pertenezca *etc* [perte'neθka] *vb ver* **pertenecer**

pértiga ['pertiɣa] *nf* pole; **salto de ~** pole vault

pertinaz [perti'naθ] *adj* (*persistente*) persistent; (*terco*) obstinate

pertinente [perti'nente] *adj* relevant, pertinent; (*apropiado*) appropriate; **~ a** concerning, relevant to

pertrechar [pertre'tʃar] *vt* (*gen*) to supply; (*Mil*) to supply with ammunition and stores; **pertrecharse** *vr*: **pertrecharse de algo** to provide o.s. with sth

pertrechos [per'tretʃos] *nmpl* (*gen*) implements; (*Mil*) supplies and stores

perturbación [perturβa'θjon] *nf* (*Pol*) disturbance; (*Med*) upset, disturbance; **~ del orden público** breach of the peace

perturbador, a [perturβa'ðor, a] *adj* (*que perturba*) perturbing, disturbing; (*subversivo*) subversive

perturbar [pertur'βar] *vt* (*el orden*) to disturb; (*Med*) to upset, disturb; (*mentalmente*) to perturb

Perú [pe'ru] *nm*: **el Perú** Peru

peruano, -a [pe'rwano, a] *adj, nm/f* Peruvian

perversión [perβer'sjon] *nf* perversion

perverso, -a [perβerso, a] *adj* perverse; (*depravado*) depraved

pervertido, -a [perβer'tiðo, a] *adj* perverted ▪ *nm/f* pervert

pervertir [perβer'tir] *vt* to pervert, corrupt

pervierta *etc* [per'βjerta], **pervirtiendo** *etc* [perβir'tjendo] *vb ver* **pervertir**

pesa ['pesa] *nf* weight; (*Deporte*) shot

pesadez [pesa'ðeθ] *nf* (*calidad de pesado*) heaviness; (*lentitud*) slowness; (*aburrimiento*) tediousness; **es una ~ tener que ...** it's a bind having to ...

pesadilla [pesa'ðiʎa] *nf* nightmare, bad dream; (*fig*) worry, obsession

pesado, -a [pe'saðo, a] *adj* (*gen*) heavy; (*lento*) slow; (*difícil, duro*) tough, hard; (*aburrido*) tedious, boring; (*bochornoso*) sultry ▪ *nm/f* bore; **tener el estómago ~** to feel bloated; **¡no seas ~!** come off it!

pesadumbre [pesa'ðumbre] *nf* grief, sorrow

pésame ['pesame] *nm* expression of condolence, message of sympathy; **dar el ~** to express one's condolences

pesar [pe'sar] *vt* to weigh; (*fig*) to weigh heavily on; (*afligir*) to grieve ▪ *vi* to weigh; (*ser pesado*) to weigh a lot, be heavy; (*fig: opinión*) to carry weight ▪ *nm* (*sentimiento*) regret; (*pena*) grief, sorrow; **a ~ de (que)** in spite of, despite; **no me pesa haberlo hecho** I'm not sorry I did it

pesca ['peska] *nf* (*acto*) fishing; (*cantidad de pescado*) catch; **~ de altura/en bajura** deep sea/coastal fishing; **ir de ~** to go fishing

pescadería [peskaðe'ria] *nf* fish shop, fishmonger's

pescadilla [peska'ðiʎa] *nf* whiting

pescado [pes'kaðo] *nm* fish

pescador, a [peska'ðor, a] *nm/f* fisherman(-woman)

pescar [pes'kar] *vt* (*coger*) to catch; (*tratar de coger*) to fish for; (*fam: lograr*) to get hold of, land; (*conseguir: trabajo*) to manage to get; (*sorprender*) to catch unawares ▪ *vi* to fish, go fishing

pescuezo [pes'kweθo] *nm* neck

pese ['pese] *prep*: **~ a** despite, in spite of

pesebre [pe'seβre] *nm* manger

peseta [pe'seta] *nf* peseta

pesetero, -a [pese'tero, a] *adj* money-grubbing

pesimismo [pesi'mismo] *nm* pessimism

pesimista [pesi'mista] *adj* pessimistic ▪ *nm/f* pessimist

pésimo, -a ['pesimo, a] *adj* abominable, vile

peso ['peso] *nm* weight; (*balanza*) scales *pl*; (*Am Com*) monetary unit; (*moneda*) peso; (*Deporte*) shot; **~ bruto/neto** gross/net weight; **~ mosca/pesado** fly-/heavyweight; **de poco ~** light(weight); **levantamiento de pesos** weightlifting; **vender a ~** to sell by weight; **argumento de ~** weighty argument; **eso cae de su ~** that goes without saying

pesque *etc* ['peske] *vb ver* **pescar**

pesquero, -a [pes'kero, a] *adj* fishing *cpd*

pesquisa [pes'kisa] *nf* inquiry, investigation

pestaña [pes'taɲa] *nf* (*Anat*) eyelash; (*borde*) rim

pestañear [pestaɲe'ar] vi to blink
peste ['peste] nf plague; (fig) nuisance; (mal olor) stink, stench; ~ **negra** Black Death; **echar pestes** to swear, fume
pesticida [pesti'θiða] nm pesticide
pestilencia [pesti'lenθja] nf (mal olor) stink, stench
pestillo [pes'tiʎo] nm bolt, latch; (cerrojo) catch; (picaporte) (door) handle
petaca [pe'taka] nf (de cigarrillos) cigarette case; (de pipa) tobacco pouch; (Am: maleta) suitcase
pétalo ['petalo] nm petal
petanca [pe'tanka] nf a game in which metal bowls are thrown at a target bowl
petardo [pe'tarðo] nm firework, firecracker
petición [peti'θjon] nf (pedido) request, plea; (memorial) petition; (Jur) plea; **a ~ de** at the request of; **~ de aumento de salarios** wage demand o claim
petirrojo [peti'rroxo] nm robin
peto ['peto] nm (corpiño) bodice; (Taur) horse's padding
pétreo, -a ['petreo, a] adj stony, rocky
petrificar [petrifi'kar] vt to petrify
petrifique etc [petri'fike] vb ver **petrificar**
PETROVEN [petro'ben] nm abr = **Petróleos de Venezuela**
petrodólar [petro'ðolar] nm petrodollar
petróleo [pe'troleo] nm oil, petroleum
petrolero, -a [petro'lero, a] adj petroleum cpd ■ nm (Com) oil man; (buque) (oil) tanker
petulancia [petu'lanθja] nf (insolencia) vanity, opinionated nature
peyorativo, -a [pejora'tiβo, a] adj pejorative
pez [peθ] nm fish; **~ de colores** goldfish; **~ espada** swordfish; **estar como el ~ en el agua** to feel completely at home
pezón [pe'θon] nm teat, nipple
pezuña [pe'θuɲa] nf hoof
piadoso, -a [pja'ðoso, a] adj (devoto) pious, devout; (misericordioso) kind, merciful
Piamonte [pja'monte] nm Piedmont
pianista [pja'nista] nm/f pianist
piano ['pjano] nm piano; **~ de cola** grand piano
piar [pjar] vi to cheep
piara ['pjara] nf (manada) herd, drove
PIB nm abr (Esp Com: = Producto Interno Bruto) GDP
pibe, -a ['piβe, a] nm/f (Am) boy/girl, kid, child
pica ['pika] nf (Mil) pike; (Taur) goad; **poner una ~ en Flandes** to bring off something difficult
picadero [pika'ðero] nm riding school
picadillo [pika'ðiʎo] nm mince, minced meat
picado, -a [pi'kaðo, a] adj pricked,

punctured; (mar) choppy; (diente) bad; (tabaco) cut; (enfadado) cross
picador [pika'ðor] nm (Taur) picador; (minero) faceworker
picadora [pika'ðora] nf mincer
picadura [pika'ðura] nf (pinchazo) puncture; (de abeja) sting; (de mosquito) bite; (tabaco picado) cut tobacco
picana [pi'kana] (Am) nf (Agr) cattle prod; (Pol: para tortura) electric prod
picante [pi'kante] adj (comida, sabor) hot; (comentario) racy, spicy
picaporte [pika'porte] nm (tirador) handle; (pestillo) latch
picar [pi'kar] vt (agujerear, perforar) to prick, puncture; (billete) to punch, clip; (abeja) to sting; (mosquito, serpiente) to bite; (persona) to nibble (at); (incitar) to incite, goad; (dañar, irritar) to annoy, bother; (quemar: lengua) to burn, sting ■ vi (pez) to bite, take the bait; (el sol) to burn, scorch; (abeja, Med) to sting; (mosquito) to bite; **picarse** vr (agriarse) to turn sour, go off; (mar) to get choppy; (ofenderse) to take offence; **me pican los ojos** my eyes sting; **me pica el brazo** my arm itches
picardía [pikar'ðia] nf villainy; (astucia) slyness, craftiness; (una picardía) dirty trick; (palabra) rude/bad word o expression
picaresco, -a [pika'resko, a] adj (travieso) roguish, rascally; (Lit) picaresque
pícaro, -a ['pikaro, a] adj (malicioso) villainous; (travieso) mischievous ■ nm (astuto) sly sort; (sinvergüenza) rascal, scoundrel
picazón [pika'θon] nf (comezón) itch; (ardor) sting(ing feeling); (remordimiento) pang of conscience
pichón, -ona [pi'tʃon, ona] nm/f (de paloma) young pigeon; (apelativo) darling, dearest
pico ['piko] nm (de ave) beak; (punta agudo) peak, sharp point; (Tec) pick, pickaxe; (Geo) peak, summit; (labia) talkativeness; **no abrir el ~** to keep quiet; **~ parásito** (Elec) spike; **y ~** and a bit; **son las tres y ~** it's just after three; **tiene 50 libros y ~** he has 50-odd books; **me costó un ~** it cost me quite a bit
picor [pi'kor] nm itch; (ardor) sting(ing feeling)
picota [pi'kota] nf pillory; **poner a algn en la ~** (fig) to ridicule sb
picotada [piko'taða] nf, **picotazo** [piko'taθo] nm (de pájaro) peck; (de insecto) sting, bite
picotear [pikote'ar] vt to peck ■ vi to nibble, pick
pictórico, -a [pik'toriko, a] adj pictorial;

p

295

tiene dotes pictóricas she has a talent for painting

picudo, -a [pi'kuðo, a] *adj* pointed, with a point

pidiendo *etc* [pi'ðjendo] *vb ver* **pedir**

pie [pje] (*pl* **pies**) *nm* (*gen, Mat*) foot; (*de cama, página, escalera*) foot, bottom; (*Teat*) cue; (*fig: motivo*) motive, basis; (*: fundamento*) foothold; **pies planos** flat feet; **ir a ~** to go on foot, walk; **estar de ~** to be standing (up); **ponerse de ~** to stand up; **al ~ de la letra** (*citar*) literally, verbatim; (*copiar*) exactly, word for word; **de pies a cabeza** from head to foot; **en ~ de guerra** on a war footing; **sin pies ni cabeza** pointless, absurd; **dar ~ a** to give cause for; **no dar ~ con bola** to be no good at anything; **saber de qué ~ cojea algn** to know sb's weak spots

piedad [pje'ðað] *nf* (*lástima*) pity, compassion; (*clemencia*) mercy; (*devoción*) piety, devotion; **tener ~ de** to take pity on

piedra ['pjeðra] *nf* stone; (*roca*) rock; (*de mechero*) flint; (*Meteorología*) hailstone; **primera ~** foundation stone; **~ de afilar** grindstone; **~ arenisca/caliza** sand-/limestone

piel [pjel] *nf* (*Anat*) skin; (*Zool*) skin, hide; (*de oso*) fur; (*cuero*) leather; (*Bot*) skin, peel ■ *nm/f*: **~ roja** redskin

pienso *etc* ['pjenso] *vb ver* **pensar** ■ *nm* (*Agr*) feed

piercing ['pjersiŋ] *nm* piercing

pierda *etc* ['pjerða] *vb ver* **perder**

pierna ['pjerna] *nf* leg; **en piernas** bare-legged

pieza ['pjeθa] *nf* piece; (*esp Am: habitación*) room; (*Mus*) piece, composition; (*Teat*) work, play; **~ de recambio o repuesto** spare (part), extra (*US*); **~ de ropa** article of clothing; **quedarse de una ~** to be dumbfounded

pigmento [piɣ'mento] *nm* pigment

pigmeo, -a [piɣ'meo, a] *adj, nm/f* pigmy

pijama [pi'xama] *nm* pyjamas *pl*

pijo, -a ['pixo, a] *nm/f* (*fam*) upper-class twit

pijotada [pixo'taða] *nf* nuisance

pila ['pila] *nf* (*Elec*) battery; (*montón*) heap, pile; (*de fuente*) sink; (*Rel: tb*: **pila bautismal**) font; **nombre de ~** Christian o first name; **tengo una ~ de cosas que hacer** (*fam*) I have heaps o stacks of things to do

pilar [pi'lar] *nm* pillar; (*de puente*) pier; (*fig*) prop, mainstay

píldora ['pildora] *nf* pill; **la ~ (anticonceptiva)** the pill; **tragarse la ~** to be taken in

pileta [pi'leta] *nf* basin, bowl; (*Am: de cocina*) sink; (*: piscina*) swimming pool

pillaje [pi'ʎaxe] *nm* pillage, plunder

pillar [pi'ʎar] *vt* (*fam: coger*) to catch; (*: agarrar*) to grasp, seize; (*: entender*) to grasp, catch on to; (*suj: coche etc*) to run over; **~ un resfriado** (*fam*) to catch a cold

pillo, -a ['piʎo, a] *adj* villainous; (*astuto*) sly, crafty ■ *nm/f* rascal, rogue, scoundrel

pilón [pi'lon] *nm* pillar, post; (*Elec*) pylon; (*bebedero*) drinking trough; (*de fuente*) basin

pilotar [pilo'tar] *vt* (*avión*) to pilot; (*barco*) to steer

piloto [pi'loto] *nm* pilot; (*Auto*) rear light, tail light; (*conductor*) driver ■ *adj inv*: **planta ~** pilot plant; **luz ~** side light

piltrafa [pil'trafa] *nf* (*carne*) poor quality meat; (*fig*) worthless object; (*: individuo*) wretch

pimentón [pimen'ton] *nm* (*polvo*) paprika

pimienta [pi'mjenta] *nf* pepper

pimiento [pi'mjento] *nm* pepper, pimiento

pimpante [pim'pante] *adj* (*encantador*) charming; (*tb*: **tan pimpante**) smug, self-satisfied

PIN *nm abr* (*Esp Com*: = *Producto Interior Neto*) net domestic product

pin (*pl* **pins**) [pin, pins] *nm* badge

pinacoteca [pinako'teka] *nf* art gallery

pinar [pi'nar] *nm* pinewood

pincel [pin'θel] *nm* paintbrush

pincelada [pinθe'laða] *nf* brushstroke; **última ~** (*fig*) finishing touch

pinchadiscos [pintʃa'diskos] *nm/f inv* disc jockey, DJ

pinchar [pin'tʃar] *vt* (*perforar*) to prick, pierce; (*neumático*) to puncture; (*incitar*) to prod ■ *vi* (*Mus fam*) to be DJ; **pincharse** *vr* (*con droga*) to inject o.s.; (*neumático*) to burst, puncture; **no ~ ni cortar** (*fam*) to cut no ice; **tener un neumático pinchado** to have a puncture o a flat tyre

pinchazo [pin'tʃaθo] *nm* (*perforación*) prick; (*de llanta*) puncture, flat (*US*)

pinche ['pintʃe] *nm* (*de cocina*) kitchen boy, scullion

pinchito [pin'tʃito] *nm* shish kebab

pincho ['pintʃo] *nm* point; (*aguijón*) spike; (*Culin*) savoury (snack); **~ moruno** shish kebab; **~ de tortilla** small slice of omelette

ping-pong ['pimpon] *nm* table tennis

pingüe ['pingwe] *adj* (*cosecha*) bumper *cpd*; (*negocio*) lucrative

pingüino [pin'gwino] *nm* penguin

pinitos [pi'nitos] *nmpl*: **hacer sus primeros ~** to take one's first steps

pino ['pino] *nm* pine (tree); **vivir en el quinto ~** to live at the back of beyond

pinta ['pinta] *nf* spot; (*gota*) spot, drop;

(*aspecto*) appearance, look(s) *pl*; (*medida*) pint; **tener buena ~** to look good, look well; **por la ~** by the look of it

pintado, -a [pin'taðo, a] *adj* spotted; (*de muchos colores*) colourful ■ *nf* piece of political graffiti; **pintados** *nfpl* political graffiti *sg*; **me sienta que ni ~, me viene que ni ~** it suits me a treat

pintar [pin'tar] *vt* to paint ■ *vi* to paint; (*fam*) to count, be important; **pintarse** *vr* to put on make-up; **pintárselas solo para hacer algo** to manage to do sth by o.s.; **no pinta nada** (*fam*) he has no say

pintor, a [pin'tor, a] *nm/f* painter; **~ de brocha gorda** house painter; (*fig*) bad painter

pintoresco, -a [pinto'resko, a] *adj* picturesque

pintura [pin'tura] *nf* painting; **~ a la acuarela** watercolour; **~ al óleo** oil painting; **~ rupestre** cave painting

pinza ['pinθa] *nf* (*Zool*) claw; (*para colgar ropa*) clothes peg, clothespin (*US*); (*Tec*) pincers *pl*; **pinzas** *nfpl* (*para depilar*) tweezers

piña ['piɲa] *nf* (*fruto del pino*) pine cone; (*fruta*) pineapple; (*fig*) group

piñón [pi'ɲon] *nm* (*Bot*) pine nut; (*Tec*) pinion

PIO *nm abr* (*Esp*: = *Patronato de Igualdad de Oportunidades*) ≈ Equal Opportunities Board

pío, -a ['pio, a] *adj* (*devoto*) pious, devout; (*misericordioso*) merciful ■ *nm*: **no decir ni ~** not to breathe a word

piojo ['pjoxo] *nm* louse

piojoso, -a [pjo'xoso, a] *adj* lousy; (*sucio*) dirty

piolet (*pl* **piolets**) [pjo'le] *nm* ice axe

pionero, -a [pjo'nero, a] *adj* pioneering ■ *nm/f* pioneer

pipa ['pipa] *nf* pipe; (*Bot*) seed, pip

pipí [pi'pi] *nm* (*fam*): **hacer pipí** to have a wee(-wee)

pipiolo [pi'pjolo] *nm* youngster; (*novato*) novice, greenhorn

pique *etc* ['pike] *vb ver* **picar** ■ *nm* (*resentimiento*) pique, resentment; (*rivalidad*) rivalry, competition; **irse a ~** to sink; (*familia*) to be ruined; **tener un ~ con algn** to have a grudge against sb

piqueta [pi'keta] *nf* pick(axe)

piquete [pi'kete] *nm* (*agujerito*) small hole; (*Mil*) squad, party; (*de obreros*) picket; **~ secundario** secondary picket

pirado, -a [pi'raðo, a] *adj* (*fam*) round the bend

piragua [pi'raɣwa] *nf* canoe

piragüismo [pira'ɣwismo] *nm* (*Deporte*) canoeing

pirámide [pi'ramiðe] *nf* pyramid

piraña [pi'raɲa] *nf* piranha

pirarse [pi'rarse] *vr*: **~(las)** (*largarse*) to beat it (*fam*); (*Escol*) to cut class

pirata [pi'rata] *adj*: **edición/disco ~** pirate edition/bootleg record ■ *nm* pirate; (*tb*: **pirata informático**) hacker

pirenaico, -a [pire'naiko, a] *adj* Pyrenean

Pirineo [piri'neo] *nm*, **Pirineos** [piri'neos] *nmpl* Pyrenees *pl*

pirómano, -a [pi'romano, a] *nm/f* (*Psico*) pyromaniac; (*Jur*) arsonist

piropo [pi'ropo] *nm* compliment, (piece of) flattery; **echar piropos a** to make flirtatious remarks to

pirueta [pi'rweta] *nf* pirouette

piruleta [piru'leta] *nf* lollipop

pirulí [piru'li] *nm* lollipop

pis [pis] *nm* (*fam*) pee; **hacer ~** to have a pee

pisada [pi'saða] *nf* (*paso*) footstep; (*huella*) footprint

pisar [pi'sar] *vt* (*caminar sobre*) to walk on, tread on; (*apretar con el pie*) to press; (*fig*) to trample on, walk all over ■ *vi* to tread, step, walk; **~ el acelerador** to step on the accelerator; **~ fuerte** (*fig*) to act determinedly

piscifactoría [pisθifakto'ria] *nf* fish farm

piscina [pis'θina] *nf* swimming pool

Piscis ['pisθis] *nm* (*Astro*) Pisces

piso ['piso] *nm* (*suelo: de edificio*) floor; (*Am*) ground; (*apartamento*) flat, apartment; **primer ~** (*Esp*) first *o* second (*US*) floor; (*Am*) ground *o* first (*US*) floor

pisotear [pisote'ar] *vt* to trample (on *o* underfoot); (*fig: humillar*) to trample on

pisotón [piso'ton] *nm* (*con el pie*) stamp

pista ['pista] *nf* track, trail; (*indicio*) clue; (*Inform*) track; **~ de auditoría** (*Com*) audit trail; **~ de aterrizaje** runway; **~ de baile** dance floor; **~ de tenis** tennis court; **~ de hielo** ice rink; **estar sobre la ~ de algn** to be on sb's trail

pisto ['pisto] *nm* (*Culin*) ratatouille; **darse ~** (*fam*) to show off

pistola [pis'tola] *nf* pistol; (*Tec*) spray-gun

pistolero, -a [pisto'lero, a] *nm/f* gunman, gangster ■ *nf* holster

pistón [pis'ton] *nm* (*Tec*) piston; (*Mus*) key

pitar [pi'tar] *vt* (*hacer sonar*) to blow; (*partido*) to referee; (*rechiflar*) to whistle at, boo; (*actor, obra*) to hiss ■ *vi* to whistle; (*Auto*) to sound *o* toot one's horn; (*Am*) to smoke; **salir pitando** to beat it

pitido [pi'tiðo] *nm* whistle; (*sonido agudo*) beep; (*sonido corto*) pip

pitillera [piti'ʎera] *nf* cigarette case

pitillo [pi'tiʎo] *nm* cigarette

p

pito ['pito] nm whistle; (de coche) horn; (cigarrillo) cigarette; (fam: de marihuana) joint; (fam!) prick (!); **me importa un ~** I don't care two hoots

pitón [pi'ton] nm (Zool) python

pitonisa [pito'nisa] nf fortune-teller

pitorrearse [pitorre'arse] vr: **~ de** to scoff at, make fun of

pitorreo [pito'rreo] nm joke, laugh; **estar de ~** to be in a joking mood

píxel ['piksel] nm (Inform) pixel

piyama [pi'jama] nm (Am) pyjamas pl, pajamas (US) pl

pizarra [pi'θarra] nf (piedra) slate; (encerado) blackboard

pizca ['piθka] nf pinch, spot; (fig) spot, speck, trace; **ni ~** not a bit

pizza ['pitsa] nf pizza

placa ['plaka] nf plate; (Med) dental plate; (distintivo) badge; **~ de matrícula** number plate; **~ madre** (Inform) mother board

placaje [pla'kaxe] nm tackle

placard [pla'kar] nm (Am) built-in cupboard, (clothes) closet (US)

placenta [pla'θenta] nf placenta, afterbirth

placentero, -a [plaθen'tero, a] adj pleasant, agreeable

placer [pla'θer] nm pleasure; **a ~** at one's pleasure

plácido, -a ['plaθiðo, a] adj placid

plafón [pla'fon] nm (Am) ceiling

plaga ['plaɣa] nf pest; (Med) plague; (fig) swarm

plagar [pla'ɣar] vt to infest, plague; (llenar) to fill; **plagado de** riddled with; **han plagado la ciudad de carteles** they have plastered the town with posters

plagiar [pla'gjar] vt to plagiarize; (Am) to kidnap

plagiario, -a [pla'gjario, a] nm/f plagiarist; (Am) kidnapper

plagio ['plaxjo] nm plagiarism; (Am) kidnap

plague etc ['plaɣe] vb ver **plagar**

plan [plan] nm (esquema, proyecto) plan; (idea, intento) idea, intention; (de curso) programme; **~ cotizable de jubilación** contributory pension scheme; **~ de estudios** curriculum, syllabus; **~ de incentivos** (Com) incentive scheme; **tener ~** (fam) to have a date; **tener un ~** (fam) to have an affair; **en ~ de cachondeo** for a laugh; **en ~ económico** (fam) on the cheap; **vamos en ~ de turismo** we're going as tourists; **si te pones en ese ~** ... if that's your attitude ...

plana ['plana] nf ver **plano**

plancha ['plantʃa] nf (para planchar) iron; (rótulo) plate, sheet; (Naut) gangway; (Culin)

grill; **pescado a la ~** grilled fish; **~ de pelo** straighteners

planchado, -a [plan'tʃaðo, a] adj (ropa) ironed; (traje) pressed ■ nm ironing

planchar [plan'tʃar] vt to iron ■ vi to do the ironing

planeador [planea'ðor] nm glider

planear [plane'ar] vt to plan ■ vi to glide

planeta [pla'neta] nm planet

planetario, -a [plane'tarjo, a] adj planetary ■ nm planetarium

planicie [pla'niθje] nf plain

planificación [planifika'θjon] nf planning; **~ corporativa** (Com) corporate planning; **~ familiar** family planning; **diagrama de ~** (Com) planner

planilla [pla'niʎa] nf (Am) form

plano, -a ['plano, a] adj flat, level, even; (liso) smooth ■ nm (Mat, Tec, Aviat) plane; (Foto) shot; (Arq) plan; (Geo) map; (de ciudad) map, street plan ■ nf sheet of paper, page; (Tec) trowel; **primer ~** close-up; **caer de ~** to fall flat; **rechazar algo de ~** to turn sth down flat; **le daba el sol de ~** (fig) the sun shone directly on it; **en primera plana** on the front page; **plana mayor** staff

planta ['planta] nf (Bot, Tec) plant; (Anat) sole of the foot, foot; **~ baja** ground floor

plantación [planta'θjon] nf (Agr) plantation; (acto) planting

plantar [plan'tar] vt (Bot) to plant; (puesto) to put in; (levantar) to erect, set up; **plantarse** vr to stand firm; **~ a algn en la calle** to chuck sb out; **dejar plantado a algn** (fam) to stand sb up; **plantarse en** to reach, get to

plantear [plante'ar] vt (problema) to pose; (dificultad) to raise; **se lo plantearé** I'll put it to him

plantel [plan'tel] nm (fig) group, set

plantilla [plan'tiʎa] nf (de zapato) insole; (personal) personnel; **ser de ~** to be on the staff

plantío [plan'tio] nm (acto) planting; (lugar) plot, bed, patch

plantón [plan'ton] nm (Mil) guard, sentry; (fam) long wait; **dar (un) ~ a algn** to stand sb up

plañir [pla'ɲir] vi to mourn

plasma ['plasma] nm plasma

plasmar [plas'mar] vt (dar forma) to mould, shape; (representar) to represent ■ vi: **~ en** to take the form of

plasta ['plasta] nf soft mass, lump; (desastre) botch, mess

plasticidad [plastiθi'ðað] nf (fig) expressiveness

plástico, -a ['plastiko, a] adj plastic ■ nf (art of) sculpture, modelling ■ nm plastic

plastificar [plastifi'kar] *vt* (*documento*) to laminate

plastifique *etc* [plasti'fike] *vb ver* **plastificar**

plastilina [plasti'lina] *nf* Plasticine®

plata ['plata] *nf* (*metal*) silver; (*cosas hechas de plata*) silverware; (*Am*) cash, dough (*fam*); **hablar en ~** to speak bluntly o frankly

plataforma [plata'forma] *nf* platform; **~ de lanzamiento/perforación** launch(ing) pad/drilling rig

plátano ['platano] *nm* (*fruta*) banana; (*árbol*) plane tree

platea [pla'tea] *nf* (*Teat*) pit

plateado, -a [plate'aðo, a] *adj* silver; (*Tec*) silver-plated

platense [pla'tense] (*fam*) = **ríoplatense**

plática ['platika] *nf* (*Am*) talk, chat; (*Rel*) sermon

platicar [plati'kar] *vi* (*Am*) to talk, chat

platillo [pla'tiʎo] *nm* saucer; (*de limosnas*) collecting bowl; **platillos** *nmpl* cymbals; **~ volador** o **volante** flying saucer; **pasar el ~** to pass the hat round

platina [pla'tina] *nf* (*Mus*) tape deck

platino [pla'tino] *nm* platinum; **platinos** *nmpl* (*Auto*) (contact) points

platique *etc* [pla'tike] *vb ver* **platicar**

plato ['plato] *nm* plate, dish; (*parte de comida*) course; (*guiso*) dish; **~ frutero/sopero** fruit/soup dish; **pagar los platos rotos** (*fam*) to carry the can (*fam*)

plató [pla'to] *nm* set

platónico, -a [pla'toniko, a] *adj* platonic

playa ['plaja] *nf* beach; (*costa*) seaside; **~ de estacionamiento** (*Am*) car park

playero, -a [pla'jero, a] *adj* beach *cpd* ▪ *nf* (*Am: camiseta*) T-shirt; **playeras** *nfpl* canvas shoes; (*Tenis*) tennis shoes

plaza ['plaθa] *nf* square; (*mercado*) market(place); (*sitio*) room, space; (*en vehículo*) seat, place; (*colocación*) post, job; **~ de abastos** food market; **~ mayor** main square; **~ de toros** bullring; **hacer la ~** to do the daily shopping; **reservar una ~** to reserve a seat; **el hotel tiene 100 plazas** the hotel has 100 beds

plazca *etc* ['plaθka] *vb ver* **placer**

plazo ['plaθo] *nm* (*lapso de tiempo*) time, period, term; (*fecha de vencimiento*) expiry date; (*pago parcial*) instalment; **a corto/largo ~** short-/long-term; **comprar a plazos** to buy on hire purchase, pay for in instalments; **nos dan un ~ de ocho días** they allow us a week

plazoleta [plaθo'leta], **plazuela** [pla'θwela] *nf* small square

pleamar [plea'mar] *nf* high tide

plebe ['pleβe] *nf:* **la ~** the common people *pl*, the masses *pl*; (*pey*) the plebs *pl*

plebeyo, -a [ple'βejo, a] *adj* plebeian; (*pey*) coarse, common

plebiscito [pleβis'θito] *nm* plebiscite

pleca ['pleka] *nf* (*Inform*) backslash

plegable [ple'ɣaβle] *adj* pliable; (*silla*) folding

plegar [ple'ɣar] *vt* (*doblar*) to fold, bend; (*Costura*) to pleat; **plegarse** *vr* to yield, submit

plegaria [ple'ɣarja] *nf* (*oración*) prayer

plegué [ple'ɣe], **pleguemos** *etc* [ple'ɣemos] *vb ver* **plegar**

pleitear [pleite'ar] *vi* (*Jur*) to plead, conduct a lawsuit; (*litigar*) to go to law

pleito ['pleito] *nm* (*Jur*) lawsuit, case; (*fig*) dispute, feud; **pleitos** *nmpl* litigation *sg*; **entablar ~** to bring an action o a lawsuit; **poner ~** to sue

plenario, -a [ple'narjo, a] *adj* plenary, full

plenilunio [pleni'lunjo] *nm* full moon

plenitud [pleni'tuð] *nf* plenitude, fullness; (*abundancia*) abundance

pleno, -a ['pleno, a] *adj* full; (*completo*) complete ▪ *nm* plenum; **en ~** as a whole; (*por unanimidad*) unanimously; **en ~ día** in broad daylight; **en ~ verano** at the height of summer; **en plena cara** full in the face

pletina *nf* (*Mus*) tape deck

pleuresía [pleure'sia] *nf* pleurisy

plexiglás [pleksi'ɣlas] *nm* acrylic

pliego *etc* ['pljeɣo] *vb ver* **plegar** ▪ *nm* (*hoja*) sheet (of paper); (*carta*) sealed letter/document; **~ de condiciones** details *pl*, specifications *pl*

pliegue *etc* ['pljeɣe] *vb ver* **plegar** ▪ *nm* fold, crease; (*de vestido*) pleat

plisado [pli'saðo] *nm* pleating

plomero [plo'mero] *nm* (*Am*) plumber

plomizo, -a [plo'miθo, a] *adj* leaden, lead-coloured

plomo ['plomo] *nm* (*metal*) lead; (*Elec*) fuse; **caer a ~** to fall heavily o flat

pluma ['pluma] *nf* (*Zool*) feather; **~ estilográfica, ~ fuente** (*Am*) fountain pen

plumazo [plu'maθo] *nm* (*lit, fig*) stroke of the pen

plumero [plu'mero] *nm* (*quitapolvos*) feather duster; **ya te veo el ~** I know what you're up to

plumón [plu'mon] *nm* (*Am*) felt-tip pen

plural [plu'ral] *adj* plural ▪ *nm:* **en ~** in the plural

pluralidad [plurali'ðað] *nf* plurality; **una ~ de votos** a majority of votes

pluriempleo [pluriem'pleo] *nm* moonlighting

plus [plus] *nm* bonus

P

plusmarquista [plusmar'kista] *nm/f* (*Deporte*) record holder

plusvalía [plusβa'lia] *nf* (*mayor valor*) appreciation, added value; (*Com*) goodwill

PM *nf abr* (*Mil*: = *Policía Militar*) MP

p.m. *abr* (= *post meridiem*) p.m.; (= *por minuto*) per minute

PMA *nm abr* (= *Programa Mundial de Alimentos*) World Food Programme

pmo. *abr* (= *próximo*) prox.

PNB *nm abr* (*Esp Com*: = *Producto Nacional Bruto*) GNP

P.N.D. *nm abr* (*Escol*: = *personal no docente*) non-teaching staff

PNN [pe'nene] *nm/f abr* (= *profesor(a) no numerario(-a)*) untenured teacher ■ *nm abr* (*Esp Com*: = *Producto Nacional Neto*) net national product

PNUD *nm abr* (= *Programa de las Naciones Unidas para el Desarrollo*) United Nations Development Programme

PNV *nm abr* (*Esp Pol*) = **Partido Nacional Vasco**

P.° *abr* (= *Paseo*) Av(e).

p.o. *abr* = **por orden**

población [poβla'θjon] *nf* population; (*pueblo, ciudad*) town, city; ~ **activa** working population

poblado, -a [po'βlaðo, a] *adj* inhabited; (*barba*) thick; (*cejas*) bushy ■ *nm* (*aldea*) village; (*pueblo*) (small) town; ~ **de** (*lleno de*) filled with; **densamente** ~ densely populated

poblador, a [poβla'ðor, a] *nm/f* settler, colonist

poblar [po'βlar] *vt* (*colonizar*) to colonize; (*fundar*) to found; (*habitar*) to inhabit; **poblarse** *vr*: **poblarse de** to fill up with; (*irse cubriendo*) to become covered with

pobre [po'βre] *adj* poor ■ *nm/f* poor person; (*mendigo*) beggar; **los pobres** the poor; **¡~!** poor thing!; ~ **diablo** (*fig*) poor wretch *o* devil

pobreza [po'βreθa] *nf* poverty; ~ **energética** fuel poverty

pocho, -a ['potʃo, a] *adj* (*flor, color*) faded, discoloured; (*persona*) pale; (*fruta*) overripe; (*deprimido*) depressed

pocilga [po'θilɣa] *nf* pigsty

pocillo [po'siʎo] *nm* (*Am*) coffee cup

pócima ['poθima], **poción** [po'θjon] *nf* potion; (*brebaje*) concoction, nasty drink

 PALABRA CLAVE

poco, -a ['poko, a] *adj* **1** (*sg*) little, not much; ~ **tiempo** little *o* not much time; **de** ~ **interés** of little interest, not very interesting; **poca cosa** not much

2 (*pl*) few, not many; **unos pocos** a few, some; **pocos niños comen lo que les conviene** few children eat what they should ■ *adv* **1** little, not much; **cuesta** ~ it doesn't cost much; ~ **más o menos** more or less

2 (+ *adj*: *negativo, antónimo*): ~ **amable/inteligente** not very nice/intelligent

3: **por** ~ **me caigo** I almost fell

4 (*tiempo*): ~ **después** soon after that; **dentro de** ~ shortly; **hace** ~ a short time ago, not long ago; **a** ~ **de haberse casado** shortly after getting married

5: ~ **a** ~ little by little

6 (*Am*): **¿a** ~ **no está divino?** isn't it just divine?; **de a** ~ gradually ■ *nm* a little, a bit; **un** ~ **triste/de dinero** a little sad/money

poda ['poða] *nf* (*acto*) pruning; (*temporada*) pruning season

podar [po'ðar] *vt* to prune

podcast ['poðkast] *nm* podcast

podcastear [poðkaste'ar] *vi* to podcast

podenco [po'ðenko] *nm* hound

 PALABRA CLAVE

poder [po'ðer] *vi* **1** (*capacidad*) can, be able to; **no puedo hacerlo** I can't do it, I'm unable to do it

2 (*permiso*) can, may, be allowed to; **¿se puede?** may I (*o* we)?; **puedes irte ahora** you may go now; **no se puede fumar en este hospital** smoking is not allowed in this hospital

3 (*posibilidad*) may, might, could; **puede llegar mañana** he may *o* might arrive tomorrow; **pudiste haberte hecho daño** you might *o* could have hurt yourself; **¡podías habérmelo dicho antes!** you might have told me before!

4: **puede (ser)** perhaps; **puede que lo sepa Tomás** Tomás may *o* might know

5: **¡no puedo más!** I've had enough!; **no pude menos que dejarlo** I couldn't help but leave it; **es tonto a más no** ~ he's as stupid as they come

6: ~ **con**: **¿puedes con eso?** can you manage that?; **no puedo con este crío** this kid's too much for me

7: **él me puede** (*fam*) he's stronger than me ■ *nm* power; **el** ~ the Government; ~ **adquisitivo** purchasing power; **detentar** *u* **ocupar** *o* **estar en el** ~ to be in power *o* office; **estar** *u* **obrar en** ~ **de** to be in the hands *o* possession of; **por** ~(**es**) by proxy

poderío [poðe'rio] *nm* power; (*autoridad*) authority

poderoso, -a [poðe'roso, a] *adj* powerful

podio ['poðjo] *nm* podium

podólogo, -a [po'ðoloɣo, a] *nm/f* chiropodist (*Brit*), podiatrist (*US*)

podré *etc* [po'ðre] *vb ver* **poder**

podrido, -a [po'ðriðo, a] *adj* rotten, bad; (*fig*) rotten, corrupt

podrir [po'ðrir] = **pudrir**

poema [po'ema] *nm* poem

poesía [poe'sia] *nf* poetry

poeta [po'eta] *nm* poet

poético, -a [po'etiko, a] *adj* poetic(al)

poetisa [poe'tisa] *nf* (woman) poet

póker ['poker] *nm* poker

polaco, -a [po'lako, a] *adj* Polish ∎ *nm/f* Pole ∎ *nm* (*Ling*) Polish

polar [po'lar] *adj* polar

polarice *etc* [pola'riθe] *vb ver* **polarizar**

polaridad [polari'ðað] *nf* polarity

polarizar [polari'θar] *vt* to polarize

polea [po'lea] *nf* pulley

polémica [po'lemika] *nf* polemics *sg*; (*una polémica*) controversy

polemice *etc* [pole'miθe] *vb ver* **polemizar**

polémico, -a [po'lemiko, a] *adj* polemic(al)

polemizar [polemi'θar] *vi* argue

polen ['polen] *nm* pollen

poleo [po'leo] *nm* pennyroyal

poli ['poli] *nm* (*fam*) cop (*fam*) ∎ *nf*: **la** ~ the cops *pl* (*fam*)

policía [poli'θia] *nm/f* policeman(-woman) ∎ *nf* police; *see note*

⊙ **POLICÍA**

⊙
⊙ There are two branches of the police,
⊙ both armed: the *policía nacional*, in charge
⊙ of national security and public order in
⊙ general, and the *policía municipal*, with
⊙ duties of regulating traffic and policing
⊙ the local community. Catalonia and the
⊙ Basque Country have their own police
⊙ forces, the *Mossos d'Esquadra* and the
⊙ *Ertzaintza* respectively.

policíaco, -a [poli'θiako, a] *adj* police *cpd*; **novela policíaca** detective story

polideportivo [poliðepor'tiβo] *nm* sports centre

poliéster [poli'ester] *nm* polyester

polietileno [polieti'leno] *nm* polythene (*Brit*), polyethylene (*US*)

polifacético, -a [polifa'θetiko, a] *adj* (*persona, talento*) many-sided, versatile

poligamia [poli'ɣamja] *nf* polygamy

polígamo, -a [po'liɣamo, a] *adj* polygamous ∎ *nm* polygamist

polígono [po'liɣono] *nm* (*Mat*) polygon; (*solar*) building lot; (*zona*) area; (*unidad vecina*) housing estate; ~ **industrial** industrial estate

polígrafo [po'liɣrafo] *nm* polygraph

polilla [po'liʎa] *nf* moth

Polinesia [poli'nesja] *nf* Polynesia

polinesio, -a [poli'nesjo, a] *adj, nm/f* Polynesian

polio ['poljo] *nf* polio

Polisario [poli'sarjo] *nm abr* (*Pol*: *tb*: **Frente Polisario**) = **Frente Político de Liberación del Sáhara y Río de Oro**

politécnico [poli'tekniko] *nm* polytechnic

político, -a [po'litiko, a] *adj* political; (*discreto*) tactful; (*pariente*) in-law ∎ *nm/f* politician ∎ *nf* politics *sg*; (*económica, agraria*) policy; **padre** ~ father-in-law; **política exterior/de ingresos y precios** foreign/prices and incomes policy

póliza ['poliθa] *nf* certificate, voucher; (*impuesto*) tax *o* fiscal stamp; ~ **de seguro(s)** insurance policy

polizón [poli'θon] *nm* (*Aviat, Naut*) stowaway

pollera [po'ʎera] *nf* (*criadero*) hencoop; (*Am*) skirt, overskirt

pollería [poʎe'ria] *nf* poulterer's (shop)

pollo ['poʎo] *nm* chicken; (*joven*) young man; (*señorito*) playboy; ~ **asado** roast chicken

polo ['polo] *nm* (*Geo, Elec*) pole; (*helado*) ice lolly; (*Deporte*) polo; (*suéter*) polo-neck; **P~ Norte/Sur** North/South Pole; **esto es el ~ opuesto de lo que dijo antes** this is the exact opposite of what he said before

Polonia [po'lonja] *nf* Poland

poltrona [pol'trona] *nf* reclining chair, easy chair

polución [polu'θjon] *nf* pollution; ~ **ambiental** environmental pollution

polvera [pol'βera] *nf* powder compact

polvo ['polβo] *nm* dust; (*Química, Culin, Med*) powder; (*fam!*) screw (!); **en** ~ powdered; ~ **de talco** talcum powder; **estar hecho** ~ to be worn out *o* exhausted; **hacer algo** ~ to smash sth; **hacer** ~ **a algn** to shatter sb; *ver tb* **polvos**

pólvora ['polβora] *nf* gunpowder; (*fuegos artificiales*) fireworks *pl*; **propagarse como la** ~ (*noticia*) to spread like wildfire

polvoriento, -a [polβo'rjento, a] *adj* (*superficie*) dusty; (*sustancia*) powdery

polvorín [polβo'rin] *nm* (*fig*) powder keg

polvorosa [polβo'rosa] *adj* (*fam*): **poner pies en** ~ to beat it

polvos ['polβos] *nmpl* powder *sg*

P

polvoso, -a [pol'βoso, a] *adj* (*Am*) dusty
pomada [po'maða] *nf* pomade
pomelo [po'melo] *nm* grapefruit
pómez ['pomeθ] *nf*: **piedra ~** pumice stone
pomo ['pomo] *nm* handle
pompa ['pompa] *nf* (*burbuja*) bubble; (*bomba*) pump; (*esplendor*) pomp, splendour; **pompas fúnebres** funeral *sg*
pomposo, -a [pom'poso, a] *adj* splendid, magnificent; (*pey*) pompous
pómulo ['pomulo] *nm* cheekbone
ponche ['pontʃe] *nm* punch
poncho ['pontʃo] *nm* (*Am*) poncho, cape
ponderar [ponde'rar] *vt* (*considerar*) to weigh up, consider; (*elogiar*) to praise highly, speak in praise of
pondré *etc* [pon'dre] *vb ver* **poner**
ponencia [po'nenθja] *nf* (*exposición*) (learned) paper, communication; (*informe*) report

 PALABRA CLAVE

poner [po'ner] *vt* **1** to put; (*colocar*) to place, set; (*ropa*) to put on; (*problema, la mesa*) to set; (*interés*) to show; (*telegrama*) to send; (*obra de teatro*) to put on; (*película*) to show; **ponlo más alto** turn it up; **¿qué ponen en el Excelsior?** what's on at the Excelsior?; **~ algo a secar** to put sth (out) to dry; **¡no pongas esa cara!** don't look at me like that!
2 (*tienda*) to open; (*instalar: gas etc*) to put in; (*radio, TV*) to switch o turn on
3 (*suponer*): **pongamos que ...** let's suppose that ...
4 (*contribuir*): **el gobierno ha puesto otro millón** the government has contributed another million
5 (*Telec*): **póngame con el Sr. López** can you put me through to Mr. López?
6 (*estar escrito*) to say; **¿qué pone aquí?** what does it say here?
7: **~ de, le han puesto de director general** they've appointed him general manager
8 (*+ adj*) to make; **me estás poniendo nerviosa** you're making me nervous
9 (*dar nombre*): **al hijo le pusieron Diego** they called their son Diego
■ *vi* (*gallina*) to lay;
ponerse *vr* **1** (*colocarse*): **se puso a mi lado** he came and stood beside me; **tú ponte en esa silla** you go and sit on that chair; **ponerse en camino** to set off
2 (*vestido, cosméticos*) to put on; **¿por qué no te pones el vestido nuevo?** why don't you put on o wear your new dress?
3 (*sol*) to set
4 (*+ adj*) to get, become; to turn; **ponerse**

enfermo/gordo/triste to get ill/fat/sad; **se puso muy serio** he got very serious; **después de lavarla la tela se puso azul** after washing it the material turned blue; **¡no te pongas así!** don't be like that!; **ponerse cómodo** to make o.s. comfortable
5: **ponerse a, se puso a llorar** he started to cry; **tienes que ponerte a estudiar** you must get down to studying
6: **ponerse a bien con algn** to make it up with sb; **ponerse a mal con algn** to get on the wrong side of sb
7 (*Am*): **se me pone que ...** it seems to me that ..., I think that ...

ponga *etc* ['ponga] *vb ver* **poner**
poniente [po'njente] *nm* west
pontevedrés, -esa [ponteβe'ðres, esa] *adj* of o from Pontevedra ■ *nm/f* native o inhabitant of Pontevedra
pontificado [pontifi'kaðo] *nm* papacy
pontífice [pon'tifiθe] *nm* pope, pontiff; **el Sumo P~** His Holiness the Pope
pontón [pon'ton] *nm* pontoon
ponzoña [pon'θoɲa] *nf* poison, venom
ponzoñoso, -a [ponθo'ɲoso, a] *adj* poisonous, venomous
pop [pop] *adj inv, nm* (*Mus*) pop
popa ['popa] *nf* stern; **a ~** astern, abaft; **de ~ a proa** fore and aft
popular [popu'lar] *adj* popular; (*del pueblo*) of the people
popularice *etc* [popula'riθe] *vb ver* **popularizarse**
popularidad [populari'ðað] *nf* popularity
popularizarse [populari'θarse] *vr* to become popular
poquísimo, -a [po'kisimo, a] *adj superlativo de* **poco** very little, very few *pl*; (*casi nada*) hardly any
poquito [po'kito] *nm*: **un ~** a little bit ■ *adv* a little, a bit; **a poquitos** bit by bit

 PALABRA CLAVE

por [por] *prep* **1** (*objetivo*) for; **luchar ~ la patria** to fight for one's country; **hazlo ~ mí** do it for my sake
2 (*+ infin*): **~ no llegar tarde** so as not to arrive late; **~ citar unos ejemplos** to give a few examples
3 (*causa*) out of, because of; **no es ~ eso** that's not the reason; **~ escasez de fondos** through o for lack of funds
4 (*tiempo*): **~ la mañana/noche** in the morning/at night; **se queda ~ una semana** she's staying (for) a week

5 (*lugar*): **pasar ~ Madrid** to pass through Madrid; **ir a Guayaquil ~ Quito** to go to Guayaquil via Quito; **caminar ~ la calle** to walk along the street; **~ allí** over there; **se va ~ ahí** we have to go that way; **¿hay un banco ~ aquí?** is there a bank near here?; **¿~ dónde?** which way?; **está ~ el norte** it's somewhere in the north; **~ todo el país** throughout the country

6 (*cambio, precio*): **te doy uno nuevo ~ el que tienes** I'll give you a new one (in return) for the one you've got; **lo vendí ~ 15 dólares** I sold it for 15 dollars

7 (*valor distributivo*): **30 euros ~ hora/cabeza** 30 euros an *o* per hour/a *o* per head; **10 ~ ciento** 10 per cent; **80 (kms) ~ hora** 80 (km) an *o* per hour

8 (*modo, medio*) by; **~ correo/avión** by post/air; **día ~ día** day by day; **~ orden** in order; **entrar ~ la entrada principal** to go in through the main entrance

9 (*agente*) by; **hecho ~ él** done by him; **"dirigido ~"** "directed by"

10: **10 ~ 10 son 100** 10 by 10 is 100

11 (*en lugar de*): **vino él ~ su jefe** he came instead of his boss

12: **~ mí que revienten** as far as I'm concerned they can drop dead

13 (*evidencia*): **~ lo que dicen** judging by *o* from what they say

14: **estar/quedar ~ hacer** to be still *o* remain to be done

15: **~ (muy) difícil que sea** however hard it is *o* may be; **~ más que lo intente** no matter how *o* however hard I try

16: **~ qué** why; **¿~ qué?** why?; **¿~?** (*fam*) why (do you ask)?

porcelana [porθe'lana] *nf* porcelain, china
porcentaje [porθen'taxe] *nm* percentage; **~ de actividad** (*Inform*) hit rate
porche ['portʃe] *nm* (*de una plaza*) arcade; (*de casa*) porch
porción [por'θjon] *nf* (*parte*) portion, share; (*cantidad*) quantity, amount
pordiosero, -a [porðjo'sero, a] *nm/f* beggar
porfía [por'fia] *nf* persistence; (*terquedad*) obstinacy
porfiado, -a [por'fjaðo, a] *adj* persistent; obstinate
porfiar [por'fjar] *vi* to persist, insist; (*disputar*) to argue stubbornly
pormenor [porme'nor] *nm* detail, particular
pormenorice *etc* [pormeno'riθe] *vb ver* **pormenorizar**
pormenorizar [pormenori'θar] *vt* to (set out in) detail ■ *vi* to go into detail

porno ['porno] *adj inv* porno ■ *nm* porn
pornografía [pornoɣra'fia] *nf* pornography
poro ['poro] *nm* pore
poroso, -a [po'roso, a] *adj* porous
poroto [po'roto] *nm* (*Am*) kidney bean
porque ['porke] *conj* (*a causa de*) because; (*ya que*) since; **~ sí** because I feel like it
porqué [por'ke] *nm* reason, cause
porquería [porke'ria] *nf* (*suciedad*) filth, muck, dirt; (*acción*) dirty trick; (*objeto*) small thing, trifle; (*fig*) rubbish
porqueriza [porke'riθa] *nf* pigsty
porra ['porra] *nf* (*arma*) stick, club; (*cachiporra*) truncheon; **¡porras!** oh heck!; **¡vete a la ~!** go to heck!
porrazo [po'rraθo] *nm* (*golpe*) blow; (*caída*) bump; **de un ~** in one go
porro ['porro] *nm* joint
porrón [po'rron] *nm* wine jar with a long spout
portaaviones [port(a)a'βjones] *nm inv* aircraft carrier
portada [por'taða] *nf* (*Tip*) title page; (*: de revista*) cover
portador, a [porta'ðor, a] *nm/f* carrier, bearer; (*Com*) bearer, payee; (*Med*) carrier; **ser ~ del virus del sida** to be HIV-positive
portaequipajes [portaeki'paxes] *nm inv* boot (*Brit*), trunk (*US*); (*baca*) luggage rack
portafolio [porta'foljo], **portafolios** [porta'foljos] *nm* (*Am*) briefcase; **~(s) de inversiones** (*Com*) investment portfolio
portal [por'tal] *nm* (*entrada*) vestibule, hall; (*pórtico*) porch, doorway; (*puerta de entrada*) main door; (*Deporte*) goal; **portales** *nmpl* arcade *sg*
portaligas [porta'liɣas] *nm inv* (*Am*) suspender belt
portamaletas [portama'letas] *nm inv* roof rack
portamonedas [portamo'neðas] *nm inv* purse
portar [por'tar] *vt* to carry, bear; **portarse** *vr* to behave, conduct o.s.; **portarse mal** to misbehave; **se portó muy bien conmigo** he treated me very well
portátil [por'tatil] *adj* portable; **(ordenador) ~** laptop (computer)
portaviones [porta'βjones] *nm inv* aircraft carrier
portavoz [porta'βoθ] *nm/f* spokesman(-woman)
portazo [por'taθo] *nm*: **dar un ~** to slam the door
porte ['porte] *nm* (*Com*) transport; (*precio*) transport charges *pl*; (*Correos*) postage; **~ debido** (*Com*) carriage forward; **~ pagado** (*Com*) carriage paid, post-paid

303

portento [por'tento] *nm* marvel, wonder

portentoso, -a [porten'toso, a] *adj* marvellous, extraordinary

porteño, -a [por'teɲo, a] *adj* of *o* from Buenos Aires ▪ *nm/f* native *o* inhabitant of Buenos Aires

portería [porte'ria] *nf* (*oficina*) porter's office; (*gol*) goal

portero, -a [por'tero, a] *nm/f* porter; (*conserje*) caretaker; (*Deporte*) goalkeeper

pórtico ['portiko] *nm* (*porche*) portico, porch; (*fig*) gateway; (*arcada*) arcade

portilla [por'tiʎa] *nf*, **portillo** [por'tiʎo] *nm* gate

portorriqueño, -a [portorri'keɲo, a] *adj, nm/f* Puerto Rican

portuario, -a [por'twarjo] *adj* (*del puerto*) port *cpd*, harbour *cpd*; (*del muelle*) dock *cpd*; **trabajador** ~ docker

Portugal [portu'ɣal] *nm* Portugal

portugués, -esa [portu'ɣes, esa] *adj, nm/f* Portuguese ▪ *nm* (*Ling*) Portuguese

porvenir [porβe'nir] *nm* future

pos [pos]: **en ~ de** *prep* after, in pursuit of

posada [po'saða] *nf* (*refugio*) shelter, lodging; (*mesón*) guest house; **dar ~ a** to give shelter to, take in

posaderas [posa'ðeras] *nfpl* backside *sg*, buttocks

posar [po'sar] *vt* (*en el suelo*) to lay down, put down; (*la mano*) to place, put gently ▪ *vi* to sit, pose; **posarse** *vr* to settle; (*pájaro*) to perch; (*avión*) to land, come down

posdata [pos'ðata] *nf* postscript

pose ['pose] *nf* (*Arte, afectación*) pose

poseedor, a [posee'ðor, a] *nm/f* owner, possessor; (*de récord, puesto*) holder

poseer [pose'er] *vt* to have, possess, own; (*ventaja*) to enjoy; (*récord, puesto*) to hold

poseído, -a [pose'iðo, a] *adj* possessed; **estar muy ~ de** to be very vain about

posesión [pose'sjon] *nf* possession; **tomar ~ (de)** to take over

posesionarse [posesjo'narse] *vr*: **~ de** to take possession of, take over

posesivo, -a [pose'siβo, a] *adj* possessive

poseyendo *etc* [pose'jendo] *vb ver* **poseer**

posgrado [pos'ɣraðo] *nm* = **postgrado**

posgraduado, -a [posɣra'ðwaðo, a] *adj, nm/f* = **postgraduado**

posguerra [pos'ɣerra] *nf* = **postguerra**

posibilidad [posiβili'ðað] *nf* possibility; (*oportunidad*) chance

posibilitar [posiβili'tar] *vt* to make possible, permit; (*hacer factible*) to make feasible

posible [po'siβle] *adj* possible; (*factible*) feasible ▪ *nm*: **posibles** means; (*bienes*)

funds, assets; **de ser** ~ if possible; **en** *o* **dentro de lo** ~ as far as possible; **lo antes** ~ as quickly as possible

posición [posi'θjon] *nf* (*gen*) position; (*rango social*) status

positivo, -a [posi'tiβo, a] *adj* positive ▪ *nf* (*Foto*) print

poso ['poso] *nm* sediment

posoperatorio, -a [posopera'torjo, a] *adj, nm* = **postoperatorio**

posponer [pospo'ner] *vt* to put behind *o* below; (*aplazar*) to postpone

posponga *etc* [pos'ponga], **pospuesto** [pos'pwesto], **pospuse** *etc* [pos'puse] *vb ver* **posponer**

post [post] *nm* (*en sitio web*) post

posta ['posta] *nf* (*de caballos*) relay, team; **a** ~ on purpose, deliberately

postal [pos'tal] *adj* postal ▪ *nf* postcard

poste ['poste] *nm* (*de telégrafos*) post, pole; (*columna*) pillar

póster (*pl* **posters**) ['poster, 'posters] *nm* poster

postergar [poster'ɣar] *vt* (*esp Am*) to put off, postpone, delay

postergue *etc* [pos'terɣe] *vb ver* **postergar**

posteridad [posteri'ðað] *nf* posterity

posterior [poste'rjor] *adj* back, rear; (*siguiente*) following, subsequent; (*más tarde*) later; **ser ~ a** to be later than

posterioridad [posterjori'ðað] *nf*: **con** ~ later, subsequently

postgrado [post'ɣraðo] *nm*: **curso de** ~ postgraduate course

postgraduado, -a [postɣra'ðwaðo, a] *adj, nm/f* postgraduate

postguerra [post'ɣerra] *nf* postwar period; **en la** ~ after the war

postigo [pos'tiɣo] *nm* (*portillo*) postern; (*contraventana*) shutter

postín [pos'tin] *nm* (*fam*) elegance; **de** ~ posh; **darse** ~ to show off

postizo, -a [pos'tiθo, a] *adj* false, artificial; (*sonrisa*) false, phoney ▪ *nm* hairpiece

postoperatorio, -a [postopera'torjo, a] *adj* postoperative ▪ *nm* postoperative period

postor, a [pos'tor, a] *nm/f* bidder; **mejor** ~ highest bidder

postrado, -a [pos'traðo, a] *adj* prostrate

postrar [pos'trar] *vt* (*derribar*) to cast down, overthrow; (*humillar*) to humble; (*Med*) to weaken, exhaust; **postrarse** *vr* to prostrate o.s.

postre ['postre] *nm* sweet, dessert ▪ *nf*: **a la** ~ in the end, when all is said and done; **para** ~ (*fam*) to crown it all; **llegar a los postres** (*fig*) to come too late

postrero, -a [pos'trero, a] adj (antes de nmsg **postrer**) (último) last; (: que viene detrás) rear
postrimerías [postrime'rias] nfpl final stages
postulado [postu'laðo] nm postulate
postulante [postu'lante] nm/f petitioner; (Rel) postulant
póstumo, -a ['postumo, a] adj posthumous
postura [pos'tura] nf (del cuerpo) posture, position; (fig) attitude, position
post-venta [pos'βenta] adj (Com) after-sales
potable [po'taβle] adj drinkable
potaje [po'taxe] nm thick vegetable soup
pote ['pote] nm pot, jar
potencia [po'tenθja] nf power; (capacidad) capacity; ~ **(en caballos)** horsepower; **en** ~ potential, in the making; **las grandes potencias** the great powers
potencial [poten'θjal] adj, nm potential
potenciar [poten'θjar] vt (promover) to promote; (fortalecer) to boost
potente [po'tente] adj powerful
potestad [potes'taŏ] nf authority; **patria** ~ paternal authority
potosí [poto'si] nm fortune; **cuesta un** ~ it costs the earth
potra ['potra] nf (Zool) filly; **tener** ~ to be lucky
potro ['potro] nm (Zool) colt; (Deporte) vaulting horse
pozo ['poθo] nm well; (de río) deep pool; (de mina) shaft; ~ **negro** cesspool; **ser un** ~ **de ciencia** (fig) to be deeply learned
PP abr (= por poderes) pp; (= porte pagado) carriage paid ■ nm abr = **Partido Popular**
p.p. abr = **por poderes**
p.p.m. abr (= palabras por minuto) wpm
práctica ['praktika] nf ver **práctico**
practicable [prakti'kaβle] adj practicable; (camino) passable, usable
prácticamente ['praktikamente] adv practically
practicante [prakti'kante] nm/f (Med: ayudante de doctor) medical assistant; (: enfermero) nurse; (el que practica algo) practitioner ■ adj practising
practicar [prakti'kar] vt to practise; (deporte) to go in for, play; (ejecutar) to carry out, perform
práctico, -a ['praktiko, a] adj (gen) practical; (conveniente) handy; (instruído: persona) skilled, expert ■ nf practice; (método) method; (arte, capacidad) skill; **en la práctica** in practice
practique etc [prak'tike] vb ver **practicar**
pradera [pra'ðera] nf meadow; (de Canadá) prairie
prado ['praðo] nm (campo) meadow, field; (pastizal) pasture; (Am) lawn

Praga ['praɣa] nf Prague
pragmático, -a [praɣ'matiko, a] adj pragmatic
preámbulo [pre'ambulo] nm preamble, introduction; **decir algo sin preámbulos** to say sth without beating about the bush
precalentamiento [prekalenta'mjento] nm (Deporte) warm-up
precalentar [prekalen'tar] vt to preheat
precaliente etc [preka'ljente] vb ver **precalentar**
precario, -a [pre'karjo, a] adj precarious
precaución [prekau'θjon] nf (medida preventiva) preventive measure, precaution; (prudencia) caution, wariness
precaver [preka'βer] vt to guard against; (impedir) to forestall; **precaverse** vr: **precaverse de** o **contra algo** to (be on one's) guard against sth
precavido, -a [preka'βiðo, a] adj cautious, wary
precedencia [preθe'ðenθja] nf precedence; (prioridad) priority; (superioridad) greater importance, superiority
precedente [preθe'ðente] adj preceding; (anterior) former ■ nm precedent; **sin ~(s)** unprecedented; **establecer** o **sentar un** ~ to establish o set a precedent
preceder [preθe'ðer] vt, vi to precede, go/come before
precepto [pre'θepto] nm precept
preceptor [preθep'tor] nm (maestro) teacher; (: particular) tutor
preciado, -a [pre'θjaðo, a] adj (estimado) esteemed, valuable
preciar [pre'θjar] vt to esteem, value; **preciarse** vr to boast; **preciarse de** to pride o.s. on
precintar [preθin'tar] vt (local) to seal off; (producto) to seal
precinto [pre'θinto] nm (Com: tb: **precinto de garantía**) seal
precio ['preθjo] nm (de mercado) price; (costo) cost; (valor) value, worth; (de viaje) fare; ~ **de coste** o **de cobertura** cost price; ~ **al contado** cash price; ~ **al detalle** o **al por menor** retail price; ~ **al detallista** trade price; ~ **de entrega inmediata** spot price; ~ **de oferta** offer price; ~ **de oportunidad** bargain price; ~ **de salida** upset price; ~ **tope** top price; ~ **unitario** unit price; **no tener** ~ (fig) to be priceless; **"no importa ~"** "cost no object"
preciosidad [preθjosi'ðað] nf (valor) (high) value, (great) worth; (encanto) charm; (cosa bonita) beautiful thing; **es una** ~ it's lovely, it's really beautiful

precioso, -a [pre'θjoso, a] *adj* precious; (*de mucho valor*) valuable; (*fam*) lovely, beautiful
precipicio [preθi'piθjo] *nm* cliff, precipice; (*fig*) abyss
precipitación [preθipita'θjon] *nf* (*prisa*) haste; (*lluvia*) rainfall; (*Química*) precipitation
precipitado, -a [preθipi'taðo, a] *adj* hasty, rash; (*salida*) hasty, sudden ■ *nm* (*Química*) precipitate
precipitar [preθipi'tar] *vt* (*arrojar*) to hurl, throw; (*apresurar*) to hasten; (*acelerar*) to speed up, accelerate; (*Química*) to precipitate; **precipitarse** *vr* to throw o.s.; (*apresurarse*) to rush; (*actuar sin pensar*) to act rashly; **precipitarse hacia** to rush towards
precisado, -a [preθi'saðo, a] *adj*: **verse ~ a hacer algo** to be obliged to do sth
precisamente [preθisa'mente] *adv* precisely; (*justo*) precisely, exactly, just; **~ por eso** for that very reason; **~ fue él quien lo dijo** as a matter of fact he said it; **no es eso ~** it's not really that
precisar [preθi'sar] *vt* (*necesitar*) to need, require; (*fijar*) to determine exactly, fix; (*especificar*) to specify; (*señalar*) to pinpoint
precisión [preθi'sjon] *nf* (*exactitud*) precision
preciso, -a [pre'θiso, a] *adj* (*exacto*) precise; (*necesario*) necessary, essential; (*estilo, lenguaje*) concise; **es ~ que lo hagas** you must do it
precocidad [prekoθi'ðað] *nf* precociousness, precocity
preconcebido, -a [prekonθe'βiðo, a] *adj* preconceived
preconice *etc* [preko'niθe] *vb ver* **preconizar**
preconizar [prekoni'θar] *vt* (*aconsejar*) to advise; (*prever*) to foresee
precoz [pre'koθ] *adj* (*persona*) precocious; (*calvicie*) premature
precursor, a [prekur'sor, a] *nm/f* precursor
predecesor, a [preðeθe'sor, a] *nm/f* predecessor
predecir [preðe'θir] *vt* to predict, foretell, forecast
predestinado, -a [preðesti'naðo, a] *adj* predestined
predeterminar [preðetermi'nar] *vt* to predetermine
predicado [preði'kaðo] *nm* predicate
predicador, a [preðika'ðor, a] *nm/f* preacher
predicar [preði'kar] *vt, vi* to preach
predicción [preðik'θjon] *nf* prediction; (*pronóstico*) forecast; **~ del tiempo** weather forecast(ing)
predicho [pre'ðitʃo], **prediga** *etc* [pre'ðiɣa], **predije** *etc* [pre'ðixe] *vb ver* **predecir**
predilecto, -a [preði'lekto, a] *adj* favourite

predique *etc* [pre'ðike] *vb ver* **predicar**
prediré *etc* [preði're] *vb ver* **predecir**
predispondré *etc* [preðispon'dre] *vb ver* **predisponer**
predisponer [preðispo'ner] *vt* to predispose; (*pey*) to prejudice
predisponga *etc* [preðis'ponga] *vb ver* **predisponer**
predisposición [preðisposi'θjon] *nf* predisposition, inclination; prejudice, bias; (*Med*) tendency
predispuesto [preðis'pwesto], **predispuse** *etc* [preðis'puse] *vb ver* **predisponer**
predominante [preðomi'nante] *adj* predominant; (*preponderante*) prevailing; (*interés*) controlling
predominar [preðomi'nar] *vt* to dominate ■ *vi* to predominate; (*prevalecer*) to prevail
predominio [preðo'minjo] *nm* predominance; prevalence
preescolar [preesko'lar] *adj* preschool
preestreno [prees'treno] *nm* preview, press view
prefabricado, -a [prefaβri'kaðo, a] *adj* prefabricated
prefacio [pre'faθjo] *nm* preface
preferencia [prefe'renθja] *nf* preference; **de ~** preferably, for preference; **localidad de ~** reserved seat
preferible [prefe'riβle] *adj* preferable
preferido, a [prefe'riðo, a] *adj, nm/f* favourite, favorite (*US*)
preferir [prefe'rir] *vt* to prefer
prefiera *etc* [pre'fjera] *vb ver* **preferir**
prefijo [pre'fixo] *nm* prefix
prefiriendo *etc* [prefi'rjendo] *vb ver* **preferir**
pregón [pre'ɣon] *nm* proclamation, announcement
pregonar [preɣo'nar] *vt* to proclaim, announce; (*mercancía*) to hawk
pregonero [preɣo'nero] *nm* town crier
pregunta [pre'ɣunta] *nf* question; **~ capciosa** catch question; **hacer una ~** to ask a question; **preguntas frecuentes** FAQs, frequently asked questions
preguntar [preɣun'tar] *vt* to ask; (*cuestionar*) to question ■ *vi* to ask; **preguntarse** *vr* to wonder; **~ por algn** to ask for sb; **~ por la salud de algn** to ask after sb's health
preguntón, -ona [preɣun'ton, ona] *adj* inquisitive
prehistórico, -a [preis'toriko, a] *adj* prehistoric
prejuicio [pre'xwiθjo] *nm* prejudgement; (*preconcepción*) preconception; (*pey*) prejudice, bias
prejuzgar [prexuθ'ɣar] *vt* (*predisponerse*) to prejudge

prejuzgue etc [pre'xuθɣe] vb ver **prejuzgar**
preliminar [prelimi'nar] adj, nm preliminary
preludio [pre'luðjo] nm (Mus, fig) prelude
premamá [prema'ma] adj: **vestido ~**
maternity dress
prematrimonial [prematrimo'njal] adj:
relaciones prematrimoniales premarital sex
prematuro, -a [prema'turo, a] adj premature
premeditación [premeðita'θjon] nf
premeditation
premeditado, -a [premeði'taðo, a] adj
premeditated, deliberate; (intencionado)
wilful
premeditar [premeði'tar] vt to premeditate
premiar [pre'mjar] vt to reward; (en un
concurso) to give a prize to
premio ['premjo] nm reward; prize; (Com)
premium; **~ gordo** first prize
premisa [pre'misa] nf premise
premonición [premoni'θjon] nf premonition
premura [pre'mura] nf (prisa) haste, urgency
prenatal [prena'tal] adj antenatal, prenatal
prenda ['prenda] nf (de ropa) garment, article
of clothing; (garantía) pledge; (fam) darling!;
prendas nfpl talents, gifts; **dejar algo en
~** to pawn sth; **no soltar ~** to give nothing
away; (fig) not to say a word
prendar [pren'dar] vt to captivate, enchant;
prendarse de algo to fall in love with sth
prendedor [prende'ðor] nm brooch
prender [pren'der] vt (captar) to catch,
capture; (detener) to arrest; (coser) to pin,
attach; (sujetar) to fasten; (Am) to switch
on ▪ vi to catch; (arraigar) to take root;
prenderse vr (encenderse) to catch fire
prendido, -a [pren'diðo, a] adj (Am: luz) on
prensa ['prensa] nf press; **la P~** the press;
tener mala ~ to have o get a bad press;
la ~ nacional the national press
prensar [pren'sar] vt to press
preñado, -a [pre'ɲaðo, a] adj (mujer)
pregnant; **~ de** pregnant with, full of
preocupación [preokupa'θjon] nf worry,
concern; (ansiedad) anxiety
preocupado, -a [preoku'paðo, a] adj
worried, concerned; anxious
preocupar [preoku'par] vt to worry;
preocuparse vr to worry; **preocuparse de
algo** (hacerse cargo de algo) to take care of sth;
preocuparse por algo to worry about sth
preparación [prepara'θjon] nf (acto)
preparation; (estado) preparedness,
readiness; (entrenamiento) training
preparado, -a [prepa'raðo, a] adj (dispuesto)
prepared; (Culin) ready (to serve) ▪ nm (Med)
preparation; **¡preparados, listos, ya!** ready,
steady, go!

preparar [prepa'rar] vt (disponer) to prepare,
get ready; (Tec: tratar) to prepare, process,
treat; (entrenar) to teach, train; **prepararse**
vr: **prepararse a o para hacer algo** to
prepare o get ready to do sth
preparativo, -a [prepara'tiβo] adj
preparatory, preliminary ▪ nm:
preparativos nmpl preparations
preparatoria [prepara'torja] nf (Am) sixth
form college (Brit), senior high school (US)
preposición [preposi'θjon] nf preposition
prepotencia [prepo'tenθja] nf abuse of
power; (Pol) high-handedness; (soberbia)
arrogance
prepotente [prepo'tente] adj (Pol) high-
handed; (soberbio) arrogant
prerrogativa [prerroɣa'tiβa] nf prerogative,
privilege
presa ['presa] nf (cosa apresada) catch; (víctima)
victim; (de animal) prey; (de agua) dam; **hacer
~ en** to clutch (on to), seize; **ser ~ de** (fig) to
be a prey to
presagiar [presa'xjar] vt to threaten
presagio [pre'saxjo] nm omen
presbítero [pres'βitero] nm priest
prescindir [presθin'dir] vi: **~ de** (privarse de)
to do without, go without; (descartar) to
dispense with; **no podemos ~ de él** we can't
manage without him
prescribir [preskri'βir] vt to prescribe
prescripción [preskrip'θjon] nf prescription;
~ facultativa medical prescription
prescrito [pres'krito] pp de **prescribir**
preseleccionar [preselekθjo'nar] vt (Deporte)
to seed
presencia [pre'senθja] nf presence; **en ~ de**
in the presence of
presencial [presen'θjal] adj: **testigo ~**
eyewitness
presenciar [presen'θjar] vt to be present at;
(asistir a) to attend; (ver) to see, witness
presentación [presenta'θjon] nf
presentation; (introducción) introduction
presentador, a [presenta'ðor, a] nm/f
compère
presentar [presen'tar] vt to present; (ofrecer)
to offer; (mostrar) to show, display; (renuncia)
to tender; (moción) to propose; (a una
persona) to introduce; **presentarse** vr (llegar
inesperadamente) to appear, turn up; (ofrecerse:
como candidato) to run, stand; (aparecer) to
show, appear; (solicitar empleo) to apply;
~ al cobro (Com) to present for payment;
presentarse a la policía to report to the
police
presente [pre'sente] adj present ▪ nm
present; (Ling) present (tense); (regalo) gift;

los presentes those present; **hacer ~** to state, declare; **tener ~** to remember, bear in mind; **la carta ~, la ~** this letter

presentimiento [presenti'mjento] *nm* premonition, presentiment

presentir [presen'tir] *vt* to have a premonition of

preservación [preserβa'θjon] *nf* protection, preservation

preservar [preser'βar] *vt* to protect, preserve

preservativo [preserβa'tiβo] *nm* sheath, condom

presidencia [presi'ðenθja] *nf* presidency; *(de comité)* chairmanship; **ocupar la ~** to preside, be in *o* take the chair

presidente [presi'ðente] *nm/f* president; chairman(-woman); *(en parlamento)* speaker; *(Jur)* presiding magistrate

presidiario [presi'ðjarjo] *nm* convict

presidio [pre'siðjo] *nm* prison, penitentiary

presidir [presi'ðir] *vt (dirigir)* to preside at, preside over; *(: comité)* to take the chair at; *(dominar)* to dominate, rule ■ *vi* to preside; to take the chair

presienta *etc* [pre'sjenta], **presintiendo** *etc* [presin'tjendo] *vb ver* **presentir**

presión [pre'sjon] *nf* pressure; **~ arterial** *o* **sanguínea** blood pressure; **a ~** under pressure

presionar [presjo'nar] *vt* to press; *(botón)* to push, press; *(fig)* to press, put pressure on ■ *vi:* **~ para** *o* **por** to press for

preso, -a ['preso, a] *adj:* **estar ~ de terror** *o* **pánico** to be panic-stricken ■ *nm/f* prisoner; **tomar** *o* **llevar ~ a algn** to arrest sb, take sb prisoner

prestación [presta'θjon] *nf (aportación)* lending; *(Inform)* capability; *(servicio)* service; *(subsidio)* benefit; **prestaciones** *nfpl (Auto)* performance features; **~ de juramento** oath-taking; **~ personal** obligatory service; **P~ Social Sustitutoria** community service for conscientious objectors; *ver tb* **mili**

prestado, -a [pres'taðo, a] *adj* on loan; **dar algo ~** to lend sth; **pedir ~** to borrow

prestamista [presta'mista] *nm/f* moneylender

préstamo ['prestamo] *nm* loan; **~ con garantía** loan against collateral; **~ hipotecario** mortgage

prestar [pres'tar] *vt* to lend, loan; *(atención)* to pay; *(ayuda)* to give; *(servicio)* to do, render; *(juramento)* to take, swear; **prestarse** *vr (ofrecerse)* to offer *o* volunteer

prestatario, -a [presta'tarjo, a] *nm/f* borrower

presteza [pres'teθa] *nf* speed, promptness

prestidigitador [prestiðixita'ðor] *nm* conjurer

prestigio [pres'tixjo] *nm* prestige; *(reputación)* face; *(renombre)* good name

prestigioso, -a [presti'xjoso, a] *adj (honorable)* prestigious; *(famoso, renombrado)* renowned, famous

presto, -a ['presto, a] *adj (rápido)* quick, prompt; *(dispuesto)* ready ■ *adv* at once, right away

presumido, -a [presu'miðo, a] *adj* conceited

presumir [presu'mir] *vt* to presume ■ *vi (darse aires)* to be conceited; **según cabe ~** as may be presumed, presumably; **~ de listo** to think o.s. very smart

presunción [presun'θjon] *nf* presumption; *(sospecha)* suspicion; *(vanidad)* conceit

presunto, -a [pre'sunto, a] *adj (supuesto)* supposed, presumed; *(así llamado)* so-called

presuntuoso, -a [presun'twoso, a] *adj* conceited, presumptuous

presupondré *etc* [presupon'dre] *vb ver* **presuponer**

presuponer [presupo'ner] *vt* to presuppose

presuponga *etc* [presu'ponga] *vb ver* **presuponer**

presupuestar [presupwes'tar] *vi* to budget ■ *vt:* **~ algo** to budget for sth

presupuestario, -a [presupwes'tarjo, a] *adj (Finanzas)* budgetary, budget *cpd*

presupuesto [presu'pwesto] *pp de* **presuponer** ■ *nm (Finanzas)* budget; *(estimación: de costo)* estimate; **asignación de ~** *(Com)* budget appropriation

presupuse *etc* [presu'puse] *vb ver* **presuponer**

presuroso, -a [presu'roso, a] *adj (rápido)* quick, speedy; *(que tiene prisa)* hasty

pretencioso, -a [preten'θjoso, a] *adj* pretentious

pretender [preten'der] *vt (intentar)* to try to, seek to; *(reivindicar)* to claim; *(buscar)* to seek, try for; *(cortejar)* to woo, court; **~ que** to expect that; **¿qué pretende usted?** what are you after?

pretendiente [preten'djente] *nm/f (candidato)* candidate, applicant; *(amante)* suitor

pretensión [preten'sjon] *nf (aspiración)* aspiration; *(reivindicación)* claim; *(orgullo)* pretension

pretérito, -a [pre'terito, a] *adj (Ling)* past; *(fig)* past, former

pretextar [preteks'tar] *vt* to plead, use as an excuse

pretexto [pre'teksto] *nm* pretext; *(excusa)* excuse; **so ~ de** under pretext of

pretil [pre'til] *nm (valla)* parapet; *(baranda)* handrail

prevalecer [preβaleˈθer] *vi* to prevail
prevaleciente [preβaleˈθjente] *adj*
prevailing, prevalent
prevalezca *etc* [preβaˈleθka] *vb ver* **prevalecer**
prevención [preβenˈθjon] *nf* (*preparación*)
preparation; (*estado*) preparedness,
readiness; (*medida*) prevention; (*previsión*)
foresight, forethought; (*precaución*)
precaution
prevendré *etc* [preβenˈdre], **prevenga** *etc*
[preˈβenga] *vb ver* **prevenir**
prevenido, -a [preβeˈniðo, a] *adj* prepared,
ready; (*cauteloso*) cautious; **estar ~** (*preparado*)
to be ready; **ser ~** (*cuidadoso*) to be cautious;
hombre ~ vale por dos forewarned is
forearmed
prevenir [preβeˈnir] *vt* (*impedir*) to prevent;
(*prever*) to foresee, anticipate; (*predisponer*) to
prejudice, bias; (*avisar*) to warn; (*preparar*)
to prepare, get ready; **prevenirse** *vr* to get
ready, prepare; **prevenirse contra** to take
precautions against
preventivo, -a [preβenˈtiβo, a] *adj*
preventive, precautionary
prever [preˈβer] *vt* to foresee; (*anticipar*) to
anticipate
previniendo *etc* [preβiˈnjendo] *vb ver*
prevenir
previo, -a [ˈpreβjo, a] *adj* (*anterior*) previous,
prior ■ *prep*: **~ acuerdo de los otros** subject
to the agreement of the others; **~ pago de
los derechos** on payment of the fees
previsible [preβiˈsiβle] *adj* foreseeable
previsión [preβiˈsjon] *nf* (*perspicacia*)
foresight; (*predicción*) forecast; (*prudencia*)
caution; **~ de ventas** (*Com*) sales forecast
previsor, a [preβiˈsor, a] *adj* (*precavido*) far-
sighted; (*prudente*) thoughtful
previsto [preˈβisto] *pp de* **prever**
P.R.I. [ˈpri] *nm abr* (*Am*: = *Partido Revolucionario
Institucional*) *political party*
prieto, -a [ˈprjeto, a] *adj* (*oscuro*) dark; (*Am*)
dark(-skinned); (*fig*) mean; (*comprimido*)
tight, compressed
prima [ˈprima] *nf ver* **primo**
primacía [primaˈθia] *nf* primacy
primar [priˈmar] *vi* (*tener primacía*) to occupy
first place; **~ sobre** to have priority over
primario, -a [priˈmarjo, a] *adj* primary ■ *nf*
primary education; *ver tb* **sistema educativo**
primavera [primaˈβera] *nf* (*temporada*) spring;
(*período*) springtime
primaveral [primaβeˈral] *adj* spring *cpd*
Primer Ministro [priˈmer-] *nm* Prime Minister
primero, -a [priˈmero, a] *adj* (*antes de nmsg*
primer) first; (*fig*) prime; (*anterior*) former;
(*básico*) fundamental ■ *adv* first; (*más bien*)

sooner, rather ■ *nf* (*Auto*) first gear; (*Ferro*)
first class; **de primera** (*fam*) first-class,
first-rate; **de buenas a primeras** suddenly;
primera dama (*Teat*) leading lady
primicia [priˈmiθja] *nf* (*Prensa*) scoop;
primicias *nfpl* (*tb fig*) first fruits
primitivo, -a [primiˈtiβo, a] *adj* primitive;
(*original*) original; (*Com: acción*) ordinary ■ *nf*:
(Lotería) Primitiva *weekly state-run lottery*; *ver
tb* **lotería**
primo, -a [ˈprimo, a] *adj* (*Mat*) prime ■ *nm/f*
cousin; (*fam*) fool, dupe ■ *nf* (*Com*) bonus;
(*de seguro*) premium; (*a la exportación*) subsidy;
~ hermano first cousin; **materias primas**
raw materials; **hacer el ~** to be taken for a ride
primogénito, -a [primoˈxenito, a] *adj* first-
born
primor [priˈmor] *nm* (*cuidado*) care; **es un ~**
it's lovely
primordial [primorˈðjal] *adj* basic,
fundamental
primoroso, -a [primoˈroso, a] *adj* exquisite,
fine
princesa [prinˈθesa] *nf* princess
principado [prinθiˈpaðo] *nm* principality
principal [prinθiˈpal] *adj* principal, main;
(*más destacado*) foremost; (*piso*) first, second
(*US*); (*Inform*) foreground ■ *nm* (*jefe*) chief,
principal
príncipe [ˈprinθipe] *nm* prince; **~ heredero**
crown prince; **P~ de Asturias** *King's son and
heir to the Spanish throne*; **~ de gales** (*tela*) check
principiante [prinθiˈpjante] *nm/f* beginner;
(*novato*) novice
principio [prinˈθipjo] *nm* (*comienzo*)
beginning, start; (*origen*) origin; (*base*)
rudiment, basic idea; (*moral*) principle; **a
principios de** at the beginning of; **desde el
~** from the first; **en un ~** at first
pringar [prinˈgar] *vt* (*Culin: pan*) to dip;
(*ensuciar*) to dirty; **pringarse** *vr* to get
splashed *o* soiled; **~ a algn en un asunto**
(*fam*) to involve sb in a matter
pringoso, -a [prinˈgoso, a] *adj* greasy;
(*pegajoso*) sticky
pringue *etc* [ˈpringe] *vb ver* **pringar** ■ *nm*
(*grasa*) grease, fat, dripping
prioridad [prioriˈðað] *nf* priority; (*Auto*) right
of way
prioritario, -a [prioriˈtarjo, a] *adj* (*Inform*)
foreground
prisa [ˈprisa] *nf* (*apresuramiento*) hurry, haste;
(*rapidez*) speed; (*urgencia*) (sense of) urgency;
correr ~ to be urgent; **darse ~** to hurry up;
estar de *o* **tener ~** to be in a hurry
prisión [priˈsjon] *nf* (*cárcel*) prison; (*período de
cárcel*) imprisonment

prisionero, -a [prisjo'nero, a] *nm/f* prisoner

prismáticos [pris'matikos] *nmpl* binoculars

privación [priβa'θjon] *nf* deprivation; (*falta*) want, privation; **privaciones** *nfpl* hardships, privations

privado, -a [pri'βaðo, a] *adj* (*particular*) private; (*Pol: favorito*) favourite (*Brit*), favorite (*US*); **en ~** privately, in private; **"~ y confidencial"** "private and confidential"

privar [pri'βar] *vt* to deprive; **privarse** *vr*: **privarse de** (*abstenerse de*) to deprive o.s. of; (*renunciar a*) to give up

privativo, -a [priβa'tiβo, a] *adj* exclusive

privatizar [priβati'θar] *vt* to privatize

privilegiado, -a [priβile'xjaðo, a] *adj* privileged; (*memoria*) very good ■ *nm/f* (*afortunado*) privileged person

privilegiar [priβile'xjar] *vt* to grant a privilege to; (*favorecer*) to favour

privilegio [priβi'lexjo] *nm* privilege; (*concesión*) concession

pro [pro] *nm o nf* profit, advantage ■ *prep*: **asociación ~ ciegos** association for the blind ■ *pref*: **~ soviético/americano** pro-Soviet/- American; **en ~ de** on behalf of, for; **los pros y los contras** the pros and cons

proa ['proa] *nf* (*Naut*) bow, prow

probabilidad [proβaβili'ðað] *nf* probability, likelihood; (*oportunidad, posibilidad*) chance, prospect

probable [pro'βaβle] *adj* probable, likely; **es ~ que** (*+subjun*) it is probable *o* likely that; **es ~ que no venga** he probably won't come

probador [proβa'ðor] *nm* (*persona*) taster (*of wine etc*); (*en una tienda*) fitting room

probar [pro'βar] *vt* (*demostrar*) to prove; (*someter a prueba*) to test, try out; (*ropa*) to try on; (*comida*) to taste ■ *vi* to try; **probarse** *vr*: **probarse un traje** to try on a suit

probeta [pro'βeta] *nf* test tube

problema [pro'βlema] *nm* problem

procaz [pro'kaθ] *adj* insolent, impudent

procedencia [proθe'ðenθja] *nf* (*principio*) source, origin; (*lugar de salida*) point of departure

procedente [proθe'ðente] *adj* (*razonable*) reasonable; (*conforme a derecho*) proper, fitting; **~ de** coming from, originating in

proceder [proθe'ðer] *vi* (*avanzar*) to proceed; (*actuar*) to act; (*ser correcto*) to be right (and proper), be fitting ■ *nm* (*comportamiento*) behaviour, conduct; **no procede obrar así** it is not right to act like that; **~ de** to come from, originate in

procedimiento [proθeði'mjento] *nm* procedure; (*proceso*) process; (*método*) means, method; (*trámite*) proceedings *pl*

prócer ['proθer] *nm* (*persona eminente*) worthy; (*líder*) great man, leader; (*esp Am*) national hero

procesado, -a [proθe'saðo, a] *nm/f* accused (person)

procesador [proθesa'ðor] *nm*: **~ de textos** (*Inform*) word processor

procesamiento [proθesa'mjento] *nm* (*Inform*) processing; **~ de datos** data processing; **~ por lotes** batch processing; **~ solapado** multiprogramming; **~ de textos** word processing

procesar [proθe'sar] *vt* to try, put on trial; (*Inform*) to process

procesión [proθe'sjon] *nf* procession; **la ~ va por dentro** he keeps his troubles to himself

proceso [pro'θeso] *nm* process; (*Jur*) trial; (*lapso*) course (of time); (*Inform*): **~ (automático) de datos** (automatic) data processing; **~ no prioritario** background process; **~ por pasadas** batch processing; **~ en tiempo real** real-time programming

proclama [pro'klama] *nf* (*acto*) proclamation; (*cartel*) poster

proclamar [prokla'mar] *vt* to proclaim

proclive [pro'kliβe] *adj*: **~ (a)** inclined *o* prone (to)

procreación [prokrea'θjon] *nf* procreation

procrear [prokre'ar] *vt, vi* to procreate

procurador, a [prokura'ðor, a] *nm/f* attorney, solicitor

procurar [proku'rar] *vt* (*intentar*) to try, endeavour; (*conseguir*) to get, obtain; (*asegurar*) to secure; (*producir*) to produce

prodigar [proði'yar] *vt* to lavish; **prodigarse** *vr*: **prodigarse en** to be lavish with

prodigio [pro'ðixjo] *nm* prodigy; (*milagro*) wonder, marvel; **niño ~** child prodigy

prodigioso, -a [proði'xjoso, a] *adj* prodigious, marvellous

pródigo, -a ['proðiyo, a] *adj* (*rico*) rich, productive; **hijo ~** prodigal son

producción [proðuk'θjon] *nf* production; (*suma de productos*) output; (*producto*) product; **~ en serie** mass production

producir [proðu'θir] *vt* to produce; (*generar*) to cause, bring about; (*impresión*) to give; (*Com: interés*) to bear; **producirse** *vr* (*gen*) to come about, happen; (*hacerse*) to be produced, be made; (*estallar*) to break out; (*accidente*) to take place

productividad [proðuktiβi'ðað] *nf* productivity

productivo, -a [proðuk'tiβo, a] *adj* productive; (*provechoso*) profitable

producto [pro'ðukto] *nm* (*resultado*) product; (*producción*) production; **~ alimenticio**

foodstuff; ~ **(nacional) bruto** gross (national) product; ~ **interno bruto** gross domestic product

productor, a [proðuk'tor, a] *adj* productive, producing ■ *nm/f* producer

produje [pro'ðuxe], **produjera** [proðu'xera], **produzca** *etc* [pro'ðuθka] *vb ver* **producir**

proeza [pro'eθa] *nf* exploit, feat

profanar [profa'nar] *vt* to desecrate, profane

profano, -a [pro'fano, a] *adj* profane ■ *nm/f* (*inexperto*) layman(-woman); **soy ~ en música** I don't know anything about music

profecía [profe'θia] *nf* prophecy

proferir [profe'rir] *vt* (*palabra, sonido*) to utter; (*injuria*) to hurl, let fly

profesar [profe'sar] *vt* (*declarar*) to profess; (*practicar*) to practise

profesión [profe'sjon] *nf* profession; (*confesión*) avowal; **abogado de ~, de ~ abogado** a lawyer by profession

profesional [profesjo'nal] *adj* professional

profesor, a [profe'sor, a] *nm/f* teacher; (*instructor*) instructor; ~ **de universidad** lecturer; ~ **adjunto** assistant lecturer, associate professor (US)

profesorado [profeso'raðo] *nm* (*profesión*) teaching profession; (*cuerpo*) teaching staff, faculty (US); (*cargo*) professorship

profeta [pro'feta] *nm/f* prophet

profetice *etc* [profe'tiθe] *vb ver* **profetizar**

profetizar [profeti'θar] *vt, vi* to prophesy

profiera *etc* [pro'fjera], **profiriendo** *etc* [profi'rjendo] *vb ver* **proferir**

profilaxis [profi'laksis] *nf inv* prevention

prófugo, -a ['profuɣo, a] *nm/f* fugitive; (*desertor*) deserter

profundice *etc* [profun'diθe] *vb ver* **profundizar**

profundidad [profundi'ðað] *nf* depth; **tener una ~ de 30 cm** to be 30 cm deep

profundizar [profundi'θar] *vt* (*fig*) to go deeply into, study in depth

profundo, -a [pro'fundo, a] *adj* deep; (*misterio, pensador*) profound; **poco ~** shallow

profusión [profu'sjon] *nf* (*abundancia*) profusion; (*prodigalidad*) wealth

progenie [pro'xenje] *nf* offspring

progenitor [proxeni'tor] *nm* ancestor; **progenitores** *nmpl* (*fam*) parents

programa [pro'ɣrama] *nm* programme; (*Inform*) program; ~ **de estudios** curriculum, syllabus; ~ **verificador de ortografía** (*Inform*) spelling checker

programación [proɣrama'θjon] *nf* (*Inform*) programming; ~ **estructurada** structured programming

programador, a [proɣrama'ðor, a] *nm/f*

(computer) programmer; ~ **de aplicaciones** applications programmer

programar [proɣra'mar] *vt* (*Inform*) to programme

progre ['proɣre] *adj* (*fam*) liberal

progresar [proɣre'sar] *vi* to progress, make progress

progresión [proɣres'jon] *nf*: ~ **geométrica/ aritmética** geometric/arithmetic progression

progresista [proɣre'sista] *adj, nm/f* progressive

progresivo, -a [proɣre'siβo, a] *adj* progressive; (*gradual*) gradual; (*continuo*) continuous

progreso [pro'ɣreso] *nm* (*tb*: **progresos**) progress; **hacer progresos** to progress, advance

prohibición [proiβi'θjon] *nf* prohibition, ban; **levantar la ~ de** to remove the ban on

prohibir [proi'βir] *vt* to prohibit, ban, forbid; **se prohíbe fumar** no smoking

prohibitivo, -a [proiβi'tiβo, a] *adj* prohibitive

prójimo, -a ['proximo, a] *nm* fellow man ■ *nm/f* (*vecino*) neighbour

prole ['prole] *nf* (*descendencia*) offspring

proletariado [proleta'rjaðo] *nm* proletariat

proletario, -a [prole'tarjo, a] *adj, nm/f* proletarian

proliferación [prolifera'θjon] *nf* proliferation; ~ **de armas nucleares** spread of nuclear arms

proliferar [prolife'rar] *vi* to proliferate

prolífico, -a [pro'lifiko, a] *adj* prolific

prolijo, -a [pro'lixo, a] *adj* long-winded, tedious; (*Am*) neat

prólogo ['proloɣo] *nm* prologue; (*preámbulo*) preface, introduction

prolongación [prolonga'θjon] *nf* extension

prolongado, -a [prolon'gaðo, a] *adj* (*largo*) long; (*alargado*) lengthy

prolongar [prolon'gar] *vt* (*gen*) to extend; (*en el tiempo*) to prolong; (*calle, tubo*) to make longer, extend; **prolongarse** *vr* (*alargarse*) to extend, go on

prolongue *etc* [pro'longe] *vb ver* **prolongar**

prom. *abr* (= *promedio*) av.

promedio [pro'meðjo] *nm* average; (*de distancia*) middle, mid-point

promesa [pro'mesa] *nf* promise ■ *adj*: **jugador ~** promising player; **faltar a una ~** to break a promise

prometer [prome'ter] *vt* to promise ■ *vi* to show promise; **prometerse** *vr* (*dos personas*) to get engaged

prometido, -a [prome'tiðo, a] *adj* promised;

engaged ∎ nm/f fiancé/fiancée

prominente [promi'nente] adj prominent

promiscuidad [promiskwi'ðað] nf promiscuity

promiscuo, -a [pro'miskwo, a] adj promiscuous

promoción [promo'θjon] nf promotion; (año) class, year; ~ **por correspondencia directa** (Com) direct mailshot; ~ **de ventas** sales promotion o drive

promocionar [promoθjo'nar] vt (Com: dar publicidad) to promote

promontorio [promon'torjo] nm promontory

promotor [promo'tor] nm promoter; (instigador) instigator

promover [promo'βer] vt to promote; (causar) to cause; (juicio) to bring; (motín) to instigate, stir up

promueva etc [pro'mweβa] vb ver **promover**

promulgar [promul'ɣar] vt to promulgate; (fig) to proclaim

promulgue etc [pro'mulɣe] vb ver **promulgar**

pronombre [pro'nombre] nm pronoun

pronosticar [pronosti'kar] vt to predict, foretell, forecast

pronóstico [pro'nostiko] nm prediction, forecast; (profecía) omen; (Med: diagnóstico) prognosis; **de ~ leve** slight, not serious; ~ **del tiempo** weather forecast

pronostique etc [pronos'tike] vb ver **pronosticar**

prontitud [pronti'tuð] nf speed, quickness

pronto, -a ['pronto, a] adj (rápido) prompt, quick; (preparado) ready ∎ adv quickly, promptly; (en seguida) at once, right away; (dentro de poco) soon; (temprano) early ∎ nm urge, sudden feeling; **tener prontos de enojo** to be quick-tempered; **al ~** at first; **de ~** suddenly; ¡**hasta ~!** see you soon!; **lo más ~ posible** as soon as possible; **por lo ~** meanwhile, for the present; **tan ~ como** as soon as

pronunciación [pronunθja'θjon] nf pronunciation

pronunciado, -a [pronun'θjaðo, a] adj (marcado) pronounced; (curva etc) sharp; (facciones) marked

pronunciamiento [pronunθja'mjento] nm (rebelión) insurrection

pronunciar [pronun'θjar] vt to pronounce; (discurso) to make, deliver; (Jur: sentencia) to pass, pronounce; **pronunciarse** vr to revolt, rise, rebel; (declararse) to declare o.s.; **pronunciarse sobre** to pronounce on

propagación [propaɣa'θjon] nf propagation; (difusión) spread(ing)

propaganda [propa'ɣanda] nf (política) propaganda; (comercial) advertising; **hacer ~ de** (Com) to advertise

propagar [propa'ɣar] vt to propagate; (difundir) to spread, disseminate; **propagarse** vr (Bio) to propagate; (fig) to spread

propague etc [pro'paɣe] vb ver **propagar**

propalar [propa'lar] vt (divulgar) to divulge; (publicar) to publish an account of

propano [pro'pano] nm propane

propasarse [propa'sarse] vr (excederse) to go too far; (sexualmente) to take liberties

propensión [propen'sjon] nf inclination, propensity

propenso, -a [pro'penso, a] adj: ~ **a** prone o inclined to; **ser ~ a hacer algo** to be inclined o have a tendency to do sth

propiamente [propja'mente] adv properly; (realmente) really, exactly; ~ **dicho** real, true

propicio, -a [pro'piθjo, a] adj favourable, propitious

propiedad [propje'ðað] nf property; (posesión) possession, ownership; (conveniencia) suitability; (exactitud) accuracy; ~ **particular** private property; ~ **pública** (Com) public ownership; **ceder algo a algn en ~** to transfer to sb the full rights over sth

propietario, -a [propje'tarjo, a] nm/f owner, proprietor

propina [pro'pina] nf tip; **dar algo de ~** to give something extra

propinar [propi'nar] vt (golpe) to strike; (azotes) to give

propio, -a ['propjo, a] adj own, of one's own; (característico) characteristic, typical; (conveniente) proper; (mismo) selfsame, very; **el ~ ministro** the minister himself; ¿**tienes casa propia?** have you a house of your own?; **eso es muy ~ de él** that's just like him; **tiene un olor muy ~** it has a smell of its own

propondré etc [propon'dre] vb ver **proponer**

proponente [propo'nente] nm proposer, mover

proponer [propo'ner] vt to propose, put forward; (candidato) to propose, nominate; (problema) to pose; **proponerse** vr to propose, plan, intend

proponga etc [pro'ponga] vb ver **proponer**

proporción [propor'θjon] nf proportion; (Mat) ratio; (razón, porcentaje) rate; **proporciones** nfpl dimensions; (fig) size sg; **en ~ con** in proportion to

proporcionado, -a [proporθjo'naðo, a] adj proportionate; (regular) medium, middling; (justo) just right; **bien ~** well-proportioned

proporcional [proporθjo'nal] adj proportional; ~ **a** proportional to

proporcionar [proporθjo'nar] *vt* (*dar*) to give, supply, provide; **esto le proporciona una renta anual de** ... this brings him in a yearly income of ...

proposición [proposi'θjon] *nf* proposition; (*propuesta*) proposal

propósito [pro'posito] *nm* (*intención*) purpose; (*intento*) aim, intention ■ *adv*: **a ~** by the way, incidentally; **a ~ de** about, with regard to

propuesto, -a [pro'pwesto, a] *pp de* **proponer** ■ *nf* proposal

propugnar [propuɣ'nar] *vt* to uphold

propulsar [propul'sar] *vt* to drive, propel; (*fig*) to promote, encourage

propulsión [propul'sjon] *nf* propulsion; **~ a chorro** *o* **por reacción** jet propulsion

propuse *etc* [pro'puse] *vb ver* **proponer**

prorrata [pro'rrata] *nf* (*porción*) share, quota, prorate (*US*) ■ *adv* (*Com*) pro rata

prorratear [prorrate'ar] *vt* (*dividir*) to share out, prorate (*US*)

prórroga ['prorroɣa] *nf* (*gen*) extension; (*Jur*) stay; (*Com*) deferment

prorrogable [prorro'ɣaβle] *adj* which can be extended

prorrogar [prorro'ɣar] *vt* (*período*) to extend; (*decisión*) to defer, postpone

prorrogue *etc* [pro'rroɣe] *vb ver* **prorrogar**

prorrumpir [prorrum'pir] *vi* to burst forth, break out; **~ en gritos** to start shouting; **~ en lágrimas** to burst into tears

prosa ['prosa] *nf* prose

prosaico, -a [pro'saiko, a] *adj* prosaic, dull

proscribir [proskri'βir] *vt* to prohibit, ban; (*desterrar*) to exile, banish; (*partido*) to proscribe

proscripción [proskrip'θjon] *nf* prohibition, ban; banishment; proscription

proscrito, -a [pros'krito, a] *pp de* **proscribir** ■ *adj* (*prohibido*) banned; (*desterrado*) outlawed ■ *nm/f* (*exilado*) exile; (*bandido*) outlaw

prosecución [proseku'θjon] *nf* continuation; (*persecución*) pursuit

proseguir [prose'ɣir] *vt* to continue, carry on, proceed with; (*investigación, estudio*) to pursue ■ *vi* to continue, go on

prosiga *etc* [pro'siɣa], **prosiguiendo** *etc* [prosi'ɣjenðo] *vb ver* **proseguir**

prosista [pro'sista] *nm/f* (*escritor*) prose writer

prospección [prospek'θjon] *nf* exploration; (*del petróleo, del oro*) prospecting

prospecto [pros'pekto] *nm* prospectus; (*folleto*) leaflet, sheet of instructions

prosperar [prospe'rar] *vi* to prosper, thrive, flourish

prosperidad [prosperi'ðað] *nf* prosperity; (*éxito*) success

próspero, -a ['prospero, a] *adj* prosperous; (*que tiene éxito*) successful

prostíbulo [pros'tiβulo] *nm* brothel

prostitución [prostitu'θjon] *nf* prostitution

prostituir [prosti'twir] *vt* to prostitute; **prostituirse** *vr* to prostitute o.s., become a prostitute

prostituta [prosti'tuta] *nf* prostitute

prostituyendo *etc* [prostitu'jendo] *vb ver* **prostituir**

protagonice *etc* [protaɣo'niθe] *vb ver* **protagonizar**

protagonista [protaɣo'nista] *nm/f* protagonist; (*Lit: personaje*) main character, hero/heroine

protagonizar [protaɣoni'θar] *vt* to head, take the chief role in

protección [protek'θjon] *nf* protection

proteccionismo [protekθjo'nismo] *nm* (*Com*) protectionism

protector, a [protek'tor, a] *adj* protective, protecting; (*tono*) patronizing ■ *nm/f* protector; (*bienhechor*) patron; (*de la tradición*) guardian

proteger [prote'xer] *vt* to protect; **~ contra grabación** *o* **contra escritura** (*Inform*) to write-protect

protegido, -a [prote'xiðo, a] *nm/f* protégé/protégée

proteína [prote'ina] *nf* protein

proteja *etc* [pro'texa] *vb ver* **proteger**

prótesis ['protesis] *nf* (*Med*) prosthesis

protesta [pro'testa] *nf* protest

protestante [protes'tante] *adj* Protestant

protestar [protes'tar] *vt* to protest, declare; (*fe*) to protest ■ *vi* to protest; (*objetar*) to object; **cheque protestado por falta de fondos** cheque referred to drawer

protocolo [proto'kolo] *nm* protocol; **sin protocolos** (*formalismo*) informal(ly)

protón [pro'ton] *nm* proton

prototipo [proto'tipo] *nm* prototype; (*ideal*) model

protuberancia [protuβe'ranθja] *nf* protuberance

prov. *abr* (= *provincia*) prov.

provecho [pro'βetʃo] *nm* advantage, benefit; (*Finanzas*) profit; **¡buen ~!** bon appétit!; **en ~ de** to the benefit of; **sacar ~ de** to benefit from, profit by

provechoso, -a [proβe'tʃoso, a] *adj* (*ventajoso*) advantageous; (*beneficioso*) beneficial, useful; (*Finanzas: lucrativo*) profitable

proveedor, a [proβee'ðor, a] *nm/f* (*abastecedor*) supplier; (*distribuidor*) dealer; **~ de (acceso a) Internet** Internet Service Provider

proveer [proβe'er] *vt* to provide, supply;

313

(*preparar*) to provide, get ready; (*vacante*) to fill; (*negocio*) to transact, dispatch ∎ vi: ~ **a** to provide for; **proveerse** vr: **proveerse de** to provide o.s. with
provendré etc [proβen'dre], **provenga** etc [pro'βenga] vb ver **provenir**
provenir [proβe'nir] vi: ~ **de** to come from
Provenza [pro'βenθa] nf Provence
proverbial [proβer'βjal] adj proverbial; (*fig*) notorious
proverbio [pro'βerβjo] nm proverb
proveyendo etc [proβe'jendo] vb ver **proveer**
providencia [proβi'ðenθja] nf providence; (*previsión*) foresight; **providencias** nfpl measures, steps
provincia [pro'βinθja] nf province; (*Esp: Admin*) ≈ county, ≈ region (*Scot*); **un pueblo de ~(s)** a country town; *see note*

⬤ **PROVINCIA**
⬤
⬤ Spain is divided up into 55 administrative
⬤ *provincias*, including the islands, and
⬤ territories in North Africa. Each one has
⬤ a *capital de provincia*, which generally bears
⬤ the same name. *Provincias* are grouped
⬤ by geography, history and culture
⬤ into *comunidades autónomas*. It should be
⬤ noted that the term *comarca* normally
⬤ has a purely geographical function in
⬤ Spanish, but in Catalonia it designates
⬤ administrative boundaries.

provinciano, -a [proβin'θjano, a] adj provincial; (*del campo*) country cpd
proviniendo etc [proβi'njendo] vb ver **provenir**
provisión [proβi'sjon] nf provision; (*abastecimiento*) provision, supply; (*medida*) measure, step
provisional [proβisjo'nal] adj provisional
provisorio, -a [proβi'sorjo, a] adj (*esp Am*) provisional
provisto, -a [pro'βisto, a] adj: ~ **de** provided o supplied with; (*que tiene*) having, possessing
provocación [proβoka'θjon] nf provocation
provocador, a [proβoka'ðor, a] adj provocative, provoking
provocar [proβo'kar] vt to provoke; (*alentar*) to tempt, invite; (*causar*) to bring about, lead to; (*promover*) to promote; (*estimular*) to rouse, stir, stimulate; (*protesta, explosión*) to cause, spark off; (*Am*): **¿te provoca un café?** would you like a coffee?
provocativo, -a [proβoka'tiβo, a] adj provocative
provoque etc [pro'βoke] vb ver **provocar**

proxeneta [prokse'neta] nm/f go-between; (*de prostitutas*) pimp/procuress
próximamente [proksima'mente] adv shortly, soon
proximidad [proksimi'ðað] nf closeness, proximity
próximo, -a ['proksimo, a] adj near, close; (*vecino*) neighbouring; (*el que viene*) next; **en fecha próxima** at an early date; **el mes ~** next month
proyección [projek'θjon] nf projection; (*Cine*) showing; (*diapositiva*) slide, transparency; (*influencia*) influence; **el tiempo de ~ es de 35 minutos** the film runs for 35 minutes
proyectar [projek'tar] vt (*objeto*) to hurl, throw; (*luz*) to cast, shed; (*Cine*) to screen, show; (*planear*) to plan
proyectil [projek'til] nm projectile, missile; ~ **(tele)dirigido** guided missile
proyecto [pro'jekto] nm plan; (*idea*) project; (*estimación de costo*) detailed estimate; **tener algo en ~** to be planning sth; ~ **de ley** (*Pol*) bill
proyector [projek'tor] nm (*Cine*) projector
prudencia [pru'ðenθja] nf (*sabiduría*) wisdom, prudence; (*cautela*) care
prudente [pru'ðente] adj sensible, wise, prudent; (*cauteloso*) careful
prueba etc ['prweβa] vb ver **probar** ∎ nf proof; (*ensayo*) test, trial; (*cantidad*) taste, sample; (*saboreo*) testing, sampling; (*de ropa*) fitting; (*Deporte*) event; **a ~** on trial; (*Com*) on approval; **a ~ de** proof against; **a ~ de agua/fuego** waterproof/fireproof; ~ **de capacitación** (*Com*) proficiency test; ~ **de fuego** (*fig*) acid test; ~ **de vallas** hurdles; **someter a ~** to put to the test; **¿tiene usted ~ de ello?** can you prove it?, do you have proof?
prurito [pru'rito] nm itch; (*de bebé*) nappy rash; (*anhelo*) urge
psico... [siko] pref psycho...
psicoanálisis [sikoa'nalisis] nm psychoanalysis
psicoanalista [sikoana'lista] nm/f psychoanalyst
psicología [sikolo'xia] nf psychology
psicológico, -a [siko'loxiko, a] adj psychological
psicólogo, -a [si'koloγo, a] nm/f psychologist
psicópata [si'kopata] nm/f psychopath
psicosis [si'kosis] nf inv psychosis
psicosomático, -a [sikoso'matiko, a] adj psychosomatic
psicoterapia [sikote'rapja] nf psychotherapy
psiquiatra [si'kjatra] nm/f psychiatrist
psiquiátrico, -a [si'kjatriko, a] adj psychiatric ∎ nm mental hospital
psíquico, -a ['sikiko, a] adj psychic(al)

PSOE [pe'soe] *nm abr* = **Partido Socialista Obrero Español**

PSS *nf abr* (= *Prestación Social Sustitutoria*) *community service for conscientious objectors*

Pta. *abr* (*Geo*: = *Punta*) Pt.

pta(s). *abr* (*Historia*) = **peseta(s)**

pts. *abr* (*Historia*) = **pesetas**

púa ['pua] *nf* sharp point; (*para guitarra*) plectrum; **alambre de púas** barbed wire

pub [puβ/paβ/paf] *nm* bar

púber, a ['puβer, a] *adj, nm/f* adolescent

pubertad [puβer'tað] *nf* puberty

publicación [puβlika'θjon] *nf* publication

publicar [puβli'kar] *vt* (*editar*) to publish; (*hacer público*) to publicize; (*divulgar*) to make public, divulge

publicidad [puβliθi'ðað] *nf* publicity; (*Com*) advertising; **dar ~ a** to publicize, give publicity to; **~ gráfica** display advertising; **~ en el punto de venta** point-of-sale advertising

publicitar [puβliθi'tar] *vt* to publicize

publicitario, -a [puβliθi'tarjo, a] *adj* publicity *cpd*; advertising *cpd*

público, -a ['puβliko, a] *adj* public ■ *nm* public; (*Teat etc*) audience; (*Deporte*) spectators *pl*, crowd; (*en restaurantes etc*) clients *pl*; **el gran ~** the general public; **hacer ~** to publish; (*difundir*) to disclose; **~ objetivo** (*Com*) target audience

publique *etc* [pu'βlike] *vb ver* **publicar**

pucherazo [putʃe'raθo] *nm* (*fraude*) electoral fiddle; **dar ~** to rig an election

puchero [pu'tʃero] *nm* (*Culin*: *olla*) cooking pot; (: *guiso*) stew; **hacer pucheros** to pout

pudibundo, -a [puði'βundo, a] *adj* bashful

púdico, -a ['puðiko, a] *adj* modest; (*pudibundo*) bashful

pudiendo *etc* [pu'ðjendo] *vb ver* **poder**

pudiente [pu'ðjente] *adj* (*opulento*) wealthy; (*poderoso*) powerful

pudín [pu'ðin] *nm* pudding

pudor [pu'ðor] *nm* modesty; (*vergüenza*) (sense of) shame

pudoroso, -a [puðo'roso, a] *adj* (*modesto*) modest; (*casto*) chaste

pudrir [pu'ðrir] *vt* to rot; (*fam*) to upset, annoy; **pudrirse** *vr* to rot, decay; (*fig*) to rot, languish

pueblerino, -a [pweβle'rino, a] *adj* (*lugareño*) small-town *cpd*; (*persona*) rustic, provincial ■ *nm/f* (*aldeano*) country person

pueblo *etc* ['pweβlo] *vb ver* **poblar** ■ *nm* people; (*nación*) nation; (*aldea*) village; (*plebe*) common people; (*población pequeña*) small town, country town

pueda *etc* ['pweða] *vb ver* **poder**

puente ['pwente] *nm* (*gen*) bridge; (*Naut*: *tb*: **puente de mando**) bridge; (: *cubierta*) deck; **~ aéreo** airlift; **~ colgante** suspension bridge; **~ levadizo** drawbridge; **hacer (el) ~** (*fam*) to take a long weekend

puenting ['pwentin] *nm* bungee jumping

puerco, -a ['pwerko, a] *adj* (*sucio*) dirty, filthy; (*obsceno*) disgusting ■ *nm/f* pig/sow

pueril [pwe'ril] *adj* childish

puerro ['pwerro] *nm* leek

puerta ['pwerta] *nf* door; (*de jardín*) gate; (*portal*) doorway; (*fig*) gateway; (*gol*) goal; (*Inform*) port; **a la ~** at the door; **a ~ cerrada** behind closed doors; **~ corredera/giratoria** sliding/swing o revolving door; **~ principal/trasera** o **de servicio** front/back door; **~ (de transmisión en) paralelo/serie** (*Inform*) parallel/serial port; **tomar la ~** (*fam*) to leave

puerto ['pwerto] *nm* (*tb Inform*) port; (*de mar*) seaport; (*paso*) pass; (*fig*) haven, refuge; **llegar a ~** (*fig*) to get over a difficulty

Puerto Rico [pwerto'riko] *nm* Puerto Rico

puertorriqueño, -a [pwertorri'keɲo, a] *adj, nm/f* Puerto Rican

pues [pwes] *adv* (*entonces*) then; (¡*entonces!*) well, well then; (*así que*) so ■ *conj* (*porque*) since; **~ ... no sé** well ... I don't know

puesto, -a ['pwesto, a] *pp de* **poner** ■ *adj* dressed ■ *nm* (*lugar, posición*) place; (*trabajo*) post, job; (*Mil*) post; (*Com*) stall; (*quiosco*) kiosk ■ *conj*: **~ que** since, as ■ *nf* (*apuesta*) bet, stake; **~ de mercado** market stall; **~ de policía** police station; **~ de socorro** first aid post; **puesta en escena** staging; **puesta en marcha** starting; **puesta del sol** sunset; **puesta a cero** (*Inform*) reset

pugna ['puɣna] *nf* battle, conflict

pugnar [puɣ'nar] *vi* (*luchar*) to struggle, fight; (*pelear*) to fight

puja ['puxa] *nf* (*esfuerzo*) attempt; (*en una subasta*) bid

pujante [pu'xante] *adj* strong, vigorous

pujar [pu'xar] *vt* (*precio*) to raise, push up ■ *vi* (*en licitación*) to bid, bid up; (*fig*: *esforzarse*) to struggle, strain

pulcro, -a ['pulkro, a] *adj* neat, tidy

pulga ['pulɣa] *nf* flea; **tener malas pulgas** to be short-tempered

pulgada [pul'ɣaða] *nf* inch

pulgar [pul'ɣar] *nm* thumb

pulgón [pul'ɣon] *nm* plant louse, greenfly

pulir [pu'lir] *vt* to polish; (*alisar*) to smooth; (*fig*) to polish up, touch up

pulla ['puʎa] *nf* cutting remark

pulmón [pul'mon] *nm* lung; **a pleno ~** (*respirar*) deeply; (*gritar*) at the top of one's voice; **~ de acero** iron lung

p

pulmonía [pulmo'nia] *nf* pneumonia
pulpa ['pulpa] *nf* pulp; (*de fruta*) flesh, soft part
pulpería [pulpe'ria] *nf* (*Am*) small grocery store
púlpito ['pulpito] *nm* pulpit
pulpo ['pulpo] *nm* octopus
pulsación [pulsa'θjon] *nf* beat, pulsation; (*Anat*) throb(bing); (*en máquina de escribir*) tap; (*de pianista, mecanógrafo*) touch; ~ (**de una tecla**) (*Inform*) keystroke; ~ **doble** (*Inform*) strikeover
pulsador [pulsa'ðor] *nm* button, push button
pulsar [pul'sar] *vt* (*tecla*) to touch, tap; (*Mus*) to play; (*botón*) to press, push ▪ *vi* to pulsate; (*latir*) to beat, throb
pulsera [pul'sera] *nf* bracelet; **reloj de** ~ wristwatch
pulso ['pulso] *nm* (*Med*) pulse; **hacer algo a** ~ to do sth unaided o by one's own efforts
pulular [pulu'lar] *vi* (*estar plagado*): ~ (**de**) to swarm (with)
pulverice *etc* [pulβe'riθe] *vb ver* **pulverizar**
pulverizador [pulβeriθa'ðor] *nm* spray, spray gun
pulverizar [pulβeri'θar] *vt* to pulverize; (*líquido*) to spray
puna ['puna] *nf* (*Am Med*) mountain sickness
punce *etc* ['punθe] *vb ver* **punzar**
punción [pun'θjon] *nf* (*Med*) puncture
pundonor [pundo'nor] *nm* (*dignidad*) self-respect
punición [puni'θjon] *nf* punishment
punitivo, -a [puni'tiβo, a] *adj* punitive
punki ['punki] *adj, nm/f* punk
punta ['punta] *nf* point, tip; (*extremidad*) end; (*promontorio*) headland; (*Costura*) corner; (*Tec*) small nail; (*fig*) touch, trace; **horas puntas** peak hours, rush hours; **sacar** ~ **a** to sharpen; **de** ~ on end; **de** ~ **a** ~ from one end to the other; **estar de** ~ to be edgy; **ir de** ~ **en blanco** to be all dressed up to the nines; **tener algo en la** ~ **de la lengua** to have sth on the tip of one's tongue; **se le pusieron los pelos de** ~ her hair stood on end
puntada [pun'taða] *nf* (*Costura*) stitch
puntal [pun'tal] *nm* prop, support
puntapié [punta'pje] *fl* (*pl* ~**s**) *nm* kick; **echar a algn a** ~**s** to kick sb out
punteado, -a [punte'aðo, a] *adj* (*moteado*) dotted; (*diseño*) of dots ▪ *nm* (*Mus*) twang
puntear [punte'ar] *vt* to tick, mark; (*Mus*) to pluck
puntería [punte'ria] *nf* (*de arma*) aim, aiming; (*destreza*) marksmanship
puntero, -a [pun'tero, a] *adj* leading ▪ *nm* (*señal, Inform*) pointer; (*dirigente*) leader
puntiagudo, -a [puntja'ɣuðo, a] *adj* sharp, pointed

puntilla [pun'tiʎa] *nf* (*Tec*) tack, braid; (*Costura*) lace edging; (**andar**) **de puntillas** (to walk) on tiptoe
puntilloso, -a [punti'ʎoso, a] *adj* (*pundonoroso*) punctilious; (*susceptible*) touchy
punto ['punto] *nm* (*gen*) point; (*señal diminuta*) spot, dot; (*lugar*) spot, place; (*momento*) point, moment; (*en un examen*) mark; (*tema*) item; (*Costura*) stitch; (*Inform: impresora*) pitch; (: *pantalla*) pixel; **a** ~ ready; **estar a** ~ **de** to be on the point of o about to; **llegar a** ~ to come just at the right moment; **al** ~ at once; **en** ~ on the dot; **estar en su** ~ (*Culin*) to be done to a turn; **hasta cierto** ~ to some extent; **hacer** ~ to knit; **poner un motor en** ~ to tune an engine; ~ **de partida/de congelación/de fusión** starting/freezing/melting point; ~ **de vista** point of view, viewpoint; ~ **muerto** dead centre; (*Auto*) neutral (gear); **puntos a tratar** matters to be discussed, agenda *sg*; ~ **final** full stop; **dos puntos** colon; ~ **y coma** semicolon; ~ **acápite** (*Am*) full stop, new paragraph; ~ **de interrogación** question mark; **puntos suspensivos** suspension points; ~ **de equilibrio/de pedido** (*Com*) breakeven/reorder point; ~ **inicial** o **de partida** (*Inform*) home; ~ **de referencia/de venta** (*Com*) benchmark point/point-of-sale
puntocom [punto'kom] *nf inv, adj inv* dotcom, dot.com
puntuación [puntwa'θjon] *nf* punctuation; (*puntos: en examen*) mark(s) *pl*; (: *Deporte*) score
puntual [pun'twal] *adj* (*a tiempo*) punctual; (*cálculo*) exact, accurate; (*informe*) reliable
puntualice *etc* [puntwa'liθe] *vb ver* **puntualizar**
puntualidad [puntwali'ðað] *nf* punctuality; exactness, accuracy; reliability
puntualizar [puntwali'θar] *vt* to fix, specify
puntuar [pun'twar] *vt* (*Ling, Tip*) to punctuate; (*examen*) to mark ▪ *vi* (*Deporte*) to score, count
punzada [pun'θaða] *nf* (*puntura*) prick; (*Med*) stitch; (*dolor*) twinge (of pain)
punzante [pun'θante] *adj* (*dolor*) shooting, sharp; (*herramienta*) sharp; (*comentario*) biting
punzar [pun'θar] *vt* to prick, pierce ▪ *vi* to shoot, stab
punzón [pun'θon] *nm* (*Tec*) punch
puñado [pu'ɲaðo] *nm* handful (*tb fig*); **a puñados** by handfuls
puñal [pu'ɲal] *nm* dagger
puñalada [puɲa'laða] *nf* stab
puñeta [pu'ɲeta] *nf*: **¡~!, ¡qué ~(s)!** (*fam!*) hell!; **mandar a algn a hacer puñetas** (*fam*) to tell sb to go to hell
puñetazo [puɲe'taθo] *nm* punch

puño ['puɲo] *nm* (*Anat*) fist; (*cantidad*) fistful, handful; (*Costura*) cuff; (*de herramienta*) handle; **como un ~** (*verdad*) obvious; (*palpable*) tangible, visible; **de ~ y letra del poeta** in the poet's own handwriting

pupila [pu'pila] *nf* (*Anat*) pupil

pupitre [pu'pitre] *nm* desk

puré [pu're ʃ] (*pl* **~s**) *nm* puree; (*sopa*) (thick) soup; **~ de patatas** mashed potatoes; **estar hecho ~** (*fig*) to be knackered

pureza [pu'reθa] *nf* purity

purga ['purɣa] *nf* purge

purgante [pur'ɣante] *adj, nm* purgative

purgar [pur'ɣar] *vt* to purge; (*Pol: depurar*) to purge, liquidate; **purgarse** *vr* (*Med*) to take a purge

purgatorio [purɣa'torjo] *nm* purgatory

purgue *etc* ['purɣe] *vb ver* **purgar**

purificar [purifi'kar] *vt* to purify; (*refinar*) to refine

purifique *etc* [puri'fike] *vb ver* **purificar**

puritano, -a [puri'tano, a] *adj* (*actitud*) puritanical; (*iglesia, tradición*) puritan ■ *nm/f* puritan

puro, -a ['puro, a] *adj* pure; (*depurado*) unadulterated; (*oro*) solid; (*cielo*) clear; (*verdad*) simple, plain ■ *adv*: **de ~ cansado** out of sheer tiredness ■ *nm* cigar; **por pura casualidad** by sheer chance

púrpura ['purpura] *nf* purple

purpúreo, -a [pur'pureo, a] *adj* purple

pus [pus] *nm* pus

puse *etc* ['puse] *vb ver* **poner**

pústula ['pustula] *nf* pimple, sore

puta ['puta] *nf* whore, prostitute

putada [pu'taða] *nf* (*fam!*): **hacer una ~ a algn** to play a dirty trick on sb; **¡qué ~!** what a pain in the arse! (!)

putería [pute'ria] *nf* (*prostitución*) prostitution; (*prostíbulo*) brothel

putrefacción [putrefak'θjon] *nf* rotting, putrefaction

pútrido, -a ['putriðo, a] *adj* rotten

puzzle ['puθle] *nm* puzzle

PVP *abr* (*Esp*: = *Precio Venta al Público*) ≈ RRP

PYME ['pime] *nf abr* (= *Pequeña y Mediana Empresa*) SME

Pza *abr* = **plaza**

p

Qq

Q, q [ku] *nf* (*letra*) Q, q; **Q de Querido** Q for Queen

q.e.p.d. *abr* (= *que en paz descanse*) R.I.P

qm *abr* = **quintal métrico**; **quintales métricos**

qts. *abr* = **quilates**

 PALABRA CLAVE

que [ke] *conj* **1** (*con oración subordinada: muchas veces no se traduce*) that; **dijo que vendría** he said (that) he would come; **espero que lo encuentres** I hope (that) you find it; **dile que me llame** ask him to call me; *ver tb* **el**

2 (*en oración independiente*): **¡que entre!** send him in; **¡que se mejore tu padre!** I hope your father gets better; **¡que lo haga él!** he can do it!; (*orden*) get him to do it!

3 (*enfático*): **¿me quieres? — ¡que sí!** do you love me? — of course!; **te digo que sí** I'm telling you

4 (*consecutivo: muchas veces no se traduce*) that; **es tan grande que no lo puedo levantar** it's so big (that) I can't lift it

5 (*comparaciones*) than; **yo que tú/él** if I were you/him; *ver tb* **más**; **menos**

6 (*valor disyuntivo*): **que le guste o no** whether he likes it or not; **que venga o que no venga** whether he comes or not

7 (*porque*): **no puedo, que tengo que quedarme en casa** I can't, I've got to stay in

8: **siguió toca que toca** he kept on playing

■ *pron* **1** (*cosa*) that, which; (+*prep*) which; **el sombrero que te compraste** the hat (that *o* which) you bought; **la cama en que dormí** the bed (that *o* which) I slept in; **el día (en) que ella nació** the day (when) she was born

2 (*persona: suj*) that, who; (: *objeto*) that, whom; **el amigo que me acompañó al museo** the friend that *o* who went to the museum with me; **la chica que invité** the girl (that *o* whom) I invited

qué [ke] *adj* what?, which? ■ *pron* what?; **¡qué divertido/asco!** how funny/revolting!; **¡qué día más espléndido!** what a glorious day!; **¿qué edad tienes?** how old are you?; **¿de qué me hablas?** what are you saying to me?; **¿qué tal?** how are you?, how are things?; **¿qué hay (de nuevo)?** what's new?; **¿qué más?** anything else?

quebrada [ke'βraða] *nf ver* **quebrado**

quebradero [keβra'ðero] *nm*: ~ **de cabeza** headache, worry

quebradizo, -a [keβra'ðiθo, a] *adj* fragile; (*persona*) frail

quebrado, -a [ke'βraðo, a] *adj* (*roto*) broken; (*terreno*) rough, uneven ■ *nm/f* bankrupt ■ *nm* (*Mat*) fraction ■ *nf* ravine; ~ **rehabilitado** discharged bankrupt

quebradura [keβra'ðura] *nf* (*fisura*) fissure; (*Med*) rupture

quebrantamiento [keβranta'mjento] *nm* (*acto*) breaking; (*de ley*) violation; (*estado*) exhaustion

quebrantar [keβran'tar] *vt* (*infringir*) to violate, transgress; **quebrantarse** *vr* (*persona*) to fail in health

quebranto [ke'βranto] *nm* damage, harm; (*decaimiento*) exhaustion; (*dolor*) grief, pain

quebrar [ke'βrar] *vt* to break, smash ■ *vi* to go bankrupt; **quebrarse** *vr* to break, get broken; (*Med*) to be ruptured

quechua ['ketʃua] *adj, nm/f* Quechua

queda ['keða] *nf*: (**toque de**) ~ curfew

quedar [ke'ðar] *vi* to stay, remain; (*encontrarse*) to be; (*restar*) to remain, be left; **quedarse** *vr* to remain, stay (behind); ~ **en** (*acordar*) to agree on/to; (*acabar siendo*) to end up as; ~ **por hacer** to be still to be done; ~ **ciego/mudo** to be left blind/dumb; **no te queda bien ese vestido** that dress doesn't suit you; **quedamos a las seis** we agreed to meet at six; **eso queda muy lejos** that's a long way (away); **nos quedan 12 kms para llegar al pueblo** there are still 12 kms before we get to the village; **no queda otra** there's no alternative; **quedarse (con) algo** to keep sth; **quedarse con algn** *(fam)* to swindle sb; **quedarse en nada** to come to nothing *o* nought; **quedarse sin** to run out of

quedo, -a ['keðo, a] *adj* still ◼ *adv* softly, gently

quehacer [kea'θer] *nm* task, job; **quehaceres (domésticos)** household chores

queja ['kexa] *nf* complaint

quejarse [ke'xarse] *vr* (*enfermo*) to moan, groan; (*protestar*) to complain; **~ de que ...** to complain (about the fact) that ...

quejica [ke'xika] *adj* grumpy, complaining ◼ *nm/f* grumbler, whinger

quejido [ke'xiðo] *nm* moan

quejoso, -a [ke'xoso, a] *adj* complaining

quema ['kema] *nf* fire; (*combustión*) burning

quemado, -a [ke'maðo, a] *adj* burnt; (*irritado*) annoyed

quemadura [kema'ðura] *nf* burn, scald; (*de sol*) sunburn; (*de fusible*) blow-out

quemar [ke'mar] *vt* to burn; (*fig: malgastar*) to burn up, squander; (*Com: precios*) to slash, cut; (*fastidiar*) to annoy, bug ◼ *vi* to be burning hot; **quemarse** *vr* (*consumirse*) to burn (up); (*del sol*) to get sunburnt

quemarropa [kema'rropa]: **a ~** *adv* point-blank

quemazón [kema'θon] *nf* burn; (*calor*) intense heat; (*sensación*) itch

quena ['kena] *nf* (*Am*) Indian flute

quepo *etc* ['kepo] *vb ver* **caber**

querella [ke'reʎa] *nf* (*Jur*) charge; (*disputa*) dispute

querellarse [kere'ʎarse] *vr* to file a complaint

querencia [ke'renθja] *nf* (*Zool*) homing instinct; (*fig*) homesickness

 PALABRA CLAVE

querer [ke'rer] *vt* **1** (*desear*) to want; **quiero más dinero** I want more money; **quisiera** *o* **querría un té** I'd like a tea; **quiero ayudar/ que vayas** I want to help/you to go; **como Vd quiera** as you wish, as you please; **ven cuando quieras** come when you like; **lo hizo sin querer** he didn't mean to do it; **no quiero** I don't want to; **le pedí que me dejara ir pero no quiso** I asked him to let me go but he refused

2 (*preguntas: para pedir u ofrecer algo*): **¿quiere abrir la ventana?** could you open the window?; **¿quieres echarme una mano?** can you give me a hand?; **¿quiere un café?** would you like some coffee?

3 (*amar*) to love; (*tener cariño a*) to be fond of;

quiere mucho a sus hijos he's very fond of his children

4 (*requerir*): **esta planta quiere más luz** this plant needs more light

5: **querer decir** to mean; **¿qué quieres decir?** what do you mean?

querido, -a [ke'riðo, a] *adj* dear ◼ *nm/f* darling; (*amante*) lover; **nuestra querida patria** our beloved country

querosén [kero'sen], **querosene** [kero'sene] *nm* (*Am*) kerosene, paraffin

querré *etc* [ke'rre] *vb ver* **querer**

quesería [kese'ria] *nf* dairy; (*fábrica*) cheese factory

quesero, -a [ke'sero, a] *adj*: **la industria quesera** the cheese industry ◼ *nm/f* cheesemaker ◼ *nf* cheese dish

queso ['keso] *nm* cheese; **~ rallado** grated cheese; **~ crema** cream cheese; **dárselas con ~ a algn** (*fam*) to take sb in

quetzal [ket'sal] *nm monetary unit of Guatemala*

quicio ['kiθjo] *nm* hinge; **estar fuera de ~** to be beside o.s.; **sacar a algn de ~** to drive sb up the wall

quid [kið] *nm* gist, crux; **dar en el ~** to hit the nail on the head

quiebra ['kjeβra] *nf* break, split; (*Com*) bankruptcy; (*Econ*) slump

quiebro *etc* ['kjeβro] *vb ver* **quebrar** ◼ *nm* (*del cuerpo*) swerve

quien [kjen] *pron relativo* (*suj*) who; (*complemento*) whom; (*indefinido*): **~ dice eso es tonto** whoever says that is a fool; **hay ~ piensa que** there are those who think that; **no hay ~ lo haga** no-one will do it; **~ más, ~ menos tiene sus problemas** everybody has problems

quién [kjen] *pron interrogativo* who; (*complemento*) whom; **¿~ es?** who is it?, who's there?; (*Telec*) who's calling?

quienquiera [kjen'kjera] (*pl* **quienesquiera**) *pron* whoever

quiera *etc* ['kjera] *vb ver* **querer**

quieto, -a ['kjeto, a] *adj* still; (*carácter*) placid; **¡estáte ~!** keep still!

quietud [kje'tuð] *nf* stillness

quijada [ki'xaða] *nf* jaw, jawbone

quijote [ki'xote] *nm* dreamer; **Don Q~** Don Quixote

quil. *abr* = **quilates**

quilate [ki'late] *nm* carat

quilla ['kiʎa] *nf* keel

quilo ... ['kilo] = **kilo...**

quimera [ki'mera] *nf* (*sueño*) pipe dream

quimérico, -a [ki'meriko, a] *adj* fantastic

químico, -a ['kimiko, a] *adj* chemical ◼ *nm/f*

q

chemist ■ *nf* chemistry

quimioterapia [kimiote'rapia] *nf* chemotherapy

quina ['kina] *nf* quinine

quincallería [kinkaʎe'ria] *nf* ironmonger's (shop), hardware store (US)

quince ['kinθe] *num* fifteen; **~ días** a fortnight

quinceañero, -a [kinθea'ɲero, a] *adj* fifteen-year-old; (*adolescente*) teenage ■ *nm/f* fifteen-year-old; (*adolescente*) teenager

quincena [kin'θena] *nf* fortnight; (*pago*) fortnightly pay

quincenal [kinθe'nal] *adj* fortnightly

quincuagésimo, -a [kinkwa'xesimo, a] *num* fiftieth

quiniela [ki'njela] *nf* football pools *pl*; **quinielas** *nfpl* pools coupon *sg*

quinientos, -as [ki'njentos, as] *num* five hundred

quinina [ki'nina] *nf* quinine

quinqué [kin'ke] *nm* oil lamp

quinquenal [kinke'nal] *adj* five-year *cpd*

quinqui ['kinki] *nm* delinquent

quinta ['kinta] *nf ver* **quinto**

quintaesencia [kintae'senθja] *nf* quintessence

quintal [kin'tal] *nm* (*Castilla: peso*) = 46kg; **~ métrico** = 100kg

quinteto [kin'teto] *nm* quintet

quinto, -a ['kinto, a] *adj* fifth ■ *nm* (*Mil*) conscript, draftee ■ *nf* country house; (*Mil*) call-up, draft

quintuplo, -a [kin'tuplo, a] *adj* quintuple, five-fold

quiosco ['kjosko] *nm* (*de música*) bandstand; (*de periódicos*) news stand (*also selling sweets,* *cigarettes etc*)

quirófano [ki'rofano] *nm* operating theatre

quiromancia [kiro'manθja] *nf* palmistry

quirúrgico, -a [ki'rurxiko, a] *adj* surgical

quise *etc* ['kise] *vb ver* **querer**

quisque ['kiske] *pron* (*fam*): **cada** *o* **todo ~** (absolutely) everyone

quisquilloso [kiski'ʎoso, a] *adj* (*susceptible*) touchy; (*meticuloso*) pernickety

quiste ['kiste] *nm* cyst

quitaesmalte [kitaes'malte] *nm* nail polish remover

quitamanchas [kita'mantʃas] *nm inv* stain remover

quitanieves [kita'njeβes] *nm inv* snowplough (*Brit*), snowplow (*US*)

quitar [ki'tar] *vt* to remove, take away; (*ropa*) to take off; (*dolor*) to relieve; (*vida*) to take; (*valor*) to reduce; (*hurtar*) to remove, steal ■ *vi*: **¡quita de ahí!** get away!; **quitarse** *vr* to withdraw; (*mancha*) to come off *o* out; (*ropa*) to take off; **me quita mucho tiempo** it takes up a lot of my time; **el café me quita el sueño** coffee stops me sleeping; **~ de en medio a algn** to get rid of sb; **quitarse algo de encima** to get rid of sth; **quitarse del tabaco** to give up smoking; **se quitó el sombrero** he took off his hat

quitasol [kita'sol] *nm* sunshade (*Brit*), parasol

quite ['kite] *nm* (*en esgrima*) parry; (*evasión*) dodge; **estar al ~** to be ready to go to sb's aid

Quito ['kito] *n* Quito

quizá [ki'θa]

quizás [ki'θas] *adv* perhaps, maybe

quórum ['kworum] (*pl* **quórums**) ['kworum] *nm* quorum

Rr

R, r ['erre] *nf* (*letra*) R, r; **R de Ramón** R for Robert (*Brit*) *o* Roger (*US*)

R. *abr* (*Rel*) = **real; reverendo; Remite, Remitente; río**

rabadilla [raβa'ðiʎa] *nf* base of the spine

rábano ['raβano] *nm* radish; **me importa un ~** I don't give a damn

rabia ['raβja] *nf* (*Med*) rabies *sg*; (*fig: ira*) fury, rage; ¡**qué ~!** isn't it infuriating!; **me da ~** it maddens me; **tener ~ a algn** to have a grudge against sb

rabiar [ra'βjar] *vi* to have rabies; to rage, be furious; **~ por algo** to long for sth

rabieta [ra'βjeta] *nf* tantrum, fit of temper

rabino [ra'βino] *nm* rabbi

rabioso, -a [ra'βjoso, a] *adj* rabid; (*fig*) furious

rabo ['raβo] *nm* tail

racanear [rakane'ar] *vi* (*fam*) to skive

rácano ['rakano] *nm* (*fam*) slacker, skiver

RACE ['raθe] *nm abr* (= *Real Automóvil Club de España*) ≈ RAC

racha ['ratʃa] *nf* gust of wind; (*serie*) string, series; **buena/mala ~** spell of good/bad luck

racial [ra'θjal] *adj* racial, race *cpd*

racimo [ra'θimo] *nm* bunch

raciocinio [raθjo'θinjo] *nm* reason; (*razonamiento*) reasoning

ración [ra'θjon] *nf* portion; **raciones** *nfpl* rations

racional [raθjo'nal] *adj* (*razonable*) reasonable; (*lógico*) rational

racionalice *etc* [raθjona'liθe] *vb ver* **racionalizar**

racionalizar [raθjonali'θar] *vt* to rationalize; (*Com*) to streamline

racionamiento [raθjona'mjento] *nm* (*Com*) rationing

racionar [raθjo'nar] *vt* to ration (out)

racismo [ra'θismo] *nm* racialism, racism

racista [ra'θista] *adj, nm/f* racist

radar [ra'ðar] *nm* radar

radiación [raðja'θjon] *nf* radiation; (*Telec*) broadcasting

radiactividad [raðjaktiβi'ðað] *nf* radioactivity

radiactivo, -a [raðjak'tiβo, a] *adj* radioactive

radiado, -a [ra'ðjaðo, a] *adj* radio *cpd*, broadcast

radiador [raðja'ðor] *nm* radiator

radial [ra'ðjal] *adj* (*Am*) radio *cpd*

radiante [ra'ðjante] *adj* radiant

radiar [ra'ðjar] *vt* to radiate; (*Telec*) to broadcast; (*Med*) to give radiotherapy to

radical [raði'kal] *adj, nm/f* radical ■ *nm* (*Ling*) root; (*Mat*) square-root sign

radicar [raði'kar] *vi* to take root; **~ en** to lie *o* consist in; **radicarse** *vr* to establish o.s., put down (one's) roots

radio ['raðjo] *nf* radio; (*aparato*) radio (set) ■ *nm* (*Mat*) radius; (*Am*) radio; (*Química*) radium; **~ de acción** extent of one's authority, sphere of influence

radioaficionado, -a [raðjoafiθjo'naðo, a] *nm/f* radio ham

radiocasete [raðjoka'sete] *nm* radiocassette (player)

radiodifusión [raðjodifu'sjon] *nf* broadcasting

radioemisora [raðjoemi'sora] *nf* transmitter, radio station

radiofónico, -a [raðjo'foniko, a] *adj* radio *cpd*

radiografía [raðjoɣra'fia] *nf* X-ray

radiólogo, -a [ra'ðjoloɣo, a] *nm/f* radiologist

radionovela [raðjono'βela] *nf* radio series

radiotaxi [raðjo'taksi] *nm* radio taxi

radioterapia [raðjote'rapja] *nf* radiotherapy

radioyente [raðjo'jente] *nm/f* listener

radique *etc* [ra'ðike] *vb ver* **radicar**

RAE ['rae] *nf abr* (= *Real Academia Española*) *ver* **real**

ráfaga ['rafaɣa] *nf* gust; (*de luz*) flash; (*de tiros*) burst

raído, -a [ra'iðo, a] *adj* (*ropa*) threadbare; (*persona*) shabby

raigambre [rai'ɣambre] *nf* (*Bot*) roots *pl*; (*fig*) tradition

r

raíz [ra'iθ] (pl **raíces**) nf root; ~ **cuadrada** square root; **a ~ de** as a result of; (después de) immediately after

raja ['raxa] nf (de melón etc) slice; (hendidura) slit, split; (grieta) crack

rajar [ra'xar] vt to split; (fam) to slash; **rajarse** vr to split, crack; **rajarse de** to back out of

rajatabla [raxa'taβla]: **a ~** adv (estrictamente) strictly, to the letter

RAL abr (Inform) = **red de área local**

ralea [ra'lea] nf (pey) kind, sort

ralenti [ra'lenti] nm (TV etc) slow motion; (Auto) neutral; **al ~** in slow motion; (Auto) ticking over

rallador [raʎa'ðor] nm grater

rallar [ra'ʎar] vt to grate

ralo, -a ['ralo, a] adj thin, sparse

RAM [ram] nf abr (= random access memory) RAM

rama ['rama] nf bough, branch; **andarse por las ramas** (fig: fam) to beat about the bush

ramaje [ra'maje] nm branches pl, foliage

ramal [ra'mal] nm (de cuerda) strand; (Ferro) branch line; (Auto) branch (road)

rambla ['rambla] nf (avenida) avenue

ramera [ra'mera] nf whore, hooker (US)

ramificación [ramifika'θjon] nf ramification

ramificarse [ramifi'karse] vr to branch out

ramifique etc [rami'fike] vb ver **ramificarse**

ramillete [rami'ʎete] nm bouquet; (fig) select group

ramo ['ramo] nm branch, twig; (sección) department, section; (sector) field, sector

rampa ['rampa] nf ramp

ramplón, -ona [ram'plon, ona] adj uncouth, coarse

rana ['rana] nf frog; **salto de ~** leapfrog; **cuando las ranas críen pelos** when pigs fly

ranchero [ran'tʃero] nm (Am) rancher; (pequeño propietario) smallholder

rancho ['rantʃo] nm (Mil) food; (Am: grande) ranch; (: pequeño) small farm

rancio, -a ['ranθjo, a] adj (comestibles) stale, rancid; (vino) aged, mellow; (fig) ancient

rango ['rango] nm rank; (prestigio) standing

ranura [ra'nura] nf groove; (de teléfono etc) slot; **~ de expansión** (Inform) expansion slot

rap [rap] nm (Mus) rap

rapacidad [rapaθi'ðað] nf rapacity

rapapolvo [rapa'polβo] nm: **echar un ~ a algn** to give sb a ticking off

rapar [ra'par] vt to shave; (los cabellos) to crop

rapaz [ra'paθ] adj (Zool) predatory ▪ nm young boy

rapaza [ra'paθa] nf young girl

rape ['rape] nm quick shave; (pez) angler (fish); **al ~** cropped

rapé [ra'pe] nm snuff

rapel [ra'pel] nm = **rappel**

rapidez [rapi'ðeθ] nf speed, rapidity

rápido, -a ['rapiðo, a] adj fast, quick ▪ adv quickly ▪ nm (Ferro) express; **rápidos** nmpl rapids

rapiña [ra'piɲa] nm robbery; **ave de ~** bird of prey

rappel [ra'pel] nm (Deporte) abseiling

raptar [rap'tar] vt to kidnap

rapto ['rapto] nm kidnapping; (impulso) sudden impulse; (éxtasis) ecstasy, rapture

raqueta [ra'keta] nf racquet

raquítico, -a [ra'kitiko, a] adj stunted; (fig) poor, inadequate

raquitismo [raki'tismo] nm rickets sg

rareza [ra'reθa] nf rarity; (fig) eccentricity

raro, -a ['raro, a] adj (poco común) rare; (extraño) odd, strange; (excepcional) remarkable; **¡qué ~!** how (very) odd!; **¡(qué cosa más rara!** how strange!

ras [ras] nm: **a ~ de** level with; **a ~ de tierra** at ground level

rasar [ra'sar] vt to level

rascacielos [raska'θjelos] nm inv skyscraper

rascar [ras'kar] vt (con las uñas etc) to scratch; (raspar) to scrape; **rascarse** vr to scratch (o.s.)

rasgar [ras'ɣar] vt to tear, rip (up)

rasgo ['rasɣo] nm (con pluma) stroke; **rasgos** nmpl features, characteristics; **a grandes rasgos** in outline, broadly

rasgue etc ['rasɣe] vb ver **rasgar**

rasguear [rasɣe'ar] vt (Mus) to strum

rasguñar [rasɣu'ɲar] vt to scratch; (bosquejar) to sketch

rasguño [ras'ɣuɲo] nm scratch

raso, -a ['raso, a] adj (liso) flat, level; (a baja altura) very low ▪ nm satin; (campo llano) flat country; **cielo ~** clear sky; **al ~** in the open

raspado [ras'paðo] nm (Med) scrape

raspador [raspa'ðor] nm scraper

raspadura [raspa'ðura] nf (acto) scrape, scraping; (marca) scratch; **raspaduras** nfpl scrapings

raspar [ras'par] vt to scrape; (arañar) to scratch; (limar) to file ▪ vi (manos) to be rough; (vino) to be sharp, have a rough taste

rasque etc ['raske] vb ver **rascar**

rastra ['rastra] nf: **a rastras** by dragging; (fig) unwillingly

rastreador [rastrea'ðor] nm tracker; **~ de minas** minesweeper

rastrear [rastre'ar] vt (seguir) to track; (minas) to sweep

rastrero, -a [ras'trero, a] adj (Bot: Zool) creeping; (fig) despicable, mean

rastrillar [rastri'ʎar] vt to rake

rastrillo [ras'triʎo] nm rake; (Am) safety razor

rastro ['rastro] nm (Agr) rake; (pista) track, trail; (vestigio) trace; (mercado) flea market; **el R~** the Madrid flea market; **perder el ~** to lose the scent; **desaparecer sin ~** to vanish without trace

rastrojo [ras'troxo] nm stubble

rasurador [rasura'ðor] nm, **rasuradora** (Am) [rasura'ðora] ■ nf electric shaver o razor

rasurarse [rasu'rarse] vr to shave

rata ['rata] nf rat

ratear [rate'ar] vt (robar) to steal

ratero, -a [ra'tero, a] adj light-fingered ■ nm/f pickpocket; (Am: de casas) burglar

ratificar [ratifi'kar] vt to ratify

ratifique etc [rati'fike] vb ver **ratificar**

rato ['rato] nm while, short time; **a ratos** from time to time; **al poco ~** shortly after, soon afterwards; **ratos libres** o **de ocio** leisure sg, spare o free time sg; **hay para ~** there's still a long way to go; **pasar el ~** to kill time; **pasar un buen/mal ~** to have a good/rough time

ratón [ra'ton] nm (tb Inform) mouse

ratonera [rato'nera] nf mousetrap

RAU nf abr (= República Árabe Unida) UAR

raudal [rau'ðal] nm torrent; **a raudales** in abundance; **entrar a raudales** to pour in

raya ['raja] nf line; (marca) scratch; (en tela) stripe; (Tip) hyphen; (de pelo) parting; (límite) boundary; (pez) ray; **a rayas** striped; **pasarse de la ~** to overstep the mark; **tener a ~** to keep in check

rayado, -a [ra'jaðo, a] adj (papel) ruled; (tela, diseño) striped

rayar [ra'jar] vt to line; to scratch; (subrayar) to underline ■ vi: **~ en** o **con** to border on; **al ~ el alba** at first light; **~ a algn >** (col) to do sb's head in (col); **está siempre rayándome con esa historia** he's doing my head in with that business (col)

rayo ['rajo] nm (del sol) ray, beam; (de luz) shaft; (en una tormenta) (flash of) lightning; **~ solar** o **de sol** sunbeam; **rayos infrarrojos** infrared rays; **rayos X** X-rays; **como un ~** like a shot; **la noticia cayó como un ~** the news was a bombshell; **pasar como un ~** to flash past

raza ['raθa] nf race; (de animal) breed; **~ humana** human race; **de pura ~** (caballo) thoroughbred; (perro etc) pedigree

razón [ra'θon] nf reason; (justicia) right, justice; (razonamiento) reasoning; (motivo) reason, motive; (proporción) rate; (Mat) ratio; **a ~ de 10 cada día** at the rate of 10 a day; **"~: ..."** "inquiries to ..."; **en ~ de** with regard to; **perder la ~** to go out of one's mind; **dar ~ a** algn to agree that sb is right; **dar ~ de** to give an account of, report on; **tener/no tener ~** to be right/wrong; **~ directa/inversa** direct/inverse proportion; **~ de ser** raison d'être

razonable [raθo'naβle] adj reasonable; (justo, moderado) fair

razonado, -a [raθo'naðo, a] adj (Com: cuenta etc) itemized

razonamiento [raθona'mjento] nm (juicio) judgement; (argumento) reasoning

razonar [raθo'nar] vt, vi to reason, argue

RDA nf abr (Historia: = República Democrática Alemana) ver **república**

Rdo. abr (Rel: = Reverendo) Rev

RDSI nf abr (= Red Digital de Servicios Integrados) ISDN

re [re] nm (Mus) D

reabierto [rea'βjerto] pp de **reabrir**

reabrir [rea'βrir] vt, **reabrirse** vr to reopen

reacción [reak'θjon] nf reaction; **avión a ~** jet plane; **~ en cadena** chain reaction

reaccionar [reakθjo'nar] vi to react

reaccionario, -a [reakθjo'narjo, a] adj reactionary

reacio, -a [re'aθjo, a] adj stubborn; **ser** o **estar ~ a** to be opposed to

reactivar [reakti'βar] vt to reactivate; **reactivarse** vr (economía) to be on the upturn

reactor [reak'tor] nm reactor; (avión) jet plane; **~ nuclear** nuclear reactor

readaptación [reaðapta'θjon] nf: **~ profesional** industrial retraining

readmitir [reaðmi'tir] vt to readmit

reafirmar [reafir'mar] vt to reaffirm

reagrupar [reaɣru'par] vt to regroup

reajustar [reaxus'tar] vt (Inform) to reset

reajuste [rea'xuste] nm readjustment; **~ salarial** wage increase; **~ de plantilla** rationalization

real [re'al] adj real; (del rey, fig) royal; (espléndido) grand ■ nm (de feria) fairground; **la R~ Academia Española** see note

r

realce *etc* [re'alθe] *vb ver* **realzar** ▪ *nm* (*Tec*) embossing; **poner de ~** to emphasize

real-decreto [re'alde'kreto] (*pl* **reales-decretos**) *nm* royal decree

realeza [rea'leθa] *nf* royalty

realice *etc* [rea'liθe] *vb ver* **realizar**

realidad [reali'ðað] *nf* reality; (*verdad*) truth; **~ virtual** virtual reality; **en ~** in fact

realismo [rea'lismo] *nm* realism

realista [rea'lista] *nm/f* realist

realización [realiθa'θjon] *nf* fulfilment, realization; (*Com*) selling up (*Brit*), conversion into money (*US*); **~ de plusvalías** profit-taking

realizador, a [realiθa'ðor, a] *nm/f* (*TV etc*) producer

realizar [reali'θar] *vt* (*objetivo*) to achieve; (*plan*) to carry out; (*viaje*) to make, undertake; (*Com*) to realize; **realizarse** *vr* to come about, come true; **realizarse como persona** to fulfil one's aims in life

realmente [real'mente] *adv* really

realojar [realo'xar] *vt* to rehouse

realquilar [realki'lar] *vt* (*subarrendar*) to sublet; (*alquilar de nuevo*) to relet

realzar [real'θar] *vt* (*Tec*) to raise; (*embellecer*) to enhance; (*acentuar*) to highlight

reanimar [reani'mar] *vt* to revive; (*alentar*) to encourage; **reanimarse** *vr* to revive

reanudar [reanu'ðar] *vt* (*renovar*) to renew; (*historia, viaje*) to resume

reaparición [reapari'θjon] *nf* reappearance; (*vuelta*) return

reapertura [reaper'tura] *nf* reopening

rearme [re'arme] *nm* rearmament

reata [re'ata] *nf* (*Am*) lasso

reavivar [reaβi'βar] *vt* (*persona*) to revive; (*fig*) to rekindle

rebaja [re'βaxa] *nf* reduction, lowering; (*Com*) discount; **"grandes rebajas"** "big reductions", "sale"

rebajar [reβa'xar] *vt* (*bajar*) to lower; (*reducir*) to reduce; (*precio*) to cut; (*disminuir*) to lessen; (*humillar*) to humble; **rebajarse** *vr*: **rebajarse a hacer algo** to stoop to doing sth

rebanada [reβa'naða] *nf* slice

rebañar [reβa'ɲar] *vt* to scrape clean

rebaño [re'βaɲo] *nm* herd; (*de ovejas*) flock

rebasar [reβa'sar] *vt* (*tb*: **rebasar de**) to exceed; (*Auto*) to overtake

rebatir [reβa'tir] *vt* to refute; (*rebajar*) to reduce; (*ataque*) to repel

rebato [re'βato] *nm* alarm; (*ataque*) surprise attack; **llamar** *o* **tocar a ~** (*fig*) to sound the alarm

rebeca [re'βeka] *nf* cardigan

rebelarse [reβe'larse] *vr* to rebel, revolt

rebelde [re'βelde] *adj* rebellious; (*niño*) unruly ▪ *nm/f* rebel; **ser ~ a** to be in revolt against, rebel against

rebeldía [reβel'dia] *nf* rebelliousness; (*desobediencia*) disobedience; (*Jur*) default

rebelión [reβe'ljon] *nf* rebellion

rebenque [re'βenke] *nm* (*Am*) whip

reblandecer [reβlande'θer] *vt* to soften

reblandezca *etc* [reβlan'deθka] *vb ver* **reblandecer**

rebobinar [reβoβi'nar] *vt* to rewind

reboce *etc* [re'βoθe] *vb ver* **rebozar**

rebosante [reβo'sante] *adj*: **~ de** (*fig*) brimming *o* overflowing with

rebosar [reβo'sar] *vi* to overflow; (*abundar*) to abound, be plentiful; **~ de salud** to be bursting *o* brimming with health

rebotar [reβo'tar] *vt* to bounce; (*rechazar*) to repel

rebote [re'βote] *nm* rebound; **de ~** on the rebound

rebozado, -a [reβo'θaðo, a] *adj* (*Culin*) fried in batter *o* breadcrumbs *o* flour

rebozar [reβo'θar] *vt* to wrap up; (*Culin*) to fry in batter *etc*

rebozo [reβo'θo] *nm*: **sin ~** openly

rebuscado, -a [reβus'kaðo, a] *adj* affected

rebuscar [reβus'kar] *vi* (*en bolsillo, cajón*) to fish; (*en habitación*) to search high and low

rebuznar [reβuθ'nar] *vi* to bray

recabar [reka'βar] *vt* (*obtener*) to manage to get; **~ fondos** to collect money

recadero [reka'ðero] *nm* messenger

recado [re'kaðo] *nm* message; **dejar/tomar un ~** (*Telec*) to leave/take a message

recaer [reka'er] *vi* to relapse; **~ en** to fall to *o* on; (*criminal etc*) to fall back into, relapse into; (*premio*) to go to

recaída [reka'iða] *nf* relapse

recaiga *etc* [re'kaiɣa] *vb ver* **recaer**

recalcar [rekal'kar] *vt* (*fig*) to stress, emphasize

recalcitrante [rekalθi'trante] *adj* recalcitrant

recalentamiento [rekalenta'mjento] *nm*: **~ global** global warming

recalentar [rekalen'tar] *vt* (*comida*) to warm up, reheat; (*demasiado*) to overheat; **recalentarse** *vr* to overheat, get too hot

recaliente *etc* [reka'ljente] *vb ver* **recalentar**

recalque *etc* [re'kalke] *vb ver* **recalcar**

recámara [re'kamara] *nf* side room; (*Am*) bedroom

recamarera [rekama'rera] *nf* (*Am*) maid

recambio [re'kambjo] *nm* spare; (*de pluma*) refill; **piezas de ~** spares

recapacitar [rekapaθi'tar] *vi* to reflect

recapitular [rekapitu'lar] vt to recap

recargable [rekar'ɣaβle] adj (batería, pila) rechargeable; (mechero, pluma) refillable

recargado, -a [rekar'ɣaðo, a] adj overloaded; (exagerado) over-elaborate

recargar [rekar'ɣar] vt to overload; (batería) to recharge; (mechero, pluma) to refill; (tarjeta de móvil) to top up

recargo [re'karɣo] nm surcharge; (aumento) increase

recargue etc [re'karɣe] vb ver **recargar**

recatado, -a [reka'taðo, a] adj (modesto) modest, demure; (prudente) cautious

recato [re'kato] nm (modestia) modesty, demureness; (cautela) caution

recauchutado, -a [rekautʃu'taðo, a] adj remould cpd

recaudación [rekauða'θjon] nf (acción) collection; (cantidad) takings pl; (en deporte) gate; (oficina) tax office

recaudador, a [rekauða'ðor, a] nm/f tax collector

recaudar [rekau'ðar] vt to collect

recaudo [re'kauðo] nm: **estar a buen ~** to be in safekeeping; **poner algo a buen ~** to put sth in a safe place

recayendo etc [reka'jendo] vb ver **recaer**

rece etc ['reθe] vb ver **rezar**

recelar [reθe'lar] vt: **~ que** (sospechar) to suspect that; (temer) to fear that ■ vi: **~(se) de** to distrust

recelo [re'θelo] nm distrust, suspicion

receloso, -a [reθe'loso, a] adj distrustful, suspicious

recepción [reθep'θjon] nf reception; (acto de recibir) receipt

recepcionista [reθepθjo'nista] nm/f receptionist

receptáculo [reθep'takulo] nm receptacle

receptivo, -a [reθep'tiβo, a] adj receptive

receptor, a [reθep'tor, a] nm/f recipient ■ nm (Telec) receiver; **descolgar el ~** to pick up the receiver

recesión [reθe'sjon] nf (Com) recession

receta [re'θeta] nf (Culin) recipe; (Med) prescription

recetar [reθe'tar] vt to prescribe

rechace etc [re'tʃaθe] vb ver **rechazar**

rechazar [retʃa'θar] vt to repel, drive back; (idea) to reject; (oferta) to turn down

rechazo [re'tʃaθo] nm (de fusil) recoil; (rebote) rebound; (negación) rebuff

rechifla [re'tʃifla] nf hissing, booing; (fig) derision

rechinar [retʃi'nar] vi to creak; (dientes) to grind; (máquina) to clank, clatter; (metal seco) to grate; (motor) to hum

rechistar [retʃis'tar] vi: **sin ~** without complaint

rechoncho, -a [re'tʃontʃo, a] adj (fam) stocky, thickset (Brit), heavy-set (US)

rechupete [retʃu'pete]: **de ~** adj (comida) delicious

recibidor [reθiβi'ðor] nm entrance hall

recibimiento [reθiβi'mjento] nm reception, welcome

recibir [reθi'βir] vt to receive; (dar la bienvenida) to welcome; (salir al encuentro de) to go and meet ■ vi to entertain; **recibirse** vr: **recibirse de** to qualify as

recibo [re'θiβo] nm receipt; **acusar ~ de** to acknowledge receipt of

reciclable [reθi'klaβle] adj recyclable

reciclaje [reθi'klaxe] nm recycling; (de trabajadores) retraining; **cursos de ~** refresher courses

reciclar [reθi'klar] vt to recycle; (trabajador) to retrain

recién [re'θjen] adv recently, newly; (Am) just, recently; **~ casado** newly-wed; **el ~ llegado** the newcomer; **el ~ nacido** the newborn child; **~ a las seis** only at six o'clock

reciente [re'θjente] adj recent; (fresco) fresh

recientemente [reθjente'mente] adv recently

recinto [re'θinto] nm enclosure; (área) area, place

recio, -a ['reθjo, a] adj strong, tough; (voz) loud ■ adv hard; loud(ly)

recipiente [reθi'pjente] nm (objeto) container, receptacle; (persona) recipient

reciprocidad [reθiproθi'ðað] nf reciprocity

recíproco, -a [re'θiproco, a] adj reciprocal

recital [reθi'tal] nm (Mus) recital; (Lit) reading

recitar [reθi'tar] vt to recite

reclamación [reklama'θjon] nf claim, demand; (queja) complaint; **libro de reclamaciones** complaints book; **~ salarial** pay claim

reclamar [rekla'mar] vt to claim, demand ■ vi: **~ contra** to complain about; **~ a algn en justicia** to take sb to court

reclamo [re'klamo] nm (anuncio) advertisement; (tentación) attraction

reclinar [rekli'nar] vt to recline, lean; **reclinarse** vr to lean back

recluir [reklu'ir] vt to intern, confine

reclusión [reklu'sjon] nf (prisión) prison; (refugio) seclusion; **~ perpetua** life imprisonment

recluso, -a [re'kluso, a] adj imprisoned; **población reclusa** prison population ■ nm/f (solitario) recluse; (Jur) prisoner

recluta [re'kluta] nm/f recruit ■ nf recruitment

325

reclutamiento [rekluta'mjento] *nm* recruitment

recluyendo *etc* [reklu'jendo] *vb ver* **recluir**

recobrar [reko'βrar] *vt* (*recuperar*) to recover; (*rescatar*) to get back; (*ciudad*) to recapture; (*tiempo*) to make up (for); **recobrarse** *vr* to recover

recochineo [rekotʃi'neo] *nm* (*fam*) mickey-taking

recodo [re'koðo] *nm* (*de río, camino*) bend

recogedor, a [rekoxe'ðor, a] *nm/f* picker, harvester

recoger [reko'xer] *vt* to collect; (*Agr*) to harvest; (*fruta*) to pick; (*levantar*) to pick up; (*juntar*) to gather; (*pasar a buscar*) to come for, get; (*dar asilo*) to give shelter to; (*faldas*) to gather up; (*mangas*) to roll up; (*pelo*) to put up; **recogerse** *vr* (*retirarse*) to retire; **me recogieron en la estación** they picked me up at the station

recogido, -a [reko'xiðo, a] *adj* (*lugar*) quiet, secluded; (*pequeño*) small ■ *nf* (*Correos*) collection; (*Agr*) harvest; **recogida de datos** (*Inform*) data capture

recogimiento [rekoxi'mjento] *nm* collection; (*Agr*) harvesting

recoja *etc* [re'koxa] *vb ver* **recoger**

recolección [rekolek'θjon] *nf* (*Agr*) harvesting; (*colecta*) collection

recomencé [rekomen'θe], **recomencemos** *etc* [rekomen'θemos] *vb ver* **recomenzar**

recomendable [rekomen'daβle] *adj* recommendable; **poco ~** inadvisable

recomendación [rekomenda'θjon] *nf* (*sugerencia*) suggestion, recommendation; (*referencia*) reference; **carta de ~ para** letter of introduction to

recomendar [rekomen'dar] *vt* to suggest, recommend; (*confiar*) to entrust

recomenzar [rekomen'θar] *vt, vi* to begin again, recommence

recomience *etc* [reko'mjenθe] *vb ver* **recomenzar**

recomiende *etc* [reko'mjende] *vb ver* **recomendar**

recomienzo *etc* [reko'mjenθo] *vb ver* **recomenzar**

recompensa [rekom'pensa] *nf* reward, recompense; (*compensación*): **~ (de una pérdida)** compensation (for a loss); **como** *o* **en ~ por** in return for

recompensar [rekompen'sar] *vt* to reward, recompense

recompondré *etc* [rekompon'dre] *vb ver* **recomponer**

recomponer [rekompo'ner] *vt* to mend; (*Inform: texto*) to reformat

recomponga *etc* [rekom'ponga], **recompuesto** [rekom'pwesto], **recompuse** *etc* [rekom'puse] *vb ver* **recomponer**

reconciliación [rekonθilja'θjon] *nf* reconciliation

reconciliar [rekonθi'ljar] *vt* to reconcile; **reconciliarse** *vr* to become reconciled

recóndito, -a [re'kondito, a] *adj* (*lugar*) hidden, secret

reconfortar [rekonfor'tar] *vt* to comfort

reconocer [rekono'θer] *vt* to recognize; **~ los hechos** to face the facts

reconocido, -a [rekono'θiðo, a] *adj* recognized; (*agradecido*) grateful

reconocimiento [rekonoθi'mjento] *nm* recognition; (*registro*) search; (*inspección*) examination; (*gratitud*) gratitude; (*confesión*) admission; **~ óptico de caracteres** (*Inform*) optical character recognition; **~ de la voz** (*Inform*) speech recognition

reconozca *etc* [reko'noθka] *vb ver* **reconocer**

reconquista [rekon'kista] *nf* reconquest

reconquistar [rekonkis'tar] *vt* (*Mil*) to reconquer; (*fig*) to recover, win back

reconstituyente [rekonstitu'jente] *nm* tonic

reconstruir [rekonstru'ir] *vt* to reconstruct

reconstruyendo *etc* [rekonstru'jendo] *vb ver* **reconstruir**

reconversión [rekomber'sjon] *nf* restructuring, reorganization; (*tb:* **reconversión industrial**) rationalization

recopilación [rekopila'θjon] *nf* (*resumen*) summary; (*compilación*) compilation

recopilar [rekopi'lar] *vt* to compile

récord ['rekorð] *adj inv* record; **cifras ~** record figures ■ *nm* (*pl* **records** *o* **récords**) ['rekorð] record; **batir el ~** to break the record

recordar [rekor'ðar] *vt* (*acordarse de*) to remember; (*traer a la memoria*) to recall; (*recordar a otro*) to remind ■ *vi* to remember; **recuérdale que me debe cinco dólares** remind him that he owes me five dollars; **que yo recuerde** as far as I can remember; **creo ~, si mal no recuerdo** if my memory serves me right

recordatorio [rekorða'torjo] *nm* (*de fallecimiento*) in memoriam card; (*de bautizo, comunión*) commemorative card

recorrer [reko'rrer] *vt* (*país*) to cross, travel through; (*distancia*) to cover; (*registrar*) to search; (*repasar*) to look over

recorrido [reko'rriðo] *nm* run, journey; **tren de largo ~** main-line *o* inter-city (*Brit*) train

recortado, -a [rekor'taðo, a] *adj* uneven, irregular

recortar [rekor'tar] *vt* (*papel*) to cut out; (*el pelo*) to trim; (*dibujar*) to draw in outline;

recortarse vr to stand out, be silhouetted

recorte [re'korte] nm (acción, de prensa) cutting; (de telas, chapas) trimming; ~ **presupuestario** budget cut; ~ **salarial** wage cut

recostado, -a [rekos'taðo, a] adj leaning; **estar** ~ to be lying down

recostar [rekos'tar] vt to lean; **recostarse** vr to lie down

recoveco [reko'βeko] nm (de camino, río etc) bend; (en casa) cubbyhole

recreación [rekrea'θjon] nf recreation

recrear [rekre'ar] vt (entretener) to entertain; (volver a crear) to recreate

recreativo, -a [rekrea'tiβo, a] adj recreational

recreo [re'kreo] nm recreation; (Escol) break, playtime

recriminar [rekrimi'nar] vt to reproach ■ vi to recriminate; **recriminarse** vr to reproach each other

recrudecer [rekruðe'θer] vt, vi, **recrudecerse** vr to worsen

recrudecimiento [rekruðeθi'mjento] nm upsurge

recrudezca etc [rekru'ðeθka] vb ver **recrudecer**

recta ['rekta] nf ver **recto**

rectangular [rektangu'lar] adj rectangular

rectángulo, -a [rek'tangulo, a] adj rectangular ■ nm rectangle

rectificable [rektifi'kaβle] adj rectifiable; **fácilmente** ~ easily rectified

rectificación [rektifika'θjon] nf correction

rectificar [rektifi'kar] vt to rectify; (volverse recto) to straighten ■ vi to correct o.s.

rectifique etc [rekti'fike] vb ver **rectificar**

rectitud [rekti'tuð] nf straightness; (fig) rectitude

recto, -a ['rekto, a] adj straight; (persona) honest, upright; (estricto) strict; (juez) fair; (juicio) sound ■ nm rectum; (Atletismo) straight ■ nf straight line; **en el sentido** ~ **de la palabra** in the proper sense of the word; **recta final** o **de llegada** home straight

rector, a [rek'tor, a] adj governing ■ nm/f head, chief; (Escol) rector, president (US)

rectorado [rekto'raðo] nm (cargo) rectorship, presidency (US); (oficina) rector's office

recuadro [re'kwaðro] nm box; (Tip) inset

recubrir [reku'βir] vt to cover

recuento [re'kwento] nm inventory; **hacer el** ~ **de** to count o reckon up

recuerdo etc [re'kwerðo] vb ver **recordar** ■ nm souvenir; **recuerdos** nmpl memories; **¡~s a tu madre!** give my regards to your mother!;

"R~ de Mallorca" "a present from Majorca"; **contar los ~s** to reminisce

recueste etc [re'kweste] vb ver **recostar**

recular [reku'lar] vi to back down

recuperable [rekupe'raβle] adj recoverable

recuperación [rekupera'θjon] nf recovery; ~ **de datos** (Inform) data retrieval

recuperar [rekupe'rar] vt to recover; (tiempo) to make up; (Inform) to retrieve; **recuperarse** vr to recuperate

recurrir [reku'rrir] vi (Jur) to appeal; ~ **a** to resort to; (persona) to turn to

recurso [re'kurso] nm resort; (medio) means pl, resource; (Jur) appeal; **como último** ~ as a last resort; **recursos económicos** economic resources; **recursos naturales** natural resources

recusar [reku'sar] vt to reject, refuse

red [reð] nf net, mesh; (Ferro: Inform) network; (Elec, de agua) mains, supply system; (de tiendas) chain; (trampa) trap; **la R~** (Internet) the Net; **estar conectado con la** ~ to be connected to the mains; ~ **local** (Inform) local area network; ~ **de transmisión** (Inform) data network

redacción [reðak'θjon] nf (acción) writing; (Escol) essay, composition; (limpieza de texto) editing; (personal) editorial staff

redactar [reðak'tar] vt to draw up, draft; (periódico, Inform) to edit

redactor, a [reðak'tor, a] nm/f writer; (en periódico) editor

redada [re'ðaða] nf (Pesca) cast, throw; (fig) catch; ~ **policial** police raid, round-up

redención [reðen'θjon] nf redemption

redentor, a [reðen'tor, a] adj redeeming ■ nm/f (Com) redeemer

redescubierto [reðesku'βjerto] pp de **redescubrir**

redescubrir [reðesku'βrir] vt to rediscover

redesignar [reðesiɣ'nar] vt (Inform) to rename

redicho, -a [re'ðitʃo, a] adj affected

redil [re'ðil] nm sheepfold

redimir [reði'mir] vt to redeem; (rehén) to ransom

redistribución [reðistriβu'θjon] nf (Com) redeployment

rédito ['reðito] nm interest, yield

redoblar [reðo'βlar] vt to redouble ■ vi (tambor) to play a roll on the drums

redoble [re'ðoβle] nm (Mus) drumroll, drumbeat; (de trueno) roll

redomado, -a [reðo'maðo, a] adj (astuto) sly, crafty; (perfecto) utter

redonda [re'ðonda] nf ver **redondo**

redondear [reðonde'ar] vt to round, round off; (cifra) to round up

redondel [reðon'del] *nm* (*círculo*) circle; (*Taur*) bullring, arena; (*Auto*) roundabout

redondo, -a [re'ðondo, a] *adj* (*circular*) round; (*completo*) complete ■ *nf*: **a la redonda** around, round about; **en muchas millas a la redonda** for many miles around; **rehusar en ~** to give a flat refusal

reducción [reðuk'θjon] *nf* reduction; **~ del activo** (*Com*) divestment; **~ de precios** (*Com*) price-cutting

reducido, -a [reðu'θiðo, a] *adj* reduced; (*limitado*) limited; (*pequeño*) small; **quedar ~ a** to be reduced to

reducir [reðu'θir] *vt* to reduce, limit; (*someter*) to bring under control; **reducirse** *vr* to diminish; (*Mat*): **~ (a)** to reduce (to), convert (into); **~ las millas a kilómetros** to convert miles into kilometres; **reducirse a** (*fig*) to come o boil down to

reducto [re'ðukto] *nm* redoubt

reduje *etc* [re'ðuxe] *vb ver* **reducir**

redundancia [reðun'danθja] *nf* redundancy

reduzca *etc* [re'ðuθka] *vb ver* **reducir**

reedición [re(e)ði'θjon] *nf* reissue

reeditar [re(e)ði'tar] *vt* to reissue

reelección [re(e)lek'θjon] *nf* re-election

reelegir [re(e)le'xir] *vt* to re-elect

reembolsable [re(e)mbol'saβle] *adj* (*Com*) redeemable, refundable

reembolsar [re(e)mbol'sar] *vt* (*persona*) to reimburse; (*dinero*) to repay, pay back; (*depósito*) to refund

reembolso [re(e)m'bolso] *nm* reimbursement; refund; **enviar algo contra ~** to send sth cash on delivery; **contra ~ del flete** freight forward; **~ fiscal** tax rebate

reemplace *etc* [re(e)m'plaθe] *vb ver* **reemplazar**

reemplazar [re(e)mpla'θar] *vt* to replace

reemplazo [re(e)m'plaθo] *nm* replacement; **de ~** (*Mil*) reserve

reencuentro [re(e)n'kwentro] *nm* reunion

reengancharse [re(e)ngan'tʃarse] *vr* (*Mil*) to re-enlist

reestreno [re(e)s'treno] *nm* rerun

reestructurar [re(e)struktu'rar] *vt* to restructure

reexportación [re(e)ksporta'θjon] *nf* (*Com*) re-export

reexportar [re(e)kspor'tar] *vt* (*Com*) to re-export

REF *nm abr* (*Esp Econ*) = **Régimen Económico Fiscal**

Ref.ª *abr* (= *referencia*) ref

refacción [refak'θjon] *nf* (*Am*) repair(s); **refacciones** *nfpl* (*piezas de repuesto*) spare parts

referencia [refe'renθja] *nf* reference; **con ~ a** with reference to; **hacer ~ a** to refer o allude to; **~ comercial** (*Com*) trade reference

referéndum [refe'rendum] (*pl* **referéndums**) *nm* referendum

referente [refe'rente] *adj*: **~ a** concerning, relating to

referir [refe'rir] *vt* (*contar*) to tell, recount; (*relacionar*) to refer, relate; **referirse** *vr*: **referirse a** to refer to; **~ al lector a un apéndice** to refer the reader to an appendix; **~ a** (*Com*) to convert into; **por lo que se refiere a eso** as for that, as regards that

refiera *etc* [re'fjera] *vb ver* **referir**

refilón [refi'lon]: **de ~** *adv* obliquely; **mirar a algn de ~** to look out of the corner of one's eye at sb

refinado, -a [refi'naðo, a] *adj* refined

refinamiento [refina'mjento] *nm* refinement; **~ por pasos** (*Inform*) stepwise refinement

refinar [refi'nar] *vt* to refine

refinería [refine'ria] *nf* refinery

refiriendo *etc* [refi'rjendo] *vb ver* **referir**

reflector [reflek'tor] *nm* reflector; (*Elec*) spotlight; (*Aviat: Mil*) searchlight

reflejar [refle'xar] *vt* to reflect; **reflejarse** *vr* to be reflected

reflejo, -a [re'flexo, a] *adj* reflected; (*movimiento*) reflex ■ *nm* reflection; (*Anat*) reflex; (*en el pelo*): **reflejos** *nmpl* highlights; **tiene el pelo castaño con reflejos rubios** she has chestnut hair with blond streaks

reflexión [reflek'sjon] *nf* reflection

reflexionar [refleksjo'nar] *vt* to reflect on ■ *vi* to reflect; (*detenerse*) to pause (to think); **¡reflexione!** you think it over!

reflexivo, -a [reflek'siβo, a] *adj* thoughtful; (*Ling*) reflexive

refluir [reflu'ir] *vi* to flow back

reflujo [re'fluxo] *nm* ebb

refluyendo *etc* [reflu'jendo] *vb ver* **refluir**

reforcé [refor'θe], **reforcemos** *etc* [refor'θemos] *vb ver* **reforzar**

reforma [re'forma] *nf* reform; (*Arq etc*) repair; **~ agraria** agrarian reform

reformar [refor'mar] *vt* to reform; (*modificar*) to change, alter; (*texto*) to revise; (*Arq*) to repair; **reformarse** *vr* to mend one's ways

reformatear [reformate'ar] *vt* (*Inform: disco*) to reformat

reformatorio [reforma'torjo] *nm* reformatory; **~ de menores** remand home

reformista [refor'mista] *adj, nm/f* reformist

reforzamiento [reforθa'mjento] *nm* reinforcement

reforzar [refor'θar] *vt* to strengthen; (*Arq*) to reinforce; (*fig*) to encourage

refractario, -a [refrak'tarjo, a] *adj* (*Tec*) heat-resistant; **ser ~ a una reforma** to resist o be opposed to a reform
refrán [re'fran] *nm* proverb, saying
refregar [refre'ɣar] *vt* to scrub
refrenar [refre'nar] *vt* to check, restrain
refrendar [refren'dar] *vt* (*firma*) to endorse, countersign; (*ley*) to approve
refrescante [refres'kante] *adj* refreshing, cooling
refrescar [refres'kar] *vt* to refresh ▪ *vi* to cool down; **refrescarse** *vr* to get cooler; (*tomar aire fresco*) to go out for a breath of fresh air; (*beber*) to have a drink
refresco [re'fresko] *nm* soft drink, cool drink; **"refrescos"** "refreshments"
refresque etc [re'freske] *vb ver* **refrescar**
refriega etc [re'frjeɣa] *vb ver* **refregar** ▪ *nf* scuffle, brawl
refriegue etc [re'frjeɣe] *vb ver* **refregar**
refrigeración [refrixera'θjon] *nf* refrigeration; (*de casa*) air-conditioning
refrigerado, -a [refrixe'raðo, a] *adj* cooled; (*sala*) air-conditioned
refrigerador [refrixera'ðor] *nm*, **refrigeradora** (*Am*) [refrixera'ðora] ▪ *nf* refrigerator, icebox (*US*)
refrigerar [refrixe'rar] *vt* to refrigerate; (*sala*) to air-condition
refrito [re'frito] *nm* (*Culin*): **un ~ de cebolla y tomate** sautéed onions and tomatoes; **un ~** (*fig*) a rehash
refuerce etc [re'fwerθe] *vb ver* **reforzar**
refuerzo etc [re'fwerθo] *vb ver* **reforzar** ▪ *nm* reinforcement; (*Tec*) support
refugiado, -a [refu'xjaðo, a] *nm/f* refugee
refugiarse [refu'xjarse] *vr* to take refuge, shelter
refugio [re'fuxjo] *nm* refuge; (*protección*) shelter; (*Auto*) street o traffic island; **~ alpino** o **de montaña** mountain hut; **~ subterráneo** (*Mil*) underground shelter
refulgencia [reful'xenθja] *nf* brilliance
refulgir [reful'xir] *vi* to shine, be dazzling
refulja etc [re'fulxa] *vb ver* **refulgir**
refundir [refun'dir] *vt* to recast; (*escrito etc*) to adapt, rewrite
refunfuñar [refunfu'ɲar] *vi* to grunt, growl; (*quejarse*) to grumble
refunfuñón, -ona [refunfu'ɲon, ona] (*fam*) *adj* grumpy ▪ *nm/f* grouch
refutación [refuta'θjon] *nf* refutation
refutar [refu'tar] *vt* to refute
regadera [reɣa'ðera] *nf* watering can; (*Am*) shower; **estar como una ~** (*fam*) to be as mad as a hatter
regadío [reɣa'ðio] *nm* irrigated land

regalado, -a [reɣa'laðo, a] *adj* comfortable, luxurious; (*gratis*) free, for nothing; **lo tuvo ~** it was handed to him on a plate
regalar [reɣa'lar] *vt* (*dar*) to give (as a present); (*entregar*) to give away; (*mimar*) to pamper, make a fuss of; **regalarse** *vr* to treat o.s. to
regalía [reɣa'lia] *nf* privilege, prerogative; (*Com*) bonus; (*de autor*) royalty
regaliz [reɣa'liθ] *nm* liquorice
regalo [re'ɣalo] *nm* (*obsequio*) gift, present; (*gusto*) pleasure; (*comodidad*) comfort
regañadientes [reɣaɲa'ðjentes]: **a ~** *adv* reluctantly
regañar [reɣa'ɲar] *vt* to scold ▪ *vi* to grumble; (*dos personas*) to fall out, quarrel
regañón, -ona [reɣa'ɲon, ona] *adj* nagging
regar [re'ɣar] *vt* to water, irrigate; (*fig*) to scatter, sprinkle
regata [re'ɣata] *nf* (*Naut*) race
regatear [reɣate'ar] *vt* (*Com*) to bargain over; (*escatimar*) to be mean with ▪ *vi* to bargain, haggle; (*Deporte*) to dribble; **no ~ esfuerzo** to spare no effort
regateo [reɣa'teo] *nm* bargaining; (*Deporte*) dribbling; (*con el cuerpo*) swerve, dodge
regazo [re'ɣaθo] *nm* lap
regencia [re'xenθja] *nf* regency
regeneración [rexenera'θjon] *nf* regeneration
regenerar [rexene'rar] *vt* to regenerate
regentar [rexen'tar] *vt* to direct, manage; (*puesto*) to hold in an acting capacity; (*negocio*) to be in charge of
regente, -a [re'xente, a] *adj* (*príncipe*) regent; (*director*) managing ▪ *nm* (*Com*) manager; (*Pol*) regent
régimen ['reximen] (*pl* **regímenes**) [re'ximenes] *nm* regime; (*reinado*) rule; (*Med*) diet; (*reglas*) (set of) rules *pl*; (*manera de vivir*) lifestyle; **estar a ~** to be on a diet
regimiento [rexi'mjento] *nm* regiment
regio, -a ['rexjo, a] *adj* royal, regal; (*fig: suntuoso*) splendid; (*Am fam*) great, terrific
región [re'xjon] *nf* region; (*área*) area
regional [rexjo'nal] *adj* regional
regir [re'xir] *vt* to govern, rule; (*dirigir*) to manage, run; (*Econ: Jur: Ling*) to govern ▪ *vi* to apply, be in force
registrador [rexistra'ðor] *nm* registrar, recorder
registrar [rexis'trar] *vt* (*buscar*) to search; (*en cajón*) to look through; (*inspeccionar*) to inspect; (*anotar*) to register, record; (*Inform: Mus*) to record; **registrarse** *vr* to register; (*ocurrir*) to happen
registro [re'xistro] *nm* (*acto*) registration;

(*Mus, libro*) register; (*lista*) list, record; (*Inform*) record; (*inspección*) inspection, search; **~ civil** registry office; **~ electoral** voting register; **~ de la propiedad** land registry (office)

regla ['reɣla] *nf* (*ley*) rule, regulation; (*de medir*) ruler, rule; (*Med: período*) period; (*regla científica*) law, principle; **no hay ~ sin excepción** every rule has its exception

reglamentación [reɣlamenta'θjon] *nf* (*acto*) regulation; (*lista*) rules *pl*

reglamentar [reɣlamen'tar] *vt* to regulate

reglamentario, -a [reɣlamen'tarjo, a] *adj* statutory; **en la forma reglamentaria** in the properly established way

reglamento [reɣla'mento] *nm* rules *pl*, regulations *pl*; **~ del tráfico** highway code

reglar [re'ɣlar] *vt* (*acciones*) to regulate; **reglarse** *vr*: **reglarse por** to be guided by

regocijarse [reɣoθi'xarse] *vr*: **~ de** *o* **por** to rejoice at, be glad about

regocijo [reɣo'θixo] *nm* joy, happiness

regodearse [reɣoðe'arse] *vr* to be glad, be delighted; (*pey*): **~ con** *o* **en** to gloat over

regodeo [reɣo'ðeo] *nm* delight; (*pey*) perverse pleasure

regresar [reɣre'sar] *vi* to come/go back, return; **regresarse** *vr* (*Am*) to return

regresivo, -a [reɣre'siβo, a] *adj* backward; (*fig*) regressive

regreso [re'ɣreso] *nm* return; **estar de ~** to be back, be home

regué [re'ɣe], **reguemos** *etc* [re'ɣemos] *vb ver* **regar**

reguero [re'ɣero] *nm* (*de sangre*) trickle; (*de humo*) trail

regulación [reɣula'θjon] *nf* regulation; (*Tec*) adjustment; (*control*) control; **~ de empleo** redundancies *pl*; **~ del tráfico** traffic control

regulador [reɣula'ðor] *nm* (*Tec*) regulator; (*de radio etc*) knob, control

regular [reɣu'lar] *adj* regular; (*normal*) normal, usual; (*común*) ordinary; (*organizado*) regular, orderly; (*mediano*) average; (*fam*) not bad, so-so ■ *adv*: **estar ~** to be so-so *o* alright ■ *vt* (*controlar*) to control, regulate; (*Tec*) to adjust; **por lo ~** as a rule

regularice *etc* [reɣula'riθe] *vb ver* **regularizar**

regularidad [reɣulari'ðað] *nf* regularity; **con ~** regularly

regularizar [reɣulari'θar] *vt* to regularize

regusto [re'ɣusto] *nm* aftertaste

rehabilitación [reaβilita'θjon] *nf* rehabilitation; (*Arq*) restoration

rehabilitar [reaβili'tar] *vt* to rehabilitate; (*Arq*) to restore; (*reintegrar*) to reinstate

rehacer [rea'θer] *vt* (*reparar*) to mend, repair; (*volver a hacer*) to redo, repeat; **rehacerse** *vr*

(*Med*) to recover

rehaga *etc* [re'aɣa], **reharé** *etc* [rea're], **rehaz** [re'aθ], **rehecho** [re'etʃo] *vb ver* **rehacer**

rehén [re'en] *nm/f* hostage

rehice *etc* [re'iθe], **rehizo** [re'iθo] *vb ver* **rehacer**

rehogar [reo'ɣar] *vt* to sauté, toss in oil

rehuir [reu'ir] *vt* to avoid, shun

rehusar [reu'sar] *vt, vi* to refuse

rehuyendo *etc* [reu'jendo] *vb ver* **rehuir**

reina ['reina] *nf* queen

reinado [rei'naðo] *nm* reign

reinante [rei'nante] *adj* (*fig*) prevailing

reinar [rei'nar] *vi* to reign; (*fig: prevalecer*) to prevail, be general

reincidir [reinθi'ðir] *vi* to relapse; (*criminal*) to repeat an offence

reincorporarse [reinkorpo'rarse] *vr*: **~ a** to rejoin

reinicializar [reiniθjali'θar] *vt* (*Inform*) to reset

reino ['reino] *nm* kingdom; **el R~ Unido** the United Kingdom

reinserción [reinser'θjon] *nf* rehabilitation

reinsertar [reinser'tar] *vt* to rehabilitate

reintegración [reinteɣra'θjon] *nf* (*Com*) reinstatement

reintegrar [reinte'ɣrar] *vt* (*reconstituir*) to reconstruct; (*persona*) to reinstate; (*dinero*) to refund, pay back; **reintegrarse** *vr*: **reintegrarse a** to return to

reintegro [rein'teɣro] *nm* refund, reimbursement; (*en banco*) withdrawal

reír [re'ir] *vi*, **reírse** *vr* to laugh; **reírse de** to laugh at

reiterado, -a [reite'raðo, a] *adj* repeated

reiterar [reite'rar] *vt* to reiterate; (*repetir*) to repeat

reivindicación [reiβindika'θjon] *nf* (*demanda*) claim, demand; (*justificación*) vindication

reivindicar [reiβindi'kar] *vt* to claim

reivindique *etc* [reiβin'dike] *vb ver* **reivindicar**

reja ['rexa] *nf* (*de ventana*) grille, bars *pl*; (*en la calle*) grating

rejilla [re'xiʎa] *nf* grating, grille; (*muebles*) wickerwork; (*de ventilación*) vent; (*de coche etc*) luggage rack

rejuvenecer [rexuβene'θer] *vt, vi* to rejuvenate

rejuvenezca *etc* [rexuβe'neθka] *vb ver* **rejuvenecer**

relación [rela'θjon] *nf* relation, relationship; (*Mat*) ratio; (*lista*) list; (*narración*) report; **~ costo-efectivo** *o* **costo-rendimiento** (*Com*) cost-effectiveness; **relaciones** *nfpl* (*enchufes*) influential friends, connections; **relaciones carnales** sexual relations; **relaciones**

comerciales business connections;
relaciones empresariales/humanas
industrial/human relations; **relaciones**
laborales/públicas labour/public relations;
con ~ a, en ~ con in relation to; **estar en** *o*
tener buenas relaciones con to be on good
terms with

relacionar [relaθjo'nar] *vt* to relate, connect;
relacionarse *vr* to be connected *o* linked

relajación [relaxa'θjon] *nf* relaxation

relajado, -a [rela'xaðo, a] *adj* (*disoluto*) loose;
(*cómodo*) relaxed; (*Med*) ruptured

relajante [rela'xante] *adj* relaxing; (*Med*)
sedative

relajar [rela'xar] *vt*, **relajarse** *vr* to relax

relamerse [rela'merse] *vr* to lick one's lips

relamido, -a [rela'miðo, a] *adj* (*pulcro*)
overdressed; (*afectado*) affected

relámpago [re'lampaɣo] *nm* flash of
lightning ■ *adj* lightning *cpd*; **como un ~** as
quick as lightning, in a flash; **visita/huelga**
~ lightning visit/strike

relampaguear [relampaɣe'ar] *vi* to flash

relanzar [relan'θar] *vt* to relaunch

relatar [rela'tar] *vt* to tell, relate

relatividad [relatiβi'ðað] *nf* relativity

relativo, -a [rela'tiβo, a] *adj* relative; **en lo ~**
a concerning

relato [re'lato] *nm* (*narración*) story, tale

relax [re'las] *nm* rest; **"R~"** (*en anuncio*)
"Personal services"

relegar [rele'ɣar] *vt* to relegate; **~ algo al**
olvido to banish sth from one's mind

relegue *etc* [re'leɣe] *vb ver* **relegar**

relevante [rele'βante] *adj* eminent,
outstanding

relevar [rele'βar] *vt* (*sustituir*) to relieve;
relevarse *vr* to relay; **~ a algn de un cargo**
to relieve sb of his post

relevo [re'leβo] *nm* relief; **carrera de relevos**
relay race; **coger** *o* **tomar el ~** to take over,
stand in

relieve [re'ljeβe] *nm* (*Arte: Tec*) relief; (*fig*)
prominence, importance; **bajo ~** bas-relief;
un personaje de ~ an important man; **dar ~**
a to highlight

religión [reli'xjon] *nf* religion

religioso, -a [reli'xjoso, a] *adj* religious
■ *nm/f* monk/nun

relinchar [relin'tʃar] *vi* to neigh

relincho [re'lintʃo] *nm* neigh; (*acto*) neighing

reliquia [re'likja] *nf* relic; **~ de familia**
heirloom

rellano [re'ʎano] *nm* (*Arq*) landing

rellenar [reʎe'nar] *vt* (*llenar*) to fill up; (*Culin*)
to stuff; (*Costura*) to pad; (*formulario etc*) to fill
in *o* out

relleno, -a [re'ʎeno, a] *adj* full up; (*Culin*)
stuffed ■ *nm* stuffing; (*de tapicería*) padding

reloj [re'lo(x)] *nm* clock; **~ de pie** grandfather
clock; **~ (de pulsera)** wristwatch; **~ de sol**
sundial; **~ despertador** alarm (clock); **como**
un ~ like clockwork; **contra (el) ~** against
the clock

relojería [reloxe'ria] (*tienda*) watchmaker's
(shop); **aparato de ~** clockwork; **bomba de**
~ time bomb

relojero, -a [relo'xero, a] *nm/f* clockmaker;
watchmaker

reluciente [relu'θjente] *adj* brilliant, shining

relucir [relu'θir] *vi* to shine; (*fig*) to excel;
sacar algo a ~ to show sth off

relumbrante [relum'brante] *adj* dazzling

relumbrar [relum'brar] *vi* to dazzle, shine
brilliantly

reluzca *etc* [re'luθka] *vb ver* **relucir**

remachar [rema'tʃar] *vt* to rivet; (*fig*) to
hammer home, drive home

remache [re'matʃe] *nm* rivet

remanente [rema'nente] *nm* remainder;
(*Com*) balance; (*de producto*) surplus

remangarse [reman'garse] *vr* to roll one's
sleeves up

remanso [re'manso] *nm* pool

remar [re'mar] *vi* to row

rematado, -a [rema'taðo, a] *adj* complete,
utter; **es un loco ~** he's a raving lunatic

rematar [rema'tar] *vt* to finish off; (*animal*) to
put out of its misery; (*Com*) to sell off cheap
■ *vi* to end, finish off; (*Deporte*) to shoot

remate [re'mate] *nm* end, finish; (*punta*) tip;
(*Deporte*) shot; (*Arq*) top; (*Com*) auction sale;
de *o* **para ~** to crown it all (*Brit*), to top it off

remediable [reme'ðjaβle] *adj*: **fácilmente ~**
easily remedied

remediar [reme'ðjar] *vt* (*gen*) to remedy;
(*subsanar*) to make good, repair; (*evitar*) to
avoid; **sin poder remediarlo** without being
able to prevent it

remedio [re'meðjo] *nm* remedy; (*Jur*)
recourse, remedy; **poner ~ a** to correct, stop;
no tener más ~ to have no alternative; **¡qué**
~! there's no other way; **como último ~** as a
last resort; **sin ~** inevitable; (*Med*) hopeless

remedo [re'meðo] *nm* imitation; (*pey*) parody

remendar [remen'dar] *vt* to repair; (*con*
parche) to patch; (*fig*) to correct

remesa [re'mesa] *nf* remittance; (*Com*)
shipment

remiendo *etc* [re'mjendo] *vb ver* **remendar**
■ *nm* mend; (*con parche*) patch; (*cosido*) darn;
(*fig*) correction

remilgado, -a [remil'ɣaðo, a] *adj* prim;
(*afectado*) affected

remilgo [re'milɣo] *nm* primness; *(afectación)* affectation

reminiscencia [reminis'θenθja] *nf* reminiscence

remirar [remi'rar] *vt (volver a mirar)* to look at again; *(examinar)* to look hard at

remisión [remi'sjon] *nf (acto)* sending, shipment; *(Rel)* forgiveness, remission; **sin ~** hopelessly

remiso, -a [re'miso, a] *adj* remiss

remite [re'mite] *nm (en sobre)* name and address of sender

remitente [remi'tente] *nm/f (Correos)* sender

remitir [remi'tir] *vt* to remit, send ■ *vi* to slacken

remo ['remo] *nm (de barco)* oar; *(Deporte)* rowing; **cruzar un río a ~** to row across a river

remoce *etc* [re'moθe] *vb ver* **remozar**

remodelación [remodela'θjon] *nf (Pol)*: **~ del gobierno** cabinet reshuffle

remojar [remo'xar] *vt* to steep, soak; *(galleta etc)* to dip, dunk; *(fam)* to celebrate with a drink

remojo [re'moxo] *nm* steeping, soaking; *(por la lluvia)* drenching, soaking; **dejar la ropa en ~** to leave clothes to soak

remojón [remo'xon] *nm* soaking; **darse un ~** *(fam)* to go (in) for a dip

remolacha [remo'latʃa] *nf* beet, beetroot *(Brit)*

remolcador [remolka'ðor] *nm (Naut)* tug; *(Auto)* breakdown lorry

remolcar [remol'kar] *vt* to tow

remolino [remo'lino] *nm* eddy; *(de agua)* whirlpool; *(de viento)* whirlwind; *(de gente)* crowd

remolón, -ona [remo'lon, ona] *adj* lazy ■ *nm/f* slacker, shirker

remolque *etc* [re'molke] *vb ver* **remolcar** ■ *nm* tow, towing; *(cuerda)* towrope; **llevar a ~** to tow

remontar [remon'tar] *vt* to mend; *(obstáculo)* to negotiate, get over; **remontarse** *vr* to soar; **remontarse a** *(Com)* to amount to; *(en tiempo)* to go back to, date from; **~ el vuelo** to soar

rémora ['remora] *nf* hindrance

remorder [remor'ðer] *vt* to distress, disturb

remordimiento [remorði'mjento] *nm* remorse

remotamente [remota'mente] *adv* vaguely

remoto, -a [re'moto, a] *adj* remote

remover [remo'βer] *vt* to stir; *(tierra)* to turn over; *(objetos)* to move round

remozar [remo'θar] *vt (Arq)* to refurbish; *(fig)* to brighten *o* polish up

remuerda *etc* [re'mwerða] *vb ver* **remorder**

remueva *etc* [re'mweβa] *vb ver* **remover**

remuneración [remunera'θjon] *nf* remuneration

remunerado, -a [remune'raðo, a] *adj*: **trabajo bien/mal ~** well-/badly-paid job

remunerar [remune'rar] *vt* to remunerate; *(premiar)* to reward

renacer [rena'θer] *vi* to be reborn; *(fig)* to revive

renacimiento [renaθi'mjento] *nm* rebirth; **el R~** the Renaissance

renacuajo [rena'kwaxo] *nm (Zool)* tadpole

renal [re'nal] *adj* renal, kidney *cpd*

Renania [re'nanja] *nf* Rhineland

renazca *etc* [re'naθka] *vb ver* **renacer**

rencilla [ren'θiʎa] *nf* quarrel; **rencillas** *nfpl* bickering *sg*

rencor [ren'kor] *nm* rancour, bitterness; *(resentimiento)* ill feeling, resentment; **guardar ~ a** to have a grudge against

rencoroso, -a [renko'roso, a] *adj* spiteful

rendición [rendi'θjon] *nf* surrender

rendido, -a [ren'diðo, a] *adj (sumiso)* submissive; *(agotado)* worn-out, exhausted; *(enamorado)* devoted

rendija [ren'dixa] *nf (hendidura)* crack; *(abertura)* aperture; *(fig)* rift, split; *(Jur)* loophole

rendimiento [rendi'mjento] *nm (producción)* output; *(Com)* yield, profit(s) *(pl)*; *(Tec: Com)* efficiency; **~ de capital** *(Com)* return on capital

rendir [ren'dir] *vt (vencer)* to defeat; *(producir)* to produce; *(dar beneficio)* to yield; *(agotar)* to exhaust ■ *vi* to pay; *(Com)* to yield, produce; **rendirse** *vr (someterse)* to surrender; *(ceder)* to yield; *(cansarse)* to wear o.s. out; **~ homenaje** *o* **culto a** to pay homage to; **el negocio no rinde** the business doesn't pay

renegado, -a [rene'ɣaðo, a] *adj, nm/f* renegade

renegar [rene'ɣar] *vt (negar)* to deny vigorously ■ *vi (blasfemar)* to blaspheme; **~ de** *(renunciar)* to renounce; *(quejarse)* to complain about

renegué [rene'ɣe], **reneguemos** *etc* [rene'ɣemos] *vb ver* **renegar**

RENFE ['renfe] *nf abr (Esp: Ferro)* = **Red Nacional de Ferrocarriles Españoles**

renglón [ren'glon] *nm (línea)* line; *(Com)* item, article; **a ~ seguido** immediately after

rengo, -a ['rengo, a] *adj (Am)* lame

reniego *etc* [re'njeɣo], **reniegue** *etc* [re'njeɣe] *vb ver* **renegar**

reno ['reno] *nm* reindeer

renombrado, -a [renom'braðo, a] *adj* renowned

renombre [re'nombre] *nm* renown

renovable [reno'βaβle] *adj* renewable

renovación [renoβa'θjon] *nf* (*de contrato*) renewal; (*Arq*) renovation

renovar [reno'βar] *vt* to renew; (*Arq*) to renovate; (*sala*) to redecorate

renquear [renke'ar] *vi* to limp; (*fam*) to get along, scrape by

renta ['renta] *nf* (*ingresos*) income; (*beneficio*) profit; (*alquiler*) rent; **~ gravable** *o* **imponible** taxable income; **~ nacional (bruta)** (gross) national income; **~ no salarial** unearned income; **~ sobre el terreno** (*Com*) ground rent; **~ vitalicia** annuity; **política de rentas** incomes policy; **vivir de sus rentas** to live on one's private income

rentabilizar [rentaβili'θar] *vt* to make profitable

rentable [ren'taβle] *adj* profitable; **no ~** unprofitable

rentar [ren'tar] *vt* to produce, yield; (*Am*) to rent

rentista [ren'tista] *nm/f* (*accionista*) shareholder (*Brit*), stockholder (*US*)

renuencia [re'nwenθja] *nf* reluctance

renuente [re'nwente] *adj* reluctant

renueve *etc* [re'nweβe] *vb ver* **renovar**

renuncia [re'nunθja] *nf* resignation

renunciar [renun'θjar] *vt* to renounce, give up ◼ *vi* to resign; **~ a hacer algo** to give up doing sth

reñido, -a [re'niðo, a] *adj* (*batalla*) bitter, hard-fought; **estar ~ con algn** to be on bad terms with sb; **está ~ con su familia** he has fallen out with his family

reñir [re'nir] *vt* (*regañar*) to scold ◼ *vi* (*estar peleado*) to quarrel, fall out; (*combatir*) to fight

reo ['reo] *nm/f* culprit, offender; (*Jur*) accused

reojo [re'oxo]: **de ~** *adv* out of the corner of one's eye

reorganizar [reorɣani'θar] *vt* to reorganize

Rep *abr* = **República**

reparación [repara'θjon] *nf* (*acto*) mending, repairing; (*Tec*) repair; (*fig*) amends, reparation; **"reparaciones en el acto"** "repairs while you wait"

reparador, -a [repara'ðor, a] *adj* refreshing; (*comida*) fortifying ◼ *nm* repairer

reparar [repa'rar] *vt* to repair; (*fig*) to make amends for; (*suerte*) to retrieve; (*observar*) to observe ◼ *vi*: **~ en** (*darse cuenta de*) to notice; (*poner atención en*) to pay attention to; **sin ~ en los gastos** regardless of the cost

reparo [re'paro] *nm* (*advertencia*) observation; (*duda*) doubt; (*dificultad*) difficulty; (*escrúpulo*) scruple, qualm; **poner reparos (a)** to raise objections (to); (*criticar*) to criticize; **no tuvo ~ en hacerlo** he did not hesitate to do it

repartición [reparti'θjon] *nf* distribution; (*división*) division

repartidor, a [reparti'ðor, a] *nm/f* distributor; **~ de leche** milkman

repartir [repar'tir] *vt* to distribute, share out; (*Com: Correos*) to deliver; (*Mil*) to partition; (*libros*) to give out; (*comida*) to serve out; (*Naipes*) to deal

reparto [re'parto] *nm* distribution; (*Com: Correos*) delivery; (*Teat, Cine*) cast; (*Am: urbanización*) housing estate (*Brit*), real estate development (*US*); **"~ a domicilio"** "home delivery service"

repasar [repa'sar] *vt* (*Escol*) to revise; (*Mecánica*) to check, overhaul; (*Costura*) to mend

repaso [re'paso] *nm* revision; (*Mecánica*) overhaul, checkup; (*Costura*) mending; **~ general** servicing, general overhaul; **curso de ~** refresher course

repatriar [repa'trjar] *vt* to repatriate; **repatriarse** *vr* to return home

repelente [repe'lente] *adj* repellent, repulsive

repeler [repe'ler] *vt* to repel; (*idea, oferta*) to reject

repensar [repen'sar] *vt* to reconsider

repente [re'pente] *nm* sudden movement; (*fig*) impulse; **de ~** suddenly; **~ de ira** fit of anger

repentice *etc* [repen'tiθe] *vb ver* **repentizar**

repentino, -a [repen'tino, a] *adj* sudden; (*imprevisto*) unexpected

repentizar [repenti'θar] *vi* (*Mus*) to sight-read

repercusión [reperku'sjon] *nf* repercussion; **de amplia** *o* **ancha ~** far-reaching

repercutir [reperku'tir] *vi* (*objeto*) to rebound; (*sonido*) to echo; **~ en** (*fig*) to have repercussions *o* effects on

repertorio [reper'torjo] *nm* list; (*Teat*) repertoire

repesca [re'peska] *nf* (*Escol fam*) resit

repetición [repeti'θjon] *nf* repetition

repetido, -a [repe'tiðo, a] *adj* repeated; **repetidas veces** repeatedly

repetir [repe'tir] *vt* to repeat; (*plato*) to have a second helping of; (*Teat*) to give as an encore, sing *etc* again ◼ *vi* to repeat; (*sabor*) to come back; **repetirse** *vr* to repeat o.s.; (*suceso*) to recur

repetitivo, -a [repeti'tiβo, a] *adj* repetitive, repetitious

repicar [repi'kar] *vi* (*campanas*) to ring (out)

repiense *etc* [re'pjense] *vb ver* **repensar**

r

repipi [re'pipi] *adj* la-di-da ▪ *nf*: **es una ~** she's a little madam
repique *etc* [re'pike] *vb ver* **repicar** ▪ *nm* pealing, ringing
repiqueteo [repike'teo] *nm* pealing; (*de tambor*) drumming
repisa [re'pisa] *nf* ledge, shelf; **~ de chimenea** mantelpiece; **~ de ventana** windowsill
repitiendo *etc* [repi'tjendo] *vb ver* **repetir**
replantear [replante'ar] *vt* (*cuestión pública*) to readdress; (*problema personal*) to reconsider; (*en reunión*) to raise again; **replantearse** *vr*: **replantearse algo** to reconsider sth
replegarse [reple'ɣarse] *vr* to fall back, retreat
replegué [reple'ɣe], **repleguemos** *etc* [reple'ɣemos] *vb ver* **replegarse**
repleto, -a [re'pleto, a] *adj* replete, full up; **~ de** filled o crammed with
réplica ['replika] *nf* answer; (*Arte*) replica; **derecho de ~** right of o to reply
replicar [repli'kar] *vi* to answer; (*objetar*) to argue, answer back
repliego *etc* [re'pljeɣo] *vb ver* **replegarse**
repliegue *etc* [re'pljeɣe] *vb ver* **replegarse** ▪ *nm* (*Mil*) withdrawal
replique *etc* [re'plike] *vb ver* **replicar**
repoblación [repoβla'θjon] *nf* repopulation; (*de río*) restocking; **~ forestal** reafforestation
repoblar [repo'βlar] *vt* to repopulate; to restock
repollo [re'poʎo] *nm* cabbage
repondré *etc* [repon'dre] *vb ver* **reponer**
reponer [repo'ner] *vt* to replace, put back; (*máquina*) to re-set; (*Teat*) to revive; **reponerse** *vr* to recover; **~ que** to reply that
reponga *etc* [re'ponga] *vb ver* **reponer**
reportaje [repor'taxe] *nm* report, article; **~ gráfico** illustrated report
reportar [repor'tar] *vt* (*traer*) to bring, carry; (*conseguir*) to obtain; (*fig*) to check; **reportarse** *vr* (*contenerse*) to control o.s.; (*calmarse*) to calm down; **la cosa no le reportó sino disgustos** the affair brought him nothing but trouble
reportero, -a [repor'tero, a] *nm/f* reporter; **~ gráfico/a** news photographer
reposacabezas [reposaka'βeθas] *nm inv* headrest
reposado, -a [repo'saðo, a] *adj* (*descansado*) restful; (*tranquilo*) calm
reposar [repo'sar] *vi* to rest, repose; (*muerto*) to lie, rest
reposición [reposi'θjon] *nf* replacement; (*Cine*) second showing; (*Teat*) revival
reposo [re'poso] *nm* rest

repostar [repos'tar] *vt* to replenish; (*Auto*) to fill up (with petrol o gasoline)
repostería [reposte'ria] *nf* (*arte*) confectionery, pastry-making; (*tienda*) confectioner's (shop)
repostero, -a [repos'tero, a] *nm/f* confectioner
reprender [repren'der] *vt* to reprimand; (*niño*) to scold
reprensión [repren'sjon] *nf* rebuke, reprimand; (*de niño*) telling-off, scolding
represa [re'presa] *nf* dam; (*lago artificial*) lake, pool
represalia [repre'salja] *nf* reprisal; **tomar represalias** to take reprisals, retaliate
representación [representa'θjon] *nf* representation; (*Teat*) performance; **en ~ de** representing; **por ~** by proxy
representante [represen'tante] *nm/f* (*Pol: Com*) representative; (*Teat*) performer
representar [represen'tar] *vt* to represent; (*significar*) to mean; (*Teat*) to perform; (*edad*) to look; **representarse** *vr* to imagine; **tal acto ~ía la guerra** such an act would mean war
representativo, -a [representa'tiβo, a] *adj* representative
represión [repre'sjon] *nf* repression
represivo, -a [repre'siβo, a] *adj* repressive
reprimenda [repri'menda] *nf* reprimand, rebuke
reprimir [repri'mir] *vt* to repress; **reprimirse** *vr*: **reprimirse de hacer algo** to stop o.s. from doing sth
reprobación [reproβa'θjon] *nf* reproval; (*culpa*) blame
reprobar [repro'βar] *vt* to censure, reprove
réprobo, -a ['reproβo, a] *nm/f* reprobate
reprochar [repro't∫ar] *vt* to reproach; (*censurar*) to condemn, censure
reproche [re'prot∫e] *nm* reproach
reproducción [reproðuk'θjon] *nf* reproduction
reproducir [reproðu'θir] *vt* to reproduce; **reproducirse** *vr* to breed; (*situación*) to recur
reproductor, a [reproðuk'tor, a] *adj* reproductive ▪ *nm*: **~ de discos compactos** CD player; **~ MP3/MP4** MP3/MP4 player
reproduje [repro'ðuxe], **reprodujera** *etc* [reproðu'xera], **reproduzca** *etc* [repro'duθka] *vb ver* **reproducir**
repruebe *etc* [re'prweβe] *vb ver* **reprobar**
reptar [rep'tar] *vi* to creep, crawl
reptil [rep'til] *nm* reptile
república [re'puβlika] *nf* republic; **R~ Dominicana** Dominican Republic; **R~ Democrática Alemana (RDA)** German

Democratic Republic; **R~ Federal Alemana
(RFA)** Federal Republic of Germany;
R~ Árabe Unida United Arab Republic
republicano, -a [repuβli'kano, a] *adj, nm/f*
republican
repudiar [repu'ðjar] *vt* to repudiate; *(fe)* to
renounce
repudio [re'puðjo] *nm* repudiation
repueble *etc* [re'pweβle] *vb ver* **repoblar**
repuesto [re'pwesto] *pp de* **reponer** ▪ *nm*
(pieza de recambio) spare (part); *(abastecimiento)*
supply; **rueda de ~** spare wheel; **y llevamos
otro de ~** and we have another as a spare *o*
in reserve
repugnancia [repuɣ'nanθja] *nf* repugnance
repugnante [repuɣ'nante] *adj* repugnant,
repulsive
repugnar [repuɣ'nar] *vt* to disgust ▪ *vi,*
repugnarse *vr* to contradict each other
repujar [repu'xar] *vt* to emboss
repulsa [re'pulsa] *nf* rebuff
repulsión [repul'sjon] *nf* repulsion, aversion
repulsivo, -a [repul'siβo, a] *adj* repulsive
repuse *etc* [re'puse] *vb ver* **reponer**
reputación [reputa'θjon] *nf* reputation
reputar [repu'tar] *vt* to consider, deem
requemado, -a [reke'maðo, a] *adj (quemado)*
scorched; *(bronceado)* tanned
requemar [reke'mar] *vt (quemar)* to scorch;
(secar) to parch; *(Culin)* to overdo, burn; *(la
lengua)* to burn, sting
requerimiento [rekeri'mjento] *nm* request;
(demanda) demand; *(Jur)* summons
requerir [reke'rir] *vt (pedir)* to ask, request;
(exigir) to require; *(ordenar)* to call for; *(llamar)*
to send for, summon
requesón [reke'son] *nm* cottage cheese
requete ... [rekete] *pref* extremely
requiebro [re'kjeβro] *nm (piropo)* compliment,
flirtatious remark
réquiem ['rekjem] *nm* requiem
requiera *etc* [re'kjera], **requiriendo** *etc*
[reki'rjendo] *vb ver* **requerir**
requisa [re'kisa] *nf (inspección)* survey,
inspection; *(Mil)* requisition
requisar [reki'sar] *vt (Mil)* to requisition;
(confiscar) to seize, confiscate
requisito [reki'sito] *nm* requirement,
requisite; **~ previo** prerequisite; **tener
los requisitos para un cargo** to have the
essential qualifications for a post
res [res] *nf* beast, animal
resabio [re'saβjo] *nm (maña)* vice, bad habit;
(dejo) (unpleasant) aftertaste
resaca [re'saka] *nf (en el mar)* undertow,
undercurrent; *(fig)* backlash; *(fam)* hangover
resaltar [resal'tar] *vi* to project, stick out;

(fig) to stand out
resarcir [resar'θir] *vt* to compensate; *(pagar)*
to repay; **resarcirse** *vr* to make up for; **~ a
algn de una pérdida** to compensate sb for
a loss; **~ a algn de una cantidad** to repay sb
a sum
resarza *etc* [re'sarθa] *vb ver* **resarcir**
resbalada [resβa'laða] *nf (Am)* slip
resbaladizo, -a [resβala'ðiθo, a] *adj* slippery
resbalar [resβa'lar] *vi,* **resbalarse** *vr* to
slip, slide; *(fig)* to slip (up); **le resbalaban
las lágrimas por las mejillas** tears were
trickling down his cheeks
resbalón [resβa'lon] *nm (acción)* slip;
(deslizamiento) slide; *(fig)* slip
rescatar [reska'tar] *vt (salvar)* to save, rescue;
(objeto) to get back, recover; *(cautivos)* to
ransom
rescate [res'kate] *nm* rescue; *(de objeto)*
recovery; **pagar un ~** to pay a ransom
rescindir [resθin'dir] *vt (contrato)* to annul,
rescind
rescisión [resθi'sjon] *nf* cancellation
rescoldo [res'koldo] *nm* embers *pl*
resecar [rese'kar] *vt* to dry off, dry
thoroughly; *(Med)* to cut out, remove;
resecarse *vr* to dry up
reseco, -a [re'seko, a] *adj* very dry; *(fig)*
skinny
resentido, -a [resen'tiðo, a] *adj* resentful;
es un ~ he's bitter
resentimiento [resenti'mjento] *nm*
resentment, bitterness
resentirse [resen'tirse] *vr (debilitarse: persona)*
to suffer; **~ con** to resent; **~ de** *(sufrir las
consecuencias de)* to feel the effects of
reseña [re'seɲa] *nf (cuenta)* account; *(informe)*
report; *(Lit)* review
reseñar [rese'ɲar] *vt* to describe; *(Lit)* to review
reseque *etc* [re'seke] *vb ver* **resecar**
reserva [re'serβa] *nf* reserve; *(reservación)*
reservation; **a ~ de que ...** unless ...; **con
toda ~** in strictest confidence; **de ~** spare;
tener algo de ~ to have sth in reserve; **~ de
indios** Indian reservation; *(Com):* **~ para
amortización** depreciation allowance; **~ de
caja** *o* **en efectivo** cash reserves; **reservas
del Estado** government stock; **reservas en
oro** gold reserves
reservación [reserβa'θjon] *nf* reservation
reservado, -a [reser'βaðo, a] *adj* reserved;
(retraído) cold, distant ▪ *nm* private room;
(Ferro) reserved compartment
reservar [reser'βar] *vt (guardar)* to keep; *(Ferro:
Teat etc)* to reserve, book; **reservarse** *vr* to
save o.s.; *(callar)* to keep to o.s.; **~ con exceso**
to overbook

r

resfriado [resˈfriaðo] *nm* cold
resfriarse [resˈfriarse] *vr* to cool off; *(Med)* to catch (a) cold
resfrío [resˈfrio] *nm (esp Am)* cold
resguardar [resɣwarˈðar] *vt* to protect, shield; **resguardarse** *vr*: **resguardarse de** to guard against
resguardo [resˈɣwarðo] *nm* defence; *(vale)* voucher; *(recibo)* receipt, slip
residencia [resiˈðenθja] *nf* residence; *(Univ)* hall of residence; **~ para ancianos** *o* **jubilados** rest home
residencial [resiðenˈθjal] *adj* residential ■ *nf (urbanización)* housing estate *(Brit)*, real estate development *(US)*
residente [resiˈðente] *adj, nm/f* resident
residir [resiˈðir] *vi* to reside, live; **~ en** to reside *o* lie in; *(consistir en)* to consist of
residual [resiˈðwal] *adj* residual; **aguas residuales** sewage
residuo [reˈsiðwo] *nm* residue; **residuos atmosféricos** *o* **radiactivos** fallout *sg*
resienta *etc* [reˈsjenta] *vb ver* **resentirse**
resignación [resiɣnaˈθjon] *nf* resignation
resignarse [resiɣˈnarse] *vr*: **~ a** *o* **con** to resign o.s. to, be resigned to
resina [reˈsina] *nf* resin
resintiendo *etc* [resinˈtjendo] *vb ver* **resentirse**
resistencia [resisˈtenθja] *nf (dureza)* endurance, strength; *(oposición, Elec)* resistance; **la R~** *(Mil)* the Resistance
resistente [resisˈtente] *adj* strong, hardy; *(Tec)* resistant; **~ al calor** heat-resistant
resistir [resisˈtir] *vt (soportar)* to bear; *(oponerse a)* to resist, oppose; *(aguantar)* to put up with ■ *vi* to resist; *(aguantar)* to last, endure; **resistirse** *vr*: **resistirse a** to refuse to, resist; **no puedo ~ este frío** I can't bear *o* stand this cold; **me resisto a creerlo** I refuse to believe it; **se le resiste la química** chemistry escapes her
resol [reˈsol] *nm* glare of the sun
resollar [resoˈʎar] *vi* to breathe noisily, wheeze
resolución [resoluˈθjon] *nf* resolution; *(decisión)* decision; *(moción)* motion; **~ judicial** legal ruling; **tomar una ~** to take a decision
resoluto, -a [resoˈluto, a] *adj* resolute
resolver [resolˈβer] *vt* to resolve; *(solucionar)* to solve, resolve; *(decidir)* to decide, settle; **resolverse** *vr* to make up one's mind
resonancia [resoˈnanθja] *nf (del sonido)* resonance; *(repercusión)* repercussion; *(fig)* wide effect, impact
resonante [resoˈnante] *adj* resonant,

resounding; *(fig)* tremendous
resonar [resoˈnar] *vi* to ring, echo
resoplar [resoˈplar] *vi* to snort; *(por cansancio)* to puff
resoplido [resoˈpliðo] *nm* heavy breathing
resorte [reˈsorte] *nm* spring; *(fig)* lever
respaldar [respalˈdar] *vt* to back (up), support; *(Inform)* to back up; **respaldarse** *vr* to lean back; **respaldarse con** *o* **en** *(fig)* to take one's stand on
respaldo [resˈpaldo] *nm (de sillón)* back; *(fig)* support, backing
respectivo, -a [respekˈtiβo, a] *adj* respective; **en lo ~ a** with regard to
respecto [resˈpekto] *nm*: **al ~** on this matter; **con ~ a, ~ de** with regard to, in relation to
respetable [respeˈtaβle] *adj* respectable
respetar [respeˈtar] *vt* to respect
respeto [resˈpeto] *nm* respect; *(acatamiento)* deference; **respetos** *nmpl* respects; **por ~ a** out of consideration for; **presentar sus respetos a** to pay one's respects to
respetuoso, -a [respeˈtwoso, a] *adj* respectful
respingo [resˈpingo] *nm* start, jump
respiración [respiraˈθjon] *nf* breathing; *(Med)* respiration; *(ventilación)* ventilation
respirar [respiˈrar] *vt, vi* to breathe; **no dejar ~ a algn** to keep on at sb; **estuvo escuchándole sin ~** he listened to him in complete silence
respiratorio, -a [respiraˈtorjo, a] *adj* respiratory
respiro [resˈpiro] *nm* breathing; *(fig: descanso)* respite, rest; *(Com)* period of grace
resplandecer [resplandeˈθer] *vi* to shine
resplandeciente [resplandeˈθjente] *adj* resplendent, shining
resplandezca *etc* [resplanˈdeθka] *vb ver* **resplandecer**
resplandor [resplanˈdor] *nm* brilliance, brightness; *(del fuego)* blaze
responder [responˈder] *vt* to answer ■ *vi* to answer; *(fig)* to respond; *(pey)* to answer back; *(corresponder)* to correspond; **~ a** *(situación etc)* to respond to; **~ a una pregunta** to answer a question; **~ a una descripción** to fit a description; **~ de** *o* **por** to answer for
respondón, -ona [responˈdon, ona] *adj* cheeky
responsabilice *etc* [responsaβiˈliθe] *vb ver* **responsabilizarse**
responsabilidad [responsaβiliˈðað] *nf* responsibility; **bajo mi ~** on my authority; **~ ilimitada** *(Com)* unlimited liability
responsabilizarse [responsaβiliˈθarse] *vr* to make o.s. responsible, take charge

responsable [respon'sable] *adj* responsible; **la persona ~** the person in charge; **hacerse ~ de algo** to assume responsibility for sth

respuesta [res'pwesta] *nf* answer, reply; *(reacción)* response

resquebrajar [reskeβra'xar] *vt*, **resquebrajarse** *vr* to crack, split

resquemor [reske'mor] *nm* resentment

resquicio [res'kiθjo] *nm* chink; *(hendidura)* crack

resta ['resta] *nf (Mat)* remainder

restablecer [restaβle'θer] *vt* to re-establish, restore; **restablecerse** *vr* to recover

restablecimiento [restaβleθi'mjento] *nm* re-establishment; *(restauración)* restoration; *(Med)* recovery

restablezca *etc* [resta'βleθka] *vb ver* **restablecer**

restallar [resta'ʎar] *vi* to crack

restante [res'tante] *adj* remaining; **lo ~** the remainder; **los restantes** the rest, those left (over)

restar [res'tar] *vt (Mat)* to subtract; *(descontar)* to deduct; *(fig)* to take away ■ *vi* to remain, be left

restauración [restaura'θjon] *nf* restoration

restaurador, a [restaura'ðor, a] *nm/f (persona)* restorer

restaurante [restau'rante] *nm* restaurant

restaurar [restau'rar] *vt* to restore

restitución [restitu'θjon] *nf* return, restitution

restituir [restitu'ir] *vt (devolver)* to return, give back; *(rehabilitar)* to restore

restituyendo *etc* [restitu'jendo] *vb ver* **restituir**

resto ['resto] *nm (residuo)* rest, remainder; *(apuesta)* stake; **restos** *nmpl* remains; *(Culin)* leftovers, scraps; **restos mortales** mortal remains

restregar [restre'ɣar] *vt* to scrub, rub

restregué [restre'ɣe], **restreguemos** *etc* [restre'ɣemos] *vb ver* **restregar**

restricción [restrik'θjon] *nf* restriction; **sin ~ de** without restrictions on *o* as to; **hablar sin restricciones** to talk freely

restrictivo, -a [restrik'tiβo, a] *adj* restrictive

restriego *etc* [res'trjeɣo], **restriegue** *etc* [res'trjeɣe] *vb ver* **restregar**

restringir [restrin'xir] *vt* to restrict, limit

restrinja *etc* [res'trinxa] *vb ver* **restringir**

resucitar [resuθi'tar] *vt, vi* to resuscitate, revive

resuello *etc* [re'sweʎo] *vb ver* **resollar** ■ *nm (aliento)* breath

resuelto, -a [re'swelto, a] *pp de* **resolver** ■ *adj* resolute, determined; **estar ~ a algo**

to be set on sth; **estar ~ a hacer algo** to be determined to do sth

resuelva *etc* [re'swelβa] *vb ver* **resolver**

resuene *etc* [re'swene] *vb ver* **resonar**

resulta [re'sulta] *nf* result; **de resultas de** as a result of

resultado [resul'taðo] *nm* result; *(conclusión)* outcome; **resultados** *nmpl (Inform)* output *sg*; **dar ~** to produce results

resultante [resul'tante] *adj* resulting, resultant

resultar [resul'tar] *vi (ser)* to be; *(llegar a ser)* to turn out to be; *(salir bien)* to turn out well; *(seguir)* to ensue; **~ a** *(Com)* to amount to; **~ de** to stem from; **~ en** to result in, produce; **resulta que ...** *(en consecuencia)* it follows that ...; *(parece que)* it seems that ...; **el conductor resultó muerto** the driver was killed; **no resultó** it didn't work *o* come off; **me resulta difícil hacerlo** it's difficult for me to do it

resumen [re'sumen] *nm* summary, résumé; **en ~** in short

resumir [resu'mir] *vt* to sum up; *(condensar)* to summarize; *(cortar)* to abridge, cut down; **resumirse** *vr*: **la situación se resume en pocas palabras** the situation can be summed up in a few words

resurgir [resur'xir] *vi (reaparecer)* to reappear

resurrección [resurrek'θjon] *nf* resurrection

retablo [re'taβlo] *nm* altarpiece

retaguardia [reta'ɣwarðja] *nf* rearguard

retahíla [reta'ila] *nf* series, string; *(de injurias)* volley, stream

retal [re'tal] *nm* remnant

retar [re'tar] *vt (gen)* to challenge; *(desafiar)* to defy, dare

retardar [retar'ðar] *vt (demorar)* to delay; *(hacer más lento)* to slow down; *(retener)* to hold back

retardo [re'tarðo] *nm* delay

retazo [re'taθo] *nm* snippet *(Brit)*, fragment

RETD *nf abr (Esp Telec)* = **Red Especial de Transmisión de Datos**

rete ... ['rete] *pref* very, extremely

retén [re'ten] *nm (Am)* roadblock, checkpoint

retención [reten'θjon] *nf* retention; *(de pago)* deduction; **~ de llamadas** *(Telec)* hold facility

retendré *etc* [reten'dre] *vb ver* **retener**

retener [rete'ner] *vt (guardar)* to retain, keep; *(intereses)* to withhold

retenga *etc* [re'tenga] *vb ver* **retener**

reticencia [reti'θenθja] *nf (insinuación)* insinuation, (malevolent) suggestion; *(verdad a medias)* half-truth

reticente [reti'θente] *adj (insinuador)*

insinuating; (*engañoso*) deceptive

retiene *etc* [re'tjene] *vb ver* **retener**

retina [re'tina] *nf* retina

retintín [retin'tin] *nm* jangle, jingle; **decir algo con ~** to say sth sarcastically

retirado, -a [reti'raðo, a] *adj* (*lugar*) remote; (*vida*) quiet; (*jubilado*) retired ▪ *nf* (*Mil*) retreat; (*de dinero*) withdrawal; (*de embajador*) recall; **batirse en retirada** to retreat

retirar [reti'rar] *vt* to withdraw; (*la mano*) to draw back; (*quitar*) to remove; (*dinero*) to take out, withdraw; (*jubilar*) to retire, pension off; **retirarse** *vr* to retreat, withdraw; (*jubilarse*) to retire; (*acostarse*) to retire, go to bed

retiro [re'tiro] *nm* retreat; (*jubilación, tb Deporte*) retirement; (*pago*) pension; (*lugar*) quiet place

reto ['reto] *nm* dare, challenge

retocar [reto'kar] *vt* to touch up, retouch

retoce *etc* [re'toθe] *vb ver* **retozar**

retoño [re'toɲo] *nm* sprout, shoot; (*fig*) offspring, child

retoque *etc* [re'toke] *vb ver* **retocar** ▪ *nm* retouching

retorcer [retor'θer] *vt* to twist; (*argumento*) to turn, twist; (*manos, lavado*) to wring; **retorcerse** *vr* to become twisted; (*persona*) to writhe; **retorcerse de dolor** to writhe in *o* squirm with pain

retorcido, -a [retor'θiðo, a] *adj* (*tb fig*) twisted

retorcimiento [retorθi'mjento] *nm* twist, twisting; (*fig*) deviousness

retórico, -a [re'toriko, a] *adj* rhetorical; (*pey*) affected, windy ▪ *nf* rhetoric; (*pey*) affectedness

retornable [retor'naβle] *adj* returnable

retornar [retor'nar] *vt* to return, give back ▪ *vi* to return, go/come back

retorno [re'torno] *nm* return; **~ del carro** (*Inform: Tip*) carriage return

retortero [retor'tero] *nm*: **andar al ~** to bustle about, have heaps of things to do; **andar al ~ por algn** to be madly in love with sb

retortijón [retorti'xon] *nm* twist, twisting; **~ de tripas** stomach cramp

retorzamos *etc* [retor'θamos] *vb ver* **retorcer**

retozar [reto'θar] *vi* (*juguetear*) to frolic, romp; (*saltar*) to gambol

retozón, -ona [reto'θon, ona] *adj* playful

retracción [retrak'θjon] *nf* retraction

retractarse [retrak'tarse] *vr* to retract; **me retracto** I take that back

retraerse [retra'erse] *vr* to retreat, withdraw

retraído, -a [retra'iðo, a] *adj* shy, retiring

retraiga *etc* [re'traiɣa] *vb ver* **retraerse**

retraimiento [retrai'mjento] *nm* retirement; (*timidez*) shyness

retraje *etc* [re'traxe], **retrajera** *etc* [retra'xera] *vb ver* **retraerse**

retransmisión [retransmi'sjon] *nf* repeat (broadcast)

retransmitir [retransmi'tir] *vt* (*mensaje*) to relay; (*TV etc*) to repeat, retransmit; (*: en vivo*) to broadcast live

retrasado, -a [retra'saðo, a] *adj* late; (*Med*) mentally retarded; (*país etc*) backward, underdeveloped; **estar ~** (*reloj*) to be slow; (*persona, industria*) to be *o* lag behind

retrasar [retra'sar] *vt* (*demorar*) to postpone, put off; (*retardar*) to slow down ▪ *vi*, **retrasarse** *vr* (*atrasarse*) to be late; (*reloj*) to be slow; (*producción*) to fall (away); (*quedarse atrás*) to lag behind

retraso [re'traso] *nm* (*demora*) delay; (*lentitud*) slowness; (*tardanza*) lateness; (*atraso*) backwardness; **retrasos** *nmpl* (*Com*) arrears; (*deudas*) deficit *sg*, debts; **llegar con ~** to arrive late; **llegar con 25 minutos de ~** to be 25 minutes late; **llevo un ~ de seis semanas** I'm six weeks behind (with my work *etc*); **~ mental** mental deficiency

retratar [retra'tar] *vt* (*Arte*) to paint the portrait of; (*fotografiar*) to photograph; (*fig*) to depict, describe; **retratarse** *vr* to have one's portrait painted; to have one's photograph taken

retratista [retra'tista] *nm/f* (*Arte*) (portrait) painter; (*Foto*) photographer

retrato [re'trato] *nm* portrait; (*Foto*) photograph; (*descripción*) portrayal, depiction; (*fig*) likeness; **ser el vivo ~ de** to be the spitting image of

retrato-robot [re'tratoro'βo(t)] (*pl* **retratos-robot**) *nm* identikit picture

retrayendo *etc* [retra'jendo] *vb ver* **retraerse**

retreta [re'treta] *nf* retreat

retrete [re'trete] *nm* toilet

retribución [retriβu'θjon] *nf* (*recompensa*) reward; (*pago*) pay, payment

retribuir [retriβu'ir] *vt* (*recompensar*) to reward; (*pagar*) to pay

retribuyendo *etc* [retriβu'jendo] *vb ver* **retribuir**

retro ... [retro] *pref* retro...

retroactivo, -a [retroak'tiβo, a] *adj* retroactive, retrospective; **dar efecto ~ a un pago** to backdate a payment

retroalimentación [retroalimenta'θjon] *nf* (*Inform*) feedback

retroceder [retroθe'ðer] *vi* (*echarse atrás*) to move back(wards); (*fig*) to back down; **no ~** to stand firm; **la policía hizo ~ a la multitud** the police forced the crowd back

retroceso [retro'θeso] *nm* backward

movement; (*Med*) relapse; (*Com*) recession, depression; (*fig*) backing down

retrógrado, -a [re'troɣraðo, a] *adj* retrograde, retrogressive; (*Pol*) reactionary

retropropulsión [retropropul'sjon] *nf* jet propulsion

retrospectivo, -a [retrospek'tiβo, a] *adj* retrospective; **mirada retrospectiva** backward glance

retrovisor [retroβi'sor] *nm* rear-view mirror

retuerce *etc* [re'twerθe], **retuerza** *etc* [re'twerθa] *vb ver* **retorcer**

retumbante [retum'bante] *adj* resounding

retumbar [retum'bar] *vi* to echo, resound; (*continuamente*) to reverberate

retuve *etc* [re'tuβe] *vb ver* **retener**

reuma ['reuma] *nm* rheumatism

reumático, -a [reu'matiko, a] *adj* rheumatic

reumatismo [reuma'tismo] *nm* rheumatism

reunificar [reunifi'kar] *vt* to reunify

reunifique *etc* [reuni'fike] *vb ver* **reunificar**

reunión [reu'njon] *nf* (*asamblea*) meeting; (*fiesta*) party; **~ en la cumbre** summit meeting; **~ de ventas** (*Com*) sales meeting

reunir [reu'nir] *vt* (*juntar*) to reunite, join (together); (*recoger*) to gather (together); (*personas*) to bring o get together; (*cualidades*) to combine; **reunirse** *vr* (*personas: en asamblea*) to meet, gather; **reunió a sus amigos para discutirlo** he got his friends together to talk it over

revalida [re'βaliða] *nf* (*Escol*) final examination

revalidar [reβali'ðar] *vt* (*ratificar*) to confirm, ratify

revalorar [reβalo'rar] *vt* to revalue, reassess

revalorización [reβaloriθa'θjon], **revaloración** [reβalora'θjon] *nf* revaluation; (*Econ*) reassessment

revancha [re'βantʃa] *nf* revenge; (*Deporte*) return match; (*Boxeo*) return fight

revelación [reβela'θjon] *nf* revelation

revelado [reβe'laðo] *nm* developing

revelador, a [reβela'ðor, a] *adj* revealing

revelar [reβe'lar] *vt* to reveal; (*secreto*) to disclose; (*mostrar*) to show; (*Foto*) to develop

revendedor, a [reβende'ðor, a] *nm/f* retailer; (*pey*) ticket tout

revendré *etc* [reβen'dre], **revenga** *etc* [re'βenga] *vb ver* **revenirse**

revenirse [reβe'nirse] *vr* to shrink; (*comida*) to go bad o off; (*vino*) to sour; (*Culin*) to get tough

reventa [re'βenta] *nf* resale; (*especulación*) speculation; (*de entradas*) touting

reventar [reβen'tar] *vt* to burst, explode; (*molestar*) to annoy, rile ■ *vi*, **reventarse** *vr* (*estallar*) to burst, explode; **me revienta**

tener que ponérmelo I hate having to wear it; **~ de** (*fig*) to be bursting with; **~ por** to be bursting to

reventón [reβen'ton] *nm* (*Auto*) blow-out (*Brit*), flat (*US*)

reverberación [reβerβera'θjon] *nf* reverberation

reverberar [reβerβe'rar] *vi* (*luz*) to play, be reflected; (*superficie*) to shimmer; (*nieve*) to glare; (*sonido*) to reverberate

reverbero [reβer'βero] *nm* play; shimmer, shine; glare; reverberation

reverencia [reβe'renθja] *nf* reverence; (*inclinación*) bow

reverenciar [reβeren'θjar] *vt* to revere

reverendo, -a [reβe'rendo, a] *adj* reverend; (*fam*) big, awful; **un ~ imbécil** an awful idiot

reverente [reβe'rente] *adj* reverent

reversible [reβer'siβle] *adj* reversible

reverso [re'βerso] *nm* back, other side; (*de moneda*) reverse

revertir [reβer'tir] *vi* to revert; **~ en beneficio de** to be to the advantage of; **~ en perjuicio de** to be to the detriment of

revés [re'βes] *nm* back, wrong side; (*fig*) reverse, setback; (*Deporte*) backhand; **al ~** the wrong way round; (*de arriba abajo*) upside down; (*ropa*) inside out; **y al ~** and vice versa; **volver algo del ~** to turn sth round; (*ropa*) to turn sth inside out; **los reveses de la fortuna** the blows of fate

revestir [reβes'tir] *vt* (*poner*) to put on; (*cubrir*) to cover, coat; (*cualidad*) to have, possess; **revestirse** *vr* (*Rel*) to put on one's vestments; (*ponerse*) to put on; **~ con o de** to arm o.s. with; **el acto revestía gran solemnidad** the ceremony had great dignity

reviejo, -a [re'βjexo, a] *adj* very old, ancient

reviene *etc* [re'βjene] *vb ver* **revenirse**

reviente *etc* [re'βjente] *vb ver* **reventar**

revierta *etc* [re'βjerta] *vb ver* **revertir**

reviniendo *etc* [reβi'njendo] *vb ver* **revenirse**

revirtiendo *etc* [reβir'tjendo] *vb ver* **revertir**

revisar [reβi'sar] *vt* (*examinar*) to check; (*texto etc*) to revise; (*Jur*) to review

revisión [reβi'sjon] *nf* revision; **~ aduanera** customs inspection; **~ de cuentas** audit

revisor, a [reβi'sor, a] *nm/f* inspector; (*Ferro*) ticket collector; **~ de cuentas** auditor

revista *etc* [re'βista] *vb ver* **revestir** ■ *nf* magazine, review; (*Teat*) revue; (*inspección*) inspection; **~ literaria** literary review; **~ de libros** book reviews (page); **pasar ~ a** to review, inspect

revivir [reβi'βir] *vt* (*recordar*) to revive memories of ■ *vi* to revive

revocación [reβoka'θjon] *nf* repeal

r

revocar [reβo'kar] *vt* (*decisión*) to revoke; (*Arq*) to plaster

revolcar [reβol'kar] *vt* to knock down, send flying; **revolcarse** *vr* to roll about

revolcón [reβol'kon] *nm* tumble

revolotear [reβolote'ar] *vi* to flutter

revoloteo [reβolo'teo] *nm* fluttering

revolqué [reβol'ke], **revolquemos** *etc* [reβol'kemos] *vb ver* **revolcar**

revoltijo [reβol'tixo] *nm* mess, jumble

revoltoso, -a [reβol'toso, a] *adj* (*travieso*) naughty, unruly

revolución [reβolu'θjon] *nf* revolution

revolucionar [reβoluθjo'nar] *vt* to revolutionize

revolucionario, -a [reβoluθjo'narjo, a] *adj*, *nm/f* revolutionary

revolver [reβol'βer] *vt* (*desordenar*) to disturb, mess up; (*agitar*) to shake; (*líquido*) to stir; (*mover*) to move about; (*Pol*) to stir up ■ *vi*: **~ en** to go through, rummage (about) in; **revolverse** *vr* (*en cama*) to toss and turn; (*Meteorología*) to break, turn stormy; **revolverse contra** to turn on *o* against; **han revuelto toda la casa** they've turned the whole house upside down

revólver [re'βolβer] *nm* revolver

revoque *etc* [re'βoke] *vb ver* **revocar**

revuelco *etc* [re'βwelko] *vb ver* **revolcar**

revuelo [re'βwelo] *nm* fluttering; (*fig*) commotion; **armar** *o* **levantar un gran ~** to cause a great stir

revuelque *etc* [re'βwelke] *vb ver* **revolcar**

revuelto, -a [re'βwelto, a] *pp de* **revolver** ■ *adj* (*mezclado*) mixed-up, in disorder; (*mar*) rough; (*tiempo*) unsettled ■ *nf* (*motín*) revolt; (*agitación*) commotion; **todo estaba ~** everything was in disorder *o* was topsy-turvy

revuelva *etc* [re'βwelβa] *vb ver* **revolver**

revulsivo [reβul'siβo] *nm*: **servir de ~** to have a salutary effect

rey [rei] *nm* king; **los Reyes** the King and Queen; *ver tb* **Baraja Española**; *see note*

The night before the 6th of January (the Epiphany), which is a holiday in Spain, children go to bed expecting *los Reyes Magos*, the Three Wise Men who visited the baby Jesus, to bring them presents. Twelfth night processions, known as *cabalgatas*, take place that evening, when 3 people dressed as *los Reyes Magos* arrive in the town by land or sea to the delight of the children.

reyerta [re'jerta] *nf* quarrel, brawl

rezagado, -a [reθa'ɣaðo, a] *adj*: **quedar ~** to be left behind; (*estar retrasado*) to be late, be behind ■ *nm/f* straggler

rezagar [reθa'ɣar] *vt* (*dejar atrás*) to leave behind; (*retrasar*) to delay, postpone; **rezagarse** *vr* (*atrasarse*) to fall behind

rezague *etc* [re'θaɣe] *vb ver* **rezagar**

rezar [re'θar] *vi* to pray; **~ con** (*fam*) to concern, have to do with

rezo ['reθo] *nm* prayer

rezongar [reθon'gar] *vi* to grumble; (*murmurar*) to mutter; (*refunfuñar*) to growl

rezongue *etc* [re'θonge] *vb ver* **rezongar**

rezumar [reθu'mar] *vt* to ooze ■ *vi* to leak; **rezumarse** *vr* to leak out

RFA *nf abr* (= *República Federal Alemana*) *ver* **república**

RI *abr* = **regimiento de infantería**

ría ['ria] *nf* estuary

riachuelo [rja'tʃwelo] *nm* stream

riada [ri'aða] *nf* flood

ribera [ri'βera] *nf* (*de río*) bank; (: *área*) riverside

ribete [ri'βete] *nm* (*de vestido*) border; (*fig*) addition

ribetear [riβete'ar] *vt* to edge, border

rice *etc* ['riθe] *vb ver* **rizar**

ricino [ri'θino] *nm*: **aceite de ~** castor oil

rico, -a ['riko, a] *adj* (*adinerado*) rich, wealthy; (*lujoso*) luxurious; (*comida*) delicious; (*niño*) lovely, cute ■ *nm/f* rich person; **nuevo ~** nouveau riche

rictus ['riktus] *nm* (*mueca*) sneer, grin; **~ de amargura** bitter smile

ridiculez [riðiku'leθ] *nf* absurdity

ridiculice *etc* [riðiku'liθe] *vb ver* **ridiculizar**

ridiculizar [riðikuli'θar] *vt* to ridicule

ridículo, -a [ri'ðikulo, a] *adj* ridiculous; **hacer el ~** to make a fool of o.s.; **poner a algn en ~** to make a fool of sb; **ponerse en ~** to make a fool of o.s.

riego *etc* ['rjeɣo] *vb ver* **regar** ■ *nm* (*aspersión*) watering; (*irrigación*) irrigation

riegue *etc* ['rjeɣe] *vb ver* **regar**

riel [rjel] *nm* rail

rienda ['rjenda] *nf* rein; (*fig*) restraint, moderating influence; **dar ~ suelta a** to give free rein to; **llevar las riendas** to be in charge

riendo ['rjendo] *vb ver* **reír**

riesgo ['rjesɣo] *nm* risk; **seguro a** *o* **contra todo ~** comprehensive insurance; **~ para la salud** health hazard; **correr el ~ de** to run the risk of

Rif [rif] *nm* Rif(f)

rifa ['rifa] *nf* (*lotería*) raffle

rifar [ri'far] *vt* to raffle
rifeño, -a [ri'feɲo, a] *adj* of the Rif(f), Rif(f)ian ■ *nm/f* Rif(f)ian, Rif(f)
rifle ['rifle] *nm* rifle
rigidez [rixi'ðeθ] *nf* rigidity, stiffness; (*fig*) strictness
rígido, -a ['rixiðo, a] *adj* rigid, stiff; (*moralmente*) strict, inflexible; (*cara*) wooden, expressionless
rigiendo *etc* [ri'xjendo] *vb ver* **regir**
rigor [ri'ɣor] *nm* strictness, rigour; (*dureza*) toughness; (*inclemencia*) harshness; (*meticulosidad*) accuracy; **el ~ del verano** the hottest part of the summer; **con todo ~ científico** with scientific precision; **de ~** de rigueur, essential; **después de los saludos de ~** after the inevitable greetings
riguroso, -a [riɣu'roso, a] *adj* rigorous; (*Meteorología*) harsh; (*severo*) severe
rija *etc* ['rixa] *vb ver* **regir** ■ *nf* quarrel
rima ['rima] *nf* rhyme; **rimas** *nfpl* verse *sg*; **~ imperfecta** assonance; **~ rimando** (*fam*) merrily
rimar [ri'mar] *vi* to rhyme
rimbombante [rimbom'bante] *adj* (*fig*) pompous
rímel, rímmel ['rimel] *nm* mascara
rimero [ri'mero] *nm* stack, pile
Rin [rin] *nm* Rhine
rincón [rin'kon] *nm* corner (*inside*)
rindiendo *etc* [rin'djendo] *vb ver* **rendir**
ring [riŋ] *nm* (*Boxeo*) ring
rinoceronte [rinoθe'ronte] *nm* rhinoceros
riña ['riɲa] *nf* (*disputa*) argument; (*pelea*) brawl
riñendo *etc* [ri'ɲendo] *vb ver* **reñir**
riñón [ri'ɲon] *nm* kidney; **me costó un ~** (*fam*) it cost me an arm and a leg; **tener riñones** to have guts
río *etc* ['rio] *vb ver* **reír** ■ *nm* river; (*fig*) torrent, stream; **~ abajo/arriba** downstream/upstream; **cuando el ~ suena, agua lleva** there's no smoke without fire
rió [ri'o] *vb ver* **reír**
Río de Janeiro ['rioðexa'neiro] *nm* Rio de Janeiro
Río de la Plata ['rioðela'plata] *nm* Rio de la Plata, River Plate
Rioja [ri'oxa] *nf*: **La ~** La Rioja ■ *nm*: **rioja** rioja wine
riojano, -a [rjo'xano, a] *adj, nm/f* Riojan
rioplatense [riopla'tense] *adj* of *o* from the River Plate region ■ *nm/f* native *o* inhabitant of the River Plate region
riqueza [ri'keθa] *nf* wealth, riches *pl*; (*cualidad*) richness
risa ['risa] *nf* laughter; (*una risa*) laugh; **¡qué**

~! what a laugh!; **caerse** *o* **morirse de ~** to split one's sides laughing, die laughing; **tomar algo a ~** to laugh sth off
risco ['risko] *nm* crag, cliff
risible [ri'sißle] *adj* ludicrous, laughable
risotada [riso'taða] *nf* guffaw, loud laugh
ristra ['ristra] *nf* string
ristre ['ristre] *nm*: **en ~** at the ready
risueño, -a [ri'sweɲo, a] *adj* (*sonriente*) smiling; (*contento*) cheerful
ritmo ['ritmo] *nm* rhythm; **a ~ lento** slowly; **trabajar a ~ lento** to go slow
rito ['rito] *nm* rite
ritual [ri'twal] *adj, nm* ritual
rival [ri'ßal] *adj, nm/f* rival
rivalice *etc* [rißa'liθe] *vb ver* **rivalizar**
rivalidad [rißali'ðað] *nf* rivalry, competition
rivalizar [rißali'θar] *vi*: **~ con** to rival, compete with
rizado, -a [ri'θaðo, a] *adj* (*pelo*) curly; (*superficie*) ridged; (*terreno*) undulating; (*mar*) choppy ■ *nm* curls *pl*
rizar [ri'θar] *vt* to curl; **rizarse** *vr* (*el pelo*) to curl; (*agua*) to ripple; (*el mar*) to become choppy
rizo ['riθo] *nm* curl; (*en agua*) ripple
Rma. *abr* (= *Reverendísima*) courtesy title
Rmo. *abr* (= *Reverendísimo*) Rt. Rev.
RNE *nf abr* = **Radio Nacional de España**
R.O. *abr* (= *Real Orden*) royal order
robar [ro'ßar] *vt* to rob; (*objeto*) to steal; (*casa etc*) to break into; (*Naipes*) to draw; (*atención*) to steal, capture; (*paciencia*) to exhaust
roble ['roßle] *nm* oak
robledal [roßle'ðal], **robledo** [ro'ßleðo] *nm* oakwood
robo ['roßo] *nm* robbery, theft; (*objeto robado*) stolen article *o* goods *pl*; **¡esto es un ~!** this is daylight robbery!
robot [ro'ßo(t)] (*pl* **robots**) *adj, nm* robot ■ *nm* (*tb*: **robot de cocina**) food processor
robótica [ro'ßotika] *nf* robotics *sg*
robustecer [roßuste'θer] *vt* to strengthen
robustezca *etc* [roßus'teθka] *vb ver* **robustecer**
robusto, -a [ro'ßusto, a] *adj* robust, strong
ROC *abr* (*Inform*: = *reconocimiento óptico de caracteres*) OCR
roca ['roka] *nf* rock; **la R~** the Rock (of Gibraltar)
roce *etc* ['roθe] *vb ver* **rozar** ■ *nm* rub, rubbing; (*caricia*) brush; (*Tec*) friction; (*en la piel*) graze; **tener ~ con** to have a brush with
rociar [ro'θjar] *vt* to sprinkle, spray
rocín [ro'θin] *nm* nag, hack
rocío [ro'θio] *nm* dew
rock [rok] *adj inv, nm* (*Mus*) rock (*cpd*)

rockero, -a [ro'kero, a] *adj* rock *cpd* ∎ *nm/f* rocker

rocoso, -a [ro'koso, a] *adj* rocky

rodado, -a [ro'ðaðo, a] *adj* (*con ruedas*) wheeled ∎ *nf* rut

rodaja [ro'ðaxa] *nf* (*raja*) slice

rodaje [ro'ðaxe] *nm* (*Cine*) shooting, filming; (*Auto*): **en ~** running in

rodamiento [roða'mjento] *nm* (*Auto*) tread

Ródano ['roðano] *nm* Rhône

rodar [ro'ðar] *vt* (*vehículo*) to wheel (along); (*escalera*) to roll down; (*viajar por*) to travel (over) ∎ *vi* to roll; (*coche*) to go, run; (*Cine*) to shoot, film; (*persona*) to move about (from place to place), drift; **echarlo todo a ~** (*fig*) to mess it all up

Rodas ['roðas] *nf* Rhodes

rodear [roðe'ar] *vt* to surround ∎ *vi* to go round; **rodearse** *vr*: **rodearse de amigos** to surround o.s. with friends

rodeo [ro'ðeo] *nm* (*ruta indirecta*) long way round, roundabout way; (*desvío*) detour; (*evasión*) evasion; (*Am*) rodeo; **dejarse de rodeos** to talk straight; **hablar sin rodeos** to come to the point, speak plainly

rodilla [ro'ðiʎa] *nf* knee; **de rodillas** kneeling

rodillo [ro'ðiʎo] *nm* roller; (*Culin*) rolling-pin; (*en máquina de escribir, impresora*) platen

rododendro [roðo'ðendro] *nm* rhododendron

roedor, a [roe'ðor, a] *adj* gnawing ∎ *nm* rodent

roer [ro'er] *vt* (*masticar*) to gnaw; (*corroer, fig*) to corrode

rogar [ro'ɣar] *vt* (*pedir*) to beg, ask for ∎ *vi* (*suplicar*) to beg, plead; **rogarse** *vr*: **se ruega no fumar** please do not smoke; **~ que** (*+subjun*) to ask to ...; **ruegue a este señor que nos deje en paz** please ask this gentleman to leave us alone; **no se hace de ~** he doesn't have to be asked twice

rogué [ro'ɣe], **roguemos** *etc* [ro'ɣemos] *vb ver* **rogar**

rojizo, -a [ro'xiθo, a] *adj* reddish

rojo, -a ['roxo, a] *adj* red ∎ *nm* red (colour); (*Pol*) red; **ponerse ~** to turn red, blush; **al ~ vivo** red-hot

rol [rol] *nm* list, roll; (*esp Am: papel*) role

rollizo, -a [ro'ʎiθo, a] *adj* (*objeto*) cylindrical; (*persona*) plump

rollo, -a ['roʎo, a] *adj* (*fam*) boring, tedious ∎ *nm* roll; (*de cuerda*) coil; (*de madera*) log; (*fam*) bore; (*discurso*) boring speech; **¡qué ~!** what a carry-on!; **la conferencia fue un ~** the lecture was a big drag

ROM [rom] *nf abr* (= *memoria de sólo lectura*) ROM

Roma ['roma] *nf* Rome; **por todas partes se va a ~** all roads lead to Rome

romance [ro'manθe] *nm* (*Ling*) Romance language; (*Lit*) ballad; **hablar en ~** to speak plainly

románico, -a [ro'maniko, a] *adj, nm* Romanesque

romano, -a [ro'mano, a] *adj* Roman, of Rome ∎ *nm/f* Roman

romanticismo [romanti'θismo] *nm* romanticism

romántico, -a [ro'mantiko, a] *adj* romantic

rombo ['rombo] *nm* (*Geom*) rhombus; (*diseño*) diamond; (*Tip*) lozenge

romería [rome'ria] *nf* (*Rel*) pilgrimage; (*excursión*) trip, outing; *see note*

ROMERÍA

Originally a pilgrimage to a shrine or church to express devotion to Our Lady or a local Saint, the *romería* has also become a rural *fiesta* which accompanies the pilgrimage. People come from all over to attend, bringing their own food and drink, and spend the day in celebration.

romero, -a [ro'mero, a] *nm/f* pilgrim ∎ *nm* rosemary

romo, -a ['romo, a] *adj* blunt; (*fig*) dull

rompecabezas [rompeka'βeθas] *nm inv* riddle, puzzle; (*juego*) jigsaw (puzzle)

rompehielos [rompe'jelos] *nm inv* icebreaker

rompeolas [rompe'olas] *nm inv* breakwater

romper [rom'per] *vt* to break; (*hacer pedazos*) to smash; (*papel, tela etc*) to tear, rip; (*relaciones*) to break off ∎ *vi* (*olas*) to break; (*sol, diente*) to break through; **~ un contrato** to break a contract; **~ a** to start (suddenly) to; **~ a llorar** to burst into tears; **~ con algn** to fall out with sb; **ha roto con su novio** she has broken up with her fiancé

rompimiento [rompi'mjento] *nm* (*acto*) breaking; (*fig*) break; (*quiebra*) crack; **~ de relaciones** breaking off of relations

ron [ron] *nm* rum

roncar [ron'kar] *vi* (*al dormir*) to snore; (*animal*) to roar

roncha ['rontʃa] *nf* (*cardenal*) bruise; (*hinchazón*) swelling

ronco, -a ['ronko, a] *adj* (*afónico*) hoarse; (*áspero*) raucous

ronda ['ronda] *nf* (*de bebidas etc*) round; (*patrulla*) patrol; (*de naipes*) hand, game; **ir de ~** to do one's round

rondar [ron'dar] *vt* to patrol; (*a una persona*) to hang round; (*molestar*) to harass; (*a una chica*) to court ∎ *vi* to patrol; (*fig*) to prowl round;

(*Mus*) to go serenading

rondeño, -a [ron'deɲo, a] *adj* of *o* from Ronda ■ *nm/f* native *o* inhabitant of Ronda

ronque *etc* ['ronke] *vb ver* **roncar**

ronquido [ron'kiðo] *nm* snore, snoring

ronronear [ronrone'ar] *vi* to purr

ronroneo [ronro'neo] *nm* purr

roña ['roɲa] *nf* (*en veterinaria*) mange; (*mugre*) dirt, grime; (*óxido*) rust

roñica [ro'ɲika] *nm/f* (*fam*) skinflint

roñoso, -a [ro'ɲoso, a] *adj* (*mugriento*) filthy; (*tacaño*) mean

ropa ['ropa] *nf* clothes *pl*, clothing; ~ **blanca** linen; ~ **de cama** bed linen; ~ **interior** underwear; ~ **lavada** *o* **para lavar** washing; ~ **planchada** ironing; ~ **sucia** dirty clothes *pl*, washing; ~ **usada** secondhand clothes

ropaje [ro'paxe] *nm* gown, robes *pl*

ropero [ro'pero] *nm* linen cupboard; (*guardarropa*) wardrobe

rosa ['rosa] *adj inv* pink ■ *nf* rose; (*Anat*) red birthmark; ~ **de los vientos** the compass; **estar como una** ~ to feel as fresh as a daisy; (**color**) **de** ~ pink

rosado, -a [ro'saðo, a] *adj* pink ■ *nm* rosé

rosal [ro'sal] *nm* rosebush

rosaleda [rosa'leða] *nf* rose bed *o* garden

rosario [ro'sarjo] *nm* (*Rel*) rosary; (*fig: serie*) string; **rezar el** ~ to say the rosary

rosbif [ros'βif] *nm* roast beef

rosca ['roska] *nf* (*de tornillo*) thread; (*de humo*) coil, spiral; (*pan, postre*) ring-shaped roll/ pastry; **hacer la** ~ **a algn** (*fam*) to suck up to sb; **pasarse de** ~ (*fig*) to go too far

Rosellón [rose'ʎon] *nm* Roussillon

rosetón [rose'ton] *nm* rosette; (*Arq*) rose window

rosquilla [ros'kiʎa] *nf* *small ring-shaped cake*; (*de humo*) ring

rosticería [rostise'ria] *nf* (*Am*) *roast chicken shop*

rostro ['rostro] *nm* (*cara*) face; (*fig*) cheek

rotación [rota'θjon] *nf* rotation; ~ **de cultivos** crop rotation

rotativo, -a [rota'tiβo, a] *adj* rotary ■ *nm* newspaper

roto, -a ['roto, a] *pp de* **romper** ■ *adj* broken; (*en pedazos*) smashed; (*tela, papel*) torn; (*vida*) shattered ■ *nm* (*en vestido*) hole, tear

rótula ['rotula] *nf* kneecap; (*Tec*) ball-and-socket joint

rotulador [rotula'ðor] *nm* felt-tip pen

rotular [rotu'lar] *vt* (*carta, documento*) to head, entitle; (*objeto*) to label

rótulo ['rotulo] *nm* (*título*) heading, title; (*etiqueta*) label; (*letrero*) sign

rotundo, -a [ro'tundo, a] *adj* round; (*enfático*) emphatic

rotura [ro'tura] *nf* (*rompimiento*) breaking; (*Med*) fracture

roturar [rotu'rar] *vt* to plough

roulote [ru'lote] *nf* caravan (*Brit*), trailer (*US*)

rozado, -a [ro'θaðo, a] *adj* worn

rozadura [roθa'ðura] *nf* abrasion, graze

rozar [ro'θar] *vt* (*frotar*) to rub; (*ensuciar*) to dirty; (*Med*) to graze; (*tocar ligeramente*) to shave, skim; (*fig*) to touch *o* border on; **rozarse** *vr* to rub (together); ~ **con** (*fam*) to rub shoulders with

Rte. *abr* = **remite, remitente**

RTVE *nf abr* (*TV*) = **Radiotelevisión Española**

Ruán [ru'an] *nm* Rouen

rubéola [ru'βeola] *nf* German measles, rubella

rubí [ru'βi] *nm* ruby; (*de reloj*) jewel

rubio, -a ['ruβjo, a] *adj* fair-haired, blond(e) ■ *nm/f* blond/blonde; **tabaco** ~ Virginia tobacco; (**cerveza**) **rubia** lager

rubor [ru'βor] *nm* (*sonrojo*) blush; (*timidez*) bashfulness

ruborice *etc* [ruβo'riθe] *vb ver* **ruborizarse**

ruborizarse [ruβori'θarse] *vr* to blush

ruboroso, -a [ruβo'roso, a] *adj* blushing

rúbrica ['ruβrika] *nf* (*título*) title, heading; (*de la firma*) flourish; **bajo la** ~ **de** under the heading of

rubricar [ruβri'kar] *vt* (*firmar*) to sign with a flourish; (*concluir*) to sign and seal

rubrique *etc* [ru'βrike] *vb ver* **rubricar**

rudeza [ru'ðeθa] *nf* (*tosquedad*) coarseness; (*sencillez*) simplicity

rudimentario, -a [ruðimen'tarjo, a] *adj* rudimentary, basic

rudo, -a ['ruðo, a] *adj* (*sin pulir*) unpolished; (*grosero*) coarse; (*violento*) violent; (*sencillo*) simple

rueda ['rweða] *nf* wheel; (*círculo*) ring, circle; (*rodaja*) slice, round; (*en impresora etc*) sprocket; ~ **delantera/trasera/de repuesto** front/ back/spare wheel; ~ **impresora** (*Inform*) print wheel; ~ **de prensa** press conference

ruedo *etc* ['rweðo] *vb ver* **rodar** ■ *nm* (*contorno*) edge, border; (*de vestido*) hem; (*círculo*) circle; (*Taur*) arena, bullring; (*esterilla*) (round) mat

ruego *etc* ['rweɣo] *vb ver* **rogar** ■ *nm* request; **a** ~ **de** at the request of; **"~s y preguntas"** "question and answer session"

ruegue *etc* ['rweɣe] *vb ver* **rogar**

rufián [ru'fjan] *nm* scoundrel

rugby ['ruɣβi] *nm* rugby

rugido [ru'xiðo] *nm* roar

rugir [ru'xir] *vi* to roar; (*toro*) to bellow; (*estómago*) to rumble

rugoso, -a [ru'ɣoso, a] *adj* (*arrugado*) wrinkled; (*áspero*) rough; (*desigual*) ridged

r

ruibarbo [rwi'βarβo] *nm* rhubarb
ruido ['rwiðo] *nm* noise; (*sonido*) sound;
(*alboroto*) racket, row; (*escándalo*) commotion,
rumpus; **~ de fondo** background noise;
hacer *o* **meter ~** to cause a stir
ruidoso, -a [rwi'ðoso, a] *adj* noisy, loud; (*fig*)
sensational
ruin [rwin] *adj* contemptible, mean
ruina ['rwina] *nf* ruin; (*hundimiento*) collapse;
(*de persona*) ruin, downfall; **estar hecho una**
~ to be a wreck; **la empresa le llevó a la ~**
the venture ruined him (financially)
ruindad [rwin'dað] *nf* lowness, meanness;
(*acto*) low *o* mean act
ruinoso, -a [rwi'noso, a] *adj* ruinous;
(*destartalado*) dilapidated, tumbledown;
(*Com*) disastrous
ruiseñor [rwise'ɲor] *nm* nightingale
ruja *etc* ['ruxa] *vb ver* **rugir**
ruleta [ru'leta] *nf* roulette
rulo ['rulo] *nm* (*para el pelo*) curler
rulot [ru'lot], **rulote** [ru'lote] *nf* caravan
(*Brit*), trailer (*US*)
Rumania [ru'manja] *nf* Rumania
rumano, -a [ru'mano, a] *adj, nm/f* Rumanian
rumba ['rumba] *nf* rumba
rumbo ['rumbo] *nm* (*ruta*) route, direction;
(*ángulo de dirección*) course, bearing; (*fig*)
course of events; **con ~ a** in the direction
of; **ir con ~ a** to be heading for; (*Naut*) to be
bound for

rumboso, -a [rum'boso, a] *adj* (*generoso*)
generous
rumiante [ru'mjante] *nm* ruminant
rumiar [ru'mjar] *vt* to chew; (*fig*) to chew
over ▪ *vi* to chew the cud
rumor [ru'mor] *nm* (*ruido sordo*) low sound;
(*murmuración*) murmur, buzz
rumorearse [rumore'arse] *vr*: **se rumorea**
que it is rumoured that
rumoroso, -a [rumo'roso, a] *adj* full of
sounds; (*arroyo*) murmuring
runrún [run'run] *nm* (*de voces*) murmur,
sound of voices; (*fig*) rumour; (*de una máquina*)
whirr
rupestre [ru'pestre] *adj* rock *cpd*; **pintura ~**
cave painting
ruptura [rup'tura] *nf* (*gen*) rupture; (*disputa*)
split; (*de contrato*) breach; (*de relaciones*)
breaking-off
rural [ru'ral] *adj* rural
Rusia ['rusja] *nf* Russia
ruso, -a ['ruso, a] *adj, nm/f* Russian ▪ *nm*
(*Ling*) Russian
rústico, -a ['rustiko, a] *adj* rustic; (*ordinario*)
coarse, uncouth ▪ *nm/f* yokel ▪ *nf*: **libro en**
rústica paperback (book)
ruta ['ruta] *nf* route
rutina [ru'tina] *nf* routine; **~ diaria** daily
routine; **por ~** as a matter of course
rutinario, -a [ruti'narjo, a] *adj* routine

Ss

S, s ['ese] *nf* (*letra*) S, s; **S de Sábado** S for Sugar

S *abr* (= *san, santo, a*) St.; (= *sur*) S

s. *abr* (*tb*: **S.**: = *siglo*) c.; (= *siguiente*) foll.

s/ *abr* (*Com*) = **su; sus**

S.Sª *abr* (= *Sierra*) Mts

S.A. *abr* (= *Sociedad Anónima*) Ltd., Inc. (US); (= *Su Alteza*) H.H.

sáb. *abr* (= *sábado*) Sat.

sábado ['saβaðo] *nm* Saturday; (*de los judíos*) Sabbath; **del ~ en ocho días** a week on Saturday; **un ~ sí y otro no, cada dos sábados** every other Saturday; **S~ Santo** Holy Saturday; *ver tb* **Semana Santa**

sabana [sa'βana] *nf* savannah

sábana ['saβana] *nf* sheet; **se le pegan las sábanas** he can't get up in the morning

sabandija [saβan'dixa] *nf* (*bicho*) bug; (*fig*) louse

sabañón [saβa'ɲon] *nm* chilblain

sabático, -a [sa'βatiko, a] *adj* (*Rel: Univ*) sabbatical

sabelotodo [saβelo'toðo] *nm/f inv* know-all

saber [sa'βer] *vt* to know; (*llegar a conocer*) to find out, learn; (*tener capacidad de*) to know how to ■ *vi*: **~ a** to taste of, taste like ■ *nm* knowledge, learning; **saberse** *vr*: **se sabe que ...** it is known that ...; **no se sabe** nobody knows; **a ~** namely; **¿sabes conducir/nadar?** can you drive/swim?; **¿sabes francés?** do you *o* can you speak French?; **~ de memoria** to know by heart; **lo sé** I know; **hacer ~** to inform, let know; **que yo sepa** as far as I know; **vete** *o* **anda a ~** your guess is as good as mine, who knows!; **¿sabe?** (*fam*) you know (what I mean)?; **le sabe mal que otro la saque a bailar** it upsets him that anybody else should ask her to dance

sabido, -a [sa'βiðo, a] *adj* (*consabido*) well-known; **como es ~** as we all know

sabiduría [saβiðu'ria] *nf* (*conocimientos*) wisdom; (*instrucción*) learning; **~ popular** folklore

sabiendas [sa'βjendas]: **a ~** *adv* knowingly; **a ~ de que ...** knowing full well that ...

sabihondo, -a [sa'βjondo, a] *adj, nm/f* know-all, know-it-all (US)

sabio, -a ['saβjo, a] *adj* (*docto*) learned; (*prudente*) wise, sensible

sablazo [sa'βlaθo] *nm* (*herida*) sword wound; (*fam*) sponging; **dar un ~ a algn** to tap sb for money

sable [sa'βle] *nm* sabre

sabor [sa'βor] *nm* taste, flavour; (*fig*) flavour; **sin ~** flavourless

saborear [saβore'ar] *vt* to taste, savour; (*fig*) to relish

sabotaje [saβo'taxe] *nm* sabotage

saboteador, a [saβotea'ðor, a] *nm/f* saboteur

sabotear [saβote'ar] *vt* to sabotage

Saboya [sa'βoja] *nf* Savoy

sabré *etc* [sa'βre] *vb ver* **saber**

sabroso, -a [sa'βroso, a] *adj* tasty; (*fig fam*) racy, salty

saca ['saka] *nf* big sack; **~ de correo(s)** mailbag; (*Com*) withdrawal

sacacorchos [saka'kortʃos] *nm inv* corkscrew

sacapuntas [saka'puntas] *nm inv* pencil sharpener

sacar [sa'kar] *vt* to take out; (*fig: extraer*) to get (out); (*quitar*) to remove, get out; (*hacer salir*) to bring out; (*fondos: de cuenta*) to draw out, withdraw; (*obtener: legado etc*) to get; (*demostrar*) to show; (*conclusión*) to draw; (*novela etc*) to publish, bring out; (*ropa*) to take off; (*obra*) to make; (*premio*) to receive; (*entradas*) to get; (*Tenis*) to serve; (*Fútbol*) to put into play; **~ adelante** (*niño*) to bring up; **~ a algn a bailar** to dance with sb; **~ a algn de sí** to infuriate sb; **~ una foto** to take a photo; **~ la lengua** to stick out one's tongue; **~ buenas/malas notas** to get good/bad marks

sacarina [saka'rina] *nf* saccharin(e)

sacerdote [saθer'ðote] *nm* priest

saciar [sa'θjar] *vt* (*hartar*) to satiate; (*fig*) to satisfy; **saciarse** *vr* (*fig*) to be satisfied

saciedad | salir

saciedad [saθje'ðað] *nf* satiety; **hasta la ~** (*comer*) one's fill; (*repetir*) ad nauseam
saco ['sako] *nm* bag; (*grande*) sack; (*contenido*) bagful; (*Am: chaqueta*) jacket; **~ de dormir** sleeping bag
sacramento [sakra'mento] *nm* sacrament
sacrificar [sakrifi'kar] *vt* to sacrifice; (*animal*) to slaughter; (*perro etc*) to put to sleep; **sacrificarse** *vr* to sacrifice o.s.
sacrificio [sakri'fiθjo] *nm* sacrifice
sacrifique *etc* [sakri'fike] *vb ver* **sacrificar**
sacrilegio [sakri'lexjo] *nm* sacrilege
sacrílego, -a [sa'krileyo, a] *adj* sacrilegious
sacristán [sakris'tan] *nm* verger
sacristía [sakris'tia] *nf* sacristy
sacro, -a ['sakro, a] *adj* sacred
sacudida [saku'ðiða] *nf* (*agitación*) shake, shaking; (*sacudimiento*) jolt, bump; (*fig*) violent change; (*Pol etc*) upheaval; **~ eléctrica** electric shock
sacudir [saku'ðir] *vt* to shake; (*golpear*) to hit; (*ala*) to flap; (*alfombra*) to beat; **~ a algn** (*fam*) to belt sb
S.A. de C.V. *abr* (*Am: = Sociedad Anónima de Capital Variable*) ≈ PLC (*Brit*), ≈ Corps (*US*), ≈ Inc. (*US*)
sádico, -a ['saðiko, a] *adj* sadistic ■ *nm/f* sadist
sadismo [sa'ðismo] *nm* sadism
sadomasoquismo [saðomaso'kismo] *nm* sadomasochism, S & M
sadomasoquista [saðomaso'kista] *adj* sadomasochistic ■ *nm/f* sadomasochist
saeta [sa'eta] *nf* (*flecha*) arrow; (*Mus*) sacred song in flamenco style
safari [sa'fari] *nm* safari
sagacidad [sayaθi'ðað] *nf* shrewdness, cleverness
sagaz [sa'yaθ] *adj* shrewd, clever
Sagitario [saxi'tarjo] *nm* (*Astro*) Sagittarius
sagrado, -a [sa'yraðo, a] *adj* sacred, holy
Sáhara ['saara] *nm*: **el ~** the Sahara (desert)
saharaui [saxa'rawi] *adj* Saharan ■ *nm/f* native o inhabitant of the Sahara
sajón, -ona [sa'xon, 'xona] *adj, nm/f* Saxon
sal [sal] *vb ver* **salir** ■ *nf* salt; (*gracia*) wit; (*encanto*) charm; **sales de baño** bath salts; **~ gorda** o **de cocina** kitchen o cooking salt
sala ['sala] *nf* (*cuarto grande*) large room; (*tb*: **sala de estar**) living room; (*Teat*) house, auditorium; (*de hospital*) ward; **~ de apelación** court; **~ de conferencias** lecture hall; **~ de espera** waiting room; **~ de embarque** departure lounge; **~ de estar** living room; **~ de fiestas** function room; **~ de juntas** (*Com*) boardroom; **~ VIP** (*en aeropuerto, discoteca*) VIP lounge
salado, -a [sa'laðo, a] *adj* salty; (*fig*) witty,

amusing; **agua salada** salt water
salar [sa'lar] *vt* to salt, add salt to
salariado, -a [sala'rjaðo, a] *adj* (*empleado*) salaried
salarial [sala'rjal] *adj* (*aumento, revisión*) wage *cpd*, salary *cpd*, pay *cpd*
salario [sa'larjo] *nm* wage, pay
salchicha [sal'tʃitʃa] *nf* (pork) sausage
salchichón [saltʃi'tʃon] *nm* (salami-type) sausage
saldar [sal'dar] *vt* to pay; (*vender*) to sell off; (*fig*) to settle, resolve
saldo ['saldo] *nm* (*pago*) settlement; (*de una cuenta*) balance; (*lo restante*) remnant(s) (*pl*), remainder; (*liquidación*) sale; (*Com*): **~ anterior** balance brought forward; **~ acreedor/deudor** o **pasivo** credit/debit balance; **~ final** final balance
saldré *etc* [sal'dre] *vb ver* **salir**
salero [sa'lero] *nm* salt cellar; (*ingenio*) wit; (*encanto*) charm
salga *etc* ['salya] *vb ver* **salir**
salida [sa'liða] *nf* (*puerta etc*) exit, way out; (*acto*) leaving, going out; (*de tren, Aviat*) departure; (*Com: Tec*) output, production; (*fig*) way out; (*resultado*) outcome; (*Com: oportunidad*) opening; (*Geo, válvula*) outlet; (*de gas*) escape; (*ocurrencia*) joke; **calle sin ~** cul-de-sac; **a la ~ del teatro** after the theatre; **dar la ~** (*Deporte*) to give the starting signal; **~ de incendios** fire escape; **~ impresa** (*Inform*) hard copy; **no hay ~** there's no way out of it; **no tenemos otra ~** we have no option; **tener salidas** to be witty
salido, -a [sa'liðo, a] *adj* (*fam*) randy
saliente [sa'ljente] *adj* (*Arq*) projecting; (*sol*) rising; (*fig*) outstanding
salina [sa'lina] *nf* salt mine; **salinas** *nfpl* saltworks *sg*

 PALABRA CLAVE

salir [sa'lir] *vi* **1** (*persona*) to come o go out; (*tren, avión*) to leave; **Juan ha salido** Juan has gone out; **salió de la cocina** he came out of the kitchen; **salimos de Madrid a las ocho** we left Madrid at eight (o'clock); **salió corriendo (del cuarto)** he ran out (of the room); **salir de un apuro** to get out of a jam
2 (*pelo*) to grow; (*diente*) to come through; (*disco, libro*) to come out; (*planta, número de lotería*) to come up; **salir a la superficie** to come to the surface; **anoche salió en la tele** she appeared o was on TV last night; **salió en todos los periódicos** it was in all the papers; **le salió un trabajo** he got a job
3 (*resultar*): **la muchacha nos salió muy**

346 · SPANISH | ENGLISH

trabajadora the girl turned out to be a very hard worker; **la comida te ha salido exquisita** the food was delicious; **sale muy caro** it's very expensive; **la entrevista que hice me salió bien/mal** the interview I did turned out *o* went well/badly; **nos salió a 5.000 ptas cada uno** it worked out at 5,000 pesetas each; **no salen las cuentas** it doesn't work out *o* add up; **salir ganando** to come out on top; **salir perdiendo** to lose out **4** (*Deporte*) to start; (*Naipes*) to lead
5: **salir con algn** to go out with sb
6: **salir adelante**: **no sé como haré para salir adelante** I don't know how I'll get by
salirse *vr* **1** (*líquido*) to spill; (*animal*) to escape **2** (*desviarse*): **salirse de la carretera** to leave *o* go off the road; **salirse de lo normal** to be unusual; **salirse del tema** to get off the point
3: **salirse con la suya** to get one's own way

saliva [sa'liβa] *nf* saliva
salivadera [saliβa'ðera] *nf* (*Am*) spittoon
salmantino, -a [salman'tino, a] *adj* of *o* from Salamanca ■ *nm/f* native *o* inhabitant of Salamanca
salmo ['salmo] *nm* psalm
salmón [sal'mon] *nm* salmon
salmonete [salmo'nete] *nm* red mullet
salmuera [sal'mwera] *nf* pickle, brine
salón [sa'lon] *nm* living-room, lounge; (*muebles*) lounge suite; **~ de belleza** beauty parlour; **~ de baile** dance hall; **~ de actos/ sesiones** assembly hall
salpicadero [salpika'ðero] *nm* (*Auto*) dashboard
salpicar [salpi'kar] *vt* (*de barro, pintura*) to splash; (*rociar*) to sprinkle, spatter; (*esparcir*) to scatter
salpicón [salpi'kon] *nm* (*acto*) splashing; (*Culin*) meat *o* fish salad
salpimentar [salpimen'tar] *vt* (*Culin*) to season
salpique *etc* [sal'pike] *vb ver* **salpicar**
salsa ['salsa] *nf* sauce; (*con carne asada*) gravy; (*fig*) spice; **~ mayonesa** mayonnaise; **estar en su ~** (*fam*) to be in one's element
saltamontes [salta'montes] *nm inv* grasshopper
saltar [sal'tar] *vt* to jump (over), leap (over); (*dejar de lado*) to skip, miss out ■ *vi* to jump, leap; (*pelota*) to bounce; (*al aire*) to fly up; (*quebrarse*) to break; (*al agua*) to dive; (*fig*) to explode, blow up; (*botón*) to come off; (*corcho*) to pop out; **saltarse** *vr* (*omitir*) to skip, miss; **salta a la vista** it's obvious; **saltarse todas las reglas** to break all the rules

salteado, -a [salte'aðo, a] *adj* (*Culin*) sauté(ed)
salteador [saltea'ðor] *nm* (*tb*: **salteador de caminos**) highwayman
saltear [salte'ar] *vt* (*robar*) to rob (in a holdup); (*asaltar*) to assault, attack; (*Culin*) to sauté
saltimbanqui [saltim'banki] *nm/f* acrobat
salto ['salto] *nm* jump, leap; (*al agua*) dive; **a saltos** by jumping; **~ de agua** waterfall; **~ de altura** high jump; **~ de cama** negligee; **~ mortal** somersault; (*Inform*): **~ de línea** line feed; **~ de línea automático** wordwrap; **~ de página** formfeed
saltón, -ona [sal'ton, ona] *adj* (*ojos*) bulging, popping; (*dientes*) protruding
salubre [sa'luβre] *adj* healthy, salubrious
salud [sa'luð] *nf* health; **estar bien/mal de ~** to be in good/poor health; **¡(a su) ~!** cheers!, good health!; **beber a la ~ de** to drink (to) the health of
saludable [salu'ðaβle] *adj* (*de buena salud*) healthy; (*provechoso*) good, beneficial
saludar [salu'ðar] *vt* to greet; (*Mil*) to salute; **ir a ~ a algn** to drop in to see sb; **salude de mi parte a X** give my regards to X; **le saluda atentamente** (*en carta*) yours faithfully
saludo [sa'luðo] *nm* greeting; **saludos** (*en carta*) best wishes, regards; **un ~ afectuoso** *o* **cordial** yours sincerely
salva ['salβa] *nf* (*Mil*) salvo; **una ~ de aplausos** thunderous applause
salvación [salβa'θjon] *nf* salvation; (*rescate*) rescue
salvado [sal'βaðo] *nm* bran
salvador [salβa'ðor] *nm* rescuer, saviour; **el S~** the Saviour; **El S~** El Salvador; **San S~** San Salvador
salvadoreño, -a [salβaðo'reɲo, a] *adj, nm/f* Salvadoran, Salvadorian
salvaguardar [salβaɣwar'ðar] *vt* to safeguard; (*Inform*) to back up, make a backup copy of
salvajada [salβa'xaða] *nf* savage deed, atrocity
salvaje [sal'βaxe] *adj* wild; (*tribu*) savage
salvajismo [salβa'xismo] *nm* savagery
salvamento [salβa'mento] *nm* (*acción*) rescue; (*de naufragio*) salvage; **~ y socorrismo** life-saving
salvapantallas [salβapan'taʎas] *nm inv* screensaver
salvar [sal'βar] *vt* (*rescatar*) to save, rescue; (*resolver*) to overcome, resolve; (*cubrir distancias*) to cover, travel; (*hacer excepción*) to except, exclude; (*un barco*) to salvage; **salvarse** *vr* to save o.s., escape; **¡sálvese el que pueda!** every man for himself!

salvavidas [salβa'βiðas] *adj inv*: **bote/ chaleco/cinturón** ~ lifeboat/lifejacket/ lifebelt

salvedad [salβe'ðað] *nf* reservation, qualification; **con la ~ de que ...** with the proviso that ...

salvia ['salβja] *nf* sage

salvo, -a ['salβo, a] *adj* safe ■ *prep* except (for), save; **~ error u omisión** (*Com*) errors and omissions excepted; **a ~** out of danger; **~ que** unless

salvoconducto [salβokon'dukto] *nm* safe-conduct

samba ['samba] *nf* samba

san [san] *n* (*apócope de* **santo**) saint; **~ Juan** St. John; *ver tb* **Juan**

sanar [sa'nar] *vt* (*herida*) to heal; (*persona*) to cure ■ *vi* (*persona*) to get well, recover; (*herida*) to heal

sanatorio [sana'torjo] *nm* sanatorium

sanción [san'θjon] *nf* sanction

sancionar [sanθjo'nar] *vt* to sanction

sancocho [san'kotʃo] *nm* (*Am*) stew

sandalia [san'dalja] *nf* sandal

sándalo ['sandalo] *nm* sandal(wood)

sandez [san'deθ] *nf* (*cualidad*) foolishness; (*acción*) stupid thing; **decir sandeces** to talk nonsense

sandía [san'dia] *nf* watermelon

sandinista [sanði'nista] *adj, nm/f* Sandinist(a)

sandwich ['sandwitʃ] (*pl* **sandwichs** *o* **sandwiches**) *nm* sandwich

saneamiento [sanea'mjento] *nm* sanitation

sanear [sane'ar] *vt* to drain; (*indemnizar*) to compensate; (*Econ*) to reorganize

sanfermines [sanfer'mines] *nmpl see note*

● **SANFERMINES**
●
● The *Sanfermines* are a week of *fiestas* in
● Pamplona, the capital of Navarre, made
● famous by Ernest Hemingway. From
● the 7th of July, the feast of San Fermín,
● crowds of mainly young people take
● to the streets drinking, singing and
● dancing. Early in the morning bulls are
● released along the narrow streets leading
● to the bullring, and people risk serious
● injury by running out in front of them,
● a custom which is also typical of many
● Spanish villages.

sangrar [san'grar] *vt, vi* to bleed; (*texto*) to indent

sangre ['sangre] *nf* blood; **~ fría** sangfroid; **a ~ fría** in cold blood

sangría [san'gria] *nf* (*Med*) bleeding; (*Culin*) sangria, *sweetened drink of red wine with fruit*, ≈ fruit cup

sangriento, -a [san'grjento, a] *adj* bloody

sanguijuela [sangi'xwela] *nf* (*Zool, fig*) leech

sanguinario, -a [sangi'narjo, a] *adj* bloodthirsty

sanguíneo, -a [san'gineo, a] *adj* blood *cpd*

sanidad [sani'ðað] *nf* sanitation; (*calidad de sano*) health, healthiness; **~ pública** public health (department)

sanitario, -a [sani'tarjo, a] *adj* sanitary; (*de la salud*) health *cpd* ■ *nm*: **sanitarios** *nmpl* toilets (*Brit*), restroom *sg* (*US*)

San Marino [sanma'rino] *nm*: **(La República de)** ~ San Marino

sano, -a ['sano, a] *adj* healthy; (*sin daños*) sound; (*comida*) wholesome; (*entero*) whole, intact; **~ y salvo** safe and sound

santanderino, -a [santande'rino, a] *adj* of *o* from Santander ■ *nm/f* native *o* inhabitant of Santander

Santiago [san'tjaɣo] *nm*: **~ (de Chile)** Santiago

santiamén [santja'men] *nm*: **en un ~** in no time at all

santidad [santi'ðað] *nf* holiness, sanctity

santificar [santifi'kar] *vt* to sanctify

santifique *etc* [santi'fike] *vb ver* **santificar**

santiguarse [santi'ɣwarse] *vr* to make the sign of the cross

santigüe *etc* [san'tiɣwe] *vb ver* **santiguarse**

santo, -a ['santo, a] *adj* holy; (*fig*) wonderful, miraculous ■ *nm/f* saint ■ *nm* saint's day; **hacer su santa voluntad** to do as one jolly well pleases; **¿a ~ de qué ...?** why on earth ...?; **se le fue el ~ al cielo** he forgot what he was about to say; **~ y seña** password; *see note*

● **SANTO**
●
● As well as celebrating their birthday
● Spaniards have traditionally celebrated
● *el santo*, their Saint's day, when the
● Saint they were called after at birth, eg
● San Pedro or la Virgen de los Dolores, is
● honoured in the Christian calendar. This
● is a custom which is gradually dying out.

santuario [san'twarjo] *nm* sanctuary, shrine

saña ['saɲa] *nf* rage, fury

sapo ['sapo] *nm* toad

saque *etc* ['sake] *vb ver* **sacar** ■ *nm* (*Tenis*) service, serve; (*Fútbol*) throw-in; **~ inicial** kick-off; **~ de esquina** corner (kick); **tener buen ~** to eat heartily

saquear [sake'ar] *vt* (*Mil*) to sack; (*robar*) to loot, plunder; (*fig*) to ransack

saqueo [sa'keo] *nm* sacking; looting, plundering; ransacking

S.A.R. *abr* (= *Su Alteza Real*) HRH

sarampión [saram'pjon] *nm* measles *sg*

sarape [sa'rape] *nm* (*Am*) blanket

sarcasmo [sar'kasmo] *nm* sarcasm

sarcástico, -a [sar'kastiko, a] *adj* sarcastic

sarcófago [sar'kofaɣo] *nm* sarcophagus

sardina [sar'ðina] *nf* sardine

sardo, -a ['sarðo, a] *adj, nm/f* Sardinian

sardónico, -a [sar'ðoniko, a] *adj* sardonic; (*irónico*) ironical, sarcastic

sargento [sar'xento] *nm* sergeant

sarmiento [sar'mjento] *nm* vine shoot

sarna ['sarna] *nf* itch; (*Med*) scabies

sarpullido [sarpu'ʎiðo] *nm* (*Med*) rash

sarro ['sarro] *nm* deposit; (*en dientes*) tartar

sarta ['sarta] *nf* (*fig*): **una ~ de mentiras** a pack of lies

sartén [sar'ten] *nf* frying pan; **tener la ~ por el mango** to rule the roost

sastre ['sastre] *nm* tailor

sastrería [sastre'ria] *nf* (*arte*) tailoring; (*tienda*) tailor's (shop)

Satanás [sata'nas] *nm* Satan

satélite [sa'telite] *nm* satellite

satinado, -a [sati'naðo, a] *adj* glossy
■ *nm* gloss, shine

sátira ['satira] *nf* satire

satírico, -a [sa'tiriko, a] *adj* satiric(al)

sátiro ['satiro] *nm* (*Mitología*) satyr; (*fig*) sex maniac

satisfacción [satisfak'θjon] *nf* satisfaction

satisfacer [satisfa'θer] *vt* to satisfy; (*gastos*) to meet; (*deuda*) to pay; (*Com: letra de cambio*) to honour (*Brit*), honor (*US*); (*pérdida*) to make good; **satisfacerse** *vr* to satisfy o.s., be satisfied; (*vengarse*) to take revenge

satisfaga *etc* [satis'faɣa], **satisfaré** *etc* [satisfa're] *vb ver* **satisfacer**

satisfecho, -a [satis'fetʃo, a] *pp de* **satisfacer**
■ *adj* satisfied; (*contento*) content(ed), happy; (*tb*: **satisfecho de sí mismo**) self-satisfied, smug

satisfice *etc* [satis'fiθe] *vb ver* **satisfacer**

saturación [satura'θjon] *nf* saturation; **llegar a la ~** to reach saturation point

saturar [satu'rar] *vt* to saturate; **saturarse** *vr* (*mercado, aeropuerto*) to reach saturation point; **¡estoy saturado de tanta televisión!** I can't take any more television!

sauce ['sauθe] *nm* willow; **~ llorón** weeping willow

saúco [sa'uko] *nm* (*Bot*) elder

saudí [sau'ði] *adj, nm/f* Saudi

sauna ['sauna] *nf* sauna

savia ['saβja] *nf* sap

saxo ['sakso] *nm* sax

saxofón [sakso'fon] *nm* saxophone

saya ['saja] *nf* (*falda*) skirt; (*enagua*) petticoat

sayo ['sajo] *nm* smock

sazón [sa'θon] *nf* (*de fruta*) ripeness; **a la ~** then, at that time

sazonado, -a [saθo'naðo, a] *adj* (*fruta*) ripe; (*Culin*) flavoured, seasoned

sazonar [saθo'nar] *vt* to ripen; (*Culin*) to flavour, season

s/c *abr* (*Com*: = *su casa*) your firm; (: = *su cuenta*) your account

Sdo. *abr* (*Com*: = *Saldo*) bal

SE *abr* (= *sudeste*) SE

○ PALABRA CLAVE

se [se] *pron* **1** (*reflexivo: sg: m*) himself; (: *f*) herself; (: *pl*) themselves; (: *cosa*) itself; (: *de Vd*) yourself; (: *de Vds*) yourselves; (*indefinido*) oneself; **se mira en el espejo** he looks at himself in the mirror; **¡siéntese!** sit down!; **se durmió** he fell asleep; **se está preparando** she's getting (herself) ready; (*para usos léxicos del pron ver el vb en cuestión, p.ej.* **arrepentirse**)

2 (*como complemento indirecto*) to him; to her; to them; to it; to you; **se lo dije ayer** (*a Vd*) I told you yesterday; **se compró un sombrero** he bought himself a hat; **se rompió la pierna** he broke his leg; **cortarse el pelo** to get one's hair cut; (*uno mismo*) to cut one's hair; **se comió un pastel** he ate a cake

3 (*uso recíproco*) each other, one another; **se miraron (el uno al otro)** they looked at each other o one another

4 (*en oraciones pasivas*): **se han vendido muchos libros** a lot of books have been sold; **"se vende coche"** "car for sale"

5 (*impers*): **se dice que** people say that, it is said that; **allí se come muy bien** the food there is very good, you can eat very well there

sé [se] *vb ver* **saber; ser**

sea *etc* ['sea] *vb ver* **ser**

SEAT ['seat] *nf abr* = **Sociedad Española de Automóviles de Turismo**

sebo ['seβo] *nm* fat, grease

Sec. *abr* (= *Secretario*) Sec

seca ['seka] *nf ver* **seco**

secado [se'kaðo] *nm* drying; **~ a mano** blow-dry

secador [seka'ðor] *nm*: **~ para el pelo** hairdryer

secadora [seka'ðora] *nf* tumble dryer; **~ centrífuga** spin-dryer

S

secano [se'kano] *nm* (*Agr*: *tb*: **tierra de secano**) dry land *o* region; **cultivo de** ~ dry farming

secante [se'kante] *adj* (*viento*) drying ∎ *nm* blotting paper

secar [se'kar] *vt* to dry; (*superficie*) to wipe dry; (*frente, suelo*) to mop; (*líquido*) to mop up; (*tinta*) to blot; **secarse** *vr* to dry (off); (*río, planta*) to dry up

sección [sek'θjon] *nf* section; (*Com*) department; ~ **deportiva** (*en periódico*) sports page(s)

seco, -a ['seko, a] *adj* dry; (*fruta*) dried; (*persona*: *magro*) thin, skinny; (*carácter*) cold; (*antipático*) disagreeable; (*respuesta*) sharp, curt ∎ *nf* dry season; **habrá pan a secas** there will be just bread; **decir algo a secas** to say sth curtly; **parar en** ~ to stop dead

secreción [sekre'θjon] *nf* secretion

secretaría [sekreta'ria] *nf* secretariat; (*oficina*) secretary's office

secretariado [sekreta'rjaðo] *nm* (*oficina*) secretariat; (*cargo*) secretaryship; (*curso*) secretarial course

secretario, -a [sekre'tarjo, a] *nm/f* secretary; ~ **adjunto** (*Com*) assistant secretary

secreto, -a [se'kreto, a] *adj* secret; (*información*) confidential; (*persona*) secretive ∎ *nm* secret; (*calidad*) secrecy

secta ['sekta] *nf* sect

sectario, -a [sek'tarjo, a] *adj* sectarian

sector [sek'tor] *nm* sector (*tb Inform*); (*de opinión*) section; (*fig*: *campo*) area, field; ~ **privado/público** (*Com*: *Econ*) private/public sector

secuela [se'kwela] *nf* consequence

secuencia [se'kwenθja] *nf* sequence

secuestrar [sekwes'trar] *vt* to kidnap; (*avión*) to hijack; (*bienes*) to seize, confiscate

secuestro [se'kwestro] *nm* kidnapping; hijack; seizure, confiscation

secular [seku'lar] *adj* secular

secundar [sekun'dar] *vt* to second, support

secundario, -a [sekun'darjo, a] *adj* secondary; (*carretera*) side *cpd*; (*Inform*) background *cpd* ∎ *nf* secondary education; *ver tb* **sistema educativo**

sed [seð] *nf* thirst; (*fig*) thirst, craving; **tener** ~ to be thirsty

seda ['seða] *nf* silk; ~ **dental** dental floss

sedal [se'ðal] *nm* fishing line

sedante [se'ðante] *nm* sedative

sede ['seðe] *nf* (*de gobierno*) seat; (*de compañía*) headquarters *pl*, head office; **Santa S**~ Holy See

sedentario, -a [seðen'tarjo, a] *adj* sedentary

SEDIC [se'ðik] *nf abr* = **Sociedad Española de Documentación e Información Científica**

sedición [seði'θjon] *nf* sedition

sediento, -a [se'ðjento, a] *adj* thirsty

sedimentar [seðimen'tar] *vt* to deposit; **sedimentarse** *vr* to settle

sedimento [seði'mento] *nm* sediment

sedoso, -a [se'ðoso, a] *adj* silky, silken

seducción [seðuk'θjon] *nf* seduction

seducir [seðu'θir] *vt* to seduce; (*sobornar*) to bribe; (*cautivar*) to charm, fascinate; (*atraer*) to attract

seductor, a [seðuk'tor, a] *adj* seductive; charming, fascinating; attractive; (*engañoso*) deceptive, misleading ∎ *nm/f* seducer

seduje *etc* [se'ðuxe], **seduzca** *etc* [se'ðuθka] *vb ver* **seducir**

sefardí [sefar'ði], **sefardita** [sefar'ðita] *adj* Sephardi(c) ∎ *nm/f* Sephardi

segador, a [seɣa'ðor, a] *nm/f* (*persona*) harvester ∎ *nf* (*Tec*) mower, reaper

segadora-trilladora [seɣa'ðoratriʎa'ðora] *nf* combine harvester

segar [se'ɣar] *vt* (*mies*) to reap, cut; (*hierba*) to mow, cut; (*esperanzas*) to ruin

seglar [se'ɣlar] *adj* secular, lay

segoviano, -a [seɣo'βjano, a] *adj* of *o* from Segovia ∎ *nm/f* native *o* inhabitant of Segovia

segregación [seɣreɣa'θjon] *nf* segregation; ~ **racial** racial segregation

segregar [seɣre'ɣar] *vt* to segregate, separate

segregue *etc* [se'ɣreɣe] *vb ver* **segregar**

segué [se'ɣe], **seguemos** *etc* [se'ɣemos] *vb ver* **segar**

seguidamente [seɣiða'mente] *adv* (*sin parar*) without a break; (*inmediatamente después*) immediately after

seguido, -a [se'ɣiðo, a] *adj* (*continuo*) continuous, unbroken; (*recto*) straight ∎ *adv* (*directo*) straight (on); (*después*) after; (*Am*: *a menudo*) often ∎ *nf*: **en seguida** at once, right away; **cinco días seguidos** five days running, five days in a row; **en seguida termino** I've nearly finished, I shan't be long now

seguimiento [seɣi'mjento] *nm* chase, pursuit; (*continuación*) continuation

seguir [se'ɣir] *vt* to follow; (*venir después*) to follow on, come after; (*proseguir*) to continue; (*perseguir*) to chase, pursue; (*indicio*) to follow up; (*mujer*) to court ∎ *vi* (*gen*) to follow; (*continuar*) to continue, carry *o* go on; **seguirse** *vr* to follow; **a** ~ to be continued; **sigo sin comprender** I still don't understand; **sigue lloviendo** it's still raining; **sigue** (*en carta*) P.T.O.; (*en libro, TV*) continued; **"hágase ~"** "please forward"; **¡siga!** (*Am: pase*) come in!

según [se'ɣun] *prep* according to ▪ *adv*: ~ **(y conforme)** it all depends ▪ *conj* as; ~ **esté el tiempo** depending on the weather; ~ **me consta** as far as I know; **está ~ lo dejaste** it is just as you left it

segundo, -a [se'ɣundo, a] *adj* second; (*en discurso*) secondly ▪ *nm* (*gen, medida de tiempo*) second; (*piso*) second floor ▪ *nf* (*sentido*) second meaning; ~ **(de a bordo)** (*Naut*) first mate; **segunda (clase)** (*Ferro*) second class; **segunda (marcha)** (*Auto*) second (gear); **de segunda mano** second hand

seguramente [seɣura'mente] *adv* surely; (*con certeza*) for sure, with certainty; (*probablemente*) probably; **¿lo va a comprar?** — ~ is he going to buy it? — I should think so

seguridad [seɣuri'ðað] *nf* safety; (*del estado, de casa etc*) security; (*certidumbre*) certainty; (*confianza*) confidence; (*estabilidad*) stability; ~ **social** social security; ~ **contra incendios** fire precautions *pl*; ~ **en sí mismo** (self-)confidence

seguro, -a [se'ɣuro, a] *adj* (*cierto*) sure, certain; (*fiel*) trustworthy; (*libre de peligro*) safe; (*bien defendido, firme*) secure; (*datos etc*) reliable; (*fecha*) firm ▪ *adv* for sure, certainly ▪ *nm* (*dispositivo*) safety device; (*de cerradura*) tumbler; (*de arma*) safety catch; (*Com*) insurance; ~ **contra accidentes/incendios** fire/accident insurance; ~ **contra terceros/ a todo riesgo** third party/comprehensive insurance; ~ **dotal con beneficios** with-profits endowment assurance; **S~ de Enfermedad** ≈ National Insurance; ~ **marítimo** marine insurance; ~ **mixto** endowment assurance; ~ **temporal** term insurance; ~ **de vida** life insurance

seis [seis] *num* six; ~ **mil** six thousand; **tiene ~ años** she is six (years old); **unos ~** about six; **hoy es el ~** today is the sixth

seiscientos, -as [seis'θjentos, as] *num* six hundred

seísmo [se'ismo] *nm* tremor, earthquake

SELA *sigla m* = **Sistema Económico Latinoamericano**

selección [selek'θjon] *nf* selection; ~ **múltiple** multiple choice; ~ **nacional** (*Deporte*) national team

seleccionador, a [selekθjona'ðor, a] *nm/f* (*Deporte*) selector

seleccionar [selekθjo'nar] *vt* to pick, choose, select

selectividad [selektiβi'ðað] *nf* (*Univ*) entrance examination; *see note*

SELECTIVIDAD

School leavers wishing to go on to University sit the dreaded *selectividad* in June, with resits in September. When student numbers are too high for a particular course only the best students get their choice. Some of the others then wait a year to sit the exam again rather than do a course they don't want.

selecto, -a [se'lekto, a] *adj* select, choice; (*escogido*) selected

sellado, -a [se'ʎaðo, a] *adj* (*documento oficial*) sealed; (*pasaporte*) stamped

sellar [se'ʎar] *vt* (*documento oficial*) to seal; (*pasaporte, visado*) to stamp; (*marcar*) to brand; (*pacto, labios*) to seal

sello ['seʎo] *nm* stamp; (*precinto*) seal; (*fig: tb*: **sello distintivo**) hallmark; ~ **fiscal** revenue stamp; **sellos de prima** (*Com*) trading stamps

selva ['selβa] *nf* (*bosque*) forest, woods *pl*; (*jungla*) jungle; **la S~ Negra** the Black Forest

S.Em. *abr* = **Su Eminencia**

semáforo [se'maforo] *nm* (*Auto*) traffic lights *pl*; (*Ferro*) signal

semana [se'mana] *nf* week; ~ **inglesa** five-day (working) week; ~ **laboral** working week; **S~ Santa** Holy Week; *see note*; **entre ~** during the week

SEMANA SANTA

Semana Santa is a holiday in Spain. All regions take *Viernes Santo*, Good Friday, *Sábado Santo*, Holy Saturday, and *Domingo de Resurrección*, Easter Sunday. Other holidays at this time vary according to each region. There are spectacular *procesiones* all over the country, with members of *cofradías* (brotherhoods) dressing in hooded robes and parading their *pasos* (religious floats or sculptures) through the streets. Seville has the most renowned celebrations, on account of the religious fervour shown by the locals.

semanal [sema'nal] *adj* weekly

semanario [sema'narjo] *nm* weekly (magazine)

semántica [se'mantika] *nf* semantics *sg*

semblante [sem'blante] *nm* face; (*fig*) look

sembrar [sem'brar] *vt* to sow; (*objetos*) to sprinkle, scatter about; (*noticias etc*) to spread

semejante [seme'xante] *adj* (*parecido*) similar; (*tal*) such; **semejantes** alike, similar ■ *nm* fellow man, fellow creature; **son muy semejantes** they are very much alike; **nunca hizo cosa** ~ he never did such a thing

semejanza [seme'xanθa] *nf* similarity, resemblance; **a** ~ **de** like, as

semejar [seme'xar] *vi* to seem like, resemble; **semejarse** *vr* to look alike, be similar

semen ['semen] *nm* semen

semental [semen'tal] *nm* (*macho*) stud

sementera [semen'tera] *nf* (*acto*) sowing; (*temporada*) seedtime; (*tierra*) sown land

semestral [semes'tral] *adj* half-yearly, bi-annual

semestre [se'mestre] *nm* period of six months; (*Univ*) semester; (*Com*) half-yearly payment

semicírculo [semi'θirkulo] *nm* semicircle

semiconductor [semikonduk'tor] *nm* semiconductor

semiconsciente [semikons'θjente] *adj* semiconscious

semidesnatado, -a [semiðesna'taðo, a] *adj* semi-skimmed

semifinal [semifi'nal] *nf* semifinal

semiinconsciente [semi(i)nkons'θjente] *adj* semiconscious

semilla [se'miʎa] *nf* seed

semillero [semi'ʎero] *nm* (*Agr etc*) seedbed; (*fig*) hotbed

seminario [semi'narjo] *nm* (*Rel*) seminary; (*Escol*) seminar

semiseco [semi'seko] *nm* medium-dry

semita [se'mita] *adj* Semitic ■ *nm/f* Semite

sémola ['semola] *nf* semolina

sempiterno, -a [sempi'terno, a] *adj* everlasting

Sena ['sena] *nm*: **el** ~ the (river) Seine

senado [se'naðo] *nm* senate; *ver tb* **Las Cortes (españolas)**

senador, a [sena'ðor, a] *nm/f* senator

sencillez [senθi'ʎeθ] *nf* simplicity; (*de persona*) naturalness

sencillo, -a [sen'θiʎo, a] *adj* simple; (*carácter*) natural, unaffected; (*billete*) single ■ *nm* (*disco*) single; (*Am*) small change

senda ['senda] *nf*, **sendero** [sen'dero] *nm* path, track; **Sendero Luminoso** the Shining Path (guerrilla movement)

senderismo [sende'rismo] *nm* trekking

sendos, -as ['sendos, as] *adj pl*: **les dio** ~ **golpes** he hit both of them

senil [se'nil] *adj* senile

seno ['seno] *nm* (*Anat*) bosom, bust; (*fig*) bosom; **senos** *nmpl* breasts; ~ **materno** womb

sensación [sensa'θjon] *nf* sensation; (*sentido*) sense; (*sentimiento*) feeling; **causar** *o* **hacer** ~ to cause a sensation

sensacional [sensaθjo'nal] *adj* sensational

sensatez [sensa'teθ] *nf* common sense

sensato, -a [sen'sato, a] *adj* sensible

sensibilidad [sensiβili'ðað] *nf* sensitivity; (*para el arte*) feel

sensibilizar [sensiβili'θar] *vt*: ~ **a la población/opinión pública** to raise public awareness

sensible [sen'sible] *adj* sensitive; (*apreciable*) perceptible, appreciable; (*pérdida*) considerable

sensiblero, -a [sensi'βlero, a] *adj* sentimental, slushy

sensitivo, -a [sensi'tiβo, a], **sensorial** [senso'rjal] *adj* sense *cpd*

sensor [sen'sor] *nm*: ~ **de fin de papel** paper out sensor

sensual [sen'swal] *adj* sensual

sentado, -a [sen'taðo, a] *adj* (*establecido*) settled; (*carácter*) sensible ■ *nf* sitting; (*Pol*) sit-in, sit-down protest; **dar por** ~ to take for granted, assume; **dejar algo** ~ to establish sth firmly; **estar** ~ to sit, be sitting (down); **de una sentada** at one sitting

sentar [sen'tar] *vt* to sit, seat; (*fig*) to establish ■ *vi* (*vestido*) to suit; (*alimento*): ~ **bien/mal a** to agree/disagree with; **sentarse** *vr* (*persona*) to sit, sit down; (*el tiempo*) to settle (down); (*los depósitos*) to settle; **¡siéntese!** (do) sit down, take a seat

sentencia [sen'tenθja] *nf* (*máxima*) maxim, saying; (*Jur*) sentence; ~ **de muerte** death sentence

sentenciar [senten'θjar] *vt* to sentence

sentido, -a [sen'tiðo, a] *adj* (*pérdida*) regrettable; (*carácter*) sensitive ■ *nm* sense; (*sentimiento*) feeling; (*significado*) sense, meaning; (*dirección*) direction; **mi más** ~ **pésame** my deepest sympathy; ~ **del humor** sense of humour; ~ **común** common sense; **en el buen** ~ **de la palabra** in the best sense of the word; **sin** ~ meaningless; **tener** ~ to make sense; ~ **único** one-way (street)

sentimental [sentimen'tal] *adj* sentimental; **vida** ~ love life

sentimiento [senti'mjento] *nm* (*emoción*) feeling, emotion; (*sentido*) sense; (*pesar*) regret, sorrow

sentir [sen'tir] *vt* to feel; (*percibir*) to perceive, sense; (*esp Am: oír*) to hear; (*lamentar*) to regret, be sorry for; (*música etc*) to have a feeling for ■ *vi* to feel; (*lamentarse*) to feel sorry ■ *nm* opinion, judgement; **sentirse** *vr* to feel; **lo siento** I'm sorry; **sentirse mejor/mal** to feel better/ill; **sentirse como en su**

casa to feel at home

seña ['seɲa] *nf* sign; (*Mil*) password; **señas** *nfpl* address *sg*; **señas personales** personal description *sg*; **por más señas** moreover; **dar señas de** to show signs of

señal [se'ɲal] *nf* sign; (*síntoma*) symptom; (*indicio*) indication; (*Ferro: Telec*) signal; (*marca*) mark; (*Com*) deposit; (*Inform*) marker, mark; **en ~ de** as a token of, as a sign of; **dar señales de** to show signs of; **~ de auxilio/de peligro** distress/danger signal; **~ de llamada** ringing tone; **~ para marcar** dialling tone

señalado, -a [seɲa'laðo, a] *adj* (*persona*) distinguished; (*pey*) notorious

señalar [seɲa'lar] *vt* to mark; (*indicar*) to point out, indicate; (*significar*) to denote; (*referirse a*) to allude to; (*fijar*) to fix, settle; (*pey*) to criticize

señalice *etc* [seɲa'liθe] *vb ver* **señalizar**

señalización [seɲaliθa'θjon] *nf* signposting; signals *pl*

señalizar [seɲali'θar] *vt* (*Auto*) to put up road signs on; (*Ferro*) to put signals on; (*Auto: ruta*): **está bien señalizada** it's well signposted

señas ['seɲas] *nfpl ver* **seña**

señor, a [se'ɲor, a] *adj* (*fam*) lordly ■ *nm* (*hombre*) man; (*caballero*) gentleman; (*dueño*) owner, master; (*trato: antes de nombre propio*) Mr; (: *hablando directamente*) sir ■ *nf* (*dama*) lady; (*trato: antes de nombre propio*) Mrs; (: *hablando directamente*) madam; (*esposa*) wife; **los señores González** Mr and Mrs González; **S~ Don Jacinto Benavente** (*en sobre*) Mr J. Benavente, J. Benavente Esq.; **S~ Director ...** (*de periódico*) Dear Sir ...; **~ juez** my lord, your worship (*US*); **~ Presidente** Mr Chairman *o* President; **Muy ~ mío** Dear Sir; **Muy señores nuestros** Dear Sirs; **Nuestro S~** (*Rel*) Our Lord; **¿está la señora?** is the lady of the house in?; **la señora de Smith** Mrs Smith; **Nuestra Señora** (*Rel*) Our Lady

señoría [seɲo'ria] *nf* rule; **su** *o* **vuestra S~** your *o* his/her lordship/ladyship

señorío [seɲo'rio] *nm* manor; (*fig*) rule

señorita [seɲo'rita] *nf* (*gen*) Miss; (*mujer joven*) young lady; (*maestra*) schoolteacher

señorito [seɲo'rito] *nm* young gentleman; (*lenguaje de criados*) master; (*pey*) toff

señuelo [se'ɲwelo] *nm* decoy

Sep. *abr* (= *septiembre*) Sept

sepa *etc* ['sepa] *vb ver* **saber**

separable [sepa'raβle] *adj* separable; (*Tec*) detachable

separación [separa'θjon] *nf* separation; (*división*) division; (*distancia*) gap, distance; **~ de bienes** division of property

separado, -a [sepa'raðo, a] *adj* separate; (*Tec*) detached; **vive ~ de su mujer** he is separated from his wife; **por ~** separately

separador [separa'ðor] *nm* (*Inform*) delimiter

separadora [separa'ðora] *nf*: **~ de hojas** burster

separar [sepa'rar] *vt* to separate; (*silla (de la mesa)*) to move away; (*Tec: pieza*) to detach; (*persona: de un cargo*) to remove, dismiss; (*dividir*) to divide; **separarse** *vr* (*parte*) to come away; (*partes*) to come apart; (*persona*) to leave, go away; (*matrimonio*) to separate

separata [sepa'rata] *nf* offprint

separatismo [separa'tismo] *nm* (*Pol*) separatism

sepelio [se'peljo] *nm* burial, interment

sepia ['sepja] *nf* cuttlefish

Sept. *abr* (= *septiembre*) Sept

septentrional [septentrjo'nal] *adj* north *cpd*, northern

septiembre [sep'tjembre] *nm* September; *ver tb* **julio**

séptimo, -a ['septimo, a] *adj, nm* seventh

septuagésimo, -a [septwa'xesimo, a] *adj* seventieth

sepulcral [sepul'kral] *adj* sepulchral; (*fig*) gloomy, dismal

sepulcro [se'pulkro] *nm* tomb, grave, sepulchre

sepultar [sepul'tar] *vt* to bury; (*en accidente*) to trap; **quedaban sepultados en la caverna** they were trapped in the cave

sepultura [sepul'tura] *nf* (*acto*) burial; (*tumba*) grave, tomb; **dar ~ a** to bury; **recibir ~** to be buried

sepulturero, -a [sepultu'rero, a] *nm/f* gravedigger

seque *etc* ['seke] *vb ver* **secar**

sequedad [seke'ðað] *nf* dryness; (*fig*) brusqueness, curtness

sequía [se'kia] *nf* drought

séquito ['sekito] *nm* (*de rey etc*) retinue; (*Pol*) followers *pl*

SER *nf abr* (*Radio*: = *Sociedad Española de Radiodifusión*) Spanish radio network

 PALABRA CLAVE

ser [ser] *vi* **1** (*descripción, identidad*) to be; **es médica/muy alta** she's a doctor/very tall; **la familia es de Cuzco** his (*o* her *etc*) family is from Cuzco; **ser de madera** to be made of wood; **soy Ana** I'm Ana
2 (*propiedad*): **es de Joaquín** it's Joaquín's, it belongs to Joaquín
3 (*horas, fechas, números*): **es la una** it's one o'clock; **son las seis y media** it's half-past

six; **es el 1 de junio** it's the first of June;
somos/son seis there are six of us/them; **2 y
2 son 4** 2 and 2 are o make 4
4 (*suceso*): **¿qué ha sido eso?** what was that?;
la fiesta es en mi casa the party's at my
house; **¿qué será de mí?** what will become
of me?; **"érase una vez ..."** "once upon a
time ..."
5 (*en oraciones pasivas*): **ha sido descubierto
ya** it's already been discovered
6: **es de esperar que ...** it is to be hoped o
I *etc* hope that ...
7 (*locuciones con sub*): **o sea** that is to say; **sea
él sea su hermana** either him or his sister;
**tengo que irme, no sea que mis hijos
estén esperándome** I have to go in case my
children are waiting for me
8: **a o de no ser por él ...** but for him ...
9: **a no ser que**: **a no ser que tenga uno ya**
unless he's got one already
■ *nm* being; **ser humano** human being;
ser vivo living creature

Serbia ['serβja] *nf* Serbia
serbio, -a ['serβjo, a] *adj* Serbian ■ *nm/f* Serb
serenarse [sere'narse] *vr* to calm down; (*mar*)
to grow calm; (*tiempo*) to clear up
serenidad [sereni'ðað] *nf* calmness
sereno, -a [se'reno, a] *adj* (*persona*) calm,
unruffled; (*tiempo*) fine, settled; (*ambiente*)
calm, peaceful ■ *nm* night watchman
serial [se'rjal] *nm* serial
serie ['serje] *nf* series; (*cadena*) sequence,
succession; (*TV etc*) serial; (*de inyecciones*)
course; **fuera de ~** out of order; (*fig*) special,
out of the ordinary; **fabricación en ~** mass
production; (*Inform*): **interface/impresora
en ~** serial interface/printer
seriedad [serje'ðað] *nf* seriousness;
(*formalidad*) reliability; (*de crisis*) gravity,
seriousness
serigrafía [seriɣra'fia] *nf* silk screen printing
serio, -a ['serjo, a] *adj* serious; reliable,
dependable; grave, serious; **poco ~** (*actitud*)
undignified; (*carácter*) unreliable; **en ~**
seriously
sermón [ser'mon] *nm* (*Rel*) sermon
sermonear [sermone'ar] *vt* (*fam*) to lecture
■ *vi* to sermonize
seropositivo, -a [seroposi'tiβo, a] *adj* HIV-
positive
serpentear [serpente'ar] *vi* to wriggle;
(*camino, río*) to wind, snake
serpentina [serpen'tina] *nf* streamer
serpiente [ser'pjente] *nf* snake; **~ boa** boa
constrictor; **~ de cascabel** rattlesnake
serranía [serra'nia] *nf* mountainous area

serrano, -a [se'rrano, a] *adj* highland *cpd*,
hill *cpd* ■ *nm/f* highlander
serrar [se'rrar] *vt* to saw
serrín [se'rrin] *nm* sawdust
serrucho [se'rrutʃo] *nm* handsaw
Servia ['serβja] *nf* Serbia
servicial [serβi'θjal] *adj* helpful, obliging
servicio [ser'βiθjo] *nm* service; (*Culin etc*) set;
servicios *nmpl* toilet(s) (*pl*); **estar de ~** to be
on duty; **~ aduanero** o **de aduana** customs
service; **~ a domicilio** home delivery service;
~ incluido (*en hotel etc*) service charge
included; **~ militar** military service;
~ público (*Com*) public utility
servidor, a [serβi'ðor, a] *nm/f* servant ■ *nm*
(*Inform*) server; **su seguro ~** (*s.s.s.*) yours
faithfully; **un ~** (*el que habla o escribe*) your
humble servant
servidumbre [serβi'ðumbre] *nf* (*sujeción*)
servitude; (*criados*) servants *pl*, staff
servil [ser'βil] *adj* servile
servilleta [serβi'ʎeta] *nf* serviette, napkin
servilletero [serβiʎe'tero] *nm* napkin ring
servir [ser'βir] *vt* to serve; (*comida*) to serve
out o up; (*Tenis etc*) to serve ■ *vi* to serve;
(*camarero*) to serve, wait; (*tener utilidad*) to be
of use, be useful; **servirse** *vr* to serve o help
o.s.; **¿en qué puedo servirle?** how can I help
you?; **~ vino a algn** to pour out wine for sb;
~ de guía to act o serve as a guide; **no sirve
para nada** it's no use at all; **servirse de algo**
to make use of sth, use sth; **sírvase pasar**
please come in
sesenta [se'senta] *num* sixty
sesentón, -ona [sesen'ton, ona] *adj, nm/f*
sixty-year-old
sesgado, -a [ses'ɣaðo, a] *adj* slanted,
slanting
sesgo ['sesɣo] *nm* slant; (*fig*) slant, twist
sesión [se'sjon] *nf* (*Pol*) session, sitting;
(*Cine*) showing; (*Teat*) performance; **abrir/
levantar la ~** to open/close o adjourn the
meeting; **la segunda ~** the second house
seso ['seso] *nm* brain; (*fig*) intelligence;
sesos *nmpl* (*Culin*) brains; **devanarse los
sesos** to rack one's brains
sesudo, -a [se'suðo, a] *adj* sensible, wise
set (*pl* **sets**) [set, sets] *nm* (*Tenis*) set
Set. *abr* (= *setiembre*) Sept.
seta ['seta] *nf* mushroom; **~ venenosa**
toadstool
setecientos, -as [sete'θjentos, as] *num* seven
hundred
setenta [se'tenta] *num* seventy
setiembre [se'tjembre] *nm* = **septiembre**; *ver
tb* **julio**
seto ['seto] *nm* fence; **~ vivo** hedge

seudo... [seuðo] *pref* pseudo...
seudónimo [seu'ðonimo] *nm* pseudonym
Seúl [se'ul] *nm* Seoul
s.e.u.o. *abr* (= *salvo error u omisión*) E & O E
severidad [seβeri'ðað] *nf* severity
severo, -a [se'βero, a] *adj* severe; (*disciplina*) strict; (*frío*) bitter
Sevilla [se'βiʎa] *nf* Seville
sevillano, -a [seβi'ʎano, a] *adj* of o from Seville ■ *nm/f* native o inhabitant of Seville
S.Exc. *abr* = **Su Excelencia**
sexagenario, -a [seksaxe'narjo, a] *adj* sixty-year-old ■ *nm/f* person in his/her sixties
sexagésimo, -a [seksa'xesimo, a] *num* sixtieth
sexo ['sekso] *nm* sex; **el ~ femenino/masculino** the female/male sex
sexto, -a ['seksto, a] *num* sixth; **Juan S~** John the Sixth
sexual [sek'swal] *adj* sexual; **vida ~** sex life
sexualidad [sekswali'ðað] *nf* sexuality
s.f. *abr* (= *sin fecha*) no date
s/f *abr* (*Com*: = *su favor*) your favour
sgte(s). *abr* (= *siguiente*) foll
si [si] *conj* if; (*en pregunta indirecta*) if, whether ■ *nm* (*Mus*) B; **si ... si ...** whether ... or ...; **me pregunto si ...** I wonder if o whether ...; **si no** if not, otherwise; **¡si fuera verdad!** if only it were true!; **por si viene** in case he comes
sí [si] *adv* yes ■ *nm* consent ■ *pron* (*uso impersonal*) oneself; (*sg: m*) himself; (: *f*) herself; (: *de cosa*) itself; (: *de usted*) yourself; (*pl*) themselves; (: *de ustedes*) yourselves; (: *recíproco*) each other; **él no quiere pero yo sí** he doesn't want to but I do; **ella sí vendrá** she will certainly come, she is sure to come; **claro que sí** of course; **creo que sí** I think so; **porque sí** because that's the way it is; (*porque lo digo yo*) because I say so; **¡sí que lo es!** I'll say it is!; **¡eso sí que no!** never!; **se ríe de sí misma** she laughs at herself; **cambiaron una mirada entre sí** they gave each other a look; **de por sí** in itself
siamés, -esa [sja'mes, esa] *adj, nm/f* Siamese
sibarita [siβa'rita] *adj* sybaritic ■ *nm/f* sybarite
sicario [si'karjo] *nm* hired killer
Sicilia [si'θilja] *nf* Sicily
siciliano, -a [siθi'ljano, a] *adj, nm/f* Sicilian ■ *nm* (*Ling*) Sicilian
SIDA ['siða] *nm abr* (= *síndrome de inmunodeficiencia adquirida*) AIDS
siderurgia [siðe'rurxja] *nf* iron and steel industry
siderúrgico, -a [siðe'rurxico, a] *adj* iron and steel *cpd*

sidra ['siðra] *nf* cider
siega *etc* ['sjeɣa] *vb ver* **segar** ■ *nf* (*el cosechar*) reaping; (*el segar*) mowing; (*época*) harvest (time)
siegue *etc* ['sjeɣe] *vb ver* **segar**
siembra *etc* ['sjembra] *vb ver* **sembrar** ■ *nf* sowing
siempre ['sjempre] *adv* always; (*todo el tiempo*) all the time; (*Am: así y todo*) still ■ *conj*: **~ que** ... (+*indic*) whenever ...; (+*subjun*) provided that ...; **es lo de ~** it's the same old story; **como ~** as usual; **para ~** forever; **~ me voy mañana** (*Am*) I'm still leaving tomorrow
sien [sjen] *nf* (*Anat*) temple
siento *etc* ['sjento] *vb ver* **sentar**; **sentir**
sierra *etc* ['sjerra] *vb ver* **serrar** ■ *nf* (*Tec*) saw; (*Geo*) mountain range; **S~ Leona** Sierra Leone
siervo, -a ['sjerβo, a] *nm/f* slave
siesta ['sjesta] *nf* siesta, nap; **dormir la o echarse una o tomar una ~** to have an afternoon nap o a doze
siete ['sjete] *num* seven ■ *excl* (*Am fam*): **¡la gran ~!** wow!, hell!; **hijo de la gran ~** (*fam!*) bastard (*!*), son of a bitch (*US!*)
sífilis ['sifilis] *nf* syphilis
sifón [si'fon] *nm* syphon; **whisky con ~** whisky and soda
siga *etc* ['siɣa] *vb ver* **seguir**
sigilo [si'xilo] *nm* secrecy; (*discreción*) discretion
sigla ['siɣla] *nf* initial, abbreviation
siglo ['siɣlo] *nm* century; (*fig*) age; **S~ de las Luces** Age of Enlightenment; **S~ de Oro** Golden Age
significación [siɣnifika'θjon] *nf* significance
significado [siɣnifi'kaðo] *nm* significance; (*de palabra etc*) meaning
significar [siɣnifi'kar] *vt* to mean, signify; (*notificar*) to make known, express
significativo, -a [siɣnifika'tiβo, a] *adj* significant
signifique *etc* [siɣni'fike] *vb ver* **significar**
signo ['siɣno] *nm* sign; **~ de admiración** o **exclamación** exclamation mark; **~ igual** equals sign; **~ de interrogación** question mark; **~ de más/de menos** plus/minus sign; **signos de puntuación** punctuation marks
siguiendo *etc* [si'ɣjendo] *vb ver* **seguir**
siguiente [si'ɣjente] *adj* following; (*próximo*) next
silbar [sil'βar] *vt, vi* to whistle; (*silbato*) to blow; (*Teat etc*) to hiss
silbato [sil'βato] *nm* (*instrumento*) whistle
silbido [sil'βiðo] *nm* whistle, whistling; (*abucheo*) hiss
silenciador [silenθja'ðor] *nm* silencer

S

silenciar [silen'θjar] vt (persona) to silence; (escándalo) to hush up

silencio [si'lenθjo] nm silence, quiet; **en el ~ más absoluto** in dead silence; **guardar ~** to keep silent

silencioso, -a [silen'θjoso, a] adj silent, quiet

sílfide ['silfiðe] nf sylph

silicio [si'liθjo] nm silicon

silla ['siʎa] nf (asiento) chair; (tb: **silla de montar**) saddle; **~ de ruedas** wheelchair

sillería [siʎe'ria] nf (asientos) chairs pl, set of chairs; (Rel) choir stalls pl; (taller) chairmaker's workshop

sillín [si'ʎin] nm saddle, seat

sillón [si'ʎon] nm armchair, easy chair

silueta [si'lweta] nf silhouette; (de edificio) outline; (figura) figure

silvestre [sil'βestre] adj (Bot) wild; (fig) rustic, rural

sima ['sima] nf abyss, chasm

simbolice etc [simbo'liθe] vb ver **simbolizar**

simbólico, -a [sim'boliko, a] adj symbolic(al)

simbolizar [simboli'θar] vt to symbolize

símbolo ['simbolo] nm symbol; **~ gráfico** (Inform) icon

simetría [sime'tria] nf symmetry

simétrico, -a [si'metriko, a] adj symmetrical

simiente [si'mjente] nf seed

similar [simi'lar] adj similar

similitud [simili'tuð] nf similarity, resemblance

simio ['simjo] nm ape

simpatía [simpa'tia] nf liking; (afecto) affection; (amabilidad) kindness; (de ambiente) friendliness; (de persona, lugar) charm, attractiveness; (solidaridad) mutual support, solidarity; **tener ~ a** to like; **la famosa ~ andaluza** that well-known Andalusian charm

simpatice etc [simpa'tiθe] vb ver **simpatizar**

simpático, -a [sim'patiko, a] adj nice, pleasant; (bondadoso) kind; **no le hemos caído muy simpáticos** she didn't much take to us

simpatiquísimo, -a [simpati'kisimo, a] adj superlativo de **simpático** ever so nice; ever so kind

simpatizante [simpati'θante] nm/f sympathizer

simpatizar [simpati'θar] vi: **~ con** to get on well with

simple ['simple] adj simple; (elemental) simple, easy; (mero) mere; (puro) pure, sheer ◾ nm/f simpleton; **un ~ soldado** an ordinary soldier

simpleza [sim'pleθa] nf simpleness; (necedad) silly thing

simplicidad [simpliθi'ðað] nf simplicity

simplificar [simplifi'kar] vt to simplify

simplifique etc [simpli'fike] vb ver **simplificar**

simplón, -ona [sim'plon, ona] adj simple, gullible ◾ nm/f simple soul

simposio [sim'posjo] nm symposium

simulacro [simu'lakro] nm (apariencia) semblance; (fingimiento) sham

simular [simu'lar] vt to simulate; (fingir) to feign, sham

simultanear [simultane'ar] vt: **~ dos cosas** to do two things simultaneously

simultáneo, -a [simul'taneo, a] adj simultaneous

sin [sin] prep without; (a no ser por) but for ◾ conj: **~ que** (+subjun) without; **~ decir nada** without a word; **~ verlo yo** without my seeing it; **platos ~ lavar** unwashed o dirty dishes; **la ropa está ~ lavar** the clothes are unwashed; **~ que lo sepa él** without his knowing; **~ embargo** however

sinagoga [sina'ɣoɣa] nf synagogue

Sinaí [sina'i] nm: **El Sinaí** Sinai, the Sinai Peninsula; **el Monte Sinaí** Mount Sinai

sinceridad [sinθeri'ðað] nf sincerity

sincero, -a [sin'θero, a] adj sincere; (persona) genuine; (opinión) frank; (felicitaciones) heartfelt

síncope ['sinkope] nm (desmayo) blackout; **~ cardíaco** (Med) heart failure

sincronice etc [sinkro'niθe] vb ver **sincronizar**

sincronizar [sinkroni'θar] vt to synchronize

sindical [sindi'kal] adj union cpd, trade-union cpd

sindicalista [sindika'lista] adj trade-union cpd ◾ nm/f trade unionist

sindicar [sindi'kar] vt (obreros) to organize, unionize; **sindicarse** vr (obrero) to join a union

sindicato [sindi'kato] nm (de trabajadores) trade(s) o labor (US) union; (de negociantes) syndicate

sindique etc [sin'dike] vb ver **sindicar**

síndrome ['sindrome] nm syndrome; **~ de abstinencia** withdrawal symptoms

sine qua non [sine'kwanon] adj: **condición ~** sine qua non

sinfín [sin'fin] nm: **un ~ de** a great many, no end of

sinfonía [sinfo'nia] nf symphony

sinfónico, -a [sin'foniko, a] adj (música) symphonic; **orquesta sinfónica** symphony orchestra

Singapur [singa'pur] nm Singapore

singular [singu'lar] adj singular; (fig) outstanding, exceptional; (pey) peculiar, odd ◾ nm (Ling) singular; **en ~** in the singular

singularice etc [singula'riθe] vb ver **singularizar**

singularidad [singulari'ðað] nf singularity, peculiarity

singularizar [singulari'θar] vt to single out; **singularizarse** vr to distinguish o.s., stand out

siniestro, -a [si'njestro, a] adj left; (fig) sinister ■ nm (accidente) accident; (desastre) natural disaster

sinnúmero [sin'numero] nm = **sinfín**

sino ['sino] nm fate, destiny ■ conj (pero) but; (salvo) except, save; **no son 8 ~ 9** there are not 8 but 9; **todos ~ él** all except him

sinónimo, -a [si'nonimo, a] adj synonymous ■ nm synonym

sinrazón [sinra'θon] nf wrong, injustice

sinsabor [sinsa'βor] nm (molestia) trouble; (dolor) sorrow; (preocupación) uneasiness

sintaxis [sin'taksis] nf syntax

síntesis ['sintesis] nf inv synthesis

sintetice etc [sinte'tiθe] vb ver **sintetizar**

sintético, -a [sin'tetiko, a] adj synthetic

sintetizador [sintetiθa'ðor] nm synthesizer

sintetizar [sinteti'θar] vt to synthesize

sintiendo etc [sin'tjendo] vb ver **sentir**

síntoma ['sintoma] nm symptom

sintomático, -a [sinto'matiko, a] adj symptomatic

sintonía [sinto'nia] nf (Radio) tuning; (melodía) signature tune

sintonice etc [sinto'niθe] vb ver **sintonizar**

sintonizador [sintoniθa'ðor] nm (Radio) tuner

sintonizar [sintoni'θar] vt (Radio) to tune (in) to, pick up

sinuoso, -a [si'nwoso, a] adj (camino) winding; (rumbo) devious

sinvergüenza [simber'ɣwenθa] nm/f rogue, scoundrel

sionismo [sjo'nismo] nm Zionism

siquiera [si'kjera] conj even if, even though ■ adv (esp Am) at least; **ni ~** not even; **~ bebe algo** at least drink something

sirena [si'rena] nf siren, mermaid; (bocina) siren, hooter

Siria ['sirja] nf Syria

sirio, -a ['sirjo, a] adj, nm/f Syrian

sirviendo etc [sir'βjendo] vb ver **servir**

sirviente, -a [sir'βjente, a] nm/f servant

sisa ['sisa] nf petty theft; (Costura) dart; (sobaquera) armhole

sisar [si'sar] vt (robar) to thieve; (Costura) to take in

sisear [sise'ar] vt, vi to hiss

sísmico, -a ['sismiko, a] adj: **movimiento ~** earthquake

sismógrafo [sis'moɣrafo] nm seismograph

sistema [sis'tema] nm system; (método) method; **~ impositivo** o **tributario** taxation, tax system; **~ pedagógico** educational system; **~ de alerta inmediata** early-warning system; **~ binario** (Inform) binary system; **~ experto** expert system; **~ de facturación** (Com) invoicing system; **~ de fondo fijo** (Com) imprest system; **~ de lógica compartida** (Inform) shared logic system; **~ métrico** metric system; **~ operativo (en disco)** (Inform) (disk-based) operating system; see note

● **SISTEMA EDUCATIVO**
●
● The reform of the Spanish sistema
● educativo (education system) begun in
● the early 90s has replaced the courses
● EGB, BUP and COU with the following:
● Primaria a compulsory 6 years; Secundaria
● a compulsory 4 years; Bachillerato an
● optional 2 year secondary school course,
● essential for those wishing to go on to
● higher education.

sistemático, -a [siste'matiko, a] adj systematic

sitiar [si'tjar] vt to besiege, lay siege to

sitio ['sitjo] nm (lugar) place; (espacio) room, space; (Mil) siege; **~ web** website; **¿hay ~?** is there any room?; **hay ~ de sobra** there's plenty of room

situación [sitwa'θjon] nf situation, position; (estatus) position, standing

situado, -a [si'twaðo, a] adj situated, placed; **estar ~** (Com) to be financially secure

situar [si'twar] vt to place, put; (edificio) to locate, situate

S.L. abr (Com: = Sociedad Limitada) Ltd

slip [es'lip] (pl **slips**) nm pants pl, briefs pl

slot [es'lot] (pl **slots**) nm: **~ de expansión** expansion slot

S.M. abr (= Su Majestad) HM

SME nm abr (= Sistema Monetario Europeo) EMS; **(mecanismo de cambios del) ~** ERM

smoking [(e)'smokin] (pl **smokings**) nm dinner jacket (Brit), tuxedo (US)

SMS nm (mensaje) text (message), SMS (message)

s/n abr (= sin número) no number

snob [es'nob] = **esnob**

SO abr (= suroeste) SW

so [so] excl whoa!; **¡so burro!** you idiot! ■ prep under

s/o abr (Com: = su orden) your order

sobaco [so'βako] nm armpit

sobado, -a [so'βaðo, a] *adj* (*ropa*) worn; (*arrugado*) crumpled; (*libro*) well-thumbed; (*Culin: bizcocho*) short

sobar [so'βar] *vt* (*tela*) to finger; (*ropa*) to rumple, mess up; (*músculos*) to rub, massage

soberanía [soβera'nia] *nf* sovereignty

soberano, -a [soβe'rano, a] *adj* sovereign; (*fig*) supreme ■ *nm/f* sovereign; **los soberanos** the king and queen

soberbio, -a [so'βerβjo, a] *adj* (*orgulloso*) proud; (*altivo*) haughty, arrogant; (*fig*) magnificent, superb ■ *nf* pride; haughtiness, arrogance; magnificence

sobornar [soβor'nar] *vt* to bribe

soborno [so'βorno] *nm* (*un soborno*) bribe; (*el soborno*) bribery

sobra ['soβra] *nf* excess, surplus; **sobras** *nfpl* left-overs, scraps; **de ~** surplus, extra; **lo sé de ~** I'm only too aware of it; **tengo de ~** I've more than enough

sobradamente [soβraða'mente] *adv* amply; (*saber*) only too well

sobrado, -a [so'βraðo, a] *adj* (*más que suficiente*) more than enough; (*superfluo*) excessive ■ *adv* too, exceedingly; **sobradas veces** repeatedly

sobrante [so'βrante] *adj* remaining, extra ■ *nm* surplus, remainder

sobrar [so'βrar] *vt* to exceed, surpass ■ *vi* (*tener de más*) to be more than enough; (*quedar*) to remain, be left (over)

sobrasada [soβra'saða] *nf* ≈ sausage spread

sobre ['soβre] *prep* (*gen*) on; (*encima*) on (top of); (*por encima de, arriba de*) over, above; (*más que*) more than; (*además*) in addition to, besides; (*alrededor de*) about; (*porcentaje*) in, out of; (*tema*) about, on ■ *nm* envelope; **~ todo** above all; **3 ~ 100** 3 in a 100, 3 out of every 100; **un libro ~ Tirso** a book about Tirso; **~ de ventanilla** window envelope

sobrecama [soβre'kama] *nf* bedspread

sobrecapitalice *etc* [soβrekapita'liθe] *vb ver* **sobrecapitalizar**

sobrecapitalizar [soβrekapitali'θar] *vi* to overcapitalize

sobrecargar [soβrekar'ɣar] *vt* (*camión*) to overload; (*Com*) to surcharge

sobrecargue *etc* [soβre'karɣe] *vb ver* **sobrecargar**

sobrecoger [soβreko'xer] *vt* (*sobresaltar*) to startle; (*asustar*) to scare; **sobrecogerse** *vr* (*sobresaltarse*) to be startled; (*asustarse*) to get scared; (*quedar impresionado*): **sobrecogerse (de)** to be overawed (by)

sobrecoja *etc* [soβre'koxa] *vb ver* **sobrecoger**

sobredosis [soβre'ðosis] *nf inv* overdose

sobreentender [soβreenten'der] *vt* to understand; (*adivinar*) to deduce, infer; **sobreentenderse** *vr*: **se sobreentiende que ...** it is implied that ...

sobreescribir [soβreeskri'βir] *vt* (*Inform*) to overwrite

sobreestimar [soβreesti'mar] *vt* to overestimate

sobregiro [soβre'xiro] *nm* (*Com*) overdraft

sobrehumano, -a [soβreu'mano, a] *adj* superhuman

sobreimprimir [soβreimpri'mir] *vt* (*Com*) to merge

sobrellevar [soβreʎe'βar] *vt* (*fig*) to bear, endure

sobremesa [soβre'mesa] *nf* (*después de comer*) sitting on after a meal; (*Inform*) desktop; **conversación de ~** table talk

sobremodo [soβre'moðo] *adv* very much, enormously

sobrenatural [soβrenatu'ral] *adj* supernatural

sobrenombre [soβre'nombre] *nm* nickname

sobrentender [soβrenten'der] *vt* = **sobreentender**

sobrepasar [soβrepa'sar] *vt* to exceed, surpass

sobrepondré *etc* [soβrepon'dre] *vb ver* **sobreponer**

sobreponer [soβrepo'ner] *vt* (*poner encima*) to put on top; (*añadir*) to add; **sobreponerse** *vr*: **sobreponerse a** to overcome

sobreponga *etc* [soβre'ponga] *vb ver* **sobreponer**

sobreprima [soβre'prima] *nf* (*Com*) loading

sobreproducción [soβreproðuk'θjon] *nf* overproduction

sobrepuesto [soβre'pwesto], **sobrepuse** *etc* [soβre'puse] *vb ver* **sobreponer**

sobresaldré *etc* [soβresal'dre], **sobresalga** *etc* [soβre'salɣa] *vb ver* **sobresalir**

sobresaliente [soβresa'ljente] *adj* projecting; (*fig*) outstanding, excellent; (*Univ etc*) first class ■ *nm* (*Univ etc*) first class (mark), distinction

sobresalir [soβresa'lir] *vi* to project, jut out; (*fig*) to stand out, excel

sobresaltar [soβresal'tar] *vt* (*asustar*) to scare, frighten; (*sobrecoger*) to startle

sobresalto [soβre'salto] *nm* (*movimiento*) start; (*susto*) scare; (*turbación*) sudden shock

sobreseer [soβrese'er] *vt*: **~ una causa** (*Jur*) to stop a case

sobrestadía [soβresta'ðia] *nf* (*Com*) demurrage

sobrestimar [soβresti'mar] *vt* = **sobreestimar**

sobretensión [soβreten'sjon] *nf* (*Elec*): **~ transitoria** surge

sobretiempo [soβre'tjempo] *nm* (*Am*) overtime
sobretodo [soβre'toðo] *nm* overcoat
sobrevendré *etc* [soβreβen'dre], **sobrevenga**
etc [soβre'βenga] *vb ver* **sobrevenir**
sobrevenir [soβreβe'nir] *vi* (*ocurrir*) to happen
(unexpectedly); (*resultar*) to follow, ensue
sobreviene *etc* [soβre'βjene], **sobrevine** *etc*
[soβre'βine] *vb ver* **sobrevenir**
sobreviviente [soβreβi'βjente] *adj* surviving
■ *nm/f* survivor
sobrevivir [soβreβi'βir] *vi* to survive; (*persona*)
to outlive; (*objeto etc*) to outlast
sobrevolar [soβreβo'lar] *vt* to fly over
sobrevuele *etc* [soβre'βwele] *vb ver*
sobrevolar
sobriedad [soβrje'ðað] *nf* sobriety, soberness;
(*moderación*) moderation, restraint
sobrino, -a [so'βrino, a] *nm/f* nephew/niece
sobrio, -a ['soβrjo, a] *adj* (*moderado*) moderate,
restrained
socarrón, -ona [soka'rron, ona] *adj*
(*sarcástico*) sarcastic, ironic(al)
socavar [soka'βar] *vt* to undermine; (*excavar*)
to dig underneath *o* below
socavón [soka'βon] *nm* (*en mina*) gallery;
(*hueco*) hollow; (*en la calle*) hole
sociable [so'θjaβle] *adj* (*persona*) sociable,
friendly; (*animal*) social
social [so'θjal] *adj* social; (*Com*) company *cpd*
socialdemócrata [soθjalde'mokrata] *adj*
social-democratic ■ *nm/f* social democrat
socialice *etc* [soθja'liθe] *vb ver* **socializar**
socialista [soθja'lista] *adj, nm/f* socialist
socializar [soθjali'θar] *vt* to socialize
sociedad [soθje'ðað] *nf* society; (*Com*)
company; ~ **de ahorro y préstamo** savings
and loan society; ~ **anónima (S.A.)** limited
company (Ltd) (*Brit*), incorporated company
(Inc) (*US*); ~ **de beneficiencia** friendly
society (*Brit*), benefit association (*US*); ~ **de
cartera** investment trust; ~ **comanditaria**
(*Com*) co-ownership; ~ **conjunta** (*Com*) joint
venture; ~ **inmobiliaria** building society
(*Brit*), savings and loan (society) (*US*); ~ **de
responsabilidad limitada** (*Com*) private
limited company
socio, -a ['soθjo, a] *nm/f* (*miembro*) member;
(*Com*) partner; ~ **activo** active partner; ~
capitalista *o* **comanditario** sleeping *o* silent
(*US*) partner
socioeconómico, -a [soθjoeko'nomiko, a]
adj socio-economic
sociología [soθjolo'xia] *nf* sociology
sociólogo, -a [so'θjoloɣo, a] *nm/f* sociologist
socorrer [soko'rrer] *vt* to help
socorrido, -a [soko'rriðo, a] *adj* (*tienda*) well-
stocked; (*útil*) handy; (*persona*) helpful

socorrismo [soko'rrismo] *nm* life-saving
socorrista [soko'rrista] *nm/f* first aider;
(*en piscina, playa*) lifeguard
socorro [so'korro] *nm* (*ayuda*) help, aid; (*Mil*)
relief; ¡~! help!
soda ['soða] *nf* (*sosa*) soda; (*bebida*) soda (water)
sódico, -a ['soðiko, a] *adj* sodium *cpd*
soez [so'eθ] *adj* dirty, obscene
sofá [so'fa] *nm* sofa, settee
sofá-cama [so'fakama] *nm* studio couch,
sofa bed
Sofia ['sofja] *nf* Sofia
sofisticación [sofistika'θjon] *nf*
sophistication
sofisticado, -a [sofisti'kaðo, a] *adj*
sophisticated
sofocado, -a [sofo'kaðo, a] *adj*: **estar** ~ (*fig*)
to be out of breath; (*ahogarse*) to feel stifled
sofocar [sofo'kar] *vt* to suffocate; (*apagar*) to
smother, put out; **sofocarse** *vr* to suffocate;
(*fig*) to blush, feel embarrassed
sofoco [so'foko] *nm* suffocation; (*azoro*)
embarrassment
sofocón [sofo'kon] *nm*: **llevarse** *o* **pasar un** ~
to have a sudden shock
sofreír [sofre'ir] *vt* to fry lightly
sofría *etc* [so'fria], **sofriendo** *etc* [so'frjendo],
sofrito [so'frito] *vb ver* **sofreír**
soft ['sof], **software** ['sofwer] *nm* (*Inform*)
software
soga ['soɣa] *nf* rope
sois [sois] *vb ver* **ser**
soja ['soxa] *nf* soya
sojuzgar [soxuθ'ɣar] *vt* to subdue, rule
despotically
sojuzgue *etc* [so'xuθɣe] *vb ver* **sojuzgar**
sol [sol] *nm* sun; (*luz*) sunshine, sunlight;
(*Mus*) G; ~ **naciente/poniente** rising/setting
sun; **tomar el** ~ to sunbathe; **hace** ~ it is
sunny
solace *etc* [so'laθe] *vb ver* **solazar**
solamente [sola'mente] *adv* only, just
solapa [so'lapa] *nf* (*de chaqueta*) lapel; (*de libro*)
jacket
solapado, -a [sola'paðo, a] *adj* sly,
underhand
solar [so'lar] *adj* solar, sun *cpd* ■ *nm* (*terreno*)
plot (of ground); (*local*) undeveloped site
solaz [so'laθ] *nm* recreation, relaxation
solazar [sola'θar] *vt* (*divertir*) to amuse;
solazarse *vr* to enjoy o.s., relax
soldada [sol'daða] *nf* pay
soldado [sol'daðo] *nm* soldier; ~ **raso** private
soldador [solda'ðor] *nm* soldering iron;
(*persona*) welder
soldar [sol'dar] *vt* to solder, weld; (*unir*) to
join, unite

soleado, -a [sole'aðo, a] *adj* sunny

soledad [sole'ðað] *nf* solitude; (*estado infeliz*) loneliness

solemne [so'lemne] *adj* solemn; (*tontería*) utter; (*error*) complete

solemnidad [solemni'ðað] *nf* solemnity

soler [so'ler] *vi* to be in the habit of, be accustomed to; **suele salir a las ocho** she usually goes out at 8 o'clock; **solíamos ir todos los años** we used to go every year

solera [so'lera] *nf* (*tradición*) tradition; **vino de ~** vintage wine

solfeo [sol'feo] *nm* singing of scales; **ir a clases de ~** to take singing lessons

solicitar [soliθi'tar] *vt* (*permiso*) to ask for, seek; (*puesto*) to apply for; (*votos*) to canvass for; (*atención*) to attract; (*persona*) to pursue, chase after

solícito, -a [so'liθito, a] *adj* (*diligente*) diligent; (*cuidadoso*) careful

solicitud [soliθi'tuð] *nf* (*calidad*) great care; (*petición*) request; (*a un puesto*) application

solidaridad [soliðari'ðað] *nf* solidarity; **por ~ con** (*Pol etc*) out of o in solidarity with

solidario, -a [soli'ðarjo, a] *adj* (*participación*) joint, common; (*compromiso*) mutually binding; **hacerse ~ de** to declare one's solidarity with

solidarizarse [soliðari'θarse] *vr*: **~ con algn** to support sb, sympathize with sb

solidez [soli'ðeθ] *nf* solidity

sólido, -a ['soliðo, a] *adj* solid; (*Tec*) solidly made; (*bien construido*) well built

soliloquio [soli'lokjo] *nm* soliloquy

solista [so'lista] *nm/f* soloist

solitario, -a [soli'tarjo, a] *adj* (*persona*) lonely, solitary; (*lugar*) lonely, desolate ■ *nm/f* (*reclusa*) recluse; (*en la sociedad*) loner ■ *nm* solitaire ■ *nf* tapeworm

soliviantar [soliβjan'tar] *vt* to stir up, rouse (to revolt); (*enojar*) to anger; (*sacar de quicio*) to exasperate

solloce *etc* [so'ʎoθe] *vb ver* **sollozar**

sollozar [soʎo'θar] *vi* to sob

sollozo [so'ʎoθo] *nm* sob

solo, -a ['solo, a] *adj* (*único*) single, sole; (*sin compañía*) alone; (*Mus*) solo; (*solitario*) lonely; **hay una sola dificultad** there is just one difficulty; **a solas** alone, by o.s.

sólo ['solo] *adv* only, just; (*exclusivamente*) solely; **tan ~** only just

solomillo [solo'miʎo] *nm* sirloin

solsticio [sols'tiθjo] *nm* solstice

soltar [sol'tar] *vt* (*dejar ir*) to let go of; (*desprender*) to unfasten, loosen; (*librar*) to release, set free; (*amarras*) to cast off; (*Auto: freno etc*) to release; (*suspiro*) to heave; (*risa etc*) to let out; **soltarse** *vr* (*desanudarse*) to come undone; (*desprenderse*) to come off; (*adquirir destreza*) to become expert; (*en idioma*) to become fluent

soltero, -a [sol'tero, a] *adj* single, unmarried ■ *nm* bachelor ■ *nf* single woman, spinster

solterón [solte'ron] *nm* confirmed bachelor

solterona [solte'rona] *nf* spinster, maiden lady; (*pey*) old maid

soltura [sol'tura] *nf* looseness, slackness; (*de los miembros*) agility, ease of movement; (*en el hablar*) fluency, ease

soluble [so'luβle] *adj* (*Química*) soluble; (*problema*) solvable; **~ en agua** soluble in water

solución [solu'θjon] *nf* solution; **~ de continuidad** break in continuity

solucionar [soluθjo'nar] *vt* (*problema*) to solve; (*asunto*) to settle, resolve

solvencia [sol'βenθja] *nf* (*Com: estado*) solvency; (: *acción*) settlement, payment

solventar [solβen'tar] *vt* (*pagar*) to settle, pay; (*resolver*) to resolve

solvente [sol'βente] *adj* solvent, free of debt

Somalia [so'malja] *nf* Somalia

sombra ['sombra] *nf* shadow; (*como protección*) shade; **sombras** *nfpl* darkness *sg*, shadows; **sin ~ de duda** without a shadow of doubt; **tener buena/mala ~** (*suerte*) to be lucky/unlucky; (*carácter*) to be likeable/disagreeable

sombrero [som'brero] *nm* hat; **~ hongo** bowler (hat), derby (*US*); **~ de copa** o **de pelo** (*Am*) top hat

sombrilla [som'briʎa] *nf* parasol, sunshade

sombrío, -a [som'brio, a] *adj* (*oscuro*) shady; (*fig*) sombre, sad; (*persona*) gloomy

somero, -a [so'mero, a] *adj* superficial

someter [some'ter] *vt* (*país*) to conquer; (*persona*) to subject to one's will; (*informe*) to present, submit; **someterse** *vr* to give in, yield, submit; **someterse a** to submit to; **someterse a una operación** to undergo an operation

sometimiento [someti'mjento] *nm* (*estado*) submission; (*acción*) presentation

somier [so'mjer] (*pl* **somiers**) *nm* spring mattress

somnífero [som'nifero] *nm* sleeping pill o tablet

somnolencia [somno'lenθja] *nf* sleepiness, drowsiness

somos ['somos] *vb ver* **ser**

son [son] *vb ver* **ser** ■ *nm* sound; **en ~ de broma** as a joke

sonado, -a [so'naðo, a] *adj* (*comentado*) talked-of; (*famoso*) famous; (*Com: pey*) hyped(-up)

sonajero [sona'xero] *nm* (baby's) rattle

sonambulismo [sonambu'lismo] *nm* sleepwalking

sonámbulo, -a [so'nambulo, a] *nm/f* sleepwalker

sonar [so'nar] *vt* (*campana*) to ring; (*trompeta, sirena*) to blow ■ *vi* to sound; (*hacer ruido*) to make a noise; (*Ling*) to be sounded, be pronounced; (*ser conocido*) to sound familiar; (*campana*) to ring; (*reloj*) to strike, chime; **sonarse** *vr*: **sonarse (la nariz)** to blow one's nose; **es un nombre que suena** it's a name that's in the news; **me suena ese nombre** that name rings a bell

sonda ['sonda] *nf* (*Naut*) sounding; (*Tec*) bore, drill; (*Med*) probe

sondear [sonde'ar] *vt* to sound; to bore (into), drill; to probe, sound; (*fig*) to sound out

sondeo [son'deo] *nm* sounding; boring, drilling; (*encuesta*) poll, enquiry; **~ de la opinión pública** public opinion poll

sónico, -a ['soniko, a] *adj* sonic, sound *cpd*

sonido [so'niðo] *nm* sound

sonoro, -a [so'noro, a] *adj* sonorous; (*resonante*) loud, resonant; (*Ling*) voiced; **efectos sonoros** sound effects

sonreír [sonre'ir] *vi*, **sonreírse** *vr* to smile

sonría *etc* [son'ria], **sonriendo** *etc* [son'rjendo] *vb ver* **sonreír**

sonriente [son'rjente] *adj* smiling

sonrisa [son'risa] *nf* smile

sonrojar [sonro'xar] *vt*: **~ a algn** to make sb blush; **sonrojarse** *vr*: **sonrojarse (de)** to blush (at)

sonrojo [son'roxo] *nm* blush

sonsacar [sonsa'kar] *vt* to wheedle, coax; **~ a algn** to pump sb for information

sonsaque *etc* [son'sake] *vb ver* **sonsacar**

sonsonete [sonso'nete] *nm* (*golpecitos*) tap(ping); (*voz monótona*) monotonous delivery, singsong (voice)

soñador, a [soɲa'ðor, a] *nm/f* dreamer

soñar [so'ɲar] *vt, vi* to dream; **~ con** to dream about *o* of; **soñé contigo anoche** I dreamed about you last night

soñoliento, -a [soɲo'ljento, a] *adj* sleepy, drowsy

sopa ['sopa] *nf* soup; **~ de fideos** noodle soup

sopero, -a [so'pero, a] *adj* (*plato, cuchara*) soup *cpd* ■ *nm* soup plate ■ *nf* soup tureen

sopesar [sope'sar] *vt* to try the weight of; (*fig*) to weigh up

sopetón [sope'ton] *nm*: **de ~** suddenly, unexpectedly

soplar [so'plar] *vt* (*polvo*) to blow away, blow off; (*inflar*) to blow up; (*vela*) to blow out; (*ayudar a recordar*) to prompt; (*birlar*) to nick; (*delatar*) to split on ■ *vi* to blow; (*delatar*) to squeal; (*beber*) to booze, bend the elbow

soplete [so'plete] *nm* blowlamp; **~ soldador** welding torch

soplo ['soplo] *nm* blow, puff; (*de viento*) puff, gust

soplón, -ona [so'plon, ona] *nm/f* (*fam: chismoso*) telltale; (*: de policía*) informer, grass

soponcio [so'ponθjo] *nm* dizzy spell

sopor [so'por] *nm* drowsiness

soporífero, -a [sopo'rifero, a] *adj* sleep-inducing; (*fig*) soporific ■ *nm* sleeping pill

soportable [sopor'taβle] *adj* bearable

soportal [sopor'tal] *nm* porch; **soportales** *nmpl* arcade *sg*

soportar [sopor'tar] *vt* to bear, carry; (*fig*) to bear, put up with

soporte [so'porte] *nm* support; (*fig*) pillar, support; (*Inform*) medium; **~ de entrada/salida** input/output medium

soprano [so'prano] *nf* soprano

sor [sor] *nf*: **S~ María** Sister Mary

sorber [sor'βer] *vt* (*chupar*) to sip; (*inhalar*) to sniff, inhale; (*absorber*) to soak up, absorb

sorbete [sor'βete] *nm* sherbet

sorbo ['sorβo] *nm* (*trago*) gulp, swallow; (*chupada*) sip; **beber a sorbos** to sip

sordera [sor'ðera] *nf* deafness

sórdido, -a ['sorðiðo, a] *adj* dirty, squalid

sordo, -a ['sorðo, a] *adj* (*persona*) deaf; (*ruido*) dull; (*Ling*) voiceless ■ *nm/f* deaf person; **quedarse ~** to go deaf

sordomudo, -a [sorðo'muðo, a] *adj* deaf and dumb ■ *nm/f* deaf-mute

soriano, -a [so'rjano, a] *adj* of *o* from Soria ■ *nm/f* native *o* inhabitant of Soria

sorna ['sorna] *nf* (*malicia*) slyness; (*tono burlón*) sarcastic tone

soroche [so'rotʃe] *nm* (*Am Med*) mountain sickness

sorprendente [sorpren'dente] *adj* surprising

sorprender [sorpren'der] *vt* to surprise; (*asombrar*) to amaze; (*sobresaltar*) to startle; (*coger desprevenido*) to catch unawares; **sorprenderse** *vr*: **sorprenderse (de)** to be surprised *o* amazed (at)

sorpresa [sor'presa] *nf* surprise

sorpresivo, -a [sorpre'siβo, a] *adj* (*Am*) surprising; (*imprevisto*) sudden

sortear [sorte'ar] *vt* to draw lots for; (*rifar*) to raffle; (*dificultad*) to dodge, avoid

sorteo [sor'teo] *nm* (*en lotería*) draw; (*rifa*) raffle

sortija [sor'tixa] *nf* ring; (*rizo*) ringlet, curl

sortilegio [sorti'lexjo] *nm* (*hechicería*) sorcery; (*hechizo*) spell

SOS *sigla m* SOS

S

sosegado, -a [sose'ɣaðo, a] *adj* quiet, calm

sosegar [sose'ɣar] *vt* to quieten, calm; (*el ánimo*) to reassure ▪ *vi* to rest

sosegué *etc* [sose'ɣe] *vb ver* **sosegar**

sosiego [so'sjeɣo] *vb ver* **sosegar** ▪ *nm* quiet(ness), calm(ness)

sosiegue *etc* [so'sjeɣe] *vb ver* **sosegar**

soslayar [sosla'jar] *vt* (*preguntas*) to get round

soslayo [sos'lajo]: **de ~** *adv* obliquely, sideways; **mirar de ~** to look out of the corner of one's eye (at)

soso, -a ['soso, a] *adj* (*Culin*) tasteless; (*fig*) dull, uninteresting

sospecha [sos'petʃa] *nf* suspicion

sospechar [sospe'tʃar] *vt* to suspect ▪ *vi*: **~ de** to be suspicious of

sospechoso, -a [sospe'tʃoso, a] *adj* suspicious; (*testimonio, opinión*) suspect ▪ *nm/f* suspect

sostén [sos'ten] *nm* (*apoyo*) support; (*sujetador*) bra; (*alimentación*) sustenance, food

sostendré *etc* [sosten'dre] *vb ver* **sostener**

sostener [soste'ner] *vt* to support; (*mantener*) to keep up, maintain; (*alimentar*) to sustain, keep going; **sostenerse** *vr* to support o.s.; (*seguir*) to continue, remain

sostenga *etc* [sos'tenga] *vb ver* **sostener**

sostenido, -a [soste'niðo, a] *adj* continuous, sustained; (*prolongado*) prolonged; (*Mus*) sharp ▪ *nm* (*Mus*) sharp

sostuve *etc* [sos'tuβe] *vb ver* **sostener**

sota ['sota] *nf* (*Naipes*) ≈ jack; *ver tb* **baraja española**

sotana [so'tana] *nf* (*Rel*) cassock

sótano ['sotano] *nm* basement

sotavento [sota'βento] *nm* (*Naut*) lee, leeward

soterrar [sote'rrar] *vt* to bury; (*esconder*) to hide away

sotierre *etc* [so'tjerre] *vb ver* **soterrar**

soviético, -a [so'βjetiko, a] *adj, nm/f* Soviet; **los soviéticos** the Soviets, the Russians

soy [soi] *vb ver* **ser**

soya ['soja] *nf* (*Am*) soya (bean)

SP *abr* (*Auto*) = **servicio público**

SPM *nm abr* (= *síndrome premenstrual*) PMS

spooling [es'pulin] *nm* (*Inform*) spooling

sport [es'por(t)] *nm* sport

spot [es'pot] (*pl* **~**) *nm* (*publicitario*) ad

squash [es'kwas] *nm* (*Deporte*) squash

Sr. *abr* (= *Señor*) Mr

Sra. *abr* (= *Señora*) Mrs

Sras. *abr* (= *Señoras*) Mrs

S.R.C. *abr* (= *se ruega contestación*) R.S.V.P.

Sres., Srs. *abr* (= *Señores*) Messrs

Sri Lanka [sri'lanka] *nm* Sri Lanka

Srta. *abr* = **Señorita**

SS *abr* (= *Santos, Santas*) SS

S.S. *abr* (*Rel*: = *Su Santidad*) H.H.; = **Seguridad Social**

ss. *abr* (= *siguientes*) foll

SSE *abr* (= *sursudeste*) SSE

SS.MM. *abr* (= *Sus Majestades*) Their Royal Highnesses

SSO *abr* (= *sursudoeste*) SSW

Sta. *abr* (= *Santa*) St; (= *Señorita*) Miss

stand (*pl* **stands**) [es'tan, es'tan(s)] *nm* (*Com*) stand

stárter [es'tarter] *nm* (*Auto*) self-starter, starting motor

statu quo [es'tatu'kuo], **status quo** [es'tatus'kuo] *nm* status quo

status ['status, es'tatus] *nm inv* status

Sto. *abr* (= *Santo*) St

stop (*pl* **stops**) [es'top, es'top(s)] *nm* (*Auto*) stop sign

su [su] *pron* (*de él*) his; (*de ella*) her; (*de una cosa*) its; (*de ellos, ellas*) their; (*de usted, ustedes*) your

suave ['swaβe] *adj* gentle; (*superficie*) smooth; (*trabajo*) easy; (*música, voz*) soft, sweet; (*clima, sabor*) mild

suavice *etc* [swa'βiθe] *vb ver* **suavizar**

suavidad [swaβi'ðað] *nf* gentleness; (*de superficie*) smoothness; (*de música*) softness, sweetness

suavizante [swaβi'θante] *nm* conditioner

suavizar [swaβi'θar] *vt* to soften; (*quitar la aspereza*) to smooth (out); (*pendiente*) to ease; (*colores*) to tone down; (*carácter*) to mellow; (*dureza*) to temper

subalimentado, -a [suβalimen'taðo, a] *adj* undernourished

subalterno, -a [suβal'terno, a] *adj* (*importancia*) secondary; (*personal*) minor, auxiliary ▪ *nm* subordinate

subarrendar [suβarren'dar] *vt* (*Com*) to lease back

subarriendo [suβa'rrjendo] *nm* (*Com*) leaseback

subasta [su'βasta] *nf* auction; **poner en** *o* **sacar a pública ~** to put up for public auction; **~ a la rebaja** Dutch auction

subastador, a [suβasta'ðor, a] *nm/f* auctioneer

subastar [suβas'tar] *vt* to auction (off)

subcampeón, -ona [suβkampe'on, ona] *nm/f* runner-up

subconsciente [suβkons'θjente] *adj* subconscious

subcontratar [suβkontra'tar] *vt* (*Com*) to subcontract

subcontrato [suβkon'trato] *nm* (*Com*) subcontract

subdesarrollado, -a [suβðesarro'ʎaðo, a] *adj* underdeveloped

subdesarrollo [suβðesa'rroʎo] *nm* underdevelopment

subdirector, a [suβðirek'tor, a] *nm/f* assistant *o* deputy manager

subdirectorio [suβðirek'torjo] *nm* (*Inform*) subdirectory

súbdito, -a ['suβðito, a] *nm/f* subject

subdividir [suβðiβi'ðir] *vt* to subdivide

subempleo [suβem'pleo] *nm* underemployment

subestimar [suβesti'mar] *vt* to underestimate, underrate

subido, -a [su'βiðo, a] *adj* (*color*) bright, strong; (*precio*) high ■ *nf* (*de montaña etc*) ascent, climb; (*de precio*) rise, increase; (*pendiente*) slope, hill

subíndice [su'βindiθe] *nm* (*Inform*, *Tip*) subscript

subir [su'βir] *vt* (*objeto*) to raise, lift up; (*cuesta, calle*) to go up; (*colina, montaña*) to climb; (*precio*) to raise, put up; (*empleado etc*) to promote ■ *vi* to go/come up; (*a un coche*) to get in; (*a un autobús, tren*) to get on; (*precio*) to rise, go up; (*en el empleo*) to be promoted; (*río, marea*) to rise; **subirse** *vr* to get up, climb; **subirse a un coche** to get in(to) a car

súbito, -a ['suβito, a] *adj* (*repentino*) sudden; (*imprevisto*) unexpected

subjetivo, -a [suβxe'tiβo, a] *adj* subjective

subjuntivo [suβxun'tiβo] *nm* subjunctive (mood)

sublevación [suβleβa'θjon] *nf* revolt, rising

sublevar [suβle'βar] *vt* to rouse to revolt; **sublevarse** *vr* to revolt, rise

sublimar [suβli'mar] *vt* (*persona*) to exalt; (*deseos etc*) to sublimate

sublime [su'βlime] *adj* sublime

subliminal [suβlimi'nal] *adj* subliminal

submarinista [suβmari'nista] *nm/f* underwater explorer

submarino, -a [suβma'rino, a] *adj* underwater ■ *nm* submarine

subnormal [suβnor'mal] *adj* subnormal ■ *nm/f* subnormal person

suboficial [suβofi'θjal] *nm* non-commissioned officer

subordinado, -a [suβorði'naðo, a] *adj*, *nm/f* subordinate

subproducto [suβpro'ðukto] *nm* by-product

subrayado [suβra'jaðo] *nm* underlining

subrayar [suβra'jar] *vt* to underline; (*recalcar*) to underline, emphasize

subrepticio, -a [suβrep'tiθjo, a] *adj* surreptitious

subrutina [suβru'tina] *nf* (*Inform*) subroutine

subsanar [suβsa'nar] *vt* (*reparar*) to make good; (*perdonar*) to excuse; (*sobreponerse a*) to overcome

subscribir [suβskri'βir] *vt* = **suscribir**

subsecretario, -a [suβsekre'tarjo, a] *nm/f* undersecretary, assistant secretary

subsidiariedad [suβsiðjarie'ðað] *nf* (*Pol*) subsidiarity

subsidiario, -a [suβsi'ðjarjo, a] *adj* subsidiary

subsidio [suβ'siðjo] *nm* (*ayuda*) aid, financial help; (*subvención*) subsidy, grant; (*de enfermedad, paro etc*) benefit, allowance

subsistencia [suβsis'tenθja] *nf* subsistence

subsistir [suβsis'tir] *vi* to subsist; (*vivir*) to live; (*sobrevivir*) to survive, endure

subsuelo [suβ'swelo] *nm* subsoil

subte *nm abr* (*CSur*) = **subterráneo**

subterfugio [suβter'fuxjo] *nm* subterfuge

subterráneo, -a [suβte'rraneo, a] *adj* underground, subterranean ■ *nm* underpass, underground passage; (*Am*) underground railway, subway (*US*)

subtitulado, -a [suβtitu'laðo, a] *adj* subtitled

subtítulo [suβ'titulo] *nm* subtitle, subheading

suburbano, -a [suβur'βano, a] *adj* suburban

suburbio [su'βurβjo] *nm* (*barrio*) slum quarter; (*afueras*) suburbs *pl*

subvención [suββen'θjon] *nf* subsidy, subvention, grant; ~ **estatal** state subsidy *o* support; ~ **para la inversión** (*Com*) investment grant

subvencionar [suββenθjo'nar] *vt* to subsidize

subversión [suββer'sjon] *nf* subversion

subversivo, -a [suββer'siβo, a] *adj* subversive

subyacente [suβja'θente] *adj* underlying

subyugar [suβju'ɣar] *vt* (*país*) to subjugate, subdue; (*enemigo*) to overpower; (*voluntad*) to dominate

subyugue *etc* [suβ'juɣe] *vb ver* **subyugar**

succión [suk'θjon] *nf* suction

succionar [sukθjo'nar] *vt* (*sorber*) to suck; (*Tec*) to absorb, soak up

sucedáneo, -a [suθe'ðaneo, a] *adj* substitute ■ *nm* substitute (food)

suceder [suθe'ðer] *vi* to happen; ~ **a** (*seguir*) to succeed, follow; **lo que sucede es que ...** the fact is that ...; ~ **al trono** to succeed to the throne

sucesión [suθe'sjon] *nf* succession; (*serie*) sequence, series; (*hijos*) issue, offspring

sucesivamente [suθesiβa'mente] *adv*: **y así** ~ and so on

sucesivo, -a [suθe'siβo, a] *adj* successive,

following; **en lo ~** in future, from now on

suceso [su'θeso] *nm* (*hecho*) event, happening; (*incidente*) incident

sucesor, a [suθe'sor, a] *nm/f* successor; (*heredero*) heir/heiress

suciedad [suθje'ðað] *nf* (*estado*) dirtiness; (*mugre*) dirt, filth

sucinto, -a [su'θinto, a] *adj* (*conciso*) succinct, concise

sucio, -a ['suθjo, a] *adj* dirty; (*mugriento*) grimy; (*manchado*) grubby; (*borroso*) smudged; (*conciencia*) bad; (*conducta*) vile; (*táctica*) dirty, unfair

Sucre ['sukre] *n* Sucre

sucre ['sukre] *nm* Ecuadorean monetary unit

suculento, -a [suku'lento, a] *adj* (*sabroso*) tasty; (*jugoso*) succulent

sucumbir [sukum'bir] *vi* to succumb

sucursal [sukur'sal] *nf* branch (office); (*filial*) subsidiary

Sudáfrica [su'ðafrika] *nf* South Africa

sudafricano, -a [suðafri'kano, a] *adj, nm/f* South African

Sudamérica [suða'merika] *nf* South America

sudamericano, -a [suðameri'kano, a] *adj, nm/f* South American

sudanés, -esa [suða'nes, esa] *adj, nm/f* Sudanese

sudar [su'ðar] *vt, vi* to sweat; (*Bot*) to ooze, give out o off

sudeste [su'ðeste] *adj* south-east(ern); (*rumbo, viento*) south-easterly ■ *nm* south-east; (*viento*) south-east wind

sudoeste [suðo'este] *adj* south-west(ern); (*rumbo, viento*) south-westerly ■ *nm* south-west; (*viento*) south-west wind

sudoku [su'ðoku] *nm* sudoku

sudor [su'ðor] *nm* sweat

sudoroso, a [suðo'roso, a] *adj* sweaty, sweating

Suecia ['sweθja] *nf* Sweden

sueco, -a ['sweko, a] *adj* Swedish ■ *nm/f* Swede ■ *nm* (*Ling*) Swedish; **hacerse el ~** to pretend not to hear o understand

suegro, -a ['sweɣro, a] *nm/f* father-/mother-in-law; **los suegros** one's in-laws

suela ['swela] *nf* (*de zapato, tb pescado*) sole

sueldo *etc* ['sweldo] *vb ver* **soldar** ■ *nm* pay, wage(s) (*pl*)

suelo *etc* ['swelo] *vb ver* **soler** ■ *nm* (*tierra*) ground; (*de casa*) floor

suelto, -a *etc* ['swelto, a] *vb ver* **soltar** ■ *adj* loose; (*libre*) free; (*separado*) detached; (*ágil*) quick, agile; (*fue corre*) fluent, flowing ■ *nm* (loose) change, small change; **está muy ~ en inglés** he is very good at o fluent in English

suene *etc* ['swene] *vb ver* **sonar**

sueño *etc* ['sweɲo] *vb ver* **soñar** ■ *nm* sleep; (*somnolencia*) sleepiness, drowsiness; (*lo soñado, fig*) dream; **~ pesado** o **profundo** deep o heavy sleep; **tener ~** to be sleepy

suero ['swero] *nm* (*Med*) serum; (*de leche*) whey

suerte ['swerte] *nf* (*fortuna*) luck; (*azar*) chance; (*destino*) fate, destiny; (*condición*) lot; (*género*) sort, kind; **lo echaron a suertes** they drew lots o tossed up for it; **tener ~** to be lucky; **de otra ~** otherwise, if not; **de ~ que** so that, in such a way that

suéter ['sweter] (*pl* **suéters**) *nm* sweater

suficiencia [sufi'θjenθja] *nf* (*cabida*) sufficiency; (*idoneidad*) suitability; (*aptitud*) adequacy

suficiente [sufi'θjente] *adj* enough, sufficient

sufijo [su'fixo] *nm* suffix

sufragar [sufra'ɣar] *vt* (*ayudar*) to help; (*gastos*) to meet; (*proyecto*) to pay for

sufragio [su'fraxjo] *nm* (*voto*) vote; (*derecho de voto*) suffrage

sufrague *etc* [su'fraɣe] *vb ver* **sufragar**

sufrido, -a [su'friðo, a] *adj* (*de carácter fuerte*) tough; (*paciente*) long-suffering; (*tela*) hard-wearing; (*color*) that does not show the dirt; (*marido*) complaisant

sufrimiento [sufri'mjento] *nm* suffering

sufrir [su'frir] *vt* (*padecer*) to suffer; (*soportar*) to bear, stand, put up with; (*apoyar*) to hold up, support ■ *vi* to suffer

sugerencia [suxe'renθja] *nf* suggestion

sugerir [suxe'rir] *vt* to suggest; (*sutilmente*) to hint; (*idea: incitar*) to prompt

sugestión [suxes'tjon] *nf* suggestion; (*sutil*) hint; (*poder*) hypnotic power

sugestionar [suxestjo'nar] *vt* to influence

sugestivo, -a [suxes'tiβo, a] *adj* stimulating; (*atractivo*) attractive; (*fascinante*) fascinating

sugiera *etc* [su'xjera], **sugiriendo** *etc* [suxi'rjendo] *vb ver* **sugerir**

suicida [sui'θiða] *adj* suicidal ■ *nm/f* suicidal person; (*muerto*) suicide, person who has committed suicide

suicidarse [suiθi'ðarse] *vr* to commit suicide, kill o.s.

suicidio [sui'θiðjo] *nm* suicide

Suiza ['swiθa] *nf* Switzerland

suizo, -a ['swiθo, a] *adj, nm/f* Swiss ■ *nm* sugared bun

sujeción [suxe'θjon] *nf* subjection

sujetador [suxeta'ðor] *nm* fastener, clip; (*prenda femenina*) bra, brassiere

sujetapapeles [suxetapa'peles] *nm inv* paper clip

sujetar [suxe'tar] *vt* (*fijar*) to fasten; (*detener*) to hold down; (*fig*) to subject, subjugate;

(*pelo etc*) to keep o hold in place; (*papeles*) to fasten together; **sujetarse** *vr* to subject o.s.
sujeto, -a [su'xeto, a] *adj* fastened, secure ■ *nm* subject; (*individuo*) individual; (*fam: tipo*) fellow, character, type, guy (*US*); ~ **a** subject to
sulfurar [sulfu'rar] *vt* (*Tec*) to sulphurate; (*sacar de quicio*) to annoy; **sulfurarse** *vr* (*enojarse*) to get riled, see red, blow up
sulfuro [sul'furo] *nm* sulphide
suma ['suma] *nf* (*cantidad*) total, sum; (*de dinero*) sum; (*acto*) adding (up), addition; **en** ~ in short; ~ **y sigue** (*Com*) carry forward
sumador [suma'ðor] *nm* (*Inform*) adder
sumamente [suma'mente] *adv* extremely, exceedingly
sumar [su'mar] *vt* to add (up); (*reunir*) to collect, gather ■ *vi* to add up
sumario, -a [su'marjo, a] *adj* brief, concise ■ *nm* summary
sumergir [sumer'xir] *vt* to submerge; (*hundir*) to sink; (*bañar*) to immerse, dip; **sumergirse** *vr* (*hundirse*) to sink beneath the surface
sumerja *etc* [su'merxa] *vb ver* **sumergir**
sumidero [sumi'ðero] *nm* drain, sewer; (*Tec*) sump
suministrador, a [suministra'ðor, a] *nm/f* supplier
suministrar [suminis'trar] *vt* to supply, provide
suministro [sumi'nistro] *nm* supply; (*acto*) supplying, providing
sumir [su'mir] *vt* to sink, submerge; (*fig*) to plunge; **sumirse** *vr* (*objeto*) to sink; **sumirse en el estudio** to become absorbed in one's studies
sumisión [sumi'sjon] *nf* (*acto*) submission; (*calidad*) submissiveness, docility
sumiso, -a [su'miso, a] *adj* submissive, docile
súmmum ['sumum] *nm inv* (*fig*) height
sumo, -a ['sumo, a] *adj* great, extreme; (*mayor*) highest, supreme ■ *nm* sumo (wrestling); **a lo** ~ at most
suntuoso, -a [sun'twoso, a] *adj* sumptuous, magnificent; (*lujoso*) lavish
sup. *abr* (= *superior*) sup
supe *etc* ['supe] *vb ver* **saber**
supeditar [supeði'tar] *vt* to subordinate; (*sojuzgar*) to subdue; (*oprimir*) to oppress; **supeditarse** *vr*: **supeditarse a** to subject o.s. to
super... [super] *pref* super..., over...
súper ['super] *adj* (*fam*) super, great
superable [supe'raßle] *adj* (*dificultad*) surmountable; (*tarea*) that can be performed
superación [supera'θjon] *nf* (*tb*: **superación personal**) self-improvement

superar [supe'rar] *vt* (*sobreponerse a*) to overcome; (*rebasar*) to surpass, do better than; (*pasar*) to go beyond; (*marca, récord*) to break; (*etapa: dejar atrás*) to get past; **superarse** *vr* to excel o.s.
superávit [supe'raßit] (*pl* **superávits**) *nm* surplus
superchería [supertʃe'ria] *nf* fraud, trick, swindle
superficial [superfi'θjal] *adj* superficial; (*medida*) surface *cpd*
superficie [super'fiθje] *nf* surface; (*área*) area; **grandes superficies** (*Com*) superstores
superfluo, -a [su'perflwo, a] *adj* superfluous
superíndice [supe'rindiθe] *nm* (*Inform: Tip*) superscript
superintendente [superinten'dente] *nm/f* supervisor, superintendent
superior [supe'rjor] *adj* (*piso, clase*) upper; (*temperatura, número, nivel*) higher; (*mejor: calidad, producto*) superior, better ■ *nm/f* superior
superiora [supe'rjora] *nf* (*Rel*) mother superior
superioridad [superjori'ðað] *nf* superiority
superlativo, -a [superla'tißo, a] *adj, nm* superlative
supermercado [supermer'kaðo] *nm* supermarket
superpoblación [superpoßla'θjon] *nf* overpopulation; (*congestionamiento*) overcrowding
superponer [superpo'ner] *vt* (*Inform*) to overstrike
superposición [superposi'θjon] *nf* (*en impresora*) overstrike
superpotencia [superpo'tenθja] *nf* superpower, great power
superproducción [superproðuk'θjon] *nf* overproduction
supersónico, -a [super'soniko, a] *adj* supersonic
superstición [supersti'θjon] *nf* superstition
supersticioso, -a [supersti'θjoso, a] *adj* superstitious
supervisar [superßi'sar] *vt* to supervise; (*Com*) to superintend
supervisor, a [superßi'sor, a] *nm/f* supervisor
supervivencia [superßi'ßenθja] *nf* survival
superviviente [superßi'ßjente] *adj* surviving ■ *nm/f* survivor
suplantar [suplan'tar] *vt* (*persona*) to supplant; (*hacerse pasar por otro*) to take the place of
suplementario, -a [suplemen'tarjo, a] *adj* supplementary

suplemento [suple'mento] *nm* supplement

suplencia [su'plenθja] *nf* substitution, replacement; (*etapa*) period during which one deputizes *etc*

suplente [su'plente] *adj* substitute; (*disponible*) reserve ■ *nm/f* substitute

supletorio, -a [suple'torjo, a] *adj* supplementary; (*adicional*) extra ■ *nm* supplement; **mesa supletoria** spare table

súplica ['suplika] *nf* request; (*Rel*) supplication; (*Jur: instancia*) petition; **súplicas** *nfpl* entreaties

suplicar [supli'kar] *vt* (*cosa*) to beg (for), plead for; (*persona*) to beg, plead with; (*Jur*) to appeal to, petition

suplicio [su'pliθjo] *nm* torture; (*tormento*) torment; (*emoción*) anguish; (*experiencia penosa*) ordeal

suplique *etc* [su'plike] *vb ver* **suplicar**

suplir [su'plir] *vt* to make good, make up for; (*reemplazar*) to replace, substitute ■ *vi*: ~ **a** to take the place of, substitute for

supo *etc* ['supo] *vb ver* **saber**

supondré *etc* [supon'dre] *vb ver* **suponer**

suponer [supo'ner] *vt* to suppose; (*significar*) to mean; (*acarrear*) to involve ■ *vi* to count, have authority; **era de ~ que ...** it was to be expected that ...

suponga *etc* [su'ponga] *vb ver* **suponer**

suposición [suposi'θjon] *nf* supposition

supositorio [suposi'torjo] *nm* suppository

supremacía [suprema'θia] *nf* supremacy

supremo, -a [su'premo, a] *adj* supreme

supresión [supre'sjon] *nf* suppression; (*de derecho*) abolition; (*de dificultad*) removal; (*de palabra etc*) deletion; (*de restricción*) cancellation, lifting

suprimir [supri'mir] *vt* to suppress; (*derecho, costumbre*) to abolish; (*dificultad*) to remove; (*palabra etc, Inform*) to delete; (*restricción*) to cancel, lift

supuestamente [supwesta'mente] *adv* supposedly

supuesto, -a [su'pwesto, a] *pp de* **suponer** ■ *adj* (*hipotético*) supposed; (*falso*) false ■ *nm* assumption, hypothesis ■ *conj*: ~ **que** since; **dar por ~ algo** to take sth for granted; **por ~** of course

supurar [supu'rar] *vi* to fester, suppurate

supuse *etc* [su'puse] *vb ver* **suponer**

sur [sur] *adj* southern; (*rumbo*) southerly ■ *nm* south; (*viento*) south wind

Suráfrica *etc* [su'rafrika] = **Sudáfrica** *etc*

Suramérica *etc* [sura'merika] = **Sudamérica** *etc*

surcar [sur'kar] *vt* to plough; (*superficie*) to cut, score

surco ['surko] *nm* groove; (*Agr*) furrow

surcoreano, -a [surkore'ano, a] *adj, nm/f* South Korean

sureño, -a [su'reɲo, a] *adj* southern ■ *nm/f* southerner

sureste [su'reste] = **sudeste**

surf [surf] *nm* surfing

surfear [surfe'ar] *vt*: ~ **el Internet** to surf the internet

surgir [sur'xir] *vi* to arise, emerge; (*dificultad*) to come up, crop up

surja *etc* ['surxa] *vb ver* **surgir**

suroeste [suro'este] = **sudoeste**

surque *etc* ['surke] *vb ver* **surcar**

surrealismo [surrea'lismo] *nm* surrealism

surrealista [surrea'lista] *adj, nm/f* surrealist

surtido, -a [sur'tiðo, a] *adj* mixed, assorted ■ *nm* (*selección*) selection, assortment; (*abastecimiento*) supply, stock

surtidor [surti'ðor] *nm* (*chorro*) jet, spout; (*fuente*) fountain; ~ **de gasolina** petrol (*Brit*) *o* gas (*US*) pump

surtir [sur'tir] *vt* to supply, provide; (*efecto*) to have, produce ■ *vi* to spout, spurt; **surtirse** *vr*: **surtirse de** to provide o.s. with

susceptible [susθep'tiβle] *adj* susceptible; (*sensible*) sensitive; ~ **de** capable of

suscitar [susθi'tar] *vt* to cause, provoke; (*discusión*) to start; (*duda, problema*) to raise; (*interés, sospechas*) to arouse

suscribir [suskri'βir] *vt* (*firmar*) to sign; (*respaldar*) to subscribe to, endorse; (*Com: acciones*) to take out an option on; **suscribirse** *vr* to subscribe; ~ **a algn a una revista** to take out a subscription to a journal for sb

suscripción [suskrip'θjon] *nf* subscription

suscrito, -a [sus'krito, a] *pp de* **suscribir** ■ *adj*: ~ **en exceso** oversubscribed

sushi ['suʃi] *nm* sushi

susodicho, -a [suso'ditʃo, a] *adj* above-mentioned

suspender [suspen'der] *vt* (*objeto*) to hang (up), suspend; (*trabajo*) to stop, suspend; (*Escol*) to fail

suspense [sus'pense] *nm* suspense

suspensión [suspen'sjon] *nf* suspension; (*fig*) stoppage, suspension; (*Jur*) stay; ~ **de fuego** *o* **de hostilidades** ceasefire, cessation of hostilities; ~ **de pagos** suspension of payments

suspensivo, -a [suspen'siβo, a] *adj*: **puntos suspensivos** dots, suspension points

suspenso, -a [sus'penso, a] *adj* hanging, suspended; (*Escol*) failed ■ *nm* (*Escol*) fail(ure); **quedar** *o* **estar en ~** to be pending

suspicacia [suspi'kaθja] *nf* suspicion, mistrust

suspicaz [suspi'kaθ] *adj* suspicious, distrustful

suspirar [suspi'rar] *vi* to sigh
suspiro [sus'piro] *nm* sigh
sustancia [sus'tanθja] *nf* substance; ~ **gris** (*Anat*) grey matter; **sin** ~ lacking in substance, shallow
sustancial [sustan'θjal] *adj* substantial
sustancioso, -a [sustan'θjoso, a] *adj* substantial; (*discurso*) solid
sustantivo, -a [sustan'tiβo, a] *adj* substantive; (*Ling*) substantival, noun *cpd* ▪ *nm* noun, substantive
sustentar [susten'tar] *vt* (*alimentar*) to sustain, nourish; (*objeto*) to hold up, support; (*idea, teoría*) to maintain, uphold; (*fig*) to sustain, keep going
sustento [sus'tento] *nm* support; (*alimento*) sustenance, food
sustituir [sustitu'ir] *vt* to substitute, replace
sustituto, -a [susti'tuto, a] *nm/f* substitute, replacement
sustituyendo *etc* [sustitu'jendo] *vb ver* **sustituir**
susto ['susto] *nm* fright, scare; **dar un ~ a algn** to give sb a fright; **darse** *o* **pegarse un ~** (*fam*) to get a fright
sustraer [sustra'er] *vt* to remove, take away; (*Mat*) to subtract
sustraiga *etc* [sus'traiɣa], **sustraje** *etc* [sus'traxe] *vb ver* **sustraer**

sustrato [sus'trato] *nm* substratum
sustrayendo *etc* [sustra'jendo] *vb ver* **sustraer**
susurrar [susu'rrar] *vi* to whisper
susurro [su'surro] *nm* whisper
sutil [su'til] *adj* (*aroma*) subtle; (*tenue*) thin; (*hilo, hebra*) fine; (*olor*) delicate; (*brisa*) gentle; (*diferencia*) fine, subtle; (*inteligencia*) sharp, keen
sutileza [suti'leθa] *nf* subtlety; (*delgadez*) thinness; (*delicadeza*) delicacy; (*agudeza*) keenness
sutura [su'tura] *nf* suture
suturar [sutu'rar] *vt* to suture; (*juntar con puntos*) to stitch
suyo, -a ['sujo, a] *adj* (*con artículo o después del verbo ser: de él*) his; (: *de ella*) hers; (: *de ellos, ellas*) theirs; (: *de usted, ustedes*) yours; (*después de un nombre: de él*) of his; (: *de ella*) of hers; (: *de ellos, ellas*) of theirs; (: *de usted, ustedes*) of yours; **lo** ~ (what is) his; (*su parte*) his share, what he deserves; **los suyos** (*su familia*) one's family *o* relations; (*sus partidarios*) one's own people *o* supporters; ~ **afectísimo** (*en carta*) yours faithfully *o* sincerely; **de** ~ in itself; **eso es muy** ~ that's just like him; **hacer de las suyas** to get up to one's old tricks; **ir a la suya, ir a lo** ~ to go one's own way; **salirse con la suya** to get one's way

S

Tt

T, t [te] *nf* (*letra*) T, t; **T de Tarragona** T for Tommy

t *abr* = **tonelada**

T. *abr* (= *Telefón, Telégrafo*) tel.; (*Com*) = **Tarifa; Tasa**

t. *abr* (= *tomo(s)*) vol(s)

TA *abr* = **traducción automática**

Tabacalera [taβaka'lera] *nf* Spanish state tobacco monopoly

tabaco [ta'βako] *nm* tobacco; (*fam*) cigarettes *pl*

tábano ['taβano] *nm* horsefly

tabaquería [tabake'ria] *nf* tobacconist's (*Brit*), cigar store (*US*)

tabarra [ta'βarra] *nf* (*fam*) nuisance; **dar la ~** to be a pain in the neck

taberna [ta'βerna] *nf* bar

tabernero, -a [taβer'nero, a] *nm/f* (*encargado*) publican; (*camarero*) barman/barmaid

tabique [ta'βike] *nm* (*pared*) thin wall; (*para dividir*) partition

tabla ['taβla] *nf* (*de madera*) plank; (*estante*) shelf; (*de anuncios*) board; (*lista, catálogo*) list; (*de vestido*) pleat; (*Arte*) panel; **tablas** *nfpl* (*Taur: Teat*) boards; **hacer tablas** to draw; **~ de consulta** (*Inform*) lookup table

tablado [ta'βlaðo] *nm* (*plataforma*) platform; (*suelo*) plank floor; (*Teat*) stage

tablao [ta'βlao] *nm* (*tb:* **tablao flamenco**) flamenco show

tablero [ta'βlero] *nm* (*de madera*) plank, board; (*pizarra*) blackboard; (*de ajedrez, damas*) board; (*Auto*) dashboard; **~ de gráficos** (*Inform*) graph pad

tableta [ta'βleta] *nf* (*Med*) tablet; (*de chocolate*) bar

tablilla [ta'βliʎa] *nf* small board; (*Med*) splint

tablón [ta'βlon] *nm* (*de suelo*) plank; (*de techo*) beam; (*de anuncios*) notice board

tabú [ta'βu] *nm* taboo

tabulación [taβula'θjon] *nf* (*Inform*) tab(bing)

tabulador [taβula'ðor] *nm* (*Inform: Tip*) tab

tabuladora [taβula'ðora] *nf:* **~ eléctrica** electric accounting machine

tabular [taβu'lar] *vt* to tabulate; (*Inform*) to tab

taburete [taβu'rete] *nm* stool

tacaño, -a [ta'kaɲo, a] *adj* (*avaro*) mean; (*astuto*) crafty

tacha ['tatʃa] *nf* (*defecto*) flaw, defect; (*Tec*) stud; **poner ~ a** to find fault with; **sin ~** flawless

tachar [ta'tʃar] *vt* (*borrar*) to cross out; (*corregir*) to correct; (*criticar*) to criticize; **~ de** to accuse of

tacho ['tatʃo] *nm* (*Am*) bucket, pail

tachón [ta'tʃon] *nm* erasure; (*tachadura*) crossing-out; (*Tec*) ornamental stud; (*Costura*) trimming

tachuela [ta'tʃwela] *nf* (*clavo*) tack

tácito, -a ['taθito, a] *adj* tacit; (*acuerdo*) unspoken; (*Ling*) understood; (*ley*) unwritten

taciturno, -a [taθi'turno, a] *adj* (*callado*) silent; (*malhumorado*) sullen

taco ['tako] *nm* (*Billar*) cue; (*libro de billetes*) book; (*manojo de billetes*) wad; (*Am*) heel; (*tarugo*) peg; (*fam: bocado*) snack; (*: palabrota*) swear word; (*: trago de vino*) swig; (*México*) filled tortilla; **armarse** *o* **hacerse un ~** to get into a mess

tacógrafo [ta'koɣrafo] *nm* (*Com*) tachograph

tacón [ta'kon] *nm* heel; **de ~ alto** high-heeled

taconear [takone'ar] *vi* (*dar golpecitos*) to tap with one's heels; (*Mil etc*) to click one's heels

taconeo [tako'neo] *nm* (*heel*) tapping *o* clicking

táctico, -a ['taktiko, a] *adj* tactical ▪ *nf* tactics *pl*

tacto ['takto] *nm* touch; (*acción*) touching; (*fig*) tact

TAE *nf abr* (= *tasa anual equivalente*) APR

tafetán [tafe'tan] *nm* taffeta; **tafetanes** *nmpl* (*fam*) frills; **~ adhesivo** *o* **inglés** sticking plaster

tafilete [tafi'lete] *nm* morocco leather

tahona [ta'ona] *nf* (*panadería*) bakery; (*molino*) flourmill

tahur [ta'ur] *nm* gambler; (*pey*) cheat

tailandés, -esa [tailan'des, esa] *adj, nm/f* Thai ▪ *nm* (*Ling*) Thai

Tailandia [tai'landja] *nf* Thailand

taimado, -a [tai'maðo, a] *adj* (*astuto*) sly; (*resentido*) sullen

taita ['taita] *nm* dad, daddy

tajada [ta'xaða] *nf* slice; (*fam*) rake-off; **sacar ~** to get one's share

tajante [ta'xante] *adj* sharp; (*negativa*) emphatic; **es una persona ~** he's an emphatic person

tajar [ta'xar] *vt* to cut, slice

Tajo ['taxo] *nm* Tagus

tajo ['taxo] *nm* (*corte*) cut; (*filo*) cutting edge; (*Geo*) cleft

tal [tal] *adj* such; **un ~ García** a man called García; **~ vez** perhaps ▪ *pron* (*persona*) someone, such a one; (*cosa*) something, such a thing; **~ como** such as; **~ para cual** tit for tat; (*dos iguales*) two of a kind; **hablábamos de que si ~ si cual** we were talking about this, that and the other ▪ *adv:* **~ como** (*igual*) just as; **~ cual** (*como es*) just as it is; **~ el padre, cual el hijo** like father, like son; **¿qué ~?** how are things?; **¿qué ~ te gusta?** how do you like it? ▪ *conj:* **con ~ (de) que** provided that

tala ['tala] *nf* (*de árboles*) tree felling

taladradora [talaðra'ðora] *nf* drill; **~ neumática** pneumatic drill

taladrar [tala'ðrar] *vt* to drill; (*fig: ruido*) to pierce

taladro [ta'laðro] *nm* (*gen*) drill; (*hoyo*) drill hole; **~ neumático** pneumatic drill

talante [ta'lante] *nm* (*humor*) mood; (*voluntad*) will, willingness

talar [ta'lar] *vt* to fell, cut down; (*fig*) to devastate

talco ['talko] *nm* (*polvos*) talcum powder; (*Mineralogía*) talc

talega [ta'leɣa] *nf* sack

talego [ta'leɣo] *nm* sack; **tener ~** (*fam*) to have money

talento [ta'lento] *nm* talent; (*capacidad*) ability; (*don*) gift

Talgo ['talɣo] *nm abr* (*Ferro: = tren articulado ligero Goicoechea-Oriol*) high-speed train

talidomida [taliðo'miða] *nm* thalidomide

talismán [talis'man] *nm* talisman

talla ['taʎa] *nf* (*estatura, fig, Med*) height, stature; (*de ropa*) size, fitting; (*palo*) measuring rod; (*Arte: de madera*) carving; (*de piedra*) sculpture

tallado, -a [ta'ʎaðo, a] *adj* carved ▪ *nm* (*de madera*) carving; (*de piedra*) sculpture

tallar [ta'ʎar] *vt* (*trabajar*) to work, carve; (*grabar*) to engrave; (*medir*) to measure; (*repartir*) to deal ▪ *vi* to deal

tallarín [taʎa'rin] *nm* noodle

talle ['taʎe] *nm* (*Anat*) waist; (*medida*) size; (*física*) build; (*: de mujer*) figure; (*fig*) appearance; **de ~ esbelto** with a slim figure

taller [ta'ʎer] *nm* (*Tec*) workshop; (*fábrica*) factory; (*Auto*) garage; (*de artista*) studio

tallo ['taʎo] *nm* (*de planta*) stem; (*de hierba*) blade; (*brote*) shoot; (*col*) cabbage; (*Culin*) candied peel

talmente [tal'mente] *adv* (*de esta forma*) in such a way; (*hasta tal punto*) to such an extent; (*exactamente*) exactly

talón [ta'lon] *nm* (*gen*) heel; (*Com*) counterfoil; (*Tec*) rim; **~ de Aquiles** Achilles heel

talonario [talo'narjo] *nm* (*de cheques*) cheque book; (*de billetes*) book of tickets; (*de recibos*) receipt book

tamaño, -a [ta'maɲo, a] *adj* (*tan grande*) such a big; (*tan pequeño*) such a small ▪ *nm* size; **de ~ natural** full-size; **¿de qué ~ es?** what size is it?

tamarindo [tama'rindo] *nm* tamarind

tambaleante [tambale'ante] *adj* (*persona*) staggering; (*mueble*) wobbly; (*vehículo*) swaying

tambalearse [tambale'arse] *vr* (*persona*) to stagger; (*mueble*) to wobble; (*vehículo*) to sway

también [tam'bjen] *adv* (*igualmente*) also, too, as well; (*además*) besides; **estoy cansado — yo ~** I'm tired — so am I *o* me too

tambor [tam'bor] *nm* drum; (*Anat*) eardrum; **~ del freno** brake drum; **~ magnético** (*Inform*) magnetic drum

tamboril [tambo'ril] *nm* small drum

tamborilear [tamborile'ar] *vi* (*Mus*) to drum; (*con los dedos*) to drum with one's fingers

tamborilero [tambori'lero] *nm* drummer

Támesis ['tamesis] *nm* Thames

tamice *etc* [ta'miθe] *vb ver* **tamizar**

tamiz [ta'miθ] *nm* sieve

tamizar [tami'θar] *vt* to sieve

tampoco [tam'poko] *adv* nor, neither; **yo ~ lo compré** I didn't buy it either

tampón [tam'pon] *nm* plug; (*Med*) tampon

tan [tan] *adv* so; **~ es así que** so much so that; **¡qué cosa ~ rara!** how strange!; **no es una idea ~ buena** it is not such a good idea

tanatorio [tana'torjo] *nm* (*privado*) funeral home *o* parlour; (*público*) mortuary

tanda ['tanda] *nf* (*gen*) series; (*de inyecciones*) course; (*juego*) set; (*turno*) shift; (*grupo*) gang

tándem ['tandem] *nm* tandem; (*Pol*) duo

tanga ['tanga] *nm* (*bikini*) tanga; (*ropa interior*) tanga briefs

t

tangente [tan'xente] *nf* tangent; **salirse por la ~** to go off at a tangent

Tánger ['tanxer] *n* Tangier

tangerino, -a [tanxe'rino, a] *adj* of o from Tangier ■ *nm/f* native o inhabitant of Tangier

tangible [tan'xiβle] *adj* tangible

tango ['tango] *nm* tango

tanino [ta'nino] *nm* tannin

tankini [tan'kini] *nm* tankini

tanque ['tanke] *nm* (*gen*) tank; (*Auto, Naut*) tanker

tanqueta [tan'keta] *nf* (*Mil*) small tank, armoured vehicle

tantear [tante'ar] *vt* (*calcular*) to reckon (up); (*medir*) to take the measure of; (*probar*) to test, try out; (*tomar la medida: persona*) to take the measurements of; (*considerar*) to weigh up ■ *vi* (*Deporte*) to score

tanteo [tan'teo] *nm* (*cálculo aproximado*) (rough) calculation; (*prueba*) test, trial; (*Deporte*) scoring; (*adivinanzas*) guesswork; **al ~** by trial and error

tantísimo, -a [tan'tisimo, a] *adj* so much; **tantísimos** so many

tanto, -a ['tanto, a] *adj* (*cantidad*) so much, as much; **tantos** so many, as many; **20 y tantos** 20-odd ■ *adv* (*cantidad*) so much, as much; (*tiempo*) so long, as long; **~ tú como yo** both you and I; **~ como eso** it's not as bad as that; **~ más ... cuanto que** it's all the more ... because; **~ mejor/peor** so much the better/the worse; **~ si viene como si va** whether he comes or whether he goes; **~ es así que** so much so that; **por ~, por lo ~** therefore; **me he vuelto ronco de o con ~ hablar** I have become hoarse with so much talking ■ *conj*: **con ~ que** provided (that); **en ~ que** while; **hasta ~ (que)** until such time as ■ *nm* (*suma*) certain amount; (*proporción*) so much; (*punto*) point; (*gol*) goal; **~ alzado** agreed price; **~ por ciento** percentage; **al ~** up to date; **estar al ~ de los acontecimientos** to be fully abreast of events; **un ~ perezoso** somewhat lazy; **al ~ de que** because of the fact that ■ *pron*: **cada uno paga ~** each one pays so much; **uno de tantos** one of many; **a tantos de agosto** on such and such a day in August; **entre ~** meanwhile

tañer [ta'ɲer] *vt* (*Mus*) to play; (*campana*) to ring

TAO *nf abr* (= *traducción asistida por ordenador*) MAT

tapa ['tapa] *nf* (*de caja, olla*) lid; (*de botella*) top; (*de libro*) cover; (*de comida*) snack

tapacubos [tapa'kuβos] *nm inv* hub cap

tapadera [tapa'ðera] *nf* lid, cover

tapado [ta'paðo] *nm* (*Am: abrigo*) coat

tapar [ta'par] *vt* (*cubrir*) to cover; (*envolver*) to wrap o cover up; (*la vista*) to obstruct; (*persona, falta*) to conceal; (*Am*) to fill; **taparse** *vr* to wrap o.s. up

tapete [ta'pete] *nm* table cover; **estar sobre el ~** (*fig*) to be under discussion

tapia ['tapja] *nf* (*garden*) wall

tapiar [ta'pjar] *vt* to wall in

tapice *etc* [ta'piθe] *vb ver* **tapizar**

tapicería [tapiθe'ria] *nf* tapestry; (*para muebles*) upholstery; (*tienda*) upholsterer's (shop)

tapicero, -a [tapi'θero, a] *nm/f* (*de muebles*) upholsterer

tapiz [ta'piθ] *nm* (*alfombra*) carpet; (*tela tejida*) tapestry

tapizar [tapi'θar] *vt* (*pared*) to wallpaper; (*suelo*) to carpet; (*muebles*) to upholster

tapón [ta'pon] *nm* (*corcho*) stopper; (*Tec*) plug; (*Med*) tampon; **~ de rosca o de tuerca** screw-top

taponar [tapo'nar] *vt* (*botella*) to cork; (*tubería*) to block

taponazo [tapo'naθo] *nm* (*de tapón*) pop

tapujo [ta'puxo] *nm* (*embozo*) muffler; (*engaño*) deceit; **sin tapujos** honestly

taquigrafía [takiɣra'fia] *nf* shorthand

taquígrafo, -a [ta'kiɣrafo, a] *nm/f* shorthand writer

taquilla [ta'kiʎa] *nf* (*de estación etc*) booking office; (*de teatro*) box office; (*suma recogida*) takings *pl*; (*archivador*) filing cabinet

taquillero, -a [taki'ʎero, a] *adj*: **función taquillera** box office success ■ *nm/f* ticket clerk

taquimecanografía [takimekanoɣra'fia] *nf* shorthand and typing

taquímetro [ta'kimetro] *nm* speedometer; (*de control*) tachymeter

tara ['tara] *nf* (*defecto*) defect; (*Com*) tare

tarado, -a [ta'raðo, a] *adj* (*Com*) defective, imperfect; (*idiota*) stupid; (*loco*) crazy, nuts ■ *nm/f* idiot, cretin

tarántula [ta'rantula] *nf* tarantula

tararear [tarare'ar] *vi* to hum

tardanza [tar'ðanθa] *nf* (*demora*) delay; (*lentitud*) slowness

tardar [tar'ðar] *vi* (*tomar tiempo*) to take a long time; (*llegar tarde*) to be late; (*demorar*) to delay; **¿tarda mucho el tren?** does the train take long?; **a más ~** at the (very) latest; **~ en hacer algo** to be slow o take a long time to do sth; **no tardes en venir** come soon, come before long

tarde ['tarðe] *adv* (*hora*) late; (*fuera de tiempo*)

too late ∎ *nf* (*de día*) afternoon; (*de noche*) evening; **~ o temprano** sooner or later; **de ~ en ~** from time to time; **¡buenas tardes!** (*de día*) good afternoon!; (*de noche*) good evening!; **a** *o* **por la ~** in the afternoon; in the evening

tardío, -a [tar'ðio, a] *adj* (*retrasado*) late; (*lento*) slow (to arrive)

tardo, -a ['tarðo, a] *adj* (*lento*) slow; (*torpe*) dull; **~ de oído** hard of hearing

tarea [ta'rea] *nf* task; **tareas** *nfpl* (*Escol*) homework *sg*; **~ de ocasión** chore

tarifa [ta'rifa] *nf* (*lista de precios*) price list; (*Com*) tariff; **~ básica** basic rate; **~ completa** all-in cost; **~ a destajo** piece rate; **~ doble** double time

tarima [ta'rima] *nf* (*plataforma*) platform

tarjeta [tar'xeta] *nf* card; **~ postal/de crédito/de Navidad** postcard/credit card/Christmas card; **~ de circuitos** (*Inform*) circuit board; **~ cliente** loyalty card; **~ comercial** (*Com*) calling card; **~ dinero** cash card; **~ gráficos** (*Inform*) graphics card; **~ monedero** electronic purse *o* wallet; **~ prepago** top-up card; **~ SIM** SIM card

tarot [ta'rot] *nm* tarot

tarraconense [tarrako'nense] *adj* of *o* from Tarragona ∎ *nm/f* native *o* inhabitant of Tarragona

tarro ['tarro] *nm* jar, pot

tarta ['tarta] *nf* (*pastel*) cake; (*torta*) tart

tartajear [tartaxe'ar] *vi* to stammer

tartamudear [tartamuðe'ar] *vi* to stutter, stammer

tartamudo, -a [tarta'muðo, a] *adj* stuttering, stammering ∎ *nm/f* stutterer, stammerer

tartárico, -a [tar'tariko, a] *adj*: **ácido ~** tartaric acid

tártaro ['tartaro] *adj*, *nm* Tartar ∎ *nm* (*Química*) tartar

tarugo, -a [ta'ruɣo, a] *adj* stupid ∎ *nm* (*de madera*) lump

tarumba [ta'rumba] *adj* (*confuso*) confused

tasa ['tasa] *nf* (*precio*) (fixed) price, rate; (*valoración*) valuation; (*medida, norma*) measure, standard; **~ básica** (*Com*) basic rate; **~ de cambio** exchange rate; **de ~ cero** (*Com*) zero-rated; **~ de crecimiento** growth rate; **~ de interés/de nacimiento** rate of interest/birth rate; **~ de rendimiento** (*Com*) rate of return; **tasas universitarias** university fees

tasación [tasa'θjon] *nf* assessment, valuation; (*fig*) appraisal

tasador, a [tasa'ðor, a] *nm/f* valuer; (*Com: de impuestos*) assessor

tasar [ta'sar] *vt* (*arreglar el precio*) to fix a price for; (*valorar*) to value, assess; (*limitar*) to limit

tasca ['taska] *nf* (*fam*) pub

tata ['tata] *nm* (*fam*) dad(dy) ∎ *nf* (*niñera*) nanny, maid

tatarabuelo, -a [tatara'βwelo, a] *nm/f* great-great-grandfather/mother; **los tatarabuelos** one's great-great-grandparents

tatuaje [ta'twaxe] *nm* (*dibujo*) tattoo; (*acto*) tattooing

tatuar [ta'twar] *vt* to tattoo

taumaturgo [tauma'turɣo] *nm* miracle-worker

taurino, -a [tau'rino, a] *adj* bullfighting *cpd*

Tauro ['tauro] *nm* Taurus

tauromaquia [tauro'makja] *nf* (art of) bullfighting

tautología [tautolo'xia] *nf* tautology

taxativo, -a [taksa'tiβo, a] *adj* (*restringido*) limited; (*sentido*) specific

taxi ['taksi] *nm* taxi

taxidermia [taksi'ðermja] *nf* taxidermy

taxímetro [tak'simetro] *nm* taximeter

taxista [tak'sista] *nm/f* taxi driver

Tayikistán [tajikis'tan] *nm* Tajikistan

taza ['taθa] *nf* cup; (*de retrete*) bowl; **~ para café** coffee cup

tazón [ta'θon] *nm* mug, large cup; (*escudilla*) basin

TCI *nf abr* (= *tarjeta de circuito impreso*) PCB

te [te] *pron* (*complemento de objeto*) you; (*complemento indirecto*) (to) you; (*reflexivo*) (to) yourself; **¿te duele mucho el brazo?** does your arm hurt a lot?; **te equivocas** you're wrong; **¡cálmate!** calm yourself!

té [te] (*pl* **tés**) *nm* tea; (*reunión*) tea party

tea ['tea] *nf* (*antorcha*) torch

teatral [tea'tral] *adj* theatre *cpd*; (*fig*) theatrical

teatro [te'atro] *nm* theatre; (*Lit*) plays *pl*, drama; **el ~** (*carrera*) the theatre, acting; **~ de aficionados/de variedades** amateur/variety theatre, vaudeville theater (*US*); **hacer ~** (*fig*) to make a fuss

tebeo [te'βeo] *nm* children's comic

techado [te'tʃaðo] *nm* (*techo*) roof; **bajo ~** under cover

techo ['tetʃo] *nm* (*externo*) roof; (*interno*) ceiling

techumbre [te'tʃumbre] *nf* roof

tecla ['tekla] *nf* (*Inform: Mus: Tip*) key; (*Inform*): **~ de anulación/de borrar** cancel/delete key; **~ de control/de edición** control/edit key; **~ con flecha** arrow key; **~ programable** user-defined key; **~ de retorno/de tabulación** return/tab key; **~ del cursor** cursor key; **teclas de control direccional del cursor** cursor control keys

371

teclado [te'klaðo] *nm* keyboard (*tb Inform*); **~ numérico** (*Inform*) numeric keypad

teclear [tekle'ar] *vi* to strum; (*fam*) to drum ▪ *vt* (*Inform*) to key (in), type in, keyboard

tecleo [te'kleo] *nm* (*Mus: sonido*) strumming; (: *forma de tocar*) fingering; (*fam*) drumming

tecnicismo [tekni'θismo] *nm* (*carácter técnico*) technical nature; (*Ling*) technical term

técnico, -a ['tekniko, a] *adj* technical ▪ *nm* technician; (*experto*) expert ▪ *nf* (*procedimientos*) technique; (*arte, oficio*) craft

tecnicolor [tekniko'lor] *nm* Technicolor®

tecnócrata [tek'nokrata] *nm/f* technocrat

tecnología [teknolo'xia] *nf* technology; **~ de estado sólido** (*Inform*) solid-state technology; **~ de la información** information technology

tecnológico, -a [tekno'loxiko, a] *adj* technological

tecnólogo, -a [tek'noloɣo, a] *nm/f* technologist

tedio ['teðjo] *nm* (*aburrimiento*) boredom; (*apatía*) apathy; (*fastidio*) depression

tedioso, -a [te'ðjoso, a] *adj* boring; (*cansado*) wearisome, tedious

Teherán [tee'ran] *nm* Teheran

teja ['texa] *nf* (*azulejo*) tile; (*Bot*) lime (tree)

tejado [te'xaðo] *nm* (tiled) roof

tejano, -a [te'xano, a] *adj, nm/f* Texan ▪ *nmpl*: **tejanos** (*vaqueros*) jeans

Tejas ['texas] *nm* Texas

tejemaneje [texema'nexe] *nm* (*actividad*) bustle; (*lío*) fuss, to-do; (*intriga*) intrigue

tejer [te'xer] *vt* to weave; (*tela de araña*) to spin; (*Am*) to knit; (*fig*) to fabricate ▪ *vi*: **~ y destejer** to chop and change

tejido [te'xiðo] *nm* fabric; (*estofa, tela*) (knitted) material; (*Anat*) tissue; (*textura*) texture

tejo ['texo] *nm* (*Bot*) yew (tree)

tel. *abr* (= *teléfono*) tel.

tela ['tela] *nf* (*material*) material; (*de fruta, en líquido*) skin; (*del ojo*) film; **hay ~ para rato** there's lots to talk about; **poner en ~ de juicio** to (call in) question; **~ de araña** cobweb, spider's web

telar [te'lar] *nm* (*máquina*) loom; (*de teatro*) gridiron; **telares** *nmpl* textile mill *sg*

telaraña [tela'raɲa] *nf* cobweb, spider's web

tele ... [tele] *pref* tele...

tele ['tele] *nf* (*fam*) TV

telecargar [telekar'ɣar] *vt* (*Inform*) to download

telecomunicación [telekomunika'θjon] *nf* telecommunication

teleconferencia [telekonfe'renθja] *nf* (*reunión*) teleconference; (*sistema*) teleconferencing

telecontrol [telekon'trol] *nm* remote control

telecopiadora [telekopja'ðora] *nf*: **~ facsímil** fax copier

telediario [tele'ðjarjo] *nm* television news

teledifusión [teleðifu'sjon] *nf* (television) broadcast

teledirigido, -a [teleðiri'xiðo, a] *adj* remote-controlled

teléf. *abr* (= *teléfono*) tel.

teleférico [tele'feriko] *nm* (*tren*) cable-railway; (*de esquí*) ski-lift

telefilm [tele'film], **telefilme** [tele'filme] *nm* TV film

telefonazo [telefo'naθo] *nm* (*fam*) telephone call; **te daré un ~** I'll give you a ring

telefonear [telefone'ar] *vi* to telephone

telefónicamente [tele'fonikamente] *adv* by (tele)phone

telefónico, -a [tele'foniko, a] *adj* telephone *cpd* ▪ *nf*: **Telefónica** (*Esp*) Spanish national telephone company, ≈ British Telecom

telefonista [telefo'nista] *nm/f* telephonist

teléfono [te'lefono] *nm* (tele)phone; **~ móvil** mobile phone; **está hablando por ~** he's on the phone

telefoto [tele'foto] *nf* telephoto

telegrafía [teleɣra'fia] *nf* telegraphy

telégrafo [te'leɣrafo] *nm* telegraph; (*fam: persona*) telegraph boy

telegrama [tele'ɣrama] *nm* telegram

teleimpresor [teleimpre'sor] *nm* teleprinter

telemática [tele'matika] *nf* telematics *sg*

telémetro [te'lemetro] *nm* rangefinder

telenovela [teleno'βela] *nf* soap (opera)

teleobjetivo [teleobxe'tiβo] *nm* telephoto lens

telepatía [telepa'tia] *nf* telepathy

telepático, -a [tele'patiko, a] *adj* telepathic

teleproceso [telepro'θeso] *nm* teleprocessing

telescópico, -a [tele'skopiko, a] *adj* telescopic

telescopio [tele'skopjo] *nm* telescope

telesilla [tele'siʎa] *nm* chairlift

telespectador, a [telespekta'ðor, a] *nm/f* viewer

telesquí [teles'ki] *nm* ski-lift

teletex [tele'teks], **teletexto** [tele'teksto] *nm* teletext

teletipista [teleti'pista] *nm/f* teletypist

teletipo [tele'tipo] *nm* teletype(writer)

teletrabajo [teletra'βaxo] *nm* teleworking

televentas [tele'βentas] *nfpl* telesales

televidente [tele'βiðente] *nm/f* viewer

televisar [teleβi'sar] *vt* to televise

televisión [teleβi'sjon] *nf* television; **~ en color/por satélite** colour/satellite television; **~ digital** digital television

televisivo, -a [teleβi'siβo, a] *adj* television *cpd*
televisor [teleβi'sor] *nm* television set
télex ['teleks] *nm* telex; **máquina ~** telex
(machine); **enviar por ~** to telex
telón [te'lon] *nm* curtain; **~ de boca/
seguridad** front/safety curtain; **~ de acero**
(*Pol*) iron curtain; **~ de fondo** backcloth,
background
telonero, -a [telo'nero, a] *nm/f* support act;
los teloneros (*Mus*) the support band
tema ['tema] *nm* (*asunto*) subject, topic; (*Mus*)
theme; **temas de actualidad** current affairs
■ *nf* (*obsesión*) obsession; (*manía*) ill-will;
tener ~ a algn to have a grudge against sb
temario [te'marjo] *nm* (*Escol*) set of topics;
(*de una conferencia*) agenda
temático, -a [te'matiko, a] *adj* thematic
■ *nf* subject matter
tembladera [tembla'ðera] *nf* shaking; (*Am*)
quagmire
temblar [tem'blar] *vi* to shake, tremble;
(*de frío*) to shiver
tembleque [tem'bleke] *adj* shaking ■ *nm*
shaking
temblón, -ona [tem'blon, ona] *adj* shaking
temblor [tem'blor] *nm* trembling; (*de tierra*)
earthquake
tembloroso, -a [temblo'roso, a] *adj*
trembling
temer [te'mer] *vt* to fear ■ *vi* to be afraid;
temo que Juan llegue tarde I am afraid
Juan may be late
temerario, -a [teme'rarjo, a] *adj* (*imprudente*)
rash; (*descuidado*) reckless; (*arbitrario*) hasty
temeridad [temeri'ðað] *nf* (*imprudencia*)
rashness; (*audacia*) boldness
temeroso, -a [teme'roso, a] *adj* (*miedoso*)
fearful; (*que inspira temor*) frightful
temible [te'miβle] *adj* fearsome
temor [te'mor] *nm* (*miedo*) fear; (*duda*)
suspicion
témpano ['tempano] *nm* (*Mus*) kettledrum;
~ de hielo ice floe
temperamento [tempera'mento] *nm*
temperament; **tener ~** to be temperamental
temperar [tempe'rar] *vt* to temper, moderate
temperatura [tempera'tura] *nf* temperature
tempestad [tempes'tað] *nf* storm; **~ en un
vaso de agua** (*fig*) storm in a teacup
tempestuoso, -a [tempes'twoso, a] *adj*
stormy
templado, -a [tem'plaðo, a] *adj* (*moderado*)
moderate; (: *en el comer*) frugal; (: *en el beber*)
abstemious; (*agua*) lukewarm; (*clima*) mild;
(*Mus*) in tune, well-tuned
templanza [tem'planθa] *nf* moderation; (*en
el beber*) abstemiousness; (*del clima*) mildness

templar [tem'plar] *vt* (*moderar*) to moderate;
(*furia*) to restrain; (*calor*) to reduce; (*solución*)
to dilute; (*afinar*) to tune (up); (*acero*) to
temper ■ *vi* to moderate; **templarse** *vr* to
be restrained
temple ['temple] *nm* (*humor*) mood; (*coraje*)
courage; (*ajuste*) tempering; (*afinación*)
tuning; (*pintura*) tempera
templo ['templo] *nm* (*iglesia*) church; (*pagano
etc*) temple; **~ metodista** Methodist chapel
temporada [tempo'raða] *nf* time, period;
(*estación, social, Deporte*) season; **en plena ~**
at the height of the season
temporal [tempo'ral] *adj* (*no permanente*)
temporary; (*Rel*) temporal ■ *nm* storm
temporario, -a [tempo'rarjo, a] *adj* (*Am*)
temporary
tempranero, -a [tempra'nero, a] *adj* (*Bot*)
early; (*persona*) early-rising
temprano, -a [tem'prano, a] *adj* early ■ *adv*
early; (*demasiado pronto*) too soon, too early;
lo más ~ posible as soon as possible
ten [ten] *vb ver* **tener**
tenacidad [tenaθi'ðað] *nf* (*gen*) tenacity;
(*dureza*) toughness; (*terquedad*) stubbornness
tenacillas [tena'θiʎas] *nfpl* (*gen*) tongs; (*para
el pelo*) curling tongs; (*Med*) forceps
tenaz [te'naθ] *adj* (*material*) tough; (*persona*)
tenacious; (*pegajoso*) sticky; (*terco*) stubborn
tenaza [te'naθa] *nf*, **tenazas** [te'naθas] *nfpl*
(*Med*) forceps; (*Tec*) pliers; (*Zool*) pincers
tendal [ten'dal] *nm* awning
tendedero [tende'ðero] *nm* (*para ropa*) drying-
place; (*cuerda*) clothes line
tendencia [ten'denθja] *nf* tendency; (*proceso*)
trend; **~ imperante** prevailing tendency;
~ del mercado run of the market; **tener ~ a**
to tend o have a tendency to
tendenciosidad [tendenθjosi'ðað] *nf*
tendentiousness
tendencioso, -a [tenden'θjoso, a] *adj*
tendentious
tender [ten'der] *vt* (*extender*) to spread out;
(*ropa*) to hang out; (*vía férrea, cable*) to lay;
(*cuerda*) to stretch; (*trampa*) to set ■ *vi* to
tend; **tenderse** *vr* to lie down; (*fig: dejarse
llevar*) to let o.s. go; (: *dejar ir*) to let things go;
~ la cama/la mesa (*Am*) to make the bed/lay
the table
ténder ['tender] *nm* (*Ferro*) tender
tenderete [tende'rete] *nm* (*puesto*) stall;
(*carretilla*) barrow; (*exposición*) display of goods
tendero, -a [ten'dero, a] *nm/f* shopkeeper
tendido, -a [ten'diðo, a] *adj* (*acostado*) lying
down, flat; (*colgado*) hanging ■ *nm* (*ropa*)
washing; (*Taur*) front rows *pl* of seats;
(*colocación*) laying; (*Arq: enyesado*) coat of

plaster; **a galope** ~ flat out

tendón [ten'don] *nm* tendon

tendré *etc* [ten'dre] *vb ver* **tener**

tenducho [ten'dutʃo] *nm* small dirty shop

tenebroso, -a [tene'βroso, a] *adj* (*oscuro*) dark; (*fig*) gloomy; (*siniestro*) sinister

tenedor [tene'ðor] *nm* (*Culin*) fork; (*poseedor*) holder; ~ **de libros** book-keeper; ~ **de acciones** shareholder; ~ **de póliza** policyholder

teneduría [teneðu'ria] *nf* keeping; ~ **de libros** book-keeping

tenencia [te'nenθja] *nf* (*de casa*) tenancy; (*de oficio*) tenure; (*de propiedad*) possession; ~ **asegurada** security of tenure; ~ **ilícita de armas** illegal possession of weapons

 PALABRA CLAVE

tener [te'ner] *vt* **1** (*poseer, gen*) to have; (*en la mano*) to hold; **¿tienes un boli?** have you got a pen?; **va a tener un niño** she's going to have a baby; **tiene los ojos azules** he's got blue eyes; **¡ten** (*o* **tenga**)!, **¡aquí tienes** (*o* **tiene**)!** here you are!

2 (*edad, medidas*) to be; **tiene siete años** she's seven (years old); **tiene 15 cm de largo** it's 15 cm long

3 (*sentimientos, sensaciones*): **tener sed/ hambre/frío/calor** to be thirsty/hungry/ cold/hot; **tener celos** to be jealous; **tener cuidado** to be careful; **tener razón** to be right; **tener suerte** to be lucky

4 (*considerar*): **lo tengo por brillante** I consider him to be brilliant; **tener en mucho a algn** to think very highly of sb

5 (+ *pp*: + *adj*: + *gerundio*): **tengo terminada ya la mitad del trabajo** I've done half the work already; **tenía el sombrero puesto** he had his hat on; **tenía pensado llamarte** I had been thinking of phoning you; **nos tiene hartos** we're fed up with him; **me ha tenido tres horas esperando** he kept me waiting three hours

6: **tener que hacer algo** to have to do sth; **tengo que acabar este trabajo hoy** I have to finish this job today

7: **¿qué tienes, estás enfermo?** what's the matter with you, are you ill?

8 (*locuciones*): **¿conque ésas tenemos?** so it's like that, then?; **no las tengo todas conmigo** I'm a bit unsure (about it); **lo tiene difícil** he'll have a hard job

tenerse *vr* **1**: **tenerse en pie** to stand up

2: **tenerse por** to think o.s.; **se tiene por un gran cantante** he thinks himself a great singer

tenga *etc* ['tenga] *vb ver* **tener**

tenia ['tenja] *nf* tapeworm

teniente [te'njente] *nm* lieutenant; ~ **coronel** lieutenant colonel

tenis ['tenis] *nm* tennis; ~ **de mesa** table tennis

tenista [te'nista] *nm/f* tennis player

tenor [te'nor] *nm* (*tono*) tone; (*sentido*) meaning; (*Mus*) tenor; **a** ~ **de** on the lines of

tenorio [te'norjo] *nm* (*fam*) ladykiller, Don Juan

tensar [ten'sar] *vt* to tauten; (*arco*) to draw

tensión [ten'sjon] *nf* tension; (*Tec*) stress; (*Med*): ~ **arterial** blood pressure; ~ **nerviosa** nervous strain; **tener la** ~ **alta** to have high blood pressure

tenso, -a ['tenso, a] *adj* tense; (*relaciones*) strained

tentación [tenta'θjon] *nf* temptation

tentáculo [ten'takulo] *nm* tentacle

tentador, a [tenta'ðor, a] *adj* tempting ◼ *nm/f* tempter/temptress

tentar [ten'tar] *vt* (*tocar*) to touch, feel; (*seducir*) to tempt; (*atraer*) to attract; (*probar*) to try (out); (*Med*) to probe; ~ **hacer algo** to try to do sth

tentativa [tenta'tiβa] *nf* attempt; ~ **de asesinato** attempted murder

tentempié [tentem'pje] *nm* (*fam*) snack

tenue ['tenwe] *adj* (*delgado*) thin, slender; (*alambre*) fine; (*insustancial*) tenuous; (*sonido*) faint; (*neblina*) light; (*lazo, vínculo*) slight

teñir [te'ɲir] *vt* to dye; (*fig*) to tinge; **teñirse el pelo** to dye one's hair

teología [teolo'xia] *nf* theology

teólogo, -a [te'oloɣo, a] *nm/f* theologist, theologian

teorema [teo'rema] *nm* theorem

teoría [teo'ria] *nf* theory; **en** ~ in theory

teóricamente [te'orikamente] *adv* theoretically

teorice *etc* [teo'riθe] *vb ver* **teorizar**

teórico, -a [te'oriko, a] *adj* theoretic(al) ◼ *nm/f* theoretician, theorist

teorizar [teori'θar] *vi* to theorize

tequila [te'kila] *nm o f* tequila

TER [ter] *nm abr* (*Ferro*) = **tren español rápido**

terapeuta [tera'peuta] *nm/f* therapist

terapéutico, -a [tera'peutiko, a] *adj* therapeutic(al) ◼ *nf* therapeutics *sg*

terapia [te'rapja] *nf* therapy; ~ **laboral** occupational therapy

tercer [ter'θer] *adj ver* **tercero**

tercermundista [terθermun'dista] *adj* Third World *cpd*

tercero, -a [ter'θero, a] *adj* third (*antes de nmsg* **tercer**) ◼ *nm* (*árbitro*) mediator; (*Jur*) third party

terceto [ter'θeto] *nm* trio

terciado, -a [ter'θjaðo, a] *adj* slanting; **azúcar ~** brown sugar

terciar [ter'θjar] *vt* (*Mat*) to divide into three; (*inclinarse*) to slope; (*llevar*) to wear across one's chest ■ *vi* (*participar*) to take part; (*hacer de árbitro*) to mediate; **terciarse** *vr* to arise

terciario, -a [ter'θjarjo, a] *adj* tertiary

tercio ['terθjo] *nm* third

terciopelo [terθjo'pelo] *nm* velvet

terco, -a ['terko, a] *adj* obstinate, stubborn; (*material*) tough

tergal® [ter'ɣal] *nm* Terylene®

tergiversación [terxiβersa'θjon] *nf* (*deformación*) distortion; (*evasivas*) prevarication

tergiversar [terxiβer'sar] *vt* to distort ■ *vi* to prevaricate

termal [ter'mal] *adj* thermal

termas ['termas] *nfpl* hot springs

térmico, -a ['termiko, a] *adj* thermic, thermal, heat *cpd*

terminación [termina'θjon] *nf* (*final*) end; (*conclusión*) conclusion, ending

terminal [termi'nal] *adj* terminal ■ *nm* (*Elec: Inform*) terminal; **~ conversacional** interactive terminal; **~ de pantalla** visual display unit ■ *nf* (*Aviat: Ferro*) terminal

terminante [termi'nante] *adj* (*final*) final, definitive; (*tajante*) categorical

terminar [termi'nar] *vt* (*completar*) to complete, finish; (*concluir*) to end ■ *vi* (*llegar a su fin*) to end; (*parar*) to stop; (*acabar*) to finish; **terminarse** *vr* to come to an end; **~ por hacer algo** to end up (by) doing sth

término ['termino] *nm* end, conclusion; (*parada*) terminus; (*límite*) boundary; (*en discusión*) point; (*Ling: Com*) term; **~ medio** average; (*fig*) middle way; **en otros términos** in other words; **en último ~** (*a fin de cuentas*) in the last analysis; (*como último recurso*) as a last resort; **en términos de** in terms of; **según los términos del contrato** according to the terms of the contract

terminología [terminolo'xia] *nf* terminology

termita [ter'mita] *nf* termite

termo ['termo] *nm* Thermos® (flask)

termodinámico, -a [termoði'namiko, a] *adj* thermodynamic ■ *nf* thermodynamics *sg*

termoimpresora [termoimpre'sora] *nf* thermal printer

termómetro [ter'mometro] *nm* thermometer

termonuclear [termonukle'ar] *adj* thermonuclear

termostato [termos'tato] *nm* thermostat

ternero, -a [ter'nero, a] *nm/f* (*animal*) calf ■ *nf* (*carne*) veal, beef

terneza [ter'neθa] *nf* tenderness

ternilla [ter'niʎa] *nf* gristle; (*cartílago*) cartilage

terno ['terno] *nm* (*traje*) three-piece suit; (*conjunto*) set of three

ternura [ter'nura] *nf* (*trato*) tenderness; (*palabra*) endearment; (*cariño*) fondness

terquedad [terke'ðað] *nf* obstinacy; (*dureza*) harshness

terrado [te'rraðo] *nm* terrace

Terranova [terra'noβa] *nf* Newfoundland

terraplén [terra'plen] *nm* (*Agr*) terrace; (*Ferro*) embankment; (*Mil*) rampart; (*cuesta*) slope

terráqueo, -a [te'rrakeo, a] *adj*: **globo ~** globe

terrateniente [terrate'njente] *nm* landowner

terraza [te'rraθa] *nf* (*balcón*) balcony; (*techo*) flat roof; (*Agr*) terrace

terremoto [terre'moto] *nm* earthquake

terrenal [terre'nal] *adj* earthly

terreno, -a [te'rreno, a] *adj* (*de la tierra*) earthly, worldly ■ *nm* (*tierra*) land; (*parcela*) plot; (*suelo*) soil; (*fig*) field; **un ~** a piece of land; **sobre el ~** on the spot; **ceder/perder ~** to give/lose ground; **preparar el ~ (a)** (*fig*) to pave the way (for)

terrestre [te'rrestre] *adj* terrestrial; (*ruta*) land *cpd*

terrible [te'rriβle] *adj* (*espantoso*) terrible; (*aterrador*) dreadful; (*tremendo*) awful

territorial [territo'rjal] *adj* territorial

territorio [terri'torjo] *nm* territory; **~ bajo mandato** mandated territory

terrón [te'rron] *nm* (*de azúcar*) lump; (*de tierra*) clod, lump; **terrones** *nmpl* land *sg*

terror [te'rror] *nm* terror

terrorífico, -a [terro'rifiko, a] *adj* terrifying

terrorismo [terro'rismo] *nm* terrorism

terrorista [terro'rista] *adj, nm/f* terrorist

terroso, -a [te'rroso, a] *adj* earthy

terruño [te'rruɲo] *nm* (*pedazo*) clod; (*parcela*) plot; (*fig*) native soil; **apego al ~** attachment to one's native soil

terso, -a ['terso, a] *adj* (*liso*) smooth; (*pulido*) polished; (*fig: estilo*) flowing

tersura [ter'sura] *nf* smoothness; (*brillo*) shine

tertulia [ter'tulja] *nf* (*reunión informal*) social gathering; (*grupo*) group, circle; (*sala*) clubroom; **~ literaria** literary circle

tesina [te'sina] *nf* dissertation

tesis ['tesis] *nf inv* thesis

tesón [te'son] *nm* (*firmeza*) firmness; (*tenacidad*) tenacity

tesorería [tesore'ria] *nf* treasurership

t

tesorero, -a [teso'rero, a] *nm/f* treasurer
tesoro [te'soro] *nm* treasure; **T~ público** (*Pol*) Exchequer
test (*pl* **tests**) [tes(t), tes(t)] *nm* test
testaferro [testa'ferro] *nm* figurehead
testamentaría [testamenta'ria] *nf* execution of a will
testamentario, -a [testamen'tarjo, a] *adj* testamentary ■ *nm/f* executor/executrix
testamento [testa'mento] *nm* will
testar [tes'tar] *vi* to make a will
testarada [testa'raða] *nf*, **testarazo** [testa'raθo] *nm*: **darse una ~** *o* **un testarazo** (*fam*) to bump one's head
testarudo, -a [testa'ruðo, a] *adj* stubborn
testículo [tes'tikulo] *nm* testicle
testificar [testifi'kar] *vt* to testify; (*fig*) to attest ■ *vi* to give evidence
testifique *etc* [testi'fike] *vb ver* **testificar**
testigo [tes'tiɣo] *nm/f* witness; **~ de cargo/descargo** witness for the prosecution/defence; **~ ocular** eye witness; **poner a algn por ~** to cite sb as a witness
testimonial [testimo'njal] *adj* (*prueba*) testimonial; (*gesto*) token
testimoniar [testimo'njar] *vt* to testify to; (*fig*) to show
testimonio [testi'monjo] *nm* testimony; **en ~ de** as a token *o* mark of; **falso ~** perjured evidence, false witness
teta ['teta] *nf* (*de biberón*) teat; (*Anat*) nipple; (*fam*) breast; (*fam!*) tit (!)
tétanos ['tetanos] *nm* tetanus
tetera [te'tera] *nf* teapot; **~ eléctrica** (electric) kettle
tetilla [te'tiʎa] *nf* (*Anat*) nipple; (*de biberón*) teat
tétrico, -a ['tetriko, a] *adj* gloomy, dismal
textear [tekste'ar] *vt* to text
textil [teks'til] *adj* textile
texto ['teksto] *nm* text
textual [teks'twal] *adj* textual; **palabras textuales** exact words
textura [teks'tura] *nf* (*de tejido*) texture; (*de mineral*) structure
tez [teθ] *nf* (*cutis*) complexion; (*color*) colouring
tfno. *abr* (= *teléfono*) tel.
ti [ti] *pron* you; (*reflexivo*) yourself
tía ['tia] *nf* (*pariente*) aunt; (*fam: mujer*) girl
Tibet [ti'βet] *nm*: **El ~** Tibet
tibetano, -a [tiβe'tano, a] *adj, nm/f* Tibetan ■ *nm* (*Ling*) Tibetan
tibia ['tiβja] *nf* tibia
tibieza [ti'βjeθa] *nf* (*temperatura*) tepidness; (*fig*) coolness
tibio, -a ['tiβjo, a] *adj* lukewarm, tepid

tiburón [tiβu'ron] *nm* shark
tic [tik] *nm* (*ruido*) click; (*de reloj*) tick; **~ nervioso** (*Med*) nervous tic
tico, -a ['tiko, a] *adj, nm/f* (*Am fam*) Costa Rican
tictac [tik'tak] *nm* (*de reloj*) tick tock
tiemble *etc* ['tjemble] *vb ver* **temblar**
tiempo ['tjempo] *nm* (*gen*) time; (*época, período*) age, period; (*Meteorología*) weather; (*Ling*) tense; (*edad*) age; (*de juego*) half; **a ~** in time; **a un** *o* **al mismo ~** at the same time; **al poco ~** very soon (after); **andando el ~** in due course; **cada cierto ~** every so often; **con ~** in time; **con el ~** eventually; **de ~ en ~** from time to time; **en mis tiempos** in my time; **en los buenos tiempos** in the good old days; **hace buen/mal ~** the weather is fine/bad; **estar a ~** to be in time; **hace ~** some time ago; **hacer ~** to while away the time; **¿qué ~ tiene?** how old is he?; **motor de 2 tiempos** two-stroke engine; **~ compartido** (*Inform*) time sharing; **~ de ejecución** (*Inform*) run time; **~ inactivo** (*Com*) downtime; **~ libre** spare time; **~ de paro** (*Com*) idle time; **a ~ partido** (*trabajar*) part-time; **~ preferencial** (*Com*) prime time; **en ~ real** (*Inform*) real time
tienda *etc* ['tjenda] *vb ver* **tender** ■ *nf* shop; (*más grande*) store; (*Naut*) awning; **~ de campaña** tent; **~ de comestibles** grocer's shop (*esp Brit*), grocery (*US*)
tiene *etc* ['tjene] *vb ver* **tener**
tienta ['tjenta] *nf* (*Med*) probe; (*fig*) tact; **andar a tientas** to grope one's way along
tiento *etc* ['tjento] *vb ver* **tentar** ■ *nm* (*tacto*) touch; (*precaución*) wariness; (*pulso*) steady hand; (*Zool*) feeler, tentacle
tierno, -a ['tjerno, a] *adj* tender; (*fresco*) fresh
tierra ['tjerra] *nf* earth; (*suelo*) soil; (*mundo*) world; (*país*) country, land; (*Elec*) earth, ground (*US*); **~ adentro** inland; **~ natal** native land; **echar ~ a un asunto** to hush an affair up; **no es de estas tierras** he's not from these parts; **la T~ Santa** the Holy Land
tieso, -a ['tjeso, a] *adj* (*rígido*) rigid; (*duro*) stiff; (*fig: testarudo*) stubborn; (*fam: orgulloso*) conceited ■ *adv* strongly
tiesto ['tjesto] *nm* flowerpot; (*pedazo*) piece of pottery
tifoidea [tifoi'ðea] *nf* typhoid
tifón [ti'fon] *nm* (*huracán*) typhoon; (*de mar*) tidal wave
tifus ['tifus] *nm* typhus; **~ icteroides** yellow fever
tigre ['tiɣre] *nm* tiger; (*Am*) jaguar
TIJ *sigla m* (= *Tribunal Internacional de Justicia*) ICJ
tijera [ti'xera] *nf* (*una tijera*) (pair of) scissors *pl*; (*Zool*) claw; (*persona*) gossip; **de ~** folding;

tijeras *nfpl* scissors; (*para plantas*) shears;
unas tijeras a pair of scissors
tijeretear [tixere'te'ar] *vt* to snip ∎ *vi* (*fig*)
to meddle
tila ['tila] *nf* (*Bot*) lime tree; (*Culin*) lime
flower tea
tildar [til'dar] *vt*: ~ **de** to brand as
tilde ['tilde] *nf* (*defecto*) defect; (*trivialidad*)
triviality; (*Tip*) tilde
tilín [ti'lin] *nm* tinkle
tilo ['tilo] *nm* lime tree
timador, a [tima'ðor, a] *nm/f* swindler
timar [ti'mar] *vt* (*robar*) to steal; (*estafar*) to
swindle; (*persona*) to con; **timarse** *vr* (*fam*):
timarse con algn to make eyes at sb
timbal [tim'bal] *nm* small drum
timbrar [tim'brar] *vt* to stamp; (*sellar*) to seal;
(*carta*) to postmark
timbrazo [tim'braθo] *nm* ring; **dar un ~**
to ring the bell
timbre ['timbre] *nm* (*sello*) stamp; (*campanilla*)
bell; (*tono*) timbre; (*Com*) stamp duty
timidez [timi'ðeθ] *nf* shyness
tímido, -a ['timiðo, a] *adj* shy, timid
timo ['timo] *nm* swindle; **dar un ~ a algn**
to swindle sb
timón [ti'mon] *nm* helm, rudder; (*Am*)
steering wheel; **coger el ~** (*fig*) to take
charge
timonel [timo'nel] *nm* helmsman
timorato, -a [timo'rato, a] *adj* God-fearing;
(*mojigato*) sanctimonious
tímpano ['timpano] *nm* (*Anat*) eardrum;
(*Mus*) small drum
tina ['tina] *nf* tub; (*Am: baño*) bath(tub)
tinaja [ti'naxa] *nf* large earthen jar
tinerfeño, -a [tiner'feɲo, a] *adj* of o from
Tenerife ∎ *nm/f* native o inhabitant of
Tenerife
tinglado [tin'glaðo] *nm* (*cobertizo*) shed; (*fig:*
truco) trick; (*intriga*) intrigue; **armar un ~**
to lay a plot
tinieblas [ti'njeβlas] *nfpl* darkness *sg*;
(*sombras*) shadows; **estamos en ~ sobre sus**
proyectos (*fig*) we are in the dark about his
plans
tino ['tino] *nm* (*habilidad*) skill; (*Mil*)
marksmanship; (*juicio*) insight; (*moderación*)
moderation; **sin ~** immoderately; **coger el ~**
to get the feel o hang of it
tinta ['tinta] *nf* ink; (*Tec*) dye; (*Arte*) colour;
~ china Indian ink; **tintas** *nfpl* (*fig*) shades;
medias tintas (*fig*) half measures; **saber**
algo de buena ~ to have sth on good
authority
tinte ['tinte] *nm* (*acto*) dyeing; (*fig*) tinge;
(*barniz*) veneer

tintero [tin'tero] *nm* inkwell; **se le quedó en**
el ~ he clean forgot about it
tintinear [tintine'ar] *vt* to tinkle
tinto, -a ['tinto, a] *adj* (*teñido*) dyed;
(*manchado*) stained ∎ *nm* red wine
tintorera [tinto'rera] *nf* shark
tintorería [tintore'ria] *nf* dry cleaner's
tintorero [tinto'rero] *nm* dry cleaner('s)
tintura [tin'tura] *nf* (*acto*) dyeing; (*Química*)
dye; (*farmacéutico*) tincture
tiña *etc* ['tiɲa] *vb ver* **teñir** ∎ *nf* (*Med*)
ringworm
tío ['tio] *nm* (*pariente*) uncle; (*fam: hombre*)
bloke, guy (*US*)
tiovivo [tio'βiβo] *nm* roundabout
típico, -a ['tipiko, a] *adj* typical; (*pintoresco*)
picturesque
tiple ['tiple] *nm* soprano (voice) ∎ *nf* soprano
tipo ['tipo] *nm* (*clase*) type, kind; (*norma*)
norm; (*patrón*) pattern; (*fam: hombre*) fellow,
bloke, guy (*US*); (*Anat*) build; (: *de mujer*)
figure; (*Imprenta*) type; **~ bancario/de**
descuento bank/discount rate; **~ de interés**
interest rate; **~ de interés vigente** (*Com*)
standard rate; **~ de cambio** exchange rate;
~ base (*Com*) base rate; **~ a término** (*Com*)
forward rate; **dos tipos sospechosos** two
suspicious characters; **~ de letra** (*Inform: Tip*)
typeface; **~ de datos** (*Inform*) data type
tipografía [tipoɣra'fia] *nf* (*tipo*) printing;
(*lugar*) printing press
tipográfico, -a [tipo'ɣrafiko, a] *adj* printing
tipógrafo, -a [ti'poɣrafo, a] *nm/f* printer
tíque, tíquet ['tike] (*pl* **~(t)s**) ['tikes] *nm*
ticket; (*en tienda*) cash slip
tiquismiquis [tikis'mikis] *nm* fussy person
∎ *nmpl* (*querellas*) squabbling *sg*; (*escrúpulos*)
silly scruples
tira ['tira] *nf* strip; (*fig*) abundance ∎ *nm*:
~ y afloja give and take; (*cautela*) caution;
la ~ de ... (*fam*) lots of ...
tirabuzón [tiraβu'θon] *nm* corkscrew; (*rizo*)
curl
tiradero [tira'ðero] *nm* (*Am*) rubbish dump
tirado, -a [ti'raðo, a] *adj* (*barato*) dirt-cheap;
(*fam: fácil*) very easy ∎ *nf* (*acto*) cast, throw;
(*distancia*) distance; (*serie*) series; (*Tip*)
printing, edition; **de una tirada** at one go;
está ~ (*fam*) it's a cinch
TIR *sigla mpl* = **Transportes internacionales**
por carretera
tirador, a [tira'ðor, a] *nm/f* (*persona*) shooter
∎ *nm* (*mango*) handle; (*Elec*) flex; **~ certero**
sniper
tiralíneas [tira'lineas] *nm inv* ruling-pen
tiranía [tira'nia] *nf* tyranny
tiránico, -a [ti'raniko, a] *adj* tyrannical

tiranizar [tirani'θar] vt (pueblo, empleado) to tyrannize

tirano, -a [ti'rano, a] adj tyrannical ▪ nm/f tyrant

tirante [ti'rante] adj (cuerda) tight, taut; (relaciones) strained ▪ nm (Arq) brace; (Tec) stay; (correa) shoulder strap; **tirantes** nmpl braces, suspenders (US)

tirantez [tiran'teθ] nf tightness; (fig) tension

tirar [ti'rar] vt to throw; (volcar) to upset; (derribar) to knock down o over; (tiro) to fire; (cohete) to launch; (bomba) to drop; (edificio) to pull down; (desechar) to throw out o away; (disipar) to squander; (imprimir) to print; (dar: golpe) to deal ▪ vi (disparar) to shoot; (dar un tirón) to pull; (fig) to draw; (interesar) to appeal; (fam: andar) to go; (tender a) to tend to; (Deporte) to shoot; **tirarse** vr to throw o.s.; (fig) to demean o.s.; (fam!) to screw (!); ~ **abajo** to bring down, destroy; **tira más a su padre** he takes more after his father; ~ **de algo** to pull o tug (on) sth; **ir tirando** to manage; ~ **a la derecha** to turn o go right; **a todo** ~ at the most

tirita [ti'rita] nf (sticking) plaster, bandaid (US)

tiritar [tiri'tar] vi to shiver

tiritona [tiri'tona] nf shivering (fit)

tiro ['tiro] nm (lanzamiento) throw; (disparo) shot; (tiroteo) shooting; (Deporte) shot; (Tenis: Golf) drive; (alcance) range; (de escalera) flight (of stairs); (golpe) blow; (engaño) hoax; ~ **al blanco** target practice; **caballo de** ~ cart-horse; **andar de tiros largos** to be all dressed up; **al** ~ (Am) at once; **de a** ~ (Am fam) completely; **se pegó un** ~ he shot himself; **le salió el** ~ **por la culata** it backfired on him

tiroides [ti'roiðes] nm inv thyroid

Tirol [ti'rol] nm: **El** ~ the Tyrol

tirolés, -esa [tiro'les, esa] adj, nm/f Tyrolean

tirón [ti'ron] nm (sacudida) pull, tug; **de un** ~ in one go; **dar un** ~ **a** to pull at, tug at

tirotear [tirote'ar] vt to shoot at; **tirotearse** vr to exchange shots

tiroteo [tiro'teo] nm exchange of shots, shooting; (escaramuza) skirmish

tirria ['tirrja] nf: **tener una** ~ **a algn** to have a grudge against sb

tísico, -a ['tisiko, a] adj, nm/f consumptive

tisis ['tisis] nf consumption, tuberculosis

tít. abr = **título**

titánico, -a [ti'taniko, a] adj titanic

títere ['titere] nm puppet; **no dejar** ~ **con cabeza** to turn everything upside-down

titilar [titi'lar] vi (luz, estrella) to twinkle; (párpado) to flutter

titiritero, -a [titiri'tero, a] nm/f (acróbata) acrobat; (malabarista) juggler

titubeante [tituβe'ante] adj (inestable) shaky, tottering; (farfullante) stammering; (dudoso) hesitant

titubear [tituβe'ar] vi to stagger; (tartamudear) to stammer; (vacilar) to hesitate

titubeo [titu'βeo] nm staggering; stammering; hesitation

titulado, -a [titu'laðo, a] adj (libro) entitled; (persona) titled

titular [titu'lar] adj titular ▪ nm/f (de oficina) occupant; (de pasaporte) holder ▪ nm headline ▪ vt to title; **titularse** vr to be entitled

título ['titulo] nm (gen) title; (de diario) headline; (certificado) professional qualification; (universitario) university degree; (Com) bond; (fig) right; **títulos** nmpl qualifications; **a** ~ **de** by way of; (en calidad de) in the capacity of; **a** ~ **de curiosidad** as a matter of interest; ~ **de propiedad** title deed; **títulos convertibles de interés fijo** (Com) convertible loan stock sg

tiza ['tiθa] nf chalk; **una** ~ a piece of chalk

tizna ['tiθna] nf grime

tiznar [tiθ'nar] vt to blacken; (manchar) to smudge, stain; (fig) to tarnish

tizón [ti'θon], **tizo** ['tiθo] nm brand; (fig) stain

TLC nm abr (= Tratado de Libre Comercio) NAFTA

Tm. abr = **tonelada(s) métrica(s)**

TNT sigla m (= trinitrotolueno) TNT

toalla [to'aʎa] nf towel

tobillo [to'βiʎo] nm ankle

tobogán [toβo'ɣan] nm toboggan; (montaña rusa) switchback; (resbaladilla) chute, slide

toca ['toka] nf headdress

tocadiscos [toka'ðiskos] nm inv record player

tocado, -a [to'kaðo, a] adj (fruta etc) rotten ▪ nm headdress; **estar** ~ **de la cabeza** (fam) to be weak in the head

tocador [toka'ðor] nm (mueble) dressing table; (cuarto) boudoir; (neceser) toilet case; (fam) ladies' room

tocante [to'kante]: ~ **a** prep with regard to; **en lo** ~ **a** as for, so far as concerns

tocar [to'kar] vt to touch; (sentir) to feel; (con la mano) to handle; (Mus) to play; (campana) to ring; (tambor) to beat; (trompeta) to blow; (topar con) to run into, strike; (referirse a) to allude to; (estar emparentado con) to be related to ▪ vi (a la puerta) to knock (on o at the door); (ser el turno) to fall to, be the turn of; (ser hora) to be due; (atañer) to concern; **tocarse** vr (cubrirse la cabeza) to cover one's head; (tener contacto) to touch (each other); **tocarle a**

algn to fall to sb's lot; **~ en** (Naut) to call at; **por lo que a mí me toca** as far as I am concerned; **esto toca en la locura** this verges on madness

tocateja [toka'texa] (fam): **a ~** adv in readies

tocayo, -a [to'kajo, a] nm/f namesake

tocino [to'θino] nm (bacon) fat; **~ de panceta** bacon

todavía [toða'βia] adv (aun) even; (aún) still, yet; **~ más** yet o still more; **~ no** not yet; **~ en 1970** as late as 1970; **está lloviendo ~** it's still raining

toditito, -a [toði'tito, a], **todito a** [to'ðito, a] adj (Am fam) (absolutely) all

 PALABRA CLAVE

todo, -a ['toðo, a] adj **1** (sg) all; **toda la carne** all the meat; **toda la noche** all night, the whole night; **todo el libro** the whole book; **toda una botella** a whole bottle; **todo lo contrario** quite the opposite; **está toda sucia** she's all dirty; **a toda velocidad** at full speed; **por todo el país** throughout the whole country; **es todo un hombre** he's every inch a man; **soy todo oídos** I'm all ears

2 (pl) all; every; **todos los libros** all the books; **todas las noches** every night; **todos los que quieran salir** all those who want to leave; **todos vosotros** all of you

■ pron **1** everything, all; **todos** everyone, everybody; **lo sabemos todo** we know everything; **todos querían más tiempo** everybody o everyone wanted more time; **nos marchamos todos** all of us left; **corriendo y todo, no llegaron a tiempo** even though they ran, they still didn't arrive in time

2 (con preposición): **a pesar de todo** even so, in spite of everything; **con todo él me sigue gustando** even so I still like him; **le llamaron de todo** they called him all the names under the sun; **no me agrada del todo** I don't entirely like it

■ adv all; **vaya todo seguido** keep straight on o ahead

■ nm: **como un todo** as a whole; **arriba del todo** at the very top; **todo a cien** ≈ pound store (Brit), ≈ dollar store (US)

todopoderoso, -a [toðopoðe'roso, a] adj all powerful; (Rel) almighty

todoterreno [toðote'rreno] nm (tb: **vehículo todoterreno**) four-by-four

toga ['toɣa] nf toga; (Escol) gown

Tokio ['tokjo] n Tokyo

toldo ['toldo] nm (para el sol) sunshade; (en tienda) marquee; (fig) pride

tole ['tole] nm (fam) commotion

toledano, -a [tole'ðano, a] adj of o from Toledo ■ nm/f native o inhabitant of Toledo

tolerable [tole'raβle] adj tolerable

tolerancia [tole'ranθja] nf tolerance

tolerante [tole'rante] adj tolerant; (fig) open-minded

tolerar [tole'rar] vt to tolerate; (resistir) to endure

Tolón [to'lon] nm Toulon

toma ['toma] nf (gen) taking; (Med) dose; (Elec: tb: **toma de corriente**) socket; (Mec) inlet; **~ de posesión** (por presidente) taking up office; **~ de tierra** (Aviat) landing

tomadura [toma'ðura] nf: **~ de pelo** hoax

tomar [to'mar] vt (gen, Cine: Foto: TV) to take; (actitud) to adopt; (aspecto) to take on; (notas) to take down; (beber) to drink ■ vi to take; (Am) to drink; **tomarse** vr to take; **tomarse por** to consider o.s. to be; **¡toma!** here you are!; **~ asiento** to sit down; **~ a algn por loco** to think sb mad; **~ a bien/a mal** to take well/badly; **~ en serio** to take seriously; **~ el pelo a algn** to pull sb's leg; **tomarla con algn** to pick a quarrel with sb; **~ por escrito** to write down; **toma y daca** give and take

tomate [to'mate] nm tomato

tomatera [toma'tera] nf tomato plant

tomavistas [toma'βistas] nm inv movie camera

tomillo [to'miʎo] nm thyme

tomo ['tomo] nm (libro) volume; (fig) importance

ton [ton] abr = **tonelada** ■ nm: **sin ~ ni son** without rhyme or reason

tonada [to'naða] nf tune

tonalidad [tonali'ðað] nf tone

tonel [to'nel] nm barrel

tonelada [tone'laða] nf ton; **~(s) métrica(s)** metric ton(s)

tonelaje [tone'laxe] nm tonnage

tonelero [tone'lero] nm cooper

tongo ['tongo] nm (Deporte) fix

tónico, -a ['toniko, a] adj tonic ■ nm (Med) tonic ■ nf (Mus) tonic; (fig) keynote

tonificador, a [tonifika'ðor, a], **tonificante** [tonifi'kante] adj invigorating, stimulating

tonificar [tonifi'kar] vt to tone up

tonifique etc [toni'fike] vb ver **tonificar**

tonillo [to'niʎo] nm monotonous voice

tono ['tono] nm (Mus) tone; (altura) pitch; (color) shade; **fuera de ~** inappropriate; **~ de llamada** ringtone; **~ de marcar** (Telec) dialling tone; **darse ~** to put on airs

tontear [tonte'ar] vi (fam) to fool about; (enamorados) to flirt

tontería [tonte'ria] *nf* (*estupidez*) foolishness; (*una tontería*) silly thing; **tonterías** *nfpl* rubbish *sg*, nonsense *sg*

tonto, -a ['tonto, a] *adj* stupid; (*ridículo*) silly ■ *nm/f* fool; (*payaso*) clown; **a tontas y a locas** anyhow; **hacer(se) el ~** to act the fool

topacio [to'paθjo] *nm* topaz

topar [to'par] *vt* (*tropezar*) to bump into; (*encontrar*) to find, come across; (*cabra etc*) to butt ■ *vi*: ~ **contra** *o* **en** to run into; ~ **con** to run up against; **el problema topa en eso** that's where the problem lies

tope ['tope] *adj* maximum ■ *nm* (*fin*) end; (*límite*) limit; (*Ferro*) buffer; (*Auto*) bumper; **al ~** end to end; **fecha ~** closing date; **precio ~** top price; **sueldo ~** maximum salary; **~ de tabulación** tab stop

tópico, -a ['topiko, a] *adj* topical; (*Med*) local ■ *nm* platitude, cliché; **de uso ~** for external application

topo ['topo] *nm* (*Zool*) mole; (*fig*) blunderer

topografía [topoɣra'fia] *nf* topography

topógrafo, -a [to'poɣrafo, a] *nm/f* topographer; (*agrimensor*) surveyor

toponimia [topo'nimja] *nf* place names *pl*; (*estudio*) study of place names

toque *etc* ['toke] *vb ver* **tocar** ■ *nm* touch; (*Mus*) beat; (*de campana*) ring, chime; (*Mil*) bugle call; (*fig*) crux; **dar un ~ a** to test; **dar el último ~ a** to put the final touch to; **~ de queda** curfew

toquetear [tokete'ar] *vt* to handle; (*fam!*) to touch up

toquilla [to'kiʎa] *nf* (*chal*) shawl

tórax ['toraks] *nm inv* thorax

torbellino [torbe'ʎino] *nm* whirlwind; (*fig*) whirl

torcedura [torθe'ðura] *nf* twist; (*Med*) sprain

torcer [tor'θer] *vt* to twist; (*la esquina*) to turn; (*Med*) to sprain; (*cuerda*) to plait; (*ropa, manos*) to wring; (*persona*) to corrupt; (*sentido*) to distort ■ *vi* (*cambiar de dirección*) to turn; **torcerse** *vr* to twist; (*doblar*) to bend; (*desviarse*) to go astray; (*fracasar*) to go wrong; **~ el gesto** to scowl; **torcerse un pie** to twist one's foot; **el coche torció a la derecha** the car turned right

torcido, -a [tor'θiðo, a] *adj* twisted; (*fig*) crooked ■ *nm* curl

tordo, -a ['torðo, a] *adj* dappled ■ *nm* thrush

torear [tore'ar] *vt* (*fig: evadir*) to dodge; (*toro*) to fight ■ *vi* to fight bulls

toreo [to'reo] *nm* bullfighting

torero, -a [to'rero, a] *nm/f* bullfighter

toril [to'ril] *nm* bullpen

tormenta [tor'menta] *nf* storm; (*fig: confusión*) turmoil

tormento [tor'mento] *nm* torture; (*fig*) anguish

tormentoso, -a [tormen'toso, a] *adj* stormy

tornar [tor'nar] *vt* (*devolver*) to return, give back; (*transformar*) to transform ■ *vi* to go back; **tornarse** *vr* (*ponerse*) to become; (*volver*) to return

tornasol [torna'sol] *nm* (*Bot*) sunflower; **papel de ~** litmus paper

tornasolado, -a [tornaso'laðo, a] *adj* (*brillante*) iridescent; (*reluciente*) shimmering

torneo [tor'neo] *nm* tournament

tornero, -a [tor'nero, a] *nm/f* machinist

tornillo [tor'niʎo] *nm* screw; **apretar los tornillos a algn** to apply pressure on sb; **le falta un ~** (*fam*) he's got a screw loose

torniquete [torni'kete] *nm* (*puerta*) turnstile; (*Med*) tourniquet

torno ['torno] *nm* (*Tec: grúa*) winch; (: *de carpintero*) lathe; (*tambor*) drum; **~ de banco** vice, vise (*US*); **en ~ (a)** round, about

toro ['toro] *nm* bull; (*fam*) he-man; **los toros** bullfighting *sg*

toronja [to'ronxa] *nf* grapefruit

torpe ['torpe] *adj* (*poco hábil*) clumsy, awkward; (*movimiento*) sluggish; (*necio*) dim; (*lento*) slow; (*indecente*) crude; (*no honrado*) dishonest

torpedo [tor'peðo] *nm* torpedo

torpemente [torpe'mente] *adv* (*sin destreza*) clumsily; (*lentamente*) slowly

torpeza [tor'peθa] *nf* (*falta de agilidad*) clumsiness; (*lentitud*) slowness; (*rigidez*) stiffness; (*error*) mistake; (*crudeza*) obscenity

torre ['torre] *nf* tower; (*de petróleo*) derrick; (*de electricidad*) pylon; (*Ajedrez*) rook; (*Aviat: Mil: Naut*) turret

torrefacto, -a [torre'fakto, a] *adj*: **café ~** high roast coffee

torrencial [torren'θjal] *adj* torrential

torrente [to'rrente] *nm* torrent

tórrido, -a ['torriðo, a] *adj* torrid

torrija [to'rrixa] *nf* fried bread; **torrijas** French toast *sg*

torsión [tor'sjon] *nf* twisting

torso ['torso] *nm* torso

torta ['torta] *nf* cake; (*fam*) slap; **~ de huevos** (*Am*) omelette; **no entendió ni ~** he didn't understand a word of it

tortazo [tor'taθo] *nm* (*bofetada*) slap; (*de coche*) crash

tortícolis [tor'tikolis] *nm inv* stiff neck

tortilla [tor'tiʎa] *nf* omelette; (*Am*) maize pancake; **~ francesa/española** plain/potato omelette; **cambiar** *o* **volver la ~ a algn** to turn the tables on sb

tortillera [torti'ʎera] *nf* (*fam!*) lesbian

tórtola ['tortola] *nf* turtledove

tortuga [tor'tuɣa] *nf* tortoise; **~ marina** turtle

tortuoso, -a [tor'twoso, a] *adj* winding

tortura [tor'tura] *nf* torture

torturar [tortu'rar] *vt* to torture

torvo, -a ['torβo, a] *adj* grim, fierce

torzamos *etc* [tor'θamos] *vb ver* **torcer**

tos [tos] *nf inv* cough; **~ ferina** whooping cough

Toscana [tos'kana] *nf*: **La ~** Tuscany

tosco, -a ['tosko, a] *adj* coarse

toser [to'ser] *vi* to cough; **no hay quien le tosa** he's in a class by himself

tostado, -a [tos'taðo, a] *adj* toasted; *(por el sol)* dark brown; *(piel)* tanned ■ *nf* tan; *(pan)* piece of toast; **tostadas** *nfpl* toast *sg*

tostador [tosta'ðor] *nm* toaster

tostar [tos'tar] *vt* to toast; *(café)* to roast; *(al sol)* to tan; **tostarse** *vr* to get brown

tostón [tos'ton] *nm*: **ser un ~** to be a drag

total [to'tal] *adj* total ■ *adv* in short; *(al fin y al cabo)* when all is said and done ■ *nm* total; **en ~** in all; **~ que** to cut a long story short; **~ de comprobación** *(Inform)* hash total; **~ debe/haber** *(Com)* debit/assets total

totalidad [totali'ðað] *nf* whole

totalitario, -a [totali'tarjo, a] *adj* totalitarian

totalmente [to'talmente] *adv* totally

tóxico, -a ['toksiko, a] *adj* toxic ■ *nm* poison

toxicómano, -a [toksi'komano, a] *adj* addicted to drugs ■ *nm/f* drug addict

toxina [to'ksina] *nf* toxin

tozudo, -a [to'θuðo, a] *adj* obstinate

traba ['traβa] *nf* bond, tie; *(cadena)* fetter; **poner trabas a** to restrain

trabajador, a [traβaxa'ðor, a] *nm/f* worker ■ *adj* hard-working

trabajar [traβa'xar] *vt* to work; *(arar)* to till; *(empeñarse en)* to work at; *(empujar: persona)* to push; *(convencer)* to persuade ■ *vi* to work; *(esforzarse)* to strive; **¡a ~!** let's get to work!; **~ por hacer algo** to strive to do sth

trabajo [tra'βaxo] *nm* work; *(tarea)* task; *(Pol)* labour; *(fig)* effort; **tomarse el ~ de** to take the trouble to; **~ por turno/a destajo** shift work/piecework; **~ en proceso** *(Com)* work-in-progress

trabajoso, -a [traβa'xoso, a] *adj* hard; *(Med)* pale

trabalenguas [traβa'lengwas] *nm inv* tongue twister

trabar [tra'βar] *vt* *(juntar)* to join, unite; *(atar)* to tie down, fetter; *(agarrar)* to seize; *(amistad)* to strike up; **trabarse** *vr* to become entangled; *(reñir)* to squabble; **se le traba la lengua** he gets tongue-tied

trabazón [traβa'θon] *nf* *(Tec)* joining, assembly; *(fig)* bond, link

trabucar [traβu'kar] *vt* *(confundir)* to confuse, mix up; *(palabras)* to misplace

trabuque *etc* [tra'βuke] *vb ver* **trabucar**

tracción [trak'θjon] *nf* traction; **~ delantera/ trasera** front-wheel/rear-wheel drive

trace *etc* ['traθe] *vb ver* **trazar**

tractor [trak'tor] *nm* tractor

trad. *abr* (= *traducido*) trans

tradición [traði'θjon] *nf* tradition

tradicional [traðiθjo'nal] *adj* traditional

traducción [traðuk'θjon] *nf* translation; **~ asistida por ordenador** computer-assisted translation

traducible [traðu'θiβle] *adj* translatable

traducir [traðu'θir] *vt* to translate; **traducirse** *vr*: **traducirse en** *(fig)* to entail, result in

traductor, a [traðuk'tor, a] *nm/f* translator

traduzca *etc* [tra'ðuθka] *vb ver* **traducir**

traer [tra'er] *vt* to bring; *(llevar)* to carry; *(ropa)* to wear; *(incluir)* to carry; *(fig)* to cause; **traerse** *vr*: **traerse algo** to be up to sth; **traerse bien/mal** to dress well/badly; **traérselas** to be annoying; **~ consigo** to involve, entail; **es un problema que se las trae** it's a difficult problem

traficante [trafi'kante] *nm/f* trader, dealer

traficar [trafi'kar] *vi* to trade; **~ con** *(pey)* to deal illegally in

tráfico ['trafiko] *nm* *(Com)* trade; *(Auto)* traffic

trafique *etc* [tra'fike] *vb ver* **traficar**

tragaderas [traɣa'ðeras] *nfpl* *(garganta)* throat *sg*, gullet *sg*; *(credulidad)* gullibility *sg*

tragaluz [traɣa'luθ] *nm* skylight

tragamonedas [traɣamo'neðas] *nm inv*, **tragaperras** [traɣa'perras] *nm inv* slot machine

tragar [tra'ɣar] *vt* to swallow; *(devorar)* to devour, bolt down; **tragarse** *vr* to swallow; *(tierra)* to absorb, soak up; **no le puedo ~** *(persona)* I can't stand him

tragedia [tra'xeðja] *nf* tragedy

trágico, -a ['traxiko, a] *adj* tragic

trago ['traɣo] *nm* *(de líquido)* drink; *(comido de golpe)* gulp; *(fam: de bebida)* swig; *(desgracia)* blow; **~ amargo** *(fig)* hard time

trague *etc* ['traɣe] *vb ver* **tragar**

traición [trai'θjon] *nf* treachery; *(Jur)* treason; *(una traición)* act of treachery

traicionar [traiθjo'nar] *vt* to betray

traicionero, -a [traiθjo'nero, a] = **traidor, a**

traída [tra'iða] *nf* carrying; **~ de aguas** water supply

traidor, a [trai'ðor, a] *adj* treacherous ■ *nm/f* traitor

traiga *etc* ['traiɣa] *vb ver* **traer**

trailer (*pl* **trailers**) ['trailer, 'trailer(s)] *nm* trailer

traje *etc* ['traxe] *vb ver* **traer** ∎ *nm* (*gen*) dress; (*de hombre*) suit; (*traje típico*) costume; (*fig*) garb; ~ **de baño** swimsuit; ~ **de luces** bullfighter's costume; ~ **hecho a la medida** made-to-measure suit

trajera *etc* [tra'xera] *vb ver* **traer**

trajín [tra'xin] *nm* haulage; (*fam: movimiento*) bustle; **trajines** *nmpl* goings-on

trajinar [traxi'nar] *vt* (*llevar*) to carry, transport ∎ *vi* (*moverse*) to bustle about; (*viajar*) to travel around

trama ['trama] *nf* (*fig*) link; (: *intriga*) plot; (*de tejido*) weft

tramar [tra'mar] *vt* to plot; (*Tec*) to weave; **tramarse** *vr* (*fig*): **algo se está tramando** there's something going on

tramitar [trami'tar] *vt* (*asunto*) to transact; (*negociar*) to negotiate; (*manejar*) to handle

trámite ['tramite] *nm* (*paso*) step; (*Jur*) transaction; **trámites** *nmpl* (*burocracia*) paperwork *sg*, procedures; (*Jur*) proceedings

tramo ['tramo] *nm* (*de tierra*) plot; (*de escalera*) flight; (*de vía*) section

tramoya [tra'moja] *nf* (*Teat*) piece of stage machinery; (*fig*) trick

tramoyista [tramo'jista] *nm/f* scene shifter; (*fig*) trickster

trampa ['trampa] *nf* trap; (*en el suelo*) trapdoor; (*prestidigitación*) conjuring trick; (*engaño*) trick; (*fam*) fiddle; **caer en la** ~ to fall into the trap; **hacer trampas** (*trampear*) to cheat

trampear [trampe'ar] *vt, vi* to cheat

trampilla [tram'piʎa] *nf* trap, hatchway

trampolín [trampo'lin] *nm* trampoline; (*de piscina etc*) diving board

tramposo, -a [tram'poso, a] *adj* crooked, cheating ∎ *nm/f* crook, cheat

tranca ['tranka] *nf* (*palo*) stick; (*viga*) beam; (*de puerta, ventana*) bar; (*borrachera*) binge; **a trancas y barrancas** with great difficulty

trancar [tran'kar] *vt* to bar ∎ *vi* to stride along

trancazo [tran'kaθo] *nm* (*golpe*) blow

trance ['tranθe] *nm* (*momento difícil*) difficult moment; (*situación crítica*) critical situation; (*estado de hipnosis*) trance; **estar en** ~ **de muerte** to be at death's door

tranco ['tranko] *nm* stride

tranque *etc* ['tranke] *vb ver* **trancar**

tranquilamente [tran'kilamente] *adv* (*sin preocupaciones: leer, trabajar*) peacefully; (*sin enfadarse: hablar, discutir*) calmly

tranquilice *etc* [tranki'liθe] *vb ver* **tranquilizar**

tranquilidad [trankili'ðað] *nf* (*calma*) calmness, stillness; (*paz*) peacefulness

tranquilizador, a [trankiliθa'ðor, a] *adj* (*música*) soothing; (*hecho*) reassuring

tranquilizante [trankili'θante] *nm* tranquillizer

tranquilizar [trankili'θar] *vt* (*calmar*) to calm (down); (*asegurar*) to reassure

tranquilo, -a [tran'kilo, a] *adj* (*calmado*) calm; (*apacible*) peaceful; (*mar*) calm; (*mente*) untroubled

Trans. *abr* (*Com*) = **transferencia**

transacción [transak'θjon] *nf* transaction

transar [tran'sar] *vi* (*Am*) = **transigir**

transatlántico, -a [transat'lantiko, a] *adj* transatlantic ∎ *nm* (ocean) liner

transbordador [transβorða'ðor] *nm* ferry

transbordar [transβor'ðar] *vt* to transfer; **transbordarse** *vr* to change

transbordo [trans'βorðo] *nm* transfer; **hacer** ~ to change (trains)

transcender [transθen'der] *vt* = **trascender**

transcribir [transkri'βir] *vt* to transcribe

transcurrir [transku'rrir] *vi* (*tiempo*) to pass; (*hecho*) to turn out

transcurso [trans'kurso] *nm* passing, lapse; **en el** ~ **de ocho días** in the course of a week

transeúnte [transe'unte] *adj* transient ∎ *nm/f* passer-by

transexual [transe'kswal] *adj, nm/f* transsexual

transferencia [transfe'renθja] *nf* transference; (*Com*) transfer; ~ **bancaria** banker's order; ~ **de crédito** (*Com*) credit transfer; ~ **electrónica de fondos** (*Com*) electronic funds transfer

transferir [transfe'rir] *vt* to transfer; (*aplazar*) to postpone

transfiera *etc* [trans'fjera] *vb ver* **transferir**

transfigurar [transfiɣu'rar] *vt* to transfigure

transfiriendo *etc* [transfi'rjendo] *vb ver* **transferir**

transformación [transforma'θjon] *nf* transformation

transformador [transforma'ðor] *nm* transformer

transformar [transfor'mar] *vt* to transform; (*convertir*) to convert

tránsfuga ['transfuɣa] *nm/f* (*Mil*) deserter; (*Pol*) turncoat

transfusión [transfu'sjon] *nf* (*tb*: **transfusión de sangre**) (blood) transfusion

transgénico, -a [trans'xeniko, a] *adj* genetically modified

transgredir [transɣre'dir] *vt* to transgress

transgresión [transɣre'sjon] *nf* transgression

transición [transi'θjon] *nf* transition;
período de ~ transitional period
transido, -a [tran'siðo, a] *adj* overcome; **~
de angustia** beset with anxiety; **~ de dolor**
racked with pain
transigir [transi'xir] *vi* to compromise;
(*ceder*) to make concessions
transija *etc* [tran'sixa] *vb ver* **transigir**
Transilvania [transil'βanja] *nf* Transylvania
transistor [transis'tor] *nm* transistor
transitable [transi'taβle] *adj* (*camino*)
passable
transitar [transi'tar] *vi* to go (from place to
place)
transitivo, -a [transi'tiβo, a] *adj* transitive
tránsito ['transito] *nm* transit; (*Auto*) traffic;
(*parada*) stop; **horas de máximo ~** rush
hours; **"se prohíbe el ~"** "no thoroughfare"
transitorio, -a [transi'torjo, a] *adj* transitory
transmisión [transmi'sjon] *nf* (*Radio*: TV)
transmission, broadcast(ing); (*transferencia*)
transfer; **~ en circuito** hookup; **~ en
directo/exterior** live/outside broadcast;
~ de datos (en paralelo/en serie)
(*Inform*) (parallel/serial) data transfer *o*
transmission; **plena/media ~ bidireccional**
(*Inform*) full/half duplex
transmitir [transmi'tir] *vt* to transmit;
(*Radio*: TV) to broadcast; (*enfermedad*) to give,
pass on
transparencia [transpa'renθja] *nf*
transparency; (*claridad*) clearness, clarity;
(*foto*) slide
transparentar [transparen'tar] *vt* to reveal
■ *vi* to be transparent
transparente [transpa'rente] *adj*
transparent; (*aire*) clear; (*ligero*) diaphanous
■ *nm* curtain
transpirar [transpi'rar] *vi* to perspire; (*fig*)
to transpire
transpondré *etc* [transpon'dre] *vb ver*
transponer
transponer [transpo'ner] *vt* to transpose;
(*cambiar de sitio*) to move about ■ *vi*
(*desaparecer*) to disappear; (*ir más allá*) to go
beyond; **transponerse** *vr* to change places;
(*ocultarse*) to hide; (*sol*) to go down
transponga *etc* [trans'ponga] *vb ver*
transponer
transportador [transporta'ðor] *nm*
(*Mecánica*): **~ de correa** belt conveyor
transportar [transpor'tar] *vt* to transport;
(*llevar*) to carry
transporte [trans'porte] *nm* transport;
(*Com*) haulage; **Ministerio de Transportes**
Ministry of Transport
transpuesto [trans'pwesto], **transpuse** *etc*

[trans'puse] *vb ver* **transponer**
transversal [transβer'sal] *adj* transverse,
cross ■ *nf* (*tb*: **calle transversal**) cross street
transversalmente [transβersal'mente] *adv*
obliquely
tranvía [tram'bia] *nm* tram, streetcar (*US*)
trapecio [tra'peθjo] *nm* trapeze
trapecista [trape'θista] *nm/f* trapeze artist
trapero, -a [tra'pero, a] *nm/f* ragman
trapicheos [trapi'tʃeos] *nmpl* (*fam*) schemes,
fiddles
trapisonda [trapi'sonda] *nf* (*jaleo*) row;
(*estafa*) swindle
trapo ['trapo] *nm* (*tela*) rag; (*de cocina*) cloth;
trapos *nmpl* (*fam*: *de mujer*) clothes, dresses;
a todo ~ under full sail; **soltar el ~** (*llorar*) to
burst into tears
tráquea ['trakea] *nf* trachea, windpipe
traqueteo [trake'teo] *nm* (*crujido*) crack;
(*golpeteo*) rattling
tras [tras] *prep* (*detrás*) behind; (*después*) after;
~ de besides; **día ~ día** day after day; **uno ~
otro** one after the other
trascendencia [trasθen'denθja] *nf*
(*importancia*) importance; (*en filosofía*)
transcendence
trascendental [trasθenden'tal] *adj*
important; transcendental
trascender [trasθen'der] *vi* (*oler*) to smell;
(*noticias*) to come out, leak out; (*sucesos,
sentimientos*) to spread, have a wide effect; **~
a** (*afectar*) to reach, have an effect on; (*oler a*)
to smack of; **en su novela todo trasciende
a romanticismo** everything in his novel
smacks of romanticism
trascienda *etc* [tras'θjenda] *vb ver* **trascender**
trasegar [trase'ɣar] *vt* (*mover*) to move about;
(*vino*) to decant
trasegué [trase'ɣe], **traseguemos** *etc*
[trase'ɣemos] *vb ver* **trasegar**
trasero, -a [tra'sero, a] *adj* back, rear ■ *nm*
(*Anat*) bottom; **traseros** *nmpl* ancestors
trasfondo [tras'fondo] *nm* background
trasgo ['trasɣo] *nm* (*duende*) goblin
trasgredir [trasɣre'ðir] *vt* to contravene
trashumante [trasu'mante] *adj* migrating
trasiego *etc* [tra'sjeɣo] *vb ver* **trasegar** ■ *nm*
(*cambiar de sitio*) move, switch; (*de vino*)
decanting; (*trastorno*) upset
trasiegue *etc* [tra'sjeɣe] *vb ver* **trasegar**
trasladar [trasla'ðar] *vt* to move; (*persona*) to
transfer; (*postergar*) to postpone; (*copiar*) to
copy; (*interpretar*) to interpret; **trasladarse** *vr*
(*irse*) to go; (*mudarse*) to move; **trasladarse a
otro puesto** to move to a new job
traslado [tras'laðo] *nm* move; (*mudanza*)
move, removal; (*de persona*) transfer; (*copia*)

copy; **~ de bloque** (*Inform*) block move, cut-and-paste

traslucir [traslu'θir] *vt* to show; **traslucirse** *vr* to be translucent; (*fig*) to be revealed

trasluz [tras'luθ] *nm* reflected light; **al ~** against o up to the light

trasluzca *etc* [tras'luθka] *vb ver* **traslucir**

trasmano [tras'mano]: **a ~** *adv* (*fuera de alcance*) out of reach; (*apartado*) out of the way

trasnochado, -a [trasno'tʃaðo, a] *adj* dated

trasnochador, a [trasnotʃa'ðor, a] *adj* given to staying up late ◾ *nm/f* (*fig*) night bird

trasnochar [trasno'tʃar] *vi* (*acostarse tarde*) to stay up late; (*no dormir*) to have a sleepless night; (*pasar la noche*) to stay the night

traspasar [traspa'sar] *vt* (*bala*) to pierce, go through; (*propiedad*) to sell, transfer; (*calle*) to cross over; (*límites*) to go beyond; (*ley*) to break; **"traspaso negocio"** "business for sale"

traspaso [tras'paso] *nm* transfer; (*fig*) anguish

traspié [tras'pje] (*pl* **~s**) *nm* (*caída*) stumble; (*tropezón*) trip; (*fig*) blunder

trasplantar [trasplan'tar] *vt* to transplant

trasplante [tras'plante] *nm* transplant

traspuesto, -a [tras'pwesto, a] *adj*: **quedarse ~** to doze off

trastada [tras'taða] *nf* (*fam*) prank

trastazo [tras'taθo] *nm* (*fam*) bump; **darse un ~** (*persona*) to bump o.s.; (*en coche*) to have a bump

traste ['traste] *nm* (*Mus*) fret; **dar al ~ con algo** to ruin sth; **ir al ~** to fall through

trastero [tras'tero] *nm* lumber room

trastienda [tras'tjenda] *nf* backshop; **obtener algo por la ~** to get sth by underhand means

trasto ['trasto] *nm* (*mueble*) piece of furniture; (*tarro viejo*) old pot; (*pey: cosa*) piece of junk; (: *persona*) dead loss; **trastos** *nmpl* (*Teat*) scenery *sg*; **tirar los trastos a la cabeza** to have a blazing row

trastocar [trasto'kar] *vt* (*papeles*) to mix up

trastornado, -a [trastor'naðo, a] *adj* (*loco*) mad; (*agitado*) crazy

trastornar [trastor'nar] *vt* to overturn, upset; (*fig: ideas*) to confuse; (: *nervios*) to shatter; (: *persona*) to drive crazy; **trastornarse** *vr* (*plan*) to fall through

trastorno [tras'torno] *nm* (*acto*) overturning; (*confusión*) confusion; (*Pol*) disturbance, upheaval; (*Med*) upset; **~ estomacal** stomach upset; **~ mental** mental disorder, breakdown

trasunto [tra'sunto] *nm* copy

trasvase [tras'βase] *nm* (*de río*) diversion

tratable [tra'taβle] *adj* friendly

tratado [tra'taðo] *nm* (*Pol*) treaty; (*Com*) agreement; (*Lit*) treatise

tratamiento [trata'mjento] *nm* treatment; (*Tec*) processing; (*de problema*) handling; **~ de datos** (*Inform*) data processing; **~ de gráficos** (*Inform*) graphics; **~ de márgenes** margin settings; **~ de textos** (*Inform*) word processing; **~ por lotes** (*Inform*) batch processing; **~ de tú** familiar address

tratante [tra'tante] *nm/f* dealer, merchandizer

tratar [tra'tar] *vt* (*ocuparse de*) to treat; (*manejar, Tec*) to handle; (*Inform*) to process; (*Med*) to treat; (*dirigirse a: persona*) to address ◾ *vi*: **~ de** (*hablar sobre*) to deal with, be about; (*intentar*) to try to; **~ con** (*Com*) to trade in; (*negociar con*) to negotiate with; (*tener tratos con*) to have dealings with; **tratarse** *vr* to treat each other; **se trata de la nueva piscina** it's about the new pool; **¿de qué se trata?** what's it about?

trato ['trato] *nm* dealings *pl*; (*relaciones*) relationship; (*comportamiento*) manner; (*Com, Jur*) agreement, contract; (*título*) (form of) address; **de ~ agradable** pleasant; **de fácil ~** easy to get on with; **~ equitativo** fair deal; **¡~ hecho!** it's a deal!; **malos tratos** ill-treatment *sg*

trauma ['trauma] *nm* trauma

traumático, -a [trau'matiko, a] *adj* traumatic

través [tra'βes] *nm* (*contratiempo*) reverse; **al ~** across, crossways; **a ~ de** across; (*sobre*) over; (*por*) through; **de ~** across; (*de lado*) sideways

travesaño [traβe'saɲo] *nm* (*Arq*) crossbeam; (*Deporte*) crossbar

travesía [traβe'sia] *nf* (*calle*) cross-street; (*Naut*) crossing

travesti [tra'βesti] *nm/f* transvestite

travesura [traβe'sura] *nf* (*broma*) prank; (*ingenio*) wit

travieso, -a [tra'βjeso, a] *adj* (*niño*) naughty; (*adulto*) restless; (*ingenioso*) witty ◾ *nf* crossing; (*Arq*) crossbeam; (*Ferro*) sleeper

trayecto [tra'jekto] *nm* (*ruta*) road, way; (*viaje*) journey; (*tramo*) stretch; (*curso*) course; **final del ~** end of the line

trayectoria [trajek'torja] *nf* trajectory; (*desarrollo*) development, path; **la ~ actual del partido** the party's present line

trayendo *etc* [tra'jendo] *vb ver* **traer**

traza ['traθa] *nf* (*Arq*) plan, design; (*aspecto*) looks *pl*; (*señal*) sign; (*engaño*) trick; (*habilidad*) skill; (*Inform*) trace

trazado, -a [tra'θaðo, a] *adj*: **bien ~** shapely, well-formed ◾ *nm* (*Arq*) plan, design; (*fig*) outline; (de carretera etc) line, route

trazador [traθa'ðor] nm plotter; **~ plano** flatbed plotter

trazar [tra'θar] vt (Arq) to plan; (Arte) to sketch; (fig) to trace; (itinerario: hacer) to plot; (plan) to follow

trazo ['traθo] nm (línea) line; (bosquejo) sketch; **trazos** nmpl (de cara) lines, features

TRB abr = **toneladas de registro bruto**

trébol ['treβol] nm (Bot) clover; **tréboles** nmpl (Naipes) clubs

trece ['treθe] num thirteen; **estar en sus ~** to stand firm

trecho ['tretʃo] nm (distancia) distance; (de tiempo) while; (fam) piece; **de ~ en ~** at intervals

tregua ['treɣwa] nf (Mil) truce; (fig) lull; **sin ~** without respite

treinta ['treinta] num thirty

treintena [trein'tena] nf (about) thirty

tremendo, -a [tre'mendo, a] adj (terrible) terrible; (imponente: cosa) imposing; (fam: fabuloso) tremendous; (divertido) entertaining

trémulo, -a ['tremulo, a] adj quivering; (luz) flickering

tren [tren] nm (Ferro) train; **~ de aterrizaje** undercarriage; **~ directo/expreso/(de) mercancías/de pasajeros/suplementario** through/fast/goods o freight/passenger/relief train; **~ de vida** way of life

trenca ['trenka] nf duffel coat

trence etc ['trenθe] vb ver **trenzar**

trenza ['trenθa] nf (de pelo) plait

trenzar [tren'θar] vt (el pelo) to plait ▪ vi (en baile) to weave in and out; **trenzarse** vr (Am) to become involved

trepa ['trepa] nf (subida) climb; (ardid) trick

trepador, a [trepa'ðor(a)] nm/f (fam): **ser un(a) ~(a)** to be on the make ▪ nf (Bot) climber

trepar [tre'par] vt, vi to climb; (Tec) to drill

trepidación [trepiða'θjon] nf shaking, vibration

trepidar [trepi'ðar] vi to shake, vibrate

tres [tres] num three; (fecha) third; **las ~** three o'clock

trescientos, -as [tres'θjentos, as] num three hundred

tresillo [tre'siʎo] nm three-piece suite; (Mus) triplet

treta ['treta] nf (Com etc) gimmick; (fig) trick

tri ... [tri] pref tri..., three-...

tríada ['triaða] nf triad

triangular [trjangu'lar] adj triangular

triángulo [tri'angulo] nm triangle

tribal [tri'βal] adj tribal

tribu ['triβu] nf tribe

tribuna [tri'βuna] nf (plataforma) platform; (Deporte) stand; (fig) public speaking; **~ de la prensa** press box; **~ del acusado** (Jur) dock; **~ del jurado** jury box

tribunal [triβu'nal] nm (en juicio) court; (comisión, fig) tribunal; (Escol: examinadores) board of examiners; **T~ Supremo** High Court, Supreme Court (US); **T~ de Justicia de las Comunidades Europeas** European Court of Justice; **~ popular** jury

tributar [triβu'tar] vt to pay; (las gracias) to give; (cariño) to show

tributario, -a [triβu'tarjo, a] adj (Geo: Pol) tributary cpd; (Econ) tax cpd, taxation cpd ▪ nm (Geo) tributary ▪ nm/f (Com) taxpayer; **sistema ~** tax system

tributo [tri'βuto] nm (Com) tax

triciclo [tri'θiklo] nm tricycle

tricornio [tri'kornjo] nm three-cornered hat

tricota [tri'kota] nf (Am) knitted sweater

tricotar [triko'tar] vi to knit

tridimensional [triðimensjo'nal] adj three-dimensional

trienal [trje'nal] adj three-year

trifulca [tri'fulka] nf (fam) row, shindy

trigal [tri'ɣal] nm wheat field

trigésimo, -a [tri'xesimo, a] num thirtieth

trigo ['triɣo] nm wheat; **trigos** nmpl wheat field(s) (pl)

trigueño, -a [tri'ɣeɲo, a] adj (pelo) corn-coloured; (piel) olive-skinned

trillado, -a [tri'ʎaðo, a] adj threshed; (fig) trite, hackneyed

trilladora [triʎa'ðora] nf threshing machine

trillar [tri'ʎar] vt (Agr) to thresh; (fig) to frequent

trillizos, -as [tri'ʎiθos, as] nmpl/nfpl triplets

trilogía [trilo'xia] nf trilogy

trimestral [trimes'tral] adj quarterly; (Escol) termly

trimestre [tri'mestre] nm (Escol) term; (Com) quarter, financial period; (: pago) quarterly payment

trinar [tri'nar] vi (Mus) to trill; (ave) to sing, warble; **está que trina** he's hopping mad

trincar [trin'kar] vt (atar) to tie up; (Naut) to lash; (agarrar) to pinion

trinchante [trin'tʃante] nm (para cortar carne) carving knife; (tenedor) meat fork

trinchar [trin'tʃar] vt to carve

trinchera [trin'tʃera] nf (fosa) trench; (para vía) cutting; (impermeable) trench-coat

trineo [tri'neo] nm sledge

trinidad [trini'ðað] nf trio; (Rel): **la T~** the Trinity

trino ['trino] nm trill

trinque etc ['trinke] vb ver **trincar**

trinquete [trin'kete] *nm* (*Tec*) pawl; (*Naut*) foremast

trío ['trio] *nm* trio

tripa ['tripa] *nf* (*Anat*) intestine; (*fig: fam*) belly; **tripas** *nfpl* (*Anat*) insides; (*Culin*) tripe *sg*; **tener mucha ~** to be fat; **me duelen las tripas** I have a stomach ache

tripartito, -a [tripar'tito, a] *adj* tripartite

triple ['triple] *adj* triple; (*tres veces*) threefold

triplicado, -a [tripli'kaðo, a] *adj*: **por ~** in triplicate

triplicar [tripli'kar] *vt* to treble

triplo ['triplo] *adj* = **triple**

trípode ['tripoðe] *nm* tripod

Trípoli ['tripoli] *nm* Tripoli

tríptico ['triptiko] *nm* (*Arte*) triptych; (*documento*) three-part document

tripulación [tripula'θjon] *nf* crew

tripulante [tripu'lante] *nm/f* crewman/woman

tripular [tripu'lar] *vt* (*barco*) to man; (*Auto*) to drive

triquiñuela [triki'ɲwela] *nf* trick

tris [tris] *nm* crack; **en un ~** in an instant; **estar en un ~ de hacer algo** to be within an inch of doing sth

triste ['triste] *adj* (*afligido*) sad; (*sombrío*) melancholy, gloomy; (*desolado*) desolate; (*lamentable*) sorry, miserable; (*viejo*) old; (*único*) single; **no queda sino un ~ penique** there's just one miserable penny left

tristeza [tris'teθa] *nf* (*aflicción*) sadness; (*melancolía*) melancholy; (*de lugar*) desolation; (*pena*) misery

tristón, -ona [tris'ton, ona] *adj* sad, downhearted

trituradora [tritura'ðora] *nf* shredder

triturar [tritu'rar] *vt* (*moler*) to grind; (*mascar*) to chew; (*documentos*) to shred

triunfador, a [triunfa'ðor, a] *adj* triumphant; (*ganador*) winning ■ *nm/f* winner

triunfal [triun'fal] *adj* triumphant; (*arco*) triumphal

triunfante [triun'fante] *adj* triumphant; (*ganador*) winning

triunfar [triun'far] *vi* (*tener éxito*) to triumph; (*ganar*) to win; (*Naipes*) to be trumps; **triunfan corazones** hearts are trumps; **~ en la vida** to succeed in life

triunfo [tri'unfo] *nm* triumph; (*Naipes*) trump

trivial [tri'βjal] *adj* trivial

trivialice *etc* [triβja'liθe] *vb ver* **trivializar**

trivializar [triβjali'θar] *vt* to minimize, play down

triza ['triθa] *nf* bit, piece; **hacer algo trizas** to smash sth to bits; (*papel*) to tear sth to shreds

trocar [tro'kar] *vt* (*Com*) to exchange; (*dinero, de lugar*) to change; (*palabras*) to exchange; (*confundir*) to confuse; **trocarse** *vr* (*confundirse*) to get mixed up; (*transformarse*): **trocarse (en)** to change (into)

trocear [troθe'ar] *vt* to cut up

trocha ['trotʃa] *nf* (*sendero*) by-path; (*atajo*) short cut

troche ['trotʃe]: **a ~ y moche** *adv* helter-skelter, pell-mell

trofeo [tro'feo] *nm* (*premio*) trophy

trola ['trola] *nf* (*fam*) fib

tromba ['tromba] *nf* whirlwind; **~ de agua** cloudburst

trombón [trom'bon] *nm* trombone

trombosis [trom'bosis] *nf inv* thrombosis

trompa ['trompa] *nf* (*Mus*) horn; (*de elefante*) trunk; (*trompo*) humming top; (*hocico*) snout; (*Anat*) tube, duct ■ *nm* (*Mus*) horn player; **~ de Falopio** Fallopian tube; **cogerse una ~** (*fam*) to get tight

trompada [trom'paða] *nf*, **trompazo** [trom'paθo] *nm* (*choque*) bump, bang; (*puñetazo*) punch

trompeta [trom'peta] *nf* trumpet; (*clarín*) bugle ■ *nm* trumpeter

trompetilla [trompe'tiʎa] *nf* ear trumpet

trompicón [trompi'kon]: **a trompicones** *adv* in fits and starts

trompo ['trompo] *nm* spinning top

trompón [trom'pon] *nm* bump

tronado, -a [tro'naðo, a] *adj* broken-down

tronar [tro'nar] *vt* (*Am*) to shoot, execute ■ *vi* to thunder; (*fig*) to rage; (*fam*) to go broke

tronchar [tron'tʃar] *vt* (*árbol*) to chop down; (*fig: vida*) to cut short; (*esperanza*) to shatter; (*persona*) to tire out; **troncharse** *vr* to fall down; **troncharse de risa** to split one's sides with laughter

tronco ['tronko] *nm* (*de árbol, Anat*) trunk; (*de planta*) stem; **estar hecho un ~** to be sound asleep

tronera [tro'nera] *nf* (*Mil*) loophole; (*Arq*) small window

trono ['trono] *nm* throne

tropa ['tropa] *nf* (*Mil*) troop; (*soldados*) soldiers *pl*; (*soldados rasos*) ranks *pl*; (*gentío*) mob

tropecé [trope'θe], **tropecemos** *etc* [trope'θemos] *vb ver* **tropezar**

tropel [tro'pel] *nm* (*muchedumbre*) crowd; (*prisa*) rush; (*montón*) throng; **acudir** *etc* **en ~** to come *etc* in a mad rush

tropelía [trope'lia] *nm* outrage

tropezar [trope'θar] *vi* to trip, stumble; (*fig*) to slip up; **tropezarse** *vr* (*dos personas*) to run into each other; **~ con** (*encontrar*) to run into; (*topar con*) to bump into

tropezón [trope'θon] *nm* trip; (*fig*) blunder; (*traspié*): **dar un ~** to trip

tropical [tropi'kal] *adj* tropical

trópico ['tropiko] *nm* tropic

tropiece *etc* [tro'pjeθe] *vb ver* **tropezar**

tropiezo *etc* [tro'pjeθo] *vb ver* **tropezar** ■ *nm* (*error*) slip, blunder; (*desgracia*) misfortune; (*revés*) setback; (*obstáculo*) snag; (*discusión*) quarrel

troqué [tro'ke], **troquemos** *etc* [tro'kemos] *vb ver* **trocar**

trotamundos [trota'mundos] *nm inv* globetrotter

trotar [tro'tar] *vi* to trot; (*viajar*) to travel about

trote ['trote] *nm* trot; (*fam*) travelling; **de mucho ~** hard-wearing

Troya ['troja] *nf* Troy; **aquí fue ~** now there's nothing but ruins

trozo ['troθo] *nm* bit, piece; (*Lit: Mus*) passage; **a trozos** in bits

trucha ['trutʃa] *nf* (*pez*) trout; (*Tec*) crane

truco ['truko] *nm* (*habilidad*) knack; (*engaño*) trick; (*Cine*) trick effect o photography; **trucos** *nmpl* billiards *sg*; **~ publicitario** advertising gimmick

trueco *etc* ['trweko] *vb ver* **trocar**

trueno *etc* ['trweno] *vb ver* **tronar** ■ *nm* (*gen*) thunder; (*estampido*) boom; (*de arma*) bang

trueque *etc* ['trweke] *vb ver* **trocar** ■ *nm* exchange; (*Com*) barter

trufa ['trufa] *nf* (*Bot*) truffle; (*fig: fam*) fib

truhán, -ana [tru'an, ana] *nm/f* rogue

truncado, -a [trun'kaðo, a] *adj* truncated

truncar [trun'kar] *vt* (*cortar*) to truncate; (*la vida etc*) to cut short; (*el desarrollo*) to stunt

trunque *etc* ['trunke] *vb ver* **truncar**

Tte. *abr* (= *Teniente*) Lt.

tu [tu] *adj* your

tú [tu] *pron* you

tubérculo [tu'βerkulo] *nm* (*Bot*) tuber

tuberculosis [tuβerku'losis] *nf inv* tuberculosis

tubería [tuβe'ria] *nf* pipes *pl*, piping; (*conducto*) pipeline

tubo ['tuβo] *nm* tube, pipe; **~ de desagüe** drainpipe; **~ de ensayo** test-tube; **~ de escape** exhaust (pipe); **~ digestivo** alimentary canal

tuerca ['twerka] *nf* (*Tec*) nut

tuerce *etc* ['twerθe] *vb ver* **torcer**

tuerto, -a ['twerto, a] *adj* (*torcido*) twisted; (*ciego*) blind in one eye ■ *nm/f* one-eyed person ■ *nm* (*ofensa*) wrong; **a tuertas** upside-down

tuerza *etc* ['twerθa] *vb ver* **torcer**

tueste *etc* ['tweste] *vb ver* **tostar**

tuétano ['twetano] *nm* (*Anat: médula*) marrow; (*Bot*) pith; **hasta los tuétanos** through and through, utterly

tufo ['tufo] *nm* vapour; (*fig: pey*) stench

tugurio [tu'ɣurjo] *nm* slum

tul [tul] *nm* tulle

tulipán [tuli'pan] *nm* tulip

tullido, -a [tu'ʎiðo, a] *adj* crippled; (*cansado*) exhausted

tumba ['tumba] *nf* (*sepultura*) tomb; (*sacudida*) shake; (*voltereta*) somersault; **ser (como) una ~** to keep one's mouth shut

tumbar [tum'bar] *vt* to knock down; (*doblar*) to knock over; (*fam: suj: olor*) to overpower ■ *vi* to fall down; **tumbarse** *vr* (*echarse*) to lie down; (*extenderse*) to stretch out

tumbo ['tumbo] *nm* (*caída*) fall; (*de vehículo*) jolt; (*momento crítico*) critical moment

tumbona [tum'bona] *nf* lounger

tumor [tu'mor] *nm* tumour

tumulto [tu'multo] *nm* turmoil; (*Pol: motín*) riot

tuna ['tuna] *nf* (*Mus*) student music group; *ver tb* **tuno**; *see note*

TUNA

A *tuna* is made up of university students, or quite often former students, who dress up in costumes from the *Edad de Oro*, the Spanish Golden Age. These musical troupes go through the town playing their guitars, lutes and tambourines and serenade the young ladies in the halls of residence, or make impromptu appearances at weddings or parties singing traditional Spanish songs for a few pesetas.

tunante [tu'nante] *adj* rascally ■ *nm* rogue, villain; **¡~!** you villain!

tunda ['tunda] *nf* (*de tela*) shearing; (*de golpes*) beating

tundir [tun'dir] *vt* (*tela*) to shear; (*hierba*) to mow; (*fig*) to exhaust; (*fam: golpear*) to beat

tunecino, -a [tune'θino, a] *adj, nm/f* Tunisian

túnel ['tunel] *nm* tunnel

Túnez ['tuneθ] *nm* Tunis

túnica ['tunika] *nf* tunic; (*vestido largo*) long dress; (*Anat: Bot*) tunic

Tunicia [tu'niθja] *nf* Tunisia

tuno, -a ['tuno, a] *nm/f* (*fam*) rogue ■ *nm* (*Mus*) member of a "tuna"

tuntún [tun'tun] : **al ~** *adv* thoughtlessly

tupamaro, -a [tupa'maro, a] *adj, nm/f* (*Am*) urban guerrilla

tupé [tu'pe] *nm* quiff

tupí [tu'pi], **tupí-guaraní** [tupigwara'ni] *adj, nm/f* Tupi-Guarani

tupido, -a [tu'piðo, a] *adj* (*denso*) dense; (*fig: torpe*) dim; (*tela*) close-woven

turba ['turβa] *nf* (*combustible*) turf; (*muchedumbre*) crowd

turbación [turβa'θjon] *nf* (*molestia*) disturbance; (*preocupación*) worry

turbado, -a [tur'βaðo, a] *adj* (*molesto*) disturbed; (*preocupado*) worried

turbante [tur'βante] *nm* turban

turbar [tur'βar] *vt* (*molestar*) to disturb; (*incomodar*) to upset; **turbarse** *vr* to be disturbed

turbina [tur'βina] *nf* turbine

turbio, -a ['turβjo, a] *adj* (*agua etc*) cloudy; (*vista*) dim, blurred; (*tema*) unclear, confused; (*negocio*) shady ▪ *adv* indistinctly

turbión [tur'βjon] *nf* downpour; (*fig*) shower, hail

turbo ['turβo] *adj inv* turbo(-charged) ▪ *nm* (*tb coche*) turbo

turbulencia [turβu'lenθja] *nf* turbulence; (*fig*) restlessness

turbulento, -a [turβu'lento, a] *adj* turbulent; (*fig: intranquilo*) restless; (: *ruidoso*) noisy

turco, -a ['turko, a] *adj* Turkish ▪ *nm/f* Turk ▪ *nm* (*Ling*) Turkish

Turena [tu'rena] *nf* Touraine

turgente [tur'xente], **túrgido, a** ['turxiðo, a] *adj* (*tirante*) turgid, swollen

Turín [tu'rin] *nm* Turin

turismo [tu'rismo] *nm* tourism; (*coche*)

saloon car; **hacer ~** to go travelling (abroad)

turista [tu'rista] *nm/f* tourist; (*vacacionista*) holidaymaker (*Brit*), vacationer (*US*)

turístico, -a [tu'ristiko, a] *adj* tourist *cpd*

Turkmenistán [turkmeni'stan] *nm* Turkmenistan

turnar [tur'nar] *vi*, **turnarse** *vr* to take (it in) turns

turno ['turno] *nm* (*oportunidad, orden de prioridad*) opportunity; (*Deporte etc*) turn; **es su ~** it's his turn (next); **~ de día/de noche** (*Industria*) day/night shift

turolense [turo'lense] *adj* of o from Teruel ▪ *nm/f* native o inhabitant of Teruel

turquesa [tur'kesa] *nf* turquoise

Turquía [tur'kia] *nf* Turkey

turrón [tu'rron] *nm* (*dulce*) nougat; (*fam*) sinecure, cushy job o number

tute ['tute] *nm* (*Naipes*) card game; **darse un ~** to break one's back

tutear [tute'ar] *vt* to address as familiar "tú"; **tutearse** *vr* to be on familiar terms

tutela [tu'tela] *nf* (*legal*) guardianship; (*instrucción*) guidance; **estar bajo la ~ de** (*fig*) to be under the protection of

tutelar [tute'lar] *adj* tutelary ▪ *vt* to protect

tutor, a [tu'tor, a] *nm/f* (*legal*) guardian; (*Escol*) tutor; **~ de curso** form master/mistress

tuve *etc* ['tuβe] *vb ver* **tener**

tuyo, -a ['tujo, a] *adj* yours, of yours ▪ *pron* yours; **los tuyos** (*fam*) your relations, your family

TVE *nf abr* = **Televisión Española**

Uu

U, u [u] *nf (letra)* U, u; **viraje en U** U-turn;
U de Ulises U for Uncle
u [u] *conj* or
u. *abr* = **unidad**
UAR [war] *nfpl abr (Esp)* = **Unidades Antiterroristas Rurales**
ubérrimo, -a [u'βerrimo, a] *adj* very rich, fertile
ubicación [uβika'θjon] *nf (esp Am)* place, position, location
ubicado, -a [uβi'kaðo, a] *adj (esp Am)* situated
ubicar [uβi'kar] *vt (esp Am)* to place, situate; *(: fig)* to install in a post; *(: encontrar)* to find; **ubicarse** *vr* to be situated, be located
ubicuo, -a [u'βikwo, a] *adj* ubiquitous
ubique *etc* [u'βike] *vb ver* **ubicar**
ubre ['uβre] *nf* udder
UCI ['uθi] *sigla f* (= *Unidad de Cuidados Intensivos*) ICU
Ucrania [u'kranja] *nf* Ukraine
ucraniano, -a [ukra'njano, a] *adj, nm/f* Ukrainian ■ *nm (Ling)* Ukrainian
ucranio [u'kranjo] *nm (Ling)* Ukrainian
Ud(s) *abr* = **usted(es)**; *ver* **usted**
UDV *sigla f* = **Unidad de Despliegue Visual**
UE *nf abr* (= *Unión Europea*) EU
UEFA [w'efa] *nf abr* (= *Unión de Asociaciones de Fútbol Europeo*) UEFA
UEO *nf abr* (= *Unión Europea Occidental*) WEU
UEP *nf abr* = **Unión Europea de Pagos**
UER *sigla f* = **Unión Europea de Radiodifusión**
uf [uf] *excl (cansancio)* phew!; *(repugnancia)* ugh!
ufanarse [ufa'narse] *vr* to boast; **~ de** to pride o.s. on
ufano, -a [u'fano, a] *adj (arrogante)* arrogant; *(presumido)* conceited
UGT *nf abr ver* **Unión General de Trabajadores**
UIT *sigla f* = **Unión Internacional de Telecomunicaciones**
ujier [u'xjer] *nm* usher; *(portero)* doorkeeper
úlcera ['ulθera] *nf* ulcer
ulcerar [ulθe'rar] *vt* to make sore; **ulcerarse** *vr* to ulcerate

ulterior [ulte'rjor] *adj (más allá)* farther, further; *(subsecuente, siguiente)* subsequent
ulteriormente [ulterjor'mente] *adv* later, subsequently
últimamente ['ultimamente] *adv (recientemente)* lately, recently; *(finalmente)* finally; *(como último recurso)* as a last resort
ultimar [ulti'mar] *vt* to finish; *(finalizar)* to finalize; *(Am: rematar)* to finish off, murder
ultimátum [ulti'matum] *nm (pl* **ultimátums***)* ultimatum
último, -a ['ultimo, a] *adj* last; *(más reciente)* latest, most recent; *(más bajo)* bottom; *(más alto)* top; *(fig)* final, extreme; **en las últimas** on one's last legs; **por último** finally
ultra ['ultra] *adj* ultra ■ *nm/f* extreme right-winger
ultracongelar [ultrakonxe'lar] *vt* to deep-freeze
ultraderecha [ultraðe'retʃa] *nf* extreme right (wing)
ultrajar [ultra'xar] *vt (escandalizar)* to outrage; *(insultar)* to insult, abuse
ultraje [ul'traxe] *nm* outrage; insult
ultraligero [ultrali'xero] *nm* microlight (Brit), microlite (US)
ultramar [ultra'mar] *nm*: **de** *o* **en ~** abroad, overseas; **los países de ~** the overseas countries
ultramarino, -a [ultrama'rino, a] *adj* overseas, foreign ■ *nmpl*: **ultramarinos** groceries; **tienda de ultramarinos** grocer's (shop)
ultranza [ul'tranθa]: **a ~** *adv* to the death; *(a toda costa)* at all costs; *(completo)* outright; *(Pol etc)* out-and-out, extreme; **un nacionalista a ~** a rabid nationalist
ultrarrojo, -a [ultra'rroxo, a] *adj* = **infrarrojo, a**
ultrasónico, -a [ultra'soniko, a] *adj* ultrasonic
ultratumba [ultra'tumba] *nf*: **la vida de ~** the next life; **una voz de ~** a ghostly voice

u

ultravioleta [ultraβjo'leta] *adj inv* ultraviolet
ulular [ulu'lar] *vi* to howl; *(búho)* to hoot
umbilical [umbili'kal] *adj:* **cordón ~** umbilical cord
umbral [um'bral] *nm (gen)* threshold; **~ de rentabilidad** *(Com)* break-even point
umbrío, -a [um'brio, a] *adj* shady
UME *nf abr* (= *Unión Monetaria y Económica*) EMU

un, una [un, 'una] *artículo indefinido* a; *(antes de vocal)* an; **una mujer/naranja** a woman/an orange
■ *adj* **1: unos** (*o* **unas**)**: hay unos regalos para ti** there are some presents for you; **hay unas cervezas en la nevera** there are some beers in the fridge
2 *(enfático):* **¡hace un frío!** it's so cold!; **¡tiene una casa!** he's got some house!

U.N.A.M. ['unam] *nf abr* = **Universidad Nacional Autónoma de México**
unánime [u'nanime] *adj* unanimous
unanimidad [unanimi'ðað] *nf* unanimity; **por ~** unanimously
unción [un'θjon] *nf* anointing
uncir [un'θir] *vt* to yoke
undécimo, -a [un'deθimo, a] *adj, nm/f* eleventh
UNED [u'ned] *nf abr* (*Esp Univ:* = *Universidad Nacional de Enseñanza a Distancia*) ≈ Open University (*Brit*)
UNEF [u'nef] *sigla f* = **Fuerzas de Urgencia de las Naciones Unidas**
UNESCO, Unesco [u'nesko] *sigla f* (= *United Nations Educational, Scientific and Cultural Organization*) UNESCO
ungir [un'xir] *vt* to rub with ointment; *(Rel)* to anoint
ungüento [un'gwento] *nm* ointment; *(fig)* salve, balm
únicamente ['unikamente] *adv* solely; *(solamente)* only
UNICEF, Unicef [uni'θef] *sigla m* (= *United Nations International Children's Emergency Fund*) ≈ UNICEF
unicidad [uniθi'ðað] *nf* uniqueness
único, -a ['uniko, a] *adj* only; *(solo)* sole, single; *(sin par)* unique; **hijo único** only child
unidad [uni'ðað] *nf* unity; *(Tec)* unit; **~ móvil** *(TV)* mobile unit; *(Inform):* **~ central** system unit, central processing unit; **~ de control** control unit; **~ de disco** disk drive; **~ de entrada/salida** input/output device; **~ de información** data item; **~ periférica** peripheral device; **~ de presentación visual**

o **de visualización** visual display unit; **~ procesadora central** central processing unit
unido, -a [u'niðo, a] *adj* joined, linked; *(fig)* united
unifamiliar [unifamil'jar] *adj:* **vivienda ~** single-family home
unificar [unifi'kar] *vt* to unite, unify
unifique *etc* [uni'fike] *vb ver* **unificar**
uniformado, -a [unifor'maðo, a] *adj* uniformed, in uniform
uniformar [unifor'mar] *vt* to make uniform; *(Tec)* to standardize
uniforme [uni'forme] *adj* uniform, equal; *(superficie)* even ■ *nm* uniform
uniformidad [uniformi'ðað] *nf* uniformity; *(llaneza)* levelness, evenness
unilateral [unilate'ral] *adj* unilateral
unión [u'njon] *nf (gen)* union; *(acto)* uniting, joining; *(calidad)* unity; *(Tec)* joint; *(fig)* closeness, togetherness; **en ~ con** (together) with, accompanied by; **~ aduanera** customs union; **U~ General de Trabajadores (UGT)** *(Esp) Socialist Union Confederation;* **U~ Europea** European Union; **la U~ Soviética** the Soviet Union; **punto de ~** *(Tec)* junction
unir [u'nir] *vt (juntar)* to join, unite; *(atar)* to tie, fasten; *(combinar)* to combine ■ *vi (ingredientes)* to mix well; **unirse** *vr* to join together, unite; *(empresas)* to merge; **les une una fuerte simpatía** they are bound by (a) strong affection; **unirse en matrimonio** to marry
unisex [uni'seks] *adj inv* unisex
unísono [u'nisono] *nm:* **al ~** in unison
unitario, -a [uni'tarjo, a] *adj* unitary; *(Rel)* Unitarian ■ *nm/f (Rel)* Unitarian
universal [uniβer'sal] *adj* universal; *(mundial)* world *cpd;* **historia ~** world history
universidad [uniβersi'ðað] *nf* university; **~ laboral** polytechnic, poly
universitario, -a [uniβersi'tarjo, a] *adj* university *cpd* ■ *nm/f (profesor)* lecturer; *(estudiante)* (university) student
universo [uni'βerso] *nm* universe
unja *etc* ['unxa] *vb ver* **ungir**

uno, -a ['uno, a] *adj* one; **es todo uno** it's all one and the same; **unos pocos** a few; **unos cien** about a hundred
■ *pron* **1** one; **quiero uno solo** I only want one; **uno de ellos** one of them; **una de dos** either one or the other; **no doy una hoy** I can't do anything right today
2 *(alguien)* somebody, someone; **conozco a**

uno que se te parece I know somebody o someone who looks like you; **unos querían quedarse** some (people) wanted to stay

3 (*impersonal*) one; **uno mismo** oneself; **uno nunca sabe qué hacer** one never knows what to do

4: **unos ... otros ...** some ... others; **una y otra son muy agradables** they're both very nice; **(los) uno(s) a (los) otro(s)** each other, one another

■ *nf* one; **es la una** it's one o'clock

■ *num* (number) one; **el día uno** the first

untar [un'tar] *vt* (*gen*) to rub; (*engrasar*) to grease, oil; (*Med*) to rub (with ointment); (*fig*) to bribe; **untarse** *vr* (*fig*) to be crooked; **~ el pan con mantequilla** to spread butter on one's bread

unto ['unto] *nm* animal fat; (*Med*) ointment

unza *etc* ['unθa] *vb ver* **uncir**

uña ['uɲa] *nf* (*Anat*) nail; (*del pie*) toenail; (*garra*) claw; (*casco*) hoof; (*arrancaclavos*) claw; **ser ~ y carne** to be as thick as thieves; **enseñar** o **mostrar** o **sacar las uñas** to show one's claws

UOE *nf abr* (*Esp Mil*) = **Unidad de Operaciones Especiales**

UPA *nf abr* = **Unión Panamericana**

UPC *nf abr* (= *unidad procesadora central*) CPU

uperizado, -a [uperi'θaðo, a] *adj*: **leche uperizada** UHT milk

Urales [u'rales] *nmpl* (*tb*: **Montes Urales**) Urals

uralita® [ura'lita] *nf* corrugated asbestos cement

uranio [u'ranjo] *nm* uranium

urbanidad [urβani'ðað] *nf* courtesy, politeness

urbanismo [urβa'nismo] *nm* town planning

urbanista [urβa'nista] *nm/f* town planner

urbanización [urβaniθa'θjon] *nf* (*colonia, barrio*) estate, housing scheme

urbanizar [urβani'θar] *vt* to develop

urbano, -a [ur'βano, a] *adj* (*de ciudad*) urban, town *cpd*; (*cortés*) courteous, polite

urbe ['urβe] *nf* large city, metropolis

urdimbre [ur'ðimbre] *nf* (*de tejido*) warp; (*intriga*) intrigue

urdir [ur'ðir] *vt* to warp; (*fig*) to plot, contrive

urgencia [ur'xenθja] *nf* urgency; (*prisa*) haste, rush; **salida de ~** emergency exit; **servicios de ~** emergency services

urgente [ur'xente] *adj* urgent; (*insistente*) insistent; **carta ~** registered (*Brit*) o special delivery (*US*) letter

urgir [ur'xir] *vi* to be urgent; **me urge** I'm in a hurry for it; **me urge terminarlo** I must finish it as soon as I can

urinario, -a [uri'narjo, a] *adj* urinary ■ *nm* urinal, public lavatory, comfort station (*US*)

urja *etc* ['urxa] *vb ver* **urgir**

urna ['urna] *nf* urn; (*Pol*) ballot box; **acudir a las urnas** (*fig*: *persona*) to (go and) vote; (: *gobierno*) to go to the country

urología [urolo'xia] *nf* urology

urólogo, -a [u'roloɣo, a] *nm/f* urologist

urraca [u'rraka] *nf* magpie

URSS *nf abr* (*Historia*: = *Unión de Repúblicas Socialistas Soviéticas*) USSR

Uruguay [uru'ɣwai] *nm*: **El ~** Uruguay

uruguayo, -a [uru'ɣwajo, a] *adj, nm/f* Uruguayan

usado, -a [u'saðo, a] *adj* (*gen*) used; (*ropa etc*) worn; **muy ~** worn out

usanza [u'sanθa] *nf* custom, usage

usar [u'sar] *vt* to use; (*ropa*) to wear; (*tener costumbre*) to be in the habit of ■ *vi*: **~ de** to make use of; **usarse** *vr* to be used; (*ropa*) to be worn o in fashion

USO ['uso] *nf abr* (*Esp*: = *Unión Sindical Obrera*) *workers' union*

uso ['uso] *nm* use; (*Mecánica etc*) wear; (*costumbre*) usage, custom; (*moda*) fashion; **al ~** in keeping with custom; **al ~ de** in the style of; **de ~ externo** (*Med*) for external application; **estar en el ~ de la palabra** to be speaking, have the floor; **~ y desgaste** (*Com*) wear and tear

usted [us'teð] *pron* (*sg formal*: *abr* **Ud** o **Vd**) you *sg*; **ustedes** (*pl formal*: *abr* **Uds** o **Vds**) you *pl*; (*Am*: *formal y fam*) you *pl*

usual [u'swal] *adj* usual

usuario, -a [usw'arjo, a] *nm/f* user; **~ final** (*Com*) end user

usufructo [usu'frukto] *nm* use; **~ vitalicio (de)** life interest (in)

usura [u'sura] *nf* usury

usurero, -a [usu'rero, a] *nm/f* usurer

usurpar [usur'par] *vt* to usurp

utensilio [uten'siljo] *nm* tool; (*Culin*) utensil

útero ['utero] *nm* uterus, womb

útil ['util] *adj* useful; (*servible*) usable, serviceable ■ *nm* tool; **día útil** working day, weekday; **es muy útil tenerlo aquí cerca** it's very handy having it here close by

utilice *etc* [uti'liθe] *vb ver* **utilizar**

utilidad [utili'ðað] *nf* usefulness, utility; (*Com*) profit; **utilidades líquidas** net profit *sg*

utilitario [utili'tarjo] *nm* (*Inform*) utility

utilizar [utili'θar] *vt* to use, utilize; (*explotar*) to harness

utopía [uto'pia] *nf* Utopia

utópico, -a [u'topiko, a] *adj* Utopian

UVA *sigla mpl* (= *ultravioleta*) UV, UVA

u

uva ['uβa] *nf* grape; ~ **pasa** raisin; ~ **de Corinto** currant; **estar de mala** ~ to be in a bad mood; *see note*

● **UVA**
●
● In Spain *Las uvas* play a big part on New
● Years' Eve (*Nochevieja*), when on the stroke
● of midnight people from every part of

● Spain, at home, in restaurants or in the
● plaza mayor eat a grape for each stroke of
● the clock of the Puerta del Sol in Madrid. It
● is said to bring luck for the following year.

uve ['uβe] *nf name of the letter* V; **en forma de** ~ V-shaped; ~ **doble** *name of the letter* W
UVI ['uβi] *nf abr* (*Esp Med*: = *unidad de vigilancia intensiva*) ICU

Vv

V, v (*Esp*) ['uβe] (*Am*) [be'korta, bet∫ika] *nf* (*letra*) V, v; **V de Valencia** V for Victor

V. *abr* = **usted**; (= *visto*) approved, passed

v. *abr* (= *voltio*) v; (= *ver, véase*) v.; (*Lit*: = *verso*) v

va [ba] *vb ver* **ir**

V.A. *abr* = **Vuestra Alteza**

vaca ['baka] *nf* (*animal*) cow; (*carne*) beef; (*cuero*) cowhide; **vacas flacas/gordas** (*fig*) bad/good times

vacaciones [baka'θjones] *nfpl* holiday(s); **estar/irse** *o* **marcharse de ~** to be/go (away) on holiday

vacante [ba'kante] *adj* vacant, empty ■ *nf* vacancy

vaciado, -a [ba'θjaðo, a] *adj* (*hecho en molde*) cast in a mould; (*hueco*) hollow ■ *nm* cast, mould(ing)

vaciar [ba'θjar] *vt* to empty (out); (*ahuecar*) to hollow out; (*moldear*) to cast; (*Inform*) to dump ■ *vi* (*río*): **~ en** to flow into; **vaciarse** *vr* to empty; (*fig*) to blab, spill the beans

vaciedad [baθje'ðað] *nf* emptiness

vacilación [baθila'θjon] *nf* hesitation

vacilante [baθi'lante] *adj* unsteady; (*habla*) faltering; (*luz*) flickering; (*fig*) hesitant

vacilar [baθi'lar] *vi* to be unsteady; to falter; to flicker; to hesitate, waver; (*persona*) to stagger, stumble; (*memoria*) to fail; (*esp Am: divertirse*) to have a great time

vacilón [baθi'lon] *nm* (*esp Am*): **estar** *o* **ir de ~** to have a great time

vacío, -a [ba'θio, a] *adj* empty; (*puesto*) vacant; (*desocupado*) idle; (*vano*) vain; (*charla etc*) light, superficial ■ *nm* emptiness; (*Física*) vacuum; (*un vacío*) (empty) space; **hacer el ~ a algn** to send sb to Coventry

vacuna [ba'kuna] *nf* vaccine

vacunar [baku'nar] *vt* to vaccinate; **vacunarse** *vr* to get vaccinated

vacuno, -a [ba'kuno, a] *adj* bovine

vacuo, -a ['bakwo, a] *adj* empty

vadear [baðe'ar] *vt* (*río*) to ford; (*problema*) to overcome; (*persona*) to sound out

vado ['baðo] *nm* ford; (*solución*) solution; (*descanso*) respite; **"~ permanente"** "keep clear"

vagabundo, -a [baɣa'βundo, a] *adj* wandering; (*pey*) vagrant ■ *nm/f* (*errante*) wanderer; (*vago*) tramp, bum (*US*)

vagamente [baɣa'mente] *adv* vaguely

vagancia [ba'ɣanθja] *nf* vagrancy

vagar [ba'ɣar] *vi* to wander; (*pasear*) to saunter up and down; (*no hacer nada*) to idle ■ *nm* leisure

vagido [ba'xiðo] *nm* wail

vagina [ba'xina] *nf* vagina

vago, -a ['baɣo, a] *adj* vague; (*perezoso*) lazy; (*ambulante*) wandering ■ *nm/f* (*vagabundo*) tramp, bum (*US*); (*perezoso*) lazybones *sg*, idler

vagón [ba'ɣon] *nm* (*de pasajeros*) carriage; (*de mercancías*) wagon; **~ cama/restaurante** sleeping/dining car

vague *etc* ['baɣe] *vb ver* **vagar**

vaguear [baɣe'ar] *vi* to laze around

vaguedad [baɣe'ðað] *nf* vagueness

vahído [ba'iðo] *nm* dizzy spell

vaho ['bao] *nm* (*vapor*) vapour, steam; (*olor*) smell; (*respiración*) breath; **vahos** *nmpl* (*Med*) inhalation *sg*

vaina ['baina] *nf* sheath ■ *nm* (*Am*) nuisance

vainilla [bai'niʎa] *nf* vanilla

vainita [bai'nita] *nf* (*Am*) green *o* French bean

vais [bais] *vb ver* **ir**

vaivén [bai'βen] *nm* to-and-fro movement; (*de tránsito*) coming and going; **vaivenes** *nmpl* (*fig*) ups and downs

vajilla [ba'xiʎa] *nf* crockery, dishes *pl*; (*una vajilla*) service; **~ de porcelana** chinaware

val [bal], **valdré** *etc* [bal'dre] *vb ver* **valer**

vale ['bale] *nm* voucher; (*recibo*) receipt; (*pagaré*) I.O.U.; **~ de regalo** gift voucher *o* token

valedero, -a [bale'ðero, a] *adj* valid

valenciano, -a [balen'θjano, a] *adj, nm/f* Valencian ■ *nm* (*Ling*) Valencian

valentía [balen'tia] *nf* courage, bravery; (*pey*) boastfulness; (*acción*) heroic deed

valentísimo, -a [balen'tisimo, a] *adj*
superlativo de **valiente** very brave, courageous
valentón, -ona [balen'ton, ona] *adj*
blustering
valer [ba'ler] *vt* to be worth; (*Mat*) to equal;
(*costar*) to cost; (*amparar*) to aid, protect ■ *vi*
(*ser útil*) to be useful; (*ser válido*) to be valid;
valerse *vr* to defend o.s. ■ *nm* worth, value;
~ **la pena** to be worthwhile; **¿vale?** O.K.?;
¡vale! (*¡basta!*) that'll do!; **¡eso no vale!** that
doesn't count!; **no vale nada** it's no good;
(*mercancía*) it's worthless; (*argumento*) it's no
use; **no vale para nada** he's no good at all;
más vale tarde que nunca better late than
never; **más vale que nos vayamos** we'd
better go; **valerse de** to make use of, take
advantage of; **valerse por sí mismo** to help
o manage by o.s.
valga *etc* ['balɣa] *vb ver* **valer**
valía [ba'lia] *nf* worth; **de gran ~** (*objeto*) very
valuable
validar [bali'ðar] *vt* to validate; (*Pol*) to ratify
validez [bali'ðeθ] *nf* validity; **dar ~ a** to
validate
válido, -a ['baliðo, a] *adj* valid
valiente [ba'ljente] *adj* brave, valiant;
(*audaz*) bold; (*pey*) boastful; (*con ironía*) fine,
wonderful ■ *nm/f* brave man/woman
valija [ba'lixa] *nf* case; (*Am*) suitcase;
(*mochila*) satchel; (*Correos*) mailbag; ~
diplomática diplomatic bag
valioso, -a [ba'ljoso, a] *adj* valuable; (*rico*)
wealthy
valla ['baʎa] *nf* fence; (*Deporte*) hurdle; (*fig*)
barrier; ~ **publicitaria** billboard
vallar [ba'ʎar] *vt* to fence in
valle ['baʎe] *nm* valley, vale
vallisoletano, -a [baʎisole'tano, a] *adj* of o
from Valladolid ■ *nm/f* native o inhabitant
of Valladolid
valor [ba'lor] *nm* value, worth; (*precio*) price;
(*valentía*) valour, courage; (*importancia*)
importance; (*cara*) nerve, cheek (*fam*); **sin**
~ worthless; ~ **adquisitivo o de compra**
purchasing power; **dar ~ a** to attach
importance to; **quitar ~ a** to minimize the
importance of; (*Com*): ~ **según balance** book
value; ~ **comercial o de mercado** market
value; ~ **contable/desglosado** asset/break-
up value; ~ **de escasez** scarcity value; ~
intrínseco intrinsic value; ~ **a la par** par
value; ~ **neto** net worth; ~ **de rescate/de**
sustitución surrender/replacement value;
ver tb **valores**
valoración [balora'θjon] *nf* valuation
valorar [balo'rar] *vt* to value; (*tasar*) to price;
(*fig*) to assess

valores [ba'lores] *nmpl* (*Com*) securities;
~ **en cartera** o **habidos** investments
vals [bals] *nm* waltz
válvula ['balβula] *nf* valve
vamos ['bamos] *vb ver* **ir**
vampiro, -iresa [bam'piro, i'resa] *nm/f*
vampire ■ *nf* (*Cine*) vamp, femme fatale
van [ban] *vb ver* **ir**
vanagloriarse [banaɣlo'rjarse] *vr* to boast
vandalismo [banda'lismo] *nm* vandalism
vándalo, -a ['bandalo, a] *nm/f* vandal
vanguardia [ban'gwardja] *nf* vanguard; **de ~**
(*Arte*) avant-garde; **estar en** o **ir a la ~ de** (*fig*)
to be in the forefront of
vanguardista [bangwar'ðista] *adj* avant-
garde
vanidad [bani'ðað] *nf* vanity; (*inutilidad*)
futility; (*irrealidad*) unreality
vanidoso, -a [bani'ðoso, a] *adj* vain,
conceited
vano, -a ['bano, a] *adj* (*irreal*) unreal;
(*irracional*) unreasonable; (*inútil*) vain, useless;
(*persona*) vain, conceited; (*frívolo*) frivolous
vapor [ba'por] *nm* vapour; (*vaho*) steam; (*de*
gas) fumes *pl*; (*neblina*) mist; **vapores** *nmpl*
(*Med*) hysterics; **al ~** (*Culin*) steamed
vaporice *etc* [bapo'riθe] *vb ver* **vaporizar**
vaporizador [baporiθa'ðor] *nm* (*de perfume*
etc) spray
vaporizar [bapori'θar] *vt* to vaporize;
(*perfume*) to spray
vaporoso, -a [bapo'roso, a] *adj* vaporous;
(*vahoso*) steamy; (*tela*) light, airy
vapulear [bapule'ar] *vt* to thrash; (*fig*) to
slate
vaquería [bake'ria] *nf* dairy
vaquero, -a [ba'kero, a] *adj* cattle *cpd* ■ *nm*
cowboy; **vaqueros** *nmpl* jeans
vaquilla [ba'kiʎa] *nf* heifer
vara ['bara] *nf* stick, pole; (*Tec*) rod; ~ **mágica**
magic wand
varado, -a [ba'raðo, a] *adj* (*Naut*) stranded;
estar ~ to be aground
varar [ba'rar] *vt* to beach ■ *vi*, **vararse** *vr* to
be beached
varear [bare'ar] *vt* to hit, beat; (*frutas*) to
knock down (with poles)
variable [ba'rjaβle] *adj, nf* variable (*tb Inform*)
variación [barja'θjon] *nf* variation; **sin ~**
unchanged
variado, -a [ba'rjaðo, a] *adj* varied; (*dulces,*
galletas) assorted; **entremeses variados** a
selection of starters
variante [ba'rjante] *adj* variant ■ *nf*
(*alternativa*) alternative; (*Auto*) bypass
variar [ba'rjar] *vt* (*cambiar*) to change; (*poner*
variedad) to vary; (*modificar*) to modify;

(*cambiar de posición*) to switch around ■ *vi* to vary; **~ de** to differ from; **~ de opinión** to change one's mind; **para ~** just for a change

varicela [bari'θela] *nf* chicken pox

varices [ba'riθes] *nfpl* varicose veins

variedad [barje'ðað] *nf* variety

varilla [ba'riʎa] *nf* stick; (*Bot*) twig; (*Tec*) rod; (*de rueda*) spoke; **~ mágica** magic wand

vario, -a ['barjo, a] *adj* (*variado*) varied; (*multicolor*) motley; (*cambiable*) changeable; **varios** various, several

variopinto, -a [barjo'pinto, a] *adj* diverse; **un público ~** a mixed audience

varita [ba'rita] *nf*: **~ mágica** magic wand

varón [ba'ron] *nm* male, man

varonil [baro'nil] *adj* manly

Varsovia [bar'soβja] *nf* Warsaw

vas [bas] *vb ver* **ir**

vasco, -a ['basko, a], **vascongado a** [baskon'gaðo, a] *adj, nm/f* Basque ■ *nm* (*Ling*) Basque ■ *nfpl*: **las Vascongadas** the Basque Country *sg o* Provinces

vascuence [bas'kwenθe] *nm* (*Ling*) Basque

vasectomía [basekto'mia] *nf* vasectomy

vaselina [base'lina] *nf* Vaseline®

vasija [ba'sixa] *nf* (earthenware) vessel

vaso ['baso] *nm* glass, tumbler; (*Anat*) vessel; (*cantidad*) glass(ful); **~ de vino** glass of wine; **~ para vino** wineglass

vástago ['bastaɣo] *nm* (*Bot*) shoot; (*Tec*) rod; (*fig*) offspring

vasto, -a ['basto, a] *adj* vast, huge

váter ['bater] *nm* lavatory, W.C.

Vaticano [bati'kano] *nm*: **el ~** the Vatican; **la Ciudad del ~** the Vatican City

vaticinar [batiθi'nar] *vt* to prophesy, predict

vaticinio [bati'θinjo] *nm* prophecy

vatio ['batjo] *nm* (*Elec*) watt

vaya *etc* ['baja] *vb ver* **ir**

Vda. *abr* (= *viuda*) = **viudo**

Vd *abr* = **usted**

Vds *abr* = **ustedes**

ve [be] *vb ver* **ir**; **ver**

vea *etc* ['bea] *vb ver* **ver**

vecinal [beθi'nal] *adj* (*camino, impuesto etc*) local

vecindad [beθin'dað] *nf*, **vecindario** [beθin'darjo] *nm* neighbourhood; (*habitantes*) residents *pl*

vecino, -a [be'θino, a] *adj* neighbouring ■ *nm/f* neighbour; (*residente*) resident; **somos vecinos** we live next door to one another

vector [bek'tor] *nm* vector

veda ['beða] *nf* prohibition; (*temporada*) close season

vedado [be'ðaðo] *nm* preserve

vedar [be'ðar] *vt* (*prohibir*) to ban, prohibit; (*idea, plan*) to veto; (*impedir*) to stop, prevent

vedette [be'ðet] *nf* (*Teat: Cine*) star(let)

vega ['beɣa] *nf* fertile plain *o* valley

vegetación [bexeta'θjon] *nf* vegetation

vegetal [bexe'tal] *adj, nm* vegetable

vegetar [bexe'tar] *vi* to vegetate

vegetariano, -a [bexeta'rjano, a] *adj, nm/f* vegetarian

vegetativo, -a [bexeta'tiβo, a] *adj* vegetative

vehemencia [bee'menθja] *nf* (*insistencia*) vehemence; (*pasión*) passion; (*fervor*) fervour; (*violencia*) violence

vehemente [bee'mente] *adj* vehement; passionate; fervent; violent

vehículo [be'ikulo] *nm* vehicle; (*Med*) carrier; **~ de servicio público** public service vehicle; **~ espacial** spacecraft

veinte ['beinte] *num* twenty; (*orden, fecha*) twentieth; **el siglo ~** the twentieth century

veintena [bein'tena] *nf*: **una ~** (about) twenty, a score

vejación [bexa'θjon] *nf* vexation; (*humillación*) humiliation

vejamen [be'xamen] *nm* satire

vejar [be'xar] *vt* (*irritar*) to annoy, vex; (*humillar*) to humiliate

vejatorio, -a [bexa'torjo, a] *adj* humiliating, degrading

vejez [be'xeθ] *nf* old age

vejiga [be'xiɣa] *nf* (*Anat*) bladder

vela ['bela] *nf* (*de cera*) candle; (*Naut*) sail; (*insomnio*) sleeplessness; (*vigilia*) vigil; (*Mil*) sentry duty; (*fam*) snot; **a toda ~** (*Naut*) under full sail; **estar a dos velas** (*fam*) to be skint; **pasar la noche en ~** to have a sleepless night

velado, -a [be'laðo, a] *adj* veiled; (*sonido*) muffled; (*Foto*) blurred ■ *nf* soirée

velador [bela'ðor] *nm* watchman; (*candelero*) candlestick; (*Am*) bedside table

velar [be'lar] *vt* (*vigilar*) to keep watch over; (*cubrir*) to veil ■ *vi* to stay awake; **~ por** to watch over, look after

velatorio [bela'torjo] *nm* (funeral) wake

veleidad [belei'ðað] *nf* (*ligereza*) fickleness; (*capricho*) whim

velero [be'lero] *nm* (*Naut*) sailing ship; (*Aviat*) glider

veleta [be'leta] *nm/f* fickle person ■ *nf* weather vane

veliz [be'lis] *nm* (*Am*) suitcase

vello ['beʎo] *nm* down, fuzz

vellón [be'ʎon] *nm* fleece

velloso, -a [be'ʎoso, a] *adj* fuzzy

velludo, -a [be'ʎuðo, a] *adj* shaggy ■ *nm* plush, velvet

velo ['belo] *nm* veil; ~ **de paladar** (*Anat*) soft palate

velocidad [beloθi'ðað] *nf* speed; (*Tec*) rate, pace, velocity; (*Mecánica: Auto*) gear; **¿a qué ~?** how fast?; **de alta ~** high-speed; **cobrar ~** to pick up *o* gather speed; **meter la segunda ~** to change into second gear; **~ máxima de impresión** (*Inform*) maximum print speed

velocímetro [belo'θimetro] *nm* speedometer

velódromo [be'loðromo] *nm* cycle track

veloz [be'loθ] *adj* fast, swift

ven [ben] *vb ver* **venir**

vena ['bena] *nf* vein; (*fig*) vein, disposition; (*Geo*) seam, vein

venablo [be'naβlo] *nm* javelin

venado [be'naðo] *nm* deer; (*Culin*) venison

venal [be'nal] *adj* (*Anat*) venous; (*pey*) venal

venalidad [benali'ðað] *nf* venality

vencedor, a [benθe'ðor, a] *adj* victorious ■ *nm/f* victor, winner

vencer [ben'θer] *vt* (*dominar*) to defeat, beat; (*derrotar*) to vanquish; (*superar, controlar*) to overcome, master ■ *vi* (*triunfar*) to win (through), triumph; (*pago*) to fall due; (*plazo*) to expire; **dejarse ~** to yield, give in

vencido, -a [ben'θiðo, a] *adj* (*derrotado*) defeated, beaten; (*Com*) payable, due ■ *adv*: **pagar ~** to pay in arrears; **le pagan por meses vencidos** he is paid at the end of the month; **darse por ~** to give up

vencimiento [benθi'mjento] *nm* collapse; (*Com: de plazo*) expiration; **a su ~** when it falls due

venda ['benda] *nf* bandage

vendaje [ben'daxe] *nm* bandage, dressing

vendar [ben'dar] *vt* to bandage; **~ los ojos** to blindfold

vendaval [benda'βal] *nm* (*viento*) gale; (*huracán*) hurricane

vendedor, a [bende'ðor, a] *nm/f* seller; **~ ambulante** hawker, pedlar (*Brit*), peddler (*US*)

vender [ben'der] *vt* to sell; (*comerciar*) to market; (*traicionar*) to sell out, betray; **venderse** *vr* to be sold; **~ al contado/al por mayor/al por menor/a plazos** to sell for cash/wholesale/retail/on credit; **"se vende"** "for sale"; **"véndese coche"** "car for sale"; **~ al descubierto** to sell short

vendimia [ben'dimja] *nf* grape harvest; **la ~ de 1973** the 1973 vintage

vendimiar [bendi'mjar] *vi* to pick grapes

vendré *etc* [ben'dre] *vb ver* **venir**

Venecia [be'neθja] *nf* Venice

veneciano, -a [bene'θjano, a] *adj, nm/f* Venetian

veneno [be'neno] *nm* poison, venom

venenoso, -a [bene'noso, a] *adj* poisonous

venerable [bene'raβle] *adj* venerable

veneración [benera'θjon] *nf* veneration

venerar [bene'rar] *vt* (*reconocer*) to venerate; (*adorar*) to worship

venéreo, -a [be'nereo, a] *adj* venereal

venezolano, -a [beneθo'lano, a] *adj, nm/f* Venezuelan

Venezuela [bene'θwela] *nf* Venezuela

venga *etc* ['benga] *vb ver* **venir**

vengador, a [benga'ðor, a] *adj* avenging ■ *nm/f* avenger

venganza [ben'ganθa] *nf* vengeance, revenge

vengar [ben'gar] *vt* to avenge; **vengarse** *vr* to take revenge

vengativo, -a [benga'tiβo, a] *adj* (*persona*) vindictive

vengue *etc* ['benge] *vb ver* **vengar**

venia ['benja] *nf* (*perdón*) pardon; (*permiso*) consent; **con su ~** by your leave

venial [be'njal] *adj* venial

venida [be'niða] *nf* (*llegada*) arrival; (*regreso*) return; (*fig*) rashness

venidero, -a [beni'ðero, a] *adj* coming, future; **en lo ~** in (the) future

venir [be'nir] *vi* to come; (*llegar*) to arrive; (*ocurrir*) to happen; **venirse** *vr*: **venirse abajo** to collapse; **~ a menos** (*persona*) to lose status; (*empresa*) to go downhill; **~ bien** to be suitable, come just right; (*ropa, gusto*) to suit; **~ mal** to be unsuitable *o* inconvenient, come awkwardly; **el año que viene** next year; **¡ven acá!** come (over) here!; **¡venga!** (*fam*) come on!

venta ['benta] *nf* (*Com*) sale; (*posada*) inn; **~ a plazos** hire purchase; **~ al contado/al por mayor/al por menor** *o* **al detalle** cash sale/wholesale/retail; **~ a domicilio** door-to-door selling; **~ y arrendamiento al vendedor** sale and lease back; **~ de liquidación** clearance sale; **estar de** *o* **en ~** to be (up) for sale *o* on the market; **ventas brutas** gross sales; **ventas a término** forward sales

ventaja [ben'taxa] *nf* advantage; **llevar la ~** (*en carrera*) to be leading *o* ahead

ventajoso, -a [benta'xoso, a] *adj* advantageous

ventana [ben'tana] *nf* window; **~ de guillotina/galería** sash/bay window; **~ de la nariz** nostril

ventanilla [benta'niʎa] *nf* (*de taquilla, tb Inform*) window

ventearse [bente'arse] *vr* (*romperse*) to crack; (*Anat*) to break wind

ventilación [bentila'θjon] *nf* ventilation; (*corriente*) draught; (*fig*) airing

ventilador [bentila'ðor] *nm* ventilator; (*eléctrico*) fan

ventilar [benti'lar] *vt* to ventilate; (*poner a secar*) to put out to dry; (*fig*) to air, discuss

ventisca [ben'tiska] *nf* blizzard

ventisquero [bentis'kero] *nm* snowdrift

ventolera [bento'lera] *nf* (*ráfaga*) gust of wind; (*idea*) whim, wild idea; **le dio la ~ de comprarlo** he had a sudden notion to buy it

ventosear [bentose'ar] *vi* to break wind

ventosidad [bentosi'ðað] *nf* flatulence

ventoso, -a [ben'toso, a] *adj* windy ∎ *nf* (*Zool*) sucker; (*instrumento*) suction pad

ventrículo [ben'trikulo] *nm* ventricle

ventrílocuo, -a [ben'trilokwo, a] *nm/f* ventriloquist

ventriloquia [bentri'lokja] *nf* ventriloquism

ventura [ben'tura] *nf* (*felicidad*) happiness; (*buena suerte*) luck; (*destino*) fortune; **a la (buena) ~** at random

venturoso, -a [bentu'roso, a] *adj* happy; (*afortunado*) lucky, fortunate

venza *etc* ['benθa] *vb ver* **vencer**

ver [ber] *vt, vi* to see; (*mirar*) to look at, watch; (*investigar*) to look into; (*entender*) to see, understand; **verse** *vr* (*encontrarse*) to meet; (*dejarse ver*) to be seen; (*hallarse: en un apuro*) to find o.s., be ∎ *nm* looks *pl*, appearance; **a ~** let's see; **a ~ si ...** I wonder if ...; **por lo que veo** apparently; **dejarse ~** to become apparent; **no tener nada que ~ con** to have nothing to do with; **a mi modo de ~** as I see it; **merece verse** it's worth seeing; **no lo veo** I can't see it; **¡nos vemos!** see you (later)!; **¡habráse visto!** did you ever! (*fam*); **¡viera(n) o hubiera(n) visto qué casa!** (*Am fam*) if only you'd seen the house!, what a house!; **ya se ve que ...** it is obvious that ...; **si te vi no me acuerdo** they *etc* just don't want to know

vera ['bera] *nf* edge, verge; (*de río*) bank; **a la ~ de** near, next to

veracidad [beraθi'ðað] *nf* truthfulness

veraneante [berane'ante] *nm/f* holidaymaker, (summer) vacationer (US)

veranear [berane'ar] *vi* to spend the summer

veraneo [bera'neo] *nm*: **estar de ~** to be away on (one's summer) holiday; **lugar de ~** holiday resort

veraniego, -a [bera'njeɣo, a] *adj* summer *cpd*

verano [be'rano] *nm* summer

veras ['beras] *nfpl* truth *sg*; **de ~** really, truly; **esto va de ~** this is serious

veraz [be'raθ] *adj* truthful

verbal [ber'βal] *adj* verbal; (*mensaje etc*) oral

verbena [ber'βena] *nf* street party

verbigracia [berβi'ɣraθja] *adv* for example

verbo ['berβo] *nm* verb

verborrea [berβo'rrea] *nf* verbosity, verbal diarrhoea

verboso, -a [ber'βoso, a] *adj* verbose

verdad [ber'ðað] *nf* (*lo verídico*) truth; (*fiabilidad*) reliability ∎ *adv* really; **¿~?, ¿no es ~?** isn't it?, aren't you?, don't you? *etc*; **de ~** *adj* real, proper; **a decir ~, no quiero** to tell (you) the truth, I don't want to; **la pura ~** the plain truth

verdaderamente [berðaðera'mente] *adv* really, indeed, truly

verdadero, -a [berða'ðero, a] *adj* (*veraz*) true, truthful; (*fiable*) reliable; (*fig*) real

verde ['berðe] *adj* green; (*fruta etc*) green, unripe; (*chiste etc*) blue, smutty, dirty ∎ *nm* green; **viejo ~** dirty old man; **poner ~ a algn** to give sb a dressing-down

verdear [berðe'ar], **verdecer** [berðe'θer] *vi* to turn green

verdezca *etc* [ber'ðeθka] *vb ver* **verdecer**

verdor [ber'ðor] *nm* (*lo verde*) greenness; (*Bot*) verdure; (*fig*) youthful vigour

verdugo [ber'ðuɣo] *nm* executioner; (*Bot*) shoot; (*cardenal*) weal

verdulero, -a [berðu'lero, a] *nm/f* greengrocer

verdura [ber'ðura] *nf* greenness; **verduras** *nfpl* (*Culin*) greens

vereda [be'reða] *nf* path; (*Am*) pavement, sidewalk (US); **meter a algn en ~** to bring sb into line

veredicto [bere'ðikto] *nm* verdict

vergel [ber'xel] *nm* lush garden

vergonzoso, -a [berɣon'θoso, a] *adj* shameful; (*tímido*) timid, bashful

vergüenza [ber'ɣwenθa] *nf* shame, sense of shame; (*timidez*) bashfulness; (*pudor*) modesty; **tener ~** to be ashamed; **me da ~ decírselo** I feel too shy o it embarrasses me to tell him; **¡qué ~!** (*de situación*) what a disgrace!; (*a persona*) shame on you!

vericueto [beri'kweto] *nm* rough track

verídico, -a [be'riðiko, a] *adj* true, truthful

verificar [berifi'kar] *vt* to check; (*corroborar*) to verify (*tb Inform*); (*testamento*) to prove; (*llevar a cabo*) to carry out; **verificarse** *vr* to occur, happen; (*mitin etc*) to be held; (*profecía etc*) to come o prove true

verifique *etc* [beri'fike] *vb ver* **verificar**

verja ['berxa] *nf* iron gate; (*cerca*) railing(s) (*pl*); (*rejado*) grating

vermut [ber'mu] (*pl* **vermuts**) *nm* vermouth ∎ *nf* (*esp Am*) matinée

verosímil [bero'simil] *adj* likely, probable; (*relato*) credible

verosimilitud [berosimili'tuð] *nf* likeliness, probability

verruga [be'rruɣa] *nf* wart

versado, -a [ber'saðo, a] *adj*: ~ **en** versed in

Versalles [ber'saʎes] *nm* Versailles

versar [ber'sar] *vi* to go round, turn; ~ **sobre** to deal with, be about

versátil [ber'satil] *adj* versatile

versículo [ber'sikulo] *nm* (Rel) verse

versión [ber'sjon] *nf* version; (*traducción*) translation

verso ['berso] *nm* verse; **un** ~ a line of poetry; ~ **libre/suelto** free/blank verse

vértebra ['berteβra] *nf* vertebra

vertebrado, -a [berte'βraðo, a] *adj, nm/f* vertebrate

vertebral [berte'βral] *adj* vertebral; **columna** ~ spine

vertedero [berte'ðero] *nm* rubbish dump, tip

verter [ber'ter] *vt* (*vaciar*) to empty, pour (out); (*tirar*) to dump ◼ *vi* to flow

vertical [berti'kal] *adj* vertical; (*postura, piano etc*) upright ◼ *nf* vertical

vértice ['bertiθe] *nm* vertex, apex

vertiente [ber'tjente] *nf* slope

vertiginoso, -a [bertixi'noso, a] *adj* giddy, dizzy

vértigo ['bertiɣo] *nm* vertigo; (*mareo*) dizziness; (*actividad*) intense activity; **de** ~ (*fam: velocidad*) giddy; (: *ruido*) tremendous; (: *talento*) fantastic

vesícula [be'sikula] *nf* blister; ~ **biliar** gall bladder

vespa® ['bespa] *nf* (motor) scooter

vespertino, -a [besper'tino, a] *adj* evening *cpd*

vespino® [bes'pino] *nm o f* ≈ moped

vestíbulo [bes'tiβulo] *nm* hall; (*de teatro*) foyer

vestido [bes'tiðo] *nm* (*ropa*) clothes *pl*, clothing; (*de mujer*) dress, frock

vestigio [bes'tixjo] *nm* (*trazo*) trace; (*señal*) sign; **vestigios** *nmpl* remains

vestimenta [besti'menta] *nf* clothing

vestir [bes'tir] *vt* (*poner: ropa*) to put on; (*llevar: ropa*) to wear; (*cubrir*) to clothe, cover; (*pagar: la ropa*) to clothe, pay for the clothing of; (*sastre*) to make clothes for ◼ *vi* (*ponerse: ropa*) to dress; (*verse bien*) to look good; **vestirse** *vr* to get dressed, dress o.s.; **traje de** ~ (*formal*) formal suit; **estar vestido de** to be dressed *o* clad in; (*como disfraz*) to be dressed as

vestuario [bes'twarjo] *nm* clothes *pl*, wardrobe; (*Teat: para actores*) dressing room; (: *para público*) cloakroom; (*Deporte*) changing room

Vesubio [be'suβjo] *nm* Vesuvius

veta ['beta] *nf* (*vena*) vein, seam; (*raya*) streak; (*de madera*) grain

vetar [be'tar] *vt* to veto

veterano, -a [bete'rano, a] *adj, nm/f* veteran

veterinario, -a [beteri'narjo, a] *nm/f* vet(erinary surgeon) ◼ *nf* veterinary science

veto ['beto] *nm* veto

vetusto, -a [be'tusto, a] *adj* ancient

vez [beθ] *nf* time; (*turno*) turn; **a la** ~ **que** at the same time as; **a su** ~ in its turn; **cada** ~ **más/menos** more and more/less and less; **una** ~ once; **dos veces** twice; **de una** ~ in one go; **de una** ~ **para siempre** once and for all; **en** ~ **de** instead of; **a veces** sometimes; **otra** ~ again; **una y otra** ~ repeatedly; **muchas veces** (*con frecuencia*) often; **pocas veces** seldom; **de** ~ **en cuando** from time to time; **7 veces 9** 7 times 9; **hacer las veces de** to stand in for; **tal** ~ perhaps; **¿lo viste alguna** ~? did you ever see it?; **¿cuántas veces?** how often?; **érase una** ~ once upon a time (there was)

v. g., v. gr. *abr* (= *verbigracia*) viz

VHF *sigla f* (= *Very High Frequency*) VHF

vía ['bia] *nf* (*calle*) road; (*ruta*) track, route; (*Ferro*) line; (*fig*) way; (*Anat*) passage, tube ◼ *prep* via, by way of; **por** ~ **bucal** orally; **por** ~ **judicial** by legal means; **por** ~ **oficial** through official channels; **por** ~ **de** by way of; **en vías de** in the process of; **un país en vías de desarrollo** a developing country; ~ **aérea** airway; **V~ Láctea** Milky Way; ~ **pública** public highway *o* thoroughfare; ~ **única** one-way street; **el tren está en la** ~ **8** the train is (standing) at platform 8

viable ['bjaβle] *adj* (Com) viable; (*plan etc*) feasible

viaducto [bja'ðukto] *nm* viaduct

viajante [bja'xante] *nm* commercial traveller, traveling salesman (US)

viajar [bja'xar] *vi* to travel, journey

viaje ['bjaxe] *nm* journey; (*gira*) tour; (*Naut*) voyage; (*Com: carga*) load; **los viajes** travel *sg*; **estar de** ~ to be on a journey; ~ **de ida y vuelta** round trip; ~ **de novios** honeymoon

viajero, -a [bja'xero, a] *adj* travelling (Brit), traveling (US); (*Zool*) migratory ◼ *nm/f* (*quien viaja*) traveller; (*pasajero*) passenger

vial [bjal] *adj* road *cpd*, traffic *cpd*

vianda ['bjanda] *nf* (*tb*: **viandas**) food

viáticos ['bjatikos] *nmpl* (Com) travelling (Brit) *o* traveling (US) expenses

víbora ['biβora] *nf* viper

vibración [biβra'θjon] *nf* vibration

vibrador [biβra'ðor] *nm* vibrator

vibrante [bi'βrante] *adj* vibrant, vibrating

vibrar [bi'βrar] *vt* to vibrate ◼ *vi* to vibrate;

(*pulsar*) to throb, beat, pulsate

vicario [bi'karjo] *nm* curate

vicecónsul [biθe'konsul] *nm* vice-consul

vicegerente [biθexe'rente] *nm/f* assistant manager

vicepresidente [biθepresi'ðente] *nm/f* vice president; (*de comité etc*) vice-chairman

viceversa [biθe'βersa] *adv* vice versa

viciado, -a [bi'θjaðo, a] *adj* (*corrompido*) corrupt; (*contaminado*) foul, contaminated

viciar [bi'θjar] *vt* (*pervertir*) to pervert; (*adulterar*) to adulterate; (*falsificar*) to falsify; (Jur) to nullify; (*estropear*) to spoil; (*sentido*) to twist; **viciarse** *vr* to become corrupted; (*aire, agua*) to be(come) polluted

vicio ['biθjo] *nm* (*libertinaje*) vice; (*mala costumbre*) bad habit; (*mimo*) spoiling; (*alabeo*) warp, warping; **de** *o* **por ~** out of sheer habit

vicioso, -a [bi'θjoso, a] *adj* (*muy malo*) vicious; (*corrompido*) depraved; (*mimado*) spoiled ■ *nm/f* depraved person; (*adicto*) addict

vicisitud [biθisi'tuð] *nf* vicissitude

víctima ['biktima] *nf* victim; (*de accidente etc*) casualty

victimario [bikti'marjo] *nm* (*Am*) killer, murderer

victoria [bik'torja] *nf* victory

victorioso, -a [bikto'rjoso, a] *adj* victorious

vicuña [bi'kuɲa] *nf* vicuna

vid [bið] *nf* vine

vida ['biða] *nf* life; (*duración*) lifetime; (*modo de vivir*) way of life; **¡~!, ¡~ mía!** (*saludo cariñoso*) my love!; **de por ~** for life; **de ~ airada** *o* **libre** loose-living; **en la/mi ~** never; **estar con ~** to be still alive; **ganarse la ~** to earn one's living; **¡esto es ~!** this is the life!; **le va la ~ en esto** his life depends on it

vidente [bi'ðente] *nm/f* (*adivino*) clairvoyant; (*no ciego*) sighted person

vídeo ['biðeo] *nm* video; (*aparato*) video (recorder); **cinta de ~** videotape; **película de ~** videofilm; **grabar en ~** to record, (video)tape; **~ compuesto/inverso** (*Inform*) composite/reverse video

videocámara [biðeo'kamara] *nf* video camera; (*pequeña*) camcorder

videocassette [biðeoka'set] *nm* video cassette

videoclip [biðeo'klip] *nm* (music) video

videoclub [biðeo'klub] *nm* video club; (*tienda*) video shop

videodatos [biðeo'ðatos] *nmpl* (*Com*) viewdata

videojuego [biðeo'xweɣo] *nm* video game

videojugador, -a [biðeoxuɣa'ðor, a] *m/f* gamer

videotex [biðeo'teks], **videotexto** [biðeo'tekso] *nm* Videotex®

vidriero, -a [bi'ðrjero, a] *nm/f* glazier ■ *nf* (*ventana*) stained-glass window; (*Am: de tienda*) shop window; (*puerta*) glass door

vidrio ['biðrjo] *nm* glass; (*Am*) window; **~ cilindrado/inastillable** plate/splinter-proof glass

vidrioso, -a [bi'ðrjoso, a] *adj* glassy; (*frágil*) fragile, brittle; (*resbaladizo*) slippery

viejo, -a ['bjexo, a] *adj* old ■ *nm/f* old man/woman; **mi ~/vieja** (*fam*) my old man/woman; **hacerse** *o* **ponerse ~** to grow *o* get old

Viena ['bjena] *nf* Vienna

viene *etc* ['bjene] *vb ver* **venir**

viento ['bjento] *nm* wind; **contra ~ y marea** at all costs; **ir ~ en popa** to go splendidly; (*negocio*) to prosper

vientre ['bjentre] *nm* belly; (*matriz*) womb; **vientres** *nmpl* bowels; **hacer de ~** to have a movement of the bowels

vier. *abr* (= *viernes*) Fri.

viernes ['bjernes] *nm inv* Friday; **V~ Santo** Good Friday; *ver tb* **Semana Santa; sábado**

vierta *etc* ['bjerta] *vb ver* **verter**

Vietnam [bjet'nam] *nm*: **el ~** Vietnam

vietnamita [bjetna'mita] *adj, nm/f* Vietnamese

viga ['biɣa] *nf* beam, rafter; (*de metal*) girder

vigencia [bi'xenθja] *nf* validity; (*de contrato etc*) term, life; **estar/entrar en ~** to be in/come into effect *o* force

vigente [bi'xente] *adj* valid, in force; (*imperante*) prevailing

vigésimo, -a [bi'xesimo, a] *num* twentieth

vigía [bi'xia] *nm* look-out ■ *nf* (*atalaya*) watchtower; (*acción*) watching

vigilancia [bixi'lanθja] *nf* vigilance

vigilante [bixi'lante] *adj* vigilant ■ *nm* caretaker; (*en cárcel*) warder; (*en almacén*) shopwalker (*Brit*), floor-walker (*US*); **~ jurado** security guard (*licensed to carry a gun*); **~ nocturno** night watchman

vigilar [bixi'lar] *vt* to watch over; (*cuidar*) to look after, keep an eye on ■ *vi* to be vigilant; (*hacer guardia*) to keep watch

vigilia [vi'xilja] *nf* wakefulness; (*Rel*) fast; **comer de ~** to fast

vigor [bi'ɣor] *nm* vigour, vitality; **en ~** in force; **entrar/poner en ~** to take/put into effect

vigoroso, -a [biɣo'roso, a] *adj* vigorous

VIH *nm abr* (= *virus de inmunodeficiencia humana*) HIV

vil [bil] *adj* vile, low

vileza [bi'leθa] *nf* vileness; (*acto*) base deed

vilipendiar [bilipen'djar] *vt* to vilify, revile

villa ['biʎa] *nf* (*pueblo*) small town;

(*municipalidad*) municipality; **la V~** (*Esp*) Madrid; **~ miseria** shanty town

villancico [biʎan'θiko] *nm* (Christmas) carol

villorrio [bi'ʎorrjo] *nm* one-horse town, dump; (*Am: barrio pobre*) shanty town

vilo ['bilo]: **en ~** *adv* in the air, suspended; (*fig*) on tenterhooks, in suspense; **estar** *o* **quedar en ~** to be left in suspense

vinagre [bi'naɣre] *nm* vinegar

vinagrera [bina'ɣrera] *nf* vinegar bottle; **vinagreras** *nfpl* cruet stand *sg*

vinagreta [bina'ɣreta] *nf* French dressing

vinatería [binate'ria] *nf* wine shop

vinatero, -a [bina'tero, a] *adj* wine *cpd* ■ *nm* wine merchant

vinculación [binkula'θjon] *nf* (*lazo*) link, bond; (*acción*) linking

vincular [binku'lar] *vt* to link, bind

vínculo ['binkulo] *nm* link, bond

vindicar [bindi'kar] *vt* to vindicate; (*vengar*) to avenge; (*Jur*) to claim

vinícola [bi'nikola] *adj* (*industria*) wine *cpd*; (*región*) wine-growing *cpd*

vinicultor, -a [binikul'tor, a] *nm/f* wine grower

vinicultura [binikul'tura] *nf* wine growing

vino *etc* ['bino] *vb ver* **venir** ■ *nm* wine; **~ de solera/seco/tinto** vintage/dry/red wine; **~ de Jerez** sherry; **~ de Oporto** port (wine)

viña ['biɲa] *nf*, **viñedo** [bi'ɲeðo] *nm* vineyard

viñeta [bi'ɲeta] *nf* (*en historieta*) cartoon

viola ['bjola] *nf* viola

violación [bjola'θjon] *nf* violation; (*Jur*) offence, infringement; (*estupro*): **~ (sexual)** rape; **~ de contrato** (*Com*) breach of contract

violar [bjo'lar] *vt* to violate; (*Jur*) to infringe; (*cometer estupro*) to rape

violencia [bjo'lenθja] *nf* (*fuerza*) violence, force; (*embarazo*) embarrassment; (*acto injusto*) unjust act

violentar [bjolen'tar] *vt* to force; (*casa*) to break into; (*agredir*) to assault; (*violar*) to violate

violento, -a [bjo'lento, a] *adj* violent; (*furioso*) furious; (*situación*) embarrassing; (*acto*) forced, unnatural; (*difícil*) awkward; **me es muy ~** it goes against the grain with me

violeta [bjo'leta] *nf* violet

violín [bjo'lin] *nm* violin

violón [bjo'lon] *nm* double bass

violoncelo [bjolon'θelo] *nm* cello

V.I.P. ['bip] *sigla m* (= *Very Important Person*) VIP

virador [bira'ðor] *nm* (*para fotocopiadora*) toner

viraje [bi'raxe] *nm* turn; (*de vehículo*) swerve; (*de carretera*) bend; (*fig*) change of direction

virar [bi'rar] *vi* to turn; to swerve; to change direction

virgen ['birxen] *adj* virgin; (*cinta*) blank

■ *nm/f* virgin; **la Santísima V~** (*Rel*) the Blessed Virgin

virginidad [birxini'ðað] *nf* virginity

Virgo ['birɣo] *nm* Virgo

viril [bi'ril] *adj* virile

virilidad [birili'ðað] *nf* virility

virrey [bi'rrei] *nm* viceroy

virtual [bir'twal] *adj* (*real*) virtual; (*en potencia*) potential

virtud [bir'tuð] *nf* virtue; **en ~ de** by virtue of

virtuoso, -a [bir'twoso, a] *adj* virtuous ■ *nm/f* virtuoso

viruela [bi'rwela] *nf* smallpox; **viruelas** *nfpl* pockmarks; **viruelas locas** chickenpox *sg*

virulento, -a [biru'lento, a] *adj* virulent

virus ['birus] *nm inv* virus

viruta [bi'ruta] *nf* wood *o* metal shaving

vis [bis] *nf*: **~ cómica** sense of humour

visa ['bisa] *nf* (*Am*), **visado** [bi'saðo] *nm* visa; **~ de permanencia** residence permit

visar [bi'sar] *vt* (*pasaporte*) to visa; (*documento*) to endorse

visceral [bisθe'ral] *adj* (*odio*) deep-rooted; **reacción ~** gut reaction

viscoso, -a [bis'koso, a] *adj* viscous

visera [bi'sera] *nf* visor

visibilidad [bisiβili'ðað] *nf* visibility

visible [bi'siβle] *adj* visible; (*fig*) obvious; **exportaciones/importaciones visibles** (*Com*) visible exports/imports

visillo [bi'siʎo] *nm* lace curtain

visión [bi'sjon] *nf* (*Anat*) vision, (eye)sight; (*fantasía*) vision, fantasy; (*panorama*) view; **ver visiones** to see *o* be seeing things

visionario, -a [bisjo'narjo, a] *adj* (*que prevé*) visionary; (*alucinado*) deluded ■ *nm/f* visionary; (*chalado*) lunatic

visita [bi'sita] *nf* call, visit; (*persona*) visitor; **horas/tarjeta de ~** visiting hours/card; **~ de cortesía/de cumplido/de despedida** courtesy/formal/farewell visit; **hacer una ~** to pay a visit; **ir de ~** to go visiting

visitante [bisi'tante] *adj* visiting ■ *nmf* visitor

visitar [bisi'tar] *vt* to visit, call on; (*inspeccionar*) to inspect

vislumbrar [bislum'brar] *vt* to glimpse, catch a glimpse of

vislumbre [bis'lumbre] *nf* glimpse; (*centelleo*) gleam; (*idea vaga*) glimmer

viso ['biso] *nm* (*de metal*) glint, gleam; (*de tela*) sheen; (*aspecto*) appearance; **hay un ~ de verdad en esto** there is an element of truth in this

visón [bi'son] *nm* mink

visor [bi'sor] *nm* (*Foto*) viewfinder

víspera ['bispera] *nf* eve, day before; **la ~** *o* **en**

vísperas de on the eve of
vista ['bista] *nf* sight, vision; (*capacidad de ver*) (eye)sight; (*mirada*) look(s) (*pl*); (*Foto etc*) view; (*Jur*) hearing ■ *nm* customs officer; **a primera ~** at first glance; **~ general** overview; **fijar** *o* **clavar la ~ en** to stare at; **hacer la ~ gorda** to turn a blind eye; **volver la ~** to look back; **está a la ~ que** it's obvious that; **a la ~** (*Com*) at sight; **en ~ de** in view of; **en ~ de que** in view of the fact that; **¡hasta la ~!** so long!, see you!; **con vistas a** with a view to; *ver tb* **visto, a**
vistazo [bis'taθo] *nm* glance; **dar** *o* **echar un ~ a** to glance at
visto, -a *etc* ['bisto, a] *vb ver* **vestir** ■ *pp de* **ver** ■ *adj* seen; (*considerado*) considered ■ *nm*: **~ bueno** approval; **"~ bueno"** "approved"; **por lo ~** evidently; **dar el ~ bueno a algo** to give sth the go-ahead; **está ~ que** it's clear that; **está bien/mal ~** it's acceptable/unacceptable; **está muy ~** it is very common; **estaba ~** it had to be; **~ que** *conj* since, considering that
vistoso, -a [bis'toso, a] *adj* colourful; (*alegre*) gay; (*pey*) gaudy
visual [bi'swal] *adj* visual
visualice *etc* [biswa'liθe] *vb ver* **visualizar**
visualizador [biswaliθa'ðor] *nm* (*Inform*) display screen, VDU
visualizar [biswali'θar] *vt* (*imaginarse*) to visualize; (*Inform*) to display
vital [bi'tal] *adj* life *cpd*, living *cpd*; (*fig*) vital; (*persona*) lively, vivacious
vitalicio, -a [bita'liθjo, a] *adj* for life
vitalidad [bitali'ðað] *nf* vitality
vitamina [bita'mina] *nf* vitamin
vitaminado, -a [bitami'naðo, a] *adj* with added vitamins
vitamínico, -a [bita'miniko, a] *adj* vitamin *cpd*; **complejos vitamínicos** vitamin compounds
viticultor, a [bitikul'tor, a] *nm/f* vine grower
viticultura [bitikul'tura] *nf* vine growing
vitorear [bitore'ar] *vt* to cheer, acclaim
vítores ['bitores] *nmpl* cheers
vitoriano, -a [bito'rjano, a] *adj* of *o* from Vitoria ■ *nm/f* native *o* inhabitant of Vitoria
vítreo, -a ['bitreo, a] *adj* vitreous
vitrina [bi'trina] *nf* glass case; (*en casa*) display cabinet; (*Am*) shop window
vituperar [bitupe'rar] *vt* to condemn
vituperio [bitu'perjo] *nm* (*condena*) condemnation; (*censura*) censure; (*insulto*) insult
viudez [bju'ðeθ] *nf* widowhood
viudo, -a ['bjuðo, a] *adj* widowed ■ *nm* widower ■ *nf* widow

viva ['biβa] *excl* hurrah! ■ *nm* cheer; **¡~ el rey!** long live the King!
vivacidad [biβaθi'ðað] *nf* (*vigor*) vigour; (*vida*) vivacity
vivamente [biβa'mente] *adv* in lively fashion; (*describir*) vividly; (*protestar*) sharply; (*emocionarse*) acutely
vivaracho, -a [biβa'ratʃo, a] *adj* jaunty, lively; (*ojos*) bright, twinkling
vivaz [bi'βaθ] *adj* (*que dura*) enduring; (*vigoroso*) vigorous; (*vivo*) lively
vivencia [bi'βenθja] *nf* experience
víveres ['biβeres] *nmpl* provisions
vivero [bi'βero] *nm* (*Horticultura*) nursery; (*para peces*) fishpond; (: *Com*) fish farm
viveza [bi'βeθa] *nf* liveliness; (*agudeza*) sharpness
vividor, a [biβi'ðor, a] *adj* (*pey*) opportunistic ■ *nm* (*aprovechado*) hustler
vivienda [bi'βjenda] *nf* (*alojamiento*) housing; (*morada*) dwelling; **viviendas protegidas** *o* **sociales** council housing *sg* (*Brit*), public housing *sg* (*US*)
viviente [bi'βjente] *adj* living
vivificar [biβifi'kar] *vt* to give life to
vivifique *etc* [biβi'fike] *vb ver* **vivificar**
vivir [bi'βir] *vt* (*experimentar*) to live *o* go through ■ *vi* (*gen*, *Com*): **~ (de)** to live (by, off, on) ■ *nm* life, living; **¡viva!** hurray!; **¡viva el rey!** long live the king!
vivo, -a ['biβo, a] *adj* living, live, alive; (*fig*) vivid; (*movimiento*) quick; (*color*) bright; (*protesta etc*) strong; (*astuto*) smart, clever; **en ~** (*TV etc*) live; **llegar a lo ~** to cut to the quick
vizcaíno, -a [biθka'ino, a] *adj*, *nm/f* Biscayan
Vizcaya [biθ'kaja] *nf* Biscay; **el Golfo de ~** the Bay of Biscay
V.M. *abr* = **Vuestra Majestad**
V.O. *abr* = **versión original**
V.°B.° *abr* = **visto bueno**
vocablo [bo'kaβlo] *nm* (*palabra*) word; (*término*) term
vocabulario [bokaβu'larjo] *nm* vocabulary, word list
vocación [boka'θjon] *nf* vocation
vocacional [bokasjo'nal] *nf* (*Am*) ≈ technical college
vocal [bo'kal] *adj* vocal ■ *nm/f* member (of a committee *etc*) ■ *nm* non-executive director ■ *nf* vowel
vocalice *etc* [boka'liθe] *vb ver* **vocalizar**
vocalizar [bokali'θar] *vt* to vocalize
voceador [bosea'ðor] *nm* (*Am*): **~ de periódicos** newspaper vendor *o* seller
vocear [boθe'ar] *vt* (*para vender*) to cry; (*aclamar*) to acclaim; (*fig*) to proclaim ■ *vi* to yell

vocerío [boθe'rio] *nm* shouting; (*escándalo*) hullabaloo

vocero, -a [bo'sero, a] *nm/f* (*Am*) spokesman/woman

vociferar [boθife'rar] *vt* to shout; (*jactarse*) to proclaim boastfully ▪ *vi* to yell

vocinglero, -a [boθin'glero, a] *adj* vociferous; (*gárrulo*) garrulous; (*fig*) blatant

vodevil [boðe'βil] *nm* music hall, variety, vaudeville (*US*)

vodka ['boðka] *nm* vodka

vodú [bo'ðu] *nm* voodoo

vol *abr* = **volumen**

volado, -a [bo'laðo, a] *adj*: **estar ~** (*fam: inquieto*) to be worried; (: *loco*) to be crazy

volador, a [bola'ðor, a] *adj* flying

voladura [bola'ðura] *nf* blowing up, demolition; (*Minería*) blasting

volandas [bo'landas]: **en ~** *adv* in o through the air; (*fig*) swiftly

volante [bo'lante] *adj* flying ▪ *nm* (*de máquina, coche*) steering wheel; (*de reloj*) balance; (*nota*) note; **ir al ~** to be at the wheel, be driving

volar [bo'lar] *vt* (*demoler*) to blow up, demolish ▪ *vi* to fly; (*fig: correr*) to rush, hurry; (*fam: desaparecer*) to disappear; **voy volando** I must dash; **¡cómo vuela el tiempo!** how time flies!

volátil [bo'latil] *adj* volatile; (*fig*) changeable

volcán [bol'kan] *nm* volcano

volcánico, -a [bol'kaniko, a] *adj* volcanic

volcar [bol'kar] *vt* to upset, overturn; (*tumbar, derribar*) to knock over; (*vaciar*) to empty out ▪ *vi* to overturn; **volcarse** *vr* to tip over; (*barco*) to capsize

voleibol [bolei'βol] *nm* volleyball

voleo [bo'leo] *nm* volley; **a(l) ~** haphazardly; **de un ~** quickly

Volga ['bolɣa] *nm* Volga

volición [boli'θjon] *nf* volition

volqué [bol'ke], **volquemos** *etc* [bol'kemos] *vb ver* **volcar**

volquete [bol'kete] *nm* dumper, dump truck (*US*)

voltaje [bol'taxe] *nm* voltage

voltear [bolte'ar] *vt* to turn over; (*volcar*) to knock over; (*doblar*) to peal ▪ *vi* to roll over; **voltearse** *vr* (*Am*) to turn round; **~ a hacer algo** (*Am*) to do sth again

voltereta [bolte'reta] *nf* somersault; **~ sobre las manos** handspring; **~ lateral** cartwheel

voltio ['boltjo] *nm* volt

voluble [bo'luβle] *adj* fickle

volumen [bo'lumen] *nm* volume; **~ monetario** money supply; **~ de negocios** turnover; **bajar el ~** to turn down the volume; **poner la radio a todo ~** to turn the radio up full

voluminoso, -a [bolumi'noso, a] *adj* voluminous; (*enorme*) massive

voluntad [bolun'taŏ] *nf* will, willpower; (*deseo*) desire, wish; (*afecto*) fondness; **a ~** at will; (*cantidad*) as much as one likes; **buena ~** goodwill; **mala ~** ill will, malice; **por causas ajenas a mi ~** for reasons beyond my control

voluntario, -a [bolun'tarjo, a] *adj* voluntary ▪ *nm/f* volunteer

voluntarioso, -a [bolunta'rjoso, a] *adj* headstrong

voluptuoso, -a [bolup'twoso, a] *adj* voluptuous

volver [bol'βer] *vt* to turn; (*boca abajo*) to turn (over); (*voltear*) to turn round, turn upside down; (*poner del revés*) to turn inside out; (*devolver*) to return; (*transformar*) to change, transform; (*manga*) to roll up ▪ *vi* to return, go/come back; **volverse** *vr* to turn round; (*llegar a ser*) to become; **~ la espalda** to turn one's back; **~ bien por mal** to return good for evil; **~ a hacer** to do again; **~ en sí** to come to o round, regain consciousness; **~ la vista atrás** to look back; **~ loco a algn** to drive sb mad; **volverse loco** to go mad

vomitar [bomi'tar] *vt, vi* to vomit

vómito ['bomito] *nm* (*acto*) vomiting; (*resultado*) vomit

voracidad [boraθi'ðað] *nf* voracity

vorágine [bo'raxine] *nf* whirlpool; (*fig*) maelstrom

voraz [bo'raθ] *adj* voracious; (*fig*) fierce

vórtice ['bortiθe] *nm* whirlpool; (*de aire*) whirlwind

VOS *abr* = **versión original subtitulada**

vos [bos] *pron* (*Am*) you

voseo [bo'seo] *nm* (*Am*) addressing a person as "vos", *familiar usage*

Vosgos ['bosɣos] *nmpl* Vosges

vosotros, -as [bo'sotros, as] *pron* you *pl*; (*reflexivo*) yourselves; **entre ~** among yourselves

votación [bota'θjon] *nf* (*acto*) voting; (*voto*) vote; **~ a mano alzada** show of hands; **someter algo a ~** to put sth to the vote

votar [bo'tar] *vt* (*Pol: partido etc*) to vote for; (*proyecto: aprobar*) to pass; (*Rel*) to vow ▪ *vi* to vote

voto ['boto] *nm* vote; (*promesa*) vow; (*maldición*) oath, curse; **votos** *nmpl* (good) wishes; **~ de bloque/de grupo** block/card vote; **~ de censura/de (des)confianza/de gracias** vote of censure/(no) confidence/thanks; **dar su ~** to cast one's vote

voy [boi] *vb ver* **ir**

voz [boθ] *nf* voice; (*grito*) shout; (*chisme*) rumour; (*Ling: palabra*) word; (: *forma*) voice; **dar voces** to shout, yell; **llamar a algn a voces** to shout to sb; **llevar la ~ cantante** (*fig*) to be the boss; **tener la ~ tomada** to be hoarse; **tener ~ y voto** to have the right to speak; **a media ~** in a low voice; **a ~ en cuello** *o* **en grito** at the top of one's voice; **de viva ~** verbally; **en ~ alta** aloud; **~ de mando** command

vozarrón [boθa'rron] *nm* booming voice

vra., vro. *abr* = **vuestra**; **vuestro**

Vto. *abr* (*Com*) = **vencimiento**

vudú [bu'ðu] *nm* voodoo

vuelco *etc* ['bwelko] *vb ver* **volcar** ■ *nm* spill, overturning; (*fig*) collapse; **mi corazón dio un ~** my heart missed a beat

vuelo *etc* ['bwelo] *vb ver* **volar** ■ *nm* flight; (*encaje*) lace, frill; (*de falda etc*) loose part; (*fig*) importance; **de altos ~s** (*fig: plan*) grandiose; (: *persona*) ambitious; **alzar el ~** to take flight; (*fig*) to dash off; **coger al ~** to catch in flight; **~ de bajo coste** low-cost flight; **~ en picado** dive; **~ libre** hang-gliding; **~ regular** scheduled flight; **falda de mucho ~** full *o* wide skirt

vuelque *etc* ['bwelke] *vb ver* **volcar**

vuelta ['bwelta] *nf* turn; (*curva*) bend, curve; (*regreso*) return; (*revolución*) revolution; (*paseo*) stroll; (*circuito*) lap; (*de papel, tela*) reverse; (*de pantalón*) turn-up (*Brit*), cuff (*US*); (*cambio*) change; **~ a empezar** back to square one; **~ al mundo** world trip; **V~ de Francia** Tour de France; **~ cerrada** hairpin bend; **a la ~** (*Esp*) on one's return; **a la ~ de la esquina, a la ~** (*Am*) round the corner; **a ~ de correo** by return of post; **dar vueltas** to turn, revolve; **dar vueltas a una idea** to turn over an idea (in one's mind); **dar una ~** to go for a walk; **dar media ~** (*Auto*) to do a U-turn; (*fam*) to beat it; **estar de ~** (*fam*) to be back; **poner a algn de ~ y media** to heap abuse on sb; **no tiene ~ de hoja** there's no alternative

vueltita [bwel'tita] *nf* (*esp Am fam*) (little) walk; (: *en coche*) (little) drive

vuelto ['bwelto] *pp de* **volver** ■ *nm* (*Am: moneda*) change

vuelva *etc* ['bwelβa] *vb ver* **volver**

vuestro, -a ['bwestro, a] *adj* your; (*después de n*) of yours ■ *pron*: **el ~/la vuestra/los vuestros/las vuestras** yours; **lo ~** (what is) yours; **un amigo ~** a friend of yours; **una idea vuestra** an idea of yours

vulgar [bul'ɣar] *adj* (*ordinario*) vulgar; (*común*) common

vulgarice *etc* [bulɣa'riθe] *vb ver* **vulgarizar**

vulgaridad [bulɣari'ðað] *nf* commonness; (*acto*) vulgarity; (*expresión*) coarse expression; **vulgaridades** *nfpl* banalities

vulgarismo [bulɣa'rismo] *nm* popular form of a word

vulgarizar [bulɣari'θar] *vt* to popularize

vulgo ['bulɣo] *nm* common people

vulnerable [bulne'raβle] *adj* vulnerable

vulnerar [bulne'rar] *vt* to harm, damage; (*derechos*) to interfere with; (*Jur: Com*) to violate

vulva ['bulβa] *nf* vulva

V

Ww

W *abr* (= *vatio(s)*) w
W, w ['uβe'doβle] (*Am*) ['doβleβe] *nf* (*letra*) W,
  w; **W de Washington** W for William
walkie-talkie [walki'talki] *nm* walkie-talkie
walkman® ['wal(k)man] *nm* Walkman®
WAP [wap] *adj, nm* WAP; **teléfono ~** WAP phone
wáter ['bater] *nm* lavatory
waterpolo [water'polo] *nm* waterpolo
web [web] *nm o nf* (*página*) website; (*red*)
  (World Wide) Web
web site ['websait] *nm* website

webcam ['webkam] *nf* webcam
web master ['webmaster] *nm/f* webmaster
whisky ['wiski] *nm* whisky
widget (*pl* **widgets**) [wi'tʃet, s] *nm* (*Inform*)
  widget
wifi ['waifai] *nm* Wi-Fi
Winchester ['wintʃester] *nm* (*Inform*): **disco ~**
  Winchester disk
windsurf ['winsurf] *nm* windsurfing
WWW *nm o nf abr* (*Inform*: = *World Wide Web*)
  WWW

X, x ['ekis] *nf* (*letra*) X, x; **X de Xiquena** X for Xmas
xenofobia [seno'foβja] *nf* xenophobia
xenófobo, -a [se'nofoβo, a] *adj* xenophobic ■ *nm/f* xenophobe

xerografía [seroɣra'fia] *nf* xerography
xilófono [si'lofono] *nm* xylophone
Xunta ['ʃunta] *nf* (*tb*: **Xunta de Galicia**) *regional government of Galicia*

Yy

Y, y [i'ɣrjeɣa] *nf* (*letra*) Y, y; **Y de Yegua** Y for
Yellow (*Brit*) o Yoke (*US*)

y [i] *conj* and; (*Am fam: pues*) well; (*hora*): **la
una y cinco** five past one; **¿y eso?** why?, how
so?; **¿y los demás?** what about the others?; **y
bueno ...** (*Am*) well ...

ya [ja] *adv* (*gen*) already; (*ahora*) now; (*en seguida*)
at once; (*pronto*) soon ■ *excl* all right!; (*por
supuesto*) of course! ■ *conj* (*ahora que*) now that;
ya no not any more, no longer; **ya lo sé** I
know; **ya dice que sí, ya dice que no** first he
says yes, then he says no; **¡ya, ya!** yes, yes!; (*con
impaciencia*) all right!, O.K.!; **¡ya voy!** (*enfático: no
se suele traducir*) coming!; **ya que** since

yacer [ja'θer] *vi* to lie

yacimiento [jaθi'mjento] *nm* bed, deposit;
~ petrolífero oilfield

Yakarta [ja'karta] *nf* Jakarta

yanqui ['janki] *adj* Yankee ■ *nm/f* Yank, Yankee

yate ['jate] *nm* yacht

yazca *etc* ['jaθka] *vb ver* **yacer**

yedra ['jeðra] *nf* ivy

yegua ['jeɣwa] *nf* mare

yema ['jema] *nf* (*del huevo*) yolk; (*Bot*) leaf bud;
(*fig*) best part; **~ del dedo** fingertip

Yemen ['jemen] *nm*: **el ~ del Norte** Yemen;
el ~ del Sur Southern Yemen

yemení [jeme'ni] *adj, nm/f* Yemeni

yendo ['jendo] *vb ver* **ir**

yerba ['jerβa] *nf* = **hierba**

yerbatero, -a [jerβa'tero, a] *adj* (*Am*) maté
■ *nm/f* (*Am*) herbal healer

yerga *etc* ['jerɣa], **yergue** *etc* ['jerɣe] *vb ver* **erguir**

yermo, -a ['jermo, a] *adj* barren; (*de gente*)
uninhabited ■ *nm* waste land

yerno ['jerno] *nm* son-in-law

yerre *etc* ['jerre] *vb ver* **errar**

yerto, -a ['jerto, a] *adj* stiff

yesca ['jeska] *nf* tinder

yeso ['jeso] *nm* (*Geo*) gypsum; (*Arq*) plaster

yo [jo] *pron personal* I; **soy yo** it's me, it is I;
yo que tú/usted if I were you

yodo ['joðo] *nm* iodine

yoga ['joɣa] *nm* yoga

yogur [jo'ɣur], **yogurt** [jo'ɣurt] *nm* yogurt

yogurtera [joɣur'tera] *nf* yogurt maker

yuca ['juka] *nf* yucca

yudo ['juðo] *nm* judo

yugo ['juɣo] *nm* yoke

Yugoslavia [juɣos'laβja] *nf* Yugoslavia

yugoslavo, -a [juɣos'laβo, a] *adj* Yugoslavian
■ *nm/f* Yugoslav

yugular [juɣu'lar] *adj* jugular

yunque ['junke] *nm* anvil

yunta ['junta] *nf* yoke

yuntero [jun'tero] *nm* ploughman

yute ['jute] *nm* jute

yuxtapondré *etc* [jukstapond're] *vb ver*
yuxtaponer

yuxtaponer [jukstapo'ner] *vt* to juxtapose

yuxtaponga *etc* [juksta'ponga] *vb ver*
yuxtaponer

yuxtaposición [jukstaposi'θjon] *nf*
juxtaposition

yuxtapuesto [juksta'pwesto], **yuxtapuse**
etc [juksta'puse] *vb ver* **yuxtaponer**

Zz

Z, z ['θeta] (*esp Am*) ['seta] *nf* (*letra*) Z, z; **Z de Zaragoza** Z for Zebra
zafar [θa'far] *vt* (*soltar*) to untie; (*superficie*) to clear; **zafarse** *vr* (*escaparse*) to escape; (*ocultarse*) to hide o.s. away; (*Tec*) to slip off; **zafarse de** (*persona*) to get away from
zafio, -a ['θafjo, a] *adj* coarse
zafiro [θa'firo] *nm* sapphire
zaga ['θaɣa] *nf* rear; **a la ~** behind, in the rear
zagal [θa'ɣal] *nm* boy, lad
zagala [θa'ɣala] *nf* girl, lass
zaguán [θa'ɣwan] *nm* hallway
zaherir [θae'rir] *vt* (*criticar*) to criticize; (*fig: herir*) to wound
zahiera *etc*, **zahiriendo** *etc* [θa'jera, θai'rjendo] *vb ver* **zaherir**
zahorí [θao'ri] *nm* clairvoyant
zaino, -a ['θaino, a] *adj* (*color de caballo*) chestnut; (*pérfido*) treacherous; (*animal*) vicious
zalamería [θalame'ria] *nf* flattery
zalamero, -a [θala'mero, a] *adj* flattering; (*relamido*) suave
zamarra [θa'marra] *nf* (*piel*) sheepskin; (*chaqueta*) sheepskin jacket
Zambeze [θam'beθe] *nm* Zambezi
zambo, -a ['θambo, a] *adj* knock-kneed ■ *nm/f* (*Am*) half-breed (*of Negro and Indian parentage*); (*mulato*) mulatto ■ *nf* samba
zambullida [θambu'ʎiða] *nf* dive, plunge
zambullirse [θambu'ʎirse] *vr* to dive; (*ocultarse*) to hide o.s.
zamorano, -a [θamo'rano, a] *adj* of *o* from Zamora ■ *nm/f* native *o* inhabitant of Zamora
zampar [θam'par] *vt* (*esconder*) to hide *o* put away (hurriedly); (*comer*) to gobble; (*arrojar*) to hurl ■ *vi* to eat voraciously; **zamparse** *vr* (*chocar*) to bump; (*fig*) to gatecrash
zanahoria [θana'orja] *nf* carrot
zancada [θan'kaða] *nf* stride
zancadilla [θanka'ðiʎa] *nf* trip; (*fig*) stratagem; **echar la ~ a algn** to trip sb up

zancajo [θan'kaxo] *nm* (*Anat*) heel; (*fig*) dwarf
zanco ['θanko] *nm* stilt
zancudo, -a [θan'kuðo, a] *adj* long-legged ■ *nm* (*Am*) mosquito
zángano ['θangano] *nm* drone; (*holgazán*) idler, slacker
zanja ['θanxa] *nf* (*fosa*) ditch; (*tumba*) grave
zanjar [θan'xar] *vt* (*fosa*) to ditch, trench; (*problema*) to surmount; (*conflicto*) to resolve
zapapico [θapa'piko] *nm* pick, pickaxe
zapata [θa'pata] *nf* half-boot; (*Mecánica*) shoe
zapateado [θapate'aðo] *nm* (*flamenco*) tap dance
zapatear [θapate'ar] *vt* (*tocar*) to tap with one's foot; (*patear*) to kick; (*fam*) to ill-treat ■ *vi* to tap with one's feet
zapatería [θapate'ria] *nf* (*oficio*) shoemaking; (*tienda*) shoe-shop; (*fábrica*) shoe factory
zapatero, -a [θapa'tero, a] *nm/f* shoemaker; **~ remendón** cobbler
zapatilla [θapa'tiʎa] *nf* slipper; (*Tec*) washer; (*de deporte*) training shoe
zapato [θa'pato] *nm* shoe
zapear [θape'ar] *vi* to flick through the channels
zapping ['θapin] *nm* channel-hopping; **hacer ~** to channel-hop
zar [θar] *nm* tsar, czar
zarabanda [θara'βanda] *nf* saraband; (*fig*) whirl
Zaragoza [θara'ɣoθa] *nf* Saragossa
zaragozano, -a [θaraɣo'θano, a] *adj* of *o* from Saragossa ■ *nm/f* native *o* inhabitant of Saragossa
zaranda [θa'randa] *nf* sieve
zarandear [θarande'ar] *vt* to sieve; (*fam*) to shake vigorously
zarpa ['θarpa] *nf* (*garra*) claw, paw; **echar la ~ a** to claw at; (*fam*) to grab
zarpar [θar'par] *vi* to weigh anchor
zarpazo [θar'paθo] *nm*: **dar un ~** to claw
zarza ['θarθa] *nf* (*Bot*) bramble
zarzal [θar'θal] *nm* (*matorral*) bramble patch

Z

zarzamora [θarθaˈmora] *nf* blackberry
zarzuela [θarˈθwela] *nf* Spanish light opera;
 la Z~ *home of the Spanish Royal Family*
zigzag [θiɣˈθaɣ] *adj* zigzag
zigzaguear [θiɣθaɣeˈar] *vi* to zigzag
zinc [θink] *nm* zinc
zíper [ˈsiper] *nm* (*Am*) zip, zipper (*US*)
zócalo [ˈθokalo] *nm* (*Arq*) plinth, base;
 (*de pared*) skirting board
zoco [ˈθoko] *nm* (Arab) market, souk
zodíaco [θoˈðiako] *nm* zodiac; **signo del ~**
 star sign
zona [ˈθona] *nf* zone; **~ cero** Ground Zero;
 ~ euro Eurozone; **los países de la ~ euro**
 the Eurozone countries; **~ fronteriza** border
 area; **~ del dólar** (*Com*) dollar area; **~ de
 fomento** *o* **de desarrollo** development area
zonzo, -a [ˈsonso, a] *adj* (*Am*) silly
zoología [θooloˈxia] *nf* zoology
zoológico, -a [θooˈloxiko, a] *adj* zoological
 ■ *nm* (*tb*: **parque zoológico**) zoo
zoólogo, -a [θoˈoloɣo, a] *nm/f* zoologist
zoom [θum] *nm* zoom lens
zopenco, -a [θoˈpenko, a] (*fam*) *adj* dull,
 stupid ■ *nm/f* clot, nitwit
zopilote [sopiˈlote] *nm* (*Am*) buzzard
zoquete [θoˈkete] *nm* (*de madera*) block;
 (*de pan*) crust; (*fam*) blockhead
zorro, -a [ˈθorro, a] *adj* crafty ■ *nm/f* fox/
 vixen ■ *nf* (*fam*) whore, tart, hooker (*US*)

zote [ˈθote] (*fam*) *adj* dim, stupid ■ *nm/f*
 dimwit
zozobra [θoˈθoβra] *nf* (*fig*) anxiety
zozobrar [θoθoˈβrar] *vi* (*hundirse*) to capsize;
 (*fig*) to fail
zueco [ˈθweko] *nm* clog
zulo [ˈθulo] *nm* (*de armas*) cache
zumbar [θumˈbar] *vt* (*burlar*) to tease; (*golpear*)
 to hit ■ *vi* to buzz; (*fam*) to be very close;
 zumbarse *vr*: **zumbarse de** to tease; **me
 zumban los oídos** I have a buzzing *o* ringing
 in my ears
zumbido [θumˈbiðo] *nm* buzzing; (*fam*)
 punch; **~ de oídos** buzzing *o* ringing in the
 ears
zumo [ˈθumo] *nm* juice; (*ganancia*) profit;
 ~ de naranja (fresh) orange juice
zurcir [θurˈθir] *vt* (*coser*) to darn; (*fig*) to put
 together; **¡que las zurzan!** to blazes with
 them!
zurdo, -a [ˈθurðo, a] *adj* (*mano*) left; (*persona*)
 left-handed
zurrar [θuˈrrar] *vt* (*Tec*) to dress; (*fam: pegar
 duro*) to wallop; (: *aplastar*) to flatten; (: *criticar*)
 to criticize harshly
zurriagazo [θurrjaˈɣaθo] *nm* lash, stroke;
 (*desgracia*) stroke of bad luck
zurrón [θuˈrron] *nm* pouch
zurza *etc* [ˈθurθa] *vb ver* **zurcir**
zutano, -a [θuˈtano, a] *nm/f* so-and-so

Aa

A, a [eɪ] *n* (*letter*) A, a; (*Scol: mark*) ≈ sobresaliente; (*Mus*): **A** la *m*; **A for Andrew,** (US) **A for Able** A de Antonio; **A road** *n* (*Brit Aut*) ≈ carretera nacional

○ **KEYWORD**

a [ə] *indef art* (*before vowel and silent h* **an**) **1** un(a); **a book** un libro; **an apple** una manzana; **she's a nurse** (ella) es enfermera; **I haven't got a car** no tengo coche
2 (*instead of the number "one"*) un(a); **a year ago** hace un año; **a hundred/thousand pounds** cien/mil libras
3 (*in expressing ratios, prices etc*): **three a day/ week** tres al día/a la semana; **10 km an hour** 10 km por hora; **£5 a person** £5 por persona; **30p a kilo** 30p el kilo; **three times a month** tres veces al mes

a. *abbr* = **acre**
A2 *n* (*Brit Scol*) *segunda parte de los "A levels"* (*módulos 4–6*)
AA *n abbr* (Brit: = *Automobile Association*) ≈ RACE *m* (SP); = **Alcoholics Anonymous** A.A.; (*US*: = *Associate in/of Arts*) *título universitario*; = **anti-aircraft**
AAA *n abbr* (= *American Automobile Association*) ≈ RACE *m* (SP) [ˈθriːˈeɪz] (Brit: = *Amateur Athletics Association*) *asociación de atletismo amateur*
A & R *n abbr* (*Mus*: = *artists and repertoire*) *nuevos artistas y canciones*; **~ man** *descubridor de jóvenes talentos*
AAUP *n abbr* (= *American Association of University Professors*) *asociación de profesores universitarios*
AB *abbr* (Brit) = **able-bodied seaman**; (*Canada*) = **Alberta**
aback [əˈbæk] *adv*: **to be taken ~** quedar(se) desconcertado
abandon [əˈbændən] *vt* abandonar; (*renounce*) renunciar a ■ *n* abandono; (*wild behaviour*): **with ~** con desenfreno; **to ~ ship**

abandonar el barco
abandoned [əˈbændənd] *adj* (*child, house etc*) abandonado; (*unrestrained: manner*) desinhibido
abase [əˈbeɪs] *vt*: **to ~ o.s. (so far as to do ...)** rebajarse (hasta el punto de hacer ...)
abashed [əˈbæʃt] *adj* avergonzado
abate [əˈbeɪt] *vi* moderarse; (*lessen*) disminuir; (*calm down*) calmarse
abatement [əˈbeɪtmənt] *n* (*of pollution, noise*) disminución *f*
abattoir [ˈæbətwɑːʳ] *n* (Brit) matadero
abbey [ˈæbɪ] *n* abadía
abbot [ˈæbət] *n* abad *m*
abbreviate [əˈbriːvɪeɪt] *vt* abreviar
abbreviation [əbriːvɪˈeɪʃən] *n* (*short form*) abreviatura; (*act*) abreviación *f*
ABC *n abbr* (= *American Broadcasting Company*) *cadena de televisión*
abdicate [ˈæbdɪkeɪt] *vt, vi* abdicar
abdication [æbdɪˈkeɪʃən] *n* abdicación *f*
abdomen [ˈæbdəmən] *n* abdomen *m*
abdominal [æbˈdɔmɪnl] *adj* abdominal
abduct [æbˈdʌkt] *vt* raptar, secuestrar
abduction [æbˈdʌkʃən] *n* rapto, secuestro
abductor [æbˈdʌktəʳ] *n* raptor(a) *m(f)*, secuestrador(a) *m(f)*
Aberdonian [æbəˈdəunɪən] *adj* de Aberdeen ■ *n* nativo(-a) *or* habitante *m/f* de Aberdeen
aberration [æbəˈreɪʃən] *n* aberración *f*; **in a moment of mental ~** en un momento de enajenación mental
abet [əˈbet] *vt see* **aid**
abeyance [əˈbeɪəns] *n*: **in ~** (*law*) en desuso; (*matter*) en suspenso
abhor [əbˈhɔːʳ] *vt* aborrecer, abominar (de)
abhorrent [əbˈhɔrənt] *adj* aborrecible, detestable
abide [əˈbaɪd] *vt*: **I can't ~ it/him** no lo/le puedo ver *or* aguantar; **to ~ by** *vt fus* atenerse a
abiding [əˈbaɪdɪŋ] *adj* (*memory etc*) perdurable
ability [əˈbɪlɪtɪ] *n* habilidad *f*, capacidad *f*;

(*talent*) talento; **to the best of my ~** lo mejor que pueda *etc*

abject ['æbdʒekt] *adj* (*poverty*) sórdido; (*apology*) rastrero; (*coward*) vil

ablaze [ə'bleɪz] *adj* en llamas, ardiendo

able ['eɪbl] *adj* capaz; (*skilled*) hábil; **to be ~ to do sth** poder hacer algo

able-bodied ['eɪbl'bɒdɪd] *adj* sano; **~ seaman** marinero de primera

ably ['eɪblɪ] *adv* hábilmente

ABM *n abbr* = **anti-ballistic missile**

abnormal [æb'nɔːməl] *adj* anormal

abnormality [æbnɔː'mælɪtɪ] *n* (*condition*) anormalidad *f*; (*instance*) anomalía

aboard [ə'bɔːd] *adv* a bordo ■ *prep* a bordo de; **~ the train** en el tren

abode [ə'bəud] *n* (*old*) morada; (*Law*) domicilio; **of no fixed ~** sin domicilio fijo

abolish [ə'bɒlɪʃ] *vt* suprimir, abolir

abolition [æbəu'lɪʃən] *n* supresión *f*, abolición *f*

abominable [ə'bɒmɪnəbl] *adj* abominable

aborigine [æbə'rɪdʒɪnɪ] *n* aborigen *m/f*

abort [ə'bɔːt] *vt* abortar; (*Comput*) interrumpir ■ *vi* (*Comput*) interrumpir el programa

abortion [ə'bɔːʃən] *n* aborto (provocado); **to have an ~** abortar

abortionist [ə'bɔːʃənɪst] *n* persona que practica abortos

abortive [ə'bɔːtɪv] *adj* fracasado

abound [ə'baund] *vi*: **to ~ (in** or **with)** abundar (de or en)

 KEYWORD

about [ə'baut] *adv* **1** (*approximately*) más o menos, aproximadamente; **about a hundred/thousand** *etc* unos (unas) or como cien/mil *etc*; **it takes about 10 hours** se tarda unas or más o menos 10 horas; **at about two o'clock** sobre las dos; **I've just about finished** casi he terminado
2 (*referring to place*) por todas partes; **to leave things lying about** dejar las cosas (tiradas) por ahí; **to run about** correr por todas partes; **to walk about** pasearse, ir y venir; **is Paul about?** ¿está por aquí Paul?; **it's the other way about** es al revés
3: **to be about to do sth** estar a punto de hacer algo; **I'm not about to do all that for nothing** no pienso hacer todo eso para nada ■ *prep* **1** (*relating to*) de, sobre, acerca de; **a book about London** un libro sobre or acerca de Londres; **what is it about?** (*book, film*) ¿de qué se trata?; **we talked about it** hablamos de eso or ello; **what** or **how about doing**

this? ¿qué tal si hacemos esto?
2 (*referring to place*) por; **to walk about the town** caminar por la ciudad

about face, about turn *n* (*Mil*) media vuelta; (*fig*) cambio radical

above [ə'bʌv] *adv* encima, por encima, arriba ■ *prep* encima de; **mentioned ~** susodicho; **~ all** sobre todo; **he's not ~ a bit of blackmail** es capaz hasta de hacer chantaje

above board *adj* legítimo

above-mentioned [əbʌv'menʃnd] *adj* susodicho

abrasion [ə'breɪʒən] *n* (*on skin*) abrasión *f*

abrasive [ə'breɪzɪv] *adj* abrasivo

abreast [ə'brest] *adv* uno al lado de otro; **to keep ~ of** mantenerse al corriente de

abridge [ə'brɪdʒ] *vt* abreviar

abroad [ə'brɔːd] *adv* (*be*) en el extranjero; (*go*) al extranjero; **there is a rumour ~ that ...** corre el rumor de que ...

abrupt [ə'brʌpt] *adj* (*sudden*: *departure*) repentino; (*manner*) brusco

abruptly [ə'brʌptlɪ] *adv* (*leave*) repentinamente; (*speak*) bruscamente

abscess ['æbsɪs] *n* absceso

abscond [əb'skɒnd] *vi* fugarse

absence ['æbsəns] *n* ausencia; **in the ~ of** (*person*) en ausencia de; (*thing*) a falta de

absent ['æbsənt] *adj* ausente; **~ without leave (AWOL)** ausente sin permiso

absentee [æbsən'tiː] *n* ausente *m/f*

absenteeism [æbsən'tiːɪzəm] *n* absentismo

absent-minded [æbsənt'maɪndɪd] *adj* distraído

absolute ['æbsəluːt] *adj* absoluto; **~ monopoly** monopolio total

absolutely [æbsə'luːtlɪ] *adv* totalmente; **oh yes, ~!** ¡claro or por supuesto que sí!

absolution [æbsə'luːʃən] *n* (*Rel*) absolución *f*

absolve [əb'zɒlv] *vt*: **to ~ sb (from)** absolver a algn (de)

absorb [əb'zɔːb] *vt* absorber; **to be absorbed in a book** estar enfrascado en un libro

absorbent [əb'zɔːbənt] *adj* absorbente

absorbent cotton *n* (*US*) algodón *m* hidrófilo

absorbing [əb'zɔːbɪŋ] *adj* absorbente; (*book etc*) interesantísimo

absorption [əb'zɔːpʃən] *n* absorción *f*

abstain [əb'steɪn] *vi*: **to ~ (from)** abstenerse (de)

abstemious [əb'stiːmɪəs] *adj* abstemio

abstention [əb'stenʃən] *n* abstención *f*

abstinence ['æbstɪnəns] *n* abstinencia

abstract ['æbstrækt] *adj* abstracto

abstruse [æb'struːs] *adj* abstruso, oscuro

absurd [əb'səːd] *adj* absurdo

absurdity [əb'sə:dɪtɪ] *n* absurdo

ABTA ['æbtə] *n abbr* = **Association of British Travel Agents**

abundance [ə'bʌndəns] *n* abundancia

abundant [ə'bʌndənt] *adj* abundante

abuse [ə'bju:s] *n* (*insults*) insultos *mpl*, improperios *mpl*; (*misuse*) abuso ■ *vt* [ə'bju:z] (*ill-treat*) maltratar; (*take advantage of*) abusar de; **open to** ~ sujeto al abuso

abusive [ə'bju:sɪv] *adj* ofensivo

abysmal [ə'bɪzməl] *adj* pésimo; (*ignorance*) supino

abyss [ə'bɪs] *n* abismo

AC *abbr* (= *alternating current*) corriente *f* alterna ■ *n abbr* (US) = **athletic club**

a/c *abbr* (*Banking etc*: = *account, account current*) c/c

academic [ækə'dɛmɪk] *adj* académico, universitario; (*pej: issue*) puramente teórico ■ *n* estudioso(-a); (*lecturer*) profesor(a) *m(f)* universitario(-a)

academic year *n* (*Univ*) año académico

academy [ə'kædəmɪ] *n* (*learned body*) academia; (*school*) instituto, colegio

academy of music *n* conservatorio

ACAS ['eɪkæs] *n abbr* (*Brit*: = *Advisory, Conciliation and Arbitration Service*) ≈ Instituto de Mediación, Arbitraje y Conciliación

accede [æk'si:d] *vi*: **to** ~ **to** acceder a

accelerate [æk'sɛləreɪt] *vt* acelerar ■ *vi* acelerarse

acceleration [æksɛlə'reɪʃən] *n* aceleración *f*

accelerator [æk'sɛləreɪtəʳ] *n* (*Brit*) acelerador *m*

accent ['æksɛnt] *n* acento

accentuate [æk'sɛntjueɪt] *vt* (*syllable*) acentuar; (*need, difference etc*) recalcar, subrayar

accept [ək'sɛpt] *vt* aceptar; (*approve*) aprobar; (*concede*) admitir

acceptable [ək'sɛptəbl] *adj* aceptable, admisible

acceptance [ək'sɛptəns] *n* aceptación *f*; aprobación *f*; **to meet with general** ~ recibir la aprobación general

access ['æksɛs] *n* acceso ■ *vt* (*Comput*) acceder a; **the burglars gained** ~ **through a window** los ladrones lograron entrar por una ventana; **to have** ~ **to** tener acceso a

accessible [æk'sɛsəbl] *adj* accesible

accession [æk'sɛʃən] *n* (*of monarch*) subida, ascenso; (*addition*) adquisición *f*

accessory [æk'sɛsərɪ] *n* accesorio; **toilet accessories** artículos *mpl* de tocador

access road *n* carretera de acceso; (*to motorway*) carril *m* de acceso

access time *n* (*Comput*) tiempo de acceso

accident ['æksɪdənt] *n* accidente *m*; (*chance*) casualidad *f*; **by** ~ (*unintentionally*) sin querer; (*by coincidence*) por casualidad; **accidents at work** accidentes *mpl* de trabajo; **to meet with** *or* **to have an** ~ tener *or* sufrir un accidente

accidental [æksɪ'dɛntl] *adj* accidental, fortuito

accidentally [æksɪ'dɛntəlɪ] *adv* sin querer; por casualidad

accident insurance *n* seguro contra accidentes

accident-prone ['æksɪdənt'prəun] *adj* propenso a los accidentes

acclaim [ə'kleɪm] *vt* aclamar, aplaudir ■ *n* aclamación *f*, aplausos *mpl*

acclamation [æklə'meɪʃən] *n* (*approval*) aclamación *f*; (*applause*) aplausos *mpl*; **by** ~ por aclamación

acclimatize [ə'klaɪmətaɪz], **acclimate** (US) [ə'klaɪmət] *vt*: **to become acclimatized** aclimatarse

accolade ['ækəuleɪd] *n* (*prize*) premio; (*praise*) alabanzas *fpl*, homenaje *m*

accommodate [ə'kɔmədeɪt] *vt* alojar, hospedar; (*oblige, help*) complacer; **this car accommodates four people comfortably** en este coche caben cuatro personas cómodamente

accommodating [ə'kɔmədeɪtɪŋ] *adj* servicial, complaciente

accommodation *n*, **accommodations** (US) ■ *npl* [əkɔmə'deɪʃən(z)] alojamiento; **"~ to let"** "se alquilan habitaciones"; **seating** ~ asientos *mpl*

accompaniment [ə'kʌmpənɪmənt] *n* acompañamiento

accompanist [ə'kʌmpənɪst] *n* (*Mus*) acompañante *m/f*

accompany [ə'kʌmpənɪ] *vt* acompañar

accomplice [ə'kʌmplɪs] *n* cómplice *m/f*

accomplish [ə'kʌmplɪʃ] *vt* (*finish*) acabar; (*aim*) realizar; (*task*) llevar a cabo

accomplished [ə'kʌmplɪʃt] *adj* experto, hábil

accomplishment [ə'kʌmplɪʃmənt] *n* (*ending*) conclusión *f*; (*bringing about*) realización *f*; (*skill*) talento

accord [ə'kɔ:d] *n* acuerdo ■ *vt* conceder; **of his own** ~ espontáneamente; **with one** ~ de *or* por común acuerdo

accordance [ə'kɔ:dəns] *n*: **in** ~ **with** de acuerdo con

according [ə'kɔ:dɪŋ]: ~ **to** *prep* según; (*in accordance with*) conforme a; **it went** ~ **to plan** salió según lo previsto

accordingly [ə'kɔ:dɪŋlɪ] *adv* (*thus*) por consiguiente

accordion [ə'kɔ:dɪən] *n* acordeón *m*
accordionist [ə'kɔ:dɪənɪst] *n* acordeonista *m/f*
accost [ə'kɔst] *vt* abordar, dirigirse a
account [ə'kaunt] *n* (*Comm*) cuenta, factura; (*report*) informe *m*; **accounts** *npl* (*Comm*) cuentas *fpl*; **"~ payee only"** "únicamente en cuenta del beneficiario"; **your ~ is still outstanding** su cuenta está todavía pendiente; **of little ~** de poca importancia; **on ~** a crédito; **to buy sth on ~** comprar algo a crédito; **on no ~** bajo ningún concepto; **on ~ of** a causa de, por motivo de; **to take into ~, take ~ of** tener en cuenta; **to keep an ~ of** llevar la cuenta de; **to bring sb to ~ for sth/ for having done sth** pedirle cuentas a algn por algo/por haber hecho algo
▸ **account for** *vt fus* (*explain*) explicar; **all the children were accounted for** no faltaba ningún niño
accountability [əkauntə'bɪlɪtɪ] *n* responsabilidad *f*
accountable [ə'kauntəbl] *adj*: **~ (for)** responsable (de)
accountancy [ə'kauntənsɪ] *n* contabilidad *f*
accountant [ə'kauntənt] *n* contable *m/f*, contador(a) *m(f)* (*LAm*)
accounting [ə'kauntɪŋ] *n* contabilidad *f*
accounting period *n* período contable, ejercicio financiero
account number *n* (*at bank etc*) número de cuenta
account payable *n* cuenta por pagar
account receivable *n* cuenta por cobrar
accoutrements [ə'ku:trəmənts] *npl* equipo, pertrechos *mpl*
accredited [ə'krɛdɪtɪd] *adj* (*agent etc*) autorizado, acreditado
accretion [ə'kri:ʃən] *n* acumulación *f*
accrue [ə'kru:] *vi* (*mount up*) aumentar, incrementarse; (*interest*) acumularse; **to ~ to** corresponder a; **accrued charges** gastos *mpl* vencidos; **accrued interest** interés *m* acumulado
accumulate [ə'kju:mjuleɪt] *vt* acumular ■ *vi* acumularse
accumulation [əkju:mju'leɪʃən] *n* acumulación *f*
accuracy ['ækjurəsɪ] *n* exactitud *f*, precisión *f*
accurate ['ækjurɪt] *adj* (*number*) exacto; (*answer*) acertado; (*shot*) certero
accurately ['ækjurɪtlɪ] *adv* (*count, shoot, answer*) con precisión
accursed [ə'kə:st] *adj* maldito
accusation [ækju'zeɪʃən] *n* acusación *f*
accusative [ə'kju:zətɪv] *n* acusativo
accuse [ə'kju:z] *vt* acusar; (*blame*) echar la culpa a

accused [ə'kju:zd] *n* acusado(-a)
accuser [ə'kju:zər] *n* acusador(a) *m(f)*
accustom [ə'kʌstəm] *vt* acostumbrar; **to ~ o.s. to sth** acostumbrarse a algo
accustomed [ə'kʌstəmd] *adj*: **~ to** acostumbrado a
AC/DC *abbr* (= *alternating current/direct current*) CA/CC
ACE [eɪs] *n abbr* = **American Council on Education**
ace [eɪs] *n* as *m*
acerbic [ə'sə:bɪk] *adj* acerbo; (*fig*) mordaz
acetate ['æsɪteɪt] *n* acetato
ache [eɪk] *n* dolor *m* ■ *vi* doler; (*yearn*): **to ~ to do sth** ansiar hacer algo; **I've got stomach ~** *or* (*US*) **a stomach ~** tengo dolor de estómago, me duele el estómago; **my head aches** me duele la cabeza
achieve [ə'tʃi:v] *vt* (*reach*) alcanzar; (*realize*) realizar; (*victory, success*) lograr, conseguir
achievement [ə'tʃi:vmənt] *n* (*completion*) realización *f*; (*success*) éxito
Achilles heel [ə'kɪli:z-] *n* talón *m* de Aquiles
acid ['æsɪd] *adj* ácido; (*bitter*) agrio ■ *n* ácido
acidity [ə'sɪdɪtɪ] *n* acidez *f*; (*Med*) acedía
acid rain *n* lluvia ácida
acid test *n* (*fig*) prueba de fuego
acknowledge [ək'nɔlɪdʒ] *vt* (*letter: also:* **acknowledge receipt of**) acusar recibo de; (*fact*) reconocer
acknowledgement [ək'nɔlɪdʒmənt] *n* acuse *m* de recibo; reconocimiento; **acknowledgements** (*in book*) agradecimientos *mpl*
ACLU *n abbr* (= *American Civil Liberties Union*) unión americana por libertades civiles
acme ['ækmɪ] *n* súmmum *m*
acne ['æknɪ] *n* acné *m*
acorn ['eɪkɔ:n] *n* bellota
acoustic [ə'ku:stɪk] *adj* acústico
acoustics [ə'ku:stɪks] *n, npl* acústica *sg*
acquaint [ə'kweɪnt] *vt*: **to ~ sb with sth** (*inform*) poner a algn al corriente de algo; **to be acquainted with** (*person*) conocer; (*fact*) estar al corriente de
acquaintance [ə'kweɪntəns] *n* conocimiento; (*person*) conocido(-a); **to make sb's ~** conocer a algn
acquiesce [ækwɪ'ɛs] *vi* (*agree*): **to ~ (in)** consentir (en), conformarse (con)
acquire [ə'kwaɪər] *vt* adquirir
acquired [ə'kwaɪəd] *adj* adquirido; **it's an ~ taste** es algo a lo que uno se aficiona poco a poco
acquisition [ækwɪ'zɪʃən] *n* adquisición *f*
acquisitive [ə'kwɪzɪtɪv] *adj* codicioso

acquit [ə'kwɪt] vt absolver, exculpar; **to ~ o.s. well** defenderse bien

acquittal [ə'kwɪtl] n absolución f, exculpación f

acre ['eɪkəʳ] n acre m

acreage ['eɪkərɪdʒ] n extensión f

acrid ['ækrɪd] adj (smell) acre; (fig) mordaz, sarcástico

acrimonious [ækrɪ'məunɪəs] adj (remark) mordaz; (argument) reñido

acrobat ['ækrəbæt] n acróbata m/f

acrobatic [ækrə'bætɪk] adj acrobático

acrobatics [ækrə'bætɪks] npl acrobacias fpl

acronym ['ækrənɪm] n siglas fpl

across [ə'krɔs] prep (on the other side of) al otro lado de; (crosswise) a través de ■ adv de un lado a otro, de una parte a otra a través, al través; **to run/swim ~** atravesar corriendo/ nadando; **~ from** enfrente de; **the lake is 12 km ~** el lago tiene 12 km de ancho; **to get sth ~ to sb** (fig) hacer comprender algo a algn

acrylic [ə'krɪlɪk] adj acrílico

ACT n abbr (= American College Test) prueba de aptitud estándar que por lo general hacen los estudiantes que quieren entrar a la universidad por primera vez

act [ækt] n acto, acción f; (Theat) acto; (in music-hall etc) número; (Law) decreto, ley f ■ vi (behave) comportarse; (Theat) actuar; (pretend) fingir; (take action) tomar medidas ■ vt (part) hacer, representar; **~ of God** fuerza mayor; **it's only an ~** es cuento; **to catch sb in the ~** coger a algn in fraganti or con las manos en la masa; **to ~ Hamlet** hacer el papel de Hamlet; **to ~ as** actuar or hacer de; **acting in my capacity as chairman, I ...** en mi calidad de presidente, yo ...; **it acts as a deterrent** sirve para disuadir; **he's only acting** está fingiendo nada más
▶ **act on** vt: **to ~ on sth** actuar sobre algo
▶ **act out** vt (event) representar; (fantasies) realizar

acting ['æktɪŋ] adj suplente ■ n: **to do some ~** hacer algo de teatro; **he is the ~ manager** es el gerente en funciones

action ['ækʃən] n acción f, acto; (Mil) acción f; (Law) proceso, demanda ■ vt (Comm) llevar a cabo; **to put a plan into ~** poner un plan en acción or en marcha; **killed in ~** (Mil) muerto en acto de servicio or en combate; **out of ~** (person) fuera de combate; (thing) averiado, descompuesto; **to take ~** tomar medidas; **to bring an ~ against sb** entablar or presentar demanda contra algn

action replay n (TV) repetición f

activate ['æktɪveɪt] vt activar

active ['æktɪv] adj activo, enérgico; (volcano)

en actividad; **to play an ~ part in** colaborar activamente en

active duty n (US Mil) servicio activo

actively ['æktɪvlɪ] adv (participate) activamente; (discourage, dislike) enérgicamente

active partner n (Comm) socio activo

activist ['æktɪvɪst] n activista m/f

activity [æk'tɪvɪtɪ] n actividad f

actor ['æktəʳ] n actor m

actress ['æktrɪs] n actriz f

actual ['æktjuəl] adj verdadero, real

actually ['æktjuəlɪ] adv realmente, en realidad

actuary ['æktjuərɪ] n (Comm) actuario(-a) (de seguros)

actuate ['æktjueɪt] vt mover, impulsar

acumen ['ækjumən] n perspicacia; **business ~** talento para los negocios

acupuncture ['ækjupʌŋktʃəʳ] n acupuntura

acute [ə'kju:t] adj agudo

acutely [ə'kju:tlɪ] adv profundamente, extremadamente

AD adv abbr (= Anno Domini) A.C. ■ n abbr (US Mil) = **active duty**

ad [æd] n abbr = **advertisement**

adage ['ædɪdʒ] n refrán m, adagio

Adam ['ædəm] n Adán; **~'s apple** n nuez f (de la garganta)

adamant ['ædəmənt] adj firme, inflexible

adapt [ə'dæpt] vt adaptar; (reconcile) acomodar ■ vi: **to ~ (to)** adaptarse (a), ajustarse (a)

adaptability [ədæptə'bɪlɪtɪ] n (of person, device etc) adaptabilidad f

adaptable [ə'dæptəbl] adj (device) adaptable; (person) acomodadizo, que se adapta

adaptation [ædæp'teɪʃən] n adaptación f

adapter, adaptor [ə'dæptəʳ] n (Elec) adaptador m

ADC n abbr (Mil: = aide-de-camp; US: = Aid to Dependent Children) ayuda para niños dependientes

add [æd] vt añadir, agregar (esp LAm); (figures: also: **add up**) sumar ■ vi: **to ~ to** (increase) aumentar, acrecentar ■ n (Internet): **thanks for the ~** gracias por agregarme
▶ **add on** vt añadir
▶ **add up** vt (figures) sumar ■ vi (fig): **it doesn't ~ up** no tiene sentido; **it doesn't ~ up to much** es poca cosa, no tiene gran or mucha importancia

addendum [ə'dɛndəm] n ad(d)enda m or f

adder ['ædəʳ] n víbora

addict ['ædɪkt] n (to drugs etc) adicto(-a); (enthusiast) aficionado(-a), entusiasta m/f; **heroin ~** heroinómano(-a)

addicted [ə'dɪktɪd] adj: **to be ~ to** ser adicto a;

413

ser aficionado a

addiction [əˈdɪkʃən] n (dependence) hábito morboso; (enthusiasm) afición f

addictive [əˈdɪktɪv] adj que causa adicción

adding machine [ˈædɪŋ-] n calculadora

Addis Ababa [ˈædɪsˈæbəbə] n Addis Abeba m

addition [əˈdɪʃən] n (adding up) adición f; (thing added) añadidura, añadido; **in ~** además, por añadidura; **in ~ to** además de

additional [əˈdɪʃənl] adj adicional

additive [ˈædɪtɪv] n aditivo

addled [ˈædld] adj (Brit: rotten) podrido; (: fig) confuso

address [əˈdrɛs] n dirección f, señas fpl; (speech) discurso; (Comput) dirección f ■ vt (letter) dirigir; (speak to) dirigirse a, dirigir la palabra a; **form of ~** tratamiento; **absolute/relative ~** (Comput) dirección f absoluta/relativa; **to ~ o.s. to sth** (issue, problem) abordar

address book n agenda (de direcciones)

addressee [ædrɛˈsiː] n destinatario(-a)

Aden [ˈeɪdn] n Adén m

adenoids [ˈædɪnɔɪdz] npl vegetaciones fpl (adenoideas)

adept [ˈædɛpt] adj: **~ at** experto or ducho en

adequacy [ˈædɪkwəsɪ] n idoneidad f

adequate [ˈædɪkwɪt] adj (satisfactory) adecuado; (enough) suficiente; **to feel ~ to a task** sentirse con fuerzas para una tarea

adequately [ˈædɪkwɪtlɪ] adv adecuadamente

adhere [ədˈhɪər] vi: **to ~ to** adherirse a; (fig: abide by) observar

adherent [ədˈhɪərənt] n partidario(-a)

adhesion [ədˈhiːʒən] n adherencia

adhesive [ədˈhiːzɪv] adj, n adhesivo

adhesive tape n (Brit) cinta adhesiva; (US Med) esparadrapo

ad hoc [ædˈhɔk] adj (decision) ad hoc; (committee) formado con fines específicos ■ adv ad hoc

adieu [əˈdjuː] excl ¡vaya con Dios!

ad inf [ˈædɪnf] adv hasta el infinito

adjacent [əˈdʒeɪsənt] adj: **~ to** contiguo a, inmediato a

adjective [ˈædʒɛktɪv] n adjetivo

adjoin [əˈdʒɔɪn] vt estar contiguo a; (land) lindar con

adjoining [əˈdʒɔɪnɪŋ] adj contiguo, vecino

adjourn [əˈdʒəːn] vt aplazar; (session) suspender, levantar; (US: end) terminar ■ vi suspenderse; **the meeting has been adjourned till next week** se ha levantado la sesión hasta la semana que viene; **they adjourned to the pub** (col) se trasladaron al bar

adjournment [əˈdʒəːnmənt] n (period)

suspensión f; (postponement) aplazamiento

Adjt. abbr (Mil) = **adjutant**

adjudicate [əˈdʒuːdɪkeɪt] vi sentenciar ■ vt (contest) hacer de árbitro en, juzgar; (claim) decidir

adjudication [ədʒuːdɪˈkeɪʃən] n fallo

adjudicator [əˈdʒuːdɪkeɪtər] n juez m, árbitro

adjust [əˈdʒʌst] vt (change) modificar; (arrange) arreglar; (machine) ajustar ■ vi: **to ~ (to)** adaptarse (a)

adjustable [əˈdʒʌstəbl] adj ajustable

adjuster [əˈdʒʌstər] n see **loss adjuster**

adjustment [əˈdʒʌstmənt] n modificación f; arreglo; (of prices, wages) ajuste m

adjutant [ˈædʒətənt] n ayudante m

ad-lib [ædˈlɪb] vt, vi improvisar ■ adv: **ad lib** a voluntad, a discreción

adman [ˈædmæn] n (col) publicista m

admin [ˈædmɪn] n abbr (col) = **administration**

administer [ədˈmɪnɪstər] vt proporcionar; (justice) administrar

administration [ədmɪnɪˈstreɪʃən] n administración f; (government) gobierno; **the A~** (US) la Administración

administrative [ədˈmɪnɪstrətɪv] adj administrativo

administrator [ədˈmɪnɪstreɪtər] n administrador(a) m(f)

admirable [ˈædmərəbl] adj admirable

admiral [ˈædmərəl] n almirante m

Admiralty [ˈædmərəltɪ] n (Brit) Ministerio de Marina, Almirantazgo

admiration [ædməˈreɪʃən] n admiración f

admire [ədˈmaɪər] vt admirar

admirer [ədˈmaɪərər] n admirador(a) m(f); (suitor) pretendiente m

admiring [ədˈmaɪərɪŋ] adj (expression) de admiración

admissible [ədˈmɪsəbl] adj admisible

admission [ədˈmɪʃən] n (to exhibition, nightclub) entrada; (enrolment) ingreso; (confession) confesión f; **"~ free"** "entrada gratis or libre"; **by his own ~** él mismo reconoce que

admit [ədˈmɪt] vt dejar entrar, dar entrada a; (permit) admitir; (acknowledge) reconocer; **"this ticket admits two"** "entrada para dos personas"; **children not admitted** se prohíbe la entrada a (los) menores de edad; **I must ~ that ...** debo reconocer que ...
▶ **admit of** vt fus admitir, permitir
▶ **admit to** vt fus confesarse culpable de

admittance [ədˈmɪtəns] n entrada; **"no ~"** "se prohíbe la entrada", "prohibida la entrada"

admittedly [ədˈmɪtədlɪ] adv de acuerdo que

admonish [ədˈmɔnɪʃ] vt amonestar; (advise) aconsejar

ad nauseam [æd'nɔːsɪæm] *adv* hasta la saciedad
ado [ə'duː] *n*: **without (any) more** ~ sin más (ni más)
adolescence [ædəʊ'lɛsns] *n* adolescencia
adolescent [ædəʊ'lɛsnt] *adj, n* adolescente *m/f*
adopt [ə'dɔpt] *vt* adoptar
adopted [ə'dɔptɪd] *adj* adoptivo
adoption [ə'dɔpʃən] *n* adopción *f*
adoptive [ə'dɔptɪv] *adj* adoptivo
adorable [ə'dɔːrəbl] *adj* adorable
adoration [ædə'reɪʃən] *n* adoración *f*
adore [ə'dɔːʳ] *vt* adorar
adoring [ə'dɔːrɪŋ] *adj*: **to his** ~ **public** a un público que le adora *or* le adoraba *etc*
adorn [ə'dɔːn] *vt* adornar
adornment [ə'dɔːnmənt] *n* adorno
ADP *n abbr* = **automatic data processing**
adrenalin [ə'drɛnəlɪn] *n* adrenalina
Adriatic [eɪdrɪ'ætɪk] *n*: **the** ~ **(Sea)** el (Mar) Adriático
adrift [ə'drɪft] *adv* a la deriva; **to come** ~ (*boat*) ir a la deriva, soltarse; (*wire, rope etc*) soltarse
adroit [ə'drɔɪt] *adj* diestro, hábil
ADSL *n abbr* (= *asymmetrical digital subscriber line*) ADSL *m*
ADT *abbr* (US: = *Atlantic Daylight Time*) hora de verano de Nueva York
adulation [ædju'leɪʃən] *n* adulación *f*
adult ['ædʌlt] *n* adulto(-a) ■ *adj*: ~ **education** educación *f* para adultos
adulterate [ə'dʌltəreɪt] *vt* adulterar
adulterer [ə'dʌltərəʳ] *n* adúltero
adulteress [ə'dʌltrɪs] *n* adúltera
adultery [ə'dʌltərɪ] *n* adulterio
adulthood ['ædʌlthud] *n* edad *f* adulta
advance [əd'vɑːns] *n* adelanto, progreso; (*money*) anticipo; (*Mil*) avance *m* ■ *vt* avanzar, adelantar; (*money*) anticipar ■ *vi* avanzar, adelantarse; **in** ~ por adelantado; (*book*) con antelación; **to make advances to sb** (*gen*) ponerse en contacto con algn; (*amorously*) insinuarse a algn
advanced *adj* avanzado; (*Scol: studies*) adelantado; ~ **in years** entrado en años
Advanced Higher *n* (*Scottish Scol*) titulación que sigue al "Higher", ≈ Bachillerato
advancement [əd'vɑːnsmənt] *n* progreso; (*in rank*) ascenso
advance notice *n* previo aviso
advance payment *n* (*part sum*) anticipo
advantage [əd'vɑːntɪdʒ] *n* (*also Tennis*) ventaja; **to take** ~ **of** aprovecharse de; **it's to our** ~ es ventajoso para nosotros
advantageous [ædvən'teɪdʒəs] *adj* ventajoso, provechoso
advent ['ædvənt] *n* advenimiento; **A**~ Adviento
adventure [əd'vɛntʃəʳ] *n* aventura
adventure playground *n* parque *m* infantil
adventurous [əd'vɛntʃərəs] *adj* aventurero; (*bold*) arriesgado
adverb ['ædvəːb] *n* adverbio
adversary ['ædvəsərɪ] *n* adversario, contrario
adverse ['ædvəːs] *adj* adverso, contrario; ~ **to** adverso a
adversity [əd'vəːsɪtɪ] *n* infortunio
advert ['ædvəːt] *n abbr* (*Brit*) = **advertisement**
advertise ['ædvətaɪz] *vi* hacer propaganda; (*in newspaper etc*) poner un anuncio, anunciarse; **to** ~ **for** (*staff*) buscar por medio de anuncios ■ *vt* anunciar
advertisement [əd'vəːtɪsmənt] *n* anuncio
advertiser ['ædvətaɪzəʳ] *n* anunciante *m/f*
advertising ['ædvətaɪzɪŋ] *n* publicidad *f*, propaganda; anuncios *mpl*
advertising agency *n* agencia de publicidad
advertising campaign *n* campaña de publicidad
advice [əd'vaɪs] *n* consejo, consejos *mpl*; (*notification*) aviso; **a piece of** ~ un consejo; **to take legal** ~ consultar a un abogado; **to ask (sb) for** ~ pedir consejo (a algn)
advice note *n* (*Brit*) nota de aviso
advisable [əd'vaɪzəbl] *adj* aconsejable, conveniente
advise [əd'vaɪz] *vt* aconsejar; **to** ~ **sb of sth** (*inform*) informar a algn de algo; **to** ~ **sb against sth/doing sth** desaconsejar algo a algn/aconsejar a algn que no haga algo; **you will be well/ill advised to go** deberías/no deberías ir
advisedly [əd'vaɪzɪdlɪ] *adv* deliberadamente
adviser [əd'vaɪzəʳ] *n* consejero(-a); (*business adviser*) asesor(a) *m(f)*
advisory [əd'vaɪzərɪ] *adj* consultivo; **in an** ~ **capacity** como asesor
advocate ['ædvəkeɪt] *vt* (*argue for*) abogar por; (*give support to*) ser partidario de ■ *n* ['ædvəkɪt] abogado(-a)
advt. *abbr* = **advertisement**
AEA *n abbr* (*Brit*: = *Atomic Energy Authority*) *consejo de energía nuclear*; (*Brit Scol*: = *Advanced Extension Award*) *titulación opcional para los alumnos mejor preparados de los "A levels"*
AEC *n abbr* (US: = *Atomic Energy Commission*) AEC *f*
Aegean [iː'dʒiːən] *n*: **the** ~ **(Sea)** el (Mar) Egeo
aegis ['iːdʒɪs] *n*: **under the** ~ **of** bajo la tutela de
aeon ['iːən] *n* eón *m*
aerial ['ɛərɪəl] *n* antena ■ *adj* aéreo
aerie ['ɛərɪ] *n* (US) aguilera

aero- ['ɛərəu] *pref* aero-

aerobatics [ɛərəu'bætɪks] *npl* acrobacia aérea

aerobics [ɛə'rəubɪks] *nsg* aerobic *m*, aerobismo (*LAm*)

aerodrome ['ɛərədrəum] *n* (*Brit*) aeródromo

aerodynamic [ɛərəudaɪ'næmɪk] *adj* aerodinámico

aeronautics [ɛərəu'nɔːtɪks] *nsg* aeronáutica

aeroplane ['ɛərəpleɪn] *n* (*Brit*) avión *m*

aerosol ['ɛərəsɔl] *n* aerosol *m*

aerospace industry ['ɛərəuspeɪs-] *n* industria aeroespacial

aesthetic [iːs'θɛtɪk] *adj* estético

aesthetics [iːs'θɛtɪks] *npl* estética

afar [ə'faːʳ] *adv* lejos; **from ~** desde lejos

AFB *n abbr* (*US*) = **Air Force Base**

AFDC *n abbr* (*US*: = *Aid to Families with Dependent Children*) ayuda a familias con hijos menores

affable ['æfəbl] *adj* afable

affair [ə'fɛəʳ] *n* asunto; (*also*: **love affair**) aventura *f* amorosa; **affairs** (*business*) asuntos *mpl*; **the Watergate ~** el asunto (de) Watergate

affect [ə'fɛkt] *vt* afectar, influir en; (*move*) conmover

affectation [æfɛk'teɪʃən] *n* afectación *f*

affected [ə'fɛktɪd] *adj* afectado

affection [ə'fɛkʃən] *n* afecto, cariño

affectionate [ə'fɛkʃənɪt] *adj* afectuoso, cariñoso

affectionately [ə'fɛkʃənɪtlɪ] *adv* afectuosamente

affidavit [æfɪ'deɪvɪt] *n* (*Law*) declaración *f* jurada

affiliated [ə'fɪlieɪtɪd] *adj* afiliado; **~ company** empresa *or* compañía filial *or* subsidiaria

affinity [ə'fɪnɪtɪ] *n* afinidad *f*

affirm [ə'fəːm] *vt* afirmar

affirmation [æfə'meɪʃən] *n* afirmación *f*

affirmative [ə'fəːmətɪv] *adj* afirmativo

affix [ə'fɪks] *vt* (*signature*) estampar; (*stamp*) pegar

afflict [ə'flɪkt] *vt* afligir

affliction [ə'flɪkʃən] *n* enfermedad *f*, aflicción *f*

affluence ['æfluəns] *n* opulencia, riqueza

affluent ['æfluənt] *adj* adinerado, acaudalado; **the ~ society** la sociedad opulenta

afford [ə'fɔːd] *vt* poder permitirse; (*provide*) proporcionar; **can we ~ a car?** ¿podemos permitirnos el gasto de comprar un coche?

affordable [ə'fɔːdəbl] *adj* asequible

affray [ə'freɪ] *n* refriega, reyerta

affront [ə'frʌnt] *n* afrenta, ofensa

affronted [ə'frʌntɪd] *adj* ofendido

Afghan ['æfgæn] *adj, n* afgano(-a) *m(f)*

Afghanistan [æf'gænɪstæn] *n* Afganistán *m*

afield [ə'fiːld] *adv*: **far ~** muy lejos

AFL-CIO *n abbr* (*US*: = *American Federation of Labor and Congress of Industrial Organizations*) confederación sindicalista

afloat [ə'fləut] *adv* (*floating*) a flote; (*at sea*) en el mar

afoot [ə'fut] *adv*: **there is something ~** algo se está tramando

aforesaid [ə'fɔːsɛd] *adj* susodicho; (*Comm*) mencionado anteriormente

afraid [ə'freɪd] *adj*: **to be ~ of** (*person*) tener miedo a; (*thing*) tener miedo de; **to be ~ to** tener miedo de, temer; **I am ~ that** me temo que; **I'm ~ so** ¡me temo que sí!, ¡lo siento, pero es así!; **I'm ~ not** me temo que no

afresh [ə'frɛʃ] *adv* de nuevo, otra vez

Africa ['æfrɪkə] *n* África

African ['æfrɪkən] *adj, n* africano(-a) *m(f)*

Afrikaans [æfrɪ'kaːns] *n* africaans *m*

Afrikaner [æfrɪ'kaːnəʳ] *n* africánder *m/f*

Afro-American ['æfrəuə'mɛrɪkən] *adj, n* afroamericano(-a) *m(f)*

AFT *n abbr* (= *American Federation of Teachers*) sindicato de profesores

aft [ɑːft] *adv* (*be*) en popa; (*go*) a popa

after ['ɑːftəʳ] *prep* (*time*) después de; (*place, order*) detrás de, tras ▪ *adv* después ▪ *conj* después (de) que; **what/who are you ~?** ¿qué/a quién buscas?; **the police are ~ him** la policía le está buscando; **~ having done/he left** después de haber hecho/después de que se marchó; **~ dinner** después de cenar *or* comer; **the day ~ tomorrow** pasado mañana; **to ask ~ sb** preguntar por algn; **~ all** después de todo, al fin y al cabo; **~ you!** ¡Vd primero!; **quarter ~ two** (*US*) las dos y cuarto

afterbirth ['ɑːftəbəːθ] *n* placenta

aftercare ['ɑːftəkɛəʳ] *n* (*Med*) asistencia postoperatoria

after-effects ['ɑːftərɪfɛkts] *npl* secuelas *fpl*, efectos *mpl*

afterlife ['ɑːftəlaɪf] *n* vida después de la muerte

aftermath ['ɑːftəmɑːθ] *n* consecuencias *fpl*, resultados *mpl*

afternoon [ɑːftə'nuːn] *n* tarde *f*; **good ~!** ¡buenas tardes!

afters ['ɑːftəz] *n* (*col*: *dessert*) postre *m*

after-sales service [ɑːftə'seɪlz-] *n* (*Brit Comm*: *for car, washing machine etc*) servicio de asistencia pos-venta

after-shave ['ɑːftəʃeɪv], **after-shave lotion** *n* loción *f* para después del afeitado, aftershave *m*

aftershock ['ɑ:ftəʃɔk] n (of earthquake) pequeño temblor m posterior

aftersun ['ɑ:ftəsʌn], **aftersun lotion** n after-sun m inv

aftertaste ['ɑ:ftəteɪst] n regusto

afterthought ['ɑ:ftəθɔ:t] n ocurrencia (tardía)

afterwards ['ɑ:ftəwədz] adv después, más tarde

again [ə'gɛn] adv otra vez, de nuevo; **to do sth** ~ volver a hacer algo; **~ and** ~ una y otra vez; **now and** ~ de vez en cuando

against [ə'gɛnst] prep (opposed) en contra de; (close to) contra, junto a; **I was leaning ~ the desk** estaba apoyado en el escritorio; **(as) ~** frente a

age [eɪdʒ] n edad f; (old age) vejez f; (period) época ■ vi envejecer(se) ■ vt envejecer; **what ~ is he?** ¿qué edad or cuántos años tiene?; **he is 20 years of** ~ tiene 20 años; **under** ~ menor de edad; **to come of** ~ llegar a la mayoría de edad; **it's been ages since I saw you** hace siglos que no te veo

aged [eɪdʒd] adj: ~ **10** de 10 años de edad ■ npl ['eɪdʒɪd]: **the** ~ los ancianos

age group n: **to be in the same** ~ tener la misma edad; **the 40 to 50** ~ las personas de 40 a 50 años

ageing ['eɪdʒɪŋ] adj que envejece; (pej) en declive ■ n envejecimiento

ageless ['eɪdʒlɪs] adj (eternal) eterno; (ever young) siempre joven

age limit n límite m de edad, edad f tope

agency ['eɪdʒənsɪ] n agencia; **through** or **by the** ~ **of** por medio de

agenda [ə'dʒɛndə] n orden m del día; **on the** ~ (Comm) en el orden del día

agent ['eɪdʒənt] n (gen) agente m/f; (representative) representante m/f delegado(-a)

aggravate ['ægrəveɪt] vt agravar; (annoy) irritar, exasperar

aggravating ['ægrəveɪtɪŋ] adj irritante, molesto

aggravation [ægrə'veɪʃən] n agravamiento

aggregate ['ægrɪgeɪt] n conjunto

aggression [ə'grɛʃən] n agresión f

aggressive [ə'grɛsɪv] adj agresivo; (vigorous) enérgico

aggressiveness [ə'grɛsɪvnɪs] n agresividad f

aggressor [ə'grɛsər] n agresor(a) m(f)

aggrieved [ə'gri:vd] adj ofendido, agraviado

aggro ['ægrəu] n (col: physical violence) bronca; (bad feeling) mal rollo; (hassle) rollo, movida

aghast [ə'gɑ:st] adj horrorizado

agile ['ædʒaɪl] adj ágil

agility [ə'dʒɪlɪtɪ] n agilidad f

agitate ['ædʒɪteɪt] vt (shake) agitar; (trouble) inquietar; **to ~ for** hacer campaña en pro de or en favor de

agitated ['ædʒɪteɪtɪd] adj agitado

agitator ['ædʒɪteɪtər] n agitador(a) m(f)

AGM n abbr = **annual general meeting**

agnostic [æg'nɔstɪk] adj, n agnóstico(-a) m(f)

ago [ə'gəu] adv: **two days** ~ hace dos días; **not long** ~ hace poco; **how long ~?** ¿hace cuánto tiempo?; **as long ~ as 1980** ya en 1980

agog [ə'gɔg] adj (anxious) ansioso; (excited): **(all)** ~ **(for)** (todo) emocionado (por)

agonize ['ægənaɪz] vi: **to ~ (over)** atormentarse (por)

agonized ['ægənaɪzd] adj angustioso

agonizing ['ægənaɪzɪŋ] adj (pain) atroz; (suspense) angustioso

agony ['ægənɪ] n (pain) dolor m atroz; (distress) angustia; **to be in** ~ retorcerse de dolor

agony aunt n (Brit col) consejera sentimental

agony column n consultorio sentimental

agree [ə'gri:] vt (price) acordar, quedar en ■ vi (statements etc) coincidir, concordar; **to ~ (with)** (person) estar de acuerdo (con), ponerse de acuerdo (con); **to ~ to do** aceptar hacer; **to ~ to sth** consentir en algo; **to ~ that** (admit) estar de acuerdo en que; **it was agreed that ...** se acordó que ...; **garlic doesn't ~ with me** el ajo no me sienta bien

agreeable [ə'gri:əbl] adj agradable; (person) simpático; (willing) de acuerdo, conforme

agreeably [ə'gri:əblɪ] adv agradablemente

agreed [ə'gri:d] adj (time, place) convenido

agreement [ə'gri:mənt] n acuerdo; (Comm) contrato; **in** ~ de acuerdo, conforme; **by mutual** ~ de común acuerdo

agricultural [ægrɪ'kʌltʃərəl] adj agrícola

agriculture ['ægrɪkʌltʃər] n agricultura

aground [ə'graund] adv: **to run** ~ encallar, embarrancar

ahead [ə'hɛd] adv delante; ~ **of** delante de; (fig: schedule etc) antes de; ~ **of time** antes de la hora; **to be** ~ **of sb** (fig) llevar ventaja or la delantera a algn; **go right** or **straight** ~ siga adelante; **they were (right)** ~ **of us** iban (justo) delante de nosotros

ahoy [ə'hɔɪ] excl ¡oiga!

AI n abbr (= Amnesty International) (Comput) = **artificial intelligence**

AIB n abbr (Brit: = Accident Investigation Bureau) oficina de investigación de accidentes

AID n abbr (= artificial insemination by donor) inseminación artificial por donante; (US: = Agency for International Development) Agencia Internacional para el Desarrollo

aid [eɪd] n ayuda, auxilio ■ vt ayudar, auxiliar; **in** ~ **of** a beneficio de; **with the** ~ **of** con la ayuda de; **to** ~ **and abet** (Law) ser cómplice

aide [eɪd] *n* (*Pol*) ayudante *m/f*

AIDS [eɪdz] *n abbr* (= *acquired immune* (*or immuno-*) *deficiency syndrome*) SIDA *m*, sida *m*

AIH *n abbr* (= *artificial insemination by husband*) inseminación artificial por esposo

ailing ['eɪlɪŋ] *adj* (*person, economy*) enfermizo

ailment ['eɪlmənt] *n* enfermedad *f*, achaque *m*

aim [eɪm] *vt* (*gun*) apuntar; (*missile, remark*) dirigir; (*blow*) asestar ■ *vi* (*also:* **take aim**) apuntar ■ *n* puntería; (*objective*) propósito, meta; **to ~ at** (*objective*) aspirar a, pretender; **to ~ to do** tener como objetivo hacer, aspirar a hacer

aimless ['eɪmlɪs] *adj* sin propósito, sin objeto

aimlessly ['eɪmlɪslɪ] *adv* sin rumbo fijo

ain't [eɪnt] (*col*) = **am not; aren't; isn't**

air [ɛəʳ] *n* aire *m*; (*appearance*) aspecto ■ *vt* (*room*) ventilar; (*clothes, bed, grievances, ideas*) airear; (*views*) hacer público ■ *cpd* aéreo; **to throw sth into the ~** (*ball etc*) lanzar algo al aire; **by ~** (*travel*) en avión; **to be on the ~** (*Radio, TV: programme*) estarse emitiendo; (: *station*) estar emitiendo

airbag ['ɛəbæg] *n* airbag *m inv*

air base *n* (*Mil*) base *f* aérea

air bed *n* (*Brit*) colchoneta inflable *or* neumática

airborne ['ɛəbɔːn] *adj* (*in the air*) en el aire; (*Mil*) aerotransportado; **as soon as the plane was ~** tan pronto como el avión estuvo en el aire

air cargo *n* carga aérea

air-conditioned ['ɛəkən'dɪʃənd] *adj* climatizado

air conditioning [-kən'dɪʃənɪŋ] *n* aire *m* acondicionado

air-cooled ['ɛəkuːld] *adj* refrigerado por aire

aircraft ['ɛəkrɑːft] *n pl inv* avión *m*

aircraft carrier *n* porta(a)viones *m inv*

air cushion *n* cojín *m* de aire; (*Aviat*) colchón *m* de aire

airdrome ['ɛədrəum] *n* (*US*) aeródromo

airfield ['ɛəfiːld] *n* campo de aviación

Air Force *n* fuerzas aéreas *fpl*, aviación *f*

air freight *n* flete *m* por avión

air freshener *n* ambientador *m*

air gun *n* escopeta de aire comprimido

air hostess (*Brit*) *n* azafata, aeromoza (*LAm*)

airily ['ɛərɪlɪ] *adv* muy a la ligera

airing ['ɛərɪŋ] *n*: **to give an ~ to** (*linen*) airear; (*room*) ventilar; (*fig: ideas etc*) airear, someter a discusión

air letter *n* (*Brit*) carta aérea

airlift ['ɛəlɪft] *n* puente *m* aéreo

airline ['ɛəlaɪn] *n* línea aérea

airliner ['ɛəlaɪnəʳ] *n* avión *m* de pasajeros

airlock ['ɛəlɔk] *n* (*in pipe*) esclusa de aire

airmail ['ɛəmeɪl] *n*: **by ~** por avión

air mattress *n* colchón *m* inflable *or* neumático

airplane ['ɛəpleɪn] *n* (*US*) avión *m*

air pocket *n* bolsa de aire

airport ['ɛəpɔːt] *n* aeropuerto

air rage *n* *conducta agresiva de pasajeros a bordo de un avión*

air raid *n* ataque *m* aéreo

air rifle *n* escopeta de aire comprimido

airsick ['ɛəsɪk] *adj*: **to be ~** marearse (en avión)

airspeed ['ɛəspiːd] *n* velocidad *f* de vuelo

airstrip ['ɛəstrɪp] *n* pista de aterrizaje

air terminal *n* terminal *f*

airtight ['ɛətaɪt] *adj* hermético

air time *n* (*Radio, TV*) tiempo en antena

air traffic control *n* control *m* de tráfico aéreo

air traffic controller *n* controlador(a) *m(f)* aéreo(-a)

airway ['ɛəweɪ] *n* (*Aviat*) vía aérea; (*Anat*) vía respiratoria

airy ['ɛərɪ] *adj* (*room*) bien ventilado; (*manners*) despreocupado

aisle [aɪl] *n* (*of church*) nave *f* lateral; (*of theatre, plane*) pasillo

ajar [ə'dʒɑːʳ] *adj* entreabierto

AK *abbr* (*US*) = **Alaska**

aka *abbr* (= *also known as*) alias

akin [ə'kɪn] *adj*: **~ to** semejante a

AL *abbr* (*US*) = **Alabama**

ALA *n abbr* = **American Library Association**

Ala. *abbr* (*US*) = **Alabama**

alabaster ['æləbɑːstəʳ] *n* alabastro

à la carte [ælæ'kɑːt] *adv* a la carta

alacrity [ə'lækrɪtɪ] *n*: **with ~** con la mayor prontitud

alarm [ə'lɑːm] *n* alarma; (*anxiety*) inquietud *f* ■ *vt* asustar, alarmar

alarm clock *n* despertador *m*

alarmed [ə'lɑːmd] *adj* (*person*) alarmado, asustado; (*house, car etc*) con alarma

alarming [ə'lɑːmɪŋ] *adj* alarmante

alarmingly [ə'lɑːmɪŋlɪ] *adv* de forma alarmante; **~ quickly** a una velocidad alarmante

alarmist [ə'lɑːmɪst] *n* alarmista *m/f*

alas [ə'læs] *adv* desgraciadamente ■ *excl* ¡ay!

Alas. *abbr* (*US*) = **Alaska**

Alaska [ə'læskə] *n* Alaska

Albania [æl'beɪnɪə] *n* Albania

Albanian [æl'beɪnɪən] *adj* albanés(-esa) ■ *n* albanés(-esa) *m(f)*; (*Ling*) albanés *m*

albatross ['ælbətrɔs] *n* albatros *m*

albeit [ɔːl'biːɪt] *conj* (*although*) aunque

album ['ælbəm] n álbum m; (L.P.) elepé m
albumen ['ælbjumɪn] n albúmina
alchemy ['ælkɪmɪ] n alquimia
alcohol ['ælkəhɔl] n alcohol m
alcohol-free adj sin alcohol
alcoholic [ælkə'hɔlɪk] adj, n alcohólico(-a) m(f)
alcoholism ['ælkəhɔlɪzəm] n alcoholismo
alcove ['ælkəuv] n nicho, hueco
Ald. abbr = **alderman**
alderman ['ɔːldəmən] n concejal m
ale [eɪl] n cerveza
alert [ə'ləːt] adj alerta inv; (sharp) despierto, despabilado ■ n alerta m, alarma ■ vt poner sobre aviso; **to ~ sb (to sth)** poner sobre aviso or alertar a algn (de algo); **to ~ sb to the dangers of sth** poner sobre aviso or alertar a algn de los peligros de algo; **to be on the ~** estar alerta or sobre aviso
alertness [ə'ləːtnɪs] n vigilancia
Aleutian Islands [ə'luːʃən-] npl Islas fpl Aleutianas
A level n abbr (Brit Scol: = Advanced level) ≈ Bachillerato
Alexandria [ælɪg'zaːndrɪə] n Alejandría
alfresco [æl'freskəu] adj, adv al aire libre
algebra ['ældʒɪbrə] n álgebra
Algeria [æl'dʒɪərɪə] n Argelia
Algerian [æl'dʒɪərɪən] adj, n argelino(-a) m(f)
Algiers [æl'dʒɪəz] n Argel m
algorithm ['ælgərɪðəm] n algoritmo
alias ['eɪlɪəs] adv alias, conocido por ■ n alias m
alibi ['ælɪbaɪ] n coartada
alien ['eɪlɪən] n (foreigner) extranjero(-a) ■ adj: **~ to** ajeno a
alienate ['eɪlɪəneɪt] vt enajenar, alejar
alienation [eɪlɪə'neɪʃən] n alejamiento m
alight [ə'laɪt] adj ardiendo ■ vi apearse, bajar
align [ə'laɪn] vt alinear
alignment [ə'laɪnmənt] n alineación f; **the desks are out of ~** los pupitres no están bien alineados
alike [ə'laɪk] adj semejantes, iguales ■ adv igualmente, del mismo modo; **to look ~** parecerse
alimony ['ælɪmənɪ] n (Law) pensión f alimenticia
alive [ə'laɪv] adj (gen) vivo; (lively) activo
alkali ['ælkəlaɪ] n álcali m

 KEYWORD

all [ɔːl] adj todo(-a) sg, todos(-as) pl; **all day** todo el día; **all night** toda la noche; **all men** todos los hombres; **all five came** vinieron los cinco; **all the books** todos los libros; **all the time/his life** todo el tiempo/toda su vida; **for all their efforts** a pesar de todos sus esfuerzos
■ pron **1** todo; **I ate it all, I ate all of it** me lo comí todo; **all of them** todos (ellos); **all of us went** fuimos todos; **all the boys went** fueron todos los chicos; **is that all?** ¿eso es todo?, ¿algo más?; (in shop) ¿algo más?, ¿alguna cosa más?
2 (in phrases): **above all** sobre todo; por encima de todo; **after all** después de todo; **at all: anything at all** lo que sea; **not at all** (in answer to question) en absoluto; (in answer to thanks) ¡de nada!, ¡no hay de qué!; **I'm not at all tired** no estoy nada cansado(-a); **anything at all will do** cualquier cosa viene bien; **all in all** a fin de cuentas
■ adv: **all alone** completamente solo(-a); **to be/feel all in** estar rendido; **it's not as hard as all that** no es tan difícil como lo pintas; **all the more/the better** tanto más/mejor; **all but** casi; **the score is two all** están empatados a dos

all-around ['ɔːlə'raund] adj (US) = **all-round**
allay [ə'leɪ] vt (fears) aquietar; (pain) aliviar
all clear n (after attack etc) fin m de la alerta; (fig) luz f verde
allegation [ælɪ'geɪʃən] n alegato
allege [ə'lɛdʒ] vt pretender; **he is alleged to have said ...** se afirma que él dijo ...
alleged [ə'lɛdʒd] adj supuesto, presunto
allegedly [ə'lɛdʒɪdlɪ] adv supuestamente, según se afirma
allegiance [ə'liːdʒəns] n lealtad f
allegory ['ælɪgərɪ] n alegoría
all-embracing ['ɔːləm'breɪsɪŋ] adj universal
allergic [ə'ləːdʒɪk] adj: **~ to** alérgico a
allergy ['ælədʒɪ] n alergia
alleviate [ə'liːvɪeɪt] vt aliviar
alleviation [əliːvɪ'eɪʃən] n alivio
alley ['ælɪ] n (street) callejuela; (in garden) paseo
alleyway ['ælɪweɪ] n callejón m
alliance [ə'laɪəns] n alianza
allied ['ælaɪd] adj aliado; (related) relacionado
alligator ['ælɪgeɪtər] n caimán m
all-important ['ɔːlɪm'pɔːtənt] adj de suma importancia
all-in ['ɔːlɪn] adj (Brit: also adv: charge) todo incluido
all-in wrestling n lucha libre
alliteration [əlɪtə'reɪʃən] n aliteración f
all-night ['ɔːl'naɪt] adj (café) abierto toda la noche; (party) que dura toda la noche
allocate ['æləkeɪt] vt (share out) repartir; (devote) asignar

allocation [ælə'keɪʃən] n (of money) ración f, cuota; (distribution) reparto

allot [ə'lɔt] vt asignar; **in the allotted time** en el tiempo asignado

allotment [ə'lɔtmənt] n porción f; (garden) parcela

all-out ['ɔːlaut] adj (effort etc) supremo ■ adv: **all out** con todas las fuerzas, a fondo

allow [ə'lau] vt (permit) permitir, dejar; (a claim) admitir; (sum to spend, time estimated) dar, conceder; (concede): **to ~ that** reconocer que; **to ~ sb to do** permitir a algn hacer; **smoking is not allowed** prohibido or se prohíbe fumar; **he is allowed to ...** se le permite ...; **we must ~ three days for the journey** debemos dejar tres días para el viaje
▶ **allow for** vt fus tener en cuenta

allowance [ə'lauəns] n concesión f; (payment) subvención f, pensión f; (discount) descuento, rebaja; **to make allowances for** (person) disculpar a; (thing: take into account) tener en cuenta

alloy ['ælɔɪ] n aleación f

all right adv (feel, work) bien; (as answer) ¡de acuerdo!, ¡está bien!

all-round ['ɔːl'raund] adj completo; (view) amplio

all-rounder ['ɔːl'raundəʳ] n: **to be a good ~** ser una persona que hace de todo

allspice ['ɔːlspaɪs] n pimienta inglesa or de Jamaica

all-time ['ɔːl'taɪm] adj (record) de todos los tiempos

allude [ə'luːd] vi: **to ~ to** aludir a

alluring [ə'ljuərɪŋ] adj seductor(a), atractivo

allusion [ə'luːʒən] n referencia, alusión f

ally n ['ælaɪ] aliado(-a) ■ vt [ə'laɪ]: **to ~ o.s. with** aliarse con

almanac ['ɔːlmənæk] n almanaque m

almighty [ɔːl'maɪtɪ] adj todopoderoso

almond ['ɑːmənd] n (fruit) almendra; (tree) almendro

almost ['ɔːlməust] adv casi; **he ~ fell** casi or por poco se cae

alms [ɑːmz] npl limosna sg

aloft [ə'lɔft] adv arriba

alone [ə'ləun] adj solo ■ adv sólo, solamente; **to leave sb ~** dejar a algn en paz; **to leave sth ~** no tocar algo; **let ~ ...** y mucho menos, y no digamos ...

along [ə'lɔŋ] prep a lo largo de, por ■ adv: **is he coming ~ with us?** ¿viene con nosotros?; **he was limping ~** iba cojeando; **~ with** junto con; **all ~** (all the time) desde el principio

alongside [ə'lɔŋ'saɪd] prep al lado de ■ adv (Naut) de costado; **we brought our boat ~** atracamos nuestro barco

aloof [ə'luːf] adj distante ■ adv: **to stand ~** mantenerse a distancia

aloud [ə'laud] adv en voz alta

alphabet ['ælfəbɛt] n alfabeto

alphabetical [ælfə'bɛtɪkəl] adj alfabético; **in ~ order** por orden alfabético

alphanumeric [ælfənjuː'mɛrɪk] adj alfanumérico

alpine ['ælpaɪn] adj alpino, alpestre

Alps [ælps] npl: **the ~** los Alpes

already [ɔːl'rɛdɪ] adv ya

alright ['ɔːl'raɪt] adv (Brit) = **all right**

Alsatian [æl'seɪʃən] n (dog) pastor m alemán

also ['ɔːlsəu] adv también, además

Alta. abbr (Canada) = **Alberta**

altar ['ɔltəʳ] n altar m

alter ['ɔltəʳ] vt cambiar, modificar ■ vi cambiarse, modificarse

alteration [ɔltə'reɪʃən] n cambio, modificación f; **alterations** npl (Arch) reformas fpl; (Sewing) arreglos mpl; **timetable subject to ~** el horario puede cambiar

altercation [ɔltə'keɪʃən] n altercado

alternate [ɔl'təːnɪt] adj alterno ■ vi ['ɔltəneɪt]: **to ~ (with)** alternar (con); **on ~ days** en días alternos

alternately [ɔl'təːnɪtlɪ] adv alternativamente, por turno

alternating ['ɔltəneɪtɪŋ] adj (current) alterno

alternative [ɔl'təːnətɪv] adj alternativo ■ n alternativa

alternatively [ɔl'təːnətɪvlɪ] adv: **~ one could ...** por otra parte se podría ...

alternative medicine n medicina alternativa

alternator ['ɔltəneɪtəʳ] n (Aut) alternador m

although [ɔːl'ðəu] conj aunque, si bien

altitude ['æltɪtjuːd] n altitud f, altura

altitude sickness n mal m de altura, soroche m (LAm)

alto ['æltəu] n (female) contralto f; (male) alto

altogether [ɔːltə'gɛðəʳ] adv completamente, del todo; (on the whole, in all) en total, en conjunto; **how much is that ~?** ¿cuánto es todo or en total?

altruism ['æltruɪzəm] n altruismo

altruistic [æltru'ɪstɪk] adj altruista

aluminium [ælju'mɪnɪəm], **aluminum** (US) [ə'luːmɪnəm] n aluminio

always ['ɔːlweɪz] adv siempre

Alzheimer's ['æltshaɪməz] n (also: **Alzheimer's disease**) enfermedad f de Alzheimer

AM abbr (= amplitude modulation) A.M. f ■ n abbr (Pol: in Wales) = **Assembly Member**

am [æm] vb see **be**

a.m. *adv abbr* (= *ante meridiem*) de la mañana

AMA *n abbr* = **American Medical Association**

amalgam [ə'mælgəm] *n* amalgama

amalgamate [ə'mælgəmeɪt] *vi* amalgamarse ∎ *vt* amalgamar

amalgamation [əmælgə'meɪʃən] *n* (*Comm*) fusión *f*

amass [ə'mæs] *vt* amontonar, acumular

amateur ['æmətər] *n* aficionado(-a), amateur *m/f*; ~ **dramatics** dramas *mpl* presentados por aficionados, representación *f* de aficionados

amateurish ['æmətərɪʃ] *adj* (*pej*) torpe, inexperto

amaze [ə'meɪz] *vt* asombrar, pasmar; **to be amazed (at)** asombrarse (de)

amazement [ə'meɪzmənt] *n* asombro, sorpresa; **to my** ~ para mi sorpresa

amazing [ə'meɪzɪŋ] *adj* extraordinario, asombroso; (*bargain, offer*) increíble

amazingly [ə'meɪzɪŋlɪ] *adv* extraordinariamente

Amazon ['æməzən] *n* (*Geo*) Amazonas *m*; (*Mythology*) amazona ∎ *cpd*: **the** ~ **basin/jungle** la cuenca/selva del Amazonas

Amazonian [æmə'zəunɪən] *adj* amazónico

ambassador [æm'bæsədər] *n* embajador(a) *m(f)*

amber ['æmbər] *n* ámbar *m*; **at** ~ (*Brit Aut*) en amarillo

ambidextrous [æmbɪ'dɛkstrəs] *adj* ambidextro

ambience ['æmbɪəns] *n* ambiente *m*

ambiguity [æmbɪ'gjuɪtɪ] *n* ambigüedad *f*; (*of meaning*) doble sentido

ambiguous [æm'bɪgjuəs] *adj* ambiguo

ambition [æm'bɪʃən] *n* ambición *f*; **to achieve one's** ~ realizar su ambición

ambitious [æm'bɪʃəs] *adj* ambicioso; (*plan*) grandioso

ambivalent [æm'bɪvələnt] *adj* ambivalente; (*pej*) equívoco

amble ['æmbl] *vi* (*gen: also:* **amble along**) deambular, andar sin prisa

ambulance ['æmbjuləns] *n* ambulancia

ambulanceman/woman ['æmbjulənsmən/wumən] *n* ambulanciero(-a)

ambush ['æmbuʃ] *n* emboscada ∎ *vt* tender una emboscada a; (*fig*) coger (*SP*) *or* agarrar (*LAm*) por sorpresa

ameba [ə'mi:bə] *n* (*US*) = **amoeba**

ameliorate [ə'mi:lɪəreɪt] *vt* mejorar

amelioration [əmi:lɪə'reɪʃən] *n* mejora

amen [ɑː'mɛn] *excl* amén

amenable [ə'mi:nəbl] *adj*: ~ **to** (*advice etc*) sensible a

amend [ə'mɛnd] *vt* (*law, text*) enmendar;

to make amends (*apologize*) enmendarlo, dar cumplida satisfacción

amendment [ə'mɛndmənt] *n* enmienda

amenities [ə'mi:nɪtɪz] *npl* comodidades *fpl*

amenity [ə'mi:nɪtɪ] *n* servicio

America [ə'mɛrɪkə] *n* América (del Norte)

American [ə'mɛrɪkən] *adj, n* (norte)americano(-a) *m(f)*, estadounidense *m/f*

Americanism [ə'mɛrɪkənɪzəm] *n* americanismo

americanize [ə'mɛrɪkənaɪz] *vt* americanizar

Amerindian [æmər'ɪndɪən] *adj, n* amerindio(-a)

amethyst ['æmɪθɪst] *n* amatista

Amex ['æmɛks] *n abbr* = **American Stock Exchange**

amiable ['eɪmɪəbl] *adj* (*kind*) amable, simpático

amicable ['æmɪkəbl] *adj* amistoso, amigable

amicably ['æmɪkəblɪ] *adv* amigablemente, amistosamente; **to part** ~ separarse amistosamente

amid [ə'mɪd], **amidst** [ə'mɪdst] *prep* entre, en medio de

amiss [ə'mɪs] *adv*: **to take sth** ~ tomar algo a mal; **there's something** ~ pasa algo

ammo ['æməu] *n abbr* (*col*) = **ammunition**

ammonia [ə'məunɪə] *n* amoníaco

ammunition [æmju'nɪʃən] *n* municiones *fpl*; (*fig*) argumentos *mpl*

ammunition dump *n* depósito de municiones

amnesia [æm'ni:zɪə] *n* amnesia

amnesty ['æmnɪstɪ] *n* amnistía; **to grant an** ~ **to** amnistiar (a); **A~ International** Amnistía Internacional

amoeba, ameba (*US*) [ə'mi:bə] *n* amiba

amok [ə'mɔk] *adv*: **to run** ~ enloquecerse, desbocarse

among [ə'mʌŋ], **amongst** [ə'mʌŋst] *prep* entre, en medio de

amoral [æ'mɔrəl] *adj* amoral

amorous ['æmərəs] *adj* cariñoso

amorphous [ə'mɔ:fəs] *adj* amorfo

amortization [əmɔ:taɪ'zeɪʃən] *n* amortización *f*

amount [ə'maunt] *n* (*gen*) cantidad *f*; (*of bill etc*) suma, importe *m* ∎ *vi*: **to** ~ **to** (*total*) sumar; (*be same as*) equivaler a, significar; **this amounts to a refusal** esto equivale a una negativa; **the total** ~ (*of money*) la suma total

amp [æmp], **ampère** ['æmpɛər] *n* amperio; **a 13** ~ **plug** un enchufe de 13 amperios

ampersand ['æmpəsænd] *n* signo &, "y" comercial

amphetamine [æmˈfɛtəmiːn] *n* anfetamina

amphibian [æmˈfɪbɪən] *n* anfibio

amphibious [æmˈfɪbɪəs] *adj* anfibio

amphitheatre, amphitheater (US) [ˈæmfɪθɪətəʳ] *n* anfiteatro

ample [ˈæmpl] *adj* (*spacious*) amplio; (*abundant*) abundante; **to have ~ time** tener tiempo de sobra

amplifier [ˈæmplɪfaɪəʳ] *n* amplificador *m*

amplify [ˈæmplɪfaɪ] *vt* amplificar, aumentar; (*explain*) explicar

amply [ˈæmplɪ] *adv* ampliamente

ampoule, ampule (US) [ˈæmpuːl] *n* (*Med*) ampolla

amputate [ˈæmpjuteɪt] *vt* amputar

amputee [æmpjuˈtiː] *n* persona que ha sufrido una amputación

Amsterdam [ˈæmstədæm] *n* Amsterdam *m*

amt *abbr* = **amount**

amuck [əˈmʌk] *adv* = **amok**

amuse [əˈmjuːz] *vt* divertir; (*distract*) distraer, entretener; **to ~ o.s. with sth/by doing sth** distraerse con algo/haciendo algo; **he was amused at the joke** le divirtió el chiste

amusement [əˈmjuːzmənt] *n* diversión *f*; (*pastime*) pasatiempo; (*laughter*) risa; **much to my ~** con gran regocijo mío

amusement arcade *n* salón *m* de juegos

amusement park *n* parque *m* de atracciones

amusing [əˈmjuːzɪŋ] *adj* divertido

an [æn, ən, n] *indef art see* **a**

ANA *n abbr* = **American Newspaper Association; American Nurses Association**

anachronism [əˈnækrənɪzəm] *n* anacronismo

anaemia [əˈniːmɪə] *n* anemia

anaemic [əˈniːmɪk] *adj* anémico; (*fig*) flojo

anaesthetic [ænɪsˈθɛtɪk] *n* anestesia; **local/general ~** anestesia local/general

anaesthetist [æˈniːsɪtɪst] *n* anestesista *m/f*

anagram [ˈænəgræm] *n* anagrama *m*

anal [ˈeɪnl] *adj* anal

analgesic [ænælˈdʒiːsɪk] *adj, n* analgésico

analogous [əˈnæləgəs] *adj*: **~ to** *or* **with** análogo a

analogue, analog [ˈænələg] *adj* (*watch*) analógico

analogy [əˈnælədʒɪ] *n* analogía; **to draw an ~ between** señalar la analogía entre

analyse [ˈænəlaɪz] *vt* (*Brit*) analizar

analysis (*pl* **analyses**) [əˈnæləsɪs, -siːz] *n* análisis *m inv*

analyst [ˈænəlɪst] *n* (*political analyst*) analista *m/f*; (*psychoanalyst*) psicoanalista *m/f*

analytic [ænəˈlɪtɪk], **analytical** [ænəˈlɪtɪkəl] *adj* analítico

analyze [ˈænəlaɪz] *vt* (US) = **analyse**

anarchic [æˈnɑːkɪk] *adj* anárquico

anarchist [ˈænəkɪst] *adj, n* anarquista *m/f*

anarchy [ˈænəkɪ] *n* anarquía, desorden *m*

anathema [əˈnæθɪmə] *n*: **that is ~ to him** eso es pecado para él

anatomical [ænəˈtɒmɪkəl] *adj* anatómico

anatomy [əˈnætəmɪ] *n* anatomía

ANC *n abbr* = **African National Congress**

ancestor [ˈænsɪstəʳ] *n* antepasado

ancestral [ænˈsɛstrəl] *adj* ancestral

ancestry [ˈænsɪstrɪ] *n* ascendencia, abolengo

anchor [ˈæŋkəʳ] *n* ancla, áncora ■ *vi* (*also:* **to drop anchor**) anclar, echar el ancla ■ *vt* (*fig*) sujetar, afianzar; **to weigh ~** levar anclas

anchorage [ˈæŋkərɪdʒ] *n* ancladero

anchor man, anchor woman *n* (*Radio, TV*) presentador(a) *m(f)*

anchovy [ˈæntʃəvɪ] *n* anchoa

ancient [ˈeɪnʃənt] *adj* antiguo; **~ monument** monumento histórico

ancillary [ænˈsɪlərɪ] *adj* (*worker, staff*) auxiliar

and [ænd] *conj* y; (*before i, hi*) e; **~ so on** etcétera; **try ~ come** procure *or* intente venir; **better ~ better** cada vez mejor

Andalusia [ændəˈluːzɪə] *n* Andalucía

Andean [ˈændɪən] *adj* andino(-a); **~ high plateau** altiplanicie *f*, altiplano (*LAm*)

Andes [ˈændiːz] *npl*: **the ~** los Andes

anecdote [ˈænɪkdəut] *n* anécdota

anemia [əˈniːmɪə] *n* (US) = **anaemia**

anemic [əˈniːmɪk] *adj* (US) = **anaemic**

anemone [əˈnɛmənɪ] *n* (*Bot*) anémone *f*; **sea ~** anémona

anesthetic [ænɪsˈθɛtɪk] *adj, n* (US) = **anaesthetic**

anesthetist [æˈniːsɪtɪst] *n* (US) = **anaesthetist**

anew [əˈnjuː] *adv* de nuevo, otra vez

angel [ˈeɪndʒəl] *n* ángel *m*

angel dust *n* polvo de ángel

angelic [ænˈdʒɛlɪk] *adj* angélico

anger [ˈæŋgəʳ] *n* ira, cólera, enojo (*LAm*) ■ *vt* enojar, enfurecer

angina [ænˈdʒaɪnə] *n* angina (del pecho)

angle [ˈæŋgl] *n* ángulo; **from their ~** desde su punto de vista

angler [ˈæŋgləʳ] *n* pescador(a) *m(f)* (de caña)

Anglican [ˈæŋglɪkən] *adj, n* anglicano(-a)

anglicize [ˈæŋglɪsaɪz] *vt* anglicanizar

angling [ˈæŋglɪŋ] *n* pesca con caña

Anglo- [ˈæŋgləu] *pref* anglo...

Angola [æŋˈgəulə] *n* Angola

Angolan [æŋˈgəulən] *adj, n* angoleño(-a) *m(f)*

angrily [ˈæŋgrɪlɪ] *adv* enojado, enfadado

angry [ˈæŋgrɪ] *adj* enfadado, enojado (*esp LAm*); **to be ~ with sb/at sth** estar enfadado con algn/por algo; **to get ~** enfadarse, enojarse (*esp LAm*)

anguish ['æŋgwɪʃ] *n* (*physical*) tormentos *mpl*; (*mental*) angustia

anguished ['æŋgwɪʃt] *adj* angustioso

angular ['æŋgjuləʳ] *adj* (*shape*) angular; (*features*) anguloso

animal ['ænɪməl] *adj, n* animal *m*

animal rights [-raɪts] *npl* derechos *mpl* de los animales

animate *vt* ['ænɪmeɪt] (*enliven*) animar; (*encourage*) estimular, alentar ■ *adj* ['ænɪmɪt] vivo, animado

animated ['ænɪmeɪtɪd] *adj* vivo, animado

animation [ænɪ'meɪʃən] *n* animación *f*

animosity [ænɪ'mɔsɪtɪ] *n* animosidad *f*, rencor *m*

aniseed ['ænɪsiːd] *n* anís *m*

Ankara ['æŋkərə] *n* Ankara

ankle ['æŋkl] *n* tobillo *m*

ankle sock *n* calcetín *m*

annex *n* ['ænɛks] (*Brit: also*: **annexe**: *building*) edificio anexo ■ *vt* [æ'nɛks] (*territory*) anexar

annihilate [ə'naɪəleɪt] *vt* aniquilar

annihilation [ənaɪə'leɪʃən] *n* aniquilación *f*

anniversary [ænɪ'vəːsərɪ] *n* aniversario

annotate ['ænəuteɪt] *vt* anotar

announce [ə'nauns] *vt* (*gen*) anunciar; (*inform*) comunicar; **he announced that he wasn't going** declaró que no iba

announcement [ə'naunsmənt] *n* (*gen*) anuncio; (*declaration*) declaración *f*; **I'd like to make an** ~ quisiera anunciar algo

announcer [ə'naunsəʳ] *n* (*Radio, TV*) locutor(a) *m(f)*

annoy [ə'nɔɪ] *vt* molestar, fastidiar, fregar (*LAm*), embromar (*LAm*); **to be annoyed (at sth/with sb)** estar enfadado *or* molesto (por algo/con algn); **don't get annoyed!** ¡no se enfade!

annoyance [ə'nɔɪəns] *n* enojo; (*thing*) molestia

annoying [ə'nɔɪɪŋ] *adj* molesto, fastidioso, fregado (*LAm*), embromado (*LAm*); (*person*) pesado

annual ['ænjuəl] *adj* anual ■ *n* (*Bot*) anual *m*; (*book*) anuario

annual general meeting *n* junta general anual

annually ['ænjuəlɪ] *adv* anualmente, cada año

annual report *n* informe *m or* memoria anual

annuity [ə'njuːɪtɪ] *n* renta *or* pensión *f* vitalicia

annul [ə'nʌl] *vt* anular; (*law*) revocar

annulment [ə'nʌlmənt] *n* anulación *f*

annum ['ænəm] *n see* **per annum**

Annunciation [ənʌnsɪ'eɪʃən] *n* Anunciación *f*

anode ['ænəud] *n* ánodo

anoint [ə'nɔɪnt] *vt* untar

anomalous [ə'nɔmələs] *adj* anómalo

anomaly [ə'nɔməlɪ] *n* anomalía

anon. [ə'nɔn] *abbr* = **anonymous**

anonymity [ænə'nɪmɪtɪ] *n* anonimato

anonymous [ə'nɔnɪməs] *adj* anónimo; **to remain** ~ quedar en el anonimato

anorak ['ænəræk] *n* anorak *m*

anorexia [ænə'rɛksɪə] *n* (*Med*) anorexia

anorexic [ænə'rɛksɪk] *adj, n* anoréxico(-a) *m(f)*

another [ə'nʌðəʳ] *adj*: ~ **book** otro libro; ~ **beer?** ¿(quieres) otra cerveza?; **in** ~ **five years** en cinco años más ■ *pron* otro; *see also* **one**

ANSI *n abbr* (= *American National Standards Institution*) oficina de normalización de EEUU

answer ['ɑːnsəʳ] *n* respuesta, contestación *f*; (*to problem*) solución *f* ■ *vi* contestar, responder ■ *vt* (*reply to*) contestar a, responder a; (*problem*) resolver; **to** ~ **the phone** contestar el teléfono; **in** ~ **to your letter** contestando *or* en contestación a su carta; **to** ~ **the bell** *or* **the door** abrir la puerta

▶ **answer back** *vi* replicar, ser respondón(-ona)

▶ **answer for** *vt fus* responder de *or* por

▶ **answer to** *vt fus* (*description*) corresponder a

answerable ['ɑːnsərəbl] *adj*: ~ **to sb for sth** responsable ante algn de algo

answering machine ['ɑːnsərɪŋ-] *n* contestador *m* automático

ant [ænt] *n* hormiga

ANTA *n abbr* = **American National Theater and Academy**

antagonism [æn'tægənɪzəm] *n* antagonismo *m*

antagonist [æn'tægənɪst] *n* antagonista *m/f*, adversario(-a)

antagonistic [æntægə'nɪstɪk] *adj* antagónico; (*opposed*) contrario, opuesto

antagonize [æn'tægənaɪz] *vt* provocar la enemistad de

Antarctic [ænt'ɑːktɪk] *adj* antártico ■ *n*: **the** ~ el Antártico

Antarctica [æn'tɑːktɪkə] *n* Antártida

Antarctic Circle *n* Círculo Polar Antártico

Antarctic Ocean *n* Océano Antártico

ante ['æntɪ] *n*: **to up the** ~ subir la apuesta

ante... ['æntɪ] *pref* ante...

anteater ['æntiːtəʳ] *n* oso hormiguero

antecedent [æntɪ'siːdənt] *n* antecedente *m*

antechamber ['æntɪtʃeɪmbəʳ] *n* antecámara

antelope ['æntɪləup] *n* antílope *m*
antenatal [æntɪ'neɪtl] *adj* prenatal
antenatal clinic *n* clínica prenatal
antenna [æn'tɛnə] (*pl* **antennae** [-niː]) *n* antena
anteroom ['æntɪrum] *n* antesala
anthem ['ænθəm] *n*: **national ~** himno nacional
anthology [æn'θɔlədʒɪ] *n* antología
anthropologist [ænθrə'pɔlədʒɪst] *n* antropólogo(-a)
anthropology [ænθrə'pɔlədʒɪ] *n* antropología
anti... [æntɪ] *pref* anti...
anti-aircraft ['æntɪ'ɛəkrɑːft] *adj* antiaéreo
antiballistic [æntɪbə'lɪstɪk] *adj* antibalístico
antibiotic [æntɪbaɪ'ɔtɪk] *adj, n* antibiótico
antibody ['æntɪbɔdɪ] *n* anticuerpo
anticipate [æn'tɪsɪpeɪt] *vt* (*foresee*) prever; (*expect*) esperar, contar con; (*forestall*) anticiparse a, adelantarse a; **this is worse than I anticipated** esto es peor de lo que esperaba; **as anticipated** según se esperaba
anticipation [æntɪsɪ'peɪʃən] *n* previsión *f*; esperanza; anticipación *f*
anticlimax [æntɪ'klaɪmæks] *n* decepción *f*
anticlockwise [æntɪ'klɔkwaɪz] *adv* en dirección contraria a la de las agujas del reloj
antics ['æntɪks] *npl* payasadas *fpl*
anticyclone [æntɪ'saɪkləun] *n* anticiclón *m*
antidepressant [æntɪdɪ'presnt] *n* antidepresivo
antidote ['æntɪdəut] *n* antídoto
antifreeze ['æntɪfriːz] *n* anticongelante *m*
anti-globalization ['æntɪgləubəlaɪ'zeɪʃən] *n* antiglobalización *f*; **~ protesters** manifestantes *m/fpl* antiglobalización
antihistamine [æntɪ'hɪstəmiːn] *n* antihistamínico
Antilles [æn'tɪliːz] *npl*: **the ~** las Antillas
antipathy [æn'tɪpəθɪ] *n* (*between people*) antipatía; (*to person, thing*) aversión *f*
antiperspirant ['æntɪpəːspɪrənt] *n* antitranspirante *m*
Antipodes [æn'tɪpədiːz] *npl*: **the ~** las Antípodas
antiquarian [æntɪ'kwɛərɪən] *n* anticuario(-a)
antiquated ['æntɪkweɪtɪd] *adj* anticuado
antique [æn'tiːk] *n* antigüedad *f* ■ *adj* antiguo
antique dealer *n* anticuario(-a)
antique shop *n* tienda de antigüedades
antiquity [æn'tɪkwɪtɪ] *n* antigüedad *f*
anti-Semitic ['æntɪsɪ'mɪtɪk] *adj* antisemita
anti-Semitism [æntɪ'semɪtɪzəm] *n* antisemitismo
antiseptic [æntɪ'septɪk] *adj, n* antiséptico

antisocial [æntɪ'səuʃəl] *adj* antisocial
antitank [æntɪ'tæŋk] *adj* antitanque
antithesis (*pl* **antitheses**) [æn'tɪθɪsɪs, -siːz] *n* antítesis *f inv*
antitrust [æntɪ'trʌst] *adj*: **~ legislation** legislación *f* antimonopolio
antiviral [æntɪ'vaɪər] *adj* (*Med*) antivírico
antivirus [æntɪ'vaɪərəs] *adj* antivirus; **~ software** antivirus *m*
antlers ['æntləz] *npl* cornamenta
anus ['eɪnəs] *n* ano
anvil ['ænvɪl] *n* yunque *m*
anxiety [æŋ'zaɪətɪ] *n* (*worry*) inquietud *f*; (*eagerness*) ansia, anhelo
anxious ['æŋkʃəs] *adj* (*worried*) inquieto; (*keen*) deseoso; **I'm very ~ about you** me tienes muy preocupado
anxiously ['æŋkʃəslɪ] *adv* con inquietud, de manera angustiada

 KEYWORD

any ['ɛnɪ] *adj* **1** (*in questions etc*) algún/alguna; **have you any butter/children?** ¿tienes mantequilla/hijos?; **if there are any tickets left** si quedan billetes, si queda algún billete
2 (*with negative*): **I haven't any money/books** no tengo dinero/libros
3 (*no matter which*) cualquier; **any excuse will do** valdrá *or* servirá cualquier excusa; **choose any book you like** escoge el libro que quieras; **any teacher you ask will tell you** cualquier profesor al que preguntes te lo dirá
4 (*in phrases*): **in any case** de todas formas, en cualquier caso; **any day now** cualquier día (de estos); **at any moment** en cualquier momento, de un momento a otro; **at any rate** en todo caso; **any time: come (at) any time** ven cuando quieras; **he might come (at) any time** podría llegar de un momento a otro
■ *pron* **1** (*in questions etc*): **have you got any?** ¿tienes alguno/a?; **can any of you sing?** ¿sabe cantar alguno de vosotros/ustedes?
2 (*with negative*): **I haven't any (of them)** no tengo ninguno
3 (*no matter which one(s)*): **take any of those books (you like)** toma el libro que quieras de ésos
■ *adv* **1** (*in questions etc*): **do you want any more soup/sandwiches?** ¿quieres más sopa/bocadillos?; **are you feeling any better?** ¿te sientes algo mejor?
2 (*with negative*): **I can't hear him any more** ya no le oigo; **don't wait any longer** no esperes más

a

anybody ['ɛnɪbɔdɪ] *pron* cualquiera, cualquier persona; (*in interrogative sentences*) alguien; (*in negative sentences*): **I don't see ~** no veo a nadie

anyhow ['ɛnɪhau] *adv* de todos modos, de todas maneras; (*carelessly*) de cualquier manera; (*haphazardly*) de cualquier modo; **I shall go ~** iré de todas maneras

anyone ['ɛnɪwʌn] = **anybody**

anyplace ['ɛnɪpleɪs] *adv* (*US*) = **anywhere**

anything ['ɛnɪθɪŋ] *pron* cualquier cosa; (*in interrogative sentences*) algo; (*in negative sentences*) nada; (*everything*) todo; **~ else?** ¿algo más?; **it can cost ~ between £15 and £20** puede costar entre 15 y 20 libras

anytime ['ɛnɪtaɪm] *adv* (*at any moment*) en cualquier momento, de un momento a otro; (*whenever*) no importa cuándo, cuando quiera

anyway ['ɛnɪweɪ] *adv* de todas maneras; de cualquier modo

anywhere ['ɛnɪwɛə'] *adv* dondequiera; (*interrogative*) en algún sitio; (*negative sense*) en ningún sitio; (*everywhere*) en *or* por todas partes; **I don't see him ~** no le veo en ningún sitio; **~ in the world** en cualquier parte del mundo

Anzac ['ænzæk] *n abbr* = **Australia-New Zealand Army Corps**

apace [ə'peɪs] *adv* aprisa

apart [ə'pɑːt] *adv* aparte, separadamente; **10 miles ~** separados por 10 millas; **to take ~** desmontar; **~ from** *prep* aparte de

apartheid [ə'pɑːteɪt] *n* apartheid *m*

apartment [ə'pɑːtmənt] *n* (*US*) piso, departamento (*LAm*), apartamento; (*room*) cuarto

apartment block *or* **building** *n* (*US*) bloque *m* de pisos

apathetic [æpə'θɛtɪk] *adj* apático, indiferente

apathy ['æpəθɪ] *n* apatía, indiferencia

APB *n abbr* (*US*: = *all points bulletin*: *police expression*) expresión usada por la policía que significa "*descubrir y aprehender al sospechoso*"

ape [eɪp] *n* mono ■ *vt* imitar, remedar

Apennines ['æpənaɪnz] *npl*: **the ~** los Apeninos *mpl*

aperitif [ə'pɛrɪtiːf] *n* aperitivo

aperture ['æpətʃuə'] *n* rendija, resquicio; (*Phot*) abertura

APEX ['eɪpɛks] *n abbr* (*Aviat*: = *advance purchase excursion*) APEX *m*

apex ['eɪpɛks] *n* ápice *m*; (*fig*) cumbre *f*

aphid ['eɪfɪd] *n* pulgón *m*

aphorism ['æfərɪzəm] *n* aforismo

aphrodisiac [æfrəu'dɪzɪæk] *adj, n* afrodisíaco

API *n abbr* = **American Press Institute**

apiece [ə'piːs] *adv* cada uno

aplomb [ə'plɔm] *n* aplomo, confianza

APO *n abbr* (*US*: = *Army Post Office*) servicio postal del ejército

Apocalypse [ə'pɔkəlɪps] *n* Apocalipsis *m*

apocryphal [ə'pɔkrɪfəl] *adj* apócrifo

apolitical [eɪpə'lɪtɪkl] *adj* apolítico

apologetic [əpɔlə'dʒɛtɪk] *adj* (*look, remark*) de disculpa

apologetically [əpɔlə'dʒɛtɪkəlɪ] *adv* con aire de disculpa, excusándose, disculpándose

apologize [ə'pɔlədʒaɪz] *vi*: **to ~ (for sth to sb)** disculparse (con algn por algo)

apology [ə'pɔlədʒɪ] *n* disculpa, excusa; **please accept my apologies** le ruego me disculpe

apoplectic [æpə'plɛktɪk] *adj* (*Med*) apoplético; (*col*): **~ with rage** furioso

apoplexy ['æpəplɛksɪ] *n* apoplejía

apostle [ə'pɔsl] *n* apóstol *m/f*

apostrophe [ə'pɔstrəfɪ] *n* apóstrofo *m*

app *n abbr* (*Comput*) = **application**

appal [ə'pɔːl] *vt* horrorizar, espantar

Appalachian Mountains [æpə'leɪʃən-] *npl*: **the ~** los (Montes) Apalaches

appalling [ə'pɔːlɪŋ] *adj* espantoso; (*awful*) pésimo; **she's an ~ cook** es una cocinera malísima

apparatus [æpə'reɪtəs] *n* aparato; (*in gymnasium*) aparatos *mpl*

apparel [ə'pærl] *n* (*US*) indumentaria

apparent [ə'pærənt] *adj* aparente; (*obvious*) manifiesto, evidente; **it is ~ that** está claro que

apparently [ə'pærəntlɪ] *adv* por lo visto, al parecer, dizque (*LAm*)

apparition [æpə'rɪʃən] *n* aparición *f*

appeal [ə'piːl] *vi* (*Law*) apelar ■ *n* (*Law*) apelación *f*; (*request*) llamamiento, llamado (*LAm*); (*plea*) súplica; (*charm*) atractivo, encanto; **to ~ for** solicitar; **to ~ to** (*person*) rogar a, suplicar a; (*thing*) atraer, interesar; **to ~ to sb for mercy** rogarle misericordia a algn; **it doesn't ~ to me** no me atrae, no me llama la atención; **right of ~** derecho de apelación

appealing [ə'piːlɪŋ] *adj* (*nice*) atractivo; (*touching*) conmovedor(a), emocionante

appear [ə'pɪə'] *vi* aparecer, presentarse; (*Law*) comparecer; (*publication*) salir (a luz), publicarse; (*seem*) parecer; **it would ~ that** parecería que

appearance [ə'pɪərəns] *n* aparición *f*; (*look, aspect*) apariencia, aspecto; **to keep up appearances** salvar las apariencias; **to all appearances** al parecer

appease [ə'piːz] *vt* (*pacify*) apaciguar; (*satisfy*) satisfacer

appeasement [ə'piːzmənt] n (Pol) apaciguamiento

append [ə'pɛnd] vt (Comput) añadir (al final)

appendage [ə'pɛndɪdʒ] n añadidura

appendicitis [əpɛndɪ'saɪtɪs] n apendicitis f

appendix (pl **appendices**) [ə'pɛndɪks, -dɪsiːz] n apéndice m; **to have one's ~ out** operarse de apendicitis

appetite ['æpɪtaɪt] n apetito; (fig) deseo, anhelo; **that walk has given me an ~** ese paseo me ha abierto el apetito

appetizer ['æpɪtaɪzər] n (drink) aperitivo; (food) tapas fpl (SP)

appetizing ['æpɪtaɪzɪŋ] adj apetitoso

applaud [ə'plɔːd] vt, vi aplaudir

applause [ə'plɔːz] n aplausos mpl

apple ['æpl] n manzana

apple tree n manzano

appliance [ə'plaɪəns] n aparato; **electrical appliances** electrodomésticos mpl

applicable [ə'plɪkəbl] adj aplicable, pertinente; **the law is ~ from January** la ley es aplicable or se pone en vigor a partir de enero; **to be ~ to** referirse a

applicant ['æplɪkənt] n candidato(-a); solicitante m/f

application [æplɪ'keɪʃən] n (also Comput) aplicación f; (for a job, a grant etc) solicitud f

application form n solicitud f

application program n (Comput) (programa m de) aplicación f

applications package n (Comput) paquete m de programas de aplicación

applied [ə'plaɪd] adj (science, art) aplicado

apply [ə'plaɪ] vt: **to ~ (to)** aplicar (a); (fig) emplear (para) ▪ vi: **to ~ to** (ask) dirigirse a; (be suitable for) ser aplicable a; (be relevant to) tener que ver con; **to ~ for** (permit, grant, job) solicitar; **to ~ the brakes** echar el freno; **to ~ o.s. to** aplicarse a, dedicarse a

appoint [ə'pɔɪnt] vt (to post) nombrar; (date, place) fijar, señalar

appointee [əpɔɪn'tiː] n persona nombrada

appointment [ə'pɔɪntmənt] n (engagement) cita; (date) compromiso; (act) nombramiento; (post) puesto; **to make an ~ (with)** (doctor) pedir hora (con); (friend) citarse (con); "**appointments**" "ofertas de trabajo"; **by ~** mediante cita

apportion [ə'pɔːʃən] vt repartir

appraisal [ə'preɪzl] n evaluación f

appraise [ə'preɪz] vt (value) tasar, valorar; (situation etc) evaluar

appreciable [ə'priːʃəbl] adj sensible

appreciably [ə'priːʃəblɪ] adv sensiblemente, de manera apreciable

appreciate [ə'priːʃɪeɪt] vt (like) apreciar, tener en mucho; (be grateful for) agradecer; (be aware of) comprender ▪ vi (Comm) aumentar en valor; **I appreciated your help** agradecí tu ayuda

appreciation [əpriːʃɪ'eɪʃən] n aprecio; reconocimiento, agradecimiento; aumento en valor

appreciative [ə'priːʃɪətɪv] adj agradecido

apprehend [æprɪ'hɛnd] vt percibir; (arrest) detener

apprehension [æprɪ'hɛnʃən] n (fear) aprensión f

apprehensive [æprɪ'hɛnsɪv] adj aprensivo

apprentice [ə'prɛntɪs] n aprendiz(a) m(f) ▪ vt: **to be apprenticed to** estar de aprendiz con

apprenticeship [ə'prɛntɪsʃɪp] n aprendizaje m; **to serve one's ~** hacer el aprendizaje

appro. ['æprəʊ] abbr (Brit Comm: col) see **approval**

approach [ə'prəʊtʃ] vi acercarse ▪ vt acercarse a; (be approximate) aproximarse a; (ask, apply to) dirigirse a; (problem) abordar ▪ n acercamiento; aproximación f; (access) acceso; (proposal) proposición f; (to problem etc) enfoque m; **to ~ sb about sth** hablar con algn sobre algo

approachable [ə'prəʊtʃəbl] adj (person) abordable; (place) accesible

approach road n vía de acceso

approbation [æprə'beɪʃən] n aprobación f

appropriate [ə'prəʊprɪɪt] adj apropiado, conveniente ▪ vt [-rɪeɪt] (take) apropiarse de; (allot): **to ~ sth for** destinar algo a; **~ for** or **to** apropiado para; **it would not be ~ for me to comment** no estaría bien or sería pertinente que yo diera mi opinión

appropriation [əprəʊprɪ'eɪʃən] n asignación f

approval [ə'pruːvəl] n aprobación f, visto bueno; **on ~** (Comm) a prueba; **to meet with sb's ~** obtener la aprobación de algn

approve [ə'pruːv] vt aprobar
▶ **approve of** vt fus aprobar

approved school n (Brit) correccional m

approx. abbr (= approximately) aprox

approximate [ə'prɒksɪmɪt] adj aproximado

approximately [ə'prɒksɪmɪtlɪ] adv aproximadamente, más o menos

approximation [əprɒksɪ'meɪʃən] n aproximación f

Apr. abbr (= April) abr

apr n abbr (= annual percentage rate) tasa de interés anual

apricot ['eɪprɪkɒt] n albaricoque m (SP), damasco (LAm)

April ['eɪprəl] n abril m; see also **July**

April Fools' Day n ≈ día m de los (Santos) Inocentes; *ver nota*

apron ['eɪprən] n delantal m; (*Aviat*) pista
apse [æps] n (*Arch*) ábside m
APT n abbr (*Brit*) = **advanced passenger train**
Apt. abbr = **apartment**
apt [æpt] adj (*to the point*) acertado, oportuno; (*appropriate*) apropiado; ~ **to do** (*likely*) propenso a hacer
aptitude ['æptɪtjuːd] n aptitud f, capacidad f
aptitude test n prueba de aptitud
aptly ['æptlɪ] adj acertadamente
aqualung ['ækwəlʌŋ] n escafandra autónoma
aquarium [əˈkwɛərɪəm] n acuario
Aquarius [əˈkwɛərɪəs] n Acuario
aquatic [əˈkwætɪk] adj acuático
aqueduct ['ækwɪdʌkt] n acueducto
AR abbr (*US*) = **Arkansas**
ARA n abbr (*Brit*) = **Associate of the Royal Academy**
Arab ['ærəb] adj, n árabe m/f
Arabia [əˈreɪbɪə] n Arabia
Arabian [əˈreɪbɪən] adj árabe, arábigo
Arabian Desert n Desierto de Arabia
Arabian Sea n Mar m de Omán
Arabic ['ærəbɪk] adj (*language, manuscripts*) árabe, arábigo ■ n árabe m; ~ **numerals** numeración f arábiga
arable ['ærəbl] adj cultivable
Aragon ['ærəgən] n Aragón m
ARAM n abbr (*Brit*) = **Associate of the Royal Academy of Music**
arbiter ['ɑːbɪtəʳ] n árbitro
arbitrary ['ɑːbɪtrərɪ] adj arbitrario
arbitrate ['ɑːbɪtreɪt] vi arbitrar
arbitration [ɑːbɪˈtreɪʃən] n arbitraje m; **the dispute went to** ~ el conflicto laboral fue sometido al arbitraje
arbitrator ['ɑːbɪtreɪtəʳ] n árbitro
ARC n abbr = **American Red Cross**
arc [ɑːk] n arco
arcade [ɑːˈkeɪd] n (*Arch*) arcada; (*round a square*) soportales mpl; (*shopping arcade*) galería comercial

arch [ɑːtʃ] n arco; (*vault*) bóveda; (*of foot*) empeine m ■ vt arquear
archaeological [ɑːkɪəˈlɒdʒɪkl] adj arqueológico
archaeologist [ɑːkɪˈɒlədʒɪst] n arqueólogo(-a)
archaeology [ɑːkɪˈɒlədʒɪ] n arqueología
archaic [ɑːˈkeɪɪk] adj arcaico
archangel ['ɑːkeɪndʒəl] n arcángel m
archbishop [ɑːtʃˈbɪʃəp] n arzobispo
arched [ɑːtʃt] adj abovedado
archenemy ['ɑːtʃɛnəmɪ] n enemigo jurado
archeology etc [ɑːkɪˈɒlədʒɪ] (*US*) see **archaeology** etc
archer ['ɑːtʃəʳ] n arquero(-a)
archery ['ɑːtʃərɪ] n tiro al arco
archetypal ['ɑːkɪtaɪpəl] adj arquetípico
archetype ['ɑːkɪtaɪp] n arquetipo
archipelago [ɑːkɪˈpɛlɪgəu] n archipiélago
architect ['ɑːkɪtɛkt] n arquitecto(-a)
architectural [ɑːkɪˈtɛktʃərəl] adj arquitectónico
architecture ['ɑːkɪtɛktʃəʳ] n arquitectura
archive ['ɑːkaɪv] n (*often pl: also Comput*) archivo
archive file n (*Comput*) fichero archivado
archives ['ɑːkaɪvz] npl archivo sg
archivist ['ɑːkɪvɪst] n archivero(-a)
archway ['ɑːtʃweɪ] n arco, arcada
ARCM n abbr (*Brit*) = **Associate of the Royal College of Music**
Arctic ['ɑːktɪk] adj ártico ■ n: **the** ~ el Ártico
Arctic Circle n Círculo Polar Ártico
Arctic Ocean n Océano (Glacial) Ártico
ARD n abbr (*US Med*) = **acute respiratory disease**
ardent ['ɑːdənt] adj (*desire*) ardiente; (*supporter, lover*) apasionado
ardour, ardor (*US*) ['ɑːdəʳ] n ardor m, pasión f
arduous ['ɑːdjuəs] adj (*gen*) arduo; (*journey*) penoso
are [ɑːʳ] vb see **be**
area ['ɛərɪə] n área; (*Math etc*) superficie f, extensión f; (*zone*) región f, zona; **the London** ~ la zona de Londres
area code n (*US Tel*) prefijo
arena [əˈriːnə] n arena; (*of circus*) pista; (*for bullfight*) plaza, ruedo
aren't [ɑːnt] = **are not**
Argentina [ɑːdʒənˈtiːnə] n Argentina
Argentinian [ɑːdʒənˈtɪnɪən] adj, n argentino(-a) m(f)
arguable ['ɑːgjuəbl] adj: **it is** ~ **whether ...** es dudoso que + subjun
arguably ['ɑːgjuəblɪ] adv: **it is** ~ **...** es discutiblemente ...
argue ['ɑːgjuː] vt (*debate: case, matter*)

mantener, argüir ■ vi (quarrel) discutir; (reason) razonar, argumentar; **to ~ that** sostener que; **to ~ about sth (with sb)** pelearse (con algn) por algo

argument ['ɑːgjumənt] n (reasons) argumento; (quarrel) discusión f; (debate) debate m; **~ for/against** argumento en pro/contra de

argumentative [ɑːgjuˈmɛntətɪv] adj discutidor(a)

aria ['ɑːrɪə] n (Mus) aria

ARIBA n abbr (Brit) = **Associate of the Royal Institute of British Architects**

arid ['ærɪd] adj árido

aridity [əˈrɪdɪtɪ] n aridez f

Aries ['ɛərɪz] n Aries m

arise [əˈraɪz] (pt **arose**, pp **arisen** [əˈrɪzn]) vi (rise up) levantarse, alzarse; (emerge) surgir, presentarse; **to ~ from** derivar de; **should the need ~** si fuera necesario

aristocracy [ærɪsˈtɔkrəsɪ] n aristocracia

aristocrat ['ærɪstəkræt] n aristócrata m/f

aristocratic [ərɪstəˈkrætɪk] adj aristocrático

arithmetic [əˈrɪθmətɪk] n aritmética

arithmetical [ærɪθˈmɛtɪkl] adj aritmético

Ariz. abbr (US) = **Arizona**

Ark [ɑːk] n: **Noah's ~** el Arca f de Noé

Ark. abbr (US) = **Arkansas**

arm [ɑːm] n (Anat) brazo ■ vt armar; **~ in ~** cogidos del brazo; see also **arms**

armaments ['ɑːməmənts] npl (weapons) armamentos mpl

armchair ['ɑːmtʃɛəʳ] n sillón m, butaca

armed [ɑːmd] adj armado; **the ~ forces** las fuerzas armadas

armed robbery n robo a mano armada

Armenia [ɑːˈmiːnɪə] n Armenia

Armenian [ɑːˈmiːnɪən] adj armenio ■ n armenio(-a); (Ling) armenio

armful ['ɑːmful] n brazada

armistice ['ɑːmɪstɪs] n armisticio

armour, armor (US) ['ɑːməʳ] n armadura

armoured car, armored car (US) n coche m or carro (LAm) blindado

armoury, armory (US) ['ɑːmərɪ] n arsenal m

armpit ['ɑːmpɪt] n sobaco, axila

armrest ['ɑːmrɛst] n reposabrazos m inv, brazo

arms [ɑːmz] npl (weapons) armas fpl; (Heraldry) escudo sg

arms control n control m de armamentos

arms race n carrera de armamentos

army ['ɑːmɪ] n ejército

aroma [əˈrəumə] n aroma m, fragancia

aromatherapy [ərəuməˈθɛrəpɪ] n aromaterapia

aromatic [ærəˈmætɪk] adj aromático, fragante

arose [əˈrəuz] pt of **arise**

around [əˈraund] adv alrededor; (in the area) a la redonda ■ prep alrededor de

arousal [əˈrauzəl] n (sexual) excitación f; (of feelings, interest) despertar m

arouse [əˈrauz] vt despertar

arrange [əˈreɪndʒ] vt arreglar, ordenar; (programme) organizar; (appointment) concertar ■ vi: **we have arranged for a taxi to pick you up** hemos organizado todo para que le recoja un taxi; **to ~ to do sth** quedar en hacer algo; **it was arranged that ...** se quedó en que ...

arrangement [əˈreɪndʒmənt] n arreglo; (agreement) acuerdo; **arrangements** npl (plans) planes mpl, medidas fpl; (preparations) preparativos mpl; **to come to an ~ (with sb)** llegar a un acuerdo (con algn); **by ~** a convenir; **I'll make arrangements for you to be met** haré los preparativos para que le estén esperando

arrant ['ærənt] adj: **~ nonsense** una verdadera tontería

array [əˈreɪ] n (Comput) matriz f; **~ of** (things) serie f or colección f de; (people) conjunto de

arrears [əˈrɪəz] npl atrasos mpl; **in ~** (Comm) en mora; **to be in ~ with one's rent** estar retrasado en el pago del alquiler

arrest [əˈrɛst] vt detener; (sb's attention) llamar ■ n detención f; **under ~** detenido

arresting [əˈrɛstɪŋ] adj (fig) llamativo

arrival [əˈraɪvəl] n llegada, arribo (LAm); **new ~** recién llegado(-a)

arrive [əˈraɪv] vi llegar, arribar (LAm)

arrogance ['ærəgəns] n arrogancia, prepotencia (LAm)

arrogant ['ærəgənt] adj arrogante, prepotente (LAm)

arrow ['ærəu] n flecha

arse [ɑːs] n (Brit col!) culo, trasero

arsenal ['ɑːsɪnl] n arsenal m

arsenic ['ɑːsnɪk] n arsénico

arson ['ɑːsn] n incendio provocado

art [ɑːt] n arte m; (skill) destreza; (technique) técnica; **Arts** npl (Scol) Letras fpl; **work of ~** obra de arte

art and design n (Brit Scol) arte m y diseño, dibujo

artefact ['ɑːtɪfækt] n artefacto

arterial [ɑːˈtɪərɪəl] adj (Anat) arterial; (road etc) principal

artery ['ɑːtərɪ] n (Med: road etc) arteria

artful ['ɑːtful] adj (cunning: person, trick) mañoso

art gallery n pinacoteca, museo de pintura; (Comm) galería de arte

arthritis [ɑ:'θraɪtɪs] n artritis f
artichoke ['ɑ:tɪtʃəuk] n alcachofa;
  Jerusalem ~ aguaturma
article ['ɑ:tɪkl] n artículo, objeto, cosa;
  (in newspaper) artículo; (Brit Law: training);
  articles npl contrato sg de aprendizaje;
  articles of clothing prendas fpl de vestir
articles of association npl (Comm) estatutos
  mpl sociales, escritura social
articulate adj [ɑ:'tɪkjulɪt] (speech) claro;
  (person) que se expresa bien ■ vi [ɑ:'tɪkjuleɪt]
  articular
articulated lorry n (Brit) trailer m
artifice ['ɑ:tɪfɪs] n artificio, truco
artificial [ɑ:tɪ'fɪʃəl] adj artificial; (teeth etc)
  postizo
artificial insemination n inseminación f
  artificial
artificial intelligence n inteligencia
  artificial
artificial respiration n respiración f
  artificial
artillery [ɑ:'tɪlərɪ] n artillería
artisan ['ɑ:tɪzæn] n artesano(-a)
artist ['ɑ:tɪst] n artista m/f; (Mus) intérprete
  m/f
artistic [ɑ:'tɪstɪk] adj artístico
artistry ['ɑ:tɪstrɪ] n arte m, habilidad f
  (artística)
artless ['ɑ:tlɪs] adj (innocent) natural, sencillo;
  (clumsy) torpe
art school n escuela de bellas artes
artwork ['ɑ:twə:k] n material m gráfico
arty ['ɑ:tɪ] adj artistoide
ARV n abbr (= American Revised Version) traducción
  americana de la Biblia
AS n abbr (US Scol) = **Associate in Science**

◯ KEYWORD

as [æz] conj **1** (referring to time: while) mientras;
  (: when) cuando; **she wept as she told her
  story** lloraba mientras contaba lo que le
  ocurrió; **as the years go by** a medida que
  pasan los años, con el paso de los años; **he
  came in as I was leaving** entró cuando me
  marchaba; **as from tomorrow** a partir de or
  desde mañana
  2 (in comparisons): **as big as** tan grande como;
  twice as big as el doble de grande que; **as
  much money/many books as** tanto dinero/
  tantos libros como; **as soon as** en cuanto, no
  bien (LAm)
  3 (since, because) como, ya que; **as I don't
  speak German I can't understand him**
  como no hablo alemán no le entiendo, no le
  entiendo ya que no hablo alemán

4 (although): **much as I like them, ...** aunque
  me gustan, ...
  5 (referring to manner, way): **do as you wish**
  haz lo que quieras; **as she said** como dijo;
  he gave it to me as a present me lo dio de
  regalo; **it's on the left as you go in** según se
  entra, a la izquierda
  6 (concerning): **as for** or **to that** por or en lo que
  respecta a eso
  7: **as if** or **though** como si; **he looked as
  if he was ill** parecía como si estuviera
  enfermo, tenía aspecto de enfermo; see also
  long; such; well
  ■ prep (in the capacity of): **he works as a
  barman** trabaja de barman; **as chairman of
  the company, he ...** como presidente de la
  compañía, ...

ASA n abbr (= American Standards Association)
  instituto de normalización; (Brit: = Advertising
  Standards Association) departamento de control de
  la publicidad; (= Amateur Swimming Association)
  federación amateur de natación
a.s.a.p. abbr (= as soon as possible) cuanto antes,
  lo más pronto posible
asbestos [æz'bɛstəs] n asbesto, amianto
ascend [ə'sɛnd] vt subir, ascender
ascendancy [ə'sɛndənsɪ] n ascendiente m,
  dominio
ascendant [ə'sɛndənt] n: **to be in the ~** estar
  en auge, ir ganando predominio
Ascension [ə'sɛnʃən] n: **the ~** la Ascensión
Ascension Island n Isla Ascensión
ascent [ə'sɛnt] n subida; (slope) cuesta,
  pendiente f; (of plane) ascenso
ascertain [æsə'teɪn] vt averiguar
ascetic [ə'sɛtɪk] adj ascético
asceticism [ə'sɛtɪsɪzəm] n ascetismo
ASCII ['æski:] n abbr (= American Standard Code
  for Information Interchange) ASCII
ascribe [ə'skraɪb] vt: **to ~ sth to** atribuir
  algo a
ASCU n abbr (US) = **Association of State
  Colleges and Universities**
ASE n abbr = **American Stock Exchange**
ASH [æʃ] n abbr (Brit: = Action on Smoking and
  Health) organización anti-tabaco
ash [æʃ] n ceniza; (tree) fresno
ashamed [ə'feɪmd] adj avergonzado; **to be ~
  of** avergonzarse de
ashcan ['æʃkæn] n (US) cubo or bote m (LAm)
  de la basura
ashen ['æʃn] adj pálido
ashore [ə'fɔ:ʳ] adv en tierra
ashtray ['æʃtreɪ] n cenicero
Ash Wednesday n miércoles m de ceniza
Asia ['eɪʃə] n Asia

Asian ['eɪʃən], **Asiatic** [eɪsɪ'ætɪk] adj, n
asiático(-a) m(f)
aside [ə'saɪd] adv a un lado ■ n aparte m;
~ from prep (as well as) aparte or además de
ask [ɑːsk] vt (question) preguntar; (demand)
pedir; (invite) invitar ■ vi: **to ~ about sth**
preguntar acerca de algo; **to ~ sb sth/to do
sth** preguntar algo a algn/pedir a algn que
haga algo; **to ~ sb about sth** preguntar
algo a algn; **to ~ (sb) a question** hacer
una pregunta (a algn); **to ~ sb the time**
preguntar la hora a algn; **to ~ sb out to
dinner** invitar a cenar a algn
  ▶ **ask after** vt fus preguntar por
  ▶ **ask for** vt fus pedir; **it's just asking for
trouble** or **for it** es buscarse problemas
askance [ə'skɑːns] adv: **to look ~ at sb** mirar
con recelo a algn
askew [ə'skjuː] adv sesgado, ladeado
asking price n (Comm) precio inicial
asleep [ə'sliːp] adj dormido; **to fall ~**
dormirse, quedarse dormido
ASLEF ['æzlɛf] n abbr (Brit: = Associated Society
of Locomotive Engineers and Firemen) sindicato de
ferroviarios
AS level n abbr (Brit Scol: = Advanced Subsidiary
level) título intermedio entre los "GCSEs" y los "A
levels"
asp [æsp] n áspid m
asparagus [əs'pærəgəs] n espárragos mpl
ASPCA n abbr = **American Society for the
Prevention of Cruelty to Animals**
aspect ['æspɛkt] n aspecto, apariencia;
(direction in which a building etc faces)
orientación f
aspersions [əs'pəːʃənz] npl: **to cast ~ on**
difamar a, calumniar a
asphalt ['æsfælt] n asfalto
asphyxiate [æs'fɪksɪeɪt] vt asfixiar
asphyxiation [aesfɪksɪ'eɪʃən] n asfixia
aspirate ['æspəreɪt] vt aspirar ■ adj
['æspɪrɪt] aspirado
aspirations [æspə'reɪʃənz] npl aspiraciones
fpl; (ambition) ambición f
aspire [əs'paɪər] vi: **to ~ to** aspirar a,
ambicionar
aspirin ['æsprɪn] n aspirina
aspiring [əs'paɪərɪŋ] adj: **an ~ actor** un
aspirante a actor
ass [æs] n asno, burro; (col) imbécil m/f; (US
col!) culo, trasero
assailant [ə'seɪlənt] n agresor(a) m(f)
assassin [ə'sæsɪn] n asesino(-a)
assassinate [ə'sæsɪneɪt] vt asesinar
assassination [əsæsɪ'neɪʃən] n asesinato
assault [ə'sɔːlt] n (gen: attack) asalto, agresión
f ■ vt asaltar, agredir; (sexually) violar

assemble [ə'sɛmbl] vt reunir, juntar; (Tech)
montar ■ vi reunirse, juntarse
assembly [ə'sɛmblɪ] n (meeting) reunión f,
asamblea; (construction) montaje m
assembly language n (Comput) lenguaje m
ensamblador
assembly line n cadena de montaje
Assembly Member n (in Wales) miembro m/f
de la Asamblea Nacional (de Gales)
assent [ə'sɛnt] n asentimiento, aprobación
f ■ vi consentir, asentir; **to ~ (to sth)**
consentir (en algo)
assert [ə'səːt] vt afirmar; (insist on) hacer
valer; **to ~ o.s.** imponerse
assertion [ə'səːʃən] n afirmación f
assertive [ə'səːtɪv] adj enérgico, agresivo,
perentorio
assess [ə'sɛs] vt valorar, calcular; (tax,
damages) fijar; (property etc: for tax) gravar
assessment [ə'sɛsmənt] n valoración f;
gravamen m; (judgment): **~ (of)** juicio (sobre)
assessor [ə'sɛsər] n asesor(a) m(f); (of tax)
tasador(a) m(f)
asset ['æsɛt] n posesión f; (quality) ventaja;
assets npl (funds) activo sg, fondos mpl
asset-stripping ['æsɛt'strɪpɪŋ] n (Comm)
acaparamiento de activos
assiduous [ə'sɪdjuəs] adj asiduo
assign [ə'saɪn] vt (date) fijar; (task) asignar;
(resources) destinar; (property) traspasar
assignment [ə'saɪnmənt] n asignación f;
(task) tarea
assimilate [ə'sɪmɪleɪt] vt asimilar
assimilation [əsɪmɪ'leɪʃən] n asimilación f
assist [ə'sɪst] vt ayudar
assistance [ə'sɪstəns] n ayuda, auxilio
assistant [ə'sɪstənt] n ayudante m/f; (Brit
also: **shop assistant**) dependiente(-a) m(f)
assistant manager n subdirector(a) m(f)
assizes [ə'saɪzɪz] npl sesión f de un tribunal
associate [adj, n ə'səuʃɪɪt, vt, vi ə'səuʃɪeɪt] adj
asociado ■ n socio(-a), colega m/f; (in crime)
cómplice m/f; (member) miembro(-a) ■ vt
asociar; (ideas) relacionar ■ vi: **to ~ with sb**
tratar con algn; **~ director** subdirector(a)
m(f); **associated company** compañía
afiliada
association [əsəusɪ'eɪʃən] n asociación f;
(Comm) sociedad f; **in ~ with** en asociación
con
association football n (Brit) fútbol m
assorted [ə'sɔːtɪd] adj surtido, variado; **in ~
sizes** en distintos tamaños
assortment [ə'sɔːtmənt] n surtido
Asst. abbr = **Assistant**
assuage [ə'sweɪdʒ] vt mitigar
assume [ə'sjuːm] vt (suppose) suponer;

assumed name n nombre m falso

assumption [ə'sʌmpʃən] n (supposition)
suposición f, presunción f; (act) asunción f;
on the ~ that suponiendo que

assurance [ə'ʃuərəns] n garantía, promesa;
(confidence) confianza, aplomo; (Brit: insurance)
seguro; **I can give you no assurances** no
puedo hacerle ninguna promesa

assure [ə'ʃuəʳ] vt asegurar

assured [ə'ʃuəd] adj seguro

assuredly [ə'ʃuərɪdlɪ] adv indudablemente

AST abbr (= Atlantic Standard Time) hora oficial del
este del Canadá

asterisk ['æstərɪsk] n asterisco

astern [ə'stə:n] adv a popa

asteroid ['æstərɔɪd] n asteroide m

asthma ['æsmə] n asma

asthmatic [æs'mætɪk] adj, n asmático(-a)
m(f)

astigmatism [ə'stɪgmətɪzəm] n
astigmatismo

astir [ə'stə:ʳ] adv en acción

astonish [ə'stɔnɪʃ] vt asombrar, pasmar

astonishing [ə'stɔnɪʃɪŋ] adj asombroso,
pasmoso; **I find it ~ that ...** me asombra or
pasma que ...

astonishingly [ə'stɔnɪʃɪŋlɪ] adv
increíblemente, asombrosamente

astonishment [ə'stɔnɪʃmənt] n asombro,
sorpresa; **to my ~** con gran sorpresa mía

astound [ə'staund] vt asombrar, pasmar

astounding [ə'staundɪŋ] adj asombroso

astray [ə'streɪ] adv: **to go ~** extraviarse; **to
lead ~** llevar por mal camino; **to go ~ in
one's calculations** equivocarse en sus
cálculos

astride [ə'straɪd] prep a caballo or horcajadas
sobre

astringent [əs'trɪndʒənt] adj, n astringente m

astrologer [əs'trɔlədʒəʳ] n astrólogo(-a)

astrology [əs'trɔlədʒɪ] n astrología

astronaut ['æstrənɔ:t] n astronauta m/f

astronomer [əs'trɔnəməʳ] n astrónomo(-a)

astronomical [æstrə'nɔmɪkəl] adj
astronómico

astronomy [aes'trɔnəmɪ] n astronomía

astrophysics ['æstrəu'fɪzɪks] n astrofísica

astute [əs'tju:t] adj astuto

asunder [ə'sʌndəʳ] adv: **to tear ~** hacer
pedazos

ASV n abbr (= American Standard Version)
traducción de la Biblia

asylum [ə'saɪləm] n (refuge) asilo; (hospital)
manicomio; **to seek political ~** pedir asilo
político

asymmetric [eɪsɪ'mɛtrɪk], **asymmetrical**
[eɪsɪ'mɛtrɪkl] adj asimétrico

○ KEYWORD

at [æt] prep **1** (referring to position) en; (direction)
a; **at the top** en lo alto; **at home/school**
en casa/la escuela; **to look at sth/sb** mirar
algo/a algn
2 (referring to time): **at four o'clock** a las
cuatro; **at night** por la noche; **at Christmas**
en Navidad; **at times** a veces
3 (referring to rates, speed etc): **at £1 a kilo** a una
libra el kilo; **two at a time** de dos en dos;
at 50 km/h a 50 km/h
4 (referring to manner): **at a stroke** de un golpe;
at peace en paz
5 (referring to activity): **to be at work** estar
trabajando; (in office) estar en el trabajo; **to
play at cowboys** jugar a los vaqueros; **to be
good at sth** ser bueno en algo
6 (referring to cause): **shocked/surprised/
annoyed at sth** asombrado/sorprendido/
fastidiado por algo; **I went at his
suggestion** fui a instancias suyas
■ n (symbol @) arroba

ate [ɛt, eɪt] pt of **eat**

atheism ['eɪθɪɪzəm] n ateísmo

atheist ['eɪθɪɪst] n ateo(-a)

Athenian [ə'θi:nɪən] adj, n ateniense m/f

Athens ['æθɪnz] n Atenas f

athlete ['æθli:t] n atleta m/f

athletic [æθ'lɛtɪk] adj atlético

athletics [æθ'lɛtɪks] n atletismo

Atlantic [ət'læntɪk] adj atlántico ■ n:
the ~ (Ocean) el (Océano) Atlántico

atlas ['ætləs] n atlas m inv

Atlas Mountains npl: **the ~** el Atlas

A.T.M. n abbr (= Automated Telling Machine) cajero
automático

atmosphere ['ætməsfɪəʳ] n (air) atmósfera;
(fig) ambiente m

atom ['ætəm] n átomo

atom bomb n bomba atómica

atomic [ə'tɔmɪk] adj atómico

atomic bomb n bomba atómica

atomic power n energía atómica

atomizer ['ætəmaɪzəʳ] n atomizador m

atone [ə'təun] vi: **to ~ for** expiar

atonement [ə'təunmənt] n expiación f

A to Z® n guía alfabética; (map) callejero

ATP n abbr (= Association of Tennis Professionals)
sindicato de jugadores de tenis profesionales

atrocious [ə'trəuʃəs] adj atroz; (fig) horrible,
infame

atrocity [ə'trɔsɪtɪ] n atrocidad f

atrophy ['ætrəfɪ] *n* atrofia ■ *vi* atrofiarse

attach [ə'tætʃ] *vt* sujetar; (*stick*) pegar; (*document, email, letter*) adjuntar; **to be attached to sb/sth** (*like*) tener cariño a algn/algo; **the attached letter** la carta adjunta

attaché [ə'tæʃeɪ] *n* agregado(-a)

attaché case *n* (*Brit*) maletín *m*

attachment [ə'tætʃmənt] *n* (*tool*) accesorio; (*Comput*) archivo o documento adjunto; (*love*): **~ (to)** apego (a), cariño (a)

attack [ə'tæk] *vt* (*Mil*) atacar; (*criminal*) agredir, asaltar; (*task etc*) emprender ■ *n* ataque *m*, asalto; (*on sb's life*) atentado; **heart ~** infarto (de miocardio)

attacker [ə'tækə'] *n* agresor(a) *m(f)*, asaltante *m/f*

attain [ə'teɪn] *vt* (*also*: **attain to**) alcanzar; (*achieve*) lograr, conseguir

attainments [ə'teɪnmənts] *npl* (*skill*) talento *sg*

attempt [ə'tɛmpt] *n* tentativa, intento; (*attack*) atentado ■ *vt* intentar, tratar de; **he made no ~ to help** ni siquiera intentó ayudar

attempted [ə'tɛmptɪd] *adj*: **~ murder/burglary/suicide** tentativa *or* intento de asesinato/robo/suicidio

attend [ə'tɛnd] *vt* asistir a; (*patient*) atender ▸ **attend to** *vt fus* (*needs, affairs etc*) ocuparse de; (*speech etc*) prestar atención a; (*customer*) atender a

attendance [ə'tɛndəns] *n* asistencia, presencia; (*people present*) concurrencia

attendant [ə'tɛndənt] *n* sirviente(-a) *m(f)*, mozo(-a); (*Theat*) acomodador(a) *m(f)* ■ *adj* concomitante

attention [ə'tɛnʃən] *n* atención *f* ■ *excl* (*Mil*) ¡firme(s)!; **for the ~ of ...** (*Admin*) a la atención de ...; **it has come to my ~ that ...** me he enterado de que ...

attentive [ə'tɛntɪv] *adj* atento; (*polite*) cortés

attenuate [ə'tɛnjueɪt] *vt* atenuar

attest [ə'tɛst] *vi*: **to ~ to** dar fe de

attic ['ætɪk] *n* desván *m*, altillo (*LAm*), entretecho (*LAm*)

attitude ['ætɪtjuːd] *n* (*gen*) actitud *f*; (*disposition*) disposición *f*

attorney [ə'tɜːnɪ] *n* (*US: lawyer*) abogado(-a); (*having proxy*) apoderado

Attorney General *n* (*Brit*) ≈ Presidente *m* del Consejo del Poder Judicial (*SP*); (*US*) ≈ ministro de justicia

attract [ə'trækt] *vt* atraer; (*attention*) llamar

attraction [ə'trækʃən] *n* (*gen*) encanto, atractivo; (*Physics*) atracción *f*; (*towards sth*) atracción *f*

attractive [ə'træktɪv] *adj* atractivo

attribute ['ætrɪbjuːt] *n* atributo ■ *vt* [ə'trɪbjuːt]: **to ~ sth to** atribuir algo a; (*accuse*) achacar algo a

attrition [ə'trɪʃən] *n*: **war of ~** guerra de agotamiento *or* desgaste

Atty. Gen. *abbr* = **Attorney General**

ATV *n abbr* (= *all terrain vehicle*) vehículo todo terreno

atypical [eɪ'tɪpɪkl] *adj* atípico

AU *n abbr* (= *African Union*) UA *f* (= Unión Africana)

aubergine ['əubəʒiːn] *n* (*Brit*) berenjena

auburn ['ɔːbən] *adj* color castaño rojizo

auction ['ɔːkʃən] *n* (*also*: **sale by auction**) subasta ■ *vt* subastar

auctioneer [ɔːkʃə'nɪə'] *n* subastador(a) *m(f)*

auction room *n* sala de subastas

audacious [ɔː'deɪʃəs] *adj* (*bold*) audaz, osado; (*impudent*) atrevido, descarado

audacity [ɔː'dæsɪtɪ] *n* audacia, atrevimiento; (*pej*) descaro

audible ['ɔːdɪbl] *adj* audible, que se puede oír

audience ['ɔːdɪəns] *n* auditorio; (*gathering*) público; (*interview*) audiencia

audio-typist ['ɔːdɪəu'taɪpɪst] *n* mecanógrafo(-a) de dictáfono

audiovisual [ɔːdɪəu'vɪzjuəl] *adj* audiovisual

audiovisual aid *n* ayuda *or* medio audiovisual

audit ['ɔːdɪt] *vt* revisar, intervenir

audition [ɔː'dɪʃən] *n* audición *f* ■ *vi*: **to ~ for the part of** hacer una audición para el papel de

auditor ['ɔːdɪtə'] *n* interventor(a) *m(f)*, censor(a) *m(f.)* de cuentas

auditorium [ɔːdɪ'tɔːrɪəm] *n* auditorio

Aug. *abbr* (= *August*) ag

augment [ɔːg'mɛnt] *vt, vi* aumentar

augur ['ɔːgə'] *vi*: **it augurs well** es de buen agüero

August ['ɔːgəst] *n* agosto; *see also* **July**

august [ɔː'gʌst] *adj* augusto

aunt [ɑːnt] *n* tía

auntie, aunty ['ɑːntɪ] *n diminutive of* **aunt**

au pair ['əu'pɛə'] *n* (*also*: **au pair girl**) chica *f* au pair

aura ['ɔːrə] *n* aura; (*atmosphere*) ambiente *m*

auspices ['ɔːspɪsɪz] *npl*: **under the ~ of** bajo los auspicios de

auspicious [ɔːs'pɪʃəs] *adj* propicio, de buen augurio

austere [ɔs'tɪə'] *adj* austero; (*manner*) adusto

austerity [ɔ'stɛrɪtɪ] *n* austeridad *f*

Australasia [ɔːstrə'leɪzɪə] *n* Australasia

Australia [ɔs'treɪlɪə] *n* Australia

Australian [ɔs'treɪlɪən] *adj, n* australiano(-a) *m(f)*

Austria ['ɔstrɪə] *n* Austria

Austrian ['ɔstrɪən] *adj, n* austríaco(-a) *m(f)*
AUT *n abbr* (Brit: = *Association of University Teachers*) *sindicato de profesores de universidad*
authentic [ɔː'θɛntɪk] *adj* auténtico
authenticate [ɔː'θɛntɪkeɪt] *vt* autentificar
authenticity [ɔːθɛn'tɪsɪtɪ] *n* autenticidad *f*
author ['ɔːθəʳ] *n* autor(a) *m(f)*
authoritarian [ɔːθɔrɪ'tɛərɪən] *adj* autoritario
authoritative [ɔː'θɔrɪtətɪv] *adj* autorizado; (*manner*) autoritario
authority [ɔː'θɔrɪtɪ] *n* autoridad *f*; **the authorities** *npl* las autoridades; **to have ~ to do sth** tener autoridad para hacer algo
authorization [ɔːθəraɪ'zeɪʃən] *n* autorización *f*
authorize ['ɔːθəraɪz] *vt* autorizar
authorized capital *n* (*Comm*) capital *m* autorizado *or* social
autistic [ɔː'tɪstɪk] *adj* autista
auto ['ɔːtəu] *n* (*US*) coche *m*, carro (*LAm*), auto (*LAm*), automóvil *m*
autobiographical [ɔːtəbaɪə'græfɪkəl] *adj* autobiográfico
autobiography [ɔːtəbaɪ'ɔgrəfɪ] *n* autobiografía
autocratic [ɔːtə'krætɪk] *adj* autocrático
Autocue® ['ɔːtəukjuː] *n* autocue *m*, teleapuntador *m*
autograph ['ɔːtəgrɑːf] *n* autógrafo ▪ *vt* firmar; (*photo etc*) dedicar
autoimmune [ɔːtəʊɪ'mjuːn] *adj* autoinmune
automat ['ɔːtəmæt] *n* (*US*) restaurante *m* de autoservicio
automate ['ɔːtəmeɪt] *vt* automatizar
automated ['ɔːtəmeɪtɪd] *adj* automatizado
automatic [ɔːtə'mætɪk] *adj* automático ▪ *n* (*gun*) pistola automática; (*washing machine*) lavadora
automatically [ɔːtə'mætɪklɪ] *adv* automáticamente
automatic data processing *n* proceso automático de datos
automation [ɔːtə'meɪʃən] *n* automatización *f*
automaton (*pl* **automata**) [ɔː'tɔmətən, -tə] *n* autómata
automobile ['ɔːtəməbiːl] *n* (*US*) coche *m*, carro (*LAm*), auto (*LAm*), automóvil *m*
autonomous [ɔː'tɔnəməs] *adj* autónomo
autonomy [ɔː'tɔnəmɪ] *n* autonomía
autopsy ['ɔːtɔpsɪ] *n* autopsia
autumn ['ɔːtəm] *n* otoño
auxiliary [ɔːg'zɪlɪərɪ] *adj* auxiliar
AV *n abbr* (= *Authorized Version*) *traducción inglesa de la Biblia* ▪ *abbr* = **audiovisual**
Av. *abbr* (= *avenue*) Av., Avda
avail [ə'veɪl] *vt*: **to ~ o.s. of** aprovechar(se) de, valerse de ▪ *n*: **to no ~** en vano, sin resultado
availability [əveɪlə'bɪlɪtɪ] *n* disponibilidad *f*

available [ə'veɪləbl] *adj* disponible; (*obtainable*) asequible; **to make sth ~ to sb** poner algo a la disposición de algn; **is the manager ~?** ¿está libre el gerente?
avalanche ['ævəlɑːnʃ] *n* alud *m*, avalancha
avant-garde ['ævãŋ'gɑːd] *adj* de vanguardia
avarice ['ævərɪs] *n* avaricia
avaricious [ævə'rɪʃəs] *adj* avaricioso
avdp. *abbr* = **avoirdupois**
Ave. *abbr* (= *avenue*) Av., Avda
avenge [ə'vɛndʒ] *vt* vengar
avenue ['ævənjuː] *n* avenida; (*fig*) camino, vía
average ['ævərɪdʒ] *n* promedio, media ▪ *adj* (*mean*) medio; (*ordinary*) regular, corriente ▪ *vt* calcular el promedio de; **on ~** por término medio
▸ **average out** *vi*: **to ~ out at** salir a un promedio de
averse [ə'vəːs] *adj*: **to be ~ to sth/doing** sentir aversión *or* antipatía por algo/por hacer
aversion [ə'vəːʃən] *n* aversión *f*, repugnancia
avert [ə'vəːt] *vt* prevenir; (*blow*) desviar; (*one's eyes*) apartar
aviary ['eɪvɪərɪ] *n* pajarera
aviation [eɪvɪ'eɪʃən] *n* aviación *f*
aviator ['eɪvɪeɪtəʳ] *n* aviador(a) *m(f)*
avid ['ævɪd] *adj* ávido, ansioso
avidly ['ævɪdlɪ] *adv* ávidamente, con avidez
avocado [ævə'kɑːdəu] *n* (*Brit*: *also*: **avocado pear**) aguacate *m*, palta (*LAm*)
avoid [ə'vɔɪd] *vt* evitar, eludir
avoidable [ə'vɔɪdəbl] *adj* evitable, eludible
avoidance [ə'vɔɪdəns] *n* evasión *f*
avow [ə'vau] *vt* prometer
avowal [ə'vauəl] *n* promesa, voto
avowed [ə'vaud] *adj* declarado
AVP *n abbr* (*US*) = **assistant vice-president**
avuncular [ə'vʌŋkjuləʳ] *adj* paternal
AWACS ['eɪwæks] *n abbr* (= *airborne warning and control system*) AWACS *m*
await [ə'weɪt] *vt* esperar, aguardar; **long awaited** largamente esperado
awake [ə'weɪk] (*pt* **awoke**, *pp* **awoken** *or* **awaked**) *adj* despierto ▪ *vt* despertar ▪ *vi* despertarse; **to be ~** estar despierto
awakening [ə'weɪknɪŋ] *n* despertar *m*
award [ə'wɔːd] *n* (*prize*) premio; (*medal*) condecoración *f*; (*Law*) fallo, sentencia; (*act*) concesión *f* ▪ *vt* (*prize*) otorgar, conceder; (*Law: damages*) adjudicar
aware [ə'wɛəʳ] *adj* consciente; (*awake*) despierto; (*informed*) enterado; **to become ~ of** darse cuenta de, enterarse de; **I am fully ~ that** sé muy bien que
awareness [ə'wɛənɪs] *n* conciencia, conocimiento
awash [ə'wɔʃ] *adj* inundado

away [ə'weɪ] *adv* (*gen*) fuera; (*far away*) lejos; **two kilometres ~** a dos kilómetros (de distancia); **two hours ~ by car** a dos horas en coche; **the holiday was two weeks ~** faltaban dos semanas para las vacaciones; **~ from** lejos de, fuera de; **he's ~ for a week** estará ausente una semana; **he's ~ in Barcelona** está en Barcelona; **to take ~** llevar(se); **to work/pedal ~** seguir trabajando/pedaleando; **to fade ~** desvanecerse; (*sound*) apagarse

away game *n* (*Sport*) partido de fuera

awe [ɔː] *n* respeto, temor *m* reverencial

awe-inspiring ['ɔːɪnspaɪərɪŋ], **awesome** ['ɔːsəm] *adj* imponente, pasmoso

awestruck ['ɔːstrʌk] *adj* pasmado

awful ['ɔːfəl] *adj* terrible; **an ~ lot of** (*people, cars, dogs*) la mar de, muchísimos

awfully ['ɔːfəlɪ] *adv* (*very*) terriblemente

awhile [ə'waɪl] *adv* (durante) un rato, algún tiempo

awkward ['ɔːkwəd] *adj* (*clumsy*) desmañado, torpe; (*shape, situation*) incómodo; (*difficult: question*) difícil; (*problem*) complicado

awkwardness ['ɔːkwədnɪs] *n* (*clumsiness*) torpeza; (*of situation*) incomodidad *f*

awl [ɔːl] *n* lezna, subilla

awning ['ɔːnɪŋ] *n* (*of shop*) toldo; (*of window etc*) marquesina

awoke [ə'wəuk], **awoken** [ə'wəukən] *pt, pp of* **awake**

AWOL ['eɪwɔl] *abbr* (*Mil etc*) *see* **absent without leave**

awry [ə'raɪ] *adv*: **to be ~** estar descolocado *or* atravesado; **to go ~** salir mal, fracasar

axe, ax (*US*) [æks] *n* hacha ■ *vt* (*employee*) despedir; (*project etc*) cortar; (*jobs*) reducir; **to have an ~ to grind** (*fig*) tener un interés creado *or* algún fin interesado

axes ['æksiːz] *npl of* **axis**

axiom ['æksɪəm] *n* axioma *m*

axiomatic [æksɪə'mætɪk] *adj* axiomático

axis (*pl* **axes**) ['æksɪs, -siːz] *n* eje *m*

axle ['æksl] *n* eje *m*, árbol *m*

ay, aye [aɪ] *excl* (*yes*) sí; **the ayes** los que votan a favor

AYH *n abbr* = **American Youth Hostels**

AZ *abbr* (*US*) = **Arizona**

azalea [ə'zeɪlɪə] *n* azalea

Azerbaijan [æzəbaɪ'dʒaːn] *n* Azerbaiyán *m*

Azerbaijani [æzəbaɪ'dʒaːnɪ], **Azeri** [ə'zɛərɪ] *adj, n* azerbaiyano(-a), azerí *m/f*

Azores [ə'zɔːz] *npl*: **the ~** las (Islas) Azores

AZT *n abbr* (= *azidothymidine*) AZT *m*

Aztec ['æztɛk] *adj, n* azteca *m/f*

azure ['eɪʒəʳ] *adj* celeste

Bb

B, b [bi:] *n* (*letter*) B, b *f*; (*Scol: mark*) N; (*Mus*) si *m*; **B for Benjamin,** (US) **B for Baker** B de Barcelona; **B road** (*Brit Aut*) ≈ carretera secundaria

b. *abbr* = **born**

BA *n abbr* = **British Academy**; (*Scol*) = **Bachelor of Arts**; *see also* **Bachelor's Degree**

babble ['bæbl] *vi* farfullar

babe [beɪb] *n* criatura

baboon [bə'bu:n] *n* mandril *m*

baby ['beɪbɪ] *n* bebé *m/f*

baby carriage *n* (US) cochecito

babyish ['beɪbɪɪʃ] *adj* infantil

baby-minder ['beɪbɪ'maɪndə'] *n* niñera *f* (cualificada)

baby-sit ['beɪbɪsɪt] *vi* hacer de canguro

baby-sitter ['beɪbɪsɪtə'] *n* canguro *m/f*

bachelor ['bætʃələ'] *n* soltero; **B~ of Arts/ Science (BA/BSc)** licenciado(-a) en Filosofía y Letras/Ciencias

bachelor's degree *n* licenciatura; *ver nota*

- **BACHELOR'S DEGREE**

  Se denomina *Bachelor's Degree* a la titulación que se recibe al finalizar el primer ciclo universitario, normalmente después de un período de estudio de tres o cuatro años. Las titulaciones más frecuentes son las de Letras, "BA (Bachelor of Arts)", Ciencias, "BSc (Bachelor of Science)", Educación, "BEd (Bachelor of Education)" y Derecho, "LLB (Bachelor of Laws)".

back [bæk] *n* (*of person*) espalda; (*of animal*) lomo; (*of hand, page*) dorso; (*as opposed to front*) parte *f* de atrás; (*of room*) fondo; (*of chair*) respaldo; (*Football*) defensa *m*; **to have one's ~ to the wall** (*fig*) estar entre la espada y la pared; **to break the ~ of a job** hacer lo más difícil de un trabajo; **~ to front** al revés; **at the ~ of my mind was the thought** that ... en el fondo tenía la idea de que ... ■ *vt* (*candidate: also:* **back up**) respaldar, apoyar; (*horse: at races*) apostar a; (*car*) dar marcha atrás a *or* con ■ *vi* (*car etc*) dar marcha atrás ■ *adj* (*in compounds*) de atrás; **~ seats/wheels** (*Aut*) asientos *mpl* traseros, ruedas *fpl* traseras; **~ garden/room** jardín *m/* habitación *f* de atrás; **~ payments** pagos *mpl* con efecto retroactivo; **~ rent** renta atrasada; **to take a ~ seat** (*fig*) pasar a segundo plano ■ *adv* (*not forward*) (hacia) atrás; **he's ~** (*returned*) ha vuelto; **he ran ~** volvió corriendo; **throw the ball ~** (*restitution*) devuelve la pelota; **can I have it ~?** ¿me lo devuelve?; **he called ~** (*again*) volvió a llamar; **~ and forth** de acá para allá; **as far ~ as the 13th century** ya en el siglo XIII; **when will you be ~?** ¿cuándo volverá?

▶ **back down** *vi* echarse atrás

▶ **back on to** *vt fus*: **the house backs on to the golf course** por atrás la casa da al campo de golf

▶ **back out** *vi* (*of promise*) volverse atrás

▶ **back up** *vt* (*support: person*) apoyar, respaldar; (*: theory*) defender; (*car*) dar marcha atrás a; (*Comput*) hacer una copia de reserva de

backache ['bækeɪk] *n* dolor *m* de espalda

backbencher ['bæk'bɛntʃə'] *n* (*Brit*) *diputado sin cargo oficial en el gobierno o la oposición*

back benches *npl* (*Brit*) *ver nota*

- **BACK BENCHES**

  Reciben el nombre genérico de the *back benches* los escaños más alejados del pasillo central en la Cámara de los Comunes del Parlamento británico, que son ocupados por los "backbenchers", los miembros de la cámara que no tienen cargo en el gobierno o en la oposición.

backbiting ['bækbaɪtɪŋ] *n* murmuración *f*

backbone ['bækbəun] n columna vertebral; **the ~ of the organization** el pilar de la organización

backchat ['bæktʃæt] n réplicas fpl

backcloth ['bækklɔθ] n telón m de fondo

backcomb ['bækkəum] vt cardar

backdate [bæk'deɪt] vt (letter) poner fecha atrasada a; **backdated pay rise** aumento de sueldo con efecto retroactivo

backdrop ['bækdrɔp] n = **backcloth**

backer ['bækə'] n partidario(-a); (Comm) promotor(a) m(f)

backfire [bæk'faɪə'] vi (Aut) petardear; (plans) fallar, salir mal

backgammon ['bækgæmən] n backgammon m

background ['bækgraund] n fondo; (of events) antecedentes mpl; (basic knowledge) bases fpl; (experience) conocimientos mpl, educación f ■ cpd (noise, music) de fondo; (Comput) secundario; ~ **reading** lectura de preparación; **family ~** origen m, antecedentes mpl familiares

backhand ['bækhænd] n (Tennis: also: **backhand stroke**) revés m

backhanded [bæk'hændɪd] adj (fig) ambiguo, equívoco

backhander [bæk'hændə'] n (Brit: bribe) soborno

backing ['bækɪŋ] n (fig) apoyo, respaldo; (Comm) respaldo financiero; (Mus) acompañamiento

backlash ['bæklæʃ] n reacción f (en contra)

backlog ['bæklɔg] n: ~ **of work** trabajo atrasado

back number n (of magazine etc) número atrasado

backpack ['bækpæk] n mochila

backpacker ['bækpækə'] n mochilero(-a)

back pay n atrasos mpl

backpedal ['bækpɛdl] vi (fig) volverse/echarse atrás

backseat driver ['bæksi:t-] n pasajero que se empeña en aconsejar al conductor

backside ['bæksaɪd] n (col) trasero

backslash ['bækslæʃ] n pleca, barra inversa

backslide ['bækslaɪd] vi reincidir, recaer

backspace ['bækspeɪs] vi (in typing) retroceder

backstage [bæk'steɪdʒ] adv entre bastidores

back-street ['bækstri:t] adj de barrio; ~ **abortionist** persona que practica abortos clandestinos

backstroke ['bækstrəuk] n espalda

backtrack ['bæktræk] vi (fig) = **backpedal**

backup ['bækʌp] adj (train, plane) suplementario; (Comput: disk, file) de reserva ■ n (support) apoyo; (also: **backup file**) copia de reserva; (US: congestion) embotellamiento, retención f

back-up lights npl (US) luces fpl de marcha atrás

backward ['bækwəd] adj (movement) hacia atrás; (person, country) atrasado; (shy) tímido

backwardness ['bækwədnɪs] n atraso

backwards ['bækwədz] adv (move, go) hacia atrás; (read a list) al revés; (fall) de espaldas; **to know sth ~** or (US) **~ and forwards** (col) saberse algo al dedillo

backwater ['bækwɔ:tə'] n (fig) lugar m atrasado or apartado

backyard [bæk'jɑ:d] n patio trasero

bacon ['beɪkən] n tocino, bacon m, beicon m

bacteria [bæk'tɪərɪə] npl bacterias fpl

bacteriology [bæktɪərɪ'ɔlədʒɪ] n bacteriología

bad [bæd] adj malo; (serious) grave; (meat, food) podrido, pasado; **to go ~** pasarse; **to have a ~ time of it** pasarlo mal; **I feel ~ about it** (guilty) me siento culpable; ~ **debt** (Comm) cuenta incobrable; **in ~ faith** de mala fe

baddie, baddy ['bædɪ] n (col: Cine etc) malo(-a)

bade [bæd] [beɪd] pt of **bid**

badge [bædʒ] n insignia; (metal badge) chapa; (of policeman) placa; (stick-on) pegatina

badger ['bædʒə'] n tejón m

badly ['bædlɪ] adv (work, dress etc) mal; ~ **wounded** gravemente herido; **he needs it ~** le hace mucha falta; **to be ~ off (for money)** andar mal de dinero; **things are going ~** las cosas van muy mal

bad-mannered ['bæd'mænəd] adj mal educado

badminton ['bædmɪntən] n bádminton m

bad-tempered ['bæd'tɛmpəd] adj de mal genio or carácter; (temporary) de mal humor

baffle ['bæfl] vt desconcertar, confundir

baffling ['bæflɪŋ] adj incomprensible

bag [bæg] n bolsa; (handbag) bolso; (satchel) mochila; (case) maleta; (of hunter) caza ■ vt (col: take) coger (SP), agarrar (LAm), pescar; **bags of** (col: lots of) un montón de; **to pack one's bags** hacer las maletas

bagful ['bægful] n saco (lleno)

baggage ['bægɪdʒ] n equipaje m

baggage claim n recogida de equipajes

baggy ['bægɪ] adj (trousers) ancho, holgado

Baghdad [bæg'dæd] n Bagdad m

bag lady n (col) mujer sin hogar cargada de bolsas

bagpipes ['bægpaɪps] npl gaita sg

bag-snatcher ['bægsnætʃə'] n (Brit) ladrón(-ona) m(f) de bolsos

bag-snatching ['bægsnætʃɪŋ] n (Brit) tirón m (de bolsos)

b

Bahamas [bə'hɑːməz] npl: **the** ~ las (Islas) Bahama

Bahrain [bɑːˈreɪn] n Bahrein m

bail [beɪl] n fianza ◼ vt (prisoner: also: **grant bail to**) poner en libertad bajo fianza; (boat: also: **bail out**) achicar; **on** ~ (prisoner) bajo fianza; **to be released on** ~ ser puesto en libertad bajo fianza; **to** ~ **sb out** pagar la fianza de algn; see also **bale**

bailiff ['beɪlɪf] n alguacil m

bait [beɪt] n cebo ◼ vt poner el cebo en

bake [beɪk] vt cocer (al horno) ◼ vi (cook) cocerse; (be hot) hacer un calor terrible

baked beans npl judías fpl en salsa de tomate

baker ['beɪkər] n panadero(-a)

baker's dozen n docena del fraile

bakery ['beɪkərɪ] n (for bread) panadería; (for cakes) pastelería

baking ['beɪkɪŋ] n (act) cocción f; (batch) hornada

baking powder n levadura (en polvo)

baking tin n molde m (para horno)

balaclava [bælə'klɑːvə] n (also: **balaclava helmet**) pasamontañas m inv

balance ['bæləns] n equilibrio; (Comm: sum) balance m; (remainder) resto; (scales) balanza ◼ vt equilibrar; (budget) nivelar; (account) saldar; (compensate) compensar; ~ **of trade/ payments** balanza de comercio/pagos; ~ **carried forward** balance m pasado a cuenta nueva; ~ **brought forward** saldo de hoja anterior; **to** ~ **the books** hacer el balance

balanced ['bælənst] adj (personality, diet) equilibrado

balance sheet n balance m

balcony ['bælkənɪ] n (open) balcón m; (closed) galería

bald [bɔːld] adj calvo; (tyre) liso

baldness ['bɔːldnɪs] n calvicie f

bale [beɪl] n (Agr) paca, fardo

▶ **bale out** vi (of a plane) lanzarse en paracaídas ◼ vt (Naut) achicar; **to** ~ **sb out of a difficulty** sacar a algn de un apuro

Balearic Islands [bælɪ'ærɪk-] npl: **the** ~ las (Islas) Baleares

baleful ['beɪlful] adj (look) triste; (sinister) funesto, siniestro

balk [bɔːk] vi: **to** ~ **(at)** resistirse (a); (horse) plantarse (ante)

Balkan ['bɔːlkən] adj balcánico ◼ n: **the Balkans** los Balcanes

ball [bɔːl] n (sphere) bola; (football) balón m; (for tennis, golf etc) pelota; (dance) baile m; **to be on the** ~ (fig: competent) ser un enterado; (: alert) estar al tanto; **to play** ~ **(with sb)** jugar a la pelota (con algn); (fig) cooperar; **to start the** ~ **rolling** (fig) empezar; **the** ~ **is in your**

court (fig) le toca a usted

ballad ['bæləd] n balada, romance m

ballast ['bæləst] n lastre m

ball bearing n cojinete m de bolas

ballcock ['bɔːlkɔk] n llave f de bola or de flotador

ballerina [bælə'riːnə] n bailarina

ballet ['bæleɪ] n ballet m

ballet dancer n bailarín(-ina) m(f) (de ballet)

ballistic [bə'lɪstɪk] adj balístico; **intercontinental** ~ **missile** misil m balístico intercontinental

ballistics [bə'lɪstɪks] n balística

balloon [bə'luːn] n globo; (in comic strip) bocadillo ◼ vi dispararse

balloonist [bə'luːnɪst] n aeróstata m/f

ballot ['bælət] n votación f

ballot box n urna (electoral)

ballot paper n papeleta

ballpark ['bɔːlpɑːk] n (US) estadio de béisbol

ball-point pen ['bɔːlpɔɪnt-] n bolígrafo

ballroom ['bɔːlrum] n salón m de baile

balm [bɑːm] n (also fig) bálsamo

balmy ['bɑːmɪ] adj (breeze, air) suave; (col) = **barmy**

BALPA ['bælpə] n abbr (= British Airline Pilots' Association) sindicato de pilotos de líneas aéreas

balsa ['bɔːlsə], **balsa wood** n (madera de) balsa

Baltic ['bɔːltɪk] adj báltico ◼ n: **the** ~ **(Sea)** el (Mar) Báltico

balustrade ['bæləstreɪd] n barandilla

bamboo [bæm'buː] n bambú m

bamboozle [bæm'buːzl] vt (col) embaucar, engatusar

ban [bæn] n prohibición f ◼ vt prohibir; (exclude) excluir; **he was banned from driving** le retiraron el carnet de conducir

banal [bə'nɑːl] adj banal, vulgar

banana [bə'nɑːnə] n plátano, banana (LAm)

band [bænd] n (group) banda; (gang) pandilla; (strip) faja, tira; (at a dance) orquesta; (Mil) banda; (rock band) grupo

▶ **band together** vi juntarse, asociarse

bandage ['bændɪdʒ] n venda, vendaje m ◼ vt vendar

Band-Aid® ['bændeɪd] n (US) tirita, curita (LAm)

B & B n abbr = **bed and breakfast**

bandit ['bændɪt] n bandido; **one-armed** ~ máquina tragaperras

bandstand ['bændstænd] n quiosco de música

bandwagon ['bændwægən] n: **to jump on the** ~ (fig) subirse al carro

bandy ['bændɪ] vt (jokes, insults) intercambiar

bandy-legged ['bændɪ'legd] adj patizambo

437

bane [beɪn] *n*: **it** (*or* **he** *etc*) **is the ~ of my life** me amarga la vida

bang [bæŋ] *n* estallido; (*of door*) portazo; (*blow*) golpe *m* ■ *vt* golpear ■ *vi* estallar ■ *adv*: **to be ~ on time** (*col*) llegar en punto; **to ~ the door** dar un portazo; **to ~ into sth** chocar con algo, golpearse contra algo; *see also* **bangs**

banger ['bæŋəᵊ] *n* (*Brit: car: also*: **old banger**) armatoste *m*, cacharro; (*Brit col: sausage*) salchicha; (*firework*) petardo

Bangkok [bæŋ'kɔk] *n* Bangkok *m*

Bangladesh [bæŋglə'dɛʃ] *n* Bangladesh *f*

bangle ['bæŋgl] *n* brazalete *m*, ajorca

bangs [bæŋz] *npl* (*US*) flequillo *sg*

banish ['bænɪʃ] *vt* desterrar

banister ['bænɪstəʳ] *n*, **banisters** ['bænɪstəz] ■ *npl* barandilla *f*, pasamanos *m inv*

banjo (*pl* **banjoes** *or* **banjos**) ['bændʒəʊ] *n* banjo

bank [bæŋk] *n* (*Comm*) banco; (*of river, lake*) ribera, orilla; (*of earth*) terraplén *m* ■ *vi* (*Aviat*) ladearse; (*Comm*): **to ~ with** tener la cuenta en

▶ **bank on** *vt fus* contar con

bank account *n* cuenta bancaria

bank balance *n* saldo

bank card *n* = **banker's card**

bank charges *npl* comisión *fsg*

bank draft *n* letra de cambio

banker ['bæŋkəʳ] *n* banquero; **~'s card** (*Brit*) tarjeta bancaria; **~'s order** orden *f* bancaria

bank giro *n* giro bancario

bank holiday *n* (*Brit*) día *m* festivo *or* de fiesta; *ver nota*

● **BANK HOLIDAY**

El término *bank holiday* se aplica en el Reino Unido a todo día festivo oficial en el que cierran bancos y comercios. Los más destacados coinciden con Navidad, Semana Santa, finales de mayo y finales de agosto. Al contrario que en los países de tradición católica, no se celebran las festividades dedicadas a los santos.

banking ['bæŋkɪŋ] *n* banca

bank loan *n* préstamo bancario

bank manager *n* director(a) *m(f)* (de sucursal) de banco

banknote ['bæŋknəʊt] *n* billete *m* de banco

bank rate *n* tipo de interés bancario

bankrupt ['bæŋkrʌpt] *n* quebrado(-a) ■ *adj* quebrado, insolvente; **to go ~** quebrar, hacer bancarrota; **to be ~** estar en quiebra

bankruptcy ['bæŋkrʌptsɪ] *n* quiebra, bancarrota

bank statement *n* extracto de cuenta

banned substance ['bænd -] *n* (*Sport*) sustancia prohibida

banner ['bænəʳ] *n* bandera; (*in demonstration*) pancarta

banns [bænz] *npl* amonestaciones *fpl*

banquet ['bæŋkwɪt] *n* banquete *m*

banter ['bæntəʳ] *n* guasa, bromas *fpl*

baptism ['bæptɪzəm] *n* bautismo; (*act*) bautizo

baptize [bæp'taɪz] *vt* bautizar

bar [bɑːʳ] *n* barra; (*on door*) tranca; (*of window, cage*) reja; (*of soap*) pastilla; (*fig: hindrance*) obstáculo; (*prohibition*) prohibición *f*; (*pub*) bar *m*, cantina (*esp LAm*); (*counter: in pub*) barra, mostrador *m*; (*Mus*) barra ■ *vt* (*road*) obstruir; (*window, door*) atrancar; (*person*) excluir; (*activity*) prohibir; **behind bars** entre rejas; **the B~** (*Law: profession*) la abogacía; (: *people*) el cuerpo de abogados; **~ none** sin excepción

Barbados [bɑː'beɪdɔs] *n* Barbados *m*

barbarian [bɑː'bɛərɪən] *n* bárbaro(-a)

barbaric [bɑː'bærɪk] *adj* bárbaro

barbarity [bɑː'bærɪtɪ] *n* barbaridad *f*

barbarous ['bɑːbərəs] *adj* bárbaro

barbecue ['bɑːbɪkjuː] *n* barbacoa, asado (*LAm*)

barbed wire ['bɑːbd -] *n* alambre *m* de espino

barber ['bɑːbəʳ] *n* peluquero, barbero

barbiturate [bɑː'bɪtjurɪt] *n* barbitúrico

Barcelona [bɑːsɪ'ləunə] *n* Barcelona

bar chart *n* gráfico de barras

bar code *n* código de barras

bare [bɛəʳ] *adj* desnudo; (*head*) descubierto ■ *vt* desnudar; **to ~ one's teeth** enseñar los dientes

bareback ['bɛəbæk] *adv* a pelo

barefaced ['bɛəfeɪst] *adj* descarado

barefoot ['bɛəfut] *adj, adv* descalzo

bareheaded [bɛə'hɛdɪd] *adj* descubierto, sin sombrero

barely ['bɛəlɪ] *adv* apenas

bareness ['bɛənɪs] *n* desnudez *f*

Barents Sea ['bærənts-] *n*: **the ~** el Mar de Barents

bargain ['bɑːgɪn] *n* pacto; (*transaction*) negocio; (*good buy*) ganga ■ *vi* negociar; (*haggle*) regatear; **into the ~** además, por añadidura

▶ **bargain for** *vt fus* (*col*): **he got more than he bargained for** le resultó peor de lo que esperaba

bargaining ['bɑːgənɪŋ] *n* negociación *f*, regateo; **~ table** mesa de negociaciones

bargaining position *n*: **to be in a strong/ weak ~** estar/no estar en una posición de fuerza para negociar

barge [bɑːdʒ] *n* barcaza
▶ **barge in** *vi* irrumpir; (*in conversation*) entrometerse
▶ **barge into** *vt fus* dar contra
baritone ['bærɪtəun] *n* barítono
barium meal ['bɛərɪəm-] *n* (*Med*) sulfato de bario
bark [bɑːk] *n* (*of tree*) corteza; (*of dog*) ladrido
■ *vi* ladrar
barley ['bɑːlɪ] *n* cebada
barley sugar *n* azúcar *m* cande
barmaid ['bɑːmeɪd] *n* camarera
barman ['bɑːmən] *n* camarero, barman *m*
barmy ['bɑːmɪ] *adj* (*col*) chiflado, chalado
barn [bɑːn] *n* granero; (*for animals*) cuadra
barnacle ['bɑːnəkl] *n* percebe *m*
barn owl *n* lechuza
barometer [bə'rɔmɪtə'] *n* barómetro
baron ['bærən] *n* barón *m*; (*fig*) magnate *m*;
the press barons los magnates de la prensa
baroness ['bærənɪs] *n* baronesa
baroque [bə'rɔk] *adj* barroco
barrack ['bærək] *vt* (*Brit*) abuchear
barracking ['bærəkɪŋ] *n*: **to give sb a ~** (*Brit*) abuchear a algn
barracks ['bærəks] *npl* cuartel *msg*
barrage ['bærɑːʒ] *n* (*Mil*) cortina de fuego;
(*dam*) presa; (*fig: of criticism etc*) lluvia, aluvión *m*; **a ~ of questions** una lluvia de preguntas
barrel ['bærəl] *n* barril *m*; (*of wine*) tonel *m*, cuba; (*of gun*) cañón *m*
barren ['bærən] *adj* estéril
barricade [bærɪ'keɪd] *n* barricada ■ *vt* cerrar con barricadas
barrier ['bærɪə'] *n* barrera; (*crash barrier*) barrera
barrier cream *n* crema protectora
barring ['bɑːrɪŋ] *prep* excepto, salvo
barrister ['bærɪstə'] *n* (*Brit*) abogado(-a);
ver nota

● **BARRISTER**

En el sistema legal inglés *barrister* es el abogado que se ocupa de defender los casos de sus clientes en los tribunales superiores. El equivalente escocés es "advocate". Normalmente actúan según instrucciones de un "solicitor", abogado de despacho que no toma parte activa en los juicios de dichos tribunales. El título de *barrister* lo otorga el órgano colegiado correspondiente, "the Inns of Court".

barrow ['bærəu] *n* (*cart*) carretilla
barstool ['bɑːstuːl] *n* taburete *m* (de bar)
Bart. *abbr* (*Brit*) = **baronet**

bartender ['bɑːtɛndə'] *n* (*US*) camarero, barman *m*
barter ['bɑːtə'] *vt*: **to ~ sth for sth** trocar algo por algo
base [beɪs] *n* base *f* ■ *vt*: **to ~ sth on** basar *or* fundar algo en ■ *adj* bajo, infame; **to ~ at** (*troops*) estacionar en; **I'm based in London** (*work*) trabajo en Londres
baseball ['beɪsbɔːl] *n* béisbol *m*
base camp *n* campamento base
Basel ['bɑːzəl] *n* Basilea
baseless ['beɪslɪs] *adj* infundado
baseline ['beɪslaɪn] *n* (*Tennis*) línea de fondo
basement ['beɪsmənt] *n* sótano
base rate *n* tipo base
bases ['beɪsiːz] *npl of* **basis** ['beɪsɪz] ■ *npl of* **base**
bash [bæʃ] *n*: **I'll have a ~ (at it)** lo intentaré
■ *vt* (*col*) golpear
▶ **bash up** *vt* (*col: car*) destrozar; (: *person*) aporrear, vapulear
bashful ['bæʃful] *adj* tímido, vergonzoso
bashing ['bæʃɪŋ] *n* (*col*) paliza; **to go Paki-/queer-~** ir a dar una paliza a los paquistaníes/a los maricas
BASIC ['beɪsɪk] *n* (*Comput*) BASIC *m*
basic ['beɪsɪk] *adj* (*salary etc*) básico; (*elementary: principles*) fundamental
basically ['beɪsɪklɪ] *adv* fundamentalmente, en el fondo
basic rate *n* (*of tax*) base *f* mínima imponible
basil ['bæzl] *n* albahaca
basin ['beɪsn] *n* (*vessel*) cuenco, tazón *m*; (*Geo*) cuenca; (*also:* **washbasin**) palangana, jofaina; (*in bathroom*) lavabo
basis ['beɪsɪs] (*pl* **-ses**) [-siːz] *n* base *f*; **on the ~ of what you've said** en base a lo que has dicho
bask [bɑːsk] *vi*: **to ~ in the sun** tomar el sol
basket ['bɑːskɪt] *n* cesta, cesto
basketball ['bɑːskɪtbɔːl] *n* baloncesto
basketball player *n* jugador(a) *m(f)* de baloncesto
basketwork ['bɑːskɪtwəːk] *n* cestería
Basle [bɑːl] *n* Basilea
basmati rice [bəz'mætɪ-] *n* arroz *m* basmati
Basque [bæsk] *adj, n* vasco(-a) *m(f)*
Basque Country *n* Euskadi *m*, País *m* Vasco
bass [beɪs] *n* (*Mus*) bajo
bass clef *n* clave *f* de fa
bassoon [bə'suːn] *n* fagot *m*
bastard ['bɑːstəd] *n* bastardo(-a); (*col!*) cabrón *m*, hijo de puta (!)
baste [beɪst] *vt* (*Culin*) rociar (con su salsa)
bastion ['bæstɪən] *n* bastión *m*, baluarte *m*
bat [bæt] *n* (*Zool*) murciélago; (*for ball games*) palo; (*for cricket, baseball*) bate *m*; (*Brit: for*

table tennis) pala; **he didn't ~ an eyelid** ni pestañeó, ni se inmutó

batch [bætʃ] *n* lote *m*, remesa; (*of bread*) hornada

bated ['beɪtɪd] *adj*: **with ~ breath** sin respirar

bath [bɑ:θ, *pl* bɑ:ðz] *n* (*act*) baño; (*bathtub*) bañera, tina (*esp LAm*) ■ *vt* bañar; **to have a ~** bañarse, darse un baño; *see also* **baths**

bathchair ['bɑ:θʃɛəʳ] *n* silla de ruedas

bathe [beɪð] *vi* bañarse; (*US*) darse un baño, bañarse ■ *vt* (*wound etc*) lavar; (*US*) bañar, dar un baño a

bather ['beɪðəʳ] *n* bañista *m/f*

bathing ['beɪðɪŋ] *n* baño

bathing cap *n* gorro de baño

bathing costume, bathing suit (*US*) *n* bañador *m*, traje *m* de baño

bathing trunks *npl* bañador *msg*

bathmat ['bɑ:θmæt] *n* alfombrilla de baño

bathrobe ['bɑ:θrəub] *n* albornoz *m*

bathroom ['bɑ:θrum] *n* (cuarto de) baño

baths [bɑ:ðz] *npl* piscina *sg*

bath towel *n* toalla de baño

bathtub ['bɑ:θtʌb] *n* bañera

batman ['bætmən] *n* (*Brit*) ordenanza *m*

baton ['bætən] *n* (*Mus*) batuta

battalion [bə'tælɪən] *n* batallón *m*

batten ['bætn] *n* (*Carpentry*) listón *m*; (*Naut*) junquillo, sable *m*

▸ **batten down** *vt* (*Naut*): **to ~ down the hatches** atrancar las escotillas

batter ['bætəʳ] *vt* maltratar; (*wind, rain*) azotar ■ *n* batido

battered ['bætəd] *adj* (*hat, pan*) estropeado

battery ['bætərɪ] *n* batería; (*of torch*) pila

battery charger *n* cargador *m* de baterías

battery farming *n* cría intensiva

battle ['bætl] *n* batalla; (*fig*) lucha ■ *vi* luchar; **that's half the ~** (*col*) ya hay medio camino andado; **to fight a losing ~** (*fig*) luchar por una causa perdida

battlefield ['bætlfi:ld] *n* campo *m* de batalla

battlements ['bætlmənts] *npl* almenas *fpl*

battleship ['bætlʃɪp] *n* acorazado

batty ['bætɪ] *adj* (*col: person*) chiflado; (: *idea*) de chiflado

bauble ['bɔ:bl] *n* chuchería

baud rate *n* (*Comput*) velocidad *f* (de transmisión) en baudios

bauxite ['bɔ:ksaɪt] *n* bauxita

Bavaria [bə'vɛərɪə] *n* Baviera

Bavarian [bə'vɛərɪən] *adj, n* bávaro(-a) *m(f)*

bawdy ['bɔ:dɪ] *adj* indecente; (*joke*) verde

bawl [bɔ:l] *vi* chillar, gritar

bay [beɪ] *n* (*Geo*) bahía; (*for parking*) parking *m*, estacionamiento; (*loading bay*) patio de carga;

(*Bot*) laurel *m* ■ *vi* aullar; **to hold sb at ~** mantener a alguien a raya

bay leaf *n* (hoja de) laurel *m*

bayonet ['beɪənɪt] *n* bayoneta

bay window *n* ventana salediza

bazaar [bə'zɑ:ʳ] *n* bazar *m*

bazooka [bə'zu:kə] *n* bazuca

BB *n abbr* (*Brit*: = *Boys' Brigade*) organización juvenil para chicos

BBB *n abbr* (*US*: = *Better Business Bureau*) organismo para la defensa del consumidor

BBC *n abbr* (= *British Broadcasting Corporation*) BBC *f*; *ver nota*

BBC

La BBC es el organismo público británico de radio y televisión, autónomo en cuanto a su política de programas pero regulado por un estatuto ("BBC charter") que ha de aprobar el Parlamento. Además de cadenas nacionales de televisión y de radio, transmite también un servicio informativo mundial ("BBC World Service"). A no tener publicidad, se financia a través de operaciones comerciales paralelas y del cobro de una licencia anual obligatoria ("TV licence") para los que tienen aparato de televisión.

BBE *n abbr* (*US*) = **Benevolent and Protective Order of Elks**

BC *adv abbr* (= *before Christ*) a. de J.C. ■ *abbr* (*Canada*) = **British Columbia**

BCG *n abbr* (= *Bacillus Calmette-Guérin*) vacuna de la tuberculosis

BD *n abbr* (= *Bachelor of Divinity*) Licenciado/a en Teología

B/D *abbr* = **bank draft**

BDS *n abbr* (= *Bachelor of Dental Surgery*) título universitario

○ **KEYWORD**

be [bi:] (*pt* **was, were**, *pp* **been**) *aux vb* **1** (*with present participle: forming continuous tenses*): **what are you doing?** ¿qué estás haciendo?, ¿qué haces?; **they're coming tomorrow** vienen mañana; **I've been waiting for you for hours** llevo horas esperándote

2 (*with pp: forming passives*) ser (*but often replaced by active or reflexive constructions*); **to be murdered** ser asesinado; **the box had been opened** habían abierto la caja; **the thief was nowhere to be seen** no se veía al ladrón por ninguna parte

3 (*in tag questions*): **it was fun, wasn't it?** fue divertido, ¿no? *or* ¿verdad?; **he's good-looking, isn't he?** es guapo, ¿no te parece?; **she's back again, is she?** entonces, ¿ha vuelto?

4 (*+to +infin*): **the house is to be sold** (*necessity*) hay que vender la casa; (*future*) van a vender la casa; **he's not to open it** no tiene que abrirlo; **he was to have come yesterday** debía de haber venido ayer; **am I to understand that ...?** ¿debo entender que ...?

■ *vb +complement* **1** (*with n or num complement*) ser; **he's a doctor** es médico; **2 and 2 are 4** 2 y 2 son 4

2 (*with adj complement: expressing permanent or inherent quality*) ser; (*: expressing state seen as temporary or reversible*) estar; **I'm English** soy inglés(-esa); **she's tall/pretty** es alta/bonita; **he's young** es joven; **be careful/good/quiet** ten cuidado/pórtate bien/cállate; **I'm tired** estoy cansado(-a); **I'm warm** tengo calor; **it's dirty** está sucio(-a)

3 (*of health*) estar; **how are you?** ¿cómo estás?; **he's very ill** está muy enfermo; **I'm better now** ya estoy mejor

4 (*of age*) tener; **how old are you?** ¿cuántos años tienes?; **I'm sixteen (years old)** tengo dieciséis años

5 (*cost*) costar; ser; **how much was the meal?** ¿cuánto fue *or* costó la comida?; **that'll be £5.75, please** son £5.75, por favor; **this shirt is £17** esta camisa cuesta £17

■ *vi* **1** (*exist, occur etc*) existir, haber; **the best singer that ever was** el mejor cantante que existió jamás; **is there a God?** ¿hay un Dios?, ¿existe Dios?; **be that as it may** sea como sea; **so be it** así sea

2 (*referring to place*) estar; **I won't be here tomorrow** no estaré aquí mañana

3 (*referring to movement*): **where have you been?** ¿dónde has estado?

■ *impers vb* **1** (*referring to time*): **it's 5 o'clock** son las 5; **it's the 28th of April** estamos a 28 de abril

2 (*referring to distance*): **it's 10 km to the village** el pueblo está a 10 km

3 (*referring to the weather*): **it's too hot/cold** hace demasiado calor/frío; **it's windy today** hace viento hoy

4 (*emphatic*): **it's me** soy yo; **it was Maria who paid the bill** fue María la que pagó la cuenta

B/E *abbr* = **bill of exchange**
beach [biːtʃ] *n* playa ■ *vt* varar
beach buggy [-bʌgɪ] *n* buggy *m*

beachcomber ['biːtʃkəʊmər] *n* raquero(-a)
beachwear ['biːtʃwɛər] *n* ropa de playa
beacon ['biːkən] *n* (*lighthouse*) faro; (*marker*) guía; (*radio beacon*) radiofaro
bead [biːd] *n* cuenta, abalorio; (*of dew, sweat*) gota; **beads** *npl* (*necklace*) collar *m*
beady ['biːdɪ] *adj* (*eyes*) pequeño y brillante
beagle ['biːgl] *n* sabueso pequeño, beagle *m*
beak [biːk] *n* pico
beaker ['biːkər] *n* vaso
beam [biːm] *n* (*Arch*) viga; (*of light*) rayo, haz *m* de luz; (*Radio*) rayo ■ *vi* brillar; (*smile*) sonreír; **to drive on full** *or* **main ~** conducir con las luces largas
beaming ['biːmɪŋ] *adj* (*sun, smile*) radiante
bean [biːn] *n* judía, frijol/frijol *m* (*esp LAm*); **runner/broad ~** habichuela/haba; **coffee ~** grano de café
beanpole ['biːnpəʊl] *n* (*col*) espárrago
beansprouts ['biːnsprauts] *npl* brotes *mpl* de soja
bear [bɛər] (*pt* **bore**, *pp* **borne**) *n* oso; (*Stock Exchange*) bajista *m* ■ *vt* (*weight etc*) llevar; (*cost*) pagar; (*responsibility*) tener; (*traces, signs*) mostrar; (*produce: fruit*) dar; (*Comm: interest*) devengar; (*endure*) soportar, aguantar; (*stand up to*) resistir a; (*children*) tener, dar a luz ■ *vi*: **to ~ right/left** torcer a la derecha/izquierda; **I can't ~ him** no le puedo ver, no lo soporto; **to bring pressure to ~ on sb** ejercer presión sobre algn
▶ **bear on** *vt fus* tener que ver con, referirse a
▶ **bear out** *vt fus* (*suspicions*) corroborar, confirmar; (*person*) confirmar lo dicho por
▶ **bear up** *vi* (*cheer up*) animarse; **he bore up well under the strain** resistió bien la presión
▶ **bear with** *vt fus* (*sb's moods, temper*) tener paciencia con
bearable ['bɛərəbl] *adj* soportable, aguantable
beard [bɪəd] *n* barba
bearded ['bɪədɪd] *adj* con barba
bearer ['bɛərər] *n* (*of news, cheque*) portador(a) *m(f)*; (*of passport*) titular *m/f*
bearing ['bɛərɪŋ] *n* porte *m*; (*connection*) relación *f*; **(ball) bearings** *npl* cojinetes *mpl* a bolas; **to take a ~** marcarse; **to find one's bearings** orientarse
bearskin ['bɛəskɪn] *n* (*Mil*) gorro militar (*de piel de oso*)
beast [biːst] *n* bestia; (*col*) bruto, salvaje *m*
beastly ['biːstlɪ] *adj* bestial; (*awful*) horrible
beat [biːt] (*pt* **~**, *pp* **beaten**) *n* (*of heart*) latido; (*Mus*) ritmo, compás *m*; (*of policeman*) ronda ■ *vt* (*hit*) golpear; (*eggs*) batir; (*defeat*) vencer, derrotar; (*better*) sobrepasar; (*drum*) tocar;

(*rhythm*) marcar ■ *vi* (*heart*) latir; **off the beaten track** aislado; **to ~ about the bush** andarse con rodeos; **to ~ it** largarse; **that beats everything!** (*col*) ¡eso es el colmo!; **to ~ on a door** dar golpes en una puerta
▶ **beat down** *vt* (*door*) derribar a golpes; (*price*) conseguir rebajar, regatear; (*seller*) hacer rebajar el precio ■ *vi* (*rain*) llover a cántaros; (*sun*) caer de plomo
▶ **beat off** *vt* rechazar
▶ **beat up** *vt* (*col: person*) dar una paliza a
beater ['biːtəʳ] *n* (*for eggs, cream*) batidora
beating ['biːtɪŋ] *n* paliza, golpiza (*LAm*); **to take a ~** recibir una paliza
beat-up ['biːt'ʌp] *adj* (*col*) destartalado
beautiful ['bjuːtɪful] *adj* hermoso, bello, lindo (*esp LAm*)
beautifully ['bjuːtɪfəlɪ] *adv* de maravilla
beautify ['bjuːtɪfaɪ] *vt* embellecer
beauty ['bjuːtɪ] *n* belleza, hermosura; (*concept, person*) belleza; **the ~ of it is that ...** lo mejor de esto es que ...
beauty contest *n* concurso de belleza
beauty queen *n* reina de la belleza
beauty salon *n* salón *m* de belleza
beauty sleep *n*: **to get one's ~** no perder horas de sueño
beauty spot *n* lunar *m* postizo; (*Brit: Tourism*) lugar *m* pintoresco
beaver ['biːvəʳ] *n* castor *m*
becalmed [bɪˈkɑːmd] *adj* encalmado
became [bɪˈkeɪm] *pt of* **become**
because [bɪˈkɔz] *conj* porque; **~ of** *prep* debido a, a causa de
beck [bɛk] *n*: **to be at the ~ and call of** estar a disposición de
beckon ['bɛkən] *vt* (*also*: **beckon to**) llamar con señas
become [bɪˈkʌm] (*irreg: like* **come**) *vi* (*+noun*) hacerse, llegar a ser; (*+adj*) ponerse, volverse ■ *vt* (*suit*) favorecer, sentar bien a; **to ~ fat** engordar; **to ~ angry** enfadarse; **it became known that ...** se descubrió que ...
becoming [bɪˈkʌmɪŋ] *adj* (*behaviour*) decoroso; (*clothes*) favorecedor(a)
becquerel [bɛkəˈrɛl] *n* becquerelio
BECTU ['bɛktuː] *n abbr* (*Brit*) = **Broadcasting Entertainment Cinematographic and Theatre Union**
BEd *n abbr* (= *Bachelor of Education*) título universitario; *see also* **Bachelor's Degree**
bed [bɛd] *n* cama; (*of flowers*) macizo; (*of sea, lake*) fondo; (*of coal, clay*) capa; **to go to ~** acostarse
▶ **bed down** *vi* acostarse
bed and breakfast *n* ≈ pensión *f*; *ver nota*

bedbug ['bɛdbʌg] *n* chinche *f*
bedclothes ['bɛdkləuðz] *npl* ropa de cama
bedding ['bɛdɪŋ] *n* ropa de cama
bedeck [bɪˈdɛk] *vt* engalanar, adornar
bedevil [bɪˈdɛvl] *vt* (*dog*) acosar; (*trouble*) fastidiar
bedfellow ['bɛdfɛləu] *n*: **they are strange bedfellows** (*fig*) hacen una pareja rara
bedlam ['bɛdləm] *n* confusión *f*
bedpan ['bɛdpæn] *n* cuña
bedraggled [bɪˈdrægld] *adj* desastrado
bedridden ['bɛdrɪdn] *adj* postrado (en cama)
bedrock ['bɛdrɔk] *n* (*Geo*) roca firme; (*fig*) pilar *m*
bedroom ['bɛdrum] *n* dormitorio, alcoba
Beds *abbr* (*Brit*) = **Bedfordshire**
bed settee *n* sofá-cama *m*
bedside ['bɛdsaɪd] *n*: **at sb's ~** a la cabecera de alguien
bedside lamp *n* lámpara de noche
bedsit ['bɛdsɪt], **bedsitter** ['bɛdsɪtəʳ] *n* (*Brit*) estudio
bedspread ['bɛdsprɛd] *n* cubrecama *m*, colcha
bedtime ['bɛdtaɪm] *n* hora de acostarse; **it's ~** es hora de acostarse *or* de irse a la cama
bee [biː] *n* abeja; **to have a ~ in one's bonnet (about sth)** tener una idea fija (de algo)
beech [biːtʃ] *n* haya
beef [biːf] *n* carne *f* de vaca; **roast ~** rosbif *m*
▶ **beef up** *vt* (*col*) reforzar
beefburger ['biːfbəːgəʳ] *n* hamburguesa
beefeater ['biːfiːtəʳ] *n* alabardero de la Torre de Londres
beehive ['biːhaɪv] *n* colmena
bee-keeping ['biːkiːpɪŋ] *n* apicultura
beeline ['biːlaɪn] *n*: **to make a ~ for** ir derecho a
been [biːn] *pp of* **be**
beep [biːp] *n* pitido ■ *vi* pitar
beeper ['biːpəʳ] *n* (*of doctor etc*) busca *m inv*
beer [bɪəʳ] *n* cerveza
beer belly *n* (*col*) barriga (*de bebedor de cerveza*)
beer can *n* bote *m or* lata de cerveza
beet [biːt] *n* (*US*) remolacha

b

beetle ['bi:tl] *n* escarabajo
beetroot ['bi:tru:t] *n* (*Brit*) remolacha
befall [bɪ'fɔ:l] *vi*, *vt* (*irreg: like* **fall**) acontecer (a)
befit [bɪ'fɪt] *vt* convenir a, corresponder a
before [bɪ'fɔ:ʳ] *prep* (*of time*) antes de; (*of space*) delante de ▪ *conj* antes (de) que ▪ *adv* (*time*) antes; (*space*) delante, adelante; **~ going** antes de marcharse; **~ she goes** antes de que se vaya; **the week ~** la semana anterior; **I've never seen it ~** no lo he visto nunca
beforehand [bɪ'fɔ:hænd] *adv* de antemano, con anticipación
befriend [bɪ'frɛnd] *vt* ofrecer amistad a
befuddled [bɪ'fʌdld] *adj* aturdido, atontado
beg [bɛg] *vi* pedir limosna, mendigar ▪ *vt* pedir, rogar; (*entreat*) suplicar; **I ~ your pardon** (*apologising*) perdóneme; (*not hearing*) ¿perdón?
began [bɪ'gæn] *pt of* **begin**
beggar ['bɛgəʳ] *n* mendigo(-a)
begin (*pt* **began**, *pp* **begun**) [bɪ'gɪn, -gæn, -gʌn] *vt*, *vi* empezar, comenzar; **to ~ doing** *or* **to do sth** empezar a hacer algo; **I can't ~ to thank you** no encuentro palabras para agradecerle; **to ~ with, I'd like to know ...** en primer lugar, quisiera saber ...; **beginning from Monday** a partir del lunes
beginner [bɪ'gɪnəʳ] *n* principiante *m/f*
beginning [bɪ'gɪnɪŋ] *n* principio, comienzo; **right from the ~** desde el principio
begrudge [bɪ'grʌdʒ] *vt*: **to ~ sb sth** tenerle envidia a alguien por algo
beguile [bɪ'gaɪl] *vt* (*enchant*) seducir
beguiling [bɪ'gaɪlɪŋ] *adj* seductor(a), atractivo
begun [bɪ'gʌn] *pp of* **begin**
behalf [bɪ'hɑ:f] *n*: **on ~ of**, (*US*) **in ~ of** en nombre de; (*for benefit of*) por
behave [bɪ'heɪv] *vi* (*person*) portarse, comportarse; (*thing*) funcionar; (*well: also*: **behave o.s.**) portarse bien
behaviour, behavior (*US*) [bɪ'heɪvjəʳ] *n* comportamiento, conducta
behead [bɪ'hɛd] *vt* decapitar
beheld [bɪ'hɛld] *pt, pp of* **behold**
behind [bɪ'haɪnd] *prep* detrás de ▪ *adv* detrás, por detrás, atrás ▪ *n* trasero; **to be ~ (schedule)** ir retrasado; **~ the scenes** (*fig*) entre bastidores; **we're ~ them in technology** (*fig*) nos dejan atrás en tecnología; **to leave sth ~** olvidar *or* dejarse algo; **to be ~ with sth** estar atrasado en algo; **to be ~ with payments (on sth)** estar atrasado en el pago (de algo)
behold [bɪ'həuld] (*irreg: like* **hold**) *vt* contemplar
beige [beɪʒ] *adj* (*color*) beige

being ['bi:ɪŋ] *n* ser *m*; **to come into ~** nacer, aparecer
Beirut [beɪ'ru:t] *n* Beirut *m*
Belarus [bɛlə'rus] *n* Bielorrusia
Belarussian [bɛlə'rʌʃən] *adj, n* bielorruso(-a) ▪ *n* (*Ling*) bielorruso
belated [bɪ'leɪtɪd] *adj* atrasado, tardío
belch [bɛltʃ] *vi* eructar ▪ *vt* (*also*: **belch out**: *smoke etc*) vomitar, arrojar
beleaguered [bɪ'li:gəd] *adj* asediado
Belfast ['bɛlfɑ:st] *n* Belfast *m*
belfry ['bɛlfrɪ] *n* campanario
Belgian ['bɛldʒən] *adj, n* belga *m/f*
Belgium ['bɛldʒəm] *n* Bélgica
Belgrade [bɛl'greɪd] *n* Belgrado
belie [bɪ'laɪ] *vt* (*give false impression of*) desmentir, contradecir
belief [bɪ'li:f] *n* (*opinion*) opinión *f*; (*trust, faith*) fe *f*; (*acceptance as true*) creencia; **it's beyond ~** es increíble; **in the ~ that** creyendo que
believable [bɪ'li:vəbl] *adj* creíble
believe [bɪ'li:v] *vt, vi* creer; **to ~ (that)** creer (que); **to ~ in** (*God, ghosts*) creer en; (*method*) ser partidario de; **he is believed to be abroad** se cree que está en el extranjero; **I don't ~ in corporal punishment** no soy partidario del castigo corporal
believer [bɪ'li:vəʳ] *n* (*in idea, activity*) partidario(-a); (*Rel*) creyente *m/f*, fiel *m/f*
belittle [bɪ'lɪtl] *vt* despreciar
Belize [bɛ'li:z] *n* Belice *f*
bell [bɛl] *n* campana; (*small*) campanilla; (*on door*) timbre *m*; (*animal's*) cencerro; (*on toy etc*) cascabel *m*; **that rings a ~** (*fig*) eso me suena
bellboy ['bɛlbɔɪ] *n*, **bellhop** (*US*) ['bɛlhɔp] ▪ *n* botones *m inv*
belligerent [bɪ'lɪdʒərənt] *adj* (*at war*) beligerante; (*fig*) agresivo
bellow ['bɛləu] *vi* bramar; (*person*) rugir ▪ *vt* (*orders*) gritar
bellows ['bɛləuz] *npl* fuelle *msg*
bell push *n* pulsador *m* de timbre
belly ['bɛlɪ] *n* barriga, panza
bellyache ['bɛlɪeɪk] *n* dolor *m* de barriga *or* de tripa ▪ *vi* (*col*) gruñir
bellyful ['bɛlɪful] *n*: **to have had a ~ of ...** (*col*) estar más que harto de ...
belong [bɪ'lɔŋ] *vi*: **to ~ to** pertenecer a; (*club etc*) ser socio de; **this book belongs here** este libro va aquí
belongings [bɪ'lɔŋɪŋz] *npl*: **personal ~** pertenencias *fpl*
Belorussia [bɛləu'rʌʃə] *n* Bielorrusia
Belorussian [bɛləu'rʌʃən] *adj, n* = **Belarussian**
beloved [bɪ'lʌvɪd] *adj, n* querido(-a) *m(f)*, amado(-a) *m(f)*

below [bɪ'ləu] *prep* bajo, debajo de ■ *adv*
abajo, (por) debajo; **see** ~ véase más abajo
belt [bɛlt] *n* cinturón *m*; (*Tech*) correa, cinta
■ *vt* (*thrash*) golpear con correa; **industrial** ~
cinturón industrial
▶ **belt out** *vt* (*song*) cantar a voz en grito *or* a
grito pelado
▶ **belt up** *vi* (*Aut*) ponerse el cinturón de
seguridad; (*fig, col*) cerrar el pico
beltway ['bɛltweɪ] *n* (*US Aut*) carretera de
circunvalación
bemoan [bɪ'məun] *vt* lamentar
bemused [bɪ'mju:zd] *adj* perplejo
bench [bɛntʃ] *n* banco; **the B~** (*Law*) el
tribunal; (*people*) la judicatura
bench mark *n* punto de referencia
bend [bɛnd] *vb* (*pt, pp* **bent**) ■ *vt* doblar; (*body,
head*) inclinar ■ *vi* inclinarse; (*road*) curvarse
■ *n* (*Brit: in road, river*) recodo; (*in pipe*) codo; *see
also* **bends**
▶ **bend down** *vi* inclinarse, doblarse
▶ **bend over** *vi* inclinarse
bends [bɛndz] *npl* (*Med*) apoplejía por cambios
bruscos de presión
beneath [bɪ'ni:θ] *prep* bajo, debajo de;
(*unworthy of*) indigno de ■ *adv* abajo, (por)
debajo
benefactor ['bɛnɪfæktə'] *n* bienhechor *m*
benefactress ['bɛnɪfæktrɪs] *n* bienhechora
beneficial [bɛnɪ'fɪʃəl] *adj*: ~ **to** beneficioso
para
beneficiary [bɛnɪ'fɪʃərɪ] *n* (*Law*)
beneficiario(-a)
benefit ['bɛnɪfɪt] *n* beneficio, provecho;
(*allowance of money*) subsidio ■ *vt* beneficiar
■ *vi*: **he'll ~ from it** le sacará provecho;
unemployment ~ subsidio de desempleo
Benelux ['bɛnɪlʌks] *n* Benelux *m*
benevolence [bɪ'nɛvələns] *n* benevolencia
benevolent [bɪ'nɛvələnt] *adj* benévolo
BEng *n abbr* (= *Bachelor of Engineering*) título
universitario
benign [bɪ'naɪn] *adj* (*person*) benigno; (*Med*)
benigno; (*smile*) afable
bent [bɛnt] *pt, pp of* **bend** ■ *n* inclinación *f*
■ *adj* (*wire, pipe*) doblado, torcido; **to be ~ on**
estar empeñado en
bequeath [bɪ'kwi:ð] *vt* legar
bequest [bɪ'kwɛst] *n* legado
bereaved [bɪ'ri:vd] *adj* afligido ■ *n*: **the** ~
los afligidos *mpl*
bereavement [bɪ'ri:vmənt] *n* aflicción *f*
beret ['bɛreɪ] *n* boina
Bering Sea ['bɛərɪŋ-] *n*: **the** ~ el Mar de
Bering
berk [bə:k] *n* (*Brit col*) capullo(-a) (!)
Berks *abbr* (*Brit*) = **Berkshire**

Berlin [bə:'lɪn] *n* Berlín *m*; **East/West** ~
Berlín del Este/Oeste
berm [bə:m] *n* (*US Aut*) arcén *m*
Bermuda [bə:'mju:də] *n* las (Islas) Bermudas
Bermuda shorts *npl* bermudas *mpl or fpl*
Bern [bə:n] *n* Berna
berry ['bɛrɪ] *n* baya
berserk [bə'sə:k] *adj*: **to go** ~ perder los
estribos
berth [bə:θ] *n* (*bed*) litera; (*cabin*) camarote *m*;
(*for ship*) amarradero ■ *vi* atracar, amarrar;
to give sb a wide ~ (*fig*) evitar encontrarse
con algn
beseech (*pt, pp* **besought**) [bɪ'si:tʃ, -'sɔ:t] *vt*
suplicar
beset (*pt, pp* ~) [bɪ'sɛt] *vt* (*person*) acosar
■ *adj*: **a policy** ~ **with dangers** una política
rodeada de peligros
besetting [bɪ'sɛtɪŋ] *adj*: **his** ~ **sin** su principal
falta
beside [bɪ'saɪd] *prep* junto a, al lado de;
(*compared with*) comparado con; **to be** ~ **o.s.
with anger** estar fuera de sí; **that's** ~ **the
point** eso no tiene nada que ver con el asunto
besides [bɪ'saɪdz] *adv* además ■ *prep* (*as well
as*) además de; (*except*) excepto
besiege [bɪ'si:dʒ] *vt* (*town*) sitiar; (*fig*) asediar
besmirch [bɪ'smə:tʃ] *vt* (*fig*) manchar,
mancillar
besotted [bɪ'sɔtɪd] *adj*: ~ **with** chiflado por
bespoke [bɪ'spəuk] *adj* (*garment*) hecho a la
medida; ~ **tailor** sastre *m* que confecciona a
la medida
best [bɛst] *adj* (el/la) mejor ■ *adv* (lo) mejor;
the ~ **part of** (*most*) la mayor parte de; **at**
~ en el mejor de los casos; **to make the** ~
of sth sacar el mejor partido de algo; **to
do one's** ~ hacer todo lo posible; **to the** ~
of my knowledge que yo sepa; **to the** ~ **of
my ability** como mejor puedo; **the** ~ **thing
to do is ...** lo mejor (que se puede hacer)
es ...; **he's not exactly patient at the** ~ **of
times** no es que tenga mucha paciencia
precisamente
bestial ['bɛstɪəl] *adj* bestial
best man *n* padrino de boda
bestow [bɪ'stəu] *vt* otorgar; (*honour, praise*)
dispensar; **to** ~ **sth on sb** conceder *or* dar
algo a algn
bestseller ['bɛst'sɛlə'] *n* éxito de ventas, best-
seller *m*
bet [bɛt] *n* apuesta ■ *vt, vi* (*pt, pp* **bet** *or*
betted); **to** ~ **(on)** apostar (a); **it's a safe** ~
(*fig*) es cosa segura
Bethlehem ['bɛθlɪhɛm] *n* Belén *m*
betray [bɪ'treɪ] *vt* traicionar; (*inform on*)
delatar

betrayal [bɪ'treɪəl] n traición f
better ['bɛtər] adj mejor ■ adv mejor ■ vt mejorar; (record etc) superar ■ n: **to get the ~ of sb** quedar por encima de algn; **you had ~ do it** más vale que lo hagas; **he thought ~ of it** cambió de parecer; **to get ~** mejorar(se); (Med) reponerse; **that's ~!** ¡eso es!; **I had ~ go** tengo que irme; **a change for the ~** una mejora; **~ off** adj más acomodado
betting ['bɛtɪŋ] n juego, apuestas fpl
betting shop n (Brit) casa de apuestas
between [bɪ'twiːn] prep entre ■ adv (also: **in between**: time) mientras tanto; (: place) en medio; **the road ~ here and London** la carretera de aquí a Londres; **we only had 5 ~ us** teníamos sólo 5 entre todos
bevel ['bɛvəl] n (also: **bevel edge**) bisel m, chaflán m
beverage ['bɛvərɪdʒ] n bebida
bevy ['bɛvɪ] n: **a ~ of** una bandada de
bewail [bɪ'weɪl] vt lamentar
beware [bɪ'wɛər] vi: **to ~ (of)** tener cuidado (con) ■ excl ¡cuidado!
bewildered [bɪ'wɪldəd] adj aturdido, perplejo
bewildering [bɪ'wɪldərɪŋ] adj desconcertante
bewitching [bɪ'wɪtʃɪŋ] adj hechicero, encantador(a)
beyond [bɪ'jɔnd] prep más allá de; (exceeding) además de, fuera de; (above) superior a ■ adv más allá, más lejos; **~ doubt** fuera de toda duda; **~ repair** irreparable
b/f abbr (= brought forward) saldo previo
BFPO n abbr (= British Forces Post Office) servicio postal del ejército
bhp n abbr (Aut: = brake horsepower) potencia al freno
bi ... [baɪ] pref bi ...
biannual [baɪ'ænjuəl] adj semestral
bias ['baɪəs] n (prejudice) prejuicio; (preference) predisposición f
biased, biassed ['baɪəst] adj parcial; **to be bias(s)ed against** tener perjuicios contra
biathlon [baɪ'æθlən] n biatlón m
bib [bɪb] n babero
Bible ['baɪbl] n Biblia
biblical ['bɪblɪkəl] adj bíblico
bibliography [bɪblɪ'ɔgrəfɪ] n bibliografía
bicarbonate of soda [baɪ'kɑ:bənɪt-] n bicarbonato de soda
bicentenary [baɪsɛn'ti:nərɪ], **bicentennial** (US) [baɪsɛn'tɛnɪəl] n bicentenario
biceps ['baɪsɛps] n bíceps m
bicker ['bɪkər] vi reñir
bickering ['bɪkərɪŋ] n riñas fpl, altercados mpl
bicycle ['baɪsɪkl] n bicicleta
bicycle path n camino para ciclistas
bicycle pump n bomba de bicicleta

bid [bɪd] n (at auction) oferta, puja, postura; (attempt) tentativa, conato ■ vi (pt, pp **bid**) hacer una oferta ■ vt (pt **bade**) [bæd] (pp **bidden**) ['bɪdn] mandar, ordenar; **to ~ sb good day** dar a algn los buenos días
bidder ['bɪdər] n: **the highest ~** el mejor postor
bidding ['bɪdɪŋ] n (at auction) ofertas fpl, puja; (order) orden f, mandato
bide [baɪd] vt: **to ~ one's time** esperar el momento adecuado
bidet ['biːdeɪ] n bidet m
bidirectional ['baɪdɪ'rɛkʃənl] adj bidireccional
biennial [baɪ'ɛnɪəl] adj, n bienal f
bier [bɪər] n féretro
bifocals [baɪ'fəuklz] npl gafas fpl or anteojos mpl (LAm) bifocales
big [bɪg] adj grande; **~ business** gran negocio; **to do things in a ~ way** hacer las cosas en grande
bigamy ['bɪgəmɪ] n bigamia
big dipper [-'dɪpər] n montaña rusa
big end n (Aut) cabeza de biela
biggish ['bɪgɪʃ] adj más bien grande; (man) más bien alto
bigheaded ['bɪg'hɛdɪd] adj engreído
bigot ['bɪgət] n fanático(-a), intolerante m/f
bigoted ['bɪgətɪd] adj fanático, intolerante
bigotry ['bɪgətrɪ] n fanatismo, intolerancia
big toe n dedo gordo (del pie)
big top n (circus) circo; (main tent) carpa principal
big wheel n (at fair) noria
bigwig ['bɪgwɪg] n (col) pez m gordo
bike [baɪk] n bici f
bike lane n carril m de bicicleta, carril m bici
bikini [bɪ'kiːnɪ] n bikini m
bilateral [baɪ'lætərl] adj (agreement) bilateral
bile [baɪl] n bilis f
bilge [bɪldʒ] n (water) agua de sentina
bilingual [baɪ'lɪŋgwəl] adj bilingüe
bilious ['bɪlɪəs] adj bilioso (also fig)
bill [bɪl] n (gen) cuenta; (invoice) factura; (Pol) proyecto de ley; (US: banknote) billete m; (of bird) pico; (notice) cartel m; (Theat) programa m ■ vt extender or pasar la factura a; **may I have the ~ please?** ¿puede traerme la cuenta, por favor?; **~ of exchange** letra de cambio; **~ of lading** conocimiento de embarque; **~ of sale** escritura de venta; **"post no bills"** "prohibido fijar carteles"
billboard ['bɪlbɔːd] n valla publicitaria
billet ['bɪlɪt] n alojamiento ■ vt: **to ~ sb (on sb)** alojar a algn (con algn)
billfold ['bɪlfəuld] n (US) cartera
billiards ['bɪljədz] n billar m

billion ['bɪljən] n (Brit) billón m; (US) mil
millones mpl
billow ['bɪləu] n (of smoke) nube f; (of sail)
ondulación f ■ vi (smoke) salir en nubes;
(sail) ondear, ondular
billy ['bɪlɪ] n (US) porra
billy goat n macho cabrío
bimbo ['bɪmbəu] n (col) tía buena sin seso
bin [bɪn] n (gen) cubo or bote m (LAm) de la
basura; **litterbin** n (Brit) papelera
binary ['baɪnərɪ] adj (Math) binario; **~ code**
código binario
bind (pt, pp bound) [baɪnd, baund] vt atar,
liar; (wound) vendar; (book) encuadernar;
(oblige) obligar
  ▸ **bind over** vt (Law) obligar por vía legal
  ▸ **bind up** vt (wound) vendar; **to be bound up
  in** (work, research etc) estar absorto en; **to be
  bound up with** (person) estar estrechamente
  ligado a
binder ['baɪndə'] n (file) archivador m
binding ['baɪndɪŋ] adj (contract) vinculante
binge [bɪndʒ] n borrachera, juerga; **to go on
a ~** ir de juerga
bingo ['bɪŋgəu] n bingo m
bin-liner ['bɪnlaɪnə'] n bolsa de la basura
binoculars [bɪ'nɔkjuləz] npl prismáticos mpl,
gemelos mpl
bio [baɪə'] adj (fam) biológico
biochemistry [baɪə'kemɪstrɪ] n bioquímica
biodegradable ['baɪəudɪ'greɪdəbl] adj
biodegradable
biodiversity ['baɪəudaɪ'və:sɪtɪ] n
biodiversidad f
biographer [baɪ'ɔgrəfə'] n biógrafo(-a)
biographical [baɪə'græfɪkəl] adj biográfico
biography [baɪ'ɔgrəfɪ] n biografía
biological [baɪə'lɔdʒɪkəl] adj biológico;
(products, foodstuffs etc) orgánico(-a)
biological clock n reloj m biológico
biologist [baɪ'ɔlədʒɪst] n biólogo(-a)
biology [baɪ'ɔlədʒɪ] n biología
biophysics ['baɪəu'fɪzɪks] nsg biofísica
biopic ['baɪəupɪk] n filme m biográfico
biopsy ['baɪɔpsɪ] n biopsia
biosphere ['baɪəsfɪə'] n biosfera
biotechnology ['baɪəutek'nɔlədʒɪ] n
biotecnología
bioterrorism ['baɪəu'terərɪzəm] n
bioterrorismo
biped ['baɪped] n bípedo
birch [bə:tʃ] n abedul m; (cane) vara
bird [bə:d] n ave f, pájaro; (Brit col: girl) chica
birdcage ['bə:dkeɪdʒ] n jaula
bird flu n gripe aviar
bird of prey n ave f de presa
bird's-eye view ['bə:dzaɪ-] n vista de pájaro

bird watcher n ornitólogo(-a)
Biro® ['baɪrəu] n bolígrafo
birth [bə:θ] n nacimiento; (Med) parto; **to
give ~ to** parir, dar a luz a; (fig) dar origen a
birth certificate n partida de nacimiento
birth control n control m de natalidad;
(methods) métodos mpl anticonceptivos
birthday ['bə:θdeɪ] n cumpleaños m inv
birthday card n tarjeta de cumpleaños
birthplace ['bə:θpleɪs] n lugar m de
nacimiento
birth rate n (tasa de) natalidad f
Biscay ['bɪskeɪ] n: **the Bay of ~** el Mar
Cantábrico, el golfo de Vizcaya
biscuit ['bɪskɪt] n (Brit) galleta
bisect [baɪ'sekt] vt (also Math) bisecar
bisexual ['baɪ'seksjuəl] adj, n bisexual m/f
bishop ['bɪʃəp] n obispo; (Chess) alfil m
bistro ['bi:strəu] n café-bar m
bit [bɪt] pt of **bite** ■ n trozo, pedazo, pedacito;
(Comput) bit m; (for horse) freno, bocado;
a ~ of un poco de; **a ~ mad** algo loco; **~ by ~**
poco a poco; **to come to bits** (break) hacerse
pedazos; **to do one's ~** aportar su granito de
arena; **bring all your bits and pieces** trae
todas tus cosas
bitch [bɪtʃ] n (dog) perra; (col!) zorra (!)
bite [baɪt] vt, vi (pt **bit**) [bɪt] (pp **bitten**) ['bɪtn]
morder; (insect etc) picar ■ n (wound: of dog,
snake etc) mordedura; (of insect) picadura;
(mouthful) bocado; **to ~ one's nails** morderse
las uñas; **let's have a ~ (to eat)** comamos
algo
biting ['baɪtɪŋ] adj (wind) que traspasa los
huesos; (criticism) mordaz
bit part n (Theat) papel m sin importancia,
papelito
bitten ['bɪtn] pp of **bite**
bitter ['bɪtə'] adj amargo; (wind, criticism)
cortante, penetrante; (icy: weather) glacial;
(battle) encarnizado ■ n (Brit: beer) cerveza
típica británica a base de lúpulos
bitterly ['bɪtəlɪ] adv (disappoint, complain,
weep) desconsoladamente; (oppose, criticise)
implacablemente; (jealous) agriamente;
it's ~ cold hace un frío glacial
bitterness ['bɪtənɪs] n amargura; (anger)
rencor m
bitty ['bɪtɪ] adj deshilvanado
bitumen ['bɪtjumɪn] n betún m
bivouac ['bɪvuæk] n vivac m, vivaque m
bizarre [bɪ'zɑ:'] adj raro, estrafalario
bk abbr = **bank**; **book**
BL n abbr (= Bachelor of Law(s), Bachelor of Letters)
título universitario; (US: = Bachelor of Literature)
título universitario
B/L abbr = **bill of lading**

blab [blæb] vi cantar ▪ vt (also: **blab out**) soltar, contar

black [blæk] adj (colour) negro; (dark) oscuro ▪ n (colour) color m negro; (person): **B~** negro(-a) ▪ vt (shoes) lustrar; (Brit Industry) boicotear; **to give sb a ~ eye** ponerle a algn el ojo morado; **~ coffee** café m solo; **there it is in ~ and white** (fig) ahí está bien claro; **to be in the ~** (in credit) tener saldo positivo; **~ and blue** adj amoratado
  ▶ **black out** vi (faint) desmayarse

black belt n (Sport) cinturón m negro; (US: area) zona negra

blackberry ['blækbərɪ] n zarzamora

blackbird ['blækbə:d] n mirlo

blackboard ['blækbɔ:d] n pizarra

black box n (Aviat) caja negra

Black Country n (Brit): **the ~** región industrial del centro de Inglaterra

blackcurrant ['blæk'kʌrənt] n grosella negra

black economy n economía sumergida

blacken ['blækən] vt ennegrecer; (fig) denigrar

Black Forest n: **the ~** la Selva Negra

blackguard ['blægɑ:d] n canalla m, pillo

black hole n (Astro) agujero negro

black ice n hielo invisible en la carretera

blackjack ['blækdʒæk] n (US) veintiuna

blackleg ['blæklɛg] n (Brit) esquirol m/f

blacklist ['blæklɪst] n lista negra ▪ vt poner en la lista negra

blackmail ['blækmeɪl] n chantaje m ▪ vt chantajear

blackmailer ['blækmeɪlər] n chantajista m/f

black market n mercado negro, estraperlo

blackness ['blæknɪs] n negrura

blackout ['blækaut] n (TV, Elec) apagón m; (fainting) desmayo, pérdida de conocimiento

Black Sea n: **the ~** el Mar Negro

black sheep n oveja negra

blacksmith ['blæksmɪθ] n herrero

black spot n (Aut) punto negro

bladder ['blædər] n vejiga

blade [bleɪd] n hoja; (cutting edge) filo; **a ~ of grass** una brizna de hierba

Blairite ['blɛərait] n, adj blairista m/f

blame [bleɪm] n culpa ▪ vt: **to ~ sb for sth** echar a algn la culpa de algo; **to be to ~ (for)** tener la culpa (de); **I'm not to ~** yo no tengo la culpa; **and I don't ~ him** y lo comprendo perfectamente

blameless ['bleɪmlɪs] adj (person) inocente

blanch [blɑ:ntʃ] vi (person) palidecer; (Culin) escaldar

bland [blænd] adj suave; (taste) soso

blank [blæŋk] adj en blanco; (shot) de fogueo; (look) sin expresión ▪ n blanco, espacio en blanco; cartucho de fogueo; **to draw a ~** (fig) no conseguir nada

blank cheque, blank check (US) n cheque m en blanco

blanket ['blæŋkɪt] n manta, frazada (LAm), cobija (LAm) ▪ adj (statement, agreement) comprensivo, general; **to give ~ cover** (insurance policy) dar póliza a todo riesgo

blankly ['blæŋklɪ] adv: **she looked at me ~** me miró sin comprender

blare [blɛər] vi (brass band, horns, radio) resonar

blasé ['blɑ:zeɪ] adj de vuelta de todo

blaspheme [blæs'fi:m] vi blasfemar

blasphemous ['blæsfɪməs] adj blasfemo

blasphemy ['blæsfɪmɪ] n blasfemia

blast [blɑ:st] n (of wind) ráfaga, soplo; (of whistle) toque m; (of explosive) carga explosiva; (force) choque m ▪ vt (blow up) volar; (blow open) abrir con carga explosiva ▪ excl (Brit col) ¡maldito sea!; **(at) full ~** (also fig) a toda marcha
  ▶ **blast off** vi (spacecraft etc) despegar

blast furnace n alto horno

blast-off ['blɑ:stɔf] n (Space) lanzamiento

blatant ['bleɪtənt] adj descarado

blatantly ['bleɪtəntlɪ] adv: **it's ~ obvious** está clarísimo

blather ['blæðər] vi decir tonterías

blaze [bleɪz] n (fire) fuego; (flames) llamarada; (glow: of fire, sun etc) resplandor m; (fig) arranque m ▪ vi (fire) arder con llamaradas; (fig) brillar ▪ vt: **to ~ a trail** (fig) abrir (un) camino; **in a ~ of publicity** bajo los focos de la publicidad

blazer ['bleɪzər] n chaqueta de uniforme de colegial o de socio de club

bleach [bli:tʃ] n (also: **household bleach**) lejía ▪ vt (linen) blanquear

bleached [bli:tʃt] adj (hair) de colorado; (clothes) blanqueado

bleachers ['bli:tʃəz] npl (US Sport) gradas fpl

bleak [bli:k] adj (countryside) desierto; (landscape) desolado, desierto; (weather) desapacible; (smile) triste; (prospect, future) poco prometedor(a)

bleary-eyed ['blɪərɪ'aɪd] adj: **to be ~** tener ojos de cansado

bleat [bli:t] vi balar

bleed (pt, pp **bled**) [bli:d, blɛd] vt sangrar; (brakes, radiator) desaguar ▪ vi sangrar

bleeding ['bli:dɪŋ] adj sangrante

bleep [bli:p] n pitido ▪ vi pitar ▪ vt llamar por el busca

bleeper ['bli:pər] n (of doctor etc) busca m

blemish ['blɛmɪʃ] n mancha, tacha

blench [blɛntʃ] vi (shrink back) acobardarse; (grow pale) palidecer

b

blend [blɛnd] n mezcla ■ vt mezclar
■ vi (colours etc) combinarse, mezclarse

blender ['blɛndəʳ] n (Culin) batidora

bless (pt, pp **blessed** or **blest**) [blɛs, blɛst] vt
bendecir

blessed ['blɛsɪd] adj (Rel: holy) santo, bendito;
(: happy) dichoso; **every ~ day** cada santo día

blessing ['blɛsɪŋ] n bendición f; (advantage)
beneficio, ventaja; **to count one's**
blessings agradecer lo que se tiene; **it was**
a ~ in disguise no hay mal que por bien no
venga

blew [blu:] pt of **blow**

blight [blaɪt] vt (hopes etc) frustrar, arruinar

blimey ['blaɪmɪ] excl (Brit col) ¡caray!

blind [blaɪnd] adj ciego ■ n (for window)
persiana ■ vt cegar; (dazzle) deslumbrar

blind alley n callejón m sin salida

blind corner n (Brit) esquina or curva sin
visibilidad

blind date n cita a ciegas

blinders ['blaɪndəz] npl (US) anteojeras fpl

blindfold ['blaɪndfəuld] n venda ■ adj, adv
con los ojos vendados ■ vt vendar los ojos a

blinding ['blaɪndɪŋ] adj (flash, light) cegador;
(pain) intenso

blindingly ['blaɪndɪŋlɪ] adv: **it's ~ obvious**
salta a la vista

blindly ['blaɪndlɪ] adv a ciegas, ciegamente

blindness ['blaɪndnɪs] n ceguera

blind spot n (Aut) ángulo muerto; **to have a ~**
about sth estar ciego para algo

blink [blɪŋk] vi parpadear, pestañear; (light)
oscilar; **to be on the ~** (col) estar
estropeado

blinkers ['blɪŋkəz] npl (esp Brit) anteojeras fpl

blinking ['blɪŋkɪŋ] adj (col): **this ~ ...** este
condenado ...

blip [blɪp] n señal f luminosa; (on graph)
pequeña desviación f; (fig) pequeña
anomalía

bliss [blɪs] n felicidad f

blissful ['blɪsful] adj dichoso; **in ~ ignorance**
feliz en la ignorancia

blissfully ['blɪsfulɪ] adv (sigh, smile) con
felicidad; **~ happy** sumamente feliz

blister ['blɪstəʳ] n ampolla ■ vi ampollarse

blistering ['blɪstərɪŋ] adj (heat) abrasador(a)

BLit, BLitt n abbr (= Bachelor of Literature) título
universitario

blithely ['blaɪðlɪ] adv alegremente,
despreocupadamente

blithering ['blɪðərɪŋ] adj (col): **this ~ idiot**
este tonto perdido

blitz [blɪts] n bombardeo aéreo; **to have a ~**
on sth (fig) emprenderla con algo

blizzard ['blɪzəd] n ventisca

BLM n abbr (US) = **Bureau of Land**
Management

bloated ['bləutɪd] adj hinchado

blob [blɔb] n (drop) gota; (stain, spot) mancha

bloc [blɔk] n (Pol) bloque m

block [blɔk] n bloque m (also Comput); (in pipes)
obstáculo; (of buildings) manzana ■ vt (gen)
obstruir, cerrar; (progress) estorbar; (Comput)
agrupar; **~ of flats** (Brit) bloque m de pisos;
mental ~ amnesia temporal; **~ and tackle**
(Tech) aparejo de polea; **3 blocks from here** a
3 manzanas or cuadras (LAm) de aquí
▶ **block up** vt tapar, obstruir; (pipe) atascar

blockade [blɔ'keɪd] n bloqueo ■ vt bloquear

blockage ['blɔkɪdʒ] n estorbo, obstrucción f

block booking n reserva en grupo

blockbuster ['blɔkbʌstəʳ] n (book) best-seller
m; (film) éxito de público

block capitals npl mayúsculas fpl

block letters npl letras fpl de molde

block release n (Brit) exención f por estudios

block vote n (Brit) voto por delegación

blog [blɔg] n (Comput) blog m ■ vi bloguear

blogger ['blɔgəʳ] n (col: person) blogger mf

blogging ['blɔgɪŋ] n blogging m

bloke [bləuk] n (Brit col) tipo, tío

blond, blonde [blɔnd] adj, n rubio(-a) m(f)

blood [blʌd] n sangre f; **new ~** (fig) gente f
nueva

blood bank n banco de sangre

blood count n recuento de glóbulos rojos y
blancos

blood donor n donante m/f de sangre

blood group n grupo sanguíneo

bloodhound ['blʌdhaund] n sabueso

bloodless ['blʌdlɪs] adj (pale) exangüe; (revolt
etc) sin derramamiento de sangre, incruento

bloodletting ['blʌdlɛtɪŋ] n (Med) sangría;
(fig) sangría, carnicería

blood poisoning n septicemia de la sangre

blood pressure n tensión f sanguínea; **to**
have high/low ~ tener la tensión alta/baja

bloodshed ['blʌdʃɛd] n baño de sangre

bloodshot ['blʌdʃɔt] adj inyectado en sangre

bloodstained ['blʌdsteɪnd] adj manchado
de sangre

bloodstream ['blʌdstri:m] n corriente f
sanguínea

blood test n análisis m de sangre

bloodthirsty ['blʌdθə:stɪ] adj sanguinario

blood transfusion n transfusión f de sangre

blood type n grupo sanguíneo

blood vessel n vaso sanguíneo

bloody ['blʌdɪ] adj sangriento; (Brit col!): **this**
~ ... este condenado or puñetero or fregado
(LAm) ... (!) ■ adv (Brit col!): **~ strong/good**
terriblemente fuerte/bueno

bloody-minded ['blʌdɪ'maɪndɪd] *adj* (*Brit col*) con malas pulgas

bloom [blu:m] *n* floración *f*; **in** ~ en flor ■ *vi* florecer

blooming ['blu:mɪŋ] *adj* (*col*): **this** ~ ... este condenado ...

blossom ['blɔsəm] *n* flor *f* ■ *vi* florecer; (*fig*) desarrollarse; **to** ~ **into** (*fig*) convertirse en

blot [blɔt] *n* borrón *m* ■ *vt* (*dry*) secar; (*stain*) manchar; **to** ~ **out** *vt* (*view*) tapar; (*memories*) borrar; **to be a** ~ **on the landscape** estropear el paisaje; **to** ~ **one's copy book** (*fig*) manchar su reputación

blotchy ['blɔtʃɪ] *adj* (*complexion*) lleno de manchas

blotter ['blɔtəʳ] *n* secante *m*

blotting paper ['blɔtɪŋ-] *n* papel *m* secante

blotto ['blɔtəu] *adj* (*col*) mamado

blouse [blauz] *n* blusa

blow [bləu] (*pt* **blew**, *pp* **blown**) *n* golpe *m* ■ *vi* soplar; (*fuse*) fundirse ■ *vt* (*glass*) soplar; (*fuse*) quemar; (*instrument*) tocar; **to come to blows** llegar a golpes; **to** ~ **one's nose** sonarse

▶ **blow away** *vt* llevarse, arrancar

▶ **blow down** *vt* derribar

▶ **blow off** *vt* arrebatar

▶ **blow out** *vt* apagar ■ *vi* apagarse; (*tyre*) reventar

▶ **blow over** *vi* amainar

▶ **blow up** *vi* estallar ■ *vt* volar; (*tyre*) inflar; (*Phot*) ampliar

blow-dry ['bləudraɪ] *n* secado con secador de mano ■ *vt* secar con secador de mano

blowlamp ['bləulæmp] *n* (*Brit*) soplete *m*, lámpara de soldar

blown [bləun] *pp of* **blow**

blow-out ['bləuaut] *n* (*of tyre*) pinchazo; (*col*: *big meal*) banquete *m*, festín *m*

blowtorch ['bləutɔ:tʃ] *n* = **blowlamp**

blow-up ['bləuʌp] *n* (*Phot*) ampliación *f*

BLS *n abbr* (*US*) = **Bureau of Labor Statistics**

blubber ['blʌbəʳ] *n* grasa de ballena ■ *vi* (*pej*) lloriquear

bludgeon ['blʌdʒən] *vt*: **to** ~ **sb into doing sth** coaccionar a algn a hacer algo

blue [blu:] *adj* azul; ~ **film** película porno; ~ **joke** chiste verde; **once in a** ~ **moon** de higos a brevas; **to come out of the** ~ (*fig*) ser completamente inesperado; *see also* **blues**

blue baby *n* niño azul *or* cianótico

bluebell ['blu:bɛl] *n* campanilla, campánula azul

blue-blooded [blu:'blʌdɪd] *adj* de sangre azul

bluebottle ['blu:bɔtl] *n* moscarda, mosca azul

blue cheese *n* queso azul

blue-chip ['blu:tʃɪp] *n*: ~ **investment** inversión *f* asegurada

blue-collar worker ['blu:kɔlər-] *n* obrero(-a)

blue jeans *npl* tejanos *mpl*, vaqueros *mpl*

blueprint ['blu:prɪnt] *n* proyecto; ~ **(for)** (*fig*) anteproyecto (de)

blues [blu:z] *npl*: **the** ~ (*Mus*) el blues; **to have the** ~ estar triste

Bluetooth® ['blu:tu:θ] *n* Bluetooth® *f*; ~ **technology**® tecnología Bluetooth®

bluff [blʌf] *vi* tirarse un farol, farolear ■ *n* bluff *m*, farol *m*; (*Geo*) precipicio, despeñadero; **to call sb's** ~ coger a algn en un renuncio

bluish ['blu:ɪʃ] *adj* azulado

blunder ['blʌndəʳ] *n* patinazo, metedura de pata ■ *vi* cometer un error, meter la pata; **to** ~ **into sb/sth** tropezar con algn/algo

blunt [blʌnt] *adj* (*knife*) desafilado; (*person*) franco, directo ■ *vt* embotar, desafilar; **this pencil is** ~ este lápiz está despuntado; ~ **instrument** (*Law*) instrumento contundente

bluntly ['blʌntlɪ] *adv* (*speak*) francamente, de modo terminante

bluntness ['blʌntnɪs] *n* (*of person*) franqueza, brusquedad *f*

blur [blə:ʳ] *n* aspecto borroso ■ *vt* (*vision*) enturbiar; (*memory*) empañar

blurb [blə:b] *n* propaganda

blurred [blə:d] *adj* borroso

blurt [blə:t]: **to** ~ **out** *vt* (*say*) descolgarse con, dejar escapar

blush [blʌʃ] *vi* ruborizarse, ponerse colorado ■ *n* rubor *m*

blusher ['blʌʃəʳ] *n* colorete *m*

bluster ['blʌstəʳ] *n* fanfarronada, bravata ■ *vi* fanfarronear, echar bravatas

blustering ['blʌstərɪŋ] *adj* (*person*) fanfarrón(-ona)

blustery ['blʌstərɪ] *adj* (*weather*) tempestuoso, tormentoso

Blvd *abbr* = **boulevard**

BM *n abbr* (= *British Museum*: *Univ*: = *Bachelor of Medicine*) título universitario

BMA *n abbr* = **British Medical Association**

BMJ *n abbr* = **British Medical Journal**

BMus *n abbr* (= *Bachelor of Music*) título universitario

BMX *n abbr* (= *bicycle motocross*) BMX *f*; ~ **bike** bici(cleta) *f* BMX

bn *abbr* = **billion**

BO *n abbr* (*col*: = *body odour*) olor *m* a sudor; (*US*) = **box office**

boa ['bəuə] *n* boa

boar [bɔ:ʳ] *n* verraco, cerdo

board [bɔ:d] *n* tabla, tablero; (*on wall*) tablón

m; (for chess etc) tablero; (committee) junta, consejo; (in firm) mesa or junta directiva; (Naut, Aviat): **on ~** a bordo ◼ vt (ship) embarcarse en; (train) subir a; **full ~** (Brit) pensión f completa; **half ~** (Brit) media pensión; **~ and lodging** alojamiento y comida; **to go by the ~** (fig) irse por la borda; **above ~** (fig) sin tapujos; **across the ~** (fig: adv) en todos los niveles; (: adj) general
▶ **board up** vt (door) tapar, cegar

boarder ['bɔːdəʳ] n huésped(a) m(f); (Scol) interno(-a)

board game n juego de tablero

boarding card ['bɔːdɪŋ-] n (Brit: Aviat, Naut) tarjeta de embarque

boarding house ['bɔːdɪŋ-] n casa de huéspedes

boarding party ['bɔːdɪŋ-] n brigada de inspección

boarding pass ['bɔːdɪŋ-] n (US) = **boarding card**

boarding school ['bɔːdɪŋ-] n internado

board meeting n reunión f de la junta directiva

board room n sala de juntas

boardwalk ['bɔːdwɔːk] n (US) paseo entablado

boast [bəust] vi: **to ~ (about** or **of)** alardear (de) ◼ vt ostentar ◼ n alarde m, baladronada

boastful ['bəustfəl] adj presumido

boastfulness ['bəustfulnɪs] n fanfarronería, jactancia

boat [bəut] n barco, buque m; (small) barca, bote m; **to go by ~** ir en barco

boater ['bəutəʳ] n (hat) canotié m

boating ['bəutɪŋ] n canotaje m

boatman ['bəutmən] n barquero

boat people npl refugiados que huyen en barca

boatswain ['bəusn] n contramaestre m

bob [bɔb] vi (boat, cork on water: also: **bob up and down**) menearse, balancearse ◼ n (Brit col) = **shilling**
▶ **bob up** vi (re)aparecer de repente

bobbin ['bɔbɪn] n (of sewing machine) carrete m, bobina

bobby ['bɔbɪ] n (Brit col) poli m/f

bobsleigh ['bɔbsleɪ] n bob m, trineo de competición f

bode [bəud] vi: **to ~ well/ill (for)** ser de buen/mal agüero (para)

bodice ['bɔdɪs] n corpiño

-bodied ['bɔdɪd] adj suff de cuerpo ...

bodily ['bɔdɪlɪ] adj (comfort, needs) corporal; (pain) corpóreo ◼ adv (in person) en persona; (carry) corporalmente; (lift) en peso

body ['bɔdɪ] n cuerpo; (corpse) cadáver m;

(of car) caja, carrocería; (also: **body stocking**) body m; (fig: organization) organización f; (: public body) organismo; (: quantity) masa; (: of speech, document) parte f principal; **ruling ~** directiva; **in a ~** todos juntos, en masa

body blow n (fig) palo

body-building ['bɔdɪˈbɪldɪŋ] n culturismo

bodyguard ['bɔdɪgɑːd] n guardaespaldas m inv

body language n lenguaje m gestual

body search n cacheo; **to carry out a ~ on sb** registrar a algn; **to submit to** or **undergo a ~** ser registrado

bodywork ['bɔdɪwəːk] n carrocería

boffin ['bɔfɪn] n (Brit) científico(-a)

bog [bɔg] n pantano, ciénaga ◼ vt: **to get bogged down** (fig) empantanarse, atascarse

boggle ['bɔgl] vi: **the mind boggles!** ¡no puedo creerlo!

Bogotá [bəugəˈtɑː] n Bogotá

bogus ['bəugəs] adj falso, fraudulento; (person) fingido

Bohemia [bəˈhiːmɪə] n Bohemia

Bohemian [bəˈhiːmɪən] adj, n bohemio(-a) m(f)

boil [bɔɪl] vt cocer; (eggs) pasar por agua ◼ vi hervir ◼ n (Med) furúnculo, divieso; **to bring to the ~** calentar hasta que hierva; **to come to the** (Brit) or **a** (US) **~** comenzar a hervir; **boiled egg** huevo pasado por agua; **boiled potatoes** patatas fpl or papas fpl (LAm) cocidas
▶ **boil down** vi (fig): **to ~ down to** reducirse a
▶ **boil over** vi (liquid) rebosar; (anger, resentment) llegar al colmo

boiler ['bɔɪləʳ] n caldera

boiler suit n (Brit) mono, overol m (LAm)

boiling ['bɔɪlɪŋ] adj: **I'm ~ (hot)** (col) estoy asado

boiling point n punto de ebullición f

boil-in-the-bag [bɔɪlɪnðəˈbæg] adj: **~ meals** platos que se cuecen en su misma bolsa

boisterous ['bɔɪstərəs] adj (noisy) bullicioso; (excitable) exuberante; (crowd) tumultuoso

bold [bəuld] adj (brave) valiente, audaz; (pej) descarado; (outline) grueso; (colour) vivo; **~ type** (Typ) negrita

boldly ['bəuldlɪ] adv audazmente

boldness ['bəuldnɪs] n valor m, audacia; (cheek) descaro

Bolivia [bəˈlɪvɪə] n Bolivia

Bolivian [bəˈlɪvɪən] adj, n boliviano(-a) m(f)

bollard ['bɔləd] n (Brit Aut) poste m

Bollywood ['bɔlɪwud] n Bollywood m

bolshy ['bɔlʃɪ] adj (Brit col) protestón(-ona); **to be in a ~ mood** tener el día protestón

bolster ['bəulstəʳ] n travesero, cabezal m

b

▸ **bolster up** *vt* reforzar; (*fig*) alentar
bolt [bəult] *n* (*lock*) cerrojo; (*with nut*) perno, tornillo ▪ *adv*: ~ **upright** rígido, erguido ▪ *vt* (*door*) echar el cerrojo a; (*food*) engullir ▪ *vi* fugarse; (*horse*) desbocarse
bomb [bɔm] *n* bomba ▪ *vt* bombardear
bombard [bɔm'bɑːd] *vt* bombardear; (*fig*) asediar
bombardment [bɔm'bɑːdmənt] *n* bombardeo
bombastic [bɔm'bæstɪk] *adj* rimbombante; (*person*) pomposo
bomb disposal *n* desactivación *f* de explosivos
bomb disposal expert *n* artificiero(-a)
bomber ['bɔmər] *n* (*Aviat*) bombardero; (*terrorist*) persona que pone bombas
bombing ['bɔmɪŋ] *n* bombardeo
bomb scare *n* amenaza de bomba
bombshell ['bɔmʃɛl] *n* obús *m*, granada; (*fig*) bomba
bomb site *n* lugar *m* donde estalló una bomba
bona fide ['bəunə'faɪdɪ] *adj* genuino, auténtico
bonanza [bə'nænzə] *n* bonanza
bond [bɔnd] *n* (*binding promise*) fianza; (*Finance*) bono; (*link*) vínculo, lazo; **in** ~ (*Comm*) en depósito bajo fianza
bondage ['bɔndɪdʒ] *n* esclavitud *f*
bonded goods ['bɔndɪd-] *npl* mercancías *fpl* en depósito de aduanas
bonded warehouse ['bɔndɪd-] *n* depósito de aduanas
bone [bəun] *n* hueso; (*of fish*) espina ▪ *vt* deshuesar; quitar las espinas a; ~ **of contention** manzana de la discordia
bone china *n* porcelana fina
bone-dry ['bəun'draɪ] *adj* completamente seco
bone idle *adj* gandul
bone marrow *n* médula; ~ **transplant** transplante *m* de médula
boner ['bəunər] *n* (*US col*) plancha, patochada
bonfire ['bɔnfaɪər] *n* hoguera, fogata
bonk [bɔŋk] *vt, vi* (*humorous, col*) chingar (!)
bonkers ['bɔŋkəz] *adj* (*Brit col*) majareta
Bonn [bɔn] *n* Bonn *m*
bonnet ['bɔnɪt] *n* gorra; (*Brit: of car*) capó *m*
bonny ['bɔnɪ] *adj* (*esp Scottish*) bonito, hermoso, lindo
bonus ['bəunəs] *n* (*at Christmas etc*) paga extraordinaria; (*merit award*) sobrepaga, prima
bony ['bəunɪ] *adj* (*arm, face*) huesudo; (*Med: tissue*) huesudo; (*meat*) lleno de huesos; (*fish*) lleno de espinas; (*thin: person*) flaco, delgado

boo [buː] *vt* abuchear
boob [buːb] *n* (*col: mistake*) disparate *m*, sandez *f*; (*: breast*) teta
booby prize ['buːbɪ-] *n* premio de consolación (*al último*)
booby trap ['buːbɪ-] *n* (*Mil etc*) trampa explosiva
book [buk] *n* libro; (*notebook*) libreta; (*of stamps etc*) librillo; **books** (*Comm*) cuentas *fpl*, contabilidad *f* ▪ *vt* (*ticket, seat, room*) reservar; (*driver*) fichar; (*Football*) amonestar; **to keep the books** llevar las cuentas *or* los libros; **by the** ~ según las reglas; **to throw the** ~ **at sb** echar un rapapolvo a algn
▸ **book in** *vi* (*at hotel*) registrarse
▸ **book up** *vt*: **all seats are booked up** todas las plazas están reservadas; **the hotel is booked up** el hotel está lleno
bookable ['bukəbl] *adj*: **seats are** ~ los asientos se pueden reservar (de antemano)
bookcase ['bukkeɪs] *n* librería, estante *m* para libros
booking office ['bukɪŋ-] *n* (*Brit: Rail*) despacho de billetes *or* boletos (*LAm*); (*: Theat*) taquilla, boletería (*LAm*)
book-keeping ['buk'kiːpɪŋ] *n* contabilidad *f*
booklet ['buklɪt] *n* folleto
bookmaker ['bukmeɪkər] *n* corredor *m* de apuestas
bookmark ['bukmɑːk] (*Comput*) favorito *m*
bookseller ['buksɛlər] *n* librero(-a)
bookshelf ['bukʃɛlf] *n* estante *m*
bookshop ['bukʃɔp] *n* librería
bookstall ['bukstɔːl] *n* quiosco de libros
book store *n* = **bookshop**
book token *n* vale *m* para libros
book value *n* (*Comm*) valor *m* contable
bookworm ['bukwəːm] *n* (*fig*) ratón *m* de biblioteca
boom [buːm] *n* (*noise*) trueno, estampido; (*in prices etc*) alza rápida; (*Econ*) boom *m*, auge *m* ▪ *vi* (*cannon*) hacer gran estruendo, retumbar; (*Econ*) estar en alza
boomerang ['buːməræŋ] *n* bumerang *m* (*also fig*) ▪ *vi*: **to** ~ **on sb** (*fig*) ser contraproducente para algn
boom town *n* ciudad *f* de crecimiento rápido
boon [buːn] *n* favor *m*, beneficio
boorish ['buərɪʃ] *adj* grosero
boost [buːst] *n* estímulo, empuje *m* ▪ *vt* estimular, empujar; (*increase: sales, production*) aumentar; **to give a** ~ **to** (*morale*) levantar; **it gave a** ~ **to his confidence** le dio confianza en sí mismo
booster ['buːstər] *n* (*Med*) reinyección *f*; (*TV*) repetidor *m*; (*Elec*) elevador *m* de tensión; (*also*: **booster rocket**) cohete *m*

boot [buːt] n bota; (ankle boot) botín m, borceguí m; (Brit: of car) maleta, maletero, baúl m (LAm) ▪ vt dar un puntapié a; (Comput) arrancar; **to** ~ (in addition) además, por añadidura; **to give sb the** ~ (col) despedir a algn, poner a algn en la calle

booth [buːð] n (at fair) barraca; (telephone booth, voting booth) cabina

bootleg ['buːtlɛg] adj de contrabando; ~ **record** disco pirata

booty ['buːtɪ] n botín m

booze [buːz] (col) n bebida ▪ vi emborracharse

boozer ['buːzəʳ] n (col: person) bebedor(a) m(f); (: Brit: pub) bar m

border ['bɔːdəʳ] n borde m, margen m; (of a country) frontera ▪ adj fronterizo; **the Borders** región fronteriza entre Escocia e Inglaterra
▶ **border on** vt fus lindar con; (fig) rayar en

borderline ['bɔːdəlaɪn] n (fig) frontera

bore [bɔːʳ] pt of **bear** ▪ vt (hole) taladrar; (person) aburrir ▪ n (person) pelmazo, pesado; (of gun) calibre m

bored [bɔːd] adj aburrido; **he's** ~ **to tears** or **to death** or **stiff** está aburrido como una ostra, está muerto de aburrimiento

boredom ['bɔːdəm] n aburrimiento

boring ['bɔːrɪŋ] adj aburrido, pesado

born [bɔːn] adj: **to be** ~ nacer; **I was** ~ **in 1960** nací en 1960

born-again [bɔːnə'gɛn] adj: ~ **Christian** evangelista m/f

borne [bɔːn] pp of **bear**

Borneo ['bɔːnɪəu] n Borneo

borough ['bʌrə] n municipio

borrow ['bɔrəu] vt: **to** ~ **sth (from sb)** tomar algo prestado (a alguien); **may I** ~ **your car?** ¿me prestas tu coche?

borrower ['bɔrəuəʳ] n prestatario(-a)

borrowing ['bɔrəuɪŋ] n préstamos mpl

borstal ['bɔːstl] n (Brit) reformatorio (de menores)

Bosnia ['bɔznɪə] n Bosnia

Bosnia-Herzegovina, Bosnia-Hercegovina ['bɔːsnɪəhɛrzə'gəuviːnə] n Bosnia-Herzegovina

Bosnian ['bɔznɪən] adj, n bosnio(-a)

bosom ['buzəm] n pecho; (fig) seno

bosom friend n amigo(-a) íntimo(-a) or del alma

boss [bɔs] n jefe(-a) m(f); (employer) patrón(-ona) m(f); (political etc) cacique m ▪ vt (also: **boss about** or **around**) mangonear; **stop bossing everyone about!** ¡deja de dar órdenes or de mangonear a todos!

bossy ['bɔsɪ] adj mandón(-ona)

bosun ['bəusn] n contramaestre m

botanical [bə'tænɪkl] adj botánico

botanist ['bɔtənɪst] n botanista m/f

botany ['bɔtənɪ] n botánica

botch [bɔtʃ] vt (also: **botch up**) arruinar, estropear

both [bəuθ] adj, pron ambos(-as), los/las dos; ~ **of us went**, **we** ~ **went** fuimos los dos, ambos fuimos ▪ adv: ~ **A and B** tanto A como B

bother ['bɔðəʳ] vt (worry) preocupar; (disturb) molestar, fastidiar, fregar (LAm), embromar (LAm) ▪ vi (gen): ~ **o.s.** molestarse ▪ n: **what a** ~! ¡qué lata! ▪ excl ¡maldita sea!, ¡caramba!; **I'm sorry to** ~ **you** perdona que te moleste; **to** ~ **doing** tomarse la molestia de hacer; **please don't** ~ no te molestes

Botswana [bɔt'swaːnə] n Botswana

bottle ['bɔtl] n botella; (small) frasco; (baby's) biberón m ▪ vt embotellar; ~ **of wine/milk** botella de vino/de leche; **wine/milk** ~ botella de vino/de leche
▶ **bottle up** vt (fig) contener, reprimir

bottle bank n contenedor m de vidrio, iglú m

bottleneck ['bɔtlnɛk] n embotellamiento

bottle-opener ['bɔtləupnəʳ] n abrebotellas m inv

bottom ['bɔtəm] n (of box, sea) fondo; (buttocks) trasero, culo; (of page, mountain, tree) pie m; (of list) final m ▪ adj (lowest) más bajo; (last) último; **to get to the** ~ **of sth** (fig) llegar al fondo de algo

bottomless ['bɔtəmlɪs] adj sin fondo, insondable

bottom line n: **the** ~ lo fundamental; **the** ~ **is he has to go** el caso es que tenemos que despedirle

botulism ['bɔtjulɪzəm] n botulismo

bough [bau] n rama

bought [bɔːt] pt, pp of **buy**

bouillon cube ['buːjɔn-] n (US) cubito de caldo

boulder ['bəuldəʳ] n canto rodado

bounce [bauns] vi (ball) (re)botar; (cheque) ser rechazado ▪ vt hacer (re)botar ▪ n (rebound) (re)bote m; **he's got plenty of** ~ (fig) tiene mucha energía

bouncer ['baunsəʳ] n (col) forzudo, gorila m

bouncy castle® ['baunsɪ-] n castillo inflable

bound [baund] pt, pp of **bind** ▪ n (leap) salto; (gen pl: limit) límite m ▪ vi (leap) saltar ▪ adj: ~ **by** rodeado de; **to be** ~ **to do sth** (obliged) tener el deber de hacer algo; **he's** ~ **to come** es seguro que vendrá; **"out of bounds to the public"** "prohibido el paso"; ~ **for** con destino a

boundary ['baundrɪ] n límite m, lindero

boundless ['baundlɪs] adj ilimitado

bountiful ['bauntɪful] adj (person) liberal,

generoso; (*God*) bondadoso; (*supply*) abundante

bounty ['baʊntɪ] *n* (*generosity*) generosidad *f*; (*reward*) prima

bounty hunter *n* cazarrecompensas *m inv*

bouquet ['bukeɪ] *n* (*of flowers*) ramo, ramillete *m*; (*of wine*) aroma *m*

bourbon ['buəbən] *n* (*US: also:* **bourbon whiskey**) whisky *m* americano, bourbon *m*

bourgeois ['buəʒwɑ:] *adj, n* burgués(-esa) *m(f)*

bout [baʊt] *n* (*of malaria etc*) ataque *m*; (*Boxing etc*) combate *m*, encuentro

boutique [bu:'ti:k] *n* boutique *f*, tienda de ropa

bow [bəʊ] *n* (*knot*) lazo; (*weapon*) arco; (*Mus*) arco [baʊ] (*of the head*) reverencia; (*Naut: also:* **bows**) proa ■ *vi* [baʊ] inclinarse, hacer una reverencia; (*yield*): **to ~ to** *or* **before** ceder ante, someterse a; **to ~ to the inevitable** resignarse a lo inevitable

bowels ['baʊəlz] *npl* intestinos *mpl*, vientre *m*

bowl [bəʊl] *n* tazón *m*, cuenco; (*for washing*) palangana, jofaina; (*ball*) bola; (*US: stadium*) estadio ■ *vi* (*Cricket*) arrojar la pelota; *see also* **bowls**

bow-legged ['bəʊ'lɛgɪd] *adj* estevado

bowler ['bəʊlər] *n* (*Cricket*) lanzador *m* (de la pelota); (*Brit: also:* **bowler hat**) hongo, bombín *m*

bowling ['bəʊlɪŋ] *n* (*game*) bolos *mpl*, bochas *fpl*

bowling alley *n* bolera

bowling green *n* pista para bochas

bowls [bəʊlz] *n* juego de los bolos, bochas *fpl*

bow tie ['bəʊ-] *n* corbata de lazo, pajarita

box [bɒks] *n* (*also:* **cardboard box**) caja, cajón *m*; (*for jewels*) estuche *m*; (*for money*) cofre *m*; (*crate*) cofre *m*, arca; (*Theat*) palco ■ *vt* encajonar ■ *vi* (*Sport*) boxear

boxer ['bɒksər] *n* (*person*) boxeador *m*; (*dog*) bóxer *m*

box file *n* fichero

boxing ['bɒksɪŋ] *n* (*Sport*) boxeo, box *m* (*LAm*)

Boxing Day *n* (*Brit*) día *m* de San Esteban; *ver nota*

BOXING DAY

El día después de Navidad es *Boxing Day*, fiesta en todo el Reino Unido, aunque si el 26 de diciembre cae en domingo el día de descanso se traslada al lunes. En dicho día solía ser tradición entregar "Christmas boxes" (aguinaldos) a empleados, proveedores a domicilio, carteros etc.

boxing gloves *npl* guantes *mpl* de boxeo

boxing ring *n* ring *m*, cuadrilátero

box number *n* (*for advertisements*) apartado

box office *n* taquilla, boletería (*LAm*)

boxroom ['bɒksrʊm] *n* trastero

boy [bɔɪ] *n* (*young*) niño; (*older*) muchacho

boycott ['bɔɪkɒt] *n* boicot *m* ■ *vt* boicotear

boyfriend ['bɔɪfrɛnd] *n* novio

boyish ['bɔɪɪʃ] *adj* de muchacho, inmaduro

boy scout *n* boy scout *m*

bp *abbr* = **bishop**

Br. *abbr* (*Rel*) = **brother**

bra [brɑ:] *n* sostén *m*, sujetador *m*, corpiño (*LAm*)

brace [breɪs] *n* refuerzo, abrazadera; (*Brit: on teeth*) corrector *m*; (*tool*) berbiquí *m* ■ *vt* asegurar, reforzar; **to ~ o.s. (for)** (*fig*) prepararse (para); *see also* **braces**

bracelet ['breɪslɪt] *n* pulsera, brazalete *m*, pulso (*LAm*)

braces ['breɪsɪz] *npl* (*Brit*) tirantes *mpl*, suspensores *mpl* (*LAm*); (*US: on teeth*) corrector *m*

bracing ['breɪsɪŋ] *adj* vigorizante, tónico

bracken ['brækən] *n* helecho

bracket ['brækɪt] *n* (*Tech*) soporte *m*, puntal *m*; (*group*) clase *f*, categoría; (*also:* **brace bracket**) soporte *m*, abrazadera; (*also:* **round bracket**) paréntesis *m inv*; (*gen*): **square ~** corchete *m* ■ *vt* (*fig: also:* **bracket together**) agrupar; **income ~** nivel *m* económico; **in brackets** entre paréntesis

brackish ['brækɪʃ] *adj* (*water*) salobre

brag [bræg] *vi* jactarse

braid [breɪd] *n* (*trimming*) galón *m*; (*of hair*) trenza

Braille [breɪl] *n* Braille *m*

brain [breɪn] *n* cerebro; **brains** *npl* sesos *mpl*; **she's got brains** es muy lista

brainchild ['breɪntʃaɪld] *n* invención *f*

braindead ['breɪndɛd] *adj* (*Med*) clínicamente muerto; (*col*) subnormal, tarado

brainless ['breɪnlɪs] *adj* estúpido, insensato

brainstorm ['breɪnstɔ:m] *n* (*fig*) ataque *m* de locura, frenesí *m*; (*US: brainwave*) idea luminosa *or* genial, inspiración *f*

brainstorming ['breɪnstɔ:mɪŋ] *n* discusión intensa para solucionar problemas

brainwash ['breɪnwɒʃ] *vt* lavar el cerebro a

brainwave ['breɪnweɪv] *n* idea luminosa *or* genial, inspiración *f*

brainy ['breɪnɪ] *adj* muy listo *or* inteligente

braise [breɪz] *vt* cocer a fuego lento

brake [breɪk] *n* (*on vehicle*) freno ■ *vt, vi* frenar

brake drum *n* tambor *m* de freno

brake fluid *n* líquido de frenos

brake light *n* luz *f* de frenado

brake pedal n pedal m de freno
bramble ['bræmbl] n (fruit) zarza
bran [bræn] n salvado
branch [brɑːntʃ] n rama; (fig) ramo; (Comm) sucursal f ■ vi ramificarse; (fig) extenderse
▶ **branch out** vi ramificarse
branch line n (Rail) ramal m, línea secundaria
branch manager n director(a) m(f) de sucursal
brand [brænd] n marca; (iron) hierro de marcar ■ vt (cattle) marcar con hierro candente
brandish ['brændɪʃ] vt blandir
brand name n marca
brand-new ['brænd'njuː] adj flamante, completamente nuevo
brandy ['brændɪ] n coñac m, brandy m
brash [bræʃ] adj (rough) tosco; (cheeky) descarado
Brasilia [brə'zɪlɪə] n Brasilia
brass [brɑːs] n latón m; **the ~** (Mus) los cobres
brass band n banda de metal
brassière ['bræsɪər] n sostén m, sujetador m, corpiño (LAm)
brass tacks npl: **to get down to ~** ir al grano
brat [bræt] n (pej) mocoso(-a)
bravado [brə'vɑːdəu] n fanfarronería
brave [breɪv] adj valiente, valeroso ■ n guerrero indio ■ vt (challenge) desafiar; (resist) aguantar
bravely ['breɪvlɪ] adv valientemente, con valor
bravery ['breɪvərɪ] n valor m, valentía
bravo [brɑː'vəu] excl ¡bravo!, ¡olé!
brawl [brɔːl] n pendencia, reyerta ■ vi pelearse
brawn [brɔːn] n fuerza muscular; (meat) carne f en gelatina
brawny ['brɔːnɪ] adj fornido, musculoso
bray [breɪ] n rebuzno ■ vi rebuznar
brazen ['breɪzn] adj descarado, cínico ■ vt: **to ~ it out** echarle cara al asunto
brazier ['breɪzɪər] n brasero
Brazil [brə'zɪl] n (el) Brasil
Brazilian [brə'zɪlɪən] adj, n brasileño(-a) m(f)
breach [briːtʃ] vt abrir brecha en ■ n (gap) brecha; (estrangement) ruptura; (breaking): **~ of confidence** abuso de confianza; **~ of contract** infracción f de contrato; **~ of the peace** perturbación f del orden público; **in ~ of** por incumplimiento or infracción de
bread [brɛd] n pan m; (col: money) pasta, lana (LAm); **~ and butter** n pan con mantequilla; (fig) pan (de cada día) ■ adj común y corriente; **to earn one's daily ~** ganarse el pan; **to know which side one's ~ is buttered (on)** saber dónde aprieta el zapato

breadbin ['brɛdbɪn] n panera
breadboard ['brɛdbɔːd] n (Comput) circuito experimental
breadbox ['brɛdbɒks] n (US) panera
breadcrumbs ['brɛdkrʌmz] npl migajas fpl; (Culin) pan msg rallado
breadline ['brɛdlaɪn] n: **on the ~** en la miseria
breadth [brɛtθ] n anchura; (fig) amplitud f
breadwinner ['brɛdwɪnər] n sostén m de la familia
break [breɪk] vb (pt **broke**, pp **broken**) ■ vt (gen) romper; (promise) no cumplir; (fall) amortiguar; (journey) interrumpir; (law) violar, infringir; (record) batir; (news) comunicar ■ vi romperse, quebrarse; (storm) estallar; (weather) cambiar ■ n (gap) abertura; (crack) grieta; (fracture) fractura; (in relations) ruptura; (rest) descanso; (time) intervalo; (: at school) (período de) recreo; (holiday) vacaciones fpl; (chance) oportunidad f; (escape) evasión f, fuga; **to ~ with sb** (fig) romper con algn; **to ~ even** vi cubrir los gastos; **to ~ free** or **loose** vi escaparse; **lucky ~** (col) chiripa, racha de buena suerte; **to have** or **take a ~** (few minutes) descansar; **without a ~** sin descanso or descansar
▶ **break down** vt (door etc) echar abajo, derribar; (resistance) vencer, acabar con; (figures, data) analizar, descomponer; (undermine) acabar con ■ vi estropearse; (Med) sufrir un colapso; (Aut) averiarse, descomponerse (LAm); (person) romper a llorar
▶ **break in** vt (horse etc) domar ■ vi (burglar) forzar una entrada
▶ **break into** vt fus (house) forzar
▶ **break off** vi (speaker) pararse, detenerse; (branch) partir ■ vt (talks) suspender; (engagement) romper
▶ **break open** vt (door etc) abrir por la fuerza, forzar
▶ **break out** vi estallar; **to ~ out in spots** salir a algn granos
▶ **break through** vi: **the sun broke through** asomó el sol ■ vt fus (defences, barrier, crowd) abrirse paso por
▶ **break up** vi (partnership) disolverse; (friends) romper ■ vt (rocks, ice etc) partir; (crowd) disolver
breakable ['breɪkəbl] adj quebradizo ■ n: **breakables** cosas fpl frágiles
breakage ['breɪkɪdʒ] n rotura; **to pay for breakages** pagar por los objetos rotos
breakaway ['breɪkəweɪ] adj (group etc) disidente
break-dancing ['breɪkdɑːnsɪŋ] n break m

breakdown ['breɪkdaun] *n* (*Aut*) avería;
(*in communications*) interrupción *f*; (*Med:*
also: **nervous breakdown**) colapso, crisis *f*
nerviosa; (*of figures*) desglose *m*
breakdown van *n* (*Brit*) (camión *m*) grúa
breaker ['breɪkə^r] *n* rompiente *m*, ola grande
breakeven ['breɪk'i:vn] *cpd:* ~ **chart** gráfico
del punto de equilibrio; ~ **point** punto de
break-even *or* de equilibrio
breakfast ['brɛkfəst] *n* desayuno
breakfast cereal *n* cereales *mpl* para el
desayuno
break-in ['breɪkɪn] *n* robo con allanamiento
de morada
breaking and entering ['breɪkɪŋənd'ɛntə
rɪŋ] *n* (*Law*) violación *f* de domicilio,
allanamiento de morada
breaking point ['breɪkɪŋ-] *n* punto de
ruptura
breakthrough ['breɪkθru:] *n* ruptura; (*fig*)
avance *m*, adelanto
break-up ['breɪkʌp] *n* (*of partnership, marriage*)
disolución *f*
break-up value *n* (*Comm*) valor *m* de
liquidación
breakwater ['breɪkwɔ:tə^r] *n* rompeolas *m inv*
breast [brɛst] *n* (*of woman*) pecho, seno; (*chest*)
pecho; (*of bird*) pechuga
breast-feed ['brɛstfi:d] *vt, vi* (*irreg: like* **feed**)
amamantar, dar el pecho
breaststroke ['brɛststrəuk] *n* braza de pecho
breath [brɛθ] *n* aliento, respiración *f*; **out of**
~ sin aliento, sofocado; **to go out for a ~ of**
air salir a tomar el fresco
Breathalyser® ['brɛθəlaɪzə^r] *n* (*Brit*)
alcoholímetro *m*; ~ **test** *n* prueba de
alcoholemia
breathe [bri:ð] *vt, vi* respirar; (*noisily*) resollar;
I won't ~ a word about it no diré ni una
palabra de ello
▶ **breathe in** *vt, vi* aspirar
▶ **breathe out** *vt, vi* espirar
breather ['bri:ðə^r] *n* respiro, descanso
breathing ['bri:ðɪŋ] *n* respiración *f*
breathing space *n* (*fig*) respiro, pausa
breathless ['brɛθlɪs] *adj* sin aliento,
jadeante; (*with excitement*) pasmado
breathtaking ['brɛθteɪkɪŋ] *adj* imponente,
pasmoso
breath test *n* prueba de la alcoholemia
-bred [brɛd] *suff:* **to be well/ill~** estar bien/
mal criado
breed [bri:d] *vb* (*pt, pp* **bred**) [brɛd] ■ *vt* criar;
(*fig: hate, suspicion*) crear, engendrar ■ *vi*
reproducirse, procrear ■ *n* raza, casta
breeder ['bri:də^r] *n* (*person*) criador(a) *m(f)*;
(*Physics: also:* **breeder reactor**) reactor *m*

breeding ['bri:dɪŋ] *n* (*of person*) educación *f*
breeze [bri:z] *n* brisa
breezeblock ['bri:zblɔk] *n* (*Brit*) bovedilla
breezy ['bri:zɪ] *adj* de mucho viento, ventoso;
(*person*) despreocupado
Breton ['brɛtən] *adj* bretón(-ona) ■ *n*
bretón(-ona) *m(f)*; (*Ling*) bretón *m*
brevity ['brɛvɪtɪ] *n* brevedad *f*
brew [bru:] *vt* (*tea*) hacer; (*beer*) elaborar;
(*plot*) tramar ■ *vi* hacerse; elaborarse;
tramarse; (*storm*) amenazar
brewer ['bru:ə^r] *n* cervecero, fabricante *m* de
cerveza
brewery ['bru:ərɪ] *n* fábrica de cerveza
briar ['braɪə^r] *n* (*thorny bush*) zarza; (*wild rose*)
escaramujo, rosa silvestre
bribe [braɪb] *n* soborno ■ *vt* sobornar,
cohechar; **to ~ sb to do sth** sobornar a algn
para que haga algo
bribery ['braɪbərɪ] *n* soborno, cohecho
bric-a-brac ['brɪkəbræk] *n inv* baratijas *fpl*
brick [brɪk] *n* ladrillo
bricklayer ['brɪkleɪə^r] *n* albañil *m*
brickwork ['brɪkwə:k] *n* enladrillado
brickworks ['brɪkwə:ks] *n* ladrillar *m*
bridal ['braɪdl] *adj* nupcial
bride [braɪd] *n* novia
bridegroom ['braɪdgru:m] *n* novio
bridesmaid ['braɪdzmeɪd] *n* dama de honor
bridge [brɪdʒ] *n* puente *m*; (*Naut*) puente *m* de
mando; (*of nose*) caballete *m*; (*Cards*) bridge *m*
■ *vt* (*river*) tender un puente sobre
bridgehead ['brɪdʒhɛd] *n* cabeza de puente
bridging loan ['brɪdʒɪŋ-] *n* crédito
provisional
bridle ['braɪdl] *n* brida, freno ■ *vt* poner la
brida a; (*fig*) reprimir, refrenar ■ *vi* (*in anger*
etc) picarse
bridle path *n* camino de herradura
brief [bri:f] *adj* breve, corto ■ *n* (*Law*)
escrito ■ *vt* (*inform*) informar; (*instruct*) dar
instrucciones a; **in ~ ...** en resumen ...; **to ~**
sb (about sth) informar a algn (sobre algo)
briefcase ['bri:fkeɪs] *n* cartera, portafolio(s)
m inv (*LAm*)
briefing ['bri:fɪŋ] *n* (*Press*) informe *m*
briefly *adv* (*smile, glance*) brevemente; (*explain,*
say) brevemente, en pocas palabras
briefs [bri:fs] *npl* (*for men*) calzoncillos *mpl*;
(*for women*) bragas *fpl*
Brig. *abbr* = **brigadier**
brigade [brɪ'geɪd] *n* (*Mil*) brigada
brigadier [brɪgə'dɪə^r] *n* general *m* de brigada
bright [braɪt] *adj* claro; (*room*) luminoso;
(*day*) de sol; (*person: clever*) listo, inteligente;
(: *lively*) alegre, animado; (*colour*) vivo; **to**
look on the ~ side mirar el lado bueno

brighten ['braɪtn] (*also*: **brighten up**) *vt* (*room*) hacer más alegre ■ *vi* (*weather*) despejarse; (*person*) animarse, alegrarse
brill [brɪl] *adj* (*Brit col*) guay
brilliance ['brɪljəns] *n* brillo, brillantez *f*; (*fig*: *of person*) inteligencia
brilliant ['brɪljənt] *adj* (*light, idea, person, success*) brillante; (*clever*) genial
brilliantly ['brɪljəntlɪ] *adv* brillantemente
brim [brɪm] *n* borde *m*; (*of hat*) ala
brimful ['brɪm'ful] *adj* lleno hasta el borde; (*fig*) rebosante
brine [braɪn] *n* (*Culin*) salmuera
bring (*pt, pp* **brought**) [brɪŋ, brɔ:t] *vt* (*thing*) traer; (*person*) conducir; **to ~ sth to an end** terminar con algo; **I can't ~ myself to sack him** no soy capaz de echarle
▶ **bring about** *vt* ocasionar, producir
▶ **bring back** *vt* volver a traer; (*return*) devolver
▶ **bring down** *vt* bajar; (*price*) rebajar
▶ **bring forward** *vt* adelantar; (*Bookkeeping*) sumar y seguir
▶ **bring in** *vt* (*harvest*) recoger; (*person*) hacer entrar *or* pasar; (*object*) traer; (*Pol*: *bill, law*) presentar; (*Law*: *verdict*) pronunciar; (*produce*: *income*) producir, rendir
▶ **bring off** *vt* (*task, plan*) lograr, conseguir; (*deal*) cerrar
▶ **bring out** *vt* (*object*) sacar; (*new product*) sacar; (*book*) publicar
▶ **bring round** *vt* (*unconscious person*) hacer volver en sí; (*convince*) convencer
▶ **bring up** *vt* (*person*) educar, criar; (*carry up*) subir; (*question*) sacar a colación; (*food*: *vomit*) devolver, vomitar
brink [brɪŋk] *n* borde *m*; **on the ~ of doing sth** a punto de hacer algo; **she was on the ~ of tears** estaba al borde de las lágrimas
brisk [brɪsk] *adj* (*walk*) enérgico, vigoroso; (*speedy*) rápido; (*wind*) fresco; (*trade*) activo, animado; (*abrupt*) brusco; **business is ~** el negocio va bien *or* a paso activo
brisket ['brɪskɪt] *n* falda de vaca
bristle ['brɪsl] *n* cerda ■ *vi* erizarse
bristly ['brɪslɪ] *adj* (*beard, hair*) erizado; **to have a ~ chin** tener la barba crecida
Brit [brɪt] *n abbr* (*col*: = *British person*) británico(-a)
Britain ['brɪtən] *n* (*also*: **Great Britain**) Gran Bretaña
British ['brɪtɪʃ] *adj* británico; **the British** *npl* los británicos; **the British Isles** *npl* las Islas Británicas
British Rail *n* ≈ RENFE *f* (*SP*)
British Summer Time *n* hora de verano británica
Briton ['brɪtən] *n* británico(-a)

brittle ['brɪtl] *adj* quebradizo, frágil
Bro. *abbr* (*Rel*) = **brother**
broach [brəutʃ] *vt* (*subject*) abordar
broad [brɔ:d] *adj* ancho, amplio; (*accent*) cerrado ■ *n* (*US col*) tía; **in ~ daylight** en pleno día; **the ~ outlines** las líneas generales
broadband ['brɔ:dbænd] *n* banda ancha
broad bean *n* haba
broadcast ['brɔ:dka:st] (*pt, pp* **~**) *n* emisión *f* ■ *vt* (*Radio*) emitir; (*TV*) transmitir ■ *vi* emitir; transmitir
broadcaster ['brɔ:dka:stər] *n* locutor(a) *m(f)*
broadcasting ['brɔ:dka:stɪŋ] *n* radiodifusión *f*, difusión *f*
broadcasting station *n* emisora
broaden ['brɔ:dn] *vt* ensanchar ■ *vi* ensancharse
broadly ['brɔ:dlɪ] *adv* en general
broad-minded ['brɔ:d'maɪndɪd] *adj* tolerante, liberal
broadsheet ['brɔ:dʃi:t] *n* (*Brit*) periódico de gran formato (*no sensacionalista*); *see also* **quality press**
brocade [brə'keɪd] *n* brocado
broccoli ['brɔkəlɪ] *n* brécol *m*, bróculi *m*
brochure ['brəuʃjuər] *n* folleto
brogue [brəug] *n* (*accent*) acento regional; (*shoe*) (*tipo de*) zapato de cuero grueso
broil [brɔɪl] *vt* (*US*) asar a la parrilla
broiler ['brɔɪlər] *n* (*fowl*) pollo (para asar)
broke [brəuk] *pt of* **break** ■ *adj* (*col*) pelado, sin una perra; **to go ~** quebrar
broken ['brəukən] *pp of* **break** ■ *adj* (*stick*) roto; (*fig*: *marriage*) deshecho; (: *promise, vow*) violado; **~ leg** pierna rota; **in ~ English** en un inglés chapurreado
broken-down ['brəukn'daun] *adj* (*car*) averiado; (*machine*) estropeado; (*house*) destartalado
broken-hearted ['brəukn'ha:tɪd] *adj* con el corazón destrozado
broker ['brəukər] *n* corredor(a) *m(f)* de bolsa
brokerage ['brəukərɪdʒ] *n* corretaje *m*
brolly ['brɔlɪ] *n* (*Brit col*) paraguas *m inv*
bronchitis [brɔŋ'kaɪtɪs] *n* bronquitis *f*
bronze [brɔnz] *n* bronce *m*
bronzed [brɔnzd] *adj* bronceado
brooch [brəutʃ] *n* broche *m*
brood [bru:d] *n* camada, cría; (*children*) progenie *f* ■ *vi* (*hen*) empollar; **to ~ over** dar vueltas a, rumiar
broody ['bru:dɪ] *adj* (*fig*) triste, melancólico
brook [bruk] *n* arroyo
broom [brum] *n* escoba; (*Bot*) retama
broomstick ['brumstɪk] *n* palo de escoba
Bros. *abbr* (*Comm*: = *Brothers*) Hnos

b

broth [brɔθ] *n* caldo
brothel ['brɔθl] *n* burdel *m*
brother ['brʌðəʳ] *n* hermano
brotherhood ['brʌðəhud] *n* hermandad *f*
brother-in-law ['brʌðərɪn'lɔ:] *n* cuñado
brotherly ['brʌðəlɪ] *adj* fraternal
brought [brɔ:t] *pt, pp of* **bring**
brow [brau] *n (forehead)* frente *f*; *(of hill)* cumbre *f*
browbeat ['braubi:t] *vt (irreg: like* **beat**) intimidar
brown [braun] *adj* marrón; *(hair)* castaño; *(tanned)* moreno ■ *n (colour)* marrón *m* ■ *vt (tan)* poner moreno; *(Culin)* dorar; **to go ~** *(person)* ponerse moreno; *(leaves)* dorarse
brown bread *n* pan *m* moreno
brownie ['braunɪ] *n* niña exploradora
brown paper *n* papel *m* de estraza
brown rice *n* arroz *m* integral
brown sugar *n* azúcar *m* moreno
browse [brauz] *vi (animal)* pacer; *(among books)* hojear libros; **to ~ through a book** hojear un libro
browser ['brauzəʳ] *n (Comput)* navegador *m*
bruise [bru:z] *n (on person)* cardenal *m*, hematoma *m* ■ *vt (leg etc)* magullar; *(fig: feelings)* herir
Brum [brʌm] *n abbr,* **Brummagem** ['brʌmədʒəm] *n (col)* = **Birmingham**
Brummie ['brʌmɪ] *n (col)* habitante *m/f* de Birmingham
brunch [brʌntʃ] *n* desayuno-almuerzo
brunette [bru:'nɛt] *n* morena, morocha *(LAm)*
brunt [brʌnt] *n:* **to bear the ~ of** llevar el peso de
brush [brʌʃ] *n* cepillo, escobilla *(LAm)*; *(large)* escoba; *(for painting, shaving etc)* brocha; *(artist's)* pincel *m*; *(Bot)* maleza ■ *vt* cepillar; *(gen):* **~ past, ~ against** rozar al pasar; **to have a ~ with the police** tener un roce con la policía
▶ **brush aside** *vt* rechazar, no hacer caso a
▶ **brush up** *vt (knowledge)* repasar, refrescar
brushed [brʌʃt] *adj (nylon, denim etc)* afelpado; *(Tech: steel, chrome etc)* cepillado
brushwood ['brʌʃwud] *n (bushes)* maleza; *(sticks)* leña
brusque [bru:sk] *adj (person, manner)* brusco; *(tone)* áspero
Brussels ['brʌslz] *n* Bruselas
Brussels sprout *n* col *f* de Bruselas
brutal ['bru:tl] *adj* brutal
brutality [bru:'tælɪtɪ] *n* brutalidad *f*
brutalize ['bru:təlaɪz] *vt (harden)* embrutecer; *(ill-treat)* tratar brutalmente a
brute [bru:t] *n* bruto; *(person)* bestia ■ *adj:*

by ~ force por la fuerza bruta
brutish ['bru:tɪʃ] *adj* brutal
BS *n abbr (US:* = *Bachelor of Science)* título universitario
bs *abbr* = **bill of sale**
BSA *n abbr (US)* = **Boy Scouts of America**
BSc *abbr* = **Bachelor of Science**; *see also* **Bachelor's Degree**
BSE *n abbr* (= *bovine spongiform encephalopathy)* encefalopatía espongiforme bovina
BSI *n abbr* (= *British Standards Institution)* institución británica de normalización
BST *n abbr* (= *British Summer Time)* hora de verano británica
Bt. *abbr (Brit)* = **baronet**
btu *n abbr* (= *British thermal unit)* = 1054.2 *julios*
BTW *abbr* (= *by the way)* por cierto
bubble ['bʌbl] *n* burbuja; *(in paint)* ampolla ■ *vi* burbujear, borbotar
bubble bath *n* espuma para el baño
bubble gum *n* chicle *m*
bubblejet printer ['bʌbldʒɛt-] *n* impresora de injección por burbujas
bubbly ['bʌblɪ] *adj (person)* vivaracho; *(liquid)* con burbujas ■ *n (col)* champán *m*
Bucharest [bu:kə'rɛst] *n* Bucarest *m*
buck [bʌk] *n* macho; *(US col)* dólar *m* ■ *vi* corcovear; **to pass the ~ (to sb)** echar (a algn) el muerto
▶ **buck up** *vi (cheer up)* animarse, cobrar ánimo ■ *vt:* **to ~ one's ideas up** poner más empeño
bucket ['bʌkɪt] *n* cubo, balde *m (esp LAm)* ■ *vi:* **the rain is bucketing (down)** *(col)* está lloviendo a cántaros
Buckingham Palace ['bʌkɪŋəm-] *n* el Palacio de Buckingham; *ver nota*

● **BUCKINGHAM PALACE**

Buckingham Palace es la residencia oficial del monarca británico en Londres. Data de 1703 y fue en principio el palacio del Duque de Buckingham, para pasar a manos de Jorge III en 1762. Fue reconstruido el siglo pasado y reformado después a principios de este siglo. Hoy en día parte del palacio está abierto al público.

buckle ['bʌkl] *n* hebilla ■ *vt* abrochar con hebilla ■ *vi* torcerse, combarse
▶ **buckle down** *vi* poner empeño
Bucks [bʌks] *abbr (Brit)* = **Buckinghamshire**
bud [bʌd] *n* brote *m*, yema; *(of flower)* capullo ■ *vi* brotar, echar brotes
Budapest [bju:də'pɛst] *n* Budapest *m*

Buddhism ['budɪzm] n Budismo
Buddhist ['budɪst] adj, n budista m/f
budding ['bʌdɪŋ] adj en ciernes, en embrión
buddy ['bʌdɪ] n (US) compañero, compinche m
budge [bʌdʒ] vt mover; (fig) hacer ceder
■ vi moverse
budgerigar ['bʌdʒərɪgɑːᵣ] n periquito
budget ['bʌdʒɪt] n presupuesto ■ vi: **to ~ for**
sth presupuestar algo; **I'm on a tight ~** no
puedo gastar mucho; **she works out her ~**
every month planea su presupuesto todos
los meses
budgie ['bʌdʒɪ] n = **budgerigar**
Buenos Aires ['bweɪnɔs'aɪrɪz] n Buenos Aires
m ■ adj bonaerense, porteño (LAm)
buff [bʌf] adj (colour) color m de ante
■ n (enthusiast) entusiasta m/f
buffalo ['bʌfələu] (pl ~ or **buffaloes**) n (Brit)
búfalo; (US: bison) bisonte m
buffer ['bʌfəᵣ] n amortiguador m; (Comput)
memoria intermedia, buffer m ■ vi (Comput)
almacenar temperalmente
buffering ['bʌfərɪŋ] n (Comput)
almacenamiento en memoria intermedia
buffer zone n zona (que sirve de) colchón
buffet ['bufeɪ] n (Brit: bar) bar m, cafetería;
(food) buffet m ■ vt ['bʌfɪt] (strike) abofetear;
(wind etc) golpear
buffet car n (Brit Rail) coche-restaurante m
buffet lunch n buffet m (almuerzo)
buffoon [bə'fuːn] n bufón m
bug [bʌg] n (insect) chinche m; (: gen) bicho,
sabandija; (germ) microbio, bacilo; (spy device)
micrófono oculto; (Comput) fallo, error m ■ vt
(annoy) fastidiar; (room) poner un micrófono
oculto en; (phone) pinchar; **I've got the**
travel ~ (fig) me encanta viajar; **it really**
bugs me me fastidia or molesta mucho
bugbear ['bʌgbɛəᵣ] n pesadilla
bugle ['bjuːgl] n corneta, clarín m
build [bɪld] n (of person) talle m, tipo ■ vt (pt, pp
built) [bɪlt] construir, edificar
▶ **build on** vt fus (fig) basar en
▶ **build up** vt (Med) fortalecer; (stocks)
acumular; (establish: business) fomentar,
desarrollar; (: reputation) crear(se); (increase:
production) aumentar; **don't ~ your hopes up**
too soon no te hagas demasiadas ilusiones
builder ['bɪldəᵣ] n constructor(a) m(f);
(contractor) contratista m/f
building ['bɪldɪŋ] n (act) construcción f;
(habitation, offices) edificio
building contractor n contratista m/f de obras
building industry n construcción f
building site n solar m (SP), obra (LAm)
building society n (Brit) sociedad f de
préstamo inmobiliario; ver nota

● **BUILDING SOCIETY**
●
● En el Reino Unido existe un tipo de
● entidad financiera llamada building
● society de la que sus clientes son también
● propietarios y cuyos servicios son
● similares a los de los bancos, aunque se
● centran fundamentalmente en créditos
● hipotecarios y cuentas de ahorro. Son la
● entidad más utilizada por el público en
● general a la hora de pedir créditos para la
● compra de la vivienda.

building trade n = **building industry**
build-up ['bɪldʌp] n (publicity): **to give sb/sth**
a good ~ hacer mucha propaganda de algn/
algo
built [bɪlt] pt, pp of **build**
built-in ['bɪlt'ɪn] adj (cupboard) empotrado;
(device) interior, incorporado; **~**
obsolescence caducidad f programada
built-up ['bɪltʌp] adj (area) urbanizado
bulb [bʌlb] n (Bot) bulbo; (Elec) bombilla,
bombillo (LAm), foco (LAm)
bulbous ['bʌlbəs] adj bulboso
Bulgaria [bʌl'gɛərɪə] n Bulgaria
Bulgarian [bʌl'gɛərɪən] adj búlgaro ■ n
búlgaro(-a); (Ling) búlgaro
bulge [bʌldʒ] n bombeo, pandeo; (in birth
rate, sales) alza, aumento ■ vi bombearse,
pandearse; (pocket etc) hacer bulto
bulimia [bə'lɪmɪə] n bulimia
bulk [bʌlk] n (mass) bulto, volumen m; (major
part) grueso; **in ~** (Comm) a granel; **the ~ of**
la mayor parte de; **to buy in ~** comprar en
grandes cantidades
bulk buying n compra a granel
bulk carrier n (buque m) granelero
bulkhead ['bʌlkhɛd] n mamparo
bulky ['bʌlkɪ] adj voluminoso, abultado
bull [bul] n toro; (Stock Exchange) alcista m/f de
bolsa; (Rel) bula
bulldog ['buldɔg] n dogo
bulldoze ['buldəuz] vt mover con excavadora;
I was bulldozed into doing it (fig col) me
obligaron a hacerlo
bulldozer ['buldəuzəᵣ] n buldozer m,
excavadora
bullet ['bulɪt] n bala; **~ wound** balazo
bulletin ['bulɪtɪn] n comunicado, parte m;
(journal) boletín m
bulletin board n (US) tablón m de anuncios;
(Comput) tablero de noticias
bulletproof ['bulɪtpruːf] adj a prueba de
balas; **~ vest** chaleco antibalas
bullfight ['bulfaɪt] n corrida de toros
bullfighter ['bulfaɪtəᵣ] n torero

bullfighting ['bulfaɪtɪŋ] n los toros mpl, el toreo; (art of bullfighting) tauromaquia
bullion ['buljən] n oro or plata en barras
bullock ['bulək] n novillo
bullring ['bulrɪŋ] n plaza de toros
bull's-eye ['bulzaɪ] n blanco, diana
bullshit ['bulʃɪt] (col!) excl chorradas ■ n chorradas fpl ■ vi decir chorradas ■ vt: **to ~ sb** quedarse con algn
bully ['bulɪ] n valentón m, matón m ■ vt intimidar, tiranizar
bum [bʌm] n (Brit: col: backside) culo; (: tramp) vagabundo; (col: esp US: idler) holgazán(-ana) m(f), flojo(-a)
bumble ['bʌmbl] vi (walk unsteadily) andar de forma vacilante; (fig) farfullar, trastabillar
bumblebee ['bʌmblbi:] n abejorro
bumbling ['bʌmblɪŋ] n divagación f
bumf [bʌmf] n (col: forms etc) papeleo
bump [bʌmp] n (blow) tope m, choque m; (jolt) sacudida; (noise) choque m, topetón m; (on road etc) bache m; (on head) chichón m ■ vt (strike) chocar contra, topetar ■ vi dar sacudidas
▶ **bump into** vt fus chocar contra, tropezar con; (person) topar con; (col: meet) tropezar con, toparse con
bumper ['bʌmpər] n (Brit) parachoques m inv ■ adj: **~ crop/harvest** cosecha abundante
bumper cars npl (US) autos or coches mpl de choque
bumph [bʌmf] n = **bumf**
bumptious ['bʌmpʃəs] adj engreído, presuntuoso
bumpy ['bʌmpɪ] adj (road) lleno de baches; (journey, flight) agitado
bun [bʌn] n (Brit: cake) pastel m; (US: bread) bollo; (of hair) moño
bunch [bʌntʃ] n (of flowers) ramo; (of keys) manojo; (of bananas) piña; (of people) grupo; (pej) pandilla
bundle ['bʌndl] n (gen) bulto, fardo; (of sticks) haz m; (of papers) legajo ■ vt (also: **bundle up**) atar, envolver; **to ~ sth/sb into** meter algo/a algn precipitadamente en
bun fight n (Brit col: tea party) merienda; (: function) fiesta oficial
bung [bʌŋ] n tapón m, bitoque m ■ vt (throw: also: **bung into**) arrojar; (also: **bung up**: pipe, hole) tapar; **my nose is bunged up** (col) tengo la nariz atascada or taponada
bungalow ['bʌŋgələu] n bungalow m, chalé m
bungee jumping ['bʌndʒi:'dʒʌmpɪŋ] n puenting m, banyi m
bungle ['bʌŋgl] vt chapucear
bunion ['bʌnjən] n juanete m

bunk [bʌŋk] n litera; **~ beds** npl literas fpl
bunker ['bʌŋkər] n (coal store) carbonera; (Mil) refugio; (Golf) bunker m
bunk off vi: **to ~ school** (Brit col) pirarse las clases; **I'll ~ at 3 this afternoon** me voy a pirar a las 3 esta tarde
bunny ['bʌnɪ] n (also: **bunny rabbit**) conejito
Bunsen burner ['bʌnsn-] n mechero Bunsen
bunting ['bʌntɪŋ] n empavesada, banderas fpl
buoy [bɔɪ] n boya
▶ **buoy up** vt mantener a flote; (fig) animar
buoyancy ['bɔɪənsɪ] n (of ship) flotabilidad f
buoyant ['bɔɪənt] adj (carefree) boyante, optimista; (Comm: market, prices etc) sostenido
BUPA ['bu:pə] n abbr (= British United Provident Association) seguro médico privado
burden ['bə:dn] n carga ■ vt cargar; **to be a ~ to sb** ser una carga para algn
bureau (pl **bureaux**) ['bjuərəu, -z] n (Brit: writing desk) escritorio, buró m; (US: chest of drawers) cómoda; (office) oficina, agencia
bureaucracy [bjuə'rɔkrəsɪ] n burocracia
bureaucrat ['bjuərəkræt] n burócrata m/f
bureaucratic [bjuərə'krætɪk] adj burocrático
burgeon ['bə:dʒən] vi (develop rapidly) crecer, incrementarse; (trade etc) florecer
burger ['bə:gər] n hamburguesa
burglar ['bə:glər] n ladrón(-ona) m(f)
burglar alarm n alarma f contra robo
burglarize ['bə:gləraɪz] vt (US) robar (con allanamiento)
burglary ['bə:glərɪ] n robo con allanamiento or fractura, robo de una casa
burgle ['bə:gl] vt robar (con allanamiento)
Burgundy ['bə:gəndɪ] n Borgoña
burial ['bɛrɪəl] n entierro
burial ground n cementerio
burlap ['bə:læp] n arpillera
burlesque [bə:'lɛsk] n parodia
burly ['bə:lɪ] adj fornido, membrudo
Burma ['bə:mə] n Birmania; see also **Myanmar**
Burmese [bə:'mi:z] adj birmano ■ n (pl inv) birmano(-a); (Ling) birmano
burn [bə:n] vb (pt, pp **burned** or **burnt**) ■ vt quemar; (house) incendiar ■ vi quemarse, arder; incendiarse; (sting) escocer ■ n (Med) quemadura; **the cigarette burnt a hole in her dress** se ha quemado el vestido con el cigarrillo; **I've burnt myself!** ¡me he quemado!
▶ **burn down** vt incendiar
▶ **burn out** vt (writer etc): **to ~ o.s. out** agotarse
burner ['bə:nər] n (gas) quemador m
burning ['bə:nɪŋ] adj ardiente; (building, forest) en llamas

Burns' Night [bə:nz-] n ver nota

ver nota

● BURNS' NIGHT

Cada veinticinco de enero los escoceses celebran la llamada *Burns' Night* (noche de Burns), en honor al poeta escocés Robert Burns (1759-1796). Es tradición hacer una cena en la que, al son de la música de la gaita escocesa, se sirve "haggis", plato tradicional de asadura de cordero cocida en el estómago del animal, acompañado de nabos y puré de patatas. Durante la misma se recitan poemas del autor y varios discursos conmemorativos de carácter festivo.

burnt [bə:nt] *pt, pp of* **burn**

burp [bə:p] (*col*) n eructo ▪ vi eructar

burqa ['bə:kə] n burka m, burqa m

burrow ['bʌrəu] n madriguera ▪ vt hacer una madriguera

bursar ['bə:səʳ] n tesorero; (*Brit: student*) becario(-a)

bursary ['bə:sərɪ] n (*Brit*) beca

burst [bə:st] vb (*pt, pp* **burst**) ▪ vt (*balloon, pipe*) reventar; (*banks etc*) romper ▪ vi reventarse; romperse; (*tyre*) pincharse; (*bomb*) ▪ n (*explosion*) estallido; (*also:* **burst pipe**) reventón m; **the river has ~ its banks** el río se ha desbordado; **to ~ into flames** estallar en llamas; **to ~ out laughing** soltar la carcajada; **to ~ into tears** deshacerse en lágrimas; **to be bursting with** reventar de; **a ~ of energy** una explosión de energía; **a ~ of applause** una salva de aplausos; **a ~ of speed** una escapada; **to ~ open** vi abrirse de golpe

▸ **burst into** vt fus (*room etc*) irrumpir en

bury ['bɛrɪ] vt enterrar; (*body*) enterrar, sepultar; **to ~ the hatchet** enterrar el hacha (de guerra), echar pelillos a la mar

bus [bʌs] n autobús m, camión m (*LAm*)

bus boy n (*US*) ayudante m/f de camarero

bush [buʃ] n arbusto; (*scrub land*) monte m bajo; **to beat about the ~** andar(se) con rodeos

bushed [buʃt] adj (*col*) molido

bushel ['buʃl] n (*measure: Brit*) = 36,36 litros; (*US*) = 35,24 litros

bush fire n incendio en el monte

bushy ['buʃɪ] adj (*beard, eyebrows*) poblado; (*hair*) espeso; (*fur*) tupido

busily ['bɪzɪlɪ] adv afanosamente

business ['bɪznɪs] n (*matter, affair*) asunto; (*trading*) comercio, negocios mpl; (*firm*) empresa, casa; (*occupation*) oficio; **to be away on ~** estar en viaje de negocios; **it's my ~ to ... me toca** or **corresponde ...; it's none of my ~** no es asunto mío; **he means ~** habla en serio; **he's in the insurance ~** se dedica a los seguros; **I'm here on ~** estoy aquí por mi trabajo; **to do ~ with sb** hacer negocios con algn

business address n dirección f comercial

business card n tarjeta de visita

businesslike ['bɪznɪslaɪk] adj (*company*) serio; (*person*) eficiente

businessman ['bɪznɪsmən] n hombre m de negocios

business trip n viaje m de negocios

businesswoman ['bɪznɪswumən] n mujer f de negocios

busker ['bʌskəʳ] n (*Brit*) músico(-a) ambulante

bus route n recorrido del autobús

bus station n estación f or terminal f de autobuses

bus-stop ['bʌsstɔp] n parada de autobús, paradero (*LAm*)

bust [bʌst] n (*Anat*) pecho ▪ adj (*col: broken*) roto, estropeado ▪ vt (*col: Police: arrest*) detener; **to go ~** quebrar

bustle ['bʌsl] n bullicio, movimiento ▪ vi menearse, apresurarse

bustling ['bʌslɪŋ] adj (*town*) animado, bullicioso

bust-up ['bʌstʌp] n (*col*) riña

busty ['bʌstɪ] adj (*col*) pechugona, con buena delantera

busy ['bɪzɪ] adj ocupado, atareado; (*shop, street*) concurrido, animado ▪ vt: **to ~ o.s. with** ocuparse en; **he's a ~ man** (*normally*) es un hombre muy ocupado; (*temporarily*) está muy ocupado; **the line's ~** (*esp US*) está comunicando

busybody ['bɪzɪbɔdɪ] n entrometido(-a)

busy signal n (*US Tel*) señal f de comunicando

 KEYWORD

but [bʌt] conj **1** pero; **he's not very bright, but he's hard-working** no es muy inteligente, pero es trabajador

2 (*in direct contradiction*) sino; **he's not English but French** no es inglés sino francés; **he didn't sing but he shouted** no cantó sino que gritó

3 (*showing disagreement, surprise etc*): **but that's far too expensive!** ¡pero eso es carísimo!; **but it does work!** ¡(pero) sí que funciona!

▪ prep (*apart from, except*) menos, salvo; **we've had nothing but trouble** no hemos tenido más que problemas; **no-one but him can**

do it nadie más que él puede hacerlo; **the last but one** el penúltimo; **who but a lunatic would do such a thing?** ¡sólo un loco haría una cosa así!; **but for you/your help** si no fuera por ti/tu ayuda; **anything but that** cualquier cosa menos eso ▪ *adv* (*just, only*): **she's but a child** no es más que una niña; **had I but known** si lo hubiera sabido; **I can but try** al menos lo puedo intentar; **it's all but finished** está casi acabado

butane ['bju:teɪn] *n* (*also:* **butane gas**) (gas *m*) butano

butch [butʃ] *adj* (*pej: woman*) machirula, marimacho; (*col: man*) muy macho

butcher ['butʃər] *n* carnicero(-a) ▪ *vt* hacer una carnicería con; (*cattle etc for meat*) matar; **~'s (shop)** carnicería

butler ['bʌtlər] *n* mayordomo

butt [bʌt] *n* (*cask*) tonel *m*; (*for rain*) tina; (*thick end*) cabo, extremo; (*of gun*) culata; (*of cigarette*) colilla; (*Brit fig: target*) blanco ▪ *vt* dar cabezadas contra, topetar
▸ **butt in** *vi* (*interrupt*) interrumpir

butter ['bʌtər] *n* mantequilla, manteca (*LAm*) ▪ *vt* untar con mantequilla

butter bean *n* judía blanca

buttercup ['bʌtəkʌp] *n* ranúnculo

butterfingers ['bʌtəfɪŋgəz] *n* (*col*) torpe *m/f*

butterfly ['bʌtəflaɪ] *n* mariposa; (*Swimming: also:* **butterfly stroke**) (braza de) mariposa

buttocks ['bʌtəks] *npl* nalgas *fpl*

button ['bʌtn] *n* botón *m* ▪ *vt* (*also:* **button up**) abotonar, abrochar ▪ *vi* abrocharse

buttonhole ['bʌtnhəul] *n* ojal *m*; (*flower*) flor *f* que se lleva en el ojal ▪ *vt* obligar a escuchar

buttress ['bʌtrɪs] *n* contrafuerte *m*; (*fig*) apoyo, sostén *m*

buxom ['bʌksəm] *adj* (*woman*) frescachona, rolliza

buy [baɪ] *vb* (*pt, pp* **bought**) ▪ *vt* comprar ▪ *n* compra; **to ~ sb sth/sth from sb** comprarle algo a algn; **to ~ sb a drink** invitar a algn a una copa; **a good/bad ~** una buena/mala compra
▸ **buy back** *vt* volver a comprar
▸ **buy in** *vt* proveerse *or* abastecerse de
▸ **buy into** *vt fus* comprar acciones en
▸ **buy off** *vt* (*col: bribe*) sobornar
▸ **buy out** *vt* (*partner*) comprar la parte de

buyer ['baɪər] *n* comprador(a) *m(f)*; **~'s market** mercado favorable al comprador

buy-out ['baɪaut] *n* (*Comm*) adquisición *f* de (la totalidad de) las acciones

buzz [bʌz] *n* zumbido; (*col: phone call*) llamada (telefónica) ▪ *vt* (*call on intercom*) llamar; (*with buzzer*) hacer sonar; (*Aviat: plane, building*)

pasar rozando ▪ *vi* zumbar; **my head is buzzing** me zumba la cabeza
▸ **buzz off** *vi* (*Brit col*) largarse

buzzard ['bʌzəd] *n* (*Brit*) águila ratonera; (*US*) buitre *m*, gallinazo (*LAm*)

buzzer ['bʌzər] *n* timbre *m*

buzz word *n* palabra que está de moda

 KEYWORD

by [baɪ] *prep* **1** (*referring to cause, agent*) por; de; **abandoned by his mother** abandonado por su madre; **surrounded by enemies** rodeado de enemigos; **a painting by Picasso** un cuadro de Picasso
2 (*referring to method, manner, means*): **by bus/car/train** en autobús/coche/tren; **to pay by cheque** pagar con cheque(s); **by moonlight/candlelight** a la luz de la luna/una vela; **by saving hard, he ...** ahorrando, ...
3 (*via, through*) por; **we came by Dover** vinimos por Dover
4 (*close to, past*): **the house by the river** la casa junto al río; **she rushed by me** pasó a mi lado como una exhalación; **I go by the post office every day** paso por delante de Correos todos los días
5 (*time: not later than*) para; (*: during*): **by daylight** de día; **by 4 o'clock** para las cuatro; **by this time tomorrow** mañana a estas horas; **by the time I got here it was too late** cuando llegué ya era demasiado tarde
6 (*amount*): **by the metre/kilo** por metro/kilo; **paid by the hour** pagado por hora
7 (*in measurements, sums*): **to divide/multiply by 3** dividir/multiplicar por 3; **a room 3 metres by 4** una habitación de 3 metros por 4; **it's broader by a metre** es un metro más ancho; **the bus missed me by inches** no me pilló el autobús por un pelo
8 (*according to*) según, de acuerdo con; **it's 3 o'clock by my watch** según mi reloj, son las tres; **it's all right by me** por mí, está bien
9: (all) by oneself *etc* todo solo; **he did it (all) by himself** lo hizo él solo; **he was standing (all) by himself in a corner** estaba de pie solo en un rincón
10: by the way a propósito, por cierto; **this wasn't my idea, by the way** pues, no fue idea mía
▪ *adv* **1** *see* **go**; **pass** *etc*
2: by and by finalmente; **they'll come back by and by** acabarán volviendo; **by and large** en líneas generales, en general

bye ['baɪ], **bye-bye** ['baɪ'baɪ] *excl* adiós, hasta luego, chao (*esp LAm*)

bye-law ['baɪlɔ:] *n see* **by-law**
by-election ['baɪɪlɛkʃən] *n* (*Brit*) elección *f*
parcial; *ver nota*

⬤ **BY-ELECTION**
⬤
⬤
⬤ Se celebra una *by-election* en el
⬤ Reino Unido y otros países de la
⬤ "Commonwealth" cuando es necesario
⬤ reemplazar a un parlamentario
⬤ ("Member of Parliament") cesado o
⬤ fallecido durante una legislatura. Dichas
⬤ elecciones tienen lugar únicamente en el
⬤ área electoral representada por el citado
⬤ parlamentario, su "constituency".

Byelorussia [bjɛləu'rʌʃə] *n* Bielorrusia
Byelorussian [bjɛləu'rʌʃən] *adj, n*

= **Belorussian**
bygone ['baɪgɔn] *adj* pasado, del pasado
■ *n*: **let bygones be bygones** lo pasado,
pasado está
by-law ['baɪlɔ:] *n* ordenanza municipal
bypass ['baɪpɑ:s] *n* carretera de,
circunvalación; (*Med*) (operación *f* de) bypass
m ■ *vt* evitar
by-product ['baɪprɔdʌkt] *n* subproducto,
derivado
bystander ['baɪstændə^r] *n* espectador(a) *m(f)*
byte [baɪt] *n* (*Comput*) byte *m*, octeto
byway ['baɪweɪ] *n* camino poco frecuentado
byword ['baɪwə:d] *n*: **to be a ~ for** ser
sinónimo de
by-your-leave ['baɪjɔ:'li:v] *n*: **without so**
much as a ~ sin decir nada, sin dar ningún
tipo de explicación

Cc

C, c [si:] *n* (*letter*) C, c *f*; (*Mus*): **C** do *m*; **C for Charlie** C de Carmen

C *abbr* (= *Celsius, centigrade*) C

c *abbr* (= *century*) S.; (= *circa*) hacia; (*US etc*) = **cent; cents**

CA *n abbr* = **Central America**; (*Brit*) = **chartered accountant**; (*US*) = **California**

ca. *abbr* (= *circa*) c

c/a *abbr* = **capital account; credit account; current account**

CAA *n abbr* (*Brit*: = *Civil Aviation Authority*) *organismo de control y desarrollo de la aviación civil;* = **Civil Aeronautics Authority**

CAB *n abbr* (*Brit*: = *Citizens' Advice Bureau*) ≈ Servicio de Información Ciudadana

cab [kæb] *n* taxi *m*; (*of truck*) cabina

cabaret ['kæbəreɪ] *n* cabaret *m*

cabbage ['kæbɪdʒ] *n* col *f*, berza

cabbie, cabby ['kæbɪ] *n* (*col*) taxista *m/f*

cab driver *n* taxista *m/f*

cabin ['kæbɪn] *n* cabaña; (*on ship*) camarote *m*

cabin cruiser *n* yate *m* de motor

cabinet ['kæbɪnɪt] *n* (*Pol*) consejo de ministros; (*furniture*) armario; (*also*: **display cabinet**) vitrina

cabinet-maker ['kæbɪnɪt'meɪkəʳ] *n* ebanista *m*

cabinet minister *n* ministro(-a) (del gabinete)

cable ['keɪbl] *n* cable *m* ■ *vt* cablegrafiar

cable-car ['keɪblkɑːʳ] *n* teleférico

cablegram ['keɪblgræm] *n* cablegrama *m*

cable television *n* televisión *f* por cable

cache [kæʃ] *n* (*of drugs*) alijo; (*of arms*) zulo

cackle ['kækl] *vi* cacarear

cactus (*pl* **cacti**) ['kæktəs, -taɪ] *n* cacto

CAD ['kæd] *n* (= *computer-aided design*) DAO *m*

caddie, caddy ['kædɪ] *n* (*Golf*) cadi *m*

cadence ['keɪdəns] *n* ritmo; (*Mus*) cadencia

cadet [kə'dɛt] *n* (*Mil*) cadete *m*; **police ~** cadete *m* de policía

cadge [kædʒ] *vt* gorronear

cadger ['kædʒəʳ] *n* gorrón(-ona) *m(f)*

cadre ['kædrɪ] *n* cuadro

Caesarean, Cesarean (*US*) [si:'zɛərɪən] *adj*: **~ (section)** cesárea

CAF *abbr* (*Brit*: = *cost and freight*) C y F

café ['kæfeɪ] *n* café *m*

cafeteria [kæfɪ'tɪərɪə] *n* cafetería (*con autoservicio para comer*)

caffeine ['kæfi:n] *n* cafeína

cage [keɪdʒ] *n* jaula ■ *vt* enjaular

cagey ['keɪdʒɪ] *adj* (*col*) cauteloso, reservado

cagoule [kə'gu:l] *n* canguro

cahoots [kə'hu:ts] *n*: **to be in ~ (with sb)** estar conchabado (con algn)

Cairo ['kaɪərəu] *n* El Cairo

cajole [kə'dʒəul] *vt* engatusar

cake [keɪk] *n* pastel *m*; (*of soap*) pastilla; **he wants to have his ~ and eat it** (*fig*) quiere estar en misa y repicando; **it's a piece of ~** (*col*) es pan comido

caked [keɪkt] *adj*: **~ with** cubierto de

cake shop *n* pastelería

Cal. *abbr* (*US*) = **California**

calamine ['kæləmaɪn] *n* calamina

calamitous [kə'læmɪtəs] *adj* calamitoso

calamity [kə'læmɪtɪ] *n* calamidad *f*

calcium ['kælsɪəm] *n* calcio

calculate ['kælkjuleɪt] *vt* (*estimate: chances, effect*) calcular

▶ **calculate on** *vt fus*: **to ~ on sth/on doing sth** contar con algo/con hacer algo

calculated ['kælkjuleɪtɪd] *adj*: **we took a ~ risk** calculamos el riesgo

calculating ['kælkjuleɪtɪŋ] *adj* (*scheming*) calculador(a)

calculation [kælkju'leɪʃən] *n* cálculo, cómputo

calculator ['kælkjuleɪtəʳ] *n* calculadora

calculus ['kælkjuləs] *n* cálculo

calendar ['kæləndəʳ] *n* calendario; **~ month/year** *n* mes *m*/año civil

calf (*pl* **calves**) [kɑ:f, kɑ:vz] *n* (*of cow*) ternero, becerro; (*of other animals*) cría; (*also*: **calfskin**) piel *f* de becerro; (*Anat*) pantorrilla, canilla (*LAm*)

caliber [ˈkælɪbəʳ] n (US) = **calibre**
calibrate [ˈkælɪbreɪt] vt (gun etc) calibrar; (scale of measuring instrument) graduar
calibre, caliber (US) [ˈkælɪbəʳ] n calibre m
calico [ˈkælɪkəu] n calicó m
Calif. abbr (US) = **California**
California [kælɪˈfɔːnɪə] n California
calipers [ˈkælɪpəz] npl (US) = **callipers**
call [kɔːl] vt (gen) llamar; (Tel) llamar; (announce: flight) anunciar; (meeting, strike) convocar ■ vi (shout) llamar; (telephone) llamar (por teléfono), telefonear; (visit: also: **call in, call round**) hacer una visita ■ n (shout) llamada, llamado (LAm); (Tel) llamada, llamado (LAm); (of bird) canto; (appeal) llamamiento, llamado (LAm); (summons: for flight etc) llamada; (fig: lure) llamada; **to be called** (person, object) llamarse; **to ~ sb names** poner verde a algn; **let's ~ it a day** (col) ¡dejémoslo!, ¡ya está bien!; **who is calling?** ¿de parte de quién?; **London calling** (Radio) aquí Londres; **on ~** (nurse, doctor etc) de guardia; **please give me a ~ at seven** despiérteme or llámeme a las siete, por favor; **long-distance ~** conferencia (interurbana); **to make a ~** llamar por teléfono; **port of ~** puerto de escala; **to pay a ~ on sb** pasarse a ver a algn; **there's not much ~ for these items** estos artículos no tienen mucha demanda
▶ **call at** vt fus (ship) hacer escala en, tocar en; (train) parar en
▶ **call back** vi (return) volver; (Tel) volver a llamar
▶ **call for** vt fus (demand) pedir, exigir; (fetch) venir por
▶ **call in** vt (doctor, expert, police) llamar
▶ **call off** vt suspender; **the strike was called off** se desconvocó la huelga
▶ **call on** vt fus (visit) ir a ver; (turn to) acudir a
▶ **call out** vi gritar, dar voces ■ vt (doctor) llamar; (police, troops) hacer intervenir
▶ **call up** vt (Mil) llamar a filas
Callanetics® [kælənˈetɪks] nsg gimnasia de repetición de pequeños ejercicios musculares
callbox [ˈkɔːlbɔks] n (Brit) cabina telefónica
call centre n (Brit) centro de llamadas
caller [ˈkɔːləʳ] n visita f; (Tel) usuario(-a); **hold the line, ~!** ¡no cuelgue!
call girl n prostituta
call-in [ˈkɔːlɪn] n (US) programa de línea abierta al público
calling [ˈkɔːlɪŋ] n vocación f; (profession) profesión f
calling card n tarjeta de visita
callipers, calipers (US) [ˈkælɪpəz] npl (Med) aparato ortopédico; (Math) calibrador m

callous [ˈkæləs] adj insensible, cruel
callousness [ˈkæləsnɪs] n insensibilidad, crueldad f
callow [ˈkæləu] adj inexperto, novato
calm [kɑːm] adj tranquilo; (sea) tranquilo, en calma ■ n calma, tranquilidad f ■ vt calmar, tranquilizar
▶ **calm down** vi calmarse, tranquilizarse ■ vt calmar, tranquilizar
calmly [ˈkɑːmlɪ] adv tranquilamente, con calma
calmness [ˈkɑːmnɪs] n calma
Calor gas® [ˈkæləʳ-] n butano, camping gas® m inv
calorie [ˈkælərɪ] n caloría; **low-~ product** producto bajo en calorías
calve [kɑːv] vi parir
calves [kɑːvz] npl of **calf**
CAM n abbr (= computer-aided manufacturing) producción f asistida por ordenador
camber [ˈkæmbəʳ] n (of road) combadura
Cambodia [kæmˈbəudjə] n Camboya
Cambodian [kæmˈbəudjən] adj, n camboyano(-a) m(f)
Cambs abbr (Brit) = **Cambridgeshire**
camcorder [ˈkæmkɔːdəʳ] n videocámara
came [keɪm] pt of **come**
camel [ˈkæməl] n camello
cameo [ˈkæmɪəu] n camafeo
camera [ˈkæmərə] n cámara or máquina fotográfica; (Cine, TV) cámara; (movie camera) cámara, tomavistas m inv; **in ~** a puerta cerrada
cameraman [ˈkæmərəmən] n cámara m
camera phone n teléfono m con cámara
Cameroon, Cameroun [kæmeˈruːn] n Camerún m
camomile tea [ˈkæməmaɪl-] n manzanilla
camouflage [ˈkæməflɑːʒ] n camuflaje m ■ vt camuflar
camp [kæmp] n campo, campamento ■ vi acampar ■ adj afectado, afeminado; **to go camping** ir de or hacer camping
campaign [kæmˈpeɪn] n (Mil, Pol etc) campaña ■ vi: **to ~ (for/against)** hacer campaña (a favor de/en contra de)
campaigner [kæmˈpeɪnəʳ] n: **~ for** defensor(a) m(f) de; **~ against** persona que hace campaña contra
campbed [ˈkæmpbed] n (Brit) cama plegable
camper [ˈkæmpəʳ] n campista m/f; (vehicle) caravana
camping [ˈkæmpɪŋ] n camping m
campsite [ˈkæmpsaɪt] n camping m
campus [ˈkæmpəs] n campus m
camshaft [ˈkæmʃɑːft] n árbol m de levas
can [kæn] (aux vb see keyword) n (of oil, water)

bidón *m*; (*tin*) lata, bote *m* ∎ *vt* enlatar; (*preserve*) conservar en lata; **a ~ of beer** una lata *or* un bote de cerveza; **to carry the ~** (*col*) pagar el pato

KEYWORD

can (*negative* **cannot, can't**, *conditional and pt* **could**) *aux vb* **1** (*be able to*) poder; **you can do it if you try** puedes hacerlo si lo intentas; **I can't see you** no te veo; **can you hear me?** (*not translated*) ¿me oyes?
2 (*know how to*) saber; **I can swim/play tennis/drive** sé nadar/jugar al tenis/conducir; **can you speak French?** ¿hablas *or* sabes hablar francés?
3 (*may*) poder; **can I use your phone?** ¿me dejas *or* puedo usar tu teléfono?; **could I have a word with you?** ¿podría hablar contigo un momento?
4 (*expressing disbelief, puzzlement etc*): **it can't be true!** ¡no puede ser (verdad)!; **what CAN he want?** ¿qué querrá?
5 (*expressing possibility, suggestion etc*): **he could be in the library** podría estar en la biblioteca; **she could have been delayed** puede que se haya retrasado

Canada ['kænədə] *n* Canadá *m*
Canadian [kə'neɪdɪən] *adj, n* canadiense *m/f*
canal [kə'næl] *n* canal *m*
canary [kə'nɛərɪ] *n* canario
Canary Islands, Canaries [kə'nɛərɪz] *npl* las (Islas) Canarias
Canberra ['kænbərə] *n* Camberra
cancel ['kænsəl] *vt* cancelar; (*train*) suprimir; (*appointment, cheque*) anular; (*cross out*) tachar
▶ **cancel out** *vt* (*Math*) anular; (*fig*) contrarrestar; **they ~ each other out** se anulan mutuamente
cancellation [kænsə'leɪʃən] *n* cancelación *f*; supresión *f*
cancer ['kænsər] *n* cáncer *m*; **C~** (*Astro*) Cáncer *m*
cancerous ['kænsərəs] *adj* canceroso
cancer patient *n* enfermo(-a) *m(f)* de cáncer
cancer research *n* investigación *f* del cáncer
C and F *abbr* (= *cost and freight*) C y F
candid ['kændɪd] *adj* franco, abierto
candidacy ['kændɪdəsɪ] *n* candidatura
candidate ['kændɪdeɪt] *n* candidato(-a)
candidature ['kændɪdətʃər] *n* (*Brit*) = **candidacy**
candidly ['kændɪdlɪ] *adv* francamente, con franqueza
candle ['kændl] *n* vela; (*in church*) cirio
candle holder *n* see **candlestick**

candlelight ['kændllaɪt] *n*: **by ~** a la luz de una vela
candlestick ['kændlstɪk] *n* (*also*: **candle holder**: *single*) candelero; (: *low*) palmatoria; (*bigger, ornate*) candelabro
candour, candor (*US*) ['kændər] *n* franqueza
C & W *n abbr* = **country and western (music)**
candy ['kændɪ] *n* azúcar *m* cande; (*US*) caramelo ∎ *vt* (*fruit*) escarchar
candy-floss ['kændɪflɔs] *n* (*Brit*) algodón *m* (azucarado)
cane [keɪn] *n* (*Bot*) caña; (*for baskets, chairs etc*) mimbre *m*; (*stick*) vara, palmeta; (*for walking*) bastón *m* ∎ *vt* (*Brit Scol*) castigar (con palmeta); **~ liquor** caña
canine ['kænaɪn] *adj* canino
canister ['kænɪstər] *n* bote *m*
cannabis ['kænəbɪs] *n* canabis *m*
canned [kænd] *adj* en lata, de lata; (*col*: *music*) grabado; (: *drunk*) mamado
cannibal ['kænɪbəl] *n* caníbal *m/f*, antropófago(-a)
cannibalism ['kænɪbəlɪzəm] *n* canibalismo
cannon (*pl ~ or* **cannons**) ['kænən] *n* cañón *m*
cannonball ['kænənbɔ:l] *n* bala (de cañón)
cannon fodder *n* carne *f* de cañón
cannot ['kænɔt] = **can not**
canny ['kænɪ] *adj* avispado
canoe [kə'nu:] *n* canoa; (*Sport*) piragua
canoeing [kə'nu:ɪŋ] *n* (*Sport*) piragüismo
canoeist [kə'nu:ɪst] *n* piragüista *m/f*
canon ['kænən] *n* (*clergyman*) canónigo; (*standard*) canon *m*
canonize ['kænənaɪz] *vt* canonizar
can opener *n* abrelatas *m inv*
canopy ['kænəpɪ] *n* dosel *m*, toldo
can't [kænt] = **can not**
Cantab. *abbr* (*Brit*: = *cantabrigiensis*) *of Cambridge*
cantankerous [kæn'tæŋkərəs] *adj* arisco, malhumorado
canteen [kæn'ti:n] *n* (*eating place*) comedor *m*; (*Brit*: *of cutlery*) juego
canter ['kæntər] *n* medio galope ∎ *vi* ir a medio galope
cantilever ['kæntɪli:vər] *n* viga voladiza
canvas ['kænvəs] *n* (*material*) lona; (*painting*) lienzo; (*Naut*) velamen *m*; **under ~** (*camping*) en tienda de campaña
canvass ['kænvəs] *vt* (*Pol*: *district*) hacer campaña (puerta a puerta) en; (: *person*) hacer campaña (puerta a puerta) a favor de; (*Comm*: *district*) sondear el mercado en; (: *citizens, opinions*) sondear
canvasser ['kænvəsər] *n* (*Pol*) representante *m/f* electoral; (*Comm*) corredor(a) *m(f)*
canyon ['kænjən] *n* cañón *m*
CAP *n abbr* (= *Common Agricultural Policy*) PAC *f*

cap [kæp] n (*hat*) gorra; (*for swimming*) gorro; (*of pen*) capuchón m; (*of bottle*) tapón m; (: *metal*) chapa; (*contraceptive*) diafragma m ◾ vt (*outdo*) superar; (*Brit Sport*) seleccionar (para el equipo nacional); **and to ~ it all, he ...** y para colmo, él ...

capability [keɪpə'bɪlɪtɪ] n capacidad f

capable ['keɪpəbl] adj capaz

capacious [kə'peɪʃəs] adj amplio

capacity [kə'pæsɪtɪ] n capacidad f; (*position*) calidad f; **filled to ~** lleno a reventar; **this work is beyond my ~** este trabajo es superior a mí; **in an advisory ~** como asesor

cape [keɪp] n capa; (*Geo*) cabo

Cape of Good Hope n Cabo de Buena Esperanza

caper ['keɪpə'] n (*Culin: also:* **capers**) alcaparra; (*prank*) travesura

Cape Town n Ciudad f del Cabo

capital ['kæpɪtl] n (*also:* **capital city**) capital f; (*money*) capital m; (*also:* **capital letter**) mayúscula

capital account n cuenta de capital

capital allowance n desgravación f sobre bienes del capital

capital assets n activo fijo

capital expenditure n inversión f de capital

capital gains tax n impuesto sobre la plusvalía

capital goods npl bienes mpl de capital

capital-intensive [kæpɪtlɪn'tɛnsɪv] adj de utilización intensiva de capital

capital investment n inversión f de capital

capitalism ['kæpɪtəlɪzəm] n capitalismo

capitalist ['kæpɪtəlɪst] adj, n capitalista m/f

capitalize ['kæpɪtəlaɪz] vt (*Comm: provide with capital*) capitalizar

▸ **capitalize on** vt fus (*fig*) sacar provecho de, aprovechar

capital punishment n pena de muerte

capital transfer tax n impuesto sobre plusvalía de cesión

Capitol ['kæpɪtl] n: **the ~** el Capitolio

　　◉ **Capitol**

　　◉ El Capitolio (*Capitol*) es el edificio en el
　　◉ que se reúne el Congreso de los Estados
　　◉ Unidos ("Congress"), situado en la ciudad
　　◉ de Washington. Por extensión, también
　　◉ se suele llamar así al edificio en el que
　　◉ tienen lugar las sesiones parlamentarias
　　◉ de la cámara de representantes de
　　◉ muchos de los estados.

capitulate [kə'pɪtjuleɪt] vi capitular, rendirse

capitulation [kəpɪtju'leɪʃən] n capitulación f, rendición f

capricious [kə'prɪʃəs] adj caprichoso

Capricorn ['kæprɪkɔ:n] n Capricornio

caps [kæps] abbr (= *capital letters*) may

capsize [kæp'saɪz] vt volcar, hacer zozobrar ◾ vi volcarse, zozobrar

capstan ['kæpstən] n cabrestante m

capsule ['kæpsju:l] n cápsula

Capt. abbr = **Captain**

captain ['kæptɪn] n capitán m ◾ vt capitanear, ser el capitán de

caption ['kæpʃən] n (*heading*) título; (*to picture*) leyenda, pie m

captivate ['kæptɪveɪt] vt cautivar, encantar

captive ['kæptɪv] adj, n cautivo(-a) m(f)

captivity [kæp'tɪvɪtɪ] n cautiverio

captor ['kæptə'] n captor(a) m(f)

capture ['kæptʃə'] vt capturar; (*place*) tomar; (*attention*) captar, llamar ◾ n captura; toma; (*Comput: also:* **data capture**) formulación f de datos

car [kɑ:'] n coche m, carro (LAm), automóvil m, auto (LAm); (*US Rail*) vagón m; **by ~** en coche

Caracas [kə'rækəs] n Caracas m

carafe [kə'ræf] n garrafa

caramel ['kærəməl] n caramelo

carat ['kærət] n quilate m; **18-~ gold** oro de 18 quilates

caravan ['kærəvæn] n (*Brit*) caravana, remolque m; (*of camels*) caravana

caravan site n (*Brit*) camping m para caravanas

caraway ['kærəweɪ] n: **~ seed** carvi m

carbohydrates [kɑ:bəu'haɪdreɪts] npl (*foods*) hidratos mpl de carbono

carbolic [kɑ:'bɔlɪk] adj: **~ acid** ácido carbólico, fenol m

car bomb n coche-bomba m

carbon ['kɑ:bən] n carbono

carbonated ['kɑ:bəneɪtɪd] adj (*drink*) con gas

carbon copy n copia al carbón

carbon dioxide n dióxido de carbono, anhídrido carbónico

carbon footprint n huella de carbono

carbon monoxide n monóxido de carbono

carbon paper n papel m carbón

carbon ribbon n cinta de carbón

car boot sale n mercadillo (*de objetos usados expuestos en el maletero del coche*)

carburettor, carburetor (US) [kɑ:bju'rɛtə'] n carburador m

carcass ['kɑ:kəs] n (*of animal*) res f muerta; (*dead body*) cadáver m

carcinogenic [kɑ:sɪnə'dʒɛnɪk] adj cancerígeno

card [kɑ:d] n (*thin cardboard*) cartulina; (*playing*

card) carta, naipe *m*; (*visiting card, greetings card etc*) tarjeta; (*index card*) ficha; **membership ~** carnet *m*; **to play cards** jugar a las cartas *or* los naipes

cardamom [ˈkɑːdəməm] *n* cardamomo

cardboard [ˈkɑːdbɔːd] *n* cartón *m*, cartulina

cardboard box *n* caja de cartón

cardboard city *n* zona de marginados sin hogar (*que se refugian entre cartones*)

card-carrying member [ˈkɑːdkærɪɪŋ-] *n* miembro con carnet

card game *n* juego de naipes *or* cartas

cardiac [ˈkɑːdɪæk] *adj* cardíaco

cardigan [ˈkɑːdɪgən] *n* chaqueta (de punto), rebeca

cardinal [ˈkɑːdɪnl] *adj* cardinal ■ *n* cardenal *m*

cardinal number *n* número cardinal

card index *n* fichero

cardphone [ˈkɑːdfəun] *n* cabina que funciona con tarjetas telefónicas

cardsharp [ˈkɑːdʃɑːp] *n* fullero(-a)

card vote *n* voto por delegación

CARE [kɛəʳ] *n abbr* (= *Cooperative for American Relief Everywhere*) sociedad benéfica

care [kɛəʳ] *n* cuidado; (*worry*) preocupación *f*; (*charge*) cargo, custodia ■ *vi*: **to ~ about** preocuparse por; **~ of (c/o)** en casa de, al cuidado de; (*on letter*) para (entregar a); **in sb's ~** a cargo de algn; **the child has been taken into ~** pusieron al niño bajo custodia del gobierno; **"with ~"** "¡frágil!"; **to take ~ to** cuidarse de, tener cuidado de; **to take ~ of** *vt* cuidar; (*details, arrangements*) encargarse de; **I don't ~** no me importa; **I couldn't ~ less** me trae sin cuidado
  ▶ **care for** *vt fus* cuidar; (*like*) querer

careen [kəˈriːn] *vi* (*ship*) inclinarse, escorar ■ *vt* carenar

career [kəˈrɪəʳ] *n* carrera (profesional); (*occupation*) profesión *f* ■ *vi* (*also*: **career along**) correr a toda velocidad

career girl *n* mujer *f* dedicada a su profesión

careers officer *n* consejero(-a) de orientación profesional

carefree [ˈkɛəfriː] *adj* despreocupado

careful [ˈkɛəful] *adj* cuidadoso; (*cautious*) cauteloso; **(be) ~!** ¡ten cuidado!; **he's very ~ with his money** mira mucho el dinero; (*pej*) es muy tacaño

carefully [ˈkɛəfəlɪ] *adv* con cuidado, cuidadosamente

careless [ˈkɛəlɪs] *adj* descuidado; (*heedless*) poco atento

carelessly [ˈkɛəlɪslɪ] *adv* sin cuidado, a la ligera

carelessness [ˈkɛəlɪsnɪs] *n* descuido, falta de atención

carer [ˈkɛərəʳ] *n* persona que cuida de enfermos, ancianos o disminuidos

caress [kəˈrɛs] *n* caricia ■ *vt* acariciar

caretaker [ˈkɛəteɪkəʳ] *n* portero(-a), conserje *m/f*

caretaker government *n* gobierno provisional

car-ferry [ˈkɑːfɛrɪ] *n* transbordador *m* para coches

cargo (*pl* **cargoes**) [ˈkɑːgəu] *n* cargamento, carga

cargo boat *n* buque *m* de carga, carguero

cargo plane *n* avión *m* de carga

car hire *n* alquiler *m* de coches

Caribbean [kærɪˈbiːən] *adj* caribe, caribeño; **the ~ (Sea)** el (Mar) Caribe

caricature [ˈkærɪkətjuəʳ] *n* caricatura

caring [ˈkɛərɪŋ] *adj* humanitario

carnage [ˈkɑːnɪdʒ] *n* matanza, carnicería

carnal [ˈkɑːnl] *adj* carnal

carnation [kɑːˈneɪʃən] *n* clavel *m*

carnival [ˈkɑːnɪvəl] *n* carnaval *m*; (*US*) parque *m* de atracciones

carnivore [ˈkɑːnɪvɔːʳ] *n* carnívoro(-a)

carnivorous [kɑːˈnɪvrəs] *adj* carnívoro

carol [ˈkærəl] *n*: **(Christmas) ~** villancico

carouse [kəˈrauz] *vi* estar de juerga

carousel [kærəˈsɛl] *n* (*US*) tiovivo, caballitos *mpl*

carp [kɑːp] *n* (*fish*) carpa
  ▶ **carp at** *or* **about** *vt fus* sacar faltas de

car park *n* (*Brit*) aparcamiento, parking *m*, playa de estacionamiento (*LAm*)

carpenter [ˈkɑːpɪntəʳ] *n* carpintero

carpentry [ˈkɑːpɪntrɪ] *n* carpintería

carpet [ˈkɑːpɪt] *n* alfombra ■ *vt* alfombrar; **fitted ~** moqueta

carpet bombing *n* bombardeo de arrasamiento

carpet slippers *npl* zapatillas *fpl*

carpet sweeper [-ˈswiːpəʳ] *n* cepillo mecánico

car phone *n* teléfono de coche

carping [ˈkɑːpɪŋ] *adj* (*critical*) criticón(-ona)

carriage [ˈkærɪdʒ] *n* coche *m*; (*Brit Rail*) vagón *m*; (*for goods*) transporte *m*; (*of typewriter*) carro; (*bearing*) porte *m*; **~ forward** porte *m* debido; **~ free** franco de porte; **~ paid** porte pagado; **~ inwards/outwards** gastos *mpl* de transporte a cargo del comprador/vendedor

carriage return *n* (*on typewriter etc*) tecla de regreso

carriageway [ˈkærɪdʒweɪ] *n* (*Brit: part of road*) calzada; **dual ~** autovía

carrier ['kærɪəʳ] n transportista m/f; (company) empresa de transportes; (Med) portador(a) m(f)
carrier bag n (Brit) bolsa de papel or plástico
carrier pigeon n paloma mensajera
carrion ['kærɪən] n carroña
carrot ['kærət] n zanahoria
carry ['kærɪ] vt (person) llevar; (transport) transportar; (a motion, bill) aprobar; (involve: responsibilities etc) entrañar, conllevar; (Comm: stock) tener en existencia; (interest) llevar; (Math: figure) llevarse ■ vi (sound) oírse; **to get carried away** (fig) entusiasmarse; **this loan carries 10% interest** este empréstito devenga un interés del 10 por ciento
  ▶ **carry forward** vt (Math, Comm) pasar a la página/columna siguiente
  ▶ **carry on** vi (continue) seguir (adelante), continuar; (fam: complain) montar el número ■ vt seguir, continuar
  ▶ **carry out** vt (orders) cumplir; (investigation) llevar a cabo, realizar
carrycot ['kærɪkɔt] n (Brit) cuna portátil, capazo
carry-on ['kærɪ'ɔn] n (col) follón m
cart [kɑːt] n carro, carreta ■ vt cargar con
carte blanche ['kɑːt'blɔnʃ] n: **to give sb ~** dar carta blanca a algn
cartel [kɑː'tɛl] n (Comm) cartel m
cartilage ['kɑːtɪlɪdʒ] n cartílago
cartographer [kɑː'tɔgrəfəʳ] n cartógrafo(-a)
carton ['kɑːtən] n caja (de cartón); (of cigarettes) cartón m
cartoon [kɑː'tuːn] n (Press) chiste m; (comic strip) historieta, tira cómica; (film) dibujos mpl animados
cartoonist [kɑː'tuːnɪst] n humorista m/f gráfico
cartridge ['kɑːtrɪdʒ] n cartucho
cartwheel ['kɑːtwiːl] n: **to turn a ~** dar una voltereta lateral
carve [kɑːv] vt (meat) trinchar; (wood) tallar; (stone) cincelar, esculpir; (on tree) grabar
  ▶ **carve up** vt dividir, repartir; (meat) trinchar
carving ['kɑːvɪŋ] n (in wood etc) escultura, talla
carving knife n trinchante m
car wash n túnel m de lavado
Casablanca [kæsə'blæŋkə] n Casablanca
cascade [kæs'keɪd] n salto de agua, cascada; (fig) chorro ■ vi caer a chorros
case [keɪs] n (container) caja; (Med) caso; (for jewels etc) estuche m; (Law) causa, proceso; (Brit: also: **suitcase**) maleta; **lower/upper ~** (Typ) caja baja/alta; **in ~ of** en caso de; **in any ~** en todo caso; **just in ~** por si acaso; **to**

have a good ~ tener buenas razones; **there's a strong ~ for reform** hay razones sólidas para exigir una reforma
case history n (Med) historial m médico, historia clínica
case study n estudio de casos prácticos
cash [kæʃ] n (dinero) efectivo; (col: money) dinero ■ vt cobrar, hacer efectivo; **to pay (in) ~** pagar al contado; **~ on delivery (COD)** entrega contra reembolso; **~ with order** paga al hacer el pedido; **to be short of ~** estar pelado, estar sin blanca
  ▶ **cash in** vt (insurance policy etc) cobrar ■ vi: **to ~ in on sth** sacar partido or aprovecharse de algo
cash account n cuenta de caja
cash and carry n cash and carry m, autoservicio mayorista
cashbook ['kæʃbuk] n libro de caja
cash box n hucha
cash card n tarjeta f de(l) cajero (automático)
cash desk n (Brit) caja
cash discount n descuento por pago al contado
cash dispenser n cajero automático
cashew [kæ'ʃuː] n (also: **cashew nut**) anacardo
cash flow n flujo de fondos, cash-flow m, movimiento de efectivo
cashier [kæ'ʃɪəʳ] n cajero(-a) ■ vt (Mil) destituir, expulsar
cashmere ['kæʃmɪəʳ] n cachemir m, cachemira
cash payment n pago al contado
cash price n precio al contado
cash register n caja
cash reserves npl reserva en efectivo
cash sale n venta al contado
casing ['keɪsɪŋ] n revestimiento
casino [kə'siːnəu] n casino
cask [kɑːsk] n tonel m, barril m
casket ['kɑːskɪt] n cofre m, estuche m; (US: coffin) ataúd m
Caspian Sea ['kæspɪən-] n: **the ~** el Mar Caspio
cassava [kə'sɑːvə] n mandioca
casserole ['kæsərəul] n (food, pot) cazuela
cassette [kæ'sɛt] n cas(s)et(t)e m or f
cassette deck n platina
cassette player, cassette recorder n cas(s)et(t)e m
cassock ['kæsək] n sotana
cast [kɑːst] vb (pt, pp **cast**) ■ vt (throw) echar, arrojar, lanzar; (skin) mudar, perder; (metal) fundir; (Theat): **to ~ sb as Othello** dar a algn el papel de Otelo ■ n (Theat) reparto; (mould) forma, molde m; (also: **plaster cast**) vaciado;

to **~ loose** soltar; to **~ one's vote** votar

▶ **cast aside** vt (reject) descartar, desechar

▶ **cast away** vt desechar

▶ **cast down** vt derribar

▶ **cast off** vi (Naut) soltar amarras; (Knitting) cerrar los puntos ■ vt (Knitting) cerrar;

to **~ sb off** abandonar a algn, desentenderse de algn

▶ **cast on** vt (Knitting) montar

castanets [kæstə'nɛts] npl castañuelas fpl

castaway ['kɑːstəwər] n náufrago(-a)

caste [kɑːst] n casta

caster sugar ['kɑːstəʳ-] n (Brit) azúcar m en polvo

Castile [kæs'tiːl] n Castilla

Castilian [kæs'tɪlɪən] adj, n castellano(-a) ■ n (Ling) castellano

casting vote ['kɑːstɪŋ-] n (Brit) voto decisivo

cast iron n hierro fundido or colado ■ adj (fig: alibi) irrebatible; (will) férreo

castle ['kɑːsl] n castillo; (Chess) torre f

castor ['kɑːstəʳ] n (wheel) ruedecilla

castor oil n aceite m de ricino

castrate [kæs'treɪt] vt castrar

casual ['kæʒjul] adj (by chance) fortuito; (irregular: work etc) eventual, temporero; (unconcerned) despreocupado; (informal: clothes) de sport

casually ['kæʒjulɪ] adv por casualidad; de manera despreocupada

casualty ['kæʒjultɪ] n víctima, herido; (dead) muerto; (Mil) baja; **heavy casualties** numerosas bajas fpl

casualty ward n urgencias fpl

cat [kæt] n gato

catacombs ['kætəkuːmz] npl catacumbas fpl

Catalan ['kætəlæn] adj, n catalán(-ana) m(f)

catalogue, catalog (US) ['kætəlɔg] n catálogo ■ vt catalogar

Catalonia [kætə'ləunɪə] n Cataluña

catalyst ['kætəlɪst] n catalizador m

catalytic converter [kætə'lɪtɪkkən'vəːtəʳ] n catalizador m

catapult ['kætəpʌlt] n tirachinas m inv

cataract ['kætərækt] n (Med) cataratas fpl

catarrh [kə'tɑːʳ] n catarro

catastrophe [kə'tæstrəfɪ] n catástrofe f

catastrophic [kætə'strɔfɪk] adj catastrófico

catcall ['kætkɔːl] n (at meeting etc) rechifla, silbido

catch [kætʃ] vb (pt, pp **caught**) ■ vt coger (SP), agarrar (LAm); (arrest) atrapar, coger (SP); (grasp) asir; (breath) recobrar; (person: by surprise) pillar; (attract: attention) captar; (Med) pillar, coger; (also: **catch up**) alcanzar ■ vi (fire) encenderse; (in branches etc) engancharse ■ n (fish etc) captura; (act of catching) cogida;

(trick) trampa; (of lock) pestillo, cerradura;

to **~ fire** prenderse; (house) incendiarse;

to **~ sight of** divisar

▶ **catch on** vi (understand) caer en la cuenta; (grow popular) tener éxito, cuajar

▶ **catch out** vt (fig: with trick question) hundir

▶ **catch up** vi (fig) ponerse al día

catching ['kætʃɪŋ] adj (Med) contagioso

catchment area ['kætʃmənt-] n (Brit) zona de captación

catch phrase n frase f de moda

catch-22 ['kætʃtwɛntɪ'tuː] n: **it's a ~ situation** es un callejón sin salida, es un círculo vicioso

catchy ['kætʃɪ] adj (tune) pegadizo

catechism ['kætɪkɪzəm] n (Rel) catecismo

categoric [kætɪ'gɔrɪk], **categorical** [kætɪ'gɔrɪkəl] adj categórico, terminante

categorically [kætɪ'gɔrɪkəlɪ] adv categóricamente, terminantemente

categorize ['kætɪgəraɪz] vt clasificar

category ['kætɪgərɪ] n categoría

cater ['keɪtəʳ] vi: to **~ for** (Brit) abastecer a; (needs) atender a; (consumers) proveer a

caterer ['keɪtərəʳ] n abastecedor(a) m(f), proveedor(a) m(f)

catering ['keɪtərɪŋ] n (trade) hostelería

caterpillar ['kætəpɪləʳ] n oruga

caterpillar track n rodado de oruga

cat flap n gatera

cathedral [kə'θiːdrəl] n catedral f

cathode-ray tube ['kæθəudreɪ'tjuːb] n tubo de rayos catódicos

catholic ['kæθəlɪk] adj católico; **C~** adj, n (Rel) católico(-a) m(f)

CAT scanner [kæt-] (Med) n abbr (= computerized axial tomography scanner) escáner m TAC

cat's-eye ['kætsaɪ] n (Brit Aut) catafaro

catsup ['kætsəp] n (US) ketchup, catsup m

cattle ['kætl] npl ganado sg

catty ['kætɪ] adj malicioso

catwalk ['kætwɔːk] n pasarela

Caucasian [kɔː'keɪzɪən] adj, n caucásico(-a) m(f)

Caucasus ['kɔːkəsəs] n Cáucaso

caucus ['kɔːkəs] n (Pol: local committee) comité m local; (: US: to elect candidates) comité m electoral; (: group) camarilla política

caught [kɔːt] pt, pp of **catch**

cauliflower ['kɔlɪflauəʳ] n coliflor f

cause [kɔːz] n causa; (reason) motivo, razón f ■ vt causar; (provoke) provocar; to **~ sb to do sth** hacer que algn haga algo

causeway ['kɔːzweɪ] n (road) carretera elevada; (embankment) terraplén m

caustic ['kɔːstɪk] adj cáustico; (fig) mordaz

cauterize ['kɔːtəraɪz] vt cauterizar
caution ['kɔːʃən] n cautela, prudencia; (warning) advertencia, amonestación f
■ vt amonestar
cautious ['kɔːʃəs] adj cauteloso, prudente, precavido
cautiously ['kɔːʃəslɪ] adv con cautela
cautiousness ['kɔːʃəsnɪs] n cautela
cavalcade [kævəl'keɪd] n cabalgata
cavalier [kævə'lɪər] n (knight) caballero
■ adj (pej: offhand: person, attitude) arrogante, desdeñoso
cavalry ['kævəlrɪ] n caballería
cave [keɪv] n cueva, caverna ■ vi: **to go caving** ir en una expedición espeleológica
▶ **cave in** vi (roof etc) derrumbarse, hundirse
caveman ['keɪvmæn] n cavernícola m
cavern ['kævən] n caverna
cavernous ['kævənəs] adj (cheeks, eyes) hundido
caviar, caviare ['kævɪɑːr] n caviar m
cavity ['kævɪtɪ] n hueco, cavidad f
cavity wall insulation n aislamiento térmico
cavort [kə'vɔːt] vi hacer cabrioladas
cayenne [keɪ'ɛn] n: ~ **pepper** pimentón m picante
CB n abbr (= Citizens' Band (Radio)) frecuencias de radio usadas para la comunicación privada; (Brit: = Companion of (the Order of) the Bath) título de nobleza
CBC n abbr (= Canadian Broadcasting Corporation) cadena de radio y televisión
CBE n abbr (Brit: = Companion of (the Order of) the British Empire) título de nobleza
CBI n abbr (= Confederation of British Industry) ≈ C.E.O.E. f (SP)
CBS n abbr (US: = Columbia Broadcasting System) cadena de radio y televisión
CC abbr (Brit) = **county council**
cc abbr (= cubic centimetres) cc, cm³; (on letter etc) = **carbon copy**
CCA n abbr (US: = Circuit Court of Appeals) tribunal de apelación itinerante
CCTV n abbr = **closed-circuit television**
CCU n abbr (esp US: = coronary care unit) unidad f de cuidados cardiológicos
CD n abbr (= compact disc) CD m; (Mil: = Civil Defence (Corps): Brit: = Civil Defense; US) ■ abbr (Brit: = Corps Diplomatique) CD
CD burner n tostadora/grabadora f de CDs
CD player n reproductor m de compact disc
CDC n abbr (US) = **center for disease control**
Cdr. abbr = **commander**
CD-ROM ['siː'diː'rɔm] n abbr (= compact disc read-only memory) CD-ROM m
CDT n abbr (US: = Central Daylight Time) hora de

verano del centro; (Brit: Scol: = Craft, Design and Technology) artesanía, diseño y tecnología
CDW n abbr = **collision damage waiver**
CD writer n tostadora/grabadora f de CDs
cease [siːs] vt cesar
ceasefire ['siːsfaɪər] n alto m el fuego
ceaseless ['siːslɪs] adj incesante
ceaselessly ['siːslɪslɪ] adv sin cesar
CED n abbr (US) = **Committee for Economic Development**
cedar ['siːdər] n cedro
cede [siːd] vt ceder
CEEB n abbr (US: = College Entrance Examination Board) tribunal para las pruebas de acceso a la universidad
ceilidh ['keɪlɪ] n baile con música y danzas tradicionales escocesas o irlandesas
ceiling ['siːlɪŋ] n techo; (fig: upper limit) límite m, tope m
celebrate ['sɛlɪbreɪt] vt celebrar; (have a party) festejar ■ vi: **let's ~!** ¡vamos a celebrarlo!
celebrated ['sɛlɪbreɪtɪd] adj célebre
celebration [sɛlɪ'breɪʃən] n celebración f, festejo
celebrity [sɪ'lɛbrɪtɪ] n celebridad f
celeriac [sə'lɛrɪæk] n apio-nabo
celery ['sɛlərɪ] n apio
celestial [sɪ'lɛstɪəl] adj (of the sky) celeste; (divine) celestial
celibacy ['sɛlɪbəsɪ] n celibato
cell [sɛl] n celda; (Biol) célula; (Elec) elemento
cellar ['sɛlər] n sótano; (for wine) bodega
cellist ['tʃɛlɪst] n violoncelista m/f
cello ['tʃɛləu] n violoncelo
cellophane ['sɛləfeɪn] n celofán m
cellphone ['sɛlfəun] n móvil m
cellular ['sɛljulər] adj celular
celluloid ['sɛljulɔɪd] n celuloide m
cellulose ['sɛljuləus] n celulosa
Celsius ['sɛlsɪəs] adj centígrado
Celt [kɛlt, sɛlt] n celta m/f
Celtic ['kɛltɪk, 'sɛltɪk] adj celta, céltico
■ n (Ling) celta m
cement [sə'mɛnt] n cemento ■ vt cementar; (fig) cimentar
cement mixer n hormigonera
cemetery ['sɛmɪtrɪ] n cementerio
cenotaph ['sɛnətɑːf] n cenotafio
censor ['sɛnsər] n censor(a) m(f) ■ vt (cut) censurar
censorship ['sɛnsəʃɪp] n censura
censure ['sɛnʃər] vt censurar
census ['sɛnsəs] n censo
cent [sɛnt] n (US: unit of dollar) centavo; (unit of euro) céntimo; see also **per**
centenary [sɛn'tiːnərɪ], **centennial** [sɛn'tɛnɪəl] (US) n centenario

center ['sɛntər] n (US) = **centre**
centigrade ['sɛntɪɡreɪd] adj centígrado
centilitre, centiliter (US) ['sɛntɪliːtər] n centilitro
centimetre, centimeter (US) ['sɛntɪmiːtər] n centímetro
centipede ['sɛntɪpiːd] n ciempiés m inv
central ['sɛntrəl] adj central; (house etc) céntrico
Central African Republic n República Centroafricana
Central America n Centroamérica
Central American adj, n centroamericano(-a) m(f)
central heating n calefacción f central
centralize ['sɛntrəlaɪz] vt centralizar
central processing unit n (Comput) unidad f procesadora central, unidad f central de proceso
central reservation n (Brit Aut) mediana
centre, center (US) ['sɛntər] n centro ■ vt centrar; **to ~ (on)** (concentrate) concentrar (en)
centrefold, centerfold (US) ['sɛntəfəuld] n página central plegable
centre-forward ['sɛntə'fɔːwəd] n (Sport) delantero centro
centre-half ['sɛntə'hɑːf] n (Sport) medio centro
centrepiece, centerpiece (US) ['sɛntəpiːs] n punto central
centre spread n (Brit) páginas fpl centrales
centre-stage n: **to take ~** pasar a primer plano
centrifuge ['sɛntrɪfjuːdʒ] n centrifugadora
century ['sɛntjurɪ] n siglo; **20th ~** siglo veinte; **in the twentieth ~** en el siglo veinte
CEO n abbr = **chief executive officer**
ceramic [sɪ'ræmɪk] adj de cerámica
ceramics [sɪ'ræmɪks] n cerámica
cereal ['siːrɪəl] n cereal m
cerebral ['sɛrɪbrəl] adj cerebral
ceremonial [sɛrɪ'məunɪəl] n ceremonial
ceremony ['sɛrɪmənɪ] n ceremonia; **to stand on ~** hacer ceremonias, andarse con cumplidos
cert [səːt] n (Brit col): **it's a dead ~** ¡es cosa segura!
certain ['səːtən] adj seguro; (correct) cierto; (particular) cierto; **for ~** a ciencia cierta
certainly ['səːtənlɪ] adv desde luego, por supuesto
certainty ['səːtəntɪ] n certeza, certidumbre f, seguridad f
certificate [sə'tɪfɪkɪt] n certificado
certified ['sə:tɪfaɪd] adj: **~ mail** (US) correo certificado

certified public accountant n (US) contable m/f diplomado(-a)
certify ['sə:tɪfaɪ] vt certificar
cervical ['sə:vɪkl] adj: **~ cancer** cáncer m cervical; **~ smear** citología
cervix ['sə:vɪks] n cerviz f, cuello del útero
Cesarean [sɪ'zɛərɪən] adj, n (US) = **Caesarean**
cessation [sə'seɪʃən] n cese m, suspensión f
cesspit ['sɛspɪt] n pozo negro
CET n abbr (= Central European Time) hora de Europa central
Ceylon [sɪ'lɔn] n Ceilán m
cf. abbr (= compare) cfr
c/f abbr (Comm) = **carried forward**
CFC n abbr (= chlorofluorocarbon) CFC m
CG n abbr (US) = **coastguard**
cg abbr (= centigram) cg
CH n abbr (Brit: = Companion of Honour) título de nobleza
ch. abbr (= chapter) cap
Chad [tʃæd] n Chad m
chafe [tʃeɪf] vt (rub) rozar; (irritate) irritar; **to ~ (against)** (fig) irritarse or enojarse (con)
chaffinch ['tʃæfɪntʃ] n pinzón m (vulgar)
chagrin ['ʃæɡrɪn] n (annoyance) disgusto; (disappointment) desazón f
chain [tʃeɪn] n cadena ■ vt (also: **chain up**) encadenar
chain reaction n reacción f en cadena
chain-smoke ['tʃeɪnsməuk] vi fumar un cigarrillo tras otro
chain store n tienda de una cadena, ≈ grandes almacenes mpl
chair [tʃɛər] n silla; (armchair) sillón m; (of university) cátedra ■ vt (meeting) presidir; **the ~** (US: electric chair) la silla eléctrica; **please take a ~** siéntese or tome asiento, por favor
chairlift ['tʃɛəlɪft] n telesilla m
chairman ['tʃɛəmən] n presidente m
chairperson ['tʃɛəpə:sn] n presidente(-a) m(f)
chairwoman ['tʃɛəwumən] n presidenta
chalet ['ʃæleɪ] n chalet m (de madera)
chalice ['tʃælɪs] n cáliz m
chalk [tʃɔːk] n (Geo) creta; (for writing) tiza, gis m (LAm)
▶ **chalk up** vt apuntar; (fig: success, victory) apuntarse
challenge ['tʃælɪndʒ] n desafío, reto ■ vt desafiar, retar; (statement, right) poner en duda; **to ~ sb to do sth** retar a algn a que haga algo
challenger ['tʃælɪndʒər] n (Sport) contrincante m/f
challenging ['tʃælɪndʒɪŋ] adj que supone un reto; (tone) de desafío
chamber ['tʃeɪmbər] n cámara, sala
chambermaid ['tʃeɪmbəmeɪd] n camarera

chamber music n música de cámara
chamber of commerce n cámara de comercio
chamberpot ['tʃeɪmbəpɔt] n orinal m
chameleon [kə'miːlɪən] n camaleón m
chamois ['ʃæmwaː] n gamuza
champagne [ʃæm'peɪn] n champaña m, champán m
champers ['ʃæmpəz] nsg (col) champán m
champion ['tʃæmpɪən] n campeón(-ona) m(f); (of cause) defensor(a) m(f), paladín m/f ■ vt defender, apoyar
championship ['tʃæmpɪənʃɪp] n campeonato
chance [tʃaːns] n (coincidence) casualidad f; (luck) suerte f; (fate) azar m; (opportunity) ocasión f, oportunidad f, chance m or f (LAm); (likelihood) posibilidad f; (risk) riesgo ■ vt arriesgar, probar ■ adj fortuito, casual; **to ~ it** arriesgarse, intentarlo; **to take a ~** arriesgarse; **by ~** por casualidad; **it's the ~ of a lifetime** es la oportunidad de su vida; **the chances are that ...** lo más probable es que ...; **to ~ to do sth** (happen) hacer algo por casualidad
  ▶ **chance (up)on** vt fus tropezar(se) con
chancel ['tʃaːnsəl] n coro y presbiterio
chancellor ['tʃaːnsələr] n canciller m; **C~ of the Exchequer** (Brit) Ministro de Economía y Hacienda; see also **Downing Street**
chancy ['tʃaːnsɪ] adj (col) arriesgado
chandelier [ʃændə'lɪər] n araña (de luces)
change [tʃeɪndʒ] vt cambiar; (clothes, house) cambiarse de, mudarse de; (transform) transformar ■ vi cambiar(se); (change trains) hacer transbordo; (be transformed): **to ~ into** transformarse en ■ n cambio; (alteration) modificación f, transformación f; (coins) suelto; (money returned) vuelta, vuelto (LAm); **to ~ one's mind** cambiar de opinión or idea; **to ~ gear** (Aut) cambiar de marcha; **she changed into an old skirt** se puso una falda vieja; **for a ~** para variar; **can you give me ~ for £1?** ¿tiene cambio de una libra?; **keep the ~** quédese con la vuelta
changeable ['tʃeɪndʒəbl] adj (weather) cambiable; (person) variable
changeless ['tʃeɪndʒlɪs] adj inmutable
change machine n máquina de cambio
changeover ['tʃeɪndʒəuvər] n (to new system) cambio
changing ['tʃeɪndʒɪŋ] adj cambiante
changing room n (Brit) vestuario
channel ['tʃænl] n (TV) canal m; (of river) cauce m; (of sea) estrecho; (groove: fig: medium) conducto, medio ■ vt (river etc) encauzar; **to ~ into** (fig: interest, energies) encauzar a, dirigir a; **the (English) C~** el Canal (de la Mancha);

the C~ Islands las Islas Anglonormandas;
channels of communication canales mpl de comunicación; **green/red ~** (Customs) pasillo verde/rojo
Channel Tunnel n: **the ~** el túnel del Canal de la Mancha, el Eurotúnel
chant [tʃaːnt] n canto; (of crowd) gritos mpl ■ vt cantar; **the demonstrators chanted their disapproval** los manifestantes corearon su desaprobación
chaos ['keɪɔs] n caos m
chaos theory n teoría del caos
chaotic [keɪ'ɔtɪk] adj caótico
chap [tʃæp] n (Brit col: man) tío, tipo; **old ~** amigo (mío)
chapel ['tʃæpəl] n capilla
chaperone ['ʃæpərəun] n carabina
chaplain ['tʃæplɪn] n capellán m
chapped [tʃæpt] adj agrietado
chapter ['tʃæptər] n capítulo
char [tʃaːr] vt (burn) carbonizar, chamuscar ■ n (Brit) = **charlady**
character ['kærɪktər] n carácter m, naturaleza, índole f; (in novel, film) personaje m; (role) papel m; (individuality) carácter m; (Comput) carácter m; **a person of good ~** una persona de buena reputación
character code n código de caracteres
characteristic [kærɪktə'rɪstɪk] adj característico ■ n característica
characterize ['kærɪktəraɪz] vt caracterizar
charade [ʃə'raːd] n farsa, comedia; **charades** (game) charadas fpl
charcoal ['tʃaːkəul] n carbón m vegetal; (Art) carboncillo
charge [tʃaːdʒ] n carga; (Law) cargo, acusación f; (cost) precio, coste m; (responsibility) cargo; (task) encargo ■ vt (Law): **to ~ (with)** acusar (de); (gun, battery) cargar; (Mil: enemy) cargar; (price) pedir; (customer) cobrar; (person: with task) encargar ■ vi precipitarse; (make pay) cobrar; **charges** npl: **bank charges** comisiones fpl bancarias; **extra ~** recargo, suplemento; **free of ~** gratis; **to reverse the charges** (Brit Tel) llamar a cobro revertido; **to take ~ of** hacerse cargo de, encargarse de; **to be in ~ of** estar encargado de; **how much do you ~?** ¿cuánto cobra usted?; **to ~ an expense (up) to sb's account** cargar algo a cuenta de algn; **~ it to my account** póngalo or cárguelo a mi cuenta
charge account n (US) cuenta abierta or a crédito
charge card n tarjeta de cuenta
chargé d'affaires ['ʃaːʒeɪdæ'feər] n encargado de negocios

chargehand ['tʃɑ:dʒhænd] *n* capataz *m*
charger ['tʃɑ:dʒəʳ] *n* (*also:* **battery charger**)
cargador *m* (de baterías)
chariot ['tʃærɪət] *n* carro
charisma [kæ'rɪzmə] *n* carisma *m*
charitable ['tʃærɪtəbl] *adj* caritativo
charity ['tʃærɪtɪ] *n* (*gen*) caridad *f*;
(*organization*) organización *f* benéfica
charlady ['tʃɑ:leɪdɪ] *n* (*Brit*) mujer *f* de la
limpieza
charlatan ['ʃɑ:lətən] *n* charlatán *m*
charm [tʃɑ:m] *n* encanto, atractivo; (*spell*)
hechizo; (*object*) amuleto ■ *vt* encantar;
hechizar
charm bracelet *n* pulsera amuleto
charming ['tʃɑ:mɪŋ] *adj* encantador(a);
(*person*) simpático
chart [tʃɑ:t] *n* (*table*) cuadro; (*graph*) gráfica;
(*map*) carta de navegación; (*weather chart*)
mapa *m* meteorológico ■ *vt* (*course*) trazar;
(*sales, progress*) hacer una gráfica de; **to be in
the charts** (*record, pop group*) estar en la lista
de éxitos
charter ['tʃɑ:təʳ] *vt* (*bus*) alquilar; (*plane, ship*)
fletar ■ *n* (*document*) estatuto, carta; **on ~** en
alquiler, alquilado
chartered accountant *n* (*Brit*) contable *m/f*
diplomado(-a)
charter flight *n* vuelo chárter
charwoman ['tʃɑ:wumən] *n* = **charlady**
chase [tʃeɪs] *vt* (*pursue*) perseguir; (*hunt*) cazar
■ *n* persecución *f*; caza; **to ~ after** correr tras
▶ **chase up** *vt* (*information*) tratar de
conseguir; **to ~ sb up about sth** recordar
algo a algn
chasm ['kæzəm] *n* abismo
chassis ['ʃæsɪ] *n* chasis *m*
chaste [tʃeɪst] *adj* casto
chastened ['tʃeɪsənd] *adj* escarmentado
chastening ['tʃeɪsnɪŋ] *adj* aleccionador(a)
chastity ['tʃæstɪtɪ] *n* castidad *f*
chat [tʃæt] *vi* (*also:* **have a chat**) charlar;
(*Internet*) chatear ■ *n* charla; (*Internet*) chat *m*
▶ **chat up** *vt* (*col: girl*) ligar con, enrollarse con
chatline ['tʃætlaɪn] *n* línea (telefónica)
múltiple, party line *f*
chat room *n* (*internet*) chat *m*, canal *m* de
charla
chat show *n* (*Brit*) programa *m* de entrevistas
chattel ['tʃætl] *n* bien *m* mueble
chatter ['tʃætəʳ] *vi* (*person*) charlar; (*teeth*)
castañetear ■ *n* (*of birds*) parloteo; (*of people*)
charla, cháchara
chatterbox ['tʃætəbɔks] *n* parlanchín(-ina)
m(f)
chattering classes ['tʃætərɪŋ'klɑ:sɪz] *npl*:
the ~ (*col, pej*) los intelectualillos

chatty ['tʃætɪ] *adj* (*style*) informal; (*person*)
hablador(a)
chauffeur ['ʃəufəʳ] *n* chófer *m*
chauvinist ['ʃəuvɪnɪst] *n* (*also:* **male
chauvinist**) machista *m*; (*nationalist*)
chovinista *m/f*, patriotero(-a) *m(f)*
ChE *abbr* = **chemical engineer**
cheap [tʃi:p] *adj* barato; (*joke*) de mal gusto,
chabacano; (*poor quality*) malo; (*reduced: ticket*)
económico; (: *fare*) barato ■ *adv* barato
cheapen ['tʃi:pn] *vt* rebajar el precio de,
abaratar
cheaply ['tʃi:plɪ] *adv* barato, a bajo precio
cheat [tʃi:t] *vi* hacer trampa; (*in exam*) copiar
■ *vt* estafar, timar ■ *n* trampa; estafa;
(*person*) tramposo(-a); **he's been cheating
on his wife** ha estado engañando a su
esposa
cheating ['tʃi:tɪŋ] *n* trampa
Chechnia ['tʃetʃni:ə] *n* Chechenia
check [tʃek] *vt* comprobar; (*count*) contar;
(*halt*) frenar; (*restrain*) refrenar, restringir
■ *vi*: **to ~ with sb** consultar con algn; (*official
etc*) informarse por ■ *n* (*inspection*) control *m*,
inspección *f*; (*curb*) freno; (*bill*) nota, cuenta;
(*US*) = **cheque**; (*pattern: gen pl*) cuadro
■ *adj* (*also:* **checked**: *pattern, cloth*) a cuadros;
to keep a ~ on sth/sb controlar algo/a algn
▶ **check in** *vi* (*in hotel*) registrarse; (*at airport*)
facturar ■ *vt* (*luggage*) facturar
▶ **check out** *vi* (*of hotel*) desocupar la
habitación ■ *vt* (*investigate: story*) comprobar;
(: *person*) informarse sobre
▶ **check up** *vi*: **to ~ up on sth** comprobar
algo; **to ~ up on sb** investigar a algn
checkbook ['tʃekbuk] *n* (*US*) = **chequebook**
checkered ['tʃekəd] *adj* (*US*) = **chequered**
checkers ['tʃekəz] *n* (*US*) damas *fpl*
check-in ['tʃekɪn] *n* (*also:* **check-in desk**: *at
airport*) mostrador *m* de facturación
checking account ['tʃekɪŋ-] *n* (*US*) cuenta
corriente
checklist ['tʃeklɪst] *n* lista
checkmate ['tʃekmeɪt] *n* jaque *m* mate
checkout ['tʃekaut] *n* (*in supermarket*) caja
checkpoint ['tʃekpɔɪnt] *n* (punto de) control
m, retén *m* (*LAm*)
checkroom ['tʃekrum] *n* (*US*) consigna
checkup ['tʃekʌp] *n* (*Med*) reconocimiento
general; (*of machine*) revisión *f*
cheek [tʃi:k] *n* mejilla; (*impudence*) descaro
cheekbone ['tʃi:kbəun] *n* pómulo
cheeky ['tʃi:kɪ] *adj* fresco, descarado
cheep [tʃi:p] *n* (*of bird*) pío ■ *vi* piar
cheer [tʃɪəʳ] *vt* vitorear, ovacionar; (*gladden*)
alegrar, animar ■ *vi* dar vivas ■ *n* viva *m*;
cheers *npl* vítores *mpl*; **cheers!** ¡salud!

▶ **cheer on** vt (person etc) animar con aplausos or gritos

▶ **cheer up** vi animarse ■ vt alegrar, animar

cheerful ['tʃɪəful] adj alegre

cheerfulness ['tʃɪəfulnɪs] n alegría

cheering ['tʃɪərɪŋ] n ovaciones fpl, vítores mpl

cheerio [tʃɪərɪ'əu] excl (Brit) ¡hasta luego!

cheerleader ['tʃɪəliːdər] n animador(a) m(f)

cheerless ['tʃɪəlɪs] adj triste, sombrío

cheese [tʃiːz] n queso

cheeseboard ['tʃiːzbɔːd] n tabla de quesos

cheeseburger ['tʃiːzbəːgər] n hamburguesa con queso

cheesecake ['tʃiːzkeɪk] n pastel m de queso

cheetah ['tʃiːtə] n guepardo

chef [ʃef] n jefe(-a) m(f) de cocina

chemical ['kemɪkəl] adj químico ■ n producto químico

chemist ['kemɪst] n (Brit: pharmacist) farmacéutico(-a); (scientist) químico(-a); ~'s (shop) n (Brit) farmacia

chemistry ['kemɪstrɪ] n química

chemotherapy [kiːməu'θerəpɪ] n quimioterapia

cheque, check (US) [tʃek] n cheque m; **to pay by** ~ pagar con cheque

chequebook, checkbook (US) ['tʃekbuk] n talonario (de cheques), chequera (LAm)

cheque card n (Brit) tarjeta de identificación bancaria

chequered, checkered (US) ['tʃekəd] adj (fig) accidentado; (pattern) de cuadros

cherish ['tʃerɪʃ] vt (love) querer, apreciar; (protect) cuidar; (hope etc) abrigar

cheroot [ʃə'ruːt] n puro (cortado en los dos extremos)

cherry ['tʃerɪ] n cereza

Ches abbr (Brit) = **Cheshire**

chess [tʃes] n ajedrez m

chessboard ['tʃesbɔːd] n tablero (de ajedrez)

chessman ['tʃesmən] n pieza (de ajedrez)

chest [tʃest] n (Anat) pecho; (box) cofre m; **to get sth off one's** ~ (col) desahogarse; **~ of drawers** n cómoda

chest measurement n talla (de chaqueta etc)

chestnut ['tʃesnʌt] n castaña; (also: **chestnut tree**) castaño; (colour) castaño ■ adj (color) castaño inv

chesty ['tʃestɪ] adj (cough) de bronquios, de pecho

chew [tʃuː] vt mascar, masticar

chewing gum ['tʃuːɪŋ-] n chicle m

chic [ʃiːk] adj elegante

chicanery [ʃɪ'keɪnərɪ] n embustes mpl, sofismas mpl

Chicano [tʃɪ'kaːnəu] adj, n chicano(-a)

chick [tʃɪk] n pollito, polluelo; (US col) chica

chicken ['tʃɪkɪn] n gallina, pollo; (food) pollo; (col: coward) gallina m/f

▶ **chicken out** vi (col) rajarse; **to ~ out of doing sth** rajarse y no hacer algo

chickenpox ['tʃɪkɪnpɔks] n varicela

chickpea ['tʃɪkpiː] n garbanzo

chicory ['tʃɪkərɪ] n (for coffee) achicoria; (salad) escarola

chide [tʃaɪd] vt: **to ~ sb for sth** reprender a algn por algo

chief [tʃiːf] n jefe(-a) m(f) ■ adj principal, esp máximo (LAm); **C~ of Staff** (esp Mil) Jefe m del Estado mayor

chief executive, chief executive officer (US) n director m general

chiefly ['tʃiːflɪ] adv principalmente

chieftain ['tʃiːftən] n jefe m, cacique m

chiffon ['ʃɪfɔn] n gasa

chilblain ['tʃɪlbleɪn] n sabañón m

child (pl **children**) [tʃaɪld, 'tʃɪldrən] n niño(-a); (offspring) hijo(-a)

child benefit n (Brit) subsidio por cada hijo pequeño

childbirth ['tʃaɪldbəːθ] n parto

childhood ['tʃaɪldhud] n niñez f, infancia

childish ['tʃaɪldɪʃ] adj pueril, infantil

childless ['tʃaɪldlɪs] adj sin hijos

childlike ['tʃaɪldlaɪk] adj de niño, infantil

child minder n (Brit) niñera, madre f de día

child prodigy n niño(-a) prodigio inv

children's home n centro de acogida para niños

child's play n (fig): **this is** ~ esto es coser y cantar

Chile ['tʃɪlɪ] n Chile m

Chilean ['tʃɪlɪən] adj, n chileno(-a) m(f)

chill [tʃɪl] n frío; (Med) resfriado ■ adj frío ■ vt enfriar; (Culin) refrigerar

▶ **chill out** vi (esp US col) tranquilizarse

chilli, chili ['tʃɪlɪ] n (Brit) chile m, ají m (LAm)

chilling ['tʃɪlɪŋ] adj escalofriante

chilly ['tʃɪlɪ] adj frío

chime [tʃaɪm] n repique m, campanada ■ vi repicar, sonar

chimney ['tʃɪmnɪ] n chimenea

chimney sweep n deshollinador m

chimpanzee [tʃɪmpæn'ziː] n chimpancé m

chin [tʃɪn] n mentón m, barbilla

China ['tʃaɪnə] n China

china ['tʃaɪnə] n porcelana; (crockery) loza

Chinese [tʃaɪ'niːz] adj chino ■ n (pl inv) chino(-a); (Ling) chino

chink [tʃɪŋk] n (opening) rendija, hendedura; (noise) tintineo

chintz [tʃɪnts] n cretona

chinwag ['tʃɪnwæg] n (Brit col): **to have a** ~ echar una parrafada

chip [tʃɪp] n (gen pl: Culin: Brit) patata or (LAm) papa frita; (: US: also: **potato chip**) patata or (LAm) papa frita; (of wood) astilla; (stone) lasca; (in gambling) ficha; (Comput) chip m ■ vt (cup, plate) desconchar; **when the chips are down** (fig) a la hora de la verdad ▶ **chip in** vi (col: interrupt) interrumpir, meterse; (: contribute) contribuir

chip and PIN n chip and PIN m (sistema de tarjetas chip con número PIN); ~ **machine** lector m de tarjetas chip and PIN

chipboard ['tʃɪpbɔːd] n madera aglomerada

chipmunk ['tʃɪpmʌŋk] n ardilla listada

chip shop n ver nota

CHIP SHOP

Se denomina chip shop o "fish-and-chip shop" a un tipo de tienda popular de comida rápida en la que se despachan platos tradicionales británicos, principalmente filetes de pescado rebozado frito y patatas fritas.

chiropodist [kɪ'rɔpədɪst] n (Brit) podólogo(-a)

chiropody [kɪ'rɔpədɪ] n podología

chirp [tʃəːp] vi gorjear; (cricket) cantar ■ n (of cricket) canto

chirpy ['tʃəːpɪ] adj alegre, animado

chisel ['tʃɪzl] n (for wood) escoplo; (for stone) cincel m

chit [tʃɪt] n nota

chitchat ['tʃɪttʃæt] n chismes mpl, habladurías fpl

chivalrous ['ʃɪvəlrəs] adj caballeroso

chivalry ['ʃɪvəlrɪ] n caballerosidad f

chives [tʃaɪvz] npl cebollinos mpl

chloride ['klɔːraɪd] n cloruro

chlorinate ['klɔːrɪneɪt] vt clorar

chlorine ['klɔːriːn] n cloro

chock-a-block ['tʃɔkə'blɔk], **chock-full** [tʃɔk'ful] adj atestado

chocolate ['tʃɔklɪt] n chocolate m

choice [tʃɔɪs] n elección f; (preference) preferencia ■ adj escogido; **I did it by** or **from** ~ lo hice de buena gana; **a wide** ~ un gran surtido, una gran variedad

choir ['kwaɪər] n coro

choirboy ['kwaɪəbɔɪ] n niño de coro

choke [tʃəuk] vi ahogarse; (on food) atragantarse ■ vt ahogar; (block) atascar ■ n (Aut) estárter m

choker ['tʃəukər] n (necklace) gargantilla

cholera ['kɔlərə] n cólera m

cholesterol [kɔ'lɛstərəl] n colesterol m

choose [tʃuːz] (pt **chose**) [tʃəuz] (pp **chosen**) [tʃəuzn] vt escoger, elegir; (team) seleccionar;

to ~ **between** elegir or escoger entre; **to** ~ **from** escoger entre

choosy ['tʃuːzɪ] adj remilgado

chop [tʃɔp] vt (wood) cortar, talar; (Culin: also: **chop up**) picar ■ n tajo, golpe m cortante; (Culin) chuleta; **chops** npl (jaws) boca sg; **to get the** ~ (col: project) ser suprimido; (: person: be sacked) ser despedido

chopper ['tʃɔpər] n (helicopter) helicóptero

choppy ['tʃɔpɪ] adj (sea) picado, agitado

chopsticks ['tʃɔpstɪks] npl palillos mpl

choral ['kɔːrəl] adj coral

chord [kɔːd] n (Mus) acorde m

chore [tʃɔːr] n faena, tarea; (routine task) trabajo rutinario

choreographer [kɔrɪ'ɔgrəfər] n coreógrafo(-a)

choreography [kɔrɪ'ɔgrəfɪ] n coreografía

chorister ['kɔrɪstər] n corista m/f

chortle ['tʃɔːtl] vi reírse satisfecho

chorus ['kɔːrəs] n coro; (repeated part of song) estribillo

chose [tʃəuz] pt of **choose**

chosen ['tʃəuzn] pp of **choose**

chowder ['tʃaudər] n (esp US) sopa de pescado

Christ [kraɪst] n Cristo

christen ['krɪsn] vt bautizar

christening ['krɪsnɪŋ] n bautizo

Christian ['krɪstɪən] adj, n cristiano(-a) m(f)

Christianity [krɪstɪ'ænɪtɪ] n cristianismo

Christian name n nombre m de pila

Christmas ['krɪsməs] n Navidad f; **Merry** ~! ¡Felices Navidades!, ¡Felices Pascuas!

Christmas card n crismas m inv, tarjeta de Navidad

Christmas Day n día m de Navidad

Christmas Eve n Nochebuena

Christmas Island n Isla Christmas

Christmas tree n árbol m de Navidad

chrome [krəum] n = **chromium plating**

chromium ['krəumɪəm] n cromo; (also: **chromium plating**) cromado

chromosome ['krəuməsəum] n cromosoma m

chronic ['krɔnɪk] adj crónico; (fig: liar, smoker) empedernido

chronicle ['krɔnɪkl] n crónica

chronological [krɔnə'lɔdʒɪkəl] adj cronológico

chrysanthemum [krɪ'sænθəməm] n crisantemo

chubby ['tʃʌbɪ] adj rechoncho

chuck [tʃʌk] vt tirar; **to** ~ (**up** or **in**) vt (Brit) dejar, mandar a paseo

chuckle ['tʃʌkl] vi reírse entre dientes

chuffed [tʃʌft] adj (col): **to be** ~ (**about sth**) estar encantado (con algo)

475

chug [tʃʌg] vi (also: **chug along**: train) ir despacio; (: fig) ir tirando

chum [tʃʌm] n amiguete(-a) m(f), coleguilla m/f

chump [tʃʌmp] n (col) tonto(-a), estúpido(-a)

chunk [tʃʌŋk] n pedazo, trozo

chunky ['tʃʌŋkɪ] adj (furniture etc) achaparrado; (person) fornido; (knitwear) de lana gorda, grueso

Chunnel [tʃʌnl] n = **Channel Tunnel**

church [tʃəːtʃ] n iglesia; **the C~ of England** la Iglesia Anglicana

churchyard ['tʃəːtʃjɑːd] n cementerio, camposanto

churlish ['tʃəːlɪʃ] adj grosero; (mean) arisco

churn [tʃəːn] n (for butter) mantequera; (for milk) lechera
▶ **churn out** vt producir en serie

chute [ʃuːt] n (also: **rubbish chute**) vertedero; (Brit: children's slide) tobogán m

chutney ['tʃʌtnɪ] n salsa picante de frutas y especias

CIA n abbr (US: = Central Intelligence Agency) CIA f, Agencia Central de Inteligencia

cicada [sɪ'kɑːdə] n cigarra

CID n abbr (Brit: = Criminal Investigation Department) ≈ B.I.C. f (SP)

cider ['saɪdəʳ] n sidra

CIF abbr (= cost, insurance, and freight) c.s.f.

cigar [sɪ'gɑːʳ] n puro

cigarette [sɪgə'rɛt] n cigarrillo, pitillo

cigarette case n pitillera

cigarette end n colilla

cigarette holder n boquilla

C-in-C abbr (= commander-in-chief) comandante mf general

cinch [sɪntʃ] n: **it's a ~** está tirado

Cinderella [sɪndə'rɛlə] n Cenicienta

cinders ['sɪndəz] npl cenizas fpl

cine-camera ['sɪnɪ'kæmərə] n (Brit) cámara cinematográfica

cine-film ['sɪnɪfɪlm] n (Brit) película de cine

cinema ['sɪnəmə] n cine m

cinnamon ['sɪnəmən] n canela

cipher ['saɪfəʳ] n clave f; (fig) cero; **in ~** en clave

circle ['səːkl] n círculo; (in theatre) anfiteatro ▪ vi dar vueltas ▪ vt (surround) rodear, cercar; (move round) dar la vuelta a

circuit ['səːkɪt] n circuito; (track) pista; (lap) vuelta

circuit board n tarjeta de circuitos

circuitous [səː'kjuɪtəs] adj indirecto

circular ['səːkjuləʳ] adj circular ▪ n circular f; (as advertisement) panfleto

circulate ['səːkjuleɪt] vi circular; (person: socially) alternar, circular ▪ vt poner en circulación

circulation [səːkju'leɪʃən] n circulación f; (of newspaper etc) tirada

circumcise ['səːkəmsaɪz] vt circuncidar

circumference [sə'kʌmfərəns] n circunferencia

circumscribe ['səːkəmskraɪb] vt circunscribir

circumspect ['səːkəmspɛkt] adj circunspecto, prudente

circumstances ['səːkəmstənsɪz] npl circunstancias fpl; (financial condition) situación f económica; **in the ~** en or dadas las circunstancias; **under no ~** de ninguna manera, bajo ningún concepto

circumstantial [səːkəm'stænʃəl] adj detallado; **~ evidence** prueba indiciaria

circumvent ['səːkəmvɛnt] vt (rule etc) burlar

circus ['səːkəs] n circo; (also: **Circus**: in place names) Plaza

cirrhosis [sɪ'rəusɪs] n (also: **cirrhosis of the liver**) cirrosis f inv

CIS n abbr (= Commonwealth of Independent States) CEI f

cissy ['sɪsɪ] n = **sissy**

cistern ['sɪstən] n tanque m, depósito; (in toilet) cisterna

citation [saɪ'teɪʃən] n cita; (Law) citación f; (Mil) mención f

cite [saɪt] vt citar

citizen ['sɪtɪzn] n (Pol) ciudadano(-a); (of city) habitante m/f

Citizens' Advice Bureau n (Brit) organización voluntaria británica que aconseja especialmente en temas legales o financieros

citizenship ['sɪtɪznʃɪp] n ciudadanía; (Brit Scol) civismo

citric ['sɪtrɪk] adj: **~ acid** ácido cítrico

citrus fruits ['sɪtrəs-] npl cítricos mpl

city ['sɪtɪ] n ciudad f; **the C~** centro financiero de Londres

city centre n centro de la ciudad

City Hall n (US) ayuntamiento

City Technology College n (Brit) ≈ Centro de formación profesional

civic ['sɪvɪk] adj cívico; (authorities) municipal

civic centre n (Brit) centro de administración municipal

civil ['sɪvɪl] adj civil; (polite) atento, cortés; (well-bred) educado

civil defence n protección f civil

civil engineer n ingeniero(-a) de caminos

civil engineering n ingeniería de caminos

civilian [sɪ'vɪlɪən] adj civil; (clothes) de paisano ▪ n civil m/f

civilization [sɪvɪlaɪ'zeɪʃən] n civilización f

civilized ['sɪvɪlaɪzd] adj civilizado

civil law n derecho civil
civil liberties npl libertades fpl civiles
civil rights npl derechos mpl civiles
civil servant n funcionario(-a) (del Estado)
Civil Service n administración f pública
civil war n guerra civil
civvies ['sɪvɪz] npl: **in ~** (col) de paisano
CJD n abbr (= Creutzfeld-Jakob disease) enfermedad de Creutzfeldt-Jakob
cl abbr (= centilitre) cl
clad [klæd] adj: **~ (in)** vestido (de)
claim [kleɪm] vt exigir, reclamar; (rights etc) reivindicar; (assert) pretender ■ vi (for insurance) reclamar ■ n (for expenses) reclamación f; (Law) demanda; (pretension) pretensión f; **to put in a ~ for sth** presentar una demanda por algo
claimant ['kleɪmənt] n (Admin, Law) demandante m/f
claim form n solicitud f
clairvoyant [klɛə'vɔɪənt] n clarividente m/f
clam [klæm] n almeja
  ▶ **clam up** vi (col) cerrar el pico
clamber ['klæmbəʳ] vi trepar
clammy ['klæmɪ] adj (cold) frío y húmedo; (sticky) pegajoso
clamour, clamor (US) ['klæməʳ] n (noise) clamor m; (protest) protesta ■ vi: **to ~ for sth** clamar por algo, pedir algo a voces
clamp [klæmp] n abrazadera; (laboratory clamp) grapa; (wheel clamp) cepo ■ vt afianzar (con abrazadera)
  ▶ **clamp down on** vt fus (government, police) poner coto a
clampdown ['klæmpdaun] n restricción f; **there has been a ~ on terrorism** se ha puesto coto al terrorismo
clan [klæn] n clan m
clandestine [klæn'dɛstɪn] adj clandestino
clang [klæŋ] n estruendo ■ vi sonar con estruendo
clanger [klæŋəʳ] n: **to drop a ~** (Brit col) meter la pata
clansman ['klænzmən] n miembro del clan
clap [klæp] vi aplaudir ■ vt (hands) batir ■ n (of hands) palmada; **to ~ one's hands** dar palmadas, batir las palmas; **a ~ of thunder** un trueno
clapping ['klæpɪŋ] n aplausos mpl
claptrap ['klæptræp] n (col) gilipolleces fpl
claret ['klærət] n burdeos m inv
clarification [klærɪfɪ'keɪʃən] n aclaración f
clarify ['klærɪfaɪ] vt aclarar
clarinet [klærɪ'nɛt] n clarinete m
clarity ['klærɪtɪ] n claridad f
clash [klæʃ] n estruendo; (fig) choque m ■ vi enfrentarse; (personalities, interests) oponerse,

chocar; (colours) desentonar; (dates, events) coincidir
clasp [klɑːsp] n broche m; (on jewels) cierre m ■ vt abrochar; (hand) apretar; (embrace) abrazar
class [klɑːs] n (gen) clase f; (group, category) clase f, categoría ■ cpd de clase ■ vt clasificar
class-conscious ['klɑːs'kɔnʃəs] adj clasista, con conciencia de clase
classic ['klæsɪk] adj clásico ■ n (work) obra clásica, clásico; **classics** npl (Univ) clásicas fpl
classical ['klæsɪkəl] adj clásico; **~ music** música clásica
classification [klæsɪfɪ'keɪʃən] n clasificación f
classified ['klæsɪfaɪd] adj (information) reservado
classified advertisement n anuncio por palabras
classify ['klæsɪfaɪ] vt clasificar
classless ['klɑːslɪs] adj: **~ society** sociedad f sin clases
classmate ['klɑːsmeɪt] n compañero(-a) de clase
classroom ['klɑːsrum] n aula
classy ['klɑːsɪ] adj (col) elegante, con estilo
clatter ['klætəʳ] n ruido, estruendo; (of hooves) trápala ■ vi hacer ruido or estruendo
clause [klɔːz] n cláusula; (Ling) oración f
claustrophobia [klɔːstrə'fəubɪə] n claustrofobia
claustrophobic [klɔːstrə'fəubɪk] adj claustrofóbico; **I feel ~** me entra claustrofobia
claw [klɔː] n (of cat) uña; (of bird of prey) garra; (of lobster) pinza; (Tech) garfio ■ vi: **to ~ at** arañar; (tear) desgarrar
clay [kleɪ] n arcilla
clean [kliːn] adj limpio; (copy) en limpio; (lines) bien definido ■ vt limpiar ■ adv: **he ~ forgot** lo olvidó por completo; **to come ~** (col: admit guilt) confesarlo todo; **to have a ~ driving licence** tener el carnet de conducir sin sanciones; **to ~ one's teeth** lavarse los dientes
  ▶ **clean off** vt limpiar
  ▶ **clean out** vt limpiar (a fondo)
  ▶ **clean up** vt limpiar, asear ■ vi (fig: make profit): **to ~ up on** sacar provecho de
clean-cut ['kliːn'kʌt] adj bien definido; (outline) nítido; (person) de buen parecer
cleaner ['kliːnəʳ] n encargado(-a) m(f) de la limpieza; (also: **dry cleaner**) tintorero(-a)
cleaning ['kliːnɪŋ] n limpieza
cleaning lady n señora de la limpieza, asistenta

cleanliness ['klɛnlınıs] n limpieza
cleanse [klɛnz] vt limpiar
cleanser ['klɛnzəʳ] n detergente m; (cosmetic) loción f or crema limpiadora
clean-shaven ['kli:n'ʃeıvn] adj bien afeitado
cleansing department ['klɛnzıŋ-] n (Brit) servicio municipal de limpieza
clean sweep n: **to make a ~** (Sport) arrasar, barrer
clear [klıəʳ] adj claro; (road, way) libre; (profit) neto; (majority) absoluto ■ vt (space) despejar, limpiar; (Law: suspect) absolver; (obstacle) salvar, saltar por encima de; (debt) liquidar; (cheque) aceptar; (site, woodland) desmontar ■ vi (fog etc) despejarse ■ n: **to be in the ~** (out of debt) estar libre de deudas; (out of suspicion) estar fuera de toda sospecha; (out of danger) estar fuera de peligro ■ adv: **~ of** a distancia de; **to make o.s. ~** explicarse claramente; **to make it ~ to sb that ...** hacer entender a algn que ...; **I have a ~ day tomorrow** mañana tengo el día libre; **to keep ~ of sth/sb** evitar algo/a algn; **to ~ a profit of ...** sacar una ganancia de ...; **to ~ the table** recoger or quitar la mesa
▶ **clear off** vi (col: leave) marcharse, mandarse mudar (LAm)
▶ **clear up** vt limpiar; (mystery) aclarar, resolver
clearance ['klıərəns] n (removal) despeje m; (permission) acreditación f
clear-cut ['klıə'kʌt] adj bien definido, claro
clearing ['klıərıŋ] n (in wood) claro
clearing bank n (Brit) banco central
clearing house n (Comm) cámara de compensación
clearly ['klıəlı] adv claramente
clearway ['klıəweı] n (Brit) carretera en la que no se puede estacionar
cleaver ['kli:və] n cuchilla (de carnicero)
clef [klɛf] n (Mus) clave f
cleft [klɛft] n (in rock) grieta, hendedura
clemency ['klɛmənsı] n clemencia
clench [klɛntʃ] vt apretar, cerrar
clergy ['klə:dʒı] n clero
clergyman ['klə:dʒımən] n clérigo
clerical ['klɛrıkəl] adj de oficina; (Rel) clerical; (error) de copia
clerk [klɑ:k] (US) [klə:k] n oficinista m/f; (US) dependiente(-a) m(f), vendedor(a) m(f); **C~ of the Court** secretario(-a) de juzgado
clever ['klɛvəʳ] adj (mentally) inteligente, listo; (skilful) hábil; (device, arrangement) ingenioso
cleverly ['klɛvəlı] adv ingeniosamente
clew [klu:] n (US) = **clue**
cliché ['kli:ʃeı] n cliché m, frase f hecha

click [klık] vt (tongue) chasquear ■ vi (Comput) hacer clic; **to ~ one's heels** taconear
clickable ['klıkəbl] adj (Comput) cliqueable
client ['klaıənt] n cliente m/f
clientele [kli:ā:n'tɛl] n clientela
cliff [klıf] n acantilado
cliffhanger ['klıfhæŋəʳ] n: **it was a ~** estuvimos etc en ascuas hasta el final
climactic [klaı'mæktık] adj culminante
climate ['klaımıt] n clima m; (fig) clima m, ambiente m
climax ['klaımæks] n punto culminante; (of play etc) clímax m; (sexual climax) orgasmo
climb [klaım] vi subir, trepar; (plane) elevarse, remontar el vuelo ■ vt (stairs) subir; (tree) trepar a; (mountain) escalar ■ n subida, ascenso; **to ~ over a wall** saltar una tapia
▶ **climb down** vi (fig) volverse atrás
climbdown ['klaımdaun] n vuelta atrás
climber ['klaıməʳ] n escalador(a) m(f)
climbing ['klaımıŋ] n escalada
clinch [klıntʃ] vt (deal) cerrar; (argument) rematar
clincher ['klıntʃəʳ] n (col): **that was the ~ for me** eso me hizo decidir
cling [klıŋ] (pt, pp **clung**) [klʌŋ] vi: **to ~ (to)** agarrarse (a); (clothes) pegarse (a)
clingfilm ['klıŋfılm] n plástico adherente
clinic ['klınık] n clínica
clinical ['klınıkl] adj clínico; (fig) frío, impasible
clink [klıŋk] vi tintinear
clip [klıp] n (for hair) horquilla; (also: **paper clip**) sujetapapeles m inv, clip m; (clamp) grapa ■ vt (cut) cortar; (hedge) podar; (also: **clip together**) unir
clippers ['klıpəz] npl (for gardening) tijeras fpl de podar; (for hair) maquinilla sg; (for nails) cortauñas m inv
clipping ['klıpıŋ] n (from newspaper) recorte m
clique [kli:k] n camarilla
cloak [kləuk] n capa, manto ■ vt (fig) encubrir, disimular
cloakroom ['kləukrum] n guardarropa m; (Brit: WC) lavabo, aseos mpl, baño (esp LAm)
clobber ['klɔbəʳ] n (col) bártulos mpl, trastos mpl ■ vt dar una paliza a
clock [klɔk] n reloj m; (in taxi) taxímetro; **to work against the ~** trabajar contra reloj; **around the ~** las veinticuatro horas; **to sleep round the ~** dormir un día entero; **30,000 on the ~** (Aut) treinta mil millas en el cuentakilómetros
▶ **clock in, clock on** vi fichar, picar
▶ **clock off, clock out** vi fichar or picar la salida
▶ **clock up** vt hacer

clockwise ['klɔkwaɪz] *adv* en el sentido de las agujas del reloj

clockwork ['klɔkwə:k] *n* aparato de relojería ▪ *adj (toy, train)* de cuerda

clog [klɔg] *n* zueco, chanclo ▪ *vt* atascar ▪ *vi* atascarse

cloister ['klɔɪstə^r] *n* claustro

clone [kləun] *n* clon *m*

close [*adj, adv* kləus, *vb, n* kləuz] *adj* cercano, próximo; *(near):* ~ **(to)** cerca (de); *(print, weave)* tupido, compacto; *(friend)* íntimo; *(connection)* estrecho; *(examination)* detallado, minucioso; *(weather)* bochornoso; *(atmosphere)* sofocante; *(room)* mal ventilado ▪ *adv* cerca; ~ **by,** ~ **at hand** *adj, adv* muy cerca; ~ **to** *prep* cerca de; **to have a ~ shave** *(fig)* escaparse por un pelo; **how ~ is Edinburgh to Glasgow?** ¿qué distancia hay de Edimburgo a Glasgow?; **at ~ quarters** de cerca ▪ *vt* cerrar; *(end)* concluir, terminar ▪ *vi (shop etc)* cerrar; *(end)* concluir(se), terminar(se) ▪ *n (end)* fin *m*, final *m*, conclusión *f*; **to bring sth to a ~** terminar algo

▸ **close down** *vi* cerrar definitivamente

▸ **close in** *vi (hunters)* acercarse rodeando, rodear; *(evening, night)* caer; *(fog)* cerrarse; **to ~ in on sb** rodear *or* cercar a algn; **the days are closing in** los días son cada vez más cortos

▸ **close off** *vt (area)* cerrar al tráfico *or* al público

closed [kləuzd] *adj (shop etc)* cerrado

closed-circuit ['kləuzd'sə:kɪt] *adj:* ~ **television** televisión *f* por circuito cerrado

closed shop *n empresa en la que todo el personal está afiliado a un sindicato*

close-knit ['kləus'nɪt] *adj (fig)* muy unido

closely ['kləuslɪ] *adv (study)* con detalle; *(listen)* con atención; *(watch)* de cerca; **we are ~ related** somos parientes cercanos; **a ~ guarded secret** un secreto rigurosamente guardado

close season [kləuz-] *n (Football)* temporada de descanso; *(Hunting)* veda

closet ['klɔzɪt] *n (cupboard)* armario, placar(d) *m (LAm)*

close-up ['kləusʌp] *n* primer plano

closing ['kləuzɪŋ] *adj (stages, remarks)* último, final; ~ **price** *(Stock Exchange)* cotización *f* de cierre

closing time *n* hora de cierre

closure ['kləuʒə^r] *n* cierre *m*

clot [klɔt] *n (gen: also:* **blood clot**) embolia; *(col: idiot)* imbécil *m/f* ▪ *vi (blood)* coagularse

cloth [klɔθ] *n (material)* tela, paño; *(table cloth)* mantel *m; (rag)* trapo

clothe [kləuð] *vt* vestir; *(fig)* revestir

clothes [kləuðz] *npl* ropa *sg*; **to put one's ~**

on vestirse, ponerse la ropa; **to take one's ~ off** desvestirse, desnudarse

clothes brush *n* cepillo (para la ropa)

clothes line *n* cuerda (para tender la ropa)

clothes peg, clothes pin *(US) n* pinza

clothing ['kləuðɪŋ] *n* = **clothes**

clotted cream ['klɔtɪd-] *n nata muy espesa*

cloud [klaud] *n* nube *f; (storm cloud)* nubarrón *m* ▪ *vt (liquid)* enturbiar; **every ~ has a silver lining** no hay mal que por bien no venga; **to ~ the issue** empañar el problema

▸ **cloud over** *vi (also fig)* nublarse

cloudburst ['klaudbə:st] *n* chaparrón *m*

cloud-cuckoo-land ['klaud'kuku:'lænd] *n* Babia

cloudy ['klaudɪ] *adj* nublado; *(liquid)* turbio

clout [klaut] *n (fig)* influencia, peso ▪ *vt* dar un tortazo a

clove [kləuv] *n* clavo; ~ **of garlic** diente *m* de ajo

clover ['kləuvə^r] *n* trébol *m*

clown [klaun] *n* payaso ▪ *vi (also:* **clown about, clown around**) hacer el payaso

cloying ['klɔɪɪŋ] *adj (taste)* empalagoso

club [klʌb] *n (society)* club *m; (weapon)* porra, cachiporra; *(also:* **golf club**) palo ▪ *vt* aporrear ▪ *vi:* **to ~ together** *(join forces)* unir fuerzas; **clubs** *npl (Cards)* tréboles *mpl*

club car *n (US Rail)* coche *m* salón

club class *n (Aviat)* clase *f* preferente

clubhouse ['klʌbhaus] *n local social, sobre todo en clubs deportivos*

club soda *n (US)* soda

cluck [klʌk] *vi* cloquear

clue [klu:] *n* pista; *(in crosswords)* indicación *f*; **I haven't a ~** no tengo ni idea

clued up, clued in *(US)* [klu:d-] *adj (col)* al tanto, al corriente

clueless ['klu:lɪs] *adj (col)* desorientado

clump [klʌmp] *n (of trees)* grupo

clumsy ['klʌmzɪ] *adj (person)* torpe; *(tool)* difícil de manejar

clung [klʌŋ] *pt, pp of* **cling**

cluster ['klʌstə^r] *n* grupo; *(Bot)* racimo ▪ *vi* agruparse, apiñarse

clutch [klʌtʃ] *n (Aut)* embrague *m; (pedal)* (pedal *m* de) embrague *m;* **to fall into sb's clutches** caer en las garras de algn ▪ *vt* agarrar

clutter ['klʌtə^r] *vt (also:* **clutter up**) atestar, llenar desordenadamente ▪ *n* desorden *m*, confusión *f*

CM *abbr (US)* = **North Mariana Islands**

cm *abbr (= centimetre)* cm

CNAA *n abbr (Brit: = Council for National Academic Awards)* organismo no universitario que otorga diplomas

CND n abbr (Brit: = Campaign for Nuclear Disarmament) plataforma pro desarme nuclear

CO n abbr = **commanding officer**; (Brit) = **Commonwealth Office** ■ abbr. (US) = **Colorado**

Co. abbr = **county**; **company**

c/o abbr (= care of) c/a, a/c

coach [kəʊtʃ] n (bus) autocar m (SP), autobús m; (horse-drawn) coche m; (ceremonial) carroza; (of train) vagón m, coche m; (Sport) entrenador(a) m(f), instructor(a) m(f) ■ vt (Sport) entrenar; (student) preparar, enseñar

coach trip n excursión f en autocar

coagulate [kəʊˈægjuleɪt] vi coagularse

coal [kəʊl] n carbón m

coal face n frente m de carbón

coalfield [ˈkəʊlfiːld] n yacimiento de carbón

coalition [kəʊəˈlɪʃən] n coalición f

coal man n carbonero

coalmine [ˈkəʊlmaɪn] n mina de carbón

coalminer [ˈkəʊlmaɪnəʳ] n minero (de carbón)

coalmining [ˈkeʊlmaɪnɪŋ] n minería (de carbón)

coarse [kɔːs] adj basto, burdo; (vulgar) grosero, ordinario

coast [kəʊst] n costa, litoral m ■ vi (Aut) ir en punto muerto

coastal [ˈkəʊstl] adj costero

coaster [ˈkəʊstəʳ] n buque m costero, barco de cabotaje

coastguard [ˈkəʊstgɑːd] n guardacostas m inv

coastline [ˈkəʊstlaɪn] n litoral m

coat [kəʊt] n (jacket) chaqueta, saco (LAm); (overcoat) abrigo; (of animal) pelo, lana; (of paint) mano f, capa ■ vt cubrir, revestir

coat hanger n percha, gancha (LAm)

coating [ˈkəʊtɪŋ] n capa, baño

coat of arms n escudo de armas

co-author [ˈkəʊˈɔːθəʳ] n coautor(a) m(f)

coax [kəʊks] vt engatusar

cob [kɒb] n see corn

cobbler [ˈkɒbləʳ] n zapatero (remendón)

cobbles [ˈkɒblz], **cobblestones** [ˈkɒblstəʊnz] npl adoquines mpl

COBOL [ˈkəʊbɒl] n COBOL m

cobra [ˈkəʊbrə] n cobra

cobweb [ˈkɒbwɛb] n telaraña

cocaine [kəˈkeɪn] n cocaína

cock [kɒk] n (rooster) gallo; (male bird) macho ■ vt (gun) amartillar

cock-a-hoop [kɒkəˈhuːp] adj: **to be ~** estar más contento que unas pascuas

cockatoo [kɒkəˈtuː] n cacatúa

cockerel [ˈkɒkərl] n gallito, gallo joven

cock-eyed [ˈkɒkaɪd] adj bizco; (fig: crooked) torcido; (: idea) disparatado

cockle [ˈkɒkl] n berberecho

cockney [ˈkɒknɪ] n habitante de ciertos barrios de Londres

cockpit [ˈkɒkpɪt] n (in aircraft) cabina

cockroach [ˈkɒkrəʊtʃ] n cucaracha

cocktail [ˈkɒkteɪl] n combinado, cóctel m; **prawn ~** cóctel m de gambas

cocktail cabinet n mueble-bar m

cocktail party n cóctel m

cocktail shaker [-ʃeɪkəʳ] n coctelera

cocky [ˈkɒkɪ] adj farruco, flamenco

cocoa [ˈkəʊkəʊ] n cacao; (drink) chocolate m

coconut [ˈkəʊkənʌt] n coco

cocoon [kəˈkuːn] n capullo

cod [kɒd] n bacalao

COD abbr = **cash on delivery**; (US) = **collect on delivery**

code [kəʊd] n código; (cipher) clave f; (Tel) prefijo; **~ of behaviour** código de conducta; **~ of practice** código profesional

codeine [ˈkəʊdiːn] n codeína

codger [kɒdʒəʳ] n (Brit col): **an old ~** un abuelo

codicil [ˈkɒdɪsɪl] n codicilo

codify [ˈkəʊdɪfaɪ] vt codificar

cod-liver oil [ˈkɒdlɪvəʳ-] n aceite m de hígado de bacalao

co-driver [ˈkəʊdraɪvəʳ] n (in race) copiloto m/f; (of lorry) segundo conductor m

co-ed [ˈkəʊɛd] adj abbr = **coeducational** ■ n abbr (US: = female student) alumna de una universidad mixta; (Brit: school) colegio mixto

coeducational [kəʊɛdjuˈkeɪʃnl] adj mixto

coerce [kəʊˈəːs] vt forzar, coaccionar

coercion [kəʊˈəːʃən] n coacción f

coexistence [ˈkəʊɪgˈzɪstəns] n coexistencia

C. of C. n abbr = **chamber of commerce**

C of E abbr = **Church of England**

coffee [ˈkɒfɪ] n café m; **white ~**, (US) **~ with cream** café con leche

coffee bar n (Brit) cafetería

coffee bean n grano de café

coffee break n descanso (para tomar café)

coffee cup n taza de café, pocillo (LAm)

coffeepot [ˈkɒfɪpɒt] n cafetera

coffee table n mesita baja

coffin [ˈkɒfɪn] n ataúd m

C of I abbr = **Church of Ireland**

C of S abbr = **Church of Scotland**

cog [kɒg] n diente m

cogent [ˈkəʊdʒənt] adj lógico, convincente

cognac [ˈkɒnjæk] n coñac m

cogwheel [ˈkɒgwiːl] n rueda dentada

cohabit [kəʊˈhæbɪt] vi (formal): **to ~ (with sb)** cohabitar (con algn)

coherent [kəʊˈhɪərənt] adj coherente

cohesion [kəʊˈhiːʒən] n cohesión f

cohesive [kəʊˈhiːsɪv] adj (fig) cohesivo, unido

COI *n abbr* (Brit: = *Central Office of Information*) servicio de información gubernamental

coil [kɔɪl] *n* rollo; (*of rope*) vuelta; (*of smoke*) espiral *f*; (*Aut, Elec*) bobina, carrete *m*; (*contraceptive*) DIU *m* ▪ *vt* enrollar

coin [kɔɪn] *n* moneda ▪ *vt* acuñar; (*word*) inventar, acuñar

coinage ['kɔɪnɪdʒ] *n* moneda

coin-box ['kɔɪnbɔks] *n* (Brit) caja recaudadora

coincide [kəʊɪn'saɪd] *vi* coincidir

coincidence [kəʊ'ɪnsɪdəns] *n* casualidad *f*, coincidencia

coin-operated ['kɔɪn'ɔpəreɪtɪd] *adj* (*machine*) que funciona con monedas

Coke® [kəʊk] *n* Coca Cola® *f*

coke [kəʊk] *n* (*coal*) coque *m*

Col. *abbr* (= *colonel*) col; (US) = **Colorado**

COLA *n abbr* (US: = *cost-of-living adjustment*) reajuste salarial de acuerdo con el coste de la vida

colander ['kɔləndə'] *n* escurridor *m*

cold [kəʊld] *adj* frío ▪ *n* frío; (*Med*) resfriado; **it's ~** hace frío; **to be ~** tener frío; **to catch a ~** coger un catarro, resfriarse, acatarrarse; **in ~ blood** a sangre fría; **the room's getting ~** está empezando a hacer frío en la habitación; **to give sb the ~ shoulder** tratar a algn con frialdad

cold-blooded ['kəʊld'blʌdɪd] *adj* (*Zool*) de sangre fría

cold cream *n* crema

coldly ['kəʊldlɪ] *adj* fríamente

cold sore *n* calentura, herpes *m* labial

cold sweat *n*: **to be in a ~ (about sth)** tener sudores fríos (por algo)

cold turkey *n* (*col*) mono

Cold War *n*: **the ~** la guerra fría

coleslaw ['kəʊlslɔː] *n* ensalada de col con zanahoria

colic ['kɔlɪk] *n* cólico

colicky ['kɔlɪkɪ] *adj*: **to be ~** tener un cólico

collaborate [kə'læbəreɪt] *vi* colaborar

collaboration [kəlæbə'reɪʃən] *n* colaboración *f*; (*Pol*) colaboracionismo

collaborator [kə'læbəreɪtə'] *n* colaborador(a) *m(f)*; (*Pol*) colaboracionista *m/f*

collage [kɔ'lɑːʒ] *n* collage *m*

collagen ['kɔlədʒən] *n* colágeno

collapse [kə'læps] *vi* (*gen*) hundirse, derrumbarse; (*Med*) sufrir un colapso ▪ *n* (*gen*) hundimiento; (*Med*) colapso; (*of government*) caída; (*of plans, scheme*) fracaso; (*of business*) ruina

collapsible [kə'læpsəbl] *adj* plegable

collar ['kɔlə'] *n* (*of coat, shirt*) cuello; (*for dog*) collar *m*; (*Tech*) collar *m* ▪ *vt* (*col: person*) agarrar; (: *object*) birlar

collarbone ['kɔləbəʊn] *n* clavícula

collate [kɔ'leɪt] *vt* cotejar

collateral [kɔ'lætərəl] *n* (*Comm*) garantía subsidiaria

collation [kə'leɪʃən] *n* colación *f*

colleague ['kɔliːg] *n* colega *m/f*, compañero(-a) *m(f)*

collect [kə'lɛkt] *vt* reunir; (*as a hobby*) coleccionar; (*Brit: call and pick up*) recoger; (*wages*) cobrar; (*debts*) recaudar; (*donations, subscriptions*) colectar ▪ *vi* (*crowd*) reunirse ▪ *adv*: **to call ~** (*US Tel*) llamar a cobro revertido; **to ~ one's thoughts** reponerse, recobrar el dominio de sí mismo; **~ on delivery (COD)** (US) entrega contra reembolso

collection [kə'lɛkʃən] *n* colección *f*; (*of fares, wages*) cobro; (*of post*) recogida

collective [kə'lɛktɪv] *adj* colectivo

collective bargaining *n* negociación *f* del convenio colectivo

collector [kə'lɛktə'] *n* coleccionista *m/f*; (*of taxes etc*) recaudador(a) *m(f)*; **~'s item** or **piece** pieza de coleccionista

college ['kɔlɪdʒ] *n* colegio; (*of technology, agriculture etc*) escuela

collide [kə'laɪd] *vi* chocar

collie ['kɔlɪ] *n* (*dog*) collie *m*, perro pastor escocés

colliery ['kɔlɪərɪ] *n* (Brit) mina de carbón

collision [kə'lɪʒən] *n* choque *m*, colisión *f*; **to be on a ~ course** (*also fig*) ir rumbo al desastre

colloquial [kə'ləʊkwɪəl] *adj* coloquial

collusion [kə'luːʒən] *n* confabulación *f*, connivencia; **in ~ with** en connivencia con

Colo. *abbr* (US) = **Colorado**

cologne [kə'ləʊn] *n* (*also*: **eau de cologne**) (agua de) colonia

Colombia [kə'lɔmbɪə] *n* Colombia

Colombian [kə'lɔmbɪən] *adj, n* colombiano(-a) *m(f)*

colon ['kəʊlən] *n* (*sign*) dos puntos; (*Med*) colon *m*

colonel ['kɜːnl] *n* coronel *m*

colonial [kə'ləʊnɪəl] *adj* colonial

colonize ['kɔlənaɪz] *vt* colonizar

colonnade [kɔlə'neɪd] *n* columnata

colony ['kɔlənɪ] *n* colonia

color ['kʌlə'] (US) = **colour**

Colorado beetle [kɔlə'rɑːdəʊ-] *n* escarabajo de la patata

colossal [kə'lɔsl] *adj* colosal

colour, color (US) ['kʌlə'] *n* color *m* ▪ *vt* colorear, pintar; (*dye*) teñir ▪ *vi* (*blush*) sonrojarse; **colours** *npl* (*of party, club*) colores *mpl*

colour bar, color bar (US) *n* segregación *f* racial

colour-blind, color-blind (US) ['kʌləblaɪnd] *adj* daltónico

coloured, colored (US) ['kʌləd] *adj* de color; (*photo*) en color; (*of race*) de color

colour film, color film (US) *n* película en color

colourful, colorful (US) ['kʌləful] *adj* lleno de color; (*person*) pintoresco

colouring, coloring (US) ['kʌlərɪŋ] *n* colorido, color; (*substance*) colorante *m*

colourless, colorless (US) ['kʌlələs] *adj* incoloro, sin color

colour scheme, color scheme (US) *n* combinación *f* de colores

colour supplement *n* (*Brit Press*) suplemento semanal *or* dominical

colour television, color television (US) *n* televisión *f* en color

colt [kəult] *n* potro

column ['kɔləm] *n* columna; (*fashion column, sports column etc*) sección *f*, columna; **the editorial ~** el editorial

columnist ['kɔləmnɪst] *n* columnista *m/f*

coma ['kəumə] *n* coma *m*

comb [kəum] *n* peine *m*; (*ornamental*) peineta ■ *vt* (*hair*) peinar; (*area*) registrar a fondo, peinar

combat ['kɔmbæt] *n* combate *m* ■ *vt* combatir

combination [kɔmbɪ'neɪʃən] *n* (*gen*) combinación *f*

combination lock *n* cerradura de combinación

combine [kəm'baɪn] *vt* combinar; (*qualities*) reunir ■ *vi* combinarse ■ *n* ['kɔmbaɪn] (*Econ*) cartel *m*; (*also:* **combine harvester**) cosechadora; **a combined effort** un esfuerzo conjunto

combine harvester *n* cosechadora

combo ['kɔmbəu] *n* (*jazz etc*) conjunto

combustion [kəm'bʌstʃən] *n* combustión *f*

🔘 KEYWORD

come [kʌm] (*pt* **came**, *pp* **come**) *vi* **1** (*movement towards*) venir; **to come running** venir corriendo; **come with me** ven conmigo **2** (*arrive*) llegar; **he's come here to work** ha venido aquí para trabajar; **to come home** volver a casa; **we've just come from Seville** acabamos de llegar de Sevilla; **coming!** ¡voy! **3** (*reach*): **to come to** llegar a; **the bill came to £40** la cuenta ascendía a cuarenta libras **4** (*occur*): **an idea came to me** se me ocurrió una idea; **if it comes to it** llegado el caso **5** (*be, become*): **to come loose/undone** *etc* aflojarse/desabrocharse, desatarse *etc*;

I've come to like him por fin ha llegado a gustarme

▶ **come about** *vi* suceder, ocurrir

▶ **come across** *vt fus* (*person*) encontrarse con; (*thing*) encontrar

■ *vi*: **to come across well/badly** causar buena/mala impresión

▶ **come away** *vi* (*leave*) marcharse; (*become detached*) desprenderse

▶ **come back** *vi* (*return*) volver; (*reply*): **can I come back to you on that one?** volvamos sobre ese punto

▶ **come by** *vt fus* (*acquire*) conseguir

▶ **come down** *vi* (*price*) bajar; (*building*) derrumbarse; (*be demolished*) ser derribado

▶ **come forward** *vi* presentarse

▶ **come from** *vt fus* (*place, source*) ser de

▶ **come in** *vi* (*visitor*) entrar; (*train, report*) llegar; (*fashion*) ponerse de moda; (*on deal etc*) entrar

▶ **come in for** *vt fus* (*criticism etc*) recibir

▶ **come into** *vt fus* (*money*) heredar; (*be involved*) tener que ver con; **to come into fashion** ponerse de moda

▶ **come off** *vi* (*button*) soltarse, desprenderse; (*attempt*) salir bien

▶ **come on** *vi* (*pupil, work, project*) marchar; (*lights*) encenderse; (*electricity*) volver; **come on!** ¡vamos!

▶ **come out** *vi* (*fact*) salir a la luz; (*book, sun*) salir; (*stain*) quitarse; **to come out (on strike)** declararse en huelga; **to come out for/against** declararse a favor/en contra de

▶ **come over** *vt fus*: **I don't know what's come over him!** ¡no sé lo que le pasa!

▶ **come round** *vi* (*after faint, operation*) volver en sí

▶ **come through** *vi* (*survive*) sobrevivir; (*telephone call*): **the call came through** recibimos la llamada

▶ **come to** *vi* (*wake*) volver en sí; (*total*) sumar; **how much does it come to?** ¿cuánto es en total?, ¿a cuánto asciende?

▶ **come under** *vt fus* (*heading*) entrar dentro de; (*influence*) estar bajo

▶ **come up** *vi* (*sun*) salir; (*problem*) surgir; (*event*) aproximarse; (*in conversation*) mencionarse

▶ **come up against** *vt fus* (*resistance etc*) tropezar con

▶ **come up to** *vt fus* llegar hasta; **the film didn't come up to our expectations** la película no fue tan buena como esperábamos

▶ **come up with** *vt fus* (*idea*) sugerir; (*money*) conseguir

▶ **come upon** *vt fus* (*find*) dar con

comeback ['kʌmbæk] n (reaction) reacción f; (response) réplica; **to make a ~** (Theat) volver a las tablas

comedian [kə'mi:dɪən] n humorista m

comedienne [kəmi:dɪ'ɛn] n humorista

comedown ['kʌmdaun] n revés m

comedy ['kɔmɪdɪ] n comedia

comet ['kɔmɪt] n cometa m

comeuppance [kʌm'ʌpəns] n: **to get one's ~** llevar su merecido

comfort ['kʌmfət] n comodidad f, confort m; (well-being) bienestar m; (solace) consuelo; (relief) alivio ▪ vt consolar; see also **comforts**

comfortable ['kʌmfətəbl] adj cómodo; (income) adecuado; (majority) suficiente; **I don't feel very ~ about it** la cosa me tiene algo preocupado

comfortably ['kʌmfətəblɪ] adv (sit) cómodamente; (live) holgadamente

comforter ['kʌmfətəʳ] n (US: pacifier) chupete m; (: bed cover) colcha

comforts ['kʌmfəts] npl comodidades fpl

comfort station n (US) servicios mpl

comic ['kɔmɪk] adj (also: **comical**) cómico, gracioso ▪ n (magazine) tebeo; (for adults) cómic m

comic strip n tira cómica

coming ['kʌmɪŋ] n venida, llegada ▪ adj que viene; (next) próximo; (future) venidero; **~(s) and going(s)** n(pl) ir y venir m, ajetreo; **in the ~ weeks** en las próximas semanas

Comintern ['kɔmɪntə:n] n Comintern m

comma ['kɔmə] n coma

command [kə'mɑ:nd] n orden f, mandato; (Mil: authority) mando; (mastery) dominio; (Comput) orden f, comando ▪ vt (troops) mandar; (give orders to) mandar, ordenar; (be able to get) disponer de; (deserve) merecer; **to have at one's ~** (money, resources etc) disponer de; **to have/take ~ of** estar al/asumir el mando de

command economy n economía dirigida

commandeer [kɔmən'dɪəʳ] vt requisar

commander [kə'mɑ:ndəʳ] n (Mil) comandante m/f, jefe(-a) m(f)

commanding [kə'mɑ:ndɪŋ] adj (appearance) imponente; (voice, tone) imperativo; (lead) abrumador(-a); (position) dominante

commanding officer n comandante m

commandment [kə'mɑ:ndmənt] n (Rel) mandamiento

command module n módulo de mando

commando [kə'mɑ:ndəu] n comando

commemorate [kə'mɛməreɪt] vt conmemorar

commemoration [kəmɛmə'reɪʃən] n conmemoración f

commemorative [kə'mɛmərətɪv] adj conmemorativo

commence [kə'mɛns] vt, vi comenzar

commend [kə'mɛnd] vt (praise) elogiar, alabar; (recommend) recomendar; (entrust) encomendar

commendable [kə'mɛndəbl] adj encomiable

commendation [kɔmɛn'deɪʃən] n (for bravery etc) elogio, encomio

commensurate [kə'mɛnʃərɪt] adj: **~ with** en proporción a

comment ['kɔmɛnt] n comentario ▪ vt: **to ~ that** comentar or observar que ▪ vi: **to ~ (on)** comentar, hacer comentarios (sobre); **"no ~"** "no tengo nada que decir", "sin comentarios"

commentary ['kɔmɛntərɪ] n comentario

commentator ['kɔmənteɪtəʳ] n comentarista m/f

commerce ['kɔmə:s] n comercio

commercial [kə'mə:ʃəl] adj comercial ▪ n (TV) anuncio

commercial bank n banco comercial

commercial break n intermedio para publicidad

commercialism [kə'mə:ʃəlɪzəm] n comercialismo

commercial television n televisión f comercial

commercial vehicle n vehículo comercial

commiserate [kə'mɪzəreɪt] vi: **to ~ with** compadecerse de, condolerse de

commission [kə'mɪʃən] n (committee, fee, order for work of art etc) comisión f; (act) perpetración f ▪ vt (Mil) nombrar; (work of art) encargar; **out of ~** (machine) fuera de servicio; **~ of inquiry** comisión f investigadora; **I get 10% ~** me dan el diez por ciento de comisión; **to ~ sb to do sth** encargar a algn que haga algo; **to ~ sth from sb** (painting etc) encargar algo a algn

commissionaire [kəmɪʃə'nɛəʳ] n (Brit) portero, conserje m

commissioner [kə'mɪʃənəʳ] n comisario; (Police) comisario m de policía

commit [kə'mɪt] vt (act) cometer; (to sb's care) entregar; **to ~ o.s. (to do)** comprometerse (a hacer); **to ~ suicide** suicidarse; **to ~ sb for trial** remitir a algn al tribunal

commitment [kə'mɪtmənt] n compromiso

committed [kə'mɪtɪd] adj (writer, politician etc) comprometido

committee [kə'mɪtɪ] n comité m; **to be on a ~** ser miembro(-a) de un comité

committee meeting n reunión f del comité

commodious [kə'məudɪəs] adj grande, espacioso

commodity [kə'mɒdɪtɪ] *n* mercancía
commodity exchange *n* bolsa de productos *or* de mercancías
commodity market *n* mercado de productos básicos
commodore ['kɒmədɔːʳ] *n* comodoro
common ['kɒmən] *adj* (*gen*) común; (*pej*) ordinario ■ *n* campo común; **in ~** en común; **in ~ use** de uso corriente
common cold *n*: **the ~** el resfriado
common denominator *n* común denominador *m*
commoner ['kɒmənəʳ] *n* plebeyo(-a)
common land *n* campo comunal, ejido
common law *n* ley *f* consuetudinaria
common-law ['kɒmənlɔː] *adj*: **~ wife** esposa de hecho
commonly ['kɒmənlɪ] *adv* comúnmente
Common Market *n* Mercado Común
commonplace ['kɒmənpleɪs] *adj* corriente
commonroom ['kɒmənrum] *n* sala de reunión
Commons ['kɒmənz] *npl* (*Brit Pol*): **the ~** (la Cámara de) los Comunes
common sense *n* sentido común
Commonwealth ['kɒmənwɛlθ] *n*: **the ~** la Comunidad (Británica) de Naciones, la Commonwealth; *ver nota*

● **COMMONWEALTH**

La *Commonwealth* es la asociación de estados soberanos independientes y territorios asociados que formaban parte del antiguo Imperio Británico. Éste pasó a llamarse así después de la Segunda Guerra Mundial, aunque ya desde 1931 se le conocía como "British Commonwealth of Nations". Todos los estados miembros reconocen al monarca británico como "Head of the Commonwealth".

commotion [kə'məuʃən] *n* tumulto, confusión *f*
communal ['kɒmjuːnl] *adj* comunal; (*kitchen*) común
commune ['kɒmjuːn] *n* (*group*) comuna ■ *vi* [kə'mjuːn]: **to ~ with** comunicarse con
communicate [kə'mjuːnɪkeɪt] *vt* comunicar ■ *vi*: **to ~ (with)** comunicarse (con)
communication [kəmjuːnɪ'keɪʃən] *n* comunicación *f*
communication cord *n* (*Brit*) timbre *m* de alarma
communications network *n* red *f* de comunicaciones
communications satellite *n* satélite *m* de comunicaciones
communicative [kə'mjuːnɪkətɪv] *adj* comunicativo
communion [kə'mjuːnɪən] *n* (*also*: **Holy Communion**) comunión *f*
communiqué [kə'mjuːnɪkeɪ] *n* comunicado, parte *m*
communism ['kɒmjunɪzəm] *n* comunismo
communist ['kɒmjunɪst] *adj, n* comunista *m/f*
community [kə'mjuːnɪtɪ] *n* comunidad *f*; (*large group*) colectividad *f*; (*local*) vecindario
community centre *n* centro social
community chest *n* (*US*) fondo social
community health centre *n* centro médico, casa de salud
community spirit *n* civismo
commutation ticket [kɒmju'teɪʃən-] *n* (*US*) billete *m* de abono
commute [kə'mjuːt] *vi* *viajar a diario de casa al trabajo* ■ *vt* conmutar
commuter [kə'mjuːtəʳ] *n* *persona que viaja a diario de casa al trabajo*
compact [kəm'pækt] *adj* compacto; (*style*) conciso; (*dense*) apretado ■ *n* ['kɒmpækt] (*pact*) pacto; (*also*: **powder compact**) polvera
compact disc *n* compact disc *m*, disco compacto
compact disc player *n* lector *m* or reproductor *m* de discos compactos
companion [kəm'pænɪən] *n* compañero(-a)
companionship [kəm'pænjənʃɪp] *n* compañerismo
companionway [kəm'pænjənweɪ] *n* (*Naut*) escalerilla
company ['kʌmpənɪ] *n* (*gen*) compañía; (*Comm*) empresa, compañía; **to keep sb ~** acompañar a algn; **Smith and C~** Smith y Compañía
company car *n* coche *m* de la empresa
company director *n* director(a) *m(f)* de empresa
company secretary *n* (*Brit*) administrador(a) *m(f)* de empresa
comparable ['kɒmpərəbl] *adj* comparable
comparative [kəm'pærətɪv] *adj* (*freedom, luxury, cost*) relativo; (*study, linguistics*) comparado
comparatively [kəm'pærətɪvlɪ] *adv* (*relatively*) relativamente
compare [kəm'pɛəʳ] *vt* comparar ■ *vi*: **to ~ (with)** poder compararse (con); **compared with** *or* **to** comparado con *or* a; **how do the prices ~?** ¿cómo son los precios en comparación?
comparison [kəm'pærɪsn] *n* comparación *f*; **in ~ (with)** en comparación (con)

compartment [kəm'pɑ:tmənt] *n* compartim(i)ento; *(Rail)* departamento, compartimento

compass ['kʌmpəs] *n* brújula; **compasses** *npl* compás *m*; **within the ~ of** al alcance de

compassion [kəm'pæʃən] *n* compasión *f*

compassionate [kəm'pæʃənɪt] *adj* compasivo; **on ~ grounds** por compasión

compassionate leave *n* permiso por asuntos familiares

compatibility [kəmpætɪ'bɪlɪtɪ] *n* compatibilidad *f*

compatible [kəm'pætɪbl] *adj* compatible

compel [kəm'pɛl] *vt* obligar

compelling [kəm'pɛlɪŋ] *adj (fig: argument)* convincente

compendium [kəm'pɛndɪəm] *n* compendio

compensate ['kɔmpənseɪt] *vt* compensar ■ *vi*: **to ~ for** compensar

compensation [kɔmpən'seɪʃən] *n (for loss)* indemnización *f*

compère ['kɔmpɛə'] *n* presentador(a) *m(f)*

compete [kəm'pi:t] *vi (take part)* competir; *(vie with)* competir, hacer la competencia

competence ['kɔmpɪtəns] *n* capacidad *f*, aptitud *f*

competent ['kɔmpɪtənt] *adj* competente, capaz

competing [kəm'pi:tɪŋ] *adj (rival)* competidor(-a); *(ideas)* contrapuesto

competition [kɔmpɪ'tɪʃən] *n (contest)* concurso; *(Sport)* competición *f*; *(Econ: rivalry)* competencia; **in ~ with** en competencia con

competitive [kəm'pɛtɪtɪv] *adj (Econ, Sport)* competitivo; *(spirit)* competidor(a), de competencia; *(selection)* por concurso

competitor [kəm'pɛtɪtə'] *n (rival)* competidor(a) *m(f)*; *(participant)* concursante *m/f*

compile [kəm'paɪl] *vt* recopilar

complacency [kəm'pleɪsnsɪ] *n* autosatisfacción *f*

complacent [kəm'pleɪsənt] *adj* autocomplaciente

complain [kəm'pleɪn] *vi (gen)* quejarse; *(Comm)* reclamar

complaint [kəm'pleɪnt] *n (gen)* queja; *(Comm)* reclamación *f*; *(Law)* demanda, querella; *(Med)* enfermedad *f*

complement ['kɔmplɪmənt] *n* complemento; *(esp ship's crew)* dotación *f* ■ *vt* ['kɔmplɪmɛnt] *(enhance)* complementar

complementary [kɔmplɪ'mɛntərɪ] *adj* complementario

complete [kəm'pli:t] *adj (full)* completo; *(finished)* acabado ■ *vt (fulfil)* completar; *(finish)* acabar; *(a form)* rellenar; **it's a ~**

disaster es un desastre total

completely [kəm'pli:tlɪ] *adv* completamente

completion [kəm'pli:ʃən] *n (gen)* conclusión *f*, terminación *f*; **to be nearing ~** estar a punto de terminarse; **on ~ of contract** cuando se realice el contrato

complex ['kɔmplɛks] *adj* complejo ■ *n (gen)* complejo

complexion [kəm'plɛkʃən] *n (of face)* tez *f*, cutis *m*; *(fig)* aspecto

complexity [kəm'plɛksɪtɪ] *n* complejidad *f*

compliance [kəm'plaɪəns] *n (submission)* sumisión *f*; *(agreement)* conformidad *f*; **in ~ with** de acuerdo con

compliant [kəm'plaɪənt] *adj* sumiso; conforme

complicate ['kɔmplɪkeɪt] *vt* complicar

complicated ['kɔmplɪkeɪtɪd] *adj* complicado

complication [kɔmplɪ'keɪʃən] *n* complicación *f*

complicity [kəm'plɪsɪtɪ] *n* complicidad *f*

compliment ['kɔmplɪmənt] *n (formal)* cumplido; *(flirtation)* piropo ■ *vt* felicitar; **compliments** *npl* saludos *mpl*; **to pay sb a ~** *(formal)* hacer cumplidos a algn; *(flirt)* piropear, echar piropos a algn; **to ~ sb (on sth/on doing sth)** felicitar a algn (por algo/por haber hecho algo)

complimentary [kɔmplɪ'mɛntərɪ] *adj* elogioso; *(copy)* de regalo; **~ ticket** invitación *f*

compliments slip *n* saluda *m*

comply [kəm'plaɪ] *vi*: **to ~ with** acatar

component [kəm'pəunənt] *adj* componente ■ *n (Tech)* pieza, componente *m*

compose [kəm'pəuz] *vt* componer; **to be composed of** componerse de, constar de; **to ~ o.s.** tranquilizarse

composed [kəm'pəuzd] *adj* sosegado

composer [kəm'pəuzə'] *n (Mus)* compositor(a) *m(f)*

composite ['kɔmpəzɪt] *adj* compuesto; **~ motion** *(Comm)* moción *f* compuesta

composition [kɔmpə'zɪʃən] *n* composición *f*

compositor [kəm'pɔzɪtə'] *n (Typ)* cajista *m/f*

compos mentis ['kɔmpəs'mɛntɪs] *adj*: **to be ~** estar en su sano juicio

compost ['kɔmpɔst] *n* abono

compost heap *n montón de basura orgánica para abono*

composure [kəm'pəuʒə'] *n* serenidad *f*, calma

compound ['kɔmpaund] *n (Chem)* compuesto; *(Ling)* término compuesto; *(enclosure)* recinto ■ *adj (gen)* compuesto; *(fracture)* complicado ■ *vt* [kəm'paund] *(fig: problem, difficulty)* agravar

comprehend [kɔmprɪ'hɛnd] *vt* comprender

comprehension [kɔmprɪ'hɛnʃən] *n*
comprensión *f*
comprehensive [kɔmprɪ'hɛnsɪv] *adj* (*broad*)
extenso; (*general*) de conjunto; **~ (school)** *n*
centro estatal de enseñanza secundaria, ≈ Instituto
Nacional de Bachillerato (*SP*); *ver nota*

○ **COMPREHENSIVE SCHOOL**
○
○   En los años 60 se creó un nuevo tipo
○   de centro educativo de enseñanza
○   secundaria (aproximadamente de los
○   once años en adelante) denominado
○   *comprehensive school*, abierto a todos los
○   alumnos independientemente de sus
○   capacidades, con el que se intentó poner
○   fin a la división tradicional entre centros
○   de enseñanzas teóricas para acceder a la
○   educación superior ("grammar schools")
○   y otros de enseñanzas básicamente
○   profesionales ("secondary modern
○   schools").

comprehensive insurance policy *n* seguro
a todo riesgo
compress [kəm'prɛs] *vt* comprimir; (*Inform*)
comprimir ▪ *n* ['kɔmprɛs] (*Med*) compresa
compression [kəm'prɛʃən] *n* compresión *f*
comprise [kəm'praɪz] *vt* (*also*: **be comprised
of**) comprender, constar de
compromise ['kɔmprəmaɪz] *n* solución
f intermedia; (*agreement*) arreglo ▪ *vt*
comprometer ▪ *vi* transigir, transar (*LAm*)
▪ *cpd* (*decision, solution*) de término medio
compulsion [kəm'pʌlʃən] *n* obligación *f*;
under ~ a la fuerza, por obligación
compulsive [kəm'pʌlsɪv] *adj* compulsivo
compulsory [kəm'pʌlsərɪ] *adj* obligatorio
compulsory purchase *n* expropiación *f*
compunction [kəm'pʌŋkʃən] *n* escrúpulo;
to have no ~ about doing sth no tener
escrúpulos en hacer algo
computer [kəm'pjuːtəʳ] *n* ordenador *m*,
computador *m*, computadora
computer game *n* juego de ordenador
computerize [kəm'pjuːtəraɪz] *vt* (*data*)
computerizar; (*system*) informatizar
computer language *n* lenguaje *m* de
ordenador *or* computadora
computer literate *adj*: **to be ~** tener
conocimientos de informática a nivel de
usuario
computer peripheral *n* periférico
computer program *n* programa *m*
informático *or* de ordenador
computer programmer *n* programador(a)
m(f)

computer programming *n* programación *f*
computer science *n* informática
computing [kəm'pjuːtɪŋ] *n* (*activity*)
informática
comrade ['kɔmrɪd] *n* compañero(-a)
comradeship ['kɔmrɪdʃɪp] *n* camaradería,
compañerismo
comsat® ['kɔmsæt] *n abbr*
= **communications satellite**
con [kɔn] *vt* timar, estafar ▪ *n* timo, estafa;
to ~ sb into doing sth (*col*) engañar a algn
para que haga algo
concave ['kɔn'keɪv] *adj* cóncavo
conceal [kən'siːl] *vt* ocultar; (*thoughts etc*)
disimular
concede [kən'siːd] *vt* reconocer; (*game*) darse
por vencido en; (*territory*) ceder ▪ *vi* darse
por vencido
conceit [kən'siːt] *n* orgullo, presunción *f*
conceited [kən'siːtɪd] *adj* orgulloso
conceivable [kən'siːvəbl] *adj* concebible;
it is ~ that ... es posible que ...
conceivably [kɔn'siːvəblɪ] *adv*: **he may ~ be
right** es posible que tenga razón
conceive [kən'siːv] *vt, vi* concebir; **to ~ of
sth/of doing sth** imaginar algo/imaginarse
haciendo algo
concentrate ['kɔnsəntreɪt] *vi* concentrarse
▪ *vt* concentrar
concentration [kɔnsən'treɪʃən] *n*
concentración *f*
concentration camp *n* campo de
concentración
concentric [kən'sɛntrɪk] *adj* concéntrico
concept ['kɔnsɛpt] *n* concepto
conception [kən'sɛpʃən] *n* (*idea*) concepto,
idea; (*Biol*) concepción *f*
concern [kən'səːn] *n* (*matter*) asunto; (*Comm*)
empresa; (*anxiety*) preocupación *f* ▪ *vt* tener
que ver con; (*affect*) atañer, concernir; **to
be concerned (about)** interesarse (por),
preocuparse (por); **to be concerned with**
tratar de; **"to whom it may ~"** "a quien
corresponda"; **the department concerned**
(*under discussion*) el departamento en cuestión;
(*relevant*) el departamento competente; **as
far as I am concerned** en cuanto a mí, por lo
que a mí se refiere
concerning [kən'səːnɪŋ] *prep* sobre, acerca de
concert ['kɔnsət] *n* concierto
concerted [kən'səːtəd] *adj* (*efforts etc*)
concertado
concert hall *n* sala de conciertos
concertina [kɔnsə'tiːnə] *n* concertina
concerto [kən'tʃəːtəu] *n* concierto
concession [kən'sɛʃən] *n* concesión *f*; (*price
concession*) descuento; **tax ~** privilegio fiscal

concessionaire [kənsɛʃə'nɛəʳ] n
concesionario(-a)
concessionary [kən'sɛʃənərɪ] adj (ticket, fare)
con descuento, a precio reducido
conciliation [kənsɪlɪ'eɪʃən] n conciliación f
conciliatory [kən'sɪlɪətrɪ] adj conciliador(a)
concise [kən'saɪs] adj conciso
conclave ['kɒnkleɪv] n cónclave m
conclude [kən'kluːd] vt (finish) concluir;
(treaty etc) firmar; (agreement) llegar a; (decide):
to ~ that ... llegar a la conclusión de que ...
■ vi (events) concluir, terminar
concluding [kən'kluːdɪŋ] adj (remarks etc)
final
conclusion [kən'kluːʒən] n conclusión f;
to come to the ~ that llegar a la conclusión
de que
conclusive [kən'kluːsɪv] adj decisivo,
concluyente
conclusively [kən'kluːsɪvlɪ] adv
concluyentemente
concoct [kən'kɒkt] vt (food, drink) preparar;
(story) inventar; (plot) tramar
concoction [kən'kɒkʃən] n (food) mezcla;
(drink) brebaje m
concord ['kɒnkɔːd] n (harmony) concordia;
(treaty) acuerdo
concourse ['kɒŋkɔːs] n (hall) vestíbulo
concrete ['kɒnkriːt] n hormigón m ■ adj
concreto
concrete mixer n hormigonera
concur [kən'kəːʳ] vi estar de acuerdo
concurrently [kən'kʌrntlɪ] adv al mismo
tiempo
concussion [kən'kʌʃən] n conmoción f
cerebral
condemn [kən'dɛm] vt condenar
condemnation [kɒndɛm'neɪʃən] n (gen)
condena; (blame) censura
condensation [kɒndɛn'seɪʃən] n
condensación f
condense [kən'dɛns] vi condensarse ■ vt
condensar; (text) abreviar
condensed milk n leche f condensada
condescend [kɒndɪ'sɛnd] vi condescender;
to ~ to sb tratar a algn con condescendencia;
to ~ to do sth dignarse hacer algo
condescending [kɒndɪ'sɛndɪŋ] adj superior
condition [kən'dɪʃən] n condición f; (of
health) estado; (disease) enfermedad f ■ vt
condicionar; **on ~ that** a condición (de)
que; **weather conditions** condiciones
atmosféricas; **in good/poor ~** en buenas/
malas condiciones, en buen/mal estado;
conditions of sale condiciones de venta
conditional [kən'dɪʃənl] adj condicional
conditioned reflex [kən'dɪʃənd-] n reflejo

condicionado
conditioner [kən'dɪʃənəʳ] n (for hair)
suavizante m, acondicionador m
condo ['kɒndəu] n abbr (US col)
= **condominium**
condolences [kən'dəulənsɪz] npl pésame msg
condom ['kɒndəm] n condón m
condominium [kɒndə'mɪnɪəm] n (US:
building) bloque m de pisos or apartamentos
(propiedad de quienes lo habitan), condominio
(LAm); (: apartment) piso or apartamento
(en propiedad), condominio (LAm)
condone [kən'dəun] vt condonar
conducive [kən'djuːsɪv] adj: **~ to**
conducente a
conduct ['kɒndʌkt] n conducta,
comportamiento ■ vt [kən'dʌkt] (lead)
conducir; (manage) llevar, dirigir; (Mus)
dirigir ■ vi (Mus) llevar la batuta; **to ~ o.s.**
comportarse
conducted tour n (Brit) visita con guía
conductor [kən'dʌktəʳ] n (of orchestra)
director(a) m(f); (US: on train) revisor(a) m(f);
(on bus) cobrador m; (Elec) conductor m
cone [kəun] n cono; (pine cone) piña; (for ice
cream) cucurucho
confectioner [kən'fɛkʃənəʳ] n (of cakes)
pastelero(-a); (of sweets) confitero(-a); **~'s
(shop)** n pastelería; confitería
confectionery [kən'fɛkʃənrɪ] n pasteles mpl;
dulces mpl
confederate [kən'fɛdrɪt] adj confederado
■ n (pej) cómplice m/f; (US History)
confederado(-a)
confederation [kənfɛdə'reɪʃən] n
confederación f
confer [kən'fəːʳ] vt: **~ (on)** otorgar (a) ■ vi
conferenciar; **to ~ (with sb about sth)**
consultar (con algn sobre algo)
conference ['kɒnfərns] n (meeting) reunión f;
(convention) congreso; **to be in ~** estar en una
reunión
conference room n sala de conferencias
confess [kən'fɛs] vt confesar ■ vi confesar;
(Rel) confesarse
confession [kən'fɛʃən] n confesión f
confessional [kən'fɛʃənl] n confesionario
confessor [kən'fɛsəʳ] n confesor m
confetti [kən'fɛtɪ] n confeti m
confide [kən'faɪd] vi: **to ~ in** confiar en
confidence ['kɒnfɪdns] n (gen: also: **self-
confidence**) confianza; (secret) confidencia;
in ~ (speak, write) en confianza; **to have
(every) ~ that** estar seguro or confiado de
que; **motion of no ~** moción f de censura;
to tell sb sth in strict ~ decir algo a algn de
manera confidencial

confidence trick n timo
confident ['kɒnfɪdənt] adj seguro de sí mismo
confidential [kɒnfɪ'dɛnʃəl] adj confidencial; (secretary) de confianza
confidentiality [kɒnfɪdɛnʃɪ'ælɪtɪ] n confidencialidad f
configuration [kənfɪgju'reɪʃən] n (Comput) configuración f
confine [kən'faɪn] vt (limit) limitar; (shut up) encerrar; **to ~ o.s. to doing sth** limitarse a hacer algo
confined [kən'faɪnd] adj (space) reducido
confinement [kən'faɪnmənt] n (prison) reclusión f; (Med) parto; **in solitary ~** incomunicado
confines ['kɒnfaɪnz] npl confines mpl
confirm [kən'fə:m] vt confirmar
confirmation [kɒnfə'meɪʃən] n confirmación f
confirmed [kən'fə:md] adj empedernido
confiscate ['kɒnfɪskeɪt] vt confiscar
confiscation [kɒnfɪs'keɪʃən] n incautación f
conflagration [kɒnflə'greɪʃən] n conflagración f
conflict ['kɒnflɪkt] n conflicto ■ vi [kən'flɪkt] (opinions) estar reñido; (reports, evidence) contradecirse
conflicting [kən'flɪktɪŋ] adj (reports, evidence, opinions) contradictorio
conform [kən'fɔ:m] vi: **to ~ to** (laws) someterse a; (usages, mores) amoldarse a; (standards) ajustarse a
conformist [kən'fɔ:mɪst] n conformista m/f
confound [kən'faund] vt confundir; (amaze) pasmar
confounded [kən'faundɪd] adj condenado
confront [kən'frʌnt] vt (problems) hacer frente a; (enemy, danger) enfrentarse con
confrontation [kɒnfrən'teɪʃən] n enfrentamiento, confrontación f
confrontational [kɒnfrən'teɪʃənəl] adj conflictivo
confuse [kən'fju:z] vt (perplex) desconcertar; (mix up) confundir
confused [kən'fju:zd] adj confuso; (person) desconcertado; **to get ~** desconcertarse; (muddled up) hacerse un lío
confusing [kən'fju:zɪŋ] adj confuso
confusion [kən'fju:ʒən] n confusión f
congeal [kən'dʒi:l] vi coagularse
congenial [kən'dʒi:nɪəl] adj agradable
congenital [kən'dʒɛnɪtl] adj congénito
congested [kən'dʒɛstɪd] adj (gen) atestado; (telephone lines) saturado
congestion [kən'dʒɛstʃən] n congestión f
congestion charge n, **congestion charges** ■ npl tasa por congestión

conglomerate [kən'glɒmərət] n (Comm, Geo) conglomerado
conglomeration [kənglɒmə'reɪʃən] n conglomeración f
Congo ['kɒŋgəu] n (state) Congo
congratulate [kən'grætjuleɪt] vt felicitar
congratulations [kəngrætju'leɪʃə nz] npl: **~ (on)** felicitaciones fpl (por); **~!** ¡enhorabuena!, ¡felicidades!
congregate ['kɒŋgrɪgeɪt] vi congregarse
congregation [kɒŋgrɪ'geɪʃən] n (in church) fieles mpl
congress ['kɒŋgrɛs] n congreso; (US Pol): **C~** el Congreso (de los Estados Unidos); ver nota

● **CONGRESS**
●
● En el Congreso de los Estados Unidos
● (Congress) se elaboran y aprueban las
● leyes federales. Consta de dos cámaras:
● la Cámara de Representantes ("House of
● Representatives"), cuyos 435 miembros
● son elegidos cada dos años por voto
● popular directo y en número proporcional
● a los habitantes de cada estado, y el
● Senado ("Senate"), con 100 senadores
● ("senators"), 2 por estado, de los que un
● tercio se elige cada dos años y el resto
● cada seis.

congressman ['kɒŋgrɛsmən] n (US) diputado, miembro del Congreso
congresswoman ['kɒŋgrɛswumən] n (US) diputada, miembro f del Congreso
conical ['kɒnɪkl] adj cónico
conifer ['kɒnɪfəʳ] n conífera
coniferous [kə'nɪfərəs] adj (forest) conífero
conjecture [kən'dʒɛktʃəʳ] n conjetura
conjugal ['kɒndʒugl] adj conyugal
conjugate ['kɒndʒugeɪt] vt conjugar
conjunction [kən'dʒʌŋkʃən] n conjunción f; **in ~ with** junto con
conjunctivitis [kəndʒʌŋktɪ'vaɪtɪs] n conjuntivitis f
conjure ['kʌndʒəʳ] vi hacer juegos de manos ▶ **conjure up** vt (ghost, spirit) hacer aparecer; (memories) evocar
conjurer ['kʌndʒərəʳ] n ilusionista m/f
conjuring trick ['kʌndʒərɪŋ-] n juego de manos
conker ['kɒŋkəʳ] n (Brit) castaño de Indias
conk out [kɒŋk-] vi (col) estropearse, fastidiarse, descomponerse (LAm)
con man n timador m
Conn. abbr (US) = **Connecticut**
connect [kə'nɛkt] vt juntar, unir; (Elec) conectar; (pipes) empalmar; (fig) relacionar,

asociar ■ *vi*: **to ~ with** (*train*) enlazar con; **to be connected with** (*associated*) estar relacionado con; (*related*) estar emparentado con; **I am trying to ~ you** (*Tel*) estoy intentando ponerle al habla

connection [kə'nɛkʃən] *n* juntura, unión *f*; (*Elec*) conexión *f*; (*Tech*) empalme *m*; (*Rail*) enlace *m*; (*Tel*) comunicación *f*; (*fig*) relación *f*; **what is the ~ between them?** ¿qué relación hay entre ellos?; **in ~ with** con respecto a, en relación a; **she has many business connections** tiene muchos contactos profesionales; **to miss/make a ~** perder/coger el enlace

connive [kə'naɪv] *vi*: **to ~ at** hacer la vista gorda a

connoisseur [kɔnɪ'səː^r] *n* experto(-a), entendido(-a)

connotation [kɔnə'teɪʃən] *n* connotación *f*

conquer ['kɔŋkə^r] *vt* (*territory*) conquistar; (*enemy, feelings*) vencer

conqueror ['kɔŋkərə^r] *n* conquistador(a) *m(f)*

conquest ['kɔŋkwɛst] *n* conquista

cons [kɔnz] *npl see* **convenience**; **pro**

conscience ['kɔnʃəns] *n* conciencia; **in all ~** en conciencia

conscientious [kɔnʃɪ'ɛnʃəs] *adj* concienzudo; (*objection*) de conciencia

conscientious objector *n* objetor *m* de conciencia

conscious ['kɔnʃəs] *adj* consciente; (*deliberate: insult, error*) premeditado, intencionado; **to become ~ of sth/that** darse cuenta de algo/de que

consciousness ['kɔnʃəsnɪs] *n* conciencia; (*Med*) conocimiento

conscript ['kɔnskrɪpt] *n* recluta *m/f*

conscription [kən'skrɪpʃən] *n* servicio militar (obligatorio)

consecrate ['kɔnsɪkreɪt] *vt* consagrar

consecutive [kən'sɛkjutɪv] *adj* consecutivo; **on 3 ~ occasions** en 3 ocasiones consecutivas

consensus [kən'sɛnsəs] *n* consenso; **the ~ of opinion** el consenso general

consent [kən'sɛnt] *n* consentimiento ■ *vi*: **to ~ to** consentir en; **by common ~** de común acuerdo

consenting adults [kən'sɛntɪŋ-] *npl* adultos con capacidad de consentir

consequence ['kɔnsɪkwəns] *n* consecuencia; **in ~** por consiguiente

consequently ['kɔnsɪkwəntlɪ] *adv* por consiguiente

conservation [kɔnsə'veɪʃən] *n* conservación *f*; (*of nature*) conservación, protección *f*

conservationist [kɔnsə'veɪʃnɪst] *n* conservacionista *m/f*

conservative [kən'sə:vətɪv] *adj* conservador(a); (*cautious*) moderado; **C~** *adj*, *n* (*Brit Pol*) conservador(a) *m(f)*; **the C~ Party** el partido conservador (británico)

conservatory [kən'sə:vətrɪ] *n* (*greenhouse*) invernadero

conserve [kən'sə:v] *vt* conservar ■ *n* conserva

consider [kən'sɪdə^r] *vt* considerar; (*take into account*) tomar en cuenta; (*study*) estudiar, examinar; **to ~ doing sth** pensar en (la posibilidad de) hacer algo; **all things considered** pensándolo bien; **~ yourself lucky** ¡date por satisfecho!

considerable [kən'sɪdərəbl] *adj* considerable

considerably [kən'sɪdərəblɪ] *adv* bastante, considerablemente

considerate [kən'sɪdərɪt] *adj* considerado

consideration [kənsɪdə'reɪʃən] *n* consideración *f*; (*reward*) retribución *f*; **to be under ~** estar estudiándose; **my first ~ is my family** mi primera consideración es mi familia

considered [kən'sɪdəd] *adj*: **it's my ~ opinion that ...** después de haber reflexionado mucho, pienso que ...

considering [kən'sɪdərɪŋ] *prep*: **~ (that)** teniendo en cuenta (que)

consign [kən'saɪn] *vt* consignar

consignee [kɔnsaɪ'niː] *n* consignatario(-a)

consignment [kɔn'saɪnmənt] *n* envío

consignment note *n* (*Comm*) talón *m* de expedición

consignor [kən'saɪnə^r] *n* remitente *m/f*

consist [kən'sɪst] *vi*: **to ~ of** consistir en

consistency [kən'sɪstənsɪ] *n* (*of person etc*) consecuencia, coherencia; (*thickness*) consistencia

consistent [kən'sɪstənt] *adj* (*person, argument*) consecuente, coherente; (*results*) constante

consolation [kɔnsə'leɪʃən] *n* consuelo

console [kən'səul] *vt* consolar ■ *n* ['kɔnsəul] (*control panel*) consola

consolidate [kən'sɔlɪdeɪt] *vt* consolidar

consols ['kɔnsɔlz] *npl* (*Brit Stock Exchange*) valores *mpl* consolidados

consommé [kən'sɔmeɪ] *n* consomé *m*, caldo

consonant ['kɔnsənənt] *n* consonante *f*

consort ['kɔnsɔ:t] *n* consorte *m/f* ■ *vi* [kən'sɔ:t]: **to ~ with sb** (*often pej*) asociarse con algn; **prince ~** príncipe *m* consorte

consortium [kən'sɔ:tɪəm] *n* consorcio

conspicuous [kən'spɪkjuəs] *adj* (*visible*) visible; (*garish etc*) llamativo; (*outstanding*) notable; **to make o.s. ~** llamar la atención

conspiracy [kən'spɪrəsɪ] *n* conjura, complot *m*

conspiratorial [kənspɪrə'tɔːrɪəl] *adj* de conspirador

conspire [kən'spaɪəʳ] *vi* conspirar

constable ['kʌnstəbl] *n* (*Brit*) agente *m/f* (de policía); **chief ~** ≈ jefe *m/f* de policía

constabulary [kən'stæbjulərɪ] *n* ≈ policía

constancy ['kɒnstənsɪ] *n* constancia; fidelidad *f*

constant ['kɒnstənt] *adj* (*gen*) constante; (*loyal*) leal, fiel

constantly ['kɒnstəntlɪ] *adv* constantemente

constellation [kɒnstə'leɪʃən] *n* constelación *f*

consternation [kɒnstə'neɪʃən] *n* consternación *f*

constipated ['kɒnstɪpeɪtəd] *adj* estreñido

constipation [kɒnstɪ'peɪʃən] *n* estreñimiento

constituency [kən'stɪtjuənsɪ] *n* (*Pol*) distrito electoral; (*people*) electorado; *ver nota*

● **CONSTITUENCY**
●
● *Constituency* es la denominación que recibe
● un distrito o circunscripción electoral y
● el grupo de electores registrados en ella
● en el sistema electoral británico. Cada
● circunscripción elige a un diputado
● ("Member of Parliament"), el cual se
● halla disponible semanalmente para las
● consultas y peticiones de sus electores
● durante ciertas horas a la semana,
● tiempo al que se llama "surgery".

constituency party *n* partido local

constituent [kən'stɪtjuənt] *n* (*Pol*) elector(a) *m(f)*; (*part*) componente *m*

constitute ['kɒnstɪtjuːt] *vt* constituir

constitution [kɒnstɪ'tjuːʃən] *n* constitución *f*

constitutional [kɒnstɪ'tjuːʃənl] *adj* constitucional; **~ monarchy** monarquía constitucional

constrain [kən'streɪn] *vt* obligar

constrained [kən'streɪnd] *adj*: **to feel ~ to …** sentirse obligado a …

constraint [kən'streɪnt] *n* (*force*) fuerza; (*limit*) restricción *f*; (*restraint*) reserva; (*embarrassment*) cohibición *f*

constrict [kən'strɪkt] *vt* oprimir

constriction [kən'strɪkʃən] *n* constricción *f*, opresión *f*

construct [kən'strʌkt] *vt* construir

construction [kən'strʌkʃən] *n* construcción *f*; (*fig: interpretation*) interpretación *f*; **under ~** en construcción

construction industry *n* industria de la construcción

constructive [kən'strʌktɪv] *adj* constructivo

construe [kən'struː] *vt* interpretar

consul ['kɒnsl] *n* cónsul *m/f*

consulate ['kɒnsjulɪt] *n* consulado

consult [kən'sʌlt] *vt*, *vi* consultar; **to ~ sb (about sth)** consultar a algn (sobre algo)

consultancy [kən'sʌltənsɪ] *n* (*Comm*) consultoría; (*Med*) puesto de especialista

consultant [kən'sʌltənt] *n* (*Brit Med*) especialista *m/f*; (*other specialist*) asesor(a) *m(f)*, consultor(a) *m(f)*

consultation [kɒnsəl'teɪʃən] *n* consulta; **in ~ with** en consulta con

consultative [kən'sʌltətɪv] *adj* consultivo

consulting room *n* (*Brit*) consulta, consultorio

consume [kən'sjuːm] *vt* (*eat*) comerse; (*drink*) beberse; (*fire etc*) consumir; (*Comm*) consumir

consumer [kən'sjuːməʳ] *n* (*of electricity, gas etc*) consumidor(a) *m(f)*

consumer association *n* asociación *f* de consumidores

consumer credit *n* crédito al consumidor

consumer durables *npl* bienes *mpl* de consumo duraderos

consumer goods *npl* bienes *mpl* de consumo

consumerism [kən'sjuːmərɪzəm] *n* consumismo

consumer society *n* sociedad *f* de consumo

consumer watchdog *n* organización *f* protectora del consumidor

consummate ['kɒnsʌmeɪt] *vt* consumar

consumption [kən'sʌmpʃən] *n* consumo; (*Med*) tisis *f*; **not fit for human ~** no apto para el consumo humano

cont. *abbr* (= *continued*) sigue

contact ['kɒntækt] *n* contacto; (*person: pej*) enchufe *m* ■ *vt* ponerse en contacto con; **~ lenses** *npl* lentes *fpl* de contacto; **to be in ~ with sb/sth** estar en contacto con algn/algo; **business contacts** relaciones *fpl* comerciales

contagious [kən'teɪdʒəs] *adj* contagioso

contain [kən'teɪn] *vt* contener; **to ~ o.s.** contenerse

container [kən'teɪnəʳ] *n* recipiente *m*; (*for shipping etc*) contenedor *m*

containerize [kən'teɪnəraɪz] *vt* transportar en contenedores

container ship *n* buque *m* contenedor, portacontenedores *m inv*

contaminate [kən'tæmɪneɪt] *vt* contaminar

contamination [kəntæmɪ'neɪʃən] *n* contaminación *f*

cont'd *abbr* (= *continued*) sigue

contemplate ['kɒntəmpleɪt] *vt* (*gen*) contemplar; (*reflect upon*) considerar; (*intend*) pensar

contemplation [kɔntəm'pleɪʃən] n
contemplación f
contemporary [kən'tɛmpərərɪ] adj, n (of the same age) contemporáneo(-a) m(f)
contempt [kən'tɛmpt] n desprecio; ~ **of court** (Law) desacato (a los tribunales or a la justicia)
contemptible [kən'tɛmptɪbl] adj
despreciable, desdeñable
contemptuous [kən'tɛmptjuəs] adj desdeñoso
contend [kən'tɛnd] vt (argue) afirmar ■ vi (struggle) luchar; **he has a lot to ~ with** tiene que hacer frente a muchos problemas
contender [kən'tɛndəʳ] n (Sport)
contendiente m/f
content [kən'tɛnt] adj (happy) contento; (satisfied) satisfecho ■ vt contentar; satisfacer ■ n ['kɔntɛnt] contenido; **contents** npl contenido msg; **(table of)**
contents índice m de materias; (in magazine) sumario; **to be ~ with** conformarse con; **to ~ o.s. with sth/with doing sth** conformarse con algo/con hacer algo
contented [kən'tɛntɪd] adj contento;
satisfecho
contentedly [kən'tɛntɪdlɪ] adv con aire satisfecho
contention [kən'tɛnʃən] n discusión f; (belief) argumento; **bone of ~** manzana de la discordia
contentious [kən'tɛnʃəs] adj discutible
contentment [kən'tɛntmənt] n satisfacción f
contest ['kɔntɛst] n contienda; (competition) concurso ■ vt [kən'tɛst] (dispute) impugnar; (Law) disputar, litigar; (Pol: election, seat) presentarse como candidato(-a) a
contestant [kən'tɛstənt] n concursante m/f; (in fight) contendiente m/f
context ['kɔntɛkst] n contexto; **in/out of ~** en/fuera de contexto
continent ['kɔntɪnənt] n continente m; **the C~** (Brit) el continente europeo, Europa; **on the C~** en el continente europeo, en Europa
continental [kɔntɪ'nɛntl] adj continental; (Brit: European) europeo
continental breakfast n desayuno estilo europeo
continental quilt n (Brit) edredón m
contingency [kən'tɪndʒənsɪ] n contingencia
contingent [kən'tɪndʒənt] n (group)
representación f
continual [kən'tɪnjuəl] adj continuo
continually [kən'tɪnjuəlɪ] adv
continuamente
continuation [kəntɪnju'eɪʃən] n
prolongación f; (after interruption)
reanudación f; (of story, episode) continuación f

continue [kən'tɪnjuː] vi, vt seguir, continuar;
continued on page 10 sigue en la página 10
continuing education [kən'tɪnjuɪŋ-] n
educación f continua de adultos
continuity [kɔntɪ'njuɪtɪ] n (also Cine)
continuidad f
continuity girl n (Cine) secretaria de continuidad
continuous [kən'tɪnjuəs] adj continuo; **~ performance** (Cine) sesión f continua
continuously [kən'tɪnjuəslɪ] adv
continuamente
contort [kən'tɔːt] vt retorcer
contortion [kən'tɔːʃən] n (movement)
contorsión f
contortionist [kən'tɔːʃənɪst] n
contorsionista m/f
contour ['kɔntuəʳ] n contorno; (also: **contour line**) curva de nivel
contraband ['kɔntrəbænd] n contrabando
■ adj de contrabando
contraception [kɔntrə'sɛpʃən] n
contracepción f
contraceptive [kɔntrə'sɛptɪv] adj, n
anticonceptivo
contract [n 'kɔntrækt, vb kɔn'trækt] n
contrato ■ cpd ['kɔntrækt] (price, date)
contratado, de contrato; (work) bajo contrato
■ vi (Comm): **to ~ to do sth** comprometerse por contrato a hacer algo; (become smaller)
contraerse, encogerse ■ vt contraer; **to be under ~ to do sth** estar bajo contrato para hacer algo; **~ of employment** or **of service**
contrato de trabajo
  ▶ **contract in** vi tomar parte
  ▶ **contract out** vi: **to ~ out (of)** optar por no tomar parte (en); **to ~ out of a pension scheme** dejar de cotizar en un plan de jubilación
contraction [kən'trækʃən] n contracción f
contractor [kən'træktəʳ] n contratista m/f
contractual [kən'træktjuəl] adj contractual
contradict [kɔntrə'dɪkt] vt (declare to be wrong)
desmentir; (be contrary to) contradecir
contradiction [kɔntrə'dɪkʃən] n
contradicción f; **to be in ~ with** contradecir
contradictory [kɔntrə'dɪktərɪ] adj
(statements) contradictorio; **to be ~ to**
contradecir
contralto [kən'træltəu] n contralto f
contraption [kən'træpʃən] n (pej) artilugio m
contrary ['kɔntrərɪ] adj (opposite, different)
contrario [kən'trɛərɪ] (perverse) terco ■ n:
on the ~ al contrario; **unless you hear to the ~** a no ser que le digan lo contrario; **~ to what we thought** al contrario de lo que pensábamos

contrast ['kɔntrɑːst] n contraste m ∎ vt
[kən'trɑːst] contrastar; **in ~ to** or **with** a
diferencia de

contrasting [kən'trɑːstɪŋ] adj (opinion)
opuesto; (colour) que hace contraste

contravene [kɔntrə'viːn] vt contravenir

contravention [kɔntrə'vɛnʃən] n: **~ (of)**
contravención f (de)

contribute [kən'trɪbjuːt] vi contribuir
∎ vt: **to ~ to** (gen) contribuir a; (newspaper)
colaborar en; (discussion) intervenir en

contribution [kɔntrɪ'bjuːʃən] n (money)
contribución f; (to debate) intervención f;
(to journal) colaboración f

contributor [kən'trɪbjutəʳ] n (to newspaper)
colaborador(a) m(f)

contributory [kən'trɪbjutərɪ] adj (cause)
contribuyente; **it was a ~ factor in ...** fue un
factor que contribuyó en ...

contributory pension scheme n plan m
cotizable de jubilación

contrivance [kən'traɪvəns] n (machine, device)
aparato, dispositivo

contrive [kən'traɪv] vt (invent) idear ∎ vi:
to ~ to do lograr hacer; (try) procurar hacer

control [kən'trəul] vt controlar; (traffic
etc) dirigir; (machinery) manejar; (temper)
dominar; (disease, fire) dominar, controlar
∎ n (command) control m; (of car) conducción
f; (check) freno; **controls** npl mandos mpl; **to
~ o.s.** controlarse, dominarse; **everything is
under ~** todo está bajo control; **to be in ~ of**
estar al mando de; **the car went out of ~** el
coche se descontroló

control group n (Med, Psych etc) grupo de
control

control key n (Comput) tecla de control

controlled economy n economía dirigida

controller [kən'trəuləʳ] n controlador(a) m(f)

controlling interest [kən'trəulɪŋ-] n
participación f mayoritaria

control panel n (on aircraft, ship, TV etc) tablero
de instrumentos

control point n (puesto de) control m

control room n (Naut, Mil) sala de mandos;
(Radio, TV) sala de control

control tower n (Aviat) torre f de control

control unit n (Comput) unidad f de control

controversial [kɔntrə'vəːʃl] adj polémico

controversy ['kɔntrəvəːsɪ] n polémica

conurbation [kɔnə'beɪʃən] n conurbación f

convalesce [kɔnvə'lɛs] vi convalecer

convalescence [kɔnvə'lɛsns] n
convalecencia

convalescent [kɔnvə'lɛsnt] adj, n
convaleciente m/f

convector [kən'vɛktəʳ] n calentador m de

convección

convene [kən'viːn] vt (meeting) convocar
∎ vi reunirse

convenience [kən'viːnɪəns] n (comfort)
comodidad f; (advantage) ventaja; **at your
earliest ~** (Comm) tan pronto como le sea
posible; **all modern conveniences,** (Brit)
all mod cons todo confort

convenience foods npl platos mpl preparados

convenient [kən'viːnɪənt] adj (useful) útil;
(place) conveniente; (time) oportuno; **if it is ~
for you** si le viene bien

conveniently [kən'viːnɪəntlɪ] adv
(happen) oportunamente; (situated)
convenientemente

convent ['kɔnvənt] n convento

convention [kən'vɛnʃən] n convención f;
(meeting) asamblea

conventional [kən'vɛnʃənl] adj convencional

convent school n colegio de monjas

converge [kən'vəːdʒ] vi converger

conversant [kən'vəːsnt] adj: **to be ~ with**
estar familiarizado con

conversation [kɔnvə'seɪʃən] n conversación f

conversational [kɔnvə'seɪʃənl] adj (familiar)
familiar; (talkative) locuaz; **~ mode** (Comput)
modo de conversación

converse ['kɔnvəːs] n inversa ∎ vi [kən'vəːs]
conversar; **to ~ (with sb about sth)**
conversar or platicar (LAm) (con algn de algo)

conversely [kɔn'vəːslɪ] adv a la inversa

conversion [kən'vəːʃən] n conversión f;
(house conversion) reforma, remodelación f

conversion table n tabla de equivalencias

convert [kən'vəːt] vt (Rel, Comm) convertir;
(alter) transformar ∎ n ['kɔnvəːt]
converso(-a)

convertible [kən'vəːtəbl] adj convertible
∎ n descapotable m; **~ loan stock**
obligaciones fpl convertibles

convex ['kɔnvɛks] adj convexo

convey [kən'veɪ] vt transportar; (thanks)
comunicar; (idea) expresar

conveyance [kən'veɪəns] n (of goods)
transporte m; (vehicle) vehículo, medio de
transporte

conveyancing [kən'veɪənsɪŋ] n (Law)
preparación f de escrituras de traspaso

conveyor belt [kən'veɪəʳ-] n cinta
transportadora

convict [kən'vɪkt] vt (gen) condenar; (find
guilty) declarar culpable a ∎ n ['kɔnvɪkt]
presidiario(-a)

conviction [kən'vɪkʃən] n condena; (belief)
creencia, convicción f

convince [kən'vɪns] vt convencer; **to ~ sb (of
sth/that)** convencer a algn (de algo/de que)

convinced [kən'vɪnst] *adj*: ~ **of/that** convencido de/de que

convincing [kən'vɪnsɪŋ] *adj* convincente

convincingly [kən'vɪnsɪŋlɪ] *adv* de modo convincente, convincentemente

convivial [kən'vɪvɪəl] *adj* (*person*) sociable; (*atmosphere*) alegre

convoluted ['kɔnvəlu:tɪd] *adj* (*argument etc*) enrevesado; (*shape*) enrollado, enroscado

convoy ['kɔnvɔɪ] *n* convoy *m*

convulse [kən'vʌls] *vt* convulsionar; **to be convulsed with laughter** dislocarse de risa

convulsion [kən'vʌlʃən] *n* convulsión *f*

coo [ku:] *vi* arrullar

cook [kuk] *vt* cocinar; (*stew etc*) guisar; (*meal*) preparar ■ *vi* hacerse; (*person*) cocinar ■ *n* cocinero(-a)
▶ **cook up** *vt* (*col: excuse, story*) inventar

cookbook ['kukbuk] *n* libro de cocina

cooker ['kukər] *n* cocina

cookery ['kukərɪ] *n* cocina

cookery book *n* (*Brit*) = **cookbook**

cookie ['kukɪ] *n* (*US*) galleta; (*Comput*) cookie *m*

cooking ['kukɪŋ] *n* cocina ■ *cpd* (*apples*) para cocinar; (*utensils, salt, foil*) de cocina

cooking chocolate *n* chocolate *m* fondant *or* de hacer

cookout ['kukaut] *n* (*US*) comida al aire libre

cool [ku:l] *adj* fresco; (*not hot*) tibio; (*not afraid*) tranquilo; (*unfriendly*) frío ■ *vt* enfriar ■ *vi* enfriarse; **it is** ~ (*weather*) hace fresco; **to keep sth** ~ *or* **in a** ~ **place** conservar algo fresco *or* en un sitio fresco
▶ **cool down** *vi* enfriarse; (*fig: person, situation*) calmarse

coolant ['ku:lənt] *n* refrigerante *m*

cool box, cooler (*US*) ['ku:lər] *n* nevera portátil

cooling ['ku:lɪŋ] *adj* refrescante

cooling-off period [ku:lɪŋ'ɔf-] *n* (*Industry*) plazo de negociaciones

cooling tower *n* torre *f* de refrigeración

coolly ['ku:lɪ] *adv* (*calmly*) con tranquilidad; (*audaciously*) descaradamente; (*unenthusiastically*) fríamente, con frialdad

coolness ['ku:lnɪs] *n* frescura; tranquilidad *f*; (*hostility*) frialdad *f*; (*indifference*) falta de entusiasmo

coop [ku:p] *n* gallinero ■ *vt*: **to** ~ **up** (*fig*) encerrar

co-op ['kəuɔp] *n abbr* (= *cooperative (society)*) cooperativa

cooperate [kəu'ɔpəreɪt] *vi* cooperar, colaborar; **will he** ~? ¿querrá cooperar?

cooperation [kəuɔpə'reɪʃən] *n* cooperación *f*, colaboración *f*

cooperative [kəu'ɔpərətɪv] *adj* cooperativo; (*person*) dispuesto a colaborar ■ *n* cooperativa

co-opt [kəu'ɔpt] *vt*: **to** ~ **sb into sth** nombrar a algn para algo

coordinate [kəu'ɔ:dɪneɪt] *vt* coordinar ■ *n* [kəu'ɔ:dɪnət] (*Math*) coordenada; **coordinates** *npl* (*clothes*) coordinados *mpl*

coordination [kəuɔ:dɪ'neɪʃən] *n* coordinación *f*

coot [ku:t] *n* focha *f* (común)

co-ownership [kəu'əunəʃɪp] *n* copropiedad *f*

cop [kɔp] *n* (*col*) poli *m*

cope [kəup] *vi*: **to** ~ **with** poder con; (*problem*) hacer frente a

Copenhagen [kəupən'heɪgən] *n* Copenhague *m*

copier ['kɔpɪər] *n* (*photocopier*) (foto)copiadora

co-pilot ['kəu'paɪlət] *n* copiloto *m/f*

copious ['kəupɪəs] *adj* copioso, abundante

copper ['kɔpər] *n* (*metal*) cobre *m*; (*col: policeman*) poli *m*; **coppers** *npl* perras *fpl*; (*small change*) calderilla

coppice ['kɔpɪs], **copse** [kɔps] *n* bosquecillo

copulate ['kɔpjuleɪt] *vi* copular

copulation [kɔpju'leɪʃən] *n* cópula

copy ['kɔpɪ] *n* copia; (*of book*) ejemplar *m*; (*of magazine*) número; (*material: for printing*) original *m* ■ *vt* copiar (*also Comput*); (*imitate*) copiar, imitar; **to make good** ~ (*fig*) ser una noticia de interés; **rough** ~ borrador *m*; **fair** ~ copia en limpio
▶ **copy out** *vt* copiar

copycat ['kɔpɪkæt] *n* (*pej*) imitador(a) *m(f)*

copyright ['kɔpɪraɪt] *n* derechos *mpl* de autor

copy typist *n* mecanógrafo(-a)

coral ['kɔrəl] *n* coral *m*

coral reef *n* arrecife *m* (de coral)

Coral Sea *n*: **the** ~ el Mar del Coral

cord [kɔ:d] *n* cuerda; (*Elec*) cable *m*; (*fabric*) pana; **cords** *npl* (*trousers*) pantalones *mpl* de pana

cordial ['kɔ:dɪəl] *adj* cordial ■ *n* cordial *m*

cordless ['kɔ:dlɪs] *adj* sin hilos; ~ **telephone** teléfono inalámbrico

cordon ['kɔ:dn] *n* cordón *m*
▶ **cordon off** *vt* acordonar

Cordova ['kɔ:dəvə] *n* Córdoba

corduroy ['kɔ:dərɔɪ] *n* pana

CORE [kɔ:r] *n abbr* (*US*) = **Congress of Racial Equality**

core [kɔ:r] *n* (*of earth, nuclear reactor*) centro, núcleo; (*of fruit*) corazón *m*; (*of problem etc*) esencia, meollo ■ *vt* quitar el corazón de

Corfu [kɔ:'fu:] *n* Corfú *m*

coriander [kɔrɪ'ændər] *n* culantro, cilantro

cork [kɔ:k] *n* corcho; (*tree*) alcornoque *m*

corkage ['kɔ:kɪdʒ] *n* precio que se cobra en un restaurante por una botella de vino traída de fuera

493

corked [kɔːkt] adj (wine) con sabor a corcho
corkscrew ['kɔːkskruː] n sacacorchos m inv
cormorant ['kɔːmərnt] n cormorán m
Corn abbr (Brit) = **Cornwall**
corn [kɔːn] n (Brit: wheat) trigo; (US: maize) maíz m, choclo (LAm); (on foot) callo; ~ **on the cob** (Culin) maíz en la mazorca
cornea ['kɔːnɪə] n córnea
corned beef ['kɔːnd-] n carne f de vaca acecinada
corner ['kɔːnə'] n (outside) esquina; (inside) rincón m; (in road) curva; (Football) córner m, saque m de esquina ▪ vt (trap) arrinconar; (Comm) acaparar ▪ vi (in car) tomar las curvas; **to cut corners** atajar
corner flag n (Football) banderola de esquina
corner kick n (Football) córner m, saque m de esquina
cornerstone ['kɔːnəstəun] n piedra angular
cornet ['kɔːnɪt] n (Mus) corneta; (Brit: of ice cream) cucurucho
cornflakes ['kɔːnfleɪks] npl copos mpl de maíz, cornflakes mpl
cornflour ['kɔːnflauə'] n (Brit) harina de maíz
cornice ['kɔːnɪs] n cornisa
Cornish ['kɔːnɪʃ] adj de Cornualles
corn oil n aceite m de maíz
cornstarch ['kɔːnstɑːtʃ] n (US) = **cornflour**
cornucopia [kɔːnjuːˈkəupɪə] n cornucopia
Cornwall ['kɔːnwəl] n Cornualles m
corny ['kɔːnɪ] adj (col) gastado
corollary [kəˈrɒlərɪ] n corolario
coronary ['kɒrənərɪ] n: ~ **(thrombosis)** infarto
coronation [kɒrəˈneɪʃən] n coronación f
coroner ['kɒrənə'] n juez m/f de instrucción
coronet ['kɒrənɪt] n corona
Corp. abbr = **corporation**
corporal ['kɔːpərl] n cabo ▪ adj: ~ **punishment** castigo corporal
corporate ['kɔːpərɪt] adj corporativo
corporate hospitality n obsequios a los clientes por cortesía de la empresa
corporate identity, corporate image n (of organization) identidad f corporativa
corporation [kɔːpəˈreɪʃən] n (of town) ayuntamiento; (Comm) corporación f
corps [kɔː'] (pl ~) [kɔːz] n cuerpo; **press ~** gabinete m de prensa
corpse [kɔːps] n cadáver m
corpulent ['kɔːpjulənt] adj corpulento(-a)
Corpus Christi ['kɔːpəsˈkrɪstɪ] n Corpus m (Christi)
corpuscle ['kɔːpʌsl] n corpúsculo
corral [kəˈrɑːl] n corral m
correct [kəˈrɛkt] adj correcto; (accurate) exacto ▪ vt corregir; **you are** ~ tiene razón

correction [kəˈrɛkʃən] n rectificación f; (erasure) tachadura
correlate ['kɒrɪleɪt] vi: **to ~ with** tener correlación con
correlation [kɒrɪˈleɪʃən] n correlación f
correspond [kɒrɪsˈpɒnd] vi (write) escribirse; (be equal to) corresponder
correspondence [kɒrɪsˈpɒndəns] n correspondencia
correspondence course n curso por correspondencia
correspondent [kɒrɪsˈpɒndənt] n corresponsal m/f
corresponding [kɒrɪsˈpɒndɪŋ] adj correspondiente
corridor ['kɒrɪdɔː'] n pasillo
corroborate [kəˈrɒbəreɪt] vt corroborar
corroboration [kərɒbəˈreɪʃən] n corroboración f, confirmación f
corrode [kəˈrəud] vt corroer ▪ vi corroerse
corrosion [kəˈrəuʒən] n corrosión f
corrosive [kəˈrəusɪv] adj corrosivo
corrugated ['kɒrəgeɪtɪd] adj ondulado
corrugated cardboard n cartón m ondulado
corrugated iron n chapa ondulada
corrupt [kəˈrʌpt] adj corrompido; (person) corrupto ▪ vt corromper; (bribe) sobornar; (Comput: data) degradar; ~ **practices** (dishonesty, bribery) corrupción f
corruption [kəˈrʌpʃən] n corrupción f; (Comput: of data) alteración f
corset ['kɔːsɪt] n faja; (old-style) corsé m
Corsica ['kɔːsɪkə] n Córcega
Corsican ['kɔːsɪkən] adj, n corso(-a) m(f)
cortège [kɔːˈteɪʒ] n cortejo, comitiva
cortisone ['kɔːtɪzəun] n cortisona
cosh [kɒʃ] n (Brit) cachiporra
cosignatory ['kəuˈsɪgnətərɪ] n cosignatario(-a)
cosine ['kəusaɪn] n coseno
cosiness ['kəuzɪnɪs] n comodidad f; (atmosphere) lo acogedor
cos lettuce [kɒs-] n lechuga romana
cosmetic [kɒzˈmɛtɪk] n cosmético ▪ adj (also fig) cosmético; (surgery) estético
cosmic ['kɒzmɪk] adj cósmico
cosmonaut ['kɒzmənɔːt] n cosmonauta m/f
cosmopolitan [kɒzməˈpɒlɪtn] adj cosmopolita
cosmos ['kɒzmɒs] n cosmos m
cosset ['kɒsɪt] vt mimar
cost [kɒst] (pt, pp ~) n (gen) coste m, costo; (price) precio; **costs** npl (Law) costas fpl ▪ vi costar, valer ▪ vt preparar el presupuesto de; **how much does it ~?** ¿cuánto cuesta?, ¿cuánto vale?; **what will it ~ to have it**

repaired? ¿cuánto costará repararlo?; **the ~ of living** el coste *or* costo de la vida; **at all costs** cueste lo que cueste

cost accountant *n* contable *m* de costos

co-star [ˈkəʊstɑːʳ] *n* coprotagonista *m/f*

Costa Rica [ˈkɔstəˈriːkə] *n* Costa Rica

Costa Rican [ˈkɔstəˈriːkən] *adj, n* costarriqueño(-a) *m(f)*, costarricense *m/f*

cost centre *n* centro (de determinación) de coste

cost control *n* control *m* de costes

cost-effective [kɔstɪˈfɛktɪv] *adj* (*Comm*) rentable

cost-effectiveness [ˈkɔstɪˈfɛktɪvnɪs] *n* relación *f* coste-rendimiento

costing [ˈkɔstɪŋ] *n* cálculo del coste

costly [ˈkɔstlɪ] *adj* (*expensive*) costoso

cost-of-living [kɔstəvˈlɪvɪŋ] *adj*: **~ allowance** *n* plus *m* de carestía de vida; **~ index** *n* índice *m* del coste de vida

cost price *n* (*Brit*) precio de coste

costume [ˈkɔstjuːm] *n* traje *m*; (*Brit: also:* **swimming costume**) traje de baño

costume jewellery *n* bisutería

cosy, cozy (*US*) [ˈkəʊzɪ] *adj* cómodo, a gusto; (*room, atmosphere*) acogedor(a)

cot [kɔt] *n* (*Brit: child's*) cuna; (*US: folding bed*) cama plegable

cot death *n* muerte *f* en la cuna

Cotswolds [ˈkɔtswəʊldz] *npl* región de colinas del suroeste inglés

cottage [ˈkɔtɪdʒ] *n* casita de campo

cottage cheese *n* requesón *m*

cottage industry *n* industria artesanal

cottage pie *n* pastel de carne cubierta de puré de patatas

cotton [ˈkɔtn] *n* algodón *m*; (*thread*) hilo
▶ **cotton on** *vi* (*col*): **to ~ on (to sth)** caer en la cuenta (de algo)

cotton candy *n* (*US*) algodón *m* (azucarado)

cotton wool *n* (*Brit*) algodón *m* (hidrófilo)

couch [kautʃ] *n* sofá *m*; (*in doctor's surgery*) camilla

couchette [kuːˈʃɛt] *n* litera

couch potato *n* (*col*) persona comodona que no se mueve en todo el día

cough [kɔf] *vi* toser ■ *n* tos *f*
▶ **cough up** *vt* escupir

cough drop *n* pastilla para la tos

cough mixture *n* jarabe *m* para la tos

could [kud] *pt of* **can**

couldn't [ˈkudnt] = **could not**

council [ˈkaunsl] *n* consejo; **city** *or* **town ~** ayuntamiento; **C~ of Europe** Consejo de Europa

council estate *n* (*Brit*) barriada de viviendas sociales de alquiler

council house *n* (*Brit*) vivienda social de alquiler

councillor [ˈkaunsləʳ] *n* concejal *m/f*

council tax *n* (*Brit*) contribución *f* municipal (*dependiente del valor de la vivienda*)

counsel [ˈkaunsl] *n* (*advice*) consejo; (*lawyer*) abogado(-a) ■ *vt* aconsejar; **~ for the defence/the prosecution** abogado(-a) defensor(a)/fiscal; **to ~ sth/sb to do sth** aconsejar algo/a algn que haga algo

counsellor, counselor (*US*) [ˈkaunsləʳ] *n* consejero(-a); (*US Law*) abogado(-a)

count [kaunt] *vt* (*gen*) contar; (*include*) incluir ■ *vi* contar ■ *n* cuenta; (*of votes*) escrutinio; (*nobleman*) conde *m*; (*sum*) total *m*, suma; **to ~ the cost of** calcular el coste de; **not counting the children** niños aparte; **10 counting him** diez incluyéndolo a él, diez con él; **~ yourself lucky** date por satisfecho; **that doesn't ~!** ¡eso no vale!; **to ~ (up) to 10** contar hasta diez; **it counts for very little** cuenta poco; **to keep ~ of sth** llevar la cuenta de algo
▶ **count on** *vt fus* contar con; **to ~ on doing sth** contar con hacer algo
▶ **count up** *vt* contar

countdown [ˈkauntdaun] *n* cuenta atrás

countenance [ˈkauntɪnəns] *n* semblante *m*, rostro ■ *vt* (*tolerate*) aprobar, consentir

counter [ˈkauntəʳ] *n* (*in shop*) mostrador *m*; (*position: in post office, bank*) ventanilla; (*in games*) ficha; (*Tech*) contador *m* ■ *vt* contrarrestar; (*blow*) parar; (*attack*) contestar a ■ *adv*: **~ to** contrario a; **to buy under the ~** (*fig*) comprar de estraperlo *or* bajo mano; **to ~ sth with sth/by doing sth** contestar algo con algo/haciendo algo

counteract [ˈkauntərˈækt] *vt* contrarrestar

counterattack [ˈkauntərəˈtæk] *n* contraataque *m* ■ *vi* contraatacar

counterbalance [ˈkauntəˈbæləns] *n* contrapeso

counter-clockwise [ˈkauntəˈklɔkwaɪz] *adv* en sentido contrario al de las agujas del reloj

counter-espionage [ˈkauntərˈɛspɪənɑːʒ] *n* contraespionaje *m*

counterfeit [ˈkauntəfɪt] *n* falsificación *f* ■ *vt* falsificar ■ *adj* falso, falsificado

counterfoil [ˈkauntəfɔɪl] *n* (*Brit*) matriz *f*, talón *m*

counterintelligence [ˈkauntərɪnˈtɛlɪdʒəns] *n* contraespionaje *m*

countermand [ˈkauntəmɑːnd] *vt* revocar

counter-measure [ˈkauntəmɛʒəʳ] *n* contramedida

counteroffensive [ˈkauntərəˈfɛnsɪv] *n* contraofensiva

counterpane ['kaʊntəpeɪn] n colcha

counterpart ['kaʊntəpɑːt] n (of person) homólogo(-a)

counter-productive [kaʊntəprə'dʌktɪv] adj contraproducente

counterproposal ['kaʊntəprə'pəʊzl] n contrapropuesta

countersign ['kaʊntəsaɪn] vt ratificar, refrendar

countess ['kaʊntɪs] n condesa

countless ['kaʊntlɪs] adj innumerable

countrified ['kʌntrɪfaɪd] adj rústico

country ['kʌntrɪ] n país m; (native land) patria; (as opposed to town) campo; (region) región f, tierra; **in the ~** en el campo; **mountainous ~** región f montañosa

country and western, country and western music n música country

country dancing n (Brit) baile m regional

country house n casa de campo

countryman ['kʌntrɪmən] n (national) compatriota m; (rural) hombre m del campo

countryside ['kʌntrɪsaɪd] n campo

countrywide ['kʌntrɪ'waɪd] adj nacional ■ adv por todo el país

county ['kaʊntɪ] n condado; see also **district council**

county council n (Brit) ≈ diputación f provincial

county town n cabeza de partido

coup [kuː] (pl **coups**) [kuːz] n golpe m; (triumph) éxito; (also: **coup d'état**) golpe de estado

coupé ['kuːpeɪ] n cupé m

couple ['kʌpl] n (of things) par m; (of people) pareja; (married couple) matrimonio ■ vt (ideas, names) unir, juntar; (machinery) acoplar; **a ~ of** un par de

couplet ['kʌplɪt] n pareado

coupling ['kʌplɪŋ] n (Rail) enganche m

coupon ['kuːpɔn] n cupón m; (pools coupon) boleto (de quiniela)

courage ['kʌrɪdʒ] n valor m, valentía

courageous [kə'reɪdʒəs] adj valiente

courgette [kuə'ʒɛt] n (Brit) calabacín m

courier ['kurɪər] n mensajero(-a); (diplomatic) correo; (for tourists) guía m/f (de turismo)

course [kɔːs] n (direction) dirección f; (of river) curso; (Scol) curso; (of ship) rumbo; (fig) proceder m; (Golf) campo; (part of meal) plato; **of ~** adv desde luego, naturalmente; **of ~!** ¡claro!, ¡cómo no! (LAm); **(no) of ~ not!** ¡claro que no!, ¡por supuesto que no!; **in due ~** a su debido tiempo; **in the ~ of the next few days** durante los próximos días; **we have no other ~ but to** ... no tenemos más remedio que ...; **there are 2 courses open**

to us se nos ofrecen dos posibilidades; **the best ~ would be to** ... lo mejor sería ...; **~ of treatment** (Med) tratamiento

court [kɔːt] n (royal) corte f; (Law) tribunal m, juzgado; (Tennis) pista, cancha (LAm) ■ vt (woman) cortejar; (fig: favour, popularity) solicitar, buscar; (: death, disaster, danger etc) buscar; **to take to ~** demandar; **~ of appeal** tribunal m de apelación

courteous ['kə:tɪəs] adj cortés

courtesan [kɔːtɪ'zæn] n cortesana

courtesy ['kə:təsɪ] n cortesía; **by ~ of** (por) cortesía de

courtesy light n (Aut) luz f interior

court-house ['kɔːthaʊs] n (US) palacio de justicia

courtier ['kɔːtɪər] n cortesano

court martial (pl **courts martial**) ['kɔːt'mɑːʃəl] n consejo de guerra ■ vt someter a consejo de guerra

courtroom ['kɔːtrum] n sala de justicia

court shoe n zapato de mujer de estilo clásico

courtyard ['kɔːtjɑːd] n patio

cousin ['kʌzn] n primo(-a); **first ~** primo(-a) carnal

cove [kəʊv] n cala, ensenada

covenant ['kʌvənənt] n convenio ■ vt: **to ~ £20 per year to a charity** concertar el pago de veinte libras anuales a una sociedad benéfica

Coventry ['kɔvəntrɪ] n: **to send sb to ~** (fig) hacer el vacío a algn

cover ['kʌvər] vt cubrir; (with lid) tapar; (chairs etc) revestir; (distance) cubrir, recorrer; (include) abarcar; (protect) abrigar; (journalist) investigar; (issues) tratar ■ n cubierta; (lid) tapa; (for chair etc) funda; (for bed) cobertor m; (envelope) sobre m; (of magazine) portada; (shelter) abrigo; (insurance) cobertura; **to take ~** (shelter) protegerse, resguardarse; **under ~** (indoors) bajo techo; **under ~ of darkness** al amparo de la oscuridad; **under separate ~** (Comm) por separado; **£10 will ~ everything** con diez libras cubriremos todos los gastos

▶ **cover up** vt (child, object) cubrir completamente, tapar; (fig: hide: truth, facts) ocultar; **to ~ up for sb** (fig) encubrir a algn

coverage ['kʌvərɪdʒ] n alcance m; (in media) reportaje m; (Insurance) cobertura

coveralls ['kʌvərɔːlz] npl (US) mono sg

cover charge n precio del cubierto

covering ['kʌvərɪŋ] n cubierta, envoltura

covering letter, cover letter (US) n carta de explicación

cover note n (Insurance) póliza provisional

cover price n precio de cubierta

covert ['kəuvət] *adj* (*secret*) secreto, encubierto; (*dissembled*) furtivo
cover-up ['kʌvərʌp] *n* encubrimiento
covet ['kʌvɪt] *vt* codiciar
covetous ['kʌvɪtəs] *adj* codicioso
cow [kau] *n* vaca ▪ *vt* intimidar
coward ['kauəd] *n* cobarde *m/f*
cowardice ['kauədɪs] *n* cobardía
cowardly ['kauədlɪ] *adj* cobarde
cowboy ['kaubɔɪ] *n* vaquero
cower ['kauə'] *vi* encogerse (de miedo)
co-worker ['kəuwə:kə'] *n* colaborador(a) *m(f)*
cowshed ['kauʃɛd] *n* establo
cowslip ['kauslɪp] *n* (*Bot*) primavera, prímula
cox ['kɔks], **coxswain** ['kɔksn] *n* timonel *m*
coy [kɔɪ] *adj* tímido
coyote [kɔɪ'əutɪ] *n* coyote *m*
cozy ['kəuzɪ] *adj* (*US*) = **cosy**
CP *n abbr* (= *Communist Party*) PC *m*
cp. *abbr* (= *compare*) cfr.
CPA *n abbr* (*US*) = **certified public accountant**
CPI *n abbr* (= *Consumer Price Index*) IPC *m*
Cpl. *abbr* (*Mil*) = **corporal**
c.p.s. *abbr* (= *characters per second*) c.p.s.
CPSA *n abbr* (Brit: = *Civil and Public Services Association*) sindicato de funcionarios
CPU *n abbr* = **central processing unit**
cr. *abbr* = **credit**; **creditor**
crab [kræb] *n* cangrejo
crab apple *n* manzana silvestre
crack [kræk] *n* grieta; (*noise*) crujido; (: *of whip*) chasquido; (*joke*) chiste *m*; (*col: drug*) crack *m*; (*attempt*): **to have a ~ at sth** intentar algo ▪ *vt* agrietar, romper; (*nut*) cascar; (*safe*) forzar; (*whip etc*) chasquear; (*knuckles*) crujir; (*joke*) contar; (*case: solve*) resolver; (*code*) descifrar ▪ *adj* (*athlete*) de primera clase; **to ~ jokes** (*col*) bromear
▸ **crack down on** *vt fus* reprimir fuertemente, adoptar medidas severas contra
▸ **crack up** *vi* sufrir una crisis nerviosa
crackdown ['krækdaun] *n*: **~ (on)** (*on crime*) campaña (contra); (*on spending*) reducción *f* (en)
cracker ['krækə'] *n* (*biscuit*) galleta salada, crácker *m*; (*Christmas cracker*) sorpresa (navideña)
crackle ['krækl] *vi* crepitar
crackling ['kræklɪŋ] *n* (*on radio, telephone*) interferencia; (*of fire*) chisporroteo, crepitación *f*; (*of leaves etc*) crujido; (*of pork*) chicharrón *m*
crackpot ['krækpɔt] (*col*) *n* pirado(-a) ▪ *adj* de pirado
cradle ['kreɪdl] *n* cuna ▪ *vt* (*child*) mecer, acunar; (*object*) abrazar

craft [krɑ:ft] *n* (*skill*) arte *m*; (*trade*) oficio; (*cunning*) astucia; (*boat*) embarcación *f*
craftsman ['krɑ:ftsmən] *n* artesano
craftsmanship ['krɑ:ftsmənʃɪp] *n* artesanía
crafty ['krɑ:ftɪ] *adj* astuto
crag [kræg] *n* peñasco
craggy ['krægɪ] *adj* escarpado
cram [kræm] *vt* (*fill*): **to ~ sth with** llenar algo (a reventar) de; (*put*): **to ~ sth into** meter algo a la fuerza en ▪ *vi* (*for exams*) empollar
crammed [kræmd] *adj* atestado
cramp [kræmp] *n* (*Med*) calambre *m*; (*Tech*) grapa ▪ *vt* (*limit*) poner trabas a
cramped [kræmpt] *adj* apretado; (*room*) minúsculo
crampon ['kræmpən] *n* crampón *m*
cranberry ['krænbərɪ] *n* arándano
crane [kreɪn] *n* (*Tech*) grúa; (*bird*) grulla ▪ *vt*, *vi*: **to ~ forward, to ~ one's neck** estirar el cuello
cranium ['kreɪnɪəm] *n* cráneo
crank [kræŋk] *n* manivela; (*person*) chiflado(-a)
crankshaft ['kræŋkʃɑ:ft] *n* cigüeñal *m*
cranky ['kræŋkɪ] *adj* (*eccentric*) maniático; (*bad-tempered*) de mal genio
cranny ['krænɪ] *n see* **nook**
crap [kræp] *n* (*col!*) mierda (!)
crappy ['kræpɪ] *adj* (*col*) chungo
craps [kræps] *n* (*US*) dados *mpl*
crash [kræʃ] *n* (*noise*) estrépito; (*of cars, plane*) accidente *m*; (*of business*) quiebra; (*Stock Exchange*) crac *m* ▪ *vt* (*plane*) estrellar ▪ *vi* (*plane*) estrellarse; (*two cars*) chocar; (*fall noisily*) caer con estrépito; **he crashed the car into a wall** estrelló el coche contra una pared *or* tapia
crash barrier *n* (*Aut*) barrera de protección
crash course *n* curso acelerado
crash helmet *n* casco (protector)
crash landing *n* aterrizaje *m* forzoso
crass [kræs] *adj* grosero, maleducado
crate [kreɪt] *n* caja, cajón *m* de embalaje; (*col*) armatoste *m*
crater ['kreɪtə'] *n* cráter *m*
cravat, cravate [krə'væt] *n* pañuelo
crave [kreɪv] *vt*, *vi*: **to ~ (for)** ansiar, anhelar
craving ['kreɪvɪŋ] *n* (*for food, cigarettes etc*) ansias *fpl*; (*during pregnancy*) antojo
crawl [krɔ:l] *vi* (*drag o.s.*) arrastrarse; (*child*) andar a gatas, gatear; (*vehicle*) avanzar (lentamente); (*col*): **to ~ to sb** dar coba a algn, hacerle la pelota a algn ▪ *n* (*Swimming*) crol *m*
crawler lane [krɔ:lə-] *n* (*Brit Aut*) carril *m* para tráfico lento

crayfish ['kreɪfɪʃ] *n pl inv* (*freshwater*) cangrejo (de río); (*saltwater*) cigala

crayon ['kreɪən] *n* lápiz *m* de color

craze [kreɪz] *n* manía; (*fashion*) moda

crazed [kreɪzd] *adj* (*look, person*) loco, demente; (*pottery, glaze*) agrietado, cuarteado

crazy ['kreɪzɪ] *adj* (*person*) loco; (*idea*) disparatado; **to go ~** volverse loco; **to be ~ about sb/sth** (*col*) estar loco por algn/algo

crazy paving *n* pavimento de baldosas irregulares

creak [kri:k] *vi* crujir; (*hinge etc*) rechinar

cream [kri:m] *n* (*of milk*) nata, crema; (*lotion*) crema; (*fig*) flor *f* y nata ■ *adj* (*colour*) color *m* crema; **whipped ~** nata batida
  ▶ **cream off** *vt* (*fig: best talents, part of profits*) separar lo mejor de

cream cake *n* pastel *m* de nata

cream cheese *n* queso fresco cremoso

creamery ['kri:mərɪ] *n* (*shop*) quesería; (*factory*) central *f* lechera

creamy ['kri:mɪ] *adj* cremoso

crease [kri:s] *n* (*fold*) pliegue *m*; (*in trousers*) raya; (*wrinkle*) arruga ■ *vt* (*fold*) doblar, plegar; (*wrinkle*) arrugar ■ *vi* (*wrinkle up*) arrugarse

crease-resistant ['kri:srɪzɪstənt] *adj* inarrugable

create [kri:'eɪt] *vt* (*also Comput*) crear; (*impression*) dar; (*fuss, noise*) hacer

creation [kri:'eɪʃən] *n* creación *f*

creative [kri:'eɪtɪv] *adj* creativo

creativity [kri:eɪ'tɪvɪtɪ] *n* creatividad *f*

creator [kri:'eɪtər] *n* creador(a) *m(f)*

creature ['kri:tʃər] *n* (*living thing*) criatura; (*animal*) animal *m*; (*insect*) bicho

creature comforts *npl* comodidades *fpl* materiales

crèche, creche [krɛʃ] *n* (*Brit*) guardería (infantil)

credence ['kri:dəns] *n*: **to lend** *or* **give ~ to** creer en, dar crédito a

credentials [krɪ'dɛnʃlz] *npl* credenciales *fpl*; (*letters of reference*) referencias *fpl*

credibility [krɛdɪ'bɪlɪtɪ] *n* credibilidad *f*

credible ['krɛdɪbl] *adj* creíble; (*witness, source*) fidedigno

credit ['krɛdɪt] *n* (*gen*) crédito; (*merit*) honor *m*, mérito ■ *vt* (*Comm*) abonar; (*believe*) creer, dar crédito a ■ *adj* crediticio; **to be in ~** (*person, bank account*) tener saldo a favor; **on ~** a crédito; (*col*) al fiado; **he's a ~ to his family** hace honor a su familia; **to ~ sb with** (*fig*) reconocer a algn el mérito de; *see also* **credits**

creditable ['krɛdɪtəbl] *adj* estimable, digno de elogio

credit account *n* cuenta de crédito

credit agency *n* agencia de informes comerciales

credit balance *n* saldo acreedor

credit card *n* tarjeta de crédito

credit control *n* control *m* de créditos

credit crunch *n* crisis *f* crediticia

credit facilities *npl* facilidades *fpl* de crédito

credit limit *n* límite *m* de crédito

credit note *n* nota de crédito

creditor ['krɛdɪtər] *n* acreedor(a) *m(f)*

credits ['krɛdɪts] *npl* (*Cine*) títulos *mpl or* rótulos *mpl* de crédito, créditos *mpl*

credit transfer *n* transferencia de crédito

creditworthy ['krɛdɪtwə:ðɪ] *adj* solvente

credulity [krɪ'dju:lɪtɪ] *n* credulidad *f*

creed [kri:d] *n* credo

creek [kri:k] *n* cala, ensenada; (*US*) riachuelo

creel [kri:l] *n* nasa

creep [kri:p] (*pt, pp* **crept**) [krɛpt] *vi* (*animal*) deslizarse; (*plant*) trepar; **to ~ up on sb** acercarse sigilosamente a algn; (*fig: old age etc*) acercarse ■ *n* (*col*): **he's a ~** ¡qué lameculos es!; **it gives me the creeps** me da escalofríos

creeper ['kri:pər] *n* enredadera

creepers ['kri:pəz] *npl* (*US: for baby*) pelele *msg*

creepy ['kri:pɪ] *adj* (*frightening*) horripilante

creepy-crawly ['kri:pɪ'krɔ:lɪ] *n* (*col*) bicho

cremate [krɪ'meɪt] *vt* incinerar

cremation [krɪ'meɪʃən] *n* incineración *f*, cremación *f*

crematorium [krɛmə'tɔ:rɪəm] (*pl* **crematoria**) [krɛmə'tɔ:rɪə] *n* crematorio

creosote ['kri:əsəut] *n* creosota

crêpe [kreɪp] *n* (*fabric*) crespón *m*; (*also*: **crêpe rubber**) crep(é) *m*

crêpe bandage *n* (*Brit*) venda elástica

crêpe paper *n* papel *m* crep(é)

crêpe sole *n* (*on shoes*) suela de crep(é)

crept [krɛpt] *pt, pp of* **creep**

crescent ['krɛsnt] *n* media luna; (*street*) calle *f* (*en forma de semicírculo*)

cress [krɛs] *n* berro

crest [krɛst] *n* (*of bird*) cresta; (*of hill*) cima, cumbre *f*; (*of helmet*) cimera; (*of coat of arms*) blasón *m*

crestfallen ['krɛstfɔ:lən] *adj* alicaído

Crete [kri:t] *n* Creta

cretin ['krɛtɪn] *n* cretino(-a)

crevasse [krɪ'væs] *n* grieta

crevice ['krɛvɪs] *n* grieta, hendedura

crew [kru:] *n* (*of ship etc*) tripulación *f*; (*Cine etc*) equipo; (*gang*) pandilla, banda; (*Mil*) dotación *f*

crew-cut ['kru:kʌt] *n* corte *m* al rape

crew-neck ['kru:nɛk] *n* cuello de caja

crib [krɪb] *n* pesebre *m* ■ *vt* (*col*) plagiar; (*Scol*) copiar

crick [krɪk] *n*: ~ **in the neck** tortícolis *f inv*
cricket ['krɪkɪt] *n* (*insect*) grillo; (*game*) críquet *m*
cricketer ['krɪkɪtəʳ] *n* jugador(a) *m(f)* de críquet
crime [kraɪm] *n* crimen *m*; (*less serious*) delito
crime wave *n* ola de crímenes *or* delitos
criminal ['krɪmɪnl] *n* criminal *m/f*, delincuente *m/f* ■ *adj* criminal; (*law*) penal
Criminal Investigation Department *n* ≈ Brigada de Investigación Criminal *f* (SP)
crimp [krɪmp] *vt* (*hair*) rizar
crimson ['krɪmzn] *adj* carmesí
cringe [krɪndʒ] *vi* encogerse
crinkle ['krɪŋkl] *vt* arrugar
crinkly ['krɪŋklɪ] *adj* (*hair*) rizado, crespo
cripple ['krɪpl] *n* lisiado(-a), cojo(-a) ■ *vt* lisiar, mutilar; (*ship, plane*) inutilizar; (*production, exports*) paralizar; **crippled with arthritis** paralizado por la artritis
crippling ['krɪplɪŋ] *adj* (*injury etc*) debilitador(a); (*prices, taxes*) devastador(a)
crisis ['kraɪsɪs] (*pl* **crises**) ['kraɪsiːz] *n* crisis *f*
crisp [krɪsp] *adj* fresco; (*toast, snow*) crujiente; (*manner*) seco
crisps [krɪsps] *npl* (Brit) patatas *fpl* fritas
crisscross ['krɪskrɔs] *adj* entrelazado, entrecruzado ■ *vt* entrecruzar(se)
criterion [kraɪ'tɪərɪən] (*pl* **criteria**) [kraɪ'tɪərɪə] *n* criterio
critic ['krɪtɪk] *n* crítico(-a)
critical ['krɪtɪkl] *adj* (*gen*) crítico; (*illness*) grave; **to be ~ of sb/sth** criticar a algn/algo
critically ['krɪtɪklɪ] *adv* (*speak etc*) en tono crítico; (*ill*) gravemente
criticism ['krɪtɪsɪzm] *n* crítica
criticize ['krɪtɪsaɪz] *vt* criticar
critique [krɪ'tiːk] *n* crítica
croak [krəuk] *vi* (*frog*) croar; (*raven*) graznar ■ *n* (*of raven*) graznido
Croat ['krəuæt] *adj*, *n* = **Croatian**
Croatia [krəu'eɪʃə] *n* Croacia
Croatian [krəu'eɪʃən] *adj*, *n* croata *m/f* ■ *n* (Ling) croata *m*
crochet ['krəuʃeɪ] *n* ganchillo
crock [krɔk] *n* cántaro; (*col: person: also:* **old crock**) carcamal *m/f*, vejestorio; (: *car etc*) cacharro
crockery ['krɔkərɪ] *n* (*plates, cups etc*) loza, vajilla
crocodile ['krɔkədaɪl] *n* cocodrilo
crocus ['krəukəs] *n* azafrán *m*
croft [krɔft] *n* granja pequeña
crofter ['krɔftəʳ] *n* pequeño granjero
croissant ['krwas] *n* croissant *m*, medialuna (*esp LAm*)
crone [krəun] *n* arpía, bruja

crony ['krəunɪ] *n* compinche *m/f*
crook [kruk] *n* (*fam*) ladrón(-ona) *m(f)*; (*of shepherd*) cayado; (*of arm*) pliegue *m*
crooked ['krukɪd] *adj* torcido; (*path*) tortuoso; (*fam*) sucio
crop [krɔp] *n* (*produce*) cultivo; (*amount produced*) cosecha; (*riding crop*) látigo de montar; (*of bird*) buche *m* ■ *vt* cortar, recortar; (*animals: grass*) pacer
▶ **crop up** *vi* surgir, presentarse
crop spraying [-'spreɪɪŋ] *n* fumigación *f* de los cultivos
croquet ['krəukeɪ] *n* croquet *m*
croquette [krə'kɛt] *n* croqueta (*de patata*)
cross [krɔs] *n* cruz *f* ■ *vt* (*street etc*) cruzar, atravesar; (*thwart: person*) contrariar, ir contra ■ *vi*: **the boat crosses from Santander to Plymouth** el barco hace la travesía de Santander a Plymouth ■ *adj* de mal humor, enojado; **it's a ~ between geography and sociology** es una mezcla de geografía y sociología; **to ~ o.s.** santiguarse; **they've got their lines crossed** (*fig*) hay un malentendido entre ellos; **to be/get ~ with sb (about sth)** estar enfadado/enfadarse con algn (por algo)
▶ **cross out** *vt* tachar
▶ **cross over** *vi* cruzar
crossbar ['krɔsbaːʳ] *n* travesaño; (*of bicycle*) barra
crossbow ['krɔsbəu] *n* ballesta
cross-Channel ferry ['krɔs'tʃænl-] *n* transbordador *m* que cruza el Canal de la Mancha
cross-check ['krɔstʃɛk] *n* verificación *f* ■ *vt* verificar
cross-country ['krɔs'kʌntrɪ], **cross-country race** *n* carrera a campo traviesa, cross *m*
cross-dressing [krɔs'drɛsɪŋ] *n* travestismo
cross-examination ['krɔsɪgzæmɪ'neɪʃən] *n* interrogatorio
cross-examine ['krɔsɪg'zæmɪn] *vt* interrogar
cross-eyed ['krɔsaɪd] *adj* bizco
crossfire ['krɔsfaɪəʳ] *n* fuego cruzado
crossing ['krɔsɪŋ] *n* (*on road*) cruce *m*; (Rail) paso a nivel; (*sea passage*) travesía; (*also:* **pedestrian crossing**) paso de peatones
crossing guard *n* (US) *persona encargada de ayudar a los niños a cruzar la calle*
crossing point *n* paso; (*at border*) paso fronterizo
cross purposes *npl*: **to be at ~ with sb** tener un malentendido con algn
cross-question ['krɔs'kwɛstʃən] *vt* interrogar
cross-reference ['krɔs'rɛfrəns] *n* remisión *f*
crossroads ['krɔsrəudz] *nsg* cruce *m*; (*fig*) encrucijada

cross section n corte m transversal; (of population) muestra (representativa)

crosswalk ['krɔswɔːk] n (US) paso de peatones

crosswind ['krɔswɪnd] n viento de costado

crossword ['krɔswəːd] n crucigrama m

crotch [krɔtʃ] n (of garment) entrepierna

crotchet ['krɔtʃɪt] n (Brit Mus) negra

crotchety ['krɔtʃɪtɪ] adj (person) arisco

crouch [krautʃ] vi agacharse

croup [kruːp] n (Med) crup m

croupier ['kruːpɪə] n crupier m/f

crouton ['kruːtɔn] n cubito de pan frito

crow [krəu] n (bird) cuervo; (of cock) canto, cacareo ■ vi (cock) cantar; (fig) jactarse

crowbar ['krəubaːʳ] n palanca

crowd [kraud] n muchedumbre f; (Sport) público; (common herd) vulgo ■ vt (gather) amontonar; (fill) llenar ■ vi (gather) reunirse; (pile up) amontonarse; **crowds of people** gran cantidad de gente

crowded ['kraudɪd] adj (full) atestado; (well-attended) concurrido

crowd scene n (Cine, Theat) escena con muchos comparsas

crown [kraun] n corona; (of head) coronilla; (of hat) copa; (of hill) cumbre f ■ vt (also tooth) coronar; **and to ~ it all ...** (fig) y para colmo or remate ...

crown court n (Law) tribunal m superior; ver nota

● **CROWN COURT**

● En el sistema legal inglés los delitos
● graves como asesinato, violación o
● atraco son juzgados por un jurado en un
● tribunal superior llamado crown court con
● sede en noventa ciudades. Los jueces de
● paz ("Justice of the Peace") juzgan delitos
● menores e infracciones de la ley en
● juzgados llamados "Magistrates' Courts".
● Es el juez de paz quien decide remitir los
● casos pertinentes a la crown court, que en
● caso de recursos se remite al tribunal de
● apelación, "Court of Appeal".

crowning ['kraunɪŋ] adj (achievement, glory) máximo

crown jewels npl joyas fpl reales

crown prince n príncipe m heredero

crow's feet ['krəuzfiːt] npl patas fpl de gallo

crucial ['kruːʃl] adj crucial, decisivo; **his approval is ~ to the success of the project** su aprobación es crucial para el éxito del proyecto

crucifix ['kruːsɪfɪks] n crucifijo

crucifixion [kruːsɪ'fɪkʃən] n crucifixión f

crucify ['kruːsɪfaɪ] vt crucificar; (fig) martirizar

crude [kruːd] adj (materials) bruto; (fig: basic) tosco; (: vulgar) ordinario ■ n (also: **crude oil**) (petróleo) crudo

crude oil n petróleo crudo

cruel ['kruəl] adj cruel

cruelty ['kruəltɪ] n crueldad f

cruet ['kruːɪt] n vinagreras fpl

cruise [kruːz] n crucero ■ vi (ship) navegar; (holidaymakers) hacer un crucero; (car) ir a velocidad constante

cruise missile n misil m de crucero

cruiser ['kruːzəʳ] n crucero

cruising speed ['kruːzɪŋ-] n velocidad f de crucero

crumb [krʌm] n miga, migaja

crumble ['krʌmbl] vt desmenuzar ■ vi (gen) desmenuzarse; (building) desmoronarse

crumbly ['krʌmblɪ] adj desmenuzable

crummy ['krʌmɪ] adj (col: poor quality) pésimo, cutre (SP); (: unwell) fatal

crumpet ['krʌmpɪt] n ≈ bollo para tostar

crumple ['krʌmpl] vt (paper) estrujar; (material) arrugar

crunch [krʌntʃ] vt (with teeth) ronzar; (underfoot) hacer crujir ■ n (fig) hora de la verdad

crunchy ['krʌntʃɪ] adj crujiente

crusade [kruː'seɪd] n cruzada ■ vi: **to ~ for/against** (fig) hacer una campaña en pro de/en contra de

crusader [kruː'seɪdəʳ] n (fig) paladín m/f

crush [krʌʃ] n (crowd) aglomeración f ■ vt (gen) aplastar; (paper) estrujar; (cloth) arrugar; (grind, break up: garlic, ice) picar; (fruit) exprimir; (grapes) exprimir, prensar; **to have a ~ on sb** estar enamorado de algn

crush barrier n barrera de seguridad

crushing ['krʌʃɪŋ] adj aplastante; (burden) agobiante

crust [krʌst] n corteza

crustacean [krʌs'teɪʃən] n crustáceo

crusty ['krʌstɪ] adj (bread) crujiente; (person) de mal carácter; (remark) brusco

crutch [krʌtʃ] n (Med) muleta; (support) apoyo

crux [krʌks] n: **the ~** lo esencial, el quid

cry [kraɪ] vi llorar; (shout: also: **cry out**) gritar ■ n grito; (of animal) aullido; (weep): **she had a good ~** lloró a lágrima viva; **what are you crying about?** ¿por qué lloras?; **to ~ for help** pedir socorro a voces; **it's a far ~ from ...** (fig) dista mucho de ...

▶ **cry off** vi retirarse

crypt [krɪpt] n cripta

cryptic ['krɪptɪk] adj enigmático

crystal ['krɪstl] n cristal m
crystal-clear ['krɪstl'klɪər] adj claro como el agua; (fig) cristalino
crystallize ['krɪstəlaɪz] vt (fig) cristalizar ▪ vi cristalizarse; **crystallized fruits** frutas fpl escarchadas
CSA n abbr (= Confederate States of America, Child Support Agency) organismo que supervisa el pago de la pensión a hijos de padres separados
CSC n abbr (= Civil Service Commission) comisión para la contratación de funcionarios
CS gas n (Brit) gas m lacrimógeno
CST n abbr (US: = Central Standard Time) huso horario
CT, Ct. abbr (US) = **Connecticut**
ct abbr = **cent**; **court**; **carat**
CTC n abbr (Brit: = city technology college) ≈ centro de formación profesional
cu. abbr = **cubic**
cub [kʌb] n cachorro; (also: **cub scout**) niño explorador
Cuba ['kju:bə] n Cuba
Cuban ['kju:bən] adj, n cubano(-a) m(f)
cubbyhole ['kʌbɪhəʊl] n cuchitril m
cube [kju:b] n cubo; (of sugar) terrón m ▪ vt (Math) elevar al cubo
cube root n raíz f cúbica
cubic ['kju:bɪk] adj cúbico; **~ capacity** (Aut) capacidad f cúbica
cubicle ['kju:bɪkl] n (at pool) caseta; (for bed) cubículo
cubism ['kju:bɪzəm] n cubismo
cuckoo ['kuku:] n cuco
cuckoo clock n reloj m de cuco
cucumber ['kju:kʌmbər] n pepino
cuddle ['kʌdl] vt abrazar ▪ vi abrazarse
cuddly ['kʌdlɪ] adj mimoso; (toy) de peluche
cudgel ['kʌdʒəl] vt: **to ~ one's brains** devanarse los sesos
cue [kju:] n (snooker cue) taco; (Theat etc) entrada
cuff [kʌf] n (Brit: of shirt, coat etc) puño; (US: of trousers) vuelta; (blow) bofetada ▪ vt bofetear; **off the ~** adv improvisado
cufflinks ['kʌflɪŋks] npl gemelos mpl
cu. ft. abbr = **cubic feet**
cu. in. abbr = **cubic inches**
cuisine [kwɪ'zi:n] n cocina
cul-de-sac ['kʌldəsæk] n callejón m sin salida
culinary ['kʌlɪnərɪ] adj culinario
cull [kʌl] vt (select) entresacar; (kill selectively: animals) matar selectivamente ▪ n matanza selectiva; **seal ~** matanza selectiva de focas
culminate ['kʌlmɪneɪt] vi: **to ~ in** culminar en
culmination [kʌlmɪ'neɪʃən] n culminación f, colmo

culottes [ku:'lɔts] npl falda f pantalón
culpable ['kʌlpəbl] adj culpable
culprit ['kʌlprɪt] n culpable m/f
cult [kʌlt] n culto; **a ~ figure** un ídolo
cultivate ['kʌltɪveɪt] vt (also fig) cultivar
cultivated ['kʌltɪveɪtɪd] adj culto
cultivation [kʌltɪ'veɪʃən] n cultivo; (fig) cultura
cultural ['kʌltʃərəl] adj cultural
culture ['kʌltʃər] n (also fig) cultura
cultured ['kʌltʃəd] adj culto
cumbersome ['kʌmbəsəm] adj voluminoso
cumin ['kʌmɪn] n (spice) comino
cummerbund ['kʌməbʌnd] n faja, fajín m
cumulative ['kju:mjulətɪv] adj cumulativo
cunning ['kʌnɪŋ] n astucia ▪ adj astuto; (clever: device, idea) ingenioso
cunt [kʌnt] n (col!) coño (!); (insult) mamonazo(-a) (!)
cup [kʌp] n taza; (prize, event) copa; **a ~ of tea** una taza de té
cupboard ['kʌbəd] n armario, placar(d) m (LAm)
cup final n (Football) final f de copa
cupful ['kʌpful] n taza
Cupid ['kju:pɪd] n Cupido
cupola ['kju:pələ] n cúpula
cuppa ['kʌpa] n (Brit col) (taza de) té m
cup-tie ['kʌptaɪ] n (Brit) partido de copa
cur [kə:r] n perro de mala raza; (person) canalla m
curable ['kjuərəbl] adj curable
curate ['kjuərɪt] n coadjutor m
curator [kjuə'reɪtər] n director(a) m(f)
curb [kə:b] vt refrenar; (powers, spending) limitar ▪ n freno; (US: kerb) bordillo
curd cheese [kə:d-] n requesón m
curdle ['kə:dl] vi cuajarse
curds [kə:dz] npl requesón msg
cure [kjuər] vt curar ▪ n cura, curación f; **to be cured of sth** curarse de algo; **to take a ~** tomar un remedio
cure-all ['kjuərɔ:l] n (also fig) panacea
curfew ['kə:fju:] n toque m de queda
curio ['kjuərɪəʊ] n curiosidad f
curiosity [kjuərɪ'ɔsɪtɪ] n curiosidad f
curious ['kjuərɪəs] adj curioso; **I'm ~ about him** me intriga
curiously ['kjuərɪəslɪ] adv curiosamente; **~ enough, ...** aunque parezca extraño ...
curl [kə:l] n rizo; (of smoke etc) espiral f, voluta ▪ vt (hair) rizar; (paper) arrollar; (lip) fruncir ▪ vi rizarse; arrollarse
▶ **curl up** vi arrollarse; (person) hacerse un ovillo; (fam) morirse de risa
curler ['kə:lər] n bigudí m
curlew ['kə:lu:] n zarapito**

curling tongs, curling irons (US) ['kəːlɪŋ-] *npl* tenacillas *fpl*

curly ['kəːlɪ] *adj* rizado

currant ['kʌrnt] *n* pasa; (*black, red*) grosella

currency ['kʌrnsɪ] *n* moneda; **to gain ~** (*fig*) difundirse

current ['kʌrnt] *n* corriente *f* ■ *adj* actual; **direct/alternating ~** corriente directa/ alterna; **the ~ issue of a magazine** el último número de una revista; **in ~ use** de uso corriente

current account *n* (*Brit*) cuenta corriente

current affairs *npl* (noticias *fpl* de) actualidad *f*

current assets *npl* (*Comm*) activo disponible

current liabilities *npl* (*Comm*) pasivo circulante

currently ['kʌrntlɪ] *adv* actualmente

curriculum (*pl* **curriculums** *or* **curricula**) [kəˈrɪkjuləm, -lə] *n* plan *m* de estudios

curriculum vitae [-ˈviːtaɪ] *n* currículum *m* (vitae)

curry ['kʌrɪ] *n* curry *m* ■ *vt:* **to ~ favour with** buscar el favor de

curry powder *n* curry *m* en polvo

curse [kəːs] *vi* echar pestes ■ *vt* maldecir ■ *n* maldición *f*; (*swearword*) palabrota

cursor ['kəːsəʳ] *n* (*Comput*) cursor *m*

cursory ['kəːsərɪ] *adj* rápido, superficial

curt [kəːt] *adj* seco

curtail [kəːˈteɪl] *vt* (*cut short*) acortar; (*restrict*) restringir

curtain ['kəːtn] *n* cortina; (*Theat*) telón *m*; **to draw the curtains** (*together*) cerrar las cortinas; (*apart*) abrir las cortinas

curtain call *n* (*Theat*) llamada a escena

curtain ring *n* anilla

curtsey, curtsy ['kəːtsɪ] *n* reverencia ■ *vi* hacer una reverencia

curve [kəːv] *n* curva ■ *vt, vi* torcer

curved [kəːvd] *adj* curvo

cushion ['kuʃən] *n* cojín *m*; (*Snooker*) banda ■ *vt* (*seat*) acolchar; (*shock*) amortiguar

cushy ['kuʃɪ] *adj* (*col*): **a ~ job** un chollo; **to have a ~ time** tener la vida arreglada

custard ['kʌstəd] *n* (*for pouring*) natillas *fpl*

custard powder *n* polvos *mpl* para natillas

custodial sentence [kʌsˈtəudɪəl-] *n* pena de prisión

custodian [kʌsˈtəudɪən] *n* guardián(-ana) *m(f)*; (*of museum etc*) conservador(a) *m(f)*

custody ['kʌstədɪ] *n* custodia; **to take sb into ~** detener a algn; **in the ~ of** al cuidado *or* cargo de

custom ['kʌstəm] *n* costumbre *f*; (*Comm*) clientela; *see also* **customs**

customary ['kʌstəmərɪ] *adj* acostumbrado;

it is ~ to do ... es la costumbre hacer ...

custom-built ['kʌstəm'bɪlt] *adj* = **custom-made**

customer ['kʌstəməʳ] *n* cliente *m/f*; **he's an awkward ~** (*col*) es un tipo difícil

customer profile *n* perfil *m* del cliente

customized ['kʌstəmaɪzd] *adj* (*car etc*) hecho a encargo

custom-made ['kʌstəm'meɪd] *adj* hecho a la medida

customs ['kʌstəmz] *npl* aduana *sg*; **to go through (the) ~** pasar la aduana

Customs and Excise *n* (*Brit*) Aduanas *fpl* y Arbitrios

customs officer *n* aduanero(-a), funcionario(-a) de aduanas

cut [kʌt] *vb* (*pt, pp* **cut**) ■ *vt* cortar; (*price*) rebajar; (*record*) grabar; (*reduce*) reducir; (*col: avoid: class, lecture*) fumarse, faltar a ■ *vi* cortar; (*intersect*) cruzarse ■ *n* corte *m*; (*in skin*) corte, cortadura; (*with sword*) tajo; (*of knife*) cuchillada; (*in salary etc*) recorte *m*; (*slice of meat*) tajada; **to ~ one's finger** cortarse un dedo; **to get one's hair ~** cortarse el pelo; **to ~ and paste** (*Comput*) cortar y pegar; **to ~ sb dead** negarle el saludo *or* cortarle (*LAm*) a algn; **it cuts both ways** (*fig*) tiene doble filo; **to ~ a tooth** echar un diente; **power ~** (*Brit*) apagón *m*
  ▶ **cut back** *vt* (*plants*) podar; (*production, expenditure*) reducir
  ▶ **cut down** *vt* (*tree*) cortar, derribar; (*consumption, expenses*) reducir; **to ~ sb down to size** (*fig*) bajarle los humos a algn
  ▶ **cut in** *vi:* **to ~ in (on)** (*interrupt: conversation*) interrumpir, intervenir (en); (*Aut*) cerrar el paso (a)
  ▶ **cut off** *vt* cortar; (*fig*) aislar; (*troops*) cercar; **we've been ~ off** (*Tel*) nos han cortado la comunicación
  ▶ **cut out** *vt* (*shape*) recortar; (*delete*) suprimir
  ▶ **cut up** *vt* cortar (en pedazos); (*chop: food*) trinchar, cortar

cut-and-dried ['kʌtən'draɪd] *adj* (*also:* **cut-and-dry**) arreglado de antemano, seguro

cutback ['kʌtbæk] *n* reducción *f*

cute [kjuːt] *adj* lindo, mono; (*shrewd*) listo

cuticle ['kjuːtɪkl] *n* cutícula

cutlery ['kʌtlərɪ] *n* cubiertos *mpl*

cutlet ['kʌtlɪt] *n* chuleta

cutoff ['kʌtɔf] *n* (*also:* **cutoff point**) límite *m*

cutout ['kʌtaut] *n* (*cardboard cutout*) recortable *m*

cut-price ['kʌt'praɪs], **cut-rate** (US) ['kʌt'reɪt] *adj* a precio reducido

cutthroat ['kʌtθrəut] *n* asesino(-a) ■ *adj* feroz; **~ competition** competencia encarnizada *or* despiadada

cutting ['kʌtɪŋ] *adj* (*gen*) cortante; (*remark*) mordaz ∎ *n* (*Brit: from newspaper*) recorte *m*; (: *Rail*) desmonte *m*; (*Cine*) montaje *m*

cutting edge *n* (*of knife*) filo; (*fig*) vanguardia; **a country on** *or* **at the ~ of space technology** un país puntero en tecnología del espacio

CV *n abbr* = **curriculum vitae**

cwo *abbr* (*Comm*) = **cash with order**

cwt. *abbr* = **hundredweight(s)**

cyanide ['saɪənaɪd] *n* cianuro

cybercafé ['saɪbə,kæfeɪ] *n* cibercafé *m*

cybernetics [saɪbə'nɛtɪks] *nsg* cibernética

cyberspace ['saɪbəspeɪs] *n* ciberespacio

cyberterrorism ['saɪbətɛrərɪzəm] *n* ciberterrorismo *m*

cyclamen ['sɪkləmən] *n* ciclamen *m*

cycle ['saɪkl] *n* ciclo; (*bicycle*) bicicleta ∎ *vi* ir en bicicleta

cycle lane *n* carril *m* de bicicleta, carril *m* bici

cycle race *n* carrera ciclista

cycle rack *n* soporte *m* para bicicletas

cycling ['saɪklɪŋ] *n* ciclismo

cycling holiday *n* vacaciones *fpl* en bicicleta

cyclist ['saɪklɪst] *n* ciclista *m/f*

cyclone ['saɪkləun] *n* ciclón *m*

cygnet ['sɪgnɪt] *n* pollo de cisne

cylinder ['sɪlɪndə^r] *n* cilindro

cylinder block *n* bloque *m* de cilindros

cylinder head *n* culata de cilindro

cylinder-head gasket *n* junta de culata

cymbals ['sɪmblz] *npl* platillos *mpl*, címbalos *mpl*

cynic ['sɪnɪk] *n* cínico(-a)

cynical ['sɪnɪkl] *adj* cínico

cynicism ['sɪnɪsɪzəm] *n* cinismo

cypress ['saɪprɪs] *n* ciprés *m*

Cypriot ['sɪprɪət] *adj, n* chipriota *m/f*

Cyprus ['saɪprəs] *n* Chipre *f*

cyst [sɪst] *n* quiste *m*

cystitis [sɪs'taɪtɪs] *n* cistitis *f*

CZ *n abbr* (*US: = Canal Zone*) *zona del Canal de Panamá*

czar [zɑː^r] *n* zar *m*

czarina [zɑː'riːnə] *n* zarina

Czech [tʃɛk] *adj* checo ∎ *n* checo(-a); (*Ling*) checo; **the ~ Republic** la República Checa

Czechoslovak [tʃɛkə'sləuvæk] *adj, n* = **Czechoslovakian**

Czechoslovakia [tʃɛkəslə'vækɪə] *n* Checoslovaquia

Czechoslovakian [tʃɛkəslə'vækɪən] *adj, n* checoslovaco(-a) *m(f)*

Dd

D, d [diː] *n* (*letter*) D, d; (*Mus*): **D** re *m*; **D for David,** (*US*) **D for Dog** D de Dolores

D *abbr* (*US Pol*) = **democrat; democratic**

d *abbr* (*Brit: old*) = **penny**

d. *abbr* = **died**

DA *n abbr* (*US*) = **district attorney**

dab [dæb] *vt*: **to ~ ointment onto a wound** aplicar pomada sobre una herida; **to ~ with paint** dar unos toques de pintura ▪ *n* (*light stroke*) toque *m*; (*small amount*) pizca

dabble ['dæbl] *vi*: **to ~ in** hacer por afición

Dacca ['dækə] *n* Dacca

dachshund ['dækshund] *n* perro tejonero

Dacron® ['deɪkrɔn] *n* (*US*) terylene *m*

dad [dæd], **daddy** ['dædɪ] *n* papá *m*

daddy-long-legs [dædɪ'lɔŋlɛgz] *n* típula

daffodil ['dæfədɪl] *n* narciso

daft [dɑːft] *adj* chiflado

dagger ['dægəʳ] *n* puñal *m*, daga; **to look daggers at sb** fulminar a algn con la mirada

dahlia ['deɪljə] *n* dalia

daily ['deɪlɪ] *adj* diario, cotidiano ▪ *n* (*paper*) diario; (*domestic help*) asistenta ▪ *adv* todos los días, cada día; **twice ~** dos veces al día

dainty ['deɪntɪ] *adj* delicado; (*tasteful*) elegante

dairy ['dɛərɪ] *n* (*shop*) lechería; (*on farm*) vaquería ▪ *adj* (*cow etc*) lechero

dairy cow *n* vaca lechera

dairy farm *n* vaquería

dairy produce *n* productos *mpl* lácteos

dais ['deɪɪs] *n* estrado

daisy ['deɪzɪ] *n* margarita

daisy-wheel printer *n* impresora de margarita

dale [deɪl] *n* valle *m*

dally ['dælɪ] *vi* entretenerse

dalmatian [dæl'meɪʃən] *n* (*dog*) (perro) dálmata *m*

dam [dæm] *n* presa; (*reservoir*) embalse ▪ *vt* embalsar

damage ['dæmɪdʒ] *n* daño; (*fig*) perjuicio; (*to machine*) avería ▪ *vt* dañar; perjudicar; averiar; **~ to property** daños materiales

damages ['dæmɪdʒɪz] *npl* (*Law*) daños y perjuicios; **to pay £5000 in ~** pagar £5000 por daños y perjuicios

damaging ['dæmɪdʒɪŋ] *adj*: **~ (to)** perjudicial (a)

Damascus [də'mɑːskəs] *n* Damasco

dame [deɪm] *n* (*title*) dama; (*US col*) tía; (*Theat*) vieja; *see also* **pantomime**

damn [dæm] *vt* condenar; (*curse*) maldecir ▪ *n* (*col*): **I don't give a ~** me importa un pito ▪ *adj* (*col: also:* **damned**) maldito, fregado (*LAm*); **~ (it)!** ¡maldito sea!

damnable ['dæmnəbl] *adj* (*col: behaviour*) detestable; (*weather*) horrible

damnation [dæm'neɪʃən] *n* (*Rel*) condenación *f* ▪ *excl* (*col*) ¡maldición!, ¡maldito sea!

damning ['dæmɪŋ] *adj* (*evidence*) irrecusable

damp [dæmp] *adj* húmedo, mojado ▪ *n* humedad *f* ▪ *vt* (*also:* **dampen**: *cloth, rag*) mojar; (*enthusiasm*) enfriar

dampcourse ['dæmpkɔːs] *n* aislante *m* hidrófugo

damper ['dæmpəʳ] *n* (*Mus*) sordina; (*of fire*) regulador *m* de tiro; **to put a ~ on things** ser un jarro de agua fría

dampness ['dæmpnɪs] *n* humedad *f*

damson ['dæmzən] *n* ciruela damascena

dance [dɑːns] *n* baile *m* ▪ *vi* bailar; **to ~ about** saltar

dance hall *n* salón *m* de baile

dancer ['dɑːnsəʳ] *n* bailador(a) *m(f)*; (*professional*) bailarín(-ina) *m(f)*

dancing ['dɑːnsɪŋ] *n* baile *m*

D and C *n abbr* (*Med:* = *dilation and curettage*) raspado

dandelion ['dændɪlaɪən] *n* diente *m* de león

dandruff ['dændrəf] *n* caspa

D and T *n abbr* (*Brit Scol*) = **design and technology**

dandy ['dændɪ] *n* dandi *m* ▪ *adj* (*US col*) estupendo

Dane [deɪn] n danés(-esa) m(f)

danger ['deɪndʒəʳ] n peligro; (risk) riesgo; ~! (on sign) ¡peligro!; **to be in ~ of** correr riesgo de; **out of ~** fuera de peligro

danger list n (Med): **to be on the ~** estar grave

dangerous ['deɪndʒərəs] adj peligroso

dangerously ['deɪndʒərəslɪ] adv peligrosamente; **~ ill** gravemente enfermo

danger zone n área or zona de peligro

dangle ['dæŋgl] vt colgar ▪ vi pender, estar colgado

Danish ['deɪnɪʃ] adj danés(-esa) ▪ n (Ling) danés m

Danish pastry n pastel m de almendra

dank [dæŋk] adj húmedo y malsano

dapper ['dæpəʳ] adj pulcro, apuesto

Dardanelles [daːdəˈnɛlz] npl Dardanelos mpl

dare [dɛəʳ] vt: **to ~ sb to do** desafiar a algn a hacer ▪ vi: **to ~ (to) do sth** atreverse a hacer algo; **I ~ say** (I suppose) puede ser, a lo mejor; **I ~ say he'll turn up** puede ser que or quizás venga; **I daren't tell him** no me atrevo a decírselo

daredevil ['dɛədɛvl] n temerario(-a), atrevido(-a)

Dar-es-Salaam ['daːrɛssəˈlaːm] n Dar es Salaam m

daring ['dɛərɪŋ] adj (person) osado; (plan, escape) atrevido ▪ n atrevimiento, osadía

dark [daːk] adj oscuro; (hair, complexion) moreno; (fig: cheerless) triste, sombrío ▪ n (gen) oscuridad f; (night) tinieblas fpl; **~ chocolate** chocolate m amargo; **it is/is getting ~** es de noche/está oscureciendo; **in the ~ about** (fig) ignorante de; **after ~** después del anochecer

darken ['daːkn] vt oscurecer; (colour) hacer más oscuro ▪ vi oscurecerse; (cloud over) nublarse

dark glasses npl gafas fpl oscuras

dark horse n (fig) incógnita

darkly ['daːklɪ] adv (gloomily) tristemente; (sinisterly) siniestramente

darkness ['daːknɪs] n (in room) oscuridad f; (night) tinieblas fpl

darkroom ['daːkrum] n cuarto oscuro

darling ['daːlɪŋ] adj, n querido(-a) m(f)

darn [daːn] vt zurcir

dart [daːt] n dardo; (in sewing) pinza ▪ vi precipitarse; **to ~ away/along** salir/marchar disparado

dartboard ['daːtbɔːd] n diana

darts [daːts] n dardos mpl

dash [dæʃ] n (small quantity: of liquid) gota, chorrito; (of solid) pizca; (sign) guión m; (: long) raya ▪ vt (break) romper, estrellar; (hopes) defraudar ▪ vi precipitarse, ir de prisa; **a ~**

of soda un poco or chorrito de sifón or soda

▸ **dash away, dash off** vi marcharse apresuradamente

dashboard ['dæʃbɔːd] n (Aut) salpicadero

dashing ['dæʃɪŋ] adj gallardo

dastardly ['dæstədlɪ] adj ruin, vil

DAT n abbr (= digital audio tape) cas(s)et(t)e m or f digital

data ['deɪtə] npl datos mpl

database ['deɪtəbeɪs] n base f de datos

data capture n recogida de datos

data link n enlace m de datos

data processing n proceso or procesamiento de datos

data transmission n transmisión f de datos

date [deɪt] n (day) fecha; (with friend) cita; (fruit) dátil m ▪ vt fechar; (col: girl etc) salir con; **what's the ~ today?** ¿qué fecha es hoy?; **~ of birth** fecha de nacimiento; **closing ~** fecha tope; **to ~** adv hasta la fecha; **out of ~** pasado de moda; **up to ~** moderno; puesto al día; **to bring up to ~** (correspondence, information) poner al día; (method) actualizar; **to bring sb up to ~** poner a algn al corriente; **letter dated 5th July** or (US) **July 5th** carta fechada el 5 de julio

dated ['deɪtɪd] adj anticuado

date rape n violación ocurrida durante una cita con un conocido

date stamp n matasellos m inv; (on fresh foods) sello de fecha

dative ['deɪtɪv] n dativo

daub [dɔːb] vt embadurnar

daughter ['dɔːtəʳ] n hija

daughter-in-law ['dɔːtərɪnlɔː] n nuera, hija política

daunting ['dɔːntɪŋ] adj desalentador(-a)

davenport ['dævnpɔːt] n escritorio; (US: sofa) sofá m

dawdle ['dɔːdl] vi (waste time) perder el tiempo; (go slowly) andar muy despacio; **to ~ over one's work** trabajar muy despacio

dawn [dɔːn] n alba, amanecer m ▪ vi amanecer; (fig): **it dawned on him that ...** cayó en la cuenta de que ...; **at ~** al amanecer; **from ~ to dusk** de sol a sol

dawn chorus n canto de los pájaros al amanecer

day [deɪ] n día m; (working day) jornada; **the ~ before** el día anterior; **the ~ after tomorrow** pasado mañana; **the ~ before yesterday** anteayer, antes de ayer; **the ~ after, the following ~** el día siguiente; **by ~** de día; **~ by ~** día a día; **(on) the ~ that ...** el día que ...; **to work an eight-hour ~** trabajar ocho horas diarias or al día; **he works eight hours a ~** trabaja ocho horas al día; **paid**

by the ~ pagado por día; **these days, in the present ~** hoy en día

daybook ['deɪbuk] n (Brit) diario or libro de entradas y salidas

daybreak ['deɪbreɪk] n amanecer m

day-care centre ['deɪkɛə-] n centro de día; (for children) guardería infantil

daydream ['deɪdri:m] n ensueño ■ vi soñar despierto

daylight ['deɪlaɪt] n luz f (del día)

daylight robbery n: **it's ~!** (fig, col) ¡es un robo descarado!

Daylight Saving Time n (US) hora de verano

day-release course [deɪrɪ'li:s-] n curso de formación de un día a la semana

day return, day return ticket n (Brit) billete m de ida y vuelta (en un día)

day shift n turno de día

daytime ['deɪtaɪm] n día m

day-to-day ['deɪtə'deɪ] adj cotidiano, diario; (expenses) diario; **on a ~ basis** día por día

day trip n excursión f (de un día)

day tripper n excursionista m/f

daze [deɪz] vt (stun) aturdir ■ n: **in a ~** aturdido

dazed [deɪzd] adj aturdido

dazzle ['dæzl] vt deslumbrar

dazzling ['dæzlɪŋ] adj (light, smile) deslumbrante; (colour) fuerte

dB abbr = **decibel**

DBS n abbr (= direct broadcasting by satellite) transmisión vía satélite

DC abbr (Elec) = **direct current**; (US) = **District of Columbia**

DCC® n abbr (= digital compact cassette) cas(s)et(t)e m digital compacto

DD n abbr (= Doctor of Divinity) título universitario ■ abbr = **direct debit**

dd. abbr (Comm) = **delivered**

D-day ['di:deɪ] n (fig) día m clave

DDS n abbr (US: = Doctor of Dental Science, Doctor of Dental Surgery) títulos universitarios

DDT n abbr (= dichlorodiphenyl trichloroethane) DDT m

DE abbr (US) = **Delaware**

DEA n abbr (US: = Drug Enforcement Administration) brigada especial dedicada a la lucha contra el tráfico de estupefacientes

deacon ['di:kən] n diácono

dead [dɛd] adj muerto; (limb) dormido; (battery) agotado ■ adv totalmente; (exactly) justo; **he was ~ on arrival** ingresó cadáver; **to shoot sb ~** matar a algn a tiros; **~ tired** muerto (de cansancio); **to stop ~** parar en seco; **the line has gone ~** (Tel) se ha cortado la línea; **the ~** npl los muertos

dead beat adj: **to be ~** (col) estar hecho polvo

deaden ['dɛdn] vt (blow, sound) amortiguar; (pain) calmar, aliviar

dead end n callejón m sin salida

dead-end ['dɛdɛnd] adj: **a ~ job** un trabajo sin porvenir

dead heat n (Sport) empate m

deadline ['dɛdlaɪn] n fecha tope; **to work to a ~** trabajar con una fecha tope

deadlock ['dɛdlɔk] n punto muerto

dead loss n (col): **to be a ~** (person) ser un inútil; (thing) ser una birria

deadly ['dɛdlɪ] adj mortal, fatal; **~ dull** aburridísimo

deadly nightshade [-'naɪtʃeɪd] n belladona

deadpan ['dɛdpæn] adj sin expresión

Dead Sea n: **the ~** el Mar Muerto

dead season n (Tourism) temporada baja

deaf [dɛf] adj sordo; **to turn a ~ ear to sth** hacer oídos sordos a algo

deaf-aid ['dɛfeɪd] n audífono

deaf-and-dumb ['dɛfən'dʌm] adj (person) sordomudo; (alphabet) para sordomudos

deafen ['dɛfn] vt ensordecer

deafening ['dɛfnɪŋ] adj ensordecedor(-a)

deaf-mute ['dɛfmju:t] n sordomudo(-a)

deafness ['dɛfnɪs] n sordera

deal [di:l] n (agreement) pacto, convenio; (business) negocio, transacción f; (Cards) reparto ■ vt (pt, pp **dealt**) (gen) dar; **a great ~ (of)** bastante, mucho; **it's a ~!** (col) ¡trato hecho!, ¡de acuerdo!; **to do a ~ with sb** hacer un trato con algn; **he got a bad/fair ~ from them** le trataron mal/bien
  ▶ **deal in** vt fus tratar en, comerciar en
  ▶ **deal with** vt fus (people) tratar con; (problem) ocuparse de; (subject) tratar de

dealer ['di:lə^r] n comerciante m/f; (Cards) mano f

dealership ['di:ləʃɪp] n concesionario

dealings ['di:lɪŋz] npl (Comm) transacciones fpl; (relations) relaciones fpl

dealt [dɛlt] pt, pp of **deal**

dean [di:n] n (Rel) deán m; (Scol) decano(-a)

dear [dɪə^r] adj querido; (expensive) caro ■ n: **my ~** querido(-a); **~ me!** ¡Dios mío!; **D~ Sir/Madam** (in letter) Muy señor mío, Estimado señor/Estimada señora, De mi/nuestra (mayor) consideración (esp LAm); **D~ Mr/Mrs X** Estimado(-a) señor(a) X

dearly ['dɪəlɪ] adv (love) mucho; (pay) caro

dearth [də:θ] n (of food, resources, money) escasez f

death [dɛθ] n muerte f

deathbed ['dɛθbɛd] n lecho de muerte

death certificate n partida de defunción

death duties npl (Brit) derechos mpl de sucesión

d

deathly ['dɛθlɪ] *adj* mortal; (*silence*) profundo
death penalty *n* pena de muerte
death rate *n* tasa de mortalidad
death row *n*: **to be on ~** (US) estar condenado a muerte
death sentence *n* condena a muerte
death squad *n* escuadrón *m* de la muerte
deathtrap ['dɛθtræp] *n* lugar *m* (*or* vehículo *etc*) muy peligroso
deb [dɛb] *n abbr* (*col*) = **debutante**
debacle [deɪ'baːkl] *n* desastre *m*, catástrofe *f*
debar [dɪ'baːʳ] *vt*: **to ~ sb from doing** prohibir a algn hacer
debase [dɪ'beɪs] *vt* degradar
debatable [dɪ'beɪtəbl] *adj* discutible; **it is ~ whether ...** es discutible si ...
debate [dɪ'beɪt] *n* debate *m* ▪ *vt* discutir
debauched [dɪ'bɔːtʃt] *adj* vicioso
debauchery [dɪ'bɔːtʃərɪ] *n* libertinaje *m*
debenture [dɪ'bɛntʃəʳ] *n* (*Comm*) bono, obligación *f*
debenture capital *n* capital *m* hipotecario
debilitate [dɪ'bɪlɪteɪt] *vt* debilitar
debilitating [dɪ'bɪlɪteɪtɪŋ] *adj* (*illness etc*) debilitante
debit ['dɛbɪt] *n* debe *m* ▪ *vt*: **to ~ a sum to sb** *or* **to sb's account** cargar una suma en cuenta a algn
debit balance *n* saldo deudor *or* pasivo
debit note *n* nota de débito *or* cargo
debonair [dɛbə'nɛəʳ] *adj* jovial, cortés(-esa)
debrief [diː'briːf] *vt* hacer dar parte
debriefing [diː'briːfɪŋ] *n* relación *f* (de un informe)
debris ['dɛbriː] *n* escombros *mpl*
debt [dɛt] *n* deuda; **to be in ~** tener deudas; **debts of £5000** deudas de cinco mil libras; **bad ~** deuda incobrable
debt collector *n* cobrador(a) *m(f)* de deudas
debtor ['dɛtəʳ] *n* deudor(a) *m(f)*
debug ['diː'bʌg] *vt* (*Comput*) depurar
debunk [diː'bʌŋk] *vt* (*col: theory*) desprestigiar, desacreditar; (*claim*) desacreditar; (*person, institution*) desenmascarar
début ['deɪbjuː] *n* presentación *f*
debutante ['dɛbjutænt] *n* debutante *f*
Dec. *abbr* (= *December*) dic
decade ['dɛkeɪd] *n* década, decenio
decadence ['dɛkədəns] *n* decadencia
decadent ['dɛkədənt] *adj* decadente
de-caff ['diːkæf] *n* (*col*) descafeinado
decaffeinated [dɪ'kæfɪneɪtɪd] *adj* descafeinado
decamp [dɪ'kæmp] *vi* (*col*) escaparse, largarse, rajarse (*LAm*)
decant [dɪ'kænt] *vt* decantar
decanter [dɪ'kæntəʳ] *n* jarra, decantador *m*

decathlon [dɪ'kæθlən] *n* decatlón *m*
decay [dɪ'keɪ] *n* (*fig*) decadencia; (*of building*) desmoronamiento; (*of tooth*) caries *f inv* ▪ *vi* (*rot*) pudrirse; (*fig*) decaer
decease [dɪ'siːs] *n* fallecimiento ▪ *vi* fallecer
deceased [dɪ'siːst] *adj* difunto
deceit [dɪ'siːt] *n* engaño
deceitful [dɪ'siːtful] *adj* engañoso
deceive [dɪ'siːv] *vt* engañar
decelerate [diː'sɛləreɪt] *vt* moderar la marcha de ▪ *vi* decelerar
December [dɪ'sɛmbəʳ] *n* diciembre *m*; *see also* **July**
decency ['diːsənsɪ] *n* decencia
decent ['diːsənt] *adj* (*proper*) decente; (*person*) amable, bueno
decently ['diːsəntlɪ] *adv* (*respectably*) decentemente; (*kindly*) amablemente
decentralization [diːsɛntrəlaɪ'zeɪʃən] *n* descentralización *f*
decentralize [diː'sɛntrəlaɪz] *vt* descentralizar
deception [dɪ'sɛpʃən] *n* engaño
deceptive [dɪ'sɛptɪv] *adj* engañoso
decibel ['dɛsɪbɛl] *n* decibel(io) *m*
decide [dɪ'saɪd] *vt* (*person*) decidir; (*question, argument*) resolver ▪ *vi*: **to ~ to do/that** decidir hacer/que; **to ~ on sth** tomar una decisión sobre algo; **to ~ against doing sth** decidir en contra de hacer algo
decided [dɪ'saɪdɪd] *adj* (*resolute*) decidido; (*clear, definite*) indudable
decidedly [dɪ'saɪdɪdlɪ] *adv* decididamente
deciding [dɪ'saɪdɪŋ] *adj* decisivo
deciduous [dɪ'sɪdjuəs] *adj* de hoja caduca
decimal ['dɛsɪməl] *adj* decimal ▪ *n* decimal *f*; **to three ~ places** con tres cifras decimales
decimalize ['dɛsɪməlaɪz] *vt* convertir al, sistema decimal
decimal point *n* coma decimal
decimal system *n* sistema *m* métrico decimal
decimate ['dɛsɪmeɪt] *vt* diezmar
decipher [dɪ'saɪfəʳ] *vt* descifrar
decision [dɪ'sɪʒən] *n* decisión *f*; **to make a ~** tomar una decisión
decisive [dɪ'saɪsɪv] *adj* (*influence*) decisivo; (*manner, person*) decidido; (*reply*) tajante
deck [dɛk] *n* (*Naut*) cubierta; (*of bus*) piso; (*of cards*) baraja; **cassette ~** platina; **to go up on ~** subir a (la) cubierta; **below ~** en la bodega
deckchair ['dɛktʃɛəʳ] *n* tumbona
deckhand ['dɛkhænd] *n* marinero de cubierta
declaration [dɛklə'reɪʃən] *n* declaración *f*
declare [dɪ'klɛəʳ] *vt* (*gen*) declarar

declassify [di:'klæsɪfaɪ] *vt* permitir que salga a la luz

decline [dɪ'klaɪn] *n* decaimiento, decadencia; (*lessening*) disminución *f* ■ *vt* rehusar ■ *vi* decaer; disminuir; **~ in living standards** disminución *f* del nivel de vida; **to ~ to do sth** rehusar hacer algo

declutch ['di:'klʌtʃ] *vi* desembragar

decode [di:'kəud] *vt* descifrar

decoder [di:'kəudəʳ] *n* (*Comput, TV*) de(s)codificador *m*

decompose [di:kəm'pəuz] *vi* descomponerse

decomposition [di:kɔmpə'zɪʃən] *n* descomposición *f*

decompression [di:kəm'prɛʃən] *n* descompresión *f*

decompression chamber *n* cámara de descompresión

decongestant [di:kən'dʒɛstənt] *n* descongestionante *m*

decontaminate [di:kən'tæmɪneɪt] *vt* descontaminar

decontrol [di:kən'trəul] *vt* (*trade*) quitar controles a; (*prices*) descongelar

décor ['deɪkɔːʳ] *n* decoración *f*; (*Theat*) decorado

decorate ['dɛkəreɪt] *vt* (*paint*) pintar; (*paper*) empapelar; (*adorn*): **to ~ (with)** adornar (de), decorar (de)

decoration [dɛkə'reɪʃən] *n* adorno; (*act*) decoración *f*; (*medal*) condecoración *f*

decorative ['dɛkərətɪv] *adj* decorativo

decorator ['dɛkəreɪtəʳ] *n* (*workman*) pintor *m* decorador

decorum [dɪ'kɔːrəm] *n* decoro

decoy ['di:kɔɪ] *n* señuelo; **police ~** trampa *or* señuelo policial

decrease [*n* 'di:kri:s] *n* disminución *f* ■ *vt* [dɪ'kri:s] disminuir, reducir ■ *vi* reducirse; **to be on the ~** ir disminuyendo

decreasing [dɪ'kri:sɪŋ] *adj* decreciente

decree [dɪ'kri:] *n* decreto ■ *vt*: **to ~ (that)** decretar (que); **~ absolute/nisi** sentencia absoluta/provisional de divorcio

decrepit [dɪ'krɛpɪt] *adj* (*person*) decrépito; (*building*) ruinoso

decry [dɪ'kraɪ] *vt* criticar, censurar

dedicate ['dɛdɪkeɪt] *vt* dedicar

dedicated ['dɛdɪkeɪtɪd] *adj* dedicado; (*Comput*) especializado; **~ word processor** procesador *m* de textos especializado *or* dedicado

dedication [dɛdɪ'keɪʃən] *n* (*devotion*) dedicación *f*; (*in book*) dedicatoria

deduce [dɪ'dju:s] *vt* deducir

deduct [dɪ'dʌkt] *vt* restar; (*from wage etc*) descontar, deducir

deduction [dɪ'dʌkʃən] *n* (*amount deducted*) descuento; (*conclusion*) deducción *f*, conclusión *f*

deed [di:d] *n* hecho, acto; (*feat*) hazaña; (*Law*) escritura; **~ of covenant** escritura de contrato

deem [di:m] *vt* (*formal*) juzgar, considerar; **to ~ it wise to do** considerar prudente hacer

deep [di:p] *adj* profundo; (*voice*) bajo; (*breath*) profundo, a pleno pulmón ■ *adv*: **the spectators stood 20 ~** los espectadores se formaron de 20 en fondo; **to be four metres ~** tener cuatro metros de profundidad

deepen ['di:pn] *vt* ahondar, profundizar ■ *vi* (*darkness*) intensificarse

deep-freeze ['di:p'fri:z] *n* arcón *m* congelador

deep-fry ['di:p'fraɪ] *vt* freír en aceite abundante

deeply ['di:plɪ] *adv* (*breathe*) profundamente, a pleno pulmón; (*interested, moved, grateful*) profundamente, hondamente; **to regret sth ~** sentir algo profundamente

deep-rooted ['di:p'ru:tɪd] *adj* (*prejudice, habit*) profundamente arraigado; (*affection*) profundo

deep-sea ['di:p'si:] *adj*: **~ diver** buzo; **~ diving** buceo de altura

deep-seated ['di:p'si:tɪd] *adj* (*beliefs*) (profundamente) arraigado

deep-set ['di:psɛt] *adj* (*eyes*) hundido

deep-vein thrombosis *n* (*Med*) trombosis *f* venosa profunda

deer (*pl ~*) [dɪəʳ] *n* ciervo

deerstalker ['dɪəstɔ:kəʳ] *n* (*hat*) gorro de cazador

deface [dɪ'feɪs] *vt* desfigurar, mutilar

defamation [dɛfə'meɪʃən] *n* difamación *f*

defamatory [dɪ'fæmətrɪ] *adj* difamatorio

default [dɪ'fɔ:lt] *vi* faltar al pago; (*Sport*) no presentarse, no comparecer ■ *n* (*Comput*) defecto; **by ~** (*Law*) en rebeldía; (*Sport*) por incomparecencia; **to ~ on a debt** dejar de pagar una deuda

defaulter [dɪ'fɔ:ltəʳ] *n* (*in debt*) moroso(-a)

default option *n* (*Comput*) opción *f* por defecto

defeat [dɪ'fi:t] *n* derrota ■ *vt* derrotar, vencer; (*fig: efforts*) frustrar

defeatism [dɪ'fi:tɪzəm] *n* derrotismo

defeatist [dɪ'fi:tɪst] *adj, n* derrotista *m/f*

defecate ['dɛfəkeɪt] *vi* defecar

defect ['di:fɛkt] *n* defecto ■ *vi* [dɪ'fɛkt]: **to ~ to the enemy** pasarse al enemigo; **physical ~** defecto físico; **mental ~** deficiencia mental

defective [dɪ'fɛktɪv] *adj* (*gen*) defectuoso; (*person*) anormal

defector [dɪ'fɛktə] n tránsfuga m/f
defence, (US) **defense** [dɪ'fɛns] n defensa;
the Ministry of D~ el Ministerio de
Defensa; witness for the ~ testigo de
descargo
defenceless [dɪ'fɛnslɪs] adj indefenso
defence spending n gasto militar
defend [dɪ'fɛnd] vt defender; (decision, action)
defender; (opinion) mantener
defendant [dɪ'fɛndənt] n acusado(-a); (in civil
case) demandado(-a)
defender [dɪ'fɛndəʳ] n defensor(a) m(f)
defending champion [dɪ'fɛndɪŋ-] n (Sport)
defensor(-a) m(f) del título
defending counsel n (Law) abogado defensor
defense [dɪ'fɛns] n (US) = **defence**
defensive [dɪ'fɛnsɪv] adj defensivo ▪ n
defensiva; on the ~ a la defensiva
defer [dɪ'fəːʳ] vt (postpone) aplazar; to ~ to
diferir a; (submit): to ~ to sb/sb's opinion
someterse a algn/a la opinión de algn
deference ['dɛfərəns] n deferencia, respeto;
out of or in ~ to por respeto a
deferential [dɛfə'rɛnʃəl] adj respetuoso
deferred [dɪ'fəːd] adj: ~ creditor acreedor m
diferido
defiance [dɪ'faɪəns] n desafío; in ~ of en
contra de
defiant [dɪ'faɪənt] adj (insolent) insolente;
(challenging) retador(a)
defiantly [dɪ'faɪəntlɪ] adv con aire de desafío
deficiency [dɪ'fɪʃənsɪ] n (lack) falta; (Comm)
déficit m; (defect) defecto
deficient [dɪ'fɪʃənt] adj (lacking) insuficiente;
(incomplete) incompleto; (defective) defectuoso;
(mentally) anormal; ~ in deficiente en
deficit ['dɛfɪsɪt] n déficit m
defile [dɪ'faɪl] vt manchar; (violate) violar
define [dɪ'faɪn] vt (Comput) definir
definite ['dɛfɪnɪt] adj (fixed) determinado;
(clear, obvious) claro; he was ~ about it no dejó
lugar a dudas (sobre ello)
definitely ['dɛfɪnɪtlɪ] adv: he's ~ mad no cabe
duda de que está loco
definition [dɛfɪ'nɪʃən] n definición f
definitive [dɪ'fɪnɪtɪv] adj definitivo
deflate [diː'fleɪt] vt (gen) desinflar; (pompous
person) quitar or rebajar los humos a; (Econ)
deflacionar
deflation [diː'fleɪʃən] n (Econ) deflación f
deflationary [diː'fleɪʃənrɪ] adj (Econ)
deflacionario
deflect [dɪ'flɛkt] vt desviar
defog [diː'fɔg] vt desempañar
defogger [diː'fɔgəʳ] n (US Aut) dispositivo
antivaho
deform [dɪ'fɔːm] vt deformar

deformed [dɪ'fɔːmd] adj deformado
deformity [dɪ'fɔːmɪtɪ] n deformación f
Defra n abbr (Brit) = **Department for
Environment, Food and Rural Affairs**
defraud [dɪ'frɔːd] vt estafar; to ~ sb of sth
estafar algo a algn
defray [dɪ'freɪ] vt: to ~ sb's expenses
reembolsar a algn los gastos
defrost [diː'frɔst] vt (frozen food, fridge)
descongelar
defroster [diː'frɔstəʳ] n (US) eliminador m
de vaho
deft [dɛft] adj diestro, hábil
defunct [dɪ'fʌŋkt] adj difunto; (organization
etc) ya desaparecido
defuse [diː'fjuːz] vt desarmar; (situation)
calmar, apaciguar
defy [dɪ'faɪ] vt (resist) oponerse a; (challenge)
desafiar; (order) contravenir
degenerate [dɪ'dʒɛnəreɪt] vi degenerar ▪ adj
[dɪ'dʒɛnərɪt] degenerado
degradation [dɛgrə'deɪʃən] n degradación f
degrade [dɪ'greɪd] vt degradar
degrading [dɪ'greɪdɪŋ] adj degradante
degree [dɪ'griː] n grado; (Scol) título; 10
degrees below freezing 10 grados bajo cero;
to have a ~ in maths ser licenciado(-a) en
matemáticas; by degrees (gradually) poco a
poco, por etapas; to some ~, to a certain ~
hasta cierto punto; a considerable ~ of risk
un gran índice de riesgo
dehydrated [diːhaɪ'dreɪtɪd] adj
deshidratado; (milk) en polvo
dehydration [diːhaɪ'dreɪʃən] n
deshidratación f
de-ice [diː'aɪs] vt (windscreen) deshelar
de-icer [diː'aɪsəʳ] n descongelador m
deign [deɪn] vi: to ~ to do dignarse hacer
deity ['diːɪtɪ] n deidad f, divinidad f
déjà vu [deɪʒɑː'vuː] n: I had a sense of ~
sentía como si ya lo hubiera vivido
dejected [dɪ'dʒɛktɪd] adj abatido,
desanimado
dejection [dɪ'dʒɛkʃən] n abatimiento
Del. abbr (US) = **Delaware**
delay [dɪ'leɪ] vt demorar, aplazar; (person)
entretener; (train) retrasar; (payment) aplazar
▪ vi tardar ▪ n demora, retraso; without ~
en seguida, sin tardar
delayed-action [dɪleɪd'ækʃən] adj (bomb etc)
de acción retardada
delectable [dɪ'lɛktəbl] adj (person)
encantador(-a); (food) delicioso
delegate ['dɛlɪgɪt] n delegado(-a) ▪ vt
['dɛlɪgeɪt] delegar; to ~ sth to sb/sb to do
sth delegar algo en algn/en algn para hacer
algo

delegation [dɛlɪˈgeɪʃən] n (of work etc) delegación f

delete [dɪˈliːt] vt suprimir, tachar; (Comput) suprimir, borrar

Delhi [ˈdɛlɪ] n Delhi m

deli [ˈdɛlɪ] n = **delicatessen**

deliberate [dɪˈlɪbərɪt] adj (intentional) intencionado; (slow) pausado, lento ■ vi [dɪˈlɪbəreɪt] deliberar

deliberately [dɪˈlɪbərɪtlɪ] adv (on purpose) a propósito; (slowly) pausadamente

deliberation [dɪlɪbəˈreɪʃən] n (consideration) reflexión f; (discussion) deliberación f, discusión f

delicacy [ˈdɛlɪkəsɪ] n delicadeza; (choice food) manjar m

delicate [ˈdɛlɪkɪt] adj (gen) delicado; (fragile) frágil

delicately [ˈdɛlɪkɪtlɪ] adv con delicadeza, delicadamente; (act, express) con discreción

delicatessen [dɛlɪkəˈtɛsn] n tienda especializada en comida exótica

delicious [dɪˈlɪʃəs] adj delicioso, rico

delight [dɪˈlaɪt] n (feeling) placer m, deleite m; (object) encanto, delicia ■ vt encantar, deleitar; **to take ~ in** deleitarse en

delighted [dɪˈlaɪtɪd] adj: **~ (at or with/to do)** encantado (con/de hacer); **to be ~ that** estar encantado de que; **I'd be ~** con mucho or todo gusto

delightful [dɪˈlaɪtful] adj encantador(a), delicioso

delimit [diːˈlɪmɪt] vt delimitar

delineate [dɪˈlɪnɪeɪt] vt delinear

delinquency [dɪˈlɪŋkwənsɪ] n delincuencia

delinquent [dɪˈlɪŋkwənt] adj, n delincuente m/f

delirious [dɪˈlɪrɪəs] adj (Med: fig) delirante; **to be ~** delirar, desvariar

delirium [dɪˈlɪrɪəm] n delirio

deliver [dɪˈlɪvəʳ] vt (distribute) repartir; (hand over) entregar; (message) comunicar; (speech) pronunciar; (blow) lanzar, dar; (Med) asistir al parto de

deliverance [dɪˈlɪvrəns] n liberación f

delivery [dɪˈlɪvərɪ] n reparto; entrega; (of speaker) modo de expresarse; (Med) parto, alumbramiento; **to take ~ of** recibir

delivery note n nota de entrega

delivery van n furgoneta de reparto

delta [ˈdɛltə] n delta m

delude [dɪˈluːd] vt engañar

deluge [ˈdɛljuːdʒ] n diluvio ■ vt (fig): **to ~ (with)** inundar (de)

delusion [dɪˈluːʒən] n ilusión f, engaño

de luxe [dəˈlʌks] adj de lujo

delve [dɛlv] vi: **to ~ into** hurgar en

Dem. abbr (US Pol) = **Democrat; Democratic**

demand [dɪˈmɑːnd] vt (gen) exigir; (rights) reclamar; (need) requerir ■ n (gen) exigencia; (claim) reclamación f; (Econ) demanda; **to ~ sth (from or of sb)** exigir algo (a algn); **to be in ~** ser muy solicitado; **on ~** a solicitud

demanding [dɪˈmɑːndɪŋ] adj (boss) exigente; (work) absorbente

demarcation [diːmɑːˈkeɪʃən] n demarcación f

demarcation dispute n conflicto de definición or demarcación del trabajo

demean [dɪˈmiːn] vt: **to ~ o.s.** rebajarse

demeanour, demeanor (US) [dɪˈmiːnəʳ] n porte m, conducta, comportamiento

demented [dɪˈmɛntɪd] adj demente

demi- [ˈdɛmɪ] pref semi..., medio...

demilitarize [diːˈmɪlɪtəraɪz] vt desmilitarizar; **demilitarized zone** zona desmilitarizada

demise [dɪˈmaɪz] n (death) fallecimiento

demist [diːˈmɪst] vt (Aut) eliminar el vaho de

demister [diːˈmɪstəʳ] n (Aut) eliminador m de vaho

demo [ˈdɛməu] n abbr (col: = demonstration) manifestación f

demobilization [diːˈməubɪlaɪˈzeɪʃən] n desmovilización f

democracy [dɪˈmɒkrəsɪ] n democracia

democrat [ˈdɛməkræt] n demócrata m/f

democratic [dɛməˈkrætɪk] adj democrático; **the D~ Party** el partido demócrata (estadounidense)

demography [dɪˈmɒgrəfɪ] n demografía

demolish [dɪˈmɒlɪʃ] vt derribar, demoler

demolition [dɛməˈlɪʃən] n derribo, demolición f

demon [ˈdiːmən] n (evil spirit) demonio ■ cpd temible

demonstrate [ˈdɛmənstreɪt] vt demostrar ■ vi manifestarse; **to ~ (for/against)** manifestarse (a favor de/en contra de)

demonstration [dɛmənˈstreɪʃən] n (Pol) manifestación f; (proof) prueba, demostración f; **to hold a ~** (Pol) hacer una manifestación

demonstrative [dɪˈmɒnstrətɪv] adj (person) expresivo; (Ling) demostrativo

demonstrator [ˈdɛmənstreɪtəʳ] n (Pol) manifestante m/f

demoralize [dɪˈmɒrəlaɪz] vt desmoralizar

demote [dɪˈməut] vt degradar

demotion [dɪˈməuʃən] n degradación f; (Comm) descenso

demur [dɪˈməːʳ] vi: **to ~ (at)** hacer objeciones (a), vacilar (ante) ■ n: **without ~** sin objeción

demure [dɪ'mjuəʳ] adj recatado

demurrage [dɪ'mʌrɪdʒ] n sobrestadía

den [dɛn] n (of animal) guarida; (study) estudio

denationalization [di:næʃnəlaɪ'zeɪʃən] n desnacionalización f

denationalize [di:'næʃnəlaɪz] vt desnacionalizar

denatured alcohol [di:'neɪtʃəd-] n (US) alcohol m desnaturalizado

denial [dɪ'naɪəl] n (refusal) negativa; (of report etc) denegación f

denier ['dɛnɪəʳ] n denier m

denim ['dɛnɪm] n tela vaquera; see also **denims**

denim jacket n chaqueta vaquera, saco vaquero (LAm)

denims ['dɛnɪms] npl vaqueros mpl

denizen ['dɛnɪzn] n (inhabitant) habitante m/f; (foreigner) residente m/f extranjero(-a)

Denmark ['dɛnmɑːk] n Dinamarca

denomination [dɪnɔmɪ'neɪʃən] n valor m; (Rel) confesión f

denominator [dɪ'nɔmɪneɪtəʳ] n denominador m

denote [dɪ'nəut] vt indicar, significar

denounce [dɪ'nauns] vt denunciar

dense [dɛns] adj (thick) espeso; (foliage etc) tupido; (stupid) torpe

densely [dɛnslɪ] adv: ~ **populated** con una alta densidad de población

density ['dɛnsɪtɪ] n densidad f; **single/double-~ disk** n disco de densidad sencilla/de doble densidad

dent [dɛnt] n abolladura ■ vt (also: **make a dent in**) abollar

dental ['dɛntl] adj dental

dental floss [-flɔs] n seda dental

dental surgeon n odontólogo(-a)

dentifrice ['dɛntɪfrɪs] n dentífrico

dentist ['dɛntɪst] n dentista m/f; **~'s surgery** (Brit) consultorio dental

dentistry ['dɛntɪstrɪ] n odontología

dentures ['dɛntʃəz] npl dentadura sg (postiza)

denude [dɪ'njuːd] vt: **to ~ of** despojar de

denunciation [dɪnʌnsɪ'eɪʃən] n denuncia, denunciación f

deny [dɪ'naɪ] vt negar; (charge) rechazar; (report) desmentir; **to ~ o.s.** privarse (de); **he denies having said it** niega haberlo dicho

deodorant [di:'əudərənt] n desodorante m

depart [dɪ'pɑːt] vi irse, marcharse; (train) salir; **to ~ from** (fig: differ from) apartarse de

departed [dɪ'pɑːtɪd] adj (bygone: days, glory) pasado; (dead) difunto ■ n: **the (dear) ~** el/la/los/las difunto/a/os/as

department [dɪ'pɑːtmənt] n (Comm) sección f; (Scol) departamento; (Pol) ministerio; **that's not my ~** (fig) no tiene que ver conmigo; **D~ of State** (US) Ministerio de Asuntos Exteriores

departmental [di:pɑː't mɛntl] adj (dispute) departamental; (meeting) departamental, de departamento; **~ manager** jefe(-a) m(f) de sección or de departamento or de servicio

department store n grandes almacenes mpl

departure [dɪ'pɑːtʃəʳ] n partida, ida; (of train) salida; **a new ~** un nuevo rumbo

departure lounge n (at airport) sala de embarque

depend [dɪ'pɛnd] vi: **to ~ (up)on** (be dependent upon) depender de; (rely on) contar con; **it depends** depende, según; **depending on the result** según el resultado

dependable [dɪ'pɛndəbl] adj (person) formal, serio

dependant [dɪ'pɛndənt] n dependiente m/f

dependence [dɪ'pɛndəns] n dependencia

dependent [dɪ'pɛndənt] adj: **to be ~ (on)** depender (de) ■ n = **dependant**

depict [dɪ'pɪkt] vt (in picture) pintar; (describe) representar

depilatory [dɪ'pɪlətrɪ] n (also: **depilatory cream**) depilatorio

depleted [dɪ'pliːtɪd] adj reducido

deplorable [dɪ'plɔːrəbl] adj deplorable

deplore [dɪ'plɔːʳ] vt deplorar

deploy [dɪ'plɔɪ] vt desplegar

depopulate [di:'pɔpjuleɪt] vt despoblar

depopulation ['di:pɔpju'leɪʃən] n despoblación f

deport [dɪ'pɔːt] vt deportar

deportation [di:pɔː'teɪʃən] n deportación f

deportation order n orden f de expulsión or deportación

deportee [di:pɔː'tiː] n deportado(-a)

deportment [dɪ'pɔːtmənt] n comportamiento

depose [dɪ'pəuz] vt deponer

deposit [dɪ'pɔzɪt] n depósito; (Chem) sedimento; (of ore, oil) yacimiento ■ vt (gen) depositar; **to put down a ~ of £50** dejar un depósito de 50 libras

deposit account n (Brit) cuenta de ahorros

depositor [dɪ'pɔzɪtəʳ] n depositante m/f, cuentacorrentista m/f

depository [dɪ'pɔzɪtərɪ] n almacén m depositario

depot ['dɛpəu] n (storehouse) depósito; (for vehicles) parque m

deprave [dɪ'preɪv] vt depravar

depraved [dɪ'preɪvd] adj depravado, vicioso

depravity [dɪ'prævɪtɪ] n depravación f, vicio

deprecate ['dɛprɪkeɪt] vt desaprobar, lamentar

d

deprecating ['dɛprɪkeɪtɪŋ] adj (disapproving) de desaprobación; (apologetic): **a ~ smile** una sonrisa de disculpa

depreciate [dɪ'priːʃɪeɪt] vi depreciarse, perder valor

depreciation [dɪpriːʃɪ'eɪʃən] n depreciación f

depress [dɪ'prɛs] vt deprimir; (press down) apretar

depressant [dɪ'prɛsnt] n (Med) calmante m, sedante m

depressed [dɪ'prɛst] adj deprimido; (Comm: market, economy) deprimido; (area) deprimido (económicamente); **to get ~** deprimirse

depressing [dɪ'prɛsɪŋ] adj deprimente

depression [dɪ'prɛʃən] n depresión f; **the economy is in a state of ~** la economía está deprimida

deprivation [dɛprɪ'veɪʃən] n privación f; (loss) pérdida

deprive [dɪ'praɪv] vt: **to ~ sb of** privar a algn de

deprived [dɪ'praɪvd] adj necesitado

dept. abbr (= department) dto

depth [dɛpθ] n profundidad f; **at a ~ of three metres** a tres metros de profundidad; **to be out of one's ~** (swimmer) perder pie; (fig) estar perdido; **to study sth in ~** estudiar algo a fondo; **in the depths of** en lo más hondo de

depth charge n carga de profundidad

deputation [dɛpju'teɪʃən] n delegación f

deputize ['dɛpjutaɪz] vi: **to ~ for sb** sustituir a algn

deputy ['dɛpjutɪ] adj: **~ head** subdirector(-a) m(f) ■ n sustituto(-a), suplente m/f; (Pol) diputado(-a); (agent) representante m/f

deputy leader n vicepresidente(-a) m(f)

derail [dɪ'reɪl] vt: **to be derailed** descarrilarse

derailment [dɪ'reɪlmənt] n descarrilamiento

deranged [dɪ'reɪndʒd] adj trastornado

derby ['dəːbɪ] n (US) hongo

deregulate [diː'rɛgjuleɪt] vt desreglamentar

deregulation [diːrɛgju'leɪʃən] n desreglamentación f

derelict ['dɛrɪlɪkt] adj abandonado

deride [dɪ'raɪd] vt ridiculizar, mofarse de

derision [dɪ'rɪʒən] n irrisión f, mofas fpl

derisive [dɪ'raɪsɪv] adj burlón(-ona)

derisory [dɪ'raɪzərɪ] adj (sum) irrisorio; (laughter, person) burlón(-ona), irónico

derivation [dɛrɪ'veɪʃən] n derivación f

derivative [dɪ'rɪvətɪv] n derivado ■ adj (work) poco original

derive [dɪ'raɪv] vt derivar ■ vi: **to ~ from** derivarse de

derived [dɪ'raɪvd] adj derivado

dermatitis [dəːmə'taɪtɪs] n dermatitis f

dermatology [dəːmə'tɔlədʒɪ] n dermatología

derogatory [dɪ'rɔgətərɪ] adj despectivo

derrick ['dɛrɪk] n torre f de perforación

derv [dəːv] n (Brit) gasoil m

descend [dɪ'sɛnd] vt, vi descender, bajar; **to ~ from** descender de; **in descending order of importance** de mayor a menor importancia
▶ **descend on** vt fus (enemy, angry person) caer sobre; (misfortune) sobrevenir; (gloom, silence) invadir; **visitors descended on us** las visitas nos invadieron

descendant [dɪ'sɛndənt] n descendiente m/f

descent [dɪ'sɛnt] n descenso; (Geo) pendiente f, declive m; (origin) descendencia

describe [dɪs'kraɪb] vt describir

description [dɪs'krɪpʃən] n descripción f; (sort) clase f, género; **of every ~** de toda clase

descriptive [dɪs'krɪptɪv] adj descriptivo

desecrate ['dɛsɪkreɪt] vt profanar

desegregation [diːsɛgrɪ'geɪʃən] n desegregación f

desert [n 'dɛzət, vb dɪ'zəːt] n desierto ■ vt abandonar, desamparar ■ vi (Mil) desertar; see also **deserts**

deserter [dɪ'zəːtər] n desertor(-a) m(f)

desertion [dɪ'zəːʃən] n deserción f

desert island n isla desierta

deserts [dɪ'zəːts] npl: **to get one's just ~** llevarse su merecido

deserve [dɪ'zəːv] vt merecer, ser digno de, ameritar (LAm)

deservedly [dɪ'zəːvɪdlɪ] adv con razón

deserving [dɪ'zəːvɪŋ] adj (person) digno; (action, cause) meritorio

desiccated ['dɛsɪkeɪtɪd] adj desecado

design [dɪ'zaɪn] n (sketch) bosquejo; (of dress, car) diseño; (pattern) dibujo ■ vt (gen) diseñar; **industrial ~** diseño industrial; **to have designs on sb** tener la(s) mira(s) puesta(s) en algn; **to be designed for sb/sth** estar hecho para algn/algo

design and technology n (Brit Scol) diseño y tecnología

designate ['dɛzɪgneɪt] vt (appoint) nombrar; (destine) designar ■ adj ['dɛzɪgnɪt] designado

designation [dɛzɪg'neɪʃən] n (appointment) nombramiento; (name) denominación f

designer [dɪ'zaɪnər] n diseñador(-a) m(f); (fashion designer) modisto(-a)

designer baby n bebé m de diseño

desirability [dɪzaɪərə'bɪlɪtɪ] n ventaja, atractivo

desirable [dɪ'zaɪərəbl] adj (proper) deseable; (attractive) atractivo; **it is ~ that** es conveniente que

desire [dɪ'zaɪər] n dèseo ■ vt desear; **to ~ sth/to do sth/that** desear algo/hacer algo/que

desirous [dɪˈzaɪərəs] *adj* deseoso
desist [dɪˈzɪst] *vi*: **to ~ (from)** desistir (de)
desk [dɛsk] *n* (*in office*) escritorio; (*for pupil*) pupitre *m*; (*in hotel, at airport*) recepción *f*; (*Brit: in shop, restaurant*) caja
desktop computer [ˈdɛsktɔp-] *n* ordenador *m* de sobremesa
desktop publishing [ˈdɛsktɔp-] *n* autoedición *f*
desolate [ˈdɛsəlɪt] *adj* (*place*) desierto; (*person*) afligido
desolation [dɛsəˈleɪʃən] *n* (*of place*) desolación *f*; (*of person*) aflicción *f*
despair [dɪsˈpɛər] *n* desesperación *f* ▪ *vi*: **to ~ of** desesperar de; **in ~** desesperado
despatch [dɪsˈpætʃ] *n, vt* = **dispatch**
desperate [ˈdɛspərɪt] *adj* desesperado; (*fugitive*) peligroso; (*measures*) extremo; **we are getting ~** estamos al borde de desesperación
desperately [ˈdɛspərɪtlɪ] *adv* desesperadamente; (*very*) terriblemente, gravemente; **~ ill** gravemente enfermo
desperation [dɛspəˈreɪʃən] *n* desesperación *f*; **in ~** desesperado
despicable [dɪsˈpɪkəbl] *adj* vil, despreciable
despise [dɪsˈpaɪz] *vt* despreciar
despite [dɪsˈpaɪt] *prep* a pesar de, pese a
despondent [dɪsˈpɔndənt] *adj* deprimido, abatido
despot [ˈdɛspɔt] *n* déspota *m/f*
dessert [dɪˈzəːt] *n* postre *m*
dessertspoon [dɪˈzəːtspuːn] *n* cuchara (de postre)
destabilize [diːˈsteɪbɪlaɪz] *vt* desestabilizar
destination [dɛstɪˈneɪʃən] *n* destino
destine [ˈdɛstɪn] *vt* destinar
destined [ˈdɛstɪnd] *adj*: **~ for London** con destino a Londres
destiny [ˈdɛstɪnɪ] *n* destino
destitute [ˈdɛstɪtjuːt] *adj* desamparado, indigente
destitution [dɛstɪˈtjuːʃən] *n* indigencia, miseria
destroy [dɪsˈtrɔɪ] *vt* destruir; (*finish*) acabar con
destroyer [dɪsˈtrɔɪər] *n* (*Naut*) destructor *m*
destruction [dɪsˈtrʌkʃən] *n* destrucción *f*; (*fig*) ruina
destructive [dɪsˈtrʌktɪv] *adj* destructivo, destructor(a)
desultory [ˈdɛsəltərɪ] *adj* (*reading*) poco metódico; (*conversation*) inconexo; (*contact*) intermitente
detach [dɪˈtætʃ] *vt* separar; (*unstick*) despegar
detachable [dɪˈtætʃəbl] *adj* separable; (*Tech*) desmontable

detached [dɪˈtætʃt] *adj* (*attitude*) objetivo, imparcial
detached house *n* chalé *m*, chalet *m*
detachment [dɪˈtætʃmənt] *n* separación *f*; (*Mil*) destacamento; (*fig*) objetividad *f*, imparcialidad *f*
detail [ˈdiːteɪl] *n* detalle *m*; (*Mil*) destacamento ▪ *vt* detallar; (*Mil*) destacar; **in ~** detalladamente; **to go into ~(s)** entrar en detalles
detailed [ˈdiːteɪld] *adj* detallado
detain [dɪˈteɪn] *vt* retener; (*in captivity*) detener
detainee [diːteɪˈniː] *n* detenido(-a)
detect [dɪˈtɛkt] *vt* (*discover*) descubrir; (*Med, Police*) identificar; (*Mil, Radar, Tech*) detectar; (*notice*) percibir
detection [dɪˈtɛkʃən] *n* descubrimiento; identificación *f*; **crime ~** investigación *f*; **to escape ~** (*criminal*) escaparse sin ser descubierto; (*mistake*) pasar inadvertido
detective [dɪˈtɛktɪv] *n* detective *m*
detective story *n* novela policíaca
detector [dɪˈtɛktər] *n* detector *m*
détente [deɪˈtɑːnt] *n* distensión *f*, detente *f*
detention [dɪˈtɛnʃən] *n* detención *f*, arresto
deter [dɪˈtəːr] *vt* (*dissuade*) disuadir; (*prevent*) impedir; **to ~ sb from doing sth** disuadir a algn de que haga algo
detergent [dɪˈtəːdʒənt] *n* detergente *m*
deteriorate [dɪˈtɪərɪəreɪt] *vi* deteriorarse
deterioration [dɪtɪərɪəˈreɪʃən] *n* deterioro
determination [dɪtəːmɪˈneɪʃən] *n* resolución *f*
determine [dɪˈtəːmɪn] *vt* determinar; **to ~ to do sth** decidir hacer algo
determined [dɪˈtəːmɪnd] *adj*: **to be ~ to do sth** estar decidido *or* resuelto a hacer algo; **a ~ effort** un esfuerzo enérgico
deterrence [dɪˈtɛrns] *n* disuasión *f*
deterrent [dɪˈtɛrənt] *n* fuerza de disuasión; **to act as a ~** servir para prevenir
detest [dɪˈtɛst] *vt* aborrecer
detestable [dɪˈtɛstəbl] *adj* aborrecible
dethrone [diːˈθrəun] *vt* destronar
detonate [ˈdɛtəneɪt] *vi* estallar ▪ *vt* hacer detonar
detonator [ˈdɛtəneɪtər] *n* detonador *m*, fulminante *m*
detour [ˈdiːtuər] *n* (*gen: US Aut: diversion*) desvío ▪ *vt* (*US: traffic*) desviar; **to make a ~** dar un rodeo
detract [dɪˈtrækt] *vt*: **to ~ from** quitar mérito a, restar valor a
detractor [dɪˈtræktər] *n* detractor(-a) *m(f)*
detriment [ˈdɛtrɪmənt] *n*: **to the ~ of** en perjuicio de; **without ~ to** sin detrimento de, sin perjuicio para

513

detrimental [dɛtrɪ'mɛntl] *adj* perjudicial

deuce [dju:s] *n* (*Tennis*) cuarenta iguales

devaluation [dɪvælju'eɪʃən] *n* devaluación *f*

devalue [dɪ'vælju:] *vt* devaluar

devastate ['dɛvəsteɪt] *vt* devastar; **he was devastated by the news** las noticias le dejaron desolado

devastating ['dɛvəsteɪtɪŋ] *adj* devastador(-a); (*fig*) arrollador(-a)

devastation [dɛvəs'teɪʃən] *n* devastación *f*, ruina

develop [dɪ'vɛləp] *vt* desarrollar; (*Phot*) revelar; (*disease*) contraer; (*habit*) adquirir ▪ *vi* desarrollarse; (*advance*) progresar; **this land is to be developed** se va a construir en este terreno; **to ~ a taste for sth** tomar gusto a algo; **to ~ into** transformarse *or* convertirse en

developer [dɪ'vɛləpəʳ] *n* (*property developer*) promotor(-a) *m(f)*

developing country *n* país *m* en (vías de) desarrollo

development [dɪ'vɛləpmənt] *n* desarrollo; (*advance*) progreso; (*of affair, case*) desenvolvimiento; (*of land*) urbanización *f*

development area *n* zona de fomento *or* desarrollo

deviant ['di:vɪənt] *adj* anómalo, pervertido

deviate ['di:vɪeɪt] *vi*: **to ~ (from)** desviarse (de)

deviation [di:vɪ'eɪʃən] *n* desviación *f*

device [dɪ'vaɪs] *n* (*scheme*) estratagema, recurso; (*apparatus*) aparato, mecanismo; (*explosive device*) artefacto explosivo

devil ['dɛvl] *n* diablo, demonio

devilish ['dɛvlɪʃ] *adj* diabólico

devil-may-care ['dɛvlmeɪ'kɛəʳ] *adj* despreocupado

devil's advocate *n*: **to play (the) ~** hacer de abogado del diablo

devious ['di:vɪəs] *adj* intricado, enrevesado; (*person*) taimado

devise [dɪ'vaɪz] *vt* idear, inventar

devoid [dɪ'vɔɪd] *adj*: **~ of** desprovisto de

devolution [di:və'lu:ʃən] *n* (*Pol*) descentralización *f*

devolve [dɪ'vɔlv] *vi*: **to ~ (up)on** recaer sobre

devote [dɪ'vəut] *vt*: **to ~ sth to** dedicar algo a

devoted [dɪ'vəutɪd] *adj* (*loyal*) leal, fiel; **the book is ~ to politics** el libro trata de política

devotee [dɛvəu'ti:] *n* devoto(-a)

devotion [dɪ'vəuʃən] *n* dedicación *f*; (*Rel*) devoción *f*

devour [dɪ'vauəʳ] *vt* devorar

devout [dɪ'vaut] *adj* devoto

dew [dju:] *n* rocío

dexterity [dɛks'tɛrɪtɪ] *n* destreza

dexterous, dextrous ['dɛkstrəs] *adj* (*skilful*) diestro, hábil; (*movement*) ágil

DfEE *n abbr* (*Brit*) = **Department for Education and Employment**

dg *abbr* (= *decigram*) dg

diabetes [daɪə'bi:ti:z] *n* diabetes *f*

diabetic [daɪə'bɛtɪk] *n* diabético(-a) ▪ *adj* diabético; (*chocolate, jam*) para diabéticos

diabolical [daɪə'bɔlɪkəl] *adj* diabólico; (*col: dreadful*) horrendo, horroroso

diagnose ['daɪəgnəuz] *vt* diagnosticar

diagnosis (*pl* **diagnoses**) [daɪəg'nəusɪs, -si:z] *n* diagnóstico

diagonal [daɪ'ægənl] *adj* diagonal ▪ *n* diagonal *f*

diagram ['daɪəgræm] *n* diagrama *m*, esquema *m*

dial ['daɪəl] *n* esfera; (*of radio*) dial *m*; (*tuner*) sintonizador *m*; (*of phone*) disco ▪ *vt* (*number*) marcar, discar (*LAm*); **to ~ a wrong number** equivocarse de número; **can I ~ London direct?** ¿puedo marcar un número de Londres directamente?

dial. *abbr* = **dialect**

dial code *n* (*US*) prefijo

dialect ['daɪəlɛkt] *n* dialecto

dialling code ['daɪəlɪŋ-] *n* (*Brit*) prefijo

dialling tone *n* (*Brit*) señal *f or* tono de marcar

dialogue, (US) dialog ['daɪəlɔg] *n* diálogo

dial tone *n* (*US*) señal *f or* tono de marcar

dialysis [daɪ'ælɪsɪs] *n* diálisis *f*

diameter [daɪ'æmɪtəʳ] *n* diámetro

diametrically [daɪə'mɛtrɪklɪ] *adv*: **~ opposed (to)** diametralmente opuesto (a)

diamond ['daɪəmənd] *n* diamante *m*; **diamonds** *npl* (*Cards*) diamantes *mpl*

diamond ring *n* anillo *or* sortija de diamantes

diaper ['daɪəpəʳ] *n* (*US*) pañal *m*

diaphragm ['daɪəfræm] *n* diafragma *m*

diarrhoea, diarrhea (*US*) [daɪə'ri:ə] *n* diarrea

diary ['daɪərɪ] *n* (*daily account*) diario; (*book*) agenda; **to keep a ~** escribir un diario

diatribe ['daɪətraɪb] *n*: **~ (against)** diatriba (contra)

dice [daɪs] *n pl inv* dados *mpl* ▪ *vt* (*Culin*) cortar en cuadritos

dicey ['daɪsɪ] *adj* (*col*): **it's a bit ~** (*risky*) es un poco arriesgado; (*doubtful*) es un poco dudoso

dichotomy [daɪ'kɔtəmɪ] *n* dicotomía

dickhead ['dɪkhɛd] *n* (*Brit col!*) gilipollas *m inv*

Dictaphone® ['dɪktəfəun] *n* dictáfono®

dictate [dɪk'teɪt] *vt* dictar ▪ *n* ['dɪkteɪt] dictado

▸ **dictate to** *vt fus* (*person*) dar órdenes a;

I won't be dictated to no recibo órdenes de nadie

dictation [dɪk'teɪʃən] *n* (*to secretary etc*) dictado; **at ~ speed** para tomar al dictado

dictator [dɪk'teɪtər] *n* dictador *m*

dictatorship [dɪk'teɪtəʃɪp] *n* dictadura

diction ['dɪkʃən] *n* dicción *f*

dictionary ['dɪkʃənrɪ] *n* diccionario

did [dɪd] *pt of* **do**

didactic [daɪ'dæktɪk] *adj* didáctico

diddle ['dɪdl] *vt* estafar, timar

didn't ['dɪdənt] = **did not**

die [daɪ] *vi* morir; **to ~ (of** *or* **from)** morirse (de); **to be dying** morirse, estar muriéndose; **to be dying for sth/to do sth** morirse por algo/de ganas de hacer algo

▶ **die away** *vi* (*sound, light*) desvanecerse

▶ **die down** *vi* (*gen*) apagarse; (*wind*) amainar

▶ **die out** *vi* desaparecer, extinguirse

diehard ['daɪhɑ:d] *n* intransigente *m/f*

diesel ['di:zl] *n* diesel *m*

diesel engine *n* motor *m* diesel

diesel fuel, diesel oil *n* gas-oil *m*

diet ['daɪət] *n* dieta; (*restricted food*) régimen *m* ■ *vi* (*also*: **be on a diet**) estar a dieta, hacer régimen; **to live on a ~ of** alimentarse de

dietician [daɪə'tɪʃən] *n* dietista *mf*

differ ['dɪfər] *vi* (*be different*) ser distinto, diferenciarse; (*disagree*) discrepar

difference ['dɪfrəns] *n* diferencia; (*quarrel*) desacuerdo; **it makes no ~ to me** me da igual *or* lo mismo; **to settle one's differences** arreglarse

different ['dɪfrənt] *adj* diferente, distinto

differential [dɪfə'renʃəl] *n* diferencial *f*

differentiate [dɪfə'renʃɪeɪt] *vt* distinguir ■ *vi* diferenciarse; **to ~ between** distinguir entre

differently ['dɪfrəntlɪ] *adv* de otro modo, en forma distinta

difficult ['dɪfɪkəlt] *adj* difícil; **~ to understand** difícil de entender

difficulty ['dɪfɪkəltɪ] *n* dificultad *f*; **to have difficulties with** (*police, landlord etc*) tener problemas con; **to be in ~** estar en apuros

diffidence ['dɪfɪdəns] *n* timidez *f*, falta de confianza en sí mismo

diffident ['dɪfɪdənt] *adj* tímido

diffuse [dɪ'fju:s] *adj* difuso ■ *vt* [dɪ'fju:z] difundir

dig [dɪg] *vt* (*pt, pp* **dug**) [dʌg] (*hole*) cavar; (*ground*) remover; (*coal*) extraer; (*nails etc*) clavar ■ *n* (*prod*) empujón *m*; (*archaeological*) excavación *f*; (*remark*) indirecta; **to ~ into** (*savings*) consumir; **to ~ into one's pockets for sth** hurgar en el bolsillo buscando algo; **to ~ one's nails into** clavar las uñas en; *see also* **digs**

▶ **dig in** *vi* (*also*: **dig o.s. in**: *Mil*) atrincherarse; (*col*: *eat*) hincar los dientes ■ *vt* (*compost*) añadir al suelo; (*knife, claw*) clavar; **to ~ in one's heels** (*fig*) mantenerse en sus trece

▶ **dig out** *vt* (*hole*) excavar; (*survivors, car from snow*) sacar

▶ **dig up** *vt* desenterrar; (*plant*) desarraigar

digest [daɪ'dʒest] *vt* (*food*) digerir; (*facts*) asimilar ■ *n* ['daɪdʒest] resumen *m*

digestible [daɪ'dʒestəbl] *adj* digerible

digestion [dɪ'dʒestʃən] *n* digestión *f*

digestive [daɪ'dʒestɪv] *adj* (*juices, system*) digestivo

digit ['dɪdʒɪt] *n* (*number*) dígito; (*finger*) dedo

digital ['dɪdʒɪtl] *adj* digital

digital camera *n* cámara digital

digital compact cassette *n* cas(s)et(t)e *m or f* digital compacto

digital TV *n* televisión *f* digital

dignified ['dɪgnɪfaɪd] *adj* grave, solemne; (*action*) decoroso

dignify ['dɪgnɪfaɪ] *vt* dignificar

dignitary ['dɪgnɪtərɪ] *n* dignatario(-a)

dignity ['dɪgnɪtɪ] *n* dignidad *f*

digress [daɪ'gres] *vi*: **to ~ from** apartarse de

digression [daɪ'greʃən] *n* digresión *f*

digs [dɪgz] *npl* (*Brit*: *col*) pensión *f*, alojamiento

dike [daɪk] *n* = **dyke**

dilapidated [dɪ'læpɪdeɪtɪd] *adj* desmoronado, ruinoso

dilate [daɪ'leɪt] *vt* dilatar ■ *vi* dilatarse

dilatory ['dɪlətərɪ] *adj* (*person*) lento; (*action*) dilatorio

dilemma [daɪ'lemə] *n* dilema *m*; **to be in a ~** estar en un dilema

dilettante [dɪlɪ'tæntɪ] *n* diletante *m/f*

diligence ['dɪlɪdʒəns] *n* diligencia

diligent ['dɪlɪdʒənt] *adj* diligente

dill [dɪl] *n* eneldo

dilly-dally ['dɪlɪ'dælɪ] *vi* (*hesitate*) vacilar; (*dawdle*) entretenerse

dilute [daɪ'lu:t] *vt* diluir

dim [dɪm] *adj* (*light*) débil; (*sight*) turbio; (*outline*) borroso; (*stupid*) lerdo; (*room*) oscuro ■ *vt* (*light*) bajar; **to take a ~ view of sth** tener una pobre opinión de algo

dime [daɪm] *n* (*US*) *moneda de diez centavos*

dimension [dɪ'menʃən] *n* dimensión *f*

-dimensional [dɪ'menʃənl] *adj suff*: **two~** de dos dimensiones

dimensions [dɪ'menʃənz] *npl* dimensiones *fpl*

diminish [dɪ'mɪnɪʃ] *vt, vi* disminuir

diminished [dɪ'mɪnɪʃt] *adj*: **~ responsibility** (*Law*) responsabilidad *f* disminuida

diminutive [dɪ'mɪnjutɪv] *adj* diminuto ■ *n* (*Ling*) diminutivo

d

dimly ['dɪmlɪ] *adv* débilmente; (*not clearly*) vagamente

dimmer ['dɪmə^r] *n* (*also*: **dimmer switch**) regulador *m* (de intensidad); (*US Aut*) interruptor *m*

dimple ['dɪmpl] *n* hoyuelo

dimwitted ['dɪm'wɪtɪd] *adj* (*col*) lerdo, de pocas luces

din [dɪn] *n* estruendo, estrépito ■ *vt*: **to ~ sth into sb** (*col*) meter algo en la cabeza a algn

dine [daɪn] *vi* cenar

diner ['daɪnə^r] *n* (*person: in restaurant*) comensal *m/f*; (*Brit Rail*) = **dining car**; (*US*) restaurante económico

dinghy ['dɪŋgɪ] *n* bote *m*; (*also*: **rubber dinghy**) lancha (neumática)

dingy ['dɪndʒɪ] *adj* (*room*) sombrío; (*dirty*) sucio; (*dull*) deslucido

dining car ['daɪnɪŋ-] *n* (*Brit*) coche-restaurante *m*

dining room ['daɪnɪŋ-] *n* comedor *m*

dinner ['dɪnə^r] *n* (*evening meal*) cena, comida (*LAm*); (*lunch*) comida; (*public*) cena, banquete *m*; **~'s ready!** ¡la cena está servida!

dinner jacket *n* smoking *m*

dinner party *n* cena

dinner time *n* hora de cenar *or* comer

dinosaur ['daɪnəsɔː^r] *n* dinosaurio

dint [dɪnt] *n*: **by ~ of (doing) sth** a fuerza de (hacer) algo

diocese ['daɪəsɪs] *n* diócesis *f*

dioxide [daɪ'ɔksaɪd] *n* bióxido; **carbon ~** bióxido de carbono

Dip. *abbr* (*Brit*) = **diploma**

dip [dɪp] *n* (*slope*) pendiente *f*; (*in sea*) chapuzón *m* ■ *vt* (*in water*) mojar; (*ladle etc*) meter; (*Brit Aut*): **to ~ one's lights** poner la luz de cruce ■ *vi* inclinarse hacia abajo

diphtheria [dɪf'θɪərɪə] *n* difteria

diphthong ['dɪfθɔŋ] *n* diptongo

diploma [dɪ'pləumə] *n* diploma *m*

diplomacy [dɪ'pləuməsɪ] *n* diplomacia

diplomat ['dɪpləmæt] *n* diplomático(-a) *m(f)*

diplomatic [dɪplə'mætɪk] *adj* diplomático; **to break off ~ relations** romper las relaciones diplomáticas

diplomatic corps *n* cuerpo diplomático

diplomatic immunity *n* inmunidad *f* diplomática

dipstick ['dɪpstɪk] *n* (*Aut*) varilla de nivel (del aceite)

dipswitch ['dɪpswɪtʃ] *n* (*Brit Aut*) interruptor *m*

dire [daɪə^r] *adj* calamitoso

direct [daɪ'rɛkt] *adj* (*gen*) directo; (*manner, person*) franco ■ *vt* dirigir; **can you ~ me to ...?** ¿puede indicarme dónde está ...?; **to ~ sb**

to do sth mandar a algn hacer algo

direct cost *n* costo directo

direct current *n* corriente *f* continua

direct debit *n* domiciliación *f* bancaria de recibos; **to pay by ~** domiciliar el pago

direct dialling *n* servicio automático de llamadas

direction [dɪ'rɛkʃən] *n* dirección *f*; **sense of ~** sentido de la orientación; **directions** *npl* (*advice*) órdenes *fpl*, instrucciones *fpl*; (*to a place*) señas *fpl*; **in the ~ of** hacia, en dirección a; **directions for use** modo de empleo; **to ask for directions** preguntar el camino

directional [dɪ'rɛkʃənl] *adj* direccional

directive [daɪ'rɛktɪv] *n* orden *f*, instrucción *f*; **a government ~** una orden del gobierno

direct labour *n* mano *f* de obra directa

directly [dɪ'rɛktlɪ] *adv* (*in straight line*) directamente; (*at once*) en seguida

direct mail *n* correspondencia personalizada

direct mailshot *n* (*Brit*) promoción *f* por correspondencia personalizada

directness [dɪ'rɛktnɪs] *n* (*of person, speech*) franqueza

director [dɪ'rɛktə^r] *n* director(a) *m(f)*; **managing ~** director(a) *m(f)* gerente

Director of Public Prosecutions *n* ≈ fiscal *m/f* general del Estado

directory [dɪ'rɛktərɪ] *n* (*Tel*) guía (telefónica); (*street directory*) callejero; (*trade directory*) directorio de comercio; (*Comput*) directorio

directory enquiries, (*US*) **directory assistance** *n* (*service*) (servicio *m* de) información

dirt [də:t] *n* suciedad *f*

dirt-cheap ['də:t'tʃi:p] *adj* baratísimo

dirt road *n* (*US*) camino sin firme

dirty ['də:tɪ] *adj* sucio; (*joke*) verde, colorado (*LAm*) ■ *vt* ensuciar; (*stain*) manchar

dirty trick *n* mala jugada, truco sucio

disability [dɪsə'bɪlɪtɪ] *n* incapacidad *f*

disability allowance *n* pensión *f* de invalidez

disable [dɪs'eɪbl] *vt* (*illness, accident*) dejar incapacitado o inválido; (*tank, gun*) inutilizar; (*Law: disqualify*) incapacitar

disabled [dɪs'eɪbld] *adj* minusválido

disabuse [dɪsə'bju:z] *vt* desengañar

disadvantage [dɪsəd'vɑ:ntɪdʒ] *n* desventaja, inconveniente *m*

disadvantaged [dɪsəd'vɑ:ntɪdʒd] *adj* (*person*) desventajado

disadvantageous [dɪsædvən'teɪdʒəs] *adj* desventajoso

disaffected [dɪsə'fɛktɪd] *adj* descontento; **to be ~ (to or towards)** estar descontento (de)

disaffection [dɪsəˈfɛkʃən] n desafecto, descontento

disagree [dɪsəˈgriː] vi (differ) discrepar; **to ~ (with)** no estar de acuerdo (con); **I ~ with you** no estoy de acuerdo contigo

disagreeable [dɪsəˈgrɪəbl] adj desagradable

disagreement [dɪsəˈgriːmənt] n (gen) desacuerdo; (quarrel) riña; **to have a ~ with sb** estar en desacuerdo con algn

disallow [ˈdɪsəˈlau] vt (goal) anular; (claim) rechazar

disappear [dɪsəˈpɪəʳ] vi desaparecer

disappearance [dɪsəˈpɪərəns] n desaparición f

disappoint [dɪsəˈpɔɪnt] vt decepcionar; (hopes) defraudar

disappointed [dɪsəˈpɔɪntɪd] adj decepcionado

disappointing [dɪsəˈpɔɪntɪŋ] adj decepcionante

disappointment [dɪsəˈpɔɪntmənt] n decepción f

disapproval [dɪsəˈpruːvəl] n desaprobación f

disapprove [dɪsəˈpruːv] vi: **to ~ of** desaprobar

disapproving [dɪsəˈpruːvɪŋ] adj de desaprobación, desaprobador(a)

disarm [dɪsˈɑːm] vt desarmar

disarmament [dɪsˈɑːməmənt] n desarme m

disarmament talks npl conversaciones fpl de or sobre desarme

disarming [dɪsˈɑːmɪŋ] adj (smile) que desarma, encantador(a)

disarray [dɪsəˈreɪ] n: **in ~** (troops) desorganizado; (thoughts) confuso; (hair, clothes) desarreglado; **to throw into ~** provocar el caos

disaster [dɪˈzɑːstəʳ] n desastre m

disaster area n zona catastrófica

disastrous [dɪˈzɑːstrəs] adj desastroso

disband [dɪsˈbænd] vt disolver ▪ vi desbandarse

disbelief [dɪsbəˈliːf] n incredulidad f; **in ~** con incredulidad

disbelieve [ˈdɪsbəˈliːv] vt (person, story) poner en duda, no creer

disc [dɪsk] n disco; (Comput) = **disk**

disc. abbr (Comm) = **discount**

discard [dɪsˈkɑːd] vt tirar; (fig) descartar

discern [dɪˈsəːn] vt percibir, discernir; (understand) comprender

discernible [dɪˈsəːnəbl] adj perceptible

discerning [dɪˈsəːnɪŋ] adj perspicaz

discharge [dɪsˈtʃɑːdʒ] vt (task, duty) cumplir; (ship etc) descargar; (patient) dar de alta; (employee) despedir; (soldier) licenciar; (defendant) poner en libertad; (settle: debt) saldar ▪ n [ˈdɪstʃɑːdʒ] (Elec) descarga;

(vaginal discharge) emisión f vaginal; (dismissal) despedida; (of duty) desempeño; (of debt) pago, descargo; (of gas, chemicals) escape m; **discharged bankrupt** quebrado/a rehabilitado/a

disciple [dɪˈsaɪpl] n discípulo(-a)

disciplinary [ˈdɪsɪplɪnərɪ] adj: **to take ~ action against sb** disciplinar a algn

discipline [ˈdɪsɪplɪn] n disciplina ▪ vt disciplinar; **to ~ o.s. to do sth** obligarse a hacer algo

disc jockey, DJ n pinchadiscos m/f inv

disclaim [dɪsˈkleɪm] vt negar tener

disclaimer [dɪsˈkleɪməʳ] n rectificación f; **to issue a ~** hacer una rectificación

disclose [dɪsˈkləuz] vt revelar

disclosure [dɪsˈkləuʒəʳ] n revelación f

Discman® [ˈdɪskmən] n Discman® m

disco [ˈdɪskəu] n abbr = **discothèque**

discolouration, discoloration (US) [dɪskʌləˈreɪʃən] n descoloramiento, decoloración f

discoloured, discolored (US) [dɪsˈkʌləd] adj descolorido

discomfort [dɪsˈkʌmfət] n incomodidad f; (unease) inquietud f; (physical) malestar m

disconcert [dɪskənˈsəːt] vt desconcertar

disconnect [dɪskəˈnɛkt] vt (gen) separar; (Elec etc) desconectar; (supply) cortar (el suministro) a

disconsolate [dɪsˈkɔnsəlɪt] adj desconsolado

discontent [dɪskənˈtɛnt] n descontento

discontented [dɪskənˈtɛntɪd] adj descontento

discontinue [dɪskənˈtɪnjuː] vt interrumpir; (payments) suspender

discord [ˈdɪskɔːd] n discordia; (Mus) disonancia

discordant [dɪsˈkɔːdənt] adj disonante

discothèque [ˈdɪskəutɛk] n discoteca

discount [ˈdɪskaunt] n descuento ▪ vt [dɪsˈkaunt] descontar; (report etc) descartar; **at a ~** con descuento; **~ for cash** descuento por pago en efectivo; **to give sb a ~ on sth** hacer un descuento a algn en algo

discount house n (Finance) banco de descuento; (Comm: also: **discount store**) ≈ tienda de saldos

discount rate n (Comm) tipo de descuento

discount store n ≈ tienda de saldos

discourage [dɪsˈkʌrɪdʒ] vt desalentar; (oppose) oponerse a; (dissuade, deter) desanimar, disuadir

discouragement [dɪsˈkʌrɪdʒmənt] n (dissuasion) disuasión f; (depression) desánimo, desaliento; **to act as a ~ to** servir para disuadir

517

discouraging [dɪsˈkʌrɪdʒɪŋ] *adj*
desalentador(a)
discourteous [dɪsˈkəːtɪəs] *adj* descortés
discover [dɪsˈkʌvəʳ] *vt* descubrir
discovery [dɪsˈkʌvərɪ] *n* descubrimiento
discredit [dɪsˈkrɛdɪt] *vt* desacreditar
discreet [dɪˈskriːt] *adj* (*tactful*) discreto;
(*careful*) circunspecto, prudente
discreetly [dɪˈskriːtlɪ] *adv* discretamente
discrepancy [dɪˈskrɛpənsɪ] *n* (*difference*)
diferencia; (*disagreement*) discrepancia
discretion [dɪˈskrɛʃən] *n* (*tact*) discreción *f*;
(*care*) prudencia, circunspección *f*; **use your
own ~** haz lo que creas oportuno
discretionary [dɪˈskrɛʃənrɪ] *adj* (*powers*)
discrecional
discriminate [dɪˈskrɪmɪneɪt] *vi*: **to ~
between** distinguir entre; **to ~ against**
discriminar contra
discriminating [dɪˈskrɪmɪneɪtɪŋ] *adj*
entendido
discrimination [dɪskrɪmɪˈneɪʃə
n] *n* (*discernment*) perspicacia; (*bias*)
discriminación *f*; **racial/sexual ~**
discriminación racial/sexual
discus [ˈdɪskəs] *n* disco
discuss [dɪˈskʌs] *vt* (*gen*) discutir; (*a theme*)
tratar
discussion [dɪˈskʌʃən] *n* discusión *f*;
under ~ en discusión
disdain [dɪsˈdeɪn] *n* desdén *m* ∎ *vt* desdeñar
disease [dɪˈziːz] *n* enfermedad *f*
diseased [dɪˈziːzd] *adj* enfermo
disembark [dɪsɪmˈbɑːk] *vt, vi* desembarcar
disembarkation [dɪsɛmbɑːˈkeɪʃən] *n*
desembarque *m*
disenchanted [dɪsɪnˈtʃɑːntɪd] *adj*: **~ (with)**
desilusionado (con)
disenfranchise [ˈdɪsɪnˈfræntʃaɪz] *vt* privar
del derecho al voto; (*Comm*) privar de
franquicias
disengage [dɪsɪnˈgeɪdʒ] *vt* soltar; **to ~ the
clutch** (*Aut*) desembragar
disentangle [dɪsɪnˈtæŋgl] *vt* desenredar
disfavour, disfavor (*US*) [dɪsˈfeɪvəʳ] *n*
desaprobación *f*
disfigure [dɪsˈfɪgəʳ] *vt* desfigurar
disgorge [dɪsˈgɔːdʒ] *vt* verter
disgrace [dɪsˈgreɪs] *n* ignominia; (*downfall*)
caída; (*shame*) vergüenza, escándalo ∎ *vt*
deshonrar
disgraceful [dɪsˈgreɪsful] *adj* vergonzoso;
(*behaviour*) escandaloso
disgruntled [dɪsˈgrʌntld] *adj* disgustado,
descontento
disguise [dɪsˈgaɪz] *n* disfraz *m* ∎ *vt* disfrazar;
(*voice*) disimular; (*feelings etc*) ocultar; **in**

~ disfrazado; **to ~ o.s. as** disfrazarse de;
there's no disguising the fact that ...
no puede ocultarse el hecho de que ...
disgust [dɪsˈgʌst] *n* repugnancia ∎ *vt*
repugnar, dar asco a
disgusting [dɪsˈgʌstɪŋ] *adj* repugnante,
asqueroso
dish [dɪʃ] *n* (*gen*) plato; **to do** *or* **wash the
dishes** fregar los platos
  ▶ **dish out** *vt* (*money, exam papers*) repartir;
  (*food*) servir; (*advice*) dar
  ▶ **dish up** *vt* servir
dishcloth [ˈdɪʃklɔθ] *n* paño de cocina, bayeta
dishearten [dɪsˈhɑːtn] *vt* desalentar
dishevelled, disheveled (*US*) [dɪˈʃɛvəld]
adj (*hair*) despeinado; (*clothes, appearance*)
desarreglado
dishonest [dɪsˈɔnɪst] *adj* (*person*) poco
honrado, tramposo; (*means*) fraudulento
dishonesty [dɪsˈɔnɪstɪ] *n* falta de honradez
dishonour, dishonor (*US*) [dɪsˈɔnəʳ] *n*
deshonra
dishonourable, dishonorable (*US*) [dɪsˈɔnə
rəbl] *adj* deshonroso
dish soap *n* (*US*) lavavajillas *m inv*
dishtowel [ˈdɪʃtauəl] *n* (*US*) trapo de fregar
dishwasher [ˈdɪʃwɔʃəʳ] *n* lavaplatos *m inv*;
(*person*) friegaplatos *m/f inv*
dishy [ˈdɪʃɪ] *adj* (*Brit col*) buenón(-ona)
disillusion [dɪsɪˈluːʒən] *vt* desilusionar;
to become disillusioned (with) quedar
desilusionado (con)
disillusionment [dɪsɪˈluːʒənmənt] *n*
desilusión *f*
disincentive [dɪsɪnˈsɛntɪv] *n* freno; **to act
as a ~ (to)** actuar de freno (a); **to be a ~ to** ser
un freno a
disinclined [ˈdɪsɪnˈklaɪnd] *adj*: **to be ~ to do
sth** estar poco dispuesto a hacer algo
disinfect [dɪsɪnˈfɛkt] *vt* desinfectar
disinfectant [dɪsɪnˈfɛktənt] *n*
desinfectante *m*
disinflation [dɪsɪnˈfleɪʃən] *n* desinflación *f*
disinformation [dɪsɪnfəˈmeɪʃən] *n*
desinformación *f*
disingenuous [dɪsɪnˈdʒɛnjuəs] *adj* poco
sincero, falso
disinherit [dɪsɪnˈhɛrɪt] *vt* desheredar
disintegrate [dɪsˈɪntɪgreɪt] *vi* disgregarse,
desintegrarse
disinterested [dɪsˈɪntrəstɪd] *adj*
desinteresado
disjointed [dɪsˈdʒɔɪntɪd] *adj* inconexo
disk [dɪsk] *n* (*Comput*) disco, disquete *m*;
single-/double-sided ~ disco de una cara/
dos caras
disk drive *n* unidad *f* (de disco)

diskette [dɪs'kɛt] *n* diskette *m*, disquete *m*, disco flexible

disk operating system *n* sistema *m* operativo de discos

dislike [dɪs'laɪk] *n* antipatía, aversión *f* ■ *vt* tener antipatía a; **to take a ~ to sb/sth** cogerle *or* (*LAm*) agarrarle antipatía a algn/algo; **I ~ the idea** no me gusta la idea

dislocate ['dɪsləkeɪt] *vt* dislocar; **he dislocated his shoulder** se dislocó el hombro

dislodge [dɪs'lɔdʒ] *vt* sacar; (*enemy*) desalojar

disloyal [dɪs'lɔɪəl] *adj* desleal

dismal ['dɪzml] *adj* (*dark*) sombrío; (*depressing*) triste; (*very bad*) fatal

dismantle [dɪs'mæntl] *vt* desmontar, desarmar

dismay [dɪs'meɪ] *n* consternación *f* ■ *vt* consternar; **much to my ~** para gran consternación mía

dismiss [dɪs'mɪs] *vt* (*worker*) despedir; (*official*) destituir; (*idea*) rechazar; (*Law*) rechazar; (*possibility*) descartar ■ *vi* (*Mil*) romper filas

dismissal [dɪs'mɪsl] *n* despedida; destitución *f*

dismount [dɪs'maunt] *vi* apearse; (*rider*) desmontar

disobedience [dɪsə'biːdɪəns] *n* desobediencia

disobedient [dɪsə'biːdɪənt] *adj* desobediente

disobey [dɪsə'beɪ] *vt* desobedecer; (*rule*) infringir

disorder [dɪs'ɔːdər] *n* desorden *m*; (*rioting*) disturbio; (*Med*) trastorno; (*disease*) enfermedad *f*; **civil ~** desorden *m* civil

disorderly [dɪs'ɔːdəlɪ] *adj* (*untidy*) desordenado; (*meeting*) alborotado; **~ conduct** (*Law*) conducta escandalosa

disorganized [dɪs'ɔːɡənaɪzd] *adj* desorganizado

disorientated [dɪs'ɔːrɪɛnteɪtəd] *adj* desorientado

disown [dɪs'əun] *vt* renegar de

disparaging [dɪs'pærɪdʒɪŋ] *adj* despreciativo; **to be ~ about sth/sb** menospreciar algo/a algn

disparate ['dɪspərɪt] *adj* dispar

disparity [dɪs'pærɪtɪ] *n* disparidad *f*

dispassionate [dɪs'pæʃnɪt] *adj* (*unbiased*) imparcial; (*unemotional*) desapasionado

dispatch [dɪs'pætʃ] *vt* enviar; (*kill*) despachar; (*deal with: business*) despachar ■ *n* (*sending*) envío; (*speed*) prontitud *f*; (*Press*) informe *m*; (*Mil*) parte *m*

dispatch department *n* (*Comm*) departamento de envíos

dispatch rider *n* (*Mil*) correo

dispel [dɪs'pɛl] *vt* disipar, dispersar

dispensary [dɪs'pɛnsərɪ] *n* dispensario

dispensation [dɪspɛn'seɪʃən] *n* (*Rel*) dispensa

dispense [dɪs'pɛns] *vt* dispensar, repartir; (*medicine*) preparar
  ▶ **dispense with** *vt fus* (*make unnecessary*) prescindir de

dispenser [dɪs'pɛnsər] *n* (*container*) distribuidor *m* automático

dispensing chemist [dɪs'pɛnsɪŋ-] *n* (*Brit*) farmacia

dispersal [dɪs'pəːsl] *n* dispersión *f*

disperse [dɪs'pəːs] *vt* dispersar ■ *vi* dispersarse

dispirited [dɪ'spɪrɪtɪd] *adj* desanimado, desalentado

displace [dɪs'pleɪs] *vt* (*person*) desplazar; (*replace*) reemplazar

displaced person *n* (*Pol*) desplazado(-a)

displacement [dɪs'pleɪsmənt] *n* cambio de sitio

display [dɪs'pleɪ] *n* (*exhibition*) exposición *f*; (*Comput*) visualización *f*; (*Mil*) desfile *m*; (*of feeling*) manifestación *f*; (*pej*) aparato, pompa ■ *vt* exponer; manifestar; (*ostentatiously*) lucir; **on ~** (*exhibits*) expuesto, exhibido; (*goods*) en el escaparate

display advertising *n* publicidad *f* gráfica

displease [dɪs'pliːz] *vt* (*offend*) ofender; (*annoy*) fastidiar; **displeased with** disgustado con

displeasure [dɪs'plɛʒər] *n* disgusto

disposable [dɪs'pəuzəbl] *adj* (*not reusable*) desechable; **~ personal income** ingresos *mpl* personales disponibles

disposable nappy *n* pañal *m* desechable

disposal [dɪs'pəuzl] *n* (*sale*) venta; (*of house*) traspaso; (*by giving away*) donación *f*; (*arrangement*) colocación *f*; (*of rubbish*) destrucción *f*; **at one's ~** a la disposición de algn; **to put sth at sb's ~** poner algo a disposición de algn

disposed [dɪs'pəuzd] *adj*: **~ to do** dispuesto a hacer

dispose of [dɪs'pəuz] *vt fus* (*time, money*) disponer de; (*unwanted goods*) deshacerse de; (*Comm: sell*) traspasar, vender; (*throw away*) tirar

disposition [dɪspə'zɪʃən] *n* disposición *f*; (*temperament*) carácter *m*

dispossess ['dɪspə'zɛs] *vt*: **to ~ sb (of)** desposeer a algn (de)

disproportion [dɪsprə'pɔːʃən] *n* desproporción *f*

disproportionate [dɪsprə'pɔːʃənət] *adj* desproporcionado

disprove [dɪs'pruːv] *vt* refutar

dispute [dɪs'pjuːt] *n* disputa; (*verbal*) discusión *f*; (*also*: **industrial dispute**) conflicto (laboral) ■ *vt* (*argue*) disputar; (*question*) cuestionar; **to be in** *or* **under ~** (*matter*) discutirse; (*territory*) estar en disputa; (*Jur*) estar en litigio

disqualification [dɪskwɔlɪfɪ'keɪʃən] *n* inhabilitación *f*; (*Sport*) descalificación *f*; (*from driving*) descalificación *f*

disqualify [dɪs'kwɔlɪfaɪ] *vt* (*Sport*) desclasificar; **to ~ sb for sth/from doing sth** incapacitar a algn para algo/para hacer algo

disquiet [dɪs'kwaɪət] *n* preocupación *f*, inquietud *f*

disquieting [dɪs'kwaɪətɪŋ] *adj* inquietante

disregard [dɪsrɪ'gɑːd] *vt* desatender; (*ignore*) no hacer caso de ■ *n* (*indifference*: *to feelings, danger, money*): **~ (for)** indiferencia (a); **~ (of)** (*non-observance*: *of law, rules*) violación *f* (de)

disrepair [dɪsrɪ'pɛər] *n*: **to fall into ~** (*building*) desmoronarse; (*street*) deteriorarse

disreputable [dɪs'rɛpjutəbl] *adj* (*person, area*) de mala fama; (*behaviour*) vergonzoso

disrepute ['dɪsrɪ'pjuːt] *n* descrédito, ignominia; **to bring into ~** desacreditar

disrespectful [dɪsrɪ'spɛktful] *adj* irrespetuoso

disrupt [dɪs'rʌpt] *vt* (*meeting, public transport, conversation*) interrumpir; (*plans*) desbaratar, alternar, trastornar

disruption [dɪs'rʌpʃən] *n* trastorno; desbaratamiento; interrupción *f*

disruptive [dɪs'rʌptɪv] *adj* (*influence*) disruptivo; (*strike action*) perjudicial

dissatisfaction [dɪssætɪs'fækʃən] *n* disgusto, descontento

dissatisfied [dɪs'sætɪsfaɪd] *adj* insatisfecho

dissect [dɪ'sɛkt] *vt* (*also fig*) disecar

disseminate [dɪ'sɛmɪneɪt] *vt* divulgar, difundir

dissent [dɪ'sɛnt] *n* disensión *f*

dissenter [dɪ'sɛntər] *n* (*Rel, Pol etc*) disidente *m/f*

dissertation [dɪsə'teɪʃən] *n* (*Univ*) tesina; *see also* **master's degree**

disservice [dɪs'səːvɪs] *n*: **to do sb a ~** perjudicar a algn

dissident ['dɪsɪdnt] *adj, n* disidente *m/f*

dissimilar [dɪ'sɪmɪlər] *adj* distinto

dissipate ['dɪsɪpeɪt] *vt* disipar; (*waste*) desperdiciar

dissipated ['dɪsɪpeɪtɪd] *adj* disoluto

dissipation [dɪsɪ'peɪʃən] *n* disipación *f* (*moral*), libertinaje *m*, vicio; (*waste*) derroche *m*

dissociate [dɪ'səuʃɪeɪt] *vt* disociar; **to ~ o.s. from** disociarse de

dissolute ['dɪsəluːt] *adj* disoluto

dissolution [dɪsə'luːʃən] *n* disolución *f*

dissolve [dɪ'zɔlv] *vt* disolver ■ *vi* disolverse

dissuade [dɪ'sweɪd] *vt*: **to ~ sb (from)** disuadir a algn (de)

distaff ['dɪstæf] *n*: **~ side** rama femenina

distance ['dɪstns] *n* distancia; **in the ~** a lo lejos; **what ~ is it to London?** ¿qué distancia hay de aquí a Londres?; **it's within walking ~** se puede ir andando

distant ['dɪstnt] *adj* lejano; (*manner*) reservado, frío

distaste [dɪs'teɪst] *n* repugnancia

distasteful [dɪs'teɪstful] *adj* repugnante, desagradable

Dist. Atty. *abbr* (*US*) = **district attorney**

distemper [dɪs'tɛmpər] *n* (*of dogs*) moquillo

distend [dɪs'tɛnd] *vt* dilatar, hinchar ■ *vi* dilatarse, hincharse

distended [dɪ'stɛndɪd] *adj* (*stomach*) hinchado

distil, distill (*US*) [dɪs'tɪl] *vt* destilar

distillery [dɪs'tɪlərɪ] *n* destilería

distinct [dɪs'tɪŋkt] *adj* (*different*) distinto; (*clear*) claro; (*unmistakeable*) inequívoco; **as ~ from** a diferencia de

distinction [dɪs'tɪŋkʃən] *n* distinción *f*; (*in exam*) sobresaliente *m*; **a writer of ~** un escritor destacado; **to draw a ~ between** hacer una distinción entre

distinctive [dɪs'tɪŋktɪv] *adj* distintivo

distinctly [dɪs'tɪŋktlɪ] *adv* claramente

distinguish [dɪs'tɪŋgwɪʃ] *vt* distinguir ■ *vi*: **to ~ (between)** distinguir (entre)

distinguished [dɪs'tɪŋgwɪʃt] *adj* (*eminent*) distinguido; (*career*) eminente; (*refined*) distinguido, de categoría

distinguishing [dɪs'tɪŋgwɪʃɪŋ] *adj* (*feature*) distintivo

distort [dɪs'tɔːt] *vt* torcer, retorcer; (*account, news*) desvirtuar, deformar

distortion [dɪs'tɔːʃən] *n* deformación *f*; (*of sound*) distorsión *f*; (*of truth etc*) tergiversación *f*; (*of facts*) falseamiento

distract [dɪs'trækt] *vt* distraer

distracted [dɪs'træktɪd] *adj* distraído

distracting [dɪs'træktɪŋ] *adj* que distrae la atención, molesto

distraction [dɪs'trækʃən] *n* distracción *f*; (*confusion*) aturdimiento; (*amusement*) diversión *f*; **to drive sb to ~** (*distress, anxiety*) volver loco a algn

distraught [dɪs'trɔːt] *adj* turbado, enloquecido

distress [dɪs'trɛs] *n* (*anguish*) angustia; (*want*) miseria; (*pain*) dolor *m*; (*danger*) peligro ■ *vt* afligir; (*pain*) doler; **in ~** (*ship etc*) en peligro

distressing [dɪs'trɛsɪŋ] *adj* angustioso; doloroso

distress signal *n* señal f de socorro

distribute [dɪs'trɪbjuːt] *vt* (*gen*) distribuir; (*share out*) repartir

distribution [dɪstrɪ'bjuːʃən] *n* distribución f

distribution cost *n* gastos *mpl* de distribución

distributor [dɪs'trɪbjutə^r] *n* (*Aut*) distribuidor *m*; (*Comm*) distribuidora

district ['dɪstrɪkt] *n* (*of country*) zona, región f; (*of town*) barrio; (*Admin*) distrito

district attorney *n* (US) fiscal *m/f*

district council *n* ≈ municipio; *ver nota*

DISTRICT COUNCIL

En Inglaterra y Gales, con la excepción de Londres, la administración local corre a cargo del *district council*, responsable de los servicios municipales como vivienda, urbanismo, recolección de basuras, salud medioambiental etc. La mayoría de sus miembros son elegidos a nivel local cada cuatro años. Hay un total de 369 "districts" (distritos), repartidos en 53 "counties" (condados), que se financian a través de los impuestos municipales y partidas presupuestarias del Estado. Éste controla sus gastos a través de una comisión independiente.

district manager *n* representante *m/f* regional

district nurse *n* (Brit) *enfermera que atiende a pacientes a domicilio*

distrust [dɪs'trʌst] *n* desconfianza ■ *vt* desconfiar de

distrustful [dɪs'trʌstful] *adj* desconfiado

disturb [dɪs'təːb] *vt* (*person: bother, interrupt*) molestar; (*meeting*) interrumpir; (*disorganize*) desordenar; **sorry to ~ you** perdone la molestia

disturbance [dɪs'təːbəns] *n* (*political etc*) disturbio; (*violence*) alboroto; (*of mind*) trastorno; **to cause a ~** causar alboroto; **~ of the peace** alteración f del orden público

disturbed [dɪs'təːbd] *adj* (*worried, upset*) preocupado, angustiado; **to be emotionally/mentally ~** tener problemas emocionales/ser un trastornado mental

disturbing [dɪs'təːbɪŋ] *adj* inquietante, perturbador(a)

disuse [dɪs'juːs] *n*: **to fall into ~** caer en desuso

disused [dɪs'juːzd] *adj* abandonado

ditch [dɪtʃ] *n* zanja; (*irrigation ditch*) acequia ■ *vt* (*col*) deshacerse de

dither ['dɪðə^r] *vi* vacilar

ditto ['dɪtəu] *adv* ídem, lo mismo

divan [dɪ'væn] *n* diván *m*

divan bed *n* cama turca

dive [daɪv] *n* (*from board*) salto; (*underwater*) buceo; (*of submarine*) inmersión f; (*Aviat*) picada ■ *vi* saltar; bucear; sumergirse; picar

diver ['daɪvə^r] *n* (*Sport*) saltador(a) *m(f)*; (*underwater*) buzo

diverge [daɪ'vəːdʒ] *vi* divergir

divergent [daɪ'vəːdʒənt] *adj* divergente

diverse [daɪ'vəːs] *adj* diversos(-as), varios(-as)

diversification [daɪvəːsɪfɪ'keɪʃən] *n* diversificación f

diversify [daɪ'vəːsɪfaɪ] *vt* diversificar

diversion [daɪ'vəːʃən] *n* (*Brit Aut*) desviación f; (*distraction*) diversión f; (*Mil*) diversión f

diversionary tactics [daɪ'vəːʃənrɪ-] *npl* tácticas *fpl* de diversión

diversity [daɪ'vəːsɪtɪ] *n* diversidad f

divert [daɪ'vəːt] *vt* (*Brit: train, plane, traffic*) desviar; (*amuse*) divertir

divest [daɪ'vɛst] *vt*: **to ~ sb of sth** despojar a algn de algo

divide [dɪ'vaɪd] *vt* dividir; (*separate*) separar ■ *vi* dividirse; (*road*) bifurcarse; **to ~ (between, among)** repartir *or* dividir (entre); **40 divided by 5** 40 dividido por 5
▶ **divide out** *vt*: **to ~ out (between, among)** (*sweets, tasks etc*) repartir (entre)

divided [dɪ'vaɪdɪd] *adj* (*country, couple*) dividido, separado; (*opinions*) en desacuerdo

divided highway *n* (US) carretera de doble calzada

dividend ['dɪvɪdɛnd] *n* dividendo; (*fig*) beneficio

dividend cover *n* cobertura de dividendo

dividers [dɪ'vaɪdəz] *npl* compás *msg* de puntas

divine [dɪ'vaɪn] *adj* divino ■ *vt* (*future*) vaticinar; (*truth*) alumbrar; (*water, metal*) descubrir, detectar

diving ['daɪvɪŋ] *n* (*Sport*) salto; (*underwater*) buceo

diving board *n* trampolín *m*

diving suit *n* escafandra

divinity [dɪ'vɪnɪtɪ] *n* divinidad f; (*Scol*) teología

divisible [dɪ'vɪzɪbl] *adj* divisible

division [dɪ'vɪʒən] *n* (*also Brit Football*) división f; (*sharing out*) repartimiento; (*Brit Pol*) votación f; **~ of labour** división f del trabajo

divisive [dɪ'vaɪsɪv] *adj* divisivo

divorce [dɪ'vɔːs] *n* divorcio ■ *vt* divorciarse de

divorced [dɪ'vɔːst] *adj* divorciado

divorcee [dɪvɔː'siː] *n* divorciado(-a)
divot ['dɪvət] *n* (*Golf*) chuleta
divulge [daɪ'vʌldʒ] *vt* divulgar, revelar
D.I.Y. *adj, n abbr* (*Brit*) = **do-it-yourself**
dizziness ['dɪzɪnɪs] *n* vértigo
dizzy ['dɪzɪ] *adj* (*person*) mareado; (*height*) vertiginoso; **to feel ~** marearse; **I feel ~** estoy mareado
DJ *n abbr see* **disc jockey**
dj *n abbr* = **dinner jacket**
Djakarta [dʒə'kɑːtə] *n* Yakarta
DJIA *n abbr* (*US Stock Exchange*) = **Dow-Jones Industrial Average**
dl *abbr* (= *decilitre(s)*) dl
DLit, DLitt *abbr* (= *Doctor of Literature, Doctor of Letters*) título universitario
dm *abbr* (= *decimetre(s)*) dm
DMus *abbr* (= *Doctor of Music*) título universitario
DMZ *n abbr* (= *demilitarized zone*) zona desmilitarizada
DNA *n abbr* (= *deoxyribonucleic acid*) ADN *m*
DNA test *n* prueba *f* del ADN

 KEYWORD

do [duː] (*pt* **did**, *pp* **done**) *n* **1** (*col: party etc*): **we're having a little do on Saturday** damos una fiestecita el sábado; **it was rather a grand do** fue un acontecimiento a lo grande
2: **the dos and don'ts** lo que se debe y no se debe hacer
■ *aux vb* **1** (*in negative constructions: not translated*): **I don't understand** no entiendo
2 (*to form questions: not translated*): **do you speak English?** ¿habla (usted) inglés?; **didn't you know?** ¿no lo sabías?; **what do you think?** ¿qué opinas?
3 (*for emphasis, in polite expressions*): **people do make mistakes sometimes** a veces sí se cometen errores; **she does seem rather late** a mí también me parece que se ha retrasado; **do sit down/help yourself** siéntate/sírvete por favor; **do take care!** ¡ten cuidado! ¿eh?; **I DO wish I could ...** ojalá (que) pudiera ...; **but I DO like it** pero, sí (que) me gusta
4 (*used to avoid repeating vb*): **she sings better than I do** canta mejor que yo; **do you agree?** — **yes, I do/no, I don't** ¿estás de acuerdo? — sí (lo estoy)/no (lo estoy); **she lives in Glasgow** — **so do I** vive en Glasgow — yo también; **he didn't like it and neither did we** no le gustó y a nosotros tampoco; **who made this mess?** — **I did** ¿quién hizo esta chapuza? — yo; **he asked me to help him and I did** me pidió que le ayudara y lo hice

5 (*in question tags*): **you like him, don't you?** te gusta, ¿verdad? *or* ¿no?; **I don't know him, do I?** creo que no le conozco; **he laughed, didn't he?** se rió ¿no?
■ *vt* **1** (*gen*): **what are you doing tonight?** ¿qué haces esta noche?; **what can I do for you?** (*in shop*) ¿en qué puedo servirle?; **what does he do for a living?** ¿a qué se dedica?; **I'll do all I can** haré todo lo que pueda; **what have you done with my slippers?** ¿qué has hecho con mis zapatillas?; **to do the washing-up/cooking** fregar los platos/cocinar; **to do one's teeth/hair/nails** lavarse los dientes/arreglarse el pelo/arreglarse las uñas
2 (*Aut etc*): **the car was doing 100** el coche iba a 100; **we've done 200 km already** ya hemos hecho 200 km; **he can do 100 in that car** puede ir a 100 en ese coche
3 (*visit: city, museum*) visitar, recorrer
4 (*cook*): **a steak – well done please** un filete bien hecho, por favor
■ *vi* **1** (*act, behave*) hacer; **do as I do** haz como yo
2 (*get on, fare*): **he's doing well/badly at school** va bien/mal en la escuela; **the firm is doing well** la empresa anda *or* va bien; **how do you do?** mucho gusto; (*less formal*) ¿qué tal?
3 (*suit*): **will it do?** ¿sirve?, ¿está *or* va bien?; **it doesn't do to upset her** cuidado en ofenderla
4 (*be sufficient*) bastar; **will £10 do?** ¿será bastante con £10?; **that'll do** así está bien; **that'll do!** (*in annoyance*) ¡ya está bien!, ¡basta ya!; **to make do (with)** arreglárselas (con)
▶ **do away with** *vt fus* (*kill*) eliminar; (*eradicate: disease*) eliminar; (*abolish: law etc*) abolir; (*withdraw*) retirar
▶ **do out of** *vt fus*: **to do sb out of sth** pisar algo a algn
▶ **do up** *vt* (*laces*) atar; (*zip, dress, shirt*) abrochar; (*renovate: room, house*) renovar
▶ **do with** *vt fus* (*need*): **I could do with a drink/some help** no me vendría mal un trago/un poco de ayuda; (*be connected with*) tener que ver con; **what has it got to do with you?** ¿qué tiene que ver contigo?
▶ **do without** *vi*: **if you're late for dinner then you'll do without** si llegas tarde tendrás que quedarte sin cenar
■ *vt fus* pasar sin; **I can do without a car** puedo pasar sin coche

do. *abbr* = **ditto**
DOA *abbr* = **dead on arrival**
d.o.b. *abbr* = **date of birth**

doc [dɔk] n (col) médico(-a)
docile ['dəusaɪl] adj dócil
dock [dɔk] n (Naut: wharf) dársena, muelle m; (Law) banquillo (de los acusados); **docks** npl muelles mpl, puerto sg ■ vi (enter dock) atracar (en el muelle) ■ vt (pay etc) descontar
dock dues npl derechos mpl de muelle
docker ['dɔkər] n trabajador m portuario, estibador m
docket ['dɔkɪt] n (on parcel etc) etiqueta
dockyard ['dɔkjɑːd] n astillero
doctor ['dɔktər] n médico; (Ph.D. etc) doctor(a) m(f) ■ vt (fig) arreglar, falsificar; (drink etc) adulterar
doctorate ['dɔktərɪt] n doctorado; ver nota

● **DOCTORATE**
●
● El grado más alto que conceden las
● universidades es el doctorado (doctorate),
● tras un período de estudio e investigación
● original no inferior a tres años que
● culmina con la presentación de una
● tesis ("thesis") en la que se exponen los
● resultados. El título más frecuente es el
● de "PhD" ("Doctor of Philosophy"), que se
● obtiene en Letras, Ciencias e Ingeniería,
● aunque también existen otros doctorados
● específicos en Música, Derecho etc.

Doctor of Philosophy n Doctor m (en Filosofía y Letras)
doctrinaire [dɔktrɪ'nɛər] adj doctrinario
doctrine ['dɔktrɪn] n doctrina
docudrama [dɔkju'drɑːmə] n (TV) docudrama m
document ['dɔkjumənt] n documento ■ vt documentar
documentary [dɔkju'mɛntərɪ] adj documental ■ n documental m
documentation [dɔkjumɛn'teɪʃən] n documentación f
DOD n abbr (US: = Department of Defense) Ministerio de Defensa
doddering ['dɔdərɪŋ] adj, **doddery** ['dɔdərɪ] ■ adj vacilante
doddle ['dɔdl] n: **it's a ~** (Brit col) es pan comido
Dodecanese [dəudɪkə'niːz], **Dodecanese Islands** npl Dodecaneso sg
dodge [dɔdʒ] n (of body) regate m; (fig) truco ■ vt (gen) evadir; (blow) esquivar ■ vi escabullirse; (Sport) hacer una finta; **to ~ out of the way** echarse a un lado; **to ~ through the traffic** esquivar el tráfico
dodgems ['dɔdʒəmz] npl (Brit) autos or coches mpl de choque

dodgy ['dɔdʒɪ] adj (col: uncertain) dudoso; (shady) sospechoso; (risky) arriesgado
DOE n abbr (Brit) = **Department of the Environment**; (US) = **Department of Energy**
doe [dəu] n (deer) cierva, gama; (rabbit) coneja
does [dʌz] vb see **do**
doesn't ['dʌznt] = **does not**
dog [dɔg] n perro ■ vt seguir (de cerca); (fig: memory etc) perseguir; **to go to the dogs** (person) echarse a perder; (nation etc) ir a la ruina
dog biscuit n galleta de perro
dog collar n collar m de perro; (fig) alzacuello(s) msg
dog-eared ['dɔgɪəd] adj sobado; (page) con la esquina doblada
dogfish ['dɔgfɪʃ] n cazón m, perro marino
dog food n comida para perros
dogged ['dɔgɪd] adj tenaz, obstinado
doggy ['dɔgɪ] n (col) perrito
doggy bag n bolsa para llevarse las sobras de la comida
dogma ['dɔgmə] n dogma m
dogmatic [dɔg'mætɪk] adj dogmático
do-gooder [duː'gudər] n (col pej): **to be a ~** ser una persona bien intencionada or un filantropista
dogsbody ['dɔgzbɔdɪ] n (Brit) burro de carga
doily ['dɔɪlɪ] n pañito de adorno
doing ['duɪŋ] n: **this is your ~** esto es obra tuya
doings ['duɪŋz] npl (events) sucesos mpl; (acts) hechos mpl
do-it-yourself [duːɪtjɔː'sɛlf] n bricolaje m
doldrums ['dɔldrəmz] npl: **to be in the ~** (person) estar abatido; (business) estar estancado
dole [dəul] n (Brit: payment) subsidio de paro; **on the ~** parado
▶ **dole out** vt repartir
doleful ['dəulful] adj triste, lúgubre
doll [dɔl] n muñeca
▶ **doll up** vt: **to ~ o.s. up** ataviarse
dollar ['dɔlər] n dólar m
dollop ['dɔləp] n buena cucharada
dolphin ['dɔlfɪn] n delfín m
domain [də'meɪn] n (fig) campo, competencia; (land) dominios mpl
dome [dəum] n (Arch) cúpula; (shape) bóveda
domestic [də'mɛstɪk] adj (animal, duty) doméstico; (flight, news, policy) nacional
domesticated [də'mɛstɪkeɪtɪd] adj domesticado; (person: home-loving) casero, hogareño
domesticity [dəumɛs'tɪsɪtɪ] n vida casera
domestic servant n sirviente(-a) m(f)
domicile ['dɔmɪsaɪl] n domicilio

dominant ['dɔmɪnənt] *adj* dominante
dominate ['dɔmɪneɪt] *vt* dominar
domination [dɔmɪ'neɪʃən] *n* dominación f
domineering [dɔmɪ'nɪərɪŋ] *adj* dominante
Dominican Republic [də'mɪnɪkən-] *n* República Dominicana
dominion [də'mɪnɪən] *n* dominio
domino (*pl* **dominoes**) ['dɔmɪnəu] *n* ficha de dominó
dominoes ['dɔmɪnəuz] *n* (*game*) dominó
don [dɔn] *n* (*Brit*) profesor(a) *m(f)* de universidad
donate [də'neɪt] *vt* donar
donation [də'neɪʃən] *n* donativo
done [dʌn] *pp of* **do**
donkey ['dɔŋkɪ] *n* burro
donkey-work ['dɔŋkɪwəːk] *n* (*Brit col*) trabajo pesado
donor ['dəunəʳ] *n* donante *m/f*
donor card *n* carnet *m* de donante de órganos
don't [dəunt] = **do not**
donut ['dəunʌt] *n* (*US*) = **doughnut**
doodle ['duːdl] *n* garabato ▪ *vi* pintar dibujitos *or* garabatos
doom [duːm] *n* (*fate*) suerte *f*; (*death*) muerte *f* ▪ *vt*: **to be doomed to failure** estar condenado al fracaso
doomsday ['duːmzdeɪ] *n* día *m* del juicio final
door [dɔːʳ] *n* puerta; (*of car*) portezuela; (*entry*) entrada; **from ~ to ~** de puerta en puerta
doorbell ['dɔːbɛl] *n* timbre *m*
door handle *n* tirador *m*; (*of car*) manija
door knocker *n* aldaba
doorman ['dɔːmən] *n* (*in hotel*) portero
doormat ['dɔːmæt] *n* felpudo, estera
doorstep ['dɔːstɛp] *n* peldaño; **on your ~** en la puerta de casa; (*fig*) al lado de casa
door-to-door ['dɔːtə'dɔːʳ] *adj*: **~ selling** venta a domicilio
doorway ['dɔːweɪ] *n* entrada, puerta; **in the ~** en la puerta
dope [dəup] *n* (*col: person*) imbécil *m/f*; (*: information*) información *f*, informes *mpl* ▪ *vt* (*horse etc*) drogar
dopey ['dəupɪ] *adj* atontado
dormant ['dɔːmənt] *adj* inactivo; (*latent*) latente
dormer ['dɔːməʳ] *n* (*also*: **dormer window**) buhardilla
dormitory ['dɔːmɪtrɪ] *n* (*Brit*) dormitorio; (*US: hall of residence*) residencia, colegio mayor
dormouse (*pl* **dormice**) ['dɔːmaus, -maɪs] *n* lirón *m*
Dors *abbr* (*Brit*) = **Dorset**
DOS [dɔs] *n abbr* = **disk operating system**

dosage ['dəusɪdʒ] *n* (*on medicine bottle*) dosis *f inv*, dosificación *f*
dose [dəus] *n* (*of medicine*) dosis *f inv*; **a ~ of flu** un ataque de gripe ▪ *vt*: **to ~ o.s. with** automedicarse con
dosser ['dɔsəʳ] *n* (*Brit col*) mendigo(-a); (*lazy person*) vago(-a)
doss house ['dɔs-] *n* (*Brit*) pensión *f* de mala muerte
dossier ['dɔsɪeɪ] *n*: **~ (on)** expediente *m* (sobre)
DOT *n abbr* (*US*: = *Department of Transportation*) ministerio de transporte
dot [dɔt] *n* punto; **dotted with** salpicado de; **on the ~** en punto
dotcom ['dɔtkɔm] *n* puntocom *f*
dot command *n* (*Comput*) instrucción *f* (precedida) de punto
dote [dəut]: **to ~ on** *vt fus* adorar, idolatrar
dot-matrix printer [dɔt'meɪtrɪks-] *n* impresora matricial *or* de matriz
dotted line ['dɔtɪd-] *n* línea de puntos; **to sign on the ~** firmar
dotty ['dɔtɪ] *adj* (*col*) disparatado, chiflado
double ['dʌbl] *adj* doble ▪ *adv* (*twice*): **to cost ~** costar el doble ▪ *n* (*gen*) doble *m* ▪ *vt* doblar; (*efforts*) redoblar ▪ *vi* doblarse; (*have two uses etc*): **to ~ as** hacer las veces de; **~ five two six (5526)** (*Telec*) cinco cinco dos seis; **spelt with a ~ "s"** escrito con dos "eses"; **on the ~**, (*Brit*) **at the ~** corriendo
  ▶ **double back** *vi* (*person*) volver sobre sus pasos
  ▶ **double up** *vi* (*bend over*) doblarse; (*share bedroom*) compartir
double bass *n* contrabajo
double bed *n* cama matrimonial
double-breasted ['dʌbl'brɛstɪd] *adj* cruzado
double-check ['dʌbltʃɛk] *vt* volver a revisar ▪ *vi*: **I'll ~** voy a revisarlo otra vez
double-click ['dʌbl,klɪk] (*Comput*) *vi* hacer doble clic
double cream *n* nata enriquecida
doublecross ['dʌbl'krɔs] *vt* (*trick*) engañar; (*betray*) traicionar
doubledecker ['dʌbl'dɛkəʳ] *n* autobús *m* de dos pisos
double glazing *n* (*Brit*) doble acristalamiento
double indemnity *n* doble indemnización *f*
double-page ['dʌblpeɪdʒ] *adj*: **~ spread** doble página
double room *n* cuarto para dos
doubles ['dʌblz] *n* (*Tennis*) juego de dobles
double time *n* tarifa doble
double whammy [-'wæmɪ] *n* (*col*) palo doble
doubly ['dʌblɪ] *adv* doblemente
doubt [daut] *n* duda ▪ *vt* dudar; (*suspect*)

dudar de; **to ~ that** dudar que; **there is no ~ that** no cabe duda de que; **without (a) ~** sin duda (alguna); **beyond ~** fuera de duda; **I ~ it very much** lo dudo mucho

doubtful ['dautful] *adj* dudoso; (*arousing suspicion: person*) sospechoso; **to be ~ about sth** tener dudas sobre algo; **I'm a bit ~** no estoy convencido

doubtless ['dautlɪs] *adv* sin duda

dough [dəu] *n* masa, pasta; (*col: money*) pasta, lana (*LAm*)

doughnut ['dəunʌt] *n* buñuelo

douse [daus] *vt* (*drench: with water*) mojar; (*extinguish: flames*) apagar

dove [dʌv] *n* paloma

Dover ['dəuvəʳ] *n* Dover

dovetail ['dʌvteɪl] *vi* (*fig*) encajar

dowager ['dauɪdʒəʳ] *n*: **~ duchess** duquesa viuda

dowdy ['daudɪ] *adj* desaliñado; (*inelegant*) poco elegante

Dow-Jones average ['daudʒəunz-] *n* (*US*) índice *m* Dow-Jones

Dow-Jones Index *n* (*US*) índice *m* Dow-Jones

down [daun] *n* (*fluff*) pelusa; (*feathers*) plumón *m*, flojel *m*; (*hill*) loma ■ *adv* (*also*: **downwards**) abajo, hacia abajo; (*on the ground*) por/en tierra ■ *prep* abajo ■ *vt* (*col: drink*) beberse, tragar(se); **~ with X!** ¡abajo X!; **~ there** allí abajo; **~ here** aquí abajo; **I'll be ~ in a minute** ahora bajo; **England is two goals ~** Inglaterra está perdiendo por dos tantos; **I've been ~ with flu** he estado con gripe; **the price of meat is ~** ha bajado el precio de la carne; **I've got it ~ in my diary** lo he apuntado en mi agenda; **to pay £2 ~** dejar £2 de depósito; **he went ~ the hill** fue cuesta abajo; **~ under** (*in Australia etc*) en Australia/Nueva Zelanda; **to ~ tools** (*fig*) declararse en huelga

down-and-out ['daunəndaut] *n* (*tramp*) vagabundo(-a)

down-at-heel ['daunət'hi:l] *adj* venido a menos; (*appearance*) desaliñado

downbeat ['daunbi:t] *n* (*Mus*) compás *m* ■ *adj* (*gloomy*) pesimista

downcast ['daunka:st] *adj* abatido

downer ['daunəʳ] *n* (*col: drug*) tranquilizante; **to be on a ~** estar pasando un mal bache

downfall ['daunfɔ:l] *n* caída, ruina

downgrade [daun'greɪd] *vt* (*job*) degradar; (*hotel*) bajar de categoría

downhearted [daun'hɑ:tɪd] *adj* desanimado

downhill [daun'hɪl] *adv*: **to go ~** ir cuesta abajo; (*business*) estar en declive

Downing Street ['daunɪŋ-] *n* (*Brit*) Downing Street *f*; *ver nota*

● **DOWNING STREET**

Downing Street es la calle de Londres en la que tienen su residencia oficial tanto el Primer Ministro ("Prime Minister") como el Ministro de Economía ("Chancellor of the Exchequer"). El primero vive en el nº10 y el segundo en el nº11. Es una calle cerrada al público que se encuentra en el barrio de Westminster, en el centro de Londres. *Downing Street* se usa también en lenguaje periodístico para referirse al jefe del gobierno británico.

download ['daunləud] *vt* (*Comput*) transferir, telecargar

downloadable [daun'ləudəbl] *adj* (*Comput*) descargable

down-market ['daun'mɑ:kɪt] *adj* de escasa calidad

down payment *n* entrada, pago al contado

downplay ['daunpleɪ] *vt* (*US*) quitar importancia a

downpour ['daunpɔ:ʳ] *n* aguacero

downright ['daunraɪt] *adj* (*nonsense, lie*) manifiesto; (*refusal*) terminante

downsize [daun'saɪz] *vt* reducir la plantilla de

Down's syndrome [daunz-] *n* síndrome *m* de Down

downstairs [daun'stɛəz] *adv* (*below*) (en el piso de) abajo; (*motion*) escaleras abajo; **to come** (*or* **go**) **~** bajar la escalera

downstream [daun'stri:m] *adv* río abajo

downtime ['dauntaɪm] *n* (*Comm*) tiempo inactivo

down-to-earth [dauntu'ə:θ] *adj* práctico

downtown [daun'taun] *adv* en el centro de la ciudad

downtrodden ['dauntrɔdn] *adj* oprimido

downward ['daunwəd] *adv* hacia abajo; **face ~** (*person*) boca abajo; (*object*) cara abajo ■ *adj*: **a ~ trend** una tendencia descendente

downwards ['daunwədz] *adv* hacia abajo

dowry ['daurɪ] *n* dote *f*

doz. *abbr* = **dozen**

doze [dəuz] *vi* dormitar
  ▶ **doze off** *vi* echar una cabezada

dozen ['dʌzn] *n* docena; **a ~ books** una docena de libros; **dozens of** cantidad de; **dozens of times** cantidad de veces; **80p a ~** 80 peniques la docena

DPh, DPhil *n abbr* (= *Doctor of Philosophy*) título universitario

DPP *n abbr* (*Brit*) = **Director of Public Prosecutions**

DPT *n abbr* (*Med*: = *diphtheria, pertussis, tetanus*) vacuna trivalente

DPW *n abbr* (*US*: = *Department of Public Works*) ministerio de obras públicas

Dr, Dr. *abbr* (= *doctor*) Dr

Dr. *abbr* (= *in street names*) = **Drive**

dr *abbr* (*Comm*) = **debtor**

drab [dræb] *adj* gris, monótono

draft [drɑːft] *n* (*first copy: of document, report*) borrador *m*; (*Comm*) giro; (*US: call-up*) quinta ■ *vt* (*write roughly*) hacer un borrador de; *see also* **draught**

draftsman *etc* ['drɑːftsmən] (*US*) = **draughtsman** *etc*

drag [dræg] *vt* arrastrar; (*river*) dragar, rastrear ■ *vi* arrastrarse por el suelo ■ *n* (*Aviat: resistance*) resistencia aerodinámica; (*col*) lata; (*women's clothing*): **in** ~ travestido; **to** ~ **and drop** (*Comput*) arrastrar y soltar
▶ **drag away** *vt*: **to** ~ **away (from)** separar a rastras (de)
▶ **drag on** *vi* ser interminable

dragnet ['drægnɛt] *n* (*Naut*) rastra; (*fig*) emboscada

dragon ['drægən] *n* dragón *m*

dragonfly ['drægənflaɪ] *n* libélula

dragoon [drə'guːn] *n* (*cavalryman*) dragón *m* ■ *vt*: **to** ~ **sb into doing sth** forzar a algn a hacer algo

drain [dreɪn] *n* desaguadero; (*in street*) sumidero; (*drain cover*) rejilla del sumidero ■ *vt* (*land, marshes*) desecar; (*Med*) drenar; (*reservoir*) desecar; (*fig*) agotar ■ *vi* escurrirse; **to be a** ~ **on** consumir, agotar; **to feel drained (of energy)** (*fig*) sentirse agotado

drainage ['dreɪnɪdʒ] *n* (*act*) desagüe *m*; (*Med, Agr*) drenaje *m*; (*sewage*) alcantarillado

draining board ['dreɪnɪŋ-], **drainboard** (*US*) ['dreɪnbɔːd] *n* escurridero, escurridor *m*

drainpipe ['dreɪnpaɪp] *n* tubo de desagüe

drake [dreɪk] *n* pato (macho)

dram [dræm] *n* (*drink*) traguito, copita

drama ['drɑːmə] *n* (*art*) teatro; (*play*) drama *m*

dramatic [drə'mætɪk] *adj* dramático

dramatist ['dræmətɪst] *n* dramaturgo(-a)

dramatize ['dræmətaɪz] *vt* (*events etc*) dramatizar; (*adapt: novel: for TV, cinema*) adaptar

drank [dræŋk] *pt of* **drink**

drape [dreɪp] *vt* cubrir

draper ['dreɪpəʳ] *n* (*Brit*) pañero, mercero

drapes [dreɪps] *npl* (*US*) cortinas *fpl*

drastic ['dræstɪk] *adj* (*measure, reduction*) severo; (*change*) radical

draught, draft (*US*) [drɑːft] *n* (*of air*) corriente *f* de aire; (*drink*) trago; (*Naut*) calado; **on** ~ (*beer*) de barril

draught beer *n* cerveza de barril

draughtboard ['drɑːftbɔːd] (*Brit*) *n* tablero de damas

draughts [drɑːfts] *n* (*Brit*) juego de damas

draughtsman, draftsman (*US*) ['drɑːftsmən] *n* proyectista *m*, delineante *m*

draughtsmanship, draftsmanship (*US*) ['drɑːftsmənʃɪp] *n* (*drawing*) dibujo lineal; (*skill*) habilidad *f* para el dibujo

draw [drɔː] *vb* (*pt* **drew**, *pp* **drawn**) ■ *vt* (*pull*) tirar; (*take out*) sacar; (*attract*) atraer; (*picture*) dibujar; (*money*) retirar; (*formulate: conclusion*): **to** ~ **(from)** sacar (de); (*comparison, distinction*): **to** ~ **(between)** hacer (entre) ■ *vi* (*Sport*) empatar ■ *n* (*Sport*) empate *m*; (*lottery*) sorteo; (*attraction*) atracción *f*; **to** ~ **near** *vi* acercarse
▶ **draw back** *vi*: **to** ~ **back (from)** echarse atrás (de)
▶ **draw in** *vi* (*car*) aparcar; (*train*) entrar en la estación
▶ **draw on** *vt* (*resources*) utilizar, servirse de; (*imagination, person*) recurrir a
▶ **draw out** *vi* (*lengthen*) alargarse
▶ **draw up** *vi* (*stop*) pararse ■ *vt* (*document*) redactar; (*plan*) trazar

drawback ['drɔːbæk] *n* inconveniente *m*, desventaja

drawbridge ['drɔːbrɪdʒ] *n* puente *m* levadizo

drawee [drɔː'iː] *n* girado, librado

drawer [drɔːʳ] *n* cajón *m*; (*of cheque*) librador(a) *m(f)*

drawing ['drɔːɪŋ] *n* dibujo

drawing board *n* tablero (de dibujante)

drawing pin *n* (*Brit*) chincheta *m*

drawing room *n* salón *m*

drawl [drɔːl] *n* habla lenta y cansina

drawn [drɔːn] *pp of* **draw** ■ *adj* (*haggard: with tiredness*) ojeroso; (: *with pain*) macilento

drawstring ['drɔːstrɪŋ] *n* cordón *m*

dread [drɛd] *n* pavor *m*, terror *m* ■ *vt* temer, tener miedo *or* pavor a

dreadful ['drɛdful] *adj* espantoso; **I feel** ~! (*ill*) ¡me siento fatal *or* malísimo!; (*ashamed*) ¡qué vergüenza!

dream [driːm] *n* sueño ■ *vt, vi* (*pt, pp* **dreamed** *or* **dreamt**) [drɛmt] soñar; **to have a** ~ **about sb/sth** soñar con algn/algo; **sweet dreams!** ¡que sueñes con los angelitos!
▶ **dream up** *vt* (*reason, excuse*) inventar; (*plan, idea*) idear

dreamer ['driːməʳ] *n* soñador(a) *m(f)*

dream world *n* mundo imaginario *or* de ensueño

dreamy ['driːmɪ] *adj* (*person*) soñador(a), distraído; (*music*) de sueño

dreary ['drɪərɪ] *adj* monótono, aburrido

dredge [drɛdʒ] vt dragar
 ▸ **dredge up** vt sacar con draga; (fig: unpleasant facts) pescar, sacar a luz
dredger ['drɛdʒəʳ] n (ship, machine) draga; (Culin) tamiz m
dregs [drɛgz] npl heces fpl
drench [drɛntʃ] vt empapar; **drenched to the skin** calado hasta los huesos
dress [drɛs] n vestido; (clothing) ropa
 ∎ vt vestir; (wound) vendar; (Culin) aliñar; (shop window) decorar, arreglar ∎ vi vestirse; **to ~ o.s., get dressed** vestirse; **she dresses very well** se viste muy bien
 ▸ **dress up** vi vestirse de etiqueta; (in fancy dress) disfrazarse
dress circle n (Brit) principal m
dress designer n modisto(-a)
dresser ['drɛsəʳ] n (furniture) aparador m; (: US) tocador m; (Theat) camarero(-a)
dressing ['drɛsɪŋ] n (Med) vendaje m; (Culin) aliño
dressing gown n (Brit) bata
dressing room n (Theat) camarín m; (Sport) vestidor m
dressing table n tocador m
dressmaker ['drɛsmeɪkəʳ] n modista, costurera
dressmaking ['drɛsmeɪkɪŋ] n costura
dress rehearsal n ensayo general
dress shirt n camisa de frac
dressy ['drɛsɪ] adj (col) elegante
drew [dru:] pt of **draw**
dribble ['drɪbl] vi gotear, caer gota a gota; (baby) babear ∎ vt (ball) driblar, regatear
dried [draɪd] adj (gen) seco; (fruit) paso; (milk) en polvo
drier ['draɪəʳ] n = **dryer**
drift [drɪft] n (of current etc) velocidad f; (of sand) montón m; (of snow) ventisquero; (meaning) significado ∎ vi (boat) ir a la deriva; (sand, snow) amontonarse; **to catch sb's ~** cogerle el hilo a algn; **to let things ~** dejar las cosas como están; **to ~ apart** (friends) seguir su camino; (lovers) disgustarse, romper
drifter ['drɪftəʳ] n vagabundo(-a)
driftwood ['drɪftwʊd] n madera flotante
drill [drɪl] n taladro; (bit) broca; (of dentist) fresa; (for mining etc) perforadora, barrena; (Mil) instrucción f ∎ vt perforar, taladrar; (soldiers) ejercitar; (pupils: in grammar) hacer ejercicios con ∎ vi (for oil) perforar
drilling ['drɪlɪŋ] n (for oil) perforación f
drilling rig n (on land) torre f de perforación; (at sea) plataforma de perforación
drily ['draɪlɪ] adv secamente
drink [drɪŋk] n bebida ∎ vt, vi (pt **drank**,

pp **drunk**) beber, tomar (LAm); **to have a ~** tomar algo; tomar una copa or un trago; **a ~ of water** un trago de agua; **to invite sb for drinks** invitar a algn a tomar unas copas; **there's food and ~ in the kitchen** hay de comer y de beber en la cocina; **would you like something to ~?** ¿quieres beber or tomar algo?
 ▸ **drink in** vt (person: fresh air) respirar; (: story, sight) beberse
drinkable ['drɪŋkəbl] adj (not poisonous) potable; (palatable) aguantable
drink-driving [drɪŋk'draɪvɪŋ] n: **to be charged with ~** ser acusado de conducir borracho or en estado de embriaguez
drinker ['drɪŋkəʳ] n bebedor(a) m(f)
drinking ['drɪŋkɪŋ] n (drunkenness) beber m
drinking fountain n fuente f de agua potable
drinking water n agua potable
drip [drɪp] n (act) goteo; (one drip) gota; (Med) gota a gota m; (sound: of water etc) goteo; (col: spineless person) soso(-a) ∎ vi gotear, caer gota a gota
drip-dry ['drɪp'draɪ] adj (shirt) de lava y pon
dripping ['drɪpɪŋ] n (animal fat) pringue m
 ∎ adj: **~ wet** calado
drive [draɪv] (pt **drove**, pp **driven**) n paseo (en coche); (journey) viaje m (en coche); (also: **driveway**) entrada; (street) calle f; (energy) energía, vigor m; (Psych) impulso; (Sport) ataque m; (Comput: also: **disk drive**) unidad f (de disco) ∎ vt (car) conducir, manejar (LAm); (nail) clavar; (push) empujar; (Tech: motor) impulsar ∎ vi (Aut: at controls) conducir, manejar (LAm); (: travel) pasearse en coche; **to go for a ~** dar una vuelta en coche; **it's three hours' ~ from London** es un viaje de tres horas en coche desde Londres; **left-/right-hand ~** conducción f a la izquierda/derecha; **front-/rear-wheel ~** tracción f delantera/trasera; **sales ~** promoción f de ventas; **to ~ sb mad** volverle loco a algn; **to ~ sb to (do) sth** empujar a algn a (hacer) algo; **he drives a taxi** es taxista; **he drives a Mercedes** tiene un Mercedes; **can you ~?** ¿sabes conducir or (LAm) manejar?; **to ~ at 50 km an hour** ir a 50km por hora
 ▸ **drive at** vt fus (fig: intend, mean) querer decir, insinuar
 ▸ **drive on** vi no parar, seguir adelante ∎ vt (incite, encourage) empujar
drive-by ['draɪvbaɪ] n: **~ shooting** tiroteo desde el coche
drive-in ['draɪvɪn] adj (esp US): **~ cinema** autocine m
drivel ['drɪvl] n (col) tonterías fpl
driven ['drɪvn] pp of **drive**

driver ['draɪvəʳ] n conductor(a) m(f), chofer m (LAm); (of taxi) taxista m/f
driver's license n (US) carnet m or permiso de conducir
driveway ['draɪvweɪ] n camino de entrada
driving ['draɪvɪŋ] n conducir m, manejar m (LAm) ■ adj (force) impulsor(a)
driving instructor n instructor(a) m(f) de autoescuela
driving lesson n clase f de conducir
driving licence n (Brit) carnet m or permiso de conducir
driving school n autoescuela
driving test n examen m de conducir
drizzle ['drɪzl] n llovizna, garúa (LAm) ■ vi lloviznar
droll [drəul] adj gracioso
dromedary ['drɒmɪdərɪ] n dromedario
drone [drəun] vi (bee, aircraft, engine) zumbar; (also: **drone on**) murmurar sin interrupción ■ n zumbido; (male bee) zángano
drool [druːl] vi babear; **to ~ over sb/sth** caérsele la baba por algn/algo
droop [druːp] vi (fig) decaer, desanimarse
drop [drɒp] n (of water) gota; (fall: in price) bajada; (: in salary) disminución f ■ vt (allow to fall) dejar caer; (voice, eyes, price) bajar; (set down from car) dejar ■ vi (price, temperature) bajar; (wind) calmarse, amainar; (numbers, attendance) disminuir; **drops** npl (Med) gotas fpl; **cough drops** pastillas fpl para la tos; **a ~ of 10%** una bajada del 10 por ciento; **to ~ anchor** echar el ancla; **to ~ sb a line** mandar unas líneas a algn
▶ **drop in** vi (col: visit): **to ~ in (on)** pasar por casa (de)
▶ **drop off** vi (sleep) dormirse ■ vt (passenger) bajar, dejar
▶ **drop out** vi (withdraw) retirarse
droplet ['drɒplɪt] n gotita
dropout ['drɒpaut] n (from society) marginado(-a); (from university) estudiante m/f que ha abandonado los estudios
dropper ['drɒpəʳ] n (Med) cuentagotas m inv
droppings ['drɒpɪŋz] npl excremento sg
dross [drɒs] n (fig) escoria
drought [draut] n sequía
drove [drəuv] pt of **drive**
drown [draun] vt (also: **drown out**: sound) ahogar ■ vi ahogarse
drowse [drauz] vi estar medio dormido
drowsy ['drauzɪ] adj soñoliento; **to be ~** tener sueño
drudge [drʌdʒ] n esclavo del trabajo
drudgery ['drʌdʒərɪ] n trabajo pesado or monótono
drug [drʌg] n (Med) medicamento, droga; (narcotic) droga ■ vt drogar; **to be on drugs** drogarse; **he's on drugs** se droga
drug addict n drogadicto(-a)
druggist ['drʌgɪst] n (US) farmacéutico(-a)
drug peddler n traficante m/f de drogas
drugstore ['drʌgstɔːʳ] n (US) tienda (de comestibles, periódicos y medicamentos)
drug trafficker n narcotraficante m/f
drum [drʌm] n tambor m; (large) bombo; (for oil, petrol) bidón m ■ vi tocar el tambor; (with fingers) tamborilear ■ vt: **to ~ one's fingers on the table** tamborilear con los dedos sobre la mesa; **drums** npl batería sg
▶ **drum up** vt (enthusiasm, support) movilizar, fomentar
drummer ['drʌməʳ] n (in military band) tambor m/f; (in jazz/pop group) batería m/f
drumstick ['drʌmstɪk] n (Mus) palillo, baqueta; (chicken leg) muslo (de pollo)
drunk [drʌŋk] pp of **drink** ■ adj borracho ■ n (also: **drunkard**) borracho(-a); **to get ~** emborracharse
drunken ['drʌŋkən] adj borracho
drunkenness ['drʌŋkənnɪs] n embriaguez f
dry [draɪ] adj seco; (day) sin lluvia; (climate) árido, seco; (humour) agudo; (uninteresting: lecture) aburrido, pesado ■ vt secar; (tears) enjugarse ■ vi secarse; **on ~ land** en tierra firme; **to ~ one's hands/hair/eyes** secarse las manos/el pelo/las lágrimas
▶ **dry up** vi (supply, imagination etc) agotarse; (in speech) atascarse
dry-clean ['draɪ'kliːn] vt limpiar or lavar en seco; **"~ only"** (on label) "limpieza or lavado en seco"
dry-cleaner's ['draɪ'kliːnəz] n tintorería
dry-cleaning ['draɪ'kliːnɪŋ] n lavado en seco
dry dock n (Naut) dique m seco
dryer ['draɪəʳ] n (for hair) secador m; (for clothes) secadora
dry goods npl (Comm) mercería sg
dry goods store n (US) mercería
dry ice n nieve f carbónica, hielo seco
dryness ['draɪnɪs] n sequedad f
dry rot n putrefacción f
dry run n (fig) ensayo
dry ski slope n pista artificial de esquí
DSc n abbr (= Doctor of Science) título universitario
DSS n abbr (Brit) = **Department of Social Security**; see **social security**
DST n abbr (US: = Daylight Saving Time) hora de verano
DT n abbr (Comput) = **data transmission**
DTI n abbr (Brit) = **Department of Trade and Industry**
DTP n abbr = **desktop publishing**; (Med) = **diphtheria, tetanus, pertussis**

DT's *n abbr* (*col*: = *delirium tremens*) delirium *m* tremens

dual ['djuəl] *adj* doble

dual carriageway *n* (*Brit*) ≈ autovía

dual-control ['djuəlkən'trəul] *adj* de doble mando

dual nationality *n* doble nacionalidad *f*

dual-purpose ['djuəl'pə:pəs] *adj* de doble uso

dubbed [dʌbd] *adj* (*Cine*) doblado

dubious ['dju:bɪəs] *adj* indeciso; (*reputation, company*) dudoso; (*character*) sospechoso; **I'm very ~ about it** tengo mis dudas sobre ello

Dublin ['dʌblɪn] *n* Dublín

Dubliner ['dʌblɪnər] *n* dublinés(-esa) *m(f)*

duchess ['dʌtʃɪs] *n* duquesa

duck [dʌk] *n* pato ■ *vi* agacharse ■ *vt* (*plunge in water*) zambullir

duckling ['dʌklɪŋ] *n* patito

duct [dʌkt] *n* conducto, canal *m*

dud [dʌd] *n* (*shell*) obús *m* que no estalla; (*object, tool*): **it's a ~** es una filfa ■ *adj*: **~ cheque** (*Brit*) cheque *m* sin fondos

due [dju:] *adj* (*proper*) debido; (*fitting*) conveniente, oportuno ■ *adv*: **~ north** derecho al norte; **dues** *npl* (*for club, union*) cuota *sg*; (*in harbour*) derechos *mpl*; **in ~ course** a su debido tiempo; **~ to** debido a; **to be ~ to** deberse a; **the train is ~ to arrive at 8.00** el tren tiene (prevista) la llegada a las ocho; **the rent's ~ on the 30th** hay que pagar el alquiler el día 30; **I am ~ six days' leave** me deben seis días de vacaciones; **she is ~ back tomorrow** ella debe volver mañana

due date *n* fecha de vencimiento

duel ['djuəl] *n* duelo

duet [dju:'ɛt] *n* dúo

duff [dʌf] *adj* sin valor

duffel bag ['dʌfl-] *n* macuto

duffel coat ['dʌfl-] *n* trenca

dug [dʌg] *pt, pp of* **dig**

dugout ['dʌgaut] *n* (*canoe*) piragua (*hecha de un solo tronco*); (*Sport*) banquillo; (*Mil*) refugio subterráneo

duke [dju:k] *n* duque *m*

dull [dʌl] *adj* (*light*) apagado; (*stupid*) torpe; (*boring*) pesado; (*sound, pain*) sordo; (*weather, day*) gris ■ *vt* (*pain, grief*) aliviar; (*mind, senses*) entorpecer

duly ['dju:lɪ] *adv* debidamente; (*on time*) a su debido tiempo

dumb [dʌm] *adj* mudo; (*stupid*) estúpido; **to be struck ~** (*fig*) quedar boquiabierto

dumbbell ['dʌmbɛl] *n* (*Sport*) pesa

dumbfounded [dʌm'faundɪd] *adj* pasmado

dummy ['dʌmɪ] *n* (*tailor's model*) maniquí *m*; (*Brit: for baby*) chupete *m* ■ *adj* falso, postizo;

~ run ensayo

dump [dʌmp] *n* (*heap*) montón *m* de basura; (*place*) basurero, vertedero; (*col*) tugurio; (*Mil*) depósito; (*Comput*) copia vaciada ■ *vt* (*put down*) dejar; (*get rid of*) deshacerse de; (*Comput*) tirar (a la papelera); (*Comm: goods*) inundar el mercado de; **to be (down) in the dumps** (*col*) tener murria, estar deprimido

dumping ['dʌmpɪŋ] *n* (*Econ*) dumping *m*; (*of rubbish*): **"no ~"** "prohibido verter basura"

dumpling ['dʌmplɪŋ] *n* bola de masa hervida

dumpy ['dʌmpɪ] *adj* regordete(-a)

dunce [dʌns] *n* zopenco

dune [dju:n] *n* duna

dung [dʌŋ] *n* estiércol *m*

dungarees [dʌŋgə'ri:z] *npl* mono *sg*, overol *msg* (*LAm*)

dungeon ['dʌndʒən] *n* calabozo

dunk [dʌŋk] *vt* mojar

duo ['dju:əu] *n* (*Mus*) dúo

duodenal [dju:ə'di:nl] *adj* (*ulcer*) de duodeno

duodenum [dju:ə'di:nəm] *n* duodeno

dupe [dju:p] *n* (*victim*) víctima ■ *vt* engañar

duplex ['dju:plɛks] *n* (*US: also*: **duplex apartment**) dúplex *m*

duplicate ['dju:plɪkət] *n* duplicado; (*copy of letter etc*) copia ■ *adj* (*copy*) duplicado ■ *vt* ['dju:plɪkeɪt] duplicar; (*on machine*) multicopiar; **in ~** por duplicado

duplicate key *n* duplicado de una llave

duplicating machine ['dju:plɪkeɪtɪŋ-], **duplicator** ['dju:plɪkeɪtər] *n* multicopista *m*

duplicity [dju:'plɪsɪtɪ] *n* doblez *f*, duplicidad *f*

Dur. *abbr* (*Brit*) = **Durham**

durability [djuərə'bɪlɪtɪ] *n* durabilidad *f*

durable ['djuərəbl] *adj* duradero

duration [djuə'reɪʃən] *n* duración *f*

duress [djuə'rɛs] *n*: **under ~** por coacción

Durex® ['djuərɛks] *n* (*Brit*) preservativo

during ['djuərɪŋ] *prep* durante

dusk [dʌsk] *n* crepúsculo, anochecer *m*

dusky ['dʌskɪ] *adj* oscuro; (*complexion*) moreno

dust [dʌst] *n* polvo ■ *vt* (*furniture*) desempolvar; (*cake etc*): **to ~ with** espolvorear de

▶ **dust off** *vt* (*also fig*) desempolvar, quitar el polvo de

dustbin ['dʌstbɪn] *n* (*Brit*) cubo de la basura, balde *m* (*LAm*)

dustbin liner *n* bolsa de basura

duster ['dʌstər] *n* paño, trapo; (*feather duster*) plumero

dust jacket *n* sobrecubierta

dustman ['dʌstmən] *n* (*Brit*) basurero

dustpan ['dʌstpæn] *n* cogedor *m*

dust storm *n* vendaval *m* de polvo

dusty ['dʌstɪ] *adj* polvoriento

d

Dutch | dystrophy

Dutch [dʌtʃ] *adj* holandés(-esa) ▪ *n* (*Ling*) holandés *m* ▪ *adv*: **to go ~** pagar a escote; **the Dutch** *npl* los holandeses

Dutch auction *n* subasta a la rebaja

Dutchman ['dʌtʃmən], **Dutchwoman** ['dʌtʃwumən] *n* holandés(-esa) *m(f)*

dutiful ['djuːtɪful] *adj* (*child*) obediente; (*husband*) sumiso; (*employee*) cumplido

duty ['djuːtɪ] *n* deber *m*; (*tax*) derechos *mpl* de aduana; (*Med: in hospital*) servicio, guardia; **on ~** de servicio; (*at night etc*) de guardia; **off ~** libre (de servicio); **to make it one's ~ to do sth** encargarse de hacer algo sin f alta; **to pay ~ on sth** pagar los derechos sobre algo

duty-free [djuːtɪ'friː] *adj* libre de derechos de aduana; **~ shop** tienda libre de impuestos

duty officer *n* (*Mil etc*) oficial *m/f* de guardia

duvet ['duːveɪ] *n* (*Brit*) edredón *m* (nórdico)

DV *abbr* (= *Deo volente*) Dios mediante

DVD *n abbr* (= *digital versatile or video disc*) DVD *m*

DVLA *n abbr* (Brit: = *Driver and Vehicle Licensing Agency*) organismo encargado de la expedición de permisos de conducir y matriculación de vehículos

DVM *n abbr* (US: = *Doctor of Veterinary Medicine*) título universitario

DVT *n abbr* = **deep-vein thrombosis**

dwarf [dwɔːf] (*pl* **dwarves**) [dwɔːvz] *n* enano ▪ *vt* empequeñecer

dwell [dwɛl] (*pt, pp* **dwelt**) [dwɛlt] *vi* morar
▸ **dwell on** *vt fus* explayarse en

dweller ['dwɛləʳ] *n* habitante *m*; **city ~** habitante *m* de la ciudad

dwelling ['dwɛlɪŋ] *n* vivienda

dwelt [dwɛlt] *pt, pp of* **dwell**

dwindle ['dwɪndl] *vi* menguar, disminuir

dwindling ['dwɪndlɪŋ] *adj* (*strength, interest*) menguante; (*resources, supplies*) en disminución

dye [daɪ] *n* tinte *m* ▪ *vt* teñir; **hair ~** tinte *m* para el pelo

dying ['daɪɪŋ] *adj* moribundo, agonizante; (*moments*) final; (*words*) último

dyke [daɪk] *n* (Brit) dique *m*; (*channel*) arroyo, acequia; (*causeway*) calzada

dynamic [daɪ'næmɪk] *adj* dinámico

dynamics [daɪ'næmɪks] *n or npl* dinámica *sg*

dynamite ['daɪnəmaɪt] *n* dinamita ▪ *vt* dinamitar

dynamo ['daɪnəməu] *n* dinamo *f*, dinamo *m* (*LAm*)

dynasty ['dɪnəstɪ] *n* dinastía

dysentery ['dɪsɪntrɪ] *n* disentería

dyslexia [dɪs'lɛksɪə] *n* dislexia

dyslexic [dɪs'lɛksɪk] *adj, n* disléxico(-a) *m(f)*

dyspepsia [dɪs'pɛpsɪə] *n* dispepsia

dystrophy ['dɪstrəfɪ] *n* distrofia; **muscular ~** distrofia muscular

Ee

E, e [iː] *n* (*letter*) E, e *f*; (*Mus*) mi *m*; **E for Edward**, (US) **E for Easy** E de Enrique
E *abbr* (= *east*) E ■ *n abbr* (= *Ecstasy*) éxtasis *m*
E111 *n abbr* (= *form* E111) impreso E111
ea. *abbr* = **each**
E.A. *abbr* (US: = *educational age*) nivel escolar
each [iːtʃ] *adj* cada *inv* ■ *pron* cada uno; (*also:* **each other**) el uno al otro; **they hate ~ other** se odian (entre ellos *or* mutuamente); **~ day** cada día; **they have two books ~** tienen dos libros cada uno; **they cost £5 ~** cuestan cinco libras cada uno; **~ of us** cada uno de nosotros
eager [ˈiːgəʳ] *adj* (*gen*) impaciente; (*hopeful*) ilusionado; (*keen*) entusiasmado; (*pupil*) apasionado; **to be ~ to do sth** estar deseoso de hacer algo; **to be ~ for** ansiar, anhelar
eagerly [ˈiːgəlɪ] *adv* con impaciencia; con ilusión; con entusiasmo
eagerness [ˈiːgənɪs] *n* impaciencia; ilusión *f*; entusiasmo
eagle [ˈiːgl] *n* águila
E & OE *abbr* = **errors and omissions excepted**
ear [ɪəʳ] *n* oreja; (*sense of hearing*) oído; (*of corn*) espiga; **up to the ears in debt** abrumado de deudas
earache [ˈɪəreɪk] *n* dolor *m* de oídos
eardrum [ˈɪədrʌm] *n* tímpano
earful [ˈɪəful] *n*: **to give sb an ~** (*col*) echar una bronca a algn
earl [əːl] *n* conde *m*
early [ˈəːlɪ] *adv* (*gen*) temprano; (*ahead of time*) con tiempo, con anticipación ■ *adj* (*gen*) temprano; (*reply*) pronto; (*man*) primitivo; (*first: Christians, settlers*) primero; **to have an ~ night** acostarse temprano; **in the ~ or ~ in the spring/19th century** a principios de primavera/del siglo diecinueve; **you're ~!** ¡has llegado temprano *or* pronto!; **~ in the morning/afternoon** a primeras horas de la mañana/tarde; **she's in her ~ forties** tiene poco más de cuarenta años; **at your earliest convenience** (*Comm*) con la mayor brevedad posible; **I can't come any earlier** no puedo llegar antes

early retirement *n* jubilación *f* anticipada
early warning system *n* sistema *m* de alerta inmediata
earmark [ˈɪəmɑːk] *vt*: **to ~ for** reservar para, destinar a
earn [əːn] *vt* (*gen*) ganar; (*interest*) devengar; (*praise*) ganarse; **to ~ one's living** ganarse la vida
earned income *n* renta del trabajo
earnest [ˈəːnɪst] *adj* serio, formal ■ *n* (*also:* **earnest money**) anticipo, señal *f*; **in ~** *adv* en serio
earnings [ˈəːnɪŋz] *npl* (*personal*) ingresos *mpl*; (*of company etc*) ganancias *fpl*
earphones [ˈɪəfəunz] *npl* auriculares *mpl*
earplugs [ˈɪəplʌgz] *npl* tapones *mpl* para los oídos
earring [ˈɪərɪŋ] *n* pendiente *m*, arete *m* (*LAm*)
earshot [ˈɪəʃɔt] *n*: **out of/within ~** fuera del/al alcance del oído
earth [əːθ] *n* (*gen*) tierra; (*Brit Elec*) toma de tierra ■ *vt* (*Brit Elec*) conectar a tierra
earthenware [ˈəːθnwɛəʳ] *n* loza (de barro)
earthly [ˈəːθlɪ] *adj* terrenal, mundano; **~ paradise** paraíso terrenal; **there is no ~ reason to think ...** no existe razón para pensar ...
earthquake [ˈəːθkweɪk] *n* terremoto
earth-shattering [ˈəːθʃætərɪŋ] *adj* trascendental
earthworm [ˈəːθwəːm] *n* lombriz *f*
earthy [ˈəːθɪ] *adj* (*fig: uncomplicated*) sencillo; (*coarse*) grosero
earwig [ˈɪəwɪg] *n* tijereta
ease [iːz] *n* facilidad *f*; (*comfort*) comodidad *f* ■ *vt* (*task*) facilitar; (*pain*) aliviar; (*loosen*) soltar; (*relieve: pressure, tension*) aflojar; (*weight*) aligerar; (*help pass*): **to ~ sth in/out** meter/sacar algo con cuidado ■ *vi* (*situation*) relajarse; **with ~** con facilidad; **to feel at ~/ill at ~** sentirse a gusto/a disgusto; **at ~!** (*Mil*) ¡descansen!

easel | edge

▶ **ease off, ease up** *vi* (*work, business*) aflojar; (*person*) relajarse
easel ['i:zl] *n* caballete *m*
easily ['i:zɪlɪ] *adv* fácilmente
easiness ['i:zɪnɪs] *n* facilidad *f*; (*of manners*) soltura
east [i:st] *n* este *m*, oriente *m* ■ *adj* del este, oriental ■ *adv* al este, hacia el este; **the E~** el Oriente; (*Pol*) el Este
Easter ['i:stə^r] *n* Pascua (de Resurrección)
Easter egg *n* huevo de Pascua
Easter holidays *npl* Semana Santa *sg*
Easter Island *n* Isla de Pascua
easterly ['i:stəlɪ] *adj* (*to the east*) al este; (*from the east*) del este
Easter Monday *n* lunes *m* de Pascua
eastern ['i:stən] *adj* del este, oriental; **E~ Europe** Europa del Este; **the E~ bloc** (*Pol*) los países del Este
Easter Sunday *n* Domingo de Resurrección
East Germany *n* (*formerly*) Alemania Oriental *or* del Este
eastward ['i:stwəd], **eastwards** ['i:stwədz] *adv* hacia el este
easy ['i:zɪ] *adj* fácil; (*life*) holgado, cómodo; (*relaxed*) natural ■ *adv*: **to take it** *or* **things ~** (*not worry*) no preocuparse; (*go slowly*) tomarlo con calma; (*rest*) descansar; **payment on ~ terms** (*Comm*) facilidades de pago; **I'm ~** (*col*) me da igual, no me importa; **easier said than done** del dicho al hecho hay buen trecho
easy chair *n* butaca
easy-going ['i:zɪ'gəuɪŋ] *adj* acomodadizo
easy touch [i:zɪ'tʌtʃ] *n*: **he's an ~** (*col*) es fácil de convencer
eat (*pt* **ate**, *pp* **eaten**) [i:t, eɪt, 'i:tn] *vt* comer
▶ **eat away** *vt* (*sea*) desgastar; (*acid*) corroer
▶ **eat into, eat away at** *vt fus* corroer
▶ **eat out** *vi* comer fuera
▶ **eat up** *vt* (*meal etc*) comerse; **it eats up electricity** devora la electricidad
eatable ['i:təbl] *adj* comestible
eau de Cologne [əudəkə'ləun] *n* (agua de) colonia
eaves [i:vz] *npl* alero *sg*
eavesdrop ['i:vzdrɔp] *vi*: **to ~ (on sb)** escuchar a escondidas *or* con disimulo (a algn)
ebb [ɛb] *n* reflujo ■ *vi* bajar; (*fig: also*: **ebb away**) decaer; **~ and flow** el flujo y reflujo; **to be at a low ~** (*fig: person*) estar de capa caída
ebb tide *n* marea menguante
ebony ['ɛbənɪ] *n* ébano
e-book ['i:buk] *n* libro electrónico
ebullient [ɪ'bʌlɪənt] *adj* entusiasta, animado
e-business [i:bɪznɪs] *n* (*commerce*) comercio electrónico; (*company*) negocio electrónico

ECB *n abbr* (= *European Central Bank*) BCE *m*
eccentric [ɪk'sɛntrɪk] *adj, n* excéntrico(-a)
ecclesiastical [ɪkli:zɪ'æstɪkəl] *adj* eclesiástico
ECG *n abbr* (= *electrocardiogram*) E.C.G. *m*
echo (*pl* **echoes**) ['ɛkəu] *n* eco *m* ■ *vt* (*sound*) repetir ■ *vi* resonar, hacer eco
ECLA *n abbr* (= *Economic Commission for Latin America*) CEPAL *f*
éclair ['eɪklɛə^r] *n* petisú *m*
eclipse [ɪ'klɪps] *n* eclipse *m* ■ *vt* eclipsar
ECM *n abbr* (*US*: = *European Common Market*) MCE *m*
eco- ['i:kəu] *pref* eco-
eco-friendly ['i:kəufrɛndlɪ] *adj* ecológico
ecological [i:kə'lɔdʒɪkl] *adj* ecológico
ecologist [ɪ'kɔlədʒɪst] *n* ecologista *m/f*; (*scientist*) ecólogo(-a) *m(f)*
ecology [ɪ'kɔlədʒɪ] *n* ecología
e-commerce ['i:ˌkɔmə:s] *n* comercio electrónico
economic [i:kə'nɔmɪk] *adj* (*profitable: price*) económico; (*business etc*) rentable
economical [i:kə'nɔmɪkl] *adj* económico
economically [i:kə'nɔmɪklɪ] *adv* económicamente
economics [i:kə'nɔmɪks] *n* economía ■ *npl* (*financial aspects*) finanzas *fpl*
economic warfare *n* guerra económica
economist [ɪ'kɔnəmɪst] *n* economista *m/f*
economize [ɪ'kɔnəmaɪz] *vi* economizar, ahorrar
economy [ɪ'kɔnəmɪ] *n* economía; **economies of scale** economías *fpl* de escala
economy class *n* (*Aviat etc*) clase *f* turista
economy class syndrome *n* síndrome *m* de la clase turista
economy size *n* tamaño familiar
ecosystem ['i:kəusɪstəm] *n* ecosistema *m*
eco-tourism [i:kəu'tuərɪzm] *n* turismo verde *or* ecológico
ECSC *n abbr* (= *European Coal and Steel Community*) CECA *f*
ecstasy ['ɛkstəsɪ] *n* éxtasis *m inv*
ecstatic [ɛks'tætɪk] *adj* extático, extasiado
ECT *n abbr* = **electroconvulsive therapy**
Ecuador ['ɛkwədɔ:^r] *n* Ecuador *m*
Ecuadoran [ɛkwə'dɔ:rən], **Ecuadorian** [ɛkwə'dɔ:rɪən] *adj, n* ecuatoriano(-a) *m(f)*
ecumenical [i:kju'mɛnɪkl] *adj* ecuménico
eczema ['ɛksɪmə] *n* eczema *m*
eddy ['ɛdɪ] *n* remolino
edge [ɛdʒ] *n* (*of knife etc*) filo; (*of object*) borde *m*; (*of lake etc*) orilla ■ *vt* (*Sewing*) ribetear ■ *vi*: **to ~ past** pasar con dificultad; **on ~** (*fig*) = **edgy**; **to ~ away from** alejarse poco a poco de; **to ~ forward** avanzar poco a poco; **to ~ up** subir lentamente

edgeways ['ɛdʒweɪz] *adv*: **he couldn't get a word in** ~ no pudo meter baza

edging ['ɛdʒɪŋ] *n* (*Sewing*) ribete *m*; (*of path*) borde *m*

edgy ['ɛdʒɪ] *adj* nervioso, inquieto

edible ['ɛdɪbl] *adj* comestible

edict ['iːdɪkt] *n* edicto

edifice ['ɛdɪfɪs] *n* edificio

edifying ['ɛdɪfaɪɪŋ] *adj* edificante

Edinburgh ['ɛdɪnbərə] *n* Edimburgo

edit ['ɛdɪt] *vt* (*be editor of*) dirigir; (*re-write*) redactar; (*cut*) cortar; (*Comput*) editar

edition [ɪ'dɪʃən] *n* (*gen*) edición *f*; (*number printed*) tirada

editor ['ɛdɪtə'] *n* (*of newspaper*) director(a) *m(f)*; (*of book*) redactor(a) *m(f)*; (*also*: **film editor**) montador(a) *m(f)*

editorial [ɛdɪ'tɔːrɪəl] *adj* editorial ▪ *n* editorial *m*; ~ **staff** redacción *f*

EDP *n abbr* (= *electronic data processing*) PED *m*

EDT *n abbr* (*US*: = *Eastern Daylight Time*) hora de verano de Nueva York

educate ['ɛdjukeɪt] *vt* (*gen*) educar; (*instruct*) instruir

educated guess ['ɛdjukeɪtɪd-] *n* hipótesis *f* sólida

education [ɛdju'keɪʃən] *n* educación *f*; (*schooling*) enseñanza; (*Scol: subject etc*) pedagogía; **primary/secondary** ~ enseñanza primaria/secundaria

educational [ɛdju'keɪʃənl] *adj* (*policy etc*) de educación, educativo; (*teaching*) docente; (*instructive*) educativo; ~ **technology** tecnología educacional

Edwardian [ɛd'wɔːdɪən] *adj* eduardiano

EE *abbr* = **electrical engineer**

EEG *n abbr* = **electroencephalogram**

eel [iːl] *n* anguila

EENT *n abbr* (*US Med*) = **eye, ear, nose and throat**

EEOC *n abbr* (*US*: = *Equal Employment Opportunity Commission*) *comisión que investiga discriminación racial o sexual en el empleo*

eerie ['ɪərɪ] *adj* (*sound, experience*) espeluznante

EET *n abbr* (= *Eastern European Time*) hora de Europa oriental

efface [ɪ'feɪs] *vt* borrar

effect [ɪ'fɛkt] *n* efecto ▪ *vt* efectuar, llevar a cabo; **effects** *npl* (*property*) efectos *mpl*; **to take** ~ (*law*) entrar en vigor *or* vigencia; (*drug*) surtir efecto; **in** ~ en realidad; **to have an** ~ **on sb/sth** hacerle efecto a algn/afectar algo; **to put into** ~ (*plan*) llevar a la práctica; **his letter is to the** ~ **that** ... su carta viene a decir que ...

effective [ɪ'fɛktɪv] *adj* (*gen*) eficaz; (*striking*: *display, outfit*) impresionante; (*real*) efectivo; **to become** ~ (*law*) entrar en vigor; ~ **date** fecha de vigencia

effectively [ɪ'fɛktɪvlɪ] *adv* (*efficiently*) eficazmente; (*strikingly*) de manera impresionante; (*in reality*) en efecto

effectiveness [ɪ'fɛktɪvnɪs] *n* eficacia

effeminate [ɪ'fɛmɪnɪt] *adj* afeminado

effervescent [ɛfə'vɛsnt] *adj* efervescente

efficacy ['ɛfɪkəsɪ] *n* eficacia

efficiency [ɪ'fɪʃənsɪ] *n* (*gen*) eficiencia; (*of machine*) rendimiento

efficient [ɪ'fɪʃənt] *adj* eficiente; (*remedy, product, system*) eficaz; (*machine, car*) de buen rendimiento

effigy ['ɛfɪdʒɪ] *n* efigie *f*

effluent ['ɛfluənt] *n* vertidos *mpl*

effort ['ɛfət] *n* esfuerzo; **to make an** ~ **to do sth** hacer un esfuerzo *or* esforzarse para hacer algo

effortless ['ɛfətlɪs] *adj* sin ningún esfuerzo

effrontery [ɪ'frʌntərɪ] *n* descaro

effusive [ɪ'fjuːsɪv] *adj* efusivo

EFL *n abbr* (*Scol*) = **English as a foreign language**

EFTA ['ɛftə] *n abbr* (= *European Free Trade Association*) EFTA *f*

e.g. *adv abbr* (= *exempli gratia*) p.ej.

egg [ɛg] *n* huevo; **hard-boiled/soft-boiled/poached** ~ huevo duro *or* (*LAm*) a la copa *or* (*LAm*) tibio /pasado por agua/escalfado; **scrambled eggs** huevos revueltos

▶ **egg on** *vt* incitar

eggcup ['ɛgkʌp] *n* huevera

eggnog [ɛg'nɔg] *n* ponche *m* de huevo

eggplant ['ɛgplɑːnt] *n* (*esp US*) berenjena

eggshell ['ɛgʃɛl] *n* cáscara de huevo

egg-timer ['ɛgtaɪmə'] *n* reloj *m* de arena (*para cocer huevos*)

egg white *n* clara de huevo

egg yolk *n* yema de huevo

ego ['iːgəu] *n* ego

egotism ['ɛgəutɪzəm] *n* egoísmo

egotist ['ɛgəutɪst] *n* egoísta *m/f*

ego trip *n*: **to be on an** ~ creerse el centro del mundo

Egypt ['iːdʒɪpt] *n* Egipto

Egyptian [ɪ'dʒɪpʃən] *adj, n* egipcio(-a) *m(f)*

eiderdown ['aɪdədaun] *n* edredón *m*

eight [eɪt] *num* ocho

eighteen [eɪ'tiːn] *num* dieciocho

eighth [eɪtθ] *adj* octavo

eighty ['eɪtɪ] *num* ochenta

Eire ['ɛərə] *n* Eire *m*

EIS *n abbr* (= *Educational Institute of Scotland*) *sindicato de profesores escoceses*

either ['aɪðəʳ] *adj* cualquiera de los dos ...;
(*both, each*) cada ■ *pron*: ~ **(of them)**
cualquiera (de los dos) ■ *adv* tampoco ■ *conj*:
~ **yes or no** o sí o no; **on** ~ **side** en ambos
lados; **I don't like** ~ no me gusta ninguno de
los dos; **no, I don't** ~ no, yo tampoco
eject [ɪ'dʒɛkt] *vt* echar; (*tenant*) desahuciar
■ *vi* eyectarse
ejector seat [ɪ'dʒɛktə-] *n* asiento proyectable
eke out [iːk-] *vt fus* (*money*) hacer que llegue
EKG *n abbr* (*US*) *see* **electrocardiogram**
el [ɛl] *n abbr* (*US col*) = **elevated railroad**
elaborate [*adj* ɪ'læbərɪt, *vb* ɪ'læbəreɪt] *adj*
(*design, pattern*) complicado ■ *vt* elaborar
■ *vi* explicarse con muchos detalles
elaborately [ɪ'læbərɪtlɪ] *adv* de manera
complicada; (*decorated*) profusamente
elaboration [ɪlæbə'reɪʃən] *n* elaboración *f*
elapse [ɪ'læps] *vi* transcurrir
elastic [ɪ'læstɪk] *adj, n* elástico
elastic band *n* (*Brit*) gomita
elated [ɪ'leɪtɪd] *adj*: **to be** ~ estar eufórico
elation [ɪ'leɪʃən] *n* euforia
elbow ['ɛlbəu] *n* codo ■ *vt*: **to** ~ **one's way
through the crowd** abrirse paso a codazos
por la muchedumbre
elbow grease *n* (*col*): **to use some** *or* **a bit of**
~ menearse
elder ['ɛldəʳ] *adj* mayor ■ *n* (*tree*) saúco;
(*person*) mayor; (*of tribe*) anciano
elderly ['ɛldəlɪ] *adj* de edad, mayor ■ *npl*:
the ~ la gente mayor, los ancianos
elder statesman *n* estadista *m* veterano; (*fig*)
figura respetada
eldest ['ɛldɪst] *adj, n* el/la mayor
elect [ɪ'lɛkt] *vt* elegir; (*choose*): **to** ~ **to do**
optar por hacer ■ *adj*: **the president** ~ el
presidente electo
election [ɪ'lɛkʃən] *n* elección *f*; **to hold an** ~
convocar elecciones
election campaign *n* campaña electoral
electioneering [ɪlɛkʃə'nɪərɪŋ] *n* campaña
electoral
elector [ɪ'lɛktəʳ] *n* elector(a) *m(f)*
electoral [ɪ'lɛktərəl] *adj* electoral
electoral college *n* colegio electoral
electoral roll *n* censo electoral
electorate [ɪ'lɛktərɪt] *n* electorado
electric [ɪ'lɛktrɪk] *adj* eléctrico
electrical [ɪ'lɛktrɪkl] *adj* eléctrico
electrical engineer *n* ingeniero(-a)
electricista
electrical failure *n* fallo eléctrico
electric blanket *n* manta eléctrica
electric chair *n* silla eléctrica
electric cooker *n* cocina eléctrica
electric current *n* corriente *f* eléctrica

electric fire *n* estufa eléctrica
electrician [ɪlɛk'trɪʃən] *n* electricista *m/f*
electricity [ɪlɛk'trɪsɪtɪ] *n* electricidad *f*;
to switch on/off the ~ conectar/desconectar
la electricidad
electricity board *n* (*Brit*) compañía eléctrica
(estatal)
electric light *n* luz *f* eléctrica
electric shock *n* electrochoque *m*
electrification [ɪlɛktrɪfɪ'keɪʃən] *n*
electrificación *f*
electrify [ɪ'lɛktrɪfaɪ] *vt* (*Rail*) electrificar;
(*fig: audience*) electrizar
electro... [ɪ'lɛktrəu] *pref* electro...
electrocardiogram [ɪ'lɛktrə'kɑːdɪəgræm] *n*
electrocardiograma *m*
electrocardiograph [ɪ'lɛktrəu'kɑːdɪəgræf] *n*
electrocardiógrafo
electro-convulsive therapy [ɪ'lɛktrə-
kən'vʌlsɪv-] *n* electroterapia
electrocute [ɪ'lɛktrəukjuːt] *vt* electrocutar
electrode [ɪ'lɛktrəud] *n* electrodo
electroencephalogram [ɪ'lɛktrəuɛn'sɛfələ-
græm] *n* electroencefalograma *m*
electrolysis [ɪlɛk'trɔlɪsɪs] *n* electrólisis *f inv*
electromagnetic [ɪ'lɛktrəmæg'nɛtɪk] *adj*
electromagnético
electron [ɪ'lɛktrɔn] *n* electrón *m*
electronic [ɪlɛk'trɔnɪk] *adj* electrónico
electronic data processing *n* tratamiento *or*
proceso electrónico de datos
electronic mail *n* correo electrónico
electronics [ɪlɛk'trɔnɪks] *n* electrónica
electron microscope *n* microscopio
electrónico
electroplated [ɪ'lɛktrə'pleɪtɪd] *adj*
galvanizado
electrotherapy [ɪ'lɛktrə'θɛrəpɪ] *n*
electroterapia
elegance ['ɛlɪgəns] *n* elegancia
elegant ['ɛlɪgənt] *adj* elegante
elegy ['ɛlɪdʒɪ] *n* elegía
element ['ɛlɪmənt] *n* (*gen*) elemento;
(*of heater, kettle etc*) resistencia
elementary [ɛlɪ'mɛntərɪ] *adj* elemental;
(*primitive*) rudimentario; (*school, education*)
primario
elementary school *n* (*US*) escuela de
enseñanza primaria; *ver nota*

⬤ **ELEMENTARY SCHOOL**

⬤ En Estados Unidos y Canadá se llama
⬤ *elementary school* al centro estatal en el que
⬤ los niños reciben los primeros seis u ocho
⬤ años de su educación, también llamado
⬤ "grade school" o "grammar school".

elephant ['ɛlɪfənt] n elefante m
elevate ['ɛlɪveɪt] vt (gen) elevar; (in rank) ascender
elevated railroad n (US) ferrocarril urbano elevado
elevation [ɛlɪ'veɪʃən] n elevación f; (rank) ascenso; (height) altitud f
elevator ['ɛlɪveɪtəʳ] n (US) ascensor m, elevador m (LAm)
eleven [ɪ'lɛvn] num once
elevenses [ɪ'lɛvnzɪz] npl (Brit) ≈ café m de media mañana
eleventh [ɪ'lɛvnθ] adj undécimo; **at the ~ hour** (fig) a última hora
elf (pl **elves**) [ɛlf, ɛlvz] n duende m
elicit [ɪ'lɪsɪt] vt: **to ~ sth (from sb)** obtener algo (de algn)
eligible ['ɛlɪdʒəbl] adj cotizado; **to be ~ for a pension** tener derecho a una pensión
eliminate [ɪ'lɪmɪneɪt] vt eliminar; (score out) suprimir; (a suspect, possibility) descartar
elimination [ɪlɪmɪ'neɪʃən] n eliminación f; supresión f; **by process of ~** por eliminación
elite [eɪ'liːt] n élite f
elitist [eɪ'liːtɪst] adj (pej) elitista
elixir [ɪ'lɪksɪəʳ] n elixir m
Elizabethan [ɪlɪzə'biːθən] adj isabelino
elm [ɛlm] n olmo
elocution [ɛlə'kjuːʃən] n elocución f
elongated ['iːlɔŋgeɪtɪd] adj alargado
elope [ɪ'ləup] vi fugarse
elopement [ɪ'ləupmənt] n fuga
eloquence ['ɛləkwəns] n elocuencia
eloquent ['ɛləkwənt] adj elocuente
else [ɛls] adv: **or ~** si no; **something ~** otra cosa or algo más; **somewhere ~** en otra parte; **everywhere ~** en los demás sitios; **everyone ~** todos los demás; **nothing ~** nada más; **is there anything ~ I can do?** ¿puedo hacer algo más?; **where ~?** ¿dónde más?, ¿en qué otra parte?; **there was little ~ to do** apenas quedaba otra cosa que hacer; **nobody ~** nadie más
elsewhere [ɛls'wɛəʳ] adv (be) en otra parte; (go) a otra parte
ELT n abbr (Scol) = **English Language Teaching**
elucidate [ɪ'luːsɪdeɪt] vt esclarecer, elucidar
elude [ɪ'luːd] vt eludir; (blow, pursuer) esquivar
elusive [ɪ'luːsɪv] adj escurridizo; (answer) difícil de encontrar; **he is very ~** no es fácil encontrarlo
elves [ɛlvz] npl of **elf**
emaciated [ɪ'meɪsɪeɪtɪd] adj escuálido
email ['iːmeɪl] n abbr (= electronic mail) email m, correo electrónico ■ vt: **to ~ sb** mandar un email or un correo electrónico a algn;
  to ~ sb sth mandar algo a algn por Internet, mandar algo a algn en un email or un correo electrónico
email account n cuenta de correo
email address n dirección f electrónica, email m
emanate ['ɛməneɪt] vi emanar, provenir
emancipate [ɪ'mænsɪpeɪt] vt emancipar
emancipated [ɪ'mænsɪpeɪtɪd] adj liberado
emancipation [ɪmænsɪ'peɪʃən] n emancipación f, liberación f
emasculate [ɪ'mæskjuleɪt] vt castrar; (fig) debilitar
embalm [ɪm'bɑːm] vt embalsamar
embankment [ɪm'bæŋkmənt] n (of railway) terraplén m; (riverside) dique m
embargo (pl **embargoes**) [ɪm'bɑːgəu] n prohibición f; (Comm, Naut) embargo; **to put an ~ on sth** poner un embargo en algo
embark [ɪm'bɑːk] vi embarcarse ■ vt embarcar; **to ~ on** (journey) comenzar, iniciar; (fig) emprender
embarkation [ɛmbɑː'keɪʃən] n (of people) embarco; (of goods) embarque m
embarrass [ɪm'bærəs] vt avergonzar, dar vergüenza a; (financially etc) poner en un aprieto
embarrassed [ɪm'bærəst] adj azorado, violento; **to be ~** sentirse azorado or violento
embarrassing [ɪm'bærəsɪŋ] adj (situation) violento; (question) embarazoso
embarrassment [ɪm'bærəsmənt] n vergüenza, azoramiento; (financial) apuros mpl
embassy ['ɛmbəsɪ] n embajada
embed [ɪm'bɛd] vt (jewel) empotrar; (teeth etc) clavar
embellish [ɪm'bɛlɪʃ] vt embellecer; (fig: story, truth) adornar
embers ['ɛmbəz] npl rescoldo sg, ascuas
embezzle [ɪm'bɛzl] vt desfalcar, malversar
embezzlement [ɪm'bɛzlmənt] n desfalco, malversación f
embezzler [ɪm'bɛzləʳ] n malversador(a) m(f)
embitter [ɪm'bɪtəʳ] vt (person) amargar; (relationship) envenenar
embittered [ɪm'bɪtəd] adj resentido, amargado
emblem ['ɛmbləm] n emblema m
embody [ɪm'bɔdɪ] vt (spirit) encarnar; (ideas) expresar
embolden [ɪm'bəuldən] vt envalentonar
embolism ['ɛmbəlɪzəm] n embolia
emboss [ɪm'bɔs] vt estampar en relieve; (metal, leather) repujar
embossed [ɪm'bɔst] adj realzado; **~ with ...** con ... en relieve
embrace [ɪm'breɪs] vt abrazar, dar un abrazo a; (include) abarcar; (adopt: idea) adherirse a ■ vi abrazarse ■ n abrazo

embroider [ɪmˈbrɔɪdəʳ] vt bordar; (fig: story) adornar, embellecer

embroidery [ɪmˈbrɔɪdərɪ] n bordado

embroil [ɪmˈbrɔɪl] vt: **to become embroiled (in sth)** enredarse (en algo)

embryo [ˈembrɪəu] n (also fig) embrión m

emcee [emˈsiː] n abbr (US: = master of ceremonies) presentador(a) m(f)

emend [ɪˈmend] vt (text) enmendar

emerald [ˈemərəld] n esmeralda

emerge [ɪˈməːdʒ] vi (gen) salir; (arise) surgir; **it emerges that** resulta que

emergence [ɪˈməːdʒəns] n (of nation) surgimiento

emergency [ɪˈməːdʒənsɪ] n (event) emergencia; (crisis) crisis f inv; **in an ~** en caso de urgencia; **(to declare a) state of ~** (declarar) estado de emergencia or de excepción

emergency cord n (US) timbre m de alarma

emergency exit n salida de emergencia

emergency landing n aterrizaje m forzoso

emergency lane n (US) arcén m

emergency meeting n reunión f extraordinaria

emergency service n servicio de urgencia

emergency stop n (Aut) parada en seco

emergent [ɪˈməːdʒənt] adj (nation) recientemente independizado

emery board [ˈemərɪ-] n lima de uñas

emetic [ɪˈmetɪk] n vomitivo, emético

emigrant [ˈemɪgrənt] n emigrante m/f

emigrate [ˈemɪgreɪt] vi emigrar

emigration [emɪˈgreɪʃən] n emigración f

émigré [ˈemɪgreɪ] n emigrado(-a)

eminence [ˈemɪnəns] n eminencia; **to gain** or **win ~** ganarse fama

eminent [ˈemɪnənt] adj eminente

eminently [ˈemɪnəntlɪ] adv eminentemente

emirate [ˈemɪrɪt] n emirato

emission [ɪˈmɪʃən] n emisión f

emit [ɪˈmɪt] vt emitir; (smell, smoke) despedir

emolument [ɪˈmɔljumənt] n (often pl: formal) honorario, emolumento

emoticon [ɪˈməutɪkɔn] n emoticón m

emotion [ɪˈməuʃən] n emoción f

emotional [ɪˈməuʃənl] adj (person) sentimental; (scene) conmovedor(a), emocionante

emotionally [ɪˈməuʃnəlɪ] adv (behave, speak) con emoción; (be involved) sentimentalmente

emotive [ɪˈməutɪv] adj emotivo

empathy [ˈempəθɪ] n empatía; **to feel ~ with sb** sentirse identificado con algn

emperor [ˈempərəʳ] n emperador m

emphasis (pl **emphases**) [ˈemfəsɪs, -siːz] n énfasis m inv; **to lay** or **place ~ on sth** (fig) hacer hincapié en algo; **the ~ is on sport** se

da mayor importancia al deporte

emphasize [ˈemfəsaɪz] vt (word, point) subrayar, recalcar; (feature) hacer resaltar

emphatic [emˈfætɪk] adj (condemnation) enérgico; (denial) rotundo

emphatically [emˈfætɪklɪ] adv con énfasis

emphysema [emfɪˈsiːmə] n (Med) enfisema m

empire [ˈempaɪəʳ] n imperio

empirical [emˈpɪrɪkl] adj empírico

employ [ɪmˈplɔɪ] vt (give job to) emplear; (make use of: thing, method) emplear, usar; **he's employed in a bank** está empleado en un banco

employee [ɪmplɔɪˈiː] n empleado(-a)

employer [ɪmˈplɔɪəʳ] n patrón(-ona) m(f); (businessman) empresario(-a)

employment [ɪmˈplɔɪmənt] n empleo; **full ~** pleno empleo; **without ~** sin empleo; **to find ~** encontrar trabajo; **place of ~** lugar m de trabajo

employment agency n agencia de colocaciones or empleo

employment exchange n bolsa de trabajo

empower [ɪmˈpauəʳ] vt: **to ~ sb to do sth** autorizar a algn para hacer algo

empress [ˈemprɪs] n emperatriz f

emptiness [ˈemptɪnɪs] n vacío

empty [ˈemptɪ] adj vacío; (street, area) desierto; (threat) vano ■ n (bottle) envase m ■ vt vaciar; (place) dejar vacío ■ vi vaciarse; (house) quedar(se) vacío or desocupado; (place) quedar(se) desierto; **to ~ into** (river) desembocar en

empty-handed [ˈemptɪˈhændɪd] adj con las manos vacías

empty-headed [ˈemptɪˈhedɪd] adj casquivano

EMS n abbr (= European Monetary System) SME m

EMT n abbr (US) = **emergency medical technician**

EMU n abbr (= European Monetary Union, Economic and Monetary Union) UME f

emulate [ˈemjuleɪt] vt emular

emulsion [ɪˈmʌlʃən] n emulsión f

enable [ɪˈneɪbl] vt: **to ~ sb to do sth** (allow) permitir a algn hacer algo; (prepare) capacitar a algn para hacer algo

enact [ɪnˈækt] vt (law) promulgar; (play, scene, role) representar

enamel [ɪˈnæməl] n esmalte m

enamel paint n esmalte m

enamoured [ɪˈnæməd] adj: **to be ~ of** (person) estar enamorado de; (activity etc) tener gran afición a; (idea) aferrarse a

enc. abbr (on letters etc: = enclosed, enclosure) adj

encampment [ɪnˈkæmpmənt] n campamento

encase [ɪn'keɪs] *vt*: **to ~ in** (*contain*) encajar; (*cover*) cubrir

encased [ɪn'keɪst] *adj*: **~ in** (*covered*) revestido de

enchant [ɪn'tʃɑ:nt] *vt* encantar

enchanting [ɪn'tʃɑ:ntɪŋ] *adj* encantador(a)

encircle [ɪn'sə:kl] *vt* (*gen*) rodear; (*waist*) ceñir

encl. *abbr* (= *enclosed*) adj

enclave ['ɛnkleɪv] *n* enclave *m*

enclose [ɪn'kləuz] *vt* (*land*) cercar; (*with letter etc*) adjuntar; (*in receptacle*): **to ~ (with)** encerrar (con); **please find enclosed** le mandamos adjunto

enclosure [ɪn'kləuʒəʳ] *n* cercado, recinto; (*Comm*) carta adjunta

encoder [ɪn'kəudəʳ] *n* (*Comput*) codificador *m*

encompass [ɪn'kʌmpəs] *vt* abarcar

encore [ɔŋ'kɔːʳ] *excl* ¡otra!, ¡bis! ■ *n* bis *m*

encounter [ɪn'kauntəʳ] *n* encuentro ■ *vt* encontrar, encontrarse con; (*difficulty*) tropezar con

encourage [ɪn'kʌrɪdʒ] *vt* alentar, animar; (*growth*) estimular; **to ~ sb (to do sth)** animar a algn (a hacer algo)

encouragement [ɪn'kʌrɪdʒmənt] *n* estímulo; (*of industry*) fomento

encouraging [ɪn'kʌrɪdʒɪŋ] *adj* alentador(a)

encroach [ɪn'krəutʃ] *vi*: **to ~ (up)on** (*gen*) invadir; (*time*) adueñarse de

encrust [ɪn'krʌst] *vt* incrustar

encrusted [ɪn'krʌstəd] *adj*: **~ with** recubierto de

encumber [ɪn'kʌmbəʳ] *vt*: **to be encumbered with** (*carry*) estar cargado de; (*debts*) estar gravado de

encyclopaedia, encyclopedia [ɛnsaɪkləu'piːdɪə] *n* enciclopedia

end [ɛnd] *n* fin *m*; (*of table*) extremo; (*of line, rope etc*) cabo; (*of pointed object*) punta; (*of town*) barrio; (*of street*) final *m*; (*Sport*) lado ■ *vt* terminar, acabar; (*also*: **bring to an end, put an end to**) acabar con ■ *vi* terminar, acabar; **to ~ (with)** terminar (con); **in the ~ al final; to be at an ~** llegar a su fin; **at the ~ of the day** (*fig*) al fin y al cabo, a fin de cuentas; **to this ~, with this ~ in view** con este propósito; **from ~ to ~** de punta a punta; **on ~** (*object*) de punta, de cabeza; **to stand on ~** (*hair*) erizarse, ponerse de punta; **for hours on ~** hora tras hora

▶ **end up** *vi*: **to ~ up in** terminar en; (*place*) ir a parar a

endanger [ɪn'deɪndʒəʳ] *vt* poner en peligro; **an endangered species** (*of animal*) una especie en peligro de extinción

endear [ɪn'dɪəʳ] *vt*: **to ~ o.s. to sb** ganarse la simpatía de algn

endearing [ɪn'dɪərɪŋ] *adj* entrañable

endearment [ɪn'dɪərmənt] *n* cariño, palabra cariñosa; **to whisper endearments** decir unas palabras cariñosas al oído; **term of ~** nombre *m* cariñoso

endeavour, endeavor (US) [ɪn'dɛvəʳ] *n* esfuerzo; (*attempt*) tentativa ■ *vi*: **to ~ to do** esforzarse por hacer; (*try*) procurar hacer

endemic [ɛn'dɛmɪk] *adj* (*poverty, disease*) endémico

ending ['ɛndɪŋ] *n* fin *m*, final *m*; (*of book*) desenlace *m*; (*Ling*) terminación *f*

endive ['ɛndaɪv] *n* (*curly*) escarola; (*smooth, flat*) endibia

endless ['ɛndlɪs] *adj* interminable, inacabable; (*possibilities*) infinito

endorse [ɪn'dɔ:s] *vt* (*cheque*) endosar; (*approve*) aprobar

endorsee [ɪndɔ:'si:] *n* endorsatario(-a)

endorsement [ɪn'dɔ:smənt] *n* (*approval*) aprobación *f*; (*signature*) endoso; (*Brit: on driving licence*) nota de sanción

endorser [ɪn'dɔ:səʳ] *n* avalista *m/f*

endow [ɪn'dau] *vt* (*provide with money*) dotar; (*found*) fundar; **to be endowed with** (*fig*) estar dotado de

endowment [ɪn'daumənt] *adj* (*amount*) donación *f*

endowment mortgage *n* hipoteca dotal

endowment policy *n* póliza dotal

end product *n* (*Industry*) producto final; (*fig*) resultado

end result *n* resultado

endurable [ɪn'djuərəbl] *adj* soportable, tolerable

endurance [ɪn'djuərəns] *n* resistencia

endurance test *n* prueba de resistencia

endure [ɪn'djuəʳ] *vt* (*bear*) aguantar, soportar; (*resist*) resistir ■ *vi* (*last*) perdurar; (*resist*) resistir

enduring [ɪn'djuərɪŋ] *adj* duradero

end user *n* (*Comput*) usuario final

enema ['ɛnɪmə] *n* (*Med*) enema *m*

enemy ['ɛnəmɪ] *adj, n* enemigo(-a) *m(f)*; **to make an ~ of sb** enemistarse con algn

energetic [ɛnə'dʒɛtɪk] *adj* enérgico

energy ['ɛnədʒɪ] *n* energía

energy crisis *n* crisis *f* energética

energy-saving ['ɛnədʒɪseɪvɪŋ] *adj* (*policy*) para ahorrar energía; (*device*) que ahorra energía ■ *n* ahorro de energía

enervating ['ɛnəveɪtɪŋ] *adj* deprimente

enforce [ɪn'fɔ:s] *vt* (*law*) hacer cumplir

enforced [ɪn'fɔ:st] *adj* forzoso, forzado

enfranchise [ɪn'fræntʃaɪz] *vt* (*give vote to*) conceder el derecho de voto a; (*set free*) emancipar

engage [ɪn'geɪdʒ] vt (attention) captar; (in conversation) abordar; (worker, lawyer) contratar ■ vi (Tech) engranar; **to ~ in** dedicarse a, ocuparse en; **to ~ sb in conversation** entablar conversación con algn; **to ~ the clutch** embragar

engaged [ɪn'geɪdʒd] adj (Brit: busy, in use) ocupado; (betrothed) prometido; **to get ~** prometerse; **he is ~ in research** se dedica a la investigación

engaged tone n (Brit Tel) señal f de comunicando

engagement [ɪn'geɪdʒmənt] n (appointment) compromiso, cita; (battle) combate m; (to marry) compromiso; (period) noviazgo; **I have a previous ~** ya tengo un compromiso

engagement ring n anillo de pedida

engaging [ɪn'geɪdʒɪŋ] adj atractivo, simpático

engender [ɪn'dʒendə'] vt engendrar

engine ['endʒɪn] n (Aut) motor m; (Rail) locomotora

engine driver n (Brit: of train) maquinista m/f

engineer [endʒɪ'nɪə'] n ingeniero(-a); (Brit: for repairs) técnico(-a); (US Rail) maquinista m/f; **civil/mechanical ~** ingeniero(-a) de caminos, canales y puertos/industrial

engineering [endʒɪ'nɪərɪŋ] n ingeniería ■ cpd (works, factory) de componentes mecánicos

engine failure, engine trouble n avería del motor

England ['ɪŋglənd] n Inglaterra

English ['ɪŋglɪʃ] adj inglés(-esa) ■ n (Ling) el inglés; **the English** npl los ingleses

English Channel n: **the ~** el Canal de la Mancha

Englishman ['ɪŋglɪʃmən], **Englishwoman** ['ɪŋglɪʃwumən] n inglés(-esa) m(f)

English-speaker ['ɪŋglɪʃspi:kə'] n persona de habla inglesa

English-speaking ['ɪŋglɪʃspi:kɪŋ] adj de habla inglesa

engraving [ɪn'greɪvɪŋ] n grabado

engrossed [ɪn'grəust] adj: **~ in** absorto en

engulf [ɪn'gʌlf] vt sumergir, hundir; (fire) devorar

enhance [ɪn'hɑːns] vt (gen) aumentar; (beauty) realzar; (position, reputation) mejorar

enigma [ɪ'nɪgmə] n enigma m

enigmatic [enɪg'mætɪk] adj enigmático

enjoy [ɪn'dʒɔɪ] vt (have: health, fortune) disfrutar de, gozar de; (food) comer con gusto; **I ~ doing ...** me gusta hacer ...; **to ~ o.s.** divertirse, pasarlo bien

enjoyable [ɪn'dʒɔɪəbl] adj (pleasant) agradable; (amusing) divertido

enjoyment [ɪn'dʒɔɪmənt] n (use) disfrute m; (joy) placer m

enlarge [ɪn'lɑːdʒ] vt aumentar; (broaden) extender; (Phot) ampliar ■ vi: **to ~ on** (subject) tratar con más detalles

enlarged [ɪn'lɑːdʒd] adj (edition) aumentado; (Med: organ, gland) dilatado

enlargement [ɪn'lɑːdʒmənt] n (Phot) ampliación f

enlighten [ɪn'laɪtn] vt informar, instruir

enlightened [ɪn'laɪtnd] adj iluminado; (tolerant) comprensivo

enlightening [ɪn'laɪtnɪŋ] adj informativo, instructivo

Enlightenment [ɪn'laɪtnmənt] n (History): **the ~** la Ilustración, el Siglo de las Luces

enlist [ɪn'lɪst] vt alistar; (support) conseguir ■ vi alistarse; **enlisted man** (US Mil) soldado raso

enliven [ɪn'laɪvn] vt (people) animar; (events) avivar, animar

enmity ['enmɪtɪ] n enemistad f

ennoble [ɪ'nəubl] vt ennoblecer

enormity [ɪ'nɔːmɪtɪ] n enormidad f

enormous [ɪ'nɔːməs] adj enorme

enough [ɪ'nʌf] adj: **~ time/books** bastante tiempo/bastantes libros ■ n: **have you got ~?** ¿tiene usted bastante? ■ adv: **big ~** bastante grande; **he has not worked ~** no ha trabajado bastante; **(that's) ~!** ¡basta ya!, ¡ya está bien!; **that's ~, thanks** con eso basta, gracias; **will five be ~?** ¿bastará con cinco?; **I've had ~** estoy harto; **he was kind ~ to lend me the money** tuvo la bondad or amabilidad de prestarme el dinero; **...** **which, funnily ~ ...** ... lo que, por extraño que parezca ...

enquire [ɪn'kwaɪə'] vt, vi = **inquire**

enrage [ɪn'reɪdʒ] vt enfurecer

enrich [ɪn'rɪtʃ] vt enriquecer

enrol, enroll (US) [ɪn'rəul] vt (member) inscribir; (Scol) matricular ■ vi inscribirse; (Scol) matricularse

enrolment, enrollment (US) [ɪn'rəulmənt] n inscripción f; matriculación f

en route [ɔn'ruːt] adv durante el viaje; **~ for/ from/to** camino de/de/a

ensconce [ɪn'skɔns] vt: **to ~ o.s.** instalarse cómodamente, acomodarse

ensemble [ɔn'sɔmbl] n (Mus) conjunto

enshrine [ɪn'ʃraɪn] vt recoger

ensign ['ensaɪn] n (flag) bandera; (Naut) alférez m

enslave [ɪn'sleɪv] vt esclavizar

ensue [ɪn'sjuː] vi seguirse; (result) resultar

ensuing [ɪn'sjuːɪŋ] adj subsiguiente

ensure [ɪn'ʃuə'] vt asegurar

ENT *n abbr* (*Med:* = *ear, nose and throat*) otorrinolaringología

entail [ɪn'teɪl] *vt* (*imply*) suponer; (*result in*) acarrear

entangle [ɪn'tæŋgl] *vt* (*thread etc*) enredar, enmarañar; **to become entangled in sth** (*fig*) enredarse en algo

entanglement [ɪn'tæŋglmənt] *n* enredo

enter ['entə^r] *vt* (*room, profession*) entrar en; (*club*) hacerse socio de; (*army*) alistarse en; (*sb for a competition*) inscribir; (*write down*) anotar, apuntar; (*Comput*) introducir ■ *vi* entrar; **to ~ for** *vt fus* presentarse a; **to ~ into** *vt fus* (*relations*) establecer; (*plans*) formar parte de; (*debate*) tomar parte en; (*negotiations*) entablar; (*agreement*) llegar a, firmar; **to ~ (up)on** *vt fus* (*career*) emprender

enteritis [entə'raɪtɪs] *n* enteritis *f*

enterprise ['entəpraɪz] *n* empresa; (*spirit*) iniciativa; **free ~** la libre empresa; **private ~** la iniciativa privada

enterprising ['entəpraɪzɪŋ] *adj* emprendedor(a)

entertain [entə'teɪn] *vt* (*amuse*) divertir; (*receive: guest*) recibir (en casa); (*idea*) abrigar

entertainer [entə'teɪnə^r] *n* artista *m/f*

entertaining [entə'teɪnɪŋ] *adj* divertido, entretenido ■ *n*: **to do a lot of ~** dar muchas fiestas, tener muchos invitados

entertainment [entə'teɪnmənt] *n* (*amusement*) diversión *f*; (*show*) espectáculo; (*party*) fiesta

entertainment allowance *n* (*Comm*) gastos *mpl* de representación

enthral [ɪn'θrɔ:l] *vt* embelesar, cautivar

enthralled [ɪn'θrɔ:ld] *adj* cautivado

enthralling [ɪn'θrɔ:lɪŋ] *adj* cautivador(a)

enthuse [ɪn'θu:z] *vi*: **to ~ about** *or* **over** entusiasmarse por

enthusiasm [ɪn'θu:zɪæzəm] *n* entusiasmo

enthusiast [ɪn'θu:zɪæst] *n* entusiasta *m/f*

enthusiastic [ɪnθu:zɪ'æstɪk] *adj* entusiasta; **to be ~ about sb/sth** estar entusiasmado con algn/algo

entice [ɪn'taɪs] *vt* tentar; (*seduce*) seducir

entire [ɪn'taɪə^r] *adj* entero, todo

entirely [ɪn'taɪəlɪ] *adv* totalmente

entirety [ɪn'taɪərətɪ] *n*: **in its ~** en su totalidad

entitle [ɪn'taɪtl] *vt*: **to ~ sb to sth** dar a algn derecho a algo

entitled [ɪn'taɪtld] *adj* (*book*) titulado; **to be ~ to sth/to do sth** tener derecho a algo/a hacer algo

entity ['entɪtɪ] *n* entidad *f*

entourage [ɔntu'rɑ:ʒ] *n* séquito

entrails ['entreɪlz] *npl* entrañas *fpl*; (*US: offal*) asadura *sg*, menudos *mpl*

entrance ['entrəns] *n* entrada ■ *vt* [ɪn'trɑ:ns] encantar, hechizar; **to gain ~ to** (*university etc*) ingresar en

entrance examination *n* (*to school*) examen *m* de ingreso

entrance fee *n* entrada

entrance ramp *n* (*US Aut*) rampa de acceso

entrancing [ɪn'trɑ:nsɪŋ] *adj* encantador(a)

entrant ['entrənt] *n* (*in race, competition*) participante *m/f*; (*in exam*) candidato(-a)

entreat [en'tri:t] *vt* rogar, suplicar

entrenched [en'trentʃd] *adj*: **~ interests** intereses *mpl* creados

entrepreneur [ɔntrəprə'nə:^r] *n* empresario(-a), capitalista *m/f*

entrepreneurial [ɔntrəprə'nə:rɪəl] *adj* empresarial

entrust [ɪn'trʌst] *vt*: **to ~ sth to sb** confiar algo a algn

entry ['entrɪ] *n* entrada; (*permission to enter*) acceso; (*in register, diary, ship's log*) apunte *m*; (*in account book, ledger, list*) partida; **no ~** prohibido el paso; (*Aut*) dirección prohibida; **single/double ~ book-keeping** contabilidad *f* simple/por partida doble

entry form *n* boletín *m* de inscripción

entry phone *n* (*Brit*) portero automático

E-number ['i:nʌmbə^r] *n* número E

enumerate [ɪ'nju:məreɪt] *vt* enumerar

enunciate [ɪ'nʌnsɪeɪt] *vt* pronunciar; (*principle etc*) enunciar

envelop [ɪn'veləp] *vt* envolver

envelope ['envələup] *n* sobre *m*

enviable ['envɪəbl] *adj* envidiable

envious ['envɪəs] *adj* envidioso; (*look*) de envidia

environment [ɪn'vaɪərnmənt] *n* medio ambiente; (*surroundings*) entorno; **Department of the E~** ministerio del medio ambiente

environmental [ɪnvaɪərn'mentl] *adj* (*medio*) ambiental; **~ studies** (*in school etc*) ecología *sg*

environmentalist [ɪnvaɪərn'mentlɪst] *n* ecologista *m/f*

environmentally [ɪnvaɪərn'mentlɪ] *adv*: **~ sound/friendly** ecológico

envisage [ɪn'vɪzɪdʒ] *vt* (*foresee*) prever; (*imagine*) concebir

envision [ɪn'vɪʒən] *vt* imaginar

envoy ['envɔɪ] *n* enviado(-a)

envy ['envɪ] *n* envidia ■ *vt* tener envidia a; **to ~ sb sth** envidiar algo a algn

enzyme ['enzaɪm] *n* enzima *m or f*

EPA *n abbr* (*US:* = *Environmental Protection Agency*) Agencia del Medio Ambiente

ephemeral [ɪ'femərl] *adj* efímero

epic ['epɪk] *n* epopeya ■ *adj* épico

539

epicentre, (US) **epicenter** ['ɛpɪsɛntə^r] n epicentro
epidemic [ɛpɪ'dɛmɪk] n epidemia
epigram ['ɛpɪgræm] n epigrama m
epilepsy ['ɛpɪlɛpsɪ] n epilepsia
epileptic [ɛpɪ'lɛptɪk] adj, n epiléptico(-a) m(f)
epilogue ['ɛpɪlɔg] n epílogo
episcopal [ɪ'pɪskəpl] adj episcopal
episode ['ɛpɪsəud] n episodio
epistle [ɪ'pɪsl] n epístola
epitaph ['ɛpɪtɑːf] n epitafio
epithet ['ɛpɪθɛt] n epíteto
epitome [ɪ'pɪtəmɪ] n arquetipo
epitomize [ɪ'pɪtəmaɪz] vt representar
epoch ['iːpɔk] n época
eponymous [ɪ'pɔnɪməs] adj epónimo
equable ['ɛkwəbl] adj (climate) estable; (character) ecuánime
equal ['iːkwl] adj (gen) igual; (treatment) equitativo ■ n igual m/f ■ vt ser igual a; (fig) igualar; **to be ~ to** (task) estar a la altura de; **the E~ Opportunities Commission** (Brit) comisión para la igualdad de la mujer en el trabajo
equality [iː'kwɔlɪtɪ] n igualdad f
equalize ['iːkwəlaɪz] vt, vi igualar; (Sport) empatar
equalizer ['iːkwəlaɪzə^r] n igualada
equally ['iːkwəlɪ] adv igualmente; (share etc) a partes iguales; **they are ~ clever** son tan listos uno como otro
equals sign n signo igual
equanimity [ɛkwə'nɪmɪtɪ] n ecuanimidad f
equate [ɪ'kweɪt] vt: **to ~ sth with** equiparar algo con
equation [ɪ'kweɪʒən] n (Math) ecuación f
equator [ɪ'kweɪtə^r] n ecuador m
equatorial [ɛkwə'tɔːrɪəl] adj ecuatorial
Equatorial Guinea n Guinea Ecuatorial
equestrian [ɪ'kwɛstrɪən] adj ecuestre ■ n jinete m/f
equilibrium [iːkwɪ'lɪbrɪəm] n equilibrio
equinox ['iːkwɪnɔks] n equinoccio
equip [ɪ'kwɪp] vt (gen) equipar; (person) proveer; **equipped with** (machinery etc) provisto de; **to be well equipped** estar bien equipado; **he is well equipped for the job** está bien preparado para este puesto
equipment [ɪ'kwɪpmənt] n equipo
equitable ['ɛkwɪtəbl] adj equitativo
equities ['ɛkwɪtɪz] npl (Brit Comm) acciones fpl ordinarias
equity ['ɛkwɪtɪ] n (fairness) equidad f; (Econ: of debtor) valor m líquido
equity capital n capital m propio, patrimonio neto
equivalent [ɪ'kwɪvəlnt] adj, n equivalente m; **to be ~ to** equivaler a

equivocal [ɪ'kwɪvəkl] adj equívoco
equivocate [ɪ'kwɪvəkeɪt] vi andarse con ambigüedades
equivocation [ɪkwɪvə'keɪʃən] n ambigüedad f
ER abbr (Brit: = Elizabeth Regina) la reina Isabel
er [əː] interj (col: in hesitation) esto, este (LAm)
ERA n abbr (US Pol: = Equal Rights Amendment) enmienda sobre la igualdad de derechos de la mujer
era ['ɪərə] n era, época
eradicate [ɪ'rædɪkeɪt] vt erradicar, extirpar
erase [ɪ'reɪz] vt (Comput) borrar
eraser [ɪ'reɪzə^r] n goma de borrar
erect [ɪ'rɛkt] adj erguido ■ vt erigir, levantar; (assemble) montar
erection [ɪ'rɛkʃən] n (of building) construcción f; (of machinery) montaje m; (structure) edificio; (Med) erección f
ergonomics [əːgə'nɔmɪks] n ergonomía
ERISA n abbr (US: = Employee Retirement Income Security Act) ley que regula las pensiones de jubilados
Eritrea [ɛrɪ'treɪə] n Eritrea
ERM n abbr (= Exchange Rate Mechanism) (mecanismo de cambios del) SME m
ermine ['əːmɪn] n armiño
ERNIE ['əːnɪ] n abbr (Brit: = Electronic Random Number Indicator Equipment) ordenador que elige al azar los números ganadores de los bonos del Estado
erode [ɪ'rəud] vt (Geo) erosionar; (metal) corroer, desgastar
erogenous zone [ɪ'rɔdʒənəs-] n zona erógena
erosion [ɪ'rəuʒən] n erosión f; desgaste m
erotic [ɪ'rɔtɪk] adj erótico
eroticism [ɪ'rɔtɪsɪzm] n erotismo
err [əː^r] vi errar; (Rel) pecar
errand ['ɛrnd] n recado, mandado; **to run errands** hacer recados; **~ of mercy** misión f de caridad
errand boy n recadero
erratic [ɪ'rætɪk] adj variable; (results etc) desigual, poco uniforme
erroneous [ɪ'rəunɪəs] adj erróneo
error ['ɛrə^r] n error m, equivocación f; **typing/ spelling ~** error de mecanografía/ortografía; **in ~** por equivocación; **errors and omissions excepted** salvo error u omisión
error message n (Comput) mensaje m de error
erstwhile ['əːstwaɪl] adj antiguo, previo
erudite ['ɛrudaɪt] adj erudito
erudition [ɛru'dɪʃən] n erudición f
erupt [ɪ'rʌpt] vi entrar en erupción; (Med) hacer erupción; (fig) estallar
eruption [ɪ'rʌpʃən] n erupción f; (fig: of anger, violence) explosión f, estallido
ESA n abbr (= European Space Agency) Agencia Espacial Europea

escalate ['ɛskəleɪt] *vi* extenderse, intensificarse; (*costs*) aumentar vertiginosamente

escalation clause [ɛskə'leɪʃən-] *n* cláusula de reajuste de los precios

escalator ['ɛskəleɪtəʳ] *n* escalera mecánica

escapade [ɛskə'peɪd] *n* aventura

escape [ɪ'skeɪp] *n* (*gen*) fuga; (*Tech*) escape *m*; (*from duties*) escapatoria; (*from chase*) evasión *f* ∎ *vi* (*gen*) escaparse; (*flee*) huir, evadirse ∎ *vt* evitar, eludir; (*consequences*) escapar a; **to ~ from** (*place*) escaparse de; (*person*) huir de; (*clutches*) librarse de; **to ~ to** (*another place, freedom, safety*) huir a; **to ~ notice** pasar desapercibido

escape artist *n* artista *m/f* de la evasión

escape clause *n* (*fig: in agreement*) cláusula de excepción

escapee [ɪskeɪ'piː] *n* fugado(-a)

escape hatch *n* (*in submarine, space rocket*) escotilla de salvamento

escape key *n* (*Comput*) tecla de escape

escape route *n* (*from fire*) vía de escape

escapism [ɪ'skeɪpɪzəm] *n* escapismo, evasión *f*

escapist [ɪ'skeɪpɪst] *adj* escapista, de evasión ∎ *n* escapista *m/f*

escapologist [ɛskə'pɒlədʒɪst] *n* (*Brit*) = **escape artist**

escarpment [ɪ'skɑːpmənt] *n* escarpa

eschew [ɪs'tʃuː] *vt* evitar, abstenerse de

escort ['ɛskɔːt] *n* acompañante *m/f*; (*Mil*) escolta; (*Naut*) convoy *m* ∎ *vt* [ɪ'skɔːt] acompañar; (*Mil, Naut*) escoltar

escort agency *n* agencia de acompañantes

Eskimo ['ɛskɪməu] *adj* esquimal ∎ *n* esquimal *m/f*; (*Ling*) esquimal *m*

ESL *n abbr* (*Scol*) = **English as a Second Language**

esophagus [iː'sɒfəgəs] *n* (*US*) = **oesophagus**

esoteric [ɛsəu'tɛrɪk] *adj* esotérico

ESP *n abbr* = **extrasensory perception**; (*Scol*: = English for Specific (or Special) Purposes) inglés especializado

esp. *abbr* = **especially**

especially [ɪ'spɛʃlɪ] *adv* (*gen*) especialmente; (*above all*) sobre todo; (*particularly*) en especial

espionage ['ɛspɪənɑːʒ] *n* espionaje *m*

esplanade [ɛsplə'neɪd] *n* (*by sea*) paseo marítimo

espouse [ɪ'spauz] *vt* adherirse a

Esq. *abbr* (= *Esquire*) D.

Esquire [ɪ'skwaɪəʳ] *n*: **J. Brown, ~** Sr. D. J. Brown

essay ['ɛseɪ] *n* (*Scol*) redacción *f*; (: *longer*) trabajo

essayist ['ɛseɪɪst] *n* ensayista *m/f*

essence ['ɛsns] *n* esencia; **in ~** esencialmente; **speed is of the ~** es esencial hacerlo con la mayor prontitud

essential [ɪ'sɛnʃl] *adj* (*necessary*) imprescindible; (*basic*) esencial ∎ *n* (*often pl*) lo esencial; **it is ~ that** es imprescindible que

essentially [ɪ'sɛnʃlɪ] *adv* esencialmente

EST *n abbr* (*US*: = Eastern Standard Time) hora de invierno de Nueva York

est. *abbr* (= *established*) fundado; (= *estimated*) aprox.

establish [ɪ'stæblɪʃ] *vt* establecer; (*prove: fact*) comprobar, demostrar; (*identity*) verificar; (*relations*) entablar

established [ɪ'stæblɪʃt] *adj* (*business*) de buena reputación; (*staff*) de plantilla

establishment [ɪ'stæblɪʃmənt] *n* establecimiento; (*also:* **the Establishment**) la clase dirigente; **a teaching ~** un centro de enseñanza

estate [ɪ'steɪt] *n* (*land*) finca, hacienda; (*property*) propiedad *f*; (*inheritance*) herencia; (*Pol*) estado; **housing ~** (*Brit*) urbanización *f*; **industrial ~** polígono industrial

estate agency *n* (*Brit*) agencia inmobiliaria

estate agent *n* (*Brit*) agente *m/f* inmobiliario(-a)

estate agent's *n* agencia inmobiliaria

estate car *n* (*Brit*) ranchera

esteem [ɪ'stiːm] *n*: **to hold sb in high ~** estimar en mucho a algn ∎ *vt* estimar

esthetic [iːs'θɛtɪk] *adj* (*US*) = **aesthetic**

estimate ['ɛstɪmət] *n* estimación *f*; (*assessment*) tasa, cálculo; (*Comm*) presupuesto ∎ *vt* ['ɛstɪmeɪt] estimar; tasar, calcular; **to give sb an ~ of** presentar a algn un presupuesto de; **at a rough ~** haciendo un cálculo aproximado; **to ~ for** (*Comm*) hacer un presupuesto de, presupuestar

estimation [ɛstɪ'meɪʃən] *n* opinión *f*, juicio; (*esteem*) aprecio; **in my ~** a mi juicio

Estonia [ɛ'stəunɪə] *n* Estonia

Estonian [ɛ'stəunɪən] *adj* estonio ∎ *n* estonio(-a); (*Ling*) estonio

estranged [ɪ'streɪndʒd] *adj* separado

estrangement [ɪ'streɪndʒmənt] *n* alejamiento, distanciamiento

estrogen ['iːstrəudʒən] *n* (*US*) = **oestrogen**

estuary ['ɛstjuərɪ] *n* estuario, ría

ET *n abbr* (*Brit*: = Employment Training) plan estatal de formación para los desempleados ∎ *abbr* (*US*) = **Eastern Time**

ETA *n abbr* = **estimated time of arrival**

e-tailing ['iːteɪlɪŋ] *n* venta en línea, venta vía or por Internet

et al. *abbr* (= *et alii: and others*) et al.

etc *abbr* (= *et cetera*) etc
etch [ɛtʃ] *vt* grabar al aguafuerte
etching ['ɛtʃɪŋ] *n* aguafuerte *m or f*
ETD *n abbr* = **estimated time of departure**
eternal [ɪ'tə:nl] *adj* eterno
eternity [ɪ'tə:nɪtɪ] *n* eternidad *f*
ether ['i:θəʳ] *n* éter *m*
ethereal [ɪ'θɪərɪəl] *adj* etéreo
ethical ['ɛθɪkl] *adj* ético; (*honest*) honrado
ethics ['ɛθɪks] *n* ética ■ *npl* moralidad *f*
Ethiopia [i:θɪ'əupɪə] *n* Etiopía
Ethiopian [i:θɪ'əupɪən] *adj*, *n* etíope *m/f*
ethnic ['ɛθnɪk] *adj* étnico
ethnic cleansing [-klɛnzɪŋ] *n* limpieza étnica
ethos ['i:θɔs] *n* (*of culture, group*) sistema *m* de valores
e-ticket ['i:tɪkɪt] *n* billete electrónico, boleto electrónico (*LAm*)
etiquette ['ɛtɪkɛt] *n* etiqueta
ETV *n abbr* (*US*: = *Educational Television*) televisión escolar
etymology [ɛtɪ'mɔlədʒɪ] *n* etimología
EU *n abbr* (= *European Union*) UE *f*
eucalyptus [ju:kə'lɪptəs] *n* eucalipto
Eucharist ['ju:kərɪst] *n* Eucaristía
eulogy ['ju:lədʒɪ] *n* elogio, encomio
eunuch ['ju:nək] *n* eunuco
euphemism ['ju:fəmɪzm] *n* eufemismo
euphemistic [ju:fə'mɪstɪk] *adj* eufemístico
euphoria [ju:'fɔ:rɪə] *n* euforia
Eurasia [juə'reɪʃə] *n* Eurasia
Eurasian [juə'reɪʃən] *adj*, *n* eurasiático(-a) *m(f)*
Euratom [juə'rætəm] *n abbr* (= *European Atomic Energy Commission*) Euratom *m*
Euro- *pref* euro-
euro ['juərəu] *n* (*currency*) euro
Eurocheque ['juərəutʃɛk] *n* Eurocheque *m*
Eurocrat ['juərəukræt] *n* eurócrata *m/f*
Eurodollar ['juərəudɔləʳ] *n* eurodólar *m*
Euroland ['juərəulænd] *n* Eurolandia
Europe ['juərəp] *n* Europa
European [juərə'pi:ən] *adj*, *n* europeo(-a) *m(f)*
European Court of Justice *n* Tribunal *m* de Justicia de las Comunidades Europeas
Euro-sceptic [juərəu'skɛptɪk] *n* euroescéptico(-a)
Eurozone ['juərəuzəun] *n* eurozona, zona euro
euthanasia [ju:θə'neɪzɪə] *n* eutanasia
evacuate [ɪ'vækjueɪt] *vt* evacuar; (*place*) desocupar
evacuation [ɪvækju'eɪʃən] *n* evacuación *f*
evacuee [ɪvækju'i:] *n* evacuado(-a)
evade [ɪ'veɪd] *vt* evadir, eludir
evaluate [ɪ'væljueɪt] *vt* evaluar; (*value*) tasar; (*evidence*) interpretar
evangelical [i:væn'dʒɛlɪkəl] *adj* evangélico

evangelist [ɪ'vændʒəlɪst] *n* evangelista *m*; (*preacher*) evangelizador(a) *m(f)*
evaporate [ɪ'væpəreɪt] *vi* evaporarse; (*fig*) desvanecerse ■ *vt* evaporar
evaporation [ɪvæpə'reɪʃən] *n* evaporación *f*
evasion [ɪ'veɪʒən] *n* evasión *f*
evasive [ɪ'veɪsɪv] *adj* evasivo
eve [i:v] *n*: **on the ~ of** en vísperas de
even ['i:vn] *adj* (*level*) llano; (*smooth*) liso; (*speed, temperature*) uniforme; (*number*) par; (*Sport*) igual(es) ■ *adv* hasta, incluso; **~ if**, **~ though** aunque + *subjun*, así + *subjun* (*LAm*); **~ more** aun más; **~ so** aun así; **not ~** ni siquiera; **~ he was there** hasta él estaba allí; **~ on Sundays** incluso los domingos; **~ faster** aún más rápido; **to break ~** cubrir los gastos; **to get ~ with sb** ajustar cuentas con algn; **to ~ out** *vi* nivelarse
even-handed [i:vn'hændɪd] *adj* imparcial
evening ['i:vnɪŋ] *n* tarde *f*; (*dusk*) atardecer *m*; (*night*) noche *f*; **in the ~** por la tarde; **this ~** esta tarde *or* noche; **tomorrow/yesterday ~** mañana/ayer por la tarde *or* noche
evening class *n* clase *f* nocturna
evening dress *n* (*man's*) traje *m* de etiqueta; (*woman's*) traje *m* de noche
evenly ['i:vnlɪ] *adv* (*distribute, space, spread*) de modo uniforme; (*divide*) equitativamente
evensong ['i:vnsɔŋ] *n* vísperas *fpl*
event [ɪ'vɛnt] *n* suceso, acontecimiento; (*Sport*) prueba; **in the ~ of** en caso de; **in the ~** en realidad; **in the course of events** en el curso de los acontecimientos; **at all events**, **in any ~** en cualquier caso
eventful [ɪ'vɛntful] *adj* azaroso; (*game*) lleno de emoción; (*journey*) lleno de incidentes
eventing [ɪ'vɛntɪŋ] *n* (*Horseriding*) competición *f*
eventual [ɪ'vɛntʃuəl] *adj* final
eventuality [ɪvɛntʃu'ælɪtɪ] *n* eventualidad *f*
eventually [ɪ'vɛntʃuəlɪ] *adv* (*finally*) por fin; (*in time*) con el tiempo
ever ['ɛvəʳ] *adv* nunca, jamás; (*at all times*) siempre; **for ~** (para) siempre; **the best ~** lo nunca visto; **did you ~ meet him?** ¿llegaste a conocerle?; **have you ~ been there?** ¿has estado allí alguna vez?; **have you ~ seen it?** ¿lo has visto alguna vez?; **better than ~** mejor que nunca; **thank you ~ so much** muchísimas gracias; **yours ~** (*in letters*) un abrazo de; **~ since** *adv* desde entonces ■ *conj* después de que
Everest ['ɛvərɪst] *n* (*also*: **Mount Everest**) el Everest *m*
evergreen ['ɛvəgri:n] *n* árbol *m* de hoja perenne
everlasting [ɛvə'lɑ:stɪŋ] *adj* eterno, perpetuo

KEYWORD

every ['εvrɪ] *adj* **1** (*each*) cada; **every one of them** (*persons*) todos ellos(-as); (*objects*) cada uno de ellos(-as); **every shop in the town was closed** todas las tiendas de la ciudad estaban cerradas
2 (*all possible*) todo(-a); **I gave you every assistance** te di toda la ayuda posible; **I have every confidence in him** tiene toda mi confianza; **we wish you every success** te deseamos toda suerte de éxitos
3 (*showing recurrence*) todo(-a); **every day/week** todos los días/todas las semanas; **every other car had been broken into** habían forzado uno de cada dos coches; **she visits me every other/third day** me visita cada dos/tres días; **every now and then** de vez en cuando

everybody ['εvrɪbɔdɪ] *pron* todos *pron pl*, todo el mundo; **~ knows about it** todo el mundo lo sabe; **~ else** todos los demás
everyday ['εvrɪdeɪ] *adj* (*daily: use, occurrence, experience*) diario, cotidiano; (*usual: expression*) corriente; (*common*) vulgar; (*routine*) rutinario
everyone ['εvrɪwʌn] = **everybody**
everything ['εvrɪθɪŋ] *pron* todo; **~ is ready** todo está dispuesto; **he did ~ possible** hizo todo lo posible
everywhere ['εvrɪwɛəʳ] *adv* (*be*) en todas partes; (*go*) a *or* por todas partes; **~ you go you meet ...** en todas partes encontrarás ...
evict [ɪ'vɪkt] *vt* desahuciar
eviction [ɪ'vɪkʃən] *n* desahucio
eviction notice *n* orden *f* de desahucio *or* desalojo (*LAm*)
evidence ['εvɪdəns] *n* (*proof*) prueba; (*of witness*) testimonio; (*facts*) datos *mpl*, hechos *mpl*; **to give ~** prestar declaración, dar testimonio
evident ['εvɪdənt] *adj* evidente, manifiesto
evidently ['εvɪdəntlɪ] *adv* (*obviously*) obviamente, evidentemente; (*apparently*) por lo visto
evil ['iːvl] *adj* malo; (*influence*) funesto; (*smell*) horrible ∎ *n* mal *m*
evildoer ['iːvldu:əʳ] *n* malhechor(a) *m(f)*
evince [ɪ'vɪns] *vt* mostrar, dar señales de
evocative [ɪ'vɔkətɪv] *adj* sugestivo, evocador(a)
evoke [ɪ'vəuk] *vt* evocar; (*admiration*) provocar
evolution [iːvə'luːʃən] *n* evolución *f*, desarrollo
evolve [ɪ'vɔlv] *vt* desarrollar ∎ *vi* evolucionar, desarrollarse

ewe [juː] *n* oveja
ex- [εks] *pref* (*former: husband, president etc*) ex-; (*out of*): **the price ~works** precio de fábrica
exacerbate [εk'sæsəbeɪt] *vt* exacerbar
exact [ɪg'zækt] *adj* exacto ∎ *vt*: **to ~ sth (from)** exigir algo (de)
exacting [ɪg'zæktɪŋ] *adj* exigente; (*conditions*) arduo
exactitude [ɪg'zæktɪtju:d] *n* exactitud *f*
exactly [ɪg'zæktlɪ] *adv* exactamente; (*time*) en punto; **~!** ¡exacto!
exactness [ɪg'zæktnɪs] *n* exactitud *f*
exaggerate [ɪg'zædʒəreɪt] *vt, vi* exagerar
exaggerated [ɪg'zædʒəreɪtɪd] *adj* exagerado
exaggeration [ɪgzædʒə'reɪʃən] *n* exageración *f*
exalt [ɪg'zɔːlt] *vt* (*praise*) ensalzar; (*elevate*) elevar
exalted [ɪg'zɔːltɪd] *adj* (*position*) elevado; (*elated*) enardecido
exam [ɪg'zæm] *n abbr* (*Scol*) = **examination**
examination [ɪgzæmɪ'neɪʃən] *n* (*gen*) examen *m*; (*Law*) interrogación *f*; (*inquiry*) investigación *f*; **to take** *or* **sit an ~** hacer un examen; **the matter is under ~** se está examinando el asunto
examine [ɪg'zæmɪn] *vt* (*gen*) examinar; (*inspect: machine, premises*) inspeccionar; (*Scol, Law: person*) interrogar; (*at customs: luggage, passport*) registrar; (*Med*) hacer un reconocimiento médico de, examinar
examiner [ɪg'zæmɪnəʳ] *n* examinador(a) *m(f)*
example [ɪg'zɑːmpl] *n* ejemplo; **for ~** por ejemplo; **to set a good/bad ~** dar buen/mal ejemplo
exasperate [ɪg'zɑːspəreɪt] *vt* exasperar, irritar; **exasperated by** *or* **at** *or* **with** exasperado por *or* con
exasperating [ɪg'zɑːspəreɪtɪŋ] *adj* irritante
exasperation [ɪgzɑːspə'reɪʃən] *n* exasperación *f*, irritación *f*
excavate ['εkskəveɪt] *vt* excavar
excavation [εkskə'veɪʃən] *n* excavación *f*
excavator ['εkskəveɪtəʳ] *n* excavadora
exceed [ɪk'siːd] *vt* exceder; (*number*) pasar de; (*speed limit*) sobrepasar; (*limits*) rebasar; (*powers*) excederse en; (*hopes*) superar
exceedingly [ɪk'siːdɪŋlɪ] *adv* sumamente, sobremanera
excel [ɪk'sεl] *vi* sobresalir; **to ~ o.s.** lucirse
excellence ['εksələns] *n* excelencia
Excellency ['εksələnsɪ] *n*: **His ~** Su Excelencia
excellent ['εksələnt] *adj* excelente
except [ɪk'sεpt] *prep* (*also:* **except for, excepting**) excepto, salvo ∎ *vt* exceptuar, excluir; **~ if/when** excepto si/cuando; **~ that** salvo que

e

exception [ɪk'sɛpʃən] n excepción f; **to take ~ to** ofenderse por; **with the ~ of** a excepción de; **to make an ~** hacer una excepción

exceptional [ɪk'sɛpʃənl] adj excepcional

excerpt ['ɛksəːpt] n extracto

excess [ɪk'sɛs] n exceso; **in ~ of** superior a; *see also* **excesses**

excess baggage n exceso de equipaje

excesses npl excesos mpl

excess fare n suplemento

excessive [ɪk'sɛsɪv] adj excesivo

excess supply n exceso de oferta

excess weight n exceso de peso

exchange [ɪks'tʃeɪndʒ] n cambio; (*of prisoners*) canje m; (*of ideas*) intercambio; (*also:* **telephone exchange**) central f (telefónica) ■ vt intercambiar; **to ~ (for)** cambiar (por); **in ~ for** a cambio de; **foreign ~** (*Comm*) divisas fpl

exchange control n control m de divisas

exchange rate n tipo de cambio

exchequer [ɪks'tʃɛkəʳ] n: **the ~** (*Brit*) Hacienda

excisable [ɛk'saɪzəbl] adj sujeto al pago de impuestos sobre el consumo

excise ['ɛksaɪz] n impuestos sobre el consumo interior

excitable [ɪk'saɪtəbl] adj excitable

excite [ɪk'saɪt] vt (*stimulate*) entusiasmar; (*anger*) suscitar, provocar; (*move*) emocionar; **to get excited** emocionarse

excitement [ɪk'saɪtmənt] n emoción f

exciting [ɪk'saɪtɪŋ] adj emocionante

excl. abbr = **excluding**; **exclusive (of)**

exclaim [ɪk'skleɪm] vi exclamar

exclamation [ɛksklə'meɪʃən] n exclamación f

exclamation mark n signo de admiración

exclude [ɪk'skluːd] vt excluir; (*except*) exceptuar

excluding [ɪks'kluːdɪŋ] prep: **~ VAT** IVA no incluido

exclusion [ɪk'skluːʒən] n exclusión f; **to the ~ of** con exclusión de

exclusion clause n cláusula de exclusión

exclusion zone n zona de exclusión

exclusive [ɪk'skluːsɪv] adj exclusivo; (*club, district*) selecto; **~ of tax** excluyendo impuestos; **~ of postage/service** franqueo/servicio no incluido; **from 1st to 13th March ~** del 1 al 13 de marzo exclusive

exclusively [ɪk'skluːsɪvlɪ] adv únicamente

excommunicate [ɛkskə'mjuːnɪkeɪt] vt excomulgar

excrement ['ɛkskrəmənt] n excremento

excrete [ɪk'skriːt] vi excretar

excruciating [ɪk'skruːʃɪeɪtɪŋ] adj (*pain*) agudísimo, atroz

excursion [ɪk'skəːʃən] n excursión f

excursion ticket n billete m (especial) de excursión

excusable [ɪk'skjuːsəbl] adj perdonable

excuse n [ɪk'skjuːs] disculpa, excusa; (*evasion*) pretexto ■ vt [ɪk'skjuːz] disculpar, perdonar; (*justify*) justificar; **to make excuses for sb** presentar disculpas por algn; **to ~ sb from doing sth** dispensar a algn de hacer algo; **to ~ o.s. (for (doing) sth)** pedir disculpas a algn (por (hacer) algo); **~ me!** ¡perdone!; (*attracting attention*) ¡oiga (, por favor)!; **if you will ~ me** con su permiso

ex-directory ['ɛksdɪ'rɛktərɪ] adj (*Brit*): **~ (phone) number** número que no figura en la guía (telefónica)

execrable ['ɛksɪkrəbl] adj execrable, abominable; (*manners*) detestable

execute ['ɛksɪkjuːt] vt. (*plan*) realizar; (*order*) cumplir; (*person*) ajusticiar, ejecutar

execution [ɛksɪ'kjuːʃən] n realización f; cumplimiento; ejecución f

executioner [ɛksɪ'kjuːʃənəʳ] n verdugo

executive [ɪg'zɛkjutɪv] n (*Comm*) ejecutivo(-a); (*Pol*) poder m ejecutivo ■ adj ejecutivo; (*car, plane, position*) de ejecutivo; (*offices, suite*) de la dirección; (*secretary*) de dirección

executive director n director(a) m(f) ejecutivo(-a)

executor [ɪg'zɛkjutəʳ] n albacea m, testamentario

exemplary [ɪg'zɛmplərɪ] adj ejemplar

exemplify [ɪg'zɛmplɪfaɪ] vt ejemplificar

exempt [ɪg'zɛmpt] adj: **~ from** exento de ■ vt: **to ~ sb from** eximir a algn de

exemption [ɪg'zɛmpʃən] n exención f; (*immunity*) inmunidad f

exercise ['ɛksəsaɪz] n ejercicio ■ vt ejercer; (*patience etc*) proceder con; (*dog*) sacar de paseo ■ vi hacer ejercicio

exercise bike n bicicleta estática

exercise book n cuaderno de ejercicios

exert [ɪg'zəːt] vt ejercer; (*strength, force*) emplear; **to ~ o.s.** esforzarse

exertion [ɪg'zəːʃən] n esfuerzo

exfoliant [ɛks'fəulɪənt] n exfoliante m

ex gratia ['ɛks'greɪʃə] adj: **~ payment** pago a título voluntario

exhale [ɛks'heɪl] vt despedir, exhalar ■ vi espirar

exhaust [ɪg'zɔːst] n (*pipe*) (tubo de) escape m; (*fumes*) gases mpl de escape ■ vt agotar; **to ~ o.s.** agotarse

exhausted [ɪg'zɔːstɪd] adj agotado

exhausting [ɪgˈzɔːstɪŋ] *adj*: **an ~ journey/day** un viaje/día agotador

exhaustion [ɪgˈzɔːstʃən] *n* agotamiento; **nervous ~** agotamiento nervioso

exhaustive [ɪgˈzɔːstɪv] *adj* exhaustivo

exhibit [ɪgˈzɪbɪt] *n* (*Art*) obra expuesta; (*Law*) objeto expuesto ■ *vt* (*show: emotions*) manifestar; (: *courage, skill*) demostrar; (*paintings*) exponer

exhibition [ɛksɪˈbɪʃən] *n* exposición *f*

exhibitionist [ɛksɪˈbɪʃənɪst] *n* exhibicionista *m/f*

exhibitor [ɪgˈzɪbɪtəʳ] *n* expositor(a) *m(f)*

exhilarating [ɪgˈzɪləreɪtɪŋ] *adj* estimulante, tónico

exhilaration [ɪgzɪləˈreɪʃən] *n* júbilo

exhort [ɪgˈzɔːt] *vt* exhortar

exile [ˈɛksaɪl] *n* exilio; (*person*) exiliado(-a) ■ *vt* desterrar, exiliar

exist [ɪgˈzɪst] *vi* existir

existence [ɪgˈzɪstəns] *n* existencia

existentialism [ɛgzɪsˈtɛnʃəlɪzəm] *n* existencialismo

existing [ɪgˈzɪstɪŋ] *adj* existente, actual

exit [ˈɛksɪt] *n* salida ■ *vi* (*Theat*) hacer mutis; (*Comput*) salir (del sistema)

exit poll *n* encuesta a la salida de los colegios electorales

exit ramp *n* (*US Aut*) vía de acceso

exit visa *n* visado de salida

exodus [ˈɛksədəs] *n* éxodo

ex officio [ˈɛksəˈfɪʃɪəu] *adj* de pleno derecho ■ *adv* ex oficio

exonerate [ɪgˈzɒnəreɪt] *vt*: **to ~ from** exculpar de

exorbitant [ɪgˈzɔːbɪtənt] *adj* (*price, demands*) exorbitante, excesivo

exorcize [ˈɛksɔːsaɪz] *vt* exorcizar

exotic [ɪgˈzɒtɪk] *adj* exótico

expand [ɪkˈspænd] *vt* ampliar, extender; (*number*) aumentar ■ *vi* (*trade etc*) ampliarse, expandirse; (*gas, metal*) dilatarse; **to ~ on** (*notes, story etc*) ampliar

expanse [ɪkˈspæns] *n* extensión *f*

expansion [ɪkˈspænʃən] *n* ampliación *f*; aumento; (*of trade*) expansión *f*

expansionism [ɪkˈspænʃənɪzəm] *n* expansionismo

expansionist [ɪkˈspænʃənɪst] *adj* expansionista

expatriate [ɛksˈpætrɪət] *n* expatriado(-a)

expect [ɪkˈspɛkt] *vt* (*gen*) esperar; (*count on*) contar con; (*suppose*) suponer ■ *vi*: **to be expecting** estar encinta; **to ~ to do sth** esperar hacer algo; **as expected** como era de esperar; **I ~ so** supongo que sí

expectancy [ɪkˈspɛktənsɪ] *n* (*anticipation*) expectación *f*; **life ~** esperanza de vida

expectantly [ɪkˈspɛktəntlɪ] *adv* (*look, listen*) con expectación

expectant mother [ɪkˈspɛktənt-] *n* futura madre *f*

expectation [ɛkspɛkˈteɪʃən] *n* esperanza, expectativa; **in ~ of** esperando; **against** *or* **contrary to all ~(s)** en contra de todas las previsiones; **to come** *or* **live up to sb's expectations** resultar tan bueno como se esperaba; **to fall short of sb's expectations** no cumplir las esperanzas de algn, decepcionar a algn

expedience [ɪkˈspiːdɪəns], **expediency** [ɪkˈspiːdɪənsɪ] *n* conveniencia

expedient [ɪkˈspiːdɪənt] *adj* conveniente, oportuno ■ *n* recurso, expediente *m*

expedite [ˈɛkspɪdaɪt] *vt* (*speed up*) acelerar; (: *progress*) facilitar

expedition [ɛkspəˈdɪʃən] *n* expedición *f*

expeditionary force [ɛkspəˈdɪʃnrɪ-] *n* cuerpo expedicionario

expel [ɪkˈspɛl] *vt* expulsar

expend [ɪkˈspɛnd] *vt* gastar; (*use up*) consumir

expendable [ɪkˈspɛndəbl] *adj* prescindible

expenditure [ɪkˈspɛndɪtʃəʳ] *n* gastos *mpl*, desembolso; (*of time, effort*) gasto

expense [ɪkˈspɛns] *n* gasto, gastos *mpl*; (*high cost*) coste *m*; **expenses** *npl* (*Comm*) gastos *mpl*; **at the ~ of** a costa de; **to meet the ~ of** hacer frente a los gastos de

expense account *n* cuenta de gastos (de representación)

expensive [ɪkˈspɛnsɪv] *adj* caro, costoso

experience [ɪkˈspɪərɪəns] *n* experiencia ■ *vt* experimentar; (*suffer*) sufrir; **to learn by ~** aprender con la experiencia

experienced [ɪkˈspɪərɪənst] *adj* experimentado

experiment [ɪkˈspɛrɪmənt] *n* experimento ■ *vi* hacer experimentos, experimentar; **to perform** *or* **carry out an ~** realizar un experimento; **as an ~** como experimento; **to ~ with a new vaccine** experimentar con una vacuna nueva

experimental [ɪkspɛrɪˈmɛntl] *adj* experimental; **the process is still at the ~ stage** el proceso está todavía en prueba

expert [ˈɛkspɜːt] *adj* experto, perito ■ *n* experto(-a), perito(-a); (*specialist*) especialista *m/f*; **~ witness** (*Law*) testigo pericial; **~ in** *or* **at doing sth** experto *or* perito en hacer algo; **an ~ on sth** un experto en algo

expertise [ɛkspəːˈtiːz] *n* pericia

expiration [ɛkspɪˈreɪʃən] *n* (*gen*) expiración *f*, vencimiento

expire [ɪkˈspaɪəʳ] *vi* (*gen*) caducar, vencerse
expiry [ɪkˈspaɪərɪ] *n* caducidad *f*,
vencimiento
explain [ɪkˈspleɪn] *vt* explicar; (*mystery*)
aclarar
▸ **explain away** *vt* justificar
explanation [ɛkspləˈneɪʃən] *n* explicación *f*;
aclaración *f*; **to find an ~ for sth** encontrarle
una explicación a algo
explanatory [ɪkˈsplænətrɪ] *adj* explicativo;
aclaratorio
expletive [ɪkˈspliːtɪv] *n* imprecación *f*
explicable [ɪkˈsplɪkəbl] *adj* explicable
explicit [ɪkˈsplɪsɪt] *adj* explícito
explicitly [ɪkˈsplɪsɪtlɪ] *adv* explícitamente
explode [ɪkˈspləud] *vi* estallar, explotar; (*with
anger*) reventar ■ *vt* hacer explotar; (*fig:
theory, myth*) demoler
exploit [ˈɛksplɔɪt] *n* hazaña ■ *vt* [ɪkˈsplɔɪt]
explotar
exploitation [ɛksplɔɪˈteɪʃən] *n* explotación *f*
exploration [ɛkspləˈreɪʃən] *n* exploración *f*
exploratory [ɪkˈsplɔrətrɪ] *adj* (*fig: talks*)
exploratorio, preliminar
explore [ɪkˈsplɔːʳ] *vt* explorar; (*fig*) examinar,
sondear
explorer [ɪkˈsplɔːrəʳ] *n* explorador(a) *m(f)*
explosion [ɪkˈspləuʒən] *n* explosión *f*
explosive [ɪkˈspləusɪv] *adj, n* explosivo
exponent [ɪkˈspəunənt] *n* partidario(-a); (*of
skill, activity*) exponente *m/f*
export *vt* [ɛkˈspɔːt] exportar ■ *n* [ˈɛkspɔːt]
exportación *f* ■ *cpd* de exportación
exportation [ɛkspɔːˈteɪʃən] *n* exportación *f*
export drive *n* campaña de exportación
exporter [ɛkˈspɔːtəʳ] *n* exportador(a) *m(f)*
export licence *n* licencia de exportación
export manager *n* gerente *m/f* de
exportación
export trade *n* comercio exterior
expose [ɪkˈspəuz] *vt* exponer; (*unmask*)
desenmascarar
exposé [ɪkˈspəuzeɪ] *n* revelación *f*
exposed [ɪkˈspəuzd] *adj* expuesto; (*land,
house*) desprotegido; (*Elec: wire*) al aire;
(*pipe, beam*) al descubierto
exposition [ɛkspəˈzɪʃən] *n* exposición *f*
exposure [ɪkˈspəuʒəʳ] *n* exposición *f*; (*Phot:
speed*) (tiempo *m* de) exposición *f*; (: *shot*)
fotografía; **to die from ~** (*Med*) morir de frío
exposure meter *n* fotómetro
expound [ɪkˈspaund] *vt* exponer; (*theory, text*)
comentar; (*one's views*) explicar
express [ɪkˈsprɛs] *adj* (*definite*) expreso,
explícito; (*Brit: letter etc*) urgente ■ *n* (*train*)
rápido ■ *adv* (*send*) por correo extraordinario
■ *vt* expresar; (*squeeze*) exprimir; **to send**

sth ~ enviar algo por correo urgente;
to ~ o.s. expresarse
expression [ɪkˈsprɛʃən] *n* expresión *f*
expressionism [ɪkˈsprɛʃənɪzm] *n*
expresionismo
expressive [ɪkˈsprɛsɪv] *adj* expresivo
expressly [ɪkˈsprɛslɪ] *adv* expresamente
expressway [ɪkˈsprɛsweɪ] *n* (*US: urban
motorway*) autopista
expropriate [ɛksˈprəuprɪeɪt] *vt* expropiar
expulsion [ɪkˈspʌlʃən] *n* expulsión *f*
expurgate [ˈɛkspəgeɪt] *vt* expurgar
exquisite [ɛkˈskwɪzɪt] *adj* exquisito
exquisitely [ɛkˈskwɪzɪtlɪ] *adv*
exquisitamente
ex-serviceman [ˈɛksˈsəːvɪsmən] *n* excombatiente *m*
ext. *abbr* (*Tel*) = **extension**
extemporize [ɪkˈstɛmpəraɪz] *vi* improvisar
extend [ɪkˈstɛnd] *vt* (*visit, street*) prolongar;
(*building*) ampliar; (*thanks, friendship etc*)
extender; (*Comm: credit*) conceder; (*deadline*)
prorrogar ■ *vi* (*land*) extenderse; **the
contract extends to/for ...** el contrato se
prolonga hasta/por ...
extension [ɪkˈstɛnʃən] *n* extensión *f*;
(*building*) ampliación *f*; (*Tel: line*) extensión
f; (: *telephone*) supletorio *m*; (*of deadline*)
prórroga; **~ 3718** extensión 3718
extension cable *n* (*Elec*) alargador *m*
extensive [ɪkˈstɛnsɪv] *adj* (*gen*) extenso;
(*damage*) importante; (*knowledge*) amplio
extensively [ɪkˈstɛnsɪvlɪ] *adv* (*altered, damaged
etc*) extensamente; **he's travelled ~** ha
viajado por muchos países
extent [ɪkˈstɛnt] *n* (*breadth*) extensión *f*;
(*scope: of knowledge, activities*) alcance *m*; (*degree:
of damage, loss*) grado; **to some ~** hasta cierto
punto; **to a certain ~** hasta cierto punto; **to
a large ~** en gran parte; **to the ~ of ...** hasta
el punto de ...; **to such an ~ that ...** hasta
tal punto que ...; **to what ~?** ¿hasta qué
punto?; **debts to the ~ of £5000** deudas por
la cantidad de £5000
extenuating [ɪkˈstɛnjueɪtɪŋ] *adj*: **~
circumstances** circunstancias *fpl*
atenuantes
exterior [ɛkˈstɪərɪəʳ] *adj* exterior, externo
■ *n* exterior *m*
exterminate [ɪkˈstəːmɪneɪt] *vt* exterminar
extermination [ɪkstəːmɪˈneɪʃən] *n*
exterminio
external [ɛkˈstəːnl] *adj* externo, exterior
■ *n*: **the externals** la apariencia exterior;
~ affairs asuntos *mpl* exteriores; **for ~ use
only** (*Med*) para uso tópico
externally [ɛkˈstəːnəlɪ] *adv* por fuera

extinct [ɪk'stɪŋkt] *adj* (*volcano*) extinguido, apagado; (*race*) extinguido

extinction [ɪk'stɪŋkʃən] *n* extinción *f*

extinguish [ɪk'stɪŋgwɪʃ] *vt* extinguir, apagar

extinguisher [ɪk'stɪŋgwɪʃəʳ] *n* extintor *m*

extol, extoll (US) [ɪk'stəul] *vt* (*merits, virtues*) ensalzar, alabar; (*person*) alabar, elogiar

extort [ɪk'stɔ:t] *vt* sacar a la fuerza; (*confession*) arrancar

extortion [ɪk'stɔ:ʃən] *n* extorsión *f*

extortionate [ɪk'stɔ:ʃnət] *adj* excesivo, exorbitante

extra ['ɛkstrə] *adj* adicional ■ *adv* (*in addition*) más ■ *n* (*addition*) extra *m*, suplemento; (*Theat*) extra *m/f*, comparsa *m/f*; (*newspaper*) edición *f* extraordinaria; **wine will cost ~** el vino se paga aparte; **~ large sizes** tallas extragrandes; *see also* **extras**

extra... ['ɛkstrə] *pref* extra...

extract *vt* [ɪk'strækt] sacar; (*tooth*) extraer; (*confession*) arrancar ■ *n* ['ɛkstrækt] fragmento; (*Culin*) extracto

extraction [ɪk'strækʃən] *n* extracción *f* (*origin*), origen *m*

extractor fan [ɪk'stræktə-] *n* extractor *m* de humos

extracurricular [ɛkstrəkə'rɪkjuləʳ] *adj* (*Scol*) extraescolar

extradite ['ɛkstrədaɪt] *vt* extraditar

extradition [ɛkstrə'dɪʃən] *n* extradición *f*

extramarital [ɛkstrə'mærɪtl] *adj* extramatrimonial

extramural [ɛkstrə'mjuərl] *adj* extra-académico

extraneous [ɪk'streɪnɪəs] *adj* extraño, ajeno

extraordinary [ɪk'strɔ:dnrɪ] *adj* extraordinario; (*odd*) raro; **the ~ thing is that ...** lo más extraordinario es que ...

extraordinary general meeting *n* junta general extraordinaria

extrapolation [ɪkstræpə'leɪʃən] *n* extrapolación *f*

extras *npl* (*additional expense*) extras *mpl*

extrasensory perception ['ɛkstrə'sɛnsərɪ-] *n* percepción *f* extrasensorial

extra time *n* (*Football*) prórroga

extravagance [ɪk'strævəgəns] *n* (*excessive spending*) derroche *m*; (*thing bought*) extravagancia

extravagant [ɪk'strævəgənt] *adj* (*wasteful*) derrochador(a); (*taste, gift*) excesivamente caro; (*price*) exorbitante; (*praise*) excesivo

extreme [ɪk'stri:m] *adj* extremo; (*poverty etc*) extremado; (*case*) excepcional ■ *n* extremo; **the ~ left/right** (*Pol*) la extrema izquierda/derecha; **extremes of temperature** temperaturas extremas

extremely [ɪk'stri:mlɪ] *adv* sumamente, extremadamente

extremist [ɪk'stri:mɪst] *adj, n* extremista *m/f*

extremity [ɪk'strɛmətɪ] *n* extremidad *f*, punta; (*need*) apuro, necesidad *f*; **extremities** *npl* (*hands and feet*) extremidades *fpl*

extricate ['ɛkstrɪkeɪt] *vt*: **to ~ o.s. from** librarse de

extrovert ['ɛkstrəvə:t] *n* extrovertido(-a)

exuberance [ɪg'zju:bərns] *n* exuberancia

exuberant [ɪg'zju:bərnt] *adj* (*person*) eufórico; (*style*) exuberante

exude [ɪg'zju:d] *vt* rezumar

exult [ɪg'zʌlt] *vi* regocijarse

exultant [ɪg'zʌltənt] *adj* (*person*) regocijado, jubiloso; (*shout, expression, smile*) de júbilo

exultation [ɛgzʌl'teɪʃən] *n* regocijo, júbilo

eye [aɪ] *n* ojo ■ *vt* mirar; **to keep an ~ on** vigilar; **as far as the ~ can see** hasta donde alcanza la vista; **with an ~ to doing sth** con vistas *or* miras a hacer algo; **to have an ~ for sth** tener mucha vista *or* buen ojo para algo; **there's more to this than meets the ~** esto tiene su miga

eyeball ['aɪbɔ:l] *n* globo ocular

eyebath ['aɪbɑ:θ] *n* baño ocular, lavaojos *m inv*

eyebrow ['aɪbrau] *n* ceja

eyebrow pencil *n* lápiz *m* de cejas

eye-catching ['aɪkætʃɪŋ] *adj* llamativo

eye cup *n* (US) = **eyebath**

eyedrops ['aɪdrɒps] *npl* gotas *fpl* para los ojos

eyeful ['aɪful] *n* (*col*): **to get an ~ of sth** ver bien algo

eyelash ['aɪlæʃ] *n* pestaña

eyelet ['aɪlɪt] *n* ojete *m*

eye-level ['aɪlɛvl] *adj* a la altura de los ojos

eyelid ['aɪlɪd] *n* párpado

eyeliner ['aɪlaɪnəʳ] *n* lápiz *m* de ojos

eye-opener ['aɪəupnəʳ] *n* revelación *f*, gran sorpresa

eyeshadow ['aɪʃædəu] *n* sombra de ojos

eyesight ['aɪsaɪt] *n* vista

eyesore ['aɪsɔ:ʳ] *n* monstruosidad *f*

eyestrain ['aɪstreɪn] *n*: **to get ~** cansar la vista *or* los ojos

eyetooth (*pl* **eyeteeth**) ['aɪtu:θ, -ti:θ] *n* colmillo; **to give one's eyeteeth for sth/to do sth** (*col, fig*) dar un ojo de la cara por algo/por hacer algo

eyewash ['aɪwɒʃ] *n* (*fig*) disparates *mpl*, tonterías *fpl*

eye witness *n* testigo *m/f* ocular

eyrie ['ɪərɪ] *n* aguilera

e

F, f [ɛf] n (letter) F, f f; (Mus) fa m; **F for Frederick,** (US) **F for Fox** F de Francia
F. abbr = **Fahrenheit**
FA n abbr (Brit: = Football Association) ≈ AFE f (SP)
FAA n abbr (US) = **Federal Aviation Administration**
fable ['feɪbl] n fábula
fabric ['fæbrɪk] n tejido, tela
fabricate ['fæbrɪkeɪt] vt fabricar; (fig) inventar
fabrication [fæbrɪ'keɪʃən] n fabricación f; (fig) invención f
fabric ribbon n (for typewriter) cinta de tela
fabulous ['fæbjuləs] adj fabuloso
façade [fə'sɑ:d] n fachada
face [feɪs] n (Anat) cara, rostro; (of clock) esfera, cara; (side) cara; (surface) superficie f ▪ vt mirar a; (fig) enfrentarse a; ~ **down** (person, card) boca abajo; **to lose ~** desprestigiarse; **to save ~** salvar las apariencias; **to make** or **pull a ~** hacer muecas; **in the ~ of** (difficulties etc) en vista de, ante; **on the ~ of it** a primera vista; **~ to ~** cara a cara; **to ~ the fact that ...** reconocer que ...
  ▸**face up to** vt fus hacer frente a, enfrentarse a
face cloth n (Brit) toallita
face cream n crema (de belleza)
faceless ['feɪslɪs] adj (fig) anónimo
face lift n lifting m, estirado facial
face powder n polvos mpl para la cara
face-saving ['feɪsseɪvɪŋ] adj para salvar las apariencias
facet ['fæsɪt] n faceta
facetious [fə'si:ʃəs] adj chistoso
facetiously [fə'si:ʃəslɪ] adv chistosamente
face value n (of stamp) valor m nominal; **to take sth at ~** (fig) tomar algo en sentido literal, aceptar las apariencias de algo
facial ['feɪʃəl] adj de la cara ▪ n (also: **beauty facial**) tratamiento facial, limpieza
facile ['fæsaɪl] adj superficial

facilitate [fə'sɪlɪteɪt] vt facilitar
facility [fə'sɪlɪtɪ] n facilidad f; **facilities** npl instalaciones fpl; **credit ~** facilidades de crédito
facing ['feɪsɪŋ] prep frente a ▪ adj de enfrente
facsimile [fæk'sɪmɪlɪ] n facsímil(e) m
fact [fækt] n hecho; **in ~** en realidad; **to know for a ~ that ...** saber a ciencia cierta que ...
fact-finding ['fæktfaɪndɪŋ] adj: **a ~ tour/mission** un viaje/una misión de reconocimiento
faction ['fækʃən] n facción f
factional ['fækʃənl] adj (fighting) entre distintas facciones
factor ['fæktəʳ] n factor m; (Comm: person) agente m/f comisionado(-a) ▪ vi (Comm) comprar deudas; **safety ~** factor de seguridad
factory ['fæktərɪ] n fábrica
factory farming n cría industrial
factory floor n (workers) trabajadores mpl, mano f de obra directa; (area) talleres mpl
factory ship n buque m factoría
factual ['fæktjuəl] adj basado en los hechos
faculty ['fækəltɪ] n facultad f; (US: teaching staff) personal m docente
fad [fæd] n novedad f, moda
fade [feɪd] vi descolorarse, desteñirse; (sound, hope) desvanecerse; (light) apagarse; (flower) marchitarse
  ▸**fade away** vi (sound) apagarse
  ▸**fade in** vt (TV, Cine) fundir; (Radio: sound) mezclar ▪ vi (TV, Cine) fundirse; (Radio) oírse por encima
  ▸**fade out** vt (TV, Cine) fundir; (Radio) apagar, disminuir el volumen de ▪ vi (TV, Cine) desvanecerse; (Radio) apagarse, dejarse de oír
faded ['feɪdɪd] adj (clothes, colour) descolorido; (flower) marchito
faeces, feces (US) ['fi:si:z] npl excremento sg, heces fpl

fag [fæg] n (Brit col: cigarette) pitillo (SP), cigarro; (US col: homosexual) maricón m
fag end n (Brit col) colilla
fagged [fægd] adj (Brit col: exhausted) rendido, agotado
Fahrenheit ['fɑːrənhaɪt] n Fahrenheit m
fail [feɪl] vt suspender; (memory etc) fallar a ▪ vi suspender; (be unsuccessful) fracasar; (strength, brakes, engine) fallar; **to ~ to do sth** (neglect) dejar de hacer algo; (be unable) no poder hacer algo; **without ~** sin falta; **words ~ me!** ¡no sé qué decir!
failing ['feɪlɪŋ] n falta, defecto ▪ prep a falta de; **~ that** de no ser posible eso
failsafe ['feɪlseɪf] adj (device etc) de seguridad
failure ['feɪljər] n fracaso; (person) fracasado(-a); (mechanical etc) fallo; (in exam) suspenso; (of crops) pérdida, destrucción f; **it was a complete ~** fue un fracaso total
faint [feɪnt] adj débil; (smell, breeze, trace) leve; (recollection) vago; (mark) apenas visible ▪ n desmayo ▪ vi desmayarse; **to feel ~** estar mareado, marearse
faintest ['feɪntɪst] adj: **I haven't the ~ idea** no tengo la más remota idea
faint-hearted ['feɪnt'hɑːtɪd] adj apocado
faintly ['feɪntlɪ] adv débilmente; (vaguely) vagamente
faintness ['feɪntnɪs] n debilidad f; vaguedad f
fair [fɛər] adj justo; (hair, person) rubio; (weather) bueno; (good enough) suficiente; (sizeable) considerable ▪ adv: **to play ~** jugar limpio ▪ n feria; (Brit: funfair) parque m de atracciones; **it's not ~!** ¡no es justo!, ¡no hay derecho!; **~ copy** copia en limpio; **~ play** juego limpio; **a ~ amount of** bastante; **~ wear and tear** desgaste m natural; **trade ~** feria de muestras
fair game n: **to be ~** ser blanco legítimo
fairground ['fɛəgraund] n recinto ferial
fair-haired [fɛə'hɛəd] adj (person) rubio
fairly ['fɛəlɪ] adv (justly) con justicia; (equally) equitativamente; (quite) bastante; **I'm ~ sure** estoy bastante seguro
fairness ['fɛənɪs] n justicia; (impartiality) imparcialidad f; **in all ~** a decir verdad
fair trade n comercio justo
fairy ['fɛərɪ] n hada
fairy godmother n hada madrina
fairyland ['fɛərɪlænd] n el país de ensueño
fairy lights npl bombillas fpl de colores
fairy tale n cuento de hadas
faith [feɪθ] n fe f; (trust) confianza; (sect) religión f; **to have ~ in sb/sth** confiar en algn/algo
faithful ['feɪθful] adj fiel
faithfully ['feɪθfulɪ] adv fielmente; **yours ~** (Brit: in letters) le saluda atentamente
faith healer n curador(a) m(f) por fe
fake [feɪk] n (painting etc) falsificación f; (person) impostor(a) m(f) ▪ adj falso ▪ vt fingir; (painting etc) falsificar
falcon ['fɔːlkən] n halcón m
Falkland Islands ['fɔːlklənd-] npl Islas fpl Malvinas
fall [fɔːl] n caída; (US) otoño; (decrease) disminución f ▪ vi (pt fell, pp fallen) ['fɔːlən] caer; (accidentally) caerse; (price) bajar; **falls** npl (waterfall) cataratas fpl, salto sg de agua; **a ~ of earth** un desprendimiento de tierra; **a ~ of snow** una nevada; **to ~ flat** vi (on one's face) caerse de bruces; (joke, story) no hacer gracia; **to ~ short of sb's expectations** decepcionar a algn; **to ~ in love (with sb/sth)** enamorarse (de algn/algo)
▶ **fall apart** vi deshacerse
▶ **fall back** vi retroceder
▶ **fall back on** vt fus (remedy etc) recurrir a; **to have sth to ~ back on** tener algo a que recurrir
▶ **fall behind** vi quedarse atrás; (fig: with payments) retrasarse
▶ **fall down** vi (person) caerse; (building) derrumbarse
▶ **fall for** vt fus (trick) tragar; (person) enamorarse de
▶ **fall in** vi (roof) hundirse; (Mil) alinearse
▶ **fall in with** vt fus: **to ~ in with sb's plans** acomodarse con los planes de algn
▶ **fall off** vi caerse; (diminish) disminuir
▶ **fall out** vi (friends etc) reñir; (Mil) romper filas
▶ **fall over** vi caer(se)
▶ **fall through** vi (plan, project) fracasar
fallacy ['fæləsɪ] n error m
fallback position ['fɔːlbæk-] n posición f de repliegue
fallen ['fɔːlən] pp of **fall**
fallible ['fæləbl] adj falible
falling ['fɔːlɪŋ] adj: **~ market** mercado en baja
falling-off ['fɔːlɪŋ'ɔf] n (reduction) disminución f
Fallopian tube [fə'ləupɪən-] n (Anat) trompa de Falopio
fallout ['fɔːlaut] n lluvia radioactiva
fallout shelter n refugio antinuclear
fallow ['fæləu] adj (land, field) en barbecho
false [fɔːls] adj (gen) falso; (teeth etc) postizo; (disloyal) desleal, traidor(a); **under ~ pretences** con engaños
false alarm n falsa alarma
falsehood ['fɔːlshud] n falsedad f
falsely ['fɔːlslɪ] adv falsamente

false teeth *npl* (*Brit*) dentadura *sg* postiza
falsify ['fɔːlsɪfaɪ] *vt* falsificar
falter ['fɔːltər] *vi* vacilar
fame [feɪm] *n* fama
familiar [fə'mɪlɪər] *adj* familiar; (*well-known*) conocido; (*tone*) de confianza; **to be ~ with** (*subject*) estar enterado de; **to make o.s. ~ with** familiarizarse con; **to be on ~ terms with sb** tener confianza con algn
familiarity [fəmɪlɪ'ærɪtɪ] *n* familiaridad *f*
familiarize [fə'mɪlɪəraɪz] *vt*: **to ~ o.s. with** familiarizarse con
family ['fæmɪlɪ] *n* familia
family allowance *n* *subsidio que se recibe por cada hijo*
family business *n* negocio familiar
family credit *n* (*Brit*) ≈ ayuda familiar
family doctor *n* médico(-a) de cabecera
family life *n* vida doméstica *or* familiar
family man *n* (*home-loving*) hombre *m* casero; (*having family*) padre *m* de familia
family planning *n* planificación *f* familiar
family planning clinic *n* clínica de planificación familiar
family tree *n* árbol *m* genealógico
famine ['fæmɪn] *n* hambre *f*, hambruna
famished ['fæmɪʃt] *adj* hambriento; **I'm ~!** (*col*) ¡estoy muerto de hambre!, ¡tengo un hambre canina!
famous ['feɪməs] *adj* famoso, célebre
famously ['feɪməslɪ] *adv* (*get on*) estupendamente
fan [fæn] *n* abanico; (*Elec*) ventilador *m*; (*person*) aficionado(-a); (*Sport*) hincha *m/f*; (*of pop star*) fan *m/f* ■ *vt* abanicar; (*fire, quarrel*) atizar
  ▶ **fan out** *vi* desplegarse
fanatic [fə'nætɪk] *n* fanático(-a)
fanatical [fə'nætɪkəl] *adj* fanático
fan belt *n* correa de ventilador
fancied ['fænsɪd] *adj* imaginario
fanciful ['fænsɪful] *adj* (*gen*) fantástico; (*imaginary*) fantasioso; (*design*) rebuscado
fan club *n* club *m* de fans
fancy ['fænsɪ] *n* (*whim*) capricho, antojo; (*imagination*) imaginación *f* ■ *adj* (*luxury*) de lujo; (*price*) exorbitado ■ *vt* (*feel like, want*) tener ganas de; (*imagine*) imaginarse, figurarse; **to take a ~ to sb** tomar cariño a algn; **when the ~ takes him** cuando se le antoja; **it took** *or* **caught my ~** me cayó en gracia; **to ~ that ...** imaginarse que ...; **he fancies her** le gusta (ella) mucho
fancy dress *n* disfraz *m*
fancy-dress ball ['fænsɪdrɛs-] *n* baile *m* de disfraces
fancy goods *n* artículos *mpl* de fantasía

fanfare ['fænfɛər] *n* fanfarria (de trompeta)
fanfold paper ['fænfəuld-] *n* papel *m* plegado en abanico *or* en acordeón
fang [fæŋ] *n* colmillo
fan heater *n* calefactor *m* de aire
fanlight ['fænlaɪt] *n* (montante *m* en) abanico
fanny ['fænɪ] *n* (*Brit col!*) chocho (!); (*US col*) pompis *m*, culo (!)
fantasize ['fæntəsaɪz] *vi* fantasear, hacerse ilusiones
fantastic [fæn'tæstɪk] *adj* fantástico
fantasy ['fæntəzɪ] *n* fantasía
fanzine ['fænziːn] *n* fanzine *m*
FAO *n abbr* (= *Food and Agriculture Organization*) OAA *f*, FAO *f*
FAQ *abbr* (= *free alongside quay*) franco sobre muelle
FAQs *npl abbr* (= *frequently asked questions*) preguntas *fpl* frecuentes
far [fɑːr] *adj* (*distant*) lejano ■ *adv* lejos; **the ~ left/right** (*Pol*) la extrema izquierda/derecha; **~ away, ~ off** (a lo) lejos; **~ better** mucho mejor; **~ from** lejos de; **by ~** con mucho; **it's by ~ the best** es con mucho el mejor; **go as ~ as the farm** vaya hasta la granja; **is it ~ to London?** ¿estamos lejos de Londres?, ¿Londres queda lejos?; **it's not ~ (from here)** no está lejos (de aquí); **as ~ as I know** que yo sepa; **how ~ have you got with your work?** ¿hasta dónde has llegado en tu trabajo?
faraway ['fɑːrəweɪ] *adj* remoto; (*look*) ausente, perdido
farce [fɑːs] *n* farsa
farcical ['fɑːsɪkəl] *adj* absurdo
fare [fɛər] *n* (*on trains, buses*) precio (del billete); (*in taxi: cost*) tarifa; (: *passenger*) pasajero; (*food*) comida; **half/full ~** medio billete *m*/billete *m* completo
Far East *n*: **the ~** el Extremo *or* Lejano Oriente
farewell [fɛə'wɛl] *excl, n* adiós *m*
far-fetched [fɑː'fɛtʃt] *adj* inverosímil
farm [fɑːm] *n* granja, finca, estancia (*LAm*), chacra (*LAm*), rancho (*LAm*) ■ *vt* cultivar
  ▶ **farm out** *vt* (*work*): **to ~ out (to sb)** mandar hacer fuera (a algn)
farmer ['fɑːmər] *n* granjero(-a), estanciero(-a) (*LAm*)
farmhand ['fɑːmhænd] *n* peón *m*
farmhouse ['fɑːmhaus] *n* granja, casa de hacienda (*LAm*)
farming ['fɑːmɪŋ] *n* (*gen*) agricultura; (*tilling*) cultivo; **sheep ~** cría de ovejas
farm labourer *n* = **farmhand**
farmland ['fɑːmlænd] *n* tierra de cultivo
farm produce *n* productos *mpl* agrícolas

farm worker *n* = **farmhand**

farmyard ['fɑːmjɑːd] *n* corral *m*

Faroe Islands ['fɛərəu-], **Faroes** ['fɛərəuz] *npl*: **the ~** las Islas Feroe

far-reaching [fɑː'riːtʃɪŋ] *adj* (*reform, effect*) de gran alcance

far-sighted [fɑː'saɪtɪd] *adj* previsor(a)

fart [fɑːt] (*col!*) *n* pedo (!) ■ *vi* tirarse un pedo (!)

farther ['fɑːðəʳ] *adv* más lejos, más allá ■ *adj* más lejano

farthest ['fɑːðɪst] *superlative of* **far**

FAS *abbr* (Brit: = *free alongside ship*) franco al costado del buque

fascinate ['fæsɪneɪt] *vt* fascinar

fascinating ['fæsɪneɪtɪŋ] *adj* fascinante

fascination [fæsɪ'neɪʃən] *n* fascinación *f*

fascism ['fæʃɪzəm] *n* fascismo

fascist ['fæʃɪst] *adj, n* fascista *m/f*

fashion ['fæʃən] *n* moda; (*manner*) manera ■ *vt* formar; **in ~** a la moda; **out of ~** pasado de moda; **in the Greek ~** a la griega, al estilo griego; **after a ~** (*finish, manage etc*) en cierto modo

fashionable ['fæʃnəbl] *adj* de moda; (*writer*) de moda, popular; **it is ~ to do ...** está de moda hacer ...

fashion designer *n* diseñador(a) *m(f)* de modas, modisto(-a)

fashionista [fæʃə'nɪstə] *n* fashionista *m/f*

fashion show *n* desfile *m* de modelos

fast [fɑːst] *adj* rápido; (*dye, colour*) sólido; (*clock*): **to be ~** estar adelantado ■ *adv* rápidamente, de prisa; (*stuck*) firmemente ■ *n* ayuno ■ *vi* ayunar; **~ asleep** profundamente dormido; **in the ~ lane** (Aut) en el carril de adelantamiento; **my watch is five minutes ~** mi reloj está adelantado cinco minutos; **as ~ as I** *etc* **can** lo más rápido posible; **to make a boat ~** amarrar una barca

fasten ['fɑːsn] *vt* asegurar, sujetar; (*coat, belt*) abrochar ■ *vi* cerrarse
  ▶ **fasten (up)on** *vt fus* (*idea*) aferrarse a

fastener ['fɑːsnəʳ] *n* cierre *m*; (*of door etc*) cerrojo; (Brit: *also*: **zip fastener**) cremallera

fastening ['fɑːsnɪŋ] *n* = **fastener**

fast food *n* comida rápida, platos *mpl* preparados

fastidious [fæs'tɪdɪəs] *adj* (*fussy*) delicado; (*demanding*) exigente

fat [fæt] *adj* gordo; (*meat*) con mucha grasa; (*greasy*) grasiento ■ *n* grasa; (*on person*) carnes *fpl*; (*lard*) manteca; **to live off the ~ of the land** vivir a cuerpo de rey

fatal ['feɪtl] *adj* (*mistake*) fatal; (*injury*) mortal; (*consequence*) funesto

fatalism ['feɪtəlɪzəm] *n* fatalismo

fatality [fə'tælɪtɪ] *n* (*road death etc*) víctima *f* mortal

fatally ['feɪtəlɪ] *adv*: **~ injured** herido de muerte

fate [feɪt] *n* destino, sino

fated ['feɪtɪd] *adj* predestinado

fateful ['feɪtful] *adj* fatídico

fat-free ['fætfriː] *adj* sin grasa

father ['fɑːðəʳ] *n* padre *m*

Father Christmas *n* Papá *m* Noel

fatherhood ['fɑːðəhud] *n* paternidad *f*

father-in-law ['fɑːðərɪnlɔː] *n* suegro

fatherland ['fɑːðəlænd] *n* patria

fatherly ['fɑːðəlɪ] *adj* paternal

fathom ['fæðəm] *n* braza ■ *vt* (*unravel*) desentrañar; (*understand*) explicarse

fatigue [fə'tiːg] *n* fatiga, cansancio; **metal ~** fatiga del metal

fatness ['fætnɪs] *n* gordura

fatten ['fætn] *vt, vi* engordar; **chocolate is fattening** el chocolate engorda

fatty ['fætɪ] *adj* (*food*) graso ■ *n* (*fam*) gordito(-a), gordinflón(-ona) *m(f)*

fatuous ['fætjuəs] *adj* fatuo, necio

faucet ['fɔːsɪt] *n* (US) grifo, llave *f*, canilla (LAm)

fault [fɔːlt] *n* (*blame*) culpa; (*defect: in character*) defecto; (*in manufacture*) desperfecto; (Geo) falla ■ *vt* criticar; **it's my ~** es culpa mía; **to find ~ with** criticar, poner peros a; **at ~** culpable

faultless ['fɔːltlɪs] *adj* (*action*) intachable; (*person*) sin defectos

faulty ['fɔːltɪ] *adj* defectuoso

fauna ['fɔːnə] *n* fauna

faux pas ['fəu'pɑː] *n* desacierto

favour, favor (US) ['feɪvəʳ] *n* favor *m*; (*approval*) aprobación *f* ■ *vt* (*proposition*) estar a favor de, aprobar; (*person etc*) preferir; (*assist*) favorecer; **to ask a ~ of** pedir un favor a; **to do sb a ~** hacer un favor a algn; **to find ~ with sb** (*person*) caerle bien a algn; (: *suggestion*) tener buena acogida por parte de algn; **in ~ of** a favor de; **to be in ~ of sth/of doing sth** ser partidario *or* estar a favor de algo/de hacer algo

favourable, favorable (US) ['feɪvərəbl] *adj* favorable

favourably, favorably (US) ['feɪvərəblɪ] *adv* favorablemente

favourite, favorite (US) ['feɪvərɪt] *adj, n* favorito(-a) *m(f)*, preferido(-a) *m(f)*

favouritism, favoritism (US) ['feɪvərɪtɪzəm] *n* favoritismo

fawn [fɔːn] *n* cervato ■ *adj* (*also*: **fawn-coloured**) de color cervato, leonado ■ *vi*: **to ~ (up)on** adular

fax [fæks] n fax m ▪ vt mandar or enviar por fax

FBI n abbr (US: = Federal Bureau of Investigation) FBI m

FCC n abbr (US) = **Federal Communications Commission**

FCO n abbr (Brit: = Foreign and Commonwealth Office) = Min. de AA. EE

FD n abbr (US) = **fire department**

FDA n abbr (US: = Food and Drug Administration) oficina que se ocupa del control de los productos alimenticios y farmacéuticos

FE n abbr = **further education**

fear [fɪəʳ] n miedo, temor m ▪ vt temer; **for ~ of** por temor a; **~ of heights** vértigo; **to ~ for/that** temer por/que

fearful ['fɪəful] adj temeroso; (awful) espantoso; **to be ~ of** (frightened) tener miedo de

fearfully ['fɪəfulɪ] adv (timidly) con miedo; (col: very) terriblemente

fearless ['fɪəlɪs] adj (gen) sin miedo or temor; (bold) audaz

fearlessly ['fɪəlɪslɪ] adv temerariamente

fearlessness ['fɪəlɪsnɪs] n temeridad f

fearsome ['fɪəsəm] adj (opponent) temible; (sight) espantoso

feasibility [fi:zə'bɪlɪtɪ] n factibilidad f, viabilidad f

feasibility study n estudio de viabilidad

feasible ['fi:zəbl] adj factible, viable

feast [fi:st] n banquete m; (Rel: also: **feast day**) fiesta ▪ vi banquetear

feat [fi:t] n hazaña

feather ['fɛðəʳ] n pluma ▪ vt: **to ~ one's nest** (fig) hacer su agosto, sacar tajada ▪ cpd (mattress, bed, pillow) de plumas

feather-weight ['fɛðəweɪt] n (Boxing) peso pluma

feature ['fi:tʃəʳ] n (gen) característica; (Anat) rasgo; (article) reportaje m ▪ vt (film) presentar ▪ vi figurar; **features** npl (of face) facciones fpl; **a (special) ~ on sth/sb** un reportaje (especial) sobre algo/algn; **it featured prominently in ...** tuvo un papel destacado en ...

feature film n largometraje m

Feb. abbr (= February) feb

February ['fɛbruərɪ] n febrero; see also **July**

feces ['fi:si:z] npl (US) = **faeces**

feckless ['fɛklɪs] adj irresponsable, irreflexivo

Fed [fɛd] abbr (US) = **federal; federation**

Fed. [fɛd] n abbr (US col) = **Federal Reserve Board**

fed [fɛd] pt, pp of **feed**

federal ['fɛdərəl] adj federal

Federal Republic of Germany n República Federal de Alemania

federation [fɛdə'reɪʃən] n federación f

fed-up [fɛd'ʌp] adj: **to be ~ (with)** estar harto (de)

fee [fi:] n (professional) honorarios mpl; (for examination) derechos mpl; (of school) matrícula; (also: **membership fee**) cuota; (also: **entrance fee**) entrada; **for a small ~** por poco dinero

feeble ['fi:bl] adj débil

feeble-minded [fi:bl'maɪndɪd] adj imbécil

feed [fi:d] n (gen) comida; (of animal) pienso; (on printer) dispositivo de alimentación ▪ vt (pp, pt **fed**) (gen) alimentar; (Brit: breastfeed) dar el pecho a; (animal, baby) dar de comer a ▪ vi (baby, animal) comer

▸ **feed back** vt (results) pasar

▸ **feed in** vt (Comput) introducir

▸ **feed into** vt (data, information) suministrar a; **to ~ sth into a machine** introducir algo en una máquina

▸ **feed on** vt fus alimentarse de

feedback ['fi:dbæk] n (from person) reacción f; (Tech) realimentación f, feedback m

feeder ['fi:dəʳ] n (bib) babero

feeding bottle ['fi:dɪŋ-] n (Brit) biberón m

feel [fi:l] n (sensation) sensación f; (sense of touch) tacto ▪ vt (pt, pp **felt**) tocar; (cold, pain etc) sentir; (think, believe) creer; **to get the ~ of sth** (fig) acostumbrarse a algo; **to ~ hungry/cold** tener hambre/frío; **to ~ lonely/better** sentirse solo/mejor; **I don't ~ well** no me siento bien; **it feels soft** es suave al tacto; **it feels colder out here** se siente más frío aquí fuera; **to ~ like** (want) tener ganas de; **I'm still feeling my way** (fig) todavía me estoy orientando; **I ~ that you ought to do it** creo que debes hacerlo; **to ~ about** or **around** vi tantear

feeler ['fi:ləʳ] n (of insect) antena; **to put out feelers** (fig) tantear el terreno

feeling ['fi:lɪŋ] n (physical) sensación f; (foreboding) presentimiento; (impression) impresión f; (emotion) sentimiento; **what are your feelings about the matter?** ¿qué opinas tú del asunto?; **to hurt sb's feelings** herir los sentimientos de algn; **feelings ran high about it** causó mucha controversia; **I got the ~ that ...** me dio la impresión de que ...; **there was a general ~ that ...** la opinión general fue que ...

fee-paying school ['fi:peɪɪŋ-] n colegio de pago

feet [fi:t] npl of **foot**

feign [feɪn] vt fingir

feigned [feɪnd] adj fingido

feline ['fi:laɪn] *adj* felino
fell [fɛl] *pt of* **fall** ■ *vt* (*tree*) talar ■ *adj*: **with one ~ blow** con un golpe feroz; **at one ~ swoop** de un solo golpe ■ *n* (*Brit: mountain*) montaña; (*moorland*): **the fells** los páramos
fellow ['fɛləu] *n* tipo, tío (*SP*); (*of learned society*) socio(-a); (*Univ*) *miembro de la junta de gobierno de un colegio* ■ *cpd*: **~ students** compañeros(-as) *m(f)pl* de curso, de curso, condiscípulos(-as) *m(f)pl*
fellow citizen *n* conciudadano(-a)
fellow countryman *n* compatriota *m*
fellow feeling *n* compañerismo
fellow men *npl* semejantes *mpl*
fellowship ['fɛləuʃɪp] *n* compañerismo; (*grant*) beca
fellow traveller *n* compañero(-a) de viaje; (*Pol: with communists*) simpatizante *m/f*
fellow worker *n* colega *m/f*
felon ['fɛlən] *n* criminal *m/f*
felony ['fɛlənɪ] *n* crimen *m*, delito mayor
felt [fɛlt] *pt, pp of* **feel** ■ *n* fieltro
felt-tip pen ['fɛlttɪp-] *n* rotulador *m*
female ['fi:meɪl] *n* (*woman*) mujer *f*; (*Zool*) hembra ■ *adj* femenino
feminine ['fɛmɪnɪn] *adj* femenino
femininity [fɛmɪ'nɪnɪtɪ] *n* feminidad *f*
feminism ['fɛmɪnɪzəm] *n* feminismo
feminist ['fɛmɪnɪst] *n* feminista *m/f*
fence [fɛns] *n* valla, cerca; (*Racing*) valla ■ *vt* (*also*: **fence in**) cercar ■ *vi* hacer esgrima; **to sit on the ~** (*fig*) nadar entre dos aguas
▶ **fence in** *vt* cercar
▶ **fence off** *vt* separar con cerca
fencing ['fɛnsɪŋ] *n* esgrima
fend [fɛnd] *vi*: **to ~ for o.s.** valerse por sí mismo
▶ **fend off** *vt* (*attack, attacker*) rechazar, repeler; (*blow*) desviar; (*awkward question*) esquivar
fender ['fɛndər] *n* pantalla; (*US Aut*) parachoques *m inv*; (*Rail*) trompa
fennel ['fɛnl] *n* hinojo
Fens [fɛnz] *npl* (*Brit*): **the ~** *las tierras bajas de Norfolk (antiguamente zona de marismas)*
ferment *vi* [fə'mɛnt] fermentar ■ *n* ['fə:mɛnt] (*fig*) agitación *f*
fermentation [fə:mɛn'teɪʃən] *n* fermentación *f*
fern [fə:n] *n* helecho
ferocious [fə'rəuʃəs] *adj* feroz
ferociously [fə'rəuʃəslɪ] *adv* ferozmente, con ferocidad
ferocity [fə'rɔsɪtɪ] *n* ferocidad *f*
ferret ['fɛrɪt] *n* hurón *m*
▶ **ferret about, ferret around** *vi* rebuscar
▶ **ferret out** *vt* (*secret, truth*) desentrañar

ferry ['fɛrɪ] *n* (*small*) barca de pasaje, balsa; (*large: also*: **ferryboat**) transbordador *m*, ferry *m* ■ *vt* transportar; **to ~ sth/sb across** or **over** transportar algo/a algn a la otra orilla; **to ~ sb to and fro** llevar a algn de un lado para otro
ferryman ['fɛrɪmən] *n* barquero
fertile ['fə:taɪl] *adj* fértil; (*Biol*) fecundo
fertility [fə'tɪlɪtɪ] *n* fertilidad *f*; fecundidad *f*
fertility drug *n* medicamento contra la infertilidad
fertilization [fə:tɪlaɪ'zeɪʃən] *n* fertilización *f*; (*Biol*) fecundación *f*
fertilize ['fə:tɪlaɪz] *vt* fertilizar; (*Biol*) fecundar; (*Agr*) abonar
fertilizer ['fə:tɪlaɪzər] *n* abono, fertilizante *m*
fervent ['fə:vənt] *adj* ferviente
fervour, fervor (*US*) ['fə:vər] *n* fervor *m*, ardor *m*
fester ['fɛstər] *vi* supurar
festival ['fɛstɪvəl] *n* (*Rel*) fiesta; (*Art, Mus*) festival *m*
festive ['fɛstɪv] *adj* festivo; **the ~ season** (*Brit: Christmas*) las Navidades
festivities [fɛs'tɪvɪtɪz] *npl* festejos *mpl*
festoon [fɛs'tu:n] *vt*: **to ~ with** festonear or engalanar de
fetch [fɛtʃ] *vt* ir a buscar; (*Brit: sell for*) venderse por; **how much did it ~?** ¿por cuánto se vendió?
▶ **fetch up** *vi* ir a parar
fetching ['fɛtʃɪŋ] *adj* atractivo
fête [feɪt] *n* fiesta
fetid ['fɛtɪd] *adj* fétido
fetish ['fɛtɪʃ] *n* fetiche *m*
fetter ['fɛtər] *vt* (*person*) encadenar, poner grillos a; (*horse*) trabar; (*fig*) poner trabas a
fetters ['fɛtəz] *npl* grillos *mpl*
fettle ['fɛtl] *n*: **in fine ~** en buenas condiciones
fetus ['fi:təs] *n* (*US*) = **foetus**
feud [fju:d] *n* (*hostility*) enemistad *f*; (*quarrel*) disputa; **a family ~** una pelea familiar
feudal ['fju:dl] *adj* feudal
feudalism ['fju:dəlɪzəm] *n* feudalismo
fever ['fi:vər] *n* fiebre *f*; **he has a ~** tiene fiebre
feverish ['fi:vərɪʃ] *adj* febril
feverishly ['fi:vərɪʃlɪ] *adv* febrilmente
few [fju:] *adj* (*not many*) pocos; (*some*) algunos, unos ■ *pron* algunos; **a ~** *adj* unos pocos; **few people, poca gente; a good ~, quite a ~** bastantes; **in** or **over the next ~ days** en los próximos días; **every ~ weeks** cada dos o tres semanas; **a ~ more days** unos días más
fewer ['fju:ər] *adj* menos
fewest ['fju:ɪst] *adj* los/las menos

FFA *n abbr* = **Future Farmers of America**
FH *abbr* (Brit) = **fire hydrant**
FHA *n abbr* (US: = *Federal Housing Administration*)
oficina federal de la vivienda
fiancé [fɪ'ɑːŋseɪ] *n* novio, prometido
fiancée [fɪ'ɑːŋseɪ] *n* novia, prometida
fiasco [fɪ'æskəʊ] *n* fiasco
fib [fɪb] *n* mentirijilla ■ *vi* decir
mentirijillas
fibre, fiber (US) ['faɪbə'] *n* fibra
fibreboard, fiberboard (US) ['faɪbəbɔːd]
n fibra vulcanizada
fibreglass, fiberglass (US) ['faɪbəglɑːs]
n fibra de vidrio
fibrositis [faɪbrə'saɪtɪs] *n* fibrositis *f inv*
FICA *n abbr* (US) = **Federal Insurance**
Contributions Act
fickle ['fɪkl] *adj* inconstante
fiction ['fɪkʃən] *n* (gen) ficción *f*
fictional ['fɪkʃənl] *adj* novelesco
fictionalize ['fɪkʃənəlaɪz] *vt* novelar
fictitious [fɪk'tɪʃəs] *adj* ficticio
fiddle ['fɪdl] *n* (Mus) violín *m*; (cheating)
trampa ■ *vt* (Brit: accounts) falsificar; **tax ~**
evasión *f* fiscal; **to work a ~** hacer trampa
▶ **fiddle with** *vt fus* juguetear con
fiddler ['fɪdlə'] *n* violinista *m/f*
fiddly ['fɪdlɪ] *adj* (task) delicado, mañoso;
(object) enrevesado
fidelity [fɪ'dɛlɪtɪ] *n* fidelidad *f*
fidget ['fɪdʒɪt] *vi* moverse (nerviosamente)
fidgety ['fɪdʒɪtɪ] *adj* nervioso
fiduciary [fɪ'duːʃɪərɪ] *n* fiduciario(-a)
field [fiːld] *n* (gen) campo; (Comput) campo;
(fig) campo, esfera; (Sport) campo, cancha
(LAm); (competitors) competidores *mpl* ■ *cpd*:
to have a ~ day (fig) ponerse las botas; **to**
lead the ~ (Sport, Comm) llevar la delantera;
to give sth a year's trial in the ~ (fig) sacar
algo al mercado a prueba por un año;
my particular ~ mi especialidad
field glasses *npl* gemelos *mpl*
field hospital *n* hospital *m* de campaña
field marshal *n* mariscal *m*
fieldwork ['fiːldwə:k] *n* (Archaeology, Geo)
trabajo de campo
fiend [fiːnd] *n* demonio
fiendish ['fiːndɪʃ] *adj* diabólico
fierce [fɪəs] *adj* feroz; (wind, attack) violento;
(heat) intenso; (fighting, enemy) encarnizado
fiercely ['fɪəslɪ] *adv* con ferocidad;
violentamente; intensamente;
encarnizadamente
fierceness ['fɪəsnɪs] *n* ferocidad *f*; violencia;
intensidad *f*; encarnizamiento
fiery ['faɪərɪ] *adj* (burning) ardiente;
(temperament) apasionado

FIFA ['fiːfə] *n abbr* (= *Fédération Internationale de*
Football Association) FIFA *f*
fifteen [fɪf'tiːn] *num* quince
fifth [fɪfθ] *adj* quinto
fiftieth ['fɪftɪɪθ] *adj* quincuagésimo
fifty ['fɪftɪ] *num* cincuenta; **the fifties** los
años cincuenta; **to be in one's fifties** andar
por los cincuenta
fifty-fifty ['fɪftɪ'fɪftɪ] *adv*: **to go ~ with sb** ir a
medias con algn ■ *adj*: **we have a ~ chance**
of success tenemos un cincuenta por ciento
de posibilidades de tener éxito
fig [fɪg] *n* higo
fight [faɪt] (pt, pp **fought**) *n* (gen) pelea; (Mil)
combate *m*; (struggle) lucha ■ *vt* luchar
contra; (cancer, alcoholism) combatir; (Law):
to ~ a case defenderse ■ *vi* pelear, luchar;
(quarrel): **to ~ (with sb)** pelear (con algn); (fig):
to ~ (for/against) luchar (por/contra)
▶ **fight back** *vi* defenderse; (after illness)
recuperarse ■ *vt* (tears) contener
▶ **fight down** *vt* (anger, anxiety, urge) reprimir
▶ **fight off** *vt* (attack, attacker) rechazar;
(disease, sleep, urge) luchar contra
▶ **fight out** *vt*: **to ~ it out** decidirlo en una
pelea
fighter ['faɪtə'] *n* combatiente *m/f*; (fig)
luchador(a) *m(f)*; (plane) caza *m*
fighter-bomber ['faɪtəbɔmə'] *n*
cazabombardero
fighter pilot *n* piloto de caza
fighting ['faɪtɪŋ] *n* (gen) el luchar; (battle)
combate *m*; (in streets) disturbios *mpl*
figment ['fɪgmənt] *n*: **a ~ of the imagination**
un producto de la imaginación
figurative ['fɪgjurətɪv] *adj* (meaning) figurado;
(Art) figurativo
figure ['fɪgə'] *n* (Drawing, Geom) figura, dibujo;
(number, cipher) cifra; (person, outline) figura;
(body shape) línea; (: attractive) tipo ■ *vt* (esp
US: think, calculate) calcular, imaginarse ■ *vi*
(appear) figurar; (esp US: make sense) ser lógico;
~ of speech (Ling) figura retórica; **public ~**
personaje *m*
▶ **figure on** *vt fus* (US) contar con
▶ **figure out** *vt* (understand) comprender
figurehead ['fɪgəhɛd] *n* (fig) figura decorativa
figure skating *n* patinaje *m* artístico
Fiji ['fiːdʒiː], **Fiji Islands** *npl* (Islas *fpl*) Fiji
filament ['fɪləmənt] *n* (Elec) filamento
filch [fɪltʃ] *vt* (col: steal) birlar
file [faɪl] *n* (tool) lima; (for nails) lima de uñas;
(dossier) expediente *m*; (folder) carpeta; (in
cabinet) archivo; (Comput) fichero; (row) fila
■ *vt* limar; (papers) clasificar; (Law: claim)
presentar; (store) archivar; **to open/close a ~**
(Comput) abrir/cerrar un fichero; **to ~ in/out**

vi entrar/salir en fila; **to ~ a suit against sb** entablar pleito contra algn; **to ~ past** desfilar ante

file name n (Comput) nombre m de fichero

filibuster ['fɪlɪbʌstəʳ] (esp US Pol) n obstruccionista m/f, filibustero(-a) ■ vi usar maniobras obstruccionistas

filing ['faɪlɪŋ] n: **to do the ~** llevar los archivos

filing cabinet n fichero, archivo

filing clerk n oficinista m/f

fill [fɪl] vt llenar; (tooth) empastar; (vacancy) cubrir ■ n: **to eat one's ~** comer hasta hartarse; **we've already filled that vacancy** ya hemos cubierto esa vacante; **filled with admiration (for)** lleno de admiración (por)
▸**fill in** vt rellenar; (details, report) completar; **to ~ sb in on sth** (col) poner a algn al corriente or al día sobre algo
▸**fill out** vt (form, receipt) rellenar
▸**fill up** vt llenar (hasta el borde) ■ vi (Aut) echar gasolina

fillet ['fɪlɪt] n filete m

fillet steak n filete m de ternera

filling ['fɪlɪŋ] n (Culin) relleno; (for tooth) empaste m

filling station n estación f de servicio

fillip ['fɪlɪp] n estímulo

filly ['fɪlɪ] n potra

film [fɪlm] n película ■ vt (scene) filmar ■ vi rodar

film script n guión m

film star n estrella de cine

filmstrip ['fɪlmstrɪp] n tira de diapositivas

film studio n estudio de cine

Filofax® ['faɪləʊfæks] n agenda (profesional)

filter ['fɪltəʳ] n filtro ■ vt filtrar
▸**filter in, filter through** vi filtrarse

filter coffee n café m (molido) para filtrar

filter lane n (Brit) carril m de selección

filter-tipped ['fɪltətɪpt] adj con filtro

filth [fɪlθ] n suciedad f

filthy ['fɪlθɪ] adj sucio; (language) obsceno

fin [fɪn] n (gen) aleta

final ['faɪnl] adj (last) final, último; (definitive) definitivo ■ n (Sport) final f; **finals** npl (Scol) exámenes mpl finales

final demand n (on invoice etc) último aviso

final dividend n dividendo final

finale [fɪ'nɑːlɪ] n final m

finalist ['faɪnəlɪst] n (Sport) finalista m/f

finality [faɪ'nælɪtɪ] n finalidad f; **with an air of ~** en tono resuelto, de modo terminante

finalize ['faɪnəlaɪz] vt ultimar

finally ['faɪnəlɪ] adv (lastly) por último, finalmente; (eventually) por fin; (irrevocably) de modo definitivo; (once and for all) definitivamente

finance [faɪ'næns] n (money, funds) fondos mpl; **finances** npl finanzas fpl ■ cpd (page, section, company) financiero ■ vt financiar

financial [faɪ'nænʃəl] adj financiero

financially [faɪ'nænʃəlɪ] adv económicamente

financial management n gestión f financiera

financial statement n estado financiero

financial year n ejercicio (financiero)

financier [faɪ'nænsɪəʳ] n financiero(-a)

find [faɪnd] vt (pt, pp **found**) [faund] (gen) encontrar, hallar; (come upon) descubrir ■ n hallazgo; descubrimiento; **to ~ sb guilty** (Law) declarar culpable a algn; **I ~ it easy** me resulta fácil
▸**find out** vt averiguar; (truth, secret) descubrir ■ vi: **to ~ out about** enterarse de

findings ['faɪndɪŋz] npl (Law) veredicto sg, fallo sg; (of report) recomendaciones fpl

fine [faɪn] adj (delicate) fino; (beautiful) hermoso ■ adv (well) bien ■ n (Law) multa ■ vt (Law) multar; **the weather is ~** hace buen tiempo; **he's ~** está muy bien; **you're doing ~** lo estás haciendo muy bien; **to cut it ~** (of time, money) calcular muy justo; **to get a ~ for (doing) sth** recibir una multa por (hacer) algo

fine arts npl bellas artes fpl

finely ['faɪnlɪ] adv (splendidly) con elegancia; (chop) en trozos pequeños, fino; (adjust) con precisión

fineness ['faɪnnɪs] n (of cloth) finura

fine print n: **the ~** la letra pequeña or menuda

finery ['faɪnərɪ] n galas fpl

finesse [fɪ'nɛs] n sutileza

fine-tooth comb ['faɪntuːθ-] n: **to go through sth with a ~** revisar algo a fondo

finger ['fɪŋgəʳ] n dedo ■ vt (touch) manosear; (Mus) puntear; **little/index ~** (dedo) meñique m/índice m

fingernail ['fɪŋgəneɪl] n uña

fingerprint ['fɪŋgəprɪnt] n huella dactilar

fingertip ['fɪŋgətɪp] n yema del dedo; **to have sth at one's fingertips** saber algo al dedillo

finicky ['fɪnɪkɪ] adj (fussy) delicado

finish ['fɪnɪʃ] n (end) fin m; (Sport) meta; (polish etc) acabado ■ vt, vi acabar, terminar; **to ~ doing sth** acabar de hacer algo; **to ~ first/second/third** (Sport) llegar el primero/segundo/tercero; **I've finished with the paper** he terminado con el periódico; **she's finished with him** ha roto or acabado con él
▸**finish off** vt acabar, terminar; (kill) rematar
▸**finish up** vt acabar, terminar ■ vi ir a parar, terminar

finished ['fɪnɪʃt] *adj* (*product*) acabado; (*performance*) pulido; (*col: tired*) rendido, hecho polvo

finishing ['fɪnɪʃɪŋ] *adj*: ~ **touches** toque *m* final

finishing line *n* línea de llegada *or* meta

finishing school *n* colegio para la educación social de señoritas

finite ['faɪnaɪt] *adj* finito

Finland ['fɪnlənd] *n* Finlandia

Finn [fɪn] *n* finlandés(-esa) *m(f)*

Finnish ['fɪnɪʃ] *adj* finlandés(-esa) ▪ *n* (*Ling*) finlandés *m*

fiord [fjɔːd] *n* fiordo

fir [fəːʳ] *n* abeto

fire ['faɪəʳ] *n* fuego; (*accidental, damaging*) incendio ▪ *vt* (*gun*) disparar; (*set fire to*) incendiar; (*excite*) exaltar; (*interest*) despertar; (*dismiss*) despedir ▪ *vi* encenderse; (*Aut: engine*) encender; **electric/gas** ~ estufa eléctrica/de gas; **on** ~ ardiendo, en llamas; **to be on** ~ estar ardiendo; **to catch** ~ prenderse fuego; **to set** ~ **to sth**, **set sth on** ~ prender fuego a algo; **insured against** ~ asegurado contra incendios; **to be/come under** ~ estar/caer bajo el fuego enemigo

fire alarm *n* alarma de incendios

firearm ['faɪərɑːm] *n* arma de fuego

fire brigade, fire department (*US*) *n* (cuerpo de) bomberos *mpl*

fire door *n* puerta contra incendios

fire drill *n* (ejercicio de) simulacro de incendio

fire engine *n* coche *m* de bomberos

fire escape *n* escalera de incendios

fire extinguisher *n* extintor *m*

fireguard ['faɪəgɑːd] *n* pantalla (guardallama)

fire hazard *n* = **fire risk**

fire hydrant *n* boca de incendios

fire insurance *n* seguro contra incendios

fireman ['faɪəmən] *n* bombero

fireplace ['faɪəpleɪs] *n* chimenea

fireplug ['faɪəplʌg] *n* (*US*) boca de incendios

fire practice *n* = **fire drill**

fireproof ['faɪəpruːf] *adj* a prueba de fuego; (*material*) incombustible

fire regulations *npl* reglamentos *mpl* contra incendios

fire risk *n* peligro de incendio

firescreen ['faɪəskriːn] *n* pantalla refractaria

fireside ['faɪəsaɪd] *n*: **by the** ~ al lado de la chimenea

fire station *n* parque *m* de bomberos

firewall ['faɪəwɔːl] *n* (*Internet*) firewall *m*

firewood ['faɪəwud] *n* leña

fireworks ['faɪəwəːks] *npl* fuegos *mpl* artificiales

firing ['faɪərɪŋ] *n* (*Mil*) disparos *mpl*, tiroteo

firing line *n* línea de fuego; **to be in the** ~ (*fig: liable to be criticised*) estar en la línea de fuego

firing squad *n* pelotón *m* de ejecución

firm [fəːm] *adj* firme; (*offer, decision*) en firme ▪ *n* empresa; **to be a** ~ **believer in sth** ser un partidario convencido de algo; **to stand** ~ *or* **take a** ~ **stand on sth** (*fig*) mantenerse firme ante algo

firmly ['fəːmlɪ] *adv* firmemente

firmness ['fəːmnɪs] *n* firmeza

first [fəːst] *adj* primero ▪ *adv* (*before others*) primero; (*when listing reasons etc*) en primer lugar, primeramente ▪ *n* (*person: in race*) primero(-a); (*Aut: also*: **first gear**) primera; **at** ~ al principio; ~ **of all** ante todo; **the** ~ **of January** el uno *or* primero de enero; **in the** ~ **instance** en primer lugar; **I'll do it** ~ **thing tomorrow** lo haré mañana a primera hora; **for the** ~ **time** por primera vez; **head** ~ de cabeza; **from the (very)** ~ desde el principio

first aid *n* primeros auxilios *mpl*

first aid kit *n* botiquín *m*

first aid post, first aid station (*US*) *n* puesto de auxilio

first-class ['fəːstklɑːs] *adj* de primera clase; ~ **ticket** (*Rail etc*) billete *m or* (*LAm*) boleto de primera clase; ~ **mail** correo de primera clase

first-hand [fəːst'hænd] *adj* de primera mano

first lady *n* (*esp US*) primera dama

firstly ['fəːstlɪ] *adv* en primer lugar

first name *n* nombre *m* de pila

first night *n* estreno

first-rate [fəːst'reɪt] *adj* de primera (clase)

first-time buyer [fəːsttaɪm-] *n* persona que compra su primera vivienda

fir tree *n* abeto

fiscal ['fɪskəl] *adj* fiscal; ~ **year** año fiscal, ejercicio

fish [fɪʃ] *n pl inv* pez *m*; (*food*) pescado ▪ *vt* pescar en ▪ *vi* pescar; **to go fishing** ir de pesca

▶ **fish out** *vt* (*from water, box etc*) sacar

fish-and-chip shop *n* = **chip shop**

fishbone ['fɪʃbəun] *n* espina

fisherman ['fɪʃəmən] *n* pescador *m*

fishery ['fɪʃərɪ] *n* pesquería

fish factory *n* fábrica de elaboración de pescado

fish farm *n* piscifactoría

fish fingers *npl* (*Brit*) palitos *mpl* de pescado (empanado)

fishing boat ['fɪʃɪŋ-] *n* barca de pesca

fishing industry *n* industria pesquera

fishing line n sedal m
fishing net n red f de pesca
fishing rod n caña (de pescar)
fishing tackle n aparejo (de pescar)
fish market n mercado de pescado
fishmonger ['fɪʃmʌŋgəʳ] n (Brit) pescadero(-a)
fishmonger's, fishmonger's shop n (Brit) pescadería
fishseller ['fɪʃsɛləʳ] n (US) = **fishmonger**
fish slice n paleta para pescado
fish sticks npl (US) = **fish fingers**
fishstore ['fɪʃstɔːʳ] n (US) = **fishmonger's**
fishy ['fɪʃɪ] adj (fig) sospechoso
fission ['fɪʃən] n fisión f; **atomic/nuclear ~** fisión f atómica/nuclear
fissure ['fɪʃəʳ] n fisura
fist [fɪst] n puño
fistfight ['fɪstfaɪt] n lucha a puñetazos
fit [fɪt] adj (Med, Sport) en (buena) forma; (proper) adecuado, apropiado ■ vt (clothes) quedar bien a; (try on: clothes) probar; (match: facts) cuadrar or corresponder or coincidir con; (: description) estar de acuerdo con; (accommodate) ajustar, adaptar ■ vi (clothes) quedar bien; (in space, gap) caber; (facts) coincidir ■ n (Med) ataque m; (outburst) arranque m; **~ to** apto para; **~ for** apropiado para; **do as you think** or **see ~** haz lo que te parezca mejor; **to keep ~** mantenerse en forma; **to be ~ for work** (after illness) estar en condiciones para trabajar; **~ of coughing** acceso de tos; **~ of anger/enthusiasm** arranque de cólera/entusiasmo; **to have** or **suffer a ~** tener un ataque or acceso; **this dress is a good ~** este vestido me queda bien; **by fits and starts** a rachas
▶ **fit in** vi encajar ■ vt (object) acomodar; (fig: appointment, visitor) encontrar un hueco para; **to ~ in with sb's plans** acomodarse a los planes de algn
▶ **fit out** vt, (Brit) **fit up** equipar
fitful ['fɪtful] adj espasmódico, intermitente
fitfully ['fɪtfəlɪ] adv irregularmente; **to sleep ~** dormir a rachas
fitment ['fɪtmənt] n mueble m
fitness ['fɪtnɪs] n (Med) forma física; (of remark) conveniencia
fitted carpet ['fɪtɪd-] n moqueta
fitted cupboards ['fɪtɪd-] npl armarios mpl empotrados
fitted kitchen ['fɪtɪd-] n cocina amueblada
fitter ['fɪtəʳ] n ajustador(a) m(f)
fitting ['fɪtɪŋ] adj apropiado ■ n (of dress) prueba; see also **fittings**
fitting room n (in shop) probador m
fittings ['fɪtɪŋz] npl instalaciones fpl
five [faɪv] num cinco; **she is ~ (years old)** tiene cinco años (de edad); **it costs ~ pounds** cuesta cinco libras; **it's ~ (o'clock)** son las cinco
five-day week ['faɪvdeɪ] n semana inglesa
fiver ['faɪvəʳ] n (col: Brit) billete m de cinco libras; (: US) billete m de cinco dólares
fix [fɪks] vt (secure) fijar, asegurar; (mend) arreglar; (make ready: meal, drink) preparar ■ n: **to be in a ~** estar en un aprieto; **to ~ sth in one's mind** fijar algo en la memoria; **the fight was a ~** (col) la pelea estaba amañada
▶ **fix on** vt (decide on) fijar
▶ **fix up** vt (arrange: date, meeting) arreglar; **to ~ sb up with sth** conseguirle algo a algn
fixation [fɪk'seɪʃən] n (Psych) fijación f
fixative ['fɪksətɪv] n fijador m
fixed [fɪkst] adj (prices etc) fijo; **how are you ~ for money?** (col) ¿qué tal andas de dinero?
fixed assets npl activo sg fijo
fixed charge n gasto fijo
fixture ['fɪkstʃəʳ] n (Sport) encuentro; **fixtures** npl instalaciones fpl fijas
fizz [fɪz] vi burbujear
fizzle out ['fɪzl-] vi apagarse; (enthusiasm, interest) decaer; (plan) quedar en agua de borrajas
fizzy ['fɪzɪ] adj (drink) gaseoso
fjord [fjɔːd] n = **fiord**
FL, Fla. abbr (US) = **Florida**
flabbergasted ['flæbəgɑːstɪd] adj pasmado
flabby ['flæbɪ] adj flojo (de carnes); (skin) fofo
flag [flæg] n bandera; (stone) losa ■ vi decaer; **~ of convenience** pabellón m de conveniencia
▶ **flag down** vt: **to ~ sb down** hacer señas a algn para que se pare
flagpole ['flægpəul] n asta de bandera
flagrant ['fleɪgrənt] adj flagrante
flagship ['flægʃɪp] n buque m insignia or almirante
flagstone ['flægstəun] n losa
flag stop n (US) parada discrecional
flair [fleəʳ] n aptitud f especial
flak [flæk] n (Mil) fuego antiaéreo; (col: criticism) lluvia de críticas
flake [fleɪk] n (of rust, paint) desconchón m; (of snow) copo; (of soap powder) escama ■ vi (also: **flake off**: paint) desconcharse; (skin) descamarse
flaky ['fleɪkɪ] adj (paintwork) desconchado; (skin) escamoso
flaky pastry n (Culin) hojaldre m
flamboyant [flæm'bɔɪənt] adj (dress) vistoso; (person) extravagante
flame [fleɪm] n llama; **to burst into flames** incendiarse; **old ~** (col) antiguo amor m/f
flamingo [flə'mɪŋgəu] n flamenco

f

flammable ['flæməbl] *adj* inflamable
flan [flæn] *n* (*Brit*) tarta
flank [flæŋk] *n* flanco; (*of person*) costado
■ *vt* flanquear
flannel ['flænl] *n* (*Brit: also*: **face flannel**)
toallita; (*fabric*) franela; **flannels** *npl*
pantalones *mpl* de franela
flannelette [flænə'lɛt] *n* franela de algodón
flap [flæp] *n* (*of pocket, envelope*) solapa; (*of table*) hoja (plegadiza); (*wing movement*)
aletazo; (*Aviat*) flap *m* ■ *vt* (*wings*) batir
■ *vi* (*sail, flag*) ondear
flapjack ['flæpdʒæk] *n* (*US: pancake*) torta,
panqueque *m* (*LAm*)
flare [flɛər] *n* llamarada; (*Mil*) bengala; (*in skirt etc*) vuelo
▶ **flare up** *vi* encenderse; (*fig: person*)
encolerizarse; (*: revolt*) estallar
flash [flæʃ] *n* relámpago; (*also*: **news flash**)
noticias *fpl* de última hora; (*Phot*) flash *m*;
(*US: torch*) linterna ■ *vt* (*light, headlights*)
lanzar destellos con; (*torch*) encender
■ *vi* destellar; **in a ~** en un santiamén; **~ of**
inspiration ráfaga de inspiración; **to ~ sth**
about (*fig, col: flaunt*) ostentar algo, presumir
con algo; **he flashed by** *or* **past** pasó como
un rayo
flashback ['flæʃbæk] *n* flashback *m*, escena
retrospectiva
flashbulb ['flæʃbʌlb] *n* bombilla de flash
flash card *n* (*Scol*) tarjeta
flasher ['flæʃər] *n* exhibicionista *m*
flashlight ['flæʃlaɪt] *n* (*US: torch*) linterna
flashpoint ['flæʃpɔɪnt] *n* punto de
inflamación; (*fig*) punto de explosión
flashy ['flæʃɪ] *adj* (*pej*) ostentoso
flask [flɑːsk] *n* petaca; (*also*: **vacuum flask**)
termo
flat [flæt] *adj* llano; (*smooth*) liso; (*tyre*)
desinflado; (*battery*) descargado; (*beer*) sin
gas; (*Mus: instrument*) desafinado ■ *n* (*Brit:
apartment*) piso (*SP*), departamento (*LAm*),
apartamento; (*Aut*) pinchazo; (*Mus*) bemol
m; (**to work**) **~ out** (trabajar) a tope; **~ rate**
of pay sueldo fijo
flatfooted [flæt'futɪd] *adj* de pies planos
flatly ['flætlɪ] *adv* rotundamente, de plano
flatmate ['flætmeɪt] *n* compañero(-a) de piso
flatness ['flætnɪs] *n* (*of land*) llanura, lo llano
flat pack *n*: **it comes in a ~** viene en un
paquete plano para su automontaje
flat-pack *adj*: **~ furniture** muebles *mpl*
automontables (*embalados en paquetes planos*)
flat-screen ['flætskriːn] *adj* de pantalla
plana
flatten ['flætn] *vt* (*also*: **flatten out**) allanar;
(*smooth out*) alisar; (*house, city*) arrasar

flatter ['flætər] *vt* adular, halagar; (*show to advantage*) favorecer
flatterer ['flætərər] *n* adulador(a) *m(f)*
flattering ['flætərɪŋ] *adj* halagador(a);
(*clothes etc*) que favorece, favorecedor(a)
flattery ['flætərɪ] *n* adulación *f*
flatulence ['flætjuləns] *n* flatulencia
flaunt [flɔːnt] *vt* ostentar, lucir
flavour, flavor (*US*) ['fleɪvər] *n* sabor *m*, gusto
■ *vt* sazonar, condimentar; **strawberry**
flavoured con sabor a fresa
flavouring, flavoring (*US*) ['fleɪvərɪŋ] *n*
(*in product*) aromatizante *m*
flaw [flɔː] *n* defecto
flawless ['flɔːlɪs] *adj* intachable
flax [flæks] *n* lino
flaxen ['flæksən] *adj* muy rubio
flea [fliː] *n* pulga
flea market *n* rastro, mercadillo
fleck [flɛk] *n* mota ■ *vt* (*with blood, mud
etc*) salpicar; **brown flecked with white**
marrón con motas blancas
fledgeling, fledgling ['flɛdʒlɪŋ] *n* (*fig*)
novato(-a), principiante *m/f*
flee [fliː] (*pt, pp* **fled**) [flɛd] *vt* huir de,
abandonar ■ *vi* huir
fleece [fliːs] *n* (*of sheep*) vellón *m*; (*wool*) lana;
(*top*) forro polar ■ *vt* (*col*) desplumar
fleecy ['fliːsɪ] *adj* (*blanket*) lanoso, lanudo;
(*cloud*) aborregado
fleet [fliːt] *n* flota; (*of cars, lorries etc*) parque *m*
fleeting ['fliːtɪŋ] *adj* fugaz
Flemish ['flɛmɪʃ] *adj* flamenco ■ *n* (*Ling*)
flamenco; **the ~** los flamencos
flesh [flɛʃ] *n* carne *f*; (*of fruit*) pulpa; **of ~ and**
blood de carne y hueso
flesh wound *n* herida superficial
flew [fluː] *pt of* **fly**
flex [flɛks] *n* cable *m* ■ *vt* (*muscles*) tensar
flexibility [flɛksɪ'bɪlɪtɪ] *n* flexibilidad *f*
flexible ['flɛksəbl] *adj* flexible; **~ working**
hours horario *sg* flexible
flexitime ['flɛksɪtaɪm] *n* horario flexible
flick [flɪk] *n* golpecito; (*with finger*) capirotazo;
(*Brit: col: film*) película ■ *vt* dar un golpecito a
▶ **flick off** *vt* quitar con el dedo
▶ **flick through** *vt fus* hojear
flicker ['flɪkər] *vi* (*light*) parpadear; (*flame*)
vacilar ■ *n* parpadeo
flick knife *n* navaja de muelle
flier ['flaɪər] *n* aviador(a) *m(f)*
flies [flaɪz] *npl of* **fly**
flight [flaɪt] *n* vuelo; (*escape*) huida, fuga;
(*also*: **flight of steps**) tramo (de escaleras);
to take ~ huir, darse a la fuga; **to put to**
~ ahuyentar; **how long does the ~ take?**
¿cuánto dura el vuelo?

flight attendant *n* (*US*) auxiliar *m/f* de vuelo
flight deck *n* (*Aviat*) cabina de mandos
flight path *n* trayectoria de vuelo
flight recorder *n* registrador *m* de vuelo
flighty ['flaɪtɪ] *adj* caprichoso
flimsy ['flɪmzɪ] *adj* (*thin*) muy ligero; (*excuse*) flojo
flinch [flɪntʃ] *vi* encogerse
fling [flɪŋ] *vt* (*pt, pp* **flung**) [flʌŋ] arrojar ▪ *n* (*love affair*) aventura amorosa
flint [flɪnt] *n* pedernal *m*; (*in lighter*) piedra
flip [flɪp] *vt*: **to ~ a coin** echar a cara o cruz
▸ **flip over** *vt* dar la vuelta a
▸ **flip through** *vt fus* (*book*) hojear; (*records*) ver de pasada
flippancy ['flɪpənsɪ] *n* ligereza
flippant ['flɪpənt] *adj* poco serio
flipper ['flɪpəʳ] *n* aleta
flip side *n* (*of record*) cara B
flirt [flə:t] *vi* coquetear, flirtear ▪ *n* coqueta *f*
flirtation [flə:'teɪʃən] *n* coqueteo, flirteo
flit [flɪt] *vi* revolotear
float [fləut] *n* flotador *m*; (*in procession*) carroza; (*sum of money*) (dinero suelto para) cambio ▪ *vi* (*Comm: currency*) flotar ▪ *vt* (*gen*) hacer flotar; (*company*) lanzar; **to ~ an idea** plantear una idea
floating ['fləutɪŋ] *adj*: **~ vote** voto indeciso; **~ voter** votante *m/f* indeciso(-a)
flock [flɔk] *n* (*of sheep*) rebaño; (*of birds*) bandada; (*of people*) multitud *f*
floe [fləu] *n*: **ice ~** témpano de hielo
flog [flɔg] *vt* azotar; (*col*) vender
flood [flʌd] *n* inundación *f*; (*of words, tears etc*) torrente *m* ▪ *vt* (*Aut: carburettor*) inundar; (*also*: **to flood the market**: *Comm*) inundar el mercado
flooding ['flʌdɪŋ] *n* inundación *f*
floodlight ['flʌdlaɪt] *n* foco ▪ *vt* (*irreg: like* **light**) iluminar con focos
floodlit ['flʌdlɪt] *pt, pp of* **floodlight** ▪ *adj* iluminado
flood tide *n* pleamar *f*
floodwater ['flʌdwɔ:təʳ] *n* aguas *fpl* (*de la inundación*)
floor [flɔ:ʳ] *n* suelo, piso (*LAm*); (*storey*) piso; (*of sea, valley*) fondo; (*dance floor*) pista ▪ *vt* (*fig: baffle*) dejar anonadado; **ground ~**, (*US*) **first ~** planta baja; **first ~**, (*US*) **second ~** primer piso; **top ~** último piso; **to have the ~** (*speaker*) tener la palabra
floorboard ['flɔ:bɔ:d] *n* tabla
flooring ['flɔ:rɪŋ] *n* suelo; (*material*) solería
floor lamp *n* (*US*) lámpara de pie
floor show *n* cabaret *m*
floorwalker ['flɔ:wɔ:kəʳ] *n* (*US Comm*) supervisor(a) *m(f)*

flop [flɔp] *n* fracaso ▪ *vi* (*fail*) fracasar
flora ['flɔ:rə] *n* flora
floral ['flɔ:rl] *adj* floral; (*dress, wallpaper*) de flores
Florence ['flɔrəns] *n* Florencia
Florentine ['flɔrəntaɪn] *adj, n* florentino(-a) *m(f)*
florid ['flɔrɪd] *adj* (*style*) florido
florist ['flɔrɪst] *n* florista *m/f*; **~'s (shop)** *n* floristería
flotation [fləu'teɪʃən] *n* (*of shares*) emisión *f*; (*of company*) lanzamiento
flounce [flauns] *n* volante *m*
▸ **flounce in** *vi* entrar con gesto exagerado
▸ **flounce out** *vi* salir con gesto airado
flounder ['flaundəʳ] *vi* tropezar ▪ *n* (*Zool*) platija
flour ['flauəʳ] *n* harina
flourish ['flʌrɪʃ] *vi* florecer ▪ *n* ademán *m*, movimiento (ostentoso)
flourishing ['flʌrɪʃɪŋ] *adj* floreciente
flout [flaut] *vt* burlarse de; (*order*) no hacer caso de, hacer caso omiso de
flow [fləu] *n* (*movement*) flujo; (*direction*) curso; (*Elec*) corriente *f* ▪ *vi* correr, fluir
flow chart *n* organigrama *m*
flow diagram *n* organigrama *m*
flower ['flauəʳ] *n* flor *f* ▪ *vi* florecer; **in ~** en flor
flower bed *n* macizo
flowerpot ['flauəpɔt] *n* tiesto
flowery ['flauərɪ] *adj* florido; (*perfume, pattern*) de flores
flowing ['fləuɪŋ] *adj* (*hair, clothes*) suelto; (*style*) fluido
flown [fləun] *pp of* **fly**
flu [flu:] *n* gripe *f*
fluctuate ['flʌktjueɪt] *vi* fluctuar
fluctuation [flʌktju'eɪʃən] *n* fluctuación *f*
flue [flu:] *n* cañón *m*
fluency ['flu:ənsɪ] *n* fluidez *f*, soltura
fluent ['flu:ənt] *adj* (*speech*) elocuente; **he speaks ~ French, he's ~ in French** domina el francés
fluently ['flu:əntlɪ] *adv* con soltura
fluff [flʌf] *n* pelusa
fluffy ['flʌfɪ] *adj* lanoso
fluid ['flu:ɪd] *adj, n* fluido, líquido; (*in diet*) líquido
fluke [flu:k] *n* (*col*) chiripa
flummox ['flʌməks] *vt* desconcertar
flung [flʌŋ] *pt, pp of* **fling**
flunky ['flʌŋkɪ] *n* lacayo
fluorescent [fluə'rɛsnt] *adj* fluorescente
fluoride ['fluəraɪd] *n* fluoruro
fluoride toothpaste *n* pasta de dientes con flúor

flurry ['flʌrɪ] n (of snow) ventisca; (haste) agitación f; ~ **of activity** frenesí m de actividad

flush [flʌʃ] n (on face) rubor m; (fig: of youth, beauty) resplandor m ▪ vt limpiar con agua; (also: **flush out**: game, birds) levantar; (fig: criminal) poner al descubierto ▪ vi ruborizarse ▪ adj: ~ **with** a ras de; **to ~ the toilet** tirar de la cadena (del wáter); **hot flushes** (Med) sofocos mpl

flushed [flʌʃt] adj ruborizado

fluster ['flʌstər] n aturdimiento ▪ vt aturdir

flustered ['flʌstəd] adj aturdido

flute [fluːt] n flauta travesera

flutter ['flʌtər] n (of wings) revoloteo, aleteo; (col: bet) apuesta ▪ vi revolotear; **to be in a ~** estar nervioso

flux [flʌks] n flujo; **in a state of ~** cambiando continuamente

fly [flaɪ] (pt **flew**, pp **flown**) n (insect) mosca; (on trousers: also: **flies**) bragueta ▪ vt (plane) pilotar; (cargo) transportar (en avión); (distance) recorrer (en avión) ▪ vi volar; (passenger) ir en avión; (escape) evadirse; (flag) ondear

▸ **fly away** vi (bird, insect) irse volando

▸ **fly in** vi (person) llegar en avión; (plane) aterrizar; **he flew in from Bilbao** llegó en avión desde Bilbao

▸ **fly off** vi irse volando

▸ **fly out** vi irse en avión

fly-fishing ['flaɪfɪʃɪŋ] n pesca con mosca

flying ['flaɪɪŋ] n (activity) (el) volar ▪ adj: ~ **visit** visita relámpago; **with ~ colours** con lucimiento

flying buttress n arbotante m

flying picket n piquete m volante

flying saucer n platillo volante

flying squad n (Police) brigada móvil

flying start n: **to get off to a ~** empezar con buen pie

flyleaf (pl **flyleaves**) ['flaɪliːf, -liːvz] n (hoja de) guarda

flyover ['flaɪəuvər] n (Brit: bridge) paso elevado or (LAm) a desnivel

flypast ['flaɪpɑːst] n desfile m aéreo

flysheet ['flaɪʃiːt] n (for tent) doble techo

flyswatter ['flaɪswɔtər] n matamoscas m inv

flyweight ['flaɪweɪt] adj de peso mosca ▪ n peso mosca

flywheel ['flaɪwiːl] n volante m (de motor)

FM abbr (Radio: = frequency modulation) FM; (Brit Mil) = **field marshal**

FMB n abbr (US) = **Federal Maritime Board**

FMCS n abbr (US: = Federal Mediation and Conciliation Services) organismo de conciliación en conflictos laborales

FO n abbr (Brit: = Foreign Office) ≈ Min. de AA. EE

foal [fəul] n potro

foam [fəum] n espuma ▪ vi hacer espuma

foam rubber n goma espuma

FOB abbr (= free on board) f.a.b.

fob [fɔb] n (also: **watch fob**) leontina ▪ vt: **to ~ sb off with sth** deshacerse de algn con algo

foc abbr (Brit: = free of charge) gratis

focal ['fəukəl] adj focal; ~ **point** punto focal; (fig) centro de atención

focus ['fəukəs] (pl **focuses**) n foco ▪ vt (field glasses etc) enfocar ▪ vi: **to ~ (on)** enfocar (a); (issue etc) centrarse en; **in/out of ~** enfocado/desenfocado

fodder ['fɔdər] n pienso

FOE n abbr (= Friends of the Earth) Amigos mpl de la Tierra; (US: = Fraternal Order of Eagles) organización benéfica

foe [fəu] n enemigo

foetus, fetus (US) ['fiːtəs] n feto

fog [fɔg] n niebla

fogbound ['fɔgbaund] adj inmovilizado por la niebla

foggy ['fɔgɪ] adj: **it's ~** hay niebla

fog lamp, fog light (US) n (Aut) faro antiniebla

foible ['fɔɪbl] n manía

foil [fɔɪl] vt frustrar ▪ n hoja; (also: **kitchen foil**) papel m (de) aluminio; (Fencing) florete m

foist [fɔɪst] vt: **to ~ sth on sb** endilgarle algo a algn

fold [fəuld] n (bend, crease) pliegue m; (Agr) redil m ▪ vt doblar; (map etc) plegar; **to ~ one's arms** cruzarse de brazos

▸ **fold up** vi plegarse, doblarse; (business) quebrar

folder ['fəuldər] n (for papers) carpeta; (binder) carpeta de anillas; (brochure) folleto

folding ['fəuldɪŋ] adj (chair, bed) plegable

foliage ['fəulɪɪdʒ] n follaje m

folio ['fəulɪəu] n folio

folk [fəuk] npl gente f ▪ adj popular, folklórico; **folks** npl familia, parientes mpl

folklore ['fəuklɔːr] n folklore m

folk music n música folk

folk singer n cantante m/f de música folk

folk song n canción f popular or folk

follow ['fɔləu] vt seguir ▪ vi seguir; (result) resultar; **he followed suit** hizo lo mismo; **to ~ sb's advice** seguir el consejo de algn; **I don't quite ~ you** no te comprendo muy bien; **to ~ in sb's footsteps** seguir los pasos de algn; **it doesn't ~ that ...** no se deduce que ....

▸ **follow on** vi seguir; (continue): **to ~ on from** ser la consecuencia lógica de

▶**follow out** vt (implement: idea, plan) realizar, llevar a cabo

▶**follow through** vt llevar hasta el fin ▪ vi (Sport) dar el remate

▶**follow up** vt (letter, offer) responder a; (case) investigar

follower ['fɔləuəʳ] n seguidor(a) m(f); (Pol) partidario(-a)

following ['fɔləuɪŋ] adj siguiente ▪ n seguidores mpl

follow-up ['fɔləuʌp] n continuación f

follow-up letter n carta recordatoria

folly ['fɔlɪ] n locura

fond [fɔnd] adj (loving) cariñoso; **to be ~ of sb** tener cariño a algn; **she's ~ of swimming** tiene afición a la natación, le gusta nadar

fondle ['fɔndl] vt acariciar

fondly ['fɔndlɪ] adv (lovingly) con cariño; **he ~ believed that ...** creía ingenuamente que ...

fondness ['fɔndnɪs] n (for things) afición f; (for people) cariño

font [fɔnt] n pila bautismal

food [fu:d] n comida

food chain n cadena alimenticia

food mixer n batidora

food poisoning n intoxicación f alimentaria

food processor n robot m de cocina

food stamp n (US) vale m para comida

foodstuffs ['fu:dstʌfs] npl comestibles mpl

fool [fu:l] n tonto(-a); (Culin) mousse m de frutas ▪ vt engañar; **to make a ~ of o.s.** ponerse en ridículo; **you can't ~ me** a mí no me engañas; see also **April Fool's Day**

▶**fool about, fool around** vi hacer el tonto

foolhardy ['fu:lhɑ:dɪ] adj temerario

foolish ['fu:lɪʃ] adj tonto; (careless) imprudente

foolishly ['fu:lɪʃlɪ] adv tontamente, neciamente

foolproof ['fu:lpru:f] adj (plan etc) infalible

foolscap ['fu:lskæp] n ≈ papel m tamaño folio

foot [fut ʃ] (pl **feet**) n (Anat) pie m; (of page, stairs, mountain) pie m; (measure) pie (=304 mm); (of animal, table) pata ▪ vt (bill) pagar; **on ~** a pie; **to find one's feet** acostumbrarse; **to put one's ~ down** (say no) plantarse; (Aut) pisar el acelerador

footage ['futɪdʒ] n (Cine) imágenes fpl

foot-and-mouth [futənd'mauθ-], **foot-and-mouth disease** n fiebre f aftosa

football ['futbɔ:l] n balón m; (game: Brit) fútbol m; (US) fútbol m americano

footballer ['futbɔ:ləʳ] n (Brit) = **football player**

football match n partido de fútbol

football player n futbolista m/f, jugador(a) m(f) de fútbol

footbrake ['futbreɪk] n freno de pie

footbridge ['futbrɪdʒ] n pasarela, puente m para peatones

foothills ['futhɪlz] npl estribaciones fpl

foothold ['futhəuld] n pie m firme

footing ['futɪŋ] n (fig) nivel m; **to lose one's ~** perder el equilibrio; **on an equal ~** en pie de igualdad

footlights ['futlaɪts] npl candilejas fpl

footman ['futmən] n lacayo

footnote ['futnəut] n nota (de pie de página)

footpath ['futpɑ:θ] n sendero

footprint ['futprɪnt] n huella, pisada

footrest ['futrɛst] n apoyapiés m inv

footsie ['futsɪ] n: **to play ~ with sb** (col) juguetear con los pies de algn

footsore ['futsɔ:ʳ] adj con los pies doloridos

footstep ['futstɛp] n paso

footwear ['futwɛəʳ] n calzado

FOR abbr (= free on rail) franco (puesto sobre) vagón

 KEYWORD

for [fɔ:] prep **1** (indicating destination, intention) para; **the train for London** el tren para Londres; (in announcements) el tren con destino a Londres; **he left for Rome** marchó para Roma; **he went for the paper** fue por el periódico; **is this for me?** ¿es esto para mí?; **it's time for lunch** es la hora de comer

2 (indicating purpose) para; **what('s it) for?** ¿para qué (es)?; **what's this button for?** ¿para qué sirve este botón?; **to pray for peace** rezar por la paz

3 (on behalf of, representing): **the MP for Hove** el diputado por Hove; **he works for the government/a local firm** trabaja para el gobierno/en una empresa local; **I'll ask him for you** se lo pediré por ti; **G for George** G de Gerona

4 (because of) por esta razón; **for fear of being criticized** por temor a ser criticado

5 (with regard to) para; **it's cold for July** hace frío para julio; **he has a gift for languages** tiene don de lenguas

6 (in exchange for) por; **I sold it for £5** lo vendí por £5; **to pay 50 pence for a ticket** pagar 50 peniques por un billete

7 (in favour of): **are you for or against us?** ¿estás con nosotros o contra nosotros?; **I'm all for it** estoy totalmente a favor; **vote for X** vote (a) X

8 (referring to distance): **there are roadworks for 5 km** hay obras en 5 km; **we walked for miles** caminamos kilómetros y kilómetros

9 (referring to time): **he was away for two**

years estuvo fuera (durante) dos años;
it hasn't rained for three weeks no ha
llovido durante *or* en tres semanas; **I have
known her for years** la conozco desde hace
años; **can you do it for tomorrow?**
¿lo podrás hacer para mañana?
10 (*with infinitive clauses*): **it is not for me to
decide** la decisión no es cosa mía; **it would
be best for you to leave** sería mejor que te
fueras; **there is still time for you to do it**
todavía te queda tiempo para hacerlo; **for
this to be possible ...** para que esto sea
posible ...
11 (*in spite of*) a pesar de; **for all his
complaints** a pesar de sus quejas
■ *conj* (*since, as: rather formal*) puesto que

forage ['fɔrɪdʒ] *n* forraje *m*
foray ['fɔreɪ] *n* incursión *f*
forbid (*pt* **forbad(e)**, *pp* **forbidden**)
[fə'bɪd, -'bæd, -'bɪdn] *vt* prohibir; **to ~ sb to
do sth** prohibir a algn hacer algo
forbidding [fə'bɪdɪŋ] *adj* (*landscape*) inhóspito;
(*severe*) severo
force [fɔ:s] *n* fuerza ■ *vt* obligar, forzar;
to ~ o.s. to do hacer un esfuerzo por hacer;
the Forces *npl* (*Brit*) las Fuerzas Armadas;
sales ~ (*Comm*) personal *m* de ventas; **a ~ 5
wind** un viento fuerza 5; **to join forces** unir
fuerzas; **in ~** (*law etc*) en vigor; **to ~ sb to do
sth** obligar a algn a hacer algo
▶ **force back** *vt* (*crowd, enemy*) hacer
retroceder; (*tears*) reprimir
▶ **force down** *vt* (*food*) tragar con esfuerzo
forced [fɔ:st] *adj* (*smile*) forzado; (*landing*)
forzoso
force-feed ['fɔ:sfi:d] *vt* (*animal, prisoner*)
alimentar a la fuerza
forceful ['fɔ:sful] *adj* enérgico
forcemeat ['fɔ:smi:t] *n* (*Culin*) relleno
forceps ['fɔ:sɛps] *npl* fórceps *m inv*
forcible ['fɔ:səbl] *adj* (*violent*) a la fuerza;
(*telling*) convincente
forcibly ['fɔ:səblɪ] *adv* a la fuerza
ford [fɔ:d] *n* vado ■ *vt* vadear
fore [fɔ:ʳ] *n*: **to bring to the ~** sacar a la
luz pública; **to come to the ~** empezar a
destacar
forearm ['fɔ:rɑ:m] *n* antebrazo
forebear ['fɔ:bɛəʳ] *n* antepasado
foreboding [fɔ:'bəudɪŋ] *n* presentimiento
forecast ['fɔ:kɑ:st] *n* pronóstico ■ *vt* (*irreg:
like* **cast**) pronosticar; **weather ~** previsión *f*
meteorológica
foreclose [fɔ:'kləuz] *vt* (*Law: also*: **foreclose
on**) extinguir el derecho de redimir
foreclosure [fɔ:'kləuʒəʳ] *n* apertura de un

juicio hipotecario
forecourt ['fɔ:kɔ:t] *n* (*of garage*) área de
entrada
forefathers ['fɔ:fɑ:ðəz] *npl* antepasados *mpl*
forefinger ['fɔ:fɪŋgəʳ] *n* (dedo) índice *m*
forefront ['fɔ:frʌnt] *n*: **in the ~ of** en la
vanguardia de
forego (*pt* **forewent**, *pp* **foregone**)
[fɔ:'gəu, -'wɛnt, -'gɔn] *vt* = **forgo**
foregoing ['fɔ:gəuɪŋ] *adj* anterior, precedente
foregone ['fɔ:gɔn] *pp of* **forego** ■ *adj*: **it's a ~
conclusion** es una conclusión inevitable
foreground ['fɔ:graund] *n* primer plano *m*
(*also Comput*)
forehand ['fɔ:hænd] *n* (*Tennis*) derechazo
directo
forehead ['fɔrɪd] *n* frente *f*
foreign ['fɔrɪn] *adj* extranjero; (*trade*) exterior
foreign currency *n* divisas *fpl*
foreigner ['fɔrɪnəʳ] *n* extranjero(-a)
foreign exchange *n* (*system*) cambio
de divisas; (*money*) divisas *fpl*, moneda
extranjera
foreign investment *n* inversión *f* en el
extranjero; (*money, stock*) inversiones *fpl*
extranjeras
Foreign Minister *n* Ministro(-a) de Asuntos
Exteriores, Canciller *m* (*LAm*)
Foreign Office *n* Ministerio de Asuntos
Exteriores
Foreign Secretary *n* (*Brit*) Ministro(-a) de
Asuntos Exteriores, Canciller *m* (*LAm*)
foreleg ['fɔ:lɛg] *n* pata delantera
foreman ['fɔ:mən] *n* capataz *m*; (*Law: of jury*)
presidente *m/f*
foremost ['fɔ:məust] *adj* principal ■ *adv*:
first and ~ ante todo, antes que nada
forename ['fɔ:neɪm] *n* nombre *m* (de pila)
forensic [fə'rɛnsɪk] *adj* forense; **~ scientist**
forense *m/f*
foreplay ['fɔ:pleɪ] *n* preámbulos *mpl* (*de
estimulación sexual*)
forerunner ['fɔ:rʌnəʳ] *n* precursor(a) *m(f)*
foresee (*pt* **foresaw**, *pp* **foreseen**)
[fɔ:'si:, -'sɔ:, -'si:n] *vt* prever
foreseeable [fɔ:'si:əbl] *adj* previsible
foreshadow [fɔ:'ʃædəu] *vt* prefigurar,
anunciar
foreshore ['fɔ:ʃɔ:ʳ] *n* playa
foreshorten [fɔ:'ʃɔ:tn] *vt* (*figure, scene*)
escorzar
foresight ['fɔ:saɪt] *n* previsión *f*
foreskin ['fɔ:skɪn] *n* (*Anat*) prepucio
forest ['fɔrɪst] *n* bosque *m*
forestall [fɔ:'stɔ:l] *vt* anticiparse a
forestry ['fɔrɪstrɪ] *n* silvicultura
foretaste ['fɔ:teɪst] *n* anticipo

foretell (*pt, pp* **foretold**) [fɔː'tɛl, -'təʊld] *vt* predecir, pronosticar

forethought ['fɔːθɔːt] *n* previsión *f*

forever [fə'rɛvəʳ] *adv* siempre; (*for good*) para siempre

forewarn [fɔː'wɔːn] *vt* avisar, advertir

forewent [fɔː'wɛnt] *pt of* **forego**

foreword ['fɔːwəːd] *n* prefacio

forfeit ['fɔːfɪt] *n* (*in game*) prenda ∎ *vt* perder (derecho a)

forgave [fə'geɪv] *pt of* **forgive**

forge [fɔːdʒ] *n* fragua; (*smithy*) herrería ∎ *vt* (*signature: Brit: money*) falsificar; (*metal*) forjar
▶ **forge ahead** *vi* avanzar mucho

forger ['fɔːdʒəʳ] *n* falsificador(a) *m(f)*

forgery ['fɔːdʒərɪ] *n* falsificación *f*

forget (*pt* **forgot**, *pp* **forgotten**) [fə'gɛt, -'gɔt, -'gɔtn] *vt* olvidar, olvidarse de ∎ *vi* olvidarse

forgetful [fə'gɛtful] *adj* olvidadizo

forget-me-not [fə'gɛtmɪnɔt] *n* nomeolvides *f inv*

forgive (*pt* **forgave**, *pp* **forgiven**) [fə'gɪv, -'geɪv, -'gɪvn] *vt* perdonar; **to ~ sb for sth/for doing sth** perdonar algo a algn/a algn por haber hecho algo

forgiveness [fə'gɪvnɪs] *n* perdón *m*

forgiving [fə'gɪvɪŋ] *adj* compasivo

forgo (*pt* **forwent**, *pp* **forgone**) [fɔː'gəʊ, -'wɛnt, -'gɔn] *vt* (*give up*) renunciar a; (*go without*) privarse de

forgot [fə'gɔt] *pt of* **forget**

forgotten [fə'gɔtn] *pp of* **forget**

fork [fɔːk] *n* (*for eating*) tenedor *m*; (*for gardening*) horca; (*of roads*) bifurcación *f*; (*in tree*) horcadura ∎ *vi* (*road*) bifurcarse
▶ **fork out** *vt* (*col: pay*) soltar

forked [fɔːkt] *adj* (*lightning*) en zigzag

fork-lift truck ['fɔːklɪft-] *n* máquina elevadora

forlorn [fə'lɔːn] *adj* (*person*) triste, melancólico; (*deserted: cottage*) abandonado; (*desperate: attempt*) desesperado

form [fɔːm] *n* forma; (*Brit Scol*) curso; (*document*) formulario, planilla (*LAm*) ∎ *vt* formar; **in the ~ of** en forma de; **in top ~** en plena forma; **to be in good ~** (*Sport: fig*) estar en plena forma; **to ~ part of sth** formar parte de algo; **to ~ a circle/a queue** hacer una curva/una cola

formal ['fɔːməl] *adj* (*offer, receipt*) por escrito; (*person etc*) correcto; (*occasion, dinner*) ceremonioso; **~ dress** traje *m* de vestir; (*evening dress*) traje *m* de etiqueta

formalities [fɔː'mælɪtɪz] *npl* formalidades *fpl*

formality [fɔː'mælɪtɪ] *n* ceremonia

formalize ['fɔːməlaɪz] *vt* formalizar

formally ['fɔːməlɪ] *adv* oficialmente

format ['fɔːmæt] *n* formato ∎ *vt* (*Comput*) formatear

formation [fɔː'meɪʃən] *n* formación *f*

formative ['fɔːmətɪv] *adj* (*years*) de formación

former ['fɔːməʳ] *adj* anterior; (*earlier*) antiguo; (*ex*) ex; **the ~ ... the latter ...** aquél ... éste ...; **the ~ president** el antiguo *or* ex presidente; **the ~ Yugoslavia/Soviet Union** la antigua *or* ex Yugoslavia/Unión Soviética

formerly ['fɔːməlɪ] *adv* antiguamente

form feed *n* (*on printer*) salto de página

Formica® [fɔː'maɪkə] *n* formica®

formidable ['fɔːmɪdəbl] *adj* formidable

formula ['fɔːmjulə] *n* fórmula; **F~ One** (*Aut*) Fórmula Uno

formulate ['fɔːmjuleɪt] *vt* formular

fornicate ['fɔːnɪkeɪt] *vi* fornicar

forsake (*pt* **forsook**, *pp* **forsaken**) [fə'seɪk, -'suk, -'seɪkən] *vt* (*gen*) abandonar; (*plan*) renunciar a

fort [fɔːt] *n* fuerte *m*; **to hold the ~** (*fig*) quedarse a cargo

forte ['fɔːtɪ] *n* fuerte *m*

forth [fɔːθ] *adv*: **back and ~** de acá para allá; **and so ~** y así sucesivamente

forthcoming [fɔːθ'kʌmɪŋ] *adj* próximo, venidero; (*character*) comunicativo

forthright ['fɔːθraɪt] *adj* franco

forthwith ['fɔːθ'wɪθ] *adv* en el acto, acto seguido

fortification [fɔːtɪfɪ'keɪʃən] *n* fortificación *f*

fortified wine ['fɔːtɪfaɪd-] *n* vino encabezado

fortify ['fɔːtɪfaɪ] *vt* fortalecer

fortitude ['fɔːtɪtjuːd] *n* fortaleza

fortnight ['fɔːtnaɪt] *n* (*Brit*) quincena; **it's a ~ since ...** hace quince días que ...

fortnightly ['fɔːtnaɪtlɪ] *adj* quincenal ∎ *adv* quincenalmente

FORTRAN ['fɔːtræn] *n* FORTRAN *m*

fortress ['fɔːtrɪs] *n* fortaleza

fortuitous [fɔː'tjuːɪtəs] *adj* fortuito

fortunate ['fɔːtʃənɪt] *adj*: **it is ~ that ...** (es una) suerte que ...

fortunately ['fɔːtʃənɪtlɪ] *adv* afortunadamente

fortune ['fɔːtʃən] *n* suerte *f*; (*wealth*) fortuna; **to make a ~** hacer un dineral

fortune-teller ['fɔːtʃəntɛləʳ] *n* adivino(-a)

forty ['fɔːtɪ] *num* cuarenta

forum ['fɔːrəm] *n* (*also fig*) foro

forward ['fɔːwəd] *adj* (*position*) avanzado; (*movement*) hacia delante; (*front*) delantero; (*not shy*) atrevido ∎ *n* (*Sport*) delantero ∎ *vt* (*letter*) remitir; (*career*) promocionar; **to move ~** avanzar; **"please ~"** "remítase al destinatario"

forward contract n contrato a término
forward exchange n cambio a término
forward planning n planificación f por anticipado
forward rate n tipo a término
forwards ['fɔːwədz] adv (hacia) adelante
forward sales npl ventas fpl a término
forwent [fɔː'wɛnt] pt of **forgo**
fossil ['fɔsl] n fósil m
fossil fuel n combustible m fósil
foster ['fɔstəʳ] vt (child) acoger en familia; (idea) fomentar
foster brother n hermano de leche
foster child n hijo(-a) adoptivo(-a)
foster mother n madre f adoptiva
fought [fɔːt] pt, pp of **fight**
foul [faul] adj (gen) sucio, puerco; (weather, smell etc) asqueroso ▪ n (Football) falta ▪ vt (dirty) ensuciar; (block) atascar; (entangle: anchor, propeller) atascar, enredarse en; (football player) cometer una falta contra
foul play n (Sport) mala jugada; (Law) muerte f violenta
found [faund] pt, pp of **find** ▪ vt (establish) fundar
foundation [faun'deɪʃən] n (act) fundación f; (basis) base f; (also: **foundation cream**) base f de maquillaje
foundations [faun'deɪʃənz] npl (of building) cimientos mpl; **to lay the ~** poner los cimientos
foundation stone n: **to lay the ~** poner la primera piedra
founder ['faundəʳ] n fundador(a) m(f) ▪ vi irse a pique
founding ['faundɪŋ] adj: **~ fathers** (esp US) fundadores mpl, próceres mpl; **~ member** miembro fundador
foundry ['faundrɪ] n fundición f
fountain ['fauntɪn] n fuente f
fountain pen n (pluma) estilográfica, plumafuente f (LAm)
four [fɔːʳ] num cuatro; **on all fours** a gatas
four-footed [fɔː'futɪd] adj cuadrúpedo
four-letter word ['fɔːlɛtə-] n taco
four-poster ['fɔː'pəustəʳ] n (also: **four-poster bed**) cama de columnas
foursome ['fɔːsəm] n grupo de cuatro personas
fourteen ['fɔː'tiːn] num catorce
fourteenth [fɔː'tiːnθ] adj decimocuarto
fourth [fɔːθ] adj cuarto ▪ n (Aut: also: **fourth gear**) cuarta (velocidad)
four-wheel drive ['fɔːwiːl-] n tracción f a las cuatro ruedas
fowl [faul] n ave f (de corral)
fox [fɔks] n zorro ▪ vt confundir

fox fur n piel f de zorro
foxglove ['fɔksglʌv] n (Bot) dedalera
fox-hunting ['fɔkshʌntɪŋ] n caza de zorros
foxtrot ['fɔkstrɔt] n fox(trot) m
foyer ['fɔɪeɪ] n vestíbulo
FPA n abbr (Brit: = Family Planning Association) asociación de planificación familiar
Fr. abbr (Rel: = father) P.; (= friar) Fr.
fracas ['frækɑː] n gresca, refriega
fraction ['frækʃən] n fracción f
fractionally ['frækʃnəlɪ] adv ligeramente
fractious ['frækʃəs] adj (person, mood) irascible
fracture ['fræktʃəʳ] n fractura ▪ vt fracturar
fragile ['frædʒaɪl] adj frágil
fragment ['frægmənt] n fragmento
fragmentary [fræg'mɛntərɪ] adj fragmentario
fragrance ['freɪgrəns] n fragancia
fragrant ['freɪgrənt] adj fragante, oloroso
frail [freɪl] adj (fragile) frágil, quebradizo; (weak) delicado
frame [freɪm] n (Tech) armazón f; (of picture, door etc) marco; (of spectacles: also: **frames**) montura ▪ vt encuadrar; (picture) enmarcar; (reply) formular; **to ~ sb** (col) inculpar por engaños a algn
frame of mind n estado de ánimo
framework ['freɪmwəːk] n marco
France [frɑːns] n Francia
franchise ['fræntʃaɪz] n (Pol) derecho al voto, sufragio; (Comm) licencia, concesión f
franchisee [fræntʃaɪ'ziː] n concesionario(-a)
franchiser ['fræntʃaɪzəʳ] n compañía concesionaria
frank [fræŋk] adj franco ▪ vt (Brit: letter) franquear
frankfurter ['fræŋkfəːtəʳ] n salchicha de Frankfurt
frankincense ['fræŋkɪnsɛns] n incienso
franking machine ['fræŋkɪŋ-] n máquina de franqueo
frankly ['fræŋklɪ] adv francamente
frankness ['fræŋknɪs] n franqueza
frantic ['fræntɪk] adj (desperate: need, desire) desesperado; (: search) frenético; (: person) desquiciado
fraternal [frə'təːnl] adj fraterno
fraternity [frə'təːnɪtɪ] n (club) fraternidad f; (US) club m de estudiantes; (guild) gremio
fraternization [frætənaɪ'zeɪʃən] n fraternización f
fraternize ['frætənaɪz] vi confraternizar
fraud [frɔːd] n fraude m; (person) impostor(a) m(f)
fraudulent ['frɔːdjulənt] adj fraudulento
fraught [frɔːt] adj (tense) tenso; **~ with** cargado de

fray [freɪ] *n* combate *m*, lucha, refriega
■ *vi* deshilacharse; **tempers were frayed**
el ambiente se ponía tenso
FRB *n abbr* (*US*) = **Federal Reserve Board**
FRCM *n abbr* (*Brit*) = **Fellow of the Royal College of Music**
FRCO *n abbr* (*Brit*) = **Fellow of the Royal College of Organists**
FRCP *n abbr* (*Brit*) = **Fellow of the Royal College of Physicians**
FRCS *n abbr* (*Brit*) = **Fellow of the Royal College of Surgeons**
freak [fri:k] *n* (*person*) fenómeno; (*event*) suceso anormal; (*col: enthusiast*) adicto(-a)
■ *adj* (*storm, conditions*) anormal; **health ~** (*col*) maniático(-a) en cuestión de salud
▶ **freak out** *vi* (*col: on drugs*) flipar
freakish ['fri:kɪʃ] *adj* (*result*) inesperado; (*appearance*) estrambótico; (*weather*) cambiadizo
freckle ['frɛkl] *n* peca
freckled ['frɛkld] *adj* pecoso, lleno de pecas
free [fri:] *adj* (*person: at liberty*) libre; (*not fixed*) suelto; (*gratis*) gratuito; (*unoccupied*) desocupado; (*liberal*) generoso ■ *vt* (*prisoner etc*) poner en libertad; (*jammed object*) soltar; **to give sb a ~ hand** dar carta blanca a algn; **~ and easy** despreocupado; **is this seat ~?** ¿está libre este asiento?; **~ of tax** libre de impuestos; **admission ~** entrada libre; **~ (of charge), for ~** *adv* gratis
freebie ['fri:bɪ] *n* (*col*): **it's a ~** es gratis
freedom ['fri:dəm] *n* libertad *f*; **~ of association** libertad de asociación
freedom fighter *n* luchador(a) *m(f)* por la libertad
free enterprise *n* libre empresa
Freefone® ['fri:fəun] *n* (*Brit*) número gratuito
free-for-all ['fri:fərɔ:l] *n* riña general
free gift *n* regalo
freehold ['fri:həuld] *n* propiedad *f* absoluta
free kick *n* tiro libre
freelance ['fri:lɑ:ns] *adj, adv* por cuenta propia; **to do ~ work** trabajar por su cuenta
freely ['fri:lɪ] *adv* libremente; (*liberally*) generosamente
free-market economy ['fri:'mɑ:kɪt-] *n* economía de libre mercado
freemason ['fri:meɪsn] *n* francmasón *m*
freemasonry ['fri:meɪsnrɪ] *n* (franc)masonería
freepost ['fri:pəust] *n* porte *m* pagado
free-range ['fri:'reɪndʒ] *adj* (*hen, egg*) de granja
free sample *n* muestra gratuita
freesia ['fri:ʒə] *n* fresia

free speech *n* libertad *f* de expresión
free trade *n* libre comercio
freeway ['fri:weɪ] *n* (*US*) autopista
freewheel [fri:'wi:l] *vi* ir en punto muerto
freewheeling [fri:'wi:lɪŋ] *adj* libre, espontáneo; (*careless*) irresponsable
free will *n* libre albedrío; **of one's own ~** por su propia voluntad
freeze [fri:z] (*pt* **froze**, *pp* **frozen**) *vi* helarse, congelarse ■ *vt* helar; (*prices, food, salaries*) congelar ■ *n* helada; congelación *f*
▶ **freeze over** *vi* (*lake, river*) helarse, congelarse; (*window, windscreen*) cubrirse de escarcha
▶ **freeze up** *vi* helarse, congelarse
freeze-dried ['fri:zdraɪd] *adj* liofilizado
freezer ['fri:zə^r] *n* congelador *m*, congeladora
freezing ['fri:zɪŋ] *adj* helado
freezing point *n* punto de congelación; **3 degrees below ~** tres grados bajo cero
freight [freɪt] *n* (*goods*) carga; (*money charged*) flete *m*
freight car *n* vagón *m* de mercancías
freighter ['freɪtə^r] *n* buque *m* de carga; (*Aviat*) avión *m* de transporte de mercancías
freight forward *n* contra reembolso del flete, flete por pagar
freight forwarder [-'fɔ:wədə^r] *n* agente *m* expedidor
freight inward *n* flete sobre compras
freight train *n* (*US*) tren *m* de mercancías
French [frɛntʃ] *adj* francés(-esa) ■ *n* (*Ling*) francés *m*; **the French** *npl* los franceses
French bean *n* judía verde
French bread *n* pan *m* francés
French Canadian *adj, n* francocanadiense *m/f*
French dressing *n* (*Culin*) vinagreta
French fried potatoes, French fries (*US*) *npl* patatas *fpl* or (*LAm*) papas *fpl* fritas
French Guiana [-gaɪ'ænə] *n* la Guayana Francesa
French loaf *n* barra de pan
Frenchman ['frɛntʃmən] *n* francés *m*
French Riviera *n*: **the ~** la Riviera, la Costa Azul
French stick *n* barra de pan
French window *n* puertaventana
Frenchwoman ['frɛntʃwumən] *n* francesa
frenetic [frə'nɛtɪk] *adj* frenético
frenzy ['frɛnzɪ] *n* frenesí *m*
frequency ['fri:kwənsɪ] *n* frecuencia
frequency modulation *n* frecuencia modulada
frequent *adj* ['fri:kwənt] frecuente
■ *vt* [frɪ'kwɛnt] frecuentar
frequently ['fri:kwəntlɪ] *adv* frecuentemente, a menudo

fresco ['freskəu] n fresco
fresh [freʃ] adj (gen) fresco; (new) nuevo; (water) dulce; **to make a ~ start** empezar de nuevo
freshen ['freʃən] vi (wind) arreciar; (air) refrescar
▸ **freshen up** vi (person) refrescarse
freshener ['freʃnər] n: **air ~** ambientador m; **skin ~** tónico
fresher ['freʃər] n (Brit Scol: col) estudiante m/f de primer año
freshly ['freʃlɪ] adv: **~ painted/arrived** recién pintado/llegado
freshman ['freʃmən] n (US Scol) = **fresher**
freshness ['freʃnɪs] n frescura
freshwater ['freʃwɔːtər] adj (fish) de agua dulce
fret [fret] vi inquietarse
fretful ['fretful] adj (child) quejumbroso
Freudian ['frɔɪdɪən] adj freudiano; **~ slip** lapsus m (freudiano)
FRG n abbr (= Federal Republic of Germany) RFA f
Fri. abbr (= Friday) vier
friar ['fraɪər] n fraile m; (before name) fray
friction ['frɪkʃən] n fricción f
friction feed n (on printer) avance m por fricción
Friday ['fraɪdɪ] n viernes m inv; see also **Tuesday**
fridge [frɪdʒ] n (Brit) nevera, frigo, refrigeradora (LAm), heladera (LAm)
fridge-freezer ['frɪdʒ'friːzər] n frigorífico-congelador m, combi m
fried [fraɪd] pt, pp of **fry** ■ adj: **~ egg** huevo frito, huevo estrellado
friend [frend] n amigo(-a) ■ vt (Internet) agregar como amigo
friendliness ['frendlɪnɪs] n simpatía
friendly ['frendlɪ] adj simpático
friendly fire n fuego amigo, disparos mpl del propio bando
friendly society n mutualidad f, montepío
friendship ['frendʃɪp] n amistad f
frieze [friːz] n friso
frigate ['frɪgɪt] n fragata
fright [fraɪt] n susto; **to take ~** asustarse
frighten ['fraɪtn] vt asustar
▸ **frighten away, frighten off** vt (birds, children etc) espantar, ahuyentar
frightened ['fraɪtnd] adj asustado
frightening ['fraɪtnɪŋ] adj: **it's ~** da miedo
frightful ['fraɪtful] adj espantoso, horrible
frightfully ['fraɪtfulɪ] adv terriblemente; **I'm ~ sorry** lo siento muchísimo
frigid ['frɪdʒɪd] adj (Med) frígido
frigidity [frɪ'dʒɪdɪtɪ] n (Med) frigidez f
frill [frɪl] n volante m; **without frills** (fig) sin adornos

frilly ['frɪlɪ] adj con volantes
fringe [frɪndʒ] n (Brit: of hair) flequillo; (edge: of forest etc) borde m, margen m
fringe benefits npl ventajas fpl complementarias
fringe theatre n teatro experimental
Frisbee® ['frɪzbɪ] n frisbee® m
frisk [frɪsk] vt cachear, registrar
frisky ['frɪskɪ] adj juguetón(-ona)
fritter ['frɪtər] n buñuelo
▸ **fritter away** vt desperdiciar
frivolity [frɪ'vɔlɪtɪ] n frivolidad f
frivolous ['frɪvələs] adj frívolo
frizzy ['frɪzɪ] adj crespo
fro [frəu] see **to**
frock [frɔk] n vestido
frog [frɔg] n rana; **to have a ~ in one's throat** tener carraspera
frogman ['frɔgmən] n hombre-rana m
frogmarch ['frɔgmɑːtʃ] vt: **to ~ sb in/out** meter/sacar a algn a rastras
frolic ['frɔlɪk] vi juguetear

🅞 **KEYWORD**

from [frɔm] prep **1** (indicating starting place) de, desde; **where do you come from?, where are you from?** ¿de dónde eres?; **where has he come from?** ¿de dónde ha venido?; **from London to Glasgow** de Londres a Glasgow; **to escape from sth/sb** escaparse de algo/algn
2 (indicating origin etc) de; **a letter/telephone call from my sister** una carta/llamada de mi hermana; **tell him from me that ...** dígale de mi parte que ...
3 (indicating time): **from one o'clock to** or **until** or **till nine** de la una a las nueve, desde la una hasta las nueve; **from January (on)** a partir de enero; **(as) from Friday** a partir del viernes
4 (indicating distance) de; **the hotel is 1 km from the beach** el hotel está a 1 km de la playa
5 (indicating price, number etc) de; **prices range from £10 to £50** los precios van desde £10 a or hasta £50; **the interest rate was increased from 9% to 10%** el tipo de interés fue incrementado de un 9% a un 10%
6 (indicating difference) de; **he can't tell red from green** no sabe distinguir el rojo del verde; **to be different from sb/sth** ser diferente a algn/algo
7 (because of, on the basis of): **from what he says** por lo que dice; **weak from hunger** debilitado por el hambre

frond [frɔnd] *n* fronda
front [frʌnt] *n* (*foremost part*) parte *f* delantera; (*of house*) fachada; (*promenade: also:* **sea front**) paseo marítimo; (*Mil, Pol, Meteorology*) frente *m*; (*fig: appearances*) apariencia ■ *adj* (*wheel, leg*) delantero; (*row, line*) primero ■ *vi:* **to ~ onto sth** dar a algo; **in ~ (of)** delante (de)
frontage ['frʌntɪdʒ] *n* (*of building*) fachada
frontal ['frʌntl] *adj* frontal
front bench *n* (*Brit: Pol*) *ver nota*

frontbencher ['frʌnt'bentʃər] *n* (*Brit*) *see* **front bench**
front desk *n* (*US*) recepción *f*
front door *n* puerta principal
frontier ['frʌntɪər] *n* frontera
frontispiece ['frʌntɪspiːs] *n* frontispicio
front page *n* primera plana
front room *n* (*Brit*) salón *m*, sala
front runner *n* favorito(-a)
front-wheel drive ['frʌntwiːl-] *n* tracción *f* delantera
frost [frɔst] *n* (*gen*) helada; (*also:* **hoarfrost**) escarcha ■ *vt* (*US Culin*) escarchar
frostbite ['frɔstbaɪt] *n* congelación *f*
frosted ['frɔstɪd] *adj* (*glass*) esmerilado; (*esp US: cake*) glaseado
frosting ['frɔstɪŋ] *n* (*esp US: icing*) glaseado
frosty ['frɔstɪ] *adj* (*surface*) cubierto de escarcha; (*welcome etc*) glacial
froth [frɔθ] *n* espuma
frothy ['frɔθɪ] *adj* espumoso
frown [fraun] *vi* fruncir el ceño ■ *n:* **with a ~** frunciendo el entrecejo
▶ **frown on** *vt fus* desaprobar
froze [frəuz] *pt of* **freeze**
frozen ['frəuzn] *pp of* **freeze** ■ *adj* (*food*) congelado; (*Comm*): **~ assets** activos *mpl* congelados *or* bloqueados
FRS *n abbr* (*Brit:* = *Fellow of the Royal Society*) *miembro de la principal asociación de investigación científica*; (*US:* = *Federal Reserve System*) *banco central de los EE. UU.*
frugal ['fruːgəl] *adj* (*person*) frugal

fruit [fruːt] *n pl inv* fruta
fruiterer ['fruːtərər] *n* frutero(-a); **~'s (shop)** frutería
fruit fly *n* mosca de la fruta
fruitful ['fruːtful] *adj* provechoso
fruition [fruː'ɪʃən] *n:* **to come to ~** realizarse
fruit juice *n* jugo *or* (*SP*) zumo de fruta
fruitless ['fruːtlɪs] *adj* (*fig*) infructuoso, inútil
fruit machine *n* (*Brit*) máquina tragaperras
fruit salad *n* macedonia *or* (*LAm*) ensalada de frutas
frump [frʌmp] *n* espantajo, adefesio
frustrate [frʌs'treɪt] *vt* frustrar
frustrated [frʌs'treɪtɪd] *adj* frustrado
frustrating [frʌs'treɪtɪŋ] *adj* (*job, day*) frustrante
frustration [frʌs'treɪʃən] *n* frustración *f*
fry (*pt, pp* **fried**) [fraɪ, -d] *vt* freír ■ *n:* **small ~** gente *f* menuda
frying pan ['fraɪɪŋ-] *n* sartén *f*, sartén *m* (*LAm*)
FT *n abbr* (*Brit:* = *Financial Times*) *periódico financiero*
ft. *abbr* = **foot; feet**
FTC *n abbr* (*US*) = **Federal Trade Commission**
FTSE 100 Index *n abbr* (= *Financial Times Stock Exchange 100 Index*) *índice bursátil del Financial Times*
fuchsia ['fjuːʃə] *n* fucsia
fuck [fʌk] (*col!*) *vt* joder (*SP*) (!), coger (*LAm*) (!) ■ *vi* joder (*SP*) (!), coger (*LAm*) (!); **~ off!** ¡vete a tomar por culo! (!)
fuddled ['fʌdld] *adj* (*muddled*) confuso, aturdido; (*col: tipsy*) borracho
fuddy-duddy ['fʌdɪdʌdɪ] (*pej*) *n* carcamal *m*, carroza *m/f* ■ *adj* chapado a la antigua
fudge [fʌdʒ] *n* (*Culin*) caramelo blando ■ *vt* (*issue, problem*) rehuir, esquivar
fuel [fjuəl] *n* (*for heating*) combustible *m*; (*coal*) carbón *m*; (*wood*) leña; (*for engine*) carburante *m* ■ *vt* (*furnace etc*) alimentar; (*aircraft, ship etc*) aprovisionar de combustible
fuel oil *n* fuel oil *m*
fuel poverty *n* pobreza energética
fuel pump *n* (*Aut*) surtidor *m* de gasolina
fuel tank *n* depósito de combustible
fug [fʌg] *n* aire *m* viciado
fugitive ['fjuːdʒɪtɪv] *n* (*from prison*) fugitivo(-a)
fulfil, fulfill (*US*) [ful'fɪl] *vt* (*function*) desempeñar; (*condition*) cumplir; (*wish, desire*) realizar
fulfilled [ful'fɪld] *adj* (*person*) realizado
fulfilment, fulfillment (*US*) [ful'fɪlmənt] *n* realización *f*; (*of promise*) cumplimiento
full [ful] *adj* lleno; (*fig*) pleno; (*complete*) completo; (*information*) detallado; (*price*) íntegro, sin descuento ■ *adv:* **~ well** perfectamente; **we're ~ up for July** estamos completos para julio; **I'm ~ (up)** estoy lleno;

~ employment pleno empleo; **~ name** nombre m completo; **a ~ two hours** dos horas enteras; **at ~ speed** a toda velocidad; **in ~** (reproduce, quote) íntegramente; **to write sth in ~** escribir algo por extenso; **to pay in ~** pagar la deuda entera

fullback ['fulbæk] n (Football) defensa m; (Rugby) zaguero

full-blooded ['ful'blʌdɪd] adj (vigorous: attack) vigoroso; (pure) puro

full-cream ['ful'kriːm] adj: **~ milk** leche f entera

full driving licence n (Brit Aut) carnet m de conducir (definitivo); see also **L-plates**

full-fledged ['fulflɛdʒd] adj (US) = **fully-fledged**

full-grown ['ful'grəun] adj maduro

full-length ['ful'lɛŋθ] adj (portrait) de cuerpo entero; (film) de largometraje

full moon n luna llena, plenilunio

fullness ['fulnɪs] n plenitud f, amplitud f

full-scale ['fulskeɪl] adj (attack, war, search, retreat) en gran escala; (plan, model) de tamaño natural

full stop n punto

full-time ['fultaɪm] adj (work) de tiempo completo ■ adv: **to work ~** trabajar a tiempo completo

fully ['fulɪ] adv completamente; (at least) al menos

fully-fledged ['fulɪ'flɛdʒd], (US) **full-fledged** adj (teacher, barrister) diplomado; (bird) con todas sus plumas, capaz de volar; (fig) de pleno derecho

fully-paid ['fulɪpeɪd] adj: **~ share** acción f liberada

fulsome ['fulsəm] adj (pej: praise, gratitude) excesivo, exagerado; (manner) obsequioso

fumble with ['fʌmbl-] vt fus manosear

fume [fjuːm] vi humear, echar humo

fumes [fjuːmz] npl humo sg, gases mpl

fumigate ['fjuːmɪgeɪt] vt fumigar

fun [fʌn] n (amusement) diversión f; (joy) alegría; **to have ~** divertirse; **for ~** por gusto; **to make ~ of** reírse de

function ['fʌŋkʃən] n función f ■ vi funcionar; **to ~ as** hacer (las veces) de, fungir de (LAm)

functional ['fʌŋkʃənl] adj funcional

function key n (Comput) tecla de función

fund [fʌnd] n fondo; (reserve) reserva; **funds** npl fondos mpl

fundamental [fʌndə'mɛntl] adj fundamental ■ n; **fundamentals** npl fundamentos mpl

fundamentalism [fʌndə'mɛntəlɪzəm] n fundamentalismo, integrismo

fundamentalist [fʌndə'mɛntəlɪst] n fundamentalista m/f, integrista m/f

fundamentally [fʌndə'mɛntəlɪ] adv fundamentalmente

funding ['fʌndɪŋ] n financiación f

fund-raising ['fʌndreɪzɪŋ] n recaudación f de fondos

funeral ['fjuːnərəl] n (burial) entierro; (ceremony) funerales mpl

funeral director n director(a) m(f) de pompas fúnebres

funeral parlour n (Brit) funeraria

funeral service n misa de cuerpo presente

funereal [fjuː'nɪərɪəl] adj fúnebre

funfair ['fʌnfɛəʳ] n (Brit) parque m de atracciones; (travelling) feria

fungus (pl **fungi**) ['fʌŋgəs, -gaɪ] n hongo

funicular [fjuː'nɪkjuləʳ] n (also: **funicular railway**) funicular m

funky ['fʌŋkɪ] adj (music) funky; (col: good) guay

funnel ['fʌnl] n embudo; (of ship) chimenea

funnily ['fʌnɪlɪ] adv de modo divertido, graciosamente; (oddly) de una manera rara; **~ enough** aunque parezca extraño

funny ['fʌnɪ] adj gracioso, divertido; (strange) curioso, raro

funny bone n hueso de la alegría

fun run n maratón m popular

fur [fəːʳ] n piel f; (Brit: on tongue etc) sarro

fur coat n abrigo de pieles

furious ['fjuərɪəs] adj furioso; (effort, argument) violento; **to be ~ with sb** estar furioso con algn

furiously ['fjuərɪəslɪ] adv con furia

furl [fəːl] vt (sail) recoger

furlong ['fəːlɔŋ] n octava parte de una milla

furlough ['fəːləu] n (US Mil) permiso

furnace ['fəːnɪs] n horno

furnish ['fəːnɪʃ] vt amueblar; (supply) proporcionar; (information) facilitar

furnished ['fəːnɪʃt] adj: **~ flat** or (US) **apartment** piso amueblado

furnishings ['fəːnɪʃɪŋz] npl mobiliario sg

furniture ['fəːnɪtʃəʳ] n muebles mpl; **piece of ~** mueble m

furniture polish n cera para muebles

furore [fjuə'rɔːrɪ] n (protests) escándalo

furrier ['fʌrɪəʳ] n peletero(-a)

furrow ['fʌrəu] n surco ■ vt (forehead) arrugar

furry ['fəːrɪ] adj peludo; (toy) de peluche

further ['fəːðəʳ] adj (new) nuevo; (place) más lejano ■ adv más lejos; (more) más; (moreover) además ■ vt hacer avanzar; **how much ~ is it?** ¿a qué distancia queda?; **~ to your letter of ...** (Comm) con referencia a su carta de ...; **to ~ one's interests** fomentar sus intereses

further education n educación f postescolar

furthermore [fəːðə'mɔːʳ] *adv* además
furthermost ['fəːðəməust] *adj* más lejano
furthest ['fəːðɪst] *superlative of* **far**
furtive ['fəːtɪv] *adj* furtivo
furtively ['fəːtɪvlɪ] *adv* furtivamente, a escondidas
fury ['fjuərɪ] *n* furia
fuse, *(US)* **fuze** [fjuːz] *n* fusible *m*; *(for bomb etc)* mecha ▪ *vt (metal)* fundir; *(fig)* fusionar ▪ *vi* fundirse; fusionarse; *(Brit Elec)*: **to ~ the lights** fundir los plomos; **a ~ has blown** se ha fundido un fusible
fuse box *n* caja de fusibles
fuselage ['fjuːzəlɑːʒ] *n* fuselaje *m*
fuse wire *n* hilo fusible
fusillade [fjuːzɪ'leɪd] *n* descarga cerrada; *(fig)* lluvia
fusion ['fjuːʒən] *n* fusión *f*
fuss [fʌs] *n (noise)* bulla; *(dispute)* lío, jaleo; *(complaining)* protesta ▪ *vi* preocuparse (por pequeñeces) ▪ *vt (person)* molestar; **to make a ~** armar jaleo

▸ **fuss over** *vt fus (person)* contemplar, mimar
fusspot ['fʌspɔt] *n (col)* quisquilloso(-a)
fussy ['fʌsɪ] *adj (person)* quisquilloso; **I'm not ~** *(col)* me da igual
fusty ['fʌstɪ] *adj (pej)* rancio; **to smell ~** oler a cerrado
futile ['fjuːtaɪl] *adj* vano
futility [fjuː'tɪlɪtɪ] *n* inutilidad *f*
futon ['fuːtɔn] *n* futón *m*
future ['fjuːtʃəʳ] *adj (gen)* futuro; *(coming)* venidero ▪ *n* futuro, porvenir; **in ~** de ahora en adelante
futures ['fjuːtʃəz] *npl (Comm)* operaciones *fpl* a término, futuros *mpl*
futuristic [fjuːtʃə'rɪstɪk] *adj* futurista
fuze [fjuːz] *(US)* = **fuse**
fuzzy ['fʌzɪ] *adj (Phot)* borroso; *(hair)* muy rizado
fwd. *abbr* = **forward**
fwy *abbr (US)* = **freeway**
FY *abbr* = **fiscal year**
FYI *abbr* = **for your information**

f

Gg

G, g [dʒiː] *n* (*letter*) G, g f; **G** (*Mus*) sol *m*; **G for George** G de Gerona

G *n abbr* (*Brit Scol: mark: = good*) N; (*US Cine: = general audience*) todos los públicos

g. *abbr* (*= gram(s), gravity*) g

G8 *n abbr* (*Pol: = Group of Eight*) G8 *m*

G20 *n abbr* (*Pol: = Group of Twenty*) G20 *m*

GA *abbr* (*US Post*) = **Georgia**

gab [gæb] *n*: **to have the gift of the ~** (*col*) tener mucha labia

gabble ['gæbl] *vi* hablar atropelladamente; (*gossip*) cotorrear

gaberdine [gæbə'diːn] *n* gabardina

gable ['geɪbl] *n* aguilón *m*

Gabon [gə'bɔn] *n* Gabón *m*

gad about [gæd-] *vi* (*col*) moverse mucho

gadget ['gædʒɪt] *n* aparato

gadgetry ['gædʒɪtrɪ] *n* chismes *mpl*

Gaelic ['geɪlɪk] *adj, n* (*Ling*) gaélico

gaffe [gæf] *n* plancha, patinazo, metedura de pata

gaffer ['gæfə^r] *n* (*Brit col*) jefe *m*; ((*old*) *man*) vejete *m*

gag [gæg] *n* (*on mouth*) mordaza; (*joke*) chiste *m* ■ *vt* (*prisoner etc*) amordazar ■ *vi* (*choke*) tener arcadas

gaga ['gɑːgɑː] *adj*: **to go ~** (*senile*) chochear; (*ecstatic*) caérsele a algn la baba

gaiety ['geɪɪtɪ] *n* alegría

gaily ['geɪlɪ] *adv* alegremente

gain [geɪn] *n* ganancia ■ *vt* ganar ■ *vi* (*watch*) adelantarse; **to ~ by sth** ganar con algo; **to ~ ground** ganar terreno; **to ~ 3 lbs (in weight)** engordar 3 libras
▶ **gain (up)on** *vt fus* alcanzar

gainful ['geɪnful] *adj* (*employment*) remunerado

gainfully ['geɪnfulɪ] *adv*: **to be ~ employed** tener un trabajo remunerado

gait [geɪt] *n* forma de andar, andares *mpl*

gala ['gɑːlə] *n* gala; **swimming ~** certamen *m* de natación

Galapagos Islands [gə'læpəgəs-] *npl*: **the ~** las Islas Galápagos

galaxy ['gæləksɪ] *n* galaxia

gale [geɪl] *n* (*wind*) vendaval *m*; **~ force 10** vendaval de fuerza 10

gall [gɔːl] *n* (*Anat*) bilis f, hiel f; (*fig: impudence*) descaro, caradura ■ *vt* molestar

gal., gall. *abbr* = **gallon**; **gallons**

gallant ['gælənt] *adj* valeroso; (*towards ladies*) galante

gallantry ['gæləntrɪ] *n* valentía; (*courtesy*) galantería

gall bladder *n* vesícula biliar

galleon ['gælɪən] *n* galeón *m*

gallery ['gælərɪ] *n* (*Theat*) galería; (*for spectators*) tribuna; (*also*: **art gallery**: *state-owned*) pinacoteca *or* museo de arte; (: *private*) galería de arte

galley ['gælɪ] *n* (*ship's kitchen*) cocina; (*ship*) galera

galley proof *n* (*Typ*) prueba de galera, galerada

Gallic ['gælɪk] *adj* galo

gallon ['gæln] *n* galón *m* (= 8 *pints*; BRIT = 4,546 *litros*; US = 3,785 *litros*)

gallop ['gæləp] *n* galope *m* ■ *vi* galopar; **galloping inflation** inflación f galopante

gallows ['gæləuz] *n* horca

gallstone ['gɔːlstəun] *n* cálculo biliar

Gallup poll ['gæləp-] *n* sondeo de opinión

galore [gə'lɔː^r] *adv* en cantidad, en abundancia

galvanize ['gælvənaɪz] *vt* (*metal*) galvanizar; (*fig*): **to ~ sb into action** mover *or* impulsar a algn a actuar

Gambia ['gæmbɪə] *n* Gambia

gambit ['gæmbɪt] *n* (*fig*): **opening ~** táctica inicial

gamble ['gæmbl] *n* (*risk*) jugada arriesgada; (*bet*) apuesta ■ *vt*: **to ~ on** apostar a; (*fig*) confiar en que ■ *vi* jugar; (*Comm*) especular; **to ~ on the Stock Exchange** jugar a la bolsa

gambler ['gæmblə^r] *n* jugador(a) *m(f)*

gambling ['gæmblɪŋ] *n* juego

gambol ['gæmbl] vi brincar, juguetear

game [geɪm] n (gen) juego; (match) partido; (of cards) partida; (Hunting) caza ▪ adj valiente; (ready): **to be ~ for anything** estar dispuesto a todo; **games** (Scol) deportes mpl; **big ~** caza mayor

game bird n ave f de caza

gamekeeper ['geɪmkiːpəʳ] n guardabosque m/f

gamely ['geɪmlɪ] adv con decisión

gamer ['geɪməʳ] n jugador(a) m(f) de videojuegos, videojugador(a) m(f)

game reserve n coto de caza

games console [geɪmz-] n consola de juegos

game show n programa m concurso inv, concurso

gamesmanship ['geɪmzmənʃɪp] n (uso de) artimañas fpl para ganar

gaming ['geɪmɪŋ] n jugar a videojuegos

gammon ['gæmən] n (bacon) tocino ahumado; (ham) jamón m ahumado

gamut ['gæmət] n (Mus) gama

gander ['gændəʳ] n ganso

gang [gæŋ] n pandilla; (of criminals etc) banda; (of kids) pandilla; (of colleagues) peña; (of workmen) brigada ▪ vi: **to ~ up on sb** conchabarse contra algn

Ganges ['gændʒiːz] n: **the ~** el Ganges

gangland ['gæŋglænd] adj: **~ bosses** cabecillas mafiosos; **~ killings** asesinatos entre bandas

gangling ['gæŋglɪn] adj larguirucho

gangly ['gæŋglɪ] adj desgarbado

gangplank ['gæŋplæŋk] n pasarela, plancha

gangrene ['gæŋgriːn] n gangrena

gangster ['gæŋstəʳ] n gángster m

gang warfare n guerra entre bandas

gangway ['gæŋweɪ] n (Brit: in theatre, bus etc) pasillo; (on ship) pasarela

gantry ['gæntrɪ] n (for crane, railway signal) pórtico; (for rocket) torre f de lanzamiento

GAO n abbr (US: = General Accounting Office) tribunal de cuentas

gaol [dʒeɪl] n, vt (Brit): **= jail**

gap [gæp] n hueco; (in trees, traffic) claro; (in market, records) laguna; (in time) intervalo

gape [geɪp] vi mirar boquiabierto

gaping ['geɪpɪŋ] adj (hole) muy abierto

gap year n año sabático

garage ['gærɑːʒ] n garaje m

garb [gɑːb] n atuendo

garbage ['gɑːbɪdʒ] n (US) basura; (nonsense) bobadas fpl; (fig: film, book etc) basura

garbage can n (US) cubo or balde m (LAm) or bote m (LAm) de la basura

garbage collector n (US) basurero(-a)

garbage disposal unit n triturador m

(de basura)

garbage man n basurero

garbage truck n (US) camión m de la basura

garbled ['gɑːbld] adj (account, explanation) confuso

garden ['gɑːdn] n jardín m; **gardens** npl (public) parque m, jardines mpl; (private) huertos mpl

garden centre n centro de jardinería

garden city n (Brit) ciudad f jardín

gardener ['gɑːdnəʳ] n jardinero(-a)

gardening ['gɑːdnɪŋ] n jardinería

garden party n recepción f al aire libre

gargle ['gɑːgl] vi hacer gárgaras, gargarear (LAm)

gargoyle ['gɑːgɔɪl] n gárgola

garish ['gɛərɪʃ] adj chillón(-ona)

garland ['gɑːlənd] n guirnalda

garlic ['gɑːlɪk] n ajo

garment ['gɑːmənt] n prenda (de vestir)

garner ['gɑːnəʳ] vt hacer acopio de

garnish ['gɑːnɪʃ] vt adornar; (Culin) aderezar

garret ['gærɪt] n desván m, buhardilla

garrison ['gærɪsn] n guarnición f ▪ vt guarnecer

garrulous ['gærjuləs] adj charlatán(-ana)

garter ['gɑːtəʳ] n (US) liga

garter belt n (US) liguero, portaligas m inv

gas [gæs] n gas m; (US: gasoline) gasolina ▪ vt asfixiar con gas; **Calor ~®** (gas m) butano

gas chamber n cámara de gas

gas cooker n (Brit) cocina de gas

gas cylinder n bombona de gas

gaseous ['gæsɪəs] adj gaseoso

gas fire n estufa de gas

gas-fired ['gæsfaɪəd] adj de gas

gash [gæʃ] n brecha, raja; (from knife) cuchillada ▪ vt rajar; (with knife) acuchillar

gasket ['gæskɪt] n (Aut) junta

gas mask n careta antigás

gas meter n contador m de gas

gasoline ['gæsəliːn] n (US) gasolina

gasp [gɑːsp] n grito sofocado ▪ vi (pant) jadear

  ▶ **gasp out** vt (say) decir jadeando

gas pedal n (esp US) acelerador m

gas ring n hornillo de gas

gas station n (US) gasolinera

gas stove n cocina de gas

gassy ['gæsɪ] adj con mucho gas

gas tank n (US Aut) depósito (de gasolina)

gas tap n llave f del gas

gastric ['gæstrɪk] adj gástrico

gastric ulcer n úlcera gástrica

gastroenteritis ['gæstrəuɛntə'raɪtɪs] n gastroenteritis f

gasworks ['gæswəːks] nsg or npl fábrica de gas

gate [geɪt] n (also at airport) puerta; (Rail: at level crossing) barrera; (metal) verja

gâteau (pl **gâteaux**) ['gætəu, z] n tarta

gatecrash ['geɪtkræʃ] vt colarse en

gatecrasher ['geɪtkræʃəʳ] n intruso(-a)

gatehouse ['geɪthaus] n casa del guarda

gateway ['geɪtweɪ] n puerta

gather ['gæðəʳ] vt (flowers, fruit) coger (SP), recoger (LAm); (assemble) reunir; (pick up) recoger; (Sewing) fruncir; (understand) sacar en consecuencia ■ vi (assemble) reunirse; (dust) acumularse; (clouds) cerrarse; **to ~ speed** ganar velocidad; **to ~ (from/that)** deducir (por/que); **as far as I can ~** por lo que tengo entendido

gathering ['gæðərɪŋ] n reunión f, asamblea

GATT [gæt] n abbr (= General Agreement on Tariffs and Trade) GATT m

gauche [gəuʃ] adj torpe

gaudy ['gɔːdɪ] adj chillón(-ona)

gauge, gage (US) [geɪdʒ] n calibre m; (Rail) ancho de vía, entrevía; (instrument) indicador m ■ vt medir; (fig: sb's capabilities, character) juzgar, calibrar; **petrol ~** indicador m (del nivel) de gasolina; **to ~ the right moment** elegir el momento (oportuno)

gaunt [gɔːnt] adj descarnado; (fig) adusto

gauntlet ['gɔːntlɪt] n (fig): **to run the ~ of sth** exponerse a algo; **to throw down the ~** arrojar el guante

gauze [gɔːz] n gasa

gave [geɪv] pt of **give**

gawk [gɔːk] vi mirar pasmado

gawky ['gɔːkɪ] adj desgarbado

gay [geɪ] adj (colour, person) alegre; (homosexual) gay

gaze [geɪz] n mirada fija ■ vi: **to ~ at sth** mirar algo fijamente

gazelle [gə'zɛl] n gacela

gazette [gə'zɛt] n (newspaper) gaceta; (official publication) boletín m oficial

gazetteer [gæzə'tɪəʳ] n índice geográfico

gazump [gə'zʌmp] vti (Brit) echarse atrás en la venta ya acordada de una casa por haber una oferta más alta

GB abbr (= Great Britain) GB

GBH n abbr (Brit Law: col) = **grievous bodily harm**

GC n abbr (Brit: = George Cross) distinción honorífica

GCE n abbr (Brit: = General Certificate of Education) ≈ certificado de bachillerato

GCHQ n abbr (Brit: = Government Communications Headquarters) centro de intercepción de las telecomunicaciones internacionales

GCSE n abbr (Brit: = General Certificate of Secondary Education) certificado del último ciclo de la enseñanza secundaria obligatoria

Gdns. abbr (= gardens) jdns

GDP n abbr (= gross domestic product) PIB m

GDR n abbr (= German Democratic Republic) RDA f

gear [gɪəʳ] n equipo; (Tech) engranaje m; (Aut) velocidad f, marcha ■ vt (fig: adapt): **to ~ sth to** adaptar or ajustar algo a; **top** or (US) **high/low ~** cuarta/primera; **in ~** con la marcha metida; **our service is geared to meet the needs of the disabled** nuestro servicio va enfocado a responder a las necesidades de los minusválidos

▶ **gear up** vi prepararse

gear box n caja de cambios

gear lever, gear shift (US) n palanca de cambio

gear wheel n rueda dentada

GED n abbr (US Scol) = **general educational development**

geese [giːs] npl of **goose**

geezer ['giːzəʳ] n (Brit col) tipo, maromo (SP)

Geiger counter ['gaɪgə-] n contador m Geiger

gel [dʒɛl] n gel m

gelatin, gelatine ['dʒɛlətiːn] n gelatina

gelignite ['dʒɛlɪgnaɪt] n gelignita

gem [dʒɛm] n gema, piedra preciosa; (fig) joya

Gemini ['dʒɛmɪnaɪ] n Géminis m

gen [dʒɛn] n (Brit col): **to give sb the ~ on sth** poner a algn al tanto de algo

Gen. abbr (Mil: = General) Gen., Gral

gen. abbr (= general) grl.; = **generally**

gender ['dʒɛndəʳ] n género

gene [dʒiːn] n gen(e) m

genealogy [dʒiːnɪ'ælədʒɪ] n genealogía

general ['dʒɛnərl] n general m ■ adj general; **in ~** en general; **~ audit** auditoría general; **the ~ public** el gran público

general anaesthetic, general anesthetic (US) n anestesia general

general delivery n (US) lista de correos

general election n elecciones fpl generales

generalization [dʒɛnrəlaɪ'zeɪʃən] n generalización f

generalize ['dʒɛnrəlaɪz] vi generalizar

generally ['dʒɛnrəlɪ] adv generalmente, en general

general manager n director(a) m(f) general

general practitioner n médico(-a) de medicina general

general strike n huelga general

generate ['dʒɛnəreɪt] vt generar

generation [dʒɛnə'reɪʃən] n (of electricity etc) generación f

generator ['dʒɛnəreɪtəʳ] n generador m

generic [dʒɪ'nɛrɪk] adj genérico

generosity [dʒɛnə'rɔsɪtɪ] n generosidad f

generous ['dʒɛnərəs] adj generoso; (copious) abundante

generously ['dʒɛnərəslı] *adv* generosamente; abundantemente

genesis ['dʒɛnɪsɪs] *n* génesis *f*

genetic [dʒɪ'nɛtɪk] *adj* genético

genetically modified organism [dʒɪ'nɛtɪkə lı] *n* organismo genéticamente modificado, organismo transgénico

genetic engineering *n* ingeniería genética

genetic fingerprinting [-'fɪŋɡəprɪntɪŋ] *n* identificación *f* genética

genetics [dʒɪ'nɛtɪks] *n* genética

Geneva [dʒɪ'niːvə] *n* Ginebra

genial ['dʒiːnɪəl] *adj* afable

genitals ['dʒɛnɪtlz] *npl* (órganos *mpl*) genitales *mpl*

genitive ['dʒɛnɪtɪv] *n* genitivo

genius ['dʒiːnɪəs] *n* genio

Genoa ['dʒɛnəuə] *n* Génova

genocide ['dʒɛnəusaɪd] *n* genocidio

gent [dʒɛnt] *n abbr* (*Brit col*) = **gentleman**

genteel [dʒɛn'tiːl] *adj* fino, distinguido

gentle ['dʒɛntl] *adj* (*sweet*) dulce; (*touch etc*) ligero, suave

gentleman ['dʒɛntlmən] *n* señor *m*; (*well-bred man*) caballero; **~'s agreement** acuerdo entre caballeros

gentlemanly ['dʒɛntlmənlı] *adj* caballeroso

gentleness ['dʒɛntlnɪs] *n* dulzura; (*of touch*) suavidad *f*

gently ['dʒɛntlı] *adv* suavemente

gentrification [dʒɛntrɪfɪ'keɪʃən] *n* aburguesamiento

gentry ['dʒɛntrı] *npl* pequeña nobleza *sg*

gents [dʒɛnts] *n* servicios *mpl* (de caballeros)

genuine ['dʒɛnjuɪn] *adj* auténtico; (*person*) sincero

genuinely ['dʒɛnjuɪnlı] *adv* sinceramente

geographer [dʒɪ'ɔɡrəfə'] *n* geógrafo(-a)

geographic [dʒɪə'ɡræfɪk], **geographical** [dʒɪə'ɡræfɪkl] *adj* geográfico

geography [dʒɪ'ɔɡrəfɪ] *n* geografía

geological [dʒɪə'lɔdʒɪkl] *adj* geológico

geologist [dʒɪ'ɔlədʒɪst] *n* geólogo(-a)

geology [dʒɪ'ɔlədʒɪ] *n* geología

geometric [dʒɪə'mɛtrɪk], **geometrical** [dʒɪə'mɛtrɪkl] *adj* geométrico

geometry [dʒɪ'ɔmətrɪ] *n* geometría

Geordie ['dʒɔːdɪ] *n* habitante *m/f* de Tyneside

Georgia ['dʒɔːdʒə] *n* Georgia

Georgian ['dʒɔːdʒən] *adj* georgiano
■ *n* georgiano(-a); (*Ling*) georgiano

geranium [dʒɪ'reɪnjəm] *n* geranio

gerbil ['dʒɛrbl] *n* gerbo

geriatric [dʒɛrɪ'ætrɪk] *adj, n* geriátrico(-a) *m(f)*

germ [dʒəːm] *n* (*microbe*) microbio, bacteria; (*seed*) germen *m*

German ['dʒəːmən] *adj* alemán(-ana)
■ *n* alemán(-ana) *m(f)*; (*Ling*) alemán *m*

German Democratic Republic *n* República Democrática Alemana

germane [dʒəː'meɪn] *adj*: ~ **(to)** pertinente (a)

German measles *n* rubeola, rubéola

German Shepherd *n* (*dog*) pastor *m* alemán

Germany ['dʒəːmənɪ] *n* Alemania; **East/West ~** Alemania Oriental *or* Democrática/Occidental *or* Federal

germination [dʒəːmɪ'neɪʃən] *n* germinación *f*

germ warfare *n* guerra bacteriológica

gesticulate [dʒɛs'tɪkjuleɪt] *vi* gesticular

gesticulation [dʒɛstɪkju'leɪʃən] *n* gesticulación *f*

gesture ['dʒɛstjə'] *n* gesto; **as a ~ of friendship** en señal de amistad

 KEYWORD

get [ɡɛt] (*pt, pp* **got**) (*US*) (*pp* **gotten**) *vi*
1 (*become, be*) ponerse, volverse; **to get old/tired** envejecer/cansarse; **to get drunk** emborracharse; **to get dirty** ensuciarse; **to get ready/washed** prepararse/lavarse; **to get married** casarse; **when do I get paid?** ¿cuándo me pagan *or* se me paga?; **it's getting late** se está haciendo tarde
2 (*go*): **to get to/from** llegar a/de; **to get home** llegar a casa; **he got under the fence** pasó por debajo de la barrera
3 (*begin*) empezar a; **to get to know sb** (llegar a) conocer a algn; **I'm getting to like him** me está empezando a gustar; **let's get going** *or* **started** ¡vamos (a empezar)!
4 (*modal aux vb*): **you've got to do it** tienes que hacerlo
■ *vt* **1**: **to get sth done** (*finish*) hacer algo; (*have done*) mandar hacer algo; **to get one's hair cut** cortarse el pelo; **to get the car going** *or* **to go** arrancar el coche; **to get sb to do sth** conseguir *or* hacer que algn haga algo; **to get sth/sb ready** preparar algo/a algn
2 (*obtain: money, permission, results*) conseguir; (*find: job, flat*) encontrar; (*fetch: person, doctor*) buscar; (*object*) ir a buscar, traer; **to get sth for sb** conseguir algo para algn; **get me Mr Jones, please** (*Tel*) póngame *or* (*LAm*) comuníqueme con el Sr. Jones, por favor; **can I get you a drink?** ¿quieres algo de beber?
3 (*receive: present, letter*) recibir; (*acquire: reputation*) alcanzar; (*: prize*) ganar; **what did you get for your birthday?** ¿qué te regalaron por tu cumpleaños?; **how much did you get for the painting?** ¿cuánto sacaste por el cuadro?

573

4 (*catch*) coger (*SP*), agarrar (*LAm*); (*hit: target etc*) dar en; **to get sb by the arm/throat** coger *or* agarrar a algn por el brazo/cuello; **get him!** ¡cógelo! (*SP*), ¡atrápalo! (*LAm*); **the bullet got him in the leg** la bala le dio en la pierna
5 (*take, move*) llevar; **to get sth to sb** hacer llegar algo a algn; **do you think we'll get it through the door?** ¿crees que lo podremos meter por la puerta?
6 (*catch, take: plane, bus etc*) coger (*SP*), tomar (*LAm*); **where do I get the train for Birmingham?** ¿dónde se coge *or* se toma el tren para Birmingham?
7 (*understand*) entender; (*hear*) oír; **I've got it!** ¡ya lo tengo!, ¡eureka!; **I don't get your meaning** no te entiendo; **I'm sorry, I didn't get your name** lo siento, no me he enterado de tu nombre
8 (*have, possess*): **to have got** tener
9 (*col: annoy*) molestar; (: *thrill*) chiflar
▸ **get about** *vi* salir mucho; (*news*) divulgarse
▸ **get across** *vt* (*message, meaning*) lograr comunicar
■ *vi*: **to get across to sb** hacer que algn comprenda
▸ **get along** *vi* (*agree*) llevarse bien; (*depart*) marcharse; (*manage*) = **get by**
▸ **get at** *vt fus* (*attack*) meterse con; (*reach*) alcanzar; (*the truth*) descubrir; **what are you getting at?** ¿qué insinúas?
▸ **get away** *vi* marcharse; (*escape*) escaparse
▸ **get away with** *vt fus* hacer impunemente
▸ **get back** *vi* (*return*) volver
■ *vt* recobrar
▸ **get back at** *vt fus* (*col*): **to get back at sb (for sth)** vengarse de algn (por algo)
▸ **get by** *vi* (*pass*) (lograr) pasar; (*manage*) arreglárselas; **I can get by in Dutch** me defiendo en holandés
▸ **get down** *vi* bajar(se)
■ *vt fus* bajar
■ *vt* bajar; (*depress*) deprimir
▸ **get down to** *vt fus* (*work*) ponerse a
▸ **get in** *vi* entrar; (*train*) llegar; (*arrive home*) volver a casa, regresar; (*political party*) salir
■ *vt* (*bring in: harvest*) recoger; (: *coal, shopping, supplies*) comprar, traer; (*insert*) meter
▸ **get into** *vt fus* entrar en; (*vehicle*) subir a; **to get into a rage** enfadarse
▸ **get off** *vi* (*from train etc*) bajar(se); (*depart: person, car*) marcharse
■ *vt* (*remove*) quitar; (*send off*) mandar; (*have as leave: day, time*) tener libre
■ *vt fus* (*train, bus*) bajar(se) de; **to get off to a good start** (*fig*) empezar muy bien *or* con buen pie

▸ **get on** *vi* (*at exam etc*): **how are you getting on?** ¿cómo te va?; (*agree*): **to get on (with)** llevarse bien (con)
■ *vt fus* subir(se) a
▸ **get on to** *vt fus* (*deal with*) ocuparse de; (*col: contact on phone etc*) hablar con
▸ **get out** *vi* salir; (*of vehicle*) bajar(se); (*news*) saberse
■ *vt* sacar
▸ **get out of** *vt fus* salir de; (*duty etc*) escaparse de; (*gain from: pleasure, benefit*) sacar de
▸ **get over** *vt fus* (*illness*) recobrarse de
▸ **get round** *vt fus* rodear; (*fig: person*) engatusar a
■ *vi*: **to get round to doing sth** encontrar tiempo para hacer algo
▸ **get through** *vt fus* (*finish*) acabar
■ *vi* (*Tel*) (lograr) comunicar
▸ **get through to** *vt fus* (*Tel*) comunicar con
▸ **get together** *vi* reunirse
■ *vt* reunir, juntar
▸ **get up** *vi* (*rise*) levantarse
■ *vt fus* subir; **to get up enthusiasm for sth** cobrar entusiasmo por algo
▸ **get up to** *vt fus* (*reach*) llegar a; (*prank*) hacer

getaway ['gɛtəweɪ] *n* fuga
getaway car *n*: **the thieves'** ~ el coche en que huyeron los ladrones
get-together ['gɛttəgɛðə ͬ] *n* reunión *f*; (*party*) fiesta
get-up ['gɛtʌp] *n* (*Brit col: outfit*) atavío, atuendo
get-well card [gɛt'wɛl-] *n* tarjeta en la que se desea a un enfermo que se mejore
geyser ['gi:zə ͬ] *n* (*water heater*) calentador *m* de agua; (*Geo*) géiser *m*
Ghana ['gɑ:nə] *n* Ghana
Ghanaian [gɑ:'neɪən] *adj, n* ghanés(-esa) *m(f)*
ghastly ['gɑ:stlɪ] *adj* horrible; (*pale*) pálido
gherkin ['gə:kɪn] *n* pepinillo
ghetto ['gɛtəu] *n* gueto
ghetto blaster [-'blɑ:stə ͬ] *n* radiocas(s)et(t)e *m* portátil (*de gran tamaño*)
ghost [gəust] *n* fantasma *m* ■ *vt* (*book*) escribir por otro
ghostly ['gəustlɪ] *adj* fantasmal
ghost story *n* cuento de fantasmas
ghostwriter ['gəustraɪtə ͬ] *n* negro(-a)
ghoul [gu:l] *n* espíritu *m* necrófago
GHQ *n abbr* (*Mil*: = *general headquarters*) cuartel *m* general
GI *n abbr* (*US col*: = *government issue*) soldado del ejército norteamericano
giant ['dʒaɪənt] *n* gigante *m/f* ■ *adj* gigantesco, gigante; ~ **(size) packet** paquete *m* (de tamaño) gigante *or* familiar

giant killer *n* (*Sport*) matagigantes *m inv*
gibber ['dʒɪbə'] *vi* farfullar
gibberish ['dʒɪbərɪʃ] *n* galimatías *m*
gibe [dʒaɪb] *n* pulla
giblets ['dʒɪblɪts] *npl* menudillos *mpl*
Gibraltar [dʒɪ'brɔːltə'] *n* Gibraltar *m*
giddiness ['gɪdɪnɪs] *n* mareo
giddy ['gɪdɪ] *adj* (*dizzy*) mareado; (*height, speed*) vertiginoso; **it makes me ~** me marea; **I feel ~** me siento mareado
gift [gɪft] *n* (*gen*) regalo; (*Comm: also*: **free gift**) obsequio; (*ability*) don *m*; **to have a ~ for sth** tener dotes para algo
gifted ['gɪftɪd] *adj* dotado
gift token, gift voucher *n* vale-regalo *m*
gig [gɪg] *n* (*col: concert*) actuación *f*
gigabyte ['dʒɪgəbaɪt] *n* gigabyte *m*
gigantic [dʒaɪ'gæntɪk] *adj* gigantesco
giggle ['gɪgl] *vi* reírse tontamente ■ *n* risilla
GIGO ['gaɪgəu] *abbr* (*Comput: col*) = **garbage in, garbage out**
gill [dʒɪl] *n* (*measure*) *0.25 pints* (*BRIT = 0,148 litros; US = 0,118 litros.*)
gills [gɪlz] *npl* (*of fish*) branquias *fpl*, agallas *fpl*
gilt [gɪlt] *adj, n* dorado
gilt-edged ['gɪltedʒd] *adj* (*Comm: stocks, securities*) de máxima garantía
gimlet ['gɪmlɪt] *n* barrena de mano
gimmick ['gɪmɪk] *n* reclamo; **sales ~** reclamo promocional
gimmicky ['gɪmɪkɪ] *adj* de reclamo
gin [dʒɪn] *n* (*liquor*) ginebra
ginger ['dʒɪndʒə'] *n* jengibre *m*
ginger ale *n* ginger ale *m*
ginger beer *n* refresco *m* de jengibre
gingerbread ['dʒɪndʒəbred] *n* pan *m* de jengibre
ginger-haired [dʒɪndʒə'hɛəd] *adj* pelirrojo
gingerly ['dʒɪndʒəlɪ] *adv* con pies de plomo
ginseng ['dʒɪnsɛŋ] *n* ginseng *m*
gipsy ['dʒɪpsɪ] *n* gitano(-a)
giraffe [dʒɪ'rɑːf] *n* jirafa
girder ['gəːdə'] *n* viga
girdle ['gəːdl] *n* (*corset*) faja ■ *vt* ceñir
girl [gəːl] *n* (*small*) niña; (*young woman*) chica, joven *f*, muchacha; **an English ~** una (chica) inglesa
girlfriend ['gəːlfrend] *n* (*of girl*) amiga; (*of boy*) novia
Girl Guide *n* exploradora
girlish ['gəːlɪʃ] *adj* de niña
Girl Scout *n* (*US*) = **Girl Guide**
giro ['dʒaɪrəu] *n* (*Brit: bank giro*) giro bancario; (*post office giro*) giro postal
girth [gəːθ] *n* circunferencia; (*of saddle*) cincha
gist [dʒɪst] *n* lo esencial

give [gɪv] (*pt* **gave**, *pp* **given**) [geɪv, 'gɪvn] *vt* dar; (*deliver*) entregar; (*as gift*) regalar ■ *vi* (*break*) romperse; (*stretch: fabric*) dar de sí; **to ~ sb sth, ~ sth to sb** dar algo a algn; **how much did you ~ for it?** ¿cuánto pagaste por él?; **12 o'clock, ~ or take a few minutes** más o menos las doce; **~ them my regards** dales recuerdos de mi parte; **I can ~ you 10 minutes** le puedo conceder 10 minutos; **to ~ way** (*Brit Aut*) ceder el paso; **to ~ way to despair** ceder a la desesperación
▶ **give away** *vt* (*give free*) regalar; (*betray*) traicionar; (*disclose*) revelar
▶ **give back** *vt* devolver
▶ **give in** *vi* ceder ■ *vt* entregar
▶ **give off** *vt* despedir
▶ **give out** *vt* distribuir ■ *vi* (*be exhausted: supplies*) agotarse; (*fail: engine*) averiarse; (*strength*) fallar
▶ **give up** *vi* rendirse, darse por vencido ■ *vt* renunciar a; **to ~ up smoking** dejar de fumar; **to ~ o.s. up** entregarse
give-and-take ['gɪvənd'teɪk] *n* (*col*) toma y daca *m*
giveaway ['gɪvəweɪ] *n* (*col*): **her expression was a ~** su expresión la delataba; **the exam was a ~!** ¡el examen estaba tirado! ■ *cpd*: **~ prices** precios *mpl* de regalo
given ['gɪvn] *pp of* **give** ■ *adj* (*fixed: time, amount*) determinado ■ *conj*: **~ (that)** ... dado (que) ...; **~ the circumstances** ... dadas las circunstancias ...
glacial ['gleɪsɪəl] *adj* glacial
glacier ['glæsɪə'] *n* glaciar *m*
glad [glæd] *adj* contento; **to be ~ about sth/ that** alegrarse de algo/de que; **I was ~ of his help** agradecí su ayuda
gladden ['glædn] *vt* alegrar
glade [gleɪd] *n* claro
gladiator ['glædɪeɪtə'] *n* gladiador *m*
gladioli [glædɪ'əulaɪ] *npl* gladiolos *mpl*
gladly ['glædlɪ] *adv* con mucho gusto
glamorous ['glæmərəs] *adj* con encanto, atractivo
glamour ['glæmə'] *n* encanto, atractivo
glance [glɑːns] *n* ojeada, mirada ■ *vi*: **to ~ at** echar una ojeada a
▶ **glance off** *vt fus* (*bullet*) rebotar en
glancing ['glɑːnsɪŋ] *adj* (*blow*) oblicuo
gland [glænd] *n* glándula
glandular ['glændjulə'] *adj*: **~ fever** mononucleosis *f* infecciosa
glare [glɛə'] *n* deslumbramiento, brillo ■ *vi* deslumbrar; **to ~ at** mirar con odio
glaring ['glɛərɪŋ] *adj* (*mistake*) manifiesto
glass [glɑːs] *n* vidrio, cristal *m*; (*for drinking*) vaso; (*with stem*) copa; (*also*: **looking glass**) espejo

glass-blowing ['glɑːsbləʊɪŋ] n soplado de vidrio

glass ceiling n (fig) techo or barrera invisible (que impide ascender profesionalmente a las mujeres o miembros de minorías étnicas)

glasses ['glɑːsəs] npl gafas fpl, anteojos mpl (LAm)

glass fibre, (US) **glass fiber** n fibra de vidrio

glasshouse ['glɑːshaus] n invernadero

glassware ['glɑːswɛəʳ] n cristalería

glassy ['glɑːsɪ] adj (eyes) vidrioso

Glaswegian [glæs'wiːdʒən] adj de Glasgow
■ n nativo(-a) or habitante m(f) de Glasgow

glaze [gleɪz] vt (window) acristalar; (pottery) vidriar; (Culin) glasear ■ n barniz m; (Culin) glaseado

glazed [gleɪzd] adj (eye) vidrioso; (pottery) vidriado

glazier ['gleɪzɪəʳ] n vidriero(-a)

gleam [gliːm] n destello ■ vi relucir; **a ~ of hope** un rayo de esperanza

gleaming ['gliːmɪŋ] adj reluciente

glean [gliːn] vt (gather: information) recoger

glee [gliː] n alegría, regocijo

gleeful ['gliːful] adj alegre

glen [glɛn] n cañada

glib [glɪb] adj (person) de mucha labia; (comment) fácil

glibly ['glɪblɪ] adv (explain) con mucha labia

glide [glaɪd] vi deslizarse; (Aviat: bird) planear

glider ['glaɪdəʳ] n (Aviat) planeador m

gliding ['glaɪdɪŋ] n (Aviat) vuelo sin motor

glimmer ['glɪməʳ] n luz f tenue

glimpse [glɪmps] n vislumbre m ■ vt vislumbrar, entrever; **to catch a ~ of** vislumbrar

glint [glɪnt] n destello; (in the eye) chispa ■ vi centellear

glisten ['glɪsn] vi relucir, brillar

glitter ['glɪtəʳ] vi relucir, brillar ■ n brillo

glittering ['glɪtərɪŋ] adj reluciente, brillante

glitz [glɪts] n (col) vistosidad f

gloat [gləʊt] vi: **to ~ over** regodearse con

global ['gləʊbl] adj (world-wide) mundial; (comprehensive) global

globalization ['gləʊbəlaɪzeɪʃən] n globalización f, mundialización f

global warming [-'wɔːmɪŋ] n (re)calentamiento global or de la tierra

globe [gləʊb] n globo, esfera; (model) bola del mundo; globo terráqueo

globetrotter ['gləʊbtrɒtəʳ] n trotamundos m inv

globule ['glɒbjuːl] n glóbulo

gloom [gluːm] n penumbra; (sadness) desaliento, melancolía

gloomily ['gluːmɪlɪ] adv tristemente;

de modo pesimista

gloomy ['gluːmɪ] adj (dark) oscuro; (sad) triste; (pessimistic) pesimista; **to feel ~** sentirse pesimista

glorification [glɔːrɪfɪ'keɪʃən] n glorificación f

glorify ['glɔːrɪfaɪ] vt glorificar

glorious ['glɔːrɪəs] adj glorioso; (weather, sunshine) espléndido

glory ['glɔːrɪ] n gloria

Glos abbr (Brit) = **Gloucestershire**

gloss [glɒs] n (shine) brillo; (also: **gloss paint**) (pintura) esmalte m
▶ **gloss over** vt fus restar importancia a; (omit) pasar por alto

glossary ['glɒsərɪ] n glosario

glossy ['glɒsɪ] adj (hair) brillante; (photograph) con brillo; (magazine) de papel satinado or cuché

glove [glʌv] n guante m

glove compartment n (Aut) guantera

glow [gləʊ] vi (shine) brillar ■ n brillo

glower ['glauəʳ] vi: **to ~ at** mirar con ceño

glowing ['gləʊɪŋ] adj (fire) vivo; (complexion) encendido; (fig: report, description) entusiasta

glow-worm ['gləʊwəːm] n luciérnaga

glucose ['gluːkəʊs] n glucosa

glue [gluː] n pegamento, cemento (LAm) ■ vt pegar

glue-sniffing ['gluːsnɪfɪŋ] n inhalación f de pegamento or (LAm) cemento

glum [glʌm] adj (mood) abatido; (person, tone) melancólico

glut [glʌt] n superabundancia

glutinous ['gluːtɪnəs] adj glutinoso, pegajoso

glutton ['glʌtn] n glotón(-ona) m(f); **~ for punishment** masoquista m/f

gluttony ['glʌtənɪ] n gula, glotonería

glycerin, glycerine ['glɪsəriːn] n glicerina

GM adj abbr (= genetically-modified) transgénico

gm abbr (= gram) g

GMAT n abbr (US: = Graduate Management Admissions Test) examen de admisión al segundo ciclo de la enseñanza superior

GMB n abbr (Brit) = **General, Municipal, and Boilermakers (Union)**

GMo n abbr (= genetically modified organism) organismo transgénico, OGM m

GMT abbr (= Greenwich Mean Time) GMT

gnarled [nɑːld] adj nudoso

gnash [næʃ] vt: **to ~ one's teeth** hacer rechinar los dientes

gnat [næt] n mosquito

gnaw [nɔː] vt roer

gnome [nəʊm] n gnomo

GNP n abbr (= gross national product) PNB m

GNVQ n abbr (Brit: = general national vocational qualification) título general de formación profesional

go [gəu] *vb* (*pt* **went**, *pp* **gone**) ■ *vi* ir; (*travel*) viajar; (*depart*) irse, marcharse; (*work*) funcionar, marchar; (*be sold*) venderse; (*time*) pasar; (*become*) ponerse; (*break etc*) estropearse, romperse; (*fit, suit*): **to go with** hacer juego con ■ *n* (*pl* **goes**); **to have a go (at)** probar suerte (con); **to be on the go** no parar; **whose go is it?** ¿a quién le toca?; **to go by car/on foot** ir en coche/a pie; **he's going to do it** va a hacerlo; **to go for a walk** ir a dar un paseo; **to go dancing** ir a bailar; **to go looking for sth/sb** ir a buscar algo/a algn; **to make sth go, get sth going** poner algo en marcha; **my voice has gone** he perdido la voz; **the cake is all gone** se acabó la tarta; **the money will go towards our holiday** el dinero es para (ayuda de) nuestras vacaciones; **how did it go?** ¿qué tal salió or resultó?, ¿cómo ha ido?; **the meeting went well** la reunión salió bien; **to go and see sb** ir a ver a algn; **to go to sleep** dormirse; **I'll take whatever is going** acepto lo que haya; **... to go** (*US: food*) ... para llevar; **to go round the back** pasar por detrás
▸ **go about** *vi* (*rumour*) propagarse; (*also*: **go round**: *wander about*) andar (de un sitio para otro) ■ *vt fus*: **how do I go about this?** ¿cómo me las arreglo para hacer esto?; **to go about one's business** ocuparse de sus asuntos
▸ **go after** *vt fus* (*pursue*) perseguir; (*job, record etc*) andar tras
▸ **go against** *vt fus* (*be unfavourable to: results*) ir en contra de; (*be contrary to: principles*) ser contrario a
▸ **go ahead** *vi* seguir adelante
▸ **go along** *vi* ir; **as you go along** sobre la marcha ■ *vt fus* bordear
▸ **go along with** *vt fus* (*accompany*) acompañar; (*agree with: idea*) estar de acuerdo con
▸ **go around** *vi* = **go round**
▸ **go away** *vi* irse, marcharse
▸ **go back** *vi* volver
▸ **go back on** *vt fus* (*promise*) faltar a
▸ **go by** *vi* (*years, time*) pasar ■ *vt fus* guiarse por
▸ **go down** *vi* bajar; (*ship*) hundirse; (*sun*) ponerse ■ *vt fus* bajar por; **that should go down well with him** eso le va a gustar; **he's gone down with flu** ha cogido la gripe
▸ **go for** *vt fus* (*fetch*) ir por; (*like*) gustar; (*attack*) atacar
▸ **go in** *vi* entrar
▸ **go in for** *vt fus* (*competition*) presentarse a
▸ **go into** *vt fus* entrar en; (*investigate*) investigar; (*embark on*) dedicarse a
▸ **go off** *vi* irse, marcharse; (*food*) pasarse; (*lights etc*) apagarse; (*explode*) estallar; (*event*) realizarse ■ *vt fus* perder el interés por; **the party went off well** la fiesta salió bien
▸ **go on** *vi* (*continue*) seguir, continuar; (*lights*) encenderse; (*happen*) pasar, ocurrir; (*be guided by: evidence etc*) partir de; **to go on doing sth** seguir haciendo algo; **what's going on here?** ¿qué pasa aquí?
▸ **go on at** *vt fus* (*nag*) soltarle el rollo a
▸ **go out** *vi* salir; (*fire, light*) apagarse; (*ebb: tide*) bajar, menguar; **to go out with sb** salir con algn
▸ **go over** *vi* (*ship*) zozobrar ■ *vt fus* (*check*) revisar; **to go over sth in one's mind** repasar algo mentalmente
▸ **go round** *vi* (*circulate: news, rumour*) correr; (*suffice*) alcanzar, bastar; (*revolve*) girar, dar vueltas; (*visit*): **to go round (to sb's)** pasar a ver (a algn); **to go round (by)** (*make a detour*) dar la vuelta (por)
▸ **go through** *vt fus* (*town etc*) atravesar; (*search through*) revisar; (*perform: ceremony*) realizar; (*examine: list, book*) repasar
▸ **go through with** *vt fus* (*plan, crime*) llevar a cabo; **I couldn't go through with it** no pude llevarlo a cabo
▸ **go together** *vi* entenderse
▸ **go under** *vi* (*sink: ship, person*) hundirse; (*fig: business, firm*) quebrar
▸ **go up** *vi* subir; **to go up in flames** estallar en llamas
▸ **go without** *vt fus* pasarse sin
goad [gəud] *vt* aguijonear
go-ahead ['gəuəhɛd] *adj* emprendedor(a) ■ *n* luz *f* verde; **to give sth/sb the ~** dar luz verde a algo/algn
goal [gəul] *n* meta, arco (*LAm*); (*score*) gol *m*
goal difference *n* diferencia por goles
goalie ['gəulɪ] *n* (*col*) = **goalkeeper**
goalkeeper ['gəulkiːpəʳ] *n* portero, guardameta *m/f*, arquero (*LAm*)
goal post *n* poste *m* (de la portería)
goat [gəut] *n* cabra *f*
gobble ['gɔbl] *vt* (*also*: **gobble down, gobble up**) engullir
go-between ['gəubɪtwiːn] *n* intermediario(-a)
Gobi Desert ['gəubɪ-] *n* Desierto de Gobi
goblet ['gɔblɪt] *n* copa
goblin ['gɔblɪn] *n* duende *m*
go-cart ['gəukɑːt] *n* = **go-kart**
god [gɔd] *n* dios *m*; **G~** Dios *m*
god-awful [gɔd'ɔːfəl] *adj* (*col*) de puta pena
godchild ['gɔdtʃaɪld] *n* ahijado(-a)
goddamn ['gɔddæm] *adj* (*col: also:* **goddamned**) maldito, puñetero ■ *excl*: **~!** ¡cagüen diez!

goddess ['gɒdɪs] n diosa
godfather ['gɒdfɑːðəʳ] n padrino
god-fearing ['gɒdfɪərɪŋ] adj temeroso de Dios
god-forsaken ['gɒdfəseɪkən] adj dejado de la mano de Dios
godmother ['gɒdmʌðəʳ] n madrina
godparents ['gɒdpɛərənts] npl: **the ~** los padrinos
godsend ['gɒdsɛnd] n: **to be a ~** venir como llovido del cielo
godson ['gɒdsʌn] n ahijado
goes [gəuz] vb see **go**
gofer ['gəufəʳ] n (col) chico(-a) para todo
go-getter ['gəugɛtəʳ] n ambicioso(-a)
goggle ['gɒgl] vi: **to ~ (at)** mirar con ojos desorbitados
goggles ['gɒglz] npl (Aut) gafas fpl, anteojos mpl (LAm); (diver's) gafas fpl submarinas
going ['gəuɪŋ] n (conditions) cosas fpl ■ adj: **the ~ rate** la tarifa corriente or en vigor; **it was slow ~** las cosas iban lentas
going-over [gəuɪŋ'əuvəʳ] n revisión f; (col: beating) paliza
goings-on ['gəuɪŋz'ɒn] npl (col) tejemanejes mpl
go-kart ['gəukɑːt] n kart m
gold [gəuld] n oro ■ adj (reserves) de oro
golden ['gəuldn] adj (made of gold) de oro; (golden in colour) dorado
Golden Age n Siglo de Oro
golden handshake n cuantiosa gratificación por los servicios prestados
golden rule n regla de oro
goldfish ['gəuldfɪʃ] n pez m de colores
gold leaf n pan m de oro
gold medal n (Sport) medalla de oro
goldmine ['gəuldmaɪn] n mina de oro
gold-plated ['gəuld'pleɪtɪd] adj chapado en oro
goldsmith ['gəuldsmɪθ] n orfebre m/f
gold standard n patrón m oro
golf [gɒlf] n golf m
golf ball n (for game) pelota de golf; (on typewriter) esfera impresora
golf club n club m de golf; (stick) palo (de golf)
golf course n campo de golf
golfer ['gɒlfəʳ] n jugador(a) m(f) de golf, golfista m/f
golfing ['gɒlfɪŋ] n: **to go ~** jugar al golf
gondola ['gɒndələ] n góndola
gondolier [gɒndə'lɪəʳ] n gondolero
gone [gɒn] pp of **go**
goner ['gɒnəʳ] n (col): **to be a ~** estar en las últimas
gong [gɒŋ] n gong m
gonorrhea [gɒnə'rɪə] n gonorrea
good [gud] adj bueno; (before m sing n) buen;

(well-behaved) educado ■ n bien m; **~!** ¡qué bien!; **he's ~ at it** se le da bien; **to be ~ for** servir para; **it's ~ for you** te hace bien; **would you be ~ enough to ...?** ¿podría hacerme el favor de ...?, ¿sería tan amable de ...?; **that's very ~ of you** es usted muy amable; **to feel ~** sentirse bien; **it's ~ to see you** me alegro de verte; **a ~ deal (of)** mucho; **a ~ many** muchos; **to make ~** reparar; **it's no ~ complaining** no sirve de nada quejarse; **is this any ~?** (will it do?) ¿sirve esto?; (what's it like?) ¿qué tal es esto?; **it's a ~ thing you were there** menos mal que estabas allí; **for ~** (for ever) para siempre, definitivamente; **~ morning/afternoon** ¡buenos días/buenas tardes!; **~ evening!** ¡buenas noches!; **~ night!** ¡buenas noches!; **he's up to no ~** está tramando algo; **for the common ~** para el bien común; see also **goods**
goodbye [gud'baɪ] excl ¡adiós!; **to say ~ (to)** (person) despedirse (de)
good faith n buena fe f
good-for-nothing ['gudfənʌθɪŋ] n inútil m/f
Good Friday n Viernes m Santo
good-humoured ['gud'hjuːməd] adj (person) afable, de buen humor; (remark, joke) bien intencionado
good-looking ['gud'lukɪŋ] adj guapo
good-natured ['gud'neɪtʃəd] adj (person) de buen carácter; (discussion) cordial
goodness ['gudnɪs] n (of person) bondad f; **for ~ sake!** ¡por Dios!; **~ gracious!** ¡madre mía!
goods [gudz] npl bienes mpl; (Comm etc) géneros mpl, mercancías fpl, artículos mpl; **all his ~ and chattels** todos sus bienes
goods train n (Brit) tren m de mercancías
goodwill [gud'wɪl] n buena voluntad f; (Comm) fondo de comercio; (customer connections) clientela
goody-goody ['gudɪgudɪ] n (pej) santurrón(-ona) m(f)
gooey ['guːɪ] adj (Brit col) pegajoso; (cake, behaviour) empalagoso
google® ['gugl] vi, vt googlear
goose, geese [guːs, giːs] n ganso, oca
gooseberry ['guzbərɪ] n grosella espinosa or silvestre
gooseflesh ['guːsfleʃ] n, **goosepimples** ['guːspɪmplz] npl carne f de gallina
goose step n (Mil) paso de la oca
GOP n abbr (US Pol: col: = Grand Old Party) Partido Republicano
gopher ['gəufəʳ] n = **gofer**
gore [gɔːʳ] vt dar una cornada a, cornear ■ n sangre f
gorge [gɔːdʒ] n garganta ■ vr: **to ~ o.s. (on)** atracarse (de)

gorgeous ['gɔːdʒəs] *adj* precioso; (*weather*) estupendo; (*person*) guapísimo

gorilla [gə'rɪlə] *n* gorila *m*

gormless ['gɔːmlɪs] *adj* (*col*) ceporro, zoquete

gorse [gɔːs] *n* tojo

gory ['gɔːrɪ] *adj* sangriento

go-slow ['gəu'sləu] *n* (*Brit*) huelga de celo

gospel ['gɔspl] *n* evangelio

gossamer ['gɔsəmər] *n* gasa

gossip ['gɔsɪp] *n* cotilleo; (*person*) cotilla *m/f* ■ *vi* cotillear, comadrear (*LAm*); **a piece of ~** un cotilleo

gossip column *n* ecos *mpl* de sociedad

got [gɔt] *pt, pp of* **get**

Gothic ['gɔθɪk] *adj* gótico

gotten ['gɔtn] (*US*) *pp of* **get**

gouge [gaudʒ] *vt* (*also:* **gouge out**: *hole etc*) excavar; (: *initials*) grabar; **to ~ sb's eyes out** sacar los ojos a algn

goulash ['guːlæʃ] *n* g(o)ulash *m*

gourd [guəd] *n* calabaza

gourmet ['guəmeɪ] *n* gastrónomo(-a) *m(f)*

gout [gaut] *n* gota

govern ['gʌvən] *vt* (*gen*) gobernar; (*event, conduct*) regir

governess ['gʌvənɪs] *n* institutriz *f*

governing ['gʌvənɪŋ] *adj* (*Pol*) de gobierno, gubernamental; **~ body** organismo de gobierno

government ['gʌvnmənt] *n* gobierno; **local ~** administración *f* municipal

governmental [gʌvn'mɛntl] *adj* gubernamental

government stock *n* papel *m* del Estado

governor ['gʌvənər] *n* gobernador(a) *m(f)*; (*of jail*) director(a) *m(f)*

Govt *abbr* (= *Government*) gobno

gown [gaun] *n* vestido; (*of teacher*: Brit: *of judge*) toga

GP *n abbr* (*Med*) = **general practitioner**

GPMU *n abbr* (Brit: = *Graphical, Paper and Media Union*) sindicato de trabajadores del sector editorial

GPO *n abbr* (Brit: old: = *General Post Office*) (US) = **Government Printing Office**

GPS *n abbr* (= *global positioning system*) GPS *m*

gr. *abbr* (Comm: = *gross*) bto

grab [græb] *vt* coger (SP) or agarrar; **to ~ at** intentar agarrar

grace [greɪs] *n* (Rel) gracia; (*gracefulness*) elegancia, gracia; (*graciousness*) cortesía, gracia ■ *vt* (*favour*) honrar; (*adorn*) adornar; **5 days' ~** un plazo de 5 días; **to say ~** bendecir la mesa; **his sense of humour is his saving ~** lo que le salva es su sentido del humor

graceful ['greɪsful] *adj* elegante

gracious ['greɪʃəs] *adj* amable ■ *excl*: **good ~!** ¡Dios mío!

grade [greɪd] *n* (*quality*) clase *f*, calidad *f*; (*in hierarchy*) grado; (*US Scol*) curso; (: *gradient*) pendiente *f*, cuesta ■ *vt* clasificar; **to make the ~** (*fig*) dar el nivel; *see also* **high school**

grade crossing *n* (US) paso a nivel

grade school *n* (US) escuela primaria; *see also* **elementary school**

gradient ['greɪdɪənt] *n* pendiente *f*

gradual ['grædjuəl] *adj* gradual

gradually ['grædjuəlɪ] *adv* gradualmente

graduate *n* ['grædjuɪt] licenciado(-a), graduado(-a), egresado(-a) (*LAm*); (*US Scol*) bachiller *m/f* ■ *vi* ['grædjueɪt] licenciarse, graduarse, recibirse (*LAm*); (US) obtener el título de bachillerato

graduated pension ['grædjueɪtɪd-] *n* pensión *f* escalonada

graduation [grædju'eɪʃən] *n* graduación *f*; (*US Scol*) entrega de los títulos de bachillerato

graffiti [grə'fiːtɪ] *npl* pintadas *fpl*

graft [graːft] *n* (*Agr, Med*) injerto; (*bribery*) corrupción *f* ■ *vt* injertar; **hard ~** (*col*) trabajo duro

grain [greɪn] *n* (*single particle*) grano; (*no pl: cereals*) cereales *mpl*; (*US: corn*) trigo; (*in wood*) veta

gram [græm] *n* (US) gramo

grammar ['græmər] *n* gramática

grammar school *n* (Brit) ≈ instituto (de segunda enseñanza); (US) escuela primaria; *see also* **comprehensive school**

grammatical [grə'mætɪkl] *adj* gramatical

gramme [græm] *n* = **gram**

gramophone ['græməfəun] *n* (Brit) gramófono

granary ['grænərɪ] *n* granero

grand [grænd] *adj* grandioso ■ *n* (*US: col*) mil dólares *mpl*

grandchildren ['græntʃɪldrən] *npl* nietos *mpl*

granddad ['grændæd] *n* yayo, abuelito

granddaughter ['grændɔːtər] *n* nieta

grandeur ['grændjər] *n* grandiosidad *f*

grandfather ['grænfɑːðər] *n* abuelo

grandiose ['grændɪəuz] *adj* grandioso; (*pej*) pomposo

grand jury *n* (US) jurado de acusación

grandma ['grænmɑː] *n* yaya, abuelita

grandmother ['grænmʌðər] *n* abuela

grandpa ['grænpɑː] *n* = **granddad**

grandparents ['grændpɛərənts] *npl* abuelos *mpl*

grand piano *n* piano de cola

Grand Prix ['grɑː'priː] *n* (Aut) gran premio, Grand Prix *m*

grandson ['grænsʌn] *n* nieto

grandstand ['grændstænd] *n* (Sport) tribuna

grand total *n* suma total, total *m*

granite ['grænɪt] n granito
granny ['grænɪ] n abuelita, yaya
grant [grɑ:nt] vt (concede) conceder; (admit):
  to ~ (that) reconocer (que) ■ n (Scol) beca;
  to take sth for granted dar algo por sentado
granulated sugar ['grænjuleɪtɪd-] n (Brit)
  azúcar m granulado
granule ['grænju:l] n gránulo
grape [greɪp] n uva; **sour grapes** (fig)
  envidia sg; **a bunch of grapes** un racimo
  de uvas
grapefruit ['greɪpfru:t] n pomelo, toronja
grape juice n jugo or (SP) zumo de uva
grapevine ['greɪpvaɪn] n vid f, parra; **I heard
  it on the ~** (fig) me enteré, me lo contaron
graph [grɑ:f] n gráfica
graphic ['græfɪk] adj gráfico
graphic designer n diseñador(a) m(f)
  gráfico(-a)
graphic equalizer n ecualizador m gráfico
graphics ['græfɪks] n (art, process) artes fpl
  gráficas ■ npl (drawings: Comput) gráficos mpl
graphite ['græfaɪt] n grafito
graph paper n papel m cuadriculado
grapple ['græpl] vi (also: **to grapple with a
  problem**) enfrentarse a un problema
grappling iron ['græplɪŋ-] n (Naut) rezón m
grasp [grɑ:sp] vt agarrar, asir; (understand)
  comprender ■ n (grip) asimiento; (reach)
  alcance m; (understanding) comprensión f;
  to have a good ~ of (subject) dominar
  ▸ **grasp at** vt fus (rope etc) tratar de agarrar;
  (fig: opportunity) aprovechar
grasping ['grɑ:spɪŋ] adj avaro
grass [grɑ:s] n hierba; (lawn) césped m;
  (pasture) pasto; (col: informer) soplón(-ona) m(f)
grasshopper ['grɑ:shɔpər] n saltamontes
  m inv
grassland ['grɑ:slænd] n pradera, pampa
  (LAm)
grass roots adj de base ■ npl (Pol) bases fpl
grass snake n culebra
grassy ['grɑ:sɪ] adj cubierto de hierba
grate [greɪt] n parrilla ■ vi chirriar, rechinar
  ■ vt (Culin) rallar
grateful ['greɪtful] adj agradecido
gratefully ['greɪtfəlɪ] adv con
  agradecimiento
grater ['greɪtər] n rallador m
gratification [grætɪfɪ'keɪʃən] n satisfacción f
gratify ['grætɪfaɪ] vt complacer; (whim)
  satisfacer
gratifying ['grætɪfaɪɪŋ] adj gratificante
grating ['greɪtɪŋ] n (iron bars) rejilla ■ adj
  (noise) chirriante
gratitude ['grætɪtju:d] n agradecimiento
gratuitous [grə'tju:ɪtəs] adj gratuito

gratuity [grə'tju:ɪtɪ] n gratificación f
grave [greɪv] n tumba ■ adj serio, grave
gravedigger ['greɪvdɪgər] n sepulturero(-a)
gravel ['grævl] n grava
gravely ['greɪvlɪ] adv seriamente; **~ ill** muy
  grave
gravestone ['greɪvstəun] n lápida
graveyard ['greɪvjɑ:d] n cementerio,
  camposanto
gravitate ['grævɪteɪt] vi gravitar
gravitation [grævɪ'teɪʃən] n gravitación f
gravity ['grævɪtɪ] n gravedad f; (seriousness)
  seriedad f
gravy ['greɪvɪ] n salsa de carne
gravy boat n salsera
gravy train n (esp US: col): **to get on the ~**
  coger un chollo
gray [greɪ] adj (US) = **grey**
graze [greɪz] vi pacer ■ vt (touch lightly, scrape)
  rozar ■ n (Med) rozadura
grazing ['greɪzɪŋ] n (for livestock) pastoreo
grease [gri:s] n (fat) grasa; (lubricant)
  lubricante m ■ vt engrasar; **to ~ the skids**
  (US: fig) engrasar el mecanismo
grease gun n pistola engrasadora
greasepaint ['gri:speɪnt] n maquillaje m
greaseproof ['gri:spru:f] adj a prueba de
  grasa; (Brit: paper) de grasa
greasy ['gri:sɪ] adj (hands, clothes) grasiento;
  (road, surface) resbaladizo
great [greɪt] adj grande; (before n sing) gran;
  (col) estupendo, macanudo (LAm), regio
  (LAm); (pain, heat) intenso; **we had a ~ time**
  nos lo pasamos muy bien; **they're ~ friends**
  son íntimos or muy amigos; **the ~ thing
  is that ...** lo bueno es que ...; **it was ~!** ¡fue
  estupendo!
Great Barrier Reef n Gran Barrera de Coral
Great Britain n Gran Bretaña
greater ['greɪtər] adj mayor; **G~ London** el
  área metropolitana de Londres
greatest ['greɪtɪst] adj (el/la) mayor
great-grandchild (pl **-children**)
  [greɪt'grændtʃaɪld, 'tʃɪldrən] n bisnieto(-a)
great-grandfather [greɪt'grændfɑ:ðər] n
  bisabuelo
great-grandmother [greɪt'grændmʌðər] n
  bisabuela
Great Lakes npl: **the ~** los Grandes Lagos
greatly ['greɪtlɪ] adv sumamente, muy
greatness ['greɪtnɪs] n grandeza
Greece [gri:s] n Grecia
greed [gri:d] n (also: **greediness**) codicia;
  (for food) gula
greedily ['gri:dɪlɪ] adv con avidez
greedy ['gri:dɪ] adj codicioso; (for food)
  glotón(-ona)

Greek [gri:k] *adj* griego ■ *n* griego(-a); (*Ling*) griego; **ancient/modern ~** griego antiguo/ moderno

green [gri:n] *adj* verde; (*inexperienced*) novato ■ *n* verde *m*; (*stretch of grass*) césped *m*; (*of golf course*) campo, "green" *m*; **the G~ party** (*Pol*) el partido verde; **greens** *npl* verduras *fpl*; **to have ~ fingers** (*fig*) tener buena mano para las plantas

green belt *n* cinturón *m* verde

green card *n* (*Aut*) carta verde

greenery ['gri:nərɪ] *n* vegetación *f*

greenfly ['gri:nflaɪ] *n* pulgón *m*

greengage ['gri:ngeɪdʒ] *n* (ciruela) claudia

greengrocer ['gri:ngrəʊsər] *n* (*Brit*) frutero(-a), verdulero(-a)

greenhouse ['gri:nhaʊs] *n* invernadero

greenhouse effect *n*: **the ~** el efecto invernadero

greenhouse gas *n* gas *m* que produce el efecto invernadero

greenish ['gri:nɪʃ] *adj* verdoso

Greenland ['gri:nlənd] *n* Groenlandia

Greenlander ['gri:nləndər] *n* groenlandés(-esa) *m(f)*

green light *n* luz *f* verde

green pepper *n* pimiento verde

greet [gri:t] *vt* saludar; (*news*) recibir

greeting ['gri:tɪŋ] *n* (*gen*) saludo; (*welcome*) bienvenida; **greetings** saludos *mpl*; **season's greetings** Felices Pascuas

greeting card, greetings card *n* tarjeta de felicitación

gregarious [grə'gɛərɪəs] *adj* gregario

grenade [grə'neɪd] *n* (*also*: **hand grenade**) granada

grew [gru:] *pt of* **grow**

grey [greɪ] *adj* gris; **to go ~** salirle canas

grey-haired [greɪ'hɛəd] *adj* canoso

greyhound ['greɪhaʊnd] *n* galgo

grid [grɪd] *n* rejilla; (*Elec*) red *f*

griddle ['grɪdl] *n* (*esp US*) plancha

gridiron ['grɪdaɪən] *n* (*Culin*) parrilla

gridlock ['grɪdlɔk] *n* (*esp US*) retención *f*

grief [gri:f] *n* dolor *m*, pena; **to come to ~** (*plan*) fracasar, ir al traste; (*person*) acabar mal, desgraciarse

grievance ['gri:vəns] *n* (*cause for complaint*) motivo de queja, agravio

grieve [gri:v] *vi* afligirse, acongojarse ■ *vt* afligir, apenar; **to ~ for** llorar por; **to ~ for sb** (*dead person*) llorar la pérdida de algn

grievous ['gri:vəs] *adj* grave; (*loss*) cruel; **~ bodily harm** (*Law*) daños *mpl* corporales graves

grill [grɪl] *n* (*on cooker*) parrilla ■ *vt* (*Brit*) asar a la parrilla; (*question*) interrogar; **grilled**

meat carne *f* (asada) a la parrilla *or* plancha

grille [grɪl] *n* rejilla

grim [grɪm] *adj* (*place*) lúgubre; (*person*) adusto

grimace [grɪ'meɪs] *n* mueca ■ *vi* hacer muecas

grime [graɪm] *n* mugre *f*

grimly ['grɪmlɪ] *adv* (*say*) sombríamente

grimy ['graɪmɪ] *adj* mugriento

grin [grɪn] *n* sonrisa abierta ■ *vi*: **to ~ (at)** sonreír abiertamente (a)

grind [graɪnd] (*pt, pp* **ground**) *vt* (*coffee, pepper etc*) moler; (*US: meat*) picar; (*make sharp*) afilar; (*polish: gem, lens*) esmerilar ■ *vi* (*car gears*) rechinar ■ *n*: **the daily ~** (*col*) la rutina diaria; **to ~ one's teeth** hacer rechinar los dientes; **to ~ to a halt** (*vehicle*) pararse con gran estruendo de frenos; (*fig: talks, scheme*) interrumpirse; (*work, production*) paralizarse

grinder ['graɪndər] *n* (*machine: for coffee*) molinillo

grindstone ['graɪndstəʊn] *n*: **to keep one's nose to the ~** trabajar sin descanso

grip [grɪp] *n* (*hold*) asimiento; (*of hands*) apretón *m*; (*handle*) asidero; (*of racquet etc*) mango; (*understanding*) comprensión *f* ■ *vt* agarrar; **to get to grips with** enfrentarse con; **to lose one's ~** (*fig*) perder el control; **he lost his ~ of the situation** la situación se le fue de las manos

gripe [graɪp] *n* (*col: complaint*) queja ■ *vi* (*col: complain*): **to ~ (about)** quejarse (de); **gripes** *npl* retortijones *mpl*

gripping ['grɪpɪŋ] *adj* absorbente

grisly ['grɪzlɪ] *adj* horripilante, horrible

gristle ['grɪsl] *n* cartílago

grit [grɪt] *n* gravilla; (*courage*) valor *m* ■ *vt* (*road*) poner gravilla en; **I've got a piece of ~ in my eye** tengo una arenilla en el ojo; **to ~ one's teeth** apretar los dientes

grits [grɪts] *npl* (*US*) maíz *msg* a medio moler

grizzle ['grɪzl] *vi* (*cry*) lloriquear

grizzly ['grɪzlɪ] *n* (*also*: **grizzly bear**) oso pardo

groan [grəʊn] *n* gemido, quejido ■ *vi* gemir, quejarse

grocer ['grəʊsər] *n* tendero (de ultramarinos); **~'s (shop)** *n* tienda de ultramarinos *or* (*LAm*) de abarrotes

groceries ['grəʊsərɪz] *npl* comestibles *mpl*

grocery ['grəʊsərɪ] *n* (*shop*) tienda de ultramarinos

grog [grɔg] *n* (*Brit*) grog *m*

groggy ['grɔgɪ] *adj* atontado

groin [grɔɪn] *n* ingle *f*

groom [gru:m] *n* mozo(-a) de cuadra; (*also*: **bridegroom**) novio ■ *vt* (*horse*) almohazar; **well-groomed** acicalado

groove [gru:v] *n* ranura; (*of record*) surco

grope [grəup] vi ir a tientas; **to ~ for** buscar a tientas

gross [grəus] adj grueso; (Comm) bruto ■ vt (Comm) recaudar en bruto

gross domestic product n producto interior bruto

gross income n ingresos mpl brutos

grossly ['grəuslɪ] adv (greatly) enormemente

gross national product n producto nacional bruto

gross profit n beneficios mpl brutos

gross sales npl ventas fpl brutas

grotesque [grə'tɛsk] adj grotesco

grotto ['grɔtəu] n gruta

grotty ['grɔtɪ] adj asqueroso

grouch [grautʃ] vi (col) refunfuñar ■ n (col: person) refunfuñón(-ona) m(f)

ground [graund] pt, pp of **grind** ■ n suelo, tierra; (Sport) campo, terreno; (reason: gen pl) motivo, razón f; (US: also: **ground wire**) tierra ■ vt (plane) mantener en tierra; (US Elec) conectar con tierra ■ vi (ship) varar, encallar ■ adj (coffee etc) molido; **grounds** npl (of coffee etc) poso sg; (gardens etc) jardines mpl, parque m; **on the ~** en el suelo; **common ~** terreno común; **to gain/lose ~** ganar/perder terreno; **to the ~** al suelo; **below ~** bajo tierra; **he covered a lot of ~ in his lecture** abarcó mucho en la clase

ground cloth n (US) = **groundsheet**

ground control n control m desde tierra

ground floor n (Brit) planta baja

grounding ['graundɪŋ] n (in education) conocimientos mpl básicos

groundkeeper ['graundkiːpəʳ] n: **groundsman**

groundless ['graundlɪs] adj infundado, sin fundamento

groundnut ['graundnʌt] n cacahuete m

ground rent n alquiler m del terreno

ground rules npl normas básicas

groundsheet ['graundʃiːt] (Brit) n tela impermeable

groundsman ['graundzmən], **groundskeeper** (US) ['graundzkiːpəʳ] n (Sport) encargado de pista de deportes

ground staff n personal m de tierra

ground swell n mar m or f de fondo; (fig) ola

ground-to-air ['grauntə'ɛə] adj tierra-aire

ground-to-ground ['grauntə'graund] adj tierra-tierra

groundwork ['graundwəːk] n trabajo preliminar

Ground Zero n zona cero

group [gruːp] n grupo; (Mus: pop group) conjunto, grupo; (vb: also: **group together**) ■ vt agrupar ■ vi agruparse

groupie ['gruːpɪ] n groupie f

group therapy n terapia de grupo

grouse [graus] n (pl inv: bird) urogallo ■ vi (complain) quejarse

grove [grəuv] n arboleda

grovel ['grɔvl] vi (fig) arrastrarse

grow (pt **grew**, pp **grown**) [grəu, gruː, grəun] vi crecer; (increase) aumentar; (expand) desarrollarse; (become) volverse ■ vt cultivar; (hair, beard) dejar crecer; **to ~ rich/weak** enriquecerse/debilitarse; **to ~ tired of waiting** cansarse de esperar
  ▸ **grow apart** vi (fig) alejarse uno del otro
  ▸ **grow away from** vt fus (fig) alejarse de
  ▸ **grow on** vt fus: **that painting is growing on me** ese cuadro me gusta cada vez más
  ▸ **grow out of** vt fus (clothes): **I've grown out of this shirt** esta camisa se me ha quedado pequeña; (habit) perder
  ▸ **grow up** vi crecer, hacerse hombre/mujer

grower ['grəuəʳ] n (Agr) cultivador(a) m(f), productor(a) m(f)

growing ['grəuɪŋ] adj creciente; **~ pains** (also fig) problemas mpl de crecimiento

growl [graul] vi gruñir

grown [grəun] pp of **grow**

grown-up [grəun'ʌp] n adulto(-a), mayor m/f

growth [grəuθ] n crecimiento, desarrollo; (what has grown) brote m; (Med) tumor m

growth rate n tasa de crecimiento

grub [grʌb] n gusano; (col: food) comida

grubby ['grʌbɪ] adj sucio, mugriento, mugroso (LAm)

grudge [grʌdʒ] n rencor ■ vt: **to ~ sb sth** dar algo a algn de mala gana; **to bear sb a ~** guardar rencor a algn; **he grudges (giving) the money** da el dinero de mala gana

grudgingly ['grʌdʒɪŋlɪ] adv de mala gana

gruelling, grueling (US) ['gruːəlɪŋ] adj agotador

gruesome ['gruːsəm] adj horrible

gruff [grʌf] adj (voice) ronco; (manner) brusco

grumble ['grʌmbl] vi refunfuñar, quejarse

grumpy ['grʌmpɪ] adj gruñón(-ona)

grunge [grʌndʒ] n (Mus: fashion) grunge m

grunt [grʌnt] vi gruñir ■ n gruñido

G-string ['dʒiːstrɪŋ] n tanga m

GSUSA n abbr = **Girl Scouts of the United States of America**

GT abbr (Aut: = gran turismo) GT

GU abbr (US Post) = **Guam**

guarantee [gærən'tiː] n garantía ■ vt garantizar; **he can't ~ (that) he'll come** no está seguro de poder venir

guarantor [gærən'tɔːʳ] n garante m/f, fiador(a) m(f)

guard [gɑːd] n guardia; (person) guarda

m/f; (*Brit Rail*) jefe *m* de tren; (*safety device: on machine*) cubierta de protección; (*protection*) protección *f*; (*fireguard*) pantalla; (*mudguard*) guardabarros *m inv* ■ *vt* guardar; **to ~ (against** *or* **from**) proteger (de); **to be on one's ~** (*fig*) estar en guardia
▶ **guard against** *vi*: **to ~ against doing sth** guardarse de hacer algo
guard dog *n* perro guardián
guarded ['gɑːdɪd] *adj* (*fig*) cauteloso
guardian ['gɑːdɪən] *n* guardián(-ana) *m(f)*; (*of minor*) tutor(a) *m(f)*
guardrail ['gɑːdreɪl] *n* pretil *m*
guard's van *n* (*Brit Rail*) furgón *m* del jefe de tren
Guatemala [gwɑːtə'mɑːlə] *n* Guatemala
Guatemalan [gwɑːtə'mɑːlən] *adj, n* guatemalteco(-a) *m(f)*
Guernsey ['gəːnzɪ] *n* Guernsey *m*
guerrilla [gə'rɪlə] *n* guerrillero(-a)
guerrilla warfare *n* guerra de guerrillas
guess [gɛs] *vi, vt* (*gen*) adivinar; (*suppose*) suponer ■ *n* suposición *f*, conjetura; **I ~ you're right** (*esp US*) supongo que tienes razón; **to keep sb guessing** mantener a algn a la expectativa; **to take** *or* **have a ~** tratar de adivinar; **my ~ is that ...** yo creo que ...
guesstimate ['gɛstɪmɪt] *n* cálculo aproximado
guesswork ['gɛswəːk] *n* conjeturas *fpl*; **I got the answer by ~** acerté a ojo de buen cubero
guest [gɛst] *n* invitado(-a); (*in hotel*) huésped(a) *m(f)*; **be my ~** (*col*) estás en tu casa
guest-house ['gɛsthaus] *n* casa de huéspedes, pensión *f*
guest room *n* cuarto de huéspedes
guff [gʌf] *n* (*col*) bobadas *fpl*
guffaw [gʌ'fɔː] *n* carcajada ■ *vi* reírse a carcajadas
guidance ['gaɪdəns] *n* (*gen*) dirección *f*; (*advice*) consejos *mpl*; **marriage/vocational ~** orientación *f* matrimonial/profesional
guide [gaɪd] *n* (*person*) guía *m/f*; (*book*) guía *f*; (*fig*) guía *f*; (*also*: **girl guide**) exploradora ■ *vt* guiar; **to be guided by sb/sth** dejarse guiar por algn/algo
guidebook ['gaɪdbuk] *n* guía
guided missile ['gaɪdɪd-] *n* misil *m* teledirigido
guide dog *n* perro guía
guidelines ['gaɪdlaɪnz] *npl* (*fig*) directrices *fpl*
guild [gɪld] *n* gremio
guildhall ['gɪldhɔːl] *n* (*Brit: town hall*) ayuntamiento
guile [gaɪl] *n* astucia

guileless ['gaɪllɪs] *adj* cándido
guillotine ['gɪlətiːn] *n* guillotina
guilt [gɪlt] *n* culpabilidad *f*
guilty ['gɪltɪ] *adj* culpable; **to feel ~ (about)** sentirse culpable (de); **to plead ~/not ~** declararse culpable/inocente
Guinea ['gɪnɪ] *n*: **Republic of ~** República de Guinea
guinea ['gɪnɪ] *n* (*Brit: old*) guinea (*21 chelines: en la actualidad ya no se usa esta moneda*)
guinea pig *n* cobaya; (*fig*) conejillo de Indias
guise [gaɪz] *n*: **in** *or* **under the ~ of** bajo la apariencia de
guitar [gɪ'tɑːʳ] *n* guitarra
guitarist [gɪ'tɑːrɪst] *n* guitarrista *m/f*
gulch [gʌltʃ] *n* (*US*) barranco
gulf [gʌlf] *n* golfo; (*abyss*) abismo; **the G~** el Golfo (Pérsico)
Gulf States *npl*: **the ~** los países del Golfo
Gulf Stream *n*: **the ~** la Corriente del Golfo
gull [gʌl] *n* gaviota
gullet ['gʌlɪt] *n* esófago
gullibility [gʌlɪ'bɪlɪtɪ] *n* credulidad *f*
gullible ['gʌlɪbl] *adj* crédulo
gully ['gʌlɪ] *n* barranco
gulp [gʌlp] *vi* tragar saliva ■ *vt* (*also*: **gulp down**) tragarse ■ *n* (*of liquid*) trago; (*of food*) bocado; **in** *or* **at one ~** de un trago
gum [gʌm] *n* (*Anat*) encía; (*glue*) goma, cemento (*LAm*); (*sweet*) gominola; (*also*: **chewing-gum**) chicle *m* ■ *vt* pegar con goma
▶ **gum up** *vt*: **to ~ up the works** (*col*) entorpecerlo todo
gumboots ['gʌmbuːts] *npl* (*Brit*) botas *fpl* de goma
gumption ['gʌmpʃən] *n* (*col*) iniciativa
gum tree *n* árbol *m* gomero
gun [gʌn] *n* (*small*) pistola; (*shotgun*) escopeta; (*rifle*) fusil *m*; (*cannon*) cañón *m* ■ *vt* (*also*: **gun down**) abatir a tiros; **to stick to one's guns** (*fig*) mantenerse firme *or* en sus trece
gunboat ['gʌnbəut] *n* cañonero
gun dog *n* perro de caza
gunfire ['gʌnfaɪəʳ] *n* disparos *mpl*
gung-ho [gʌŋ'həu] *adj* (*col*) patriotero
gunk [gʌŋk] *n* (*col*) masa viscosa
gunman ['gʌnmən] *n* pistolero
gunner ['gʌnəʳ] *n* artillero
gunpoint ['gʌnpɔɪnt] *n*: **at ~** a mano armada
gunpowder ['gʌnpaudəʳ] *n* pólvora
gunrunner ['gʌnrʌnəʳ] *n* traficante *m/f* de armas
gunrunning ['gʌnrʌnɪŋ] *n* tráfico de armas
gunshot ['gʌnʃɒt] *n* disparo
gunsmith ['gʌnsmɪθ] *n* armero

g

gurgle ['gə:gl] vi gorgotear
guru ['gu:ru:] n guru m
gush [gʌʃ] vi chorrear; (fig) deshacerse en efusiones
gushing ['gʌʃɪŋ] adj efusivo
gusset ['gʌsɪt] n (in tights, pants) escudete m
gust [gʌst] n (of wind) ráfaga
gusto ['gʌstəu] n entusiasmo
gusty ['gʌstɪ] adj racheado
gut [gʌt] n intestino; (Mus etc) cuerda de tripa ■ vt (poultry, fish) destripar; (building): **the blaze gutted the entire building** el fuego destruyó el edificio entero
gut reaction n reacción f instintiva
guts [gʌts] npl (courage) agallas fpl, valor m; (col: innards: of people, animals) tripas fpl; **to hate sb's ~** odiar a algn (a muerte)
gutsy ['gʌtsɪ] adj: **to be ~** (col) tener agallas
gutted ['gʌtɪd] adj (col: disappointed): **I was ~** me quedé hecho polvo
gutter ['gʌtəʳ] n (of roof) canalón m; (in street) cuneta; **the ~** (fig) el arroyo
gutter press n (col): **the ~** la prensa sensacionalista or amarilla; see also **tabloid press**
guttural ['gʌtərl] adj gutural
guy [gaɪ] n (also: **guyrope**) viento, cuerda; (col: man) tío (SP), tipo
Guyana [gaɪ'ænə] n Guayana
Guy Fawkes' Night [gaɪ'fɔ:ks-] n

guzzle ['gʌzl] vi tragar ■ vt engullir
gym [dʒɪm] n (also: **gymnasium**) gimnasio; (also: **gymnastics**) gimnasia
gymkhana [dʒɪm'kɑ:nə] n gincana
gymnast ['dʒɪmnæst] n gimnasta m/f
gymnastics [dʒɪm'næstɪks] n gimnasia
gym shoes npl zapatillas fpl de gimnasia
gym slip n (Brit) pichi m
gynaecologist, (US) **gynecologist** [gaɪnɪ'kɔlədʒɪst] n ginecólogo(-a)
gynaecology, (US) **gynecology** [gaɪnə'kɔlədʒɪ] n ginecología
gypsy ['dʒɪpsɪ] n = **gipsy**
gyrate [dʒaɪ'reɪt] vi girar
gyroscope ['dʒaɪrəskəup] n giroscopio

Hh

H, h [eɪtʃ] *n* (*letter*) H, h *f*; **H for Harry,**
(*US*) **H for How** H de Historia
habeas corpus [ˈheɪbɪəsˈkɔːpəs] *n* (*Law*)
hábeas corpus *m*
haberdashery [ˈhæbəˈdæʃərɪ] *n* (*Brit*) mercería;
(*US: men's clothing*) prendas *fpl* de caballero
habit [ˈhæbɪt] *n* hábito, costumbre *f*; **to get**
out of/into the ~ of doing sth perder la
costumbre de/acostumbrarse a hacer algo
habitable [ˈhæbɪtəbl] *adj* habitable
habitat [ˈhæbɪtæt] *n* hábitat *m*
habitation [hæbɪˈteɪʃən] *n* habitación *f*
habitual [həˈbɪtjuəl] *adj* acostumbrado,
habitual; (*drinker, liar*) empedernido
habitually [həˈbɪtjuəlɪ] *adv* por costumbre
hack [hæk] *vt* (*cut*) cortar; (*slice*) tajar
■ *n* corte *m*; (*axe blow*) hachazo; (*pej: writer*)
escritor(a) *m(f)* a sueldo; (*old horse*) jamelgo
hacker [ˈhækəʳ] *n* (*Comput*) pirata *m* informático
hackles [ˈhæklz] *npl*: **to make sb's ~ rise** (*fig*)
poner furioso a algn
hackney cab [ˈhæknɪ-] *n* coche *m* de alquiler
hackneyed [ˈhæknɪd] *adj* trillado, gastado
hacksaw [ˈhæksɔː] *n* sierra para metales
had [hæd] *pt, pp of* **have**
haddock (*pl ~ or* **haddocks**) [ˈhædək] *n especie*
de merluza
hadn't [ˈhædnt] = **had not**
haematology, hematology (*US*)
[ˈhiːməˈtɔlədʒɪ] *n* hematología
haemoglobin, hemoglobin (*US*)
[ˈhiːməˈɡləubɪn] *n* hemoglobina
haemophilia, hemophilia (*US*) [ˈhiːməˈfɪlɪə]
n hemofilia
haemorrhage, hemorrhage (*US*)
[ˈhɛmərɪdʒ] *n* hemorragia
haemorrhoids, hemorrhoids (*US*) [ˈhɛmə-
rɔɪdz] *npl* hemorroides *fpl*, almorranas *fpl*
hag [hæg] *n* (*ugly*) vieja fea, tarasca; (*nasty*)
bruja; (*witch*) hechicera
haggard [ˈhæɡəd] *adj* ojeroso
haggis [ˈhæɡɪs] *n* (*Scottish*) asadura de cordero

cocida; *see also* **Burns' Night**
haggle [ˈhæɡl] *vi* (*argue*) discutir; (*bargain*)
regatear
haggling [ˈhæɡlɪŋ] *n* regateo
Hague [heɪɡ] *n*: **The ~** La Haya
hail [heɪl] *n* (*weather*) granizo ■ *vt* saludar;
(*call*) llamar a ■ *vi* granizar; **to ~ (as)**
aclamar (como), celebrar (como); **he hails**
from Scotland es natural de Escocia
hailstone [ˈheɪlstəun] *n* (piedra de) granizo
hailstorm [ˈheɪlstɔːm] *n* granizada
hair [hɛəʳ] *n* (*gen*) pelo, cabellos *mpl*; (*one hair*)
pelo, cabello; (*head of hair*) pelo, cabellera; (*on*
legs etc) vello; **to do one's ~** arreglarse el pelo;
grey ~ canas *fpl*
hairbrush [ˈhɛəbrʌʃ] *n* cepillo (para el pelo)
haircut [ˈhɛəkʌt] *n* corte *m* de pelo
hairdo [ˈhɛəduː] *n* peinado
hairdresser [ˈhɛədrɛsəʳ] *n* peluquero(-a);
~'s peluquería
hair-dryer [ˈhɛədraɪəʳ] *n* secador *m* (de pelo)
-haired [hɛəd] *adj suff*: **fair/long~** (de pelo)
rubio *or* (*LAm*) güero/de pelo largo
hairgrip [ˈhɛəɡrɪp] *n* horquilla
hairline [ˈhɛəlaɪn] *n* nacimiento del pelo
hairline fracture *n* fractura muy fina
hairnet [ˈhɛənɛt] *n* redecilla
hair oil *n* brillantina
hairpiece [ˈhɛəpiːs] *n* trenza postiza
hairpin [ˈhɛəpɪn] *n* horquilla
hairpin bend, (*US*) **hairpin curve** *n* curva
muy cerrada
hair-raising [ˈhɛəreɪzɪŋ] *adj* espeluznante
hair remover *n* depilatorio
hair's breadth *n*: **by a ~** por un pelo
hair spray *n* laca
hairstyle [ˈhɛəstaɪl] *n* peinado
hairy [ˈhɛərɪ] *adj* peludo, velludo
Haiti [ˈheɪtɪ] *n* Haití *m*
hake [heɪk] *n* merluza
halcyon [ˈhælsɪən] *adj* feliz
hale [heɪl] *adj*: **~ and hearty** sano y fuerte

half [hɑːf] n (pl **halves**) [hɑːvz] mitad f; (Sport: of match) tiempo, parte f; (: of ground) campo ■ adj medio ■ adv medio, a medias; **~-an-hour** media hora; **two and a ~** dos y media; **~ a dozen** media docena; **~ a pound** media libra, ≈ 250 gr.; **to cut sth in ~** cortar algo por la mitad; **to go halves (with sb)** ir a medias (con algn); **halfempty/closed** medio vacío/ entreabierto; **~ asleep** medio dormido; **~ past 3** las 3 y media

half-back ['hɑːfbæk] n (Sport) medio

half-baked ['hɑːfˈbeɪkt] adj (col: idea, scheme) mal concebido or pensado

half-breed ['hɑːfbriːd] n = **half-caste**

half-brother ['hɑːfbrʌðə'] n hermanastro

half-caste ['hɑːfkɑːst] n mestizo(-a)

half-hearted ['hɑːfˈhɑːtɪd] adj indiferente, poco entusiasta

half-hour [hɑːfˈauə'] n media hora

half-mast ['hɑːfmɑːst] n: **at ~** (flag) a media asta

halfpenny ['heɪpnɪ] n medio penique m

half-price ['hɑːfˈpraɪs] adj a mitad de precio

half term n (Brit Scol) vacaciones de mediados del trimestre

half-time [hɑːfˈtaɪm] n descanso

halfway ['hɑːfˈweɪ] adv a medio camino; **to meet sb ~** (fig) llegar a un acuerdo con algn

halfway house n centro de readaptación de antiguos presos; (fig) solución f intermedia

half-wit ['hɑːfwɪt] n (col) zoquete m

half-yearly [hɑːfˈjɪəlɪ] adv semestralmente ■ adj semestral

halibut ['hælɪbət] n (pl inv) halibut m

halitosis [hælɪˈtəusɪs] n halitosis f

hall [hɔːl] n (for concerts) sala; (entrance way) entrada, vestíbulo

hallmark ['hɔːlmɑːk] n (mark) rasgo distintivo; (seal) sello

hallo [həˈləu] excl = **hello**

hall of residence n (Brit) colegio mayor, residencia universitaria

Hallowe'en [hæləuˈiːn] n víspera de Todos los Santos; ver nota

● **HALLOWE'EN**

La tradición anglosajona dice que en la noche del 31 de octubre, Hallowe'en, víspera de Todos los Santos, es fácil ver a brujas y fantasmas. Es una ocasión festiva en la que los niños se disfrazan y van de puerta en puerta llevando un farol hecho con una calabaza en forma de cabeza humana. Cuando se les abre la puerta gritan "trick or treat" para indicar que gastarán una broma a quien no les dé un pequeño regalo (como golosinas o dinero).

hallucination [həluːsɪˈneɪʃən] n alucinación f

hallucinogenic [həluːsɪnəuˈdʒɛnɪk] adj alucinógeno

hallway ['hɔːlweɪ] n vestíbulo

halo ['heɪləu] n (of saint) aureola

halt [hɔːlt] n (stop) alto, parada, (Rail) apeadero ■ vt parar ■ vi pararse; (process) interrumpirse; **to call a ~ (to sth)** (fig) poner fin (a algo)

halter ['hɔːltə'] n (for horse) cabestro

halterneck ['hɔːltənɛk] adj de espalda escotada

halve [hɑːv] vt partir por la mitad

halves [hɑːvz] pl of **half**

ham [hæm] n jamón m (cocido); (col: also: **radio ham**) radioaficionado(-a) m(f); (: also: **ham actor**) comicastro

hamburger ['hæmbəgə'] n hamburguesa

ham-fisted ['hæmˈfɪstɪd] adj torpe, desmañado

hamlet ['hæmlɪt] n aldea

hammer ['hæmə'] n martillo ■ vt (nail) clavar; **to ~ a point home to sb** remacharle un punto a algn
▶ **hammer out** vt (metal) forjar a martillo; (fig: solution, agreement) elaborar (trabajosamente)

hammock ['hæmək] n hamaca

hamper ['hæmpə'] vt estorbar ■ n cesto

hamster ['hæmstə'] n hámster m

hand [hænd] n mano f; (of clock) aguja, manecilla; (writing) letra; (worker) obrero; (measurement: of horse) palmo ■ vt (give) dar, pasar; (deliver) entregar; **to give sb a ~** echar una mano a algn, ayudar a algn; **to force sb's ~** forzarle la mano a algn; **at ~** a mano; **in ~** entre manos; **we have the matter in ~** tenemos el asunto entre manos; **to have in one's ~** (knife, victory) tener en la mano; **to have a free ~** tener carta blanca; **on ~** (person, services) a mano, al alcance; **to ~** (information etc) a mano; **on the one ~ ...**, **on the other ~** ... por una parte ... por otra (parte) ...
▶ **hand down** vt pasar, bajar; (tradition) transmitir; (heirloom) dejar en herencia; (US: sentence, verdict) imponer
▶ **hand in** vt entregar
▶ **hand out** vt (leaflets, advice) repartir, distribuir
▶ **hand over** vt (deliver) entregar; (surrender) ceder
▶ **hand round** vt (Brit: information, papers) pasar (de mano en mano); (: chocolates etc) ofrecer

handbag ['hændbæg] n bolso, cartera (LAm)

hand baggage n = **hand luggage**
handball ['hændbɔ:l] n balonmano
handbasin ['hændbeɪsn] n lavabo
handbook ['hændbʊk] n manual m
handbrake ['hændbreɪk] n freno de mano
hand cream n crema para las manos
handcuffs ['hændkʌfs] npl esposas fpl
handful ['hændfʊl] n puñado
hand-held ['hænd'hɛld] adj de mano
handicap ['hændɪkæp] n desventaja; (Sport) hándicap m ■ vt estorbar
handicapped ['hændɪkæpt] adj: **to be mentally ~** ser deficiente m/f mental; **to be physically ~** ser minusválido(-a)
handicraft ['hændɪkrɑ:ft] n artesanía
handiwork ['hændɪwə:k] n manualidad(es) f(pl); (fig) obra; **this looks like his ~** (pej) es obra de él, parece
handkerchief ['hæŋkətʃɪf] n pañuelo
handle ['hændl] n (of door etc) pomo; (of cup etc) asa; (of knife etc) mango; (for winding) manivela ■ vt (touch) tocar; (deal with) encargarse de; (treat: people) manejar; **"~ with care"** "(manéjese) con cuidado"; **to fly off the ~** perder los estribos
handlebar ['hændlbɑ:ʳ] n, **handlebars** ['hændlbɑ:z] npl manillar msg
handling ['hændlɪŋ] n (Aut) conducción f; **his ~ of the matter** su forma de llevar el asunto
handling charges npl gastos mpl de tramitación
hand luggage n equipaje m de mano
handmade ['hændmeɪd] adj hecho a mano
handout ['hændaʊt] n (distribution) repartición f; (charity) limosna; (leaflet) folleto, octavilla; (press handout) nota
hand-picked ['hænd'pɪkt] adj (produce) escogido a mano; (staff etc) seleccionado cuidadosamente
handrail ['hændreɪl] n (on staircase etc) pasamanos m inv, barandilla
handset ['hændsɛt] n (Tel) auricular m
handsfree ['hændzfri:] adj (Tel: telephone, kit) manos libres
handshake ['hændʃeɪk] n apretón m de manos; (Comput) coloquio
handsome ['hænsəm] adj guapo
hands-on ['hændz'ɔn] adj práctico; **she has a very ~ approach** le gusta tomar parte activa; **~ experience** (Comput) experiencia práctica
handstand ['hændstænd] n voltereta, salto mortal
hand-to-mouth ['hændtə'maʊθ] adj (existence) precario
handwriting ['hændraɪtɪŋ] n letra
handwritten ['hændrɪtn] adj escrito a mano, manuscrito

handy ['hændɪ] adj (close at hand) a mano; (useful: machine, tool etc) práctico; (skilful) hábil, diestro; **to come in ~** venir bien
handyman ['hændɪmæn] n manitas m inv
hang (pt, pp **hung**) [hæŋ, hʌŋ] vt colgar; (head) bajar; (criminal) (pt, pp **hanged**) ahorcar; **to get the ~ of sth** (col) coger el tranquillo a algo
▶**hang about** vi haraganear
▶**hang back** vi (hesitate): **to ~ back (from doing)** vacilar (en hacer)
▶**hang on** vi (wait) esperar ■ vt fus (depend on: decision etc) depender de; **to ~ on to** (keep) guardar, quedarse con
▶**hang out** vt (washing) tender, colgar ■ vi (col: live) vivir; (: often be found) moverse; **to ~ out of sth** colgar fuera de algo
▶**hang together** vi (cohere: argument etc) sostenerse
▶**hang up** vt (coat) colgar ■ vi (Tel) colgar; **to ~ up on sb** colgarle a algn
hangar ['hæŋəʳ] n hangar m
hangdog ['hæŋdɔg] adj (guilty: look, expression) avergonzado
hanger ['hæŋəʳ] n percha
hanger-on [hæŋər'ɔn] n parásito
hang-glider ['hæŋglaɪdəʳ] n ala delta
hang-gliding ['hæŋglaɪdɪŋ] n vuelo con ala delta
hanging ['hæŋɪŋ] n (execution) ejecución f (en la horca)
hangman ['hæŋmən] n verdugo
hangover ['hæŋəʊvəʳ] n (after drinking) resaca
hang-up ['hæŋʌp] n complejo
hanker ['hæŋkəʳ] vi: **to ~ after** (miss) echar de menos; (long for) añorar
hankie, hanky ['hæŋkɪ] n abbr = **handkerchief**
Hansard ['hænsɑ:d] n actas oficiales de las sesiones del parlamento británico
Hants abbr (Brit) = **Hampshire**
haphazard [hæp'hæzəd] adj fortuito
hapless ['hæplɪs] adj desventurado
happen ['hæpən] vi suceder, ocurrir; (take place) tener lugar, realizarse; **as it happens** da la casualidad de que; **what's happening?** ¿qué pasa?
▶**happen (up)on** vt fus tropezar or dar con
happening ['hæpnɪŋ] n suceso, acontecimiento
happily ['hæpɪlɪ] adv (luckily) afortunadamente; (cheerfully) alegremente
happiness ['hæpɪnɪs] n (contentment) felicidad f; (joy) alegría
happy ['hæpɪ] adj feliz; (cheerful) alegre; **to be ~ (with)** estar contento (con); **yes, I'd be ~ to** sí, con mucho gusto; **H~ Christmas!** ¡Feliz

Navidad!; **H~ New Year!** ¡Feliz Año Nuevo!;
~ birthday! ¡felicidades!, ¡feliz cumpleaños!
happy-go-lucky ['hæpɪɡəu'lʌkɪ] *adj*
despreocupado
happy hour *n horas en las que la bebida es más
barata en un bar*
harangue [hə'ræŋ] *vt* arengar
harass ['hærəs] *vt* acosar, hostigar
harassed ['hærəst] *adj* agobiado, presionado
harassment ['hærəsmənt] *n* persecución *f*,
acoso; (*worry*) preocupación *f*
harbour, harbor (US) ['hɑ:bə'] *n* puerto ■ *vt*
(*hope etc*) abrigar; (*hide*) dar abrigo a; (*retain:
grudge etc*) guardar
harbour dues, harbor dues (US) *npl*
derechos *mpl* portuarios
hard [hɑ:d] *adj* duro; (*difficult*) difícil; (*person*)
severo ■ *adv* (*work*) mucho, duro; (*think*)
profundamente; **to look ~ at sb/sth** clavar
los ojos en algn/algo; **to try ~** esforzarse;
no ~ feelings! ¡sin rencor(es)!; **to be ~ of
hearing** ser duro de oído; **to be ~ done by**
ser tratado injustamente; **to be ~ on sb** ser
muy duro con algn; **I find it ~ to believe
that ...** me cuesta trabajo creer que ...
hard-and-fast ['hɑ:dən'fɑ:st] *adj* rígido,
definitivo
hardback ['hɑ:dbæk] *n* libro de tapas duras
hard cash *n* dinero en efectivo
hard copy *n* (*Comput*) copia impresa
hard-core ['hɑ:d'kɔ:'] *adj* (*pornography*) duro;
(*supporters*) incondicional
hard court *n* (*Tennis*) pista *or* cancha (de tenis)
de cemento
hard disk *n* (*Comput*) disco duro
harden ['hɑ:dn] *vt* endurecer; (*steel*) templar;
(*fig*) curtir; (: *determination*) fortalecer ■ *vi*
(*substance*) endurecerse
hardened ['hɑ:dnd] *adj* (*criminal*) habitual;
to be ~ to sth estar acostumbrado a algo
hard-headed ['hɑ:d'hɛdɪd] *adj* poco
sentimental, realista
hard-hearted ['hɑ:d'hɑ:tɪd] *adj* insensible
hard-hitting ['hɑ:d'hɪtɪŋ] *adj* (*speech, article*)
contundente
hard labour *n* trabajos *mpl* forzados
hardliner [hɑ:d'laɪnə'] *n* partidario(-a) de la
línea dura
hard-luck story ['hɑ:dlʌk-] *n* dramón *m*
hardly ['hɑ:dlɪ] *adv* (*scarcely*) apenas; **that can
~ be true** eso difícilmente puede ser cierto;
~ ever casi nunca; **I can ~ believe it** apenas
me lo puedo creer
hardness ['hɑ:dnɪs] *n* dureza
hard-nosed ['hɑ:d'nəuzd] *adj* duro, sin
contemplaciones
hard-pressed ['hɑ:d'prest] *adj* en apuros

hard sell *n* publicidad *f* agresiva; **~
techniques** técnicas *fpl* agresivas de venta
hardship ['hɑ:dʃɪp] *n* (*troubles*) penas *fpl*;
(*financial*) apuro
hard shoulder *n* (*Aut*) arcén *m*
hard-up [hɑ:d'ʌp] *adj* (*col*) sin un duro (SP),
sin plata (LAm)
hardware ['hɑ:dwɛə'] *n* ferretería; (*Comput*)
hardware *m*
hardware shop *n* ferretería
hard-wearing [hɑ:d'wɛərɪŋ] *adj* resistente,
duradero; (*shoes*) resistente
hard-won ['hɑ:d'wʌn] *adj* ganado con
esfuerzo
hard-working [hɑ:d'wə:kɪŋ] *adj*
trabajador(a)
hardy ['hɑ:dɪ] *adj* fuerte; (*plant*) resistente
hare [hɛə'] *n* liebre *f*
hare-brained ['hɛəbreɪnd] *adj* atolondrado
harelip ['hɛəlɪp] *n* labio leporino
harem [hɑ:'ri:m] *n* harén *m*
haricot ['hærɪkəu], **haricot bean** *n* alubia
hark back [hɑ:k-] *vi*: **to ~ to** (*former days, earlier
occasion*) recordar
harm [hɑ:m] *n* daño, mal *m* ■ *vt* (*person*)
hacer daño a; (*health, interests*) perjudicar;
(*thing*) dañar; **out of ~'s way** a salvo; **there's
no ~ in trying** no se pierde nada con
intentar
harmful ['hɑ:mful] *adj* (*gen*) dañino;
(*reputation*) perjudicial
harmless ['hɑ:mlɪs] *adj* (*person*) inofensivo;
(*drug*) inocuo
harmonica [hɑ:'mɒnɪkə] *n* armónica
harmonious [hɑ:'məunɪəs] *adj* armonioso
harmonize ['hɑ:mənaɪz] *vt, vi* armonizar
harmony ['hɑ:mənɪ] *n* armonía
harness ['hɑ:nɪs] *n* arreos *mpl* ■ *vt* (*horse*)
enjaezar; (*resources*) aprovechar
harp [hɑ:p] *n* arpa ■ *vi*: **to ~ on (about)**
machacar (con)
harpoon [hɑ:'pu:n] *n* arpón *m*
harrow ['hærəu] *n* grada ■ *vt* gradar
harrowing ['hærəuɪŋ] *adj* angustioso
harry ['hærɪ] *vt* (*Mil*) acosar; (*person*) hostigar
harsh [hɑ:ʃ] *adj* (*cruel*) duro, cruel; (*severe*)
severo; (*words*) hosco; (*colour*) chillón(-ona);
(*contrast*) violento
harshly ['hɑ:ʃlɪ] *adv* (*say*) con aspereza; (*treat*)
con mucha dureza
harshness ['hɑ:ʃnɪs] *n* dureza
harvest ['hɑ:vɪst] *n* cosecha; (*of grapes*)
vendimia ■ *vt, vi* cosechar
harvester ['hɑ:vɪstə'] *n* (*machine*)
cosechadora; (*person*) segador(a) *m(f)*;
combine ~ segadora trilladora
has [hæz] *vb see* **have**

has-been ['hæzbi:n] *n* (*col: person*) persona acabada; (*: thing*) vieja gloria

hash [hæʃ] *n* (*Culin*) picadillo; (*fig: mess*) lío

hashish ['hæʃɪʃ] *n* hachís *m*

hasn't ['hæznt] = **has not**

hassle ['hæsl] *n* (*col*) lío, rollo ■ *vt* incordiar

haste [heɪst] *n* prisa

hasten ['heɪsn] *vt* acelerar ■ *vi* darse prisa; **I ~ to add that ...** me apresuro a añadir que ...

hastily ['heɪstɪlɪ] *adv* de prisa

hasty ['heɪstɪ] *adj* apresurado

hat [hæt] *n* sombrero

hatbox ['hætbɔks] *n* sombrerera

hatch [hætʃ] *n* (*Naut: also:* **hatchway**) escotilla ■ *vi* salir del cascarón ■ *vt* incubar; (*fig: scheme, plot*) idear, tramar

hatchback ['hætʃbæk] *n* (*Aut*) tres or cinco puertas *m*

hatchet ['hætʃɪt] *n* hacha

hatchet job *n* (*col*) varapalo

hatchet man *n* (*col*) ejecutor de faenas desagradables por cuenta de otro

hate [heɪt] *vt* odiar, aborrecer ■ *n* odio; **I ~ to trouble you, but ...** siento or lamento molestarle, pero ...

hateful ['heɪtful] *adj* odioso

hater ['heɪtə^r] *n*: **cop-hater** persona que siente aversión a la policía; **woman-hater** misógino

hatred ['heɪtrɪd] *n* odio

hat trick *n*: **to score a ~** (*Brit Sport*) marcar tres tantos (or triunfos) seguidos

haughty ['hɔːtɪ] *adj* altanero, arrogante

haul [hɔːl] *vt* tirar, jalar (*LAm*) ■ *n* (*of fish*) redada; (*of stolen goods etc*) botín *m*

haulage ['hɔːlɪdʒ] *n* (*Brit*) transporte *m*; (*costs*) gastos *mpl* de transporte

haulage contractor *n* (*firm*) empresa de transportes; (*person*) transportista *m/f*

haulier ['hɔːlɪə^r], **hauler** (*US*) ['hɔːlə^r] *n* transportista *m/f*

haunch [hɔːntʃ] *n* anca; (*of meat*) pierna

haunt [hɔːnt] *vt* (*ghost*) aparecer en; (*frequent*) frecuentar; (*obsess*) obsesionar ■ *n* guarida

haunted ['hɔːntɪd] *adj* (*castle etc*) embrujado; (*look*) de angustia

haunting ['hɔːntɪŋ] *adj* (*sight, music*) evocativo

Havana [hə'vɑːnə] *n* La Habana

 KEYWORD

have [hæv] (*pt, pp* **had**) *aux vb* **1** (*gen*) haber; **to have arrived/eaten** haber llegado/comido; **having finished** or **when he had finished, he left** cuando hubo acabado, se fue
2 (*in tag questions*): **you've done it, haven't you?** lo has hecho, ¿verdad? or ¿no?
3 (*in short answers and questions*): **I haven't** no;

so I have pues, es verdad; **we haven't paid — yes we have!** no hemos pagado — ¡sí que hemos pagado!; **I've been there before, have you?** he estado allí antes, ¿y tú?
■ *modal aux vb* (*be obliged*): **to have (got) to do sth** tener que hacer algo; **you haven't to tell her** no hay que or no debes decírselo
■ *vt* **1** (*possess*) tener; **he has (got) blue eyes/dark hair** tiene los ojos azules/el pelo negro
2 (*referring to meals etc*): **to have breakfast/lunch/dinner** desayunar/comer/cenar; **to have a drink/a cigarette** tomar algo/fumar un cigarrillo
3 (*receive*) recibir; (*obtain*) obtener; **may I have your address?** ¿puedes darme tu dirección?; **you can have it for £5** te lo puedes quedar por £5; **I must have it by tomorrow** lo necesito para mañana; **to have a baby** tener un niño or bebé
4 (*maintain, allow*): **I won't have it!** ¡no lo permitiré!; **I won't have this nonsense!** ¡no permitiré estas tonterías!; **we can't have that** no podemos permitir eso
5: **to have sth done** hacer or mandar hacer algo; **to have one's hair cut** cortarse el pelo; **to have sb do sth** hacer que algn haga algo
6 (*experience, suffer*): **to have a cold/flu** tener un resfriado/la gripe; **she had her bag stolen/her arm broken** le robaron el bolso/se rompió un brazo; **to have an operation** operarse
7 (*+ noun*): **to have a swim/walk/bath/rest** nadar/dar un paseo/darse un baño/descansar; **let's have a look** vamos a ver; **to have a meeting/party** celebrar una reunión/una fiesta; **let me have a try** déjame intentarlo
▶ **have in** *vt*: **to have it in for sb** (*col*) tenerla tomada con algn
▶ **have on** *vt*: **have you anything on tomorrow?** ¿vas a hacer algo mañana?; **I don't have any money on me** no llevo dinero (encima); **to have sb on** (*Brit col*) tomarle el pelo a algn
▶ **have out** *vt*: **to have it out with sb** (*settle a problem etc*) dejar las cosas en claro con algn

haven ['heɪvn] *n* puerto; (*fig*) refugio

haven't ['hævnt] = **have not**

haversack ['hævəsæk] *n* macuto

haves [hævz] *npl*: **the ~ and the have-nots** los ricos y los pobres

havoc ['hævək] *n* estragos *mpl*; **to play ~ with sth** hacer estragos en algo

Hawaii [hə'waɪiː] *n* (Islas *fpl*) Hawai *m*

Hawaiian [hə'waɪjən] *adj, n* hawaiano(-a) *m(f)*

hawk [hɔːk] *n* halcón *m* ■ *vt* (*goods for sale*) pregonar

hawkish ['hɔːkɪʃ] *adj* beligerante

hawthorn ['hɔːθɔːn] *n* espino

hay [heɪ] *n* heno

hay fever *n* fiebre *f* del heno

haystack ['heɪstæk] *n* almiar *m*

haywire ['heɪwaɪəʳ] *adj* (*col*): **to go ~** (*person*) volverse loco; (*plan*) irse al garete

hazard ['hæzəd] *n* riesgo; (*danger*) peligro ■ *vt* (*remark*) aventurar; (*one's life*) arriesgar; **to be a health ~** ser un peligro para la salud; **to ~ a guess** aventurar una respuesta *or* hipótesis

hazardous ['hæzədəs] *adj* (*dangerous*) peligroso; (*risky*) arriesgado

hazard warning lights *npl* (*Aut*) señales *fpl* de emergencia

haze [heɪz] *n* neblina

hazel ['heɪzl] *n* (*tree*) avellano ■ *adj* (*eyes*) color *m* de avellano

hazelnut ['heɪzlnʌt] *n* avellana

hazy ['heɪzɪ] *adj* brumoso; (*idea*) vago

H-bomb ['eɪtʃbɔm] *n* bomba H

h & c *abbr* (*Brit*) = **hot and cold (water)**

HD *abbr* (= **high definition**) HD *m*

HDTV *abbr* (= **high definition television**) HDTV *f*

HE *abbr* = **high explosive**; (*Rel, Diplomacy*: = *His (or Her) Excellency*) S. Excª

he [hiː] *pron* él; **he who** ... aquél que ..., quien ...

head [hed] *n* cabeza; (*leader*) jefe(-a) *m(f)* ■ *vt* (*list*) encabezar; (*group*) capitanear; **heads (or taiis)** cara (o cruz); **~ first** de cabeza; **~ over heels** patas arriba; **~ over heels in love** perdidamente enamorado; **it was above** *or* **over their heads** no alcanzaron a entenderlo; **to come to a ~** (*fig: situation etc*) llegar a un punto crítico; **to have a ~ for business** tener talento para los negocios; **to have no ~ for heights** no resistir las alturas; **to lose/keep one's ~** perder la cabeza/mantener la calma; **to sit at the ~ of the table** sentarse a la cabecera de la mesa; **to ~ the ball** cabecear (el balón)

▸ **head for** *vt fus* dirigirse a

▸ **head off** *vt* (*threat, danger*) evitar

headache ['hedeɪk] *n* dolor *m* de cabeza; **to have a ~** tener dolor de cabeza

headband ['hedbænd] *n* cinta (para la cabeza), vincha (*LAm*)

headboard ['hedbɔːd] *n* cabecera

headdress ['heddres] *n* (*of bride, Indian*) tocado

headed notepaper ['hedɪd-] *n* papel *m* con membrete

header ['hedəʳ] *n* (*Brit col: Football*) cabezazo; (: *fall*) caída de cabeza

headfirst [hed'fəːst] *adv* de cabeza

headhunt ['hedhʌnt] *vt*: **to be headhunted** ser seleccionado por un cazatalentos

headhunter ['hedhʌntəʳ] *n* (*fig*) cazaejecutivos *m inv*

heading ['hedɪŋ] *n* título

headlamp ['hedlæmp] *n* (*Brit*) = **headlight**

headland ['hedlənd] *n* promontorio

headlight ['hedlaɪt] *n* faro

headline ['hedlaɪn] *n* titular *m*

headlong ['hedlɔŋ] *adv* (*fall*) de cabeza; (*rush*) precipitadamente

headmaster/mistress [hed'mɑːstəʳ/mɪstrɪs] *n* director(a) *m(f)* (de escuela)

head office *n* oficina central, central *f*

head-on [hed'ɔn] *adj* (*collision*) de frente

headphones ['hedfəunz] *npl* auriculares *mpl*

headquarters ['hedkwɔːtəz] *npl* sede *f* central; (*Mil*) cuartel *m* general

head-rest ['hedrest] *n* reposa-cabezas *m inv*

headroom ['hedrum] *n* (*in car*) altura interior; (*under bridge*) (límite *m* de) altura

headscarf ['hedskɑːf] *n* pañuelo

headset ['hedset] *n* cascos *mpl*

headstone ['hedstəun] *n* lápida

headstrong ['hedstrɔŋ] *adj* testarudo

head waiter *n* maître *m*

headway ['hedweɪ] *n*: **to make ~** (*fig*) hacer progresos

headwind ['hedwɪnd] *n* viento contrario

heady ['hedɪ] *adj* (*experience, period*) apasionante; (*wine*) fuerte

heal [hiːl] *vt* curar ■ *vi* cicatrizar

health [helθ] *n* salud *f*

health care *n* asistencia sanitaria

health centre *n* ambulatorio, centro médico

health food *n*, **health foods** *npl* alimentos *mpl* orgánicos

health hazard *n* riesgo para la salud

Health Service *n* (*Brit*) servicio de salud pública, ≈ Insalud *m* (*SP*)

healthy ['helθɪ] *adj* (*gen*) sano; (*economy, bank balance*) saludable

heap [hiːp] *n* montón *m* ■ *vt* amontonar; (*plate*) colmar; **heaps (of)** (*col: lots*) montones (de); **to ~ favours/praise/gifts** *etc* **on sb** colmar a algn de favores/elogios/regalos *etc*

hear (*pt, pp heard*) [hɪəʳ, həːd] *vt* oír; (*perceive*) sentir; (*listen to*) escuchar; (*lecture*) asistir a; (*Law: case*) ver ■ *vi* oír; **to ~ about** oír hablar de; **to ~ from sb** tener noticias de algn; **I've never heard of that book** nunca he oído hablar de ese libro

▸ **hear out** *vt*: **to ~ sb out** dejar que algn termine de hablar

hearing ['hɪərɪŋ] *n* (*sense*) oído; (*Law*) vista; **to give sb a ~** dar a algn la oportunidad de

hablar, escuchar a algn
hearing aid n audífono
hearsay ['hɪəseɪ] n rumores mpl, habladurías fpl
hearse [hə:s] n coche m fúnebre
heart [hɑːt] n corazón m; **hearts** npl (Cards) corazones mpl; **at ~** en el fondo; **by ~** (learn, know) de memoria; **to have a weak ~** tener el corazón débil; **to set one's ~ on sth/on doing sth** anhelar algo/hacer algo; **I did not have the ~ to tell her** no tuve valor para decírselo; **to take ~** cobrar ánimos; **the ~ of the matter** lo esencial or el meollo del asunto
heartache ['hɑːteɪk] n angustia
heart attack n infarto (de miocardio)
heartbeat ['hɑːtbiːt] n latido (del corazón)
heartbreak ['hɑːtbreɪk] n angustia, congoja
heartbreaking ['hɑːtbreɪkɪŋ] adj desgarrador(a)
heartbroken ['hɑːtbrəukən] adj: **she was ~ about it** le partió el corazón
heartburn ['hɑːtbəːn] n acedía
-hearted ['hɑːtɪd] adj suff: **a kind~ person** una persona bondadosa
heartening ['hɑːtnɪŋ] adj alentador(a)
heart failure n (Med) paro cardíaco
heartfelt ['hɑːtfɛlt] adj (cordial) cordial; (deeply felt) sincero
hearth [hɑːθ] n (gen) hogar m; (fireplace) chimenea
heartily ['hɑːtɪlɪ] adv sinceramente, cordialmente; (laugh) a carcajadas; (eat) con buen apetito; **to be ~ sick of** estar completamente harto de
heartland ['hɑːtlænd] n zona interior or central; (fig) corazón m
heartless ['hɑːtlɪs] adj despiadado
heartstrings ['hɑːtstrɪŋz] npl: **to tug (at) sb's ~** tocar la fibra sensible de algn
heart-throb ['hɑːtθrɔb] n ídolo
heart-to-heart ['hɑːttə'hɑːt] n (also: **heart-to-heart talk**) conversación f íntima
heart transplant n transplante m de corazón
hearty ['hɑːtɪ] adj cordial
heat [hiːt] n (gen) calor m; (Sport: also: **qualifying heat**) prueba eliminatoria; (Zool): **in** or **on ~** en celo ▪ vt calentar
  ▶ **heat up** vi (gen) calentarse
heated ['hiːtɪd] adj caliente; (fig) acalorado
heater ['hiːtəʳ] n calentador m
heath [hiːθ] n (Brit) brezal m
heathen ['hiːðn] adj, n pagano(-a) m(f)
heather ['hɛðəʳ] n brezo
heating ['hiːtɪŋ] n calefacción f
heat-resistant ['hiːtrɪzɪstənt] adj refractario
heat-seeking ['hiːtsiːkɪŋ] adj guiado por infrarrojos, termoguiado

heatstroke ['hiːtstrəuk] n insolación f
heatwave ['hiːtweɪv] n ola de calor
heave [hiːv] vt (pull) tirar; (push) empujar con esfuerzo; (lift) levantar (con esfuerzo) ▪ vi (water) subir y bajar ▪ n tirón m; empujón m; (effort) esfuerzo; (throw) echada; **to ~ a sigh** dar or echar un suspiro, suspirar
  ▶ **heave to** vi (Naut) ponerse al pairo
heaven ['hɛvn] n cielo; (Rel) paraíso; **thank ~!** ¡gracias a Dios!; **for ~'s sake!** (pleading) ¡por el amor de Dios!, ¡por lo que más quiera!; (protesting) ¡por Dios!
heavenly ['hɛvnlɪ] adj celestial; (Rel) divino
heavenly body n cuerpo celeste
heavily ['hɛvɪlɪ] adv pesadamente; (drink, smoke) en exceso; (sleep, sigh) profundamente
heavy ['hɛvɪ] adj pesado; (work) duro; (sea, rain, meal) fuerte; (drinker, smoker) empedernido; (eater) comilón(-ona)
heavy-duty ['hɛvɪ'djuːtɪ] adj resistente
heavy goods vehicle n (Brit) vehículo pesado
heavy-handed ['hɛvɪ'hændɪd] adj (clumsy, tactless) torpe
heavy industry n industria pesada
heavy metal n (Mus) heavy m (metal)
heavy-set [hɛvɪ'sɛt] adj (esp US) corpulento, fornido
heavy user n consumidor m intensivo
heavyweight ['hɛvɪweɪt] n (Sport) peso pesado
Hebrew ['hiːbruː] adj, n (Ling) hebreo
Hebrides ['hɛbrɪdiːz] npl: **the ~** las Hébridas
heck [hɛk] n (col): **why the ~ ...?** ¿por qué porras ...?; **a ~ of a lot of** cantidad de
heckle ['hɛkl] vt interrumpir
heckler ['hɛkləʳ] n el/la que interrumpe a un orador
hectare ['hɛktaːʳ] n (Brit) hectárea
hectic ['hɛktɪk] adj agitado; (busy) ocupado
hector ['hɛktəʳ] vt intimidar con bravatas
he'd [hiːd] = **he would; he had**
hedge [hɛdʒ] n seto ▪ vt cercar (con un seto) ▪ vi contestar con evasivas; **as a ~ against inflation** como protección contra la inflación; **to ~ one's bets** (fig) cubrirse
hedgehog ['hɛdʒhɔg] n erizo
hedgerow ['hɛdʒrəu] n seto vivo
hedonism ['hiːdənɪzəm] n hedonismo
heed [hiːd] vt (also: **take heed of**: pay attention) hacer caso de; (bear in mind) tener en cuenta; **to pay (no) ~ to, take (no) ~ of** (no) hacer caso a, (no) tener en cuenta
heedless ['hiːdlɪs] adj desatento
heel [hiːl] n talón m ▪ vt (shoe) poner tacón a; **to take to one's heels** (col) poner pies en polvorosa; **to bring to ~** meter en cintura; see also **dig**
hefty ['hɛftɪ] adj (person) fornido; (piece) grande; (price) alto

heifer ['hɛfəʳ] n novilla, ternera
height [haɪt] n (of person) talla f; (of building) altura; (high ground) cerro; (altitude) altitud f; **what ~ are you?** ¿cuánto mides?; **of average ~** de estatura mediana; **to be afraid of heights** tener miedo a las alturas; **it's the ~ of fashion** es el último grito en moda
heighten ['haɪtn] vt elevar; (fig) aumentar
heinous ['heɪnəs] adj atroz, nefasto
heir [ɛəʳ] n heredero
heir apparent n presunto heredero
heiress ['ɛərɛs] n heredera
heirloom ['ɛəluːm] n reliquia de familia
heist [haɪst] n (col: hold-up) atraco a mano armada
held [hɛld] pt, pp of **hold**
helicopter ['hɛlɪkɔptəʳ] n helicóptero
heliport ['hɛlɪpɔːt] n (Aviat) helipuerto
helium ['hiːlɪəm] n helio
hell [hɛl] n infierno; **oh ~!** (col) ¡demonios!, ¡caramba!
he'll [hiːl] = **he will; he shall**
hellbent [hɛl'bɛnt] adj (col): **he was ~ on going** se le metió entre ceja y ceja ir
hellish ['hɛlɪʃ] adj infernal; (col) horrible
hello [hə'ləu] excl ¡hola!; (surprise) ¡caramba!; (Tel) ¡dígame! (esp SP), ¡aló! (LAm)
helm [hɛlm] n (Naut) timón m
helmet ['hɛlmɪt] n casco
helmsman ['hɛlmzmən] n timonel m
help [hɛlp] n ayuda; (charwoman) criada, asistenta ■ vt ayudar; **~!** ¡socorro!; **with the ~ of** con la ayuda de; **can I ~ you?** (in shop) ¿qué desea?; **to be of ~ to sb** servir a algn; **to ~ sb (to) do sth** echarle una mano or ayudar a algn a hacer algo; **~ yourself** sírvete; **he can't ~ it** no lo puede evitar
helper ['hɛlpəʳ] n ayudante m/f
helpful ['hɛlpful] adj útil; (person) servicial
helping ['hɛlpɪŋ] n ración f
helping hand n: **to give sb a ~** echar una mano a algn
helpless ['hɛlplɪs] adj (incapable) incapaz; (defenceless) indefenso
helpline ['hɛlplaɪn] n teléfono de asistencia al público
Helsinki ['hɛlsɪŋkɪ] n Helsinki m
helter-skelter ['hɛltə'skɛltəʳ] n (in funfair) tobogán m
hem [hɛm] n dobladillo ■ vt poner or coser el dobladillo a
▶ **hem in** vt cercar; **to feel hemmed in** (fig) sentirse acosado
he-man ['hiːmæn] n macho
hematology [hiːmə'tɔlədʒɪ] n (US) = **haematology**
hemisphere ['hɛmɪsfɪəʳ] n hemisferio

hemline ['hɛmlaɪn] n bajo (del vestido)
hemlock ['hɛmlɔk] n cicuta
hemoglobin [hiːmə'gləubɪn] n (US) = **haemoglobin**
hemophilia [hiːmə'fɪlɪə] n (US) = **haemophilia**
hemorrhage ['hɛmərɪdʒ] n (US) = **haemorrhage**
hemorrhoids ['hɛmərɔɪdz] npl (US) = **haemorrhoids**
hemp [hɛmp] n cáñamo
hen [hɛn] n gallina; (female bird) hembra
hence [hɛns] adv (therefore) por lo tanto; **two years ~** de aquí a dos años
henceforth [hɛns'fɔːθ] adv de hoy en adelante
henchman ['hɛntʃmən] n (pej) secuaz m
henna ['hɛnə] n alheña
hen night n (col) despedida de soltera
hen party n (col) reunión f de mujeres
henpecked ['hɛnpɛkt] adj: **to be ~** ser un calzonazos
hepatitis [hɛpə'taɪtɪs] n hepatitis f inv
her [həːʳ] pron (direct) la; (indirect) le; (stressed, after prep) ella ■ adj su; see also **me; my**
herald ['hɛrəld] n (forerunner) precursor(a) m(f) ■ vt anunciar
heraldic [hɛ'rældɪk] adj heráldico
heraldry ['hɛrəldrɪ] n heráldica
herb [həːb] n hierba
herbaceous [hə'beɪʃəs] adj herbáceo
herbal ['həːbl] adj de hierbas
herbicide ['həːbɪsaɪd] n herbicida m
herd [həːd] n rebaño; (of wild animals, swine) piara ■ vt (drive, gather: animals) llevar en manada; (: people) reunir
▶ **herd together** vt agrupar, reunir ■ vi apiñarse, agruparse
here [hɪəʳ] adv aquí; **~!** (present) ¡presente!; **~ is/are** aquí está/están; **~ she is** aquí está; **come ~!** ¡ven aquí or acá!; **~ and there** aquí y allá
hereabouts ['hɪərə'bauts] adv por aquí (cerca)
hereafter [hɪər'ɑːftəʳ] adv en el futuro ■ n: **the ~** el más allá
hereby [hɪə'baɪ] adv (in letter) por la presente
hereditary [hɪ'rɛdɪtrɪ] adj hereditario
heredity [hɪ'rɛdɪtɪ] n herencia
heresy ['hɛrəsɪ] n herejía
heretic ['hɛrətɪk] n hereje m/f
heretical [hɪ'rɛtɪkəl] adj herético
herewith [hɪə'wɪð] adv: **I send you ~ ...** le mando adjunto ...
heritage ['hɛrɪtɪdʒ] n (gen) herencia; (fig) patrimonio; **our national ~** nuestro patrimonio nacional

hermetically [hə:'mɛtɪkəlɪ] *adv*: ~ **sealed** herméticamente cerrado
hermit ['hə:mɪt] *n* ermitaño(-a)
hernia ['hə:nɪə] *n* hernia
hero (*pl* **heroes**) ['hɪərəu] *n* héroe *m*; (*in book, film*) protagonista *m*
heroic [hɪ'rəuɪk] *adj* heroico
heroin ['hɛrəuɪn] *n* heroína
heroin addict *n* heroinómano(-a), adicto(-a) a la heroína
heroine ['hɛrəuɪn] *n* heroína; (*in book, film*) protagonista
heroism ['hɛrəuɪzm] *n* heroísmo
heron ['hɛrən] *n* garza
hero worship *n* veneración *f*
herring ['hɛrɪŋ] *n* arenque *m*
hers [hə:z] *pron* (el) suyo/(la) suya *etc*; **a friend of** ~ un amigo suyo; **this is** ~ esto es suyo *or* de ella; *see also* **mine**
herself [hə:'sɛlf] *pron* (*reflexive*) se; (*emphatic*) ella misma; (*after prep*) sí (misma); *see also* **oneself**
Herts *abbr* (*Brit*) = **Hertfordshire**
he's [hi:z] = **he is**; **he has**
hesitant ['hɛzɪtənt] *adj* indeciso; **to be** ~ **about doing sth** no decidirse a hacer algo
hesitate ['hɛzɪteɪt] *vi* dudar, vacilar; **don't** ~ **to ask (me)** no dudes en pedírmelo
hesitation [hɛzɪ'teɪʃən] *n* indecisión *f*; **I have no** ~ **in saying (that)** ... no tengo el menor reparo en afirmar que ...
hessian ['hɛsɪən] *n* arpillera
heterogeneous ['hɛtərə'dʒi:nɪəs] *adj* heterogéneo
heterosexual [hɛtərəu'sɛksjuəl] *adj*, *n* heterosexual *m/f*
het up [hɛt'ʌp] *adj* (*col*) agitado, nervioso
HEW *n abbr* (*US*: = *Department of Health, Education, and Welfare*) ministerio de sanidad, educación y bienestar público
hew [hju:] *vt* cortar
hex [hɛks] (*US*) *n* maleficio, mal *m* de ojo ▪ *vt* embrujar
hexagon ['hɛksəgən] *n* hexágono
hexagonal [hɛk'sægənl] *adj* hexagonal
hey [heɪ] *excl* ¡oye!, ¡oiga!
heyday ['heɪdeɪ] *n*: **the** ~ **of** el apogeo de
HF *n abbr* = **high frequency**
HGV *n abbr* = **heavy goods vehicle**
HI *abbr* (*US*) = **Hawaii**
hi [haɪ] *excl* ¡hola!
hiatus [haɪ'eɪtəs] *n* vacío, interrupción *f*; (*Ling*) hiato
hibernate ['haɪbəneɪt] *vi* invernar
hibernation [haɪbə'neɪʃən] *n* hibernación *f*
hiccough, hiccup ['hɪkʌp] *vi* hipar; **hiccoughs** *npl* hipo *sg*
hick [hɪk] *n* (*US col*) paleto(-a)

hid [hɪd] *pt of* **hide**
hidden ['hɪdn] *pp of* **hide** ▪ *adj*: **there are no** ~ **extras** no hay suplementos ocultos; ~ **agenda** plan *m* encubierto
hide [haɪd] (*pt* **hid**, *pp* **hidden**) *n* (*skin*) piel *f* ▪ *vt* esconder, ocultar; (*feelings, truth*) encubrir, ocultar ▪ *vi*: **to** ~ **(from sb)** esconderse *or* ocultarse (de algn)
hide-and-seek ['haɪdən'si:k] *n* escondite *m*
hideaway ['haɪdəweɪ] *n* escondite *m*
hideous ['hɪdɪəs] *adj* horrible
hideously ['hɪdɪəslɪ] *adv* horriblemente
hide-out ['haɪdaut] *n* escondite *m*, refugio
hiding ['haɪdɪŋ] *n* (*beating*) paliza; **to be in** ~ (*concealed*) estar escondido
hiding place *n* escondrijo
hierarchy ['haɪərɑ:kɪ] *n* jerarquía
hieroglyphic [haɪərə'glɪfɪk] *adj* jeroglífico ▪ *n*: **hieroglyphics** jeroglíficos *mpl*
hi-fi ['haɪfaɪ] *abbr* (= *high fidelity*) *n* estéreo, hifi *m* ▪ *adj* de alta fidelidad
higgledy-piggledy ['hɪgldɪ'pɪgldɪ] *adv* en desorden, de cualquier modo
high [haɪ] *adj* alto; (*speed, number*) grande, alto; (*price*) elevado; (*wind*) fuerte; (*voice*) agudo; (*col: on drugs*) colocado; (: *on drink*) borracho; (*Culin: meat, game*) pasado; (: *spoilt*) estropeado ▪ *adv* alto, a gran altura ▪ *n*: **exports have reached a new** ~ las exportaciones han alcanzado niveles inusitados; **it is 20 m** ~ tiene 20 m de altura; ~ **in the air** en las alturas; **to pay a** ~ **price for sth** pagar algo muy caro
highball ['haɪbɔ:l] *n* (*US: drink*) whisky *m* soda, highball *m* (*LAm*), jaibol *m* (*LAm*)
highboy ['haɪbɔɪ] *n* (*US*) cómoda alta
highbrow ['haɪbrau] *adj* culto
highchair ['haɪtʃɛər] *n* silla alta (para niños)
high-class ['haɪ'klɑ:s] *adj* (*neighbourhood*) de alta sociedad; (*hotel*) de lujo; (*person*) distinguido, de categoría; (*food*) de alta categoría
High Court *n* (*Law*) tribunal *m* supremo; *ver nota*

● **HIGH COURT**
●
● En el sistema legal de Inglaterra y Gales
● *High Court* es la forma abreviada de "High
● Court of Justice", tribunal superior que
● junto con el de apelación ("Court of
● Appeal") forma el Tribunal Supremo
● ("Supreme Court of Judicature"). En
● el sistema legal escocés es la forma
● abreviada de "High Court of Justiciary",
● tribunal con jurado que juzga los delitos
● más serios, que pueden dar lugar a una
● pena de gran severidad.

h

higher ['haɪəʳ] *adj (form of life, study etc)* superior ∎ *adv* más alto ∎ *n (Scottish Scol):* H~ *cada una de las asignaturas que se estudian entre los 16 y los 17 años generalmente, así como el certificado de haberlas probado*

higher education *n* educación *f* or enseñanza superior

high explosive *n* explosivo de gran potencia

highfalutin [haɪfə'lu:tɪn] *adj (col)* de altos vuelos, encopetado

high finance *n* altas finanzas *fpl*

high-flier, high-flyer [haɪ'flaɪəʳ] *n* ambicioso(-a)

high-handed [haɪ'hændɪd] *adj* despótico

high-heeled [haɪ'hi:ld] *adj* de tacón alto

highjack ['haɪdʒæk] = **hijack**

high jump *n (Sport)* salto de altura

highlands ['haɪləndz] *npl* tierras *fpl* altas; **the H~** *(in Scotland)* las Tierras Altas de Escocia

high-level ['haɪlɛvl] *adj (talks etc)* de alto nivel

highlight ['haɪlaɪt] *n (fig: of event)* punto culminante ∎ *vt* subrayar

highly ['haɪlɪ] *adv* sumamente; ~ **paid** muy bien pagado; **to speak ~ of** hablar muy bien de; ~ **strung** muy excitable

High Mass *n* misa mayor

highness ['haɪnɪs] *n* altura; **Her** or **His H~** Su Alteza

high-pitched [haɪ'pɪtʃt] *adj* agudo

high point *n*: **the ~** el punto culminante

high-powered ['haɪ'pauəd] *adj (engine)* de gran potencia; *(fig: person)* importante

high-pressure ['haɪprɛʃəʳ] *adj* de alta presión; *(fig: salesman etc)* enérgico

high-rise ['haɪraɪz] *n (also:* **high-rise block, high-rise building)** torre *f* de pisos

high school *n* centro de enseñanza secundaria, ≈ Instituto Nacional de Bachillerato *(SP)*, liceo *(LAm)*; *ver nota*

○ **HIGH SCHOOL**
○
○
○ El término *high school* se aplica en
○ Estados Unidos a dos tipos de centros
○ de educación secundaria: "Junior
○ High Schools", en los que se imparten
○ normalmente del 7° al 9° curso (llamado
○ "grade") y "Senior High Schools", que
○ abarcan los cursos 10°, 11° y 12° y en
○ ocasiones el 9°. Aquí pueden estudiarse
○ asignaturas tanto de contenido
○ académico como profesional. En
○ Gran Bretaña también se llaman *high*
○ *school* algunos centros de enseñanza
○ secundaria.

high season *n (Brit)* temporada alta

high-speed ['haɪspi:d] *adj* de alta velocidad

high-spirited [haɪ'spɪrɪtɪd] *adj* animado

high spirits *npl* ánimos *mpl*

high street *n (Brit)* calle *f* mayor

high tide *n* marea alta

highway ['haɪweɪ] *n* carretera; *(US)* autopista

Highway Code *n (Brit)* código de la circulación

highwayman ['haɪweɪmən] *n* salteador *m* de caminos

hijack ['haɪdʒæk] *vt* secuestrar ∎ *n (also:* **hijacking)** secuestro

hijacker ['haɪdʒækəʳ] *n* secuestrador(a) *m(f)*

hike [haɪk] *vi (go walking)* ir de excursión (a pie); *(tramp)* caminar ∎ *n* caminata; *(col: in prices etc)* aumento
▶ **hike up** *vt (raise)* aumentar

hiker ['haɪkəʳ] *n* excursionista *m/f*

hilarious [hɪ'lɛərɪəs] *adj* divertidísimo

hilarity [hɪ'lærɪtɪ] *n (laughter)* risas *fpl*, carcajadas *fpl*

hill [hɪl] *n* colina; *(high)* montaña; *(slope)* cuesta

hillbilly ['hɪlbɪlɪ] *n (US)* rústico(-a) montañés(-esa); *(pej)* palurdo(-a)

hillock ['hɪlək] *n* montecillo, altozano

hillside ['hɪlsaɪd] *n* ladera

hilltop ['hɪltɔp] *n* cumbre *f*

hilly ['hɪlɪ] *adj* montañoso; *(uneven)* accidentado

hilt [hɪlt] *n (of sword)* empuñadura; **to the ~** *(fig: support)* incondicionalmente; **to be in debt up to the ~** estar hasta el cuello de deudas

him [hɪm] *pron (direct)* le, lo; *(indirect)* le; *(stressed, after prep)* él; *see also* **me**

Himalayas [hɪmə'leɪəz] *npl:* **the ~** el Himalaya

himself [hɪm'sɛlf] *pron (reflexive)* se; *(emphatic)* él mismo; *(after prep)* sí (mismo); *see also* **oneself**

hind [haɪnd] *adj* posterior ∎ *n* cierva

hinder ['hɪndəʳ] *vt* estorbar, impedir

hindquarters ['haɪndkwɔ:təz] *npl (Zool)* cuartos *mpl* traseros

hindrance ['hɪndrəns] *n* estorbo, obstáculo

hindsight ['haɪndsaɪt] *n* percepción *f* tardía or retrospectiva; **with the benefit of ~** con la perspectiva del tiempo transcurrido

Hindu ['hɪndu:] *n* hindú *m/f*

hinge [hɪndʒ] *n* bisagra, gozne *m* ∎ *vi (fig):* **to ~ on** depender de

hint [hɪnt] *n* indirecta; *(advice)* consejo ∎ *vt:* **to ~ that** insinuar que ∎ *vi:* **to ~ at** aludir a; **to drop a ~** soltar or tirar una indirecta; **give me a ~** dame una pista

hip [hɪp] *n* cadera; *(Bot)* escaramujo

hip flask n petaca
hip-hop ['hɪphɔp] n hip hop m
hippie ['hɪpɪ] n hippie m/f, jipi m/f
hip pocket n bolsillo de atrás
hippopotamus (pl **hippopotamuses** or **hippopotami**) n [hɪpə'pɔtəməs, -'pɔtəmaɪ] hipopótamo
hippy ['hɪpɪ] n = **hippie**
hire ['haɪəʳ] vt (Brit: car, equipment) alquilar; (worker) contratar ■ n alquiler m; **for** ~ se alquila; (taxi) libre; **on** ~ de alquiler
  ▶ **hire out** vt alquilar, arrendar
hire car, hired car n (Brit) coche m de alquiler
hire purchase n (Brit) compra a plazos; **to buy sth on** ~ comprar algo a plazos
his [hɪz] pron (el) suyo/(la) suya etc ■ adj su; **this is** ~ esto es suyo or de él; see also **my**; **mine**
Hispanic [hɪs'pænɪk] adj hispánico
hiss [hɪs] vi sisear; (in protest) silbar ■ n siseo; silbido
histogram ['hɪstəgræm] n histograma m
historian [hɪ'stɔːrɪən] n historiador(a) m(f)
historic [hɪ'stɔrɪk], **historical** [hɪ'stɔrɪkl] adj histórico
history ['hɪstərɪ] n historia; **there's a long** ~ **of that illness in his family** esa enfermedad corre en su familia
histrionics [hɪstrɪ'ɔnɪks] npl histrionismo
hit [hɪt] vt (pt, pp **hit**) (strike) golpear, pegar; (reach: target) alcanzar; (collide with: car) chocar contra; (fig: affect) afectar ■ n golpe m; (success) éxito; **to** ~ **the headlines** salir en primera plana; **to** ~ **the road** (col) largarse; **to** ~ **it off with sb** llevarse bien con algn
  ▶ **hit back** vi defenderse; (fig) devolver golpe por golpe
  ▶ **hit out at** vt fus asestar un golpe a; (fig) atacar
  ▶ **hit (up)on** vt fus (answer) dar con; (solution) hallar, encontrar
hit and miss adj: **it's very** ~, **it's a** ~ **affair** es cuestión de suerte
hit-and-run driver ['hɪtən'rʌn-] n conductor que tras atropellar a algn se da a la fuga
hitch [hɪtʃ] vt (fasten) atar, amarrar; (also: **hitch up**) arremangarse ■ n (difficulty) problema, pega; **to** ~ **a lift** hacer autostop; **technical** ~ problema m técnico
  ▶ **hitch up** vt (horse, cart) enganchar, uncir
hitch-hike ['hɪtʃhaɪk] vi hacer autostop
hitch-hiker ['hɪtʃhaɪkəʳ] n autostopista m/f
hi-tech [haɪ'tɛk] adj de alta tecnología
hitherto ['hɪðə'tuː] adv hasta ahora, hasta aquí
hit list n lista negra
hitman ['hɪtmæn] n asesino a sueldo
hit or miss ['hɪtə'mɪs] adj = **hit and miss**
hit parade n: **the** ~ los cuarenta principales

HIV n abbr (= human immunodeficiency virus) VIH m; ~-**negative** no portador(a) del virus del sida, no seropositivo; ~-**positive** portador(a) del virus del sida, seropositivo
hive [haɪv] n colmena; **the shop was a** ~ **of activity** (fig) la tienda era una colmena humana
  ▶ **hive off** vt (col: separate) separar; (: privatize) privatizar
hl abbr (= hectolitre) hl
HM abbr (= His (or Her) Majesty) S.M.
HMG abbr (Brit) = **His (**or **Her) Majesty's Government**
HMI n abbr (Brit Scol) = **His (**or **Her) Majesty's Inspector**
HMO n abbr (US: = Health Maintenance Organization) seguro médico global
HMS abbr = **His (**or **Her) Majesty's Ship**
HMSO n abbr (Brit: = His (or Her) Majesty's Stationery Office) distribuidor oficial de las publicaciones del gobierno del Reino Unido
HNC n abbr (Brit: = Higher National Certificate) título académico
HND n abbr (Brit: = Higher National Diploma) título académico
hoard [hɔːd] n (treasure) tesoro; (stockpile) provisión f ■ vt acumular
hoarding ['hɔːdɪŋ] n (for posters) valla publicitaria
hoarfrost ['hɔːfrɔst] n escarcha
hoarse [hɔːs] adj ronco
hoax [həʊks] n engaño
hob [hɔb] n quemador m
hobble ['hɔbl] vi cojear
hobby ['hɔbɪ] n pasatiempo, afición f
hobby-horse ['hɔbɪhɔːs] n (fig) tema preferido
hobnob ['hɔbnɔb] vi: **to** ~ **(with)** alternar (con)
hobo ['həʊbəʊ] n (US) vagabundo
hock [hɔk] n corvejón m; (col): **to be in** ~ (person) estar empeñado or endeudado; (object) estar empeñado
hockey ['hɔkɪ] n hockey m
hocus-pocus [həʊkəs'pəʊkəs] n (trickery) engañifa; (words: of magician) abracadabra m
hod [hɔd] n capacho
hodge-podge ['hɔdʒpɔdʒ] n (US) = **hotchpotch**
hoe [həʊ] n azadón m ■ vt azadonar
hog [hɔg] n cerdo, puerco ■ vt (fig) acaparar; **to go the whole** ~ echar el todo por el todo
Hogmanay [hɔgmə'neɪ] n (Scottish) Nochevieja
hoist [hɔɪst] n (crane) grúa ■ vt levantar, alzar
hoity-toity [hɔɪtɪ'tɔɪtɪ] adj (col): **to be** ~ darse humos

h

hold [həuld] (*pt, pp* **held**) *vt* tener; (*contain*) contener; (*keep back*) retener; (*believe*) sostener; (*take hold of*) coger (SP), agarrar (LAm); (*bear: weight*) soportar; (*meeting*) celebrar ■ *vi* (*withstand: pressure*) resistir; (*be valid*) ser válido; (*stick*) pegarse ■ *n* (*grasp*) asimiento; (*fig*) dominio; (*Wrestling*) presa; (*Naut*) bodega; ~ **the line!** (*Tel*) ¡no cuelgue!; **to ~ one's own** (*fig*) defenderse; **to ~ office** (*Pol*) ocupar un cargo; **to ~ firm** or **fast** mantenerse firme; **he holds the view that ...** opina *or* es su opinión que ...; **to ~ sb responsible for sth** culpar *or* echarle la culpa a algn de algo; **where can I get ~ of ...?** ¿dónde puedo encontrar (a) ...?; **to catch** or **get (a) ~ of** agarrarse *or* asirse de

▶ **hold back** *vt* retener; (*secret*) ocultar; **to ~ sb back from doing sth** impedir a algn hacer algo, impedir que algn haga algo

▶ **hold down** *vt* (*person*) sujetar; (*job*) mantener

▶ **hold forth** *vi* perorar

▶ **hold off** *vt* (*enemy*) rechazar ■ *vi*: **if the rain holds off** si no llueve

▶ **hold on** *vi* agarrarse bien; (*wait*) esperar

▶ **hold on to** *vt fus* agarrarse a; (*keep*) guardar

▶ **hold out** *vt* ofrecer ■ *vi* (*resist*) resistir; **to ~ out (against)** resistir (a), sobrevivir

▶ **hold over** *vt* (*meeting etc*) aplazar

▶ **hold up** *vt* (*raise*) levantar; (*support*) apoyar; (*delay*) retrasar; (: *traffic*) demorar; (*rob: bank*) asaltar, atracar

holdall ['həuldɔːl] *n* (*Brit*) bolsa

holder ['həuldəʳ] *n* (*of ticket, record*) poseedor(a) *m(f)*; (*of passport, post, office, title etc*) titular *m/f*

holding ['həuldɪŋ] *n* (*share*) participación *f*

holding company *n* holding *m*

holdup ['həuldʌp] *n* (*robbery*) atraco; (*delay*) retraso; (*Brit: in traffic*) embotellamiento

hole [həul] *n* agujero ■ *vt* agujerear; **~ in the heart** (*Med*) boquete *m* en el corazón; **to pick holes in** (*fig*) encontrar defectos en; **the ship was holed** se abrió una vía de agua en el barco

▶ **hole up** *vi* esconderse

holiday ['hɔlədɪ] *n* vacaciones *fpl*; (*day off*) (día *m* de) fiesta, día *m* festivo *or* feriado (LAm); **on ~** de vacaciones; **to be on ~** estar de vacaciones

holiday camp *n* colonia *or* centro vacacional; (*for children*) colonia veraniega infantil

holiday home *n* residencia vacacional

holiday job *n* (*Brit*) trabajo para las vacaciones

holidaymaker ['hɔlədɪmeɪkəʳ] *n* (*Brit*) turista *m/f*

holiday pay *n* paga de las vacaciones

holiday resort *n* centro turístico

holiday season *n* temporada de vacaciones

holiness ['həulɪnɪs] *n* santidad *f*

holistic [həu'lɪstɪk] *adj* holístico

Holland ['hɔlənd] *n* Holanda

holler ['hɔləʳ] *vi* (*col*) gritar, vocear

hollow ['hɔləu] *adj* hueco; (*fig*) vacío; (*eyes*) hundido; (*sound*) sordo ■ *n* (*gen*) hueco; (*in ground*) hoyo ■ *vt*: **to ~ out** ahuecar

holly ['hɔlɪ] *n* acebo

hollyhock ['hɔlɪhɔk] *n* malva loca

Hollywood ['hɔlɪwud] Hollywood *m*

holocaust ['hɔləkɔːst] *n* holocausto

hologram ['hɔləgræm] *n* holograma *m*

holster ['həulstəʳ] *n* pistolera

holy ['həulɪ] *adj* (*gen*) santo, sagrado; (*water*) bendito; **the H~ Father** el Santo Padre

Holy Communion *n* Sagrada Comunión *f*

Holy Ghost, Holy Spirit *n* Espíritu *m* Santo

homage ['hɔmɪdʒ] *n* homenaje *m*; **to pay ~ to** rendir homenaje a

home [həum] *n* casa; (*country*) patria; (*institution*) asilo; (*Comput*) punto inicial *or* de partida ■ *adj* (*domestic*) casero, de casa; (*Econ, Pol*) nacional; (*Sport: team*) de casa; (: *match, win*) en casa ■ *adv* (*direction*) a casa; **at ~** en casa; **to go/come ~** ir/volver a casa; **make yourself at ~** ¡estás en tu casa!; **it's near my ~** está cerca de mi casa

▶ **home in on** *vt fus* (*missile*) dirigirse hacia

home address *n* domicilio

home-brew [həum'bruː] *n* cerveza *etc* casera

homecoming ['həumkʌmɪŋ] *n* regreso (al hogar)

home computer *n* ordenador *m* doméstico

Home Counties *npl* condados que rodean Londres

home economics *n* economía doméstica

home ground *n*: **to be on ~** estar en su *etc* terreno

home-grown ['həumgrəun] *adj* de cosecha propia

home help *n* (*Brit*) trabajador(a) *m(f)* del servicio de atención domiciliaria

homeland ['həumlænd] *n* tierra natal

homeless ['həumlɪs] *adj* sin hogar, sin casa ■ *npl*: **the ~** las personas sin hogar

home loan *n* préstamo para la vivienda

homely ['həumlɪ] *adj* (*domestic*) casero; (*simple*) sencillo

home-made [həum'meɪd] *adj* hecho en casa

Home Office *n* (*Brit*) Ministerio del Interior

homeopathy *etc* [həumɪ'ɔpəθɪ] (US) = **homoeopathy** *etc*

home page *n* (*Comput*) página de inicio

home rule *n* autonomía

Home Secretary *n* (*Brit*) Ministro del Interior

homesick ['həumsɪk] *adj*: **to be ~** tener morriña *or* nostalgia

homestead ['həumstɛd] *n* hacienda

home town *n* ciudad *f* natal

home truth *n*: **to tell sb a few home truths** decir cuatro verdades a algn

homeward ['həumwəd] *adj* (*journey*) de vuelta ■ *adv* hacia casa

homewards ['həumwədz] *adv* hacia casa

homework ['həumwə:k] *n* deberes *mpl*

homicidal [hɔmɪ'saɪdl] *adj* homicida

homicide ['hɔmɪsaɪd] *n* (US) homicidio

homily ['hɔmɪlɪ] *n* homilía

homing ['həumɪŋ] *adj* (*device, missile*) buscador(a); **~ pigeon** paloma mensajera

homoeopath, homeopath (US) ['həumɪəupæθ] *n* homeópata *m/f*

homoeopathic, homeopathic (US) [həumɪəu'pæθɪk] *adj* homeopático

homoeopathy, homeopathy (US) [həumɪ'ɔpəθɪ] *n* homeopatía

homogeneous [hɔmə'dʒi:nɪəs] *adj* homogéneo

homogenize [hə'mɔdʒənaɪz] *vt* homogeneizar

homosexual [hɔməu'sɛksjuəl] *adj, n* homosexual *m/f*

Hon *abbr* (= honourable, honorary) en títulos

Honduras [hɔn'djuərəs] *n* Honduras *fpl*

hone [həun] *vt* (*sharpen*) afilar; (*fig*) perfeccionar

honest ['ɔnɪst] *adj* honrado; (*sincere*) franco, sincero; **to be quite ~ with you ...** para serte franco ...

honestly ['ɔnɪstlɪ] *adv* honradamente; francamente, de verdad

honesty ['ɔnɪstɪ] *n* honradez *f*

honey ['hʌnɪ] *n* miel *f*; (US col) cariño; (: *to strangers*) guapo, linda

honeycomb ['hʌnɪkəum] *n* panal *m*; (*fig*) laberinto

honeymoon ['hʌnɪmu:n] *n* luna de miel

honeysuckle ['hʌnɪsʌkl] *n* madreselva

Hong Kong ['hɔŋ'kɔŋ] *n* Hong-Kong *m*

honk [hɔŋk] *vi* (Aut) tocar la bocina

Honolulu [hɔnə'lu:lu:] *n* Honolulú *m*

honorary ['ɔnərərɪ] *adj* no remunerado; (*duty, title*) honorario

honour, honor (US) ['ɔnər] *vt* honrar ■ *n* honor *m*, honra; **in ~ of** en honor de; **it's a great ~** es un gran honor

honourable, honorable (US) ['ɔnərəbl] *adj* honrado, honorable

honour-bound, honor-bound (US) ['ɔnə'baund] *adj* moralmente obligado

honours degree *n* (Univ) licenciatura superior; ver nota

HONOURS DEGREE

Tras un período de estudios de tres años normalmente (cuatro en Escocia), los universitarios obtienen una licenciatura llamada *honours degree*. La calificación global que se recibe, en una escala de mayor a menor es la siguiente: "first class" (I), "upper-second class" (II:1), "lower-second class" (II:2) y "third class" (III). El licenciado puede añadir las letras "Hons" al título obtenido tras su nombre y apellidos, por ejemplo "BA Hons" *see also* **ordinary degree**

honours list *n* (Brit) lista de distinciones honoríficas que entrega la reina; *ver nota*

HONOURS LIST

A la lista con los títulos honoríficos y condecoraciones que el monarca británico otorga en Año Nuevo y en el día de su cumpleaños se la conoce con el nombre de *honours list*. Las personas que reciben dichas distinciones suelen ser miembros destacados de la vida pública (ámbito empresarial, ejército, deportes, espectáculos), aunque últimamente también se reconoce con ellas el trabajo abnegado y anónimo de la gente de la calle.

Hons. [ɔnz] *abbr* (Univ) = **hono(u)rs degree**

hood [hud] *n* capucha; (Brit Aut) capota; (US Aut) capó *m*; (US col) matón *m*

hooded ['hudɪd] *adj* (*robber*) encapuchado

hoodie ['hudɪ] *n* (*pullover*) sudadera *f* con capucha; (*young person*) capuchero(-a) *m(f)*

hoodlum ['hu:dləm] *n* matón *m*

hoodwink ['hudwɪŋk] *vt* (Brit) timar, engañar

hoof (*pl* **hoofs** *or* **hooves**) [hu:f, hu:vz] *n* pezuña

hook [huk] *n* gancho; (*on dress*) corchete *m*, broche *m*; (*for fishing*) anzuelo ■ *vt* enganchar; **hooks and eyes** corchetes *mpl*, macho y hembra *m*; **by ~ or by crook** por las buenas o por las malas, cueste lo que cueste; **to be hooked on** (*col*) estar enganchado a
▸ **hook up** *vt* (Radio, TV) transmitir en cadena

hooligan ['hu:lɪgən] *n* gamberro

hooliganism ['hu:lɪgənɪzəm] *n* gamberrismo

hoop [hu:p] *n* aro

hoot [hu:t] *vi* (Brit Aut) tocar la bocina; (*siren*) sonar; (*owl*) ulular ■ *n* bocinazo, toque *m* de sirena; **to ~ with laughter** morirse de risa

hooter ['huːtəʳ] n (Brit Aut) bocina; (of ship, factory) sirena
hoover® ['huːvəʳ] (Brit) n aspiradora ∎ vt pasar la aspiradora por
hooves [huːvz] pl of **hoof**
hop [hɔp] vi saltar, brincar; (on one foot) saltar con un pie ∎ n salto, brinco; see also **hops**
hope [həup] vt, vi esperar ∎ n esperanza; **I ~ so/not** espero que sí/no
hopeful ['həupful] adj (person) optimista; (situation) prometedor(a); **I'm ~ that she'll manage to come** confío en que podrá venir
hopefully ['həupfulɪ] adv con optimismo, con esperanza
hopeless ['həuplɪs] adj desesperado
hopelessly ['həuplɪslɪ] adv (live etc) sin esperanzas; **I'm ~ confused/lost** estoy totalmente despistado/perdido
hopper ['hɔpəʳ] n (chute) tolva
hops [hɔps] npl lúpulo sg
horde [hɔːd] n horda
horizon [həˈraɪzn] n horizonte m
horizontal [hɔrɪˈzɔntl] adj horizontal
hormone ['hɔːməun] n hormona
hormone replacement therapy n terapia hormonal sustitutiva
horn [hɔːn] n cuerno, cacho (LAm); (Mus: also: **French horn**) trompa; (Aut) bocina, claxon m
horned [hɔːnd] adj con cuernos
hornet ['hɔːnɪt] n avispón m
horny ['hɔːnɪ] adj (material) córneo; (hands) calloso; (US col) cachondo
horoscope ['hɔrəskəup] n horóscopo
horrendous [hɔˈrɛndəs] adj horrendo
horrible ['hɔrɪbl] adj horrible
horribly ['hɔrɪblɪ] adv horriblemente
horrid ['hɔrɪd] adj horrible, horroroso
horridly ['hɔrɪdlɪ] adv (behave) tremendamente mal
horrific [hɔˈrɪfɪk] adj (accident) horroroso; (film) horripilante
horrify ['hɔrɪfaɪ] vt horrorizar
horrifying ['hɔrɪfaɪɪŋ] adj horroroso
horror ['hɔrəʳ] n horror m
horror film n película de terror or miedo
horror-struck ['hɔrəstrʌk], **horror-stricken** ['hɔrəstrɪkn] adj horrorizado
hors d'œuvre [ɔːˈdəːvrə] n entremeses mpl
horse [hɔːs] n caballo
horseback ['hɔːsbæk] n: **on ~** a caballo
horsebox ['hɔːsbɔks] n remolque m para transportar caballos
horse chestnut n (tree) castaño de Indias
horsedrawn ['hɔːsdrɔːn] adj de tracción animal
horsefly ['hɔːsflaɪ] n tábano
horseman ['hɔːsmən] n jinete m

horsemanship ['hɔːsmənʃɪp] n equitación f, manejo del caballo
horseplay ['hɔːspleɪ] n pelea amistosa
horsepower ['hɔːspauəʳ] n caballo (de fuerza), potencia en caballos
horse-racing ['hɔːsreɪsɪŋ] n carreras fpl de caballos
horseradish ['hɔːsrædɪʃ] n rábano picante
horseshoe ['hɔːsʃuː] n herradura
horse show n concurso hípico
horse-trader ['hɔːstreɪdəʳ] n chalán(-ana) m(f)
horse trials npl = **horse show**
horsewhip ['hɔːswɪp] vt azotar
horsewoman ['hɔːswumən] n amazona
horsey ['hɔːsɪ] adj (col: person) aficionado a los caballos
horticulture ['hɔːtɪkʌltʃəʳ] n horticultura
hose [həuz] n (also: **hosepipe**) manguera
▶ **hose down** vt limpiar con manguera
hosiery ['həuzɪərɪ] n calcetería
hospice ['hɔspɪs] n hospicio
hospitable ['hɔspɪtəbl] adj hospitalario
hospital ['hɔspɪtl] n hospital m
hospitality [hɔspɪˈtælɪtɪ] n hospitalidad f
hospitalize ['hɔspɪtəlaɪz] vt hospitalizar
host [həust] n anfitrión m; (TV, Radio) presentador(a) m(f); (of inn etc) mesonero; (Rel) hostia; (large number): **a ~ of** multitud de
hostage ['hɔstɪdʒ] n rehén m
hostel ['hɔstl] n hostal m; (for students, nurses etc) residencia; (also: **youth hostel**) albergue m juvenil; (for homeless people) hospicio
hostelling ['hɔstlɪŋ] n: **to go (youth) ~** hospedarse en albergues
hostess ['həustɪs] n anfitriona; (Brit: air hostess) azafata; (in night-club) señorita de compañía
hostile ['hɔstaɪl] adj hostil
hostility [hɔˈstɪlɪtɪ] n hostilidad f
hot [hɔt] adj caliente; (weather) caluroso, de calor; (as opposed to only warm) muy caliente; (spicy) picante; (fig) ardiente, acalorado; **to be ~** (person) tener calor; (object) estar caliente; (weather) hacer calor
▶ **hot up** vi (col: situation) ponerse difícil or apurado; (: party) animarse ∎ vt (col: pace) apretar; (: engine) aumentar la potencia de
hot air n (col) palabras fpl huecas
hot-air balloon [hɔtˈɛə-] n (Aviat) globo aerostático or de aire caliente
hotbed ['hɔtbɛd] n (fig) semillero
hot-blooded [hɔtˈblʌdɪd] adj impetuoso
hotchpotch ['hɔtʃpɔtʃ] n mezcolanza, baturrillo
hot dog n perrito caliente
hotel [həuˈtɛl] n hotel m

hotelier [həu'tɛlɪəʳ] *n* hotelero
hotel industry *n* industria hotelera
hotel room *n* habitación *f* de hotel
hot flush *n* (*Brit*) sofoco
hotfoot ['hɔtfut] *adv* a toda prisa
hothead ['hɔthɛd] *n* (*fig*) exaltado(-a)
hotheaded [hɔt'hɛdɪd] *adj* exaltado
hothouse ['hɔthaus] *n* invernadero
hot line *n* (*Pol*) teléfono rojo, línea directa
hotly ['hɔtlɪ] *adv* con pasión, apasionadamente
hotplate ['hɔtpleɪt] *n* (*on cooker*) hornillo
hotpot ['hɔtpɔt] *n* (*Brit Culin*) estofado
hot potato *n* (*Brit col*) asunto espinoso;
  to drop sth/sb like a ~ no querer saber ya nada de algo/algn
hot seat *n* primera fila
hotspot ['hɔt'spɔt] *n* (*Comput: also:* **wireless hotspot**) punto de acceso inalámbrico
hot spot *n* (*trouble spot*) punto caliente; (*night club etc*) lugar *m* popular
hot spring *n* terma, fuente *f* de aguas termales
hot-tempered ['hɔt'tɛmpəd] *adj* de mal genio *or* carácter
hot-water bottle [hɔt'wɔːtə-] *n* bolsa de agua caliente
hot-wire ['hɔtwaɪəʳ] *vt* (*col: car*) hacer el puente en
hound [haund] *vt* acosar ▪ *n* perro de caza
hour ['auəʳ] *n* hora; **at 30 miles an ~** a 30 millas por hora; **lunch ~** la hora del almuerzo *or* de comer; **to pay sb by the ~** pagar a algn por horas
hourly ['auəlɪ] *adj* (de) cada hora; (*rate*) por hora ▪ *adv* cada hora
house *n* [haus] (*pl* **houses** ['hauzɪz]) casa; (*Pol*) cámara; (*Theat*) sala ▪ *vt* [hauz] (*person*) alojar; **at/to my ~** en/a mi casa; **the H~ (of Commons/Lords)** (*Brit*) la Cámara de los Comunes/Lores; **the H~ (of Representatives)** (*US*) la Cámara de Representantes; **it's on the ~** (*fig*) la casa invita
house arrest *n* arresto domiciliario
houseboat ['hausbəut] *n* casa flotante
housebound ['hausbaund] *adj* confinado en casa
housebreaking ['hausbreɪkɪŋ] *n* allanamiento de morada
house-broken ['hausbrəukən] *adj* (*US*) = **house-trained**
housecoat ['hauskəut] *n* bata
household ['haushəuld] *n* familia
householder ['haushəuldəʳ] *n* propietario(-a); (*head of house*) cabeza de familia
househunting ['haushʌntɪŋ] *n*: **to go ~** ir en busca de vivienda

housekeeper ['hauskiːpəʳ] *n* ama de llaves
housekeeping ['hauskiːpɪŋ] *n* (*work*) trabajos *mpl* domésticos; (*Comput*) gestión *f* interna; (*also:* **housekeeping money**) dinero para gastos domésticos
houseman ['hausmən] *n* (*Brit Med*) médico residente
house-owner ['hausəunəʳ] *n* propietario(a) de una vivienda
house plant *n* planta de interior
house-proud ['hauspraud] *adj* preocupado por el embellecimiento de la casa
house-to-house ['haustə'haus] *adj*; (*search*) casa por casa; (*collection*) de casa en casa
house-train ['haustreɪn] *vt* (*pet*) enseñar (*a hacer sus necesidades en el sitio apropiado*)
house-trained ['haustreɪnd] *adj* (*Brit: animal*) enseñado
house-warming ['hauswɔːmɪŋ] *n* (*also:* **house-warming party**) fiesta de estreno de una casa
housewife ['hauswaɪf] *n* ama de casa
housework ['hauswəːk] *n* faenas *fpl* (de la casa)
housing ['hauzɪŋ] *n* (*act*) alojamiento; (*houses*) viviendas *fpl* ▪ *cpd* (*problem, shortage*) de (la) vivienda
housing association *n* asociación *f* de la vivienda
housing benefit *n* (*Brit*) subsidio por alojamiento
housing conditions *npl* condiciones *fpl* de habitabilidad
housing development, (*Brit*) **housing estate** *n* urbanización *f*
hovel ['hɔvl] *n* casucha
hover ['hɔvəʳ] *vi* flotar (en el aire); (*helicopter*) cernerse; **to ~ on the brink of disaster** estar al borde mismo del desastre
hovercraft ['hɔvəkrɑːft] *n* aerodeslizador *m*, hovercraft *m*
hoverport ['hɔvəpɔːt] *n* puerto de aerodeslizadores
how [hau] *adv* cómo; **~ are you?** ¿cómo está usted?, ¿cómo estás?; **~ do you do?** encantado, mucho gusto; **~ far is it to ...?** ¿qué distancia hay de aquí a ...?; **~ long have you been here?** ¿cuánto (tiempo) hace que estás aquí?, ¿cuánto (tiempo) llevas aquí?; **~ lovely!** ¡qué bonito!; **~ many/much?** ¿cuántos/cuánto?; **~ old are you?** ¿cuántos años tienes?; **~ is school?** ¿qué tal la escuela?; **~ about a drink?** ¿te gustaría algo de beber?, ¿qué te parece una copa?
however [hau'ɛvəʳ] *adv* de cualquier manera; (+ *adjective*) por muy ... que; (*in questions*) cómo ▪ *conj* sin embargo, no obstante

howitzer ['hauɪtsəʳ] *n* (*Mil*) obús *m*
howl [haul] *n* aullido ■ *vi* aullar
howler ['hauləʳ] *n* plancha, falta garrafal
howling ['haulɪŋ] *adj* (*wind*) huracanado
HP *n abbr* (*Brit*) = **hire purchase**
hp *abbr* (*Aut*) = **horsepower**
HQ *n abbr* = **headquarters**
HR *n abbr* (*US*) = **House of Representatives**; **human resources**
hr, hrs *abbr* (= *hour(s)*) h
HRH *abbr* (= *His (or Her) Royal Highness*) S.A.R.
HRT *n abbr* = **hormone replacement therapy**
HS *abbr* (*US*) = **high school**
HST *abbr* (*US*: = *Hawaiian Standard Time*) hora de Hawai
HT *abbr* = **high tension**
HTML *n abbr* (*Comput*: = *hypertext markup language*) HTML *m*
hub [hʌb] *n* (*of wheel*) cubo; (*fig*) centro
hubbub ['hʌbʌb] *n* barahúnda, barullo
hubcap ['hʌbkæp] *n* tapacubos *m inv*
HUD *n abbr* (*US*: = *Department of Housing and Urban Development*) ministerio de la vivienda y urbanismo
huddle ['hʌdl] *vi*: **to ~ together** amontonarse
hue [hju:] *n* color *m*, matiz *m*; **~ and cry** *n* protesta
huff [hʌf] *n*: **in a ~** enojado
huffy ['hʌfɪ] *adj* (*col*) mosqueado
hug [hʌg] *vt* abrazar ■ *n* abrazo
huge [hju:dʒ] *adj* enorme
hulk [hʌlk] *n* (*ship*) barco viejo; (*person, building etc*) mole *f*
hulking ['hʌlkɪŋ] *adj* pesado
hull [hʌl] *n* (*of ship*) casco
hullabaloo ['hʌləbə'lu:] *n* (*col: noise*) algarabía, jaleo
hullo [hə'ləu] *excl* = **hello**
hum [hʌm] *vt* tararear, canturrear ■ *vi* tararear, canturrear; (*insect*) zumbar ■ *n* (*Elec*) zumbido; (*of traffic, machines*) zumbido, ronroneo; (*of voices etc*) murmullo
human ['hju:mən] *adj* humano ■ *n* (*also*: **human being**) ser *m* humano
humane [hju:'meɪn] *adj* humano, humanitario
humanism ['hju:mənɪzəm] *n* humanismo
humanitarian [hju:mænɪ'tɛərɪən] *adj* humanitario
humanity [hju:'mænɪtɪ] *n* humanidad *f*
humanly ['hju:mənlɪ] *adv* humanamente
humanoid ['hju:mənɔɪd] *adj, n* humanoide *m/f*
human relations *npl* relaciones *fpl* humanas
human rights *npl* derechos *mpl* humanos
humble ['hʌmbl] *adj* humilde ■ *vt* humillar
humbly ['hʌmblɪ] *adv* humildemente

humbug ['hʌmbʌg] *n* patrañas *fpl*; (*Brit: sweet*) caramelo de menta
humdrum ['hʌmdrʌm] *adj* (*boring*) monótono, aburrido; (*routine*) rutinario
humid ['hju:mɪd] *adj* húmedo
humidifier [hju:'mɪdɪfaɪəʳ] *n* humectador *m*
humidity [hju:'mɪdɪtɪ] *n* humedad *f*
humiliate [hju:'mɪlɪeɪt] *vt* humillar
humiliation [hju:mɪlɪ'eɪʃən] *n* humillación *f*
humility [hju:'mɪlɪtɪ] *n* humildad *f*
humorist ['hju:mərɪst] *n* humorista *m/f*
humorous ['hju:mərəs] *adj* gracioso, divertido
humour, humor (*US*) ['hju:məʳ] *n* humorismo, sentido del humor; (*mood*) humor *m* ■ *vt* (*person*) complacer; **sense of ~** sentido del humor; **to be in a good/bad ~** estar de buen/mal humor
humourless, humorless (*US*) ['hju:məlɪs] *adj* serio
hump [hʌmp] *n* (*in ground*) montículo; (*camel's*) giba
humus ['hju:məs] *n* (*Bio*) humus *m*
hunch [hʌntʃ] *n* (*premonition*) presentimiento; **I have a ~ that** tengo la corazonada *or* el presentimiento de que
hunchback ['hʌntʃbæk] *n* jorobado(-a)
hunched [hʌntʃt] *adj* jorobado
hundred ['hʌndrəd] *num* ciento; (*before n*) cien; **about a ~ people** unas cien personas, alrededor de cien personas; **hundreds of** centenares de; **hundreds of people** centenares de personas; **I'm a ~ per cent sure** estoy completamente seguro
hundredweight ['hʌndrədweɪt] *n* (*Brit*) = 50.8 *kg*; 112 *lb*; (*US*) = 45.3 *kg*; 100 *lb*
hung [hʌŋ] *pt, pp of* **hang**
Hungarian [hʌŋ'gɛərɪən] *adj* húngaro ■ *n* húngaro(-a) *m(f)*; (*Ling*) húngaro
Hungary ['hʌŋgərɪ] *n* Hungría
hunger ['hʌŋgəʳ] *n* hambre *f* ■ *vi*: **to ~ for** (*fig*) tener hambre de, anhelar
hunger strike *n* huelga de hambre
hungover [hʌŋ'əuvəʳ] *adj* (*col*): **to be ~** tener resaca
hungrily ['hʌŋgrəlɪ] *adv* ávidamente, con ganas
hungry ['hʌŋgrɪ] *adj* hambriento; **to be ~** tener hambre; **~ for** (*fig*) sediento de
hunk [hʌŋk] *n* (*of bread etc*) trozo, pedazo
hunt [hʌnt] *vt* (*seek*) buscar; (*Sport*) cazar ■ *vi* cazar ■ *n* caza, cacería
▶ **hunt down** *vt* acorralar, seguir la pista a
hunter ['hʌntəʳ] *n* cazador(a) *m(f)*; (*horse*) caballo de caza
hunting ['hʌntɪŋ] *n* caza
hurdle ['hə:dl] *n* (*Sport*) valla; (*fig*) obstáculo

hurl [həːl] *vt* lanzar, arrojar
hurling ['həːlɪŋ] *n* (*Sport*) *juego irlandés semejante al hockey*
hurly-burly ['həːlɪ'bəːlɪ] *n* jaleo, follón *m*
hurrah [hu'rɑː], **hurray** [hu'reɪ] *n* ¡viva!, ¡hurra!
hurricane ['hʌrɪkən] *n* huracán *m*
hurried ['hʌrɪd] *adj* (*fast*) apresurado; (*rushed*) hecho de prisa
hurriedly ['hʌrɪdlɪ] *adv* con prisa, apresuradamente
hurry ['hʌrɪ] *n* prisa ◾ *vb* (*also*: **hurry up**)
◾ *vi* apresurarse, darse prisa, apurarse (*LAm*)
◾ *vt* (*person*) dar prisa a; (*work*) apresurar, hacer de prisa; **to be in a ~** tener prisa, tener apuro (*LAm*), estar apurado (*LAm*); **to ~ back/ home** darse prisa en volver/volver a casa
▸ **hurry along** *vi* pasar de prisa
▸ **hurry away, hurry off** *vi* irse corriendo
▸ **hurry on** *vi*: **to ~ on to say** apresurarse a decir
▸ **hurry up** *vi* darse prisa, apurarse (*LAm*)
hurt [həːt] (*pl* **hurt**) *vt* hacer daño a; (*business, interests etc*) perjudicar ◾ *vi* doler ◾ *adj* lastimado; **I ~ my arm** me lastimé el brazo; **where does it ~?** ¿dónde te duele?
hurtful ['həːtful] *adj* (*remark etc*) hiriente, dañino
hurtle ['həːtl] *vi*: **to ~ past** pasar como un rayo
husband ['hʌzbənd] *n* marido
hush [hʌʃ] *n* silencio ◾ *vt* hacer callar; (*cover up*) encubrir; **~!** ¡chitón!, ¡cállate!
▸ **hush up** *vt* (*fact*) encubrir, callar
hushed [hʌʃt] *adj* (*voice*) bajo
hush-hush [hʌʃ'hʌʃ] *adj* (*col*) muy secreto
husk [hʌsk] *n* (*of wheat*) cáscara
husky ['hʌskɪ] *adj* ronco; (*burly*) fornido ◾ *n* perro esquimal
hustings ['hʌstɪŋz] *npl* (*Pol*) mítin *msg* preelectoral
hustle ['hʌsl] *vt* (*push*) empujar; (*hurry*) dar prisa a ◾ *n* bullicio, actividad *f* febril; **~ and bustle** ajetreo
hut [hʌt] *n* cabaña; (*shed*) cobertizo
hutch [hʌtʃ] *n* conejera
hyacinth ['haɪəsɪnθ] *n* jacinto
hybrid ['haɪbrɪd] *adj, n* híbrido
hydrant ['haɪdrənt] *n* (*also*: **fire hydrant**) boca de incendios
hydraulic [haɪ'drɔːlɪk] *adj* hidráulico

hydraulics [haɪ'drɔːlɪks] *n* hidráulica
hydrochloric ['haɪdrəu'klɔrɪk] *adj*: **~ acid** ácido clorhídrico
hydroelectric [haɪdrəuɪ'lɛktrɪk] *adj* hidroeléctrico
hydrofoil ['haɪdrəfɔɪl] *n* aerodeslizador *m*
hydrogen ['haɪdrədʒən] *n* hidrógeno
hydrogen bomb *n* bomba de hidrógeno
hydrophobia [haɪdrə'fəubɪə] *n* hidrofobia
hydroplane ['haɪdrəpleɪn] *n* hidroavión *m*, hidroavioneta
hyena [haɪ'iːnə] *n* hiena
hygiene ['haɪdʒiːn] *n* higiene *f*
hygienic [haɪ'dʒiːnɪk] *adj* higiénico
hymn [hɪm] *n* himno
hype [haɪp] *n* (*col*) bombo
hyperactive [haɪpər'æktɪv] *adj* hiperactivo
hyperlink ['haɪpəlɪŋk] *n* hiperlink *m*
hypermarket ['haɪpəmɑːkɪt] *n* hipermercado
hypertension ['haɪpə'tɛnʃən] *n* hipertensión *f*
hypertext ['haɪpə'tɛkst] *n* (*Comput*) hipertexto *m*
hyphen ['haɪfn] *n* guión *m*
hypnosis [hɪp'nəusɪs] *n* hipnosis *f*
hypnotic [hɪp'nɔtɪk] *adj* hipnótico
hypnotism ['hɪpnətɪzəm] *n* hipnotismo
hypnotist ['hɪpnətɪst] *n* hipnotista *m/f*
hypnotize ['hɪpnətaɪz] *vt* hipnotizar
hypoallergenic ['haɪpəuælə'dʒɛnɪk] *adj* hipoalérgeno
hypochondriac [haɪpəu'kɔndrɪæk] *n* hipocondríaco(-a)
hypocrisy [hɪ'pɔkrɪsɪ] *n* hipocresía
hypocrite ['hɪpəkrɪt] *n* hipócrita *m/f*
hypocritical [hɪpə'krɪtɪkl] *adj* hipócrita
hypodermic [haɪpə'dəːmɪk] *adj* hipodérmico ◾ *n* (*syringe*) aguja hipodérmica
hypotenuse [haɪ'pɔtɪnjuːz] *n* hipotenusa
hypothermia [haɪpəu'θəːmɪə] *n* hipotermia
hypothesis, hypotheses [haɪ'pɔθɪsɪs, -siːz] *n* hipótesis *finv*
hypothetical [haɪpə'θɛtɪkl] *adj* hipotético
hysterectomy [hɪstə'rɛktəmɪ] *n* histerectomía
hysteria [hɪ'stɪərɪə] *n* histeria
hysterical [hɪ'stɛrɪkl] *adj* histérico
hysterics [hɪ'stɛrɪks] *npl* histeria *sg*, histerismo *sg*; **to have ~** ponerse histérico
Hz *abbr* (= *Hertz*) Hz

h

I i

I, i [aɪ] n (letter) I, i f; **I for Isaac,** (US) **I for Item** I de Inés, I de Israel

I [aɪ] pron yo ▪ abbr = **island; isle**

IA, Ia. abbr (US) = **Iowa**

IAEA n abbr = **International Atomic Energy Agency**

ib., ibid. abbr (= ibidem: from the same source) ibídem

IBA n abbr (Brit: = Independent Broadcasting Authority) see **ITV**

Iberian [aɪ'bɪərɪən] adj ibero, ibérico

Iberian Peninsula n: **the ~** la Península Ibérica

IBEW n abbr (US: = International Brotherhood of Electrical Workers) sindicato internacional de electricistas

i/c abbr (Brit) = **in charge**

ICBM n abbr (= intercontinental ballistic missile) misil m balístico intercontinental

ICC n abbr (= International Chamber of Commerce) CCI f; (US) = **Interstate Commerce Commission**

ice [aɪs] n hielo ▪ vt (cake) alcorzar ▪ vi (also: **ice over, ice up**) helarse; **to keep sth on ~** (fig: plan, project) tener algo en reserva

ice age n período glaciar

ice axe n piqueta (de alpinista)

iceberg ['aɪsbəːg] n iceberg m; **the tip of the ~** la punta del iceberg

icebox ['aɪsbɔks] n (Brit) congelador m; (US) nevera, refrigeradora (LAm)

icebreaker ['aɪsbreɪkə^r] n rompehielos m inv

ice bucket n cubo para el hielo

icecap ['aɪskæp] n casquete m polar

ice-cold [aɪs'kəuld] adj helado

ice cream n helado

ice-cream soda n soda mezclada con helado

ice cube n cubito de hielo

iced [aɪst] adj (drink) con hielo; (cake) escarchado

ice hockey n hockey m sobre hielo

Iceland ['aɪslənd] n Islandia

Icelander ['aɪsləndə^r] n islandés(-esa) m(f)

Icelandic [aɪs'lændɪk] adj islandés(-esa) ▪ n (Ling) islandés m

ice lolly n (Brit) polo

ice pick n piolet m

ice rink n pista de hielo

ice-skate ['aɪsskeɪt] n patín m de hielo ▪ vi patinar sobre hielo

ice-skating ['aɪsskeɪtɪŋ] n patinaje m sobre hielo

icicle ['aɪsɪkl] n carámbano

icing ['aɪsɪŋ] n (Culin) alcorza; (Aviat etc) formación f de hielo

icing sugar n (Brit) azúcar m glas(eado)

ICJ n abbr = **International Court of Justice**

icon ['aɪkɔn] n (gen) icono; (Comput) icono

ICR n abbr (US) = **Institute for Cancer Research**

ICT n abbr (= Information and Communication(s) Technology) TIC f, tecnología de la información; (Brit Scol) informática

ICU n abbr (= intensive care unit) UVI f

icy ['aɪsɪ] adj (road) helado; (fig) glacial

ID abbr (US: Post) = **Idaho**

I'd [aɪd] = **I would; I had**

Ida. abbr (US: Post) = **Idaho**

ID card n (identity card) DNI m

IDD n abbr (Brit Tel: = international direct dialling) servicio automático internacional

idea [aɪ'dɪə] n idea; **good ~!** ¡buena idea!; **to have an ~ that ...** tener la impresión de que ...; **I haven't the least ~** no tengo ni (la más remota) idea

ideal [aɪ'dɪəl] n ideal m ▪ adj ideal

idealism [aɪ'dɪəlɪzəm] n idealismo

idealist [aɪ'dɪəlɪst] n idealista m/f

ideally [aɪ'dɪəlɪ] adv perfectamente; **~, the book should have ...** idealmente, el libro debería tener ...

identical [aɪ'dɛntɪkl] adj idéntico

identification [aɪdentɪfɪ'keɪʃən] n identificación f; **means of ~** documentos mpl personales

identify [aɪ'dɛntɪfaɪ] *vt* identificar ■ *vi*:
to ~ with identificarse con

Identikit® [aɪ'dɛntɪkɪt] *n*: ~ (picture)
retrato-robot *m*

identity [aɪ'dɛntɪtɪ] *n* identidad *f*

identity card *n* carnet *m* de identidad, cédula
(de identidad) (*LAm*)

identity papers *npl* documentos *mpl* (de
identidad), documentación *fsg*

identity parade *n* identificación *f* de
acusados

ideological [aɪdɪə'lɔdʒɪkəl] *adj* ideológico

ideology [aɪdɪ'ɔlədʒɪ] *n* ideología

idiocy ['ɪdɪəsɪ] *n* idiotez *f*; (*stupid act*)
estupidez *f*

idiom ['ɪdɪəm] *n* modismo; (*style of speaking*)
lenguaje *m*

idiomatic [ɪdɪə'mætɪk] *adj* idiomático

idiosyncrasy [ɪdɪəu'sɪŋkrəsɪ] *n* idiosincrasia

idiot ['ɪdɪət] *n* (*gen*) idiota *m/f*; (*fool*) tonto(-a)

idiotic [ɪdɪ'ɔtɪk] *adj* idiota; tonto

idle ['aɪdl] *adj* (*lazy*) holgazán(-ana);
(*unemployed*) parado, desocupado; (*talk*)
frívolo ■ *vi* (*machine*) funcionar *or* marchar
en vacío; ~ **capacity** (*Comm*) capacidad *f*
sin utilizar; ~ **money** (*Comm*) capital *m*
improductivo; ~ **time** (*Comm*) tiempo de paro
▶ **idle away** *vt*: to ~ away one's time
malgastar *or* desperdiciar el tiempo

idleness ['aɪdlnɪs] *n* holgazanería; paro,
desocupación *f*

idler ['aɪdlə^r] *n* holgazán(-ana) *m(f)*, vago(-a)

idol ['aɪdl] *n* ídolo

idolize ['aɪdəlaɪz] *vt* idolatrar

idyllic [ɪ'dɪlɪk] *adj* idílico

i.e. *abbr* (= *id est*: *that is*) es decir

if [ɪf] *conj* si ■ *n*: there are a lot of ifs and
buts hay muchas dudas sin resolver; (even)
if aunque, si bien; I'd be pleased if you
could do it yo estaría contento si pudieras
hacerlo; if necessary si resultase necesario;
if only si solamente; as if como si

iffy ['ɪfɪ] *adj* (*col*) dudoso

igloo ['ɪɡluː] *n* iglú *m*

ignite [ɪɡ'naɪt] *vt* (*set fire to*) encender
■ *vi* encenderse

ignition [ɪɡ'nɪʃən] *n* (*Aut*) encendido; to
switch on/off the ~ arrancar/apagar el
motor

ignition key *n* (*Aut*) llave *f* de contacto

ignoble [ɪɡ'nəubl] *adj* innoble, vil

ignominious [ɪɡnə'mɪnɪəs] *adj* ignominioso,
vergonzoso

ignoramus [ɪɡnə'reɪməs] *n* ignorante *m/f*,
inculto(-a)

ignorance ['ɪɡnərəns] *n* ignorancia; to keep
sb in ~ of sth ocultarle algo a algn

ignorant ['ɪɡnərənt] *adj* ignorante; to be ~ of
(*subject*) desconocer; (*events*) ignorar

ignore [ɪɡ'nɔː^r] *vt* (*person*) no hacer caso de;
(*fact*) pasar por alto

ikon ['aɪkɔn] *n* = **icon**

IL *abbr* (*US*: *Post*) = **Illinois**

ILA *n abbr* (*US*: = *International Longshoremen's
Association*) sindicato internacional de trabajadores
portuarios

ill [ɪl] *adj* enfermo, malo ■ *n* mal *m*; (*fig*)
infortunio ■ *adv* mal; to take *or* be taken
~ caer *or* ponerse enfermo; to feel ~ (with)
encontrarse mal (de); to speak/think ~ of
sb hablar/pensar mal de algn; *see also* ills

Ill. *abbr* (*US*: *Post*) = **Illinois**

I'll [aɪl] = I will; I shall

ill-advised [ɪləd'vaɪzd] *adj* poco
recomendable; he was ~ to go se equivocaba
al ir

ill-at-ease [ɪlət'iːz] *adj* incómodo

ill-considered [ɪlkən'sɪdəd] *adj* (*plan*) poco
pensado

ill-disposed [ɪldɪs'pəuzd] *adj*: to be ~
towards sb/sth estar maldispuesto hacia
algn/algo

illegal [ɪ'liːɡl] *adj* ilegal

illegible [ɪ'lɛdʒɪbl] *adj* ilegible

illegitimate [ɪlɪ'dʒɪtɪmət] *adj* ilegítimo

ill-fated [ɪl'feɪtɪd] *adj* malogrado

ill-favoured, ill-favored (*US*) [ɪl'feɪvəd] *adj*
poco agraciado

ill feeling *n* rencor *m*

ill-gotten ['ɪlɡɔtn] *adj* (*gains etc*) mal
adquirido

ill health *n* mala salud *f*; to be in ~ estar mal
de salud

illicit [ɪ'lɪsɪt] *adj* ilícito

ill-informed [ɪlɪn'fɔːmd] *adj* (*judgement*)
erróneo; (*person*) mal informado

illiterate [ɪ'lɪtərət] *adj* analfabeto

ill-mannered [ɪl'mænəd] *adj* mal educado

illness ['ɪlnɪs] *n* enfermedad *f*

illogical [ɪ'lɔdʒɪkl] *adj* ilógico

ills [ɪlz] *npl* males *mpl*

ill-suited [ɪl'suːtɪd] *adj* (*couple*) incompatible;
he is ~ to the job no es la persona indicada
para el trabajo

ill-timed [ɪl'taɪmd] *adj* inoportuno

ill-treat [ɪl'triːt] *vt* maltratar

ill-treatment [ɪl'triːtmənt] *n* malos tratos
mpl

illuminate [ɪ'luːmɪneɪt] *vt* (*room, street*)
iluminar, alumbrar; (*subject*) aclarar;
illuminated sign letrero luminoso

illuminating [ɪ'luːmɪneɪtɪŋ] *adj* revelador(a)

illumination [ɪluːmɪ'neɪʃən] *n* alumbrado;
illuminations *npl* luminarias *fpl*, luces *fpl*

illusion [ɪ'luːʒən] n ilusión f; **to be under the ~ that ...** estar convencido de que ...
illusive [ɪ'luːsɪv], **illusory** [ɪ'luːsərɪ] adj ilusorio
illustrate ['ɪləstreɪt] vt ilustrar
illustration [ɪlə'streɪʃən] n (example) ejemplo, ilustración f; (in book) lámina, ilustración f
illustrator ['ɪləstreɪtər] n ilustrador(a) m(f)
illustrious [ɪ'lʌstrɪəs] adj ilustre
ill will n rencor m
ILO n abbr (= International Labour Organization) OIT f
IM n abbr (= instant messaging) IM f ■ vt enviar un mensaje instantáneo
I'm [aɪm] = I am
image ['ɪmɪdʒ] n imagen f
imagery ['ɪmɪdʒərɪ] n imágenes fpl
imaginable [ɪ'mædʒɪnəbl] adj imaginable
imaginary [ɪ'mædʒɪnərɪ] adj imaginario
imagination [ɪmædʒɪ'neɪʃən] n imaginación f; (inventiveness) inventiva; (illusion) fantasía
imaginative [ɪ'mædʒɪnətɪv] adj imaginativo
imagine [ɪ'mædʒɪn] vt imaginarse; (suppose) suponer
imbalance [ɪm'bæləns] n desequilibrio
imbecile ['ɪmbəsiːl] n imbécil m/f
imbue [ɪm'bjuː] vt: **to ~ sth with** imbuir algo de
IMF n abbr (= International Monetary Fund) FMI m
imitate ['ɪmɪteɪt] vt imitar
imitation [ɪmɪ'teɪʃən] n imitación f; (copy) copia; (pej) remedo
imitator ['ɪmɪteɪtər] n imitador(a) m(f)
immaculate [ɪ'mækjulət] adj limpísimo, inmaculado; (Rel) inmaculado
immaterial [ɪmə'tɪərɪəl] adj incorpóreo; **it is ~ whether ...** no importa si ...
immature [ɪmə'tjuər] adj (person) inmaduro; (of one's youth) joven
immaturity [ɪmə'tjuərɪtɪ] n inmadurez f
immeasurable [ɪ'mɛʒrəbl] adj inconmensurable
immediacy [ɪ'miːdɪəsɪ] n urgencia, proximidad f
immediate [ɪ'miːdɪət] adj inmediato; (pressing) urgente, apremiante; **in the ~ future** en un futuro próximo
immediately [ɪ'miːdɪətlɪ] adv (at once) en seguida; **~ next to** justo al lado de
immense [ɪ'mɛns] adj inmenso, enorme
immensity [ɪ'mɛnsɪtɪ] n (of size, difference) inmensidad f; (of problem) enormidad f
immerse [ɪ'məːs] vt (submerge) sumergir; **to be immersed in** (fig) estar absorto en
immersion heater [ɪ'məːʃən-] n (Brit) calentador m de inmersión
immigrant ['ɪmɪgrənt] n inmigrante m/f
immigrate ['ɪmɪgreɪt] vi inmigrar

immigration [ɪmɪ'greɪʃən] n inmigración f
immigration authorities npl servicio sg de inmigración
immigration laws npl leyes fpl de inmigración
imminent ['ɪmɪnənt] adj inminente
immobile [ɪ'məubaɪl] adj inmóvil
immobilize [ɪ'məubɪlaɪz] vt inmovilizar
immoderate [ɪ'mɔdərɪt] adj (person) desmesurado; (opinion, demand) excesivo
immodest [ɪ'mɔdɪst] adj (indecent) desvergonzado, impúdico; (boasting) jactancioso
immoral [ɪ'mɔrl] adj inmoral
immorality [ɪmə'rælɪtɪ] n inmoralidad f
immortal [ɪ'mɔːtl] adj inmortal
immortality [ɪmɔː'tælɪtɪ] n inmortalidad f
immortalize [ɪ'mɔːtlaɪz] vt inmortalizar
immovable [ɪ'muːvəbl] adj (object) imposible de mover; (person) inconmovible
immune [ɪ'mjuːn] adj: **~ (to)** inmune (a)
immune system n sistema m inmunitario
immunity [ɪ'mjuːnɪtɪ] n (Med, of diplomat) inmunidad f; (Comm) exención f
immunization [ɪmjunaɪ'zeɪʃən] n inmunización f
immunize ['ɪmjunaɪz] vt inmunizar
imp [ɪmp] n (small devil, child) diablillo
impact ['ɪmpækt] n (gen) impacto
impair [ɪm'pɛər] vt perjudicar
-impaired [ɪm'pɛəd] suff: **visually-impaired** con defectos de visión
impale [ɪm'peɪl] vt (with sword) atravesar
impart [ɪm'pɑːt] vt comunicar; (make known) participar; (bestow) otorgar
impartial [ɪm'pɑːʃl] adj imparcial
impartiality [ɪmpɑːʃɪ'ælɪtɪ] n imparcialidad f
impassable [ɪm'pɑːsəbl] adj (barrier) infranqueable; (road) intransitable
impasse [ɪm'pɑːs] n callejón m sin salida; **to reach an ~** llegar a un punto muerto
impassioned [ɪm'pæʃənd] adj apasionado, exaltado
impassive [ɪm'pæsɪv] adj impasible
impatience [ɪm'peɪʃəns] n impaciencia
impatient [ɪm'peɪʃənt] adj impaciente; **to get** or **grow ~** impacientarse
impatiently [ɪm'peɪʃəntlɪ] adv con impaciencia
impeachment [ɪm'piːtʃmənt] n denuncia, acusación f
impeccable [ɪm'pɛkəbl] adj impecable
impecunious [ɪmpɪ'kjuːnɪəs] adj sin dinero
impede [ɪm'piːd] vt estorbar, dificultar
impediment [ɪm'pɛdɪmənt] n obstáculo, estorbo; (also: **speech impediment**) defecto (del habla)

impel [ɪm'pɛl] vt (force): **to ~ sb (to do sth)** obligar a algn (a hacer algo)

impending [ɪm'pɛndɪŋ] adj inminente

impenetrable [ɪm'pɛnɪtrəbl] adj (jungle, fortress) impenetrable; (unfathomable) insondable

imperative [ɪm'pɛrətɪv] adj (tone) imperioso; (necessary) imprescindible ■ n (Ling) imperativo

imperceptible [ɪmpə'sɛptɪbl] adj imperceptible

imperfect [ɪm'pə:fɪkt] adj imperfecto; (goods etc) defectuoso

imperfection [ɪmpə'fɛkʃən] n (blemish) desperfecto; (fault, flaw) defecto

imperial [ɪm'pɪərɪəl] adj imperial

imperialism [ɪm'pɪərɪəlɪzəm] n imperialismo

imperil [ɪm'pɛrɪl] vt poner en peligro

imperious [ɪm'pɪərɪəs] adj señorial, apremiante

impersonal [ɪm'pə:sənl] adj impersonal

impersonate [ɪm'pə:səneɪt] vt hacerse pasar por

impersonation [ɪmpə:sə'neɪʃən] n imitación f

impersonator [ɪm'pə:səneɪtər] n (Theat etc) imitador(a) m(f)

impertinence [ɪm'pə:tɪnəns] n impertinencia, insolencia

impertinent [ɪm'pə:tɪnənt] adj impertinente, insolente

imperturbable [ɪmpə'tə:bəbl] adj imperturbable, impasible

impervious [ɪm'pə:vɪəs] adj impermeable; (fig): ~ **to** insensible a

impetuous [ɪm'pɛtjuəs] adj impetuoso

impetus ['ɪmpətəs] n ímpetu m; (fig) impulso

impinge [ɪm'pɪndʒ]: **to ~ on** vt fus (affect) afectar a

impish ['ɪmpɪʃ] adj travieso

implacable [ɪm'plækəbl] adj implacable

implant [ɪm'plɑ:nt] vt (Med) injertar, implantar; (fig: idea, principle) inculcar

implausible [ɪm'plɔ:zɪbl] adj implausible

implement n ['ɪmplɪmənt] instrumento, herramienta ■ vt ['ɪmplɪmɛnt] hacer efectivo; (carry out) realizar

implicate ['ɪmplɪkeɪt] vt (compromise) comprometer; (involve) enredar; **to ~ sb in sth** comprometer a algn en algo

implication [ɪmplɪ'keɪʃən] n consecuencia; **by ~** indirectamente

implicit [ɪm'plɪsɪt] adj (gen) implícito; (complete) absoluto

implicitly [ɪm'plɪsɪtlɪ] adv implícitamente

implore [ɪm'plɔ:r] vt (person) suplicar

imploring [ɪm'plɔ:rɪŋ] adj de súplica

imply [ɪm'plaɪ] vt (involve) implicar, suponer; (hint) insinuar

impolite [ɪmpə'laɪt] adj mal educado

impolitic [ɪm'pɔlɪtɪk] adj poco diplomático

imponderable [ɪm'pɔndərəbl] adj imponderable

import vt [ɪm'pɔ:t] importar ■ n ['ɪmpɔ:t] (Comm) importación f; (meaning) significado, sentido ■ cpd (duty, licence etc) de importación

importance [ɪm'pɔ:təns] n importancia; **to be of great/little ~** tener mucha/poca, importancia

important [ɪm'pɔ:tənt] adj importante; **it's not ~** no importa, no tiene importancia; **it is ~ that** es importante que

importantly [ɪm'pɔ:təntlɪ] adv (pej) dándose importancia; **but, more ~ ...** pero, lo que es aún más importante ...

import duty n derechos mpl de importación

imported [ɪm'pɔ:tɪd] adj importado

importer [ɪm'pɔ:tər] n importador(a) m(f)

import licence, import license (US) n licencia de importación

impose [ɪm'pəuz] vt imponer ■ vi: **to ~ on sb** abusar de algn

imposing [ɪm'pəuzɪŋ] adj imponente, impresionante

imposition [ɪmpə'zɪʃn] n (of tax etc) imposición f; **to be an ~** (on person) molestar

impossibility [ɪmpɔsə'bɪlɪtɪ] n imposibilidad f

impossible [ɪm'pɔsɪbl] adj imposible; (person) insoportable; **it is ~ for me to leave now** me es imposible salir ahora

impossibly [ɪm'pɔsɪblɪ] adv imposiblemente

impostor [ɪm'pɔstər] n impostor(a) m(f)

impotence ['ɪmpətəns] n impotencia

impotent ['ɪmpətənt] adj impotente

impound [ɪm'paund] vt embargar

impoverished [ɪm'pɔvərɪʃt] adj necesitado; (land) agotado

impracticable [ɪm'præktɪkəbl] adj no factible, irrealizable

impractical [ɪm'præktɪkl] adj (person) poco práctico

imprecise [ɪmprɪ'saɪs] adj impreciso

impregnable [ɪm'prɛgnəbl] adj invulnerable; (castle) inexpugnable

impregnate ['ɪmprɛgneɪt] vt (gen) impregnar; (soak) empapar; (fertilize) fecundar

impresario [ɪmprɪ'sɑ:rɪəu] n empresario(-a)

impress [ɪm'prɛs] vt impresionar; (mark) estampar ■ vi causar buena impresión; **to ~ sth on sb** convencer a algn de la importancia de algo

impression [ɪm'prɛʃən] *n* impresión *f*; (*footprint etc*) huella; (*print run*) edición *f*; **to be under the ~ that** tener la idea de que; **to make a good/bad ~ on sb** causar buena/mala impresión a algn

impressionable [ɪm'prɛʃnəbl] *adj* impresionable

impressionist [ɪm'prɛʃənɪst] *n* impresionista *m/f*

impressive [ɪm'prɛsɪv] *adj* impresionante

imprint ['ɪmprɪnt] *n* (*Publishing*) pie *m* de imprenta; (*fig*) sello

imprison [ɪm'prɪzn] *vt* encarcelar

imprisonment [ɪm'prɪznmənt] *n* encarcelamiento; (*term of imprisonment*) cárcel *f*; **life ~** cadena perpetua

improbable [ɪm'prɔbəbl] *adj* improbable, inverosímil

impromptu [ɪm'prɔmptjuː] *adj* improvisado ■ *adv* de improviso

improper [ɪm'prɔpəʳ] *adj* (*incorrect*) impropio; (*unseemly*) indecoroso; (*indecent*) indecente

impropriety [ɪmprə'praɪətɪ] *n* falta de decoro; (*indecency*) indecencia; (*of language*) impropiedad *f*

improve [ɪm'pruːv] *vt* mejorar; (*foreign language*) perfeccionar ■ *vi* mejorar
▶ **improve (up)on** *vt fus* (*offer*) mejorar

improvement [ɪm'pruːvmənt] *n* mejora; perfeccionamiento; **to make improvements to** mejorar

improvise ['ɪmprəvaɪz] *vt, vi* improvisar

imprudence [ɪm'pruːdns] *n* imprudencia

imprudent [ɪm'pruːdnt] *adj* imprudente

impudent ['ɪmpjudnt] *adj* descarado, insolente

impugn [ɪm'pjuːn] *vt* impugnar

impulse ['ɪmpʌls] *n* impulso; **to act on ~** actuar sin reflexionar, dejarse llevar por el impulso

impulse buying *n* compra impulsiva

impulsive [ɪm'pʌlsɪv] *adj* irreflexivo, impulsivo

impunity [ɪm'pjuːnɪtɪ] *n*: **with ~** impunemente

impure [ɪm'pjuəʳ] *adj* (*adulterated*) adulterado; (*morally*) impuro

impurity [ɪm'pjuərɪtɪ] *n* impureza

IN *abbr* (*US: Post*) = **Indiana**

 KEYWORD

in [ɪn] *prep* **1** (*indicating place, position, with place names*) en; **in the house/garden** en (la) casa/el jardín; **in here/there** aquí/ahí *or* allí dentro; **in London/England** en Londres/Inglaterra; **in town** en el centro (de la ciudad)

2 (*indicating time*) en; **in spring** en (la) primavera; **in 1988/May** en 1988/mayo; **in the afternoon** por la tarde; **at four o'clock in the afternoon** a las cuarto de la tarde; **I did it in three hours/days** lo hice en tres horas/días; **I'll see you in two weeks** *or* **in two weeks' time** te veré dentro de dos semanas; **once in a hundred years** una vez cada cien años

3 (*indicating manner etc*) en; **in a loud/soft voice** en voz alta/baja; **in pencil/ink** a lápiz/bolígrafo; **the boy in the blue shirt** el chico de la camisa azul; **in writing** por escrito; **to pay in dollars** pagar en dólares

4 (*indicating circumstances*): **in the sun/shade** al sol/a la sombra; **in the rain** bajo la lluvia; **a change in policy** un cambio de política; **a rise in prices** un aumento de precios

5 (*indicating mood, state*): **in tears** llorando; **in anger/despair** enfadado/desesperado; **to live in luxury** vivir lujosamente

6 (*with ratios, numbers*): **1 in 10 households**, **1 household in 10** una de cada 10 familias; **20 pence in the pound** 20 peniques por libra; **they lined up in twos** se alinearon de dos en dos; **in hundreds** a *or* por centenares

7 (*referring to people, works*) en; entre; **the disease is common in children** la enfermedad es común entre los niños; **in (the works of) Dickens** en (las obras de) Dickens

8 (*indicating profession etc*): **to be in teaching** dedicarse a la enseñanza

9 (*after superlative*) de; **the best pupil in the class** el/la mejor alumno(-a) de la clase

10 (*with present participle*): **in saying this** al decir esto

■ *adv*: **to be in** (*person: at home*) estar en casa; (*: at work*) estar; (*train, ship, plane*) haber llegado; (*in fashion*) estar de moda; **she'll be in later today** llegará más tarde hoy; **to ask sb in** hacer pasar a algn; **to run/limp** *etc* **in** entrar corriendo/cojeando *etc*; **in that** *conj* ya que

■ *npl*: **the ins and outs** (*of proposal, situation etc*) los detalles

in., ins *abbr* = **inch**; **inches**

inability [ɪnə'bɪlɪtɪ] *n* incapacidad *f*; **~ to pay** insolvencia en el pago

inaccessible [ɪnək'sɛsɪbl] *adj* inaccesible

inaccuracy [ɪn'ækjurəsɪ] *n* inexactitud *f*

inaccurate [ɪn'ækjurət] *adj* inexacto, incorrecto

inaction [ɪn'ækʃən] *n* inacción *f*

inactive [ɪn'æktɪv] *adj* inactivo

inactivity [ɪnæk'tɪvɪtɪ] *n* inactividad *f*

inadequacy [ɪnˈædɪkwəsɪ] *n* insuficiencia; incapacidad *f*
inadequate [ɪnˈædɪkwət] *adj* (*insufficient*) insuficiente; (*unsuitable*) inadecuado; (*person*) incapaz
inadmissible [ɪnədˈmɪsəbl] *adj* improcedente, inadmisible
inadvertent [ɪnədˈvəːtənt] *adj* descuidado, involuntario
inadvertently [ɪnədˈvəːtntlɪ] *adv* por descuido
inadvisable [ɪnədˈvaɪzəbl] *adj* poco aconsejable
inane [ɪˈneɪn] *adj* necio, fatuo
inanimate [ɪnˈænɪmət] *adj* inanimado
inapplicable [ɪnˈæplɪkəbl] *adj* inaplicable
inappropriate [ɪnəˈprəuprɪət] *adj* inadecuado
inapt [ɪnˈæpt] *adj* impropio
inaptitude [ɪnˈæptɪtjuːd] *n* incapacidad *f*
inarticulate [ɪnɑːˈtɪkjulət] *adj* (*person*) incapaz de expresarse; (*speech*) mal pronunciado
inartistic [ɪnɑːˈtɪstɪk] *adj* antiestético
inasmuch as [ɪnəzˈmʌtʃ-] *adv* en la medida en que
inattention [ɪnəˈtɛnʃən] *n* desatención *f*
inattentive [ɪnəˈtɛntɪv] *adj* distraído
inaudible [ɪnˈɔːdɪbl] *adj* inaudible
inaugural [ɪˈnɔːgjurəl] *adj* inaugural; (*speech*) de apertura
inaugurate [ɪˈnɔːgjureɪt] *vt* inaugurar; (*president, official*) investir
inauguration [ɪnɔːgjuˈreɪʃən] *n* inauguración *f*; (*of official*) investidura; (*of event*) ceremonia de apertura
inauspicious [ɪnɔːsˈpɪʃəs] *adj* poco propicio, inoportuno
in-between [ɪnbɪˈtwiːn] *adj* intermedio
inborn [ɪnˈbɔːn] *adj* (*feeling*) innato
inbred [ɪnˈbrɛd] *adj* innato; (*family*) consanguíneo
inbreeding [ɪnˈbriːdɪŋ] *n* endogamia
Inc. *abbr* = **incorporated**
Inca [ˈɪŋkə] *adj* (*also*: **Incan**) inca, de los incas
■ *n* inca *m/f*
incalculable [ɪnˈkælkjuləbl] *adj* incalculable
incapability [ɪnkeɪpəˈbɪlɪtɪ] *n* incapacidad *f*
incapable [ɪnˈkeɪpəbl] *adj*: **~ (of doing sth)** incapaz (de hacer algo)
incapacitate [ɪnkəˈpæsɪteɪt] *vt*: **to ~ sb** incapacitar a algn
incapacitated [ɪnkəˈpæsɪteɪtɪd] *adj* incapacitado
incapacity [ɪnkəˈpæsɪtɪ] *n* (*inability*) incapacidad *f*
incarcerate [ɪnˈkɑːsəreɪt] *vt* encarcelar

incarnate *adj* [ɪnˈkɑːnɪt] en persona
■ *vt* [ˈɪnkɑːneɪt] encarnar
incarnation [ɪnkɑːˈneɪʃən] *n* encarnación *f*
incendiary [ɪnˈsɛndɪərɪ] *adj* incendiario
■ *n* (*bomb*) bomba incendiaria
incense *n* [ˈɪnsɛns] incienso ■ *vt* [ɪnˈsɛns] (*anger*) indignar, encolerizar
incentive [ɪnˈsɛntɪv] *n* incentivo, estímulo
incentive bonus *n* prima
incentive scheme *n* plan *m* de incentivos
inception [ɪnˈsɛpʃən] *n* comienzo, principio
incessant [ɪnˈsɛsnt] *adj* incesante, continuo
incessantly [ɪnˈsɛsəntlɪ] *adv* constantemente
incest [ˈɪnsɛst] *n* incesto
inch [ɪntʃ] *n* pulgada; **to be within an ~ of** estar a dos dedos de; **he didn't give an ~** no hizo la más mínima concesión; **a few inches** unas pulgadas
▶ **inch forward** *vi* avanzar palmo a palmo
incidence [ˈɪnsɪdns] *n* (*of crime, disease*) incidencia
incident [ˈɪnsɪdnt] *n* incidente *m*; (*in book*) episodio
incidental [ɪnsɪˈdɛntl] *adj* circunstancial, accesorio; (*unplanned*) fortuito; **~ to** relacionado con; **~ expenses** (gastos *mpl*) imprevistos *mpl*
incidentally [ɪnsɪˈdɛntəlɪ] *adv* (*by the way*) por cierto
incidental music *n* música de fondo
incident room *n* (*Police*) centro de coordinación
incinerate [ɪnˈsɪnəreɪt] *vt* incinerar, quemar
incinerator [ɪnˈsɪnəreɪtəʳ] *n* incinerador *m*, incineradora
incipient [ɪnˈsɪpɪənt] *adj* incipiente
incision [ɪnˈsɪʒən] *n* incisión *f*
incisive [ɪnˈsaɪsɪv] *adj* (*mind*) penetrante; (*remark etc*) incisivo
incisor [ɪnˈsaɪzəʳ] *n* incisivo
incite [ɪnˈsaɪt] *vt* provocar, incitar
incl. *abbr* = **including; inclusive (of)**
inclement [ɪnˈklɛmənt] *adj* inclemente
inclination [ɪnklɪˈneɪʃən] *n* (*tendency*) tendencia, inclinación *f*
incline [*n* ˈɪnklaɪn, *vb* ɪnˈklaɪn] *n* pendiente *f*, cuesta ■ *vt* (*slope*) inclinar; (*head*) poner de lado ■ *vi* inclinarse; **to be inclined to** (*tend*) ser propenso a; (*be willing*) estar dispuesto a
include [ɪnˈkluːd] *vt* incluir, comprender; (*in letter*) adjuntar; **the tip is/is not included** la propina está/no está incluida
including [ɪnˈkluːdɪŋ] *prep* incluso, inclusive; **~ tip** propina incluida
inclusion [ɪnˈkluːʒən] *n* inclusión *f*
inclusive [ɪnˈkluːsɪv] *adj* inclusivo ■ *adv*

inclusive; ~ **of tax** incluidos los impuestos; **$50, ~ of all surcharges** 50 dólares, incluidos todos los recargos

incognito [ɪnkɔg'niːtəu] *adv* de incógnito

incoherent [ɪnkəu'hɪərənt] *adj* incoherente

income ['ɪnkʌm] *n* (*personal*) ingresos *mpl*; (*from property etc*) renta; (*profit*) rédito; **gross/ net** ~ ingresos *mpl* brutos/netos; **~ and expenditure account** cuenta de gastos e ingresos

income bracket *n* categoría económica

income support *n* (*Brit*) ≈ ayuda familiar

income tax *n* impuesto sobre la renta

income tax inspector *n* inspector(a) *m(f)* de Hacienda

income tax return *n* declaración *f* de ingresos

incoming ['ɪnkʌmɪŋ] *adj* (*passengers, flight*) de llegada; (*government*) entrante; (*tenant*) nuevo

incommunicado ['ɪnkəmjunɪ'kaːdəu] *adj*: **to hold sb** ~ mantener incomunicado a algn

incomparable [ɪn'kɔmpərəbl] *adj* incomparable, sin par

incompatible [ɪnkəm'pætɪbl] *adj* incompatible

incompetence [ɪn'kɔmpɪtəns] *n* incompetencia

incompetent [ɪn'kɔmpɪtənt] *adj* incompetente

incomplete [ɪnkəm'pliːt] *adj* incompleto; (*unfinished*) sin terminar

incomprehensible [ɪnkɔmprɪ'hɛnsɪbl] *adj* incomprensible

inconceivable [ɪnkən'siːvəbl] *adj* inconcebible

inconclusive [ɪnkən'kluːsɪv] *adj* sin resultado (definitivo); (*argument*) poco convincente

incongruity [ɪnkɔŋ'gruːɪtɪ] *n* incongruencia

incongruous [ɪn'kɔŋgruəs] *adj* discordante

inconsequential [ɪnkɔnsɪ'kwɛnʃl] *adj* intranscendente

inconsiderable [ɪnkən'sɪdərəbl] *adj* insignificante

inconsiderate [ɪnkən'sɪdərət] *adj* desconsiderado; **how ~ of him!** ¡qué falta de consideración (de su parte)!

inconsistency [ɪnkən'sɪstənsɪ] *n* inconsecuencia; (*of actions etc*) falta de lógica; (*of work*) carácter *m* desigual, inconsistencia; (*of statement etc*) contradicción *f*

inconsistent [ɪnkən'sɪstnt] *adj* inconsecuente; **~ with** que no concuerda con

inconsolable [ɪnkən'səuləbl] *adj* inconsolable

inconspicuous [ɪnkən'spɪkjuəs] *adj* (*discreet*) discreto; (*person*) que llama poco la atención

inconstancy [ɪn'kɔnstənsɪ] *n* inconstancia

inconstant [ɪn'kɔnstənt] *adj* inconstante

incontinence [ɪn'kɔntɪnəns] *n* incontinencia

incontinent [ɪn'kɔntɪnənt] *adj* incontinente

incontrovertible [ɪnkɔntrə'vəːtəbl] *adj* incontrovertible

inconvenience [ɪnkən'viːnjəns] *n* (*gen*) inconvenientes *mpl*; (*trouble*) molestia ■ *vt* incomodar; **to put sb to great** ~ causar mucha molestia a algn; **don't ~ yourself** no se moleste

inconvenient [ɪnkən'viːnjənt] *adj* incómodo, poco práctico; (*time, place*) inoportuno; **that time is very ~ for me** esa hora me es muy inconveniente

incorporate [ɪn'kɔːpəreɪt] *vt* incorporar; (*contain*) comprender; (*add*) agregar

incorporated [ɪn'kɔːpəreɪtɪd] *adj*: **~ company** (*US*) ≈ Sociedad *f* Anónima (S.A.)

incorrect [ɪnkə'rɛkt] *adj* incorrecto

incorrigible [ɪn'kɔrɪdʒəbl] *adj* incorregible

incorruptible [ɪnkə'rʌptɪbl] *adj* incorruptible

increase [*n* 'ɪnkriːs, *vb* ɪn'kriːs] *n* aumento ■ *vi* aumentar; (*grow*) crecer; (*price*) subir ■ *vt* aumentar; **an ~ of 5%** un aumento de 5%; **to be on the** ~ ir en aumento

increasing [ɪn'kriːsɪŋ] *adj* (*number*) creciente, que va en aumento

increasingly [ɪn'kriːsɪŋlɪ] *adv* cada vez más

incredible [ɪn'krɛdɪbl] *adj* increíble

incredibly [ɪn'krɛdɪblɪ] *adv* increíblemente

incredulity [ɪnkrɪ'djuːlɪtɪ] *n* incredulidad *f*

incredulous [ɪn'krɛdjuləs] *adj* incrédulo

increment ['ɪnkrɪmənt] *n* aumento, incremento

incriminate [ɪn'krɪmɪneɪt] *vt* incriminar

incriminating [ɪn'krɪmɪneɪtɪŋ] *adj* incriminatorio

incrust [ɪn'krʌst] *vt* = **encrust**

incubate ['ɪnkjubeɪt] *vt* (*egg*) incubar, empollar ■ *vi* (*egg, disease*) incubar

incubation [ɪnkju'beɪʃən] *n* incubación *f*

incubation period *n* período de incubación

incubator ['ɪnkjubeɪtəʳ] *n* incubadora

inculcate ['ɪnkʌlkeɪt] *vt*: **to ~ sth in sb** inculcar algo en algn

incumbent [ɪn'kʌmbənt] *n* ocupante *m/f* ■ *adj*: **it is ~ on him to ...** le incumbe ...

incur [ɪn'kəːʳ] *vt* (*expenses*) incurrir en; (*loss*) sufrir

incurable [ɪn'kjuərəbl] *adj* incurable

incursion [ɪn'kəːʃən] *n* incursión *f*

Ind. *abbr* (*US*) = **Indiana**

indebted [ɪn'dɛtɪd] *adj*: **to be ~ to sb** estar agradecido a algn

indecency [ɪn'diːsnsɪ] *n* indecencia

indecent [ɪn'diːsnt] *adj* indecente
indecent assault *n* (*Brit*) atentado contra el pudor
indecent exposure *n* exhibicionismo
indecipherable [ɪndɪ'saɪfərəbl] *adj* indescifrable
indecision [ɪndɪ'sɪʒən] *n* indecisión *f*
indecisive [ɪndɪ'saɪsɪv] *adj* indeciso; (*discussion*) no resuelto, inconcluyente
indeed [ɪn'diːd] *adv* efectivamente, en realidad; **yes ~!** ¡claro que sí!
indefatigable [ɪndɪ'fætɪgəbl] *adj* incansable, infatigable
indefensible [ɪndɪ'fɛnsəbl] *adj* (*conduct*) injustificable
indefinable [ɪndɪ'faɪnəbl] *adj* indefinible
indefinite [ɪn'dɛfɪnɪt] *adj* indefinido; (*uncertain*) incierto
indefinitely [ɪn'dɛfɪnɪtlɪ] *adv* (*wait*) indefinidamente
indelible [ɪn'dɛlɪbl] *adj* imborrable
indelicate [ɪn'dɛlɪkɪt] *adj* (*tactless*) indiscreto, inoportuno; (*not polite*) poco delicado
indemnify [ɪn'dɛmnɪfaɪ] *vt* indemnizar, resarcir
indemnity [ɪn'dɛmnɪtɪ] *n* (*insurance*) indemnidad *f*; (*compensation*) indemnización *f*
indent [ɪn'dɛnt] *vt* (*text*) sangrar
indentation [ɪndɛn'teɪʃən] *n* mella; (*Typ*) sangría
indenture [ɪn'dɛntʃəʳ] *n* escritura, instrumento
independence [ɪndɪ'pɛndns] *n* independencia
Independence Day *n* Día *m* de la Independencia

● **INDEPENDENCE DAY**
●
● El cuatro de julio es la fiesta nacional
● de los Estados Unidos, *Independence Day*,
● en conmemoración de la Declaración
● de Independencia escrita por Thomas
● Jefferson y adoptada en 1776. En ella se
● proclamaba la ruptura total con Gran
● Bretaña de las trece colonias americanas
● que fueron el origen de los Estados
● Unidos de América.

independent [ɪndɪ'pɛndənt] *adj* independiente; **to become ~** independizarse
in-depth ['ɪndɛpθ] *adj* en profundidad, a fondo
indescribable [ɪndɪ'skraɪbəbl] *adj* indescriptible
indestructible [ɪndɪs'trʌktəbl] *adj* indestructible

indeterminate [ɪndɪ'təːmɪnɪt] *adj* indeterminado
index ['ɪndɛks] *n* (*pl* **indexes**) (*in book*) índice *m*; (*in library etc*) catálogo; (*pl* **indices**) ['ɪndɪsiːz] (*ratio, sign*) exponente *m*
index card *n* ficha
index finger *n* índice *m*
index-linked ['ɪndɛks'lɪŋkt], (*US*) **indexed** ['ɪndɛkst] *adj* indexado
India ['ɪndɪə] *n* la India
Indian ['ɪndɪən] *adj, n* indio(-a) *m(f)*; (*also:* **American Indian**) indio(-a) *m(f)* de América, amerindio(-a) *m(f)*; (*pej*): **Red ~** piel roja *m/f*
Indian Ocean *n*: **the ~** el Océano Índico, el Mar de las Indias
Indian summer *n* (*fig*) veranillo de San Martín
india rubber *n* caucho
indicate ['ɪndɪkeɪt] *vt* indicar ■ *vi* (*Brit Aut*): **to ~ left/right** indicar a la izquierda/a la derecha
indication [ɪndɪ'keɪʃən] *n* indicio, señal *f*
indicative [ɪn'dɪkətɪv] *adj*: **to be ~ of sth** indicar algo ■ *n* (*Ling*) indicativo
indicator ['ɪndɪkeɪtəʳ] *n* (*gen*) indicador *m*; (*Aut*) intermitente *m*, direccional *m* (*LAm*)
indices ['ɪndɪsiːz] *npl of* **index**
indict [ɪn'daɪt] *vt* acusar
indictable [ɪn'daɪtəbl] *adj*: **~ offence** delito procesable
indictment [ɪn'daɪtmənt] *n* acusación *f*
indifference [ɪn'dɪfrəns] *n* indiferencia
indifferent [ɪn'dɪfrənt] *adj* indiferente; (*poor*) regular
indigenous [ɪn'dɪdʒɪnəs] *adj* indígena
indigestible [ɪndɪ'dʒɛstɪbl] *adj* indigesto
indigestion [ɪndɪ'dʒɛstʃən] *n* indigestión *f*
indignant [ɪn'dɪgnənt] *adj*: **to be ~ about sth** indignarse por algo
indignation [ɪndɪg'neɪʃən] *n* indignación *f*
indignity [ɪn'dɪgnɪtɪ] *n* indignidad *f*
indigo ['ɪndɪgəu] *adj* (*colour*) (de color) añil ■ *n* añil *m*
indirect [ɪndɪ'rɛkt] *adj* indirecto
indirectly [ɪndɪ'rɛktlɪ] *adv* indirectamente
indiscernible [ɪndɪ'səːnəbl] *adj* imperceptible
indiscreet [ɪndɪ'skriːt] *adj* indiscreto, imprudente
indiscretion [ɪndɪ'skrɛʃən] *n* indiscreción *f*, imprudencia
indiscriminate [ɪndɪ'skrɪmɪnət] *adj* indiscriminado
indispensable [ɪndɪ'spɛnsəbl] *adj* indispensable, imprescindible
indisposed [ɪndɪ'spəuzd] *adj* (*unwell*) indispuesto

indisposition [ɪndɪspə'zɪʃən] *n* indisposición *f*

indisputable [ɪndɪ'spju:təbl] *adj* incontestable

indistinct [ɪndɪ'stɪŋkt] *adj* indistinto

indistinguishable [ɪndɪ'stɪŋgwɪʃəbl] *adj* indistinguible

individual [ɪndɪ'vɪdjuəl] *n* individuo ■ *adj* individual; (*personal*) personal; (*for/of one only*) particular

individualist [ɪndɪ'vɪdjuəlɪst] *n* individualista *m/f*

individuality [ɪndɪvɪdju'ælɪtɪ] *n* individualidad *f*

individually [ɪndɪ'vɪdjuəlɪ] *adv* individualmente; particularmente

indivisible [ɪndɪ'vɪzəbl] *adj* indivisible

Indo-China ['ɪndəu'tʃaɪnə] *n* Indochina

indoctrinate [ɪn'dɔktrɪneɪt] *vt* adoctrinar

indoctrination [ɪndɔktrɪ'neɪʃən] *n* adoctrinamiento

indolence ['ɪndələns] *n* indolencia

indolent ['ɪndələnt] *adj* indolente, perezoso

Indonesia [ɪndə'ni:zɪə] *n* Indonesia

Indonesian [ɪndə'ni:zɪən] *adj* indonesio ■ *n* indonesio(-a); (*Ling*) indonesio

indoor ['ɪndɔ:ʳ] *adj* (*swimming pool*) cubierto; (*plant*) de interior; (*sport*) bajo cubierta

indoors [ɪn'dɔ:z] *adv* dentro; (*at home*) en casa

indubitable [ɪn'dju:bɪtəbl] *adj* indudable

indubitably [ɪn'dju:bɪtəblɪ] *adv* indudablemente

induce [ɪn'dju:s] *vt* inducir, persuadir; (*bring about*) producir; **to ~ sb to do sth** persuadir a algn a que haga algo

inducement [ɪn'dju:smənt] *n* (*incentive*) incentivo, aliciente *m*

induct [ɪn'dʌkt] *vt* iniciar; (*in job, rank, position*) instalar

induction [ɪn'dʌkʃən] *n* (*Med: of birth*) inducción *f*

induction course *n* (*Brit*) cursillo introductorio *or* de iniciación

indulge [ɪn'dʌldʒ] *vt* (*whim*) satisfacer; (*person*) complacer; (*child*) mimar ■ *vi*: **to ~ in** darse el gusto de

indulgence [ɪn'dʌldʒəns] *n* vicio

indulgent [ɪn'dʌldʒənt] *adj* indulgente

industrial [ɪn'dʌstrɪəl] *adj* industrial

industrial action *n* huelga

industrial estate *n* (*Brit*) polígono *or* (*LAm*) zona industrial

industrial goods *npl* bienes *mpl* de producción

industrialist [ɪn'dʌstrɪəlɪst] *n* industrial *m/f*

industrialize [ɪn'dʌstrɪəlaɪz] *vt* industrializar

industrial park *n* (*US*) = **industrial estate**

industrial relations *npl* relaciones *fpl* empresariales

industrial tribunal *n* magistratura de trabajo, tribunal *m* laboral

industrial unrest *n* (*Brit*) agitación *f* obrera

industrious [ɪn'dʌstrɪəs] *adj* (*gen*) trabajador(a); (*student*) aplicado

industry ['ɪndəstrɪ] *n* industria; (*diligence*) aplicación *f*

inebriated [ɪ'ni:brɪeɪtɪd] *adj* borracho

inedible [ɪn'ɛdɪbl] *adj* incomible; (*plant etc*) no comestible

ineffective [ɪnɪ'fɛktɪv], **ineffectual** [ɪnɪ'fɛktʃuəl] *adj* ineficaz, inútil

inefficiency [ɪnɪ'fɪʃənsɪ] *n* ineficacia

inefficient [ɪnɪ'fɪʃənt] *adj* ineficaz, ineficiente

inelegant [ɪn'ɛlɪgənt] *adj* poco elegante

ineligible [ɪn'ɛlɪdʒɪbl] *adj* inelegible

inept [ɪ'nɛpt] *adj* incompetente, incapaz

ineptitude [ɪ'nɛptɪtju:d] *n* incapacidad *f*, ineptitud *f*

inequality [ɪnɪ'kwɔlɪtɪ] *n* desigualdad *f*

inequitable [ɪn'ɛkwɪtəbl] *adj* injusto

ineradicable [ɪnɪ'rædɪkəbl] *adj* inextirpable

inert [ɪ'nə:t] *adj* inerte, inactivo; (*immobile*) inmóvil

inertia [ɪ'nə:ʃə] *n* inercia; (*laziness*) pereza

inertia-reel seat-belt [ɪ'nə:ʃə'ri:l-] *n* cinturón *m* de seguridad retráctil

inescapable [ɪnɪ'skeɪpəbl] *adj* ineludible, inevitable

inessential [ɪnɪ'sɛnʃl] *adj* no esencial

inestimable [ɪn'ɛstɪməbl] *adj* inestimable

inevitability [ɪnɛvɪtə'bɪlɪtɪ] *n* inevitabilidad *f*

inevitable [ɪn'ɛvɪtəbl] *adj* inevitable; (*necessary*) forzoso

inevitably [ɪn'ɛvɪtəblɪ] *adv* inevitablemente; **as ~ happens ...** como siempre pasa ...

inexact [ɪnɪg'zaekt] *adj* inexacto

inexcusable [ɪnɪks'kju:zəbl] *adj* imperdonable

inexhaustible [ɪnɪg'zɔ:stɪbl] *adj* inagotable

inexorable [ɪn'ɛksərəbl] *adj* inexorable, implacable

inexpensive [ɪnɪk'spɛnsɪv] *adj* económico

inexperience [ɪnɪk'spɪərɪəns] *n* falta de experiencia

inexperienced [ɪnɪk'spɪərɪənst] *adj* inexperto; **to be ~ in sth** no tener experiencia en algo

inexplicable [ɪnɪk'splɪkəbl] *adj* inexplicable

inexpressible [ɪnɪk'sprɛsəbl] *adj* inexpresable

inextricable [ɪnɪks'trɪkəbl] *adj* inseparable

inextricably [ɪnɪks'trɪkəblɪ] *adv* indisolublemente

infallibility [ɪnfælə'bɪlɪtɪ] n infalibilidad f
infallible [ɪn'fælɪbl] adj infalible
infamous ['ɪnfəməs] adj infame
infamy ['ɪnfəmɪ] n infamia
infancy ['ɪnfənsɪ] n infancia
infant ['ɪnfənt] n niño(-a)
infantile ['ɪnfəntaɪl] adj infantil; (pej)
aniñado
infant mortality n mortalidad f infantil
infantry ['ɪnfəntrɪ] n infantería
infantryman ['ɪnfəntrɪmən] n soldado de
infantería
infant school n (Brit) escuela de párvulos; see
also **primary school**
infatuated [ɪn'fætjueɪtɪd] adj: ~ **with**
(in love) loco por; **to become ~ (with sb)**
enamoriscarse (de algn), encapricharse
(con algn)
infatuation [ɪnfætju'eɪʃən] n
enamoramiento
infect [ɪn'fɛkt] vt (wound) infectar; (person)
contagiar; (fig: pej) corromper; **infected
with** (illness) contagiado de; **to become
infected** (wound) infectarse
infection [ɪn'fɛkʃən] n infección f; (fig)
contagio
infectious [ɪn'fɛkʃəs] adj contagioso; (fig)
infeccioso
infer [ɪn'fəːʳ] vt deducir, inferir; **to ~ (from)**
inferir (de), deducir (de)
inference ['ɪnfərəns] n deducción f,
inferencia
inferior [ɪn'fɪərɪəʳ] adj, n inferior m/f; **to feel ~**
sentirse inferior
inferiority [ɪnfɪərɪ'ɔrətɪ] n inferioridad f
inferiority complex n complejo de
inferioridad
infernal [ɪn'fəːnl] adj infernal
inferno [ɪn'fəːnəu] n infierno; (fig) hoguera
infertile [ɪn'fəːtaɪl] adj estéril; (person)
infecundo
infertility [ɪnfəː'tɪlɪtɪ] n esterilidad f;
infecundidad f
infest [ɪn'fɛst] vt infestar
infested [ɪn'fɛstɪd] adj: ~ **(with)** plagado (de)
infidel ['ɪnfɪdəl] n infiel m/f
infidelity [ɪnfɪ'dɛlɪtɪ] n infidelidad f
in-fighting ['ɪnfaɪtɪŋ] n (fig) lucha(s) f(pl)
interna(s)
infiltrate ['ɪnfɪltreɪt] vt (troops etc) infiltrarse
en ■ vi infiltrarse
infinite ['ɪnfɪnɪt] adj infinito; **an ~ amount
of money/time** un sinfín de dinero/tiempo
infinitely ['ɪnfɪnɪtlɪ] adv infinitamente
infinitesimal [ɪnfɪnɪ'tɛsɪməl] adj
infinitésimo
infinitive [ɪn'fɪnɪtɪv] n infinitivo

infinity [ɪn'fɪnɪtɪ] n (Math) infinito; **an ~**
infinidad f
infirm [ɪn'fəːm] adj enfermizo, débil
infirmary [ɪn'fəːmərɪ] n hospital m
infirmity [ɪn'fəːmɪtɪ] n debilidad f; (illness)
enfermedad f, achaque m
inflame [ɪn'fleɪm] vt inflamar
inflamed [ɪn'fleɪmd] adj: **to become ~**
inflamarse
inflammable [ɪn'flæməbl] adj (Brit)
inflamable; (situation etc) explosivo
inflammation [ɪnflə'meɪʃən] n inflamación f
inflammatory [ɪn'flæmətərɪ] adj (speech)
incendiario
inflatable [ɪn'fleɪtəbl] adj inflable
inflate [ɪn'fleɪt] vt (tyre) inflar; (fig) hinchar
inflated [ɪn'fleɪtɪd] adj (tyre etc) inflado; (price,
self-esteem etc) exagerado
inflation [ɪn'fleɪʃən] n (Econ) inflación f
inflationary [ɪn'fleɪʃnərɪ] adj inflacionario
inflationary spiral n espiral f inflacionista
inflexible [ɪn'flɛksɪbl] adj inflexible
inflict [ɪn'flɪkt] vt: **to ~ on** infligir en; (tax etc)
imponer a
in-flight ['ɪnflaɪt] adj durante el vuelo
inflow ['ɪnfləu] n afluencia
influence ['ɪnfluəns] n influencia ■ vt
influir en, influenciar; **under the ~ of
alcohol** en estado de embriaguez
influential [ɪnflu'ɛnʃl] adj influyente
influenza [ɪnflu'ɛnzə] n gripe f
influx ['ɪnflʌks] n afluencia
inform [ɪn'fɔːm] vt: **to ~ sb of sth** informar
a algn sobre or de algo; (warn) avisar a algn
de algo; (communicate) comunicar algo a algn
■ vi: **to ~ on sb** delatar a algn
informal [ɪn'fɔːml] adj (manner, tone)
desenfadado; (dress, occasion) informal
informality [ɪnfɔː'mælɪtɪ] n falta de
ceremonia; (intimacy) intimidad f; (familiarity)
familiaridad f; (ease) afabilidad f
informally [ɪn'fɔːməlɪ] adv sin ceremonia;
(invite) informalmente
informant [ɪn'fɔːmənt] n informante m/f
informatics [ɪnfɔː'mætɪks] n informática
information [ɪnfə'meɪʃən] n información f;
(news) noticias fpl; (knowledge) conocimientos
mpl; (Law) delación f; **a piece of ~** un dato;
for your ~ para su información
**information and communication
technology, information and
communications technology** n (gen)
tecnología de la información y de las
comunicaciones; (Brit Scol) informática
information bureau n oficina de información
information processing n procesamiento
de datos

611

information retrieval | inlet

information retrieval n recuperación f de información

information science n gestión f de la información

information technology n informática

informative [ɪnˈfɔːmətɪv] adj informativo

informed [ɪnˈfɔːmd] adj (observer) informado, al corriente; **an ~ guess** una opinión bien fundamentada

informer [ɪnˈfɔːməʳ] n delator(a) m(f); (also: **police informer**) soplón(-ona) m(f)

infra dig [ˈɪnfrəˈdɪɡ] adj abbr (col: = infra dignitatem: = beneath one's dignity) denigrante

infra-red [ɪnfrəˈrɛd] adj infrarrojo

infrastructure [ˈɪnfrəstrʌktʃəʳ] n infraestructura

infrequent [ɪnˈfriːkwənt] adj infrecuente

infringe [ɪnˈfrɪndʒ] vt infringir, violar ■ vi: **to ~ on** invadir

infringement [ɪnˈfrɪndʒmənt] n infracción f; (of rights) usurpación f; (Sport) falta

infuriate [ɪnˈfjuərɪeɪt] vt: **to become infuriated** ponerse furioso

infuriating [ɪnˈfjuərɪeɪtɪŋ] adj: **I find it ~** me saca de quicio

infuse [ɪnˈfjuːz] vt (with courage, enthusiasm): **to ~ sb with sth** infundir algo a algn

infusion [ɪnˈfjuːʒən] n (tea etc) infusión f

ingenious [ɪnˈdʒiːnjəs] adj ingenioso

ingenuity [ɪndʒɪˈnjuːɪtɪ] n ingeniosidad f

ingenuous [ɪnˈdʒɛnjuəs] adj ingenuo

ingot [ˈɪŋɡət] n lingote m, barra

ingrained [ɪnˈɡreɪnd] adj arraigado

ingratiate [ɪnˈɡreɪʃɪeɪt] vt: **to ~ o.s. with** congraciarse con

ingratiating [ɪnˈɡreɪʃɪeɪtɪŋ] adj (smile, speech) insinuante; (person) zalamero, congraciador(a)

ingratitude [ɪnˈɡrætɪtjuːd] n ingratitud f

ingredient [ɪnˈɡriːdɪənt] n ingrediente m

ingrowing [ˈɪnɡrəʊɪŋ] adj: **~ (toe)nail** uña encarnada

inhabit [ɪnˈhæbɪt] vt vivir en; (occupy) ocupar

inhabitable [ɪnˈhæbɪtəbl] adj habitable

inhabitant [ɪnˈhæbɪtənt] n habitante m/f

inhale [ɪnˈheɪl] vt inhalar ■ vi (in smoking) tragar

inhaler [ɪnˈheɪləʳ] n inhalador m

inherent [ɪnˈhɪərənt] adj: **~ in** or **to** inherente a

inherently [ɪnˈhɪərəntlɪ] adv intrínsecamente

inherit [ɪnˈhɛrɪt] vt heredar

inheritance [ɪnˈhɛrɪtəns] n herencia; (fig) patrimonio

inhibit [ɪnˈhɪbɪt] vt inhibir, impedir; **to ~ sb from doing sth** impedir a algn hacer algo

inhibited [ɪnˈhɪbɪtɪd] adj (person) cohibido

inhibition [ɪnhɪˈbɪʃən] n cohibición f

inhospitable [ɪnhɔsˈpɪtəbl] adj (person) inhospitalario; (place) inhóspito

in-house [ˈɪnhaus] adj dentro de la empresa

inhuman [ɪnˈhjuːmən] adj inhumano

inhumane [ɪnhjuːˈmeɪn] adj inhumano

inimitable [ɪˈnɪmɪtəbl] adj inimitable

iniquity [ɪˈnɪkwɪtɪ] n iniquidad f; (injustice) injusticia

initial [ɪˈnɪʃl] adj inicial; (first) primero ■ n inicial f ■ vt firmar con las iniciales; **initials** npl iniciales fpl; (abbreviation) siglas fpl

initialize [ɪˈnɪʃəlaɪz] vt (Comput) inicializar

initially [ɪˈnɪʃəlɪ] adv en un principio

initiate [ɪˈnɪʃɪeɪt] vt (start) iniciar; **to ~ sb into a secret** iniciar a algn en un secreto; **to ~ proceedings against sb** (Law) poner una demanda contra algn

initiation [ɪnɪʃɪˈeɪʃən] n (into secret etc) iniciación f; (beginning) comienzo

initiative [ɪˈnɪʃətɪv] n iniciativa; **to take the ~** tomar la iniciativa

inject [ɪnˈdʒɛkt] vt inyectar; (money, enthusiasm) aportar

injection [ɪnˈdʒɛkʃən] n inyección f; **to have an ~** ponerse una inyección

injudicious [ɪndʒuˈdɪʃəs] adj imprudente, indiscreto

injunction [ɪnˈdʒʌŋkʃən] n entredicho, interdicto

injure [ˈɪndʒəʳ] vt herir; (hurt) lastimar; (fig: reputation etc) perjudicar; (feelings) herir; **to ~ o.s.** hacerse daño, lastimarse

injured [ˈɪndʒəd] adj (also fig) herido; **~ party** (Law) parte f perjudicada

injurious [ɪnˈdʒuərɪəs] adj: **~ (to)** perjudicial (para)

injury [ˈɪndʒərɪ] n herida, lesión f; (wrong) perjuicio, daño; **to escape without ~** salir ileso

injury time n (Sport) descuento

injustice [ɪnˈdʒʌstɪs] n injusticia; **you do me an ~** usted es injusto conmigo

ink [ɪŋk] n tinta

ink-jet printer [ˈɪŋkdʒɛt-] n impresora de chorro de tinta

inkling [ˈɪŋklɪŋ] n sospecha; (idea) idea

inkpad [ˈɪŋkpæd] n almohadilla

inlaid [ˈɪnleɪd] adj (wood) taraceado; (tiles) entarimado

inland adj [ˈɪnlənd] interior; (town) del interior ■ adv [ɪnˈlænd] tierra adentro

Inland Revenue n (Brit) ≈ Hacienda

in-laws [ˈɪnlɔːz] npl suegros mpl

inlet [ˈɪnlɛt] n (Geo) ensenada, cala; (Tech) admisión f, entrada

inmate ['ınmeıt] *n* (*in prison*) preso(-a), presidiario(-a); (*in asylum*) internado(-a)
inmost ['ınməust] *adj* más íntimo, más secreto
inn [ın] *n* posada, mesón *m*; **the Inns of Court** *see* **barrister**
innards ['ınədz] *npl* (*col*) tripas *fpl*
innate [ı'neıt] *adj* innato
inner ['ınə'] *adj* interior, interno
inner city *n* barrios deprimidos del centro de una ciudad
innermost ['ınəməust] *adj* más íntimo, más secreto
inner tube *n* (*of tyre*) cámara, llanta (*LAm*)
innings ['ınıŋz] *n* (*Cricket*) entrada, turno
innocence ['ınəsns] *n* inocencia
innocent ['ınəsnt] *adj* inocente
innocuous [ı'nɔkjuəs] *adj* inocuo
innovation [ınəu'veıʃən] *n* novedad *f*
innuendo (*pl* **innuendoes**) [ınju'ɛndəu, -əuz] *n* indirecta
innumerable [ı'nju:mrəbl] *adj* innumerable
inoculate [ı'nɔkjuleıt] *vt*: **to ~ sb with sth/ against sth** inocular *or* vacunar a algn con algo/contra algo
inoculation [ınɔkju'leıʃən] *n* inoculación *f*
inoffensive [ınə'fɛnsıv] *adj* inofensivo
inopportune [ın'ɔpətju:n] *adj* inoportuno
inordinate [ı'nɔ:dınət] *adj* excesivo, desmesurado
inordinately [ı'nɔ:dınətlı] *adv* excesivamente, desmesuradamente
inorganic [ınɔ:'gaenık] *adj* inorgánico
in-patient ['ınpeıʃənt] *n* (paciente *m/f*) interno(-a)
input ['ınput] *n* (*Elec*) entrada; (*Comput*) entrada de datos ■ *vt* (*Comput*) introducir, entrar
inquest ['ınkwɛst] *n* (*coroner's*) investigación *f* post-mortem
inquire [ın'kwaıə'] *vi* preguntar ■ *vt*: **to ~ when/where/whether** preguntar cuándo/ dónde/si; **to ~ about** (*person*) preguntar por; (*fact*) informarse de
  ▶ **inquire into** *vt fus*: **to ~ into sth** investigar *or* indagar algo
inquiring [ın'kwaıərıŋ] *adj* (*mind*) inquieto; (*look*) interrogante
inquiry [ın'kwaıərı] *n* pregunta; (*Law*) investigación *f*, pesquisa; (*commission*) comisión *f* investigadora; **to hold an ~ into sth** emprender una investigación sobre algo
inquiry desk *n* mesa de información
inquiry office *n* (*Brit*) oficina de información
inquisition [ınkwı'zıʃən] *n* inquisición *f*
inquisitive [ın'kwızıtıv] *adj* (*mind*) inquisitivo; (*person*) fisgón(-ona)

inroad ['ınrəud] *n* incursión *f*; (*fig*) invasión *f*; **to make inroads into** (*time*) ocupar parte de; (*savings, supplies*) agotar parte de
insane [ın'seın] *adj* loco; (*Med*) demente
insanitary [ın'sænıtərı] *adj* insalubre
insanity [ın'sænıtı] *n* demencia, locura
insatiable [ın'seıʃəbl] *adj* insaciable
inscribe [ın'skraıb] *vt* inscribir; (*book etc*): **to ~ (to sb)** dedicar (a algn)
inscription [ın'skrıpʃən] *n* (*gen*) inscripción *f*; (*in book*) dedicatoria
inscrutable [ın'skru:təbl] *adj* inescrutable, insondable
inseam measurement ['ınsi:m-] *n* (*US*) = **inside leg measurement**
insect ['ınsɛkt] *n* insecto
insect bite *n* picadura
insecticide [ın'sɛktısaıd] *n* insecticida *m*
insect repellent *n* loción *f* contra los insectos
insecure [ınsı'kjuə'] *adj* inseguro
insecurity [ınsı'kjuərıtı] *n* inseguridad *f*
insemination [ınsɛmı'neıʃn] *n*: **artificial ~** inseminación *f* artificial
insensible [ın'sɛnsıbl] *adj* inconsciente; (*unconscious*) sin conocimiento
insensitive [ın'sɛnsıtıv] *adj* insensible
insensitivity [ınsɛnsı'tıvıtı] *n* insensibilidad *f*
inseparable [ın'sɛprəbl] *adj* inseparable; **they were ~ friends** los unía una estrecha amistad
insert *vt* [ın'sə:t] (*into sth*) introducir; (*Comput*) insertar ■ *n* ['ınsə:t] encarte *m*
insertion [ın'sə:ʃən] *n* inserción *f*
in-service [ın'sə:vıs] *adj* (*training, course*) en el trabajo, a cargo de la empresa
inshore [ın'ʃɔ:'] *adj*: **~ fishing** pesca *f* costera ■ *adv* (*fish*) a lo largo de la costa; (*move*) hacia la orilla
inside ['ın'saıd] *n* interior *m*; (*lining*) forro; (*of road: Brit*) izquierdo; (: *in US, Europe etc*) derecho ■ *adj* interior, interno ■ *adv* (*within*) (por) dentro, adentro (*esp LAm*); (*with movement*) hacia dentro; (*col: in prison*) en chirona ■ *prep* dentro de; (*of time*): **~ 10 minutes** en menos de 10 minutos; **insides** *npl* (*col*) tripas *fpl*; **~ out** *adv* (*turn*) al revés; (*know*) a fondo
inside forward *n* (*Sport*) interior *m*
inside information *n* información *f* confidencial
inside lane *n* (*Aut: Brit*) carril *m* izquierdo; (: *in US, Europe etc*) carril *m* derecho
inside leg measurement *n* medida de pernera
insider [ın'saıdə'] *n* enterado(-a)
insider dealing, insider trading *n* (*Stock Exchange*) abuso de información privilegiada

inside story n historia íntima

insidious [ɪn'sɪdɪəs] adj insidioso

insight ['ɪnsaɪt] n perspicacia, percepción f; **to gain** or **get an ~ into sth** comprender algo mejor

insignia [ɪn'sɪgnɪə] npl insignias fpl

insignificant [ɪnsɪg'nɪfɪknt] adj insignificante

insincere [ɪnsɪn'sɪə^r] adj poco sincero

insincerity [ɪnsɪn'sɛrɪtɪ] n falta de sinceridad, doblez f

insinuate [ɪn'sɪnjueɪt] vt insinuar

insinuation [ɪnsɪnju'eɪʃən] n insinuación f

insipid [ɪn'sɪpɪd] adj soso, insulso

insist [ɪn'sɪst] vi insistir; **to ~ on doing** empeñarse en hacer; **to ~ that** insistir en que; (claim) exigir que

insistence [ɪn'sɪstəns] n insistencia; (stubbornness) empeño

insistent [ɪn'sɪstənt] adj insistente; empeñado

insofar as [ɪnsəʊ'fɑ:-] conj en la medida en que, en tanto que

insole ['ɪnsəʊl] n plantilla

insolence ['ɪnsələns] n insolencia, descaro

insolent ['ɪnsələnt] adj insolente, descarado

insoluble [ɪn'sɔljubl] adj insoluble

insolvency [ɪn'sɔlvənsɪ] n insolvencia

insolvent [ɪn'sɔlvənt] adj insolvente

insomnia [ɪn'sɔmnɪə] n insomnio

insomniac [ɪn'sɔmnɪæk] n insomne m/f

inspect [ɪn'spɛkt] vt inspeccionar, examinar; (troops) pasar revista a

inspection [ɪn'spɛkʃən] n inspección f, examen m

inspector [ɪn'spɛktə^r] n inspector(a) m(f); (Brit: on buses, trains) revisor(a) m(f)

inspiration [ɪnspə'reɪʃən] n inspiración f

inspire [ɪn'spaɪə^r] vt inspirar; **to ~ sb (to do sth)** alentar a algn (a hacer algo)

inspired [ɪn'spaɪəd] adj (writer, book etc) inspirado, genial, iluminado; **in an ~ moment** en un momento de inspiración

inspiring [ɪn'spaɪərɪŋ] adj inspirador(a)

inst. [ɪnst] abbr (Brit Comm: = instant, of the present month) cte

instability [ɪnstə'bɪlɪtɪ] n inestabilidad f

install [ɪn'stɔ:l] vt instalar

installation [ɪnstə'leɪʃən] n instalación f

installment plan n (US) compra a plazos

instalment, (US) **installment** [ɪn'stɔ:lmənt] n plazo; (of story) entrega; (of TV serial etc) capítulo; **in instalments** (pay, receive) a plazos; **to pay in instalments** pagar a plazos or por abonos

instance ['ɪnstəns] n ejemplo, caso; **for ~** por ejemplo; **in the first ~** en primer lugar; **in**

that ~ en ese caso

instant ['ɪnstənt] n instante m, momento
■ adj inmediato; (coffee) instantáneo

instantaneous [ɪnstən'teɪnɪəs] adj instantáneo

instantly ['ɪnstəntlɪ] adv en seguida, al instante

instant messaging [-'mɛsədʒɪŋ] n mensajería instantánea

instant replay n (US TV) repetición f de la jugada

instead [ɪn'stɛd] adv en cambio; **~ of** en lugar de, en vez de

instep ['ɪnstɛp] n empeine m

instigate ['ɪnstɪgeɪt] vt (rebellion, strike, crime) instigar; (new ideas etc) fomentar

instigation [ɪnstɪ'geɪʃən] n instigación f; **at sb's ~** a instigación de algn

instil [ɪn'stɪl] vt: **to ~ into** inculcar a

instinct ['ɪnstɪŋkt] n instinto

instinctive [ɪn'stɪŋktɪv] adj instintivo

instinctively [ɪn'stɪŋktɪvlɪ] adv por instinto

institute ['ɪnstɪtjuːt] n instituto; (professional body) colegio ■ vt (begin) iniciar, empezar; (proceedings) entablar

institution [ɪnstɪ'tjuːʃən] n institución f; (beginning) iniciación f; (Med: home) asilo; (asylum) manicomio; (custom) costumbre f arraigada

institutional [ɪnstɪ'tjuːʃənl] adj institucional

instruct [ɪn'strʌkt] vt: **to ~ sb in sth** instruir a algn en or sobre algo; **to ~ sb to do sth** dar instrucciones a algn de or mandar a algn hacer algo

instruction [ɪn'strʌkʃən] n (teaching) instrucción f; **instructions** npl órdenes fpl; **instructions (for use)** modo sg de empleo

instruction book n manual m

instructive [ɪn'strʌktɪv] adj instructivo

instructor [ɪn'strʌktə^r] n instructor(a) m(f)

instrument ['ɪnstrəmənt] n instrumento

instrumental [ɪnstrə'mɛntl] adj (Mus) instrumental; **to be ~ in** ser el artífice de; **to be ~ in sth/in doing sth** ser responsable de algo/de hacer algo

instrumentalist [ɪnstrə'mɛntəlɪst] n instrumentista m/f

instrument panel n tablero (de instrumentos)

insubordinate [ɪnsə'bɔːdənɪt] adj insubordinado

insubordination [ɪnsəbɔːdə'neɪʃən] n insubordinación f

insufferable [ɪn'sʌfrəbl] adj insoportable

insufficient [ɪnsə'fɪʃənt] adj insuficiente

insular ['ɪnsjulə^r] adj insular; (outlook) estrecho de miras

insularity [ɪnsjuˈlærɪtɪ] n insularidad f
insulate [ˈɪnsjuleɪt] vt aislar
insulating tape [ˈɪnsjuleɪtɪŋ-] n cinta aislante
insulation [ɪnsjuˈleɪʃən] n aislamiento
insulator [ˈɪnsjuleɪtəʳ] n aislante m
insulin [ˈɪnsjulɪn] n insulina
insult n [ˈɪnsʌlt] insulto; (offence) ofensa ■ vt [ɪnˈsʌlt] insultar; ofender
insulting [ɪnˈsʌltɪŋ] adj insultante; ofensivo
insuperable [ɪnˈsjuːprəbl] adj insuperable
insurance [ɪnˈʃuərəns] n seguro; **fire/life** ~ seguro de incendios/vida; **to take out ~ (against)** hacerse un seguro (contra)
insurance agent n agente m/f de seguros
insurance broker n corredor(a) m(f) or agente m/f de seguros
insurance policy n póliza (de seguros)
insurance premium n prima de seguros
insure [ɪnˈʃuəʳ] vt asegurar; **to ~ sb** or **sb's life** hacer un seguro de vida a algn; **to ~ (against)** asegurar (contra); **to be insured for £5000** tener un seguro de 5000 libras
insured [ɪnˈʃuəd] n: **the ~** el/la asegurado(-a)
insurer [ɪnˈʃuərəʳ] n asegurador(a)
insurgent [ɪnˈsəːdʒənt] adj, n insurgente m/f, insurrecto(-a) m(f)
insurmountable [ɪnsəˈmauntəbl] adj insuperable
insurrection [ɪnsəˈrɛkʃən] n insurrección f
intact [ɪnˈtækt] adj íntegro; (untouched) intacto
intake [ˈɪnteɪk] n (Tech) entrada, toma; (: pipe) tubo de admisión; (of food) ingestión f; (Brit Scol): **an ~ of 200 a year** 200 matriculados al año
intangible [ɪnˈtændʒɪbl] adj intangible
integer [ˈɪntɪdʒəʳ] n (número) entero
integral [ˈɪntɪɡrəl] adj (whole) íntegro; (part) integrante
integrate [ˈɪntɪɡreɪt] vt integrar ■ vi integrarse
integrated circuit [ˈɪntɪɡreɪtɪd-] n (Comput) circuito integrado
integration [ɪntɪˈɡreɪʃən] n integración f; **racial ~** integración de razas
integrity [ɪnˈtɛɡrɪtɪ] n honradez f, rectitud f; (Comput) integridad f
intellect [ˈɪntəlɛkt] n intelecto
intellectual [ɪntəˈlɛktjuəl] adj, n intelectual m/f
intelligence [ɪnˈtɛlɪdʒəns] n inteligencia
intelligence quotient n coeficiente m intelectual
Intelligence Service n Servicio de Inteligencia
intelligence test n prueba de inteligencia

intelligent [ɪnˈtɛlɪdʒənt] adj inteligente
intelligently [ɪnˈtɛlɪdʒəntlɪ] adv inteligentemente
intelligentsia [ɪntɛlɪˈdʒɛntsɪə] n intelectualidad f
intelligible [ɪnˈtɛlɪdʒɪbl] adj inteligible, comprensible
intemperate [ɪnˈtɛmpərət] adj inmoderado
intend [ɪnˈtɛnd] vt (gift etc): **to ~ sth for** destinar algo a; **to ~ to do sth** tener intención de or pensar hacer algo
intended [ɪnˈtɛndɪd] adj (effect) deseado
intense [ɪnˈtɛns] adj intenso; **to be ~** (person) tomárselo todo muy en serio
intensely [ɪnˈtɛnslɪ] adv intensamente; (very) sumamente
intensify [ɪnˈtɛnsɪfaɪ] vt intensificar; (increase) aumentar
intensity [ɪnˈtɛnsɪtɪ] n (gen) intensidad f
intensive [ɪnˈtɛnsɪv] adj intensivo
intensive care n: **to be in ~** estar bajo cuidados intensivos; **~ unit** n unidad f de vigilancia intensiva
intensively [ɪnˈtɛnsɪvlɪ] adv intensivamente
intent [ɪnˈtɛnt] n propósito ■ adj (absorbed) absorto; (attentive) atento; **to all intents and purposes** a efectos prácticos; **to be ~ on doing sth** estar resuelto or decidido a hacer algo
intention [ɪnˈtɛnʃən] n intención f, propósito
intentional [ɪnˈtɛnʃənl] adj deliberado
intentionally [ɪnˈtɛnʃnəlɪ] adv a propósito
intently [ɪnˈtɛntlɪ] adv atentamente, fijamente
inter [ɪnˈtəːʳ] vt enterrar, sepultar
inter- [ˈɪntəʳ] pref inter-
interact [ɪntərˈækt] vi (substances) influirse mutuamente; (people) relacionarse
interaction [ɪntərˈækʃən] n interacción f, acción f recíproca
interactive [ɪntərˈæktɪv] adj (Comput) interactivo
intercede [ɪntəˈsiːd] vi (also: **to intercede (with)**) interceder (con); **to ~ with sb/on behalf of sb** interceder con algn/en nombre de algn
intercept [ɪntəˈsɛpt] vt interceptar; (stop) detener
interception [ɪntəˈsɛpʃən] n interceptación f; detención f
interchange n [ˈɪntətʃeɪndʒ] intercambio; (on motorway) intersección f ■ vt [ɪntəˈtʃeɪndʒ] intercambiar
interchangeable [ɪntəˈtʃeɪndʒəbl] adj intercambiable
intercity [ɪntəˈsɪtɪ] adj: **~ (train)** (tren m) intercity m

intercom ['ıntəkɔm] n interfono
interconnect [ıntəkə'nɛkt] vi (rooms)
comunicar(se)
intercontinental ['ıntəkɔntı'nɛntl] adj
intercontinental
intercourse ['ıntəkɔːs] n (also: **sexual
intercourse**) relaciones fpl sexuales, contacto
sexual; (social) trato
interdependence [ıntədı'pɛndəns] n
interdependencia
interdependent [ıntədı'pɛndənt] adj
interdependiente
interest ['ıntrıst] n (Comm) interés m ■ vt
interesar; **compound/simple** ~ interés
compuesto/simple; **business interests**
negocios mpl; **British interests in the
Middle East** los intereses británicos en el
Medio Oriente
interested ['ıntrıstıd] adj interesado; **to be ~
in** interesarse por
interest-free ['ıntrıst'friː] adj libre de interés
interesting ['ıntrıstıŋ] adj interesante
interest rate n tipo de interés
interface ['ıntəfeıs] n (Comput) junción f,
interface m
interfere [ıntə'fıəʳ] vi: **to ~ in** (quarrel, other
people's business) entrometerse en; **to ~ with**
(hinder) estorbar; (damage) estropear; (Radio)
interferir con
interference [ıntə'fıərəns] n (gen)
intromisión f; (Radio, TV) interferencia
interfering [ıntə'fıərıŋ] adj entrometido
interim ['ıntərım] adj: ~ **dividend** dividendo
parcial ■ n: **in the ~** en el ínterin
interior [ın'tıərıəʳ] n interior m ■ adj interior
interior decorator, interior designer
n interiorista m/f, diseñador(a) m(f) de
interiores
interjection [ıntə'dʒɛkʃən] n interrupción f
interlock [ıntə'lɔk] vi entrelazarse; (wheels
etc) endentarse
interloper ['ıntələupəʳ] n intruso(-a)
interlude ['ıntəluːd] n intervalo; (rest)
descanso; (Theat) intermedio
intermarriage [ıntə'mærıdʒ] n endogamia
intermarry [ıntə'mærı] vi casarse (entre
parientes)
intermediary [ıntə'miːdıərı] n
intermediario(-a)
intermediate [ıntə'miːdıət] adj intermedio
interminable [ın'təːmınəbl] adj inacabable
intermission [ıntə'mıʃən] n (Theat) descanso
intermittent [ıntə'mıtnt] adj intermitente
intermittently [ıntə'mıtntlı] adv
intermitentemente
intern vt [ın'təːn] internar; (enclose) encerrar
■ n ['ıntəːn] (US) médico(-a) m(f) interno(-a)

internal [ın'təːnl] adj interno, interior;
~ **injuries** heridas fpl or lesiones fpl internas
internally [ın'təːnəlı] adv interiormente;
"not to be taken ~" "uso externo"
Internal Revenue Service n (US) ≈ Hacienda
international [ıntə'næʃənl] adj
internacional; ~ **(game)** partido
internacional; ~ **(player)** jugador(a) m(f)
internacional
International Atomic Energy Agency
n Organismo Internacional de Energía
Atómica
International Chamber of Commerce n
Cámara de Comercio Internacional
International Court of Justice n Corte f
Internacional de Justicia
international date line n línea de cambio
de fecha
internationally [ıntə'næʃnəlı] adv
internacionalmente
International Monetary Fund n Fondo
Monetario Internacional
internecine [ıntə'niːsaın] adj de
aniquilación mutua
internee [ıntəː'niː] n interno(-a), recluso(-a)
Internet ['ıntənɛt] n: **the ~** (el or la) Internet
Internet café n cibercafé m
Internet Service Provider n proveedor m de
(acceso a) Internet
Internet user n internauta m/f
internment [ın'təːnmənt] n internamiento
interplanetary [ıntə'plænıtərı] adj
interplanetario
interplay ['ıntəpleı] n interacción f
Interpol ['ıntəpɔl] n Interpol f
interpret [ın'təːprıt] vt interpretar; (translate)
traducir; (understand) entender ■ vi hacer de
intérprete
interpretation [ıntəːprı'teıʃən] n
interpretación f; traducción f
interpreter [ın'təːprıtəʳ] n intérprete m/f
interrelated [ıntərı'leıtıd] adj
interrelacionado
interrogate [ın'tɛrəugeıt] vt interrogar
interrogation [ıntɛrəu'geıʃən] n
interrogatorio
interrogative [ıntə'rɔgətıv] adj interrogativo
interrupt [ıntə'rʌpt] vt, vi interrumpir
interruption [ıntə'rʌpʃən] n interrupción f
intersect [ıntə'sɛkt] vt cruzar ■ vi (roads)
cruzarse
intersection [ıntə'sɛkʃən] n intersección f;
(of roads) cruce m
intersperse [ıntə'spəːs] vt: **to ~ with** salpicar
de
intertwine [ıntə'twaın] vt entrelazar ■ vi
entrelazarse

interval ['ɪntəvl] n intervalo; (Brit Theat, Sport) descanso; **at intervals** a ratos, de vez en cuando; **sunny intervals** (Meteorology) claros mpl

intervene [ɪntə'viːn] vi intervenir; (take part) participar; (occur) sobrevenir

intervening [ɪntə'viːnɪŋ] adj intermedio

intervention [ɪntə'vɛnʃən] n intervención f

interview ['ɪntəvjuː] n (Radio, TV etc) entrevista ■ vt entrevistar a

interviewee [ɪntəvjuː'iː] n entrevistado(-a)

interviewer ['ɪntəvjuːəʳ] n entrevistador(a) m(f)

intestate [ɪn'tɛstɛɪt] adj intestado

intestinal [ɪn'tɛstɪnl] adj intestinal

intestine [ɪn'tɛstɪn] n: **large/small ~** intestino grueso/delgado

intimacy ['ɪntɪməsɪ] n intimidad f; (relations) relaciones fpl íntimas

intimate adj ['ɪntɪmət] íntimo; (friendship) estrecho; (knowledge) profundo ■ vt ['ɪntɪmeɪt] (announce) dar a entender

intimately ['ɪntɪmətlɪ] adv íntimamente

intimidate [ɪn'tɪmɪdeɪt] vt intimidar, amedrentar

intimidation [ɪntɪmɪ'deɪʃən] n intimidación f

into ['ɪntuː] prep (gen) en; (towards) a; (inside) hacia el interior de; **~ three pieces/French** en tres pedazos/al francés; **to change pounds ~ euros** cambiar libras por euros

intolerable [ɪn'tɔlərəbl] adj intolerable, insoportable

intolerance [ɪn'tɔlərəns] n intolerancia

intolerant [ɪn'tɔlərənt] adj: **~ (of)** intolerante (con)

intonation [ɪntəu'neɪʃən] n entonación f

intoxicate [ɪn'tɔksɪkeɪt] vt embriagar

intoxicated [ɪn'tɔksɪkeɪtɪd] adj embriagado

intoxication [ɪntɔksɪ'keɪʃən] n embriaguez f

intractable [ɪn'træktəbl] adj (person) intratable; (problem) irresoluble; (illness) incurable

intranet ['ɪntrənɛt] n intranet f

intransigence [ɪn'trænsɪdʒəns] n intransigencia

intransigent [ɪn'trænsɪdʒənt] adj intransigente

intransitive [ɪn'trænsɪtɪv] adj intransitivo

intravenous [ɪntrə'viːnəs] adj intravenoso

in-tray ['ɪntreɪ] n bandeja de entrada

intrepid [ɪn'trɛpɪd] adj intrépido

intricacy ['ɪntrɪkəsɪ] n complejidad f

intricate ['ɪntrɪkət] adj intrincado; (plot, problem) complejo

intrigue [ɪn'triːg] n intriga ■ vt fascinar ■ vi andar en intrigas

intriguing [ɪn'triːgɪŋ] adj fascinante

intrinsic [ɪn'trɪnsɪk] adj intrínseco

introduce [ɪntrə'djuːs] vt introducir, meter; **to ~ sb (to sb)** presentar algn (a algn); **to ~ sb to** (pastime, technique) introducir a algn a; **may I ~ ...?** permítame presentarle a ...

introduction [ɪntrə'dʌkʃən] n introducción f; (of person) presentación f; **a letter of ~** una carta de recomendación

introductory [ɪntrə'dʌktərɪ] adj introductorio; **an ~ offer** una oferta introductoria; **~ remarks** comentarios mpl preliminares

introspection [ɪntrəu'spɛkʃən] n introspección f

introspective [ɪntrəu'spɛktɪv] adj introspectivo

introvert ['ɪntrəuvəːt] adj, n introvertido(-a) m(f)

intrude [ɪn'truːd] vi (person) entrometerse; **to ~ on** estorbar

intruder [ɪn'truːdəʳ] n intruso(-a)

intrusion [ɪn'truːʒən] n invasión f

intrusive [ɪn'truːsɪv] adj intruso

intuition [ɪntjuː'ɪʃən] n intuición f

intuitive [ɪn'tjuːɪtɪv] adj intuitivo

intuitively [ɪn'tjuːɪtɪvlɪ] adv por intuición, intuitivamente

inundate ['ɪnʌndeɪt] vt: **to ~ with** inundar de

inure [ɪn'juəʳ] vt: **to ~ (to)** acostumbrar or habituar (a)

invade [ɪn'veɪd] vt invadir

invader [ɪn'veɪdəʳ] n invasor(a) m(f)

invalid n ['ɪnvəlɪd] minusválido(-a) ■ adj [ɪn'vælɪd] (not valid) inválido, nulo

invalidate [ɪn'vælɪdeɪt] vt invalidar, anular

invalid chair n silla de ruedas

invaluable [ɪn'væljuəbl] adj inestimable

invariable [ɪn'vɛərɪəbl] adj invariable

invariably [ɪn'vɛərɪəblɪ] adv sin excepción, siempre; **she is ~ late** siempre llega tarde

invasion [ɪn'veɪʒən] n invasión f

invective [ɪn'vɛktɪv] n invectiva

inveigle [ɪn'viːgl] vt: **to ~ sb into (doing) sth** embaucar or engatusar a algn para (que haga) algo

invent [ɪn'vɛnt] vt inventar

invention [ɪn'vɛnʃən] n invento; (inventiveness) inventiva; (lie) invención f

inventive [ɪn'vɛntɪv] adj inventivo

inventiveness [ɪn'vɛntɪvnɪs] n ingenio, inventiva

inventor [ɪn'vɛntəʳ] n inventor(a) m(f)

inventory ['ɪnvəntrɪ] n inventario

inventory control n control m de existencias

inverse [ɪn'vəːs] adj, n inverso; **in ~ proportion (to)** en proporción inversa (a)

inversely [ɪn'vəːslɪ] *adv* a la inversa
invert [ɪn'vəːt] *vt* invertir
invertebrate [ɪn'vəːtɪbrət] *n* invertebrado
inverted commas [ɪn'vəːtɪd-] *npl* (*Brit*)
comillas *fpl*
invest [ɪn'vɛst] *vt* invertir; (*fig: time, effort*)
dedicar ▪ *vi* invertir; **to ~ sb with sth**
conferir algo a algn
investigate [ɪn'vɛstɪɡeɪt] *vt* investigar;
(*study*) estudiar, examinar
investigation [ɪnvɛstɪ'ɡeɪʃən] *n*
investigación *f*, pesquisa; examen *m*
investigative journalism [ɪn'vɛstɪɡətɪv-] *n*
periodismo de investigación
investigator [ɪn'vɛstɪɡeɪtə']
n investigador(a) *m(f)*; **private ~**
investigador(a) *m(f)* privado(-a)
investiture [ɪn'vɛstɪtʃə'] *n* investidura
investment [ɪn'vɛstmənt] *n* inversión *f*
investment grant *n* subvención *f* para la
inversión
investment income *n* ingresos *mpl*
procedentes de inversiones
investment portfolio *n* cartera de
inversiones
investment trust *n* compañía inversionista,
sociedad *f* de cartera
investor [ɪn'vɛstə'] *n* inversor(a) *m(f)*
inveterate [ɪn'vɛtərət] *adj* empedernido
invidious [ɪn'vɪdɪəs] *adj* odioso
invigilate [ɪn'vɪdʒɪleɪt] *vt, vi* (*in exam*) vigilar
invigilator [ɪn'vɪdʒɪleɪtə'] *n* celador(a) *m(f)*
invigorating [ɪn'vɪɡəreɪtɪŋ] *adj* vigorizante
invincible [ɪn'vɪnsɪbl] *adj* invencible
inviolate [ɪn'vaɪələt] *adj* inviolado
invisible [ɪn'vɪzɪbl] *adj* invisible
invisible assets *npl* activo invisible
invisible ink *n* tinta simpática
invisible mending *n* puntada invisible
invitation [ɪnvɪ'teɪʃən] *n* invitación *f*; **by ~
only** solamente por invitación
invite [ɪn'vaɪt] *vt* invitar; (*opinions etc*)
solicitar, pedir; (*trouble*) buscarse; **to ~ sb
(to do)** invitar a algn (a hacer); **to ~ sb to
dinner** invitar a algn a cenar
▶ **invite out** *vt* invitar a salir
▶ **invite over** *vt* invitar a casa
inviting [ɪn'vaɪtɪŋ] *adj* atractivo; (*look*)
provocativo; (*food*) apetitoso
invoice ['ɪnvɔɪs] *n* factura ▪ *vt* facturar; **to ~
sb for goods** facturar a algn las mercancías
invoicing ['ɪnvɔɪsɪŋ] *n* facturación *f*
invoke [ɪn'vəuk] *vt* invocar; (*aid*) pedir; (*law*)
recurrir a
involuntary [ɪn'vɔləntrɪ] *adj* involuntario
involve [ɪn'vɔlv] *vt* (*entail*) suponer, implicar;
to ~ sb (in) involucrar a algn (en)

involved [ɪn'vɔlvd] *adj* complicado;
to be/become ~ in sth estar involucrado/
involucrarse en algo
involvement [ɪn'vɔlvmənt] *n* (*gen*) enredo;
(*obligation*) compromiso; (*difficulty*) apuro
invulnerable [ɪn'vʌlnərəbl] *adj* invulnerable
inward ['ɪnwəd] *adj* (*movement*) interior,
interno; (*thought, feeling*) íntimo ▪ *adv* hacia
dentro
inwardly ['ɪnwədlɪ] *adv* (*feel, think etc*) para sí,
para dentro
inwards ['ɪnwədz] *adv* hacia dentro
I/O *abbr* (*Comput*: = *input/output*) E/S; **~ error**
error *m* de E/S
IOC *n abbr* (= *International Olympic Committee*)
COI *m*
iodine ['aɪəudiːn] *n* yodo
IOM *abbr* (*Brit*) = **Isle of Man**
ion ['aɪən] *n* ion *m*
Ionian Sea [aɪ'əunɪən-] *n*: **the ~** el Mar Jónico
ioniser ['aɪənaɪzə'] *n* ionizador *m*
iota [aɪ'əutə] *n* (*fig*) jota, ápice *m*
IOU *n abbr* (= *I owe you*) pagaré *m*
IOW *abbr* (*Brit*) = **Isle of Wight**
IPA *n abbr* (= *International Phonetic Alphabet*) AFI
m
iPod® ['aɪpɔd] *n* iPod® *m*
IQ *n abbr* (= *intelligence quotient*) C.I. *m*
IRA *n abbr* (= *Irish Republican Army*) IRA *m*; (*US*)
= **individual retirement account**
Iran [ɪ'rɑːn] *n* Irán *m*
Iranian [ɪ'reɪnɪən] *adj* iraní ▪ *n* iraní *m/f*;
(*Ling*) iraní *m*
Iraq [ɪ'rɑːk] *n* Irak *m*
Iraqi [ɪ'rɑːkɪ] *adj, n* irakí *m/f*
irascible [ɪ'ræsɪbl] *adj* irascible
irate [aɪ'reɪt] *adj* enojado, airado
Ireland ['aɪələnd] *n* Irlanda; **Republic of ~**
República de Irlanda
iris (*pl* **irises**) ['aɪrɪs, -ɪz] *n* (*Anat*) iris *m*; (*Bot*)
lirio
Irish ['aɪrɪʃ] *adj* irlandés(-esa) ▪ *n* (*Ling*)
irlandés *m*; **the ~** *npl* los irlandeses
Irishman ['aɪrɪʃmən] *n* irlandés *m*
Irish Sea *n*: **the ~** el Mar de Irlanda
Irishwoman ['aɪrɪʃwumən] *n* irlandesa
irk [əːk] *vt* fastidiar
irksome ['əːksəm] *adj* fastidioso
IRN *n abbr* (= *Independent Radio News*) *servicio de
noticias en las cadenas de radio privadas*
IRO *n abbr* (*US*) = **International Refugee
Organization**
iron ['aɪən] *n* hierro; (*for clothes*) plancha ▪ *adj*
de hierro ▪ *vt* (*clothes*) planchar; **irons** *npl*
(*chains*) grilletes *mpl*
▶ **iron out** *vt* (*crease*) quitar; (*fig*) allanar,
resolver

Iron Curtain *n*: **the ~** el Telón de Acero
iron foundry *n* fundición *f*, fundidora
ironic [aɪ'rɔnɪk], **ironical** [aɪ'rɔnɪkl] *adj*
irónico
ironically [aɪ'rɔnɪklɪ] *adv* irónicamente
ironing ['aɪənɪŋ] *n* (*act*) planchado; (*ironed clothes*) ropa planchada; (*clothes to be ironed*) ropa por planchar
ironing board *n* tabla de planchar
iron lung *n* (*Med*) pulmón *m* de acero
ironmonger ['aɪənmʌŋgəʳ] *n* (*Brit*) ferretero(-a); **~'s (shop)** ferretería
iron ore *n* mineral *m* de hierro
ironworks ['aɪənwɜːks] *n* fundición *f*
irony ['aɪrənɪ] *n* ironía; **the ~ of it is that ...** lo irónico del caso es que ...
irrational [ɪ'ræʃənl] *adj* irracional
irreconcilable [ɪrɛkən'saɪləbl] *adj* inconciliable; (*enemies*) irreconciliable
irredeemable [ɪrɪ'diːməbl] *adj* irredimible
irrefutable [ɪrɪ'fjuːtəbl] *adj* irrefutable
irregular [ɪ'rɛgjuləʳ] *adj* irregular; (*surface*) desigual
irregularity [ɪrɛgju'lærɪtɪ] *n* irregularidad *f*; desigualdad *f*
irrelevance [ɪ'rɛləvəns] *n* irrelevancia
irrelevant [ɪ'rɛləvənt] *adj* irrelevante; **to be ~** estar fuera de lugar, no venir al caso
irreligious [ɪrɪ'lɪdʒəs] *adj* irreligioso
irreparable [ɪ'rɛprəbl] *adj* irreparable
irreplaceable [ɪrɪ'pleɪsəbl] *adj* irremplazable
irrepressible [ɪrɪ'prɛsəbl] *adj* incontenible
irreproachable [ɪrɪ'prəutʃəbl] *adj* irreprochable
irresistible [ɪrɪ'zɪstɪbl] *adj* irresistible
irresolute [ɪ'rɛzəluːt] *adj* indeciso
irrespective [ɪrɪ'spɛktɪv]: **~ of** *prep* sin tener en cuenta, no importa
irresponsibility [ɪrɪspɔnsɪ'bɪlɪtɪ] *n* irresponsabilidad *f*
irresponsible [ɪrɪ'spɔnsɪbl] *adj* (*act*) irresponsable; (*person*) poco serio
irretrievable [ɪrɪ'triːvəbl] *adj* (*object*) irrecuperable; (*loss, damage*) irremediable, irreparable
irretrievably [ɪrɪ'triːvəblɪ] *adv* irremisiblemente
irreverence [ɪ'rɛvərns] *n* irreverencia
irreverent [ɪ'rɛvərnt] *adj* irreverente, irrespetuoso
irrevocable [ɪ'rɛvəkəbl] *adj* irrevocable
irrigate ['ɪrɪgeɪt] *vt* regar
irrigation [ɪrɪ'geɪʃən] *n* riego
irritability [ɪrɪtə'bɪlɪtɪ] *n* irritabilidad *f*
irritable ['ɪrɪtəbl] *adj* (*person: temperament*) irritable; (: *mood*) de mal humor
irritant ['ɪrɪtənt] *n* agente *m* irritante

irritate ['ɪrɪteɪt] *vt* fastidiar; (*Med*) picar
irritating ['ɪrɪteɪtɪŋ] *adj* fastidioso
irritation [ɪrɪ'teɪʃən] *n* fastidio; picazón *f*, picor *m*
IRS *n abbr* (*US*) = **Internal Revenue Service**
is [ɪz] *vb see* **be**
ISA ['aɪsə] *n abbr* (*Brit*: = *individual savings account*) plan de ahorro personal para pequeños inversores con fiscalidad cero
ISBN *n abbr* (= *International Standard Book Number*) ISBN *m*
ISDN *n abbr* (= *Integrated Services Digital Network*) RDSI *f*
Islam ['ɪzlɑːm] *n* Islam *m*
island ['aɪlənd] *n* isla; (*also*: **traffic island**) isleta
islander ['aɪləndəʳ] *n* isleño(-a)
isle [aɪl] *n* isla
isn't ['ɪznt] = **is not**
isobar ['aɪsəubɑːʳ] *n* isobara
isolate ['aɪsəleɪt] *vt* aislar
isolated ['aɪsəleɪtɪd] *adj* aislado
isolation [aɪsə'leɪʃən] *n* aislamiento
isolationism [aɪsə'leɪʃənɪzəm] *n* aislacionismo
isolation ward *n* pabellón *m* de aislamiento
isotope ['aɪsəutəup] *n* isótopo
ISP *n abbr* = **Internet service provider**
Israel ['ɪzreɪl] *n* Israel *m*
Israeli [ɪz'reɪlɪ] *adj, n* israelí *m/f*
issue ['ɪsjuː] *n* cuestión *f*, asunto; (*outcome*) resultado; (*of banknotes etc*) emisión *f*; (*of newspaper etc*) número; (*offspring*) sucesión *f*, descendencia ▪ *vt* (*rations, equipment*) distribuir, repartir; (*orders*) dar; (*certificate, passport*) expedir; (*decree*) promulgar; (*magazine*) publicar; (*cheque*) extender; (*banknotes, stamp*) emitir ▪ *vi*: **to ~ (from)** derivar (de), brotar (de); **at ~** en cuestión; **to take ~ with sb (over)** disentir con algn (en); **to avoid the ~** andarse con rodeos; **to confuse** *or* **obscure the ~** confundir las cosas; **to make an ~ of sth** dar a algo más importancia de lo necesario; **to ~ sth to sb, ~ sb with sth** entregar algo a algn
Istanbul [ɪstæn'buːl] *n* Estambul *m*
isthmus ['ɪsməs] *n* istmo
IT *n abbr* = **information technology**

 KEYWORD

it [ɪt] *pron* **1** (*specific: subject: not generally translated*) él/ella; (: *direct object*) lo/la; (: *indirect object*) le; (*after prep*) él/ella; (*abstract concept*)

ello; **it's on the table** está en la mesa;
I can't find it no lo (or la) encuentro; **give
it to me** dámelo (or dámela); **I spoke to
him about it** le hablé del asunto; **what did
you learn from it?** ¿qué aprendiste de él
(or ella)?; **did you go to it?** (party, concert etc)
¿fuiste?
2 (impersonal): **it's raining** llueve, está
lloviendo; **it's 6 o'clock/the 10th of
August** son las 6/es el 10 de agosto; **how far
is it? — it's 10 miles/2 hours on the
train** ¿a qué distancia está? — a 10 millas/
2 horas en tren; **who is it? — it's me** ¿quién
es? — soy yo

ITA n abbr (Brit: = initial teaching alphabet)
alfabeto parcialmente fonético, ayuda para enseñar
a leer
Italian [ɪ'tæljən] adj italiano ■ n
italiano(-a); (Ling) italiano
italic [ɪ'tælɪk] adj cursivo; **italics** npl
cursiva sg
Italy ['ɪtəlɪ] n Italia
ITC n abbr (Brit) = **Independent Television
Commission**
itch [ɪtʃ] n picazón f; (fig) prurito ■ vi (person)
sentir or tener comezón; (part of body) picar;
to be itching to do sth rabiar por or morirse
de ganas de hacer algo
itching ['ɪtʃɪŋ] n picazón f, comezón f
itchy ['ɪtʃɪ] adj: **to be ~** picar
it'd ['ɪtd] = **it would; it had**
item ['aɪtəm] n artículo; (on agenda) asunto
(a tratar); (in programme) número; (also: **news
item**) noticia; **items of clothing** prendas fpl
de vestir
itemize ['aɪtəmaɪz] vt detallar
itemized bill ['aɪtəmaɪzd-] n recibo detallado
itinerant [ɪ'tɪnərənt] adj ambulante
itinerary [aɪ'tɪnərərɪ] n itinerario
it'll ['ɪtl] = **it will; it shall**
ITN n abbr (Brit) = **Independent Television News**

its [ɪts] adj su
it's [ɪts] = **it is; it has**
itself [ɪt'sɛlf] pron (reflexive) sí mismo(-a);
(emphatic) él/ella mismo(-a)
ITV n abbr (Brit: = Independent Television) ver nota

ITV

En el Reino Unido la ITV ("Independent
Television") es una cadena de
emisoras comerciales regionales con
licencia exclusiva para emitir en su
región. Suelen producir sus propios
programas, se financian con publicidad
y están bajo el control del organismo
oficial independiente "Independent
Broadcasting Authority" ("IBA").
El servicio de noticias nacionales e
internacionales, "ITN" ("Independent
Television News"), funciona como
una compañía productora para toda la
cadena.

IUD n abbr (= intra-uterine device) DIU m
I've [aɪv] = **I have**
ivory ['aɪvərɪ] n marfil m
Ivory Coast n: **the ~** la Costa de Marfil
ivory tower n (fig) torre f de marfil
ivy ['aɪvɪ] n hiedra
Ivy League n (US) ver nota

IVY LEAGUE

Las ocho universidades más prestigiosas
del nordeste de los Estados Unidos
reciben el nombre colectivo de Ivy
League, por sus muros cubiertos de
hiedra. Son: Brown, Columbia, Cornell,
Dartmouth College, Harvard, Princeton,
la universidad de Pennsylvania y Yale.
También se llaman así las competiciones
deportivas que celebran entre ellas.

J j

J, j [dʒeɪ] n (letter) J, j f; **J for Jack,** (US) **J for Jig** J de José

JA n abbr = **judge advocate**

J/A abbr = **joint account**

jab [dʒæb] vt (elbow) dar un codazo a; (punch) dar un golpe rápido a ■ vi: **to ~ at** intentar golpear a; **to ~ sth into sth** clavar algo en algo ■ n codazo; golpe m (rápido); (Med: col) pinchazo

jabber ['dʒæbə'] vt, vi farfullar

jack [dʒæk] n (Aut) gato; (Bowls) boliche m; (Cards) sota
  ▸ **jack in** vt (col) dejar
  ▸ **jack up** vt (Aut) levantar con el gato

jackal ['dʒækl] n (Zool) chacal m

jackass ['dʒækæs] n (also fig) asno, burro

jackdaw ['dʒækdɔː] n grajo(-a), chova

jacket ['dʒækɪt] n chaqueta, americana, saco (LAm); (of boiler etc) camisa; (of book) sobrecubierta

jacket potato n patata asada (con piel)

jack-in-the-box ['dʒækɪnðəbɔks] n caja sorpresa, caja de resorte

jack-knife ['dʒæknaɪf] vi colear

jack-of-all-trades ['dʒækəv'ɔːltreɪdz] n aprendiz m de todo

jack plug n (Elec) enchufe m de clavija

jackpot ['dʒækpɔt] n premio gordo

Jacuzzi® [dʒə'kuːzɪ] n jacuzzi® m

jade [dʒeɪd] n (stone) jade m

jaded ['dʒeɪdɪd] adj (tired) cansado; (fed up) hastiado

jagged ['dʒægɪd] adj dentado

jaguar ['dʒægjuə'] n jaguar m

jail [dʒeɪl] n cárcel f ■ vt encarcelar

jailbird ['dʒeɪlbəːd] n preso(-a) reincidente

jailbreak ['dʒeɪlbreɪk] n fuga or evasión f (de la cárcel)

jailer ['dʒeɪlə'] n carcelero(-a)

jalopy [dʒə'lɔpɪ] n (col) cacharro, armatoste m

jam [dʒæm] n mermelada; (also: **traffic jam**) atasco, embotellamiento; (difficulty) apuro ■ vt (passage etc) obstruir; (mechanism, drawer etc) atascar; (Radio) interferir ■ vi atascarse, trabarse; **to get sb out of a ~** sacar a algn del paso or de un apuro; **to ~ sth into sth** meter algo a la fuerza en algo; **the telephone lines are jammed** las líneas están saturadas

Jamaica [dʒə'meɪkə] n Jamaica

Jamaican [dʒə'meɪkən] adj, n jamaicano(-a) m(f)

jamb [dʒæm] n jamba

jamboree [dʒæmbə'riː] n congreso de niños exploradores

jam-packed [dʒæm'pækt] adj: **~ (with)** atestado (de)

jam session n concierto improvisado de jazz/rock etc

Jan abbr (= January) ene

jangle ['dʒæŋgl] vi sonar (de manera) discordante

janitor ['dʒænɪtə'] n (caretaker) portero, conserje m

January ['dʒænjuərɪ] n enero; see also **July**

Japan [dʒə'pæn] n (el) Japón

Japanese [dʒæpə'niːz] adj japonés(-esa) ■ n (pl inv) japonés(-esa) m(f); (Ling) japonés m

jar [dʒɑː'] n (glass: large) jarra; (: small) tarro ■ vi (sound) chirriar; (colours) desentonar

jargon ['dʒɑːgən] n jerga

jarring ['dʒɑːrɪŋ] adj (sound) discordante, desafinado; (colour) chocante

Jas. abbr = **James**

jasmine, jasmin ['dʒæzmɪn] n jazmín m

jaundice ['dʒɔːndɪs] n ictericia

jaundiced ['dʒɔːndɪst] adj (fig: embittered) amargado; (: disillusioned) desilusionado

jaunt [dʒɔːnt] n excursión f

jaunty ['dʒɔːntɪ] adj alegre; (relaxed) desenvuelto

Java ['dʒɑːvə] n Java

javelin ['dʒævlɪn] n jabalina

jaw [dʒɔː] n mandíbula; **jaws** npl (Tech: of vice etc) mordaza sg

jawbone ['dʒɔːbəun] n mandíbula, quijada

jay [dʒeɪ] n (Zool) arrendajo

jaywalker ['dʒeɪwɔːkə'] n peatón(-ona) m(f) imprudente

jazz [dʒæz] n jazz m
▶jazz up vt (liven up) animar
jazz band n orquesta de jazz
jazzy ['dʒæzɪ] adj de colores llamativos
JCB® n abbr excavadora
JCS n abbr (US) = **Joint Chiefs of Staff**
JD n abbr (US: = Doctor of Laws) título universitario; (= Justice Department) Ministerio de Justicia
jealous ['dʒɛləs] adj (gen) celoso; (envious) envidioso; **to be ~** tener celos
jealously ['dʒɛləslɪ] adv (enviously) envidiosamente; (watchfully) celosamente
jealousy ['dʒɛləsɪ] n celos mpl; envidia
jeans [dʒiːnz] npl (pantalones mpl) vaqueros mpl or tejanos mpl, bluejean m inv (LAm)
Jeep® [dʒiːp] n jeep m
jeer [dʒɪər] vi: **to ~ (at)** (boo) abuchear; (mock) mofarse (de)
jeering ['dʒɪərɪŋ] adj (crowd) insolente, ofensivo ■ n protestas fpl; (mockery) burlas fpl
jelly ['dʒɛlɪ] n gelatina, jalea
jellyfish ['dʒɛlɪfɪʃ] n medusa
jemmy ['dʒɛmɪ] n palanqueta
jeopardize ['dʒɛpədaɪz] vt arriesgar, poner en peligro
jeopardy ['dʒɛpədɪ] n: **to be in ~** estar en peligro
jerk [dʒəːk] n (jolt) sacudida; (wrench) tirón m; (US col) imbécil m/f, pendejo(-a) (LAm) ■ vt dar una sacudida a; tirar bruscamente de ■ vi (vehicle) dar una sacudida
jerkin ['dʒəːkɪn] n chaleco
jerky ['dʒəːkɪ] adj espasmódico
jerry-built ['dʒɛrɪbɪlt] adj mal construido
jerry can ['dʒɛrɪ-] n bidón m
Jersey ['dʒəːzɪ] n Jersey m
jersey ['dʒəːzɪ] n jersey m; (fabric) tejido de punto
Jerusalem [dʒəˈruːsləm] n Jerusalén m
jest [dʒɛst] n broma
jester ['dʒɛstər] n bufón m
Jesus ['dʒiːzəs] n Jesús m; **~ Christ** Jesucristo
jet [dʒɛt] n (of gas, liquid) chorro; (Aviat) avión m a reacción
jet-black ['dʒɛt'blæk] adj negro como el azabache
jet engine n motor m a reacción
jet lag n desorientación f por desfase horario
jetsam ['dʒɛtsəm] n echazón f
jet-setter ['dʒɛtsɛtər] n personaje m de la jet
jettison ['dʒɛtɪsn] vt desechar
jetty ['dʒɛtɪ] n muelle m, embarcadero
Jew [dʒuː] n judío
jewel ['dʒuːəl] n joya; (in watch) rubí m
jeweller, jeweler (US) ['dʒuːələr] n joyero(-a); **~'s (shop)** joyería

jewellery, jewelry (US) ['dʒuːəlrɪ] n joyas fpl, alhajas fpl
Jewess ['dʒuːɪs] n judía
Jewish ['dʒuːɪʃ] adj judío
JFK n abbr (US) = **John Fitzgerald Kennedy International Airport**
jib [dʒɪb] vi (horse) plantarse; **to ~ at doing sth** resistirse a hacer algo
jibe [dʒaɪb] n mofa
jiffy ['dʒɪfɪ] n (col): **in a ~** en un santiamén
jig [dʒɪg] n (dance, tune) giga
jigsaw ['dʒɪgsɔː] n (also: **jigsaw puzzle**) rompecabezas m inv; (tool) sierra de vaivén
jilt [dʒɪlt] vt dejar plantado a
jingle ['dʒɪŋgl] n (advert) musiquilla ■ vi tintinear
jingoism ['dʒɪŋgəuɪzəm] n patriotería, jingoísmo
jinx [dʒɪŋks] n: **there's a ~ on it** está gafado
jitters ['dʒɪtəz] npl (col): **to get the ~** ponerse nervioso
jittery ['dʒɪtərɪ] adj (col) agitado
jiujitsu [dʒuːˈdʒɪtsuː] n jiujitsu m
job [dʒɔb] n trabajo; (task) tarea; (duty) deber m; (post) empleo; (col: difficulty) dificultad f; **it's a good ~ that ...** menos mal que ...; **just the ~!** ¡justo lo que necesito!; **a part-time/full-time ~** un trabajo a tiempo parcial/tiempo completo; **that's not my ~** eso no me incumbe or toca a mí; **he's only doing his ~** está cumpliendo nada más
job centre n (Brit) oficina de empleo
job creation scheme n plan m de creación de puestos de trabajo
job description n descripción f del puesto de trabajo
jobless ['dʒɔblɪs] adj sin trabajo ■ n: **the ~** los parados
job lot n lote m de mercancías, saldo
job satisfaction n satisfacción f en el trabajo
job security n garantía de trabajo
job specification n especificación f del trabajo, profesiograma m
Jock n (col: Scotsman) escocés m
jockey ['dʒɔkɪ] n jockey m/f ■ vi: **to ~ for position** maniobrar para sacar delantera
jockey box n (US Aut) guantera
jockstrap ['dʒɔkstræp] n suspensorio
jocular ['dʒɔkjulər] adj (humorous) gracioso; (merry) alegre
jodhpurs ['dʒɔdpəːz] npl pantalón msg de montar
jog [dʒɔg] vt empujar (ligeramente) ■ vi (run) hacer footing; **to ~ along** (fig) ir tirando; **to ~ sb's memory** refrescar la memoria a algn
jogger ['dʒɔgər] n corredor(a) m(f)
jogging ['dʒɔgɪŋ] n footing m

john [dʒɒn] *n* (*US col*) wáter *m*
join [dʒɔɪn] *vt* (*things*) unir, juntar; (*become member of: club*) hacerse socio de; (*Pol: party*) afiliarse a; (*meet: people*) reunirse con; (*fig*) unirse a ▪ *vi* (*roads*) empalmar; (*rivers*) confluir ▪ *n* juntura; **will you ~ us for dinner?** ¿quieres cenar con nosotros?; **I'll ~ you later** me reuniré contigo luego; **to ~ forces (with)** aliarse (con)
  ▸**join in** *vi* tomar parte, participar ▪ *vt fus* tomar parte *or* participar en
  ▸**join up** *vi* unirse; (*Mil*) alistarse
joiner ['dʒɔɪnəʳ] *n* carpintero(-a)
joinery ['dʒɔɪnərɪ] *n* carpintería
joint [dʒɔɪnt] *n* (*Tech*) juntura, unión *f*; (*Anat*) articulación *f*; (*Brit Culin*) pieza de carne (para asar); (*col: place*) garito ▪ *adj* (*common*) común; (*combined*) conjunto; (*responsibility*) compartido; (*committee*) mixto
joint account *n* (*with bank etc*) cuenta común
jointly ['dʒɔɪntlɪ] *adv* (*gen*) en común; (*together*) conjuntamente
joint owners *npl* copropietarios *mpl*
joint ownership *n* copropiedad *f*, propiedad *f* común
joint-stock bank ['dʒɔɪntstɔk-] *n* banco por acciones
joint-stock company ['dʒɔɪntstɔk-] *n* sociedad *f* anónima
joint venture *n* empresa conjunta
joist [dʒɔɪst] *n* viga
joke [dʒəuk] *n* chiste *m*; (*also:* **practical joke**) broma ▪ *vi* bromear; **to play a ~ on** gastar una broma a
joker ['dʒəukəʳ] *n* chistoso(-a), bromista *m/f*; (*Cards*) comodín *m*
joking ['dʒəukɪŋ] *n* bromas *fpl*
jokingly ['dʒəukɪŋlɪ] *adv* en broma
jollity ['dʒɔlɪtɪ] *n* alegría
jolly ['dʒɔlɪ] *adj* (*merry*) alegre; (*enjoyable*) divertido ▪ *adv* (*col*) muy, la mar de ▪ *vt*: **to ~ sb along** animar *or* darle ánimos a algn; **~ good!** ¡estupendo!
jolt [dʒəult] *n* (*shake*) sacudida; (*blow*) golpe *m*; (*shock*) susto ▪ *vt* sacudir
Jordan ['dʒɔːdən] *n* (*country*) Jordania; (*river*) Jordán *m*
joss stick [dʒɔs-] *n* barrita de incienso, pebete *m*
jostle ['dʒɔsl] *vt* dar empujones *or* empellones a
jot [dʒɔt] *n*: **not one ~** ni pizca, ni un ápice
  ▸**jot down** *vt* apuntar
jotter ['dʒɔtəʳ] *n* (*Brit*) bloc *m*
journal ['dʒəːnl] *n* (*paper*) periódico; (*magazine*) revista; (*diary*) diario

journalese [dʒəːnə'liːz] *n* (*pej*) lenguaje *m* periodístico
journalism ['dʒəːnəlɪzəm] *n* periodismo
journalist ['dʒəːnəlɪst] *n* periodista *m/f*
journey ['dʒəːnɪ] *n* viaje *m*; (*distance covered*) trayecto ▪ *vi* viajar; **return ~** viaje de regreso; **a five-hour ~** un viaje de cinco horas
jovial ['dʒəuvɪəl] *adj* risueño, alegre
jowl [dʒaul] *n* quijada
joy [dʒɔɪ] *n* alegría
joyful ['dʒɔɪful] *adj* alegre
joyfully ['dʒɔɪfulɪ] *adv* alegremente
joyous ['dʒɔɪəs] *adj* alegre
joyride ['dʒɔɪraɪd] *n*: **to go for a ~** darse una vuelta en un coche robado
joyrider ['dʒɔɪraɪdəʳ] *n* persona que se da una vuelta en un coche robado
joystick ['dʒɔɪstɪk] *n* (*Aviat*) palanca de mando; (*Comput*) palanca de control
JP *n abbr see* **Justice of the Peace**
Jr *abbr* = **junior**
JTPA *n abbr* (*US: = Job Training Partnership Act*) programa gubernamental de formación profesional
jubilant ['dʒuːbɪlnt] *adj* jubiloso
jubilation [dʒuːbɪ'leɪʃən] *n* júbilo
jubilee ['dʒuːbɪliː] *n* aniversario; **silver ~** vigésimo quinto aniversario
judge [dʒʌdʒ] *n* juez *m/f* ▪ *vt* juzgar; (*competition*) actuar de *or* ser juez en; (*estimate*) considerar; (*: weight, size etc*) calcular ▪ *vi*: **judging** *or* **to ~ by his expression** a juzgar por su expresión; **as far as I can ~** por lo que puedo entender, a mi entender; **I judged it necessary to inform him** consideré necesario informarle
judge advocate *n* (*Mil*) auditor *m* de guerra
judgment, judgement ['dʒʌdʒmənt] *n* juicio; (*punishment*) sentencia, fallo; **to pass judg(e)ment (on)** (*Law*) pronunciar *or* dictar sentencia (sobre); (*fig*) emitir un juicio crítico *or* dictaminar (sobre); **in my judg(e)ment** a mi juicio
judicial [dʒuː'dɪʃl] *adj* judicial
judiciary [dʒuː'dɪʃɪərɪ] *n* poder *m* judicial, magistratura
judicious [dʒuː'dɪʃəs] *adj* juicioso
judo ['dʒuːdəu] *n* judo
jug [dʒʌg] *n* jarro
jugged hare [dʒʌgd-] *n* (*Brit*) estofado de liebre
juggernaut ['dʒʌgənɔːt] *n* (*Brit: huge truck*) camión *m* de carga pesada
juggle ['dʒʌgl] *vi* hacer juegos malabares
juggler ['dʒʌgləʳ] *n* malabarista *m/f*
Jugoslav *etc* ['juːgəuslɑːv] = **Yugoslav** *etc*
jugular ['dʒʌgjuləʳ] *adj*: **~ vein** (vena) yugular *f*

juice [dʒuːs] *n* jugo, zumo (*SP*); (*of meat*) jugo; (*col: petrol*): **we've run out of ~** se nos acabó la gasolina
juiciness ['dʒuːsɪnɪs] *n* jugosidad *f*
juicy ['dʒuːsɪ] *adj* jugoso
juijitsu, jujitsu [dʒuː'dʒɪtsuː] *n* jujitsu *m*
jukebox ['dʒuːkbɔks] *n* máquina de discos
Jul. *abbr* (= *July*) jul
July [dʒuː'laɪ] *n* julio; **the first of ~** el uno *or* primero de julio; **during ~** en el mes de julio; **in ~ of next year** en julio del año que viene
jumble ['dʒʌmbl] *n* revoltijo ■ *vt* (*also*: **jumble together, jumble up**: *mix up*) revolver; (: *disarrange*) mezclar
jumble sale *n* (*Brit*) mercadillo; *ver nota*

● **JUMBLE SALE**
●
● En cada *jumble sale* pueden comprarse
● todo tipo de objetos baratos de segunda
● mano, especialmente ropa, juguetes,
● libros, vajillas y muebles. Suelen
● organizarse en los locales de un colegio,
● iglesia, ayuntamiento o similar, con
● fines benéficos, bien en ayuda de una
● organización benéfica conocida o para
● solucionar problemas más concretos de la
● comunidad.

jumbo ['dʒʌmbəu], **jumbo jet** *n* jumbo
jump [dʒʌmp] *vi* saltar, dar saltos; (*start*) sobresaltarse; (*increase*) aumentar ■ *vt* saltar ■ *n* salto; (*fence*) obstáculo; (*increase*) aumento; **to ~ the queue** (*Brit*) colarse
▸ **jump about** *vi* dar saltos, brincar
▸ **jump at** *vt fus* (*fig*) apresurarse a aprovechar; **he jumped at the offer** se apresuró a aceptar la oferta
▸ **jump down** *vi* bajar de un salto, saltar a tierra
▸ **jump up** *vi* levantarse de un salto
jumped-up ['dʒʌmptʌp] *adj* (*pej*) engreído
jumper ['dʒʌmpə'] *n* (*Brit: pullover*) jersey *m*, suéter *m*; (*US: pinafore dress*) pichi *m*; (*Sport*) saltador(a) *m(f)*
jump leads, (*US*) **jumper cables** *npl* cables *mpl* puente de batería
jump-start ['dʒʌmpstɑːt] *vt* (*car*) arrancar con ayuda de otra batería *or* empujando; (*fig: economy*) reactivar
jump suit *n* mono
jumpy ['dʒʌmpɪ] *adj* nervioso
Jun. *abbr* = **junior**; (= *June*) jun
junction ['dʒʌŋkʃən] *n* (*Brit: of roads*) cruce *m*; (*Rail*) empalme *m*
juncture ['dʒʌŋktʃə'] *n*: **at this ~** en este momento, en esta coyuntura

June [dʒuːn] *n* junio; *see also* **July**
jungle ['dʒʌŋgl] *n* selva, jungla
junior ['dʒuːnɪə'] *adj* (*in age*) menor, más joven; (*competition*) juvenil; (*position*) subalterno ■ *n* menor *m/f*, joven *m/f*; **he's ~ to me** es menor que yo
junior executive *n* ejecutivo/a subalterno/a
junior high school *n* (*US*) *centro de educación secundaria*; *see also* **high school**
junior school *n* (*Brit*) escuela primaria; *see also* **primary school**
junk [dʒʌŋk] *n* (*cheap goods*) baratijas *fpl*; (*lumber*) trastos *mpl* viejos; (*rubbish*) basura; (*ship*) junco ■ *vt* (*esp US*) deshacerse de
junk bond *n* (*Comm*) obligación *f* basura *inv*
junk dealer *n* vendedor(a) *m(f)* de objetos usados
junket ['dʒʌŋkɪt] *n* (*Culin*) *dulce de leche cuajada*; (*Brit col*): **to go on a ~, go junketing** viajar a costa ajena *or* del erario público
junk food *n* comida basura *or* de plástico
junkie ['dʒʌŋkɪ] *n* (*col*) yonqui *m/f*, heroinómano(-a)
junk mail *n* propaganda (buzoneada), correo *m* basura *inv*
junk room *n* trastero
junk shop *n* tienda de objetos usados
junta ['dʒʌntə] *n* junta militar
Jupiter ['dʒuːpɪtə'] *n* (*Mythology, Astro*) Júpiter *m*
jurisdiction [dʒuərɪs'dɪkʃən] *n* jurisdicción *f*; **it falls** *or* **comes within/outside our ~** es/no es de nuestra competencia
jurisprudence [dʒuərɪs'pruːdəns] *n* jurisprudencia
juror ['dʒuərə'] *n* jurado
jury ['dʒuərɪ] *n* jurado
jury box *n* tribuna del jurado
juryman ['dʒuərɪmən] *n* miembro del jurado
just [dʒʌst] *adj* justo ■ *adv* (*exactly*) exactamente; (*only*) sólo, solamente, no más (*LAm*); **he's ~ done it/left** acaba de hacerlo/irse; **I've ~ seen him** acabo de verle; **~ right** perfecto; **~ two o'clock** las dos en punto; **she's ~ as clever as you** es tan lista como tú; **~ as well that ...** menos mal que ...; **it's ~ as well you didn't go** menos mal que no fuiste; **it's ~ as good (as)** es igual (que), es tan bueno (como); **~ as he was leaving** en el momento en que se marchaba; **we were ~ going** ya nos íbamos; **I was ~ about to phone** estaba a punto de llamar; **~ before/enough** justo antes/lo suficiente; **~ here** aquí mismo; **he ~ missed** falló por poco; **~ listen to this** escucha esto un momento; **~ ask someone the way** simplemente

pregúntale a alguien por dónde se va; **not ~ now** ahora no

justice ['dʒʌstɪs] *n* justicia; **this photo doesn't do you ~** esta foto no te favorece

Justice of the Peace *n* juez *m/f* de paz; *see also* **Crown Court**

justifiable [dʒʌstɪ'faɪəbl] *adj* justificable, justificado

justifiably [dʒʌstɪ'faɪəblɪ] *adv* justificadamente, con razón

justification [dʒʌstɪfɪ'keɪʃən] *n* justificación *f*

justify ['dʒʌstɪfaɪ] *vt* justificar; (*text*) alinear, justificar; **to be justified in doing sth**

tener motivo para *or* razón al hacer algo

justly ['dʒʌstlɪ] *adv* (*gen*) justamente; (*with reason*) con razón

justness ['dʒʌstnɪs] *n* justicia

jut [dʒʌt] *vi* (*also*: **jut out**) sobresalir

jute [dʒuːt] *n* yute *m*

juvenile ['dʒuːvənaɪl] *adj* juvenil; (*court*) de menores ▪ *n* joven *m/f*, menor *m/f* de edad

juvenile delinquency *n* delincuencia juvenil

juvenile delinquent *n* delincuente *m/f* juvenil

juxtapose ['dʒʌkstəpəuz] *vt* yuxtaponer

juxtaposition ['dʒʌkstəpə'zɪʃən] *n* yuxtaposición *f*

Kk

K, k [keɪ] *n* (*letter*) K, k *f*; **K for King** K de Kilo
K *n abbr* (= *one thousand*) mille ■ *abbr* (*Brit*:
  = *Knight*) titolo; (= *kilobyte*) K
kaftan ['kæftæn] *n* caftán *m*
Kalahari Desert [kælə'hɑ:rɪ-] *n* desierto de
  Kalahari
kale [keɪl] *n* col *f* rizada
kaleidoscope [kə'laɪdəskəup] *n* calidoscopio
kamikaze [kæmɪ'kɑ:zɪ] *adj* kamikaze
Kampala [kæm'pɑ:lə] *n* Kampala
Kampuchea [kæmpu'tʃɪə] *n* Kampuchea
kangaroo [kæŋgə'ru:] *n* canguro
Kans. *abbr* (*US*) = **Kansas**
kaput [kə'put] *adj* (*col*) roto, estropeado
karaoke [kɑ:rə'əukɪ] *n* karaoke
karate [kə'rɑ:tɪ] *n* karate *m*
Kashmir [kæʃ'mɪəʳ] *n* Cachemira
kayak ['kaɪæk] *n* kayak *m*
Kazakhstan [kɑ:zɑ:k'stæn] *n* Kazajstán *m*
KC *n abbr* (*Brit Law*: = *King's Counsel*) título
  concedido a determinados abogados
kebab [kə'bæb] *n* pincho moruno, brocheta
keel [ki:l] *n* quilla; **on an even ~** (*fig*)
  en equilibrio
  ▶ **keel over** *vi* (*Naut*) zozobrar, volcarse;
  (*person*) desplomarse
keen [ki:n] *adj* (*interest, desire*) grande, vivo;
  (*eye, intelligence*) agudo; (*competition*) intenso;
  (*edge*) afilado; (*Brit*: *eager*) entusiasta; **to be
  ~ to do** *or* **on doing sth** tener muchas ganas
  de hacer algo; **to be ~ on sth/sb** interesarse
  por algo/algn; **I'm not ~ on going** no tengo
  ganas de ir
keenly ['ki:nlɪ] *adv* (*enthusiastically*) con
  entusiasmo; (*acutely*) vivamente; (*intensely*)
  intensamente
keenness ['ki:nnɪs] *n* (*eagerness*) entusiasmo,
  interés *m*
keep [ki:p] (*pt, pp* **kept**) *vt* (*retain, preserve*)
  guardar; (*hold back*) quedarse con; (*shop*) ser
  propietario de; (*feed: family etc*) mantener;
  (*promise*) cumplir; (*chickens, bees etc*) criar ■ *vi*
  (*food*) conservarse; (*remain*) seguir, continuar

■ *n* (*of castle*) torreón *m*; (*food etc*) comida,
sustento; **to ~ doing sth** seguir haciendo
algo; **to ~ sb from doing sth** impedir a
algn hacer algo; **to ~ sth from happening**
impedir que algo ocurra; **to ~ sb happy**
tener a algn contento; **to ~ sb waiting** hacer
esperar a algn; **to ~ a place tidy** mantener
un lugar limpio; **to ~ sth to o.s.** no decirle
algo a nadie; **to ~ time** (*clock*) mantener la
hora exacta; **~ the change** quédese con la
vuelta; **to ~ an appointment** acudir a una
cita; **to ~ a record** *or* **note of sth** tomar nota
de *or* apuntar algo; *see also* **keeps**
▶ **keep away** *vt*: **to ~ sth/sb away from sb**
mantener algo/a algn apartado de algn ■ *vi*:
to ~ away (from) mantenerse apartado (de)
▶ **keep back** *vt* (*crowd, tears*) contener; (*money*)
quedarse con; (*conceal: information*): **to ~ sth
back from sb** ocultar algo a algn
■ *vi* hacerse a un lado
▶ **keep down** *vt* (*control: prices, spending*)
controlar; (*retain: food*) retener ■ *vi* seguir
agachado, no levantar la cabeza
▶ **keep in** *vt* (*invalid, child*) impedir que salga,
no dejar salir; (*Scol*) castigar (a quedarse en el
colegio) ■ *vi* (*col*): **to ~ in with sb** mantener
la relación con algn
▶ **keep off** *vt* (*dog, person*) mantener a distancia
■ *vi* evitar; **~ your hands off!** ¡no toques!;
"~ off the grass" "prohibido pisar el césped"
▶ **keep on** *vi* seguir, continuar
▶ **keep out** *vi* (*stay out*) permanecer fuera;
"~ out" "prohibida la entrada"
▶ **keep up** *vt* mantener, conservar ■ *vi* no
rezagarse; (*fig: in comprehension*) seguir (el
hilo); **to ~ up with** (*pace*) ir al paso de; (*level*)
mantenerse a la altura de; **to ~ up with sb**
seguir el ritmo a algn; (*fig*) seguir a algn
keeper ['ki:pəʳ] *n* guarda *m/f*
keep-fit [ki:p'fɪt] *n* gimnasia (de
  mantenimiento)
keeping ['ki:pɪŋ] *n* (*care*) cuidado; **in ~ with**
  de acuerdo con

keeps [kiːps] *n*: **for ~** (*col*) para siempre
keepsake ['kiːpseɪk] *n* recuerdo
keg [kɛg] *n* barrilete *m*, barril *m*
Ken. *abbr* (*US*) = **Kentucky**
kennel ['kɛnl] *n* perrera; **kennels** *npl* perrera
Kenya ['kɛnjə] *n* Kenia
Kenyan ['kɛnjən] *adj*, *n* keniata *m/f*, keniano(-a) *m(f)*
kept [kɛpt] *pt*, *pp of* **keep**
kerb [kəːb] *n* (*Brit*) bordillo
kerb crawler [-krɔːlə] *n* *conductor en busca de prostitutas desde su coche*
kernel ['kəːnl] *n* (*nut*) fruta; (*fig*) meollo
kerosene ['kɛrəsiːn] *n* keroseno
kestrel ['kɛstrəl] *n* cernícalo
ketchup ['kɛtʃəp] *n* salsa de tomate, ketchup *m*
kettle ['kɛtl] *n* hervidor *m*
kettle drum *n* (*Mus*) timbal *m*
key [kiː] *n* (*gen*) llave *f*; (*Mus*) tono; (*of piano, typewriter*) tecla; (*on map*) clave *f* ■ *cpd* (*vital: position, industry etc*) clave ■ *vt* (*also*: **key in**) teclear
keyboard ['kiːbɔːd] *n* teclado ■ *vt* (*text*) teclear
keyboarder ['kiːbɔːdə] *n* teclista *m/f*
keyed up [kiːd-] *adj* (*person*) nervioso; **to be (all) ~** estar nervioso *or* emocionado
keyhole ['kiːhəul] *n* ojo (de la cerradura)
keyhole surgery *n* cirugía cerrada *or* no invasiva
key man *n* hombre *m* clave
keynote ['kiːnəut] *n* (*Mus*) tónica; (*fig*) idea fundamental
keynote speech *n* discurso de apertura
keypad ['kiːpæd] *n* teclado numérico
keyring ['kiːrɪŋ] *n* llavero
keystone ['kiːstəun] *n* piedra clave
keystroke ['kiːstrəuk] *n* pulsación *f* (de una tecla)
kg *abbr* (= *kilogram*) kg
KGB *n abbr* KGB *m*
khaki ['kɑːkɪ] *n* caqui
kibbutz, kibbutzim [kɪ'buts, -ɪm] *n* kibutz *m*
kick [kɪk] *vt* (*person*) dar una patada a; (*ball*) dar un puntapié a ■ *vi* (*horse*) dar coces ■ *n* patada; puntapié *m*, tiro; (*of rifle*) culetazo; (*col: thrill*): **he does it for kicks** lo hace por pura diversión
  ▶ **kick around** *vt* (*idea*) dar vueltas a; (*person*) tratar a patadas a
  ▶ **kick off** *vi* (*Sport*) hacer el saque inicial
kick-start ['kɪkstɑːt] *n* (*also*: **kick-starter**) (pedal *m* de) arranque *m*
kid [kɪd] *n* (*col: child*) niño(-a), chiquillo(-a); (*animal*) cabrito; (*leather*) cabritilla ■ *vi* (*col*) bromear

kid gloves *npl*: **to treat sb with ~** andarse con pies de plomo con algn
kidnap ['kɪdnæp] *vt* secuestrar
kidnapper ['kɪdnæpə] *n* secuestrador(a) *m(f)*
kidnapping ['kɪdnæpɪŋ] *n* secuestro
kidney ['kɪdnɪ] *n* riñón *m*
kidney bean *n* judía, alubia
kidney machine *n* riñón *m* artificial
kill [kɪl] *vt* matar; (*murder*) asesinar; (*fig: rumour, conversation*) acabar con ■ *n* matanza; **to ~ time** matar el tiempo
  ▶ **kill off** *vt* exterminar, terminar con; (*fig*) echar por tierra
killer ['kɪlə] *n* asesino(-a)
killer app [- 'æp] *n abbr* (*col*: = *killer application*) aplicación *f* rompedora, aplicación *f* excelente rendimiento
killer instinct *n*: **to have the ~** ir a por todas
killing ['kɪlɪŋ] *n* (*one*) asesinato; (*several*) matanza; (*Comm*): **to make a ~** tener un gran éxito financiero
killjoy ['kɪldʒɔɪ] *n* (*Brit*) aguafiestas *m/f inv*
kiln [kɪln] *n* horno
kilo ['kiːləu] *n abbr* (= *kilogram(me)*) kilo
kilobyte ['kɪləubaɪt] *n* (*Comput*) kilobyte *m*
kilogram, kilogramme ['kɪləugræm] *n* kilogramo
kilometre, (*US*) **kilometer** ['kɪləmiːtə] *n* kilómetro
kilowatt ['kɪləuwɔt] *n* kilovatio
kilt [kɪlt] *n* falda escocesa
kilter ['kɪltə] *n*: **out of ~** desbaratado
kimono [kɪ'məunəu] *n* quimono
kin [kɪn] *n* parientes *mpl*
kind [kaɪnd] *adj* (*treatment*) bueno, cariñoso; (*person, act, word*) amable, atento ■ *n* clase *f*, especie *f*; (*species*) género; **in ~** (*Comm*) en especie; **a ~ of** una especie de; **to be two of a ~** ser tal para cual; **would you be ~ enough to ...?**, **would you be so ~ as to ...?** ¿me hace el favor de ...?; **it's very ~ of you (to do)** le agradezco mucho (el que haya hecho)
kindergarten ['kɪndəgɑːtn] *n* jardín *m* de infancia
kind-hearted [kaɪnd'hɑːtɪd] *adj* bondadoso, de buen corazón
kindle ['kɪndl] *vt* encender
kindliness ['kaɪndlɪnəs] *n* bondad *f*, amabilidad *f*
kindling ['kɪndlɪŋ] *n* leña (menuda)
kindly ['kaɪndlɪ] *adj* bondadoso; (*gentle*) cariñoso ■ *adv* bondadosamente, amablemente; **will you ~ ...** sería usted tan amable de ...
kindness ['kaɪndnɪs] *n* bondad *f*, amabilidad *f*
kindred ['kɪndrɪd] *n* familia, parientes *mpl*
  ■ *adj*: **~ spirits** almas *fpl* gemelas

k

kinetic [kɪˈnɛtɪk] *adj* cinético
king [kɪŋ] *n* rey *m*
kingdom [ˈkɪŋdəm] *n* reino
kingfisher [ˈkɪŋfɪʃəʳ] *n* martín *m* pescador
kingpin [ˈkɪŋpɪn] *n* (*Tech*) perno real *or* pinzote; (*fig*) persona clave
king-size [ˈkɪŋsaɪz], **king-sized** [ˈkɪŋsaɪzd] *adj* de tamaño gigante; (*cigarette*) extra largo
kink [kɪŋk] *n* (*in rope etc*) enroscadura; (*in hair*) rizo; (*fig: emotional, psychological*) manía
kinky [ˈkɪŋkɪ] *adj* (*pej*) perverso
kinship [ˈkɪnʃɪp] *n* parentesco; (*fig*) afinidad *f*
kinsman [ˈkɪnzmən] *n* pariente *m*
kinswoman [ˈkɪnzwumən] *n* parienta
kiosk [ˈkiːɔsk] *n* quiosco; (*Brit Tel*) cabina; **newspaper ~** quiosco, kiosco
kipper [ˈkɪpəʳ] *n* arenque *m* ahumado
Kirghizia [kəˈgɪzɪə] *n* Kirguizistán *m*
kiss [kɪs] *n* beso ■ *vt* besar; **~ of life** (*artificial respiration*) respiración *f* artificial; **to ~ sb goodbye** dar un beso de despedida a algn; **to ~ (each other)** besarse
kissogram [ˈkɪsəgræm] *n* servicio de felicitaciones mediante el que se envía a una persona vestida de manera sugerente para besar a algn
kit [kɪt] *n* equipo; (*set of tools etc*) (caja de) herramientas *fpl*; (*assembly kit*) juego de armar; **tool ~** juego *or* estuche *m* de herramientas
  ▶ **kit out** *vt* equipar
kitbag [ˈkɪtbæg] *n* (*Mil*) macuto
kitchen [ˈkɪtʃɪn] *n* cocina
kitchen garden *n* huerto
kitchen sink *n* fregadero
kitchen unit *n* módulo de cocina
kitchenware [ˈkɪtʃɪnwɛəʳ] *n* batería de cocina
kite [kaɪt] *n* (*toy*) cometa
kith [kɪθ] *n*: **~ and kin** parientes *mpl* y allegados
kitten [ˈkɪtn] *n* gatito(-a)
kitty [ˈkɪtɪ] *n* (*pool of money*) fondo común; (*Cards*) bote *m*
kiwi [ˈkiːwiː] *n* (*col: New Zealander*) neozelandés(-esa) *m(f)*; (*also*: **kiwi fruit**) kiwi *m*
KKK *n abbr* (*US*) = **Ku Klux Klan**
kleptomaniac [klɛptəuˈmeɪnɪæk] *n* cleptómano(-a)
km *abbr* (= *kilometre*) km
km/h *abbr* (= *kilometres per hour*) km/h
knack [næk] *n*: **to have the ~ of doing sth** tener facilidad para hacer algo
knackered [ˈnækəd] *adj* (*col*) hecho polvo
knapsack [ˈnæpsæk] *n* mochila
knead [niːd] *vt* amasar
knee [niː] *n* rodilla
kneecap [ˈniːkæp] *vt* destrozar a tiros la

rótula de ■ *n* rótula
knee-deep [ˈniːˈdiːp] *adj*: **the water was ~** el agua llegaba hasta la rodilla
kneel [niːl] (*pt, pp* **knelt** [nɛlt]) *vi* (*also*: **kneel down**) arrodillarse
kneepad [ˈniːpæd] *n* rodillera
knell [nɛl] *n* toque *m* de difuntos
knelt [nɛlt] *pt, pp of* **kneel**
knew [njuː] *pt of* **know**
knickers [ˈnɪkəz] *npl* (*Brit*) bragas *fpl*, calzones *mpl* (*LAm*)
knick-knack [ˈnɪknæk] *n* chuchería, baratija
knife [naɪf] (*pl* **knives**) *n* cuchillo ■ *vt* acuchillar; **~, fork and spoon** cubiertos *mpl*
knife edge *n*: **to be on a ~** estar en la cuerda floja
knight [naɪt] *n* caballero; (*Chess*) caballo
knighthood [ˈnaɪthud] *n* (*title*): **to get a ~** recibir el título de Sir
knit [nɪt] *vt* tejer, tricotar; (*brows*) fruncir; (*fig*): **to ~ together** unir, juntar ■ *vi* hacer punto, tejer, tricotar; (*bones*) soldarse
knitted [ˈnɪtɪd] *adj* de punto
knitting [ˈnɪtɪŋ] *n* labor *f* de punto
knitting machine *n* máquina de tricotar
knitting needle, knit pin (*US*) *n* aguja de hacer punto *or* tejer
knitting pattern *n* patrón *m* para tricotar
knitwear [ˈnɪtwɛəʳ] *n* prendas *fpl* de punto
knives [naɪvz] *pl of* **knife**
knob [nɔb] *n* (*of door*) pomo; (*of stick*) puño; (*lump*) bulto; (*fig*): **a ~ of butter** (*Brit*) un pedazo de mantequilla
knobbly [ˈnɔblɪ], **knobby** (*US*) [ˈnɔbɪ] *adj* (*wood, surface*) nudoso; (*knee*) huesudo
knock [nɔk] *vt* (*strike*) golpear; (*bump into*) chocar contra; (*fig: col*) criticar ■ *vi* (*at door etc*): **to ~ at/on** llamar a ■ *n* golpe *m*; (*on door*) llamada; **he knocked at the door** llamó a la puerta
  ▶ **knock down** *vt* (*pedestrian*) atropellar; (*price*) rebajar
  ▶ **knock off** *vi* (*col: finish*) salir del trabajo ■ *vt* (*col: steal*) birlar; (*strike off*) quitar; (*fig: from price, record*): **to ~ off £10** rebajar en £10
  ▶ **knock out** *vt* dejar sin sentido; (*Boxing*) poner fuera de combate, dejar K.O.; (*stop*) estropear, dejar fuera de servicio
  ▶ **knock over** *vt* (*object*) derribar, tirar; (*pedestrian*) atropellar
knockdown [ˈnɔkdaun] *adj* (*price*) de saldo
knocker [ˈnɔkəʳ] *n* (*on door*) aldaba
knocking [ˈnɔkɪŋ] *n* golpes *mpl*, golpeteo
knock-kneed [nɔkˈniːd] *adj* patizambo
knockout [ˈnɔkaut] *n* (*Boxing*) K.O. *m*, knockout *m*
knock-up [ˈnɔkʌp] *n* (*Tennis*) peloteo

knot [nɔt] n (gen) nudo ▪ vt anudar; **to tie a** ~ hacer un nudo
knotted ['nɔtɪd] adj anudado
knotty ['nɔtɪ] adj (fig) complicado
know [nəu] (pt **knew**, pp **known**) [njuː, nəun] vt (gen) saber; (person, author, place) conocer ▪ vi: **as far as I** ~ ... que yo sepa ...; **yes, I** ~ sí, ya lo sé; **I don't** ~ no lo sé; **to** ~ **how to do** saber hacer; **to** ~ **how to swim** saber nadar; **to** ~ **about** or **of sb/sth** saber de algn/algo; **to get to** ~ **sth** enterarse de algo; **I** ~ **nothing about it** no sé nada de eso; **I don't** ~ **him** no lo or le conozco; **to** ~ **right from wrong** saber distinguir el bien del mal
know-all ['nəuɔːl] n (Brit pej) sabelotodo m/f inv, sabihondo(-a)
know-how ['nəuhau] n conocimientos mpl
knowing ['nəuɪŋ] adj (look etc) de complicidad
knowingly ['nəuɪŋlɪ] adv (purposely) a sabiendas; (smile, look) con complicidad
know-it-all ['nəuɪtɔːl] n (US) = **know-all**
knowledge ['nɔlɪdʒ] n (gen) conocimiento; (learning) saber m, conocimientos mpl; **to have no** ~ **of** no saber nada de; **with my** ~ con mis conocimientos, sabiéndolo; **to (the best of) my** ~ a mi entender, que yo sepa; **not to my** ~ que yo sepa, no; **it is common** ~ **that** ... es del dominio público que ...; **it has come to my** ~ **that** ... me he enterado de que ...; **to have a working** ~ **of Spanish** defenderse con el español
knowledgeable ['nɔlɪdʒəbl] adj entendido, erudito

known [nəun] pp of **know** ▪ adj (thief, facts) conocido; (expert) reconocido
knuckle ['nʌkl] n nudillo
▶ **knuckle down** vi (col) ponerse a trabajar en serio
▶ **knuckle under** vi someterse
knuckleduster ['nʌkldʌstəʳ] n puño de hierro
KO abbr (= knock out) K.O. m ▪ vt (knock out) dejar K.O.
koala [kəu'ɑːlə] n (also: **koala bear**) koala m
kook [kuːk] n (US col) chiflado(-a) m(f), majareta m/f
Koran [kɔ'rɑːn] n Corán m
Korea [kə'rɪə] n Corea; **North/South** ~ Corea del Norte/Sur
Korean [kə'rɪən] adj, n coreano(-a) m(f)
kosher ['kəuʃəʳ] adj autorizado por la ley judía
Kosovan ['kɒsəvən], **Kosovar** ['kɒsəvɑːʳ] adj kosovar
Kosovo ['kɒsəvəu] n Kosovo m
kowtow ['kau'tau] vi: **to** ~ **to sb** humillarse ante algn
KS abbr (US) = **Kansas**
Kt abbr (Brit: = Knight) caballero de una orden
Kuala Lumpur ['kwɑːlə'lumpuəʳ] n Kuala Lumpur m
kudos ['kjuːdɔs] n gloria, prestigio
Kurd [kəːd] n kurdo(-a)
Kuwait [ku'weɪt] n Kuwait m
Kuwaiti [ku'weɪtɪ] adj, n Kuwaití m/f
kW abbr (= kilowatt) Kv
KY, Ky. abbr (US) = **Kentucky**

Ll

L, l [ɛl] n (letter) L, l f; **L for Lucy,** (US) **L for Love** L de Lorenzo

L abbr (on maps etc) = **lake; large;** (= left) izq.; (Brit Aut: = learner) L

l abbr = **litre**

LA n abbr (US: = Los Angeles) ▪ abbr (US) = **Louisiana**

La. abbr (US) = **Louisiana**

lab [læb] n abbr = **laboratory**

Lab. abbr (Canada) = **Labrador**

label ['leɪbl] n etiqueta; (brand: of record) sello (discográfico) ▪ vt poner una etiqueta a, etiquetar

labor ['leɪbəʳ] (US) = **labour**

laboratory [lə'bɔrətərɪ] n laboratorio

Labor Day n (US) día m de los trabajadores (primer lunes de septiembre)

laborious [lə'bɔːrɪəs] adj penoso

laboriously [lə'bɔːrɪəslɪ] adv penosamente

labor union n (US) sindicato

labor unrest n (US) conflictividad f laboral

Labour ['leɪbəʳ] n (Brit Pol: also: **the Labour Party**) el partido laborista, los laboristas

labour, labor (US) ['leɪbəʳ] n (task) trabajo; (also: **labour force**) mano f de obra; (workers) trabajadores mpl; (Med) (dolores mpl de) parto ▪ vi: **to ~ (at)** trabajar (en) ▪ vt insistir en; **hard ~** trabajos mpl forzados; **to be in ~** estar de parto

labour cost, labor cost (US) n costo de la mano de obra

labour dispute, labor dispute (US) n conflicto laboral

laboured, labored (US) ['leɪbəd] adj (breathing) fatigoso; (style) forzado, pesado

labourer, laborer (US) ['leɪbərəʳ] n peón m; (on farm) peón m, obrero; (day labourer) jornalero

labour force, labor force (US) n mano f de obra

labour-intensive, labor-intensive (US) [leɪbərɪn'tɛnsɪv] adj que necesita mucha mano de obra

labour relations, labor relations (US) npl relaciones fpl laborales

labour-saving, labor-saving (US) ['leɪbəseɪvɪŋ] adj que ahorra trabajo

laburnum [lə'bəːnəm] n codeso

labyrinth ['læbɪrɪnθ] n laberinto

lace [leɪs] n encaje m; (of shoe etc) cordón m ▪ vt (shoes: also: **lace up**) atarse; (drink: fortify with spirits) echar licor a

lacemaking ['leɪsmeɪkɪŋ] n obra de encaje

lacerate ['læsəreɪt] vt lacerar

laceration [læsə'reɪʃən] n laceración f

lace-up ['leɪsʌp] adj (shoes etc) con cordones

lack [læk] n (absence) falta, carencia; (scarcity) escasez f ▪ vt faltarle a algn, carecer de; **through** or **for ~ of** por falta de; **to be lacking** faltar, no haber

lackadaisical [lækə'deɪzɪkl] adj (careless) descuidado; (indifferent) indiferente

lackey ['lækɪ] n (also fig) lacayo

lacklustre, lackluster (US) ['læklʌstəʳ] adj (surface) deslustrado, deslucido; (style) inexpresivo; (eyes) apagado

laconic [lə'kɔnɪk] adj lacónico

lacquer ['lækəʳ] n laca; **hair ~** laca para el pelo

lacrosse [lə'krɔs] n lacrosse f

lacy ['leɪsɪ] adj (like lace) parecido al encaje

lad [læd] n muchacho, chico; (in stable etc) mozo

ladder ['lædəʳ] n escalera (de mano); (Brit: in tights) carrera ▪ vt (Brit: tights) hacer una carrera en

laden ['leɪdn] adj: **~ (with)** cargado (de); **fully ~** (truck, ship) cargado hasta el tope

ladle ['leɪdl] n cucharón m

lady ['leɪdɪ] n señora; (distinguished, noble) dama; **young ~** señorita; **the ladies' (room)** los servicios de señoras

ladybird ['leɪdɪbəːd], **ladybug** (US) ['leɪdɪbʌg] n mariquita

lady doctor n médica, doctora

lady-in-waiting ['leɪdɪɪn'weɪtɪŋ] n dama de honor

ladykiller ['leɪdɪkɪləʳ] n robacorazones m inv
ladylike ['leɪdɪlaɪk] adj fino
Ladyship ['leɪdɪʃɪp] n: **your ~** su Señoría
LAFTA n abbr (= Latin American Free Trade Association) ALALC f
lag [læg] vi (also: **lag behind**) retrasarse, quedarse atrás ▪ vt (pipes) revestir
lager ['lɑːgəʳ] n cerveza (rubia)
lager lout n (Brit col) gamberro borracho
lagging ['lægɪŋ] n revestimiento
lagoon [lə'guːn] n laguna
Lagos ['leɪgɔs] n Lagos m
laid [leɪd] pt, pp of **lay**
laid-back [leɪd'bæk] adj (col) tranquilo, relajado
laid up adj: **to be ~** (person) tener que guardar cama
lain [leɪn] pp of **lie**
lair [lɛəʳ] n guarida
laissez-faire [lɛseɪ'fɛəʳ] n laissez-faire m
laity ['leɪtɪ] n laicado
lake [leɪk] n lago
Lake District n (Brit): **the ~** la Región de los Lagos
lamb [læm] n cordero; (meat) carne f de cordero
lamb chop n chuleta de cordero
lambswool ['læmzwul] n lana de cordero
lame [leɪm] adj cojo, rengo (LAm); (weak) débil, poco convincente; **~ duck** (fig: person) inútil m/f; (: firm) empresa en quiebra
lamely ['leɪmlɪ] adv (fig) sin convicción
lament [lə'mɛnt] n lamento ▪ vt lamentarse de
lamentable ['læməntəbl] adj lamentable
lamentation [læmən'teɪʃən] n lamento
laminated ['læmɪneɪtɪd] adj laminado
lamp [læmp] n lámpara
lamplight ['læmplaɪt] n: **by ~** a la luz de la lámpara
lampoon [læm'puːn] vt satirizar
lamppost ['læmppəust] n (Brit) farola
lampshade ['læmpʃeɪd] n pantalla
lance [lɑːns] n lanza ▪ vt (Med) abrir con lanceta
lance corporal n (Brit) soldado de primera clase
lancet ['lɑːnsɪt] n (Med) lanceta
Lancs [læŋks] abbr (Brit) = **Lancashire**
land [lænd] n tierra; (country) país m; (piece of land) terreno; (estate) tierras fpl, finca; (Agr) campo ▪ vi (from ship) desembarcar; (Aviat) aterrizar; (fig: fall) caer ▪ vt (obtain) conseguir; (passengers, goods) desembarcar; **to go/travel by ~** ir/viajar por tierra; **to own ~** ser dueño de tierras; **to ~ on one's feet** caer de pie; (fig: to be lucky) salir bien parado

▶ **land up** vi: **to ~ up in/at** ir a parar a/en
landed ['lændɪd] adj: **~ gentry** terratenientes mpl
landfill site ['lændfɪl-] n vertedero
landing ['lændɪŋ] n desembarco; aterrizaje m; (of staircase) rellano
landing card n tarjeta de desembarque
landing craft n lancha de desembarco
landing gear n (Aviat) tren m de aterrizaje
landing stage n (Brit) desembarcadero
landing strip n pista de aterrizaje
landlady ['lændleɪdɪ] n (of boarding house) patrona; (owner) dueña
landlocked ['lændlɔkt] adj cercado de tierra
landlord ['lændlɔːd] n propietario; (of pub etc) patrón m
landlubber ['lændlʌbəʳ] n marinero de agua dulce
landmark ['lændmɑːk] n lugar m conocido; **to be a ~** (fig) hacer época
landowner ['lændəunəʳ] n terrateniente m/f
landscape ['lænskeɪp] n paisaje m
landscape architecture n arquitectura paisajista
landscaped ['lænskeɪpt] adj reformado artísticamente
landscape gardener n diseñador(-a) m(f) de paisajes
landscape gardening n jardinería paisajista
landscape painting n (Art) paisaje m
landslide ['lændslaɪd] n (Geo) corrimiento de tierras; (fig: Pol) victoria arrolladora
lane [leɪn] n (in country) camino; (in town) callejón m; (Aut) carril m; (in race) calle f; (for air or sea traffic) ruta; **shipping ~** ruta marina
language ['læŋgwɪdʒ] n lenguaje m; (national tongue) idioma m, lengua; **bad ~** palabrotas fpl
language laboratory n laboratorio de idiomas
language studies npl estudios mpl filológicos
languid ['læŋgwɪd] adj lánguido
languish ['læŋgwɪʃ] vi languidecer
languor ['læŋgəʳ] n languidez f
languorous ['læŋgərəs] adj lánguido
lank [læŋk] adj (hair) lacio
lanky ['læŋkɪ] adj larguirucho
lanolin, lanoline ['lænəlɪn] n lanolina
lantern ['læntn] n linterna, farol m
lanyard ['lænjed] n acollador m
Laos [laus] n Laos m
lap [læp] n (of track) vuelta; (of body): **to sit on sb's ~** sentarse en las rodillas de algn ▪ vt (also: **lap up**) beber a lengüetadas or con la lengua ▪ vi (waves) chapotear
▶ **lap up** vt beber a lengüetadas or con la lengua; (fig: compliments, attention) disfrutar; (: lies etc) tragarse

La Paz [læ'pæz] *n* La Paz
lapdog ['læpdɔg] *n* perro faldero
lapel [lə'pɛl] *n* solapa
Lapland ['læplænd] *n* Laponia
Laplander ['læplændə^r] *n* lapón(-ona) *m(f)*
lapse [læps] *n* (*fault*) error *m*, fallo; (*moral*) desliz *m* ■ *vi* (*expire*) caducar; (*morally*) cometer un desliz; (*time*) pasar, transcurrir; **to ~ into bad habits** volver a las andadas; **~ of time** lapso, período; **a ~ of memory** un lapsus de memoria
laptop ['læptɔp] *n* (*also*: **laptop computer**) (ordenador *m*) portátil *m*
larceny ['lɑ:sənı] *n* latrocinio
lard [lɑ:d] *n* manteca (de cerdo)
larder ['lɑ:də^r] *n* despensa
large [lɑ:dʒ] *adj* grande ■ *adv*: **by and ~** en general, en términos generales; **at ~** (*free*) en libertad; (*generally*) en general; **to make ~(r)** hacer mayor *or* más extenso; **a ~ number of people** una gran cantidad de personas; **on a ~ scale** a gran escala
largely ['lɑ:dʒlı] *adv* en gran parte
large-scale ['lɑ:dʒ'skeıl] *adj* (*map, drawing*) a gran escala; (*reforms, business activities*) importante
largesse [lɑ:'ʒɛs] *n* generosidad *f*
lark [lɑ:k] *n* (*bird*) alondra; (*joke*) broma
▶ **lark about** *vi* bromear, hacer el tonto
larva (*pl* **larvae**) ['lɑ:və, -i:] *n* larva
laryngitis [lærın'dʒaıtıs] *n* laringitis *f*
larynx ['lærıŋks] *n* laringe *f*
lasagne [lə'zænjə] *n* lasaña
lascivious [lə'sıvıəs] *adj* lascivo
laser ['leızə^r] *n* láser *m*
laser beam *n* rayo láser
laser printer *n* impresora láser
lash [læʃ] *n* latigazo; (*punishment*) azote *m*; (*also*: **eyelash**) pestaña ■ *vt* azotar; (*tie*) atar
▶ **lash down** *vt* sujetar con cuerdas ■ *vi* (*rain*) caer a trombas
▶ **lash out** *vi* (*col: spend*) gastar a la loca; **to ~ out at** *or* **against sb** (*fig*) lanzar invectivas contra algn
lashing ['læʃıŋ] *n* (*beating*) azotaina, flagelación *f*; **lashings of** (*col*) montones *mpl* de
lass [læs] *n* chica
lassitude ['læsıtju:d] *n* lasitud *f*
lasso [læ'su:] *n* lazo ■ *vt* coger con lazo
last [lɑ:st] *adj* (*gen*) último; (*final*) último, final ■ *adv* por último ■ *vi* (*endure*) durar; (*continue*) continuar, seguir; **~ night** anoche; **~ week** la semana pasada; **at ~** por fin; **~ but one** penúltimo; **~ time** la última vez; **it lasts (for) two hours** dura dos horas
last-ditch ['lɑ:st'dıtʃ] *adj* (*attempt*) de último recurso, último, desesperado

lasting ['lɑ:stıŋ] *adj* duradero
lastly ['lɑ:stlı] *adv* por último, finalmente
last-minute ['lɑ:stmınıt] *adj* de última hora
latch [lætʃ] *n* picaporte *m*, pestillo
▶ **latch on to** *vt fus* (*cling to: person*) pegarse a; (: *idea*) agarrarse de
latchkey ['lætʃki:] *n* llavín *m*
latchkey child *n* niño cuyos padres trabajan
late [leıt] *adj* (*not on time*) tarde, atrasado; (*towards end of period, life*) tardío; (*hour*) avanzado; (*deceased*) fallecido ■ *adv* tarde; (*behind time, schedule*) con retraso; **to be (10 minutes) ~** llegar con (10 minutos de) retraso; **to be ~ with** estar atrasado con; **~ delivery** entrega tardía; **~ in life** a una edad avanzada; **of ~** últimamente; **in ~ May** hacia fines de mayo; **the ~ Mr X** el difunto Sr. X; **to work ~** trabajar hasta tarde
latecomer ['leıtkʌmə^r] *n* recién llegado(-a)
lately ['leıtlı] *adv* últimamente
lateness ['leıtnıs] *n* (*of person*) demora; (*of event*) tardanza
latent ['leıtnt] *adj* latente; **~ defect** defecto latente
later ['leıtə^r] *adj* (*date etc*) posterior; (*version etc*) más reciente ■ *adv* más tarde, después; **~ on today** hoy más tarde
lateral ['lætərl] *adj* lateral
latest ['leıtıst] *adj* último; **at the ~** a más tardar
latex ['leıtɛks] *n* látex *m*
lathe [leıð] *n* torno
lather ['lɑ:ðə^r] *n* espuma (de jabón) ■ *vt* enjabonar
Latin ['lætın] *n* latín *m* ■ *adj* latino
Latin America *n* América Latina, Latinoamérica
Latin American *adj, n* latinoamericano(-a) *m(f)*
Latino [læ'ti:nəu] *adj, n* latino(-a) *m(f)*
latitude ['lætıtju:d] *n* latitud *f*; (*fig: freedom*) libertad *f*
latrine [lə'tri:n] *n* letrina
latter ['lætə^r] *adj* último; (*of two*) segundo ■ *n*: **the ~** el último, éste
latter-day ['lætədeı] *adj* moderno
latterly ['lætəlı] *adv* últimamente
lattice ['lætıs] *n* enrejado
lattice window *n* ventana enrejada *or* de celosía
lattice work *n* enrejado
Latvia ['lætvıə] *n* Letonia
Latvian ['lætvıən] *adj* letón(-ona) ■ *n* letón(-ona) *m(f)*; (*Ling*) letón *m*
laudable ['lɔ:dəbl] *adj* loable
laugh [lɑ:f] *n* risa; (*loud*) carcajada ■ *vi* reírse, reír; reírse a carcajadas

▶ **laugh at** *vt fus* reírse de
▶ **laugh off** *vt* tomar a risa
laughable ['lɑːfəbl] *adj* ridículo
laughing ['lɑːfɪŋ] *adj* risueño ■ *n*: **it's no ~ matter** no es cosa de risa
laughing gas *n* gas *m* hilarante
laughing stock *n*: **to be the ~ of the town** ser el hazmerreír de la ciudad
laughter ['lɑːftəʳ] *n* risa
launch [lɔːntʃ] *n* (*boat*) lancha; *see also* **launching** ■ *vt* (*ship*) botar; (*rocket, plan*) lanzar
▶ **launch forth** *vi*: **to ~ forth (into)** lanzarse a *or* en, emprender
▶ **launch out** *vi* = **launch forth**
launching ['lɔːntʃɪŋ] *n* (*of rocket etc*) lanzamiento; (*inauguration*) estreno
launching pad, launch pad *n* plataforma de lanzamiento
launder ['lɔːndəʳ] *vt* lavar
Launderette® [lɔːn'drɛt], **Laundromat**® (*US*) ['lɔːndrəmæt] *n* lavandería (automática)
laundry ['lɔːndrɪ] *n* lavandería; (*clothes*) ropa sucia; **to do the ~** hacer la colada
laureate ['lɔːrɪət] *adj see* **poet**
laurel ['lɔrl] *n* laurel *m*; **to rest on one's laurels** dormirse en *or* sobre los laureles
lava ['lɑːvə] *n* lava
lavatory ['lævətərɪ] *n* wáter *m*; **lavatories** *npl* servicios *mpl*, aseos *mpl*, sanitarios *mpl* (*LAm*)
lavatory paper *n* papel *m* higiénico
lavender ['lævəndəʳ] *n* lavanda
lavish ['lævɪʃ] *adj* abundante; (*giving freely*): **~ with** pródigo en ■ *vt*: **to ~ sth on sb** colmar a algn de algo
lavishly ['lævɪʃlɪ] *adv* (*give, spend*) generosamente; (*furnished*) lujosamente
law [lɔː] *n* ley *f*; (*study*) derecho; (*of game*) regla; **against the ~** contra la ley; **to study ~** estudiar derecho; **to go to ~** recurrir a la justicia
law-abiding ['lɔːəbaɪdɪŋ] *adj* respetuoso con la ley
law and order *n* orden *m* público
lawbreaker ['lɔːbreɪkəʳ] *n* infractor(a) *m(f)* de la ley
law court *n* tribunal *m* (de justicia)
lawful ['lɔːful] *adj* legítimo, lícito
lawfully ['lɔːfulɪ] *adv* legalmente
lawless ['lɔːlɪs] *adj* (*act*) ilegal; (*person*) rebelde; (*country*) ingobernable
Law Lord *n* (*Brit*) *miembro de la Cámara de los Lores y del más alto tribunal de apelación*
lawmaker ['lɔːmeɪkəʳ] *n* legislador(a) *m(f)*
lawn [lɔːn] *n* césped *m*

lawnmower ['lɔːnməuəʳ] *n* cortacésped *m*
lawn tennis *n* tenis *m* sobre hierba
law school *n* (*US*) facultad *f* de derecho
law student *n* estudiante *m/f* de derecho
lawsuit ['lɔːsuːt] *n* pleito; **to bring a ~ against** entablar un pleito contra
lawyer ['lɔːjəʳ] *n* abogado(-a); (*for sales, wills etc*) notario(-a)
lax [læks] *adj* (*discipline*) relajado; (*person*) negligente
laxative ['læksətɪv] *n* laxante *m*
laxity ['læksɪtɪ] *n* flojedad *f*; (*moral*) relajamiento; (*negligence*) negligencia
lay [leɪ] *pt of* **lie** ■ *adj* laico; (*not expert*) lego ■ *vt* (*pt, pp* **laid** [leɪd]) (*place*) colocar; (*eggs, table*) poner; (*trap*) tender; **to ~ the facts/one's proposals before sb** presentar los hechos/sus propuestas a algn
▶ **lay aside, lay by** *vt* dejar a un lado
▶ **lay down** *vt* (*pen etc*) dejar; (*arms*) rendir; (*policy*) trazar; **to ~ down the law** imponer las normas
▶ **lay in** *vt* abastecerse de
▶ **lay into** *vt fus* (*col: attack, scold*) arremeter contra
▶ **lay off** *vt* (*workers*) despedir
▶ **lay on** *vt* (*water, gas*) instalar; (*meal, facilities*) proveer
▶ **lay out** *vt* (*plan*) trazar; (*display*) exponer; (*spend*) gastar
▶ **lay up** *vt* (*store*) guardar; (*ship*) desarmar; (*illness*) obligar a guardar cama
layabout ['leɪəbaut] *n* vago(-a)
lay-by ['leɪbaɪ] *n* (*Brit Aut*) apartadero
lay days *npl* días *mpl* de inactividad
layer ['leɪəʳ] *n* capa
layette [leɪ'ɛt] *n* ajuar *m* (de niño)
layman ['leɪmən] *n* lego
lay-off ['leɪɔf] *n* despido, paro forzoso
layout ['leɪaut] *n* (*design*) plan *m*, trazado; (*disposition*) disposición *f*; (*Press*) composición *f*
laze [leɪz] *vi* no hacer nada; (*pej*) holgazanear
lazily ['leɪzɪlɪ] *adv* perezosamente
laziness ['leɪzɪnɪs] *n* pereza
lazy ['leɪzɪ] *adj* perezoso, vago, flojo (*LAm*)
LB *abbr* (*Canada*) = **Labrador**
lb. *abbr* = **pound** (*weight*)
lbw *abbr* (*Cricket*) = **leg before wicket**
LC *n abbr* (*US*) = **Library of Congress**
lc *abbr* (*Typ*: = *lower case*) min
L/C *abbr* = **letter of credit**
LCD *n abbr see* **liquid crystal display**
Ld *abbr* (*Brit*: = *Lord*) título de nobleza
LDS *n abbr* (= *Licentiate in Dental Surgery*) diploma universitario; (= *Latter-day Saints*) Iglesia de Jesucristo de los Santos del último día

LEA n abbr (Brit: = local education authority) organismo local encargado de la enseñanza

lead [li:d] (pt, pp **led** [lɛd]) n (front position) delantera; (distance, time ahead) ventaja; (clue) pista; (Elec) cable m; (for dog) correa; (Theat) papel m principal; (metal) plomo; (in pencil) mina ■ vt conducir; (life) llevar; (be leader of) dirigir; (Sport) ir en cabeza de; (orchestra: Brit) ser el primer violín en; (: US) dirigir ■ vi ir primero; **to be in the ~** (Sport) llevar la delantera; (fig) ir a la cabeza; **to take the ~** (Sport) tomar la delantera; (fig) tomar la iniciativa; **to ~ sb to believe that ...** hacer creer a algn que ...; **to ~ sb to do sth** llevar a algn a hacer algo

▶ **lead astray** vt llevar por mal camino
▶ **lead away** vt llevar
▶ **lead back** vt hacer volver
▶ **lead off** vt llevar ■ vi (in game) abrir
▶ **lead on** vt (tease) engañar; **to ~ sb on to** (induce) incitar a algn a
▶ **lead to** vt fus producir, provocar
▶ **lead up to** vt fus conducir a

leaded ['lɛdɪd] adj: **~ windows** ventanas fpl emplomadas

leaden ['lɛdn] adj (sky, sea) plomizo; (heavy: footsteps) pesado

leader ['li:dər] n jefe(-a) m(f), líder m; (of union etc) dirigente m/f; (guide) guía m/f; (of newspaper) editorial m; **they are leaders in their field** (fig) llevan la delantera en su especialidad

leadership ['li:dəʃɪp] n dirección f; **qualities of ~** iniciativa sg; **under the ~ of ...** bajo la dirección de ..., al mando de ...

lead-free ['lɛdfri:] adj sin plomo

leading ['li:dɪŋ] adj (main) principal; (outstanding) destacado; (first) primero; (front) delantero; **a ~ question** una pregunta tendenciosa

leading lady n (Theat) primera actriz f

leading light n (fig: person) figura principal

leading man n (Theat) primer actor m

leading role n papel m principal

lead pencil n lápiz m

lead poisoning n envenenamiento plúmbico

lead time n (Comm) plazo de entrega

lead-up ['li:dʌp] n: **in the ~ to the election** cuando falta etc poco para las elecciones

lead weight n peso de plomo

leaf (pl **leaves**) [li:f, li:vz] n hoja; **to turn over a new ~** (fig) volver la hoja, hacer borrón y cuenta nueva; **to take a ~ out of sb's book** (fig) seguir el ejemplo de algn
▶ **leaf through** vt fus (book) hojear

leaflet ['li:flɪt] n folleto

leafy ['li:fɪ] adj frondoso

league [li:g] n sociedad f; (Football) liga; **to be in ~ with** estar confabulado con

league table n clasificación f

leak [li:k] n (of liquid, gas) escape m, fuga; (in pipe) agujero; (in roof) gotera; (fig: of information, in security) filtración f ■ vi (ship) hacer agua; (shoes) tener un agujero; (pipe) tener un escape; (roof) tener goteras; (also: **leak out**: liquid, gas) escaparse, salirse; (fig: news) trascender, divulgarse ■ vt (gen) dejar escapar; (fig: information) filtrar

leakage ['li:kɪdʒ] n (of water, gas etc) escape m, fuga

leaky ['li:kɪ] adj (roof) con goteras; (bucket, shoe) con agujeros; (pipe) con un escape; (boat) que hace agua

lean [li:n] (pt, pp **leaned** or **leant**) adj (thin) flaco; (meat) magro ■ vt: **to ~ sth on sth** apoyar algo en algo ■ vi (slope) inclinarse; (rest): **to ~ against** apoyarse contra; **to ~ on** apoyarse en
▶ **lean back** vi inclinarse hacia atrás
▶ **lean forward** vi inclinarse hacia adelante
▶ **lean out** vi: **to ~ out (of)** asomarse (a)
▶ **lean over** vi inclinarse

leaning ['li:nɪŋ] adj inclinado ■ n: **~ (towards)** inclinación f (hacia); **the L~ Tower of Pisa** la Torre Inclinada de Pisa

leant [lɛnt] pt, pp of **lean**

lean-to ['li:ntu:] n (roof) tejado de una sola agua; (building) cobertizo

leap [li:p] n salto ■ vi (pt, pp **leaped** or **leapt**) [lɛpt] saltar; **to ~ at an offer** apresurarse a aceptar una oferta
▶ **leap up** vi (person) saltar

leapfrog ['li:pfrɒg] n pídola ■ vi: **to ~ over sb/sth** saltar por encima de algn/algo

leapt [lɛpt] pt, pp of **leap**

leap year n año bisiesto

learn (pt, pp **learned** or **learnt**) [lə:n, -t] vt (gen) aprender; (come to know of) enterarse de ■ vi aprender; **to ~ how to do sth** aprender a hacer algo; **to ~ that ...** enterarse or informarse de que ...; **to ~ about sth** (Scol) aprender algo; (hear) enterarse or informarse de algo; **we were sorry to ~ that ...** nos dio tristeza saber que ...

learned ['lə:nɪd] adj erudito

learner ['lə:nər] n principiante m/f; (Brit: also: **learner driver**) conductor(a) m(f) en prácticas; see also **L-plates**

learning ['lə:nɪŋ] n saber m, conocimientos mpl

learnt [lə:nt] pp of **learn**

lease [li:s] n arriendo ■ vt arrendar; **on ~** en arriendo
▶ **lease back** vt subarrendar

leaseback ['li:sbæk] n subarriendo
leasehold ['li:shəuld] n (contract) derechos
mpl de arrendamiento ■ adj arrendado
leash [li:ʃ] n correa
least [li:st] adj (slightest) menor, más
pequeño; (smallest amount of) mínimo ■ adv
menos ■ n: **the ~** lo menos; **the ~ expensive
car** el coche menos caro; **at ~** por lo menos,
al menos; **not in the ~** en absoluto
leather ['lɛðəʳ] n cuero ■ cpd: **~ goods**
artículos mpl de cuero or piel
leathery ['lɛðərɪ] adj (skin) curtido
leave [li:v] (pt, pp **left**) vt dejar; (go away
from) abandonar ■ vi irse; (train) salir ■ n
permiso; **to ~ school** dejar la escuela or
el colegio; **~ it to me!** ¡yo me encargo!;
he's already left for the airport ya se ha
marchado al aeropuerto; **to be left** quedar,
sobrar; **there's some milk left over** sobra
or queda algo de leche; **on ~** de permiso; **to
take one's ~ of** despedirse de
▶ **leave behind** vt (on purpose) dejar (atrás);
(accidentally) olvidar
▶ **leave off** vt (lid) no poner; (switch) no
encender; (col: stop): **to ~ off doing sth** dejar
de hacer algo
▶ **leave on** vt (lid) dejar puesto; (light, fire,
cooker) dejar encendido
▶ **leave out** vt omitir
▶ **leave over** vt (postpone) dejar, aplazar
leave of absence n excedencia
leaves [li:vz] pl of **leaf**
leavetaking ['li:vteɪkɪŋ] n despedida
Lebanon ['lɛbənən] n: **the ~** el Líbano
lecherous ['lɛtʃərəs] adj lascivo
lectern ['lɛktə:n] n atril m
lecture ['lɛktʃəʳ] n conferencia; (Scol) clase
f ■ vi dar clase(s) ■ vt (scold) sermonear;
(reprove) echar una reprimenda a; **to give
a ~ on** dar una conferencia sobre
lecture hall n sala de conferencias; (Univ)
aula
lecturer ['lɛktʃərəʳ] n conferenciante m/f;
(Brit: at university) profesor(a) m(f)
lecture theatre n = **lecture hall**
LED n abbr (Elec: = light-emitting diode) LED m
led [lɛd] pt, pp of **lead**
ledge [lɛdʒ] n (of window, on wall) repisa,
reborde m; (of mountain) saliente m
ledger ['lɛdʒəʳ] n libro mayor
lee [li:] n sotavento; **in the ~ of** al abrigo de
leech [li:tʃ] n sanguijuela
leek [li:k] n puerro
leer [lɪəʳ] vi: **to ~ at sb** mirar de manera
lasciva a algn
leeway ['li:weɪ] n (fig): **to have some ~** tener
cierta libertad de acción

left [lɛft] pt, pp of **leave** ■ adj izquierdo ■ n
izquierda ■ adv a la izquierda; **on** or **to the ~**
a la izquierda; **the L~** (Pol) la izquierda
left-click ['lɛftklɪk] vi clicar con el botón
izquierdo del ratón ■ vt: **to ~ an icon** clicar
en un icono con el botón izquierdo del ratón
left-hand drive ['lɛfthænd-] n conducción f
por la izquierda
left-handed [lɛft'hændɪd] adj zurdo;
~ scissors tijeras fpl zurdas or para zurdos
left-hand side ['lɛfthænd-] n izquierda
leftie ['lɛftɪ] n = **lefty**
leftist ['lɛftɪst] adj (Pol) izquierdista
left-luggage [lɛft'lʌgɪdʒ], **left-luggage
office** n (Brit) consigna
left-overs ['lɛftəuvəz] npl sobras fpl
left-wing [lɛft'wɪŋ] adj (Pol) de izquierda(s),
izquierdista
left-winger ['lɛft'wɪŋəʳ] n (Pol) izquierdista
m/f
lefty ['lɛftɪ] n (col: Pol) rojillo(-a)
leg [lɛg] n pierna; (of animal, chair) pata; (Culin:
of meat) pierna; (of journey) etapa; **lst/2nd ~**
(Sport) partido de ida/de vuelta; **to pull sb's ~**
tomar el pelo a algn; **to stretch one's legs**
dar una vuelta
legacy ['lɛgəsɪ] n herencia; (fig) herencia,
legado
legal ['li:gl] adj (permitted by law) lícito; (of law)
legal; (inquiry etc) jurídico; **to take ~ action** or
proceedings against sb entablar or levantar
un pleito contra algn
legal adviser n asesor(a) m(f) jurídico(-a)
legal holiday n (US) fiesta oficial
legality [lɪ'gælɪtɪ] n legalidad f
legalize ['li:gəlaɪz] vt legalizar
legally ['li:gəlɪ] adv legalmente; **~ binding**
con fuerza legal
legal tender n moneda de curso legal
legend ['lɛdʒənd] n leyenda
legendary ['lɛdʒəndərɪ] adj legendario
-legged ['lɛgɪd] suff: **two~** (table etc) de dos
patas
leggings ['lɛgɪŋz] npl mallas fpl, leggins mpl
leggy ['lɛgɪ] adj de piernas largas
legibility [lɛdʒɪ'bɪlɪtɪ] n legibilidad f
legible ['lɛdʒəbl] adj legible
legibly ['lɛdʒəblɪ] adv legiblemente
legion ['li:dʒən] n legión f
legionnaire [li:dʒə'nɛəʳ] n legionario
legionnaire's disease n enfermedad f del
legionario
legislation [lɛdʒɪs'leɪʃən] n legislación f;
a piece of ~ (bill) un proyecto de ley; (act)
una ley
legislative ['lɛdʒɪslətɪv] adj legislativo
legislator ['lɛdʒɪsleɪtəʳ] n legislador(a) m(f)

legislature ['lɛdʒɪslətʃəʳ] n cuerpo legislativo
legitimacy [lɪ'dʒɪtɪməsɪ] n legitimidad f
legitimate [lɪ'dʒɪtɪmət] adj legítimo
legitimize [lɪ'dʒɪtɪmaɪz] vt legitimar
legless ['lɛglɪs] adj (Brit col) mamado
leg-room ['lɛgruːm] n espacio para las piernas
Leics abbr (Brit) = **Leicestershire**
leisure ['lɛʒəʳ] n ocio, tiempo libre; **at ~** con tranquilidad
leisure centre n centro recreativo
leisurely ['lɛʒəlɪ] adj sin prisa; lento
leisure suit n conjunto tipo chandal
lemon ['lɛmən] n limón m
lemonade [lɛmə'neɪd] n (fruit juice) limonada; (fizzy) gaseosa
lemon cheese, lemon curd n queso de limón
lemon juice n zumo de limón
lemon tea n té m con limón
lend [lɛnd] (pt, pp **lent** [lɛnt]) vt: **to ~ sth to sb** prestar algo a algn
lender ['lɛndəʳ] n prestamista m/f
lending library ['lɛndɪŋ-] n biblioteca de préstamo
length [lɛŋθ] n (size) largo, longitud f; (section: of road, pipe) tramo; (: of rope etc) largo; **at ~** (at last) por fin, finalmente; (lengthily) largamente; **it is two metres in ~** tiene dos metros de largo; **what ~ is it?** ¿cuánto tiene de largo?; **to fall full ~** caer de bruces; **to go to any ~(s) to do sth** ser capaz de hacer cualquier cosa para hacer algo
lengthen ['lɛŋθn] vt alargar ▪ vi alargarse
lengthways ['lɛŋθweɪz] adv a lo largo
lengthy ['lɛŋθɪ] adj largo, extenso; (meeting) prolongado
lenient ['liːnɪənt] adj indulgente
lens [lɛnz] n (of spectacles) lente f; (of camera) objetivo
Lent [lɛnt] n Cuaresma
lent [lɛnt] pt, pp of **lend**
lentil ['lɛntl] n lenteja
Leo ['liːəu] n Leo
leopard ['lɛpəd] n leopardo
leotard ['liːətɑːd] n leotardo
leper ['lɛpəʳ] n leproso(-a)
leper colony n colonia de leprosos
leprosy ['lɛprəsɪ] n lepra
lesbian ['lɛzbɪən] adj lesbiano ▪ n lesbiana
lesion ['liːʒən] n (Med) lesión f
Lesotho [lɪ'suːtuː] n Lesotho
less [lɛs] adj (in size, degree etc) menor; (in quantity) menos ▪ pron, adv menos; **~ than half** menos de la mitad; **~ than £1/a kilo/3 metres** menos de una libra/un kilo/3 metros; **~ than ever** menos que nunca; **~ 5%**

menos el cinco por ciento; **~ and ~** cada vez menos; **the ~ he works ...** cuanto menos trabaja ...
lessee [lɛ'siː] n inquilino(-a), arrendatario(-a)
lessen ['lɛsn] vi disminuir, reducirse ▪ vt disminuir, reducir
lesser ['lɛsəʳ] adj menor; **to a ~ extent or degree** en menor grado
lesson ['lɛsn] n clase f; **a maths ~** una clase de matemáticas; **to give lessons in** dar clases de; **it taught him a ~** (fig) le sirvió de lección
lessor ['lɛsɔːʳ, lɛ'sɔːʳ] n arrendador(a) m(f)
lest [lɛst] conj: **~ it happen** para que no pase
let (pt, pp **let**) [lɛt] vt (allow) dejar, permitir; (Brit: lease) alquilar; **to ~ sb do sth** dejar que algn haga algo; **to ~ sb have sth** dar algo a algn; **to ~ sb know sth** comunicar algo a algn; **~'s go** ¡vamos!; **~ him come** que venga; **"to ~"** "se alquila"
▶ **let down** vt (lower) bajar; (dress) alargar; (tyre) desinflar; (hair) soltar; (disappoint) defraudar
▶ **let go** vi soltar; (fig) dejarse ir ▪ vt soltar
▶ **let in** vt dejar entrar; (visitor etc) hacer pasar; **what have you ~ yourself in for?** ¿en qué te has metido?
▶ **let off** vt dejar escapar; (firework etc) disparar; (bomb) accionar; (passenger) dejar, bajar; **to ~ off steam** (fig, col) desahogarse, desfogarse
▶ **let on** vi: **to ~ on that ...** revelar que ...
▶ **let out** vt dejar salir; (dress) ensanchar; (rent out) alquilar
▶ **let up** vi disminuir; (rain etc) amainar
let-down ['lɛtdaun] n (disappointment) decepción f
lethal ['liːθl] adj (weapon) mortífero; (poison, wound) mortal
lethargic [lɛ'θɑːdʒɪk] adj aletargado
lethargy ['lɛθədʒɪ] n letargo
letter ['lɛtəʳ] n (of alphabet) letra; (correspondence) carta; **letters** npl (literature, learning) letras fpl; **small/capital ~** minúscula/mayúscula; **covering ~** carta adjunta
letter bomb n carta-bomba
letterbox ['lɛtəbɔks] n (Brit) buzón m
letterhead ['lɛtəhɛd] n membrete m, encabezamiento
lettering ['lɛtərɪŋ] n letras fpl
letter of credit n carta de crédito; **documentary ~** carta de crédito documentaria; **irrevocable ~** carta de crédito irrevocable
letter-opener ['lɛtərəupnəʳ] n abrecartas m inv

letterpress ['lɛtəprɛs] n (method) prensa de copiar; (printed page) impresión f tipográfica
letter quality n calidad f de correspondencia
letters patent npl letra sg de patente
lettuce ['lɛtɪs] n lechuga
let-up ['lɛtʌp] n descanso, tregua
leukaemia, (US) **leukemia** [luː'kiːmɪə] n leucemia
level ['lɛvl] adj (flat) llano; (flattened) nivelado; (uniform) igual ■ adv a nivel ■ n nivel m ■ vt nivelar, allanar; (gun) apuntar; (accusation): **to ~ (against)** levantar (contra) ■ vi (col): **to ~ with sb** ser franco con algn; **to be ~ with** estar a nivel de; **a ~ spoonful** (Culin) una cucharada rasa; **to draw ~ with** (team) igualar; (runner, car) alcanzar a; **O levels** npl (Brit: formerly) ≈ bachillerato sg elemental, octavo sg de Básica; **on the ~** (fig: honest) en serio; **talks at ministerial ~** charlas fpl a nivel ministerial
▶ **level off** or **out** vi (prices etc) estabilizarse; (ground) nivelarse; (aircraft) ponerse en una trayectoria horizontal
level crossing n (Brit) paso a nivel
level-headed [lɛvl'hɛdɪd] adj sensato
levelling, leveling (US) ['lɛvlɪŋ] adj (process, effect) de nivelación ■ n igualación f, allanamiento
level playing field n situación f de igualdad; **to compete on a ~** competir en igualdad de condiciones
lever ['liːvəʳ] n palanca ■ vt: **to ~ up** levantar con palanca
leverage ['liːvərɪdʒ] n (fig: influence) influencia
levity ['lɛvɪtɪ] n frivolidad f, informalidad f
levy ['lɛvɪ] n impuesto ■ vt exigir, recaudar
lewd [luːd] adj lascivo, obsceno, colorado (LAm)
lexicographer [lɛksɪ'kɔgrəfəʳ] n lexicógrafo(-a) m(f)
lexicography [lɛksɪ'kɔgrəfɪ] n lexicografía
LGV n abbr (= Large Goods Vehicle) vehículo pesado
LI abbr (US) = **Long Island**
liabilities [laɪə'bɪlətɪz] npl obligaciones fpl; pasivo sg
liability [laɪə'bɪlətɪ] n responsabilidad f; (handicap) desventaja
liable ['laɪəbl] adj (subject): **~ to** sujeto a; (responsible): **~ for** responsable de; (likely): **~ to do** propenso a hacer; **to be ~ to a fine** exponerse a una multa
liaise [liː'eɪz] vi: **to ~ (with)** colaborar (con); **to ~ with sb** mantener informado a algn

liaison [liː'eɪzɔn] n (coordination) enlace m; (affair) relación f
liar ['laɪəʳ] n mentiroso(-a)
libel ['laɪbl] n calumnia ■ vt calumniar
libellous ['laɪbləs] adj difamatorio, calumnioso
liberal ['lɪbərl] adj (gen) liberal; (generous): **~ with** generoso con ■ n: **L~** (Pol) liberal m/f
Liberal Democrat n (Brit) demócrata m/f liberal
liberality [lɪbə'rælɪtɪ] n (generosity) liberalidad f, generosidad f
liberalize ['lɪbərəlaɪz] vt liberalizar
liberally ['lɪbərəlɪ] adv liberalmente
liberal-minded ['lɪbərl'maɪndɪd] adj de miras anchas, liberal
liberate ['lɪbəreɪt] vt liberar
liberation [lɪbə'reɪʃən] n liberación f
liberation theology n teología de la liberación
Liberia [laɪ'bɪərɪə] n Liberia
Liberian [laɪ'bɪərɪən] adj, n liberiano(-a) m(f)
liberty ['lɪbətɪ] n libertad f; **to be at ~ to do** estar libre para hacer; **to take the ~ of doing sth** tomarse la libertad de hacer algo
libido [lɪ'biːdəu] n libido
Libra ['liːbrə] n Libra
librarian [laɪ'brɛərɪən] n bibliotecario(-a)
library ['laɪbrərɪ] n biblioteca
library book n libro de la biblioteca
libretto [lɪ'brɛtəu] n libreto
Libya ['lɪbɪə] n Libia
Libyan ['lɪbɪən] adj, n libio(-a) m(f)
lice [laɪs] pl of **louse**
licence, license (US) ['laɪsns] n licencia; (permit) permiso; (also: **driving licence,** (US) **driver's license**) carnet m de conducir; (excessive freedom) libertad f; **import ~** licencia or permiso de importación; **produced under ~** elaborado bajo licencia
licence number n (número de) matrícula
licence plate n (placa de) matrícula
license ['laɪsns] (US) = **licence**; vt autorizar, dar permiso a; (car) sacar la matrícula de or (LAm) la patente de
licensed ['laɪsnst] adj (for alcohol) autorizado para vender bebidas alcohólicas
licensed trade n comercio or negocio autorizado
licensee [laɪsən'siː] n (in a pub) concesionario(-a), dueño(-a) de un bar
licentious [laɪ'sɛnʃəs] adj licencioso
lichen ['laɪkən] n liquen m
lick [lɪk] vt lamer; (col: defeat) dar una paliza a ■ n lamedura; **a ~ of paint** una mano de pintura
licorice ['lɪkərɪs] n = **liquorice**

lid | lightness

lid [lɪd] n (of box, case) tapa; (of pan) cobertera; **to take the ~ off sth** (fig) exponer algo a la luz pública

lido ['laɪdəu] n (Brit) piscina, alberca (LAm)

lie [laɪ] n mentira ■ vi mentir; (pt **lay**, pp **lain**) [leɪ, leɪn] (rest) estar echado, estar acostado; (of object: be situated) estar, encontrarse; **to tell lies** mentir; **to ~ low** (fig) mantenerse a escondidas
▸ **lie about, lie around** vi (things) estar tirado; (Brit: people) estar acostado or tumbado
▸ **lie back** vi recostarse
▸ **lie down** vi echarse, tumbarse
▸ **lie up** vi (hide) esconderse

Liechtenstein ['lɪktənstaɪn] n Liechtenstein m

lie detector n detector m de mentiras

lie-down ['laɪdaun] n (Brit): **to have a ~** echarse (una siesta)

lie-in ['laɪɪn] n (Brit): **to have a ~** quedarse en la cama

lieu [luː]: **in ~ of** prep en lugar de

Lieut. abbr = **lieutenant**

lieutenant [lɛf'tɛnənt, (US) luː'tɛnənt] n (Mil) teniente m

lieutenant colonel n teniente m coronel

life (pl **lives**) [laɪf, laɪvz] n vida; (of licence etc) vigencia; **to be sent to prison for ~** ser condenado a cadena perpetua; **country/city ~** la vida en el campo/en la ciudad; **true to ~** fiel a la realidad; **to paint from ~** pintar del natural; **to put** or **breathe new ~ into** (person) reanimar; (project, area etc) infundir nueva vida a

life assurance n (Brit) seguro de vida

lifebelt ['laɪfbɛlt] n (Brit) cinturón m salvavidas

lifeblood ['laɪfblʌd] n (fig) alma, nervio

lifeboat ['laɪfbəut] n lancha de socorro

life-buoy ['laɪfbɔɪ] n boya or guindola salvavidas

life coach n profesional encargado de mejorar la situación laboral y personal de sus clientes

life expectancy n esperanza de vida

lifeguard ['laɪfgɑːd] n vigilante m/f

life imprisonment n cadena perpetua

life insurance n = **life assurance**

life jacket n chaleco salvavidas

lifeless ['laɪflɪs] adj sin vida; (dull) soso

lifelike ['laɪflaɪk] adj natural

lifeline ['laɪflaɪn] n (fig) cordón m umbilical

lifelong ['laɪflɔŋ] adj de toda la vida

life preserver n (US) = **lifebelt**

lifer ['laɪfər] n (col) condenado(-a) m(f) a cadena perpetua

life-saver ['laɪfseɪvər] n socorrista m/f

life sentence n cadena perpetua

life-sized ['laɪfsaɪzd] adj de tamaño natural

life span n vida

lifestyle ['laɪfstaɪl] n estilo de vida

life support system n (Med) sistema m de respiración asistida

lifetime ['laɪftaɪm] n: **in his ~** durante su vida; **once in a ~** una vez en la vida; **the chance of a ~** una oportunidad única

lift [lɪft] vt levantar; (copy) plagiar ■ vi (fog) disiparse ■ n (Brit: elevator) ascensor m, elevador m (LAm); **to give sb a ~** (Brit) llevar a algn en coche
▸ **lift off** vt levantar, quitar ■ vi (rocket, helicopter) despegar
▸ **lift out** vt sacar; (troops, evacuees etc) evacuar
▸ **lift up** vt levantar

lift-off ['lɪftɔf] n despegue m

ligament ['lɪgəmənt] n ligamento

light [laɪt] n luz f; (flame) lumbre f; (lamp) luz f, lámpara; (daylight) luz f del día; (headlight) faro; (rear light) luz f trasera; (for cigarette etc): **have you got a ~?** ¿tienes fuego? ■ vt (pt, pp **lighted**, pt, pp **lit** [lɪt]) (candle, cigarette, fire) encender; (room) alumbrar ■ adj (colour) claro ligero, liviano (LAm); (room) alumbrado ■ adv (travel) con poco equipaje; **to turn the ~ on/off** encender/apagar la luz; **in the ~ of** a la luz de; **to come to ~** salir a la luz; **to cast** or **shed** or **throw ~ on** arrojar luz sobre; **to make ~ of sth** (fig) no dar importancia a algo
▸ **light up** vi (smoke) encender un cigarrillo; (face) iluminarse ■ vt (illuminate) iluminar, alumbrar

light bulb n bombilla, bombillo (LAm), foco (LAm)

lighten ['laɪtn] vi (grow light) clarear ■ vt (give light to) iluminar; (make lighter) aclarar; (make less heavy) aligerar

lighter ['laɪtər] n (also: **cigarette lighter**) encendedor m (LAm), mechero

light-fingered [laɪt'fɪŋgəd] adj de manos largas

light-headed [laɪt'hɛdɪd] adj (dizzy) mareado; (excited) exaltado; (by nature) atolondrado

light-hearted [laɪt'hɑːtɪd] adj alegre

lighthouse ['laɪthaus] n faro

lighting ['laɪtɪŋ] n (act) iluminación f; (system) alumbrado

lighting-up time [laɪtɪŋ'ʌp-] n (Brit) hora de encendido del alumbrado

lightly ['laɪtlɪ] adv ligeramente; (not seriously) con poca seriedad; **to get off ~** ser castigado con poca severidad

light meter n (Phot) fotómetro

lightness ['laɪtnɪs] n claridad f; (in weight) ligereza

lightning ['laɪtnɪŋ] n relámpago, rayo
lightning conductor, lightning rod (US) n
pararrayos m inv
lightning strike n huelga relámpago
lightweight ['laɪtweɪt] adj (suit) ligero
■ n (Boxing) peso ligero
light year n año luz
like [laɪk] vt (person) querer a; (thing):
I ~ **swimming/apples** me gusta nadar/me
gustan las manzanas ■ prep como ■ adj
parecido, semejante ■ n: **did you ever see
the ~ (of it)?** ¿has visto cosa igual?; **his likes
and dislikes** sus gustos y aversiones; **the
likes of him** personas como él; **I would ~,
I'd ~** me gustaría; (for purchase) quisiera;
would you ~ a coffee? ¿te apetece un café?;
to be or **look ~ sb/sth** parecerse a algn/algo;
that's just ~ him es muy de él, es típico de él;
do it ~ this hazlo así; **it is nothing ~** ... no
tiene parecido alguno con ...; **what's he ~?**
¿cómo es (él)?; **what's the weather ~?** ¿qué
tiempo hace?; **something ~ that** algo así or
por el estilo; **I feel ~ a drink** me apetece algo
de beber; **if you ~** si quieres
likeable ['laɪkəbl] adj simpático, agradable
likelihood ['laɪklɪhud] n probabilidad f; **in
all ~** según todas las probabilidades
likely ['laɪklɪ] adj probable, capaz (LAm); **he's
~ to leave** es probable or (LAm) capaz que se
vaya; **not ~!** ¡ni hablar!
like-minded [laɪk'maɪndɪd] adj de la misma
opinión
liken ['laɪkən] vt: **to ~ to** comparar con
likeness ['laɪknɪs] n (similarity) semejanza,
parecido
likewise ['laɪkwaɪz] adv igualmente
liking ['laɪkɪŋ] n: ~ **(for)** (person) cariño (a);
(thing) afición (a); **to take a ~ to sb** tomar
cariño a algn; **to be to sb's ~** ser del gusto
de algn
lilac ['laɪlək] n lila ■ adj (colour) de color lila
Lilo® ['laɪləu] n colchoneta inflable
lilt [lɪlt] n deje m
lilting ['lɪltɪŋ] adj melodioso
lily ['lɪlɪ] n lirio, azucena
lily of the valley n lirio de los valles
Lima ['liːmə] n Lima
limb [lɪm] n miembro; (of tree) rama; **to be
out on a ~** (fig) estar aislado
limber up ['lɪmbər-] vi (fig) entrenarse; (Sport)
hacer (ejercicios de) precalentamiento
limbo ['lɪmbəu] n: **to be in ~** (fig) quedar a la
expectativa
lime [laɪm] n (tree) limero; (fruit) lima; (Geo) cal f
lime juice n zumo (SP) or jugo de lima
limelight ['laɪmlaɪt] n: **to be in the ~** (fig) ser
el centro de atención

limerick ['lɪmərɪk] n quintilla humorística
limestone ['laɪmstəun] n piedra caliza
limit ['lɪmɪt] n límite m ■ vt limitar;
weight/speed ~ peso máximo/velocidad f
máxima; **within limits** entre límites
limitation [lɪmɪ'teɪʃən] n limitación f
limited ['lɪmɪtɪd] adj limitado; **to be ~ to**
limitarse a; ~ **edition** edición limitada
**limited company, limited liability
company** n (Brit) sociedad f anónima
limitless ['lɪmɪtlɪs] adj sin límites
limousine ['lɪməziːn] n limusina
limp [lɪmp] n: **to have a ~** tener cojera
■ vi cojear, renguear (LAm) ■ adj flojo
limpet ['lɪmpɪt] n lapa
limpid ['lɪmpɪd] adj (poetic) límpido, cristalino
limply ['lɪmplɪ] adv desmayadamente; **to say**
~ decir débilmente
linchpin ['lɪntʃpɪn] n pezonera; (fig) eje m
Lincs [lɪŋks] abbr (Brit) = **Lincolnshire**
line [laɪn] n (Comm) línea; (straight line) raya;
(rope) cuerda; (for fishing) sedal m; (wire) hilo;
(row, series) fila, hilera; (of writing) renglón m;
(on face) arruga; (speciality) rama ■ vt (Sewing):
to ~ (with) forrar (de); **to ~ the streets**
ocupar las aceras; **in ~ with** de acuerdo con;
she's in ~ for promotion (fig) tiene muchas
posibilidades de que la asciendan; **to bring
sth into ~ with sth** poner algo de acuerdo
con algo; ~ **of research/business** campo
de investigación/comercio; **to take the ~
that** ... ser de la opinión que ...; **hold the ~
please** (Tel) no cuelgue usted, por favor; **to
draw the ~ at doing sth** negarse a hacer
algo; no permitir que se haga algo; **on the
right lines** por buen camino; **a new ~ in
cosmetics** una nueva línea en cosméticos;
see also **lines**
▶ **line up** vi hacer cola ■ vt alinear, poner
en fila; **to have sth lined up** tener algo
arreglado
linear ['lɪnɪər] adj lineal
lined [laɪnd] adj (face) arrugado; (paper)
rayado; (clothes) forrado
line editing n (Comput) corrección f por líneas
line feed n (Comput) avance m de línea
lineman ['laɪnmən] n (US) técnico de las
líneas; (Football) delantero
linen ['lɪnɪn] n ropa blanca; (cloth) lino
line printer n impresora de línea
liner ['laɪnər] n vapor m de línea
transatlántico; **dustbin ~** bolsa de la basura
lines [laɪnz] npl (Rail) vía sg, raíles mpl
linesman ['laɪnzmən] n (Sport) juez m de línea
line-up ['laɪnʌp] n alineación f
linger ['lɪŋgər] vi retrasarse, tardar en
marcharse; (smell, tradition) persistir

639

lingerie ['lænʒəri:] n ropa interior or íntima (de mujer)

lingering ['lɪŋgərɪŋ] adj persistente; (death) lento

lingo (pl lingoes) ['lɪŋgəu, -gəuz] n (pej) jerga

linguist ['lɪŋgwɪst] n lingüista m/f

linguistic [lɪŋ'gwɪstɪk] adj lingüístico

linguistics [lɪŋ'gwɪstɪks] n lingüística

liniment ['lɪnɪmənt] n linimento

lining ['laɪnɪŋ] n forro; (Tech) revestimiento; (of brake) guarnición f

link [lɪŋk] n (of chain) eslabón m; (connection) conexión f; (bond) vínculo, lazo; (Internet) enlace m ■ vt vincular, unir; **rail ~** línea de ferrocarril, servicio de trenes
▸ **link up** vt acoplar ■ vi unirse

links [lɪŋks] npl (Golf) campo sg de golf

link-up ['lɪŋkʌp] n (gen) unión f; (meeting) encuentro, reunión f; (of roads) empalme m; (of spaceships) acoplamiento; (Radio, TV) enlace m

lino ['laɪnəu], (Brit) **linoleum** [lɪ'nəulɪəm] n linóleo

linseed oil ['lɪnsi:d-] n aceite m de linaza

lint [lɪnt] n gasa

lintel ['lɪntl] n dintel m

lion ['laɪən] n león m

lioness ['laɪənɪs] n leona

lip [lɪp] n labio; (of jug) pico; (of cup etc) borde m

liposuction ['lɪpəusʌkʃən] n liposucción f

lipread ['lɪpri:d] vi leer los labios

lip salve n crema protectora para labios

lip service n: **to pay ~ to sth** alabar algo pero sin hacer nada

lipstick ['lɪpstɪk] n lápiz m or barra de labios, carmín m

liquefy ['lɪkwɪfaɪ] vt licuar ■ vi licuarse

liqueur [lɪ'kjuəʳ] n licor m

liquid ['lɪkwɪd] adj, n líquido

liquidate ['lɪkwɪdeɪt] vt liquidar

liquidation [lɪkwɪ'deɪʃən] n liquidación f; **to go into ~** entrar en liquidación

liquid crystal display n pantalla de cristal líquido

liquidity [lɪ'kwɪdɪtɪ] n (Comm) liquidez f

liquidize ['lɪkwɪdaɪz] vt (Culin) licuar

liquidizer ['lɪkwɪdaɪzəʳ] n (Culin) licuadora

liquor ['lɪkəʳ] n licor m, bebidas fpl alcohólicas

liquorice ['lɪkərɪs] n regaliz m

liquor store n (US) bodega, tienda de vinos y bebidas alcohólicas

Lisbon ['lɪzbən] n Lisboa

lisp [lɪsp] n ceceo

lissom ['lɪsəm] adj ágil

list [lɪst] n lista; (of ship) inclinación f ■ vt (write down) hacer una lista de; (enumerate) catalogar; (Comput) hacer un listado de ■ vi (ship) inclinarse; **shopping ~** lista de las compras; see also **lists**

listed building ['lɪstɪd-] n (Arch) edificio de interés histórico-artístico

listed company ['lɪstɪd-] n compañía cotizable

listen ['lɪsn] vi escuchar, oír; (pay attention) atender

listener ['lɪsnəʳ] n oyente m/f

listeria [lɪs'tɪərɪə] n listeria

listing ['lɪstɪŋ] n (Comput) listado

listless ['lɪstlɪs] adj apático, indiferente

listlessly ['lɪstlɪslɪ] adv con indiferencia

listlessness ['lɪstlɪsnɪs] n indiferencia, apatía

list price n precio de catálogo

lists [lɪsts] npl (History) liza sg; **to enter the ~ (against sb/sth)** salir a la palestra (contra algn/algo)

lit [lɪt] pt, pp of **light**

litany ['lɪtənɪ] n letanía

liter ['li:təʳ] n (US) = **litre**

literacy ['lɪtərəsɪ] n capacidad f de leer y escribir

literacy campaign n campaña de alfabetización

literal ['lɪtərl] adj literal

literally ['lɪtrəlɪ] adv literalmente

literary ['lɪtərərɪ] adj literario

literate ['lɪtərət] adj que sabe leer y escribir; (fig) culto

literature ['lɪtərɪtʃəʳ] n literatura; (brochures etc) folletos mpl

lithe [laɪð] adj ágil

lithography [lɪ'θɒgrəfɪ] n litografía

Lithuania [lɪθju'eɪnɪə] n Lituania

Lithuanian [lɪθju'eɪnɪən] adj lituano ■ n lituano(-a); (Ling) lituano

litigate ['lɪtɪgeɪt] vi litigar

litigation [lɪtɪ'geɪʃən] n litigio

litmus paper ['lɪtməs-] n papel m de tornasol

litre, liter (US) ['li:təʳ] n litro

litter ['lɪtəʳ] n (rubbish) basura; (paper) papeles mpl (tirados); (young animals) camada, cría

litter bin n (Brit) papelera

littered ['lɪtəd] adj: **~ with** lleno de

litter lout, litterbug (US) ['lɪtəbʌg] n persona que tira papeles usados en la vía pública

little ['lɪtl] adj (small) pequeño, chico (LAm); (not much) poco; (often translated by suffix, eg): **~ house** casita ■ adv poco; **a ~** un poco (de); **~ by ~** poco a poco; **~ finger** (dedo) meñique m; **for a ~ while** (durante) un rato; **with ~ difficulty** sin problema or dificultad; **as ~ as possible** lo menos posible

little-known ['lɪtl'nəun] adj poco conocido

liturgy ['lɪtədʒɪ] n liturgia

live [*vb* lɪv, *adj* laɪv] *vi* vivir ■ *vt* (*a life*) llevar; (*experience*) vivir ■ *adj* (*animal*) vivo; (*wire*) conectado; (*broadcast*) en directo; (*issue*) de actualidad; (*unexploded*) sin explotar; **to ~ in London** vivir en Londres; **to ~ together** vivir juntos
▶ **live down** *vt* hacer olvidar
▶ **live off** *vt fus* (*land, fish etc*) vivir de; (*pej: parents etc*) vivir a costa de
▶ **live on** *vt fus* (*food*) vivir de, alimentarse de; **to ~ on £50 a week** vivir con 50 libras semanales o a la semana
▶ **live out** *vi* (*student*) ser externo ■ *vt*: **to ~ out one's days** *or* **life** pasar el resto de la vida
▶ **live up** *vt*: **to ~ it up** (*col*) tirarse la gran vida
▶ **live up to** *vt fus* (*fulfil*) cumplir con; (*justify*) justificar

live-in ['lɪvɪn] *adj*: **~ partner** pareja, compañero(-a) sentimental; **~ maid** asistenta interna
livelihood ['laɪvlɪhud] *n* sustento
liveliness ['laɪvlɪnɪs] *n* viveza
lively ['laɪvlɪ] *adj* (*gen*) vivo; (*talk*) animado; (*pace*) rápido; (*party, tune*) alegre
liven up ['laɪvn-] *vt* (*discussion, evening*) animar
liver ['lɪvəʳ] *n* hígado
liverish ['lɪvərɪʃ] *adj*: **to feel ~** sentirse *or* encontrarse mal, no estar muy católico
Liverpudlian [lɪvə'pʌdlɪən] *adj* de Liverpool ■ *n* nativo(-a) *or* habitante *m(f)* de Liverpool
livery ['lɪvərɪ] *n* librea
lives [laɪvz] *npl of* **life**
livestock ['laɪvstɔk] *n* ganado
live wire [laɪv-] *n* (*fig, col*): **he's a real ~!** ¡tiene una marcha!
livid ['lɪvɪd] *adj* lívido; (*furious*) furioso
living ['lɪvɪŋ] *adj* (*alive*) vivo ■ *n*: **to earn** *or* **make a ~** ganarse la vida; **cost of ~** coste *m* de la vida; **in ~ memory** que se recuerde *or* recuerda
living conditions *npl* condiciones *fpl* de vida
living expenses *npl* gastos *mpl* de mantenimiento
living room *n* sala (de estar), living *m* (*LAm*)
living standards *npl* nivel *msg* de vida
living wage *n* sueldo suficiente para vivir
lizard ['lɪzəd] *n* lagartija
llama ['lɑːmə] *n* llama
LLB *n abbr* (= *Bachelor of Laws*) Ldo.(-a.) en Dcho.; *see also* **Bachelor's Degree**
LLD *n abbr* (= *Doctor of Laws*) Dr(a). en Dcho.
LMT *n abbr* (US: = *Local Mean Time*) hora local
load [ləud] *n* (*gen*) carga; (*weight*) peso ■ *vt* (*Comput*) cargar; (*also*: **load up**): **to ~ (with)** cargar (con *or* de); **a ~ of**, **loads of** (*fig*) (gran) cantidad de, montones de

loaded ['ləudɪd] *adj* (*dice*) cargado; (*question*) intencionado; (*col: rich*) forrado (de dinero)
loading ['ləudɪŋ] *n* (*Comm*) sobreprima
loading bay *n* área de carga y descarga
loaf (*pl* **loaves**) [ləuf, ləuvz] *n* (barra de) pan *m* ■ *vi* (*also*: **loaf about, loaf around**) holgazanear
loam [ləum] *n* marga
loan [ləun] *n* préstamo; (*Comm*) empréstito ■ *vt* prestar; **on ~** (*book, painting*) prestado; **to raise a ~** (*money*) procurar un empréstito
loan account *n* cuenta de crédito
loan capital *n* empréstito
loan shark *n* (*col: pej*) prestamista *m/f* sin escrúpulos
loath [ləuθ] *adj*: **to be ~ to do sth** ser reacio a hacer algo
loathe [ləuð] *vt* aborrecer; (*person*) odiar
loathing ['ləuðɪŋ] *n* aversión *f*; odio
loathsome ['ləuðsəm] *adj* asqueroso, repugnante; (*person*) odioso
loaves [ləuvz] *pl of* **loaf**
lob [lɔb] *vt* (*ball*) volear por alto
lobby ['lɔbɪ] *n* vestíbulo, sala de espera; (*Pol: pressure group*) grupo de presión ■ *vt* presionar
lobbyist ['lɔbɪɪst] *n* cabildero(-a)
lobe [ləub] *n* lóbulo
lobster ['lɔbstəʳ] *n* langosta
lobster pot *n* nasa, langostera
local ['ləukl] *adj* local ■ *n* (*pub*) bar *m*; **the locals** *npl* los vecinos, los del lugar
local anaesthetic *n* (*Med*) anestesia local
local authority *n* municipio, ayuntamiento (*SP*)
local call *n* (*Tel*) llamada local
local government *n* gobierno municipal
locality [ləu'kælɪtɪ] *n* localidad *f*
localize ['ləukəlaɪz] *vt* localizar
locally ['ləukəlɪ] *adv* en la vecindad
locate [ləu'keɪt] *vt* (*find*) localizar; (*situate*) situar, ubicar (*LAm*)
location [ləu'keɪʃən] *n* situación *f*; **on ~** (*Cine*) en exteriores, fuera del estudio
loch [lɔx] *n* lago
lock [lɔk] *n* (*of door, box*) cerradura, chapa (*LAm*); (*of canal*) esclusa; (*of hair*) mechón *m* ■ *vt* (*with key*) cerrar con llave; (*immobilize*) inmovilizar ■ *vi* (*door etc*) cerrarse con llave; (*wheels*) trabarse; **~, stock and barrel** (*fig*) por completo *or* entero; **on full ~** (*Aut*) con el volante girado al máximo
▶ **lock away** *vt* (*valuables*) guardar bajo llave; (*criminal*) encerrar
▶ **lock out** *vt*: **the workers were locked out** los trabajadores tuvieron que enfrentarse con un cierre patronal

▶ **lock up** vi echar la llave

locker ['lɔkəʳ] n casillero

locker-room ['lɔkərum] n (US Sport) vestuario

locket ['lɔkɪt] n medallón m

lockout ['lɔkaut] n (Industry) paro or cierre m patronal, lockout m

locksmith ['lɔksmɪθ] n cerrajero(-a)

lock-up ['lɔkʌp] n (prison) cárcel f; (cell) jaula; (also: **lock-up garage**) jaula, cochera

locomotive [ləukə'məutɪv] n locomotora

locum ['ləukəm] n (Med) (médico(-a)) suplente m(f)

locust ['ləukəst] n langosta

lodge [lɔdʒ] n casa del guarda; (porter's) portería; (Freemasonry) logia ▪ vi (person): **to ~ (with)** alojarse (en casa de) ▪ vt (complaint) presentar

lodger ['lɔdʒəʳ] n huésped(a) m(f)

lodging house ['lɔdʒɪŋ-] n pensión f, casa de huéspedes

lodgings ['lɔdʒɪŋz] npl alojamiento sg; (house) casa sg de huéspedes

loft [lɔft] n desván m

lofty ['lɔftɪ] adj alto; (haughty) altivo, arrogante; (sentiments, aims) elevado, noble

log [lɔg] n (of wood) leño, tronco; (book) = **logbook** ▪ n abbr (= logarithm) log ▪ vt anotar, registrar

▶ **log in**, **log on** vi (Comput) iniciar la (or una) sesión

▶ **log off**, **log out** vi (Comput) finalizar la sesión

logarithm ['lɔgərɪðəm] n logaritmo

logbook ['lɔgbuk] n (Naut) diario de a bordo; (Aviat) libro de vuelo; (of car) documentación f (del coche)

log cabin n cabaña de troncos

log fire n fuego de leña

logger ['lɔgəʳ] n leñador(a) m(f)

loggerheads ['lɔgəhɛdz] npl: **at ~ (with)** de pique (con)

logic ['lɔdʒɪk] n lógica

logical ['lɔdʒɪkl] adj lógico

logically ['lɔdʒɪkəlɪ] adv lógicamente

login ['lɔgɪn] n login m

logistics [lɔ'dʒɪstɪks] n logística

log jam n: **to break the ~** poner fin al estancamiento

logo ['ləugəu] n logotipo

loin [lɔɪn] n (Culin) lomo, solomillo; **loins** npl lomos mpl

loin cloth n taparrabos m inv

loiter ['lɔɪtəʳ] vi vagar; (pej) merodear

lol abbr (Internet, Tel: = laugh out loud) lol (muerto de risa)

loll [lɔl] vi (also: **loll about**) repantigarse

lollipop ['lɔlɪpɔp] n pirulí m; (iced) polo

lollipop man/lady n (Brit) ver nota

---

lollop ['lɔləp] vi (Brit) moverse desgarbadamente

lolly ['lɔlɪ] n (col: ice cream) polo; (: lollipop) piruleta; (: money) guita

London ['lʌndən] n Londres m

Londoner ['lʌndənəʳ] n londinense m/f

lone [ləun] adj solitario

loneliness ['ləunlɪnɪs] n soledad f, aislamiento

lonely ['ləunlɪ] adj solitario, solo

lonely hearts adj: **~ ad** anuncio de la sección de contactos; **~ column** sección f de contactos

lone parent family n familia monoparental

loner ['ləunəʳ] n solitario(-a)

lonesome ['ləunsəm] adj (esp US) = **lonely**

long [lɔŋ] adj largo ▪ adv mucho tiempo, largamente ▪ vi: **to ~ for sth** anhelar algo ▪ n: **the ~ and the short of it is that ...** (fig) en resumidas cuentas ...; **in the ~ run** a la larga; **so** or **as ~ as** mientras, con tal de que; **don't be ~!** ¡no tardes!, ¡vuelve pronto!; **how ~ is the street?** ¿cuánto tiene la calle de largo?; **how ~ is the lesson?** ¿cuánto dura la clase?; **six metres ~** que mide seis metros, de seis metros de largo; **six months ~** que dura seis meses, de seis meses de duración; **all night ~** toda la noche; **~ ago** hace mucho (tiempo); **he no longer comes** ya no viene; **~ before** mucho antes; **before ~** (+ future) dentro de poco; (+ past) poco tiempo después; **at ~ last** al fin, por fin; **I shan't be ~** termino pronto

long-distance [lɔŋ'dɪstəns] adj (race) de larga distancia; (call) interurbano

longevity [lɔn'dʒɛvɪtɪ] n longevidad f

long-haired ['lɔŋ'hɛəd] adj de pelo largo

longhand ['lɔŋhænd] n escritura (corriente)

longing ['lɔŋɪŋ] n anhelo, ansia; (nostalgia) nostalgia ▪ adj anhelante

longingly ['lɔŋɪŋlɪ] adv con ansia

longitude ['lɔŋgɪtjuːd] n longitud f

long jump n salto de longitud

long-lost ['lɔŋlɔst] adj desaparecido hace mucho tiempo

long-playing record ['lɒŋpleɪɪŋ-] n elepé m, disco de larga duración

long-range ['lɒŋ'reɪndʒ] adj de gran alcance; (weather forecast) a largo plazo

longshoreman ['lɒŋʃɔ:mən] n (US) estibador m

long-sighted ['lɒŋ'saɪtɪd] adj (Brit) présbita

long-standing ['lɒŋ'stændɪŋ] adj de mucho tiempo

long-suffering [lɒŋ'sʌfərɪŋ] adj sufrido

long-term ['lɒŋtə:m] adj a largo plazo

long wave n onda larga

long-winded [lɒŋ'wɪndɪd] adj prolijo

loo [lu:] n (Brit: col) wáter m

loofah ['lu:fə] n esponja de lufa

look [luk] vi mirar; (seem) parecer; (building etc): **to ~ south/on to the sea** dar al sur/al mar ■ n mirada; (glance) vistazo; (appearance) aire m, aspecto; **looks** npl físico sg, belleza sg; **to ~ ahead** mirar hacia delante; **it looks about four metres long** yo calculo que tiene unos cuarto metros de largo; **it looks all right to me** a mí me parece que está bien; **to have a ~ at sth** echar un vistazo a algo; **to have a ~ for sth** buscar algo
▶ **look after** vt fus cuidar
▶ **look around** vi echar una mirada alrededor
▶ **look at** vt fus mirar; (consider) considerar
▶ **look back** vi mirar hacia atrás; **to ~ back at sb/sth** mirar hacia atrás algo/a algn; **to ~ back on** (event, period) recordar
▶ **look down on** vt fus (fig) despreciar, mirar con desprecio
▶ **look for** vt fus buscar
▶ **look forward to** vt fus esperar con ilusión; (in letters): **we ~ forward to hearing from you** quedamos a la espera de su respuesta or contestación; **I'm not looking forward to it** no tengo ganas de eso, no me hace ilusión
▶ **look in** vi: **to ~ in on sb** (visit) pasar por casa de algn
▶ **look into** vt fus investigar
▶ **look on** vi mirar (como espectador)
▶ **look out** vi (beware): **to ~ out (for)** tener cuidado (de)
▶ **look out for** vt fus (seek) buscar; (await) esperar
▶ **look over** vt (essay) revisar; (town, building) inspeccionar, registrar; (person) examinar
▶ **look round** vi (turn) volver la cabeza; **to ~ round for sth** buscar algo
▶ **look through** vt fus (papers, book) hojear; (briefly) echar un vistazo a; (telescope) mirar por
▶ **look to** vt fus ocuparse de; (rely on) contar con
▶ **look up** vi mirar hacia arriba; (improve)

mejorar ■ vt (word) buscar; (friend) visitar
▶ **look up to** vt fus admirar

look-out ['lukaut] n (tower etc) puesto de observación; (person) vigía m/f; **to be on the ~ for sth** estar al acecho de algo

look-up table ['lukʌp-] n (Comput) tabla de consulta

loom [lu:m] n telar m ■ vi (threaten) amenazar

loony ['lu:nɪ] adj, n (col) loco(-a) m(f)

loop [lu:p] n lazo; (bend) vuelta, recodo; (Comput) bucle m

loophole ['lu:phəul] n laguna

loose [lu:s] adj (gen) suelto; (not tight) flojo; (wobbly etc) movedizo; (clothes) ancho; (morals, discipline) relajado ■ vt (free) soltar; (slacken) aflojar; (also: **loose off**: arrow) disparar, soltar; **~ connection** (Elec) hilo desempalmado; **to be at a ~ end** or (US) **at ~ ends** no saber qué hacer; **to tie up ~ ends** (fig) no dejar ningún cabo suelto, atar cabos

loose change n cambio

loose chippings [-'tʃɪpɪŋz] npl (on road) gravilla sg suelta

loose-fitting ['lu:sfɪtɪŋ] adj suelto

loose-leaf ['lu:sli:f] adj: **~ binder** or **folder** carpeta de anillas

loose-limbed ['lu:slɪmd] adj ágil, suelto

loosely ['lu:slɪ] adv libremente, aproximadamente

loosely-knit [-nɪt] adj de estructura abierta

loosen ['lu:sn] vt (free) soltar; (untie) desatar; (slacken) aflojar
▶ **loosen up** vi (before game) hacer (ejercicios de) precalentamiento; (col: relax) soltarse, relajarse

looseness ['lu:snɪs] n soltura; flojedad f

loot [lu:t] n botín m ■ vt saquear

looter ['lu:tər] n saqueador(a) m(f)

looting ['lu:tɪŋ] n pillaje m

lop [lɒp]: **to ~ off** vt cortar; (branches) podar

lop-sided ['lɒp'saɪdɪd] adj desequilibrado

lord [lɔ:d] n señor m; **L~ Smith** Lord Smith; **the L~** el Señor; **the (House of) Lords** (Brit) la Cámara de los Lores

lordly ['lɔ:dlɪ] adj señorial

Lordship ['lɔ:dʃɪp] n: **your ~** su Señoría

lore [lɔ:r] n saber m popular, tradiciones fpl

lorry ['lɒrɪ] n (Brit) camión m

lorry driver n camionero(-a)

lorry load n carga

lose (pt, pp lost) [lu:z, lɒst] vt perder ■ vi perder, ser vencido; **to ~ (time)** (clock) atrasarse; **to ~ no time (in doing sth)** no tardar (en hacer algo); **to get lost** (object) extraviarse; (person) perderse
▶ **lose out** vi salir perdiendo

loser ['luːzə^r] *n* perdedor(a) *m(f)*; **to be a bad ~** no saber perder

losing ['luːzɪŋ] *adj* (*team etc*) vencido, perdedor(a)

loss [lɔs] *n* pérdida; **heavy losses** (*Mil*) grandes pérdidas *fpl*; **to be at a ~** no saber qué hacer; **to be a dead ~** ser completamente inútil; **to cut one's losses** reducir las pérdidas; **to sell sth at a ~** vender algo perdiendo dinero

loss adjuster *n* (*Insurance*) perito(-a) *m(f)* or tasador(-a) *m/f* de pérdidas

loss leader *n* (*Comm*) artículo de promoción

lost [lɔst] *pt, pp of* **lose** ■ *adj* perdido; **~ in thought** absorto, ensimismado

lost and found *n* (*US*) = **lost property**; **lost property office** or **department**

lost cause *n* causa perdida

lost property *n* (*Brit*) objetos *mpl* perdidos

lost property office or **department** *n* (*Brit*) departamento de objetos perdidos

lot [lɔt] *n* (*at auction*) lote *m*; (*destiny*) suerte *f*; **the ~** el todo, todos *mpl*, todas *fpl*; **a ~** mucho, bastante; **a ~ of, lots of** muchos(-as), mucho(-a) *adj sg*; **I read a ~** leo bastante; **to draw lots (for sth)** echar suertes (para decidir algo)

lotion ['ləʊʃən] *n* loción *f*

lottery ['lɔtərɪ] *n* lotería

loud [laud] *adj* (*voice, sound*) fuerte; (*laugh, shout*) estrepitoso; (*gaudy*) chillón(-ona) ■ *adv* (*speak etc*) fuerte; **out ~** en voz alta

loudhailer [laud'heɪlə^r] *n* (*Brit*) megáfono

loudly ['laudlɪ] *adv* (*noisily*) fuerte; (*aloud*) en alta voz

loudness ['laudnɪs] *n* (*of sound etc*) fuerza

loudspeaker [laud'spiːkə^r] *n* altavoz *m*

lounge [laundʒ] *n* salón *m*, sala de estar; (*of hotel*) salón *m*; (*of airport*) sala de embarque ■ *vi* (*also*: **lounge about, lounge around**) holgazanear, no hacer nada; *see also* **pub**

lounge bar *n* salón *m*

lounge suit *n* (*Brit*) traje *m* de calle

louse (*pl* **lice**) [laus, laɪs] *n* piojo
▶ **louse up** *vt* (*col*) echar a perder

lousy ['lauzɪ] *adj* (*fig*) vil, asqueroso

lout [laut] *n* gamberro(-a)

louvre, louver (*US*) ['luːvə^r] *adj*: **~ door** puerta de rejilla; **~ window** ventana de libro

lovable ['lʌvəbl] *adj* amable, simpático

love [lʌv] *n* amor *m* ■ *vt* amar, querer; **to send one's ~ to sb** dar sus recuerdos a algn; **~ from Anne** (*in letter*) con cariño de Anne; **I ~ to read** me encanta leer; **to be in ~ with** estar enamorado de; **to make ~** hacer el amor; **for the ~ of** por amor a; "**15 ~**" (*Tennis*) "15 a cero"; **I ~ paella** me encanta la paella; **I'd ~**

to come me gustaría muchísimo venir

love affair *n* aventura sentimental or amorosa

love child *n* hijo(-a) natural

loved ones ['lʌvdwʌnz] *npl* seres *mpl* queridos

love-hate relationship ['lʌvheɪt-] *n* relación *f* de amor y odio

love letter *n* carta de amor

love life *n* vida sentimental

lovely ['lʌvlɪ] *adj* (*delightful*) precioso, encantador(a), lindo (*esp LAm*); (*beautiful*) hermoso, lindo (*esp LAm*); **we had a ~ time** lo pasamos estupendo

lovemaking ['lʌvmeɪkɪŋ] *n* relaciones *fpl* sexuales

lover ['lʌvə^r] *n* amante *m/f*; (*amateur*): **a ~ of** un(a) aficionado(-a) or un(a) amante de

lovesick ['lʌvsɪk] *adj* enfermo de amor, amartelado

lovesong ['lʌvsɔŋ] *n* canción *f* de amor

loving ['lʌvɪŋ] *adj* amoroso, cariñoso

lovingly ['lʌvɪŋlɪ] *adv* amorosamente, cariñosamente

low [ləu] *adj, adv* bajo ■ *n* (*Meteorology*) área de baja presión ■ *vi* (*cow*) mugir; **to feel ~** sentirse deprimido; **to turn (down) ~** bajar; **to reach a new** or **an all-time ~** llegar a su punto más bajo

low-alcohol [ləu'ælkəhɔl] *adj* bajo en alcohol

lowbrow ['ləubrau] *adj* (*person*) de poca cultura

low-calorie ['ləu'kælərɪ] *adj* bajo en calorías

low-cut ['ləukʌt] *adj* (*dress*) escotado

low-down ['ləudaun] *n* (*col*): **he gave me the ~ on it** me puso al corriente ■ *adj* (*mean*) vil, bajo

lower ['ləuə^r] *vt* bajar; (*reduce: price*) reducir, rebajar; (: *resistance*) debilitar; **to ~ o.s. to** (*fig*) rebajarse a ■ *vi* ['lauə^r]: **to ~ (at sb)** fulminar (a algn) con la mirada

lower case *n* (*Typ*) minúscula

Lower House *n* (*Pol*): **the ~** la Cámara baja

lowering ['lauərɪŋ] *adj* (*sky*) amenazador(a)

low-fat ['ləu'fæt] *adj* (*milk, yoghurt*) desnatado; (*diet*) bajo en calorías

low-key ['ləu'kiː] *adj* de mínima intensidad; (*operation*) de poco perfil

lowland ['ləulənd] *n* tierra baja

low-level ['ləulevl] *adj* de bajo nivel; (*flying*) a poca altura

low-loader ['ləuləudə^r] *n* camión *m* de caja a bajo nivel

lowly ['ləulɪ] *adj* humilde

low-lying [ləu'laɪɪŋ] *adj* bajo

low-rise ['ləuraɪz] *adj* bajo

low-tech ['ləutɛk] *adj* de baja tecnología, tradicional

loyal ['lɔɪəl] *adj* leal
loyalist ['lɔɪəlɪst] *n* legitimista *m/f*
loyally ['lɔɪəlɪ] *adv* lealmente
loyalty ['lɔɪəltɪ] *n* lealtad *f*
loyalty card *n* (*Brit*) tarjeta cliente
lozenge ['lɔzɪndʒ] *n* (*Med*) pastilla
LP *n abbr* (= *long-playing record*) elepé *m*
LPG *n abbr* (= *liquefied petroleum gas*) GLP *m*
    (= *Gas Licuado de Petróleo*)
L-plates ['ɛlpleɪts] *npl* (*Brit*) (placas *fpl* de)
    la L; *ver nota*

● L-PLATES

En el Reino Unido las personas que
están aprendiendo a conducir han de
llevar indicativos blancos con una L en
rojo llamados normalmente *L-plates* (de
"learner") en la parte delantera y trasera
de los automóviles que conducen. No
tienen que ir a clases teóricas, sino que
desde el principio se les entrega un carnet
de conducir provisional ("provisional
driving licence") para que realicen sus
prácticas, que han de estar supervisadas
por un conductor con carnet definitivo
("full driving licence"). Tampoco se les
permite hacer prácticas en autopistas
aunque vayan acompañados.

LPN *n abbr* (US: = *Licensed Practical Nurse*)
    enfermero(-a) practicante
LRAM *n abbr* (*Brit*) = **Licentiate of the Royal
    Academy of Music**
LSAT *n abbr* (US) = **Law School Admissions
    Test**
LSD *n abbr* (= *lysergic acid diethylamide*) LSD
    m; (*Brit*: = *pounds, shillings and pence*) sistema
    monetario usado en Gran Bretaña hasta 1971
LSE *n abbr* = **London School of Economics**
LT *abbr* (*Elec*) = **low tension**
Lt. *abbr* (= *lieutenant*) Tte.
Ltd *abbr* (*Comm*) = **limited**
lubricant ['lu:brɪkənt] *n* lubricante *m*
lubricate ['lu:brɪkeɪt] *vt* lubricar, engrasar
lubrication [lu:brɪ'keɪʃən] *n* lubricación *f*
lucid ['lu:sɪd] *adj* lúcido
lucidity [lu:'sɪdɪtɪ] *n* lucidez *f*
lucidly ['lu:sɪdlɪ] *adv* lúcidamente
luck [lʌk] *n* suerte *f*; **good/bad ~** buena/mala
    suerte; **good ~!** ¡(que tengas) suerte!; **to be
    in ~** estar de suerte; **to be out of ~** tener
    mala suerte
luckily ['lʌkɪlɪ] *adv* afortunadamente
luckless ['lʌklɪs] *adj* desafortunado
lucky ['lʌkɪ] *adj* afortunado
lucrative ['lu:krətɪv] *adj* lucrativo

ludicrous ['lu:dɪkrəs] *adj* absurdo
ludo ['lu:dəu] *n* parchís *m*
lug [lʌg] *vt* (*drag*) arrastrar
luggage ['lʌgɪdʒ] *n* equipaje *m*
luggage rack *n* (*in train*) rejilla, redecilla;
    (*on car*) baca, portaequipajes *m inv*
luggage van *n* furgón *m or* vagón *m* de
    equipaje
lugubrious [lu'gu:brɪəs] *adj* lúgubre
lukewarm ['lu:kwɔ:m] *adj* tibio, templado
lull [lʌl] *n* tregua ■ *vt* (*child*) acunar; (*person,
    fear*) calmar
lullaby ['lʌləbaɪ] *n* nana
lumbago [lʌm'beɪgəu] *n* lumbago
lumber ['lʌmbəʳ] *n* (*junk*) trastos *mpl* viejos;
    (*wood*) maderos *mpl* ■ *vt* (*Brit col*): **to ~ sb
    with sth/sb** hacer que algn cargue con algo/
    algn ■ *vi* (*also*: **lumber about, lumber along**)
    moverse pesadamente
lumberjack ['lʌmbədʒæk] *n* maderero
lumber room *n* (*Brit*) cuarto trastero
lumber yard *n* (US) almacén *m* de madera
luminous ['lu:mɪnəs] *adj* luminoso
lump [lʌmp] *n* terrón *m*; (*fragment*) trozo;
    (*in sauce*) grumo; (*in throat*) nudo; (*swelling*)
    bulto ■ *vt* (*also*: **lump together**) juntar;
    (*persons*) poner juntos
lump sum *n* suma global
lumpy ['lʌmpɪ] *adj* (*sauce*) lleno de grumos
lunacy ['lu:nəsɪ] *n* locura
lunar ['lu:nəʳ] *adj* lunar
lunatic ['lu:nətɪk] *adj, n* loco(-a) *m(f)*
lunatic asylum *n* manicomio
lunch [lʌntʃ] *n* almuerzo, comida ■ *vi*
    almorzar; **to invite sb to** *or* **for ~** invitar a
    algn a almorzar
lunch break, lunch hour *n* hora del
    almuerzo
luncheon ['lʌntʃən] *n* almuerzo
luncheon meat *n* tipo de fiambre
luncheon voucher *n* vale *m* de comida
lunchtime ['lʌntʃtaɪm] *n* hora del almuerzo
    or de comer
lung [lʌŋ] *n* pulmón *m*
lung cancer *n* cáncer *m* del pulmón
lunge [lʌndʒ] *vi* (*also*: **lunge forward**)
    abalanzarse; **to ~ at** arremeter contra
lupin ['lu:pɪn] *n* altramuz *m*
lurch [lə:tʃ] *vi* dar sacudidas ■ *n* sacudida;
    to leave sb in the ~ dejar a algn plantado
lure [luəʳ] *n* (*bait*) cebo; (*decoy*) señuelo ■ *vt*
    convencer con engaños
lurid ['luərɪd] *adj* (*colour*) chillón(-ona);
    (*account*) sensacional; (*detail*) horripilante
lurk [lə:k] *vi* (*hide*) esconderse; (*wait*) estar al
    acecho
luscious ['lʌʃəs] *adj* delicioso

lush [lʌʃ] *adj* exuberante
lust [lʌst] *n* lujuria; (*greed*) codicia
▶ **lust after** *vt fus* codiciar
lustful ['lʌstful] *adj* lascivo, lujurioso
lustre, luster (*US*) ['lʌstə'] *n* lustre *m*, brillo
lustrous ['lʌstrəs] *adj* brillante
lusty ['lʌstɪ] *adj* robusto, fuerte
lute [luːt] *n* laúd *m*
Luxembourg ['lʌksəmbəːg] *n* Luxemburgo
luxuriant [lʌg'zjuərɪənt] *adj* exuberante
luxurious [lʌg'zjuərɪəs] *adj* lujoso
luxury ['lʌkʃərɪ] *n* lujo ■ *cpd* de lujo

luxury tax *n* impuesto de lujo
LV *n abbr* (*Brit*) = **luncheon voucher**
LW *abbr* (*Radio*) = **long wave**
Lycra® ['laɪkrə] *n* licra®
lying ['laɪɪŋ] *n* mentiras *fpl* ■ *adj* (*statement, story*) falso; (*person*) mentiroso
lynch [lɪntʃ] *vt* linchar
lynx [lɪnks] *n* lince *m*
Lyons ['laɪənz] *n* Lyón *m*
lyre ['laɪə'] *n* lira
lyric ['lɪrɪk] *adj* lírico; **lyrics** *npl* (*of song*) letra *sg*
lyrical ['lɪrɪkl] *adj* lírico

Mm

M, m [ɛm] n (letter) M, m f; **M for Mary,**
   (US) **M for Mike** M de Madrid
M n abbr (Brit: = motorway): **the M8** ≈ la A8;
   = **million; millions** ■ abbr (= medium) M
m abbr (= metre) m.; = **mile; miles**
MA n abbr (Scol) see **Master of Arts;**
   (US) = **Military Academy** ■ abbr (US)
   = **Massachusetts**
mac [mæk] n (Brit) impermeable m
macabre [mə'kɑ:brə] adj macabro
macaroni [mækə'rəʊnɪ] n macarrones mpl
macaroon [mækə'ru:n] n macarrac m,
   mostachón m
mace [meɪs] n (weapon, ceremonial) maza;
   (spice) macis f
Macedonia [mæsɪ'dəʊnɪə] n Macedonia
Macedonian [mæsɪ'dəʊnɪən] adj
   macedonio ■ n macedonio(-a); (Ling)
   macedonio
machinations [mækɪ'neɪʃənz] npl intrigas fpl,
   maquinaciones fpl
machine [mə'ʃi:n] n máquina ■ vt (dress etc)
   coser a máquina; (Tech) trabajar a máquina
machine code n (Comput) código máquina
machine gun n ametralladora
machine language n (Comput) lenguaje m
   máquina
machine readable adj (Comput) legible por
   máquina
machinery [mə'ʃi:nərɪ] n maquinaria; (fig)
   mecanismo
machine shop n taller m de máquinas
machine tool n máquina herramienta
machine translation n traducción f
   automática
machine washable adj lavable a máquina
machinist [mə'ʃi:nɪst] n operario(-a) m(f) (de
   máquina)
macho ['mætʃəʊ] adj macho
mackerel ['mækrl] n pl inv caballa
mackintosh ['mækɪntɒʃ] n (Brit)
   impermeable m
macro ... ['mækrəʊ] pref macro...

macro-economics ['mækrəʊi:kə'nɒmɪks] n
   macroeconomía
mad [mæd] adj loco; (idea) disparatado;
   (angry) furioso, enojado (LAm); ~ **(at or with
   sb)** furioso (con algn); **to be ~ (keen) about**
   or **on sth** estar loco por algo; **to go ~** volverse
   loco, enloquecer(se)
madam ['mædəm] n señora; **can I help you,
   ~?** ¿le puedo ayudar, señora?; **M~ Chairman**
   señora presidenta
madcap ['mædkæp] adj (col) alocado,
   disparatado
mad cow disease n encefalopatía
   espongiforme bovina
madden ['mædn] vt volver loco
maddening ['mædnɪŋ] adj enloquecedor(a)
made [meɪd] pt, pp of **make**
Madeira [mə'dɪərə] n (Geo) Madeira; (wine)
   madeira m
made-to-measure ['meɪdtəmɛʒəʳ] adj (Brit)
   hecho a la medida
made-up ['meɪdʌp] adj (story) ficticio
madhouse ['mædhaʊs] n (also fig)
   manicomio
madly ['mædlɪ] adv locamente
madman ['mædmən] n loco
madness ['mædnɪs] n locura
Madonna [mə'dɒnə] n Virgen f
Madrid [mə'drɪd] n Madrid m
madrigal ['mædrɪɡəl] n madrigal m
Mafia ['mæfɪə] n Mafia
mag [mæg] n abbr (Brit col) = **magazine**
magazine [mæɡə'zi:n] n revista; (Mil: store)
   almacén m; (of firearm) recámara
maggot ['mæɡət] n gusano
magic ['mædʒɪk] n magia ■ adj mágico
magical ['mædʒɪkəl] adj mágico
magician [mə'dʒɪʃən] n mago(-a)
magistrate ['mædʒɪstreɪt] n juez m/f
   (municipal); **Magistrates' Court** (Brit)
   see **crown court**
magnanimity [mæɡnə'nɪmɪtɪ] n
   magnanimidad f

magnanimous [mæg'nænɪməs] *adj* magnánimo

magnate ['mægneɪt] *n* magnate *m/f*

magnesium [mæg'niːzɪəm] *n* magnesio

magnet ['mægnɪt] *n* imán *m*

magnetic [mæg'nɛtɪk] *adj* magnético

magnetic disk *n* (*Comput*) disco magnético

magnetic tape *n* cinta magnética

magnetism ['mægnɪtɪzəm] *n* magnetismo

magnification [mægnɪfɪ'keɪʃən] *n* aumento

magnificence [mæg'nɪfɪsns] *n* magnificencia

magnificent [mæg'nɪfɪsnt] *adj* magnífico

magnificently [mæg'nɪfɪsntlɪ] *adv* magníficamente

magnify ['mægnɪfaɪ] *vt* aumentar; (*fig*) exagerar

magnifying glass ['mægnɪfaɪɪŋ-] *n* lupa

magnitude ['mægnɪtjuːd] *n* magnitud *f*

magnolia [mæg'nəʊlɪə] *n* magnolia

magpie ['mægpaɪ] *n* urraca

maharajah [mɑːhə'rɑːdʒə] *n* maharajá *m*

mahogany [mə'hɒgənɪ] *n* caoba ■ *cpd* de caoba

maid [meɪd] *n* criada; **old ~** (*pej*) solterona

maiden ['meɪdn] *n* doncella ■ *adj* (*aunt etc*) solterona; (*speech, voyage*) inaugural

maiden name *n* apellido de soltera

mail [meɪl] *n* correo; (*letters*) cartas *fpl* ■ *vt* (*post*) echar al correo; (*send*) mandar por correo; **by ~** por correo

mailbox ['meɪlbɒks] *n* (*US: for letters etc*: *Comput*) buzón *m*

mailing list ['meɪlɪŋ-] *n* lista de direcciones

mailman ['meɪlmæn] *n* (*US*) cartero

mail-order ['meɪlɔːdəʳ] *n* pedido postal; (*business*) venta por correo ■ *adj*: **~ firm** or **house** casa de venta por correo

mailshot ['meɪlʃɒt] *n* mailing *m inv*

mailtrain ['meɪltreɪn] *n* tren *m* correo

mail van, mail truck (*US*) *n* (*Aut*) camioneta de correos or de reparto

maim [meɪm] *vt* mutilar, lisiar

main [meɪn] *adj* principal, mayor ■ *n* (*pipe*) cañería principal or maestra; (*US*) red *f* eléctrica; **the mains** (*Brit Elec*) la red eléctrica; **in the ~** en general

main course *n* (*Culin*) plato principal

mainframe ['meɪnfreɪm] *n* (*also*: **mainframe computer**) ordenador *m* or computadora central

mainland ['meɪnlənd] *n* continente *m*

main line *n* línea principal

mainly ['meɪnlɪ] *adv* principalmente, en su mayoría

main road *n* carretera principal

mainstay ['meɪnsteɪ] *n* (*fig*) pilar *m*

mainstream ['meɪnstriːm] *n* (*fig*) corriente *f* principal

main street *n* calle *f* mayor

maintain [meɪn'teɪn] *vt* mantener; (*affirm*) sostener; **to ~ that ...** mantener or sostener que ...

maintenance ['meɪntənəns] *n* mantenimiento; (*alimony*) pensión *f* alimenticia

maintenance contract *n* contrato de mantenimiento

maintenance order *n* (*Law*) obligación *f* de pagar una pensión alimenticia al cónyuge

maisonette [meɪzə'nɛt] *n* dúplex *m*

maize [meɪz] *n* (*Brit*) maíz *m*, choclo (*LAm*)

Maj. *abbr* (*Mil*) = **major**

majestic [mə'dʒɛstɪk] *adj* majestuoso

majesty ['mædʒɪstɪ] *n* majestad *f*

major ['meɪdʒəʳ] *n* (*Mil*) comandante *m* ■ *adj* principal; (*Mus*) mayor ■ *vi* (*US Univ*): **to ~ in** especializarse en; **a ~ operation** una operación or intervención de gran importancia

Majorca [mə'jɔːkə] *n* Mallorca

major general *n* (*Mil*) general *m* de división

majority [mə'dʒɒrɪtɪ] *n* mayoría ■ *cpd* (*verdict*) mayoritario

majority holding *n* (*Comm*): **to have a ~** tener un interés mayoritario

make [meɪk] *vt* (*pt, pp* **made** [meɪd]) hacer; (*manufacture*) hacer, fabricar; (*cause to be*): **to ~ sb sad** poner triste or entristecer a algn; (*force*): **to ~ sb do sth** obligar a algn a hacer algo; (*equal*): **2 and 2 ~ 4** 2 y 2 son 4 ■ *n* marca; **to ~ a fool of sb** poner a algn en ridículo; **to ~ a profit/loss** obtener ganancias/sufrir pérdidas; **to ~ a profit of £500** sacar una ganancia de 500 libras; **to ~ it** (*arrive*) llegar; (*achieve sth*) tener éxito; **what time do you ~ it?** ¿qué hora tienes?; **to ~ do with** contentarse con

▶ **make for** *vt fus* (*place*) dirigirse a

▶ **make off** *vi* largarse

▶ **make out** *vt* (*decipher*) descifrar; (*understand*) entender; (*see*) distinguir; (*write: cheque*) extender; **to ~ out (that)** (*claim, imply*) dar a entender (que); **to ~ out a case for sth** dar buenas razones en favor de algo

▶ **make over** *vt* (*assign*): **to ~ over (to)** ceder or traspasar (a)

▶ **make up** *vt* (*invent*) inventar; (*parcel*) hacer ■ *vi* reconciliarse; (*with cosmetics*) maquillarse; **to be made up of** estar compuesto de

▶ **make up for** *vt fus* compensar

make-believe ['meɪkbɪliːv] *n* ficción *f*, fantasía

makeover ['meɪkəuvəʳ] n cambio de imagen; **to give sb a ~** hacerle a algn un cambio de imagen

maker ['meɪkəʳ] n fabricante m/f

makeshift ['meɪkʃɪft] adj improvisado

make-up ['meɪkʌp] n maquillaje m

make-up bag n bolsita del maquillaje or de los cosméticos

make-up remover n desmaquillador m

making ['meɪkɪŋ] n (fig): **in the ~** en vías de formación; **to have the makings of** (person) tener madera de

maladjusted [mælə'dʒʌstɪd] adj inadaptado

maladroit [maelə'drɔɪt] adj torpe

malaise [mæ'leɪz] n malestar m

malaria [mə'lɛərɪə] n malaria

Malawi [mə'lɑːwɪ] n Malawi m

Malay [mə'leɪ] adj malayo ■ n malayo(-a); (Ling) malayo

Malaya [mə'leɪə] n Malaya, Malaca

Malayan [mə'leɪən] adj, n = **Malay**

Malaysia [mə'leɪzɪə] n Malaisia, Malaysia

Malaysian [mə'leɪzɪən] adj, n malaisio(-a) m(f), malaysio(-a) m(f)

Maldives ['mɔːldɪːvz] npl: **the ~** las Maldivas

male [meɪl] n (Biol, Elec) macho ■ adj (sex, attitude) masculino; (child etc) varón

male chauvinist n machista m

male nurse n enfermero

malevolence [mə'lɛvələns] n malevolencia

malevolent [mə'lɛvələnt] adj malévolo

malfunction [mæl'fʌŋkʃən] n mal funcionamiento

malice ['mælɪs] n (ill will) malicia; (rancour) rencor m

malicious [mə'lɪʃəs] adj malicioso; rencoroso

maliciously [mə'lɪʃəslɪ] adv con malevolencia, con malicia; rencorosamente

malign [mə'laɪn] vt difamar, calumniar ■ adj maligno

malignant [mə'lɪgnənt] adj (Med) maligno

malinger [mə'lɪŋgəʳ] vi fingirse enfermo

malingerer [mə'lɪŋgərəʳ] n enfermo(-a) fingido(-a)

mall [mɔːl] n (US: also: **shopping mall**) centro comercial

malleable ['mælɪəbl] adj maleable

mallet ['mælɪt] n mazo

malnutrition [mælnjuː'trɪʃən] n desnutrición f

malpractice [mæl'præktɪs] n negligencia profesional

malt [mɔːlt] n malta

Malta ['mɔːltə] n Malta

Maltese [mɔːl'tiːz] adj maltés(-esa) ■ n (pl inv) maltés(-esa) m(f); (Ling) maltés m

maltreat [mæl'triːt] vt maltratar

mammal ['mæml] n mamífero

mammoth ['mæməθ] n mamut m ■ adj gigantesco

man (pl men) [mæn, mɛn] n hombre m; (Chess) pieza ■ vt (Naut) tripular; (Mil) defender; **an old ~** un viejo; **~ and wife** marido y mujer

Man. abbr (Canada) = **Manitoba**

manacle ['mænəkl] n esposa, manilla; **manacles** npl grillos mpl

manage ['mænɪdʒ] vi arreglárselas ■ vt (be in charge of) dirigir; (person etc) manejar; **to ~ to do sth** conseguir hacer algo; **to ~ without sth/sb** poder prescindir de algo/algn

manageable ['mænɪdʒəbl] adj manejable

management ['mænɪdʒmənt] n dirección f, administración f; **"under new ~"** "bajo nueva dirección"

management accounting n contabilidad f de gestión

management buyout n adquisición f por parte de la dirección

management consultant n consultor(a) m(f) en dirección de empresas

manager ['mænɪdʒəʳ] n director(a) m(f); (Sport) entrenador(a) m(f); **sales ~** jefe(-a) m(f) de ventas

manageress ['mænɪdʒərɛs] n directora; (Sport) entrenadora

managerial [mænə'dʒɪərɪəl] adj directivo

managing director ['mænɪdʒɪŋ-] n director(a) m(f) general

Mancunian [mæŋ'kjuːnɪən] adj de Manchester ■ n nativo(-a) or habitante m(f) de Manchester

mandarin ['mændərɪn] n (also: **mandarin orange**) mandarina; (person) mandarín m

mandate ['mændeɪt] n mandato

mandatory ['mændətərɪ] adj obligatorio

mandolin, mandoline ['mændəlɪn] n mandolina

mane [meɪn] n (of horse) crin f; (of lion) melena

maneuver [mə'nuːvəʳ] (US) = **manoeuvre**

manful ['mænful] adj resuelto

manfully ['mænfəlɪ] adv resueltamente

mangetout [mɔnʒ'tuː] n tirabeque m

mangle ['mæŋgl] vt mutilar, destrozar ■ n escurridor m

mango (pl mangoes) ['mæŋgəu] n mango

mangrove ['mæŋgrəuv] n mangle m

mangy ['meɪndʒɪ] adj roñoso; (Med) sarnoso

manhandle ['mænhændl] vt maltratar; (move by hand: goods) manipular

manhole ['mænhəul] n boca de acceso

manhood ['mænhud] n edad f viril; (manliness) virilidad f

man-hour ['mæn'auəʳ] n hora-hombre f

manhunt ['mænhʌnt] n caza de hombre

m

mania ['meɪnɪə] n manía
maniac ['meɪnɪæk] n maníaco(-a); (fig) maniático
manic ['mænɪk] adj (behaviour, activity) frenético
manic-depressive ['mænɪkdɪ'prɛsɪv] adj, n maniacodepresivo(-a) m(f)
manicure ['mænɪkjuəʳ] n manicura
manicure set n estuche m de manicura
manifest ['mænɪfɛst] vt manifestar, mostrar ■ adj manifiesto ■ n manifiesto
manifestation [mænɪfɛs'teɪʃən] n manifestación f
manifestly ['mænɪfɛstlɪ] adv evidentemente
manifesto [mænɪ'fɛstəu] n manifiesto
manifold ['mænɪfəuld] adj múltiples ■ n (Aut etc): **exhaust** ~ colector m de escape
Manila [mə'nɪlə] n Manila
manila, manilla [mə'nɪlə] n (paper, envelope) manila
manipulate [mə'nɪpjuleɪt] vt manipular
manipulation [mənɪpju'leɪʃən] n manipulación f, manejo
mankind [mæn'kaɪnd] n humanidad f, género humano
manliness ['mænlɪnɪs] n virilidad f, hombría
manly ['mænlɪ] adj varonil
man-made ['mæn'meɪd] adj artificial
manna ['mænə] n maná m
mannequin ['mænɪkɪn] n (dummy) maniquí m; (fashion model) maniquí m/f
manner ['mænəʳ] n manera, modo; (behaviour) conducta, manera de ser; (type) clase f; **manners** npl modales mpl, educación fsg; (**good**) **manners** (buena) educación fsg, (buenos) modales mpl; **bad manners** falta sg de educación, pocos modales mpl; **all ~ of** toda clase or suerte de
mannerism ['mænərɪzəm] n gesto típico
mannerly ['mænəlɪ] adj bien educado, formal
manoeuvrable, maneuvrable (US) [mə'nu:vrəbl] adj (car etc) manejable
manoeuvre, maneuver (US) [mə'nu:vəʳ] vt, vi maniobrar ■ n maniobra; **to ~ sb into doing sth** manipular a algn para que haga algo
manor ['mænəʳ] n (also: **manor house**) casa solariega
manpower ['mænpauəʳ] n mano f de obra
Manpower Services Commission n (Brit) comisión para el aprovechamiento de los recursos humanos
manservant ['mænsə:vənt] n criado
mansion ['mænʃən] n mansión f
manslaughter ['mænslɔ:təʳ] n homicidio involuntario

mantelpiece ['mæntlpi:s] n repisa de la chimenea
mantle ['mæntl] n manto
man-to-man ['mæntə'mæn] adj de hombre a hombre
manual ['mænjuəl] adj manual ■ n manual m; ~ **worker** obrero(-a), trabajador(a) m(f) manual
manufacture [mænju'fæktʃəʳ] vt fabricar ■ n fabricación f
manufactured goods [mænju'fæktʃəd-] npl manufacturas fpl, bienes mpl manufacturados
manufacturer [mænju'fæktʃərəʳ] n fabricante m/f
manufacturing industries [mænju'fæktʃərɪŋ-] npl industrias fpl manufactureras
manure [mə'njuəʳ] n estiércol m, abono
manuscript ['mænjuskrɪpt] n manuscrito
Manx [mæŋks] adj de la Isla de Man
many ['mɛnɪ] adj muchos(-as) ■ pron muchos(-as); **a great** ~ muchísimos, un buen número de; ~ **a time** muchas veces; **too** ~ **difficulties** demasiadas dificultades; **twice as** ~ el doble; **how** ~? ¿cuántos?
Maori ['maurɪ] adj, n maorí m/f
map [mæp] n mapa m ■ vt trazar el mapa de
▶ **map out** vt (fig: career, holiday, essay) proyectar, planear
maple ['meɪpl] n arce m, maple m (LAm)
mar [mɑ:ʳ] vt estropear
Mar abbr (= March) mar
marathon ['mærəθən] n maratón m ■ adj: **a** ~ **session** una sesión maratoniana
marathon runner n corredor(a) m(f) de maratones
marauder [mə'rɔ:dəʳ] n merodeador(a) m(f)
marble ['mɑ:bl] n mármol m; (toy) canica
March [mɑ:tʃ] n marzo; see also **July**
march [mɑ:tʃ] vi (Mil) marchar; (fig) caminar con resolución ■ n marcha; (demonstration) manifestación f
marcher ['mɑ:tʃəʳ] n manifestante m/f
marching ['mɑ:tʃɪŋ] n: **to give sb his ~ orders** (fig) mandar a paseo a algn; (employee) poner de patitas en la calle a algn
march-past ['mɑ:tʃpɑ:st] n desfile m
mare [mɛəʳ] n yegua
margarine [mɑ:dʒə'ri:n] n margarina
marg(e) [mɑ:dʒ] n abbr (col) = **margarine**
margin ['mɑ:dʒɪn] n margen m
marginal ['mɑ:dʒɪnl] adj marginal
marginally ['mɑ:dʒɪnəlɪ] adv ligeramente
marginal seat n (Pol) circunscripción f políticamente no definida
marigold ['mærɪgəuld] n caléndula

marijuana [mærɪ'wɑːnə] *n* marihuana
marina [mə'riːnə] *n* marina
marinade [mærɪ'neɪd] *n* adobo
marinate ['mærɪneɪt] *vt* adobar
marine [mə'riːn] *adj* marino ■ *n* soldado de infantería de marina
marine insurance *n* seguro marítimo
mariner ['mærɪnəʳ] *n* marinero, marino
marionette [mærɪə'nɛt] *n* marioneta, títere *m*
marital ['mærɪtl] *adj* matrimonial; ~ **status** estado civil
maritime ['mærɪtaɪm] *adj* marítimo
marjoram ['mɑːdʒərəm] *n* mejorana
mark [mɑːk] *n* marca, señal *f*; (*imprint*) huella; (*stain*) mancha; (*Brit Scol*) nota; (*currency*) marco ■ *vt* (*Sport: player*) marcar; (*stain*) manchar; (*Brit Scol*) calificar, corregir; **punctuation marks** signos *mpl* de puntuación; **to be quick off the ~** (*fig*) ser listo; **up to the ~** (*in efficiency*) a la altura de las circunstancias; **to ~ time** marcar el paso
▶ **mark down** *vt* (*reduce: prices, goods*) rebajar
▶ **mark off** *vt* (*tick*) indicar, señalar
▶ **mark out** *vt* trazar
▶ **mark up** *vt* (*price*) aumentar
marked [mɑːkt] *adj* marcado, acusado
markedly ['mɑːkɪdlɪ] *adv* marcadamente, apreciablemente
marker ['mɑːkəʳ] *n* (*sign*) marcador *m*; (*bookmark*) registro
market ['mɑːkɪt] *n* mercado ■ *vt* (*Comm*) comercializar; (*promote*) publicitar; **open ~** mercado libre; **to be on the ~** estar en venta; **to play the ~** jugar a la bolsa
marketable ['mɑːkɪtəbl] *adj* comerciable
market analysis *n* análisis *m* del mercado
market day *n* día *m* de mercado
market demand *n* demanda de mercado
market economy *n* economía de mercado
market forces *npl* tendencias *fpl* del mercado
market garden *n* (*Brit*) huerto
marketing ['mɑːkɪtɪŋ] *n* marketing *m*, mercadotecnia
marketing manager *n* director *m* de marketing
market leader *n* líder *m* de ventas
marketplace ['mɑːkɪtpleɪs] *n* mercado
market price *n* precio de mercado
market research *n* (*Comm*) estudios *mpl* de mercado
market value *n* valor *m* en el mercado
marking ['mɑːkɪŋ] *n* (*on animal*) pinta; (*on road*) señal *f*
marking ink *n* tinta indeleble *or* de marcar
marksman ['mɑːksmən] *n* tirador *m*
marksmanship ['mɑːksmənʃɪp] *n* puntería
mark-up ['mɑːkʌp] *n* (*Comm: margin*) margen

m de beneficio; (: *increase*) aumento
marmalade ['mɑːməleɪd] *n* mermelada de naranja
maroon [mə'ruːn] *vt*: **to be marooned** (*shipwrecked*) naufragar; (*fig*) quedar abandonado ■ *adj* granate *inv*
marquee [mɑː'kiː] *n* carpa, entoldado
marquess, marquis ['mɑːkwɪs] *n* marqués *m*
Marrakech, Marrakesh [mærə'kɛʃ] *n* Marrakech *m*
marriage ['mærɪdʒ] *n* (*state*) matrimonio; (*wedding*) boda; (*act*) casamiento
marriage bureau *n* agencia matrimonial
marriage certificate *n* partida de casamiento
marriage guidance, marriage counseling (US) *n* orientación *f* matrimonial
marriage of convenience *n* matrimonio de conveniencia
married ['mærɪd] *adj* casado; (*life, love*) conyugal
marrow ['mærəu] *n* médula; (*vegetable*) calabacín *m*
marry ['mærɪ] *vt* casarse con; (*father, priest etc*) casar ■ *vi* (*also*: **get married**) casarse
Mars [mɑːz] *n* Marte *m*
Marseilles [mɑː'seɪ] *n* Marsella
marsh [mɑːʃ] *n* pantano; (*salt marsh*) marisma
marshal ['mɑːʃl] *n* (*Mil*) mariscal *m*; (*at sports meeting, demonstration etc*) oficial *m*; (*US: of police, fire department*) jefe(-a) *m(f)* ■ *vt* (*facts*) ordenar; (*soldiers*) formar
marshalling yard ['mɑːʃəlɪŋ-] *n* (*Rail*) estación *f* clasificadora
marshmallow ['mɑːʃmæləu] *n* (*Bot*) malvavisco; (*sweet*) esponja, dulce *m* de merengue blando
marshy ['mɑːʃɪ] *adj* pantanoso
marsupial [mɑː'suːpɪəl] *adj, n* marsupial *m*
martial ['mɑːʃl] *adj* marcial
martial arts *npl* artes *fpl* marciales
martial law *n* ley *f* marcial
martin ['mɑːtɪn] *n* (*also*: **house martin**) avión *m*
martyr ['mɑːtəʳ] *n* mártir *m/f* ■ *vt* martirizar
martyrdom ['mɑːtədəm] *n* martirio
marvel ['mɑːvl] *n* maravilla, prodigio ■ *vi*: **to ~ (at)** maravillarse (de)
marvellous, (US) marvelous ['mɑːvləs] *adj* maravilloso
marvellously, (US) marvelously ['mɑːvləslɪ] *adv* maravillosamente
Marxism ['mɑːksɪzəm] *n* marxismo
Marxist ['mɑːksɪst] *adj, n* marxista *m/f*
marzipan ['mɑːzɪpæn] *n* mazapán *m*
mascara [mæs'kɑːrə] *n* rímel *m*
mascot ['mæskət] *n* mascota

m

masculine ['mæskjulɪn] *adj* masculino
masculinity [mæskju'lɪnɪtɪ] *n* masculinidad *f*
MASH [mæʃ] *n abbr* (*US Mil*) = **mobile army surgical hospital**
mash [mæʃ] *n* (*mix*) mezcla; (*Culin*) puré *m*; (*pulp*) amasijo
mashed potatoes [mæʃt-] *npl* puré *m* de patatas *or* (*LAm*) papas
mask [mɑːsk] *n* (*Elec*) máscara ■ *vt* enmascarar
masochism ['mæsəkɪzəm] *n* masoquismo
masochist ['mæsəukɪst] *n* masoquista *m/f*
mason ['meɪsn] *n* (*also*: **stonemason**) albañil *m*; (*also*: **freemason**) masón *m*
masonic [mə'sɔnɪk] *adj* masónico
masonry ['meɪsnrɪ] *n* masonería; (*building*) mampostería
masquerade [mæskə'reɪd] *n* baile *m* de máscaras; (*fig*) mascarada ■ *vi*: **to ~ as** disfrazarse de, hacerse pasar por
mass [mæs] *n* (*people*) muchedumbre *f*; (*Physics*) masa; (*Rel*) misa; (*great quantity*) montón *m* ■ *vi* reunirse; (*Mil*) concentrarse; **the masses** las masas; **to go to ~** ir a *or* oír misa
Mass. *abbr* (*US*) = **Massachusetts**
massacre ['mæsəkəʳ] *n* masacre *f* ■ *vt* masacrar
massage ['mæsɑːʒ] *n* masaje *m* ■ *vt* dar masajes *or* un masaje a
masseur [mæ'səːʳ] *n* masajista *m*
masseuse [mæ'səːz] *n* masajista *f*
massive ['mæsɪv] *adj* enorme; (*support, intervention*) masivo
mass media *npl* medios *mpl* de comunicación de masas
mass meeting *n* (*of everyone concerned*) reunión *f* en masa; (*huge*) mitin *m*
mass-produce ['mæsprə'djuːs] *vt* fabricar en serie
mass-production ['mæsprə'dʌkʃən] *n* fabricación *f or* producción *f* en serie
mast [mɑːst] *n* (*Naut*) mástil *m*; (*Radio etc*) torre *f*, antena
mastectomy [mæs'tɛktəmɪ] *n* mastectomía
master ['mɑːstəʳ] *n* (*of servant, animal*) amo; (*fig: of situation*) dueño; (*Art, Mus*) maestro; (*in secondary school*) profesor *m*; (*title for boys*): **M~ X** Señorito X ■ *vt* dominar
master disk *n* (*Comput*) disco maestro
masterful ['mɑːstəful] *adj* magistral, dominante
master key *n* llave *f* maestra
masterly ['mɑːstəlɪ] *adj* magistral
mastermind ['mɑːstəmaɪnd] *n* inteligencia superior ■ *vt* dirigir, planear
Master of Arts *n* licenciatura superior en

Letras; *see also* **master's degree**
Master of Ceremonies *n* encargado de protocolo
Master of Science *n* licenciatura superior en Ciencias; *see also* **master's degree**
masterpiece ['mɑːstəpiːs] *n* obra maestra
master plan *n* plan *m* rector
master's degree *n* máster *m*

● **MASTER'S DEGREE**
●
● Los estudios de postgrado británicos
● que llevan a la obtención de un *master's*
● *degree* consisten generalmente en una
● combinación de curso(s) académico(s)
● y tesina ("dissertation") sobre un
● tema original, o bien únicamente la
● redacción de una tesina. El primer caso
● es el más frecuente para los títulos
● de "MA" ("Master of Arts") y "MSc"
● ("Master of Science"), mientras que
● los de "MLitt" ("Master of Letters") o
● "MPhil" ("Master of Philosophy") se
● obtienen normalmente mediante tesina.
● En algunas universidades, como las
● escocesas, el título de *master's degree* no es
● de postgrado, sino que corresponde a la
● licenciatura.

master stroke *n* golpe *m* maestro
mastery ['mɑːstərɪ] *n* maestría
mastiff ['mæstɪf] *n* mastín *m*
masturbate ['mæstəbeɪt] *vi* masturbarse
masturbation [mæstə'beɪʃən] *n* masturbación *f*
mat [mæt] *n* alfombrilla; (*also*: **doormat**) felpudo ■ *adj* = **matt**
MAT *n abbr* (= *machine-assisted translation*) TAO
match [mætʃ] *n* cerilla, fósforo; (*game*) partido; (*fig*) igual *m/f* ■ *vt* emparejar; (*go well with*) hacer juego con; (*equal*) igualar ■ *vi* hacer juego; **to be a good ~** hacer buena pareja
matchbox ['mætʃbɔks] *n* caja de cerillas
matching ['mætʃɪŋ] *adj* que hace juego
matchless ['mætʃlɪs] *adj* sin par, incomparable
matchmaker ['mætʃmeɪkəʳ] *n* casamentero
mate [meɪt] *n* (*workmate*) compañero(-a), colega *m/f*; (*col: friend*) amigo(-a), compadre *m/f* (*LAm*); (*animal*) macho/hembra; (*in merchant navy*) primer oficial *m* ■ *vi* acoplarse, parearse ■ *vt* acoplar, parear
maté ['mɑːteɪ] *n* mate *m* (cocido), yerba mate
material [mə'tɪərɪəl] *n* (*substance*) materia; (*equipment*) material *m*; (*cloth*) tela, tejido ■ *adj* material; (*important*) esencial;

materials *npl* materiales *mpl*; (*equipment etc*) artículos *mpl*
materialistic [mətɪərɪə'lɪstɪk] *adj* materialista
materialize [mə'tɪərɪəlaɪz] *vi* materializarse
materially [mə'tɪərɪəlɪ] *adv* materialmente
maternal [mə'tɜːnl] *adj* maternal; ~ **grandmother** abuela materna
maternity [mə'tɜːnɪtɪ] *n* maternidad *f*
maternity benefit *n* subsidio por maternidad
maternity dress *n* vestido premamá
maternity hospital *n* hospital *m* de maternidad
maternity leave *n* baja por maternidad
math [mæθ] *n abbr* (US: = *mathematics*) matemáticas *fpl*
mathematical [mæθə'mætɪkl] *adj* matemático
mathematically [mæθɪ'mætɪklɪ] *adv* matemáticamente
mathematician [mæθəmə'tɪʃən] *n* matemático
mathematics [mæθə'mætɪks] *n* matemáticas *fpl*
maths [mæθs] *n abbr* (Brit: = *mathematics*) matemáticas *fpl*
matinée ['mætɪneɪ] *n* función *f* de la tarde, vermú(t) *m* (*LAm*)
mating ['meɪtɪŋ] *n* aparejamiento
mating call *n* llamada del macho
mating season *n* época de celo
matins ['mætɪnz] *n* maitines *mpl*
matriarchal [meɪtrɪ'ɑːkl] *adj* matriarcal
matrices ['meɪtrɪsiːz] *pl of* **matrix**
matriculation [mətrɪkju'leɪʃən] *n* matriculación *f*, matrícula
matrimonial [mætrɪ'məunɪəl] *adj* matrimonial
matrimony ['mætrɪmənɪ] *n* matrimonio
matrix (*pl* **matrices**) ['meɪtrɪks, 'meɪtrɪsiːz] *n* matriz *f*
matron ['meɪtrən] *n* (*in hospital*) enfermera jefe; (*in school*) ama de llaves
matronly ['meɪtrənlɪ] *adj* de matrona; (*fig: figure*) corpulento
matt [mæt] *adj* mate
matted ['mætɪd] *adj* enmarañado
matter ['mætər] *n* cuestión *f*, asunto; (*Physics*) sustancia, materia; (*content*) contenido; (*Med: pus*) pus *m* ■ *vi* importar; **it doesn't ~** no importa; **what's the ~?** ¿qué pasa?; **no ~ what** pase lo que pase; **as a ~ of course** por rutina; **as a ~ of fact** en realidad; **printed ~** impresos *mpl*; **reading ~** material *m* de lectura, lecturas *fpl*
matter-of-fact ['mætərəv'fækt] *adj* (*style*) prosaico; (*person*) práctico; (*voice*) neutro

mattress ['mætrɪs] *n* colchón *m*
mature [mə'tjuər] *adj* maduro ■ *vi* madurar
mature student *n* estudiante de más de 21 años
maturity [mə'tjuərɪtɪ] *n* madurez *f*
maudlin ['mɔːdlɪn] *adj* llorón(-ona)
maul [mɔːl] *vt* magullar
Mauritania [mɔːrɪ'teɪnɪə] *n* Mauritania
Mauritius [mə'rɪʃəs] *n* Mauricio
mausoleum [mɔːsə'lɪəm] *n* mausoleo
mauve [məuv] *adj* de color malva
maverick ['mævrɪk] *n* (*fig*) inconformista *m/f*, persona independiente
mawkish ['mɔːkɪʃ] *adj* sensiblero, empalagoso
max *abbr* = **maximum**
maxim ['mæksɪm] *n* máxima
maxima ['mæksɪmə] *pl of* **maximum**
maximize ['mæksɪmaɪz] *vt* (*profits etc*) llevar al máximo; (*chances*) maximizar
maximum ['mæksɪməm] *adj* máximo ■ *n* (*pl* **maxima**) ['mæksɪmə] máximo
May [meɪ] *n* mayo; *see also* **July**
may [meɪ] *vi* (*conditional* **might**) (*indicating possibility*): **he ~ come** puede que venga; (*be allowed to*): ~ **I smoke?** ¿puedo fumar?; (*wishes*): ~ **God bless you!** ¡que Dios le bendiga!; ~ **I sit here?** ¿me puedo sentar aquí?
maybe ['meɪbiː] *adv* quizá(s); ~ **not** quizá(s) no
May Day *n* el primero de Mayo
mayday ['meɪdeɪ] *n* señal *f* de socorro
mayhem ['meɪhɛm] *n* caos *m* total
mayonnaise [meɪə'neɪz] *n* mayonesa
mayor [mɛər] *n* alcalde *m*
mayoress ['mɛərɛs] *n* alcaldesa
maypole ['meɪpəul] *n* mayo
maze [meɪz] *n* laberinto
MB *abbr* (*Comput*) = **megabyte**; (*Canada*) = **Manitoba**
MBA *n abbr* (= *Master of Business Administration*) título universitario
MBBS, MBChB *n abbr* (Brit: = *Bachelor of Medicine and Surgery*) título universitario
MBE *n abbr* (Brit: = *Member of the Order of the British Empire*) título ceremonial
MBO *n abbr see* **management buyout**
MC *n abbr* (= *master of ceremonies*) e.p.; (US: = *Member of Congress*) diputado del Congreso de los Estados Unidos
MCAT *n abbr* (US: = *Medical College Admissions Test*) examen de ingreso en los estudios superiores de Medicina
MD *n abbr* (= *Doctor of Medicine*) título universitario; (*Comm*) = **managing director**; (= *MiniDisc®*) MiniDisc® *m*, minidisc *m* ■ *abbr* (US) = **Maryland**

Md. *abbr* (US) = **Maryland**
MD player *n* MiniDisc® *m*, minidisc *m*
MDT *n abbr* (US: = *Mountain Daylight Time*) hora de verano de las Montañas Rocosas
ME *abbr* (US Post: = *Maine*) ■ *n abbr* (US *Med*: = *medical examiner*); (*Med*: = *myalgic encephalomyelitis*) encefalomielitis *f* miálgica
me [mi:] *pron* (*direct*) me; (*stressed, after pronoun*) mí; **can you hear me?** ¿me oyes?; **he heard ME!** me oyó a mí; **it's me** soy yo; **give them to me** dámelos; **with/without me** conmigo/sin mí; **it's for me** es para mí
meadow ['mɛdəu] *n* prado, pradera
meagre, (US) **meager** ['mi:gəʳ] *adj* escaso, pobre
meal [mi:l] *n* comida; (*flour*) harina; **to go out for a ~** salir a comer
meals on wheels *nsg* (Brit) servicio de alimentación a domicilio para necesitados y tercera edad
mealtime ['mi:ltaɪm] *n* hora de comer
mealy-mouthed ['mi:lɪmauðd] *adj*: **to be ~** no decir nunca las cosas claras
mean [mi:n] *adj* (*with money*) tacaño; (*unkind*) mezquino, malo; (*average*) medio; (US: *vicious: animal*) resabiado; (: *person*) malicioso ■ *vt* (*pt, pp* **meant** [mɛnt]) (*signify*) querer decir, significar; (*intend*): **to ~ to do sth** tener la intención de *or* pensar hacer algo ■ *n* medio, término medio; **do you ~ it?** ¿lo dices en serio?; **what do you ~?** ¿qué quiere decir?; **to be meant for sb/sth** ser para algn/algo; *see also* **means**
meander [mɪ'ændəʳ] *vi* (*river*) serpentear; (*person*) vagar
meaning ['mi:nɪŋ] *n* significado, sentido
meaningful ['mi:nɪŋful] *adj* significativo
meaningless ['mi:nɪŋlɪs] *adj* sin sentido
meanness ['mi:nnɪs] *n* (*with money*) tacañería; (*unkindness*) maldad *f*, mezquindad *f*
means [mi:nz] *npl* medio *sg*, manera *sg*; (*resource*) recursos *mpl*, medios *mpl*; **by ~ of** mediante, por medio de; **by all ~!** ¡naturalmente!, ¡claro que sí!
means test *n* control *m* de los recursos económicos
meant [mɛnt] *pt, pp of* **mean**
meantime ['mi:ntaɪm], **meanwhile** ['mi:nwaɪl] *adv* (*also*: **in the meantime**) mientras tanto
measles ['mi:zlz] *n* sarampión *m*
measly ['mi:zlɪ] *adj* (*col*) miserable
measurable ['mɛʒərəbl] *adj* mensurable, que se puede medir
measure ['mɛʒəʳ] *vt* medir; (*for clothes etc*) tomar las medidas a ■ *vi* medir ■ *n*

medida; (*ruler*) cinta métrica, metro; **a litre ~** una medida de un litro; **some ~ of success** cierto éxito; **to take measures to do sth** tomar medidas para hacer algo
▶ **measure up** *vi*: **to ~ up (to)** estar a la altura (de)
measured ['mɛʒəd] *adj* moderado; (*tone*) mesurado
measurement ['mɛʒəmənt] *n* (*measure*) medida; (*act*) medición *f*; **to take sb's measurements** tomar las medidas a algn
meat [mi:t] *n* carne *f*; **cold meats** fiambres *mpl*; **crab ~** carne *f* de cangrejo
meatball ['mi:tbɔ:l] *n* albóndiga
meat pie *n* pastel *m* de carne
meaty ['mi:tɪ] *adj* (*person*) fuerte, corpulento; (*role*) sustancioso; **a ~ meal** una comida con bastante carne
Mecca ['mɛkə] *n* (*city*) la Meca; (*fig*) meca
mechanic [mɪ'kænɪk] *n* mecánico(-a)
mechanical [mɪ'kænɪkl] *adj* mecánico
mechanical engineering *n* (*science*) ingeniería mecánica; (*industry*) construcción *f* mecánica
mechanics [mə'kænɪks] *n* mecánica ■ *npl* mecanismo *sg*
mechanism ['mɛkənɪzəm] *n* mecanismo
mechanization [mɛkənaɪ'zeɪʃən] *n* mecanización *f*
mechanize ['mɛkənaɪz] *vt* mecanizar; (*factory etc*) automatizar
MEd *n abbr* (= *Master of Education*) título universitario
medal ['mɛdl] *n* medalla
medallion [mɪ'dælɪən] *n* medallón *m*
medallist, (US) **medalist** ['mɛdlɪst] *n* (*Sport*) medallista *m/f*
meddle ['mɛdl] *vi*: **to ~ in** entrometerse en; **to ~ with sth** manosear algo
meddlesome ['mɛdlsəm], **meddling** ['mɛdlɪŋ] *adj* (*interfering*) entrometido; (*touching things*) curioso
media ['mi:dɪə] *npl* medios *mpl* de comunicación
media circus *n* excesivo despliegue informativo
mediaeval [mɛdɪ'i:vl] *adj* = **medieval**
median ['mi:dɪən] *n* (US: *also*: **median strip**) mediana
media research *n* estudio de los medios de publicidad
mediate ['mi:dɪeɪt] *vi* mediar
mediation [mi:dɪ'eɪʃən] *n* mediación *f*
mediator ['mi:dɪeɪtəʳ] *n* mediador(a) *m(f)*
Medicaid ['mɛdɪkeɪd] *n* (US) programa de ayuda médica
medical ['mɛdɪkl] *adj* médico ■ *n* (*also*: **medical examination**) reconocimiento médico

medical certificate n certificado m médico
Medicare ['mɛdɪkɛəʳ] n (US) seguro médico del Estado
medicated ['mɛdɪkeɪtɪd] adj medicinal
medication [mɛdɪ'keɪʃən] n (drugs etc) medicación f
medicinal [mɛ'dɪsɪnl] adj medicinal
medicine ['mɛdsɪn] n medicina; (drug) medicamento
medicine chest n botiquín m
medicine man n hechicero
medieval [mɛdɪ'iːvl] adj medieval
mediocre [miːdɪ'əʊkəʳ] adj mediocre
mediocrity [miːdɪ'ɔkrɪtɪ] n mediocridad f
meditate ['mɛdɪteɪt] vi meditar
meditation [mɛdɪ'teɪʃən] n meditación f
Mediterranean [mɛdɪtə'reɪnɪən] adj mediterráneo; **the ~ (Sea)** el (Mar m) Mediterráneo
medium ['miːdɪəm] adj mediano; (level, height) medio ■ n (pl **media**) (means) medio (pl **mediums**) (person) médium m/f; **happy ~** punto justo
medium-dry ['miːdɪəm'draɪ] adj semiseco
medium-sized ['miːdɪəm'saɪzd] adj de tamaño mediano; (clothes) de (la) talla mediana
medium wave n onda media
medley ['mɛdlɪ] n mezcla; (Mus) popurrí m
meek [miːk] adj manso, sumiso
meekly ['miːklɪ] adv mansamente, dócilmente
meet [miːt] (pt, pp **met**) vt encontrar; (accidentally) encontrarse con; (by arrangement) reunirse con; (for the first time) conocer; (go and fetch) ir a buscar; (opponent) enfrentarse con; (obligations) cumplir; (bill, expenses) pagar, costear ■ vi encontrarse; (in session) reunirse; (join: objects) unirse; (get to know) conocerse ■ n (Brit Hunting) cacería; (US Sport) encuentro; **pleased to ~ you!** ¡encantado (de conocerle)!, ¡mucho gusto!
▶ **meet up** vi: **to ~ up with sb** reunirse con algn
▶ **meet with** vt fus reunirse con; (difficulty) tropezar con
meeting ['miːtɪŋ] n (also Sport: rally) encuentro; (arranged) cita, compromiso (LAm); (formal session, business meeting) reunión f; (Pol) mitin m; **to call a ~** convocar una reunión
meeting place n lugar m de reunión or encuentro
megabyte ['mɛgə'baɪt] n (Comput) megabyte m, megaocteto
megalomaniac [mɛgələʊ'meɪnɪæk] adj, n megalómano(-a) m(f)

megaphone ['mɛgəfəʊn] n megáfono
megawatt ['mɛgəwɔt] n megavatio
meh [mɛ] excl ¡bah!
melancholy ['mɛlənkəlɪ] n melancolía ■ adj melancólico
melee ['mɛleɪ] n refriega
mellow ['mɛləʊ] adj (wine) añejo; (sound, colour) suave; (fruit) maduro ■ vi (person) madurar
melodious [mɪ'ləʊdɪəs] adj melodioso
melodrama ['mɛləʊdrɑːmə] n melodrama m
melodramatic [mɛləʊdrə'mætɪk] adj melodramático
melody ['mɛlədɪ] n melodía
melon ['mɛlən] n melón m
melt [mɛlt] vi (metal) fundirse; (snow) derretirse; (fig) ablandarse ■ vt (also: **melt down**) fundir; **melted butter** mantequilla derretida
▶ **melt away** vi desvanecerse
meltdown ['mɛltdaʊn] n (in nuclear reactor) fusión f (de un reactor nuclear)
melting point ['mɛltɪŋ-] n punto de fusión
melting pot ['mɛltɪŋ-] n (fig) crisol m; **to be in the ~** estar sobre el tapete
member ['mɛmbəʳ] n (of political party) miembro; (of club) socio(-a); **M~ of Parliament (MP)** (Brit) diputado(-a); **M~ of the European Parliament (MEP)** (Brit) eurodiputado(-a); **M~ of the House of Representatives (MHR)** (US) diputado(-a) del Congreso de los Estados Unidos; **M~ of the Scottish Parliament (MSP)** (Brit) diputado(-a) m(f) del Parlamento escocés
membership ['mɛmbəʃɪp] n (members) miembros mpl; socios mpl; (numbers) número de miembros or socios; **to seek ~ of** pedir el ingreso a
membership card n carnet m de socio
membrane ['mɛmbreɪn] n membrana
memento [mə'mɛntəʊ] n recuerdo
memo ['mɛməʊ] n abbr (= memorandum) nota (de servicio)
memoirs ['mɛmwɑːz] npl memorias fpl
memo pad n bloc m de notas
memorable ['mɛmərəbl] adj memorable
memorandum (memoranda) [mɛmə'rændəm, -də] n nota (de servicio); (Pol) memorándum m
memorial [mɪ'mɔːrɪəl] n monumento conmemorativo ■ adj conmemorativo
Memorial Day n (US) día de conmemoración de los caídos en la guerra
memorize ['mɛməraɪz] vt aprender de memoria
memory ['mɛmərɪ] n memoria; (recollection) recuerdo; (Comput) memoria; **to have a**

m

good/bad ~ tener buena/mala memoria; **loss of ~** pérdida de memoria

memory stick n (Comput) barra de memoria

men [mɛn] pl of **man**

menace ['mɛnəs] n amenaza; (col: nuisance) lata ▪ vt amenazar; **a public ~** un peligro público

menacing ['mɛnɪsɪŋ] adj amenazador(-a)

menacingly ['mɛnɪsɪŋlɪ] adv amenazadoramente

menagerie [mɪ'nædʒərɪ] n casa de fieras

mend [mɛnd] vt reparar, arreglar; (darn) zurcir ▪ vi reponerse ▪ n (gen) remiendo; (darn) zurcido; **to be on the ~** ir mejorando

mending ['mɛndɪŋ] n arreglo, reparación f; (clothes) ropa por remendar

menial ['miːnɪəl] adj (pej) bajo, servil

meningitis [mɛnɪn'dʒaɪtɪs] n meningitis f

menopause ['mɛnəupɔːz] n menopausia

men's room n (US): **the ~** el servicio de caballeros

menstrual ['mɛnstruəl] adj menstrual

menstruate ['mɛnstrueɪt] vi menstruar

menstruation [mɛnstru'eɪʃən] n menstruación f

menswear ['mɛnzwɛə'] n confección f de caballero

mental ['mɛntl] adj mental; **~ illness** enfermedad f mental

mental hospital n (hospital m) psiquiátrico

mentality [mɛn'tælɪtɪ] n mentalidad f

mentally ['mɛntlɪ] adv: **to be ~ handicapped** ser un disminuido mental

menthol ['mɛnθɔl] n mentol m

mention ['mɛnʃən] n mención f ▪ vt mencionar; (speak of) hablar de; **don't ~ it!** ¡de nada!; **I need hardly ~ that ...** huelga decir que ...; **not to ~, without mentioning** sin contar

mentor ['mɛntɔː'] n mentor m

menu ['mɛnjuː] n (set menu) menú m; (printed) carta; (Comput) menú m

menu-driven ['mɛnjuːdrɪvn] adj (Comput) guiado por menú

MEP n abbr = **Member of the European Parliament**

mercantile ['məːkəntaɪl] adj mercantil

mercenary ['məːsɪnərɪ] adj, n mercenario(-a)

merchandise ['məːtʃəndaɪz] n mercancías fpl

merchandiser ['məːtʃəndaɪzə'] n comerciante m/f, tratante m

merchant ['məːtʃənt] n comerciante m/f

merchant bank n (Brit) banco comercial

merchantman ['məːtʃəntmən] n buque m mercante

merchant navy, (US) **merchant marine** n marina mercante

merciful ['məːsɪful] adj compasivo

mercifully ['məːsɪfulɪ] adv con compasión; (fortunately) afortunadamente

merciless ['məːsɪlɪs] adj despiadado

mercilessly ['məːsɪlɪslɪ] adv despiadadamente, sin piedad

mercurial [məː'kjuərɪəl] adj veleidoso, voluble

mercury ['məːkjurɪ] n mercurio

mercy ['məːsɪ] n compasión f; (Rel) misericordia; **at the ~ of** a la merced de

mercy killing n eutanasia

mere [mɪə'] adj simple, mero

merely ['mɪəlɪ] adv simplemente, sólo

merge [məːdʒ] vt (join) unir; (mix) mezclar; (fuse) fundir; (Comput: files, text) intercalar ▪ vi unirse; (Comm) fusionarse

merger ['məːdʒə'] n (Comm) fusión f

meridian [mə'rɪdɪən] n meridiano

meringue [mə'ræŋ] n merengue m

merit ['mɛrɪt] n mérito ▪ vt merecer

meritocracy [mɛrɪ'tɔkrəsɪ] n meritocracia

mermaid ['məːmeɪd] n sirena

merriment ['mɛrɪmənt] n alegría

merry ['mɛrɪ] adj alegre; **M~ Christmas!** ¡Felices Pascuas!

merry-go-round ['mɛrɪgəuraund] n tiovivo

mesh [mɛʃ] n malla; (Tech) engranaje m ▪ vi (gears) engranar; **wire ~** tela metálica

mesmerize ['mɛzməraɪz] vt hipnotizar

mess [mɛs] n confusión f; (of objects) revoltijo; (tangle) lío; (Mil) comedor m; **to be (in) a ~** (room) estar revuelto; **to be/get o.s. in a ~** estar/meterse en un lío

▸ **mess about, mess around** vi (col) perder el tiempo; (pass the time) pasar el rato

▸ **mess about** or **around with** vt fus (col: play with) divertirse con; (: handle) manosear

▸ **mess up** vt (disarrange) desordenar; (spoil) estropear; (dirty) ensuciar

message ['mɛsɪdʒ] n recado, mensaje m; **to get the ~** (fig, col) enterarse

message switching n (Comput) conmutación f de mensajes

messenger ['mɛsɪndʒə'] n mensajero(-a)

Messiah [mɪ'saɪə] n Mesías m

Messrs, Messrs. abbr (on letters: = Messieurs) Sres

messy ['mɛsɪ] adj (dirty) sucio; (untidy) desordenado; (confused: situation etc) confuso

Met [mɛt] n abbr (US) = **Metropolitan Opera**

met [mɛt] pt, pp of **meet** ▪ adj abbr = **meteorological**

metabolism [mɛ'tæbəlɪzəm] n metabolismo

metal ['mɛtl] n metal m

metallic [mɛ'tælɪk] adj metálico

metallurgy [mɛ'tælədʒɪ] n metalurgia

metalwork ['mɛtlwəːk] n (craft) metalistería
metamorphosis (pl **metamorphoses**)
[mɛtə'mɔːfəsɪs, -siːz] n metamorfosis f inv
metaphor ['mɛtəfəʳ] n metáfora
metaphorical [mɛtə'fɔrɪkl] adj metafórico
metaphysics [mɛtə'fɪzɪks] n metafísica
mete [miːt]: **to ~ out** vt fus (punishment)
imponer
meteor ['miːtɪəʳ] n meteoro
meteoric [miːtɪ'ɒrɪk] adj (fig) meteórico
meteorite ['miːtɪəraɪt] n meteorito
meteorological [miːtɪərə'lɒdʒɪkl] adj
meteorológico
meteorology [miːtɪə'rɒlədʒɪ] n meteorología
meter ['miːtəʳ] n (instrument) contador m;
(US: unit) = **metre** ■ vt (US Post) franquear;
parking ~ parquímetro
methane ['miːθeɪn] n metano
method ['mɛθəd] n método; **~ of payment**
método de pago
methodical [mɪ'θɒdɪkl] adj metódico
Methodist ['mɛθədɪst] adj, n metodista m/f
methodology [mɛθə'dɒlədʒɪ] n metodología
meths [mɛθs] n (Brit) = **methylated spirit**
methylated spirit ['mɛθɪleɪtɪd-] n (Brit)
alcohol m metilado or desnaturalizado
meticulous [mɛ'tɪkjuləs] adj meticuloso
metre, meter (US) ['miːtəʳ] n metro
metric ['mɛtrɪk] adj métrico; **to go ~** pasar al
sistema métrico
metrication [mɛtrɪ'keɪʃən] n conversión f al
sistema métrico
metric system n sistema m métrico
metric ton n tonelada métrica
metronome ['mɛtrənəum] n metrónomo
metropolis [mɪ'trɒpəlɪs] n metrópoli(s) f
metropolitan [mɛtrə'pɒlɪtən] adj
metropolitano
Metropolitan Police n (Brit): **the ~** la policía
londinense
mettle ['mɛtl] n valor m, ánimo
mew [mjuː] vi (cat) maullar
mews [mjuːz] (Brit) n: **~ cottage** casa
acondicionada en antiguos establos o cocheras;
~ flat piso en antiguos establos o cocheras
Mexican ['mɛksɪkən] adj, n mejicano(-a) m(f),
mexicano(-a) m(f) (LAm)
Mexico ['mɛksɪkəu] n Méjico, México (LAm)
Mexico City n Ciudad f de Méjico or (LAm)
México
mezzanine ['mɛtsəniːn] n entresuelo
MFA n abbr (US: = Master of Fine Arts) título
universitario
mfr abbr (= manufacturer) fab; = **manufacture**
mg abbr (= milligram) mg
Mgr abbr (= Monseigneur, Monsignor) Mons;
(Comm) = **manager**

mgr abbr = **manager**
MHR n abbr (US) see **Member of the House of
Representatives**
MHz abbr (= megahertz) MHz
MI abbr (US) = **Michigan**
MI5 n abbr (Brit: = Military Intelligence, section five)
servicio de contraespionaje del gobierno británico
MI6 n abbr (Brit: = Military Intelligence, section six)
servicio de inteligencia del gobierno británico
MIA abbr (Mil: = missing in action) desaparecido
miaow [miː'au] vi maullar
mice [maɪs] pl of **mouse**
Mich. abbr (US) = **Michigan**
mickey ['mɪkɪ] n: **to take the ~ out of sb**
tomar el pelo a algn
micro ['maɪkrəu] n = **microcomputer**
micro... [maɪkrəu] pref micro...
microbe ['maɪkrəub] n microbio
microbiology [maɪkrəubaɪ'ɒlədʒɪ] n
microbiología
microchip ['maɪkrəutʃɪp] n microchip m,
microplaqueta
microcomputer ['maɪkrəukəm'pjuːtəʳ] n
microordenador m, microcomputador m
(LAm)
microcosm ['maɪkrəukɔzəm] n microcosmo
microeconomics ['maɪkrəuiːkə'nɔmɪks] n
microeconomía
microfiche ['maɪkrəufiːʃ] n microficha
microfilm ['maɪkrəufɪlm] n microfilm m
microlight ['maɪkrəulaɪt] n ultraligero
micrometer [maɪ'krɔmɪtəʳ] n micrómetro
microphone ['maɪkrəfəun] n micrófono
microprocessor ['maɪkrəu'prəusɛsəʳ] n
microprocesador m
microscope ['maɪkrəskəup] n microscopio;
under the ~ al microscopio
microscopic [maɪkrə'skɔpɪk] adj
microscópico
microwave ['maɪkrəuweɪv] n (also:
microwave oven) horno microondas
mid [mɪd] adj: **in ~ May** a mediados de mayo;
in ~ afternoon a media tarde; **in ~ air** en
el aire; **he's in his ~ thirties** tiene unos
treinta y cinco años
midday [mɪd'deɪ] n mediodía m
middle ['mɪdl] n medio, centro; (waist)
cintura ■ adj de en medio; **in the ~ of
the night** en plena noche; **I'm in the ~ of
reading it** lo estoy leyendo ahora mismo
middle-aged [mɪdl'eɪdʒd] adj de mediana
edad
Middle Ages npl: **the ~** la Edad sg Media
middle class n: **the ~(es)** la clase media
■ adj: **middle-class** de clase media
Middle East n Oriente m Medio
middleman ['mɪdlmæn] n intermediario

m

middle management n dirección f de nivel medio

middle name n segundo nombre m

middle-of-the-road ['mɪdləvðə'rəud] adj moderado

middleweight ['mɪdlweɪt] n (Boxing) peso medio

middling ['mɪdlɪŋ] adj mediano

Middx abbr (Brit) = **Middlesex**

midge [mɪdʒ] n mosquito

midget ['mɪdʒɪt] n enano(-a)

midi system n cadena midi

Midlands ['mɪdləndz] npl región central de Inglaterra

midnight ['mɪdnaɪt] n medianoche f; **at ~** a medianoche

midriff ['mɪdrɪf] n diafragma m

midst [mɪdst] n: **in the ~ of** entre, en medio de

midsummer [mɪd'sʌmə^r] n: **a ~ day** un día de pleno verano

Midsummer's Day n Día m de San Juan

midway [mɪd'weɪ] adj, adv: **~ (between)** a mitad de camino or a medio camino (entre)

midweek [mɪd'wiːk] adv entre semana

midwife (pl **midwives**) ['mɪdwaɪf, -waɪvz] n comadrona

midwifery ['mɪdwɪfərɪ] n tocología

midwinter [mɪd'wɪntə^r] n: **in ~** en pleno invierno

miffed [mɪft] adj (col) mosqueado

might [maɪt] vb see **may** ■ n fuerza, poder m; **he ~ be there** puede que esté allí, a lo mejor está allí; **I ~ as well go** más vale que vaya; **you ~ like to try** podría intentar

mightily ['maɪtɪlɪ] adv fuertemente, poderosamente; **I was ~ surprised** me sorprendí enormemente

mightn't ['maɪtnt] = **might not**

mighty ['maɪtɪ] adj fuerte, poderoso

migraine ['miːgreɪn] n jaqueca

migrant ['maɪgrənt] adj migratorio ■ n (bird) ave f migratoria; (worker) emigrante m/f

migrate [maɪ'greɪt] vi emigrar

migration [maɪ'greɪʃən] n emigración f

mike [maɪk] n abbr (= microphone) micro

Milan [mɪ'læn] n Milán m

mild [maɪld] adj (person) apacible; (climate) templado; (slight) ligero; (taste) suave; (illness) leve

mildew ['mɪldjuː] n moho

mildly ['maɪldlɪ] adv ligeramente; suavemente; **to put it ~** por no decir algo peor

mildness ['maɪldnɪs] n suavidad f; (of illness) levedad f

mile [maɪl] n milla; **to do 20 miles per gallon** hacer 20 millas por galón

mileage ['maɪlɪdʒ] n número de millas; (Aut) kilometraje m

mileage allowance n ≈ asignación f por kilometraje

mileometer [maɪ'lɔmɪtə^r] n (Brit) = **milometer**

milestone ['maɪlstəun] n mojón m; (fig) hito

milieu ['miːljəː] n (medio) ambiente m, entorno

militant ['mɪlɪtnt] adj, n militante m/f

militarism ['mɪlɪtərɪzəm] n militarismo

militaristic [mɪlɪtə'rɪstɪk] adj militarista

military ['mɪlɪtərɪ] adj militar

military service n servicio militar

militate ['mɪlɪteɪt] vi: **to ~ against** militar en contra de

militia [mɪ'lɪʃə] n milicia

milk [mɪlk] n leche f ■ vt (cow) ordeñar; (fig) chupar

milk chocolate n chocolate m con leche

milk float n (Brit) furgoneta de la leche

milking ['mɪlkɪŋ] n ordeño

milkman ['mɪlkmən] n lechero, repartidor m de la leche

milk shake n batido, malteada (LAm)

milk tooth n diente m de leche

milk truck n (US) = **milk float**

milky ['mɪlkɪ] adj lechoso

Milky Way n Vía Láctea

mill [mɪl] n (windmill etc) molino; (coffee mill) molinillo; (factory) fábrica; (spinning mill) hilandería ■ vt moler ■ vi (also: **mill about**) arremolinarse

milled [mɪld] (grain) molido; (coin, edge) acordonado

millennium (pl **millenniums** or **millennia**) [mɪ'lɛnɪəm, 'lɛnɪə] n milenio, milenario

millennium bug n (Comput): **the ~** el (problema del) efecto 2000

miller ['mɪlə^r] n molinero

millet ['mɪlɪt] n mijo

milli... ['mɪlɪ] pref mili...

milligram, milligramme ['mɪlɪgraem] n miligramo

millilitre, (US) **milliliter** ['mɪlɪliːtə^r] n mililitro

millimetre, (US) **millimeter** ['mɪlɪmiːtə^r] n milímetro

milliner ['mɪlɪnə^r] n sombrerero(-a)

millinery ['mɪlɪnərɪ] n sombrerería

million ['mɪljən] n millón m; **a ~ times** un millón de veces

millionaire [mɪljə'nɛə^r] n millonario(-a)

millipede ['mɪlɪpiːd] n milpiés m inv

millstone ['mɪlstəun] n piedra de molino

millwheel ['mɪlwiːl] n rueda de molino

milometer [maɪˈlɒmɪtəʳ] n (Brit) cuentakilómetros m inv

mime [maɪm] n mímica; (actor) mimo(-a) ■ vt remedar ■ vi actuar de mimo

mimic [ˈmɪmɪk] n imitador(a) m(f) ■ adj mímico ■ vt remedar, imitar

mimicry [ˈmɪmɪkrɪ] n imitación f

Min abbr (Brit Pol: = Ministry) Min

min. abbr (= minute(s)) m.; := **minimum**

minaret [mɪnəˈrɛt] n alminar m, minarete m

mince [mɪns] vt picar ■ vi (in walking) andar con pasos menudos ■ n (Brit Culin) carne f picada, picadillo

mincemeat [ˈmɪnsmiːt] n conserva de fruta picada

mince pie n pastelillo relleno de fruta picada

mincer [ˈmɪnsəʳ] n picadora de carne

mincing [ˈmɪnsɪŋ] adj afectado

mind [maɪnd] n (gen) mente f; (contrasted with matter) espíritu m ■ vt (attend to, look after) ocuparse de, cuidar; (be careful of) tener cuidado con; (object to): **I don't ~ the noise** no me molesta el ruido; **it is on my ~** me preocupa; **to my ~** a mi parecer or juicio; **to change one's ~** cambiar de idea or de parecer; **to bring** or **call sth to ~** recordar algo; **to have sth/sb in ~** tener algo/a algn en mente; **to be out of one's ~** haber perdido el juicio; **to bear sth in ~** tomar or tener algo en cuenta; **to make up one's ~** decidirse; **it went right out of my ~** se me fue por completo (de la cabeza); **to be in two minds about sth** estar indeciso or dudar ante algo; **I don't ~** me es igual; **~ you, ...** te advierto que ...; **never ~!** ¡es igual!, ¡no importa!; (don't worry) ¡no te preocupes!; '**~ the step**' 'cuidado con el escalón'

mind-boggling [ˈmaɪndbɒglɪŋ] adj (col) alucinante, increíble

-minded [-maɪndɪd] adj: **fair~** imparcial; **an industrially~ nation** una nación orientada a la industria

minder [ˈmaɪndəʳ] n guardaespaldas m inv

mindful [ˈmaɪndful] adj: **~ of** consciente de

mindless [ˈmaɪndlɪs] adj (violence, crime) sin sentido; (work) de autómata

mine [maɪn] pron (el) mío/(la) mía etc; **a friend of ~** un(a) amigo(-a) mío/mía ■ adj: **this book is ~** este libro es mío ■ n mina ■ vt (coal) extraer; (ship, beach) minar

mine detector n detector m de minas

minefield [ˈmaɪnfiːld] n campo de minas

miner [ˈmaɪnəʳ] n minero(-a)

mineral [ˈmɪnərəl] adj mineral ■ n mineral m; **minerals** npl (Brit: soft drinks) refrescos mpl con gas

mineral water n agua mineral

minesweeper [ˈmaɪnswiːpəʳ] n dragaminas m inv

mingle [ˈmɪŋgl] vi: **to ~ with** mezclarse con

mingy [ˈmɪndʒɪ] adj (col) tacaño

mini ... [mɪnɪ] pref mini..., micro...

miniature [ˈmɪnətʃəʳ] adj (en) miniatura ■ n miniatura

minibus [ˈmɪnɪbʌs] n microbús m

minicab [ˈmɪnɪkæb] n taxi m (que sólo puede pedirse por teléfono)

minicomputer [ˈmɪnɪkəmˈpjuːtəʳ] n miniordenador m, minicomputador m (LAm)

MiniDisc® [ˈmɪnɪdɪsk] n MiniDisc® m

minim [ˈmɪnɪm] n (Brit Mus) blanca

minimal [ˈmɪnɪml] adj mínimo

minimalist [ˈmɪnɪməlɪst] adj, n minimalista m/f

minimize [ˈmɪnɪmaɪz] vt minimizar

minimum [ˈmɪnɪməm] n (pl **minima**) [ˈmɪnɪmə] mínimo ■ adj mínimo; **to reduce to a ~** reducir algo al mínimo; **~ wage** salario mínimo

minimum lending rate n tipo de interés mínimo

mining [ˈmaɪnɪŋ] n minería ■ adj minero

minion [ˈmɪnjən] n secuaz m

mini-series [ˈmɪnɪsɪəriːz] n serie f de pocos capítulos, miniserie f

miniskirt [ˈmɪnɪskəːt] n minifalda

minister [ˈmɪnɪstəʳ] n (Brit Pol) ministro(-a); (Rel) pastor m ■ vi: **to ~ to** atender a

ministerial [mɪnɪsˈtɪərɪəl] adj (Brit Pol) ministerial

ministry [ˈmɪnɪstrɪ] n (Brit Pol) ministerio; (Rel) sacerdocio; **M~ of Defence** Ministerio de Defensa

mink [mɪŋk] n visón m

mink coat n abrigo de visón

Minn. abbr (US) = **Minnesota**

minnow [ˈmɪnəu] n pececillo (de agua dulce)

minor [ˈmaɪnəʳ] adj (unimportant) secundario; (Mus) menor ■ n (Law) menor m/f de edad

Minorca [mɪˈnɔːkə] n Menorca

minority [maɪˈnɒrɪtɪ] n minoría; **to be in a ~** estar en or ser minoría

minority interest n participación f minoritaria

minster [ˈmɪnstəʳ] n catedral f

minstrel [ˈmɪnstrəl] n juglar m

mint [mɪnt] n (plant) menta, hierbabuena; (sweet) caramelo de menta ■ vt (coins) acuñar; **the (Royal) M~**, (US) **the (US) M~** la Casa de la Moneda; **in ~ condition** en perfecto estado

mint sauce n salsa de menta

minuet [mɪnjuˈɛt] n minué m

minus [ˈmaɪnəs] n (also: **minus sign**) signo menos ■ prep menos

m

minuscule ['mɪnəskjuːl] *adj* minúsculo
minute *n* ['mɪnɪt] minuto; (*fig*) momento;
minutes *npl* (*of meeting*) actas *fpl* ■ *adj*
[maɪ'njuːt] diminuto; (*search*) minucioso;
it is 5 minutes past 3 son las 3 y 5 (minutos);
at the last ~ a última hora; **wait a ~!** ¡espera
un momento!; **up to the ~** de última hora;
in ~ detail con todo detalle
minute book *n* libro de actas
minute hand *n* minutero
minutely [maɪ'njuːtlɪ] *adv* (*by a small amount*)
por muy poco; (*in detail*) detalladamente,
minuciosamente
minutiae [mɪ'njuːʃiiː] *npl* minucias *fpl*
miracle ['mɪrəkl] *n* milagro
miracle play *n* auto, milagro
miraculous [mɪ'rækjuləs] *adj* milagroso
miraculously [mɪ'rækjuləslɪ] *adv*
milagrosamente
mirage ['mɪrɑːʒ] *n* espejismo
mire [maɪə^r] *n* fango, lodo
mirror ['mɪrə^r] *n* espejo; (*in car*) retrovisor *m*
■ *vt* reflejar
mirror image *n* reflejo inverso
mirth [məːθ] *n* alegría; (*laughter*) risa, risas *fpl*
misadventure [mɪsəd'vɛntʃə^r] *n* desventura;
death by ~ muerte *f* accidental
misanthropist [mɪ'zænθrəpɪst] *n*
misántropo(-a)
misapply [mɪsə'plaɪ] *vt* emplear mal
misapprehension ['mɪsæprɪ'hɛnʃən] *n*
equivocación *f*
misappropriate [mɪsə'prəuprɪeɪt] *vt* (*funds*)
malversar
misappropriation ['mɪsəprəuprɪ'eɪʃən] *n*
malversación *f*, desfalco
misbehave [mɪsbɪ'heɪv] *vi* portarse mal
misbehaviour, misbehavior (*US*)
[mɪsbɪ'heɪvjə^r] *n* mala conducta
misc. *abbr* = **miscellaneous**
miscalculate [mɪs'kælkjuleɪt] *vt* calcular mal
miscalculation [mɪskælkju'leɪʃən] *n* error *m*
(de cálculo)
miscarriage ['mɪskærɪdʒ] *n* (*Med*) aborto (no
provocado); **~ of justice** error *m* judicial
miscarry [mɪs'kærɪ] *vi* (*Med*) abortar
(de forma natural); (*fail: plans*) fracasar,
malograrse
miscellaneous [mɪsɪ'leɪnɪəs] *adj* varios(-as),
diversos(-as); **~ expenses** gastos diversos
miscellany [mɪ'sɛlənɪ] *n* miscelánea
mischance [mɪs'tʃɑːns] *n* desgracia, mala
suerte *f*; **by (some) ~** por (alguna) desgracia
mischief ['mɪstʃɪf] *n* (*naughtiness*) travesura;
(*harm*) mal *m*, daño; (*maliciousness*) malicia
mischievous ['mɪstʃɪvəs] *adj* travieso;
dañino; (*playful*) malicioso

mischievously ['mɪstʃɪvəslɪ] *adv* por
travesura; maliciosamente
misconception ['mɪskən'sɛpʃən] *n* concepto
erróneo; equivocación *f*
misconduct [mɪs'kɔndʌkt] *n* mala conducta;
professional ~ falta profesional
misconstrue [mɪskən'struː] *vt* interpretar
mal
miscount [mɪs'kaunt] *vt*, *vi* contar mal
misdeed [mɪs'diːd] *n* (*old*) fechoría, delito
misdemeanour, misdemeanor (*US*)
[mɪsdɪ'miːnə^r] *n* delito, ofensa
misdirect [mɪsdɪ'rɛkt] *vt* (*person*) informar
mal; (*letter*) poner señas incorrectas en
miser ['maɪzə^r] *n* avaro(-a)
miserable ['mɪzərəbl] *adj* (*unhappy*) triste,
desgraciado; (*wretched*) miserable; **to feel ~**
sentirse triste
miserably ['mɪzərəblɪ] *adv* (*smile, answer*)
tristemente; (*fail*) rotundamente; **to pay ~**
pagar una miseria
miserly ['maɪzəlɪ] *adj* avariento, tacaño
misery ['mɪzərɪ] *n* (*unhappiness*) tristeza;
(*wretchedness*) miseria, desdicha
misfire [mɪs'faɪə^r] *vi* fallar
misfit ['mɪsfɪt] *n* (*person*) inadaptado(-a)
misfortune [mɪs'fɔːtʃən] *n* desgracia
misgiving [mɪs'gɪvɪŋ] *n*, **misgivings**
[mɪs'gɪvɪŋz] *npl* (*mistrust*) recelo;
(*apprehension*) presentimiento; **to have
misgivings about sth** tener dudas sobre
algo
misguided [mɪs'gaɪdɪd] *adj* equivocado
mishandle [mɪs'hændl] *vt* (*treat roughly*)
maltratar; (*mismanage*) manejar mal
mishap ['mɪshæp] *n* desgracia, contratiempo
mishear [mɪs'hɪə^r] *vt*, *vi* (*irreg: like* **hear**) oír
mal
mishmash ['mɪʃmæʃ] *n* (*col*) revoltijo
misinform [mɪsɪn'fɔːm] *vt* informar mal
misinterpret [mɪsɪn'təːprɪt] *vt* interpretar
mal
misinterpretation ['mɪsɪntəːprɪ'teɪʃən] *n*
mala interpretación *f*
misjudge [mɪs'dʒʌdʒ] *vt* juzgar mal
mislay [mɪs'leɪ] *vt* (*irreg: like* **lay**) extraviar,
perder
mislead [mɪs'liːd] *vt* (*irreg: like* **lead**) llevar a
conclusiones erróneas; (*deliberately*) engañar
misleading [mɪs'liːdɪŋ] *adj* engañoso
misled [mɪs'lɛd] *pt*, *pp of* **mislead**
mismanage [mɪs'mænɪdʒ] *vt* administrar
mal
mismanagement [mɪs'mænɪdʒmənt] *n*
mala administración *f*
misnomer [mɪs'nəumə^r] *n* término
inapropiado *or* equivocado

misogynist [mɪ'sɔdʒɪnɪst] n misógino
misplace [mɪs'pleɪs] vt (lose) extraviar;
misplaced (trust etc) inmerecido
misprint ['mɪsprɪnt] n errata, error m de
imprenta
mispronounce [mɪsprə'naʊns] vt
pronunciar mal
misquote ['mɪs'kwəʊt] vt citar
incorrectamente
misread [mɪs'riːd] vt (irreg: like **read**) leer mal
misrepresent [mɪsrɛprɪ'zɛnt] vt falsificar
misrepresentation [mɪsrɛprɪzɛn'teɪʃən] n
(Law) falsa declaración f
Miss [mɪs] n Señorita; **Dear ~ Smith**
Estimada Señorita Smith
miss [mɪs] vt (train etc) perder; (shot) errar,
fallar; (appointment, class) faltar a; (escape,
avoid) evitar; (notice loss of: money etc) notar la
falta de, echar en falta; (regret the absence of): **I
~ him** le echo de menos ■ vi fallar ■ n (shot)
tiro fallido; **the bus just missed the wall**
faltó poco para que el autobús se estrella
contra el muro; **you're missing the point**
no has entendido la idea
▶ **miss out** vt (Brit) omitir
▶ **miss out on** vt fus (fun, party, opportunity)
perderse
Miss. abbr (US) = **Mississippi**
missal ['mɪsl] n misal m
misshapen [mɪs'ʃeɪpən] adj deforme
missile ['mɪsaɪl] n (Aviat) misil m; (object
thrown) proyectil m
missile base n base f de misiles
missile launcher n lanzamisiles m inv
missing ['mɪsɪŋ] adj (pupil) ausente, que falta;
(thing) perdido; (Mil) desaparecido; **to be ~**
faltar; **~ person** desaparecido(-a)
mission ['mɪʃən] n misión f; **on a ~ for sb** en
una misión para algn
missionary ['mɪʃənrɪ] n misionero(-a)
misspell [mɪs'spɛl] vt (irreg: like **spell**) escribir
mal
misspent ['mɪs'spɛnt] adj: **his ~ youth** su
juventud disipada
mist [mɪst] n (light) neblina; (heavy) niebla;
(at sea) bruma ■ vi (also: **mist over, mist up**:
weather) nublarse; (Brit: windows) empañarse
mistake [mɪs'teɪk] n error m ■ vt (irreg: like
take) entender mal; **by ~** por equivocación;
to make a ~ (about sb/sth) equivocarse; (in
writing, calculating etc) cometer un error; **to ~ A
for B** confundir A con B
mistaken [mɪs'teɪkən] pp of **mistake** ■ adj
(idea etc) equivocado; **to be ~** equivocarse,
engañarse; **~ identity** identificación f
errónea
mistakenly [mɪs'teɪkənlɪ] adv erróneamente

mister ['mɪstər] n (col) señor m; see **Mr**
mistletoe ['mɪsltəʊ] n muérdago
mistook [mɪs'tʊk] pt of **mistake**
mistranslation [mɪstræns'leɪʃən] n mala
traducción f
mistreat [mɪs'triːt] vt maltratar, tratar mal
mistress ['mɪstrɪs] n (lover) amante f; (of
house) señora (de la casa); (Brit: in primary
school) maestra; (in secondary school) profesora;
see also **Mrs**
mistrust [mɪs'trʌst] vt desconfiar de ■ n:
~ (of) desconfianza (de)
mistrustful [mɪs'trʌstful] adj: **~ (of)**
desconfiado (de), receloso (de)
misty ['mɪstɪ] adj nebuloso, brumoso; (day) de
niebla; (glasses) empañado
misty-eyed ['mɪstɪ'aɪd] adj sentimental
misunderstand [mɪsʌndə'stænd] vt, vi (irreg:
like **understand**) entender mal
misunderstanding [mɪsʌndə'stændɪŋ] n
malentendido
misunderstood [mɪsʌndə'stʊd] pt,
pp of **misunderstand** ■ adj (person)
incomprendido
misuse n [mɪs'juːs] mal uso; (of power) abuso
■ vt [mɪs'juːz] abusar de; (funds) malversar
MIT n abbr (US) = **Massachusetts Institute of
Technology**
mite [maɪt] n (small quantity) pizca; **poor ~!**
¡pobrecito!
mitigate ['mɪtɪgeɪt] vt mitigar; **mitigating
circumstances** circunstancias fpl
atenuantes
mitigation [mɪtɪ'geɪʃən] n mitigación f,
alivio
mitre, (US) **miter** ['maɪtər] n mitra
mitt ['mɪt], **mitten** ['mɪtn] n manopla
mix [mɪks] vt (gen) mezclar; (combine) unir
■ vi mezclarse; (people) llevarse bien ■ n
mezcla; **to ~ sth with sth** mezclar algo
con algo; **to ~ business with pleasure**
combinar los negocios con el placer; **cake ~**
preparado para pastel
▶ **mix in** vt (eggs etc) añadir
▶ **mix up** vt mezclar; (confuse) confundir;
to be mixed up in sth estar metido en algo
mixed [mɪkst] adj (assorted) variado, surtido;
(school, marriage etc) mixto
mixed-ability ['mɪkstə'bɪlɪtɪ] adj (class etc) de
alumnos de distintas capacidades
mixed blessing n: **it's a ~** tiene su lado bueno
y su lado malo
mixed doubles n (Sport) mixtos mpl
mixed economy n economía mixta
mixed grill n (Brit) parrillada mixta
mixed-up [mɪkst'ʌp] adj (confused) confuso,
revuelto

m

mixer ['mɪksəʳ] n (for food) batidora; (person): **he's a good ~** tiene don de gentes
mixer tap n (grifo) monomando
mixture ['mɪkstʃəʳ] n mezcla
mix-up ['mɪksʌp] n confusión f
Mk abbr (Brit Tech: = mark) Mk
mkt abbr = **market**
MLA n abbr (Brit Pol: Northern Ireland: = Member of the Legislative Assembly) miembro de la asamblea legislativa
MLitt n abbr (= Master of Literature, Master of Letters) título universitario de postgrado; see also **master's degree**
MLR n abbr (Brit) = **minimum lending rate**
mm abbr (= millimetre) mm
MMR vaccine n (against measles, mumps, rubella) vacuna triple vírica
MMS n abbr (= multimedia messaging service) MMS m
MN abbr (Brit) = **Merchant Navy**; (US) = **Minnesota**
MO n abbr (Med) = **medical officer**; (US col) = **modus operandi** ■ abbr (US) = **Missouri**
Mo. abbr (US) = **Missouri**
m.o. abbr (= money order) g/
moan [məun] n gemido ■ vi gemir; (col: complain): **to ~ (about)** quejarse (de)
moaning ['məunɪŋ] n gemidos mpl; quejas fpl
moat [məut] n foso
mob [mɔb] n multitud f; (pej): **the ~** el populacho ■ vt acosar
mobile ['məubaɪl] adj móvil ■ n móvil m
mobile home n caravana
mobile phone n teléfono móvil
mobility [məu'bɪlɪtɪ] n movilidad f; **~ of labour** or (US) **labor** movilidad f de la mano de obra
mobilize ['məubɪlaɪz] vt movilizar
moccasin ['mɔkəsɪn] n mocasín m
mock [mɔk] vt (make ridiculous) ridiculizar; (laugh at) burlarse de ■ adj fingido
mockery ['mɔkərɪ] n burla; **to make a ~ of** desprestigiar
mocking ['mɔkɪŋ] adj (tone) burlón(-ona)
mockingbird ['mɔkɪŋbəːd] n sinsonte m (LAm), zenzontle m (LAm)
mock-up ['mɔkʌp] n maqueta
MOD n abbr (Brit) = **Ministry of Defence**; see **defence**
mod cons ['mɔd'kɔnz] npl abbr (= modern conveniences) see **convenience**
mode [məud] n modo; (of transport) medio; (Comput) modo, modalidad f
model ['mɔdl] n (gen) modelo; (Arch) maqueta; (person: for fashion, art) modelo m/f ■ adj modelo inv ■ vt modelar ■ vi ser modelo; **~ railway** ferrocarril m de juguete;

to ~ clothes pasar modelos, ser modelo; **to ~ on** crear a imitación de
modelling, (US) **modeling** ['mɔdlɪŋ] n (modelmaking) modelado
modem ['məudəm] n módem m
moderate [adj, n 'mɔdərət, vb 'mɔdəreɪt] adj, n moderado(-a) m(f) ■ vi moderarse, calmarse ■ vt moderar
moderately ['mɔdərətlɪ] adv (act) con moderación; (expensive, difficult) medianamente; (pleased, happy) bastante
moderation [mɔdə'reɪʃən] n moderación f; **in ~** con moderación
moderator ['mɔdəreɪtəʳ] n (mediator) moderador(a) m(f)
modern ['mɔdən] adj moderno; **~ languages** lenguas fpl modernas
modernity [mə'dəːnɪtɪ] n modernidad f
modernization [mɔdənaɪ'zeɪʃən] n modernización f
modernize ['mɔdənaɪz] vt modernizar
modest ['mɔdɪst] adj modesto
modestly ['mɔdɪstlɪ] adv modestamente
modesty ['mɔdɪstɪ] n modestia
modicum ['mɔdɪkəm] n: **a ~ of** un mínimo de
modification [mɔdɪfɪ'keɪʃən] n modificación f; **to make modifications** hacer cambios or modificaciones
modify ['mɔdɪfaɪ] vt modificar
modish ['məudɪʃ] adj de moda
Mods [mɔdz] n abbr (Brit: = (Honour) Moderations) examen de licenciatura de la universidad de Oxford
modular ['mɔdjuləʳ] adj (filing, unit) modular
modulate ['mɔdjuleɪt] vt modular
modulation [mɔdju'leɪʃən] n modulación f
module ['mɔdju:l] n módulo
modus operandi ['məudəsɔpə'rændi:] n manera de actuar
Mogadishu [mɔgə'dɪʃu:] n Mogadiscio
mogul ['məugəl] n (fig) magnate m
MOH n abbr (Brit) = **Medical Officer of Health**
mohair ['məuhɛəʳ] n mohair m
Mohammed [mə'hæmɛd] n Mahoma m
moist [mɔɪst] adj húmedo
moisten ['mɔɪsn] vt humedecer
moisture ['mɔɪstʃəʳ] n humedad f
moisturize ['mɔɪstʃəraɪz] vt (skin) hidratar
moisturizer ['mɔɪstʃəraɪzəʳ] n crema hidratante
molar ['məuləʳ] n muela
molasses [məu'læsɪz] n melaza
mold [məuld] n, vt (US) = **mould**
Moldavia [mɔl'deɪvɪə], **Moldova** [mɔl'dəuvə] n Moldavia, Moldova
Moldavian [mɔl'deɪvɪən], **Moldovan** [mɔl'dəuvən] adj, n moldavo(-a) m(f)

mole [məʊl] n (animal) topo; (spot) lunar m
molecular [məˈlɛkjʊləʳ] adj molecular
molecule [ˈmɒlɪkjuːl] n molécula
molest [məʊˈlɛst] vt importunar; (sexually) abordar con propósitos deshonestos
moll [mɒl] n (slang) amiga
mollusc, mollusk (US) [ˈmɒləsk] n molusco
mollycoddle [ˈmɒlɪkɒdl] vt mimar
Molotov cocktail [ˈmɒlətɒf-] n cóctel m Molotov
molt [məʊlt] vi (US) = **moult**
molten [ˈməʊltən] adj fundido; (lava) líquido
mom [mɒm] n (US) = **mum**
moment [ˈməʊmənt] n momento; **at** or **for the ~** de momento, por el momento, por ahora; **in a ~** dentro de un momento
momentarily [ˈməʊməntrɪlɪ] adv momentáneamente; (US: very soon) de un momento a otro
momentary [ˈməʊməntərɪ] adj momentáneo
momentous [məʊˈmɛntəs] adj trascendental, importante
momentum [məʊˈmɛntəm] n momento; (fig) ímpetu m; **to gather ~** cobrar velocidad; (fig) cobrar fuerza
mommy [ˈmɒmɪ] n (US) = **mummy**
Mon abbr (= Monday) lun
Monaco [ˈmɒnəkəʊ] n Mónaco
monarch [ˈmɒnək] n monarca m/f
monarchist [ˈmɒnəkɪst] n monárquico(-a)
monarchy [ˈmɒnəkɪ] n monarquía
monastery [ˈmɒnəstərɪ] n monasterio
monastic [məˈnæstɪk] adj monástico
Monday [ˈmʌndɪ] n lunes m inv; see also **Tuesday**
Monegasque [mɒnɪˈgæsk] adj, n monegasco(-a) m(f)
monetarist [ˈmʌnɪtərɪst] n monetarista m/f
monetary [ˈmʌnɪtərɪ] adj monetario
monetary policy n política monetaria
money [ˈmʌnɪ] n dinero, plata (LAm); **to make ~** ganar dinero; **I've got no ~ left** no me queda dinero
moneyed [ˈmʌnɪd] adj adinerado
moneylender [ˈmʌnɪlɛndəʳ] n prestamista m/f
moneymaker [ˈmʌnɪmeɪkəʳ] n (Brit col: business) filón m
moneymaking [ˈmʌnɪmeɪkɪŋ] adj rentable
money market n mercado monetario
money order n giro
money-spinner [ˈmʌnɪspɪnəʳ] n (col: person, idea, business) filón m
money supply n oferta monetaria, medio circulante, volumen m monetario
Mongol [ˈmɒŋgəl] n mongol(a) m(f); (Ling)

mongol m
mongol [ˈmɒŋgəl] adj, n (Med) mongólico
Mongolia [mɒŋˈgəʊlɪə] n Mongolia
Mongolian [mɒŋˈgəʊlɪən] adj mongol(a) ■ n mongol(a) m(f); (Ling) mongol m
mongoose [ˈmɒŋguːs] n mangosta
mongrel [ˈmʌŋgrəl] n (dog) perro cruzado
monitor [ˈmɒnɪtəʳ] n monitor m ■ vt controlar; (foreign station) escuchar
monk [mʌŋk] n monje m
monkey [ˈmʌŋkɪ] n mono
monkey business n, **monkey tricks** ■ npl tejemanejes mpl
monkey nut n (Brit) cacahuete m, maní m (LAm)
monkey wrench n llave f inglesa
mono [ˈmɒnəʊ] adj (broadcast etc) mono inv
mono... [mɒnəʊ] pref mono ...
monochrome [ˈmɒnəʊkrəʊm] adj monocromo
monocle [ˈmɒnəkl] n monóculo
monogamous [məˈnɒgəməs] adj monógamo
monogram [ˈmɒnəgræm] n monograma m
monolith [ˈmɒnəlɪθ] n monolito
monolithic [mɒnəˈlɪθɪk] adj monolítico
monologue [ˈmɒnəlɒg] n monólogo
monoplane [ˈmɒnəpleɪn] n monoplano
monopolist [məˈnɒpəlɪst] n monopolista m/f
monopolize [məˈnɒpəlaɪz] vt monopolizar
monopoly [məˈnɒpəlɪ] n monopolio; **Monopolies and Mergers Commission** (Brit) comisión reguladora de monopolios y fusiones
monorail [ˈmɒnəʊreɪl] n monocarril m, monorraíl m
monosodium glutamate [mɒnəˈsəʊdɪəm ˈgluːtəmeɪt] n glutamato monosódico
monosyllabic [mɒnəsɪˈlæbɪk] adj monosílabo
monosyllable [ˈmɒnəsɪləbl] n monosílabo
monotone [ˈmɒnətəʊn] n voz f (or tono) monocorde
monotonous [məˈnɒtənəs] adj monótono
monotony [məˈnɒtənɪ] n monotonía
monoxide [məˈnɒksaɪd] n: **carbon ~** monóxido de carbono
monseigneur [mɒnsɛnˈjəːʳ], **monsignor** [mɒnˈsiːnjəʳ] n monseñor m
monsoon [mɒnˈsuːn] n monzón m
monster [ˈmɒnstəʳ] n monstruo
monstrosity [mɒnsˈtrɒsɪtɪ] n monstruosidad f
monstrous [ˈmɒnstrəs] adj (huge) enorme; (atrocious) monstruoso
Mont. abbr (US) = **Montana**
montage [mɒnˈtɑːʒ] n montaje m
Mont Blanc [mɔ̃ˈblɑ̃] n Mont Blanc m
month [mʌnθ] n mes m; **300 dollars a ~** 300 dólares al mes; **every ~** cada mes

m

monthly ['mʌnθlı] *adj* mensual ■ *adv* mensualmente ■ *n* (*magazine*) revista, mensual; **twice** ~ dos veces al mes; ~ **instalment** mensualidad *f*

monument ['mɔnjumənt] *n* monumento

monumental [mɔnju'mɛntl] *adj* monumental

moo [mu:] *vi* mugir

mood [mu:d] *n* humor *m*; **to be in a good/ bad** ~ estar de buen/mal humor

moodily ['mu:dɪlɪ] *adv* malhumoradamente

moodiness ['mu:dɪnɪs] *n* humor *m* cambiante; (*bad mood*) mal humor *m*

moody ['mu:dɪ] *adj* (*variable*) de humor variable; (*sullen*) malhumorado

moon [mu:n] *n* luna

moonbeam ['mu:nbi:m] *n* rayo de luna

moon landing *n* alunizaje *m*

moonless ['mu:nlɪs] *adj* sin luna

moonlight ['mu:nlaɪt] *n* luz *f* de la luna ■ *vi* hacer pluriempleo

moonlighting ['mu:nlaɪtɪŋ] *n* pluriempleo

moonlit ['mu:nlɪt] *adj*: **a** ~ **night** una noche de luna

moonshot ['mu:nʃɔt] *n* lanzamiento de una astronave a la luna

moonstruck ['mu:nstrʌk] *adj* chiflado

moony ['mu:nɪ] *adj*: **to have** ~ **eyes** estar soñando despierto, estar pensando en las musarañas

Moor [muəʳ] *n* moro(-a)

moor [muəʳ] *n* páramo ■ *vt* (*ship*) amarrar ■ *vi* echar las amarras

moorings ['muərɪŋz] *npl* (*chains*) amarras *fpl*; (*place*) amarradero *sg*

Moorish ['muərɪʃ] *adj* moro; (*architecture*) árabe

moorland ['muələnd] *n* páramo, brezal *m*

moose [mu:s] *n pl inv* alce *m*

moot [mu:t] *vt* proponer para la discusión, sugerir ■ *adj*: ~ **point** punto discutible

mop [mɔp] *n* fregona; (*of hair*) greñas *fpl* ■ *vt* fregar
▶ **mop up** *vt* limpiar

mope [məup] *vi* estar deprimido
▶ **mope about, mope around** *vi* andar abatido

moped ['məupɛd] *n* ciclomotor *m*

moquette [mɔ'kɛt] *n* moqueta

MOR *adj abbr* (*Mus*: = *middle-of-the-road*) para el gran público

moral ['mɔrl] *adj* moral ■ *n* moraleja; **morals** *npl* moralidad *f*, moral *f*

morale [mɔ'rɑ:l] *n* moral *f*

morality [mə'rælɪtɪ] *n* moralidad *f*

moralize ['mɔrəlaɪz] *vi*: **to** ~ (**about**) moralizar (sobre)

morally ['mɔrəlɪ] *adv* moralmente

moral victory *n* victoria moral

morass [mə'ræs] *n* pantano

moratorium [mɔrə'tɔ:rɪəm] *n* moratoria

morbid ['mɔ:bɪd] *adj* (*interest*) morboso; (*Med*) mórbido

 KEYWORD

more [mɔ:ʳ] *adj* **1** (*greater in number etc*) más; **more people/work than before** más gente/ trabajo que antes

2 (*additional*) más; **do you want (some) more tea?** ¿quieres más té?; **is there any more wine?** ¿queda vino?; **it'll take a few more weeks** tardará unas semanas más; **it's 2 kms more to the house** faltan 2 kms para la casa; **more time/letters than we expected** más tiempo del que/más cartas de las que esperábamos; **I have no more money, I don't have any more money** (ya) no tengo más dinero

■ *pron* (*greater amount, additional amount*) más; **more than 10** más de 10; **it cost more than the other one/than we expected** costó más que el otro/más de lo que esperábamos; **is there any more?** ¿hay más?; **I want more** quiero más; **and what's more ...** y además ...; **many/much more** muchos(-as)/ mucho(-a) más

■ *adv* más; **more dangerous/easily (than)** más peligroso/fácilmente (que); **more and more expensive** cada vez más caro; **more or less** más o menos; **more than ever** más que nunca; **she doesn't live here any more** ya no vive aquí

moreover [mɔ:'rəuvəʳ] *adv* además, por otra parte

morgue [mɔ:g] *n* depósito de cadáveres

MORI ['mɔ:rɪ] *n abbr* (*Brit*) = **Market and Opinion Research Institute**

moribund ['mɔrɪbʌnd] *adj* moribundo

Mormon ['mɔ:mən] *n* mormón(-ona) *m(f)*

morning ['mɔ:nɪŋ] *n* (*gen*) mañana; (*early morning*) madrugada; **in the** ~ por la mañana; **7 o'clock in the** ~ las 7 de la mañana; **this** ~ esta mañana

morning-after pill ['mɔ:nɪŋ'ɑ:ftə-] *n* píldora del día después

morning sickness *n* (*Med*) náuseas *fpl* del embarazo

Moroccan [mə'rɔkən] *adj, n* marroquí *m/f*

Morocco [mə'rɔkəu] *n* Marruecos *m*

moron ['mɔ:rɔn] *n* imbécil *m/f*

morose [mə'rəus] *adj* hosco, malhumorado

morphine ['mɔ:fi:n] *n* morfina

morris dancing ['mɔrɪs-] n (Brit) baile tradicional inglés en el que se llevan cascabeles en la ropa
Morse [mɔːs] n (also: **Morse code**) (alfabeto) morse m
morsel ['mɔːsl] n (of food) bocado
mortal ['mɔːtl] adj, n mortal m
mortality [mɔːˈtælɪtɪ] n mortalidad f
mortality rate n tasa de mortalidad
mortally ['mɔːtəlɪ] adv mortalmente
mortar ['mɔːtəʳ] n argamasa; (implement) mortero
mortgage ['mɔːgɪdʒ] n hipoteca ▪ vt hipotecar; **to take out a ~** sacar una hipoteca
mortgage company n (US) ≈ banco hipotecario
mortgagee [mɔːgəˈdʒiː] n acreedor(a) m(f) hipotecario(-a)
mortgager ['mɔːgədʒəʳ] n deudor(a) m(f) hipotecario(-a)
mortice ['mɔːtɪs] = **mortise**
mortician [mɔːˈtɪʃən] n (US) director(a) m(f) de pompas fúnebres
mortification ['mɔːtɪfɪˈkeɪʃən] n mortificación f, humillación f
mortified ['mɔːtɪfaɪd] adj: **I was ~** me dio muchísima vergüenza
mortise ['mɔːtɪs], **mortise lock** n cerradura de muesca
mortuary ['mɔːtjuərɪ] n depósito de cadáveres
mosaic [məuˈzeɪɪk] n mosaico
Moscow ['mɔskəu] n Moscú m
Moslem ['mɔzləm] adj, n = **Muslim**
mosque [mɔsk] n mezquita
mosquito (pl **mosquitoes**) [mɔsˈkiːtəu] n mosquito
moss [mɔs] n musgo
mossy ['mɔsɪ] adj musgoso, cubierto de musgo
most [məust] adj la mayor parte de, la mayoría de ▪ pron la mayor parte, la mayoría ▪ adv el más; (very) muy; **the ~** (also: + adjective) el más; **~ of them** la mayor parte de ellos; **I saw the ~** yo fui el que más vi; **at the (very) ~** a lo sumo, todo lo más; **to make the ~ of** aprovechar (al máximo); **a ~ interesting book** un libro interesantísimo
mostly ['məustlɪ] adv en su mayor parte, principalmente
MOT n abbr (Brit: = Ministry of Transport): **the ~ (test)** ≈ la ITV
motel [məuˈtɛl] n motel m
moth [mɔθ] n mariposa nocturna; (clothes moth) polilla
mothball ['mɔθbɔːl] n bola de naftalina

moth-eaten ['mɔθiːtn] adj apolillado
mother ['mʌðəʳ] n madre f ▪ adj materno ▪ vt (care for) cuidar (como una madre)
mother board n (Comput) placa madre
motherhood ['mʌðəhud] n maternidad f
mother-in-law ['mʌðərɪnlɔː] n suegra
motherly ['mʌðəlɪ] adj maternal
mother-of-pearl ['mʌðərəv'pəːl] n nácar m
mother's help n niñera
mother-to-be ['mʌðətə'biː] n futura madre
mother tongue n lengua materna
mothproof ['mɔθpruːf] adj a prueba de polillas
motif [məuˈtiːf] n motivo; (theme) tema m
motion ['məuʃən] n movimiento; (gesture) ademán m, señal f; (at meeting) moción f; (Brit: also: **bowel motion**) evacuación f intestinal ▪ vt, vi: **to ~ (to) sb to do sth** hacer señas a algn para que haga algo; **to be in ~** (vehicle) estar en movimiento; **to set in ~** poner en marcha; **to go through the motions of doing sth** (fig) hacer algo mecánicamente or sin convicción
motionless ['məuʃənlɪs] adj inmóvil
motion picture n película
motivate ['məutɪveɪt] vt motivar
motivated ['məutɪveɪtɪd] adj motivado
motivation [məutɪˈveɪʃən] n motivación f
motivational research [məutɪˈveɪʃənl-] n estudios mpl de motivación
motive ['məutɪv] n motivo; **from the best motives** con las mejores intenciones
motley ['mɔtlɪ] adj variopinto
motor ['məutəʳ] n motor m; (Brit: col: vehicle) coche m, carro (LAm), automóvil m, auto m (LAm) ▪ adj motor/motora, motriz
motorbike ['məutəbaɪk] n moto f
motorboat ['məutəbəut] n lancha motora
motorcade ['məutəkeɪd] n desfile m de automóviles
motorcar ['məutəkɑːʳ] n (Brit) coche m, carro (LAm), automóvil m, auto m (LAm)
motorcoach ['məutəkəutʃ] n autocar m, autobús m, camión m (LAm)
motorcycle ['məutəsaɪkl] n motocicleta
motorcycle racing n motociclismo
motorcyclist ['məutəsaɪklɪst] n motociclista m/f
motoring ['məutərɪŋ] n (Brit) automovilismo ▪ adj (accident, offence) de tráfico or tránsito
motorist ['məutərɪst] n conductor(a) m(f), automovilista m/f
motorize ['məutəraɪz] vt motorizar
motor oil n aceite m para motores
motor racing n (Brit) carreras fpl de coches, automovilismo

motor scooter n vespa®
motor vehicle n automóvil m
motorway ['məutəwei] n (Brit) autopista
mottled ['mɔtld] adj moteado
motto (pl **mottoes**) ['mɔtəu] n lema m;
(watchword) consigna
mould, mold (US) [məuld] n molde m;
(mildew) moho ■ vt moldear; (fig) formar
moulder, molder (US) ['məuldər] vi (decay)
decaer
moulding, molding (US) ['məuldɪŋ] n (Arch)
moldura
mouldy, moldy (US) ['məuldɪ] adj
enmohecido
moult, molt (US) [məult] vi mudar la piel;
(bird) mudar las plumas
mound [maund] n montón m, montículo
mount [maunt] n monte m; (horse) montura;
(for jewel etc) engarce m; (for picture) marco ■ vt
montar en, subir a; (stairs) subir; (exhibition)
montar; (attack) lanzar; (stamp) pegar, fijar;
(picture) enmarcar ■ vi (also: **mount up**)
subirse, montarse
mountain ['mauntɪn] n montaña ■ cpd de
montaña; **to make a ~ out of a molehill**
hacer una montaña de un grano de arena
mountain bike n bicicleta de montaña
mountaineer [mauntɪ'nɪər] n
montañero(-a), alpinista m/f, andinista m/f
(LAm)
mountaineering [mauntɪ'nɪərɪŋ] n
montañismo, alpinismo, andinismo (LAm)
mountainous ['mauntɪnəs] adj montañoso
mountain range n sierra
mountain rescue team n equipo de rescate
de montaña
mountainside ['mauntɪnsaɪd] n ladera de la
montaña
mounted ['mauntɪd] adj montado
Mount Everest n Monte m Everest
mourn [mɔːn] vt llorar, lamentar ■ vi: **to ~**
for llorar la muerte de, lamentarse por
mourner ['mɔːnər] n doliente m/f
mournful ['mɔːnful] adj triste, lúgubre
mourning ['mɔːnɪŋ] n luto ■ cpd (dress) de
luto; **in ~** de luto
mouse (pl **mice**) [maus, maɪs] n (also Comput)
ratón m
mouse mat, mouse pad n (Comput)
alfombrilla, almohadilla
mousetrap ['maustræp] n ratonera
mousse [muːs] n (Culin) mousse f; (for hair)
espuma (moldeadora)
moustache [məs'tɑːʃ], (US) **mustache**
['mʌstæʃ] n bigote m
mousy ['mausɪ] adj (person) tímido; (hair)
pardusco

mouth (pl **mouths**) [mauθ, -ðz] n boca; (of
river) desembocadura
mouthful ['mauθful] n bocado
mouth organ n armónica
mouthpiece ['mauθpiːs] n (of musical
instrument) boquilla; (Tel) micrófono;
(spokesman) portavoz m/f
mouth-to-mouth ['mauθtə'mauθ] adj (also:
mouth-to-mouth resuscitation) boca a
boca m
mouthwash ['mauθwɔʃ] n enjuague m bucal
mouth-watering ['mauθwɔːtərɪŋ] adj
apetitoso
movable ['muːvəbl] adj movible
move [muːv] n (movement) movimiento; (in
game) jugada; (: turn to play) turno; (change of
house) mudanza ■ vt mover; (emotionally)
conmover; (Pol: resolution etc) proponer ■ vi
(gen) moverse; (traffic) circular; (Brit: also:
move house) trasladarse, mudarse; **to ~ sb**
to do sth mover a algn a hacer algo; **to be**
moved estar conmovido; **to get a ~ on** darse
prisa
▶ **move about** or **around** vi moverse; (travel)
viajar
▶ **move along** vi (stop loitering) circular; (along
seat etc) correrse
▶ **move away** vi (leave) marcharse
▶ **move back** vi (return) volver
▶ **move down** vt (demote) degradar
▶ **move forward** vi avanzar ■ vt adelantar
▶ **move in** vi (to a house) instalarse
▶ **move off** vi ponerse en camino
▶ **move on** vi seguir viaje ■ vt (onlookers)
hacer circular
▶ **move out** vi (of house) mudarse
▶ **move over** vi hacerse a un lado, correrse
▶ **move up** vi subir; (employee) ascender
movement ['muːvmənt] n movimiento;
(Tech) mecanismo; **~ (of the bowels)** (Med)
evacuación f
mover ['muːvər] n proponente m/f
movie ['muːvɪ] n película; **to go to the**
movies ir al cine
movie camera n cámara cinematográfica
moviegoer ['muːvɪɡəuər] n (US)
aficionado(-a) al cine
moving ['muːvɪŋ] adj (emotional)
conmovedor(a); (that moves) móvil;
(instigating) motor(a)
mow (pt **mowed**, pp **mowed** or **mown**)
[məu, -n] vt (grass) cortar; (corn) segar; (also:
mow down: shoot) acribillar
mower ['məuər] n (also: **lawnmower**)
cortacésped m
Mozambique [məuzæm'biːk] n
Mozambique m

MP n abbr (= Military Police) PM; (Brit)
= **Member of Parliament**; (Canada)
= **Mounted Police**
mpg n abbr (= miles per gallon) 30 mpg = 9.4 l. per
100 km
mph abbr (= miles per hour) 60 mph = 96 km/h
MPhil n abbr (= Master of Philosophy) título
universitario de postgrado; see also **master's
degree**
MPS n abbr (Brit) = **Member of the
Pharmaceutical Society**
MP3 ['ɛmpiː'θriː] n MP3 m
MP3 player n reproductor m MP3
Mr, Mr. ['mɪstər] n: **Mr Smith** (el) Sr. Smith
MRC n abbr (Brit: = Medical Research Council)
departamento estatal que controla la investigación
médica
MRCP n abbr (Brit) = **Member of the Royal
College of Physicians**
MRCS n abbr (Brit) = **Member of the Royal
College of Surgeons**
MRCVS n abbr (Brit) = **Member of the Royal
College of Veterinary Surgeons**
Mrs, Mrs. ['mɪsɪz] n: ~ **Smith** (la) Sra. de
Smith
MS n abbr (= manuscript) MS; = **multiple
sclerosis**; (US: = Master of Science) título
universitario ▪ abbr (US) = **Mississippi**
Ms, Ms. [mɪz] n (Miss or Mrs) abreviatura con la
que se evita hacer expreso el estado civil de una mujer
MSA n abbr (US: = Master of Science in Agriculture)
título universitario
MSc abbr see **Master of Science**
MSG n abbr = **monosodium glutamate**
MSP n abbr (Brit) = **Member of the Scottish
Parliament**
MST abbr (US: = Mountain Standard Time) hora de
invierno de las Montañas Rocosas
MSW n abbr (US: = Master of Social Work) título
universitario
MT abbr (US: = Montana) ▪ n abbr = **machine
translation**
Mt abbr (Geo: = mount) m
mth abbr (= month) m
MTV n abbr = **music television**
much [mʌtʃ] adj mucho ▪ adv, n, pron mucho;
(before pp) muy; **how ~ is it?** ¿cuánto es?,
¿cuánto cuesta?; **too ~** demasiado; **so ~**
tanto; **it's not ~** no es mucho; **as ~ as** tanto
como; **however ~ he tries** por mucho que
se esfuerce; **I like it very/so ~** me gusta
mucho/tanto; **thank you very ~** muchas
gracias, muy agradecido
muck [mʌk] n (dirt) suciedad f; (fig) porquería
▸ **muck about** or **around** vi (col) perder el
tiempo; (enjoy o.s.) entretenerse; (tinker)
manosear

▸ **muck in** vi (col) arrimar el hombro
▸ **muck out** vt (stable) limpiar
▸ **muck up** vt (col: dirty) ensuciar; (: spoil)
echar a perder; (: ruin) estropear
muckraking ['mʌkreɪkɪŋ] (fig col) n
amarillismo ▪ adj especializado en
escándalos
mucky ['mʌkɪ] adj (dirty) sucio
mucus ['mjuːkəs] n mucosidad f, moco
mud [mʌd] n barro, lodo
muddle ['mʌdl] n desorden m, confusión f;
(mix-up) embrollo, lío ▪ vt (also: **muddle up**)
embrollar, confundir
▸ **muddle along, muddle on** vi
arreglárselas de alguna manera
▸ **muddle through** vi salir del paso
muddle-headed [mʌdl'hɛdɪd] adj (person)
despistado, confuso
muddy ['mʌdɪ] adj fangoso, cubierto de lodo
mudguard ['mʌdgɑːd] n guardabarros m inv
mudpack ['mʌdpæk] n mascarilla
mud-slinging ['mʌdslɪŋɪŋ] n injurias fpl,
difamación f
muesli ['mjuːzlɪ] n muesli m
muff [mʌf] n manguito ▪ vt (chance)
desperdiciar; (lines) estropear; (shot, catch etc)
fallar; **to ~ it** fracasar
muffin ['mʌfɪn] n bollo
muffle ['mʌfl] vt (sound) amortiguar; (against
cold) abrigar
muffled ['mʌfld] adj sordo, apagado
muffler ['mʌflər] n (scarf) bufanda; (US Aut)
silenciador m; (on motorbike) silenciador m,
mofle m
mufti ['mʌftɪ] n: **in ~** (vestido) de paisano
mug [mʌg] n (cup) taza alta; (for beer) jarra;
(col: face) jeta; (: fool) bobo ▪ vt (assault)
atracar; **it's a ~'s game** es cosa de bobos
▸ **mug up** vt (col: also: **mug up on**) empollar
mugger ['mʌgər] n atracador(a) m(f)
mugging ['mʌgɪŋ] n atraco callejero
muggins ['mʌgɪnz] nsg (col) tonto(-a) el bote
muggy ['mʌgɪ] adj bochornoso
mug shot n (col) foto f (para la ficha policial)
mulatto (pl **mulattoes**) [mjuː'lætəu] n
mulato(-a)
mulberry ['mʌlbrɪ] n (fruit) mora; (tree)
morera, moral m
mule [mjuːl] n mula
mull [mʌl]: **to ~ over** vt meditar sobre
mulled [mʌld] adj: ~ **wine** vino caliente (con
especias)
mullioned ['mʌlɪənd] adj (window) dividido
por parteluces
multi... [mʌltɪ] pref multi...
multi-access ['mʌltɪ'æksɛs] adj (Comput)
multiacceso, de acceso múltiple

m

667

multicoloured, (US) **multicolored**
['mʌltɪkʌləd] adj multicolor

multifarious [mʌltɪ'fɛərɪəs] adj múltiple,
vario

multilateral [mʌltɪ'lætərl] adj (Pol)
multilateral

multi-level [mʌltɪ'lɛvl] adj (US) = **multistorey**

multimillionaire [mʌltɪmɪljə'nɛəʳ] n
multimillonario(-a)

multinational [mʌltɪ'næʃənl] n
multinacional f ■ adj multinacional

multiple ['mʌltɪpl] adj múltiple ■ n
múltiplo; (Brit: also: **multiple store**) (cadena
de) grandes almacenes mpl

multiple choice n examen m de tipo test

multiple crash n colisión f en cadena

multiple sclerosis [-sklɪ'rəusɪs] n esclerosis
f múltiple

multiplex ['mʌltɪplɛks] n (also: **multiplex
cinema**) multicines m inv

multiplication [mʌltɪplɪ'keɪʃən] n
multiplicación f

multiplication table n tabla de multiplicar

multiplicity [mʌltɪ'plɪsɪtɪ] n multiplicidad f

multiply ['mʌltɪplaɪ] vt multiplicar ■ vi
multiplicarse

multiracial [mʌltɪ'reɪʃl] adj multirracial

multistorey [mʌltɪ'stɔːrɪ] adj (Brit: building, car
park) de muchos pisos

multi-tasking ['mʌltɪtɑːskɪŋ] n (Comput)
ejecución f de tareas múltiples, multitarea

multitude ['mʌltɪtjuːd] n multitud f

mum [mʌm] n (Brit) mamá ■ adj: **to keep ~
(about sth)** no decir ni mu (de algo)

mumble ['mʌmbl] vt decir entre dientes
■ vi hablar entre dientes, musitar

mumbo jumbo ['mʌmbəu-] n (col)
galimatías m inv

mummify ['mʌmɪfaɪ] vt momificar

mummy ['mʌmɪ] n (Brit: mother) mamá;
(embalmed) momia

mumps [mʌmps] n paperas fpl

munch [mʌntʃ] vt, vi mascar

mundane [mʌn'deɪn] adj mundano

municipal [mju:'nɪsɪpl] adj municipal

municipality [mju:nɪsɪ'pælɪtɪ] n municipio

munificence [mu:'nɪfɪsns] n munificencia

munitions [mju:'nɪʃənz] npl municiones fpl

mural ['mjuərl] n (pintura) mural m

murder ['mə:dəʳ] n asesinato; (in law)
homicidio ■ vt asesinar, matar; **to commit
~** cometer un asesinato or homicidio

murderer ['mə:dərəʳ] n asesino

murderess ['mə:dərɪs] n asesina

murderous ['mə:dərəs] adj homicida

murk [mə:k] n oscuridad f, tinieblas fpl

murky ['mə:kɪ] adj (water, past) turbio; (room)
sombrío

murmur ['mə:məʳ] n murmullo ■ vt, vi
murmurar; **heart ~** soplo cardíaco

MusB, MusBac n abbr (= Bachelor of Music)
título universitario

muscle ['mʌsl] n músculo
▶ **muscle in** vi entrometerse

muscular ['mʌskjuləʳ] adj muscular; (person)
musculoso

muscular dystrophy n distrofia muscular

MusD, MusDoc n abbr (= Doctor of Music) título
universitario

muse [mju:z] vi meditar ■ n musa

museum [mju:'zɪəm] n museo

mush [mʌʃ] n gachas fpl

mushroom ['mʌʃrum] n (gen) seta, hongo;
(small) champiñón m ■ vi (fig) crecer de la
noche a la mañana

mushy ['mʌʃɪ] adj (vegetables) casi hecho puré;
(story) sentimentaloide

music ['mju:zɪk] n música

musical ['mju:zɪkl] adj melodioso; (person)
musical ■ n (show) (comedia) musical m

musical box n = **music box**

musical chairs n juego de las sillas; (fig):
to play ~ cambiar de puesto continuamente

musical instrument n instrumento musical

musically ['mju:zɪklɪ] adv melodiosamente,
armoniosamente

music box n caja de música

music centre n equipo de música

music hall n teatro de variedades

musician [mju:'zɪʃən] n músico(-a)

music stand n atril m

musk [mʌsk] n (perfume m de) almizcle m

musket ['mʌskɪt] n mosquete m

musk rat n ratón m almizclero

musk rose n (Bot) rosa almizcleña

Muslim ['mʌzlɪm] adj, n musulmán(-ana) m(f)

muslin ['mʌzlɪn] n muselina

musquash ['mʌskwɔʃ] n (fur) piel f del ratón
almizclero

muss [mʌs] vt (col: hair) despeinar; (: dress)
arrugar

mussel ['mʌsl] n mejillón m

must [mʌst] aux vb (obligation): **I ~ do it** debo
hacerlo, tengo que hacerlo; (probability):
he ~ be there by now ya debe (de) estar allí
■ n: **it's a ~** es imprescindible

mustache ['mʌstæʃ] n (US) = **moustache**

mustard ['mʌstəd] n mostaza

mustard gas n gas m mostaza

muster ['mʌstəʳ] vt juntar, reunir; (also:
muster up) reunir; (: courage) armarse de

mustiness ['mʌstɪnɪs] n olor m a cerrado

mustn't ['mʌsnt] = **must not**

musty ['mʌstɪ] *adj* mohoso, que huele a humedad
mutant ['mju:tənt] *adj, n* mutante *m*
mutate [mju:'teɪt] *vi* sufrir mutación, transformarse
mutation [mju:'teɪʃən] *n* mutación *f*
mute [mju:t] *adj, n* mudo(-a) *m(f)*
muted ['mju:tɪd] *adj (noise)* sordo; *(criticism)* callado
mutilate ['mju:tɪleɪt] *vt* mutilar
mutilation [mju:tɪ'leɪʃən] *n* mutilación *f*
mutinous ['mju:tɪnəs] *adj (troops)* amotinado; *(attitude)* rebelde
mutiny ['mju:tɪnɪ] *n* motín *m* ▪ *vi* amotinarse
mutter ['mʌtəʳ] *vt, vi* murmurar
mutton ['mʌtn] *n* (carne *f* de) cordero
mutual ['mju:tʃuəl] *adj* mutuo; *(friend)* común
mutually ['mju:tʃuəlɪ] *adv* mutuamente
Muzak® ['mju:zæk] *n* hilo musical
muzzle ['mʌzl] *n* hocico; *(protective device)* bozal *m*; *(of gun)* boca ▪ *vt* amordazar; *(dog)* poner un bozal a
MV *abbr* = **motor vessel**
MVP *n abbr (US Sport)* = **most valuable player**
MW *abbr* (Radio: = *medium wave*) onda media
my [maɪ] *adj* mi(s); **my house/brother/**

sisters mi casa/hermano/mis hermanas;
I've washed my hair/cut my finger me he lavado el pelo/cortado un dedo; **is this my pen or yours?** ¿este bolígrafo es mío o tuyo?
Myanmar ['maɪænmɑːʳ] *n* Myanmar
myopic [maɪ'ɔpɪk] *adj* miope
myriad ['mɪrɪəd] *n (of people, things)* miríada
myrrh [məːʳ] *n* mirra
myself [maɪ'sɛlf] *pron (reflexive)* me; *(emphatic)* yo mismo; *(after prep)* mí (mismo); *see also* **oneself**
mysterious [mɪs'tɪərɪəs] *adj* misterioso
mysteriously [mɪs'tɪərɪəslɪ] *adv* misteriosamente
mystery ['mɪstərɪ] *n* misterio
mystery play *n* auto, misterio
mystic ['mɪstɪk] *adj, n* místico(-a) *m(f)*
mystical ['mɪstɪkl] *adj* místico
mysticism ['mɪstɪsɪzəm] *n* misticismo
mystification [mɪstɪfɪ'keɪʃən] *n* perplejidad *f*; desconcierto
mystify ['mɪstɪfaɪ] *vt (perplex)* dejar perplejo; *(disconcert)* desconcertar
mystique [mɪs'ti:k] *n* misterio
myth [mɪθ] *n* mito
mythical ['mɪθɪkl] *adj* mítico
mythological [mɪθə'lɔdʒɪkl] *adj* mitológico
mythology [mɪ'θɔlədʒɪ] *n* mitología

m

Nn

N, n [ɛn] *n* (*letter*) N, n *f*; **N for Nellie**, (US) **N for Nan** N de Navarra

N *abbr* (= *North*) N

NA *n abbr* (US: = *Narcotics Anonymous*) organización de ayuda a los drogadictos; (US) = **National Academy**

n/a *abbr* (= *not applicable*) no interesa; (*Comm etc*) = **no account**

NAACP *n abbr* (US) = **National Association for the Advancement of Colored People**

NAAFI ['næfɪ] *n abbr* (Brit: = *Navy, Army & Air Force Institutes*) servicio de cantinas etc para las fuerzas armadas

nab [næb] *vt* (*col: grab*) coger (SP), agarrar (LAm); (: *catch out*) pillar

NACU *n abbr* (US) = **National Association of Colleges and Universities**

nadir ['neɪdɪə^r] *n* (*Astro*) nadir *m*; (*fig*) punto más bajo

NAFTA ['næftə] *n abbr* (= *North Atlantic Free Trade Agreement*) TLC *m*

nag [næg] *n* (*pej: horse*) rocín *m* ▪ *vt* (*scold*) regañar; (*annoy*) fastidiar

nagging ['nægɪŋ] *adj* (*doubt*) persistente; (*pain*) continuo ▪ *n* quejas *fpl*

nail [neɪl] *n* (*human*) uña; (*metal*) clavo ▪ *vt* clavar; (*fig: catch*) coger (SP), pillar; **to pay cash on the ~** pagar a tocateja; **to ~ sb down to a date/price** hacer que algn se comprometa a una fecha/un precio

nailbrush ['neɪlbrʌʃ] *n* cepillo para las uñas

nailfile ['neɪlfaɪl] *n* lima para las uñas

nail polish *n* esmalte *m* or laca para las uñas

nail polish remover *n* quitaesmalte *m*

nail scissors *npl* tijeras *fpl* para las uñas

nail varnish *n* (Brit) = **nail polish**

Nairobi [naɪˈrəubɪ] *n* Nairobi *m*

naïve [naɪˈiːv] *adj* ingenuo

naïvely [naɪˈiːvlɪ] *adv* ingenuamente

naïveté [naɪˈiːvteɪ], **naivety** [naɪˈiːvɪtɪ] *n* ingenuidad *f*, candidez *f*

naked ['neɪkɪd] *adj* (*nude*) desnudo; (*flame*) expuesto al aire; **with the ~ eye** a simple vista

NAM *n abbr* (US) = **National Association of Manufacturers**

name [neɪm] *n* (*gen*) nombre *m*; (*surname*) apellido; (*reputation*) fama, renombre *m* ▪ *vt* (*child*) poner nombre a; (*appoint*) nombrar; **by ~** de nombre; **in the ~ of** en nombre de; **what's your ~?** ¿cómo se llama usted?; **my ~ is Peter** me llamo Pedro; **to give one's ~ and address** dar sus señas; **to take sb's ~ and address** apuntar las señas de algn; **to make a ~ for o.s.** hacerse famoso; **to get (o.s.) a bad ~** forjarse una mala reputación

name-drop ['neɪmdrɔp] *vi*: **he's always name-dropping** siempre está presumiendo de la gente que conoce

nameless ['neɪmlɪs] *adj* anónimo, sin nombre

namely ['neɪmlɪ] *adv* a saber

nameplate ['neɪmpleɪt] *n* (*on door etc*) placa

namesake ['neɪmseɪk] *n* tocayo(-a)

nan bread [nɑː-] *n* pan indio sin apenas levadura

nanny ['nænɪ] *n* niñera

nap [næp] *n* (*sleep*) sueñecito, siesta; **they were caught napping** les pilló desprevenidos

NAPA *n abbr* (US: = *National Association of Performing Artists*) sindicato de trabajadores del espectáculo

napalm ['neɪpɑːm] *n* napalm *m*

nape [neɪp] *n*: **~ of the neck** nuca, cogote *m*

napkin ['næpkɪn] *n* (*also*: **table napkin**) servilleta

Naples ['neɪplz] *n* Nápoles

nappy ['næpɪ] *n* (Brit) pañal *m*

nappy liner *n* gasa

nappy rash *n* prurito

narcissism [nɑːˈsɪsɪzəm] *n* narcisismo

narcissus (*pl* **narcissi**) [nɑːˈsɪsəs, -saɪ] *n* narciso

narcotic [nɑːˈkɔtɪk] *adj, n* narcótico

narrate [nəˈreɪt] *vt* narrar, contar

narration [nəˈreɪʃən] *n* narración *f*, relato

narrative ['nærətɪv] *n* narrativa ▪ *adj* narrativo

narrator [nəˈreɪtəʳ] *n* narrador(a) *m(f)*

narrow [ˈnærəu] *adj* estrecho; *(resources, means)* escaso ∎ *vi* estrecharse; *(diminish)* reducirse; **to have a ~ escape** escaparse por los pelos; **to ~ sth down** reducir algo

narrow gauge *adj* *(Rail)* de vía estrecha

narrowly [ˈnærəlɪ] *adv* *(miss)* por poco

narrow-minded [nærəuˈmaɪndɪd] *adj* de miras estrechas

narrow-mindedness [ˈnærəuˈmaɪndɪdnɪs] *n* estrechez *f* de miras

NAS *n abbr* *(US)* = **National Academy of Sciences**

NASA *n abbr* *(US: = National Aeronautics and Space Administration)* NASA *f*

nasal [ˈneɪzl] *adj* nasal

Nassau [ˈnæsɔː] *n* *(in Bahamas)* Nassau *m*

nastily [ˈnɑːstɪlɪ] *adv* *(unpleasantly)* de mala manera; *(spitefully)* con rencor

nastiness [ˈnɑːstɪnɪs] *n* *(malice)* malevolencia; *(rudeness)* grosería; *(of person, remark)* maldad *f*; *(spitefulness)* rencor *m*

nasturtium [nəsˈtəːʃəm] *n* capuchina

nasty [ˈnɑːstɪ] *adj* *(remark)* feo; *(person)* antipático; *(revolting: taste, smell)* asqueroso; *(wound, disease etc)* peligroso, grave; **to turn ~** *(situation)* ponerse feo; *(weather)* empeorar; *(person)* ponerse negro

NAS/UWT *n abbr* *(Brit: = National Association of Schoolmasters/Union of Women Teachers)* sindicato de profesores

nation [ˈneɪʃən] *n* nación *f*

national [ˈnæʃənl] *adj* nacional ∎ *n* súbdito(-a)

national anthem *n* himno nacional

National Curriculum *n* *(Brit)* plan *m* general de estudios *(en Inglaterra y Gales)*

national debt *n* deuda pública

national dress *n* traje *m* típico del país

National Guard *n* *(US)* Guardia Nacional

National Health Service *n* *(Brit)* servicio nacional de sanidad, ≈ INSALUD *m* *(SP)*

National Insurance *n* *(Brit)* seguro social nacional, ≈ Seguridad *f* Social

nationalism [ˈnæʃnəlɪzəm] *n* nacionalismo

nationalist [ˈnæʃnəlɪst] *adj, n* nacionalista *m/f*

nationality [næʃəˈnælɪtɪ] *n* nacionalidad *f*

nationalization [næʃnəlaɪˈzeɪʃən] *n* nacionalización *f*

nationalize [ˈnæʃnəlaɪz] *vt* nacionalizar; **nationalized industry** industria nacionalizada

nationally [ˈnæʃnəlɪ] *adv* *(nationwide)* a escala nacional; *(as a nation)* como nación

national press *n* prensa nacional

national service *n* *(Mil)* servicio militar

National Trust *n* *(Brit)* organización encargada de preservar el patrimonio histórico británico

nationwide [ˈneɪʃənwaɪd] *adj* a escala nacional

native [ˈneɪtɪv] *n* *(local inhabitant)* natural *m/f*; *(in colonies)* indígena *m/f*, nativo(-a) ∎ *adj* *(indigenous)* indígena; *(country)* natal; *(innate)* natural, innato; **a ~ of Russia** un(a) natural de Rusia; **~ language** lengua materna; **a ~ speaker of French** un hablante nativo de francés

Native American *adj, n* americano(-a) indígena *m(f)*, amerindio(-a) *m(f)*

Nativity [nəˈtɪvɪtɪ] *n*: **the ~** Navidad *f*

nativity play *n* auto del nacimiento

NATO [ˈneɪtəu] *n abbr* (= *North Atlantic Treaty Organization*) OTAN *f*

natter [ˈnætəʳ] *vi* *(Brit)* charlar ∎ *n*: **to have a ~** charlar

natural [ˈnætʃrəl] *adj* natural; **death from ~ causes** *(Law)* muerte *f* por causas naturales

natural childbirth *n* parto natural

natural gas *n* gas *m* natural

natural history *n* historia natural

naturalist [ˈnætʃrəlɪst] *n* naturalista *m/f*

naturalization [nætʃrəlaɪˈzeɪʃən] *n* naturalización *f*

naturalize [ˈnætʃrəlaɪz] *vt*: **to become naturalized** *(person)* naturalizarse; *(plant)* aclimatarse

naturally [ˈnætʃrəlɪ] *adv* *(speak etc)* naturalmente; *(of course)* desde luego, por supuesto, ¡cómo no! *(LAm)*; *(instinctively)* por naturaleza

naturalness [ˈnætʃrəlnɪs] *n* naturalidad *f*

natural resources *npl* recursos *mpl* naturales

natural selection *n* selección *f* natural

natural wastage *n* *(Industry)* desgaste *m* natural

nature [ˈneɪtʃəʳ] *n* naturaleza; *(group, sort)* género, clase *f*; *(character)* modo de ser, carácter *m*; **by ~** por naturaleza; **documents of a confidential ~** documentos *mpl* de tipo confidencial

-natured [ˈneɪtʃəd] *suff*: **ill~** malhumorado

nature reserve *n* reserva natural

nature trail *n* camino forestal educativo

naturist [ˈneɪtʃərɪst] *n* naturista *m/f*

naught [nɔːt] = **nought**

naughtily [ˈnɔːtɪlɪ] *adv* *(behave)* mal; *(say)* con malicia

naughtiness [ˈnɔːtɪnɪs] *n* travesuras *fpl*

naughty [ˈnɔːtɪ] *adj* *(child)* travieso; *(story, film)* picante, escabroso, colorado *(LAm)*

nausea [ˈnɔːsɪə] *n* náusea

nauseate [ˈnɔːsɪeɪt] *vt* dar náuseas a; *(fig)* dar asco a

n

nauseating ['nɔːsɪeɪtɪŋ] *adj* nauseabundo; (*fig*) asqueroso, repugnante

nauseous ['nɔːsɪəs] *adj* nauseabundo; **to feel ~** sentir náuseas

nautical ['nɔːtɪkl] *adj* náutico, marítimo; **~ mile** milla marina

naval ['neɪvl] *adj* naval, de marina

naval officer *n* oficial *m/f* de marina

nave [neɪv] *n* nave *f*

navel ['neɪvl] *n* ombligo

navigable ['nævɪgəbl] *adj* navegable

navigate ['nævɪgeɪt] *vt* (*ship*) gobernar; (*river etc*) navegar por ▪ *vi* navegar; (*Aut*) hacer de copiloto

navigation [nævɪ'geɪʃən] *n* (*action*) navegación *f*; (*science*) náutica

navigator ['nævɪgeɪtər] *n* navegante *m/f*

navvy ['nævɪ] *n* (*Brit*) peón *m* caminero

navy ['neɪvɪ] *n* marina de guerra; (*ships*) armada, flota ▪ *adj* azul marino

navy-blue ['neɪvɪ'bluː] *adj* azul marino

Nazareth ['næzərɪθ] *n* Nazaret *m*

Nazi ['nɑːtsɪ] *adj, n* nazi *m/f*

NB *abbr* (= *nota bene*) nótese; (*Canada*) = **New Brunswick**

NBA *n abbr* (*US*) = **National Basketball Association; National Boxing Association**

NBC *n abbr* (*US*: = *National Broadcasting Company*) *cadena de televisión*

NBS *n abbr* (*US*: = *National Bureau of Standards*) ≈ Oficina Nacional de Normalización

NC *abbr* (*Comm etc*: = *no charge*: *US*) = **North Carolina**

NCC *n abbr* (*Brit*: = *Nature Conservancy Council*) ≈ ICONA *m*; (*US*) = **National Council of Churches**

NCCL *n abbr* (*Brit*: = *National Council for Civil Liberties*) *asociación para la defensa de las libertades públicas*

NCO *n abbr* = **non-commissioned officer**

ND, N. Dak. *abbr* (*US*) = **North Dakota**

NE *abbr* (*US*) = **Nebraska; New England**

NEA *n abbr* (*US*) = **National Education Association**

Neapolitan [nɪə'pɔlɪtən] *adj, n* napolitano(-a) *m(f)*

neap tide [niːp-] *n* marea muerta

near [nɪər] *adj* (*place, relation*) cercano; (*time*) próximo ▪ *adv* cerca ▪ *prep* (*also*: **near to**: *space*) cerca de, junto a; (: *time*) cerca de ▪ *vt* acercarse a, aproximarse a; **~ here/there** cerca de aquí/de allí; **£25,000 or nearest offer** 25,000 libras o precio a discutir; **in the ~ future** en fecha próxima; **the building is nearing completion** el edificio está casi terminado

nearby [nɪə'baɪ] *adj* cercano, próximo

▪ *adv* cerca

nearly ['nɪəlɪ] *adv* casi, por poco; **I ~ fell** por poco me caigo; **not ~** ni mucho menos, ni con mucho

near miss *n* (*shot*) tiro casi en el blanco; (*Aviat*) accidente evitado por muy poco

nearness ['nɪənɪs] *n* cercanía, proximidad *f*

nearside ['nɪəsaɪd] *n* (*Aut*: *right-hand drive*) lado izquierdo; (: *left-hand drive*) lado derecho

near-sighted [nɪə'saɪtɪd] *adj* miope, corto de vista

neat [niːt] *adj* (*place*) ordenado, bien cuidado; (*person*) pulcro; (*plan*) ingenioso; (*spirits*) solo

neatly ['niːtlɪ] *adv* (*tidily*) con esmero; (*skilfully*) ingeniosamente

neatness ['niːtnɪs] *n* (*tidiness*) orden *m*; (*skilfulness*) destreza, habilidad *f*

Nebr. *abbr* (*US*) = **Nebraska**

nebulous ['nɛbjuləs] *adj* (*fig*) vago, confuso

necessarily ['nɛsɪsrɪlɪ] *adv* necesariamente; **not ~** no necesariamente

necessary ['nɛsɪsrɪ] *adj* necesario, preciso; **he did all that was ~** hizo todo lo necesario; **if ~** si es necesario

necessitate [nɪ'sɛsɪteɪt] *vt* necesitar, precisar

necessity [nɪ'sɛsɪtɪ] *n* necesidad *f*; **necessities** *npl* artículos *mpl* de primera necesidad; **in case of ~** en caso de urgencia

neck [nɛk] *n* (*Anat*) cuello; (*of animal*) pescuezo ▪ *vi* besuquearse; **~ and ~** parejos; **to stick one's ~ out** (*col*) arriesgarse

necklace ['nɛklɪs] *n* collar *m*

neckline ['nɛklaɪn] *n* escote *m*

necktie ['nɛktaɪ] *n* (*US*) corbata

nectar ['nɛktər] *n* néctar *m*

nectarine ['nɛktərɪn] *n* nectarina

née [neɪ] *adj*: **~ Scott** de soltera Scott

need [niːd] *n* (*lack*) escasez *f*, falta; (*necessity*) necesidad *f* ▪ *vt* (*require*) necesitar; **in case of ~** en caso de necesidad; **there's no ~ for ...** no hace(n) falta ...; **to be in ~ of, have ~ of** necesitar; **10 will meet my immediate needs** 10 satisfacerán mis necesidades más apremiantes; **the needs of industry** las necesidades de la industria; **I ~ it** lo necesito; **a signature is needed** se requiere una firma; **I ~ to do it** tengo que hacerlo; **you don't ~ to go** no hace falta que vayas

needle ['niːdl] *n* aguja ▪ *vt* (*fig: col*) picar, fastidiar

needless ['niːdlɪs] *adj* innecesario, inútil; **~ to say** huelga decir que

needlessly ['niːdlɪslɪ] *adv* innecesariamente, inútilmente

needlework ['niːdlwəːk] *n* (*activity*) costura, labor *f* de aguja

needn't ['niːdnt] = **need not**

needy ['niːdɪ] *adj* necesitado

negation [nɪ'geɪʃən] *n* negación *f*

negative ['nɛgətɪv] *n* (*Phot*) negativo; (*answer*) negativa; (*Ling*) negación *f* ■ *adj* negativo

negative cash flow *n* flujo negativo de efectivo

negative equity *n* situación en la que el valor de la vivienda es menor que el de la hipoteca que pesa sobre ella

neglect [nɪ'glɛkt] *vt* (*one's duty*) faltar a, no cumplir con; (*child*) descuidar, desatender ■ *n* (*state*) abandono; (*personal*) dejadez *f*; (*of duty*) incumplimiento; **to ~ to do sth** olvidarse de hacer algo

neglected [nɪ'glɛktɪd] *adj* abandonado

neglectful [nɪ'glɛktful] *adj* negligente; **to be ~ of sth/sb** desatender algo/a algn

negligee ['nɛglɪʒeɪ] *n* salto de cama

negligence ['nɛglɪdʒəns] *n* negligencia

negligent ['nɛglɪdʒənt] *adj* negligente; (*casual*) descuidado

negligently ['nɛglɪdʒəntlɪ] *adv* negligentemente; (*casually*) con descuido

negligible ['nɛglɪdʒɪbl] *adj* insignificante, despreciable

negotiable [nɪ'gəʊʃɪəbl] *adj* negociable; **not ~** (*cheque*) no trasferible

negotiate [nɪ'gəʊʃɪeɪt] *vt* (*treaty, loan*) negociar; (*obstacle*) franquear; (*bend in road*) tomar ■ *vi*: **to ~ (with)** negociar (con); **to ~ with sb for sth** tratar *or* negociar con algn por algo

negotiating table [nɪ'gəʊʃɪeɪtɪŋ-] *n* mesa de negociaciones

negotiation [nɪgəʊʃɪ'eɪʃən] *n* negociación *f*, gestión *f*; **to enter into negotiations with sb** entrar en negociaciones con algn

negotiator [nɪ'gəʊʃɪeɪtəʳ] *n* negociador(a) *m(f)*

Negress ['niːgrɪs] *n* negra

Negro ['niːgrəʊ] *adj, n* negro

neigh [neɪ] *n* relincho ■ *vi* relinchar

neighbour, neighbor (US) ['neɪbəʳ] *n* vecino(-a)

neighbourhood, neighborhood (US) ['neɪbəhud] *n* (*place*) vecindad *f*, barrio; (*people*) vecindario

neighbourhood watch *n* (Brit: *also*: **neighbourhood watch scheme**) vigilancia del barrio por los propios vecinos

neighbouring, neighboring (US) ['neɪbərɪŋ] *adj* vecino

neighbourly, neighborly (US) ['neɪbəlɪ] *adj* amigable, sociable

neither ['naɪðəʳ] *adj* ni ■ *conj*: **I didn't move and ~ did John** no me he movido, ni

Juan tampoco ■ *pron* ninguno; **~ is true** ninguno(-a) de los/las dos es cierto(-a) ■ *adv*: **~ good nor bad** ni bueno ni malo

neo ... [niːəu] *pref* neo...

neolithic [niːəu'lɪθɪk] *adj* neolítico

neologism [nɪ'ɔlədʒɪzəm] *n* neologismo

neon ['niːɔn] *n* neón *m*

neon light *n* lámpara de neón

Nepal [nɪ'pɔːl] *n* Nepal *m*

nephew ['nɛvjuː] *n* sobrino

nepotism ['nɛpətɪzəm] *n* nepotismo

nerd [nəːd] *n* (*col*) primo(-a)

nerve [nəːv] *n* (*Anat*) nervio; (*courage*) valor *m*; (*impudence*) descaro, frescura; **a fit of nerves** un ataque de nervios; **to lose one's ~** (*self-confidence*) perder el valor

nerve centre *n* (*Anat*) centro nervioso; (*fig*) punto neurálgico

nerve gas *n* gas *m* nervioso

nerve-racking ['nəːvrækɪŋ] *adj* angustioso

nervous ['nəːvəs] *adj* (*anxious*) nervioso; (*Anat*) nervioso; (*timid*) tímido, miedoso

nervous breakdown *n* crisis *f* nerviosa

nervously ['nəːvəslɪ] *adv* nerviosamente; tímidamente

nervousness ['nəːvəsnɪs] *n* nerviosismo; timidez *f*

nervous wreck *n* (*col*): **to be a ~** estar de los nervios

nervy ['nəːvɪ] *adj*: **to be ~** estar nervioso

nest [nɛst] *n* (*of bird*) nido ■ *vi* anidar

nest egg *n* (*fig*) ahorros *mpl*

nestle ['nɛsl] *vi*: **to ~ down** acurrucarse

nestling ['nɛstlɪŋ] *n* pajarito

Net ['nɛt] *n* (*Comput*) Internet *m or f*

net [nɛt] *n* (*gen*) red *f*; (*fabric*) tul *m* ■ *adj* (*Comm*) neto, líquido; (*weight, price, salary*) neto ■ *vt* coger (SP) *or* agarrar (LAm) con red; (*money: person*) cobrar; (*: deal, sale*) conseguir; (*Sport*) marcar; **~ of tax** neto; **he earns £10,000 ~ per year** gana 10,000 libras netas por año; **the N~** (*Internet*) la Red

netball ['nɛtbɔːl] *n* básquet *m*

net curtain *n* visillo

Netherlands ['nɛðələndz] *npl*: **the ~** los Países Bajos

net income *n* renta neta

netiquette ['nɛtɪkɛt] *n* netiqueta

net loss *n* pérdida neta

net profit *n* beneficio neto

nett [nɛt] *adj* = **net**

netting ['nɛtɪŋ] *n* red *f*, redes *fpl*

nettle ['nɛtl] *n* ortiga

network ['nɛtwəːk] *n* red *f* ■ *vt* (*Radio, TV*) difundir por la red de emisores; **local area ~** red local; **there's no ~ coverage here** (*Tel*) aquí no hay cobertura

n

neuralgia [njuə'rældʒə] *n* neuralgia
neurological [njuərə'lɔdʒɪkl] *adj* neurológico
neurosis (*pl* -**ses**) [njuə'rəusɪs, -si:z] *n* neurosis *f inv*
neurotic [njuə'rɔtɪk] *adj, n* neurótico(-a) *m(f)*
neuter ['nju:tər] *adj* (*Ling*) neutro ▪ *vt* castrar, capar
neutral ['nju:trəl] *adj* (*person*) neutral; (*colour etc*) neutro; (*Elec*) neutro ▪ *n* (*Aut*) punto muerto
neutrality [nju:'trælɪtɪ] *n* neutralidad *f*
neutralize ['nju:trəlaɪz] *vt* neutralizar
neutron ['nju:trɔn] *n* neutrón *m*
neutron bomb *n* bomba de neutrones
Nev. *abbr* (*US*) = **Nevada**
never ['nɛvər] *adv* nunca, jamás; **I ~ went** no fui nunca; **~ in my life** jamás en la vida; *see also* **mind**
never-ending [nɛvər'ɛndɪŋ] *adj* interminable, sin fin
nevertheless [nɛvəðə'lɛs] *adv* sin embargo, no obstante
New Age *n* Nueva era
new [nju:] *adj* nuevo; (*recent*) reciente; **as good as ~** como nuevo
newbie ['nju:bɪ] *n* recién llegado(-a) *m(f)*
newborn ['nju:bɔ:n] *adj* recién nacido
newcomer ['nju:kʌmər] *n* recién venido *or* llegado
new-fangled ['nju:fæŋgld] *adj* (*pej*) modernísimo
new-found ['nju:faund] *adj* (*friend*) nuevo; (*enthusiasm*) recién adquirido
New Guinea *n* Nueva Guinea
newly ['nju:lɪ] *adv* recién
newly-weds ['nju:lɪwɛdz] *npl* recién casados
new moon *n* luna nueva
newness ['nju:nɪs] *n* novedad *f*; (*fig*) inexperiencia
news [nju:z] *n* noticias *fpl*; **a piece of ~** una noticia; **the ~** (*Radio, TV*) las noticias *fpl*, el telediario; **good/bad ~** buenas/malas noticias *fpl*; **financial ~** noticias *fpl* financieras
news agency *n* agencia de noticias
newsagent ['nju:zeɪdʒənt] *n* (*Brit*) vendedor(a) *m(f)* de periódicos
news bulletin *n* (*Radio, TV*) noticiario
newscaster ['nju:zkɑ:stər] *n* presentador(a) *m(f)*, locutor(a) *m(f)*
news dealer *n* (*US*) = **newsagent**
news flash *n* noticia de última hora
newsletter ['nju:zlɛtər] *n* hoja informativa, boletín *m*
newspaper ['nju:zpeɪpər] *n* periódico, diario; **daily ~** diario; **weekly ~** periódico semanal
newsprint ['nju:zprɪnt] *n* papel *m* de periódico

newsreader ['nju:zri:dər] *n* = **newscaster**
newsreel ['nju:zri:l] *n* noticiario
newsroom ['nju:zru:m] *n* (*Press, Radio, TV*) sala de redacción
news stand *n* quiosco *or* puesto de periódicos
newsworthy ['nju:zwə:ðɪ] *adj*: **to be ~** ser de interés periodístico
newt [nju:t] *n* tritón *m*
new town *n* (*Brit*) ciudad *f* nueva
New Year *n* Año Nuevo; **Happy ~!** ¡Feliz Año Nuevo!; **to wish sb a happy ~** desear a algn un feliz año nuevo
New Year's Day *n* Día *m* de Año Nuevo
New Year's Eve *n* Nochevieja
New York [-'jɔ:k] *n* Nueva York
New Zealand [-'zi:lənd] *n* Nueva Zelanda (*SP*), Nueva Zelandia (*LAm*) ▪ *adj* neozelandés(-esa)
New Zealander [-'zi:ləndər] *n* neozelandés(-esa) *m(f)*
next [nɛkst] *adj* (*house, room*) vecino, de al lado; (*meeting*) próximo; (*page*) siguiente ▪ *adv* después; **the ~ day** el día siguiente; **~ time** la próxima vez; **~ year** el año próximo *or* que viene; **~ month** el mes que viene *or* entrante; **the week after ~** no la semana que viene sino la otra; **"turn to the ~ page"** "vuelva a la página siguiente"; **you're ~** le toca; **~ to** *prep* junto a, al lado de; **~ to nothing** casi nada
next door *adv* en la casa de al lado ▪ *adj* vecino, de al lado
next-of-kin ['nɛkstəv'kɪn] *n* pariente(s) *m(pl)* más cercano(s)
NF *n abbr* (*Brit Pol*: = *National Front*) *partido político de la extrema derecha* ▪ *abbr* (*Canada*) = **Newfoundland**
NFL *n abbr* (*US*) = **National Football League**
Nfld. *abbr* (*Canada*) = **Newfoundland**
NG *abbr* (*US*) = **National Guard**
NGO *n abbr* (= *non-governmental organization*) ONG *f*
NH *abbr* (*US*) = **New Hampshire**
NHL *n abbr* (*US*) = **National Hockey League**
NHS *n abbr* (*Brit*) = **National Health Service**
NI *abbr* = **Northern Ireland**; (*Brit*) = **National Insurance**
nib [nɪb] *n* plumilla
nibble ['nɪbl] *vt* mordisquear
Nicaragua [nɪkə'rægjuə] *n* Nicaragua
Nicaraguan [nɪkə'rægjuən] *adj, n* nicaragüense *m/f*, nicaragüeño(-a) *m(f)*
Nice [ni:s] *n* Niza
nice [naɪs] *adj* (*likeable*) simpático, majo; (*kind*) amable; (*pleasant*) agradable; (*attractive*) bonito, mono; (*distinction*) fino; (*taste, smell, meal*) rico

nice-looking ['naɪslʊkɪŋ] *adj* guapo
nicely ['naɪslɪ] *adv* amablemente; (*of health etc*) bien; **that will do ~** perfecto
niceties ['naɪsɪtɪz] *npl* detalles *mpl*
niche [niːʃ] *n* (*Arch*) nicho, hornacina
nick [nɪk] *n* (*wound*) rasguño; (*cut, indentation*) mella, muesca ■ *vt* (*cut*) cortar; (*col*) birlar, mangar; (: *arrest*) pillar; **in the ~ of time** justo a tiempo; **in good ~** en buen estado; **to ~ o.s.** cortarse
nickel ['nɪkl] *n* níquel *m*; (*US*) *moneda de 5 centavos*
nickname ['nɪkneɪm] *n* apodo, mote *m* ■ *vt* apodar
Nicosia [nɪkə'siːə] *n* Nicosia
nicotine ['nɪkətiːn] *n* nicotina
nicotine patch *n* parche *m* de nicotina
niece [niːs] *n* sobrina
nifty ['nɪftɪ] *adj* (*col: car, jacket*) elegante, chulo; (: *gadget, tool*) ingenioso
Niger ['naɪdʒəʳ] *n* (*country, river*) Níger *m*
Nigeria [naɪ'dʒɪərɪə] *n* Nigeria
Nigerian [naɪ'dʒɪərɪən] *adj, n* nigeriano(-a) *m(f)*
niggardly ['nɪgədlɪ] *adj* (*person*) avaro, tacaño, avariento; (*allowance, amount*) miserable
nigger ['nɪgəʳ] *n* (*col!: highly offensive*) negro(-a)
niggle ['nɪgl] *vt* preocupar ■ *vi* (*complain*) quejarse; (*fuss*) preocuparse por minucias
niggling ['nɪglɪŋ] *adj* (*detail: trifling*) nimio, insignificante; (*annoying*) molesto; (*doubt, pain*) constante
night [naɪt] *n* (*gen*) noche *f*; (*evening*) tarde *f*; **last ~** anoche; **the ~ before last** anteanoche, antes de ayer por la noche; **at ~**, **by ~** de noche, por la noche; **in the ~**, **during the ~** durante la noche, por la noche
night-bird ['naɪtbəd] *n* (*fig*) trasnochador(a) *m(f)*, madrugador(a) *m(f)* (*LAm*)
nightcap ['naɪtkæp] *n* (*drink*) *bebida que se toma antes de acostarse*
night club *n* club nocturno, discoteca
nightdress ['naɪtdrɛs] *n* (*Brit*) camisón *m*
nightfall ['naɪtfɔːl] *n* anochecer *m*
nightgown ['naɪtgaun], **nightie** ['naɪtɪ] (*Brit*) *n* = **nightdress**
nightingale ['naɪtɪŋgeɪl] *n* ruiseñor *m*
night life *n* vida nocturna
nightly ['naɪtlɪ] *adj* de todas las noches ■ *adv* todas las noches, cada noche
nightmare ['naɪtmɛəʳ] *n* pesadilla
night porter *n* guardián *m* nocturno
night safe *n* caja fuerte
night school *n* clase(s) *f(pl)* nocturna(s)
nightshade ['naɪtʃeɪd] *n*: **deadly ~** (*Bot*) belladona
night shift *n* turno nocturno *or* de noche

night-time ['naɪttaɪm] *n* noche *f*
night watchman *n* vigilante *m* nocturno, sereno
nihilism ['naɪɪlɪzəm] *n* nihilismo
nil [nɪl] *n* (*Brit Sport*) cero, nada
Nile [naɪl] *n*: **the ~** el Nilo
nimble ['nɪmbl] *adj* (*agile*) ágil, ligero; (*skilful*) diestro
nimbly ['nɪmblɪ] *adv* ágilmente; con destreza
nine [naɪn] *num* nueve
9-11, Nine-Eleven [naɪnɪ'lɛvn] *n* 11-S *m*
nineteen ['naɪn'tiːn] *num* diecinueve
nineteenth [naɪn'tiːnθ] *adj* decimonoveno, decimonono
ninety ['naɪntɪ] *num* noventa
ninth [naɪnθ] *adj* noveno
nip [nɪp] *vt* (*pinch*) pellizcar; (*bite*) morder ■ *vi* (*Brit col*): **to ~ out/down/up** salir/bajar/subir un momento ■ *n* (*drink*) trago
nipple ['nɪpl] *n* (*Anat*) pezón *m*; (*of bottle*) tetilla; (*Tech*) boquilla, manguito
nippy ['nɪpɪ] *adj* (*Brit: person*) rápido; (*taste*) picante; **it's a very ~ car** es un coche muy potente para el tamaño que tiene
nit [nɪt] *n* (*of louse*) liendre *f*; (*col: idiot*) imbécil *m/f*
nit-pick ['nɪtpɪk] *vi* (*col*) sacar punta a todo
nitrogen ['naɪtrədʒən] *n* nitrógeno
nitroglycerin, nitroglycerine ['naɪtrəu'glɪsəriːn] *n* nitroglicerina
nitty-gritty ['nɪtɪ'grɪtɪ] *n* (*col*): **to get down to the ~** ir al grano
nitwit ['nɪtwɪt] *n* cretino(-a)
NJ *abbr* (*US*) = **New Jersey**
NLF *n abbr* (= *National Liberation Front*) FLN *m*
NLRB *n abbr* (*US*: = *National Labor Relations Board*) *organismo de protección al trabajador*
NM, N. Mex. *abbr* (*US*) = **New Mexico**

 KEYWORD

no [nəu] (*pl* **noes**) *adv* (*opposite of "yes"*) no; **are you coming? — no (I'm not)** ¿vienes? — no; **would you like some more? — no thank you** ¿quieres más? — no gracias
 ■ *adj* (*not any*): **I have no money/time/books** no tengo dinero/tiempo/libros; **no other man would have done it** ningún otro lo hubiera hecho; **"no entry"** "prohibido el paso"; **"no smoking"** "prohibido fumar"
 ■ *n* no *m*

no. *abbr* (= *number*) nº, núm
nobble ['nɔbl] *vt* (*Brit col: bribe*) sobornar; (: *catch*) pescar; (: *Racing*) drogar
Nobel prize [nəu'bɛl-] *n* premio Nobel
nobility [nəu'bɪlɪtɪ] *n* nobleza

noble ['nəubl] *adj* (*person*) noble; (*title*) de nobleza
nobleman ['nəublmən] *n* noble *m*
nobly ['nəublɪ] *adv* (*selflessly*) noblemente
nobody ['nəubədɪ] *pron* nadie
no-claims bonus ['nəukleɪmz-] *n* bonificación *f* por carencia de reclamaciones
nocturnal [nɔk'tə:nl] *adj* nocturno
nod [nɔd] *vi* saludar con la cabeza; (*in agreement*) asentir con la cabeza ■ *vt*:
to ~ one's head inclinar la cabeza ■ *n* inclinación *f* de cabeza; **they nodded their agreement** asintieron con la cabeza
▶ **nod off** *vi* cabecear
no-fly zone [nəu'flaɪ-] *n* zona de exclusión aérea
noise [nɔɪz] *n* ruido; (*din*) escándalo, estrépito
noisily ['nɔɪzɪlɪ] *adv* ruidosamente, estrepitosamente
noisy ['nɔɪzɪ] *adj* (*gen*) ruidoso; (*child*) escandaloso
nomad ['nəumæd] *n* nómada *m/f*
nomadic [nəu'mædɪk] *adj* nómada
no man's land *n* tierra de nadie
nominal ['nɔmɪnl] *adj* nominal
nominate ['nɔmɪneɪt] *vt* (*propose*) proponer; (*appoint*) nombrar
nomination [nɔmɪ'neɪʃən] *n* propuesta; nombramiento
nominee [nɔmɪ'ni:] *n* candidato(-a)
non... [nɔn] *pref* no, des..., in...
nonalcoholic [nɔnælkə'hɔlɪk] *adj* sin alcohol
nonaligned [nɔnə'laɪnd] *adj* no alineado
nonarrival [nɔnə'raɪvl] *n* falta de llegada
nonce word [nɔns-] *n* hápax *m*
nonchalant ['nɔnʃələnt] *adj* indiferente
noncommissioned [nɔnkə'mɪʃənd] *adj*: ~ **officer** suboficial *m/f*
noncommittal ['nɔnkə'mɪtl] *adj* (*reserved*) reservado; (*uncommitted*) evasivo
nonconformist [nɔnkən'fɔ:mɪst] *adj* inconformista ■ *n* inconformista *m/f*; (*Brit Rel*) no conformista *m/f*
noncontributory [nɔnkən'trɪbjutərɪ] *adj*: ~ **pension scheme** *or* (*US*) **plan** fondo de pensiones no contributivo
noncooperation ['nɔnkəuəpə'reɪʃən] *n* no cooperación *f*
nondescript ['nɔndɪskrɪpt] *adj* anodino, soso
none [nʌn] *pron* ninguno(-a) ■ *adv* de ninguna manera; ~ **of you** ninguno de vosotros; **I've ~ left** no me queda ninguno(-a); **he's ~ the worse for it** no le ha perjudicado; **I have ~** no tengo ninguno; ~ **at all** (*not one*) ni uno
nonentity [nɔ'nɛntɪtɪ] *n* cero a la izquierda, nulidad *f*

nonessential [nɔnɪ'sɛnʃl] *adj* no esencial ■ *n*: **nonessentials** cosas *fpl* secundarias *or* sin importancia
nonetheless [nʌnðə'lɛs] *adv* sin embargo, no obstante, aún así
non-EU [nɔni:'ju:] *adj* (*citizen, passport*) no comunitario; (*imports*) de fuera de la Unión Europea
non-event [nɔnɪ'vɛnt] *n* acontecimiento sin importancia; **it was a ~** no pasó absolutamente nada
nonexecutive [nɔnɪg'zɛkjutɪv] *adj*: ~ **director** director *m* no ejecutivo
nonexistent [nɔnɪg'zɪstənt] *adj* inexistente
nonfiction [nɔn'fɪkʃən] *n* no ficción *f*
nonintervention [nɔnɪntə'vɛnʃən] *n* no intervención *f*
no-no ['nəunəu] *n* (*col*): **it's a ~** de eso ni hablar
non obst. *abbr* (= *non obstante*: *notwithstanding*) no obstante
no-nonsense [nəu'nɔnsəns] *adj* sensato
nonpayment [nɔn'peɪmənt] *n* falta de pago
nonplussed [nɔn'plʌst] *adj* perplejo
non-profit-making [nɔn'prɔfitmeɪkɪŋ] *adj* no lucrativo
nonsense ['nɔnsəns] *n* tonterías *fpl*, disparates *fpl*; ~! ¡qué tonterías!; **it is ~ to say that ...** es absurdo decir que ...
nonsensical [nɔn'sɛnsɪkl] *adj* disparatado, absurdo
nonshrink [nɔn'ʃrɪŋk] *adj* que no encoge
nonskid [nɔn'skɪd] *adj* antideslizante
nonsmoker ['nɔn'sməukəʳ] *n* no fumador(a) *m(f)*
nonstarter [nɔn'stɑ:təʳ] *n*: **it's a ~** no tiene futuro
nonstick ['nɔn'stɪk] *adj* (*pan, surface*) antiadherente
nonstop ['nɔn'stɔp] *adj* continuo; (*Rail*) directo ■ *adv* sin parar
nontaxable [nɔn'tæksəbl] *adj*: ~ **income** renta no imponible
non-U ['nɔnju:] *adj abbr* (*Brit col*: = *non-upper class*) que no pertenece a la clase alta
nonvolatile [nɔn'vɔlətaɪl] *adj*: ~ **memory** (*Comput*) memoria permanente
nonvoting [nɔn'vəutɪŋ] *adj*: ~ **shares** acciones *fpl* sin derecho a voto
nonwhite [nɔn'waɪt] *adj* de color ■ *n* (*person*) persona de color
noodles ['nu:dlz] *npl* tallarines *mpl*
nook [nuk] *n* rincón *m*; **nooks and crannies** escondrijos *mpl*
noon [nu:n] *n* mediodía *m*
no-one ['nəuwʌn] *pron* = **nobody**
noose [nu:s] *n* lazo corredizo

nor [nɔːʳ] *conj* = **neither** ■ *adv see* **neither**
Norf *abbr* (*Brit*) = **Norfolk**
norm [nɔːm] *n* norma
normal ['nɔːml] *adj* normal; **to return to ~**
volver a la normalidad
normality [nɔː'mælɪtɪ] *n* normalidad *f*
normally ['nɔːməlɪ] *adv* normalmente
Normandy ['nɔːməndɪ] *n* Normandía
north [nɔːθ] *n* norte *m* ■ *adj* del norte ■ *adv*
al *or* hacia el norte
North Africa *n* África del Norte
North African *adj, n* norteafricano(-a) *m(f)*
North America *n* América del Norte
North American *adj, n* norteamericano(-a)
m(f)
Northants [nɔː'θænts] *abbr* (*Brit*)
= **Northamptonshire**
northbound ['nɔːθbaund] *adj* (*traffic*) que
se dirige al norte; (*carriageway*) de dirección
norte
Northd *abbr* (*Brit*) = **Northumberland**
north-east [nɔːθ'iːst] *n* nor(d)este *m*
northerly ['nɔːðəlɪ] *adj* (*point, direction*) hacia
el norte, septentrional; (*wind*) del norte
northern ['nɔːðən] *adj* norteño, del norte
Northern Ireland *n* Irlanda del Norte
North Korea *n* Corea del Norte
North Pole *n*: **the ~** el Polo Norte
North Sea *n*: **the ~** el Mar del Norte
North Sea oil *n* petróleo del Mar del Norte
northward ['nɔːθwəd], **northwards**
['nɔːθwədz] *adv* hacia el norte
north-west [nɔːθ'wɛst] *n* noroeste *m*
Norway ['nɔːweɪ] *n* Noruega
Norwegian [nɔː'wiːdʒən] *adj* noruego
■ *n* noruego(-a); (*Ling*) noruego
nos. *abbr* (= *numbers*) núms.
nose [nəuz] *n* (*Anat*) nariz *f*; (*Zool*) hocico;
(*sense of smell*) olfato ■ *vi* (*also*: **nose one's
way**) avanzar con cautela; **to pay through
the ~ (for sth)** (*col*) pagar un dineral (por algo)
▶ **nose about, nose around** *vi* curiosear
nosebleed ['nəuzbliːd] *n* hemorragia, nasal
nose-dive ['nəuzdaɪv] *n* picado vertical
nose drops *npl* gotas *fpl* para la nariz
nosey ['nəuzɪ] *adj* curioso, fisgón(-ona)
nostalgia [nɔs'tældʒɪə] *n* nostalgia
nostalgic [nɔs'tældʒɪk] *adj* nostálgico
nostril ['nɔstrɪl] *n* ventana *or* orificio de la
nariz
nosy ['nəuzɪ] *adj* = **nosey**
not [nɔt] *adv* no; **~ at all** no ... en absoluto; **~
that ...** no es que ...; **it's too late, isn't it?** es
demasiado tarde, ¿verdad?; **~ yet** todavía no;
~ now ahora no; **why ~?** ¿por qué no?; **I hope
~** espero que no; **~ at all** no ... nada; (*after
thanks*) de nada

notable ['nəutəbl] *adj* notable
notably ['nəutəblɪ] *adv* especialmente;
(*in particular*) sobre todo
notary ['nəutərɪ] *n* (*also*: **notary public**)
notario(-a)
notation [nəu'teɪʃən] *n* notación *f*
notch [nɔtʃ] *n* muesca, corte *m*
▶ **notch up** *vt* (*score, victory*) apuntarse
note [nəut] *n* (*Mus, record, letter*) nota;
(*banknote*) billete *m*; (*tone*) tono ■ *vt* (*observe*)
notar, observar; (*write down*) apuntar,
anotar; **delivery ~** nota de entrega; **to
compare notes** (*fig*) cambiar impresiones;
of ~ conocido, destacado; **to take ~** prestar
atención a; **just a quick ~ to let you know
that ...** sólo unas líneas para informarte
que ...
notebook ['nəutbuk] *n* libreta, cuaderno;
(*for shorthand*) libreta
notecase ['nəutkeɪs] *n* (*Brit*) cartera, billetero
noted ['nəutɪd] *adj* célebre, conocido
notepad ['nəutpæd] *n* bloc *m*
notepaper ['nəutpeɪpə] *n* papel *m* para cartas
noteworthy ['nəutwəːðɪ] *adj* notable, digno
de atención
nothing ['nʌθɪŋ] *n* nada; (*zero*) cero; **he does
~** no hace nada; **~ new** nada nuevo; **for ~**
(*free*) gratis; (*in vain*) en balde; **~ at all** nada
en absoluto
notice ['nəutɪs] *n* (*announcement*) anuncio;
(*dismissal*) despido; (*resignation*) dimisión *f*;
(*review: of play etc*) reseña ■ *vt* (*observe*) notar,
observar; **to take ~ of** hacer caso de, prestar
atención a; **at short ~** con poca antelación;
without ~ sin previo aviso; **advance ~** previo
aviso; **until further ~** hasta nuevo aviso; **to
give sb ~ of sth** avisar a algn de algo; **to give
~, hand in one's ~** dimitir, renunciar; **it has
come to my ~ that ...** he llegado a saber que
...; **to escape** *or* **avoid ~** pasar inadvertido
noticeable ['nəutɪsəbl] *adj* evidente, obvio
notice board *n* (*Brit*) tablón *m* de anuncios
notification [nəutɪfɪ'keɪʃən] *n* aviso;
(*announcement*) anuncio
notify ['nəutɪfaɪ] *vt*: **to ~ sb (of sth)**
comunicar (algo) a algn
notion ['nəuʃən] *n* noción *f*, concepto;
(*opinion*) opinión *f*
notions ['nəuʃənz] *npl* (*US*) mercería
notoriety [nəutə'raɪətɪ] *n* notoriedad *f*, mala
fama
notorious [nəu'tɔːrɪəs] *adj* notorio,
tristemente célebre
notoriously [nəu'tɔːrɪəslɪ] *adv* notoriamente
Notts [nɔts] *abbr* (*Brit*) = **Nottinghamshire**
notwithstanding [nɔtwɪθ'stændɪŋ] *adv* no
obstante, sin embargo; **~ this** a pesar de esto

n

nougat ['nuːgaː] n turrón m
nought [nɔːt] n cero
noun [naun] n nombre m, sustantivo
nourish ['nʌrɪʃ] vt nutrir, alimentar; (fig) fomentar, nutrir
nourishing ['nʌrɪʃɪŋ] adj nutritivo, rico
nourishment ['nʌrɪʃmənt] n alimento, sustento
Nov. abbr (= November) nov
novel ['nɔvl] n novela ■ adj (new) nuevo, original; (unexpected) insólito
novelist ['nɔvəlɪst] n novelista m/f
novelty ['nɔvəltɪ] n novedad f
November [nəu'vɛmbəʳ] n noviembre m; see also **July**
novice ['nɔvɪs] n principiante m/f, novato(-a); (Rel) novicio(-a)
NOW [nau] n abbr (US) = **National Organization for Women**
now [nau] adv (at the present time) ahora; (these days) actualmente, hoy día ■ conj: ~ **(that)** ya que, ahora que; **right** ~ ahora mismo; **by** ~ ya; **just** ~: **I'll do it just now** ahora mismo lo hago; ~ **and then**, ~ **and again** de vez en cuando; **from** ~ **on** de ahora en adelante; **between** ~ **and Monday** entre hoy y el lunes; **in 3 days from** ~ de hoy en 3 días; **that's all for** ~ eso es todo por ahora
nowadays ['nauədeɪz] adv hoy (en) día, actualmente
nowhere ['nəuwɛəʳ] adv (direction) a ninguna parte; (location) en ninguna parte; ~ **else** en or a ninguna otra parte
no-win situation [nəu'wɪn-] n: **I'm in a** ~ haga lo que haga, llevo las de perder
noxious ['nɔkʃəs] adj nocivo
nozzle ['nɔzl] n boquilla
NP n abbr = **notary public**
NS abbr (Canada) = **Nova Scotia**
NSC n abbr (US) = **National Security Council**
NSF n abbr (US) = **National Science Foundation**
NSPCC n abbr (Brit) = **National Society for the Prevention of Cruelty to Children**
NSW abbr (Australia) = **New South Wales**
NT n abbr (= New Testament) ■ abbr (Canada) = **Northwest Territories**
nth [ɛnθ] adj: **for the** ~ **time** (col) por enésima vez
nuance ['njuːɑːns] n matiz m
nubile ['njuːbaɪl] adj núbil
nuclear ['njuːklɪəʳ] adj nuclear
nuclear disarmament n desarme m nuclear
nuclear family n familia nuclear
nuclear-free zone ['njuːklɪə'friː-] n zona desnuclearizada
nucleus (pl **nuclei**) ['njuːklɪəs, 'njuːklɪaɪ] n núcleo

NUCPS n abbr (Brit: = National Union of Civil and Public Servants) sindicato de funcionarios
nude [njuːd] adj, n desnudo(-a) m(f); **in the** ~ desnudo
nudge [nʌdʒ] vt dar un codazo a
nudist ['njuːdɪst] n nudista m/f
nudist colony n colonia de desnudistas
nudity ['njuːdɪtɪ] n desnudez f
nugget ['nʌgɪt] n pepita
nuisance ['njuːsns] n molestia, fastidio; (person) pesado, latoso; **what a** ~! ¡qué lata!
NUJ n abbr (Brit: = National Union of Journalists) sindicato de periodistas
nuke [njuːk] (col) n bomba atómica ■ vt atacar con arma nuclear
null [nʌl] adj: ~ **and void** nulo y sin efecto
nullify ['nʌlɪfaɪ] vt anular, invalidar
NUM n abbr (Brit: = National Union of Mineworkers) sindicato de mineros
numb [nʌm] adj entumecido; (fig) insensible ■ vt quitar la sensación a, entumecer, entorpecer; **to be** ~ **with cold** estar entumecido de frío; ~ **with fear/grief** paralizado de miedo/dolor
number ['nʌmbəʳ] n número; (numeral) número, cifra ■ vt (pages etc) numerar, poner número a; (amount to) sumar, ascender a; **reference** ~ número de referencia; **telephone** ~ número de teléfono; **wrong** ~ (Tel) número equivocado; **opposite** ~ (person) homólogo(-a); **to be numbered among** figurar entre; **a** ~ **of** varios, algunos; **they were ten in** ~ eran diez
number plate n (Brit) matrícula, placa
Number Ten n (Brit: 10 Downing Street) residencia del primer ministro
numbness ['nʌmnɪs] n insensibilidad f, parálisis f inv; (due to cold) entumecimiento
numbskull ['nʌmskʌl] n (col) papanatas m/f inv
numeral ['njuːmərəl] n número, cifra
numerate ['njuːmərɪt] adj competente en aritmética
numerical [njuː'mɛrɪkl] adj numérico
numerous ['njuːmərəs] adj numeroso, muchos
nun [nʌn] n monja, religiosa
nunnery ['nʌnərɪ] n convento de monjas
nuptial ['nʌpʃəl] adj nupcial
nurse [nəːs] n enfermero(-a); (nanny) niñera ■ vt (patient) cuidar, atender; (baby: Brit) mecer; (: US) criar, amamantar; **male** ~ enfermero
nursery ['nəːsərɪ] n (institution) guardería infantil; (room) cuarto de los niños; (for plants) criadero, semillero
nursery rhyme n canción f infantil
nursery school n escuela de preescolar

nursery slope n (Brit Ski) cuesta para principiantes

nursing ['nə:sɪŋ] n (profession) profesión f de enfermera; (care) asistencia, cuidado ∎ adj (mother) lactante

nursing home n clínica de reposo

nurture ['nə:tʃəʳ] vt (child, plant) alimentar, nutrir

NUS n abbr (Brit: = National Union of Students) sindicato de estudiantes

NUT n abbr (Brit: = National Union of Teachers) sindicato de profesores

nut [nʌt] n (Tech) tuerca; (Bot) nuez f ∎ adj (chocolate etc) con nueces; **nuts** (Culin) frutos secos

nutcrackers ['nʌtkrækəz] npl cascanueces m inv

nutmeg ['nʌtmɛg] n nuez f moscada

nutrient ['nju:trɪənt] adj nutritivo ∎ n elemento nutritivo

nutrition [nju:'trɪʃən] n nutrición f, alimentación f

nutritionist [nju:'trɪʃənɪst] n dietista m/f

nutritious [nju:'trɪʃəs] adj nutritivo

nuts [nʌts] adj (col) chiflado

nutshell ['nʌtʃɛl] n cáscara de nuez; **in a ~** en resumidas cuentas

nutty ['nʌtɪ] adj (flavour) a frutos secos; (col: foolish) chalado

nuzzle ['nʌzl] vi: **to ~ up to** arrimarse a

NV abbr (US) = **Nevada**

NVQ n abbr (Brit: = national vocational qualification) título de formación profesional

NWT abbr (Canada) = **Northwest Territories**

NY abbr (US) = **New York**

NYC abbr (US) = **New York City**

nylon ['naɪlɔn] n nylon m, nilón m ∎ adj de nylon or nilón

nymph [nɪmf] n ninfa

nymphomaniac ['nɪmfəu'meɪnɪæk] adj, n ninfómana

NYSE n abbr (US) = **New York Stock Exchange**

n

Oo

O, o [əu] *n* (*letter*) O, o *f*; **O for Oliver,** (*US*) **O for Oboe** O de Oviedo

oaf [əuf] *n* zoquete *m/f*

oak [əuk] *n* roble *m* ▪ *adj* de roble

O & M *n abbr* = **organization and method**

OAP *n abbr* (*Brit*) = **old-age pensioner**

oar [ɔːʳ] *n* remo; **to put** *or* **shove one's ~ in** (*fig col*) entrometerse

oarsman ['ɔːzmən] *n* remero

OAS *n abbr* (= *Organization of American States*) OEA *f*

oasis (*pl* **oases**) [əu'eɪsɪs, əu'eɪsiːz] *n* oasis *m inv*

oath [əuθ] *n* juramento; (*swear word*) palabrota; **on** (*Brit*) *or* **under ~** bajo juramento

oatmeal ['əutmiːl] *n* harina de avena

oats [əuts] *n* avena

OAU *n abbr* (= *Organization of African Unity*) OUA *f*

obdurate ['ɔbdjurɪt] *adj* (*stubborn*) terco, obstinado; (*sinner*) empedernido; (*unyielding*) inflexible, firme

OBE *n abbr* (*Brit*: = *Order of the British Empire*) título ceremonial

obedience [ə'biːdɪəns] *n* obediencia; **in ~ to** de acuerdo con

obedient [ə'biːdɪənt] *adj* obediente

obelisk ['ɔbɪlɪsk] *n* obelisco

obese [əu'biːs] *adj* obeso

obesity [əu'biːsɪtɪ] *n* obesidad *f*

obey [ə'beɪ] *vt* obedecer; (*instructions*) cumplir

obituary [ə'bɪtjuərɪ] *n* necrología

object ['ɔbdʒɪkt] *n* (*gen*) objeto; (*purpose*) objeto, propósito; (*Ling*) objeto, complemento ▪ *vi* [əb'dʒɛkt]: **to ~ to** (*attitude*) protestar contra; (*proposal*) oponerse a; **expense is no ~** no importan los gastos; **I ~!** ¡protesto!; **to ~ that** objetar que

objection [əb'dʒɛkʃən] *n* objeción *f*; **I have no ~ to ...** no tengo inconveniente en, que ...

objectionable [əb'dʒɛkʃənəbl] *adj* (*gen*) desagradable; (*conduct*) censurable

objective [əb'dʒɛktɪv] *adj, n* objetivo

objectively [əb'dʒɛktɪvlɪ] *adv* objetivamente

objectivity [ɔbdʒɪk'tɪvɪtɪ] *n* objetividad *f*

object lesson *n* (*fig*) (buen) ejemplo

objector [əb'dʒɛktəʳ] *n* objetor(a) *m(f)*

obligation [ɔblɪ'geɪʃən] *n* obligación *f*; (*debt*) deber *m*; **"without ~"** "sin compromiso"; **to be under an ~ to sb/to do sth** estar comprometido con algn/a hacer algo

obligatory [ə'blɪgətərɪ] *adj* obligatorio

oblige [ə'blaɪdʒ] *vt* (*do a favour for*) complacer, hacer un favor a; **to ~ sb to do sth** obligar a algn a hacer algo; **to be obliged to sb for sth** estarle agradecido a algn por algo; **anything to ~!** todo sea por complacerte

obliging [ə'blaɪdʒɪŋ] *adj* servicial, atento

oblique [ə'bliːk] *adj* oblicuo; (*allusion*) indirecto ▪ *n* (*Typ*) barra

obliterate [ə'blɪtəreɪt] *vt* arrasar; (*memory*) borrar

oblivion [ə'blɪvɪən] *n* olvido

oblivious [ə'blɪvɪəs] *adj*: **~ of** inconsciente de

oblong ['ɔblɔŋ] *adj* rectangular ▪ *n* rectángulo

obnoxious [əb'nɔkʃəs] *adj* odioso, detestable; (*smell*) nauseabundo

o.b.o. *abbr* (*US*: = *or best offer: in classified ads*) abierto ofertas

oboe ['əubəu] *n* oboe *m*

obscene [əb'siːn] *adj* obsceno

obscenity [əb'sɛnɪtɪ] *n* obscenidad *f*

obscure [əb'skjuəʳ] *adj* oscuro ▪ *vt* oscurecer; (*hide: sun*) ocultar

obscurity [əb'skjuərɪtɪ] *n* oscuridad *f*; (*obscure point*) punto oscuro; **to rise from ~** salir de la nada

obsequious [əb'siːkwɪəs] *adj* servil

observable [əb'zəːvəbl] *adj* observable, perceptible

observance [əb'zəːvns] *n* observancia, cumplimiento; (*ritual*) práctica; **religious observances** prácticas *fpl* religiosas

observant [əb'zəːvnt] *adj* observador(a)

observation [ɔbzə'veɪʃən] *n* (*Med*) observación *f*; (*by police etc*) vigilancia

observation post n (Mil) puesto de observación

observatory [əb'zɜːvətrɪ] n observatorio

observe [əb'zɜːv] vt (gen) observar; (rule) cumplir

observer [əb'zɜːvəʳ] n observador(a) m(f)

obsess [əb'sɛs] vt obsesionar; **to be obsessed by** or **with sb/sth** estar obsesionado con algn/algo

obsession [əb'sɛʃən] n obsesión f

obsessive [əb'sɛsɪv] adj obsesivo

obsolescence [ɔbsə'lɛsns] n obsolescencia

obsolescent [ɔbsə'lɛsnt] adj que está cayendo en desuso

obsolete ['ɔbsəliːt] adj obsoleto

obstacle ['ɔbstəkl] n obstáculo; (nuisance) estorbo

obstacle race n carrera de obstáculos

obstetrician [ɔbstə'trɪʃən] n obstetra m/f

obstetrics [ɔb'stɛtrɪks] n obstetricia

obstinacy ['ɔbstɪnəsɪ] n terquedad f, obstinación f; tenacidad f

obstinate ['ɔbstɪnɪt] adj terco, obstinado; (determined) tenaz

obstinately ['ɔbstɪnɪtlɪ] adv tercamente, obstinadamente

obstreperous [əb'strɛpərəs] adj ruidoso; (unruly) revoltoso

obstruct [əb'strʌkt] vt (block) obstruir; (hinder) estorbar, obstaculizar

obstruction [əb'strʌkʃən] n obstrucción f; estorbo, obstáculo

obstructive [əb'strʌktɪv] adj obstruccionista; **stop being ~!** ¡deja de poner peros!

obtain [əb'teɪn] vt (get) obtener; (achieve) conseguir; **to ~ sth (for o.s.)** conseguir or adquirir algo

obtainable [əb'teɪnəbl] adj asequible

obtrusive [əb'truːsɪv] adj (person) importuno; (: interfering) entrometido; (building etc) demasiado visible

obtuse [əb'tjuːs] adj obtuso

obverse ['ɔbvɜːs] n (of medal) anverso; (fig) complemento

obviate ['ɔbvɪeɪt] vt obviar, evitar

obvious ['ɔbvɪəs] adj (clear) obvio, evidente; (unsubtle) poco sutil; **it's ~ that ...** está claro que ..., es evidente que ...

obviously ['ɔbvɪəslɪ] adv obviamente, evidentemente; **~ not!** ¡por supuesto que no!; **he was ~ not drunk** era evidente que no estaba borracho; **he was not ~ drunk** no se le notaba que estaba borracho

OCAS n abbr (= Organization of Central American States) ODECA f

occasion [ə'keɪʒən] n oportunidad f, ocasión f; (event) acontecimiento ■ vt ocasionar, causar; **on that ~** esa vez, en aquella ocasión; **to rise to the ~** ponerse a la altura de las circunstancias

occasional [ə'keɪʒənl] adj poco frecuente, ocasional

occasionally [ə'keɪʒənlɪ] adv de vez en cuando; **very ~** muy de tarde en tarde, en muy contadas ocasiones

occasional table n mesita

occult [ɔ'kʌlt] adj (gen) oculto

occupancy ['ɔkjupənsɪ] n ocupación f

occupant ['ɔkjupənt] n (of house) inquilino(-a); (of boat, car) ocupante m/f

occupation [ɔkju'peɪʃən] n (of house) tenencia; (job) trabajo; (calling) oficio

occupational accident [ɔkju'peɪʃənl-] n accidente m laboral

occupational guidance n orientación f profesional

occupational hazard n gajes mpl del oficio

occupational pension scheme n plan m profesional de jubilación

occupational therapy n terapia ocupacional

occupier ['ɔkjupaɪəʳ] n inquilino(-a)

occupy ['ɔkjupaɪ] vt (seat, post, time) ocupar; (house) habitar; **to ~ o.s. with** or **by doing** (as job) dedicarse a hacer; (to pass time) entretenerse haciendo; **to be occupied with sth/in doing sth** estar ocupado con algo/haciendo algo

occur [ə'kɜːʳ] vi ocurrir, suceder; **to ~ to sb** ocurrírsele a algn

occurrence [ə'kʌrəns] n suceso

ocean ['əuʃən] n océano; **oceans of** (col) la mar de

ocean bed n fondo del océano

ocean-going ['əuʃəngəuɪŋ] adj de alta mar

Oceania [əuʃɪ'ɑːnɪə] n Oceanía

ocean liner n buque m transoceánico

ochre, (US) **ocher** ['əukəʳ] n ocre m

o'clock [ə'klɔk] adv: **it is five ~** son las cinco

OCR n abbr = **optical character recognition/ reader**

Oct. abbr (= October) oct

octagonal [ɔk'tægənl] adj octagonal

octane ['ɔkteɪn] n octano; **high ~ petrol** or (US) **gas** gasolina de alto octanaje

octave ['ɔktɪv] n octava

October [ɔk'təubəʳ] n octubre m; see also **July**

octogenarian ['ɔktəudʒɪ'nɛərɪən] n octogenario(-a)

octopus ['ɔktəpəs] n pulpo

oculist ['ɔkjulɪst] n oculista m/f

odd [ɔd] adj (strange) extraño, raro; (number) impar; (left over) sobrante, suelto; **60~** 60 y pico; **at ~ times** de vez en cuando; **to be**

the ~ **one out** estar de más; **if you have the ~ minute** si tienes unos minutos libres; *see also* **odds**

oddball ['ɔdbɔːl] *n* (*col*) bicho raro

oddity ['ɔdɪtɪ] *n* rareza; (*person*) excéntrico(-a)

odd-job man [ɔd'dʒɔb-] *n* hombre *m* que hace chapuzas

odd jobs *npl* chapuzas *fpl*

oddly ['ɔdlɪ] *adv* extrañamente

oddments ['ɔdmənts] *npl* (*Brit Comm*) restos *mpl*

odds [ɔdz] *npl* (*in betting*) puntos *mpl* de ventaja; **it makes no ~** da lo mismo; **at ~** reñidos(-as); **to succeed against all the ~** tener éxito contra todo pronóstico; **~ and ends** cachivaches *mpl*

odds-on [ɔdz'ɔn] *adj* (*col*): **the ~ favourite** el máximo favorito; **it's ~ he'll come** seguro que viene

ode [əud] *n* oda

odious ['əudɪəs] *adj* odioso

odometer [ɔ'dɔmɪtər] *n* (*US*) cuentakilómetros *m inv*

odour, odor (*US*) ['əudər] *n* olor *m*; (*perfume*) perfume *m*

odourless, odorless (*US*) ['əudəlɪs] *adj* sin olor

OECD *n abbr* (= *Organization for Economic Cooperation and Development*) OCDE *f*

oesophagus, esophagus (*US*) [iː'sɔfəgəs] *n* esófago

oestrogen, estrogen (*US*) ['iːstrədʒən] *n* estrógeno

 KEYWORD

of [ɔv, əv] *prep* **1** (*gen*) de; **a friend of ours** un amigo nuestro; **a boy of 10** un chico de 10 años; **that was kind of you** eso fue muy amable de tu parte
2 (*expressing quantity, amount, dates etc*) de; **a kilo of flour** un kilo de harina; **there were three of them** había tres; **three of us went** tres de nosotros fuimos; **the 5th of July** el 5 de julio; **a quarter of four** (*US*) las cuarto menos cuarto
3 (*from, out of*) de; **made of wood** (hecho) de madera

Ofcom ['ɔfkɔm] *n abbr* (*Brit*) = **Office of Communications**

off [ɔf] *adj, adv* (*engine, light*) apagado; (*tap*) cerrado; (*Brit: food: bad*) pasado, malo; (: *milk*) cortado; (*cancelled*) suspendido; (*removed*): **the lid was ~** no estaba puesta la tapadera ■ *prep* de; **to be ~** (*leave*) irse, marcharse; **to be ~ sick** estar enfermo *or* de baja; **a day ~** un día libre; **to have an ~ day** tener un mal día;

he **had his coat ~** se había quitado el abrigo; **10% ~** (*Comm*) (con el) 10% de descuento; **it's a long way ~** está muy lejos; **5 km ~ (the road)** a 5 km (de la carretera); **~ the coast** frente a la costa; **I'm ~ meat** (*no longer eat/like it*) paso de la carne; **on the ~ chance** por si acaso; **~ and on, on and ~** de vez en cuando; **I must be ~** tengo que irme; **to be well/badly ~** andar bien/mal de dinero; **I'm afraid the chicken is ~** desgraciadamente ya no queda pollo; **that's a bit ~, isn't it?** (*fig, col*) ¡eso no se hace!

offal ['ɔfl] *n* (*Brit Culin*) menudillos *mpl*, asaduras *fpl*

off-centre, (*US*) **off-center** [ɔf'sɛntər] *adj* descentrado, ladeado

off-colour ['ɔf'kʌlər] *adj* (*Brit: ill*) indispuesto; **to feel ~** sentirse *or* estar mal

offence, offense (*US*) [ə'fɛns] *n* (*crime*) delito; (*insult*) ofensa; **to take ~ at** ofenderse por; **to commit an ~** cometer un delito

offend [ə'fɛnd] *vt* (*person*) ofender ■ *vi*: **to ~ against** (*law, rule*) infringir

offender [ə'fɛndər] *n* delincuente *m/f*; (*against regulations*) infractor(a) *m(f)*

offending [ə'fɛndɪŋ] *adj* culpable; (*object*) molesto; (*word*) problemático

offense [ə'fɛns] *n* (*US*) = **offence**

offensive [ə'fɛnsɪv] *adj* ofensivo; (*smell etc*) repugnante ■ *n* (*Mil*) ofensiva

offer ['ɔfər] *n* (*gen*) oferta, ofrecimiento; (*proposal*) propuesta ■ *vt* ofrecer; **"on ~"** (*Comm*) "en oferta"; **to make an ~ for sth** hacer una oferta por algo; **to ~ sth to sb, ~ sb sth** ofrecer algo a algn; **to ~ to do sth** ofrecerse a hacer algo

offering ['ɔfərɪŋ] *n* (*Rel*) ofrenda

offer price *n* precio de oferta

offertory ['ɔfətrɪ] *n* (*Rel*) ofertorio

offhand [ɔf'hænd] *adj* informal; (*brusque*) desconsiderado ■ *adv* de improviso, sin pensarlo; **I can't tell you ~** no te lo puedo decir así de improviso *or* (*LAm*) así nomás

office ['ɔfɪs] *n* (*place*) oficina; (*room*) despacho; (*position*) cargo, oficio; **doctor's ~** (*US*) consultorio; **to take ~** entrar en funciones; **through his good offices** gracias a sus buenos oficios; **O~ of Fair Trading** (*Brit*) oficina que regula normas comerciales

office automation *n* ofimática, buromática

office bearer *n* (*of club etc*) titular *m/f* (de una cartera)

office block, office building (*US*) *n* bloque *m* de oficinas

office boy *n* ordenanza *m*

office hours *npl* horas *fpl* de oficina; (*US Med*) horas *fpl* de consulta

office manager n jefe(-a) m(f) de oficina
officer ['ɔfɪsəʳ] n (Mil etc) oficial m/f; (of organization) director(a) m(f); (also: **police officer**) agente m/f de policía
office work n trabajo de oficina
office worker n oficinista m/f
official [əˈfɪʃl] adj (authorized) oficial, autorizado; (strike) oficial ∎ n funcionario(-a)
officialdom [əˈfɪʃldəm] n burocracia
officially [əˈfɪʃəlɪ] adv oficialmente
official receiver n síndico
officiate [əˈfɪʃɪeɪt] vi (Rel) oficiar; **to ~ as Mayor** ejercer las funciones de alcalde; **to ~ at a marriage** celebrar una boda
officious [əˈfɪʃəs] adj oficioso
offing ['ɔfɪŋ] n: **in the ~** (fig) en perspectiva
off-key [ɔfˈkiː] adj desafinado ∎ adv desafinadamente
off-licence ['ɔflaɪsns] n (Brit: shop) tienda de bebidas alcohólicas; ver nota

⬤ **OFF-LICENCE**

⬤ En el Reino Unido una off-licence es una
⬤ tienda especializada en la venta de
⬤ bebidas alcohólicas para el consumo
⬤ fuera del establecimiento. De ahí su
⬤ nombre, pues se necesita un permiso
⬤ especial para tal venta, que está
⬤ estrictamente regulada. Suelen vender
⬤ además bebidas sin alcohol, tabaco,
⬤ chocolate, patatas fritas etc y a menudo
⬤ son parte de grandes cadenas nacionales.

off-limits [ɔfˈlɪmɪts] adj (US Mil) prohibido al personal militar
off line adj, adv (Comput) fuera de línea; (switched off) desconectado
off-load ['ɔfləud] vt descargar, desembarcar
off-peak ['ɔfpiːk] adj (holiday) de temporada baja; (electricity) de banda económica
off-putting ['ɔfputɪŋ] adj (Brit: person) poco amable, difícil; (behaviour) chocante
off-season ['ɔfsiːzn] adj, adv fuera de temporada
offset ['ɔfsɛt] vt (irreg: like **set**) (counteract) contrarrestar, compensar ∎ n (also: **offset printing**) offset m
offshoot ['ɔfʃuːt] n (Bot) vástago; (fig) ramificación f
offshore [ɔfˈʃɔːʳ] adj (breeze, island) costero; (fishing) de bajura; **~ oilfield** campo petrolífero submarino
offside ['ɔfsaɪd] n (Aut: with right-hand drive) lado derecho; (: with left-hand drive) lado izquierdo ∎ adj (Sport) fuera de juego; (Aut)

del lado derecho; del lado izquierdo
offspring ['ɔfsprɪŋ] n descendencia
offstage [ɔfˈsteɪdʒ] adv entre bastidores
off-the-cuff [ɔfðəˈkʌf] adj espontáneo
off-the-job [ɔfðəˈdʒɔb] adj: **~ training** formación f fuera del trabajo
off-the-peg [ɔfðəˈpɛg], (US) **off-the-rack** [ɔfðəˈræk] adv confeccionado
off-the-record ['ɔfðəˈrɛkɔːd] adj extraoficial, confidencial ∎ adv extraoficialmente, confidencialmente
off-white ['ɔfwaɪt] adj blanco grisáceo
Ofgas ['ɔfgæs] n abbr (Brit: = Office of Gas Supply) organismo que controla a las empresas del gas en Gran Bretaña
Ofgem ['ɔfdʒɛm] n abbr (Brit) = **Office of Gas and Electricity Markets**
Oftel ['ɔftɛl] n abbr (Brit: = Office of Telecommunications) organismo que controla las telecomunicaciones británicas
often ['ɔfn] adv a menudo, con frecuencia, seguido (LAm); **how ~ do you go?** ¿cada cuánto vas?
Ofwat ['ɔfwɔt] n abbr (Brit: = Office of Water Services) organismo que controla a las empresas suministradoras del agua en Inglaterra y Gales
ogle ['əugl] vt comerse con los ojos a
ogre ['əugəʳ] n ogro
OH abbr (US) = **Ohio**
oh [əu] excl ¡ah!
OHMS abbr (Brit) = **On His (or Her) Majesty's Service**
oil [ɔɪl] n aceite m; (petroleum) petróleo ∎ vt (machine) engrasar; **fried in ~** frito en aceite
oilcan ['ɔɪlkæn] n lata de aceite
oilfield ['ɔɪlfiːld] n campo petrolífero
oil filter n (Aut) filtro de aceite
oil-fired ['ɔɪlfaɪəd] adj de fuel-oil
oil gauge n indicador m del aceite
oil industry n industria petrolífera
oil level n nivel m del aceite
oil painting n pintura al óleo
oil refinery n refinería de petróleo
oil rig n torre f de perforación
oilskins ['ɔɪlskɪnz] npl impermeable msg, chubasquero sg
oil tanker n petrolero
oil well n pozo (de petróleo)
oily ['ɔɪlɪ] adj aceitoso; (food) grasiento
ointment ['ɔɪntmənt] n ungüento
OK abbr (US) = **Oklahoma**
O.K., okay ['əuˈkeɪ] excl O.K., ¡está bien!, ¡vale! ∎ adj bien ∎ n: **to give sth one's O.K.** dar el visto bueno a or aprobar algo ∎ vt dar el visto bueno a; **it's O.K. with** or **by me** estoy de acuerdo, me parece bien; **are you O.K. for money?** ¿andas or vas bien de dinero?

O

Okla. *abbr* (*US*) = **Oklahoma**

old [əʊld] *adj* viejo; (*former*) antiguo; **how ~ are you?** ¿cuántos años tienes?, ¿qué edad tienes?; **he's 10 years ~** tiene 10 años; **older brother** hermano mayor; **any ~ thing will do** sirve cualquier cosa

old age *n* vejez *f*

old-age pension ['əʊldeɪdʒ-] *n* (*Brit*) jubilación *f*, pensión *f*

old-age pensioner ['əʊldeɪdʒ-] *n* (*Brit*) jubilado(-a)

olden ['əʊldən] *adj* antiguo

old-fashioned ['əʊld'fæʃənd] *adj* anticuado, pasado de moda

old maid *n* solterona

old-style ['əʊldstaɪl] *adj* tradicional, chapado a la antigua

old-time ['əʊld'taɪm] *adj* antiguo, de antaño

old-timer [əʊld'taɪməʳ] *n* veterano(-a); (*old person*) anciano(-a)

old wives' tale *n* cuento de viejas, patraña

olive ['ɔlɪv] *n* (*fruit*) aceituna; (*tree*) olivo ■ *adj* (*also*: **olive-green**) verde oliva *inv*

olive branch *n* (*fig*): **to offer an ~ to sb** ofrecer hacer las paces con algn

olive oil *n* aceite *m* de oliva

Olympic [əʊ'lɪmpɪk] *adj* olímpico; **the ~ Games**, **the Olympics** *npl* las Olimpíadas

OM *n abbr* (*Brit*: = *Order of Merit*) título ceremonial

Oman [əʊ'mɑːn] *n* Omán *m*

OMB *n abbr* (*US*: = *Office of Management and Budget*) servicio que asesora al presidente en materia presupuestaria

omelette, omelet ['ɔmlɪt] *n* tortilla, tortilla de huevo (*LAm*)

omen ['əʊmən] *n* presagio

ominous ['ɔmɪnəs] *adj* de mal agüero, amenazador(a)

omission [əʊ'mɪʃən] *n* omisión *f*; (*error*) descuido

omit [əʊ'mɪt] *vt* omitir; (*by mistake*) olvidar, descuidar; **to ~ to do sth** olvidarse *or* dejar de hacer algo

omnivorous [ɔm'nɪvərəs] *adj* omnívoro

ON *abbr* (*Canada*) = **Ontario**

 KEYWORD

on [ɔn] *prep* **1** (*indicating position*) en; sobre; **on the wall** en la pared; **it's on the table** está sobre *or* en la mesa; **on the left** a la izquierda; **I haven't got any money on me** no llevo dinero encima

2 (*indicating means, method, condition etc*): **on foot** a pie; **on the train/plane** (*go*) en tren/avión; (*be*) en el tren/el avión; **on the radio/television** por *or* en la radio/televisión; **on the telephone** al teléfono; **to be on drugs** drogarse; (*Med*) estar a tratamiento; **to be on holiday/business** estar de vacaciones/en viaje de negocios; **we're on irregular verbs** estamos con los verbos irregulares

3 (*referring to time*): **on Friday** el viernes; **on Fridays** los viernes; **on June 20th** el 20 de junio; **a week on Friday** del viernes en una semana; **on arrival** al llegar; **on seeing this** al ver esto

4 (*about, concerning*) sobre, acerca de; **a book on physics** un libro de *or* sobre física

5 (*at the expense of*): **this round's on me** esta ronda la pago yo, invito yo a esta ronda; (*earning*): **he's on sixteen thousand pounds a year** gana dieciséis mil libras al año

■ *adv* **1** (*referring to dress*): **to have one's coat on** tener *or* llevar el abrigo puesto; **she put her gloves on** se puso los guantes

2 (*referring to covering*): **"screw the lid on tightly"** "cerrar bien la tapa"

3 (*further, continuously*): **to walk/run** *etc* **on** seguir caminando/corriendo *etc*; **from that day on** desde aquel día; **it was well on in the evening** estaba ya entrada la tarde

4 (*in phrases*): **I'm on to sth** creo haber encontrado algo; **my father's always on at me to get a job** (*col*) mi padre siempre me está dando la lata para que me ponga a trabajar

■ *adj* **1** (*functioning, in operation: machine, radio, TV, light*) encendido(-a) (*SP*), prendido(-a) (*LAm*); (: *tap*) abierto(-a); (: *brakes*) echado(-a), puesto(-a); **is the meeting still on?** (*in progress*) ¿todavía continúa la reunión?; (*not cancelled*) ¿va a haber reunión al fin?; **there's a good film on at the cinema** ponen una buena película en el cine

2: **that's not on!** (*col: not possible*) ¡eso ni hablar!; (: *not acceptable*) ¡eso no se hace!

ONC *n abbr* (*Brit*: = *Ordinary National Certificate*) título escolar

once [wʌns] *adv* una vez; (*formerly*) antiguamente ■ *conj* una vez que; **~ he had left/it was done** una vez que se había marchado/se hizo; **at ~** en seguida, inmediatamente; (*simultaneously*) a la vez; **~ a week** una vez a la semana; **~ more** otra vez; **~ and for all** de una vez por todas; **~ upon a time** érase una vez; **I knew him ~** le conocía hace tiempo

oncoming ['ɔnkʌmɪŋ] *adj* (*traffic*) que viene de frente

OND *n abbr* (*Brit*: = *Ordinary National Diploma*) título escolar

● KEYWORD

one [wʌn] *num* un/una; **one hundred and fifty** ciento cincuenta; **one by one** uno a uno; **it's one (o'clock)** es la una
■ *adj* **1** (*sole*) único; **the one book which** el único libro que; **the one man who** el único que
2 (*same*) mismo(-a); **they came in the one car** vinieron en un solo coche
■ *pron* **1**: **this one** éste/ésta; **that one** ése/ésa; (*more remote*) aquél/aquélla; **I've already got (a red) one** ya tengo uno(-a) (rojo(-a)); **one by one** uno(-a) por uno(-a); **to be one up on sb** llevar ventaja a algn; **to be at one (with sb)** estar completamente de acuerdo (con algn)
2: **one another** (US) nos; (*you*) os (SP); (*you: polite: them*) se; **do you two ever see one another?** ¿os veis alguna vez? (SP), ¿se ven alguna vez?; **the two boys didn't dare look at one another** los dos chicos no se atrevieron a mirarse (el uno al otro); **they all kissed one another** se besaron unos a otros
3 (*impers*): **one never knows** nunca se sabe; **to cut one's finger** cortarse el dedo; **one needs to eat** hay que comer

one-armed bandit ['wʌnɑːmd-] *n* máquina tragaperras
one-day excursion ['wʌndeɪ-] *n* (US) billete *m* de ida y vuelta en un día
One-hundred share index ['wʌnhʌndrəd-] *n* índice *m* bursátil (*del Financial Times*)
one-man ['wʌnmæn] *adj* (*business*) individual
one-man band *n* hombre-orquesta *m*
one-off [wʌnˈɔf] *n* (*Brit col: object*) artículo único; (*: event*) caso especial
one-parent family ['wʌnpɛərənt-] *n* familia monoparental
one-piece ['wʌnpiːs] *adj* (*bathing suit*) de una pieza
onerous ['ɔnərəs] *adj* (*task, duty*) pesado; (*responsibility*) oneroso
oneself [wʌnˈsɛlf] *pron* uno mismo; (*after prep, also emphatic*) sí (mismo(-a)); **to do sth by ~** hacer algo solo *or* por sí solo
one-shot [wʌnˈʃɔt] *n* (US) = **one-off**
one-sided [wʌnˈsaɪdɪd] *adj* (*argument*) parcial; (*decision, view*) unilateral; (*game, contest*) desigual
one-time ['wʌntaɪm] *adj* antiguo, ex-
one-to-one ['wʌntəwʌn] *adj* (*relationship*) individualizado
one-upmanship [wʌnˈʌpmənʃɪp] *n*: **the art of ~** el arte de quedar siempre por encima

one-way ['wʌnweɪ] *adj* (*street, traffic*) de dirección única; (*ticket*) sencillo
ongoing ['ɔngəuɪŋ] *adj* continuo
onion ['ʌnjən] *n* cebolla
online *adj, adv* (*Comput*) en línea; (*switched on*) conectado
onlooker ['ɔnlukər] *n* espectador(a) *m(f)*
only ['əunlɪ] *adv* solamente, sólo, nomás (*LAm*) ■ *adj* único, solo ■ *conj* solamente que, pero; **an ~ child** un hijo único; **not ~ ... but also ...** no sólo ... sino también ...; **I'd be ~ too pleased to help** encantado de ayudarles; **I saw her ~ yesterday** le vi ayer mismo; **I would come, ~ I'm very busy** iría, sólo que estoy muy atareado
ono *abbr* (= *or nearest offer: in classified ads*) abierto ofertas
onset ['ɔnsɛt] *n* comienzo
onshore ['ɔnʃɔːr] *adj* (*wind*) que sopla del mar hacia la tierra
onslaught ['ɔnslɔːt] *n* ataque *m*, embestida
Ont. *abbr* (*Canada*) = **Ontario**
on-the-job ['ɔnðəˈdʒɔb] *adj*: **~ training** formación *f* en el trabajo *or* sobre la práctica
onto ['ɔntu] *prep* = **on to**
onus ['əunəs] *n* responsabilidad *f*; **the ~ is upon him to prove it** le incumbe a él demostrarlo
onward ['ɔnwəd], **onwards** ['ɔnwədz] *adv* (*move*) (hacia) adelante
onyx ['ɔnɪks] *n* ónice *m*, onyx *m*
oops [ups] *excl* (*also*: **oops-a-daisy!**) ¡huy!
ooze [uːz] *vi* rezumar
opal ['əupl] *n* ópalo
opaque [əuˈpeɪk] *adj* opaco
OPEC ['əupɛk] *n abbr* (= *Organization of Petroleum-Exporting Countries*) OPEP *f*
open ['əupn] *adj* abierto; (*car*) descubierto; (*road, view*) despejado; (*meeting*) público; (*admiration*) manifiesto ■ *vt* abrir ■ *vi* (*flower, eyes, door, debate*) abrirse; (*book etc: commence*) comenzar; **in the ~ (air)** al aire libre; **~ verdict** veredicto inconcluso; **~ ticket** billete *m* sin fecha; **~ ground** (*among trees*) claro; (*waste ground*) solar *m*; **to have an ~ mind (on sth)** estar sin decidirse aún (sobre algo); **to ~ a bank account** abrir una cuenta en el banco
▶ **open on to** *vt fus* (*room, door*) dar a
▶ **open out** *vt* abrir ■ *vi* (*person*) abrirse
▶ **open up** *vt* abrir; (*blocked road*) despejar ■ *vi* abrirse
open-and-shut ['əupənənˈʃʌt] *adj*: **~ case** caso claro *or* evidente
open day *n* (*Brit*) jornada de puertas abiertas *or* acceso público

o

open-ended [əupn'ɛndɪd] adj (fig) indefinido, sin definir

opener ['əupnər] n (also: **can opener, tin opener**) abrelatas m inv

open-heart surgery [əupn'hɑːt-] n cirugía a corazón abierto

opening ['əupnɪŋ] n abertura; (beginning) comienzo; (opportunity) oportunidad f; (job) puesto vacante, vacante f

opening night n estreno

open learning n enseñanza flexible a tiempo parcial

openly ['əupnlɪ] adv abiertamente

open-minded [əupn'maɪndɪd] adj de amplias miras, sin prejuicios

open-necked ['əupnnɛkt] adj sin corbata

openness ['əupnnɪs] n (frankness) franqueza

open-plan ['əupn'plæn] adj sin tabiques, de plan abierto

open prison n centro penitenciario de régimen abierto

open return n vuelta con fecha abierta

open shop n empresa que contrata a mano de obra no afiliada a ningún sindicato

Open University n (Brit) ≈ Universidad f Nacional de Enseñanza a Distancia, UNED f; ver nota

OPEN UNIVERSITY

La Open University, fundada en 1969, está especializada en impartir cursos a distancia y a tiempo parcial con sus propios materiales de apoyo diseñados para tal fin, entre ellos programas de radio y televisión emitidos por la "BBC". Los trabajos se envían por correo y se complementan con la asistencia obligatoria a cursos de verano. Para obtener la licenciatura es necesario estudiar un mínimo de módulos y alcanzar un determinado número de créditos.

opera ['ɔpərə] n ópera

opera glasses npl gemelos mpl

opera house n teatro de la ópera

opera singer n cantante m/f de ópera

operate ['ɔpəreɪt] vt (machine) hacer funcionar; (company) dirigir ▪ vi funcionar; (drug) hacer efecto; **to ~ on sb** (Med) operar a algn

operatic [ɔpə'rætɪk] adj de ópera

operating costs ['ɔpəreɪtɪŋ-] npl gastos mpl operacionales

operating profit n beneficio de explotación

operating room n (US) quirófano, sala de operaciones

operating table n mesa de operaciones

operating theatre n quirófano, sala de operaciones

operation [ɔpə'reɪʃən] n (gen) operación f; (of machine) funcionamiento; **to be in ~** estar funcionando or en funcionamiento; **to have an ~** (Med) ser operado; **to have an ~ for** operarse de; **the company's operations during the year** las actividades de la compañía durante el año

operational [ɔpə'reɪʃənl] adj operacional, en buen estado; (Comm) en condiciones de servicio; (ready for use or action) en condiciones de funcionar; **when the service is fully ~** cuando el servicio esté en pleno funcionamiento

operative ['ɔpərətɪv] adj (measure) en vigor; **the ~ word** la palabra clave

operator ['ɔpəreɪtər] n (of machine) operario(-a); (Tel) operador(a) m(f), telefonista m/f

operetta [ɔpə'rɛtə] n opereta

ophthalmic [ɔf'θælmɪk] adj oftálmico

ophthalmologist [ɔfθæl'mɔlədʒɪst] n oftalmólogo(-a)

opinion [ə'pɪnjən] n (gen) opinión f; **in my ~** en mi opinión, a mi juicio; **to seek a second ~** pedir una segunda opinión

opinionated [ə'pɪnjəneɪtɪd] adj testarudo

opinion poll n encuesta, sondeo

opium ['əupɪəm] n opio

opponent [ə'pəunənt] n adversario(-a), contrincante m/f

opportune ['ɔpətjuːn] adj oportuno

opportunism [ɔpə'tjuːnɪzm] n oportunismo

opportunist [ɔpə'tjuːnɪst] n oportunista m/f

opportunity [ɔpə'tjuːnɪtɪ] n oportunidad f, chance m or f (LAm); **to take the ~ to do** or **of doing** aprovechar la ocasión para hacer

oppose [ə'pəuz] vt oponerse a; **to be opposed to sth** oponerse a algo; **as opposed to** en vez de; (unlike) a diferencia de

opposing [ə'pəuzɪŋ] adj (side) opuesto, contrario

opposite ['ɔpəzɪt] adj opuesto, contrario; (house etc) de enfrente ▪ adv en frente ▪ prep en frente de, frente a ▪ n lo contrario; **the ~ sex** el otro sexo, el sexo opuesto

opposite number n (Brit) homólogo(-a)

opposition [ɔpə'zɪʃən] n oposición f

oppress [ə'prɛs] vt oprimir

oppression [ə'prɛʃən] n opresión f

oppressive [ə'prɛsɪv] adj opresivo

opprobrium [ə'prəubrɪəm] n (formal) oprobio

opt [ɔpt] vi: **to ~ for** optar por; **to ~ to do** optar por hacer; **to ~ out** (of NHS etc) salirse

optical ['ɔptɪkl] *adj* óptico
optical character reader *n* lector *m* óptico de caracteres
optical character recognition *n* reconocimiento *m* óptico de caracteres
optical fibre *n* fibra óptica
optician [ɔp'tɪʃən] *n* óptico *m/f*
optics ['ɔptɪks] *n* óptica
optimism ['ɔptɪmɪzəm] *n* optimismo
optimist ['ɔptɪmɪst] *n* optimista *m/f*
optimistic [ɔptɪ'mɪstɪk] *adj* optimista
optimum ['ɔptɪməm] *adj* óptimo
option ['ɔpʃən] *n* opción *f*; **to keep one's options open** (*fig*) mantener las opciones abiertas; **I have no ~** no tengo más *or* otro remedio
optional ['ɔpʃənl] *adj* opcional; (*course*) optativo; **~ extras** opciones *fpl* extras
opulence ['ɔpjuləns] *n* opulencia
opulent ['ɔpjulənt] *adj* opulento
OR *abbr* (*US*) = **Oregon**
or [ɔːʳ] *conj* o; (*before o, ho*) u; (*with negative*): **he hasn't seen or heard anything** no ha visto ni oído nada; **or else** si no; **let me go or I'll scream!** ¡suélteme, o me pongo a gritar!
oracle ['ɔrəkl] *n* oráculo
oral ['ɔːrəl] *adj* oral ■ *n* examen *m* oral
orange ['ɔrɪndʒ] *n* (*fruit*) naranja ■ *adj* (de color) naranja
orangeade [ɔrɪndʒ'eɪd] *n* naranjada, refresco de naranja
orange squash *n* zumo (*SP*) *or* jugo de naranja
orang-outang, orang-utan [ɔ'ræŋuː'tæn] *n* orangután *m*
oration [ɔː'reɪʃən] *n* discurso solemne; **funeral ~** oración *f* fúnebre
orator ['ɔrətəʳ] *n* orador(a) *m(f)*
oratorio [ɔrə'tɔːrɪəu] *n* oratorio
orbit ['ɔːbɪt] *n* órbita ■ *vt, vi* orbitar; **to be in/go into ~ (round)** estar en/entrar en órbita (alrededor de)
orbital ['ɔːbɪtl] *n* (*also*: **orbital motorway**) autopista de circunvalación
orchard ['ɔːtʃəd] *n* huerto; **apple ~** manzanar *m*, manzanal *m*
orchestra ['ɔːkɪstrə] *n* orquesta; (*US: seating*) platea
orchestral [ɔː'kɛstrəl] *adj* de orquesta
orchestrate ['ɔːkɪstreɪt] *vt* orquestar
orchid ['ɔːkɪd] *n* orquídea
ordain [ɔː'deɪn] *vt* (*Rel*) ordenar
ordeal [ɔː'diːl] *n* experiencia terrible
order ['ɔːdəʳ] *n* orden *m*; (*command*) orden *f*; (*type, kind*) clase *f*; (*state*) estado; (*Comm*) pedido, encargo ■ *vt* (*also*: **put in order**) ordenar, poner en orden; (*Comm*) encargar,

pedir; (*command*) mandar, ordenar; **in ~** (*gen*) en orden; (*of document*) en regla; **in (working) ~** en funcionamiento; **a machine in working ~** una máquina en funcionamiento; **to be out of ~** (*machine, toilets*) estar estropeado *or* (*LAm*) descompuesto; **in ~ to do** para hacer; **in ~ that** para que + *subjun*; **on ~** (*Comm*) pedido; **to be on ~** estar pedido; **we are under orders to do it** tenemos orden de hacerlo; **a point of ~** una cuestión de procedimiento; **to place an ~ for sth with sb** hacer un pedido de algo a algn; **made to ~** hecho a la medida; **his income is of the ~ of £24,000 per year** sus ingresos son del orden de 24 mil libras al año; **to the ~ of** (*Banking*) a la orden de; **to ~ sb to do sth** mandar a algn hacer algo
order book *n* cartera de pedidos
order form *n* hoja de pedido
orderly ['ɔːdəlɪ] *n* (*Mil*) ordenanza *m*; (*Med*) auxiliar *m/f* (de hospital) ■ *adj* ordenado
orderly officer *n* (*Mil*) oficial *m* del día
order number *n* número de pedido
ordinal ['ɔːdɪnl] *adj* ordinal
ordinarily ['ɔːdnrɪlɪ] *adv* por lo común
ordinary ['ɔːdnrɪ] *adj* corriente, normal; (*pej*) común y corriente; **out of the ~** fuera de lo común, extraordinario
ordinary degree *n* (*Brit*) diploma *m*; *ver nota*

O

🔵 **ORDINARY DEGREE**
⚪
🔵 Después de tres años de estudios, algunos
🔵 universitarios obtienen la titulación
🔵 de *ordinary degree*. Esto ocurre en el caso
🔵 poco frecuente de que no aprueben los
🔵 exámenes que conducen al título de
🔵 "honours degree" pero sus examinadores
🔵 consideren que a lo largo de la carrera
🔵 han logrado unos resultados mínimos
🔵 satisfactorios. También es una opción
🔵 que tienen los estudiantes de las
🔵 universidades escocesas no interesados
🔵 en estudiar en la universidad más de tres
🔵 años.

ordinary seaman *n* (*Brit*) marinero
ordinary shares *npl* acciones *fpl* ordinarias
ordination [ɔːdɪ'neɪʃən] *n* ordenación *f*
ordnance ['ɔːdnəns] *n* (*Mil: unit*) artillería
ordnance factory *n* fábrica de artillería
Ordnance Survey *n* (*Brit*) *servicio oficial de topografía y cartografía*
ore [ɔːʳ] *n* mineral *m*
Ore., Oreg. *abbr* (*US*) = **Oregon**
organ ['ɔːgən] *n* órgano

organic | out

organic [ɔːˈɡænɪk] *adj* orgánico; *(vegetables, produce)* biológico
organism [ˈɔːɡənɪzəm] *n* organismo
organist [ˈɔːɡənɪst] *n* organista *m/f*
organization [ɔːɡənaɪˈzeɪʃən] *n* organización *f*
organization chart *n* organigrama *m*
organize [ˈɔːɡənaɪz] *vt* organizar; **to get organized** organizarse
organized crime *n* crimen organizado
organizer [ˈɔːɡənaɪzəʳ] *n* organizador(-a) *m(f)*
orgasm [ˈɔːɡæzəm] *n* orgasmo
orgy [ˈɔːdʒɪ] *n* orgía
Orient [ˈɔːrɪənt] *n* Oriente *m*
oriental [ɔːrɪˈɛntl] *adj* oriental
orientate [ˈɔːrɪənteɪt] *vt* orientar
origin [ˈɒrɪdʒɪn] *n* origen *m*; *(point of departure)* procedencia
original [əˈrɪdʒɪnl] *adj* original; *(first)* primero; *(earlier)* primitivo ▪ *n* original *m*
originality [ərɪdʒɪˈnælɪtɪ] *n* originalidad *f*
originally [əˈrɪdʒɪnəlɪ] *adv* *(at first)* al principio; *(with originality)* con originalidad
originate [əˈrɪdʒɪneɪt] *vi*: **to ~ from, to ~ in** surgir de, tener su origen en
originator [əˈrɪdʒɪneɪtəʳ] *n* inventor(a) *m(f)*, autor(a) *m(f)*
Orkneys [ˈɔːknɪz] *npl*: **the ~** *(also*: **the Orkney Islands)** las Orcadas
ornament [ˈɔːnəmənt] *n* adorno
ornamental [ɔːnəˈmɛntl] *adj* decorativo, de adorno
ornamentation [ɔːnəmɛnˈteɪʃən] *n* ornamentación *f*
ornate [ɔːˈneɪt] *adj* recargado
ornithologist [ɔːnɪˈθɒlədʒɪst] *n* ornitólogo(-a)
ornithology [ɔːnɪˈθɒlədʒɪ] *n* ornitología
orphan [ˈɔːfn] *n* huérfano(-a) ▪ *vt*: **to be orphaned** quedar huérfano(-a)
orphanage [ˈɔːfənɪdʒ] *n* orfanato
orthodox [ˈɔːθədɒks] *adj* ortodoxo
orthodoxy [ˈɔːθədɒksɪ] *n* ortodoxia
orthopaedic, orthopedic (US) [ɔːθəˈpiːdɪk] *adj* ortopédico
orthopaedics, orthopedics (US) [ɔːθəˈpiːdɪks] *n* ortopedia
OS *abbr* (Brit: = *Ordnance Survey)* servicio oficial de topografía y cartografía; (: *Dress)* = **outsize**
O.S. *abbr* = **out of stock**
Oscar [ˈɒskəʳ] *n* óscar *m*
oscillate [ˈɒsɪleɪt] *vi* oscilar; *(person)* vacilar
oscillation [ɒsɪˈleɪʃən] *n* oscilación *f*; *(of prices)* fluctuación *f*
OSHA *n abbr* (US: = *Occupational Safety and Health Administration)* oficina de la higiene y la seguridad en el trabajo
Oslo [ˈɒzləu] *n* Oslo

ostensible [ɒsˈtɛnsɪbl] *adj* aparente
ostensibly [ɒsˈtɛnsɪblɪ] *adv* aparentemente
ostentatious [ɒstɛnˈteɪʃəs] *adj* pretencioso, aparatoso; *(person)* ostentativo
osteopath [ˈɒstɪəpæθ] *n* osteópata *m/f*
ostracize [ˈɒstrəsaɪz] *vt* hacer el vacío a
ostrich [ˈɒstrɪtʃ] *n* avestruz *m*
OT *n abbr* (= *Old Testament)* A.T. *m*
OTB *n abbr* (US: = *off-track betting)* apuestas hechas fuera del hipódromo
OTE *abbr* (= *on-target earnings)* beneficios según objetivos
other [ˈʌðəʳ] *adj* otro ▪ *pron*: **the ~** *(one)* el/la otro(-a); **others** *(other people)* otros; **~ than** *(apart from)* aparte de; **the ~ day** el otro día; **some ~ people have still to arrive** quedan por llegar otros; **some actor or ~** un actor cualquiera; **somebody or ~** alguien, alguno; **it was no ~ than the bishop** no era otro que el obispo
otherwise [ˈʌðəwaɪz] *adv, conj* de otra manera; *(if not)* si no; **an ~ good piece of work** un trabajo que, quitando eso, es bueno
OTT *abbr* (col) = **over the top**; *see* **top**
otter [ˈɒtəʳ] *n* nutria
OU *n abbr* (Brit) = **Open University**
ouch [autʃ] *excl* ¡ay!
ought *(pt* **ought)** [ɔːt] *aux vb*: **I ~ to do it** debería hacerlo; **this ~ to have been corrected** esto debiera de haberse corregido; **he ~ to win** *(probability)* debiera ganar; **you ~ to go and see it** vale la pena ir a verlo
ounce [auns] *n* onza *(28.35g: 16 in a pound)*
our [ˈauəʳ] *adj* nuestro; *see also* **my**
ours [ˈauəz] *pron* (el) nuestro/(la) nuestra *etc*; *see also* **mine**
ourselves [auəˈsɛlvz] *pron pl (reflexive, after prep)* nosotros; *(emphatic)* nosotros mismos; **we did it (all) by ~** lo hicimos nosotros solos; *see also* **oneself**
oust [aust] *vt* desalojar
out [aut] *adv* fuera, afuera; *(not at home)* fuera (de casa); *(light, fire)* apagado; *(on strike)* en huelga ▪ *vt*: **to ~ sb** revelar públicamente la homosexualidad de algn; **~ there** allí (fuera); **he's ~** *(absent)* no está, ha salido; **to be ~ in one's calculations** equivocarse (en sus cálculos); **to run ~** salir corriendo; **~ loud** en alta voz; **~ of** *prep (outside)* fuera de; *(because of: anger etc)* por; **to look ~ of the window** mirar por la ventana; **to drink ~ of a cup** beber de una taza; **made ~ of wood** de madera; **~ of petrol** sin gasolina; **"~ of order"** "no funciona"; **it's ~ of stock** (Comm) está agotado; **to be ~ and about again** estar repuesto y levantado; **the journey ~** el viaje de ida; **the boat was 10**

688 · ENGLISH | SPANISH

out-and-out ['autəndaut] *adj* (*liar, thief etc*) redomado, empedernido

outback ['autbæk] *n* interior *m*

outbid [aut'bɪd] *vt* pujar más alto que, sobrepujar

outboard ['autbɔːd] *adj*: ~ **motor** (motor *m*) fuera borda *m*

outbound ['autbaund] *adj*: ~ **from/for** con salida de/hacia

outbreak ['autbreɪk] *n* (*of war*) comienzo; (*of disease*) epidemia; (*of violence etc*) ola

outbuilding ['autbɪldɪŋ] *n* dependencia; (*shed*) cobertizo

outburst ['autbəːst] *n* explosión *f*, arranque *m*

outcast ['autkɑːst] *n* paria *m/f*

outclass [aut'klɑːs] *vt* aventajar, superar

outcome ['autkʌm] *n* resultado

outcrop ['autkrɔp] *n* (*of rock*) afloramiento

outcry ['autkraɪ] *n* protestas *fpl*

outdated [aut'deɪtɪd] *adj* anticuado

outdistance [aut'dɪstəns] *vt* dejar atrás

outdo [aut'duː] *vt* (*irreg: like* **do**) superar

outdoor [aut'dɔːʳ] *adj* al aire libre

outdoors [aut'dɔːz] *adv* al aire libre

outer ['autəʳ] *adj* exterior, externo

outer space *n* espacio exterior

outfit ['autfɪt] *n* equipo; (*clothes*) traje *m*; (*col: organization*) grupo, organización *f*

outfitter's ['autfɪtəz] *n* (*Brit*) sastrería

outgoing ['autgəuɪŋ] *adj* (*president, tenant*) saliente; (*means of transport*) que sale; (*character*) extrovertido

outgoings ['autgəuɪŋz] *npl* (*Brit*) gastos *mpl*

outgrow [aut'grəu] *vt* (*irreg: like* **grow**) **he has outgrown his clothes** su ropa le queda pequeña ya

outhouse ['authaus] *n* dependencia

outing ['autɪŋ] *n* excursión *f*, paseo

outlandish [aut'lændɪʃ] *adj* estrafalario

outlast [aut'lɑːst] *vt* durar más tiempo que, sobrevivir a

outlaw ['autlɔː] *n* proscrito(-a) ■ *vt* (*person*) declarar fuera de la ley; (*practice*) declarar ilegal

outlay ['autleɪ] *n* inversión *f*

outlet ['autlɛt] *n* salida; (*of pipe*) desagüe *m*; (*US Elec*) toma de corriente; (*for emotion*) desahogo; (*also*: **retail outlet**) punto de venta

outline ['autlaɪn] *n* (*shape*) contorno, perfil *m*; **in ~** (*fig*) a grandes rasgos

outlive [aut'lɪv] *vt* sobrevivir a

outlook ['autluk] *n* perspectiva; (*opinion*) punto de vista

outlying ['autlaɪɪŋ] *adj* remoto, aislado

outmanoeuvre, (*US*) **outmaneuver** [autmə'nuːvəʳ] *vt* (*Mil: fig*) superar en la estrategia

outmoded [aut'məudɪd] *adj* anticuado, pasado de moda

outnumber [aut'nʌmbəʳ] *vt* exceder *or* superar en número

out of bounds [autəv'baundz] *adj*: **it's** ~ está prohibido el paso

out-of-court [autəv'kɔːt] *adj, adv* sin ir a juicio

out-of-date [autəv'deɪt] *adj* (*passport*) caducado, vencido; (*theory, idea*) anticuado; (*clothes, customs*) pasado de moda

out-of-doors [autəv'dɔːz] *adv* al aire libre

out-of-the-way [autəvðə'weɪ] *adj* (*remote*) apartado; (*unusual*) poco común *or* corriente

out-of-touch [autəv'tʌtʃ] *adj*: **to be** ~ estar desconectado

outpatient ['autpeɪʃənt] *n* paciente *m/f* externo(-a)

outpost ['autpəust] *n* puesto avanzado

outpouring ['autpɔːrɪŋ] *n* (*fig*) efusión *f*

output ['autput] *n* (volumen *m* de) producción *f*, rendimiento; (*Comput*) salida ■ *vt* (*Comput: to power*) imprimir

outrage ['autreɪdʒ] *n* (*scandal*) escándalo; (*atrocity*) atrocidad *f* ■ *vt* ultrajar

outrageous [aut'reɪdʒəs] *adj* (*clothes*) extravagante; (*behaviour*) escandaloso

outright [aut'raɪt] *adv* (*win*) de manera absoluta; (*be killed*) en el acto; (*ask*) abiertamente; (*completely*) completamente ■ *adj* ['autraɪt] completo; (*winner*) absoluto; (*refusal*) rotundo

outrun [aut'rʌn] *vt* (*irreg: like* **run**) correr más que, dejar atrás

outset ['autsɛt] *n* principio

outshine [aut'ʃaɪn] *vt* (*irreg: like* **shine**) (*fig*) eclipsar, brillar más que

outside [aut'saɪd] *n* exterior *m* ■ *adj* exterior, externo ■ *adv* fuera, afuera (*LAm*) ■ *prep* fuera de; (*beyond*) más allá de; **at the** ~ (*fig*) a lo sumo; **an** ~ **chance** una posibilidad remota; ~ **left/right** (*esp Football*) extremo izquierdo/derecho

outside broadcast *n* (*Radio, TV*) emisión *f* exterior

outside contractor *n* contratista *m/f* independiente

outside lane *n* (*Aut*) carril *m* de adelantamiento

outside line *n* (*Tel*) línea (exterior)

outsider [aut'saɪdəʳ] *n* (*stranger*) forastero(-a)

outsize ['autsaɪz] *adj* (*clothes*) de talla grande

outskirts ['autskəːts] *npl* alrededores *mpl*, afueras *fpl*

outsmart [aut'smɑːt] vt ser más listo que

outspoken [aut'spəukən] adj muy franco

outspread [aut'sprɛd] adj extendido; (wings) desplegado

outstanding [aut'stændɪŋ] adj excepcional, destacado; (unfinished) pendiente

outstay [aut'steɪ] vt: **to ~ one's welcome** quedarse más de la cuenta

outstretched [aut'strɛtʃt] adj (arm) extendido

outstrip [aut'strɪp] vt (competitors, demand: also fig) dejar atrás, aventajar

out-tray ['auttreɪ] n bandeja de salida

outvote [aut'vəut] vt: **it was outvoted (by ...)** fue rechazado en el voto (por ...)

outward ['autwəd] adj (sign, appearances) externo; (journey) de ida

outwardly ['autwədlɪ] adv por fuera

outweigh [aut'weɪ] vt pesar más que

outwit [aut'wɪt] vt ser más listo que

outworn [aut'wɔːn] adj (expression) cansado

oval ['əuvl] adj ovalado ■ n óvalo

ovarian [əu'vɛərɪən] adj ovárico; (cancer) de ovario

ovary ['əuvərɪ] n ovario

ovation [əu'veɪʃən] n ovación f

oven ['ʌvn] n horno

ovenproof ['ʌvnpruːf] adj refractario, resistente al horno

oven-ready ['ʌvnrɛdɪ] adj listo para el horno

ovenware ['ʌvnwɛəʳ] n artículos mpl para el horno

over ['əuvəʳ] adv encima, por encima ■ adj (finished) terminado; (surplus) de sobra; (excessively) demasiado ■ prep (por) encima de; (above) sobre; (on the other side of) al otro lado de; (more than) más de; (during) durante; (about, concerning): **they fell out ~ money** riñeron por una cuestión de dinero; **~ here** (por) aquí; **~ there** (por) allí or allá; **all ~** (everywhere) por todas partes; **~ and ~ (again)** una y otra vez; **~ and above** además de; **to ask sb ~** invitar a algn a casa; **to bend ~** inclinarse; **now ~ to our Paris correspondent** damos la palabra a nuestro corresponsal de París; **the world ~** en todo el mundo, en el mundo entero; **she's not ~ intelligent** no es muy lista que digamos

over... [əuvəʳ] pref sobre..., super...

overact [əuvər'ækt] vi (Theat) exagerar el papel

overall ['əuvərɔːl] adj (length) total; (study) de conjunto ■ adv [əuvər'ɔːl] en conjunto ■ n (Brit) guardapolvo; **overalls** npl mono sg, overol msg (LAm)

overall majority n mayoría absoluta

overanxious [əuvər'æŋkʃəs] adj demasiado preocupado or ansioso

overawe [əuvər'ɔː] vt intimidar

overbalance [əuvə'bæləns] vi perder el equilibrio

overbearing [əuvə'bɛərɪŋ] adj autoritario, imperioso

overboard ['əuvəbɔːd] adv (Naut) por la borda; **to go ~ for sth** (fig) enloquecer por algo

overbook [əuvə'buk] vt sobrereservar, reservar con exceso

overcapitalize [əuvə'kæpɪtəlaɪz] vi sobrecapitalizar

overcast ['əuvəkɑːst] adj encapotado

overcharge [əuvə'tʃɑːdʒ] vt: **to ~ sb** cobrar un precio excesivo a algn

overcoat ['əuvəkəut] n abrigo

overcome [əuvə'kʌm] vt (irreg: like **come**) (gen) vencer; (difficulty) superar; **she was quite ~ by the occasion** la ocasión le conmovió mucho

overconfident [əuvə'kɔnfɪdənt] adj demasiado confiado

overcrowded [əuvə'kraudɪd] adj atestado de gente; (city, country) superpoblado

overcrowding [əuvə'kraudɪŋ] n (in town, country) superpoblación f; (in bus etc) hacinamiento, apiñamiento

overdo [əuvə'duː] vt (irreg: like **do**) exagerar; (overcook) cocer demasiado; **to ~ it, ~ things** (work too hard) trabajar demasiado

overdose ['əuvədəus] n sobredosis f inv

overdraft ['əuvədrɑːft] n saldo deudor

overdrawn [əuvə'drɔːn] adj (account) en descubierto

overdrive ['əuvədraɪv] n (Aut) sobremarcha, superdirecta

overdue [əuvə'djuː] adj retrasado; (recognition) tardío; (bill) vencido y no pagado; **that change was long ~** ese cambio tenía que haberse hecho hace tiempo

overemphasis [əuvər'ɛmfəsɪs] n: **to put an ~ on** poner énfasis excesivo en

overenthusiastic ['əuvərənθuːzɪ'æstɪk] adj demasiado entusiasta

overestimate [əuvər'ɛstɪmeɪt] vt sobreestimar

overexcited [əuvərɪk'saɪtɪd] adj sobreexcitado

overexertion [əuvərɪg'zəːʃən] n agotamiento, fatiga

overexpose [əuvərɪk'spəuz] vt (Phot) sobreexponer

overflow [əuvə'fləu] vi desbordarse ■ n ['əuvəfləu] (excess) exceso; (of river) desbordamiento; (also: **overflow pipe**) (cañería de) desagüe m

overfly [əuvə'flaɪ] vt (irreg: like **fly**) sobrevolar

overgenerous [əuvəˈdʒɛnərəs] *adj*
demasiado generoso

overgrown [əuvəˈgrəun] *adj* (*garden*) cubierto
de hierba; **he's just an ~ schoolboy** es un
niño en grande

overhang [əuvəˈhæŋ] *vt* (*irreg: like* **hang**)
sobresalir por encima de ■ *vi* sobresalir

overhaul *vt* [əuvəˈhɔ:l] revisar, repasar ■ *n*
[ˈəuvəhɔ:l] revisión *f*

overhead *adv* [əuvəˈhɛd] por arriba *or*
encima ■ *adj* [ˈəuvəhɛd] (*cable*) aéreo;
(*railway*) elevado, aéreo ■ *n* [ˈəuvəhɛd] (*US*)
= **overheads**

overheads [ˈəuvəhɛdz] *npl* (*Brit*) gastos *mpl*
generales

overhear [əuvəˈhɪəʳ] *vt* (*irreg: like* **hear**) oír por
casualidad

overheat [əuvəˈhi:t] *vi* (*engine*) recalentarse

overjoyed [əuvəˈdʒɔɪd] *adj* encantado, lleno
de alegría

overkill [ˈəuvəkɪl] *n* (*Mil*) capacidad *f* excesiva
de destrucción; (*fig*) exceso

overland [ˈəuvəlænd] *adj, adv* por tierra

overlap *vi* [əuvəˈlæp] superponerse ■ *n*
[ˈəuvəlæp] superposición *f*

overleaf [əuvəˈli:f] *adv* al dorso

overload [əuvəˈləud] *vt* sobrecargar

overlook [əuvəˈluk] *vt* (*have view of*) dar a,
tener vistas a; (*miss*) pasar por alto; (*forgive*)
hacer la vista gorda a

overlord [ˈəuvəlɔ:d] *n* señor *m*

overmanning [əuvəˈmænɪŋ] *n* exceso de
mano de obra; (*in organization*) exceso de
personal

overnight [əuvəˈnaɪt] *adv* durante la noche;
(*fig*) de la noche a la mañana ■ *adj* de noche;
to stay ~ pasar la noche

overnight bag *n* fin *m* de semana, neceser
m de viaje

overnight stay *n* estancia de una noche

overpass [ˈəuvəpɑ:s] *n* (*US*) paso elevado *or* a
desnivel

overpay [əuvəˈpeɪ] *vt*: **to ~ sb by £50** pagar
50 libras de más a algn

overplay [əuvəˈpleɪ] *vt* exagerar; **to ~ one's
hand** desmedirse

overpower [əuvəˈpauəʳ] *vt* dominar; (*fig*)
embargar

overpowering [əuvəˈpauərɪŋ] *adj* (*heat*)
agobiante; (*smell*) penetrante

overproduction [əuvəprəˈdʌkʃən] *n*
superproducción *f*

overrate [əuvəˈreɪt] *vt* sobrevalorar

overreach [əuvəˈri:tʃ] *vt*: **to ~ o.s.** ir
demasiado lejos, pasarse

override [əuvəˈraɪd] *vt* (*irreg: like* **ride**) (*order,
objection*) no hacer caso de

overriding [əuvəˈraɪdɪŋ] *adj* predominante

overrule [əuvəˈru:l] *vt* (*decision*) anular;
(*claim*) denegar

overrun [əuvəˈrʌn] *vt* (*irreg: like* **run**) (*Mil:
country*) invadir; (*time limit*) rebasar, exceder
■ *vi* rebasar el límite previsto; **the town is
~ with tourists** el pueblo está inundado de
turistas

overseas [əuvəˈsi:z] *adv* en ultramar; (*abroad*)
en el extranjero ■ *adj* (*trade*) exterior; (*visitor*)
extranjero

oversee [əuvəˈsi:] *vt* supervisar

overseer [ˈəuvəsɪəʳ] *n* (*in factory*) supervisor(a)
m(f); (*foreman*) capataz *m*

overshadow [əuvəˈʃædəu] *vt* (*fig*) eclipsar

overshoot [əuvəˈʃu:t] *vt* (*irreg: like* **shoot**)
excederse

oversight [ˈəuvəsaɪt] *n* descuido; **due to an ~**
a causa de un descuido *or* una equivocación

oversimplify [əuvəˈsɪmplɪfaɪ] *vt* simplificar
demasiado

oversleep [əuvəˈsli:p] *vi* (*irreg: like* **sleep**)
dormir más de la cuenta, no despertarse a
tiempo

overspend [əuvəˈspɛnd] *vi* gastar más de la
cuenta; **we have overspent by five dollars**
hemos excedido el presupuesto en cinco
dólares

overspill [ˈəuvəspɪl] *n* exceso de población

overstaffed [əuvəˈstɑ:ft] *adj*: **to be ~** tener
exceso de plantilla

overstate [əuvəˈsteɪt] *vt* exagerar

overstatement [ˈəuvəsteɪtmənt] *n*
exageración *f*

overstay [əuvəˈsteɪ] *vt*: **to ~ one's time** *or*
welcome quedarse más de lo conveniente

overstep [əuvəˈstɛp] *vt*: **to ~ the mark** *or* **the
limits** pasarse de la raya

overstock [əuvəˈstɔk] *vt* abarrotar

overstretched [əuvəˈstrɛtʃt] *adj* utilizado por
encima de su capacidad

overstrike *n* [ˈəuvəstraɪk] (*on printer*)
superposición *f* ■ *vt* (*irreg: like* **strike**)
[əuvəˈstraɪk] superponer

oversubscribed [əuvəsəbˈskraɪbd] *adj*
suscrito en exceso

overt [əuˈvə:t] *adj* abierto

overtake [əuvəˈteɪk] *vt* (*irreg: like* **take**)
sobrepasar; (*Brit Aut*) adelantar

overtax [əuvəˈtæks] *vt* (*Econ*) exigir
contribuciones *fpl* excesivas *or* impuestos
mpl excesivos a; (*fig: strength*) poner a prueba;
(*patience*) agotar, abusar de; **to ~ o.s.** fatigarse
demasiado

overthrow [əuvəˈθrəu] *vt* (*irreg: like* **throw**)
(*government*) derrocar

overtime [ˈəuvətaɪm] *n* horas *fpl*

extraordinarias; **to do** or **work** ~ hacer or trabajar horas extraordinarias or extras

overtime ban n prohibición f de (hacer) horas extraordinarias

overtone ['əuvətəun] n (fig) tono

overture ['əuvətʃuəʳ] n (Mus) obertura; (fig) propuesta

overturn [əuvə'tə:n] vt, vi volcar

overview ['əuvəvju:] n visión f de conjunto

overweight [əuvə'weɪt] adj demasiado gordo or pesado

overwhelm [əuvə'wɛlm] vt aplastar

overwhelming [əuvə'wɛlmɪŋ] adj (victory, defeat) arrollador(a); (desire) irresistible; **one's ~ impression is of heat** lo que más impresiona es el calor

overwhelmingly [əuvə'wɛlmɪŋlɪ] adv abrumadoramente

overwork [əuvə'wə:k] n trabajo excesivo ▪ vt hacer trabajar demasiado ▪ vi trabajar demasiado

overwrite [əuvə'raɪt] vt (irreg: like **write**) (Comput) sobreescribir

overwrought [əuvə'rɔ:t] adj sobreexcitado

ovulation [ɔvju'leɪʃən] n ovulación f

owe [əu] vt deber; **to ~ sb sth, ~ sth to sb** deber algo a algn

owing to ['əuɪŋtu:] prep debido a, por causa de

owl [aul] n (also: **long-eared owl**) búho; (also: **barn owl**) lechuza

own [əun] vt tener, poseer ▪ vi: **to ~ to sth/ to having done sth** confesar or reconocer algo/haber hecho algo ▪ adj propio; **a room of my ~** mi propia habitación; **to get one's ~ back** tomarse la revancha; **on one's ~** solo, a solas; **can I have it for my (very) ~?** ¿puedo quedarme con él?; **to come into one's ~** llegar a realizarse
  ▸ **own up** vi confesar

own brand n (Comm) marca propia

owner ['əunəʳ] n dueño(-a)

owner-occupier ['əunər'ɔkjupaɪəʳ] n ocupante propietario(-a) m(f)

ownership ['əunəʃɪp] n posesión f; **it's under new ~** está bajo nueva dirección

own goal n (Sport) autogol m; **to score an ~** marcar un gol en propia puerta, marcar un autogol

ox (pl **oxen**) [ɔks, 'ɔksn] n buey m

Oxbridge ['ɔksbrɪdʒ] n universidades de Oxford y Cambridge; ver nota

● **OXBRIDGE**

El término Oxbridge es una fusión de Ox(ford) y (Cam)bridge, las dos universidades británicas más antiguas y con mayor prestigio académico y social. Muchos miembros destacados de la clase dirigente del país son antiguos alumnos de una de las dos. El mismo término suele aplicarse a todo lo que ambas representan en cuestión de prestigio y privilegios sociales.

Oxfam ['ɔksfæm] n abbr (Brit: = Oxford Committee for Famine Relief) OXFAM

oxide ['ɔksaɪd] n óxido

Oxon. ['ɔksn] abbr (Brit) = **Oxoniensis; of Oxford**

oxtail ['ɔksteɪl] n: ~ **soup** sopa de rabo de buey

oxyacetylene ['ɔksɪə'sɛtɪli:n] adj oxiacetilénico; ~ **burner**, ~ **torch** soplete m oxiacetilénico

oxygen ['ɔksɪdʒən] n oxígeno

oxygen mask n máscara de oxígeno

oxygen tent n tienda de oxígeno

oyster ['ɔɪstəʳ] n ostra

oz. abbr = **ounce; ounces**

ozone ['əuzəun] n ozono

ozone layer n capa de ozono

Pp

P, p [pi:] *n* (*letter*) P, p *f*; **P for Peter** P de París

P *abbr* = **president; prince**

p *abbr* (= *page*) pág.; (*Brit*) = **penny; pence**

PA *n abbr see* **personal assistant; public address system** ■ *abbr* (*US*) = **Pennsylvania**

pa [pɑ:] *n* (*col*) papá *m*

p.a. *abbr* = **per annum**

PAC *n abbr* (*US*) = **political action committee**

pace [peɪs] *n* paso; (*rhythm*) ritmo ■ *vi*: **to ~ up and down** pasearse de un lado a otro; **to keep ~ with** llevar el mismo paso que; (*events*) mantenerse a la altura de *or* al corriente de; **to set the ~** (*running*) marcar el paso; (*fig*) marcar la pauta; **to put sb through his paces** (*fig*) poner a algn a prueba

pacemaker ['peɪsmeɪkə'] *n* (*Med*) marcapasos *m inv*

pacific [pə'sɪfɪk] *adj* pacífico ■ *n*: **the P~ (Ocean)** el (Océano) Pacífico

pacification [pæsɪfɪ'keɪʃən] *n* pacificación *f*

pacifier ['pæsɪfaɪə'] *n* (*US: dummy*) chupete *m*

pacifism ['pæsɪfɪzəm] *n* pacifismo

pacifist ['pæsɪfɪst] *n* pacifista *m/f*

pacify ['pæsɪfaɪ] *vt* (*soothe*) apaciguar; (*country*) pacificar

pack [pæk] *n* (*packet*) paquete *m*; (*Comm*) embalaje *m*; (*of hounds*) jauría; (*of wolves*) manada; (*of thieves etc*) banda; (*of cards*) baraja; (*bundle*) fardo; (*US: of cigarettes*) paquete *m*, cajetilla ■ *vt* (*wrap*) empaquetar; (*fill*) llenar; (*in suitcase etc*) meter, poner; (*cram*) llenar, atestar; (*fig: meeting etc*) llenar de partidarios; (*Comput*) comprimir; **to ~ (one's bags)** hacer las maletas; **to ~ sb off** despachar a algn; **the place was packed** el local estaba (lleno) hasta los topes; **to send sb packing** (*col*) echar a algn con cajas destempladas

▶ **pack in** *vi* (*break down: watch, car*) estropearse ■ *vt* (*col*) dejar; **~ it in!** ¡para!, ¡basta ya!

▶ **pack up** *vi* (*col: machine*) estropearse; (*person*) irse ■ *vt* (*belongings, clothes*) recoger; (*goods, presents*) empaquetar, envolver

package ['pækɪdʒ] *n* paquete *m*; (*bulky*) bulto; (*Comput*) paquete *m* (*de software*); (*also*: **package deal**) acuerdo global ■ *vt* (*Comm: goods*) envasar, embalar

package holiday *n* viaje *m* organizado (con todo incluido)

package tour *n* viaje *m* organizado

packaging ['pækɪdʒɪŋ] *n* envase *m*

packed lunch [pækt-] *n* almuerzo frío

packer ['pækə'] *n* (*person*) empacador(a) *m(f)*

packet ['pækɪt] *n* paquete *m*

packet switching [-'swɪtʃɪŋ] *n* (*Comput*) conmutación *f* por paquetes

packhorse ['pækhɔ:s] *n* caballo de carga

pack ice *n* banco de hielo

packing ['pækɪŋ] *n* embalaje *m*

packing case *n* cajón *m* de embalaje

pact [pækt] *n* pacto

pad [pæd] *n* (*of paper*) bloc *m*; (*cushion*) cojinete *m*; (*launching pad*) plataforma (de lanzamiento); (*col: flat*) casa ■ *vt* rellenar

padded cell ['pædɪd-] *n* celda acolchada

padding ['pædɪŋ] *n* relleno; (*fig*) paja

paddle ['pædl] *n* (*oar*) canalete *m*, pala; (*US: for table tennis*) pala ■ *vt* remar ■ *vi* (*with feet*) chapotear

paddle steamer *n* vapor *m* de ruedas

paddling pool ['pædlɪŋ-] *n* (*Brit*) piscina para niños

paddock ['pædək] *n* (*field*) potrero

paddy field ['pædɪ-] *n* arrozal *m*

padlock ['pædlɔk] *n* candado ■ *vt* cerrar con candado

padre ['pɑ:drɪ] *n* capellán *m*

paediatrician, (*US*) **pediatrician** [pi:dɪə'trɪʃən] *n* pediatra *m/f*

paediatrics, (*US*) **pediatrics** [pi:dɪ'ætrɪks] *n* pediatría

paedophile, (*US*) **pedophile** ['pi:dəufaɪl] *adj* de pedófilos ■ *n* pedófilo(-a)

pagan ['peɪgən] *adj, n* pagano(-a) *m(f)*

page [peɪdʒ] *n* página; (*also*: **page boy**) paje *m* ■ *vt* (*in hotel etc*) llamar por altavoz a

pageant ['pædʒənt] n (procession) desfile m; (show) espectáculo
pageantry ['pædʒəntrɪ] n pompa
page break n límite m de la página
pager ['peɪdʒəʳ] n busca m
paginate ['pædʒɪneɪt] vt paginar
pagination [pædʒɪ'neɪʃən] n paginación f
pagoda [pə'gəudə] n pagoda
paid [peɪd] pt, pp of **pay** ■ adj (work) remunerado; (official) asalariado; **to put ~ to** (Brit) acabar con
paid-up ['peɪdʌp], **paid-in** (US) ['peɪdɪn] adj (member) con sus cuotas pagadas or al día; (share) liberado; **~ capital** capital m desembolsado
pail [peɪl] n cubo, balde m
pain [peɪn] n dolor m; **to be in ~** sufrir; **on ~ of death** so or bajo pena de muerte; see also **pains**
pained [peɪnd] adj (expression) afligido
painful ['peɪnful] adj doloroso; (difficult) penoso; (disagreeable) desagradable
painfully ['peɪnfəlɪ] adv (fig: very) terriblemente
painkiller ['peɪnkɪləʳ] n analgésico
painless ['peɪnlɪs] adj sin dolor; (method) fácil
pains [peɪnz] npl (efforts) esfuerzos mpl; **to take ~ to do sth** tomarse trabajo en hacer algo
painstaking ['peɪnzteɪkɪŋ] adj (person) concienzudo, esmerado
paint [peɪnt] n pintura ■ vt pintar; **a tin of ~** un bote de pintura; **to ~ the door blue** pintar la puerta de azul
paintbox ['peɪntbɒks] n caja de pinturas
paintbrush ['peɪntbrʌʃ] n (artist's) pincel m; (decorator's) brocha
painter ['peɪntəʳ] n pintor(a) m(f)
painting ['peɪntɪŋ] n pintura
paintwork ['peɪntwəːk] n pintura
pair [pɛəʳ] n (of shoes, gloves etc) par m; (of people) pareja; **a ~ of scissors** unas tijeras; **a ~ of trousers** unos pantalones, un pantalón
  ▶ **pair off** vi: **to ~ off (with sb)** hacer pareja (con algn)
pajamas [pɪ'dʒɑːməz] npl (US) pijama msg, piyama msg (LAm)
Pakistan [pɑːkɪ'stɑːn] n Paquistán m
Pakistani [pɑːkɪ'stɑːnɪ] adj, n paquistaní m/f
PAL [pæl] n abbr (TV) = **phase alternation line**
pal [pæl] n (col) amiguete(-a) m(f), colega m/f
palace ['pæləs] n palacio
palatable ['pælɪtəbl] adj sabroso; (acceptable) aceptable
palate ['pælɪt] n paladar m
palatial [pə'leɪʃəl] adj (surroundings, residence) suntuoso, espléndido

palaver [pə'lɑːvəʳ] n (fuss) lío
pale [peɪl] adj (gen) pálido; (colour) claro ■ n: **to be beyond the ~** pasarse de la raya ■ vi palidecer; **to grow** or **turn ~** palidecer; **to ~ into insignificance (beside)** no poderse comparar (con)
paleness ['peɪlnɪs] n palidez f
Palestine ['pælɪstaɪn] n Palestina
Palestinian [pælɪs'tɪnɪən] adj, n palestino(-a) m(f)
palette ['pælɪt] n paleta
paling ['peɪlɪŋ] n (stake) estaca; (fence) valla
palisade [pælɪ'seɪd] n palizada
pall [pɔːl] n (of smoke) cortina ■ vi cansar
pallbearer ['pɔːlbɛərəʳ] n portador m del féretro
pallet ['pælɪt] n (for goods) pallet m
palletization [pælɪtaɪ'zeɪʃən] n paletización f
palliative ['pælɪətɪv] n paliativo
pallid ['pælɪd] adj pálido
pallor ['pæləʳ] n palidez f
pally ['pælɪ] adj (col): **to be very ~ with sb** ser muy amiguete de algn
palm [pɑːm] n (Anat) palma; (also: **palm tree**) palmera, palma ■ vt: **to ~ sth off on sb** (Brit col) endosarle algo a algn
palmist ['pɑːmɪst] n quiromántico(-a), palmista m/f
Palm Sunday n Domingo de Ramos
palpable ['pælpəbl] adj palpable
palpably ['pælpəblɪ] adv obviamente
palpitation [pælpɪ'teɪʃən] n palpitación f
paltry ['pɔːltrɪ] adj (amount etc) miserable; (insignificant: person) insignificante
pamper ['pæmpəʳ] vt mimar
pamphlet ['pæmflət] n folleto; (political: handed out in street) panfleto
pan [pæn] n (also: **saucepan**) cacerola, cazuela, olla; (also: **frying pan**) sartén m; (of lavatory) taza ■ vi (Cine) tomar panorámicas; **to ~ for gold** cribar oro
pan- [pæn] pref pan-
panacea [pænə'sɪə] n panacea
panache [pə'næʃ] n gracia, garbo
Panama ['pænəmɑː] n Panamá m
Panama Canal n el Canal de Panamá
pancake ['pænkeɪk] n crepe f, panqueque m (LAm)
Pancake Day n martes m de carnaval
pancake roll n rollito de primavera
pancreas ['pæŋkrɪəs] n páncreas m
panda ['pændə] n panda m
panda car n (Brit) coche m de la policía
pandemic [pæn'dɛmɪk] n pandemia
pandemonium [pændɪ'məunɪəm] n (noise): **there was ~** se armó un tremendo jaleo; (mess) caos m
pander ['pændəʳ] vi: **to ~ to** complacer a

p & h *abbr* (US: = *postage and handling*) gastos de envío

P & L *abbr* = **profit and loss**

p & p *abbr* (Brit: = *postage and packing*) gastos de envío

pane [peɪn] *n* cristal *m*

panel ['pænl] *n* (*of wood*) panel *m*; (*of cloth*) paño; (*Radio, TV*) panel *m* de invitados

panel game *n* (*TV*) programa *m* concurso para equipos

panelling, (US) **paneling** ['pænəlɪŋ] *n* paneles *mpl*

panellist, panelist (US) ['pænəlɪst] *n* miembro del jurado

pang [pæŋ] *n*: **pangs of conscience** remordimientos *mpl*; **pangs of hunger** dolores *mpl* del hambre

panhandler ['pænhændlə r] *n* (US col) mendigo(-a)

panic ['pænɪk] *n* pánico ■ *vi* dejarse llevar por el pánico

panic buying [-baɪɪŋ] *n* compras masivas por miedo a futura escasez

panicky ['pænɪkɪ] *adj* (*person*) asustadizo

panic-stricken ['pænɪkstrɪkən] *adj* preso del pánico

pannier ['pænɪə r] *n* (*on bicycle*) cartera; (*on mule etc*) alforja

panorama [pænə'rɑːmə] *n* panorama *m*

panoramic [pænə'ræmɪk] *adj* panorámico

pansy ['pænzɪ] *n* (*Bot*) pensamiento; (*col: pej*) maricón *m*

pant [pænt] *vi* jadear

panther ['pænθə r] *n* pantera

panties ['pæntɪz] *npl* bragas *fpl*

pantihose ['pæntɪhəuz] *n* (US) medias *fpl*, panties *mpl*

panto ['pæntəu] *n* (*Brit col*) = **pantomime**

pantomime ['pæntəmaɪm] *n* (Brit) representación musical navideña *ver nota*

● **PANTOMIME**

En época navideña los teatros británicos ponen en escena representaciones llamadas *pantomimes*, versiones libres de cuentos tradicionales como Aladino o El gato con botas. En ella nunca faltan personajes como la dama ("dame"), papel que siempre interpreta un actor; el protagonista joven ("principal boy"), normalmente interpretado por una actriz, y el malvado ("villain"). Es un espectáculo familiar dirigido a los niños pero con grandes dosis de humor para adultos en el que se alienta la participación del público.

pantry ['pæntrɪ] *n* despensa

pants [pænts] *npl* (Brit: *underwear: woman's*) bragas *fpl*; (: *man's*) calzoncillos *mpl*; (US: *trousers*) pantalones *mpl*

pantsuit ['pæntsjuːt] *n* (US) traje *m* de chaqueta y pantalón

papal ['peɪpəl] *adj* papal

paparazzi [pæpə'rætsɪ] *npl* paparazzi *mpl*

paper ['peɪpə r] *n* papel *m*; (*also*: **newspaper**) periódico, diario; (*study, article*) artículo; (*exam*) examen *m* ■ *adj* de papel ■ *vt* empapelar; (**identity**) **papers** *npl* papeles *mpl*, documentos *mpl*; **a piece of** ~ un papel; **to put sth down on** ~ poner algo por escrito

paper advance *n* (*on printer*) avance *m* de papel

paperback ['peɪpəbæk] *n* libro de bolsillo

paper bag *n* bolsa de papel

paperboy ['peɪpəbɔɪ] *n* (*selling*) vendedor *m* de periódicos; (*delivering*) repartidor *m* de periódicos

paper clip *n* clip *m*

paper hankie *n* pañuelo de papel

paper money *n* papel *m* moneda

paper profit *n* beneficio no realizado

paper shop *n* (Brit) tienda de periódicos

paperweight ['peɪpəweɪt] *n* pisapapeles *m inv*

paperwork ['peɪpəwəːk] *n* trabajo administrativo; (*pej*) papeleo

papier-mâché ['pæpɪeɪ'mæʃeɪ] *n* cartón *m* piedra

paprika ['pæprɪkə] *n* pimentón *m*

Pap test ['pæp-] *n* (*Med*) frotis *m* (cervical)

papyrus [pə'paɪərəs] *n* papiro

par [pɑː r] *n* par *f*; (*Golf*) par *m* ■ *adj* a la par; **to be on a** ~ **with** estar a la par con; **at** ~ a la par; **to be above/below** ~ estar sobre/bajo par; **to feel under** ~ sentirse en baja forma

parable ['pærəbl] *n* parábola

parachute ['pærəʃuːt] *n* paracaídas *m inv* ■ *vi* lanzarse en paracaídas

parachutist ['pærəʃuːtɪst] *n* paracaidista *m/f*

parade [pə'reɪd] *n* desfile *m* ■ *vt* (*gen*) recorrer, desfilar por; (*show off*) hacer alarde de ■ *vi* desfilar; (*Mil*) pasar revista; **a fashion** ~ un desfile de modelos

parade ground *n* plaza de armas

paradise ['pærədaɪs] *n* paraíso

paradox ['pærədɔks] *n* paradoja

paradoxical [pærə'dɔksɪkl] *adj* paradójico

paradoxically [pærə'dɔksɪklɪ] *adv* paradójicamente

paraffin ['pærəfɪn] *n* (Brit): ~ (**oil**) parafina

paraffin heater *n* estufa de parafina

paraffin lamp *n* quinqué *m*

paragon ['pærəgən] *n* modelo

paragraph ['pærəgrɑːf] *n* párrafo, acápite *m*

p

(LAm); **new ~** punto y aparte, punto acápite (LAm)

Paraguay ['pærəgwaɪ] n Paraguay m

Paraguayan [pærə'gwaɪən] adj, n paraguayo(-a) m(f), paraguayano(-a) m(f)

parallel ['pærəlɛl] adj: **~ (with/to)** en paralelo (con/a); (fig) semejante (a) ■ n (line) paralela; (fig) paralelo; (Geo) paralelo

paralysis [pə'rælɪsɪs] n parálisis f inv

paralytic [pærə'lɪtɪk] adj paralítico

paralyze ['pærəlaɪz] vt paralizar

paramedic [pærə'mɛdɪk] n auxiliar m/f sanitario(-a)

parameter [pə'ræmɪtər] n parámetro

paramilitary [pærə'mɪlɪtərɪ] adj (organization, operations) paramilitar

paramount ['pærəmaunt] adj: **of ~ importance** de suma importancia

paranoia [pærə'nɔɪə] n paranoia

paranoid ['pærənɔɪd] adj (person, feeling) paranoico

paranormal [pærə'nɔːml] adj paranormal

parapet ['pærəpɪt] n parapeto

paraphernalia [pærəfə'neɪlɪə] n parafernalia

paraphrase ['pærəfreɪz] vt parafrasear

paraplegic [pærə'pliːdʒɪk] n parapléjico(-a)

parapsychology [pærəsaɪ'kɔlədʒɪ] n parasicología

parasite ['pærəsaɪt] n parásito(-a)

parasol ['pærəsɔl] n sombrilla, quitasol m

paratrooper ['pærətruːpər] n paracaidista m/f

parcel ['pɑːsl] n paquete m ■ vt (also: **parcel up**) empaquetar, embalar; **to be part and ~ of** ser parte integrante de
▶ **parcel out** vt parcelar, repartir

parcel bomb n paquete m bomba

parcel post n servicio de paquetes postales

parch [pɑːtʃ] vt secar, resecar

parched [pɑːtʃt] adj (person) muerto de sed

parchment ['pɑːtʃmənt] n pergamino

pardon ['pɑːdn] n perdón m; (Law) indulto ■ vt perdonar; indultar; **~ me!, I beg your ~!** ¡perdone usted!; **(I beg your) ~?,** (US) **~ me?** ¿cómo (dice)?

pare [pɛər] vt (nails) cortar; (fruit etc) pelar

parent ['pɛərənt] n: **parents** npl padres mpl

parentage ['pɛərəntɪdʒ] n familia, linaje m; **of unknown ~** de padres desconocidos

parental [pə'rɛntl] adj paternal/maternal

parent company n casa matriz

parenthesis (pl **parentheses**) [pə'rɛnθɪsɪs, -θɪsiːz] n paréntesis m inv; **in parentheses** entre paréntesis

parenthood ['pɛərənthud] n el ser padres

parent ship n buque m nodriza

Paris ['pærɪs] n París m

parish ['pærɪʃ] n parroquia

parish council n consejo parroquial

parishioner [pə'rɪʃənər] n feligrés(-esa) m(f)

Parisian [pə'rɪzɪən] adj, n parisino(-a) m(f), parisiense m/f

parity ['pærɪtɪ] n paridad f, igualdad f

park [pɑːk] n parque m, jardín m público ■ vt aparcar, estacionar ■ vi aparcar, estacionar

parka ['pɑːkə] n parka

parking ['pɑːkɪŋ] n aparcamiento, estacionamiento; **"no ~"** "prohibido aparcar or estacionarse"

parking lights npl luces fpl de estacionamiento

parking lot n (US) parking m, aparcamiento, playa f de estacionamiento (LAm)

parking meter n parquímetro

parking offence, (US) **parking violation** n ofensa por aparcamiento indebido

parking place n sitio para aparcar, aparcamiento

parking ticket n multa de aparcamiento

Parkinson's n (also: **Parkinson's disease**) (enfermedad f de) Parkinson m

parkway ['pɑːkweɪ] n (US) alameda

parlance ['pɑːləns] n lenguaje m; **in common/modern ~** en lenguaje corriente/moderno

parliament ['pɑːləmənt] n parlamento; (Spanish) las Cortes fpl; ver nota

PARLIAMENT

El Parlamento británico (Parliament) tiene como sede el palacio de Westminster, también llamado "Houses of Parliament". Consta de dos cámaras: la Cámara de los Comunes ("House of Commons") está formada por 650 diputados ("Members of Parliament") que acceden a ella tras ser elegidos por sufragio universal en su respectiva área o circunscripción electoral ("constituency"). Se reúne 175 días al año y sus sesiones son presididas y moderadas por el Presidente de la Cámara ("Speaker"). La cámara alta es la Cámara de los Lores ("House of Lords") y sus miembros son nombrados por el monarca o bien han heredado su escaño. Su poder es limitado, aunque actúa como tribunal supremo de apelación, excepto en Escocia.

parliamentary [pɑːlə'mɛntərɪ] adj parlamentario

parlour, parlor (US) ['pɑːlər] n salón m, living m (LAm)

parlous ['pɑːləs] *adj* peligroso, alarmante
Parmesan [pɑːmɪ'zæn] *n* (*also:* **Parmesan cheese**) queso parmesano
parochial [pə'rəukɪəl] *adj* parroquial; (*pej*) de miras estrechas
parody ['pærədɪ] *n* parodia ■ *vt* parodiar
parole [pə'rəul] *n*: **on ~** en libertad condicional
paroxysm ['pærəksɪzəm] *n* (*Med*) paroxismo, ataque *m*; (*of anger, laughter, coughing*) ataque *m*; (*of grief*) crisis *f*
parquet ['pɑːkeɪ] *n*: **~ floor(ing)** parquet *m*
parrot ['pærət] *n* loro, papagayo
parrot fashion *adv* como un loro
parry ['pærɪ] *vt* parar
parsimonious [pɑːsɪ'məunɪəs] *adj* tacaño
parsley ['pɑːslɪ] *n* perejil *m*
parsnip ['pɑːsnɪp] *n* chirivía
parson ['pɑːsn] *n* cura *m*
part [pɑːt] *n* (*gen*) parte *f*; (*Mus*) parte *f*; (*bit*) trozo; (*of machine*) pieza; (*Theat etc*) papel *m*; (*of serial*) entrega; (*US: in hair*) raya ■ *adv* = **partly** ■ *vt* separar; (*break*) partir ■ *vi* (*people*) separarse; (*roads*) bifurcarse; (*crowd*) apartarse; (*break*) romperse; **to take ~ in** participar *or* tomar parte en; **to take sb's ~** tomar partido por algn; **for my ~** por mi parte; **for the most ~** en su mayor parte; (*people*) en su mayoría; **for the better ~ of the day** durante la mayor parte del día; **~ of speech** (*Ling*) categoría gramatical, parte *f* de la oración; **to take sth in good/bad ~** aceptar algo bien/tomarse algo a mal
▶ **part with** *vt fus* ceder, entregar; (*money*) pagar; (*get rid of*) deshacerse de
partake [pɑː'teɪk] *vi* (*irreg: like* **take**) (*formal*): **to ~ of sth** (*food*) comer algo; (*drink*) tomar *or* beber algo
part exchange *n* (*Brit*): **in ~** como parte del pago
partial ['pɑːʃl] *adj* parcial; **to be ~ to** (*like*) ser aficionado a
partially ['pɑːʃəlɪ] *adv* en parte, parcialmente
participant [pɑː'tɪsɪpənt] *n* (*in competition*) concursante *m/f*
participate [pɑː'tɪsɪpeɪt] *vi*: **to ~ in** participar en
participation [pɑːtɪsɪ'peɪʃən] *n* participación *f*
participle ['pɑːtɪsɪpl] *n* participio
particle ['pɑːtɪkl] *n* partícula; (*of dust*) mota; (*fig*) pizca
particular [pə'tɪkjulə^r] *adj* (*special*) particular; (*concrete*) concreto; (*given*) determinado; (*detailed*) detallado, minucioso; (*fussy*) quisquilloso, exigente; **particulars** *npl* (*information*) datos *mpl*, detalles *mpl*; (*details*)

pormenores *mpl*; **in ~** en particular; **to be very ~ about** ser muy exigente en cuanto a; **I'm not ~** me es *or* da igual
particularly [pə'tɪkjuləlɪ] *adv* especialmente, en particular
parting ['pɑːtɪŋ] *n* (*act of*) separación *f*; (*farewell*) despedida; (*Brit: in hair*) raya ■ *adj* de despedida; **~ shot** (*fig*) golpe *m* final
partisan [pɑːtɪ'zæn] *adj* partidista ■ *n* partidario(-a); (*fighter*) partisano(-a)
partition [pɑː'tɪʃən] *n* (*Pol*) división *f*; (*wall*) tabique *m* ■ *vt* dividir; dividir con tabique
partly ['pɑːtlɪ] *adv* en parte
partner ['pɑːtnə^r] *n* (*Comm*) socio(-a); (*Sport*) pareja; (*at dance*) pareja; (*spouse*) cónyuge *m/f*; (*friend etc*) compañero(-a) ■ *vt* acompañar
partnership ['pɑːtnəʃɪp] *n* (*gen*) asociación *f*; (*Comm*) sociedad *f*; **to go into ~ (with), form a ~ (with)** asociarse (con)
part payment *n* pago parcial
partridge ['pɑːtrɪdʒ] *n* perdiz *f*
part-time ['pɑːt'taɪm] *adj, adv* a tiempo parcial
part-timer [pɑːt'taɪmə^r] *n* trabajador(a) *m(f)* a tiempo parcial
party ['pɑːtɪ] *n* (*Pol*) partido; (*celebration*) fiesta; (*group*) grupo; (*Law*) parte *f*, interesado ■ *adj* (*Pol*) de partido; (*dress etc*) de fiesta, de gala; **to have** *or* **give** *or* **throw a ~** organizar una fiesta; **dinner ~** cena; **to be a ~ to a crime** ser cómplice *m/f* de un crimen
party line *n* (*Pol*) línea política del partido; (*Tel*) línea compartida
party piece *n*: **to do one's ~** hacer su numerito (de fiesta)
party political broadcast *n* ≈ espacio electoral
pass [pɑːs] *vt* (*time, object*) pasar; (*place*) pasar por; (*exam, law*) aprobar; (*overtake, surpass*) rebasar; (*approve*) aprobar ■ *vi* pasar; (*Scol*) aprobar ■ *n* (*permit*) permiso, pase *m*; (*membership card*) carnet *m*; (*in mountains*) puerto; (*Sport*) pase *m*; (*Scol: also:* **pass mark**) aprobado; **to ~ sth through sth** pasar algo por algo; **to ~ the time of day with sb** pasar el rato con algn; **things have come to a pretty ~!** ¡hasta dónde hemos llegado!; **to make a ~ at sb** (*col*) insinuársele a algn
▶ **pass away** *vi* fallecer
▶ **pass by** *vi* pasar ■ *vt* (*ignore*) pasar por alto
▶ **pass down** *vt* (*customs, inheritance*) pasar, transmitir
▶ **pass for** *vt fus* pasar por; **she could ~ for 25** se podría creer que sólo tiene 25 años
▶ **pass on** *vi* (*die*) fallecer, morir ■ *vt* (*hand on*): **to ~ on (to)** transmitir (a); (*cold, illness*) pegar (a); (*benefits*) dar (a); (*price rises*) pasar (a)

P

▶ **pass out** *vi* desmayarse; *(Mil)* graduarse
▶ **pass over** *vi* *(die)* fallecer ■ *vt* omitir, pasar por alto
▶ **pass up** *vt* *(opportunity)* dejar pasar, no aprovechar
passable ['pɑːsəbl] *adj* *(road)* transitable; *(tolerable)* pasable
passably ['pɑːsəblɪ] *adv* pasablemente
passage ['pæsɪdʒ] *n* pasillo; *(act of passing)* tránsito; *(fare, in book)* pasaje *m*; *(by boat)* travesía
passageway ['pæsɪdʒweɪ] *n* *(in house)* pasillo, corredor *m*; *(between buildings etc)* pasaje *m*, pasadizo
passenger ['pæsɪndʒəʳ] *n* pasajero(-a), viajero(-a)
passer-by [pɑːsə'baɪ] *n* transeúnte *m/f*
passing ['pɑːsɪŋ] *adj* *(fleeting)* pasajero; **in ~** de paso
passing place *n* *(Aut)* apartadero
passion ['pæʃən] *n* pasión *f*
passionate ['pæʃənɪt] *adj* apasionado
passionately ['pæʃənɪtlɪ] *adv* apasionadamente, con pasión
passion fruit *n* fruta de la pasión, granadilla
passion play *n* drama *m* de la Pasión
passive ['pæsɪv] *adj* *(also Ling)* pasivo
passive smoking *n* *efectos del tabaco en fumadores pasivos*
passkey ['pɑːskiː] *n* llave *f* maestra
Passover ['pɑːsəuvəʳ] *n* Pascua (de los judíos)
passport ['pɑːspɔːt] *n* pasaporte *m*
passport control *n* control *m* de pasaporte
password ['pɑːswɜːd] *n* *(also Comput)* contraseña
past [pɑːst] *prep* *(further than)* más allá de; *(later than)* después de ■ *adj* pasado; *(president etc)* antiguo ■ *n* *(time)* pasado; *(of person)* antecedentes *mpl*; **quarter/half ~ four** las cuatro y cuarto/media; **he's ~ forty** tiene más de cuarenta años; **I'm ~ caring** ya no me importa; **to be ~ it** *(col: person)* estar acabado; **for the ~ few/three days** durante los últimos días/últimos tres días; **to run ~** pasar corriendo por; **in the ~** en el pasado, antes
pasta ['pæstə] *n* pasta
paste [peɪst] *n* *(gen)* pasta; *(glue)* engrudo ■ *vt* *(stick)* pegar; *(glue)* engomar; **tomato ~** tomate concentrado
pastel ['pæstl] *adj* pastel; *(painting)* al pastel
pasteurized ['pæstəraɪzd] *adj* pasteurizado
pastille ['pæstl] *n* pastilla
pastime ['pɑːstaɪm] *n* pasatiempo
past master *n*: **to be a ~ at** ser un maestro en
pastor ['pɑːstəʳ] *n* pastor *m*
pastoral ['pɑːstərl] *adj* pastoral

pastry ['peɪstrɪ] *n* *(dough)* pasta; *(cake)* pastel *m*
pasture ['pɑːstʃəʳ] *n* *(grass)* pasto
pasty *n* ['pæstɪ] empanada ■ *adj* ['peɪstɪ] pastoso; *(complexion)* pálido
pat [pæt] *vt* dar una palmadita a; *(dog etc)* acariciar ■ *n* *(of butter)* porción *f* ■ *adj*: **he knows it (off) ~** se lo sabe de memoria or al dedillo; **to give sb/o.s. a ~ on the back** *(fig)* felicitar a algn/felicitarse
patch [pætʃ] *n* *(of material)* parche *m*; *(mended part)* remiendo; *(of land)* terreno; *(Comput)* ajuste *m* ■ *vt* *(clothes)* remendar; **(to go through) a bad ~** (pasar por) una mala racha
▶ **patch up** *vt* *(mend temporarily)* reparar; **to ~ up a quarrel** hacer las paces
patchwork ['pætʃwəːk] *n* labor *f* de retales
patchy ['pætʃɪ] *adj* desigual
pate [peɪt] *n*: **bald ~** calva
pâté ['pæteɪ] *n* paté *m*
patent ['peɪtnt] *n* patente *f* ■ *vt* patentar ■ *adj* patente, evidente
patent leather *n* charol *m*
patently ['peɪtntlɪ] *adv* evidentemente
patent medicine *n* específico
patent office *n* oficina de patentes y marcas
patent rights *npl* derechos *mpl* de patente
paternal [pə'təːnl] *adj* paternal; *(relation)* paterno
paternalistic [pətə:nə'lɪstɪk] *adj* paternalista
paternity [pə'təːnɪtɪ] *n* paternidad *f*
paternity suit *n* *(Law)* caso de paternidad
path [pɑːθ] *n* camino, sendero; *(trail, track)* pista; *(of missile)* trayectoria
pathetic [pə'θεtɪk] *adj* *(pitiful)* penoso, patético; *(very bad)* malísimo; *(moving)* conmovedor(a)
pathetically [pə'θεtɪklɪ] *adv* penosamente, patéticamente; *(very badly)* malísimamente mal, de pena
pathological [pæθə'lɒdʒɪkəl] *adj* patológico
pathologist [pə'θɒlədʒɪst] *n* patólogo(-a)
pathology [pə'θɒlədʒɪ] *n* patología
pathos ['peɪθɔs] *n* patetismo
pathway ['pɑːθweɪ] *n* sendero, vereda
patience ['peɪʃns] *n* paciencia; *(Brit Cards)* solitario; **to lose one's ~** perder la paciencia
patient ['peɪʃnt] *n* paciente *m/f* ■ *adj* paciente, sufrido; **to be ~ with sb** tener paciencia con algn
patiently ['peɪʃəntlɪ] *adv* pacientemente, con paciencia
patio ['pætɪəu] *n* patio
patriot ['peɪtrɪət] *n* patriota *m/f*
patriotic [pætrɪ'ɔtɪk] *adj* patriótico
patriotism ['pætrɪətɪzəm] *n* patriotismo
patrol [pə'trəul] *n* patrulla ■ *vt* patrullar por; **to be on ~** patrullar, estar de patrulla

patrol boat n patrullero, patrullera
patrol car n coche m patrulla
patrolman [pə'trəulmən] n (US) policía m
patron ['peɪtrən] n (in shop) cliente m/f; (of charity) patrocinador(a) m(f); **~ of the arts** mecenas m
patronage ['pætrənɪdʒ] n patrocinio, protección f
patronize ['pætrənaɪz] vt (shop) ser cliente de; (look down on) tratar con condescendencia a
patronizing ['pætrənaɪzɪŋ] adj condescendiente
patron saint n santo(-a) patrón(-ona)
patter ['pætər] n golpeteo; (sales talk) labia ■ vi (rain) tamborilear
pattern ['pætən] n (Sewing) patrón m; (design) dibujo; (behaviour, events) esquema m; **~ of events** curso de los hechos; **behaviour patterns** modelos mpl de comportamiento
patterned ['pætənd] adj (material) estampado
paucity ['pɔːsɪtɪ] n escasez f
paunch [pɔːntʃ] n panza, barriga
pauper ['pɔːpər] n pobre m/f
pause [pɔːz] n pausa; (interval) intervalo ■ vi hacer una pausa; **to ~ for breath** detenerse para tomar aliento
pave [peɪv] vt pavimentar; **to ~ the way for** preparar el terreno para
pavement ['peɪvmənt] n (Brit) acera, vereda (LAm), andén m (LAm), banqueta (LAm); (US) calzada, pavimento
pavilion [pə'vɪlɪən] n pabellón m; (Sport) vestuarios mpl
paving ['peɪvɪŋ] n pavimento
paving stone n losa
paw [pɔː] n pata; (claw) garra ■ vt (animal) tocar con la pata; (pej: touch) tocar, manosear
pawn [pɔːn] n (Chess) peón m; (fig) instrumento ■ vt empeñar
pawnbroker ['pɔːnbrəukər] n prestamista m/f
pawnshop ['pɔːnʃɔp] n casa de empeños
pay [peɪ] (pt, pp **paid**) n paga; (wage etc) sueldo, salario ■ vt pagar; (visit) hacer; (respect) ofrecer ■ vi pagar; (be profitable) rendir, compensar, ser rentable; **to be in sb's ~** estar al servicio de algn; **to ~ attention (to)** prestar atención (a); **I paid £5 for that record** pagué 5 libras por ese disco; **how much did you ~ for it?** ¿cuánto pagaste por él?; **to ~ one's way** (contribute one's share) pagar su parte; (remain solvent: company) ser solvente; **to ~ dividends** (Comm) pagar dividendos; (fig) compensar; **it won't ~ you to do that** no te merece la pena hacer eso; **to put paid to** (plan, person) acabar con
▶ **pay back** vt (money) devolver, reembolsar; (person) pagar

▶ **pay for** vt fus pagar
▶ **pay in** vt ingresar
▶ **pay off** vt liquidar; (person) pagar; (debts) liquidar, saldar; (creditor) cancelar, redimir; (workers) despedir; (mortgage) cancelar, redimir ■ vi (scheme, decision) dar resultado; **to ~ sth off in instalments** pagar algo a plazos
▶ **pay out** vt (rope) ir dando; (money) gastar, desembolsar
▶ **pay up** vt pagar
payable ['peɪəbl] adj pagadero; **to make a cheque ~ to sb** extender un cheque a favor de algn
pay-as-you-go [peɪəzjə'gəu] adj (mobile phone) (de) prepago
pay award n aumento de sueldo
pay day n día m de paga
PAYE n abbr (Brit: = pay as you earn) sistema de retención fiscal en la fuente de ingresos
payee [peɪ'iː] n portador(a) m(f)
pay envelope n (US) = **pay packet**
paying ['peɪɪŋ] adj: **~ guest** huésped(a) m(f) que la paga
payload ['peɪləud] n carga útil
payment ['peɪmənt] n pago; **advance ~** (part sum) anticipo, adelanto; (total sum) saldo; **monthly ~** mensualidad f; **deferred ~, ~ by instalments** pago a plazos or diferido; **on ~ of £5** mediante pago de or pagando £5; **in ~ for** en pago de
pay packet n (Brit) sobre m (de la paga)
pay-phone ['peɪfəun] n teléfono público
payroll ['peɪrəul] n nómina; **to be on a firm's ~** estar en la nómina de una compañía
pay slip n hoja del sueldo
pay station n (US) teléfono público
PBS n abbr (US: = Public Broadcasting Service) agrupación de ayuda a la realización de emisiones para la TV pública
PBX abbr (Tel) = **private branch exchange**
PC n abbr (= personal computer) PC m, OP m; (Brit) = **police constable** ■ abbr (Brit) = **Privy Councillor** ■ adj abbr = **politically correct**
pc abbr = **per cent; postcard**
p/c abbr = **petty cash**
PCB n abbr (= printed circuit board) TCI f
pcm abbr = **per calendar month**
PD n abbr (US) = **police department**
pd abbr = **paid**
PDA n abbr (= personal digital assistant) agenda electrónica
PDSA n abbr (Brit) = **People's Dispensary for Sick Animals**
PDT n abbr (US: = Pacific Daylight Time) hora de verano del Pacífico

PE *n abbr* (= *physical education*) ed. física ■ *abbr*
(*Canada*) = **Prince Edward Island**
pea [pi:] *n* guisante *m*, chícharo (*LAm*), arveja
(*LAm*)
peace [pi:s] *n* paz *f*; (*calm*) paz *f*, tranquilidad
f; **to be at ~ with sb/sth** estar en paz
con algn/algo; **to keep the ~** (*policeman*)
mantener el orden; (*citizen*) guardar el orden
peaceable ['pi:səbl] *adj* pacífico
peaceably [pɪ:səblɪ] *adv* pacíficamente
peaceful ['pi:sful] *adj* (*gentle*) pacífico; (*calm*)
tranquilo, sosegado
peacekeeping ['pi:ski:pɪŋ] *adj* de
pacificación ■ *n* pacificación *f*
peacekeeping force *n* fuerza de pacificación
peace offering *n* (*fig*) prenda de paz
peacetime ['pi:staɪm] *n*: **in ~** en tiempo de
paz
peach [pi:tʃ] *n* melocotón *m*, durazno (*LAm*)
peacock ['pi:kɔk] *n* pavo real
peak [pi:k] *n* (*of mountain: top*) cumbre *f*, cima;
(: *point*) pico; (*of cap*) visera; (*fig*) cumbre *f*
peak-hour ['pi:kauəʳ] *adj* (*traffic etc*) de horas
punta
peak hours *npl*, **peak period** ■ *n* horas *fpl*
punta
peak rate *n* tarifa máxima
peaky ['pi:kɪ] *adj* (*Brit col*) pálido, paliducho;
I'm feeling a bit ~ estoy malucho, no me
encuentro bien
peal [pi:l] *n* (*of bells*) repique *m*; **~ of laughter**
carcajada
peanut ['pi:nʌt] *n* cacahuete *m*, maní *m* (*LAm*)
peanut butter *n* mantequilla de cacahuete
pear [pɛəʳ] *n* pera
pearl [pə:l] *n* perla
peasant ['pɛznt] *n* campesino(-a)
peat [pi:t] *n* turba
pebble ['pɛbl] *n* guijarro
peck [pɛk] *vt* (*also*: **peck at**) picotear; (*food*)
comer sin ganas ■ *n* picotazo; (*kiss*) besito
pecking order ['pɛkɪŋ-] *n* orden *m* de
jerarquía
peckish ['pɛkɪʃ] *adj* (*Brit col*): **I feel ~** tengo
ganas de picar algo
peculiar [pɪˈkju:lɪəʳ] *adj* (*odd*) extraño, raro;
(*typical*) propio, característico; (*particular*:
importance, qualities) particular; **~ to** propio de
peculiarity [pɪkju:lɪˈærɪtɪ] *n* peculiaridad *f*,
característica
peculiarly [pɪˈkju:lɪəlɪ] *adv* extrañamente;
particularmente
pedal ['pɛdl] *n* pedal *m* ■ *vi* pedalear
pedal bin *n* cubo de la basura con pedal
pedant ['pɛdənt] *n* pedante *m/f*
pedantic [pɪˈdæntɪk] *adj* pedante
pedantry ['pɛdəntrɪ] *n* pedantería

peddle ['pɛdl] *vt* (*goods*) ir vendiendo *or*
vender de puerta en puerta; (*drugs*) traficar
con; (*gossip*) divulgar
peddler ['pɛdləʳ] *n* vendedor(a) *m(f)*
ambulante
pedestal ['pɛdəstl] *n* pedestal *m*
pedestrian [pɪˈdɛstrɪən] *n* peatón *m* ■ *adj*
pedestre
pedestrian crossing *n* (*Brit*) paso de
peatones
pedestrian precinct *n* zona reservada para
peatones
pediatrics [pi:dɪˈætrɪks] *n* (*US*) = **paediatrics**
pedigree ['pɛdɪgri:] *n* genealogía; (*of animal*)
pedigrí *m* ■ *cpd* (*animal*) de raza, de casta
pedlar ['pɛdləʳ] *n* (*Brit*) = **peddler**
pee [pi:] *vi* (*col*) mear
peek [pi:k] *vi* mirar a hurtadillas; (*Comput*)
inspeccionar
peel [pi:l] *n* piel *f*; (*of orange, lemon*) cáscara;
(: *removed*) peladuras *fpl* ■ *vt* pelar ■ *vi* (*paint
etc*) desconcharse; (*wallpaper*) despegarse,
desprenderse
  ▶ **peel back** *vt* pelar
peeler ['pi:ləʳ] *n*: **potato ~** mondador *m or*
pelador *m* de patatas, pelapatatas *m inv*
peep [pi:p] *n* (*Brit: look*) mirada furtiva;
(*sound*) pío ■ *vi* (*Brit*) piar
  ▶ **peep out** *vi* asomar la cabeza
peephole ['pi:phəul] *n* mirilla
peer [pɪəʳ] *vi*: **to ~ at** escudriñar ■ *n* (*noble*)
par *m*; (*equal*) igual *m*
peerage ['pɪərɪdʒ] *n* nobleza
peerless ['pɪəlɪs] *adj* sin par, incomparable,
sin igual
peeved [pi:vd] *adj* enojado
peevish ['pi:vɪʃ] *adj* malhumorado
peevishness ['pi:vɪʃnɪs] *n* mal humor *m*
peg [pɛg] *n* clavija; (*for coat etc*) gancho,
colgador *m*; (*Brit: also*: **clothes peg**) pinza;
(*also*: **tent peg**) estaca ■ *vt* (*clothes*) tender;
(*groundsheet*) fijar con estacas; (*fig: wages,
prices*) fijar
pejorative [pɪˈdʒɔrətɪv] *adj* peyorativo
Pekin [pi:ˈkɪn], **Peking** [pi:ˈkɪŋ] *n* Pekín *m*
pekinese [pi:kɪˈni:z] *n* pequinés(-esa) *m(f)*
pelican ['pɛlɪkən] *n* pelícano
pelican crossing *n* (*Brit Aut*) paso de peatones
señalizado
pellet ['pɛlɪt] *n* bolita; (*bullet*) perdigón *m*
pell-mell ['pɛl'mɛl] *adv* en tropel
pelmet ['pɛlmɪt] *n* galería
pelt [pɛlt] *vt*: **to ~ sb with sth** arrojarle algo
a algn ■ *vi* (*rain: also*: **pelt down**) llover a
cántaros ■ *n* pellejo
pelvis ['pɛlvɪs] *n* pelvis *f*
pen [pɛn] *n* (*also*: **ballpoint pen**) bolígrafo;

(also: **fountain pen**) pluma; (for sheep) redil m; (US col: prison) cárcel f, chirona; **to put ~ to paper** tomar la pluma
penal ['pi:nl] adj penal; **~ servitude** trabajos mpl forzados
penalize ['pi:nəlaɪz] vt (punish) castigar; (Sport) sancionar, penalizar
penalty ['pɛnltɪ] n (gen) pena; (fine) multa; (Sport) sanción f; (also: **penalty kick**: Football) penalty m
penalty area n (Brit Sport) área de castigo
penalty clause n cláusula de penalización
penalty shoot-out [-'ʃu:taʊt] n (Football) tanda de penaltis
penance ['pɛnəns] n penitencia
pence [pɛns] pl of **penny**
penchant ['pã:ʃã:ŋ] n predilección f, inclinación f
pencil ['pɛnsl] n lápiz m, lapicero (LAm) ▪ vt (also: **pencil in**) escribir con lápiz
pencil case n estuche m
pencil sharpener n sacapuntas m inv
pendant ['pɛndnt] n pendiente m
pending ['pɛndɪŋ] prep antes de ▪ adj pendiente; **~ the arrival of ...** hasta que llegue ..., hasta llegar ...
pendulum ['pɛndjuləm] n péndulo
penetrate ['pɛnɪtreɪt] vt penetrar
penetrating ['pɛnɪtreɪtɪŋ] adj penetrante
penetration [pɛnɪ'treɪʃən] n penetración f
penfriend ['pɛnfrɛnd] n (Brit) amigo(-a) por correspondencia
penguin ['pɛŋgwɪn] n pingüino
penicillin [pɛnɪ'sɪlɪn] n penicilina
peninsula [pə'nɪnsjulə] n península
penis ['pi:nɪs] n pene m
penitence ['pɛnɪtns] n penitencia
penitent ['pɛnɪtnt] adj arrepentido; (Rel) penitente
penitentiary [pɛnɪ'tɛnʃərɪ] n (US) cárcel f, presidio
penknife ['pɛnnaɪf] n navaja
Penn., Penna. abbr (US) = **Pennsylvania**
pen name n seudónimo
pennant ['pɛnənt] n banderola; banderín m
penniless ['pɛnɪlɪs] adj sin dinero
Pennines ['pɛnaɪnz] npl (Montes mpl) Peninos mpl
penny (pl **pennies** or (BRIT) **pence**) ['pɛnɪ, 'pɛnɪz, pɛns] n (Brit) penique m; (US) centavo
penpal ['pɛnpæl] n amigo(-a) por correspondencia
penpusher ['pɛnpuʃər] n (pej) chupatintas m/f inv
pension ['pɛnʃən] n (allowance, state payment) pensión f; (old-age) jubilación f
▶ **pension off** vt jubilar

pensioner ['pɛnʃənər] n (Brit) jubilado(-a)
pension fund n fondo de pensiones
pensive ['pɛnsɪv] adj pensativo; (withdrawn) preocupado
pentagon ['pɛntəgən] n pentágono; **the P~** (US Pol) el Pentágono

● **PENTAGON**

Se conoce como el Pentágono (the Pentagon) al edificio de planta pentagonal que acoge las dependencias del Ministerio de Defensa estadounidense ("Department of Defense") en Arlington, Virginia. En lenguaje periodístico se aplica también a la dirección militar del país.

Pentecost ['pɛntɪkɔst] n Pentecostés m
penthouse ['pɛnthaʊs] n ático (de lujo)
pent-up ['pɛntʌp] adj (feelings) reprimido
penultimate [pɛ'nʌltɪmət] adj penúltimo
penury ['pɛnjurɪ] n miseria, pobreza
people ['pi:pl] npl gente f; (citizens) pueblo sg, ciudadanos mpl ▪ n (nation, race) pueblo, nación f ▪ vt poblar; **several ~ came** vinieron varias personas; **~ say that ...** dice la gente que ...; **old/young ~** los ancianos/jóvenes; **~ at large** la gente en general; **a man of the ~** un hombre del pueblo
PEP [pɛp] n abbr (= personal equity plan) plan personal de inversión con desgravación fiscal
pep [pɛp] n (col) energía
▶ **pep up** vt animar
pepper ['pɛpər] n (spice) pimienta; (vegetable) pimiento, ají m (LAm), chile m (LAm) ▪ vt (fig) salpicar
peppermint ['pɛpəmɪnt] n menta; (sweet) pastilla de menta
pepperoni [pɛpə'rəunɪ] n ≈ salchichón m picante
pepperpot ['pɛpəpɔt] n pimentero
peptalk ['pɛptɔ:k] n (col): **to give sb a ~** darle a algn una inyección de ánimo
per [pər] prep por; **~ day/person** por día/persona; **as ~ your instructions** de acuerdo con sus instrucciones
per annum adv al año
per capita adj, adv per cápita
perceive [pə'si:v] vt percibir; (realize) darse cuenta de
per cent, (US) **percent** [pə'sɛnt] n por ciento; **a 20 ~ discount** un descuento del 20 por ciento
percentage [pə'sɛntɪdʒ] n porcentaje m; **to get a ~ on all sales** percibir un tanto por ciento sobre todas las ventas; **on a ~ basis** a porcentaje

P

percentage point n punto (porcentual)
perceptible [pə'sɛptəbl] adj perceptible;
(notable) sensible
perception [pə'sɛpʃən] n percepción f;
(insight) perspicacia
perceptive [pə'sɛptɪv] adj perspicaz
perch [pə:tʃ] n (fish) perca; (for bird) percha
■ vi posarse
percolate ['pə:kəleɪt] vt (coffee) filtrar ■ vi
(coffee) filtrarse; (fig) filtrarse
percolator ['pə:kəleɪtəʳ] n cafetera de filtro
percussion [pə'kʌʃən] n percusión f
percussionist [pə'kʌʃənɪst] n percusionista
m/f
peremptory [pə'rɛmptərɪ] adj perentorio
perennial [pə'rɛnɪəl] adj perenne
perfect adj ['pə:fɪkt] perfecto ■ n (also:
perfect tense) perfecto ■ vt [pə'fɛkt]
perfeccionar; **he's a ~ stranger to me** no
le conozco de nada, me es completamente
desconocido
perfection [pə'fɛkʃən] n perfección f
perfectionist [pə'fɛkʃənɪst] n perfeccionista
m/f
perfectly ['pə:fɪktlɪ] adv perfectamente;
I'm ~ happy with the situation estoy muy
contento con la situación; **you know ~ well**
lo sabes muy bien or perfectamente
perforate ['pə:fəreɪt] vt perforar
perforated ulcer n úlcera perforada
perforation [pə:fə'reɪʃən] n perforación f
perform [pə'fɔ:m] vt (carry out) realizar,
llevar a cabo; (Theat) representar; (piece of
music) interpretar ■ vi (Theat) actuar; (Tech)
funcionar
performance [pə'fɔ:məns] n (of task)
realización f; (of a play) representación f; (of
player etc) actuación f; (of engine) rendimiento;
(of car) prestaciones fpl; (of function)
desempeño; **the team put up a good ~**
el equipo se defendió bien
performer [pə'fɔ:məʳ] n (actor) actor m,
actriz f; (Mus) intérprete m/f
performing [pə'fɔ:mɪŋ] adj (animal)
amaestrado
performing arts npl: **the ~** las artes teatrales
perfume ['pə:fju:m] n perfume m
perfunctory [pə'fʌŋktərɪ] adj superficial
perhaps [pə'hæps] adv quizá(s), tal vez; **~ so/
not** puede que sí/no
peril ['pɛrɪl] n peligro, riesgo
perilous ['pɛrɪləs] adj peligroso
perilously ['pɛrɪləslɪ] adv: **they came ~
close to being caught** por poco les cogen or
agarran
perimeter [pə'rɪmɪtəʳ] n perímetro
period ['pɪərɪəd] n período, periodo; (History)

época; (Scol) clase f; (full stop) punto; (Med)
regla, periodo; (US Sport) tiempo ■ adj
(costume, furniture) de época; **for a ~ of three
weeks** durante (un período de) tres semanas;
the holiday ~ el período de vacaciones
periodic [pɪərɪ'ɔdɪk] adj periódico
periodical [pɪərɪ'ɔdɪkl] adj periódico ■ n
revista, publicación f periódica
periodically [pɪərɪ'ɔdɪklɪ] adv de vez en
cuando, cada cierto tiempo
period pains npl dolores mpl de la regla or de
la menstruación
peripatetic [pɛrɪpə'tɛtɪk] adj (salesman)
ambulante; (teacher) con trabajo en varios
colegios
peripheral [pə'rɪfərəl] adj periférico ■ n
(Comput) periférico, unidad f periférica
periphery [pə'rɪfərɪ] n periferia
periscope ['pɛrɪskəup] n periscopio
perish ['pɛrɪʃ] vi perecer; (decay) echarse a
perder
perishable ['pɛrɪʃəbl] adj perecedero
perishables ['pɛrɪʃəblz] npl productos mpl
perecederos
peritonitis [pɛrɪtə'naɪtɪs] n peritonitis f
perjure ['pə:dʒəʳ] vt: **to ~ o.s.** perjurar
perjury ['pə:dʒərɪ] n (Law) perjurio
perk [pə:k] n beneficio, extra m
▶ **perk up** vi (cheer up) animarse
perky ['pə:kɪ] adj alegre, animado
perm [pə:m] n permanente f ■ vt:
to have one's hair permed hacerse una
permanente
permanence ['pə:mənəns] n permanencia
permanent ['pə:mənənt] adj permanente;
(job, position) fijo; (dye, ink) indeleble;
~ address domicilio permanente; **I'm not
~ here** no estoy fijo aquí
permanently ['pə:mənəntlɪ] adv (lastingly)
para siempre, de modo definitivo; (all the
time) permanentemente
permeate ['pə:mɪeɪt] vi penetrar, trascender
■ vt penetrar, trascender a
permissible [pə'mɪsɪbl] adj permisible, lícito
permission [pə'mɪʃən] n permiso; **to give sb
~ to do sth** autorizar a algn para que haga
algo; **with your ~** con su permiso
permissive [pə'mɪsɪv] adj permisivo
permit n ['pə:mɪt] permiso, licencia; (entrance
pass) pase m ■ vt [pə'mɪt] permitir; (accept)
tolerar ■ vi [pə'mɪt]: **weather permitting**
si el tiempo lo permite; **fishing ~** permiso de
pesca; **building/export ~** licencia or permiso
de construcción/exportación
permutation [pə:mju'teɪʃən] n permutación f
pernicious [pə:'nɪʃəs] adj nocivo; (Med)
pernicioso

pernickety [pə'nɪkɪtɪ] *adj* (*col: person*) quisquilloso; (: *task*) delicado

perpendicular [pə:pən'dɪkjuləʳ] *adj* perpendicular

perpetrate ['pə:pɪtreɪt] *vt* cometer

perpetual [pə'pɛtjuəl] *adj* perpetuo

perpetually [pə'pɛtjuəlɪ] *adv* (*eternally*) perpetuamente; (*continuously*) constantemente, continuamente

perpetuate [pə'pɛtjueɪt] *vt* perpetuar

perpetuity [pə:pɪ'tjuɪtɪ] *n:* **in ~** a perpetuidad

perplex [pə'plɛks] *vt* dejar perplejo

perplexed [pə'plɛkst] *adj* perplejo, confuso

perplexing [pə'plɛksɪŋ] *adj* que causa perplejidad

perplexity [pə'plɛksɪtɪ] *n* perplejidad *f*, confusión *f*

perquisites ['pə:kwɪzɪts] *npl* (*also:* **perks**) beneficios *mpl*

persecute ['pə:sɪkju:t] *vt* (*pursue*) perseguir; (*harass*) acosar

persecution [pə:sɪ'kju:ʃən] *n* persecución *f*

perseverance [pə:sɪ'vɪərəns] *n* perseverancia

persevere [pə:sɪ'vɪəʳ] *vi* perseverar

Persia ['pə:ʃə] *n* Persia

Persian ['pə:ʃən] *adj, n* persa *m/f* ■ *n* (*Ling*) persa *m*; **the ~ Gulf** el Golfo Pérsico

Persian cat *n* gato persa

persist [pə'sɪst] *vi* persistir; **to ~ in doing sth** empeñarse en hacer algo

persistence [pə'sɪstəns] *n* empeño

persistent [pə'sɪstənt] *adj* (*lateness, rain*) persistente; (*determined*) porfiado; (*continuing*) constante; **~ offender** (*Law*) multirreincidente *m/f*

persistently [pə'sɪstəntlɪ] *adv* persistentemente; (*continually*) constantemente

persnickety [pə'snɪkətɪ] *adj* (*US col*) = **pernickety**

person ['pə:sn] *n* persona; **in ~** en persona; **on** *or* **about one's ~** encima; **a ~ to ~ call** una llamada (de) persona a persona

personable ['pə:snəbl] *adj* atractivo

personal ['pə:snl] *adj* personal, individual; (*visit*) en persona; (*Brit Tel*) (de) persona a persona

personal allowance *n* desgravación *f* personal

personal assistant *n* ayudante *m/f* personal

personal belongings *npl* efectos *mpl* personales

personal column *n* anuncios *mpl* personales

personal computer *n* ordenador *m* personal

personal effects *npl* efectos *mpl* personales

personal identification number *n* número personal de identificación

personality [pə:sə'nælɪtɪ] *n* personalidad *f*

personally ['pə:snəlɪ] *adv* personalmente

personal organizer *n* agenda (profesional); (*electronic*) organizador *m* personal

personal property *n* bienes *mpl* muebles

personal, social and health education *n* (*Brit Scol*) formación social y sanitaria para la vida adulta

personal stereo *n* walkman® *m*

personification [pə:sɔnɪfɪ'keɪʃən] *n* personificación *f*

personify [pə'sɔnɪfaɪ] *vt* encarnar, personificar

personnel [pə:sə'nɛl] *n* personal *m*

personnel department *n* departamento de personal

personnel management *n* gestión *f* de personal

personnel manager *n* jefe *m* de personal

perspective [pə'spɛktɪv] *n* perspectiva; **to get sth into ~** ver algo en perspectiva *or* como es

Perspex® ['pə:spɛks] *n* (*Brit*) vidrio acrílico, plexiglás® *m*

perspiration [pə:spɪ'reɪʃən] *n* transpiración *f*, sudor *m*

perspire [pə'spaɪəʳ] *vi* transpirar, sudar

persuade [pə'sweɪd] *vt:* **to ~ sb to do sth** persuadir a algn para que haga algo; **to ~ sb of sth/that** persuadir *or* convencer a algn de algo/de que; **I am persuaded that ...** estoy convencido de que ...

persuasion [pə'sweɪʒən] *n* persuasión *f*; (*persuasiveness*) persuasiva; (*creed*) creencia

persuasive [pə'sweɪsɪv] *adj* persuasivo

persuasively [pə'sweɪsɪvlɪ] *adv* de modo persuasivo

pert [pə:t] *adj* impertinente, fresco, atrevido

pertaining [pə:'teɪnɪŋ]: **~ to** *prep* relacionado con

pertinent ['pə:tɪnənt] *adj* pertinente, a propósito

perturb [pə'tə:b] *vt* perturbar

perturbing [pə'tə:bɪŋ] *adj* inquietante, perturbador(a)

Peru [pə'ru:] *n* el Perú

perusal [pə'ru:zəl] *n* (*quick*) lectura somera; (*careful*) examen *m*

peruse [pə'ru:z] *vt* (*examine*) leer con detención, examinar; (*glance at*) mirar por encima

Peruvian [pə'ru:vɪən] *adj, n* peruano(-a) *m(f)*

pervade [pə'veɪd] *vt* impregnar; (*influence, ideas*) extenderse por

pervasive [pə'veɪsɪv] *adj* (*smell*) penetrante;

P

(*influence*) muy extendido; (*gloom, feelings, ideas*) reinante

perverse [pə'və:s] *adj* perverso; (*stubborn*) terco; (*wayward*) travieso

perversely [pə'və:slı] *adv* perversamente; tercamente; traviesamente

perverseness [pə'və:snıs] *n* perversidad *f*; terquedad *f*; travesura

perversion [pə'və:ʃən] *n* perversión *f*

pervert *n* ['pə:və:t] pervertido(-a) ▪ *vt* [pə'və:t] pervertir

pessary ['pɛsərı] *n* pesario

pessimism ['pɛsımızəm] *n* pesimismo

pessimist ['pɛsımıst] *n* pesimista *m/f*

pessimistic [pɛsı'mıstık] *adj* pesimista

pest [pɛst] *n* (*insect*) insecto nocivo; (*fig*) lata, molestia; **pests** *npl* plaga

pest control *n* control *m* de plagas

pester ['pɛstə*r*] *vt* molestar, acosar

pesticide ['pɛstısaıd] *n* pesticida *m*

pestilence ['pɛstıləns] *n* pestilencia

pestle ['pɛsl] *n* mano *f* de mortero *or* de almirez

pet [pɛt] *n* animal *m* doméstico; (*favourite*) favorito(-a) ▪ *vt* acariciar ▪ *vi* (*col*) besuquearse ▪ *cpd*: **my ~ aversion** mi manía

petal ['pɛtl] *n* pétalo

peter ['pi:tə*r*]: **to ~ out** *vi* agotarse, acabarse

petite [pə'ti:t] *adj* menuda, chiquita

petition [pə'tıʃən] *n* petición *f* ▪ *vt* presentar una petición a ▪ *vi*: **to ~ for divorce** pedir el divorcio

pet name *n* nombre *m* cariñoso, apodo

petrified ['pɛtrıfaıd] *adj* (*fig*) pasmado, horrorizado

petrochemical [pɛtrə'kɛmıkl] *adj* petroquímico

petrodollars ['pɛtrəudɔləz] *npl* petrodólares *mpl*

petrol ['pɛtrəl] (*Brit*) *n* gasolina; (*for lighter*) bencina; **two/four-star ~** gasolina normal/súper

petrol bomb *n* cóctel *m* Molotov

petrol can *n* bidón *m* de gasolina

petrol engine *n* (*Brit*) motor *m* de gasolina

petroleum [pə'trəulıəm] *n* petróleo

petroleum jelly *n* vaselina

petrol pump *n* (*Brit: in car*) bomba de gasolina; (*in garage*) surtidor *m* de gasolina

petrol station *n* (*Brit*) gasolinera

petrol tank *n* (*Brit*) depósito (de gasolina)

petticoat ['pɛtıkəut] *n* combinación *f*, enagua(s) *f(pl)* (*LAm*)

pettifogging ['pɛtıfɔgıŋ] *adj* quisquilloso

pettiness ['pɛtınıs] *n* mezquindad *f*

petty ['pɛtı] *adj* (*mean*) mezquino; (*unimportant*) insignificante

petty cash *n* dinero para gastos menores

petty cash book *n* libro de caja auxiliar

petty officer *n* contramaestre *m*

petulant ['pɛtjulənt] *adj* malhumorado

pew [pju:] *n* banco

pewter ['pju:tə*r*] *n* peltre *m*

Pfc *abbr* (*US Mil*) = **private first class**

PG *n abbr* (*Cine*) = **parental guidance**

PG 13 *abbr* (*US: Cine*: = *Parental Guidance* 13) no apto para menores de 13 años

PGA *n abbr* = **Professional Golfers' Association**

PH *n abbr* (*US Mil*: = *Purple Heart*) decoración otorgada a los heridos de guerra

pH *n abbr* (= *pH value*) pH

PHA *n abbr* (*US*) = **Public Housing Administration**

phallic ['fælık] *adj* fálico

phantom ['fæntəm] *n* fantasma *m*

Pharaoh ['fɛərəu] *n* faraón *m*

pharmaceutical [fɑ:mə'sju:tıkl] *adj* farmacéutico

pharmacist ['fɑ:məsıst] *n* farmacéutico(-a)

pharmacy ['fɑ:məsı] *n* (*US*) farmacia

phase [feız] *n* fase *f* ▪ *vt*: **to ~ sth in/out** introducir/retirar algo por etapas; **phased withdrawal** retirada progresiva

PhD *abbr* = **Doctor of Philosophy**

pheasant ['fɛznt] *n* faisán *m*

phenomenal [fı'nɔmınl] *adj* fenomenal, extraordinario

phenomenally [fı'nɔmınlı] *adv* extraordinariamente

phenomenon (*pl* **phenomena**) [fə'nɔmınən, -nə] *n* fenómeno

phial ['faıəl] *n* ampolla

philanderer [fı'lændərə*r*] *n* donjuán *m*, don Juan *m*

philanthropic [fılən'θrɔpık] *adj* filantrópico

philanthropist [fı'lænθrəpıst] *n* filántropo(-a)

philatelist [fı'lætəlıst] *n* filatelista *m/f*

philately [fı'lætəlı] *n* filatelia

Philippines ['fılıpi:nz] *npl*: **the ~** (las Islas) Filipinas

philosopher [fı'lɔsəfə*r*] *n* filósofo(-a)

philosophical [fılə'sɔfıkl] *adj* filosófico

philosophy [fı'lɔsəfı] *n* filosofía

phishing ['fıʃıŋ] *n* phishing *m*, *método de estafa a través de Internet*

phlegm [flɛm] *n* flema

phlegmatic [flɛg'mætık] *adj* flemático

phobia ['fəubjə] *n* fobia

phone [fəun] *n* teléfono ▪ *vt* telefonear, llamar por teléfono; **to be on the ~** tener teléfono; (*be calling*) estar hablando por teléfono

▶ **phone back** *vt, vi* volver a llamar
▶ **phone up** *vt, vi* llamar por teléfono
phone book *n* guía telefónica
phone box, phone booth *n* cabina telefónica
phone call *n* llamada (telefónica)
phonecard ['fəunkɑːd] *n* tarjeta telefónica
phone-in ['fəunɪn] *n* (*Brit Radio, TV*) *programa de radio o televisión con las líneas abiertas al público*
phone tapping [-tæpɪŋ] *n* escuchas telefónicas
phonetics [fə'nɛtɪks] *n* fonética
phoney ['fəunɪ] *adj* = **phony**
phonograph ['fəunəgræf] *n* (*US*) fonógrafo, tocadiscos *m inv*
phonology [fəu'nɔlədʒɪ] *n* fonología
phony ['fəunɪ] *adj* falso ▪ *n* (*person*) farsante *m/f*
phosphate ['fɔsfeɪt] *n* fosfato
phosphorus ['fɔsfərəs] *n* fósforo
photo ['fəutəu] *n* foto *f*
photo... ['fəutəu] *pref* foto...
photocall ['fəutəukɔːl] *n* sesión *f* fotográfica para la prensa
photocopier ['fəutəukɔpɪə'] *n* fotocopiadora
photocopy ['fəutəukɔpɪ] *n* fotocopia ▪ *vt* fotocopiar
photoelectric [fəutəuɪ'lɛktrɪk] *adj*: **~ cell** célula fotoeléctrica
photo finish *n* resultado comprobado por fotocontrol
Photofit® ['fəutəufɪt] *n* (*also*: **Photofit picture**) retrato robot
photogenic [fəutəu'dʒɛnɪk] *adj* fotogénico
photograph ['fəutəgræf] *n* fotografía ▪ *vt* fotografiar; **to take a ~ of sb** sacar una foto de algn
photographer [fə'tɔgrəfə'] *n* fotógrafo
photographic [fəutə'græfɪk] *adj* fotográfico
photography [fə'tɔgrəfɪ] *n* fotografía
photo opportunity *n* *oportunidad de salir en la foto*
Photostat® ['fəutəustæt] ·*n* fotóstato
photosynthesis [fəutəu'sɪnθəsɪs] *n* fotosíntesis *f*
phrase [freɪz] *n* frase *f* ▪ *vt* (*letter*) expresar, redactar
phrase book *n* libro de frases
physical ['fɪzɪkl] *adj* físico; **~ examination** reconocimiento médico; **~ exercises** ejercicios *mpl* físicos
physical education *n* educación *f* física
physically ['fɪsɪklɪ] *adv* físicamente
physical training *n* gimnasia
physician [fɪ'zɪʃən] *n* médico(-a)
physicist ['fɪzɪsɪst] *n* físico(-a)
physics ['fɪzɪks] *n* física

physiological [fɪzɪə'lɔdʒɪkl] *adj* fisiológico
physiology [fɪzɪ'ɔlədʒɪ] *n* fisiología
physiotherapy [fɪzɪəu'θɛrəpɪ] *n* fisioterapia
physique [fɪ'ziːk] *n* físico
pianist ['pɪənɪst] *n* pianista *m/f*
piano [pɪ'ænəu] *n* piano
piano accordion *n* (*Brit*) acordeón-piano *m*
piccolo ['pɪkələu] *n* (*Mus*) flautín *m*
pick [pɪk] *n* (*tool: also*: **pick-axe**) pico, piqueta ▪ *vt* (*select*) elegir, escoger; (*gather*) coger (*SP*), recoger (*LAm*); (*lock*) abrir con ganzúa; (*scab, spot*) rascar ▪ *vi*: **to ~ and choose** ser muy exigente; **take your ~** escoja lo que quiera; **the ~ of** lo mejor de; **to ~ one's nose/teeth** hurgarse las narices/escarbarse los dientes; **to ~ pockets** ratear, ser carterista; **to ~ one's way through** andar a tientas, abrirse camino; **to ~ a fight/quarrel with sb** buscar pelea/camorra con algn; **to ~ sb's brains** aprovecharse de los conocimientos de algn
▶ **pick at** *vt fus*: **to ~ at one's food** comer con poco apetito
▶ **pick off** *vt* (*kill*) matar de un tiro
▶ **pick on** *vt fus* (*person*) meterse con
▶ **pick out** *vt* escoger; (*distinguish*) identificar
▶ **pick up** *vi* (*improve: sales*) ir mejor; (: *patient*) reponerse; (: *Finance*) recobrarse ▪ *vt* (*from floor*) recoger; (*buy*) comprar; (*find*) encontrar; (*learn*) aprender; (*Radio, TV, Tel*) captar; **to ~ up speed** acelerarse; **to ~ o.s. up** levantarse; **to ~ up where one left off** volver a empezar algo donde lo había dejado
pickaxe, pickax (*US*) ['pɪkæks] *n* pico, zapapico
picket ['pɪkɪt] *n* (*in strike*) piquete *m* ▪ *vt* hacer un piquete en, piquetear; **to be on ~ duty** estar de piquete
picketing ['pɪkɪtɪŋ] *n* organización *f* de piquetes
picket line *n* piquete *m*
pickings ['pɪkɪŋz] *npl* (*pilferings*): **there are good ~ to be had here** se pueden sacar buenas ganancias de aquí
pickle ['pɪkl] *n* (*also*: **pickles**: *as condiment*) escabeche *m*; (*fig: mess*) apuro ▪ *vt* conservar en escabeche; (*in vinegar*) conservar en vinagre; **in a ~** en un lío, en apuros
pick-me-up ['pɪkmɪʌp] *n* reconstituyente *m*
pickpocket ['pɪkpɔkɪt] *n* carterista *m/f*
pickup ['pɪkʌp] *n* (*also*: **pickup truck, pickup van**) furgoneta
picnic ['pɪknɪk] *n* picnic *m*, merienda ▪ *vi* merendar en el campo
pictorial [pɪk'tɔːrɪəl] *adj* pictórico; (*magazine etc*) ilustrado
picture ['pɪktʃə'] *n* cuadro; (*painting*) pintura; (*photograph*) fotografía; (*film*) película; (*TV*)

p

imagen f ■ vt pintar; **the pictures** (Brit) el cine; **we get a good ~ here** captamos bien la imagen aquí; **to take a ~ of sb/sth** hacer or sacar una foto a algn/de algo; **the garden is a ~ in June** el jardín es una preciosidad en junio; **the overall ~** la impresión general; **to put sb in the ~** poner a algn al corriente or al tanto

picture book n libro de dibujos

picture message n mensaje m con foto

picture messaging n (envío de) mensajes mpl con imágenes

picturesque [pɪktʃəˈrɛsk] adj pintoresco

piddling [ˈpɪdlɪŋ] adj insignificante

pidgin [ˈpɪdʒɪn] adj: **~ English** lengua franca basada en el inglés

pie [paɪ] n (of meat etc: large) pastel m; (: small) empanada; (sweet) tarta

piebald [ˈpaɪbɔːld] adj pío

piece [piːs] n pedazo, trozo; (of cake) trozo; (Draughts etc) ficha; (Chess) pieza; (part of a set) pieza; (item): **a ~ of furniture/advice** un mueble/un consejo ■ vt: **to ~ together** juntar; (Tech) armar; **to take to pieces** desmontar; **a ~ of news** una noticia; **a 10p ~** una moneda de 10 peniques; **a six-~ band** un conjunto de seis (músicos); **in one ~** (object) de una sola pieza; **~ by ~** pieza por or a pieza; **to say one's ~** decir su parecer

piecemeal [ˈpiːsmiːl] adv poco a poco

piece rate n tarifa a destajo

piecework [ˈpiːswəːk] n trabajo a destajo

pie chart n gráfico de sectores or de tarta

pier [pɪər] n muelle m, embarcadero

pierce [pɪəs] vt penetrar en, perforar; **to have one's ears pierced** hacerse los agujeros de las orejas

piercing [ˈpɪəsɪŋ] adj (cry) penetrante ■ n (body art) piercing m

piety [ˈpaɪətɪ] n piedad f

pig [pɪg] n cerdo, puerco, chancho (LAm); (person: greedy) tragón(-ona) m(f), comilón(-ona) m(f); (nasty) cerdo(-a)

pigeon [ˈpɪdʒən] n paloma; (as food) pichón m

pigeonhole [ˈpɪdʒənhəul] n casilla

piggy bank [ˈpɪgɪbæŋk] n hucha (en forma de cerdito)

pigheaded [pɪgˈhɛdɪd] adj terco, testarudo

piglet [ˈpɪglɪt] n cerdito, cochinillo

pigment [ˈpɪgmənt] n pigmento

pigmentation [pɪgmənˈteɪʃən] n pigmentación f

pigmy [ˈpɪgmɪ] n = **pygmy**

pigskin [ˈpɪgskɪn] n piel f de cerdo

pigsty [ˈpɪgstaɪ] n pocilga

pigtail [ˈpɪgteɪl] n (girl's) trenza; (Chinese) coleta; (Taur) coleta

pike [paɪk] n (spear) pica; (fish) lucio

pilchard [ˈpɪltʃəd] n sardina

pile [paɪl] n (heap) montón m; (of carpet) pelo; (vb: also: **pile up**) ■ vt amontonar; (fig) acumular ■ vi amontonarse; **in a ~** en un montón; **to ~ into** (car) meterse en
▶ **pile on** vt: **to ~ it on** (col) exagerar

piles [paɪlz] npl (Med) almorranas fpl, hemorroides mpl

pile-up [ˈpaɪlʌp] n (Aut) accidente m múltiple

pilfer [ˈpɪlfər] vt, vi ratear, robar, sisar

pilfering [ˈpɪlfərɪŋ] n ratería

pilgrim [ˈpɪlgrɪm] n peregrino(-a); **the P~ Fathers** or **Pilgrims** los primeros colonos norteamericanos; see also **Thanksgiving**

pilgrimage [ˈpɪlgrɪmɪdʒ] n peregrinación f, romería

pill [pɪl] n píldora; **the ~** la píldora; **to be on the ~** tomar la píldora (anticonceptiva)

pillage [ˈpɪlɪdʒ] vt pillar, saquear

pillar [ˈpɪlər] n pilar m, columna

pillar box n (Brit) buzón m

pillion [ˈpɪljən] n (of motorcycle) asiento trasero; **to ride ~** ir en el asiento trasero

pillion passenger n pasajero que va detrás

pillory [ˈpɪlərɪ] vt poner en ridículo

pillow [ˈpɪləu] n almohada

pillowcase [ˈpɪləukeɪs], **pillowslip** [ˈpɪləuslɪp] n funda (de almohada)

pilot [ˈpaɪlət] n piloto inv ■ adj (scheme etc) piloto ■ vt pilotar; (fig) guiar, conducir

pilot light n piloto

pimento [pɪˈmɛntəu] n pimiento morrón

pimp [pɪmp] n chulo, cafiche m (LAm)

pimple [ˈpɪmpl] n grano

pimply [ˈpɪmplɪ] adj lleno de granos

PIN n abbr (= personal identification number) NPI m

pin [pɪn] n alfiler m; (Elec: of plug) clavija; (Tech) perno; (: wooden) clavija; (drawing pin) chincheta; (in grenade) percutor m ■ vt prender con (alfiler); sujetar con perno; **pins and needles** hormigueo sg; **to ~ sth on sb** (fig) cargar a algn con la culpa de algo
▶ **pin down** vt (fig): **there's something strange here, but I can't quite ~ it down** aquí hay algo raro pero no puedo precisar qué es; **to ~ sb down** hacer que algn concrete

pinafore [ˈpɪnəfɔːr] n delantal m

pinafore dress n (Brit) pichi m

pinball [ˈpɪnbɔːl] n (also: **pinball machine**) millón m, fliper m

pincers [ˈpɪnsəz] npl pinzas fpl, tenazas fpl

pinch [pɪntʃ] n pellizco; (of salt etc) pizca ■ vt pellizcar; (col: steal) birlar ■ vi (shoe) apretar; **at a ~** en caso de apuro; **to feel the ~** (fig) pasar apuros or estrecheces

pinched [pɪntʃt] adj (drawn) cansado; **~ with**

cold transido de frío; **~ for money/space** mal or falto de dinero/espacio or sitio

pincushion ['pɪnkuʃən] n acerico

pine [paɪn] n (also: **pine tree**) pino ■ vi: **to ~ for** suspirar por
▸ **pine away** vi morirse de pena

pineapple ['paɪnæpl] n piña, ananá(s) m (LAm)

pine cone n piña

pine needle n aguja de pino

Ping-Pong® ['pɪŋpɔn] n pingpong m

pink [pɪŋk] adj (de color) rosa ■ n (colour) rosa; (Bot) clavel m

pinking shears ['pɪŋkɪŋ-] npl tijeras fpl dentadas

pin money n dinero para gastos extra

pinnacle ['pɪnəkl] n cumbre f

pinpoint ['pɪnpɔɪnt] vt precisar

pinstripe ['pɪnstraɪp] adj: **~ suit** traje m a rayas

pint [paɪnt] n (Brit) pinta (= 0,57 l); (US) pinta (= 0,47 l); (Brit col: of beer) pinta de cerveza, ≈ jarra (SP)

pin-up ['pɪnʌp] n (picture) fotografía de mujer u hombre medio desnudos; **~ (girl)** ≈ chica de calendario

pioneer [paɪə'nɪər] n pionero(-a) ■ vt promover

pious ['paɪəs] adj piadoso, devoto

pip [pɪp] n (seed) pepita; **the pips** (Brit Tel) la señal

pipe [paɪp] n tubería, cañería; (for smoking) pipa, cachimba (LAm), cachimbo (LAm) ■ vt conducir en cañerías; **(bag)pipes** npl gaita sg
▸ **pipe down** vi (col) callarse

pipe cleaner n limpiapipas m inv

piped music [paɪpt-] n música ambiental

pipe dream n sueño imposible

pipeline ['paɪplaɪn] n tubería, cañería; (for oil) oleoducto; (for natural gas) gaseoducto; **it is in the ~** (fig) está en trámite

piper ['paɪpər] n (gen) flautista m/f; (with bagpipes) gaitero(-a)

pipe tobacco n tabaco de pipa

piping ['paɪpɪŋ] adv: **to be ~ hot** estar calentito

piquant ['piːkənt] adj picante

pique [piːk] n pique m, resentimiento

pirate ['paɪərət] n pirata m/f ■ vt (record, video, book) hacer una copia pirata de

pirated ['paɪərətɪd] adj (book, record etc) pirata inv

pirate radio n (Brit) emisora pirata

pirouette [pɪru'et] n pirueta ■ vi piruetear

Pisces ['paɪsiːz] n Piscis m

piss [pɪs] vi (col) mear

pissed [pɪst] adj (col: drunk) mamado

pistol ['pɪstl] n pistola

piston ['pɪstən] n pistón m, émbolo

pit [pɪt] n hoyo; (also: **coal pit**) mina; (in garage) foso de inspección; (also: **orchestra pit**) foso de la orquesta; (quarry) cantera ■ vt (chickenpox) picar; (rust) comer; **to ~ A against B** oponer A a B; **pits** npl (Aut) box msg; **pitted with** (chickenpox) picado de

pitapat ['pɪtə'pæt] adv: **to go ~** (heart) latir rápidamente; (rain) golpetear

pitch [pɪtʃ] n (throw) lanzamiento; (Mus) tono; (Brit Sport) campo, terreno; (tar) brea; (in market etc) puesto; (fig: degree) nivel m, grado ■ vt (throw) arrojar, lanzar ■ vi (fall) caer(se); (Naut) cabecear; **I can't keep working at this ~** no puedo seguir trabajando a este ritmo; **at its (highest) ~** en su punto máximo; **his anger reached such a ~ that ...** su ira or cólera llegó a tal extremo que ...; **to ~ a tent** montar una tienda (de campaña); **to ~ one's aspirations too high** tener ambiciones desmesuradas

pitch-black ['pɪtʃ'blæk] adj negro como boca de lobo

pitched battle [pɪtʃt-] n batalla campal

pitcher ['pɪtʃər] n cántaro, jarro

pitchfork ['pɪtʃfɔːk] n horca

piteous ['pɪtɪəs] adj lastimoso

pitfall ['pɪtfɔːl] n riesgo

pith [pɪθ] n (of orange) piel f blanca; (fig) meollo

pithead ['pɪthɛd] n (Brit) bocamina

pithy ['pɪθɪ] adj jugoso

pitiful ['pɪtɪful] adj (touching) lastimoso, conmovedor(a); (contemptible) lamentable

pitifully ['pɪtɪfəlɪ] adv: **it's ~ obvious** es tan evidente que da pena

pitiless ['pɪtɪlɪs] adj despiadado, implacable

pitilessly ['pɪtɪlɪslɪ] adv despiadadamente, implacablemente

pittance ['pɪtns] n miseria

pity ['pɪtɪ] n (compassion) compasión f, piedad f; (shame) lástima ■ vt compadecer(se de); **to have** or **take ~ on sb** compadecerse de algn; **what a ~!** ¡qué pena!; **it is a ~ that you can't come** ¡qué pena que no puedas venir!

pitying ['pɪtɪɪŋ] adj compasivo, de lástima

pivot ['pɪvət] n eje m ■ vi: **to ~ on** girar sobre; (fig) depender de

pixel ['pɪksl] n (Comput) pixel m, punto

pixie ['pɪksɪ] n duendecillo

pizza ['piːtsə] n pizza

placard ['plækɑːd] n (in march etc) pancarta

placate [plə'keɪt] vt apaciguar

place [pleɪs] n lugar m, sitio; (rank) rango; (seat) plaza, asiento; (post) puesto; (in street names) plaza; (home): **at/to his ~** en/a su casa ■ vt (object) poner, colocar; (identify) reconocer; (find a post for) dar un puesto a, colocar; (goods) vender; **to take ~** tener lugar; **to be placed** (in race, exam) colocarse; **out of ~** (not suitable) fuera de lugar; **in the first ~** (first of all) en primer lugar; **to change places with sb** cambiarse de sitio con algn; **from ~ to ~** de un sitio a or para otro; **all over the ~** por todas partes; **he's going places** (fig, col) llegará lejos; **I feel rather out of ~ here** me encuentro algo desplazado; **to put sb in his ~** (fig) poner a algn en su lugar; **it is not my ~ to do it** no me incumbe a mí hacerlo; **to ~ an order with sb (for)** hacer un pedido a algn (de); **we are better placed than a month ago** estamos en mejor posición que hace un mes

placebo [plə'si:bəu] n placebo

place mat n (wooden etc) salvamanteles m inv; (in linen etc) mantel m individual

placement ['pleɪsmənt] n colocación f

place name n topónimo

placid ['plæsɪd] adj apacible, plácido

placidity [plæ'sɪdɪtɪ] n placidez f

plagiarism ['pleɪdʒərɪzm] n plagio

plagiarist ['pleɪdʒərɪst] n plagiario(-a)

plagiarize ['pleɪdʒəraɪz] vt plagiar

plague [pleɪg] n plaga; (Med) peste f ■ vt (fig) acosar, atormentar; **to ~ sb with questions** acribillar a algn a preguntas

plaice [pleɪs] n pl inv platija

plaid [plæd] n (material) tela de cuadros

plain [pleɪn] adj (clear) claro, evidente; (simple) sencillo; (frank) franco, abierto; (not handsome) poco atractivo; (pure) natural, puro ■ adv claramente ■ n llano, llanura; **in ~ clothes** (police) vestido de paisano; **to make sth ~ to sb** dejar algo en claro a algn

plain chocolate n chocolate m oscuro or amargo

plainly ['pleɪnlɪ] adv claramente, evidentemente; (frankly) francamente

plainness ['pleɪnnɪs] n (clarity) claridad f; (simplicity) sencillez f; (of face) falta de atractivo

plain speaking n: **there has been some ~** se ha hablado claro

plaintiff ['pleɪntɪf] n demandante m/f

plaintive ['pleɪntɪv] adj (cry, voice) lastimero, quejumbroso; (look) que da lástima

plait [plæt] n trenza ■ vt trenzar

plan [plæn] n (drawing) plano; (scheme) plan m, proyecto ■ vt (think) pensar; (prepare) proyectar, planear; (intend) pensar, tener la intención de ■ vi hacer proyectos; **have you any plans for today?** ¿piensas hacer algo hoy?; **to ~ to do** pensar hacer; **how long**

do you ~ to stay? ¿cuánto tiempo piensas quedarte?; **to ~ (for)** planear, proyectar
▶ **plan out** vt planear detalladamente

plane [pleɪn] n (Aviat) avión m; (tree) plátano; (tool) cepillo; (Math) plano

planet ['plænɪt] n planeta m

planetarium [plænɪ'tɛərɪəm] n planetario

planetary ['plænɪtərɪ] adj planetario

plank [plæŋk] n tabla

plankton ['plæŋktən] n plancton m

planned economy [plænd-] n economía planificada

planner ['plænər] n planificador(-a) m(f); (chart) diagrama m de planificación; **town ~** urbanista m/f

planning ['plænɪŋ] n (Pol, Econ) planificación f; **family ~** planificación familiar

planning committee n (in local government) comité m de planificación

planning permission n licencia de obras

plant [plɑ:nt] n planta; (machinery) maquinaria; (factory) fábrica ■ vt plantar; (field) sembrar; (bomb) colocar

plantain ['plæntɪn] n llantén m

plantation [plæn'teɪʃən] n plantación f; (estate) hacienda

planter ['plɑ:ntər] n hacendado

plant pot n maceta, tiesto

plaque [plæk] n placa

plasma ['plæzmə] n plasma m

plaster ['plɑ:stər] n (for walls) yeso; (also: **plaster of Paris**) yeso mate; (Med: for broken leg etc) escayola; (Brit: also: **sticking plaster**) tirita, esparadrapo ■ vt enyesar; (cover): **to ~ with** llenar or cubrir de; **to be plastered with mud** estar cubierto de barro

plasterboard ['plɑ:stəbɔ:d] n cartón m yeso

plaster cast n (Med) escayola; (model, statue) vaciado de yeso

plastered ['plɑ:stəd] adj (col) borracho

plasterer ['plɑ:stərər] n yesero

plastic ['plæstɪk] n plástico ■ adj de plástico

plastic bag n bolsa de plástico

plastic bullet n bala de goma

plastic explosive n goma 2®

plasticine® ['plæstɪsi:n] n (Brit) plastilina®

plastic surgery n cirugía plástica

plastinate ['plæstɪneɪt] vt plastinar

plate [pleɪt] n (dish) plato; (metal, in book) lámina; (Phot) placa; (on door) placa; (Aut: also: **number plate**) matrícula

plateau (pl **plateaus** or **plateaux**) ['plætəu, -z] n meseta, altiplanicie f

plateful ['pleɪtful] n plato

plate glass n vidrio or cristal m cilindrado

platen ['plætən] n (on typewriter, printer) rodillo

plate rack n escurreplatos m inv

platform ['plætfɔːm] n (Rail) andén m; (stage) plataforma; (at meeting) tribuna; (Pol) programa m (electoral); **the train leaves from ~ seven** el tren sale del andén número siete

platform ticket n (Brit) billete m de andén

platinum ['plætɪnəm] n platino

platitude ['plætɪtjuːd] n tópico, lugar m común

platonic [plə'tɒnɪk] adj platónico

platoon [plə'tuːn] n pelotón m

platter ['plætəʳ] n fuente f

plaudits ['plɔːdɪts] npl aplausos mpl

plausibility [plɔːzɪ'bɪlɪtɪ] n verosimilitud f, credibilidad f

plausible ['plɔːzɪbl] adj verosímil; (person) convincente

play [pleɪ] n (gen) juego; (Theat) obra ■ vt (game) jugar; (instrument) tocar; (Theat) representar; (: part) hacer el papel de; (fig) desempeñar ■ vi jugar; (frolic) juguetear; **to ~ safe** ir a lo seguro; **to bring** or **call into ~** poner en juego; **to ~ a trick on sb** gastar una broma a algn; **they're playing at soldiers** están jugando a (los) soldados; **to ~ for time** (fig) tratar de ganar tiempo; **to ~ into sb's hands** (fig) hacerle el juego a algn; **a smile played on his lips** una sonrisa le bailaba en los labios

▸ **play about, play around** vi (person) hacer el tonto; **to ~ about** or **around with** (fiddle with) juguetear con; (idea) darle vueltas a

▸ **play along** vi: **to ~ along with** seguirle el juego a ■ vt: **to ~ sb along** (fig) jugar con algn

▸ **play back** vt poner

▸ **play down** vt quitar importancia a

▸ **play on** vt fus (sb's feelings, credulity) aprovecharse de; **to ~ on sb's nerves** atacarle los nervios a algn

▸ **play up** vi (cause trouble) dar guerra

playact ['pleɪækt] vi (fig) hacer comedia or teatro

play-acting ['pleɪæktɪŋ] n teatro

playboy ['pleɪbɔɪ] n playboy m

player ['pleɪəʳ] n jugador(a) m(f); (Theat) actor m, actriz f; (Mus) músico(-a) m(f)

playful ['pleɪful] adj juguetón(-ona)

playground ['pleɪgraund] n (in school) patio de recreo

playgroup ['pleɪgruːp] n jardín m de infancia

playing card ['pleɪɪŋ-] n naipe m, carta

playing field n campo de deportes

playmaker ['pleɪmeɪkəʳ] n (Sport) jugador encargado de facilitar buenas jugadas a sus compañeros

playmate ['pleɪmeɪt] n compañero(-a) de juego

play-off ['pleɪɔf] n (Sport) (partido de) desempate m

playpen ['pleɪpɛn] n corral m

playroom ['pleɪruːm] n cuarto de juego

playschool ['pleɪskuːl] n = **playgroup**

plaything ['pleɪθɪŋ] n juguete m

playtime ['pleɪtaɪm] n (Scol) (hora de) recreo

playwright ['pleɪraɪt] n dramaturgo(-a)

plc abbr (Brit: = public limited company) S.A.

plea [pliː] n (request) súplica, petición f; (excuse) pretexto, disculpa; (Law) alegato, defensa

plea bargaining n (Law) acuerdo entre fiscal y defensor para agilizar los trámites judiciales

plead [pliːd] vt (Law): **to ~ sb's case** defender a alguien; (give as excuse) poner como pretexto ■ vi (Law) declararse; (beg): **to ~ with sb** suplicar or rogar a algn; **to ~ guilty/not guilty** (defendant) declararse culpable/ inocente; **to ~ for sth** (beg for) suplicar algo

pleasant ['plɛznt] adj agradable

pleasantly ['plɛzntlɪ] adv agradablemente

pleasantries ['plɛzntrɪz] npl (polite remarks) cortesías fpl; **to exchange ~** conversar amablemente

please [pliːz] vt (give pleasure to) dar gusto a, agradar ■ vi (think fit): **do as you ~** haz lo que quieras or lo que te dé la gana; **to ~ o.s.** hacer lo que le parezca; **~!** ¡por favor!; **~ yourself!** ¡haz lo que quieras!, ¡como quieras!; **~ don't cry!** ¡no llores! te lo ruego

pleased [pliːzd] adj (happy) alegre, contento; (satisfied): **~ (with)** satisfecho (de); **~ to meet you** (col) ¡encantado!, ¡tanto or mucho gusto!; **to be ~ (about sth)** alegrarse (de algo); **we are ~ to inform you that ...** tenemos el gusto de comunicarle que ...

pleasing ['pliːzɪŋ] adj agradable, grato

pleasurable ['plɛʒərəbl] adj agradable, grato

pleasurably ['plɛʒərəblɪ] adv agradablemente, gratamente

pleasure ['plɛʒəʳ] n placer m, gusto; (will) voluntad f ■ cpd de recreo; **"it's a ~"** "el gusto es mío"; **it's a ~ to see him** da gusto verle; **I have much ~ in informing you that ...** tengo el gran placer de comunicarles que ...; **with ~** con mucho or todo gusto; **is this trip for business or ~?** ¿este viaje es de negocios o de placer?

pleasure cruise n crucero de placer

pleasure ground n parque m de atracciones

pleasure-seeking ['plɛʒəsiːkɪŋ] adj hedonista

pleat [pliːt] n pliegue m

pleb [plɛb] n: **the plebs** la gente baja, la plebe

plebeian [plɪˈbiːən] n plebeyo(-a) ■ adj plebeyo; (pej) ordinario
plebiscite [ˈplɛbɪsɪt] n plebiscito
plectrum [ˈplɛktrəm] n plectro
pledge [plɛdʒ] n (object) prenda; (promise) promesa, voto ■ vt (pawn) empeñar; (promise) prometer; **to ~ support for sb** prometer su apoyo a algn; **to ~ sb to secrecy** hacer jurar a algn que guardará el secreto
plenary [ˈpliːnərɪ] adj: **in ~ session** en sesión plenaria
plentiful [ˈplɛntɪful] adj copioso, abundante
plenty [ˈplɛntɪ] n abundancia; **~ of** mucho(s)(-a(s)); **we've got ~ of time to get there** tenemos tiempo de sobra para llegar
plethora [ˈplɛθərə] n plétora
pleurisy [ˈpluərɪsɪ] n pleuresía
pliability [plaɪəˈbɪlɪtɪ] n flexibilidad f
pliable [ˈplaɪəbl] adj flexible
pliers [ˈplaɪəz] npl alicates mpl, tenazas fpl
plight [plaɪt] n condición f or situación f difícil
plimsolls [ˈplɪmsəlz] npl (Brit) zapatillas fpl de tenis
plinth [plɪnθ] n plinto
PLO n abbr (= Palestine Liberation Organization) OLP f
plod [plɔd] vi caminar con paso pesado; (fig) trabajar laboriosamente
plodder [ˈplɔdər] n trabajador(a) diligente pero lento/a
plodding [ˈplɔdɪŋ] adj (student) empollón(-ona); (worker) más aplicado que brillante
plonk [plɔŋk] (col) n (Brit: wine) vino peleón ■ vt: **to ~ sth down** dejar caer algo
plot [plɔt] n (scheme) complot m, conjura; (of story, play) argumento; (of land) terreno, parcela ■ vt (mark out) trazar; (conspire) tramar, urdir ■ vi conspirar; **a vegetable ~** un cuadro de hortalizas
plotter [ˈplɔtər] n (instrument) trazador m (de gráficos)
plotting [ˈplɔtɪŋ] n conspiración f, intrigas fpl
plough, plow (US) [plau] n arado ■ vt (earth) arar
▶ **plough back** vt (Comm) reinvertir
▶ **plough through** vt fus (crowd) abrirse paso a la fuerza por
ploughing [ˈplauɪŋ] n labranza
ploughman [ˈplaumən] n: **~'s lunch** pan m con queso y cebolla
plow [plau] (US) = **plough**
ploy [plɔɪ] n truco, estratagema
pluck [plʌk] vt (fruit) coger (SP), recoger (LAm); (musical instrument) puntear; (bird) desplumar ■ n valor m, ánimo; **to ~ up courage** hacer

de tripas corazón; **to ~ one's eyebrows** depilarse las cejas
plucky [ˈplʌkɪ] adj valiente
plug [plʌg] n tapón m; (Elec) enchufe m, clavija; (Aut: also: **spark(ing) plug**) bujía ■ vt (hole) tapar; (col: advertise) dar publicidad a; **to give sb/sth a ~** dar publicidad a algn/algo; **to ~ a lead into a socket** enchufar un hilo en una toma
▶ **plug in** vt, vi (Elec) enchufar
plughole [ˈplʌghəul] n desagüe m
plum [plʌm] n (fruit) ciruela; (also: **plum job**) chollo
plumage [ˈpluːmɪdʒ] n plumaje m
plumb [plʌm] adj vertical ■ n plomo ■ adv (exactly) exactamente, en punto ■ vt sondar; (fig) sondear
▶ **plumb in** vt (washing machine) conectar
plumber [ˈplʌmər] n fontanero(-a), plomero(-a) (LAm)
plumbing [ˈplʌmɪŋ] n (trade) fontanería, plomería (LAm); (piping) cañerías
plume [pluːm] n (gen) pluma; (on helmet) penacho
plummet [ˈplʌmɪt] vi: **to ~ (down)** caer a plomo
plump [plʌmp] adj rechoncho, rollizo ■ vt: **to ~ sth (down) on** dejar caer algo en
▶ **plump for** vt fus (col: choose) optar por
▶ **plump up** vt ahuecar
plumpness [ˈplʌmpnɪs] n gordura
plunder [ˈplʌndər] n pillaje m; (loot) botín m ■ vt saquear, pillar
plunge [plʌndʒ] n zambullida ■ vt sumergir, hundir ■ vi (fall) caer; (dive) saltar; (person) arrojarse; (sink) hundirse; **to take the ~** lanzarse; **to ~ a room into darkness** sumir una habitación en la oscuridad
plunger [ˈplʌndʒər] n émbolo; (for drain) desatascador m
plunging [ˈplʌndʒɪŋ] adj (neckline) escotado
pluperfect [pluːˈpəːfɪkt] n pluscuamperfecto
plural [ˈpluərl] n plural m
plus [plʌs] n (also: **plus sign**) signo más; (fig) punto a favor ■ adj: **a ~ factor** (fig) un factor m a favor ■ prep más, y, además de; **ten/twenty ~** más de diez/veinte
plush [plʌʃ] adj de felpa
plutonium [pluːˈtəunɪəm] n plutonio
ply [plaɪ] vt (a trade) ejercer ■ vi (ship) ir y venir; (for hire) ofrecerse (para alquilar); **three ~** (wool) de tres cabos; **to ~ sb with drink** no dejar de ofrecer copas a algn
plywood [ˈplaɪwud] n madera contrachapada
PM n abbr (Brit) see **Prime Minister**
p.m. adv abbr (= post meridiem) de la tarde or noche

PMS *n abbr* (= *premenstrual syndrome*) SPM *m*
PMT *n abbr* (= *premenstrual tension*) SPM *m*
pneumatic [nju:'mætɪk] *adj* neumático
pneumatic drill *n* taladradora neumática
pneumonia [nju:'məunɪə] *n* pulmonía, neumonía
PO *n abbr* (= *Post Office*) Correos *mpl*; (*Naut*) = **petty officer**
po *abbr* = **postal order**
POA *n abbr* (*Brit*) = **Prison Officers' Association**
poach [pəutʃ] *vt* (*cook*) escalfar; (*steal*) cazar/pescar en vedado ■ *vi* cazar/pescar en vedado
poached [pəutʃt] *adj* (*egg*) escalfado
poacher ['pəutʃər] *n* cazador(a) *m(f)* furtivo(-a)
poaching ['pəutʃɪŋ] *n* caza/pesca furtiva
PO Box *n abbr see* **Post Office Box**
pocket ['pɔkɪt] *n* bolsillo; (*of air, Geo*) bolsa; (*fig*) bolsa; (*Billiards*) tronera ■ *vt* meter en el bolsillo; (*steal*) embolsarse; (*Billiards*) entronerar; **breast ~** bolsillo de pecho; **~ of resistance** foco de resistencia; **~ of warm air** bolsa de aire caliente; **to be out of ~** salir perdiendo; **to be £5 in/out of ~** salir ganando/perdiendo 5 libras
pocketbook ['pɔkɪtbuk] *n* (*US: wallet*) cartera; (: *handbag*) bolso
pocketful ['pɔkɪtful] *n* bolsillo lleno
pocket knife *n* navaja
pocket money *n* asignación *f*
pockmarked ['pɔkmɑ:kt] *adj* (*face*) picado de viruelas
pod [pɔd] *n* vaina
podcast ['pɔdkɑ:st] *n* podcast *m* ■ *vi* podcastear
podcasting ['pɔdkɑ:stɪŋ] *n* podcasting *m*
podgy ['pɔdʒɪ] *adj* gordinflón(-ona)
podiatrist [pɔ'di:ətrɪst] *n* (*US*) podólogo(-a)
podiatry [pɔ'di:ətrɪ] *n* (*US*) podología
podium ['pəudɪəm] *n* podio
POE *n abbr* = **port of embarkation; port of entry**
poem ['pəuɪm] *n* poema *m*
poet ['pəuɪt] *n* poeta *m/f*
poetic [pəu'ɛtɪk] *adj* poético
poet laureate [-'lɔ:rɪɪt] *n* poeta *m* laureado; *ver nota*

● oficiales, aunque hoy día esto es poco
● frecuente. El primer poeta así distinguido
● fue Ben Jonson, en 1616.

poetry ['pəuɪtrɪ] *n* poesía
poignant ['pɔɪnjənt] *adj* conmovedor(a)
poignantly ['pɔɪnjəntlɪ] *adv* de modo conmovedor
point [pɔɪnt] *n* punto; (*tip*) punta; (*purpose*) fin *m*, propósito; (*Brit Elec: also:* **power point**) toma de corriente, enchufe *m*; (*use*) utilidad *f*; (*significant part*) lo esencial; (*place*) punto, lugar *m*; (*also:* **decimal point**): **2 ~ 3 (2.3)** dos coma tres (2,3) ■ *vt* (*gun etc*): **to ~ sth at sb** apuntar con algo a algn ■ *vi* señalar con el dedo; **points** *npl* (*Aut*) contactos *mpl*; (*Rail*) agujas *fpl*; **to be on the ~ of doing sth** estar a punto de hacer algo; **to make a ~ of doing sth** poner empeño en hacer algo; **to get the ~** comprender; **to come to the ~** ir al meollo; **there's no ~ (in doing)** no tiene sentido (hacer); **~ of departure** (*also fig*) punto de partida; **~ of order** cuestión *f* de procedimiento; **~ of sale** (*Comm*) punto de venta; **~-of-sale advertising** publicidad *f* en el punto de venta; **the train stops at Carlisle and all points south** el tren para en Carlisle, y en todas las estaciones al sur; **when it comes to the ~** a la hora de la verdad; **in ~ of fact** en realidad; **that's the whole ~!** ¡de eso se trata!; **to be beside the ~** no venir al caso; **you've got a ~ there!** ¡tienes razón!
▶ **point out** *vt* señalar
▶ **point to** *vt fus* indicar con el dedo; (*fig*) indicar, señalar
point-blank ['pɔɪnt'blæŋk] *adv* (*also:* **at point-blank range**) a quemarropa
point duty *n* (*Brit*) control *m* de circulación
pointed ['pɔɪntɪd] *adj* (*shape*) puntiagudo, afilado; (*remark*) intencionado
pointedly ['pɔɪntɪdlɪ] *adv* intencionadamente
pointer ['pɔɪntər] *n* (*stick*) puntero; (*needle*) aguja, indicador *m*; (*clue*) indicación *f*, pista; (*advice*) consejo
pointless ['pɔɪntlɪs] *adj* sin sentido
pointlessly ['pɔɪntlɪslɪ] *adv* inútilmente, sin motivo
point of view *n* punto de vista
poise [pɔɪz] *n* (*of head, body*) porte *m*; (*calmness*) aplomo
poised [pɔɪzd] *adj* (*in temperament*) sereno
poison ['pɔɪzn] *n* veneno ■ *vt* envenenar
poisoning ['pɔɪznɪŋ] *n* envenenamiento
poisonous ['pɔɪznəs] *adj* venenoso; (*fumes etc*) tóxico; (*fig: ideas, literature*) pernicioso; (: *rumours, individual*) nefasto

p

poke [pəuk] vt (fire) hurgar, atizar; (jab with finger, stick etc) dar; (Comput) almacenar; (put): **to ~ sth in(to)** introducir algo en ■ n (jab) empujoncito; (with elbow) codazo; **to ~ one's head out of the window** asomar la cabeza por la ventana; **to ~ fun at sb** ridiculizar a algn; **to give the fire a ~** atizar el fuego
▶ **poke about** vi fisgonear

poker ['pəukə^r] n atizador m; (Cards) póker m

poker-faced ['pəukə'feist] adj de cara impasible

poky ['pəuki] adj estrecho

Poland ['pəulənd] n Polonia

polar ['pəulə^r] adj polar

polar bear n oso polar

polarization [pəulərai'zeiʃən] n polarización f

polarize ['pəuləraiz] vt polarizar

Pole [pəul] n polaco(-a)

pole [pəul] n palo; (Geo) polo; (Tel) poste m; (flagpole) asta; (tent pole) mástil m

poleaxe ['pəulæks] vt (fig) desnucar

pole bean n (US) judía trepadora

polecat ['pəulkæt] n (Brit) turón m; (US) mofeta

Pol. Econ. ['pɔlikɔn] n abbr = **political economy**

polemic [pɔ'lɛmik] n polémica

polemicist [pɔ'lɛmisist] n polemista m/f

pole star n estrella polar

pole vault n salto con pértiga

police [pə'li:s] n policía ■ vt (streets, city, frontier) vigilar

police car n coche-patrulla m

police constable n (Brit) guardia m, policía m

police department n (US) policía

police force n cuerpo de policía

policeman [pə'li:smən] n guardia m, policía m, agente m (LAm)

police officer n guardia m, policía m

police record n: **to have a ~** tener antecedentes penales

police state n estado policial

police station n comisaría

policewoman [pə'li:swumən] n mujer f policía

policy ['pɔlisi] n política; (also: **insurance policy**) póliza; (of newspaper, company) política; **it is our ~ to do that** tenemos por norma hacer eso; **to take out a ~** sacar una póliza, hacerse un seguro

policy holder n asegurado(-a)

policy-making ['pɔlisimeikiŋ] n elaboración f de directrices generales

policy-making body n organismo encargado de elaborar las directrices generales

polio ['pəuliəu] n polio f

Polish ['pəuliʃ] adj polaco ■ n (Ling) polaco

polish ['pɔliʃ] n (for shoes) betún m; (for floor) cera (de lustrar); (for nails) esmalte m; (shine) brillo, lustre m; (fig: refinement) refinamiento ■ vt (shoes) limpiar; (make shiny) pulir, sacar brillo a; (fig: improve) perfeccionar, refinar
▶ **polish off** vt (work) terminar; (food) despachar
▶ **polish up** vt (shoes, furniture etc) limpiar, sacar brillo a; (fig: language) perfeccionar

polished ['pɔliʃt] adj (fig: person) refinado

polite [pə'lait] adj cortés, atento; (formal) correcto; **it's not ~ to do that** es de mala educación hacer eso

politely [pə'laitli] adv cortésmente

politeness [pə'laitnis] n cortesía

politic ['pɔlitik] adj prudente

political [pə'litikl] adj político

political asylum n asilo político

politically [pə'litikəli] adv políticamente

politically correct adj políticamente correcto

politician [pɔli'tiʃən] n político(-a)

politics ['pɔlitiks] n política

polka ['pɔlkə] n polca

polka dot n lunar m

poll [pəul] n (votes) votación f, votos mpl; (also: **opinion poll**) sondeo, encuesta ■ vt (votes) obtener; (in opinion poll) encuestar; **to go to the polls** (voters) votar; (government) acudir a las urnas

pollen ['pɔlən] n polen m

pollen count n índice m de polen

pollination [pɔli'neiʃən] n polinización f

polling ['pəuliŋ] n (Brit Pol) votación f; (Tel) interrogación f

polling booth n cabina de votar

polling day n día m de elecciones

polling station n centro electoral

pollster ['pəulstə^r] n (person) encuestador(a) m(f); (organization) empresa de encuestas or sondeos

poll tax n (Brit) contribución f municipal (no progresiva)

pollutant [pə'lu:tənt] n (agente m) contaminante m

pollute [pə'lu:t] vt contaminar

pollution [pə'lu:ʃən] n contaminación f, polución f

polo ['pəuləu] n (sport) polo

polo-neck ['pəuləunɛk] adj de cuello vuelto ■ n (sweater) suéter m de cuello vuelto

poly ['pɔli] n abbr (Brit) = **polytechnic**

poly... [pɔli] pref poli...

poly bag n (Brit col) bolsa de plástico

polyester [pɔli'ɛstə^r] n poliéster m

polyethylene [pɔli'ɛθili:n] n (US) polietileno

polygamy [pə'lıgəmı] *n* poligamia
polygraph ['pɔlıgrɑːf] *n* polígrafo
Polynesia [pɔlı'niːzıə] *n* Polinesia
Polynesian [pɔlı'niːzıən] *adj, n* polinesio(-a) *m(f)*
polyp ['pɔlıp] *n* (*Med*) pólipo
polystyrene [pɔlı'staırıːn] *n* poliestireno
polytechnic [pɔlı'tɛknık] *n* escuela politécnica
polythene ['pɔlıθiːn] *n* (*Brit*) polietileno
polythene bag *n* bolsa de plástico
polyurethane [pɔlı'juərıθeın] *n* poliuretano
pomegranate ['pɔmıgrænıt] *n* granada
pommel ['pɔml] *n* pomo ∎ *vt* = **pummel**
pomp [pɔmp] *n* pompa
pompom ['pɔmpɔm] *n* borla
pompous ['pɔmpəs] *adj* pomposo; (*person*) presumido
pond [pɔnd] *n* (*natural*) charca; (*artificial*) estanque *m*
ponder ['pɔndəʳ] *vt* meditar
ponderous ['pɔndərəs] *adj* pesado
pong [pɔŋ] *n* (*Brit col*) peste *f* ∎ *vi* (*Brit col*) apestar
pontiff ['pɔntıf] *n* pontífice *m*
pontificate [pɔn'tıfıkeıt] *vi* (*fig*): **to ~ (about)** pontificar (sobre)
pontoon [pɔn'tuːn] *n* pontón *m*; (*Brit: card game*) veintiuna
pony ['pəunı] *n* poney *m*, potro
ponytail ['pəunıteıl] *n* coleta, cola de caballo
pony trekking *n* (*Brit*) excursión *f* a caballo
poodle ['puːdl] *n* caniche *m*
pool [puːl] *n* (*natural*) charca; (*pond*) estanque *m*; (*also:* **swimming pool**) piscina, alberca (*LAm*); (*billiards*) billar *m* americano; (*Comm: consortium*) consorcio; (: *US: monopoly trust*) trust *m* ∎ *vt* juntar; **typing ~** servicio de mecanografía; (**football**) **pools** *npl* quinielas *fpl*
poor [puəʳ] *adj* pobre; (*bad*) malo ∎ *npl*: **the ~** los pobres
poorly ['puəlı] *adj* mal, enfermo
pop [pɔp] *n* ¡pum!; (*sound*) ruido seco; (*Mus*) (música) pop *m*; (*US col: father*) papá *m*; (*col: drink*) gaseosa ∎ *vt* (*burst*) hacer reventar ∎ *vi* reventar; (*cork*) saltar; **she popped her head out (of the window)** sacó de repente la cabeza (por la ventana)
▸ **pop in** *vi* entrar un momento
▸ **pop out** *vi* salir un momento
▸ **pop up** *vi* aparecer inesperadamente
pop concert *n* concierto pop
popcorn ['pɔpkɔːn] *n* palomitas *fpl* (de maíz)
pope [pəup] *n* papa *m*
poplar ['pɔpləʳ] *n* álamo
poplin ['pɔplın] *n* popelina

popper ['pɔpəʳ] *n* corchete *m*, botón *m* automático
poppy ['pɔpı] *n* amapola; *see also* **Remembrance Sunday**
poppycock ['pɔpıkɔk] *n* (*col*) tonterías *fpl*
Popsicle® ['pɔpsıkl] *n* (*US*) polo
populace ['pɔpjuləs] *n* pueblo
popular ['pɔpjuləʳ] *adj* popular; **a ~ song** una canción popular; **to be ~ (with)** (*person*) caer bien (a); (*decision*) ser popular (entre)
popularity [pɔpju'lærıtı] *n* popularidad *f*
popularize ['pɔpjuləraız] *vt* popularizar; (*disseminate*) vulgarizar
populate ['pɔpjuleıt] *vt* poblar
population [pɔpju'leıʃən] *n* población *f*
population explosion *n* explosión *f* demográfica
populous ['pɔpjuləs] *adj* populoso
pop-up menu ['pɔpʌp-] *n* (*Comput*) menú *m* emergente
porcelain ['pɔːslın] *n* porcelana
porch [pɔːtʃ] *n* pórtico, entrada
porcupine ['pɔːkjupaın] *n* puerco *m* espín
pore [pɔːʳ] *n* poro ∎ *vi*: **to ~ over** enfrascarse en
pork [pɔːk] *n* (carne *f* de) cerdo *or* chancho (*LAm*)
pork chop *n* chuleta de cerdo
porn [pɔːn] *adj* (*col*) porno *inv* ∎ *n* porno
pornographic [pɔːnə'græfık] *adj* pornográfico
pornography [pɔː'nɔgrəfı] *n* pornografía
porous ['pɔːrəs] *adj* poroso
porpoise ['pɔːpəs] *n* marsopa
porridge ['pɔrıdʒ] *n* gachas *fpl* de avena
port [pɔːt] *n* (*harbour*) puerto; (*Naut: left side*) babor *m*; (*wine*) oporto; (*Comput*) puerta, puerto, port *m*; **~ of call** puerto de escala
portable ['pɔːtəbl] *adj* portátil
portal ['pɔːtl] *n* puerta (grande), portalón *m*
port authorities *npl* autoridades *fpl* portuarias
portcullis [pɔːt'kʌlıs] *n* rastrillo
portend [pɔː'tɛnd] *vt* presagiar, anunciar
portent ['pɔːtɛnt] *n* presagio, augurio
porter ['pɔːtəʳ] *n* (*for luggage*) maletero; (*doorkeeper*) portero(-a), conserje *m/f*; (*US Rail*) mozo de los coches-cama
portfolio [pɔːt'fəulıəu] *n* (*case, of artist*) cartera, carpeta; (*Pol, Finance*) cartera
porthole ['pɔːthəul] *n* portilla
portico ['pɔːtıkəu] *n* pórtico
portion ['pɔːʃən] *n* porción *f*; (*helping*) ración *f*
portly ['pɔːtlı] *adj* corpulento
portrait ['pɔːtreıt] *n* retrato
portray [pɔː'treı] *vt* retratar; (*in writing*) representar

p

713

portrayal [pɔːˈtreɪəl] *n* representación *f*
Portugal [ˈpɔːtjʊgl] *n* Portugal *m*
Portuguese [pɔːtjuˈgiːz] *adj* portugués(-esa)
■ *n pl inv* portugués(-esa) *m(f)*; (*Ling*)
portugués *m*
Portuguese man-of-war [-mænəuˈwɔːʳ] *n*
(*jellyfish*) *especie de medusa*
pose [pəuz] *n* postura, actitud *f*; (*pej*)
afectación *f*, pose *f* ■ *vi* posar; (*pretend*): **to ~
as** hacerse pasar por ■ *vt* (*question*) plantear;
to strike a ~ tomar *or* adoptar una pose *or*
actitud
poser [ˈpəuzəʳ] *n* problema *m*/pregunta
difícil; (*person*) = **poseur**
poseur [pəuˈzəːʳ] *n* presumido(-a), persona
afectada
posh [pɔʃ] *adj* (*col*) elegante, de lujo ■ *adv*
(*col*): **to talk ~** hablar con acento afectado
position [pəˈzɪʃən] *n* posición *f*; (*job*) puesto
■ *vt* colocar; **to be in a ~ to do sth** estar en
condiciones de hacer algo
positive [ˈpɔzɪtɪv] *adj* positivo; (*certain*)
seguro; (*definite*) definitivo; **we look
forward to a ~ reply** (*Comm*) esperamos que
pueda darnos una respuesta en firme;
~ cash flow (*Comm*) flujo positivo de efectivo
positively [ˈpɔzɪtɪvlɪ] *adv* (*affirmatively,
enthusiastically*) de forma positiva; (*col: really*)
absolutamente
posse [ˈpɔsɪ] *n* (*US*) pelotón *m*
possess [pəˈzɛs] *vt* poseer; **like one
possessed** como un poseído; **whatever can
have possessed you?** ¿cómo se te ocurrió?
possessed [pəˈzɛst] *adj* poseso, poseído
possession [pəˈzɛʃən] *n* posesión *f*; **to take ~
of sth** tomar posesión de algo
possessive [pəˈzɛsɪv] *adj* posesivo
possessiveness [pəˈzɛsɪvnɪs] *n* posesividad *f*
possessor [pəˈzɛsəʳ] *n* poseedor(a) *m(f)*,
dueño(-a)
possibility [pɔsɪˈbɪlɪtɪ] *n* posibilidad *f*; **he's
a ~ for the part** es uno de los posibles para
el papel
possible [ˈpɔsɪbl] *adj* posible; **as big as ~**
lo más grande posible; **it is ~ to do it** es
posible hacerlo; **as far as ~** en la medida
de lo posible; **a ~ candidate** un(a) posible
candidato(-a)
possibly [ˈpɔsɪblɪ] *adv* (*perhaps*) posiblemente,
tal vez; **I cannot ~ come** me es imposible
venir; **could you ~ ...?** ¿podrías ...?
post [pəust] *n* (*Brit: letters, delivery*) correo;
(*job, situation*) puesto; (*trading post*) factoría;
(*pole*) poste *m*; (*on internet forum*) anuncio, post
m ■ *vt* (*Brit: send by post*) mandar por correo;
(: *put in mailbox*) echar al correo; (*Mil*) apostar;
(*bills*) fijar, pegar; (*to internet*) colgar; (*Brit:*

appoint): **to ~ to** destinar a; **by ~** por correo;
by return of ~ a vuelta de correo; **to keep sb
posted** tener a algn al corriente
post ... [pəust] *pref* post..., pos...; **post 1950**
pos(t) 1950
postage [ˈpəustɪdʒ] *n* porte *m*, franqueo
postage stamp *n* sello (de correo)
postal [ˈpəustl] *adj* postal, de correos
postal order *n* giro postal
postbag [ˈpəustbæg] *n* (*Brit*)
correspondencia, cartas *fpl*
postbox [ˈpəustbɔks] *n* (*Brit*) buzón *m*
postcard [ˈpəustkɑːd] *n* (tarjeta) postal *f*
postcode [ˈpəustkəud] *n* (*Brit*) código postal
postdate [pəustˈdeɪt] *vt* (*cheque*) poner fecha
adelantada a
poster [ˈpəustəʳ] *n* cartel *m*, afiche *m* (*LAm*)
poste restante [pəustˈrɛstɔ̃nt] *n* (*Brit*) lista
de correos
posterior [pɔsˈtɪərɪəʳ] *n* (*col*) trasero
posterity [pɔsˈtɛrɪtɪ] *n* posteridad *f*
poster paint *n* pintura al agua
post-free [pəustˈfriː] *adj* (*con*) porte pagado
postgraduate [ˈpəustˈgrædjuɪt] *n*
posgraduado(-a)
posthumous [ˈpɔstjuməs] *adj* póstumo
posthumously [ˈpɔstjuməslɪ] *adv*
póstumamente, con carácter póstumo
posting [ˈpəustɪŋ] *n* destino
postman [ˈpəustmən] *n* cartero
postmark [ˈpəustmɑːk] *n* matasellos *m inv*
postmaster [ˈpəustmɑːstəʳ] *n* administrador
m de correos
Postmaster General *n* director *m* general
de correos
postmistress [ˈpəustmɪstrɪs] *n*
administradora de correos
post-mortem [pəustˈmɔːtəm] *n* autopsia
postnatal [ˈpəustˈneɪtl] *adj* postnatal,
postparto
post office *n* (*building*) (oficina de)
correos *m*; (*organization*): **the Post Office**
Administración *f* General de Correos
Post Office Box *n* apartado postal, casilla de
correos (*LAm*)
post-paid [ˈpəustˈpeɪd] *adj* porte pagado
postpone [pəsˈpəun] *vt* aplazar, postergar
(*LAm*)
postponement [pəsˈpəunmənt] *n*
aplazamiento
postscript [ˈpəustskrɪpt] *n* posdata
postulate [ˈpɔstjuleɪt] *vt* postular
posture [ˈpɔstʃəʳ] *n* postura, actitud *f*
postwar [ˈpəustˈwɔːʳ] *adj* de la posguerra
posy [ˈpəuzɪ] *n* ramillete *m* (de flores)
pot [pɔt] *n* (*for cooking*) olla; (*for flowers*)
maceta; (*for jam*) tarro, pote *m* (*LAm*); (*piece of*

pottery) cacharro; (*col: marijuana*) costo ■ *vt*
(*plant*) poner en tiesto; (*conserve*) conservar
(en tarros); **pots of** (*col*) montones de; **to go
to ~** (*col: work, performance*) irse al traste
potash ['pɔtæʃ] *n* potasa
potassium [pə'tæsɪəm] *n* potasio
potato (*pl* **potatoes**) [pə'teɪtəu] *n* patata,
papa (*LAm*)
potato crisps, potato chips (US) *npl*
patatas *fpl* or papas *fpl* (*LAm*)
potato peeler *n* pelapatatas *m inv*
potbellied ['pɔtbelɪd] *adj* (*from overeating*)
barrigón(-ona); (*from malnutrition*) con el
vientre hinchado
potency ['pəutnsɪ] *n* potencia
potent ['pəutnt] *adj* potente, poderoso;
(*drink*) fuerte
potentate ['pəutnteɪt] *n* potentado
potential [pə'tɛnʃl] *adj* potencial, posible
■ *n* potencial *m*; **to have ~** prometer
potentially [pə'tɛnʃəlɪ] *adv* en potencia
pothole ['pɔthəul] *n* (*in road*) bache *m*; (*Brit:
underground*) gruta
potholer ['pɔthəulər] *n* (*Brit*) espeleólogo(-a)
potholing ['pɔthəulɪŋ] *n* (*Brit*): **to go ~**
dedicarse a la espeleología
potion ['pəuʃən] *n* poción *f*, pócima
potluck [pɔt'lʌk] *n*: **to take ~** conformarse
con lo que haya
pot roast *n* carne *f* asada
potshot ['pɔtʃɔt] *n*: **to take a ~ at sth** tirar a
algo sin apuntar
potted ['pɔtɪd] *adj* (*food*) en conserva; (*plant*)
en tiesto or maceta; (*fig: shortened*) resumido
potter ['pɔtər] *n* alfarero(-a) ■ *vi*: **to ~
around, ~ about** entretenerse haciendo
cosillas; **to ~ round the house** estar en
casa haciendo cosillas; **~'s wheel** torno de
alfarero
pottery ['pɔtərɪ] *n* cerámica, alfarería; **a
piece of ~** un objeto de cerámica
potty ['pɔtɪ] *adj* (*col: mad*) chiflado ■ *n* orinal
m de niño
potty-trained ['pɔtɪtreɪnd] *adj* que ya no
necesita pañales
pouch [pautʃ] *n* (*Zool*) bolsa; (*for tobacco*)
petaca
pouf, pouffe [pu:f] *n* (*stool*) pouf *m*
poultry ['pəultrɪ] *n* aves *fpl* de corral; (*dead*)
pollos *mpl*
poultry farm *n* granja avícola
poultry farmer *n* avicultor(-a) *m(f)*
pounce [pauns] *vi*: **to ~ on** precipitarse sobre
■ *n* salto, ataque *m*
pound [paund] *n* libra; (*for dogs*) perrera;
(*for cars*) depósito ■ *vt* (*beat*) golpear; (*crush*)
machacar ■ *vi* (*beat*) dar golpes; **half a ~**

media libra; **a one ~ note** un billete de una
libra
pounding ['paundɪŋ] *n*: **to take a ~** (*team*)
recibir una paliza
pound sterling *n* libra esterlina
pour [pɔːr] *vt* echar; (*tea*) servir ■ *vi* correr,
fluir; (*rain*) llover a cántaros
▸ **pour away, pour off** *vt* vaciar, verter
▸ **pour in** *vi* (*people*) entrar en tropel; **to
come pouring in** (*water*) entrar a raudales;
(*letters*) llegar a montones; (*cars, people*) llegar
en tropel
▸ **pour out** *vi* (*people*) salir en tropel ■ *vt*
(*drink*) echar, servir
pouring ['pɔːrɪŋ] *adj*: **~ rain** lluvia torrencial
pout [paut] *vi* hacer pucheros
poverty ['pɔvətɪ] *n* pobreza, miseria; (*fig*)
falta, escasez *f*
poverty line *n*: **below the ~** por debajo del
umbral de pobreza
poverty-stricken ['pɔvətɪstrɪkn] *adj*
necesitado
poverty trap *n* trampa de la pobreza
POW *n abbr* = **prisoner of war**
powder ['paudər] *n* polvo; (*also:* **face powder**)
polvos *mpl*; (*also:* **gun powder**) pólvora ■ *vt*
empolvar; **to ~ one's face** ponerse polvos;
to ~ one's nose empolvarse la nariz, ponerse
polvos; (*euphemism*) ir al baño
powder compact *n* polvera
powdered milk ['paudəd-] *n* leche *f* en polvo
powder keg *n* (*fig*) polvorín *m*
powder puff *n* borla (para empolvarse)
powder room *n* aseos *mpl*
powdery ['paudərɪ] *adj* polvoriento
power ['pauər] *n* poder *m*; (*strength*) fuerza;
(*nation*) potencia; (*drive*) empuje *m*; (*Tech*)
potencia; (*Elec*) energía ■ *vt* impulsar; **to be
in ~** (*Pol*) estar en el poder; **to do all in one's
~ to help sb** hacer todo lo posible por ayudar
a algn; **the world powers** las potencias
mundiales
powerboat ['pauəbəut] *n* lancha a motor
power cut *n* (*Brit*) apagón *m*
powered ['pauəd] *adj*: **~ by** impulsado por;
nuclear-~ submarine submarino nuclear
power failure *n* = **power cut**
powerful ['pauəful] *adj* poderoso; (*engine*)
potente; (*strong*) fuerte; (*play, speech*)
conmovedor(a)
powerhouse ['pauəhaus] *n* (*fig: person*) fuerza
motriz; **a ~ of ideas** una cantera de ideas
powerless ['pauəlɪs] *adj* impotente, ineficaz
power line *n* línea de conducción eléctrica
power of attorney *n* poder *m*, procuración *f*
power point *n* (*Brit*) enchufe *m*
power station *n* central *f* eléctrica

p

power steering n (Aut) dirección f asistida
powwow ['pauwau] n conferencia ■ vi
conferenciar
pp abbr (= per procurationem: by proxy) p.p.;
= **pages**
PPE n abbr (Brit Scol) = **philosophy, politics,
and economics**
PPS n abbr (= post postscriptum) posdata adicional;
(Brit: = Parliamentary Private Secretary) ayudante
de un ministro
PQ abbr (Canada) = **Province of Quebec**
PR n abbr see **proportional representation**;
(= public relations) relaciones fpl públicas
■ abbr (US) = **Puerto Rico**
Pr. abbr (= prince) P
practicability [præktɪkə'bɪlɪtɪ] n
factibilidad f
practicable ['præktɪkəbl] adj (scheme) factible
practical ['præktɪkl] adj práctico
practicality [præktɪ'kælɪtɪ] n (of situation etc)
aspecto práctico
practical joke n broma pesada
practically ['præktɪklɪ] adv (almost) casi,
prácticamente
practice ['præktɪs] n (habit) costumbre f;
(exercise) práctica; (training) adiestramiento;
(Med) clientela ■ vt, vi (US) = **practise**;
in ~ (in reality) en la práctica; **out of ~**
desentrenado; **to put sth into ~** poner algo
en práctica; **it's common ~** es bastante
corriente; **target ~** práctica de tiro; **he has a
small ~** (doctor) tiene pocos pacientes; **to set
up in ~ as** establecerse como
practise, practice (US) ['præktɪs] vt (carry
out) practicar; (profession) ejercer; (train at)
practicar ■ vi ejercer; (train) practicar
practised, (US) practiced ['præktɪst] adj
(person) experto; (performance) bien ensayado;
(liar) consumado; **with a ~ eye** con ojo
experto
practising, practicing (US) ['præktɪsɪŋ] adj
(Christian etc) practicante; (lawyer) que ejerce;
(homosexual) activo
practitioner [præk'tɪʃənəʳ] n practicante m/f;
(Med) médico(-a)
pragmatic [præg'mætɪk] adj pragmático
pragmatism ['prægmətɪzəm] n
pragmatismo
pragmatist ['prægmətɪst] n pragmatista m/f
Prague [prɑːg] n Praga
prairie ['prɛərɪ] n (US) pampa
praise [preɪz] n alabanza(s) f(pl), elogio(s)
m(pl)
praiseworthy ['preɪzwəːðɪ] adj loable
pram [præm] n (Brit) cochecito de niño
prance [prɑːns] vi (horse) hacer cabriolas
prank [præŋk] n travesura

prat [præt] n (Brit col) imbécil m/f
prattle ['prætl] vi parlotear; (child) balbucear
prawn [prɔːn] n gamba
pray [preɪ] vi rezar; **to ~ for forgiveness**
pedir perdón
prayer [prɛəʳ] n oración f, rezo; (entreaty)
ruego, súplica
prayer book n devocionario, misal m
pre- ['priː] pref pre..., ante-; **~1970** pre 1970
preach [priːtʃ] vi predicar
preacher ['priːtʃəʳ] n predicador(a) m(f); (US:
minister) pastor(a) m(f)
preamble [prɪ'æmbl] n preámbulo
prearrange [priːə'reɪndʒ] vt organizar or
acordar de antemano
prearrangement [priːə'reɪndʒmənt] n: **by ~**
por previo acuerdo
precarious [prɪ'kɛərɪəs] adj precario
precariously [prɪ'kɛərɪəslɪ] adv
precariamente
precaution [prɪ'kɔːʃən] n precaución f
precautionary [prɪ'kɔːʃənrɪ] adj (measure) de
precaución
precede [prɪ'siːd] vt, vi preceder
precedence ['prɛsɪdəns] n precedencia;
(priority) preferencia
precedent ['prɛsɪdənt] n precedente m;
to establish or **set a ~** sentar un precedente
preceding [prɪ'siːdɪŋ] adj precedente
precept ['priːsɛpt] n precepto
precinct ['priːsɪŋkt] n recinto; (US: district)
distrito, barrio; **precincts** npl recinto;
pedestrian ~ (Brit) zona peatonal; **shopping
~** (Brit) centro comercial
precious ['prɛʃəs] adj precioso; (treasured)
querido; (stylized) afectado ■ adv (col):
~ little/few muy poco/pocos; **your ~ dog**
(ironic) tu querido perro
precipice ['prɛsɪpɪs] n precipicio
precipitate adj [prɪ'sɪpɪtɪt] (hasty) precipitado
■ vt [prɪ'sɪpɪteɪt] precipitar
precipitation [prɪsɪpɪ'teɪʃən] n
precipitación f
precipitous [prɪ'sɪpɪtəs] adj (steep) escarpado;
(hasty) precipitado
précis ['preɪsiː] n resumen m
precise [prɪ'saɪs] adj preciso, exacto; (person)
escrupuloso
precisely [prɪ'saɪslɪ] adv exactamente,
precisamente
precision [prɪ'sɪʒən] n precisión f
preclude [prɪ'kluːd] vt excluir
precocious [prɪ'kəʊʃəs] adj precoz
preconceived [priːkən'siːvd] adj (idea)
preconcebido
preconception [priːkən'sɛpʃən] n (idea) idea
preconcebida

precondition [priːkənˈdɪʃən] *n* condición *f* previa
precursor [priːˈkəːsəʳ] *n* precursor(a) *m(f)*
predate [priːˈdeɪt] *vt* (*precede*) preceder
predator [ˈprɛdətəʳ] *n* depredador *m*
predatory [ˈprɛdətərɪ] *adj* depredador(a)
predecessor [ˈpriːdɪsesəʳ] *n* antecesor(a) *m(f)*
predestination [priːdɛstɪˈneɪʃən] *n* predestinación *f*
predestine [priːˈdɛstɪn] *vt* predestinar
predetermine [priːdɪˈtəːmɪn] *vt* predeterminar
predicament [prɪˈdɪkəmənt] *n* apuro
predicate [ˈprɛdɪkɪt] *n* predicado
predict [prɪˈdɪkt] *vt* predecir, pronosticar
predictable [prɪˈdɪktəbl] *adj* previsible
predictably [prɪˈdɪktəblɪ] *adv* (*behave, react*) de forma previsible; ~ **she didn't arrive** como era de prever, no llegó
prediction [prɪˈdɪkʃən] *n* pronóstico, predicción *f*
predispose [ˈpriːdɪsˈpəuz] *vt* predisponer
predominance [prɪˈdɔmɪnəns] *n* predominio
predominant [prɪˈdɔmɪnənt] *adj* predominante
predominantly [prɪˈdɔmɪnəntlɪ] *adv* en su mayoría
predominate [prɪˈdɔmɪneɪt] *vi* predominar
pre-eminent [priːˈɛmɪnənt] *adj* preeminente
pre-empt [priːˈɛmt] *vt* (*Brit*) adelantarse a
pre-emptive [priːˈɛmtɪv] *adj*: ~ **strike** ataque *m* preventivo
preen [priːn] *vt*: **to ~ itself** (*bird*) limpiarse las plumas; **to ~ o.s.** pavonearse
prefab [ˈpriːfæb] *n* casa prefabricada
prefabricated [priːˈfæbrɪkeɪtɪd] *adj* prefabricado
preface [ˈprɛfəs] *n* prefacio
prefect [ˈpriːfɛkt] *n* (*Brit: in school*) monitor(a) *m(f)*
prefer [prɪˈfəːʳ] *vt* preferir; (*Law: charges, complaint*) presentar; (*: action*) entablar; **to ~ coffee to tea** preferir el café al té
preferable [ˈprɛfrəbl] *adj* preferible
preferably [ˈprɛfrəblɪ] *adv* preferentemente, más bien
preference [ˈprɛfrəns] *n* preferencia; **in ~ to sth** antes que algo
preference shares *npl* acciones *fpl* privilegiadas
preferential [prɛfəˈrɛnʃəl] *adj* preferente
prefix [ˈpriːfɪks] *n* prefijo
pregnancy [ˈprɛgnənsɪ] *n* embarazo
pregnancy test *n* prueba del embarazo
pregnant [ˈprɛgnənt] *adj* embarazada; **3**

months ~ embarazada de tres meses; ~ **with meaning** cargado de significado
prehistoric [ˈpriːhɪsˈtɔrɪk] *adj* prehistórico
prehistory [priːˈhɪstərɪ] *n* prehistoria
prejudge [priːˈdʒʌdʒ] *vt* prejuzgar
prejudice [ˈprɛdʒudɪs] *n* (*bias*) prejuicio; (*harm*) perjuicio ■ *vt* (*bias*) predisponer; (*harm*) perjudicar; **to ~ sb in favour of/against** (*bias*) predisponer a algn a favor de/en contra de
prejudiced [ˈprɛdʒudɪst] *adj* (*person*) predispuesto; (*view*) parcial, interesado; **to be ~ against sb/sth** estar predispuesto en contra de algn/algo
prelate [ˈprɛlət] *n* prelado
preliminaries [prɪˈlɪmɪnərɪz] *npl* preliminares *mpl*, preparativos *mpl*
preliminary [prɪˈlɪmɪnərɪ] *adj* preliminar
prelude [ˈprɛljuːd] *n* preludio
premarital [ˈpriːˈmærɪtl] *adj* prematrimonial, premarital
premature [ˈprɛmətʃuəʳ] *adj* (*arrival etc*) prematuro; **you are being a little ~** te has adelantado
prematurely [prɛməˈtʃuəlɪ] *adv* prematuramente, antes de tiempo
premeditate [priːˈmɛdɪteɪt] *vt* premeditar
premeditated [priːˈmɛdɪteɪtɪd] *adj* premeditado
premeditation [priːmɛdɪˈteɪʃən] *n* premeditación *f*
premenstrual [priːˈmɛnstruəl] *adj* premenstrual
premenstrual tension *n* (*Med*) tensión *f* premenstrual
premier [ˈprɛmɪəʳ] *adj* primero, principal ■ *n* (*Pol*) primer(a) ministro(-a)
première [ˈprɛmɪɛəʳ] *n* estreno
premise [ˈprɛmɪs] *n* premisa
premises [ˈprɛmɪsɪs] *npl* local *msg*; **on the ~** en el lugar mismo; **business ~** locales *mpl* comerciales
premium [ˈpriːmɪəm] *n* prima; **to be at a ~** estar muy solicitado; **to sell at a ~** (*shares*) vender caro
premium bond *n* (*Brit*) *bono del estado que participa en una lotería nacional; ver nota*

● **PREMIUM BOND**

Se conoce como *Premium Bonds* o *Premium Savings Bonds* a los bonos emitidos por el Ministerio de Economía británico (*Treasury*) en los que se pueden invertir los ahorros. No producen intereses, pero dan acceso a un sorteo mensual de premios en metálico.

premium deal n (*Comm*) oferta extraordinaria

premium gasoline n (*US*) (gasolina) súper m

premonition [prɛmə'nɪʃən] n presentimiento

preoccupation [priːɔkju'peɪʃən] n preocupación f

preoccupied [priː'ɔkjupaɪd] adj (*worried*) preocupado; (*absorbed*) ensimismado

prep [prɛp] adj abbr: ~ **school** = **preparatory school** ■ n abbr (*Scol*: = **preparation**) deberes mpl

prepaid [priː'peɪd] adj porte pagado; ~ **envelope** sobre m de porte pagado

preparation [prɛpə'reɪʃən] n preparación f; **preparations** npl preparativos mpl; **in ~ for sth** en preparación para algo

preparatory [prɪ'pærətərɪ] adj preparatorio, preliminar; ~ **to sth/to doing sth** como preparación para algo/para hacer algo

preparatory school n (*Brit*) colegio privado de enseñanza primaria; (*US*) colegio privado de enseñanza secundaria; see also **public school**

prepare [prɪ'pɛəʳ] vt preparar, disponer ■ vi: **to ~ for** prepararse or disponerse para; (*make preparations*) hacer preparativos para

prepared [prɪ'pɛəd] adj (*willing*): **to be ~ to help sb** estar dispuesto a ayudar a algn

preponderance [prɪ'pɔndərns] n preponderancia, predominio

preposition [prɛpə'zɪʃən] n preposición f

prepossessing [priː'pə'zɛsɪŋ] adj agradable, atractivo

preposterous [prɪ'pɔstərəs] adj absurdo, ridículo

prerecorded ['priː'rɪ'kɔːdɪd] adj: ~ **broadcast** programa m grabado de antemano; ~ **cassette** cassette f pregrabada

prerequisite [priː'rɛkwɪzɪt] n requisito previo

prerogative [prɪ'rɔgətɪv] n prerrogativa

Presbyterian [prɛzbɪ'tɪərɪən] adj, n presbiteriano(-a) m(f)

presbytery ['prɛzbɪtərɪ] n casa parroquial

preschool ['priː'skuːl] adj (*child, age*) preescolar

prescribe [prɪ'skraɪb] vt prescribir; (*Med*) recetar; **prescribed books** (*Brit Scol*) libros mpl del curso

prescription [prɪ'skrɪpʃən] n (*Med*) receta; **to make up** or (*US*) **fill a ~** preparar una receta; **only available on ~** se vende solamente con receta (médica)

prescription charges npl (*Brit*) precio sg de las recetas

prescriptive [prɪ'skrɪptɪv] adj normativo

presence ['prɛzns] n presencia; (*attendance*) asistencia

presence of mind n aplomo

present adj ['prɛznt] (*in attendance*) presente; (*current*) actual ■ n (*gift*) regalo; (*actuality*) actualidad f, presente m ■ vt [prɪ'zɛnt] (*introduce*) presentar; (*expound*) exponer; (*give*) presentar, dar, ofrecer; (*Theat*) representar; **to be ~ at** asistir a, estar presente en; **those ~** los presentes; **to give sb a ~, make sb a ~ of sth** regalar algo a algn; **at ~** actualmente; **to ~ o.s. for an interview** presentarse a una entrevista; **may I ~ Miss Clark** permítame presentarle or le presento a la Srta Clark

presentable [prɪ'zɛntəbl] adj: **to make o.s. ~** arreglarse

presentation [prɛzn'teɪʃən] n presentación f; (*gift*) obsequio; (*of case*) exposición f; (*Theat*) representación f; **on ~ of the voucher** al presentar el vale

present-day ['prɛzntdeɪ] adj actual

presenter [prɪ'zɛntəʳ] n (*Radio, TV*) locutor(a) m(f)

presently ['prɛzntlɪ] adv (*soon*) dentro de poco; (*US: now*) ahora

present participle n participio (de) presente

present tense n (tiempo) presente m

preservation [prɛzə'veɪʃən] n conservación f

preservative [prɪ'zəːvətɪv] n conservante m

preserve [prɪ'zəːv] vt (*keep safe*) preservar, proteger; (*maintain*) mantener; (*food*) conservar; (*in salt*) salar ■ n (*for game*) coto, vedado; (*often pl: jam*) confitura

preshrunk [priː'ʃrʌŋk] adj inencogible

preside [prɪ'zaɪd] vi presidir

presidency ['prɛzɪdənsɪ] n presidencia

president ['prɛzɪdənt] n presidente m/f; (*US: of company*) director(a) m(f)

presidential [prɛzɪ'dɛnʃl] adj presidencial

press [prɛs] n (*tool, machine, newspapers*) prensa; (*printer's*) imprenta; (*of hand*) apretón m ■ vt (*push*) empujar; (*squeeze*) apretar; (*grapes*) pisar; (*clothes: iron*) planchar; (*pressure*) presionar; (*doorbell*) apretar, pulsar, tocar; (*insist*): **to ~ sth on sb** insistir en que algn acepte algo ■ vi (*squeeze*) apretar; (*pressurize*) ejercer presión; **to go to ~** (*newspaper*) entrar en prensa; **to be in the ~** (*being printed*) estar en prensa; (*in the newspapers*) aparecer en la prensa; **we are pressed for time** tenemos poco tiempo; **to ~ sb to do** or **into doing sth** (*urge, entreat*) presionar a algn para que haga algo; **to ~ sb for an answer** insistir a algn para que conteste; **to ~ charges against sb** (*Law*) demandar a algn
▶ **press ahead** vi seguir adelante
▶ **press on** vi avanzar; (*hurry*) apretar el paso

press agency n agencia de prensa

press clipping n = **press cutting**

press conference n rueda de prensa
press cutting n recorte m (de periódico)
pressing ['prɛsɪŋ] adj apremiante
pressman ['prɛsmæn] n periodista m
press officer n jefe(-a) m(f) de prensa
press release n comunicado de prensa
press stud n (Brit) botón m de presión
press-up ['prɛsʌp] n (Brit) flexión f
pressure ['prɛʃəʳ] n presión f; (urgency)
apremio, urgencia; (influence) influencia;
high/low ~ alta/baja presión; **to put ~ on sb**
presionar a algn, hacer presión sobre algn
pressure cooker n olla a presión
pressure gauge n manómetro
pressure group n grupo de presión
pressurize ['prɛʃəraɪz] vt presurizar; **to ~ sb**
(into doing sth) presionar a algn (para que
haga algo)
pressurized ['prɛʃəraɪzd] adj (container) a
presión
Prestel® ['prɛstɛl] n videotex m
prestige [prɛs'tiːʒ] n prestigio
prestigious [prɛs'tɪdʒəs] adj prestigioso
presumably [prɪ'zjuːməblɪ] adv es de
suponer que, cabe presumir que; **~ he did it**
es de suponer que lo hizo él
presume [prɪ'zjuːm] vt suponer, presumir;
to ~ to do (dare) atreverse a hacer
presumption [prɪ'zʌmpʃən] n suposición f;
(pretension) presunción f
presumptuous [prɪ'zʌmptjuəs] adj
presumido
presuppose [priːsə'pəuz] vt presuponer
presupposition [priːsʌpə'zɪʃən] n
presuposición f
pre-tax [priː'tæks] adj anterior al impuesto
pretence, pretense (US) [prɪ'tɛns] n (claim)
pretensión f; (pretext) pretexto; (make-believe)
fingimiento; **on** or **under the ~ of doing sth**
bajo or con el pretexto de hacer algo; **she is**
devoid of all ~ no es pretenciosa
pretend [prɪ'tɛnd] vt (feign) fingir ■ vi (feign)
fingir; (claim): **to ~ to sth** pretender a algo
pretense [prɪ'tɛns] n (US) = **pretence**
pretension [prɪ'tɛnʃən] n (claim) pretensión f;
to have no pretensions to sth/to being sth
no engañarse en cuanto a algo/a ser algo
pretentious [prɪ'tɛnʃəs] adj pretencioso
pretext ['priːtɛkst] n pretexto; **on** or **under**
the ~ of doing sth con el pretexto de hacer
algo
prettily ['prɪtɪlɪ] adv encantadoramente, con
gracia
pretty ['prɪtɪ] adj (gen) bonito, lindo (LAm)
■ adv bastante
prevail [prɪ'veɪl] vi (gain mastery) prevalecer;
(be current) predominar; (persuade): **to ~**

(up)on sb to do sth persuadir a algn para
que haga algo
prevailing [prɪ'veɪlɪŋ] adj (dominant)
predominante
prevalent ['prɛvələnt] adj (dominant)
dominante; (widespread) extendido;
(fashionable) de moda
prevarication [prɪværɪ'keɪʃən] n evasivas fpl
prevent [prɪ'vɛnt] vt: **to ~ (sb) from doing**
sth impedir (a algn) hacer algo
preventable [prɪ'vɛntəbl] adj evitable
preventative [prɪ'vɛntətɪv] adj preventivo
prevention [prɪ'vɛnʃən] n prevención f
preventive [prɪ'vɛntɪv] adj preventivo
preview ['priːvjuː] n (of film) preestreno
previous ['priːvɪəs] adj previo, anterior;
he has no ~ experience in that field no
tiene experiencia previa en ese campo;
I have a ~ engagement tengo un
compromiso anterior
previously ['priːvɪəslɪ] adv antes
prewar [priː'wɔːʳ] adj antes de la guerra
prey [preɪ] n presa ■ vi: **to ~ on** vivir a costa
de; (feed on) alimentarse de; **it was preying**
on his mind le obsesionaba
price [praɪs] n precio; (Betting: odds) puntos
mpl de ventaja ■ vt (goods) fijar el precio de;
to go up or **rise in ~** subir de precio; **what**
is the ~ of …? ¿qué precio tiene …?; **to put**
a ~ on sth poner precio a algo; **what ~ his**
promises now? ¿para qué sirven ahora sus
promesas?; **he regained his freedom,**
but at a ~ recobró su libertad, pero le había
costado caro; **to be priced out of the**
market (article) no encontrar comprador por
ese precio; (nation) no ser competitivo
price control n control m de precios
price-cutting ['praɪskʌtɪŋ] n reducción f de
precios
priceless ['praɪslɪs] adj que no tiene precio;
(col: amusing) divertidísimo
price list n tarifa
price range n gama de precios; **it's within**
my ~ está al alcance de mi bolsillo
price tag n etiqueta
price war n guerra de precios
pricey ['praɪsɪ] adj (Brit col) caro
prick [prɪk] n pinchazo; (with pin) alfilerazo;
(sting) picadura ■ vt pinchar; picar; **to ~ up**
one's ears aguzar el oído
prickle ['prɪkl] n (sensation) picor m; (Bot)
espina; (Zool) púa
prickly ['prɪklɪ] adj espinoso; (fig: person)
enojadizo
prickly heat n sarpullido causado por exceso
de calor
prickly pear n higo chumbo

P

pride [praɪd] n orgullo; (pej) soberbia ■ vt:
to ~ o.s. on enorgullecerse de; **to take (a)
~ in** enorgullecerse de; **her ~ and joy** su
orgullo; **to have ~ of place** tener prioridad
priest [priːst] n sacerdote m
priestess ['priːstɪs] n sacerdotisa
priesthood ['priːsthud] n (practice)
sacerdocio; (priests) clero
prig [prɪg] n gazmoño(-a)
prim [prɪm] adj (demure) remilgado; (prudish)
gazmoño
primacy ['praɪməsɪ] n primacía
prima donna ['priːmə'dɔnə] n primadonna,
diva
prima facie ['praɪmə'feɪʃɪ] adj: **to have a ~
case** (Law) tener razón a primera vista
primal ['praɪməl] adj original; (important)
principal
primarily ['praɪmərɪlɪ] adv (above all) ante
todo, primordialmente
primary ['praɪmərɪ] adj primario; (first in
importance) principal ■ n (US: also: **primary
election**) (elección f) primaria; ver nota

● **PRIMARY**

Las elecciones primarias (primaries) sirven
para preseleccionar a los candidatos de
los partidos Demócrata ("Democratic")
y Republicano ("Republican") durante
la campaña que precede a las elecciones
a presidente de los Estados Unidos. Se
inician en New Hampshire y tienen
lugar en 35 estados de febrero a junio.
El número de votos obtenidos por cada
candidato determina el número de
delegados que votarán en el congreso
general ("National Convention") de julio
y agosto, cuando se decide el candidato
definitivo de cada partido.

primary colour, (US) **primary color** n color
m primario
primary education n enseñanza primaria
primary school n (Brit) escuela primaria; ver
nota

● **PRIMARY SCHOOL**

En el Reino Unido la escuela a la que
van los niños entre cinco y once años se
llama primary school, a menudo dividida en
"infant school" (entre cinco y siete años
de edad) y "junior school" (entre siete y
once).

primate n ['praɪmɪt] (Rel) primado;

['praɪmeɪt] (Zool) primate m
prime [praɪm] adj primero, principal; (basic)
fundamental; (excellent) selecto, de primera
clase ■ n: **in the ~ of life** en la flor de la vida
■ vt (gun, pump) cebar; (fig) preparar
Prime Minister n primer(a) ministro(-a);
see also **Downing Street**
primer ['praɪmər] n (book) texto elemental;
(paint) capa preparatoria
prime time n (Radio, TV) horas fpl de mayor
audiencia
primeval [praɪ'miːvəl] adj primitivo
primitive ['prɪmɪtɪv] adj primitivo; (crude)
rudimentario; (uncivilized) inculto
primly ['prɪmlɪ] adv remilgadamente; con
gazmoñería
primrose ['prɪmrəuz] n primavera, prímula
primus® ['praɪməs], **primus stove** n (Brit)
hornillo de camping
prince [prɪns] n príncipe m
prince charming n príncipe m azul
princess [prɪn'sɛs] n princesa
principal ['prɪnsɪpl] adj principal ■ n
director(a) m(f); (in play) protagonista
principal m/f; (Comm) capital m, principal m;
see also **pantomime**
principality [prɪnsɪ'pælɪtɪ] n principado
principle ['prɪnsɪpl] n principio; **in ~** en
principio; **on ~** por principio
print [prɪnt] n (impression) marca, impresión
f; huella; (letters) letra de molde; (fabric)
estampado; (Art) grabado; (Phot) impresión
f ■ vt (gen) imprimir; (on mind) grabar; (write
in capitals) escribir en letras de molde; **out of
~** agotado
▶ **print out** vt (Comput) imprimir
printed circuit ['prɪntɪd-] n circuito
impreso
printed circuit board n tarjeta de circuito
impreso
printed matter n impresos mpl
printer ['prɪntər] n (person) impresor(a) m(f);
(machine) impresora
printhead ['prɪnthed] n cabeza impresora
printing ['prɪntɪŋ] n (art) imprenta; (act)
impresión f; (quantity) tirada
printing press n prensa
printout ['prɪntaut] n (Comput) printout m
print wheel n rueda impresora
prior ['praɪər] adj anterior, previo ■ n prior m;
~ to doing antes de or hasta hacer; **without
~ notice** sin previo aviso; **to have a ~ claim
to sth** tener prioridad en algo
prioress [praɪə'rɛs] n priora
priority [praɪ'ɔrɪtɪ] n prioridad f; **to have or
take ~ over sth** tener prioridad sobre algo
priory ['praɪərɪ] n priorato

prise, prize (US) [praɪz] vt: **to ~ open** abrir con palanca
prism ['prɪzəm] n prisma m
prison ['prɪzn] n cárcel f, prisión f ■ cpd carcelario
prison camp n campamento para prisioneros
prisoner ['prɪznəʳ] n (in prison) preso(-a); (under arrest) detenido(-a); (in dock) acusado(-a); **the ~ at the bar** el/la acusado(-a); **to take sb ~** hacer or tomar prisionero a algn
prisoner of war n prisionero(-a) or preso(-a) de guerra
prissy ['prɪsɪ] adj remilgado
pristine ['prɪstiːn] adj pristino
privacy ['prɪvəsɪ] n (seclusion) soledad f; (intimacy) intimidad f; **in the strictest ~** con el mayor secreto
private ['praɪvɪt] adj (personal) particular; (confidential) secreto, confidencial; (intimate) privado, íntimo; (sitting etc) a puerta cerrada ■ n soldado raso; **"~"** (on envelope) "confidencial"; (on door) "privado"; **in ~** en privado; **in (his) ~ life** en su vida privada; **to be in ~ practice** tener consulta particular
private enterprise n la empresa privada
private eye n detective m/f privado(-a)
private hearing n (Law) vista a puerta cerrada
private limited company n (Brit) sociedad f de responsabilidad limitada
privately ['praɪvɪtlɪ] adv en privado; (in o.s.) en secreto
private parts npl partes fpl pudendas
private property n propiedad f privada
private school n colegio privado
privation [praɪ'veɪʃən] n (state) privación f; (hardship) privaciones fpl, estrecheces fpl
privatize ['praɪvɪtaɪz] vt privatizar
privet ['prɪvɪt] n alheña
privilege ['prɪvɪlɪdʒ] n privilegio; (prerogative) prerrogativa
privileged ['prɪvɪlɪdʒd] adj privilegiado; **to be ~ to do sth** gozar del privilegio de hacer algo
privy ['prɪvɪ] adj: **to be ~ to** estar enterado de
Privy Council n consejo privado (de la Corona); ver nota

● **PRIVY COUNCIL**
●
● El consejo de asesores de la Corona
● conocido como Privy Council tuvo su origen
● en la época de los normandos, y fue
● adquiriendo mayor importancia hasta
● ser substituido en 1688 por el actual
● Consejo de Ministros ("Cabinet"). Hoy
● día sigue existiendo con un carácter

● fundamentalmente honorífico y
● los ministros del gobierno y otras
● personalidades políticas, eclesiásticas
● y jurídicas adquieren el rango de "privy
● councillors" de manera automática.

prize [praɪz] n premio ■ adj (first class) de primera clase ■ vt apreciar, estimar; (US) = **prise**
prize fighter n boxeador m profesional
prize fighting n boxeo m profesional
prize-giving ['praɪzgɪvɪŋ] n distribución f de premios
prize money n (Sport) bolsa
prizewinner ['praɪzwɪnəʳ] n premiado(-a)
prizewinning ['praɪzwɪnɪŋ] adj (novel, essay) premiado
PRO n abbr = **public relations officer**
pro [prəu] n (Sport) profesional m/f; **the pros and cons** los pros y los contras
pro- [prəu] pref (in favour of) pro, en pro de; **~Soviet** pro-soviético
proactive [prəu'æktɪv] adj: **to be ~** impulsar la actividad
probability [prɔbə'bɪlɪtɪ] n probabilidad f; **in all ~** lo más probable
probable ['prɔbəbl] adj probable; **it is ~/ hardly ~ that** es probable/poco probable que
probably ['prɔbəblɪ] adv probablemente
probate ['prəubeɪt] n (Law) legalización f de un testamento
probation [prə'beɪʃən] n: **on ~** (employee) a prueba; (Law) en libertad condicional
probationary [prə'beɪʃənrɪ] adj: **~ period** período de prueba
probationer [prə'beɪʃənəʳ] n (Law) persona en libertad condicional; (nurse) ≈ ATS m/f (SP) or enfermero(-a) en prácticas
probation officer n persona a cargo de los presos en libertad condicional
probe [prəub] n (Med, Space) sonda; (enquiry) investigación f ■ vt sondar; (investigate) investigar
probity ['prəubɪtɪ] n probidad f
problem ['prɔbləm] n problema m; **what's the ~?** ¿cuál es el problema?, ¿qué pasa?; **no ~!** ¡por supuesto!; **to have problems with the car** tener problemas con el coche
problematic [prɔblə'mætɪk], **problematical** [prɔblə'mætɪkl] adj problemático
problem-solving [prɔbləm'sɔlvɪŋ] n resolución f de problemas; **~ skills** técnicas de resolución de problemas
procedural [prəu'siːdʒərəl] adj de procedimiento; (Law) procesal
procedure [prə'siːdʒəʳ] n procedimiento; (bureaucratic) trámites mpl; **cashing a cheque**

is a simple ~ cobrar un cheque es un trámite sencillo

proceed [prə'siːd] *vi* proceder; (*continue*): **to ~ (with)** continuar (con); **to ~ against sb** (*Law*) proceder contra algn; **I am not sure how to ~** no sé cómo proceder; *see also* **proceeds**

proceedings [prə'siːdɪŋz] *npl* acto *sg*, actos *mpl*; (*Law*) proceso *sg*; (*meeting*) función *fsg*; (*records*) actas *fpl*

proceeds ['prəusiːdz] *npl* ganancias *fpl*, ingresos *mpl*

process ['prəusɛs] *n* proceso; (*method*) método, sistema *m*; (*proceeding*) procedimiento ■ *vt* tratar, elaborar ■ *vi* [prə'sɛs] (*Brit: formal: go in procession*) desfilar; **in ~** en curso; **we are in the ~ of moving to ...** estamos en vías de mudarnos a ...

processed cheese ['prəusɛst-], (*US*) **process cheese** *n* queso fundido

processing ['prəusɛsɪŋ] *n* elaboración *f*

procession [prə'sɛʃən] *n* desfile *m*; **funeral ~** cortejo fúnebre

pro-choice [prəu'tʃɔɪs] *adj* en favor del derecho de elegir de la madre

proclaim [prə'kleɪm] *vt* proclamar; (*announce*) anunciar

proclamation [prɔklə'meɪʃən] *n* proclamación *f*; (*written*) proclama

proclivity [prə'klɪvɪtɪ] *n* propensión *f*, inclinación *f*

procrastinate [prəu'kræstɪneɪt] *vi* demorarse

procrastination [prəukræstɪ'neɪʃən] *n* dilación *f*

procreation [prəukrɪ'eɪʃən] *n* procreación *f*

Procurator Fiscal ['prɔkjureɪtə-] *n* (*Scottish*) fiscal *m/f*

procure [prə'kjuər] *vt* conseguir, obtener

procurement [prə'kjuəmənt] *n* obtención *f*

prod [prɔd] *vt* (*push*) empujar; (*with elbow*) dar un codazo a ■ *n* empujoncito; codazo

prodigal ['prɔdɪgl] *adj* pródigo

prodigious [prə'dɪdʒəs] *adj* prodigioso

prodigy ['prɔdɪdʒɪ] *n* prodigio

produce *n* ['prɔdjuːs] (*Agr*) productos *mpl* agrícolas ■ *vt* [prə'djuːs] producir; (*yield*) rendir; (*bring*) sacar; (*show*) presentar, mostrar; (*proof of identity*) enseñar, presentar; (*Theat*) presentar, poner en escena; (*offspring*) dar a luz

produce dealer *n* (*US*) verdulero(-a)

producer [prə'djuːsər] *n* (*Theat*) director(a) *m(f)*; (*Agr, Cine*) productor(a) *m(f)*

product ['prɔdʌkt] *n* producto

production [prə'dʌkʃən] *n* (*act*) producción *f*; (*Theat*) representación *f*, montaje *m*; **to put**

into ~ lanzar a la producción

production agreement *n* (*US*) acuerdo de productividad

production line *n* línea de producción

production manager *n* jefe/jefa *m/f* de producción

productive [prə'dʌktɪv] *adj* productivo

productivity [prɔdʌk'tɪvɪtɪ] *n* productividad *f*

productivity agreement *n* (*Brit*) acuerdo de productividad

productivity bonus *n* bono de productividad

Prof. [prɔf] *abbr* (= *professor*) Prof

profane [prə'feɪn] *adj* profano

profess [prə'fɛs] *vt* profesar; **I do not ~ to be an expert** no pretendo ser experto

professed [prə'fɛst] *adj* (*self-declared*) declarado

profession [prə'fɛʃən] *n* profesión *f*

professional [prə'fɛʃnl] *n* profesional *m/f* ■ *adj* profesional; (*by profession*) de profesión; **to take ~ advice** buscar un consejo profesional

professionalism [prə'fɛʃnəlɪzm] *n* profesionalismo

professionally [prə'fɛʃnəlɪ] *adv*: **I only know him ~** sólo le conozco por nuestra relación de trabajo

professor [prə'fɛsər] *n* (*Brit*) catedrático(-a) *m(f)*; (*US: teacher*) profesor(a) *m(f)*

professorship [prə'fɛsəʃɪp] *n* cátedra

proffer ['prɔfər] *vt* ofrecer

proficiency [prə'fɪʃənsɪ] *n* capacidad *f*, habilidad *f*

proficiency test *n* prueba de capacitación

proficient [prə'fɪʃənt] *adj* experto, hábil

profile ['prəufaɪl] *n* perfil *m*; **to keep a high/low ~** tratar de llamar la atención/pasar inadvertido

profit ['prɔfɪt] *n* (*Comm*) ganancia; (*fig*) provecho ■ *vi*: **to ~ by** *or* **from** aprovechar *or* sacar provecho de; **~ and loss account** cuenta de ganancias y pérdidas; **with profits endowment assurance** seguro dotal con beneficios; **to sell sth at a ~** vender algo con ganancia

profitability [prɔfɪtə'bɪlɪtɪ] *n* rentabilidad *f*

profitable ['prɔfɪtəbl] *adj* (*Econ*) rentable; (*beneficial*) provechoso, útil

profitably ['prɔfɪtəblɪ] *adv* rentablemente; provechosamente

profit centre, (*US*) **profit center** *n* centro de beneficios

profiteering [prɔfɪ'tɪərɪŋ] *n* (*pej*) explotación *f*

profit-making ['prɔfɪtmeɪkɪŋ] *adj* rentable

profit margin *n* margen *m* de ganancia

profit-sharing ['prɔfɪtʃɛərɪŋ] n participación f de empleados en los beneficios
profits tax n impuesto sobre los beneficios
profligate ['prɔflɪgɪt] adj (dissolute: behaviour, act) disoluto; (: person) libertino; (extravagant): **he's very ~ with his money** es muy derrochador
pro forma ['prəu'fɔːmə] adj: **~ invoice** factura pro-forma
profound [prə'faund] adj profundo
profoundly [prə'faundlɪ] adv profundamente
profusely [prə'fjuːslɪ] adv profusamente
profusion [prə'fjuːʒən] n profusión f, abundancia
progeny ['prɔdʒɪnɪ] n progenie f
programme, program (US) ['prəugræm] n programa m ▪ vt programar
programmer, program (US) ['prəugræmər] n programador(a) m(f)
programming, program (US) ['prəugræmɪŋ] n programación f
programming language, programing language (US) n lenguaje m de programación
progress n ['prəugrɛs] progreso; (development) desarrollo ▪ vi [prə'grɛs] progresar, avanzar; desarrollarse; **in ~** (meeting, work etc) en curso; **as the match progressed** a medida que avanzaba el partido
progression [prə'grɛʃən] n progresión f
progressive [prə'grɛsɪv] adj progresivo; (person) progresista
progressively [prə'grɛsɪvlɪ] adv progresivamente, poco a poco
progress report n (Med) informe m sobre el estado del paciente; (Admin) informe m sobre la marcha del trabajo
prohibit [prə'hɪbɪt] vt prohibir; **to ~ sb from doing sth** prohibir a algn hacer algo; **"smoking prohibited"** "prohibido fumar"
prohibition [prəuɪ'bɪʃən] n (US) prohibicionismo
prohibitive [prə'hɪbɪtɪv] adj (price etc) prohibitivo
project [n 'prɔdʒɛkt, vb prə'dʒɛkt] n proyecto; (Scol, Univ: research) trabajo, proyecto ▪ vt proyectar ▪ vi (stick out) salir, sobresalir
projectile [prə'dʒɛktaɪl] n proyectil m
projection [prə'dʒɛkʃən] n proyección f; (overhang) saliente m
projectionist [prə'dʒɛkʃənɪst] n (Cine) operador(a) m(f) de cine
projection room n (Cine) cabina de proyección
projector [prə'dʒɛktər] n proyector m

proletarian [prəulɪ'tɛərɪən] adj proletario
proletariat [prəulɪ'tɛərɪət] n proletariado
pro-life [prəu'laɪf] adj pro-vida
proliferate [prə'lɪfəreɪt] vi proliferar, multiplicarse
proliferation [prəlɪfə'reɪʃən] n proliferación f
prolific [prə'lɪfɪk] adj prolífico
prologue, (US) prolog ['prəulɔg] n prólogo
prolong [prə'lɔn] vt prolongar, extender
prom [prɔm] n abbr (Brit) = **promenade**; **promenade concert**; (US: ball) baile m de gala; ver nota

● **PROM**
●
● Los conciertos de música clásica más
● conocidos en Inglaterra son los llamados
● Proms (o promenade concerts), que tienen
● lugar en el "Royal Albert Hall" de Londres,
● aunque también se llama así a cualquier
● concierto de esas características. Su
● nombre se debe al hecho de que en un
● principio el público paseaba durante las
● actuaciones; en la actualidad parte de
● la gente que acude a ellos permanece de
● pie. En Estados Unidos se llama prom a un
● baile de gala en un colegio o universidad.

promenade [prɔmə'nɑːd] n (by sea) paseo marítimo ▪ vi (stroll) pasearse
promenade concert n concierto (en que parte del público permanece de pie)
promenade deck n cubierta de paseo
prominence ['prɔmɪnəns] n (fig) importancia
prominent ['prɔmɪnənt] adj (standing out) saliente; (important) eminente, importante; **he is ~ in the field of ...** destaca en el campo de ...
prominently ['prɔmɪnəntlɪ] adv (display, set) muy a la vista; **he figured ~ in the case** desempeñó un papel destacado en el juicio
promiscuity [prɔmɪs'kjuːɪtɪ] n promiscuidad f
promiscuous [prə'mɪskjuəs] adj (sexually) promiscuo
promise ['prɔmɪs] n promesa ▪ vt, vi prometer; **to make sb a ~** prometer algo a algn; **a young man of ~** un joven con futuro; **to ~ (sb) to do sth** prometer (a algn) hacer algo; **to ~ well** ser muy prometedor
promising ['prɔmɪsɪŋ] adj prometedor(a)
promissory note ['prɔmɪsərɪ-] n pagaré m
promontory ['prɔməntrɪ] n promontorio
promote [prə'məut] vt promover; (new product) dar publicidad a, lanzar; (Mil) ascender; **the team was promoted to the second division** (Brit Football) el equipo ascendió a la segunda división

P

723

promoter [prə'məutər] n (of sporting event) promotor(a) m(f); (of company, business) patrocinador(a) m(f)

promotion [prə'məuʃən] n (gen) promoción f; (Mil) ascenso

prompt [prɔmpt] adj pronto ■ adv: **at six o'clock ~** a las seis en punto ■ n (Comput) aviso, guía ■ vt (urge) mover, incitar; (Theat) apuntar; **to ~ sb to do sth** instar a algn a hacer algo; **to be ~ to do sth** no tardar en hacer algo; **they're very ~** (punctual) son muy puntuales

prompter ['prɔmptər] n (Theat) apuntador(a) m(f)

promptly ['prɔmptlɪ] adv (punctually) puntualmente; (rapidly) rápidamente

promptness ['prɔmptnɪs] n puntualidad f; rapidez f

promulgate ['prɔməlgeɪt] vt promulgar

prone [prəun] adj (lying) postrado; **~ to** propenso a

prong [prɔŋ] n diente m, punta

pronoun ['prəunaun] n pronombre m

pronounce [prə'nauns] vt pronunciar; (declare) declarar ■ vi: **to ~ (up)on** pronunciarse sobre; **they pronounced him unfit to plead** le declararon incapaz de defenderse

pronounced [prə'naunst] adj (marked) marcado

pronouncement [prə'naunsmənt] n declaración f

pronunciation [prənʌnsɪ'eɪʃən] n pronunciación f

proof [pru:f] n prueba; **70° ~** graduación f del 70 por 100 ■ adj: **~ against** a prueba de ■ vt (tent, anorak) impermeabilizar

proofreader ['pru:fri:dər] n corrector(a) m(f) de pruebas

prop [prɔp] n apoyo; (fig) sostén m ■ vt (also: **prop up**) apoyar; (lean): **to ~ sth against** apoyar algo contra

Prop. abbr (Comm) = **proprietor**

propaganda [prɔpə'gændə] n propaganda

propagate ['prɔpəgeɪt] vt propagar

propagation [prɔpə'geɪʃən] n propagación f

propel [prə'pɛl] vt impulsar, propulsar

propeller [prə'pɛlər] n hélice f

propelling pencil [prə'pɛlɪŋ-] n (Brit) lapicero

propensity [prə'pɛnsɪtɪ] n propensión f

proper ['prɔpər] adj (suited, right) propio; (exact) justo; (apt) apropiado, conveniente; (timely) oportuno; (seemly) correcto, decente; (authentic) verdadero; (col: real) auténtico; **to go through the ~ channels** (Admin) ir por la vía oficial

properly ['prɔpəlɪ] adv (adequately) correctamente; (decently) decentemente

proper noun n nombre m propio

properties ['prɔpətɪz] npl (Theat) accesorios mpl, atrezzo msg

property ['prɔpətɪ] n propiedad f; (estate) finca; **lost ~** objetos mpl perdidos; **personal ~** bienes mpl muebles

property developer n promotor(a) m(f) de construcciones

property owner n dueño(-a) de propiedades

property tax n impuesto sobre la propiedad

prophecy ['prɔfɪsɪ] n profecía

prophesy ['prɔfɪsaɪ] vt profetizar; (fig) predecir

prophet ['prɔfɪt] n profeta m/f

prophetic [prə'fɛtɪk] adj profético

proportion [prə'pɔ:ʃən] n proporción f; (share) parte f; **to be in/out of ~ to or with sth** estar en/no guardar proporción con algo; **to see sth in ~** (fig) ver algo en su justa medida

proportional [prə'pɔ:ʃənl] adj proporcional

proportionally [prəpɔ:ʃnəlɪ] adv proporcionalmente, en proporción

proportional representation n (Pol) representación f proporcional

proportional spacing n (on printer) espaciado proporcional

proportionate [prə'pɔ:ʃənɪt] adj proporcionado

proportionately [prə'pɔ:ʃnɪtlɪ] adv proporcionadamente, en proporción

proportioned [prə'pɔ:ʃənd] adj proporcionado

proposal [prə'pəuzl] n propuesta; (offer of marriage) oferta de matrimonio; (plan) proyecto; (suggestion) sugerencia

propose [prə'pəuz] vt proponer; (have in mind): **to ~ sth/to do or doing sth** proponer algo/proponerse hacer algo ■ vi declararse

proposer [prə'pəuzər] n (of motion) proponente m/f

proposition [prɔpə'zɪʃən] n propuesta, proposición f; **to make sb a ~** proponer algo a algn

propound [prə'paund] vt (theory) exponer

proprietary [prə'praɪətərɪ] adj (Comm): **~ article** artículo de marca; **~ brand** marca comercial

proprietor [prə'praɪətər] n propietario(-a), dueño(-a)

propriety [prə'praɪətɪ] n decoro

propulsion [prə'pʌlʃən] n propulsión f

pro rata [prəu'rɑ:tə] adv a prorrata

prosaic [prəu'zeɪɪk] adj prosaico

Pros. Atty. abbr (US) = **prosecuting attorney**

proscribe [prə'skraɪb] vt proscribir

prose [prəuz] n prosa; (Scol) traducción f inversa
prosecute ['prɔsɪkju:t] vt (Law) procesar; **"trespassers will be prosecuted"** (Law) "se procesará a los intrusos"
prosecution [prɔsɪ'kju:ʃən] n proceso, causa; (accusing side) acusación f
prosecutor ['prɔsɪkju:təʳ] n acusador(a) m(f); (also: **public prosecutor**) fiscal m/f
prospect [n 'prɔspɛkt, vb prə'spɛkt] n (chance) posibilidad f; (outlook) perspectiva; (hope) esperanza ∎ vt explorar ∎ vi buscar; **prospects** npl (for work etc) perspectivas fpl; **to be faced with the ~ of** tener que enfrentarse a la posibilidad de que ...; **we were faced with the ~ of leaving early** se nos planteó la posibilidad de marcharnos pronto; **there is every ~ of an early victory** hay buenas perspectivas de una pronta victoria
prospecting [prə'spɛktɪŋ] n prospección f
prospective [prə'spɛktɪv] adj (possible) probable, eventual; (certain) futuro; (buyer) presunto; (legislation, son-in-law) futuro
prospector [prə'spɛktəʳ] n explorador(a) m(f); **gold ~** buscador m de oro
prospectus [prə'spɛktəs] n prospecto
prosper ['prɔspəʳ] vi prosperar
prosperity [prɔ'spɛrɪtɪ] n prosperidad f
prosperous ['prɔspərəs] adj próspero
prostate ['prɔsteɪt] n (also: **prostate gland**) próstata
prostitute ['prɔstɪtju:t] n prostituta; **male ~** prostituto
prostitution [prɔstɪ'tju:ʃən] n prostitución f
prostrate ['prɔstreɪt] adj postrado; (fig) abatido ∎ vt: **to ~ o.s.** postrarse
protagonist [prə'tægənɪst] n protagonista m/f
protect [prə'tɛkt] vt proteger
protection [prə'tɛkʃən] n protección f; **to be under sb's ~** estar amparado por algn
protectionism [prə'tɛkʃənɪzəm] n proteccionismo
protection racket n chantaje m
protective [prə'tɛktɪv] adj protector(a); **~ custody** (Law) detención f preventiva
protector [prə'tɛktəʳ] n protector(a) m(f)
protégé ['prəutɛʒeɪ] n protegido(-a)
protein ['prəuti:n] n proteína
pro tem [prəu'tɛm] adv abbr (= pro tempore: for the time being) provisionalmente
protest [n 'prəutɛst, vb prə'tɛst] n protesta ∎ vi protestar ∎ vt (affirm) afirmar, declarar; **to do sth under ~** hacer algo bajo protesta; **to ~ against/about** protestar en contra de/por
Protestant ['prɔtɪstənt] adj, n protestante m/f

protester, protestor [prə'tɛstəʳ] n (in demonstration) manifestante m/f
protest march n manifestación f or marcha (de protesta)
protocol ['prəutəkɔl] n protocolo
prototype ['prəutətaɪp] n prototipo
protracted [prə'træktɪd] adj prolongado
protractor [prə'træktəʳ] n (Geom) transportador m
protrude [prə'tru:d] vi salir, sobresalir
protuberance [prə'tju:bərəns] n protuberancia
proud [praud] adj orgulloso; (pej) soberbio, altanero ∎ adv: **to do sb ~** tratar a algn a cuerpo de rey; **to do o.s. ~** no privarse de nada; **to be ~ to do sth** estar orgulloso de hacer algo
proudly ['praudlɪ] adv orgullosamente, con orgullo; (pej) con soberbia, con altanería
prove [pru:v] vt probar; (verify) comprobar; (show) demostrar ∎ vi: **to ~ correct** resultar correcto; **to ~ o.s.** ponerse a prueba; **he was proved right in the end** al final se vio que tenía razón
proverb ['prɔvə:b] n refrán m
proverbial [prə'və:bɪəl] adj proverbial
proverbially [prə'və:bɪəlɪ] adv proverbialmente
provide [prə'vaɪd] vt proporcionar, dar; **to ~ sb with sth** proveer a algn de algo; **to be provided with** ser provisto de
▸ **provide for** vt fus (person) mantener a; (problem etc) tener en cuenta
provided [prə'vaɪdɪd] conj: **~ (that)** con tal de que, a condición de que
Providence ['prɔvɪdəns] n Divina Providencia
providing [prə'vaɪdɪŋ] conj a condición de que, con tal de que
province ['prɔvɪns] n provincia; (fig) esfera
provincial [prə'vɪnʃəl] adj provincial; (pej) provinciano
provision [prə'vɪʒən] n provisión f; (supply) suministro, abastecimiento; **provisions** npl provisiones fpl, víveres mpl; **to make ~ for** (one's family, future) atender las necesidades de
provisional [prə'vɪʒənl] adj provisional, provisorio (LAm); (temporary) interino ∎ n: **P~** (Ireland Pol) Provisional m (miembro de la tendencia activista del IRA)
provisional driving licence n (Brit Aut) carnet m de conducir provisional; see also **L-plates**
proviso [prə'vaɪzəu] n condición f, estipulación f; **with the ~ that** a condición de que
Provo ['prɔvəu] n abbr (col) = **Provisional**

provocation | publican

provocation [prɔvə'keɪʃən] *n* provocación *f*
provocative [prə'vɔkətɪv] *adj* provocativo
provoke [prə'vəuk] *vt* (*arouse*) provocar, incitar; (*cause*) causar, producir; (*anger*) enojar; **to ~ sb to sth/to do** *or* **into doing sth** provocar a algn a algo/a hacer algo
provoking [prə'vəukɪŋ] *adj* provocador(a)
provost ['prɔvəst] *n* (*Brit: of university*) rector(a) *m(f)*; (*Scottish*) alcalde(-esa) *m(f)*
prow [prau] *n* proa
prowess ['prauɪs] *n* (*skill*) destreza, habilidad *f*; (*courage*) valor *m*; **his ~ as a footballer** (*skill*) su habilidad como futbolista
prowl [praul] *vi* (*also:* **prowl about, prowl around**) merodear ■ *n*: **on the ~** de merodeo, merodeando
prowler ['praulə'] *n* merodeador(a) *m(f)*
proximity [prɔk'sɪmɪtɪ] *n* proximidad *f*
proxy ['prɔksɪ] *n* poder *m*; (*person*) apoderado(-a); **by ~** por poderes
PRP *n abbr* (= *performance related pay*) retribución en función del rendimiento en el trabajo
prude [pru:d] *n* gazmoño(-a), mojigato(-a)
prudence ['pru:dns] *n* prudencia
prudent ['pru:dnt] *adj* prudente
prudently ['pru:dntlɪ] *adv* prudentemente, con prudencia
prudish ['pru:dɪʃ] *adj* gazmoño
prudishness [pru:dɪʃnɪs] *n* gazmoñería
prune [pru:n] *n* ciruela pasa ■ *vt* podar
pry [praɪ] *vi*: **to ~ into** entrometerse en
PS *abbr* (= *postscript*) P.D.
psalm [sɑ:m] *n* salmo
PSAT *n abbr* (*US*) = **Preliminary Scholastic Aptitude Test**
PSBR *n abbr* (*Brit*: = *public sector borrowing requirement*) necesidades de endeudamiento del sector público
pseud [sju:d] *n* (*Brit col: intellectually*) farsante *m/f*; (*: socially*) pretencioso(-a)
pseudo... [sju:dəu] *pref* seudo...
pseudonym ['sju:dənɪm] *n* seudónimo
PSHE *n abbr* (*Brit Scol:* = *personal, social, and health education*) formación social y sanitaria para la vida adulta
PST *n abbr* (*US:* = *Pacific Standard Time*) hora de invierno del Pacífico
PSV *n abbr* (*Brit*) *see* **public service vehicle**
psyche ['saɪkɪ] *n* psique *f*
psychiatric [saɪkɪ'ætrɪk] *adj* psiquiátrico
psychiatrist [saɪ'kaɪətrɪst] *n* psiquiatra *m/f*
psychiatry [saɪ'kaɪətrɪ] *n* psiquiatría
psychic ['saɪkɪk] *adj* (*also:* **psychical**) psíquico
psycho ['saɪkəu] *n* (*col*) psicópata *m/f*, pirado(-a)
psychoanalyse, psychoanalyze [saɪkəu'ænəlaɪz] *vt* psicoanalizar

psychoanalysis (*pl* **psychoanalyses**) [saɪkəuə'nælɪsɪs, -siːz] *n* psicoanálisis *m inv*
psychoanalyst [saɪkəu'ænəlɪst] *n* psicoanalista *m/f*
psychological [saɪkə'lɔdʒɪkl] *adj* psicológico
psychologically [saɪkə'lɔdʒɪklɪ] *adv* psicológicamente
psychologist [saɪ'kɔlədʒɪst] *n* psicólogo(-a)
psychology [saɪ'kɔlədʒɪ] *n* psicología
psychopath ['saɪkəupæθ] *n* psicópata *m/f*
psychosis (*pl* **psychoses**) [saɪ'kəusɪs, -siːz] *n* psicosis *f inv*
psychosomatic ['saɪkəusə'mætɪk] *adj* psicosomático
psychotherapy [saɪkəu'θɛrəpɪ] *n* psicoterapia
psychotic [saɪ'kɔtɪk] *adj, n* psicótico(-a)
PT *n abbr* (*Brit*: = *physical training*) Ed. Fís.
pt *abbr* = **pint; pints; point; points**
Pt. *abbr* (*Geo: in place names*: = *Point*) Pta
PTA *n abbr* (*Brit*: = *Parent-Teacher Association*) ≈ Asociación *f* de Padres de Alumnos
Pte. *abbr* (*Brit Mil*) = **private**
PTO *abbr* (= *please turn over*) sigue
PTV *n abbr* (*US*) = **pay television; public television**
pub [pʌb] *n abbr* (= *public house*) pub *m*, bar *m*; *ver nota*

● **PUB**
●
● En un *pub* (o *public house*) se pueden
● consumir fundamentalmente bebidas
● alcohólicas, aunque en la actualidad
● también se sirven platos ligeros durante
● el almuerzo. Es, además, un lugar de
● encuentro donde se juega a los dardos o al
● billar, entre otras actividades. La estricta
● regulación sobre la venta de alcohol
● controla las horas de apertura, aunque
● éstas son más flexibles desde hace unos
● años. No se puede servir alcohol a los
● menores de 18 años.

pub crawl *n* (*col*): **to go on a ~** ir a recorrer bares
puberty ['pju:bətɪ] *n* pubertad *f*
pubic ['pju:bɪk] *adj* púbico
public ['pʌblɪk] *adj, n* público; **in ~** en público; **to make sth ~** revelar *or* hacer público algo; **to be ~ knowledge** ser del dominio público; **to go ~** (*Comm*) proceder a la venta pública de acciones
public address system *n* megafonía, sistema *m* de altavoces
publican ['pʌblɪkən] *n* dueño(-a) *or* encargado(-a) de un bar

publication [pʌblɪˈkeɪʃən] *n* publicación *f*
public company *n* sociedad *f* anónima
public convenience *n* (Brit) aseos *mpl* públicos, sanitarios *mpl* (LAm)
public holiday *n* día *m* de fiesta, (día) feriado (LAm)
public house *n* (Brit) bar *m*, pub *m*
publicity [pʌbˈlɪsɪtɪ] *n* publicidad *f*
publicize [ˈpʌblɪsaɪz] *vt* publicitar; (advertise) hacer propaganda para
public limited company *n* sociedad *f* anónima (S.A.)
publicly [ˈpʌblɪklɪ] *adv* públicamente, en público
public opinion *n* opinión *f* pública
public ownership *n* propiedad *f* pública; **to be taken into ~** ser nacionalizado
Public Prosecutor *n* Fiscal *m/f* del Estado
public relations *n* relaciones *fpl* públicas
public relations officer *n* encargado(-a) de relaciones públicas
public school *n* (Brit) colegio privado; (US) instituto; ver nota

● **PUBLIC SCHOOL**
●
● En Inglaterra el término *public school* se
● usa para referirse a un colegio privado
● de pago, generalmente de alto prestigio
● social y en régimen de internado.
● Algunos de los más conocidos son Eton
○ o Harrow. Muchos de sus alumnos
● estudian previamente hasta los 13 años
● en un centro privado de pago llamado
● "prep(aratory) school" y al terminar
● el bachiller pasan a estudiar en las
● universidades de Oxford y Cambridge.
● En otros lugares como Estados Unidos
● el mismo término se refiere a una
● escuela pública de enseñanza gratuita
● administrada por el Estado.

public sector *n* sector *m* público
public service vehicle *n* vehículo de servicio público
public-spirited [pʌblɪkˈspɪrɪtɪd] *adj* cívico
public transport, public transportation (US) *n* transporte *m* público
public utility *n* servicio público
public works *npl* obras *fpl* públicas
publish [ˈpʌblɪʃ] *vt* publicar
publisher [ˈpʌblɪʃəʳ] *n* (person) editor(a) *m(f)*; (firm) editorial *f*
publishing [ˈpʌblɪʃɪŋ] *n* (industry) industria del libro
publishing company *n* (casa) editorial *f*
puce [pjuːs] *adj* de color pardo rojizo

puck [pʌk] *n* (ice hockey) puck *m*
pucker [ˈpʌkəʳ] *vt* (pleat) arrugar; (brow etc) fruncir
pudding [ˈpudɪŋ] *n* pudín *m*; (Brit: sweet) postre *m*; **black ~** morcilla; **rice ~** arroz *m* con leche
puddle [ˈpʌdl] *n* charco
puerile [ˈpjuəraɪl] *adj* pueril
Puerto Rican [ˈpwəːtəuˈriːkən] *adj, n* puertorriqueño(-a) *m(f)*
Puerto Rico [-ˈriːkəu] *n* Puerto Rico
puff [pʌf] *n* soplo; (of smoke) bocanada; (of breathing, engine) resoplido; (also: **powder puff**) borla ■ *vt*: **to ~ one's pipe** dar chupadas a la pipa; (also: **puff out**: sails, cheeks) hinchar, inflar ■ *vi* (gen) soplar; (pant) jadear; **to ~ out smoke** echar humo
puffed [pʌft] *adj* (col: out of breath) sin aliento
puffin [ˈpʌfɪn] *n* frailecillo
puff pastry, puff paste (US) *n* hojaldre *m*
puffy [ˈpʌfɪ] *adj* hinchado
pull [pul] *n* (tug): **to give sth a ~** dar un tirón a algo; (fig: advantage) ventaja; (: influence) influencia ■ *vt* tirar de, jalar (LAm); (haul) tirar, jalar (LAm), arrastrar; (strain): **to ~ a muscle** sufrir un tirón ■ *vi* tirar, jalar (LAm); **to ~ to pieces** hacer pedazos; **to ~ one's punches** andarse con bromas; **to ~ one's weight** hacer su parte; **to ~ o.s. together** tranquilizarse; **to ~ sb's leg** tomar el pelo a algn; **to ~ strings (for sb)** enchufar (a algn)
▶ **pull about** *vt* (handle roughly: object) manosear; (: person) maltratar
▶ **pull apart** *vt* (take apart) desmontar
▶ **pull down** *vt* (house) derribar
▶ **pull in** *vi* (Aut: at the kerb) parar (junto a la acera); (Rail) llegar
▶ **pull off** *vt* (deal etc) cerrar
▶ **pull out** *vi* irse, marcharse; (Aut: from kerb) salir ■ *vt* sacar, arrancar
▶ **pull over** *vi* (Aut) hacerse a un lado
▶ **pull round, pull through** *vi* salvarse; (Med) recobrar la salud
▶ **pull up** *vi* (stop) parar ■ *vt* (uproot) arrancar, desarraigar; (stop) parar
pulley [ˈpulɪ] *n* polea
pull-out [ˈpulaut] *n* suplemento ■ *cpd* (pages, magazine) separable
pullover [ˈpuləuvəʳ] *n* jersey *m*, suéter *m*
pulp [pʌlp] *n* (of fruit) pulpa; (for paper) pasta; (pej: also: **pulp magazines** etc) prensa amarilla; **to reduce sth to ~** hacer algo papilla
pulpit [ˈpulpɪt] *n* púlpito
pulsate [pʌlˈseɪt] *vi* pulsar, latir
pulse [pʌls] *n* (Anat) pulso; (of music, engine) pulsación *f*; (Bot) legumbre *f*; **to feel** or **take sb's ~** tomar el pulso a algn

727

pulverize ['pʌlvəraɪz] vt pulverizar; (fig) hacer polvo

puma ['pju:mə] n puma m

pumice ['pʌmɪs], **pumice stone** n piedra pómez

pummel ['pʌml] vt aporrear

pump [pʌmp] n bomba; (shoe) zapatilla de tenis ■ vt sacar con una bomba; (fig: col) (son)sacar; **to ~ sb for information** (son)sacarle información a algn
▶ **pump up** vt inflar

pumpkin ['pʌmpkɪn] n calabaza

pun [pʌn] n juego de palabras

punch [pʌntʃ] n (blow) golpe m, puñetazo; (tool) punzón m; (for paper) perforadora; (for tickets) taladro; (drink) ponche m ■ vt (hit): **to ~ sb/sth** dar un puñetazo or golpear a algn/algo; (make a hole in) punzar; perforar

punch card, punched card [pʌntʃt-] n tarjeta perforada

punch-drunk ['pʌntʃdrʌŋk] adj (Brit) grogui, sonado

punch line n (of joke) remate m

punch-up ['pʌntʃʌp] n (Brit col) riña

punctual ['pʌŋktjuəl] adj puntual

punctuality [pʌŋktju'ælɪtɪ] n puntualidad f

punctually ['pʌŋktjuəlɪ] adv: **it will start ~ at six** empezará a las seis en punto

punctuate ['pʌŋktjueɪt] vt puntuar; (fig) interrumpir

punctuation [pʌŋktju'eɪʃən] n puntuación f

punctuation mark n signo de puntuación

puncture ['pʌŋktʃər] (Brit) n pinchazo ■ vt pinchar; **to have a ~** tener un pinchazo

pundit ['pʌndɪt] n experto(-a)

pungent ['pʌndʒənt] adj acre

punish ['pʌnɪʃ] vt castigar; **to ~ sb for sth/for doing sth** castigar a algn por algo/por haber hecho algo

punishable ['pʌnɪʃəbl] adj punible, castigable

punishing ['pʌnɪʃɪŋ] adj (fig: exhausting) agotador(a)

punishment ['pʌnɪʃmənt] n castigo; (fig, col): **to take a lot of ~** (boxer) recibir una paliza; (car) ser maltratado

punitive ['pju:nɪtɪv] adj punitivo

punk [pʌŋk] n (also: **punk rocker**) punki m/f; (also: **punk rock**) música punk; (US col: hoodlum) matón m

punt [pʌnt] n (boat) batea; (Ireland) libra irlandesa ■ vi (bet) apostar

punter ['pʌntər] n (gambler) jugador(a) m(f)

puny ['pju:nɪ] adj enclenque

pup [pʌp] n cachorro

pupil ['pju:pl] n alumno(-a); (of eye) pupila

puppet ['pʌpɪt] n títere m

puppet government n gobierno títere

puppy ['pʌpɪ] n cachorro, perrito

purchase ['pə:tʃɪs] n compra; (grip) agarre m, asidero ■ vt comprar

purchase order n orden f de compra

purchase price n precio de compra

purchaser ['pə:tʃɪsər] n comprador(a) m(f)

purchase tax n (Brit) impuesto sobre la venta

purchasing power ['pə:tʃɪsɪŋ-] n poder m adquisitivo

pure [pjuər] adj puro; **a ~ wool jumper** un jersey de pura lana; **it's laziness, ~ and simple** es pura vagancia

purebred ['pjuəbred] adj de pura sangre

purée ['pjuəreɪ] n puré m

purely ['pjuəlɪ] adv puramente

purgatory ['pə:gətərɪ] n purgatorio

purge [pə:dʒ] n (Med, Pol) purga ■ vt purgar

purification [pjuərɪfɪ'keɪʃən] n purificación f, depuración f

purify ['pjuərɪfaɪ] vt purificar, depurar

purist ['pjuərɪst] n purista m/f

puritan ['pjuərɪtən] n puritano(-a)

puritanical [pjuərɪ'tænɪkl] adj puritano

purity ['pjuərɪtɪ] n pureza

purl [pə:l] n punto del revés

purloin [pə:'lɔɪn] vt hurtar, robar

purple ['pə:pl] adj morado

purport [pə:'pɔ:t] vi: **to ~ to be/do** dar a entender que es/hace

purpose ['pə:pəs] n propósito; **on ~** a propósito, adrede; **to no ~** para nada, en vano; **for teaching purposes** con fines pedagógicos; **for the purposes of this meeting** para los fines de esta reunión

purpose-built ['pə:pəs'bɪlt] adj (Brit) construido especialmente

purposeful ['pə:pəsful] adj resuelto, determinado

purposely ['pə:pəslɪ] adv a propósito, adrede

purr [pə:r] n ronroneo ■ vi ronronear

purse [pə:s] n monedero; (US: handbag) bolso ■ vt fruncir

purser ['pə:sər] n (Naut) comisario(-a)

purse snatcher [-snætʃər] n (US) persona que roba por el procedimiento del tirón

pursue [pə'sju:] vt seguir; (harass) perseguir; (profession) ejercer; (pleasures) buscar; (inquiry, matter) seguir

pursuer [pə'sju:ər] n perseguidor(a) m(f)

pursuit [pə'sju:t] n (chase) caza; (of pleasure etc) busca; (occupation) actividad f; **in (the) ~ of sth** en busca de algo

purveyor [pə'veɪər] n proveedor(a) m(f)

pus [pʌs] n pus m

push [pʊʃ] n empujón m; (Mil) ataque m; (drive) empuje m ■ vt empujar; (button) apretar; (*promote*) promover; (*fig: press, advance: views*) fomentar; (*thrust*): **to ~ sth (into)** meter algo a la fuerza (en) ■ *vi* empujar; (*fig*) hacer esfuerzos; **at a ~** (*col*) a duras penas; **she is pushing 50** (*col*) raya en los 50; **to be pushed for time/money** andar justo de tiempo/escaso de dinero; **to ~ a door open/shut** abrir/cerrar una puerta empujándola; **to ~ for** (*better pay, conditions*) reivindicar; **"~"** (*on door*) "empujar"; (*on bell*) "pulse"

▶ **push aside** *vt* apartar con la mano
▶ **push in** *vi* colarse
▶ **push off** *vi* (*col*) largarse
▶ **push on** *vi* (*continue*) seguir adelante
▶ **push through** *vt* (*measure*) despachar
▶ **push up** *vt* (*total, prices*) hacer subir

push-bike ['puʃbaɪk] *n* (*Brit*) bicicleta
push-button ['puʃbʌtn] *adj* con botón de mando
pushchair ['puʃtʃɛər] *n* (*Brit*) silla de niño
pusher ['puʃər] *n* (*also*: **drug pusher**) traficante *m/f* de drogas
pushover ['puʃəuvər] *n* (*col*): **it's a ~** está tirado
push-up ['puʃʌp] *n* (*US*) flexión *f*
pushy ['puʃɪ] *adj* (*pej*) agresivo
puss [pus], **pussy** ['pusɪ], **pussy-cat** ['pusɪkæt] *n* minino
put [put] (*pt, pp* **put**) *vt* (*place*) poner, colocar; (*put into*) meter; (*express, say*) expresar; (*a question*) hacer; (*estimate*) calcular; (*cause to be*): **to ~ sb in a good/bad mood** poner a algn de buen/mal humor; **to ~ a lot of time into sth** dedicar mucho tiempo a algo; **to ~ money on a horse** apostar dinero en un caballo; **to ~ money into a company** invertir dinero en una compañía; **to ~ sb to a lot of trouble** causar mucha molestia a algn; **we ~ the children to bed** acostamos a los niños; **how shall I ~ it?** ¿cómo puedo explicarlo *or* decirlo?; **I ~ it to you that ...** le sugiero que ...; **to stay ~** no moverse
▶ **put about** *vi* (*Naut*) virar ■ *vt* (*rumour*) hacer correr
▶ **put across** *vt* (*ideas etc*) comunicar
▶ **put aside** *vt* (*lay down: book etc*) dejar *or* poner a un lado; (*save*) ahorrar; (*in shop*) guardar
▶ **put away** *vt* (*store*) guardar
▶ **put back** *vt* (*replace*) devolver a su lugar; (*postpone*) posponer; (*set back: watch, clock*) retrasar; **this will ~ us back 10 years** esto nos retrasará 10 años
▶ **put by** *vt* (*money*) guardar
▶ **put down** *vt* (*on ground*) poner en el suelo; (*animal*) sacrificar; (*in writing*) apuntar;

(*suppress: revolt etc*) sofocar; (*attribute*) atribuir; **~ me down for £15** apúntame por 15 libras; **~ it down on my account** (*Comm*) póngalo en mi cuenta
▶ **put forward** *vt* (*ideas*) presentar, proponer; (*date*) adelantar
▶ **put in** *vt* (*application, complaint*) presentar
▶ **put in for** *vt fus* (*job*) solicitar; (*promotion*) pedir
▶ **put off** *vt* (*postpone*) aplazar; (*discourage*) desanimar, quitar las ganas a
▶ **put on** *vt* (*clothes, lipstick etc*) ponerse; (*light etc*) encender; (*play etc*) presentar; (*brake*) echar; (*assume: accent, manner*) afectar, fingir; (*airs*) adoptar, darse; (*concert, exhibition etc*) montar; (*extra bus, train etc*) poner; (*col: kid, have on: esp US*) tomar el pelo a; (*inform, indicate*): **to ~ sb on to sb/sth** informar a algn de algn/algo; **to ~ on weight** engordar
▶ **put out** *vt* (*fire, light*) apagar; (*one's hand*) alargar; (*news, rumour*) hacer circular; (*tongue etc*) sacar; (*person: inconvenience*) molestar, fastidiar; (*dislocate: shoulder, vertebra, knee*) dislocar(se); (*vi: Naut*): **to ~ out to sea** hacerse a la mar; **to ~ out from Plymouth** salir de Plymouth
▶ **put through** *vt* (*call*) poner; **~ me through to Mr Low** póngame *or* comuníqueme (*LAm*) con el Señor Low
▶ **put together** *vt* unir, reunir; (*assemble: furniture*) armar, montar; (*meal*) preparar
▶ **put up** *vt* (*raise*) levantar, alzar; (*hang*) colgar; (*build*) construir; (*increase*) aumentar; (*accommodate*) alojar; (*incite*): **to ~ sb up to doing sth** instar *or* incitar a algn a hacer algo; **to ~ sth up for sale** poner algo a la venta
▶ **put upon** *vt fus*: **to be ~ upon** (*imposed upon*) dejarse explotar
▶ **put up with** *vt fus* aguantar

putrid ['pju:trɪd] *adj* podrido
putsch [putʃ] *n* golpe *m* de estado
putt [pʌt] *vt* hacer un putt ■ *n* putt *m*
putter ['pʌtər] *n* putter *m*
putting green ['pʌtɪŋ-] *n* green *m*, minigolf *m*
putty ['pʌtɪ] *n* masilla
put-up ['putʌp] *adj*: **~ job** (*Brit*) estafa
puzzle ['pʌzl] *n* (*riddle*) acertijo; (*jigsaw*) rompecabezas *m inv*; (*also*: **crossword puzzle**) crucigrama *m*; (*mystery*) misterio ■ *vt* dejar perplejo, confundir ■ *vi*: **to ~ about** quebrar la cabeza por; **to ~ over** (*sb's actions*) quebrarse la cabeza por; (*mystery, problem*) devanarse los sesos sobre; **to be puzzled about sth** no llegar a entender algo
puzzling ['pʌzlɪŋ] *adj* (*question*) misterioso, extraño; (*attitude, instructions*) extraño

729

PVC *n abbr* (= *polyvinyl chloride*) P.V.C. *m*
Pvt. *abbr* (*US Mil*) = **private**
PW *n abbr* (*US*) = **prisoner of war**
pw *abbr* (= *per week*) por semana
PX *n abbr* (*US Mil*: = *post exchange*) economato
  militar
pygmy ['pɪgmɪ] *n* pigmeo(-a)
pyjamas, pajamas (*US*) [pɪ'dʒɑːməz] *npl*
  pijama *m*, piyama *m* (*LAm*); **a pair of** ~ un
  pijama
pylon ['paɪlən] *n* torre *f* de conducción
  eléctrica
pyramid ['pɪrəmɪd] *n* pirámide *f*
Pyrenean [pɪrə'niːən] *adj* pirenaico
Pyrenees [pɪrə'niːz] *npl*: **the** ~ los Pirineos
Pyrex® ['paɪreks] *n* pírex *m* ▪ *cpd*: ~
  casserole cazuela de pírex
python ['paɪθən] *n* pitón *m*

Qq

Q, q [kju:] *n* (*letter*) Q, q *f*; **Q for Queen** Q de Quebec

Qatar [kæ'tɑ:] *n* Qatar *m*

QC *n abbr* (*Brit*: = *Queen's Counsel*) título concedido a determinados abogados

QCA *n abbr* (*Brit*: = *Qualifications and Curriculum Authority*) organismo que se encarga del currículum educativo en Inglaterra

QED *abbr* (= *quod erat demonstrandum*) Q.E.D.

QM *n abbr see* **quartermaster**

q.t. *n abbr* (*col*: = *quiet*): **on the q.t.** a hurtadillas

qty *abbr* (= *quantity*) cantidad

quack [kwæk] *n* (*of duck*) graznido; (*pej: doctor*) curandero(-a), matasanos *m inv* ■ *vi* graznar

quad [kwɔd] *abbr* = **quadrangle**; **quadruple**; **quadruplet**

quadrangle ['kwɔdræŋgl] *n* (*Brit: courtyard: abbr: quad*) patio

quadruple [kwɔ'dru:pl] *vt, vi* cuadruplicar

quadruplet [kwɔ'dru:plɪt] *n* cuatrillizo

quagmire ['kwægmaɪə'] *n* lodazal *m*, cenegal *m*

quail [kweɪl] *n* (*bird*) codorniz *f* ■ *vi* amedrentarse

quaint [kweɪnt] *adj* extraño; (*picturesque*) pintoresco

quaintly ['kweɪntlɪ] *adv* extrañamente; pintorescamente

quaintness ['kweɪntnɪs] *n* lo pintoresco, tipismo

quake [kweɪk] *vi* temblar ■ *n abbr* = **earthquake**

Quaker ['kweɪkə'] *n* cuáquero(-a)

qualification [kwɔlɪfɪ'keɪʃən] *n* (*reservation*) reserva; (*modification*) modificación *f*; (*act*) calificación *f*; (*paper qualification*) título; **what are your qualifications?** ¿qué títulos tienes?

qualified ['kwɔlɪfaɪd] *adj* (*trained*) cualificado; (*fit*) capacitado; (*limited*) limitado; (*professionally*) titulado; **~ for/to do sth** capacitado para/para hacer algo; **he's not ~ for the job** no está capacitado para ese trabajo; **it was a ~ success** fue un éxito relativo

qualify ['kwɔlɪfaɪ] *vt* (*Ling*) calificar a; (*capacitate*) capacitar; (*modify*) matizar; (*limit*) moderar ■ *vi* (*Sport*) clasificarse; **to ~ (as)** calificarse (de), graduarse (en), recibirse (de) (*LAm*); **to ~ (for)** reunir los requisitos (para); **to ~ as an engineer** sacar el título de ingeniero

qualifying ['kwɔlɪfaɪɪŋ] *adj* (*exam, round*) eliminatorio

qualitative ['kwɔlɪtətɪv] *adj* cualitativo

quality ['kwɔlɪtɪ] *n* calidad *f*; (*moral*) cualidad *f*; **of good/poor ~** de buena *or* alta/poca calidad

quality control *n* control *m* de calidad

quality of life *n* calidad *f* de vida

quality press *n* prensa seria; *ver nota*

qualm [kwɑ:m] *n* escrúpulo; **to have qualms about sth** sentir escrúpulos por algo

quandary ['kwɔndrɪ] *n*: **to be in a ~** verse en un dilema

quango ['kwæŋgəu] *n abbr* (*Brit*: = *quasi-autonomous non-governmental organization*) organismo semiautónomo de subvención estatal

quantifiable [kwɔntɪ'faɪəbl] *adj* cuantificable

quantitative ['kwɔntɪtətɪv] *adj* cuantitativo

quantity ['kwɔntɪtɪ] *n* cantidad *f*; **in ~** en grandes cantidades

quantity surveyor *n* aparejador(a) *m(f)*

q

quantum leap ['kwɔntəm-] n (fig) avance m espectacular

quarantine ['kwɔrntiːn] n cuarentena

quark [kwɑːk] n cuark m

quarrel ['kwɔrl] n riña, pelea ▪ vi reñir, pelearse; **to have a ~ with sb** reñir or pelearse con algn; **I can't ~ with that** no le veo pegas

quarrelsome ['kwɔrəlsəm] adj pendenciero

quarry ['kwɔrɪ] n (for stone) cantera; (animal) presa

quart [kwɔːt] n cuarto de galón = 1.136 l

quarter ['kwɔːtə^r] n cuarto, cuarta parte f; (of year) trimestre m; (district) barrio; (US, Canada: 25 cents) cuarto de dólar ▪ vt dividir en cuartos; (Mil: lodge) alojar; **quarters** npl (barracks) cuartel m; (living quarters) alojamiento sg; **a ~ of an hour** un cuarto de hora; **to pay by the ~** pagar trimestralmente or cada tres meses; **it's a ~ to** or (US) **of three** son las tres menos cuarto; **it's a ~ past** or (US) **after three** son las tres y cuarto; **from all quarters** de todas partes; **at close quarters** de cerca

quarterback ['kwɔːtəbæk] n (US: football) mariscal m de campo

quarter-deck ['kwɔːtədɛk] n (Naut) alcázar m

quarter final n cuarto de final

quarterly ['kwɔːtəlɪ] adj trimestral ▪ adv cada 3 meses, trimestralmente

quartermaster ['kwɔːtəmɑːstə^r] n (Mil) comisario, intendente m militar

quartet, quartette [kwɔːˈtɛt] n cuarteto

quarto ['kwɔːtəu] n tamaño holandés ▪ adj de tamaño holandés

quartz [kwɔːts] n cuarzo

quash [kwɔʃ] vt (verdict) anular, invalidar

quasi- ['kweɪzaɪ] pref cuasi

quaver ['kweɪvə^r] n (Brit Mus) corchea ▪ vi temblar

quay [kiː] n (also: **quayside**) muelle m

Que. abbr (Canada) = **Quebec**

queasiness ['kwiːzɪnɪs] n malestar m, náuseas fpl

queasy ['kwiːzɪ] adj: **to feel ~** tener náuseas

Quebec [kwɪˈbɛk] n Quebec m

queen [kwiːn] n reina; (Cards etc) dama

queen mother n reina madre

Queen's Speech n ver nota

● **QUEEN'S SPEECH**

● Se llama Queen's Speech (o "King's
● Speech") al discurso que pronuncia el
● monarca durante la sesión de apertura
● del Parlamento británico, en el que
● se expresan las líneas generales de la

política del gobierno para la nueva
legislatura. El Primer Ministro se encarga
de redactarlo con la ayuda del Consejo
de Ministros y es leído en la Cámara
de los Lores ("House of Lords") ante los
miembros de ambas cámaras.

queer [kwɪə^r] adj (odd) raro, extraño ▪ n (pej: col) marica m

quell [kwɛl] vt calmar; (put down) sofocar

quench [kwɛntʃ] vt (flames) apagar; **to ~ one's thirst** apagar la sed

querulous ['kwɛruləs] adj (person, voice) quejumbroso

query ['kwɪərɪ] n (question) pregunta; (doubt) duda ▪ vt preguntar; (disagree with, dispute) no estar conforme con, dudar de

quest [kwɛst] n busca, búsqueda

question ['kwɛstʃən] n pregunta; (matter) asunto, cuestión f ▪ vt (doubt) dudar de; (interrogate) interrogar, hacer preguntas a; **to ask sb a ~, put a ~ to sb** hacerle una pregunta a algn; **the ~ is ...** el asunto es ...; **to bring** or **call sth into ~** poner algo en (tela de) duda; **beyond ~** fuera de toda duda; **it's out of the ~** imposible, ni hablar

questionable ['kwɛstʃənəbl] adj discutible; (doubtful) dudoso

questioner ['kwɛstʃənə^r] n interrogador(a) m(f)

questioning ['kwɛstʃənɪŋ] adj inquisitivo ▪ n preguntas fpl; (by police etc) interrogatorio

question mark n punto de interrogación

questionnaire [kwɛstʃəˈnɛə^r] n cuestionario

queue [kjuː] (Brit) n cola ▪ vi hacer cola; **to jump the ~** colarse

quibble ['kwɪbl] vi andarse con sutilezas

quick [kwɪk] adj rápido; (temper) vivo; (agile) ágil; (mind) listo; (eye) agudo; (ear) fino ▪ n: **cut to the ~** (fig) herido en lo más vivo; **be ~!** ¡date prisa!; **to be ~ to act** obrar con prontitud; **she was ~ to see that** se dio cuenta de eso en seguida

quicken ['kwɪkən] vt apresurar ▪ vi apresurarse, darse prisa

quick-fire ['kwɪkfaɪə^r] adj (questions etc) rápido, (hecho) a quemarropa

quick fix n (pej) parche m

quickly ['kwɪklɪ] adv rápidamente, de prisa; **we must act ~** tenemos que actuar cuanto antes

quickness ['kwɪknɪs] n rapidez f; (of temper) viveza; (agility) agilidad f; (of mind, eye etc) agudeza

quicksand ['kwɪksænd] n arenas fpl movedizas

quickstep ['kwɪkstɛp] n baile de ritmo rápido

quick-tempered [kwɪk'tɛmpəd] *adj* de genio vivo

quick-witted [kwɪk'wɪtɪd] *adj* listo, despabilado

quid [kwɪd] *n pl inv* (*Brit: col*) libra

quid pro quo ['kwɪdprəu'kwəu] *n* quid pro quo *m*, compensación *f*

quiet ['kwaɪət] *adj* (*not busy: day*) tranquilo; (*silent*) callado; (*reserved*) reservado; (*discreet*) discreto; (*not noisy: engine*) silencioso ■ *n* tranquilidad *f* ■ *vt, vi* (*US*) = **quieten; keep ~!** ¡cállate!, ¡silencio!; **business is ~ at this time of year** hay poco movimiento en esta época

quieten ['kwaɪətn] (*also:* **quieten down**) *vi* (*grow calm*) calmarse; (*grow silent*) callarse ■ *vt* calmar; hacer callar

quietly ['kwaɪətlɪ] *adv* tranquilamente; (*silently*) silenciosamente

quietness ['kwaɪətnɪs] *n* (*silence*) silencio; (*calm*) tranquilidad *f*

quill [kwɪl] *n* (*of porcupine*) púa; (*pen*) pluma

quilt [kwɪlt] *n* (*Brit*) edredón *m*

quin [kwɪn] *n abbr* = **quintuplet**

quince [kwɪns] *n* membrillo

quinine [kwɪ'ni:n] *n* quinina

quintet, quintette [kwɪn'tɛt] *n* quinteto

quintuplet [kwɪn'tju:plɪt] *n* quintillizo

quip [kwɪp] *n* ocurrencia ■ *vi* decir con.ironía

quire ['kwaɪəʳ] *n* mano *f* de papel

quirk [kwə:k] *n* peculiaridad *f*; **by some ~ of fate** por algún capricho del destino

quit (*pt, pp* **~** *or* **quitted**) [kwɪt] *vt* dejar, abandonar; (*premises*) desocupar; (*Comput*) abandonar ■ *vi* (*give up*) renunciar; (*go away*) irse; (*resign*) dimitir; **~ stalling!** (*US col*)

¡déjate de evasivas!

quite [kwaɪt] *adv* (*rather*) bastante; (*entirely*) completamente; **~ a few of them** un buen número de ellos; **~ (so)!** ¡así es!, ¡exactamente!; **~ new** bastante nuevo; **that's not ~ right** eso no está del todo bien; **not ~ as many as last time** no tantos como la última vez; **she's ~ pretty** es bastante guapa

Quito ['ki:təu] *n* Quito

quits [kwɪts] *adj:* **~ (with)** en paz (con); **let's call it ~** quedamos en paz

quiver ['kwɪvəʳ] *vi* estremecerse ■ *n* (*for arrows*) carcaj *m*

quiz [kwɪz] *n* (*game*) concurso; (*: TV, Radio*) programa-concurso; (*questioning*) interrogatorio ■ *vt* interrogar

quizzical ['kwɪzɪkl] *adj* burlón(-ona)

quoits [kwɔits] *npl* juego de aros

quorum ['kwɔ:rəm] *n* quórum *m*

quota ['kwəutə] *n* cuota

quotation [kwəu'teɪʃən] *n* cita; (*estimate*) presupuesto

quotation marks *npl* comillas *fpl*

quote [kwəut] *n* cita ■ *vt* (*sentence*) citar; (*Comm: sum, figure*) cotizar ■ *vi:* **to ~ from** citar de; **quotes** *npl* (*inverted commas*) comillas *fpl*; **in quotes** entre comillas; **the figure quoted for the repairs** el presupuesto dado para las reparaciones; **~ ... unquote** (*in dictation*) comillas iniciales ... finales

quotient ['kwəuʃənt] *n* cociente *m*

qv *n abbr* (= *quod vide: which see*) q.v.

qwerty keyboard ['kwə:tɪ-] *n* teclado QWERTY

q

Rr

R, r [ɑːˈr] *n* (*letter*) R, r *f*; **R for Robert,** (US)
R **for Roger** R de Ramón

R *abbr* (= *right*) dcha.; (= *river*) R.; (= *Réaumur*
(*scale*)) R; (*US Cine*: = *restricted*) *sólo mayores*; (*US
Pol*: = *republican*; *Brit*: = *Rex, Regina*) R

RA *abbr* = **rear admiral** ■ *n abbr* (*Brit*) = **Royal
Academy; Royal Academician**

RAAF *n abbr* = **Royal Australian Air Force**

Rabat [rəˈbɑːt] *n* Rabat *m*

rabbi [ˈræbaɪ] *n* rabino

rabbit [ˈræbɪt] *n* conejo ■ *vi*: **to ~ (on)** (*Brit
col*) hablar sin ton ni son

rabbit hutch *n* conejera

rabble [ˈræbl] *n* (*pej*) chusma, populacho

rabies [ˈreɪbiːz] *n* rabia

RAC *n abbr* (*Brit*: = *Royal Automobile Club*) ≈ RACE
m (*SP*)

raccoon [rəˈkuːn] *n* mapache *m*

race [reɪs] *n* carrera; (*species*) raza ■ *vt* (*horse*)
hacer correr; (*person*) competir contra;
(*engine*) acelerar ■ *vi* (*compete*) competir;
(*run*) correr; (*pulse*) latir a ritmo acelerado;
the arms ~ la carrera armamentista; **the
human ~** el género humano; **he raced
across the road** cruzó corriendo la carretera;
to ~ in/out entrar/salir corriendo

race car *n* (*US*) = **racing car**

race car driver *n* (*US*) = **racing driver**

racecourse [ˈreɪskɔːs] *n* hipódromo

racehorse [ˈreɪshɔːs] *n* caballo de carreras

race meeting *n* concurso hípico

race relations *npl* relaciones *fpl* raciales

racetrack [ˈreɪstræk] *n* hipódromo; (*for cars*)
circuito de carreras

racial [ˈreɪʃl] *adj* racial

racial discrimination *n* discriminación *f*
racial

racial integration *n* integración *f* racial

racialism [ˈreɪʃəlɪzəm] *n* racismo

racialist [ˈreɪʃəlɪst] *adj, n* racista *m/f*

racing [ˈreɪsɪŋ] *n* carreras *fpl*

racing car *n* (*Brit*) coche *m* de carreras

racing driver *n* (*Brit*) corredor(a) *m(f)* de coches

racism [ˈreɪsɪzəm] *n* racismo

racist [ˈreɪsɪst] *adj, n* racista *m/f*

rack [ræk] *n* (*also*: **luggage rack**) rejilla
(portaequipajes); (*shelf*) estante *m*; (*also*:
roof rack) baca; (*also*: **clothes rack**) perchero
■ *vt* (*cause pain to*) atormentar; **to go to ~
and ruin** venirse abajo; **to ~ one's brains**
devanarse los sesos

▶ **rack up** *vt* conseguir, ganar

racket [ˈrækɪt] *n* (*for tennis*) raqueta; (*noise*)
ruido, estrépito; (*swindle*) estafa, timo

racketeer [rækɪˈtɪər] *n* (*esp US*) estafador(a)
m(f)

racoon [rəˈkuːn] *n* = **raccoon**

racquet [ˈrækɪt] *n* raqueta

racy [ˈreɪsɪ] *adj* picante, subido

RADA [ˈrɑːdə] *n abbr* (*Brit*) = **Royal Academy
of Dramatic Art**

radar [ˈreɪdɑːr] *n* radar *m*

radar trap *n* trampa radar

radial [ˈreɪdɪəl] *adj* (*tyre*: *also*: **radial-ply**) radial

radiance [ˈreɪdɪəns] *n* brillantez *f*, resplandor *m*

radiant [ˈreɪdɪənt] *adj* brillante,
resplandeciente

radiate [ˈreɪdɪeɪt] *vt* (*heat*) radiar, irradiar
■ *vi* (*lines*) extenderse

radiation [reɪdɪˈeɪʃən] *n* radiación *f*

radiation sickness *n* enfermedad *f* de
radiación

radiator [ˈreɪdɪeɪtər] *n* (*Aut*) radiador *m*

radiator cap *n* tapón *m* de radiador

radiator grill *n* (*Aut*) rejilla del radiador

radical [ˈrædɪkl] *adj* radical

radically [ˈrædɪkəlɪ] *adv* radicalmente

radii [ˈreɪdɪaɪ] *npl of* **radius**

radio [ˈreɪdɪəu] *n* radio *f* or *m* (*LAm*) ■ *vi*:
to ~ to sb mandar un mensaje por radio a
algn ■ *vt* (*information*) radiar, transmitir por
radio; (*one's position*) indicar por radio; (*person*)
llamar por radio; **on the ~** en *or* por la radio

radioactive [reɪdɪəuˈæktɪv] *adj* radi(o)activo

radioactivity [reɪdɪəuækˈtɪvɪtɪ] *n*
radi(o)actividad *f*

radio announcer n locutor(a) m(f) de radio
radio-controlled [reɪdɪəukən'trəuld] adj
teledirigido
radiographer [reɪdɪ'ɔgrəfə^r] n radiógrafo(-a)
radiography [reɪdɪ'ɔgrəfɪ] n radiografía
radiology [reɪdɪ'ɔlədʒɪ] n radiología
radio station n emisora
radio taxi n radio taxi m
radiotelephone [reɪdɪəu'tɛlɪfəun] n
radioteléfono
radiotelescope [reɪdɪəu'tɛlɪskəup] n
radiotelescopio
radiotherapist [reɪdɪəu'θɛrəpɪst] n
radioterapeuta m/f
radiotherapy ['reɪdɪəuθɛrəpɪ] n radioterapia
radish ['rædɪʃ] n rábano
radium ['reɪdɪəm] n radio
radius (pl **radii**) ['reɪdɪəs, -ɪaɪ] n radio; **within
a ~ of 50 miles** en un radio de 50 millas
RAF n abbr (Brit) see **Royal Air Force**
raffia ['ræfɪə] n rafia
raffle ['ræfl] n rifa, sorteo ▪ vt (object) rifar
raft [rɑːft] n (craft) balsa; (also: **life raft**) balsa
salvavidas
rafter ['rɑːftə^r] n viga
rag [ræg] n (piece of cloth) trapo; (torn cloth)
harapo; (pej: newspaper) periodicucho; (for
charity) actividades estudiantiles benéficas ▪ vt
(Brit) tomar el pelo a; **rags** npl harapos mpl;
in rags en harapos, hecho jirones
rag-and-bone man [rægən'bəunmæn] n
(Brit) trapero
rag doll n muñeca de trapo
rage [reɪdʒ] n (fury) rabia, furor m ▪ vi (person)
rabiar, estar furioso; (storm) bramar; **to fly
into a ~** montar en cólera; **it's all the ~** es
lo último
ragged ['rægɪd] adj (edge) desigual,
mellado; (cuff) roto; (appearance) andrajoso,
harapiento; **~ left/right** (text) margen m
izquierdo/derecho irregular
raging ['reɪdʒɪŋ] adj furioso; **in a ~ temper**
de un humor de mil demonios
rag trade n: **the ~** (col) el ramo de la
confección
rag week n ver nota

RAG WEEK

En la universidad los estudiantes suelen
organizar cada año lo que llaman rag week.
Consiste en una serie de actos festivos y
de participación general como teatro en
la calle, marchas patrocinadas etc, para
hacer colectas con fines benéficos. En
ocasiones hacen también una revista
("rag mag"), que consiste básicamente en

chistes más bien picantes para vender a
los transeúntes, e incluso un baile de gala
("rag ball").

raid [reɪd] n (Mil) incursión f; (criminal) asalto;
(by police) redada, allanamiento (LAm) ▪ vt
invadir, atacar; asaltar
raider ['reɪdə^r] n invasor(a) m(f)
rail [reɪl] n (on stair) barandilla, pasamanos
m inv; (on bridge) pretil m; (of balcony, ship)
barandilla; (for train) riel m, carril m; **rails** npl
vía sg; **by ~** por ferrocarril, en tren
railcard ['reɪlkɑːd] n (Brit) tarjeta para obtener
descuentos en el tren; **Young Person's ~**
≈ Tarjeta joven (SP)
railing ['reɪlɪŋ] n, **railings** ['reɪlɪŋz] npl
verja sg
railway ['reɪlweɪ], (US) **railroad** ['reɪlrəud] n
ferrocarril m, vía férrea
railway engine n (máquina) locomotora
railway line n (Brit) línea (de ferrocarril)
railwayman ['reɪlweɪmən] n (Brit) ferroviario
railway station n (Brit) estación f de
ferrocarril
rain [reɪn] n lluvia ▪ vi llover; **in the ~** bajo
la lluvia; **it's raining** llueve, está lloviendo;
it's raining cats and dogs está lloviendo a
cántaros or a mares
rainbow ['reɪnbəu] n arco iris
raincoat ['reɪnkəut] n impermeable m
raindrop ['reɪndrɔp] n gota de lluvia
rainfall ['reɪnfɔːl] n lluvia
rainforest ['reɪnfɔrɪst] n selva tropical
rainproof ['reɪnpruːf] adj impermeable,
a prueba de lluvia
rainstorm ['reɪnstɔːm] n temporal m (de
lluvia)
rainwater ['reɪnwɔːtə^r] n agua de lluvia
rainy ['reɪnɪ] adj lluvioso
raise [reɪz] n aumento ▪ vt (lift) levantar;
(build) erigir, edificar; (increase) aumentar;
(doubts) suscitar; (a question) plantear; (cattle,
family) criar; (crop) cultivar; (army) reclutar;
(funds) reunir; (loan) obtener; (end: embargo)
levantar; **to ~ one's voice** alzar la voz; **to ~
one's glass to sb/sth** brindar por algn/algo;
to ~ a laugh/a smile provocar risa/una
sonrisa; **to ~ sb's hopes** dar esperanzas a
algn
raisin ['reɪzn] n pasa de Corinto
rake [reɪk] n (tool) rastrillo; (person) libertino
▪ vt (garden) rastrillar; (fire) hurgar; (with
machine gun) barrer
▸ **rake in, rake together** vt sacar
rake-off ['reɪkɔf] n (col) comisión f, tajada
rakish ['reɪkɪʃ] adj (dissolute) libertino; **at a ~
angle** (hat) echado a un lado, de lado

735

rally ['rælɪ] n reunión f; (Pol) mitin m; (Aut) rallye m; (Tennis) peloteo ■ vt reunir ■ vi reunirse; (sick person) recuperarse; (Stock Exchange) recuperarse
▶ **rally round** vt fus (fig) dar apoyo a
rallying point ['rælɪɪŋ-] n (Pol, Mil) punto de reunión
RAM [ræm] n abbr (Comput: = random access memory) RAM f
ram [ræm] n carnero; (Tech) pisón m ■ vt (crash into) dar contra, chocar con; (tread down) apisonar
Ramadan ['ræmədæn] n Ramadán m
ramble ['ræmbl] n caminata, excursión f en el campo ■ vi (pej: also: **ramble on**) divagar
rambler ['ræmblər] n excursionista m/f; (Bot) trepadora
rambling ['ræmblɪŋ] adj (speech) inconexo; (Bot) trepador(a); (house) laberíntico
rambunctious [ræm'bʌŋkʃəs] adj (US) = **rumbustious**
RAMC n abbr (Brit) = **Royal Army Medical Corps**
ramification [ræmɪfɪ'keɪʃən] n ramificación f
ramp [ræmp] n rampa; **on/off ~** n (US Aut) vía de acceso/salida; "**~**" (Aut) "rampa"
rampage [ræm'peɪdʒ] n: **to be on the ~** desmandarse
rampant ['ræmpənt] adj (disease etc): **to be ~** estar muy extendido
rampart ['ræmpɑːt] n terraplén m; (wall) muralla
ram raid vt atracar (rompiendo el escaparate con un coche)
ramshackle ['ræmʃækl] adj destartalado
RAN n abbr = **Royal Australian Navy**
ran [ræn] pt of **run**
R & B n abbr = **rhythm and blues**
ranch [rɑːntʃ] n (US) hacienda, estancia
rancher ['rɑːntʃər] n ganadero
rancid ['rænsɪd] adj rancio
rancour, rancor (US) ['ræŋkər] n rencor m
R & D n abbr (= research and development) I + D
random ['rændəm] adj fortuito, sin orden; (Comput, Math) aleatorio ■ n: **at ~** al azar
random access n (Comput) acceso aleatorio
R & R n abbr (also US Mil) = **rest and recreation**
randy ['rændɪ] adj (Brit col) cachondo, caliente
rang [ræŋ] pt of **ring**
range [reɪndʒ] n (of mountains) cadena de montañas, cordillera; (of missile) alcance m; (of voice) registro; (series) serie f; (of products) surtido; (Mil: also: **shooting range**) campo de tiro; (also: **kitchen range**) fogón m ■ vt (place) colocar; (arrange) arreglar ■ vi: **to ~ over** (wander) recorrer; (extend) extenderse

por; **within (firing) ~** a tiro;
do you have anything else in this price ~? ¿tiene algo más de esta gama de precios?; **intermediate-/short-~ missile** proyectil m de medio/corto alcance; **to ~ from ... to ...** oscilar entre ... y ...; **ranged left/right** (text) alineado a la izquierda/derecha
ranger [reɪndʒər] n guardabosques m inv
Rangoon [ræŋ'guːn] n Rangún m
rangy ['reɪndʒɪ] adj alto y delgado
rank [ræŋk] n (row) fila; (Mil) rango; (status) categoría; (Brit: also: **taxi rank**) parada ■ vi: **to ~ among** figurar entre ■ adj (stinking) fétido, rancio; (hypocrisy, injustice etc) manifiesto; **the ~ and file** (fig) las bases; **to close ranks** (Mil) cerrar filas; (fig) hacer un frente común; **~ outsider** participante m/f sin probabilidades de vencer; **I ~ him sixth** yo le pongo en sexto lugar
rankle ['ræŋkl] vi (insult) doler
ransack ['rænsæk] vt (search) registrar; (plunder) saquear
ransom ['rænsəm] n rescate m; **to hold sb to ~** (fig) poner a algn entre la espada y la pared
rant [rænt] vi despotricar
ranting ['ræntɪŋ] n desvaríos mpl
rap [ræp] vt golpear, dar un golpecito en
rape [reɪp] n violación f; (Bot) colza ■ vt violar
rape oil, rapeseed oil ['reɪpsiːd-] n aceite m de colza
rapid ['ræpɪd] adj rápido
rapidity [rə'pɪdɪtɪ] n rapidez f
rapidly ['ræpɪdlɪ] adv rápidamente
rapids ['ræpɪdz] npl (Geo) rápidos mpl
rapier ['reɪpɪər] n estoque m
rapist ['reɪpɪst] n violador m
rapport [ræ'pɔːr] n entendimiento
rapprochement [ræ'prɔʃmɑːŋ] n acercamiento
rapt [ræpt] adj (attention) profundo; **to be ~ in contemplation** estar ensimismado
rapture ['ræptʃər] n éxtasis m
rapturous ['ræptʃərəs] adj extático; (applause) entusiasta; **a ~ (party)** macrofiesta con música máquina; **~ music** música máquina
rare [rɛər] adj raro, poco común; (Culin: steak) poco hecho; **it is ~ to find that ...** es raro descubrir que ...
rarefied ['rɛərɪfaɪd] adj (air, atmosphere) enrarecido
rarely ['rɛəlɪ] adv rara vez, pocas veces
raring ['rɛərɪŋ] adj: **to be ~ to go** (col) tener muchas ganas de empezar
rarity ['rɛərɪtɪ] n rareza
rascal ['rɑːskl] n pillo(-a), pícaro(-a)

rash [ræʃ] *adj* imprudente, precipitado ■ *n* (*Med*) salpullido, erupción *f* (cutánea); **to come out in a ~** salir salpullidos
rasher ['ræʃəʳ] *n* loncha
rashly ['ræʃlɪ] *adv* imprudentemente, precipitadamente
rashness ['ræʃnɪs] *n* imprudencia, precipitación *f*
rasp [rɑːsp] *n* (*tool*) escofina ■ *vt* (*speak: also:* **rasp out**) decir con voz áspera
raspberry ['rɑːzbərɪ] *n* frambuesa
rasping ['rɑːspɪŋ] *adj*: **a ~ noise** un ruido áspero
Rastafarian [ræstə'fɛərɪən] *adj, n* rastafari *m/f*
rat [ræt] *n* rata
ratchet ['rætʃɪt] *n* (*Tech*) trinquete *m*
rate [reɪt] *n* (*ratio*) razón *f*; (*percentage*) tanto por ciento; (*price*) precio; (: *of hotel*) tarifa; (*of interest*) tipo; (*speed*) velocidad *f* ■ *vt* (*value*) tasar; (*estimate*) estimar; **to ~ as** ser considerado como; **rates** *npl* (*Brit*) impuesto *sg* municipal; (*fees*) tarifa *sg*; **failure ~** porcentaje *m* de fallos; **pulse ~** pulsaciones *fpl* por minuto; **~ of pay** tipos *mpl* de sueldo; **at a ~ of 60 kph** a una velocidad de 60 kph; **~ of growth** ritmo de crecimiento; **~ of return** (*Comm*) tasa de rendimiento; **bank ~** tipo *or* tasa de interés bancario; **at any ~** en todo caso; **to ~ sb/sth highly** tener a algn/ algo en alta estima; **the house is rated at £84 per annum** (*Brit*) la casa está tasada en 84 libras al año
rateable value ['reɪtəbl-] *n* (*Brit*) valor *m* impuesto
rate-capping ['reɪtkæpɪŋ] *n* (*Brit*) fijación *f* de las contribuciones
ratepayer ['reɪtpeɪəʳ] *n* (*Brit*) contribuyente *m/f*
rather ['rɑːðəʳ] *adv* antes, más bien; (*somewhat*) algo, un poco; (*quite*) bastante; **it's ~ expensive** es algo caro; (*too much*) es demasiado caro; **there's ~ a lot** hay bastante; **I would** *or* **I'd ~ go** preferiría ir; **I'd ~ not** prefiero que no; **I ~ think he won't come** me inclino a creer que no vendrá; **or ~** (*more accurately*) o mejor dicho
ratification [rætɪfɪ'keɪʃən] *n* ratificación *f*
ratify ['rætɪfaɪ] *vt* ratificar
rating ['reɪtɪŋ] *n* (*valuation*) tasación *f*; (*standing*) posición *f*; (*Brit Naut: sailor*) marinero; **ratings** *npl* (*Radio, TV*) clasificación *f*
ratio ['reɪʃɪəu] *n* razón *f*; **in the ~ of 100 to 1** a razón de *or* en la proporción de 100 a 1
ration ['ræʃən] *n* ración *f*; **rations** *npl* víveres *mpl* ■ *vt* racionar

rational ['ræʃənl] *adj* racional; (*solution, reasoning*) lógico, razonable; (*person*) cuerdo, sensato
rationale [ræʃə'nɑːl] *n* razón *f* fundamental
rationalism ['ræʃnəlɪzəm] *n* racionalismo
rationalization [ræʃnəlaɪ'zeɪʃən] *n* racionalización *f*
rationalize ['ræʃnəlaɪz] *vt* (*reorganize: industry*) racionalizar
rationally ['ræʃnəlɪ] *adv* racionalmente; (*logically*) lógicamente
rationing ['ræʃnɪŋ] *n* racionamiento
ratpack ['rætpæk] *n* (*Brit col*) periodistas que persiguen a los famosos
rat race *n* lucha incesante por la supervivencia
rattan [ræ'tæn] *n* rota, caña de Indias
rattle ['rætl] *n* golpeteo; (*of train etc*) traqueteo; (*object: of baby*) sonaja, sonajero; (: *of sports fan*) matraca ■ *vi* sonar, golpear; traquetear; (*small objects*) castañetear ■ *vt* hacer sonar agitando; (*col: disconcert*) poner nervioso a
rattlesnake ['rætlsneɪk] *n* serpiente *f* de cascabel
ratty ['rætɪ] *adj* (*col*) furioso; **to get ~** mosquearse
raucous ['rɔːkəs] *adj* estridente, ronco
raucously ['rɔːkəslɪ] *adv* de modo estridente, roncamente
raunchy ['rɔːntʃɪ] *adj* (*col*) lascivo
ravage ['rævɪdʒ] *vt* hacer estragos en, destrozar; **ravages** *npl* estragos *mpl*
rave [reɪv] *vi* (*in anger*) encolerizarse; (*with enthusiasm*) entusiasmarse; (*Med*) delirar, desvariar ■ *cpd*: **~ review** reseña entusiasta; **a ~ (party)** macrofiesta con música máquina; **~ music** música máquina
raven ['reɪvən] *n* cuervo
ravenous ['rævənəs] *adj*: **to be ~** tener un hambre canina
ravine [rə'viːn] *n* barranco
raving ['reɪvɪŋ] *adj*: **~ lunatic** loco de atar
ravings ['reɪvɪŋz] *npl* desvaríos *mpl*
ravioli [rævɪ'əulɪ] *n* ravioles *mpl*, ravioli *mpl*
ravish ['rævɪʃ] *vt* (*charm*) encantar, embelesar; (*rape*) violar
ravishing ['rævɪʃɪŋ] *adj* encantador(a)
raw [rɔː] *adj* (*uncooked*) crudo; (*not processed*) bruto; (*sore*) vivo; (*inexperienced*) novato, inexperto
Rawalpindi [rɔːl'pɪndɪ] *n* Rawalpindi *m*
raw data *n* (*Comput*) datos *mpl* en bruto
raw deal *n* (*col: bad deal*) mala pasada *or* jugada; (: *harsh treatment*) injusticia
raw material *n* materia prima
ray [reɪ] *n* rayo; **~ of hope** (rayo de) esperanza
rayon ['reɪɔn] *n* rayón *m*

raze [reɪz] *vt* (*also*: **raze to the ground**) arrasar, asolar

razor ['reɪzəʳ] *n* (*open*) navaja; (*safety razor*) máquina de afeitar

razor blade *n* hoja de afeitar

razzle ['ræzl], **razzle-dazzle** ['ræzl'dæzl] *n* (*Brit col*): **to be/go on the ~(-dazzle)** estar/irse de juerga

razzmatazz ['ræzmə'tæz] *n* (*col*) animación *f*, bullicio

RC *abbr* = **Roman Catholic**

RCAF *n abbr* = **Royal Canadian Air Force**

RCMP *n abbr* = **Royal Canadian Mounted Police**

RCN *n abbr* = **Royal Canadian Navy**

RD *abbr* (*US Post*) = **rural delivery**

Rd *abbr* = **road**

RDC *n abbr* (*Brit*) = **rural district council**

RE *n abbr* (*Brit*: = *religious education*) (*Brit Mil*) = **Royal Engineers**

re [riː] *prep* con referencia a

re... [riː] *pref* re...

reach [riːtʃ] *n* alcance *m*; (*Boxing*) envergadura; (*of river etc*) extensión *f* entre dos recodos ■ *vt* alcanzar, llegar a; (*achieve*) lograr ■ *vi* extenderse; (*stretch out hand*: *also*: **reach down, reach over**: *also*: **reach across** *etc*) tender la mano; **within ~** al alcance (de la mano); **out of ~** fuera del alcance; **to ~ out for sth** alargar *or* tender la mano para tomar algo; **can I ~ you at your hotel?** ¿puedo localizarte en tu hotel?; **to ~ sb by phone** comunicarse con algn por teléfono

react [riː'ækt] *vi* reaccionar

reaction [riː'ækʃən] *n* reacción *f*

reactionary [riː'ækʃənrɪ] *adj*, *n* reaccionario(-a) *m(f)*

reactor [riː'æktəʳ] *n* reactor *m*

read (*pt*, *pp* ~) [riːd, rɛd] *vi* leer ■ *vt* leer; (*understand*) entender; (*study*) estudiar; **to take sth as ~** (*fig*) dar algo por sentado; **do you ~ me?** (*Tel*) ¿me escucha?; **to ~ between the lines** leer entre líneas
  ▸ **read out** *vt* leer en alta voz
  ▸ **read over** *vt* repasar
  ▸ **read through** *vt* (*quickly*) leer rápidamente, echar un vistazo a; (*thoroughly*) leer con cuidado *or* detenidamente
  ▸ **read up** *vt*, **read up on** *vt fus* documentarse sobre

readable ['riːdəbl] *adj* (*writing*) legible; (*book*) que merece la pena leer

reader ['riːdəʳ] *n* lector(a) *m(f)*; (*book*) libro de lecturas; (*Brit*: *at university*) profesor(a) *m(f)*

readership ['riːdəʃɪp] *n* (*of paper etc*) número de lectores

readily ['rɛdɪlɪ] *adv* (*willingly*) de buena gana; (*easily*) fácilmente; (*quickly*) en seguida

readiness ['rɛdɪnɪs] *n* buena voluntad; (*preparedness*) preparación *f*; **in ~** (*prepared*) listo, preparado

reading ['riːdɪŋ] *n* lectura; (*understanding*) comprensión *f*; (*on instrument*) indicación *f*

reading lamp *n* lámpara portátil

reading matter *n* lectura

reading room *n* sala de lectura

readjust [riːə'dʒʌst] *vt* reajustar ■ *vi* (*person*): **to ~ to** reajustarse a

readjustment [riːə'dʒʌstmənt] *n* reajuste *m*

ready ['rɛdɪ] *adj* listo, preparado; (*willing*) dispuesto; (*available*) disponible ■ *n*: **at the ~** (*Mil*) listo para tirar; **~ for use** listo para usar; **to be ~ to do sth** estar listo para hacer algo; **to get ~** *vi* prepararse ■ *vt* preparar

ready cash *n* efectivo

ready-made ['rɛdɪ'meɪd] *adj* confeccionado

ready money *n* dinero contante

ready reckoner *n* tabla de cálculos hechos

ready-to-wear ['rɛdɪtə'wɛəʳ] *adj* confeccionado

reaffirm [riːə'fəːm] *vt* reafirmar

reagent [riː'eɪdʒənt] *n* reactivo

real [rɪəl] *adj* verdadero, auténtico; **in ~ terms** en términos reales; **in ~ life** en la vida real, en la realidad

real ale *n* cerveza elaborada tradicionalmente

real estate *n* bienes *mpl* raíces

real estate agency *n* = **estate agency**

realism ['rɪəlɪzəm] *n* (*also Art*) realismo

realist ['rɪəlɪst] *n* realista *m/f*

realistic [rɪə'lɪstɪk] *adj* realista

realistically [rɪə'lɪstɪklɪ] *adv* de modo realista

reality [riː'ælɪtɪ] *n* realidad *f*; **in ~** en realidad

reality TV *n* telerrealidad *f*

realization [rɪəlaɪ'zeɪʃən] *n* comprensión *f*; (*of a project*) realización *f*; (*Comm*: *of assets*) realización *f*

realize ['rɪəlaɪz] *vt* (*understand*) darse cuenta de; (*a project*) realizar; (*Comm*: *asset*) realizar; **I ~ that ...** comprendo *or* entiendo que ...

really ['rɪəlɪ] *adv* realmente; **~?** ¿de veras?

realm [rɛlm] *n* reino; (*fig*) esfera

real time *n* (*Comput*) tiempo real

Realtor® ['rɪəltɔːʳ] *n* (*US*) corredor(a) *m(f)* de bienes raíces

ream [riːm] *n* resma; **reams** (*fig*, *col*) montones *mpl*

reap [riːp] *vt* segar; (*fig*) cosechar, recoger

reaper ['riːpəʳ] *n* segador(a) *m(f)*

reappear [riːə'pɪəʳ] *vi* reaparecer

reappearance [riːə'pɪərəns] *n* reaparición *f*

reapply [riːə'plaɪ] *vi* volver a presentarse, hacer *or* presentar una nueva solicitud

reappoint [riːəˈpɔɪnt] vt volver a nombrar
reappraisal [riːəˈpreɪzl] n revaluación f
rear [rɪəʳ] adj trasero ▪ n parte f trasera ▪ vt (cattle, family) criar ▪ vi (also: **rear up**: animal) encabritarse
rear-engined [ˈrɪərˈɛndʒɪnd] adj (Aut) con motor trasero
rearguard [ˈrɪəɡɑːd] n retaguardia
rearm [riːˈɑːm] vt rearmar ▪ vi rearmarse
rearmament [riːˈɑːməmənt] n rearme m
rearrange [riːəˈreɪndʒ] vt ordenar or arreglar de nuevo
rear-view [ˈrɪəvjuː]: ~ **mirror** n (Aut) espejo retrovisor
reason [ˈriːzn] n razón f ▪ vi: **to ~ with sb** tratar de que algn entre en razón; **it stands to ~ that** es lógico que; **the ~ for/why** la causa de/la razón por la cual; **she claims with good ~ that she's underpaid** dice con razón que está mal pagada; **all the more ~ why you should not sell it** razón de más para que no lo vendas
reasonable [ˈriːznəbl] adj razonable; (sensible) sensato
reasonably [ˈriːznəblɪ] adv razonablemente; **a ~ accurate report** un informe bastante exacto
reasoned [ˈriːznd] adj (argument) razonado
reasoning [ˈriːznɪŋ] n razonamiento, argumentos mpl
reassemble [riːəˈsɛmbl] vt volver a reunir; (machine) montar de nuevo ▪ vi volver a reunirse
reassert [riːəˈsəːt] vt reafirmar, reiterar
reassurance [riːəˈʃuərəns] n consuelo
reassure [riːəˈʃuəʳ] vt tranquilizar; **to ~ sb that** tranquilizar a algn asegurándole que
reassuring [riːəˈʃuərɪŋ] adj tranquilizador(a)
reawakening [riːəˈweɪknɪŋ] n despertar m
rebate [ˈriːbeɪt] n (on product) rebaja; (on tax etc) desgravación f; (repayment) reembolso
rebel [ˈrɛbl] n rebelde m/f ▪ vi [rɪˈbɛl] rebelarse, sublevarse
rebellion [rɪˈbɛljən] n rebelión f, sublevación f
rebellious [rɪˈbɛljəs] adj rebelde; (child) revoltoso
rebirth [riːˈbəːθ] n renacimiento
rebound [rɪˈbaund] vi (ball) rebotar ▪ n [ˈriːbaund] rebote m
rebuff [rɪˈbʌf] n desaire m, rechazo ▪ vt rechazar
rebuild [riːˈbɪld] vt (irreg: like **build**) reconstruir
rebuke [rɪˈbjuːk] n reprimenda ▪ vt reprender
rebut [rɪˈbʌt] vt rebatir

recalcitrant [rɪˈkælsɪtrənt] adj reacio
recall [rɪˈkɔːl] vt (remember) recordar; (ambassador etc) retirar; (Comput) volver a llamar ▪ n recuerdo
recant [rɪˈkænt] vi retractarse
recap [ˈriːkæp] vt, vi recapitular
recapitulate [riːkəˈpɪtjuleɪt] vt, vi = **recap**
recapture [riːˈkæptʃəʳ] vt (town) reconquistar; (atmosphere) hacer revivir
recd., rec'd abbr (= received) recibido
recede [rɪˈsiːd] vi retroceder
receding [rɪˈsiːdɪŋ] adj (forehead, chin) hundido; ~ **hairline** entradas fpl
receipt [rɪˈsiːt] n (document) recibo; (act of receiving) recepción f; **receipts** npl (Comm) ingresos mpl; **to acknowledge ~ of** acusar recibo de; **we are in ~ of ...** obra en nuestro poder ...
receivable [rɪˈsiːvəbl] adj (Comm) a cobrar
receive [rɪˈsiːv] vt recibir; (guest) acoger; (wound) sufrir; **"received with thanks"** "recibí"
Received Pronunciation [rɪˈsiːvd-] n see **RP**
receiver [rɪˈsiːvəʳ] n (Tel) auricular m; (Radio) receptor m; (of stolen goods) perista m/f; (Law) administrador m jurídico
receivership [rɪˈsiːvəʃɪp] n: **to go into ~** entrar en liquidación
recent [ˈriːsnt] adj reciente; **in ~ years** en los últimos años
recently [ˈriːsntlɪ] adv recientemente, recién (LAm); ~ **arrived** recién llegado; **until ~** hasta hace poco
receptacle [rɪˈsɛptɪkl] n receptáculo
reception [rɪˈsɛpʃən] n (in building, office etc) recepción f; (welcome) acogida
reception centre n (Brit) centro de recepción
reception desk n recepción f
receptionist [rɪˈsɛpʃənɪst] n recepcionista m/f
receptive [rɪˈsɛptɪv] adj receptivo
recess [rɪˈsɛs] n (in room) hueco; (for bed) nicho; (secret place) escondrijo; (Pol etc: holiday) período vacacional; (US Law: short break) descanso; (Scol: esp US) recreo
recession [rɪˈsɛʃən] n recesión f, depresión f
recessionista [rɪsɛʃəˈnɪstə] n recesionista m/f
recharge [riːˈtʃɑːdʒ] vt (battery) recargar
rechargeable [riːˈtʃɑːdʒəbl] adj recargable
recipe [ˈrɛsɪpɪ] n receta
recipient [rɪˈsɪpɪənt] n recibidor(a) m(f); (of letter) destinatario(-a)
reciprocal [rɪˈsɪprəkl] adj recíproco
reciprocate [rɪˈsɪprəkeɪt] vt devolver, corresponder a ▪ vi corresponder
recital [rɪˈsaɪtl] n (Mus) recital m
recitation [rɛsɪˈteɪʃən] n (of poetry) recitado; (of complaints etc) enumeración f, relación f

r

739

recite [rɪ'saɪt] *vt* (*poem*) recitar; (*complaints etc*) enumerar

reckless ['rɛkləs] *adj* temerario, imprudente; (*speed*) peligroso

recklessly ['rɛkləslɪ] *adv* imprudentemente; de modo peligroso

recklessness ['rɛkləsnɪs] *n* temeridad *f*, imprudencia

reckon ['rɛkən] *vt* (*count*) contar; (*consider*) considerar ■ *vi*: **to ~ without sb/sth** dejar de contar con algn/algo; **he is somebody to be reckoned with** no se le puede descartar; **I ~ that ...** me parece que ..., creo que ...
  ▸ **reckon on** *vt fus* contar con

reckoning ['rɛkənɪŋ] *n* (*calculation*) cálculo

reclaim [rɪ'kleɪm] *vt* (*land*) recuperar; (: *from sea*) rescatar; (*demand back*) reclamar

reclamation [rɛklə'meɪʃən] *n* recuperación *f*; rescate *m*

recline [rɪ'klaɪn] *vi* reclinarse

reclining [rɪ'klaɪnɪŋ] *adj* (*seat*) reclinable

recluse [rɪ'kluːs] *n* recluso(-a)

recognition [rɛkəg'nɪʃən] *n* reconocimiento; **transformed beyond ~** irreconocible; **in ~ of** en reconocimiento de

recognizable ['rɛkəgnaɪzəbl] *adj*: **~ (by)** reconocible (por)

recognize ['rɛkəgnaɪz] *vt* reconocer, conocer; **to ~ (by/as)** reconocer (por/como)

recoil [rɪ'kɔɪl] *vi* (*person*): **to ~ from doing sth** retraerse de hacer algo ■ *n* (*of gun*) retroceso

recollect [rɛkə'lɛkt] *vt* recordar, acordarse de

recollection [rɛkə'lɛkʃən] *n* recuerdo; **to the best of my ~** que yo recuerde

recommend [rɛkə'mɛnd] *vt* recomendar; **she has a lot to ~ her** tiene mucho a su favor

recommendation [rɛkəmɛn'deɪʃən] *n* recomendación *f*

recommended retail price *n* (*Brit*) precio (recomendado) de venta al público

recompense ['rɛkəmpɛns] *vt* recompensar ■ *n* recompensa

reconcilable ['rɛkənsaɪləbl] *adj* (re)conciliable

reconcile ['rɛkənsaɪl] *vt* (*two people*) reconciliar; (*two facts*) conciliar; **to ~ o.s. to sth** resignarse *or* conformarse a algo

reconciliation [rɛkənsɪlɪ'eɪʃən] *n* reconciliación *f*

recondite [rɪ'kɔndaɪt] *adj* recóndito

recondition [riːkən'dɪʃən] *vt* (*machine*) reparar, reponer

reconditioned [riːkən'dɪʃənd] *adj* renovado, reparado

reconnaissance [rɪ'kɔnɪsns] *n* (*Mil*) reconocimiento

reconnoitre, (*US*) **reconnoiter** [rɛkə'nɔɪtə^r] *vt*, *vi* (*Mil*) reconocer

reconsider [riːkən'sɪdə^r] *vt* repensar

reconstitute [riː'kɔnstɪtjuːt] *vt* reconstituir

reconstruct [riːkən'strʌkt] *vt* reconstruir

reconstruction [riːkən'strʌkʃən] *n* reconstrucción *f*

reconvene [riːkən'viːn] *vt* volver a convocar ■ *vi* volver a reunirse

record *n* ['rɛkɔːd] (*Mus*) disco; (*of meeting etc*) relación *f*; (*register*) registro, partida; (*file*) archivo; (*also*: **police** *or* **criminal record**) antecedentes *mpl* penales; (*written*) expediente *m*; (*Sport*) récord *m*; (*Comput*) registro ■ *vt* [rɪ'kɔːd] (*set down*) registrar; (*Comput*) registrar; (*relate*) hacer constar; (*Mus: song etc*) grabar; **in ~ time** en un tiempo récord; **public records** archivos *mpl* nacionales; **he is on ~ as saying that ...** hay pruebas de que ha dicho públicamente que ...; **Spain's excellent ~** el excelente historial de España; **off the ~** *adj* no oficial ■ *adv* confidencialmente

record card *n* (*in file*) ficha

recorded delivery letter [rɪ'kɔːdɪd-] *n* (*Brit Post*) carta de entrega con acuse de recibo

recorded music *n* música grabada

recorder [rɪ'kɔːdə^r] *n* (*Mus*) flauta de pico; (*Tech*) contador *m*

record holder *n* (*Sport*) actual poseedor(a) *m(f)* del récord

recording [rɪ'kɔːdɪŋ] *n* (*Mus*) grabación *f*

recording studio *n* estudio de grabación

record library *n* discoteca

record player *n* tocadiscos *m inv*

recount *vt* [rɪ'kaunt] contar

re-count ['riːkaunt] *n* (*Pol: of votes*) segundo escrutinio, recuento ■ *vt* [riː'kaunt] volver a contar

recoup [rɪ'kuːp] *vt*: **to ~ one's losses** recuperar las pérdidas

recourse [rɪ'kɔːs] *n* recurso; **to have ~ to** recurrir a

recover [rɪ'kʌvə^r] *vt* recuperar; (*rescue*) rescatar ■ *vi* recuperarse

recovery [rɪ'kʌvərɪ] *n* recuperación *f*; rescate *m*; (*Med*): **to make a ~** restablecerse

recreate [riːkrɪ'eɪt] *vt* recrear

recreation [rɛkrɪ'eɪʃən] *n* recreación *f*; (*amusement*) recreo

recreational [rɛkrɪ'eɪʃənl] *adj* de, recreo

recreational drug *n* droga recreativa

recreational vehicle *n* (*US*) caravana *or* roulotte *f* pequeña

recrimination [rɪkrɪmɪ'neɪʃən] *n* recriminación *f*

recruit [rɪ'kruːt] *n* recluta *m/f* ■ *vt* reclutar; (*staff*) contratar

recruiting office [rɪ'kruːtɪŋ-] *n* caja de reclutas

recruitment [rɪˈkruːtmənt] n reclutamiento
rectangle [ˈrɛktæŋgl] n rectángulo
rectangular [rɛkˈtæŋgjuləʳ] adj rectangular
rectify [ˈrɛktɪfaɪ] vt rectificar
rector [ˈrɛktəʳ] n (Rel) párroco; (Scol) rector(a) m(f)
rectory [ˈrɛktərɪ] n casa del párroco
rectum [ˈrɛktəm] n (Anat) recto
recuperate [rɪˈkuːpəreɪt] vi reponerse, restablecerse
recur [rɪˈkəːʳ] vi repetirse; (pain, illness) producirse de nuevo
recurrence [rɪˈkəːrns] n repetición f
recurrent [rɪˈkəːrnt] adj repetido
recyclable [riːˈsaɪkləbl] adj reciclable
recycle [riːˈsaɪkl] vt reciclar
recycling [riːˈsaɪklɪŋ] vt reciclaje m
red [rɛd] n rojo ■ adj rojo; **to be in the ~** (account) estar en números rojos; (business) tener un saldo negativo; **to give sb the ~ carpet treatment** recibir a algn con todos los honores
red alert n alerta roja
red-blooded [ˈrɛdˈblʌdɪd] adj (col) viril
redbrick university [ˈrɛdbrɪk-] n ver nota

● **REDBRICK UNIVERSITY**

El término redbrick university se aplica a las universidades construidas en los grandes centros urbanos industriales como Birmingham, Liverpool o Manchester a finales del siglo XIX o principios del XX. Deben su nombre a que sus edificios son normalmente de ladrillo, a diferencia de las universidades tradicionales de Oxford y Cambridge, cuyos edificios suelen ser de piedra.

Red Cross n Cruz f Roja
redcurrant [ˈrɛdkʌrənt] n grosella
redden [ˈrɛdn] vt enrojecer ■ vi enrojecerse
reddish [ˈrɛdɪʃ] adj (hair) rojizo
redecorate [riːˈdɛkəreɪt] vt pintar de nuevo; volver a decorar
redecoration [riːdɛkəˈreɪʃən] n renovación f
redeem [rɪˈdiːm] vt (sth in pawn) desempeñar; (Rel) rescatar; (fig) rescatar
redeemable [rɪˈdiːməbl] adj canjeable
redeeming [rɪˈdiːmɪŋ] adj: **~ feature** punto bueno or favorable
redefine [riːdɪˈfaɪn] vt redefinir
redemption [rɪˈdɛmpʃən] n (Rel) redención f; **to be past** or **beyond ~** no tener remedio
redeploy [riːdɪˈplɔɪ] vt disponer de nuevo
redeployment [riːdɪˈplɔɪmənt] n redistribución f

redevelop [riːdɪˈvɛləp] vt reorganizar
redevelopment [riːdɪˈvɛləpmənt] n reorganización f
red-handed [rɛdˈhændɪd] adj: **he was caught ~** le pillaron con las manos en la masa
redhead [ˈrɛdhɛd] n pelirrojo(-a)
red herring n (fig) pista falsa
red-hot [rɛdˈhɔt] adj candente
redirect [riːdaɪˈrɛkt] vt (mail) reexpedir
rediscover [riːdɪsˈkʌvəʳ] vt redescubrir
rediscovery [riːdɪsˈkʌvərɪ] n redescubrimiento
redistribute [riːdɪsˈtrɪbjuːt] vt redistribuir, hacer una nueva distribución de
red-letter day [rɛdˈlɛtə-] n día m señalado, día m especial
red light n: **to go through** or **jump a ~** (Aut) saltarse un semáforo
red-light district n barrio chino, zona de tolerancia
red meat n carne f roja
redness [ˈrɛdnɪs] n rojez f
redo [riːˈduː] vt (irreg: like **do**) rehacer
redolent [ˈrɛdələnt] adj: **~ of** (smell) con fragancia a; **to be ~ of** (fig) evocar
redouble [riːˈdʌbl] vt: **to ~ one's efforts** redoblar los esfuerzos
redraft [riːˈdrɑːft] vt volver a redactar
redress [rɪˈdrɛs] n reparación f ■ vt reparar, corregir; **to ~ the balance** restablecer el equilibrio
Red Sea n: **the ~** el mar Rojo
redskin [ˈrɛdskɪn] n piel roja m/f
red tape n (fig) trámites mpl, papeleo (fam)
reduce [rɪˈdjuːs] vt reducir; (lower) rebajar; **to ~ sth by/to** reducir algo en/a; **to ~ sb to silence/despair/tears** hacer callar/desesperarse/llorar a algn; **"~ speed now"** (Aut) "reduzca la velocidad"
reduced [rɪˈdjuːst] adj (decreased) reducido, rebajado; **at a ~ price** con rebaja or descuento; **"greatly ~ prices"** "grandes rebajas"
reduction [rɪˈdʌkʃən] n reducción f; (of price) rebaja; (discount) descuento
redundancy [rɪˈdʌndənsɪ] n despido; (unemployment) desempleo; **voluntary ~** baja voluntaria
redundancy payment n indemnización f por desempleo
redundant [rɪˈdʌndənt] adj (Brit: worker) parado, sin trabajo; (detail, object) superfluo; **to be made ~** quedar(se) sin trabajo, perder el empleo
reed [riːd] n (Bot) junco, caña; (Mus: of clarinet etc) lengüeta

r

re-educate [riːˈɛdjukeɪt] *vt* reeducar
reedy [ˈriːdɪ] *adj* (*voice, instrument*) aflautado
reef [riːf] *n* (*at sea*) arrecife *m*
reek [riːk] *vi*: **to ~ (of)** oler *or* apestar (a)
reel [riːl] *n* carrete *m*, bobina; (*of film*) rollo
■ *vt* (*Tech*) devanar; (*also*: **reel in**) sacar ■ *vi*
(*sway*) tambalear(se); **my head is reeling** me
da vueltas la cabeza
▶ **reel off** *vt* recitar de memoria
re-election [riːɪˈlɛkʃən] *n* reelección *f*
re-engage [riːɪnˈgeɪdʒ] *vt* contratar de
nuevo
re-enter [riːˈɛntəʳ] *vt* reingresar en, volver a
entrar en
re-entry [riːˈɛntrɪ] *n* reingreso, reentrada
re-examine [riːɪgˈzæmɪn] *vt* reexaminar
re-export *vt* [ˈriːɪksˈpɔːt] reexportar ■ *n*
[riːˈɛkspɔːt] reexportación *f*
ref [rɛf] *n abbr* (*col*) = **referee**
ref. *abbr* (*Comm*: = *with reference to*) Ref
refectory [rɪˈfɛktərɪ] *n* comedor *m*
refer [rɪˈfəːʳ] *vt* (*send*) remitir; (*ascribe*) referir
a, relacionar con ■ *vi*: **to ~ to** (*allude to*)
referirse a, aludir a; (*apply to*) relacionarse
con; (*consult*) remitirse a; **he referred me to
the manager** me envió al gerente
referee [rɛfəˈriː] *n* árbitro; (*Brit: for job
application*) persona que da referencias de otro
■ *vt* (*match*) arbitrar en
reference [ˈrɛfrəns] *n* (*mention: in book*)
referencia; (*sending*) remisión *f*; (*relevance*)
relación *f*; (*for job application: letter*) carta de
recomendación; **with ~ to** con referencia a;
(*Comm: in letter*) me remito a
reference book *n* libro de consulta
reference library *n* biblioteca de consulta
reference number *n* número de referencia
referendum (*pl* **referenda**) [rɛfəˈrɛndəm, -də]
n referéndum *m*
referral [rɪˈfəːrəl] *n* remisión *f*
refill *vt* [riːˈfɪl] rellenar ■ *n* [ˈriːfɪl] repuesto,
recambio
refine [rɪˈfaɪn] *vt* (*sugar, oil*) refinar
refined [rɪˈfaɪnd] *adj* (*person, taste*) refinado,
culto
refinement [rɪˈfaɪnmənt] *n* (*of person*)
cultura, educación *f*
refinery [rɪˈfaɪnərɪ] *n* refinería
refit (*also Naut*) *n* [ˈriːfɪt] reparación *f* ■ *vt*
[riːˈfɪt] reparar
reflate [riːˈfleɪt] *vt* (*economy*) reflacionar
reflation [riːˈfleɪʃən] *n* reflación *f*
reflationary [riːˈfleɪʃənrɪ] *adj* reflacionario
reflect [rɪˈflɛkt] *vt* (*light, image*) reflejar ■ *vi*
(*think*) reflexionar, pensar; **it reflects badly/
well on him** le perjudica/le hace honor
reflection [rɪˈflɛkʃən] *n* (*act*) reflexión *f*;

(*image*) reflejo; (*discredit*) crítica; **on ~**
pensándolo bien
reflector [rɪˈflɛktəʳ] *n* (*Aut*) catafaros *m inv*;
(*telescope*) reflector *m*
reflex [ˈriːflɛks] *adj, n* reflejo
reflexive [rɪˈflɛksɪv] *adj* (*Ling*) reflexivo
reform [rɪˈfɔːm] *n* reforma ■ *vt* reformar
reformat [riːˈfɔːmæt] *vt* (*Comput*) recomponer
Reformation [rɛfəˈmeɪʃən] *n*: **the ~** la
Reforma
reformatory [rɪˈfɔːmətərɪ] *n* (*US*)
reformatorio
reformer [rɪˈfɔːməʳ] *n* reformador(a) *m(f)*
refrain [rɪˈfreɪn] *vi*: **to ~ from doing**
abstenerse de hacer ■ *n* (*Mus etc*) estribillo
refresh [rɪˈfrɛʃ] *vt* refrescar
refresher course [rɪˈfrɛʃə-] *n* (*Brit*) curso de
repaso
refreshing [rɪˈfrɛʃɪŋ] *adj* (*drink*) refrescante;
(*sleep*) reparador; (*change etc*) estimulante;
(*idea, point of view*) estimulante, interesante
refreshments [rɪˈfrɛʃmənts] *npl* (*drinks*)
refrescos *mpl*
refrigeration [rɪfrɪdʒəˈreɪʃən] *n*
refrigeración *f*
refrigerator [rɪˈfrɪdʒəreɪtəʳ] *n* frigorífico,
refrigeradora (*LAm*), heladera (*LAm*)
refuel [riːˈfjuəl] *vi* repostar (combustible)
refuelling, (*US*) **refueling** [riːˈfjuəlɪŋ] *n*
reabastecimiento de combustible
refuge [ˈrɛfjuːdʒ] *n* refugio, asilo; **to take ~
in** refugiarse en
refugee [rɛfjuˈdʒiː] *n* refugiado(-a)
refugee camp *n* campamento para
refugiados
refund *n* [ˈriːfʌnd] reembolso ■ *vt* [rɪˈfʌnd]
devolver, reembolsar
refurbish [riːˈfəːbɪʃ] *vt* restaurar, renovar
refurnish [riːˈfəːnɪʃ] *vt* amueblar de nuevo
refusal [rɪˈfjuːzəl] *n* negativa; **first ~** primera
opción; **to have first ~ on sth** tener la
primera opción a algo
refuse [*n* ˈrɛfjuːs, *vb* rɪˈfjuːz] *n* basura ■ *vt*
(*reject*) rehusar; (*say no to*) negarse a ■ *vi*
negarse; (*horse*) rehusar; **to ~ to do sth**
negarse a *or* rehusar hacer algo
refuse bin *n* cubo *or* bote *m* (*LAm*) *or* balde *m*
(*LAm*) de la basura
refuse collection *n* recogida de basuras
refuse disposal *n* eliminación *f* de basuras
refusenik [rɪˈfjuːznɪk] *n* judío/a que tenía
prohibido emigrar de la ex Unión Soviética
refuse tip *n* vertedero
refute [rɪˈfjuːt] *vt* refutar, rebatir
regain [rɪˈgeɪn] *vt* recobrar, recuperar
regal [ˈriːgl] *adj* regio, real
regale [rɪˈgeɪl] *vt* agasajar, entretener

regalia [rɪˈgeɪlɪə] *n* galas *fpl*

regard [rɪˈgɑːd] *n* (*gaze*) mirada; (*aspect*) respecto; (*esteem*) respeto, consideración *f* ▪ *vt* (*consider*) considerar; (*look at*) mirar; **to give one's regards to** saludar de su parte a; **"(kind) regards"** "muy atentamente"; **"with kindest regards"** "con muchos recuerdos"; **regards to María, please give my regards to María** recuerdos a María, dele recuerdos a María de mi parte; **as regards, with ~ to** con respecto a, en cuanto a

regarding [rɪˈgɑːdɪŋ] *prep* con respecto a, en cuanto a

regardless [rɪˈgɑːdlɪs] *adv* a pesar de todo; **~ of** sin reparar en

regatta [rɪˈgætə] *n* regata

regency [ˈriːdʒənsɪ] *n* regencia

regenerate [rɪˈdʒɛnəreɪt] *vt* regenerar

regent [ˈriːdʒənt] *n* regente *m/f*

reggae [ˈrɛgeɪ] *n* reggae *m*

régime [reɪˈʒiːm] *n* régimen *m*

regiment *n* [ˈrɛdʒɪmənt] regimiento ▪ *vt* [ˈrɛdʒɪmɛnt] reglamentar

regimental [rɛdʒɪˈmɛntl] *adj* militar

regimentation [rɛdʒɪmɛnˈteɪʃən] *n* regimentación *f*

region [ˈriːdʒən] *n* región *f*; **in the ~ of** (*fig*) alrededor de

regional [ˈriːdʒənl] *adj* regional

regional development *n* desarrollo, regional

register [ˈrɛdʒɪstər] *n* registro ▪ *vt* registrar; (*birth*) declarar; (*letter*) certificar; (*instrument*) marcar, indicar ▪ *vi* (*at hotel*) registrarse; (*sign on*) inscribirse; (*make impression*) producir impresión; **to ~ a protest** presentar una queja; **to ~ for a course** matricularse *or* inscribirse en un curso

registered [ˈrɛdʒɪstəd] *adj* (*design*) registrado; (*Brit: letter*) certificado; (*student*) matriculado; (*voter*) registrado

registered company *n* sociedad *f* legalmente constituida

registered nurse *n* (*US*) enfermero(-a) titulado(-a)

registered office *n* domicilio social

registered trademark *n* marca registrada

registrar [ˈrɛdʒɪstrɑːr] *n* secretario(-a) (del registro civil)

registration [rɛdʒɪsˈtreɪʃən] *n* (*act*) declaración *f*; (*Aut: also:* **registration number**) matrícula

registry [ˈrɛdʒɪstrɪ] *n* registro

registry office *n* (*Brit*) registro civil; **to get married in a ~** casarse por lo civil

regret [rɪˈgrɛt] *n* sentimiento, pesar *m*; (*remorse*) remordimiento ▪ *vt* sentir, lamentar; (*repent of*) arrepentirse de; **we ~ to inform you that ...** sentimos informarle que ...

regretful [rɪˈgrɛtful] *adj* pesaroso, arrepentido

regretfully [rɪˈgrɛtfəlɪ] *adv* con pesar, sentidamente

regrettable [rɪˈgrɛtəbl] *adj* lamentable; (*loss*) sensible

regrettably [rɪˈgrɛtəblɪ] *adv* desgraciadamente

regroup [riːˈgruːp] *vt* reagrupar ▪ *vi* reagruparse

regt *abbr* = **regiment**

regular [ˈrɛgjulər] *adj* regular; (*soldier*) profesional; (*col: intensive*) verdadero; (*listener, reader*) asiduo, habitual ▪ *n* (*client etc*) cliente(-a) *m(f)* habitual

regularity [rɛgjuˈlærɪtɪ] *n* regularidad *f*

regularly [ˈrɛgjuləlɪ] *adv* con regularidad

regulate [ˈrɛgjuleɪt] *vt* (*gen*) controlar; (*Tech*) regular, ajustar

regulation [rɛgjuˈleɪʃən] *n* (*rule*) regla, reglamento; (*adjustment*) regulación *f*

rehabilitate [riːəˈbɪlɪteɪt] *vt* rehabilitar

rehabilitation [ˈriːəbɪlɪˈteɪʃən] *n* rehabilitación *f*

rehash [riːˈhæʃ] *vt* (*col*) hacer un refrito de

rehearsal [rɪˈhəːsəl] *n* ensayo; **dress ~** ensayo general *or* final

rehearse [rɪˈhəːs] *vt* ensayar

rehouse [riːˈhauz] *vt* dar nueva vivienda a

reign [reɪn] *n* reinado; (*fig*) predominio ▪ *vi* reinar; (*fig*) imperar

reigning [ˈreɪnɪŋ] *adj* (*monarch*) reinante, actual; (*predominant*) imperante

reiki [ˈreɪkɪ] *n* reiki *m*

reimburse [riːɪmˈbəːs] *vt* reembolsar

rein [reɪn] *n* (*for horse*) rienda; **to give sb free ~** dar rienda suelta a algn

reincarnation [riːɪnkɑːˈneɪʃən] *n* reencarnación *f*

reindeer [ˈreɪndɪər] *n* (*pl inv*) reno

reinforce [riːɪnˈfɔːs] *vt* reforzar

reinforced concrete [riːɪnˈfɔːst-] *n* hormigón *m* armado

reinforcement [riːɪnˈfɔːsmənt] *n* (*action*) refuerzo; **reinforcements** *npl* (*Mil*) refuerzos *mpl*

reinstate [riːɪnˈsteɪt] *vt* (*worker*) reintegrar (a su puesto)

reinstatement [riːɪnˈsteɪtmənt] *n* reintegración *f*

reissue [riːˈɪʃuː] *vt* (*record, book*) reeditar

reiterate [riːˈɪtəreɪt] *vt* reiterar, repetir

reject *n* [ˈriːdʒɛkt] (*thing*) desecho ▪ *vt* [rɪˈdʒɛkt] rechazar; (*proposition, offer etc*) descartar

r

rejection [rɪ'dʒɛkʃən] n rechazo
rejoice [rɪ'dʒɔɪs] vi: **to ~ at** or **over** regocijarse or alegrarse de
rejoinder [rɪ'dʒɔɪndə'] n (retort) réplica
rejuvenate [rɪ'dʒu:vəneɪt] vt rejuvenecer
rekindle [ri:'kɪndl] vt volver a encender; (fig) despertar
relapse [rɪ'læps] n (Med) recaída; (into crime) reincidencia
relate [rɪ'leɪt] vt (tell) contar, relatar; (connect) relacionar ■ vi relacionarse; **to ~ to** (connect) relacionarse or tener que ver con
related [rɪ'leɪtɪd] adj afín; (person) emparentado; **~ to** con referencia a, relacionado con
relating [rɪ'leɪtɪŋ]: **~ to** prep referente a
relation [rɪ'leɪʃən] n (person) pariente m/f; (link) relación f; **in ~ to** en relación con, en lo que se refiere a; **to bear a ~ to** guardar relación con; **diplomatic relations** relaciones fpl diplomáticas
relationship [rɪ'leɪʃənʃɪp] n relación f; (personal) relaciones fpl; (also: **family relationship**) parentesco
relative ['rɛlətɪv] n pariente m/f, familiar m/f ■ adj relativo
relatively ['rɛlətɪvlɪ] adv (fairly, rather) relativamente
relative pronoun n pronombre m relativo
relax [rɪ'læks] vi descansar; (quieten down) relajarse ■ vt relajar; (grip) aflojar; **~!** (calm down) ¡tranquilo!
relaxation [ri:læk'seɪʃən] n (rest) descanso; (easing) relajación f, relajamiento m; (amusement) recreo; (entertainment) diversión f
relaxed [rɪ'lækst] adj relajado; (tranquil) tranquilo
relaxing [rɪ'læksɪŋ] adj relajante
relay n ['ri:leɪ] (race) carrera de relevos ■ vt [rɪ'leɪ] (Radio, TV) retransmitir; (pass on) retransmitir
release [rɪ'li:s] n (liberation) liberación f; (discharge) puesta en libertad f; (of gas etc) escape m; (of film etc) estreno ■ vt (prisoner) poner en libertad; (film) estrenar; (book) publicar; (piece of news) difundir; (gas etc) despedir, arrojar; (free: from wreckage etc) liberar; (Tech: catch, spring etc) desenganchar; (let go) soltar, aflojar
relegate ['rɛləgeɪt] vt relegar; (Sport): **to be relegated to** bajar a
relent [rɪ'lɛnt] vi ceder, ablandarse; (let up) descansar
relentless [rɪ'lɛntlɪs] adj implacable
relentlessly [rɪ'lɛntlɪslɪ] adv implacablemente
relevance ['rɛləvəns] n relación f

relevant ['rɛləvənt] adj (fact) pertinente; **~ to** relacionado con
reliability [rɪlaɪə'bɪlɪtɪ] n fiabilidad f; seguridad f; veracidad f
reliable [rɪ'laɪəbl] adj (person, firm) de confianza, de fiar; (method, machine) seguro; (source) fidedigno
reliably [rɪ'laɪəblɪ] adv: **to be ~ informed that ...** saber de fuente fidedigna que ...
reliance [rɪ'laɪəns] n: **~ (on)** dependencia (de)
reliant [rɪ'laɪənt] adj: **to be ~ on sth/sb** depender de algo/algn
relic ['rɛlɪk] n (Rel) reliquia; (of the past) vestigio
relief [rɪ'li:f] n (from pain, anxiety) alivio, desahogo; (help, supplies) socorro, ayuda; (Art, Geo) relieve m; **by way of light ~** a modo de diversión
relief road n carretera de descongestionamiento
relieve [rɪ'li:v] vt (pain, patient) aliviar; (bring help to) ayudar, socorrer; (burden) aligerar; (take over from: gen) sustituir a; (: guard) relevar; **to ~ sb of sth** quitar algo a algn; **to ~ sb of his command** (Mil) relevar a algn de su mando; **to ~ o.s.** hacer sus necesidades; **I am relieved to hear you are better** me alivia saber que estás or te encuentras mejor
religion [rɪ'lɪdʒən] n religión f
religious [rɪ'lɪdʒəs] adj religioso
religious education n educación f religiosa
religiously [rɪ'lɪdʒəslɪ] adv religiosamente
relinquish [rɪ'lɪŋkwɪʃ] vt abandonar; (plan, habit) renunciar a
relish ['rɛlɪʃ] n (Culin) salsa; (enjoyment) entusiasmo; (flavour) sabor m, gusto ■ vt (food, challenge etc) saborear; **to ~ doing** gozar haciendo
relive [ri:'lɪv] vt vivir de nuevo, volver a vivir
relocate [ri:ləu'keɪt] vt trasladar ■ vi trasladarse
reluctance [rɪ'lʌktəns] n desgana, renuencia
reluctant [rɪ'lʌktənt] adj reacio; **to be ~ to do sth** resistirse a hacer algo
reluctantly [rɪ'lʌktəntlɪ] adv de mala gana
rely [rɪ'laɪ]: **to ~ on** vt fus confiar en, fiarse de; (be dependent on) depender de; **you can ~ on my discretion** puedes contar con mi discreción
remain [rɪ'meɪn] vi (survive) quedar; (be left) sobrar; (continue) quedar(se), permanecer; **to ~ silent** permanecer callado; **I ~, yours faithfully** (in letters) le saluda atentamente
remainder [rɪ'meɪndə'] n resto
remaining [rɪ'meɪnɪŋ] adj sobrante
remains [rɪ'meɪnz] npl restos mpl

remand [rɪ'mɑːnd] n: **on ~** detenido (bajo custodia) ■ vt: **to ~ in custody** mantener bajo custodia
remand home n (Brit) reformatorio
remark [rɪ'mɑːk] n comentario ■ vt comentar; **to ~ on sth** hacer observaciones sobre algo
remarkable [rɪ'mɑːkəbl] adj notable; (outstanding) extraordinario
remarkably [rɪ'mɑːkəblɪ] adv extraordinariamente
remarry [riː'mærɪ] vi casarse por segunda vez, volver a casarse
remedial [rɪ'miːdɪəl] adj: **~ education** educación f de los niños atrasados
remedy ['rɛmədɪ] n remedio ■ vt remediar, curar
remember [rɪ'mɛmbə^r] vt recordar, acordarse de; (bear in mind) tener presente; **I ~ seeing it, I ~ having seen it** recuerdo haberlo visto; **she remembered doing it** se acordó de hacerlo; **~ me to your wife and children!** ¡déle recuerdos a su familia!
remembrance [rɪ'mɛmbrəns] n (memory, souvenir) recuerdo; **in ~ of** en conmemoración de
Remembrance Day, Remembrance Sunday n (Brit) ver nota

● **REMEMBRANCE DAY**
●
● En el Reino Unido el domingo más
● cercano al 11 de noviembre es Remembrance
● Day o Remembrance Sunday, aniversario
● de la firma del armisticio de 1918 que
● puso fin a la Primera Guerra Mundial.
● Tal día se recuerda a todos aquellos
● que murieron en las dos guerras
● mundiales con dos minutos de silencio
● a las once de la mañana hora en que se
● firmó el armisticio durante los actos
● de conmemoración celebrados en los
● monumentos a los caídos. Allí se colocan
● coronas de amapolas, flor que también
● se suele llevar prendida en el pecho tras
● pagar un donativo para los inválidos de
● guerra.

remind [rɪ'maɪnd] vt: **to ~ sb to do sth** recordar a algn que haga algo; **to ~ sb of sth** recordar algo a algn; **she reminds me of her mother** me recuerda a su madre; **that reminds me!** ¡a propósito!
reminder [rɪ'maɪndə^r] n notificación f; (memento) recuerdo
reminisce [rɛmɪ'nɪs] vi recordar (viejas historias)

reminiscences [rɛmɪ'nɪsnsɪz] npl reminiscencias fpl, recuerdos mpl
reminiscent [rɛmɪ'nɪsnt] adj: **to be ~ of sth** recordar algo
remiss [rɪ'mɪs] adj descuidado; **it was ~ of me** fue un descuido de mi parte
remission [rɪ'mɪʃən] n remisión f; (of sentence) reducción f de la pena
remit [rɪ'mɪt] vt (send: money) remitir, enviar
remittance [rɪ'mɪtns] n remesa, envío
remnant ['rɛmnənt] n resto; (of cloth) retal m, retazo; **remnants** npl (Comm) restos de serie
remonstrate ['rɛmənstreɪt] vi protestar
remorse [rɪ'mɔːs] n remordimientos mpl
remorseful [rɪ'mɔːsful] adj arrepentido
remorseless [rɪ'mɔːslɪs] adj (fig) implacable, inexorable
remorselessly [rɪ'mɔːslɪslɪ] adv implacablemente, inexorablemente
remote [rɪ'məut] adj remoto; (distant) lejano; (person) distante; **there is a ~ possibility that ...** hay una posibilidad remota de que ...
remote control n mando a distancia
remote-controlled [rɪ'məutkən'trəuld] adj teledirigido, con mando a distancia
remotely [rɪ'məutlɪ] adv remotamente; (slightly) levemente
remoteness [rɪ'məutnɪs] n alejamiento; distancia
remould ['riːməuld] n (Brit: tyre) neumático or llanta (LAm) recauchutado(-a)
removable [rɪ'muːvəbl] adj (detachable) separable
removal [rɪ'muːvəl] n (taking away) (el) quitar; (Brit: from house) mudanza; (from office: dismissal) destitución f; (Med) extirpación f
removal van n (Brit) camión m de mudanzas
remove [rɪ'muːv] vt quitar; (employee) destituir; (name: from list) tachar, borrar; (doubt) disipar; (Tech) retirar, separar; (Med) extirpar; **first cousin once removed** (parent's cousin) tío(-a) segundo(-a); (cousin's child) sobrino(-a) segundo(-a)
remover [rɪ'muːvə^r] n: **make-up ~** desmaquilladora
remunerate [rɪ'mjuːnəreɪt] vt remunerar
remuneration [rɪmjuːnə'reɪʃən] n remuneración f
Renaissance [rɪ'neɪsõns] n: **the ~** el Renacimiento
rename [riː'neɪm] vt poner nuevo nombre a
render ['rɛndə^r] vt (thanks) dar; (aid) proporcionar; (honour) dar, conceder; (assistance) dar, prestar; **to ~ sth** (+ adj) volver algo + adj
rendering ['rɛndərɪŋ] n (Mus etc) interpretación f

r

rendez-vous ['rɔndɪvu:] n cita ▪ vi reunirse, encontrarse; (spaceship) efectuar una reunión espacial

rendition [rɛn'dɪʃən] n (Mus) interpretación f

renegade ['rɛnɪgeɪd] n renegado(-a)

renew [rɪ'nju:] vt renovar; (resume) reanudar; (extend date) prorrogar; (negotiations) volver a

renewable [rɪ'nju:əbl] adj renovable; ~ energy, renewables energías renovables

renewal [rɪ'nju:əl] n renovación f; reanudación f; prórroga

renounce [rɪ'nauns] vt renunciar a; (right, inheritance) renunciar

renovate ['rɛnəveɪt] vt renovar

renovation [rɛnə'veɪʃən] n renovación f

renown [rɪ'naun] n renombre m

renowned [rɪ'naund] adj renombrado

rent [rɛnt] n alquiler m; (for house) arriendo, renta ▪ vt (also: rent out) alquilar

rental ['rɛntl] n (for television, car) alquiler m

rent boy n (Brit col) chapero

renunciation [rɪnʌnsɪ'eɪʃən] n renuncia

reopen [ri:'əupən] vt volver a abrir, reabrir

reorder [ri:'ɔ:dəʳ] vt volver a pedir, repetir el pedido de; (rearrange) volver a ordenar or arreglar

reorganization [ri:ɔ:gənaɪ'zeɪʃən] n reorganización f

reorganize [ri:'ɔ:gənaɪz] vt reorganizar

Rep abbr (US Pol) = representative; Republican

rep [rɛp] n abbr (Comm) = representative; (Theat) = repertory

repair [rɪ'pɛəʳ] n reparación f, arreglo; (patch) remiendo ▪ vt reparar, arreglar; in good/ bad ~ en buen/mal estado; under ~ en obras

repair kit n caja de herramientas

repair man n mecánico

repair shop n taller m de reparaciones

repartee [rɛpɑ:'ti:] n réplicas fpl agudas

repast [rɪ'pɑ:st] n (formal) comida

repatriate [ri:'pætrɪeɪt] vt repatriar

repay [ri:'peɪ] vt (irreg: like pay) (money) devolver, reembolsar; (person) pagar; (debt) liquidar; (sb's efforts) devolver, corresponder a

repayment [ri:'peɪmənt] n reembolso, devolución f; (sum of money) recompensa

repeal [rɪ'pi:l] n revocación f ▪ vt revocar

repeat [rɪ'pi:t] n (Radio, TV) reposición f ▪ vt repetir ▪ vi repetirse

repeatedly [rɪ'pi:tɪdlɪ] adv repetidas veces

repeat order n (Comm): to place a ~ for renovar un pedido de

repel [rɪ'pɛl] vt repugnar

repellent [rɪ'pɛlənt] adj repugnante ▪ n: insect ~ crema/loción f antiinsectos

repent [rɪ'pɛnt] vi: to ~ (of) arrepentirse (de)

repentance [rɪ'pɛntəns] n arrepentimiento

repercussion [ri:pə'kʌʃən] n (consequence) repercusión f; to have repercussions repercutir

repertoire ['rɛpətwɑ:ʳ] n repertorio

repertory ['rɛpətərɪ] n (also: repertory theatre) teatro de repertorio

repertory company n compañía de repertorio

repetition [rɛpɪ'tɪʃən] n repetición f

repetitious [rɛpɪ'tɪʃəs] adj repetidor(a), que se repite

repetitive [rɪ'pɛtɪtɪv] adj (movement, work) repetitivo, reiterativo; (speech) lleno de repeticiones

rephrase [ri:'freɪz] vt decir or formular de otro modo

replace [rɪ'pleɪs] vt (put back) devolver a su sitio; (take the place of) reemplazar, sustituir

replacement [rɪ'pleɪsmənt] n reemplazo; (act) reposición f; (thing) recambio; (person) suplente m/f

replacement cost n costo de sustitución

replacement part n repuesto

replacement value n valor m de sustitución

replay ['ri:pleɪ] n (Sport) partido de desempate; (TV: playback) repetición f

replenish [rɪ'plɛnɪʃ] vt (tank etc) rellenar; (stock etc) reponer; (with fuel) repostar

replete [rɪ'pli:t] adj repleto, lleno

replica ['rɛplɪkə] n réplica, reproducción f

reply [rɪ'plaɪ] n respuesta, contestación f ▪ vi contestar, responder; in ~ en respuesta; there's no ~ (Tel) no contestan

reply coupon n cupón-respuesta m

reply-paid [rɪ'plaɪ'peɪd] adj: ~ postcard tarjeta postal con respuesta pagada

report [rɪ'pɔ:t] n informe m; (Press etc) reportaje m; (Brit: also: school report) informe m escolar; (of gun) detonación f ▪ vt informar sobre; (Press etc) hacer un reportaje sobre; (notify: accident, culprit) denunciar ▪ vi (make a report) presentar un informe; (present o.s.): to ~ (to sb) presentarse (ante algn); annual ~ (Comm) informe m anual; to ~ (on) hacer un informe (sobre); it is reported from Berlin that ... se informa desde Berlín que ...

report card n (US, Scottish) cartilla escolar

reportedly [rɪ'pɔ:tɪdlɪ] adv según se dice, según se informa

reporter [rɪ'pɔ:təʳ] n (Press) periodista m/f, reportero(-a); (Radio, TV) locutor(a) m(f)

repose [rɪ'pəuz] n: in ~ (face, mouth) en reposo

repossess [ri:pə'zɛs] vt recuperar

repossession order [ri:pə'zɛʃən-] n orden de devolución de la vivienda por el impago de la hipoteca

reprehensible [rɛprɪ'hɛnsɪbl] *adj* reprensible, censurable

represent [rɛprɪ'zɛnt] *vt* representar; (*Comm*) ser agente de

representation [rɛprɪzɛn'teɪʃən] *n* representación *f*; (*petition*) petición *f*; **representations** *npl* (*protest*) quejas *fpl*

representative [rɛprɪ'zɛntətɪv] *n* (*US Pol*) representante *m/f*, diputado(-a); (*Comm*) representante *m/f* ■ *adj*: ~ **(of)** representativo (de)

repress [rɪ'prɛs] *vt* reprimir

repression [rɪ'prɛʃən] *n* represión *f*

repressive [rɪ'prɛsɪv] *adj* represivo

reprieve [rɪ'priːv] *n* (*Law*) indulto; (*fig*) alivio ■ *vt* indultar; (*fig*) salvar

reprimand ['rɛprɪmɑːnd] *n* reprimenda ■ *vt* reprender

reprint ['riːprɪnt] *n* reimpresión *f* ■ *vt* [riː'prɪnt] reimprimir

reprisal [rɪ'praɪzl] *n* represalia; **to take reprisals** tomar represalias

reproach [rɪ'prəʊtʃ] *n* reproche *m* ■ *vt*: **to ~ sb with sth** reprochar algo a algn; **beyond ~** intachable

reproachful [rɪ'prəʊtʃful] *adj* de reproche, de acusación

reproduce [riːprə'djuːs] *vt* reproducir ■ *vi* reproducirse

reproduction [riːprə'dʌkʃən] *n* reproducción *f*

reproductive [riːprə'dʌktɪv] *adj* reproductor(a)

reproof [rɪ'pruːf] *n* reproche *m*

reprove [rɪ'pruːv] *vt*: **to ~ sb for sth** reprochar algo a algn

reptile ['rɛptaɪl] *n* reptil *m*

Repub. *abbr* (*US Pol*) = **Republican**

republic [rɪ'pʌblɪk] *n* república

republican [rɪ'pʌblɪkən] *adj*, *n* republicano(-a) *m(f)*

repudiate [rɪ'pjuːdɪeɪt] *vt* (*accusation*) rechazar; (*obligation*) negarse a reconocer

repudiation [rɪpjuːdɪ'eɪʃən] *n* incumplimiento

repugnance [rɪ'pʌgnəns] *n* repugnancia

repugnant [rɪ'pʌgnənt] *adj* repugnante

repulse [rɪ'pʌls] *vt* rechazar

repulsion [rɪ'pʌlʃən] *n* repulsión *f*, repugnancia

repulsive [rɪ'pʌlsɪv] *adj* repulsivo

repurchase [riː'pəːtʃəs] *vt* volver a comprar, readquirir

reputable ['rɛpjutəbl] *adj* (*make etc*) de renombre

reputation [rɛpju'teɪʃən] *n* reputación *f*; **he has a ~ for being awkward** tiene fama de difícil

repute [rɪ'pjuːt] *n* reputación *f*, fama

reputed [rɪ'pjuːtɪd] *adj* supuesto; **to be ~ to be rich/intelligent** *etc* tener fama de rico/inteligente *etc*

reputedly [rɪ'pjuːtɪdlɪ] *adv* según dicen *or* se dice

request [rɪ'kwɛst] *n* solicitud *f*, petición *f* ■ *vt*: **to ~ sth of** *or* **from sb** solicitar algo a algn; **at the ~ of** a petición de; **"you are requested not to smoke"** "se ruega no fumar"

request stop *n* (*Brit*) parada discrecional

requiem ['rɛkwɪəm] *n* réquiem *m*

require [rɪ'kwaɪəʳ] *vt* (*need: person*) necesitar, tener necesidad de; (: *thing, situation*) exigir, requerir; (*want*) pedir; (*demand*) insistir en que; **to ~ sb to do sth/sth of sb** exigir que algn haga algo; **what qualifications are required?** ¿qué títulos se requieren?; **required by law** requerido por la ley

requirement [rɪ'kwaɪəmənt] *n* requisito; (*need*) necesidad *f*

requisite ['rɛkwɪzɪt] *n* requisito ■ *adj* necesario, requerido

requisition [rɛkwɪ'zɪʃən] *n* solicitud *f*; (*Mil*) requisa ■ *vt* (*Mil*) requisar

reroute [riː'ruːt] *vt* desviar

resale ['riːseɪl] *n* reventa

resale price maintenance *n* mantenimiento del precio de venta

rescind [rɪ'sɪnd] *vt* (*Law*) abrogar; (*contract*) rescindir; (*order etc*) anular

rescue ['rɛskjuː] *n* rescate *m* ■ *vt* rescatar; **to come/go to sb's ~** ir en auxilio de uno, socorrer a algn; **to ~ from** librar de

rescue party *n* equipo de salvamento

rescuer ['rɛskjuəʳ] *n* salvador(a) *m(f)*

research [rɪ'səːtʃ] *n* investigaciones *fpl* ■ *vt* investigar; **a piece of ~** un trabajo de investigación; **to ~ (into sth)** investigar (algo)

research and development *n* investigación *f* y desarrollo

researcher [rɪ'səːtʃəʳ] *n* investigador(a) *m(f)*

research work *n* investigación *f*

resell [riː'sɛl] *vt* revender

resemblance [rɪ'zɛmbləns] *n* parecido; **to bear a strong ~ to** parecerse mucho a

resemble [rɪ'zɛmbl] *vt* parecerse a

resent [rɪ'zɛnt] *vt* resentirse por, ofenderse por; **he resents my being here** le molesta que esté aquí

resentful [rɪ'zɛntful] *adj* resentido

resentment [rɪ'zɛntmənt] *n* resentimiento

reservation [rɛzə'veɪʃən] *n* reserva; (*Brit: also*: **central reservation**) mediana; **with reservations** con reservas

r

reservation desk n (US: in hotel) recepción f
reserve [rɪ'zəːv] n reserva; (Sport) suplente m/f ■ vt (seats etc) reservar; **reserves** npl (Mil) reserva sg; **in ~** en reserva
reserve currency n divisa de reserva
reserved [rɪ'zəːvd] adj reservado
reserve price n (Brit) precio mínimo
reserve team n (Sport) equipo de reserva
reservist [rɪ'zəːvɪst] n (Mil) reservista m
reservoir ['rɛzəvwaːʳ] n (artificial lake) embalse m, represa; (small) depósito
reset [riː'sɛt] vt (Comput) reinicializar
reshape [riː'ʃeɪp] vt (policy) reformar, rehacer
reshuffle [riː'ʃʌfl] n: **Cabinet ~** (Pol) remodelación f del gabinete
reside [rɪ'zaɪd] vi residir
residence ['rɛzɪdəns] n residencia; (formal: home) domicilio; (length of stay) permanencia; **in ~** (doctor) residente; **to take up ~** instalarse
residence permit n (Brit) permiso de residencia
resident ['rɛzɪdənt] n vecino(-a); (in hotel) huésped(a) m(f) ■ adj residente; (population) permanente
residential [rɛzɪ'dɛnʃəl] adj residencial
residue ['rɛzɪdjuː] n resto, residuo
resign [rɪ'zaɪn] vt (gen) renunciar a ■ vi: **to ~ (from)** dimitir (de), renunciar (a); **to ~ o.s. to** (endure) resignarse a
resignation [rɛzɪg'neɪʃən] n dimisión f; (state of mind) resignación f; **to tender one's ~** presentar la dimisión
resigned [rɪ'zaɪnd] adj resignado
resilience [rɪ'zɪlɪəns] n (of material) elasticidad f; (of person) resistencia
resilient [rɪ'zɪlɪənt] adj (person) resistente
resin ['rɛzɪn] n resina
resist [rɪ'zɪst] vt resistirse a; (temptation, damage) resistir
resistance [rɪ'zɪstəns] n resistencia
resistant [rɪ'zɪstənt] adj: **~ (to)** resistente (a)
resolute ['rɛzəluːt] adj resuelto
resolutely ['rɛzəluːtlɪ] adv resueltamente
resolution [rɛzə'luːʃən] n (gen) resolución f; (purpose) propósito; (Comput) definición f; **to make a ~** tomar una resolución
resolve [rɪ'zɔlv] n (determination) resolución f; (purpose) propósito ■ vt resolver ■ vi resolverse; **to ~ to do** resolver hacer
resolved [rɪ'zɔlvd] adj resuelto
resonance ['rɛzənəns] n resonancia
resonant ['rɛzənənt] adj resonante
resort [rɪ'zɔːt] n (town) centro turístico; (recourse) recurso ■ vi: **to ~ to** recurrir a; **in the last ~** como último recurso; **seaside/ winter sports ~** playa, estación f balnearia/

centro de deportes de invierno
resound [rɪ'zaund] vi: **to ~ (with)** resonar (con)
resounding [rɪ'zaundɪŋ] adj sonoro; (fig) clamoroso
resource [rɪ'sɔːs] n recurso; **resources** npl recursos mpl; **natural resources** recursos mpl naturales; **to leave sb to his/her own resources** (fig) abandonar a algn/a sus propios recursos
resourceful [rɪ'sɔːsful] adj ingenioso
resourcefulness [rɪ'sɔːsfulnɪs] n inventiva, iniciativa
respect [rɪs'pɛkt] n (consideration) respeto; (relation) respecto; **respects** npl recuerdos mpl, saludos mpl ■ vt respetar; **with ~ to** con respecto a; **in this ~** en cuanto a eso; **to have** or **show ~ for** tener or mostrar respeto a; **out of ~ for** por respeto a; **in some respects** en algunos aspectos; **with due ~ I still think you're wrong** con el respeto debido, sigo creyendo que está equivocado
respectability [rɪspɛktə'bɪlɪtɪ] n respetabilidad f
respectable [rɪs'pɛktəbl] adj respetable; (quite big: amount etc) apreciable; (passable) tolerable; (quite good: player, result etc) bastante bueno
respected [rɪs'pɛktɪd] adj respetado, estimado
respectful [rɪs'pɛktful] adj respetuoso
respectfully [rɪs'pɛktfulɪ] adv respetuosamente; **Yours ~** Le saluda atentamente
respecting [rɪs'pɛktɪŋ] prep (con) respecto a, en cuanto a
respective [rɪs'pɛktɪv] adj respectivo
respectively [rɪs'pɛktɪvlɪ] adv respectivamente
respiration [rɛspɪ'reɪʃən] n respiración f
respiratory [rɛs'pɪrətərɪ] adj respiratorio
respite ['rɛspaɪt] n respiro; (Law) prórroga
resplendent [rɪs'plɛndənt] adj resplandeciente
respond [rɪs'pɔnd] vi responder; (react) reaccionar
respondent [rɪs'pɔndənt] n (Law) demandado(-a)
response [rɪs'pɔns] n respuesta; (reaction) reacción f; **in ~ to** como respuesta a
responsibility [rɪspɔnsɪ'bɪlɪtɪ] n responsabilidad f; **to take ~ for sth/sb** admitir responsabilidad por algo/uno
responsible [rɪs'pɔnsɪbl] adj (liable): **~ (for)** responsable (de); (character) serio, formal; (job) de responsabilidad; **to be ~ to sb (for sth)** ser responsable ante algn (de algo)

responsibly [rɪs'pɔnsɪblɪ] *adv* con seriedad
responsive [rɪs'pɔnsɪv] *adj* sensible
rest [rɛst] *n* descanso, reposo; (*Mus*) pausa, silencio; (*support*) apoyo; (*remainder*) resto ▪ *vi* descansar; (*be supported*): **to ~ on** apoyarse en ▪ *vt* (*lean*): **to ~ sth on/against** apoyar algo en or sobre/contra; **the ~ of them** (*people, objects*) los demás; **to set sb's mind at ~** tranquilizar a algn; **to ~ one's eyes** or **gaze on** fijar la mirada en; **it rests with him** depende de él; **~ assured that ...** tenga por seguro que ...
restaurant ['rɛstərɔŋ] *n* restaurante *m*
restaurant car *n* (*Brit*) coche-comedor *m*
restaurant owner *n* dueño(-a) or propietario(-a) de un restaurante
rest cure *n* cura de reposo
restful ['rɛstful] *adj* descansado, tranquilo
rest home *n* residencia de ancianos
restitution [rɛstɪ'tjuːʃən] *n*: **to make ~ to sb for sth** restituir algo a algn; (*paying*) indemnizar a algn por algo
restive ['rɛstɪv] *adj* inquieto; (*horse*) rebelón(-ona)
restless ['rɛstlɪs] *adj* inquieto; **to get ~** impacientarse
restlessly ['rɛstlɪslɪ] *adv* inquietamente, con inquietud *f*
restlessness ['rɛstlɪsnɪs] *n* inquietud *f*
restock [riː'stɔk] *vt* reaprovisionar
restoration [rɛstə'reɪʃən] *n* restauración *f*; (*giving back*) devolución *f*, restitución *f*
restorative [rɪ'stɔːrətɪv] *adj* reconstituyente, fortalecedor(a) ▪ *n* reconstituyente *m*
restore [rɪ'stɔːʳ] *vt* (*building*) restaurar; (*sth stolen*) devolver, restituir; (*health*) restablecer
restorer [rɪ'stɔːrəʳ] *n* (*Art etc*) restaurador(a) *m(f)*
restrain [rɪs'treɪn] *vt* (*feeling*) contener, refrenar; (*person*): **to ~ (from doing)** disuadir (de hacer)
restrained [rɪs'treɪnd] *adj* (*style*) reservado
restraint [rɪs'treɪnt] *n* (*restriction*) freno, control *m*; (*of style*) reserva; **wage ~** control *m* de los salarios
restrict [rɪs'trɪkt] *vt* restringir, limitar
restricted [rɪs'trɪktɪd] *adj* restringido, limitado
restriction [rɪs'trɪkʃən] *n* restricción *f*, limitación *f*
restrictive [rɪs'trɪktɪv] *adj* restrictivo
restrictive practices *npl* (*Industry*) prácticas *fpl* restrictivas
rest room *n* (*US*) aseos *mpl*
restructure [riː'strʌktʃəʳ] *vt* reestructurar
result [rɪ'zʌlt] *n* resultado ▪ *vi*: **to ~ in** terminar en, tener por resultado; **as a ~**

of a or como consecuencia de; **to ~ (from)** resultar (de)
resultant [rɪ'zʌltənt] *adj* resultante
resume [rɪ'zjuːm] *vt* (*work, journey*) reanudar; (*sum up*) resumir ▪ *vi* (*meeting*) continuar
résumé ['reɪzjuːmeɪ] *n* resumen *m*
resumption [rɪ'zʌmpʃən] *n* reanudación *f*
resurgence [rɪ'səːdʒəns] *n* resurgimiento
resurrection [rɛzə'rɛkʃən] *n* resurrección *f*
resuscitate [rɪ'sʌsɪteɪt] *vt* (*Med*) resucitar
resuscitation [rɪsʌsɪ'teɪʃn] *n* resucitación *f*
retail ['riːteɪl] *n* venta al por menor ▪ *cpd* al por menor ▪ *vt* vender al por menor or al detalle ▪ *vi*: **to ~ at** (*Comm*) tener precio de venta al público de
retailer ['riːteɪləʳ] *n* minorista *m/f*, detallista *m/f*
retail outlet *n* punto de venta
retail price *n* precio de venta al público, precio al detalle or al por menor
retail price index *n* índice *m* de precios al por menor
retain [rɪ'teɪn] *vt* (*keep*) retener, conservar; (*employ*) contratar
retainer [rɪ'teɪnəʳ] *n* (*servant*) criado; (*fee*) anticipo
retaliate [rɪ'tælɪeɪt] *vi*: **to ~ (against)** tomar represalias (contra)
retaliation [rɪtælɪ'eɪʃən] *n* represalias *fpl*; **in ~ for** como represalia por
retaliatory [rɪ'tælɪətərɪ] *adj* de represalia
retarded [rɪ'tɑːdɪd] *adj* retrasado
retch [rɛtʃ] *vi* darle a algn arcadas
retentive [rɪ'tɛntɪv] *adj* (*memory*) retentivo
rethink [riː'θɪŋk] *vt* repensar
reticence ['rɛtɪsns] *n* reticencia, reserva
reticent ['rɛtɪsnt] *adj* reticente, reservado
retina ['rɛtɪnə] *n* retina
retinue ['rɛtɪnjuː] *n* séquito, comitiva
retire [rɪ'taɪəʳ] *vi* (*give up work*) jubilarse; (*withdraw*) retirarse; (*go to bed*) acostarse
retired [rɪ'taɪəd] *adj* (*person*) jubilado
retirement [rɪ'taɪəmənt] *n* jubilación *f*; **early ~** jubilación *f* anticipada
retiring [rɪ'taɪərɪŋ] *adj* (*departing: chairman*) saliente; (*shy*) retraído
retort [rɪ'tɔːt] *n* (*reply*) réplica ▪ *vi* replicar
retrace [riː'treɪs] *vt*: **to ~ one's steps** volver sobre sus pasos, desandar lo andado
retract [rɪ'trækt] *vt* (*statement*) retirar; (*claws*) retraer; (*undercarriage, aerial*) replegar ▪ *vi* retractarse
retractable [rɪ'træktəbl] *adj* replegable
retrain [riː'treɪn] *vt* reciclar
retraining [riː'treɪnɪŋ] *n* reciclaje *m*, readaptación *f* profesional
retread ['riːtrɛd] *n* neumático or llanta (*LAm*) recauchutado(-a)

r

retreat [rɪˈtriːt] n (place) retiro; (Mil) retirada ■ vi retirarse; (flood) bajar; **to beat a hasty ~** (fig) retirarse en desbandada

retrial [ˈriːtraɪəl] n nuevo proceso

retribution [rɛtrɪˈbjuːʃən] n desquite m

retrieval [rɪˈtriːvəl] n recuperación f; **information retrieval** recuperación f de datos

retrieve [rɪˈtriːv] vt recobrar; (situation, honour) salvar; (Comput) recuperar; (error) reparar

retriever [rɪˈtriːvəʳ] n perro cobrador

retroactive [rɛtrəuˈæktɪv] adj retroactivo

retrograde [ˈrɛtrəgreɪd] adj retrógrado

retrospect [ˈrɛtrəspɛkt] n: **in ~** retrospectivamente

retrospective [rɛtrəˈspɛktɪv] adj retrospectivo; (law) retroactivo ■ n exposición f retrospectiva

return [rɪˈtəːn] n (going or coming back) vuelta, regreso; (of sth stolen etc) devolución f; (recompense) recompensa; (Finance: from land, shares) ganancia, ingresos mpl; (Comm: of merchandise) devolución f ■ cpd (journey) de regreso; (Brit: ticket) de ida y vuelta; (match) de vuelta ■ vi (person etc: come or go back) volver, regresar; (symptoms etc) reaparecer ■ vt devolver; (favour, love etc) corresponder a; (verdict) pronunciar; (Pol: candidate) elegir; **returns** npl (Comm) ingresos mpl; **tax ~** declaración f de la renta; **in ~ (for)** a cambio (de); **by ~ of post** a vuelta de correo; **many happy returns (of the day)!** ¡feliz cumpleaños!

returnable [rɪˈtəːnəbl] adj: **~ bottle** envase m retornable

returner [rɪˈtəːnəʳ] n mujer que vuelve a trabajar tras un tiempo dedicada a la familia

returning officer [rɪˈtəːnɪŋ-] n (Brit Pol) escrutador(a) m(f)

return key n (Comput) tecla de retorno

reunion [riːˈjuːnɪən] n reencuentro

reunite [riːjuːˈnaɪt] vt reunir; (reconcile) reconciliar

rev [rɛv] n abbr (Aut: = revolution) revolución f ■ vt (also: **rev up**) acelerar

Rev., Revd. abbr (= reverend) R., Rvdo

revaluation [riːvæljuːˈeɪʃən] n revalorización f

revamp [riːˈvæmp] vt renovar

reveal [rɪˈviːl] vt (make known) revelar

revealing [rɪˈviːlɪŋ] adj revelador(a)

reveille [rɪˈvælɪ] n (Mil) diana

revel [ˈrɛvl] vi: **to ~ in sth/in doing sth** gozar de algo/haciendo algo

revelation [rɛvəˈleɪʃən] n revelación f

reveller, (US) **reveler** [ˈrɛvləʳ] n jaranero, juerguista m/f

revelry [ˈrɛvlrɪ] n jarana, juerga

revenge [rɪˈvɛndʒ] n venganza; (in sport) revancha; **to take ~ on** vengarse de; **to get one's ~ (for sth)** vengarse (de algo)

revengeful [rɪˈvɛndʒful] adj vengativo

revenue [ˈrɛvənjuː] n ingresos mpl, rentas fpl

revenue account n cuenta de ingresos presupuestarios

revenue expenditure n gasto corriente

reverberate [rɪˈvəːbəreɪt] vi (sound) resonar, retumbar

reverberation [rɪvəːbəˈreɪʃən] n resonancia

revere [rɪˈvɪəʳ] vt reverenciar, venerar

reverence [ˈrɛvərəns] n reverencia

Reverend [ˈrɛvərənd] adj (in titles): **the ~ John Smith** (Anglican) el Reverendo John Smith; (Catholic) el Padre John Smith; (Protestant) el Pastor John Smith

reverent [ˈrɛvərənt] adj reverente

reverie [ˈrɛvərɪ] n ensueño

reversal [rɪˈvəːsl] n (of order) inversión f; (of policy) cambio de rumbo; (of decision) revocación f

reverse [rɪˈvəːs] n (opposite) contrario; (back: of cloth) revés m; (: of coin) reverso; (: of paper) dorso; (Aut: also: **reverse gear**) marcha atrás ■ adj (order) inverso; (direction) contrario ■ vt (decision) dar marcha atrás a; (Aut) dar marcha atrás a; (position, function) invertir ■ vi (Brit Aut) poner en marcha atrás; **in ~ order** en orden inverso; **the ~** lo contrario; **to go into ~** dar marcha atrás

reverse-charge call [rɪˈvəːstʃɑːdʒ-] n (Brit) llamada a cobro revertido

reverse video n vídeo inverso

reversible [rɪˈvəːsəbl] adj (garment, procedure) reversible

reversing lights [rɪˈvəːsɪŋ-] npl (Brit Aut) luces fpl de marcha atrás

revert [rɪˈvəːt] vi: **to ~ to** volver or revertir a

review [rɪˈvjuː] n (magazine) revista; (Mil) revista; (of book, film) reseña; (US: examination) repaso, examen m ■ vt repasar, examinar; (Mil) pasar revista a; (book, film) reseñar; **to come under ~** ser examinado

reviewer [rɪˈvjuːəʳ] n crítico(-a)

revile [rɪˈvaɪl] vt injuriar, vilipendiar

revise [rɪˈvaɪz] vt (manuscript) corregir; (opinion) modificar; (Brit: study: subject) repasar; (look over) revisar; **revised edition** edición f corregida

revision [rɪˈvɪʒən] n corrección f; modificación f; (of subject) repaso; (revised version) revisión f

revisit [riːˈvɪzɪt] vt volver a visitar

revitalize [riːˈvaɪtəlaɪz] vt revivificar

revival [rɪˈvaɪvəl] n (recovery) reanimación f;

(Pol) resurgimiento; (of interest) renacimiento; (Theat) reestreno; (of faith) despertar m

revive [rɪ'vaɪv] vt resucitar; (custom) restablecer; (hope, courage) reanimar; (play) reestrenar ■ vi (person) volver en sí; (from tiredness) reponerse; (business) reactivarse

revoke [rɪ'vəuk] vt revocar

revolt [rɪ'vəult] n rebelión f ■ vi rebelarse, sublevarse ■ vt dar asco a, repugnar; **to ~ (against sb/sth)** rebelarse (contra algn/algo)

revolting [rɪ'vəultɪŋ] adj asqueroso, repugnante

revolution [rɛvə'luːʃən] n revolución f

revolutionary [rɛvə'luːʃənrɪ] adj, n revolucionario(-a) m(f)

revolutionize [rɛvə'luːʃənaɪz] vt revolucionar

revolve [rɪ'vɔlv] vi dar vueltas, girar

revolver [rɪ'vɔlvər] n revólver m

revolving [rɪ'vɔlvɪŋ] adj (chair, door etc) giratorio

revue [rɪ'vjuː] n (Theat) revista

revulsion [rɪ'vʌlʃən] n asco, repugnancia

reward [rɪ'wɔːd] n premio, recompensa ■ vt: **to ~ (for)** recompensar or premiar (por)

rewarding [rɪ'wɔːdɪŋ] adj (fig) gratificante; **financially ~** económicamente provechoso

rewind [riː'waɪnd] vt (watch) dar cuerda a; (wool etc) devanar

rewire [riː'waɪər] vt (house) renovar la instalación eléctrica de

reword [riː'wəːd] vt expresar en otras palabras

rewritable [riː'raɪtəbl] adj reescribible

rewrite [riː'raɪt] vt (irreg: like **write**) reescribir

Reykjavik ['reɪkjəviːk] n Reykjavik m

RFD abbr (US Post) = **rural free delivery**

RGN n abbr (Brit) = **Registered General Nurse**

Rh abbr (= rhesus) Rh m

rhapsody ['ræpsədɪ] n (Mus) rapsodia; (fig): **to go into rhapsodies over** extasiarse por

rhesus negative ['riːsəs-] adj (Med) Rh negativo

rhesus positive adj (Med) Rh positivo

rhetoric ['rɛtərɪk] n retórica

rhetorical [rɪ'tɔrɪkl] adj retórico

rheumatic [ruː'mætɪk] adj reumático

rheumatism ['ruːmətɪzəm] n reumatismo, reúma

rheumatoid arthritis ['ruːmətɔɪd-] n reúma m articular

Rhine [raɪn] n: **the ~** el (río) Rin

rhinestone ['raɪnstəun] n diamante m de imitación

rhinoceros [raɪ'nɔsərəs] n rinoceronte m

Rhodes [rəudz] n Rodas f

rhododendron [rəudə'dɛndrn] n rododendro

Rhone [rəun] n: **the ~** el (río) Ródano

rhubarb ['ruːbɑːb] n ruibarbo

rhyme [raɪm] n rima; (verse) poesía ■ vi: **to ~ (with)** rimar (con); **without ~ or reason** sin ton ni son

rhythm ['rɪðm] n ritmo

rhythmic ['rɪðmɪk], **rhythmical** ['rɪðmɪkl] adj rítmico

rhythmically ['rɪðmɪklɪ] adv rítmicamente

rhythm method n método (de) Ogino

RI n abbr (Brit: = religious instruction) ed. religiosa ■ abbr (US: Post) = **Rhode Island**

rib [rɪb] n (Anat) costilla ■ vt (mock) tomar el pelo a

ribald ['rɪbəld] adj escabroso

ribbon ['rɪbən] n cinta; **in ribbons** (torn) hecho trizas

rice [raɪs] n arroz m

ricefield ['raɪsfiːld] n arrozal m

rice pudding n arroz m con leche

rich [rɪtʃ] adj rico; (soil) fértil; (food) pesado; (: sweet) empalagoso; **the rich** npl los ricos; **riches** npl riqueza sg; **to be ~ in sth** abundar en algo

richly ['rɪtʃlɪ] adv ricamente

richness ['rɪtʃnɪs] n riqueza; (of soil) fertilidad f

rickets ['rɪkɪts] n raquitismo

rickety ['rɪkɪtɪ] adj (old) desvencijado; (shaky) tambaleante

rickshaw ['rɪkʃɔː] n carro de culí

ricochet ['rɪkəʃeɪ] n rebote m ■ vi rebotar

rid (pt, pp ~) [rɪd] vt: **to ~ sb of sth** librar a algn de algo; **to get ~ of** deshacerse or desembarazarse de

riddance ['rɪdns] n: **good ~!** ¡y adiós muy buenas!

ridden ['rɪdn] pp of **ride**

-ridden ['rɪdn] suff: **disease~** plagado de enfermedades; **inflation~** minado por la inflación

riddle ['rɪdl] n (conundrum) acertijo; (mystery) enigma m, misterio ■ vt: **to be riddled with** ser lleno or plagado de

ride [raɪd] (pt **rode**, pp **ridden**) n paseo; (distance covered) viaje m, recorrido ■ vi (on horse: as sport) montar; (go somewhere: on horse, bicycle) dar un paseo, pasearse; (journey: on bicycle, motorcycle, bus) viajar ■ vt (a horse) montar a; (distance) viajar; **to ~ a bicycle** andar en bicicleta; **to ~ at anchor** (Naut) estar fondeado; **can you ~ a bike?** ¿sabes montar en bici(cleta)?; **to go for a ~** dar un paseo; **to take sb for a ~** (fig) tomar el pelo a algn

▶ **ride out** vt: **to ~ out the storm** (fig) capear el temporal

rider ['raɪdə'] n (on horse) jinete m; (on bicycle) ciclista m/f; (on motorcycle) motociclista m/f
ridge [rɪdʒ] n (of hill) cresta; (of roof) caballete m; (wrinkle) arruga
ridicule ['rɪdɪkju:l] n irrisión f, burla ■ vt poner en ridículo a, burlarse de; **to hold sth/sb up to ~** poner algo/a algn en ridículo
ridiculous [rɪ'dɪkjuləs] adj ridículo
ridiculously [rɪ'dɪkjuləslɪ] adv ridículamente, de modo ridículo
riding ['raɪdɪŋ] n equitación f; **I like ~** me gusta montar a caballo
riding habit n traje m de montar
riding school n escuela de equitación
rife [raɪf] adj: **to be ~** ser muy común; **to be ~ with** abundar en
riffraff ['rɪfræf] n chusma, gentuza
rifle ['raɪfl] n rifle m, fusil m ■ vt saquear
  ▶ **rifle through** vt fus saquear
rifle range n campo de tiro; (at fair) tiro al blanco
rift [rɪft] n (fig: between friends) desavenencia; (: in party) escisión f
rig [rɪg] n (also: **oil rig**: on land) torre f de perforación; (: at sea) plataforma petrolera ■ vt (election etc) amañar los resultados de
  ▶ **rig out** vt (Brit) ataviar
  ▶ **rig up** vt improvisar
rigging ['rɪgɪŋ] n (Naut) aparejo
right [raɪt] adj (true, correct) correcto, exacto; (suitable) indicado, debido; (proper) apropiado, propio; (just) justo; (morally good) bueno; (not left) derecho ■ n (title, claim) derecho; (not left) derecha ■ adv (correctly) bien, correctamente; (straight) derecho, directamente; (not on the left) a la derecha; (to the right) hacia la derecha ■ vt (put straight) enderezar ■ excl ¡bueno!, ¡está bien!; **to be ~** (person) tener razón; **to get sth ~** acertar en algo; **you did the ~ thing** hiciste bien; **let's get it ~ this time!** ¡a ver si esta vez nos sale bien!; **to put a mistake ~** corregir un error; **the ~ time** la hora exacta; (fig) el momento oportuno; **by rights** en justicia; **~ and wrong** el bien y el mal; **film rights** derechos mpl de la película; **on the ~** a la derecha; **to be in the ~** tener razón; **~ now** ahora mismo; **~ before/after** inmediatamente antes/después; **~ in the middle** exactamente en el centro; **~ away** en seguida; **to go ~ to the end of sth** llegar hasta el final de algo; **~, who's next?** bueno, ¿quién sigue?; **all ~!** ¡vale!; **I'm/I feel all ~ now** ya estoy bien
right angle n ángulo recto
right-click ['raɪtklɪk] vi clicar con el botón derecho del ratón ■ vt: **to ~ an icon** clicar en un icono con el botón derecho del ratón

righteous ['raɪtʃəs] adj justo, honrado; (anger) justificado
righteousness ['raɪtʃəsnɪs] n justicia
rightful ['raɪtful] adj (heir) legítimo
right-hand ['raɪthænd] adj (drive, turn) por la derecha
right-handed [raɪt'hændɪd] adj (person) que usa la mano derecha
right-hand man n brazo derecho
right-hand side n derecha
rightly ['raɪtlɪ] adv correctamente, debidamente; (with reason) con razón; **if I remember ~** si recuerdo bien
right-minded ['raɪt'maɪndɪd] adj (sensible) sensato; (decent) honrado
right of way n (on path etc) derecho de paso; (Aut) prioridad f de paso
right-wing [raɪt'wɪŋ] adj (Pol) de derechas, derechista
right-winger [raɪt'wɪŋə'] n (Pol) persona de derechas, derechista m/f; (Sport) extremo derecha
rigid ['rɪdʒɪd] adj rígido; (person, ideas) inflexible
rigidity [rɪ'dʒɪdɪtɪ] n rigidez f; inflexibilidad f
rigidly ['rɪdʒɪdlɪ] adv rígidamente; (inflexibly) inflexiblemente
rigmarole ['rɪgmərəul] n galimatías m inv
rigor mortis ['rɪgə'mɔ:tɪs] n rigidez f cadavérica
rigorous ['rɪgərəs] adj riguroso
rigorously ['rɪgərəslɪ] adv rigurosamente
rigour, rigor (US) ['rɪgə'] n rigor m, severidad f
rile [raɪl] vt irritar
rim [rɪm] n borde m; (of spectacles) montura, aro; (of wheel) llanta
rimless ['rɪmlɪs] adj (spectacles) sin aros
rimmed [rɪmd] adj: **~ with** con un borde de, bordeado de
rind [raɪnd] n (of bacon, cheese) corteza; (of lemon etc) cáscara
ring [rɪŋ] n (pt **rang**, pp **rung**) (of metal) aro; (on finger) anillo; (of people) corro; (of objects) círculo; (gang) banda; (for boxing) cuadrilátero; (of circus) pista; (bull ring) ruedo, plaza; (sound of bell) toque m; (telephone call) llamada ■ vi (on telephone) llamar por teléfono; (large bell) repicar; (also: **ring out**: voice, words) sonar; (ears) zumbar ■ vt (Brit Tel: also: **ring up**) llamar; (bell etc) hacer sonar; (doorbell) tocar; **that has the ~ of truth about it** eso suena a verdad; **to give sb a ~** (Brit Tel) llamar por teléfono a algn, dar un telefonazo a algn; **the name doesn't ~ a bell (with me)** el nombre no me suena; **to ~ sb (up)** llamar a algn

▶ **ring back** *vt, vi* (*Tel*) devolver la llamada

▶ **ring off** *vi* (*Brit Tel*) colgar, cortar la comunicación

ring binder *n* carpeta de anillas

ring finger *n* (dedo) anular *m*

ringing ['rɪŋɪŋ] *n* (*of bell*) toque *m*, tañido; (*of large bell*) repique *m*; (*in ears*) zumbido

ringing tone *n* (*Tel*) tono de llamada

ringleader ['rɪŋli:dəʳ] *n* cabecilla *m/f*

ringlets ['rɪŋlɪts] *npl* tirabuzones *mpl*, bucles *mpl*

ring road *n* (*Brit*) carretera periférica *or* de circunvalación

ringtone ['rɪŋtəun] *n* tono de llamada

rink [rɪŋk] *n* (*also*: **ice rink**) pista de hielo; (*for roller-skating*) pista de patinaje

rinse [rɪns] *n* (*of dishes*) enjuague *m*; (*of clothes*) aclarado; (*of hair*) reflejo ■ *vt* enjuagar; aclarar; dar reflejos a

Rio ['ri:əu], **Rio de Janeiro** ['ri:əudədʒə'nɪərəu] *n* Río de Janeiro

riot ['raɪət] *n* motín *m*, disturbio ■ *vi* amotinarse; **to run ~** desmandarse

rioter ['raɪətəʳ] *n* amotinado(-a)

riot gear *n* uniforme *m* antidisturbios *inv*

riotous ['raɪətəs] *adj* alborotado; (*party*) bullicioso; (*uncontrolled*) desenfrenado

riotously ['raɪətəslɪ] *adv* bulliciosamente

riot police *n* policía antidisturbios

RIP *abbr* (= *requiescat or requiescant in pace: rest in peace*) q.e.p.d.

rip [rɪp] *n* rasgón *m*, desgarrón *m* ■ *vt* rasgar, desgarrar ■ *vi* rasgarse

▶ **rip up** *vt* hacer pedazos

ripcord ['rɪpkɔ:d] *n* cabo de desgarre

ripe [raɪp] *adj* (*fruit*) maduro

ripen ['raɪpən] *vt, vi* madurar

ripeness ['raɪpnɪs] *n* madurez *f*

rip-off ['rɪpɔf] *n* (*col*): **it's a ~!** ¡es una estafa!, ¡es un timo!

riposte [rɪ'pɔst] *n* respuesta aguda, réplica

ripple ['rɪpl] *n* onda, rizo; (*sound*) murmullo ■ *vi* rizarse ■ *vt* rizar

rise [raɪz] *n* (*slope*) cuesta, pendiente *f*; (*hill*) altura; (*increase: in wages: Brit*) aumento; (: *in prices, temperature*) subida, alza; (*fig: to power etc*) ascenso; (: *ascendancy*) auge *m* ■ *vi* (*pt* **rose**, *pp* **risen**) [rəuz, 'rɪzn] (*gen*) elevarse; (*prices*) subir; (*waters*) crecer; (*river*) nacer; (*sun*) salir; (*person: from bed etc*) levantarse; (*also*: **rise up**: *rebel*) sublevarse; (*in rank*) ascender; **~ to power** ascenso al poder; **to give ~ to** dar lugar *or* origen a; **to ~ to the occasion** ponerse a la altura de las circunstancias

rising ['raɪzɪŋ] *adj* (*increasing: number*) creciente; (: *prices*) en aumento *or* alza; (*tide*) creciente; (*sun, moon*) naciente ■ *n* (*uprising*) sublevación *f*

rising damp *n* humedad *f* de paredes

rising star *n* (*fig*) figura en alza

risk [rɪsk] *n* riesgo, peligro ■ *vt* (*gen*) arriesgar; (*dare*) atreverse a; **to take** *or* **run the ~ of doing** correr el riesgo de hacer; **at ~** en peligro; **at one's own ~** bajo su propia responsabilidad; **fire/health/security ~** peligro de incendio/para la salud/para la seguridad

risk capital *n* capital *m* de riesgo

risky ['rɪskɪ] *adj* arriesgado, peligroso

risqué ['ri:skeɪ] *adj* (*joke*) subido de color

rissole ['rɪsəul] *n* croqueta

rite [raɪt] *n* rito; **last rites** últimos sacramentos *mpl*

ritual ['rɪtjuəl] *adj* ritual ■ *n* ritual *m*, rito

rival ['raɪvl] *n* rival *m/f*; (*in business*) competidor(a) *m(f)* ■ *adj* rival, opuesto ■ *vt* competir con

rivalry ['raɪvlrɪ] *n* rivalidad *f*, competencia

river ['rɪvəʳ] *n* río ■ *cpd* (*port, traffic*) de río, del río; **up/down ~** río arriba/abajo

riverbank ['rɪvəbæŋk] *n* orilla (del río)

riverbed ['rɪvəbɛd] *n* lecho, cauce *m*

rivet ['rɪvɪt] *n* roblón *m*, remache *m* ■ *vt* remachar; (*fig*) fascinar

riveting ['rɪvɪtɪŋ] *adj* (*fig*) fascinante

Riviera [rɪvɪ'ɛərə] *n*: **the (French) ~** la Costa Azul, la Riviera (francesa); **the Italian ~** la Riviera italiana

Riyadh [rɪ'jɑːd] *n* Riyadh *m*

RMT *n abbr* (= *National Union of Rail, Maritime and Transport Workers*) *sindicato de transportes*

RN *n abbr* (*Brit*) = **Royal Navy**; (*US*) = **registered nurse**

RNA *n abbr* (= *ribonucleic acid*) ARN *m*, RNA *m*

RNLI *n abbr* (*Brit*: = *Royal National Lifeboat Institution*) *organización benéfica que proporciona un servicio de lanchas de socorro*

RNZAF *n abbr* = **Royal New Zealand Air Force**

RNZN *n abbr* = **Royal New Zealand Navy**

road [rəud] *n* (*gen*) camino; (*motorway etc*) carretera; (*in town*) calle *f*; **major/minor ~** carretera general/secundaria; **main ~** carretera; **it takes four hours by ~** se tarda cuarto horas por carretera; **on the ~ to success** camino del éxito

roadblock ['rəudblɔk] *n* barricada, control *m*, retén *m* (*LAm*)

road haulage *n* transporte *m* por carretera

roadhog ['rəudhɔg] *n* loco(-a) del volante

road map *n* mapa *m* de carreteras

road rage *n* *conducta agresiva de los conductores*

road safety *n* seguridad *f* vial

roadside ['rəudsaɪd] *n* borde *m* (del camino)

r

■ *cpd* al lado de la carretera; **by the ~** al borde del camino

roadsign ['rəudsaɪn] *n* señal *f* de tráfico

roadsweeper ['rəudswiːpəʳ] *n* (*Brit*: *person*) barrendero(-a)

road user *n* usuario(-a) de la vía pública

roadway ['rəudweɪ] *n* calzada

roadworks ['rəudwəːks] *npl* obras *fpl*

roadworthy ['rəudwəːðɪ] *adj* (*car*) en buen estado para circular

roam [rəum] *vi* vagar ■ *vt* vagar por

roar [rɔːʳ] *n* (*of animal*) rugido, bramido; (*of crowd*) clamor *m*, rugido; (*of vehicle, storm*) estruendo; (*of laughter*) carcajada ■ *vi* rugir, bramar; hacer estruendo; **to ~ with laughter** reírse a carcajadas

roaring ['rɔːrɪŋ] *adj*: **a ~ success** un tremendo éxito; **to do a ~ trade** hacer buen negocio

roast [rəust] *n* carne *f* asada, asado ■ *vt* (*meat*) asar; (*coffee*) tostar

roast beef *n* rosbif *m*

roasting ['rəustɪŋ] *n*: **to give sb a ~** (*col*) echar una buena bronca a algn

rob [rɔb] *vt* robar; **to ~ sb of sth** robar algo a algn; (*fig*: *deprive*) quitar algo a algn

robber ['rɔbəʳ] *n* ladrón(-ona) *m(f)*

robbery ['rɔbərɪ] *n* robo

robe [rəub] *n* (*for ceremony etc*) toga; (*also*: **bath robe**) bata

robin ['rɔbɪn] *n* petirrojo

robot ['rəubɔt] *n* robot *m*

robotics [rəu'bɔtɪks] *n* robótica

robust [rəu'bʌst] *adj* robusto, fuerte

rock [rɔk] *n* (*gen*) roca; (*boulder*) peña, peñasco; (*Brit*: *sweet*) ≈ pirulí *m* ■ *vt* (*swing gently*) mecer; (*shake*) sacudir ■ *vi* mecerse, balancearse; sacudirse; **on the rocks** (*drink*) con hielo; **their marriage is on the rocks** su matrimonio se está yendo a pique; **to ~ the boat** (*fig*) crear problemas

rock and roll *n* rock and roll *m*, rocanrol *m*

rock-bottom ['rɔk'bɔtəm] *adj* (*fig*) por los suelos; **to reach** *or* **touch ~** (*price*) estar por los suelos; (*person*) tocar fondo

rock cake *n* (*Brit*) *bollito de pasas con superficie rugosa*

rock climber *n* escalador(a) *m(f)*

rock climbing *n* (*Sport*) escalada

rockery ['rɔkərɪ] *n* cuadro alpino

rocket ['rɔkɪt] *n* cohete *m* ■ *vi* (*prices*) dispararse, ponerse por las nubes

rocket launcher *n* lanzacohetes *m inv*

rock face *n* pared *f* de roca

rocking chair ['rɔkɪŋ-] *n* mecedora

rocking horse *n* caballo de balancín

rocky ['rɔkɪ] *adj* (*gen*) rocoso; (*unsteady*: *table*) inestable

Rocky Mountains *npl*: **the ~** las Montañas Rocosas

rococo [rə'kəukəu] *adj* rococó *inv* ■ *n* rococó

rod [rɔd] *n* vara, varilla; (*Tech*) barra; (*also*: **fishing rod**) caña

rode [rəud] *pt of* **ride**

rodent ['rəudnt] *n* roedor *m*

rodeo ['rəudɪəu] *n* rodeo

roe [rəu] *n* (*species*: *also*: **roe deer**) corzo; (*of fish*): **hard/soft ~** hueva/lecha

rogue [rəug] *n* pícaro, pillo

roguish ['rəugɪʃ] *adj* (*child*) travieso; (*smile etc*) pícaro

role [rəul] *n* papel *m*, rol *m*

role-model ['rəulmɔdl] *n* modelo a imitar

role play *n* (*also*: **role playing**) juego de papeles *or* roles

roll [rəul] *n* rollo; (*of bank notes*) fajo; (*also*: **bread roll**) panecillo; (*register*) lista, nómina; (*sound*: *of drums etc*) redoble *m*; (*movement*: *of ship*) balanceo ■ *vt* hacer rodar; (*also*: **roll up**: *string*) enrollar; (: *sleeves*) arremangar; (*cigarettes*) liar; (*also*: **roll out**: *pastry*) aplanar ■ *vi* (*gen*) rodar; (*drum*) redoblar; (*in walking*) bambolearse; (*ship*) balancearse; **cheese ~** panecillo de queso

▶ **roll about, roll around** *vi* (*person*) revolcarse

▶ **roll by** *vi* (*time*) pasar

▶ **roll in** *vi* (*mail, cash*) entrar a raudales

▶ **roll over** *vi* dar una vuelta

▶ **roll up** *vi* (*col*: *arrive*) presentarse, aparecer ■ *vt* (*carpet, cloth, map*) arrollar; (*sleeves*) arremangar; **to ~ o.s. up into a ball** acurrucarse, hacerse un ovillo

roll call *n*: **to take a ~** pasar lista

rolled [rəuld] *adj* (*umbrella*) plegado

roller ['rəuləʳ] *n* rodillo; (*wheel*) rueda

roller blind *n* (*Brit*) persiana (enrollable)

roller coaster *n* montaña rusa

roller skates *npl* patines *mpl* de rueda

rollicking ['rɔlɪkɪŋ] *adj*: **we had a ~ time** nos divertimos una barbaridad

rolling ['rəulɪŋ] *adj* (*landscape*) ondulado

rolling mill *n* taller *m* de laminación

rolling pin *n* rodillo (de cocina)

rolling stock *n* (*Rail*) material *m* rodante

ROM [rɔm] *n abbr* (*Comput*: = *read-only memory*) (memoria) ROM *f*

Roman ['rəumən] *adj, n* romano(-a) *m(f)*

Roman Catholic *adj, n* católico(-a) *m(f)* (romano(-a))

romance [rə'mæns] *n* (*love affair*) amor *m*, idilio; (*charm*) lo romántico; (*novel*) novela de amor

romanesque [rəumə'nɛsk] *adj* románico

Romania [ruː'meɪnɪə] *n* = **Rumania**

Romanian [ru:'meɪnɪən] *adj, n* = **Rumanian**
Roman numeral *n* número romano
romantic [rə'mæntɪk] *adj* romántico
romanticism [rə'mæntɪsɪzəm] *n* romanticismo
Romany ['rəumənɪ] *adj* gitano ▪ *n* (*person*) gitano(-a); (*Ling*) lengua gitana, caló (*SP*)
Rome [rəum] *n* Roma
romp [rɔmp] *n* retozo, jugueteo ▪ *vi* (*also*: **romp about**) juguetear; **to ~ home** (*horse*) ganar fácilmente
rompers ['rɔmpəz] *npl* pelele *m*
roof [ru:f] *n* (*gen*) techo; (*of house*) tejado ▪ *vt* techar, poner techo a; **~ of the mouth** paladar *m*
roofing ['ru:fɪŋ] *n* techumbre *f*
roof rack *n* (*Aut*) baca
rook [ruk] *n* (*bird*) graja; (*Chess*) torre *f*
rookie ['rukɪ] *n* (*col*) novato(-a); (*Mil*) chivo
room [ru:m] *n* (*in house*) cuarto, habitación *f*, pieza (*esp LAm*); (*also*: **bedroom**) dormitorio; (*in school etc*) sala; (*space*) sitio; **rooms** *npl* (*lodging*) alojamiento *sg*; **"rooms to let"**, (*US*) **"rooms for rent"** "se alquilan pisos or cuartos"; **single/double ~** habitación individual/doble *or* para dos personas; **is there ~ for this?** ¿cabe esto?; **to make ~ for sb** hacer sitio para algn; **there is ~ for improvement** podría mejorarse
roominess ['ru:mɪnɪs] *n* amplitud *f*, espaciosidad *f*
rooming house ['ru:mɪŋ-] *n* (*US*) pensión *f*
roommate ['ru:mmeɪt] *n* compañero(-a) de cuarto
room service *n* servicio de habitaciones
room temperature *n* temperatura ambiente
roomy ['ru:mɪ] *adj* espacioso
roost [ru:st] *n* percha ▪ *vi* pasar la noche
rooster ['ru:stəʳ] *n* gallo
root [ru:t] *n* (*Bot, Math*) raíz *f* ▪ *vi* (*plant, belief*) arraigar(se); **to take ~** (*plant*) echar raíces; (*idea*) arraigar(se); **the ~ of the problem is that ...** la raíz del problema es que ...
  ▶ **root about** *vi* (*fig*) rebuscar
  ▶ **root for** *vt fus* apoyar a
  ▶ **root out** *vt* desarraigar
root beer *n* (*US*) *refresco sin alcohol de extractos de hierbas*
rooted ['ru:tɪd] *adj* enraizado; (*opinions etc*) arraigado
rope [rəup] *n* cuerda; (*Naut*) cable *m* ▪ *vt* (*box*) atar *or* amarrar con (una) cuerda; (*climbers: also*: **rope together**) encordarse; **to ~ sb in** (*fig*) persuadir a algn a tomar parte; **to know the ropes** (*fig*) conocer los trucos (del oficio)
rope ladder *n* escala de cuerda

ropey ['rəupɪ] *adj* (*col*) chungo
rosary ['rəuzərɪ] *n* rosario
rose [rəuz] *pt of* **rise** ▪ *n* rosa; (*also*: **rosebush**) rosal *m*; (*on watering can*) roseta ▪ *adj* color de rosa
rosé ['rəuzeɪ] *n* vino rosado, clarete *m*
rosebed ['rəuzbed] *n* rosaleda
rosebud ['rəuzbʌd] *n* capullo de rosa
rosebush ['rəuzbuʃ] *n* rosal *m*
rosemary ['rəuzmərɪ] *n* romero
rosette [rəu'zɛt] *n* rosetón *m*
ROSPA ['rɔspə] *n abbr* (*Brit*) = **Royal Society for the Prevention of Accidents**
roster ['rɔstəʳ] *n*: **duty ~** lista de tareas
rostrum ['rɔstrəm] *n* tribuna
rosy ['rəuzɪ] *adj* rosado, sonrosado; **the future looks ~** el futuro parece prometedor
rot [rɔt] *n* (*decay*) putrefacción *f*, podredumbre *f*; (*fig: pej*) tonterías *fpl* ▪ *vt* pudrir, corromper ▪ *vi* pudrirse, corromperse; **it has rotted** está podrido; **to stop the ~** (*fig*) poner fin a las pérdidas
rota ['rəutə] *n* lista (de tareas)
rotary ['rəutərɪ] *adj* rotativo
rotate [rəu'teɪt] *vt* (*revolve*) hacer girar, dar vueltas a; (*change round: crops*) cultivar en rotación; (*:jobs*) alternar ▪ *vi* (*revolve*) girar, dar vueltas
rotating [rəu'teɪtɪŋ] *adj* (*movement*) rotativo
rotation [rəu'teɪʃən] *n* rotación *f*; **in ~** por turno
rote [rəut] *n*: **by ~** de memoria
rotor ['rəutəʳ] *n* rotor *m*
rotten ['rɔtn] *adj* (*decayed*) podrido; (*: wood*) carcomido; (*fig*) corrompido; (*col: bad*) pésimo; **to feel ~** (*ill*) sentirse fatal; **~ to the core** completamente podrido
rotund [rəu'tʌnd] *adj* rotundo
rouble, ruble (*US*) ['ru:bl] *n* rublo
rouge [ru:ʒ] *n* colorete *m*
rough [rʌf] *adj* (*skin, surface*) áspero; (*terrain*) accidentado; (*road*) desigual; (*voice*) bronco; (*person, manner: coarse*) tosco, grosero; (*weather*) borrascoso; (*treatment*) brutal; (*sea*) embravecido; (*cloth*) basto; (*plan*) preliminar; (*guess*) aproximado; (*violent*) violento ▪ *n* (*Golf*): **in the ~** en las hierbas altas; **to ~ it** vivir sin comodidades; **to sleep ~** (*Brit*) pasar la noche al raso; **the sea is ~ today** el mar está agitado hoy; **to have a ~ time (of it)** pasar una mala racha; **~ estimate** cálculo aproximado
roughage ['rʌfɪdʒ] *n* fibra(s) *f(pl)*, forraje *m*
rough-and-ready ['rʌfən'rɛdɪ] *adj* improvisado, tosco
rough-and-tumble ['rʌfən'tʌmbl] *n* pelea
roughcast ['rʌfkɑ:st] *n* mezcla gruesa

r

rough copy, rough draft n borrador m
roughen ['rʌfn] vt (a surface) poner áspero
roughly ['rʌflɪ] adv (handle) torpemente;
(make) toscamente; (approximately)
aproximadamente; ~ **speaking** más o menos
roughness ['rʌfnɪs] n aspereza; tosquedad f;
brutalidad f
roughshod ['rʌfʃɒd] adv: **to ride ~ over**
(person) pisotear a; (objections) hacer caso
omiso de
rough work n (Scol etc) borrador m
roulette [ruː'lɛt] n ruleta
Roumania [ruː'meɪnɪə] n = **Rumania**
round [raund] adj redondo ■ n círculo;
(of policeman) ronda; (of milkman) recorrido;
(of doctor) visitas fpl; (game: in competition, cards)
partida; (of ammunition) cartucho; (Boxing)
asalto; (of talks) ronda ■ vt (corner) doblar
■ prep alrededor de ■ adv: **all ~** por todos
lados; **the long way ~** por el camino menos
directo; **all the year ~** durante todo el año;
it's just ~ the corner (fig) está a la vuelta
de la esquina; **to ask sb ~** invitar a algn a
casa; **I'll be ~ at six o'clock** llegaré a eso de
las seis; **she arrived ~ (about) noon** llegó
alrededor del mediodía; **~ the clock** adv las
24 horas; **to go ~ to sb's (house)** ir a casa de
algn; **to go ~ the back** pasar por atrás; **to
go ~ a house** visitar una casa; **enough to
go ~** bastante (para todos); **in ~ figures** en
números redondos; **to go the rounds** (story)
divulgarse; **a ~ of applause** una salva de
aplausos; **a ~ of drinks/sandwiches** una
ronda de bebidas/bocadillos; **a ~ of toast**
(Brit) una tostada; **the daily ~** la rutina
cotidiana
▸ **round off** vt (speech etc) acabar, poner
término a
▸ **round up** vt (cattle) acorralar; (people)
reunir; (prices) redondear
roundabout ['raundəbaut] n (Brit: Aut)
glorieta, rotonda; (: at fair) tiovivo ■ adj
(route, means) indirecto
rounded ['raundɪd] adj redondeado, redondo
rounders ['raundəz] n (Brit: game) juego similar
al béisbol
roundly ['raundlɪ] adv (fig) rotundamente
round-robin ['raundrɒbɪn] n (Sport: also:
round-robin tournament) liguilla
round-shouldered ['raund'ʃəuldəd] adj
cargado de espaldas
round trip n viaje m de ida y vuelta
roundup ['raundʌp] n rodeo; (of criminals)
redada; **a ~ of the latest news** un resumen
de las últimas noticias
rouse [rauz] vt (wake up) despertar; (stir up)
suscitar

rousing ['rauzɪŋ] adj (applause) caluroso;
(speech) conmovedor(a)
rout [raut] n (Mil) derrota; (flight) desbandada
■ vt derrotar
route [ruːt] n ruta, camino; (of bus) recorrido;
(of shipping) rumbo, derrota; **the best ~ to
London** el mejor camino or la mejor ruta
para ir a Londres; **en ~ from ... to** en el viaje
de ... a; **en ~ for** rumbo a, con destino en
route map n (Brit: for journey) mapa m de
carreteras
routine [ruː'tiːn] adj (work) rutinario ■ n
rutina; (Theat) número; (Comput) rutina; ~
procedure trámite m rutinario
rover ['rəuvər] n vagabundo(-a)
roving ['rəuvɪŋ] adj (wandering) errante;
(salesman) ambulante; (reporter) volante
row [rəu] n (line) fila, hilera; (Knitting) vuelta
[rau] (noise) escándalo; (dispute) bronca,
pelea; (fuss) jaleo; (scolding) reprimenda ■ vi
(in boat) remar; [rau] reñir(se) ■ vt (boat)
conducir remando; **four days in a ~** cuarto
días seguidos; **to make a ~** armar un lío; **to
have a ~** pelearse, reñir
rowboat ['rəubəut] n (US) bote m de remos
rowdy ['raudɪ] adj (person: noisy) ruidoso;
(: quarrelsome) pendenciero; (occasion)
alborotado ■ n pendenciero
rowdyism ['raudɪɪzəm] n gamberrismo
row houses npl (US) casas fpl adosadas
rowing ['rəuɪŋ] n remo
rowing boat n (Brit) bote m or barco de remos
rowlock ['rɒlək] n (Brit) chumacera
royal ['rɔɪəl] adj real
Royal Academy, Royal Academy of Arts
n (Brit) la Real Academia (de Bellas Artes);
ver nota

● **ROYAL ACADEMY (OF ARTS)**
●
● La Royal Academy (of Arts), fundada en
● 1768 durante el reinado de Jorge III, es
● una institución dedicada al fomento de
● la pintura, escultura y arquitectura en
● el Reino Unido. Además de dar cursos
● de arte, presenta una exposición anual
● de artistas contemporáneos en su sede
● de Burlington House, en el centro de
● Londres. No existe una institución
● equivalente a la Real Academia de la
● Lengua.

Royal Air Force n Fuerzas Aéreas Británicas
fpl
royal blue n azul m marino
royalist ['rɔɪəlɪst] adj, n monárquico(-a) m(f)
Royal Navy n (Brit) Marina Británica

royalty ['rɔɪəltɪ] *n* (*royal persons*) (miembros *mpl* de la) familia real; (*payment to author*) derechos *mpl* de autor

RP (*n abbr: Brit: = Received Pronunciation*) *ver nota*

R P

El acento con el que suelen hablar las clases medias y altas de Inglaterra se denomina RP (o *Received Pronunciation*). Es el acento estándar, sin variaciones regionales, que aún usan los locutores en los informativos nacionales de la "BBC". También suele tomarse como norma en la enseñanza del inglés británico como lengua extranjera. Todavía conserva un gran prestigio, aunque la gran mayoría de la población habla con el acento de su región, que puede ser más o menos fuerte según su educación o clase social.

rpm (*abbr: = revolutions per minute*) r.p.m.

RR *abbr* (*US*) = **railroad**

RRP *n abbr* (*Brit: = recommended retail price*) PVP *m*

RSA *n abbr* (*Brit*) = **Royal Society of Arts**; **Royal Scottish Academy**

RSI *n abbr* (*Med: = repetitive strain injury*) *traumatismo producido por un esfuerzo continuado* (*como el de las mecanógrafas*)

RSPB *n abbr* (*Brit*) = **Royal Society for the Protection of Birds**

RSPCA *n abbr* (*Brit*) = **Royal Society for the Prevention of Cruelty to Animals**

RSVP *abbr* (*= répondez s'il vous plaît*) SRC

RTA *n abbr* (*= road traffic accident*) accidente *m* de carretera

Rt. Hon. *abbr* (*Brit: = Right Honourable*) *tratamiento honorífico de diputado*

Rt. Rev. *abbr* (*= Right Reverend*) Rvdo.

rub [rʌb] *vt* (*gen*) frotar; (*hard*) restregar ■ *n* (*gen*) frotamiento; (*touch*) roce *m*; **to ~ sb up** *or* (*US*) **~ sb the wrong way** sacar de quicio a algn

▶ **rub down** *vt* (*body*) secar frotando; (*horse*) almohazar

▶ **rub in** *vt* (*ointment*) frotar

▶ **rub off** *vt* borrarse ■ *vi* quitarse (frotando); **to ~ off on sb** influir en algn, pegársele a algn

▶ **rub out** *vt* borrar ■ *vi* borrarse

rubber ['rʌbəʳ] *n* caucho, goma; (*Brit: eraser*) goma de borrar

rubber band *n* goma, gomita

rubber bullet *n* bala de goma

rubber plant *n* ficus *m*

rubber ring *n* (*for swimming*) flotador *m*

rubber stamp *n* sello (de caucho) ■ *vt:*

rubber-stamp (*fig*) aprobar maquinalmente

rubbery ['rʌbərɪ] *adj* (como) de goma

rubbish ['rʌbɪʃ] (*Brit*) *n* (*from household*) basura; (*waste*) desperdicios *mpl*; (*fig: pej*) tonterías *fpl*; (*trash*) basura, porquería ■ *vt* (*col*) poner por los suelos; **what you've just said is ~** lo que acabas de decir es una tontería

rubbish bin *n* cubo *or* bote *m* (*LAm*) de la basura

rubbish dump *n* (*in town*) vertedero, basurero

rubbishy ['rʌbɪʃɪ] *adj* de mala calidad, de pacotilla

rubble ['rʌbl] *n* escombros *mpl*

ruby ['ru:bɪ] *n* rubí *m*

RUC *n abbr* (*= Royal Ulster Constabulary*) *fuerza de policía en Irlanda del Norte*

rucksack ['rʌksæk] *n* mochila

ructions ['rʌkʃənz] *npl*: **there will be ~** se va a armar la gorda

ruddy ['rʌdɪ] *adj* (*face*) rubicundo; (*col: damned*) condenado

rude [ru:d] *adj* (*impolite: person*) grosero, maleducado; (: *word, manners*) rudo, grosero; (*indecent*) indecente; **to be ~ to sb** ser grosero con algn

rudeness ['ru:dnɪs] *n* grosería, tosquedad *f*

rudiment ['ru:dɪmənt] *n* rudimento

rudimentary [ru:dɪ'mɛntərɪ] *adj* rudimentario

rue [ru:] *vt* arrepentirse de

rueful ['ru:ful] *adj* arrepentido

ruffian ['rʌfɪən] *n* matón *m*, criminal *m*

ruffle ['rʌfl] *vt* (*hair*) despeinar; (*clothes*) arrugar; (*fig: person*) agitar

rug [rʌg] *n* alfombra; (*Brit: for knees*) manta

rugby ['rʌgbɪ] *n* (*also: rugby football*) rugby *m*

rugged ['rʌgɪd] *adj* (*landscape*) accidentado; (*features*) robusto

rugger ['rʌgəʳ] *n* (*Brit col*) rugby *m*

ruin ['ru:ɪn] *n* ruina ■ *vt* arruinar; (*spoil*) estropear; **ruins** *npl* ruinas *fpl*, restos *mpl*; **in ruins** en ruinas

ruinous ['ru:ɪnəs] *adj* ruinoso

rule [ru:l] *n* (*norm*) norma, costumbre *f*; (*regulation, ruler*) regla; (*government*) dominio; (*dominion etc*): **under British ~** bajo el dominio británico ■ *vt* (*country, person*) gobernar; (*decide*) disponer; (*draw lines*) trazar ■ *vi* gobernar; (*Law*) fallar; **to ~ against/in favour of/on** fallar en contra de/a favor de/ sobre; **to ~ that ...** (*umpire, judge*) fallar que ...; **it's against the rules** está prohibido; **as a ~** por regla general, generalmente; **by ~ of thumb** por experiencia; **majority ~** (*Pol*) gobierno mayoritario

▶ **rule out** *vt* excluir

ruled [ru:ld] *adj* (*paper*) rayado

r

ruler ['ru:lə^r] n (sovereign) soberano; (for measuring) regla

ruling ['ru:lɪŋ] adj (party) gobernante; (class) dirigente ■ n (Law) fallo, decisión f

rum [rʌm] n ron m

Rumania [ru:'meɪnɪə] n Rumanía

Rumanian [ru:'meɪnɪən] adj, n rumano(-a) m(f)

rumble ['rʌmbl] n ruido sordo; (of thunder) redoble m ■ vi retumbar, hacer un ruido sordo; (stomach, pipe) sonar

rumbustious [rʌm'bʌstʃəs] adj (person) bullicioso

rummage ['rʌmɪdʒ] vi revolverlo todo

rumour, rumor (US) ['ru:mə^r] n rumor m ■ vt: **it is rumoured that ...** se rumorea que ...; **~ has it that ...** corre la voz de que ...

rump [rʌmp] n (of animal) ancas fpl, grupa

rumple ['rʌmpl] vt (clothes) arrugar; (hair) despeinar

rump steak n filete m de lomo

rumpus ['rʌmpəs] n (col) lío, jaleo; (quarrel) pelea, riña; **to kick up a ~** armar un follón or armar bronca

run [rʌn] (pt **ran**, pp **~**) n (Sport) carrera; (outing) paseo, excursión f; (distance travelled) trayecto; (series) serie f; (Theat) temporada; (Ski) pista; (in tights, stockings) carrera ■ vt (operate: business) dirigir; (: competition, course) organizar; (: hotel, house) administrar, llevar; (Comput: program) ejecutar; (to pass: hand) pasar; (bath): **to ~ a bath** llenar la bañera ■ vi (gen) correr; (work: machine) funcionar, marchar; (bus, train: operate) circular, ir; (: travel) ir; (continue: play) seguir en cartel; (: contract) ser válido; (flow: river, bath) fluir; (colours, washing) desteñirse; (in election) ser candidato; **to go for a ~** ir a correr; **to make a ~ for it** echar(se) a correr, escapar(se), huir; **to have the ~ of sb's house** tener el libre uso de la casa de algn; **a ~ of luck** una racha de suerte; **there was a ~ on** (meat, tickets) hubo mucha demanda de; **in the long ~** a la larga; **on the ~** en fuga; **I'll ~ you to the station** te llevaré a la estación en coche; **to ~ a risk** correr un riesgo; **to ~ errands** hacer recados; **it's very cheap to ~** es muy económico; **to be ~ off one's feet** estar ocupadísimo; **to ~ for the bus** correr tras el autobús; **we shall have to ~ for it** tendremos que escapar; **the train runs between Gatwick and Victoria** el tren circula entre Gatwick y Victoria; **the bus runs every 20 minutes** el autobús pasa cada 20 minutos; **to ~ on petrol/on diesel/off batteries** funcionar con gasolina/gasoil/baterías; **my salary won't ~ to a car** mi sueldo no me da para comprarme un coche;

the car ran into the lamppost el coche chocó contra el farol

▶ **run about, run around** vi (children) correr por todos lados

▶ **run across** vt fus (find) dar or topar con

▶ **run away** vi huir

▶ **run down** vi (clock) pararse ■ vt (reduce: production) ir reduciendo; (factory) restringir la producción de; (Aut) atropellar; (criticize) criticar; **to be ~ down** (person: tired) encontrarse agotado

▶ **run in** vt (Brit: car) rodar

▶ **run into** vt fus (meet: person, trouble) tropezar con; (collide with) chocar con; **to ~ into debt** contraer deudas, endeudarse

▶ **run off** vt (water) dejar correr ■ vi huir corriendo

▶ **run out** vi (person) salir corriendo; (liquid) irse; (lease) caducar, vencer; (money) acabarse

▶ **run out of** vt fus quedar sin; **I've ~ out of petrol** se me acabó la gasolina

▶ **run over** vt (Aut) atropellar ■ vt fus (revise) repasar

▶ **run through** vt fus (instructions) repasar

▶ **run up** vt (debt) incurrir en; **to ~ up against** (difficulties) tropezar con

run-around ['rʌnəraund] n: **to give sb the ~** traer a algn al retortero

runaway ['rʌnəweɪ] adj (horse) desbocado; (truck) sin frenos; (person) fugitivo

rundown ['rʌndaun] n (Brit: of industry etc) cierre m gradual

rung [rʌn] pp of **ring** ■ n (of ladder) escalón m, peldaño

run-in ['rʌnɪn] n (col) altercado

runner ['rʌnə^r] n (in race: person) corredor(a) m(f); (: horse) caballo; (on sledge) patín m; (wheel) ruedecilla

runner bean n (Brit) judía escarlata

runner-up [rʌnər'ʌp] n subcampeón(-ona) m(f)

running ['rʌnɪŋ] n (sport) atletismo; (race) carrera ■ adj (costs, water) corriente; (commentary) en directo; **to be in/out of the ~ for sth** tener/no tener posibilidades de ganar algo; **6 days** ~ 6 días seguidos

running costs npl (of business) gastos mpl corrientes; (of car) gastos mpl de mantenimiento

running head n (Typ) encabezamiento normal

running mate n (US Pol) candidato(-a) a la vicepresidencia

runny ['rʌnɪ] adj derretido

run-off ['rʌnɔf] n (in contest, election) desempate m; (extra race) carrera de desempate

run-of-the-mill ['rʌnəvðə'mɪl] adj común y corriente

runt [rʌnt] *n* (*also pej*) enano
run-up ['rʌnʌp] *n*: ~ **to** (*election etc*) período previo a
runway ['rʌnweɪ] *n* (*Aviat*) pista (de aterrizaje)
rupee [ruː'piː] *n* rupia
rupture ['rʌptʃəʳ] *n* (*Med*) hernia ∎ *vt*: **to ~ o.s.** causarse una hernia
rural ['ruərl] *adj* rural
ruse [ruːz] *n* ardid *m*
rush [rʌʃ] *n* ímpetu *m*; (*hurry*) prisa, apuro (*LAm*); (*Comm*) demanda repentina; (*Bot*) junco; (*current*) corriente *f* fuerte, ráfaga ∎ *vt* apresurar; (*work*) hacer de prisa; (*attack: town etc*) asaltar ∎ *vi* correr, precipitarse; **gold ~** fiebre *f* del oro; **we've had a ~ of orders** ha habido una gran demanda; **I'm in a ~ (to do)** tengo prisa *or* apuro (*LAm*) (por hacer); **is there any ~ for this?** ¿te corre prisa esto?; **to ~ sth off** hacer algo de prisa y corriendo
▶**rush through** *vt fus* (*meal*) comer de prisa; (*book*) leer de prisa; (*work*) hacer de prisa;

(*town*) atravesar a toda velocidad ∎ *vt sep* (*Comm: order*) despachar rápidamente
rush hour *n* horas *fpl* punta
rush job *n* (*urgent*) trabajo urgente
rusk [rʌsk] *n* bizcocho tostado
Russia ['rʌʃə] *n* Rusia
Russian ['rʌʃən] *adj* ruso ∎ *n* ruso(-a); (*Ling*) ruso
rust [rʌst] *n* herrumbre *f*, moho ∎ *vi* oxidarse
rustic ['rʌstɪk] *adj* rústico
rustle ['rʌsl] *vi* susurrar ∎ *vt* (*paper*) hacer crujir; (*US: cattle*) hurtar, robar
rustproof ['rʌstpruːf] *adj* inoxidable
rusty ['rʌstɪ] *adj* oxidado
rut [rʌt] *n* surco; (*Zool*) celo; **to be in a ~** ser esclavo de la rutina
ruthless ['ruːθlɪs] *adj* despiadado
RV *abbr* (= *revised version*) traducción inglesa de la Biblia de 1855 ∎ *n abbr* (*US*) = **recreational vehicle**
rye [raɪ] *n* centeno
rye bread *n* pan de centeno

Ss

S, s [ɛs] n (letter) S, s f; **S for Sugar** S de sábado
S abbr (= Saint) Sto.(-a.); (US Scol: mark:
= satisfactory) suficiente; (= south) S; (on clothes)
= **small**
SA n abbr = **South Africa**; **South America**
sabbath ['sæbəθ] n domingo; (Jewish) sábado
sabbatical [sə'bætɪkl] adj: ~ **year** año
sabático
sabotage ['sæbətɑːʒ] n sabotaje m ■ vt
sabotear
sabre, saber (US) ['seɪbəʳ] n sable m
saccharin, saccharine ['sækərɪn] n sacarina
sachet ['sæʃeɪ] n sobrecito
sack [sæk] n (bag) saco, costal m ■ vt (dismiss)
despedir, echar; (plunder) saquear; **to get the
~** ser despedido; **to give sb the ~** despedir or
echar a algn
sackful ['sækful] n saco
sacking ['sækɪŋ] n (material) arpillera
sacrament ['sækrəmənt] n sacramento
sacred ['seɪkrɪd] adj sagrado, santo
sacred cow n (fig) vaca sagrada
sacrifice ['sækrɪfaɪs] n sacrificio ■ vt
sacrificar; **to make sacrifices (for sb)**
sacrificarse (por algn)
sacrilege ['sækrɪlɪdʒ] n sacrilegio
sacrosanct ['sækrəusæŋkt] adj sacrosanto
sad [sæd] adj (unhappy) triste; (deplorable)
lamentable
sadden ['sædn] vt entristecer
saddle ['sædl] n silla (de montar); (of cycle)
sillín m ■ vt (horse) ensillar; **to ~ sb with
sth** (col: task, bill, name) cargar a algn con algo;
(responsibility) gravar a algn con algo; **to be
saddled with sth** (col) quedar cargado con
algo
saddlebag ['sædlbæg] n alforja
sadism ['seɪdɪzm] n sadismo
sadist ['seɪdɪst] n sádico(-a)
sadistic [sə'dɪstɪk] adj sádico
sadly ['sædlɪ] adv tristemente; (regrettably)
desgraciadamente; **~ lacking (in)** muy
deficiente (en)

sadness ['sædnɪs] n tristeza
sado-masochism [seɪdəu'mæsəkɪzɪm] n
sadomasoquismo
sae abbr (Brit: = stamped addressed envelope) sobre
con las propias señas de uno y con sello
safari [sə'fɑːrɪ] n safari m
safari park n safari m
safe [seɪf] adj (out of danger) fuera de peligro;
(not dangerous, sure) seguro; (unharmed) ileso;
(trustworthy) digno de confianza ■ n caja de
caudales, caja fuerte; **~ and sound** sano y
salvo; **(just) to be on the ~ side** para mayor
seguridad; **~ journey!** ¡buen viaje!; **it is ~
to say that …** se puede decir con confianza
que …
safe bet n apuesta segura; **it's a ~ she'll
turn up** seguro que viene
safe-breaker ['seɪfbreɪkəʳ] n (Brit)
ladrón(-ona) m(f) de cajas fuertes
safe-conduct [seɪf'kɔndʌkt] n salvoconducto
safe-cracker ['seɪfkrækəʳ] n (US) = **safe-
breaker**
safe-deposit ['seɪfdɪpɔzɪt] n (vault) cámara
acorazada; (box) caja de seguridad or de
caudales
safeguard ['seɪfgɑːd] n protección f, garantía
■ vt proteger, defender
safe haven n refugio
safekeeping ['seɪf'kiːpɪŋ] n custodia
safely ['seɪflɪ] adv seguramente, con
seguridad; (without mishap) sin peligro;
I can ~ say puedo decir or afirmar con toda
seguridad
safeness ['seɪfnɪs] n seguridad f
safe passage n garantías fpl para marcharse
en libertad
safe sex n sexo seguro or sin riesgo
safety ['seɪftɪ] n seguridad f ■ cpd de
seguridad; **road ~** seguridad f en carretera;
~ first! ¡precaución!
safety belt n cinturón m (de seguridad)
safety catch n seguro
safety net n red f (de seguridad)

safety pin n imperdible m, seguro (LAm)
safety valve n válvula de seguridad or de escape
saffron ['sæfrən] n azafrán m
sag [sæg] vi aflojarse
saga ['sɑːgə] n (History) saga; (fig) epopeya
sage [seɪdʒ] n (herb) salvia; (man) sabio
Sagittarius [sædʒɪ'tɛərɪəs] n Sagitario
sago ['seɪgəu] n sagú m
Sahara [sə'hɑːrə] n: the ~ (**Desert**) el Sáhara
Sahel [sæ'hɛl] n Sahel m
said [sɛd] pt, pp of **say**
Saigon [saɪ'gɔn] n Saigón m
sail [seɪl] n (on boat) vela ∎ vt (boat) gobernar ∎ vi (travel: ship) navegar; (passenger) pasear en barco; (set off: also: **to set sail**) zarpar; **to go for a** ~ dar un paseo en barco; **they sailed into Copenhagen** arribaron a Copenhague
▶ **sail through** vt fus (exam) aprobar fácilmente
sailboat ['seɪlbəut] n (US) velero, barco de vela
sailing ['seɪlɪŋ] n (Sport) balandrismo; **to go** ~ salir en balandro
sailing ship n barco de vela
sailor ['seɪlər] n marinero, marino
saint [seɪnt] n santo; **S~ John** San Juan
saintliness ['seɪntlɪnɪs] n santidad f
saintly ['seɪntlɪ] adj santo
sake [seɪk] n: **for the ~ of** por; **for the ~ of argument** digamos, es un decir; **art for art's** ~ el arte por el arte
salad ['sæləd] n ensalada; **tomato** ~ ensalada de tomate
salad bowl n ensaladera
salad cream n (Brit) mayonesa
salad dressing n aliño
salad oil n aceite m para ensalada
salami [sə'lɑːmɪ] n salami m, salchichón m
salaried ['sælərɪd] adj asalariado
salary ['sælərɪ] n sueldo
salary earner n asalariado(-a)
salary scale n escala salarial
sale [seɪl] n venta; (at reduced prices) liquidación f, saldo; **"for ~"** "se vende"; **on** ~ en venta; **on** ~ **or return** (goods) venta por reposición; **closing-down** or (US) **liquidation** ~ liquidación f; ~ **and lease back** venta y arrendamiento al vendedor
saleroom ['seɪlruːm] n sala de subastas
sales assistant n (Brit) dependiente(-a) m(f)
sales campaign n campaña de venta
sales clerk n (US) dependiente(-a) m(f)
sales conference n conferencia de ventas
sales drive n promoción f de ventas
sales figures npl cifras fpl de ventas
sales force n personal m de ventas

salesman ['seɪlzmən] n vendedor m; (in shop) dependiente m; (representative) viajante m
sales manager n gerente m/f de ventas
salesmanship ['seɪlzmənʃɪp] n arte m de vender
sales meeting n reunión f de ventas
sales tax n (US) = **purchase tax**
saleswoman ['seɪlzwumən] n vendedora; (in shop) dependienta; (representative) viajante f
salient ['seɪlɪənt] adj (features, points) sobresaliente
saline ['seɪlaɪn] adj salino
saliva [sə'laɪvə] n saliva
sallow ['sæləu] adj cetrino
sally forth, sally out ['sælɪ-] vi salir, ponerse en marcha
salmon ['sæmən] n (pl inv) salmón m
salon ['sælɔn] n (hairdressing salon, beauty salon) salón m
saloon [sə'luːn] n (US) bar m, taberna; (Brit Aut) (coche m de) turismo; (ship's lounge) cámara, salón m
SALT [sɔːlt] n abbr (= Strategic Arms Limitation Talks/Treaty) tratado SALT
salt [sɔːlt] n sal f ∎ vt salar; (put salt on) poner sal en; **an old** ~ un lobo de mar
▶ **salt away** vt (col: money) ahorrar
salt cellar n salero
salt mine n mina de sal
saltwater ['sɔːlt'wɔːtər] adj (fish etc) de agua salada, de mar
salty ['sɔːltɪ] adj salado
salubrious [sə'luːbrɪəs] adj sano; (fig: district etc) atractivo
salutary ['sæljutərɪ] adj saludable
salute [sə'luːt] n saludo; (of guns) salva ∎ vt saludar
salvage ['sælvɪdʒ] n (saving) salvamento, recuperación f; (things saved) objetos mpl salvados ∎ vt salvar
salvage vessel n buque m de salvamento
salvation [sæl'veɪʃən] n salvación f
Salvation Army n Ejército de Salvación
salve [sælv] n (cream etc) ungüento, bálsamo
salvo ['sælvəu] n (Mil) salva
Samaritan [sə'mærɪtən] n: **to call the Samaritans** llamar al teléfono de la esperanza
same [seɪm] adj mismo ∎ pron: **the** ~ el mismo/la misma; **the** ~ **book as** el mismo libro que; **on the** ~ **day** el mismo día; **at the** ~ **time** (at the same moment) al mismo tiempo; (yet) sin embargo; **all** or **just the** ~ sin embargo, aun así; **they're one and the** ~ (person) son la misma persona; (thing) son iguales; **to do the** ~ (**as sb**) hacer lo mismo (que otro); **and the** ~ **to you!** ¡igualmente!;

~ **here!** ¡yo también!; **the ~ again** (in bar etc) otro igual

sampan ['sæmpæn] n sampán m

sample ['sɑːmpl] n muestra ■ vt (food, wine) probar; **to take a ~** tomar una muestra; **free ~** muestra gratuita

sanatorium (pl **sanatoria**) [sænə'tɔːrɪəm, -rɪə] n (Brit) sanatorio

sanctify ['sæŋktɪfaɪ] vt santificar

sanctimonious [sæŋktɪ'məunɪəs] adj santurrón(-ona)

sanction ['sæŋkʃən] n sanción f ■ vt sancionar; **to impose economic sanctions on** or **against** imponer sanciones económicas a or contra

sanctity ['sæŋktɪtɪ] n (gen) santidad f; (inviolability) inviolabilidad f

sanctuary ['sæŋktjuərɪ] n (gen) santuario; (refuge) asilo, refugio

sand [sænd] n arena; (beach) playa ■ vt (also: **sand down**: wood etc) lijar

sandal ['sændl] n sandalia

sandalwood ['sændlwud] n sándalo

sandbag ['sændbæg] n saco de arena

sandblast ['sændblɑːst] vt limpiar con chorro de arena

sandbox ['sændbɔks] n (US) = **sandpit**

sandcastle ['sændkɑːsl] n castillo de arena

sand dune n duna

sander ['sændər] n pulidora

sandpaper ['sændpeɪpər] n papel m de lija

sandpit ['sændpɪt] n (for children) cajón m de arena

sands [sændz] npl playa sg de arena

sandstone ['sændstəun] n piedra arenisca

sandstorm ['sændstɔːm] n tormenta de arena

sandwich ['sændwɪtʃ] n bocadillo (SP), sandwich m (LAm) ■ vt (also: **sandwich in**) intercalar; **to be sandwiched between** estar apretujado entre; **cheese/ham ~** sandwich de queso/jamón

sandwich board n cartelón m

sandwich course n (Brit) programa que intercala períodos de estudio con prácticas profesionales

sandy ['sændɪ] adj arenoso; (colour) rojizo

sane [seɪn] adj cuerdo, sensato

sang [sæŋ] pt of **sing**

sanitarium [sænɪ'tɛərɪəm] n (US) = **sanatorium**

sanitary ['sænɪtərɪ] adj (system, arrangements) sanitario; (clean) higiénico

sanitary towel, sanitary napkin (US) n paño higiénico, compresa

sanitation [sænɪ'teɪʃən] n (in house) servicios mpl higiénicos; (in town) servicio de desinfección

sanitation department n (US) departamento de limpieza y recogida de basuras

sanity ['sænɪtɪ] n cordura; (of judgment) sensatez f

sank [sæŋk] pt of **sink**

San Marino ['sænmə'riːnəu] n San Marino

Santa Claus [sæntə'klɔːz] n San Nicolás m, Papá Noel m

Santiago [sæntɪ'ɑːgəu] n (also: **Santiago de Chile**) Santiago (de Chile)

sap [sæp] n (of plants) savia ■ vt (strength) minar, agotar

sapling ['sæplɪŋ] n árbol nuevo or joven

sapphire ['sæfaɪər] n zafiro

Saragossa [særə'gɔsə] n Zaragoza

sarcasm ['sɑːkæzm] n sarcasmo

sarcastic [sɑː'kæstɪk] adj sarcástico; **to be ~** ser sarcástico

sarcophagus, sarcophagi [sɑː'kɔfəgəs, -gaɪ] n sarcófago

sardine [sɑː'diːn] n sardina

Sardinia [sɑː'dɪnɪə] n Cerdeña

Sardinian [sɑː'dɪnɪən] adj, n sardo(-a) m(f)

sardonic [sɑː'dɔnɪk] adj sardónico

sari ['sɑːrɪ] n sari m

SARS ['sɑːz] n abbr (= severe acute respiratory syndrome) neumonía asiática, SARS m

SAS n abbr (Brit Mil: = Special Air Service) cuerpo del ejército británico encargado de misiones clandestinas

SASE n abbr (US: = self-addressed stamped envelope) sobre con las propias señas de uno y con sello

sash [sæʃ] n faja

Sask. abbr (Canada) = **Saskatchewan**

SAT n abbr (US) = **Scholastic Aptitude Test**

Sat. abbr (= Saturday) sáb

sat [sæt] pt, pp of **sit**

Satan ['seɪtn] n Satanás m

satanic [sə'tænɪk] adj satánico

satchel ['sætʃl] n bolsa; (child's) cartera, mochila (LAm)

sated ['seɪtɪd] adj (appetite, person) saciado

satellite ['sætəlaɪt] n satélite m

satellite dish n (antena) parabólica

satellite navigation system n sistema m de navegación por satélite

satellite television n televisión f por satélite

satiate ['seɪʃɪeɪt] vt saciar, hartar

satin ['sætɪn] n raso ■ adj de raso; **with a ~ finish** satinado

satire ['sætaɪər] n sátira

satirical [sə'tɪrɪkl] adj satírico

satirist ['sætɪrɪst] n (writer etc) escritor(a) m(f) satírico(-a); (cartoonist) caricaturista m/f

satirize ['sætɪraɪz] vt satirizar

satisfaction [sætɪs'fækʃən] n satisfacción f; **it gives me great ~** es para mí una gran satisfacción; **has it been done to your ~?** ¿se ha hecho a su satisfacción?

satisfactorily [sætɪs'fæktərɪlɪ] *adv* satisfactoriamente, de modo satisfactorio

satisfactory [sætɪs'fæktərɪ] *adj* satisfactorio

satisfied ['sætɪsfaɪd] *adj* satisfecho; **to be ~ (with sth)** estar satisfecho (de algo)

satisfy ['sætɪsfaɪ] *vt* satisfacer; *(pay)* liquidar; *(convince)* convencer; **to ~ the requirements** llenar los requisitos; **to ~ sb that** convencer a algn de que; **to ~ o.s. of sth** convencerse de algo

satisfying ['sætɪsfaɪɪŋ] *adj* satisfactorio

satsuma [sæt'suːmə] *n* satsuma

saturate ['sætʃəreɪt] *vt*: **to ~ (with)** empapar *or* saturar (de)

saturated fat [sætʃəreɪtɪd-] *n* grasa saturada

saturation [sætʃə'reɪʃən] *n* saturación *f*

Saturday ['sætədɪ] *n* sábado; *see also* **Tuesday**

sauce [sɔːs] *n* salsa; *(sweet)* crema; *(fig: cheek)* frescura

saucepan ['sɔːspən] *n* cacerola, olla

saucer ['sɔːsəʳ] *n* platillo

saucily ['sɔːsɪlɪ] *adv* con frescura, descaradamente

sauciness ['sɔːsɪnɪs] *n* frescura, descaro

saucy ['sɔːsɪ] *adj* fresco, descarado

Saudi ['saudɪ] *adj, n* saudí *m/f*, saudita *m/f*

Saudi Arabia *n* Arabia Saudí *or* Saudita

Saudi Arabian *adj, n* = **Saudi**

sauna ['sɔːnə] *n* sauna

saunter ['sɔːntəʳ] *vi* deambular

sausage ['sɔsɪdʒ] *n* salchicha; *(salami etc)* salchichón *m*

sausage roll *n* empanadilla

sauté ['səuteɪ] *adj* *(Culin: potatoes)* salteado; *(: onions)* dorado, rehogado ■ *vt* saltear; dorar

savage ['sævɪdʒ] *adj* *(cruel, fierce)* feroz, furioso; *(primitive)* salvaje ■ *n* salvaje *m/f* ■ *vt* *(attack)* embestir

savagely ['sævɪdʒlɪ] *adv* con ferocidad, furiosamente; de modo salvaje

savagery ['sævɪdʒrɪ] *n* ferocidad *f*; salvajismo

save [seɪv] *vt* *(rescue)* salvar, rescatar; *(money, time)* ahorrar; *(put by)* guardar; *(Comput)* salvar (y guardar); *(avoid: trouble)* evitar ■ *vi* *(also: **save up**)* ahorrar ■ *n* *(Sport)* parada ■ *prep* salvo, excepto; **to ~ face** salvar las apariencias; **God ~ the Queen!** ¡Dios guarde a la Reina!, ¡Viva la Reina!; **I saved you a piece of cake** te he guardado un trozo de tarta; **it will ~ me an hour** con ello ganaré una hora

saving ['seɪvɪŋ] *n* *(on price etc)* economía ■ *adj*: **the ~ grace of** el único mérito de;

savings *npl* ahorros *mpl*; **to make savings** economizar

savings account *n* cuenta de ahorros

savings bank *n* caja de ahorros

saviour, savior *(US)* ['seɪvjəʳ] *n* salvador(a) *m(f)*

savoir-faire ['sævwɑː'fɛəʳ] *n* don *m* de gentes

savour, savor *(US)* ['seɪvəʳ] *n* sabor *m*, gusto ■ *vt* saborear

savoury, savory *(US)* ['seɪvərɪ] *adj* sabroso; *(dish: not sweet)* salado

savvy ['sævɪ] *n* *(col)* conocimiento, experiencia

saw [sɔː] *pt of* **see** ■ *n* *(tool)* sierra ■ *vt* *(pt sawed, pp sawed or sawn* [sɔːn]*)* serrar; **to ~ sth up** (a)serrar algo

sawdust ['sɔːdʌst] *n* (a)serrín *m*

sawmill ['sɔːmɪl] *n* aserradero

sawn [sɔːn] *pp of* **saw**

sawn-off ['sɔːnɔf], **sawed-off** *(US)* ['sɔːdɔf] *adj*: **~ shotgun** escopeta de cañones recortados

saxophone ['sæksəfəun] *n* saxófono

say [seɪ] *n*: **to have one's ~** expresar su opinión; **to have a** *or* **some ~ in sth** tener voz y voto en algo ■ *vt, vi* *(pt, pp said* [sɛd]*)* decir; **to ~ yes/no** decir que sí/no; **my watch says 3 o'clock** mi reloj marca las tres; **that is to ~** es decir; **that goes without saying** ni que decir tiene; **she said (that) I was to give you this** me pidió que te diera esto; **I should ~ it's worth about £100** yo diría que vale unas 100 libras; **~ after me** repite lo que yo diga; **shall we ~ Tuesday?** ¿quedamos, por ejemplo, el martes?; **that doesn't ~ much for him** eso no dice nada a su favor; **when all is said and done** al fin y al cabo, a fin de cuentas; **there is something** *or* **a lot to be said for it** hay algo *or* mucho que decir a su favor

saying ['seɪɪŋ] *n* dicho, refrán *m*

say-so ['seɪsəu] *n* *(col)* autorización *f*

SBA *n abbr* *(US)* = **Small Business Administration**

SC *n abbr* *(US)* = **Supreme Court** ■ *abbr* *(US)* = **South Carolina**

s/c *abbr* = **self-contained**

scab [skæb] *n* costra; *(pej)* esquirol(a) *m(f)*

scaffold ['skæfəld] *n* *(for execution)* cadalso

scaffolding ['skæfəldɪŋ] *n* andamio, andamiaje *m*

scald [skɔːld] *n* escaldadura ■ *vt* escaldar

scalding ['skɔːldɪŋ] *adj* *(also: **scalding hot**)* hirviendo, que arde

scale [skeɪl] *n* *(gen)* escala; *(Mus)* escala; *(of fish)* escama; *(of salaries, fees etc)* escalafón *m* ■ *vt* *(mountain)* escalar; *(tree)* trepar; **scales**

npl (*small*) balanza *sg*; (*large*) báscula *sg*; **on a large ~** a gran escala; **~ of charges** tarifa, lista de precios; **pay ~** escala salarial; **to draw sth to ~** dibujar algo a escala
▸ **scale down** *vt* reducir

scaled-down [skeɪld'daun] *adj* reducido proporcionalmente

scale model *n* modelo a escala

scallop ['skɔləp] *n* (*Zool*) venera; (*Sewing*) festón *m*

scalp [skælp] *n* cabellera ▪ *vt* escalpar

scalpel ['skælpl] *n* bisturí *m*

scam [skæm] *n* (*col*) estafa, timo

scamper ['skæmpəʳ] *vi*: **to ~ away, ~ off** escabullirse

scampi ['skæmpɪ] *npl* gambas *fpl*

scan [skæn] *vt* (*examine*) escudriñar; (*glance at quickly*) dar un vistazo a; (*TV, Radar*) explorar, registrar; (*Comput*) escanear ▪ *n* (*Med*) examen *m* ultrasónico

scandal ['skændl] *n* escándalo; (*gossip*) chismes *mpl*

scandalize ['skændəlaɪz] *vt* escandalizar

scandalous ['skændələs] *adj* escandaloso

Scandinavia [skændɪ'neɪvɪə] *n* Escandinavia

Scandinavian [skændɪ'neɪvɪən] *adj, n* escandinavo(-a) *m(f)*

scanner ['skænəʳ] *n* (*Radar, Med, Comput*) escáner *m*

scant [skænt] *adj* escaso

scantily ['skæntɪlɪ] *adv*: **~ clad** *or* **dressed** ligero de ropa

scantiness ['skæntɪnɪs] *n* escasez *f*, insuficiencia

scanty ['skæntɪ] *adj* (*meal*) insuficiente; (*clothes*) ligero

scapegoat ['skeɪpgəut] *n* cabeza de turco, chivo expiatorio

scar [skɑ:] *n* cicatriz *f* ▪ *vt* marcar con una cicatriz ▪ *vi* cicatrizarse

scarce [skɛəs] *adj* escaso

scarcely ['skɛəslɪ] *adv* apenas; **~ anybody** casi nadie; **I can ~ believe it** casi no puedo creerlo

scarceness ['skɛəsnɪs], **scarcity** ['skɛəsɪtɪ] *n* escasez *f*

scarcity value *n* valor *m* de escasez

scare [skɛəʳ] *n* susto, sobresalto; (*panic*) pánico ▪ *vt* asustar, espantar; **to ~ sb stiff** dar a algn un susto de muerte; **bomb ~** amenaza de bomba
▸ **scare away, scare off** *vt* espantar, ahuyentar

scarecrow ['skɛəkrəu] *n* espantapájaros *m inv*

scared [skɛəd] *adj*: **to be ~** asustarse, estar asustado

scaremonger ['skɛəmʌŋgəʳ] *n* alarmista *m/f*

scarf (*pl* **scarves**) [skɑ:f, skɑ:vz] *n* (*long*) bufanda; (*square*) pañuelo

scarlet ['skɑ:lɪt] *adj* escarlata

scarlet fever *n* escarlatina

scarper ['skɑ:pəʳ] *vi* (*Brit col*) largarse

scarred [skɑ:d] *adj* lleno de cicatrices

scarves [skɑ:vz] *npl of* **scarf**

scary ['skɛərɪ] *adj* (*col*) de miedo; **it's ~** da miedo

scathing ['skeɪðɪŋ] *adj* mordaz; **to be ~ about sth** criticar algo duramente

scatter ['skætəʳ] *vt* (*spread*) esparcir, desparramar; (*put to flight*) dispersar ▪ *vi* desparramarse; dispersarse

scatterbrained ['skætəbreɪnd] *adj* ligero de cascos

scavenge ['skævɪndʒ] *vi*: **to ~ (for)** (*person*) revolver entre la basura (para encontrar); **to ~ for food** (*hyenas etc*) nutrirse de carroña

scavenger ['skævɪndʒəʳ] *n* (*person*) mendigo/a que rebusca en la basura; (*Zool: animal*) animal *m* de carroña; (: *bird*) ave *f* de carroña

SCE *n abbr* = **Scottish Certificate of Education**

scenario [sɪ'nɑ:rɪəu] *n* (*Theat*) argumento; (*Cine*) guión *m*; (*fig*) escenario

scene [si:n] *n* (*Theat*) escena; (*of crime, accident*) escenario; (*sight, view*) vista, perspectiva; (*fuss*) escándalo; **the political ~ in Spain** el panorama político español; **behind the scenes** (*also fig*) entre bastidores; **to appear** *or* **come on the ~** (*also fig*) aparecer, presentarse; **to make a ~** (*col: fuss*) armar un escándalo

scenery ['si:nərɪ] *n* (*Theat*) decorado; (*landscape*) paisaje *m*

scenic ['si:nɪk] *adj* (*picturesque*) pintoresco

scent [sɛnt] *n* perfume *m*, olor *m*; (*fig: track*) rastro, pista; (*sense of smell*) olfato ▪ *vt* perfumar; (*suspect*) presentir; **to put** *or* **throw sb off the ~** (*fig*) despistar a algn

sceptic, skeptic (US) ['skɛptɪk] *n* escéptico(-a)

sceptical, skeptical (US) ['skɛptɪkl] *adj* escéptico

scepticism, skepticism (US) ['skɛptɪsɪzm] *n* escepticismo

sceptre, scepter (US) ['sɛptəʳ] *n* cetro

schedule ['ʃɛdju:l], (US) ['skɛdju:l] *n* (*of trains*) horario; (*of events*) programa *m*; (*list*) lista ▪ *vt* (*timetable*) establecer el horario de; (*list*) catalogar; (*visit*) fijar la hora de; **on ~** a la hora, sin retraso; **to be ahead of/behind ~** estar adelantado/retrasado; **we are working to a very tight ~** tenemos un programa de trabajo muy apretado; **everything went according to ~** todo salió según lo previsto;

the meeting is scheduled for seven or to begin at seven la reunión está fijada para las siete

scheduled ['ʃɛdju:ld], (US) ['skɛdju:ld] adj (date, time) fijado; (visit, event, bus, train) programado; (stop) previsto; ~ **flight** vuelo regular

schematic [skɪ'mætɪk], adj (diagram etc) esquemático

scheme [ski:m] n (plan) plan m, proyecto; (method) esquema m; (plot) intriga; (trick) ardid m; (arrangement) disposición f; (pension scheme etc) sistema m ▪ vt proyectar ▪ vi (plan) hacer proyectos; (intrigue) intrigar; **colour** ~ combinación f de colores

scheming ['ski:mɪŋ] adj intrigante

schism ['skɪzəm] n cisma m

schizophrenia [skɪtsə'fri:nɪə] n esquizofrenia

schizophrenic [skɪtsə'frenɪk] adj esquizofrénico

scholar ['skɔlə'] n (pupil) alumno(-a), estudiante m/f; (learned person) sabio(-a), erudito(-a)

scholarly ['skɔləlɪ] adj erudito

scholarship ['skɔləʃɪp] n erudición f; (grant) beca

school [sku:l] n (gen) escuela, colegio; (in university) facultad f; (of fish) banco ▪ vt (animal) amaestrar; **to be at** or **go to** ~ ir al colegio or a la escuela

school age n edad f escolar

schoolbook ['sku:lbuk] n libro de texto

schoolboy ['sku:lbɔɪ] n alumno

schoolchild (pl **schoolchildren**) ['sku:ltʃaɪld, -tʃɪldrən] n alumno(-a)

schooldays ['sku:ldeɪz] npl años mpl del colegio

schoolgirl ['sku:lgə:l] n alumna

schooling ['sku:lɪŋ] n enseñanza

school-leaver ['sku:lli:və'] n (Brit) joven que ha terminado la educación secundaria

schoolmaster ['sku:lmɑ:stə'] n (primary) maestro; (secondary) profesor m

schoolmistress ['sku:lmɪstrɪs] n (primary) maestra; (secondary) profesora

schoolroom ['sku:lrum] n clase f

schoolteacher ['sku:lti:tʃə'] n (primary) maestro(-a); (secondary) profesor(a) m(f)

schoolyard ['sku:ljɑ:d] n (US) patio del colegio

schooner ['sku:nə'] n (ship) goleta

sciatica [saɪ'ætɪkə] n ciática

science ['saɪəns] n ciencia; **the sciences** las ciencias

science fiction n ciencia-ficción f

scientific [saɪən'tɪfɪk] adj científico

scientist ['saɪəntɪst] n científico(-a)

sci-fi ['saɪfaɪ] n abbr (col) = **science fiction**

Scilly Isles ['sɪlɪ-], **Scillies** ['sɪlɪz] npl: **the** ~ las Islas Sorlingas

scintillating ['sɪntɪleɪtɪŋ] adj (wit, conversation, company) brillante, chispeante, ingenioso

scissors ['sɪzəz] npl tijeras fpl; **a pair of** ~ unas tijeras

scoff [skɔf] vt (Brit col: eat) engullir ▪ vi: **to** ~ **(at)** (mock) mofarse (de)

scold [skəuld] vt regañar

scolding ['skəuldɪŋ] n riña, reprimenda

scone [skɔn] n pastel de pan

scoop [sku:p] n cucharón m; (for flour etc) pala; (Press) exclusiva ▪ vt (Comm: market) adelantarse a; (: profit) sacar; (Comm, Press: competitors) adelantarse a
  ▸ **scoop out** vt excavar
  ▸ **scoop up** vt recoger

scooter ['sku:tə'] n (motor cycle) Vespa®; (toy) patinete m

scope [skəup] n (of plan, undertaking) ámbito; (reach) alcance m; (of person) competencia; (opportunity) libertad f (de acción); **there is plenty of** ~ **for improvement** hay bastante campo para efectuar mejoras

scorch [skɔ:tʃ] vt (clothes) chamuscar; (earth, grass) quemar, secar

scorcher ['skɔ:tʃə'] n (col: hot day) día m abrasador

scorching ['skɔ:tʃɪŋ] adj abrasador(a)

score [skɔ:'] n (points etc) puntuación f; (Mus) partitura; (reckoning) cuenta; (twenty) veintena ▪ vt (goal, point) ganar; (mark, cut) rayar ▪ vi marcar un tanto; (Football) marcar un gol; (keep score) llevar el tanteo; **to keep (the)** ~ llevar la cuenta; **to have an old** ~ **to settle with sb** (fig) tener cuentas pendientes con algn; **on that** ~ en lo que se refiere a eso; **scores of people** (fig) muchísima gente, cantidad de gente; **to** ~ **6 out of 10** obtener una puntuación de 6 sobre 10
  ▸ **score out** vt tachar

scoreboard ['skɔ:bɔ:d] n marcador m

scoreline ['skɔ:laɪn] n (Sport) resultado final

scorer ['skɔ:rə'] n marcador m; (keeping score) encargado(-a) del marcador

scorn [skɔ:n] n desprecio ▪ vt despreciar

scornful ['skɔ:nful] adj desdeñoso, despreciativo

scornfully ['skɔ:nfulɪ] adv desdeñosamente, con desprecio

Scorpio ['skɔ:pɪəu] n Escorpión m

scorpion ['skɔ:pɪən] n alacrán m, escorpión m

Scot [skɔt] n escocés(-esa) m(f)

Scotch [skɔtʃ] n whisky m escocés

S

765

scotch [skɔtʃ] vt (rumour) desmentir; (plan) frustrar

Scotch tape® n (US) cinta adhesiva, celo, scotch® m

scot-free [skɔt'fri:] adv: **to get off ~** (unpunished) salir impune; (unhurt) salir ileso

Scotland ['skɔtlənd] n Escocia

Scots [skɔts] adj escocés(-esa)

Scotsman ['skɔtsmən] n escocés m

Scotswoman ['skɔtswumən] n escocesa

Scottish ['skɔtiʃ] adj escocés(-esa); **the ~ National Party** partido político independista escocés; **the ~ Parliament** el Parlamento escocés

scoundrel ['skaundrəl] n canalla m/f, sinvergüenza m/f

scour ['skauər] vt (clean) fregar, estregar; (search) recorrer, registrar

scourer ['skauərər] n (pad) estropajo; (powder) limpiador m

scourge [skəːdʒ] n azote m

scout [skaut] n explorador m
▶ **scout around** vi reconocer el terreno

scowl [skaul] vi fruncir el ceño; **to ~ at sb** mirar con ceño a algn

scrabble ['skræbl] vi (claw): **to ~ (at)** arañar ■ n: **S~**® Scrabble® m, Intelect® m; **to ~ around for sth** revolver todo buscando algo

scraggy ['skrægi] adj flaco, delgaducho

scram [skræm] vi (col) largarse

scramble ['skræmbl] n (climb) subida (difícil); (struggle) pelea ■ vi: **to ~ out/through** salir/abrirse paso con dificultad; **to ~ for** pelear por; **to go scrambling** (Sport) hacer motocrós

scrambled eggs ['skræmbld-] npl huevos mpl revueltos

scrap [skræp] n (bit) pedacito; (fig) pizca; (fight) riña, bronca; (also: **scrap iron**) chatarra, hierro viejo ■ vt (discard) desechar, descartar ■ vi reñir, armar (una) bronca; **scraps** npl (waste) sobras fpl, desperdicios mpl; **to sell sth for ~** vender algo como chatarra

scrapbook ['skræpbuk] n álbum m de recortes

scrap dealer n chatarrero(-a)

scrape [skreip] n (fig) lío, apuro ■ vt raspar; (skin etc) rasguñar; (also: **scrape against**) rozar
▶ **scrape through** vi (succeed) salvarse por los pelos; (exam) aprobar por los pelos

scraper ['skreipər] n raspador m

scrap heap n (fig): **on the ~** desperdiciado; **to throw sth on the ~** desechar or descartar algo

scrap iron n chatarra

scrap merchant n (Brit) chatarrero(-a)

scrap metal n chatarra, desecho de metal

scrap paper n pedazos mpl de papel

scrappy ['skræpi] adj (essay etc) deshilvanado; (education) incompleto

scrap yard n depósito de chatarra; (for cars) cementerio de coches

scratch [skrætʃ] n rasguño; (from claw) arañazo ■ adj: **~ team** equipo improvisado ■ vt (record) rayar; (with claw, nail) rasguñar, arañar; (Comput) borrar ■ vi rascarse; **to start from ~** partir de cero; **to be up to ~** cumplir con los requisitos

scratchpad ['skrætʃpæd] n (US) bloc m de notas

scrawl [skrɔːl] n garabatos mpl ■ vi hacer garabatos

scrawny ['skrɔːni] adj (person, neck) flaco

scream [skriːm] n chillido ■ vi chillar; **it was a ~** (fig, col) fue para morirse de risa or muy divertido; **he's a ~** (fig, col) es muy divertido or de lo más gracioso; **to ~ at sb (to do sth)** gritarle a algn (para que haga algo)

scree [skriː] n cono de desmoronamiento

screech [skriːtʃ] vi chirriar

screen [skriːn] n (Cine, TV) pantalla; (movable) biombo; (wall) tabique m; (also: **windscreen**) parabrisas m inv ■ vt (conceal) tapar; (from the wind etc) proteger; (film) proyectar; (fig: person: for security) investigar; (: for illness) hacer una exploración a

screen editing n (Comput) corrección f en pantalla

screenful ['skriːnful] n pantalla

screening ['skriːniŋ] n (of film) proyección f; (for security) investigación f; (Med) exploración f

screen memory n (Comput) memoria de la pantalla

screenplay ['skriːnplei] n guión m

screen saver [-seivər] n (Comput) salvapantallas m inv

screen test n prueba de pantalla

screw [skruː] n tornillo; (propeller) hélice f ■ vt atornillar; **to ~ sth to the wall** fijar algo a la pared con tornillos
▶ **screw up** vt (paper, material etc) arrugar; (col: ruin) fastidiar; **to ~ up one's eyes** arrugar el entrecejo; **to ~ up one's face** torcer or arrugar la cara

screwdriver ['skruːdraivər] n destornillador m

screwed-up ['skruːd'ʌp] adj (col): **she's totally ~** está trastornada

screwy ['skruːi] adj (col) chiflado

scribble ['skribl] n garabatos mpl ■ vt escribir con prisa; **to ~ sth down** garabatear algo

script [skrɪpt] n (Cine etc) guión m; (writing) escritura, letra

scripted ['skrɪptɪd] adj (Radio, TV) escrito

Scripture ['skrɪptʃəʳ] n Sagrada Escritura

scriptwriter ['skrɪptraɪtəʳ] n guionista m/f

scroll [skrəʊl] n rollo ▪ vt (Comput) desplazar

scrotum ['skrəʊtəm] n escroto

scrounge [skraʊndʒ] (col) vt: **to ~ sth off** or **from sb** gorronear algo a algn ▪ vi: **to ~ on sb** vivir a costa de algn

scrounger ['skraʊndʒəʳ] n gorrón(-ona) m(f)

scrub [skrʌb] n (clean) fregado; (land) maleza ▪ vt fregar, restregar; (reject) cancelar, anular

scrubbing brush ['skrʌbɪŋ-] n cepillo de fregar

scruff [skrʌf] n: **by the ~ of the neck** por el pescuezo

scruffy ['skrʌfɪ] adj desaliñado, desaseado

scrum ['skrʌm], **scrummage** ['skrʌmɪdʒ] n (Rugby) melée f

scruple ['skruːpl] n escrúpulo; **to have no scruples about doing sth** no tener reparos en or escrúpulos para hacer algo

scrupulous ['skruːpjʊləs] adj escrupuloso

scrupulously ['skruːpjʊləslɪ] adv escrupulosamente; **to be ~ fair/honest** ser sumamente justo/honesto

scrutinize ['skruːtɪnaɪz] vt escudriñar; (votes) escrutar

scrutiny ['skruːtɪnɪ] n escrutinio, examen m; **under the ~ of sb** bajo la mirada or el escrutinio de algn

scuba ['skuːbə] n escafandra autónoma

scuba diving n submarinismo

scuff [skʌf] vt (shoes, floor) rayar

scuffle ['skʌfl] n refriega

scullery ['skʌlərɪ] n trascocina

sculptor ['skʌlptəʳ] n escultor(a) m(f)

sculpture ['skʌlptʃəʳ] n escultura

scum [skʌm] n (on liquid) espuma; (pej: people) escoria

scupper ['skʌpəʳ] vt (Brit: boat) hundir; (: fig: plans etc) acabar con

scurrilous ['skʌrɪləs] adj difamatorio, calumnioso

scurry ['skʌrɪ] vi: **to ~ off** escabullirse

scurvy ['skəːvɪ] n escorbuto

scuttle ['skʌtl] n (also: **coal scuttle**) cubo, carbonera ▪ vt (ship) barrenar ▪ vi (scamper): **to ~ away, ~ off** escabullirse

scythe [saɪð] n guadaña

SD, S. Dak. abbr (US) = **South Dakota**

SDI n abbr (= Strategic Defense Initiative) IDE f

SDLP n abbr (Brit Pol) = **Social Democratic and Labour Party**

sea [siː] n mar m/f; **by ~** (travel) en barco; **on the ~** (boat) en el mar; (town) junto al mar; **to be all at ~** (fig) estar despistado; **out to** or **at ~** en alta mar; **to go by ~** ir en barco; **heavy** or **rough seas** marejada; **by** or **beside the ~** (holiday) en la playa; (village) a orillas del mar; **a ~ of faces** una multitud de caras

sea bed n fondo del mar

sea bird n ave f marina

seaboard ['siːbɔːd] n litoral m

sea breeze n brisa de mar

seadog ['siːdɔg] n lobo de mar

seafarer ['siːfɛərəʳ] n marinero

seafaring ['siːfɛərɪŋ] adj (community) marinero; (life) de marinero

seafood ['siːfuːd] n mariscos mpl

sea front n (beach) playa; (prom) paseo marítimo

seagoing ['siːgəʊɪŋ] adj (ship) de alta mar

seagull ['siːgʌl] n gaviota

seal [siːl] n (animal) foca; (stamp) sello ▪ vt (close) cerrar; (: with seal) sellar; (decide: sb's fate) decidir; (: bargain) cerrar; **~ of approval** sello de aprobación

▶ **seal off** vt obturar

seal cull n matanza de crías de foca

sea level n nivel m del mar

sealing wax ['siːlɪŋ-] n lacre m

sea lion n león m marino

sealskin ['siːlskɪn] n piel f de foca

seam [siːm] n costura; (of metal) juntura; (of coal) veta, filón m; **the hall was bursting at the seams** la sala rebosaba de gente

seaman ['siːmən] n marinero

seamanship ['siːmənʃɪp] n náutica

seamy ['siːmɪ] adj sórdido

seance ['seɪɔns] n sesión f de espiritismo

seaplane ['siːpleɪn] n hidroavión m

seaport ['siːpɔːt] n puerto de mar

search [səːtʃ] n (for person, thing) busca, búsqueda; (of drawer, pockets) registro; (inspection) reconocimiento ▪ vt (look in) buscar en; (examine) examinar; (person, place) registrar; (Comput) buscar ▪ vi: **to ~ for** buscar; **in ~ of** en busca de; **"~ and replace"** (Comput) "buscar y reemplazar"

▶ **search through** vt fus registrar

search engine n (Comput: Internet) buscador m

searcher ['səːtʃəʳ] n buscador(a) m(f)

searching ['səːtʃɪŋ] adj (question) penetrante

searchlight ['səːtʃlaɪt] n reflector m

search party n equipo de salvamento

search warrant n mandamiento judicial

searing ['sɪərɪŋ] adj (heat) abrasador(a); (pain) agudo

seashore ['siːʃɔʳ] n playa, orilla del mar; **on the ~** a la orilla del mar

seasick ['siːsɪk] adj mareado; **to be ~** marearse

seaside ['siːsaɪd] n playa, orilla del mar; **to go to the ~** ir a la playa

seaside resort n playa

season ['siːzn] n (of year) estación f; (sporting etc) temporada; (gen) época, período ■ vt (food) sazonar; **to be in/out of ~** estar en sazón/fuera de temporada; **the busy ~** (for shops, hotels etc) la temporada alta; **the open ~** (Hunting) la temporada de caza or de pesca

seasonal ['siːznl] adj estacional

seasoned ['siːznd] adj (wood) curado; (fig: worker, actor) experimentado; (troops) curtido; **~ campaigner** veterano(-a)

seasoning ['siːznɪŋ] n condimento

season ticket n abono

seat [siːt] n (in bus, train: place) asiento; (chair) silla; (Parliament) escaño; (buttocks) trasero; (centre: of government etc) sede f ■ vt sentar; (have room for) tener cabida para; **are there any seats left?** ¿quedan plazas?; **to take one's ~** sentarse, tomar asiento; **to be seated** estar sentado, sentarse

seat belt n cinturón m de seguridad

seating ['siːtɪŋ] n asientos mpl

seating arrangements npl distribución fsg de los asientos

seating capacity n número de asientos, aforo

SEATO ['siːtəʊ] n abbr (= Southeast Asia Treaty Organization) OTASE f

sea water n agua m del mar

seaweed ['siːwiːd] n alga marina

seaworthy ['siːwəːðɪ] adj en condiciones de navegar

SEC n abbr (US: = Securities and Exchange Commission) comisión de operaciones bursátiles

sec. abbr = **second; seconds**

secateurs [sɛkə'təːz] npl podadera sg

secede [sɪ'siːd] vi: **to ~ (from)** separarse (de)

secluded [sɪ'kluːdɪd] adj retirado

seclusion [sɪ'kluːʒən] n retiro

second ['sɛkənd] adj segundo ■ adv (in race etc) en segundo lugar ■ n (gen) segundo; (Aut: also: **second gear**) segunda; (Comm) artículo con algún desperfecto; (Brit Scol: degree) título universitario de segunda clase ■ vt (motion) apoyar [sɪ'kɒnd] (employee) trasladar temporalmente; **~ floor** (Brit) segundo piso; (US) primer piso; **Charles the S~** Carlos Segundo; **to ask for a ~ opinion** (Med) pedir una segunda opinión; **just a ~!** ¡un momento!; **to have ~ thoughts** cambiar de opinión; **on ~ thoughts** or (US) **thought** pensándolo bien; **~ mortgage** segunda hipoteca

secondary ['sɛkəndərɪ] adj secundario

secondary education n enseñanza secundaria

secondary school n escuela secundaria; ver nota

● SECONDARY SCHOOL
●
● En el Reino Unido se llama secondary school
● a un centro educativo para alumnos de
● 11 a 18 años, si bien muchos estudiantes
● acaban a los 16, edad mínima de
● escolarización obligatoria. La mayor
● parte de estos centros funcionan como
● "comprehensive schools", aunque aún
● existen algunos de tipo selectivo.

second-best [sɛkənd'bɛst] n segundo

second-class ['sɛkənd'klɑːs] adj de segunda clase ■ adv: **to send sth ~** enviar algo por correo de segunda clase; **to travel ~** viajar en segunda; **~ citizen** ciudadano(-a) de segunda (clase)

second cousin n primo(-a) segundo(-a)

seconder ['sɛkəndər] n el/la que apoya una moción

second-guess ['sɛkənd'gɛs] vt (evaluate) juzgar (a posteriori); (anticipate): **to ~ sth/sb** (intentar) adivinar algo/lo que va a hacer algn

secondhand ['sɛkənd'hænd] adj de segunda mano, usado ■ adv: **to buy sth ~** comprar algo de segunda mano; **to hear sth ~** oír algo indirectamente

second hand n (on clock) segundero

second-in-command ['sɛkəndɪnkə'mɑːnd] n (Mil) segundo en el mando; (Admin) segundo(-a), ayudante m/f

secondly ['sɛkəndlɪ] adv en segundo lugar

secondment [sɪ'kɒndmənt] n (Brit) traslado temporal

second-rate ['sɛkənd'reɪt] adj de segunda categoría

secrecy ['siːkrəsɪ] n secreto

secret ['siːkrɪt] adj, n secreto; **in ~** adv en secreto; **to keep sth ~ (from sb)** ocultarle algo (a algn); **to make no ~ of sth** no ocultar algo

secret agent n agente m/f secreto(-a), espía m/f

secretarial [sɛkrɪ'tɛərɪəl] adj (course) de secretariado; (staff) de secretaría; (work, duties) de secretaria

secretariat [sɛkrɪ'tɛərɪət] n secretaría

secretary ['sɛkrətərɪ] n secretario(-a); **S~ of State** (Brit Pol) Ministro (con cartera)

secretary-general ['sɛkrətərɪ'dʒenərl] n secretario(-a) general

secretary pool n (US) = **typing pool**
secrete [sɪ'kri:t] vt (Med, Anat, Bio) secretar; (hide) ocultar, esconder
secretion [sɪ'kri:ʃən] n secreción f
secretive ['si:krətɪv] adj reservado, sigiloso
secretly ['si:krɪtlɪ] adv en secreto
secret police n policía secreta
secret service n servicio secreto
sect [sɛkt] n secta
sectarian [sɛk'tɛərɪən] adj sectario
section ['sɛkʃən] n sección f; (part) parte f; (of document) artículo; (of opinion) sector m; **business ~** (Press) sección f de economía
sectional ['sɛkʃənl] adj (regional) regional, local
sector ['sɛktəʳ] n sector m
secular ['sɛkjuləʳ] adj secular, seglar
secure [sɪ'kjuəʳ] adj (free from anxiety) seguro; (firmly fixed) firme, fijo ▪ vt (fix) asegurar, afianzar; (get) conseguir; (Comm: loan) garantizar; **to make sth ~** afianzar algo; **to ~ sth for sb** conseguir algo para algn
secured creditor [sɪ'kjuəd-] n acreedor(a) m(f) con garantía
securely [sɪ'kjuəlɪ] adv firmemente; **it is ~ fastened** está bien sujeto
security [sɪ'kjuərɪtɪ] n seguridad f; (for loan) fianza; (: object) prenda; **securities** npl (Comm) valores mpl, títulos mpl; **~ of tenure** tenencia asegurada; **to increase/tighten ~** aumentar/estrechar las medidas de seguridad; **job ~** seguridad f en el empleo
Security Council n: **the ~** el Consejo de Seguridad
security forces npl fuerzas fpl de seguridad
security guard n guardia m/f de seguridad
security risk n riesgo para la seguridad
secy. abbr (= secretary) Sec.
sedan [sɪ'dæn] n (US Aut) sedán m
sedate [sɪ'deɪt] adj tranquilo ▪ vt administrar sedantes a, sedar
sedation [sɪ'deɪʃən] n (Med) sedación f; **to be under ~** estar bajo sedación
sedative ['sɛdɪtɪv] n sedante m, calmante m
sedentary ['sɛdntrɪ] adj sedentario
sediment ['sɛdɪmənt] n sedimento
sedimentary [sɛdɪ'mɛntərɪ] adj (Geo) sedimentario
sedition [sɪ'dɪʃən] n sedición f
seduce [sɪ'dju:s] vt (gen) seducir
seduction [sɪ'dʌkʃən] n seducción f
seductive [sɪ'dʌktɪv] adj seductor(-a)
see [si:] (pt **saw**, pp **seen**) vt (gen) ver; (understand) ver, comprender; (look at) mirar ▪ vi ver ▪ n sede f; **to ~ sb to the door** acompañar a algn a la puerta; **to ~ that** (ensure) asegurarse de que; **~ you soon/later/**

tomorrow! ¡hasta pronto/luego/mañana!; **as far as I can ~** por lo visto or por lo que veo; **there was nobody to be seen** no se veía a nadie; **let me ~** (show me) a ver; (let me think) vamos a ver; **to go and ~ sb** ir a ver a algn; **~ for yourself** compruébalo tú mismo; **I don't know what she sees in him** no sé qué le encuentra
▶ **see about** vt fus atender a, encargarse de
▶ **see off** vt despedir
▶ **see through** vt fus calar ▪ vt llevar a cabo
▶ **see to** vt fus atender a, encargarse de
seed [si:d] n semilla; (in fruit) pepita; (fig) germen m; (Tennis) preseleccionado(-a); **to go to ~** (plant) granar; (fig) descuidarse
seedless ['si:dlɪs] adj sin semillas or pepitas
seedling ['si:dlɪŋ] n planta de semillero
seedy ['si:dɪ] adj (person) desaseado; (place) sórdido
seeing ['si:ɪŋ] conj: **~ (that)** visto que, en vista de que
seek (pt, pp **sought**) [si:k, sɔ:t] vt (gen) buscar; (post) solicitar; **to ~ advice/help from sb** pedir consejos/solicitar ayuda a algn
▶ **seek out** vt (person) buscar
seem [si:m] vi parecer; **there seems to be ...** parece que hay ...; **it seems (that) ...** parece que ...; **what seems to be the trouble?** ¿qué pasa?; **I did what seemed best** hice lo que parecía mejor
seemingly ['si:mɪŋlɪ] adv aparentemente, según parece
seen [si:n] pp of **see**
seep [si:p] vi filtrarse
seer [sɪəʳ] n vidente m/f, profeta m/f
seersucker [sɪə'sʌkəʳ] n sirsaca
seesaw ['si:sɔ:] n balancín m, subibaja m
seethe [si:ð] vi hervir; **to ~ with anger** enfurecerse
see-through ['si:θru:] adj transparente
segment ['sɛgmənt] n segmento
segregate ['sɛgrɪgeɪt] vt segregar
segregation [sɛgrɪ'geɪʃən] n segregación f
Seine [seɪn] n Sena m
seismic ['saɪzmɪk] adj sísmico
seize [si:z] vt (grasp) agarrar, asir; (take possession of) secuestrar; (: territory) apoderarse de; (opportunity) aprovecharse de
▶ **seize up** vi (Tech) agarrotarse
▶ **seize (up)on** vt fus valerse de
seizure ['si:ʒəʳ] n (Med) ataque m; (Law) incautación f
seldom ['sɛldəm] adv rara vez
select [sɪ'lɛkt] adj selecto, escogido; (hotel, restaurant, clubs) exclusivo ▪ vt escoger, elegir; (Sport) seleccionar; **a ~ few** una minoría selecta

769

selection [sɪ'lɛkʃən] *n* selección *f*, elección *f*; (*Comm*) surtido

selection committee *n* comisión *f* de nombramiento

selective [sɪ'lɛktɪv] *adj* selectivo

self [sɛlf] *n* (*pl* **selves**) [sɛlvz] uno mismo
  ■ *pref* auto...; **the ~** el yo

self-addressed ['sɛlfə'drɛst] *adj*: **~ envelope** sobre *m* con la dirección propia

self-adhesive [sɛlfəd'hi:zɪv] *adj* autoadhesivo, autoadherente

self-appointed [sɛlfə'pɔɪntɪd] *adj* autonombrado

self-assurance [sɛlfə'ʃuərəns] *n* confianza en sí mismo

self-assured [sɛlfə'ʃuəd] *adj* seguro de sí mismo

self-catering [sɛlf'keɪtərɪŋ] *adj* (*Brit*) sin pensión *or* servicio de comida; **~ apartment** apartamento con cocina propia

self-centred, self-centered (*US*) [sɛlf'sɛntəd] *adj* egocéntrico

self-cleaning [sɛlf'kli:nɪŋ] *adj* autolimpiador

self-confessed [sɛlfkən'fɛst] *adj* (*alcoholic etc*) confeso

self-confidence [sɛlf'kɒnfɪdns] *n* confianza en sí mismo

self-confident [sɛlf'kɒnfɪdnt] *adj* seguro de sí (mismo), lleno de confianza en sí mismo

self-conscious [sɛlf'kɒnʃəs] *adj* cohibido

self-contained [sɛlfkən'teɪnd] *adj* (*gen*) independiente; (*Brit*: *flat*) con entrada particular

self-control [sɛlfkən'trəul] *n* autodominio

self-defeating [sɛlfdɪ'fi:tɪŋ] *adj* contraproducente

self-defence, self-defense (*US*) [sɛlfdɪ'fɛns] *n* defensa propia

self-discipline [sɛlf'dɪsɪplɪn] *n* autodisciplina

self-employed [sɛlfɪm'plɔɪd] *adj* que trabaja por cuenta propia, autónomo

self-esteem [sɛlfɪ'sti:m] *n* amor *m* propio

self-evident [sɛlf'ɛvɪdnt] *adj* patente

self-explanatory [sɛlfɪks'plænətərɪ] *adj* que no necesita explicación

self-financing [sɛlffaɪ'nænsɪŋ] *adj* autofinanziado

self-governing [sɛlf'gʌvənɪŋ] *adj* autónomo

self-help ['sɛlf'hɛlp] *n* autosuficiencia, ayuda propia

self-importance [sɛlfɪm'pɔ:tns] *n* presunción *f*, vanidad *f*

self-important [sɛlfɪm'pɔ:tnt] *adj* vanidoso

self-indulgent [sɛlfɪn'dʌldʒənt] *adj* indulgente consigo mismo

self-inflicted [sɛlfɪn'flɪktɪd] *adj* infligido a sí mismo

self-interest [sɛlf'ɪntrɪst] *n* egoísmo

selfish ['sɛlfɪʃ] *adj* egoísta

selfishly ['sɛlfɪʃlɪ] *adv* con egoísmo, de modo egoísta

selfishness ['sɛlfɪʃnɪs] *n* egoísmo

selfless ['sɛlflɪs] *adj* desinteresado

selflessly ['sɛlflɪslɪ] *adv* desinteresadamente

self-made man ['sɛlfmeɪd-] *n hombre que ha triunfado por su propio esfuerzo*

self-pity [sɛlf'pɪtɪ] *n* lástima de sí mismo

self-portrait [sɛlf'pɔ:treɪt] *n* autorretrato

self-possessed [sɛlfpə'zɛst] *adj* sereno, dueño de sí mismo

self-preservation ['sɛlfprɛzə'veɪʃən] *n* propia conservación *f*

self-propelled [sɛlfprə'pɛld] *adj* autopropulsado, automotor(-triz)

self-raising [sɛlf'reɪzɪŋ], **self-rising** (*US*) [sɛlf'raɪzɪŋ] *adj*: **~ flour** harina con levadura

self-reliant [sɛlfrɪ'laɪənt] *adj* independiente, autosuficiente

self-respect [sɛlfrɪ'spɛkt] *n* amor *m* propio

self-respecting [sɛlfrɪ'spɛktɪŋ] *adj* que tiene amor propio

self-righteous [sɛlf'raɪtʃəs] *adj* santurrón(-ona)

self-rising [sɛlf'raɪzɪŋ] *adj* (*US*) = **self-raising**

self-sacrifice [sɛlf'sækrɪfaɪs] *n* abnegación *f*

self-same [sɛlfseɪm] *adj* mismo, mismísimo

self-satisfied [sɛlf'sætɪsfaɪd] *adj* satisfecho de sí mismo

self-service [sɛlf'sə:vɪs] *adj* de autoservicio

self-styled ['sɛlfstaɪld] *adj* supuesto, sedicente

self-sufficient [sɛlfsə'fɪʃənt] *adj* autosuficiente

self-supporting [sɛlfsə'pɔ:tɪŋ] *adj* económicamente independiente

self-tanning [sɛlf'tænɪŋ] *adj* autobronceador

self-taught [sɛlf'tɔ:t] *adj* autodidacta

self-test ['sɛlftɛst] *n* (*Comput*) autocomprobación *f*

sell (*pt, pp* **sold**) [sɛl, səuld] *vt* vender ■ *vi* venderse; **to ~ at** *or* **for £10** venderse a 10 libras; **to ~ sb an idea** (*fig*) convencer a algn de una idea
  ▶ **sell off** *vt* liquidar
  ▶ **sell out** *vi* transigir, transar (*LAm*); **to ~ out** (**to sb/sth**) (*Comm*) vender su negocio (a algn/algo) ■ *vt* agotar las existencias de, venderlo todo; **the tickets are all sold out** las entradas están agotadas
  ▶ **sell up** *vi* (*Comm*) liquidarse

sell-by date ['sɛlbaɪ-] *n* fecha de caducidad

seller ['sɛlər] n vendedor(a) m(f); **~'s market** mercado de demanda

selling price ['sɛlɪŋ-] n precio de venta

Sellotape® ['sɛləuteɪp] n (Brit) cinta adhesiva, celo, scotch® m

sellout ['sɛlaut] n traición f; **it was a ~** (Theat etc) fue un éxito de taquilla

selves [sɛlvz] npl of **self**

semantic [sɪ'mæntɪk] adj semántico

semaphore ['sɛməfɔː'] n semáforo

semblance ['sɛmbləns] n apariencia

semen ['siːmən] n semen m

semester [sɪ'mɛstər] n (US) semestre m

semi ['sɛmɪ] n = **semidetached house**

semi... [sɛmɪ] pref semi..., medio...

semicircle ['sɛmɪsəːkl] n semicírculo

semicircular ['sɛmɪ'səːkjulər] adj semicircular

semicolon [sɛmɪ'kəulən] n punto y coma

semiconductor [sɛmɪkən'dʌktər] n semiconductor m

semiconscious [sɛmɪ'kɒnʃəs] adj semiconsciente

semidetached [sɛmɪdɪ'tætʃt], **semidetached house** n casa adosada

semi-final [sɛmɪ'faɪnl] n semifinal f

seminar ['sɛmɪnɑː'] n seminario

seminary ['sɛmɪnərɪ] n (Rel) seminario

semiprecious stone [sɛmɪ'prɛʃəs-] n piedra semipreciosa

semiquaver ['sɛmɪkweɪvə'] n (Brit) semicorchea

semiskilled ['sɛmɪskɪld] adj (work, worker) semicualificado

semi-skimmed adj semidesnatado

semitone ['sɛmɪtəun] n semitono

semolina [sɛmə'liːnə] n sémola

Sen., sen. abbr = **senator; senior**

senate ['sɛnɪt] n senado; see also **Congress**

senator ['sɛnɪtər] n senador(a) m(f)

send (pt, pp **sent**) [sɛnd, sɛnt] vt mandar, enviar; **to ~ by post** mandar por correo; **to ~ sb for sth** mandar a algn a buscar algo; **to ~ word that** ... avisar or mandar aviso de que ...; **she sends (you) her love** te manda or envía cariñosos recuerdos; **to ~ sb to sleep/into fits of laughter** dormir/hacer reír a algn; **to ~ sb flying** echar a algn; **to ~ sth flying** tirar algo

▶ **send away** vt (letter, goods) despachar

▶ **send away for** vt fus pedir

▶ **send back** vt devolver

▶ **send for** vt fus mandar traer; (by post) escribir pidiendo algo

▶ **send in** vt (report, application, resignation) mandar

▶ **send off** vt (goods) despachar; (Brit Sport: player) expulsar

▶ **send on** vt (letter) mandar, expedir; (luggage etc: in advance) facturar

▶ **send out** vt (invitation) mandar; (emit: light, heat) emitir, difundir; (signal) emitir

▶ **send round** vt (letter, document etc) hacer circular

▶ **send up** vt (person, price) hacer subir; (Brit: parody) parodiar

sender ['sɛndər] n remitente m/f

send-off ['sɛndɒf] n: **a good ~** una buena despedida

send-up ['sɛndʌp] n (col) parodia, sátira

Senegal [sɛnɪ'gɔːl] n Senegal m

Senegalese [sɛnɪgə'liːz] adj, n senegalés(-esa) m(f)

senile ['siːnaɪl] adj senil

senility [sɪ'nɪlɪtɪ] n senilidad f

senior ['siːnɪə'] adj (older) mayor, más viejo; (: on staff) más antiguo; (of higher rank) superior ■ n mayor m; **P. Jones ~** P. Jones padre

senior citizen n persona de la tercera edad

senior high school n (US) ≈ instituto de enseñanza media; see also **high school**

seniority [siːnɪ'ɔrɪtɪ] n antigüedad f; (in rank) rango superior

sensation [sɛn'seɪʃən] n (physical feeling, impression) sensación f

sensational [sɛn'seɪʃənl] adj sensacional

sense [sɛns] n (faculty, meaning) sentido; (feeling) sensación f; (good sense) sentido común, juicio ■ vt sentir, percibir; **~ of humour** sentido del humor; **it makes ~** tiene sentido; **there is no ~ in (doing) that** no tiene sentido (hacer) eso; **to come to one's senses** (regain consciousness) volver en sí, recobrar el sentido; **to take leave of one's senses** perder el juicio

senseless ['sɛnslɪs] adj estúpido, insensato; (unconscious) sin conocimiento

senselessly ['sɛnslɪslɪ] adv estúpidamente, insensatamente

sensibility [sɛnsɪ'bɪlɪtɪ] n sensibilidad f; **sensibilities** npl delicadeza sg

sensible ['sɛnsɪbl] adj sensato; (reasonable) razonable, lógico

sensibly ['sɛnsɪblɪ] adv sensatamente; razonablemente, de modo lógico

sensitive ['sɛnsɪtɪv] adj sensible; (touchy) susceptible; **he is very ~ about it** es muy susceptible acerca de eso

sensitivity [sɛnsɪ'tɪvɪtɪ] n sensibilidad f; susceptibilidad f

sensual ['sɛnsjuəl] adj sensual

sensuous ['sɛnsjuəs] adj sensual

sent [sɛnt] pt, pp of **send**

S

sentence ['sɛntəns] n (Ling) frase f, oración f; (Law) sentencia, fallo ■ vt: **to ~ sb to death/ to five years** condenar a algn a muerte/a cinco años de cárcel; **to pass ~ on sb** (also fig) sentenciar or condenar a algn

sentiment ['sɛntɪmənt] n sentimiento; (opinion) opinión f

sentimental [sɛntɪ'mɛntl] adj sentimental

sentimentality [sɛntɪmɛn'tælɪtɪ] n sentimentalismo, sensiblería

sentinel ['sɛntɪnl] n centinela m

sentry ['sɛntrɪ] n centinela m

sentry duty n: **to be on ~** estar de guardia, hacer guardia

Seoul [səʊl] n Seúl m

separable ['sɛpərəbl] adj separable

separate [adj 'sɛprɪt, vb 'sɛpəreɪt] adj separado; (distinct) distinto ■ vt separar; (part) dividir ■ vi separarse; **~ from** separado or distinto de; **under ~ cover** (Comm) por separado; **to ~ into** dividir or separar en; **he is separated from his wife, but not divorced** está separado de su mujer, pero no (está) divorciado

separately ['sɛprɪtlɪ] adv por separado

separates ['sɛprɪts] npl (clothes) coordinados mpl

separation [sɛpə'reɪʃən] n separación f

sepia ['si:pɪə] adj color sepia inv

Sept. abbr (= September) sep

September [sɛp'tɛmbəʳ] n se(p)tiembre m; see also **July**

septic ['sɛptɪk] adj séptico; **to go ~** ponerse séptico

septicaemia, septicemia (US) [sɛptɪ'si:mɪə] n septicemia

septic tank n fosa séptica

sequel ['si:kwl] n consecuencia, resultado; (of story) continuación f

sequence ['si:kwəns] n sucesión f, serie f; (Cine) secuencia; **in ~** en orden or serie

sequential [sɪ'kwɛnʃəl] adj: **~ access** (Comput) acceso en serie

sequin ['si:kwɪn] n lentejuela

Serb [sə:b] adj, n = **Serbian**

Serbia ['sə:bɪə] n Serbia

Serbian ['sə:bɪən] adj serbio ■ n serbio(-a); (Ling) serbio

Serbo-Croat ['sə:bəʊ'krəʊæt] n (Ling) serbocroata m

serenade [sɛrə'neɪd] n serenata ■ vt dar serenata a

serene [sɪ'ri:n] adj sereno, tranquilo

serenely [sɪ'ri:nlɪ] adv serenamente, tranquilamente

serenity [sə'rɛnɪtɪ] n serenidad f, tranquilidad f

sergeant ['sɑ:dʒənt] n sargento

sergeant major n sargento mayor

serial ['sɪərɪəl] n novela por entregas; (TV) telenovela

serial access n (Comput) acceso en serie

serial interface n (Comput) interface m en serie

serialize ['sɪərɪəlaɪz] vt publicar/televisar por entregas

serial killer n asesino(-a) múltiple

serial number n número de serie

series ['sɪəri:z] n (pl inv) serie f

serious ['sɪərɪəs] adj serio; (grave) grave; **are you ~ (about it)?** ¿lo dices en serio?

seriously ['sɪərɪəslɪ] adv en serio; (ill, wounded etc) gravemente; (col: extremely) de verdad; **to take sth/sb ~** tomar algo/a algn en serio; **he's ~ rich** es una pasada de rico

seriousness ['sɪərɪəsnɪs] n seriedad f; gravedad f

sermon ['sə:mən] n sermón m

serpent ['sə:pənt] n serpiente f

serrated [sɪ'reɪtɪd] adj serrado, dentellado

serum ['sɪərəm] n suero

servant ['sə:vənt] n (gen) servidor(a) m(f); (also: **house servant**) criado(-a) m(f)

serve [sə:v] vt servir; (customer) atender; (train) tener parada en; (apprenticeship) hacer; (prison term) cumplir ■ vi (servant, soldier etc) servir; (Tennis) sacar ■ n (Tennis) saque m; **it serves him right** se lo merece, se lo tiene merecido; **to ~ a summons on sb** entregar una citación a algn; **it serves my purpose** me sirve para lo que quiero; **are you being served?** ¿le atienden?; **the power station serves the entire region** la central eléctrica abastece a toda la región; **to ~ as/for/to do** servir de/para/para hacer; **to ~ on a committee/a jury** ser miembro de una comisión/un jurado

▶ **serve out, serve up** vt (food) servir

service ['sə:vɪs] n (gen) servicio; (Rel: Catholic) misa; (: other) oficio (religioso); (Aut) mantenimiento; (of dishes) juego ■ vt (car, washing machine) mantener; (: repair) reparar; **the Services** las fuerzas armadas; **funeral ~** exequias fpl; **to hold a ~** celebrar un oficio religioso; **the essential services** los servicios esenciales; **medical/social services** servicios mpl médicos/sociales; **the train ~ to London** los trenes a Londres; **to be of ~ to sb** ser útil a algn

serviceable ['sə:vɪsəbl] adj servible, utilizable

service area n (on motorway) área de servicios

service charge n (Brit) servicio

service industries *npl* industrias *fpl* del servicio

serviceman ['sə:vɪsmən] *n* militar *m*

service station *n* estación *f* de servicio

servicing ['sə:vɪsɪŋ] *n* (*of car*) revisión *f*; (*of washing machine etc*) servicio de reparaciones

serviette [sə:vɪ'ɛt] *n* (*Brit*) servilleta

servile ['sə:vaɪl] *adj* servil

session ['sɛʃən] *n* (*sitting*) sesión *f*; **to be in ~** estar en sesión

session musician *n* músico *m/f* de estudio

set [sɛt] (*pt, pp ~*) *n* juego; (*Radio*) aparato; (*TV*) televisor *m*; (*of utensils*) batería; (*of cutlery*) cubierto; (*of books*) colección *f*; (*Tennis*) set *m*; (*group of people*) grupo; (*Cine*) plató *m*; (*Theat*) decorado; (*Hairdressing*) marcado ■ *adj* (*fixed*) fijo; (*ready*) listo; (*resolved*) resuelto, decidido ■ *vt* (*place*) poner, colocar; (*fix*) fijar; (*adjust*) ajustar, arreglar; (*decide: rules etc*) establecer, decidir; (*assign: task*) asignar; (*: homework*) poner ■ *vi* (*sun*) ponerse; (*jam, jelly*) cuajarse; (*concrete*) fraguar; **a ~ of false teeth** una dentadura postiza; **a ~ of dining-room furniture** muebles *mpl* de comedor; **~ in one's ways** con costumbres arraigadas; **a ~ phrase** una frase hecha; **to be all ~ to do sth** estar listo para hacer algo; **to be ~ on doing sth** estar empeñado en hacer algo; **a novel ~ in Valencia** una novela ambientada en Valencia; **to ~ to music** poner música a; **to ~ on fire** incendiar, prender fuego a; **to ~ free** poner en libertad; **to ~ sth going** poner algo en marcha; **to ~ sail** zarpar, hacerse a la mar
  ▶ **set about** *vt fus*: **to ~ about doing sth** ponerse a hacer algo
  ▶ **set aside** *vt* poner aparte, dejar de lado
  ▶ **set back** *vt* (*progress*): **to ~ back (by)** retrasar (por); **a house ~ back from the road** una casa apartada de la carretera
  ▶ **set down** *vt* (*bus, train*) dejar; (*record*) poner por escrito
  ▶ **set in** *vi* (*infection*) declararse; (*complications*) comenzar; **the rain has ~ in for the day** parece que va a llover todo el día
  ▶ **set off** *vi* partir ■ *vt* (*bomb*) hacer estallar; (*cause to start*) poner en marcha; (*show up well*) hacer resaltar
  ▶ **set out** *vi*: **to ~ out to do sth** proponerse hacer algo ■ *vt* (*arrange*) disponer; (*state*) exponer; **to ~ out (from)** salir (de)
  ▶ **set up** *vt* (*organization*) establecer

setback ['sɛtbæk] *n* (*hitch*) revés *m*, contratiempo; (*in health*) recaída

set menu *n* menú *m*

set phrase *n* frase *f* hecha

set square *n* cartabón *m*

settee [sɛ'ti:] *n* sofá *m*

setting ['sɛtɪŋ] *n* (*scenery*) marco; (*of jewel*) engaste *m*, montadura

setting lotion *n* fijador *m* (para el pelo)

settle ['sɛtl] *vt* (*argument, matter*) resolver; (*pay: bill, accounts*) pagar, liquidar; (*colonize: land*) colonizar; (*Med: calm*) calmar, sosegar ■ *vi* (*dust etc*) depositarse; (*weather*) estabilizarse; (*also*: **settle down**) instalarse; (*calm down*) tranquilizarse; **to ~ for sth** convenir en aceptar algo; **to ~ on sth** decidirse por algo; **that's settled then** bueno, está arreglado; **to ~ one's stomach** asentar el estómago
  ▶ **settle in** *vi* instalarse
  ▶ **settle up** *vi*: **to ~ up with sb** ajustar cuentas con algn

settlement ['sɛtlmənt] *n* (*payment*) liquidación *f*; (*agreement*) acuerdo, convenio; (*village etc*) poblado; **in ~ of our account** (*Comm*) en pago *or* liquidación de nuestra cuenta

settler ['sɛtləʳ] *n* colono(-a), colonizador(a) *m(f)*

setup ['sɛtʌp] *n* sistema *m*

seven ['sɛvn] *num* siete

seventeen [sɛvn'ti:n] *num* diez y siete, diecisiete

seventh ['sɛvnθ] *adj* séptimo

seventy ['sɛvntɪ] *num* setenta

sever ['sɛvəʳ] *vt* cortar; (*relations*) romper

several ['sɛvərl] *adj, pron* varios(-as) *m(f)pl*, algunos(-as) *m(f)pl*; **~ of us** varios de nosotros; **~ times** varias veces

severance ['sɛvərəns] *n* (*of relations*) ruptura

severance pay *n* indemnización *f* por despido

severe [sɪ'vɪəʳ] *adj* severo; (*serious*) grave; (*hard*) duro; (*pain*) intenso

severely [sɪ'vɪəlɪ] *adv* severamente; (*wounded, ill*) de gravedad, gravemente

severity [sɪ'vɛrɪtɪ] *n* severidad *f*; gravedad *f*; intensidad *f*

Seville [sə'vɪl] *n* Sevilla

sew (*pt* **sewed**, *pp* **sewn**) [səu, səud, səun] *vt, vi* coser
  ▶ **sew up** *vt* coser

sewage ['su:ɪdʒ] *n* (*effluence*) aguas *fpl* residuales; (*system*) alcantarillado

sewage works *n* estación *f* depuradora (de aguas residuales)

sewer ['su:əʳ] *n* alcantarilla, cloaca

sewing ['səuɪŋ] *n* costura

sewing machine *n* máquina de coser

sewn [səun] *pp of* **sew**

sex [sɛks] *n* sexo; **the opposite ~** el sexo opuesto; **to have ~ with sb** tener relaciones (sexuales) con algn

S

773

sex act n acto sexual, coito
sex appeal n sex-appeal m, gancho
sex education n educación f sexual
sexism ['sɛksɪzəm] n sexismo
sexist ['sɛksɪst] adj, n sexista m/f
sex life n vida sexual
sex object n objeto sexual
sextant ['sɛkstənt] n sextante m
sextet [sɛks'tɛt] n sexteto
sexual ['sɛksjuəl] adj sexual; **~ assault**
atentado contra el pudor; **~ harassment**
acoso sexual; **~ intercourse** relaciones fpl
sexuales
sexually ['sɛksjuəlɪ] adv sexualmente
sexy ['sɛksɪ] adj sexy
Seychelles [seɪ'ʃɛlz] npl: **the ~** las Seychelles
SF n abbr = **science fiction**
SG n abbr (US: = Surgeon General) jefe del servicio
federal de sanidad
Sgt. abbr (= sergeant) Sgto.
shabbily ['ʃæbɪlɪ] adv (treat) injustamente;
(dressed) pobremente
shabbiness ['ʃæbɪnɪs] n (of dress, person)
aspecto desharrapado; (of building) mal
estado
shabby ['ʃæbɪ] adj (person) desharrapado;
(clothes) raído, gastado
shack [ʃæk] n choza, chabola
shackle ['ʃækl] vt encadenar; (fig): **to be
shackled by sth** verse obstaculizado por
algo
shackles ['ʃæklz] npl grillos mpl, grilletes mpl
shade [ʃeɪd] n sombra; (for lamp) pantalla;
(for eyes) visera; (of colour) tono m, tonalidad f;
(US: window shade) persiana ■ vt dar sombra
a; **shades** npl (US: sunglasses) gafas fpl de sol;
in the ~ a la sombra; (small quantity): **a ~ of**
un poquito de; **a ~ smaller** un poquito más
pequeño
shadow ['ʃædəu] n sombra ■ vt (follow)
seguir y vigilar; **without** or **beyond a ~ of
doubt** sin lugar a dudas
shadow cabinet n (Brit Pol) gobierno en la
oposición
shadowy ['ʃædəuɪ] adj oscuro; (dim)
indistinto
shady ['ʃeɪdɪ] adj sombreado; (fig: dishonest)
sospechoso; (deal) turbio
shaft [ʃɑːft] n (of arrow, spear) astil m; (Aut, Tech)
eje m, árbol m; (of mine) pozo; (of lift) hueco,
caja; (of light) rayo; **ventilator ~** chimenea de
ventilación
shaggy ['ʃægɪ] adj peludo
shake [ʃeɪk] (pt **shook**, pp **shaken**) ['ʃeɪkn] vt
sacudir; (building) hacer temblar; (perturb)
inquietar, perturbar; (weaken) debilitar;
(alarm) trastornar ■ vi estremecerse;

(tremble) temblar ■ n (movement) sacudida;
to ~ one's head (in refusal) negar con la
cabeza; (in dismay) mover or menear la cabeza,
incrédulo; **to ~ hands with sb** estrechar
la mano a algn; **to ~ in one's shoes** (fig)
temblar de miedo
▸ **shake off** vt sacudirse; (fig) deshacerse de
▸ **shake up** vt agitar
shake-up ['ʃeɪkʌp] n reorganización f
shakily ['ʃeɪkɪlɪ] adv (reply) con voz temblorosa
or trémula; (walk) con paso vacilante; (write)
con mano temblorosa
shaky ['ʃeɪkɪ] adj (unstable) inestable, poco
firme; (trembling) tembloroso; (health)
delicado; (memory) defectuoso; (person: from
illness) temblando; (premise etc) incierto
shale [ʃeɪl] n esquisto
shall [ʃæl] aux vb: **I ~ go** iré
shallot [ʃə'lɔt] n (Brit) cebollita, chalote m
shallow ['ʃæləu] adj poco profundo; (fig)
superficial
shallows ['ʃæləuz] npl bajío sg, bajos mpl
sham [ʃæm] n fraude m, engaño ■ adj falso,
fingido ■ vt fingir, simular
shambles ['ʃæmblz] n desorden m, confusión
f; **the economy is (in) a complete ~** la
economía está en un estado desastroso
shambolic [ʃæm'bɔlɪk] adj (col) caótico
shame [ʃeɪm] n vergüenza; (pity) lástima,
pena ■ vt avergonzar; **it is a ~ that/to do**
es una lástima or pena que/hacer; **what a ~!**
¡qué lástima or pena!; **to put sth/sb to ~** (fig)
ridiculizar algo/a algn
shamefaced ['ʃeɪmfeɪst] adj avergonzado
shameful ['ʃeɪmful] adj vergonzoso
shamefully ['ʃeɪmfulɪ] adv vergonzosamente
shameless ['ʃeɪmlɪs] adj descarado
shampoo [ʃæm'puː] n champú m ■ vt lavar
con champú
shampoo and set n lavado y marcado
shamrock ['ʃæmrɔk] n trébol m
shandy ['ʃændɪ], **shandygaff** (US)
['ʃændɪgæf] n clara, cerveza con gaseosa
shan't [ʃɑːnt], **shall not**
shanty town ['ʃæntɪ-] n barrio de chabolas
SHAPE [ʃeɪp] n abbr (= Supreme Headquarters
Allied Powers, Europe) cuartel general de las fuerzas
aliadas en Europa
shape [ʃeɪp] n forma ■ vt formar, dar forma
a; (clay) modelar; (stone) labrar; (sb's ideas)
formar; (sb's life) determinar ■ vi (also: **shape
up**: events) desarrollarse; (person) formarse;
to take ~ tomar forma; **to get o.s. into ~**
ponerse en forma or en condiciones; **in the ~
of a heart** en forma de corazón; **I can't bear
gardening in any ~ or form** no aguanto la
jardinería de ningún modo

-shaped *suff*: **heart~** en forma de corazón

shapeless ['ʃeɪplɪs] *adj* informe, sin forma definida

shapely ['ʃeɪplɪ] *adj* bien formado o proporcionado

share [ʃɛəʳ] *n* (*part*) parte *f*, porción *f*; (*contribution*) cuota; (*Comm*) acción *f* ■ *vt* dividir; (*fig*: *have in common*) compartir; **to have a ~ in the profits** tener una proporción de las ganancias; **he has a 50% ~ in a new business venture** tiene una participación del 50% en un nuevo negocio; **to ~ in** participar en; **to ~ out (among** or **between)** repartir (entre)

share capital *n* (*Comm*) capital *m* social en acciones

share certificate *n* certificado *or* título de una acción

shareholder ['ʃɛəhəʊldəʳ] *n* (*Brit*) accionista *m/f*

share index *n* (*Comm*) índice *m* de la bolsa

share issue *n* emisión *f* de acciones

share price *n* (*Comm*) cotización *f*

shark [ʃɑːk] *n* tiburón *m*

sharp [ʃɑːp] *adj* (*razor, knife*) afilado; (*point*) puntiagudo; (*outline*) definido; (*pain*) intenso; (*Mus*) desafinado; (*contrast*) marcado; (*voice*) agudo; (*curve, bend*) cerrado; (*person: quick-witted*) avispado; (: *dishonest*) poco escrupuloso ■ *n* (*Mus*) sostenido ■ *adv*: **at two o'clock ~** a las dos en punto; **to be ~ with sb** hablar a algn de forma brusca y tajante; **turn ~ left** tuerce del todo a la izquierda

sharpen ['ʃɑːpn] *vt* afilar; (*pencil*) sacar punta a; (*fig*) agudizar

sharpener ['ʃɑːpnəʳ] *n* (*gen*) afilador *m*; (*also*: **pencil sharpener**) sacapuntas *m inv*

sharp-eyed [ʃɑːp'aɪd] *adj* de vista aguda

sharpish ['ʃɑːpɪʃ] *adv* (*Brit col: quickly*) prontito, bien pronto

sharply ['ʃɑːplɪ] *adv* (*abruptly*) bruscamente; (*clearly*) claramente; (*harshly*) severamente

sharp-tempered [ʃɑːp'tɛmpəd] *adj* de genio arisco

sharp-witted [ʃɑːp'wɪtɪd] *adj* listo, despabilado

shatter ['ʃætəʳ] *vt* hacer añicos *or* pedazos; (*fig: ruin*) destruir, acabar con ■ *vi* hacerse añicos

shattered ['ʃætəd] *adj* (*grief-stricken*) destrozado, deshecho; (*exhausted*) agotado, hecho polvo

shattering ['ʃætərɪŋ] *adj* (*experience*) devastador(a), anonadante

shatterproof ['ʃætəpruːf] *adj* inastillable

shave [ʃeɪv] *vt* afeitar, rasurar ■ *vi* afeitarse ■ *n*: **to have a ~** afeitarse

shaven ['ʃeɪvn] *adj* (*head*) rapado

shaver ['ʃeɪvəʳ] *n* (*also*: **electric shaver**) máquina de afeitar (eléctrica)

shaving ['ʃeɪvɪŋ] *n* (*action*) afeitado; **shavings** *npl* (*of wood etc*) virutas *fpl*

shaving brush *n* brocha (de afeitar)

shaving cream *n* crema (de afeitar)

shaving point *n* enchufe *m* para máquinas de afeitar

shaving soap *n* jabón *m* de afeitar

shawl [ʃɔːl] *n* chal *m*

she [ʃiː] *pron* ella; **there ~ is** allí está; **~-cat** gata, NB: *for ships, countries follow the gender of your translation*

sheaf (*pl* **sheaves**) [ʃiːf, ʃiːvz] *n* (*of corn*) gavilla; (*of arrows*) haz *m*; (*of papers*) fajo

shear [ʃɪəʳ] *vt* (*pt, pp* **sheared** *or* **shorn**) [ʃɔːn] (*sheep*) esquilar, trasquilar
▶ **shear off** *vi* romperse

shears ['ʃɪəz] *npl* (*for hedge*) tijeras *fpl* de jardín

sheath [ʃiːθ] *n* vaina; (*contraceptive*) preservativo

sheath knife *n* cuchillo de monte

sheaves [ʃiːvz] *npl of* **sheaf**

shed [ʃed] *n* cobertizo; (*Industry, Rail*) nave *f* ■ *vt* (*pt, pp* **shed**) (*skin*) mudar; (*tears*) derramar; **to ~ light on** (*problem, mystery*) aclarar, arrojar luz sobre

she'd [ʃiːd] = **she had; she would**

sheen [ʃiːn] *n* brillo, lustre *m*

sheep [ʃiːp] *n* (*pl inv*) oveja

sheepdog ['ʃiːpdɔg] *n* perro pastor

sheep farmer *n* ganadero (de ovejas)

sheepish ['ʃiːpɪʃ] *adj* tímido, vergonzoso

sheepskin ['ʃiːpskɪn] *n* piel *f* de carnero

sheepskin jacket *n* zamarra

sheer [ʃɪəʳ] *adj* (*utter*) puro, completo; (*steep*) escarpado; (*material*) diáfano ■ *adv* verticalmente; **by ~ chance** de pura casualidad

sheet [ʃiːt] *n* (*on bed*) sábana; (*of paper*) hoja; (*of glass, metal*) lámina

sheet feed *n* (*on printer*) alimentador *m* de papel

sheet lightning *n* relámpago (difuso)

sheet metal *n* metal *m* en lámina

sheet music *n* hojas *fpl* de partitura

sheik, sheikh [ʃeɪk] *n* jeque *m*

shelf (*pl* **shelves**) [ʃelf, ʃelvz] *n* estante *m*

shelf life *n* (*Comm*) periodo de conservación antes de la venta

shell [ʃel] *n* (*on beach*) concha, caracol (*LAm*); (*of egg, nut etc*) cáscara; (*explosive*) proyectil *m*, obús *m*; (*of building*) armazón *m* ■ *vt* (*peas*) desenvainar; (*Mil*) bombardear

▶ **shell out** vi (col): **to ~ out (for)** soltar el dinero (para), desembolsar (para)

she'll [ʃi:l] = **she will; she shall**

shellfish ['ʃelfɪʃ] n pl inv crustáceo; (pl: as food) mariscos mpl

shellsuit ['ʃelsu:t] n chándal m (de tactel®)

shelter ['ʃeltəʳ] n abrigo, refugio ■ vt (aid) amparar, proteger; (give lodging to) abrigar; (hide) esconder ■ vi abrigarse, refugiarse; **to take ~ (from)** refugiarse or asilarse (de); **bus ~** parada de autobús cubierta

sheltered ['ʃeltəd] adj (life) protegido; (spot) abrigado

shelve [ʃelv] vt (fig) dar carpetazo a

shelves [ʃelvz] npl of **shelf**

shelving ['ʃelvɪŋ] n estantería

shepherd ['ʃepəd] n pastor m ■ vt (guide) guiar, conducir

shepherdess ['ʃepədɪs] n pastora

shepherd's pie n pastel de carne y puré de patatas

sherbert ['ʃə:bət] n (Brit: powder) polvos mpl azucarados; (US: water ice) sorbete m

sheriff ['ʃerɪf] n (US) sheriff m

sherry ['ʃerɪ] n jerez m

she's [ʃi:z] = **she is; she has**

Shetland ['ʃetlənd] n (also: **the Shetlands, the Shetland Isles**) las Islas fpl Shetland

Shetland pony n pony m de Shetland

shield [ʃi:ld] n escudo; (Tech) blindaje m ■ vt: **to ~ (from)** proteger (de)

shift [ʃɪft] n (change) cambio; (at work) turno ■ vt trasladar; (remove) quitar ■ vi moverse; (change place) cambiar de sitio; **the wind has shifted to the south** el viento ha virado al sur; **a ~ in demand** (Comm) un desplazamiento de la demanda

shift key n (on typewriter) tecla de mayúsculas

shiftless ['ʃɪftlɪs] adj (person) vago

shift work n (Brit) trabajo por turnos; **to do ~** trabajar por turnos

shifty ['ʃɪftɪ] adj tramposo; (eyes) furtivo

Shiite ['ʃi:aɪt] adj, n shiíta m/f

shilling ['ʃɪlɪŋ] n (Brit) chelín m (= 12 old pence; 20 in a pound)

shilly-shally ['ʃɪlɪʃælɪ] vi titubear, vacilar

shimmer ['ʃɪməʳ] n reflejo trémulo ■ vi relucir

shimmering ['ʃɪmərɪŋ] adj reluciente; (haze) trémulo; (satin etc) lustroso

shin [ʃɪn] n espinilla ■ vi: **to ~ down/up a tree** bajar de/trepar un árbol

shindig ['ʃɪndɪg] n (col) fiesta, juerga

shine [ʃaɪn] (pt, pp **shone**) n brillo, lustre m ■ vi brillar, relucir ■ vt (shoes) lustrar, sacar brillo a; **to ~ a torch on sth** dirigir una linterna hacia algo

shingle ['ʃɪŋgl] n (on beach) guijarras fpl

shingles ['ʃɪŋglz] n (Med) herpes msg

shining ['ʃaɪnɪŋ] adj (surface, hair) lustroso; (light) brillante

shiny ['ʃaɪnɪ] adj brillante, lustroso

ship [ʃɪp] n buque m, barco ■ vt (goods) embarcar; (oars) desarmar; (send) transportar or enviar por vía marítima; **~'s manifest** manifiesto del buque; **on board ~** a bordo

shipbuilder ['ʃɪpbɪldəʳ] n constructor(a) m(f) naval

shipbuilding ['ʃɪpbɪldɪŋ] n construcción f naval

ship canal n canal m de navegación

ship chandler [-'tʃɑ:ndləʳ] n proveedor m de efectos navales

shipment ['ʃɪpmənt] n (act) embarque m; (goods) envío

shipowner ['ʃɪpəunəʳ] n naviero, armador m

shipper ['ʃɪpəʳ] n compañía naviera

shipping ['ʃɪpɪŋ] n (act) embarque m; (traffic) buques mpl

shipping agent n agente m/f marítimo(-a)

shipping company n compañía naviera

shipping lane n ruta de navegación

shipping line n = **shipping company**

shipshape ['ʃɪpʃeɪp] adj en buen orden

shipwreck ['ʃɪprek] n naufragio ■ vt: **to be shipwrecked** naufragar

shipyard ['ʃɪpjɑ:d] n astillero

shire ['ʃaɪəʳ] n (Brit) condado

shirk [ʃə:k] vt eludir, esquivar; (obligations) faltar a

shirt [ʃə:t] n camisa; **in ~ sleeves** en mangas de camisa

shirty ['ʃə:tɪ] adj (Brit col): **to be ~** estar de malas pulgas

shit [ʃɪt] (col!) n mierda (!); (nonsense) chorradas fpl; **to be a ~** ser un cabrón (!) ■ excl ¡mierda! (!); **tough ~!** ¡te jodes! (!)

shiver ['ʃɪvəʳ] vi temblar, estremecerse; (with cold) tiritar

shoal [ʃəul] n (of fish) banco

shock [ʃɔk] n (impact) choque m; (Elec) descarga (eléctrica); (emotional) conmoción f; (start) sobresalto, susto; (Med) postración f nerviosa ■ vt dar un susto a; (offend) escandalizar; **to get a ~** (Elec) sentir una sacudida eléctrica; **to give sb a ~** dar un susto a algn; **to be suffering from ~** padecer una postración nerviosa; **it came as a ~ to hear that ...** me etc asombró descubrir que ...

shock absorber [-əbsɔ:bəʳ] n amortiguador m

shocker ['ʃɔkəʳ] n (col): **it was a real ~** fue muy fuerte

shocking ['ʃɔkɪŋ] adj (awful: weather, handwriting) espantoso, horrible; (improper) escandaloso; (result) inesperado

shock therapy, shock treatment n (Med) terapia de choque
shock wave n onda expansiva or de choque
shod [ʃɒd] pt, pp of **shoe** ■ adj calzado
shoddiness [ˈʃɒdɪnɪs] n baja calidad f
shoddy [ˈʃɒdɪ] adj de pacotilla
shoe [ʃuː] n zapato; (for horse) herradura; (brake shoe) zapata ■ vt (pt, pp **shod**) [ʃɒd] (horse) herrar
shoebrush [ˈʃuːbrʌʃ] n cepillo para zapatos
shoehorn [ˈʃuːhɔːn] n calzador m
shoelace [ˈʃuːleɪs] n cordón m
shoemaker [ˈʃuːmeɪkər] n zapatero(-a)
shoe polish n betún m
shoeshop [ˈʃuːʃɒp] n zapatería
shoestring [ˈʃuːstrɪŋ] n (shoelace) cordón m; (fig): **on a ~** con muy poco dinero, a lo barato
shone [ʃɒn] pt, pp of **shine**
shoo [ʃuː] excl ¡fuera!; (to animals) ¡zape! ■ vt (also: **shoo away, shoo off**) ahuyentar
shook [ʃʊk] pt of **shake**
shoot [ʃuːt] (pt, pp **shot**) n (on branch, seedling) retoño, vástago; (shooting party) cacería; (competition) concurso de tiro; (preserve) coto de caza ■ vt disparar; (kill) matar a tiros; (execute) fusilar; (Cine: film, scene) rodar, filmar ■ vi (Football) chutar; **to ~ (at)** tirar (a); **to ~ past** pasar como un rayo; **to ~ in/out** vi entrar corriendo/salir disparado
▶ **shoot down** vt (plane) derribar
▶ **shoot up** vi (prices) dispararse
shooting [ˈʃuːtɪŋ] n (shots) tiros mpl, tiroteo; (Hunting) caza con escopeta; (act: murder) asesinato (a tiros); (Cine) rodaje m
shooting star n estrella fugaz
shop [ʃɒp] n tienda; (workshop) taller m ■ vi (also: **go shopping**) ir de compras; **to talk ~** (fig) hablar del trabajo; **repair ~** taller m de reparaciones
▶ **shop around** vi comparar precios
shopaholic [ˈʃɒpəˈhɒlɪk] n (col) adicto(-a) a las compras
shop assistant n (Brit) dependiente(-a) m(f)
shop floor n (Brit fig) taller m, fábrica
shopkeeper [ˈʃɒpkiːpər] n (Brit) tendero(-a)
shoplift [ˈʃɒplɪft] vi robar en las tiendas
shoplifter [ˈʃɒplɪftər] n ratero(-a)
shoplifting [ˈʃɒplɪftɪŋ] n ratería, robo (en las tiendas)
shopper [ˈʃɒpər] n comprador(a) m(f)
shopping [ˈʃɒpɪŋ] n (goods) compras fpl
shopping bag n bolsa (de compras)
shopping centre, shopping center (US) n centro comercial
shopping mall n centro comercial
shop-soiled [ˈʃɒpsɔɪld] adj (Brit) usado

shop steward n (Brit Industry) enlace m/f sindical
shop window n escaparate m, vidriera (LAm)
shopworn [ˈʃɒpwɔːn] adj (US) usado
shore [ʃɔːr] n (of sea, lake) orilla ■ vt: **to ~ (up)** reforzar; **on ~** en tierra
shore leave n (Naut) permiso para bajar a tierra
shorn [ʃɔːn] pp of **shear**
short [ʃɔːt] adj (not long) corto; (in time) breve, de corta duración; (person) bajo; (curt) brusco, seco ■ vi (Elec) ponerse en cortocircuito ■ n (also: **short film**) cortometraje m; (a pair of) **shorts** (unos) pantalones mpl cortos; **to be ~ of sth** estar falto de algo; **in ~** en pocas palabras; **a ~ time ago** hace poco (tiempo); **in the ~ term** a corto plazo; **to be in ~ supply** escasear, haber escasez de; **I'm ~ of time** me falta tiempo; **~ of doing ...** a menos que hagamos etc ...; **everything ~ of ...** todo menos ...; **it is ~ for** es la forma abreviada de; **to cut ~** (speech, visit) interrumpir, terminar inesperadamente; **to fall ~ of** no alcanzar; **to run ~ of sth** acabársele algo; **to stop ~** parar en seco; **to stop ~ of** detenerse antes de
shortage [ˈʃɔːtɪdʒ] n escasez f, falta
shortbread [ˈʃɔːtbred] n pasta de mantequilla
short-change [ʃɔːtˈtʃeɪndʒ] vt: **to ~ sb** no dar el cambio completo a algn
short-circuit [ʃɔːtˈsəːkɪt] n cortocircuito ■ vt poner en cortocircuito ■ vi ponerse, en cortocircuito
shortcoming [ˈʃɔːtkʌmɪŋ] n defecto, deficiencia
shortcrust pastry [ˈʃɔːtkrʌst-], **short pastry** n (Brit) pasta quebradiza
shortcut [ˈʃɔːtkʌt] n atajo
shorten [ˈʃɔːtn] vt acortar; (visit) interrumpir
shortfall [ˈʃɔːtfɔːl] n déficit m, deficiencia
shorthand [ˈʃɔːthænd] n (Brit) taquigrafía; **to take sth down in ~** taquigrafiar algo
shorthand notebook n cuaderno de taquigrafía
shorthand typist n (Brit) taquimecanógrafo(-a)
short list n (Brit: for job) lista de candidatos pre-seleccionados
short-lived [ˈʃɔːtˈlɪvd] adj efímero
shortly [ˈʃɔːtlɪ] adv en breve, dentro de poco
shortness [ˈʃɔːtnɪs] n (of distance) cortedad f; (of time) brevedad f; (manner) brusquedad f
short-sighted [ʃɔːtˈsaɪtɪd] adj (Brit) miope, corto de vista; (fig) imprudente
short-sightedness [ʃɔːtˈsaɪtɪdnɪs] n miopía; (fig) falta de previsión, imprudencia

short-staffed [ʃɔːtˈstɑːft] *adj* falto de personal

short story *n* cuento

short-tempered [ʃɔːtˈtɛmpəd] *adj* enojadizo

short-term [ˈʃɔːttəːm] *adj* (*effect*) a corto plazo

short time *n*: **to work ~, be on ~** (*Industry*) trabajar con sistema de horario reducido

short-time working [ˈʃɔːttaɪm-] *n* trabajo de horario reducido

short wave *n* (*Radio*) onda corta

shot [ʃɔt] *pt, pp of* **shoot** ■ *n* (*sound*) tiro, disparo; (*person*) tirador(a) *m(f)*; (*try*) tentativa; (*injection*) inyección *f*; (*Phot*) toma, fotografía; (*shotgun pellets*) perdigones *mpl*; **to fire a ~ at sb/sth** tirar *or* disparar contra algn/algo; **to have a ~ at (doing) sth** probar suerte con algo; **like a ~** (*without any delay*) como un rayo; **a big ~** (*col*) un pez gordo; **to get ~ of sth/sb** (*col*) deshacerse de algo/algn, quitarse algo/a algn de encima

shotgun [ˈʃɔtgʌn] *n* escopeta

should [ʃud] *aux vb*: **I ~ go now** debo irme ahora; **he ~ be there now** debe de haber llegado (ya); **I ~ go if I were you** yo en tu lugar me iría; **I ~ like to** me gustaría; **~ he phone ...** si llamara ..., en caso de que llamase ...

shoulder [ˈʃəʊldəʳ] *n* hombro; (*Brit: of road*): **hard ~** arcén *m* ■ *vt* (*fig*) cargar con; **to look over one's ~** mirar hacia atrás; **to rub shoulders with sb** (*fig*) codearse con algn; **to give sb the cold ~** (*fig*) dar de lado a algn

shoulder bag *n* bolso de bandolera

shoulder blade *n* omóplato

shoulder strap *n* tirante *m*

shouldn't [ˈʃudnt] = **should not**

shout [ʃaut] *n* grito ■ *vt* gritar ■ *vi* gritar, dar voces

▶ **shout down** *vt* hundir a gritos

shouting [ˈʃautɪŋ] *n* griterío

shouting match *n* (*col*) discusión *f* a voz en grito

shove [ʃʌv] *n* empujón *m* ■ *vt* empujar; (*col: put*): **to ~ sth in** meter algo a empellones; **he shoved me out of the way** me quitó de en medio de un empujón

▶ **shove off** *vi* (*Naut*) alejarse del muelle; (*fig: col*) largarse

shovel [ˈʃʌvl] *n* pala; (*mechanical*) excavadora ■ *vt* mover con pala

show [ʃəu] (*pt* **showed**, *pp* **shown**) *n* (*of emotion*) demostración *f*; (*semblance*) apariencia; (*Comm, Tech: exhibition*) exhibición *f*, exposición *f*; (*Theat*) función *f*, espectáculo; (*organization*) negocio, empresa ■ *vt* mostrar, enseñar; (*courage etc*) mostrar, manifestar; (*exhibit*) exponer; (*film*) proyectar ■ *vi*

mostrarse; (*appear*) aparecer; **on ~** (*exhibits etc*) expuesto; **to be on ~** estar expuesto; **it's just for ~** es sólo para impresionar; **to ask for a ~ of hands** pedir una votación a mano alzada; **who's running the ~ here?** ¿quién manda aquí?; **to ~ a profit/loss** (*Comm*) arrojar un saldo positivo/negativo; **I have nothing to ~ for it** no saqué ningún provecho (de ello); **to ~ sb to his seat/to the door** acompañar a algn a su asiento/a la puerta; **as shown in the illustration** como se ve en el grabado; **it just goes to ~ that ...** queda demostrado que ...; **it doesn't ~** no se ve *or* nota

▶ **show in** *vt* (*person*) hacer pasar

▶ **show off** *vi* (*pej*) presumir ■ *vt* (*display*) lucir; (*pej*) hacer alarde de

▶ **show out** *vt*: **to ~ sb out** acompañar a algn a la puerta

▶ **show up** *vi* (*stand out*) destacar; (*col: turn up*) presentarse ■ *vt* descubrir; (*unmask*) desenmascarar

showbiz [ˈʃəubɪz] *n* (*col*) = **show business**

show business *n* el mundo del espectáculo

showcase [ˈʃəukeɪs] *n* vitrina; (*fig*) escaparate *m*

showdown [ˈʃəudaun] *n* crisis *f*, momento decisivo

shower [ˈʃauəʳ] *n* (*rain*) chaparrón *m*, chubasco; (*of stones etc*) lluvia; (*also:* **shower bath**) ducha ■ *vi* llover ■ *vt*: **to ~ sb with sth** colmar a algn de algo; **to have** *or* **take a ~** ducharse

shower cap *n* gorro de baño

shower gel *n* gel de ducha

showerproof [ˈʃauəpruːf] *adj* impermeable

showery [ˈʃauərɪ] *adj* (*weather*) lluvioso

showground [ˈʃəugraund] *n* ferial *m*, real *m* (de la feria)

showing [ˈʃəuɪŋ] *n* (*of film*) proyección *f*

show jumping *n* hípica

showman [ˈʃəumən] *n* (*at fair, circus*) empresario (de espectáculos); (*fig*) actor *m* consumado

showmanship [ˈʃəumənʃɪp] *n* dotes *fpl* teatrales

shown [ʃəun] *pp of* **show**

show-off [ˈʃəuɔf] *n* (*col: person*) fantasmón(-ona) *m(f)*

showpiece [ˈʃəupiːs] *n* (*of exhibition etc*) objeto más valioso, joya; **that hospital is a ~** ese hospital es un modelo del género

showroom [ˈʃəuruːm] *n* sala de muestras

show trial *n* juicio propagandístico

showy [ˈʃəuɪ] *adj* ostentoso

shrank [ʃræŋk] *pt of* **shrink**

shrapnel [ˈʃræpnl] *n* metralla

shred [ʃrɛd] n (gen pl) triza, jirón m; (fig: of truth, evidence) pizca, chispa ■ vt hacer trizas; (documents) triturar; (Culin) desmenuzar

shredder ['ʃrɛdəʳ] n (vegetable shredder) picadora; (document shredder) trituradora (de papel)

shrewd [ʃru:d] adj astuto

shrewdly ['ʃru:dlɪ] adv astutamente

shrewdness ['ʃru:dnɪs] n astucia

shriek [ʃri:k] n chillido ■ vt, vi chillar

shrill [ʃrɪl] adj agudo, estridente

shrimp [ʃrɪmp] n camarón m

shrine [ʃraɪn] n santuario, sepulcro

shrink (pt **shrank**, pp **shrunk**) [ʃrɪŋk, ʃræŋk, ʃrʌŋk] vi encogerse; (be reduced) reducirse ■ vt encoger; **to ~ from (doing) sth** no atreverse a hacer algo

▶ **shrink away** vi retroceder, retirarse

shrinkage ['ʃrɪŋkɪdʒ] n encogimiento; reducción f; (Comm: in shops) pérdidas fpl

shrink-wrap ['ʃrɪŋkræp] vt empaquetar en envase termoretráctil

shrivel ['ʃrɪvl] (also: **shrivel up**) vt (dry) secar; (crease) arrugar ■ vi secarse; arrugarse

shroud [ʃraud] n sudario ■ vt: **shrouded in mystery** envuelto en el misterio

Shrove Tuesday ['ʃrəuv-] n martes m de carnaval

shrub [ʃrʌb] n arbusto

shrubbery ['ʃrʌbərɪ] n arbustos mpl

shrug [ʃrʌg] n encogimiento de hombros ■ vt, vi: **to ~ (one's shoulders)** encogerse de hombros

▶ **shrug off** vt negar importancia a; (cold, illness) deshacerse de

shrunk [ʃrʌŋk] pp of **shrink**

shrunken ['ʃrʌŋkn] adj encogido

shudder ['ʃʌdəʳ] n estremecimiento, escalofrío ■ vi estremecerse

shuffle ['ʃʌfl] vt (cards) barajar; **to ~ (one's feet)** arrastrar los pies

shun [ʃʌn] vt rehuir, esquivar

shunt [ʃʌnt] vt (Rail) maniobrar

shunting yard ['ʃʌntɪŋ-] n estación f de maniobras

shut (pt, pp **~**) [ʃʌt] vt cerrar ■ vi cerrarse

▶ **shut down** vt, vi cerrar; (machine) parar

▶ **shut off** vt (stop: power, water supply etc) interrumpir, cortar; (engine) parar

▶ **shut out** vt (person) excluir, dejar fuera; (noise, cold) no dejar entrar; (block: view) tapar; (memory) tratar de olvidar

▶ **shut up** vi (col: keep quiet) callarse ■ vt (close) cerrar; (silence) callar

shutdown ['ʃʌtdaun] n cierre m

shutter ['ʃʌtəʳ] n contraventana; (Phot) obturador m

shuttle ['ʃʌtl] n lanzadera; (also: **shuttle service**: Aviat) puente m aéreo ■ vi (vehicle, person) ir y venir ■ vt (passengers) transportar, trasladar

shuttlecock ['ʃʌtlkɔk] n volante m

shuttle diplomacy n viajes mpl diplomáticos

shy [ʃaɪ] adj tímido ■ vi: **to ~ away from doing sth** (fig) rehusar hacer algo; **to be ~ of doing sth** esquivar hacer algo

shyly ['ʃaɪlɪ] adv tímidamente

shyness ['ʃaɪnɪs] n timidez f

Siam [saɪ'æm] n Siam m

Siamese [saɪə'mi:z] adj siamés(-esa) ■ n (person) siamés(-esa) m(f); (Ling) siamés m; **~ cat** gato siamés; **~ twins** gemelos(-as) m(f)pl siameses(-as)

Siberia [saɪ'bɪərɪə] n Siberia

sibling ['sɪblɪŋ] n (formal) hermano(-a)

Sicilian [sɪ'sɪlɪən] adj, n siciliano(-a) m(f)

Sicily ['sɪsɪlɪ] n Sicilia

sick [sɪk] adj (ill) enfermo; (nauseated) mareado; (humour) morboso; **to be ~** (Brit) vomitar; **to feel ~** estar mareado; **to be ~ of** (fig) estar harto de; **a ~ person** un(a) enfermo(-a); **to be (off) ~** estar ausente por enfermedad; **to fall** or **take ~** ponerse enfermo

sickbag ['sɪkbæg] n bolsa para el mareo

sick bay n enfermería

sickbed ['sɪkbɛd] n lecho de enfermo

sick building syndrome n enfermedad causada por falta de ventilación y luz natural en un edificio

sicken ['sɪkn] vt dar asco a ■ vi enfermar; **to be sickening for** (cold, flu etc) mostrar síntomas de

sickening ['sɪknɪŋ] adj (fig) asqueroso

sickle ['sɪkl] n hoz f

sick leave n baja por enfermedad

sickle-cell anaemia ['sɪklsɛl-] n anemia de células falciformes, drepanocitosis f

sick list n: **to be on the ~** estar de baja

sickly ['sɪklɪ] adj enfermizo; (taste) empalagoso

sickness ['sɪknɪs] n enfermedad f, mal m; (vomiting) náuseas fpl

sickness benefit n subsidio de enfermedad

sick pay n prestación por enfermedad pagada por la empresa

sickroom ['sɪkru:m] n cuarto del enfermo

side [saɪd] n (gen) lado; (face, surface) cara; (of paper) cara; (slice of bread) rebanada; (of body) costado; (of animal) ijar m, ijada; (of lake) orilla; (part) lado; (aspect) aspecto; (team: Sport) equipo; (: Pol etc) partido; (of hill) ladera ■ adj (door, entrance) lateral ■ vi: **to ~ with sb** ponerse de parte de algn; **by the ~ of** al lado de; **~ by ~** juntos(-as); **from all sides**

S

de todos lados; **to take sides (with)** tomar partido (por); ~ **of beef** flanco de vaca; **the right/wrong** ~ el derecho/revés; **from ~ to ~** de un lado a otro

sideboard ['saɪdbɔːd] n aparador m

sideboards ['saɪdbɔːdz], (Brit) **sideburns** ['saɪdbəːnz] npl patillas fpl

sidecar ['saɪdkɑːʳ] n sidecar m

side dish n entremés m

side drum n (Mus) tamboril m

side effect n efecto secundario

sidekick ['saɪdkɪk] n compinche m

sidelight ['saɪdlaɪt] n (Aut) luz f lateral

sideline ['saɪdlaɪn] n (Sport) línea lateral; (fig) empleo suplementario

sidelong ['saɪdlɔŋ] adj de soslayo; **to give a ~ glance at sth** mirar algo de reojo

side plate n platito

side road n (Brit) calle f lateral

sidesaddle ['saɪdsædl] adv a la amazona

side show n (stall) caseta; (fig) atracción f secundaria

sidestep ['saɪdstɛp] vt (question) eludir; (problem) esquivar ▪ vi (Boxing etc) dar un quiebro

side street n calle f lateral

sidetrack ['saɪdtræk] vt (fig) desviar (de su propósito)

sidewalk ['saɪdwɔːk] n (US) acera, vereda (LAm), andén m (LAm), banqueta (LAm)

sideways ['saɪdweɪz] adv de lado

siding ['saɪdɪŋ] n (Rail) apartadero, vía muerta

sidle ['saɪdl] vi: **to ~ up (to)** acercarse furtivamente (a)

SIDS [sɪdz] n abbr (= sudden infant death syndrome) (síndrome m de la) muerte f súbita

siege [siːdʒ] n cerco, sitio; **to lay ~ to** cercar, sitiar

siege economy n economía de sitio or de asedio

Sierra Leone [sɪˈɛrəlɪˈəun] n Sierra Leona

siesta [sɪˈɛstə] n siesta

sieve [sɪv] n colador m ▪ vt cribar

sift [sɪft] vt cribar ▪ vi: **to ~ through** pasar por una criba; (information) analizar cuidadosamente

sigh [saɪ] n suspiro ▪ vi suspirar

sight [saɪt] n (faculty) vista; (spectacle) espectáculo; (on gun) mira, alza ▪ vt ver, divisar; **in ~** a la vista; **out of ~** fuera de (la) vista; **at ~** a la vista; **at first ~** a primera vista; **to lose ~ of sth/sb** perder algo/a algn de vista; **to catch ~ of sth/sb** divisar algo/a algn; **I know her by ~** la conozco de vista; **to set one's sights on (doing) sth** aspirar a or ambicionar (hacer) algo

sighted ['saɪtɪd] adj vidente, de vista normal; **partially ~** de vista limitada

sightseeing ['saɪtsiːɪŋ] n excursionismo, turismo; **to go ~** visitar monumentos

sightseer ['saɪtsiːəʳ] n excursionista m/f, turista m/f

sign [saɪn] n (with hand) señal f, seña; (trace) huella, rastro; (notice) letrero; (written) signo; (also: **road sign**) indicador m; (: with instructions) señal f de tráfico ▪ vt firmar; **as a ~ of** en señal de; **it's a good/bad ~ es** buena/mala señal; **plus/minus ~** signo de más/de menos; **to ~ one's name** firmar

  ▸ **sign away** vt (rights etc) ceder

  ▸ **sign off** vi (Radio, TV) cerrar el programa

  ▸ **sign on** vi (Mil) alistarse; (as unemployed) apuntarse al paro; (employee) firmar un contrato ▪ vt (Mil) alistar; (employee) contratar; **to ~ on for a course** matricularse en un curso

  ▸ **sign out** vi firmar el registro (al salir)

  ▸ **sign over** vt: **to ~ sth over to sb** traspasar algo a algn

  ▸ **sign up** vi (Mil) alistarse ▪ vt (contract) contratar

signal ['sɪgnl] n señal f ▪ vi (Aut) señalizar ▪ vt (person) hacer señas a; (message) transmitir; **the engaged ~** (Tel) la señal de comunicando; **the ~ is very weak** (TV) no captamos bien el canal; **to ~ a left/right turn** (Aut) indicar que se va a doblar a la izquierda/derecha; **to ~ to sb (to do sth)** hacer señas a algn (para que haga algo)

signal box n (Rail) garita de señales

signalman ['sɪgnlmən] n (Rail) guardavía m

signatory ['sɪgnətərɪ] n firmante m/f

signature ['sɪgnətʃəʳ] n firma

signature tune n sintonía

signet ring ['sɪgnət-] n (anillo de) sello

significance [sɪgˈnɪfɪkəns] n significado; (importance) trascendencia; **that is of no ~** eso no tiene importancia

significant [sɪgˈnɪfɪkənt] adj significativo; trascendente; **it is ~ that ...** es significativo que ...

significantly [sɪgˈnɪfɪkəntlɪ] adv (smile) expresivamente; (improve, increase) sensiblemente; **and, ~ ...** y debe notarse que ...

signify ['sɪgnɪfaɪ] vt significar

sign language n mímica, lenguaje m por or de señas

signpost ['saɪnpəust] n indicador m

silage ['saɪlɪdʒ] n ensilaje m

silence ['saɪlns] n silencio ▪ vt hacer callar; (guns) reducir al silencio

silencer ['saɪlnsə^r] *n* silenciador *m*
silent ['saɪlnt] *adj* (*gen*) silencioso; (*not speaking*) callado; (*film*) mudo; **to keep** *or* **remain ~** guardar silencio
silently ['saɪlntlɪ] *adv* silenciosamente, en silencio
silent partner *n* (*Comm*) socio(-a) comanditario(-a)
silhouette [sɪlu:'ɛt] *n* silueta; **silhouetted against** destacado sobre *or* contra
silicon ['sɪlɪkən] *n* silicio
silicon chip *n* chip *m*, plaqueta de silicio
silicone ['sɪlɪkəun] *n* silicona
silk [sɪlk] *n* seda ▪ *cpd* de seda
silky ['sɪlkɪ] *adj* sedoso
sill [sɪl] *n* (*also*: **windowsill**) alféizar *m*; (*Aut*) umbral *m*
silliness ['sɪlɪnɪs] *n* (*of person*) necedad *f*; (*of idea*) lo absurdo
silly ['sɪlɪ] *adj* (*person*) tonto; (*idea*) absurdo; **to do sth ~** hacer una tontería
silo ['saɪləu] *n* silo
silt [sɪlt] *n* sedimento
silver ['sɪlvə^r] *n* plata; (*money*) moneda suelta ▪ *adj* de plata
silver paper, (*Brit*) **silver foil** *n* papel *m* de plata
silver-plated [sɪlvə'pleɪtɪd] *adj* plateado
silversmith ['sɪlvəsmɪθ] *n* platero(-a)
silverware ['sɪlvəwɛə^r] *n* plata
silver wedding, silver wedding anniversary *n* (*Brit*) bodas *fpl* de plata
silvery ['sɪlvrɪ] *adj* plateado
SIM card ['sɪm-] *n* (*Tel*) SIM card *m o f*, tarjeta SIM
similar ['sɪmɪlə^r] *adj*: **~ to** parecido *or* semejante a
similarity [sɪmɪ'lærɪtɪ] *n* parecido, semejanza
similarly ['sɪmɪləlɪ] *adv* del mismo modo; (*in a similar way*) de manera parecida; (*equally*) igualmente
simile ['sɪmɪlɪ] *n* símil *m*
simmer ['sɪmə^r] *vi* hervir a fuego lento
▶ **simmer down** *vi* (*fig, col*) calmarse, tranquilizarse
simpering ['sɪmpərɪŋ] *adj* afectado; (*foolish*) bobo
simple ['sɪmpl] *adj* (*easy*) sencillo; (*foolish*) simple; (*Comm*) simple; **the ~ truth** la pura verdad
simple interest *n* (*Comm*) interés *m* simple
simple-minded [sɪmpl'maɪndɪd] *adj* simple, ingenuo
simpleton ['sɪmpltən] *n* inocentón(-ona) *m(f)*
simplicity [sɪm'plɪsɪtɪ] *n* sencillez *f*; (*foolishness*) ingenuidad *f*

simplification [sɪmplɪfɪ'keɪʃən] *n* simplificación *f*
simplify ['sɪmplɪfaɪ] *vt* simplificar
simply ['sɪmplɪ] *adv* (*in a simple way: live, talk*) sencillamente; (*just, merely*) sólo
simulate ['sɪmjuleɪt] *vt* simular
simulation [sɪmju'leɪʃən] *n* simulación *f*
simultaneous [sɪməl'teɪnɪəs] *adj* simultáneo
simultaneously [sɪməl'teɪnɪəslɪ] *adv* simultáneamente, a la vez
sin [sɪn] *n* pecado ▪ *vi* pecar
since [sɪns] *adv* desde entonces ▪ *prep* desde ▪ *conj* (*time*) desde que; (*because*) ya que, puesto que; **~ then** desde entonces; **~ Monday** desde el lunes; (**ever**) **~ I arrived** desde que llegué
sincere [sɪn'sɪə^r] *adj* sincero
sincerely [sɪn'sɪəlɪ] *adv* sinceramente; **yours ~** (*in letters*) le saluda (afectuosamente); **~ yours** (*US: in letters*) le saluda atentamente
sincerity [sɪn'sɛrɪtɪ] *n* sinceridad *f*
sinecure ['saɪnɪkjuə^r] *n* chollo
sinew ['sɪnju:] *n* tendón *m*
sinful ['sɪnful] *adj* (*thought*) pecaminoso; (*person*) pecador(a)
sing (*pt* **sang**, *pp* **sung**) [sɪŋ, sæŋ, sʌŋ] *vt* cantar ▪ *vi* (*gen*) cantar; (*bird*) trinar; (*ears*) zumbar
Singapore [sɪŋə'pɔ:^{r}] *n* Singapur *m*
singe [sɪndʒ] *vt* chamuscar
singer ['sɪŋə^r] *n* cantante *m/f*
Singhalese [sɪŋə'li:z] *adj* = **Sinhalese**
singing ['sɪŋɪŋ] *n* (*of person, bird*) canto; (*songs*) canciones *fpl*; (*in the ears*) zumbido; (*of kettle*) silbido
single ['sɪŋgl] *adj* único, solo; (*unmarried*) soltero; (*not double*) individual, sencillo ▪ *n* (*Brit: also*: **single ticket**) billete *m* sencillo; (*record*) sencillo, single *m*; **singles** *npl* (*Tennis*) individual *msg*; **not a ~ one was left** no quedaba ni uno; **every ~ day** todos los días (sin excepción)
▶ **single out** *vt* (*choose*) escoger; (*point out*) singularizar
single bed *n* cama individual
single-breasted [sɪŋgl'brɛstɪd] *adj* (*jacket, suit*) recto, sin cruzar
single-entry book-keeping ['sɪŋglɛntrɪ-] *n* contabilidad *f* por partida simple
Single European Market *n*: **the ~** el Mercado Único Europeo
single file *n*: **in ~** en fila de uno
single-handed [sɪŋgl'hændɪd] *adv* sin ayuda
single-minded [sɪŋgl'maɪndɪd] *adj* resuelto, firme
single parent *n* (*mother*) madre *f* soltera; (*father*) padre *m* soltero

single-parent family ['sɪŋglpɛərənt-] *n* familia monoparental

single room *n* habitación *f* individual

singles bar *n* (*esp US*) bar *m* para solteros

single-sex school ['sɪŋglsɛks-] *n* escuela no mixta

single-sided [sɪŋgl'saɪdɪd] *adj* (*Comput: disk*) de una cara

single spacing *n* (*Typ*): **in ~** a un espacio

singlet ['sɪŋglɪt] *n* camiseta

singly ['sɪŋglɪ] *adv* uno por uno

singsong ['sɪŋsɔn] *adj* (*tone*) cantarín(-ina) ■ *n* (*songs*): **to have a ~** tener un concierto improvisado

singular ['sɪŋgjulər] *adj* singular, extraordinario; (*odd*) extraño; (*Ling*) singular ■ *n* (*Ling*) singular *m*; **in the feminine ~** en femenino singular

singularly ['sɪŋgjulǝlɪ] *adv* singularmente, extraordinariamente

Sinhalese [sɪnhǝ'liːz] *adj* singhalese

sinister ['sɪnɪstər] *adj* siniestro

sink [sɪŋk] (*pt* **sank**, *pp* **sunk**) *n* fregadero ■ *vt* (*ship*) hundir, echar a pique; (*foundations*) excavar; (*piles etc*): **to ~ sth into** hundir algo en ■ *vi* (*gen*) hundirse; **he sank into a chair/the mud** se dejó caer en una silla/se hundió en el barro; **the shares** *or* **share prices have sunk to three dollars** las acciones han bajado a tres dólares
  ▶ **sink in** *vi* (*fig*) penetrar, calar; **the news took a long time to ~ in** la noticia tardó mucho en hacer mella en él (*or* mí *etc*)

sinking ['sɪŋkɪŋ] *adj*: **that ~ feeling** la sensación esa de desmoralización

sinking fund *n* fondo de amortización

sink unit *n* fregadero

sinner ['sɪnǝr] *n* pecador(a) *m(f)*

Sinn Féin [ʃɪn'feɪn] *n* partido político republicano de Irlanda del Norte

sinuous ['sɪnjuǝs] *adj* sinuoso

sinus ['saɪnǝs] *n* (*Anat*) seno

sip [sɪp] *n* sorbo ■ *vt* sorber, beber a sorbitos

siphon ['saɪfǝn] *n* sifón *m* ■ *vt* (*also*: **siphon off**: *funds*) desviar

sir [sǝːr] *n* señor *m*; **S~ John Smith** el Señor John Smith; **yes ~** sí, señor; **Dear S~** (*in letter*) Muy señor mío, Estimado Señor; **Dear Sirs** Muy señores nuestros, Estimados Señores

siren ['saɪǝrn] *n* sirena

sirloin ['sǝːlɔɪn] *n* solomillo

sirloin steak *n* filete *m* de solomillo

sisal ['saɪsǝl] *n* pita, henequén *m* (*LAm*)

sissy ['sɪsɪ] *n* (*col*) marica *m*

sister ['sɪstǝr] *n* hermana; (*Brit: nurse*) enfermera jefe

sister-in-law ['sɪstǝrɪnlɔː] *n* cuñada

sister organization *n* organización *f* hermana

sister ship *n* barco gemelo

sit (*pt, pp* **sat**) [sɪt, sæt] *vi* sentarse; (*be sitting*) estar sentado; (*assembly*) reunirse; (*dress etc*) caer, sentar ■ *vt* (*exam*) presentarse a; **that jacket sits well** esa chaqueta sienta bien; **to ~ on a committee** ser miembro de una comisión *or* un comité
  ▶ **sit about, sit around** *vi* holgazanear
  ▶ **sit back** *vi* (*in seat*) recostarse
  ▶ **sit down** *vi* sentarse; **to be sitting down** estar sentado
  ▶ **sit in on** *vt fus*: **to ~ in on a discussion** asistir a una discusión
  ▶ **sit up** *vi* incorporarse; (*not go to bed*) no acostarse

sitcom ['sɪtkɔm] *n abbr* (*TV*: = *situation comedy*) telecomedia

sit-down ['sɪtdaun] *adj*: **~ strike** huelga de brazos caídos; **a ~ meal** una comida sentada

site [saɪt] *n* sitio; (*also*: **building site**) solar *m* ■ *vt* situar

sit-in ['sɪtɪn] *n* (*demonstration*) sentada *f*

siting ['saɪtɪŋ] *n* (*location*) situación *f*, emplazamiento

sitter ['sɪtǝr] *n* (*Art*) modelo *m/f*; (*babysitter*) canguro *m/f*

sitting ['sɪtɪŋ] *n* (*of assembly etc*) sesión *f*; (*in canteen*) turno

sitting member *n* (*Pol*) titular *m/f* de un escaño

sitting room *n* sala de estar

sitting tenant *n* inquilino con derechos de estancia en una vivienda

situate ['sɪtjueɪt] *vt* situar, ubicar (*LAm*)

situated ['sɪtjueɪtɪd] *adj* situado, ubicado (*LAm*)

situation [sɪtju'eɪʃǝn] *n* situación *f*; **"situations vacant"** (*Brit*) "ofertas de trabajo"

situation comedy *n* (*TV, Radio*) serie *f* cómica, comedia de situación

six [sɪks] *num* seis

six-pack ['sɪkspæk] *n* (*esp US*) paquete *m* de seis cervezas

sixteen [sɪks'tiːn] *num* dieciséis

sixth [sɪksθ] *adj* sexto; **the upper/lower ~** (*Scol*) el séptimo/sexto año

sixty ['sɪkstɪ] *num* sesenta

size [saɪz] *n* (*gen*) tamaño; (*extent*) extensión *f*; (*of clothing*) talla; (*of shoes*) número; **I take ~ 5 shoes** calzo el número cinco; **I take ~ 14** mi talla es la 42; **I'd like the small/large ~** (*of soap powder etc*) quisiera el tamaño pequeño/grande
  ▶ **size up** *vt* formarse una idea de

sizeable ['saɪzəbl] *adj* importante, considerable

sizzle ['sɪzl] *vi* crepitar

SK *abbr* (*Canada*) = **Saskatchewan**

skate [skeɪt] *n* patín *m*; (*fish: pl inv*) raya ▪ *vi* patinar

▶ **skate over, skate round** *vt fus* (*problem, issue*) pasar por alto

skateboard ['skeɪtbɔ:d] *n* monopatín *m*

skater ['skeɪtər] *n* patinador(a) *m(f)*

skating ['skeɪtɪŋ] *n* patinaje *m*

skating rink *n* pista de patinaje

skeleton ['skelɪtn] *n* esqueleto; (*Tech*) armazón *m*; (*outline*) esquema *m*

skeleton key *n* llave *f* maestra

skeleton staff *n* personal *m* reducido

skeptic *etc* ['skeptɪk] (*US*) = **sceptic** *etc*

sketch [sketʃ] *n* (*drawing*) dibujo; (*outline*) esbozo, bosquejo; (*Theat*) pieza corta ▪ *vt* dibujar; esbozar

sketch book *n* bloc *m* de dibujo

sketch pad *n* bloc *m* de dibujo

sketchy ['sketʃɪ] *adj* incompleto

skewer ['skju:ər] *n* broqueta

ski [ski:] *n* esquí *m* ▪ *vi* esquiar

ski boot *n* bota de esquí

skid [skɪd] *n* patinazo ▪ *vi* patinar; **to go into a ~** comenzar a patinar

skid mark *n* señal *f* de patinazo

skier ['ski:ər] *n* esquiador(a) *m(f)*

skiing ['ski:ɪŋ] *n* esquí *m*; **to go ~** practicar el esquí, (ir a) esquiar

ski instructor *n* instructor(a) *m(f)* de esquí

ski jump *n* pista para salto de esquí

● **skilful, skillful** (*US*) ['skɪlful] *adj* diestro, experto

skilfully, skillfully (*US*) ['skɪlfulɪ] *adv* hábilmente, con destreza

ski lift *n* telesilla *m*, telesquí *m*

skill [skɪl] *n* destreza, pericia; (*technique*) arte *m*, técnica; **there's a certain ~ to doing it** se necesita cierta habilidad para hacerlo

skilled [skɪld] *adj* hábil, diestro; (*worker*) cualificado

skillet ['skɪlɪt] *n* sartén *f* pequeña

skillful *etc* ['skɪlful] (*US*) = **skilful** *etc*

skim [skɪm] *vt* (*milk*) desnatar; (*glide over*) rozar, rasar ▪ *vi*: **to ~ through** (*book*) hojear

skimmed milk [skɪmd-] *n* leche *f* desnatada *or* descremada

skimp [skɪmp] *vt* (*work*) chapucear; (*cloth etc*) escatimar; **to ~ on** (*material etc*) economizar; (*work*) escatimar

skimpy ['skɪmpɪ] *adj* (*meagre*) escaso; (*skirt*) muy corto

skin [skɪn] *n* (*gen*) piel *f*; (*complexion*) cutis *m*; (*of fruit, vegetable*) piel *f*, cáscara; (*crust: on pudding, paint*) nata ▪ *vt* (*fruit etc*) pelar; (*animal*) despellejar; **wet** *or* **soaked to the ~** calado hasta los huesos

skin cancer *n* cáncer *m* de piel

skin-deep ['skɪn'di:p] *adj* superficial

skin diver *n* buceador(a) *m(f)*

skin diving *n* buceo

skinflint ['skɪnflɪnt] *n* tacaño(-a), roñoso(-a)

skinhead ['skɪnhed] *n* cabeza *m/f* rapada, skin(head) *m/f*

skinny ['skɪnɪ] *adj* flaco, magro

skintight ['skɪntaɪt] *adj* (*dress etc*) muy ajustado

skip [skɪp] *n* brinco, salto; (*container*) contenedor *m* ▪ *vi* brincar; (*with rope*) saltar a la comba ▪ *vt* (*pass over*) omitir, saltar

ski pants *npl* pantalones *mpl* de esquí

ski pole *n* bastón *m* de esquiar

skipper ['skɪpər] *n* (*Naut, Sport*) capitán *m*

skipping rope ['skɪpɪŋ-] *n* (*Brit*) comba, cuerda (de saltar)

ski resort *n* estación *f* de esquí

skirmish ['skə:mɪʃ] *n* escaramuza

skirt [skə:t] *n* falda, pollera (*LAm*) ▪ *vt* (*surround*) ceñir, rodear; (*go round*) ladear

skirting board ['skə:tɪŋ-] *n* (*Brit*) rodapié *m*

ski run *n* pista de esquí

ski suit *n* traje *m* de esquiar

skit [skɪt] *n* sátira, parodia

ski tow *n* arrastre *m* (de esquí)

skittle ['skɪtl] *n* bolo; **skittles** (*game*) boliche *m*

skive [skaɪv] *vi* (*Brit: col*) gandulear

skulk [skʌlk] *vi* esconderse

skull [skʌl] *n* calavera; (*Anat*) cráneo

skullcap ['skʌlkæp] *n* (*worn by Jews*) casquete *m*; (*worn by Pope*) solideo

skunk [skʌŋk] *n* mofeta

sky [skaɪ] *n* cielo; **to praise sb to the skies** poner a algn por las nubes

sky-blue [skaɪ'blu:] *adj* (azul) celeste

skydiving ['skaɪdaɪvɪŋ] *n* paracaidismo acrobático

sky-high ['skaɪ'haɪ] *adj* (*col*) por las nubes ▪ *adv* (*throw*) muy alto; **prices have gone ~** (*col*) los precios están por las nubes

skylark ['skaɪlɑ:k] *n* (*bird*) alondra

skylight ['skaɪlaɪt] *n* tragaluz *m*, claraboya

skyline ['skaɪlaɪn] *n* (*horizon*) horizonte *m*; (*of city*) perfil *m*

Skype® ['skaɪp] (*Internet, Tel*) *n* skype® *m* ▪ *vt* hablar con algn a través de skype

skyscraper ['skaɪskreɪpər] *n* rascacielos *m inv*

slab [slæb] *n* (*stone*) bloque *m*; (*of wood*) tabla, plancha; (*flat*) losa; (*of cake*) trozo; (*of meat, cheese*) tajada, trozo

slack [slæk] *adj* (*loose*) flojo; (*slow*) de poca

S

actividad; (*careless*) descuidado; (*Comm: market*) poco activo; (: *demand*) débil; (*period*) bajo; **business is** ~ hay poco movimiento en el negocio

slacken ['slækn] (*also*: **slacken off**) *vi* aflojarse ■ *vt* aflojar; (*speed*) disminuir

slackness ['slæknıs] *n* flojedad *f*; negligencia

slacks [slæks] *npl* pantalones *mpl*

slag [slæg] *n* escoria, escombros *mpl*

slag heap *n* escorial *m*, escombrera

slain [sleın] *pp of* **slay**

slake [sleık] *vt* (*one's thirst*) apagar

slalom ['sla:ləm] *n* eslálom *m*

slam [slæm] *vt* (*door*) cerrar de golpe; (*throw*) arrojar (violentamente); (*criticize*) vapulear, vituperar ■ *vi* cerrarse de golpe

slammer [slæmə^r] *n* (*col*): **the** ~ la trena, el talego

slander ['sla:ndə^r] *n* calumnia, difamación *f* ■ *vt* calumniar, difamar

slanderous ['sla:ndərəs] *adj* calumnioso, difamatorio

slang [slæŋ] *n* argot *m*; (*jargon*) jerga

slanging match ['slæŋıŋ-] *n* (*Brit col*) bronca gorda

slant [sla:nt] *n* sesgo, inclinación *f*; (*fig*) punto de vista; **to get a new ~ on sth** obtener un nuevo punto de vista sobre algo

slanted ['sla:ntıd], **slanting** ['sla:ntıŋ] *adj* inclinado

slap [slæp] *n* palmada; (*in face*) bofetada ■ *vt* dar una palmada/bofetada a ■ *adv* (*directly*) de lleno

slapdash ['slæpdæʃ] *adj* chapucero

slaphead ['slæphɛd] *n* (*Brit col*) colgado(-a)

slapstick ['slæpstık] *n*: ~ **comedy** comedia de payasadas

slap-up ['slæpʌp] *adj*: **a ~ meal** (*Brit*) un banquetazo, una comilona

slash [slæʃ] *vt* acuchillar; (*fig: prices*) quemar

slat [slæt] *n* (*of wood, plastic*) tablilla, listón *m*

slate [sleıt] *n* pizarra ■ *vt* (*Brit: fig: criticize*) vapulear

slaughter ['slɔ:tə^r] *n* (*of animals*) matanza; (*of people*) carnicería ■ *vt* matar

slaughterhouse ['slɔ:təhaus] *n* matadero

Slav [sla:v] *adj* eslavo

slave [sleıv] *n* esclavo(-a) ■ *vi* (*also*: **slave away**) trabajar como un negro; **to ~ (away) at sth** trabajar como un negro en algo

slave driver *n* (*col, pej*) tirano(-a)

slave labour, slave labor (*US*) *n* trabajo de esclavos

slaver ['slævə^r] *vi* (*dribble*) babear

slavery ['sleıvərı] *n* esclavitud *f*

slavish ['sleıvıʃ] *adj* (*devotion*) de esclavo; (*imitation*) servil

slay (*pt* **slew**, *pp* **slain**) [sleı, slu:, sleın] *vt* (*literary*) matar

sleazy ['sli:zı] *adj* (*fig: place*) sórdido

sledge [slɛdʒ], **sled** (*US*) [slɛd] *n* trineo

sledgehammer ['slɛdʒhæmə^r] *n* mazo

sleek [sli:k] *adj* (*shiny*) lustroso

sleep [sli:p] (*pt, pp* **slept**) *n* sueño ■ *vi* dormir ■ *vt*: **we can ~ 4** podemos alojar a 4, tenemos cabida para 4; **to go to ~** dormirse; **to have a good night's ~** dormir toda la noche; **to put to ~** (*patient*) dormir; (*animal: euphemism: kill*) sacrificar; **to ~ lightly** tener el sueño ligero; **to ~ with sb** (*euphemism*) acostarse con algn
▶ **sleep in** *vi* (*oversleep*) quedarse dormido

sleeper ['sli:pə^r] *n* (*person*) durmiente *m/f*; (*Brit Rail: on track*) traviesa; (: *train*) coche-cama *m*

sleepiness ['sli:pınıs] *n* somnolencia

sleeping bag ['sli:pıŋ-] *n* saco de dormir

sleeping car *n* coche-cama *m*

sleeping partner *n* (*Comm*) socio(-a) comanditario(-a)

sleeping pill *n* somnífero

sleeping sickness *n* enfermedad *f* del sueño

sleepless ['sli:plıs] *adj*: **a ~ night** una noche en blanco

sleeplessness ['sli:plısnıs] *n* insomnio

sleepover ['sli:pəuvə^r] *n*: **we're having a ~ at Fiona's** pasamos la noche en casa de Fiona

sleepwalk ['sli:pwɔ:k] *vi* caminar dormido; (*habitually*) ser sonámbulo

sleepwalker ['sli:pwɔ:kə^r] *n* sonámbulo(-a)

sleepy ['sli:pı] *adj* soñoliento; **to be** *or* **feel ~** tener sueño

sleet [sli:t] *n* aguanieve *f*

sleeve [sli:v] *n* manga; (*Tech*) manguito; (*of record*) funda

sleeveless ['sli:vlıs] *adj* (*garment*) sin mangas

sleigh [sleı] *n* trineo

sleight [slaıt] *n*: ~ **of hand** prestidigitación *f*

slender ['slɛndə^r] *adj* delgado; (*means*) escaso

slept [slɛpt] *pt, pp of* **sleep**

sleuth [slu:θ] *n* (*col*) detective *m/f*

slew [slu:] *vi* (*veer*) torcerse ■ *pt of* **slay**

slice [slaıs] *n* (*of meat*) tajada; (*of bread*) rebanada; (*of lemon*) rodaja; (*utensil*) paleta ■ *vt* cortar, tajar; rebanar; **sliced bread** pan *m* de molde

slick [slık] *adj* (*skilful*) hábil, diestro ■ *n* (*also*: **oil slick**) capa de aceite

slid [slıd] *pt, pp of* **slide**

slide [slaıd] (*pt, pp* **slid**) *n* (*in playground*) tobogán *m*; (*Phot*) diapositiva; (*microscope slide*) portaobjetos *m inv*, plaquilla de vidrio; (*Brit: also*: **hair slide**) pasador *m* ■ *vt* correr, deslizar ■ *vi* (*slip*) resbalarse; (*glide*) deslizarse; **to let things ~** (*fig*) dejar que ruede la bola

slide projector *n* (*Phot*) proyector *m* de diapositivas

slide rule *n* regla de cálculo

sliding ['slaɪdɪŋ] *adj* (*door*) corredizo; **~ roof** (*Aut*) techo de corredera

sliding scale *n* escala móvil

slight [slaɪt] *adj* (*slim*) delgado; (*frail*) delicado; (*pain etc*) leve; (*trifling*) insignificante; (*small*) pequeño ▪ *n* desaire *m* ▪ *vt* (*offend*) ofender, desairar; **a ~ improvement** una ligera mejora; **not in the slightest** en absoluto; **there's not the slightest possibility** no hay la menor *or* más mínima posibilidad

slightly ['slaɪtlɪ] *adv* ligeramente, un poco; **~ built** delgado

slim [slɪm] *adj* delgado, esbelto ▪ *vi* adelgazar

slime [slaɪm] *n* limo, cieno

slimming ['slɪmɪŋ] *n* adelgazamiento ▪ *adj* (*diet, pills*) adelgazante

slimness ['slɪmnɪs] *n* delgadez *f*

slimy ['slaɪmɪ] *adj* limoso; (*covered with mud*) fangoso; (*also fig: person*) adulón, zalamero

sling [slɪŋ] *n* (*Med*) cabestrillo; (*weapon*) honda ▪ *vt* (*pt, pp* **slung**) [slʌŋ] tirar, arrojar; **to have one's arm in a ~** llevar el brazo en cabestrillo

slink (*pt, pp* **slunk**) [slɪŋk, slʌŋk] *vi*: **to ~ away, ~ off** escabullirse

slinky ['slɪŋkɪ] *adj* (*clothing*) pegado al cuerpo, superajustado

slip [slɪp] *n* (*slide*) resbalón *m*; (*mistake*) descuido; (*underskirt*) combinación *f*; (*of paper*) papelito ▪ *vt* (*slide*) deslizar ▪ *vi* (*slide*) deslizarse; (*stumble*) resbalar(se); (*decline*) decaer; (*move smoothly*): **to ~ into/out of** (*room etc*) colarse en/salirse de; **to let a chance ~ by** dejar escapar la oportunidad; **to ~ sth on/ off** ponerse/quitarse algo; **to ~ on a jumper** ponerse un jersey *or* un suéter; **it slipped from her hand** se la cayó de la mano; **to give sb the ~** dar esquinazo a algn; **wages ~** (*Brit*) hoja del sueldo; **a ~ of the tongue** un lapsus
  ▸ **slip away** *vi* escabullirse
  ▸ **slip in** *vt* meter ▪ *vi* meterse, colarse
  ▸ **slip out** *vi* (*go out*) salir (un momento)

slip-on ['slɪpɔn] *adj* de quita y pon; (*shoes*) sin cordones

slipped disc [slɪpt-] *n* vértebra dislocada

slipper ['slɪpəʳ] *n* zapatilla, pantufla

slippery ['slɪpərɪ] *adj* resbaladizo

slip road *n* (*Brit*) carretera de acceso

slipshod ['slɪpʃɔd] *adj* descuidado, chapucero

slipstream ['slɪpstriːm] *n* viento de la hélice

slip-up ['slɪpʌp] *n* (*error*) desliz *m*

slipway ['slɪpweɪ] *n* grada, gradas *fpl*

slit [slɪt] *n* raja; (*cut*) corte *m* ▪ *vt* (*pt, pp* **slit**) rajar, cortar; **to ~ sb's throat** cortarle el pescuezo a algn

slither ['slɪðəʳ] *vi* deslizarse

sliver ['slɪvəʳ] *n* (*of glass, wood*) astilla; (*of cheese, sausage*) lonja, loncha

slob [slɔb] *n* (*col*) patán(-ana) *m(f)*, palurdo(-a) *m(f)*

slog [slɔg] (*Brit*) *vi* sudar tinta ▪ *n*: **it was a ~** costó trabajo (hacerlo)

slogan ['sləugən] *n* eslogan *m*, lema *m*

slop [slɔp] *vi* (*also*: **slop over**) derramarse, desbordarse ▪ *vt* derramar, verter

slope [sləup] *n* (*up*) cuesta, pendiente *f*; (*down*) declive *m*; (*side of mountain*) falda, vertiente *f* ▪ *vi*: **to ~ down** estar en declive; **to ~ up** subir (en pendiente)

sloping ['sləupɪŋ] *adj* en pendiente; en declive

sloppily ['slɔpɪlɪ] *adv* descuidadamente; con descuido *or* desaliño

sloppiness ['slɔpɪnɪs] *n* descuido; desaliño

sloppy ['slɔpɪ] *adj* (*work*) descuidado; (*appearance*) desaliñado

slosh [slɔʃ] *vi*: **to ~ about** *or* **around** chapotear

sloshed [slɔʃt] *adj* (*col: drunk*): **to get ~** agarrar una trompa

slot [slɔt] *n* ranura; (*fig: in timetable*) hueco; (*Radio, TV*) espacio ▪ *vt*: **to ~ into** encajar en

sloth [sləuθ] *n* (*vice*) pereza; (*Zool*) oso perezoso

slot machine *n* (*Brit: vending machine*) máquina expendedora; (*for gambling*) máquina tragaperras

slot meter *n* contador *m*

slouch [slautʃ] *vi*: **to ~ about, ~ around** (*laze*) gandulear

Slovak ['sləuvæk] *adj* eslovaco ▪ *n* eslovaco(-a); (*Ling*) eslovaco; **the ~ Republic** Eslovaquia

Slovakia [sləu'vækɪə] *n* Eslovaquia

Slovakian [sləu'vækɪən] *adj, n* = **Slovak**

Slovene [sləu'viːn] *adj* esloveno ▪ *n* esloveno(-a); (*Ling*) esloveno

Slovenia [sləu'viːnɪə] *n* Eslovenia

Slovenian [sləu'viːnɪən] *adj, n* = **Slovene**

slovenly ['slʌvənlɪ] *adj* (*dirty*) desaliñado, desaseado; (*careless*) descuidado

slow [sləu] *adj* lento; (*watch*): **to be ~** estar atrasado ▪ *adv* lentamente, despacio ▪ *vt* (*also*: **slow down, slow up**) retardar; (*engine, machine*) reducir la marcha de ▪ *vi* (*also*: **slow down, slow up**) ir más despacio; **"~"** (*road sign*) "disminuir la velocidad"; **at a ~**

S

speed a una velocidad lenta; **the ~ lane** el carril derecho; **business is ~** (*Comm*) hay poca actividad; **my watch is 20 minutes ~** mi reloj lleva 20 minutos de retraso; **bake in a ~ oven** cocer *or* asar en el horno a fuego lento; **to be ~ to act/decide** tardar en obrar/decidir; **to go ~** (*driver*) conducir despacio; (*in industrial dispute*) trabajar a ritmo lento

slow-acting [sləuˈæktɪŋ] *adj* de efecto retardado

slowcoach [ˈsləukəutʃ] *n* (*Brit col*) tortuga

slowdown [ˈsləudaun] *n* (*US*) huelga de celo

slowly [ˈsləulɪ] *adv* lentamente, despacio; **to drive ~** conducir despacio; **~ but surely** lento pero seguro

slow motion *n*: **in ~** a cámara lenta

slow-moving [ˈsləuˈmuːvɪŋ] *adj* lento

slowpoke [ˈsləupəuk] *n* (*US col*) = **slowcoach**

sludge [slʌdʒ] *n* lodo, fango

slug [slʌɡ] *n* babosa; (*bullet*) posta

sluggish [ˈslʌɡɪʃ] *adj* (*slow*) lento; (*lazy*) perezoso; (*business, market, sales*) inactivo

sluggishly [ˈslʌɡɪʃlɪ] *adv* lentamente

sluggishness [ˈslʌɡɪʃnɪs] *n* lentitud *f*

sluice [sluːs] *n* (*gate*) esclusa; (*channel*) canal *m* ■ *vt*: **to ~ down** *or* **out** regar

slum [slʌm] *n* (*area*) barrios *mpl* bajos; (*house*) casucha

slumber [ˈslʌmbəʳ] *n* sueño

slum clearance, slum clearance programme *n* (programa *m* de) deschabolización *f*

slump [slʌmp] *n* (*economic*) depresión *f* ■ *vi* hundirse; **the ~ in the price of copper** la baja repentina del precio del cobre; **he was slumped over the wheel** se había desplomado encima del volante

slung [slʌŋ] *pt, pp of* **sling**

slunk [slʌŋk] *pt, pp of* **slink**

slur [sləːʳ] *n* calumnia ■ *vt* calumniar, difamar; (*word*) pronunciar mal; **to cast a ~ on sb** manchar la reputación de algn, difamar a algn

slurp [sləːp] *vt, vi* sorber ruidosamente

slurred [sləːd] *adj* (*pronunciation*) poco claro

slush [slʌʃ] *n* nieve *f* a medio derretir

slush fund *n* fondos *mpl* para sobornar

slushy [ˈslʌʃɪ] *adj* (*col: poetry etc*) sentimentaloide

slut [slʌt] *n* marrana

sly [slaɪ] *adj* (*clever*) astuto; (*nasty*) malicioso

slyly [ˈslaɪlɪ] *adv* astutamente; taimadamente

slyness [ˈslaɪnɪs] *n* astucia

SM *n abbr* = **sadomasochism**

smack [smæk] *n* (*slap*) manotada; (*blow*) golpe *m* ■ *vt* dar una manotada a; golpear con la mano ■ *vi*: **to ~ of** saber a, oler a ■ *adv*: **it fell ~ in the middle** (*col*) cayó justo en medio

smacker [ˈsmækəʳ] *n* (*col: kiss*) besazo; (: *Brit: pound note*) billete *m* de una libra; (: *US: dollar bill*) billete *m* de un dólar

small [smɔːl] *adj* pequeño, chico (*LAm*); (*in height*) bajo, chaparro (*LAm*); (*letter*) en minúscula ■ *n*: **~ of the back** región *f* lumbar; **~ shopkeeper** pequeño(-a) comerciante *m(f)*; **to get** *or* **grow smaller** (*stain, town*) empequeñecer; (*debt, organization, numbers*) reducir, disminuir; **to make smaller** (*amount, income*) reducir; (*garden, object, garment*) achicar

small ads *npl* (*Brit*) anuncios *mpl* por palabras

small arms *npl* armas *fpl* cortas

small business *n* pequeño negocio; **small businesses** la pequeña empresa

small change *n* suelto, cambio

smallholder [ˈsmɔːlhəuldəʳ] *n* (*Brit*) granjero(-a), parcelero(-a)

smallholding [ˈsmɔːlhəuldɪŋ] *n* parcela, minifundio

small hours *npl*: **in the ~** a altas horas de la noche

smallish [ˈsmɔːlɪʃ] *adj* más bien pequeño

small-minded [smɔːlˈmaɪndɪd] *adj* mezquino, de miras estrechas

smallness [ˈsmɔːlnɪs] *n* pequeñez *f*

smallpox [ˈsmɔːlpɔks] *n* viruela

small print *n* letra pequeña *or* menuda

small-scale [ˈsmɔːlskeɪl] *adj* (*map, model*) a escala reducida; (*business, farming*) en pequeña escala

small talk *n* cháchara

small-time [ˈsmɔːltaɪm] *adj* (*col*) de poca categoría *or* monta; **a ~ thief** un(a) ratero(-a)

small-town [ˈsmɔːltəun] *adj* de provincias

smarmy [ˈsmɑːmɪ] *adj* (*Brit pej*) pelotillero (*fam*)

smart [smɑːt] *adj* elegante; (*clever*) listo, inteligente; (*quick*) rápido, vivo; (*weapon*) inteligente ■ *vi* escocer, picar; **the ~ set** la gente de buen tono; **to look ~** estar elegante; **my eyes are smarting** me pican los ojos

smartcard [ˈsmɑːtkɑːd] *n* tarjeta inteligente

smarten up [ˈsmɑːtn-] *vi* arreglarse ■ *vt* arreglar

smartness [ˈsmɑːtnɪs] *n* elegancia; (*cleverness*) inteligencia

smart phone *n* smartphone *m*

smash [smæʃ] *n* (*also:* **smash-up**) choque *m*; (*sound*) estrépito ■ *vt* (*break*) hacer pedazos; (*car etc*) estrellar; (*Sport: record*) batir ■ *vi* hacerse pedazos; (*against wall etc*) estrellarse

▶ **smash up** vt (car) hacer pedazos; (room) destrozar

smash hit n exitazo

smashing ['smæʃɪŋ] adj (col) cojonudo

smattering ['smætərɪŋ] n: **a ~ of Spanish** algo de español

smear [smɪəʳ] n mancha; (Med) frotis m inv (cervical); (insult) calumnia ▪ vt untar; (fig) calumniar, difamar; **his hands were smeared with oil/ink** tenía las manos manchadas de aceite/tinta

smear campaign n campaña de calumnias

smear test n (Med) citología, frotis m inv (cervical)

smell [smɛl] (pt, pp smelt or smelled) n olor m; (sense) olfato ▪ vt, vi oler; **it smells good/of garlic** huele bien/a ajo

smelly ['smɛlɪ] adj maloliente

smelt [smɛlt] vt (ore) fundir ▪ pt, pp of smell

smile [smaɪl] n sonrisa ▪ vi sonreír

smiley ['smaɪlɪ] n (in email etc) smiley m, emoticón m

smiling ['smaɪlɪŋ] adj sonriente, risueño

smirk [smə:k] n sonrisa falsa or afectada

smith [smɪθ] n herrero

smitten ['smɪtn] adj: **he's really ~ with her** está totalmente loco por ella

smock [smɔk] n blusón; (children's) babi m; (US: overall) guardapolvo, bata

smog [smɔg] n smog m

smoke [sməuk] n humo ▪ vi fumar; (chimney) echar humo ▪ vt (cigarettes) fumar; **to go up in ~** quemarse; (fig) quedar en agua de borrajas

smoked [sməukt] adj (bacon, glass) ahumado

smokeless fuel ['sməuklɪs-] n combustible m sin humo

smokeless zone ['sməuklɪs-] n zona libre de humo

smoker ['sməukəʳ] n fumador(a) m(f)

smoke screen n cortina de humo

smoke shop n (US) estanco, tabaquería

smoking ['sməukɪŋ] n: **"no ~"** "prohibido fumar"; **he's given up ~** ha dejado de fumar

smoking compartment, smoking car (US) n departamento de fumadores

smoky ['sməukɪ] adj (room) lleno de humo

smolder ['sməuldəʳ] vi (US) = smoulder

smoochy ['smu:tʃɪ] adj (col) blandengue

smooth [smu:ð] adj liso; (sea) tranquilo; (flavour, movement) suave; (person: pej) meloso ▪ vt alisar; (also: smooth out: creases) alisar; (difficulties) allanar

▶ **smooth over** vt: **to ~ things over** (fig) limar las asperezas

smoothly ['smu:ðlɪ] adv (easily) fácilmente; **everything went ~** todo fue sobre ruedas

smoothness ['smu:ðnɪs] n (of skin, cloth) tersura; (of surface, flavour, movement) suavidad f

smother ['smʌðəʳ] vt sofocar; (repress) contener

smoulder, smolder (US) ['sməuldəʳ] vi arder sin llama

SMS n abbr (= short message service) SMS m

smudge [smʌdʒ] n mancha ▪ vt manchar

smug [smʌg] adj engreído

smuggle ['smʌgl] vt pasar de contrabando; **to ~ in/out** (goods etc) meter/sacar de contrabando

smuggler ['smʌgləʳ] n contrabandista m/f

smuggling ['smʌglɪŋ] n contrabando

smugly ['smʌglɪ] adv con suficiencia

smugness ['smʌgnɪs] n suficiencia

smut [smʌt] n (grain of soot) carbonilla, hollín m; (mark) tizne m; (in conversation etc) obscenidades fpl

smutty ['smʌtɪ] adj (fig) verde, obsceno

snack [snæk] n bocado, tentempié m; **to have a ~** tomar un bocado

snack bar n cafetería

snag [snæg] n problema m; **to run into or hit a ~** encontrar inconvenientes, dar con un obstáculo

snail [sneɪl] n caracol m

snake [sneɪk] n (gen) serpiente f; (harmless) culebra; (poisonous) víbora

snap [snæp] n (sound) chasquido; golpe m seco; (photograph) foto f ▪ adj (decision) instantáneo ▪ vt (fingers etc) castañetear; (break) partir, quebrar; (photograph) tomar una foto de ▪ vi (break) partirse, quebrarse; (fig: person) contestar bruscamente; **to ~ (at sb)** (person) hablar con brusquedad (a algn); (dog) intentar morder (a algn); **to ~ shut** cerrarse de golpe; **to ~ one's fingers at sth/sb** (fig) burlarse de algo/uno; **a cold ~** (of weather) una ola de frío

▶ **snap off** vi (break) partirse

▶ **snap up** vt agarrar

snap fastener n (US) botón m de presión

snappy ['snæpɪ] adj (col: answer) instantáneo; (slogan) conciso; **make it ~!** (hurry up) ¡date prisa!

snapshot ['snæpʃɒt] n foto f (instantánea)

snare [snɛəʳ] n trampa ▪ vt cazar con trampa; (fig) engañar

snarl [snɑ:l] n gruñido ▪ vi gruñir; **to get snarled up** (wool, plans) enmarañarse, enredarse; (traffic) quedar atascado

snatch [snætʃ] n (fig) robo; **snatches of** trocitos mpl de ▪ vt (snatch away) arrebatar; (grasp) coger (SP), agarrar; **snatches of conversation** fragmentos mpl de

conversación; **to ~ a sandwich** comer un bocadillo a prisa; **to ~ some sleep** buscar tiempo para dormir; **don't ~!** ¡no me lo quites!
▸ **snatch up** *vt* agarrar
snazzy ['snæzɪ] *adj* (*col*) guapo
sneak [sniːk] *vi*: **to ~ in/out** entrar/salir a hurtadillas ▪ *vt*: **to ~ a look at sth** mirar algo de reojo ▪ *n* (*fam*) soplón(-ona) *m(f)*
sneakers ['sniːkəz] *npl* (US) zapatos *mpl* de lona, zapatillas *fpl*
sneaking ['sniːkɪŋ] *adj*: **to have a ~ feeling/suspicion that ...** tener la sensación/sospecha de que ...
sneaky ['sniːkɪ] *adj* furtivo
sneer [snɪəʳ] *n* sonrisa de desprecio ▪ *vi* sonreír con desprecio; **to ~ at sth/sb** burlarse *or* mofarse de algo/uno
sneeze [sniːz] *n* estornudo ▪ *vi* estornudar
snide [snaɪd] *adj* (*col: sarcastic*) sarcástico
sniff [snɪf] *vi* sorber (por la nariz) ▪ *vt* husmear, oler; (*glue, drug*) esnifar
▸ **sniff at** *vt fus*: **it's not to be sniffed at** no es de despreciar
sniffer dog ['snɪfə-] *n* (*for drugs*) perro antidroga; (*for explosives*) perro antiexplosivos
snigger ['snɪgəʳ] *n* risa disimulada ▪ *vi* reírse con disimulo
snip [snɪp] *n* (*piece*) recorte *m*; (*bargain*) ganga ▪ *vt* tijeretear
sniper ['snaɪpəʳ] *n* francotirador(a) *m(f)*
snippet ['snɪpɪt] *n* retazo
snivelling, sniveling (US) ['snɪvlɪŋ] *adj* llorón(-ona)
snob [snɔb] *n* (e)snob *m/f*
snobbery ['snɔbərɪ] *n* (e)snobismo
snobbish ['snɔbɪʃ] *adj* (e)snob
snobbishness ['snɔbɪʃnɪs] *n* (e)snobismo
snog [snɔg] *vi* (*Brit col*) besuquearse, morrear; **to ~ sb** besuquear a algn
snooker ['snuːkəʳ] *n* snooker *m*
snoop [snuːp] *vi*: **to ~ about** fisgonear
snooper ['snuːpəʳ] *n* fisgón(-ona) *m(f)*
snooty ['snuːtɪ] *adj* (e)snob
snooze [snuːz] *n* siesta ▪ *vi* echar una siesta
snore [snɔːʳ] *vi* roncar ▪ *n* ronquido
snoring ['snɔːrɪŋ] *n* ronquidos *mpl*
snorkel ['snɔːkl] *n* tubo de respiración
snort [snɔːt] *n* bufido ▪ *vi* bufar ▪ *vt* (*col: drugs*) esnifar
snotty ['snɔtɪ] *adj* (*col*) creído
snout [snaut] *n* hocico, morro
snow [snəu] *n* nieve *f* ▪ *vi* nevar ▪ *vt*: **to be snowed under with work** estar agobiado de trabajo
snowball ['snəubɔːl] *n* bola de nieve ▪ *vi* ir aumentándose

snow-blind ['snəublaɪnd] *adj* cegado por la nieve
snowbound ['snəubaund] *adj* bloqueado por la nieve
snow-capped ['snəukæpt] *adj* (*peak*) cubierto de nieve, nevado
snowdrift ['snəudrɪft] *n* ventisquero
snowdrop ['snəudrɔp] *n* campanilla
snowfall ['snəufɔːl] *n* nevada
snowflake ['snəufleɪk] *n* copo de nieve
snowline ['snəulaɪn] *n* límite *m* de las nieves perpetuas
snowman ['snəumæn] *n* figura de nieve
snowplough, snowplow (US) ['snəuplau] *n* quitanieves *m inv*
snowshoe ['snəuʃuː] *n* raqueta (de nieve)
snowstorm ['snəustɔːm] *n* tormenta de nieve, nevasca
Snow White *n* Blancanieves *f*
snowy ['snəuɪ] *adj* de (mucha) nieve
SNP *n abbr* (*Brit Pol*) = **Scottish National Party**
snub [snʌb] *vt*: **to ~ sb** desairar a algn ▪ *n* desaire *m*, repulsa
snub-nosed [snʌb'nəuzd] *adj* chato
snuff [snʌf] *n* rapé *m* ▪ *vt* (*also:* **snuff out**: *candle*) apagar
snuffbox ['snʌfbɔks] *n* caja de rapé
snuff movie *n* (*col*) película porno (*que acaba con un asesinato real*)
snug [snʌg] *adj* (*cosy*) cómodo; (*fitted*) ajustado
snuggle ['snʌgl] *vi*: **to ~ down in bed** hacerse un ovillo *or* acurrucarse en la cama; **to ~ up to sb** acurrucarse junto a algn
snugly ['snʌglɪ] *adv* cómodamente; **it fits ~** (*object in pocket etc*) cabe perfectamente; (*garment*) ajusta perfectamente
SO *abbr* (*Banking*) = **standing order**

 KEYWORD

so [səu] *adv* **1** (*thus, likewise*) así, de este modo; **if so** de ser así; **I like swimming — so do I** a mí me gusta nadar — a mí también; **I've got work to do — so has Paul** tengo trabajo que hacer — Paul también; **it's five o'clock — so it is!** son las cinco — ¡pues es verdad!; **I hope/think so** espero/creo que sí; **so far** hasta ahora; (*in past*) hasta este momento; **so to speak** por decirlo así
2 (*in comparisons etc: to such a degree*) tan; **so quickly (that)** tan rápido (que); **so big (that)** tan grande (que); **she's not so clever as her brother** no es tan lista como su hermano; **we were so worried** estábamos preocupadísimos
3: **so much** *adj* tanto(-a)

■ *adv* tanto; **so many** tantos(-as)
4 (*phrases*): **10 or so** unos 10, 10 o así; **so long!**
(*col: goodbye*) ¡hasta luego!; **so (what)?** (*col*)
¿y (qué)?
■ *conj* **1** (*expressing purpose*): **so as to do**
para hacer; **so (that)** para que + *subjun*; **we**
hurried so (that) we wouldn't be late nos
dimos prisa para no llegar tarde
2 (*expressing result*) así que; **so you see, I**
could have gone así que ya ves, (yo) podría
haber ido; **so that's the reason!** ¡así que es
por eso *or* por eso es!

soak [səʊk] *vt* (*drench*) empapar; (*put in water*)
remojar ■ *vi* remojarse, estar a remojo
▶ **soak in** *vi* penetrar
▶ **soak up** *vt* absorber
soaking ['səʊkɪŋ] *adj* (*also*: **soaking wet**)
calado *or* empapado (hasta los huesos *or* el
tuétano)
so-and-so ['səʊənsəʊ] *n* (*somebody*) fulano(-a)
de tal
soap [səʊp] *n* jabón *m*
soapbox ['səʊpbɔks] *n* tribuna improvisada
soapflakes ['səʊpfleɪks] *npl* jabón *msg* en
escamas
soap opera *n* (*TV*) telenovela; (*Radio*)
radionovela
soap powder *n* jabón *m* en polvo
soapsuds ['səʊpsʌdz] *npl* espuma *sg*
soapy ['səʊpɪ] *adj* jabonoso
soar [sɔːʳ] *vi* (*on wings*) remontarse; (*building*
etc) elevarse; (*price*) subir vertiginosamente;
(*morale*) elevarse
soaring ['sɔːrɪŋ] *adj* (*flight*) por lo alto; (*prices*)
en alza *or* aumento; ~ **inflation** inflación *f*
altísima *or* en aumento
sob [sɔb] *n* sollozo ■ *vi* sollozar
s.o.b. *n abbr* (*US col!*: = *son of a bitch*) hijo de
puta (!)
sober ['səʊbəʳ] *adj* (*moderate*) moderado;
(*serious*) serio; (*not drunk*) sobrio; (*colour, style*)
discreto
▶ **sober up** *vi* pasársele a algn la borrachera
soberly ['səʊbəlɪ] *adv* sobriamente
sobriety [sə'braɪətɪ] *n* (*not being drunk*)
sobriedad *f*; (*seriousness, sedateness*) seriedad *f*,
sensatez *f*
sob story *n* (*col, pej*) dramón *m*
Soc. *abbr* (= *society*) S
so-called ['səʊ'kɔːld] *adj* presunto, supuesto
soccer ['sɔkəʳ] *n* fútbol *m*
soccer pitch *n* campo *or* cancha (*LAm*) de
fútbol
soccer player *n* jugador(a) *m(f)* de fútbol
sociability [səʊʃə'bɪlɪtɪ] *n* sociabilidad *f*
sociable ['səʊʃəbl] *adj* sociable

social ['səʊʃl] *adj* social ■ *n* velada, fiesta
social class *n* clase *f* social
social climber *n* arribista *m/f*
social club *n* club *m*
Social Democrat *n* socialdemócrata *m/f*
social insurance *n* (*US*) seguro social
socialism ['səʊʃəlɪzəm] *n* socialismo
socialist ['səʊʃəlɪst] *adj, n* socialista *m/f*
socialite ['səʊʃəlaɪt] *n persona que alterna con la*
buena sociedad
socialize ['səʊʃəlaɪz] *vi* hacer vida social; **to ~**
with (*colleagues*) salir con
social life *n* vida social
socially ['səʊʃəlɪ] *adv* socialmente
social networking [-'nɛtwə:kɪŋ] *n*
interacción *f* social a través de la red
social science *n*, **social sciences** *npl*
ciencias *fpl* sociales
social security *n* seguridad *f* social
social services *npl* servicios *mpl* sociales
social welfare *n* asistencia social
social work *n* asistencia social
social worker *n* asistente(-a) *m(f)* social
society [sə'saɪətɪ] *n* sociedad *f*; (*club*)
asociación *f*; (*also*: **high society**) buena
sociedad ■ *cpd* (*party, column*) social, de
sociedad
socio-economic ['səʊsɪəui:kə'nɔmɪk] *adj*
socioeconómico
sociological [səʊsɪə'lɔdʒɪkəl] *adj* sociológico
sociologist [səʊsɪ'ɔlədʒɪst] *n* sociólogo(-a)
sociology [səʊsɪ'ɔlədʒɪ] *n* sociología
sock [sɔk] *n* calcetín *m*, media (*LAm*); **to**
pull one's socks up (*fig*) hacer esfuerzos,
despabilarse
socket ['sɔkɪt] *n* (*Elec*) enchufe *m*
sod [sɔd] *n* (*of earth*) césped *m*; (*col!*)
cabrón(-ona) *m(f)* (!) ■ *excl*: ~ **off!** (*col!*) ¡vete
a la porra!
soda ['səʊdə] *n* (*Chem*) sosa; (*also*: **soda water**)
soda; (*US: also*: **soda pop**) gaseosa
sodden ['sɔdn] *adj* empapado
sodium ['səʊdɪəm] *n* sodio
sodium chloride *n* cloruro sódico *or* de sodio
sofa ['səʊfə] *n* sofá *m*
Sofia ['səʊfɪə] *n* Sofía
soft [sɔft] *adj* (*teacher, parent*) blando; (*gentle,*
not loud) suave; (*stupid*) bobo; ~ **currency**
divisa blanda *or* débil
soft-boiled ['sɔftbɔɪld] *adj* (*egg*) pasado por
agua
soft copy *n* (*Comput*) copia transitoria
soft drink *n* bebida no alcohólica
soft drugs *npl* drogas *fpl* blandas
soften ['sɔfn] *vt* ablandar; suavizar ■ *vi*
ablandarse; suavizarse
softener ['sɔfnəʳ] *n* suavizante *m*

S

soft fruit n bayas fpl
soft furnishings npl tejidos mpl para el hogar
soft-hearted [sɔft'hɑ:tɪd] adj bondadoso
softly ['sɔftlɪ] adv suavemente; (gently) delicadamente, con delicadeza
softness ['sɔftnɪs] n blandura; suavidad f
soft option n alternativa fácil
soft sell n venta persuasiva
soft target n blanco or objetivo fácil
soft toy n juguete m de peluche
software ['sɔftwɛəʳ] n (Comput) software m
soft water n agua blanda
soggy ['sɔgɪ] adj empapado
soil [sɔɪl] n (earth) tierra, suelo ■ vt ensuciar
soiled [sɔɪld] adj sucio, manchado
sojourn ['sɔdʒə:n] n (formal) estancia
solace ['sɔlɪs] n consuelo
solar ['səuləʳ] adj solar
solarium (pl **solaria**) [sə'lɛərɪəm, -rɪə] n solario
solar panel n panel m solar
solar plexus [-'plɛksəs] n (Anat) plexo solar
solar power n energía solar
solar system n sistema m solar
sold [səuld] pt, pp of **sell**
solder ['səuldəʳ] vt soldar ■ n soldadura
soldier ['səuldʒəʳ] n (gen) soldado; (army man) militar m ■ vi: **to ~ on** seguir adelante; **toy ~** soldadito de plomo
sold out adj (Comm) agotado
sole [səul] n (of foot) planta; (of shoe) suela; (fish: pl inv) lenguado ■ adj único; **the ~ reason** la única razón
solely ['səullɪ] adv únicamente, sólo, solamente; **I will hold you ~ responsible** le consideraré el único responsable
solemn ['sɔləm] adj solemne
sole trader n (Comm) comerciante m/f exclusivo(-a)
solicit [sə'lɪsɪt] vt (request) solicitar ■ vi (prostitute) abordar clientes
solicitor [sə'lɪsɪtəʳ] n abogado(-a); see also **barrister**
solid ['sɔlɪd] adj sólido; (gold etc) macizo; (line) continuo; (vote) unánime ■ n sólido; **we waited two ~ hours** esperamos dos horas enteras; **to be on ~ ground** estar en tierra firme; (fig) estar seguro
solidarity [sɔlɪ'dærɪtɪ] n solidaridad f
solid fuel n combustible m sólido
solidify [sə'lɪdɪfaɪ] vi solidificarse
solidity [sə'lɪdɪtɪ] n solidez f
solidly ['sɔlɪdlɪ] adv sólidamente; (fig) unánimemente
solid-state ['sɔlɪdsteɪt] adj (Elec) estado sólido
soliloquy [sə'lɪləkwɪ] n soliloquio

solitaire [sɔlɪ'tɛəʳ] n (game, gem) solitario
solitary ['sɔlɪtərɪ] adj solitario, solo; (isolated) apartado, aislado; (only) único
solitary confinement n incomunicación f; **to be in ~** estar incomunicado
solitude ['sɔlɪtju:d] n soledad f
solo ['səuləu] n solo
soloist ['səuləuɪst] n solista m/f
Solomon Islands ['sɔləmən-] npl: **the ~** las Islas Salomón
solstice ['sɔlstɪs] n solsticio
soluble ['sɔljubl] adj soluble
solution [sə'lu:ʃən] n solución f
solve [sɔlv] vt resolver, solucionar
solvency ['sɔlvənsɪ] n (Comm) solvencia
solvent ['sɔlvənt] adj (Comm) solvente ■ n (Chem) solvente m
solvent abuse n uso indebido de disolventes
Som. abbr (Brit) = **Somerset**
Somali [sə'mɑ:lɪ] adj, n somalí m/f
Somalia [sə'mɑ:lɪə] n Somalia
Somaliland [sə'mɑ:lɪlænd] n Somaliland f
sombre, somber (US) ['sɔmbəʳ] adj sombrío

◯ KEYWORD

some [sʌm] adj **1** (a certain amount or number of): **some tea/water/biscuits** té/agua/(unas) galletas; **have some tea** tómese un té; **there's some milk in the fridge** hay leche en el frigo; **there were some people outside** había algunas personas fuera; **I've got some money, but not much** tengo algo de dinero, pero no mucho
2 (certain: in contrasts) algunos(-as); **some people say that ...** hay quien dice que ...; **some films were excellent, but most were mediocre** hubo películas excelentes, pero la mayoría fueron mediocres
3 (unspecified): **some woman was asking for you** una mujer estuvo preguntando por ti; **some day** algún día; **some day next week** un día de la semana que viene; **he was asking for some book (or other)** pedía no se qué libro; **in some way or other** de alguna que otra manera
4 (considerable amount of) bastante; **some days ago** hace unos cuantos días; **after some time** pasado algún tiempo; **at some length** con mucho detalle
5 (col: intensive): **that was some party!** ¡menuda fiesta!
■ pron **1** (a certain number): **I've got some** (books etc) tengo algunos(-as)
2 (a certain amount) algo; **I've got some** (money, milk) tengo algo; **would you like some?** (coffee etc) ¿quiere un poco?; (books

etc) ¿quiere alguno?; **could I have some of that cheese?** ¿me puede dar un poco de ese queso?; **I've read some of the book** he leído parte del libro
■ *adv*: **some 10 people** unas 10 personas, una decena de personas

somebody ['sʌmbədɪ] *pron* alguien; **~ or other** alguien

someday ['sʌmdeɪ] *adv* algún día

somehow ['sʌmhau] *adv* de alguna manera; (*for some reason*) por una u otra razón

someone ['sʌmwʌn] *pron* = **somebody**

someplace ['sʌmpleɪs] *adv* (*US*) = **somewhere**

somersault ['sʌməsɔːlt] *n* (*deliberate*) salto mortal; (*accidental*) vuelco ■ *vi* dar un salto mortal; dar vuelcos

something ['sʌmθɪŋ] *pron* algo ■ *adv*: **he's ~ like me** es un poco como yo; **~ to do** algo que hacer; **it's ~ of a problem** es bastante problemático

sometime ['sʌmtaɪm] *adv* (*in future*) algún día, en algún momento; **~ last month** durante el mes pasado; **I'll finish it ~** lo terminaré un día de éstos

sometimes ['sʌmtaɪmz] *adv* a veces

somewhat ['sʌmwɔt] *adv* algo

somewhere ['sʌmwɛər] *adv* (*be*) en alguna parte; (*go*) a alguna parte; **~ else** (*be*) en otra parte; (*go*) a otra parte

son [sʌn] *n* hijo

sonar ['səunɑːr] *n* sonar *m*

sonata [sə'nɑːtə] *n* sonata

song [sɔŋ] *n* canción *f*

songwriter ['sɔŋraɪtər] *n* compositor(a) *m(f)* de canciones

sonic ['sɔnɪk] *adj* (*boom*) sónico

son-in-law ['sʌnɪnlɔː] *n* yerno

sonnet ['sɔnɪt] *n* soneto

sonny ['sʌnɪ] *n* (*col*) hijo

soon [suːn] *adv* pronto, dentro de poco; **~ afterwards** poco después; **very/quite ~** muy/bastante pronto; **how ~ can you be ready?** ¿cuánto tardas en prepararte?; **it's too ~ to tell** es demasiado pronto para saber; **see you ~!** ¡hasta pronto!; *see also* **as**

sooner ['suːnər] *adv* (*time*) antes, más temprano; **I would ~ do that** preferiría hacer eso; **~ or later** tarde o temprano; **no ~ said than done** dicho y hecho; **the ~ the better** cuanto antes mejor; **no ~ had we left than ...** apenas nos habíamos marchado cuando ...

soot [sut] *n* hollín *m*

soothe [suːð] *vt* tranquilizar; (*pain*) aliviar

soothing ['suːðɪŋ] *adj* (*ointment etc*) sedante;

(*tone, words etc*) calmante, tranquilizante

SOP *n abbr* = **standard operating procedure**

sophisticated [sə'fɪstɪkeɪtɪd] *adj* sofisticado

sophistication [səfɪstɪ'keɪʃən] *n* sofisticación *f*

sophomore ['sɔfəmɔːr] *n* (*US*) estudiante *m/f* de segundo año

soporific [sɔpə'rɪfɪk] *adj* soporífero

sopping ['sɔpɪŋ] *adj*: **~ (wet)** empapado

soppy ['sɔpɪ] *adj* (*pej*) bobo, tonto

soprano [sə'prɑːnəu] *n* soprano *f*

sorbet ['sɔːbeɪ] *n* sorbete *m*

sorcerer ['sɔːsərər] *n* hechicero

sordid ['sɔːdɪd] *adj* (*place etc*) sórdido; (*motive etc*) mezquino

sore [sɔːr] *adj* (*painful*) doloroso, que duele; (*offended*) resentido ■ *n* llaga; **~ throat** dolor *m* de garganta; **my eyes are ~, I have ~ eyes** me duelen los ojos; **it's a ~ point** es un asunto delicado *or* espinoso

sorely *adv*: **I am ~ tempted to (do it)** estoy muy tentado a (hacerlo)

soreness ['sɔːnɪs] *n* dolor *m*

sorrel ['sɔrəl] *n* (*Bot*) acedera

sorrow ['sɔrəu] *n* pena, dolor *m*

sorrowful ['sɔrəuful] *adj* afligido, triste

sorrowfully ['sɔrəfulɪ] *adv* tristemente

sorry ['sɔrɪ] *adj* (*regretful*) arrepentido; (*condition, excuse*) lastimoso; (*sight, failure*) triste; **~!** ¡perdón!, ¡perdone!; **I am ~** lo siento; **I feel ~ for him** me da lástima *or* pena; **I'm ~ to hear that ...** siento saber que ...; **to be ~ about sth** lamentar algo

sort [sɔːt] *n* clase *f*, género, tipo; (*make: of coffee, car etc*) marca ■ *vt* (*also*: **sort out**: *papers*) clasificar; (: *problems*) arreglar, solucionar; (*Comput*) clasificar; **what ~ do you want?** (*make*) ¿qué marca quieres?; **what ~ of car?** ¿qué tipo de coche?; **I shall do nothing of the ~** no pienso hacer nada parecido; **it's ~ of awkward** (*col*) es bastante difícil

sortie ['sɔːtɪ] *n* salida

sorting office ['sɔːtɪŋ-] *n* oficina de clasificación del correo

SOS *n* SOS *m*

so-so ['səusəu] *adv* regular, así así

soufflé ['suːfleɪ] *n* suflé *m*

sought [sɔːt] *pt, pp of* **seek**

sought-after ['sɔːtɑːftər] *adj* solicitado, codiciado

soul [səul] *n* alma *f*; **God rest his ~** Dios le reciba en su seno *or* en su gloria; **I didn't see a ~** no vi a nadie; **the poor ~ had nowhere to sleep** el pobre no tenía dónde dormir

soul-destroying ['səuldɪstrɔɪŋ] *adj* (*work*) deprimente

soulful ['səulful] *adj* lleno de sentimiento
soulmate ['səulmeɪt] *n* compañero(-a) del
alma
soul-searching ['səulsə:tʃɪŋ] *n*: **after much**
~ después de pensarlo mucho, después de
darle muchas vueltas
sound [saund] *adj* (*healthy*) sano; (*safe, not
damaged*) en buen estado; (*valid: argument,
policy, claim*) válido; (: *move*) acertado;
(*dependable: person*) de fiar; (*sensible*) sensato,
razonable ■ *adv*: ~ **asleep** profundamente
dormido ■ *n* (*noise*) sonido, ruido; (*Geo*)
estrecho ■ *vt* (*alarm*) sonar; (*also:* **sound
out**: *opinions*) consultar, sondear ■ *vi* sonar,
resonar; (*fig: seem*) parecer; **to ~ like** sonar a;
to be of ~ mind estar en su sano juicio;
I don't like the ~ of it no me gusta nada;
it sounds as if ... parece que ...
▶ **sound off** *vi* (*col*): **to ~ off (about)** (*give one's
opinions*) despotricar (contra)
sound barrier *n* barrera del sonido
sound bite *n* cita jugosa
sound effects *npl* efectos *mpl* sonoros
sound engineer *n* ingeniero(-a) del sonido
sounding ['saundɪŋ] *n* (*Naut etc*) sondeo
sounding board *n* caja de resonancia
soundly ['saundlɪ] *adv* (*sleep*)
profundamente; (*beat*) completamente
soundproof ['saundpru:f] *adj* insonorizado
sound system *n* equipo de sonido
soundtrack ['saundtræk] *n* (*of film*) banda
sonora
sound wave *n* (*Physics*) onda sonora
soup [su:p] *n* (*thick*) sopa; (*thin*) caldo; **in the
~** (*fig*) en apuros
soup kitchen *n* comedor *m* de beneficencia
soup plate *n* plato sopero
soupspoon ['su:pspu:n] *n* cuchara sopera
sour ['sauəʳ] *adj* agrio; (*milk*) cortado; **it's
just ~ grapes!** (*fig*) ¡pura envidia!, ¡están
verdes!; **to go** *or* **turn ~** (*milk*) cortarse; (*wine*)
agriarse; (*fig: relationship*) agriarse; (: *plans*)
irse a pique
source [sɔ:s] *n* fuente *f*; **I have it from a
reliable ~ that ...** sé de fuente fidedigna
que ...
source language *n* (*Comput*) lenguaje *m*
fuente *or* de origen
south [sauθ] *n* sur *m* ■ *adj* del sur ■ *adv* al
sur, hacia el sur; (**to the) ~ of** al sur de; **the
S~ of France** el Sur de Francia; **to travel ~**
viajar hacia el sur
South Africa *n* Sudáfrica
South African *adj, n* sudafricano(-a) *m(f)*
South America *n* América del Sur,
Sudamérica
South American *adj, n* sudamericano(-a) *m(f)*

southbound ['sauθbaund] *adj* (con) rumbo
al sur
south-east [sauθ'i:st] *n* sudeste *m* ■ *adj*
(*counties etc*) (del) sudeste
Southeast Asia *n* Sudeste *m* asiático
southerly ['sʌðəlɪ] *adj* sur; (*from the south*)
del sur
southern ['sʌðən] *adj* del sur, meridional;
the ~ hemisphere el hemisferio sur
South Korea *n* Corea del Sur
South Pole *n* Polo Sur
South Sea Islands *npl*: **the ~** Oceanía
South Seas *npl*: **the ~** los Mares del Sur
South Vietnam *n* Vietnam *m* del Sur
southward ['sauθwəd], **southwards**
['sauθwədz] *adv* hacia el sur
south-west [sauθ'wɛst] *n* suroeste *m*
souvenir [su:və'nɪəʳ] *n* recuerdo
sovereign ['sɔvrɪn] *adj, n* soberano(-a) *m(f)*
sovereignty ['sɔvrɪntɪ] *n* soberanía
soviet ['səuvɪət] *adj* soviético
Soviet Union *n*: **the ~** la Unión Soviética
sow [sau] *n* cerda, puerca ■ *vt* [səu] (*pt
sowed, pp* **sown**) [səun] (*gen*) sembrar;
(*spread*) esparcir
soya ['sɔɪə], **soy** (*US*) [sɔɪ] *n* soja
soya bean, soy bean (*US*) *n* semilla de soja
soya sauce, soy sauce (*US*) *n* salsa de soja
sozzled ['sɔzld] *adj* (*Brit col*) mamado
spa [spɑ:] *n* balneario
space [speɪs] *n* espacio; (*room*) sitio ■ *vt*
(*also:* **space out**) espaciar; **to clear a ~ for
sth** hacer sitio para algo; **in a confined ~**
en un espacio restringido; **in a short ~
of time** en poco *or* un corto espacio de
tiempo; (**with)in the ~ of an hour/three
generations** en el espacio de una hora/tres
generaciones
space bar *n* (*on typewriter*) barra espaciadora
spacecraft ['speɪskrɑ:ft] *n* nave *f* espacial,
astronave *f*
spaceman ['speɪsmæn] *n* astronauta *m*,
cosmonauta *m*
spaceship ['speɪsʃɪp] *n* = **spacecraft**
space shuttle *n* transportador *m* espacial
spacesuit ['speɪssu:t] *n* traje *m* espacial
spacewoman ['speɪswumən] *n* astronauta,
cosmonauta
spacing ['speɪsɪŋ] *n* espacio
spacious ['speɪʃəs] *adj* amplio
spade [speɪd] *n* (*tool*) pala; **spades** *npl* (*Cards:
British*) picas *fpl*; (*Spanish*) espadas *fpl*
spadework ['speɪdwə:k] *n* (*fig*) trabajo
preliminar
spaghetti [spə'gɛtɪ] *n* espaguetis *mpl*
Spain [speɪn] *n* España
spam [spæm] *n* (*junk email*) correo basura

span [spæn] *n* (*of bird, plane*) envergadura; (*of hand*) palmo; (*of arch*) luz *f*; (*in time*) lapso ■ *vt* extenderse sobre, cruzar; (*fig*) abarcar

Spaniard ['spænjəd] *n* español(a) *m(f)*

spaniel ['spænjəl] *n* perro de aguas

Spanish ['spænɪʃ] *adj* español(a) ■ *n* (*Ling*) español *m*, castellano; **the Spanish** *npl* (*people*) los españoles; **~ omelette** tortilla española *or* de patata

spank [spæŋk] *vt* zurrar, dar unos azotes a

spanner ['spænə^r] *n* (*Brit*) llave *f* inglesa

spar [spɑː^r] *n* palo, verga ■ *vi* (*Boxing*) entrenarse (en el boxeo)

spare [spɛə^r] *adj* de reserva; (*surplus*) sobrante, de más ■ *n* (*part*) pieza de repuesto ■ *vt* (*do without*) pasarse sin; (*afford to give*) tener de sobra; (*refrain from hurting*) perdonar; (*details etc*) ahorrar; **to ~** (*surplus*) sobrante, de sobra; **there are two going ~** sobran *or* quedan dos; **to ~ no expense** no escatimar gastos; **can you ~ (me) £10?** ¿puedes prestarme *or* darme 10 libras?; **can you ~ the time?** ¿tienes tiempo?; **I've a few minutes to ~** tengo unos minutos libres; **there is no time to ~** no hay tiempo que perder

spare part *n* pieza de repuesto

spare room *n* cuarto de los invitados

spare time *n* ratos *mpl* de ocio, tiempo libre

spare tyre, spare tire (US) *n* (*Aut*) neumático *or* llanta (*LAm*) de recambio

spare wheel *n* (*Aut*) rueda de recambio

sparing ['spɛərɪŋ] *adj*: **to be ~ with** ser parco en

sparingly ['spɛərɪŋlɪ] *adv* escasamente

spark [spɑːk] *n* chispa; (*fig*) chispazo

sparking plug ['spɑːkɪŋ-] *n* = **spark plug**

sparkle ['spɑːkl] *n* centelleo, destello ■ *vi* centellear; (*shine*) relucir, brillar

sparkler ['spɑːklə^r] *n* bengala

sparkling ['spɑːklɪŋ] *adj* centelleante; (*wine*) espumoso

spark plug *n* bujía

sparring partner ['spɑːrɪŋ-] *n* sparring *m*; (*fig*) contrincante *m/f*

sparrow ['spærəu] *n* gorrión *m*

sparse [spɑːs] *adj* esparcido, escaso

sparsely ['spɑːslɪ] *adv* escasamente; **a ~ furnished room** un cuarto con pocos muebles

spartan ['spɑːtən] *adj* (*fig*) espartano

spasm ['spæzəm] *n* (*Med*) espasmo; (*fig*) arranque *m*, ataque *m*

spasmodic [spæz'mɔdɪk] *adj* espasmódico

spastic ['spæstɪk] *n* espástico(-a)

spat [spæt] *pt, pp of* **spit** ■ *n* (US) riña

spate [speɪt] *n* (*fig*): **~ of** torrente *m* de; **in ~** (*river*) crecido

spatial ['speɪʃl] *adj* espacial

spatter ['spætə^r] *vt*: **to ~ with** salpicar de

spatula ['spætjulə] *n* espátula

spawn [spɔːn] *vt* (*pej*) engendrar ■ *vi* desovar, frezar ■ *n* huevas *fpl*

SPCA *n abbr* (US) = **Society for the Prevention of Cruelty to Animals**

SPCC *n abbr* (US) = **Society for the Prevention of Cruelty to Children**

speak (*pt* **spoke**, *pp* **spoken**) [spiːk, spəuk, 'spəukn] *vt* (*language*) hablar; (*truth*) decir ■ *vi* hablar; (*make a speech*) intervenir; **to ~ one's mind** hablar claro *or* con franqueza; **to ~ to sb/of** *or* **about sth** hablar con algn/de *or* sobre algo; **to ~ at a conference/in a debate** hablar en un congreso/un debate; **he has no money to ~ of** no tiene mucho dinero que digamos; **speaking!** ¡al habla!; **~ up!** ¡habla más alto!

▶ **speak for** *vt fus*: **to ~ for sb** hablar por *or* en nombre de algn; **that picture is already spoken for** (*in shop*) ese cuadro está reservado

speaker ['spiːkə^r] *n* (*in public*) orador(a) *m(f)*; (*also*: **loudspeaker**) altavoz *m*; (*for stereo etc*) bafle *m*; (*Pol*): **the S~** (*Brit*) el Presidente de la Cámara de los Comunes; (US) el Presidente del Congreso; **are you a Welsh ~?** ¿habla Ud galés?

speaking ['spiːkɪŋ] *adj* hablante

-speaking ['spiːkɪŋ] *suff* -hablante; **Spanish~ people** los hispanohablantes

spear [spɪə^r] *n* lanza; (*for fishing*) arpón *m* ■ *vt* alancear; arponear

spearhead ['spɪəhɛd] *vt* (*attack etc*) encabezar ■ *n* punta de lanza, vanguardia

spearmint ['spɪəmɪnt] *n* menta verde

spec [spɛk] *n* (*col*): **on ~** por si acaso; **to buy on ~** arriesgarse a comprar

special ['spɛʃl] *adj* especial; (*edition etc*) extraordinario; (*delivery*) urgente ■ *n* (*train*) tren *m* especial; **nothing ~** nada de particular, nada extraordinario

special agent *n* agente *m/f* especial

special correspondent *n* corresponsal *m/f* especial

special delivery *n* (*Post*): **by ~** por entrega urgente

special effects *npl* (*Cine*) efectos *mpl* especiales

specialist ['spɛʃəlɪst] *n* especialista *m/f*; **a heart ~** (*Med*) un(-a) especialista del corazón

speciality [spɛʃɪ'ælɪtɪ], **specialty** (US) ['spɛʃəltɪ] *n* especialidad *f*

specialize ['spɛʃəlaɪz] *vi*: **to ~ (in)** especializarse (en)

specially ['spɛʃlɪ] *adv* especialmente

S

special offer n (*Comm*) oferta especial
special train n tren m especial
specialty ['spɛʃəltɪ] n (*US*) = **speciality**
species ['spi:ʃi:z] n especie f
specific [spə'sɪfɪk] adj específico
specifically [spə'sɪfɪklɪ] adv (*explicitly: state, warn*) específicamente, expresamente; (*especially: design, intend*) especialmente
specification [spɛsɪfɪ'keɪʃən] n especificación f; **specifications** npl (*plan*) presupuesto sg; (*of car, machine*) descripción f técnica; (*for building*) plan msg detallado
specify ['spɛsɪfaɪ] vt, vi especificar, precisar; **unless otherwise specified** salvo indicaciones contrarias
specimen ['spɛsɪmən] n ejemplar m; (*Med: of urine*) espécimen m; (*: of blood*) muestra
specimen copy n ejemplar m de muestra
specimen signature n muestra de firma
speck [spɛk] n grano, mota
speckled ['spɛkld] adj moteado
specs [spɛks] npl (*col*) gafas fpl (SP), anteojos mpl
spectacle ['spɛktəkl] n espectáculo
spectacle case n estuche m or funda (de gafas)
spectacles ['spɛktəklz] npl (*Brit*) gafas fpl (SP), anteojos mpl
spectacular [spɛk'tækjuləʳ] adj espectacular; (*success*) impresionante
spectator [spɛk'teɪtəʳ] n espectador(a) m(f)
spectator sport n deporte m espectáculo
spectra ['spɛktrə] npl of **spectrum**
spectre, specter (*US*) ['spɛktəʳ] n espectro, fantasma m
spectrum (*pl* **spectra**) ['spɛktrəm, -trə] n espectro
speculate ['spɛkjuleɪt] vi especular; (*try to guess*): **to ~ about** especular sobre
speculation [spɛkju'leɪʃən] n especulación f
speculative ['spɛkjulətɪv] adj especulativo
speculator ['spɛkjuleɪtəʳ] n especulador(a) m(f)
sped [spɛd] pt, pp of **speed**
speech [spi:tʃ] n (*faculty*) habla; (*formal talk*) discurso; (*words*) palabras fpl; (*manner of speaking*) forma de hablar; (*language*) idioma m, lenguaje m
speech day n (*Brit Scol*) ≈ día de reparto de premios
speech impediment n defecto del habla
speechless ['spi:tʃlɪs] adj mudo, estupefacto
speech therapy n logopedia
speed [spi:d] n (*also Aut, Tech: gear*) velocidad f; (*haste*) prisa; (*promptness*) rapidez f ■ vi (*pt, pp* **sped**) [spɛd] (*Aut: exceed speed limit*) conducir con exceso de velocidad; **at full** or **top ~**

a máxima velocidad; **at a ~ of 70 km/h** a una velocidad de 70 km por hora; **at ~** a gran velocidad; **a five-~ gearbox** una caja de cambios de cinco velocidades; **shorthand/ typing ~** rapidez f en taquigrafía/ mecanografía; **the years sped by** los años pasaron volando
▸ **speed up** vi acelerarse ■ vt acelerar
speedboat ['spi:dbəut] n lancha motora
speedily ['spi:dɪlɪ] adv rápido, rápidamente
speeding ['spi:dɪŋ] n (*Aut*) exceso de velocidad
speed limit n límite m de velocidad, velocidad f máxima
speedometer [spɪ'dɔmɪtəʳ] n velocímetro
speed trap n (*Aut*) control m de velocidades
speedway ['spi:dweɪ] n (*Sport*) pista de carrera
speedy ['spi:dɪ] adj (*fast*) veloz, rápido; (*prompt*) pronto
spell [spɛl] n (*also:* **magic spell**) encanto, hechizo; (*period of time*) rato, período; (*turn*) turno ■ vt (*pt, pp* **spelt** or **spelled**) [spɛlt, spɛld] (*also:* **spell out**) deletrear; (*fig*) anunciar, presagiar; **to cast a ~ on sb** hechizar a algn; **he can't ~** no sabe escribir bien, comete faltas de ortografía; **can you ~ it for me?** ¿cómo se deletrea or se escribe?; **how do you ~ your name?** ¿cómo se escribe tu nombre?
spellbound ['spɛlbaund] adj embelesado, hechizado
spellchecker n (*Comput*) corrector m (ortográfico)
spelling ['spɛlɪŋ] n ortografía
spelling mistake n falta de ortografía
spelt [spɛlt] pt, pp of **spell**
spend (*pt, pp* **spent**) [spɛnd, spɛnt] vt (*money*) gastar; (*time*) pasar; (*life*) dedicar; **to ~ time/ money/effort on sth** gastar tiempo/dinero/ energías en algo
spending ['spɛndɪŋ] n: **government ~** gastos mpl del gobierno
spending money n dinero para gastos
spending power n poder m adquisitivo
spendthrift ['spɛndθrɪft] n derrochador(a) m(f) manirroto(-a)
spent [spɛnt] pt, pp of **spend** ■ adj (*cartridge, bullets, match*) usado
sperm [spə:m] n esperma
sperm bank n banco de esperma
sperm whale n cachalote m
spew [spju:] vt vomitar, arrojar
sphere [sfɪəʳ] n esfera
spherical ['sfɛrɪkl] adj esférico
sphinx [sfɪŋks] n esfinge f
spice [spaɪs] n especia ■ vt especiar

spiciness ['spaɪsɪnɪs] *n* lo picante
spick-and-span ['spɪkən'spæn] *adj* impecable
spicy ['spaɪsɪ] *adj* picante
spider ['spaɪdəʳ] *n* araña
spider's web *n* telaraña
spiel [ʃpi:l] *n* (*col*) rollo
spike [spaɪk] *n* (*point*) punta; (*Zool*) pincho, púa; (*Bot*) espiga; (*Elec*) pico parásito ▪ *vt*: **to ~ a quote** cancelar una cita; **spikes** *npl* (*Sport*) zapatillas *fpl* con clavos
spiky ['spaɪkɪ] *adj* (*bush, branch*) cubierto de púas; (*animal*) erizado
spill (*pt, pp* **spilt** *or* **spilled**) [spɪl, spɪlt, spɪld] *vt* derramar, verter; (*blood*) derramar ▪ *vi* derramarse; **to ~ the beans** (*col*) descubrir el pastel
  ▸ **spill out** *vi* derramarse, desparramarse
  ▸ **spill over** *vi* desbordarse
spillage ['spɪlɪdʒ] *n* (*event*) derrame *m*; (*substance*) vertidos
spin [spɪn] (*pt, pp* **spun**) *n* (*revolution of wheel*) vuelta, revolución *f*; (*Aviat*) barrena; (*trip in car*) paseo (en coche) ▪ *vt* (*wool etc*) hilar; (*wheel*) girar ▪ *vi* girar, dar vueltas; **the car spun out of control** el coche se descontroló y empezó a dar vueltas
  ▸ **spin out** *vt* alargar, prolongar
spina bifida ['spaɪnə'bɪfɪdə] *n* espina *f* bífida
spinach ['spɪnɪtʃ] *n* espinacas *fpl*
spinal ['spaɪnl] *adj* espinal
spinal column *n* columna vertebral
spinal cord *n* médula espinal
spin class *n* (*Sport*) clase *f* de spinning
spindly ['spɪndlɪ] *adj* (*leg*) zanquivano
spin doctor *n* (*col*) informador(a) parcial al servicio de un partido político
spin-dry ['spɪn'draɪ] *vt* centrifugar
spin-dryer [spɪn'draɪəʳ] *n* (*Brit*) secadora centrífuga
spine [spaɪn] *n* espinazo, columna vertebral; (*thorn*) espina
spine-chilling ['spaɪntʃɪlɪŋ] *adj* terrorífico
spineless ['spaɪnlɪs] *adj* (*fig*) débil, flojo
spinet [spɪ'nɛt] *n* espineta
spinning ['spɪnɪŋ] *n* (*of thread*) hilado; (*art*) hilandería; (*Sport*) spinning *m*
spinning top *n* peonza
spinning wheel *n* rueca, torno de hilar
spin-off ['spɪnɔf] *n* derivado, producto secundario
spinster ['spɪnstəʳ] *n* soltera; (*pej*) solterona
spiral ['spaɪərl] *n* espiral *f* ▪ *adj* en espiral ▪ *vi* (*prices*) dispararse; **the inflationary ~** la espiral inflacionista
spiral staircase *n* escalera de caracol
spire ['spaɪəʳ] *n* aguja, chapitel *m*

spirit ['spɪrɪt] *n* (*soul*) alma *f*; (*ghost*) fantasma *m*; (*attitude*) espíritu *m*; (*courage*) valor *m*, ánimo; **spirits** *npl* (*drink*) alcohol *msg*, bebidas *fpl* alcohólicas; **in good spirits** alegre, de buen ánimo; **Holy S~** Espíritu *m* Santo; **community ~, public ~** civismo
spirit duplicator *n* copiadora al alcohol
spirited ['spɪrɪtɪd] *adj* enérgico, vigoroso
spirit level *n* nivel *m* de aire
spiritual ['spɪrɪtjuəl] *adj* espiritual ▪ *n* (*also:* **Negro spiritual**) canción *f* religiosa, espiritual *m*
spiritualism ['spɪrɪtjuəlɪzəm] *n* espiritualismo
spit [spɪt] *n* (*for roasting*) asador *m*, espetón *m*; (*spittle*) esputo, escupitajo; (*saliva*) saliva ▪ *vi* (*pt, pp* **spat**) [spæt] escupir; (*sound*) chisporrotear
spite [spaɪt] *n* rencor *m*, ojeriza ▪ *vt* fastidiar; **in ~ of** a pesar de, pese a
spiteful ['spaɪtful] *adj* rencoroso, malévolo
spitting ['spɪtɪŋ] *n*: **"~ prohibited"** "se prohíbe escupir" ▪ *adj*: **to be the ~ image of sb** ser la viva imagen de algn
spittle ['spɪtl] *n* saliva, baba
splash [splæʃ] *n* (*sound*) chapoteo; (*of colour*) mancha ▪ *vt* salpicar de ▪ *vi* (*also:* **splash about**) chapotear; **to ~ paint on the floor** manchar el suelo de pintura
splashdown ['splæʃdaun] *n* amaraje *m*, amerizaje *m*
spleen [spli:n] *n* (*Anat*) bazo
splendid ['splɛndɪd] *adj* espléndido
splendidly ['splɛndɪdlɪ] *adv* espléndidamente; **everything went ~** todo fue a las mil maravillas
splendour, splendor (*US*) ['splɛndəʳ] *n* esplendor *m*; (*fig*) brillo, gloria
splice [splaɪs] *vt* empalmar
splint [splɪnt] *n* tablilla
splinter ['splɪntəʳ] *n* astilla ▪ *vi* astillarse, hacer astillas
splinter group *n* grupo disidente, facción *f*
split [splɪt] (*pt, pp* **~**) *n* hendedura, raja; (*fig*) división *f*; (*Pol*) escisión *f* ▪ *vt* partir, rajar; (*party*) dividir; (*work, profits*) repartir ▪ *vi* (*divide*) dividirse, escindirse; **to ~ the difference** partir la diferencia; **to do the splits** hacer el spagat; **to ~ sth down the middle** (*also fig*) dividir algo en dos
  ▸ **split up** *vi* (*couple*) separarse, romper; (*meeting*) acabarse
split-level ['splɪtlɛvl] *adj* (*house*) dúplex
split peas *npl* guisantes *mpl* secos
split personality *n* doble personalidad *f*
split second *n* fracción *f* de segundo
splitting ['splɪtɪŋ] *adj* (*headache*) horrible

S

splutter ['splʌtəʳ] vi chisporrotear; (person) balbucear

spoil (pt, pp **spoilt** or **spoiled**) [spɔɪl, spɔɪlt, spɔɪld] vt (damage) dañar; (ruin) estropear, echar a perder; (child) mimar, consentir; (ballot paper) invalidar ■ vi: **to be spoiling for a fight** estar con ganas de lucha, andar con ganas de pelea

spoiled [spɔɪld] adj (US: food: bad) pasado, malo; (milk) cortado

spoils [spɔɪlz] npl despojo sg, botín msg

spoilsport ['spɔɪlspɔːt] n aguafiestas m inv

spoilt [spɔɪlt] pt, pp of **spoil** ■ adj (child) mimado, consentido; (ballot paper) invalidado

spoke [spəuk] pt of **speak** ■ n rayo, radio

spoken ['spəukn] pp of **speak**

spokesman ['spəuksmən] n portavoz m, vocero (LAm)

spokesperson ['spəukspə:sn] n portavoz m/f, vocero(-a) (LAm)

spokeswoman ['spəukswumən] n portavoz f, vocera (LAm)

sponge [spʌndʒ] n esponja; (Culin: also: **sponge cake**) bizcocho ■ vt (wash) lavar con esponja ■ vi: **to ~ on** or (US) **off sb** vivir a costa de algn

sponge bag n (Brit) neceser m

sponge cake n bizcocho, pastel m

sponger ['spʌndʒəʳ] n gorrón(-ona) m(f)

spongy ['spʌndʒɪ] adj esponjoso

sponsor ['spɔnsəʳ] n (Radio, TV) patrocinador(a) m(f); (for membership) padrino/madrina; (Comm) fiador(a) m(f), avalador(a) m(f) ■ vt patrocinar; apadrinar; (parliamentary bill) apoyar, respaldar; (idea etc) presentar, promover; **I sponsored him at 3p a mile** (in fund-raising race) me apunté para darle 3 peniques la milla

sponsorship ['spɔnsəʃɪp] n patrocinio

spontaneity [spɔntə'neɪɪtɪ] n espontaneidad f

spontaneous [spɔn'teɪnɪəs] adj espontáneo

spontaneously [spɔn'teɪnɪəslɪ] adv espontáneamente

spooky ['spu:kɪ] adj (col: place, atmosphere) espeluznante, horripilante

spool [spu:l] n carrete m; (of sewing machine) canilla

spoon [spu:n] n cuchara

spoon-feed ['spu:nfi:d] vt dar de comer con cuchara a; (fig) dárselo todo mascado a

spoonful ['spu:nful] n cucharada

sporadic [spə'rædɪk] adj esporádico

sport [spɔːt] n deporte m; (person) buen(a) perdedor(a) m/f; (amusement) juego, diversión f; **indoor/outdoor sports** deportes mpl en sala cubierta/al aire libre; **to say sth in ~** decir algo en broma

sport coat n (US) = **sports jacket**

sporting ['spɔːtɪŋ] adj deportivo; **to give sb a ~ chance** darle a algn su oportunidad

sports car n coche m sport

sports coat n (US) = **sports jacket**

sports ground n campo de deportes, centro deportivo

sports jacket, sport jacket (US) n chaqueta deportiva

sportsman ['spɔːtsmən] n deportista m

sportsmanship ['spɔːtsmənʃɪp] n deportividad f

sports pages npl páginas fpl deportivas

sportswear ['spɔːtswɛəʳ] n ropa de deporte

sportswoman ['spɔːtswumən] n deportista

sporty ['spɔːtɪ] adj deportivo

spot [spɔt] n sitio, lugar m; (dot: on pattern) punto, mancha; (pimple) grano; (also: **advertising spot**) spot m; (small amount): **a ~ of** un poquito de ■ vt (notice) notar, observar ■ adj (Comm) inmediatamente efectivo; **on the ~** en el acto, acto seguido; (in difficulty) en un aprieto; **to do sth on the ~** hacer algo en el acto; **to put sb on the ~** poner a algn en un apuro

spot check n reconocimiento rápido

spotless ['spɔtlɪs] adj (clean) inmaculado; (reputation) intachable

spotlessly ['spɔtlɪslɪ] adv: **~ clean** limpísimo

spotlight ['spɔtlaɪt] n foco, reflector m; (Aut) faro auxiliar

spot-on [spɔt'ɔn] adj (Brit col) exacto

spot price n precio de entrega inmediata

spotted ['spɔtɪd] adj (pattern) de puntos

spotty ['spɔtɪ] adj (face) con granos

spouse [spauz] n cónyuge m/f

spout [spaut] n (of jug) pico; (pipe) caño ■ vi chorrear

sprain [spreɪn] n torcedura, esguince m ■ vt: **to ~ one's ankle** torcerse el tobillo

sprang [spræŋ] pt of **spring**

sprawl [sprɔːl] vi tumbarse ■ n: **urban ~** crecimiento urbano descontrolado; **to send sb sprawling** tirar a algn al suelo

sprawling ['sprɔːlɪŋ] adj (town) desparramado

spray [spreɪ] n rociada; (of sea) espuma; (container) atomizador m; (of paint) pistola rociadora; (of flowers) ramita ■ vt rociar; (crops) regar ■ cpd (deodorant) en atomizador

spread [sprɛd] (pt, pp **~**) n extensión f; (of idea) diseminación f; (col: food) comilona; (Press, Typ: two pages) plana ■ vt extender; diseminar; (butter) untar; (wings, sails) desplegar; (scatter) esparcir ■ vi extenderse; diseminarse; untarse; desplegarse;

esparcirse; **middle-age** ~ gordura de la mediana edad; **repayments will be** ~ **over 18 months** los pagos se harán a lo largo de 18 meses

spread-eagled ['sprɛdiːgld] *adj*: **to be** ~ estar despatarrado

spreadsheet ['sprɛdʃiːt] *n* (*Comput*) hoja de cálculo

spree [spriː] *n*: **to go on a** ~ ir de juerga *or* farra (*LAm*)

sprightly ['spraɪtlɪ] *adj* vivo, enérgico

spring [sprɪŋ] (*pt* **sprang**, *pp* **sprung**) *n* (*season*) primavera; (*leap*) salto, brinco; (*coiled metal*) resorte *m*; (*of water*) fuente *f*, manantial *m*; (*bounciness*) elasticidad *f* ▪ *vi* (*arise*) brotar, nacer; (*leap*) saltar, brincar ▪ *vt*: **to** ~ **a leak** (*pipe etc*) empezar a hacer agua; **he sprang the news on me** de repente me soltó la noticia; **in (the)** ~ en (la) primavera; **to walk with a** ~ **in one's step** andar dando saltos *or* brincos; **to** ~ **into action** lanzarse a la acción
▶ **spring up** *vi* (*problem*) surgir

springboard ['sprɪŋbɔːd] *n* trampolín *m*

spring-clean [sprɪŋ'kliːn] *n* (*also*: **spring-cleaning**) limpieza general

spring onion *n* cebolleta

spring roll *n* rollito de primavera

springtime ['sprɪŋtaɪm] *n* primavera

springy ['sprɪŋɪ] *adj* elástico; (*grass*) mullido

sprinkle ['sprɪŋkl] *vt* (*pour*) rociar; **to** ~ **water on**, ~ **with water** rociar *or* salpicar de agua

sprinkler ['sprɪŋklər] *n* (*for lawn*) aspersor *m*; (*to put out fire*) aparato de rociadura automática

sprinkling ['sprɪŋklɪŋ] *n* (*of water*) rociada; (*of salt, sugar*) un poco de

sprint [sprɪnt] *n* (e)sprint *m* ▪ *vi* (*gen*) correr a toda velocidad; (*Sport*) esprintar; **the 200 metres** ~ el (e)sprint de 200 metros

sprinter ['sprɪntər] *n* velocista *m/f*

spritzer ['sprɪtsər] *n* vino blanco con soda

sprocket ['sprɔkɪt] *n* (*on printer etc*) rueda dentada

sprocket feed *n* avance *m* por rueda dentada

sprout [spraʊt] *vi* brotar, retoñar ▪ *n*: **(Brussels) sprouts** *npl* coles *fpl* de Bruselas

spruce [spruːs] *n* (*Bot*) pícea ▪ *adj* aseado, pulcro
▶ **spruce up** *vt* (*tidy*) arreglar, acicalar; (*smarten up: room etc*) ordenar; **to** ~ **o.s. up** arreglarse

sprung [sprʌŋ] *pp of* **spring**

spry [spraɪ] *adj* ágil, activo

SPUC *n abbr* (= *Society for the Protection of Unborn Children*) ≈ Federación *f* Española de Asociaciones Provida

spun [spʌn] *pt, pp of* **spin**

spur [spəːr] *n* espuela; (*fig*) estímulo, aguijón *m* ▪ *vt* (*also*: **spur on**) estimular, incitar; **on the** ~ **of the moment** de improviso

spurious ['spjʊərɪəs] *adj* falso

spurn [spəːn] *vt* desdeñar, rechazar

spurt [spəːt] *n* chorro; (*of energy*) arrebato ▪ *vi* chorrear; **to put in** *or* **on a** ~ (*runner*) acelerar; (*fig: in work etc*) hacer un gran esfuerzo

sputter ['spʌtər] *vi* = **splutter**

spy [spaɪ] *n* espía *m/f* ▪ *vi*: **to** ~ **on** espiar a ▪ *vt* (*see*) divisar, lograr ver ▪ *cpd* (*film, story*) de espionaje

spying ['spaɪɪŋ] *n* espionaje *m*

Sq. *abbr* (*in address*: = *Square*) Pl.

sq. *abbr* (*Math etc*) = **square**

squabble ['skwɔbl] *n* riña, pelea ▪ *vi* reñir, pelear

squad [skwɔd] *n* (*Mil*) pelotón *m*; (*Police*) brigada; (*Sport*) equipo; **flying** ~ (*Police*) brigada móvil

squad car *n* (*Police*) coche-patrulla *m*

squaddie ['skwɔdɪ] *n* (*Mil: col*) chivo

squadron ['skwɔdrn] *n* (*Mil*) escuadrón *m*; (*Aviat, Naut*) escuadra

squalid ['skwɔlɪd] *adj* miserable

squall [skwɔːl] *n* (*storm*) chubasco; (*wind*) ráfaga

squalor ['skwɔlər] *n* miseria

squander ['skwɔndər] *vt* (*money*) derrochar, despilfarrar; (*chances*) desperdiciar

square [skwɛər] *n* cuadro; (*in town*) plaza; (*US: block of houses*) manzana, cuadra (*LAm*) ▪ *adj* cuadrado ▪ *vt* (*arrange*) arreglar; (*Math*) cuadrar; (*reconcile*): **can you** ~ **it with your conscience?** ¿cómo se justifica ante sí mismo? ▪ *vi* cuadrar, conformarse; **all** ~ igual(es); **a** ~ **meal** una comida decente; **two metres** ~ dos metros por dos; **one** ~ **metre** un metro cuadrado; **to get one's accounts** ~ dejar las cuentas claras; **I'll** ~ **it with him** (*col*) yo lo arreglo con él; **we're back to** ~ **one** (*fig*) hemos vuelto al punto de partida
▶ **square up** *vi* (*settle*): **to** ~ **up (with sb)** ajustar cuentas (con algn)

square bracket *n* (*Typ*) corchete *m*

squarely ['skwɛəlɪ] *adv* (*fully*) de lleno; (*honestly, fairly*) honradamente, justamente

square root *n* raíz *f* cuadrada

squash [skwɔʃ] *n* (*vegetable*) calabaza; (*Sport*) squash *m*; (*Brit: drink*): **lemon/orange** ~ zumo (*SP*) *or* jugo (*LAm*) de limón/naranja ▪ *vt* aplastar

squat [skwɔt] *adj* achaparrado ▪ *vi* agacharse, sentarse en cuclillas; (*on property*) ocupar ilegalmente

squatter ['skwɔtər] *n* ocupante *m/f* ilegal, okupa *m/f*

S

squawk [skwɔ:k] vi graznar
squeak [skwi:k] vi (hinge, wheel) chirriar,
rechinar; (shoe, wood) crujir ■ n (of hinge,
wheel etc) chirrido, rechinamiento; (of shoes)
crujir m; (of mouse etc) chillido
squeaky ['skwi:kı] adj que cruje; **to be ~
clean** (fig) ser superhonrado
squeal [skwi:l] vi chillar, dar gritos agudos
squeamish ['skwi:mıʃ] adj delicado,
remilgado
squeeze [skwi:z] n presión f; (of hand)
apretón m; (Comm: credit squeeze) restricción f
■ vt (lemon etc) exprimir; (hand, arm) apretar;
a ~ of lemon unas gotas de limón; **to ~
past/under sth** colarse al lado de/por debajo
de algo
▶ **squeeze out** vt exprimir; (fig) excluir
▶ **squeeze through** vi abrirse paso con
esfuerzos
squelch [skwɛltʃ] vi chapotear
squid [skwıd] n calamar m
squiggle ['skwıgl] n garabato
squint [skwınt] vi entrecerrar los ojos ■ n
(Med) estrabismo; **to ~ at sth** mirar algo
entornando los ojos
squire ['skwaıəʳ] n (Brit) terrateniente m
squirm [skwə:m] vi retorcerse, revolverse
squirrel ['skwırəl] n ardilla
squirt [skwə:t] vi salir a chorros
Sr abbr = **senior**; (Rel) = **sister**
SRC n abbr (Brit: = Students' Representative Council)
consejo de estudiantes
Sri Lanka [srı'læŋkə] n Sri Lanka m
SRO abbr (US) = **standing room only**
SS abbr (= steamship) M.V.
SSA n abbr (US: = Social Security Administration)
≈ Seguro Social
SST n abbr (US) = **supersonic transport**
ST abbr (US: = Standard Time) hora oficial
St abbr (= saint) Sto.(-a); (= street) c/
stab [stæb] n (with knife etc) puñalada; (of pain)
pinchazo; **to have a ~ at (doing) sth** (col)
probar (a hacer) algo ■ vt apuñalar; **to ~ sb
to death** matar a algn a puñaladas
stabbing ['stæbıŋ] n: **there's been a ~** han
apuñalado a alguien ■ adj (pain) punzante
stability [stə'bılıtı] n estabilidad f
stabilization [steıbəlaı'zeıʃən] n
estabilización f
stabilize ['steıbəlaız] vt estabilizar ■ vi
estabilizarse
stabilizer ['steıbəlaızəʳ] n (Aviat, Naut)
estabilizador m
stable ['steıbl] adj estable ■ n cuadra,
caballeriza; **riding stables** escuela hípica
staccato [stə'kɑ:təu] adj, adv staccato
stack [stæk] n montón m, pila; (col) mar f

■ vt amontonar, apilar; **there's stacks of
time to finish it** hay cantidad de tiempo
para acabarlo
stacker ['stækəʳ] n (for printer) apiladora
stadium ['steıdıəm] n estadio
staff [stɑ:f] n (work force) personal m, plantilla;
(Brit Scol: also: **teaching staff**) cuerpo docente;
(stick) bastón m ■ vt proveer de personal;
to be staffed by Asians/women tener una
plantilla asiática/femenina
staffroom ['stɑ:fru:m] n sala de profesores
Staffs abbr (Brit) = **Staffordshire**
stag [stæg] n ciervo, venado; (Brit Stock
Exchange) especulador m con nuevas
emisiones
stage [steıdʒ] n escena; (point) etapa;
(platform) plataforma; **the ~** el escenario,
el teatro ■ vt (play) poner en escena,
representar; (organize) montar, organizar;
(fig: perform: recovery etc) efectuar; **in stages**
por etapas; **in the early/final stages** en las
primeras/últimas etapas; **to go through
a difficult ~** pasar una fase or etapa mala
stagecoach ['steıdʒkəutʃ] n diligencia
stage door n entrada de artistas
stagehand ['steıdʒhænd] n tramoyista m/f
stage-manage ['steıdʒmænıdʒ] vt (fig)
manipular
stage manager n director(a) m(f) de escena
stagger ['stægəʳ] vi tambalear ■ vt (amaze)
asombrar; (hours, holidays) escalonar
staggering ['stægərıŋ] adj (amazing)
asombroso, pasmoso
staging post ['steıdʒıŋ-] n escala
stagnant ['stægnənt] adj estancado
stagnate [stæg'neıt] vi estancarse; (fig:
economy, mind) quedarse estancado
stagnation [stæg'neıʃən] n estancamiento
stag night, stag party n despedida de
soltero
staid [steıd] adj (clothes) serio, formal
stain [steın] n mancha; (colouring) tintura
■ vt manchar; (wood) teñir
stained glass window [steınd-] n vidriera
de colores
stainless ['steınlıs] adj (steel) inoxidable
stain remover n quitamanchas m inv
stair [steəʳ] n (step) peldaño, escalón m; **stairs**
npl escaleras fpl
staircase ['steəkeıs], **stairway** ['steəweı] n
escalera
stairwell ['steəwɛl] n hueco or caja de la
escalera
stake [steık] n estaca, poste m; (Betting)
apuesta ■ vt (bet) apostar; (also: **stake out**:
area) cercar con estacas; **to be at ~** estar
en juego; **to have a ~ in sth** tener interés

en algo; **to ~ a claim to (sth)** presentar reclamación por or reclamar (algo)

stake-out ['steɪkaut] n vigilancia; **to be on a ~** estar de vigilancia

stalactite ['stæləktaɪt] n estalactita

stalagmite ['stæləgmaɪt] n estalagmita

stale [steɪl] adj (bread) duro; (food) pasado

stalemate ['steɪlmeɪt] n tablas fpl; **to reach ~** (fig) estancarse, alcanzar un punto muerto

stalk [stɔːk] n tallo, caña ▪ vt acechar, cazar al acecho; **to ~ off** irse airado

stall [stɔːl] n (in market) puesto; (in stable) casilla (de establo) ▪ vt (Aut) parar, calar ▪ vi (Aut) pararse, calarse; (fig) buscar evasivas; **stalls** npl (Brit: in cinema, theatre) butacas fpl; **a newspaper ~** un quiosco (de periódicos); **a flower ~** un puesto de flores

stallholder ['stɔːlhəuldəʳ] n dueño(-a) de un puesto

stallion ['stælɪən] n semental m, garañón m

stalwart ['stɔːlwət] n partidario(-a) incondicional

stamen ['steɪmən] n estambre m

stamina ['stæmɪnə] n resistencia

stammer ['stæməʳ] n tartamudeo, balbuceo ▪ vi tartamudear, balbucir

stamp [stæmp] n sello, estampilla (LAm); (mark) marca, huella; (on document) timbre m ▪ vi (also: **stamp one's foot**) patear ▪ vt patear, golpear con el pie; (letter) poner sellos en; (with rubber stamp) marcar con sello; **stamped addressed envelope (sae)** sobre m sellado con las señas propias
▶ **stamp out** vt (fire) apagar con el pie; (crime, opposition) acabar con

stamp album n álbum m para sellos

stamp collecting n filatelia

stamp duty n (Brit) derecho de timbre

stampede [stæm'piːd] n (of cattle) estampida

stamp machine n máquina (expendedora) de sellos

stance [stæns] n postura

stand [stænd] (pt, pp **stood**) n (attitude) posición f, postura; (for taxis) parada; (also: **music stand**) atril m; (Sport) tribuna; (at exhibition) stand m ▪ vi (be) estar, encontrarse; (be on foot) estar de pie; (rise) levantarse; (remain) quedar en pie ▪ vt (place) poner, colocar; (tolerate, withstand) aguantar, soportar; **to make a ~** resistir; (fig) mantener una postura firme; **to take a ~ on an issue** adoptar una actitud hacia una cuestión; **to ~ for parliament** (Brit) presentarse (como candidato) a las elecciones; **nothing stands in our way** nada nos lo impide; **to ~ still** quedarse inmóvil; **to let sth ~ as it is** dejar algo como está; **as things ~** tal como están

las cosas; **to ~ sb a drink/meal** invitar a algn a una copa/a comer; **the company will have to ~ the loss** la empresa tendrá que hacer frente a las pérdidas; **I can't ~ him** no le aguanto, no le puedo ver; **to ~ guard** or **watch** (Mil) hacer guardia
▶ **stand aside** vi apartarse, mantenerse aparte
▶ **stand by** vi (be ready) estar listo ▪ vt fus (opinion) mantener
▶ **stand down** vi (withdraw) ceder el puesto; (Mil, Law) retirarse
▶ **stand for** vt fus (signify) significar; (tolerate) aguantar, permitir
▶ **stand in for** vt fus suplir a
▶ **stand out** vi (be prominent) destacarse
▶ **stand up** vi (rise) levantarse, ponerse de pie
▶ **stand up for** vt fus defender
▶ **stand up to** vt fus hacer frente a

stand-alone ['stændələun] adj (Comput) autónomo

standard ['stændəd] n patrón m, norma; (flag) estandarte m ▪ adj (size etc) normal, corriente, estándar; **standards** npl (morals) valores mpl morales; **the gold ~** (Comm) el patrón oro; **high/low ~** de alto/bajo nivel; **below** or **not up to ~** (work) de calidad inferior; **to be** or **come up to ~** satisfacer los requisitos; **to apply a double ~** aplicar un doble criterio

Standard Grade n (Scottish Scol) certificado del último ciclo de la enseñanza secundaria obligatoria

standardization [stændədaɪ'zeɪʃən] n normalización f

standardize ['stændədaɪz] vt estandarizar

standard lamp n (Brit) lámpara de pie

standard model n modelo estándar

standard of living n nivel m de vida

standard practice n norma, práctica común

standard rate n tasa de imposición

standard time n hora oficial

stand-by ['stændbaɪ] n (alert) alerta, aviso; (also: **stand-by ticket**: Theat) entrada reducida de última hora; (: Aviat) billete m standby; **to be on ~** estar preparado; (doctor) estar listo para acudir; (Aviat) estar en la lista de espera

stand-by generator n generador m de reserva

stand-by passenger n (Aviat) pasajero(-a) en lista de espera

stand-by ticket n (Aviat) (billete m) standby m

stand-in ['stændɪn] n suplente m/f; (Cine) doble m/f

standing ['stændɪŋ] adj (upright) derecho; (on foot) de pie, en pie; (permanent: committee) permanente; (: rule) fijo; (: army) permanente, regular; (grievance) constante, viejo ■ *n* reputación *f*; (*duration*): **of six months'** ~ que lleva seis meses; **of many years'** ~ que lleva muchos años; **he was given a ~ ovation** le dieron una calurosa ovación de pie; ~ **joke** motivo constante de broma; **a man of some ~** un hombre de cierta posición *or* categoría

standing order *n* (*Brit*: *at bank*) giro bancario; **standing orders** *npl* (*Mil*) reglamento *sg* general

standing room *n* sitio para estar de pie

stand-off ['stændɔf] *n* punto muerto

stand-offish [stænd'ɔfɪʃ] *adj* distante

standpipe ['stændpaɪp] *n* tubo vertical

standpoint ['stændpɔɪnt] *n* punto de vista

standstill ['stændstɪl] *n*: **at a ~** paralizado, en un punto muerto; **to come to a ~** pararse, quedar paralizado

stank [stæŋk] *pt of* **stink**

staple ['steɪpl] *n* (*for papers*) grapa; (*product*) producto *or* artículo de primeva necesidad ■ *adj* (*crop, industry, food etc*) básico ■ *vt* grapar

stapler ['steɪplə'] *n* grapadora

star [stɑː'] *n* estrella; (*celebrity*) estrella, astro ■ *vi*: **to ~ in** ser la estrella de; **four-~ hotel** hotel *m* de cuatro estrellas; **4-~ petrol** gasolina extra

star attraction *n* atracción *f* principal

starboard ['stɑːbəd] *n* estribor *m*

starch [stɑːtʃ] *n* almidón *m*

starchy ['stɑːtʃɪ] *adj* (*food*) feculento

stardom ['stɑːdəm] *n* estrellato

stare [stɛə'] *n* mirada fija ■ *vi*: **to ~ at** mirar fijo

starfish ['stɑːfɪʃ] *n* estrella de mar

stark [stɑːk] *adj* (*bleak*) severo, escueto; (*simplicity, colour*) austero; (*reality, truth*) puro; (*poverty*) absoluto ■ *adv*: ~ **naked** en cueros

starkers ['stɑːkəz] *adj* (*Brit col*): **to be ~** estar en cueros

starlet ['stɑːlɪt] *n* (*Cine*) actriz *f* principiante

starling ['stɑːlɪŋ] *n* estornino

starry ['stɑːrɪ] *adj* estrellado

starry-eyed [stɑːrɪ'aɪd] *adj* (*gullible, innocent*) inocentón(-ona), ingenuo; (*idealistic*) idealista; (*from wonder*) asombrado; (*from love*) enamoradísimo

Stars and Stripes *npl*: **the ~** las barras y las estrellas, la bandera de EEUU

star sign *n* signo del zodíaco

star-studded ['stɑːstʌdɪd] *adj*: **a ~ cast** un elenco estelar

start [stɑːt] *n* (*beginning*) principio, comienzo; (*departure*) salida; (*sudden movement*) sobresalto; (*advantage*) ventaja ■ *vt* empezar, comenzar; (*cause*) causar; (*found: business,* *newspaper*) establecer, fundar; (*engine*) poner en marcha ■ *vi* (*begin*) comenzar, empezar; (*with fright*) asustarse, sobresaltarse; (*train etc*) salir; **to give sb a ~** dar un susto a algn; **at the ~** al principio; **for a ~** en primer lugar; **to make an early ~** ponerse en camino temprano; **the thieves had three hours' ~** los ladrones llevaban tres horas de ventaja; **to ~ a fire** provocar un incendio; **to ~ doing** *or* **to do sth** empezar a hacer algo; **to ~ (off) with ...** (*firstly*) para empezar; (*at the beginning*) al principio

▶ **start off** *vi* empezar, comenzar; (*leave*) salir, ponerse en camino

▶ **start over** *vi* (*US*) volver a empezar

▶ **start up** *vi* comenzar; (*car*) ponerse en marcha ■ *vt* comenzar; (*car*) poner en marcha

starter ['stɑːtə'] *n* (*Aut*) botón *m* de arranque; (*Sport: official*) juez *m/f* de salida; (: *runner*) corredor(a) *m(f)*; (*Brit Culin*) entrada

starting point ['stɑːtɪŋ-] *n* punto de partida

starting price *n* (*Comm*) precio inicial

startle ['stɑːtl] *vt* asustar, sobresaltar

startling ['stɑːtlɪŋ] *adj* alarmante

star turn *n* (*Brit*) atracción *f* principal

starvation [stɑː'veɪʃən] *n* hambre *f*, hambruna (*LAm*); (*Med*) inanición *f*

starvation wages *npl* sueldo *sg* de hambre

starve [stɑːv] *vi* pasar hambre; (*to death*) morir de hambre ■ *vt* hacer pasar hambre; (*fig*) privar; **I'm starving** estoy muerto de hambre

stash [stæʃ] *vt*: **to ~ sth away** (*col*) poner algo a buen recaudo

state [steɪt] *n* estado; (*pomp*): **in ~** con mucha ceremonia ■ *vt* (*say, declare*) afirmar; (*a case*) presentar, exponer; ~ **of emergency** estado de excepción *or* emergencia; ~ **of mind** estado de ánimo; **to lie in ~** (*corpse*) estar de cuerpo presente; **to be in a ~** estar agitado

State Department *n* (*US*) Ministerio de Asuntos Exteriores

state education *n* (*Brit*) enseñanza pública

stateless ['steɪtlɪs] *adj* desnacionalizado

stately ['steɪtlɪ] *adj* majestuoso, imponente

statement ['steɪtmənt] *n* afirmación *f*; (*Law*) declaración *f*; (*Comm*) estado; **official ~** informe *m* oficial; ~ **of account, bank ~** estado de cuenta

state-of-the-art ['steɪtəvðɪ'ɑːt] *adj* (*technology etc*) puntero

state-owned ['steɪtəund] *adj* estatal, del estado

States [steɪts] *npl*: **the ~** los Estados Unidos

state school *n* escuela *or* colegio estatal

statesman ['steɪtsmən] *n* estadista *m*

statesmanship ['steɪtsmənʃɪp] *n* habilidad *f* política, arte *m* de gobernar

static ['stætɪk] *n* (*Radio*) parásitos *mpl* ■ *adj* estático

static electricity *n* electricidad *f* estática

station ['steɪʃən] *n* (*gen*) estación *f*; (*place*) puesto, sitio; (*Radio*) emisora; (*rank*) posición *f* social ■ *vt* colocar, situar; (*Mil*) apostar; **action stations!** ¡a los puestos de combate!; **to be stationed in** (*Mil*) estar estacionado en

stationary ['steɪʃnərɪ] *adj* estacionario, fijo

stationer ['steɪʃənəʳ] *n* papelero(-a)

stationer's, stationer's shop *n* (*Brit*) papelería

stationery ['steɪʃənərɪ] *n* (*writing paper*) papel *m* de escribir; (*writing materials*) artículos *mpl* de escritorio

station master *n* (*Rail*) jefe *m* de estación

station wagon *n* (*US*) coche *m* familiar con ranchera

statistic [stə'tɪstɪk] *n* estadística

statistical [stə'tɪstɪkl] *adj* estadístico

statistics [stə'tɪstɪks] *n* (*science*) estadística

statue ['stætjuː] *n* estatua

statuette [stætju'ɛt] *n* figurilla

stature ['stætʃəʳ] *n* estatura; (*fig*) talla

status ['steɪtəs] *n* condición *f*, estado; (*reputation*) reputación *f*, estatus *m*; **the ~ quo** el statu quo

status line *n* (*Comput*) línea de situación or de estado

status symbol *n* símbolo de prestigio

statute ['stætjuːt] *n* estatuto, ley *f*

statute book *n* código de leyes

statutory ['stætjutrɪ] *adj* estatutario; **~ meeting** junta ordinaria

staunch [stɔːntʃ] *adj* leal, incondicional ■ *vt* (*flow, blood*) restañar

stave [steɪv] *vt*: **to ~ off** (*attack*) rechazar; (*threat*) evitar

stay [steɪ] *n* (*period of time*) estancia; (*Law*): **~ of execution** aplazamiento de una sentencia ■ *vi* (*remain*) quedar(se); (*as guest*) hospedarse; **to ~ put** seguir en el mismo sitio; **to ~ the night/5 days** pasar la noche/ estar or quedarse 5 días

▶ **stay behind** *vi* quedar atrás

▶ **stay in** *vi* (*at home*) quedarse en casa

▶ **stay on** *vi* quedarse

▶ **stay out** *vi* (*of house*) no volver a casa; (*strikers*) no volver al trabajo

▶ **stay up** *vi* (*at night*) velar, no acostarse

staying power ['steɪɪŋ-] *n* resistencia, aguante *m*

STD *n abbr* (Brit: = *subscriber trunk dialling*) servicio de conferencias automáticas; (= *sexually transmitted disease*) ETS *f*

stead [stɛd] *n*: **in sb's ~** en lugar de algn; **to stand sb in good ~** ser muy útil a algn

steadfast ['stɛdfɑːst] *adj* firme, resuelto

steadily ['stɛdɪlɪ] *adv* (*firmly*) firmemente; (*unceasingly*) sin parar; (*fixedly*) fijamente; (*walk*) normalmente; (*drive*) a velocidad constante

steady ['stɛdɪ] *adj* (*fixed*) firme, fijo; (*regular*) regular; (*boyfriend etc*) formal, fijo; (*person, character*) sensato, juicioso ■ *vt* (*hold*) mantener firme; (*stabilize*) estabilizar; (*nerves*) calmar; **to ~ o.s. on** or **against sth** afirmarse en algo

steak [steɪk] *n* (*gen*) filete *m*; (*beef*) bistec *m*

steal (*pt* **stole**, *pp* **stolen**) [stiːl, stəul, 'stəuln] *vt, vi* robar

▶ **steal away, steal off** *vi* marcharse furtivamente, escabullirse

stealth [stɛlθ] *n*: **by ~** a escondidas, sigilosamente

stealthy ['stɛlθɪ] *adj* cauteloso, sigiloso

steam [stiːm] *n* vapor *m*; (*mist*) vaho, humo ■ *vt* (*Culin*) cocer al vapor ■ *vi* echar vapor; (*ship*): **to ~ along** avanzar, ir avanzando; **under one's own ~** (*fig*) por sus propios medios or propias fuerzas; **to run out of ~** (*fig: person*) quedar(se) agotado, quemarse; **to let off ~** (*fig*) desahogarse

▶ **steam up** *vi* (*window*) empañarse; **to get steamed up about sth** (*fig*) ponerse negro por algo

steam engine *n* máquina de vapor

steamer ['stiːməʳ] *n* (buque *m* de) vapor *m*; (*Culin*) recipiente para cocinar al vapor

steam iron *n* plancha de vapor

steamroller ['stiːmrəuləʳ] *n* apisonadora

steamship ['stiːmʃɪp] *n* = **steamer**

steamy ['stiːmɪ] *adj* (*room*) lleno de vapor; (*window*) empañado

steel [stiːl] *n* acero ■ *adj* de acero

steel band *n* banda de percusión del Caribe

steel industry *n* industria siderúrgica

steel mill *n* fábrica de acero

steelworks ['stiːlwəːks] *n* acería, fundición *f* de acero

steely ['stiːlɪ] *adj* (*determination*) inflexible; (*gaze*) duro; (*eyes*) penetrante; **~ grey** gris *m* metálico

steelyard ['stiːljɑːd] *n* romana

steep [stiːp] *adj* escarpado, abrupto; (*stair*) empinado; (*price*) exorbitante, excesivo ■ *vt* empapar, remojar

steeple ['stiːpl] *n* aguja, campanario

steeplechase ['stiːpltʃeɪs] *n* carrera de obstáculos

S

steeplejack ['sti:pldʒæk] n reparador(a) m(f) de chimeneas or de campanarios

steer [stɪəʳ] vt (car) conducir (SP), manejar (LAm); (person) dirigir, guiar ■ vi conducir; **to ~ clear of sb/sth** (fig) esquivar a algn/evadir algo

steering ['stɪərɪŋ] n (Aut) dirección f

steering committee n comisión f directiva

steering wheel n volante m

stellar ['stɛləʳ] adj estelar

stem [stɛm] n (of plant) tallo; (of glass) pie m; (of pipe) cañón m ■ vt detener; (blood) restañar
▶ **stem from** vt fus ser consecuencia de

stem cell n célula madre

stench [stɛntʃ] n hedor m

stencil ['stɛnsl] n (typed) cliché m, clisé m; (lettering) plantilla ■ vt hacer un cliché de

stenographer [stɛ'nɔgrəfəʳ] n (US) taquígrafo(-a)

step [stɛp] n paso; (sound) paso, pisada; (stair) peldaño, escalón m ■ vi: **to ~ forward** dar un paso adelante; **steps** npl (Brit) = **stepladder**; **~ by ~** paso a paso; (fig) poco a poco; **to keep in ~ (with)** llevar el paso de; (fig) llevar el paso de, estar de acuerdo con; **to be in/out of ~ with** estar acorde con/estar en disonancia con; **to take steps to solve a problem** tomar medidas para resolver un problema
▶ **step down** vi (fig) retirarse
▶ **step in** vi entrar; (fig) intervenir
▶ **step off** vt fus bajar de
▶ **step on** vt fus pisar
▶ **step over** vt fus pasar por encima de
▶ **step up** vt (increase) aumentar

step aerobics npl step m

stepbrother ['stɛpbrʌðəʳ] n hermanastro

stepdaughter ['stɛpdɔ:təʳ] n hijastra

stepfather ['stɛpfɑ:ðəʳ] n padrastro

stepladder ['stɛplædəʳ] n escalera doble or de tijera

stepmother ['stɛpmʌðəʳ] n madrastra

stepping stone ['stɛpɪŋ-] n pasadera

step Reebok® [-'ri:bɔk] n step m

stepsister ['stɛpsɪstəʳ] n hermanastra

stepson ['stɛpsʌn] n hijastro

stereo ['stɛrɪəu] n estéreo ■ adj (also: **stereophonic**) estéreo, estereofónico; **in ~** en estéreo

stereotype ['stɪərɪətaɪp] n estereotipo ■ vt estereotipar

sterile ['stɛraɪl] adj estéril

sterilization [stɛrɪlaɪ'zeɪʃən] n esterilización f

sterilize ['stɛrɪlaɪz] vt esterilizar

sterling ['stə:lɪŋ] adj (silver) de ley ■ n (Econ) libras fpl esterlinas; **a pound ~** una libra esterlina; **he is of ~ character** tiene un carácter excelente

stern [stə:n] adj severo, austero ■ n (Naut) popa

sternum ['stə:nəm] n esternón m

steroid ['stɪərɔɪd] n esteroide m

stethoscope ['stɛθəskəup] n estetoscopio

stevedore ['sti:vədɔ:ʳ] n estibador m

stew [stju:] n cocido, estofado, guisado (LAm) ■ vt, vi estofar, guisar; (fruit) cocer; **stewed fruit** compota de fruta

steward ['stju:əd] n (Brit: gen) camarero; (shop steward) enlace m/f sindical

stewardess ['stju:ədəs] n azafata

stewardship ['stju:ədʃɪp] n tutela

stewing steak ['stju:ɪŋ-], **stew meat** (US) n carne f de vaca

St. Ex. abbr = **stock exchange**

stg abbr (= sterling) ester

stick [stɪk] (pt, pp **stuck**) n palo; (as weapon) porra; (also: **walking stick**) bastón m ■ vt (glue) pegar; (col: put) meter; (: tolerate) aguantar, soportar ■ vi pegarse; (come to a stop) quedarse parado; (get jammed: door, lift) atascarse; **to get hold of the wrong end of the ~** entender al revés; **to ~ to** (word, principles) atenerse a, ser fiel a; (promise) cumplir; **it stuck in my mind** se me quedó grabado; **to ~ sth into** clavar or hincar algo en
▶ **stick around** vi (col) quedarse
▶ **stick out** vi sobresalir ■ vt: **to ~ it out** (col) aguantar
▶ **stick up** vi sobresalir
▶ **stick up for** vt fus defender

sticker ['stɪkəʳ] n (label) etiqueta adhesiva; (with slogan) pegatina

sticking plaster ['stɪkɪŋ-] n (Brit) esparadrapo

sticking point n (fig) punto de fricción

stick insect n insecto palo

stickler ['stɪkləʳ] n: **to be a ~ for** insistir mucho en

stick shift n (US Aut) palanca de cambios

stick-up ['stɪkʌp] n asalto, atraco

sticky ['stɪkɪ] adj pegajoso; (label) adhesivo; (fig) difícil

stiff [stɪf] adj rígido, tieso; (hard) duro; (difficult) difícil; (person) inflexible; (price) exorbitante; **to have a ~ neck/back** tener tortícolis/dolor de espalda; **the door's ~** la puerta está atrancada

stiffen ['stɪfn] vt hacer más rígido; (limb) entumecer ■ vi endurecerse; (grow stronger) fortalecerse

stiffness ['stɪfnɪs] n rigidez f

stifle ['staɪfl] *vt* ahogar, sofocar
stifling ['staɪflɪŋ] *adj* (*heat*) sofocante, bochornoso
stigma *n* (*Bot, Med, Rel*) (*pl* **stigmata**) (*fig*) (*pl* **stigmas**) ['stɪɡmə, stɪɡ'mɑːtə] ▪ *n* estigma *m*
stile [staɪl] *n* escalera (*para pasar una cerca*)
stiletto [stɪ'lɛtəu] *n* (*Brit: also:* **stiletto heel**) tacón *m* de aguja
still [stɪl] *adj* inmóvil, quieto; (*orange juice etc*) sin gas ▪ *adv* (*up to this time*) todavía; (*even*) aún; (*nonetheless*) sin embargo, aun así ▪ *n* (*Cine*) foto *f* fija; **keep ~!** ¡estate quieto!, ¡no te muevas!; **he ~ hasn't arrived** todavía no ha llegado
stillborn ['stɪlbɔːn] *adj* nacido muerto
still life *n* naturaleza muerta
stilt [stɪlt] *n* zanco; (*pile*) pilar *m*, soporte *m*
stilted ['stɪltɪd] *adj* afectado, artificial
stimulant ['stɪmjulənt] *n* estimulante *m*
stimulate ['stɪmjuleɪt] *vt* estimular
stimulating ['stɪmjuleɪtɪŋ] *adj* estimulante
stimulation [stɪmju'leɪʃən] *n* estímulo
stimulus (*pl* **stimuli**) ['stɪmjuləs, -laɪ] *n* estímulo, incentivo
sting [stɪŋ] (*pt, pp* **stung**) *n* (*wound*) picadura; (*pain*) escozor *m*, picazón *m*; (*organ*) aguijón *m*; (*col: confidence trick*) timo ▪ *vt* picar ▪ *vi* picar, escocer; **my eyes are stinging** me pican *or* escuecen los ojos
stingy ['stɪndʒɪ] *adj* tacaño
stink [stɪŋk] *n* hedor *m*, tufo ▪ *vi* (*pt* **stank**, *pp* **stunk**) [stæŋk, stʌŋk] heder, apestar
stinking ['stɪŋkɪŋ] *adj* hediondo, fétido; (*fig: col*) horrible
stint [stɪnt] *n* tarea, destajo; **to do one's ~ (at sth)** hacer su parte (de algo), hacer lo que corresponde (de algo) ▪ *vi*: **to ~ on** escatimar
stipend ['staɪpɛnd] *n* salario, remuneración *f*
stipendiary [staɪ'pɛndɪərɪ] *adj*: **~ magistrate** magistrado(-a) estipendiario(-a)
stipulate ['stɪpjuleɪt] *vt* estipular
stipulation [stɪpju'leɪʃən] *n* estipulación *f*
stir [stəː] *n* (*fig: agitation*) conmoción *f* ▪ *vt* (*tea etc*) remover; (*fire*) atizar; (*move*) agitar; (*fig: emotions*) conmover ▪ *vi* moverse; **to give sth a ~** remover algo; **to cause a ~** causar conmoción *or* sensación
▸ **stir up** *vt* excitar; (*trouble*) fomentar
stir-fry ['stəːfraɪ] *vt* sofreír removiendo ▪ *n* plato preparado sofriendo y removiendo los ingredientes
stirrup ['stɪrəp] *n* estribo
stitch [stɪtʃ] *n* (*Sewing*) puntada; (*Knitting*) punto; (*Med*) punto (de sutura); (*pain*) punzada ▪ *vt* coser; (*Med*) suturar
stoat [stəut] *n* armiño

stock [stɔk] *n* (*Comm: reserves*) existencias *fpl*, stock *m*; (*: selection*) surtido; (*Agr*) ganado, ganadería; (*Culin*) caldo; (*fig: lineage*) estirpe *f*, cepa; (*Finance*) capital *m*; (*: shares*) acciones *fpl*; (*Rail: rolling stock*) material *m* rodante ▪ *adj* (*Comm: goods, size*) normal, de serie; (*fig: reply etc*) clásico, trillado; (*: greeting*) acostumbrado ▪ *vt* (*have in stock*) tener existencias de; (*supply*) proveer, abastecer; **in ~** en existencia *or* almacén; **to have sth in ~** tener existencias de algo; **out of ~** agotado; **to take ~ of** (*fig*) considerar, examinar; **stocks** *npl* (*History: punishment*) cepo *sg*; **stocks and shares** acciones y valores; **government ~** papel *m* del Estado
▸ **stock up with** *vt fus* abastecerse de
stockbroker ['stɔkbrəukə] *n* agente *m/f or* corredor(a) *m/f* de bolsa
stock control *n* (*Comm*) control *m* de existencias
stock cube *n* pastilla *or* cubito de caldo
stock exchange *n* bolsa
stockholder ['stɔkhəuldə] *n* (*US*) accionista *m/f*
Stockholm ['stɔkhəum] *n* Estocolmo
stocking ['stɔkɪŋ] *n* media
stock-in-trade ['stɔkɪn'treɪd] *n* (*tools etc*) herramientas *fpl*; (*stock*) existencia de mercancías; (*fig*): **it's his ~** es su especialidad
stockist ['stɔkɪst] *n* (*Brit*) distribuidor(a) *m(f)*
stock market *n* bolsa (de valores)
stock phrase *n* vieja frase *f*
stockpile ['stɔkpaɪl] *n* reserva ▪ *vt* acumular, almacenar
stockroom ['stɔkruːm] *n* almacén *m*, depósito
stocktaking ['stɔkteɪkɪŋ] *n* (*Brit Comm*) inventario, balance *m*
stocky ['stɔkɪ] *adj* (*strong*) robusto; (*short*) achaparrado
stodgy ['stɔdʒɪ] *adj* indigesto, pesado
stoical ['stəuɪkəl] *adj* estoico
stoke [stəuk] *vt* atizar
stole [stəul] *pt of* **steal** ▪ *n* estola
stolen ['stəuln] *pp of* **steal**
stolid ['stɔlɪd] *adj* (*person*) imperturbable, impasible
stomach ['stʌmək] *n* (*Anat*) estómago; (*belly*) vientre *m* ▪ *vt* tragar, aguantar
stomach ache *n* dolor *m* de estómago
stomach pump *n* bomba gástrica
stomach ulcer *n* úlcera de estómago
stomp [stɔmp] *vi*: **to ~ in/out** entrar/salir con pasos ruidosos
stone [stəun] *n* piedra; (*in fruit*) hueso; (*Brit: weight*) = 6.348 kg; 14 pounds ▪ *adj* de piedra ▪ *vt*

apedrear; **within a ~'s throw of the station**
a tiro de piedra or a dos pasos de la estación
Stone Age n: **the ~** la Edad de Piedra
stone-cold ['stəun'kəuld] adj helado
stoned [stəund] adj (col: drunk) trompa,
borracho, colocado
stone-deaf ['stəun'dɛf] adj sordo como una
tapia
stonemason ['stəunmeɪsən] n albañil m
stonewall [stəun'wɔ:l] vi alargar la cosa
innecesariamente ■ vt dar largas a
stonework ['stəunwə:k] n (art) cantería
stony ['stəunɪ] adj pedregoso; (glance) glacial
stood [stud] pt, pp of **stand**
stooge [stu:dʒ] n (col) hombre m de paja
stool [stu:l] n taburete m
stoop [stu:p] vi (also: **have a stoop**) ser
cargado de espaldas; (bend) inclinarse,
encorvarse; **to ~ to (doing) sth** rebajarse a
(hacer) algo
stop [stɔp] n parada, alto; (in punctuation)
punto ■ vt parar, detener; (break off)
suspender; (block) tapar, cerrar; (prevent)
impedir; (also: **put a stop to**) poner término
a ■ vi pararse, detenerse; (end) acabarse;
to ~ doing sth dejar de hacer algo; **to ~ sb
(from) doing sth** impedir a algn hacer algo;
to ~ dead pararse en seco; **~ it!** ¡basta ya!,
¡párate!
▶ **stop by** vi pasar por
▶ **stop off** vi interrumpir el viaje
▶ **stop up** vt (hole) tapar
stopcock ['stɔpkɔk] n llave f de paso
stopgap ['stɔpgæp] n interino; (person)
sustituto(-a); (measure) medida provisional
■ cpd (situation) provisional
stoplights ['stɔplaɪts] npl (Aut) luces fpl de
detención
stopover ['stɔpəuvə^r] n parada intermedia;
(Aviat) escala
stoppage ['stɔpɪdʒ] n (strike) paro; (temporary
stop) interrupción f; (of pay) suspensión f;
(blockage) obstrucción f
stopper ['stɔpə^r] n tapón m
stop press n noticias fpl de última hora
stopwatch ['stɔpwɔtʃ] n cronómetro
storage ['stɔ:rɪdʒ] n almacenaje m; (Comput)
almacenamiento
storage capacity n espacio de almacenaje
store [stɔ:^r] n (stock) provisión f; (depot)
almacén m; (Brit: large shop) almacén m; (US)
tienda; (reserve) reserva, repuesto ■ vt (gen)
almacenar; (Comput) almacenar; (keep)
guardar; (in filing system) archivar; **stores** npl
víveres mpl; **who knows what is in ~ for us**
quién sabe lo que nos espera; **to set great/
little ~ by sth** dar mucha/poca importancia

a algo, valorar mucho/poco algo
▶ **store up** vt acumular
storehouse ['stɔ:haus] n almacén m, depósito
storekeeper ['stɔ:ki:pə^r] n (US) tendero(-a)
storeroom ['stɔ:ru:m] n despensa
storey, story (US) ['stɔ:rɪ] n piso
stork [stɔ:k] n cigüeña
storm [stɔ:m] n tormenta; (wind) vendaval m;
(fig) tempestad f ■ vi (fig) rabiar ■ vt tomar
por asalto, asaltar; **to take a town by ~** (Mil)
tomar una ciudad por asalto
storm cloud n nubarrón m
storm door n contrapuerta
stormy ['stɔ:mɪ] adj tempestuoso
story ['stɔ:rɪ] n historia; (Press) artículo;
(joke) cuento, chiste m; (plot) argumento; (lie)
cuento; (US) = **storey**
storybook ['stɔ:rɪbuk] n libro de cuentos
storyteller ['stɔ:rɪtɛlə^r] n cuentista m/f
stout [staut] adj (strong) sólido; (fat) gordo,
corpulento ■ n cerveza negra
stove [stəuv] n (for cooking) cocina; (for heating)
estufa; **gas/electric ~** cocina de gas/eléctrica
stow [stəu] vt meter, poner; (Naut) estibar
stowaway ['stəuəweɪ] n polizón(-ona) m(f)
straddle ['strædl] vt montar a horcajadas
straggle ['strægl] vi (wander) vagar en
desorden; (lag behind) rezagarse
straggler ['stræglə^r] n rezagado(-a)
straggling ['stræglɪŋ], **straggly** ['stræglɪ]
adj (hair) desordenado
straight [streɪt] adj (direct) recto, derecho;
(plain, uncomplicated) sencillo; (frank) franco,
directo; (in order) en orden; (continuous)
continuo; (Theat: part, play) serio; (person:
conventional) recto, convencional;
(: heterosexual) heterosexual ■ adv derecho,
directamente; (drink) solo; **to put** or **get sth
~** dejar algo en claro; **10 ~ wins** 10 victorias
seguidas; **to be (all) ~** (tidy) estar en orden;
(clarified) estar claro; **I went ~ home** (me) fui
directamente a casa; **~ away, ~ off** (at once)
en seguida
straighten ['streɪtn] vt (also: **straighten out**)
enderezar, poner derecho; **to ~ things out**
poner las cosas en orden
straighteners ['streɪtnə] npl (for hair) plancha
de pelo
straight-faced [streɪt'feɪst] adj serio ■ adv
sin mostrar emoción, impávido
straightforward [streɪt'fɔ:wəd] adj (simple)
sencillo; (honest) sincero
strain [streɪn] n (gen) tensión f; (Tech)
esfuerzo; (Med) distensión f, torcedura;
(breed) raza; (lineage) linaje m; (of virus)
variedad f ■ vt (back etc) distender, torcerse;
(tire) cansar; (stretch) estirar; (filter) filtrar;

(*meaning*) tergiversar ■ vi esforzarse; **strains** npl (*Mus*) son m; **she's under a lot of ~** está bajo mucha tensión

strained [streɪnd] adj (*muscle*) torcido; (*laugh*) forzado; (*relations*) tenso

strainer ['streɪnəʳ] n colador m

strait [streɪt] n (*Geo*) estrecho; **to be in dire straits** (*fig*) estar en un gran aprieto

straitjacket ['streɪtdʒækɪt] n camisa de fuerza

strait-laced [streɪt'leɪst] adj mojigato, gazmoño

strand [strænd] n (*of thread*) hebra; (*of rope*) ramal m; **a ~ of hair** un pelo

stranded ['strændɪd] adj (*person*) colgado

strange [streɪndʒ] adj (*not known*) desconocido; (*odd*) extraño, raro

stranger ['streɪndʒəʳ] n desconocido(-a); (*from another area*) forastero(-a); **I'm a ~ here** no soy de aquí

strangle ['stræŋgl] vt estrangular

stranglehold ['stræŋglhəʊld] n (*fig*) dominio completo

strangulation [stræŋgju'leɪʃən] n estrangulación f

strap [stræp] n correa; (*of slip, dress*) tirante m ■ vt atar con correa

straphanging ['stræphæŋɪŋ] n viajar m de pie or parado (*LAm*)

strapless ['stræplɪs] adj (*bra, dress*) sin tirantes

strapped [stræpt] adj: **to be ~ for cash** (*col*) andar mal de dinero

strapping ['stræpɪŋ] adj robusto, fornido

Strasbourg ['stræzbəːg] n Estrasburgo

strata ['strɑːtə] npl of **stratum**

stratagem ['strætɪdʒəm] n estratagema

strategic [strə'tiːdʒɪk] adj estratégico

strategy ['strætɪdʒɪ] n estrategia

stratum, strata ['strɑːtəm, 'strɑːtə] n estrato

straw [strɔː] n paja; (*also*: **drinking straw**) caña, pajita; **that's the last ~!** ¡eso es el colmo!

strawberry ['strɔːbərɪ] n fresa, frutilla (*LAm*)

stray [streɪ] adj (*animal*) extraviado; (*bullet*) perdido; (*scattered*) disperso ■ vi extraviarse, perderse; (*wander: walker*) vagar, ir sin rumbo fijo; (*: speaker*) desvariar

streak [striːk] n raya; (*fig: of madness etc*) vena ■ vt rayar ■ vi: **to ~ past** pasar como un rayo; **to have streaks in one's hair** tener vetas en el pelo; **a winning/losing ~** una racha de buena/mala suerte

streaker ['striːkəʳ] n corredor(a) m(f) desnudo(-a)

streaky ['striːkɪ] adj rayado

stream [striːm] n riachuelo, arroyo; (*jet*) chorro; (*flow*) corriente f; (*of people*) oleada ■ vt (*Scol*) dividir en grupos por habilidad ■ vi correr, fluir; **to ~ in/out** (*people*) entrar/salir en tropel; **against the ~** a contracorriente; **on ~** (*new power plant etc*) en funcionamiento

streamer ['striːməʳ] n serpentina

stream feed n (*on photocopier etc*) alimentación f continua

streamline ['striːmlaɪn] vt aerodinamizar; (*fig*) racionalizar

streamlined ['striːmlaɪnd] adj aerodinámico

street [striːt] n calle f ■ adj callejero; **the back streets** las callejuelas; **to be on the streets** (*homeless*) estar sin vivienda; (*as prostitute*) hacer la calle

streetcar ['striːtkɑː] n (*US*) tranvía m

street cred [-krɛd] n (*col*) imagen de estar en la onda

street lamp n farol m

street lighting n alumbrado público

street market n mercado callejero

street plan n plano callejero

streetwise ['striːtwaɪz] adj (*col*) pícaro

strength [strɛŋθ] n fuerza; (*of girder, knot etc*) resistencia; (*of chemical solution*) potencia; (*of wine*) graduación f de alcohol; **on the ~ of** a base de, en base a; **to be at full/below ~** tener/no tener completo el cupo

strengthen ['strɛŋθn] vt fortalecer, reforzar

strenuous ['strɛnjuəs] adj (*tough*) arduo; (*energetic*) enérgico; (*opposition*) firme, tenaz; (*efforts*) intensivo

stress [strɛs] n (*force, pressure*) presión f; (*mental strain*) estrés m, tensión f; (*accent, emphasis*) énfasis m, acento; (*Ling, Poetry*) acento; (*Tech*) tensión f, carga ■ vt subrayar, recalcar; **to be under ~** estar estresado; **to lay great ~ on sth** hacer hincapié en algo

stressful ['strɛsful] adj (*job*) estresante

stretch [strɛtʃ] n (*of sand etc*) trecho; (*of road*) tramo; (*of time*) período, tiempo ■ vi estirarse; (*extend*): **to ~ to** or **as far as** extenderse hasta; (*be enough: money, food*): **to ~ to** alcanzar para, dar de sí para ■ vt extender, estirar; (*make demands of*) exigir el máximo esfuerzo a; **to ~ one's legs** estirar las piernas

▶ **stretch out** vi tenderse ■ vt (*arm etc*) extender; (*spread*) estirar

stretcher ['strɛtʃəʳ] n camilla

stretcher-bearer ['strɛtʃəbɛərəʳ] n camillero(-a)

stretch marks npl estrías fpl

strewn [struːn] adj: **~ with** cubierto or sembrado de

stricken ['strɪkən] *adj* (*person*) herido; (*city, industry etc*) condenado; ~ **with** (*arthritis, disease*) afligido por; **grief-~** destrozado por el dolor

strict [strɪkt] *adj* (*order, rule etc*) estricto; (*discipline, ban*) severo; **in ~ confidence** en la más absoluta confianza

strictly ['strɪktlɪ] *adv* estrictamente; (*totally*) terminantemente; ~ **confidential** estrictamente confidencial; ~ **speaking** en (el) sentido estricto (de la palabra); ~ **between ourselves** ... entre nosotros ...

stridden ['strɪdn] *pp of* **stride**

stride [straɪd] *n* zancada, tranco ■ *vi* (*pt* **strode**, *pp* **stridden**) [strəud, 'strɪdn] dar zancadas, andar a trancos; **to take in one's ~** (*fig: changes etc*) tomar con calma

strident ['straɪdnt] *adj* estridente; (*colour*) chillón(-ona)

strife [straɪf] *n* lucha

strike [straɪk] (*pt, pp* **struck**) *n* huelga; (*of oil etc*) descubrimiento; (*attack*) ataque *m*; (*Sport*) golpe *m* ■ *vt* golpear, pegar; (*oil etc*) descubrir; (*obstacle*) topar con; (*produce: coin, medal*) acuñar; (: *agreement, deal*) concertar ■ *vi* declarar la huelga; (*attack: Mil etc*) atacar; (*clock*) dar la hora; **on ~** (*workers*) en huelga; **to call a ~** declarar una huelga; **to go on** *or* **come out on ~** ponerse *or* declararse en huelga; **to ~ a match** encender una cerilla; **to ~ a balance** (*fig*) encontrar un equilibrio; **to ~ a bargain** cerrar un trato; **the clock struck nine o'clock** el reloj dio las nueve
  ▸ **strike back** *vi* (*Mil*) contraatacar; (*fig*) devolver el golpe
  ▸ **strike down** *vt* derribar
  ▸ **strike off** *vt* (*from list*) tachar; (*doctor etc*) suspender
  ▸ **strike out** *vt* borrar, tachar
  ▸ **strike up** *vt* (*Mus*) empezar a tocar; (*conversation*) entablar; (*friendship*) trabar

strikebreaker ['straɪkbreɪkəʳ] *n* rompehuelgas *m/f inv*

striker ['straɪkəʳ] *n* huelguista *m/f*; (*Sport*) delantero

striking ['straɪkɪŋ] *adj* (*colour*) llamativo; (*obvious*) notorio

Strimmer® ['strɪməʳ] *n* cortacéspedes *m inv* (*especial para los bordes*)

string [strɪŋ] *n* (*gen*) cuerda; (*row*) hilera; (*Comput*) cadena ■ *vt* (*pt, pp* **strung**) [strʌŋ]: **to ~ together** ensartar; **to ~ out** extenderse; **the strings** *npl* (*Mus*) los instrumentos de cuerda; **to pull strings** (*fig*) mover palancas; **to get a job by pulling strings** conseguir un trabajo por enchufe; **with no strings attached** (*fig*) sin compromiso

string bean *n* judía verde, habichuela

stringed instrument [strɪŋ(d)-], **string instrument** *n* (*Mus*) instrumento de cuerda

stringent ['strɪndʒənt] *adj* riguroso, severo

string quartet *n* cuarteto de cuerdas

strip [strɪp] *n* tira; (*of land*) franja; (*of metal*) cinta, lámina ■ *vt* desnudar; (*also*: **strip down**: *machine*) desmontar ■ *vi* desnudarse

strip cartoon *n* tira cómica, historieta (*LAm*)

stripe [straɪp] *n* raya; (*Mil*) galón *m*; **white with green stripes** blanco con rayas verdes

striped [straɪpt] *adj* a rayas, rayado

strip lighting *n* alumbrado fluorescente

stripper ['strɪpəʳ] *n* artista *m/f* de striptease

strip-search ['strɪpsə:tʃ] *vt*: **to ~ sb** desnudar y registrar a algn

striptease ['strɪpti:z] *n* striptease *m*

strive (*pt* **strove**, *pp* **striven**) [straɪv, strəuv, 'strɪvn] *vi*: **to ~ to do sth** esforzarse *or* luchar por hacer algo

strobe [strəub] *n* (*also*: **strobe light**) luz *f* estroboscópica

strode [strəud] *pt of* **stride**

stroke [strəuk] *n* (*blow*) golpe *m*; (*Med*) apoplejía; (*caress*) caricia; (*of pen*) trazo; (*Swimming: style*) estilo; (*of piston*) carrera ■ *vt* acariciar; **at a ~** de golpe; **a ~ of luck** un golpe de suerte; **two-~ engine** motor *m* de dos tiempos

stroll [strəul] *n* paseo, vuelta ■ *vi* dar un paseo *or* una vuelta; **to go for a ~**, **have** *or* **take a ~** dar un paseo

stroller ['strəuləʳ] *n* (*US: pushchair*) cochecito

strong [strɔŋ] *adj* fuerte; (*bleach, acid*) concentrado ■ *adv*: **to be going ~** (*company*) marchar bien; (*person*) conservarse bien; **they are 50 ~** son 50

strong-arm ['strɔŋa:m] *adj* (*tactics, methods*) represivo

strongbox ['strɔŋbɔks] *n* caja fuerte

strong drink *n* bebida cargada *or* fuerte

stronghold ['strɔŋhəuld] *n* fortaleza; (*fig*) baluarte *m*

strong language *n* lenguaje *m* fuerte

strongly ['strɔŋlɪ] *adv* fuertemente, con fuerza; (*believe*) firmemente; **to feel ~ about sth** tener una opinión firme sobre algo

strongman ['strɔŋmæn] *n* forzudo; (*fig*) hombre *m* robusto

strongroom ['strɔŋru:m] *n* cámara acorazada

stroppy ['strɔpɪ] *adj* (*Brit col*) borde; **to get ~** ponerse borde

strove [strəuv] *pt of* **strive**

struck [strʌk] *pt, pp of* **strike**

structural ['strʌktʃərəl] *adj* estructural

structure ['strʌktʃəʳ] n estructura; (building) construcción f

struggle ['strʌgl] n lucha ■ vi luchar; **to have a ~ to do sth** esforzarse por hacer algo

strum [strʌm] vt (guitar) rasguear

strung [strʌŋ] pt, pp of **string**

strut [strʌt] n puntal m ■ vi pavonearse

strychnine ['strɪkni:n] n estricnina

stub [stʌb] n (of ticket etc) matriz f; (of cigarette) colilla ■ vt: **to ~ one's toe on sth** dar con el dedo del pie contra algo
  ▶ **stub out** vt (cigarette) apagar

stubble ['stʌbl] n rastrojo; (on chin) barba (incipiente)

stubborn ['stʌbən] adj terco, testarudo

stucco ['stʌkəu] n estuco

stuck [stʌk] pt, pp of **stick** ■ adj (jammed) atascado

stuck-up [stʌk'ʌp] adj engreído, presumido

stud [stʌd] n (shirt stud) corchete m; (of boot) taco; (of horses) caballeriza; (also: **stud horse**) caballo semental ■ vt (fig): **studded with** salpicado de

student ['stju:dənt] n estudiante m/f ■ adj estudiantil; **a law/medical ~** un(a) estudiante de derecho/medicina

student driver n (US Aut) aprendiz(a) m(f) de conductor

students' union n (Brit: association) sindicato de estudiantes; (: building) centro de estudiantes

studio ['stju:dɪəu] n estudio; (artist's) taller m

studio flat, studio apartment (US) n estudio

studious ['stju:dɪəs] adj estudioso; (studied) calculado

studiously ['stju:dɪəslɪ] adv (carefully) con esmero

study ['stʌdɪ] n estudio ■ vt estudiar; (examine) examinar, investigar ■ vi estudiar; **to make a ~ of sth** realizar una investigación de algo; **to ~ for an exam** preparar un examen

stuff [stʌf] n materia; (cloth) tela; (substance) material m, sustancia; (things, belongings) cosas fpl ■ vt llenar; (Culin) rellenar; (animal: for exhibition) disecar; **my nose is stuffed up** tengo la nariz tapada; **stuffed toy** juguete m or muñeco de trapo

stuffing ['stʌfɪŋ] n relleno

stuffy ['stʌfɪ] adj (room) mal ventilado; (person) de miras estrechas

stumble ['stʌmbl] vi tropezar, dar un traspié
  ▶ **stumble across** vt fus (fig) tropezar con

stumbling block ['stʌmblɪŋ-] n tropiezo, obstáculo

stump [stʌmp] n (of tree) tocón m; (of limb) muñón m ■ vt: **to be stumped** quedarse perplejo; **to be stumped for an answer** quedarse sin saber qué contestar

stun [stʌn] vt aturdir

stung [stʌŋ] pt, pp of **sting**

stunk [stʌŋk] pp of **stink**

stunning ['stʌnɪŋ] adj (fig) pasmoso

stunt [stʌnt] n (Aviat) vuelo acrobático; (also: **publicity stunt**) truco publicitario

stunted ['stʌntɪd] adj enano, achaparrado

stuntman ['stʌntmæn] n especialista m

stupefaction [stju:pɪ'fækʃən] n estupefacción f

stupefy ['stju:pɪfaɪ] vt dejar estupefacto

stupendous [stju:'pɛndəs] adj estupendo, asombroso

stupid ['stju:pɪd] adj estúpido, tonto

stupidity [stju:'pɪdɪtɪ] n estupidez f

stupor ['stju:pəʳ] n estupor m

sturdy ['stə:dɪ] adj robusto, fuerte

stutter ['stʌtəʳ] n tartamudeo ■ vi tartamudear

sty [staɪ] n (for pigs) pocilga

stye [staɪ] n (Med) orzuelo

style [staɪl] n estilo; (fashion) moda; (of dress etc) hechura; (hairstyle) corte m; **in the latest ~** en el último modelo

stylish ['staɪlɪʃ] adj elegante, a la moda

stylist ['staɪlɪst] n (hair stylist) peluquero(-a)

stylus (pl **styli** or **styluses**) ['staɪləs, -laɪ] n (of record player) aguja

Styrofoam® ['staɪrəfəum] n (US) poliestireno ■ adj (cup) de poliestireno

suave [swɑ:v] adj cortés, fino

sub [sʌb] n abbr = **submarine**; **subscription**

sub... [sʌb] pref sub...

subcommittee ['sʌbkəmɪtɪ] n subcomisión f

subconscious [sʌb'kɔnʃəs] adj subconsciente ■ n subconsciente m

subcontinent [sʌb'kɔntɪnənt] n: **the Indian ~** el subcontinente (de la India)

subcontract n ['sʌb'kɔntrækt] subcontrato ■ vt ['sʌbkən'trækt] subcontratar

subcontractor [sʌbkən'træktəʳ] n subcontratista m/f

subdivide [sʌbdɪ'vaɪd] vt subdividir

subdue [səb'dju:] vt sojuzgar; (passions) dominar

subdued [səb'dju:d] adj (light) tenue; (person) sumiso, manso

sub-editor ['sʌb'ɛdɪtəʳ] n (Brit) redactor(a) m(f)

subject n ['sʌbdʒɪkt] súbdito; (Scol) tema m, materia ■ vt [səb'dʒɛkt]: **to ~ sb to sth** someter a algn a algo ■ adj ['sʌbdʒɪkt]: **to be ~ to** (law) estar sujeto a; **~ to confirmation**

in writing sujeto a confirmación por escrito; **to change the ~** cambiar de tema

subjective [səb'dʒɛktɪv] *adj* subjetivo

subject matter *n* materia; *(content)* contenido

sub judice [sʌb'djuːdɪsɪ] *adj (Law)* pendiente de resolución

subjugate ['sʌbdʒugeɪt] *vt* subyugar, sojuzgar

subjunctive [səb'dʒʌŋktɪv] *adj, n* subjuntivo

sublet [sʌb'lɛt] *vt, vi* subarrendar, realquilar

sublime [sə'blaɪm] *adj* sublime

subliminal [sʌb'lɪmɪnl] *adj* subliminal

submachine gun ['sʌbmə'ʃiːn-] *n* metralleta

submarine [sʌbmə'riːn] *n* submarino

submerge [səb'məːdʒ] *vt* sumergir; *(flood)* inundar ▪ *vi* sumergirse

submersion [səb'məːʃən] *n* submersión *f*

submission [səb'mɪʃən] *n* sumisión *f*; *(to committee etc)* ponencia

submissive [səb'mɪsɪv] *adj* sumiso

submit [səb'mɪt] *vt* someter; *(proposal, claim)* presentar ▪ *vi* someterse; **I ~ that ...** me permito sugerir que ...

subnormal [sʌb'nɔːməl] *adj* subnormal

subordinate [sə'bɔːdɪnət] *adj, n* subordinado(-a) *m(f)*

subpoena [səb'piːnə] *(Law) n* citación *f* ▪ *vt* citar

subroutine [sʌbruː'tiːn] *n (Comput)* subrutina

subscribe [səb'skraɪb] *vi* suscribir; **to ~ to** *(fund)* suscribir, aprobar; *(opinion)* estar de acuerdo con; *(newspaper)* suscribirse a

subscribed capital [səb'skraɪbd-] *n* capital *m* suscrito

subscriber [səb'skraɪbəʳ] *n (to periodical)* suscriptor(a) *m(f)*; *(to telephone)* abonado(-a)

subscript ['sʌbskrɪpt] *n (Typ)* subíndice *m*

subscription [səb'skrɪpʃən] *n (to club)* abono; *(to magazine)* suscripción *f*; **to take out a ~ to** suscribirse a

subsequent ['sʌbsɪkwənt] *adj* subsiguiente, posterior; **~ to** posterior a

subsequently ['sʌbsɪkwəntlɪ] *adv* posteriormente, más tarde

subservient [səb'səːvɪənt] *adj*: **~ (to)** servil (a)

subside [səb'saɪd] *vi* hundirse; *(flood)* bajar; *(wind)* amainar

subsidence [səb'saɪdns] *n* hundimiento; *(in road)* socavón *m*

subsidiarity [səbsɪdɪ'ærɪtɪ] *n (Pol)* subsidiariedad *f*

subsidiary [səb'sɪdɪərɪ] *n* sucursal *f*, filial *f* ▪ *adj (Univ: subject)* secundario

subsidize ['sʌbsɪdaɪz] *vt* subvencionar

subsidy ['sʌbsɪdɪ] *n* subvención *f*

subsist [səb'sɪst] *vi*: **to ~ on sth** subsistir a base de algo, sustentarse con algo

subsistence [səb'sɪstəns] *n* subsistencia

subsistence allowance *n* dietas *fpl*

subsistence level *n* nivel *m* de subsistencia

subsistence wage *n* sueldo de subsistencia

substance ['sʌbstəns] *n* sustancia; *(fig)* esencia; **to lack ~** *(argument)* ser poco convincente; *(accusation)* no tener fundamento; *(film, book)* tener poca profundidad

substance abuse *n* uso indebido de sustancias tóxicas

substandard [sʌb'stændəd] *adj (goods)* inferior; *(housing)* deficiente

substantial [səb'stænʃl] *adj* sustancial, sustancioso; *(fig)* importante

substantially [səb'stænʃəlɪ] *adv* sustancialmente; **~ bigger** bastante más grande

substantiate [səb'stænʃɪeɪt] *vt* comprobar

substitute ['sʌbstɪtjuːt] *n (person)* suplente *m/f*; *(thing)* sustituto ▪ *vt*: **to ~ A for B** sustituir B por A, reemplazar A por B

substitution [sʌbstɪ'tjuːʃən] *n* sustitución *f*

subterfuge ['sʌbtəfjuːdʒ] *n* subterfugio

subterranean [sʌbtə'reɪnɪən] *adj* subterráneo

subtitle ['sʌbtaɪtl] *n* subtítulo

subtle ['sʌtl] *adj* sutil

subtlety ['sʌtltɪ] *n* sutileza

subtly ['sʌtlɪ] *adv* sutilmente

subtotal [sʌb'təutl] *n* subtotal *m*

subtract [səb'trækt] *vt* restar; sustraer

subtraction [səb'trækʃən] *n* resta; sustracción *f*

suburb ['sʌbəːb] *n* barrio residencial; **the suburbs** las afueras (de la ciudad)

suburban [sə'bəːbən] *adj* suburbano; *(train etc)* de cercanías

suburbia [sə'bəːbɪə] *n* barrios *mpl* residenciales

subversion [səb'vəːʃən] *n* subversión *f*

subversive [səb'vəːsɪv] *adj* subversivo

subway ['sʌbweɪ] *n (Brit)* paso subterráneo *or* inferior; *(US)* metro

sub-zero [sʌb'zɪərəu] *adj*: **~ temperatures** temperaturas *fpl* por debajo del cero

succeed [sək'siːd] *vi (person)* tener éxito; *(plan)* salir bien ▪ *vt* suceder a; **to ~ in doing** lograr hacer

succeeding [sək'siːdɪŋ] *adj (following)* sucesivo; **~ generations** generaciones *fpl* futuras

success [sək'sɛs] *n* éxito; *(gain)* triunfo

successful [sək'sɛsful] *adj (venture)* de éxito, exitoso *(esp LAm)*; **to be ~ (in doing)** lograr (hacer)

successfully [sək'sɛsfulɪ] *adv* con éxito
succession [sək'sɛʃən] *n* (*series*) sucesión
f, serie f; (*descendants*) descendencia; **in ~**
sucesivamente
successive [sək'sɛsɪv] *adj* sucesivo,
consecutivo; **on three ~ days** tres días
seguidos
successor [sək'sɛsəʳ] *n* sucesor(a) m(f)
succinct [sək'sɪŋkt] *adj* sucinto
succulent ['sʌkjulənt] *adj* suculento ◾ *n*
(*Bot*); **succulents** *npl* plantas *fpl* carnosas
succumb [sə'kʌm] *vi* sucumbir
such [sʌtʃ] *adj* tal, semejante; (*of that kind*):
~ a book tal libro; **~ books** tales libros; (*so much*): **~ courage** tanto valor ◾ *adv* tan; **~ a long trip** un viaje tan largo; **~ a lot of** tanto; **~ as** (*like*) tal como; **a noise ~ as to** un ruido tal que; **~ books as I have** cuantos libros tengo; **I said no ~ thing** no dije tal cosa; **it's ~ a long time since we saw each other** hace tanto tiempo que no nos vemos; **~ a long time ago** hace tantísimo tiempo; **as ~** *adv* como tal
such-and-such ['sʌtʃənsʌtʃ] *adj* tal o cual
suchlike ['sʌtʃlaɪk] *pron* (*col*): **and ~** y cosas por el estilo
suck [sʌk] *vt* chupar; (*bottle*) sorber; (*breast*) mamar; (*pump, machine*) aspirar
sucker ['sʌkəʳ] *n* (*Bot*) serpollo; (*Zool*) ventosa; (*col*) bobo, primo
sucrose ['su:krəuz] *n* sacarosa
suction ['sʌkʃən] *n* succión f
suction pump *n* bomba aspirante *or* de succión
Sudan [su'dæn] *n* Sudán m
Sudanese [su:də'ni:z] *adj, n* sudanés(-esa) m(f)
sudden ['sʌdn] *adj* (*rapid*) repentino, súbito; (*unexpected*) imprevisto; **all of a ~** de repente
sudden-death [sʌdn'dɛθ] *n* (*also*: **sudden-death play off**) desempate m instantáneo, muerte f súbita
suddenly ['sʌdnlɪ] *adv* de repente
sudoku [su'dəuku:] *n* sudoku m
suds [sʌdz] *npl* espuma *sg* de jabón
sue [su:] *vt* demandar; **to ~ (for)** demandar (por); **to ~ for divorce** solicitar *or* pedir el divorcio; **to ~ for damages** demandar por daños y perjuicios
suede [sweɪd] *n* ante m, gamuza (*LAm*)
suet ['suɪt] *n* sebo
Suez Canal ['su:ɪz-] *n* Canal m de Suez
Suff. *abbr* (*Brit*) = **Suffolk**
suffer ['sʌfəʳ] *vt* sufrir, padecer; (*tolerate*) aguantar, soportar; (*undergo: loss, setback*) experimentar ◾ *vi* sufrir, padecer; **to ~**

from sufrir, tener; **to ~ from the effects of alcohol/a fall** sufrir los efectos del alcohol/ resentirse de una caída
sufferance ['sʌfərns] *n*: **he was only there on ~** estuvo allí sólo porque se lo toleraron
sufferer ['sʌfərəʳ] *n* víctima f; (*Med*): **~ from** enfermo(-a) de
suffering ['sʌfərɪŋ] *n* (*hardship, deprivation*) sufrimiento; (*pain*) dolor m
suffice [sə'faɪs] *vi* bastar, ser suficiente
sufficient [sə'fɪʃənt] *adj* suficiente, bastante
sufficiently [sə'fɪʃəntlɪ] *adv* suficientemente, bastante
suffix ['sʌfɪks] *n* sufijo
suffocate ['sʌfəkeɪt] *vi* ahogarse, asfixiarse
suffocation [sʌfə'keɪʃən] *n* sofocación f, asfixia
suffrage ['sʌfrɪdʒ] *n* sufragio
suffuse [sə'fju:z] *vt*: **to ~ (with)** (*colour*) bañar (de); **her face was suffused with joy** su cara estaba llena de alegría
sugar ['ʃugəʳ] *n* azúcar m ◾ *vt* echar azúcar a, azucarar
sugar basin *n* (*Brit*) = **sugar bowl**
sugar beet *n* remolacha
sugar bowl *n* azucarero
sugar cane *n* caña de azúcar
sugar-coated [ʃugə'kəutɪd] *adj* azucarado
sugar lump *n* terrón m de azúcar
sugar refinery *n* refinería de azúcar
sugary ['ʃugərɪ] *adj* azucarado
suggest [sə'dʒɛst] *vt* sugerir; (*recommend*) aconsejar; **what do you ~ I do?** ¿qué sugieres que haga?; **this suggests that ...** esto hace pensar que ...
suggestion [sə'dʒɛstʃən] *n* sugerencia; **there's no ~ of ...** no hay indicación *or* evidencia de ...
suggestive [sə'dʒɛstɪv] *adj* sugestivo; (*pej: indecent*) indecente
suicidal ['suɪsaɪdl] *adj* suicida
suicide ['suɪsaɪd] *n* suicidio; (*person*) suicida m/f; **to commit ~** suicidarse
suicide attempt, suicide bid *n* intento de suicidio
suicide bomber *n* terrorista m/f suicida
suicide bombing *n* atentado m suicida
suit [su:t] *n* (*man's*) traje m; (*woman's*) traje de chaqueta; (*Law*) pleito; (*Cards*) palo ◾ *vt* convenir; (*clothes*) sentar bien a, ir bien a; (*adapt*): **to ~ sth to** adaptar *or* ajustar algo a; **to be suited to sth** (*suitable for*) ser apto para algo; **well suited** (*couple*) hechos el uno para el otro; **to bring a ~ against sb** entablar demanda contra algn; **to follow ~** (*Cards*) seguir el palo; (*fig*) seguir el ejemplo (de algn); **that suits me** me va bien

suitable ['su:təbl] *adj* conveniente; *(apt)* indicado

suitably ['su:təblɪ] *adv* convenientemente; *(appropriately)* en forma debida

suitcase ['su:tkeɪs] *n* maleta, valija *(LAm)*

suite [swi:t] *n* *(of rooms)* suite *f*; *(Mus)* suite *f*; *(furniture)*: **bedroom/dining room ~** (juego de) dormitorio/comedor *m*; **a three-piece ~** un tresillo

suitor ['su:təʳ] *n* pretendiente *m*

sulfate ['sʌlfeɪt] *n* *(US)* = **sulphate**

sulfur ['sʌlfəʳ] *n* *(US)* = **sulphur**

sulk [sʌlk] *vi* estar de mal humor

sulky ['sʌlkɪ] *adj* malhumorado

sullen ['sʌlən] *adj* hosco, malhumorado

sulphate, sulfate *(US)* ['sʌlfeɪt] *n* sulfato; **copper ~** sulfato de cobre

sulphur, sulfur *(US)* ['sʌlfəʳ] *n* azufre *m*

sulphur dioxide *n* dióxido de azufre

sultan ['sʌltən] *n* sultán *m*

sultana [sʌl'tɑ:nə] *n* *(fruit)* pasa de Esmirna

sultry ['sʌltrɪ] *adj* *(weather)* bochornoso; *(seductive)* seductor(a)

sum [sʌm] *n* suma; *(total)* total *m*
▶ **sum up** *vt* resumir; *(evaluate rapidly)* evaluar ▪ *vi* hacer un resumen

Sumatra [su'mɑ:trə] *n* Sumatra

summarize ['sʌməraɪz] *vt* resumir

summary ['sʌmərɪ] *n* resumen *m* ▪ *adj* *(justice)* sumario

summer ['sʌməʳ] *n* verano ▪ *adj* de verano; **in (the) ~** en (el) verano

summerhouse ['sʌməhaus] *n* *(in garden)* cenador *m*, glorieta

summertime ['sʌmətaɪm] *n* *(season)* verano

summer time *n* *(by clock)* hora de verano

summery ['sʌmərɪ] *adj* veraniego

summing-up [sʌmɪŋ'ʌp] *n* *(Law)* resumen *m*

summit ['sʌmɪt] *n* cima, cumbre *f*; *(also:* **summit conference)** (conferencia) cumbre *f*

summit conference *n* conferencia cumbre *f*

summon ['sʌmən] *vt* *(person)* llamar; *(meeting)* convocar; **to ~ a witness** citar a un testigo
▶ **summon up** *vt* *(courage)* armarse de

summons ['sʌmənz] *n* llamamiento, llamada ▪ *vt* citar, emplazar; **to serve a ~ on sb** citar a algn ante el juicio

sumo ['su:məu] *n* *(also:* **sumo wrestling)** sumo

sump [sʌmp] *n* *(Brit Aut)* cárter *m*

sumptuous ['sʌmptjuəs] *adj* suntuoso

sun [sʌn] *n* sol *m*; **they have everything under the ~** no les falta nada, tienen de todo

Sun. *abbr* (= *Sunday*) dom

sunbathe ['sʌnbeɪð] *vi* tomar el sol

sunbeam ['sʌnbi:m] *n* rayo de sol

sunbed ['sʌnbɛd] *n* cama solar

sunburn ['sʌnbə:n] *n* *(painful)* quemadura del sol; *(tan)* bronceado

sunburnt ['sʌnbə:nt], **sunburned** ['sʌnbə:nd] *adj* *(tanned)* bronceado; *(painfully)* quemado por el sol

sundae ['sʌndeɪ] *n* helado con frutas y nueces

Sunday ['sʌndɪ] *n* domingo; *see also* **Tuesday**

Sunday paper *n* (periódico) dominical *m*

Sunday school *n* catequesis *f*

sundial ['sʌndaɪəl] *n* reloj *m* de sol

sundown ['sʌndaun] *n* anochecer *m*, puesta de sol

sundries ['sʌndrɪz] *npl* géneros *mpl* diversos

sundry ['sʌndrɪ] *adj* varios, diversos; **all and ~** todos sin excepción

sunflower ['sʌnflauəʳ] *n* girasol *m*

sung [sʌŋ] *pp of* **sing**

sunglasses ['sʌnglɑ:sɪz] *npl* gafas *fpl* de sol

sunk [sʌŋk] *pp of* **sink**

sunken ['sʌŋkn] *adj* *(bath)* hundido

sunlamp ['sʌnlæmp] *n* lámpara solar ultravioleta

sunlight ['sʌnlaɪt] *n* luz *f* del sol

sunlit ['sʌnlɪt] *adj* iluminado por el sol

sunny ['sʌnɪ] *adj* soleado; *(day)* de sol; *(fig)* alegre; **it is ~** hace sol

sunrise ['sʌnraɪz] *n* salida del sol

sun roof *n* *(Aut)* techo corredizo *or* solar; *(on building)* azotea, terraza

sunscreen ['sʌnskri:n] *n* protector *m* solar

sunset ['sʌnsɛt] *n* puesta del sol

sunshade ['sʌnʃeɪd] *n* *(over table)* sombrilla

sunshine ['sʌnʃaɪn] *n* sol *m*

sunstroke ['sʌnstrəuk] *n* insolación *f*

suntan ['sʌntæn] *n* bronceado

suntanned ['sʌntænd] *adj* bronceado

suntan oil *n* aceite *m* bronceador

super ['su:pəʳ] *adj* *(col)* bárbaro

superannuation [su:pərænju'eɪʃən] *n* jubilación *f*, pensión *f*

superb [su:'pə:b] *adj* magnífico, espléndido

Super Bowl *n* *(US Sport)* super copa de fútbol americano

supercilious [su:pə'sɪlɪəs] *adj* *(disdainful)* desdeñoso; *(haughty)* altanero

superconductor [su:pəkən'dʌktəʳ] *n* superconductor *m*

superficial [su:pə'fɪʃəl] *adj* superficial

superfluous [su'pə:fluəs] *adj* superfluo, de sobra

superglue ['su:pəglu:] *n* cola de contacto, supercola

superhighway ['su:pəhaɪweɪ] *n* *(US)* superautopista; **the information ~** la superautopista de la información

superhuman [su:pə'hju:mən] *adj* sobrehumano

superimpose ['su:pərɪm'pəuz] vt sobreponer
superintend [su:pərɪn'tɛnd] vt supervisar
superintendent [su:pərɪn'tɛndənt] n
  director(a) m(f); (also: **police superintendent**)
  subjefe(-a) m(f)
superior [su'pɪərɪəʳ] adj superior; (smug:
  person) altivo, desdeñoso; (: smile, air) de
  suficiencia; (: remark) desdeñoso ■ n
  superior m; **Mother S~** (Rel) madre f
  superiora
superiority [supɪərɪ'ɔrɪtɪ] n superioridad f;
  desdén m
superlative [su'pə:lətɪv] adj, n superlativo
superman ['su:pəmæn] n superhombre m
supermarket ['su:pəmɑ:kɪt] n supermercado
supermodel ['su:pəmɔdl] n top model f,
  supermodelo f
supernatural [su:pə'nætʃərəl] adj
  sobrenatural
supernova [su:pə'nəuvə] n supernova
superpower ['su:pəpauəʳ] n (Pol)
  superpotencia
supersede [su:pə'si:d] vt suplantar
supersonic ['su:pə'sɔnɪk] adj supersónico
superstar ['su:pəstɑ:ʳ] n superestrella ■ adj
  de superestrella
superstition [su:pə'stɪʃən] n superstición f
superstitious [su:pə'stɪʃəs] adj supersticioso
superstore ['su:pəstɔ:ʳ] n (Brit) hipermercado
supertanker ['su:pətæŋkəʳ] n superpetrolero
supertax ['su:pətæks] n sobretasa,
  sobreimpuesto
supervise ['su:pəvaɪz] vt supervisar
supervision [su:pə'vɪʒən] n supervisión f
supervisor ['su:pəvaɪzəʳ] n supervisor(a) m(f)
supervisory ['su:pəvaɪzərɪ] adj de
  supervisión
supper ['sʌpəʳ] n cena; **to have ~** cenar
supplant [sə'plɑ:nt] vt suplantar, reemplazar
supple ['sʌpl] adj flexible
supplement n ['sʌplɪmənt] suplemento ■ vt
  [sʌplɪ'mɛnt] suplir
supplementary [sʌplɪ'mɛntərɪ] adj
  suplementario
supplementary benefit n (Brit) subsidio
  adicional de la seguridad social
supplier [sə'plaɪəʳ] n suministrador(a) m(f);
  (Comm) distribuidor(a) m(f)
supply [sə'plaɪ] vt (provide) suministrar;
  (information) facilitar; (fill: need, want) suplir,
  satisfacer; (equip): **to ~ (with)** proveer (de)
  ■ n provisión f; (of gas, water etc) suministro
  ■ adj (Brit: teacher etc) suplente; **supplies** npl
  (food) víveres mpl; (Mil) pertrechos mpl; **office
  supplies** materiales mpl para oficina; **to be
  in short ~** escasear, haber escasez de; **the
  electricity/water/gas ~** el suministro de

electricidad/agua/gas; **~ and demand** la
oferta y la demanda
support [sə'pɔ:t] n (moral, financial etc) apoyo;
  (Tech) soporte m ■ vt apoyar; (financially)
  mantener; (uphold) sostener; (Sport: team)
  seguir, ser hincha de; **they stopped work
  in ~ (of)** pararon de trabajar en apoyo (de);
  to ~ o.s. (financially) ganarse la vida
support buying [-'baɪɪŋ] n compra
  proteccionista
supporter [sə'pɔ:təʳ] n (Pol etc) partidario(-a);
  (Sport) aficionado(-a); (Football) hincha m/f
supporting [sə'pɔ:tɪŋ] adj (wall) de apoyo;
  ~ role papel m secundario; **~ actor/actress**
  actor/actriz m/f secundario(-a)
supportive [sə'pɔ:tɪv] adj de apoyo; **I have a
  ~ family/wife** mi familia/mujer me apoya
suppose [sə'pəuz] vt, vi suponer; (imagine)
  imaginarse; **to be supposed to do sth** deber
  hacer algo; **I don't ~ she'll come** no creo que
  venga; **he's supposed to be an expert** se le
  supone un experto
supposedly [sə'pəuzɪdlɪ] adv según cabe
  suponer
supposing [sə'pəuzɪŋ] conj en caso de que;
  always ~ (that) he comes suponiendo que
  venga
supposition [sʌpə'zɪʃən] n suposición f
suppository [sə'pɔzɪtrɪ] n supositorio
suppress [sə'prɛs] vt suprimir; (yawn) ahogar
suppression [sə'prɛʃən] n represión f
supremacy [su'prɛməsɪ] n supremacía
supreme [su'pri:m] adj supremo
Supreme Court n (US) Tribunal m Supremo,
  Corte f Suprema
supremo [su'pri:məu] n autoridad f máxima
Supt. abbr (Police) = **superintendent**
surcharge ['sə:tʃɑ:dʒ] n sobretasa, recargo
sure [ʃuəʳ] adj seguro; (definite, convinced)
  cierto; (aim) certero ■ adv: **that ~ is pretty**,
  that's ~ pretty (US) ¡qué bonito es!; **to be ~
  of sth** estar seguro de algo; **to be ~ of
  o.s.** estar seguro de sí mismo; **to make ~
  of sth/that** asegurarse de algo/asegurar
  que; **I'm not ~ how/why/when** no estoy
  seguro de cómo/por qué/cuándo; **~!** (of
  course) ¡claro!, ¡por supuesto!; **~ enough**
  efectivamente
sure-fire ['ʃuəfaɪəʳ] adj (col) infalible
sure-footed [ʃuə'futɪd] adj de pie firme
surely ['ʃuəlɪ] adv (certainly) seguramente;
  ~ you don't mean that! ¡no lo dices en serio!
surety ['ʃuərətɪ] n fianza; (person) fiador(a)
  m(f); **to go** or **stand ~ for sb** ser fiador de
  algn, salir garante por algn
surf [sə:f] n olas fpl ■ vi hacer surf ■ vt
  (Internet): **to ~ the Net** navegar por Internet

S

surface ['sə:fɪs] n superficie f ▪ vt (road) revestir ▪ vi salir a la superficie ▪ cpd (Mil, Naut) de (la) superficie; **on the ~ it seems that ...** (fig) a primera vista parece que ...

surface area n área de la superficie

surface mail n vía terrestre

surface-to-air ['sə:fɪstə'ɛəʳ] adj (Mil) tierra-aire

surface-to-surface ['sə:fɪstə'sə:fɪs] adj (Mil) tierra-tierra

surfboard ['sə:fbɔ:d] n plancha (de surf)

surfeit ['sə:fɪt] n: **a ~ of** un exceso de

surfer ['sə:fəʳ] n súrfer m/f

surfing ['sə:fɪŋ] n surf m

surge [sə:dʒ] n oleada, oleaje m; (Elec) sobretensión f transitoria ▪ vi avanzar a tropel; **to ~ forward** avanzar rápidamente

surgeon ['sə:dʒən] n cirujano(-a)

surgery ['sə:dʒərɪ] n cirugía; (Brit: room) consultorio; (: Pol) horas en las que los electores pueden reunirse personalmente con su diputado; **to undergo ~** operarse; see also **constituency**

surgery hours npl (Brit) horas fpl de consulta

surgical ['sə:dʒɪkl] adj quirúrgico

surgical spirit n (Brit) alcohol m

surly ['sə:lɪ] adj hosco, malhumorado

surmount [sə:'maunt] vt superar, vencer

surname ['sə:neɪm] n apellido

surpass [sə:'pɑ:s] vt superar, exceder

surplus ['sə:pləs] n excedente m; (Comm) superávit m ▪ adj (Comm) excedente, sobrante; **to have a ~ of sth** tener un excedente de algo; **it is ~ to our requirements** nos sobra; **~ stock** saldos mpl

surprise [sə'praɪz] n sorpresa ▪ vt sorprender; **to take by ~** (person) coger desprevenido or por sorpresa a, sorprender a; (Mil: town, fort) atacar por sorpresa

surprising [sə'praɪzɪŋ] adj sorprendente

surprisingly [sə'praɪzɪŋlɪ] adv (easy, helpful) de modo sorprendente; **(somewhat) ~, he agreed** para sorpresa de todos, aceptó

surrealism [sə'rɪəlɪzəm] n surrealismo

surrender [sə'rɛndəʳ] n rendición f, entrega ▪ vi rendirse, entregarse ▪ vt renunciar

surrender value n valor m de rescate

surreptitious [sʌrəp'tɪʃəs] adj subrepticio

surrogate ['sʌrəgɪt] n (Brit) sustituto(-a)

surrogate mother n madre f de alquiler

surround [sə'raund] vt rodear, circundar; (Mil etc) cercar

surrounding [sə'raundɪŋ] adj circundante

surroundings [sə'raundɪŋz] npl alrededores mpl, cercanías fpl

surtax ['sə:tæks] n sobretasa, sobreimpuesto

surveillance [sə:'veɪləns] n vigilancia

survey n ['sə:veɪ] inspección f

reconocimiento; (inquiry) encuesta; (comprehensive view: of situation etc) vista de conjunto ▪ vt [sə:'veɪ] examinar, inspeccionar; (Surveying: building) inspeccionar; (: land) hacer un reconocimiento de, reconocer; (look at) mirar, contemplar; (make inquiries about) hacer una encuesta de; **to carry out a ~ of** inspeccionar, examinar

surveyor [sə'veɪəʳ] n (Brit: of building) perito m/f; (of land) agrimensor(a) m(f)

survival [sə'vaɪvl] n supervivencia

survival course n curso de supervivencia

survival kit n equipo de emergencia

survive [sə'vaɪv] vi sobrevivir; (custom etc) perdurar ▪ vt sobrevivir a

survivor [sə'vaɪvəʳ] n superviviente m/f

susceptibility [səsɛptə'bɪlɪtɪ] n (to illness) propensión f

susceptible [sə'sɛptəbl] adj (easily influenced) influenciable; (to disease, illness): **~ to** propenso a

sushi [su:ʃɪ] n sushi m

suspect adj, n ['sʌspɛkt] sospechoso(-a) m(f) ▪ vt [səs'pɛkt] sospechar

suspected [səs'pɛktɪd] adj presunto; **to have a ~ fracture** tener una posible fractura

suspend [səs'pɛnd] vt suspender

suspended animation [səs'pɛndəd-] n: **in a state of ~** en (estado de) hibernación

suspended sentence n (Law) libertad f condicional

suspender belt [səs'pɛndəʳ-] n (Brit) liguero, portaligas m inv (LAm)

suspenders [səs'pɛndəz] npl (Brit) ligas fpl; (US) tirantes mpl

suspense [səs'pɛns] n incertidumbre f, duda; (in film etc) suspense m

suspension [səs'pɛnʃən] n (gen) suspensión f; (of driving licence) privación f

suspension bridge n puente m colgante

suspension file n archivador m colgante

suspicion [səs'pɪʃən] n sospecha; (distrust) recelo; (trace) traza; **to be under ~** estar bajo sospecha; **arrested on ~ of murder** detenido bajo sospecha de asesinato

suspicious [səs'pɪʃəs] adj (suspecting) receloso; (causing suspicion) sospechoso; **to be ~ of or about sb/sth** tener sospechas de algn/algo

suss out [sʌs-] vt (Brit col) calar

sustain [səs'teɪn] vt sostener, apoyar; (suffer) sufrir, padecer

sustainable [səs'teɪnəbl] adj sostenible; **~ development** desarrollo sostenible

sustained [səs'teɪnd] adj (effort) sostenido

sustenance ['sʌstɪnəns] n sustento

suture ['su:tʃəʳ] n sutura

SUV [ɛsˈjuːˈviː] *n abbr* (= *sports utility vehicle*) todoterreno *m inv*

SVQ *n abbr* (= *Scottish Vocational Qualification*) titulación de formación profesional en Escocia

SW *abbr* = **short wave**

swab [swɔb] *n* (*Med*) algodón *m*, frotis *m inv* ■ *vt* (*Naut: also:* **swab down**) limpiar, fregar

swagger [ˈswægəʳ] *vi* pavonearse

swallow [ˈswɔləu] *n* (*bird*) golondrina; (*of food*) bocado; (*of drink*) trago ■ *vt* tragar
  ▶ **swallow up** *vt* (*savings etc*) consumir

swam [swæm] *pt of* **swim**

swamp [swɔmp] *n* pantano, ciénaga ■ *vt* abrumar, agobiar

swampy [ˈswɔmpɪ] *adj* pantanoso

swan [swɔn] *n* cisne *m*

swank [swæŋk] (*col*) *n* (*vanity, boastfulness*) fanfarronada ■ *vi* fanfarronear, presumir

swan song *n* (*fig*) canto del cisne

swap [swɔp] *n* canje *m*, trueque *m* ■ *vt:* **to ~ (for)** canjear (por)

SWAPO [ˈswɑːpəu] *n abbr* (= *South-West Africa People's Organization*) SWAPO *f*

swarm [swɔːm] *n* (*of bees*) enjambre *m*; (*fig*) multitud *f* ■ *vi* (*fig*) hormiguear, pulular

swarthy [ˈswɔːðɪ] *adj* moreno

swashbuckling [ˈswɔʃbʌklɪŋ] *adj* (*person*) aventurero; (*film*) de capa y espada

swastika [ˈswɔstɪkə] *n* esvástica, cruz *f* gamada

swat [swɔt] *vt* aplastar ■ *n* (*also:* **fly swat**) matamoscas *m inv*

SWAT [swɔt] *n abbr* (*US:* = *Special Weapons and Tactics*) unidad especial de la policía

swathe [sweɪð] *vt:* **to ~ in** (*blankets*) envolver en; (*bandages*) vendar en

sway [sweɪ] *vi* mecerse, balancearse ■ *vt* (*influence*) mover, influir en ■ *n* (*rule, power*): **~ (over)** dominio (sobre); **to hold ~ over sb** dominar a algn, mantener el dominio sobre algn

Swaziland [ˈswɑːzɪlænd] *n* Swazilandia

swear (*pt* **swore**, *pp* **sworn**) [sweəʳ, swɔːʳ, swɔːn] *vi* jurar; (*with swearwords*) decir tacos ■ *vt:* **to ~ an oath** prestar juramento, jurar; **to ~ to sth** declarar algo bajo juramento
  ▶ **swear in** *vt* tomar juramento (a)

swearword [ˈsweəwəːd] *n* taco, palabrota

sweat [swɛt] *n* sudor *m* ■ *vi* sudar

sweatband [ˈswɛtbænd] *n* (*Sport: on head*) banda; (*: on wrist*) muñequera

sweater [ˈswɛtəʳ] *n* suéter *m*

sweatshirt [ˈswɛtʃəːt] *n* sudadera

sweatshop [ˈswɛtʃɔp] *n* fábrica donde se explota al obrero

sweaty [ˈswɛtɪ] *adj* sudoroso

Swede [swiːd] *n* sueco(-a)

swede [swiːd] *n* (*Brit*) nabo

Sweden [ˈswiːdn] *n* Suecia

Swedish [ˈswiːdɪʃ] *adj, n* (*Ling*) sueco

sweep [swiːp] (*pt, pp* **swept**) *n* (*act*) barrida; (*of arm*) manotazo *m*; (*curve*) curva, alcance *m*; (*also:* **chimney sweep**) deshollinador(a) *m(f)* ■ *vt* barrer; (*disease, fashion*) recorrer ■ *vi* barrer
  ▶ **sweep away** *vt* barrer; (*rub out*) borrar
  ▶ **sweep past** *vi* pasar rápidamente; (*brush by*) rozar
  ▶ **sweep up** *vi* barrer

sweeper [ˈswiːpəʳ] *n* (*person*) barrendero(-a); (*machine*) barredora; (*Football*) líbero, libre *m*

sweeping [ˈswiːpɪŋ] *adj* (*gesture*) dramático; (*generalized*) generalizado; (*changes, reforms*) radical

sweepstake [ˈswiːpsteɪk] *n* lotería

sweet [swiːt] *n* (*candy*) dulce *m*, caramelo; (*Brit: pudding*) postre *m* ■ *adj* dulce; (*sugary*) azucarado; (*charming: person*) encantador(a); (*: smile, character*) dulce, amable, agradable ■ *adv:* **to smell/taste ~** oler/saber dulce

sweet and sour *adj* agridulce

sweetcorn [ˈswiːtkɔːn] *n* maíz *m* (dulce)

sweeten [ˈswiːtn] *vt* (*person*) endulzar; (*add sugar to*) poner azúcar a

sweetener [ˈswiːtnəʳ] *n* (*Culin*) edulcorante *m*

sweetheart [ˈswiːthɑːt] *n* amor *m*, novio(-a); (*in speech*) amor, cariño

sweetness [ˈswiːtnɪs] *n* (*gen*) dulzura

sweet pea *n* guisante *m* de olor

sweet potato *n* batata, camote *m* (*LAm*)

sweetshop [ˈswiːtʃɔp] *n* (*Brit*) confitería, bombonería

swell [swɛl] (*pt* **swelled**, *pp* **swollen** *or* **swelled**) *n* (*of sea*) marejada, oleaje *m* ■ *adj* (*US: col: excellent*) estupendo, fenomenal ■ *vt* hinchar, inflar ■ *vi* hincharse, inflarse

swelling [ˈswɛlɪŋ] *n* (*Med*) hinchazón *f*

sweltering [ˈswɛltərɪŋ] *adj* sofocante, de mucho calor

swept [swɛpt] *pt, pp of* **sweep**

swerve [swəːv] *n* regate *m*; (*in car*) desvío brusco ■ *vi* desviarse bruscamente

swift [swɪft] *n* (*bird*) vencejo ■ *adj* rápido, veloz

swiftly [ˈswɪftlɪ] *adv* rápidamente

swiftness [ˈswɪftnɪs] *n* rapidez *f*, velocidad *f*

swig [swɪg] *n* (*col: drink*) trago

swill [swɪl] *n* bazofia ■ *vt* (*also:* **swill out, swill down**) lavar, limpiar con agua

swim [swɪm] (*pt* **swam**, *pp* **swum**) *n:* **to go for a ~** ir a nadar *or* a bañarse ■ *vi* nadar; (*head, room*) dar vueltas ■ *vt* pasar a nado; **to go swimming** ir a nadar; **to ~ a length** nadar *or* hacer un largo

S

swimmer ['swɪmə^r] *n* nadador(a) *m(f)*
swimming ['swɪmɪŋ] *n* natación *f*
swimming cap *n* gorro de baño
swimming costume *n* bañador *m*, traje *m* de baño
swimmingly ['swɪmɪŋlɪ] *adv*: **to go ~** (*wonderfully*) ir como una seda *or* sobre ruedas
swimming pool *n* piscina, alberca (*LAm*)
swimming trunks *npl* bañador *msg*
swimsuit ['swɪmsuːt] *n* = **swimming costume**
swindle ['swɪndl] *n* estafa ▪ *vt* estafar
swine [swaɪn] *n pl inv* cerdo, puerco; (*col!*) canalla *m* (*!*)
swine flu *n* gripe *f* porcina
swing [swɪŋ] (*pt, pp* **swung**) *n* (*in playground*) columpio; (*movement*) balanceo, vaivén *m*; (*change of direction*) viraje *m*; (*rhythm*) ritmo; (*Pol: in votes etc*): **there has been a ~ towards/away from Labour** ha habido un viraje en favor/en contra del Partido Laborista ▪ *vt* balancear; (*on a swing*) columpiar; (*also*: **swing round**) voltear, girar ▪ *vi* balancearse, columpiarse; (*also*: **swing round**) dar media vuelta; **a ~ to the left** un movimiento hacia la izquierda; **to be in full ~** estar en plena marcha; **to get into the ~ of things** meterse en situación; **the road swings south** la carretera gira hacia el sur
swing bridge *n* puente *m* giratorio
swing door, swinging door (*US*) ['swɪŋɪŋ-] *n* puerta giratoria
swingeing ['swɪndʒɪŋ] *adj* (*Brit*) abrumador(a)
swipe [swaɪp] *n* golpe *m* fuerte ▪ *vt* (*hit*) golpear fuerte; (*col: steal*) guindar; (*credit card etc*) pasar
swirl [swəːl] *vi* arremolinarse
swish [swɪʃ] *n* (*sound: of whip*) chasquido; (: *of skirts*) frufrú *m*; (: *of grass*) crujido ▪ *adj* (*col: smart*) elegante ▪ *vi* chasquear
Swiss [swɪs] *adj, n* (*pl inv*) suizo(-a) *m(f)*
switch [swɪtʃ] *n* (*for light, radio etc*) interruptor *m*; (*change*) cambio ▪ *vt* (*change*) cambiar de; (*invert: also*: **switch round, switch over**) intercambiar
▸ **switch off** *vt* apagar; (*engine*) parar
▸ **switch on** *vt* (*Aut: ignition*) encender, prender (*LAm*); (*engine, machine*) arrancar; (*water supply*) conectar
switchboard ['swɪtʃbɔːd] *n* (*Tel*) centralita (de teléfonos), conmutador *m* (*LAm*)
Switzerland ['swɪtsələnd] *n* Suiza
swivel ['swɪvl] *vi* (*also*: **swivel round**) girar
swollen ['swəʊlən] *pp of* **swell**
swoon [swuːn] *vi* desmayarse
swoop [swuːp] *n* (*by police etc*) redada; (*of bird etc*) descenso en picado, calada ▪ *vi* (*also*:

swoop down) caer en picado
swop [swɔp] = **swap**
sword [sɔːd] *n* espada
swordfish ['sɔːdfɪʃ] *n* pez *m* espada
swore [swɔː^r] *pt of* **swear**
sworn [swɔːn] *pp of* **swear**
swot [swɔt] (*Brit*) *vt, vi* empollar ▪ *n* empollón(-ona) *m(f)*
swum [swʌm] *pp of* **swim**
swung [swʌŋ] *pt, pp of* **swing**
sycamore ['sɪkəmɔː^r] *n* sicomoro
sycophant ['sɪkəfænt] *n* adulador(a) *m(f)* pelotillero(-a)
Sydney ['sɪdnɪ] *n* Sidney *m*
syllable ['sɪləbl] *n* sílaba
syllabus ['sɪləbəs] *n* programa *m* de estudios; **on the ~** en el programa de estudios
symbol ['sɪmbl] *n* símbolo
symbolic [sɪm'bɔlɪk], **symbolical** [sɪm'bɔlɪkl] *adj* simbólico; **to be ~(al) of sth** simbolizar algo
symbolism ['sɪmbəlɪzəm] *n* simbolismo
symbolize ['sɪmbəlaɪz] *vt* simbolizar
symmetrical [sɪ'mɛtrɪkl] *adj* simétrico
symmetry ['sɪmɪtrɪ] *n* simetría
sympathetic [sɪmpə'θɛtɪk] *adj* compasivo; (*understanding*) comprensivo; **to be ~ to a cause** (*well-disposed*) apoyar una causa; **to be ~ towards** (*person*) ser comprensivo con
sympathize ['sɪmpəθaɪz] *vi*: **to ~ with sb** compadecerse de algn; (*understand*) comprender a algn
sympathizer ['sɪmpəθaɪzə^r] *n* (*Pol*) simpatizante *m/f*
sympathy ['sɪmpəθɪ] *n* (*pity*) compasión *f*; (*understanding*) comprensión *f*; **with our deepest ~** nuestro más sentido pésame
symphony ['sɪmfənɪ] *n* sinfonía
symposium [sɪm'pəuzɪəm] *n* simposio
symptom ['sɪmptəm] *n* síntoma *m*, indicio
symptomatic [sɪmptə'mætɪk] *adj*: **~ (of)** sintomático (de)
synagogue ['sɪnəgɔg] *n* sinagoga
sync [sɪŋk] *n* (*col*): **to be in/out of ~ (with)** ir/no ir al mismo ritmo (que); (*fig: people*) conectar/no conectar con
synchromesh ['sɪŋkrəumɛʃ] *n* cambio sincronizado de velocidades
synchronize ['sɪŋkrənaɪz] *vt* sincronizar ▪ *vi*: **to ~ with** sincronizarse con
synchronized swimming ['sɪŋkrənaɪzd-] *n* natación *f* sincronizada
syncopated ['sɪŋkəpeɪtɪd] *adj* sincopado
syndicate ['sɪndɪkɪt] *n* (*gen*) sindicato; (*Press*) agencia (de noticias)
syndrome ['sɪndrəum] *n* síndrome *m*
synonym ['sɪnənɪm] *n* sinónimo

synonymous [sɪ'nɒnɪməs] *adj*: ~ **(with)** sinónimo (con)

synopsis, synopses [sɪ'nɒpsɪs, -siːz] *n* sinopsis *f inv*

syntax ['sɪntæks] *n* sintaxis *f*

syntax error *n* (*Comput*) error *m* sintáctico

synthesis, syntheses ['sɪnθəsɪs, -siːz] *n* síntesis *f inv*

synthesizer ['sɪnθəsaɪzəʳ] *n* sintetizador *m*

synthetic [sɪn'θɛtɪk] *adj* sintético ■ *n* sintético

syphilis ['sɪfɪlɪs] *n* sífilis *f*

syphon ['saɪfən] = **siphon**

Syria ['sɪrɪə] *n* Siria

Syrian ['sɪrɪən] *adj, n* sirio(-a) *m(f)*

syringe [sɪ'rɪndʒ] *n* jeringa

syrup ['sɪrəp] *n* jarabe *m*, almíbar *m*

system ['sɪstəm] *n* sistema *m*; (*Anat*) organismo; **it was quite a shock to his ~** fue un golpe para él

systematic [sɪstə'mætɪk] *adj* sistemático; metódico

system disk *n* (*Comput*) disco del sistema

systems analyst *n* analista *m/f* de sistemas

S

Tt

T, t [tiː] *n* (*letter*) T, t *f*; **T for Tommy** T de Tarragona

TA *n abbr* (*Brit*) = **Territorial Army**

ta [tɑː] *excl* (*Brit: col*) ¡gracias!

tab [tæb] *n abbr* = **tabulator** ■ *n* lengüeta; (*label*) etiqueta; **to keep tabs on** (*fig*) vigilar

tabby ['tæbɪ] *n* (*also*: **tabby cat**) gato atigrado

tabernacle ['tæbənækl] *n* tabernáculo

table ['teɪbl] *n* mesa; (*chart: of statistics etc*) cuadro, tabla ■ *vt* (*Brit: motion etc*) presentar; **to lay** *or* **set the ~** poner la mesa; **to clear the ~** quitar *or* levantar la mesa; **league ~** (*Football, Rugby*) clasificación *f* del campeonato; **~ of contents** índice *m* de materias

tablecloth ['teɪblklɔθ] *n* mantel *m*

table d'hôte [tɑːblˈdəut] *n* menú *m*

table lamp *n* lámpara de mesa

tablemat ['teɪblmæt] *n* salvamanteles *m inv*, posaplatos *m inv*

tablespoon ['teɪblspuːn] *n* cuchara grande; (*also*: **tablespoonful**: *as measurement*) cucharada

tablet ['tæblɪt] *n* (*Med*) pastilla, comprimido; (*for writing*) bloc *m*; (*of stone*) lápida; **~ of soap** pastilla de jabón

table talk *n* conversación *f* de sobremesa

table tennis *n* ping-pong *m*, tenis *m* de mesa

table wine *n* vino de mesa

tabloid ['tæblɔɪd] *n* (*newspaper*) periódico popular sensacionalista

tabloid press *n* ver nota

taboo [tə'buː] *adj, n* tabú *m*

tabulate ['tæbjuleɪt] *vt* disponer en tablas

tabulator ['tæbjuleɪtəʳ] *n* tabulador *m*

tachograph ['tækəgrɑːf] *n* tacógrafo

tachometer [tæ'kɔmɪtəʳ] *n* taquímetro

tacit ['tæsɪt] *adj* tácito

tacitly ['tæsɪtlɪ] *adv* tácitamente

taciturn ['tæsɪtəːn] *adj* taciturno

tack [tæk] *n* (*nail*) tachuela; (*stitch*) hilván *m*; (*Naut*) bordada ■ *vt* (*nail*) clavar con tachuelas; (*stitch*) hilvanar ■ *vi* virar; **to ~ sth on to (the end of) sth** (*of letter, book*) añadir algo a(l final de) algo

tackle ['tækl] *n* (*gear*) equipo; (*fishing tackle, for lifting*) aparejo; (*Football*) entrada, tackle *m*; (*Rugby*) placaje *m* ■ *vt* (*difficulty*) enfrentarse a, abordar; (*grapple with*) agarrar; (*Football*) entrar a; (*Rugby*) placar

tacky ['tækɪ] *adj* pegajoso; (*fam*) hortera *inv*

tact [tækt] *n* tacto, discreción *f*

tactful ['tæktful] *adj* discreto, diplomático; **to be ~** tener tacto, actuar discretamente

tactfully ['tæktfulɪ] *adv* diplomáticamente, con tacto

tactical ['tæktɪkl] *adj* táctico

tactical voting *n* voto útil

tactician [tæk'tɪʃən] *n* táctico(-a)

tactics ['tæktɪks] *n, npl* táctica *sg*

tactless ['tæktlɪs] *adj* indiscreto

tactlessly ['tæktlɪslɪ] *adv* indiscretamente, sin tacto

tadpole ['tædpəul] *n* renacuajo

taffy ['tæfɪ] *n* (*US*) melcocha

tag [tæg] *n* (*label*) etiqueta; **price/name ~** etiqueta del precio/con el nombre
  ▶ **tag along** *vi*: **to ~ along with sb** engancharse a algn

tag question *n* pregunta coletilla

Tahiti [tɑːˈhiːtɪ] n Tahití m
tail [teɪl] n cola; (Zool) rabo; (of shirt, coat) faldón m ■ vt (follow) vigilar a; **heads or tails** cara o cruz; **to turn ~** volver la espalda
▶ **tail away, tail off** vi (in size, quality etc) ir disminuyendo
tailback [ˈteɪlbæk] n (Brit Aut) cola
tail coat n frac m
tail end n cola, parte f final
tailgate [ˈteɪlgeɪt] n (Aut) puerta trasera
tail light n (Aut) luz f trasera
tailor [ˈteɪləʳ] n sastre m ■ vt: **to ~ sth (to)** confeccionar algo a medida (para); **~'s (shop)** sastrería
tailoring [ˈteɪlərɪŋ] n (cut) corte m; (craft) sastrería
tailor-made [ˈteɪləˈmeɪd] adj (also fig) hecho a (la) medida
tailwind [ˈteɪlwɪnd] n viento de cola
taint [teɪnt] vt (meat, food) contaminar; (fig: reputation) manchar, tachar (LAm)
tainted [ˈteɪntɪd] adj (water, air) contaminado; (fig) manchado
Taiwan [taɪˈwɑːn] n Taiwán m
Tajikistan [tɑːdʒɪkɪˈstɑːn] n Tayikistán m
take [teɪk] (pt **took**, pp **taken**) vt tomar; (grab) coger (SP), agarrar (LAm); (gain: prize) ganar; (require: effort, courage) exigir; (support weight of) aguantar; (hold: passengers etc) tener cabida para; (accompany, bring, carry) llevar; (exam) presentarse a; (conduct: meeting) presidir ■ vi (fire) prender; (dye) coger (SP), agarrar, tomar ■ n (Cine) toma; **to ~ sth from** (drawer etc) sacar algo de; (person) coger algo a (SP); **to ~ sb's hand** tomar de la mano a algn; **to ~ notes** tomar apuntes; **to be taken ill** ponerse enfermo; **~ the first on the left** toma la primera a la izquierda; **I only took Russian for one year** sólo estudié ruso un año; **I took him for a doctor** le tenía por médico; **it won't ~ long** durará poco; **it will ~ at least five litres** tiene cabida por lo menos para cinco litros; **to be taken with sb/sth** (attracted) tomarle cariño a algn/ tomarle gusto a algo; **I ~ it that ...** supongo que ...
▶ **take after** vt fus parecerse a
▶ **take apart** vt desmontar
▶ **take away** vt (remove) quitar; (carry off) llevar ■ vi: **to ~ away from** quitar mérito a
▶ **take back** vt (return) devolver; (one's words) retractar
▶ **take down** vt (building) derribar; (dismantle: scaffolding) desmantelar; (message etc) apuntar, tomar nota de
▶ **take in** vt (Brit: deceive) engañar; (understand) entender; (include) abarcar; (lodger) acoger,

recibir; (orphan, stray dog) recoger; (Sewing) achicar
▶ **take off** vi (Aviat) despegar, decolar (LAm) ■ vt (remove) quitar; (imitate) imitar, remedar
▶ **take on** vt (work) emprender; (employee) contratar; (opponent) desafiar
▶ **take out** vt sacar; (remove) quitar; **don't ~ it out on me!** ¡no te desquites conmigo!
▶ **take over** vt (business) tomar posesión de ■ vi: **to ~ over from sb** reemplazar a algn
▶ **take to** vt fus (person) coger cariño a (SP), encariñarse con (LAm); (activity) aficionarse a; **to ~ to doing sth** aficionarse a (hacer) algo
▶ **take up** vt (a dress) acortar; (occupy: time, space) ocupar; (engage in: hobby etc) dedicarse a; (absorb: liquids) absorber; (accept: offer, challenge) aceptar ■ vi: **to ~ up with sb** hacerse amigo de algn
▶ **take upon** vt: **to ~ it upon o.s. to do sth** encargarse de hacer algo
takeaway [ˈteɪkəweɪ] adj (Brit: food) para llevar
take-home pay [ˈteɪkhəum-] n salario neto
taken [ˈteɪkən] pp of **take**
takeoff [ˈteɪkɔf] n (Aviat) despegue m, decolaje m (LAm)
takeover [ˈteɪkəuvəʳ] n (Comm) absorción f
takeover bid n oferta pública de adquisición
takings [ˈteɪkɪŋz] npl (Comm) ingresos mpl
talc [tælk] n (also: **talcum powder**) talco
tale [teɪl] n (story) cuento; (account) relación f; **to tell tales** (fig) contar chismes
talent [ˈtælnt] n talento
talented [ˈtæləntɪd] adj talentoso, de talento
talisman [ˈtælɪzmən] n talismán m
talk [tɔːk] n charla; (gossip) habladurías fpl, chismes mpl; (conversation) conversación f ■ vi (speak) hablar; (chatter) charlar; **talks** npl (Pol etc) conversaciones fpl; **to give a ~** dar una charla or conferencia; **to ~ about** hablar de; **to ~ sb into doing sth** convencer a algn para que haga algo; **to ~ sb out of doing sth** disuadir a algn de que haga algo; **to ~ shop** hablar del trabajo; **talking of films, have you seen ...?** hablando de películas, ¿has visto ...?
▶ **talk over** vt discutir
talkative [ˈtɔːkətɪv] adj hablador(a)
talker [ˈtɔːkəʳ] n hablador(a) m(f)
talking point [ˈtɔːkɪŋ-] n tema m de conversación
talking-to [ˈtɔːkɪŋtuː] n: **to give sb a good ~** echar una buena bronca a algn
talk show n programa m magazine
tall [tɔːl] adj alto; (tree) grande; **to be 6 feet ~** ≈ medir 1 metro 80, tener 1 metro 80 de alto; **how ~ are you?** ¿cuánto mides?

tallboy ['tɔːlbɔɪ] n (Brit) cómoda alta
tallness ['tɔːlnɪs] n altura
tall story n cuento chino
tally ['tælɪ] n cuenta ∎ vi: **to ~ (with)**
concordar (con), cuadrar (con); **to keep a ~
of sth** llevar la cuenta de algo
talon ['tælən] n garra
tambourine [tæmbə'riːn] n pandereta
tame [teɪm] adj (mild) manso; (tamed)
domesticado; (fig: story, style, person) soso,
anodino
tameness ['teɪmnɪs] n mansedumbre f
Tamil ['tæmɪl] adj tamil ∎ n tamil m/f; (Ling)
tamil m
tamper ['tæmpəʳ] vi: **to ~ with** (lock etc)
intentar forzar; (papers) falsificar
tampon ['tæmpən] n tampón m
tan [tæn] n (also: **suntan**) bronceado ∎ vt
broncear ∎ vi ponerse moreno ∎ adj (colour)
marrón; **to get a ~** broncearse, ponerse
moreno
tandem ['tændəm] n tándem m
tandoori [tæn'duərɪ] adj, n tandoori m (asado a
la manera hindú, en horno de barro)
tang [tæŋ] n sabor m fuerte
tangent ['tændʒənt] n (Math) tangente f;
to go off at a ~ (fig) salirse por la tangente
tangerine [tændʒə'riːn] n mandarina
tangible ['tændʒəbl] adj tangible; **~ assets**
bienes mpl tangibles
Tangier [tæn'dʒɪəʳ] n Tánger m
tangle ['tæŋgl] n enredo; **to get in(to) a ~**
enredarse
tango ['tæŋgəu] n tango
tank [tæŋk] n (also: **water tank**) depósito,
tanque m; (for fish) acuario; (Mil) tanque m
tankard ['tæŋkəd] n bock m
tanker ['tæŋkəʳ] n (ship) petrolero; (truck)
camión m cisterna
tankful ['tæŋkful] n: **to get a ~ of petrol**
llenar el depósito de gasolina
tankini [tæŋ'kiːnɪ] tankini m
tanned [tænd] adj (skin) moreno, bronceado
tannin ['tænɪn] n tanino
tanning ['tænɪŋ] n (of leather) curtido
tannoy® ['tænɔɪ] n: **over the ~** por el altavoz
tantalizing ['tæntəlaɪzɪŋ] adj tentador(a)
tantamount ['tæntəmaunt] adj: **~ to**
equivalente a
tantrum ['tæntrəm] n rabieta; **to throw a ~**
coger una rabieta
Tanzania [tænzə'nɪə] n Tanzania
Tanzanian [tænzə'nɪən] adj, n tanzano(-a) m(f)
tap [tæp] n (Brit: on sink etc) grifo, canilla
(LAm); (gentle blow) golpecito; (gas tap) llave
f ∎ vt (table etc) tamborilear; (shoulder etc) dar
palmaditas en; (resources) utilizar, explotar;

(telephone conversation) intervenir, pinchar;
on ~ (fig: resources) a mano; **beer on ~** cerveza
de barril
tap-dancing ['tæpdɑːnsɪŋ] n claqué m
tape [teɪp] n cinta; (also: **magnetic tape**)
cinta magnética; (sticky tape) cinta adhesiva
∎ vt (record) grabar (en cinta); **on ~** (song etc)
grabado (en cinta)
tape deck n pletina
tape measure n cinta métrica, metro
taper ['teɪpəʳ] n cirio ∎ vi afilarse
tape-record ['teɪprɪkɔːd] vt grabar (en cinta)
tape recorder n grabadora
tapered ['teɪpəd], **tapering** ['teɪpərɪŋ] adj
terminado en punta
tapestry ['tæpɪstrɪ] n (object) tapiz m; (art)
tapicería
tape-worm ['teɪpwəːm] n solitaria, tenia
tapioca [tæpɪ'əukə] n tapioca
tappet ['tæpɪt] n excéntrica
tar [tɑːʳ] n alquitrán m, brea; **low/middle ~
cigarettes** cigarrillos con contenido bajo/
medio de alquitrán
tarantula [tə'ræntjulə] n tarántula
tardy ['tɑːdɪ] adj (late) tardío; (slow) lento
tare [tɛəʳ] n (Comm) tara
target ['tɑːgɪt] n (gen) blanco; **to be on ~**
(project) seguir el curso previsto
target audience n público al que va destinado un
programa etc
target market n (Comm) mercado al que va
destinado un producto etc
target practice n tiro al blanco
tariff ['tærɪf] n tarifa
tariff barrier n (Comm) barrera arancelaria
tarmac ['tɑːmæk] n (Brit: on road)
alquitranado; (Aviat) pista (de aterrizaje)
tarn [tɑːn] n lago pequeño de montaña
tarnish ['tɑːnɪʃ] vt deslustrar
tarot ['tærəu] n tarot m
tarpaulin [tɑː'pɔːlɪn] n alquitranado
tarragon ['tærəgən] n estragón m
tarry ['tærɪ] vi entretenerse, quedarse atrás
tart [tɑːt] n (Culin) tarta; (Brit col: pej: woman)
fulana ∎ adj (flavour) agrio, ácido
▶ **tart up** vt (room, building) dar tono a
tartan ['tɑːtn] n tartán m ∎ adj de tartán
tartar ['tɑːtəʳ] n (on teeth) sarro
tartar sauce n salsa tártara
tartly ['tɑːtlɪ] adv (answer) ásperamente
task [tɑːsk] n tarea; **to take to ~** reprender
task force n (Mil, Police) grupo de operaciones
taskmaster ['tɑːskmɑːstəʳ] n: **he's a hard ~**
es muy exigente
tassel ['tæsl] n borla
taste [teɪst] n sabor m, gusto; (also:
aftertaste) dejo; (sip) sorbo; (fig: glimpse, idea)

muestra, idea ■ *vt* probar ■ *vi*: **to ~ of** *or*
like *(fish etc)* saber a; **you can ~ the garlic
(in it)** se nota el sabor a ajo; **can I have a ~
of this wine?** ¿puedo probar este vino?; **to
have a ~ for sth** ser aficionado a algo; **in
good/bad ~** de buen/mal gusto; **to be in bad**
or **poor ~** ser de mal gusto
taste bud *n* papila gustativa *or* del gusto
tasteful ['teɪstful] *adj* de buen gusto
tastefully ['teɪstfulɪ] *adv* elegantemente, con
buen gusto
tasteless ['teɪstlɪs] *adj (food)* soso; *(remark)* de
mal gusto
tastelessly ['teɪstlɪslɪ] *adv* con mal gusto
tastily ['teɪstɪlɪ] *adv* sabrosamente
tastiness ['teɪstɪnɪs] *n* (buen) sabor *m*, lo
sabroso
tasty ['teɪstɪ] *adj* sabroso, rico
ta-ta ['tæ'tɑː] *interj (Brit col)* hasta luego, adiós
tatters ['tætəz] *npl*: **in ~** *(also:* **tattered**)
hecho jirones
tattoo [tə'tuː] *n* tatuaje *m*; *(spectacle)*
espectáculo militar ■ *vt* tatuar
tatty ['tætɪ] *adj (Brit col)* cochambroso
taught [tɔːt] *pt, pp of* **teach**
taunt [tɔːnt] *n* pulla ■ *vt* lanzar pullas a
Taurus ['tɔːrəs] *n* Tauro
taut [tɔːt] *adj* tirante, tenso
tavern ['tævən] *n (old)* posada, fonda
tawdry ['tɔːdrɪ] *adj* de mal gusto
tawny ['tɔːnɪ] *adj* leonado
tax [tæks] *n* impuesto ■ *vt* gravar (con
un impuesto); *(fig: test)* poner a prueba;
(: patience) agotar; **before/after ~** impuestos
excluidos/incluidos; **free of ~** libre de
impuestos
taxable ['tæksəbl] *adj (income)* imponible,
sujeto a impuestos
tax allowance *n* desgravación *f* fiscal
taxation [tæk'seɪʃən] *n* impuestos *mpl*;
system of ~ sistema *m* tributario
tax avoidance *n* evasión *f* de impuestos
tax collector *n* recaudador(a) *m(f)*
tax disc *n (Brit Aut)* pegatina del impuesto de
circulación
tax evasion *n* evasión *f* fiscal
tax exemption *n* exención *f* de impuestos
tax-free ['tæksfriː] *adj* libre de impuestos
tax haven *n* paraíso fiscal
taxi ['tæksɪ] *n* taxi *m* ■ *vi (Aviat)* rodar por la
pista
taxidermist ['tæksɪdəːmɪst] *n* taxidermista
m/f
taxi driver *n* taxista *m/f*
tax inspector *n* inspector(a) *m(f)* de
Hacienda
taxi rank, *(Brit)* **taxi stand** *n* parada de taxis

tax payer *n* contribuyente *m/f*
tax rebate *n* devolución *f* de impuestos,
reembolso fiscal
tax relief *n* desgravación *f* fiscal
tax return *n* declaración *f* de la renta
tax shelter *n* protección *f* fiscal
tax year *n* año fiscal
TB *n abbr* = **tuberculosis**
tbc *abbr (= to be confirmed)* por confirmar
TD *n abbr (US)* = **Treasury Department**;
(: Football) = **touchdown**
tea [tiː] *n* té *m*; *(Brit: snack)* ≈ merienda; **high ~**
(Brit) ≈ merienda-cena
tea bag *n* bolsita de té
tea break *n (Brit)* descanso para el té
teacake ['tiːkeɪk] *n* bollito, queque *m (LAm)*
teach *(pt, pp* **taught**) [tiːtʃ, tɔːt] *vt*: **to ~ sb sth**,
~ sth to sb enseñar algo a algn ■ *vi* enseñar;
(be a teacher) ser profesor(a); **it taught him a
lesson** (eso) le sirvió de escarmiento
teacher ['tiːtʃəʳ] *n (in secondary school)*
profesor(a) *m(f)*; *(in primary school)*
maestro(-a); **Spanish ~** profesor(a) *m(f)* de
español
teacher training college *n (for primary schools)*
escuela normal; *(for secondary schools)* centro
de formación del profesorado
teach-in ['tiːtʃɪn] *n* seminario
teaching ['tiːtʃɪŋ] *n* enseñanza
teaching aids *npl* materiales *mpl*
pedagógicos
teaching hospital *n* hospital universitario
tea cosy *n* cubretetera *m*
teacup ['tiːkʌp] *n* taza de té
teak [tiːk] *n* (madera de) teca
tea leaves *npl* hojas *fpl* de té
team [tiːm] *n* equipo; *(of animals)* pareja
▶ **team up** *vi* asociarse
team spirit *n* espíritu *m* de equipo
teamwork ['tiːmwəːk] *n* trabajo en equipo
tea party *n* té *m*
teapot ['tiːpɔt] *n* tetera
tear [tɛəʳ] *(pt* **tore**, *pp* **torn**) *n* rasgón *m*,
desgarrón *m* [tɪəʳ] lágrima ■ *vb* [tɛəʳ] ■ *vt*
romper, rasgar ■ *vi* rasgarse; **in tears**
llorando; **to burst into tears** deshacerse
en lágrimas; **to ~ to pieces** *or* **to bits** *or* **to
shreds** *(also fig)* hacer pedazos, destrozar
▶ **tear along** *vi (rush)* precipitarse
▶ **tear apart** *vt (also fig)* hacer pedazos
▶ **tear away** *vt*: **to ~ o.s. away (from sth)**
alejarse (de algo)
▶ **tear out** *vt (sheet of paper, cheque)* arrancar
▶ **tear up** *vt (sheet of paper etc)* romper
tearaway ['tɛərəweɪ] *n (col)* gamberro(-a)
teardrop ['tɪədrɔp] *n* lágrima
tearful ['tɪəful] *adj* lloroso

tear gas n gas m lacrimógeno
tearing ['tɛərɪŋ] adj: **to be in a ~ hurry** tener muchísima prisa
tearoom ['ti:ru:m] n salón m de té
tease [ti:z] n bromista m/f ■ vt tomar el pelo a
tea set n servicio de té
teashop ['ti:ʃɔp] n café m, cafetería
Teasmaid® ['ti:zmeɪd] n tetera automática
teaspoon ['ti:spu:n] n cucharita; (also: **teaspoonful**: as measurement) cucharadita
tea strainer n colador m de té
teat [ti:t] n (of bottle) boquilla, tetilla
teatime ['ti:taɪm] n hora del té
tea towel n (Brit) paño de cocina
tea urn n tetera grande
tech [tɛk] n abbr (col) = **technology; technical college**
technical ['tɛknɪkl] adj técnico
technical college n centro de formación profesional
technicality [tɛknɪ'kælɪtɪ] n detalle m técnico; **on a legal ~** por una cuestión formal
technically ['tɛknɪklɪ] adv técnicamente
technician [tɛk'nɪʃn] n técnico(-a)
technique [tɛk'ni:k] n técnica
techno ['tɛknəu] n (Mus) (música) tecno
technocrat ['tɛknəkræt] n tecnócrata m/f
technological [tɛknə'lɔdʒɪkl] adj tecnológico
technologist [tɛk'nɔlədʒɪst] n tecnólogo(-a)
technology [tɛk'nɔlədʒɪ] n tecnología
teddy ['tɛdɪ], **teddy bear** n osito de peluche
tedious ['ti:dɪəs] adj pesado, aburrido
tedium ['ti:dɪəm] n tedio
tee [ti:] n (Golf) tee m
teem [ti:m] vi: **to ~ with** rebosar de; **it is teeming (with rain)** llueve a mares
teenage ['ti:neɪdʒ] adj (fashions etc) juvenil
teenager ['ti:neɪdʒər] n adolescente m/f, quinceañero(-a)
teens [ti:nz] npl: **to be in one's ~** ser adolescente
tee-shirt ['ti:ʃə:t] n = **T-shirt**
teeter ['ti:tər] vi balancearse
teeth [ti:θ] npl of **tooth**
teethe [ti:ð] vi echar los dientes
teething ring ['ti:ðɪŋ-] n mordedor m
teething troubles ['ti:ðɪŋ-] npl (fig) dificultades fpl iniciales
teetotal ['ti:'təutl] adj (person) abstemio
teetotaller, teetotaler (US) ['ti:'təutlər] n (person) abstemio(-a)
TEFL ['tɛfl] n abbr (= Teaching of English as a Foreign Language, TEFL qualification) título para la enseñanza del inglés como lengua extranjera
Teflon® ['tɛflɔn] n teflón® m

Teheran [tɛə'rɑ:n] n Teherán m
tel. abbr (= telephone) tel
Tel Aviv ['tɛlə'vi:v] n Tel Aviv m
telecast ['tɛlɪkɑ:st] vt, vi transmitir por televisión
telecommunications ['tɛlɪkəmju:nɪ] n telecomunicaciones fpl
teleconferencing ['tɛlɪkɒnfərənsɪŋ] n teleconferencias fpl
telefax ['tɛlɪfæks] n telefax m
telegram ['tɛlɪgræm] n telegrama m
telegraph ['tɛlɪgrɑ:f] n telégrafo
telegraphic [tɛlɪ'græfɪk] adj telegráfico
telegraph pole n poste m telegráfico
telegraph wire n hilo telegráfico
telepathic [tɛlɪ'pæθɪk] adj telepático
telepathy [tə'lɛpəθɪ] n telepatía
telephone ['tɛlɪfəun] n teléfono ■ vt llamar por teléfono, telefonear; **to be on the ~** (subscriber) tener teléfono; (be speaking) estar hablando por teléfono
telephone booth, (Brit) **telephone box** n cabina telefónica
telephone call n llamada telefónica
telephone directory n guía telefónica
telephone exchange n central f telefónica
telephone number n número de teléfono
telephonist [tə'lɛfənɪst] n (Brit) telefonista m/f
telephoto ['tɛlɪ'fəutəu] adj: **~ lens** teleobjetivo
teleprinter ['tɛlɪprɪntər] n teletipo, teleimpresora
teleprompter® ['tɛlɪprɔmptər] n teleapuntador m
telesales ['tɛlɪseɪlz] npl televentas fpl
telescope ['tɛlɪskəup] n telescopio
telescopic [tɛlɪ'skɔpɪk] adj telescópico; (umbrella) plegable
Teletext® ['tɛlɪtɛkst] n teletexto m
telethon ['tɛlɪθɔn] n telemaratón m, maratón m televisivo (con fines benéficos)
televise ['tɛlɪvaɪz] vt televisar
television ['tɛlɪvɪʒən] n televisión f; **to watch ~** mirar or ver la televisión
television licence n impuesto por uso de televisor
television set n televisor m
teleworking ['tɛlɪwɜ:kɪŋ] n teletrabajo
telex ['tɛlɛks] n télex m ■ vt (message) enviar por télex; (person) enviar un télex a ■ vi enviar un télex
tell (pt, pp **told**) [tɛl, təuld] vt decir; (relate: story) contar; (distinguish): **to ~ sth from** distinguir algo de ■ vi (talk): **to ~ (of)** contar; (have effect) tener efecto; **to ~ sb to do sth** decir a algn que haga algo; **to ~ sb about**

sth contar algo a algn; **to ~ the time** dar
or decir la hora; **can you ~ me the time?**
¿me puedes decir la hora?; **(I) ~ you what ...**
fíjate ...; **I couldn't ~ them apart** no podía
distinguirlos
▶ **tell off** vt: **to ~ sb off** regañar a algn
▶ **tell on** vt fus: **to ~ on sb** chivarse de algn
teller ['tɛləʳ] n (in bank) cajero(-a)
telling ['tɛlɪŋ] adj (remark, detail) revelador(a)
telltale ['tɛlteɪl] adj (sign) indicador(a)
telly ['tɛlɪ] n (Brit col) tele f
temerity [tə'mɛrɪtɪ] n temeridad f
temp [tɛmp] n abbr (Brit: = temporary office
worker) empleado(-a) eventual ▪ vi trabajar
como empleado(-a) eventual
temper ['tɛmpəʳ] n (mood) humor m; (bad
temper) (mal) genio; (fit of anger) ira; (of child)
rabieta ▪ vt (moderate) moderar; **to be in a
~** estar furioso; **to lose one's ~** enfadarse,
enojarse (LAm); **to keep one's ~** contenerse,
no alterarse
temperament ['tɛmprəmənt] n (nature)
temperamento
temperamental [tɛmprə'mɛntl] adj
temperamental
temperance ['tɛmpərns] n moderación f; (in
drinking) sobriedad f
temperate ['tɛmprət] adj moderado; (climate)
templado
temperature ['tɛmprətʃəʳ] n temperatura;
to have or **run a ~** tener fiebre
tempered ['tɛmpəd] adj (steel) templado
tempest ['tɛmpɪst] n tempestad f
tempestuous [tɛm'pɛstjuəs] adj (relationship,
meeting) tempestuoso
tempi ['tɛmpi:] npl of **tempo**
template ['tɛmplɪt] n plantilla
temple ['tɛmpl] n (building) templo; (Anat)
sien f
templet ['tɛmplɪt] n = **template**
tempo (pl **tempos** or **tempi**) ['tɛmpəu,
'tɛmpi:] n tempo; (fig: of life etc) ritmo
temporal ['tɛmpərl] adj temporal
temporarily ['tɛmpərərɪlɪ] adv
temporalmente
temporary ['tɛmpərərɪ] adj provisional,
temporal; (passing) transitorio; (worker)
eventual; **~ teacher** maestro(-a) interino(-a)
tempt [tɛmpt] vt tentar; **to ~ sb into doing
sth** tentar or inducir a algn a hacer algo;
to be tempted to do sth (person) sentirse
tentado de hacer algo
temptation [tɛmp'teɪʃən] n tentación f
tempting ['tɛmptɪŋ] adj tentador(a)
ten [tɛn] num diez; **tens of thousands**
decenas fpl de miles
tenable ['tɛnəbl] adj sostenible

tenacious [tə'neɪʃəs] adj tenaz
tenaciously [tə'neɪʃəslɪ] adv tenazmente
tenacity [tə'næsɪtɪ] n tenacidad f
tenancy ['tɛnənsɪ] n alquiler m
tenant ['tɛnənt] n (rent-payer) inquilino(-a);
(occupant) habitante m/f
tend [tɛnd] vt (sick etc) cuidar, atender; (cattle,
machine) vigilar, cuidar ▪ vi: **to ~ to do sth**
tener tendencia a hacer algo
tendency ['tɛndənsɪ] n tendencia
tender ['tɛndəʳ] adj tierno, blando; (delicate)
delicado; (sore) sensible; (affectionate) tierno,
cariñoso ▪ n (Comm: offer) oferta; (money):
legal ~ moneda de curso legal ▪ vt ofrecer;
to put in a ~ (for) hacer una oferta (para);
to put work out to ~ ofrecer un trabajo a
contrata; **to ~ one's resignation** presentar
la dimisión
tenderize ['tɛndəraɪz] vt (Culin) ablandar
tenderly ['tɛndəlɪ] adv tiernamente
tenderness ['tɛndənɪs] n ternura; (of meat)
blandura
tendon ['tɛndən] n tendón m
tendril ['tɛndrɪl] n zarcillo
tenement ['tɛnəmənt] n casa or bloque m de
pisos or vecinos (LAm)
Tenerife [tɛnə'ri:f] n Tenerife m
tenet ['tɛnət] n principio
Tenn. abbr (US) = **Tennessee**
tenner ['tɛnəʳ] n (billete m de) diez libras fpl
tennis ['tɛnɪs] n tenis m
tennis ball n pelota de tenis
tennis club n club m de tenis
tennis court n cancha de tenis
tennis elbow n (Med) sinovitis f del codo
tennis match n partido de tenis
tennis player n tenista m/f
tennis racket n raqueta de tenis
tennis shoes npl zapatillas fpl de tenis
tenor ['tɛnəʳ] n (Mus) tenor m
tenpin bowling ['tɛnpɪn-] n bolos mpl
tense [tɛns] adj tenso; (stretched) tirante;
(stiff) rígido, tieso; (person) nervioso ▪ n (Ling)
tiempo ▪ vt (tighten: muscles) tensar
tensely ['tɛnslɪ] adv: **they waited ~**
esperaban tensos
tenseness ['tɛnsnɪs] n tirantez f, tensión f
tension ['tɛnʃən] n tensión f
tent [tɛnt] n tienda (de campaña), carpa
(LAm)
tentacle ['tɛntəkl] n tentáculo
tentative ['tɛntətɪv] adj (person) indeciso;
(provisional) provisional
tentatively ['tɛntətɪvlɪ] adv con indecisión;
(provisionally) provisionalmente
tenterhooks ['tɛntəhuks] npl: **on ~** sobre
ascuas

tenth [tɛnθ] *adj* décimo
tent peg *n* clavija, estaca
tent pole *n* mástil *m*
tenuous ['tɛnjuəs] *adj* tenue
tenure ['tɛnjuəʳ] *n* posesión *f*, tenencia; **to have ~** tener posesión *or* título de propiedad
tepid ['tɛpɪd] *adj* tibio
Ter. *abbr* = **terrace**
term [tə:m] *n* (*limit*) límite *m*; (*Comm*) plazo; (*word*) término; (*period*) período; (*Scol*) trimestre *m* ▪ *vt* llamar, calificar de; **terms** *npl* (*conditions*) condiciones *fpl*; (*Comm*) precio, tarifa; **in the short/long ~** a corto/largo plazo; **during his ~ of office** bajo su mandato; **to be on good terms with sb** llevarse bien con algn; **to come to terms with** (*problem*) aceptar; **in terms of ...** en cuanto a ..., en términos de ...
terminal ['tə:mɪnl] *adj* terminal ▪ *n* (*Elec*) borne *m*; (*Comput*) terminal *m*; (*also:* **air terminal**) terminal *f*; (*Brit: also:* **coach terminal**) (estación *f*) terminal *f*
terminate ['tə:mɪneɪt] *vt* poner término a; (*pregnancy*) interrumpir ▪ *vi:* **to ~ in** acabar en
termination [tə:mɪ'neɪʃən] *n* fin *m*; (*of contract*) terminación *f*; **~ of pregnancy** interrupción *f* del embarazo
termini ['tə:mɪnaɪ] *npl of* **terminus**
terminology [tə:mɪ'nɔlədʒɪ] *n* terminología
terminus (*pl* **termini**) ['tə:mɪnəs, 'tə:mɪnaɪ] *n* término, (estación *f*) terminal *f*
termite ['tə:maɪt] *n* termita, comején *m*
term paper *n* (*US Univ*) trabajo escrito trimestral *or* semestral
terrace ['tɛrəs] *n* terraza; (*Brit: row of houses*) hilera de casas adosadas; **the terraces** (*Brit Sport*) las gradas *fpl*
terraced ['tɛrəst] *adj* (*garden*) escalonado; (*house*) adosado
terracotta [tɛrə'kɔtə] *n* terracota
terrain [tɛ'reɪn] *n* terreno
terrible ['tɛrɪbl] *adj* terrible, horrible; (*fam*) malísimo
terribly ['tɛrɪblɪ] *adv* terriblemente; (*very badly*) malísimamente
terrier ['tɛrɪəʳ] *n* terrier *m*
terrific [tə'rɪfɪk] *adj* fantástico, fenomenal, macanudo (*LAm*); (*wonderful*) maravilloso
terrify ['tɛrɪfaɪ] *vt* aterrorizar; **to be terrified** estar aterrado *or* aterrorizado
terrifying ['tɛrɪfaɪɪŋ] *adj* aterrador(a)
territorial [tɛrɪ'tɔ:rɪəl] *adj* territorial
territorial waters *npl* aguas *fpl* jurisdiccionales
territory ['tɛrɪtərɪ] *n* territorio
terror ['tɛrəʳ] *n* terror *m*
terror attack *n* atentado (terrorista)

terrorism ['tɛrərɪzəm] *n* terrorismo
terrorist ['tɛrərɪst] *n* terrorista *m/f*
terrorize ['tɛrəraɪz] *vt* aterrorizar
terse [tə:s] *adj* (*style*) conciso; (*reply*) brusco
tertiary ['tə:ʃərɪ] *adj* terciario; **~ education** enseñanza superior
Terylene® ['tɛrəli:n] *n* (*Brit*) terylene® *m*
TESL [tɛsl] *n abbr* = **Teaching of English as a Second Language**
TESSA ['tɛsə] *n abbr* (*Brit:* = *Tax Exempt Special Savings Account*) plan de ahorro por el que se invierte a largo plazo a cambio de intereses libres de impuestos
test [tɛst] *n* (*trial, check*) prueba, ensayo; (: *of goods in factory*) control *m*; (*of courage etc*) prueba; (*Chem, Med*) prueba; (*of blood, urine*) análisis *m inv*; (*exam*) examen *m*, test *m*; (*also:* **driving test**) examen *m* de conducir ▪ *vt* probar, poner a prueba; (*Med*) examinar; (: *blood*) analizar; **to put sth to the ~** someter algo a prueba; **to ~ sth for sth** analizar algo en busca de algo
testament ['tɛstəmənt] *n* testamento; **the Old/New T~** el Antiguo/Nuevo Testamento
test ban *n* (*also:* **nuclear test ban**) suspensión *f* de pruebas nucleares
test card *n* (*TV*) carta de ajuste
test case *n* juicio que sienta precedente
testes ['tɛsti:z] *npl* testes *mpl*
test flight *n* vuelo de ensayo
testicle ['tɛstɪkl] *n* testículo
testify ['tɛstɪfaɪ] *vi* (*Law*) prestar declaración; **to ~ to sth** atestiguar algo
testimonial [tɛstɪ'məunɪəl] *n* (*of character*) (carta de) recomendación *f*
testimony ['tɛstɪmənɪ] *n* (*Law*) testimonio, declaración *f*
testing ['tɛstɪŋ] *adj* (*difficult: time*) duro
test match *n* partido internacional
testosterone [tɛs'tɔstərəun] *n* testosterona
test paper *n* examen *m*, test *m*
test pilot *n* piloto *m/f* de pruebas
test tube *n* probeta
test-tube baby *n* bebé *m* probeta *inv*
testy ['tɛstɪ] *adj* irritable
tetanus ['tɛtənəs] *n* tétano
tetchy ['tɛtʃɪ] *adj* irritable
tether ['tɛðəʳ] *vt* atar ▪ *n:* **to be at the end of one's ~** no aguantar más
Tex. *abbr* (*US*) = **Texas**
text [tɛkst] *n* texto; (*on mobile*) mensaje *m* de texto ▪ *vt:* **to ~ sb** enviar un mensaje (de texto) a algn
textbook ['tɛkstbuk] *n* libro de texto
textiles ['tɛkstaɪlz] *npl* tejidos *mpl*
text message *n* mensaje *m* de texto
text messaging [-'mɛsɪdʒɪŋ] *n* (envío de) mensajes *mpl* de texto

textual ['tɛkstjuəl] *adj* del texto, textual
texture ['tɛkstʃəʳ] *n* textura
TGIF *abbr (col)* = **thank God it's Friday**
TGWU *n abbr* (Brit: = *Transport and General Workers' Union*) sindicato de transportistas
Thai [taɪ] *adj, n* tailandés(-esa) *m(f)*
Thailand ['taɪlænd] *n* Tailandia
thalidomide® [θə'lɪdəmaɪd] *n* talidomida®
Thames [tɛmz] *n*: **the ~** el (río) Támesis
than [ðæn, ðən] *conj* que; (*with numerals*): **more ~ 10/once** más de 10/una vez; **I have more/less ~ you** tengo más/menos que tú; **it is better to phone ~ to write** es mejor llamar por teléfono que escribir; **no sooner did he leave ~ the phone rang** en cuanto se marchó, sonó el teléfono
thank [θæŋk] *vt* dar las gracias a, agradecer; **~ you (very much)** muchas gracias; **~ heavens, ~ God!** ¡gracias a Dios!, ¡menos mal!
thankful ['θæŋkful] *adj*: **~ for** agradecido (por)
thankfully ['θæŋkfəlɪ] *adv* (*gratefully*) con agradecimiento; (*with relief*) por suerte; **~ there were few victims** afortunadamente hubo pocas víctimas
thankless ['θæŋklɪs] *adj* ingrato
thanks [θæŋks] *npl* gracias *fpl* ■ *excl* ¡gracias!; **~ to** *prep* gracias a
Thanksgiving ['θæŋksgɪvɪŋ], **Thanksgiving Day** *n* día *m* de Acción de Gracias; *ver nota*

⬤ **THANKSGIVING DAY**
⬤
⬤ En Estados Unidos el cuarto jueves de
⬤ noviembre es *Thanksgiving Day*, fiesta
⬤ oficial en la que se conmemora la
⬤ celebración que tuvieron los primeros
⬤ colonos norteamericanos ("Pilgrims"
⬤ o "Pilgrim Fathers") tras la estupenda
⬤ cosecha de 1621, por la que se dan gracias
⬤ a Dios. En Canadá se celebra una fiesta
⬤ semejante el segundo lunes de octubre,
⬤ aunque no está relacionada con dicha
⬤ fecha histórica.

⬤ **KEYWORD**

that [ðæt] (*pl* **those**) *adj* (*demonstrative*) ese(-a), esos(-as) *pl*; (*more remote*) aquel/aquella *m/f*, aquellos(-as) *m(f)pl*; **leave those books on the table** deja esos libros sobre la mesa; **that one** ése/ésa; (*more remote*) aquél/aquélla; **that one over there** ése/ésa de ahí; aquél/aquélla de allí
■ *pron* **1** (*demonstrative*) ése(-a), ésos(-as) *pl*; (*neuter*) eso; (*more remote*) aquél/aquélla *m/f*,

aquéllos(-as) *m(f)pl*, aquello *neuter*; **what's that?** ¿qué es eso (*or* aquello)?; **who's that?** ¿quién es?; (*pointing etc*) ¿quién es ése/a?; **is that you?** ¿eres tú?; **will you eat all that?** ¿vas a comer todo eso?; **that's my house** ésa es mi casa; **that's what he said** eso es lo que dijo; **that is (to say)** es decir; **at** *or* **with that she ...** en eso, ella ...; **do it like that** hazlo así
2 (*relative: subject, object*) que; (*with preposition*) (el/la) que, el/la cual; **the book (that) I read** el libro que leí; **the books that are in the library** los libros que están en la biblioteca; **all (that) I have** todo lo que tengo; **the box (that) I put it in** la caja en la que *or* donde lo puse; **the people (that) I spoke to** la gente con la que hablé; **not that I know of** que yo sepa, no
3 (*relative: of time*) que; **the day (that) he came** el día (en) que vino
■ *conj* que; **he thought that I was ill** creyó que yo estaba enfermo
■ *adv* (*demonstrative*): **I can't work that much** no puedo trabajar tanto; **I didn't realize it was that bad** no creí que fuera tan malo; **that high** así de alto

thatched [θætʃt] *adj* (*roof*) de paja; **~ cottage** casita con tejado de paja
Thatcherism ['θætʃərɪzəm] *n* thatcherismo
thaw [θɔ:] *n* deshielo ■ *vi* (*ice*) derretirse; (*food*) descongelarse ■ *vt* descongelar

⬤ **KEYWORD**

the [ði:, ðə] *def art* **1** (*gen*) el, la *f*, los *pl*, las *fpl* (NB =*el* immediately before feminine noun beginning with stressed (h)a; a+el = al; de + el = del): **the boy/girl** el chico/la chica; **the books/flowers** los libros/las flores; **to the postman/from the drawer** al cartero/del cajón; **I haven't the time/money** no tengo tiempo/dinero; **1.10 euros to the dollar** 1,10 euros por dólar; **paid by the hour** pagado por hora
2 (*+adj to form noun*) los; lo; **the rich and the poor** los ricos y los pobres; **to attempt the impossible** intentar lo imposible
3 (*in titles, surnames*): **Elizabeth the First** Isabel Primera; **Peter the Great** Pedro el Grande; **do you know the Smiths?** ¿conoce a los Smith?
4 (*in comparisons*): **the more he works the more he earns** cuanto más trabaja más gana

theatre, theater (US) ['θɪətəʳ] *n* teatro
theatre-goer, theater-goer (US) ['θɪətəgəuəʳ] *n* aficionado(-a) al teatro

823

theatrical [θɪ'ætrɪkl] *adj* teatral
theft [θɛft] *n* robo
their [ðɛəʳ] *adj* su
theirs [ðɛəz] *pron* (el) suyo/(la) suya *etc*; *see also* **my**; **mine**
them [ðɛm, ðəm] *pron* (*direct*) los/las; (*indirect*) les; (*stressed, after prep*) ellos/ellas; **I see ~** los veo; **both of ~** ambos(-as), los/las dos; **give me a few of ~** dame algunos(-as); *see also* **me**
theme [θiːm] *n* tema *m*
theme park *n* parque *m* temático
theme song *n* tema *m* (*musical*)
themselves [ðəm'sɛlvz] *pl pron* (*subject*) ellos mismos/ellas mismas; (*complement*) se; (*after prep*) sí (mismos(-as)); *see also* **oneself**
then [ðɛn] *adv* (*at that time*) entonces; (*next*) pues; (*later*) luego, después; (*and also*) además ■ *conj* (*therefore*) en ese caso, entonces ■ *adj*: **the ~ president** el entonces presidente; **from ~ on** desde entonces; **until ~** hasta entonces; **and ~ what?** y luego, ¿qué?; **what do you want me to do, ~?** ¿entonces, qué quiere que haga?
theologian [θɪə'ləudʒən] *n* teólogo(-a)
theological [θɪə'lɔdʒɪkl] *adj* teológico
theology [θɪ'ɔlədʒɪ] *n* teología
theorem ['θɪərəm] *n* teorema *m*
theoretical [θɪə'rɛtɪkl] *adj* teórico
theoretically [θɪə'rɛtɪklɪ] *adv* teóricamente, en teoría
theorize ['θɪəraɪz] *vi* teorizar
theory ['θɪərɪ] *n* teoría
therapeutic [θɛrə'pjuːtɪk], **therapeutical** [θɛrə'pjuːtɪkl] *adj* terapéutico
therapist ['θɛrəpɪst] *n* terapeuta *m/f*
therapy ['θɛrəpɪ] *n* terapia

 KEYWORD

there ['ðɛəʳ] *adv* **1**: **there is, there are** hay; **there is no-one here** no hay nadie aquí; **there is no bread left** no queda pan; **there has been an accident** ha habido un accidente
2 (*referring to place*) ahí; (*distant*) allí; **it's there** está ahí; **put it in/on/up/down there** ponlo ahí dentro/encima/arriba/abajo; **I want that book there** quiero ese libro de ahí; **there he is!** ¡ahí está!; **there's the bus** ahí *or* ya viene el autobús; **back/down there** allí atrás/abajo; **over there, through there** por allí
3: **there, there** (*esp to child*) ¡venga, venga!

thereabouts ['ðɛərə'bauts] *adv* por ahí
thereafter [ðɛər'ɑːftəʳ] *adv* después
thereby ['ðɛəbaɪ] *adv* así, de ese modo

therefore ['ðɛəfɔːʳ] *adv* por lo tanto
there's [ðɛəz] = **there is; there has**
thereupon [ðɛərə'pɔn] *adv* (*at that point*) en eso, en seguida
thermal ['θəːml] *adj* termal
thermal paper *n* papel *m* térmico
thermal printer *n* termoimpresora
thermodynamics ['θəːmədaɪnæmɪks] *n* termodinámica
thermometer [θə'mɔmɪtəʳ] *n* termómetro
thermonuclear [θə:məu'njuːklɪəʳ] *adj* termonuclear
Thermos® ['θəːməs] *n* (*also*: **Thermos flask**) termo
thermostat ['θəːməustæt] *n* termostato
thesaurus [θɪ'sɔːrəs] *n* tesoro, diccionario de sinónimos
these [ðiːz] *pl adj* estos(-as) ■ *pl pron* éstos(-as)
thesis (*pl* **theses**) ['θiːsɪs, -siːz] *n* tesis *f inv*; *see also* **doctorate**
they [ðeɪ] *pl pron* ellos/ellas; **~ say that ...** (*it is said that*) se dice que ...
they'd [ðeɪd] = **they had; they would**
they'll [ðeɪl] = **they shall; they will**
they're [ðɛəʳ] = **they are**
they've [ðeɪv] = **they have**
thick [θɪk] *adj* (*wall, slice*) grueso; (*dense: liquid, smoke etc*) espeso; (*vegetation, beard*) tupido; (*stupid*) torpe ■ *n*: **in the ~ of the battle** en lo más reñido de la batalla; **it's 20 cm ~** tiene 20 cm de espesor
thicken ['θɪkn] *vi* espesarse ■ *vt* (*sauce etc*) espesar
thicket ['θɪkɪt] *n* espesura
thickly ['θɪklɪ] *adv* (*spread*) en capa espesa; (*cut*) en rebanada gruesa; (*populated*) densamente
thickness ['θɪknɪs] *n* espesor *m*, grueso
thickset [θɪk'sɛt] *adj* fornido
thickskinned [θɪk'skɪnd] *adj* (*fig*) insensible
thief (*pl* **thieves**) [θiːf, θiːvz] *n* ladrón(-ona) *m(f)*
thieving ['θiːvɪŋ] *n* tobo, hurto ■ *adj* ladrón(-ona)
thigh [θaɪ] *n* muslo
thighbone ['θaɪbəun] *n* fémur *m*
thimble ['θɪmbl] *n* dedal *m*
thin [θɪn] *adj* delgado; (*wall, layer*) fino; (*watery*) aguado; (*light*) tenue; (*hair*) escaso; (*fog*) ligero; (*crowd*) disperso ■ *vt*: **to ~ (down)** (*sauce, paint*) diluir ■ *vi* (*fog*) aclararse; (*also*: **thin out**: *crowd*) dispersarse; **his hair is thinning** se está quedando calvo
thing [θɪŋ] *n* cosa; (*object*) objeto, artículo; (*contraption*) chisme *m*; (*mania*) manía; **things** *npl* (*belongings*) cosas *fpl*; **the best ~ would**

be to ... lo mejor sería ...; **the main ~ is** ... lo principal es ...; **first ~ (in the morning)** a primera hora (de la mañana); **last ~ (at night)** a última hora (de la noche); **the ~ is** ... lo que pasa es que ...; **how are things?** ¿qué tal van las cosas?; **she's got a ~ about mice** le dan no sé qué los ratones; **poor ~!** ¡pobre! *m/f*, ¡pobrecito(-a)!

think (*pl* **thought**) [θɪŋk, θɔːt] *vi* pensar ■ *vt* pensar, creer; (*imagine*) imaginar; **what did you ~ of it?** ¿qué te parece?; **what did you ~ of them?** ¿qué te parecieron?; **to ~ about sth/sb** pensar en algo/uno; **I'll ~ about it** lo pensaré; **to ~ of doing sth** pensar en hacer algo; **I ~ so/not** creo que sí/no; **~ again!** ¡piénsalo bien!; **to ~ aloud** pensar en voz alta; **to ~ well of sb** tener buen concepto de algn

▶ **think out** *vt* (*plan*) elaborar, tramar; (*solution*) encontrar

▶ **think over** *vt* reflexionar sobre, meditar; **I'd like to ~ things over** me gustaría pensármelo

▶ **think through** *vt* pensar bien

▶ **think up** *vt* imaginar

thinking ['θɪŋkɪŋ] *n*: **to my (way of) ~** a mi parecer

think tank *n* grupo de expertos

thinly ['θɪnlɪ] *adv* (*cut*) en lonchas finas; (*spread*) en una capa fina

thinness ['θɪnnɪs] *n* delgadez *f*

third [θəːd] *adj* (*before nmsg*) tercer; tercero(-a) ■ *n* tercero(-a); (*fraction*) tercio; (*Brit Scol: degree*) título universitario de tercera clase

third degree *adj* (*burns*) de tercer grado

thirdly ['θəːdlɪ] *adv* en tercer lugar

third party insurance *n* (*Brit*) seguro a terceros

third-rate ['θəːd'reɪt] *adj* de poca calidad

Third World *n*: **the ~** el Tercer Mundo ■ *cpd* tercermundista

thirst [θəːst] *n* sed *f*

thirsty ['θəːstɪ] *adj* (*person*) sediento; **to be ~** tener sed

thirteen [θəː'tiːn] *num* trece

thirteenth [θəː'tiːnθ] *adj* decimotercero ■ *n* (*in series*) decimotercero(-a); (*fraction*) decimotercio

thirtieth ['θəːtɪəθ] *adj* trigésimo ■ *n* (*in series*) trigésimo(-a); (*fraction*) treintavo

thirty ['θəːtɪ] *num* treinta

○ **KEYWORD**

this [ðɪs] (*pl* **these**) *adj* (*demonstrative*) este(-a), estos(-as) *pl*, esto *neuter*; **this man/woman** este hombre/esta mujer; **these children/**

flowers estos chicos/estas flores; **this way** por aquí; **this time last year** hoy hace un año; **this one (here)** éste(-a), esto (de aquí) ■ *pron* (*demonstrative*) éste(-a), éstos(-as) *pl*, esto *neuter*; **who is this?** ¿quién es éste/ésta?; **what is this?** ¿qué es esto?; **this is where I live** aquí vivo; **this is what he said** esto es lo que dijo; **this is Mr Brown** (*in introductions*) le presento al Sr. Brown; (*photo*) éste es el Sr. Brown; (*on telephone*) habla el Sr. Brown; **they were talking of this and that** hablaban de esto y lo otro

■ *adv* (*demonstrative*): **this high/long** así de alto/largo; **this far** hasta aquí

thistle ['θɪsl] *n* cardo

thong [θɔŋ] *n* correa

thorn [θɔːn] *n* espina

thorny ['θɔːnɪ] *adj* espinoso

thorough ['θʌrə] *adj* (*search*) minucioso; (*knowledge*) profundo; (*research*) a fondo

thoroughbred ['θʌrəbrɛd] *adj* (*horse*) de pura sangre

thoroughfare ['θʌrəfɛəʳ] *n* calle *f*; **"no ~"** "prohibido el paso"

thoroughgoing ['θʌrəgəuɪŋ] *adj* a fondo

thoroughly ['θʌrəlɪ] *adv* minuciosamente; a fondo

thoroughness ['θʌrənɪs] *n* minuciosidad *f*

those [ðəuz] *pl pron* ésos/ésas; (*more remote*) aquéllos(-as) ■ *pl adj* esos/esas; aquellos(-as)

though [ðəu] *conj* aunque ■ *adv* sin embargo, aún así; **even ~** aunque; **it's not so easy, ~** sin embargo no es tan fácil

thought [θɔːt] *pt, pp of* **think** ■ *n* pensamiento; (*opinion*) opinión *f*; (*intention*) intención *f*; **to give sth some ~** pensar algo detenidamente; **after much ~** después de pensarlo bien; **I've just had a ~** se me acaba de ocurrir una idea

thoughtful ['θɔːtful] *adj* pensativo; (*considerate*) atento

thoughtfully ['θɔːtfəlɪ] *adv* pensativamente; atentamente

thoughtless ['θɔːtlɪs] *adj* desconsiderado

thoughtlessly ['θɔːtlɪslɪ] *adv* insensatamente

thought-provoking ['θɔːtprəvəukɪŋ] *adj* estimulante

thousand ['θauzənd] *num* mil; **two ~** dos mil; **thousands of** miles de

thousandth ['θauzəntθ] *num* milésimo

thrash [θræʃ] *vt* dar una paliza a

▶ **thrash about** *vi* revolverse

▶ **thrash out** *vt* discutir a fondo

thrashing ['θræʃɪŋ] *n*: **to give sb a ~** dar una paliza a algn

t

thread [θrɛd] n hilo; (of screw) rosca ■ vt (needle) enhebrar

threadbare ['θrɛdbɛəʳ] adj raído

threat [θrɛt] n amenaza; **to be under ~ of** estar amenazado de

threaten ['θrɛtn] vi amenazar ■ vt: **to ~ sb with sth/to do** amenazar a algn con algo/con hacer

threatening ['θrɛtnɪŋ] adj amenazador(a), amenazante

three [θriː] num tres

three-dimensional [θriːdɪ'mɛnʃənl] adj tridimensional

threefold ['θriːfəuld] adv: **to increase ~** triplicar

three-piece ['θriːpiːs]: **~ suit** n traje m de tres piezas

three-piece suite n tresillo

three-ply [θriː'plaɪ] adj (wood) de tres capas; (wool) triple

three-quarter [θriː'kwɔːtəʳ] adj: **~ length sleeves** mangas fpl tres cuartos

three-quarters [θriː'kwɔːtəz] npl tres cuartas partes; **~ full** tres cuartas partes lleno

three-wheeler [θriː'wiːləʳ] n (car) coche m cabina

thresh [θrɛʃ] vt (Agr) trillar

threshing machine ['θrɛʃɪŋ-] n trilladora

threshold ['θrɛʃhəuld] n umbral m; **to be on the ~ of** (fig) estar al borde de

threshold agreement n convenio de nivel crítico

threw [θruː] pt of **throw**

thrift [θrɪft] n economía

thrifty ['θrɪftɪ] adj económico

thrill [θrɪl] n (excitement) emoción f ■ vt emocionar; **to be thrilled** (with gift etc) estar encantado

thriller ['θrɪləʳ] n película/novela de suspense

thrilling ['θrɪlɪŋ] adj emocionante

thrive (pt **thrived, throve**, pp **thrived, thriven**) [θraɪv, θrəuv, 'θrɪvn] vi (grow) crecer; (do well) prosperar

thriving ['θraɪvɪŋ] adj próspero

throat [θrəut] n garganta; **I have a sore ~** me duele la garganta

throb [θrɔb] n (of heart) latido; (of engine) vibración f ■ vi latir; vibrar; (with pain) dar punzadas; **my head is throbbing** la cabeza me da punzadas

throes [θrəuz] npl: **in the ~ of** en medio de

thrombosis [θrɔm'bəusɪs] n trombosis f

throne [θrəun] n trono

throng [θrɔŋ] n multitud f, muchedumbre f ■ vt, vi apiñarse, agolparse

throttle ['θrɔtl] n (Aut) acelerador m ■ vt estrangular

through [θruː] prep por, a través de; (time) durante; (by means of) por medio de, mediante; (owing to) gracias a ■ adj (ticket, train) directo ■ adv completamente, de parte a parte; de principio a fin; **(from) Monday ~ Friday** (US) de lunes a viernes; **to go ~ sb's papers** mirar entre los papeles de algn; **I am halfway ~ the book** voy por la mitad del libro; **the soldiers didn't let us ~** los soldados no nos dejaron pasar; **to put sb ~ to sb** (Tel) poner or pasar a algn con algn; **to be ~** (Tel) tener comunicación; (have finished) haber terminado; **"no ~ road"** (Brit) "calle sin salida"

throughout [θruː'aut] prep (place) por todas partes de, por todo; (time) durante todo ■ adv por or en todas partes

throughput ['θruːput] n (of goods, materials) producción f; (Comput) capacidad f de procesamiento

throve [θrəuv] pt of **thrive**

throw [θrəu] n tiro; (Sport) lanzamiento ■ vt (pt **threw**, pp **thrown**) [θruː, θrəun] tirar, echar, botar (LAm); (Sport) lanzar; (rider) derribar; (fig) desconcertar; **to ~ a party** dar una fiesta

▶ **throw about, throw around** vt (litter etc) tirar, esparcir

▶ **throw away** vt tirar

▶ **throw off** vt deshacerse de

▶ **throw open** vt (doors, windows) abrir de par en par; (house, gardens etc) abrir al público; (competition, race) abrir a todos

▶ **throw out** vt tirar, botar (LAm)

▶ **throw together** vt (clothes) amontonar; (meal) preparar a la carrera; (essay) hacer sin cuidado

▶ **throw up** vi vomitar, devolver

throwaway ['θrəuəweɪ] adj para tirar, desechable

throwback ['θrəubæk] n: **it's a ~ to** (fig) eso nos lleva de nuevo a

throw-in ['θrəuɪn] n (Sport) saque m de banda

thrown [θrəun] pp of **throw**

thru [θruː] (US) = **through**

thrush [θrʌʃ] n zorzal m, tordo; (Med) candiasis f

thrust [θrʌst] n (Tech) empuje m ■ vt (pt, pp **thrust**) empujar; (push in) introducir

thrusting ['θrʌstɪŋ] adj (person) dinámico, con empuje

thud [θʌd] n golpe m sordo

thug [θʌg] n gamberro(-a)

thumb [θʌm] n (Anat) pulgar m ■ vt: **to ~ a lift** hacer dedo; **to give sth/sb the thumbs up/down** aprobar/desaprobar algo/a algn

▶ **thumb through** vt fus (book) hojear

thumb index n uñero, índice m recortado

thumbnail ['θʌmneɪl] n uña del pulgar

thumbnail sketch n esbozo

thumbtack ['θʌmtæk] n (US) chincheta, chinche f

thump [θʌmp] n golpe m; (sound) ruido seco or sordo ■ vt, vi golpear

thumping ['θʌmpɪŋ] adj (col: huge) descomunal

thunder ['θʌndə^r] n trueno; (of applause etc) estruendo ■ vi tronar; (train etc): **to ~ past** pasar como un trueno

thunderbolt ['θʌndəbəult] n rayo

thunderclap ['θʌndəklæp] n trueno

thunderous ['θʌndərəs] adj ensordecedor(a), estruendoso

thunderstorm ['θʌndəstɔːm] n tormenta

thunderstruck ['θʌndəstrʌk] adj pasmado

thundery ['θʌndərɪ] adj tormentoso

Thur., Thurs. abbr (= Thursday) juev

Thursday ['θəːzdɪ] n jueves m inv; see also **Tuesday**

thus [ðʌs] adv así, de este modo

thwart [θwɔːt] vt frustrar

thyme [taɪm] n tomillo

thyroid ['θaɪrɔɪd] n tiroides m inv

tiara [tɪˈɑːrə] n tiara, diadema

Tiber ['taɪbə^r] n Tíber m

Tibet [tɪˈbɛt] n el Tibet

Tibetan [tɪˈbɛtən] adj tibetano ■ n tibetano(-a); (Ling) tibetano

tibia ['tɪbɪə] n tibia

tic [tɪk] n tic m

tick [tɪk] n (sound: of clock) tictac m; (mark) señal f (de visto bueno), palomita (LAm); (Zool) garrapata; (Brit col): **in a ~** en un instante; (Brit col: credit): **to buy sth on ~** comprar algo a crédito ■ vi hacer tictac ■ vt marcar, señalar; **to put a ~ against sth** poner una señal en algo
  ▶ **tick off** vt marcar; (person) reñir
  ▶ **tick over** vi (Brit: engine) girar en marcha lenta; (: fig) ir tirando

ticker tape ['tɪkə-] n cinta perforada

ticket ['tɪkɪt] n billete m, tíquet m, boleto (LAm); (for cinema etc) entrada, boleto (LAm); (in shop: on goods) etiqueta; (for library) tarjeta; (US Pol) lista (de candidatos);
  to get a parking ~ (Aut) ser multado por estacionamiento ilegal

ticket agency n (Theat) agencia de venta de entradas

ticket collector n revisor(a) m(f)

ticket holder n poseedor(a) m(f) de billete or entrada

ticket inspector n revisor(a) m(f), inspector(a) m(f) de boletos (LAm)

ticket office n (Theat) taquilla, boletería (LAm); (Rail) despacho de billetes or boletos (LAm)

ticking-off ['tɪkɪŋ'ɔf] n (col): **to give sb a ~** echarle una bronca a algn

tickle ['tɪkl] n: **to give sb a ~** hacer cosquillas a algn ■ vt hacer cosquillas a

ticklish ['tɪklɪʃ] adj (which tickles: blanket) que pica; (: cough) irritante; **to be ~** tener cosquillas

tidal ['taɪdl] adj de marea

tidal wave n maremoto

tidbit ['tɪdbɪt] (US) = **titbit**

tiddlywinks ['tɪdlɪwɪŋks] n juego de la pulga

tide [taɪd] n marea; (fig: of events) curso, marcha ■ vt: **to ~ sb over or through (until)** sacar a algn del apuro (hasta); **high/low ~** marea alta/baja; **the ~ of public opinion** la tendencia de la opinión pública

tidily ['taɪdɪlɪ] adv bien, ordenadamente; **to arrange ~** ordenar; **to dress ~** vestir bien

tidiness ['taɪdɪnɪs] n (order) orden m; (cleanliness) aseo

tidy ['taɪdɪ] adj (room) ordenado; (drawing, work) limpio; (person) (bien) arreglado; (: in character) metódico; (mind) claro, metódico ■ vt (also: **tidy up**) ordenar, poner en orden

tie [taɪ] n (string etc) atadura; (Brit: necktie) corbata; (fig: link) vínculo, lazo; (Sport: draw) empate m ■ vt atar ■ vi (Sport) empatar; **family ties** obligaciones fpl familiares; **cup ~** (Sport: match) partido de copa; **to ~ in a bow** hacer un lazo; **to ~ a knot in sth** hacer un nudo en algo
  ▶ **tie down** vt atar; (fig): **to ~ sb down to** obligar a algn a
  ▶ **tie in** vi: **to ~ in (with)** (correspond) concordar (con)
  ▶ **tie on** vt (Brit: label etc) atar
  ▶ **tie up** vt (parcel) envolver; (dog) atar; (boat) amarrar; (arrangements) concluir; **to be tied up** (busy) estar ocupado

tie-break ['taɪbreɪk], **tie-breaker** ['taɪbreɪkə^r] n (Tennis) tiebreak m, muerte f súbita; (in quiz) punto decisivo

tie-on ['taɪɔn] adj (Brit: label) para atar

tie-pin ['taɪpɪn] n (Brit) alfiler m de corbata

tier [tɪə^r] n grada; (of cake) piso

tie tack n (US) alfiler m de corbata

tiff [tɪf] n (col) pelea, riña

tiger ['taɪgə^r] n tigre m

tight [taɪt] adj (rope) tirante; (money) escaso; (clothes, budget) ajustado; (programme) apretado; (col: drunk) borracho ■ adv (squeeze) muy fuerte; (shut) herméticamente; **to be packed ~** (suitcase) estar completamente lleno; (people) estar apretados; **everybody hold ~!** ¡agárrense bien!

tighten ['taɪtn] *vt* (*rope*) tensar, estirar; (*screw*) apretar ∎ *vi* estirarse; apretarse

tight-fisted [taɪt'fɪstɪd] *adj* tacaño

tight-lipped ['taɪt'lɪpt] *adj*: **to be ~** (*silent*) rehusar hablar; (*angry*) apretar los labios

tightly ['taɪtlɪ] *adv* (*grasp*) muy fuerte

tightness ['taɪtnɪs] *n* (*of rope*) tirantez *f*; (*of clothes*) estrechez *f*; (*of budget*) lo ajustado

tightrope ['taɪtrəup] *n* cuerda floja

tightrope walker *n* equilibrista *m/f*, funambulista *m/f*

tights [taɪts] *npl* (Brit) medias *fpl*, panties *mpl*

tigress ['taɪgrɪs] *n* tigresa

tilde ['tɪldə] *n* tilde *f*

tile [taɪl] *n* (*on roof*) teja; (*on floor*) baldosa; (*on wall*) azulejo ∎ *vt* (*floor*) poner baldosas en; (*wall*) alicatar

tiled [taɪld] *adj* (*floor*) embaldosado; (*wall, bathroom*) alicatado; (*roof*) con tejas

till [tɪl] *n* caja (registradora) ∎ *vt* (*land*) cultivar ∎ *prep, conj* = **until**

tiller ['tɪləʳ] *n* (Naut) caña del timón

tilt [tɪlt] *vt* inclinar ∎ *vi* inclinarse ∎ *n* (*slope*) inclinación *f*; **to wear one's hat at a ~** llevar el sombrero echado a un lado *or* terciado; **(at) full ~** a toda velocidad *or* carrera

timber [tɪmbəʳ] *n* (*material*) madera; (*trees*) árboles *mpl*

time [taɪm] *n* tiempo; (*epoch: often pl*) época; (*by clock*) hora; (*moment*) momento; (*occasion*) vez *f*; (*Mus*) compás *m* ∎ *vt* calcular *or* medir el tiempo de; (*race*) cronometrar; (*remark etc*) elegir el momento para; **a long ~** mucho tiempo; **four at a ~** cuarto a la vez; **for the ~ being** de momento, por ahora; **at times** a veces, a ratos; **~ after ~**, **~ and again** repetidas veces, una y otra vez; **from ~ to ~** de vez en cuando; **in ~** (*soon enough*) a tiempo; (*after some time*) con el tiempo; (*Mus*) al compás; **in a week's ~** dentro de una semana; **in no ~** en un abrir y cerrar de ojos; **any ~** cuando sea; **on ~** a la hora; **to be 30 minutes behind/ahead of ~** llevar media hora de retraso/adelanto; **to take one's ~** tomárselo con calma; **he'll do it in his own ~** (*without being hurried*) lo hará sin prisa; (*out of working hours*) lo hará en su tiempo libre; **by the ~ he arrived** cuando llegó; **5 times 5** 5 por 5; **what ~ is it?** ¿qué hora es?; **what ~ do you make it?** ¿qué hora es *or* tiene?; **to be behind the times** estar atrasado; **to carry three boxes at a ~** llevar tres cajas a la vez; **to keep ~** llevar el ritmo *or* el compás; **to have a good ~** pasarlo bien, divertirse; **to ~ sth well/badly** elegir un buen/mal momento para algo; **the bomb was timed**

to explode five minutes later la bomba estaba programada para explotar cinco minutos más tarde

time-and-motion expert ['taɪmənd'mə ʊʃən-] *n* experto(-a) en la ciencia de la producción

time-and-motion study ['taɪmənd'məʊʃən-] *n* estudio de desplazamientos y tiempos

time bomb *n* bomba de relojería

time card *n* tarjeta de registro horario

time clock *n* reloj *m* registrador

time-consuming ['taɪmkənsju:mɪŋ] *adj* que requiere mucho tiempo

time frame *n* plazo

time-honoured, time-honored (US) ['taɪmɔnəd] *adj* consagrado

timekeeper ['taɪmki:pəʳ] *n* (Sport) cronómetro

time lag *n* desfase *m*

timeless ['taɪmlɪs] *adj* eterno

time limit *n* (*gen*) límite *m* de tiempo; (*Comm*) plazo

timely ['taɪmlɪ] *adj* oportuno

time off *n* tiempo libre

timer ['taɪməʳ] *n* (*also*: **timer switch**) interruptor *m*; (*in kitchen*) temporizador *m*; (*Tech*) temporizador *m*

time-saving ['taɪmseɪvɪŋ] *adj* que ahorra tiempo

time scale *n* escala de tiempo

time sharing *n* (Comput) tiempo compartido

time sheet *n* = **time card**

time signal *n* señal *f* horaria

time switch *n* (Brit) interruptor *m* (horario)

timetable ['taɪmteɪbl] *n* horario; (*programme of events etc*) programa *m*

time zone *n* huso horario

timid ['tɪmɪd] *adj* tímido

timidity [tɪ'mɪdɪtɪ] *n* timidez *f*

timidly ['tɪmɪdlɪ] *adv* tímidamente

timing ['taɪmɪŋ] *n* (Sport) cronometraje *m*; **the ~ of his resignation** el momento que eligió para dimitir

timpani ['tɪmpənɪ] *npl* tímpanos *mpl*

tin [tɪn] *n* estaño; (*also*: **tin plate**) hojalata; (Brit: *can*) lata

tinfoil ['tɪnfɔɪl] *n* papel *m* de estaño

tinge [tɪndʒ] *n* matiz *m* ∎ *vt*: **tinged with** teñido de

tingle ['tɪŋgl] *n* hormigueo ∎ *vi* (*cheeks, skin: from cold*) sentir comezón; (: *from bad circulation*) sentir hormigueo

tinker ['tɪŋkəʳ] *n* calderero(-a); (*gipsy*) gitano(-a)

▶ **tinker with** *vt fus* jugar con, tocar

tinkle ['tɪŋkl] *vi* tintinear

tin mine *n* mina de estaño

tinned [tɪnd] *adj* (*Brit: food*) en lata, en conserva

tinnitus ['tɪnɪtəs] *n* (*Med*) acufeno

tinny ['tɪnɪ] *adj* (*sound, taste*) metálico; (*pej: car*) poco sólido, de pacotilla

tin opener [-əupnəʳ] *n* (*Brit*) abrelatas *m inv*

tinsel ['tɪnsl] *n* oropel *m*

tint [tɪnt] *n* matiz *m*; (*for hair*) tinte *m* ■ *vt* (*hair*) teñir

tinted ['tɪntɪd] *adj* (*hair*) teñido; (*glass, spectacles*) ahumado

tiny ['taɪnɪ] *adj* minúsculo, pequeñito

tip [tɪp] *n* (*end*) punta; (*gratuity*) propina; (*Brit: for rubbish*) vertedero; (*advice*) consejo ■ *vt* (*waiter*) dar una propina a; (*tilt*) inclinar; (*empty: also:* **tip out**) vaciar, echar; (*predict: winner*) pronosticar; (: *horse*) recomendar; **he tipped out the contents of the box** volcó el contenido de la caja
▶ **tip off** *vt* avisar, poner sobre aviso a
▶ **tip over** *vt* volcar ■ *vi* volcarse

tip-off ['tɪpɔf] *n* (*hint*) advertencia

tipped [tɪpt] *adj* (*Brit: cigarette*) con filtro

Tipp-Ex® ['tɪpɛks] *n* Tipp-Ex® *m*

tipple ['tɪpl] *n* (*Brit*): **his ~ is Cointreau** bebe Cointreau

tipster ['tɪpstəʳ] *n* (*Racing*) pronosticador(a) *m(f)*

tipsy ['tɪpsɪ] *adj* alegre, achispado

tiptoe ['tɪptəu] *n* (*Brit*): **on ~** de puntillas

tiptop ['tɪptɔp] *adj*: **in ~ condition** en perfectas condiciones

tirade [taɪ'reɪd] *n* diatriba

tire ['taɪəʳ] *n* (*US*) = **tyre** ■ *vt* cansar ■ *vi* (*gen*) cansarse; (*become bored*) aburrirse
▶ **tire out** *vt* agotar, rendir

tired ['taɪəd] *adj* cansado; **to be ~ of sth** estar harto de algo; **to be/feel/look ~** estar/sentirse/parecer cansado

tiredness ['taɪədnɪs] *n* cansancio

tireless ['taɪəlɪs] *adj* incansable

tirelessly ['taɪəlɪslɪ] *adv* incansablemente

tiresome ['taɪəsəm] *adj* aburrido

tiring ['taɪrɪŋ] *adj* cansado

tissue ['tɪʃuː] *n* tejido; (*paper handkerchief*) pañuelo de papel, kleenex® *m*

tissue paper *n* papel *m* de seda

tit [tɪt] *n* (*bird*) herrerillo común; **to give ~ for tat** dar ojo por ojo

titbit ['tɪtbɪt], **tidbit** (*US*) ['tɪdbɪt] *n* (*food*) golosina; (*news*) pedazo

titillate ['tɪtɪleɪt] *vt* estimular, excitar

titillation [tɪtɪ'leɪʃən] *n* estimulación *f*, excitación *f*

titivate ['tɪtɪveɪt] *vt* emperejilar

title ['taɪtl] *n* título; (*Law: right*): **~ (to)** derecho (a)

title deed *n* (*Law*) título de propiedad

title page *n* portada

title role *n* papel *m* principal

titter ['tɪtəʳ] *vi* reírse entre dientes

tittle-tattle ['tɪtltætl] *n* chismes *mpl*

titular ['tɪtjuləʳ] *adj* (*in name only*) nominal

T-junction ['tiːdʒʌŋkʃən] *n* cruce *m* en T

TM *abbr* (= *trademark*) marca de fábrica; = **transcendental meditation**

TN *abbr* (*US*) = **Tennessee**

TNT *n abbr* (= *trinitrotoluene*) TNT *m*

 KEYWORD

to [tuː, tə] *prep* **1** (*direction*) a; **to go to France/London/school/the station** ir a Francia/Londres/al colegio/a la estación; **to go to Claude's/the doctor's** ir a casa de Claude/al médico; **the road to Edinburgh** la carretera de Edimburgo; **to the left/right** a la izquierda/derecha

2 (*as far as*) hasta, a; **from here to London** de aquí a *or* hasta Londres; **to count to 10** contar hasta 10; **from 40 to 50 people** entre 40 y 50 personas

3 (*with expressions of time*): **a quarter/twenty to five** las cuarto menos cuarto/veinte

4 (*for, of*): **the key to the front door** la llave de la puerta principal; **she is secretary to the director** es la secretaria del director; **a letter to his wife** una carta a *or* para su mujer

5 (*expressing indirect object*) a; **to give sth to sb** darle algo a algn; **give it to me** dámelo; **to talk to sb** hablar con algn; **to be a danger to sb** ser un peligro para algn; **to carry out repairs to sth** hacer reparaciones en algo

6 (*in relation to*): **3 goals to 2** 3 goles a 2; **30 miles to the gallon** ≈ 9,4 litros a los cien (kilómetros); **8 apples to the kilo** 8 manzanas por kilo

7 (*purpose, result*): **to come to sb's aid** venir en auxilio *or* ayuda de algn; **to sentence sb to death** condenar a algn a muerte; **to my great surprise** con gran sorpresa mía

■ *infin particle* **1** (*simple infin*): **to go/eat** ir/comer

2 (*following another vb; see also relevant vb*): **to want/try/start to do** querer/intentar/empezar a hacer

3 (*with vb omitted*): **I don't want to** no quiero

4 (*purpose, result*) para; **I did it to help you** lo hice para ayudarte; **he came to see you** vino a verte

5 (*equivalent to relative clause*): **I have things to do** tengo cosas que hacer; **the main thing is to try** lo principal es intentarlo

t

6 (*after adj etc*): **ready to go** listo para irse; **too old to ...** demasiado viejo (como) para ... ■ *adv*: **pull/push the door to** tirar de/empujar la puerta; **to go to and fro** ir y venir

toad [təud] *n* sapo
toadstool ['təudstu:l] *n* seta venenosa
toady ['təudɪ] *n* pelota *m/f* ■ *vi*: **to ~ to sb** hacer la pelota *or* dar coba a algn
toast [təust] *n* (*Culin: also:* **piece of toast**) tostada; (*drink, speech*) brindis *m inv* ■ *vt* (*Culin*) tostar; (*drink to*) brindar
toaster ['təustə'] *n* tostador *m*
toastmaster ['təustmɑ:stə'] *n persona que propone brindis y anuncia a los oradores en un banquete*
toast rack *n* rejilla para tostadas
tobacco [tə'bækəu] *n* tabaco; **pipe ~** tabaco de pipa
tobacconist [tə'bækənɪst] *n* estanquero(-a), tabaquero(-a) (*LAm*); **~'s (shop)** (*Brit*) estanco, tabaquería (*LAm*)
tobacco plantation *n* plantación *f* de tabaco, tabacal *m*
Tobago [tə'beɪgəu] *n see* **Trinidad and Tobago**
toboggan [tə'bɔgən] *n* tobogán *m*
today [tə'deɪ] *adv, n* (*also fig*) hoy *m*; **what day is it ~?** ¿qué día es hoy?; **what date is it ~?** ¿a qué fecha estamos hoy?; **~ is the 4th of March** hoy es el 4 de marzo; **~'s paper** el periódico de hoy; **a fortnight ~** de hoy en 15 días, dentro de 15 días
toddle ['tɔdl] *vi* empezar a andar, dar los primeros pasos
toddler ['tɔdlə'] *n* niño(-a) (que empieza a andar)
toddy ['tɔdɪ] *n* ponche *m*
to-do [tə'du:] *n* (*fuss*) lío
toe [təu] *n* dedo (del pie); (*of shoe*) punta ■ *vt*: **to ~ the line** (*fig*) acatar las normas; **big/little ~** dedo gordo/pequeño del pie
TOEFL ['təufl] *n abbr* = **Test(ing) of English as a Foreign Language**
toehold ['təuhəuld] *n* punto de apoyo (para el pie)
toenail ['təuneɪl] *n* uña del pie
toffee ['tɔfɪ] *n* caramelo
toffee apple *n* (*Brit*) manzana de caramelo
tofu ['təufu:] *n* tofu *m*
toga ['təugə] *n* toga
together [tə'gɛðə'] *adv* juntos; (*at same time*) al mismo tiempo, a la vez; **~ with** junto con
togetherness [tə'gɛðənɪs] *n* compañerismo
toggle switch ['tɔgl-] *n* (*Comput*) conmutador *m* de palanca
Togo ['təugəu] *n* Togo

togs [tɔgz] *npl* (*col: clothes*) atuendo, ropa
toil [tɔɪl] *n* trabajo duro, labor *f* ■ *vi* esforzarse
toilet ['tɔɪlət] *n* (*Brit: lavatory*) servicios *mpl*, wáter *m* ■ *cpd* (*bag, soap etc*) de aseo; **to go to the ~** ir al baño; *see also* **toilets**
toilet bag *n* neceser *m*, bolsa de aseo
toilet bowl *n* taza (de retrete)
toilet paper *n* papel *m* higiénico
toiletries ['tɔɪlətrɪz] *npl* artículos *mpl* de aseo; (*make-up etc*) artículos *mpl* de tocador
toilet roll *n* rollo de papel higiénico
toilets ['tɔɪləts] *npl* (*Brit*) servicios *mpl*
toilet soap *n* jabón *m* de tocador
toilet water *n* (agua de) colonia
to-ing and fro-ing ['tuɪŋən'frəuɪŋ] *n* vaivén *m*
token ['təukən] *n* (*sign*) señal *f*, muestra; (*souvenir*) recuerdo; (*voucher*) vale *m*; (*disc*) ficha ■ *cpd* (*fee, strike*) nominal, simbólico; **book/record ~** (*Brit*) vale *m* para comprar libros/discos; **by the same ~** (*fig*) por la misma razón
tokenism ['təukənɪzəm] *n* (*Pol*) política simbólica *or* de fachada
Tokyo ['təukjəu] *n* Tokio, Tokío
told [təuld] *pt, pp of* **tell**
tolerable ['tɔlərəbl] *adj* (*bearable*) soportable; (*fairly good*) pasable
tolerably ['tɔlərəblɪ] *adv* (*good, comfortable*) medianamente
tolerance ['tɔlərns] *n* (*also Tech*) tolerancia
tolerant ['tɔlərnt] *adj*: **~ of** tolerante con
tolerantly ['tɔlərntlɪ] *adv* con tolerancia
tolerate ['tɔləreɪt] *vt* tolerar
toleration [tɔlə'reɪʃən] *n* tolerancia
toll [təul] *n* (*of casualties*) número de víctimas; (*tax, charge*) peaje *m* ■ *vi* (*bell*) doblar
toll bridge *n* puente *m* de peaje
toll call *n* (*US Telec*) conferencia, llamada interurbana
toll-free *adj, adv* (*US*) gratis
toll road *n* carretera de peaje
tomato (*pl* **tomatoes**) [tə'mɑ:təu] *n* tomate *m*
tomato puree *n* puré *m* de tomate
tomb [tu:m] *n* tumba
tombola [tɔm'bəulə] *n* tómbola
tomboy ['tɔmbɔɪ] *n* marimacho
tombstone ['tu:mstəun] *n* lápida
tomcat ['tɔmkæt] *n* gato
tomorrow [tə'mɔrəu] *adv, n* (*also fig*) mañana; **the day after ~** pasado mañana; **~ morning** mañana por la mañana; **a week ~** de mañana en ocho (días)
ton [tʌn] *n* tonelada; **tons of** (*col*) montones de
tonal ['təunl] *adj* tonal

tone [təun] *n* tono ■ *vi* armonizar; **dialling ~** (*Tel*) señal *f* para marcar
▸ **tone down** *vt* (*criticism*) suavizar; (*colour*) atenuar
▸ **tone up** *vt* (*muscles*) tonificar
tone-deaf [təun'dɛf] *adj* sin oído musical
toner ['təunəʳ] *n* (*for photocopier*) virador *m*
Tonga ['tɔŋə] *n* Islas *fpl* Tonga
tongs [tɔŋz] *npl* (*for coal*) tenazas *fpl*; (*for hair*) tenacillas *fpl*
tongue [tʌŋ] *n* lengua; **~ in cheek** *adv* en plan de broma
tongue-tied ['tʌŋtaɪd] *adj* (*fig*) mudo
tongue-twister ['tʌŋtwɪstəʳ] *n* trabalenguas *m inv*
tonic ['tɔnɪk] *n* (*Med*) tónico; (*Mus*) tónica; (*also:* **tonic water**) (agua) tónica
tonight [tə'naɪt] *adv, n* esta noche; **I'll see you ~** nos vemos esta noche
tonnage ['tʌnɪdʒ] *n* (*Naut*) tonelaje *m*
tonsil ['tɔnsl] *n* amígdala; **to have one's tonsils out** sacarse las amígdalas *or* anginas
tonsillitis [tɔnsɪ'laɪtɪs] *n* amigdalitis *f*
too [tu:] *adv* (*excessively*) demasiado; (*very*) muy; (*also*) también; (*also:* **it's too sweet**) está demasiado dulce; **I'm not ~ sure about that** no estoy muy seguro de eso; **I went ~** yo también fui; **~ much** *adv, adj* demasiado; **~ many** *adj* demasiados(-as); **~ bad!** ¡mala suerte!
took [tuk] *pt of* **take**
tool [tu:l] *n* herramienta; (*fig: person*) instrumento
toolbar ['tu:lbɑːʳ] *n* barra de herramientas
tool box *n* caja de herramientas
tool kit *n* juego de herramientas
tool shed *n* cobertizo (para herramientas)
toot [tu:t] *n* (*of horn*) bocinazo; (*of whistle*) silbido ■ *vi* (*with car horn*) tocar la bocina
tooth (*pl* **teeth**) [tu:θ, ti:θ] *n* (*Anat, Tech*) diente *m*; (*molar*) muela; **to clean one's teeth** lavarse los dientes; **to have a ~ out** sacarse una muela; **by the skin of one's teeth** por un pelo
toothache ['tu:θeɪk] *n* dolor *m* de muelas
toothbrush ['tu:θbrʌʃ] *n* cepillo de dientes
toothpaste ['tu:θpeɪst] *n* pasta de dientes
toothpick ['tu:θpɪk] *n* palillo
tooth powder *n* polvos *mpl* dentífricos
top [tɔp] *n* (*of mountain*) cumbre *f*, cima; (*of head*) coronilla; (*of ladder*) (lo) alto; (*of cupboard, table*) superficie *f*; (*lid: of box, jar*) tapa; (*: of bottle*) tapón *m*; (*of list, table, queue, page*) cabeza; (*toy*) peonza; (*Dress: blouse*) blusa; (*: T-shirt*) camiseta; (*: of pyjamas*) chaqueta ■ *adj* de arriba; (*in rank*) principal, primero; (*best*) mejor ■ *vt* (*exceed*) exceder; (*be first in*)

encabezar; **on ~ of** sobre, encima de; **from ~ to bottom** de pies a cabeza; **the ~ of the milk** la nata; **at the ~ of the stairs** en lo alto de la escalera; **at the ~ of the street** al final de la calle; **at the ~ of one's voice** (*fig*) a voz en grito; **at ~ speed** a máxima velocidad; **a ~ surgeon** un cirujano eminente; **over the ~** (*col*) excesivo, desmesurado; **to go over the ~** pasarse
▸ **top up**, (*US*) **top off** *vt* volver a llenar
topaz ['təupæz] *n* topacio
top-class ['tɔp'klɑːs] *adj* de primera clase
topcoat ['tɔpkəut] *n* sobretodo, abrigo
topflight ['tɔpflaɪt] *adj* de primera (categoría *or* clase)
top floor *n* último piso
top hat *n* sombrero de copa
top-heavy [tɔp'hɛvɪ] *adj* (*object*) con más peso en la parte superior
topic ['tɔpɪk] *n* tema *m*
topical ['tɔpɪkl] *adj* actual
topless ['tɔplɪs] *adj* (*bather etc*) topless
top-level ['tɔplɛvl] *adj* (*talks*) al más alto nivel
topmost ['tɔpməust] *adj* más alto
top-notch ['tɔp'nɔtʃ] *adj* (*col*) de primerísima categoría
topography [tə'pɔgrəfɪ] *n* topografía
topping ['tɔpɪŋ] *n* (*Culin*): **with a ~ of cream** con nata por encima
topple ['tɔpl] *vt* volcar, derribar ■ *vi* caerse
top-ranking ['tɔpræŋkɪŋ] *adj* de alto rango
top-secret [tɔp'siːkrɪt] *adj* de alto secreto
top-security ['tɔpsɪ'kjuərɪtɪ] *adj* (*Brit*) de máxima seguridad
topsy-turvy ['tɔpsɪ'təːvɪ] *adj, adv* patas arriba
top-up ['tɔpʌp] *n*: **would you like a ~?** ¿quiere que se lo vuelva a llenar?
top-up loan *n* (*Brit*) préstamo complementario
torch [tɔːtʃ] *n* antorcha; (*Brit: electric*) linterna
tore [tɔːʳ] *pt of* **tear**
torment *n* ['tɔːmɛnt] tormento ■ *vt* [tɔː'mɛnt] atormentar; (*fig: annoy*) fastidiar
torn [tɔːn] *pp of* **tear**
tornado (*pl* **tornadoes**) [tɔː'neɪdəu] *n* tornado
torpedo (*pl* **torpedoes**) [tɔː'piːdəu] *n* torpedo
torpedo boat *n* torpedero, lancha torpedera
torpor ['tɔːpəʳ] *n* letargo
torrent ['tɔrnt] *n* torrente *m*
torrential [tɔ'rɛnʃl] *adj* torrencial
torrid ['tɔrɪd] *adj* tórrido; (*fig*) apasionado
torso ['tɔːsəu] *n* torso
tortoise ['tɔːtəs] *n* tortuga
tortoiseshell ['tɔːtəʃɛl] *adj* de carey
tortuous ['tɔːtjuəs] *adj* tortuoso
torture ['tɔːtʃəʳ] *n* tortura ■ *vt* torturar; (*fig*) atormentar

t

torturer ['tɔ:tʃərər] n torturador(a) m(f)

Tory ['tɔ:rɪ] adj, n (Brit Pol) conservador(a) m(f)

toss [tɔs] vt tirar, echar; (head) sacudir ◼ n (movement: of head etc) sacudida; (of coin) tirada, echada (LAm); **to ~ a coin** echar a cara o cruz; **to ~ up for sth** jugar algo a cara o cruz; **to ~ and turn** (in bed) dar vueltas (en la cama); **to win/lose the ~** (also Sport) ganar/perder (a cara o cruz)

tot [tɔt] n (Brit: drink) copita; (child) nene(-a) m(f)

▶ **tot up** vt sumar

total ['təutl] adj total, entero ◼ n total m, suma ◼ vt (add up) sumar; (amount to) ascender a; **grand ~** cantidad f total; (cost) importe m total; **in ~** en total, en suma

totalitarian [təutælɪ'tɛərɪən] adj totalitario

totality [təu'tælɪtɪ] n totalidad f

total loss n siniestra total

totally ['təutəlɪ] adv totalmente

tote bag n bolsa

totem pole ['təutəm-] n poste m totémico

totter ['tɔtər] vi tambalearse

touch [tʌtʃ] n (sense) tacto; (contact) contacto; (Football) fuera de juego ◼ vt tocar; (emotionally) conmover; **a ~ of** (fig) una pizca or un poquito de; **to get in ~ with sb** ponerse en contacto con algn; **I'll be in ~** le llamaré/escribiré; **to lose ~** (friends) perder contacto; **to be out of ~ with events** no estar al corriente (de los acontecimientos); **the personal ~** el toque personal; **to put the finishing touches to sth** dar el último toque a algo

▶ **touch on** vt fus (topic) aludir (brevemente) a

▶ **touch up** vt (paint) retocar

touch-and-go ['tʌtʃən'gəu] adj arriesgado

touchdown ['tʌtʃdaun] n aterrizaje m; (US Football) ensayo

touched [tʌtʃt] adj conmovido; (col) chiflado

touchiness ['tʌtʃɪnɪs] n susceptibilidad f

touching ['tʌtʃɪŋ] adj conmovedor(a)

touchline ['tʌtʃlaɪn] n (Sport) línea de banda

touch screen n (Tech) pantalla táctil; **~ mobile** móvil m con pantalla táctil; **~ technology** tecnología táctil

touch-sensitive ['tʌtʃsɛnsɪtɪv] adj sensible al tacto

touch-type ['tʌtʃtaɪp] vi mecanografiar al tacto

touchy ['tʌtʃɪ] adj (person) quisquilloso

tough [tʌf] adj (meat) duro; (journey) penoso; (task, problem, situation) difícil; (resistant) resistente; (person) fuerte; (: pej) bruto ◼ n (gangster etc) gorila m; **they got ~ with the workers** se pusieron muy duros con los trabajadores

toughen ['tʌfn] vt endurecer

toughness ['tʌfnɪs] n dureza; (resistance) resistencia; (strictness) inflexibilidad f

toupée ['tu:peɪ] n peluquín m

tour ['tuər] n viaje m; (also: **package tour**) viaje m con todo incluido; (of town, museum) visita ◼ vt viajar por; **to go on a ~ of** (region, country) ir de viaje por; (museum, castle) visitar; **to go on ~** partir or ir de gira

touring ['tuərɪŋ] n viajes mpl turísticos, turismo

tourism ['tuərɪzm] n turismo

tourist ['tuərɪst] n turista m/f ◼ cpd turístico; **the ~ trade** el turismo

tourist class n (Aviat) clase f turista

tourist office n oficina de turismo

tournament ['tuənəmənt] n torneo

tourniquet ['tuənɪkeɪ] n (Med) torniquete m

tour operator n touroperador(a) m(f), operador(a) m(f) turístico(-a)

tousled ['tauzld] adj (hair) despeinado

tout [taut] vi: **to ~ for business** solicitar clientes ◼ n: **ticket ~** revendedor(a) m(f)

tow [təu] n: **to give sb a ~** (Aut) remolcar a algn ◼ vt remolcar; **"on** or (US) **in ~"** (Aut) "a remolque"

toward [tə'wɔ:d], **towards** [tə'wɔ:dz] prep hacia; (of attitude) respecto a, con; (of purpose) para; **~(s) noon** alrededor de mediodía; **~(s) the end of the year** hacia finales de año; **to feel friendly ~(s) sb** sentir amistad hacia algn

towel ['tauəl] n toalla; **to throw in the ~** (fig) darse por vencido, renunciar

towelling ['tauəlɪŋ] n (fabric) felpa

towel rail, towel rack (US) n toallero

tower ['tauər] n torre f ◼ vi (building, mountain) elevarse; **to ~ above** or **over sth/sb** dominar algo/destacarse sobre algn

tower block n (Brit) bloque m de pisos

towering ['tauərɪŋ] adj muy alto, imponente

town [taun] n ciudad f; **to go to ~** ir a la ciudad; (fig) tirar la casa por la ventana; **in the ~** en la ciudad; **to be out of ~** estar fuera de la ciudad

town centre n centro de la ciudad

town clerk n secretario(-a) del Ayuntamiento

town council n Ayuntamiento, consejo municipal

town crier [-kraɪər] n (Brit) pregonero

town hall n ayuntamiento

townie ['taunɪ] n (Brit col) persona de la ciudad

town plan n plano de la ciudad

town planner n urbanista m/f

town planning n urbanismo

township ['taʊnʃɪp] n municipio habitado sólo por negros en Sudáfrica
townspeople ['taʊnzpi:pl] npl gente f de ciudad
towpath ['təʊpɑ:θ] n camino de sirga
towrope ['təʊrəʊp] n cable m de remolque
tow truck n (US) camión m grúa
toxic ['tɒksɪk] adj tóxico
toxic asset n (Econ) activo tóxico
toxic bank n (Econ) banco malo
toxin ['tɒksɪn] n toxina
toy [tɔɪ] n juguete m
▶ **toy with** vt fus jugar con; (idea) acariciar
toyshop ['tɔɪʃɒp] n juguetería
trace [treɪs] n rastro ■ vt (draw) trazar, delinear; (locate) encontrar; **there was no ~ of it** no había ningún indicio de ello
trace element n oligoelemento
trachea [trə'kɪə] n (Anat) tráquea
tracing paper ['treɪsɪŋ-] n papel m de calco
track [træk] n (mark) huella, pista; (path: gen) camino, senda; (: of bullet etc) trayectoria; (: of suspect, animal) pista, rastro; (Rail) vía; (Comput, Sport) pista; (on album) canción f ■ vt seguir la pista de; **to keep ~ of** mantenerse al tanto de, seguir; **a four-~ tape** una cinta de cuarto pistas; **the first ~ on the record/tape** la primera canción en el disco/la cinta; **to be on the right ~** (fig) ir por buen camino
▶ **track down** vt (person) localizar; (sth lost) encontrar
tracker dog ['trækə-] n (Brit) perro rastreador
track events npl (Sport) pruebas fpl en pista
tracking station ['trækɪŋ-] n (Space) estación f de seguimiento
track meet n (US) concurso de carreras y saltos
track record n: **to have a good ~** (fig) tener un buen historial
tracksuit ['træksu:t] n chandal m
tract [trækt] n (Geo) región f; (pamphlet) folleto
traction ['trækʃən] n (Aut: power) tracción f; **in ~** (Med) en tracción
traction engine n locomotora de tracción
tractor ['træktər] n tractor m
trade [treɪd] n comercio, negocio; (skill, job) oficio, empleo; (industry) industria ■ vi negociar, comerciar; **foreign ~** comercio exterior
▶ **trade in** vt (old car etc) ofrecer como parte del pago
trade barrier n barrera comercial
trade deficit n déficit m comercial
Trade Descriptions Act n (Brit) ley sobre descripciones comerciales
trade discount n descuento comercial

trade fair n feria de muestras
trade-in ['treɪdɪn] adj: ~ **price/value** precio/valor de un artículo usado que se descuenta del precio de otro nuevo
trademark ['treɪdmɑ:k] n marca de fábrica
trade mission n misión f comercial
trade name n marca registrada
trade-off n: **a ~ (between)** un equilibrio (entre)
trade price n precio al detallista
trader ['treɪdər] n comerciante m/f
trade reference n referencia comercial
trade secret n secreto profesional
tradesman ['treɪdzmən] n (shopkeeper) comerciante m/f
trade union n sindicato
trade unionist [-'ju:njənɪst] n sindicalista m/f
trade wind n viento alisio
trading ['treɪdɪŋ] n comercio
trading account n cuenta de compraventa
trading estate n (Brit) polígono industrial
trading stamp n cupón m, sello de prima
tradition [trə'dɪʃən] n tradición f
traditional [trə'dɪʃənl] adj tradicional
traditionally [trə'dɪʃənlɪ] adv tradicionalmente
traffic ['træfɪk] n tráfico, circulación f, tránsito ■ vi: **to ~ in** (pej: liquor, drugs) traficar en; **air ~** tráfico aéreo
traffic calming [-'kɑ:mɪŋ] n reducción f de la velocidad de la circulación
traffic circle n (US) glorieta de tráfico
traffic island n refugio, isleta
traffic jam n embotellamiento, atasco
trafficker ['træfɪkər] n traficante m/f
traffic lights npl semáforo sg
traffic offence, traffic violation (US) n infracción f de tráfico
traffic warden n guardia m/f de tráfico
tragedy ['trædʒədɪ] n tragedia
tragic ['trædʒɪk] adj trágico
tragically ['trædʒɪkəlɪ] adv trágicamente
trail [treɪl] n (tracks) rastro, pista; (path) camino, sendero; (dust, smoke) estela ■ vt (drag) arrastrar; (follow) seguir la pista de; (follow closely) vigilar ■ vi arrastrarse; **to be on sb's ~** seguir la pista de algn
▶ **trail away, trail off** vi (sound) desvanecerse; (interest, voice) desaparecer
▶ **trail behind** vi quedar a la zaga
trailer ['treɪlər] n (Aut) remolque m; (caravan) caravana; (Cine) trailer m, avance m
trailer truck n (US) camión articulado m
train [treɪn] n tren m; (of dress) cola; (series): **~ of events** curso de los acontecimientos ■ vt (educate) formar; (teach skills to) adiestrar;

(*sportsman*) entrenar; (*dog*) amaestrar; (*point: gun etc*): **to ~ on** apuntar a ■ vi (*Sport*) entrenarse; (*be educated, learn a skill*) formarse; **to go by ~** ir en tren; **one's ~ of thought** el razonamiento de algn; **to ~ sb to do sth** enseñar a algn a hacer algo

train attendant n (*US Rail*) empleado(-a) de coches-cama

trained [treɪnd] adj (*worker*) cualificado; (*animal*) amaestrado

trainee [treɪ'niː] n trabajador(a) m(f) en prácticas ■ cpd: **he's a ~ teacher** (*primary*) es estudiante de magisterio; (*secondary*) está haciendo las prácticas del I.C.E.

trainer ['treɪnər] n (*Sport*) entrenador(a) m(f); (*of animals*) domador(a) m(f); **trainers** npl (*shoes*) zapatillas fpl (de deporte)

training ['treɪnɪŋ] n formación f; entrenamiento; **to be in ~** (*Sport*) estar entrenando; (*: fit*) estar en forma

training college n (*gen*) colegio de formación profesional; (*for teachers*) escuela normal

training course n curso de formación

train wreck n (*fig*) destrozo; **he's a complete ~** está completamente destrozado

traipse [treɪps] vi andar penosamente

trait [treɪt] n rasgo

traitor ['treɪtər] n traidor(a) m(f)

trajectory [trə'dʒɛktərɪ] n trayectoria, curso

tram [træm] n (*Brit: also:* **tramcar**) tranvía m

tramline ['træmlaɪn] n carril m de tranvía

tramp [træmp] n (*person*) vagabundo(-a); (*col: offensive: woman*) puta ■ vi andar con pasos pesados

trample ['træmpl] vt: **to ~ (underfoot)** pisotear

trampoline ['træmpəliːn] n trampolín m

trance [trɑːns] n trance m; **to go into a ~** entrar en trance

tranquil ['træŋkwɪl] adj tranquilo

tranquillity, tranquility (*US*) [træŋ'kwɪlɪtɪ] n tranquilidad f

tranquillizer, tranquilizer (*US*) ['træŋkwɪlaɪzər] n (*Med*) tranquilizante m

trans- [trænz] pref trans-, tras-

transact [træn'zækt] vt (*business*) tramitar

transaction [træn'zækʃən] n transacción f, operación f; **cash transactions** transacciones al contado

transatlantic ['trænzət'læntɪk] adj transatlántico

transcend [træn'sɛnd] vt rebasar

transcendental [trænsɛn'dɛntl] adj: **~ meditation** meditación f transcendental

transcribe [træn'skraɪb] vt transcribir, copiar

transcript ['trænskrɪpt] n copia

transcription [træn'skrɪpʃən] n transcripción f

transept ['trænsɛpt] n crucero

transfer n ['trænsfər] transferencia; (*Sport*) traspaso; (*picture, design*) calcomanía ■ vt [træns'fəːr] trasladar, pasar; **to ~ the charges** (*Brit Tel*) llamar a cobro revertido; **by bank ~** por transferencia bancaria or giro bancario; **to ~ money from one account to another** transferir dinero de una cuenta a otra; **to ~ sth to sb's name** transferir algo al nombre de algn

transferable [træns'fəːrəbl] adj: **not ~** intransferible

transfix [træns'fɪks] vt traspasar; (*fig*): **transfixed with fear** paralizado por el miedo

transform [træns'fɔːm] vt transformar

transformation [trænsfə'meɪʃən] n transformación f

transformer [træns'fɔːmər] n (*Elec*) transformador m

transfusion [træns'fjuːʒən] n transfusión f

transgress [træns'grɛs] vt (*go beyond*) traspasar; (*violate*) violar, infringir

tranship [træn'ʃɪp] vt trasbordar

transient ['trænzɪənt] adj transitorio

transistor [træn'zɪstər] n (*Elec*) transistor m

transistorized [træn'zɪstəraɪzd] adj (*circuit*) transistorizado

transistor radio n transistor m

transit ['trænzɪt] n: **in ~** en tránsito

transit camp n campamento de tránsito

transition [træn'zɪʃən] n transición f

transitional [træn'zɪʃənl] adj transitorio

transition period n período de transición

transitive ['trænzɪtɪv] adj (*Ling*) transitivo

transitively ['trænzɪtɪvlɪ] adv transitivamente

transitory ['trænzɪtərɪ] adj transitorio

transit visa n visado de tránsito

translate [trænz'leɪt] vt: **to ~ (from/into)** traducir (de/a)

translation [trænz'leɪʃən] n traducción f

translator [trænz'leɪtər] n traductor(a) m(f)

translucent [trænz'luːsnt] adj traslúcido

transmission [trænz'mɪʃən] n transmisión f

transmit [trænz'mɪt] vt transmitir

transmitter [trænz'mɪtər] n transmisor m; (*station*) emisora

transparency [træns'pɛərnsɪ] n (*Brit Phot*) diapositiva

transparent [træns'pærnt] adj transparente

transpire [træns'paɪər] vi (*turn out*) resultar (ser); (*happen*) ocurrir, suceder; (*become known*): **it finally transpired that ...** por fin se supo que ...

transplant vt [træns'plɑ:nt] transplantar
  ■ n ['trænsplɑ:nt] (Med) transplante m;
  to have a heart ~ hacerse un transplante
  de corazón

transport n ['trænspɔ:t] transporte m ■ vt
  [træns'pɔ:t] transportar; **public ~** transporte
  m público

transportable [træns'pɔ:təbl] adj
  transportable

transportation [trænspɔ:'teɪʃən] n
  transporte m; (of prisoners) deportación f

transport café n (Brit) bar-restaurante m de
  carretera

transpose [træns'pəuz] vt transponer

transsexual [trænz'sɛksjuəl] adj, n
  transexual m/f

transverse ['trænzvə:s] adj transverso,
  transversal

transvestite [trænz'vɛstaɪt] n travesti m/f

trap [træp] n (snare, trick) trampa; (carriage)
  cabriolé m ■ vt coger (SP) or agarrar (LAm)
  en una trampa; (immobilize) bloquear; (jam)
  atascar; **to set** or **lay a ~ (for sb)** poner(le)
  una trampa (a algn); **to ~ one's finger in
  the door** pillarse el dedo en la puerta

trap door n escotilla

trapeze [trə'pi:z] n trapecio

trapper ['træpər] n trampero, cazador m

trappings ['træpɪŋz] npl adornos mpl

trash [træʃ] n basura; (nonsense) tonterías fpl

trash can n (US) cubo, balde m (LAm) or bote m
  (LAm) de la basura

trash can liner n (US) bolsa de basura

trashy ['træʃɪ] adj (col) chungo

trauma ['trɔ:mə] n trauma m

traumatic [trɔ:'mætɪk] adj traumático

travel ['trævl] n viaje m ■ vi viajar ■ vt
  (distance) recorrer; **this wine doesn't ~ well**
  este vino pierde con los viajes

travel agency n agencia de viajes

travel agent n agente m/f de viajes

travel brochure n folleto turístico

traveller, traveler (US) ['trævlər] n
  viajero(-a); (Comm) viajante m/f

traveller's cheque, traveler's check (US) n
  cheque m de viaje

travelling, traveling (US) ['trævlɪŋ] n
  los viajes, el viajar ■ adj (circus, exhibition)
  ambulante ■ cpd (bag, clock) de viaje

travelling expenses, traveling expenses
  (US) npl dietas fpl

travelling salesman, traveling salesman
  (US) n viajante m

travelogue ['trævəlɔg] n (book) relación f de
  viajes; (film) documental m de viajes; (talk)
  recuento de viajes

travel sickness n mareo

traverse ['trævəs] vt atravesar

travesty ['trævəstɪ] n parodia

trawler ['trɔ:lər] n pesquero de arrastre

tray [treɪ] n (for carrying) bandeja; (on desk)
  cajón m

treacherous ['trɛtʃərəs] adj traidor(a); **road
  conditions are ~** el estado de las carreteras
  es peligroso

treachery ['trɛtʃərɪ] n traición f

treacle ['tri:kl] n (Brit) melaza

tread [trɛd] n paso, pisada; (of tyre) banda de
  rodadura ■ vi (pt **trod**, pp **trodden**) [trɔd,
  'trɔdn] pisar
  ▶ **tread on** vt fus pisar

treas. abbr = **treasurer**

treason ['tri:zn] n traición f

treasure ['trɛʒər] n tesoro ■ vt (value)
  apreciar, valorar

treasure hunt n caza del tesoro

treasurer ['trɛʒərər] n tesorero(-a)

treasury ['trɛʒərɪ] n: **the T~**, (US) **the T~
  Department** ≈ el Ministerio de Economía y
  de Hacienda

treasury bill n bono del Tesoro

treat [tri:t] n (present) regalo; (pleasure) placer
  m ■ vt tratar; (consider) considerar; **to give
  sb a ~** hacer un regalo a algn; **to ~ sb to
  sth** invitar a algn a algo; **to ~ sth as a joke**
  tomar algo a broma

treatise ['tri:tɪz] n tratado

treatment ['tri:tmənt] n tratamiento; **to
  have ~ for sth** recibir tratamiento por algo

treaty ['tri:tɪ] n tratado

treble ['trɛbl] adj triple ■ vt triplicar ■ vi
  triplicarse

treble clef n (Mus) clave f de sol

tree [tri:] n árbol m

tree-lined ['tri:laɪnd] adj bordeado de árboles

tree trunk n tronco de árbol

trek [trɛk] n (long journey) expedición f; (tiring
  walk) caminata

trellis ['trɛlɪs] n enrejado

tremble ['trɛmbl] vi temblar

trembling ['trɛmblɪŋ] n temblor m ■ adj
  tembloroso

tremendous [trɪ'mɛndəs] adj tremendo;
  (enormous) enorme; (excellent) estupendo

tremendously [trɪ'mɛndəslɪ] adv
  enormemente, sobremanera; **he enjoyed it
  ~** lo disfrutó de lo lindo

tremor ['trɛmər] n temblor m; (also: **earth
  tremor**) temblor m de tierra

trench [trɛntʃ] n zanja; (Mil) trinchera

trench coat n trinchera

trench warfare n guerra de trincheras

trend [trɛnd] n (tendency) tendencia; (of events)
  curso; (fashion) moda; **~ towards/away from**

sth tendencia hacia/en contra de algo; **to set the ~** marcar la pauta

trendy ['trɛndɪ] *adj* de moda

trepidation [trɛpɪ'deɪʃən] *n* inquietud *f*

trespass ['trɛspəs] *vi*: **to ~ on** entrar sin permiso en; **"no trespassing"** "prohibido el paso"

trespasser ['trɛspəsər] *n* intruso(-a) *m(f)*; **"trespassers will be prosecuted"** "se procesará a los intrusos"

tress [trɛs] *n* guedeja

trestle ['trɛsl] *n* caballete *m*

trestle table *n* mesa de caballete

tri- [traɪ] *pref* tri-

trial ['traɪəl] *n* (*Law*) juicio, proceso; (*test: of machine etc*) prueba; (*hardship*) desgracia; **trials** *npl* (*Athletics*) pruebas *fpl*; (*of horses*) pruebas *fpl*; **to bring sb to ~ (for a crime)** llevar a algn a juicio (por un delito); **~ by jury** juicio ante jurado; **to be sent for ~** ser remitido al tribunal; **by ~ and error** a fuerza de probar

trial balance *n* balance *m* de comprobación

trial basis *n*: **on a ~** a modo de prueba

trial offer *n* oferta de prueba

trial run *n* prueba

triangle ['traɪæŋgl] *n* (*Math, Mus*) triángulo

triangular [traɪ'æŋgjulər] *adj* triangular

triathlon [traɪ'æθlən] *n* triatlón *m*

tribal ['traɪbəl] *adj* tribal

tribe [traɪb] *n* tribu *f*

tribesman ['traɪbzmən] *n* miembro de una tribu

tribulation [trɪbju'leɪʃən] *n* tribulación *f*

tribunal [traɪ'bjuːnl] *n* tribunal *m*

tributary ['trɪbjuːtərɪ] *n* (*river*) afluente *m*

tribute ['trɪbjuːt] *n* homenaje *m*, tributo; **to pay ~ to** rendir homenaje a

trice [traɪs] *n*: **in a ~** en un santiamén

trick [trɪk] *n* trampa; (*conjuring trick, deceit*) truco; (*joke*) broma; (*Cards*) baza ■ *vt* engañar; **it's a ~ of the light** es una ilusión óptica; **to play a ~ on sb** gastar una broma a algn; **that should do the ~** eso servirá; **to ~ sb out of sth** quitarle algo a algn con engaños; **to ~ sb into doing sth** hacer que algn haga algo con engaños

trickery ['trɪkərɪ] *n* engaño

trickle ['trɪkl] *n* (*of water etc*) hilo ■ *vi* gotear

trick question *n* pregunta capciosa

trickster ['trɪkstər] *n* estafador(a) *m(f)*

tricky ['trɪkɪ] *adj* difícil; (*problem*) delicado

tricycle ['traɪsɪkl] *n* triciclo

tried [traɪd] *adj* probado

trifle ['traɪfl] *n* bagatela; (*Culin*) dulce de bizcocho, gelatina, fruta y natillas ■ *adv*: **a ~ long** un pelín largo ■ *vi*: **to ~ with** jugar con

trifling ['traɪflɪŋ] *adj* insignificante

trigger ['trɪgər] *n* (*of gun*) gatillo ▶ **trigger off** *vt* desencadenar

trigonometry [trɪgə'nɔmətrɪ] *n* trigonometría

trilby ['trɪlbɪ] *n* (*also*: **trilby hat**) sombrero flexible *or* tirolés

trill [trɪl] *n* (*of bird*) gorjeo; (*Mus*) trino

trilogy ['trɪlədʒɪ] *n* trilogía

trim [trɪm] *adj* (*elegant*) aseado; (*house, garden*) en buen estado; (*figure*): **to be ~** tener buen talle ■ *n* (*haircut etc*) recorte *m* ■ *vt* (*neaten*) arreglar; (*cut*) recortar; (*decorate*) adornar; (*Naut: a sail*) orientar; **to keep in (good) ~** mantener en buen estado

trimmings ['trɪmɪŋz] *npl* (*extras*) accesorios *mpl*; (*cuttings*) recortes *mpl*

Trinidad and Tobago ['trɪnɪdæd-] *n* Trinidad *f* y Tobago

Trinity ['trɪnɪtɪ] *n*: **the ~** la Trinidad

trinket ['trɪŋkɪt] *n* chuchería, baratija

trio ['triːəu] *n* trío

trip [trɪp] *n* viaje *m*; (*excursion*) excursión *f*; (*stumble*) traspié *m* ■ *vi* (*stumble*) tropezar; (*go lightly*) andar a paso ligero; **on a ~** de viaje ▶ **trip over** *vt fus* tropezar con ▶ **trip up** *vi* tropezar, caerse ■ *vt* hacer tropezar *or* caer

tripartite [traɪ'pɑːtaɪt] *adj* (*agreement, talks*) tripartito

tripe [traɪp] *n* (*Culin*) callos *mpl*; (*pej: rubbish*) bobadas *fpl*

triple ['trɪpl] *adj* triple ■ *adv*: **~ the distance/the speed** 3 veces la distancia/la velocidad

triple jump *n* triple salto

triplets ['trɪplɪts] *npl* trillizos(-as) *m(f)pl*

triplicate ['trɪplɪkət] *n*: **in ~** por triplicado

tripod ['traɪpɔd] *n* trípode *m*

Tripoli ['trɪpəlɪ] *n* Trípoli *m*

tripper ['trɪpər] *n* turista *m/f*, excursionista *m/f*

tripwire ['trɪpwaɪər] *n* cable *m* de trampa

trite [traɪt] *adj* trillado

triumph ['traɪʌmf] *n* triunfo ■ *vi*: **to ~ (over)** vencer

triumphal [traɪ'ʌmfl] *adj* triunfal

triumphant [traɪ'ʌmfənt] *adj* triunfante

triumphantly [traɪ'ʌmfəntlɪ] *adv* triunfalmente, en tono triunfal

trivia ['trɪvɪə] *npl* trivialidades *fpl*

trivial ['trɪvɪəl] *adj* insignificante, trivial

triviality [trɪvɪ'ælɪtɪ] *n* insignificancia, trivialidad *f*

trivialize ['trɪvɪəlaɪz] *vt* trivializar

trod [trɔd] *pt of* **tread**

trodden ['trɔdn] *pp of* **tread**

trolley ['trɔlɪ] *n* carrito; (*in hospital*) camilla

trolley bus n trolebús m
trombone [trɔm'bəun] n trombón m
troop [tru:p] n grupo, banda; see also **troops**
▶ **troop in** vi entrar en tropel
▶ **troop out** vi salir en tropel
troop carrier n (plane) transporte m
(militar); (Naut: also: **troopship**) (buque m de)
transporte m
trooper ['tru:pəʳ] n (Mil) soldado (de
caballería); (US: policeman) policía m/f
montado(-a)
trooping the colour ['tru:pɪŋ-] n (ceremony)
presentación f de la bandera
troopship ['tru:pʃɪp] n (buque m de)
transporte m
trophy ['trəufɪ] n trofeo
tropic ['trɔpɪk] n trópico; **the tropics** los
trópicos, la zona tropical; **T~ of Cancer/
Capricorn** trópico de Cáncer/Capricornio
tropical ['trɔpɪkl] adj tropical
trot [trɔt] n trote m ▪ vi trotar; **on the ~**
(Brit fig) seguidos(-as)
▶ **trot out** vt (excuse, reason) volver a usar;
(names, facts) sacar a relucir
trouble ['trʌbl] n problema m, dificultad
f; (worry) preocupación f; (bother, effort)
molestia, esfuerzo; (unrest) inquietud f;
(with machine etc) fallo, avería; (Med):
stomach ~ problemas mpl gástricos ▪ vt
molestar; (worry) preocupar, inquietar ▪ vi:
to ~ to do sth molestarse en hacer algo;
troubles npl (Pol etc) conflictos mpl; **to be
in ~** estar en un apuro; (for doing wrong) tener
problemas; **to have ~ doing sth** tener
dificultad en or para hacer algo; **to go to the
~ of doing sth** tomarse la molestia de hacer
algo; **what's the ~?** ¿qué pasa?; **the ~ is ...**
el problema es ..., lo que pasa es ...; **please
don't ~ yourself** por favor no se moleste
troubled ['trʌbld] adj (person) preocupado;
(epoch, life) agitado
trouble-free ['trʌblfri:] adj sin problemas or
dificultades
troublemaker ['trʌblmeɪkəʳ] n agitador(a)
m(f)
troubleshooter ['trʌblʃu:təʳ] n (in conflict)
mediador(a) m(f)
troublesome ['trʌblsəm] adj molesto,
inoportuno
trouble spot n centro de fricción, punto
caliente
troubling ['trʌblɪŋ] adj (thought) preocupante;
these are ~ times son malos tiempos
trough [trɔf] n (also: **drinking trough**)
abrevadero; (also: **feeding trough**) comedero;
(channel) canal m
trounce [trauns] vt dar una paliza a

troupe [tru:p] n grupo
trouser press n prensa para pantalones
trousers ['trauzəz] npl pantalones mpl; **short
~** pantalones mpl cortos
trouser suit n traje m de chaqueta y pantalón
trousseau (pl **trousseaux** or **trousseaus**)
['tru:səu, -z] n ajuar m
trout [traut] n (pl inv) trucha
trowel ['trauəl] n paleta
truant ['truənt] n: **to play ~** (Brit) hacer
novillos
truce [tru:s] n tregua
truck [trʌk] n (US) camión m; (Rail) vagón m
truck driver n camionero(-a)
trucker ['trʌkəʳ] n (esp US) camionero(-a)
truck farm n (US) huerto de hortalizas
trucking ['trʌkɪŋ] n (esp US) transporte m en
camión
trucking company n (US) compañía de
transporte por carretera
truckload ['trʌkləud] n camión m lleno
truculent ['trʌkjulənt] adj agresivo
trudge [trʌdʒ] vi caminar penosamente
true [tru:] adj verdadero; (accurate) exacto;
(genuine) auténtico; (faithful) fiel; (wheel)
centrado; (wall) a plomo; (beam) alineado;
~ to life verídico; **to come ~** realizarse,
cumplirse
truffle ['trʌfl] n trufa
truly ['tru:lɪ] adv realmente; (faithfully)
fielmente; **yours ~** (in letter-writing)
atentamente
trump [trʌmp] n (Cards) triunfo; **to turn up
trumps** (fig) salir or resultar bien
trump card n triunfo; (fig) baza
trumped-up ['trʌmptʌp] adj inventado
trumpet ['trʌmpɪt] n trompeta
truncated [trʌŋ'keɪtɪd] adj truncado
truncheon ['trʌntʃən] n (Brit) porra
trundle ['trʌndl] vt, vi: **to ~ along** rodar
haciendo ruido
trunk [trʌŋk] n (of tree, person) tronco; (of
elephant) trompa; (case) baúl m; (US Aut)
maletero, baúl m (LAm); see also **trunks**
trunk call n (Brit Tel) llamada interurbana
trunk road n carretera principal
trunks [trʌŋks] npl (also: **swimming trunks**)
bañador m
truss [trʌs] n (Med) braguero ▪ vt: **to ~ (up)**
atar
trust [trʌst] n confianza; (Comm) trust
m; (Law) fideicomiso ▪ vt (rely on) tener
confianza en; (entrust): **to ~ sth to sb** confiar
algo a algn; (hope): **to ~ (that)** esperar (que);
in ~ en fideicomiso; **you'll have to take it
on ~** tienes que aceptarlo a ojos cerrados
trust company n banco fideicomisario

t

trusted ['trʌstɪd] *adj* de confianza, fiable, de fiar
trustee [trʌs'tiː] *n* (*Law*) fideicomisario
trustful ['trʌstful] *adj* confiado
trust fund *n* fondo fiduciario *or* de fideicomiso
trusting ['trʌstɪŋ] *adj* confiado
trustworthy ['trʌstwə:ðɪ] *adj* digno de confianza, fiable, de fiar
trusty ['trʌstɪ] *adj* fiel
truth, truths [truː:θ, truː:ðz] *n* verdad *f*
truthful ['truː:θfəl] *adj* (*person*) sincero; (*account*) fidedigno
truthfully ['truː:θfulɪ] *adv* (*answer*) con sinceridad
truthfulness ['truː:θfulnɪs] *n* (*of account*) verdad *f*; (*of person*) sinceridad *f*
try [traɪ] *n* tentativa, intento; (*Rugby*) ensayo ■ *vt* (*Law*) juzgar, procesar; (*test: sth new*) probar, someter a prueba; (*attempt*) intentar; (*strain: patience*) hacer perder ■ *vi* probar; **to give sth a ~** intentar hacer algo; **to ~ one's (very) best** *or* **hardest** poner todo su empeño, esmerarse; **to ~ to do sth** intentar hacer algo
▶ **try on** *vt* (*clothes*) probarse
▶ **try out** *vt* probar, poner a prueba
trying ['traɪɪŋ] *adj* cansado; (*person*) pesado
tsar [zɑ:ʳ] *n* zar *m*
T-shirt ['tiː:ʃə:t] *n* camiseta
TSO *n abbr* (*Brit*) = **The Stationery Office**
T-square ['tiː:skwɛəʳ] *n* regla en T
tsunami [tsʊ'nɑ:mɪ] *n* tsunami *m*
TT *adj abbr* (*Brit col*) = **teetotal** ■ *abbr* (*US*) = **Trust Territory**
tub [tʌb] *n* cubo (*SP*), balde *m* (*LAm*); (*bath*) bañera, tina (*LAm*)
tuba ['tjuː:bə] *n* tuba
tubby ['tʌbɪ] *adj* regordete
tube [tjuː:b] *n* tubo; (*Brit: underground*) metro; (*US col: television*) tele *f*
tubeless ['tjuː:blɪs] *adj* (*tyre*) sin cámara
tuber ['tjuː:bəʳ] *n* (*Bot*) tubérculo
tuberculosis [tjubə:kju'ləusɪs] *n* tuberculosis *f inv*
tube station *n* (*Brit*) estación *f* de metro
tubing ['tjuː:bɪŋ] *n* tubería (*SP*), cañería; **a piece of** ~ un trozo de tubo
tubular ['tjuː:bjuləʳ] *adj* tubular
TUC *n abbr* (*Brit*: = *Trades Union Congress*) *federación nacional de sindicatos*
tuck [tʌk] *n* (*Sewing*) pliegue *m* ■ *vt* (*put*) poner
▶ **tuck away** *vt* esconder
▶ **tuck in** *vt* meter; (*child*) arropar ■ *vi* (*eat*) comer con apetito
▶ **tuck up** *vt* (*child*) arropar

tuck shop *n* (*Scol*) tienda de golosinas
Tue., Tues. *abbr* (= *Tuesday*) mart
Tuesday ['tjuː:zdɪ] *n* martes *m inv*; **on** ~ el martes; **on Tuesdays** los martes; **every** ~ todos los martes; **every other** ~ cada dos martes, un martes sí y otro no; **last/next** ~ el martes pasado/próximo; **a week/fortnight on** ~, ~ **week/fortnight** del martes en 8/15 días, del martes en una semana/dos semanas
tuft [tʌft] *n* mechón *m*; (*of grass etc*) manojo
tug [tʌg] *n* (*ship*) remolcador *m* ■ *vt* remolcar
tug-of-love [tʌgəv'lʌv] *n*: ~ **children** hijos envueltos en el litigio de los padres por su custodia
tug-of-war [tʌgəv'wɔ:ʳ] *n* juego de la cuerda
tuition [tjuː:'ɪʃən] *n* (*Brit*) enseñanza; (: *private tuition*) clases *fpl* particulares; (*US: school fees*) matrícula
tulip ['tjuː:lɪp] *n* tulipán *m*
tumble ['tʌmbl] *n* (*fall*) caída ■ *vi* caerse, tropezar; **to ~ to sth** (*col*) caer en la cuenta de algo
tumbledown ['tʌmbldaun] *adj* ruinoso
tumble dryer *n* (*Brit*) secadora
tumbler ['tʌmbləʳ] *n* vaso
tummy ['tʌmɪ] *n* (*col*) barriga, vientre *m*
tumour, tumor (*US*) ['tjuː:məʳ] *n* tumor *m*
tumult ['tjuː:mʌlt] *n* tumulto
tumultuous [tjuː:'mʌltjuəs] *adj* tumultuoso
tuna ['tjuː:nə] *n* (*pl inv: also:* **tuna fish**) atún *m*
tundra ['tʌndrə] *n* tundra
tune [tjuː:n] *n* (*melody*) melodía ■ *vt* (*Mus*) afinar; (*Radio, TV, Aut*) sintonizar; **to be in/out of** ~ (*instrument*) estar afinado/desafinado; (*singer*) afinar/desafinar; **to be in/out of** ~ **with** (*fig*) armonizar/desentonar con; **to the** ~ **of** (*fig: amount*) por (la) cantidad de
▶ **tune in** *vi* (*Radio, TV*): **to ~ in (to)** sintonizar (con)
▶ **tune up** *vi* (*musician*) afinar (su instrumento)
tuneful ['tjuː:nful] *adj* melodioso
tuner ['tjuː:nəʳ] *n* (*radio set*) sintonizador *m*; **piano** ~ afinador(a) *m(f)* de pianos
tungsten ['tʌŋstn] *n* tungsteno
tunic ['tjuː:nɪk] *n* túnica
tuning ['tjuː:nɪŋ] *n* sintonización *f*; (*Mus*) afinación *f*
tuning fork *n* diapasón *m*
Tunis ['tjuː:nɪs] *n* Túnez *m*
Tunisia [tjuː:'nɪzɪə] *n* Túnez *m*
Tunisian [tjuː:'nɪzɪən] *adj, n* tunecino(-a) *m(f)*
tunnel ['tʌnl] *n* túnel *m*; (*in mine*) galería ■ *vi* construir un túnel/una galería
tunnel vision *n* (*Med*) visión *f* periférica restringida; (*fig*) estrechez *f* de miras

tunny ['tʌnɪ] n atún m
turban ['tə:bən] n turbante m
turbid ['tə:bɪd] adj turbio
turbine ['tə:baɪn] n turbina
turbo ['tə:bəu] n turbo
turboprop ['tə:bəuprɔp] n turbohélice m
turbot ['tə:bət] n (pl inv) rodaballo
turbulence ['tə:bjuləns] n (Aviat) turbulencia
turbulent ['tə:bjulənt] adj turbulento
tureen [tə'ri:n] n sopera
turf [tə:f] n césped m; (clod) tepe m ▪ vt cubrir con césped
 ▶ **turf out** vt (col) echar a la calle
turf accountant n corredor(a) m(f) de apuestas
turgid ['tə:dʒɪd] adj (prose) pesado
Turin [tjuə'rɪn] n Turín m
Turk [tə:k] n turco(-a)
Turkey ['tə:kɪ] n Turquía
turkey ['tə:kɪ] n pavo
Turkish ['tə:kɪʃ] adj turco ▪ n (Ling) turco
Turkish bath n baño turco
turmeric ['tə:mərɪk] n cúrcuma
turmoil ['tə:mɔɪl] n desorden m, alboroto
turn [tə:n] n turno; (in road) curva; (Theat) número; (Med) ataque m ▪ vt girar, volver, voltear (LAm); (collar, steak) dar la vuelta a; (shape: wood, metal) tornear; (change): **to ~ sth into** convertir algo en ▪ vi volver, voltearse (LAm); (person: look back) volverse; (reverse direction) dar la vuelta, voltear (LAm); (milk) cortarse; (change) cambiar; (become): **to ~ into sth** convertirse or transformarse en algo; **a good ~** un favor; **it gave me quite a ~** me dio un susto; **"no left ~"** (Aut) "prohibido girar a la izquierda"; **it's your ~** te toca a ti; **in ~** por turnos; **to take turns** turnarse; **at the ~ of the year/century** a fin de año/a finales de siglo; **to take a ~ for the worse** (situation, patient) empeorar; **they turned him against us** le pusieron en contra nuestra; **the car turned the corner** el coche dobló la esquina; **to ~ left** (Aut) torcer or girar a la izquierda; **she has no-one to ~ to** no tiene a quién recurrir
 ▶ **turn away** vi apartar la vista ▪ vt (reject: person, business) rechazar
 ▶ **turn back** vi volverse atrás
 ▶ **turn down** vt (refuse) rechazar; (reduce) bajar; (fold) doblar
 ▶ **turn in** vi (col: go to bed) acostarse ▪ vt (fold) doblar hacia dentro
 ▶ **turn off** vi (from road) desviarse ▪ vt (light, radio etc) apagar; (engine) parar
 ▶ **turn on** vt (light, radio etc) encender, prender (LAm); (engine) poner en marcha
 ▶ **turn out** vt (light, gas) apagar; (produce: goods, novel etc) producir ▪ vi (attend: troops)

presentarse; (: doctor) atender; **to ~ out to be ... resultar ser ...**
 ▶ **turn over** vi (person) volverse ▪ vt (mattress, card) dar la vuelta a; (page) volver
 ▶ **turn round** vi volverse; (rotate) girar
 ▶ **turn to** vt fus: **to ~ to sb** acudir a algn
 ▶ **turn up** vi (person) llegar, presentarse; (lost object) aparecer ▪ vt (radio) subir, poner más alto; (heat, gas) poner más fuerte
turnabout ['tə:nəbaut], **turnaround** ['tə:nəraund] n (fig) giro total
turncoat ['tə:nkəut] n renegado(-a)
turned-up ['tə:ndʌp] adj (nose) respingón(-ona)
turning ['tə:nɪŋ] n (side road) bocacalle f; (bend) curva; **the first ~ on the right** la primera bocacalle a la derecha
turning point n (fig) momento decisivo
turnip ['tə:nɪp] n nabo
turnkey system ['tə:nki:-] n (Comput) sistema m de seguridad
turnout ['tə:naut] n asistencia, número de asistentes, público
turnover ['tə:nəuvər] n (Comm: amount of money) facturación f; (of goods) movimiento; **there is a rapid ~ in staff** hay mucho movimiento de personal
turnpike ['tə:npaɪk] n (US) autopista de peaje
turnstile ['tə:nstaɪl] n torniquete m
turntable ['tə:nteɪbl] n plato
turn-up ['tə:nʌp] n (Brit: on trousers) vuelta
turpentine ['tə:pəntaɪn] n (also: **turps**) trementina
turquoise ['tə:kwɔɪz] n (stone) turquesa ▪ adj color turquesa
turret ['tʌrɪt] n torreón m
turtle ['tə:tl] n tortuga (marina)
turtleneck ['tə:tlnɛk], **turtleneck sweater** n (jersey m de) cuello cisne
Tuscany ['tʌskənɪ] n Toscana
tusk [tʌsk] n colmillo
tussle ['tʌsl] n lucha, pelea
tutor ['tju:tər] n profesor(a) m(f)
tutorial [tju:'tɔ:rɪəl] n (Scol) seminario
tuxedo [tʌk'si:dəu] n (US) smóking m, esmoquin m
TV [ti:'vi:] n abbr (= television) televisión f
TV dinner n cena precocinada
TV licence n licencia que se paga por el uso del televisor, destinada a financiar la BBC
twaddle ['twɔdl] n (col) tonterías fpl
twang [twæŋ] n (of instrument) tañido; (of voice) timbre m nasal
tweak [twi:k] vt (nose, ear) pellizcar; (hair) tirar
tweed [twi:d] n tweed m
tweezers ['twi:zəz] npl pinzas fpl (de depilar)

twelfth [twɛlfθ] *num* duodécimo
Twelfth Night *n* (Día *m* de) Reyes *mpl*
twelve [twɛlv] *num* doce; **at ~ o'clock**
(*midday*) a mediodía; (*midnight*) a medianoche
twentieth ['twɛntιιθ] *num* vigésimo
twenty ['twɛntι] *num* veinte
twerp [twə:p] *n* (*col*) idiota *m/f*
twice [twaιs] *adv* dos veces; ~ **as much** dos
veces más, el doble; **she is ~ your age** ella
te dobla edad; **~ a week** dos veces a la *or* por
semana
twiddle ['twιdl] *vt, vi*: **to ~ (with) sth** dar
vueltas a algo; **to ~ one's thumbs** (*fig*) estar
de brazos cruzados
twig [twιg] *n* ramita ▪ *vi* (*col*) caer en la
cuenta
twilight ['twaιlaιt] *n* crepúsculo; (*morning*)
madrugada; **in the ~** en la media luz
twill [twιl] *n* sarga, estameña
twin [twιn] *adj, n* gemelo(-a) *m(f)* ▪ *vt*
hermanar
twin-bedded room ['twιn'bɛdιd-] *n* = **twin**
room
twin beds *npl* camas *fpl* gemelas
twin-carburettor ['twιnkɑ:bju'rɛtəʳ] *adj* de
dos carburadores
twine [twaιn] *n* bramante *m* ▪ *vi* (*plant*)
enroscarse
twin-engined [twιn'ɛndʒιnd] *adj* bimotor;
~ aircraft avión *m* bimotor
twinge [twιndʒ] *n* (*of pain*) punzada; (*of
conscience*) remordimiento
twinkle ['twιŋkl] *n* centelleo ▪ *vi* centellear;
(*eyes*) parpadear
twin room *n* habitación *f* con dos camas
twin town *n* ciudad *f* hermanada *or* gemela
twirl [twə:l] *n* giro ▪ *vt* dar vueltas a ▪ *vi*
piruetear
twist [twιst] *n* (*action*) torsión *f*; (*in road, coil*)
vuelta; (*in wire, flex*) doblez *f*; (*in story*) giro
▪ *vt* torcer, retorcer; (*roll around*) enrollar; (*fig*)
deformar ▪ *vi* serpentear; **to ~ one's ankle/
wrist** (*Med*) torcerse el tobillo/la muñeca
twisted ['twιstιd] *adj* (*wire, rope*) trenzado,
enroscado; (*ankle, wrist*) torcido; (*fig: logic,
mind*) retorcido
twit [twιt] *n* (*col*) tonto
twitch [twιtʃ] *n* sacudida; (*nervous*) tic *m*
nervioso ▪ *vi* moverse nerviosamente
Twitter® ['twιtəʳ] *n* Twitter® *m* ▪ *vi*
conectarse a Twitter
two [tu:] *num* dos; **~ by ~, in twos** de dos en
dos; **to put ~ and ~ together** (*fig*) atar cabos
two-bit [tu:'bιt] *adj* (*esp US: col, pej*) de poca
monta, de tres al cuarto
two-door [tu:'dɔ:ʳ] *adj* (*Aut*) de dos puertas

two-faced [tu:'feιst] *adj* (*pej: person*) falso,
hipócrita
twofold ['tu:fəuld] *adv*: **to increase ~**
duplicarse ▪ *adj* (*increase*) doble; (*reply*) en
dos partes
two-piece [tu:'pi:s] *n* (*also*: **two-piece suit**)
traje *m* de dos piezas; (*also*: **two-piece
swimsuit**) dos piezas *m inv*, bikini *m*
two-seater [tu:'si:təʳ] *n* (*plane, car*) avión *m*/
coche *m* de dos plazas, biplaza *m*
twosome ['tu:səm] *n* (*people*) pareja
two-stroke ['tu:strəuk] *n* (*also*: **two-stroke
engine**) motor *m* de dos tiempos ▪ *adj* de dos
tiempos
two-tone ['tu:təun] *adj* (*colour*) bicolor, de
dos tonos
two-way ['tu:weι] *adj*: **~ traffic** circulación
f de dos sentidos; **~ radio** radio *f* emisora y
receptora
TX *abbr* (*US*) = **Texas**
tycoon [taι'ku:n] *n*: **(business) ~** magnate
m/f
type [taιp] *n* (*category*) tipo, género; (*model*)
modelo; (*Typ*) tipo, letra ▪ *vt* (*letter etc*)
escribir a máquina; **what ~ do you want?**
¿qué tipo quieres?; **in bold/italic ~** en
negrita/cursiva
type-cast ['taιpkɑ:st] *adj* (*actor*) encasillado
typeface ['taιpfeιs] *n* tipo de letra
typescript ['taιpskrιpt] *n* texto
mecanografiado
typeset ['taιpsɛt] *vt* (*irreg: like* **set**) componer
typesetter ['taιpsɛtəʳ] *n* cajista *m/f*
typewriter ['taιpraιtəʳ] *n* máquina de
escribir
typewritten ['taιprιtn] *adj* mecanografiado
typhoid ['taιfɔιd] *n* (*fiebre f*) tifoidea
typhoon [taι'fu:n] *n* tifón *m*
typhus ['taιfəs] *n* tifus *m*
typical ['tιpιkl] *adj* típico
typically ['tιpιklι] *adv* típicamente
typify ['tιpιfaι] *vt* tipificar
typing ['taιpιŋ] *n* mecanografía
typing pool *n* (*Brit*) servicio de mecanógrafos
typist ['taιpιst] *n* mecanógrafo(-a)
typography [taι'pɔgrəfι] *n* tipografía
tyranny ['tιrənι] *n* tiranía
tyrant ['taιərənt] *n* tirano(-a)
tyre, tire (*US*) ['taιəʳ] *n* neumático, llanta
(*LAm*)
tyre pressure *n* presión *f* de los neumáticos
Tyrol [tι'rəul] *n* Tirol *m*
Tyrolean [tιrə'lιən], **Tyrolese** [tιrə'li:z] *adj*
tirolés(-esa)
Tyrrhenian Sea [tι'ri:nιən-] *n* Mar *m* Tirreno
tzar [zɑ:ʳ] *n* = **tsar**

Uu

U, u [juː] *n* (*letter*) U, u f; **U for Uncle** U de
Uruguay

U *n abbr* (*Brit Cine*: = *universal*) todos los públicos

UAW *n abbr* (*US*) = **United Automobile
Workers**

UB40 *n abbr* (*Brit*: = *unemployment benefit form 40*)
número de referencia en la solicitud de inscripción en
la lista de parados por extensión, la tarjeta del paro o
su beneficiario

U-bend [ˈjuːbɛnd] *n* recodo

ubiquitous [juːˈbɪkwɪtəs] *adj* omnipresente,
ubicuo

UCAS [ˈjuːkæs] *n abbr* (*Brit*) = **Universities and
Colleges Admissions Service**

UDA *n abbr* (*Brit*: = *Ulster Defence Association*)
organización paramilitar protestante de Irlanda del
Norte

UDC *n abbr* (*Brit*) = **Urban District Council**

udder [ˈʌdəʳ] *n* ubre f

UDI *n abbr* (*Brit Pol*) = **unilateral declaration of
independence**

UDR *n abbr* (*Brit*: = *Ulster Defence Regiment*) fuerza
de seguridad de Irlanda del Norte

UEFA [juːˈeɪfə] *n abbr* (= *Union of European
Football Associations*) U.E.F.A. f

UFO [ˈjuːfəu] *n abbr* (= *unidentified flying object*)
OVNI m

Uganda [juːˈgændə] *n* Uganda

Ugandan [juːˈgændən] *adj* de Uganda

UGC *n abbr* (*Brit*: = *University Grants Committee*)
entidad gubernamental que controla las finanzas de
las universidades

ugh [əːh] *excl* ¡uf!

ugliness [ˈʌglɪnɪs] *n* fealdad f

ugly [ˈʌglɪ] *adj* feo; (*dangerous*) peligroso

UHF *abbr* (= *ultra-high frequency*) UHF f

UHT *adj abbr* (= *ultra heat treated*): ~ **milk** leche
f uperizada

UK *n abbr* (= *United Kingdom*) Reino Unido, R.U.

Ukraine [juːˈkreɪn] *n* Ucrania

Ukrainian [juːˈkreɪnɪən] *adj* ucraniano ∎ *n*
ucraniano(-a); (*Ling*) ucraniano

ulcer [ˈʌlsəʳ] *n* úlcera; **mouth** ~ úlcera bucal

Ulster [ˈʌlstəʳ] *n* Ulster m

ulterior [ʌlˈtɪərɪəʳ] *adj* ulterior; ~ **motive**
segundas intenciones *fpl*

ultimate [ˈʌltɪmət] *adj* último, final;
(*greatest*) mayor ∎ *n*: **the ~ in luxury** el
colmo del lujo

ultimately [ˈʌltɪmətlɪ] *adv* (*in the end*) por
último, al final; (*fundamentally*) a fin de
cuentas

ultimatum (*pl* **ultimatums** *or* **ultimata**)
[ʌltɪˈmeɪtəm, -tə] *n* ultimátum m

ultra- [ˈʌltrə] *pref* ultra-

ultrasonic [ʌltrəˈsɔnɪk] *adj* ultrasónico

ultrasound [ˈʌltrəsaund] *n* (*Med*) ultrasonido

ultraviolet [ˈʌltrəˈvaɪəlɪt] *adj* ultravioleta

um [ʌm] *interj* (*col*: *in hesitation*) esto, este (*LAm*)

umbilical cord [ʌmbɪˈlaɪkl-] *n* cordón m
umbilical

umbrage [ˈʌmbrɪdʒ] *n*: **to take ~ (at)**
ofenderse (por)

umbrella [ʌmˈbrɛlə] *n* paraguas m inv; **under
the ~ of** (*fig*) bajo la protección de

umlaut [ˈumlaut] *n* diéresis f inv

umpire [ˈʌmpaɪəʳ] *n* árbitro ∎ *vt* arbitrar

umpteen [ʌmpˈtiːn] *num* enésimos(-as);
for the umpteenth time por enésima vez

UMW *n abbr* (= *United Mineworkers of America*)
sindicato de mineros

UN *n abbr* (= *United Nations*) ONU f

un- [ʌn] *pref* in-; des-; no ...; (*XX*) poco ...; nada ...

unabashed [ʌnəˈbæʃt] *adj* nada avergonzado

unabated [ʌnəˈbeɪtɪd] *adj*: **to continue ~**
seguir con la misma intensidad

unable [ʌnˈeɪbl] *adj*: **to be ~ to do sth** no
poder hacer algo; (*not know how to*) ser incapaz
de hacer algo, no saber hacer algo

unabridged [ʌnəˈbrɪdʒd] *adj* íntegro

unacceptable [ʌnəkˈsɛptəbl] *adj* (*proposal,
behaviour, price*) inaceptable; **it's ~ that** no se
puede aceptar que

unaccompanied [ʌnəˈkʌmpənɪd] *adj*
no acompañado; (*singing, song*) sin
acompañamiento

u

unaccountably [ˌʌnəˈkaʊntəblɪ] *adv* inexplicablemente

unaccounted [ˌʌnəˈkaʊntɪd] *adj*: **two passengers are ~ for** faltan dos pasajeros

unaccustomed [ˌʌnəˈkʌstəmd] *adj*: **to be ~ to** no estar acostumbrado a

unacquainted [ˌʌnəˈkweɪntɪd] *adj*: **to be ~ with** (*facts*) desconocer, ignorar

unadulterated [ˌʌnəˈdʌltəreɪtɪd] *adj* (*gen*) puro; (*wine*) sin mezcla

unaffected [ˌʌnəˈfɛktɪd] *adj* (*person, behaviour*) sin afectación, sencillo; (*emotionally*): **to be ~ by** no estar afectado por

unafraid [ˌʌnəˈfreɪd] *adj*: **to be ~** no tener miedo

unaided [ʌnˈeɪdɪd] *adj* sin ayuda, por sí solo

unanimity [juːnəˈnɪmɪtɪ] *n* unanimidad *f*

unanimous [juːˈnænɪməs] *adj* unánime

unanimously [juːˈnænɪməslɪ] *adv* unánimemente

unanswered [ʌnˈɑːnsəd] *adj* (*question, letter*) sin contestar; (*criticism*) incontestado

unappetizing [ʌnˈæpɪtaɪzɪŋ] *adj* poco apetitoso

unappreciative [ˌʌnəˈpriːʃɪətɪv] *adj* desagradecido

unarmed [ʌnˈɑːmd] *adj* (*person*) desarmado; (*combat*) sin armas

unashamed [ˌʌnəˈʃeɪmd] *adj* desvergonzado

unassisted [ˌʌnəˈsɪstɪd] *adj, adv* sin ayuda

unassuming [ˌʌnəˈsjuːmɪŋ] *adj* modesto, sin pretensiones

unattached [ˌʌnəˈtætʃt] *adj* (*person*) soltero; (*part etc*) suelto

unattended [ˌʌnəˈtɛndɪd] *adj* (*car, luggage*) sin atender

unattractive [ˌʌnəˈtræktɪv] *adj* poco atractivo

unauthorized [ʌnˈɔːθəraɪzd] *adj* no autorizado

unavailable [ˌʌnəˈveɪləbl] *adj* (*article, room, book*) no disponible; (*person*) ocupado

unavoidable [ˌʌnəˈvɔɪdəbl] *adj* inevitable

unavoidably [ˌʌnəˈvɔɪdəblɪ] *adv* (*detained*) por causas ajenas a su voluntad

unaware [ˌʌnəˈwɛəʳ] *adj*: **to be ~ of** ignorar

unawares [ˌʌnəˈwɛəz] *adv* de improviso

unbalanced [ʌnˈbælənst] *adj* desequilibrado; (*mentally*) trastornado

unbearable [ʌnˈbɛərəbl] *adj* insoportable

unbeatable [ʌnˈbiːtəbl] *adj* (*gen*) invencible; (*price*) inmejorable

unbeaten [ʌnˈbiːtn] *adj* (*team*) imbatido; (*army*) invicto; (*record*) no batido

unbecoming [ˌʌnbɪˈkʌmɪŋ] *adj* (*unseemly: language, behaviour*) indecoroso, impropio; (*unflattering: garment*) poco favorecedor(a)

unbeknown [ˌʌnbɪˈnəun], **unbeknownst** [ˌʌnbɪˈnəunst] *adv*: **~(st) to me** sin saberlo yo

unbelief [ˌʌnbɪˈliːf] *n* incredulidad *f*

unbelievable [ˌʌnbɪˈliːvəbl] *adj* increíble

unbelievingly [ˌʌnbɪˈliːvɪŋlɪ] *adv* sin creer

unbend [ʌnˈbɛnd] (*irreg: like* **bend**) *vi* (*fig: person*) relajarse ■ *vt* (*wire*) enderezar

unbending [ʌnˈbɛndɪŋ] *adj* (*fig*) inflexible

unbiased, unbiassed [ʌnˈbaɪəst] *adj* imparcial

unblemished [ʌnˈblɛmɪʃt] *adj* sin mancha

unblock [ʌnˈblɔk] *vt* (*pipe*) desatascar; (*road*) despejar

unborn [ʌnˈbɔːn] *adj* que va a nacer

unbounded [ʌnˈbaundɪd] *adj* ilimitado, sin límite

unbreakable [ʌnˈbreɪkəbl] *adj* irrompible

unbridled [ʌnˈbraɪdld] *adj* (*fig*) desenfrenado

unbroken [ʌnˈbrəukən] *adj* (*seal*) intacto; (*series*) continuo, ininterrumpido; (*record*) no batido; (*spirit*) indómito

unbuckle [ʌnˈbʌkl] *vt* desabrochar

unburden [ʌnˈbəːdn] *vt*: **to ~ o.s.** desahogarse

unbusinesslike [ʌnˈbɪznɪslaɪk] *adj* (*trader*) poco profesional; (*transaction*) incorrecto; (*fig: person*) poco práctico; (: *without method*) desorganizado

unbutton [ʌnˈbʌtn] *vt* desabrochar

uncalled-for [ʌnˈkɔːldfɔːʳ] *adj* gratuito, inmerecido

uncanny [ʌnˈkænɪ] *adj* extraño, extraordinario

unceasing [ʌnˈsiːsɪŋ] *adj* incesante

unceremonious [ˈʌnsɛrɪˈməunɪəs] *adj* (*abrupt, rude*) brusco, hosco

uncertain [ʌnˈsəːtn] *adj* incierto; (*indecisive*) indeciso; **it's ~ whether** no se sabe si; **in no ~ terms** sin dejar lugar a dudas

uncertainty [ʌnˈsəːtntɪ] *n* incertidumbre *f*

unchallenged [ʌnˈtʃælɪndʒd] *adj* (*Law etc*) incontestado; **to go ~** no encontrar respuesta

unchanged [ʌnˈtʃeɪndʒd] *adj* sin cambiar *or* alterar

uncharitable [ʌnˈtʃærɪtəbl] *adj* (*remark, behaviour*) demasiado duro

uncharted [ʌnˈtʃɑːtɪd] *adj* inexplorado

unchecked [ʌnˈtʃɛkt] *adj* desenfrenado

uncivil [ʌnˈsɪvɪl] *adj* descortés, grosero

uncivilized [ʌnˈsɪvɪlaɪzd] *adj* (*gen*) inculto, poco civilizado; (*fig: behaviour etc*) bárbaro

uncle [ˈʌŋkl] *n* tío

unclear [ʌnˈklɪəʳ] *adj* poco claro; **I'm still ~ about what I'm supposed to do** todavía no tengo muy claro lo que tengo que hacer

uncoil [ʌnˈkɔɪl] *vt* desenrollar ■ *vi* desenrollarse

uncomfortable [ʌn'kʌmfətəbl] *adj* incómodo; *(uneasy)* inquieto

uncomfortably [ʌn'kʌmfətəblɪ] *adv* *(uneasily: say)* con inquietud; *(: think)* con remordimiento *or* nerviosismo

uncommitted [ʌnkə'mɪtɪd] *adj (attitude, country)* no comprometido; **to remain ~ to** *(policy, party)* no comprometerse a

uncommon [ʌn'kɔmən] *adj* poco común, raro

uncommunicative [ʌnkə'mjuːnɪkətɪv] *adj* poco comunicativo, reservado

uncomplicated [ʌn'kɔmplɪkeɪtɪd] *adj* sin complicaciones

uncompromising [ʌn'kɔmprəmaɪzɪŋ] *adj* intransigente

unconcerned [ʌnkən'səːnd] *adj* indiferente; **to be ~ about** ser indiferente a, no preocuparse de

unconditional [ʌnkən'dɪʃənl] *adj* incondicional

uncongenial [ʌnkən'dʒiːnɪəl] *adj* desagradable

unconnected [ʌnkə'nɛktɪd] *adj (unrelated)*: **to be ~ with** no estar relacionado con

unconscious [ʌn'kɔnʃəs] *adj* sin sentido; *(unaware)* inconsciente ▪ *n*: **the ~** el inconsciente; **to knock sb ~** dejar a algn sin sentido

unconsciously [ʌn'kɔnʃəslɪ] *adv* inconscientemente

unconsciousness [ʌn'kɔnʃəsnɪs] *n* inconsciencia

unconstitutional [ʌnkɔnstɪ'tjuːʃənl] *adj* anticonstitucional

uncontested [ʌnkən'tɛstɪd] *adj (champion)* incontestado; *(Parliament: seat)* ganado sin oposición

uncontrollable [ʌnkən'trəuləbl] *adj (temper)* indomable; *(laughter)* incontenible

uncontrolled [ʌnkən'trəuld] *adj (child, dog, emotion)* incontrolado; *(inflation, price rises)* desenfrenado

unconventional [ʌnkən'vɛnʃənl] *adj* poco convencional

unconvinced [ʌnkən'vɪnst] *adj*: **to be** *or* **remain ~** seguir sin convencerse

unconvincing [ʌnkən'vɪnsɪŋ] *adj* poco convincente

uncork [ʌn'kɔːk] *vt* descorchar

uncorroborated [ʌnkə'rɔbəreɪtɪd] *adj* no confirmado

uncouth [ʌn'kuːθ] *adj* grosero, inculto

uncover [ʌn'kʌvəʳ] *vt (gen)* descubrir; *(take lid off)* destapar

undamaged [ʌn'dæmɪdʒd] *adj (goods)* en buen estado; *(fig: reputation)* intacto

undaunted [ʌn'dɔːntɪd] *adj*: **~ by** sin dejarse desanimar por

undecided [ʌndɪ'saɪdɪd] *adj (person)* indeciso; *(question)* no resuelto, pendiente

undelivered [ʌndɪ'lɪvəd] *adj* no entregado al destinatario; **if ~ return to sender** en caso de no llegar a su destino devolver al, remitente

undeniable [ʌndɪ'naɪəbl] *adj* innegable

undeniably [ʌndɪ'naɪəblɪ] *adv* innegablemente

under ['ʌndəʳ] *prep* debajo de; *(less than)* menos de; *(according to)* según, de acuerdo con ▪ *adv* debajo, abajo; **~ there** ahí debajo; **~ construction** en construcción; en obras; **~ the circumstances** dadas las circunstancias; **in ~ 2 hours** en menos de dos horas; **~ anaesthetic** bajo los efectos de la anestesia; **~ discussion** en discusión, sobre el tapete

under... [ʌndəʳ] *pref* sub...

under-age [ʌndər'eɪdʒ] *adj* menor de edad

underarm ['ʌndərɑːm] *n* axila, sobaco ▪ *cpd*: **~ deodorant** desodorante *m* corporal

undercapitalised [ʌndə'kæpɪtəlaɪzd] *adj* descapitalizado

undercarriage ['ʌndəkærɪdʒ] *n (Brit Aviat)* tren *m* de aterrizaje

undercharge [ʌndə'tʃɑːdʒ] *vt* cobrar de menos

underclass ['ʌndəklɑːs] *n* clase *f* marginada

underclothes ['ʌndəkləuðz] *npl* ropa *sg* interior *or* íntima *(LAm)*

undercoat ['ʌndəkəut] *n (paint)* primera mano

undercover [ʌndə'kʌvəʳ] *adj* clandestino

undercurrent ['ʌndəkʌrnt] *n* corriente *f* submarina; *(fig)* tendencia oculta

undercut ['ʌndəkʌt] *vt (irreg: like cut)* vender más barato que; fijar un precio más barato que

underdeveloped [ʌndədɪ'vɛləpt] *adj* subdesarrollado

underdog ['ʌndədɔg] *n* desvalido(-a)

underdone [ʌndə'dʌn] *adj (Culin)* poco hecho

underemployment [ʌndərɪm'plɔɪmənt] *n* subempleo

underestimate [ʌndər'ɛstɪmeɪt] *vt* subestimar

underexposed [ʌndərɪks'pəuzd] *adj (Phot)* subexpuesto

underfed [ʌndə'fɛd] *adj* subalimentado

underfoot [ʌndə'fut] *adv*: **it's wet ~** el suelo está mojado

underfunded [ʌndə'fʌndɪd] *adj* infradotado (económicamente)

undergo [ʌndə'gəu] *vt (irreg: like go)* sufrir;

(*treatment*) recibir, someterse a; **the car is undergoing repairs** están reparando el coche

undergraduate [ˈʌndəˈgrædjuət] *n* estudiante *m/f* ▪ *cpd*: **~ courses** cursos *mpl* de licenciatura

underground [ˈʌndəgraund] *n* (*Brit: railway*) metro; (*Pol*) movimiento clandestino ▪ *adj* subterráneo

undergrowth [ˈʌndəgrəuθ] *n* maleza

underhand [ʌndəˈhænd], **underhanded** [ʌndəˈhændɪd] *adj* (*fig*) poco limpio

underinsured [ʌndərɪnˈʃuəd] *adj* insuficientemente asegurado

underlie [ʌndəˈlaɪ] *vt* (*irreg: like* **lie**) (*fig*) ser la razón fundamental de; **the underlying cause** la causa fundamental

underline [ʌndəˈlaɪn] *vt* subrayar

underling [ˈʌndəlɪŋ] *n* (*pej*) subalterno(-a)

undermanning [ʌndəˈmænɪŋ] *n* falta de personal

undermentioned [ʌndəˈmɛnʃənd] *adj* abajo citado

undermine [ʌndəˈmaɪn] *vt* socavar, minar

underneath [ʌndəˈniːθ] *adv* debajo ▪ *prep* debajo de, bajo

undernourished [ʌndəˈnʌrɪʃt] *adj* desnutrido

underpaid [ʌndəˈpeɪd] *adj* mal pagado

underpants [ˈʌndəpænts] *npl* calzoncillos *mpl*

underpass [ˈʌndəpɑːs] *n* (*Brit*) paso subterráneo

underpin [ʌndəˈpɪn] *vt* (*argument, case*) secundar, sostener

underplay [ʌndəˈpleɪ] *vt* (*Brit*) minimizar

underpopulated [ʌndəˈpɔpjuleɪtɪd] *adj* poco poblado

underprice [ʌndəˈpraɪs] *vt* vender demasiado barato

underpriced [ʌndəˈpraɪst] *adj* con precio demasiado bajo

underprivileged [ʌndəˈprɪvɪlɪdʒd] *adj* desvalido

underrate [ʌndəˈreɪt] *vt* infravalorar, subestimar

underscore [ˈʌndəskɔːr] *vt* subrayar, sostener

underseal [ʌndəˈsiːl] *vt* (*Aut*) proteger contra la corrosión

undersecretary [ʌndəˈsɛkrətrɪ] *n* subsecretario(-a)

undersell [ʌndəˈsɛl] *vt* (*competitors*) vender más barato que

undershirt [ˈʌndəʃɜːt] *n* (*US*) camiseta

undershorts [ˈʌndəʃɔːts] *npl* (*US*) calzoncillos *mpl*

underside [ˈʌndəsaɪd] *n* parte *f* inferior, revés *m*

undersigned [ˈʌndəsaɪnd] *adj, n*: **the ~** el/la *etc* abajo firmante

underskirt [ˈʌndəskəːt] *n* (*Brit*) enaguas *fpl*

understaffed [ʌndəˈstɑːft] *adj* falto de personal

understand [ʌndəˈstænd] (*irreg: like* **stand**) *vt, vi* entender, comprender; (*assume*) tener entendido; **to make o.s. understood** hacerse entender; **I ~ you have been absent** tengo entendido que (usted) ha estado ausente

understandable [ʌndəˈstændəbl] *adj* comprensible

understanding [ʌndəˈstændɪŋ] *adj* comprensivo ▪ *n* comprensión *f*, entendimiento; (*agreement*) acuerdo; **to come to an ~ with sb** llegar a un acuerdo con algn; **on the ~ that** a condición de que + *subjun*

understate [ʌndəˈsteɪt] *vt* minimizar

understatement [ʌndəˈsteɪtmənt] *n* subestimación *f*; (*modesty*) modestia (excesiva); **to say it was good is quite an ~** decir que estuvo bien es quedarse corto

understood [ʌndəˈstud] *pt, pp of* **understand** ▪ *adj* entendido; (*implied*): **it is ~ that** se sobreentiende que

understudy [ˈʌndəstʌdɪ] *n* suplente *m/f*

undertake [ʌndəˈteɪk] *vt* (*irreg: like* **take**) emprender; **to ~ to do sth** comprometerse a hacer algo

undertaker [ˈʌndəteɪkər] *n* director(a) *m(f)* de pompas fúnebres

undertaking [ˈʌndəteɪkɪŋ] *n* empresa; (*promise*) promesa

undertone [ˈʌndətəun] *n* (*of criticism*) connotación *f*; (*low voice*): **in an ~** en voz baja

undervalue [ʌndəˈvæljuː] *vt* (*fig*) subestimar, infravalorar; (*Comm etc*) valorizar por debajo de su precio

underwater [ʌndəˈwɔːtər] *adv* bajo el agua ▪ *adj* submarino

underwear [ˈʌndəwɛər] *n* ropa interior *or* íntima (*LAm*)

underweight [ʌndəˈweɪt] *adj* de peso insuficiente; (*person*) demasiado delgado

underworld [ˈʌndəwəːld] *n* (*of crime*) hampa, inframundo

underwrite [ʌndəˈraɪt] *vt* (*irreg: like* **write**) (*Comm*) suscribir; (*Insurance*) asegurar (*contra riesgos*)

underwriter [ˈʌndəraɪtər] *n* (*Insurance*) asegurador(a) *m(f)*

undeserving [ʌndɪˈzəːvɪŋ] *adj*: **to be ~ of** no ser digno de

undesirable [ʌndɪˈzaɪərəbl] *adj* indeseable

undeveloped [ʌndɪˈvɛləpt] *adj* (*land, resources*) sin explotar

undies ['ʌndɪz] npl (col) paños mpl menores
undiluted [ʌndaɪ'luːtɪd] adj (concentrate) concentrado
undiplomatic [ʌndɪplə'mætɪk] adj poco diplomático
undischarged [ʌndɪs'tʃɑːdʒd] adj:
~ **bankrupt** quebrado(-a) no rehabilitado(-a)
undisciplined [ʌn'dɪsɪplɪnd] adj indisciplinado
undiscovered [ʌndɪs'kʌvəd] adj no descubierto; (unknown) desconocido
undisguised [ʌndɪs'gaɪzd] adj franco, abierto
undisputed [ʌndɪ'spjuːtɪd] adj incontestable
undistinguished [ʌndɪs'tɪŋgwɪʃt] adj mediocre
undisturbed [ʌndɪs'təːbd] adj (sleep) ininterrumpido; **to leave sth** ~ dejar algo tranquilo or como está
undivided [ʌndɪ'vaɪdɪd] adj: **I want your** ~ **attention** quiero su completa atención
undo [ʌn'duː] vt (irreg: like **do**) deshacer
undoing [ʌn'duːɪŋ] n ruina, perdición f
undone [ʌn'dʌn] pp of **undo** ■ adj: **to come** ~ (clothes) desabrocharse; (parcel) desatarse
undoubted [ʌn'dautɪd] adj indudable
undoubtedly [ʌn'dautɪdlɪ] adv indudablemente, sin duda
undress [ʌn'drɛs] vi desnudarse, desvestirse (esp LAm)
undrinkable [ʌn'drɪŋkəbl] adj (unpalatable) imbebible; (poisonous) no potable
undue [ʌn'djuː] adj indebido, excesivo
undulating ['ʌndjuleɪtɪŋ] adj ondulante
unduly [ʌn'djuːlɪ] adv excesivamente, demasiado
undying [ʌn'daɪɪŋ] adj eterno
unearned [ʌn'əːnd] adj (praise, respect) inmerecido; ~ **income** ingresos mpl no ganados, renta no ganada or salarial
unearth [ʌn'əːθ] vt desenterrar
unearthly [ʌn'əːθlɪ] adj: ~ **hour** (col) hora intempestiva
unease [ʌn'iːz] n malestar m
uneasy [ʌn'iːzɪ] adj intranquilo; (worried) preocupado; **to feel** ~ **about doing sth** sentirse incómodo con la idea de hacer algo
uneconomic ['ʌniːkə'nɔmɪk], **uneconomical** ['ʌniːkə'nɔmɪkl] adj no económico
uneducated [ʌn'ɛdjukeɪtɪd] adj ignorante, inculto
unemployed [ʌnɪm'plɔɪd] adj parado, sin trabajo ■ n: **the** ~ los parados
unemployment [ʌnɪm'plɔɪmənt] n paro, desempleo, cesantía (LAm)
unemployment benefit n (Brit) subsidio de desempleo or paro

unending [ʌn'ɛndɪŋ] adj interminable
unenviable [ʌn'ɛnvɪəbl] adj poco envidiable
unequal [ʌn'iːkwəl] adj (length, objects etc) desigual; (amounts) distinto; (division of labour) poco justo
unequalled, unequaled (US) [ʌn'iːkwəld] adj inigualado, sin par
unequivocal [ʌnɪ'kwɪvəkəl] adj (answer) inequívoco, claro; (person) claro
unerring [ʌn'əːrɪŋ] adj infalible
UNESCO [juː'nɛskəu] n abbr (= United Nations Educational, Scientific and Cultural Organization) UNESCO f
unethical [ʌn'ɛθɪkəl] adj (methods) inmoral; (doctor's behaviour) que infringe la ética profesional
uneven [ʌn'iːvn] adj desigual; (road etc) con baches
uneventful [ʌnɪ'vɛntful] adj sin incidentes
unexceptional [ʌnɪk'sɛpʃənl] adj sin nada de extraordinario, corriente
unexciting [ʌnɪk'saɪtɪŋ] adj (news) sin interés; (film, evening) aburrido
unexpected [ʌnɪk'spɛktɪd] adj inesperado
unexpectedly [ʌnɪk'spɛktɪdlɪ] adv inesperadamente
unexplained [ʌnɪks'pleɪnd] adj inexplicado
unexploded [ʌnɪks'pləudɪd] adj sin explotar
unfailing [ʌn'feɪlɪŋ] adj (support) indefectible; (energy) inagotable
unfair [ʌn'fɛəʳ] adj: ~ **(to sb)** injusto (con algn); **it's** ~ **that ...** es injusto que ..., no es justo que ...
unfair dismissal n despido improcedente
unfairly [ʌn'fɛəlɪ] adv injustamente
unfaithful [ʌn'feɪθful] adj infiel
unfamiliar [ʌnfə'mɪlɪəʳ] adj extraño, desconocido; **to be** ~ **with sth** desconocer or ignorar algo
unfashionable [ʌn'fæʃnəbl] adj (clothes) pasado or fuera de moda; (district) poco elegante
unfasten [ʌn'fɑːsn] vt desatar
unfathomable [ʌn'fæðəməbl] adj insondable
unfavourable, unfavorable (US) [ʌn'feɪvərəbl] adj desfavorable
unfavourably, unfavorably (US) [ʌn'feɪvrəblɪ] adv: **to look** ~ **upon** ser adverso a
unfeeling [ʌn'fiːlɪŋ] adj insensible
unfinished [ʌn'fɪnɪʃt] adj inacabado, sin terminar
unfit [ʌn'fɪt] adj en baja forma; (incompetent) incapaz; ~ **for work** no apto para trabajar
unflagging [ʌn'flægɪŋ] adj incansable
unflappable [ʌn'flæpəbl] adj imperturbable
unflattering [ʌn'flætərɪŋ] adj (dress, hairstyle) poco favorecedor

u

unflinching [ʌn'flɪntʃɪŋ] *adj* impávido
unfold [ʌn'fəuld] *vt* desdoblar; (*fig*) revelar ▪ *vi* abrirse; revelarse
unforeseeable [ʌnfɔ:'si:əbl] *adj* imprevisible
unforeseen ['ʌnfɔ:'si:n] *adj* imprevisto
unforgettable [ʌnfə'gɛtəbl] *adj* inolvidable
unforgivable [ʌnfə'gɪvəbl] *adj* imperdonable
unformatted [ʌn'fɔ:mætɪd] *adj* (*disk*, *text*) sin formatear
unfortunate [ʌn'fɔ:tʃnət] *adj* desgraciado; (*event*, *remark*) inoportuno
unfortunately [ʌn'fɔ:tʃnətlɪ] *adv* desgraciadamente, por desgracia
unfounded [ʌn'faundɪd] *adj* infundado
unfriendly [ʌn'frɛndlɪ] *adj* antipático
unfulfilled [ʌnful'fɪld] *adj* (*ambition*) sin realizar; (*prophecy*, *promise*, *terms of contract*) incumplido; (*desire*, *person*) insatisfecho
unfurl [ʌn'fə:l] *vt* desplegar
unfurnished [ʌn'fə:nɪʃt] *adj* sin amueblar
ungainly [ʌn'geɪnlɪ] *adj* (*walk*) desgarbado
ungodly [ʌn'gɔdlɪ] *adj*: **at an ~ hour** a una hora intempestiva
ungrateful [ʌn'greɪtful] *adj* ingrato
unguarded [ʌn'gɑ:dɪd] *adj* (*moment*) de descuido
unhappily [ʌn'hæpɪlɪ] *adv* (*unfortunately*) desgraciadamente
unhappiness [ʌn'hæpɪnɪs] *n* tristeza
unhappy [ʌn'haepɪ] *adj* (*sad*) triste; (*unfortunate*) desgraciado; (*childhood*) infeliz; **~ with** (*arrangements etc*) poco contento con, descontento de
unharmed [ʌn'hɑ:md] *adj* (*person*) ileso
UNHCR *n abbr* (= *United Nations High Commission for Refugees*) ACNUR *m*
unhealthy [ʌn'hɛlθɪ] *adj* (*gen*) malsano, insalubre; (*person*) enfermizo; (*interest*) morboso
unheard-of [ʌn'hə:dɔv] *adj* inaudito, sin precedente
unhelpful [ʌn'hɛlpful] *adj* (*person*) poco servicial; (*advice*) inútil
unhesitating [ʌn'hezɪteɪtɪŋ] *adj* (*loyalty*) automático; (*reply*, *offer*) inmediato; (*person*) resuelto
unholy [ʌn'həulɪ] *adj*: **an ~ alliance** una alianza nefasta; **he returned at an ~ hour** volvió a una hora intempestiva
unhook [ʌn'huk] *vt* desenganchar; (*from wall*) descolgar; (*undo*) desabrochar
unhurt [ʌn'hə:t] *adj* ileso
unhygienic [ʌnhaɪ'dʒi:nɪk] *adj* antihigiénico
UNICEF ['ju:nɪsɛf] *n abbr* (= *United Nations International Children's Emergency Fund*) UNICEF *f*
unidentified [ʌnaɪ'dɛntɪfaɪd] *adj* no identificado; **~ flying object (UFO)** objeto volante no identificado

unification [ju:nɪfɪ'keɪʃən] *n* unificación *f*
uniform ['ju:nɪfɔ:m] *n* uniforme *m* ▪ *adj* uniforme
uniformity [ju:nɪ'fɔ:mɪtɪ] *n* uniformidad *f*
unify ['ju:nɪfaɪ] *vt* unificar, unir
unilateral [ju:nɪ'lætərəl] *adj* unilateral
unimaginable [ʌnɪ'mædʒɪnəbl] *adj* inconcebible, inimaginable
unimaginative [ʌnɪ'mædʒɪnətɪv] *adj* falto de imaginación
unimpaired [ʌnɪm'pɛəd] *adj* (*unharmed*) intacto; (*not lessened*) no disminuido; (*unaltered*) inalterado
unimportant [ʌnɪm'pɔ:tənt] *adj* sin importancia
unimpressed [ʌnɪm'prɛst] *adj* poco impresionado
uninhabited [ʌnɪn'hæbɪtɪd] *adj* desierto; (*country*) despoblado; (*house*) deshabitado, desocupado
uninhibited [ʌnɪn'hɪbɪtɪd] *adj* nada cohibido, desinhibido
uninjured [ʌn'ɪndʒəd] *adj* (*person*) ileso
uninspiring [ʌnɪn'spaɪərɪŋ] *adj* anodino
unintelligent [ʌnɪn'tɛlɪdʒənt] *adj* poco inteligente
unintentional [ʌnɪn'tɛnʃənəl] *adj* involuntario
unintentionally [ʌnɪn'tɛnʃnəlɪ] *adv* sin querer
uninvited [ʌnɪn'vaɪtɪd] *adj* (*guest*) sin invitación
uninviting [ʌnɪn'vaɪtɪŋ] *adj* (*place*, *offer*) poco atractivo; (*food*) poco apetecible
union ['ju:njən] *n* unión *f*; (*also*: **trade union**) sindicato ▪ *cpd* sindical; **the U~** (*US*) la Unión
union card *n* carnet *m* de sindicato
unionize ['ju:njənaɪz] *vt* sindicalizar
Union Jack *n* bandera del Reino Unido
Union of Soviet Socialist Republics *n* Unión *f* de Repúblicas Socialistas Soviéticas
union shop *n* (*US*) *empresa de afiliación sindical obligatoria*
unique [ju:'ni:k] *adj* único
unisex ['ju:nɪsɛks] *adj* unisex
Unison ['ju:nɪsn] *n* (*trade union*) *gran sindicato de funcionarios*
unison ['ju:nɪsn] *n*: **in ~** en armonía
unissued capital [ʌn'ɪʃu:d-] *n* capital *m* no emitido
unit ['ju:nɪt] *n* unidad *f*; (*team*, *squad*) grupo; **kitchen ~** módulo de cocina; **production ~** taller *m* de fabricación; **sink ~** fregadero
unit cost *n* costo unitario
unite [ju:'naɪt] *vt* unir ▪ *vi* unirse
united [ju:'naɪtɪd] *adj* unido

United Arab Emirates *npl* Emiratos *mpl* Árabes Unidos
United Kingdom *n* Reino Unido
United Nations, United Nations Organization *n* Naciones Unidas *fpl*
United States, United States of America *n* Estados Unidos *mpl* (de América)
unit price *n* precio unitario
unit trust *n* (*Brit*) bono fiduciario
unity ['ju:nɪtɪ] *n* unidad *f*
Univ. *abbr* = **university**
universal [ju:nɪ'və:sl] *adj* universal
universally [ju:nɪ'və:səlɪ] *adv* universalmente
universe ['ju:nɪvə:s] *n* universo
university [ju:nɪ'və:sɪtɪ] *n* universidad *f* ■ *cpd* (*student, professor, education, degree*) universitario; (*year*) académico; **to be at/go to** ~ estudiar en/ir a la universidad
unjust [ʌn'dʒʌst] *adj* injusto
unjustifiable [ʌndʒʌstɪ'faɪəbl] *adj* injustificable
unjustified [ʌn'dʒʌstɪfaɪd] *adj* (*text*) no alineado *or* justificado
unkempt [ʌn'kɛmpt] *adj* descuidado; (*hair*) despeinado
unkind [ʌn'kaɪnd] *adj* poco amable; (*comment etc*) cruel
unkindly [ʌn'kaɪndlɪ] *adv* (*speak*) severamente; (*treat*) cruelmente, mal
unknown [ʌn'nəun] *adj* desconocido ■ *adv*: ~ **to me** sin saberlo yo; ~ **quantity** incógnita
unladen [ʌn'leɪdən] *adj* (*weight*) vacío, sin cargamento
unlawful [ʌn'lɔ:ful] *adj* ilegal, ilícito
unleaded [ʌn'lɛdɪd] *n* (*also*: **unleaded petrol**) gasolina sin plomo
unleash [ʌn'li:ʃ] *vt* desatar
unleavened [ʌn'lɛvənd] *adj* ácimo, sin levadura
unless [ʌn'lɛs] *conj* a menos que; ~ **he comes** a menos que venga; ~ **otherwise stated** salvo indicación contraria; ~ **I am mistaken** si no mi equivoco
unlicensed [ʌn'laɪsənst] *adj* (*Brit*: *to sell alcohol*) no autorizado
unlike [ʌn'laɪk] *adj* distinto ■ *prep* a diferencia de
unlikelihood [ʌn'laɪklɪhud] *n* improbabilidad *f*
unlikely [ʌn'laɪklɪ] *adj* improbable
unlimited [ʌn'lɪmɪtɪd] *adj* ilimitado; ~ **liability** responsabilidad *f* ilimitada
unlisted [ʌn'lɪstɪd] *adj* (*US Tel*) que no figura en la guía; ~ **company** empresa sin cotización en bolsa
unlit [ʌn'lɪt] *adj* (*room*) oscuro, sin luz

unload [ʌn'ləud] *vt* descargar
unlock [ʌn'lɔk] *vt* abrir (con llave)
unlucky [ʌn'lʌkɪ] *adj* desgraciado; (*object, number*) que da mala suerte; **to be** ~ (*person*) tener mala suerte
unmanageable [ʌn'mænɪdʒəbl] *adj* (*unwieldy*: *tool, vehicle*) difícil de manejar; (*situation*) incontrolable
unmanned [ʌn'mænd] *adj* (*spacecraft*) sin tripulación
unmannerly [ʌn'mænəlɪ] *adj* mal educado, descortés
unmarked [ʌn'mɑ:kt] *adj* (*unstained*) sin mancha; ~ **police car** vehículo policial camuflado
unmarried [ʌn'mærɪd] *adj* soltero
unmask [ʌn'mɑ:sk] *vt* desenmascarar
unmatched [ʌn'mætʃt] *adj* incomparable
unmentionable [ʌn'mɛnʃnəbl] *adj* (*topic, vice*) indecible; (*word*) que no se debe decir
unmerciful [ʌn'mə:sɪful] *adj* despiadado
unmistakable [ʌnmɪs'teɪkəbl] *adj* inconfundible
unmistakably [ʌnmɪs'teɪkəblɪ] *adv* de modo inconfundible
unmitigated [ʌn'mɪtɪgeɪtɪd] *adj* rematado, absoluto
unnamed [ʌn'neɪmd] *adj* (*nameless*) sin nombre; (*anonymous*) anónimo
unnatural [ʌn'nætʃrəl] *adj* (*gen*) antinatural; (*manner*) afectado; (*habit*) perverso
unnecessary [ʌn'nɛsəsərɪ] *adj* innecesario, inútil
unnerve [ʌn'nə:v] *vt* (*accident*) poner nervioso; (*hostile attitude*) acobardar; (*long wait, interview*) intimidar
unnoticed [ʌn'nəutɪst] *adj*: **to go** *or* **pass** ~ pasar desapercibido
UNO ['ju:nəu] *n abbr* (= *United Nations Organization*) ONU *f*
unobservant [ʌnəb'zə:vnt] *adj*: **to be** ~ ser poco observador, ser distraído
unobtainable [ʌnəb'teɪnəbl] *adj* inasequible; (*Tel*) inexistente
unobtrusive [ʌnəb'tru:sɪv] *adj* discreto
unoccupied [ʌn'ɔkjupaɪd] *adj* (*house etc*) libre, desocupado
unofficial [ʌnə'fɪʃl] *adj* no oficial; ~ **strike** huelga no oficial
unopened [ʌn'əupənd] *adj* (*letter, present*) sin abrir
unopposed [ʌnə'pəuzd] *adv* (*enter, be elected*) sin oposición
unorthodox [ʌn'ɔ:θədɔks] *adj* poco ortodoxo
unpack [ʌn'pæk] *vi* deshacer las maletas, desempacar (*LAm*)
unpaid [ʌn'peɪd] *adj* (*bill, debt*) sin pagar,

u

impagado; (*Comm*) pendiente; (*holiday*) sin sueldo; (*work*) sin pago, voluntario

unpalatable [ʌnˈpælətəbl] *adj* (*truth*) desagradable

unparalleled [ʌnˈpærəlɛld] *adj* (*unequalled*) sin par; (*unique*) sin precedentes

unpatriotic [ʌnpætrɪˈɔtɪk] *adj* (*person*) poco patriota; (*speech, attitude*) antipatriótico

unplanned [ʌnˈplænd] *adj* (*visit*) imprevisto; (*baby*) no planeado

unpleasant [ʌnˈplɛznt] *adj* (*disagreeable*) desagradable; (*person, manner*) antipático

unplug [ʌnˈplʌg] *vt* desenchufar, desconectar

unpolluted [ʌnpəˈluːtɪd] *adj* impoluto, no contaminado

unpopular [ʌnˈpɔpjuləʳ] *adj* poco popular; **to be ~ with sb** (*person, law*) no ser popular con algn; **to make o.s. ~ (with)** hacerse impopular (con)

unprecedented [ʌnˈprɛsɪdəntɪd] *adj* sin precedentes

unpredictable [ʌnprɪˈdɪktəbl] *adj* imprevisible

unprejudiced [ʌnˈprɛdʒudɪst] *adj* (*not biased*) imparcial; (*having no prejudices*) sin prejuicio

unprepared [ʌnprɪˈpɛəd] *adj* (*person*) desprevenido; (*speech*) improvisado

unprepossessing [ʌnpriːpəˈzɛsɪŋ] *adj* poco atractivo

unprincipled [ʌnˈprɪnsɪpld] *adj* sin escrúpulos

unproductive [ʌnprəˈdʌktɪv] *adj* improductivo; (*discussion*) infructuoso

unprofessional [ʌnprəˈfɛʃənl] *adj* poco profesional; **~ conduct** negligencia

unprofitable [ʌnˈprɔfɪtəbl] *adj* poco provechoso, no rentable

UNPROFOR *n abbr* (= *United Nations Protection Force*) FORPRONU *f*, Unprofor *f*

unprotected [ˈʌnprəˈtɛktɪd] *adj* (*sex*) sin protección

unprovoked [ʌnprəˈvəukt] *adj* no provocado

unpunished [ʌnˈpʌnɪʃt] *adj*: **to go ~** quedar sin castigo, salir impune

unqualified [ʌnˈkwɔlɪfaɪd] *adj* sin título, no cualificado; (*success*) total, incondicional

unquestionably [ʌnˈkwɛstʃənəblɪ] *adv* indiscutiblemente

unquestioning [ʌnˈkwɛstʃənɪŋ] *adj* (*obedience, acceptance*) incondicional

unravel [ʌnˈrævl] *vt* desenmarañar

unreal [ʌnˈrɪəl] *adj* irreal

unrealistic [ʌnrɪəˈlɪstɪk] *adj* poco realista

unreasonable [ʌnˈriːznəbl] *adj* irrazonable; **to make ~ demands on sb** hacer demandas excesivas a algn

unrecognizable [ʌnˈrɛkəgnaɪzəbl] *adj* irreconocible

unrecognized [ʌnˈrɛkəgnaɪzd] *adj* (*talent, genius*) ignorado; (*Pol: regime*) no reconocido

unrecorded [ʌnrɪˈkɔːdɪd] *adj* no registrado

unrefined [ʌnrɪˈfaɪnd] *adj* (*sugar, petroleum*) sin refinar

unrehearsed [ʌnrɪˈhəːst] *adj* (*Theat etc*) improvisado; (*spontaneous*) espontáneo

unrelated [ʌnrɪˈleɪtɪd] *adj* sin relación; (*family*) no emparentado

unrelenting [ʌnrɪˈlɛntɪŋ] *adj* implacable

unreliable [ʌnrɪˈlaɪəbl] *adj* (*person*) informal; (*machine*) poco fiable

unrelieved [ʌnrɪˈliːvd] *adj* (*monotony*) constante

unremitting [ʌnrɪˈmɪtɪŋ] *adj* incesante

unrepeatable [ʌnrɪˈpiːtəbl] *adj* irrepetible

unrepentant [ʌnrɪˈpɛntənt] *adj* (*smoker, sinner*) impenitente; **to be ~ about sth** no arrepentirse de algo

unrepresentative [ʌnrɛprɪˈzɛntətɪv] *adj* (*untypical*) poco representativo

unreserved [ʌnrɪˈzəːvd] *adj* (*seat*) no reservado; (*approval, admiration*) total

unreservedly [ʌnrɪˈzəːvɪdlɪ] *adv* sin reserva

unresponsive [ʌnrɪˈspɔnsɪv] *adj* insensible

unrest [ʌnˈrɛst] *n* inquietud *f*, malestar *m*; (*Pol*) disturbios *mpl*

unrestricted [ʌnrɪˈstrɪktɪd] *adj* (*power, time*) sin restricción; (*access*) libre

unrewarded [ʌnrɪˈwɔːdɪd] *adj* sin recompensa

unripe [ʌnˈraɪp] *adj* verde, inmaduro

unrivalled, unrivaled (*US*) [ʌnˈraɪvəld] *adj* incomparable, sin par

unroll [ʌnˈrəul] *vt* desenrollar

unruffled [ʌnˈrʌfld] *adj* (*person*) imperturbable; (*hair*) liso

unruly [ʌnˈruːlɪ] *adj* indisciplinado

unsafe [ʌnˈseɪf] *adj* (*journey*) peligroso; (*car etc*) inseguro; (*method*) arriesgado; **~ to drink/eat** no apto para el consumo humano

unsaid [ʌnˈsɛd] *adj*: **to leave sth ~** dejar algo sin decir

unsaleable, unsalable (*US*) [ʌnˈseɪləbl] *adj* invendible

unsatisfactory [ˈʌnsætɪsˈfæktərɪ] *adj* poco satisfactorio

unsatisfied [ʌnˈsætɪsfaɪd] *adj* (*desire, need etc*) insatisfecho

unsavoury, unsavory (*US*) [ʌnˈseɪvərɪ] *adj* (*fig*) repugnante

unscathed [ʌnˈskeɪðd] *adj* ileso

unscientific [ʌnsaɪənˈtɪfɪk] *adj* poco científico

unscrew [ʌnˈskruː] *vt* destornillar

unscrupulous [ʌnˈskruːpjuləs] *adj* sin escrúpulos

unseat [ʌn'si:t] *vt* (*rider*) hacer caerse de la silla a; (*fig: official*) hacer perder su escaño a

unsecured [ʌnsɪ'kjuəd] *adj:* ~ **creditor** acreedor(a) *m(f)* común

unseeded [ʌn'si:dɪd] *adj* (*Sport*) no preseleccionado

unseen [ʌn'si:n] *adj* (*person, danger*) oculto

unselfish [ʌn'sɛlfɪʃ] *adj* generoso, poco egoísta; (*act*) desinteresado

unsettled [ʌn'sɛtld] *adj* inquieto; (*situation*) inestable; (*weather*) variable

unsettling [ʌn'sɛtlɪŋ] *adj* perturbador(a), inquietante

unshakable, unshakeable [ʌn'ʃeɪkəbl] *adj* inquebrantable

unshaven [ʌn'ʃeɪvn] *adj* sin afeitar

unsightly [ʌn'saɪtlɪ] *adj* desagradable

unskilled [ʌn'skɪld] *adj:* ~ **workers** mano *f* de obra no cualificada

unsociable [ʌn'səuʃəbl] *adj* insociable

unsocial [ʌn'səuʃl] *adj:* ~ **hours** horario nocturno

unsold [ʌn'səuld] *adj* sin vender

unsolicited [ʌnsə'lɪsɪtɪd] *adj* no solicitado

unsophisticated [ʌnsə'fɪstɪkeɪtɪd] *adj* (*person*) sencillo, ingenuo; (*method*) poco sofisticado

unsound [ʌn'saund] *adj* (*health*) malo; (*in construction: floor, foundations*) defectuoso; (*policy, advice, judgment*) erróneo; (*investment*) poco seguro

unspeakable [ʌn'spi:kəbl] *adj* indecible; (*awful*) incalificable

unspoken [ʌn'spəukn] *adj* (*words*) sobreentendido; (*agreement, approval*) tácito

unstable [ʌn'steɪbl] *adj* inestable

unsteady [ʌn'stɛdɪ] *adj* inestable

unstinting [ʌn'stɪntɪŋ] *adj* (*support etc*) pródigo

unstuck [ʌn'stʌk] *adj:* **to come** ~ despegarse; (*fig*) fracasar

unsubscribe [ʌnsəb'skraɪb] *vt* (*Internet*) borrarse

unsubstantiated [ʌnsəb'stænʃieɪtɪd] *adj* (*rumour, accusation*) no comprobado

unsuccessful [ʌnsək'sɛsful] *adj* (*attempt*) infructuoso; (*writer, proposal*) sin éxito; **to be** ~ (*in attempting sth*) no tener éxito, fracasar

unsuccessfully [ʌnsək'sɛsfulɪ] *adv* en vano, sin éxito

unsuitable [ʌn'su:təbl] *adj* inconveniente, inapropiado; (*time*) inoportuno

unsuited [ʌn'su:tɪd] *adj:* **to be** ~ **for** *or* **to** no ser apropiado para

unsung ['ʌnsʌŋ] *adj:* **an** ~ **hero** un héroe desconocido

unsupported [ʌnsə'pɔ:tɪd] *adj* (*claim*) sin

fundamento; (*theory*) sin base firme

unsure [ʌn'ʃuəʳ] *adj* inseguro, poco seguro; **to be** ~ **of o.s.** estar poco seguro de sí mismo

unsuspecting [ʌnsə'spɛktɪŋ] *adj* confiado

unsweetened [ʌn'swi:tnd] *adj* sin azúcar

unsympathetic [ʌnsɪmpə'θɛtɪk] *adj* (*attitude*) poco comprensivo; (*person*) sin compasión; ~ **(to)** indiferente (a)

untangle [ʌn'tæŋgl] *vt* desenredar

untapped [ʌn'tæpt] *adj* (*resources*) sin explotar

untaxed [ʌn'tækst] *adj* (*goods*) libre de impuestos; (*income*) antes de impuestos

unthinkable [ʌn'θɪŋkəbl] *adj* inconcebible, impensable

unthinkingly [ʌn'θɪŋkɪŋlɪ] *adv* irreflexivamente

untidy [ʌn'taɪdɪ] *adj* (*room*) desordenado, en desorden; (*appearance*) desaliñado

untie [ʌn'taɪ] *vt* desatar

until [ən'tɪl] *prep* hasta ■ *conj* hasta que; ~ **he comes** hasta que venga; ~ **now** hasta ahora; ~ **then** hasta entonces; **from morning** ~ **night** de la mañana a la noche

untimely [ʌn'taɪmlɪ] *adj* inoportuno; (*death*) prematuro

untold [ʌn'təuld] *adj* (*story*) nunca contado; (*suffering*) indecible; (*wealth*) incalculable

untouched [ʌn'tʌtʃt] *adj* (*not used etc*) intacto, sin tocar; (*safe: person*) indemne, ileso; (*unaffected*): ~ **by** insensible a

untoward [ʌntə'wɔ:d] *adj* (*behaviour*) impropio; (*event*) adverso

untrained [ʌn'treɪnd] *adj* (*worker*) sin formación; (*troops*) no entrenado; **to the** ~ **eye** para los no entendidos

untrammelled, untrammeled (*US*) [ʌn'træməld] *adj* ilimitado

untranslatable [ʌntrænz'leɪtəbl] *adj* intraducible

untried [ʌn'traɪd] *adj* (*plan*) no probado

untrue [ʌn'tru:] *adj* (*statement*) falso

untrustworthy [ʌn'trʌstwə:ðɪ] *adj* (*person*) poco fiable

unusable [ʌn'ju:zəbl] *adj* inservible

unused [ʌn'ju:zd] *adj* sin usar, nuevo; **to be** ~ **to (doing) sth** no estar acostumbrado a (hacer) algo

unusual [ʌn'ju:ʒuəl] *adj* insólito, poco común

unusually [ʌn'ju:ʒuəlɪ] *adv:* **he arrived** ~ **early** llegó más temprano que de costumbre

unveil [ʌn'veɪl] *vt* (*statue*) descubrir

unwanted [ʌn'wɔntɪd] *adj* (*person, effect*) no deseado

unwarranted [ʌn'wɔrəntɪd] *adj* injustificado

unwary [ʌn'wɛərɪ] *adj* imprudente, incauto

unwavering [ʌn'weɪvərɪŋ] *adj* inquebrantable

u

unwelcome [ʌn'wɛlkəm] *adj* (*at a bad time*) inoportuno, molesto; **to feel ~** sentirse incómodo

unwell [ʌn'wɛl] *adj*: **to feel ~** estar indispuesto, sentirse mal

unwieldy [ʌn'wiːldɪ] *adj* difícil de manejar

unwilling [ʌn'wɪlɪŋ] *adj*: **to be ~ to do sth** estar poco dispuesto a hacer algo

unwillingly [ʌn'wɪlɪŋlɪ] *adv* de mala gana

unwind [ʌn'waɪnd] (*irreg: like* **wind**) *vt* desenvolver ■ *vi* (*relax*) relajarse

unwise [ʌn'waɪz] *adj* imprudente

unwitting [ʌn'wɪtɪŋ] *adj* inconsciente

unworkable [ʌn'wəːkəbl] *adj* (*plan*) impracticable

unworthy [ʌn'wəːðɪ] *adj* indigno; **to be ~ of sth/to do sth** ser indigno de algo/de hacer algo

unwrap [ʌn'ræp] *vt* deshacer

unwritten [ʌn'rɪtn] *adj* (*agreement*) tácito; (*rules, law*) no escrito

unzip [ʌn'zɪp] *vt* abrir la cremallera de; (*Comput*) descomprimir

● KEYWORD

up [ʌp] *prep*: **to go/be up sth** subir/estar subido en algo; **he went up the stairs/the hill** subió las escaleras/la colina; **we walked/climbed up the hill** subimos la colina; **they live further up the street** viven más arriba en la calle; **go up that road and turn left** sigue por esa calle y gira a la izquierda
■ *adv* **1** (*upwards, higher*) más arriba; **up in the mountains** en lo alto (de la montaña); **put it a bit higher up** ponlo un poco más arriba *or* alto; **to stop halfway up** pararse a la mitad del camino *or* de la subida; **up there** ahí *or* allí arriba; **up above** en lo alto, por encima, arriba; **"this side up"** "este lado hacia arriba"; **to live/go up North** vivir en el norte/ir al norte
2: **to be up** (*out of bed*) estar levantado; (*prices, level*) haber subido; (*building*) estar construido; (*tent*) estar montado; (*curtains, paper etc*) estar puesto; **time's up** se acabó el tiempo; **when the year was up** al terminarse el año; **he's well up in** *or* **on politics** (*Brit: knowledgeable*) está muy al día en política; **what's up?** (*wrong*) ¿qué pasa?; **what's up with him?** ¿qué le pasa?; **prices are up on last year** los precios han subido desde el año pasado
3: **up to** (*as far as*) hasta; **up to now** hasta ahora *or* la fecha
4: **to be up to** (*depending on*): **it's up to you** depende de ti; **he's not up to it** (*job, task etc*) no es capaz de hacerlo; **I don't feel up to it** no me encuentro con ánimos para ello; **his work is not up to the required standard** su trabajo no da la talla; (*col: be doing*): **what is he up to?** ¿qué estará tramando?
■ *vi* (*col*): **she upped and left** se levantó y se marchó
■ *vt* (*col: price*) subir
■ *n*: **ups and downs** altibajos *mpl*

up-and-coming [ʌpənd'kʌmɪŋ] *adj* prometedor(a)

upbeat ['ʌpbiːt] *n* (*Mus*) tiempo no acentuado; (*in economy, prosperity*) aumento
■ *adj* (*col*) optimista, animado

upbraid [ʌp'breɪd] *vt* censurar, reprender

upbringing ['ʌpbrɪŋɪŋ] *n* educación *f*

upcoming ['ʌpkʌmɪŋ] *adj* próximo

update [ʌp'deɪt] *vt* poner al día

upend [ʌp'ɛnd] *vt* poner vertical

upfront [ʌp'frʌnt] *adj* claro, directo ■ *adv* a las claras; (*pay*) por adelantado; **to be ~ about sth** admitir algo claramente

upgrade [ʌp'greɪd] *vt* ascender; (*Comput*) modernizar

upheaval [ʌp'hiːvl] *n* trastornos *mpl*; (*Pol*) agitación *f*

uphill [ʌp'hɪl] *adj* cuesta arriba; (*fig: task*) penoso, difícil ■ *adv*: **to go ~** ir cuesta arriba

uphold [ʌp'həuld] *vt* (*irreg: like* **hold**) sostener

upholstery [ʌp'həulstərɪ] *n* tapicería

upkeep ['ʌpkiːp] *n* mantenimiento

upmarket [ʌp'mɑːkɪt] *adj* (*product*) de categoría

upon [ə'pɔn] *prep* sobre

upper ['ʌpəʳ] *adj* superior, de arriba ■ *n* (*of shoe: also*: **uppers**) pala

upper case *n* (*Typ*) mayúsculas *fpl*

upper-class [ʌpə'klɑːs] *adj* (*district, people, accent*) de clase alta; (*attitude*) altivo

uppercut ['ʌpəkʌt] *n* uppercut *m*, gancho a la cara

upper hand *n*: **to have the ~** tener la sartén por el mango

Upper House *n* (*Pol*): **the ~** la Cámara alta

uppermost ['ʌpəməust] *adj* el más alto; **what was ~ in my mind** lo que me preocupaba más

Upper Volta [-'vəultə] *n* Alto Volta *m*

upright ['ʌpraɪt] *adj* vertical; (*fig*) honrado

uprising ['ʌpraɪzɪŋ] *n* sublevación *f*

uproar ['ʌprɔːʳ] *n* tumulto, escándalo

uproarious [ʌp'rɔːrɪəs] *adj* escandaloso; (*hilarious*) graciosísimo

uproot [ʌp'ruːt] *vt* desarraigar

upset *n* ['ʌpsɛt] (*to plan etc*) revés *m*,

contratiempo; (*Med*) trastorno ∎ *vt*
[ʌp'sɛt] (*irreg: like* **set**) (*glass etc*) volcar; (*spill*)
derramar; (*plan*) alterar; (*person*) molestar,
perturbar ∎ *adj* [ʌp'sɛt] preocupado,
perturbado; (*stomach*) revuelto; **to have a**
stomach ~ (*Brit*) tener el estómago revuelto;
to get ~ molestarse, llevarse un disgusto

upset price *n* (*US, Scottish*) precio mínimo *or*
de reserva

upsetting [ʌp'sɛtɪŋ] *adj* (*worrying*)
inquietante; (*offending*) ofensivo; (*annoying*)
molesto

upshot ['ʌpʃɔt] *n* resultado

upside-down ['ʌpsaɪd'daun] *adv* al revés

upstage ['ʌp'steɪdʒ] *vt* robar protagonismo a

upstairs [ʌp'stɛəz] *adv* arriba ∎ *adj* (*room*) de
arriba ∎ *n* el piso superior

upstart ['ʌpstɑːt] *n* advenedizo

upstream [ʌp'striːm] *adv* río arriba

upsurge ['ʌpsəːdʒ] *n* (*of enthusiasm etc*) arrebato

uptake ['ʌpteɪk] *n*: **he is quick/slow on the ~**
es muy listo/torpe

uptight [ʌp'taɪt] *adj* tenso, nervioso

up-to-date ['ʌptə'deɪt] *adj* moderno, actual;
to bring sb ~ (on sth) poner a algn al
corriente/tanto (de algo)

upturn ['ʌptəːn] *n* (*in luck*) mejora; (*Comm: in*
market) resurgimiento económico; (: *in value of*
currency) aumento

upturned ['ʌptəːnd] *adj*: **~ nose** nariz *f*
respingona

upward ['ʌpwəd] *adj* ascendente ∎ *adv* hacia
arriba

upwardly-mobile ['ʌpwədlɪ'məubaɪl] *adj*:
to be ~ mejorar socialmente

upwards ['ʌpwədz] *adv* hacia arriba

URA *n abbr* (*US*) = **Urban Renewal**
Administration

Ural Mountains ['juərəl-] *npl*: **the ~** (*also*: **the**
Urals) los Montes Urales

uranium [juə'reɪnɪəm] *n* uranio

Uranus [juə'reɪnəs] *n* (*Astro*) Urano

urban ['əːbən] *adj* urbano

urbane [əː'beɪn] *adj* cortés, urbano

urbanization ['əːbənaɪ'zeɪʃən] *n*
urbanización *f*

urchin ['əːtʃɪn] *n* pilluelo, golfillo

Urdu ['uəduː] *n* urdu *m*

urge [əːdʒ] *n* (*force*) impulso; (*desire*) deseo
∎ *vt*: **to ~ sb to do** animar a algn a hacer
▸ **urge on** *vt* animar

urgency ['əːdʒənsɪ] *n* urgencia

urgent ['əːdʒənt] *adj* (*earnest, persistent: plea*)
insistente; (: *tone*) urgente

urgently ['əːdʒəntlɪ] *adv* con urgencia,
urgentemente

urinal ['juərɪnl] *n* (*building*) urinario; (*vessel*)

orinal *m*

urinate ['juərɪneɪt] *vi* orinar

urine ['juərɪn] *n* orina

URL *n abbr* (= *uniform resource locator*) URL *m*

urn [əːn] *n* urna; (*also*: **tea urn**) tetera
(grande)

Uruguay ['juərəgwaɪ] *n* el Uruguay

Uruguayan [juərə'gwaɪən] *adj, n*
uruguayo(-a) *m(f)*

US *n abbr* (= *United States*) EE.UU.

us [ʌs] *pron* nos; (*after prep*) nosotros(-as); (*col*:
me): **give us a kiss** dame un beso; *see also* **me**

USA *n abbr* = **United States of America**; (*Mil*)
= **United States Army**

usable ['juːzəbl] *adj* utilizable

USAF *n abbr* = **United States Air Force**

usage ['juːzɪdʒ] *n* (*Ling*) uso; (*utilization*)
utilización *f*

USB key *n* llave *f* USB, memoria *f* USB

USCG *n abbr* = **United States Coast Guard**

USDA *n abbr* = **United States Department of**
Agriculture

USDAW ['ʌzdɔː] *n abbr* (*Brit*: = *Union of Shop,*
Distributive, and Allied Workers) *sindicato de*
empleados de comercio

USDI *n abbr* = **United States Department of**
the Interior

use *n* [juːs] uso, empleo; (*usefulness*) utilidad
f ∎ *vt* [juːz] usar, emplear; **in ~** en uso; **out**
of ~ en desuso; **to be of ~** servir; **ready**
for ~ listo (para usar); **to make ~ of sth**
aprovecharse *or* servirse de algo; **it's no**
~ (*pointless*) es inútil; (*not useful*) no sirve;
what's this used for? ¿para qué sirve esto?;
to be used to estar acostumbrado a (SP),
acostumbrar; **to get used to** acostumbrarse
a; **she used to do it** (ella) solía *or*
acostumbraba hacerlo
▸ **use up** *vt* agotar

used [juːzd] *adj* (*car*) usado

useful ['juːsful] *adj* útil; **to come in ~** ser útil

usefulness ['juːsfəlnɪs] *n* utilidad *f*

useless ['juːslɪs] *adj* inútil; (*unusable: object*)
inservible

uselessly ['juːslɪslɪ] *adv* inútilmente, en vano

uselessness ['juːslɪsnɪs] *n* inutilidad *f*

user ['juːzəʳ] *n* usuario(-a); (*of petrol, gas etc*)
consumidor(a) *m(f)*

user-friendly ['juːzə'frɛndlɪ] *adj* (*Comput*) fácil
de utilizar

USES *n abbr* = **United States Employment**
Service

usher ['ʌʃəʳ] *n* (*at wedding*) ujier *m*; (*in cinema*
etc) acomodador *m* ∎ *vt*: **to ~ sb in** (*into room*)
hacer pasar a algn; **it ushered in a new era**
(*fig*) inició una nueva era

usherette [ʌʃə'rɛt] *n* (*in cinema*) acomodadora

u

USIA *n abbr* = **United States Information Agency**

USM *n abbr* = **United States Mail; United States Mint**

USN *n abbr* = **United States Navy**

USP *n abbr* = **unique selling point** *or* **proposition**

USPHS *n abbr* = **United States Public Health Service**

USPO *n abbr* = **United States Post Office**

USS *abbr* = **United States Ship (or Steamer)**

USSR *n abbr* (History): **the (former)** ~ la (antigua) U.R.S.S.; *see* **Union of Soviet Socialist Republics**

usu. *abbr* = **usually**

usual ['juːʒuəl] *adj* normal, corriente; **as** ~ como de costumbre, como siempre

usually ['juːʒuəlɪ] *adv* normalmente

usurer ['juːʒərəʳ] *n* usurero

usurp [juːˈzəːp] *vt* usurpar

usury ['juːʒərɪ] *n* usura

UT *abbr* (US) = **Utah**

utensil [juːˈtɛnsl] *n* utensilio; **kitchen utensils** batería de cocina

uterus ['juːtərəs] *n* útero

utilitarian [juːtɪlɪˈtɛərɪən] *adj* utilitario

utility [juːˈtɪlɪtɪ] *n* utilidad *f*

utility room *n* trascocina

utilization [juːtɪlaɪˈzeɪʃən] *n* utilización *f*

utilize ['juːtɪlaɪz] *vt* utilizar

utmost ['ʌtməust] *adj* mayor ■ *n*: **to do one's** ~ hacer todo lo posible; **it is of the** ~ **importance that ...** es de la mayor importancia que ...

utter ['ʌtəʳ] *adj* total, completo ■ *vt* pronunciar, proferir

utterance ['ʌtərns] *n* palabras *fpl*, declaración *f*

utterly ['ʌtəlɪ] *adv* completamente, totalmente

U-turn ['juːtəːn] *n* cambio de sentido; (*fig*) giro de 180 grados

Uzbekistan [ʌzbɛkɪˈstaːn] *n* Uzbekistán *m*

Vv

V, v [viː] *n* (*letter*) V, v *f*; **V for Victor** V de
Valencia

v. *abbr* (= *verse*) vers.°; (= *vide: see*) V, vid., vide;
(= *versus*) vs.; = **volt**

VA, Va. *abbr* (*US*) = **Virginia**

vac [væk] *n abbr* (*Brit col*) = **vacation**

vacancy ['veɪkənsɪ] *n* (*Brit: job*) vacante *f*; (*room*)
cuarto libro; **have you any vacancies?** ¿tiene
or hay alguna habitación *or* algún cuarto libre?

vacant ['veɪkənt] *adj* desocupado, libre;
(*expression*) distraído

vacant lot *n* (*US*) solar *m*

vacate [və'keɪt] *vt* (*house*) desocupar; (*job*)
dejar (vacante)

vacation [və'keɪʃən] *n* vacaciones *fpl*; **on ~**
de vacaciones; **to take a ~** (*esp US*) tomarse
unas vacaciones

vacation course *n* curso de vacaciones

vacationer [və'keɪʃənəʳ], **vacationist**
[və'keɪʃənɪst] *n* (*US*) turista *m/f*

vaccinate ['væksɪneɪt] *vt* vacunar

vaccination [væksɪ'neɪʃən] *n* vacunación *f*

vaccine ['væksiːn] *n* vacuna

vacuum ['vækjum] *n* vacío

vacuum bottle *n* (*US*) = **vacuum flask**

vacuum cleaner *n* aspiradora

vacuum flask *n* (*Brit*) termo

vacuum-packed ['vækjum'pækt] *adj*
envasado al vacío

vagabond ['vægəbɔnd] *n* vagabundo(-a)

vagary ['veɪgərɪ] *n* capricho

vagina [və'dʒaɪnə] *n* vagina

vagrancy ['veɪgrənsɪ] *n* vagabundeo

vagrant ['veɪgrənt] *n* vagabundo(-a)

vague [veɪg] *adj* vago; (*blurred: memory*)
borroso; (*uncertain*) incierto, impreciso;
(*person*) distraído; **I haven't the vaguest
idea** no tengo la más remota idea

vaguely ['veɪglɪ] *adv* vagamente

vagueness ['veɪgnɪs] *n* vaguedad *f*;
imprecisión *f*; (*absent-mindedness*) despiste *m*

vain [veɪn] *adj* (*conceited*) presumido; (*useless*)
vano, inútil; **in ~** en vano

vainly ['veɪnlɪ] *adv* (*to no effect*) en vano;
(*conceitedly*) vanidosamente

valance ['væləns] *n* (*for bed*) volante alrededor de
la colcha o sábana que cuelga hasta el suelo

valedictory [vælɪ'dɪktərɪ] *adj* de despedida

valentine ['væləntaɪn] *n* (*also:* **valentine
card**) tarjeta del Día de los Enamorados

valet ['væleɪ] *n* ayuda *m* de cámara

valet service *n* (*for clothes*) planchado

valiant ['væljənt] *adj* valiente

valiantly ['væljəntlɪ] *adv* valientemente,
con valor

valid ['vælɪd] *adj* válido; (*ticket*) valedero;
(*law*) vigente

validate ['vælɪdeɪt] *vt* (*contract, document*)
convalidar; (*argument, claim*) dar validez a

validity [və'lɪdɪtɪ] *n* validez *f*; vigencia

valise [və'liːz] *n* maletín *m*

valley ['vælɪ] *n* valle *m*

valour, valor (*US*) ['væləʳ] *n* valor *m*, valentía

valuable ['væljuəbl] *adj* (*jewel*) de valor; (*time*)
valioso; **valuables** *npl* objetos *mpl* de valor

valuation [vælju'eɪʃən] *n* tasación *f*, valuación *f*

value ['væljuː] *n* valor *m*; (*importance*)
importancia ■ *vt* (*fix price of*) tasar, valorar;
(*esteem*) apreciar; **values** *npl* (*moral*) valores
mpl morales; **to lose (in) ~** (*currency*) bajar;
(*property*) desvalorizarse; **to gain (in) ~**
(*currency*) subir; (*property*) revalorizarse; **you
get good ~ (for money) in that shop** la
relación calidad-precio es muy buena en
esa tienda; **to be of great ~ to sb** ser de
gran valor para algn; **it is valued at £8** está
valorado en ocho libras

value added tax *n* (*Brit*) impuesto sobre el
valor añadido *or* agregado (*LAm*)

valued ['væljuːd] *adj* (*appreciated*) apreciado

valueless ['væljuːlɪs] *adj* sin valor

valuer ['væljuːəʳ] *n* tasador(a) *m(f)*

valve [vælv] *n* (*Anat, Tech*) válvula

vampire ['væmpaɪəʳ] *n* vampiro

van [væn] *n* (*Aut*) furgoneta, camioneta (*LAm*); (*Brit Rail*) furgón *m* (de equipajes)

V and A *n abbr* (*Brit*) = **Victoria and Albert Museum**

vandal ['vændl] *n* vándalo(-a)

vandalism ['vændəlɪzəm] *n* vandalismo

vandalize ['vændələɪz] *vt* dañar, destruir, destrozar

vanguard ['vænɡɑːd] *n* vanguardia

vanilla [və'nɪlə] *n* vainilla

vanish ['vænɪʃ] *vi* desaparecer, esfumarse

vanity ['vænɪtɪ] *n* vanidad *f*

vanity case *n* neceser *m*

vantage point ['vɑːntɪdʒ-] *n* posición *f* ventajosa

vaporize ['veɪpəraɪz] *vt* vaporizar ∎ *vi* vaporizarse

vapour, vapor (*US*) ['veɪpə'] *n* vapor *m*; (*on breath, window*) vaho

vapour trail, vapor trail (*US*) *n* (*Aviat*) estela

variable ['vɛərɪəbl] *adj* variable ∎ *n* variable *f*

variance ['vɛərɪəns] *n*: **to be at ~ (with)** estar en desacuerdo (con), no cuadrar (con)

variant ['vɛərɪənt] *n* variante *f*

variation [vɛərɪ'eɪʃən] *n* variación *f*

varicose ['værɪkəus] *adj*: **~ veins** varices *fpl*

varied ['vɛərɪd] *adj* variado

variety [və'raɪətɪ] *n* variedad *f*, diversidad *f*; (*quantity*) surtido; **for a ~ of reasons** por varias *or* diversas razones

variety show *n* espectáculo de variedades

various ['vɛərɪəs] *adj* varios(-as), diversos(-as); **at ~ times** (*different*) en distintos momentos; (*several*) varias veces

varnish ['vɑːnɪʃ] *n* (*gen*) barniz *m*; (*also*: **nail varnish**) esmalte *m* ∎ *vt* (*gen*) barnizar; (*nails*) pintar (con esmalte)

vary ['vɛərɪ] *vt* variar; (*change*) cambiar ∎ *vi* variar; (*disagree*) discrepar; **to ~ with** *or* **according to** variar según *or* de acuerdo con

varying ['vɛərɪɪŋ] *adj* diversos(-as)

vase [vɑːz] *n* florero

vasectomy [və'sɛktəmɪ] *n* vasectomía

Vaseline® ['væsɪliːn] *n* vaselina®

vast [vɑːst] *adj* enorme; (*success*) abrumador(a), arrollador(a)

vastly ['vɑːstlɪ] *adv* enormemente

vastness ['vɑːstnɪs] *n* inmensidad *f*

VAT [væt] *n abbr* (*Brit*: = *value added tax*) IVA *m*

vat [væt] *n* tina, tinaja

Vatican ['vætɪkən] *n*: **the ~** el Vaticano

vatman ['vætmæn] *n* (*Brit col*) inspector *m or* recaudador *m* del IVA; **"how to avoid the ~"** "cómo evitar pagar el IVA"

vaudeville ['vəudəvɪl] *n* (*US*) vodevil *m*

vault [vɔːlt] *n* (*of roof*) bóveda; (*tomb*) tumba; (*in bank*) cámara acorazada ∎ *vt* (*also*: **vault over**) saltar (por encima de)

vaunted ['vɔːntɪd] *adj*: **much ~** cacareado

VC *n abbr* = **vice-chairman**; **vice-chancellor**; (*Brit*: = *Victoria Cross*) condecoración militar

VCR *n abbr* = **video cassette recorder**

VD *n abbr see* **venereal disease**

VDU *n abbr see* **visual display unit**

veal [viːl] *n* ternera

veer [vɪə'] *vi* (*ship*) virar

veg. [vɛdʒ] *n abbr* (*Brit col*) = **vegetable(s)**

vegan ['viːɡən] *n* vegetariano(-a) estricto(-a)

vegeburger, veggieburger ['vɛdʒɪbəːɡə'] *n* hamburguesa vegetal

vegetable ['vɛdʒtəbl] *n* (*Bot*) vegetal *m*; (*edible plant*) legumbre *f*, hortaliza ∎ *adj* vegetal; **vegetables** *npl* (*cooked*) verduras *fpl*

vegetable garden *n* huerta, huerto

vegetarian [vɛdʒɪ'tɛərɪən] *adj*, *n* vegetariano(-a) *m(f)*

vegetate ['vɛdʒɪteɪt] *vi* vegetar

vegetation [vɛdʒɪ'teɪʃən] *n* vegetación *f*

vegetative ['vɛdʒɪtətɪv] *adj* vegetativo; (*Bot*) vegetal

vehemence ['viːɪməns] *n* vehemencia; violencia

vehement ['viːɪmənt] *adj* vehemente, apasionado; (*dislike, hatred*) violento

vehicle ['viːɪkl] *n* vehículo; (*fig*) vehículo, medio

vehicular [vɪ'hɪkjulə'] *adj*: **~ traffic** circulación *f* rodada

veil [veɪl] *n* velo ∎ *vt* velar; **under a ~ of secrecy** (*fig*) en el mayor secreto

veiled [veɪld] *adj* (*also fig*) disimulado, velado

vein [veɪn] *n* vena; (*of ore etc*) veta

Velcro® ['vɛlkrəu] *n* velcro® *m*

vellum ['vɛləm] *n* (*writing paper*) papel *m* vitela

velocity [vɪ'lɔsɪtɪ] *n* velocidad *f*

velour [və'luə'] *n* terciopelo

velvet ['vɛlvɪt] *n* terciopelo ∎ *adj* aterciopelado

vendetta [vɛn'dɛtə] *n* vendetta

vending machine ['vɛndɪŋ-] *n* máquina expendedora, expendedor *m*

vendor ['vɛndə'] *n* vendedor(a) *m(f)*; **street ~** vendedor(a) *m(f)* callejero(-a)

veneer [və'nɪə'] *n* chapa, enchapado; (*fig*) barniz *m*

venereal [vɪ'nɪərɪəl] *adj*: **~ disease (VD)** enfermedad *f* venérea

Venetian blind [vɪ'niːʃən-] *n* persiana

Venezuela [vɛnɛ'zweɪlə] *n* Venezuela

Venezuelan [vɛnɛ'zweɪlən] *adj*, *n* venezolano(-a) *m(f)*

vengeance ['vɛndʒəns] *n* venganza; **with a ~** (*fig*) con creces

vengeful ['vɛndʒful] *adj* vengativo
Venice ['vɛnɪs] *n* Venecia
venison ['vɛnɪsn] *n* carne *f* de venado
venom ['vɛnəm] *n* veneno
venomous ['vɛnəməs] *adj* venenoso
venomously ['vɛnəməslɪ] *adv* con odio
vent [vɛnt] *n* (*opening*) abertura; (*air-hole*) respiradero; (*in wall*) rejilla (de ventilación) ■ *vt* (*fig: feelings*) desahogar
ventilate ['vɛntɪleɪt] *vt* ventilar
ventilation [vɛntɪ'leɪʃən] *n* ventilación *f*
ventilation shaft *n* pozo de ventilación
ventilator ['vɛntɪleɪtəʳ] *n* ventilador *m*
ventriloquist [vɛn'trɪləkwɪst] *n* ventrílocuo(-a)
venture ['vɛntʃəʳ] *n* empresa ■ *vt* arriesgar; (*opinion*) ofrecer ■ *vi* arriesgarse, lanzarse; **a business ~** una empresa comercial; **to ~ to do sth** aventurarse a hacer algo
venture capital *n* capital *m* arriesgado
venue ['vɛnjuː] *n* (*meeting place*) lugar *m* de reunión; (*for concert*) local *m*
Venus ['viːnəs] *n* (*Astro*) Venus *m*
veracity [və'ræsɪtɪ] *n* veracidad *f*
veranda, verandah [və'rændə] *n* terraza; (*with glass*) galería
verb [vəːb] *n* verbo
verbal ['vəːbl] *adj* verbal
verbally ['vəːbəlɪ] *adv* verbalmente, de palabra
verbatim [vəː'beɪtɪm] *adj, adv* al pie de la letra, palabra por palabra
verbose [vəː'bəus] *adj* prolijo
verdict ['vəːdɪkt] *n* veredicto, fallo; (*fig: opinion*) opinión *f*, juicio; **~ of guilty/not guilty** veredicto de culpabilidad/inocencia
verge [vəːdʒ] *n* (*Brit*) borde *m*; **to be on the ~ of doing sth** estar a punto de hacer algo
  ▶ **verge on** *vt fus* rayar en
verger ['vəːdʒəʳ] *n* sacristán *m*
verification [vɛrɪfɪ'keɪʃən] *n* comprobación *f*, verificación *f*
verify ['vɛrɪfaɪ] *vt* comprobar, verificar; (*prove the truth of*) confirmar
veritable ['vɛrɪtəbl] *adj* verdadero, auténtico
vermin ['vəːmɪn] *npl* (*animals*) bichos *mpl*; (*insects*) sabandijas *fpl*; (*fig*) sabandijas *fpl*
vermouth ['vəːməθ] *n* vermut *m*
vernacular [və'nækjuləʳ] *n* lengua vernácula
versatile ['vəːsətaɪl] *adj* (*person*) polifacético; (*machine, tool etc*) versátil
versatility [vəːsə'tɪlɪtɪ] *n* versatilidad *f*
verse [vəːs] *n* versos *mpl*, poesía; (*stanza*) estrofa; (*in bible*) versículo; **in ~** en verso
versed [vəːst] *adj*: **(well-)~ in** versado en
version ['vəːʃən] *n* versión *f*
versus ['vəːsəs] *prep* contra

vertebra (*pl* **vertebrae**) ['vəːtɪbrə, briː] *n* vértebra
vertebrate ['vəːtɪbrɪt] *n* vertebrado
vertical ['vəːtɪkl] *adj* vertical
vertically ['vəːtɪkəlɪ] *adv* verticalmente
vertigo ['vəːtɪgəu] *n* vértigo; **to suffer from ~** tener vértigo
verve [vəːv] *n* brío
very ['vɛrɪ] *adv* muy ■ *adj*: **the ~ book which** el mismo libro que; **the ~ last** el último (de todos); **at the ~ least** al menos; **~ much** muchísimo; **~ well/little** muy bien/poco; **~ high frequency** (*Radio*) frecuencia muy alta; **it's ~ cold** hace mucho frío; **the ~ thought (of it) alarms me** con sólo pensarlo me entra miedo
vespers ['vɛspəz] *npl* vísperas *fpl*
vessel ['vɛsl] *n* (*Anat*) vaso; (*ship*) barco; (*container*) vasija
vest [vɛst] *n* (*Brit*) camiseta; (*US: waistcoat*) chaleco
vested interests ['vɛstɪd-] *npl* (*Comm*) intereses *mpl* creados
vestibule ['vɛstɪbjuːl] *n* vestíbulo
vestige ['vɛstɪdʒ] *n* vestigio, rastro
vestry ['vɛstrɪ] *n* sacristía
Vesuvius [vɪ'suːvɪəs] *n* Vesubio
vet [vɛt] *n abbr* = **veterinary surgeon**; (*US: col*) = **veteran** ■ *vt* revisar; **to ~ sb for a job** someter a investigación a algn para un trabajo
veteran ['vɛtərn] *n* veterano(-a) ■ *adj*: **she is a ~ campaigner for ...** es una veterana de la campaña de ...
veteran car *n* coche *m* antiguo
veterinarian [vɛtrɪ'nɛərɪən] *n* (*US*) = **veterinary surgeon**
veterinary ['vɛtrɪnərɪ] *adj* veterinario
veterinary surgeon *n* (*Brit*) veterinario(-a)
veto ['viːtəu] *n* (*pl* **vetoes**) veto ■ *vt* prohibir, vedar; **to put a ~ on** vetar
vetting ['vɛtɪŋ] *n*: **positive ~** *investigación gubernamental de los futuros altos cargos de la Administración*
vex [vɛks] *vt* (*irritate*) fastidiar; (*make impatient*) impacientar
vexed [vɛkst] *adj* (*question*) controvertido
vexing ['vɛksɪŋ] *adj* molesto, engorroso
VFD *n abbr* (*US*) = **voluntary fire department**
VG *n abbr* (*Brit Scol etc*: = *very good*) S (= *sobresaliente*)
VHF *abbr* (= *very high frequency*) VHF *f*
VI *abbr* (*US*) = **Virgin Islands**
via ['vaɪə] *prep* por, por vía de
viability [vaɪə'bɪlɪtɪ] *n* viabilidad *f*
viable ['vaɪəbl] *adj* viable
viaduct ['vaɪədʌkt] *n* viaducto

V

vial ['vaɪəl] n frasco pequeño
vibes [vaɪbz] npl (col): **I got good/bad ~** me dio buen/mal rollo
vibrant ['vaɪbrənt] adj (lively, bright) vivo; (full of emotion: voice) vibrante; (colour) fuerte
vibraphone ['vaɪbrəfəʊn] n vibráfono
vibrate [vaɪ'breɪt] vi vibrar
vibration [vaɪ'breɪʃən] n vibración f
vibrator [vaɪ'breɪtəʳ] n vibrador m
vicar ['vɪkəʳ] n párroco
vicarage ['vɪkərɪdʒ] n parroquia
vicarious [vɪ'kɛərɪəs] adj indirecto; (responsibility) delegado
vice [vaɪs] n (evil) vicio; (Tech) torno de banco
vice- [vaɪs] pref vice...
vice-chairman ['vaɪs'tʃɛəmən] n vicepresidente m
vice-chancellor [vaɪs'tʃɑːnsələʳ] n (Brit Univ) rector(a) m(f)
vice-president [vaɪs'prɛzɪdənt] n vicepresidente(-a) m(f)
viceroy ['vaɪsrɔɪ] n virrey m
vice versa ['vaɪsɪ'vəːsə] adv viceversa
vicinity [vɪ'sɪnɪtɪ] n (area) vecindad f; (nearness) proximidad f; **in the ~ (of)** cercano (a)
vicious ['vɪʃəs] adj (remark) malicioso; (blow) brutal; **a ~ circle** un círculo vicioso
viciousness ['vɪʃəsnɪs] n brutalidad f
vicissitudes [vɪ'sɪsɪtjuːdz] npl vicisitudes fpl, peripecias fpl
victim ['vɪktɪm] n víctima; **to be the ~ of** ser víctima de
victimization [vɪktɪmaɪ'zeɪʃən] n persecución f; (of striker etc) represalias fpl
victimize ['vɪktɪmaɪz] vt (strikers etc) tomar represalias contra
victor ['vɪktəʳ] n vencedor(a) m(f)
Victorian [vɪk'tɔːrɪən] adj victoriano
victorious [vɪk'tɔːrɪəs] adj vencedor(a)
victory ['vɪktərɪ] n victoria; **to win a ~ over sb** obtener una victoria sobre algn
video ['vɪdɪəʊ] cpd de vídeo ■ n vídeo ■ vt grabar (en vídeo)
video call n llamada de vídeo
video camera n videocámara, cámara de vídeo
video cassette n videocassette f
video cassette recorder n = **video recorder**
videodisk ['vɪdɪəʊdɪsk] n videodisco
video game n videojuego
video nasty n vídeo de violencia y/o porno duro
videophone ['vɪdɪəʊfəʊn] n videoteléfono, videófono
video recorder n vídeo, videocassette f
video recording n videograbación f
video tape n cinta de vídeo

vie [vaɪ] vi: **to ~ with** competir con
Vienna [vɪ'ɛnə] n Viena
Viennese [vɪə'niːz] adj, n vienés(-esa) m(f)
Vietnam, Viet Nam [vjɛt'næm] n Vietnam m
Vietnamese [vjɛtnə'miːz] adj vietnamita ■ n (pl inv) vietnamita m/f; (Ling) vietnamita m
view [vjuː] n vista; (landscape) paisaje m; (opinion) opinión f, criterio ■ vt (look at) mirar; (examine) examinar; **on ~** (in museum etc) expuesto; **in full ~ of sb** a la vista de algn; **to be within ~ (of sth)** estar a la vista (de algo); **an overall ~ of the situation** una visión de conjunto de la situación; **in ~ of the fact that** en vista de que; **to take or hold the ~ that ...** opinar or pensar que ...; **with a ~ to doing sth** con miras or vistas a hacer algo
viewdata ['vjuːdeɪtə] n (Brit) videodatos mpl
viewer ['vjuːəʳ] n (small projector) visionadora; (TV) televidente m/f, telespectador(a) m(f)
viewfinder ['vjuːfaɪndəʳ] n visor m de imagen
viewpoint ['vjuːpɔɪnt] n punto de vista
vigil ['vɪdʒɪl] n vigilia; **to keep ~** velar
vigilance ['vɪdʒɪləns] n vigilancia
vigilance committee n (US) comité m de autodefensa
vigilant ['vɪdʒɪlənt] adj vigilante
vigilante [vɪdʒɪ'læntɪ] n vecino/a que se toma la justicia por su mano
vigorous ['vɪɡərəs] adj enérgico, vigoroso
vigorously ['vɪɡərəslɪ] adv enérgicamente, vigorosamente
vigour, vigor (US) ['vɪɡəʳ] n energía, vigor m
vile [vaɪl] adj (action) vil, infame; (smell) repugnante
vilify ['vɪlɪfaɪ] vt denigrar, vilipendiar
villa ['vɪlə] n (country house) casa de campo; (suburban house) chalet m
village ['vɪlɪdʒ] n aldea
villager ['vɪlɪdʒəʳ] n aldeano(-a)
villain ['vɪlən] n (scoundrel) malvado(-a); (criminal) maleante m/f; see also **pantomime**
VIN n abbr (US) = **vehicle identification number**
vinaigrette [vɪneɪ'ɡrɛt] n vinagreta
vindicate ['vɪndɪkeɪt] vt vindicar, justificar
vindication [vɪndɪ'keɪʃən] n: **in ~ of** en justificación de
vindictive [vɪn'dɪktɪv] adj vengativo
vine [vaɪn] n vid f
vinegar ['vɪnɪɡəʳ] n vinagre m
vine-growing ['vaɪnɡrəʊɪŋ] adj (region) viticultor(a)
vineyard ['vɪnjɑːd] n viña, viñedo
vintage ['vɪntɪdʒ] n (year) vendimia, cosecha; **the 1970 ~** la cosecha de 1970
vintage car n coche m antiguo or de época

vintage wine *n* vino añejo
vintage year *n*: **it's been a ~ for plays** ha sido un año destacado en lo que a teatro se refiere
vinyl ['vaɪnl] *n* vinilo
viola [vɪ'əʊlə] *n* (*Mus*) viola
violate ['vaɪəleɪt] *vt* violar
violation [vaɪə'leɪʃən] *n* violación *f*; **in ~ of sth** en violación de algo
violence ['vaɪələns] *n* violencia; **acts of ~** actos *mpl* de violencia
violent ['vaɪələnt] *adj* (*gen*) violento; (*pain*) intenso; **a ~ dislike of sb/sth** una profunda antipatía *or* manía a algn/algo
violently ['vaɪələntlɪ] *adv* (*severely: ill, angry*) muy
violet ['vaɪələt] *adj* violado, violeta ∎ *n* (*plant*) violeta
violin [vaɪə'lɪn] *n* violín *m*
violinist [vaɪə'lɪnɪst] *n* violinista *m/f*
VIP *n abbr* (= *very important person*) VIP *m*
viper ['vaɪpəʳ] *n* víbora
viral ['vaɪərəl] *adj* vírico
virgin ['vɜːdʒɪn] *n* virgen *m/f* ∎ *adj* virgen; **the Blessed V~** la Santísima Virgen
virginity [vɜː'dʒɪnɪtɪ] *n* virginidad *f*
Virgo ['vɜːgəʊ] *n* Virgo
virile ['vɪraɪl] *adj* viril
virility [vɪ'rɪlɪtɪ] *n* virilidad *f*
virtual ['vɜːtjʊəl] *adj* (*also Comput, Phys*) virtual
virtually ['vɜːtjʊəlɪ] *adv* (*almost*) prácticamente, virtualmente; **it is ~ impossible** es prácticamente imposible
virtual reality *n* (*Comput*) realidad *f* virtual
virtue ['vɜːtjuː] *n* virtud *f*; **by ~ of** en virtud de
virtuosity [vɜːtjʊ'ɒsɪtɪ] *n* virtuosismo
virtuoso [vɜːtjʊ'əʊsəʊ] *n* virtuoso
virtuous ['vɜːtjʊəs] *adj* virtuoso
virulence ['vɪrʊləns] *n* virulencia
virulent ['vɪrʊlənt] *adj* virulento, violento
virus ['vaɪərəs] *n* virus *m inv*
visa ['viːzə] *n* visado, visa (*LAm*)
vis-à-vis [viːzə'viː] *prep* con respecto a
viscount ['vaɪkaʊnt] *n*. vizconde *m*
viscous ['vɪskəs] *adj* viscoso
vise [vaɪs] *n* (*US Tech*) = **vice**
visibility [vɪzɪ'bɪlɪtɪ] *n* visibilidad *f*
visible ['vɪzəbl] *adj* visible; **~ exports/imports** exportaciones *fpl*/importaciones *fpl* visibles
visibly ['vɪzɪblɪ] *adv* visiblemente
vision ['vɪʒən] *n* (*sight*) vista; (*foresight: in dream*) visión *f*
visionary ['vɪʒənrɪ] *n* visionario(-a)
visit ['vɪzɪt] *n* visita ∎ *vt* (*person*) visitar, hacer una visita a; (*place*) ir a, (ir a) conocer; **to pay**

a ~ **to** (*person*) visitar a; **on a private/official ~** en visita privada/oficial
visiting ['vɪzɪtɪŋ] *adj* (*speaker, professor*) invitado; (*team*) visitante
visiting card *n* tarjeta de visita
visiting hours *npl* (*in hospital etc*) horas *fpl* de visita
visitor *n* (*gen*) visitante *m/f*; (*to one's house*) visita; (*tourist*) turista *m/f*; (*tripper*) excursionista *m/f*; **to have visitors** (*at home*) tener visita
visitors' book *n* libro de visitas
visor ['vaɪzəʳ] *n* visera
VISTA ['vɪstə] *n abbr* (= *Volunteers In Service to America*) *programa de ayuda voluntaria a los necesitados*
vista ['vɪstə] *n* vista, panorama
visual ['vɪzjʊəl] *adj* visual
visual aid *n* medio visual
visual arts *npl* artes *fpl* plásticas
visual display unit *n* unidad *f* de despliegue visual, monitor *m*
visualize ['vɪzjʊəlaɪz] *vt* imaginarse; (*foresee*) prever
visually ['vɪzjʊəlɪ] *adv*: **~ handicapped** con visión deficiente
vital ['vaɪtl] *adj* (*essential*) esencial, imprescindible; (*crucial*) crítico; (*person*) enérgico, vivo; (*of life*) vital; **of ~ importance (to sb/sth)** de suma importancia (para algn/algo)
vitality [vaɪ'tælɪtɪ] *n* energía, vitalidad *f*
vitally ['vaɪtəlɪ] *adv*: **~ important** de suma importancia
vital statistics *npl* (*of population*) estadísticas *fpl* demográficas; (*col: of woman*) medidas *fpl* (corporales)
vitamin ['vɪtəmɪn] *n* vitamina
vitamin pill *n* pastilla de vitaminas
vitreous ['vɪtrɪəs] *adj* (*china, enamel*) vítreo
vitriolic [vɪtrɪ'ɒlɪk] *adj* mordaz
viva ['vaɪvə] *n* (*also:* **viva voce**) examen *m* oral
vivacious [vɪ'veɪʃəs] *adj* vivaz, alegre
vivacity [vɪ'væsɪtɪ] *n* vivacidad *f*
vivid ['vɪvɪd] *adj* (*account*) gráfico; (*light*) intenso; (*imagination*) vivo
vividly ['vɪvɪdlɪ] *adv* (*describe*) gráficamente; (*remember*) como si fuera hoy
vivisection [vɪvɪ'sɛkʃən] *n* vivisección *f*
vixen ['vɪksn] *n* (*Zool*) zorra, raposa; (*pej: woman*) arpía, bruja
viz *abbr* (= *vide licet: namely*) v.gr.
VLF *abbr* = **very low frequency**
V-neck ['viːnɛk] *n* cuello de pico
VOA *n abbr* (= *Voice of America*) Voz *f* de América
vocabulary [vəʊ'kæbjʊlərɪ] *n* vocabulario
vocal ['vəʊkl] *adj* vocal; (*articulate*) elocuente

V

vocal cords *npl* cuerdas *fpl* vocales
vocalist ['vəukəlɪst] *n* cantante *m/f*
vocation [vəu'keɪʃən] *n* vocación *f*
vocational [vəu'keɪʃənl] *adj* vocacional; ~ **guidance** orientación *f* profesional; ~ **training** formación *f* profesional
vociferous [və'sɪfərəs] *adj* vociferante
vociferously [və'sɪfərəslɪ] *adv* a gritos
vodka ['vɒdkə] *n* vodka *m*
vogue [vəug] *n* boga, moda; **to be in** ~, **be the** ~ estar de moda *or* en boga
voice [vɔɪs] *n* voz *f* ■ *vt* (*opinion*) expresar; **in a loud/soft** ~ en voz alta/baja; **to give** ~ **to** expresar
voice mail *n* (*Tel*) fonobuzón *m*
voice-over ['vɔɪsəuvə'] *n* voz *f* en off
void [vɔɪd] *n* vacío; (*hole*) hueco ■ *adj* (*invalid*) nulo, inválido; (*empty*): ~ **of** carente *or* desprovisto de
voile [vɔɪl] *n* gasa
vol. *abbr* (= *volume*) t
volatile ['vɒlətaɪl] *adj* volátil; (*Comput: memory*) no permanente
volcanic [vɒl'kænɪk] *adj* volcánico
volcano (*pl* **volcanoes**) [vɒl'keɪnəu] *n* volcán *m*
volition [və'lɪʃən] *n*: **of one's own** ~ por su propia voluntad
volley ['vɒlɪ] *n* (*of gunfire*) descarga; (*of stones etc*) lluvia; (*Tennis etc*) volea
volleyball *n* voleibol *m*, balonvolea *m*
volt [vəult] *n* voltio
voltage ['vəultɪdʒ] *n* voltaje *m*; **high/low** ~ alto/bajo voltaje, alta/baja tensión
volte-face ['vɒlt'fɑːs] *n* viraje *m*
voluble ['vɒljubl] *adj* locuaz, hablador(a)
volume ['vɒljuːm] *n* (*of tank*) volumen *m*; (*book*) tomo; ~ **one/two** (*of book*) tomo primero/segundo; **volumes** *npl* (*great quantities*) cantidad *fsg*; **his expression spoke volumes** su expresión (lo) decía todo
volume control *n* (*Radio, TV*) (botón *m* del) volumen *m*
volume discount *n* (*Comm*) descuento por volumen de compras
voluminous [və'luːmɪnəs] *adj* (*large*) voluminoso; (*prolific*) prolífico
voluntarily ['vɒləntrɪlɪ] *adv* libremente, voluntariamente
voluntary ['vɒləntərɪ] *adj* voluntario, espontáneo
voluntary liquidation *n* (*Comm*) liquidación *f* voluntaria
voluntary redundancy *n* (*Brit*) despido voluntario
volunteer [vɒlən'tɪə'] *n* voluntario(-a) ■ *vi* ofrecerse (de voluntario); **to** ~ **to do** ofrecerse a hacer
voluptuous [və'lʌptjuəs] *adj* voluptuoso
vomit ['vɒmɪt] *n* vómito ■ *vt, vi* vomitar
voracious [və'reɪʃəs] *adj* voraz; (*reader*) ávido
vote [vəut] *n* voto; (*votes cast*) votación *f*; (*right to vote*) derecho a votar; (*franchise*) sufragio ■ *vt* (*chairman*) elegir ■ *vi* votar, ir a votar; ~ **of thanks** voto de gracias; **to put sth to the** ~, **to take a** ~ **on sth** someter algo a votación; ~ **for** *or* **in favour of/against** voto a favor de/en contra de; **to** ~ **to do sth** votar por hacer algo; **he was voted secretary** fue elegido secretario por votación; **to pass a** ~ **of confidence/no confidence** aprobar un voto de confianza/de censura
voter ['vəutə'] *n* votante *m/f*
voting ['vəutɪŋ] *n* votación *f*
voting paper *n* (*Brit*) papeleta de votación
voting right *n* derecho a voto
vouch [vautʃ] : **to** ~ **for** *vt fus* garantizar, responder de
voucher ['vautʃə'] *n* (*for meal, petrol*) vale *m*; **luncheon/travel** ~ vale *m* de comida/de viaje
vow [vau] *n* voto ■ *vi* hacer voto; **to take** *or* **make a** ~ **to do sth** jurar hacer algo, comprometerse a hacer algo
vowel ['vauəl] *n* vocal *f*
voyage ['vɔɪɪdʒ] *n* (*journey*) viaje *m*; (*crossing*) travesía
voyeur [vwɑː'jəː'] *n* voyeur *m/f*, mirón(-ona) *m(f)*
VP *n abbr* (= *vice-president*) V.P.
vs *abbr* (= *versus*) vs
VSO *n abbr* (*Brit*: = *Voluntary Service Overseas*) organización que envía jóvenes voluntarios a trabajar y enseñar en los países del Tercer Mundo
VT, Vt. *abbr* (*US*) = **Vermont**
vulgar ['vʌlgə'] *adj* (*rude*) ordinario, grosero; (*in bad taste*) de mal gusto
vulgarity [vʌl'gærɪtɪ] *n* grosería; mal gusto
vulnerability [vʌlnərə'bɪlɪtɪ] *n* vulnerabilidad *f*
vulnerable ['vʌlnərəbl] *adj* vulnerable
vulture ['vʌltʃə'] *n* buitre *m*, gallinazo (*LAm*)

W, w ['dʌblju:] n (letter) W, w f; **W for William** W de Washington
W abbr (= west) O; (Elec: = watt) v
WA abbr (US) = **Washington**
wad [wɔd] n (of cotton wool, paper) bolita; (of banknotes etc) fajo
wadding ['wɔdɪŋ] n relleno
waddle ['wɔdl] vi andar como un pato
wade [weɪd] vi: **to ~ through** caminar por el agua; (fig: a book) leer con dificultad
wading pool ['weɪdɪŋ-] n (US) piscina para niños
wafer ['weɪfə'] n (biscuit) barquillo; (Rel) oblea; (: consecrated) hostia; (Comput) oblea, microplaqueta
wafer-thin ['weɪfə'θɪn] adj finísimo
waffle ['wɔfl] n (Culin) gofre m ■ vi meter el rollo
waffle iron n molde m para hacer gofres
waft [wɔft] vt llevar por el aire ■ vi flotar
wag [wæg] vt menear, agitar ■ vi moverse, menearse; **the dog wagged its tail** el perro meneó la cola
wage [weɪdʒ] n (also: **wages**) sueldo, salario ■ vt: **to ~ war** hacer la guerra; **a day's ~** el sueldo de un día
wage claim n reivindicación f salarial
wage differential n diferencia salarial
wage earner n asalariado(-a)
wage freeze n congelación f de salarios
wage packet n sobre m de la paga
wager ['weɪdʒə'] n apuesta ■ vt apostar
waggle ['wægl] vt menear, mover
wagon, waggon ['wægən] n (horse-drawn) carro; (Brit Rail) vagón m
wail [weɪl] n gemido ■ vi gemir
waist [weɪst] n cintura, talle m
waistcoat ['weɪstkəut] n (Brit) chaleco
waistline ['weɪstlaɪn] n talle m
wait [weɪt] n espera; (interval) pausa ■ vi esperar; **to lie in ~ for** acechar a; **I can't ~ to** (fig) estoy deseando; **to ~ for** esperar (a); **to keep sb waiting** hacer esperar a algn; **~ a**

moment! ¡un momento!, ¡un momentito!; **"repairs while you ~"** "reparaciones en el acto"
▶ **wait behind** vi quedarse
▶ **wait on** vt fus servir a
▶ **wait up** vi esperar levantado
waiter ['weɪtə'] n camarero
waiting ['weɪtɪŋ] n: **"no ~"** (Brit Aut) "prohibido estacionarse"
waiting list n lista de espera
waiting room n sala de espera
waitress ['weɪtrɪs] n camarera
waive [weɪv] vt suspender
waiver ['weɪvə'] n renuncia
wake [weɪk] (pt **woke** or **waked**, pp **woken** or **waked**) vt (also: **wake up**) despertar ■ vi (also: **wake up**) despertarse ■ n (for dead person) velatorio; (Naut) estela; **to ~ up to sth** (fig) darse cuenta de algo; **in the ~ of** tras, después de; **to follow in sb's ~** (fig) seguir las huellas de algn
waken ['weɪkn] vt, vi = **wake**
Wales [weɪlz] n País m de Gales
walk [wɔ:k] n (stroll) paseo; (hike) excursión f a pie, caminata; (gait) paso, andar m; (in park etc) paseo ■ vi andar, caminar; (for pleasure, exercise) pasearse ■ vt (distance) recorrer a pie, andar; (dog) (sacar a) pasear; **to go for a ~** ir a dar un paseo; **10 minutes' ~ from here** a 10 minutos de aquí andando; **people from all walks of life** gente de todas las esferas; **to ~ in one's sleep** ser sonámbulo(-a); **I'll ~ you home** te acompañaré a casa
▶ **walk out** vi (go out) salir; (as protest) marcharse, salirse; (strike) declararse en huelga; **to ~ out on sb** abandonar a algn
walkabout ['wɔ:kəbaut] n: **to go (on a) ~** darse un baño de multitudes
walker ['wɔ:kə'] n (person) paseante m/f, caminante m/f
walkie-talkie ['wɔ:kɪ'tɔ:kɪ] n walkie-talkie m
walking ['wɔ:kɪŋ] n (el) andar; **it's within ~ distance** se puede ir andando or a pie

W

walking stick _n_ bastón _m_

Walkman® ['wɔːkmən] _n_ walkman® _m_

walk-on ['wɔːkɔn] _adj_ (_Theat: part_) de comparsa

walkout ['wɔːkaut] _n_ (_of workers_) huelga

walkover ['wɔːkəuvə^r] _n_ (_col_) pan _m_ comido

walkway ['wɔːkweɪ] _n_ paseo

wall [wɔːl] _n_ pared _f_; (_exterior_) muro; (_city wall etc_) muralla; **to go to the ~** (_fig: firm etc_) quebrar, ir a la bancarrota
  ▶ **wall in** _vt_ (_garden etc_) cercar con una tapia

walled [wɔːld] _adj_ (_city_) amurallado; (_garden_) con tapia

wallet ['wɔlɪt] _n_ cartera, billetera (_esp LAm_)

wallflower ['wɔːlflauə^r] _n_ alhelí _m_; **to be a ~** (_fig_) comer pavo

wall hanging _n_ tapiz _m_

wallop ['wɔləp] _vt_ (_col_) zurrar

wallow ['wɔləu] _vi_ revolcarse; **to ~ in one's grief** sumirse en su pena

wallpaper ['wɔːlpeɪpə^r] _n_ (_for walls_) papel _m_ pintado; (_Comput_) fondo de escritorio

wall-to-wall ['wɔːltə'wɔːl] _adj_: **~ carpeting** moqueta

wally ['wɔlɪ] _n_ (_col_) majadero(-a)

walnut ['wɔːlnʌt] _n_ nuez _f_; (_tree_) nogal _m_

walrus (_pl ~ or_ **walruses**) ['wɔːlrəs] _n_ morsa

waltz [wɔːlts] _n_ vals _m_ ■ _vi_ bailar el vals

wan [wɔn] _adj_ pálido

wand [wɔnd] _n_ (_also:_ **magic wand**) varita (mágica)

wander ['wɔndə^r] _vi_ (_person_) vagar; deambular; (_thoughts_) divagar; (_get lost_) extraviarse ■ _vt_ recorrer, vagar por

wanderer ['wɔndərə^r] _n_ vagabundo(-a)

wandering ['wɔndərɪŋ] _adj_ (_tribe_) nómada; (_minstrel, actor_) ambulante; (_path, river_) sinuoso; (_glance, mind_) distraído

wane [weɪn] _vi_ menguar

wangle ['wæŋgl] (_Brit col_) _vt_: **to ~ sth** agenciarse _or_ conseguir algo ■ _n_ chanchullo

wanker ['wæŋkə^r] _n_ (_col!_) pajero(-a) (!); (_as insult_) mamón(-ona) (!) _m/f_

want [wɔnt] _vt_ (_wish for_) querer, desear; (_need_) necesitar; (_lack_) carecer de ■ _n_ (_poverty_) pobreza; **for ~ of** por falta de; **wants** _npl_ (_needs_) necesidades _fpl_; **to ~ to do** querer hacer; **to ~ sb to do sth** querer que algn haga algo; **you're wanted on the phone** te llaman al teléfono; **to be in ~** estar necesitado; **"cook wanted"** "se necesita cocinero(-a)"

want ads _npl_ (_US_) anuncios _mpl_ por palabras

wanting ['wɔntɪŋ] _adj_: **to be ~ (in)** estar falto (de); **to be found ~** no estar a la altura de las circunstancias

wanton ['wɔntn] _adj_ (_licentious_) lascivo

WAP [wæp] _n abbr_ (= _wireless application protocol_) WAP _f_

WAP phone _n_ teléfono WAP

war [wɔː^r] _n_ guerra; **to make ~** hacer la guerra; **the First/Second World W~** la primera/segunda guerra mundial

warble ['wɔːbl] _n_ (_of bird_) trino, gorjeo ■ _vi_ (_bird_) trinar

war cry _n_ grito de guerra

ward [wɔːd] _n_ (_in hospital_) sala; (_Pol_) distrito electoral; (_Law: child_) pupilo(-a)
  ▶ **ward off** _vt_ desviar, parar; (_attack_) rechazar

warden ['wɔːdn] _n_ (_Brit: of institution_) director(a) _m(f)_; (_of park, game reserve_) guardián(-ana) _m(f)_; (_Brit: also:_ **traffic warden**) guardia _m/f_

warder ['wɔːdə^r] _n_ (_Brit_) guardián(-ana) _m(f)_, carcelero(-a) _m(f)_

wardrobe ['wɔːdrəub] _n_ armario, guardarropa, ropero, clóset/closet _m_ (_LAm_)

warehouse ['wɛəhaus] _n_ almacén _m_, depósito

wares [wɛəz] _npl_ mercancías _fpl_

warfare ['wɔːfɛə^r] _n_ guerra

war game _n_ juego de estrategia militar

warhead ['wɔːhɛd] _n_ cabeza armada; **nuclear warheads** cabezas _fpl_ nucleares

warily ['wɛərɪlɪ] _adv_ con cautela, cautelosamente

warlike ['wɔːlaɪk] _adj_ guerrero

warm [wɔːm] _adj_ caliente; (_person, greeting, heart_) afectuoso, cariñoso; (_supporter_) entusiasta; (_thanks, congratulations, apologies_) efusivo; (_clothes etc_) que abriga; (_welcome, day_) caluroso; **it's ~** hace calor; **I'm ~** tengo calor; **to keep sth ~** mantener algo caliente
  ▶ **warm up** _vi_ (_room_) calentarse; (_person_) entrar en calor; (_athlete_) hacer ejercicios de calentamiento; (_discussion_) acalorarse ■ _vt_ calentar

warm-blooded ['wɔːm'blʌdɪd] _adj_ de sangre caliente

war memorial _n_ monumento a los caídos

warm-hearted [wɔːm'hɑːtɪd] _adj_ afectuoso

warmly ['wɔːmlɪ] _adv_ afectuosamente

warmonger ['wɔːmʌŋgə^r] _n_ belicista _m/f_

warmongering ['wɔːmʌŋgrɪŋ] _n_ belicismo

warmth [wɔːmθ] _n_ calor _m_

warm-up ['wɔːmʌp] _n_ (_Sport_) ejercicios _mpl_ de calentamiento

warn [wɔːn] _vt_ avisar, advertir; **to ~ sb not to do sth** _or_ **against doing sth** aconsejar a algn que no haga algo

warning ['wɔːnɪŋ] _n_ aviso, advertencia; **gale ~** (_Meteorology_) aviso de vendaval; **without (any) ~** sin aviso _or_ avisar

warning light _n_ luz _f_ de advertencia

warning triangle n (Aut) triángulo señalizador

warp [wɔ:p] vi (wood) combarse

warpath ['wɔ:pɑ:θ] n: **to be on the ~** (fig) estar en pie de guerra

warped [wɔ:pt] adj (wood) alabeado; (fig: character, sense of humour etc) pervertido

warrant ['wɔrnt] n (Law: to arrest) orden f de detención; (: to search) mandamiento de registro ■ vt (justify, merit) merecer

warrant officer n (Mil) brigada m; (Naut) contramaestre m

warranty ['wɔrəntɪ] n garantía; **under ~** (Comm) bajo garantía

warren ['wɔrən] n (of rabbits) madriguera; (fig) laberinto

warring ['wɔ:rɪŋ] adj (interests etc) opuesto; (nations) en guerra

warrior ['wɔrɪəʳ] n guerrero(-a)

Warsaw ['wɔ:sɔ:] n Varsovia

warship ['wɔ:ʃɪp] n buque m or barco de guerra

wart [wɔ:t] n verruga

wartime ['wɔ:taɪm] n: **in ~** en tiempos de guerra, en la guerra

wary ['wɛərɪ] adj cauteloso; **to be ~ about** or **of doing sth** tener cuidado con hacer algo

was [wɔz] pt of **be**

wash [wɔʃ] vt lavar; (sweep, carry: sea etc) llevar ■ vi lavarse ■ n (clothes etc) lavado; (bath) baño; (of ship) estela; **he was washed overboard** fue arrastrado del barco por las olas; **to have a ~** lavarse
 ▶ **wash away** vt (stain) quitar lavando; (river etc) llevarse; (fig) limpiar
 ▶ **wash down** vt lavar
 ▶ **wash off** vt quitar lavando
 ▶ **wash up** vi (Brit) fregar los platos; (US: have a wash) lavarse

Wash. abbr (US) = **Washington**

washable ['wɔʃəbl] adj lavable

washbasin ['wɔʃbeɪsn], **washbowl** (US) ['wɔʃbəul] n lavabo

washcloth ['wɔʃklɔθ] n (US) manopla

washer ['wɔʃəʳ] n (Tech) arandela

washing ['wɔʃɪŋ] n (dirty) ropa sucia; (clean) colada

washing line n cuerda de (colgar) la ropa

washing machine n lavadora

washing powder n (Brit) detergente m (en polvo)

Washington ['wɔʃɪŋtən] n (city, state) Washington m

washing-up [wɔʃɪŋ'ʌp] n fregado; (dishes) platos mpl (para fregar); **to do the ~** fregar los platos

washing-up liquid n lavavajillas m inv

wash leather n gamuza

wash-out ['wɔʃaut] n (col) fracaso

washroom ['wɔʃrum] n servicios mpl

wasn't ['wɔznt] = **was not**

WASP, Wasp [wɔsp] n abbr (US col: = White Anglo-Saxon Protestant) sobrenombre, en general peyorativo, que se da a los americanos de origen anglosajón, acomodados y de tendencia conservadora

wasp [wɔsp] n avispa

waspish ['wɔspɪʃ] adj (character) irascible; (comment) mordaz, punzante

wastage ['weɪstɪdʒ] n desgaste m; (loss) pérdida; **natural ~** desgaste natural

waste [weɪst] n derroche m, despilfarro; (misuse) desgaste m; (of time) pérdida; (food) sobras fpl; (rubbish) basura, desperdicios mpl ■ adj (material) de desecho; (left over) sobrante; (energy, heat) desperdiciado; (land, ground: in city) sin construir; (: in country) baldío ■ vt (squander) malgastar, derrochar; (time) perder; (opportunity) desperdiciar; **wastes** npl (area of land) tierras fpl baldías; **to lay ~** devastar, arrasar; **it's a ~ of money** es tirar el dinero; **to go to ~** desperdiciarse
 ▶ **waste away** vi consumirse

wastebasket ['weɪstbɑ:skɪt] n (esp US) = **wastepaper basket**

waste disposal, waste disposal unit n (Brit) triturador m de basura

wasteful ['weɪstful] adj derrochador(a); (process) antieconómico

wastefully ['weɪstfulɪ] adv: **to spend money ~** derrochar dinero

waste ground n (Brit) terreno baldío

wasteland ['weɪstlənd] n (urban) descampados mpl

wastepaper basket ['weɪstpeɪpə-] n papelera; (Comput) papelera de reciclaje

waste pipe n tubo de desagüe

waste products npl (Industry) residuos mpl

waster ['weɪstəʳ] n (col) gandul m/f

watch [wɔtʃ] n reloj m; (vigil) vigilia; (vigilance) vigilancia; (Mil: guard) centinela m; (Naut: spell of duty) guardia ■ vt (look at) mirar, observar; (: match, programme) ver; (spy on, guard) vigilar; (be careful of) cuidar, tener cuidado de ■ vi ver, mirar; (keep guard) montar guardia; **to keep a close ~ on sth/sb** vigilar algo/a algn de cerca; **~ how you drive/what you're doing** ten cuidado al conducir/con lo que haces
 ▶ **watch out** vi cuidarse, tener cuidado

watch band n (US) pulsera (de reloj)

watchdog ['wɔtʃdɔg] n perro guardián; (fig) organismo de control

watchful ['wɔtʃful] adj vigilante, sobre aviso

watchfully ['wɔtʃfulɪ] adv: **to stand ~** permanecer vigilante

w

watchmaker ['wɒtʃmeɪkə^r] n relojero(-a)
watchman n guardián m; (also: **night watchman**) sereno, vigilante m; (in factory) vigilante m nocturno
watch stem n (US) cuerda
watch strap n pulsera (de reloj)
watchword ['wɒtʃwə:d] n consigna, contraseña
water ['wɔ:tə^r] n agua ▪ vt (plant) regar ▪ vi (eyes) llorar; **I'd like a drink of ~** quisiera un vaso de agua; **in British waters** en aguas británicas; **to pass ~** orinar; **his mouth watered** se le hizo la boca agua
▶ **water down** vt (milk etc) aguar
water closet n wáter m
watercolour, watercolor (US) ['wɔ:təkʌlə^r] n acuarela
water-cooled ['wɔ:təku:ld] adj refrigerado (por agua)
watercress ['wɔ:təkrɛs] n berro
waterfall ['wɔ:təfɔ:l] n cascada, salto de agua
waterfront ['wɔ:təfrʌnt] n (seafront) parte f que da al mar; (at docks) muelles mpl
water heater n calentador m de agua
water hole n abrevadero
watering can ['wɔ:tərɪŋ-] n regadera
water level n nivel m del agua
water lily n nenúfar m
waterline ['wɔ:təlaɪn] n (Naut) línea de flotación
waterlogged ['wɔ:təlɒgd] adj (boat) anegado; (ground) inundado
water main n cañería del agua
watermark ['wɔ:təmɑ:k] n (on paper) filigrana
watermelon ['wɔ:təmɛlən] n sandía
water polo n waterpolo, polo acuático
waterproof ['wɔ:təpru:f] adj impermeable
water-repellent ['wɔ:tərɪ'pɛlənt] adj hidrófugo
watershed ['wɔ:təʃɛd] n (Geo) cuenca; (fig) momento crítico
water-skiing ['wɔ:təski:ɪŋ] n esquí m acuático
water softener n ablandador m de agua
water tank n depósito de agua
watertight ['wɔ:tətaɪt] adj hermético
water vapour, water vapor (US) n vapor m de agua
waterway ['wɔ:təweɪ] n vía fluvial or navegable
waterworks ['wɔ:təwə:ks] npl central fsg depuradora
watery ['wɔ:tərɪ] adj (colour) desvaído; (coffee) aguado; (eyes) lloroso
watt [wɒt] n vatio
wattage ['wɒtɪdʒ] n potencia en vatios

wattle ['wɒtl] n zarzo
wave [weɪv] n ola; (of hand) señal f con la mano; (Radio) onda; (in hair) onda; (fig: of enthusiasm, strikes) oleada ▪ vi agitar la mano; (flag) ondear ▪ vt (handkerchief, gun) agitar; **short/medium/long ~** (Radio) onda corta/media/larga; **the new ~** (Cine, Mus) la nueva ola; **to ~ goodbye to sb** decir adiós a algn con la mano; **he waved us over to his table** nos hizo señas (con la mano) para que nos acercásemos a su mesa
▶ **wave aside, wave away** vt (person): **to ~ sb aside** apartar a algn con la mano; (fig: suggestion, objection) rechazar; (doubts) desechar
waveband ['weɪvbænd] n banda de ondas
wavelength ['weɪvlɛŋθ] n longitud f de onda
waver ['weɪvə^r] vi oscilar; (confidence) disminuir; (faith) flaquear
wavy ['weɪvɪ] adj ondulado
wax [wæks] n cera ▪ vt encerar ▪ vi (moon) crecer
waxen ['wæksn] adj (fig: pale) blanco como la cera
waxworks ['wækswə:ks] npl museo sg de cera
way [weɪ] n camino; (distance) trayecto, recorrido; (direction) dirección f, sentido; (manner) modo, manera; (habit) costumbre f; **which ~? — this ~** ¿por dónde? or ¿en qué dirección? — por aquí; **on the ~** (en route) en (el) camino; (expected) en camino; **to be on one's ~** estar en camino; **you pass it on your ~ home** está de camino a tu casa; **to be in the ~** bloquear el camino; (fig) estorbar; **to keep out of sb's ~** esquivar a algn; **to make ~ (for sb/sth)** dejar paso (a algn/algo); (fig) abrir camino (a algn/algo); **to go out of one's ~ to do sth** desvivirse por hacer algo; **to lose one's ~** perderse, extraviarse; **to be the wrong ~ round** estar del or al revés; **in a ~** en cierto modo or sentido; **by the ~** a propósito; **by ~ of** (via) pasando por; (as a sort of) como, a modo de; **"~ in"** (Brit) "entrada"; **"~ out"** (Brit) "salida"; **the ~ back** el camino de vuelta; **the village is rather out of the ~** el pueblo está un poco apartado or retirado; **it's a long ~ away** está muy lejos; **to get one's own ~** salirse con la suya; **"give ~"** (Brit Aut) "ceda el paso"; **no ~!** (col) ¡ni pensarlo!; **put it the right ~ up** ponlo boca arriba; **he's in a bad ~** está grave; **to be under ~** (work, project) estar en marcha
waybill ['weɪbɪl] n (Comm) hoja de ruta, carta de porte
waylay [weɪ'leɪ] vt (irreg: like **lay**) atacar
wayside ['weɪsaɪd] n borde m del camino; **to fall by the ~** (fig) fracasar

way station n (US Rail) apeadero
wayward ['weɪwəd] adj díscolo, caprichoso
WC ['dʌblju:si:] n abbr (Brit: = water closet) wáter m
WCC n abbr = **World Council of Churches**
we [wi:] pl pron nosotros(-as); **we understand** (nosotros) entendemos; **here we are** aquí estamos
weak [wi:k] adj débil, flojo; (tea, coffee) flojo, aguado; **to grow ~(er)** debilitarse
weaken ['wi:kən] vi debilitarse; (give way) ceder ▪ vt debilitar
weak-kneed [wi:k'ni:d] adj (fig) sin voluntad or carácter
weakling ['wi:klɪŋ] n debilucho(-a)
weakly ['wi:klɪ] adj enfermizo, débil ▪ adv débilmente
weakness ['wi:knɪs] n debilidad f; (fault) punto débil
wealth [wɛlθ] n (money, resources) riqueza; (of details) abundancia
wealth tax n impuesto sobre el patrimonio
wealthy ['wɛlθɪ] adj rico
wean [wi:n] vt destetar
weapon ['wɛpən] n arma; **weapons of mass destruction** armas de destrucción masiva
wear [wɛəʳ] (pt **wore**, pp **worn**) n (use) uso; (deterioration through use) desgaste m; (clothing): **sports/babywear** ropa de deportes/de niños ▪ vt (clothes, beard) llevar; (shoes) calzar; (look, smile) tener; (damage: through use) gastar, usar ▪ vi (last) durar; (rub through etc) desgastarse; **evening ~** (man's) traje m de etiqueta; (woman's) traje m de noche; **to ~ a hole in sth** hacer un agujero en algo
▶ **wear away** vt gastar ▪ vi desgastarse
▶ **wear down** vt gastar; (strength) agotar
▶ **wear off** vi (pain, excitement etc) pasar, desaparecer
▶ **wear out** vt desgastar; (person, strength) agotar
wearable ['wɛərəbl] adj que se puede llevar, ponible
wear and tear n desgaste m
wearer ['wɛərəʳ] n: **the ~ of this jacket** el/la que lleva puesta esta chaqueta
wearily ['wɪərɪlɪ] adv con cansancio
weariness ['wɪərɪnɪs] n cansancio; abatimiento
wearisome ['wɪərɪsəm] adj (tiring) cansado, pesado; (boring) aburrido
weary ['wɪərɪ] adj (tired) cansado; (dispirited) abatido ▪ vt cansar ▪ vi: **to ~ of** cansarse de, aburrirse de
weasel ['wi:zl] n (Zool) comadreja
weather ['wɛðəʳ] n tiempo ▪ vt (storm, crisis) hacer frente a; **under the ~** (fig: ill) mal, pachucho; **what's the ~ like?** ¿qué tiempo

hace?, ¿cómo hace?
weather-beaten ['wɛðəbi:tn] adj curtido
weathercock ['wɛðəkɔk] n veleta
weather forecast n boletín m meteorológico
weatherman ['wɛðəmæn] n hombre m del tiempo
weatherproof ['wɛðəpru:f] adj (garment) impermeable
weather report n parte m meteorológico
weather vane n = **weathercock**
weave (pt **wove**, pp **woven**) [wi:v, wəuv, 'wəuvn] vt (cloth) tejer; (fig) entretejer ▪ vi (fig) (pt, pp **weaved**) (move in and out) zigzaguear
weaver ['wi:vəʳ] n tejedor(a) m(f)
weaving ['wi:vɪŋ] n tejeduría
web [wɛb] n (of spider) telaraña; (on foot) membrana; (Comput: network) red f; **the (World Wide) W~** el or la Web
web address n dirección f de página web
webbed [wɛbd] adj (foot) palmeado
webbing ['wɛbɪŋ] n (on chair) cinchas fpl
webcam ['wɛbkæm] n webcam f
weblog ['wɛblɔg] n weblog m
web page n página web
website ['wɛbsaɪt] n sitio web
wed [wɛd] vt (pt, pp **wedded**) casar ▪ n: **the newly-weds** los recién casados
Wed. abbr (= Wednesday) miérc
we'd [wi:d] = **we had**; **we would**
wedded ['wɛdɪd] pt, pp of **wed**
wedding ['wɛdɪŋ] n boda, casamiento
wedding anniversary n aniversario de boda; **silver/golden ~** bodas fpl de plata/de oro
wedding day n día m de la boda
wedding dress n traje m de novia
wedding present n regalo de boda
wedding ring n alianza
wedge [wɛdʒ] n (of wood etc) cuña; (of cake) trozo ▪ vt acuñar; (push) apretar
wedge-heeled [wɛdʒ'hi:ld] adj con suela de cuña
wedlock ['wɛdlɔk] n matrimonio
Wednesday ['wɛdnzdɪ] n miércoles m inv; see also **Tuesday**
wee [wi:] adj (Scottish) pequeñito
weed [wi:d] n mala hierba, maleza ▪ vt escardar, desherbar
▶ **weed out** vt eliminar
weedkiller ['wi:dkɪləʳ] n herbicida m
weedy ['wi:dɪ] adj (person) debilucho
week [wi:k] n semana; **a ~ today** de hoy en ocho días; **Tuesday ~, a ~ on Tuesday** del martes en una semana; **once/twice a ~** una vez/dos veces a la semana; **this ~** esta semana; **in two weeks' time** dentro de dos semanas; **every other ~** cada dos semanas

W

weekday ['wi:kdeɪ] *n* día *m* laborable; **on weekdays** entre semana, en días laborables
weekend [wi:k'ɛnd] *n* fin *m* de semana
weekend case *n* neceser *m*
weekly ['wi:klɪ] *adv* semanalmente, cada semana ■ *adj* semanal ■ *n* semanario; **~ newspaper** semanario
weep (*pt, pp* **wept**) [wi:p, wɛpt] *vi, vt* llorar; (*Med: wound etc*) supurar
weeping willow ['wi:pɪŋ-] *n* sauce *m* llorón
weepy ['wi:pɪ] *n* (*col: film*) película lacrimógena; (: *story*) historia lacrimógena
weft [wɛft] *n* (*Textiles*) trama
weigh [weɪ] *vt, vi* pesar; **to ~ anchor** levar anclas; **to ~ the pros and cons** pesar los pros y los contras
▶ **weigh down** *vt* sobrecargar; (*fig: with worry*) agobiar
▶ **weigh out** *vt* (*goods*) pesar
▶ **weigh up** *vt* pesar
weighbridge ['weɪbrɪdʒ] *n* báscula para camiones
weighing machine ['weɪɪŋ-] *n* báscula, peso
weight [weɪt] *n* peso; (*on scale*) pesa; **to lose/put on ~** adelgazar/engordar; **weights and measures** pesas y medidas
weighting ['weɪtɪŋ] *n* (*allowance*): **(London) ~** dietas (*por residir en Londres*)
weightlessness ['weɪtlɪsnɪs] *n* ingravidez *f*
weight lifter *n* levantador(a) *m(f)* de pesas
weight limit *n* límite *m* de peso
weight training *n* musculación *f* (con pesas)
weighty ['weɪtɪ] *adj* pesado
weir [wɪəʳ] *n* presa
weird [wɪəd] *adj* raro, extraño
weirdo ['wɪədəu] *n* (*col*) tío(-a) raro(-a)
welcome ['wɛlkəm] *adj* bienvenido ■ *n* bienvenida ■ *vt* dar la bienvenida a; (*be glad of*) alegrarse de; **to make sb ~** recibir *or* acoger bien a algn; **thank you — you're ~** gracias — de nada; **you're ~ to try** puede intentar cuando quiera; **we ~ this step** celebramos esta medida
weld [wɛld] *n* soldadura ■ *vt* soldar
welding ['wɛldɪŋ] *n* soldadura
welfare ['wɛlfɛəʳ] *n* bienestar *m*; (*social aid*) asistencia social; **W~** (*US*) subsidio de paro; **to look after sb's ~** cuidar del bienestar de algn
welfare state *n* estado del bienestar
welfare work *n* asistencia social
well [wɛl] *n* pozo ■ *adv* bien ■ *adj*: **to be ~** estar bien (de salud) ■ *excl* ¡vaya!, ¡bueno!; **as ~** (*in addition*) además, también; **as ~ as** además de; **you might as ~ tell me** más vale que me lo digas; **it would be as ~ to ask** más valdría preguntar; **~ done!** ¡bien

hecho!; **get ~ soon!** ¡que te mejores pronto!; **to do ~** (*business*) ir bien; **I did ~ in my exams** me han salido bien los exámenes; **they are doing ~ now** les va bien ahora; **to think ~ of sb** pensar bien de algn; **I don't feel ~** no me encuentro *or* siento bien; **~, as I was saying** ... bueno, como decía ...
▶ **well up** *vi* brotar
we'll [wi:l] = **we will**; **we shall**
well-behaved ['wɛlbɪ'heɪvd] *adj*: **to be ~** portarse bien
well-being ['wɛl'bi:ɪŋ] *n* bienestar *m*
well-bred ['wɛl'brɛd] *adj* bien educado
well-built ['wɛl'bɪlt] *adj* (*person*) fornido
well-chosen ['wɛl'tʃəuzn] *adj* (*remarks, words*) acertado
well-deserved ['wɛldɪ'zə:vd] *adj* merecido
well-developed ['wɛldɪ'vɛləpt] *adj* (*arm, muscle etc*) bien desarrollado; (*sense*) agudo, fino
well-disposed ['wɛldɪs'pəuzd] *adj*: **~ to(wards)** bien dispuesto a
well-dressed ['wɛl'drɛst] *adj* bien vestido
well-earned ['wɛl'ə:nd] *adj* (*rest*) merecido
well-groomed ['wɛl'gru:md] *adj* de apariencia cuidada
well-heeled ['wɛl'hi:ld] *adj* (*col: wealthy*) rico
well-informed ['wɛlɪn'fɔ:md] *adj* (*having knowledge of sth*) enterado, al corriente
Wellington ['wɛlɪŋtən] *n* Wellington *m*
wellingtons ['wɛlɪŋtənz] *npl* (*also:* **Wellington boots**) botas *fpl* de goma
well-kept ['wɛl'kɛpt] *adj* (*secret*) bien guardado; (*hair, hands, house, grounds*) bien cuidado
well-known ['wɛl'nəun] *adj* (*person*) conocido
well-mannered ['wɛl'mænəd] *adj* educado
well-meaning ['wɛl'mi:nɪŋ] *adj* bienintencionado
well-nigh ['wɛl'naɪ] *adv*: **~ impossible** casi imposible
well-off ['wɛl'ɔf] *adj* acomodado
well-read ['wɛl'rɛd] *adj* culto
well-spoken ['wɛl'spəukən] *adj* bienhablado
well-stocked ['wɛl'stɔkt] *adj* (*shop, larder*) bien surtido
well-timed ['wɛl'taɪmd] *adj* oportuno
well-to-do ['wɛltə'du:] *adj* acomodado
well-wisher ['wɛlwɪʃəʳ] *n* admirador(a) *m(f)*
well-woman clinic ['wɛlwumən-] *n* centro de prevención médica para mujeres
Welsh [wɛlʃ] *adj* galés(-esa) ■ *n* (*Ling*) galés *m*; **the Welsh** *npl* los galeses; **the ~ Assembly** el Parlamento galés
Welshman ['wɛlʃmən] *n* galés *m*
Welsh rarebit [-'rɛəbɪt] *n* pan *m* con queso tostado

Welshwoman ['wɛlʃwumən] *n* galesa
welter ['wɛltə^r] *n* mescolanza, revoltijo
went [wɛnt] *pt of* **go**
wept [wɛpt] *pt, pp of* **weep**
were [wəː^r] *pt of* **be**
we're [wɪə^r] = **we are**
weren't [wəːnt] = **were not**
werewolf (*pl* **werewolves**) ['wɪəwulf, -wulvz] *n* hombre *m* lobo
west [wɛst] *n* oeste *m* ■ *adj* occidental, del oeste ■ *adv* al *or* hacia el oeste; **the W~** Occidente *m*
westbound ['wɛstbaund] *adj* (*traffic, carriageway*) con rumbo al oeste
West Country *n*: **the ~** el suroeste de Inglaterra
westerly ['wɛstəlɪ] *adj* (*wind*) del oeste
western ['wɛstən] *adj* occidental ■ *n* (*Cine*) película del oeste
westerner ['wɛstənə^r] *n* (*Pol*) occidental *m/f*
westernized ['wɛstənaɪzd] *adj* occidentalizado
West German (*formerly*) *adj* de Alemania Occidental ■ *n* alemán(-ana) *m(f)* (de Alemania Occidental)
West Germany *n* (*formerly*) Alemania Occidental
West Indian *adj, n* antillano(-a) *m(f)*
West Indies [-'ɪndɪz] *npl*: **the ~** las Antillas
Westminster ['wɛstmɪnstə^r] *n* el parlamento británico, Westminster *m*
westward ['wɛstwəd], **westwards** ['wɛstwədz] *adv* hacia el oeste
wet [wɛt] *adj* (*damp*) húmedo; (*wet through*) mojado; (*rainy*) lluvioso ■ *vt*: **to ~ one's pants** *or* **o.s.** mearse; **to get ~** mojarse; **"~ paint"** "recién pintado"
wet blanket *n*: **to be a ~** (*fig*) ser un/una aguafiestas
wetness ['wɛtnɪs] *n* humedad *f*
wet rot *n* putrefacción *f* por humedad
wet suit *n* traje *m* de buzo
we've [wiːv] = **we have**
whack [wæk] *vt* dar un buen golpe a
whale [weɪl] *n* (*Zool*) ballena
whaler ['weɪlə^r] *n* (*ship*) ballenero
whaling ['weɪlɪŋ] *n* pesca de ballenas
wharf (*pl* **wharves**) [wɔːf, wɔːvz] *n* muelle *m*

○ **KEYWORD**

what [wɔt] *adj* **1** (*in direct/indirect questions*) qué; **what size is he?** ¿qué talla usa?; **what colour/shape is it?** ¿de qué color/forma es?; **what books do you need?** ¿qué libros necesitas?
2 (*in exclamations*): **what a mess!** ¡qué

desastre!; **what a fool I am!** ¡qué tonto soy!
■ *pron* **1** (*interrogative*) qué; **what are you doing?** ¿qué haces *or* estás haciendo?; **what is happening?** ¿qué pasa *or* está pasando?; **what is it called?** ¿cómo se llama?; **what about me?** ¿y yo qué?; **what about doing ...?** ¿qué tal si hacemos ...?; **what is his address?** ¿cuáles son sus señas?; **what will it cost?** ¿cuánto costará?
2 (*relative*) lo que; **I saw what you did/was on the table** vi lo que hiciste/había en la mesa; **what I want is a cup of tea** lo que quiero es una taza de té; **I don't know what to do** no sé qué hacer; **tell me what you're thinking about** dime en qué estás pensando
3 (*reported questions*): **she asked me what I wanted** me preguntó qué quería
■ *excl* (*disbelieving*) ¡cómo!; **what, no coffee!** ¡que no hay café!

whatever [wɔt'ɛvə^r] *adj*: **~ book you choose** cualquier libro que elijas ■ *pron*: **do ~ is necessary** haga lo que sea necesario; **no reason ~** ninguna razón en absoluto; **nothing ~** nada en absoluto; **~ it costs** cueste lo que cueste
wheat [wiːt] *n* trigo
wheatgerm ['wiːtdʒəːm] *n* germen *m* de trigo
wheatmeal ['wiːtmiːl] *n* harina de trigo
wheedle ['wiːdl] *vt*: **to ~ sb into doing sth** engatusar a algn para que haga algo; **to ~ sth out of sb** sonsacar algo a algn
wheel [wiːl] *n* rueda; (*Aut: also:* **steering wheel**) volante *m*; (*Naut*) timón *m* ■ *vt* (*pram etc*) empujar ■ *vi* (*also:* **wheel round**) dar la vuelta, girar; **four-~ drive** tracción *f* en las cuatro ruedas; **front-/rear-~ drive** tracción *f* delantera/trasera
wheelbarrow ['wiːlbærəu] *n* carretilla
wheelbase ['wiːlbeɪs] *n* batalla
wheelchair ['wiːltʃɛə^r] *n* silla de ruedas
wheel clamp *n* (*Aut*) cepo
wheeler-dealer ['wiːlə'diːlə^r] *n* chanchullero(-a)
wheelie-bin ['wiːlɪbɪn] *n* (*Brit*) contenedor *m* de basura
wheeling ['wiːlɪŋ] *n*: **~ and dealing** (*col*) chanchullos *mpl*
wheeze [wiːz] *vi* resollar
wheezy ['wiːzɪ] *adj* silbante

○ **KEYWORD**

when [wɛn] *adv* cuando; **when did it happen?** ¿cuándo ocurrió?; **I know when it happened** sé cuándo ocurrió

■ *conj* **1** (*at, during, after the time that*) cuando; **be careful when you cross the road** ten cuidado al cruzar la calle; **that was when I needed you** entonces era cuando te necesitaba; **I'll buy you a car when you're 18** te compraré un coche cuando cumplas 18 años **2** (*on, at which*): **on the day when I met him** el día en qué le conocí **3** (*whereas*) cuando; **you said I was wrong when in fact I was right** dijiste que no tenía razón, cuando en realidad sí la tenía

whenever [wɛnˈɛvəʳ] *conj* cuando; (*every time*) cada vez que; **I go ~ I can** voy siempre *or* todas las veces que puedo

where [wɛəʳ] *adv* dónde ■ *conj* donde; **this is ~** aquí es donde; **~ possible** donde sea posible; **~ are you from?** ¿de dónde es usted?

whereabouts [ˈwɛərəbauts] *adv* dónde ■ *n*: **nobody knows his ~** nadie conoce su paradero

whereas [wɛərˈæz] *conj* mientras

whereby [wɛəˈbaɪ] *adv* mediante el/la cual *etc*

whereupon [wɛərəˈpɔn] *conj* con lo cual, después de lo cual

wherever [wɛərˈɛvəʳ] *adv* dondequiera que; (*interrogative*) dónde; **sit ~ you like** siéntese donde quiera

wherewithal [ˈwɛəwɪðɔːl] *n* recursos *mpl*; **the ~ (to do sth)** los medios económicos (para hacer algo)

whet [wɛt] *vt* estimular; (*appetite*) abrir

whether [ˈwɛðəʳ] *conj* si; **I don't know ~ to accept or not** no sé si aceptar o no; **~ you go or not** vayas o no vayas

whey [weɪ] *n* suero

 KEYWORD

which [wɪtʃ] *adj* **1** (*interrogative: direct, indirect*) qué; **which picture(s) do you want?** ¿qué cuadro(s) quieres?; **which one?** ¿cuál?; **which one of you?** ¿cuál de vosotros?; **tell me which one you want** dime cuál (es el que) quieres **2**: **in which case** en cuyo caso; **we got there at eight pm, by which time the cinema was full** llegamos allí a las ocho, cuando el cine estaba lleno ■ *pron* (*interrogative*) cuál; **I don't mind which** el(-la) que sea; **which do you want?** ¿cuál quieres? **3** (*relative: replacing noun*) que; (: *replacing clause*) lo que; (: *after preposition*) (el(-la)) que, el(-la) cual; **the apple which you ate/which is on the table** la manzana que comiste/que está en la mesa; **the chair on which you**

are sitting la silla en la que estás sentado; **he didn't believe it, which upset me** no se lo creyó, lo cual *or* lo que me disgustó; **after which** después de lo cual

whichever [wɪtʃˈɛvəʳ] *adj*: **take ~ book you prefer** coja el libro que prefiera; **~ book you take** cualquier libro que coja

whiff [wɪf] *n* bocanada; **to catch a ~ of sth** oler algo

while [waɪl] *n* rato, momento ■ *conj* durante; (*whereas*) mientras; (*although*) aunque ■ *vt*: **to ~ away the time** pasar el rato; **for a ~** durante algún tiempo; **in a ~** dentro de poco; **all the ~** todo el tiempo; **we'll make it worth your ~** te compensaremos generosamente

whilst [waɪlst] *conj* = **while**

whim [wɪm] *n* capricho

whimper [ˈwɪmpəʳ] *n* (*weeping*) lloriqueo; (*moan*) quejido ■ *vi* lloriquear; quejarse

whimsical [ˈwɪmzɪkl] *adj* (*person*) caprichoso

whine [waɪn] *n* (*of pain*) gemido; (*of engine*) zumbido ■ *vi* gemir; zumbar

whip [wɪp] *n* látigo; (*Brit: Pol*) *diputado encargado de la disciplina del partido en el parlamento* ■ *vt* azotar; (*snatch*) arrebatar; (*US Culin*) batir
▶ **whip up** *vt* (*cream etc*) batir (rápidamente); (*col: meal*) preparar rápidamente; (: *stir up: support, feeling*) avivar; *ver nota*

WHIP

En el Parlamento británico la disciplina de partido (en concreto de voto y de asistencia a la Cámara de los Comunes) está a cargo de un grupo de parlamentarios llamados *whips*, encabezados por el "Chief Whip". Por lo general todos ellos tienen también altos cargos en la Administración del Estado si pertenecen al partido en el poder.

whiplash [ˈwɪplæʃ] *n* (*Med: also:* **whiplash injury**) latigazo

whipped cream [wɪpt-] *n* nata montada

whipping boy [ˈwɪpɪŋ-] *n* (*fig*) cabeza de turco

whip-round [ˈwɪpraund] *n* (*Brit*) colecta

whirl [wəːl] *n* remolino ■ *vt* hacer girar, dar vueltas a ■ *vi* (*dancers*) girar, dar vueltas; (*leaves, dust, water etc*) arremolinarse

whirlpool [ˈwəːlpuːl] *n* remolino

whirlwind [ˈwəːlwɪnd] *n* torbellino

whirr [wəːʳ] *vi* zumbar

whisk [wɪsk] *n* (*Brit Culin*) batidor *m* ■ *vt* (*Brit Culin*) batir; **to ~ sb away** *or* **off** llevarse volando a algn

whiskers [ˈwɪskəz] npl (of animal) bigotes mpl; (of man) patillas fpl

whisky, whiskey (US, Ireland) [ˈwɪskɪ] n whisky m

whisper [ˈwɪspəʳ] n cuchicheo; (rumour) rumor m; (fig) susurro, murmullo ▪ vi cuchichear, hablar bajo; (fig) susurrar ▪ vt decir en voz muy baja; **to ~ sth to sb** decirle algo al oído a algn

whispering [ˈwɪspərɪŋ] n cuchicheo

whist [wɪst] n (Brit) whist m

whistle [ˈwɪsl] n (sound) silbido; (object) silbato ▪ vi silbar; **to ~ a tune** silbar una melodía

whistle-stop [ˈwɪslstɔp] adj: **~ tour** (US Pol) gira electoral rápida; (fig) recorrido rápido

Whit [wɪt] n Pentecostés m

white [waɪt] adj blanco; (pale) pálido ▪ n blanco; (of egg) clara; **to turn** or **go ~** (person) palidecer, ponerse blanco; (hair) encanecer; **the whites** (washing) la ropa blanca; **tennis whites** ropa f de tenis

whitebait [ˈwaɪtbeɪt] n chanquetes mpl

whiteboard [ˈwaɪtbɔːd] n pizarra blanca; **interactive ~** pizarra interactiva

white coffee n (Brit) café m con leche

white-collar worker [ˈwaɪtkɔlə-] n oficinista m/f

white elephant n (fig) maula

white goods npl (appliances) electrodomésticos mpl de línea blanca; (linen etc) ropa blanca

white-hot [waɪtˈhɔt] adj (metal) candente, calentado al (rojo) blanco

white lie n mentirijilla

whiteness [ˈwaɪtnɪs] n blancura

white noise n sonido blanco

whiteout [ˈwaɪtaut] n resplandor m sin sombras; (fig) masa confusa

white paper n (Pol) libro blanco

whitewash [ˈwaɪtwɔʃ] n (paint) cal f, jalbegue m ▪ vt encalar, blanquear; (fig) encubrir

whiting [ˈwaɪtɪŋ] n (pl inv: fish) pescadilla

Whit Monday n lunes m de Pentecostés

Whitsun [ˈwɪtsn] n (Brit) Pentecostés m

whittle [ˈwɪtl] vt: **to ~ away: whittle down** ir reduciendo

whizz [wɪz] vi: **to ~ past** or **by** pasar a toda velocidad

whizz kid n (col) prodigio(-a)

WHO n abbr (= World Health Organization) OMS f

 KEYWORD

who [huː] pron 1 (interrogative) quién; **who is it?, who's there?** ¿quién es?; **who are you looking for?** ¿a quién buscas?; **I told her**

who I was le dije quién era yo
2 (relative) que; **the man/woman who spoke to me** el hombre/la mujer que habló conmigo; **those who can swim** los que saben or sepan nadar

whodunit, whodunnit [huːˈdʌnɪt] n (col) novela policíaca

whoever [huːˈɛvəʳ] pron: **~ finds it** cualquiera or quienquiera que lo encuentre; **ask ~ you like** pregunta a quien quieras; **~ he marries** se case con quien se case

whole [həul] adj (complete) todo, entero; (not broken) intacto ▪ n (total) total m; (sum) conjunto; **~ villages were destroyed** pueblos enteros fueron destruídos; **the ~ of the town** toda la ciudad, la ciudad entera; **on the ~, as a ~** en general

wholehearted [həulˈhaːtɪd] adj (support, approval) total; (sympathy) todo

wholeheartedly [həulˈhaːtɪdlɪ] adv con entusiasmo

wholemeal [ˈhəulmiːl] adj (Brit: flour, bread) integral

wholesale [ˈhəulseɪl] n venta al por mayor ▪ adj al por mayor; (destruction) sistemático

wholesaler [ˈhəulseɪləʳ] n mayorista m/f

wholesome [ˈhəulsəm] adj sano

wholewheat [ˈhəulwiːt] adj = **wholemeal**

wholly [ˈhəulɪ] adv totalmente, enteramente

KEYWORD

whom [huːm] pron 1 (interrogative): **whom did you see?** ¿a quién viste?; **to whom did you give it?** ¿a quién se lo diste?; **tell me from whom you received it** dígame de quién lo recibiste
2 (relative) que; **to whom** a quien(es); **of whom** de quien(es), del/de la que; **the man whom I saw** el hombre qui vi; **the man to whom I wrote** el hombre a quien escribí; **the lady about whom I was talking** la señora de (la) que hablaba; **the lady with whom I was talking** la señora con quien or (la) que hablaba

whooping cough [ˈhuːpɪŋ-] n tos f ferina

whoops [wuːps] excl (also: **whoops-a-daisy!**) ¡huy!

whoosh [wuʃ] n: **it came out with a ~** (sauce etc) salió todo de repente; (air) salió con mucho ruido

whopper [ˈwɔpəʳ] n (col: lie) embuste m; (: large thing): **a ~** uno(-a) enorme

whopping [ˈwɔpɪŋ] adj (col) enorme

whore [hɔːʳ] n (col: pej) puta

W

KEYWORD

whose [huːz] *adj* **1** (*possessive: interrogative*) de quién; **whose book is this?**, **whose is this book?** ¿de quién es este libro?; **whose pencil have you taken?** ¿de quién es el lápiz que has cogido?; **whose daughter are you?** ¿de quién eres hija?
2 (*possessive: relative*) cuyo(-a) *m(f)*, cuyos(-as) *m(f)pl*; **the man whose son they rescued** el hombre cuyo hijo rescataron; **the girl whose sister he was speaking to** la chica con cuya hermana estaba hablando; **those whose passports I have** aquellas personas cuyos pasaportes tengo; **the woman whose car was stolen** la mujer a quien le robaron el coche
■ *pron* de quién; **whose is this?** ¿de quién es esto?; **I know whose it is** sé de quién es

 KEYWORD

why [waɪ] *adv* por qué; **why not?** ¿por qué no?; **why not do it now?** ¿por qué no lo haces (*or* hacemos ahora?
■ *conj*: **I wonder why he said that** me pregunto por qué dijo eso; **that's not why I'm here** no es por eso (por lo) que estoy aquí; **the reason why** la razón por la que
■ *excl* (*expressing surprise, shock, annoyance*) ¡hombre!, ¡vaya!; (*explaining*): **why, it's you!** ¡hombre, eres tú!; **why, that's impossible** ¡pero si eso es imposible!

whyever [waɪ'ɛvəʳ] *adv* por qué
WI *n abbr* (*Brit*: = *Women's Institute*) asociación de amas de casa ■ *abbr* (*Geo*) = **West Indies**; (*US*) = **Wisconsin**
wick [wɪk] *n* mecha
wicked ['wɪkɪd] *adj* malvado, cruel
wicker ['wɪkəʳ] *n* mimbre *m*
wickerwork ['wɪkəwəːk] *n* artículos *mpl* de mimbre
wicket ['wɪkɪt] *n* (*Cricket*) palos *mpl*
wicket keeper *n* guardameta *m*
wide [waɪd] *adj* ancho; (*area, knowledge*) vasto, grande; (*choice*) grande ■ *adv*: **to open ~** abrir de par en par; **to shoot ~** errar el tiro; **it is three metres ~** tiene tres metros de ancho
wide-angle lens ['waɪdæŋgl-] *n* (objetivo) gran angular *m*
wide-awake [waɪdə'weɪk] *adj* bien despierto
wide-eyed [waɪd'aɪd] *adj* con los ojos muy abiertos; (*fig*) ingenuo
widely ['waɪdlɪ] *adv* (*differing*) muy; **it is ~ believed that ...** existe la creencia generalizada de que ...; **to be ~ read** (*author*)

ser muy leído; (*reader*) haber leído mucho
widen ['waɪdn] *vt* ensanchar
wideness ['waɪdnɪs] *n* anchura; amplitud *f*
wide open *adj* abierto de par en par
wide-ranging [waɪd'reɪndʒɪŋ] *adj* (*survey, report*) de gran alcance; (*interests*) muy diversos
widespread ['waɪdsprɛd] *adj* (*belief etc*) extendido, general
widget ['wɪdʒɪt] *n* (*Comput*) mini aplicación *f*, widget *m*
widow ['wɪdəu] *n* viuda
widowed ['wɪdəud] *adj* viudo
widower ['wɪdəuəʳ] *n* viudo
width [wɪdθ] *n* anchura; (*of cloth*) ancho; **it's seven metres in ~** tiene siete metros de ancho
widthways ['wɪdθweɪz] *adv* a lo ancho
wield [wiːld] *vt* (*sword*) manejar; (*power*) ejercer
wife (*pl* **wives**) [waɪf, waɪvz] *n* mujer *f*, esposa
WiFi ['waɪfaɪ] *n abbr* (= *wireless fidelity*) wi-fi *m*
■ *adj* (*hot spot, network etc*) wi-fi
wig [wɪg] *n* peluca
wigging ['wɪgɪŋ] *n* (*Brit col*) rapapolvo, bronca
wiggle ['wɪgl] *vt* menear ■ *vi* menearse
wiggly ['wɪglɪ] *adj* (*line*) ondulado
wigwam ['wɪgwæm] *n* tipi *m*, tienda india
wild [waɪld] *adj* (*animal*) salvaje; (*plant*) silvestre; (*rough*) furioso, violento; (*idea*) descabellado; (*col: angry*) furioso ■ *n*: **the ~** la naturaleza; **wilds** *npl* regiones *fpl* salvajes, tierras *fpl* vírgenes; **to be ~ about** (*enthusiastic*) estar *or* andar loco por; **in its ~ state** en estado salvaje
wild card *n* (*Comput*) comodín *m*
wildcat ['waɪldkæt] *n* gato montés
wildcat strike *n* huelga salvaje
wilderness ['wɪldənɪs] *n* desierto; (*jungle*) jungla
wildfire ['waɪldfaɪəʳ] *n*: **to spread like ~** correr como un reguero de pólvora
wild-goose chase [waɪld'guːs-] *n* (*fig*) búsqueda inútil
wildlife ['waɪldlaɪf] *n* fauna
wildly ['waɪldlɪ] *adv* (*roughly*) violentamente; (*foolishly*) locamente; (*rashly*) descabelladamente
wiles [waɪlz] *npl* artimañas *fpl*, ardides *mpl*
wilful, willful (*US*) ['wɪlful] *adj* (*action*) deliberado; (*obstinate*) testarudo

 KEYWORD

will [wɪl] *aux vb* **1** (*forming future tense*): **I will finish it tomorrow** lo terminaré *or* voy a terminar mañana; **I will have finished it by tomorrow** lo habré terminado para mañana; **will you do it? — yes I will/no I**

won't ¿lo harás? — sí/no; **you won't lose it, will you?** no lo vayas a perder *or* no lo perderás ¿verdad?

2 (*in conjectures, predictions*): **he will** *or* **he'll be there by now** ya habrá llegado, ya debe (de) haber llegado; **that will be the postman** será el cartero, debe ser el cartero

3 (*in commands, requests, offers*): **will you be quiet!** ¿quieres callarte?; **will you help me?** ¿quieres ayudarme?; **will you have a cup of tea?** ¿te apetece un té?; **I won't put up with it!** ¡no lo soporto!

4 (*habits, persistence*): **the car won't start** el coche no arranca; **accidents will happen** son cosas que pasan

■ *vt* (*pt, pp* **willed**); **to will sb to do sth** desear que algn haga algo; **he willed himself to go on** con gran fuerza de voluntad, continuó

■ *n* **1** (*desire*) voluntad *f*; **against sb's will** contra la voluntad de algn; **he did it of his own free will** lo hizo por su propia voluntad **2** (*Law*) testamento; **to make a** *or* **one's will** hacer su testamento

willful ['wɪful] *adj* (*US*) = **wilful**

willing ['wɪlɪŋ] *adj* (*with goodwill*) de buena voluntad; complaciente; **he's ~ to do it** está dispuesto a hacerlo; **to show ~** mostrarse dispuesto

willingly ['wɪlɪŋlɪ] *adv* con mucho gusto

willingness ['wɪlɪŋnɪs] *n* buena voluntad

will-o'-the-wisp ['wɪləðə'wɪsp] *n* fuego fatuo; (*fig*) quimera

willow ['wɪləu] *n* sauce *m*

willpower ['wɪlpauəʳ] *n* fuerza de voluntad

willy-nilly [wɪlɪ'nɪlɪ] *adv* quiérase o no

wilt [wɪlt] *vi* marchitarse

Wilts *abbr* (*Brit*) = **Wiltshire**

wily ['waɪlɪ] *adj* astuto

wimp [wɪmp] *n* (*col*) enclenque *m/f*; (*character*) calzonazos *m inv*

win [wɪn] (*pt, pp* **won**) *n* (*in sports etc*) victoria, triunfo ■ *vt* ganar; (*obtain: contract etc*) conseguir, lograr ■ *vi* ganar

▶ **win over, win round** (*Brit*) *vt* convencer a

wince [wɪns] *vi* encogerse

winch [wɪntʃ] *n* torno

Winchester disk® ['wɪntʃɪstə-] *n* (*Comput*) disco Winchester®

wind [*n* wɪnd, *vb* waɪnd] (*pt, pp* **wound**) *n* viento; (*Med*) gases *mpl*; (*breath*) aliento ■ *vt* enrollar; (*wrap*) envolver; (*clock, toy*) dar cuerda a [waɪnd] (*take breath away from*) dejar sin aliento a ■ *vi* (*road, river*) serpentear; **into** *or* **against the ~** contra el viento; **to get ~ of sth** enterarse de algo; **to break ~** ventosear

▶ **wind down** *vt* (*car window*) bajar; (*fig:*

production, business) disminuir

▶ **wind up** *vt* (*clock*) dar cuerda a; (*debate*) concluir, terminar

windbreak ['wɪndbreɪk] *n* barrera contra el viento

windcheater ['wɪndtʃiːtəʳ], **windbreaker** (*US*) ['wɪndbreɪkəʳ] *n* cazadora

winder ['waɪndəʳ] *n* (*on watch*) cuerda

wind erosion *n* erosión *f* del viento

windfall ['wɪndfɔːl] *n* golpe *m* de suerte

wind farm *n* parque *m* eólico

winding ['waɪndɪŋ] *adj* (*road*) tortuoso

wind instrument *n* (*Mus*) instrumento de viento

windmill ['wɪndmɪl] *n* molino de viento

window ['wɪndəu] *n* ventana; (*in car, train*) ventana; (*in shop etc*) escaparate *m*, vitrina (*LAm*), vidriera (*LAm*); (*Comput*) ventana

window box *n* jardinera (de ventana)

window cleaner *n* (*person*) limpiacristales *m inv*

window dressing *n* decoración *f* de escaparates

window envelope *n* sobre *m* de ventanilla

window frame *n* marco de ventana

window ledge *n* alféizar *m*, repisa

window pane *n* cristal *m*

window-shopping [wɪndəu'ʃɔpɪŋ] *n*: **to go ~** ir a ver *or* mirar escaparates

windowsill ['wɪndəusɪl] *n* alféizar *m*, repisa

windpipe ['wɪndpaɪp] *n* tráquea

wind power *n* energía eólica

windscreen ['wɪndskriːn], **windshield** (*US*) ['wɪndʃiːld] *n* parabrisas *m inv*

windscreen washer, windshield washer (*US*) *n* lavaparabrisas *m inv*

windscreen wiper, windshield wiper (*US*) *n* limpiaparabrisas *m inv*

windsurfing ['wɪndsəːfɪŋ] *n* windsurf *m*

windswept ['wɪndswept] *adj* azotado por el viento

wind tunnel *n* túnel *m* aerodinámico

windy ['wɪndɪ] *adj* de mucho viento; **it's ~** hace viento

wine [waɪn] *n* vino ■ *vt*: **to ~ and dine sb** agasajar *or* festejar a algn

wine bar *n* bar especializado en vinos

wine cellar *n* bodega

wine glass *n* copa (de *or* para vino)

wine list *n* lista de vinos

wine merchant *n* vinatero

wine tasting *n* degustación *f* de vinos

wine waiter *n* escanciador *m*

wing [wɪŋ] *n* ala; (*Brit Aut*) aleta; **wings** *npl* (*Theat*) bastidores *mpl*

winger ['wɪŋəʳ] *n* (*Sport*) extremo

wing mirror *n* (espejo) retrovisor *m*

W

wing nut n tuerca (de) mariposa
wingspan ['wɪŋspæn], **wingspread** ['wɪŋsprɛd] n envergadura
wink [wɪŋk] n guiño; (blink) pestañeo ▪ vi guiñar; (blink) pestañear; (light etc) parpadear
winkle ['wɪŋkl] n bígaro, bigarro
winner ['wɪnəʳ] n ganador(a) m(f)
winning ['wɪnɪŋ] adj (team) ganador(a); (goal) decisivo; (charming) encantador(a)
winning post n meta
winnings ['wɪnɪŋz] npl ganancias fpl
winter ['wɪntəʳ] n invierno ▪ vi invernar
winter sports npl deportes mpl de invierno
wintry ['wɪntrɪ] adj invernal
wipe [waɪp] n: **to give sth a ~** pasar un trapo sobre algo ▪ vt limpiar; **to ~ one's nose** limpiarse la nariz
   ▸ **wipe off** vt limpiar con un trapo
   ▸ **wipe out** vt (debt) liquidar; (memory) borrar; (destroy) destruir
   ▸ **wipe up** vt limpiar
wire ['waɪəʳ] n alambre m; (Elec) cable m (eléctrico); (Tel) telegrama m ▪ vt (house) poner la instalación eléctrica en; (also: **wire up**) conectar
wire cutters npl cortaalambres msg inv
wireless ['waɪəlɪs] n (Brit) radio f ▪ adj inalámbrico
wireless technology n tecnología inalámbrica
wire mesh, wire netting n tela metálica
wire service n (US) agencia de noticias
wire-tapping ['waɪə'tæpɪŋ] n intervención f telefónica
wiring ['waɪərɪŋ] n instalación f eléctrica
wiry ['waɪərɪ] adj enjuto y fuerte
Wis., Wisc. abbr (US) = **Wisconsin**
wisdom ['wɪzdəm] n sabiduría, saber m; (good sense) cordura
wisdom tooth n muela del juicio
wise [waɪz] adj sabio; (sensible) juicioso; **I'm none the wiser** sigo sin entender
   ▸ **wise up** vi (col): **to ~ up (to sth)** enterarse (de algo)
...wise [waɪz] suff: **timewise** en cuanto a or respecto al tiempo
wisecrack ['waɪzkræk] n broma
wish [wɪʃ] n (desire) deseo ▪ vt desear; (want) querer; **best wishes** (on birthday etc) felicidades fpl; **with best wishes** (in letter) saludos mpl, recuerdos mpl; **he wished me well** me deseó mucha suerte; **to ~ sth on sb** imponer algo a algn; **to ~ to do/sb to do sth** querer hacer/que algn haga algo; **to ~ for** desear
wishbone ['wɪʃbəun] n espoleta (de la que tiran dos personas quien se quede con el hueso más largo pide un deseo)
wishful ['wɪʃful] adj: **it's ~ thinking** eso es hacerse ilusiones
wishy-washy ['wɪʃɪwɔʃɪ] adj (col: colour) desvaído; (: ideas, thinking) flojo
wisp [wɪsp] n mechón m; (of smoke) voluta
wistful ['wɪstful] adj pensativo; (nostalgic) nostálgico
wit [wɪt] n (wittiness) ingenio, gracia; (intelligence: also: **wits**) inteligencia; (person) chistoso(-a); **to have** or **keep one's wits about one** no perder la cabeza
witch [wɪtʃ] n bruja
witchcraft ['wɪtʃkrɑ:ft] n brujería
witch doctor n hechicero
witch-hunt ['wɪtʃhʌnt] n (Pol) caza de brujas

 KEYWORD

with [wɪð, wɪθ] prep **1** (accompanying, in the company of) con (con +mí, ti, sí = conmigo, contigo, consigo); **I was with him** estaba con él; **we stayed with friends** nos quedamos en casa de unos amigos
2 (descriptive, indicating manner etc) con; de; **a room with a view** una habitación con vistas; **the man with the grey hat/blue eyes** el hombre del sombrero gris/de los ojos azules; **red with anger** rojo de ira; **to shake with fear** temblar de miedo; **to fill sth with water** llenar algo de agua
3: **I'm with you/I'm not with you** (understand) ya te entiendo/no te entiendo; **I'm not really with it today** no doy pie con bola hoy

withdraw [wɪθ'drɔ:] (irreg: like **draw**) vt retirar ▪ vi retirarse; (go back on promise) retractarse; **to ~ money (from the bank)** retirar fondos (del banco); **to ~ into o.s.** ensimismarse
withdrawal [wɪθ'drɔ:əl] n retirada
withdrawal symptoms npl síndrome m de abstinencia
withdrawn [wɪθ'drɔ:n] adj (person) reservado, introvertido ▪ pp of **withdraw**
wither ['wɪðəʳ] vi marchitarse
withered ['wɪðəd] adj marchito, seco
withhold [wɪθ'həuld] vt (irreg: like **hold**) (money) retener; (decision) aplazar; (permission) negar; (information) ocultar
within [wɪð'ɪn] prep dentro de ▪ adv dentro; **~ reach** al alcance de la mano; **~ sight of** a la vista de; **~ the week** antes de que acabe la semana; **to be ~ the law** atenerse a la legalidad; **~ an hour from now** dentro de una hora

without [wɪð'aut] *prep* sin; **to go** *or* **do ~ sth** prescindir de algo; **~ anybody knowing** sin saberlo nadie
withstand [wɪθ'stænd] *vt* (*irreg: like* **stand**) resistir a
witness ['wɪtnɪs] *n* (*person*) testigo *m/f*; (*evidence*) testimonio ■ *vt* (*event*) presenciar, ser testigo de; (*document*) atestiguar la veracidad de; **~ for the prosecution/ defence** testigo de cargo/descargo; **to ~ to (having seen) sth** dar testimonio de (haber visto) algo
witness box, witness stand (*US*) *n* tribuna de los testigos
witticism ['wɪtɪsɪzm] *n* dicho ingenioso
wittily ['wɪtɪlɪ] *adv* ingeniosamente
witty ['wɪtɪ] *adj* ingenioso
wives [waɪvz] *npl of* **wife**
wizard ['wɪzəd] *n* hechicero
wizened ['wɪznd] *adj* arrugado, marchito
wk *abbr* = **week**
Wm. *abbr* = **William**
WMD *n abbr see* **weapons of mass destruction**
WO *n abbr* = **warrant officer**
wobble ['wɔbl] *vi* tambalearse
wobbly ['wɔblɪ] *adj* (*hand, voice*) tembloroso; (*table, chair*) tambaleante, cojo
woe [wəu] *n* desgracia
woeful ['wəuful] *adj* (*bad*) lamentable; (*sad*) apesadumbrado
wok [wɔk] *n* wok *m*
woke [wəuk] *pt of* **wake**
woken ['wəukn] *pp of* **wake**
wolf (*pl* **wolves**) [wulf, wulvz] *n* lobo
woman (*pl* **women**) ['wumən, 'wɪmɪn] *n* mujer *f*; **young ~** (mujer *f*) joven *f*; **women's page** (*Press*) sección *f* de la mujer
woman doctor *n* doctora
woman friend *n* amiga
womanize ['wumənaɪz] *vi* ser un mujeriego
womanly ['wumənlɪ] *adj* femenino
womb [wu:m] *n* (*Anat*) matriz *f*, útero
women ['wɪmɪn] *npl of* **woman**
Women's Liberation Movement, Women's Movement *n* (*also:* **women's lib**) Movimiento de liberación de la mujer
won [wʌn] *pt, pp of* **win**
wonder ['wʌndər] *n* maravilla, prodigio; (*feeling*) asombro ■ *vi*: **to ~ whether** preguntarse si; **to ~ at** asombrarse de; **to ~ about** pensar sobre *or* en; **it's no ~ that** no es de extrañar que
wonderful ['wʌndəful] *adj* maravilloso
wonderfully ['wʌndəfəlɪ] *adv* maravillosamente, estupendamente
wonky ['wɔŋkɪ] *adj* (*Brit col: unsteady*) poco seguro, cojo; (: *broken down*) estropeado

wont [wɔnt] *n*: **as is his/her ~** como tiene por costumbre
won't [wəunt] = **will not**
woo [wu:] *vt* (*woman*) cortejar
wood [wud] *n* (*timber*) madera; (*forest*) bosque *m* ■ *cpd* de madera
wood alcohol *n* (*US*) alcohol *m* desnaturalizado
wood carving *n* tallado en madera
wooded ['wudɪd] *adj* arbolado
wooden ['wudn] *adj* de madera; (*fig*) inexpresivo
woodland ['wudlənd] *n* bosque *m*
woodpecker ['wudpɛkər] *n* pájaro carpintero
wood pigeon *n* paloma torcaz
woodwind ['wudwɪnd] *n* (*Mus*) instrumentos *mpl* de viento de madera
woodwork ['wudwə:k] *n* carpintería
woodworm ['wudwə:m] *n* carcoma
woof [wuf] *n* (*of dog*) ladrido ■ *vi* ladrar; **~, ~!** ¡guau, guau!
wool [wul] *n* lana; **knitting ~** lana (de hacer punto); **to pull the ~ over sb's eyes** (*fig*) dar a algn gato por liebre
woollen, woolen (*US*) ['wulən] *adj* de lana ■ *n*: **woollens** géneros *mpl* de lana
woolly, wooly (*US*) ['wulɪ] *adj* de lana; (*fig: ideas*) confuso
woozy ['wu:zɪ] *adj* (*col*) mareado
word [wə:d] *n* palabra; (*news*) noticia; (*promise*) palabra (de honor) ■ *vt* redactar; **~ for ~** palabra por palabra; **what's the ~ for "pen" in Spanish?** ¿cómo se dice "pen" en español?; **to put sth into words** expresar algo en palabras; **to have a ~ with sb** hablar (dos palabras) con algn; **in other words** en otras palabras; **to break/keep one's ~** faltar a la palabra/cumplir la promesa; **to leave ~ (with/for sb) that ...** dejar recado (con/para algn) de que ...; **to have words with sb** (*quarrel with*) discutir *or* reñir con algn
wording ['wə:dɪŋ] *n* redacción *f*
word-of-mouth [wə:dəv'mauθ] *n*: **by** *or* **through ~** de palabra, por el boca a boca
word-perfect ['wə:d'pə:fɪkt] *adj* (*speech etc*) sin faltas de expresión
word processing *n* procesamiento *or* tratamiento de textos
word processor [-'prəusɛsər] *n* procesador *m* de textos
wordwrap ['wə:dræp] *n* (*Comput*) salto de línea automático
wordy ['wə:dɪ] *adj* verboso, prolijo
wore [wɔ:r] *pt of* **wear**
work [wə:k] *n* trabajo; (*job*) empleo, trabajo; (*Art, Lit*) obra ■ *vi* trabajar; (*mechanism*) funcionar, marchar; (*medicine*) ser eficaz,

W

surtir efecto ■ *vt* (*shape*) trabajar; (*stone etc*)
tallar; (*mine etc*) explotar; (*machine*) manejar,
hacer funcionar; (*cause*) producir; **to go to**
~ ir a trabajar *or* al trabajo; **to be at ~ (on**
sth) estar trabajando (en algo); **to set to**
~, **start** ~ ponerse a trabajar; **to be out of**
~ estar parado, no tener trabajo; **his life's**
~ el trabajo de su vida; **to ~ hard** trabajar
mucho *or* duro; **to ~ to rule** (*Industry*)
hacer una huelga de celo; **to ~ loose** (*part*)
desprenderse; (*knot*) aflojarse; *see also* **works**
▶ **work off** *vt*: **to ~ off one's feelings**
desahogarse
▶ **work on** *vt fus* trabajar en, dedicarse a;
(*principle*) basarse en; **he's working on the**
car está reparando el coche
▶ **work out** *vi* (*plans etc*) salir bien, funcionar;
(*Sport*) hacer ejercicios ■ *vt* (*problem*) resolver;
(*plan*) elaborar; **it works out at £100**
asciende a 100 libras
▶ **work up** *vt*: **he worked his way up in**
the company ascendió en la compañía
mediante sus propios esfuerzos
workable ['wə:kəbl] *adj* (*solution*) práctico,
factible
workaholic [wə:kə'hɔlɪk] *n* adicto(-a) al
trabajo
workbench ['wə:kbɛntʃ] *n* banco *or* mesa de
trabajo
worked up [wə:kt-] *adj*: **to get ~** excitarse
worker ['wə:kəʳ] *n* trabajador(a) *m(f)*,
obrero(-a) *m(f)*; **office ~** oficinista *m/f*
work force *n* mano *f* de obra
work-in ['wə:kɪn] *n* (*Brit*) ocupación *f* (de la
empresa sin interrupción del trabajo)
working ['wə:kɪŋ] *adj* (*day, week*) laborable;
(*tools, conditions, clothes*) de trabajo; (*wife*) que
trabaja; (*partner*) activo
working capital *n* (*Comm*) capital *m*
circulante
working class *n* clase *f* obrera ■ *adj*:
working-class obrero
working knowledge *n* conocimientos *mpl*
básicos
working man *n* obrero
working order *n*: **in ~** en funcionamiento
working party *n* comisión *f* de
investigación, grupo de trabajo
working week *n* semana laboral
work-in-progress ['wə:kɪn'prəugrɛs] *n*
(*Comm*) trabajo en curso
workload ['wə:kləud] *n* cantidad *f* de trabajo
workman ['wə:kmən] *n* obrero
workmanship ['wə:kmənʃɪp] *n* (*art*) hechura;
(*skill*) habilidad *f*
workmate ['wə:kmeɪt] *n* compañero(-a) de
trabajo

workout ['wə:kaut] *n* (*Sport*) sesión *f* de
ejercicios
work permit *n* permiso de trabajo
works [wə:ks] *nsg* (*Brit: factory*) fábrica ■ *npl*
(*of clock, machine*) mecanismo; **road ~** obras *fpl*
works council *n* comité *m* de empresa
worksheet ['wə:kʃi:t] *n* (*Comput*) hoja de
trabajo; (*Scol*) hoja de ejercicios
workshop ['wə:kʃɔp] *n* taller *m*
work station *n* estación *f* de trabajo
work study *n* estudio del trabajo
worktop ['wə:ktɔp] *n* encimera
work-to-rule ['wə:ktə'ru:l] *n* (*Brit*) huelga
de celo
world [wə:ld] *n* mundo ■ *cpd* (*champion*) del
mundo; (*power, war*) mundial; **all over the**
~ por todo el mundo, en el mundo entero;
the business ~ el mundo de los negocios;
what in the ~ is he doing? ¿qué diablos está
haciendo?; **to think the ~ of sb** (*fig*) tener
un concepto muy alto de algn; **to do sb a ~ of**
good sentar muy bien a algn; **W~ War One/**
Two la primera/segunda Guerra Mundial
World Cup *n* (*Football*): **the ~** el Mundial, los
Mundiales
world-famous [wə:ld'feɪməs] *adj* de fama
mundial, mundialmente famoso
worldly ['wə:ldlɪ] *adj* mundano
world music *n* música étnica
World Series *n*: **the ~** (*US Baseball*) el
campeonato nacional de béisbol de EEUU
World Service *n see* **BBC**
world-wide ['wə:ldwaɪd] *adj* mundial,
universal
worm [wə:m] *n* gusano; (*earthworm*) lombriz *f*
worn [wɔ:n] *pp of* **wear** ■ *adj* usado
worn-out ['wɔ:naut] *adj* (*object*) gastado;
(*person*) rendido, agotado
worried ['wʌrɪd] *adj* preocupado; **to be ~**
about sth estar preocupado por algo
worrisome ['wʌrɪsəm] *adj* preocupante,
inquietante
worry ['wʌrɪ] *n* preocupación *f* ■ *vt*
preocupar, inquietar ■ *vi* preocuparse;
to ~ about *or* **over sth/sb** preocuparse por
algo/algn
worrying ['wʌrɪɪŋ] *adj* inquietante
worse [wə:s] *adj, adv* peor ■ *n* el peor, lo peor;
a change for the ~ un empeoramiento; **so**
much the ~ for you tanto peor para ti; **he is**
none the ~ for it se ha quedado tan fresco *or*
tan tranquilo; **to get ~, to grow ~** empeorar
worsen ['wə:sn] *vt, vi* empeorar
worse off *adj* (*fig*): **you'll be ~ this way** de
esta forma estarás peor que antes
worship ['wə:ʃɪp] *n* (*organized worship*) culto;
(*act*) adoración *f* ■ *vt* adorar; **Your W~** (*Brit*:

to mayor) su Ilustrísima; (: *to judge*) su señoría

worshipper, worshiper (US) ['wəːʃɪpəʳ] *n*
devoto(-a)

worst [wəːst] *adj* (el/la) peor ■ *adv* peor ■ *n*
lo peor; **at** ~ en el peor de los casos; **to come
off** ~ llevar la peor parte; **if the** ~ **comes to
the** ~ en el peor de los casos

worst-case ['wəːstkeɪs] *adj*: **the** ~ **scenario** el
peor de los casos

worsted ['wustɪd] *n*: (**wool**) ~ estambre *m*

worth [wəːθ] *n* valor *m* ■ *adj*: **to be** ~ valer;
how much is it ~? ¿cuánto vale?; **it's** ~ **it**
vale *or* merece la pena; **to be** ~ **one's while
(to do)** merecer la pena (hacer); **it's not** ~
the trouble no vale *or* merece la pena

worthless ['wəːθlɪs] *adj* sin valor; (*useless*)
inútil

worthwhile ['wəːθwaɪl] *adj* (*activity*) que
merece la pena; (*cause*) loable

worthy ['wəːðɪ] *adj* (*person*) respetable;
(*motive*) honesto; ~ **of** digno de

 KEYWORD

would [wud] *aux vb* **1** (*conditional tense*): **if you
asked him he would do it** si se lo pidieras,
lo haría; **if you had asked him he would
have done it** si se lo hubieras pedido, lo
habría *or* hubiera hecho
2 (*in offers, invitations, requests*): **would you like
a biscuit?** ¿quieres una galleta?; (*formal*)
¿querría una galleta?; **would you ask him
to come in?** ¿quiere hacerle pasar?; **would
you open the window please?** ¿quiere *or*
podría abrir la ventana, por favor?
3 (*in indirect speech*): **I said I would do it** dije
que lo haría
4 (*emphatic*): **it WOULD have to snow today!**
¡tenía que nevar precisamente hoy!
5 (*insistence*): **she wouldn't behave** no quiso
comportarse bien
6 (*conjecture*): **it would have been midnight**
sería medianoche; **it would seem so** parece
ser que sí
7 (*indicating habit*): **he would go there on
Mondays** iba allí los lunes

would-be ['wudbiː] *adj* (*pej*) presunto
wouldn't ['wudnt] = **would not**
wound [*n* wuːnd, *vb* waund] *pt, pp of* **wind** ■ *n*
herida ■ *vt* herir
wove [wəuv] *pt of* **weave**
woven ['wəuvən] *pp of* **weave**
WP *n abbr* = **word processing**; **word processor**
■ *abbr* (Brit col: = *weather permitting*) si lo
permite el tiempo
WPC *n abbr* (Brit) = **woman police constable**

wpm *abbr* (= *words per minute*) p.p.m.
WRAC *n abbr* (Brit: = *Women's Royal Army Corps*)
cuerpo auxiliar femenino del ejército de tierra
WRAF *n abbr* (Brit: = *Women's Royal Air Force*)
cuerpo auxiliar femenino del ejército del aire
wrangle ['ræŋgl] *n* riña ■ *vi* reñir
wrap [ræp] *n* (*stole*) chal *m* ■ *vt* (*also*: **wrap
up**) envolver; **under wraps** (*fig*: *plan, scheme*)
oculto, tapado
wrapper ['ræpəʳ] *n* (Brit: *of book*)
sobrecubierta; (*on chocolate etc*) envoltura
wrapping paper ['ræpɪŋ-] *n* papel *m* de
envolver
wrath [rɔθ] *n* cólera
wreak [riːk] *vt* (*destruction*) causar; **to** ~ **havoc
(on)** hacer *or* causar estragos (en); **to** ~
vengeance (on) vengarse (en)
wreath (*pl* **wreaths**) [riːθ, riːðz] *n* (*also*:
funeral wreath) corona; (*of flowers*) guirnalda
wreck [rɛk] *n* (*ship*: *destruction*) naufragio;
(: *remains*) restos *mpl* del barco; (*pej*: *person*)
ruina ■ *vt* destrozar; **to be wrecked** (*Naut*)
naufragar
wreckage ['rɛkɪdʒ] *n* (*remains*) restos *mpl*;
(*of building*) escombros *mpl*
wrecker ['rɛkəʳ] *n* (US: *breakdown van*) camión-
grúa *m*
WREN [rɛn] *n abbr* (Brit) miembro del WRNS
wren [rɛn] *n* (*Zool*) reyezuelo
wrench [rɛntʃ] *n* (*Tech*) llave *f* inglesa; (*tug*)
tirón *m* ■ *vt* arrancar; **to** ~ **sth from sb**
arrebatar algo violentamente a algn
wrest [rɛst] *vt*: **to** ~ **sth from sb** arrebatar *or*
arrancar algo a algn
wrestle ['rɛsl] *vi*: **to** ~ **(with sb)** luchar (con *or*
contra algn)
wrestler ['rɛsləʳ] *n* luchador(a) *m(f)* (de lucha
libre)
wrestling ['rɛslɪŋ] *n* lucha libre
wrestling match *n* combate *m* de lucha libre
wretch [rɛtʃ] *n* desgraciado(-a), miserable
m/f; **little** ~! (*often humorous*) ¡granuja!
wretched ['rɛtʃɪd] *adj* miserable
wriggle ['rɪgl] *vi* serpentear
wring (*pt, pp* **wrung**) [rɪŋ, rʌŋ] *vt* torcer,
retorcer; (*wet clothes*) escurrir; (*fig*): **to** ~ **sth
out of sb** sacar algo por la fuerza a algn
wringer ['rɪŋəʳ] *n* escurridor *m*
wringing ['rɪŋɪŋ] *adj* (*also*: **wringing wet**)
empapado
wrinkle ['rɪŋkl] *n* arruga ■ *vt* arrugar ■ *vi*
arrugarse
wrinkled ['rɪŋkld], **wrinkly** ['rɪŋklɪ] *adj*
(*fabric, paper etc*) arrugado
wrist [rɪst] *n* muñeca
wristband ['rɪstbænd] *n* (Brit: *of shirt*) puño;
(: *of watch*) correa

W

wrist watch *n* reloj *m* de pulsera
writ [rɪt] *n* mandato judicial; **to serve a ~ on sb** notificar un mandato judicial a algn
writable ['raɪtəbl] *adj* (CD, DVD) escribible
write (*pt* **wrote**, *pp* **written**) [raɪt, rəʊt, 'rɪtn] *vt, vi* escribir; **to ~ sb a letter** escribir una carta a algn
  ▸ **write away** *vi*: **to ~ away for** (*information, goods*) pedir por escrito *or* carta
  ▸ **write down** *vt* escribir; (*note*) apuntar
  ▸ **write off** *vt* (*debt*) borrar (como incobrable); (*fig*) desechar por inútil; (*smash up: car*) destrozar
  ▸ **write out** *vt* escribir
  ▸ **write up** *vt* redactar
write-off ['raɪtɔf] *n* siniestro total; **the car is a ~** el coche es pura chatarra
write-protect ['raɪtprə'tɛkt] *vt* (*Comput*) proteger contra escritura
writer ['raɪtər] *n* escritor(a) *m(f)*
write-up ['raɪtʌp] *n* (*review*) crítica, reseña
writhe [raɪð] *vi* retorcerse
writing ['raɪtɪŋ] *n* escritura; (*handwriting*) letra; (*of author*) obras *fpl*; **in ~** por escrito; **to put sth in ~** poner algo por escrito; **in my own ~** escrito por mí; *see also* **writings**
writing case *n* estuche *m* de papel de escribir
writing desk *n* escritorio
writing paper *n* papel *m* de escribir
writings *npl* obras *fpl*
written ['rɪtn] *pp of* **write**
WRNS *n abbr* (Brit: = Women's Royal Naval Service) cuerpo auxiliar femenino de la armada
wrong [rɔŋ] *adj* (*wicked*) malo; (*unfair*) injusto; (*incorrect*) equivocado, incorrecto; (*not suitable*) inoportuno, inconveniente ▪ *adv* mal ▪ *n*

mal *m*; (*injustice*) injusticia ▪ *vt* ser injusto con; (*hurt*) agraviar; **to be ~** (*answer*) estar equivocado; (*in doing, saying*) equivocarse; **it's ~ to steal, stealing is ~** es mal robar; **you are ~ to do it** haces mal en hacerlo; **you are ~ about that, you've got it ~** en eso estás equivocado; **to be in the ~** no tener razón; (*guilty*) tener la culpa; **what's ~?** ¿qué pasa?; **what's ~ with the car?** ¿qué le pasa al coche?; **there's nothing ~** no pasa nada; **you have the ~ number** (*Tel*) se ha equivocado de número; **to go ~** (*person*) equivocarse; (*plan*) salir mal; (*machine*) estropearse
wrongdoer ['rɔŋduər] *n* malhechor(a) *m(f)*
wrong-foot [rɔŋ'fʊt] *vt* (*Sport*) hacer perder el equilibrio a; (*fig*) poner en un aprieto a
wrongful ['rɔŋful] *adj* injusto; **~ dismissal** (*Industry*) despido improcedente
wrongly ['rɔŋlɪ] *adv* (*answer, do, count*) incorrectamente; (*treat*) injustamente
wrote [rəʊt] *pt of* **write**
wrought [rɔːt] *adj*: **~ iron** hierro forjado
wrung [rʌŋ] *pt, pp of* **wring**
WRVS *n abbr* (Brit: = Women's Royal Voluntary Service) cuerpo de voluntarias al servicio de la comunidad
wry [raɪ] *adj* irónico
wt. *abbr* = **weight**
WV, W.Va. *abbr* (US) = **West Virginia**
WWW *n abbr* (= World Wide Web) WWW *m or f*
WY, Wyo. *abbr* (US) = **Wyoming**
WYSIWYG ['wɪzɪwɪg] *abbr* (Comput: = what you see is what you get) tipo de presentación en un procesador de textos

X, x [eks] *n* (*letter*) X, x *f*; (*Brit Cine: formerly*) no apto para menores de 18 años; **X for Xmas** X de Xiquena; **if you earn X dollars a year** si ganas X dólares al año

X-certificate ['ɛkssə'tɪfɪkɪt] *adj* (*Brit: film: formerly*) no apto para menores de 18 años

Xerox® ['zɪərɔks] *n* (*also:* **Xerox machine**) fotocopiadora; (*photocopy*) fotocopia ■ *vt* fotocopiar

XL *abbr* = **extra large**

Xmas ['ɛksməs] *n abbr* = **Christmas**

X-rated ['eks'reɪtɪd] *adj* (*US: film*) no apto para menores de 18 años

X-ray [ɛks'reɪ] *n* radiografía; **X-rays** *npl* rayos *mpl* X ■ *vt* radiografiar

xylophone ['zaɪləfəun] *n* xilófono

Yy

Y, y [waɪ] n (letter) Y, y f; **Y for Yellow**, (US) Y for Yoke Y de Yegua

Y2K [ˌwaɪtuːˈkeɪ] abbr (= Year 2000): **the ~ problem** (Comput) el efecto 2000

yacht [jɔt] n yate m

yachting [ˈjɔtɪŋ] n (sport) balandrismo

yachtsman [ˈjɔtsmən] n balandrista m

yachtswoman [ˈjɔtswumən] n balandrista

yam [jæm] n ñame m; (sweet potato) batata, camote m (LAm)

Yank [jæŋk], **Yankee** [ˈjæŋkɪ] n (pej) yanqui m/f

yank [jæŋk] vt tirar de, jalar de (LAm) ■ n tirón m

yap [jæp] vi (dog) aullar

yard [jɑːd] n patio; (US: garden) jardín m; (measure) yarda; **builder's ~** almacén m

yardstick [ˈjɑːdstɪk] n (fig) criterio, norma

yarn [jɑːn] n hilo; (tale) cuento (chino), historia

yawn [jɔːn] n bostezo ■ vi bostezar

yawning [ˈjɔːnɪŋ] adj (gap) muy abierto

yd. abbr (= yard) yda

yeah [jɛə] adv (col) sí

year [jɪəʳ] n año; (Scol, Univ) curso; **this ~** este año; **~ in, ~ out** año tras año; **a** or **per ~** al año; **to be eight years old** tener ocho años; **she's three years old** tiene tres años; **an eight-~-old child** un niño de ocho años (de edad)

yearbook [ˈjɪəbuk] n anuario

yearling [ˈjɪəlɪŋ] n (racehorse) potro de un año

yearly [ˈjɪəlɪ] adj anual ■ adv anualmente, cada año; **twice ~** dos veces al año

yearn [jəːn] vi: **to ~ for sth** añorar algo, suspirar por algo

yearning [ˈjəːnɪŋ] n ansia; (longing) añoranza

yeast [jiːst] n levadura

yell [jɛl] n grito, alarido ■ vi gritar

yellow [ˈjɛləu] adj, n amarillo

yellow fever n fiebre f amarilla

yellowish [ˈjɛləuɪʃ] adj amarillento

Yellow Pages® npl páginas fpl amarillas

Yellow Sea n: **the ~** el Mar Amarillo

yelp [jɛlp] n aullido ■ vi aullar

Yemen [ˈjɛmən] n Yemen m

Yemeni [ˈjɛmənɪ] adj, n yemení m/f, yemenita m/f

yen [jɛn] n (currency) yen m

yeoman [ˈjəumən] n: **Y~ of the Guard** alabardero de la Casa Real

yes [jɛs] adv, n sí m; **to say/answer ~** decir/contestar que sí; **to say ~ (to)** decir que sí (a), conformarse (con)

yes man n pelotillero

yesterday [ˈjɛstədɪ] adv, n ayer m; **~ morning/evening** ayer por la mañana/tarde; **all day ~** todo el día de ayer; **the day before ~** antes de ayer, anteayer

yet [jɛt] adv todavía ■ conj sin embargo, a pesar de todo; **~ again** de nuevo; **it is not finished ~** todavía no está acabado; **the best ~** el/la mejor hasta ahora; **as ~** hasta ahora, todavía

yew [juː] n tejo

Y-fronts® [ˈwaɪfrʌnts] npl (Brit) calzoncillos mpl, eslip msg tradicional

YHA n abbr (Brit: = Youth Hostel Association) ≈ Red f Española de Albergues Juveniles

Yiddish [ˈjɪdɪʃ] n yiddish m

yield [jiːld] n producción f; (Agr) cosecha; (Comm) rendimiento ■ vt producir, dar; (profit) rendir ■ vi rendirse, ceder; (US Aut) ceder el paso; **a ~ of 5%** un rédito del 5 por ciento

YMCA n abbr (= Young Men's Christian Association) Asociación f de Jóvenes Cristianos

yob [ˈjɔb], **yobbo** [ˈjɔbbəu] n (Brit col) gamberro

yodel [ˈjəudl] vi cantar a la tirolesa

yoga [ˈjəugə] n yoga m

yoghurt, yogurt [ˈjəugət] n yogur m

yoke [jəuk] n (of oxen) yunta; (on shoulders) balancín m; (fig) yugo ■ vt (also: **yoke together**: oxen) uncir

yolk [jəuk] n yema (de huevo)

yonder [ˈjɔndəʳ] adv allá (a lo lejos)

yonks [jɔŋks] *npl* (*col*): **I haven't seen him for** ~ hace siglos que no lo veo
Yorks [jɔ:ks] *abbr* (*Brit*) = **Yorkshire**

 KEYWORD

you [ju:] *pron* **1** (*subject: familiar*) tú, vosotros(-as) (*SP*) *pl*, ustedes (*LAm*); (*polite*) usted, ustedes *pl*; **you are very kind** eres/es *etc* muy amable; **you French enjoy your food** a vosotros (*or* ustedes) los franceses os (*or* les) gusta la comida; **you and I will go** iremos tú y yo
2 (*object: direct: familiar*) te, os *pl* (*SP*), les (*LAm*); (*polite*) lo *or* le; (*pl*) los *or* les; (*f*) la; (*pl*) las; **I know you** te/le *etc* conozco
3 (*object: indirect: familiar*) te, os *pl* (*SP*), les (*LAm*); (*polite*) le, les *pl*; **I gave the letter to you yesterday** te/os *etc* di la carta ayer
4 (*stressed*): **I told YOU to do it** te dije a ti que lo hicieras, es a ti a quien dije que lo hicieras; *see also* **3, 5**
5 (*after prep*: NB: *con* +*ti* = *contigo: familiar*) ti, vosotros(-as) *pl* (*SP*), ustedes *pl* (*LAm*); (: *polite*) usted, ustedes *pl*; **it's for you** es para ti/ vosotros *etc*
6 (*comparisons: familiar*) tú, vosotros(-as) *pl* (*SP*), ustedes *pl* (*LAm*); (: *polite*) usted, ustedes *pl*; **she's younger than you** es más joven que tú/vosotros *etc*
7 (*impersonal: one*): **fresh air does you good** el aire puro (te) hace bien; **you never know** nunca se sabe; **you can't do that!** ¡eso no se hace!

you'd [ju:d] = **you had**; **you would**
you'll [ju:l] = **you will**; **you shall**
young [jʌŋ] *adj* joven ■ *npl* (*of animal*) cría; (*people*): **the** ~ los jóvenes, la juventud; **a** ~ **man/lady** un(a) joven; **my younger brother** mi hermano menor *or* pequeño; **the younger generation** la nueva generación
youngster ['jʌŋstəʳ] *n* joven *m/f*
your [jɔ:ʳ] *adj* tu, vuestro *pl*; (*formal*) su; ~ **house** tu *etc* casa; *see also* **my**
you're [juəʳ] = **you are**
yours [jɔ:z] *pron* tuyo, vuestro *pl*; (*formal*) suyo; **a friend of** ~ un amigo tuyo *etc*; *see also* **faithfully**; **mine**; **sincerely**
yourself [jɔ:'sɛlf] *pron* (*reflexive*) tú mismo; (*complement*) te; (*after prep*) ti (mismo); (*formal*) usted mismo; (: *complement*) se; (: *after prep*) sí (mismo); **you** ~ **told me** me lo dijiste tú mismo; (**all**) **by** ~ sin ayuda de nadie, solo; *see also* **oneself**
yourselves [jɔ:'sɛlvz] *pl pron* vosotros mismos; (*after prep*) vosotros (mismos); (*formal*) ustedes (mismos); (: *complement*) se; (: *after prep*) sí mismos
youth [ju:θ] *n* juventud *f*; (*young man*) (*pl* **youths**) [ju:ðz] joven *m*; **in my** ~ en mi juventud
youth club *n* club *m* juvenil
youthful ['ju:θful] *adj* juvenil
youthfulness ['ju:θfəlnɪs] *n* juventud *f*
youth hostel *n* albergue *m* juvenil
youth movement *n* movimiento juvenil
you've [ju:v] = **you have**
yowl [jaul] *n* (*of animal, person*) aullido ■ *vi* aullar
yr *abbr* (= *year*) a
YT *abbr* (*Canada*) = **Yukon Territory**
Yugoslav ['ju:gəuslɑ:v] *adj, n* yugoslavo(-a) *m(f)*
Yugoslavia [ju:gəu'slɑ:vɪə] *n* Yugoslavia
Yugoslavian [ju:gəu'slɑ:vɪən] *adj* yugoslavo(-a)
yuppie ['jʌpɪ] (*col*) *adj, n* yuppie *m/f*
YWCA *n abbr* (= *Young Women's Christian Association*) Asociación *f* de Jóvenes Cristianas

y

Zz

Z, z [zɛd] (US) [ziː] *n* (*letter*) Z, z f; **Z for Zebra** Z de Zaragoza
Zaire [zɑːˈiːəʳ] *n* Zaire *m*
Zambia [ˈzæmbɪə] *n* Zambia
Zambian [ˈzæmbɪən] *adj, n* zambiano(-a) *m(f)*
zany [ˈzeɪnɪ] *adj* estrafalario
zap [zæp] *vt* (*Comput*) borrar
zeal [ziːl] *n* celo, entusiasmo
zealot [ˈzɛlət] *n* fanático(-a)
zealous [ˈzɛləs] *adj* celoso, entusiasta
zebra [ˈziːbrə] *n* cebra
zebra crossing *n* (*Brit*) paso de peatones
zenith [ˈzɛnɪθ] *n* (*Astro*) cénit *m*; (*fig*) apogeo
zero [ˈzɪərəu] *n* cero; **5 degrees below ~** 5 grados bajo cero
zero hour *n* hora cero
zero option *n* (*Pol*) opción *f* cero
zero-rated [ˈzɪərəureɪtɪd] *adj* (*Brit*) de tasa cero
zest [zɛst] *n* entusiasmo; **~ for living** brío
zigzag [ˈzɪgzæg] *n* zigzag *m* ▪ *vi* zigzaguear
Zimbabwe [zɪmˈbɑːbwɪ] *n* Zimbabwe *m*
Zimbabwean [zɪmˈbɑːbwɪən] *adj, n* zimbabuo(-a) *m(f)*
Zimmer® [ˈzɪməʳ] *n* (*also*: **Zimmer frame**) andador *m*, andaderas *fpl*

zinc [zɪŋk] *n* cinc *m*, zinc *m*
Zionism [ˈzaɪənɪzm] *n* sionismo
Zionist [ˈzaɪənɪst] *adj, n* sionista *m/f*
zip [zɪp] *n* (*also*: **zip fastener**: US: *also*: **zipper**) cremallera, cierre *m* relámpago (*LAm*); (*energy*) energía, vigor *m* ▪ *vt* (*Comput*) comprimir; (*also*: **zip up**) cerrar la cremallera de ▪ *vi*: **to ~ along to the shops** ir de compras volando
zip code *n* (US) código postal
zip file *n* (*Comput*) archivo *m* comprimido
zither [ˈzɪðəʳ] *n* cítara
zodiac [ˈzəudɪæk] *n* zodíaco
zombie [ˈzɒmbɪ] *n* zombi *m*
zone [zəun] *n* zona
zonked [zɒŋkt] *adj* (*col*) hecho polvo
zoo [zuː] *n* zoo, (parque *m*) zoológico
zoological [zuːəˈlɒdʒɪkəl] *adj* zoológico
zoologist [zuˈɒlədʒɪst] *n* zoólogo(-a)
zoology [zuːˈɒlədʒɪ] *n* zoología
zoom [zuːm] *vi*: **to ~ past** pasar zumbando; **to ~ in (on sth/sb)** (*Phot, Cine*) enfocar (algo/a algn) con el zoom
zoom lens *n* zoom *m*
zucchini [zuːˈkiːnɪ] *n(pl)* (US) calabacín(ines) *m(pl)*

Grammar
Gramática

Grammar
Gramática

Using the grammar

The Grammar section deals systematically and comprehensively with all the information you will need in order to communicate accurately in Spanish. The user-friendly layout explains the grammar point on a left hand page, leaving the facing page free for illustrative examples. The circled numbers, → ❶ etc, direct you to the relevant example in every case. Another strong point of the Grammar section is its comprehensive treatment of verbs. Regular verbs are fully explained, and 80 major irregular verbs are conjugated in their simple tenses. The irregular verbs are given in alphabetical order and laid out in tables, making them easy and efficient to consult. In addition, a verb index lists every Spanish verb in this dictionary each cross-referred to the appropriate conjugation model.

The Grammar section also provides invaluable guidance on the danger of translating English structures by identical structures in Spanish. Use of Numbers and Punctuation are important areas covered towards the end of the section. Finally, the index lists the main words and grammatical terms in both English and Spanish.

Abbreviations

cond.	conditional
fem.	feminine
masc.	masculine
plur.	plural
sing.	singular
subj	subjunctive
algn	alguien
sb	somebody
sth	something

Contents

Verbs

Simple Tenses: Formation

In Spanish the simple tenses are:
Present → ❶
Imperfect → ❷
Future → ❸
Conditional → ❹
Preterite → ❺
Present Subjunctive → ❻
Imperfect Subjunctive → ❼

They are formed by adding endings to a verb stem. The endings show the number and person of the subject of the verb → ❽

The stem and endings of regular verbs are totally predictable. The following sections show all the patterns for regular verbs. For irregular verbs see page 80 onwards.

Regular Verbs

There are three regular verb patterns (called conjugations), each identifiable by the ending of the infinitive:

First conjugation verbs end in **-ar** e.g. **hablar** to speak.

Second conjugation verbs end in **-er** e.g. **comer** to eat.

Third conjugation verbs end in **-ir** e.g. **vivir** to live.

These three conjugations are treated in order on the following pages. The subject pronouns will appear in brackets because they are not always necessary in Spanish (see page 230).

Examples

1 (yo) hablo

    I speak
    I am speaking
    I do speak

2 (yo) hablaba

    I spoke
    I was speaking
    I used to speak

3 (yo) hablaré

    I shall speak
    I shall be speaking

4 (yo) hablaría

    I should/would speak
    I should/would be speaking

5 (yo) hablé

    I spoke

6 (que) (yo) hable

    (that) I speak

7 (que) (yo) hablara *or* hablase

    (that) I spoke

8 (yo) hablo

    I speak
(nosotros) hablamos   we speak
(yo) hablaría   I would speak
(nosotros) hablaríamos   we would speak

Verbs

Simple Tenses: First Conjugation

The stem is formed as follows:

TENSE	FORMATION	EXAMPLE
Present		
Imperfect		
Preterite	infinitive minus **-ar**	**habl-**
Present Subjunctive	For irregular verbs see page 80	
Imperfect Subjunctive		
Future	infinitive	**hablar-**
Conditional		

To the appropriate stem add the following endings:

		❶ PRESENT	❷ IMPERFECT	❸ PRETERITE
sing.	1ˢᵗ person	**-o**	**-aba**	**-é**
	2ⁿᵈ person	**-as**	**-abas**	**-aste**
	3ʳᵈ person	**-a**	**-aba**	**-ó**
plur.	1ˢᵗ person	**-amos**	**-ábamos**	**-amos**
	2ⁿᵈ person	**-áis**	**-abais**	**-asteis**
	3ʳᵈ person	**-an**	**-aban**	**-aron**

		❹ PRESENT SUBJUNCTIVE	❺ IMPERFECT SUBJUNCTIVE
sing.	1ˢᵗ person	**-e**	**-ara** or **-ase**
	2ⁿᵈ person	**-es**	**-aras** or **-ases**
	3ʳᵈ person	**-e**	**-ara** or **-ase**
plur.	1ˢᵗ person	**-emos**	**-áramos** or **-ásemos**
	2ⁿᵈ person	**-éis**	**-arais** or **-aseis**
	3ʳᵈ person	**-en**	**-aran** or **-asen**

		❻ FUTURE	❼ CONDITIONAL
sing.	1ˢᵗ person	**-é**	**-ía**
	2ⁿᵈ person	**-ás**	**-ías**
	3ʳᵈ person	**-á**	**-ía**
plur.	1ˢᵗ person	**-emos**	**-íamos**
	2ⁿᵈ person	**-éis**	**-íais**
	3ʳᵈ person	**-án**	**-ían**

Examples

❶ PRESENT

(yo)	hablo
(tú)	hablas
(él/ella/Vd)	habla
(nosotros/as)	hablamos
(vosotros/as)	habláis
(ellos/as/Vds)	hablan

❷ IMPERFECT

hablaba
hablabas
hablaba
hablábamos
hablabais
hablaban

❸ PRETERITE

hablé
hablaste
habló
hablamos
hablasteis
hablaron

❹ PRESENT SUBJUNCTIVE

(yo)	hable
(tú)	hables
(él/ella/Vd)	hable
(nosotros/as)	hablemos
(vosotros/as)	habléis
(ellos/as/Vds)	hablen

❺ IMPERFECT SUBJUNCTIVE

hablara *or* hablase
hablaras *or* hablases
hablara *or* hablase
habláramos *or* hablásemos
hablarais *or* hablaseis
hablaran *or* hablasen

❻ FUTURE

(yo)	hablaré
(tú)	hablarás
(él/ella/Vd)	hablará
(nosotros/as)	hablaremos
(vosotros/as)	hablaréis
(ellos/as/Vds)	hablarán

❼ CONDITIONAL

hablaría
hablarías
hablaría
hablaríamos
hablaríais
hablarían

Simple Tenses: Second Conjugation

The stem is formed as follows:

TENSE	FORMATION	EXAMPLE
Present		
Imperfect		
Preterite	infinitive minus **-er**	**com-**
Present Subjunctive	For irregular verbs see page 80	
Imperfect Subjunctive		
Future	infinitive	**comer-**
Conditional		

To the appropriate stem add the following endings:

		❶ PRESENT	❷ IMPERFECT	❸ PRETERITE
sing.	1ˢᵗ person	-o	-ía	-í
	2ⁿᵈ person	-es	-ías	-iste
	3ʳᵈ person	-e	-ía	-ió
plur.	1ˢᵗ person	-emos	-íamos	-imos
	2ⁿᵈ person	-éis	-íais	-isteis
	3ʳᵈ person	-en	-ían	-ieron

		❹ PRESENT SUBJUNCTIVE	❺ IMPERFECT SUBJUNCTIVE
sing.	1ˢᵗ person	-a	-iera or -iese
	2ⁿᵈ person	-as	-ieras or -ieses
	3ʳᵈ person	-a	-iera or -iese
plur.	1ˢᵗ person	-amos	-iéramos or -iésemos
	2ⁿᵈ person	-áis	-ierais or -ieseis
	3ʳᵈ person	-an	-ieran or -iesen

		❻ FUTURE	❼ CONDITIONAL
sing.	1ˢᵗ person	-é	-ía
	2ⁿᵈ person	-ás	-ías
	3ʳᵈ person	-á	-ía
plur.	1ˢᵗ person	-emos	-íamos
	2ⁿᵈ person	-éis	-íais
	3ʳᵈ person	-án	-ían

Examples

1 PRESENT

(yo)	como
(tú)	comes
(él/ella/Vd)	come
(nosotros/as)	comemos
(vosotros/as)	coméis
(ellos/as/Vds)	comen

2 IMPERFECT

comía
comías
comía
comíamos
comíais
comían

3 PRETERITE

comí
comiste
comió
comimos
comisteis
comieron

4 PRESENT SUBJUNCTIVE

(yo)	coma
(tú)	comas
(él/ella/Vd)	coma
(nosotros/as)	comamos
(vosotros/as)	comáis
(ellos/as/Vds)	coman

5 IMPERFECT SUBJUNCTIVE

comiera *or* comiese
comieras *or* comieses
comiera *or* comiese
comiéramos *or* comiésemos
comierais *or* comieseis
comieran *or* comiesen

6 FUTURE

(yo)	comeré
(tú)	comerás
(él/ella/Vd)	comerá
(nosotros/as)	comeremos
(vosotros/as)	comeréis
(ellos/as/Vds)	comerán

7 CONDITIONAL

comería
comerías
comería
comeríamos
comeríais
comerían

Simple Tenses: Third Conjugation

The stem is formed as follows:

TENSE	FORMATION	EXAMPLE
Present		
Imperfect		
Preterite	infinitive minus **-ir**	**viv-**
Present Subjunctive	For irregular verbs see page 80	
Imperfect Subjunctive		
Future		
Conditional	infinitive	**vivir-**

To the appropriate stem add the following endings:

		❶ PRESENT	❷ IMPERFECT	❸ PRETERITE
	1st person	**-o**	**-ía**	**-í**
sing.	2nd person	**-es**	**-ías**	**-iste**
	3rd person	**-e**	**-ía**	**-ió**
	1st person	**-imos**	**-íamos**	**-imos**
plur.	2nd person	**-ís**	**-íais**	**-isteis**
	3rd person	**-en**	**-ían**	**-ieron**

		❹ PRESENT SUBJUNCTIVE	❺ IMPERFECT SUBJUNCTIVE
	1st person	**-a**	**-iera** or **-iese**
sing.	2nd person	**-as**	**-ieras** or **-ieses**
	3rd person	**-a**	**-iera** or **-iese**
	1st person	**-amos**	**-iéramos** or **-iésemos**
plur.	2nd person	**-áis**	**-ierais** or **-ieseis**
	3rd person	**-an**	**-ieran** or **-iesen**

		❻ FUTURE	❼ CONDITIONAL
	1st person	**-é**	**-ía**
sing.	2nd person	**-ás**	**-ías**
	3rd person	**-á**	**-ía**
	1st person	**-emos**	**-íamos**
plur.	2nd person	**-éis**	**-íais**
	3rd person	**-án**	**-ían**

Examples

1 PRESENT

(yo)	vivo
(tú)	vives
(él/ella/Vd)	vive
(nosotros/as)	vivimos
(vosotros/as)	vivís
(ellos/as/Vds)	viven

2 IMPERFECT

vivía
vivías
vivía
vivíamos
vivíais
vivían

3 PRETERITE

viví
viviste
vivió
vivimos
vivisteis
vivieron

4 PRESENT SUBJUNCTIVE

(yo)	viva
(tú)	vivas
(él/ella/Vd)	viva
(nosotros/as)	vivamos
(vosotros/as)	viváis
(ellos/as/Vds)	vivan

5 IMPERFECT SUBJUNCTIVE

viviera *or* viviese
vivieras *or* vivieses
viviera *or* viviese
viviéramos *or* viviésemos
vivierais *or* vivieseis
vivieran *or* viviesen

6 FUTURE

(yo)	viviré
(tú)	vivirás
(él/ella/Vd)	vivirá
(nosotros/as)	viviremos
(vosotros/as)	viviréis
(ellos/as/Vds)	vivirán

7 CONDITIONAL

viviría
vivirías
viviría
viviríamos
viviríais
vivirían

The Imperative

The imperative is the form of the verb used to give commands or orders. It can be used politely, as in English 'Shut the door, please'.

In *positive* commands, the imperative forms for **Vd**, **Vds** and **nosotros** are the same as the subjunctive. The other forms are as follows:

> **tú** (same as 3rd person singular present indicative)
> **vosotros** (final **-r** of infinitive changes to **-d**) → ❶

(tú)	**habla** speak	**come** eat	**vive** live
(Vd)	**hable** speak	**coma** eat	**viva** live
(nosotros)	**hablemos** let's speak	**comamos** let's eat	**vivamos** let's live
(vosotros)	**hablad** speak	**comed** eat	**vivid** live
(Vds)	**hablen** speak	**coman** eat	**vivan** live

In *negative* commands, all the imperative forms are exactly the same as the present subjunctive.

The imperative of irregular verbs is given in the verb tables, pages 82 to 160.

Position of object pronouns with the imperative:
- in *positive* commands: they follow the verb and are attached to it. An accent is needed to show the correct position for stress (see page 296) → ❷
- in *negative* commands: they precede the verb and are not attached to it → ❸

For the order of object pronouns, see page 236.

Examples

1 cantar — to sing
cantad — sing

2 Perdóneme — Excuse me
Enviémoselos — Let's send them to him/her/them

Elíjanos — Choose us
Explíquemelo — Explain it to me

Esperémosla — Let's wait for her/it
Devuélvaselo — Give it back to him/her/them

3 No me molestes — Don't disturb me
No se la devolvamos — Let's not give it back to him/her/them

No les castiguemos — Let's not punish them
No me lo mandes — Don't send it to me
No las conteste — Don't answer them
No nos lo hagan — Don't do it to us

The Imperative *continued*

For reflexive verbs – e.g. **levantarse** to get up – the object pronoun is the reflexive pronoun. It should be noted that the imperative forms need an accent to show the correct position for stress (see page 296). The forms **nosotros** and **vosotros** also drop the final **-s** and **-d** respectively before the pronoun → **❶**

> BUT: **idos (vosotros)** go

ⓘ Note: For general instructions, the infinitive is used instead of the imperative → **❷**, but when it is preceded by **vamos a** it often translates *let's* ... → **❸**

Examples

1 Levántate — Get up
No te levantes — Don't get up
Levántese (Vd) — Get up
No se levante (Vd) — Don't get up
Levantémonos — Let's get up
No nos levantemos — Let's not get up
Levantaos — Get up
No os levantéis — Don't get up
Levántense (Vds) — Get up
No se levanten (Vds) — Don't get up

2 Ver pág … — See page
No pasar — Do not pass …

3 Vamos a ver — Let's see
Vamos a empezar — Let's start

17

Compound Tenses: formation

In Spanish the compound tenses are:

> Perfect → ❶
> Pluperfect → ❷
> Future Perfect → ❸
> Conditional Perfect → ❹
> Past Anterior → ❺
> Perfect Subjunctive → ❻
> Pluperfect Subjunctive → ❼

They consist of the past participle of the verb together with the auxiliary verb **haber**.

Compound tenses are formed in exactly the same way for both regular and irregular verbs, the only difference being that irregular verbs may have an irregular past participle.

The Past Participle

For all compound tenses you need to know how to form the past participle of the verb. For regular verbs this is as follows:

> First conjugation: replace the **-ar** of the infinitive by **-ado** → ❽

> Second conjugation: replace the **-er** of the infinitive by **-ido** → ❾

> Third conjugation: replace the **-ir** of the infinitive by **-ido** → ❿

Examples

1 (yo) he hablado   I have spoken

2 (yo) había hablado   I had spoken

3 (yo) habré hablado   I shall have spoken

4 (yo) habría hablado   I should/would have spoken

5 (yo) hube hablado   I had spoken

6 (que) (yo) haya hablado   (that) I spoke, have spoken

7 (que) (yo) hubiera/hubiese   (that) I had spoken
      hablado

8 **cantar** to sing → **cantado** sung

9 **comer** to eat → **comido** eaten

10 **vivir** to live → **vivido** lived

Compound Tenses: formation *continued*

PERFECT TENSE
The present tense of **haber** plus the past participle → ❶

PLUPERFECT TENSE
The imperfect tense of **haber** plus the past participle → ❷

FUTURE PERFECT
The future tense of **haber** plus the past participle → ❸

CONDITIONAL PERFECT
The conditional of **haber** plus the past participle → ❹

Examples

❶ PERFECT

(yo)	**he** hablado
(tú)	**has** hablado
(él/ella/Vd)	**ha** hablado
(nosotros/as)	**hemos** hablado
(vosotros/as)	**habéis** hablado
(ellos/as/Vds)	**han** hablado

❷ PLUPERFECT

(yo)	**había** hablado
(tú)	**habías** hablado
(él/ella/Vd)	**había** hablado
(nosotros/as)	**habíamos** hablado
(vosotros/as)	**habíais** hablado
(ellos/as/Vds)	**habían** hablado

❸ FUTURE PERFECT

(yo)	**habré** hablado
(tú)	**habrás** hablado
(él/ella/Vd)	**habrá** hablado
(nosotros/as)	**habremos** hablado
(vosotros/as)	**habréis** hablado
(ellos/as/Vds)	**habrán** hablado

❹ CONDITIONAL PERFECT

(yo)	**habría** hablado
(tú)	**habrías** hablado
(él/ella/Vd)	**habría** hablado
(nosotros/as)	**habríamos** hablado
(vosotros/as)	**habríais** hablado
(ellos/as/Vds)	**habrían** hablado

Compound Tenses: Formation *continued*

PAST ANTERIOR

The preterite of **haber** plus the past participle → ❶

PERFECT SUBJUNCTIVE

The present subjunctive of **haber** plus the past participle → ❷

PLUPERFECT SUBJUNCTIVE

The imperfect subjunctive of **haber** plus the past participle → ❸

For how to form the past participle of regular verbs see page 18. The past participle of irregular verbs is given for each verb in the verb tables, pages 82 to 160.

Examples

① PAST ANTERIOR

(yo)	**hube** hablado
(tú)	**hubiste** hablado
(él/ella/Vd)	**hubo** hablado
(nosotros/as)	**hubimos** hablado
(vosotros/as)	**hubisteis** hablado
(ellos/as/Vds)	**hubieron** hablado

② PERFECT SUBJUNCTIVE

(yo)	**haya** hablado
(tú)	**hayas** hablado
(él/ella/Vd)	**haya** hablado
(nosotros/as)	**hayamos** hablado
(vosotros/as)	**hayáis** hablado
(ellos/as/Vds)	**hayan** hablado

③ PLUPERFECT SUBJUNCTIVE

(yo)	**hubiera** or **hubiese** hablado
(tú)	**hubieras** or **hubieses** hablado
(él/ella/Vd)	**hubiera** or **hubiese** hablado
(nosotros/as)	**hubiéramos** or **hubiésemos** hablado
(vosotros/as)	**hubierais** or **hubieseis** hablado
(ellos/as/Vds)	**hubieran** or **hubiesen** hablado

Reflexive Verbs

A reflexive verb is one accompanied by a reflexive pronoun. The infinitive of a reflexive verb ends with the pronoun **se**, which is added to the verb form e.g. **levantarse** to get up; **lavarse** to wash (oneself)
The reflexive pronouns are:

	SINGULAR	PLURAL
1st person	me	nos
2nd person	te	os
3rd person	se	se

The reflexive pronoun 'reflects back' to the subject, but it is not always translated in English → ❶

The plural pronouns are sometimes translated as 'one another', 'each other' (the *reciprocal* meaning) → ❷

The reciprocal meaning may be emphasized by **el uno al otro/ la una a la otra (los unos a los otros/las unas a las otras)** → ❸

Both simple and compound tenses of reflexive verbs are conjugated in exactly the same way as those of non-reflexive verbs, except that the reflexive pronoun is always used.

The only irregularity is in the 1st and 2nd person plural of the affirmative imperative (see page 16). A sample reflexive verb is conjugated in full on pages 28 to 31.

Position of reflexive pronouns

Except with the infinitive, gerund and positive commands, the pronoun comes before the verb → ❹

In the infinitive, gerund and positive commands, the pronoun follows the verb and is attached to it (but see also page 232) → ❺

Examples

1 Me visto — I'm dressing (myself)
Nos lavamos — We're washing (ourselves)
Se levanta — He gets up

2 Nos queremos — We love each other
Se parecen — They resemble one another

3 Se miraban el uno al otro — They were looking at each other

4 Me acuesto temprano — I go to bed early
¿Cómo se llama Vd? — What is your name?
No se ha despertado — He hasn't woken up
No te levantes — Don't get up

5 Quiero irme — I want to go away
Estoy levantándome — I am getting up
Siéntense — Sit down
Vámonos — Let's go

Reflexive Verbs *continued*

Some verbs have both a reflexive and non-reflexive form. When used reflexively, they have a different but closely related meaning, as shown in the following examples.

NON-REFLEXIVE	REFLEXIVE
acostar to put to bed	**acostarse** to go to bed
casar to marry (off)	**casarse** to get married
detener to stop	**detenerse** to come to a halt
dormir to sleep	**dormirse** to go to sleep
enfadar to annoy	**enfadarse** to get annoyed
hacer to make	**hacerse** to become
ir to go	**irse** to leave, go away
lavar to wash	**lavarse** to get washed
levantar to raise	**levantarse** to get up
llamar to call	**llamarse** to be called
poner to put	**ponerse** to put on (clothing), to become
sentir to feel (something)	**sentirse** to feel (sick, tired, *etc*)
vestir to dress (someone)	**vestirse** to get dressed
volver to return	**volverse** to turn round

Some other verbs exist only in the reflexive:

arrepentirse to repent   **jactarse** to boast
atreverse to dare   **quejarse** to complain

Some verbs acquire a different nuance when used reflexively:
caer to fall → ❶   **caerse** to fall down (by accident) → ❷

morir to die, be killed (by accident or on purpose) → ❸   **morirse** to die (from natural causes) → ❹

Often a reflexive verb can be used:
- to avoid the passive (see page 32) → ❺
- in impersonal expressions (see page 40) → ❻

Examples

1 El agua caía desde las rocas — Water fell from the rocks

2 Me caí y me rompí el brazo — I fell and broke my arm

3 Tres personas han muerto en un accidente/atentado terrorista — Three people were killed in an accident/a terrorist attack

4 Mi abuelo se murió a los ochenta años — My grandfather died at the age of eighty

5 Se perdió la batalla — The battle was lost
No se veían las casas — The houses could not be seen

6 Se dice que ... — (It is said that) People say that ...
No se puede entrar — You/One can't go in
No se permite — It is not allowed

Reflexive Verbs *continued*

Conjugation of: **lavarse** to wash oneself

1 SIMPLE TENSES

PRESENT

(yo)	**me** lavo
(tú)	**te** lavas
(él/ella/Vd)	**se** lava
(nosotros/as)	**nos** lavamos
(vosotros/as)	**os** laváis
(ellos/as/Vds)	**se** lavan

IMPERFECT

(yo)	**me** lavaba
(tú)	**te** lavabas
(él/ella/Vd)	**se** lavaba
(nosotros/as)	**nos** lavábamos
(vosotros/as)	**os** lavabais
(ellos/as/Vds)	**se** lavaban

FUTURE

(yo)	**me** lavaré
(tú)	**te** lavarás
(él/ella/Vd)	**se** lavará
(nosotros/as)	**nos** lavaremos
(vosotros/as)	**os** lavaréis
(ellos/as/Vds)	**se** lavarán

CONDITIONAL

(yo)	**me** lavaría
(tú)	**te** lavarías
(él/ella/Vd)	**se** lavaría
(nosotros/as)	**nos** lavaríamos
(vosotros/as)	**os** lavaríais
(ellos/as/Vds)	**se** lavarían

Reflexive Verbs *continued*

Conjugation of: **lavarse** to wash oneself

1 SIMPLE TENSES

PRETERITE

(yo)	**me** lavé
(tú)	**te** lavaste
(él/ella/Vd)	**se** lavó
(nosotros/as)	**nos** lavamos
(vosotros/as)	**os** lavasteis
(ellos/as/Vds)	**se** lavaron

PRESENT SUBJUNCTIVE

(yo)	**me** lave
(tú)	**te** laves
(él/ella/Vd)	**se** lave
(nosotros/as)	**nos** lavemos
(vosotros/as)	**os** lavéis
(ellos/as/Vds)	**se** laven

IMPERFECT SUBJUNCTIVE

(yo)	**me** lavara *or* lavase
(tú)	**te** lavaras *or* lavases
(él/ella/Vd)	**se** lavara *or* lavase
(nosotros/as)	**nos** laváramos *or* lavásemos
(vosotros/as)	**os** lavarais *or* lavaseis
(ellos/as/Vds)	**se** lavaran *or* lavasen

ReflexiveVerbs *continued*

Conjugation of: **lavarse** to wash oneself

2 COMPOUND TENSES

PERFECT

(yo)	**me he** lavado
(tú)	**te has** lavado
(él/ella/Vd)	**se ha** lavado
(nosotros/as)	**nos hemos** lavado
(vosotros/as)	**os habéis** lavado
(ellos/as/Vds)	**se han** lavado

PLUPERFECT

(yo)	**me había** lavado
(tú)	**te habías** lavado
(él/ella/Vd)	**se había** lavado
(nosotros/as)	**nos habíamos** lavado
(vosotros/as)	**os habíais** lavado
(ellos/as/Vds)	**se habían** lavado

FUTURE PERFECT

(yo)	**me habré** lavado
(tú)	**te habrás** lavado
(él/ella/Vd)	**se habrá** lavado
(nosotros/as)	**nos habremos** lavado
(vosotros/as)	**os habréis** lavado
(ellos/as/Vds)	**se habrán** lavado

ReflexiveVerbs *continued*

Conjugation of: **lavarse** to wash oneself

2 COMPOUND TENSES

PAST ANTERIOR

(yo)	**me hube** lavado
(tú)	**te hubiste** lavado
(él/ella/Vd)	**se hubo** lavado
(nosotros/as)	**nos hubimos** lavado
(vosotros/as)	**os hubisteis** lavado
(ellos/as/Vds)	**se hubieron** lavado

PERFECT SUBJUNCTIVE

(yo)	**me haya** lavado
(tú)	**te hayas** lavado
(él/ella/Vd)	**se haya** lavado
(nosotros/as)	**nos hayamos** lavado
(vosotros/as)	**os hayáis** lavado
(ellos/as/Vds)	**se hayan** lavado

PLUPERFECT SUBJUNCTIVE

(yo)	**me hubiera** *or* **hubiese** lavado
(tú)	**te hubieras** *or* **hubieses** lavado
(él/ella/Vd)	**se hubiera** *or* **hubiese** lavado
(nosotros/as)	**nos hubiéramos** *or* **hubiésemos** lavado
(vosotros/as)	**os hubierais** *or* **hubieseis** lavado
(ellos/as/Vds)	**se hubieran** *or* **hubiesen** lavado

The Passive

In active sentences, the subject of a verb carries out the action of that verb, but in passive sentences the subject receives the action. Compare the following:

> The car hit Jane (*subject*: the car)
> Jane was hit by the car (*subject*: Jane)

English uses the verb 'to be' with the past participle to form passive · sentences. Spanish forms them in the same way, i.e.:
    a tense of **ser** + *past participle*.

The past participle agrees in number and gender with the subject → **1**

A sample verb is conjugated in the passive voice on pages 36 to 39.

In English, the word 'by' usually introduces the agent through which the action of a passive sentence is performed. In Spanish this agent is preceded by **por** → **2**

The passive voice is used much less frequently in Spanish than English. It is, however, often used in expressions where the identity of the agent is unknown or unimportant → **3**

Examples

1. Pablo ha sido despedido — Paul has been sacked
   Su madre era muy admirada — His mother was greatly admired
   El palacio será vendido — The palace will be sold
   Las puertas habían sido cerradas — The doors had been closed

2. La casa fue diseñada por mi hermano — The house was designed by my brother

3. La ciudad fue conquistada tras un largo asedio — The city was conquered after a long siege
   Ha sido declarado el estado de excepción — A state of emergency has been declared

Verbs

The Passive *continued*

In English the indirect object in an active sentence can become the subject of the related passive sentence, e.g.

> 'His mother gave him the book' (*indirect object*: him)
> He was given the book by his mother

This is not possible in Spanish. The indirect object remains as such, while the object of the active sentence becomes the subject of the passive sentence → ❶

Other ways to express a passive meaning

Since modern Spanish tends to avoid the passive, it uses various other constructions to replace it:

If the agent (person or object performing the action) is known, the active is often preferred where English might prefer the passive → ❷

The 3rd person plural of the active voice can be used. The meaning is equivalent to 'they' + *verb* → ❸

When the action of the sentence is performed on a person, the reflexive form of the verb can be used in the 3rd person singular, and the person becomes the object → ❹

When the action is performed on a thing, this becomes the subject of the sentence and the verb is made reflexive, agreeing in number with the subject → ❺

34 | Grammar Guide

Examples

1. Su madre le regaló el libro
   BECOMES:
   El libro le fue regalado por su madre

   His mother gave him the book

   The book was given to him by his mother

2. La policía interrogó al sospechoso
   RATHER THAN:
   El sospechoso fue interrogado por la policía

   The police questioned the suspect

3. Usan demasiada publicidad en la televisión

   Too much advertising is used on television

4. Últimamente no se le/les ha visto mucho en público

   He has/they have not been seen much in public recently

5. Esta palabra ya no se usa
   Todos los libros se han vendido

   This word is no longer used
   All the books have been sold

The Passive *continued*

Conjugation of: **ser amado** to be loved

PRESENT

(yo)	**soy** amado(a)
(tú)	**eres** amado(a)
(él/ella/Vd)	**es** amado(a)
(nosotros/as)	**somos** amado(a)s
(vosotros/as)	**sois** amado(a)s
(ellos/as/Vds)	**son** amado(a)s

IMPERFECT

(yo)	**era** amado(a)
(tú)	**eras** amado(a)
(él/ella/Vd)	**era** amado(a)
(nosotros/as)	**éramos** amado(a)s
(vosotros/as)	**erais** amado(a)s
(ellos/as/Vds)	**eran** amado(a)s

FUTURE

(yo)	**seré** amado(a)
(tú)	**serás** amado(a)
(él/ella/Vd)	**será** amado(a)
(nosotros/as)	**seremos** amado(a)s
(vosotros/as)	**seréis** amado(a)s
(ellos/as/Vds)	**serán** amado(a)s

CONDITIONAL

(yo)	**sería** amado(a)
(tú)	**serías** amado(a)
(él/ella/Vd)	**sería** amado(a)
(nosotros/as)	**seríamos** amado(a)s
(vosotros/as)	**seríais** amado(a)s
(ellos/as/Vds)	**serían** amado(a)s

The Passive *continued*

Conjugation of: **ser amado** to be loved

PRETERITE

(yo)	**fui** am**ado(a)**
(tú)	**fuiste** am**ado(a)**
(él/ella/Vd)	**fue** am**ado(a)**
(nosotros/as)	**fuimos** am**ado(a)s**
(vosotros/as)	**fuisteis** am**ado(a)s**
(ellos/as/Vds)	**fueron** am**ado(a)s**

PRESENT SUBJUNCTIVE

(yo)	**sea** am**ado(a)**
(tú)	**seas** am**ado(a)**
(él/ella/Vd)	**sea** am**ado(a)**
(nosotros/as)	**seamos** am**ado(a)s**
(vosotros/as)	**seáis** am**ado(a)s**
(ellos/as/Vds)	**sean** am**ado(a)s**

IMPERFECT SUBJUNCTIVE

(yo)	**fuera** *or* **fuese** am**ado(a)**
(tú)	**fueras** *or* **fueses** am**ado(a)**
(él/ella/Vd)	**fuera** *or* **fuese** am**ado(a)**
(nosotros/as)	**fuéramos** *or* **fuésemos** am**ado(a)s**
(vosotros/as)	**fuerais** *or* **fueseis** am**ado(a)s**
(ellos/as/Vds)	**fueran** *or* **fuesen** am**ado(a)s**

The Passive *continued*

Conjugation of: **ser amado** to be loved

PERFECT

(yo)	**he sido** amado(a)
(tú)	**has sido** amado(a)
(él/ella/Vd)	**ha sido** amado(a)
(nosotros/as)	**hemos sido** amado(a)s
(vosotros/as)	**habéis sido** amado(a)s
(ellos/as/Vds)	**han sido** amado(a)s

PLUPERFECT

(yo)	**había sido** amado(a)
(tú)	**habías sido** amado(a)
(él/ella/Vd)	**había sido** amado(a)
(nosotros/as)	**habíamos sido** amado(a)s
(vosotros/as)	**habíais sido** amado(a)s
(ellos/as/Vds)	**habían sido** amado(a)s

FUTURE PERFECT

(yo)	**habré sido** amado(a)
(tú)	**habrás sido** amado(a)
(él/ella/Vd)	**habrá sido** amado(a)
(nosotros/as)	**habremos sido** amado(a)s
(vosotros/as)	**habréis sido** amado(a)s
(ellos/as/Vds)	**habrán sido** amado(a)s

CONDITIONAL PERFECT

(yo)	**habría sido** amado(a)
(tú)	**habrías sido** amado(a)
(él/ella/Vd)	**habría sido** amado(a)
(nosotros/as)	**habríamos sido** amado(a)s
(vosotros/as)	**habríais sido** amado(a)s
(ellos/as/Vds)	**habrían sido** amado(a)s

The Passive *continued*

Conjugation of: **ser amado** to be loved

PAST ANTERIOR

(yo)	**hube sido** amado(a)
(tú)	**hubiste sido** amado(a)
(él/ella/Vd)	**hubo sido** amado(a)
(nosotros/as)	**hubimos sido** amado(a)s
(vosotros/as)	**hubisteis sido** amado(a)s
(ellos/as/Vds)	**hubieron sido** amado(a)s

PERFECT SUBJUNCTIVE

(yo)	**haya sido** amado(a)
(tú)	**hayas sido** amado(a)
(él/ella/Vd)	**haya sido** amado(a)
(nosotros/as)	**hayamos sido** amado(a)s
(vosotros/as)	**hayáis sido** amado(a)s
(ellos/as/Vds)	**hayan sido** amado(a)s

PLUPERFECT SUBJUNCTIVE

(yo)	**hubiera/-se sido** amado(a)
(tú)	**hubieras/-ses sido** amado(a)
(él/ella/Vd)	**hubiera/-se sido** amado(a)
(nosotros/as)	**hubiéramos/-semos sido** amado(a)s
(vosotros/as)	**hubierais/-seis sido** amado(a)s
(ellos/as/Vds)	**hubieran/-sen sido** amado(a)s

Impersonal Verbs

Impersonal verbs are used only in the infinitive, the gerund, and in the 3rd person (usually singular); unlike English, Spanish does not use the subject pronoun with impersonal verbs, e.g.

>**llueve** it's raining
>**es fácil decir que ...** it's easy to say that ...

The most common impersonal verbs are:

INFINITIVE	CONSTRUCTION
amanecer	amanece/está amaneciendo it's daybreak
anochecer	anochece/está anocheciendo it's getting dark
granizar	graniza/está granizando it's hailing
llover	llueve/está lloviendo it's raining → ❶
lloviznar	llovizna/está lloviznando it's drizzling
nevar	nieva/está nevando it's snowing → ❶
tronar	truena/está tronando it's thundering

Some reflexive verbs are also used impersonally.
The most common are:

INFINITIVE	CONSTRUCTION
creerse	se cree que* + *indicative* → ❷ it is thought that; people think that
decirse	se dice que* + *indicative* → ❸ it is said that; people say that

Examples

1 Llovía a cántaros

It was raining cats and dogs

Estaba nevando cuando salieron

It was snowing when they left

2 Se cree que llegarán mañana

It is thought they will arrive tomorrow

3 Se dice que ha sido el peor invierno en 50 años

People say it's been the worst winter in 50 years

Impersonal Verbs *continued*

INFINITIVE	CONSTRUCTION
poderse	**se puede** + *infinitive* → ❶ one/people can, it is possible to
tratarse de	**se trata de** + *noun* → ❷ it's a question/matter of something it's about something
	se trata de + *infinitive* → ❸ it's a question/matter of doing; somebody must do
venderse	**se vende*** + *noun* → ❹ to be sold; for sale

* This impersonal construction conveys the same meaning as the 3rd person plural of these verbs; **creen que**, **dicen que**, **venden**

The following verbs are also commonly used in impersonal constructions:

INFINITIVE	CONSTRUCTION
bastar	**basta con** + *infinitive* → ❺ it is enough to do **basta con** + *noun* → ❻ something is enough, it only takes something
faltar	**falta** + *infinitive* → ❼ we still have to/one still has to
haber	**hay** + *noun* → ❽ there is/are **hay que** + *infinitive* → ❾ one has to/we have to
hacer	**hace** + *noun/adjective depicting weather/dark/light* *etc* → ❿ it is **hace** + *time expression* + **que** + *indicative* → ⓫ somebody has done *or* been doing something since ... **hace** + *time expression* + **que** + *negative indicative* → ⓬ it is ... since

Examples

1. Aquí se puede aparcar — One can park here

2. No se trata de dinero — It isn't a question/matter of money

3. Se trata de poner fin al asunto — We must put an end to the matter

4. Se vende coche — Car for sale

5. Basta con telefonear para reservar un asiento — You need only phone to reserve a seat

6. Basta con un error para que todo se estropee — One single error is enough to ruin everything

7. Aún falta cerrar las maletas — We/One still have/has to close the suitcases

8. Hay una habitación libre — There is one spare room
   No había cartas esta mañana — There were no letters this morning

9. Hay que cerrar las puertas — We have/One has to shut the doors

10. Hace calor/viento/sol — It is hot/windy/sunny
    Mañana hará bueno — It'll be nice (weather) tomorrow

11. Hace seis meses que vivo/vivimos aquí — I/We have lived or been living here for six months

12. Hace tres años que no le veo — It is three years since I last saw him

Impersonal Verbs *continued*

INFINITIVE	CONSTRUCTION
hacer falta	**hace falta** + *noun object* (+ *indirect object*) → ❶ (somebody) needs something; something is necessary (to somebody) **hace falta** + *infinitive* (+ *indirect object*) → ❷ it is necessary to do **hace falta que** + *subjunctive* → ❸ it is necessary to do, somebody must do
parecer	**parece que** (+ *indirect object*) + *indicative* → ❹ it seems/appears that
ser	**es/son** + *time expression* → ❺ it is **es** + **de día/noche** → ❻ it is **es** + *adjective* + *infinitive* → ❼ it is
ser mejor	**es mejor** + *infinitive* → ❽ it's better to do **es mejor que** + *subjunctive* → ❾ it's better if/that
valer más	**más vale** + *infinitive* → ❿ it's better to do **más vale que** + *subjunctive* → ⓫ it's better to do/that somebody does

Examples

1. Hace falta valor para hacer eso — One needs courage to do that/ Courage is needed to do that

   Me hace falta otro vaso más — I need an extra glass

2. Hace falta volver — It is necessary to return/ We/I/You must return*

   Me hacía falta volver — I had to return

3. Hace falta que Vd se vaya — You have to/must leave

4. (Me) parece que estás equivocado — It seems (to me) you are wrong

5. Son las tres y media — It is half past three
   Ya es primavera — It is spring now

6. Era de noche cuando llegamos — It was night when we arrived

7. Era inútil protestar — It was useless to complain

8. Es mejor no decir nada — It's better to keep quiet

9. Es mejor que lo pongas aquí — It's better if/that you put it here

10. Más vale prevenir que curar — Prevention is better than cure

11. Más valdría que no fuéramos — It would be better if we didn't go/ We'd better not go

*The translation here obviously depends on context

The Infinitive

The infinitive is the form of the verb found in dictionary entries meaning 'to ...', e.g. **hablar** to speak, **vivir** to live.

The infinitive is used in the following ways:

After a preposition → ❶

As a verbal noun → ❷
In this use the article may precede the infinitive, especially when the infinitive is the subject and begins the sentence → ❸

As a dependent infinitive, in the following verbal constructions:
- with no linking preposition → ❹
- with the linking preposition **a** → ❺
  (see also page 66)
- with the linking preposition **de** → ❻
  (see also page 66)
- with the linking preposition **en** → ❼
  (see also page 66)
- with the linking preposition **con** → ⑧
  (see also page 66)
- with the linking preposition **por** → ⑨
  (see also page 66)

The following construction should also be noted:
    indefinite pronoun + **que** + *infinitive* → ⑩

The object pronouns generally follow the infinitive and are attached to it. For exceptions see page 232.

Examples

1 Después de acabar el desayuno, salió de casa

After finishing her breakfast she went out

Al enterarse de lo ocurrido se puso furiosa

When she found out what had happened she was furious

Me hizo daño sin saberlo

She hurt me without her knowing

2 Su deporte preferido es montar a caballo

Her favourite sport is horse riding

Ver es creer

Seeing is believing

3 El viajar tanto me resulta cansado

I find so much travelling tiring

4 ¿Quiere Vd esperar?

Would you like to wait?

5 Aprenderán pronto a nadar

They will soon learn to swim

6 Pronto dejará de llover

It'll stop raining soon

7 La comida tarda en hacerse

The meal is taking a long time to cook

8 Amenazó con denunciarles

He threatened to report them (to the police)

9 Comience Vd por decirme su nombre

Please start by giving me your name

10 Tengo algo que decirte

I have something to tell you

The Infinitive *continued*

The verbs set out below are followed by the infinitive with no linking preposition.

deber, **poder**, **saber**, **querer** and **tener que** (**hay que** in impersonal constructions) → ❶

valer más, **hacer falta**: see Impersonal Verbs, page 44.

verbs of seeing or hearing, e.g. **ver** to see, **oír** to hear → ❷

hacer → ❸

dejar to let, allow → ❸

The following common verbs:

    aconsejar to advise → ❹
    conseguir to manage to → ❺
    decidir to decide
    desear to wish, want → ❻
    esperar to hope → ❼
    evitar to avoid → ❽
    impedir to prevent → ❾
    intentar to try → ❿
    lograr to manage to → ❺

    necesitar to need → ⓫
    odiar to hate
    olvidar to forget → ⓬
    pensar to think → ⓭
    preferir to prefer → ⓮
    procurar to try → ❿
    prohibir to forbid → ⓯
    prometer to promise → ⓰
    proponer to propose → ⓱

Examples

1. ¿Quiere Vd esperar? Would you like to wait?
   No puede venir She can't come

2. Nos ha visto llegar She saw us arriving
   Se les oye cantar You can hear them singing

3. No me hagas reír Don't make me laugh
   Déjeme pasar Let me past

4. Le aconsejamos dejarlo para mañana We advise you to leave it until tomorrow

5. Aún no he conseguido/logrado entenderlo I still haven't managed to understand it

6. No desea tener más hijos She doesn't want to have any more children

7. Esperamos ir de vacaciones este verano We are hoping to go on holiday this summer

8. Evite beber cuando conduzca Avoid drinking and driving

9. No pudo impedirle hablar He couldn't prevent him from speaking

10. Intentamos/procuramos pasar desapercibidos We tried not to be noticed

11. Necesitaba salir a la calle I/he/she needed to go out

12. Olvidó dejar su dirección He/she forgot to leave his/her address

13. ¿Piensan venir por Navidad? Are you thinking of coming for Christmas?

14. Preferiría elegirlo yo mismo I'd rather choose it myself

15. Prohibió fumar a los alumnos He forbade the pupils to smoke

16. Prometieron volver pronto They promised to come back soon

17. Propongo salir cuanto antes I propose to leave as soon as possible

The Infinitive: Set Expressions

The following are set in Spanish with the meaning shown:

> **dejar caer** to drop → ❶
> **hacer entrar** to show in → ❷
> **hacer saber** to let know, make known → ❸
> **hacer salir** to let out → ❹
> **hacer venir** to send for → ❺
> **ir(se) a buscar** to go for, go and get → ❻
> **mandar hacer** to order → ❼
> **mandar llamar** to send for → ❽
> **oír decir que** to hear it said that → ❾
> **oír hablar de** to hear of/about → ❿
> **querer decir** to mean → ⓫

The Perfect Infinitive

The perfect infinitive is formed using the auxiliary verb **haber** with the past participle of the verb → ⓬

The perfect infinitive is found:
- following certain prepositions, especially **después de** after → ⓭
- following certain verbal constructions → ⓮

Examples

1 Al verlo, dejó caer lo que llevaba en las manos — When he saw him he dropped what he was carrying

2 Haz entrar a nuestros invitados — Show our guests in

3 Quiero hacerles saber que no serán bien recibidos — I want to let them know that they won't be welcome

4 Hágale salir, por favor — Please let him out

5 Le he hecho venir a Vd porque ... — I sent for you because ...

6 Vete a buscar los guantes — Go and get your gloves

7 Me he mandado hacer un traje — I have ordered a suit

8 Mandaron llamar al médico — They sent for the doctor

9 He oído decir que está enfermo — I've heard it said that he's ill

10 No he oído hablar más de él — I haven't heard anything more (said) of him

11 ¿Qué quiere decir eso? — What does that mean?

12 haber terminado — to have finished
haberse vestido — to have got dressed

13 Después de haber comprado el regalo, volvió a casa — After buying/having bought the present, he went back home
Después de haber madrugado tanto, el taxi se retrasó — After she got up so early, the taxi arrived late

14 perdonar a alguien por haber hecho — to forgive somebody for doing/having done
dar las gracias a alguien por haber hecho — to thank somebody for doing/having done
pedir perdón por haber hecho — to be sorry for doing/having done

The Gerund

Formation

First conjugation:
- replace the **-ar** of the infinitive by **-ando** → **❶**

Second conjugation:
- replace the **-er** of the infinitive by **-iendo** → **❷**

Third conjugation:
- replace the **-ir** of the infinitive by **-iendo** → **❸**

For irregular gerunds, see irregular verbs, page 80 onwards.

Uses

After the verb **estar**, to form the continuous tenses → **❹**

After the verbs **seguir** and **continuar** *to continue*, and **ir** when meaning to *happen gradually* → **❺**

In time constructions, after **llevar** → **❻**

When the action in the main clause needs to be complemented by another action → **❼**

The position of object pronouns is the same as for the infinitive (see page 46).

The gerund is invariable and strictly verbal in sense.

The Present Participle

It is formed by replacing the **-ar** of the infinitive of 1st conjugation verbs by **-ante**, and the **-er** and **-ir** of the 2nd and 3rd conjugations by **-iente** → **❽**

A very limited number of verbs have a present participle used either as an adjective or a noun → **❾/❿**

Examples

1 cantar to sing → cantando singing

2 temer to fear → temiendo fearing

3 partir to leave → partiendo leaving

4 Estoy escribiendo una carta   I am writing a letter
Estaban esperándonos   They were waiting for us

5 Sigue viniendo todos los días   He/she is still coming every day
Continuarán subiendo los precios   Prices will continue to go up
El ejército iba avanzando poco   The army was gradually
  a poco   advancing

6 Lleva dos años estudiando inglés   He/she has been studying
                                  English for two years

7 Pasamos el día tomando el sol   We spent the day sunbathing
  en la playa   on the beach
Iba cojeando   He/she/I was limping
Salieron corriendo   They ran out

8 cantar to sing → cantante singing/singer
pender to hang → pendiente hanging
seguir to follow → siguiente following

9 agua corriente   running water

10 un estudiante   a student

Verbs

Use of Tenses

The Present

Unlike English, Spanish often uses the same verb form for the simple present (e.g. I smoke, he reads, we live) and the continuous present (e.g. I am smoking, he is reading, we are living) → **❶**

Normally, however, the continuous present is used to translate the Spanish:
estar haciendo to be doing → **❷**

Spanish uses the present tense where English uses the perfect in the following cases:
- with certain prepositions of time – notably **desde** for/since – when an action begun in the past is continued in the present → **❸**
  ⓘ Note: The perfect can be used as in English when the verb is negative → **❹**
- in the construction **acabar de hacer** to have just done → **❺**

Like English, Spanish often uses the present where a future action is implied → **❻**

The Future

The future is generally used as in English → **❼**, but note the following:

Immediate future time is often expressed by means of the present tense of **ir** + **a** + infinitive → **❽**

When 'will' or 'shall' mean 'wish to', 'are willing to', **querer** is used → **❾**

The Future Perfect

Used as in English shall/will have done → **❿**

It can also express conjecture, usually about things in the recent past → **⓫**

Examples

1 Fumo   I smoke *or* I am smoking
Lee   He reads *or* He is reading
Vivimos   We live *or* We are living

2 Está fumando

He is smoking

3 Linda estudia español desde
hace seis meses
Estoy de pie desde las siete
¿Hace mucho que esperan?
Ya hace dos semanas que
estamos aquí

Linda's been learning Spanish for
six months (and still is)
I've been up since seven
Have you been waiting long?
That's two weeks we've been
here (now)

4 No se han visto desde hace
meses

They haven't seen each other for
months

5 Isabel acaba de salir

Isabel has just left

6 Mañana voy a Madrid

I am going to Madrid tomorrow

7 Lo haré mañana

I'll do it tomorrow

8 Te vas a caer si no tienes cuidado
Va a perder el tren
Va a llevar una media hora

You'll fall if you're not careful
He's going to miss the train
It'll take about half an hour

9 ¿Me quieres esperar un
momento, por favor?

Will you wait for me a second,
please?

10 Lo habré acabado para mañana

I will have finished it for
tomorrow

11 Ya habrán llegado a casa

They must have arrived home by
now

Use of Tenses *continued*

The Imperfect

The imperfect describes:
- an action or state in the past without definite limits in time → ❶
- habitual action(s) in the past (often expressed in English by means of would or used to) → ❷

Spanish uses the imperfect tense where English uses the pluperfect in the following cases:
- with certain prepositions of time – notably **desde** for/since – when an action begun in the remoter past was continued in the more recent past → ❸
  - ⓘ Note: The pluperfect is used as in English when the verb is negative or the action has been completed → ❹
- in the construction **acabar de hacer** to have just done → ❺

Both the continuous and simple forms in English can be translated by the Spanish simple imperfect, but the continuous imperfect is used when the emphasis is on the fact that an action was going on at a precise moment in the past → ❻

The Perfect

The perfect is generally used as in English → ❼

The Preterite

The preterite generally corresponds to the English simple past in both written and spoken Spanish → ❽

However, while English can use the simple past to describe habitual actions or settings, Spanish uses the imperfect (see above) → ❾

The Past Anterior

This tense is only ever used in written, literary Spanish, to replace the pluperfect in time clauses where the verb in the main clause is in the preterite → ❿

Examples

1. Todos mirábamos en silencio
   Nuestras habitaciones daban a la playa

   We were all watching in silence
   Our rooms overlooked the beach

2. En su juventud se levantaba de madrugada
   Hablábamos sin parar durante horas
   Mi hermano siempre me tomaba el pelo

   In his youth he got up at dawn
   We would talk non-stop for hours on end
   My brother always used to tease me

3. Hacía dos años que vivíamos en Irlanda
   Estaba enfermo desde 1990
   Hacía mucho tiempo que salían juntos

   We had been living in Ireland for two years
   He had been ill since 1990
   They had been going out together for a long time

4. Hacía un año que no le había visto
   Hacía una hora que había llegado

   I hadn't seen him for a year
   She had arrived an hour before

5. Acababa de encontrármelos

   I had just met them

6. Cuando llegué, todos estaban fumando

   When I arrived, they were all smoking

7. Todavía no han salido

   They haven't come out yet

8. Me desperté y salté de la cama

   I woke up and jumped out of bed

9. Siempre iban en coche al trabajo

   They always travelled to work by car

10. Apenas hubo acabado, se oyeron unos golpes en la puerta

    She had scarcely finished when there was a knock at the door

The Subjunctive: when to use it

For how to form the subjunctive see page 6 onwards.

After verbs of:

- 'wishing'
  querer que ⎤
  desear que ⎦   to wish that, want → **❶**

- 'emotion' (e.g. regret, surprise, shame, pleasure, etc)
  sentir que   to be sorry that → **❷**
  sorprender que   to be surprised that → **❸**
  alegrarse de que   to be pleased that → **❹**

- 'asking' and 'advising'
  pedir que   to ask that → **❺**
  aconsejar que   to advise that → **❻**

In all the above constructions, when the subject of the verbs in the main and subordinate clause is the same, the infinitive is used, and the conjunction **que** omitted → **❼**

- 'ordering', 'forbidding', 'allowing'
  mandar que* ⎤
  ordenar que ⎦   to order that → **❽**

  permitir que* ⎤
  dejar que*   ⎦   to allow that → **❾**

  prohibir que*   to forbid that → **❿**
  impedir que*   to prevent that → **⓫**

  *With these verbs either the subjunctive or the infinitive is used when the object of the main verb is the subject of the subordinate verb → **⓬**

Always after verbs expressing doubt or uncertainty, and verbs of opinion used negatively.

  dudar que   to doubt that → **⓭**

  no creer que ⎤
  no pensar que ⎦   not to think that → **⓮**

Examples

1. Queremos que esté contenta — We want her to be happy (*literally*: We want that she is happy)

   ¿Desea Vd que lo haga yo? — Do you want me to do it?

2. Sentí mucho que no vinieran — I was very sorry that they didn't come

3. Nos sorprendió que no les vieran Vds — We were surprised you didn't see them

4. Me alegro de que te gusten — I'm pleased that you like them

5. Sólo les pedimos que tengan cuidado — We're only asking you to take care

6. Le aconsejé que no llegara tarde — I advised him not to be late

7. Quiero que lo termines pronto — I want you to finish it soon
   BUT:
   Quiero terminarlo pronto — I want to finish it soon

8. Ha mandado que vuelvan — He has ordered them to come back
   Ordenó que fueran castigados — He ordered them to be punished

9. No permitas que te tomen el pelo — Don't let them pull your leg
   No me dejó que la llevara a casa — She didn't allow me to take her home

10. Te prohíbo que digas eso — I forbid you to say that

11. No les impido que vengan — I am not preventing them from coming

12. Les ordenó que salieran *or* Les ordenó salir — She ordered them to go out

13. Dudo que lo sepan hacer — I doubt they can do it

14. No creo que sean tan listos — I don't think they are as clever as that

The Subjunctive: when to use it *continued*

In impersonal constructions which express necessity, possibility, etc:

hace falta que ⎤ **es necesario que** ⎦	it is necessary that → ❶
es posible que	it is possible that → ❷
más vale que	it is better that → ❸
es una lástima que	it is a pity that → ❹

ⓘ Note: In impersonal constructions which state a fact or express certainty the indicative is used when the impersonal verb is affirmative. When it is negative, the subjunctive is used → ❺

After certain conjunctions:

para que ⎤ **a fin de que*** ⎦	so that → ❻
como si	as if → ❼
sin que*	without → ❽
a condición de que* ⎤ **con tal (de) que*** **siempre que** ⎦	provided that, on condition that → ❾
a menos que ⎤ **a no ser que** ⎦	unless → ❿
antes (de) que*	before → ⓫
no sea que	lest/in case → ⓬
mientras (que) ⎤ **siempre que** ⎦	as long as → ⓭
(el) que	the fact that → ⓮

* When the subject of both verbs is the same, the infinitive is used, and the final **que** is omitted → ❽

Examples

1. ¿Hace falta que vaya Jaime?   Does James have to go?

2. Es posible que tengan razón   It's possible that they are right

3. Más vale que se quede Vd en su casa   It's better that you stay at home

4. Es una lástima que haya perdido su perrito   It's a shame/pity that she has lost her puppy

5. Es verdad que va a venir   It's true that he's coming
   BUT:
   No es verdad que vayan a hacerlo   It's not true that they are going to do it

6. Átalas bien para que no se caigan   Tie them up tightly so that they won't fall

7. Hablaba como si no creyera en sus propias palabras   He talked as if he didn't believe in his own words

8. Salimos sin que nos vieran   We left without them seeing us
   BUT:
   Me fui sin esperarla   I went without waiting for her

9. Lo haré con tal de que me cuentes todo lo que pasó   I'll do it provided you tell me all that happened

10. Saldremos de paseo a menos que esté lloviendo   We'll go for a walk unless it's raining

11. Avísale antes de que sea demasiado tarde   Warn him before it's too late

12. Habla en voz baja, no sea que alguien nos oiga   Speak softly in case anyone hears us

13. Eso no pasará mientras yo sea el jefe aquí   That won't happen as long as I am the boss here

14. El que no me escribiera no me importaba demasiado   The fact that he didn't write didn't matter to me too much

The Subjunctive: when to use it *continued*

After the conjunctions:
> **de modo que**
> **de forma que**   so that (*indicating a purpose*) → ❶
> **de manera que**

> ⓘ Note: When these conjunctions introduce a result and not a purpose the subjunctive is not used → ❷

In relative clauses with an antecedent which is:
- negative → ❸
- indefinite → ❹
- non-specific → ❺

In main clauses, to express a wish or exhortation. The verb may be preceded by expressions like **ojalá** or **que** → ❻

In the **si** clause of conditions where the English sentence contains a conditional tense → ❼

In set expressions → ❽

In the following constructions which translate however:
- **por** + *adjective* + *subjunctive* → ❾
- **por** + *adverb* + *subjunctive* → ❿
- **por** + **mucho** + *subjunctive* → ⓫

Examples

1. Vuélvanse de manera que les vea bien

   Turn round so that I can see you properly

2. No quieren hacerlo, de manera que tendré que hacerlo yo

   They won't do it, so I'll have to do it myself

3. No he encontrado a nadie que la conociera

   I haven't met anyone who knows her

   No dijo nada que no supiéramos ya

   He/she didn't say anything we didn't already know

4. Necesito alguien que sepa conducir

   I need someone who can drive

   Busco algo que me distraiga

   I'm looking for something to take my mind off it

5. Busca una casa que tenga calefacción central

   He/she's looking for a house which has central heating (*subjunctive used since such a house may or may not exist*)

   El que lo haya visto tiene que decírmelo

   Anyone who has seen it must tell me (*subjunctive used since it is not known who has seen it*)

6. ¡Ojalá haga buen tiempo!

   Let's hope the weather will be good!

   ¡Que te diviertas!

   Have a good time!

7. Si fuéramos en coche llegaríamos a tiempo

   If we went by car we'd be there in time

8. Diga lo que diga ...

   Whatever he may say ...

   Sea lo que sea ...

   Be that as it may ...

   Pase lo que pase ...

   Come what may ...

   Sea como sea ...

   One way or another ...

9. Por cansado que esté, seguirá trabajando

   No matter how/however tired he may be, he'll go on working

10. Por lejos que viva, iremos a buscarle

    No matter how/however far away he lives, we'll go and look for him

11. Por mucho que lo intente, nunca lo conseguirá

    No matter how/however hard he tries, he'll never succeed

The Subjunctive: when to use it *continued*

Clauses taking either a subjunctive or an indicative

In certain constructions, a subjunctive is needed when the action refers to future events or hypothetical situations, whereas an indicative is used when stating a fact or experience → ❶

The commonest of these are:

The conjunctions:

cuando	when → ❶
en cuanto	as soon as → ❷
tan pronto como	
después (de) que*	after → ❸
hasta que	until → ❹
mientras	while → ❺
siempre que	whenever → ❻
aunque	even though → ❼

All conjunctions and pronouns ending in **-quiera** (*-ever*) → ❽

* ⓘ Note: If the subject of both verbs is the same, the subjunctive introduced by **después (de) que** may be replaced by **después de** + *infinitive* → ❾

Sequence of tenses in Subordinate Clauses

If the verb in the main clause is in the present, future or imperative, the verb in the dependent clause will be in the present or perfect subjunctive → ❿

If the verb in the main clause is in the conditional or any past tense, the verb in the dependent clause will be in the imperfect or pluperfect subjunctive → ⓫

Examples

1. Le aconsejé que oyera música cuando estuviera nervioso — I advised him to listen to music when he felt nervous
   Me gusta nadar cuando hace calor — I like to swim when it is warm

2. Te devolveré el libro tan pronto como lo haya leído — I'll give you back the book as soon as I have read it

3. Te lo diré después de que te hayas sentado — I'll tell you after you've sat down

4. Quédate aquí hasta que volvamos — Stay here until we come back

5. No hablen en voz alta mientras estén ellos aquí — Don't speak loudly while they are here

6. Vuelvan por aquí siempre que quieran — Come back whenever you wish to

7. No le creeré aunque diga la verdad — I won't believe him even if he tells the truth

8. La encontraré dondequiera que esté — I will find her wherever she might be

9. Después de cenar nos fuimos al cine — After dinner we went to the cinema
   Quiero que lo hagas (*pres + pres subj*) — I want you to do it
   Temo que no haya venido (*pres + perf subj*) — I fear he hasn't come (might not have come)
   Iremos por aquí para que no nos vean (*future + pres subj*) — We'll go this way so that they won't see us
   Me gustaría que llegaras temprano (*cond + imperf subj*) — I'd like you to arrive early
   Les pedí que me esperaran (*preterite + imperf subj*) — I asked them to wait for me
   Sentiría mucho que hubiese muerto (*cond + pluperf subj*) — I would be very sorry if he were dead

Verbs governing a, de, con, en, por and para

The following lists (pages 66 to 73) contain common verbal constructions using the prepositions **a**, **de**, **con**, **en**, **por** and **para**.

Note the following abbreviations:

infin.	*infinitive*
perf. infin.	*perfect infinitive**
algn	alguien
sb	somebody
sth	something

* For information see page 50.

aburrirse de + *infin.*	to get bored with doing → **1**
acabar con algo/algn	to put an end to sth/finish with sb → **2**
acabar de * + *infin.*	to have just done → **3**
acabar por + *infin.*	to end up doing → **4**
acercarse a algo/algn	to approach sth/sb
acordarse de algo/algn/de + *infin.*	to remember sth/sb/doing → **5**
acostumbrarse a algo/algn/a + *infin.*	to get used to sth/sb/to doing → **6**
acusar a algn de algo/de + *perf. infin*	to accuse sb of sth/of doing, having done. → **7**
advertir a algn de algo	to notify, warn sb about sth → **8**
aficionarse a algo/a + *infin.*	to grow fond of sth/of doing → **9**
alegrarse de algo/de + *perf. infin.*	to be glad about sth/of doing, having done → **10**
alejarse de algn/algo	to move away from sb/sth
amenazar a algn con algo/con + *infin.*	to threaten sb with sth/to do → **11**
animar a algn a + *infin.*	to encourage sb to do
apresurarse a + *infin.*	to hurry to do → **12**

* See also Use of Tenses, pages 54 and 56

Examples

1. Me aburría de no poder salir de casa — I used to get bored with not being able to leave the house

2. Quiso acabar con su vida — He wanted to put an end to his life

3. Acababan de llegar cuando ... — They had just arrived when ...

4. El acusado acabó por confesarlo todo — The accused ended up by confessing everything

5. Nos acordamos muy bien de aquellas vacaciones — We remember that holiday very well

6. Me he acostumbrado a levantarme temprano — I've got used to getting up early

7. Le acusó de haber mentido — She accused him of lying

8. Advertí a mi amigo del peligro que corría — I warned my friend about the danger he was in

9. Nos hemos aficionado a la música clásica — We've grown fond of classical music

10. Me alegro de haberle conocido — I'm glad I met him

11. Amenazó con denunciarles — He threatened to report them

12. Se apresuraron a coger sitio — They hurried to find a seat

Verbs governing a, de, con, en, por and para *continued*

aprender a + *infin.*	to learn to do → ❶
aprovecharse de algo/algn	to take advantage of sth/sb
aproximarse a algn/algo	to approach sb/sth
asistir a algo	to attend sth, be at sth
asomarse a/por	to lean out of → ❷
asombrarse de + *infin.*	to be surprised at doing → ❸
atreverse a + *infin.*	to dare to do
avergonzarse de algo/algn/de + *perf. infin.*	to be ashamed of sth/sb/of doing, having done → ❹
ayudar a algn a + *infin.*	to help sb to do → ❺
bajarse de (+ *place/vehicle*)	to get off/out of → ❻
burlarse de algn	to make fun of sb
cansarse de algo/algn/de + *infin.*	to tire of sth/sb/of doing
carecer de algo	to lack sth → ❼
cargar de algo	to load with sth → ❽
casarse con algn	to get married to sb → ❾
cesar de + *infin.*	to stop doing
chocar con algo	to crash/bump into sth → ❿
comenzar a + *infin.*	to begin to do
comparar con algn/algo	to compare with sb/sth
consentir en + *infin.*	to agree to do
consistir en + *infin.*	to consist of doing → ⓫
constar de algo	to consist of sth → ⓬
contar con algn/algo	to rely on sb/sth → ⓭
convenir en + *infin.*	to agree to do → ⓮
darse cuenta de algo	to realize sth
dejar de + *infin.*	to stop doing → ⓯
depender de algo/algn	to depend on sth/sb → ⓰
despedirse de algn	to say goodbye to sb
dirigirse a algn/+ place	to address sb/head for
disponerse a + *infin.*	to get ready to do
empezar a + *infin.*	to begin to do
empezar por + *infin.*	to begin by doing → ⓱

Examples

1. Me gustaría aprender a nadar — I'd like to learn to swim

2. No te asomes a la ventana — Don't lean out of the window

3. Nos asombramos mucho de verles ahí — We were very surprised at seeing them there

4. No me avergüenzo de haberlo hecho — I'm not ashamed of having done it

5. Ayúdeme a llevar estas maletas — Help me to carry these cases

6. Se bajó del coche — He got out of the car

7. La casa carecía de jardín — The house lacked (did not have) a garden

8. El carro iba cargado de paja — The cart was loaded with straw

9. Se casó con Andrés — She married Andrew

10. Enciende la luz, o chocarás con la puerta — Turn the light on, or you'll bump into the door

11. Mi plan consistía en vigilarles de cerca — My plan consisted of keeping a close eye on them

12. El examen consta de tres partes — The exam consists of three parts

13. Cuento contigo para que me ayudes a hacerlo — I rely on you to help me do it

14. Convinieron en reunirse al día siguiente — They agreed to meet the following day

15. ¿Quieres dejar de hablar? — Will you stop talking?

16. No depende de mí — It doesn't depend on me

17. Empieza por enterarte de lo que se trata — Begin by finding out what it is about

Verbs governing a, de, con, en, por and para *continued*

encontrarse con algn	to meet sb (by chance) → ❶
enfadarse con algn	to get annoyed with sb
enseñar a algn a + *infin.*	to teach sb to → ❷
enterarse de algo	to find out about sth → ❸
entrar en (+ *place*)	to enter, go into
esperar a + *infin.*	to wait until → ❹
estar de acuerdo con algn/algo	to agree with sb/sth
fiarse de algn/algo	to trust sb/sth
fijarse en algo/algn	to notice sth/sb → ❺
hablar con algn	to talk to sb → ❻
hacer caso a algn	to pay attention to sb
hartarse de algo/algn/de + *infin.*	to get fed up with sth/sb/with doing → ❼
interesarse por algo/algn	to be interested in sth/sb → ❽
invitar a algn a + *infin.*	to invite sb to do
jugar a (+ sports, games)	to play
luchar por algo/por + *infin.*	to fight, strive for/to do → ❾
llegar a + *infin.*/(place)	to manage to do/to reach → ❿
llenar de algo	to fill with sth
negarse a + *infin.*	to refuse to do → ⓫
obligar a algn a + *infin.*	to make sb do → ⓬
ocuparse de algn/algo	to take care of sb/attend to sth
oler a algo	to smell of sth → ⓭
olvidarse de algo/algn/de + *infin.*	to forget sth/sb/to do → ⓮
oponerse a algo/a + *infin.*	to be opposed to sth/to doing
parecerse a algn/algo	to resemble sb/sth
pensar en algo/algn/en + *infin.*	to think about sth/sb/about doing → ⓯
preguntar por algn	to ask for/about sb
preocuparse de *or* por algo/algn	to worry about sth/sb → ⓰

Examples

1. Me encontré con ella al entrar en el banco — I met her as I was entering the bank

2. Le estoy enseñando a nadar — I am teaching him to swim

3. ¿Te has enterado del sitio adonde hay que ir? — Have you found out where we have to go?

4. Espera a saber lo que quiere antes de comprar el regalo — Wait until you know what he wants before buying the present

5. Me fijé en él cuando subía a su coche — I noticed him when he was getting into his car

6. ¿Puedo hablar con Vd un momento? — May I talk to you for a moment?

7. Me he hartado de escribirle — I've got fed up with writing to him

8. Me interesaba mucho por la arqueología — I was very interested in archaeology

9. Hay que luchar por mantener la paz — One must strive to preserve peace

10. Lo intenté sin llegar a conseguirlo — I tried without managing to do it

11. Se negó a hacerlo — He refused to do it

12. Le obligó a sentarse — He made him sit down

13. Este perfume huele a jazmín — This perfume smells of jasmine

14. Siempre me olvido de cerrar la puerta — I always forget to shut the door

15. No quiero pensar en eso — I don't want to think about that

16. Se preocupa mucho de/por su apariencia — He worries a lot about his appearance

Verbs governing a, de, con, en, por and para *continued*

prepararse a + *infin.*	to prepare to do
probar a + *infin.*	to try to do
quedar en + *infin.*	to agree to do → ❶
quedar por + *infin.*	to remain to be done → ❷
quejarse de algo	to complain of sth
referirse a algo	to refer to sth
reírse de algo/algn	to laugh at sth/sb
rodear de	to surround with → ❸
romper a + *infin.*	to (suddenly) start to do → ❹
salir de (+ *place*)	to leave
sentarse a (+ *table etc*)	to sit down at
subir(se) a (+ *vehicle/place*)	to get on, into/to climb → ❺
servir de algo a algn	to be useful to/serve sb as sth → ❻
servir para algo/para + *infin.*	to be good as sth/for doing → ❼
servirse de algo	to use sth → ❽
soñar con algn/algo/con + *infin.*	to dream about/of sb/sth/of doing
sorprenderse de algo	to be surprised at sth
tardar en + *infin.*	to take time to do → ❾
tener ganas de algo/de + *infin.*	to want sth/to do → ❿
tener miedo de algo	to be afraid of sth → ⓫
tener miedo a algn	to be afraid of sb → ⓬
terminar por + *infin.*	to end by doing
tirar de algo/algn	to pull sth/sb
trabajar de (+ *occupation*)	to work as → ⓭
trabajar en (+ *place of work*)	to work at/in → ⓮
traducir a (+ *language*)	to translate into
tratar de + *infin.*	to try to do → ⓯
tratarse de algo/algn/de + *infin.*	to be a question of sth/about sb/ about doing → ⓰
vacilar en + *infin.*	to hesitate to do → ⓱
volver a + *infin.*	to do again → ⓲

Examples

1. Habíamos quedado en encontrarnos a las 8 — We had agreed to meet at 8

2. Queda por averiguar dónde se ocultan — It remains to be discovered where they are hiding

3. Habían rodeado el jardín de un seto de cipreses — They had surrounded the garden with a hedge of cypress trees

4. Al apagarse la luz, el niño rompió a llorar — When the lights went out, the little boy suddenly started to cry

5. ¡De prisa, sube al coche! — Get into the car, quick!

6. Esto me servirá de bastón — This will serve me as a walking stick

7. No sirvo para (ser) jardinero — I'm no good as a gardener

8. Se sirvió de un destornillador para abrirlo — She used a screwdriver to open it

9. Tardaron mucho en salir — They took a long time to come out

10. Tengo ganas de volver a España — I want to go back to Spain

11. Mi hija tiene miedo de la oscuridad — My daughter is afraid of the dark

12. Nunca tuvieron miedo a su padre — They were never afraid of their father

13. Pedro trabaja de camarero en Londres — Peter works as a waiter in London

14. Trabajaba en una oficina — I used to work in an office

15. No trates de engañarme — Don't try to fool me

16. Se trata de nuestro nuevo vecino — It's about our new neighbour

17. Nunca vacilaban en pedir dinero — They never hesitated to borrow money

18. No vuelvas a hacerlo nunca más — Don't ever do it again

Ser and Estar

Spanish has two verbs – **ser** and **estar** – for 'to be'.

They are not interchangeable and each one is used in defined contexts.

ser is used:
- with an adjective, to express a permanent or inherent quality → **1**
- to express occupation or nationality → **2**
- to express possession → **3**
- to express origin or the material from which something is made → **4**
- with a noun, pronoun or infinitive following the verb → **5**
- to express the time and date → **6**
- to form the passive, with the past participle (see page 32).

  (i) Note: This use emphasizes the action of the verb. If, however, the resultant state or condition needs to be emphasized, **estar** is used. The past participle then functions as an adjective (see page 208) and has to agree in gender and in number with the noun → **7**

estar is used:
- always, to indicate place or location → **8**
- with an adjective or adjectival phrase, to express a quality or state seen by the speaker as subject to change or different from expected → **9**
- when speaking of a person's state of health → **10**
- to form the continuous tenses, used with the gerund (see page 52) → **11**
- with **de** + *noun*, to indicate a temporary occupation → **12**

Examples

① Mi hermano es alto
My brother is tall
María es inteligente
Mary is intelligent

② Javier es aviador
Javier is an airman
Sus padres son italianos
His parents are Italian

③ La casa es de Miguel
The house belongs to Michael

④ Mi hermana es de Granada
My sister is from Granada
Las paredes son de ladrillo
The walls are made of brick

⑤ Andrés es un niño travieso
Andrew is a naughty boy
Soy yo, Enrique
It's me, Henry
Todo es proponérselo
It's all a question of putting your mind to it

⑥ Son las tres y media
It's half past three
Mañana es sábado
Tomorrow is Saturday

⑦ Las puertas eran cerradas sigilosamente
The doors were being silently closed
Las puertas estaban cerradas
The doors were closed (resultant action)

⑧ La comida está en la mesa
The meal is on the table

⑨ Su amigo está enfermo
Her friend is ill
El lavabo está ocupado
The toilet is engaged
Hoy estoy de mal humor
I'm in a bad mood today
Las tiendas están cerradas
The shops are closed

⑩ ¿Cómo están Vds?
How are you?
Estamos todos bien
We are all well

⑪ Estamos aprendiendo mucho
We are learning a great deal

⑫ Mi primo está de médico en un pueblo
My cousin works as a doctor in a village

Ser and Estar *continued*

With certain adjectives, both ser and estar can be used, although they are not interchangeable when used in this way:
- **ser** will express a permanent or inherent quality → ❶
- **estar** will express a temporary state or quality → ❷

Both **ser** and **estar** may also be used in set expressions.

The commonest of these are:

With **ser**

Sea como sea	Be that as it may
Es igual/Es lo mismo	It's all the same
llegar a ser	to become
¿Cómo fue eso?	How did that happen?
¿Qué ha sido de él?	What has become of him?
ser para (*with the idea of purpose*)	to be for → ❸

With **estar**

estar de pie/de rodillas	to be standing/kneeling
estar de viaje	to be travelling
estar de vacaciones	to be on holiday
estar de vuelta	to be back
estar de moda	to be in fashion
Está bien	It's all right
estar para	to be about to do sth/to be in a mood for → ❹
estar por	to be inclined to/to be (all) for → ❺
estar a punto de	to be just about to do sth → ❻

Examples

1 Su hermana es muy joven/vieja — His sister is very young/old
Son muy ricos/pobres — They are very rich/poor
Su amigo era un enfermo — His friend was an invalid
Es un borracho — He is a drunkard
Mi hijo es bueno/malo — My son is good/naughty
Viajar es cansado — Travelling is tiring

2 Está muy joven/vieja con ese vestido — She looks very young/old in that dress
Ahora están muy ricos/pobres — They have become very rich/poor lately
Estaba enfermo — He was ill
Está borracho — He is drunk
Está bueno/malo — He is well/ill
Hoy estoy cansada — I am tired today

3 Este paquete es para Vd — This parcel is for you
Esta caja es para guardar semillas — This box is for keeping seeds in

4 Están para llegar — They're about to arrive

5 Estoy por irme a vivir a España — I'm inclined to go and live in Spain

6 Las rosas están a punto de salir — The roses are about to come out

Verbal Idioms

Special Intransitive Verbs

With the following verbs the Spanish construction is the opposite of the English. The subject in English becomes the indirect object of the Spanish verb, while the object in English becomes the subject of the Spanish verb. Compare the following:

> I like that house (subject: I, object: that house)
> **Esa casa me gusta** (subject: **esa casa**, indirect object: **me**)

The commonest of these verbs are:

gustar	to like →	❶
gustar más	to prefer →	❷
encantar	(colloquial) to love →	❸
faltar	to need/to be short of/to have missing →	❹
quedar	to be/have left →	❺
doler	to have a pain in/to hurt, ache →	❻
interesar	to be interested in →	❼
importar	to mind →	❽

Examples

① Me gusta este vestido

I like this dress (This dress pleases me)

② Me gustan más éstas

I prefer these

③ Nos encanta hacer deporte

We love sport

④ Me faltaban 100 euros

I was short of 100 euros

Sólo le falta el toque final

It just needs the finishing touch

Le faltaban tres dientes

He/she had three teeth missing

⑤ Sólo nos quedan dos kilómetros

We only have two kilometres (left) to go

⑥ Me duele la cabeza

I have a headache

⑦ Nos interesa mucho la política

We are very interested in politics

⑧ No me importa la lluvia

I don't mind the rain

Irregular Verbs

The verbs listed opposite and conjugated on pages 82 to 160 provide the main patterns for irregular verbs. The verbs are grouped opposite according to their infinitive ending and are shown in the following tables in alphabetical order.

In the tables, the most important irregular verbs are given in their most common simple tenses, together with the imperative and the gerund.

The past participle is also shown for each verb, to enable you to form all the compound tenses, as on pages 18 to 23.

The pronouns **ella** and **Vd** take the same verb endings as **él**, while **ellas** and **Vds** take the same endings as **ellos**.

> All the verbs included in the tables differ from the three conjugations set out on pages 8 to 13. Many – e.g. **contar** – serve as models for groups of verbs, while others – e.g. **ir** – are unique. On pages 161–190 you will find every verb in this dictionary listed alphabetically and cross-referred either to the relevant basic conjugation or to the appropriate model in the verb tables.

Imperfect Subjunctive of Irregular Verbs

For verbs with an irregular root form in the preterite tense – e.g. **andar** → **anduvieron** – the imperfect subjunctive is formed by using the root form of the 3rd person plural of the preterite tense, and adding the imperfect subjunctive endings **-iera/-iese** etc where the verb has an 'i' in the preterite ending – e.g. anduv**ieron** → anduv**iera/iese**. Where the verb has no 'i' in the preterite ending, add **-era/-ese** etc – e.g. produj**eron** → produj**era/ese**.

Irregular Verbs

'-ar':			
	actuar		saber
	almorzar		satisfacer
	andar		ser
	aullar		tener
	avergonzar		torcer
	averiguar		traer
	contar		valer
	cruzar		vencer
	dar		ver
	empezar		volver
	enviar		
	errar	'-ir':	abolir
	estar		abrir
	jugar		adquirir
	negar		bendecir
	pagar		conducir
	pensar		construir
	rehusar		decir
	rogar		dirigir
	sacar		distinguir
	volcar		dormir
			elegir
'-er':	caber		erguir
	caer		escribir
	cocer		freír
	coger		gruñir
	crecer		ir
	entender		lucir
	haber		morir
	hacer		oír
	hay		pedir
	leer		prohibir
	llover		reír
	mover		reñir
	nacer		reunir
	oler		salir
	poder		seguir
	poner		sentir
	querer		venir
	resolver		zurcir
	romper		

abolir (to abolish)

	PRESENT*			IMPERFECT
nosotros	abol**imos**		yo	abol**ía**
vosotros	abol**ís**		tú	abol**ías**
			él	abol**ía**
			nosotros	abol**íamos**
			vosotros	abol**íais**
			ellos	abol**ían**

* Present tense only used in persons shown

	FUTURE			CONDITIONAL
yo	abolir**é**		yo	abolir**ía**
tú	abolir**ás**		tú	abolir**ías**
él	abolir**á**		él	abolir**ía**
nosotros	abolir**emos**		nosotros	abolir**íamos**
vosotros	abolir**éis**		vosotros	abolir**íais**
ellos	abolir**án**		ellos	abolir**ían**

	PRESENT SUBJUNCTIVE			PRETERITE
	not used		yo	abol**í**
			tú	abol**iste**
			él	abol**ió**
			nosotros	abol**imos**
			vosotros	abol**isteis**
			ellos	abol**ieron**

PAST PARTICIPLE	IMPERATIVE
abol**ido**	abol**id**

GERUND
abol**iendo**

abrir (to open)

	PRESENT		IMPERFECT
yo	abro	yo	abría
tú	abres	tú	abrías
él	abre	él	abría
nosotros	abrimos	nosotros	abríamos
vosotros	abrís	vosotros	abríais
ellos	abren	ellos	abrían

	FUTURE		CONDITIONAL
yo	abriré	yo	abriría
tú	abrirás	tú	abrirías
él	abrirá	él	abriría
nosotros	abriremos	nosotros	abriríamos
vosotros	abriréis	vosotros	abriríais
ellos	abrirán	ellos	abrirían

	PRESENT SUBJUNCTIVE		PRETERITE
yo	abra	yo	abrí
tú	abras	tú	abriste
él	abra	él	abrió
nosotros	abramos	nosotros	abrimos
vosotros	abráis	vosotros	abristeis
ellos	abran	ellos	abrieron

PAST PARTICIPLE
abierto

IMPERATIVE
abre
abrid

GERUND
abriendo

actuar (to act)

	PRESENT		IMPERFECT
yo	**actúo**	yo	actu**aba**
tú	**actúas**	tú	actu**abas**
él	**actúa**	él	actu**aba**
nosotros	actu**amos**	nosotros	actu**ábamos**
vosotros	actu**áis**	vosotros	actu**abais**
ellos	**actúan**	ellos	actu**aban**

	FUTURE		CONDITIONAL
yo	actuar**é**	yo	actuar**ía**
tú	actuar**ás**	tú	actuar**ías**
él	actuar**á**	él	actuar**ía**
nosotros	actuar**emos**	nosotros	actuar**íamos**
vosotros	actuar**éis**	vosotros	actuar**íais**
ellos	actuar**án**	ellos	actuar**ían**

	PRESENT SUBJUNCTIVE		PRETERITE
yo	**actúe**	yo	actu**é**
tú	**actúes**	tú	actu**aste**
él	**actúe**	él	actu**ó**
nosotros	actu**emos**	nosotros	actu**amos**
vosotros	actu**éis**	vosotros	actu**asteis**
ellos	**actúen**	ellos	actu**aron**

PAST PARTICIPLE	IMPERATIVE
actu**ado**	**actúa**
	actua**d**

GERUND
actu**ando**

adquirir (to acquire)

	PRESENT		IMPERFECT
yo	adquiero	yo	adquiría
tú	adquieres	tú	adquirías
él	adquiere	él	adquiría
nosotros	adquirimos	nosotros	adquiríamos
vosotros	adquirís	vosotros	adquiríais
ellos	adquieren	ellos	adquirían

	FUTURE		CONDITIONAL
yo	adquiriré	yo	adquiriría
tú	adquirirás	tú	adquirirías
él	adquirirá	él	adquiriría
nosotros	adquiriremos	nosotros	adquiriríamos
vosotros	adquiriréis	vosotros	adquiriríais
ellos	adquirirán	ellos	adquirirían

	PRESENT SUBJUNCTIVE		PRETERITE
yo	adquiera	yo	adquirí
tú	adquieras	tú	adquiriste
él	adquiera	él	adquirió
nosotros	adquiramos	nosotros	adquirimos
vosotros	adquiráis	vosotros	adquiristeis
ellos	adquieran	ellos	adquirieron

PAST PARTICIPLE	IMPERATIVE
adquirido	adquiere
	adquirid

GERUND
adquiriendo

almorzar (to have lunch)

	PRESENT		IMPERFECT
yo	**almuerzo**	yo	almorz**aba**
tú	**almuerzas**	tú	almorz**abas**
él	**almuerza**	él	almorz**aba**
nosotros	almorz**amos**	nosotros	almorz**ábamos**
vosotros	almorz**áis**	vosotros	almorz**abais**
ellos	**almuerzan**	ellos	almorz**aban**

	FUTURE		CONDITIONAL
yo	almorzar**é**	yo	almorzar**ía**
tú	almorzar**ás**	tú	almorzar**ías**
él	almorzar**á**	él	almorzar**ía**
nosotros	almorzar**emos**	nosotros	almorzar**íamos**
vosotros	almorzar**éis**	vosotros	almorzar**íais**
ellos	almorzar**án**	ellos	almorzar**ían**

	PRESENT SUBJUNCTIVE		PRETERITE
yo	**almuerce**	yo	**almorcé**
tú	**almuerces**	tú	almorz**aste**
él	**almuerce**	él	almorz**ó**
nosotros	**almorcemos**	nosotros	almorz**amos**
vosotros	**almorcéis**	vosotros	almorz**asteis**
ellos	**almuercen**	ellos	almorz**aron**

PAST PARTICIPLE
almorz**ado**

IMPERATIVE
almuerza
almorza**d**

GERUND
almorz**ando**

andar (to walk)

	PRESENT		IMPERFECT
yo	ando	yo	andaba
tú	andas	tú	andabas
él	anda	él	andaba
nosotros	andamos	nosotros	andábamos
vosotros	andáis	vosotros	andabais
ellos	andan	ellos	andaban

	FUTURE		CONDITIONAL
yo	andaré	yo	andaría
tú	andarás	tú	andarías
él	andará	él	andaría
nosotros	andaremos	nosotros	andaríamos
vosotros	andaréis	vosotros	andaríais
ellos	andarán	ellos	andarían

	PRESENT SUBJUNCTIVE		PRETERITE
yo	ande	yo	anduve
tú	andes	tú	anduviste
él	ande	él	anduvo
nosotros	andemos	nosotros	anduvimos
vosotros	andéis	vosotros	anduvisteis
ellos	anden	ellos	anduvieron

PAST PARTICIPLE
andado

IMPERATIVE
anda
andad

GERUND
andando

aullar (to howl)

	PRESENT		IMPERFECT
yo	**aúllo**	yo	aull**aba**
tú	**aúllas**	tú	aull**abas**
él	**aúlla**	él	aull**aba**
nosotros	aull**amos**	nosotros	aull**ábamos**
vosotros	aull**áis**	vosotros	aull**abais**
ellos	**aúllan**	ellos	aull**aban**

	FUTURE		CONDITIONAL
yo	aullar**é**	yo	aullar**ía**
tú	aullar**ás**	tú	aullar**ías**
él	aullar**á**	él	aullar**ía**
nosotros	aullar**emos**	nosotros	aullar**íamos**
vosotros	aullar**éis**	vosotros	aullar**íais**
ellos	aullar**án**	ellos	aullar**ían**

	PRESENT SUBJUNCTIVE		PRETERITE
yo	**aúlle**	yo	aull**é**
tú	**aúlles**	tú	aull**aste**
él	**aúlle**	él	aull**ó**
nosotros	aull**emos**	nosotros	aull**amos**
vosotros	aull**éis**	vosotros	aull**asteis**
ellos	**aúllen**	ellos	aull**aron**

PAST PARTICIPLE	IMPERATIVE
aull**ado**	**aúlla**
	aulla**d**

GERUND
aull**ando**

avergonzar (to shame)

	PRESENT		IMPERFECT
yo	**avergüenzo**	yo	avergonz**aba**
tú	**avergüenzas**	tú	avergonz**abas**
él	**avergüenza**	él	avergonz**aba**
nosotros	avergonz**amos**	nosotros	avergonz**ábamos**
vosotros	avergonz**áis**	vosotros	avergonz**abais**
ellos	**avergüenzan**	ellos	avergonz**aban**

	FUTURE		CONDITIONAL
yo	avergonzar**é**	yo	avergonzar**ía**
tú	avergonzar**ás**	tú	avergonzar**ías**
él	avergonzar**á**	él	avergonzar**ía**
nosotros	avergonzar**emos**	nosotros	avergonzar**íamos**
vosotros	avergonzar**éis**	vosotros	avergonzar**íais**
ellos	avergonzar**án**	ellos	avergonzar**ían**

	PRESENT SUBJUNCTIVE		PRETERITE
yo	**avergüence**	yo	**avergoncé**
tú	**avergüences**	tú	avergonz**aste**
él	**avergüence**	él	avergonz**ó**
nosotros	**avergoncemos**	nosotros	avergonz**amos**
vosotros	**avergoncéis**	vosotros	avergonz**asteis**
ellos	**avergüencen**	ellos	avergonz**aron**

PAST PARTICIPLE	IMPERATIVE
avergonz**ado**	**avergüenza**
	avergonza**d**

GERUND
avergonz**ando**

averiguar (to find out)

	PRESENT		IMPERFECT
yo	averigu**o**	yo	averigu**aba**
tú	averigu**as**	tú	averigu**abas**
él	averigu**a**	él	averigu**aba**
nosotros	averigu**amos**	nosotros	averigu**ábamos**
vosotros	averigu**áis**	vosotros	averigu**abais**
ellos	averigu**an**	ellos	averigu**aban**

	FUTURE		CONDITIONAL
yo	averiguar**é**	yo	averiguar**ía**
tú	averiguar**ás**	tú	averiguar**ías**
él	averiguar**á**	él	averiguar**ía**
nosotros	averiguar**emos**	nosotros	averiguar**íamos**
vosotros	averiguar**éis**	vosotros	averiguar**íais**
ellos	averiguar**án**	ellos	averiguar**ían**

	PRESENT SUBJUNCTIVE		PRETERITE
yo	**averigüe**	yo	**averigüé**
tú	**averigües**	tú	averigu**aste**
él	**averigüe**	él	averigu**ó**
nosotros	**averigüemos**	nosotros	averigu**amos**
vosotros	**averigüéis**	vosotros	averigu**asteis**
ellos	**averigüen**	ellos	averigu**aron**

PAST PARTICIPLE	IMPERATIVE
averigu**ado**	averigu**a**
	averigu**ad**

GERUND
averigu**ando**

bendecir (to bless)

	PRESENT		IMPERFECT
yo	bendigo	yo	bendecía
tú	bendices	tú	bendecías
él	bendice	él	bendecía
nosotros	bendecimos	nosotros	bendecíamos
vosotros	bendecís	vosotros	bendecíais
ellos	bendicen	ellos	bendecían

	FUTURE		CONDITIONAL
yo	bendeciré	yo	bendeciría
tú	bendecirás	tú	bendecirías
él	bendecirá	él	bendeciría
nosotros	bendeciremos	nosotros	bendeciríamos
vosotros	bendeciréis	vosotros	bendeciríais
ellos	bendecirán	ellos	bendecirían

	PRESENT SUBJUNCTIVE		PRETERITE
yo	bendiga	yo	bendije
tú	bendigas	tú	bendijiste
él	bendiga	él	bendijo
nosotros	bendigamos	nosotros	bendijimos
vosotros	bendigáis	vosotros	bendijisteis
ellos	bendigan	ellos	bendijeron

PAST PARTICIPLE	IMPERATIVE
bendecido	bendice
	bendecid

GERUND
bendiciendo

caber (to fit)

	PRESENT		IMPERFECT
yo	**quepo**	yo	cab**ía**
tú	cab**es**	tú	cab**ías**
él	cab**e**	él	cab**ía**
nosotros	cab**emos**	nosotros	cab**íamos**
vosotros	cab**éis**	vosotros	cab**íais**
ellos	cab**en**	ellos	cab**ían**

	FUTURE		CONDITIONAL
yo	**cabré**	yo	**cabría**
tú	**cabrás**	tú	**cabrías**
él	**cabrá**	él	**cabría**
nosotros	**cabremos**	nosotros	**cabríamos**
vosotros	**cabréis**	vosotros	**cabríais**
ellos	**cabrán**	ellos	**cabrían**

	PRESENT SUBJUNCTIVE		PRETERITE
yo	**quepa**	yo	**cupe**
tú	**quepas**	tú	**cupiste**
él	**quepa**	él	**cupo**
nosotros	**quepamos**	nosotros	**cupimos**
vosotros	**quepáis**	vosotros	**cupisteis**
ellos	**quepan**	ellos	**cupieron**

PAST PARTICIPLE	IMPERATIVE
cab**ido**	cab**e**
	cab**ed**

GERUND
cab**iendo**

caer (to fall)

	PRESENT		IMPERFECT
yo	**caigo**	yo	ca**ía**
tú	ca**es**	tú	ca**ías**
él	ca**e**	él	ca**ía**
nosotros	ca**emos**	nosotros	ca**íamos**
vosotros	ca**éis**	vosotros	ca**íais**
ellos	ca**en**	ellos	ca**ían**

	FUTURE		CONDITIONAL
yo	caer**é**	yo	caer**ía**
tú	caer**ás**	tú	caer**ías**
él	caer**á**	él	caer**ía**
nosotros	caer**emos**	nosotros	caer**íamos**
vosotros	caer**éis**	vosotros	caer**íais**
ellos	caer**án**	ellos	caer**ían**

	PRESENT SUBJUNCTIVE		PRETERITE
yo	**caiga**	yo	**caí**
tú	**caigas**	tú	**caíste**
él	**caiga**	él	**cayó**
nosotros	**caigamos**	nosotros	**caímos**
vosotros	**caigáis**	vosotros	**caísteis**
ellos	**caigan**	ellos	**cayeron**

PAST PARTICIPLE	IMPERATIVE
caído	ca**e**
	ca**ed**

GERUND
cayendo

cocer (to boil)

	PRESENT			IMPERFECT
yo	**cuezo**		yo	cocía
tú	**cueces**		tú	cocías
él	**cuece**		él	cocía
nosotros	coc**emos**		nosotros	cocíamos
vosotros	coc**éis**		vosotros	cocíais
ellos	**cuecen**		ellos	cocían

	FUTURE			CONDITIONAL
yo	cocer**é**		yo	cocer**ía**
tú	cocer**ás**		tú	cocer**ías**
él	cocer**á**		él	cocer**ía**
nosotros	cocer**emos**		nosotros	cocer**íamos**
vosotros	cocer**éis**		vosotros	cocer**íais**
ellos	cocer**án**		ellos	cocer**ían**

	PRESENT SUBJUNCTIVE			PRETERITE
yo	**cueza**		yo	coc**í**
tú	**cuezas**		tú	coc**iste**
él	**cueza**		él	coc**ió**
nosotros	**cozamos**		nosotros	coc**imos**
vosotros	**cozáis**		vosotros	coc**isteis**
ellos	**cuezan**		ellos	coc**ieron**

PAST PARTICIPLE	IMPERATIVE
coc**ido**	**cuece**
	coc**ed**

GERUND
coc**iendo**

coger (to take)

	PRESENT		IMPERFECT
yo	**cojo**	yo	cog**ía**
tú	cog**es**	tú	cog**ías**
él	cog**e**	él	cog**ía**
nosotros	cog**emos**	nosotros	cog**íamos**
vosotros	cog**éis**	vosotros	cog**íais**
ellos	cog**en**	ellos	cog**ían**

	FUTURE		CONDITIONAL
yo	coger**é**	yo	coger**ía**
tú	coger**ás**	tú	coger**ías**
él	coger**á**	él	coger**ía**
nosotros	coger**emos**	nosotros	coger**íamos**
vosotros	coger**éis**	vosotros	coger**íais**
ellos	coger**án**	ellos	coger**ían**

	PRESENT SUBJUNCTIVE		PRETERITE
yo	**coja**	yo	cog**í**
tú	**cojas**	tú	cog**iste**
él	**coja**	él	cog**ió**
nosotros	**cojamos**	nosotros	cog**imos**
vosotros	**cojáis**	vosotros	cog**isteis**
ellos	**cojan**	ellos	cog**ieron**

PAST PARTICIPLE	IMPERATIVE
cog**ido**	cog**e**
	cog**ed**

GERUND

cog**iendo**

conducir (to drive, to lead)

	PRESENT		IMPERFECT
yo	**conduzco**	yo	conducía
tú	conduces	tú	conducías
él	conduce	él	conducía
nosotros	conducimos	nosotros	conducíamos
vosotros	conducís	vosotros	conducíais
ellos	conducen	ellos	conducían

	FUTURE		CONDITIONAL
yo	conduciré	yo	conduciría
tú	conducirás	tú	conducirías
él	conducirá	él	conduciría
nosotros	conduciremos	nosotros	conduciríamos
vosotros	conduciréis	vosotros	conduciríais
ellos	conducirán	ellos	conducirían

	PRESENT SUBJUNCTIVE		PRETERITE
yo	**conduzca**	yo	**conduje**
tú	**conduzcas**	tú	**condujiste**
él	**conduzca**	él	**condujo**
nosotros	**conduzcamos**	nosotros	**condujimos**
vosotros	**conduzcáis**	vosotros	**condujisteis**
ellos	**conduzcan**	ellos	**condujeron**

PAST PARTICIPLE	IMPERATIVE
conducido	conduce
	conducid

GERUND
conduciendo

construir (to build)

	PRESENT		IMPERFECT
yo	construyo	yo	construía
tú	construyes	tú	construías
él	construye	él	construía
nosotros	construimos	nosotros	construíamos
vosotros	construís	vosotros	construíais
ellos	construyen	ellos	construían

	FUTURE		CONDITIONAL
yo	construiré	yo	construiría
tú	construirás	tú	construirías
él	construirá	él	construiría
nosotros	construiremos	nosotros	construiríamos
vosotros	construiréis	vosotros	construiríais
ellos	construirán	ellos	construirían

	PRESENT SUBJUNCTIVE		PRETERITE
yo	construya	yo	construí
tú	construyas	tú	construiste
él	construya	él	construyó
nosotros	construyamos	nosotros	construimos
vosotros	construyáis	vosotros	construisteis
ellos	construyan	ellos	construyeron

PAST PARTICIPLE	IMPERATIVE
construido	construye
	construid

GERUND
construyendo

contar (to tell, to count)

	PRESENT		IMPERFECT
yo	**cuento**	yo	contaba
tú	**cuentas**	tú	contabas
él	**cuenta**	él	contaba
nosotros	contamos	nosotros	contábamos
vosotros	contáis	vosotros	contabais
ellos	**cuentan**	ellos	contaban

	FUTURE		CONDITIONAL
yo	contaré	yo	contaría
tú	contarás	tú	contarías
él	contará	él	contaría
nosotros	contaremos	nosotros	contaríamos
vosotros	contaréis	vosotros	contaríais
ellos	contarán	ellos	contarían

	PRESENT SUBJUNCTIVE		PRETERITE
yo	**cuente**	yo	conté
tú	**cuentes**	tú	contaste
él	**cuente**	él	contó
nosotros	contemos	nosotros	contamos
vosotros	contéis	vosotros	contasteis
ellos	**cuenten**	ellos	contaron

PAST PARTICIPLE	IMPERATIVE
contado	**cuenta**
	contad

GERUND
contando

crecer (to grow)

	PRESENT		IMPERFECT
yo	crezco	yo	crecía
tú	creces	tú	crecías
él	crece	él	crecía
nosotros	crecemos	nosotros	crecíamos
vosotros	crecéis	vosotros	crecíais
ellos	crecen	ellos	crecían

	FUTURE		CONDITIONAL
yo	creceré	yo	crecería
tú	crecerás	tú	crecerías
él	crecerá	él	crecería
nosotros	creceremos	nosotros	creceríamos
vosotros	creceréis	vosotros	creceríais
ellos	crecerán	ellos	crecerían

	PRESENT SUBJUNCTIVE		PRETERITE
yo	crezca	yo	crecí
tú	crezcas	tú	creciste
él	crezca	él	creció
nosotros	crezcamos	nosotros	crecimos
vosotros	crezcáis	vosotros	crecisteis
ellos	crezcan	ellos	crecieron

PAST PARTICIPLE
crecido

IMPERATIVE
crece
creced

GERUND
creciendo

cruzar (to cross)

	PRESENT		IMPERFECT
yo	cruzo	yo	cruzaba
tú	cruzas	tú	cruzabas
él	cruza	él	cruzaba
nosotros	cruzamos	nosotros	cruzábamos
vosotros	cruzáis	vosotros	cruzabais
ellos	cruzan	ellos	cruzaban

	FUTURE		CONDITIONAL
yo	cruzaré	yo	cruzaría
tú	cruzarás	tú	cruzarías
él	cruzará	él	cruzaría
nosotros	cruzaremos	nosotros	cruzaríamos
vosotros	cruzaréis	vosotros	cruzaríais
ellos	cruzarán	ellos	cruzarían

	PRESENT SUBJUNCTIVE		PRETERITE
yo	cruce	yo	crucé
tú	cruces	tú	cruzaste
él	cruce	él	cruzó
nosotros	crucemos	nosotros	cruzamos
vosotros	crucéis	vosotros	cruzasteis
ellos	crucen	ellos	cruzaron

PAST PARTICIPLE	IMPERATIVE
cruzado	cruza
	cruzad

GERUND
cruzando

dar (to give)

	PRESENT		IMPERFECT
yo	**doy**	yo	d**aba**
tú	d**as**	tú	d**abas**
él	d**a**	él	d**aba**
nosotros	d**amos**	nosotros	d**ábamos**
vosotros	d**ais**	vosotros	d**abais**
ellos	d**an**	ellos	d**aban**

	FUTURE		CONDITIONAL
yo	dar**é**	yo	dar**ía**
tú	dar**ás**	tú	dar**ías**
él	dar**á**	él	dar**ía**
nosotros	dar**emos**	nosotros	dar**íamos**
vosotros	dar**éis**	vosotros	dar**íais**
ellos	dar**án**	ellos	dar**ían**

	PRESENT SUBJUNCTIVE		PRETERITE
yo	**dé**	yo	**di**
tú	d**es**	tú	**diste**
él	**dé**	él	**dio**
nosotros	d**emos**	nosotros	**dimos**
vosotros	d**eis**	vosotros	**disteis**
ellos	d**en**	ellos	**dieron**

PAST PARTICIPLE	IMPERATIVE
d**ado**	d**a**
	d**ad**

GERUND
d**ando**

decir (to say)

	PRESENT		IMPERFECT
yo	**digo**	yo	dec**ía**
tú	**dices**	tú	dec**ías**
él	**dice**	él	dec**ía**
nosotros	dec**imos**	nosotros	dec**íamos**
vosotros	dec**ís**	vosotros	dec**íais**
ellos	**dicen**	ellos	dec**ían**

	FUTURE		CONDITIONAL
yo	**diré**	yo	**diría**
tú	**dirás**	tú	**dirías**
él	**dirá**	él	**diría**
nosotros	**diremos**	nosotros	**diríamos**
vosotros	**diréis**	vosotros	**diríais**
ellos	**dirán**	ellos	**dirían**

	PRESENT SUBJUNCTIVE		PRETERITE
yo	**diga**	yo	**dije**
tú	**digas**	tú	**dijiste**
él	**diga**	él	**dijo**
nosotros	**digamos**	nosotros	**dijimos**
vosotros	**digáis**	vosotros	**dijisteis**
ellos	**digan**	ellos	**dijeron**

PAST PARTICIPLE	IMPERATIVE
dicho	**di**
	dec**d**

GERUND
diciendo

dirigir (to direct)

	PRESENT		IMPERFECT
yo	**dirijo**	yo	dirig**ía**
tú	dirig**es**	tú	dirig**ías**
él	dirig**e**	él	dirig**ía**
nosotros	dirig**imos**	nosotros	dirig**íamos**
vosotros	dirig**ís**	vosotros	dirig**íais**
ellos	dirig**en**	ellos	dirig**ían**

	FUTURE		CONDITIONAL
yo	dirigir**é**	yo	dirigir**ía**
tú	dirigir**ás**	tú	dirigir**ías**
él	dirigir**á**	él	dirigir**ía**
nosotros	dirigir**emos**	nosotros	dirigir**íamos**
vosotros	dirigir**éis**	vosotros	dirigir**íais**
ellos	dirigir**án**	ellos	dirigir**ían**

	PRESENT SUBJUNCTIVE		PRETERITE
yo	**dirija**	yo	dirig**í**
tú	**dirijas**	tú	dirig**iste**
él	**dirija**	él	dirig**ió**
nosotros	**dirijamos**	nosotros	dirig**imos**
vosotros	**dirijáis**	vosotros	dirig**isteis**
ellos	**dirijan**	ellos	dirig**ieron**

PAST PARTICIPLE
dirig**ido**

IMPERATIVE
dirig**e**
dirig**id**

GERUND
dirig**iendo**

distinguir (to distinguish)

	PRESENT		IMPERFECT
yo	**distingo**	yo	distinguía
tú	distingues	tú	distinguías
él	distingue	él	distinguía
nosotros	distinguimos	nosotros	distinguíamos
vosotros	distinguís	vosotros	distinguíais
ellos	distinguen	ellos	distinguían

	FUTURE		CONDITIONAL
yo	distinguiré	yo	distinguiría
tú	distinguirás	tú	distinguirías
él	distinguirá	él	distinguiría
nosotros	distinguiremos	nosotros	distinguiríamos
vosotros	distinguiréis	vosotros	distinguiríais
ellos	distinguirán	ellos	distinguirían

	PRESENT SUBJUNCTIVE		PRETERITE
yo	**distinga**	yo	distinguí
tú	**distingas**	tú	distinguiste
él	**distinga**	él	distinguió
nosotros	**distingamos**	nosotros	distinguimos
vosotros	**distingáis**	vosotros	distinguisteis
ellos	**distingan**	ellos	distinguieron

PAST PARTICIPLE
distinguido

IMPERATIVE
distingue
distinguid

GERUND
distinguiendo

dormir (to sleep)

	PRESENT		IMPERFECT
yo	**duermo**	yo	dorm**ía**
tú	**duermes**	tú	dorm**ías**
él	**duerme**	él	dorm**ía**
nosotros	dorm**imos**	nosotros	dorm**íamos**
vosotros	dorm**ís**	vosotros	dorm**íais**
ellos	**duermen**	ellos	dorm**ían**

	FUTURE		CONDITIONAL
yo	dormir**é**	yo	dormir**ía**
tú	dormir**ás**	tú	dormir**ías**
él	dormir**á**	él	dormir**ía**
nosotros	dormir**emos**	nosotros	dormir**íamos**
vosotros	dormir**éis**	vosotros	dormir**íais**
ellos	dormir**án**	ellos	dormir**ían**

	PRESENT SUBJUNCTIVE		PRETERITE
yo	**duerma**	yo	dorm**í**
tú	**duermas**	tú	dorm**iste**
él	**duerma**	él	**durmió**
nosotros	**durmamos**	nosotros	dorm**imos**
vosotros	**durmáis**	vosotros	dorm**isteis**
ellos	**duerman**	ellos	**durmieron**

PAST PARTICIPLE	IMPERATIVE
dorm**ido**	**duerme**
	dorm**id**

GERUND
durmiendo

elegir (to choose)

	PRESENT		IMPERFECT
yo	elijo	yo	elegía
tú	eliges	tú	elegías
él	elige	él	elegía
nosotros	elegimos	nosotros	elegíamos
vosotros	elegís	vosotros	elegíais
ellos	eligen	ellos	elegían

	FUTURE		CONDITIONAL
yo	elegiré	yo	elegiría
tú	elegirás	tú	elegirías
él	elegirá	él	elegiría
nosotros	elegiremos	nosotros	elegiríamos
vosotros	elegiréis	vosotros	elegiríais
ellos	elegirán	ellos	elegirían

	PRESENT SUBJUNCTIVE		PRETERITE
yo	elija	yo	elegí
tú	elijas	tú	elegiste
él	elija	él	eligió
nosotros	elijamos	nosotros	elegimos
vosotros	elijáis	vosotros	elegisteis
ellos	elijan	ellos	eligieron

PAST PARTICIPLE
elegido

IMPERATIVE
elige
elegid

GERUND
eligiendo

empezar (to begin)

	PRESENT		IMPERFECT
yo	empiezo	yo	empezaba
tú	empiezas	tú	empezabas
él	empieza	él	empezaba
nosotros	empezamos	nosotros	empezábamos
vosotros	empezáis	vosotros	empezabais
ellos	empiezan	ellos	empezaban

	FUTURE		CONDITIONAL
yo	empezaré	yo	empezaría
tú	empezarás	tú	empezarías
él	empezará	él	empezaría
nosotros	empezaremos	nosotros	empezaríamos
vosotros	empezaréis	vosotros	empezaríais
ellos	empezarán	ellos	empezarían

	PRESENT SUBJUNCTIVE		PRETERITE
yo	empiece	yo	empecé
tú	empieces	tú	empezaste
él	empiece	él	empezó
nosotros	empecemos	nosotros	empezamos
vosotros	empecéis	vosotros	empezasteis
ellos	empiecen	ellos	empezaron

PAST PARTICIPLE
empezado

IMPERATIVE
empieza
empezad

GERUND
empezando

entender (to understand)

	PRESENT		IMPERFECT
yo	entiendo	yo	entendía
tú	entiendes	tú	entendías
él	entiende	él	entendía
nosotros	entendemos	nosotros	entendíamos
vosotros	entendéis	vosotros	entendíais
ellos	entienden	ellos	entendían

	FUTURE		CONDITIONAL
yo	entenderé	yo	entendería
tú	entenderás	tú	entenderías
él	entenderá	él	entendería
nosotros	entenderemos	nosotros	entenderíamos
vosotros	entenderéis	vosotros	entenderíais
ellos	entenderán	ellos	entenderían

	PRESENT SUBJUNCTIVE		PRETERITE
yo	entienda	yo	entendí
tú	entiendas	tú	entendiste
él	entienda	él	entendió
nosotros	entendamos	nosotros	entendimos
vosotros	entendáis	vosotros	entendisteis
ellos	entiendan	ellos	entendieron

PAST PARTICIPLE
entendido

IMPERATIVE
entiende
entended

GERUND
entendiendo

enviar (to send)

	PRESENT		IMPERFECT
yo	envío	yo	enviaba
tú	envías	tú	enviabas
él	envía	él	enviaba
nosotros	enviamos	nosotros	enviábamos
vosotros	enviáis	vosotros	enviabais
ellos	envían	ellos	enviaban

	FUTURE		CONDITIONAL
yo	enviaré	yo	enviaría
tú	enviarás	tú	enviarías
él	enviará	él	enviaría
nosotros	enviaremos	nosotros	enviaríamos
vosotros	enviaréis	vosotros	enviaríais
ellos	enviarán	ellos	enviarían

	PRESENT SUBJUNCTIVE		PRETERITE
yo	envíe	yo	envié
tú	envíes	tú	enviaste
él	envíe	él	envió
nosotros	enviemos	nosotros	enviamos
vosotros	enviéis	vosotros	enviasteis
ellos	envíen	ellos	enviaron

PAST PARTICIPLE
enviado

IMPERATIVE
envía
enviad

GERUND
enviando

erguir (to erect)

	PRESENT		IMPERFECT
yo	yergo	yo	erguía
tú	yergues	tú	erguías
él	yergue	él	erguía
nosotros	erguimos	nosotros	erguíamos
vosotros	erguís	vosotros	erguíais
ellos	yerguen	ellos	erguían

	FUTURE		CONDITIONAL
yo	erguiré	yo	erguiría
tú	erguirás	tú	erguirías
él	erguirá	él	erguiría
nosotros	erguiremos	nosotros	erguiríamos
vosotros	erguiréis	vosotros	erguiríais
ellos	erguirán	ellos	erguirían

	PRESENT SUBJUNCTIVE		PRETERITE
yo	yerga	yo	erguí
tú	yergas	tú	erguiste
él	yerga	él	irguió
nosotros	irgamos	nosotros	erguimos
vosotros	irgáis	vosotros	erguisteis
ellos	yergan	ellos	irguieron

PAST PARTICIPLE
erguido

IMPERATIVE
yergue
erguid

GERUND
irguiendo

errar (to err)

	PRESENT		IMPERFECT
yo	**yerro**	yo	erraba
tú	**yerras**	tú	errabas
él	**yerra**	él	erraba
nosotros	erramos	nosotros	errábamos
vosotros	erráis	vosotros	errabais
ellos	**yerran**	ellos	erraban

	FUTURE		CONDITIONAL
yo	erraré	yo	erraría
tú	errarás	tú	errarías
él	errará	él	erraría
nosotros	erraremos	nosotros	erraríamos
vosotros	erraréis	vosotros	erraríais
ellos	errarán	ellos	errarían

	PRESENT SUBJUNCTIVE		PRETERITE
yo	**yerre**	yo	erré
tú	**yerres**	tú	erraste
él	**yerre**	él	erró
nosotros	erremos	nosotros	erramos
vosotros	erréis	vosotros	errasteis
ellos	**yerren**	ellos	erraron

PAST PARTICIPLE
errado

IMPERATIVE
yerra
errad

GERUND
errando

escribir (to write)

	PRESENT			IMPERFECT
yo	escribo		yo	escribía
tú	escribes		tú	escribías
él	escribe		él	escribía
nosotros	escribimos		nosotros	escribíamos
vosotros	escribís		vosotros	escribíais
ellos	escriben		ellos	escribían

	FUTURE			CONDITIONAL
yo	escribiré		yo	escribiría
tú	escribirás		tú	escribirías
él	escribirá		él	escribiría
nosotros	escribiremos		nosotros	escribiríamos
vosotros	escribiréis		vosotros	escribiríais
ellos	escribirán		ellos	escribirían

	PRESENT SUBJUNCTIVE			PRETERITE
yo	escriba		yo	escribí
tú	escribas		tú	escribiste
él	escriba		él	escribió
nosotros	escribamos		nosotros	escribimos
vosotros	escribáis		vosotros	escribisteis
ellos	escriban		ellos	escribieron

PAST PARTICIPLE
escrito

IMPERATIVE
escribe
escribid

GERUND
escribiendo

estar (to be)

	PRESENT		IMPERFECT
yo	**estoy**	yo	est**aba**
tú	**estás**	tú	est**abas**
él	**está**	él	est**aba**
nosotros	est**amos**	nosotros	est**ábamos**
vosotros	est**áis**	vosotros	est**abais**
ellos	**están**	ellos	est**aban**

	FUTURE		CONDITIONAL
yo	estar**é**	yo	estar**ía**
tú	estar**ás**	tú	estar**ías**
él	estar**á**	él	estar**ía**
nosotros	estar**emos**	nosotros	estar**íamos**
vosotros	estar**éis**	vosotros	estar**íais**
ellos	estar**án**	ellos	estar**ían**

	PRESENT SUBJUNCTIVE		PRETERITE
yo	**esté**	yo	**estuve**
tú	**estés**	tú	**estuviste**
él	**esté**	él	**estuvo**
nosotros	est**emos**	nosotros	**estuvimos**
vosotros	est**éis**	vosotros	**estuvisteis**
ellos	**estén**	ellos	**estuvieron**

PAST PARTICIPLE
est**ado**

IMPERATIVE
est**á**
esta**d**

GERUND
est**ando**

freír (to fry)

	PRESENT		IMPERFECT
yo	frío	yo	freía
tú	fríes	tú	freías
él	fríe	él	freía
nosotros	freímos	nosotros	freíamos
vosotros	freís	vosotros	freíais
ellos	fríen	ellos	freían

	FUTURE		CONDITIONAL
yo	freiré	yo	freiría
tú	freirás	tú	freirías
él	freirá	él	freiría
nosotros	freiremos	nosotros	freiríamos
vosotros	freiréis	vosotros	freiríais
ellos	freirán	ellos	freirían

	PRESENT SUBJUNCTIVE		PRETERITE
yo	fría	yo	freí
tú	frías	tú	freíste
él	fría	él	frió
nosotros	friamos	nosotros	freímos
vosotros	friáis	vosotros	freísteis
ellos	frían	ellos	frieron

PAST PARTICIPLE
frito

IMPERATIVE
fríe
freíd

GERUND
friendo

gruñir (to grunt)

	PRESENT		IMPERFECT
yo	gruño	yo	gruñía
tú	gruñes	tú	gruñías
él	gruñe	él	gruñía
nosotros	gruñimos	nosotros	gruñíamos
vosotros	gruñís	vosotros	gruñíais
ellos	gruñen	ellos	gruñían

	FUTURE		CONDITIONAL
yo	gruñiré	yo	gruñiría
tú	gruñirás	tú	gruñirías
él	gruñirá	él	gruñiría
nosotros	gruñiremos	nosotros	gruñiríamos
vosotros	gruñiréis	vosotros	gruñiríais
ellos	gruñirán	ellos	gruñirían

	PRESENT SUBJUNCTIVE		PRETERITE
yo	gruña	yo	gruñí
tú	gruñas	tú	gruñíste
él	gruña	él	gruñó
nosotros	gruñamos	nosotros	gruñimos
vosotros	gruñáis	vosotros	gruñisteis
ellos	gruñan	ellos	gruñeron

PAST PARTICIPLE
gruñido

IMPERATIVE
gruñe
gruñid

GERUND
gruñendo

haber (to have, *auxiliary*)

	PRESENT			IMPERFECT
yo	**he**		yo	hab**ía**
tú	**has**		tú	hab**ías**
él	**ha**		él	hab**ía**
nosotros	**hemos**		nosotros	hab**íamos**
vosotros	hab**éis**		vosotros	hab**íais**
ellos	**han**		ellos	hab**ían**

	FUTURE			CONDITIONAL
yo	**habré**		yo	**habría**
tú	**habrás**		tú	**habrías**
él	**habrá**		él	**habría**
nosotros	**habremos**		nosotros	**habríamos**
vosotros	**habréis**		vosotros	**habríais**
ellos	**habrán**		ellos	**habrían**

	PRESENT SUBJUNCTIVE			PRETERITE
yo	**haya**		yo	**hube**
tú	**hayas**		tú	**hubiste**
él	**haya**		él	**hubo**
nosotros	**hayamos**		nosotros	**hubimos**
vosotros	**hayáis**		vosotros	**hubisteis**
ellos	**hayan**		ellos	**hubieron**

PAST PARTICIPLE	IMPERATIVE
hab**ido**	*not used*

GERUND
hab**iendo**

hacer (to do, to make)

	PRESENT		IMPERFECT
yo	**hago**	yo	hac**ía**
tú	hac**es**	tú	hac**ías**
él	hac**e**	él	hac**ía**
nosotros	hac**emos**	nosotros	hac**íamos**
vosotros	hac**éis**	vosotros	hac**íais**
ellos	hac**en**	ellos	hac**ían**

	FUTURE		CONDITIONAL
yo	**haré**	yo	**haría**
tú	**harás**	tú	**harías**
él	**hará**	él	**haría**
nosotros	**haremos**	nosotros	**haríamos**
vosotros	**haréis**	vosotros	**haríais**
ellos	**harán**	ellos	**harían**

	PRESENT SUBJUNCTIVE		PRETERITE
yo	**haga**	yo	**hice**
tú	**hagas**	tú	**hiciste**
él	**haga**	él	**hizo**
nosotros	**hagamos**	nosotros	**hicimos**
vosotros	**hagáis**	vosotros	**hicisteis**
ellos	**hagan**	ellos	**hicieron**

PAST PARTICIPLE	IMPERATIVE
hecho	**haz**
	hac**ed**

GERUND
hac**iendo**

hay (there is, there are)

PRESENT
hay

IMPERFECT
había

FUTURE
habrá

CONDITIONAL
habría

PRESENT SUBJUNCTIVE
haya

PRETERITE
hubo

PAST PARTICIPLE
hab**ido**

IMPERATIVE
not used

GERUND
hab**iendo**

ir (to go)

	PRESENT		IMPERFECT
yo	voy	yo	iba
tú	vas	tú	ibas
él	va	él	iba
nosotros	vamos	nosotros	íbamos
vosotros	vais	vosotros	ibais
ellos	van	ellos	iban

	FUTURE		CONDITIONAL
yo	iré	yo	iría
tú	irás	tú	irías
él	irá	él	iría
nosotros	iremos	nosotros	iríamos
vosotros	iréis	vosotros	iríais
ellos	irán	ellos	irían

	PRESENT SUBJUNCTIVE		PRETERITE
yo	vaya	yo	fui
tú	vayas	tú	fuiste
él	vaya	él	fue
nosotros	vayamos	nosotros	fuimos
vosotros	vayáis	vosotros	fuisteis
ellos	vayan	ellos	fueron

PAST PARTICIPLE	IMPERATIVE
ido	ve
	id

GERUND
yendo

jugar (to play)

	PRESENT		IMPERFECT
yo	**juego**	yo	jug**aba**
tú	**juegas**	tú	jug**abas**
él	**juega**	él	jug**aba**
nosotros	jug**amos**	nosotros	jug**ábamos**
vosotros	jug**áis**	vosotros	jug**abais**
ellos	**juegan**	ellos	jug**aban**

	FUTURE		CONDITIONAL
yo	jugar**é**	yo	jugar**ía**
tú	jugar**ás**	tú	jugar**ías**
él	jugar**á**	él	jugar**ía**
nosotros	jugar**emos**	nosotros	jugar**íamos**
vosotros	jugar**éis**	vosotros	jugar**íais**
ellos	jugar**án**	ellos	jugar**ían**

	PRESENT SUBJUNCTIVE		PRETERITE
yo	**juegue**	yo	**jugué**
tú	**juegues**	tú	jug**aste**
él	**juegue**	él	jug**ó**
nosotros	**juguemos**	nosotros	jug**amos**
vosotros	**juguéis**	vosotros	jug**asteis**
ellos	**jueguen**	ellos	jug**aron**

PAST PARTICIPLE	IMPERATIVE
jug**ado**	**juega**
	jug**ad**

GERUND
jug**ando**

leer (to read)

	PRESENT		IMPERFECT
yo	leo	yo	leía
tú	lees	tú	leías
él	lee	él	leía
nosotros	leemos	nosotros	leíamos
vosotros	leéis	vosotros	leíais
ellos	leen	ellos	leían

	FUTURE		CONDITIONAL
yo	leeré	yo	leería
tú	leerás	tú	leerías
él	leerá	él	leería
nosotros	leeremos	nosotros	leeríamos
vosotros	leeréis	vosotros	leeríais
ellos	leerán	ellos	leerían

	PRESENT SUBJUNCTIVE		PRETERITE
yo	lea	yo	leí
tú	leas	tú	leíste
él	lea	él	leyó
nosotros	leamos	nosotros	leímos
vosotros	leáis	vosotros	leísteis
ellos	lean	ellos	leyeron

PAST PARTICIPLE
leído

IMPERATIVE
lee
leed

GERUND
leyendo

lucir (to shine)

	PRESENT		IMPERFECT
yo	luzco	yo	lucía
tú	luces	tú	lucías
él	luce	él	lucía
nosotros	lucimos	nosotros	lucíamos
vosotros	lucís	vosotros	lucíais
ellos	lucen	ellos	lucían

	FUTURE		CONDITIONAL
yo	luciré	yo	luciría
tú	lucirás	tú	lucirías
él	lucirá	él	luciría
nosotros	luciremos	nosotros	luciríamos
vosotros	luciréis	vosotros	luciríais
ellos	lucirán	ellos	lucirían

	PRESENT SUBJUNCTIVE		PRETERITE
yo	luzca	yo	lucí
tú	luzcas	tú	luciste
él	luzca	él	lució
nosotros	luzcamos	nosotros	lucimos
vosotros	luzcáis	vosotros	lucisteis
ellos	luzcan	ellos	lucieron

PAST PARTICIPLE
lucido

IMPERATIVE
luce
lucid

GERUND
luciendo

llover (to rain)

PRESENT	IMPERFECT
llueve	llov**ía**

FUTURE	CONDITIONAL
llover**á**	llover**ía**

PRESENT SUBJUNCTIVE	PRETERITE
llueva	llov**ió**

PAST PARTICIPLE	IMPERATIVE
llov**ido**	*not used*

GERUND
llov**iendo**

morir (to die)

	PRESENT		IMPERFECT
yo	muero	yo	moría
tú	mueres	tú	morías
él	muere	él	moría
nosotros	morimos	nosotros	moríamos
vosotros	morís	vosotros	moríais
ellos	mueren	ellos	morían

	FUTURE		CONDITIONAL
yo	moriré	yo	moriría
tú	morirás	tú	morirías
él	morirá	él	moriría
nosotros	moriremos	nosotros	moriríamos
vosotros	moriréis	vosotros	moriríais
ellos	morirán	ellos	morirían

	PRESENT SUBJUNCTIVE		PRETERITE
yo	muera	yo	morí
tú	mueras	tú	moriste
él	muera	él	murió
nosotros	muramos	nosotros	morimos
vosotros	muráis	vosotros	moristeis
ellos	mueran	ellos	murieron

PAST PARTICIPLE	IMPERATIVE
muerto	muere
	morid

GERUND
muriendo

mover (to move)

	PRESENT		IMPERFECT
yo	**muevo**	yo	mov**ía**
tú	**mueves**	tú	mov**ías**
él	**mueve**	él	mov**ía**
nosotros	mov**emos**	nosotros	mov**íamos**
vosotros	mov**éis**	vosotros	mov**íais**
ellos	**mueven**	ellos	mov**ían**

	FUTURE		CONDITIONAL
yo	mover**é**	yo	mover**ía**
tú	mover**ás**	tú	mover**ías**
él	mover**á**	él	mover**ía**
nosotros	mover**emos**	nosotros	mover**íamos**
vosotros	mover**éis**	vosotros	mover**íais**
ellos	mover**án**	ellos	mover**ían**

	PRESENT SUBJUNCTIVE		PRETERITE
yo	**mueva**	yo	mov**í**
tú	**muevas**	tú	mov**iste**
él	**mueva**	él	mov**ió**
nosotros	mov**amos**	nosotros	mov**imos**
vosotros	mov**áis**	vosotros	mov**isteis**
ellos	**muevan**	ellos	mov**ieron**

PAST PARTICIPLE	IMPERATIVE
mov**ido**	**mueve**
	mov**ed**

GERUND
mov**iendo**

nacer (to be born)

	PRESENT		IMPERFECT
yo	**nazco**	yo	nac**ía**
tú	nac**es**	tú	nac**ías**
él	nac**e**	él	nac**ía**
nosotros	nac**emos**	nosotros	nac**íamos**
vosotros	nac**éis**	vosotros	nac**íais**
ellos	nac**en**	ellos	nac**ían**

	FUTURE		CONDITIONAL
yo	nacer**é**	yo	nacer**ía**
tú	nacer**ás**	tú	nacer**ías**
él	nacer**á**	él	nacer**ía**
nosotros	nacer**emos**	nosotros	nacer**íamos**
vosotros	nacer**éis**	vosotros	nacer**íais**
ellos	nacer**án**	ellos	nacer**ían**

	PRESENT SUBJUNCTIVE		PRETERITE
yo	**nazca**	yo	nac**í**
tú	**nazcas**	tú	nac**iste**
él	**nazca**	él	nac**ió**
nosotros	**nazcamos**	nosotros	nac**imos**
vosotros	**nazcáis**	vosotros	nac**isteis**
ellos	**nazcan**	ellos	nac**ieron**

PAST PARTICIPLE	IMPERATIVE
nac**ido**	nac**e**
	nac**ed**

GERUND

nac**iendo**

negar (to deny)

	PRESENT		IMPERFECT
yo	niego	yo	negaba
tú	niegas	tú	negabas
él	niega	él	negaba
nosotros	negamos	nosotros	negábamos
vosotros	negáis	vosotros	negabais
ellos	niegan	ellos	negaban

	FUTURE		CONDITIONAL
yo	negaré	yo	negaría
tú	negarás	tú	negarías
él	negará	él	negaría
nosotros	negaremos	nosotros	negaríamos
vosotros	negaréis	vosotros	negaríais
ellos	negarán	ellos	negarían

	PRESENT SUBJUNCTIVE		PRETERITE
yo	niegue	yo	negué
tú	niegues	tú	negaste
él	niegue	él	negó
nosotros	nieguemos	nosotros	negamos
vosotros	nieguéis	vosotros	negasteis
ellos	nieguen	ellos	negaron

PAST PARTICIPLE	IMPERATIVE
negado	niega
	negad

GERUND
negando

oír (to hear)

	PRESENT		IMPERFECT
yo	oigo	yo	oía
tú	oyes	tú	oías
él	oye	él	oía
nosotros	oímos	nosotros	oíamos
vosotros	oís	vosotros	oíais
ellos	oyen	ellos	oían

	FUTURE		CONDITIONAL
yo	oiré	yo	oiría
tú	oirás	tú	oirías
él	oirá	él	oiría
nosotros	oiremos	nosotros	oiríamos
vosotros	oiréis	vosotros	oiríais
ellos	oirán	ellos	oirían

	PRESENT SUBJUNCTIVE		PRETERITE
yo	oiga	yo	oí
tú	oigas	tú	oíste
él	oiga	él	oyó
nosotros	oigamos	nosotros	oímos
vosotros	oigáis	vosotros	oísteis
ellos	oigan	ellos	oyeron

PAST PARTICIPLE	IMPERATIVE
oído	oye
	oíd

GERUND

oyendo

oler (to smell)

	PRESENT			IMPERFECT
yo	huelo		yo	olía
tú	hueles		tú	olías
él	huele		él	olía
nosotros	olemos		nosotros	olíamos
vosotros	oléis		vosotros	olíais
ellos	huelen		ellos	olían

	FUTURE			CONDITIONAL
yo	oleré		yo	olería
tú	olerás		tú	olerías
él	olerá		él	olería
nosotros	oleremos		nosotros	oleríamos
vosotros	oleréis		vosotros	oleríais
ellos	olerán		ellos	olerían

	PRESENT SUBJUNCTIVE			PRETERITE
yo	huela		yo	olí
tú	huelas		tú	oliste
él	huela		él	olió
nosotros	olamos		nosotros	olimos
vosotros	oláis		vosotros	olisteis
ellos	huelan		ellos	olieron

PAST PARTICIPLE
olido

IMPERATIVE
huele
oled

GERUND
oliendo

pagar (to pay)

	PRESENT		IMPERFECT
yo	pago	yo	pagaba
tú	pagas	tú	pagabas
él	paga	él	pagaba
nosotros	pagamos	nosotros	pagábamos
vosotros	pagáis	vosotros	pagabais
ellos	pagan	ellos	pagaban

	FUTURE		CONDITIONAL
yo	pagaré	yo	pagaría
tú	pagarás	tú	pagarías
él	pagará	él	pagaría
nosotros	pagaremos	nosotros	pagaríamos
vosotros	pagaréis	vosotros	pagaríais
ellos	pagarán	ellos	pagarían

	PRESENT SUBJUNCTIVE		PRETERITE
yo	pague	yo	pagué
tú	pagues	tú	pagaste
él	pague	él	pagó
nosotros	paguemos	nosotros	pagamos
vosotros	paguéis	vosotros	pagasteis
ellos	paguen	ellos	pagaron

PAST PARTICIPLE	IMPERATIVE
pagado	paga
	pagad

GERUND

pagando

pedir (to ask for)

	PRESENT		IMPERFECT
yo	pido	yo	pedía
tú	pides	tú	pedías
él	pide	él	pedía
nosotros	pedimos	nosotros	pedíamos
vosotros	pedís	vosotros	pedíais
ellos	piden	ellos	pedían

	FUTURE		CONDITIONAL
yo	pediré	yo	pediría
tú	pedirás	tú	pedirías
él	pedirá	él	pediría
nosotros	pediremos	nosotros	pediríamos
vosotros	pediréis	vosotros	pediríais
ellos	pedirán	ellos	pedirían

	PRESENT SUBJUNCTIVE		PRETERITE
yo	pida	yo	pedí
tú	pidas	tú	pediste
él	pida	él	pidió
nosotros	pidamos	nosotros	pedimos
vosotros	pidáis	vosotros	pedisteis
ellos	pidan	ellos	pidieron

PAST PARTICIPLE	IMPERATIVE
pedido	pide
	pedid

GERUND
pidiendo

pensar (to think)

	PRESENT			IMPERFECT
yo	**pienso**		yo	pens**aba**
tú	**piensas**		tú	pens**abas**
él	**piensa**		él	pens**aba**
nosotros	pens**amos**		nosotros	pens**ábamos**
vosotros	pens**áis**		vosotros	pens**abais**
ellos	**piensan**		ellos	pens**aban**

	FUTURE			CONDITIONAL
yo	pensar**é**		yo	pensar**ía**
tú	pensar**ás**		tú	pensar**ías**
él	pensar**á**		él	pensar**ía**
nosotros	pensar**emos**		nosotros	pensar**íamos**
vosotros	pensar**éis**		vosotros	pensar**íais**
ellos	pensar**án**		ellos	pensar**ían**

	PRESENT SUBJUNCTIVE			PRETERITE
yo	**piense**		yo	pens**é**
tú	**pienses**		tú	pens**aste**
él	**piense**		él	pens**ó**
nosotros	pens**emos**		nosotros	pens**amos**
vosotros	pens**éis**		vosotros	pens**asteis**
ellos	**piensen**		ellos	pens**aron**

PAST PARTICIPLE	IMPERATIVE
pens**ado**	**piensa**
	pensa**d**

GERUND
pens**ando**

poder (to be able)

	PRESENT		IMPERFECT
yo	**puedo**	yo	pod**ía**
tú	**puedes**	tú	pod**ías**
él	**puede**	él	pod**ía**
nosotros	pod**emos**	nosotros	pod**íamos**
vosotros	pod**éis**	vosotros	pod**íais**
ellos	**pueden**	ellos	pod**ían**

	FUTURE		CONDITIONAL
yo	**podré**	yo	**podría**
tú	**podrás**	tú	**podrías**
él	**podrá**	él	**podría**
nosotros	**podremos**	nosotros	**podríamos**
vosotros	**podréis**	vosotros	**podríais**
ellos	**podrán**	ellos	**podrían**

	PRESENT SUBJUNCTIVE		PRETERITE
yo	**pueda**	yo	**pude**
tú	**puedas**	tú	**pudiste**
él	**pueda**	él	**pudo**
nosotros	pod**amos**	nosotros	**pudimos**
vosotros	pod**áis**	vosotros	**pudisteis**
ellos	**puedan**	ellos	**pudieron**

PAST PARTICIPLE
pod**ido**

IMPERATIVE
puede
pod**ed**

GERUND
pudiendo

poner (to put)

	PRESENT		IMPERFECT
yo	pongo	yo	ponía
tú	pones	tú	ponías
él	pone	él	ponía
nosotros	ponemos	nosotros	poníamos
vosotros	ponéis	vosotros	poníais
ellos	ponen	ellos	ponían

	FUTURE		CONDITIONAL
yo	pondré	yo	pondría
tú	pondrás	tú	pondrías
él	pondrá	él	pondría
nosotros	pondremos	nosotros	pondríamos
vosotros	pondréis	vosotros	pondríais
ellos	pondrán	ellos	pondrían

	PRESENT SUBJUNCTIVE		PRETERITE
yo	ponga	yo	puse
tú	pongas	tú	pusiste
él	ponga	él	puso
nosotros	pongamos	nosotros	pusimos
vosotros	pongáis	vosotros	pusisteis
ellos	pongan	ellos	pusieron

PAST PARTICIPLE	IMPERATIVE
puesto	pon
	poned

GERUND
poniendo

prohibir (to forbid)

	PRESENT		IMPERFECT
yo	prohíbo	yo	prohibía
tú	prohíbes	tú	prohibías
él	prohíbe	él	prohibía
nosotros	prohibimos	nosotros	prohibíamos
vosotros	prohibís	vosotros	prohibíais
ellos	prohíben	ellos	prohibían

	FUTURE		CONDITIONAL
yo	prohibiré	yo	prohibiría
tú	prohibirás	tú	prohibirías
él	prohibirá	él	prohibiría
nosotros	prohibiremos	nosotros	prohibiríamos
vosotros	prohibiréis	vosotros	prohibiríais
ellos	prohibirán	ellos	prohibirían

	PRESENT SUBJUNCTIVE		PRETERITE
yo	prohíba	yo	prohibí
tú	prohíbas	tú	prohibiste
él	prohíba	él	prohibió
nosotros	prohibamos	nosotros	prohibimos
vosotros	prohibáis	vosotros	prohibisteis
ellos	prohíban	ellos	prohibieron

PAST PARTICIPLE	IMPERATIVE
prohibido	prohíbe
	prohibid

GERUND
prohibiendo

querer (to want)

	PRESENT		IMPERFECT
yo	quiero	yo	quería
tú	quieres	tú	querías
él	quiere	él	quería
nosotros	queremos	nosotros	queríamos
vosotros	queréis	vosotros	queríais
ellos	quieren	ellos	querían

	FUTURE		CONDITIONAL
yo	querré	yo	querría
tú	querrás	tú	querrías
él	querrá	él	querría
nosotros	querremos	nosotros	querríamos
vosotros	querréis	vosotros	querríais
ellos	querrán	ellos	querrían

	PRESENT SUBJUNCTIVE		PRETERITE
yo	quiera	yo	quise
tú	quieras	tú	quisiste
él	quiera	él	quiso
nosotros	queramos	nosotros	quisimos
vosotros	queráis	vosotros	quisisteis
ellos	quieran	ellos	quisieron

PAST PARTICIPLE
querido

IMPERATIVE
quiere
quered

GERUND
queriendo

rehusar (to refuse)

	PRESENT		IMPERFECT
yo	rehúso	yo	rehusaba
tú	rehúsas	tú	rehusabas
él	rehúsa	él	rehusaba
nosotros	rehusamos	nosotros	rehusábamos
vosotros	rehusáis	vosotros	rehusabais
ellos	rehúsan	ellos	rehusaban

	FUTURE		CONDITIONAL
yo	rehusaré	yo	rehusaría
tú	rehusarás	tú	rehusarías
él	rehusará	él	rehusaría
nosotros	rehusaremos	nosotros	rehusaríamos
vosotros	rehusaréis	vosotros	rehusaríais
ellos	rehusarán	ellos	rehusarían

	PRESENT SUBJUNCTIVE		PRETERITE
yo	rehúse	yo	rehusé
tú	rehúses	tú	rehusaste
él	rehúse	él	rehusó
nosotros	rehusemos	nosotros	rehusamos
vosotros	rehuséis	vosotros	rehusasteis
ellos	rehúsen	ellos	rehusaron

PAST PARTICIPLE
rehusado

IMPERATIVE
rehúsa
rehusad

GERUND
rehusando

reír (to laugh)

	PRESENT		IMPERFECT
yo	río	yo	reía
tú	ríes	tú	reías
él	ríe	él	reía
nosotros	reímos	nosotros	reíamos
vosotros	reís	vosotros	reíais
ellos	ríen	ellos	reían

	FUTURE		CONDITIONAL
yo	reiré	yo	reiría
tú	reirás	tú	reirías
él	reirá	él	reiría
nosotros	reiremos	nosotros	reiríamos
vosotros	reiréis	vosotros	reiríais
ellos	reirán	ellos	reirían

	PRESENT SUBJUNCTIVE		PRETERITE
yo	ría	yo	reí
tú	rías	tú	reíste
él	ría	él	rió
nosotros	riamos	nosotros	reímos
vosotros	riáis	vosotros	reísteis
ellos	rían	ellos	rieron

PAST PARTICIPLE
reído

IMPERATIVE
ríe
reíd

GERUND
riendo

reñir (to scold)

	PRESENT		IMPERFECT
yo	riño	yo	reñía
tú	riñes	tú	reñías
él	riñe	él	reñía
nosotros	reñimos	nosotros	reñíamos
vosotros	reñís	vosotros	reñíais
ellos	riñen	ellos	reñían

	FUTURE		CONDITIONAL
yo	reñiré	yo	reñiría
tú	reñirás	tú	reñirías
él	reñirá	él	reñiría
nosotros	reñiremos	nosotros	reñiríamos
vosotros	reñiréis	vosotros	reñiríais
ellos	reñirán	ellos	reñirían

	PRESENT SUBJUNCTIVE		PRETERITE
yo	riña	yo	reñí
tú	riñas	tú	reñiste
él	riña	él	riñó
nosotros	riñamos	nosotros	reñimos
vosotros	riñáis	vosotros	reñisteis
ellos	riñan	ellos	riñeron

PAST PARTICIPLE
reñido

IMPERATIVE
riñe
reñid

GERUND
riñendo

resolver (to solve)

	PRESENT		IMPERFECT
yo	resuelvo	yo	resolvía
tú	resuelves	tú	resolvías
él	resuelve	él	resolvía
nosotros	resolvemos	nosotros	resolvíamos
vosotros	resolvéis	vosotros	resolvíais
ellos	resuelven	ellos	resolvían

	FUTURE		CONDITIONAL
yo	resolveré	yo	resolvería
tú	resolverás	tú	resolverías
él	resolverá	él	resolvería
nosotros	resolveremos	nosotros	resolveríamos
vosotros	resolveréis	vosotros	resolveríais
ellos	resolverán	ellos	resolverían

	PRESENT SUBJUNCTIVE		PRETERITE
yo	resuelva	yo	resolví
tú	resuelvas	tú	resolviste
él	resuelva	él	resolvió
nosotros	resolvamos	nosotros	resolvimos
vosotros	resolváis	vosotros	resolvisteis
ellos	resuelvan	ellos	resolvieron

PAST PARTICIPLE
resuelto

IMPERATIVE
resuelve
resolved

GERUND
resolviendo

reunir (to put together, to gather)

	PRESENT		IMPERFECT
yo	reúno	yo	reunía
tú	reúnes	tú	reunías
él	reúne	él	reunía
nosotros	reunimos	nosotros	reuníamos
vosotros	reunís	vosotros	reuníais
ellos	reúnen	ellos	reunían

	FUTURE		CONDITIONAL
yo	reuniré	yo	reuniría
tú	reunirás	tú	reunirías
él	reunirá	él	reuniría
nosotros	reuniremos	nosotros	reuniríamos
vosotros	reuniréis	vosotros	reuniríais
ellos	reunirán	ellos	reunirían

	PRESENT SUBJUNCTIVE		PRETERITE
yo	reúna	yo	reuní
tú	reúnas	tú	reuniste
él	reúna	él	reunió
nosotros	reunamos	nosotros	reunimos
vosotros	reunáis	vosotros	reunisteis
ellos	reúnan	ellos	reunieron

PAST PARTICIPLE
reunido

IMPERATIVE
reúne
reunid

GERUND
reuniendo

rogar (to beg)

	PRESENT		IMPERFECT
yo	ruego	yo	rogaba
tú	ruegas	tú	rogabas
él	ruega	él	rogaba
nosotros	rogamos	nosotros	rogábamos
vosotros	rogáis	vosotros	rogabais
ellos	ruegan	ellos	rogaban

	FUTURE		CONDITIONAL
yo	rogaré	yo	rogaría
tú	rogarás	tú	rogarías
él	rogará	él	rogaría
nosotros	rogaremos	nosotros	rogaríamos
vosotros	rogaréis	vosotros	rogaríais
ellos	rogarán	ellos	rogarían

	PRESENT SUBJUNCTIVE		PRETERITE
yo	ruegue	yo	rogué
tú	ruegues	tú	rogaste
él	ruegue	él	rogó
nosotros	roguemos	nosotros	rogamos
vosotros	roguéis	vosotros	rogasteis
ellos	rueguen	ellos	rogaron

PAST PARTICIPLE
rogado

IMPERATIVE
ruega
rogad

GERUND
rogando

romper (to break)

	PRESENT		IMPERFECT
yo	romp**o**	yo	romp**ía**
tú	romp**es**	tú	romp**ías**
él	romp**e**	él	romp**ía**
nosotros	romp**emos**	nosotros	romp**íamos**
vosotros	romp**éis**	vosotros	romp**íais**
ellos	romp**en**	ellos	romp**ían**

	FUTURE		CONDITIONAL
yo	romper**é**	yo	romper**ía**
tú	romper**ás**	tú	romper**ías**
él	romper**á**	él	romper**ía**
nosotros	romper**emos**	nosotros	romper**íamos**
vosotros	romper**éis**	vosotros	romper**íais**
ellos	romper**án**	ellos	romper**ían**

	PRESENT SUBJUNCTIVE		PRETERITE
yo	romp**a**	yo	romp**í**
tú	romp**as**	tú	romp**iste**
él	romp**a**	él	romp**ió**
nosotros	romp**amos**	nosotros	romp**imos**
vosotros	romp**áis**	vosotros	romp**isteis**
ellos	romp**an**	ellos	romp**ieron**

PAST PARTICIPLE	IMPERATIVE
roto	romp**e**
	romp**ed**

GERUND
romp**iendo**

saber (to know)

	PRESENT		IMPERFECT
yo	sé	yo	sabía
tú	sabes	tú	sabías
él	sabe	él	sabía
nosotros	sabemos	nosotros	sabíamos
vosotros	sabéis	vosotros	sabíais
ellos	saben	ellos	sabían

	FUTURE		CONDITIONAL
yo	sabré	yo	sabría
tú	sabrás	tú	sabrías
él	sabrá	él	sabría
nosotros	sabremos	nosotros	sabríamos
vosotros	sabréis	vosotros	sabríais
ellos	sabrán	ellos	sabrían

	PRESENT SUBJUNCTIVE		PRETERITE
yo	sepa	yo	supe
tú	sepas	tú	supiste
él	sepa	él	supo
nosotros	sepamos	nosotros	supimos
vosotros	sepáis	vosotros	supisteis
ellos	sepan	ellos	supieron

PAST PARTICIPLE	IMPERATIVE
sabido	sabe
	sabed

GERUND

sabiendo

sacar (to take out)

	PRESENT		IMPERFECT
yo	saco	yo	sacaba
tú	sacas	tú	sacabas
él	saca	él	sacaba
nosotros	sacamos	nosotros	sacábamos
vosotros	sacáis	vosotros	sacabais
ellos	sacan	ellos	sacaban

	FUTURE		CONDITIONAL
yo	sacaré	yo	sacaría
tú	sacarás	tú	sacarías
él	sacará	él	sacaría
nosotros	sacaremos	nosotros	sacaríamos
vosotros	sacaréis	vosotros	sacaríais
ellos	sacarán	ellos	sacarían

	PRESENT SUBJUNCTIVE		PRETERITE
yo	saque	yo	saqué
tú	saques	tú	sacaste
él	saque	él	sacó
nosotros	saquemos	nosotros	sacamos
vosotros	saqueís	vosotros	sacasteis
ellos	saquen	ellos	sacaron

PAST PARTICIPLE
sacado

IMPERATIVE
saca
sacad

GERUND
sacando

salir (to go out)

	PRESENT		IMPERFECT
yo	salgo	yo	salía
tú	sales	tú	salías
él	sale	él	salía
nosotros	salimos	nosotros	salíamos
vosotros	salís	vosotros	salíais
ellos	salen	ellos	salían

	FUTURE		CONDITIONAL
yo	saldré	yo	saldría
tú	saldrás	tú	saldrías
él	saldrá	él	saldría
nosotros	saldremos	nosotros	saldríamos
vosotros	saldréis	vosotros	saldríais
ellos	saldrán	ellos	saldrían

	PRESENT SUBJUNCTIVE		PRETERITE
yo	salga	yo	salí
tú	salgas	tú	saliste
él	salga	él	salió
nosotros	salgamos	nosotros	salimos
vosotros	salgáis	vosotros	salisteis
ellos	salgan	ellos	salieron

PAST PARTICIPLE
salido

IMPERATIVE
sal
salid

GERUND
saliendo

satisfacer (to satisfy)

PRESENT
yo	satisfago
tú	satisfaces
él	satisface
nosotros	satisfacemos
vosotros	satisfacéis
ellos	satisfacen

IMPERFECT
yo	satisfacía
tú	satisfacías
él	satisfacía
nosotros	satisfacíamos
vosotros	satisfacíais
ellos	satisfacían

FUTURE
yo	satisfaré
tú	satisfarás
él	satisfará
nosotros	satisfaremos
vosotros	satisfaréis
ellos	satisfarán

CONDITIONAL
yo	satisfaría
tú	satisfarías
él	satisfaría
nosotros	satisfaríamos
vosotros	satisfaríais
ellos	satisfarían

PRESENT SUBJUNCTIVE
yo	satisfaga
tú	satisfagas
él	satisfaga
nosotros	satisfagamos
vosotros	satisfagáis
ellos	satisfagan

PRETERITE
yo	satisfice
tú	satisficiste
él	satisfizo
nosotros	satisficimos
vosotros	satisficisteis
ellos	satisficieron

PAST PARTICIPLE
satisfecho

IMPERATIVE
satisfaz/satisface
satisfaced

GERUND
satisfaciendo

seguir (to follow)

	PRESENT		IMPERFECT
yo	sigo	yo	seguía
tú	sigues	tú	seguías
él	sigue	él	seguía
nosotros	seguimos	nosotros	seguíamos
vosotros	seguís	vosotros	seguíais
ellos	siguen	ellos	seguían

	FUTURE		CONDITIONAL
yo	seguiré	yo	seguiría
tú	seguirás	tú	seguirías
él	seguirá	él	seguiría
nosotros	seguiremos	nosotros	seguiríamos
vosotros	seguiréis	vosotros	seguiríais
ellos	seguirán	ellos	seguirían

	PRESENT SUBJUNCTIVE		PRETERITE
yo	siga	yo	seguí
tú	sigas	tú	seguiste
él	siga	él	siguió
nosotros	sigamos	nosotros	seguimos
vosotros	sigáis	vosotros	seguisteis
ellos	sigan	ellos	siguieron

PAST PARTICIPLE
seguido

IMPERATIVE
sigue
seguid

GERUND
siguiendo

sentir (to feel)

	PRESENT		IMPERFECT
yo	siento	yo	sentía
tú	sientes	tú	sentías
él	siente	él	sentía
nosotros	sentimos	nosotros	sentíamos
vosotros	sentís	vosotros	sentíais
ellos	sienten	ellos	sentían

	FUTURE		CONDITIONAL
yo	sentiré	yo	sentiría
tú	sentirás	tú	sentirías
él	sentirá	él	sentiría
nosotros	sentiremos	nosotros	sentiríamos
vosotros	sentiréis	vosotros	sentiríais
ellos	sentirán	ellos	sentirían

	PRESENT SUBJUNCTIVE		PRETERITE
yo	sienta	yo	sentí
tú	sientas	tú	sentiste
él	sienta	él	sintió
nosotros	sintamos	nosotros	sentimos
vosotros	sintáis	vosotros	sentisteis
ellos	sientan	ellos	sintieron

PAST PARTICIPLE
sentido

IMPERATIVE
siente
sentid

GERUND
sintiendo

ser (to be)

	PRESENT		IMPERFECT
yo	**soy**	yo	**era**
tú	**eres**	tú	**eras**
él	**es**	él	**era**
nosotros	**somos**	nosotros	**éramos**
vosotros	**sois**	vosotros	**erais**
ellos	**son**	ellos	**eran**

	FUTURE		CONDITIONAL
yo	ser**é**	yo	ser**ía**
tú	ser**ás**	tú	ser**ías**
él	ser**á**	él	ser**ía**
nosotros	ser**emos**	nosotros	ser**íamos**
vosotros	ser**éis**	vosotros	ser**íais**
ellos	ser**án**	ellos	ser**ían**

	PRESENT SUBJUNCTIVE		PRETERITE
yo	**sea**	yo	**fui**
tú	**seas**	tú	**fuiste**
él	**sea**	él	**fue**
nosotros	**seamos**	nosotros	**fuimos**
vosotros	**seáis**	vosotros	**fuisteis**
ellos	**sean**	ellos	**fueron**

PAST PARTICIPLE	IMPERATIVE
sido	**sé**
	se**d**

GERUND
siendo

tener (to have)

	PRESENT		IMPERFECT
yo	**tengo**	yo	**tenía**
tú	**tienes**	tú	**tenías**
él	**tiene**	él	**tenía**
nosotros	**tenemos**	nosotros	**teníamos**
vosotros	**tenéis**	vosotros	**teníais**
ellos	**tienen**	ellos	**tenían**

	FUTURE		CONDITIONAL
yo	**tendré**	yo	**tendría**
tú	**tendrás**	tú	**tendrías**
él	**tendrá**	él	**tendría**
nosotros	**tendremos**	nosotros	**tendríamos**
vosotros	**tendréis**	vosotros	**tendríais**
ellos	**tendrán**	ellos	**tendrían**

	PRESENT SUBJUNCTIVE		PRETERITE
yo	**tenga**	yo	**tuve**
tú	**tengas**	tú	**tuviste**
él	**tenga**	él	**tuvo**
nosotros	**tengamos**	nosotros	**tuvimos**
vosotros	**tengáis**	vosotros	**tuvisteis**
ellos	**tengan**	ellos	**tuvieron**

PAST PARTICIPLE	IMPERATIVE
tenido	**ten**
	tened

GERUND
teniendo

torcer (to twist)

	PRESENT		IMPERFECT
yo	**tuerzo**	yo	torcía
tú	**tuerces**	tú	torcías
él	**tuerce**	él	torcía
nosotros	torc**emos**	nosotros	torcíamos
vosotros	toc**éis**	vosotros	torcíais
ellos	**tuercen**	ellos	torcían

	FUTURE		CONDITIONAL
yo	torcer**é**	yo	torcería
tú	torcer**ás**	tú	torcerías
él	torcer**á**	él	torcería
nosotros	torcer**emos**	nosotros	torceríamos
vosotros	torcer**éis**	vosotros	torceríais
ellos	torcer**án**	ellos	torcerían

	PRESENT SUBJUNCTIVE		PRETERITE
yo	**tuerza**	yo	torc**í**
tú	**tuerzas**	tú	torc**iste**
él	**tuerza**	él	torc**ió**
nosotros	**tuerzamos**	nosotros	torc**imos**
vosotros	**tuerzáis**	vosotros	torc**isteis**
ellos	**tuerzan**	ellos	torc**ieron**

PAST PARTICIPLE
torc**ido**

IMPERATIVE
tuerce
torc**ed**

GERUND
torc**iendo**

traer (to bring)

	PRESENT		IMPERFECT
yo	**traigo**	yo	traía
tú	tra**es**	tú	traías
él	tra**e**	él	traía
nosotros	tra**emos**	nosotros	traíamos
vosotros	tra**éis**	vosotros	traíais
ellos	tra**en**	ellos	traían

	FUTURE		CONDITIONAL
yo	traer**é**	yo	traer**ía**
tú	traer**ás**	tú	traer**ías**
él	traer**á**	él	traer**ía**
nosotros	traer**emos**	nosotros	traer**íamos**
vosotros	traer**éis**	vosotros	traer**íais**
ellos	traer**án**	ellos	traer**ían**

	PRESENT SUBJUNCTIVE		PRETERITE
yo	**traiga**	yo	**traje**
tú	**traigas**	tú	**trajiste**
él	**traiga**	él	**trajo**
nosotros	**traigamos**	nosotros	**trajimos**
vosotros	**traigáis**	vosotros	**trajisteis**
ellos	**traigan**	ellos	**trajeron**

PAST PARTICIPLE	IMPERATIVE
traído	tra**e**
	tra**ed**

GERUND
trayendo

valer (to be worth)

	PRESENT		IMPERFECT
yo	**valgo**	yo	val**ía**
tú	val**es**	tú	val**ías**
él	val**e**	él	val**ía**
nosotros	val**emos**	nosotros	val**íamos**
vosotros	val**éis**	vosotros	val**íais**
ellos	val**en**	ellos	val**ían**

	FUTURE		CONDITIONAL
yo	**valdré**	yo	**valdría**
tú	**valdrás**	tú	**valdrías**
él	**valdrá**	él	**valdría**
nosotros	**valdremos**	nosotros	**valdríamos**
vosotros	**valdréis**	vosotros	**valdríais**
ellos	**valdrán**	ellos	**valdrían**

	PRESENT SUBJUNCTIVE		PRETERITE
yo	**valga**	yo	val**í**
tú	**valgas**	tú	val**iste**
él	**valga**	él	val**ió**
nosotros	**valgamos**	nosotros	val**imos**
vosotros	**valgáis**	vosotros	val**isteis**
ellos	**valgan**	ellos	val**ieron**

PAST PARTICIPLE	IMPERATIVE
val**ido**	val**e**
	val**ed**

GERUND

val**iendo**

vencer (to win)

	PRESENT		IMPERFECT
yo	venzo	yo	vencía
tú	vences	tú	vencías
él	vence	él	vencía
nosotros	vencemos	nosotros	vencíamos
vosotros	vencéis	vosotros	vencíais
ellos	vencen	ellos	vencían

	FUTURE		CONDITIONAL
yo	venceré	yo	vencería
tú	vencerás	tú	vencerías
él	vencerá	él	vencería
nosotros	venceremos	nosotros	venceríamos
vosotros	venceréis	vosotros	venceríais
ellos	vencerán	ellos	vencerían

	PRESENT SUBJUNCTIVE		PRETERITE
yo	venza	yo	vencí
tú	venzas	tú	venciste
él	venza	él	venció
nosotros	venzamos	nosotros	vencimos
vosotros	venzáis	vosotros	vencisteis
ellos	venzan	ellos	vencieron

PAST PARTICIPLE
vencido

IMPERATIVE
vence
venced

GERUND
venciendo

666

Irregular Verbs

venir (to come)

	PRESENT			IMPERFECT
yo	vengo		yo	venía
tú	vienes		tú	venías
él	viene		él	venía
nosotros	venimos		nosotros	veníamos
vosotros	venís		vosotros	veníais
ellos	vienen		ellos	venían

	FUTURE			CONDITIONAL
yo	vendré		yo	vendría
tú	vendrás		tú	vendrías
él	vendrá		él	vendría
nosotros	vendremos		nosotros	vendríamos
vosotros	vendréis		vosotros	vendríais
ellos	vendrán		ellos	vendrían

	PRESENT SUBJUNCTIVE			PRETERITE
yo	venga		yo	vine
tú	vengas		tú	viniste
él	venga		él	vino
nosotros	vengamos		nosotros	vinimos
vosotros	vengáis		vosotros	vinisteis
ellos	vengan		ellos	vinieron

PAST PARTICIPLE
venido

IMPERATIVE
ven
venid

GERUND
viniendo

ver (to see)

	PRESENT		IMPERFECT
yo	veo	yo	veía
tú	ves	tú	veías
él	ve	él	veía
nosotros	vemos	nosotros	veíamos
vosotros	veis	vosotros	veíais
ellos	ven	ellos	veían

	FUTURE		CONDITIONAL
yo	veré	yo	vería
tú	verás	tú	verías
él	verá	él	vería
nosotros	veremos	nosotros	veríamos
vosotros	veréis	vosotros	veríais
ellos	verán	ellos	verían

	PRESENT SUBJUNCTIVE		PRETERITE
yo	vea	yo	vi
tú	veas	tú	viste
él	vea	él	vio
nosotros	veamos	nosotros	vimos
vosotros	veáis	vosotros	visteis
ellos	vean	ellos	vieron

PAST PARTICIPLE	IMPERATIVE
visto	ve
	ved

GERUND
viendo

volcar (to overturn)

	PRESENT		IMPERFECT
yo	**vuelco**	yo	volc**aba**
tú	**vuelcas**	tú	volc**abas**
él	**vuelca**	él	volc**aba**
nosotros	volc**amos**	nosotros	volc**ábamos**
vosotros	volc**áis**	vosotros	volc**abais**
ellos	**vuelcan**	ellos	volc**aban**

	FUTURE		CONDITIONAL
yo	volcar**é**	yo	volcar**ía**
tú	volcar**ás**	tú	volcar**ías**
él	volcar**á**	él	volcar**ía**
nosotros	volcar**emos**	nosotros	volcar**íamos**
vosotros	volcar**éis**	vosotros	volcar**íais**
ellos	volcar**án**	ellos	volcar**ían**

	PRESENT SUBJUNCTIVE		PRETERITE
yo	**vuelque**	yo	**volqué**
tú	**vuelques**	tú	volc**aste**
él	**vuelque**	él	volc**ó**
nosotros	**volquemos**	nosotros	volc**amos**
vosotros	**volquéis**	vosotros	volc**asteis**
ellos	**vuelquen**	ellos	volc**aron**

PAST PARTICIPLE	IMPERATIVE
volc**ado**	**vuelca**
	volc**ad**

GERUND
volc**ando**

volver (to return)

	PRESENT		IMPERFECT
yo	**vuelvo**	yo	volv**ía**
tú	**vuelves**	tú	volv**ías**
él	**vuelve**	él	volv**ía**
nosotros	volv**emos**	nosotros	volv**íamos**
vosotros	volv**éis**	vosotros	volv**íais**
ellos	**vuelven**	ellos	volv**ían**

	FUTURE		CONDITIONAL
yo	volver**é**	yo	volver**ía**
tú	volver**ás**	tú	volver**ías**
él	volver**á**	él	volver**ía**
nosotros	volver**emos**	nosotros	volver**íamos**
vosotros	volver**éis**	vosotros	volver**íais**
ellos	volver**án**	ellos	volver**ían**

	PRESENT SUBJUNCTIVE		PRETERITE
yo	**vuelva**	yo	volv**í**
tú	**vuelvas**	tú	volv**iste**
él	**vuelva**	él	volv**ió**
nosotros	volv**amos**	nosotros	volv**imos**
vosotros	volv**áis**	vosotros	volv**isteis**
ellos	**vuelvan**	ellos	volv**ieron**

PAST PARTICIPLE	IMPERATIVE
vuelto	**vuelve**
	volve**d**

GERUND
volv**iendo**

159

zurcir (to darn)

	PRESENT		IMPERFECT
yo	zurzo	yo	zurcía
tú	zurces	tú	zurcías
él	zurce	él	zurcía
nosotros	zurcimos	nosotros	zurcíamos
vosotros	zurcís	vosotros	zurcíais
ellos	zurcen	ellos	zurcían

	FUTURE		CONDITIONAL
yo	zurciré	yo	zurciría
tú	zurcirás	tú	zurcirías
él	zurcirá	él	zurciría
nosotros	zurciremos	nosotros	zurciríamos
vosotros	zurciréis	vosotros	zurciríais
ellos	zurcirán	ellos	zurcirían

	PRESENT SUBJUNCTIVE		PRETERITE
yo	zurza	yo	zurcí
tú	zurzas	tú	zurciste
él	zurza	él	zurció
nosotros	zurzamos	nosotros	zurcimos
vosotros	zurzáis	vosotros	zurcisteis
ellos	zurzan	ellos	zurcieron

PAST PARTICIPLE
zurcido

IMPERATIVE
zurce
zurcid

GERUND
zurciendo

Verb Index

The following pages, 162 to 190, contain an index of all the Spanish verbs in this dictionary cross-referred to the appropriate conjugation model:

- Regular verbs belonging to the first, second and third conjugation are numbered 1, 2 and 3 respectively. For the regular conjugations see pages 6 to 13.

- Irregular verbs are numerically cross-referred to the appropriate model as conjugated on pages 82 to 160. Thus, **alzar** is cross-referred to page 100 where **cruzar**, the model for this verb group, is conjugated.

- Verbs which are most commonly used in the reflexive form – e.g. **amodorrarse** – have been cross-referred to the appropriate non-reflexive model. For the full conjugation of a reflexive verb, see pages 28 to 31.

- Verbs printed in **bold** – e.g. **abrir** – are themselves models.

- Superior numbers refer you to notes on page 191 which indicate how the verb differs from its model.

Verb Index

adicionar	1	agachar	1	ahumar	1
adiestrar	1	agarrar	1	ahuyentar	1
adivinar	1	agarrotar	1	airar	1
adjudicar	145	agasajar	1	airear	1
adjuntar	1	agazapar	1	aislar	88
administrar	1	agenciar	1	ajar	1
admirar	1	agilizar	100	ajetrearse	1
admitir	3	agitar	1	ajustar	1
adobar	1	aglomerar	1	alabar	1
adoctrinar	1	agobiar	1	alambicar	143
adolecer	99	agolparse	1	alardear	1
adoptar	1	agonizar	100	alargar	130
adorar	1	agostar	1	alarmar	1
adormecer	99	agotar	1	albergar	130
adormilarse	1	agraciar	1	alborear	1
adornar	1	agradar	1	alborotar	1
adquirir	85	agradecer	99	alborozar	100
adscribir	112	agrandar	1	alcanzar	100
aducir	96	agravar	1	alcoholizarse	100
adueñarse	1	agraviar	1	aleccionar	1
adular	1	agredir	3	alegar	130
adulterar	1	agregar	130	alegrar	1
advertir	149	agriar	109	alejar	1
afanar	1	agrietarse	1	alelar	1
afear	1	agrupar	1	alentar	132
afectar	1	aguaitar	1	aletargar	130
afeitar	1	aguantar	1	aletear	1
aferrar	1	aguar	90	alfombrar	1
afianzar	100	aguardar	1	aliar	109
aficionar	1	agudizar	100	alicatar	1
afilar	1	aguijar	1	aligerar	1
afiliarse	1	aguijonear	1	alimentar	1
afinar	1	agujerear	1	alinear	1
afincarse	1	aguzar	100	aliñar	1
afirmar	1	aherrumbrarse	1	alisar	1
afligir	103	ahijar	1	alistar	1
aflojar	1	ahogar	130	aliviar	1
aflorar	1	ahondar	1	allanar	1
afluir	97	ahorcar	145	almacenar	1
aforar	1	ahorrar	1	almidonar	1
afrontar	1	ahuecar	145	**almorzar**	86

Verb Index

alojar	1	amotinar	1	apalear	1
alquilar	1	amparar	1	apañar	1
alterar	1	ampliar	109	aparcar	145
alternar	1	amplificar	145	aparear	1
alucinar	1	amputar	1	aparecer	99
aludir	3	amueblar	1	aparejar	1
alumbrar	1	amurallar	1	aparentar	1
alunizar	100	analizar	100	apartar	1
alzar	100	anatematizar	100	apasionar	1
amaestrar	1	anclar	1	apearse	1
amagar	130	**andar**	87	apechugar	130
amainar	1	anegar	130	apedrear	1
amalgamar	1	anestesiar	1	apegarse	1
amamantar	1	anexar	1	apelar	1
amancebarse	1	anexionar	1	apellidar	1
amanecer[1]	99	angustiar	1	apelotonar	1
amansar	1	anhelar	1	apenar	1
amañar	1	anidar	1	apercibir	3
amar	1	animar	1	apesadumbrar	1
amargar	130	aniquilar	1	apestar	1
amarrar	1	anochecer[1]	99	apetecer	99
amartillar	1	anonadar	1	apiadarse	1
amasar	1	anotar	1	apilar	1
ambicionar	1	anquilosarse	1	apiñar	1
ambientar	1	ansiar	109	aplacar	145
amedrentar	1	anteceder	2	aplanar	1
amenazar	100	anteponer	134	aplastar	1
amerizar	100	anticipar	1	aplatanarse	1
amilanar	1	antojarse	1	aplaudir	3
aminorar	1	anudar	1	aplazar	100
amnistiar	109	anular	1	aplicar	145
amodorrarse	1	anunciar	1	apocarse	145
amolar	1	añadir	3	apocopar	1
amoldar	1	añorar	1	apodar	1
amonestar	1	aovar	1	apoderar	1
amontonar	1	apabullar	1	apolillarse	1
amordazar	100	apacentar	132	apoltronarse	1
amortajar	1	apaciguar	90	apoquinar	1
amortiguar	90	apadrinar	1	aporrear	1
amortizar	100	apagar	130	aportar	1
amoscarse	145	apalabrar	1	aposentar	1

Verb Index

apostar	98	arrebañar	1	aserrar	132
apostatar	1	arrebatar	1	asesinar	1
apoyar	1	arrebolar	1	asesorar	1
apreciar	1	arrebujar	1	asestar	1
aprehender	2	arrechar	1	aseverar	1
apremiar	1	arreciar	1	asfixiar	1
aprender	2	arredrar	1	asignar	1
apresar	1	arreglar	1	asimilar	1
aprestar	1	arrellanarse	1	asir[2]	3
apresurarse	1	arremangar	130	asistir	3
apretar	132	arremeter	2	asociar	1
aprisionar	1	arremolinarse	1	asolar	1
aprobar	98	arrendar	132	asolear	1
apropiarse	1	arrepentirse	149	asomar	1
aprovechar	1	arrestar	1	asombrar	1
aprovisionar	1	arriar	109	asorocharse	1
aproximar	1	arribar	1	aspirar	1
apuntalar	1	arriesgar	130	asquear	1
apuntar	1	arrimar	1	astillarse	1
apuñalar	1	arrinconar	1	asumir	3
apurar	1	arrobar	1	asustar	1
aquejar	1	arrodillarse	1	atacar	145
aquietar	1	arrojar	1	atajar	1
arañar	1	arrollar	1	atañer[3]	2
arar	1	arropar	1	atar	1
arbitrar	1	arrostrar	1	atardecer	99
arbolar	1	arrugar	130	atascar	145
archivar	1	arruinar	1	ataviar	109
arder	2	arrullar	1	atemorizar	100
arengar	1	arrumbar	1	atender	108
argüir	97	articular	1	atenerse	151
argumentar	1	asaetear	1	atentar	1
armar	1	asaltar	1	atenuar	84
armonizar	100	asar	1	aterrar	1
arquear	1	ascender	108	aterrizar	100
arracimarse	1	asear	1	aterrorizar	100
arraigar	130	asediar	1	atesorar	1
arrancar	145	asegurar	1	atestar	1
arrasar	1	asemejarse	1	atestiguar	90
arrastrar	1	asentar	132	atiborrar	1
arrear	1	asentir	149	atildar	1

Verb Index

atinar	1	avecinarse	1	batallar	1
atisbar	1	avejentar	1	batir	3
atizar	100	avenir	156	bautizar	100
atollarse	1	aventajar	1	beatificar	145
atontar	1	aventar	132	beber	2
atorar	1	aventurar	1	befarse	1
atormentar	1	**avergonzar**	89	**bendecir**	91
atornillar	1	averiar	109	beneficiar	1
atosigar	130	**averiguar**	90	berrear	1
atracar	145	aviar	109	besar	1
atraer	153	avinagrarse	1	besuquear	1
atragantarse	1	avisar	1	bifurcarse	145
atrancar	145	avistar	1	birlar	1
atrapar	1	avituallar	1	bisbisar	1
atrasar	1	avivar	1	biselar	1
atravesar	132	avizorar	1	bizquear	1
atreverse	2	ayudar	1	blandir	3
atribuir	97	ayunar	1	blanquear	1
atribular	1	azorar	1	blasfemar	1
atrincherarse	1	azotar	1	blasonar	1
atrofiarse	1	azuzar	100	bloquear	1
atropellar	1	babear	1	bogar	130
atufar	1	bailar	1	boicotear	1
aturdir	3	bajar	1	bombardear	1
aturrullar	1	balancear	1	bombear	1
atusar	1	balar	1	boquear	1
augurar	1	balbucear	1	barbollar	1
aullar	88	balbucir[4]	3	borbotar	1
aumentar	1	baldar	1	bordar	1
aupar	1	balear	1	bordear	1
auscultar	1	bambolearse	1	borrar	1
ausentarse	1	bañar	1	bosquejar	1
auspiciar	1	barajar	1	bostezar	100
autenticar	145	barbotar	1	botar	1
autentificar	145	barbullar	1	boxear	1
automatizar	100	barnizar	100	bracear	1
autorizar	100	barrenar	1	bramar	1
auxiliar	1	barrer	2	bregar	130
avalar	1	barruntar	1	brillar	1
avanzar	100	basar	1	brincar	145
avasallar	1	bastar	1	brindar	1

Verb Index

Verb Index

Verb Index

congelar	1	contemporizar	100	corroborar	1
congeniar	1	contender	108	corroer	93
congestionar	1	contener	151	corromper	2
congraciarse	1	contentar	1	cortar	1
congratular	1	contestar	1	cortejar	1
congregar	130	continuar	84	cosechar	1
conjeturar	1	contonearse	1	coser	2
conjugar	130	contradecir	102	costar	98
conjurar	1	contraer	153	costear	1
conllevar	1	contrahacer	117	cotejar	1
conmemorar	1	contrapesar	1	cotillear	1
conminar	1	contraponer	134	cotizar	100
conmover	125	contrariar	109	crear	1
conmutar	1	contrarrestar	1	**crecer**	99
conocer	99	contrastar	1	creer	121
conquistar	1	contratar	1	crepitar	1
consagrar	1	contravenir	156	criar	109
conseguir	148	contribuir	97	cribar	1
consentir	149	controlar	1	crispar	1
conservar	1	convalecer	99	cristalizar	100
considerar	1	convalidar	1	criticar	145
consignar	1	convencer	99	croar	1
consistir	3	convenir	156	cronometrar	1
consolar	98	converger	95	crucificar	145
consolidar	1	conversar	1	crujir	3
conspirar	1	convertir	149	**cruzar**	100
constar	1	convidar	1	cuadrar	1
constatar	1	convivir	3	cuadruplicarse	145
constiparse	1	convocar	145	cuajar	1
constituir	97	cooperar	1	cuartear	1
constreñir	139	coordinar	1	cubrir	83
construir	97	copar	1	cuchichear	1
consultar	1	copiar	1	cuidar	1
consumar	1	copular	1	culebrear	1
consumir	3	coquetear	1	culminar	1
contabilizar	100	corear	1	culpar	1
contactar	1	coronar	1	cultivar	1
contagiar	1	corregir	106	cumplimentar	1
contaminar	1	correr	2	cumplir	3
contar	98	corresponder	2	cundir	3
contemplar	1	corretear	1	curar	1

Verb Index

curiosear	1	dejar	1	derrotar	1
currar	1	delatar	1	derruir	97
cursar	1	delegar	130	derrumbar	1
curtir	3	deleitar	1	desabotonar	1
custodiar	1	deletrear	1	desabrigar	130
damnificar	145	deliberar	1	desabrochar	1
danzar	100	delimitar	1	desacatar	1
dañar	1	delinear	1	desaconsejar	1
dar	101	delinquir[7]	3	desacoplar	1
datar	1	delirar	1	desacreditar	1
deambular	1	demandar	1	desactivar	1
debatir	3	demoler	125	desafiar	109
deber	2	demorar	1	desafinar	1
debilitar	1	demostrar	98	desagradar	1
debutar	1	demudar	1	desagraviar	1
decaer	93	denegar	127	desahogar	130
decantar	1	denigrar	1	desahuciar	1
decapitar	1	denostar	98	desairar	1
decepcionar	1	denotar	1	desajustar	1
decidir	3	denunciar	1	desalentar	132
decir	102	deparar	1	desalojar	1
declamar	1	departir	3	desalquilar	1
declarar	1	depender	2	desamarrar	1
declinar	1	depilar	1	desamparar	1
decolorarse	1	deplorar	1	desandar	87
decomisar	1	deponer	134	desangrar	1
decorar	1	deportar	1	desanimar	1
decrecer	99	depositar	1	desanudar	1
decretar	1	depravar	1	desaparecer	99
dedicar	145	depreciar	1	desaprobar	98
deducir	96	depredar	1	desaprovechar	1
defender	108	deprimir	3	desarmar	1
deferir	131	depurar	1	desarraigar	130
definir	3	derivar	1	desarreglar	1
deformar	1	derogar	142	desarrollar	1
defraudar	1	derramar	1	desarrugar	130
degenerar	1	derrapar	1	desarticular	1
deglutir	3	derretir	131	desasir[8]	3
degollar[6]	98	derribar	1	desasosegar	127
degradar	1	derrocar	145	desatar	1
deificar	145	derrochar	1	desatascar	145

Verb Index

Verb Index

Verb index

educar	145	embrollar	1	emular	1
efectuar	84	embromar	1	enajenar	1
egresar	1	embrutecer	99	enamorar	1
ejecutar	1	embutir	3	enarbolar	1
ejemplificar	145	emerger	95	enardecer	99
ejercer	155	emigrar	1	encabezar	100
ejercitar	1	emitir	3	encadenar	1
elaborar	1	emocionar	1	encajar	1
electrificar	145	empacar	145	encajonar	1
electrizar	100	empacharse	1	encalar	1
electrocutar	1	empadronarse	1	encallar	1
elegir	106	empalagar	130	encaminar	1
elevar	1	empalmar	1	encandilar	1
eliminar	1	empanar	1	encanecer	99
elogiar	1	empantanarse	1	encantar	1
eludir	3	empañarse	1	encapricharse	1
emanar	1	empapar	1	encaramar	1
emancipar	1	empapelar	1	encararse	1
embadurnar	1	empaquetar	1	encarcelar	1
embalar	1	emparejar	1	encarecer	99
embalsamar	1	emparentar	1	encargar	130
embalsar	1	empastar	1	encariñarse	1
embarazar	100	empatar	1	encarnar	1
embarcar	145	empedrar	132	encarrilar	1
embargar	130	empeñar	1	encasillar	1
embarrancar	145	empeorar	1	encasquetar	1
embarullar	1	empequeñecer	99	encausar	1
embaular	88	emperrarse	1	encauzar	100
embeber	2	**empezar**	107	encender	108
embelesar	1	empinar	1	encerar	1
embellecer	99	emplazar	100	encerrar	132
embestir	131	emplear	1	encestar	1
emblanquecer	99	emplumar	1	encharcar	1
embobar	1	empobrecer	99	enchufar	1
embolsar	1	empollar	1	encoger	95
emborrachar	1	empolvar	1	encolar	1
embotar	1	emponzoñar	1	encolerizar	100
embotellar	1	empotrar	1	encomendar	132
embragar	130	emprender	2	encomiar	1
embravecer	99	empujar	1	encontrar	98
embriagar	130	empuñar	1	encorvar	1

Verb Index

Verb Index

enzarzarse	100	escrutar	1	**estar**	113
equilibrar	1	escuchar	1	estereotipar	1
equipar	1	escudarse	1	esterilizar	100
equiparar	1	escudriñar	1	estibar	1
equivaler	154	esculpir	3	estigmatizar	100
equivocarse	145	escupir	3	estilarse	1
erguir	110	escurrir	3	estilizar	100
erigir	103	esforzarse	86	estimar	1
erizarse	100	esfumarse	1	estimular	1
erosionar	1	esgrimir	3	estipular	1
erradicar	145	eslabonar	1	estirar	1
errar	111	esmaltar	1	estofar	1
eructar	1	esmerarse	1	estorbar	1
esbozar	100	espabilar	1	estornudar	1
escabullirse	115	espachurrar	1	estrangular	1
escacharrar	1	espaciar	1	estratificar	145
escalar	1	espantar	1	estrechar	1
escaldar	1	españolizar	100	estrellar	1
escalfar	1	esparcir	160	estremecer	99
escalonar	1	especificar	145	estrenar	1
escamar	1	especular	1	estreñir	139
escamotear	1	esperanzar	100	estribar	1
escampar[1]	1	esperar	1	estropear	1
escanciar	1	espesar	1	estrujar	1
escandalizar	100	espetar	1	estudiar	1
escapar	1	espiar	109	eternizarse	100
escaquearse	1	espirar	1	europeizar	100
escarbar	1	espolear	1	evacuar	1
escarmentar	1	espolvorear	1	evadir	3
escasear	1	esposar	1	evaluar	84
escatimar	1	esquiar	109	evaporar	1
escayolar	1	esquilar	1	evidenciar	1
escindir	3	esquivar	1	evitar	1
esclarecer	99	estabilizar	100	evocar	145
esclavizar	100	establecer	99	evolucionar	1
escocer	94	estacionar	1	exacerbar	1
escoger	95	estafar	1	exagerar	1
escoltar	1	estallar	1	exaltar	1
esconder	2	estampar	1	examinar	1
escotar	1	estancar	145	exasperar	1
escribir	112	estandarizar	100	excarcelar	1

Verb Index

Verb Index

Verb Index

Verb Index

notificar	145	ordenar	1	parir	3
nublar	1	ordeñar	1	parlamentar	1
numerar	1	orear	1	parlar	1
nutrir	3	organizar	100	parlotear	1
obcecarse	145	orientar	1	parodiar	1
obedecer	99	originar	1	parpadear	1
objetar	1	orillar	1	participar	1
obligar	130	orinar	1	particularizar	100
obrar	1	ornamentar	1	partir	3
obsequiar	1	ornar	1	pasar	1
observar	1	orquestar	1	pasear	1
obsesionar	1	osar	1	pasmar	1
obstaculizar	100	oscilar	1	pastar	1
obstinarse	1	oscurecer	99	patalear	1
obstruir	97	ostentar	1	patear	1
obtener	151	otear	1	patentar	1
obviar	1	otorgar	130	patinar	1
ocasionar	1	ovacionar	1	patrocinar	1
ocultar	1	oxidar	1	patrullar	1
ocupar	1	oxigenar	1	pavonearse	1
ocurrir	3	pacer	99	pecar	145
odiar	1	pacificar	145	pedalear	1
ofender	2	pactar	1	**pedir**	131
oficiar	1	padecer	99	pegar	130
ofrecer	99	**pagar**	130	peinar	1
ofrendar	1	paginar	1	pelar	1
ofuscar	145	paladear	1	pelear	1
oír	128	paliar	1	peligrar	1
oler	129	palidecer	99	pellizcar	145
olfatear	1	palmar	1	penalizar	100
olvidar	1	palmear	1	penar	1
omitir	3	palmotear	1	pender	2
ondear	1	palpar	1	penetrar	1
ondular	1	palpitar	1	**pensar**	132
operar	1	papear	1	pepenar	1
opinar	1	parafrasear	1	percatarse	1
oponer	134	paralizar	100	percibir	3
opositar	1	parapetarse	1	perder	108
oprimir	3	parar	1	perdonar	1
optar	1	parear	1	perdurar	1
orar	1	parecer	99	perecer	99

Verb Index

Verb Index

Verb Index

remorder	125	repujar	1	retar	1
remover	125	reputar	1	retardar	1
remozar	100	requemar	1	retener	151
remunerar	1	requerir	149	retirar	1
renacer	126	requisar	1	retocar	145
rendir	131	resaltar	1	retorcer	152
renegar	127	resarcir	160	retornar	1
renovar	98	resbalar	1	retozar	100
renquear	1	rescatar	1	retractarse	1
rentabilizar	100	rescindir	3	retraerse	153
rentar	1	resecar	145	retransmitir	3
renunciar	1	resentirse	149	retrasar	1
reñir	139	reseñar	1	retratar	1
reorganizar	100	reservar	1	retribuir	97
reparar	1	resfriarse	109	retroceder	2
repartir	3	resguardar	1	retumbar	1
repasar	1	residir	3	reunificar	145
repatriar	109	resignarse	1	**reunir**	141
repeler	2	resistir	3	revalidar	1
repensar	132	resollar	98	revalorar	1
repentizar	100	**resolver**	140	revelar	1
repercutir	3	resonar	98	revenirse	156
repetir	131	resoplar	1	reventar	132
repicar	145	respaldar	1	reverberar	1
replantear	1	respetar	1	reverenciar	1
replegarse	127	respirar	1	revertir	149
replicar	145	resplandecer	99	revestir	131
repoblar	98	responder	2	revisar	1
reponer	134	responsabilizarse	100	revivir	3
reportar	1	resquebrajar	1	revocar	145
reposar	1	restablecer	99	revolcar	158
repostar	1	restallar	1	revolotear	1
reprender	2	restar	1	revolucionar	1
representar	1	restaurar	1	revolver	159
reprimir	3	restituir	97	rezagar	130
reprobar	98	restregar	130	rezar	100
reprochar	1	restringir	103	rezongar	130
reproducir	96	resucitar	1	rezumar	1
reptar	1	resultar	1	ribetear	1
repudiar	1	resumir	3	ridiculizar	100
repugnar	1	resurgir	103	rifar	1

Verb Index

Verb Index

Verb Index

Notes

The notes below indicate special peculiarities of individual verbs.
When only some forms of a given tense are affected, all these are shown.
When all forms of the tense are affected, only the 1st and 2nd persons are
shown, followed by *etc*.

1 Gerund 2 Past Participle 3 Present 4 Preterite 5 Present Subjunctive
6 Imperfect Subjunctive

1 **acaecer, acontecer, amanecer, anochecer, competer, deshelar,
   escampar, granizar, helar, nevar, nublar, relampaguear, tronar,
   verdear**: used almost exclusively in infinitive and 3rd person singular
2 **asir** 3 asgo 5 asga, asgar *etc*
3 **atañer, -tañer** 1 atañendo 4 atañó: see also 1 above
4 **balbucir** 3 balbuceo 5 balbucee, balbucees *etc*
5 **concernir** 3 concierne, conciernen 5 concierna, conciernan:
   only used in 3rd person
6 **degollar** 3 degüello, degüellas, degüella, degüellan 5 degüelle,
   degüelles, degüellen
7 **delinquir** 3 delinco 5 delinca, delincas *etc*
8 **desasir** 3 desasgo 5 desasga, desasgas *etc*
9 **discernir** 3 discierno, disciernes, discierne, disciernen 5 discierna,
   disciernas, disciernan
10 **enraizar** 3 enraízo, enraízas, enraíza, enraízan 5 enraíce, enraíces,
   enraícen
11 **pudrir** 2 podrido
12 **rehuir** 3 rehúyo, rehúyes, rehúye, rehúyen 5 rehúya, rehúyas,
   rehúyan
13 **roer** 4 royó, royeron 6 royera, royeras *etc*
14 **soler**: used only in present and imperfect indicative
15 **yacer** 3 yazgo *or* yazco *or* yago 5 yazga *etc* or yazca *etc* or yaga *etc*

The Gender of Nouns

In Spanish, all nouns are either masculine or feminine, whether denoting people, animals or things. Gender is largely unpredictable and has to be learnt for each noun. However, the following guidelines will help you determine the gender for certain types of nouns:

Nouns denoting male people and animals are usually – but not always – masculine, e.g.
un hombre a man
un toro a bull
un enfermero a (*male*) nurse
un semental a stallion

Nouns denoting female people and animals are usually – but not always – feminine, e.g.
una niña a girl
una vaca a cow
una enfermera a nurse
una yegua a mare

Some nouns are masculine *or* feminine depending on the sex of the person to whom they refer, e.g.
un camarada a (*male*) comrade
una camarada a (*female*) comrade
un belga a Belgian (*man*)
una belga a Belgian (*woman*)
un marroquí a Moroccan (*man*)
una marroquí a Moroccan (*woman*)

Other nouns referring to either men *or* women have only one gender which applies to both, e.g.
una persona a person
una visita a visitor
una víctima a victim
una estrella a star

Often the ending of a noun indicates its gender. Shown opposite are some of the most important to guide you.

Nouns

Often the ending of the noun indicates its gender. Shown below are some of the most important to guide you:

Masculine endings

-o	un **clavo** a nail, **un plátano** a banana EXCEPTIONS: **mano** hand, **foto** photograph, **moto(cicleta)** motorbike
-l	un **tonel** a barrel, **un hotel** a hotel EXCEPTIONS: **cal** lime, **cárcel** prison, **catedral** cathedral, **col** cabbage, **miel** honey, **piel** skin, **sal** salt, **señal** sign
-r	un **tractor** a tractor, **el altar** the altar EXCEPTIONS: **coliflor** cauliflower, **flor** flower, **labor** task
-y	**el rey** the king, **un buey** an ox EXCEPTION: **ley** law

Feminine endings

-a	un **casa** a house, **la cara** the face EXCEPTIONS: **día** day, **mapa** map, **planeta** planet, **tranvía** tram, and most words ending in **-ma** (**tema** subject, **problema** problem, *etc*)
-ión	una **canción** a song, **una procesión** a procession EXCEPTIONS: most nouns not ending in **-ción** or **-sión**, e.g. **avión** aeroplane, **camión** lorry, **gorrión** sparrow
-dad, -tad, -tud	una **ciudad** a town, **la libertad** freedom, una **multitud** a crowd
-ed	una **pared** a wall, **la sed** thirst EXCEPTION: **césped** lawn
-itis	una **faringitis** pharyngitis, **la celulitis** cellulitis
-iz	una **perdiz** a partridge, **una matriz** a matrix EXCEPTIONS: **lápiz** pencil, **maíz** corn, **tapiz** tapestry
-sis	una **tesis** a thesis, **una dosis** a dose EXCEPTIONS: **análisis** analysis, **énfasis** emphasis, **paréntesis** parenthesis
-umbre	**la podredumbre** rot, **la muchedrume** crowd

The Gender of Nouns *continued*

Some nouns change meaning according to gender. The most common are set out below:

	MASCULINE	FEMININE
capital	capital (*money*)	capital (*city*) → ❶
clave	harpsichord	clue
cólera	cholera	anger → ❷
cometa	comet	kite
corriente	current month	current
corte	cut	court (*royal*) → ❸
coma	coma	comma → ❹
cura	priest	cure → ❺
frente	front (*in war*)	forehead → ❻
guardia	guard(sman)	guard → ❼
guía	guide (*person*)	guide(book) → ❽
moral	mulberry tree	morals
orden	order (*arrangement*)	order (*command*) → ❾
ordenanza	office boy	ordinance
papa	Pope	potato
parte	dispatch	part → ❿
pendiente	earring	slope
pez	fish	pitch
policía	policeman	police
radio	radius, radium	radio

Examples

1. Invirtieron mucho capital — They invested a lot of capital
   La capital es muy fea — The capital city is very ugly

2. Es difícil luchar contra el cólera — Cholera is difficult to combat
   Montó en cólera — He got angry

3. Me encanta tu corte de pelo — I love your haircut
   Se trasladó la corte a Madrid — The court was moved to Madrid

4. Entró en un coma profundo — He went into a deep coma
   Aquí hace falta una coma — You need to put a comma here

5. ¿Quién es? – El cura — Who is it? – The priest
   No tiene cura — It's hopeless

6. Han mandado a su hijo al frente — Her son has been sent to the front
   Tiene la frente muy ancha — She has a very broad forehead

7. Vino un guardia de tráfico — A traffic policeman came
   Están relevando la guardia ahora — They're changing the guard now

8. Nuestro guía nos hizo reír a carcajadas — Our guide had us falling about laughing
   Busco una guía turística — I'm looking for a guidebook

9. Están en orden alfabético — They're in alphabetical order
   No hemos recibido la orden de pago — We haven't had the payment order

10. Le mandó un parte al general — He sent a dispatch to the general
    En alguna parte debe estar — It must be somewhere or other

Gender: the Formation of Feminines

As in English, male and female are sometimes differentiated by the use of two quite separate words, e.g.

mi marido my husband
mi mujer my wife
un toro a bull
una vaca a cow

There are, however, some words in Spanish which show this distinction by the form of their ending:

Nouns ending in **-o** change to **-a** to form the feminine → **1**

If the masculine singular form already ends in **-a**, no further **-a** is added to the feminine → **2**

If the last letter of the masculine singular form is a consonant, an **-a** is normally added in the feminine* → **3**

Feminine forms to note

MASCULINE	FEMININE	
el abad	**la abadesa**	abbot/abbess
un actor	**una actriz**	actor/actress
el alcalde	**la alcaldesa**	mayor/mayoress
el conde	**la condesa**	count/countess
el duque	**la duquesa**	duke/duchess
el emperador	**la emperatriz**	emperor/empress
un poeta	**una poetisa**	poet/poetess
el príncipe	**la princesa**	prince/princess
el rey	**la reina**	king/queen
un sacerdote	**una sacerdotisa**	priest/priestess
un tigre	**una tigresa**	tiger/tigress
el zar	**la zarina**	tzar/tzarina

* If the last syllable has an accent, it disappears in the feminine (see page 296) → **4**

Examples

❶ un amigo a (*male*) friend
un empleado a (*male*) employee
un gato a cat

una amiga a (*female*) friend
una empleada a (*female*) employee
una gata a (*female*) cat

❷ un deportista a sportsman
un colega a (*male*) colleague
un camarada a (*male*) comrade

una deportista a sportswoman
una colega a (*female*) colleague
una camarada a (*female*) comrade

❸ un español a Spaniard,
  a Spanish man
un vendedor a salesman
un jugador a (*male*) player

una española a Spanish woman

una vendedora a saleswoman
una jugadora a (*female*) player

❹ un lapón a Laplander (*man*)
un león a lion
un neocelandés
  a New Zealander (*man*)

una lapona a Laplander (*woman*)
una leona a lioness
una neocelandesa
  a New Zealander (*woman*)

The Formation of Plurals

Nouns ending in an unstressed vowel add **-s** to the singular form → **❶**

Nouns ending in a consonant or a stressed vowel add **-es** to the singular form → **❷**

> ⓘ BUT: **café** coffee shop   (*plural*: **cafés**)
>   **mamá** mummy   (*plural*: **mamás**)
>   **papá** daddy   (*plural*: **papás**)
>   **pie** foot   (*plural*: **pies**)
>   **sofá** sofa   (*plural*: **sofás**)
>   **té** tea   (*plural*: **tes**)

and words of foreign origin ending in a consonant, e.g.:

> **coñac** brandy   (*plural*: **coñacs**)
> **jersey** jumper   (*plural*: **jerseys**)

ⓘ Note:

- nouns ending in **-n** or **-s** with an accent on the last syllable drop this accent in the plural (see page 296) → **❸**
- nouns ending in **-n** with the stress on the second-last syllable in the singular add an accent to that syllable in the plural in order to show the correct position for stress (see page 296) → **❹**
- nouns ending in **-z** change this to **c** in the plural → **❺**

Nouns with an unstressed final syllable ending in **-s** do not change in the plural → **❻**

Examples

1   la casa   the house   las casas   the houses
     el libro   the book   los libros   the books

2   un rumor   a rumour   unos rumores   (some) rumours
     un jabalí   a boar   unos jabalíes   (some) boars

3   la canción   the song   las canciones   the songs
     el autobús   the bus   los autobuses   the buses

4   un examen   an exam   unos exámenes   (some) exams
     un crimen   a crime   unos crímenes   (some) crimes

5   la luz   the light   las luces   the lights

6   un paraguas   an umbrella   unos paraguas   (some) umbrellas
     la dosis   the dose   las dosis   the doses
     el lunes   Monday   los lunes   Mondays

Nouns

The Definite Article

	WITH MASC. NOUN	WITH FEM. NOUN	
SING.	el	la	the
PLUR.	los	las	the

The gender and number of the noun determine the form of the article → **1**

> ⓘ Note: However, if the article comes directly before a feminine singular noun which starts with a stressed **a-** or **ha-**, the masculine form **el** is used instead of the feminine **la** → **2**

For uses of the definite article see page 203.

a + **el** becomes **al** → **3**

de + **el** becomes **del** → **4**

Examples

①   el tren the train   la estación the station
        el actor the actor   la actriz the actress
        los hoteles the hotels   las escuelas the schools
        los profesores the teachers   las mujeres the women

②   el agua   the water
        BUT:
        la misma agua   the same water

        el hacha   the axe
        BUT:
        la mejor hacha   the best axe

③   al cine   to the cinema
        al empleado   to the employee
        al hospital   to the hospital

④   del departamento   from/of the department
        del autor   from/of the author
        del presidente   from/of the president

Uses of the Definite Article

While the definite article is used in much the same way in Spanish as it is in English, its use is more widespread in Spanish. Unlike English the definite article is also used:

> with abstract nouns, except when following certain prepositions → **1**

> in generalizations, especially with plural or uncountable* nouns → **2**

> with parts of the body → **3**
> 'Ownership' is often indicated by an indirect object pronoun or a reflexive pronoun → **4**

> with titles/ranks/professions followed by a proper name → **5**
> EXCEPTIONS: with **Don/Doña**, **San/Santo(a)** → **6**

> before nouns of official, academic and religious buildings, and names of meals and games → **7**

> The definite article is *not* used with nouns in apposition unless those nouns are individualized → **8**

* An uncountable noun is one which cannot be used in the plural or with an indefinite article, e.g. **el acero** steel; **la leche** milk.

Examples

1 Los precios suben — Prices are rising
El tiempo es oro — Time is money
BUT:
con pasión — with passion
sin esperanza — without hope

2 No me gusta el café — I don't like coffee
Los niños necesitan ser queridos — Children need to be loved

3 Vuelva la cabeza hacia la izquierda — Turn your head to the left
No puedo mover las piernas — I can't move my legs

4 La cabeza me da vueltas — My head is spinning
Lávate las manos — Wash your hands

5 El rey Jorge III — King George III
el capitán Menéndez — Captain Menéndez
el doctor Ochoa — Doctor Ochoa
el señor Ramírez — Mr Ramírez

6 Don Arturo Ruiz — Mr Arturo Ruiz
Santa Teresa — Saint Teresa

7 en la cárcel — in prison
en la universidad — at university
en la iglesia — at church
la cena — dinner
el tenis — tennis
el ajedrez — chess

8 Madrid, capital de España, — Madrid, the capital of Spain,
es la ciudad que ... — is the city which ...
BUT:
Maria Callas, la famosa cantante — Maria Callas, the famous opera
de ópera ... — singer ...

The Indefinite Article

	WITH MASC. NOUN	WITH FEM. NOUN	
SING.	un	una	a
PLUR.	unos	unas	some

The indefinite article is used in Spanish largely as it is in English.

BUT:

There is no article when a person's profession is being stated → **1**

The article is used, however, when the profession is qualified by an adjective → **2**

The article is not used with the following words:

otro	another	→ **3**
cierto	certain	→ **4**
semejante	such (a)	→ **5**
tal	such (a)	→ **6**
cien	a hundred	→ **7**
mil	a thousand	→ **8**
sin	without	→ **9**
qué	what a	→ **10**

There is no article with a noun in apposition → **11**. When an abstract noun is qualified by an adjective, the indefinite article is used, but is not translated in English → **12**

Examples

1 Es profesor
Mi madre es enfermera

He's a teacher
My mother is a nurse

2 Es un buen médico
Se hizo una escritora célebre

He's a good doctor
She became a famous writer

3 otro libro

another book

4 cierta calle

a certain street

5 semejante ruido

such a noise

6 tal mentira

such a lie

7 cien soldados

a hundred soldiers

8 mil años

a thousand years

9 sin casa

without a house

10 ¡Qué sorpresa!

What a surprise!

11 Baroja, gran escritor de la
Generación del 98

Baroja, a great writer of the
'Generación del 98'

12 con una gran sabiduría/un valor
admirable
Dieron pruebas de una sangre
fría increíble
una película de un mal gusto
espantoso

with great wisdom/admirable
courage
They showed incredible coolness

a film in appallingly bad taste

The Article 'lo'

This is never used with a noun. Instead, it is used in the following ways:

as an intensifier before an adjective or adverb in the construction

lo + adjective/adverb + **que** → **❶**

ⓘ Note: The adjective agrees with the noun it refers to → **❷**

With an adjective or participle to form an abstract noun → **❸**

In the phrase **lo de** to refer to a subject of which speaker and listener are already aware. It can often be translated as *the business/affair of/ about* ... → **❹**

In set expressions, the commonest of which are:

a lo mejor	maybe, perhaps	→ ❺
a lo lejos	in the distance	→ ❻
a lo largo de	along, through	→ ❼
por lo menos	at least	→ ❽
por lo tanto	therefore, so	→ ❾
por lo visto	apparently	→ ❿

Examples

1 No sabíamos lo pequeña que era la casa

We didn't know how small the house was

Sé lo mucho que te gusta la música

I know how much you like music

2 No te imaginas lo simpáticos que son

You can't imagine how nice they are

Ya sabes lo buenas que son estas manzanas

You already know how good these apples are

3 Lo bueno de eso es que ...

The good thing about it is that ...

Sentimos mucho lo ocurrido

We are very sorry about what happened

4 Lo de ayer es mejor que lo olvides

It's better if you forget what happened yesterday

Lo de tu hermano me preocupa mucho

The business about your brother worries me very much

5 A lo mejor ha salido

Perhaps he's gone out

6 A lo lejos se veían unas casas

Some houses could be seen in the distance

7 A lo largo de su vida

Throughout his life

A lo largo de la carretera

Along the road

8 Hubo por lo menos cincuenta heridos

At least fifty people were injured

9 No hemos recibido ninguna instrucción al respecto, y por lo tanto no podemos ...

We have not received any instructions about it, therefore we cannot ...

10 Por lo visto, no viene

Apparently he's not coming *or:* He's not coming, it seems

Adjectives

Most adjectives agree in number and in gender with the noun or pronoun.

ⓘ Note that:

- if the adjective refers to two or more singular nouns of the same gender, a plural ending of that gender is required → ❶
- if the adjective refers to two or more singular nouns of different genders, a masculine plural ending is required → ❷

The formation of feminines

Adjectives ending in **-o** change to **-a** → ❸

Some groups of adjectives add **-a**:
- adjectives of nationality or geographical origin → ❹
- adjectives ending in **-or** (except irregular comparatives: see page 214), **-án**, **-ón**, **-ín** → ❺

ⓘ Note: When there is an accent on the last syllable, it disappears in the feminine (see page 296).

Other adjectives do not change → ❻

The formation of plurals

Adjectives ending in an unstressed vowel add **-s** → ❼

Adjectives ending in a stressed vowel or a consonant add **-es** → ❽

ⓘ Note:

- if there is an accent on the last syllable of a word ending in a consonant, it will disappear in the plural (see page 296) → ❾
- if the last letter is a **z** it will become a **c** in the plural → ❿

Examples

1 la lengua y la literatura españolas — (the) Spanish language and literature

2 Nunca había visto árboles y flores tan raros — I had never seen such strange trees and flowers

3 mi hermano pequeño — my little brother
mi hermana pequeña — my little sister

4 un chico español — a Spanish boy
una chica española — a Spanish girl
el equipo barcelonés — the team from Barcelona
la vida barcelonesa — the Barcelona way of life

5 un niño encantador — a charming little boy
una niña encantadora — a charming little girl
un hombre holgazán — an idle man
una mujer holgazana — an idle woman
un gesto burlón — a mocking gesture
una sonrisa burlona — a mocking smile
un chico cantarín — a boy fond of singing
una chica cantarina — a girl fond of singing

6 un final feliz — a happy ending
una infancia feliz — a happy childhood
mi amigo belga — my Belgian (*male*) friend
mi amiga belga — my Belgian (*female*) friend
el vestido verde — the green dress
la blusa verde — the green blouse

7 el último tren — the last train
los últimos trenes — the last trains
una casa vieja — an old house
unas casas viejas — (some) old houses

8 un médico iraní — an Iranian doctor
unos médicos iraníes — (some) Iranian doctors
un examen fácil — easy exam
unos exámenes fáciles — (some) easy exams

9 un río francés — a French river
unos ríos franceses — (some) French rivers

10 un día feliz — a happy day
unos días felices — (some) happy days

Adjectives

Invariable Adjectives

Some adjectives and other parts of speech when used adjectivally never change in the feminine or plural.

The commonest of these are:
- nouns denoting colour → **1**
- compound adjectives → **2**
- nouns used as adjectives → **3**

Shortening of adjectives

The following drop the final **-o** before a masculine singular noun:
bueno good → **4**
malo bad
alguno* some → **5**
ninguno* none ·
uno one → **6**
primero first → **7**
tercero third
postrero last → **8**

  * ⓘ Note: An accent is required to show the correct position for stress.

Grande *big, great* is usually shortened to **gran** before a masculine or feminine singular noun → **9**

Santo *Saint* changes to **San** except with saints' names beginning with **Do-** *or* **To-** → **10**

Ciento *a hundred* is shortened to **cien** before a masculine *or* feminine plural noun → **11**

Cualquiera drops the final **-a** before a masculine *or* feminine singular noun → **12**

Examples

1 los vestidos naranja — the orange dresses

2 las chaquetas azul marino — the navy blue jackets

3 bebés probeta — test-tube babies
mujeres soldado — women soldiers

4 un buen libro — a good book

5 algún libro — some book

6 cuarenta y un años — forty-one years

7 el primer hijo — the first child

8 un postrer deseo — a last wish

9 un gran actor — a great actor
una gran decepción — a great disappointment

10 San Antonio — Saint Anthony
Santo Tomás — Saint Thomas

11 cien años — a hundred years
cien millones — a hundred million

12 cualquier día — any day
a cualquier hora — any time

Comparatives and Superlatives

Comparatives

These are formed using the following constructions:

más ... (que) more ... (than) → ❶
menos ... (que) less ... (than) → ❷
tanto ... como as ... as → ❸
tan ... como as ... as → ❹
tan ... que so ... that → ❺

demasiado ... ⎤   too ... ⎤
bastante ... ⎬ **para** enough ... ⎬ to → ❻
suficiente ... ⎦   enough ... ⎦

'Than' followed by a clause is translated by **de lo que** → ❼

Superlatives

These are formed using the following constructions:

el/la/los/las más ... (que) the most ... (that) → ❽
el/la/los/las menos ... (que) the least ... (that) → ❾

After a superlative the preposition **de** is often translated as 'in' → ❿

The absolute superlative (*very, most, extremely + adjective*) is expressed in Spanish by **muy** + adjective, or by adding **-ísimo/a/os/as** to the adjective when it ends in a consonant, or to its stem (adjective minus final vowel) when it ends in a vowel → ⓫

ⓘ Note: It is sometimes necessary to change the spelling of the adjective when **-ísimo** is added, in order to maintain the same sound (see page 300) → ⓬

Examples

1. una razón más seria · a more serious reason
   Es más alto que mi hermano · He's taller than my brother

2. una película menos conocida · a less well known film
   Luis es menos tímido que tú · Luis is less shy than you

3. Pablo tenía tanto miedo como yo · Paul was as frightened as I was

4. No es tan grande como creía · It isn't as big as I thought

5. El examen era tan difícil que · The exam was so difficult that
   nadie aprobó · nobody passed

6. No tengo suficiente dinero para · I haven't got enough money to
   comprarlo · buy it

7. Está más cansada de lo que parece · She is more tired than she seems

8. el caballo más veloz · the fastest horse
   la casa más pequeña · the smallest house
   los días más lluviosos · the wettest days
   las manzanas más maduras · the ripest apples

9. el hombre menos simpático · the least likeable man
   la niña menos habladora · the least talkative girl
   los cuadros menos bonitos · the least attractive paintings
   las camisas menos viejas · the least old shirts

10. la estación más ruidosa de Londres · the noisiest station in London

11. Este libro es muy interesante · This book is very interesting

12. Tienen un coche rapidísimo · They have an extremely fast car
    Era facilísimo de hacer · It was very easy to make
    Mi tío era muy rico · My uncle was very rich
    Se hizo riquísimo · He became extremely rich
    un león muy feroz · a very ferocious lion
    un tigre ferocísimo · an extremely ferocious tiger

213

Comparatives and Superlatives *continued*

Adjectives with irregular comparatives/superlatives

ADJECTIVE	COMPARATIVE	SUPERLATIVE
bueno	**mejor**	**el mejor**
good	better	the best
malo	**peor**	**el peor**
bad	worse	the worst
grande	**mayor** *or* **más grande**	**el más grande**
big	bigger; older	the biggest; the oldest
pequeño	**menor** *or* **más pequeño**	**el más pequeño**
small	smaller; younger; lesser	the smallest; the youngest; the least

The irregular comparative and superlative forms of **grande** and **pequeño** are used mainly to express:
- age, in which case they come after the noun → ❶
- abstract size and degrees of importance, in which case they come before the noun → ❷

The regular forms are used mainly to express physical size → ❸

Irregular comparatives and superlatives have one form for both masculine and feminine, but always agree in number with the noun → ❶

Examples

① mis hermanos mayores
   la hija menor

     my older brothers
     the youngest daughter

② el menor ruido
   las mayores dificultades

     the slightest sound
     the biggest difficulties

③ Este plato es más grande que
    aquél
   Mi casa es más pequeña que
    la tuya

     This plate is bigger than that
      one
     My house is smaller than yours

Demonstrative Adjectives

	MASCULINE	FEMININE	
SING.	este	esta	this
	ese	esa	that
	aquel	aquella	
PLUR.	estos	estas	these
	esos	esas	those
	aquellos	aquellas	

Demonstrative adjectives normally precede the noun and always agree in number and in gender → ❶

The forms **ese/a/os/as** are used:
- to indicate distance from the speaker but proximity to the person addressed → ❷
- to indicate a not too remote distance → ❸

The forms **aquel/la/los/las** are used to indicate distance, in space or time → ❹

Examples

1 Este bolígrafo no escribe — This pen is not working
Esa revista es muy mala — That is a very bad magazine
Aquella montaña es muy alta — That mountain (over there) is very high

¿Conoces a esos señores? — Do you know those gentlemen?
Siga Vd hasta aquellos edificios — Carry on until you come to those buildings

¿Ves aquellas personas? — Can you see those people (over there)?

2 Ese papel en donde escribes ... — That paper you are writing on ...

3 No me gustan esos cuadros — I don't like those pictures

4 Aquella calle parece muy ancha — That street (over there) looks very wide

Aquellos años sí que fueron felices — Those were really happy years

Adjectives

Interrogative Adjectives

	MASCULINE	FEMININE	
SING.	¿qué?	¿qué?	what?, which?
	¿cuánto?	¿cuánta?	how much?, how many?
PLUR.	¿qué?	¿qué?	what?, which?
	¿cuántos?	¿cuántas?	how much?, how many?

Interrogative adjectives, when not invariable, agree in number and gender with the noun → **1**

The forms shown above are also used in indirect questions → **2**

Exclamatory Adjectives

	MASCULINE	FEMININE	
SING.	¡qué!	¡qué!	what (a)
	¡cuánto!	¡cuánta!	what (a lot of)
PLUR.	¡qué!	¡qué!	what
	¡cuántos!	¡cuántas!	what (a lot of)

Exclamatory adjectives, when not invariable, agree in number and gender with the noun → **3**

Examples

❶ ¿Qué libro te gustó más?
Which book did you like most?

¿Qué clase de hombre es?
What type of man is he?

¿Qué instrumentos toca Vd?
What instruments do you play?

¿Qué ofertas ha recibido Vd?
What offers have you received?

¿Cuánto dinero te queda?
How much money have you got left?

¿Cuánta lluvia ha caído?
How much rain have we had?

¿Cuántos vestidos quieres comprar?
How many dresses do you want to buy?

¿Cuántas personas van a venir?
How many people are coming?

❷ No sé a qué hora llegó
I don't know at what time she arrived

Dígame cuántas postales quiere
Tell me how many postcards you'd like

❸ ¡Qué pena!
What a pity!

¡Qué tiempo tan/más malo!
What lousy weather!

¡Cuánto tiempo!
What a long time!

¡Cuánta pobreza!
What poverty!

¡Cuántos autobuses!
What a lot of buses!

¡Cuántas mentiras!
What a lot of lies!

Possessive Adjectives

Weak forms

WITH SING. NOUN		WITH PLUR. NOUN		
MASC.	FEM.	MASC.	FEM.	
mi	mi	mis	mis	my
tu	tu	tus	tus	your
su	su	sus	sus	his; her; its; your
				(of **Vd**)
nuestro	nuestra	nuestros	nuestras	our
vuestro	vuestra	vuestros	vuestras	your
su	su	sus	sus	their; your
				(of **Vds**)

All possessive adjectives agree in number and (when applicable) in gender with the noun, not with the owner → **1**
The weak forms always precede the noun → **1**

Since the form **su(s)** can mean his, her, your (of **Vd**, **Vds**) or their, clarification is often needed. This is done by adding **de él**, **de ella**, **de Vds** etc to the noun, and usually (but not always) changing the possessive to a definite article → **2**

Examples

1 Pilar no ha traído nuestros libros   Pilar hasn't brought our books
Antonio irá a vuestra casa   Anthony will go to your house
¿Han vendido su coche tus   Have your neighbours sold their
  vecinos?   car?
Mi hermano y tu primo no se   My brother and your cousin
  llevan bien   don't get on

2 su casa → la casa de él   his house
sus amigos → los amigos de Vd   your friends
sus coches → los coches de ellos   their cars
su abrigo → el abrigo de ella   her coat

Adjectives

Possessive Adjectives *continued*

Strong forms

WITH SING. NOUN		WITH PLUR. NOUN		
MASC.	FEM.	MASC.	FEM.	
mío	mía	míos	mías	my
tuyo	tuya	tuyos	tuyas	your
suyo	suya	suyos	suyas	his; her; its; your (of **Vd**)
nuestro	nuestra	nuestros	nuestras	our
vuestro	vuestra	vuestros	vuestras	your
suyo	suya	suyos	suyas	their; your (of **Vds**)

The strong forms agree in the same way as the weak forms (see page 220)

The strong forms always follow the noun, and they are used:
- to translate the English *of mine, of yours*, etc → **❶**
- to address people → **❷**

Examples

1 Es un capricho suyo   It's a whim of hers
un amigo nuestro   a friend of ours
una revista tuya   a magazine of yours

2 Muy señor mío (in letters)   Dear Sir
hija mía   my daughter
¡Dios mío!   My God!
Amor mío   Darling/My love

Adjectives

Indefinite Adjectives

alguno(a)s	some
ambos(as)	both
cada	each; every
cierto(a)s	certain; definite
cualquiera plural **cualesquiera**	some; any
los (las) demás	the others; the remainder
mismo(a)s	same; -self
mucho(a)s	many; much
ningún, ninguna plural **ningunos, ningunas**	any; no
otro(a)s	other; another
poco(a)s	few; little
tal(es)	such (a)
tanto(a)s	so much; so many
todo(a)s	all; every
varios(as)	several; various

Unless invariable, all indefinite adjectives agree in number and gender with the noun → **❶**

alguno
Before a masculine singular noun, this drops the final **-o** and adds an accent to show the correct position for stress → **❷** (see also page 296)

ambos
This is usually only used in written Spanish. The spoken language prefers the form **los dos/las dos** → **❸**

cierto and mismo
These change their meaning according to their position in relation to the noun (see also Position of Adjectives, page 228) → **❹**

cualquiera
This drops the final **-a** before a masculine or feminine noun → **❺**

Examples

1 el mismo día   the same day
las mismas películas   the same films
mucha/poca gente   many/few people
mucho/poco dinero   much/little money

2 algún día   some day
alguna razón   some reason

3 Me gustan los dos cuadros   I like both pictures
¿Conoces a las dos enfermeras?   Do you know both nurses?

4 cierto tiempo   a certain time
BUT:
éxito cierto   sure success
el mismo color   the same colour
BUT:
en la iglesia misma   in the church itself

5 cualquier casa   any house
BUT:
una revista cualquiera   any magazine

Indefinite Adjectives *continued*

ningún is only used in negative sentences or phrases → **1**

otro is never preceded by an indefinite article → **2**

tal is never followed by an indefinite article → **3**

todo can be followed by a definite article, a demonstrative or possessive adjective or a place name → **4**

> EXCEPTIONS:
> - when **todo** in the singular means any, every, or each → **5**
> - in some set expressions → **6**

Examples

1 No es ninguna tonta
¿No tienes parientes?
— No, ninguno

She's no fool
Haven't you any relatives?
— No, none

2 ¿Me das otra manzana?
Prefiero estos otros zapatos

Will you give me another apple?
I prefer these other shoes

3 Nunca dije tal cosa

I never said such a thing

4 Estudian durante toda la noche
Ha llovido toda esta semana
Pondré en orden todos mis libros
Lo sabe todo Madrid

They study all night
It has rained all this week
I'll sort out all my books
All Madrid knows it

5 Podrá entrar toda persona que
  lo desee
BUT:
Vienen todos los días

Any person who wishes to enter
  may do so

They come every day

6 de todos modos
a toda velocidad
por todas partes
por todos lados
a/en todas partes
a/en todos lados

anyway
at full/top speed

everywhere

Position of Adjectives

Spanish adjectives usually follow the noun → **❶**, **❷**

Note that when used figuratively or to express a quality already inherent in the noun, adjectives can precede the noun → **❸**

As in English, demonstrative, possessive (weak forms), numerical, interrogative and exclamatory adjectives precede the noun → **❹**

Indefinite adjectives also usually precede the noun → **❺**

> ⓘ Note: **alguno** *some* in negative expressions follows the noun → **❻**

Some adjectives can precede or follow the noun, but their meaning varies according to their position:

	BEFORE NOUN	AFTER NOUN
antiguo	former	old, ancient → ❼
diferente	various	different → ❽
grande	great	big → ❾
medio	half	average → ❿
mismo	same	-self, very/precisely → ⓫
nuevo	new, another, fresh	brand new → ⓬
pobre	poor (wretched)	poor (not rich) → ⓭
puro	sheer, mere	pure (clear) → ⓮
varios	several	various, different → ⓯
viejo	old (long known, etc)	old (aged) → ⓰

Adjectives following the noun are linked by **y** → ⓱

Examples

1. la página siguiente — the following page
   la hora exacta — the right time

2. una corbata azul — a blue tie
   una palabra española — a Spanish word

3. un dulce sueño — a sweet dream
   un terrible desastre — a terrible disaster
   (*all disasters are terrible*)

4. este sombrero — this hat
   mi padre — my father
   ¿qué hombre? — what man?

5. cada día — every day
   otra vez — another time
   poco dinero — little money

6. sin duda alguna — without any doubt

7. un antiguo colega — a former colleague
   la historia antigua — ancient history

8. diferentes capítulos — various chapters
   personas diferentes — different people

9. un gran pintor — a great painter
   una casa grande — a big house

10. medio melón — half a melon
    velocidad media — average speed

11. la misma respuesta — the same answer
    yo mismo — myself
    eso mismo — precisely that

12. mi nuevo coche — my new car
    unos zapatos nuevos — (some) brand new shoes

13. esa pobre mujer — that poor woman
    un país pobre — a poor country

14. la pura verdad — the plain truth
    aire puro — fresh air

15. varios caminos — several ways/paths
    artículos varios — various items

16. un viejo amigo — an old friend
    esas toallas viejas — those old towels

17. una acción cobarde y falsa — a cowardly, deceitful act

Personal Pronouns

SUBJECT PRONOUNS		
SINGULAR	PLURAL	
1st person **yo** I	**nosotros** we	(*masc./masc.* *+ fem.*)
	nosotras we	(*all fem.*)
2nd person **tú** you	**vosotros** you	(*masc./masc.* *+ fem.*)
	vosotras you	(*all fem.*)
3rd person **él** he; it	**ellos** they	(*masc./masc.* *+ fem.*)
ella she; it	**ellas** they	(*all fem.*)
usted (Vd) you	**ustedes (Vds)** you	

Subject pronouns have a limited usage in Spanish. Normally they are only used:

- for emphasis → **❶**
- for clarity → **❷**

BUT: **Vd** and **Vds** should always be used for politeness, whether they are otherwise needed or not → **❸**

It as subject and *they*, referring to things, are never translated into Spanish → **❹**

tú/usted
As a general rule, you should use **tú** (or **vosotros**, if plural) when addressing a friend, a child, a relative, someone you know well, or when invited to do so. In all other cases, use **usted** (or **ustedes**).

nosotros/as; vosotros/as; él/ella; ellos/ellas
All these forms reflect the number and gender of the noun(s) they replace. **Nosotros**, **vosotros** and **ellos** also replace a combination of masculine and feminine nouns.

230 | Grammar Guide

Examples

1 Ellos sí que llegaron tarde
   Tú no tienes por qué venir

   Ella jamás creería eso

2 Yo estudio español pero él
   estudia francés
   Ella era muy deportista pero
   él prefería jugar a las cartas
   Vosotros saldréis primero y
   nosotros os seguiremos

3 Pase Vd por aquí
   ¿Habían estado Vds antes en
   esta ciudad?

4 ¿Qué es? — Es una sorpresa
   ¿Qué son? — Son abrelatas

They really did arrive late
There is no reason for you to
   come

She would never believe that

I study Spanish but he studies
   French
She was a sporty type but he
   preferred to play cards
You leave first and we will
   follow you

Please come this way
Had you been to this town
   before?

What is it? — It's a surprise
What are they? — They are
   tin-openers

Personal Pronouns *continued*

	DIRECT OBJECT PRONOUNS	
	SINGULAR	PLURAL
1st person	**me** me	**nos** us
2nd person	**te** you	**os** you
3rd person (*masc.*)	**lo** him; it; you (of **Vd**)	**los** them; you (of **Vds**)
(*fem.*)	**la** her; it; you (of **Vd**)	**las** them; you (of **Vds**)

lo sometimes functions as a 'neuter' pronoun, referring to an idea or information contained in a previous statement or question. It is often not translated → **1**

Position of direct object pronouns

In constructions other than the imperative affirmative, infinitive or gerund, the pronoun always comes before the verb → **2**

In the imperative affirmative, infinitive and gerund, the pronoun follows the verb and is attached to it. An accent is needed in certain cases to show the correct position for stress (see also page 296) → **3**

Where an infinitive or gerund depends on a previous verb, the pronoun may be used either after the infinitive or gerund, or before the main verb → **4**

ⓘ Note: see how this applies to reflexive verbs → **4**

For further information, see Order of Object Pronouns, page 236.

Reflexive Pronouns

These are dealt with under reflexive verbs, page 24.

Examples

1 ¿Va a venir María? — No lo sé | Is Maria coming? — I don't know
Hay que regar las plantas — Yo lo haré | The plants need watering — I'll do it
Habían comido ya pero no nos lo dijeron | They had already eaten, but they didn't tell us
Yo conduzco de prisa pero él lo hace despacio | I drive fast but he drives slowly

2 Te quiero | I love you
¿Las ve Vd? | Can you see them?
¿No me oyen Vds? | Can't you hear me?
Tu hija no nos conoce | Your daughter doesn't know us
No los toques | Don't touch them

3 Ayúdame | Help me
Acompáñenos | Come with us
Quiero decirte algo | I want to tell you something
Estaban persiguiéndonos | They were coming after us

4 Lo está comiendo *or* Está comiéndolo | She is eating it
Nos vienen a ver *or* Vienen a vernos | They are coming to see us
No quería levantarse *or* No se quería levantar | He didn't want to get up
Estoy afeitándome *or* Me estoy afeitando | I'm shaving

Personal Pronouns *continued*

	INDIRECT OBJECT PRONOUNS	
	SINGULAR	PLURAL
1st person	me	nos
2nd person	te	os
3rd person	le	les

The pronouns shown in the above table replace the preposition **a** + noun → **①**

Position of indirect object pronouns

In constructions other than the imperative affirmative, the infinitive or the gerund, the pronoun comes before the verb → **②**

> In the imperative affirmative, infinitive and gerund, the pronoun follows the verb and is attached to it. An accent is needed in certain cases to show the correct position for stress (see also page 296) → **③**

Where an infinitive or gerund depends on a previous verb, the pronoun may be used either after the infinitive or gerund, or before the main verb → **④**

For further information, see Order of Object Pronouns, page 236.

Reflexive Pronouns

These are dealt with under reflexive verbs, page 24.

Examples

❶
Estoy escribiendo a Teresa	I am writing to Teresa
Le estoy escribiendo	I am writing to her
Da de comer al gato	Give the cat some food
Dale de comer	Give it some food

❷
Sofía os ha escrito	Sophie has written to you
¿Os ha escrito Sofía?	Has Sophie written to you?
Carlos no nos habla	Charles doesn't speak to us
¿Qué te pedían?	What were they asking you for?
No les haga caso Vd	Don't take any notice of them

❸
Respóndame Vd	Answer me
Díganos Vd la respuesta	Tell us the answer
No quería darte la noticia todavía	I didn't want to tell you the news yet
Llegaron diciéndome que ...	They came telling me that ...

❹
Estoy escribiéndole *or*	I am writing to him/her
Le estoy escribiendo	
Les voy a hablar *or*	I'm going to talk to them
Voy a hablarles	

Personal Pronouns *continued*

Order of object pronouns

When two object pronouns of different persons are combined, the order
is: indirect before direct, i.e.

me			lo	
te		before	la	→ **1**
nos			los	
os			las	

> ⓘ Note: When two 3rd person object pronouns are combined, the
> first (i.e. the indirect object pronoun) becomes **se** → **2**

Points to note on object pronouns

As **le/les** can refer to either gender, and **se** to either gender, singular or
plural, sometimes clarification is needed. This is done by adding **a él** *to
him*, **a ella** *to her*, **a Vd** *to you* etc to the phrase, usually after the verb → **3**

When a noun object precedes the verb, the corresponding object pronoun
must be used too → **4**

Indirect object pronouns are often used instead of possessive adjectives
with parts of the body or clothing to indicate 'ownership', and also
in certain common constructions involving reflexive verbs (see also
The Indefinite Article, page 202) → **5**

Le and **les** are often used in Spanish instead of **lo** and **los** when referring
to people. Equally **la** is sometimes used instead of **le** when referring to a
feminine person or animal, although this usage is considered incorrect
by some speakers of Spanish → **6**

Examples

❶ Paloma os lo mandará mañana
Paloma is sending it to you tomorrow

¿Te los ha enseñado mi hermana?
Has my sister shown them to you?

No me lo digas
Don't tell me (that)

Todos estaban pidiéndotelo
They were all asking you for it

No quiere prestárnosla
He won't lend it to us

❷ Se lo di ayer
I gave it to him/her/them yesterday

❸ Le escriben mucho a ella
They write to her often

Se lo van a mandar pronto a ellos
They will be sending it to them soon

❹ A tu hermano lo conozco bien
I know your brother well

A María la vemos algunas veces
We sometimes see Maria

❺ La chaqueta le estaba ancha
His jacket was too loose

Me duele el tobillo
My ankle is aching

Se me ha perdido el bolígrafo
I have lost my pen

❻ Le/lo encontraron en el cine
They met him at the cinema

Les/los oímos llegar
We heard them coming

Le/la escribimos una carta
We wrote a letter to her

Personal Pronouns *continued*

Pronouns after prepositions

These are the same as the subject pronouns, except for the forms **mí** me, **ti** you (*singular*), and the reflexive **sí** himself, herself, themselves, yourselves → **❶**

Con with combines with **mí**, **ti** and **sí** to form

conmigo	with me → **❷**
contigo	with you
consigo	with himself/herself *etc*

The following prepositions always take a subject pronoun:

entre	between, among → **❸**
hasta ⎤	even, including → **❹**
incluso ⎦	
salvo ⎤	except → **❺**
menos ⎦	
según	according to → **❻**

These pronouns are used for emphasis, especially where contrast is involved → **❼**

Ello it, that is used after a preposition when referring to an idea already mentioned, but never to a concrete noun → **❼**

A él, **de él** never contract → **❾**

Examples

1 Pienso en ti   I think about you
   ¿Son para mí?   Are they for me?
   Es para ella   This is for her
   Iban hacia ellos   They were going towards them
   Volveréis sin nosotros   You'll come back without us
   Volaban sobre vosotros   They were flying above you
   Hablaba para si   He was talking to himself

2 Venid conmigo   Come with me
   Lo trajeron consigo   They brought it/him with them
   BUT:
   ¿Hablaron con vosotros?   Did they talk to you?

3 entre tú y ella   between you and her

4 Hasta yo puedo hacerlo   Even I can do it

5 todos menos yo   everybody except me

6 según tú   according to you

7 ¿A ti no te escriben?   Don't they write to you?
   Me lo manda a mí, no a ti   She is sending it to me, not to you

8 Nunca pensaba en ello   He never thought about it
   Por todo ello me parece que ...   For all those reasons it seems to
                             me that ...

9 A él no lo conozco   I don't know him
   No he sabido nada de él   I haven't heard from him

Indefinite Pronouns

algo	something, anything → ❶
alguien	somebody, anybody → ❷
alguno/a/os/as	some, a few → ❸
cada uno/a	each (one) → ❹
	everybody
cualquiera	anybody; any → ❺
los/las demás	the others
	the rest → ❻
mucho/a/os/as	many; much → ❼
nada	nothing → ❽
nadie	nobody → ❾
ninguno/a	none, not any → ❿
poco/a/os/as	few; little → ⓫
tanto/a/os/as	so much; so many → ⓬
todo/a/os/as	all; everything → ⓭
uno ... (el) otro **una ... (la) otra**	(the) one ... the other
unos ... (los) otros **unas ... (las) otras**	some ... (the) others → ⓮
varios/as	several → ⓯

algo, alguien, alguno

They can never be used after a negative. The appropriate negative pronouns are used instead: **nada**, **nadie**, **ninguno** (see also negatives, page 276) → ⓰

Examples

1. Tengo algo para ti   I have something for you
   ¿Viste algo?   Did you see anything?

2. Alguien me lo ha dicho   Somebody said it to me
   ¿Has visto a alguien?   Have you seen anybody?

3. Algunos de los niños ya sabían leer   Some of the children could read already

4. Le dió una manzana a cada uno   She gave each of them an apple
   !Cada uno a su casa!   Everybody go home!

5. Cualquiera puede hacerlo   Anybody can do it
   Cualquiera de las explicaciones vale   Any of the explanations is a valid one

6. Yo me fui, los demás se quedaron   I went, the others stayed

7. Muchas de las casas no tenían jardín   Many of the houses didn't have a garden

8. ¿Qué tienes en la mano?   What have you got in your hand?
   — Nada   — Nothing

9. ¡A quién ves? — A nadie   Who can you see? — Nobody

10. ¿Cuántas tienes? — Ninguna   How many have you got? — None

11. Había muchos cuadros, pero vi pocos que me gustaran   There were many pictures, but I saw few I liked

12. ¿Se oía mucho ruido? — No tanto   Was it very noisy? — Not so very

13. Lo ha estropeado todo   He has spoiled everything
    Todo va bien   All is going well

14. Unos cuestan 30 euros, los otros 40 euros   Some cost 30 euros, the others 40 euros

15. Varios de ellos me gustaron mucho   I liked several of them very much

16. Veo a alguien   I can see somebody
    No veo a nadie   I can't see anybody
    Tengo algo que hacer   I have something to do
    No tengo nada que hacer   I don't have anything to do

Relative Pronouns

PEOPLE		
SINGULAR	PLURAL	
que	que	who, that (*subject*) → ❶
que	que	who(m), that (*direct object*) → ❷
a quien	a quienes	
a quien	a quienes	to whom, that → ❸
de que	de que	of whom, that → ❹
de quien	de quienes	
cuyo/a	cuyos/as	whose → ❺

THINGS	
SINGULAR AND PLURAL	
que	which, that (*subject*) → ❻
que	which, that (*direct object*) → ❼
a que	to which, that → ❽
de que	of which, that → ❾
cuyo	whose → ❿

ⓘ Note: These forms can also refer to people.

cuyo agrees with the noun it accompanies, not with the owner → ❺/❿

You cannot omit the relative pronoun in Spanish as you can in English → ❷/❼

Examples

1. Mi hermano, que tiene veinte años, es el más joven

   My brother, who is twenty, is the youngest

2. Los amigos que más quiero son ...

   The friends (that) I like best are ...

   María, a quien Daniel admira tanto, es ...

   Maria, whom Daniel admires so much, is ...

3. Mis abogados, a quienes he escrito hace poco, están ...

   My lawyers, to whom I wrote recently, are ...

4. La chica de que te hablé llega mañana

   The girl (that) I told you about is coming tomorrow

   los niños de quienes se ocupa Vd

   the children (that) you look after

5. Vendrá la mujer cuyo hijo está enfermo

   The woman whose son is ill will be coming

6. Hay una escalera que lleva a la buhardilla

   There's a staircase which leads to the loft

7. La casa que hemos comprado tiene ...

   The house (which) we've bought has ...

   Este es el regalo que me ha mandado mi amiga

   This is the present (that) my friend has sent to me

8. la tienda a que siempre va

   the shop (which) she always goes to

9. las injusticias de que se quejan

   the injustices (that) they're complaining about

10. la ventana cuyas cortinas están corridas

    the window whose curtains are drawn

Relative Pronouns *continued*

el cual, el que

These are used when the relative is separated from the word it refers to, or when it would otherwise be unclear which word it referred to. The pronouns always agree in number and gender with the noun → ❶

> **El cual** may also be used when the verb in the relative clause is separated from the relative pronoun → ❷

lo que, lo cual

The neuter form **lo** is normally used when referring to an idea, statement or abstract noun. In certain expressions, the form **lo cual** may also be used as the subject of the relative clause → ❸

Relative pronouns after prepositions

Que and **quienes** are generally used after the prepositions:

a	to	→ ❹
con	with	→ ❺
de	from, about, of	→ ❻
en	in, on, into	→ ❼

It should be noted that **en que** can sometimes be translated by:
- *where*. In this case it can also be replaced by **en donde** or **donde** → ❽
- *when*. Sometimes here it can be replaced by **cuando** → ❾

El que or **el cual** are used after other prepositions, and they always agree → ❿

Examples

1 El padre de Elena, el cual tiene mucho dinero, es ...

Elena's father, who has a lot of money, is ...

(el cual *is used here since* que *or* quien *might equally refer to Elena*)

Su hermana, a la cual/la que hacía mucho que no veía, estaba también allí

His sister, whom I hadn't seen for a long time, was also there

2 Vieron a su tio, el cual, después de levantarse, salió

They saw their uncle, who, after having got up, went out

3 No sabe lo que hace

He doesn't know what he is doing

Lo que dijiste fue una tontería

What you said was foolish

Todo estaba en silencio, lo que (*or* lo cual) me pareció muy raro

All was silent, which I thought most odd

4 las tiendas a (las) que íbamos

the shops we used to go to

5 la chica con quien (or la que) sale

the girl he's going out with

6 el libro de(l) que te hablé

the book I told you about

7 el lío en (el) que te has metido

the trouble you've got yourself into

8 el sitio en que (en donde/donde) se escondía

the place where he/she was hiding

9 el año en que naciste

the year (when) you were born

10 el puente debajo del que/cual pasa el río

the bridge under which the river flows

las obras por las cuales/que es famosa

the plays for which she is famous

Relative Pronouns *continued*

el que, la que; los que, las que
These mean *the one(s) who/which, those who* → ❶

> ⓘ Note: **quien(es)** can replace **el que** *etc* when used in a general sense → ❷

todos los que, todas las que
These mean *all who, all those/the ones which* → ❸

todo lo que
This translates *all that, everything that* → ❹

el de, la de; los de, las de
These can mean:
- *the one(s) of, that/those of* → ❺
- *the one(s) with* → ❻

Examples

1 Esa película es la que quiero ver
¿Te acuerdas de ese amigo?
  El que te presenté ayer

  Los que quieran entrar tendrán
  que pagar

That film is the one I want to see
Do you remember that friend?
  The one I introduced you to
  yesterday
Those who want to go in will
  have to pay

2 Quien (or el que) llegue antes
  ganará el premio

He who arrives first will win the
  prize

3 Todos los que salían iban de negro

¿Qué autobuses puedo tomar?
  – Todos los que pasen por aquí

All those who were coming out
  were dressed in black
Which buses can I take?
  – Any (All those) that come this
  way

4 Quiero saber todo lo que ha
  pasado

I want to know all that has
  happened

5 Trae la foto de tu novio y la de
  tu hermano
Viajamos en mi coche y en el
  de María
Te doy estos libros y también
  los de mi hermana

Bring the photo of your boyfriend
  and the one of your brother
We travelled in my car and Maria's

I'll give you these books and my
  sister's too

6 Tu amigo, el de las gafas,
  me lo contó

Your friend, the one with glasses,
  told me

Interrogative Pronouns

¿qué? what?; which?
¿cuál(es)? which?; what?
¿quién(es)? who?

qué

It always translates *what* → ❶

ⓘ Note: **por** + **qué** is normally translated by *why* → ❷

cuál

It normally implies a choice, and translates *which* → ❸

ⓘ EXCEPT: when no choice is implied or more specific information is required → ❹

ⓘ Note: Whilst the pronoun **qué** can also work as an adjective, **cuál** only works as a pronoun → ❺

quién

SUBJECT *or* AFTER PREPOSITION	**quién(es)**	who → ❻
OBJECT	**a quién(es)**	whom → ❼
	de quién(es)	whose → ❽

All the forms shown above are also used in indirect questions → ❾

Examples

1 ¿Qué estan haciendo? What are they doing?
¿Qué dices? What are you saying?
¿Para qué lo quieres? What do you want it for?

2 ¿Por qué no llegaron Vds antes? Why didn't you arrive earlier?

3 ¿Cuál de estos vestidos te gusta más? Which of these dresses do you like best?
¿Cuáles viste? Which ones did you see?

4 ¿Cuál es la capital de España? What is the capital of Spain?
¿Cuál es tu consejo? What is your advice?
¿Cuál es su fecha de nacimiento? What is your date of birth?

5 ¿Qué libro es más interesante? Which book is more interesting?
¿Cuál (de estos libros) es más interesante? Which (of these books) is more interesting?

6 ¿Quién ganó la carrera? Who won the race?
¿Con quiénes los viste? Who did you see them with?

7 ¿A quiénes ayudaste? Who(m) did you help?
¿A quién se lo diste? Who did you give it to?

8 ¿De quién es este libro? Whose is this book?

9 Le pregunté para qué lo quería I asked him/her what he/she wanted it for

No me dijeron cuáles preferían They didn't tell me which ones they preferred

No sabía a quién acudir I didn't know who to turn to

Possessive Pronouns

These are the same as the strong forms of the possessive adjectives, but they are always accompanied by the definite article.

Singular:

MASCULINE	FEMININE	
el mío	la mía	mine
el tuyo	la tuya	yours (of **tú**)
el suyo	la suya	his; hers; its; yours (of **Vd**)
el nuestro	la nuestra	ours
el vuestro	la vuestra	yours (of **vosotros**)
el suyo	la suya	theirs; yours (of **Vds**)

Plural:

MASCULINE	FEMININE	
los míos	las mías	mine
los tuyos	las tuyas	yours (of **tú**)
los suyos	las suyas	his; hers; its; yours (of **Vd**)
los nuestros	las nuestras	ours
los vuestros	las vuestras	yours (of **vosotros**)
los suyos	las suyas	theirs; yours (of **Vds**)

The pronoun agrees in number and gender with the noun it replaces, not with the owner → **1**

Alternative translations are 'my own', 'your own' *etc* → **2**

After the prepositions **a** and **de** the article **el** is contracted in the normal way (see page 200):

> a + el mío → al mío → **3**
> de + el mío → del mío → **4**

Examples

1 Pregunta a Cristina si este bolígrafo es el suyo — Ask Christine if this pen is hers

¿Qué equipo ha ganado, el suyo o el nuestro? — Which team won – theirs or ours?

Mi perro es más joven que el tuyo — My dog is younger than yours

Daniel pensó que esos libros eran los suyos — Daniel thought those books were his

Si no tienes discos, te prestaré los míos — If you don't have any records, I'll lend you mine

Las habitaciones son menos amplias que las vuestras — The rooms are smaller than yours

2 ¿Es su familia tan grande como la tuya? — Is his/her/their family as big as your own?

Sus precios son más bajos que los nuestros — Their prices are lower than our own

3 ¿Por qué prefieres este sombrero al mío? — Why do you prefer this hat to mine?

Su coche se parece al vuestro — His/her/their car looks like yours

4 Mi libro está encima del tuyo — My book is on top of yours

Su padre vive cerca del nuestro — His/her/their father lives near ours

Demonstrative Pronouns

	MASCULINE	FEMININE	NEUTER	
SING.	éste	ésta	esto	this
	ése	ésa	eso	that
	aquél	aquélla	aquello	
PLUR.	éstos	éstas		these
	ésos	ésas		those
	aquéllos	aquéllas		

The pronoun agrees in number and gender with the noun it replaces → ❶

The difference in meaning between the forms **ése** and **aquél** is the same as between the corresponding adjectives (see page 216).

The masculine and feminine forms have an accent, which is the only thing that differentiates them from the corresponding adjectives.

The neuter forms always refer to an idea or a statement or to an object when we want to identify it, etc, but never to specified nouns → ❷

An additional meaning of **aquél** is *the former*, and of **éste** *the latter* → ❸

Examples

1 ¿Qué abrigo te gusta más?
   — Éste de aquí
Aquella casa era más grande
   que ésta
estos libros y aquéllos

Quiero estas sandalias y ésas

Which coat do you like best?
   — This one here
That house was bigger than
   this one
these books and those (over
   there)
I'd like these sandals and those
   ones

2 No puedo creer que esto me
   esté pasando a mí
Eso de madrugar es algo que
   no le gusta

Aquello sí que me gustó
Esto es una bicicleta

I can't believe this is really
   happening to me
(This business of) getting up
   early is something she doesn't
   like
I really did like that
This is a bicycle

3 Hablaban Jaime y Andrés, éste a
   voces y aquél casi en un susurro

James and Andrew were talking,
   the latter in a loud voice and
   the former almost in a whisper

Adverbs

Formation

Most adverbs are formed by adding **-mente** to the feminine form of the adjective. Accents on the adjective are not affected since the suffix **-mente** is stressed independently → **1**

> ⓘ Note: **-mente** is omitted:
> - in the first of two or more of these adverbs when joined by a conjunction → **2**
> - in **recientemente** *recently* when immediately preceding a past participle → **3**
>   An accent is then needed on the last syllable (see page 296)

The following adverbs are formed in an irregular way:

bueno	→	**bien**
good		well
malo	→	**mal**
bad		badly

Adjectives used as adverbs

Certain adjectives are used adverbially. These include:
alto, **bajo**, **barato**, **caro**, **claro**, **derecho**, **fuerte** and **rápido** → **4**

> ⓘ Note: Other adjectives used as adverbs agree with the subject, and can normally be replaced by the adverb ending in **-mente** or an adverbial phrase → **5**

Position of adverbs

When the adverb accompanies a verb, it may either immediately follow it or precede it for emphasis → **6**

> ⓘ Note: The adverb can never be placed between **haber** and the past participle in compound tenses → **7**

When the adverb accompanies an adjective or another adverb, it generally precedes the adjective or adverb → **8**

Examples

❶ FEM ADJECTIVE

lenta slow
franca frank
feliz happy
fácil easy

ADVERB

lentamente slowly
francamente frankly
felizmente happily
fácilmente easily

❷ Lo hicieron lenta pero eficazmente

They did it slowly but efficiently

❸ El pan estaba recién hecho

The bread had just been baked

❹ hablar alto/bajo
cortar derecho
costar barato/caro
Habla muy fuerte
ver claro
correr rápido

to speak loudly/softly
to cut (in a) straight (line)
to be cheap/expensive
He talks very loudly
to see clearly
to run fast

❺ Esperaban impacientes
   (or impacientemente/
   con impaciencia)
Vivieron muy felices (or muy
   felizmente)

They were waiting impatiently

They lived very happily

❻ No conocemos aún al nuevo
   médico
Aún estoy esperando
Han hablado muy bien
Siempre le regalaban flores

We still haven't met the new
   doctor
I'm still waiting
They have spoken very well
They always gave her flowers

❼ Lo he hecho ya
No ha estado nunca en Italia

I've already done it
She's never been to Italy

❽ un sombrero muy bonito
hablar demasiado alto
mañana temprano
hoy mismo

a very nice hat
to talk too loud
early tomorrow
today

Adverbs

Comparatives and Superlatives

Comparatives

These are formed using the following constructions:

        más ... (que) more ... (than) → **1**
        menos ... (que) less ... (than) → **2**
        tanto como as much as → **3**
        tan ... como as ... as → **4**
        tan ... que so ... that → **5**
        demasiado ... para too ... to → **6**
        (lo) bastante ...
                            para enough to → **7**
        (lo) suficientemente ...
        cada vez más/menos more and more/less and less → **8**

Superlatives

These are formed by placing **más/menos** *the most/the least* before the adverb → **9**

lo is added before a superlative which is qualified → **10**

The absolute superlative (*very, most, extremely* + adverb) is formed by placing **muy** before the adverb. The form **-ísimo** (see also page 296) is also occasionally found → **11**

Adverbs with irregular comparatives/superlatives

ADVERB	COMPARATIVE	SUPERLATIVE
bien well	**mejor*** better	**(lo) mejor** (the) best
mal badly	**peor** worse	**(lo) peor** (the) worst
mucho a lot	**más** more	**(lo) más** (the) most
poco little	**menos** less	**(io) menos** (the) least

* **más bien** also exists, meaning *rather* → **12**

Examples

1. más de prisa — more quickly
   más abiertamente — more openly
   Mi hermana canta más fuerte que yo — My sister sings louder than me

2. menos fácilmente — less easily
   menos a menudo — less often
   Nos vemos menos frecuentemente que antes — We see each other less frequently than before

3. Daniel no lee tanto como Andrés — Daniel doesn't read as much as Andrew

4. Hágalo tan rápido como le sea posible — Do it as quickly as you can
   Ganan tan poco como nosotros — They earn as little as we do

5. Llegaron tan pronto que tuvieron que esperarnos — They arrived so early that they had to wait for us

6. Es demasiado tarde para ir al cine — It's too late to go to the cinema

7. Eres (lo) bastante grande para hacerlo solo — You're old enough to do it by yourself

8. Me gusta el campo cada vez más — I like the countryside more and more

9. María es la que corre más rápido — Maria is the one who runs fastest
   El que llegó menos tarde fue Miguel — Miguel was the one to arrive the least late

10. Lo hice lo más de prisa que pude — I did it as quickly as I could

11. muy lentamente — very slowly
    tempranísimo — extremely early
    muchísimo — very much

12. Era un hombre más bien bajito — He was a rather short man
    Estaba más bien inquieta que impaciente — I was restless rather than impatient

Common Adverbs and their Usage

Some common adverbs:

bastante	enough; quite → ❶
bien	well → ❷
cómo	how → ❸
cuánto	how much → ❹
demasiado	too much; too → ❺
más	more → ❻
menos	less → ❼
mucho	a lot; much → ❽
poco	little, not much; not very → ❾
siempre	always → ❿
también	also, too → ⓫
tan	as → ⓬
tanto	as much → ⓭
todavía/aún	still; yet; even → ⓮
ya	already → ⓯

bastante, **cuánto**, **demasiado**, **mucho**, **poco** and **tanto** are also used as adjectives that agree with the noun they qualify (see indefinite adjectives, page 224 and interrogative adjectives, page 218)

Examples

1. Es bastante tarde   It's quite late

2. ¡Bien hecho!   Well done!

3. ¡Cómo me ha gustado!   How I liked it!

4. ¿Cuánto cuesta este libro?   How much is this book?

5. He comido demasiado   I've eaten too much
   Es demasiado caro   It's too expensive

6. Mi hermano trabaja más ahora   My brother works more now
   Es más tímida que Sofía   She is shyer than Sophie

7. Se debe beber menos   One must drink less
   Estoy menos sorprendida que tú   I'm less surprised than you are

8. ¿Lees mucho?   Do you read a lot?
   ¿Está mucho más lejos?   Is it much further?

9. Comen poco   They don't eat (very) much
   María es poco decidida   Maria is not very daring

10. Siempre dicen lo mismo   They always say the same (thing)

11. A mí también me gusta   I like it too

12. Ana es tan alta como yo   Ana is as tall as I am

13. Nos aburrimos tanto como   We got as bored as you did
    vosotros

14. Todavía/aún tengo dos   I've still got two
    Todavía/aún no han llegado   They haven't arrived yet
    Mejor aún/todavía   Even better

15. Ya lo he hecho   I've done it already

Prepositions

On the following pages you will find some of the most frequent uses of prepositions in Spanish. Particular attention is paid to cases where usage differs markedly from English. It is often difficult to give an English equivalent for Spanish prepositions, since usage *does* vary so much between the two languages. In the list below, the broad meaning of the preposition is given on the left, with examples of usage following. Prepositions are dealt with in alphabetical order, except **a**, **de**, **en** and **por** which are shown first.

a

at	**echar algo a algn** to throw sth at sb
	a 50 euros el kilo (at) 50 euros a kilo
	a 100 km por hora at 100 km per hour
	sentarse a la mesa to sit down at the table
in	**al sol** in the sun
	a la sombra in the shade
onto	**cayeron al suelo** they fell onto the floor
	pegar una foto al álbum to stick a photo into the album
to	**ir al cine** to go to the cinema
	dar algo a algn to give sth to sb
	venir a hacer to come to do
from	**quitarle algo a algn** to take sth from sb
	robarle algo a algn to steal sth from sb
	arrebatarle algo a algn to snatch sth from sb
	comprarle algo a algn to buy sth from/for sb*
	esconderle algo a algn to hide sth from sb
means	**a mano** by hand
	a caballo on horseback
	(*but note other forms of transport used with* **en** *and* **por**)
	a pie on foot

* The translation here obviously depends on the context.

manner	**a la inglesa** in the English manner
	a pasos lentos with slow steps
	poco a poco little by little
	a ciegas blindly
time, date:	**a medianoche** at midnight
at, on	**a las dos y cuarto** at quarter past two
	a tiempo on time
	a final/fines de mes at the end of the month
	a veces at times
distance	**a 8 km de aquí** (at a distance of) 8 kms from here
	a dos pasos de mi casa just a step from my house
	a lo lejos in the distance
*with **el** + infin.*	**al levantarse** on getting up
	al abrir la puerta on opening the door
after certain adjectives	**dispuesto a todo** ready for anything
	parecido a esto similar to this
	obligado a ello obliged to (do) that
after certain verbs	see page 66

Personal a

When the direct object of a verb is a person or pet animal, **a** must always be placed immediately before it.

EXAMPLES: **querían mucho a sus hijos**
    they loved their children dearly
el niño miraba a su perro con asombro
    the boy kept looking at his dog in astonishment

EXCEPTIONS: **tener**
    to have
tienen dos hijos
    they have two children

Prepositions

de

from	**venir de Londres** to come from London
	un médico de Valencia a doctor from Valencia
	de la mañana a la noche from morning till night
	de 10 a 15 from 10 to 15
belonging to, of	**el sombrero de mi padre** my father's hat
	las lluvias de abril April showers
contents, composition, material	**una caja de cerillas** a box of matches
	una taza de té a cup of tea; a tea-cup
	un vestido de seda a silk dress
destined for	**una silla de cocina** a kitchen chair
	un traje de noche an evening dress
descriptive	**la mujer del sombrero verde** the woman with the green hat
	el vecino de al lad/lado the next door neighbour
manner	**de manera irregular** in an irregular way
	de una puñalada by stabbing
quality	**una mujer de edad** an aged lady
	objetos de valor valuable items
comparative + a number	**había más/menos de 100 personas** there were more/fewer than 100 people
in (after superlatives)	**la ciudad más/menos bonita del mundo** the most/least beautiful city in the world
after certain adjectives	**contento de ver** pleased to see
	fácil/difícil de entender easy/difficult to understand
	capaz de hacer capable of doing
after certain verbs	see page 66

Prepositions

en

in, at	**en el campo** in the country
	en Londres in London
	en la cama in bed
	con un libro en la mano with a book in his hand
	en voz baja in a low voice
	en la escuela in/at school
into	**entra en la casa** go into the house
	metió la mano en su bolso
	she put her hand into her handbag
on	**un cuadro en la pared** a picture on the wall
	sentado en una silla sitting on a chair
	en la planta baja on the ground floor
time, dates, months: at, in	**en este momento** at this moment
	en 1994 in 1994
	en enero in January
transport: by	**en coche** by car
	en avión by plane
	en tren by train (but see also **por**)
language	**en español** in Spanish
duration	**lo haré en una semana** I'll do it in one week
after certain adjectives	**es muy buena/mala en geografía**
	she is very good/bad at geography
	fueron los primeros/últimos/únicos en + *infin.*
	they were the first/last/only ones + *infin.*
after certain verbs	see page 66

Prepositions

por

motion: along, through, around	**vaya por ese camino** go along that path **por el túnel** through the tunnel **pasear por el campo** to walk around the countryside
vague location	**tiene que estar por aquí** it's got to be somewhere around here **le busqué por todas partes** I looked for him everywhere
vague time	**por la tarde** in the afternoon **por aquellos días** in those days
rate	**90 km por hora** 90 km per hour **un cinco por ciento** five per cent **ganaron por 3 a 0** they won by 3 to 0
by (*agent of passive*)	**descubierto por unos niños** discovered by some children **odiado por sus enemigos** hated by his enemies
by (*means of*)	**por barco** by boat **por tren** by train (freight) **por correo aéreo** by airmail **llamar por teléfono** to telephone
cause, reason: for, because	**¿por qué?** why?, for what reason? **por todo eso** because of all that **por lo que he oído** judging by what I've heard
+ *infinitive*: to	**libros por leer** books to be read **cuentas por pagar** bills to be paid
equivalence	**¿me tienes por tonto?** do you think I'm stupid?
+ *adjective*/+ *adverb* + **que**: however	**por buenos que sean** however good they are **por mucho que lo quieras** however much you want it

Prepositions

for	**¿cuanto me darán por este libro?** how much will they give me for this book?
	te lo cambio por éste I'll swap you this one for it
	no siento nada por ti I feel nothing for you
	si no fuera por ti if it weren't for you
	¡Por Dios! For God's sake!
for the benefit of	**lo hago por ellos** I do it for their benefit
on behalf of	**firma por mí** sign on my behalf

por also combines with other prepositions to form double prepositions usually conveying the idea of movement. The commonest of these are:

over	**saltó por encima de la mesa** she jumped over the table
under	**nadamos por debajo del puente** we swam under the bridge
past	**pasaron por delante de Correos** they went past the post office
behind	**por detrás de la puerta** behind the door
through	**la luz entraba por entre las cortinas** light was coming in through the curtains
+ **donde**	**¿por dónde has venido?** which way did you come?

ante

faced with, before	**lo hicieron ante mis propios ojos** they did it before my very eyes
	ante eso no se puede hacer nada one can't do anything when faced with that
preference	**la salud ante todo** health above all things

antes de

before (*time*)	**antes de las 5** before 5 o'clock

Prepositions

bajo/debajo de

These are usually equivalent, although **bajo** is used more frequently in a figurative sense and with temperatures.

under	**bajo/debajo de la cama** under the bed
	bajo el dominio romano under Roman rule
below	**un grado bajo cero** one degree below zero

con

with	**vino con su amigo** she came with her friend
after certain adjectives	**enfadado con ellos** angry with them
	magnánimo con sus súbditos
	magnanimous with his subjects

contra

against	**no tengo nada contra ti** I've nothing against you
	apoyado contra la pared leaning against the wall

delante de

in front of	**iba delante de mí** she was walking in front of me

desde

from	**desde aquí se puede ver** you can see it from here
	llamaban desde España
	they were phoning from Spain
	desde otro punto de vista
	from a different point of view
	desde la 1 hasta las 6 from 1 till 6
	desde entonces from then onwards
since	**desde que volvieron** since they returned

Prepositions

for
    viven en esa casa desde hace 3 años
      they've been living in that house for 3 years
      (*note tense*)

detrás de

behind
    están detrás de la puerta they are behind the door

durante

during
    durante la guerra during the war

for
    anduvieron durante 3 días they walked for 3 days

entre

between
    entre 8 y 10 between 8 and 10

among
    María y Elena, entre otras
      Maria and Elena, among others

reciprocal
    ayudarse entre sí to help each other

excepto

except (for)
    todos excepto tú everybody except you

hacia

towards
    van hacia ese edificio
      they're going towards that building

around (*time*)
    hacia las 3 at around 3 (o'clock)
    hacia fines de enero around the end of January

Prepositions

Hacia can also combine with some adverbs to convey a sense of motion in a particular direction:

hacia arriba upwards
hacia abajo downwards
hacia adelante forwards
hacia atrás backwards
hacia adentro inwards
hacia afuera outwards

hasta

until	**hasta la noche** until night
as far as	**viajaron hasta Sevilla** they travelled as far as Seville
up to	**conté hasta 300 ovejas** I counted up to 300 lambs **hasta ahora no los había visto** up to now I hadn't seen them
even	**hasta un tonto lo entendería** even an imbecile would understand that

para

for	**es para ti** it's for you **es para mañana** it's for tomorrow **una habitación para dos noches** a room for two nights **para ser un niño, lo hace muy bien** for a child he is very good at it **salen para Cádiz** they are leaving for Cádiz **se conserva muy bien para sus años** he keeps very well for his age
+ *infinitive*: (in order) to	**es demasiado torpe para comprenderlo** he's too stupid to understand
+ **sí**: to oneself	**hablar para sí** to talk to oneself **reír para sí** to laugh to oneself
with time	**todavía tengo para 1 hora** I'll be another hour (at it) yet

Prepositions

salvo

except (for)	**todos salvo él** all except him **salvo cuando llueve** except when it's raining
barring	**salvo imprevistos** barring the unexpected **salvo contraorden** unless you hear to the contrary

según

according to	**según su consejo** according to her advice **según lo que me dijiste** according to what you told me

sin

without	**sin agua/dinero** without water/money **sin mi marido** without my husband
+ *infinitive*	**sin contar a los otros** without counting the others

sobre

on	**sobre la cama** on the bed **sobre el armario** on (top of) the wardrobe
on (to)	**póngalo sobre la mesa** put it on the table
about, on	**un libro sobre Eva Perón** a book about Eva Perón
above, over	**volábamos sobre el mar** we were flying over the sea **la nube sobre aquella montaña** the cloud above that mountain
approximately	**vendré sobre las 4** I'll come about 4 o'clock
about	**Madrid tiene sobre 4 millones de habitantes** Madrid has about 4 million inhabitants

tras

behind	**está tras el asiento** it's behind the seat
after	**uno tras otro** one after another **día tras día** day after day **corrieron tras el ladrón** they ran after the thief

Conjunctions

There are conjunctions which introduce a main clause, such as **y** (*and*), **pero** (*but*), **si** (*if*), **o** (*or*) etc, and those which introduce subordinate clauses like **porque** (*because*), **mientras que** (*while*), **después de que** (*after*) etc. They are all used in much the same way as in English, but the following points are of note:

Some conjunctions in Spanish require a following subjunctive, see pages 60 to 63.

Some conjunctions are 'split' in Spanish like 'both ... and', 'either ... or' in English:

tanto ... como both ... and → **1**
ni ... ni neither ... nor → **2**
o (bien) ... o (bien) either ... or (else) → **3**
sea ... sea either ... or, whether ... or → **4**

y
- Before words beginning with **i-** or **hi-** + consonant it becomes **e** → **5**

o
- Before words beginning with **o-** or **ho-** it becomes **u** → **6**
- Between numerals it becomes **ó** → **7**

que
- meaning *that* → **8**
- in comparisons, meaning *than* → **9**
- followed by the subjunctive, see page 58.

porque (Not to be confused with **por qué** *why*)
- como should be used instead at the beginning of a sentence → **10**

pero, sino
- pero normally translates *but* → **11**
- sino is used when there is a direct contrast after a negative → **12**

Examples

1 Estas flores crecen tanto en verano como en invierno

These flowers grow in both summer and winter

2 Ni él ni ella vinieron
No tengo ni dinero ni comida

Neither he nor she came
I have neither money nor food

3 Debe de ser o ingenua o tonta

She must be either naïve or stupid

O bien me huyen o bien no me reconocen

Either they're avoiding me or else they don't recognize me

4 Sea en verano, sea en invierno, siempre me gusta andar

I always like walking, whether in summer or in winter

5 Diana e Isabel
madre e hija
BUT:
árboles y hierba

Diana and Isabel
mother and daughter

trees and grass

6 diez u once
minutos u horas

ten or eleven
minutes or hours

7 37 ó 38

37 or 38

8 Dicen que te han visto
¿Sabías que estábamos allí?

They say (that) they've seen you
Did you know that we were there?

9 Le gustan más que nunca
María es menos guapa que su hermana

He likes them more than ever
Maria is less attractive than her sister

10 Como estaba lloviendo no pudimos salir
(*Compare with*: No pudimos salir porque estaba lloviendo)

Because/As it was raining we couldn't go out

11 Me gustaría ir, pero estoy muy cansada

I'd like to go, but I am very tired

12 No es escocesa sino irlandesa

She is not Scottish but Irish

Suffixes

Augmentative, Diminutive and Pejorative Suffixes

These can be used after nouns, adjectives and some adverbs. They are attached to the end of the word after any final vowel has been removed:

    e.g.   **puerta** → **puertita**
           doctor → **doctorcito**

   ⓘ Note: Further changes sometimes take place (see page 300).

Augmentatives

These are used mainly to imply largeness, but they can also suggest clumsiness, ugliness or grotesqueness. The commonest augmentatives are:
    ón/ona → ❶
    azo/a → ❷
    ote/a → ❸

Diminutives

These are used mainly to suggest smallness or to express a feeling of affection. Occasionally they can be used to express ridicule or contempt. The commonest diminutives are:
    ito/a → ❹
    (e)cito/a → ❺
    (ec)illo/a → ❻
    (z)uelo/a → ❼

Pejoratives

These are used to convey the idea that something is unpleasant or to express contempt. The commonest suffixes are:
    ucho/a → ❽
    acho/a → ❾
    uzo/a → ❿
    uco/a → ⓫
    astro/a → ⓬

Examples

ORIGINAL WORD	DERIVED FORM
1 un hombre a man	un hombrón a big man
2 bueno good	buenazo (person) easily imposed on
un perro a dog	un perrazo a really big dog
gripe flu	un gripazo a really bad bout of flu
3 grande big	grandote huge
palabra word	palabrota swear word
amigo friend	amigote old pal
4 una casa a house	una casita a cottage
un poco a little	un poquito a little bit
un rato a while	un ratito a little while
mi hija my daughter	mi hijita my dear sweet daughter
despacio slowly	despacito nice and slowly
5 un viejo an old man	un viejecito a little old man
un pueblo a village	un pueblecito a small village
una voz a voice	una vocecita a sweet little voice
6 una ventana a window	una ventanilla a small window (car, train etc)
un chico a boy	un chiquillo a small boy
una campana a bell	una campanilla a small bell
un palo a stick	un palillo a toothpick
un médico a doctor	un mediquillo a quack (doctor)
7 los pollos the chickens	los polluelos the little chicks
hoyos hollows	hoyuelos dimples
un ladrón a thief	un ladronzuelo a petty thief
una mujer a woman	una mujerzuela a whore
8 un animal an animal	un animalucho a wretched animal
un cuarto a room	un cuartucho a poky little room
una casa a house	una casucha a shack
9 rico rich	ricacho nouveau riche
10 gente people	gentuza scum
11 una ventana a window	un ventanuco a miserable little window
12 un político a politician	un politicastro a third-rate politician

Sentence structure

Word Order

Word order in Spanish is much more flexible than in English. You can often find the subject placed after the verb or the object before the verb, either for emphasis or for stylistic reasons → ❶

There are some cases, however, where the order is always different from English. Most of these have already been dealt with under the appropriate part of speech, but are summarized here along with other instances not covered elsewhere.

> Object pronouns nearly always come before the verb → ❷
> For details, see pages 232 to 235.
>
> Qualifying adjectives nearly always come after the noun → ❸
> For details, see page 228.
>
> Following direct speech the subject always follows the verb → ❹

For word order in negative sentences, see page 276.

For word order in interrogative sentences, see page 280 → ❶

Examples

1 Ese libro te lo di yo   I gave you that book
No nos vio nadie   Nobody saw us

2 Ya los veo   I can see them now
Me lo dieron ayer   They gave it to me yesterday

3 Ya los veo   I can see them now
Me lo dieron ayer   They gave it to me yesterday

4 una ciudad española   a Spanish town
vino tinto   red wine

5 – Pienso que sí – dijo María   'I think so,' said Maria
– No importa – replicó Daniel   'It doesn't matter,' Daniel replied

Negatives

A sentence is made negative by adding **no** between the subject and the verb (and any preceding object pronouns) → ❶

There are, however, some points to note:
- in phrases like *not her, not now*, etc the Spanish **no** usually comes after the word it qualifies → ❷
- with verbs of saying, hoping, thinking etc *not* is translated by **que no** → ❸

Double negatives

The following are the most common negative pairs:

no ... nada nothing (*not ... anything*)
no ... nadie nobody (*not ... anybody*)
no ... más no longer (*not ... any more*)
no ... nunca never (*not ... ever*)
no ... jamás never (stronger) (*not ... ever*)
no ... más que only (*not ... more than*)
no ... ningún(o)(a) no (*not any*)
no ... tampoco not ... either
no ... ni ... ni neither ... nor
no ... ni siquiera not even

Word order

No precedes the verb (and any object pronouns) in both simple and compound tenses, and the second element follows the verb → ❹

Sometimes the above negatives are placed before the verb (with the exception of **más** and **más que**), and **no** is then dropped → ❺

For use of **nada**, **nadie** and **ninguno** as pronouns, see page 240.

Examples

AFFIRMATIVE		NEGATIVE
1 El coche es suyo	→	El coche no es suyo
The car is his		The car is not his
Yo me lo pondré	→	Yo no me lo pondré
I will put it on		I will not put it on

2 ¿Quién lo ha hecho? — Ella no   Who did it? — Not her
¿Quieres un cigarrillo?   Do you want a cigarette?
   — Ahora no   — Not now
Dame ese libro, el que está a tu   Give me that book, not the one
   lado no, el otro   near you, the other one

3 Opino que no   I think not
Dijeron que no   They said not

4 No dicen nada   They don't say anything
No han visto a nadie   They haven't seen anybody
No me veréis más   You won't see me any more
No te olvidaré nunca/jamás   I'll never forget you
No habían recorrido más que   They hadn't travelled more than
   40 kms cuando ...   40 kms when ...
No se me ha ocurrido ninguna idea   I haven't had any ideas
No les estaban esperando ni mi   Neither my son nor my daughter
   hijo ni mi hija   were waiting for them
No ha venido ni siquiera Juan   Even John hasn't come

5 Nadie ha venido hoy   Nobody came today
Nunca me han gustado   I've never liked them
Ni mi hermano ni mi hermana   Neither my brother nor my sister
   fuman   smokes

Sentence structure

Negatives *continued*

Negatives in short replies

No *no* is the usual negative response to a question → **1**

> (i) Note: It is often translated as 'not' → **2**
> (see also page 276)

Nearly all the other negatives listed on page 276 may be used without a verb in a short reply → **3**

Combination of negatives

These are the most common combinations of negative particles:
    no … nunca más → **4**
    no … nunca a nadie → **5**
    no … nunca nada/nada nunca → **6**
    no … nunca más que → **7**
    no … ni … nunca … → **8**

Examples

1 ¿Quieres venir con nosotros? — No

Do you want to come with us? — No

2 ¿Vienes o no?

Are you coming or not?

3 ¿Ha venido alguien? — ¡Nadie! ¿Has ido al Japón alguna vez? — Nunca

Has anyone come? — Nobody! Have you ever been to Japan? — Never

4 No lo haré nunca más

I'll never do it again

5 No se ve nunca a nadie por allí

You never see anybody around there

6 No cambiaron nada nunca

They never changed anything

7 No he hablado nunca más que con su mujer

I've only ever spoken to his wife

8 No me ha escrito ni llamado por teléfono nunca

He/she has never written to me or phoned me

Sentence structure

Question Forms

Direct

There are two ways of forming direct questions in Spanish:

by inverting the normal word order so that
subject + verb → *verb + subject* → ❶

by maintaining the word order *subject + verb*, but by using a rising
intonation at the end of the sentence → ❷

ⓘ Note: In compound tenses the auxiliary may never be
separated from the past participle, as happens in English → ❸

Indirect

An indirect question is one that is 'reported', e.g. he asked me 'what the
time was', tell me 'which way to go'. Word order in indirect questions can
adopt one of the two following patterns:

interrogative word + subject + verb → ❹

interrogative word + verb + subject → ❺

¿verdad?, ¿no?

These are used wherever English would use 'isn't it?', 'don't they?', 'weren't
we?', 'is it?' etc tagged on to the end of a sentence → ❻

sí

Sí is the word for 'yes' in answer to a question put either in the affirmative
or in the negative → ❼

Examples

1
¿Vendrá tu madre?
¿Lo trajo Vd?
¿Es posible eso?
¿Cuándo volverán Vds?

Will your mother come?
Did you bring it?
Is it possible?
When will you come back?

2
El gato, ¿se bebió toda la leche?
Andrés, ¿va a venir?

Did the cat drink up all his milk?
Is Andrew coming?

3
¿Lo ha terminado Vd?
¿Había llegado tu amigo?

Have you finished it?
Had your friend arrived?

4
Dime qué autobuses pasan por aquí
No sé cuántas personas vendrán

Tell me which buses come this way
I don't know how many people will turn up

5
Me preguntó dónde trabajaba mi hermano
No sabemos a qué hora empieza la película

He asked me where my brother worked
We don't know what time the film starts

6
Hace calor, ¿verdad?
No se olvidará Vd, ¿verdad?
Estaréis cansados, ¿no?
Te lo dijo María, ¿no?

It's warm, isn't it?
You won't forget, will you?
You will be tired, won't you?
Maria told you, didn't she?

7
¿Lo has hecho? — Sí
¿No lo has hecho? — Sí

Have you done it? — Yes (I have)
Haven't you done it? — Yes (I have)

Translation problems

Beware of translating word by word. While on occasions this is possible, quite often it is not. The need for caution is illustrated by the following:

English phrasal verbs (i.e. verbs followed by a preposition), e.g. 'to run away', 'to fall down', are often translated by one word in Spanish → ❶

English verbal constructions often contain a preposition where none exists in Spanish, or vice versa → ❷

Two or more prepositions in English may have a single rendering in Spanish → ❸

A word which is singular in English may be plural in Spanish, or vice versa → ❹

Spanish has no equivalent of the possessive construction denoted by ...'s/...s' → ❺

Problems

-ing

This is translated in a variety of ways in Spanish:

'to be ... -ing' can sometimes be translated by a simple tense (see also pages 54 to 56) → ❻
But, when a physical position is denoted, a past participle is used → ❼

in the construction 'to see/hear sb ... -ing', use an infinitive → ❽
'-ing' can also be translated by:
- an infinitive, see page 46 → ❾
- a perfect infinitive, see page 50 → ❿
- a gerund, see page 52 → ⓫
- a noun → ⓬

Examples

1. huir — to run away
   caerse — to fall down
   ceder — to give in

2. pagar — to pay for
   mirar — to look at
   escuchar — to listen to
   encontrarse con — to meet
   fijarse en — to notice
   servirse de — to use

3. extrañarse de — to be surprised at
   harto de — fed up with
   soñar con — to dream of
   contar con — to count on

4. unas vacaciones — a holiday
   sus cabellos — his/her hair
   la gente — people
   mi pantalón — my trousers

5. el coche de mi hermano — my brother's car
      (*literally*: ... of my brother)

   el cuarto de las niñas — the children's bedroom
      (*literally*: ... of the children)

6. Se va mañana — He/she is leaving tomorrow
   ¿Qué haces? — What are you doing?

7. Está sentado ahí — He is sitting over there
   Estaba tendida en el suelo — She was lying on the ground

8. Les veo venir — I can see them coming
   La he oído cantar — I've heard her singing

9. Me gusta ir al cine — I like going to the cinema

10. ¡Deja de hablar! — Stop talking!
    En vez de contestar — Instead of answering
    Antes de salir — Before leaving
    Después de haber abierto la caja, María ... — After opening the box, Maria ...

11. Pasamos la tarde fumando y charlando — We spent the afternoon smoking and chatting

12. El esquí me mantiene en forma — Skiing keeps me fit

Translation problems

to be (*See also Verbal Idioms*, pages 74 to 76)

In set expressions, describing physical and emotional conditions, **tener** is used:

> **tener calor/frío** to be warm/cold
> **tener hambre/sed** to be hungry/thirsty
> **tener miedo** to be afraid
> **tener razón** to be right

Describing the weather, e.g. 'what's the weather like?', 'it's windy/sunny', use **hacer** → ❶

For ages, e.g. 'he is 6', use **tener** (see also page 310) → ❷

there is/there are

Both are translated by **hay** → ❸

can, be able

Physical ability is expressed by **poder** → ❹

If the meaning is 'to know how to', use **saber** → ❺

'Can' + a 'verb of hearing or seeing etc' in English is not translated in Spanish → ❻

to

Generally translated by **a** → ❼

In time expressions, e.g. 10 to 6, use **menos** → ❽

When the meaning is 'in order to', use **para** → ❾

Following a verb, as in 'to try to do', 'to like to do', see pages 46 and 48.

'easy/difficult/impossible' etc 'to do' are translated by **fácil/difícil/imposible** etc **de hacer** → ❿

Examples

1 ¿Qué tiempo hace?
Hace bueno/malo/viento

What's the weather like?
It's lovely/miserable/windy

2 ¿Cuántos años tienes?
Tengo quince (años)

How old are you?
I'm fifteen

3 Hay un señor en la puerta
Hay cinco libros en la mesa

There's a gentleman at the door
There are five books on the table

4 No puedo salir contigo

I can't go out with you

5 ¿Sabes nadar?

Can you swim?

6 No veo nada
¿Es que no me oyes?

I can't see anything
Can't you hear me?

7 Dale el libro a Isabel

Give the book to Isabel

8 las diez menos cinco
a las siete menos cuarto

five to ten
at a quarter to seven

9 Lo hice para ayudaros
Se inclinó para atarse el cordón
  de zapato

I did it to help you
He bent down to tie his
  shoe-lace

10 Este libro es fácil/difícil de leer

This book is easy/difficult to read

must

When *must* expresses an assumption, **deber de** is often used → **①**

> ⓘ Note: This meaning is also often expressed by **deber** directly followed by the infinitive → **②**

When it expresses obligation, there are three possible translations:
- **tener que** → **③**
- **deber** → **④**
- **hay que** (impersonal) → **⑤**

may

If *may* expresses possibility, it can be translated by:
- **poder** → **⑥**
- **puede (ser) que** + *subjunctive*

To express permission, use **poder** → **⑦**

will

If *will* expresses willingness or desire rather than the future, the present tense of **querer** is used → **⑧**

would

If *would* expresses willingness, use the preterite or imperfect of **querer** → **⑨**

When a repeated or habitual action in the past is referred to, use
- the imperfect → **⑩**
- the imperfect of **soler** + *infinitive* → **⑪**

Examples

1 Ha debido de mentir
He must have lied
Debe de gustarle
She must like it

2 Debe estar por aquí cerca
It must be near here
Debo haberlo dejado en el tren
I must have left it on the train

3 Tenemos que salir temprano mañana
We must leave early tomorrow
Tengo que irme
I must go

4 Debo visitarles
I must visit them
Debéis escuchar lo que se os dice
You must listen to what is said to you

5 Hay que entrar por ese lado
One (We etc) must get in that way

6 Todavía puede cambiar de opinión
He may still change his mind
Creo que puede llover esta tarde
I think it may rain this afternoon
Puede (ser) que no lo sepa
She may not know

7 ¿Puedo irme?
May I go?
Puede sentarse
You may sit down

8 Quiere Vd esperar un momento, por favor?
Will you wait a moment, please?
No quiere ayudarme
He won't help me

9 No quisieron venir
They wouldn't come

10 Las miraba hora tras hora
She would watch them for hours on end

11 Últimamente solía comer muy poco
Latterly he would eat very little

Pronunciation of Vowels

Spanish vowels are always clearly pronounced and not relaxed in unstressed syllables as happens in English.

	EXAMPLES	HINTS ON PRONUNCIATION
[a]	casa	Between English *a* as in *hat* and *u* as in *hut*
[e]	pensar	Similar to English *e* in *pet*
[i]	filo	Between English *i* as in *pin* and *ee* as in *been*
[o]	loco	Similar to English *o* in *hot*
[u]	luna	Between English *ew* as in *few* and *u* as in *put*

Pronunciation of Diphthongs

All these diphthongs are shorter than similar English diphthongs.

[ai]	baile hay	Like *i* in *side*
[au]	causa	Like *ou* in *sound*
[ei]	peine rey	Like *ey* in *grey*
[eu]	deuda	Like the vowel sounds in English *may you*, but without the sound of the *y*
[oi]	boina voy	Like *oy* in *boy*

Semi-consonants

[j]	hacia ya tiene yeso labio yo	*i* following a consonant and preceding a vowel, and **y** preceding a vowel are pronounced as *y* in English *yet*
[w]	agua bueno arduo ruido	*u* following a consonant and preceding a vowel is pronounced as *w* in English *walk*

EXCEPTIONS: **gue, gui** (see page 290)

Pronunciation

Pronunciation of Consonants

Some consonants are pronounced almost exactly as in English:
[l, m, n, f, k, and in some cases g].

Others, listed below, are similar to English, but differences should be noted.

	EXAMPLES	HINTS ON PRONUNCIATION
[p]	**p**adre	They are not aspirated, unlike
[k]	**c**o**c**o	English *p*ot, *c*ook and ten.
[t]	**t**an	
[t]	**t**odo **t**ú	Pronounced with the tip of the
[d]	**d**oy bal**d**e	tongue touching the upper front teeth and not the roof of the mouth as in English.

The following consonants are not heard in English:

[β]	la**b**io	This is pronounced between upper and lower lips, which do not touch, unlike English *b* as in *b*end.
[ɣ]	ha**g**a	Similar to English *g* as in *g*ate, but tongue does not touch the soft palate.
[ɲ]	a**ñ**o	Similar to *ni* in o*ni*on
[x]	**j**ota	Like the guttural *ch* in lo*ch*
[ɾ]	pe**r**a	A single trill with the tip of the tongue against the teeth ridge.
[rr]	**r**ojo pe**rr**o	A multiple trill with the tip of the tongue against the teeth ridge.

From Spelling to Sounds

Note the pronunciation of the following (groups of) letters.

LETTER	PRONOUNCED	EXAMPLES
b,v	[b]	These letters have the same value. At the start of a breath group, and after written **m** and **n**, the sound is similar to English *boy* → ❶
	[β]	in all other positions, the sound is unknown in English (see page 289) → ❷
c	[k]	Before **a**, **o**, **u** or a consonant, like English *keep*, but not aspirated → ❸
	[θ/s]	Before **e**, **i** like English *thin*, or, in Latin America and parts of Spain, like English *same* → ❹
ch	[tʃ]	Like English *church* → ❺
d	[d]	At the start of the breath group and after **l** or **n**, it is pronounced similar to English *deep* (see page 289) → ❻
	[ð]	Between vowels and after consonants (except **l** or **n**), it is pronounced very like English *though* → ❼
	[(ð)]	At the end of words, and in the verb ending **-ado**, it is often not pronounced → ❽
g	[x]	Before **e**, **i**, pronounced gutturally, similar to English lo*ch* → ❾
	[g]	At the start of the breath group and after **n**, it is pronounced like English *get* → ❿
	[ɣ]	In other positions the sound is unknown in English → ⓫
gue	[ge/ɣe]	The **u** is silent → ⓬
gui	[gi/ɣi]	
güe	[gwe/ɣwe]	The **u** is pronounced like English
güi	[gwi/ɣwi]	*walk* → ⓭

Examples

1 bomba ['bomba]   voy [boi]   vicio ['biθjo]

2 hubo ['uβo]   de veras [de 'βeras]   lavar [la'βar]

3 casa ['kasa]   coco ['koko]   cumbre ['kumbre]

4 cero ['θero/'sero]   cinco ['θiŋko/'siŋko]

5 mucho ['mutʃo]   chuchería [tʃutʃe'ria]

6 doy [doi]   balde ['balde]   bondad [bon'dað]

7 modo ['moðo]   ideal [iðe'al]

8 Madrid [ma'ðri(ð)]   comprado [kom'pra(ð)o]

9 gente ['xente]   giro ['xiro]   general [xene'ral]

10 ganar [ga'nar]   pongo ['poŋgo]

11 agua ['aɣwa]   agrícola [a'ɣrikola]

12 guija ['gixa]   guerra ['gerra]   pague ['paɣe]

13 agüero [a'ɣwero]   argüir [ar'ɣwir]

From Spelling to Sounds *continued*

LETTER	PRONOUNCED	EXAMPLES
h	[-]	This is always silent → ❶
j	[x]	Like the guttural sound in English lo*ch*, but often aspirated at the end of a word → ❷
ll	[ʎ]	Similar to English -*ll*- in mi*lli*on → ❸
	[j/ʒ]	In some parts of Spain and in Latin America, like English yet or pleasure → ❹
-nv-	[mb]	This combination of letters is pronounced as in English i*mb*ibe → ❺
ñ	[ɲ]	As in English o*ni*on → ❻
q	[k]	Always followed by silent letter **u**, and pronounced as in English keep, but not aspirated → ❼
s	[s]	Except where mentioned below, like English sing → ❽
	[z]	When followed by **b, d, g, l, m, n** like English zoo → ❾
w	[w]	Like English v, w → ❿
x	[ks]	Between vowels, often like English exit → ⓫
	[s]	Before a consonant, and, increasingly, even between vowels, like English send → ⓬
y	[j]	Like English yes → ⓭
	[ʒ]	In some parts of Latin America, like English leisure → ⓮
z	[θ]	Like English thin → ⓯
	[s]	In some parts of Spain and in Latin America, like English send → ⓰

Examples

① hombre ['ombre]   hoja ['oxa]   ahorrar [ao'rrar]

② jota ['xota]   tejer [te'xer]   reloj [re'lo(h)]

③ calle ['kaʎe]   llamar [ʎa'mar]

④ pillar [pi'jar/pi'ʒar] olla ['oja/'oʒa]

⑤ enviar [em'bjar]   sin valor ['sim ba'lor]

⑥ uña ['uɲa]   bañar [ba'ɲar]

⑦ aquel [a'kel]   querer [ke'rer]

⑧ está [es'ta]   serio ['serjo]

⑨ desde ['dezðe]   mismo ['mizmo]   asno ['azno]

⑩ wáter ['bater]   Walkman® [wak'man]

⑪ éxito ['eksito]   máximo ['maksimo]

⑫ extra ['estra]   sexto ['sesto]

⑬ yo [jo]   yedra ['jeðra]

⑭ yeso ['ʒeso]   yerno ['ʒerno]

⑮ zapato [θa'pato]   zona ['θona]   luz [luθ]

⑯ zaguán [sa'ʎwan]   zueco ['sweko]   pez [pes]

Normal Word Stress

There are simple rules to establish which syllable in a Spanish word is stressed. When an exception to these rules occurs an acute accent (stress-mark) is needed (see page 296). These rules are as follows:

- words ending in a vowel or combination of vowels, or with the consonants **-s** or **-n** are stressed on the next to last syllable. The great majority of Spanish words fall into this category → **❶**
- words ending in a consonant other than **-s** or **-n** bear the stress on the last syllable → **❷**
- a minority of words bear the stress on the second to last syllable, and these always need an accent → **❸**
- some nouns change their stress from singular to plural → **❹**

Stress in Diphthongs

In the case of diphthongs there are rules to establish which of the vowels is stressed (see page 288 for pronunciation). These rules are as follows:

- diphthongs formed by the combination of a 'weak' vowel (**i**, **u**) and a 'strong' vowel (**a**, **e** or **o**) bear the stress on the strong vowel → **❺**
- diphthongs formed by the combination of two 'weak' vowels bear the stress on the second vowel → **❻**

  ⓘ Note: Two 'strong' vowels don't form a diphthong but are pronounced as two separate vowels. In these cases stress follows the normal rules → **❼**

Examples

1 **ca**sa house
corre he runs
pala**bra** word
crisis crisis

casas houses
corren they run
pala**bra**s words
crisis crises

2 rel**oj** watch
ver**dad** truth
bati**dor** beater

3 mur**cié**lago bat
pájaro bird

4 car**á**cter character
r**é**gimen regime

caract**e**res characters
reg**í**menes regimes

5 **ba**ile dance
boina beret
peine comb
causa cause
reina queen

6 f**ui** I went
vi**u**do widower

7 me ma**re**o I feel dizzy
ca**er** to fall
caos chaos
co**rrea** leash

Spelling

The Acute Accent (´)

This is used in writing to show that a word is stressed contrary to the normal rules for stress (see page 294) → ❶

The following points should be noted:

The same syllable is stressed in the plural form of adjectives and nouns as in the singular. To show this, it is necessary to
- add an accent in the case of unaccented nouns and adjectives ending in **-n** → ❷
- drop the accent from nouns and adjectives ending in **-n** or **-s** which have an accent on the last syllable → ❸

The feminine form of accented nouns or adjectives does not have an accent → ❹

When object pronouns are added to certain verb forms an accent is required to show that the syllable stressed in the verb form does not change. These verb forms are:
- the gerund → ❺
- the infinitive, when followed by two pronouns → ❻
- imperative forms, except for the 2nd person plural → ❼

The absolute superlative forms of adjectives are always accented → ❽

Accents on adjectives are not affected by the addition of the adverbial suffix **-mente** → ❾

Examples

❶ autobús
bus
relámpago
lightning

revolución
revolution
árboles
trees

❷ orden → órdenes
order orders
examen → exámenes
examination examinations
joven → jóvenes
young young

❸ revolución → revoluciones
revolution revolutions
autobús → autobuses
bus buses
parlanchín → parlanchines
chatty chatty

❹ marqués → marquesa
marquis marchioness
francés → francesa
French (*masc*) French (*fem*)

❺ comprando → comprándo(se)lo
buying buying it (for him/her/them)

❻ vender → vendérselas
to sell to sell them to him/her/them

❼ compra → cómpralo
buy buy it
hagan → hágenselo
do do it for him/her/them

❽ viejo → viejísimo
old ancient
caro → carísimo
expensive very expensive

❾ fácil → fácilmente
easy easily

The Acute Accent *continued*

It is also used to distinguish between the written forms of words which are pronounced the same but have a different meaning or function. These are as follows:

Possessive adjectives/personal pronouns → **❶**

Demonstrative adjectives/demonstrative pronouns → **❷**

Interrogative and exclamatory forms of adverbs, pronouns and adjectives → **❸**

ⓘ Note: The accent is used in indirect as well as direct questions and exclamations → **❹**

The pronoun **él** and the article **el** → **❺**

A small group of words which could otherwise be confused. These are:

de	of, from	**dé**	give (*pres. subj.*)
mas	but	**más**	more
si	if	**sí**	yes; himself etc → **❻**
solo/a	alone	**sólo**	only → **❼**
te	you	**té**	tea

The Dieresis (¨)

This is used only in the combinations **güi** or **güe** to show that the **u** is pronounced as a semi-consonant (see page 288) → **❽**

Examples

① Han robado mi coche — They've stolen my car
A mí no me vio — He didn't see me
¿Te gusta tu trabajo? — Do you like your job?
Tú, ¿que opinas? — What do you think?

② Me gusta esta casa — I like this house
Me quedo con ésta — I'll take this one
¿Ves aquellos edificios? — Can you see those buildings?
Aquéllos son más bonitos — Those are prettier

③ El chico con quien viajé — The boy I travelled with
¿Con quién viajaste? — Who did you travel with?
Donde quieras — Wherever you want
¿Dónde encontraste eso? — Where did you find that?

④ ¿Cómo se abre? — How does it open?
No sé cómo se abre — I don't know how it opens

⑤ El puerto queda cerca — The harbour's nearby
Él no quiso hacerlo — *He* refused to do it

⑥ si no viene — if he doesn't come
Sí que lo sabe — Yes he *does* know

⑦ Vino solo — He came by himself
Sólo lo sabe él — Only he knows

⑧ ¡Qué vergüenza! — How shocking!
En seguida averigüé dónde estaba — I found out straight away where it was

Spelling

Regular Spelling Changes

The consonants **c**, **g** and **z** are modified by the addition of certain verb or plural endings and by some suffixes. Most of the cases where this occurs have already been dealt with under the appropriate part of speech, but are summarized here along with other instances not covered elsewhere.

Verbs

The changes set out below occur so that the consonant of the verb stem is always pronounced the same as in the infinitive. For verbs affected by these changes see the list of verbs on page 81.

INFINITIVE	CHANGE			TENSES AFFECTED	
-car	c + e	→	-que	Present subj, pret →	❶
-cer, -cir	c + a, o	→	-za, -zo	Present, pres subj →	❷
-gar	g + e, i	→	-gue	Present subj, pret →	❸
-guar	gu + e	→	-güe	Present subj, pret →	❹
-ger, -gir	g + a, o	→	-ja, -jo	Present, pres subj →	❺
-guir	gu + a, o	→	-ga, -go	Present, pres subj →	❻
-zar	z + e	→	-ce	Present subj, pret →	❼

Noun and adjective plurals

SINGULAR			PLURAL	
vowel + z	→		-ces →	❽

Nouns and adjectives + suffixes

ENDING	SUFFIX	NEW ENDING	
vowel + z +	-cito	-cecito →	❾
-go, -ga +	-ito, -illo	-guito/a, -guillo/a →	❿
-co, -ca +	-ito, -illo	-quito/a, -quillo/a →	⓫

Adjective absolute superlatives

ENDING	SUPERLATVE	
-co	-quísimo →	⓬
-go	-guísimo →	�13
vowel + z	-císimo →	�14

Examples

1 Es inútil que lo busques aquí — It's no good looking for it here
Saqué dos entradas — I got two tickets

2 Hace falta que venzas tu miedo — You must overcome your fear

3 No creo que lleguemos antes — I don't think we'll be there any sooner

Ya le pagué — I've already paid her

4 Averigüé dónde estaba la casa — I found out where the house was

5 Cojo el autobús, es más barato — I take the bus, it's cheaper

6 ¿Sigo? — Shall I go on?

7 No permiten que se cruce la frontera — They don't allow people to cross the border
Nunca simpaticé mucho con él — I never got on very well with him

8
voz	→	voces	luz	→	luces
voice		voices	light		lights
veloz	→	veloces	capaz	→	capaces
quick			capable		

9 luz → lucecita
light   little light

10 amigo → amiguito
friend   chum

11 chico → chiquillo
boy   little boy

12 rico → riquísimo
rich   extremely rich

13 largo → larguísimo
long   very, very long

14 feroz → ferocísimo
fierce   extremely fierce

The Alphabet

A, a [a]	J, j ['xota]	R, r ['erre]
B, b [be]	K, k [ka]	S, s ['ese]
C, c [θe]	L, l ['ele]	T, t [te]
Ch, ch [tʃe]	Ll, ll ['eʎe]	U, u [u]
D, d [de]	M, m ['eme]	V, v ['uβe]
E, e [e]	N, n ['ene]	W, w ['uβe'doble]
F, f ['efe]	Ñ, ñ ['eɲe]	X, x ['ekis]
G, g [xe]	O, o [o]	Y, y [i'ɣrjeɣa]
H, h ['atʃe]	P, p [pe]	Z, z ['θeta]
I, i [i]	Q, q [ku]	

The letters are feminine and you therefore talk of **una a**, or **la a**.

Capital letters are used as in English except for the following:

adjectives of nationality:
e.g. **una ciudad alemana** a German town
un autor español a Spanish author

languages:
e.g. **¿Habla Vd inglés?** Do you speak English?
Hablan español e italiano They speak Spanish and Italian

days of the week:

lunes Monday	**viernes** Friday
martes Tuesday	**sábado** Saturday
miércoles Wednesday	**domingo** Sunday
jueves Thursday	

months of the year:

enero January	**julio** July
febrero February	**agosto** August
marzo March	**se(p)tiembre** September
abril April	**octubre** October
mayo May	**noviembre** November
junio June	**diciembre** December

Punctuation

Spanish punctuation differs from English in the following ways:

Question marks

There are inverted question marks and exclamation marks at the beginning of a question or exclamation, as well as upright ones at the end.

Indications of dialogue

Dashes are used to indicate dialogue, and are equivalent to the English inverted commas:

> – **¿Vendrás conmigo? – le preguntó María**
> 'Will you come with me?' Maria asked him

ⓘ Note: When no expression of saying, replying etc follows, only one dash is used at the beginning:
– **Sí.** 'Yes.'

Letter headings

At the beginning of a letter, a colon is used instead of the English comma:
Querida Cristina: Dear Cristina, Muy Sr. mío: Dear Sir,

Punctuation terms in Spanish

.	**punto**		!	**se cierra admiración**
,	**coma**		" "	**comillas** (used as '...')
;	**punto y coma**		"	**se abren comillas**
:	**dos puntos**		"	**se cierran comillas**
...	**puntos suspensivos**		( )	**paréntesis**
¿?	**interrogación**		(	**se abre paréntesis**
¿	**se abre interrogación**		)	**se cierra paréntesis**
?	**se cierra interrogación**		–	**guión**
¡!	**admiración**			
¡	**se abre admiración**	**punto y aparte**	new paragraph	
		punto final	last full stop	

Numbers

Cardinal (one, two, three *etc*)

cero	0	setenta	70
uno (un, una)	1	ochenta	80
dos	2	noventa	90
tres	3	cien (ciento)	100
cuatro	4	ciento uno(una)	101
cinco	5	ciento dos	102
seis	6	ciento diez	110
siete	7	ciento cuarenta y dos	142
ocho	8	doscientos(as)	200
nueve	9	doscientos(as) uno(una)	201
diez	10	doscientos(as) dos	202
once	11	trescientos(as)	300
doce	12	cuatrocientos(as)	400
trece	13	quinientos(as)	500
catorce	14	seiscientos(as)	600
quince	15	setecientos(as)	700
dieciséis	16	ochocientos(as)	800
diecisiete	17	novecientos(as)	900
dieciocho	18	mil	1.000
diecinueve	19	mil uno(una)	1.001
veinte	20	mil dos	1.002
veintiuno	21	mil doscientos veinte	1.220
veintidós	22	dos mil	2.000
treinta	30	cien mil	100.000
treinta y uno	31	doscientos(as) mil	200.000
cuarenta	40	un millón	1.000.000
cincuenta	50	dos millones	2.000.000
sesenta	60	un billón	1.000.000.000.000

Fractions

un medio; medio(a)	½
un tercio	⅓
dos tercios	⅔
un cuarto	¼
tres cuartos	¾
un quinto	⅕
cinco y tres cuartos	5¾

Others

cero coma cinco	0,5
uno coma tres	1,3
(el, un) diez por ciento	10%
dos más/y dos	2 + 2
dos menos dos	2 − 2
dos por dos	2 × 2
dos dividido por dos	2 ÷ 2

Numbers

Points to note on cardinals

uno drops the **o** before masculine nouns, and the same applies when in compound numerals:
- **un libro** 1 book, **treinta y un niños** 31 children

1, 21, 31 etc and 200, 300, 400 etc have feminine forms:
- **cuarenta y una euros** 41 euros, **quinientas libras** £500

ciento is used before numbers smaller than 100, otherwise **cien** is used:
- **ciento cuatro** 104 but **cien euros** 100 euros, **cien mil** 100,000 (see also page 210)

millón takes **de** before a noun:
- **un millón de personas** 1,000,000 people

mil is only found in the plural when meaning thousands of:
- **miles de solicitantes** thousands of applicants

cardinals normally precede ordinals:
- **los tres primeros pisos** the first three floors

ⓘ Note: The full stop is used with numbers over one thousand and the comma with decimals i.e. the opposite of English usage.

Numbers

Ordinal Numbers (first, second, third *etc*)

primero (primer, primera)	$1°,1^a$	undécimo(a)	$11°,11^a$
segundo(a)	$2°,2^a$	duodécimo(a)	$12°,12^a$
tercero (tercer, tercera)	$3°,3^a$	decimotercer(o)(a)	$13°,13^a$
cuarto(a)	$4°,4^a$	decimocuarto(a)	$14°,14^a$
quinto(a)	$5°,5^a$	decimoquinto(a)	$15°,15^a$
sexto(a)	$6°,6^a$	decimosexto(a)	$16°,16^a$
séptimo(a)	$7°,7^a$	decimoséptimo(a)	$17°,17^a$
octavo(a)	$8°,8^a$	decimoctavo(a)	$18°,18^a$
noveno(a)	$9°,9^a$	decimonoveno(a)	$19°,19^a$
décimo(a)	$10°,10^a$	vigésimo(a)	$20°,20^a$

Points to note on ordinals

They agree in gender and in number with the noun, which they normally precede, except with royal titles:

> **la primera vez** the first time
> **Felipe segundo** Philip II

primero and **tercero** drop the **o** before a masculine singular noun:

> **el primer premio** the first prize
> **el tercer día** the third day

Beyond **décimo** ordinal numbers are rarely used, and they are replaced by the cardinal number placed immediately after the noun:

> **el siglo diecisiete** the seventeenth century
> **Alfonso doce** Alfonso XII
> **en el piso trece** on the 13th floor

> BUT: **vigésimo(a)** 20th
> (but not with royal titles or centuries)
> **centésimo(a)** 100th
> **milésimo(a)** 1,000th
> **millonésimo(a)** 1,000,000th

Numbers

Other Uses

collective numbers:

un par	2, a couple
una decena (de personas)	about 10 (people)
una docena (de niños)	(about) a dozen (children)
una quincena (de hombres)	about fifteen (men)
una veintena* (de coches)	about twenty (cars)
un centenar, una centena (de casas)	about a hundred (houses)
cientos/centenares de personas	hundreds of people
un millar (de soldados)	about a thousand (soldiers)
miles/millares de moscas	thousands of flies

* 20, 30, 40, 50 can also be converted in the same way.

measurements:

veinte metros cuadrados 20 square metres
veinte metros cúbicos 20 cubic metres
un puente de cuarenta metros de largo/longitud a bridge 40 metres long

distance:

De aquí a Madrid hay 400 km Madrid is 400 km away
a siete km de aquí 7 km from here

Telephone numbers

Póngame con Madrid, el cuatro, cincuenta y ocho, veintidós, noventa y tres
 I would like Madrid 458 22 93
Me da Valencia, el veinte, cincuenta y uno, setenta y tres
 Could you get me Valencia 20 51 73
Extensión tres, tres, cinco/trescientos treinta y cinco
 Extension number 335

(i) Note: In Spanish telephone numbers may be read out individually, but more frequently they are broken down into groups of two. They are written in groups of two or three numbers (never four).

The Time

¿Qué hora es? *What time is it?*
Es ... *(1 o'clock, midnight, noon)* ⎤
Son las ... *(other times)* ⎦   It's ...
Es la una y cuarto   It's 1.15
Son las diez menos cinco   It's 9.55

00.00	**medianoche; las doce (de la noche)** midnight, twelve o'clock
00.10	**las doce y diez (de la noche)**
00.15	**las doce y cuarto**
00.30	**las doce y media**
00.45	**la una menos cuarto**
01.00	**la una (de la madrugada)** one a.m., one o'clock in the morning
01.10	**la una y diez (de la madrugada)**
02.45	**las tres menos cuarto**
07.00	**las siete (de la mañana)**
07.50	**las ocho menos diez**
12.00	**mediodía; las doce (de la mañana)** noon, twelve o'clock
13.00	**la una (de la tarde)** one p.m., one o'clock in the afternoon
19.00	**las siete (de la tarde)** seven p.m., seven o'clock in the evening
21.00	**las nueve (de la noche)** nine p.m., nine o'clock at night

ⓘ Note: When referring to a timetable, the 24 hour clock is used:

las dieciséis cuarenta y cinco   16.45
las veintiuna quince   21.15

Examples

¿A qué hora vas a venir?
— A las siete

What time are you coming?
— At seven o'clock

Las oficinas cierran de dos a
cuatro

The offices are closed from two
until four

Vendré a eso de/hacia las siete y
media

I'll come at around 7.30

a las seis y pico

just after 6 o'clock

a las cinco en punto

at 5 o'clock sharp

entre las ocho y las nueve

between 8 and 9 o'clock

Son más de las tres y media

It's after half past three

Hay que estar allí lo más tarde a
las diez

You have to be there by ten
o'clock at the latest

Tiene para media hora

He'll be half an hour (at it)

Estuvo sin conocimiento durante
un cuarto de hora

She was unconscious for a
quarter of an hour

Les estoy esperando desde hace
una hora/desde las dos

I've been waiting for them for
an hour/since two o'clock

Se fueron hace unos minutos

They left a few minutes ago

Lo hice en veinte minutos

I did it in twenty minutes

El tren llega dentro de una hora

The train arrives in an
hour('s time)

¿Cuánto (tiempo) dura la película?

How long does the film last?

por la mañana/tarde/noche

in the morning/afternoon or
evening/at night

mañana por la mañana

tomorrow morning

ayer por la tarde

yesterday afternoon *or* evening

anoche

last night

anteayer

the day before yesterday

pasado mañana

the day after tomorrow

Calendar

Dates

¿Qué día es hoy?	What's the date today?
¿A qué día estamos?	
Es (el) ...	It's the ...
Estamos a ...	
uno/primero de mayo	1st of May
dos de mayo	2nd of May
veintiocho de mayo	28th of May
lunes tres de octubre	Monday the 3rd of October
Vienen el siete de marzo	They're coming on the 7th of March

ⓘ Note: Use cardinal numbers for dates. Only for the first of the month can the ordinal number sometimes be used.

Years

Nací en 1970	I was born in 1970
el veinte de enero de mil novecientos setenta	(on) 20th January 1970

Other expressions

en los años cincuenta	during the fifties
en el siglo veinte	in the twentieth century
en mayo	in May
lunes (quince)	Monday (the 15th)
el quince de marzo	on March the 15th
el/los lunes	on Monday/Mondays
dentro de diez días	in 10 days' time
hace diez días	10 days ago

Age

¿Qué edad tiene?	How old is he/she?
¿Cuántos años tiene?	
Tiene 23 (años)	He/She is 23
Tiene unos 40 años	He/She is around 40
A los 21 años	At the age of 21

Index

The following index lists comprehensively both grammatical terms and key words in English and Spanish.

Index

Index

Index

Index

Index

Index

Index

Index

Index

INGLÉS PRÁCTICO

ÍNDICE

▼ Pedir aclaraciones

Could you repeat that please?	¿Me podrías repetir eso, por favor?
I'm sorry, I don't understand	Lo siento, pero no entiendo
Please can you explain what it says here?	¿Me podrías explicar lo que pone aquí, por favor?
Could you speak a little more slowly, please?	¿Podrías hablar un poquito más despacio, por favor?
Please excuse me; I'm afraid my English isn't very good	Lo siento, pero es que no hablo muy bien inglés
Please could you write that down for me?	¿Me podrías escribir eso, por favor?
How do you spell that, please?	¿Podrías deletrear eso, por favor?
Does anyone here speak Spanish?	¿Hay aquí alguien que hable español?

▼ Gustos y preferencias

► Preguntar preferencias

Do you like chips/swimming?	¿te gustan/gusta …?
Would you like to come with us?	¿te gustaría …?
What's your favourite film?	¿cuál es tu … preferida?
Which of the two colours **do you prefer**?	¿cuál de los dos … prefieres?

► Gustos

I like/love cooking	me gusta/me encanta
I'm very keen on gardening	me gusta mucho
I really enjoyed the film	me gustó mucho
I don't mind being on my own	no me importa

► Desagrado

I don't like his attitude **(at all)**	no me gusta (nada)
I hate shopping	odio
I can't stand o **bear** the thought of seeing him	no soporto
I'm not keen on seafood	no me entusiasma
Rock climbing **doesn't appeal to me**	no me atrae

► Preferencias

I like the blue T-shirt **better than** the white one	me gusta … más que
What I like best about Barcelona **is** the atmosphere	lo que más me gusta de … es
My favourite city **is** Paris	mi … preferida es
I prefer red wine **to** white	prefiero … a
I'd prefer (not) to wait o **I'd rather (not)** wait	prefiero (no)

▶ **Indiferencia**

I don't care	*me da igual*
It's all the same to me	*me da exactamente igual*
I don't mind (at all)	*me da (exactamente) lo mismo*
It doesn't matter	*no importa*

▼ Opiniones

▶ **Pedir opinión**

What do you think of the new doctor?	*¿qué te parece … ?*
What 's your opinion o **view on** the subject?	*¿qué opinas sobre …?*
What do you think about the monarchy?	*¿qué piensas de …?*

▶ **Dar su opinión**

You're right	*tienes razón*
He was right/wrong to resign	*hizo bien/mal en*
Personally, I believe that education is a right	*yo personalmente creo que*
I'm sure he doesn't mean it	*estoy seguro de que*
I think you are mistaken	*creo que*
I'm convinced that he did it	*estoy convencido de que*
In my opinion o **view** it should be legalized	*en mi opinión*
As far as I'm concerned, Barnes deserved it	*en lo que a mí respecta*

▶ **Responder sin dar opinión**

It (all) depends on your point of view	*(todo) depende de tu punto de vista*
I'd rather not comment on it	*preferiría no pronunciarme sobre*
I don't know anything about it	*no sé nada sobre*
I've never thought about it	*nunca lo he pensado*

▼ Acuerdo

I (quite) agree	*estoy (totalmente) de acuerdo*
I totally agree with you	*estoy totalmente de acuerdo contigo*
I agree up to a point	*estoy de acuerdo hasta cierto punto*
You were right to leave	*hiciste bien en*
What a good idea!	*¡qué buena idea!*
It's a great idea	*es una idea estupenda*
I'll be happy to organize it for you	*estaré encantado de*
We should be delighted to accept your offer	*… con mucho gusto …*

▼ Desacuerdo

I (totally) disagree (with you)	*no estoy (en absoluto) de acuerdo (contigo)*

I cannot agree with you on this point	no estoy de acuerdo contigo
It isn't true that people care less about poverty	no es cierto que
I entirely reject his claims	rechazo totalmente
I don't think much of this idea	no me convence mucho
It's quite out of the question	no puede ser
I'm afraid you are mistaken	creo o me temo que está usted equivocado

▼ Aprobación y desaprobación

► Aprobación

This is exactly what I had in mind	es justo lo que yo tenía pensado
I'm in favour of higher taxation	estoy a favor de
I think it's a great idea	creo que es una idea estupenda

► Desaprobación

I don't think much of what this government has done	no tengo muy buena opinión de
I can't bear o **stand** people who smoke on buses	no soporto
I think he was quite wrong to repeat what I said	creo que hizo muy mal en
We are opposed to nuclear testing	nos oponemos a
I am against animal experiments	estoy en contra de
You shouldn't have done that	no deberías haber
It's a most regrettable situation	es … muy de lamentar

▼ Disculpas

► Disculparse

Sorry	lo siento
I'm really sorry but we've got to go	de verdad lo siento pero
Sorry to disturb you	siento
I do apologize for what happened	pido disculpas por
Please forgive me for being so thoughtless	perdóname por
Please accept our apologies	les rogamos acepten nuestras disculpas

► Asumir la responsabilidad

It's my fault	es culpa mía
I shouldn't have lost my temper	no debería haber
If only I hadn't lost the keys	ojalá no hubiera
It was a mistake to come here	fue un error

► Lamentarse

It's a shame that you should feel like that	es una pena que
I'm sorry, but that's the way it is	lo siento
I'm afraid I can't help you very much	(me temo que) no puedo

I'm afraid not	me temo que no
We regret to inform you that the post has been filled	lamentamos tener que informarle que

It wasn't my fault	no fue culpa mía
I didn't do it **on purpose**	no lo hice a propósito
I didn't mean to upset you	no era mi intención
I had no choice o **option**	no me quedaba otro remedio
I had **nothing to do with it**	no tuve nada que ver con ello
We have no alternative but to accept	no nos queda otra alternativa que

▼ Explicaciones

I didn't have any lunch **because** I wasn't hungry	porque
I was held up **because of** the traffic	por
He has given in **as a result of** public pressure	como consecuencia de
We were not allowed out **for** security **reasons**	por razones de
The match was called off **owing to** o **due to** bad weather	debido a
Thanks to their efforts, productivity has increased	gracias a
I refused to leave **out of** stubbornness	por
He was very tired **as** he had been up since 4 a.m.	como
Since you've been so kind, I really can't refuse	ya que
I couldn't find you, **so** I left	así que
Given the scale of the problem, any help is welcome	dada
Given that she's only young, she's done very well	dado que

I've got to go shortly, **so** we'll have to hurry	así que
I put the oven on too hot, **with the result that** everything was burned to a frazzle	y el resultado fue que
I need some money **so that** we can pay the rent	para que
He doesn't listen. **That's why** people think he's stupid	por eso

▼ Comparaciones

This dessert **is like** a soufflé	es como
People **compare him to** Robert Redford	lo compara con
She reminds me of my old headmistress	me recuerda a
She and her son **were very alike**	había un gran parecido entre … y
The new computerized system costs **(much) the same as** a more conventional one	(prácticamente) lo mismo que

► **Diferencias**

If you compare today's team **to** o **with** that of the 1980s, you will find few similarities	*si comparas … con*
The streets are narrow **compared to** o **with** British ones	*comparadas con*
The bomb was small **in** o **by comparison with** modern ones	*en comparación con*
No catastrophe **can compare to** o **with** Chernobyl	*no hay … que se pueda comparar a*
There's no comparison between my photos **and** hers	*no hay comparación entre … y*
In contrast to the rest of the world, Asia is not experiencing a recession	*en contraste con*
Only 30% of the females died **as opposed to** 57% of the males	*frente a*
The two leaders **differ in** their approach	*difieren en*
Real ale is **better than** lager	*mejor que*
Whereas o **While** some people like to go to the cinema, others prefer to stay in and watch videos	*mientras que*
My old flat **was nowhere near as** nice **as** my new one	*no era ni mucho menos tan … como*
We may be twins, but **we have nothing in common**	*no tenemos nada en común*

▼ **Peticiones**

I'd like two lagers and a packet of crisps, **please**	*¿me pone …?*
Could you give me a hand with this?	*¿puedes …?*
Can you pass on the message **to** Eddie?	*¿le pasas … a …?*
Would you mind looking after Hannah tomorrow?	*¿te importaría …?*
Do you mind if I smoke?	*¿te importa que …?*
Could I borrow the car on Sunday?	*¿me dejas …?*
Let me know if you need any help	*si … dímelo*
I'd be (most) grateful if you could help	*le agradecería que*

▼ **Propuestas**

I could pick you up on my way home, **if you like**	*podría … si quieres*
Can I give you a hand with that?	*¿te echo una mano …?*
How would you like to go and live in California?	*¿qué te parecería …?*
How about a nice hot bath/a gin and tonic?	*¿qué tal …?*
Would you like to watch a video?	*¿te gustaría …?*
It would be nice if you could come too	*estaría bien que*
Do you want o **Would you like me to** come up?	*¿quieres que …?*

▼ **Consejos y sugerencias**

► **Pedir consejo**

What would you do **if you were me**?	*en mi lugar*
I don't know any of these wines – **what would you recommend?**	*¿cuál me recomiendas?*

Do you think I ought to tell the truth?   *¿crees que debería …?*
What do you think?   *¿tú qué crees?*
What would you advise me to do?   *¿qué me aconsejas que haga?*

I'm not sure what to do. **What do you suggest?**   *¿qué sugieres tú?*

► Aconsejar

If I were you, I'd be moving on   *yo que tú, me pondría a*
I think you ought to o **should** seek advice   *creo que deberías*
Perhaps you should speak to your boss about it   *a lo mejor deberías*
I suggest that you go to bed and try to sleep   *te aconsejo que*
It would be better to wait and see what happens   *sería mejor*
It might be as well to change the locks   *quizá(s) lo mejor sería*
It might be a good idea to tell her about this   *sería una buena idea*
What if o **Suppose** o **Supposing you** went away?   *¿y si …?*
Why don't you come with us?   *¿por qué no …?*
You could (always) try again next year   *(siempre) puedes*
What you need is a change of scene   *lo que necesitas es*
You'd better take some extra cash   *es mejor que*

► Advertir

I don't think you should get involved   *creo que no deberías*
I should warn you that he can be very awkward   *te advierto que*
Watch you don't trip over your shoelaces   *cuidado no*
Make sure that o **See that you don't** miss your bus   *ten cuidado no vayas a*
Whatever you do, don't drink the local schnapps   *no se te ocurra*

▼ Intenciones y deseos

► Preguntar intenciones y planes

Will you take the job?   *¿vas a …?*
What are you going to do when you leave school?   *¿qué vas a hacer …?*
What will you do if you can't find a job?   *¿qué vas a hacer si …?*
Are you planning on staying o **to** stay long?   *¿tienes pensado …?*
Are you thinking of going on holiday this year?   *¿tienes pensado …?*
What do you intend doing o **to do**?   *¿qué piensas hacer?*

► Expresar intenciones

I'm thinking of retiring next year   *estoy pensando en*
I'm hoping to go and see her when I'm in Paris   *espero*
I was planning to visit her later this month   *había pensado*
I am going to sell the car as soon as possible   *voy a*
I intend to put the house on the market   *tengo la intención de*
I've made up my mind to o **I've decided to** sell   *he decidido*
I have no intention of accepting the post   *no tengo intención de*

► Expresar deseos

I'd like to work in publishing   *me gustaría*

INGLÉS PRÁCTICO

I want to work abroad when I leave college — *quiero*
I hope to find a job in advertising — *espero*
I'd have liked to be an actress — *me habría gustado*

▼ Obligación

You have to o **You've got to** o **You must** be eighteen to join — *tienes que*
You really ought to o **should** talk to him about it — *tendrías que*
You need to have a valid passport to go abroad — *hay que*
I must try to see her — *debo*
It is essential to know what the career options are — *es esencial*
School **is compulsory** up to the age of 16 — *es obligatorio*
We have no alternative o **option** o **choice but to** fight — *no nos queda otro remedio más que*
Three passport photos **are required** — *se necesitan*
I don't have to o **I haven't got to** work late — *no tengo que*
You don't have to o **You needn't** go if you don't want to — *no hace falta que*
You cannot sit the exam more than twice — *no puedes*
You're not supposed to o **meant to** use this room — *no puedes*
You mustn't show this document to anyone — *no debes*
Smoking **is not permitted** in the lounge — *está prohibido*

▼ Permiso

► Pedir permiso

May I o **Could I** o **Can I borrow** your car this afternoon? — *¿me dejas ...?*
May I o **Could I** o **Can I** use the telephone, please? — *¿puedo ...?*
Are we allowed to smoke in here? — *¿podemos ...?*
Would it be all right if I arrived on Monday instead? — *¿te importaría que ...?*
We leave tomorrow. **Is that all right by you?** — *¿te parece bien?*
Do you mind if I come to the meeting next week? — *¿te importa que ...?*

► Dar permiso

You can have anything you want — *puedes*
I don't mind if you read my letter — *no me importa que*
That's fine by me — *me parece bien*
Yes, by all means — *sí, por supuesto*

► Denegar permiso

No. **You can't** swim here — *no puedes*
I'm afraid **it's not allowed** — *no está permitido*
You mustn't enter the premises without permission — *no puede*
Smoking **is (strictly) forbidden** at all times — *está (terminantemente) prohibido*

▼ Certeza, probabilidad y posibilidad

► Certeza

He is, **undoubtedly** o **without doubt**, a good chef — *sin duda*

She has **obviously** changed her mind	*obviamente*
I'm sure o **certain** (**that**) he'll keep his word	*estoy seguro de que*
I'm positive o **convinced** (**that**) it was her	*estoy convencido de que*
We now know for certain o **for sure that** he was right	*sabemos ya con seguridad que*

▶ Probabilidad

I'll **probably** go next week	*seguramente*
You'll **very probably** be met at the airport	*es muy probable que*
It seems (highly) likely that they had met before	*parece (muy) probable que*
He must have forgotten to turn off the lights	*debe de haber*
The cheque **should** reach you by Saturday	*debería*
It looks as though o **as if** it might rain	*parece que*

▶ Posibilidad

It's possible	*es posible*
Possibly	*posiblemente*
The situation **could** change	*podría*
In a few months everything **may** have changed	*puede que*
She **may** be ill	*es posible que*
Perhaps I am mistaken	*quizá(s)*
It is possible that psychological factors play a part	*es posible que*
It may be that we will have to redo the work	*puede ser que*

▼ Incertidumbre, improbabilidad e imposibilidad

▶ Incertidumbre

I'm not sure o **certain that** I really know the answer	*no estoy seguro de que*
We can't say for sure what time we'll arrive	*no podemos decir con seguridad*
Will he come? **I doubt it**	*lo dudo*
I doubt whether o **if** he'll have any problems	*dudo que*
It's doubtful whether the match will take place	*no es seguro que*

▶ Improbabilidad

He **probably** won't come	*seguramente*
It's unlikely that we'll stay in touch	*es bastante improbable que*
It's (very) doubtful whether they can succeed	*es (bastante) dudoso que*

▶ Imposibilidad

It's impossible	*es imposible*
I couldn't possibly invite George and not his wife	*¿cómo voy a …?*
There is no possibility of a ceasefire	*no hay posibilidades de*
There is no question of us getting this finished	*es imposible que*

INGLÉS PRÁCTICO

▼ Fórmulas de encabezamiento y despedida

▶ **Correspondencia formal a destinatarios desconocidos**

Dear Sir or Madam
Dear Sir/Madam
Dear Sirs
Dear Sir
Dear Madam

Yours faithfully (*BRIT*)
Sincerely (yours) (*US*)
Yours sincerely (*US*)
Respectfully yours (*US*)

▶ **Correspondencia formal a destinatarios conocidos**

Dear Mr Palmer
Dear Mr and Mrs Palmer
Dear Mrs Palmer
Dear Ms Palmer
Dear Miss Palmer
Dear Sandra Palmer
Dear Dr Palmer

Yours sincerely
Sincerely (yours) (*US*)

O, menos formal:

Best wishes
Regards
Kind regards

Mr se usa para dirigirse a un hombre de cualquier edad
Mrs se usa para dirigirse a una mujer casada
Miss se usa para dirigirse a una mujer soltera
Ms se usa para dirigirse a una mujer de cualquier edad, casada o no

En Estados Unidos, los títulos abreviados van seguidos de punto: Mr., Mrs., Ms., Dr.

▶ **Correspondencia informal**

Dear Bob
Dear Alice
Dear Bob and Alice
Dear Uncle Bob/Mum
Dear Uncle Bob and Aunt
 Jean/Mum and Dad

Best wishes
Kind regards
Regards
Con amigos y familiares:
Best wishes
Love/Lots of love/With love

NOTA: Normalmente se emplea una coma tanto después del encabezamiento, como después de la despedida, en las cartas escritas a mano. Sin embargo, en inglés **británico**, la coma suele omitirse en las cartas escritas a máquina u ordenador. En inglés **norteamericano**, se usan a veces los dos puntos en lugar de la coma en el encabezamiento.

▶ **Diferencias en la forma de escribir la fecha en inglés**

En inglés **británico**, se puede utilizar cualquiera de las siguientes fórmulas:

   6th March   6 March   March 6th   March 6

En cambio, en inglés **norteamericano**, sólo se utilizan las siguientes:

   March 6th   March 6

Con el fin de evitar confusión, se recomienda no escribir la fecha de esta manera: **12.03.03**, ya que en inglés **británico** se leería como **12 de marzo de 2003** mientras en inglés **norteamericano** se leería como **3 de diciembre de 2003**.

▼ Carta a una oficina de turismo

2 North Park Road
Southampton
S09 1IZ

Department of Tourism   2 April 2003
Isle of Man

Dear Sir or Madam

Re: hotels/places to visit/things to do

My wife and I and our two children (aged 10 and 14) are hoping to visit the Island in August 2003 and would be very grateful if you would send us details of hotels and guest houses as well as of car hire firms. Any information on prices would also be much appreciated.

It would also be extremely useful if you could send us a list of places of special interest and tourist activities. My son and daughter are particularly keen on anything involving cycling, riding or walking, while my wife and I very much enjoy visiting castles, museums and places of historical interest. We should also like to find out about organizations helping people trace their roots, as I believe my ancestors came from the Island.

I enclose a large stamped addressed envelope.

Thanking you in advance for your help in this matter.

Yours faithfully

William Christian
William Christian

INGLÊS PRÁCTICO

▶ **Expresiones útiles**

Re:
Tema:

I am hoping to come to Britain/be in Manchester in August
Espero poder visitar el Reino Unido/estar en Manchester en agosto

I would be (very) grateful if you would send me ...
Le quedaría muy agradecido si me pudiera enviar ...

Any information on prices would be much appreciated
Le agradecería cualquier información sobre los precios

It would be extremely useful if you could send us ...
Sería de tremenda utilidad si nos pudiera enviar ...

I enclose/Please find enclosed a (large) stamped addressed envelope
Le adjunto/Adjunto le envío un sobre (grande) con dirección y sello

Thank you o **Thanking you in advance for your help in this matter**
Muchas gracias de antemano por su ayuda en esta cuestión

▼ E-mail para reservar una habitación de hotel

To: info@miltonhotel.co.uk
From: gb@linkup.co.uk
Subject: Accommodation
Attachments:

En inglés la dirección de correo se lee así: **info at milton hotel dot co dot u k**

Dear Sir/Madam

My wife and I will be visiting Milton from 25 to 29 April and a colleague has recommended the Milton Hotel. I would like to book a double room with en suite facilities, preferably with a sea view.

Please confirm at your earliest convenience that suitable accommodation is available for these dates, and that the charge for the room is £90 per night. I would be grateful if you could also send details of your menu, along with information about how to reach the hotel.

I look forward to hearing from you.

Yours faithfully

Gerald Baird

▶ **Expresiones útiles**

I would like to book o **reserve ...**
Quisiera reservar ...
details of your prices/menu
información sobre los precios/las comidas
single room/double room/twin room/family room
habitación individual/habitación doble/habitación doble (con dos camas)/ suite familiar
with en suite facilities (BRIT) o **with a bathroom**
con baño
disabled access/disabled toilets
acceso para minusválidos/baños para minusválidos
Internet access
acceso a Internet
parking facilities
aparcamiento
Is breakfast included?
¿El desayuno está incluido?
tourist information/places of interest
información turística/lugares de interés turístico
Please confirm as soon as possible/at your earliest convenience
Le ruego que me lo confirme tan pronto como pueda/en cuanto le sea posible
I look forward to hearing from you
Quedo a la espera de sus noticias

INGLÉS PRÁCTICO

▼ Carta formal de queja

29 Beech Rd
Ambleton
CB24 9PQ

The Manager
Sergio's
88 Bottle St
Coombes
CB5 8NY

5 October 2002

Dear Sir or Madam

I am writing to complain about the poor service I received at Sergio's recently.

On 25 September, I booked a table for six for 2 October at 8.00 p.m. in the non-smoking section of the restaurant, and at the same time checked that a range of vegetarian and vegan meals would be available.

We arrived on 2 October at 7.50 p.m. and were shown to a table for four in the smoking section, then had to wait half an hour at the bar while the table we had booked was prepared. During our wait, the attitude of the staff was extremely offhand and on occasions bordered on rudeness.

When we finally sat down and ordered our food, we were informed that the only vegetarian option available that evening was omelette. Again, the staff were extremely unhelpful and at this stage we decided to eat elsewhere.

I would be very interested to hear your comments on both the poor service at your establishment and the unhelpful attitude of your staff.

Yours faithfully

V Meldrew

V Meldrew

INGLÉS PRÁCTICO

▶ Expresiones útiles

I am writing to complain about/to make a (formal) complaint about …
Le escribo para quejarme de/presentar una queja (formal) sobre …

I am extremely dissatisfied with/disappointed with …
Estoy tremendamente descontento con/decepcionado con …

I regard this situation as unacceptable/unsatisfactory
Considero esta situación inaceptable/poco satisfactoria

I would like to know/I would like you to explain …
Me gustaría saber/Me gustaría que me explicara …

what you plan to do about this situation/state of affairs
lo que pretende hacer al respecto de esta situación/este estado de cosas

I would be interested to hear your comments on …
Estaría interesado en conocer su opinión sobre …

▼ Carta en inglés norteamericano

76 Newton Lane
Oak Ridge, Tennessee
38097

January 23, 2003

Dr. Michael Townsend
Director of Admissions
Brightwater Institute
89 Lincoln Avenue
Hartford, Illinois
87498

Dear Dr. Townsend:

Re: Application for History Course #176

I have looked through your recent catalog, and I am very interested in the Brightwater Institute's Summer Program for 2003. I am particularly interested in your History Course #176, "Early American History", taught by Dr. Leigh Thorne, as described on page 82 of your catalog. I heard Dr. Thorne speak in Charleston, South Carolina last April and I am fascinated by her work.

Could you please send me the institute's application form for this course? I would also be grateful if you could send me further details of the essay requirements for this application.

I look forward to hearing from you, and thank you for your help. I hope that my application will be successful, and that I will see you at the Brightwater Institute this summer.

Yours sincerely,

Gwyneth Young

Gwyneth Young

▶ **Expresiones útiles**

I am very interested in ...
Me interesa mucho ...
I am particularly interested in ...
Me interesa particularmente ...
as described on page ...
tal como se describe en la página ...
Could you please send me further details of ... ?
Por favor, ¿me podría enviar más información sobre ...?
I look forward to hearing from you
Quedo a la espera de sus noticias
Thank you for your help
Gracias por su ayuda

INGLÉS PRÁCTICO

▼ **Carta de disculpa informal**

> 76 Oak Ave
> Riverdale
> CB65 9VF
>
> 10/5/08
>
> Dear Janice,
>
> I'm really sorry about forgetting your birthday – I feel terrible about it. We went away to London to stay with Dave and Sue for a few days over Easter and I completely forgot about it in the rush to get everything ready. I hope you had a great time, and that you like your present – so sorry it's late! Will phone you soon to catch up on things.
>
> Love,
> Anne

▶ **Expresiones útiles**

I'm (so o **really) sorry about …**
Siento (mucho) lo de …
I'm (so o **really) sorry that …**
Siento (mucho) lo de que …
I feel really terrible o **awful about forgetting your birthday**
Me siento fatal por haberme olvidado de tu cumpleaños
I feel really terrible about it
Me siento fatal por eso
I hope you didn't mind (too much) that …
Espero que no te importara (demasiado) que …

▼ E-mail informal de agradecimiento

From:	ianp@quickmail.com ◄------------------
To:	bob.savage@savage.linkup.co.uk
Subject:	CD
Attachments:	

> En inglés la dirección de correo se lee así: **ian p at quick mail dot com**

Hi Bob

This is just a few lines to say thanks for the CD you sent me for my birthday. I haven't heard anything else by the Pixies, but 'Bossanova' is amazing and I want to hear more.

I had a pretty quiet birthday, with pizza and a bottle of wine at home with Karen and the kids - we had the wine; they had to make do with water! I must be getting old because I no longer feel like clubs and late nights at times like this :-)

Regards

Ian

► Expresiones útiles

Hi Bob/Dear Bob/Bob
Hola Bob/Querido Bob/Bob
This is just a few lines/quick note to say ...
Tan solo unas líneas/una nota para decirte ...
Thanks (very much o a lot) for o Thank you (very much) for ...
(Muchas) gracias por ...
Regards/Love/Best wishes
Saludos/Besos/Un abrazo
Speak to you soon/Take care (of yourself)/Bye for now
Hablamos pronto/Cuídate/Hasta la próxima
That's all for now
Esto es todo por el momento

INGLÉS PRÁCTICO

► **Expresiones útiles**

Re:
Tema:

reference number/our ref/your ref
número de referencia/nuestra referencia/su referencia

Thank you for your letter of 12 April 2003
Gracias por su carta de fecha 12 de abril de 2003

With reference to …
Con referencia a …

In reply to your letter of …
En respuesta a su carta de …

Further to my previous letter/correspondence …
Como continuación a mi carta/correspondencia anterior …

Further to our recent telephone conversation …
Como continuación a nuestra reciente conversación telefónica …

I would be (very) grateful if you could …
Le quedaría muy agradecido si pudiera …

I acknowledge receipt of …
Acuso recibo de …

I am writing to enquire about …
Le escribo para solicitarle información sobre …

Please find enclosed o **attached …**
Adjunto le envío …

I am sending you … as arranged
Tal como quedamos, le envío …

As you can see from the enclosed/attached brochure …
Como puede observar en el folleto adjunto …

Nigel Palmer has suggested that I contact you about o **regarding …**
Me pongo en contacto con usted por indicación de Nigel Palmer en relación a …

I am sorry/I am pleased to inform you that …
Siento/Me complace informarle de que …

For further information, please visit our website at …
Para más información, por favor, visite nuestra página web en …

If you require further information, please do not hesitate to contact me
Si necesita más información, por favor, no dude en ponerse en contacto conmigo

Please reply at your earliest convenience
Le ruego una respuesta en cuanto le sea posible

I can be contacted on 304 3443 during office hours, or on my mobile (07844 123 123) at any other time
Me puede localizar en el 304 3443 en horario de oficina, o en el móvil (07844 123 123) en cualquier otro momento

Please note that …
Le ruego tenga en cuenta que …

Thank you o **Thanking you in advance for your help**
Muchas gracias de antemano por su ayuda

I look forward to hearing from you
Quedo a la espera de sus noticias

enc o **enc.**
inc.

INGLÉS PRÁCTICO

▼ Fax solicitando un catálogo

FAX

**Panchester School,
Woodlands Road,
Panchester, PA6 7JV**

To: Collins Dictionaries
Fax Number: 0141 306 3388

From: Julia Hall, Head of Modern Languages
Fax Number: 0196 225 347

Date: 17 March 2003
Subject: Dictionary catalogue

Number of Pages (including this one): one

Dear Sir/Madam

Please would you be so kind as to send me two copies of your dictionary catalogue together with details of discounts for bulk orders?

It would also be good if you could send me sample copies of any French dictionaries that you consider suitable for children aged between 11 and 14, as we are shortly going to have to replace some old reference books.

Thanking you for your help in this matter.

Yours faithfully

Julia Hall (Mrs)

If you have any difficulties receiving this message, please phone Clare Franks on 0196 333 456

▶ **Expresiones útiles**

Please would you be so kind as to send me ...?
Le quedaría muy agradecido si fuera tan amable de enviarme ...

together with details of discounts for bulk orders
junto con la información sobre las ofertas para pedidos al por mayor

It would also be good if you could send me ...
También convendría que me enviase ...

Thank you o **Thanking you for your help in this matter**
Muchas gracias por su ayuda

▼ **Carta de pedido de mercancías**

---

9 Waterside Road
Liverpool
L19 1TZ

Melody Makers Ltd
35 Ogden Square
Little Granton
M96 3EZ

18 February 2003

Dear Mr Wright

Re: Fantasy Tree (CD by The Cave Dwellers)

Further to my telephone conversation with you earlier this morning, I now enclose my cheque for the sum of £15.69 to cover the cost of the above CD together with postage and packing.

I look forward to hearing from you and receiving my CD.

Yours sincerely

Patrick Tully

INGLÉS PRÁCTICO

► **Expresiones útiles**

Re:
Tema:
Further to my letter of …/our telephone conversation
Como continuación a mi carta de … /nuestra conversación telefónica
I enclose/Please find enclosed …
Le adjunto …/Adjunto le envío …
my cheque (BRIT) o **check** (US) **for the sum of**
mi cheque por la cantidad de
to cover the cost of
para cubrir los gastos de
postage and packing
gastos de envío
I look forward to hearing from you
Quedo a la espera de sus noticias

▼ Carta en relación a un pedido de mercancías

14 Campsie View Road
Lennoxtown
Glasgow
G75 1NQ

Health Products Ltd
15 Park Industrial Estate
Portsmouth
P17 5RP

3 March 2003

Dear Sir or Madam

**Re: Dispatch no 30096, dated 25 February 2003,
your ref: 12678/SL/25.2**

Many thanks for sending off my above-mentioned order so promptly.

The carton was unfortunately damaged in transit, however, causing two bottles of peppermint oil to break and one bottle of vitamin C tablets (200 x 1000mg) to spill out inside the packaging. Please could you therefore replace these products as soon as possible?

I look forward to hearing from you and to receiving my replacement goods.

Thanking you in advance for your help in this matter.

Yours faithfully

Penelope Stevenage

Penelope Stevenage

▶ **Expresiones útiles**

Many thanks for your letter of February 19, 2003/for sending off my order so promptly
Muchas gracias por su carta de fecha 19 de febrero de 2003/por enviarme el pedido tan rápido

my above-mentioned order/account
el pedido/la cuenta que aparece arriba

The carton was unfortunately damaged in transit
Desgraciadamente, la caja se ha dañado durante el transporte

Please could you therefore replace it?
Por tanto, le rogaría que lo cambiase, si es posible

I look forward to hearing from you
Quedo a la espera de sus noticias

Thank you o **Thanking you in advance for your help in this matter**
Muchas gracias de antemano por su ayuda

▼ Carta formal de presentación de una oferta

EnviroEmbrace
Dynamo House
Disraeli St
Downes
DH38 9JK

B Godfrey
Personnel Manager
ComputAid
456 Gladstone Rd
Coombes
CB66 7HF

14 June 2003

Dear Mr Godfrey

On the recommendation of Ian Fortescue at OJDC Computing, I am writing to tell you about the range of office products and services my company can provide, all designed to make offices happier, healthier places and to boost morale and productivity.

At EnviroEmbrace, we have devoted a great deal of time and effort to finding out what the key features of a happy, productive office are, and we now have a long list of satisfied clients who are willing to testify to our success.

Attached is a brochure describing what we can do for companies like ComputAid, together with typical costings for goods and services. You may be surprised to see the outstanding value for money we offer.

As you will see, services range from fitness advice and massage to 24-hour staff helplines, while our product range encompasses everything from ergonomic chairs and environmentally friendly paper to plants which benefit the atmosphere.

To find out more, you can visit our website at www.enviroembrace.com, or phone me on 041 - 848 1357. Needless to say, we will be only too glad to arrange for a consultant to visit you to make a free assessment of the situation at ComputAid.

I look forward to hearing from you.

Yours sincerely

Nigel Palmer

Nigel Palmer
nigel.palmer@enviroembrace.co.uk

INGLÉS PRÁCTICO

▶ Expresiones útiles

on the recommendation of ...
siguiendo la sugerencia de ...

I am writing to tell you about ...
Le escribo para comunicarle acerca de ...

In addition to ... we also offer ...
Además de ... también le ofrecemos ...

outstanding value for money
excelente relación calidad/precio

To find out more about ...
Si necesita más información sobre ...

▼ E-mail para concertar una cita formal

From:	bobg@computaid.co.uk
To:	nigel.palmer@enviro-embrace.co.uk
Subject:	Meeting
Attachments:	

> En inglés la dirección de correo se lee así: **bob g at computaid dot co dot u k**

Dear Nigel Palmer

Many thanks for your very interesting letter of 14 June, 2003, describing the services and goods offered by EnviroEmbrace.

Perhaps you could arrange a time for one of your consultants to visit us? Any time between three o'clock and five thirty on a Friday is usually good for me.

I look forward to hearing from you and to learning what EnviroEmbrace can offer ComputAid.

Regards

Bob Godfrey
Personnel Manager
ComputAid

▶ **Expresiones útiles**

Many thanks for your very interesting letter
Muchas gracias por su carta, que ha despertado nuestro interés
Perhaps you could arrange a time to visit us
¿Le sería posible encontrar un momento para hacernos una visita?
Perhaps you could contact ...
Quizás convendría que se pusiera en contacto con ...
How about some time after 2 p.m. on Thursday?
¿Qué le parece en algún momento después de las 2 de la tarde del jueves?
Any time between three o'clock and five thirty on a Friday is good for me
Cualquier hora entre las tres y las cinco y media de la tarde de un viernes me viene bien

▼ **Orden del día de una reunión**

Office Improvements and Staff Services

AGENDA

1 Presentation by Bob Godfrey on problems identified by EnviroEmbrace consultant and the recommendations made to deal with these
2 Comparison of EnviroEmbrace services and costings with those of HappyAmbi by Tim Wall
3 Group evaluation
4 Any other business

Copies to – Bob Godfrey, Tim Wall, Sarah Hutton, Bill Rhodes

▼ **Actas/Conclusiones**

State of Office, Staff Services

Thursday May 13, 3.00 p.m.

Present – Bob Godfrey, Tim Wall, Sarah Hutton, Bill Rhodes

MINUTES

1 BG outlined the problems identified by the EnviroEmbrace consultant, namely inadequate ventilation and lighting, dingy surroundings, excessive noise, poor quality chairs and uninspiring pictures.

2 BG outlined the solutions recommended by EnviroEmbrace

3 Tim Wall compared the services and costings provided by EnviroEmbrace with those of HappyAmbi, its main competitor.

4 Group discussion, during which SH pointed out that while prices and services were comparable, EnviroEmbrace seemed to be able to provide a much more impressive list of satisfied clients. BR said that he had been very impressed by the thoroughness of the EnviroEmbrace report and the willingness of the consultant to listen to staff suggestions.

ACTION POINTS

1 SH to contact some of EnviroEmbrace's previous customers for an assessment of services and goods and to pass on any information to BG, TW and BR

2 BR to canvass staff on their views

3 BG to set up a further meeting with NP and to provide evidence of the improvements brought about by EnviroEmbrace

▶ **Expresiones útiles**

agenda *orden del día*
any other business *o* **AOB** *otros puntos (a tratar) o ruegos y preguntas*
minutes *actas*
action points *conclusiones*

INGLÉS PRÁCTICO

▼ E-mail posterior a la reunión

From:	bobg@computaid.co.uk ◄------------¬
To:	nigel.palmer@enviro-embrace.co.uk
Subject:	Presentation
Attachments:	

> En inglés la dirección de correo se lee así: **bob g at computaid dot co dot u k**

Dear Nigel

Thank you for your very informative report on the state of our office and on ways to improve both the office environment and the morale of staff.

I have passed on your comments to other members of the team and they are keen to find out more about what EnviroEmbrace can do for us.

Please can you therefore arrange a presentation for us all on what you have achieved elsewhere, complete with the videoed interviews you mentioned?

We could perhaps devote one Friday afternoon to this.

I look forward to hearing from you.

Regards
Bob Godfrey

► **Expresiones útiles**

Thank you for your very informative report
Gracias por su informe y por la cantidad de información que contiene
I have passed on your comments to the other members of the team
He transmitido sus comentarios a los otros miembros del equipo
He is keen to find out more about ...
Tiene interés en saber más cosas sobre ...
Please can you arrange a presentation for us on ...?
¿Podría organizarnos una presentación sobre ...?

INGLÉS PRÁCTICO

CYBEROKI
www.cyberoki.com

Trainee Software Support Manager

Cyberoki is a successful company offering a range of office systems and support services to suit the needs of clients ranging from small businesses to multinationals. We thrive on our ability to satisfy all our clients with our friendly, down-to-earth approach, our attention to detail and our outstanding value for money.

Due to expansion, we are seeking a trainee software support manager. The successful candidate will be confident, imaginative, willing to travel and will have sound qualifications and training in computing.

To apply, send a CV and covering letter to:

Fiona Parker
Personnel Manager
Cyberoki
Virtual House
Disraeli St
Downes
DH38 9JK

▶ **Expresiones útiles**

We are seeking/looking for …
Se selecciona/Se busca …

The successful candidate will …
El candidato deberá tener los siguientes requisitos …

To apply …
Para solicitar (el empleo) …

CV *(BRIT)* o **résumé** *(US)* **and covering letter** *(BRIT)* o **cover letter** *(US)*
CV y carta de presentación

For an application form, please phone 0569 74 357 or write to …/or visit our website at …
Para pedir el formulario de solicitud, llamar al 0569 74 357 o escribir a …/o visitar nuestra página web en …

Applicants should preferably have a minimum of 2 years' work experience
Los candidatos deben tener preferiblemente un mínimo de dos años de experiencia

Cyberoki is an equal opportunities employer
Cyberoki es una empresa que ofrece igualdad de oportunidades para todos

Closing date *(esp BRIT)* o **Final date** *(esp US)* **for applications is …**
El plazo para la presentación de solicitudes acaba …

Interviews will be held in Edinburgh on Monday
Las entrevistas se celebrarán el lunes en Edimburgo

We offer a competitive salary/benefits package/opportunities for career development
Le ofrecemos una retribución altamente competitiva/un paquete de beneficios/posibilidades de desarrollo profesional

37 Elm Rd
Hackforth
Nethersage
NS66 4HG

Ms Fiona Parker
Personnel Manager
Cyberoki
Virtual House
Disraeli Street
Downes
DH38 9JK

16 April 2003

Dear Ms Parker

Re: Post of Trainee software support manager

I am writing to apply for the post of trainee software support manager advertised in the Nethersage Guardian.

Although I am happy with my current employer, I am seeking a more challenging position and Cyberoki offers an excellent career opportunity.

As you will see from my enclosed CV, I am qualified to HND level in computing and have also obtained a Level 3 certificate in desktop publishing, which I put to good use publishing a monthly newsletter for the Cat Protection Society.

I enjoy the challenge of new situations, and travelled by myself around Australia following graduation, supporting myself through a range of casual jobs. I recently passed my advanced driving test and am now a member of the Institute of Advanced Motorists. Having already worked as a delivery driver, I am keen to put my driving skills to good use.

I am available for interview, but will need to take time off work so would be grateful for some advance notice of any interview. I look forward to hearing from you.

Yours faithfully

Susan Ferris

▶ **Expresiones útiles**

I am writing/I wish to apply for the post of ... that was advertised recently in ...
Le escribo para/Me gustaría solicitar el puesto de ... que apareció recientemente en ...

I wish to be considered for the post of ...
Me gustaría ser tenido en cuenta para el puesto de ...

As you will see from my enclosed CV (BRIT) o **curriculum vitae** (BRIT) o **résumé** (US) **...**
Como puede observar en el CV adjunto ...

I am available for interview (from/between ...)
Estoy disponible para la entrevista (desde/entre ...)

I look forward to hearing from you
Quedo a la espera de sus noticias

▼ **Currículum vitae británico**

CV

Personal details

Name: Susan Ferris
Address: 37 Elm Rd, Hackforth, Nethersage, NS66 4HG
Telephone: 0866 734 8384
E-mail: susanf@ferris.linkup.co.uk
Date of birth: 12 October 1978
Nationality: British
Marital Status: single

Qualifications

1994: 8 GCSEs (English, Maths, Physics, Chemistry, Biology, French, Computing, Art), Hackforth School
1996: 4 A Levels (Biology A, Physics B, Chemistry B, Maths B), Hackforth College
1999: HND Computing, Nethersage University

Employment

September 2001 – present: Trainee Manager, Roboservu, Thorness
October 2000 – September 2001: Administrative Assistant, Housing Department, Nethersage Council
Christmas, Easter, Summer 1998: Delivery Driver, Pizza Home

Training, skills and experience

Desktop Publishing, Level 3, Hackforth Community College
Spent the year after graduation working and travelling in Australia
Advanced driving skills

Interests

Playing the violin
Weekend work for the Cat Protection Society

Referees

Mr John Bowles, Housing Manager, Housing Department, Nethersage Council, Industry St, Nethersage, NS34 7GT

Ms Andrea Patel, Senior Lecturer, Department of Computing, Nethersage University, Albion Rd, Nethersage, NS7 9JE

▼ Currículum vitae norteamericano

RÉSUMÉ

EVE DEACON

Apartment 3b, 76 Chestnut Hill Road
Somerville, Massachusetts 02144
Telephone: 1-617-556-782
E-mail: evedeacon@paisleyshawl.com

EDUCATION

1995 — 1999 **UNIVERSITY OF PENNSYLVANIA**, Philadelphia, PA
Bachelor of Arts in English Literature, May 1999

1993 — 1999 **INTERLOCHEN CAMP**, Interlochen, MI
Summer courses (June through August) in piano music technique and performance, and theatrical adaptation

WORK EXPERIENCE

Aug. 1999 — Present **HARPERCOLLINS PUBLISHERS**, New York, NY

Oct. 2000 — Present **Assistant Editor**, *Children's Books Division*: Evaluate fiction and non-fiction children's book manuscripts for publication. Proofread and collate editorial changes throughout all stages of production. Check and prepare manuscripts for typesetting and printing.

Aug. 1999 — Oct. 2000 **Editorial Assistant**, *Children's Book Division*: Proofread and collated editorial changes throughout all stages of production. Answered author and agent enquiries. Organized new filing system and handled correspondence for Editorial Director.

Sept. 1996 — May 1999 **HOGAN'S HEROES**, Philadelphia, PA
Sandwich Maker: Responsible for fulfilling special orders and closing shop. Stocked ingredients and made sandwiches to customer specifications. Baked bread.

SKILLS
Proofreading. Editing. Typing at 70 words per minute.
Experience in using a variety of word-processing and desktop-publishing software.
Fluency in French.

INTERESTS
Children's books, classical piano music and French films.

References available upon request.

▶ **Expresiones útiles**

Directory enquiries *(BRIT)* o **Information** *(US)* — **which town, please?**
Información — ¿con qué ciudad desea hablar?

Hello, there's no one in at the moment, but please leave a message after the tone
Hola, en estos momentos no hay nadie, pero puede dejar su mensaje después de oír la señal

Hello Ian, this is Joe, can you call o **phone me back when you've got a minute? My number is** ...
Hola Ian, soy Joe, ¿me puedes llamar cuando tengas un momento? Mi número es el ...

I'm just calling o **phoning to** ...
Llamaba sólo para ...

Thank you o **Thanks for calling**
Gracias por llamar

Thank you for calling Alan Paul hair salon. Michelle speaking. How may I help you?
Gracias por llamar a la peluquería Alan Paul. Le atiende Michelle. ¿En qué puedo ayudarle?

Can you say that again/repeat that, please?
¿Puedes decir eso otra vez/repetir eso, por favor?

Can you speak (a bit) more slowly, please? My English isn't very good
¿Puedes hablar (un poco) más despacio, por favor? No hablo muy bien inglés

Can you give me your number and I'll call you back?
¿Me puedes dar tu número y te llamo?

(I'm afraid) he's not here/in/available at the moment
(Me temo que) no está aquí/no está/no está disponible en este momento

Would you like to leave a message/Can I take a message?
¿Quieres dejar un mensaje?/¿Quieres que le diga algo?

Would you like to/Can you call o **phone back (in half an hour)?**
Si quieres, puedes volver a llamar (dentro de media hora)/¿Puedes volver a llamar (dentro de media hora)?

Extension 121
(Con la) Extensión 121

May I speak to ...?
¿Puedo hablar con ...?

Can I have an outside line, please?
¿Me da línea con el exterior, por favor?

Please press hash/the star button on your telephone keypad
Por favor, pulse almohadilla/asterisco en el teclado de su teléfono

Please hold the line
Por favor, no cuelgue

I'd like to make a reverse charge call *(BRIT)* o **collect call** *(US)*
Quisiera hacer una llamada a cobro revertido

The person you are calling is not available at the moment
La persona a quien ha llamado no se encuentra disponible en este momento

► Los Números Cardinales

0	zero, nought*	12	twelve	30	thirty
1	one	13	thirteen	31	thirty-one
2	two	14	fourteen	40	forty
3	three	15	fifteen	50	fifty
4	four	16	sixteen	60	sixty
5	five	17	seventeen	70	seventy
6	six	18	eighteen	80	eighty
7	seven	19	nineteen	90	ninety
8	eight	20	twenty	100	one o a hundred
9	nine	21	twenty-one	101	one o a hundred and one
10	ten	22	twenty-two	212	two hundred and twelve
11	eleven	23	twenty-three	999	nine hundred and ninety-nine

1,000	one o a thousand	100,000	one o a hundred thousand
1,001	one o a thousand and one	1,000,000	one o a million
2,500	two thousand five hundred	1,000,000,000	one o a billion

NOTA: en inglés los miles y millones se separan con una coma y no con un punto.

► Los Números Ordinales

1st	first		19th	nineteenth
2nd	second		20th	twentieth
3rd	third		21st	twenty-first
4th	fourth		22nd	twenty-second
5th	fifth		23rd	twenty-third
6th	sixth		30th	thirtieth
7th	seventh		31st	thirty-first
8th	eighth		40th	fortieth
9th	ninth		50th	fiftieth
10th	tenth		60th	sixtieth
11th	eleventh		70th	seventieth
12th	twelfth		80th	eightieth
13th	thirteenth		90th	ninetieth
14th	fourteenth		100th	hundredth
15th	fifteenth		101st	hundred and first
16th	sixteenth		1,000th	thousandth
17th	seventeenth		1,000,000th	millionth
18th	eighteenth		1,000,000,000th	billionth

► Las Fracciones y Porcentajes

½	a half		0.5	zero point five o nought* point five
⅓	a o one third		3.5	three point five
¼	a o one quarter		6.89	six point eight nine
¹⁄₁₀	a o one tenth		10%	ten per cent
⅔	two thirds		100%	one o a hundred percent

NOTA: en inglés se separan los decimales con un punto y no con una coma.

* **Nought** se emplea sobre todo en inglés británico.

What time is it?

¿Qué hora es?

It's one o'clock

It's (a) quarter past one
o It's one fifteen

It's ten to two o
It's one fifty

It's half past three o
It's three thirty

It's twenty to six o
It's five forty

It's (a) quarter to eight o
It's seven forty-five

It's nine o'clock

It's twelve o'clock

▶ **Cómo preguntar la hora**

What time do you make it?	¿Qué hora tienes?
Can you tell me the time?	¿Me dices la hora?
Do you have the time (on you)?	¿Tienes hora?

▶ **Cómo contestar**

I make it 2.20 o **twenty past two**	Yo tengo las dos y veinte
It must be about eleven	Serán las once
It's three o'clock exactly	Son las tres en punto
It's just past five o'clock	Son las cinco y pico
It's nearly four o'clock	Falta (un) poco para las cuatro

▶ **¿A qué hora?**

What time does it start?	¿A qué hora empieza?
At midnight	A medianoche
In twenty minutes	Dentro de veinte minutos
At around eight o'clock	A eso de las ocho
It leaves at seven thirty	Sale a las siete y media

INGLÉS PRÁCTICO

INGLÉS PRÁCTICO

▶ Los días de la semana

Monday	*lunes*
Tuesday	*martes*
Wednesday	*miércoles*
Thursday	*jueves*
Friday	*viernes*
Saturday	*sábado*
Sunday	*domingo*

▶ Los meses del año

January	*enero*
February	*febrero*
March	*marzo*
April	*abril*
May	*mayo*
June	*junio*
July	*julio*
August	*agosto*
September	*septiembre*
October	*octubre*
November	*noviembre*
December	*diciembre*

NOTA: en inglés, los días de la semana y los meses del año siempre se escriben con mayúscula.

▶ Las estaciones

spring	*primavera*
summer	*verano*
autumn	*otoño*
winter	*invierno*

▶ Cómo expresar la fecha

What day is it today?	*¿Qué día es hoy?*
It's Saturday	*Es sábado o Estamos a sábado*
1st/24th October 2002	*1/24 de octubre de 2002*

Ver también **CORRESPONDENCIA**, *p.10*

▶ ¿Cuándo?

today/yesterday/tomorrow	*hoy/ayer/mañana*
the day after tomorrow	*pasado mañana*
the day before yesterday	*antes de ayer*
the next o **following day**	*el o al día siguiente*
yesterday afternoon/evening	*ayer por la tarde*
last night	*ayer por la noche*
tomorrow morning	*mañana por la mañana*
on Saturday/on Saturdays	*el sábado/los sábados*
next Sunday	*el domingo que viene*
last Tuesday	*el martes pasado*
a week ago	*hace una semana*
last year	*el año pasado*
in two days	*dentro de/en dos días*
a fortnight ago	*hace quince días*
at the beginning of the year	*a principios de año*
in the middle of o **halfway through May**	*a mediados de mayo*
at the end of the month	*a finales de mes*
at the latest	*a más tardar*
at the earliest	*lo más pronto*
no later than	*no más tarde de*
in 1999	*en 1999*
in the nineteenth century	*en el siglo diecinueve*
in the (nineteen) nineties	*en los años noventa*
44 BC/14 AD	*44 a. de C./14 d. de C.*

PRACTICAL SPANISH

CONTENTS

▼ Expressing language difficulties

¿Me podrías repetir eso, por favor?	*could you repeat that please?*
Lo siento, pero no entiendo	*I'm sorry, I don't understand*
¿Podrías hablar un poquito más despacio, por favor?	*could you speak a little more slowly, please?*
Lo siento, pero es que no hablo muy bien español	*sorry, I'm afraid my Spanish isn't very good*
¿Me podrías escribir eso, por favor?	*please could you write that down for me?*
¿Podrías deletrear eso, por favor?	*how do you spell that, please?*
¿Hay aquí alguien que hable inglés?	*does anyone here speak English?*

▼ Likes, dislikes and preferences

▶ Asking people what they like

¿Te gusta el cine?/**¿Te gustan** las peras?	*do you like …?*
¿Cuál de las tres camisas **te gusta más**?	*which of … do you like best?*
¿Te gustaría viajar a otra época?	*would you like to …?*

▶ Saying what you like or dislike

Me ha gustado mucho el regalo que me has enviado	*I was delighted with*
El chocolate **me vuelve loco** *or* **me chifla**	*I'm mad about*
Me encanta el mar	*I love*
Soy muy aficionado a la danza contemporánea	*I'm very keen on*
No me gusta nada comer fuera/que me mientan	*I really dislike*
Me molesta que me miren	*it annoys me when*
Mi vecina **me cae muy mal** *or* **no me cae nada bien**	*I don't like … at all*
Me horrorizan las corridas de toros	*I really hate*

▶ Saying what you prefer

Prefiero la lectura **a** la televisión	*I prefer … to*
Prefiero que vengas ahora **a que** lo hagas más tarde	*I'd rather you … than*
Es mejor *or* **preferible** hablar en el idioma del cliente	*it's better* or *preferable to*
Nos vendría mejor *or* **Nos convendría más** el lunes	*… would suit us better*

▶ Expressing indifference

Me da igual *or* **Me da lo mismo** vivir aquí **que** allí	*it's all the same to me whether … or*
Me es (completamente) indiferente que venga **o** no	*it makes (absolutely) no difference to me whether … or*
¿Vendrás también mañana? – **Como quieras**	*if you like*

▼ Opinions

▶ Asking for someone's opinion

¿Qué piensas de su actitud?	*what do you think of …?*
¿Qué te parece mi trabajo?	*what do you think of …?*
En tu opinión, ¿cuáles son sus posibilidades?	*in your opinion*

▶ Expressing your opinion

Creo *or* **Pienso** *or* **Me parece que** le gustará	*I think that*
Imagino que *or* **Supongo que** también les gustará	*I imagine* or *suppose that*
Lo que es yo, no lo veo necesario	*personally*
Estoy totalmente seguro de que nos lo van a devolver	*I'm quite sure that*
Si quieres que te diga la verdad, no me gusta nada	*to tell you the truth*
Tengo la impresión de que algo marcha mal	*I have the impression that*

▶ Replying without giving an opinion

No sé qué decirte	*I don't know what to say*
Depende	*it depends*
No puedo opinar sobre ese tema	*I can't express an opinion on*

▼ Agreement

▶ Agreeing with a statement

¡Claro que sí! *or* **¡Naturalmente!** ¡Ya lo creo que iré!	*of course*
¡Exacto! Ahí está la raíz del problema	*exactly*
Tienes (toda la) razón	*you're (quite) right*
Estoy de acuerdo (contigo)	*I agree (with you)*
Por supuesto que no está bien	*of course*
En eso tienes *or* **te doy toda la razón**	*you're quite right there*
Es cierto que es un tema delicado	*it is true that*
Admito que estaba equivocado	*I admit that*

▶ Agreeing to a proposal or request

¡Me apunto!	*count me in!*
¡Vale! *or* **¡Perfecto!** *or* **¡De acuerdo!**	*fine!*
Me parece una idea estupenda	*I think it's a great idea*
Me parece perfecto. Podemos empezar ya	*that seems fine to me*
Será un placer colaborar con ustedes	*it will be a pleasure to*
Estamos conformes con el precio que piden	*we agree to*
¿Que si iré? **¡Por supuesto** *or* **Claro que sí!**	*of course I will!*
Estaré encantado de participar en ese intercambio	*I'll be delighted to*
No tengo ningún inconveniente en que vengan ellos	*I have no objection to*

▼ Disagreement

▶ Disagreeing with what someone has said

¡No digas tonterías!	*don't talk nonsense!*
Yo no lo veo así	*that's not how I see it*

PRACTICAL SPANISH

No estoy de acuerdo contigo en ese punto — *I disagree with you on*
Yo opino de manera distinta — *I see it differently*

▶ **Disagreeing with what someone proposes**

¡De ninguna manera! — *no way!*
Me niego a votar sin estar debidamente informado — *I refuse to*
Me temo que no me será posible aceptar tu oferta — *I'm afraid I shall not be able to*

▶ **Refusing a request**

¡Ni hablar! — *no chance!*
¡Ni pensarlo! — *it's out of the question!*

▼ Approving and disapproving

▶ **Approval**

¡Buena idea! Yo también me voy a bañar — *good idea!*
Has hecho bien en decírmelo — *you were right to*
Me alegro mucho de que des un paso tan importante — *I'm so pleased that*

▶ **Disapproval**

¡Menuda ocurrencia! — *what a ridiculous idea!*
Me parece fatal que la gente fume — *I think it's awful that*
No deberías haber hablado así — *you shouldn't have*
No estamos conformes con tu versión de los hechos — *we're not happy with*

▼ Apologies

▶ **Apologizing**

¡Perdón! *or* **¡Lo siento!** — *sorry!*
Perdona por lo que dije/**por** no haber contestado antes — *I'm sorry about/for*
Lamentamos profundamente que haya ocurrido esto — *we are very sorry that*
Perdonen las molestias — *sorry for any inconvenience*

Disculpen si les he causado alguna molestia — *I apologize if*
Siento mucho no haber podido conseguir la información — *I'm so sorry that I wasn't able to*
Siento comunicarle que me es totalmente imposible — *I regret to tell you that*

▶ **Admitting or disclaiming responsibility**

Es culpa mía *or* **Yo tengo la culpa** — *it's my fault*
Me responsabilizo plenamente de todo — *I take full responsibility for*
Ha sido sin querer — *it was an accident*

▶ **Replying to an apology**

No pasa nada *or* **No te preocupes,** ya compraré otro — *don't worry about it*

No importa or **No tiene importancia**, ya lo sabíamos   *it doesn't matter*
No es ninguna molestia   *it's no trouble*

▼ Explanations

Tuvimos que marcharnos **porque** se puso a llover   *because*
Como tardabas en llegar, decidimos irnos   *as*
Las plantas se han marchitado **por** exceso de riego   *due to*
Tiene ahorros **gracias a** una herencia que recibió   *thanks to*
Con la nevada que ha caído no ha venido el cartero   *what with*
Ha sido desafortunado. **Por eso** le tengo tanta pena   *that's why*
En vista de que or **Dado que** no llegaban, nos fuimos   *seeing that* or *given that*
Debido al mal tiempo, decidieron cancelar la regata   *owing to*
El problema es grave, **ya que** no tienen más dinero   *for*
Ve pronto, **puesto que** or **pues** habrá mucha gente   *since*
Se cansa mucho **a causa de** su enfermedad   *because of*
No había autobuses **a** or **como consecuencia de** la huelga   *as a result of*
Tenía hambre, **así que** piqué unas aceitunas   *so*
Llamé antes de salir, **de modo que** sabían que íbamos para allá   *so*

▼ Comparisons

▶ Contrasting facts

La gente cena muy tarde, **comparado con** el Reino Unido   *compared with*
En comparación con mi país, el clima **no es tan** frío aquí   *in comparison with … is not so*
A mí me gusta el cine, **mientras que** ella prefiere el teatro   *while*

▶ Comparing similar things or facts

Su programa político **es igual que** el de la oposición   *is the same as*
Recibimos **casi tantos** turistas **como** en Grecia   *almost as many … as*
El paisaje es **tan** bello **como** lo describió el poeta   *as … as*
Ha vuelto a suceder **lo mismo que** hace unos años   *the same thing that*
El clima **es muy parecido** or **similar al** de mi país   *is very similar to*

▶ Comparing dissimilar things or facts

Los pros **son (muchos) más/menos que** los contras   *there are (far) more/fewer … than*
Es **más** inteligente **de lo que** parece   *more … than*
Este vino **es muy superior al** otro   *is vastly superior to*
No es lo mismo estar a dieta **que** ser anoréxico   *… is not the same as*
Esa canción ya **no** suena **tanto como** el año pasado   *not … as much as*
Este premio **no es tan** importante **como** el anterior   *is not as … as*
Este hotel es **mucho mejor/peor que** el otro   *much better/worse than*

▼ Offers

¿Te ayudo?   *shall I help (you)?*
¿Cierro la ventana?   *shall I close …?*

¿Necesitas ayuda?	*do you need any help?*
Si quieres, te acompaño	*... if you like*

▼ Requests

¿Me traes un vaso de agua?	*would you fetch me ...?*
¿Me dejas tu chaqueta?	*can I borrow ...?*
¿Quieres *or* **Te importa(ría)** cambiarme el turno?	*would you mind ...?*
¿Te puedo pedir un favor?	*can I ask you a favour?*
Por favor, házmelo cuanto antes	*please can you do it for me ...?*
Haz el favor de no poner los pies en el asiento	*please don't*
Vuelva a llamar en cinco minutos, **si es tan amable**	*if you don't mind*
Le agradecería que me ayudara a resolver el problema	*I'd be grateful if you would*
Tenga la amabilidad de respondernos	*please*
Le quedaría muy agradecido si me la diera	*I would be grateful if*

▼ Suggestions and advice

► Making suggestions

¿Y si organizáramos una fiesta para darle una sorpresa?	*what if ...?*
¿Te parece bien que la invitemos a la fiesta?	*do you think we should ...?*
¿Qué te parece decírselo por carta?	*how about ...?*
Lo que podríamos hacer es hablar con él	*what we could do is*
Propongo que busquemos ayuda profesional	*I suggest that*
Quizás habría que ser un poco más firmes con ellos	*perhaps you/we should*
Convendría *or* **Sería conveniente que** vinieras	*you would do well to*
Si me permite una sugerencia, creo que debería aplazarse	*if I may make a suggestion*

► Asking for suggestions or advice

¿Alguna idea? *or* **¿Se te ocurre algo?**	*any ideas?*
¿Tú qué dices? *or* **¿Cómo lo ves?**	*what do you think?*
¿Tú qué me aconsejas que haga?	*what would you advise me to do?*
¿Tú qué harías (si estuvieras) en mi lugar?	*what would you do if you were me?*
¿Qué restaurante **me recomiendas?**	*which ... would you recommend?*

► Giving advice or warnings

Yo que tú *or* **Yo en tu lugar** no haría nada por ahora	*if I were you*
Deberías mostrarte más abierto	*you should*
¿Por qué no la llamas por teléfono?	*why not ...?*
¿Y si fueras a su casa y le pidieras perdón?	*what if ...?*
Yo te aconsejaría un cambio de aires	*I'd recommend*
Más vale *or* **Sería mejor no** decir nada	*it would be better not to*
No sería mala idea enviarlo todo por correo	*it wouldn't be a bad idea to*
Lo mejor que puedes hacer es pedir más información	*the best thing you can do is*

Les advierto que no vamos a dar ninguna información	*I should warn you that*
No te fíes de lo que te digan	*don't believe*
No te olvides de cerrar la puerta al salir	*don't forget to*
¡Ni se te ocurra (hacerlo)!	*don't even think about (doing) it!*

▼ Intentions and desires

▶ Asking what someone intends to do

¿Qué piensas hacer?	*what do you intend or are you going to do?*
¿Qué planes tienes para la familia?	*what plans do you have …?*

▶ Saying what you intend to do

Voy a/Pienso tomar el tren de las siete	*I'm going to/I intend to*
Haremos los preparativos para la fiesta la noche antes	*we'll get everything ready for*
Tenemos previsto or **pensado** casarnos	*we're planning to*
Estoy decidido or **resuelto a** hacerlo como sea	*I'm determined to*

▶ Saying what you would like

Me gustaría or **Quisiera que** me atendieras	*I would like … to*
Me encantaría poder trabajar con él	*I'd love to be able to*
Ojalá no lloviera tanto	*if only it didn't rain*
Esperemos que todo salga bien	*let's hope that*

▶ Saying what you don't intend or don't want to do

No quiero que vayas a pensar otra cosa	*I don't want you to*
No pienso hacerle caso	*I don't intend to*
Me niego (rotundamente) a entrar en la polémica	*I (categorically) refuse to*
No desearíamos causarles molestias	*we would not wish to*

▼ Obligations

▶ Saying what someone must do

Tenemos que levantarnos a primera hora de la mañana	*we have to*
Las circunstancias políticas **me obligaron a** emigrar	*forced me to*
En verano **hay que** or **es preciso** proteger más la piel	*you must* or *have to*
Es obligatorio que figure la fecha de caducidad	*it is compulsory for … to*
Es imprescindible or **indispensable** leerlo	*it is essential to*
Se exige que todo el mundo lleve el DNI	*… is required to*

▶ Asking what you are obliged to do

¿Qué debo hacer para hacerme socio?	*what must I do to …?*
¿Se necesita carnet de conducir?	*do I need …?*
¿(De verdad) tengo que or **es obligatorio** pagar?	*do I (really) have to …?*

PRACTICAL SPANISH

▶ Saying what someone is not obliged to do

No hace falta or **No es necesario que** lo hagas **si no quieres**	you needn't … if you don´t want to
No estás obligado a contestar si no quieres	you're not obliged to
No tienes por qué aceptar una oferta que no te interesa	there is no reason for you to

▶ Saying what someone must not do

No se puede or **No puedes** fumar	you cannot
No te permito que me hables de ese modo	I won't have you
Está prohibido fumar	… is prohibited

▼ Permission

▶ Asking for permission

¿Puedo pasar?	may I …?
¿Me dejas que lo use **yo** antes?	will you let me …?
¿Se puede aparcar aquí?	can I …?
¿Te importa si subo la tele un poco?	do you mind if …?
¿Podría hacerte unas preguntas?	could I …?
¿Te molesta que abra la ventana?	do you mind if …?
¿Tendrían inconveniente en que tomáramos unas fotos?	would you mind if …?

▶ Giving or refusing permission

¡Naturalmente or **Claro que** puedes ir!	of course
Haz lo que quieras	do what you like
No tengo ningún inconveniente en responder	I don't have any objection to
¡Ni pensarlo!	no way!
No se puede fumar aquí	you can't
Lo siento, pero no está permitido el acceso a menores	I'm sorry, but … aren't allowed in
Te prohíbo (terminantemente) que hables así	I (absolutely) forbid you to

▶ Saying that permission is granted or refused

La dejan acostarse a la hora que quiera	she's allowed to
Me dijo que podía venir cuando quisiera	he said I could
Nuestros padres **nos dieron permiso para** ir	gave us permission to
No me dejan or **No me está permitido** or **Tengo prohibido** participar en la carrera	I'm not allowed to
No estoy autorizado a hacer declaraciones	I'm not authorized to

▼ Certainty, probability and possibility

▶ Certainty

Seguro que no está en casa	I'm sure
Está claro que no tienen intención de votar	it is obvious that

Es obvio or **evidente que** será todo un éxito	it is clear that
Por supuesto que siempre va a haber quien le crea	of course
Será, casi con toda or **total seguridad**, este domingo	it will almost certainly be
Sin lugar a dudas or **Sin duda alguna**, es una estafa	without a doubt

▶ **Probability**

Seguramente se ha retrasado por el camino	… probably …
Debe (de) haberse olvidado de su compromiso	he must have
Lo más seguro or **probable es que** no venga	… almost certainly …
Probablemente sea ella	… probably …
Parece ser que han decidido no publicar la noticia	it seems that
Hay muchas posibilidades de que lo consigamos	it is very likely that

▶ **Possibility**

Igual tengo suerte y apruebo	I may
A lo mejor hago escala en Tenerife	… may …
Quizá(s) or **Tal vez** tengamos que volver antes	perhaps
Puede que la situación se convierta en irreversible	… may …
Dicho grupo **podría ser** el autor del robo	could be
Posiblemente sea él	… may …

▼ Doubt, improbability and impossibility

▶ **Doubt**

No sé si debemos discutir ese tema ahora	I don't know if
No estoy seguro de que or **No tengo muy claro que** sea lo mejor	I'm not sure if …
No es seguro que venga	… won't necessarily …
No está claro quién va a salir ganando de todo esto	it isn't clear who
Dudo que vuelva a haber otra oferta similar	I doubt if

▶ **Improbability**

Es difícil que el actual campeón participe este año	… is unlikely to …
Dudo mucho que el cambio implique una mejora de la calidad	I very much doubt whether
No parece que vaya a hacer buen tiempo	it doesn't look as if
Me extrañaría or **Me sorprendería (mucho) que** fuera ella	I should be (very) surprised if
Es (muy) poco probable que suba el precio	… is (very) unlikely to …
Tiene muy pocas posibilidades de ascender de puesto	he doesn't have much chance of

▶ **Impossibility**

No es posible que sea or **No puede ser** verdad	it can't be
Es totalmente or **completamente imposible que** fuera él	it can't possibly
No existe ninguna posibilidad de que construyan un museo	there isn't the slightest chance of
Me es imposible llamarla hasta mañana	I can't

▼ Standard letter openings and closings

► In formal correspondence to someone you do not know

Estimado/a señor/a *or* Sr./Sra.
Estimados señores *or* Sres.   (Muy) atentamente
Estimado/a amigo/a
Distinguido/a cliente
Muy señor *or* Sr. mío   Reciba un cordial saludo
Muy señores *or* Sres. míos

► In formal correspondence to officials

Excmo. Sr.   (Muy) atentamente
Ilmo. Sr.   Reciba un (muy) cordial saludo
                  Sin otro particular, aprovecho la ocasión
                     para saludarle (cordialmente)
                  Aprovecho la ocasión para enviarle mi
                     más distinguida consideración

► With title and surname in formal or fairly formal correspondence

Estimado Sr. González   (Muy) cordialmente
Estimados Sr. y Sra. González   Reciba un (muy) cordial saludo
Estimada Sra. González   *or quite a lot less formal:*
Estimado Dr. Gónzalez   Un afectuoso saludo
                             Saludos cordiales
                             Saludos

► To friends and family

Querido *or* Estimado Luis   Un (fuerte) abrazo
Querida *or* Estimada Ana   Muchos besos
Queridos *or* Estimados primos   Muchos besos y abrazos de ...
Queridos *or* Estimados mamá y papá Con todo mi cariño
Queridos *or* Estimados abuelos   ¡Hasta pronto!
Querida *or* Estimada tía Rosario
¡Hola Lidia!

NOTES:
1 In Spanish, a colon rather than a comma, is usually used after the opening formula.
2 When addressing envelopes, it is common to use **Sr. D.** before a man's forename and surnames and **Sra. Dña.** before a woman's.

▼ Letter to a tourist office

José María Aguilar
C/ Joaquín María López 5, 8º A
Madrid 28005

Oficina de Turismo
Granada 18003   Madrid, 3 de abril de 2003

Estimados Sres.:

Me pongo en contacto con ustedes porque estoy organizando una visita a Granada de dos días para un grupo de diez turistas coreanos que estarán de paso por varias ciudades españolas entre los días 5 y 12 de julio de este año.

Dado su gran atractivo turístico, Granada es una de las ciudades que desean visitar y me gustaría que me enviaran, si es posible, algunos folletos sobre los monumentos de interés de la ciudad, así como alguna información sobre restaurantes de calidad y hoteles de categoría superior a tres estrellas, a fin de poder realizar la reserva con la debida antelación. Sería bueno saber también cuáles de estos hoteles disponen de piscina, ya que imagino que por esas fechas las temperaturas ya deben de ser muy altas.

Por otra parte, me gustaría que me informaran sobre la posibilidad de comprar con antelación las entradas para visitar la Alhambra, pues me han dicho que es necesario realizar reserva, debido al gran número de visitas del monumento. Además hace poco me pareció leer en la prensa que existía un bono turístico que incluía la entrada a otros monumentos además de la Alhambra y me gustaría saber si es posible adquirirlo desde Madrid con anterioridad a la visita.

Por último, hay un par de personas interesadas en conocer los lugares relacionados con la vida de Federico García Lorca, por lo que le quedaría muy agradecido si también me pudiera enviar información sobre este tema.

Muchas gracias por su atención.

Atentamente,

José María Aguilar
José María Aguilar

▶ Useful expressions

Me pongo en contacto con ustedes porque ...
I am writing to you because ...

Sería bueno saber también cuáles ...
It would also be good to know which ...

Me gustaría que me informaran sobre la posibilidad de ...
Please could you give me any information about the possibility of ... ?

Me gustaría saber si es posible ...
I would like to know if it is possible ...

Le quedaría muy agradecido si me pudiera enviar información sobre ...
I would be very grateful if you could send me information about ...

▼ Formal e-mail booking a hotel

De: silvia@liberia.com
Para: info@marinahotels.com
Asunto: Reserva

In Spanish, when telling someone your e-mail address, you say: **silvia arroba liberia punto com**

Estimados Sres.:

Por la presente quisiera confirmar la reserva telefónica de alojamiento durante los días 20 y 21 de mayo en su hotel de Carmona (Sevilla), en régimen de habitación y desayuno.

Les ruego que me confirmen que el precio de la habitación doble con desayuno incluido es de 115 euros más el 16% de IVA. Asimismo, les agradecería que me informasen de si es posible disfrutar de un régimen de media pensión o de pensión completa y cuál sería el coste de ésta. Mi esposo es diabético, por lo que necesita una dieta especial y querríamos saber si cuentan con este tipo de servicios en su establecimiento.

Por otro lado, he visto en el folleto que el hotel tiene una estupenda piscina exterior, pero no sé si por estas fechas estará ya abierta al público.

Finalmente, dado que viajaremos en coche desde Madrid y que llegaremos bastante tarde a Carmona, le agradecería también que nos tuviera reservada una plaza en el parking.

Sin otro particular, quedo a la espera de su respuesta y le envío un cordial saludo

Silvia Llompart

▶ Useful expressions

Por la presente quisiera confirmar la reserva telefónica
I am writing to confirm my telephone booking
Les ruego que me confirmen ...
Please can you confirm ...?
habitación individual/habitación doble (con una cama/con dos camas)/suite familiar
single room/double room (with double bed/twin beds)/family room
con baño
with bathroom
acceso para minusválidos
disabled access
régimen de media pensión/pensión completa
half board/full board
¿El desayuno está incluido?
Is breakfast included?
Quedo a la espera de su respuesta
I look forward to hearing from you

▼ Formal letter of complaint

Manuel Lugo Iglesias
C/ Sedeño 23
18006 Granada

3 de octubre de 2002

Gerente
Restaurante Sodakoff
C/ Málaga 35
18002 Granada

Estimado Sr.:

Por la presente quisiera manifestar mi descontento en relación al servicio de su restaurante en el día 9 de septiembre pasado, en una reciente visita a Granada.

Habíamos confirmado una reserva para 11 personas en la mesa más grande, la que queda un poco más apartada del resto del comedor, pero al llegar allí nos dicen que esa mesa está ya ocupada porque ha llegado un grupo de 10 y tienen que ponerlos allí, ante lo cual ni siquiera nos pidieron disculpas.

Cuando nos sentamos, todo se complicó a la hora de pedir los platos, pues ya no quedaban de la mayoría de los que aparecían en la carta, a pesar de que eran sólo las 10 de la noche. Al final tuvimos que conformarnos con elegir entre dos opciones, ninguna de los cuales era vegetariana, a pesar de que había sido la oferta de platos sin carne uno de los motivos por los que fuimos allí a cenar. De nuevo, ni una sola disculpa por parte de los camareros que nos atendían.

Tengo que decir que la calidad de los pocos platos que ofrecían era correcta, pero cuando llegamos a los postres, el helado estaba prácticamente derretido y además nos dijeron que no podían hacernos un café porque la máquina ya estaba apagada. Para colmo de males, tanto la cerveza como el cava que nos sirvieron durante la cena no estaban a la temperatura adecuada.

Por todo ello, le agradecería que me diera alguna explicación sobre estos fallos del restaurante y, ya que es un sitio que nos agrada y al que nos gustaría volver, esperamos que mejoren el trato en el futuro.

Atentamente,

Manuel Lugo

Manuel Lugo

PRACTICAL SPANISH

▶ **Useful expressions**

Por la presente quisiera hacer constar una reclamación formal en relación a/manifestar mi descontento en relación a …
I am writing to make a formal complaint about/to bring to your attention my dissatisfaction regarding …
Al final tuvimos que …
In the end we had to …
Le agradecería que …
I would be grateful if you …

▼ Holiday e-mail

De : jmcrespo@liberia.com ◄--------

Para : marifranta@perilis.com

CC :

Asunto : vacaciones caribeñas

> In Spanish, when telling someone your e-mail address, you say: **j m crespo arroba liberia punto com**

Queridos Mari y Paco:

Hace tanto tiempo que no nos vemos que seguro que no teníais ni idea de que este verano teníamos planeado un viaje largo. Pues así ha sido, sin pensarlo dos veces, hemos venido a Cuba, que hacía ya tiempo que teníamos ganas. Primero estuvimos una semana en Santiago de Cuba y ahora estamos pasando unos días en la Habana, que es una ciudad maravillosa, con todo lo decadente que pueden parecer algunos rincones.

Además, estamos teniendo mucha suerte con el tiempo pues, aunque habían anunciado un huracán, de momento hace un sol espléndido y parece que se trataba sólo de una falsa alarma.

Nos lo estamos pasando muy bien, la gente es muy acogedora y estamos comiendo cada día en un sitio distinto, todo muy rico. No me extraña que la gente quede enamorada de esta isla y que cada vez vengan más españoles. Fíjate, el otro día vimos por la calle a un presentador de la tele y le saludamos y todo. El encuentro fue muy divertido y el tío era muy simpático.

¿Y por allí, qué tal? ¿Habéis ido a algún sitio este verano? El otro día vimos en las noticias que no para de llover en Europa, así que menos mal que hemos elegido venir a un sitio tropical, en vez de ir a Praga, que era adonde teníamos planeado ir en principio.

Espero que nos veamos pronto a la vuelta. Tenemos mucho que contar y estamos haciendo muchas fotos con la nueva cámara digital, que es una maravilla, así que un día hacemos una cena en casa y nos ponemos al día, ¿vale?

Muchos besos de vuestros amigos,

José María y Carmen

▶ Useful expressions

Estamos pasando las vacaciones/unos días en la Habana
We're having our holiday/spending a few days in Havana

Estamos teniendo mucha suerte con el tiempo
We've been very lucky with the weather

Hace un sol espléndido
It's lovely and sunny

Ayer nos cruzamos con/vimos por la calle a …
Yesterday we bumped into … /we saw … in the road

Nos lo estamos pasando muy bien
We're having a great time

¿Y por allí qué tal?
How are things with you?

▼ Informal letter of apology

Barcelona, 5 de enero de 2003

Querida Francis:

Lo primero es pedirte disculpas por la forma en que desaparecí de vuestra boda. La verdad es que pensaba que iba a aguantar mejor, aunque sólo fuera la media hora de la ceremonia. Sin embargo, al final me emocioné al ver que ya no estaba allí Antonio con nosotros y luego perdí el control de las lágrimas. Lo siento mucho, de verdad.

Espero que lo hayáis pasado muy bien en la luna de miel y que hayáis tenido una buena entrada en vuestra nueva etapa. Yo me quedé tres días más en Madrid y allí tuve ocasión de visitar sitios en los que hacía tiempo que no estaba y también quedé con Julia y con Justino, que hacía mucho que no los veía.

Veréis, también os escribo con relación a vuestro regalo de bodas. La verdad es que estoy encantada con que hayáis aceptado la invitación de venir a Barcelona, pero lo que pasa es que al final he tenido un montón de gastos este mes con el coche y luego, con lo de la compra del piso, me he quedado sin un duro. Me siento fatal por esto, pero este mes no voy a poder pagaros el viaje como os prometí, así que lo vamos a tener que dejar para más adelante, si no quiero acabar pidiendo en las Ramblas. Espero que no os importe mucho esperar, pero en cuanto pueda, os envío el dinero para el vuelo, es una promesa.

De nuevo, os pido disculpas por todo y espero que me escribáis muy pronto.

Un fuerte abrazo de vuestra amiga,

Maripaz

PRACTICAL SPANISH

▶ **Useful expressions**

Lo primero es pedir disculpas por …
Firstly, I must apologize for …
Lo siento mucho, de verdad
I'm really or *so sorry*
Me siento fatal por esto
I feel terrible about it
Espero que no os importe mucho esperar
I hope you won't mind too much having to wait

▼ Informal thank you e-mail

de: octavio@hitmail.com
a: diana@wanadu.es

> In Spanish, when telling someone your e-mail address, you say: **octavio arroba hitmail punto com**

¡Hola Diana!

Oye, muchas gracias por el CD que me has regalado para mi cumpleaños. Desde luego, has dado en el clavo, pues hace tiempo que tenía ganas de tener la versión de Josep Pons de El amor brujo, desde que lo oí en concierto hace un par de años.

Me vino muy bien oírlo al día siguiente del cumpleaños y relajarme un poco, después de tanta marcha. Al final salimos hasta las tantas y luego tuve una resaca de muerte. Nada mejor que oír a Carmen Linares interpretando a Falla con ese pedazo de voz. Se me ponía la carne de gallina, tía.

Creo que el próximo cumpleaños lo celebraré de una forma más tranquila yendo a un concierto, en vez de tanto jaleo.

Nos vemos pronto,

Octavio

▶ Useful expressions

¡Hola Diana!
Hi Diana
Oye, muchas gracias
Thanks so much
hasta las tantas
until really late
una resaca de muerte
an almighty hangover
ese pedazo de voz
that really powerful voice
se me pone la carne de gallina
it gives me goose bumps
tanta marcha
all that partying
Nos vemos pronto
See you soon

▼ Letter to a newspaper

POR UN COLEGIO MEJOR

La asociación de padres de alumnos del colegio público La Rosaleda envió hace unos meses un escrito al alcalde y al delegado de educación haciendo constar su profundo malestar e inquietud por el mal estado en que se encuentra el centro.

La realidad del problema que estamos exponiendo se refleja en las siguientes cifras: los niños de primaria disponen apenas de un metro de espacio por niño. A partir de secundaria, la situación se agrava aún más, ya que el recreo lo tienen que hacer en la calle, entre los coches y en una zona en la que es habitual encontrar jeringuillas usadas.

Acudimos a este diario, porque la única respuesta institucional que han recibido nuestras demandas ha sido que no se dispone de presupuesto para la adquisición de otro centro. Esperamos que no tenga que suceder una desgracia para llegar a denunciar a unas instituciones que incumplen las normas que ellas mismas emiten. José Vázquez Carrasco. Sevilla

▶ **Useful expressions**

hacer constar
to put on record
nuestro profundo malestar e inquietud por …
our deep unease and concern regarding …
La realidad del problema se refleja en …
The extent of the problem is shown by …
no se dispone de presupuesto para …
there's no budget for …
Esperamos que no tenga que suceder una desgracia para …
Let's hope there doesn't have to be tragedy for …

PRACTICAL SPANISH

▶ **Useful expressions**

Muchas gracias por su carta/fax/mensaje de fecha …
Many thanks for your letter/fax/message of …

Con referencia a …
With reference to …

En respuesta a su carta de …
In reply to your letter of …

En relación a mi carta/correspondencia anterior
Further to my previous letter/correspondence

Continuando con nuestra conversación telefónica de fecha 3 de mayo …
Further to our telephone conversation of May 3 …

Le quedaría muy agradecido si pudiera …
I would be very grateful if you could …

Acuso recibo de su carta de fecha …
I acknowledge receipt of your letter dated …

Le escribo para solicitar información sobre …
I am writing to you to enquire about …

Adjunto le envío copia de la carta
Please find enclosed a copy of the letter

Tal como quedamos, le envío …
I am sending you …, as agreed

El folleto adjunto muestra …
The attached brochure shows …

Como se puede ver en el folleto adjunto …
As you will see from the attached brochure …

Le ruego me permita presentarme
Please allow me to introduce myself

Enrique Gómez me sugirió que me pusiera en contacto con usted en relación a/con vistas a …
Enrique Gomez suggested that I contact you regarding/with a view to …

Lamento/Siento/Me complace informarle de que …
I regret/I am sorry/I am pleased to inform you that …

Para más información, por favor, visite nuestra página web en …
For further information, please visit our website at …

Si necesita más información, por favor, no dude en contactar conmigo
If you need further information, please do not hesitate to contact me

Puede localizarme durante las horas de oficina en el número 987 245 345, o en el móvil (670 123 123) en cualquier otro momento
You can contact me on 987 245 345 during office hours or on my mobile (670 123 123) at any other time

Le ruego tenga en cuenta que …
Please note that …

Le ruego una pronta respuesta
Please reply at your earliest convenience

Muchas gracias por …
Thanking you for …

Sin otro particular, quedo a la espera de sus noticias/de nuestro futuro encuentro
I look forward to hearing from you/to seeing you

▼ Fax ordering a catalogue

FAX

**Centro de estudios Enseñanza Activa,
Avda. de Aragón 5, 74003 Huesca**

Para: Grupo Editorial Sonrisas y Lágrimas S.A.
Fax: 93 666 666

De: Julia Castellano, Sección de referencias
Fax: 974 432 532

Fecha: 17 de marzo de 2003
Asunto: Catálogo de libros infantiles

Nº de páginas (incluida ésta): 1

Estimados Sres.:

Les ruego que sean tan amables de enviarme un par de ejemplares de su catálogo de libros infantiles a la dirección que aparece arriba en este fax, junto con una lista de precios que incluya los descuentos para pedidos de grandes cantidades.

Asimismo, si es posible, les agradecería que me enviaran un ejemplar de algún diccionario ilustrativo que consideren adecuado para alumnos de primaria, ya que estamos pensando en sustituir los que tenemos actualmente.

Muchas gracias por su atención y les envío un atento saludo,

Julia Castellano

P.D. Si tiene algún problema para leer este fax, por favor, póngase en contacto con Clara Fernández en el 974 432 533

▶ **Useful expressions**

Les ruego que sean tan amables de …
Please would you be so kind as to …
Asimismo, les agradecería que …
Also, I should be grateful if you …
Muchas gracias por su atención
Thank you for your help in this matter
P.D.
PS
Si tienen algún problema para …
If you have any problem …
Por favor, pónganse en contacto con … en el …
Please contact … on …

▼ Order

Comestibles Vintage
Plaza Lalla 6
08002 Barcelona

Ricardo Bonell
Vinos y Cavas S.L.
Avda. de Barcelona 7
77004 Tarragona

REF: pedido 210/02

Barcelona, 15 de noviembre de 2002

Estimado Sr. Bonell:

Con referencia a las muestras que recibimos de su nueva gama de vinos tintos y según la lista de precios que nos enviaron, quisieramos realizar el siguiente pedido:

Cantidad/unidades	Producto	Año	Precio/caja
20 cajas de 12 botellas	Riberas	99	85 euros/caja
12 cajas de 12 botellas	Conde Robles	00	63.2 euros/caja
10 cajas de 12 botellas	Altares	99	80 euros/caja

Les rogamos que nos hagan llegar la mercancía antes del 1 de diciembre, a ser posible.

Por otro lado, como ya habíamos acordado por teléfono, le confirmo que al precio de la caja se le sumará el 7% del IVA correspondiente, mientras que el porte quedaría incluido en el precio total. En cuanto recibamos la mercancía y la factura les realizaremos el pago a la cuenta que nos indiquen.

Sin otro particular, quedo a la espera de sus noticias y les envío un muy cordial saludo,

María Ramírez Aguileño

María Ramírez Aguileño

▶ Useful expressions

Con referencia a ...
With reference to ...
quisieramos realizar el siguiente pedido
we should like to place the following order
Les rogamos que nos hagan llegar ...
We would be grateful if you would arrange delivery ...
a ser posible
if possible
Como ya habíamos acordado por teléfono
As agreed over the telephone

▼ Letter relating to an order

Luis Martínez Moreno
C/ Nicaragua 23 5º izda.
28345 Alcalá de Henares
Madrid

Autoprinsa S.L.
C/ Antonio Machado 30
08024 Barcelona

Alcalá de Henares, 25 de enero de 2003

Estimados Sres.:

Esta mañana he recibido el paquete con los altavoces del radiocasete del coche modelo X-3232 que les había pedido por teléfono. Sin embargo, no sé si se ha debido a un malentendido o si se han perdido durante el transporte, pero en lugar de los cuatro altavoces que les había pedido, sólo me han llegado dos.

Dado que ya les había abonado por adelantado la cantidad correspondiente a los cuatro altavoces, les ruego me los hagan llegar a la mayor brevedad a la dirección que aparece arriba en la carta.

Muchas gracias y les envío un cordial saludo,

Luis Martínez

Luis Martínez

▶ Useful expressions

el modelo ... que les había pedido por teléfono
model number ... as ordered by telephone
No sé si se ha debido a un malentendido o si ...
I don't know whether this is due to a misunderstanding or whether ...
se han perdido durante el transporte
they have been lost in transit
Dado que ...
As ...
la cantidad correspondiente a ...
the sum corresponding to ...
Les ruego me los hagan llegar ...
I would be grateful if you would arrange delivery ...
a la mayor brevedad
at your earliest convenience

▼ Letter introducing a product

CIBERTÉCNICA S.L.
C/ Lonas 35
Polígono Industrial Central
Barcelona 08356

HIPERHISPANIA S. L.
C/ Pelayo 35
Barcelona 08001

Barcelona, 5 de octubre de 2002

Estimado Sr. Gómez:

Tengo el gusto de escribirle para ofrecerles la posibilidad de mejorar el software de su oficina sin el inconveniente de tener que ir buscando cuál es la mejor oferta y sin necesidad de tener que encontrar la ayuda técnica más adecuada para su negocio en cada momento.

En Cibertécnica siempre hemos pensado que el cliente es lo más importante y nuestros servicios y nuestra cifra de negocios así lo demuestran. Desde las pequeñas empresas hasta las multinacionales, nuestro propósito es el de satisfacer a nuestros clientes por medio de la eliminación de los obstáculos en cualquier situación, nuestro cuidado de los detalles y nuestra excelente relación calidad-precio.

Le adjuntamos a esta carta un folleto en el que se describe el tipo de atención personalizada que podemos prestar a HIPERHISPANIA S.L., así como todos nuestros productos informáticos. Además de una completa gama de servicios informáticos, también le ofrecemos una asistencia 24 horas al día de lunes a viernes y un servicio de asistencia al instante. Para mayor información, puede visitar también nuestra página web (www.cibertecnica.com) o llamar a nuestro servicio de atención al cliente (902 333434).

Le agradezco mucho su atención y le envío un cordial saludo,

Miguel Romero

Miguel Romero

Gerente

► **Useful expressions**

Tengo el gusto de escribirle para ...
I have the pleasure of writing to you to ...
Nuestro propósito principal es el de satisfacer a nuestros clientes ...
Our main aim is to satisfy our clients ...
Le adjuntamos a esta carta un folleto en el que ...
Enclosed, please find a brochure in which ...
Le ofrecemos una asistencia 24 horas al día
We can provide you with 24-hour support
excelente relación calidad-precio
outstanding value for money
Para mayor información, puede ...
For further information, you can ...

▼ Formal e-mail setting up a meeting

De: joseg@hiperhispania.com

Para: luisma@tranzine.com

Asunto: Futura reunión

> In Spanish, when telling someone your e-mail address, you say: **josé g arroba hiperhispania punto com**

Estimado Sr. Martín:

Hace tiempo que quería escribirle, pero desde aquella presentación que nos hizo de los nuevos servicios de traducción de su empresa, no me había sido posible ponerme en contacto con usted.

En realidad, me parecieron muy interesante tanto los servicios como los presupuestos que nos ofreció, pero hasta estos días no había tenido ocasión de hablar más detenidamente con el responsable del servicio de traducciones de la editorial. Parece que los dos estamos de acuerdo en que podríamos empezar a enviarles textos durante un período de prueba y, si todo va bien, seguir trabajando con ustedes.

De momento tenemos varios capítulos de un libro sobre salud pública que será publicado por una editorial francesa. La traducción es del inglés al español y no parece demasiado difícil. El único problema es que lo necesitamos con bastante urgencia, así que espero que me pueda confirmar pronto que les es posible hacerse cargo del trabajo.

También me gustaría comentar con usted con más detalle las tarifas para los servicios de interpretación, ya que pronto tendremos que organizar un congreso y necesitaremos gente que hable inglés y ruso. Por ello, si le es posible, me gustaría que tuviéramos un encuentro en persona el lunes que viene para hablar más detenidamente del tema. Si no le va bien esa fecha, podemos vernos otro día que me sugiera.

Quedo a la espera de sus noticias.

Saludos,

José García

► **Useful expressions**

Hace tiempo que quería escribirle
I have been meaning to write to you for some time
Me gustaría que tuviéramos un encuentro en persona
It would be good to have a meeting in person
para hablar más detenidamente del tema de ...
to discuss the matter of ... in more depth
si no le va bien esa fecha
if this date is not convenient for you
podemos vernos otro día que me sugiera
we can meet on any other day you care to suggest
Saludos
Regards

▼ Agenda for meeting

Asistencia de software – Robomática y Cibertécnica

ORDEN DEL DÍA

1 Presentación del producto de Cibertécnica por Miguel Romero
2 Resumen del proveedor actual, Robomática, por Carlos León
3 Comparación entre Robomática y Cibertécnica
4 Otros puntos

Copias para – José Gómez, Luis Romeral, Pedro Ramos y Pilar Toro

Asistencia de software Robomática y Cibertécnica

Jueves 12 de octubre de 2002, 18:00

Asistentes: José Gómez, Luis Romeral, Pedro Ramos, Pilar Toro, Carlos León y Miguel Romero

Actas

1 MR expuso la propuesta de servicios profesionales de Cibertécnica y aportó la documentación informativa adjunta.

2 CL describió en qué consistía el paquete actual de la oferta de Robomática.

3 JG manifestó su postura crítica ante la lenta reacción de Robomática durante la avería del mes de julio. LR, PR y PT estaban de acuerdo. PT manifestó también su preocupación sobre algunos asuntos relacionados con la seguridad que afectan a Robomática. JG, PR y MR estaban de acuerdo. Como consecuencia y en relación con estos problemas de seguridad, todos acordaron que la oferta de Cibermática debía ser aceptada, si cumplían estos requisitos de seguridad.

4 PT hizo una anotación sobre el nuevo software de reconocimiento de voz que había sido producido por Intervox y sugirió que se probara.

Conclusiones

1 LR debe resolver las cuestiones de seguridad con MN de Cibertécnica e informar del resultado a JG.

2 PT debe conseguir el software de Intervox durante un período de prueba.

► **Useful expressions**

orden del día *agenda*
otros puntos (a tratar) *any other business*
actas *minutes*
conclusiones *action points*
asistentes: *present:*

▼ Follow up e-mail

De: joseg@hiperhispania.com
Para: pedrog@liberia.com
Asunto: Cambio de proveedor

> In Spanish, when telling someone your e-mail address, you say: **josé g arroba hiperhispania punto com**

¡Hola Pedro!

Como continuación de la reunión que tuvimos el jueves pasado, quería informarte de que he estado en contacto con Miguel Núñez de Cibertécnica y me ha confirmado que los problemas de seguridad pueden resolverse. Además el otro día tuvimos una reunión de empresa y ya se decidió que seguiríamos adelante con estos nuevos proveedores.

Quería comunicártelo para que, como tenías tus dudas al respecto, supieras que hemos hablado de los problemas con ellos y parece que son fáciles de resolver.

Una cosa que nos han dicho es que dentro de tres meses pasarán un test de calidad para comprobar la satisfacción de los programas. Espero que tanto los colaboradores que utilizáis estos programas desde casa, como los que estamos en la oficina, quedemos satisfechos con los resultados.

De todas formas, no dudes en hacerme llegar cualquier comentario que se te ocurra sobre el funcionamiento del nuevo software.

Espero verte pronto por aquí.

Un saludo,

Jose García

PRACTICAL SPANISH

▶ **Useful expressions**

Como continuación a la reunión que tuvimos …
Following the meeting we had …
Quería informarte de que …
I wanted to let you know that …
Quería comunicártelo para que …
I wanted to let you know so that …
Una cosa que nos han dicho es que …
One thing they've said is that …
No dudes en hacerme llegar cualquier comentario que se te ocurra
Don't hesitate to pass on any comments you may have

PUBLICIDAD HIPERHISPANIA
http://www.hiperhispania.com

Hiperhispania, una de las empresas de publicidad líderes del sector, perteneciente a un importante grupo internacional y con una sólida presencia nacional, precisa incorporar en su sede de Barcelona:

Director de publicidad

Dependiendo de la dirección comercial, se responsabilizará de la gestión personalizada de los clientes y de asegurar el correcto cumplimiento de los objetivos y políticas establecidos, atendiendo tanto al mercado nacional como al de las ventas dirigidas al mercado europeo.

Buscamos profesionales con las siguientes cualidades:

* Experiencia de al menos 3 años en puesto similar
* Titulación universitaria, con formación adicional en el área de tratamiento de textos e imágenes
* Buenos conocimientos de inglés y alemán

Nuestra oferta:

* Incorporación a una compañía sólida con inmejorables posibilidades de promoción y desarrollo profesional futuro
* Entorno de trabajo innovador y dinámico
* Vehículo de la empresa
* Retribución negociable según experiencia y valores aportados

Presentación de solicitudes con CV y carta de presentación a:

info@hiperhispania.com

O por correo a:

HIPERHISPANIA S.L.
C/ Pelayo 35
Barcelona 08001

► **Useful expressions**

Buscamos profesionales con las siguientes cualidades
We are seeking professionals who meet the following requirements

buenos conocimientos de inglés
a good knowledge of English

experiencia de al menos 3 años
at least 3 years' experience

incorporación a una compañía sólida
the opportunity to join an established company

vehículo de la empresa
company car

currículum y carta de presentación
CV (BRIT) or résumé (US) and covering letter (BRIT) or cover letter (US)

El plazo de presentación de solicitudes acaba el ...
The closing date (esp BRIT) or final date for applications is ...

Las entrevistas tendrán lugar a partir del día 1 de noviembre
Interviews will take place from November 1

Carmen Piñero Collat
C/ Consell de Cent 65 2º 4ª
08006 Barcelona

3 de octubre de 2002

HIPERHISPANIA S.L.
C/ Pelayo 35
Barcelona 08001

Estimados Sres.:

En respuesta al anuncio publicado en el periódico *El mundo de hoy* con fecha 1 de octubre, en el que se solicita un director de publicidad, quisiera presentar mi solicitud para el puesto que se anuncia.

Como se puede ver en el currículum vitae adjunto, llevo varios años como editora especializada en publicidad y creo que cumplo con los requisitos necesarios para este tipo de trabajo.

Tengo perfecto dominio de los idiomas inglés y alemán, así como sólidos conocimientos de informáticas y de herramientas de diseño gráfico. Asimismo tengo bastante habilidad para el trato con clientes externos y con contactos extranjeros.

Quedo a su disposición para ampliar cualquier información que necesite al respecto, así como para asistir a una entrevista, si fuera necesario.

Muchas gracias por su atención y, sin otro particular, le saluda atentamente,

Carmen Piñero

▶ **Useful expressions**

En respuesta a su anuncio publicado en ...
Further to your advertisement in ...
Como se puede ver en ...
As you will see from ...
Tengo perfecto dominio de ...
I speak excellent ...
Quedo a su disposición para asistir a una entrevista/una reunión
I am available to attend an interview/a meeting
Muchas gracias por su atención
Thank you for your help in this matter
Quedo a la espera de su respuesta
I look forward to hearing from you

PRACTICAL SPANISH

PRACTICAL SPANISH

Datos personales:

Nombre: Carmen Piñero Collat
Dirección: C/ Consell de Cent 65 2° 4ª
08006 Barcelona
Teléfono: 93 4374499
Dirección electrónica: capico@yal.com
Edad: 30
Nacionalidad: española
Estado civil: soltera
Carnet de conducir: sí

Estudios universitarios:

1990–1995:	Universidad de Barcelona: Licenciatura en Filología Hispánica
1996:	Universidad de Glasgow: Máster en Publicidad y Comunicación

Experiencia profesional:

1999–presente:	Subdirectora del Departamento de Diseño y Producción en el diario *La Red de Barcelona*
1998–1999:	Ayudante en la sección de publicidad de la revista *¡Adiós!*
1997	Estancia en Bonn como lectora en el Departamento de Lenguas Extranjeras de la Universidad Autónoma

Otros datos de interés:

Informática:
Conocimientos avanzados a nivel de usuario de Internet, Windows y UNIX
Procesadores de texto: Word Perfect, Microsoft Word
Hojas de cálculo: Excel, Lotus 123
Bases de datos: Access

Idiomas:
Castellano – nativa
Catalán – nativa
Inglés – nivel alto
Alemán – nivel alto

Referencias:

Carlos Vaca	Josep Puig Cantallops
Editor jefe	Director
¡Adiós!	*La Red de Barcelona*

► **Useful expressions**

Datos personales *Personal details*
Estudios universitarios *University education*
Experiencia profesional *Professional experience*
Referencias *Referees*

► Useful expressions

Información – ¿con qué ciudad desea hablar?
Directory enquiries (BRIT) or Information (US) – which town, please?

Hola, en estos momentos no le puedo atender, pero deje su mensaje después de oír la señal
Hello, there's no one available to speak to you at the moment, but please leave a message after the tone

Hola Manuel, soy Lourdes, ¿me puedes llamar cuando tengas un momento? Mi número es el …
Hello Manuel. This is Lourdes. Can you call or phone me back when you've got a minute? My number is …

Llamaba para …
I was just calling to …

Gracias por llamar
Thank you for calling

Gracias por llamar a la peluquería Reflejo. Le habla Pilar, ¿en qué puedo ayudarle?
Thank you for calling the Reflejo hair salon. Pilar speaking. How may I help you?

¿Puedes repetir eso, por favor?
Can you repeat that please?

¿Puedes hablar un poco más despacio, por favor? No hablo muy bien español
Can you speak a bit more slowly, please? My Spanish isn't very good

¿Me dejas tu número y te llamo en cuanto pueda?
Can you give me your number and I'll call you back as soon as I can?

Me temo que no está aquí en este momento
I'm afraid she's not here at the moment

¿Desea dejar algún mensaje?
Can I take a message?

¿Le importaría volver a llamar dentro de media hora?
Could you call back in half an hour?

Con la extensión 123
Extension 123 please

¿Puedo hablar con …?
May I speak to …?

¿Puedo hacer una llamada al exterior, por favor?
Can I have an outside line, please?

Pulse la tecla almohadilla/asterisco de su teléfono
Please press hash/the star button on your telephone keypad

Por favor, espere
Please hold the line

Quisiera hacer una llamada a cobro revertido
I'd like to make a reverse charge (BRIT) or collect call (US)

La persona a quien llama está ocupada en estos momentos
The person you are calling is not available at the moment

PRACTICAL SPANISH

▶ Cardinal numbers

0	cero	14	catorce	28	veintiocho
1	uno (un, una)*	15	quince	29	veintinueve
2	dos	16	dieciséis	30	treinta
3	tres	17	diecisiete	31	treinta y uno (un, una)*
4	cuatro	18	dieciocho	42	cuarenta y dos
5	cinco	19	diecinueve	54	cincuenta y cuatro
6	seis	20	veinte	65	sesenta y cinco
7	siete	21	veintiuno (-ún, -una)*	76	setenta y seis
8	ocho	22	veintidós	88	ochenta y ocho
9	nueve	23	veintitrés	99	noventa y nueve
10	diez	24	veinticuatro	100	cien (ciento)**
11	once	25	veinticinco	101	ciento uno (un, una)*
12	doce	26	veintiséis	212	doscientos/as doce
13	trece	27	veintisiete	990	novecientos/as noventa

1.000	mil	1.000.000	un millón
1.001	mil (y) uno (un, una)*	1.000.000.000	mil millones
2.500	dos mil quinientos/as	1.000.000.000.000	un billón

NOTE: A full stop, not a comma, separates thousands and millions.

▶ Ordinal numbers

1º, 1er/1ª	primero (primer, primera)†	13º/13ª	decimotercero/a or decimotercio/a
2º/2ª	segundo/a	14º/14ª	decimocuarto/a
3º, 3er/3ª	tercero (tercer, tercera)†	15º/15ª	decimoquinto/a
4º/4ª	cuarto/a	16º/16ª	decimosexto/a
5º/5ª	quinto/a	17º/17ª	decimoséptimo/a
6º/6ª	sexto/a	18º/18ª	decimoctavo/a
7º/7ª	séptimo/a	19º/19ª	decimonoveno/a or decimonono/a
8º/8ª	octavo/a	20º/20ª	vigésimo/a
9º/9ª	noveno/a	21º/21ª	vigésimo primero/a
10º/10ª	décimo/a	30º/30ª	trigésimo/a
11º/11ª	undécimo/a	100º/100ª	centésimo/a
12º/12ª	duodécimo/a	1000º/1000ª	milésimo/a

▶ Fractions and percentages

½	medio/a	1/10	un décimo, una décima parte
⅓	un tercio, una tercera parte	6,89	seis coma ochenta y nueve
¼	un cuarto, una cuarta parte	10%	un diez por cien(to)

NOTE: A comma, not a full stop, is used to show decimal places.

* **Uno** (+ **treinta y uno** etc) agrees in gender (but not number) with its noun: *treinta y una personas*; the masculine form is shortened to **un** before a noun: *treinta y un caballos*.

** **Ciento** is used in compound numbers, except when it multiplies: *ciento diez*, but *cien mil*. **Cien** is used before nouns: *cien hombres, cien casas*.

† **Primero** and **tercero** are shortened to **primer** and **tercer** when they directly precede a masculine singular noun: *en el primer capítulo*, but *los primeros coches en llegar*.

¿Qué hora es?   *What time is it?*

Es la una

Es la una y cuarto

Son las dos menos diez

Son las tres y media

Son las seis menos veinte

Son las ocho menos cuarto

Son las nueve

Son las doce

► Asking the time

¿Qué hora tienes?	*What time do you make it?*
¿Me dices la hora?	*Can you tell me the time?*
¿Tienes hora?	*Do you have the time (on you)?*

► Telling the time

Yo tengo las dos y veinte	*I make it twenty past two*
Serán las once	*It must be about eleven*
Son las tres en punto	*It's three o'clock exactly*
Son las cinco y pico	*It's just past five o'clock*
Falta (un) poco para las cuatro	*It's nearly four o'clock*

► What time?

¿A qué hora empieza?	*What time does it start?*
A medianoche	*At midnight*
Dentro de veinte minutos	*In twenty minutes*
A eso de las ocho	*At around eight o'clock*
Sale a las siete y media	*It leaves at 7.30*

▶ The days of the week

lunes	*Monday*
martes	*Tuesday*
miércoles	*Wednesday*
jueves	*Thursday*
viernes	*Friday*
sábado	*Saturday*
domingo	*Sunday*

▶ The months of the year

enero	*January*
febrero	*February*
marzo	*March*
abril	*April*
mayo	*May*
junio	*June*
julio	*July*
agosto	*August*
septiembre	*September*
octubre	*October*
noviembre	*November*
diciembre	*December*

NOTE: in Spanish, the days of the week and months of the year always begin with a small letter.

▶ The seasons

primavera	*spring*
verano	*summer*
otoño	*autumn*
invierno	*winter*

▶ Talking about the date

¿Qué día es hoy?	*What day is it today?*
Es sábado or **Estamos a sábado**	*It's Saturday*
1/24 de octubre de 2003	*1st/24th October 2003*

▶ When?

hoy/ayer/mañana	*today/yesterday/tomorrow*
pasado mañana	*the day after tomorrow*
antes de ayer	*the day before yesterday*
el día siguiente	*the next or following day*
ayer por la tarde	*yesterday afternoon/evening*
mañana por la mañana	*tomorrow morning*
el sábado/los sábados	*on Saturday/on Saturdays*
el domingo que viene	*next Sunday*
el martes pasado	*last Tuesday*
hace una semana	*a week ago*
el año pasado	*last year*
dentro de dos días	*in two days' time*
hace quince días	*a fortnight ago*
a principios de año	*at the beginning of the year*
a mediados de mayo	*in the middle of May*
a finales de mes	*at the end of the month*
a más tardar	*at the latest*
lo más pronto	*at the earliest*
no más tarde de	*no later than*
en 1999	*in 1999*
en el siglo diecinueve	*in the nineteenth century*
en los años noventa	*in the (nineteen) nineties*
44 a. de C.	*44 BC*
14 d. de C.	*14 AD*

PRACTICAL SPANISH